Oxford
ENGLISH-
HINDI
Dictionary

अंग्रेज़ी–हिंदी शब्दकोश

Oxford
ENGLISH-
HINDI
Dictionary

अंग्रेज़ी–हिंदी शब्दकोश

Editors

S.K. VERMA
R.N. SAHAI

OXFORD
UNIVERSITY PRESS

OXFORD
UNIVERSITY PRESS

YMCA Library Building, Jai Singh Road, New Delhi 110001

Oxford University Press is a department of the University of Oxford.
It furthers the University's objective of excellence in research, scholarship,
and education by publishing worldwide in

Oxford   New York
Auckland   Cape Town   Dar es Salaam   Hong Kong   Karachi
Kuala Lumpur   Madrid   Melbourne   Mexico City   Nairobi
New Delhi   Shanghai   Taipei   Toronto

With offices in
Argentina   Austria   Brazil   Chile   Czech Republic   France   Greece
Guatemala   Hungary   Italy   Japan   Poland   Portugal   Singapore
South Korea   Switzerland   Thailand   Turkey   Ukraine   Vietnam

Oxford is a registered trademark of Oxford University Press
in the UK and in certain other countries.

Published in India
by Oxford University Press

First published 2003
Published by arrangement with
Oxford University Press, Oxford
(for sale throughout the world)
Eleventh impression July 2005

ISBN-13: 978-0-19-564819-5
ISBN-10: 0-19-564819-6

Typeset by Neographics, New Delhi 110019
Printed in India by Gopsons, Noida 201301
and published by Manzar Khan, Oxford University Press
YMCA Library Building, Jai Singh Road, New Delhi 110001

विषय-सूची

भूमिका

अंग्रेज़ी भाषा के शिक्षण में, विशेषत: माध्यमिक तथा उच्च-माध्यमिक स्तर कक्षा के विद्यार्थियों के लिए, प्रयोक्ता-अनुकूल अंग्रेज़ी-हिंदी कोश की उपदेयता निर्विवाद रही है और ऐसे कोश की कमी प्राय: सभी शिक्षाविद्, अध्यापक और माता-पिता अनुभव करते आ रहे थे। इस रिक्ति को देखते हुए ऑक्सफोर्ड यूनिवर्सिटी प्रेस ने एक शब्दकोश संपादित करवाने का निर्णय लिया और प्रस्तुत अंग्रेज़ी-हिंदी शब्दकोश उसकी परिणति है।

इस शब्दकोश का संकलन दोहरे उद्देश्य से किया गया है। दूसरी भाषा के रूप में अंग्रेज़ी सीख रहे हिंदी-भाषी और अतिरिक्त भाषा के रूप में हिंदी सीख रहे अंग्रेज़ी-भाषी इस कोश को अत्यंत उपयोगी पाएँगे। यद्यपि इस कोश का निर्माण मुख्यत: उच्च-माध्यमिक स्तर के शिक्षार्थियों की आवश्यकताओं को ध्यान में रखकर किया गया है, यह पूरा विश्वास है कि यह अंग्रेज़ी की पुस्तकों तथा पत्र-पत्रिकाओं के सामान्य पाठकों, कार्यालयों में अंग्रेज़ी में कार्य करने वालों और हिंदी-अनुवादकों के लिए भी उपदेय सिद्ध होगा।

इस शब्दकोश में शब्दों के अर्थों को भेद-उपभेद सहित सुपरिभाषित किया गया है और उपयुक्त उदाहरणों से समझाया गया है। शब्दकोश का मूल दिग्दर्शक ग्रंथ *Oxford Advanced Learner's Dictionary 5/e* है। प्रस्तुत द्वैभाषिक कोश में प्रयोक्ताओं की दृष्टि से प्रविष्टियों को अपनी स्थानसीमा के भीतर आत्मसात् किया गया है और भारतीय परिप्रेक्ष्य में निखारा गया है।

वर्तमान शब्दकोश में लगभग 25,000 शीर्षशब्दों, उपशीर्षशब्दों और उपवाक्यों को समाविष्ट किया गया है। शब्दावली अंग्रेज़ी साहित्य तथा परंपरागत ज्ञानविषयों तक ही सीमित नहीं है, इसमें नवीनतम और वर्तमान में प्रचलित विषयों (जैसे कंप्यूटर, सूचना प्रौद्योगिकी, वाणिज्यविषयक विश्वीकरण और सूक्ष्मजैविकी) से संबंधित शब्दों का भी समावेश किया गया है। ये शब्द अब सामान्य परिधि में आ गए हैं और इनकी उपेक्षा कोश को अधूरा बना देती।

शब्द के आगे उच्चारण (देवनागरी लिपि में), व्याकरणिक कोटि, शब्दप्रयोग परास आदि अर्थ के पहले दिए गए हैं। 'प्रयोगविधि' शीर्षक के अंतर्गत शब्दप्रविष्टि के इन सभी पहलुओं को उदाहरण सहित समझाया गया है। इस शब्दकोश में प्रविष्टियों को किसी न किसी शीर्षशब्द के अधीन दिया गया है किंतु ऐसा नहीं है कि केवल 'शब्द' के ही अर्थ दिए गए हैं। क्रिया शब्द के आगे क्रिया पदबंध की

व्याख्या, उदाहरण आदि दिए गए हैं। संबद्ध मुहावरों और लोकोक्तियों को भी प्रविष्टि में समाविष्ट किया गया है।

अंग्रेज़ी शब्द के अर्थ को हिंदी के एक शब्द द्वारा केवल तभी समझाया गया है जब उनमें अर्थतादात्म्य हो। ऐसा विरल ही होता है, इसलिए इस शब्दकोश में अर्थ को प्राय: विवरण द्वारा, कभी-कभी पूरे-पूरे वाक्य द्वारा, समझाया गया है। उदाहरण देने में कभी संकोच नहीं किया गया है क्योंकि इससे अर्थ की जानकारी गहराई से मिलती है। इसके अतिरिक्त यदि शब्द के एक से अधिक अर्थ प्रयोग में दृष्टिगोचर हैं, तो 1, 2, 3 आदि अंक लगाकर इन अर्थों को यथासंभव उदाहरणों के साथ दिया गया है।

अमेरिकन अंग्रेज़ी के बढ़ते प्रचलन और लोकप्रियता को ध्यान में रखते हुए शब्दों की ब्रिटिश वर्तनी के आगे अमेरिकन वर्तनी दी गई है तथा कुछ शब्दों के अमेरिकन अंग्रेज़ी में प्रयुक्त पर्याय शब्द भी दिए गए हैं। इसी प्रकार ब्रिटिश उच्चारण के साथ-साथ अमेरिकन उच्चारण भी दिया गया है।

आशा है कि इन सब अधुनातन प्रयुक्तियों से संपादित यह शब्दकोश प्रयोक्ताओं की लगभग सभी बोधन और अभिव्यक्ति संबंधी कठिनाइओं को दूर करेगा और उनकी अंग्रेज़ी समझने, बोलने एवं लिखने की क्षमता बढ़ाएगा। कोश को अधिक उपयोगी बनाने के लिए सुझावों का सदैव स्वागत है।

अंत में हम अपने अध्ययन सहायक, श्री प्रदीप शर्मा, के प्रति आभार प्रकट करना चाहेंगे।

शिवेन्द्र किशोर वर्मा
रमानाथ सहाय

प्रयोग विधि

शीर्षशब्द

शीर्षशब्द अंग्रेज़ी में स्थूल अक्षरों में दिए गए हैं (**1** देखिए)। जहाँ अमेरिकन वर्तनी में भिन्नता मिलती है वहाँ कोष्ठक में *US* संकेत के बाद अमेरिकन शीर्षशब्द दिया गया है (**2** देखिए)।

शीर्षशब्द सामान्यतया छोटे अक्षर से शुरू होते हैं किंतु व्यक्तिवाचक संज्ञा के रूप में आए शीर्षशब्द बड़े अक्षर से शुरू होते हैं (**3** देखिए)।

कहीं-कहीं शीर्षशब्द के ठीक ऊपर 1, 2, 3 आदि लगे हुए मिलेंगे। इसका तात्पर्य यह है कि लिपि के अनुसार ये शब्द एक-से दिखाई पड़ते हैं किंतु उच्चारण या/और अर्थ की दृष्टि से वे भिन्न हैं (**4** देखिए)।

कुछ शीर्षशब्द एक से ज़्यादा शब्दभेदों के रूप में प्रयुक्त होते हैं। यदि इनका विस्तृत विवरण देने से प्रविष्टि का आकार बहुत बड़ा हो जाता है तो इन शब्दभेदों को अलग-अलग प्रविष्टियाँ बना दी गई हैं और इन्हें संख्यांकित किया गया है (**5** देखिए)।

कुछ अंग्रेज़ी शब्दों के एक से ज़्यादा रूप या वर्तनी हो सकते हैं। सामान्य तौर पर प्रयुक्त होने वाला रूप/वर्तनी शीर्षशब्द बनाया गया है। अतिरिक्त रूप/वर्तनी कोष्ठक में दी गई है (**6** देखिए)।

उच्चारण शैली

शीर्षशब्द के ठीक बाद दो तिर्यक् रेखाओं के बीच उच्चारण देवनागरी में दिया गया है (**7** देखिए)। उच्चारण शैली में प्रयुक्त चिह्नों की पूर्ण सूची पृष्ठ xii-xiii पर दी गई है।

neighbour (*US* neighbor) / 'नेबर् / *noun* 1 पड़ोसी 2 पड़ोसी देश या क्षेत्र ▸ neighbourhood (*US* neighborhood) *noun* 1 घर के आस-पास, समीपता की स्थिति 2 आस-पास के क्षेत्र के निवासी neighbouring (*US* neighboring) *adj* समीपवर्ती neighbourly (*US* neighborly) *adj* मैत्रीपूर्ण, मिलनसार।

October / ऑक् 'टोबर् / *noun* (*संक्षि* Oct) अक्तूबर (महीना)।

row¹ / रो / *noun* (व्यक्तियों या वस्तुओं की) पंक्ति : *a row of books* ■ in a row लगातार, बिना अंतराल के।
row² / रो / *verb* (नाव) खेना; खेते हुए नाव में सैर करना/कराना : *He rowed us across the river.* ▸ row *noun* (प्राय: *sing*) नौका-विहार : *go for a row.*
row³ / राउ / *noun* (अनौप) 1 (बहस) झगड़ा 2 [*sing*] उपद्रव, अप्रिय शोर : *What a row they're making!* ▸ row *verb* row (with sb) झगड़ा करना।

net² (nett भी) / नेट् / *adj* (धन) शेष, जिसके बाद अब कुछ निकालना नहीं है; (क़ीमत) कुल, संपूर्ण; (वज़न, भार, आदि) डिब्बे या पैकिंग को छोड़कर (सिर्फ़ सामान का भार)।

obedient / अ'बीडिअन्ट् / *adj* obedient (to sb/sth) आज्ञाकारी ▸ obedience / अ'बीडिअन्स् / *noun* आज्ञाकारिता obediently *adv*.

उच्चारण में भिन्नताओं, विशेषत: अमेरिकन, का समावेश किया गया है (**8** देखिए)।

व्याकरणिक सूचना

उच्चारण के तुरंत बाद शब्द की व्याकरणिक कोटि (*noun, adj, prep* आदि) का उल्लेख अंग्रेज़ी में तिर्यक् अक्षरों में है (**9** देखिए)। कुछ शब्दभेदों का संक्षिप्त रूप दिया गया है। संक्षिप्त रूपों का पूर्ण रूप संक्षिप्ति सूची में पृष्ठ xiv पर दिया गया है।

रूप-रचना में संज्ञा के अनियमित रूप कोष्ठक में दिए गए हैं (**10** देखिए)। कुछ संज्ञाओं के स्त्रीलिंग/पुलिंग रूप कोष्ठक में दिए गए हैं (**11** देखिए)।

कहीं-कहीं संज्ञा के बाद [*sing*] या [*pl*] दिया गया है; इसका अर्थ यह है कि यह शब्द केवल एकवचन या बहुवचन में प्रयोग योग्य है (**12** देखिए)।

क्रिया के अनियमित रूप दिए गए हैं और वर्तनी में जहाँ अंतिम व्यंजन का द्वित्व होता है वहाँ कोष्ठक में संकेत दिया गया है (**13** देखिए)।

विशेषण के तुलनात्मक और उत्तमावस्था रूप दिए गए हैं (**14** देखिए)।

लेबल

विषय-लेबल शब्द के विशिष्ट अर्थ के प्रयोग या व्यवहार क्षेत्र को दर्शाते हैं। ये लेबल शब्द के अर्थ से पहले कोष्ठक में संक्षिप्त रूप और तिर्यक् अक्षरों में दिए गए हैं (**15** देखिए)। पूर्ण लेबल-सूची पृष्ठ xv पर दी गई है।

⑧ **narrate** / न'रेट्; *US* 'नैरेट् / *verb* (किसी घटना/कथा का) वर्णन करना ▸ **narration** *noun* विवरण, कथन **narrative** / 'नैरटिव्/ *adj, noun* कथनात्मक/विवरणात्मक वर्णन **narrator** *noun* कथावाचक; वर्णन करने वाला।

⑨ **dairy** /'डेअरि/ *noun* ⑩(*pl* **dairies**) 1 डेरी, जहाँ दूध इकट्ठा किया जाता है और दुग्ध उत्पाद जैसे मक्खन, दही आदि बनाए जाते हैं 2 दूध-मक्खन की दुकान ▸ **dairy** *adj* 1 दूध से बना : *dairy products* 2 दुग्ध उत्पादन से संबंधित : *the dairy industry.*

⑪ **fiancé** (*fem* **fiancée**) / फ़ि'ऑन्से; *US* ,फ़ीआन्'से / *noun* वह आदमी या औरत जिससे विवाह होने जा रहा है।

⑫ **nemesis** /'नेमसिस्/ *noun* [*sing*] (*औप*) दंड या पतन जिससे बच नहीं सकते : *He met his nemesis.*

⑬ **shed²** / शेड्/ *verb* (**-dd-**; *pt, pp* **shed**) 1 गिराना, गिरने देना : *Many trees shed their leaves in autumn.* 2 (*औप*) बहाना, बहने देना : *shed tears* 3 उतारना, फेंकना; छुटकारा पाना 4 **shed sth** (**on/over sb/sth**) फैलाना : *The candle shed a soft glow over the room.*

⑭ **pretty¹** / 'प्रिटि / *adj* (**-ier, -iest**) मनोरम और आकर्षक : *a pretty girl* ▸ **prettily** *adv* अच्छी तरह, आकर्षक ढंग से : *She decorated the room very prettily.*

⑮ **magnitude** /'मैग्निट्यूड्; *US* 'मैग्निट्यूड् / *noun* 1 (*औप*) (आकार की) विशालता 2 महत्ता 3 (*खगोल*) किसी तारे की चमक की तीव्रता : *a star of the first magnitude.*

अर्थ

अर्थ को अधिकतर अनेक शब्दों या वाक्यों से समझाया गया है—एक शब्द में अर्थ तभी व्यक्त किया गया है जब उसकी अर्थछाया बिलकुल अंग्रेज़ी शब्द की अर्थछाया से मिलती हो। प्राय:, अर्थ को अधिक स्पष्ट करने के लिए कोष्ठक में अतिरिक्त जानकारी दी गई है (**16** और **17** देखिए)।

एक ही शब्द के एक से अधिक अर्थ हो सकते हैं। ऐसी स्थिति में अर्थों को 1, 2, 3 आदि संख्याएँ लगाकर पृथक् किया गया है (**17** देखिए)।

उदाहरण

अर्थों को अधिकतर समुपयुक्त अंग्रेज़ी उदाहरणों से स्पष्ट किया गया है। उदाहरणों का मुद्रण तिर्यक् अक्षरों में हैं। दो या ज़्यादा उदाहरणों को ○ चिह्न द्वारा अलग किया गया है (**18** देखिए)।

विशिष्ट शब्द प्रयोग

शीर्षशब्द से संबंधित उपवाक्यों, मुहावरों और कहावतों को ■ चिह्न के बाद स्थूल वर्णरूप में दिया गया है (**19** देखिए)।

उपशीर्षशब्द

शीर्षशब्द से व्युत्पन्न (प्रत्ययजनित) अथवा समासजनित शब्द, उपशीर्ष शब्द के रूप में ▶ चिह्न के बाद स्थूल अक्षरों में दिए गए हैं। आवश्यकता पड़ने पर इनके उच्चारण, उच्चारणभेद, वर्तनीभेद, व्याकरण, प्रयोग क्षेत्र आदि की सूचना शीर्षशब्द के समान दी गई है (**20** देखिए)।

---

⑯
nephew / 'नेफ़्यू; 'नेव्यू / *noun* भतीजा; भाँजा।

⑰
needle / 'नीड्ल् / *noun* **1** सूई (कपड़ा सिलने की) **2** सलाई (जैसे ऊन बुनने की) **3** (घड़ी या सूचक यंत्रों की) सूई **4** इंजेक्शन की सूई; सूई के आकार की वस्तु ▶ **needle-work** *noun* सिलाई–कढ़ाई का काम।

⑱
cabinet / 'कैबिनट् / *noun* **1** ड्राअर वाली अलमारी : *a filing cabinet* ○ *a medicine cabinet* **2** (**the cabinet** भी) (राज्य या शासन से संबद्ध) मंत्रिमंडल, मंत्रि-परिषद।

fish² / फ़िश् / *verb* **fish** (**for sth**) **1** मछली पकड़ना **2** कुछ ढूँढ़ना, विशेषत: किसी अंधेरे एवं छुपे हुए स्थान में : *She* ⑲ *fished (around) in her bag for the keys.* ■ **fish sth out** (**of sth**) पाना, खोज निकालना ▶ **fishing** *noun* मछली पकड़ना **fishing-line** *noun* मछली पकड़ने की लग्गी (डोरी)।

⑳
magic / 'मैजिक् / *noun* **1** जादू **2** जादूगरी **3** बाज़ीगरी के करिश्मे, इंद्रजाल **4** आकर्षक एवं आश्चर्यजनक गुण : *the magic of Shakespeare's poetry* ▶ **magic** *adj* **1** जादू में प्रयुक्त; जादूभरा **2** विशिष्ट एवं महत्त्वपूर्ण **3** आश्चर्यजनक **magical** *adj* **magician** / म'जिश्न् / *noun* जादूगर, बाज़ीगर।

उच्चारण शैली

Consonants

IPA* symbol	Usage	Hindi symbol	Usage
p	cap /kæp/	प्	/ कैप् /
b	rub /rʌb/	ब्	/ रब् /
t	fit /fɪt/	ट्	/ फ़िट् /
d	red /red/	ड्	/ रेड् /
k	flak /flæk/	क्	/ फ़्लैक् /
g	rig /rɪg/	ग्	/ रिग् /
tʃ	rich /rɪtʃ/	च्	/ रिच् /
dʒ	pledge /pledʒ/	ज्	/ प्लेज् /
f	life /laɪf/	फ़्	/ लाइफ़् /
v	wave /weɪv/	व़्	/ वेव़् /
θ	filth /fɪlθ/	थ़्	/ फ़िल्थ़् /
δ	bathe /beɪδ/	द़्	/ बेद़् /
s	fuss /fʌs/	स्	/ फ़स् /
z	filings / 'faɪlɪŋz/	ज़्	/'फ़ाइलिङ्ज़् /
ʃ	fish /fɪʃ/	श्	/ फ़िश् /
ʒ	fuselage / 'fju:zəla:ʒ/	श़्	/'फ़्यूज़्लाश़् /
h	hunk /hʌŋk/	ह	/ हङ्क् /
m	fame /feɪm/	म्	/ फ़ेम् /
n	fin /fɪn/	न्	/ फ़िन् /
ŋ	ring /rɪŋ/	ङ्	/ रिङ्/
l	file /faɪl /	ल्	/ फ़ाइल् /
r	run /rʌn/	र्	/ रन् /
(r)	for /fɔ:(r)/	र्	/ फ़ॉर् /
j	granular / 'grænjələ(r)/	य	/'ग्रैन्यलर् /
w	won /wʌn/	व	/ वन् /

Vowels and diphthongs

i	happy /hæpi/	इ / ि	/ हैपि /
ɪ	fig /fɪg/	इ / ि	/ फ़िग् /
i:	see /si:/	ई / ी	/ सी /
e	ten /ten/	ए / ॆ	/ टेन् /
æ	cat /kæt/	ऐ / ॅ	/ कैट् /
ɑ:	far /fɑ:(r)/	आ / ा	/ फ़ार् /
ɒ	lot /lɒt/	ऑ / ॉ	/ लॉट् /
ɔ:	saw /sɔ:/	ऑ / ॉ	/ सॉ /
ʊ	put /pʊt/	उ / ु	/ पुट् /
u	actual / ˈæktʃuəl/	उ / ु	/ ˈऐक्चुअल् /
u:	too /tu:/	ऊ / ू	/ टू /
ʌ	cut /kʌt/	अ	/ कट् /
ɜ:	bird /bɜ:d/	अ+र् / अ+ʿ	/ बईं /
ə	about; paper /əˈbaʊt; ˈpeɪpə(r)/	अ	/अ ˈबाउट्; पेपर्/
eɪ	fade /feɪd/	ए / ॆ	/ फ़ेड् /
əʊ	go /gəʊ/	ओ / ो	/ गो /
aɪ	five /faɪv/	आ+इ / ा+इ	/ फ़ाइव् /
ɔɪ	boy /bɔɪ/	ऑ+इ / ॉ+इ	/ बॉइ /
aʊ	now /naʊ/	आ+उ / ा+उ	/ नाउ /
ɪə	near /nɪə(r)/	इ+अ / ि+अ	/ निअर् /
eə	flair /fleə(r)/	ए+अ / ॆ+अ	/ फ़्लेअर् /
ʊə	pure /pjʊə(r)/	उ+अ /ु+अ	/ प्युअर /

इस शब्दकोश में दी गई उच्चारण शैली *Oxford Advanced Learner's Dictionary* में दी गई शैली के यथासंभव समान है। यथार्थ उच्चारण के लिए *Oxford Advanced Learner's Dictionary* देखिए।

*International Phonetic Alphabet

abbr	abbreviation
adj	adjective
adv	adverb
adv part	adverbial particle
art	article
aux verb	auxiliary verb
def art	definite article
det	determiner
emph	emphatic
fem	feminine
indef det	indefinite determiner
indef pron	indefinite pronoun
interj	interjection
interrog adv	interrogative adverb
interrog det	interrogative determiner
interrog pron	interrogative pronoun
masc	masculine
modal verb	modal verb
neg	negative
noun	noun
pers pron	personal pronoun
[pl]	plural noun
possess pron	possessive pronoun
pp	past participle
pref	prefix
pres p	present participle
pres t	present tense
pron	pronoun
pt	past tense
reflex	reflexive
rel adv	relative adverb
rel det	relative determiner
rel pron	relative pronoun
sb	somebody
sth	something
verb	verb
[sing]	singular noun
suff	suffix
US	American usage
3rd per sing	3rd person singular

लेबल-सूची

abbreviation	(संक्षि)	संक्षिप्त रूप
archaic	(प्रा)	प्राचीन प्रयोग
astronomy	(खगोल)	खगोल विज्ञान
biology	(जीव विज्ञान)	जीव विज्ञान
botany	(वनस्पति विज्ञान)	वनस्पति विज्ञान
chemistry	(रसा)	रसायन शास्त्र
colloquial (also *slang*)	(अप)	अपभाषा
commerce/finance	(वाणिज्य)	वाणिज्य
dated	(अप्र)	अप्रचलित
derogatory	(अपमा)	अपमानजनक
figurative	(अलं)	अलंकारिक
formal	(औप)	औपचारिक
French	(फ़्रेंच)	फ़्रेंच
geography	(भूगोल)	भूगोल
geology	(भूविज्ञान)	भूविज्ञान
geometry	(ज्यामिति)	ज्यामिति
grammar	(व्या)	व्याकरण
informal	(अनौप)	अनौपचारिक
jocular	(परि)	परिहासिक
Latin	(लैटिन)	लैटिन
law	(क़ानून)	क़ानूनी प्रयोग
linguistics	(भाषा विज्ञान)	भाषा विज्ञान
literary	(साहि)	साहित्यिक
mathematics	(गणित)	गणित
medicine	(चिकि)	चिकित्सा
music	(संगीत)	संगीत
philosophy	(दर्शन)	दर्शनशास्त्र
phonetics	(स्वर विद्या)	स्वर विद्या
physics	(भौतिकी)	भौतिकी विज्ञान
political	(राज)	राजनीतिक
prefix	(पूर्वपद)/(उपसर्ग)	पूर्वपद/उपसर्ग
psychology	(मनो)	मनोविज्ञान
saying	(कहा)	कहावत
short form	(लघु रूप)	लघु रूप
suffix	(प्रत्यय)	प्रत्यय
symbol	(प्रतीक)	प्रतीक
technical	(तक)	तकनीकी
trademark	(ट्रेडमार्क)	ट्रेडमार्क

Aa

a /अ; ए/ (an / अन्; ऐन्/ भी) *indef art* (व्यंजन ध्वनियों से आरंभ होने वाले शब्दों से पहले **a** का प्रयोग और स्वर ध्वनियों से आरंभ होने वाले शब्दों से पहले **an** का प्रयोग होता है) **1** एक; कोई : *a girl/a teacher/a unit; an hour/an aunt/an iceberg* **2** प्रत्येक, हर एक : *A horse is a quadruped.* ○ *An owl can see in the dark.* **3** (नकारात्मक पद के साथ) एक, अकेला; कुछ भी : *He didn't tell us a thing about his trip.* **4** विशेष संख्याओं (भिन्न आदि) व अंशों के पूर्व : *a fifth of the population* ○ *A thousand people attended the concert.* **5** प्रत्येक/ हर एक के लिए : *write 800 words a day* ○ *pay Rs 80 a litre* **6** व्यक्तियों या वस्तुओं की उनके वर्ग की सदस्यता प्रदर्शित करने के लिए: *My mother is a doctor.* ○ *The car was a Mercedez, not a Rolls Royce.* **7** एक इकाई के रूप में माने जाने वाली दो संज्ञाओं से पहले प्रयुक्त: *a cup and saucer* ○ *a knife and fork.*

aback / अ'बैक्/ *adv* ■ **taken aback; take sb aback** चकित हो जाना; चकित कर देना।

abandon/अं'बैन्डन्/ *verb* **1 abandon sb/sth (to sb/sth)** सदैव के लिए छोड़ना, परित्याग करना : *The order came : 'Abandon ship!'* ○ *a baby abandoned by its parents* **2** (पूरा होने से पहले) छोड़ देना, त्याग देना : *The match was abandoned because of bad weather.* **3 abandon oneself to sth** (साहि) वशीभूत हो जाना; (भावनाओं) के वश में आ जाना : *He abandoned himself to despair.* ▶ **abandon** (**abandonment** भी) *noun* बेफ़िक्री; स्वच्छंदता, असंयम : *dance with gay abandon* **abandoned** *adj* बिगड़ा हुआ व्यक्ति, दुश्चरित्र; त्यागा हुआ **abandon-**

ment / अ'बैन्डन्मन्ट् / *noun* परित्याग, उससे उत्पन्न अकेलापन : *the fear of abandonment in old age.*

abase / अ'बेस्/ *verb* **abase oneself/ sb** (औप)(स्वयं का या दूसरों का) अपमान करना, आत्मसम्मान से नीचे गिराना, अनादर करना ▶ **abasement** *noun*.

abashed/ अ'बैश्ट्/ *adj* शर्मिंदा, लज्जित: *His boss's criticism left him feeling rather abashed.*

abate / अ'बेट्/ *verb* (वायु, शोर, दर्द आदि की तीव्रता का) कम या शांत होना : *Public interest in this issue seems to have abated.*

abattoir / 'ऐबट्वार्/ *noun* (ब्रिटेन में) बूचड़ख़ाना, वधशाला।

abbey / 'ऐबि / *noun* (*pl* **abbeys**) ईसाई मठ, महामठ।

abbreviate / अ'ब्रीव़िएट्/ *verb* (शब्द, कहानी आदि को) संक्षिप्त या छोटा करना : *In writing, the title 'Doctor' is abbreviated to 'Dr'.* ▶ **abbrevia-tion** / अ, ब्रीव़ि'एश्न्/ *noun* **1** संक्षेप, संक्षिप्त रूप : *'GB' is the abbreviation of/for 'Great Britain'.* **2** संक्षेपण करने की प्रक्रिया।

abdicate / 'ऐब्डिकेट्/ *verb* **1** किसी पद अथवा अधिकार (प्राय: राजगद्दी) को त्यागना: *King Edward VIII abdicated in 1936.* **2** (औप) कोई कर्तव्य या ज़िम्मेदारी न निबाहने का निर्णय करना : *This government will not abdicate its responsibility to beat inflation.* ▶ **ab-dication** / 'ऐब्डि'केश्न्/ *noun* राज-त्याग, पद-त्याग।

abdomen / 'ऐब्डमन्/ *noun* पेट, उदर आँत ▶ **abdominal** / ऐब्'डॉमिन्ल्/ *adj* उदर-संबंधी।

abduct / ऐब्'डक्ट्/ *verb* ज़बरदस्ती भगा ले जाना, बलपूर्वक भगाना, अपहरण करना :

He was abducted by four gunmen.
▸ **abduction** / ऐब्'डक्शन् / *noun* अप-
हरण।

aberration / ऐब'रेशन् / *noun* सन्मार्ग या
सत्यपथ से (संभवत: अस्थायी) विचलन या
हटना : *steal something in a moment*
of aberration.

abet / अ'बेट् / *verb* (-tt-) **abet sb (in**
sth) पाप के लिए उकसाना; (अपराध में)
सहायता और प्रोत्साहन देना : *He was*
abetted (in the deception) by his
wife.

abeyance / अ'बेअन्स् / *noun* स्थगित
रहने, रोके रखने की स्थिति : *The scheme*
is/has been put in abeyance until
sufficient funds can be found.

abhor / अब्'हॉर् / *verb* (-rr-) घृणा या
नफरत करना, घृणित समझना : *abhor*
terrorism/terrorists ▸ **abhorrence**
/ अब्'हॉरन्स् / *noun* [*sing*] अत्यधिक
घृणा, जुगुप्सा : *have an abhorrence of*
war.

abide / अ'बाइड् / *verb* (*pt, pp* **abided**)
1 (विशेषत: can/could, नकारात्मक वाक्यों
एवं प्रश्नों के साथ) सहना; बर्दाश्त करना :
She can't abide that man. 2 (*pt, pp*
abode / अ'बोड्/) (प्रा या औप) स्थान पर
बना रहना, रहना : *the right to enter*
and abide in a country ∎ **abide by**
sth दृढ़ता और निष्ठा से नियम का पालन
करना, वादा निभाना : *abide by a deci-*
sion/verdict ▸ **abiding** *adj* स्थायी;
अटूट : *an abiding friendship.*

ability / अ'बिलटि / *noun* (*pl* **abilities**)
ability (to do sth) काम करने की शारीरिक
या मानसिक योग्यता, क्षमता, सामर्थ्य : *I try*
to do my job to the best of my ability.

abject / 'ऐजेक्ट् / *adj* 1 (व्यक्ति) नीच;
स्वाभिमान रहित, अधम : *an abject cow-*
ard ∘ *an abject apology* 2 दीन-हीन
दशा : *living in abject poverty.*

ablaze / अ'ब्लेज़् / *adj* 1 प्रज्वलित, जलता

हुआ : *The whole building was soon*
well ablaze. 2 **ablaze (with sth)**
दमकता हुआ, उत्तेजित अवस्था में : *The*
palace was ablaze with lights.
∘ *Her face was ablaze with anger.*

able[1] / 'एब्ल् / *adj* **be able to do sth**
किसी काम को करने की शक्ति, सामर्थ्य आदि
रखना : *I wasn't able to lift the*
suitcase.

able[2] / 'एब्ल् / *adj* (-r / 'एब्लर् /, -st
/ 'एब्लिस्ट्/) निपुण, कुशल, समर्थ: *an able*
worker ∘ *the ablest student in the*
class ▸ **able-bodied** *adj* स्वस्थ, हृष्ट-
पुष्ट **ably** *adv* कुशलतापूर्वक।

abnormal / ऐब्'नॉर्मल् / *adj* सामान्य से
अलग; अस्वाभाविक, अनियमित; अप-
सामान्य : *abnormal behaviour/*
weather conditions ▸ **abnormality**
/ ऐब्नॉर्'मैलटि / *noun* (*pl* **abnormali-**
ties) असामान्यता, व्यतिक्रम **abnormally**
/ ऐब्'नॉर्मलि / *adv* असाधारण रूप से।

aboard / अ'बॉर्ड् / *adv part, prep*
जहाज़/हवाई जहाज़/बस या ट्रेन में सवार।

abode / अ'बोड् / *noun* (प्राय: *sing*)
(औप या *साहि* या *परि*) घर, आवास;
निवास-स्थान, अधिवास : *Welcome to*
our humble abode!

abolish / अ'बॉलिश् / *verb* (किसी प्रथा,
स्थिति या क़ानून को) समाप्त करना, (का)
उन्मूलन करना : *Should the death*
penalty be abolished? ▸ **abolition**
/ ऐब'लिशन् / *noun* उन्मूलन; समापन।

abominable / अ'बॉमिनब्ल् / *adj*
1 (औप) डरावना और घिनौना : *an abomi-*
nable crime 2 (अनौप) भद्दा; निकृष्ट,
अप्रिय : *abominable food/weather/*
music/people ▸ **Abominable Snow-**
man (Yeti भी) *noun* येति **abominably**
adv घिनौनेपन से।

aboriginal / ऐब'रिजनल् / *adj* (किसी
स्थान/देश का) मूल निवासी, आदिवासी :
aboriginal tribes ∘ *aboriginal cul-*

ture ▸ **aboriginal** (प्रायः Aboriginal) *noun* (ऑस्ट्रेलियाई) आदिवासी।

aborigine / ‚ऐब ˈरिजनि / (प्रायः **Aborigine**) *noun* किसी देश के (विशेषतः ऑस्ट्रेलिया के) आदि-निवासी, आदिवासी जातियाँ।

abort / अ ˈबॉर्ट् / *verb* **1** (चिकि) गर्भपात होना/कराना : *In this age group more than half of all pregnancies are aborted.* **2** निष्फल या व्यर्थ होने की संभावना के कारण किसी कार्य को समयपूर्व समाप्त करना : *abort a space mission* ○ *Peace talks had to be aborted.*

abortion / अ ˈबॉर्शन् / *noun* **1** गर्भपात, भ्रूण हत्या : *Her parents don't approve of abortion.* **2** गर्भपात होना : *She had an abortion.* → **miscarriage** देखिए।

abortive / अ ˈबॉर्टिव् / *adj* निष्फल (प्रयत्न/ क्रिया) : *an abortive attempt/coup/ mission.*

abound / अ ˈबाउन्ड् / *verb* **1** खूब या भरपूर होना या मिलना : *Oranges abound here all the year round.* **2 abound in/with sth** कोई वस्तु आदि बड़ी मात्रा या संख्या में होना : *The river abounds in/ with fish.* → **abundance, abundant** देखिए।

about¹ / अ ˈबाउट् / *prep* **1** विषय में, बारे में; के संबंध में : *a book about flowers* ○ *There's something strange about the whole affair.* **2** (**around** भी) भर, में, इधर-उधर : *walking about the town* **3** (**around** भी) यहाँ-वहाँ, जहाँ-तहाँ : *papers strewn about the room* **4** (**around** भी) कहीं पास में : *I dropped the key somewhere about here.* **5** (**around** भी) विभिन्न दिशाओं में; विभिन्न स्थानों पर : *He came out of the door and looked about him.* ■ **be about to do sth** (किसी क्रिया के) आरंभ मात्र के क्षण, बस करने को : *We are about to*

start. **how/what about ...?** **1** सूचना जानने या मत जानने में प्रयुक्त : *What about his qualifications?* **2** सुझाव देना : *What about a cup of tea?*

about² / अ ˈबाउट् / *adv* **1** (**around** भी) लगभग (मात्रा में), आसपास (समय में) : *He's about the same height as you.* ○ *They waited (for) about an hour.*

about³ / अ ˈबाउट् / *adv part* **1** (विशेषतः US **around** भी) (दिशा बोधक) यहाँ-वहाँ; किसी एक दिशा में न होकर, यत्र-तत्र : *The boys were climbing about on the rocks.* **2** (विशेषतः US **around** भी) (पास में ही) : *She's somewhere about.* **3** (विशेषतः US **around** भी) फैला हुआ/घूमता हुआ : *There is a lot of flu about.* **4** उल्टे, घूमकर : *It is the wrong way about.* ▸ **about-turn** (**about-face** भी) *noun* रंग बदलना, पलटी खाना : *These new measures indicate an about-turn in government policy.*

above¹ / अ ˈबव् / *adv* **1** ऊँचाई पर (से); ऊँचे : *Seen from above, the fields looked like a geometrical pattern.* **2** (किताब आदि में) पहले कहा या लिखा हुआ : *As was stated above...* **3** संख्या, स्तर या आयु से अधिक : *The competition is open to anyone aged 18 and above.* ▸ **above-mentioned** *adj* उपर्युक्त, ऊपर कहा हुआ।

above² / अ ˈबव् / *prep* **1** ऊँचे पर, से ऊँचा : *The sun rose above the horizon.* **2** संख्या, मूल्य, भार, स्तर, आयु आदि में अधिक : *Temperatures have been above average recently.* **3** (पद या स्थान में) ऊपर, पहले : *A captain in the Navy ranks above a captain in the Army.* **4** से अधिक : *Should a soldier value honour above life?* **5** के परे, पहुँच के बाहर (बहुत अच्छा/सच्चा/निष्कपट

होने के कारण) : *His conduct has always been above suspicion.* ■ **above all** सर्वोपरि, अन्य सब से अधिक **over and above** के अतिरिक्त।

abrasion / अ'ब्रेश्न् / *noun* 1 अपघर्षण, घिसाई : *wood that is resistant to abrasion* 2 खरोंच, ख़राश : *suffer cuts and abrasions.*

abrasive / अ'ब्रेसिव् / *adj* 1 अपघर्षक, अपघर्षी : *abrasive substances/materials* 2 दूसरों की भावनाओं को ठेस पहुँचाने की प्रवृत्ति वाला; कटु, कठोर : *an abrasive person/personality/tone of voice* ▶ **abrasive** *noun* सतह को घिसने, रगड़ने, चिकना बनाने में प्रयुक्त पदार्थ **abrasively** *adv* कटुता से **abrasiveness** *noun.*

abreast / अ'ब्रेस्ट् / *adv* **abreast (of sb/ sth)** एक ही दिशा में और अगल-बगल में : *The boat came abreast of us and signalled us to stop.* ■ **be/keep abreast of sth** नवीनतम विचारों, गतिविधियों से अपने को हमेशा परिचित रखना : *Reading the newspapers keeps me abreast of current affairs.*

abridge / अ'ब्रिज् / *verb* संक्षिप्त करना : *an abridged edition/version of 'War and Peace'* ▶ **abridgement (abridgment** भी) *noun* काट-छाँट, संक्षिप्तीकरण; (किसी पुस्तक या नाटक आदि का) संक्षिप्त रूप, सार-संग्रह।

abroad / अ'ब्रॉड् / *adv* 1 विदेश में, घर से दूर : *visitors (who have come) from abroad* 2 सर्वत्र, चारों ओर : *There is a rumour abroad that....*

abrupt / अ'ब्रप्ट् / *adj* 1 आकस्मिक, अप्रत्याशित : *a road with many abrupt turns* 2 (भाषण, लेख आदि) असंबद्ध, विषम; (व्यवहार) रूखा : *short abrupt sentences* ○ *He has an abrupt manner.* ▶ **abruptly** *adv* एकाएक,

अचानक : *The interview ended abruptly.* **abruptness** *noun* रुक्षता।

abscess / 'ऐब्सेस् / *noun* फोड़ा, व्रण; शरीर के किसी भाग में मवाद भर जाना।

abscond / अब्'स्कॉन्ड् / *verb* (औप) चुपके से भाग जाना (विशेषत: पकड़े जाने के डर से), पलायन कर जाना : *He absconded (from police custody) on the way to court.*

absence / 'ऐब्सन्स् / *noun* 1 **absence (from...)** अनुपस्थिति, ग़ैरहाज़िरी : *His repeated absence (from school) is worrying.* ○ *It happened in my absence.* 2 **absence (from...)** अनुपस्थिति का अवसर या अवधि : *numerous absences from school* 3 अभाव; न होने की स्थिति : *in the absence of definite proof.*

absent[1] / 'ऐब्सन्ट् / *adj* 1 **absent(from sth)** अनुपस्थित, ग़ैरहाज़िर : *be absent from work* 2 अविद्यमान, नामौजूद : *Love was totally absent from his childhood.* ▶ **absently** *adv* खोए-खोए **absent-minded** *adj* भुलक्कड़, खोया-खोया **absent-mindedly** *adv* अनमनेपन से।

absent[2] / ऐब्'सेन्ट् / *verb* **absent oneself(from sth)** (औप) उपस्थित न रहना : *He deliberately absented himself (from the meeting).*

absentee / ऐब्सन्'टी / *noun* ग़ैरहाज़िर व्यक्ति; दूरस्थ; (क़ानून) अनुपस्थाता ▶ **absenteeism** / ऐब्सन्'टीइज़म् / *noun* कार्य से आदतन अनुपस्थिति।

absolute / 'ऐब्सलूट् / *adj* 1 पूरा, संपूर्ण : *have absolute trust in a person* 2 असीमित; पूर्ण शक्तिमान : *absolute authority* ○ *an absolute ruler* 3 पक्का, असंदिग्ध : *have absolute proof* 4 स्वतंत्र रूप से विद्यमान ओर बिना किसी से संबंधित : *There is no absolute standard for beauty.*

absolutely / ˈऐब्सलूट्लि / *adv* 1 पूर्ण-तया, नितांत : *You're absolutely right.* 2 बिना प्रतिबंध के : *It's absolutely pouring.* 3 निश्चित रूप से : *'Don't you agree?' 'Oh, absolutely !'*

absolutism / ˈऐब्सलुटिज़्म्/ *noun* (राज) तानाशाही, निरंकुशता।

absolve / अब्ˈज़ॉल्व् / *verb* **absolve sb (from/of sth)** (औप) अपराध या पाप से मुक्त करना; निरपराध सिद्ध करना : *The inquiry absolved the driver (of all responsibility for the accident).*

absorb / अब्ˈसॉर्ब् / *verb* 1 सोख लेना, अवशोषित करना : *Plants absorb oxygen.* 2 अपने में मिला लेना, आत्मसात् करना, अंतर्लीन करना : *The larger firm gradually absorbed its smaller competitors.* 3 तन्मय या तल्लीन होना : *His business absorbs him.* ▸ **absorbed** *adj* तल्लीन : *She seemed totally absorbed in her book.* **absorbent** *adj* अवशोषक, सोख लेने वाला **absorbing** *adj* पूर्णतः तल्लीन करने वाला : *an absorbing film* **absorption** / अब्ˈसॉर्प्श्न्/ *noun* **absorption (in sth)** अवशोषण, तन्मयता, तल्लीनता।

abstain / अब्ˈस्टेन् / *verb* **abstain (from sth)** 1 (औप या परि) परहेज़ रखना; अपने को संयम में रखना : *He has been advised to abstain from alcohol.* 2 मतदान न करने का निर्णय लेना : *At the last elections he abstained (from voting).* ▸ **abstainer** *noun* परहेज़ करने वाला, मद्यत्यागी।

abstention / अब्ˈस्टेन्श्न् / *noun* **abstention (from sth)** (मतदान में) तटस्थता; तटस्थ मत : *five votes in favour of the proposal, three against and two abstentions.*

abstinence / ˈऐब्स्टिनन्स् / *noun* **abstinence (from sth)** खाने-पीने एवं भोग-विलास से दूर रहने का आचरण ▸ **abstinent** *adj* संयमी, मिताहारी।

abstract¹ / ˈऐब्स्ट्रैक्ट् / *adj* 1 अमूर्त, निराकार : *We may talk of beautiful things, but beauty itself is abstract.* 2 सामान्य, किसी विशेष व्यक्ति / स्थिति पर आधारित नहीं : *talk about something in abstract terms* ▸ **abstractly** *adv* **abstract noun** *noun* भाववाचक संज्ञा।

abstract² / ˈऐब्स्ट्रैक्ट् / *noun* 1 अव्याव-हारिक गुण या विचार/भावना 2 सारांश, सार, संक्षेप : *an abstract of a lecture* ■ **in the abstract** सामान्य तौर पर, बिना किसी विशेष व्यक्ति / स्थिति के संदर्भ में : *Consider the problem in the abstract.*

abstract³ / ऐब्ˈस्ट्रैक्ट्/ *verb* 1 **abstract sth (from sth)** पृथक करना, सार निकाल-ना : *Two other points must be abstracted from the argument.* 2 संक्षिप्त करना, सार तैयार करना।

abstracted / ऐब्ˈस्ट्रैक्टिड् / *adj* पृथक; अनमना, ध्यान न देने वाला : *an abstracted gaze/smile* ▸ **abstractedly** *adv.*

abstraction / ऐब्ˈस्ट्रैक्श्न्/ *noun* पृथक-करण, सारांशन, सारग्रहण।

abstruse / ऐब्ˈस्ट्रूस्/ *adj* (औप) दुर्बोध, जिसका अर्थ या उत्तर छिपा हो, अव्यक्त।

absurd / अब्ˈसर्ड् / *adj* 1 बेतुका; अ-संगत : *What an absurd idea!* 2 मूर्खतापूर्ण, हास्यास्पद : *That uniform makes them look absurd.* ▸ **absurdity** *noun* बेतुकापन, असंगति **absurdly** *adv* मूर्खतापूर्वक **the absurd** *noun* [*sing*] बेतुकी या असंगत वस्तु/ विचार : *Some of his criticisms verge on the absurd.*

abundance / अˈबन्डन्स्/ *noun* [*sing*] बहुतायत, प्रचुरता, बाहुल्य, आधिक्य, बहु-लता : *There was good food in abundance.*

abundant / अˈबन्डन्ट् / *adj* पर्याप्त से

अधिक, प्रचुर : *an abundant supply of fruit* ▸ **abundantly** *adv.*

abuse¹ / अं'ब्यूस् / *noun* **1** अधिकार, पद आदि का दुरुपयोग : *an abuse of trust/privilege/authority* **2** दुष्प्रयोग : *drug/solvent abuse* **3** कुप्रथा : *put a stop to political abuses* **4** कठोर, बुरा और हानिजनक व्यवहार : *child/sex abuse*ᵒ *physical abuse of horses* **5** गाली, अपशब्द, दुर्वचन : *hurl (a stream/torrent of) abuses at sb.*

abuse² / अं'ब्यूज़् / *verb* **1** दुरुपयोग करना : *abuse sb's hospitality* **2** दुर्व्यवहार करना : *a hostel for abused and battered women* **3** गाली देना, भला-बुरा सुनाना : *Journalists had been threatened and abused.*

abusive / अं'ब्यूसिव् / *adj* अपमानजनक: *abusive language/remarks* ▸ **abusively** *adv.*

abysmal / अं'बिज़्मल् / *adj* (अनौप) एकदम घटिया : *live in abysmal conditions.*

abyss / अं'बिस् / *noun* बहुत गहरा गड्ढा (जिसका तला मालूम न पड़े) : *(अलं) an abyss of ignorance/despair.*

academic / ऐक'डेमिक् / *adj* **1** शैक्षिक, अध्ययन-अध्यापन संबंधी : *the academic year* **2** अव्यावहारिक, शास्त्रीय; पांडित्यपूर्ण: *The issue/question is purely academic.* ▸ **academic** *noun* विश्वविद्या-लय प्राध्यापक।

academician / अकैड'मिश्न्; *US* ऐकड 'मिश्न् / *noun* अकादमी का सदस्य।

academy / अ'कैडमि / *noun* (*pl* **academies**) **1** विशेष विषय या प्रयोजन के लिए उच्चतर अध्ययन का स्कूल/संस्थान : *a naval/military academy* **2** (प्राय: **Academy**) विद्वानों की समिति, अकादमी।

accede / अक्'सीड् / *verb* **accede (to sth)** (औप) **1** सहमति देना, किसी के अनुरोध को स्वीकार करना : *They will not*

lightly accede *to his request/demand.* **2** पद या कार्यभार ग्रहण करना : *accede to the chancellorship.*

accelerate / अक्'सेलेरेट् / *verb* **1** (वाहन या व्यक्ति) गति या चाल बढ़ाना : *He accelerated away from the traffic light.* **2** गतिशील बनाना, शीघ्र घटित करना : *accelerating the rate of growth* ▸ **acceleration** *noun* त्वरण, गतिवर्धन **accelerator** / अक्'सेलेरटर् / *noun* त्वरित करने का यंत्र, मोटरकार आदि की चाल बढ़ाने के लिए पुर्ज़ा।

accent / 'ऐक्सन्ट्; 'ऐक्सेन्ट् / *noun* **1** (बोलने में) शब्द के किसी अक्षर पर या वाक्य के कुछ शब्दों पर अधिक बल देना, बलाघात, स्वराघात: *In the word 'today' the accent is on the second syllable.* **2** किसी भाषा को बोलने का लहजा, उच्चारण : *speak English with a foreign accent* **3** किसी बात पर ज़ोर देना : *In all our products the accent is on quality.*

accentuate / अक्'सेन्चुएट् / *verb* अधिक महत्त्व या बल देना ▸ **accentuation** / अक्सेन्चु'एश्न् / *noun* स्वराघात; स्वरांकन।

accept / अक्'सेप्ट् / *verb* **1** (दी हुई वस्तु को) ग्रहण करना, लेना : *accept a gift / piece of advice* **2** पर्याप्त या अनुकूल समझ कर स्वीकार करना : *Will you accept a cheque?* **3** मंज़ूर करना, हामी भरना : *She offered me a lift so I accepted (it).* **4** ज़िम्मेदारी स्वीकार करना : *He accepts blame for the accident.* **5** **accept sth (as sth)** किसी बात को सत्य मानना, विश्वास कर लेना : *I cannot accept that he is to blame.*

acceptable / अक्'सेप्टब्ल् / *adj* स्वीकार्य, ग्राह्य : *socially acceptable behaviour* ▸ **acceptability** *noun* स्वीकार्यता।

acceptance / अक्'सेप्टन्स् / *noun*

1 मंजूरी, अनुमोदन, सहमति : *her grudging acceptance of his explanation* 2 स्वीकृति : *a short speech of acceptance.*

access / 'ऐक्सेस् / *noun* 1 **access (to sth)** प्रवेश-मार्ग, रास्ता : *The only access to the farmhouse is across the fields.* 2 **access (to sth/sb)** कुछ प्रयोग करने या किसी तक पहुँचने का अवसर या अधिकार : *Students must have access to a good library.*

accessible / अक्'सेसबल् / *adj* सुगम : *documents not accessible to the public* ▸ **accessibility** *noun* प्रवेश-अधिकार, सुगम्यता।

accession / ऐक्'सेश्न् / *noun* **accession (to sth)** 1 अधिकार या पद पर पहुँचना, पदग्रहण; आरोहण, राज्यारोहण : *celebrating the queen's accession (to the throne)* 2 अभिवृद्धि, बढ़ती; इस तरह की बढ़ोतरी का उदाहरण : *recent accessions to the art gallery.*

accessory / अक्'सेसरि / *noun* (*pl* **accessories**) 1 (प्राय: *pl*) सहायक, उपयोगी और अतिरिक्त (पर अनिवार्य नहीं) गौण साधन, उपसाधन : *bicycle accessories* 2 **accessory to sth** (*क़ानून*) अपराध में सहायक या साथी : *He was charged with being an accessory to the murder.*

accident / 'ऐक्सिडन्ट् / *noun* 1 दुर्घटना; दुर्घटनाग्रस्त होना : *be killed in a car/road accident* 2 आकस्मिक घटना, अप्रत्याशित घटना : *Their early arrival was just an accident.* ▸ **accident-prone** *adj* (क्षेत्र या व्यक्ति) दुर्घटना संभावित।

accidental / ऐक्सि'डेन्टल् / *adj* आकस्मिक, संयोगवश ▸ **accidentally** *adv* संयोग से; बिना जाने-बूझे; अनजाने में : *The carpet accidentally caught fire.*

acclaim / अ'क्लेम् / *verb* **acclaim sb/**

sth **(as sth)** (जय-जयकार से) स्वागत करना, प्रशंसा/अनुमोदन करना : *It was acclaimed as a great discovery.* ▸ **acclaim** *noun* प्रशंसा; साधुवाद : *The play received great critical acclaim.*

acclamation / ऐक्ल'मेश्न् / *noun* प्रशंसा या तृप्तिसूचक जयघोष; अभिनंदन : *She collected her prize amid great acclamation.*

acclimatize, -ise / अ'क्लाइमटाइज़् / *verb* **acclimatize (oneself/sb/sth) (to sth)** नए वातावरण, जलवायु का अभ्यस्त बनाना; स्वयं को नई परिस्थितियों के अनुकूल ढालना : *It takes many months to acclimatize (yourself) to life in the tropics.* ▸ **acclimatization, -isation** *noun* परिस्थिति-अनुकूलन।

accommodate / अ'कॉमडेट् / *verb* 1 आवास-स्थान देना, ठहराना : *The hotel can accommodate up to 500 guests.* 2 सुविधा या जगह होना : *The garden isn't big enough to accommodate livestock.* 3 (*औप*) ध्यान में रखना, समायोजित करना : *accommodate the special needs of minority groups* ▸ **accommodating** *adj* (व्यक्ति) सहायता देने के लिए तैयार; मिलनसार : *I found the officials extremely accommodating to foreign visitors.*

accommodation / अकॉम'डेश्न् / *noun* 1 आवास : *Wanted—furnished accommodation for a young married couple.* 2 **accommodations** [*pl*] (*US*) आवास; (कभी-कभी खाने की सुविधा सहित) आवासीय कमरे 3 (*औप*) समायोजन, समझौता : *It's a matter of mutual accommodation.*

accompaniment / अ'कम्पनिमन्ट् / *noun* **accompaniment (to sth)** 1 संलग्न वस्तु, आनुषंगिक वस्तु/यंत्र; साथ

में : *She made her speech to the accompaniment of loud laughter.* 2 (संगीत) संगत : *singing with a piano accompaniment* ▸ **accompanist** / अ'कम्पनिस्ट / *noun* संगतकार (संगीत में)।

accompany / अ'कम्पनि / *verb (pt, pp* **accompanied**) 1 (औप) (किसी के) साथ-साथ जाना या रहना : *He was accompanied on the expedition by his wife.* 2 साथ-साथ विद्यमान रहना या घटित होना : *strong winds accompanied by heavy rain* 3 साथ में जोड़ना, संलग्न करना : *Each application should be accompanied by a stamped addressed envelope.*

accomplice / अं'कम्प्लिस्; *US* अं'कॉम्-प्लिस् / *noun* (अपराध आदि में) सहायक, साथी, सहापराधी : *The police arrested him and his two accomplices.*

accomplish / अं'कम्प्लिश्; *US* अं'कॉम्-प्लिश् / *verb* सफलतापूर्वक पूरा या संपन्न करना : *I don't feel I've accomplished very much today.* ▸ **accomplished** *adj* कुशल; (विशेषतः संगीत, चित्रकला आदि कलाओं में) निपुण : *an accomplished young lady.*

accomplishment / अं'कम्प्लिश्मन्ट; *US* अं'कॉम्प्लिश्मन्ट/ *noun* 1 सफलतापूर्वक कार्य संपादन 2 उपलब्धि, प्राप्ति 3 दक्षता, प्रवीणता : *a poet of rare accomplishment.*

accord¹ / अं'कॉर्ड / *noun* औपचारिक समझौता, संधि (जैसे दो देशों के बीच) : *a peace accord* ■ **of one's own accord** स्वेच्छा से, अपनी ही इच्छा से **with one accord** सर्वसम्मति से : *With one accord they all stood up and cheered.*

accord² / अं'कॉर्ड / *verb* 1 **accord (with sth)** (औप) से मेल खाना, के अनुरूप होना : *This information does not accord with the evidence of earlier witnesses.* 2 **accord sth to sb** (औप) देना, प्रदान करना : *the powers accorded to the government.*

accordance / अं'कॉर्डन्स् / *noun* ■ **in accordance with sth** के अनुसार : *in accordance with sb's wishes.*

according / अं'कॉर्डिंङ् / **according to** *prep* 1 के अनुसार : *According to Jaya, you were in Allahabad last week.* 2 के अनुपात में : *salary according to qualifications and experience* ▸ **accordingly** *adv* 1 इस कारण से, अतः, इसलिए : *The cost of materials rose sharply last year. Accordingly, this increase was passed on to the consumer in higher prices.* 2 तदनुसार, के अनुसार : *I have told you the circumstances, so you must act accordingly.*

accordion / अं'कॉर्डिअन् / (**piano accordion** भी) *noun* दोनों हाथों से बजाया जाने वाला हार्मोनियम जैसा छोटा वाद्ययंत्र।

accost / अं'कॉस्ट् / *verb* अनिच्छुक व्यक्ति से बात करना, को संबोधित करना या टोकना : *She was accosted in the street by a complete stranger.*

account¹ / अं'काउन्ट् / *noun* 1 (संक्षि **a/c**) लेखा-जोखा, हिसाब-किताब : *The accounts show a profit of Rs 90,000.* 2 (बैंक में) खाता : *open/ close an account* 3 वर्णन, विवरण : *Don't believe the newspaper account* (*of what happened*). ■ **by/ from all accounts** जैसा कहा गया है उसके अनुसार **on account of sth; on this/that account** इस/उस कारण से **take account of sth; take sth into account** (किसी विशेष चीज़/परिणाम आदि को) ध्यान में रखना, महत्त्व देना : *You must take his age into* *account when you judge his performance.*

account² / अं'काउन्ट् / *verb* ■ **account for sth 1** स्पष्टीकरण देना; कारण बताना : *He has been asked to account for his conduct.* **2** कुछ निर्धारित मात्रा या अनुपात होना।

accountable / अं'काउन्टब्ल् / *adj* **accountable (to sb) (for sth)** उत्तरदायी, ज़िम्मेदार होना : *Who are you accountable to in the organization?* ▸ **accountability** *noun* उत्तरदायित्व, जवाबदेही : *proposals for greater accountability on part of the police.*

accountant / अं'काउन्टन्ट् / *noun* एकाउंटेंट, लेखाकार, मुनीम ▸ **accountancy** *noun* लेखाकर्म, लेखाविधि।

accredit / अ'क्रेडिट् / *verb* (औप) **1 accredit sb to...** प्राधिकृत करना, (दूत को) अधिकार-पत्र के साथ भेजना : *He was accredited to Madrid.* **2 accredit sth to sb/accredit sb with sth** किसी को कुछ कहने/करने के लिए ज़िम्मेदार समझना ▸ **accredited** *adj* प्रामाणिक, सरकारी तौर पर नियुक्त : *our accredited representative.*

accrue / अ'क्रू / *verb* **accrue (to sb) (from sth)** बढ़ना; बढ़ाना; समय के दौरान वृद्धि : *Interest will accrue if you keep your money in a savings account.*

accumulate / अं'क्यूमुलेट् / *verb* **1** इकट्ठा करना, संचित करना : *I seem to have accumulated a lot of books.* **2** मात्रा में बढ़ जाना, जमा हो जाना : *Dust and dirt soon accumulate if a house is not cleaned regularly.* ▸ **accumulation** / अ'क्यूम्यु'लेश्न् / *noun* ढेर, समूह, जमा; संचय : *the accumulation of wealth/debt* **accumulative** *adj.*

accuracy / 'ऐक्यरसि / *noun* परिशुद्धि,

यथार्थता : *doubt the accuracy of government statistics.*

accurate / 'ऐक्यरट् / *adj* **1** (काम करने में) सावधान, यथार्थ और सही : *Journalists are not always accurate in what they write.* **2** त्रुटिहीन, सही : *an accurate clock/map* ▸ **accurately** *adv* ठीक-ठीक।

accusation / 'एक्यु'ज़ेश्न् / *noun* **1** दोषारोपण, इल्ज़ाम लगाने की प्रक्रिया : *There was a hint of accusation in her voice.* **2** अभियोग, अभियोजन : *Accusations of corruption have been made/brought/laid against him.*

accusative / अं'क्यूज़टिव् / *adj, noun* (व्या) कर्मकारक; द्वितीया विभक्ति : *The accusative forms of the pronouns 'I', 'we' and 'she' are 'me', 'us' and 'her'.*

accuse / अं'क्यूज़् / *verb* **accuse sb (of sth)** (किसी व्यक्ति को) दोषी ठहराना, आरोप लगाना : *accuse sb of theft/murder* ▸ **accusatory** / अं'क्यूज़टरि; ,एक्यु'ज़ेटरि; *US* ,एक्यु'ज़ेटॉरि / *adj* अभियोगात्मक **accusing** *adj* दोषपूर्ण : *a slightly accusing look/stare/face* **the accused** *noun* (*pl* अपरिवर्तित) (न्यायालय में) अभियुक्त, दोषी व्यक्ति, अपराधी।

accustom / अं'कस्टम् / *verb* ■ **accustom oneself/sb to sth** किसी चीज़ की आदत डालना, अभ्यस्त बनना : *He quickly accustomed himself to this new way of life.* ▸ **accustomed** *adj* अभ्यस्त, आदी; सामान्य : *I soon became/got accustomed to his strange ways.*

ace / एस् / *noun* **1** (ताश में) इक्का **2** (अनौप) अपने क्षेत्र में सर्वश्रेष्ठ व्यक्ति।

ache / एक् / *noun* दर्द, पीड़ा, वेदना या शूल : *He has an ache in his chest.* ○ *backache* ○ *toothache* ○ *head-*

ache ▸ **ache** *verb* 1 दर्द होना, टीसना, शूल होना : *My head aches/is aching.* 2 **ache for sb/sth** लालायित होना, तीव्र लालसा रखना, उत्कंठित होना : *He was aching for home.*

achieve / अ'चीव़् / *verb* 1 मान्य/लक्ष्य आदि प्राप्त करना (विशेषतः बल, मेहनत, साहस आदि द्वारा) : *achieve success/ peace of mind* 2 सफल होना; अच्छा प्रदर्शन करना ▸ **achievable** *adj* प्राप्त करने योग्य, प्राप्य **achievement** *noun* 1 संपादित कार्य, विशेषतः प्रयास और निपुणता से किया गया; उपलब्धि : *the greatest scientific achievement of the decade* 2 कुछ सफलतापूर्वक करने की प्रक्रिया : *celebrate the achievement of one's aims.*

Achilles / अ'किलीज़् / *noun* ■ **an/ one's Achilles' heel** व्यक्ति के चरित्र का कमज़ोर बिंदु जिसका कोई फ़ायदा उठा सकता हो।

acid / 'ऐसिड् / *noun* (रसा)अम्ल, तेज़ाब : *Some acids burn holes in wood.* ▸ **acid** *adj* 1 खट्टा, तीखा, चटपटा : *Vinegar has an acid taste.* 2 (**acidic** भी) (रसा) अम्लीय, अम्ल के गुण वाला पदार्थ **acidity** *noun* खट्टापन, अम्लता, गैस रहना (पेट में) : *suffer from acidity of the stomach.*

acknowledge / अक्'नॉलिज़् / *verb* 1 (किसी चीज़ को) क़बूलना, मान लेना, (सत्यता) स्वीकार करना : *She refused to acknowledge what had happened.* 2 प्राप्ति सूचना या पावती भेजना : *acknowledge (receipt of) a letter* 3 आभार मानना, धन्यवाद ज्ञापन करना : *He is always ready to acknowledge his debt to his teachers.* 4 अभिवादन करके या मुस्कराकर पहचान प्रदर्शित करना : *I was standing right next to her but she didn't even acknowledge me.* ▸ **acknowledgement (acknowl-**

edgment भी) *noun* 1 मानने/स्वीकार करने की क्रिया 2 पाने की सूचना; स्वीकृति; पावती : *I didn't receive an acknowledgement of my application.* 3 लेखक द्वारा धन्यवाद ज्ञापन, आभारकथन : *a page of acknowledgements.*

acne / 'ऐक्नि / *noun* मुँहासा।

acorn / 'ऐकॉर्न् / *noun* बलूत के पेड़ का फल।

acoustic / अं'कूस्टिक्/ *adj* श्रवण-विषयक, ध्वनि-विषयक : *the acoustic proper- ties of the music room* ▸ **acoustics** *noun* 1 [pl] (**acoustic** [sing] भी) सभा-भवन आदि का श्रवण गुण जो ध्वनि एवं गुंजन की दृष्टि से अच्छा या बुरा हो : *The acoustics of the new concert hall are excellent.* 2 ध्वनि का वैज्ञानिक अध्ययन।

acquaint / अ'क्वेन्ट् / *verb* **acquaint sb/oneself with sth** (औप) परिचित होना या करना; जानकारी प्राप्त करना : *Please acquaint me with the facts of the case.* ▸ **acquainted** *adj* **ac- quainted (with sb)** व्यक्तिगत रूप से परिचित होना : *I am not acquainted with the lady.*

acquaintance / अ'क्वेन्टन्स् / *noun* 1 **acquaintance with sth** जानकारी, परिचय : *I have little acquaintance with the Japanese language.* 2 **acquaintance (with sb)** हलकी मैत्री 3 परिचित व्यक्ति परंतु घनिष्ठ मित्र नहीं : *He has a wide circle of acquaint- ances.*

acquiesce / ऐक्वि'एस् / *verb* **acqui- esce in sth** (औप) बिना विरोध किए कुछ भी मानने को सहमत होना : *Her parents will never acquiesce (in such an unsuitable marriage).*

acquire / अं'क्वाइर्/ *verb* (औप) 1 अर्जित करना; योग्यता, दक्षता आदि से कुछ पाना : *acquire a good knowledge of*

English 2 पाना, प्राप्त करना : *The company has just acquired a further 5% of the shares.* ■ **an acquired taste** अभ्यास से अर्जित रुचि : *Abstract art is an acquired taste.*

acquisition / ˌऐकि'ज़िश्न् / *noun* 1 अधिग्रहण, कौशल-अर्जन की क्रिया : *acquisition of knowledge* 2 अर्जित वस्तु: *the library's most recent acquisitions.*

acquisitive / अ'क्विज़टिव् / *adj* (प्रायः अपमा) अर्जन की लालसा रखने वाला; संग्रहणशील।

acquit / अ'क्विट् / *verb* (-tt-) **acquit sb (of sth)** (क़ानून) निर्दोष ठहराना; रिहा करना : *The jury acquitted him of (the charge of) murder.* ▸ **acquittal** / अ'क्विट्ल् / *noun* (क़ानून) दोषमोचन, छुटकारा : *Lack of evidence resulted in their acquittal.*

acre / एकर् / *noun* एकड़, लगभग 4,050 वर्गमीटर का भूखंड ▸ **acreage** / 'एक-रिज़् / *noun* भूमि की एकड़ में नाप।

acrimony / 'ऐक्रिमनि ; *US* 'ऐक्रिमोनि / *noun* (औप) (व्यवहार, स्वभाव, बातचीत आदि में) रुखाई, कटुता : *The dispute was settled without acrimony.* ▸ **acrimonious** / ˌऐक्रि'मोनिअस् / *adj* (औप) (वाद-विवाद आदि) क्रोध एवं कटुता युक्त : *an acrimonious meeting.*

acrobat / 'ऐक्रबैट् / *noun* नट, कलाबाज़ ▸ **acrobatic** / ˌऐक्र'बैटिक् / *adj* नट विष-यक, कलाबाज़ी संबंधी **acrobatics** *noun* [*pl*] कलाबाज़ी।

acronym / 'ऐक्रनिम् / *noun* शब्दों के आदि-अक्षरों से बना संक्षिप्त शब्द जैसे *WHO* यानि *World Health Organization.*

across¹ / अ'क्रॉस् / *adv* *part* उस पार; आर-पार; आड़े-तिरछे : *Can you swim across?* ○ *I helped the blind man*

across. ○ *The river is half a mile across.* ▸ **across from** *prep* (*US*) सामने : *Just across from our house there's a school.*

across² / अ'क्रॉस् / *prep* 1 एक ओर से दूसरी ओर : *walk across the street* 2 दूसरी तरफ़, परली तरफ़ : *My house is just across the street.* 3 हर तरफ़, सब ओर: *an interview broadcast across the world.*

acrylic / अ'क्रिलिक् / *adj* एक्रिलिक, स्वे-टर या कपड़ों में प्रयुक्त पालीमर।

act¹ / ऐक्ट् / *noun* 1 कार्य, कर्म : *It is an act of kindness to help a blind man across the street.* 2 संसद द्वारा पारित क़ानून, अधिनियम 3 (अनौप) स्वाँग, ढोंग, अभिनय : *Don't take him seriously— it's all an act.* 4 नाटक का अंक : *a play in five acts* 5 (मनोरंजक) प्रदर्शन: *a circus/song and dance act.*

act² / ऐक्ट् / *verb* 1 करना, कार्य करना, कोई क्रिया करना : *The time for talking is past: we must act at once.* 2 कर्तव्य पूरा करना : *The police refused to act until they had more evidence.* 3 अभिनय करना : *Who is acting (the part of) Hamlet?* ■ **act as sb/sth** किसी अन्य का/अन्य के स्थान पर कार्य करना : *I don't understand their language, you'll have to act as interpreter.* **act for/on behalf of sb** किसी अन्य के बदले में काम करना **act on/upon sth** फलस्वरूप कार्य करना; कुछ प्रभाव छोड़ना : *Acting on the information received, the police raided the club.* **act sth out** किसी ख़ास मतलब से वास्तविक जीवन में अभिनय करना : *She acted out the role of wronged lover to make him feel guilty.*

acting / ऐक्टिङ् / *noun* अभिनय करने की कला या व्यवसाय ▸ **acting** *adj* कार्य-कारी, दूसरे के कार्यभार को अस्थायी

रूप से संभालने वाला : *the acting manager.*

action / 'ऐक्शन् / *noun* **1** गतिविधि, क्रिया; शक्ति या प्रभाव आदि को काम में लाना : *The time has come for action.* ○ *a man of action* (कर्मठ व्यक्ति) **2** किया हुआ कार्य : *Her quick action saved his life.* **3** क्रियाविधि, कार्यशैली: *study the action of the liver* **4** (क़ानून) न्यायालय में कार्रवाई चलाना, वाद : *a court action* ■ **actions speak louder than words** (कहा) बातों से कर्म ज़्यादा महत्त्वपूर्ण है **into action** व्यवहार में लाना : *put a plan into action* **out of action** काम के लायक न होना, बेकार : *This machine is out of action.*

activate / 'ऐक्टिवेट् / *verb* सक्रिय करना, क्रियाशील बना देना : *The gene is activated by a specific protein.*

active / 'ऐक्टिव् / *adj* **1** सक्रिय; क्रियाशील : *an active volcano* **2** फुरतीला, चपल **3** असरदार, प्रभावशाली **4** (व्या) कर्तृवाचक जैसे '*He was driving the car.*' में ▸ **actively** *adv* सक्रियता से : *Your proposal is being actively considered.*

activist / 'ऐक्टिविस्ट् / *noun* सक्रिय कार्यकर्ता : *anti-nuclear/feminist activists.*

activity / ऐक्'टिवटि / *noun* (*pl* **activities**) **1** सक्रियता, क्रियाशीलता : *electrical/volcanic activity* **2** क्रियाकलाप, गतिविधि, व्यवसाय : *The house has been full of activity all day.*

actor / 'ऐक्टर् / *noun* **1** (रंगमंच, फ़िल्म आदि में) अभिनेता; पात्र।

actress / 'ऐक्ट्रस् / *noun* अभिनेत्री।

actual / 'ऐक्चुअल/ *adj* असली, वास्तविक; यथार्थ : *What were his actual words?* ▸ **actually** *adv* वास्तव में, वस्तुत:, सच-मुच में : *What did he actually say?*

actuality / ऐक्चु'ऐलटि / *noun* **1** सचाई,

असलियत, वास्तविकता : *In actuality, I knew about the plan already.* **2** **actualities** [*pl*] वर्तमान परिस्थितियाँ, वास्तविकताएँ: *the grim actualities of prison life.*

acumen / 'ऐक्यमन; अ'क्यूमन/ *noun* विदग्धता, कुशाग्र बुद्धि : *business acumen.*

acupuncture / 'ऐक्युपङ्क्चर् / *noun* (चिकि) शरीर में बारीक सूइयों से छेद करके रोग ठीक करने का उपाय, ऐक्युपंक्चर (चीन में प्रचलित एक चिकित्सा पद्धति)।

acute / अ'क्यूट् / *adj* **1** बहुत अधिक, घोर : *suffer acute hardship* **2** (भाव, संवेदन) तीक्ष्ण, प्रखर, तेज़ : *Dogs have an acute sense of smell.* **3** (बुद्धि, समझ) कुशाग्र, तीव्र; होशियार (व्यक्ति) : *He is an acute observer of the social scene.* **4** (बीमारी, रोग आदि) प्रचंड, निर्णायक चरण पर : *acute appendicitis* ▸ **acute angle** *noun* (ज्यामिति) 90° से कम का कोण, न्यूनकोण **acutely** *adv* तीव्रता से **acuteness** *noun* तीक्ष्णता।

AD / ‚ऐ'डी / *abbr* (लैटिन **anno domini** का संक्षिप्त रूप) ईसवी सन् : *in (the year) 1998 AD* → **BC** देखिए।

ad / ऐड् / *noun* (अनौप) = **advertisement.**

Adam / 'ऐडम् / *noun* आदि पुरुष; आदम ▸ **Adam's apple** *noun* गले के बीच में हड्डी का उभार।

adamant / 'ऐडमन्ट् / *adj* अपने निर्णय पर दृढ़, अटल : *an adamant refusal* ▸ **adamantly** *adv.*

adapt / अ'डैप्ट् / *verb* **1 adapt sth (for sth)** (नए काम में लाने के लिए) फेर बदल कर अनुकूल बनाना : *This machine has been specially adapted for use under water.* **2 adapt sth (for sth) (from sth)** के लिए रूपांतरित करना : *This novel has been adapted for radio from the Marathi original.* **3 adapt**

(oneself) (to sth) (स्वयं को) परिस्थिति अनुसार अनुकूलित करना : She adapted herself quickly to the new climate.

▶ adaptable adj अनुकूलनीय adaptability noun अनुकूलनशीलता adaptation / ऐडैप्'टेश्न् / noun अनुकूलन।

add / ऐड् / verb 1 add A and B together; add A to B (दो या अनेक संख्याओं को) जोड़ना, योग करना या योग निकालना : If you add 5 and 5 (together) you get 10. 2 add sth (to sth) (एक को दूसरे में) मिलाना, मात्रा बढ़ाना : If the tea is too strong, add some more water. ■ add fuel to the flames क्रोधाग्नि को और भड़काना add insult to injury जले पर नमक छिड़कना add to sth बढ़ाना : The bad weather only added to our difficulties. add up (अनौप) तर्कसंगत लगना, ठीक प्रतीत होना : His story just doesn't add up—he must be lying. add up to sth कुल होना, के बराबर होना : The numbers add up to exactly 100.

addendum / अ'ड्रेन्डम् / noun (pl addenda / अ'ड्रेन्डा /) सूची जिसमें मुख्य भाग से छूटी सूचनाएँ दी जाती हैं (प्रायः अंत में)।

adder / ऐडर् / noun एक छोटा ज़हरीला साँप, गेहुँअन।

addict / ऐडिक्ट् / noun व्यसनी, नशीली वस्तुएँ सेवन करने का आदी व्यक्ति : a heroin addict ▶ addicted / अ'डिक्टिड् / adj addicted (to sth) 1 व्यसनी, आसक्त : addicted to tobacco 2 किसी रुचि में अधिक समय गुज़ारना : be hopelessly addicted to computer games addiction noun व्यसन, लत, आसक्ति।

addition / अ'डिश्न् / noun 1 जोड़ने की क्रिया, संयोजन : children learning addition and subtraction 2 addition (to sth) योग, जोड़; वृद्धि : They've just had an addition to the family. ○ the latest addition to our range of furniture ▶ additional / अ'डि-शन्ल् / adj अतिरिक्त : additional resources additionally adv के अतिरिक्त/अलावा; अधिकतर।

additive / 'ऐडिटिव् / noun विशेष उद्देश्य से थोड़ी मात्रा में मिलाया गया पदार्थ; मिश्रित पदार्थ : additive-free orange juice.

address¹ / अ'ड्रेस्; US 'ऐड्रेस् / noun 1 पता, ठिकाना 2 भाषण, अभिभाषण : tonight's televised presidential address.

address² / अ'ड्रेस् / verb 1 भाषण देना : The chairman will now address the meeting. 2 address sth (to sb/sth) पता लिखना (चिट्ठी आदि पर) : The letter was wrongly addressed to our old home. 3 address sb as sth संबोधित करना : How should I address the judge? 4 address sth to sb/sth (औप) लिखित या मौखिक संदेश देना या शिकायतें आदि लिखना : Please address all enquiries to this office.

▶ addressee / ऐड्रे'सी / noun पाने वाला, प्रेषिती।

adept / अ'ड्रेप्ट् / adj adept (at/in sth/doing sth) कुशल, दक्ष, निपुण : an adept ball player.

adequate / 'ऐडिक्वट् / adj adequate (to/for sth) काफ़ी, पर्याप्त; अभीष्ट गुणों से युक्त; समुचित : adequate car parking facilities ▶ adequacy / 'ऐडि-क्वसि / noun पर्याप्तता; उपयुक्तता : He questioned the adequacy of the security arrangements. adequately adv पर्याप्त रूप से।

adhere / अड्'हिअर् / verb 1 adhere (to sth) चिपके रहना, जुड़ जाना, संसक्त होना : The gold leaf will adhere to any clean metal surface. 2 किसी का साथ देते रहना; किसी विचारधारा का अनुसरण

करते रहना : *adhere strictly to the terms of a treaty/to a schedule.*

adherent / अड्'हिअरन्ट् / *noun* (किसी दल/संघ या विचारधारा का) अनुचर (व्यक्ति), समर्थक ▸ **adherence** / अड्'हिअरन्स् / *noun* जुड़ाव, संसक्ति; निष्ठा, समर्थन।

adhesion / अड्'हीश़न् / *noun* 1 **adhesion (to sth)** चिपकाव, जुड़ाव, आसंजन 2 (औप) योजना आदि के लिए समर्थन, निष्ठा।

adhesive / अड्'हीसिव् / *adj* चिपचिपा, चिपकने वाला : *the adhesive side of a stamp* ▸ **adhesive** *noun* आसंजन-शील पदार्थ, गोंद।

ad hoc / ,ऐड् 'हॉक् / *adj, adv* 1 किसी विशेष कार्य के लिए बनाया गया; तदर्थ (नियुक्ति) 2 ज़रूरत के अनुसार होने वाला, अनौपचारिक : *Problems were solved on an ad hoc basis.*

adieu / अं'ड्यू; *US* अं'डू / *interj* (प्रा या साहि) विदाई, विदाई के समय का अभि-वादन : *bid sb adieu.*

ad infinitum / ,ऐड् 'इन्फ़ि'नाइटम् / *adv* (लैटिन) निरवधि, अनंत तक।

adjacent / अं'जेसन्ट् / *adj* **adjacent (to sth)** निकटवर्ती, सन्निकट; पड़ोस या बग़ल में स्थित : *We work in adjacent rooms.* ▸ **adjacent angles** *noun* [pl] (ज्या-मिति) आसन्न/संलग्न कोण।

adjective / 'ऐजिक्टिव् / *noun* (व्या) विशेषण ▸ **adjectival** / ,ऐजे़क्'टाइवल् / *adj* विशेषणात्मक, विशेषणयुक्त।

adjoin / अं'जॉइन् / *verb* बहुत पास होना; साथ लगा हुआ होना : *The playing-field adjoins the school.*

adjourn / अं'जर्न् / *verb* 1 किसी बैठक या कार्य को कुछ निश्चित समय के लिए स्थगित करना : *The trial was adjourned for a week.* 2 कुछ समय के लिए कार्य रोक देना : *The court will adjourn for lunch.* ▸ **adjournment** *noun* स्थगन।

adjudicate / अं'जूडिकेट् / *verb* 1 **adju-**

dicate (between/on sth) (औप) (अदालत द्वारा) निर्णय देना, फ़ैसला सुनाना 2 किसी प्रतियोगिता में निर्णायक के रूप में कार्य करना : *We would like you to adjudicate at the local flower show.* ▸ **adjudication** / अ,जूडि'केश़न् / *noun* (औप) न्यायनिर्णय, अधि-निर्णय निर्णयादेश : *The case was referred to a higher court for adjudication.*

adjudicator *noun* न्यायनिर्णायक, किसी प्रतियोगिता आदि में जज।

adjunct / 'ऐजङ्क्ट् / *noun* 1 **adjunct (to/of sth)** अनुबंधक, अनुलग्नक : *The scheme was designed as an adjunct to existing health care facilities.* 2 (व्या) अनुबंध।

adjust / अं'जस्ट् / *verb* **adjust (one-self/sth) (to sth)** समायोजित/अनुकूलित करना : *The body quickly adjusts itself to changes in temperature.* ▸ **adjustable** *adj* समंजनीय, समायोज्य : *The height of the chair is adjustable.* **adjustment** *noun* सामंजस्य, समायोजन, समाधान : *a period of emotional adjustment* ○ *I've made a few minor adjustments to the seating plan.*

ad lib / ,ऐड् 'लिब् / *adj, adv* (अनौप) (विशेषकर जनता में बोलने या भाषण करने में) बिना पूर्व तैयारी के; स्वत: प्रवाह में : *He spoke entirely ad lib.*

administer / अड्'मिनिस्टर् / *verb* 1 प्रबंध या व्यवस्था करना; संचालन या देखभाल करना; नियंत्रित करना : *administer a charity/a school/a project* 2 (औप) (क़ानून आदि) प्रयुक्त करना, लागू करना : *administer the law.*

administration / अड्,मिनि'स्ट्रेश़न् / *noun* 1 प्रबंध, संचालन : *the day-to-day administration of a company* 2 प्रशासन, शासन-तंत्र, सरकार : *Succes-*

sive administrations failed to solve the country's economic problems.
▸ **administrative**/ अड्'मिनिस्ट्रटिव़्; US अड्'मिनिस्ट्रेटिव़् / *adj* प्रशासनिक, प्रबंध-कीय : *an administrative post* **administratively** *adv* **administrator** *noun* प्रशासक, प्रबंधक।

admirable / 'ऐड्मरबल् / *adj* (औप) प्रशंसनीय, अत्युत्तम ▸ **admirably** *adv* उत्तम रीति से।

admiral / 'ऐड्मरल् / *noun* ऐडमिरल, नौ-सेना अध्यक्ष।

admiration /,ऐड्म'रेशन् / *noun* **admiration (for sb/sth)** आह्लाद, संतृप्ति और आदर की भावना; श्लाघा : *I have great admiration for his courage.*

admire / अड्'माइअर् / *verb* **admire sb/sth (for sth)** आह्लाद और समादर की दृष्टि से देखना; पसंद करना : *We've been admiring your garden.* ▸ **admirer** *noun* प्रशंसक।

admissible /अड्'मिसबल्/ *adj* स्वीकृति/अनुमति देने लायक; ग्राह्य : *Such behaviour is not admissible among our staff.* ▸ **admissibility** *noun* ग्राह्यता।

admission / अड्'मिशन् / *noun* **1 admission (to sth)** प्रवेश, भर्ती : *Admission to university depends on examination results.* **2 admission (of sth); admission (that...)** स्वीकृति; स्वीकरण : *Her resignation amounts to an admission of failure.*

admit / अड्'मिट् / *verb* (-tt-) **1 admit sb/sth (to sth)** प्रवेश करने देना, आने देना; (कक्षा/अस्पताल आदि में) भर्ती करना : *Each ticket admits two people to the party.* **2 admit to sth/doing sth** क़बूलना, स्वीकार करना : *I admit my mistake/ (that) I was wrong.* **3 admit of sth** (औप) (संदेह आदि की) गुंजाइश रखना : *The question admits of only one answer.* ▸ **admittedly**

adv बिना इनकार के; निस्संदेह; सर्वसम्मति से : *The plan, admittedly, is not without its difficulties.*

admittance / अड्'मिट्न्स् / *noun* **admittance to sth** (किसी स्थान में) प्रवेश करने की अनुमति; अंदर जाने का अधिकार।

admonish / अड्'मॉनिश् / *verb* (औप) **admonish sb (for sth/doing sth)** (औप) हल्की-सी चेतावनी देना, सावधान करना : *He was frequently admonished by his teachers.* ▸ **admonition** /,ऐड्म'निश्न् / *noun* (औप) चेतावनी, भर्त्सना, डाँट-फटकार : *a letter full of the gravest admonitions.*

adolescence /,ऐड्'लेसन्स् / *noun* किशोरावस्था : *a happy childhood and adolescence* ▸ **adolescent** /,ऐड्'लेसन्ट् / *noun* किशोर, 13-17 वर्ष का लड़का या लड़की।

adopt / अ'डॉप्ट् / *verb* **1** किसी बच्चे को क़ानूनन गोद लेना : *As they had no children of their own, they were hoping to adopt an orphan.* **2** किसी विधि को अपनाना, अंगीकार करना : *adopt an idea/a style of dress* **3** विशेषत: औपचारिक रूप से प्रस्ताव आदि स्वीकार करना : *Parliament voted to adopt the new measures.* ▸ **adoption** *noun* दत्तक ग्रहण; अंगीकरण।

adorable / अ'डॉरबल् / *adj* आराधना योग्य; अति आकर्षक, प्यारा : *Your dress is absolutely adorable.*

adore / अ'डॉर् / *verb* **1** बहुत प्यार और आदर देना **2** (अनौप) बहुत पसंद करना : *I simply adore that dress!* ▸ **adoration** /,ऐड'रेशन् / *noun* आराधना, श्रद्धा; प्यार।

adorn / अ'डॉर्न् / *verb* **adorn sth/sb/oneself (with sth)** शृंगार करना; शोभा बढ़ाना : *admire the paintings that adorn the walls* ▸ **adornment** *noun* सजावट, शृंगार, अलंकरण।

adrenalin / अ'ड्रेनलिन् / noun (चिकि) क्रोधित, उत्तेजित आदि होने के कारण अधिवृक्क ग्रंथि द्वारा स्रावित हॉर्मोन।

adrift / अ'ड्रिफ़्ट् / adj (जहाज़, नाव आदि) बिना नियंत्रण के तैरता : The survivors were adrift on a raft for six days.

adulation / ˌऐड्यु'लेश्न्; US ˌएज्'लेश्न् / noun ख़ुशामद, चाटुकारी।

adult / 'ऐडल्ट्; अ'डल्ट् / adj 1 वयस्क, बालिग 2 (क़ानून) शादी करने या मत दे सकने की आयु वाला ▶ **adult** noun वयस्क (व्यक्ति या जीव) **adulthood** noun वयस्क होने की अवस्था।

adulterate / अ'डल्टरेट् / verb किसी चीज़ में मिलावट करना : adulterated milk ▶ **adulteration** / अˌडल्ट'रेश्न् / noun मिलावट, अपमिश्रण।

adultery / अ'डल्टरि / noun पति या पत्नी से भिन्न व्यक्ति से अनैतिक (यौन) संबंध ▶ **adulterer** / अ'डल्टरर् / noun (fem **adulteress** / अ'डल्टरस् /) व्यभिचारी व्यक्ति (स्त्री या पुरुष)।

advance¹ / अड्'वान्स्; US अड्'वैन्स् / noun 1 प्रगति, विकास, उन्नति : the continued advance of civilization 2 **advance (in sth)** प्रगति, विकास आदि की घटना : recent advances in medical science 3 अग्रिम राशि, पेशगी : She asked for an advance on her salary. ■ **in advance (of sth)** समय से पहले : Send your luggage on in advance. ▶ **advance** adj अग्रिम, पहले से : give sb advance warning/ notice of sth.

advance² / अड्'वान्स्; US अड्'वैन्स् / verb 1 **advance (on/towards sb/ sth)** आगे रखना, आगे बढ़ना या बढ़ाना (प्राय: आक्रामक रूप से) : The general advanced his troops at night. ○ The mob advanced on/towards us shouting angrily. 2 (और) चर्चा के लिए विचार, सुझाव आदि प्रस्तुत करना,

सामने रखना : Scientists have advanced a new theory to explain this phenomenon. 3 प्रगति करना, उन्नति करना : Has civilization advanced in this century? 4 **advance sth (to sb)** अग्रिम राशि या पेशगी देना : He asked his employer to advance him a month's salary. 5 (किसी घटना या कार्यक्रम आदि की तारीख़ या समय को) पहले रखना, आगे कर देना : The date of the meeting has been advanced from 10 to 3 June. ▶ **advanced** adj 1 उच्च स्तर का 2 अंतिम चरणों में 3 प्रगतिशील, उन्नतिशील : have advanced ideas.

advancement / अड्'वान्स्मन्ट् / noun प्रगति, उन्नति : the advancement of learning.

advantage / अड्'वान्टिज्; US अड्'वैन्टिज् / noun 1 **advantage (over sb)** लाभ या फ़ायदे की स्थिति; अनुकूल या लाभदायक वस्तु : gain an advantage over an opponent 2 लाभ, फ़ायदा : Is there any advantage in learning Sanskrit nowadays? ▶ **advantaged** adj अच्छी सामाजिक और वित्तीय स्थिति में होना : improve opportunities for the less advantaged groups **advantageous** / ˌऐड्वन्'टेजस् / adj **advantageous (to sb)** सहायक; उपयोगी; लाभदायक।

advent / 'ऐड्वेन्ट् / noun [sing] the **advent of sb/sth** (किसी महत्त्वपूर्ण व्यक्ति या घटना का) शुभागमन : the advent of modern technology.

adventure / अड्'वेन्चर् / noun 1 असाधारण, उत्तेजक और संकटपूर्ण कार्य/अनुभव: her adventures in Africa 2 साहस, जोखिम, ख़तरा : a life full of adventure ▶ **adventurer** / अड्'वेन्चरर् / noun (fem **adventuress**) साहसिक व्यक्ति, जोखिमभरे कार्य करने वाला; जीवट

वाला **adventurous** adj 1 ख़तरे उठाने, नए विचारों को परखने को तैयार : *More adventurous investors should look overseas.* 2 साहसिक, जोखिम उठाने को उत्सुक : *adventurous children* 3 जोखिम भरा, ख़तरनाक और उत्तेजनापूर्ण : *an adventurous trip/ life.*

adverb / 'ऐड्वर्ब् / noun (व्या) क्रिया-विशेषण ▸ **adverbial** / एड्'वर्बिअल् / adj क्रियाविशेषणात्मक।

adversary / 'ऐड्वर्सरि / noun (pl ad-versaries) किसी भी मामले में विरोधी ▸ **adversarial** adj विरोधात्मक; शत्रुतापूर्ण।

adverse / 'ऐड्वर्स; अड्'वर्स् / adj प्रति-कूल, विरुद्ध; हानिप्रद : *adverse weather conditions/winds* ▸ **adversely** adv प्रतिकूल रूप से : *His health was adversely affected by the climate.*

adversity / अड्'वर्सटि / noun (pl ad-versities) मुसीबत; विपत्ति; दुर्भाग्य : *re-main cheerful in adversity.*

advertise / 'ऐड्वर्टाइज़् / verb 1 विज्ञापन करना/देना : *advertise soap powder* 2 सार्वजनिक सूचना देना : *The post has been advertised.* ▸ **advertisement** / अड्'वर्टिस्मन्ट्; US ,ऐड्वर्'टाइज़्मन्ट् / noun (अनौप ad भी) **advertisement (for sb/sth)** विज्ञापन; सार्वजनिक सूचना : *If you want to sell your old sofa, why not put/place an advertise-ment in the local paper?* **adver-tiser** noun विज्ञापक।

advice / अड्'वाइस् / noun 1 परामर्श, राय, सम्मति : *act on/follow/take sb's advice* 2 (वाणिज्य) औपचारिक सूचना, संज्ञापन : *We received advice that the goods had been dispatched.*

advisable / अड्'वाइज़ब्ल् / adj **advis-able (to do sth)** उचित, उपयुक्त ▸ **ad-visability** noun औचित्य।

advise / अड्'वाइज़् / verb **advise (sb)**

against sth/doing sth; advise sb (on sth) सलाह या परामर्श देना; उपयुक्त बताना : *The doctor advised (me to take) a complete rest.* ▸ **adviser** (विशेषत: US **advisor** भी) noun **ad-viser (to sb) (on sth)** सलाहकार, परामर्श-दाता।

advisory / अड्'वाइज़रि / adj सलाहकारी, परामर्शी : *an advisory committee.*

advocacy / 'ऐड्वकसि / noun समर्थन, हिमायत; वकालत।

advocate / 'ऐड्वकेट् / verb (औप) (किसी बात की) वकालत करना; समर्थन करना : *I advocate a policy of gradual reform.* ▸ **advocate** noun 1 वकील, अधिवक्ता 2 **advocate (of sth)** समर्थन करने वाला व्यक्ति।

aegis / 'ईजिस् / noun ■ **under the aegis of sb/sth** के तत्त्वावधान में : *Medical supplies are being flown in under the aegis of the Red Cross.*

aerate / 'एअरेट् / verb हवा भरना, हवा में रखना; गैस भरना, तरल पदार्थ में कार्बन डाइऑक्साइड घोलना : *aerate the soil by digging it* ○ *aerated water.*

aerial / 'एअरिअल् / adj 1 वायवीय, आकाशीय, हवाई : *an aerial railway* 2 हवाई जहाज़ से, हवाई : *aerial bom-bardment/photography* ▸ **aerial** (US **antenna**) noun एरियल (जिससे रेडियो आदि तरंग ग्रहण करते हैं)।

aero- pref (पूर्वपद) वायु अथवा हवाई जहाज़ से संबंधित।

aerobics / एअ'रोबिक्स् / noun [pl] प्राणायाम पर आधारित शारीरिक व्यायाम।

aerodrome / 'एअरड्रोम् / noun (अप्र) छोटा हवाई-अड्डा।

aerodynamics / ,एअरोडाइ'नैमिक्स् / noun [pl] वायुगति शास्त्र।

aeronautics / ,एअर्'नॉटिक्स् / noun [pl] विमान शास्त्र।

aeroplane /'एअरप्लेन्/ (plane भी)(US airplane) noun हवाई जहाज़, वायुयान।

aerosol /'एअरसॉल्/ noun द्रव पदार्थों को दाब में रखकर और बहुत बारीक धार या फ़व्वारे के रूप में छिड़कने वाला यंत्र।

aerospace /'एअरोस्पेस / noun हवाई-जहाज़, अंतरिक्ष यान, मिसाइल आदि बनाने में प्रयुक्त प्रौद्योगिकी।

aesthete / 'ईस्थीट् / (US esthete /'एस्थीट्/ भी) noun (कभी-कभी अपमा) सौंदर्यसंवेदी, सौंदर्यवादी।

aesthetic / ईस्'थेटिक् / (US esthetic /एस्'थेटिक् / भी) adj सौंदर्यपरक, सौंदर्य-विषयक : an aesthetic sense ▸ aesthetics noun सौंदर्य शास्त्र; रस-सिद्धांत, रस शास्त्र।

afar / अं'फ़ार् / adv ■ from afar बहुत दूर से।

affable /'ऐफ़्ब्ल्/ adj मिलनसार, मित्रता-पूर्ण; अच्छे स्वभाव वाला (व्यक्ति) : He found her parents very affable. ▸ affability /,ऐफ़्'बिलटि/ noun सौ-जन्यतापूर्ण, मिलनसारिता affably /'ऐफ़्ब्लि/ adv.

affair / अं'फ़ेअर् / noun 1 [sing] मामला, विचारणीय विषय, कार्य; कार्य-कलाप : It's not my affair. 2 affairs [pl] निजी कार्य या व्यवसाय 3 सामाजिक एवं महत्त्वपूर्ण कार्य-कलाप/घटनाएँ : world affairs 4 [sing] घटना; सुघटित सामाजिक घटना/कार्य : The wedding was a very grand affair. 5 प्रेम संबंध : She's having an affair with her boss.

affect[1] / अं'फ़ेक्ट्/ verb 1 प्रभावित करना, असर डालना : The change in climate may affect your health. 2 दुख/सहानुभूति की भावना उभारना : We were deeply affected by the news of her death. 3 (बीमारी, रोग आदि) लग जाना, आक्रांत करना : Cancer had affected his lungs.

affect[2] / अं'फ़ेक्ट् / verb कुछ करने या होने का ढोंग रचाना, अभिनय करना : He affected an air of innocence. ▸ affected adj (प्राय: अपमा) बनावटी कृत्रिम, दिखावटी : an affected politeness.

affectation /,ऐफ़्क्'टेश्न् / noun (प्राय: अपमा) बनावटी व्यवहार या भावना : I detest all affectation.

affection / अं'फ़ेक्श्न् / noun affection (for sb/sth) अनुराग, स्नेह : He felt great affection for his sister. ▸ affectionate / अं'फ़ेक्शनट् / adj स्नेही, स्नेहशील : He is very affectionate towards his children. affectionately adv स्नेह से, प्रेम से।

affidavit / ऐफ़्'डेविट् / noun (क़ानून) सौगंध खाकर किसी तथ्य को (क़ानूनी रूप में) लिखित पत्र पर देना; हलफ़नामा, शपथ-पत्र।

affiliate / अं'फ़िलिएट् / verb affiliate sb/sth (to/with sb/sth) किसी संस्था की शाखा बनकर संबद्ध होना या सदस्यता स्वीकार करना : The college is affiliated to the university. ▸ affiliation /अ,फ़िलि 'एश्न् / noun संबद्धता।

affinity / अं'फ़िनटि / noun (pl affinities) affinity (for/with sb/sth); affinity (between A and B) घनिष्ठ संबंध, सजातीयता; सादृश्यता : There is (a) close affinity between Italian and Spanish. ○ Early man shows certain affinities with the ape.

affirm / अं'फ़र्म्/ verb (औप) निश्चय-पूर्वक या दृढ़तापूर्वक किसी बात को सच या सही बताना : She continued to affirm her innocence. ▸ affirmation /,ऐफ़र् 'मेश्न् / noun 1 कुछ निश्चयपूर्वक कहने की क्रिया; धारणा, विश्वास 2 (क़ानून) शपथ न लेने वाले व्यक्ति का औपचारिक कथन, अभिकथन।

affirmative / अं'फ़र्मटिव्/ adj स्वीकृति, हामी व्यक्त करते हुए (शब्द) : an af-

firmative reply/reaction ▸ **affirmatively** *adv.*

affix¹ /अं'फ़िक्स् / *verb* **affix sth (to/on sth)** (औप) संबद्ध करना, जोड़ना, अनुलग्न करना : *affix a stamp (to an envelope).*

affix² / 'ऐफ़िक्स् / *noun* (व्या) प्रत्यय या उपसर्ग।

afflict / अं'फ़्लिक्ट् / *verb* **afflict sb/sth (with sth)** दुख देना, सताना; पीड़ित करना : *She is afflicted with arthritis.* ▸ **affliction** / अं'फ़्लिक्श्न् / *noun* (औप) 1 दुख, वेदना, मनस्ताप 2 पीड़ा का कारण या अवसर।

affluent / 'ऐफ़्लुअन्ट् / *adj* समृद्ध; खुशहाल, धनाढ्य : *His parents were very affluent.* ▸ **affluence** / 'ऐफ़्लुअन्स् / *noun* बहुतायत; अमीरी; प्रवाह।

afford / अं'फ़ॉर्ड् / *verb* 1 खर्च कर सकना; पर्याप्त धन या समय निकाल सकना : *They walked because they could not afford (to take) a taxi.* 2 हानि या कष्ट उठाने की स्थिति में होना : *I can't afford to lose my job.* ▸ **affordable** / अं'फ़ॉर्डब्ल् / *adj.*

afforest / अं'फ़ॉरिस्ट् / *verb* वृक्ष लगाकर जंगल बनाना ▸ **afforestation** / अ,फ़ॉरि'स्टेश्न् / *noun* वनरोपण, वन लगाना।

affront / अं'फ़्रन्ट् / *noun* (प्रायः : *sing*) **affront to (sb/sth)** कथन या क्रिया जो खुले तौर पर अपमानजनक हो : *His speech was an affront to all decent members of the community.* ▸ **affront** *verb* जानबूझकर खुले तौर पर अपमान करना।

aflame / अं'फ़्लेम् / *adj* प्रज्वलित; प्रदीप्त : *The whole building was soon aflame.* ○ (अलं) *The woods were aflame with autumn colours.*

afloat / अं'फ़्लोट् / *adj* 1 द्रव पर तिरता हुआ : *The life-jacket kept him afloat.* 2 ऋणमुक्त या कठिनाइयों से मुक्त : *keep the economy afloat.*

afoot / अं'फ़ुट् / *adj* तैयार किया जा रहा; योजना बनाई जा रही : *Great changes are afoot.* ○ *He sensed that something was afoot.*

aforementioned / अ,फ़ॉर'मेन्शन्ड् / (**aforesaid** / अं'फ़ॉर्सेड् / भी) *adj* (औप) पूर्वकथित, पूर्वोल्लिखित : *The aforementioned person was acting suspiciously.*

afraid / अं'फ़्रेड् / *adj* 1 **afraid (of sb/sth); afraid (of doing sth/to do sth)** डरा हुआ, भयभीत : *Are you afraid of snakes?* 2 **afraid of doing sth; afraid (that) ...** संभावित परिणाम, प्रभाव आदि के बारे में सशंकित : *I didn't mention it because I was afraid of upsetting him.* ■ **I'm afraid (that)...** कुछ न कर पाने/न होने की अभिव्यक्ति का नम्र ढंग : *I'm afraid we can't come.*

afresh / अं'फ़्रेश् / *adv* फिर से, दुबारा, नए सिरे से : *Let's start afresh.*

after¹ / 'आफ़्टर; *US* 'ऐफ़्टर / *prep* 1 पश्चात्, बाद में : *leave after lunch* ○ *the day after tomorrow* 2 क्रम से अगला, परवर्ती : *C comes after B in the alphabet.* 3 के पीछे, की तलाश में : *The police are after him.* 4 पीछे : *Shut the door after you when you go out.* 5 किसी की ओर : *The boys stared after us.* 6 (आश्चर्य दर्शाते हुए) के बावजूद; सब होते हुए भी : *After everything I've done for him, he still ignores me.* 7 (अनौप) उत्कंठा से किसी चीज़ को प्राप्त करने की कोशिश में : *She's after a job in publishing.* 8 बारे में, के विषय में : *They inquired after you.* 9 के नाम पर; की शैली में : *We've named the baby after you.* ○ *a painting after Rubens* 10 **sth after sth** बारंबार, बार-बार : *day after day/week after week* ■ **after all** के बावजूद, आखिरकार : *So you've come after all!*

after² / 'आफ़्टर; US 'ऐफ़्टर / conj (समय की दृष्टि से) बाद में; के बाद : *I arrived after he (had) started.*

after³ / 'आफ़्टर; US 'ऐफ़्टर / adv (समय की दृष्टि से) बाद में, पीछे, पश्चात् : *They lived happily ever after.*

aftermath / 'आफ़्टरमैथ; US 'ऐफ़्टरमैथ / noun (प्राय: sing) परिणाम (विशेषत: किसी दुर्घटना के बाद) : *the rebuilding which took place in the aftermath of the war.*

afternoon / ,आफ़्टर'नून; US ,ऐफ़्टर'नून / noun तीसरा पहर, अपराह्न : *in/during the afternoon.*

aftershave / 'आफ़्टरशेव; US 'ऐफ़्टरशेव/ noun शेव (हजामत) के बाद चेहरे पर लगाने वाला सुगंधित द्रव।

afterthought / 'आफ़्टरथॉट; US 'ऐफ़्टर-थॉट/ noun अनुबोध, घटना के बाद दिमाग़ में उठा विचार।

afterwards / 'आफ़्टरवर्ड्ज़; US 'ऐफ़्टर-वर्ड्ज़ / adv बाद में : *Let's go to the theatre first and eat afterwards.*

again / अ'गेन; अ'गेन/ adv 1 एक बार फिर; दुबारा : *Try again.* ○ *This must never happen again.* 2 पहले की स्थिति में, पूर्ववत् : *He was glad to be home again.* 3 इसके अतिरिक्त, इसके साथ ही : *Again, we have to consider the legal implications.*

against / अ'गेन्स्ट; अ'गेन्स्ट / prep 1 के विरोध (में); के विपरीत, विरुद्ध, प्रतिकूल, ख़िलाफ़ : *fight against enemy forces* 2 हानि या क्षति से बचने के लिए : *take precautions against fire* 3 की तुलना में; के संबंध में : *check your receipts against the statement* 4 समीप, साथ-साथ और छूते हुए : *Put the piano there, with its back against the wall.*

age¹ / एज / noun 1 उम्र, आयु, अवस्था : *He is six years of age.* 2 उम्र का अंतिम पड़ाव—वृद्धावस्था (जवानी के विपरीत) : *His face was wrinkled with age.* 3 (प्राय: pl) (अनौप) समय की एक बड़ी अवधि : *It took (us) ages to find a place to park.* 4 विशेष घटनाओं वाला ऐतिहासिक समय : *the modern age* ■ **be/come of age** वयस्क होना **look one's age** अपनी ही उम्र का लगना : *She doesn't look her age at all.* ▸ **age-less** adj चिरयुवा, चिरनूतन **age-long** adj चिरकालीन, दीर्घकालिक।

age² / एज / verb (pres p **ageing** या **aging**; pp **aged** / एज्ड /) बूढ़ा होना; बूढ़ा लगना : *He's aged a lot recently.* ▸ **aged** adj 1 / एज्ड / अमुक आयु का : *The boy was aged ten.* 2 / 'एजिड / (औप) अतिशय वृद्ध : *an aged man* **ageing (aging** भी) noun बूढ़े होने की प्रक्रिया : *signs/effects of ageing.*

agency / 'एजन्सि/ noun (pl **agencies**) एजेंसी, एजेंट का कार्य या कार्यस्थान : *a travel agency* ■ **by/through the agency of sth/sb** (औप) के माध्यम से : *He obtained his position by/ through the agency of his friends.*

agenda / अ'जेन्डा / noun (pl **agendas**) (बैठक में) विचारणीय विषयों की सूची, कार्य विवरण : *What is the next item on the agenda?*

agent / 'एजन्ट / noun 1 एजेंट, अभिकर्ता; दूसरे की ओर से उसके कारोबार को करने वाला व्यक्ति : *an insurance agent* ○ *a travel agent* 2 प्रभाव पैदा करने वाला पदार्थ; कारक (कारण या व्यक्ति) : *cleaning agent* ○ *an agent of his own ruin.*

aggravate / 'ऐग्रवेट / verb (स्थिति को) बिगाड़ देना, बदतर होना या करना : *He aggravated his condition by leaving hospital too soon.* ▸ **aggrava-tion** / ऐग्र'वेश्न / noun स्थिति को तीव्र करने या बिगाड़ देने की प्रक्रिया।

aggregate¹ / 'ऐग्रिग्ट् / noun पूर्ण योग, कुल जोड़, संकलन : the complete aggregate of unemployment figures.

aggregate² / 'ऐग्रिगेट् / verb (औप)एकत्र हो जाना या करना; जोड़ना ▸ **aggregation** noun संकलन : the aggregation of funds.

aggression / अ'ग्रेश्न् / noun उपद्रवी या शत्रुतापूर्ण भाव या आचरण; बिना उचित कारणों के आक्रमण : an act of open aggression ▸ **aggressor** / अ'ग्रेसर् / noun आक्रामक, हमलावर व्यक्ति या देश।

aggressive / अ'ग्रेसिव् / adj 1 लड़ाकू, लड़ाका, सहज में हमला करने वाला : dogs trained to be aggressive 2 उत्साही, उद्यमशील : an aggressive advertising campaign ▸ **aggressively** adv आक्रामकता से; ज़ोर-शोर से।

aggrieved / अ'ग्रीव्ड् / adj aggrieved (at/by sth) अपमानित; अत्याचार-पीड़ित; उद्विग्न : feel aggrieved at losing one's job.

aghast / अ'गास्ट; US अं'गैस्ट् / adj aghast (at sth) विस्मित, भयचकित : He stood aghast at the terrible sight.

agile / 'ऐजाइल; US 'ऐज्ल् / adj फुर्तीला, चपल : as agile as a monkey ○ (अलं) an agile mind/brain ▸ **agility** / अ 'जिलटि / noun फुर्ती, चपलता।

agitate / 'ऐजिटेट् / verb 1 (किसी व्यक्ति की) भावनाओं को उभारना, उत्तेजित करना : His appearance at the party had clearly agitated her. 2 **agitate for/ against sth** (किसी मुद्दे को लेकर) आंदोलन करना : agitate against nuclear weapons 3 (द्रवों को) कसकर हिलाना : Agitate the mixture to dissolve the powder. ▸ **agitated** adj उत्तेजित; परेशानहाल **agitation** / ऐजि 'टेश्न् / noun आंदोलन; उत्तेजना, अशांति : She was in a state of great agita-

tion. **agitator** noun आंदोलनकर्ता, उत्पाती।

aglow / अ'ग्लो / adv, adj चमकदार, उज्ज्वल रोशनी और गरमी देता हुआ : Christmas trees aglow with coloured lights.

agnostic / ऐग्'नॉस्टिक् / noun अज्ञेयवादी; जो इस विचार को मानता हो कि ईश्वर के अस्तित्व के बारे में कुछ निश्चितता से नहीं कहा जा सकता, संशयवादी।

ago / अ'गो / adv कुछ निश्चित समय से पहले; अतीत काल में : ten years ago.

agog / अ'गॉग् / adj उत्तेजित, उत्सुक; आतुर : agog with curiosity.

agonize, -ise / 'ऐगनाइज़् / verb **agonize (about/over sth)** अत्यधिक चिंता करना, तड़पना ▸ **agonized, -ised** adj वेदनाग्रस्त, पीड़ाग्रस्त **agonizing, -ising** adj व्यथाकारक, पीड़ाकारक : an agonizing pain/delay/decision.

agony / 'ऐगनि / noun (pl agonies) तीव्र वेदना, अत्यधिक मानसिक या शारीरिक पीड़ा; व्यथा की पराकाष्ठा : The wounded man was in agony.

agrarian / अ'ग्रेअरिअन् / adj भूसंपदा-विषयक (विशेषत: कृषिभूमि) : agrarian laws/problems/reforms.

agree / अ'ग्री / verb 1 **agree (to sth)** 'हाँ' करना; बात मानना : I asked for a pay rise and she agreed. 2 **agree (with sb) (about/on sth); agree (with sth)** सहमत होना : I agree with his analysis of the situation. 3 **agree (with sth)** से मेल खाना, के अनुकूल होना : Your account of the affair does not agree with hers. 4 सुखद और अनुकूल होना, स्वास्थ्यवर्धक होना : The climate doesn't agree with me. 5 **agree (with sth)** (व्या) वचन या पुरुष से अन्वय होना : a verb that agrees with its subject ■ **agree to differ** मतभेद स्वीकार कर लेना : We must just agree to differ on this. ▸ **agree-able** / अ'ग्रीअब्ल् / adj रुचिकर, सुखद, सहमत : agreeable weather **agree-ably** adv प्रसन्नता से, चाव से।

agreement / अ'ग्रीमन्ट् / noun 1 सम-झौता, अनुबंध 2 किसी व्यक्ति/वस्तु से सहमति व्यक्त करना; सहमति : Are we in agreement over the price?

agriculture / 'ऐग्रिकल्चर् / noun खेती-बाड़ी, कृषि, कृषि शास्त्र ▸ **agricultural** / ऐग्रि'कल्चरल् / adj कृषि-संबंधी, कृषि-योग्य : agricultural land **agricultur-ist** noun कृषक, किसान।

aground / अ'ग्राउन्ड् / adv, adj (जहाज़ों का) छिछले पानी में फँस जाना : The tanker ran aground.

ahead / अ'हेड् / adv part 1 (समय या स्थान में) आगे, सामने : look straight ahead ○ run ahead 2 पहले से; पूर्व में ही : She likes to plan her dinner parties several days ahead. 3 (किसी से) आगे; बढ़त में : Our team was ahead by six points.

aid / एड् / noun 1 सहायता, मदद : legal aid 2 सहायक सामग्री : a hearing-aid ○ teaching-aids 3 किसी क्षेत्र की सहा-यता के लिए भेजी गई भोजन सामग्री, धन आदि : How much overseas/foreign aid does India give? ■ **in aid of sth/sb** के सहायतार्थ : collect money in aid of charity ▸ **aid** verb **aid sb/sth** (विशेषत: और) सहायता करना, मदद पहुँ-चाना : His absence aided the rebels to gain control of the city.

aide / एड् / noun (विशेषत: US) सहायक; वरिष्ठ अधिकारी का परिसहायक : one of the President's closest aides.

AIDS (**Aids** भी) / एड्ज़् / abbr (चिकि): Acquired Immune Deficiency Syndrome (अक्वायर्ड इम्यून डेफ़िशंसी सिंड्रोम) विशेष वायरस से होने वाली एक घातक बीमारी जिससे शरीर की रोग-प्रतिरोधक

क्षमता नष्ट हो जाती है : AIDS is spread mainly by sexual contact.

ail / एल् / verb (प्रा) परेशानी, कष्ट पहुँचाना या होना, बीमार होना : What ails him? ▸ **ailing** adj बीमार : My wife is ail-ing.

ailment / 'ऐल्मन्ट् / noun (हलकी) बीमारी: the treatment of minor ailments.

aim^1 / एम् / verb 1 **aim (at/for sth)**; **aim (at doing sth)** लक्ष्य में रखना, उद्देश्य बनाना : We must aim at increasing/ aim to increase exports. 2 **aim (sth)** **(at sb/sth)** (पिस्तल आदि का) निशाना लगाना : He aimed (his gun) at the target, fired and missed it. 3 **aim sth at sb** (किसी को लक्ष्य बनाकर) कुछ कहना : My remarks were not aimed at you.

aim^2 / एम् / noun 1 अभिप्राय, लक्ष्य, उद्देश्य : The aim is to increase sales in India. 2 निशाना लगाने की क्रिया : Take careful aim at the target.

aimless / 'एम्लस् / adj निरुद्देश्य, लक्ष्य-हीन : lead an aimless life ▸ **aim-lessly** adv.

air^1 / एअर् / noun 1 वायु, हवा : Let's go out for some fresh air. 2 **the air** भूसतह के ऊपर ख़ाली स्थान : kick a ball high in the air 3 वायुमंडल (विशेषत: जहाँ से वायुयान गुज़रते हैं) : air travel/ transport 4 व्यवहार, रंग-ढंग : She had a triumphant air. 5 **airs** [pl] (अपमा) हाव-भाव, चोंचला, नख़रे : Stop putting on airs. ■ **on/off the air** रेडियो/टी.वी. पर प्रसारित होना/न होना : The channel comes on the air every morning at 7 am. ▸ **airbase** noun (सेना के हवाई जहाज़ों के लिए) हवाई अड्डा **airbed** noun हवा भरा गद्दा **Air-bus** noun (ट्रेडमार्क) एक प्रकार का हवाई जहाज़, एअरबस **air-conditioned** adj वातानुकूलित **airconditioning** noun

वातानुकूलन **airhostess** *noun* विमान परिचारिका **airline** *noun* हवाई जहाज़ की कंपनी/सेवा **airliner** *noun* नियमित यात्रा-सेवा का बड़ा हवाई जहाज़ **airmail** *noun* हवाई डाक **airport** *noun* हवाई अड्डा **air raid** *noun* हवाई हमला **airtight** *adj* वायुरुद्ध **air traffic controller** *noun* - वायु यातायात नियंत्रक।

air² / एअर् / *verb* 1 कपड़ों को सुखाना, हवा देना : *air the sheets* 2 (अपने विचारों को दूसरों पर) प्रकट करना : *air one's views/ opinions/grievances* ▸ **airing** / 'एअ-रिङ् / *noun* [sing] : *give the bed a good airing.*

airborne / 'एअर्बॉर्न् / *adj* हवा से फैलने वाले (रोग); पृथ्वी तल से ऊपर; विमानवाहित।

aircraft / 'एअर्क्राफ्ट् / *noun* (*pl* अपरि-वर्तित) हवाई जहाज़।

airless / 'एअर्लस् / 1 (कमरा) घुटन भरा; (मौसम) उमसदार 2 वायुरहित : *It was a hot, airless evening.*

airy / 'एअरि / *adj* (-ier, -iest) 1 हवादार (स्थान) : *The office was light and airy.* 2 लापरवाह, चंचल, चपल; उपेक्षा-पूर्ण : *an airy manner.*

aisle / आइल् / *noun* 1 संकरा रास्ता, गलि-यारा; सीटों के बीच का मार्ग (विशेषत: चर्च/ रेलगाड़ी आदि में) 2 (प्रेक्षागृह, सभाभवन, चर्च आदि में) पार्श्ववीथी।

ajar / अ'जार् / *adj* अधखुला (दरवाज़ा) : *leave the door ajar.*

akin / अ'किन् / *adj* **akin (to sth)** समान जाति या गुण वाले : *Pity and love are closely akin.*

à la carte /, आ ला'कार्ट् / *adv, adj* (फ्रेंच) (होटल, रेस्तराँ आदि में) मेन्यू से अलग-अलग चुनिंदा व्यंजन मँगवाना : *We only have an à la carte menu.*

alacrity / अ'लैक्रटि / *noun* (औप या साहि) तत्परता; फुर्ती : *He accepted her offer with alacrity.*

alarm / अ'लार्म् / *noun* 1 संत्रास, भय और घबराहट : *There's no cause for alarm.* 2 (प्राय: *sing*) संकट आदि की चेतावनी देती हुई ध्वनि, सिगनल : *give/sound the alarm* 3 चेतावनी की घंटी : *set off a burglar/smoke alarm* 4 (**alarm clock** भी) एलार्म घड़ी ▸ **alarm** *verb* आने वाले संकट की चेतावनी देना, सतर्क करना : *I don't want to alarm you, but there's a stranger in your garden.* **alarmed** *adj* **alarmed (at/by sth)** चिंतित या भयभीत **alarming** *adj* भयप्रद, चिंताजनक : *an alarming increase in the number of car thefts* **alarmingly** *adv.*

alas / अ'लैस् / *interj* (अप्र या साहि) दुख या चिंता का उद्गार : *Alas, we never seem to learn from our mistakes.*

albatross / 'ऐल्बट्रॉस् / *noun* एक श्वेत रंग की बड़ी समुद्री चिड़िया।

albino / ऐल्'बीनो; *US* ऐल्'बाइनो / *noun* (*pl* **albinos**) रंजकहीन (व्यक्ति अथवा अन्य प्राणी); जिसकी प्राकृतिक त्वचा जन्म से रंगहीन या सफ़ेद हो : *an albino rabbit.*

album / 'ऐल्बम् / *noun* 1 एल्बम 2 किसी कलाकार की विभिन्न प्रस्तुतियों का संग्रह, रिकॉर्ड, टेप आदि : *This is one of the songs from/on her latest album.*

alchemy / 'ऐल्कमि / *noun* प्राचीनकालिक रसायनशास्त्र; कीमिया : *The chief aim of alchemy was to discover how to change ordinary metals into gold.*

alcohol / 'ऐल्कहॉल् / *noun* 1 शराब में विद्यमान रंगहीन मादक द्रव्य 2 शराब, बिअर आदि मादक द्रव्य : *prohibit the sale of alcohol* ▸ **alcoholic** / ,ऐल्क'हॉलिक् / *adj* मादक, शराबी : *alcoholic drinks* **alcoholism** / 'ऐल्क'हॉलिज़म् / *noun* शराबखोरी के कारण उत्पन्न शारीरिक अक्षमता।

alcove / 'ऐल्कोव् / *noun* कमरे की दीवार में मेहराबदार ताख, आला।

ale / एल् / *noun* एक प्रकार की बिअर; ऐसी बिअर की बोतल या गिलास।

alert / अ'लर्ट् / adj alert (to sth) सतर्क, चौकन्ना : The alert listener will have noticed the error. ▸ **alert** noun 1 [sing] स्थिति जिसमें लोग सतर्क, सावधान रहते हैं : The police were put on (full) alert. 2 चेतावनी : a bomb/fire alert **alert** verb सावधान करना; आगाह करना : alert staff to the crisis facing the company **alertness** noun सतर्कता, चौकसी।

algae / 'ऐल्जी; 'ऐल्गी / noun [pl] जल-शैवाल, प्रायः पानी में उगने वाला पौधा।

algebra / 'ऐल्जिब्रा / noun बीजगणित ▸ **algebraic** adj.

algorithm / 'ऐल्गरिद्म् / noun गणितीय समस्याएँ हल करने के लिए कुछ निर्धारित नियम; ऐलगोरिद्म।

alias / 'एलिअस् / noun (विशेषतः अपराधियों का) उपनाम; छद्मनाम : The swindler used a series of aliases.

alibi / 'ऐलबाइ / noun (pl alibis / 'ऐल्बाइज़्/) 1 (क़ानून) (अपराध घटित होने के समय) अन्यत्र उपस्थित होने का तर्क 2 (अनौप) किसी भी तरह की बहानेबाज़ी : Late again, Laxmi? What's your alibi this time?

alien / 'एलिअन् / noun 1 (क़ानून या औप) विदेशी (व्यक्ति), अन्यदेशी 2 अन्य-लोकवासी : aliens from outer space ▸ **alien** adj 1 विजातीय, विदेशी : an alien environment 2 विचित्र, अन-जान : alien concepts/customs 3 alien to sb/sth बेमेल, प्रतिकूल, अ-संगत : Such principles are alien to our religion.

alienate / 'एलिअनेट् / verb alienate sb (from sb/sth) 1 अपनों को पराया कर देना, अपने से दूर करना : The Prime Minister's policy alienated many of his supporters. 2 लोगों से या समूह से किसी को भिन्न अनुभव करना : Many artists feel alienated from society.

▸ **alienation** / ,एलिअ'नेश्न् / noun हस्तांतरण; विलगाव; विमुखीकरण : His criminal activities led to complete alienation from his family.

alight[1] / अ'लाइट् / adj प्रदीप्त, जलता हुआ : A cigarette set the dry grass alight.

alight[2] / अ'लाइट् / verb alight (from sth) (औप) (बस, हवाई जहाज़, घोड़े आदि से) उतरना : Passengers should never alight from a moving bus.

align / अ'लाइन् / verb align sth (with sth) 1 पंक्तिबद्ध करना, सीध मिलाना : The columns of printed text are aligned with the edge of each page. ■ align oneself with sb किसी दल में सम्मिलित होना, किसी के साथ हो जाना : The Communist Party has aligned itself with the Socialists. ▸ **align-ment** noun 1 सीध, संरेखण : The bathroom tiles are clearly out of alignment. 2 (राज) सम्मिलन : the alignment of Japan with the West.

alike / अ'लाइक् / adj समान, सदृश, तुल्य : These two photographs are almost alike. ▸ **alike** adv समान रूप से; समान रीति से।

alimentary canal / ,ऐलिमेन्टरि क'नैल्/ noun आहारनली।

alimony / 'ऐलिमनि; US 'ऐलिमोनि / noun तलाक़ के बाद भूतपूर्व पति या पत्नी को नियमित रूप से दी जाने वाली राशि।

alive / अ'लाइव्/ adj 1 जीवित, ज़िंदा : She was still alive when I reached the hospital. 2 सजीव, फुरतीला : Her eyes were alive and full of fun. 3 alive to sth (मानसिक दृष्टि से) जागरूक, स-चेत : He is fully alive to the possible dangers. ■ alive and kicking (अनौप) स्वस्थ एवं सक्रिय : You'll be glad to hear that Bindu is alive and kicking.

alkali / 'ऐल्कलाइ / *noun* (*pl* **alkalis** / 'ऐल्कलाइज़् /) (*रसा*) क्षार ▶ **alkaline** *adj* क्षारीय।

all[1] / ऑल् / *indef det* 1 सभी, समस्त : *All my plants have died.* 2 सारा का सारा, सब, संपूर्ण : *He has lost all his money.* 3 अधिकतम, यथासंभव : *with all speed/haste* ○ *in all honesty/ frankness* ■ **not all that good, well, etc** विशेष अच्छा नहीं : *He doesn't sing all that well.* ○ *Her writing isn't all that accurate.* ▶ **all-night** *adj* रात-भर चलने वाला : *an all-night party* **all-time** *adj* अब तक के समय का : *an all-time record.*

all[2] / ऑल् / *indef adv* पूर्णतया, बिल्कुल : *She lives all alone/all by herself.* ■ **all along** बराबर, शुरू से ही : *I realized I'd had it in my pocket all along.* **all over** सर्वत्र, प्रत्येक भाग में : *We looked all over for the ring.* **all right** (*अनौप* **alright**) 1 ठीक, स्वीकार्य : *Is the coffee all right?* 2 कुशल-मंगल : *I hope the children are all right.* 3 बस ठीक-ठाक : *Your work is all right but I'm sure you could do better.* **be all about sth** मुख्य विषय, के विषय में : *This book is all about ancient Greece.* **be all for sth** किसी ख़ास चीज़ के पीछे पड़ जाना, किसी चीज़ को बहुत अधिक वांछित मानना : *She's all for more nursery schools being built.*

all[3] / ऑल् / *indef pron* 1 **all (of it/ them/us/you)** सर्वस्व, सब (कुछ) : *I invited my five sisters, but not all (of them) can come.* 2 **all of sth/sb** प्रत्येक, हर एक : *All of the toys were broken.* ■ **all in all** कुल मिलाकर : *All in all it had been a great success.* **all in one** बहुत-से उपयोग वाली वस्तु : *It's a corkscrew and bottle-opener*

all in one. (not) at all किसी भी तरह (नहीं); ज़रा-सा भी (नहीं) : *I didn't enjoy it at all.*

all- *pref* (*पूर्वपद*) 1 पूर्णतया : *an all-electric kitchen* 2 उत्तम श्रेणी का : *all-important* ○ *all-powerful.*

Allah / अल्'लाह / *noun* अल्लाह।

allay / अं'ले / *verb* (*औप*) (पीड़ा, कष्ट, भय आदि को) कम करना।

allege / अ'लेज़् / *verb* (*औप*) आरोप लगाना, निश्चयपूर्वक किंतु बिना प्रमाण के कहना : *The prisoner alleges (that) he was at home on the night of the crime.* ▶ **allegation** / ऐल'गेश्न् / *noun* अभिकथन, प्रमाण रहित कथन, आरोप, दावा : *These are serious allegations.* **alleged** *adj* तथाकथित, जिस पर आरोप लगा हो : *an alleged criminal* **allegedly** / अं'लेजिड्लि / *adv* तथाकथित रूप से : *The novel was allegedly written by a computer.*

allegiance / अं'लीजन्स् / *noun* (*औप*) **allegiance (to sb/sth)** (*औप*) (राज्य अथवा स्वामी के प्रति) निष्ठा; समर्थन : *swear (an oath of) allegiance to the flag.*

allegory / 'ऐलगरि / *noun* (*pl* **allegories**) प्रतीक कथा जिसमें अमूर्त भाव जैसे सत्य, प्रेम, धैर्य आदि सजीव पात्र के रूप में आते हैं : *His writings are full of allegory.* ▶ **allegorical** / ऐल'गॉरिक्ल् / *adj* प्रतीक कथात्मक, अन्योक्ति-परक : *an allegorical figure* ○ *allegorical poetry.*

allergy / 'ऐलर्जि / *noun* (*pl* **allergies**) (*चिकि*) **allergy (to sth)** ऐसी स्थिति जब किसी व्यक्ति को किसी वस्तु के संपर्क अथवा सेवन से शरीर पर बुरा असर पड़ता है, एलर्जी : *I have an allergy to certain milk products.* ▶ **allergic** / अंलर्जिक् / *adj* 1 **allergic (to sth)** एलर्जी होना : *I like cats but unfortunately I'm al-*

lergic to them. 2 एलर्जी से उत्पन्न : *an allergic rash/reaction* 3 **allergic to sth** (*अनौप या परि*) अति घृणा, अरुचि या चिढ़ होना : *He's allergic to hard work!*

alleviate / अ'लीवि़एट् / *verb* (पीड़ा या कष्ट को) कम करना, सहने लायक बनाना : *The doctor gave her an injection to alleviate the pain.* ▸ **alleviation** / अ,लीवि़'एश्न् / *noun* आराम; उपशयन।

alley / 'ऐलि / *noun* 1 (**alleyway** भी) गली : *a back alley* 2 (बाग़, उपवन आदि में) वीथि, वीथिका।

alliance / अ'लाइअन्स् / *noun* 1 साहचर्य, सहबंध : *We are working in alliance with our European partners.* 2 मैत्री; संधि; समझौता : *enter into/break off an alliance with a neighbouring state.*

alligator / 'ऐलिगेट् / *noun* घड़ियाल (मगरमच्छ की एक जाति)।

alliteration / अ,लिट्'रेश्न् / *noun* अनुप्रास अलंकार (जिसमें एक ध्वनि बार-बार आती है जैसे 'चार चंद्र की चंचल किरणें' में) ▸ **alliterative** *adj* सानुप्रास।

allocate / 'ऐलकेट् / *verb* **allocate sth (to sb/sth)** (किसी कार्य के लिए) धन आदि निर्धारित करना; विनिहित करना, कार्य की ज़िम्मेदारी सौंपना : *allocate funds for repair work* ० *He allocated tasks to each of us.* ▸ **allocation** / ,ऐल'केश्न् / *noun* 1 आवंटन, बँटवारा : *housing allocation* 2 नियतन, निर्धारण, विनिधान : *We've spent our entire allocation for the year.*

allopathy / ऐ'लॉपथि / *noun* एलोपैथी एक प्रकार की आधुनिक चिकित्सा प्रणाली (जो प्रायः अस्पतालों में सर्वाधिक प्रचलित है)।

allot / अ'लॉट् / *verb* (**-tt-**) **allot sth (to sb/sth)** उपलब्ध समय, राशि, ज़िम्मेदारियाँ हिस्सों में बाँटना; हिस्सा नियत करना; अंश

देना : *How much cash has been allotted?* ० *Who will she allot the easy jobs to?* ▸ **allotment** *noun* आवंटन; नियतन।

allow / अ'लाउ / *verb* 1 (होने या करने) देना, कुछ करने की आज्ञा या अनुमति देना : *My boss doesn't allow me to use the telephone for private calls.* ० (*अलं*) *She allowed her mind to wander.* 2 किसी की सत्यता स्वीकार करना, मान लेना : *The judge allowed the claim.* 3 (*औप*) मान लेना : *Even if we allow that the poet was mad....*

allowance / अ'लाउअन्स् / *noun* 1 भत्ता : *an allowance of Rs 100 per day* ० *be paid a travel allowance* 2 छूट; कटौती ■ **make allowance (s) for sth** निर्णय लेते समय अन्य बातों को भी ध्यान में रखना : *You must make allowances for him because he has been ill.*

alloy / 'ऐलॉइ / *noun* दो धातुओं का मिश्रण, मिश्रधातु; खोट : *Brass is an alloy of copper and zinc.* ▸ **alloy** / अ'लॉइ / *verb* **alloy sth (with sth)** धातुओं का मिश्रण करना; खोट मिलाना।

allude / अ'लूड् / *verb* **allude to sb/sth** (*औप*) घुमा-फिराकर कहना या लिखना, संकेत मात्र देना : *You alluded in your speech to certain developments— what exactly did you mean?* ▸ **allusion** / अ'लूश्न् / *noun* **allusion (to sb/sth)** संकेत, इशारा : *His writing is full of obscure literary allusions.*

allusive / अ'लूसिव़् / *adj* सांकेतिक : *Her allusive style is difficult to follow.*

allure / अ'लुअर् / *noun* प्रलोभन, आकर्षण : *the false allure of big-city life* ▸ **alluring** *adj* सम्मोहक; आकर्षक।

alluvial / अ'लूवि़अल / *adj* नदियों से बहाकर लाई मिट्टी-रेती से बनी (भूमि),

जलोढ़, कछारी (भूमि) : *alluvial deposits/soil/plains.*

ally / अॅ'लाइ / *verb (pt, pp allied)* ally (sb/oneself) with/to sb/sth जुड़ना/जोड़ना, संबद्ध करना, मिलाना, मित्रता का संबंध रखना : *The prince allied himself with the Mughal ruler in Agra.*
▸ **ally** / 'ऐलाइ / *noun* संधिबद्ध व्यक्ति या देश : *a close ally and friend of the prime minister* **allied** / अॅ'लाइड्; ऐ-लाइड् / *adj* allied (to sth) समझौते से संबद्ध; सहबद्ध, समवर्गी : *a union of allied trades.*

Alma Mater / ऐल्मा 'माटर् / *noun* (लैटिन) (औपचारिक) कॉलेज या विद्यालय जहाँ से शिक्षा प्राप्त की गई हो।

almanac (almanack भी) / 'ऑल्मनैक् / *noun* 1 सूचना-कोश 2 पंचांग, जंत्री।

almighty / ऑल्'माइटि / *adj* असीम शक्ति वाला, सर्वशक्ति संपन्न ▸ **the Almighty** *noun* [*sing*] सर्वशक्तिमान्ईश्वर, परमेश्वर।

almond / 'आमन्ड् / *noun* बादाम।

almost / 'ऑल्मोस्ट् / *adv* लगभग, क़रीब-क़रीब : *It's a mistake they almost always make.*

alms / आम्ज़् / *noun* [*pl*] (अप्र) भीख, भिक्षा; (ग़रीबों को) दान।

aloft / अॅ'लॉफ्ट् / *adv* ऊँचे पर, सिर के ऊपर, बहुत ऊँचे पर : *flags flying aloft.*

alone / अॅ'लोन् / *adj, adv* 1 अकेले, निर्जनता की स्थिति : *I don't like going out alone after dark.* 2 बिना किसी अन्य की सहायता के : *She raised her family quite alone.* 3 एकाकी, अकेला और (बहुधा) अप्रसन्न : *It was my first experience of living away from home and I felt terribly alone.* ■ **let alone** को तो जाने दीजिए, को तो छोड़िए : *There isn't enough room for us, let alone a dog and two cats.* **leave/let sb/sth alone** अकेले रहने देना, न छेड़ना, प्रभाव डालना या बदलने

का प्रयास न करना : *She's asked to be left alone but the press keep pestering her.*

along / अॅ'लॉङ् / *prep* 1 एक सिरे से दूसरे सिरे तक/की ओर : *walk along the street* 2 लंबाई के समानांतर : *Flowers grow along the side of the wall.*
▸ **along** *adv part* 1 आगे : *The policeman told the crowd to move along.* 2 (अनौप) किसी के साथ, साथ-साथ : *Come to the party and bring some friends along.* ■ **along with sb/sth** किसी व्यक्ति/वस्तु के अतिरिक्त; के ही समान, की तरह ही : *Tobacco is taxed in most countries, along with alcohol.*

alongside / अॅ,लॉङ्'साइड् / *prep* बग़ल में, बराबर में : *The car drew up alongside the kerb.*

aloof / अॅ'लूफ़् / *adj* aloof (from sb/sth) अलग; दूर, अलग-थलग; शांत और उदासीन : *Throughout the conversation he remained quiet and aloof.* ■ **keep (oneself)/hold (oneself)/stand aloof from sb/sth** बातचीत या काम में हिस्सा न लेना, अलग खड़े रहना : *She kept herself aloof from her fellow students.* ▸ **aloofness** *noun* अलगाव, बिलगाव।

aloud / अॅ'लाउड् / *adv* 1 ऊँचे स्वर से : *He read his sister's letter aloud.* 2 ज़ोर से : *He called aloud for help.*

alphabet / 'ऐल्फ़बेट् / *noun* वर्णमाला : *There are 26 letters in the English alphabet, which begins A, B, C, D, etc.* ▸ **alphabetical** / ,ऐल्फ़'बेटिकल् / *adj* वर्ण क्रम से, अकार आदि क्रम से : *a dictionary listing words in alphabetical order* **alphabetically** *adv* : *books arranged alphabetically.*

alpine / 'ऐल्पाइन् / *adj* ऊँचे पहाड़ों का य

ऊँचे पहाड़ों पर पाया जाने वाला : *alpine village/flowers.*

already / ऑल् 'रेडि / *adv* इससे पहले; पहले से ही : *She had already left when I phoned.* ○ *There are far too many people here already.*

Alsatian / ऐल् 'सेशन् / (*US* **German shepherd**) *noun* अलसेशन (कुत्ता)।

also / 'ऑल्सो / *adv* भी; साथ ही : *She speaks French and German and also a little Russian.* ○ *It is my favourite restaurant and hers also.*

altar / 'ऑल्टर / *noun* 1 वेदी, वेदिका 2 (ईसाई चर्च में) चबूतरा : *an altar cloth* ■ **at/on the altar of sth** की बलिवेदी; की भेंट : *Moral considerations were sacrificed on the altar of profit.*

alter / 'ऑल्टर / *verb* परिवर्तन करना या होना : *She had to alter her clothes after losing weight.* ▸ **alteration** / ‚ऑल्ट' रेशन् / *noun* 1 परिवर्तन प्रक्रिया : *How much alteration will be necessary?* 2 परिवर्तन : *a drastic/radical alteration of the law* ○ *We are making a few alterations to the house.*

altercation / ‚आल्टर 'केशन् / *noun* (औप) अनबन, कहा-सुनी : *Just before half-time there was a brief altercation with the referee.*

alternate¹ / 'ऑल् 'टर्नट् / *adj* 1 बारी-बारी से, पहले एक फिर दूसरा : *alternate triumph and despair* 2 दो में से एक, एक-एक छोड़कर : *I visit them on alternate Sundays.* ▸ **alternately** *adv* बारी-बारी से।

alternate² / 'ऑल्टर्नेट् / *verb* 1 **alternate A and B/alternate A with B** (दो प्रकार की वस्तुओं को) बारी-बारी से रखना या करना : *He alternated blue beads with white.* 2 **alternate between A and B; alternate (with sth)** एक अवस्था से दूसरी में जाना और पुन: पहली अवस्था में लौट आना : *Rainy days alternated with dry ones.* ▸ **alternating current** *noun* (संक्षि AC) प्रत्यावर्ती विद्युतधारा

alternation / ‚ऑल्टर 'नेशन् / *noun* प्रत्यावर्तन, एकांतरण।

alternative / ऑल् 'टर्नटिव् / *adj* 1 वैकल्पिक; विकल्प या दूसरी संभावना वाला : *find alternative means of transport* ▸ **alternative** *noun* विकल्प : *One of the alternatives open to you is to resign.* **alternatively** *adv* विकल्पत: : *We could take the train or alternatively go by car.*

although / ऑल् 'द्रो / *conj* यद्यपि, हालाँकि : *Although he had only entered the contest for fun, he won first prize.*

altimeter / 'ऐल्टिमीटर / *noun* समुद्र तल से ऊँचाई मापने का यंत्र।

altitude / 'ऐल्टिट्यूड्; *US* 'ऐल्टिट्यूड् / *noun* 1 ऊँचाई (विशेषत: समुद्र तल से) : *What is the altitude of this town?* 2 (प्राय: *pl*) ऊँचा स्थान : *There is snow at high altitudes.*

altogether / ‚ऑल्ट 'गेदर् / *adv* 1 पूरी तरह से; बिलकुल : *I'm not altogether happy about the decision.* 2 सब मिलाकर, कुल : *You owe me Rs 2,500 altogether.*

altruism / 'ऐल्टूइज़म् / *noun* परोपकारिता, परहितवाद ▸ **altruist** / 'ऐल्टूइस्ट् / *noun* परहितवादी (व्यक्ति) **altruistic** *adj* परोपकारी, परहितवादी।

alum / 'ऐलम् / *noun* फिटकिरी।

aluminium / ‚ऐल्य 'मिनिअम्; ऐल् 'मिनिअम् / (*US* **aluminum** / अ'लूमिनम् /) *noun* (प्रतीक AI) अलूमिनियम, एक हलकी धातु।

always / 'ऑल्वेज़् / *adv* 1 सदा, हमेशा; बिना अपवाद के : *The sun always rises in the east.* 2 बार-बार; लगातार : *He*

was always asking for money.
■ **as always** हमेशा की तरह : *As always he was late and had to run to catch the bus.*

am / ऐम् / → be देखिए।

a.m. / ए एम् / (*US* **A.M.**) *abbr* (लैटिन *ante meridiem*) मध्याह्नपूर्व, दोपहर के 12 बजे तक का समय : *It starts at 10 a.m.*

amalgam / अ मैल्गम् / *noun* 1 (प्राय: *sing*) सम्मिश्रण, विलयन, योग : *an amalgam of several political groups* 2 पारे का अन्य धातुओं से मिश्रण; पारद-मिश्रण।

amalgamate / अ मैल्गमेट् / *verb* **amalgamate (sb/sth) (with sb/sth)** एक को दूसरे से मिलाकर एक कर देना, मिश्रण करना : *Several colleges were amalgamated into the new university.* ▸ **amalgamation** / अ मैल्ग मे शन् / *noun* एकीकरण, सम्मिश्रण : *a process of political amalgamation.*

amass / अ मैस् / *verb* (विशेषत: धन-दौलत को) बड़ी मात्रा में इकट्ठा या संचित करना : *They amassed enough evidence to convict him.*

amateur / ऐमटर; ऐमचर / *noun* 1 केवल शौक के लिए किसी कला, खेल-कूद, संगीत आदि में भाग लेने वाला; अव्यवसायी : *an amateur painter/photographer* 2 (प्राय: *अपमा*) कच्चा खिलाड़ी, अनाड़ी : *The whole house needs rewiring—it's not a job for amateurs.* ▸ **amateurish** / ऐमटरिश; ऐम चरिश् / *adj* (अक्सर *अपमा*) अनाड़ी, अदक्ष : *Detectives described the burglary as 'crude and amateurish'.* **amateurishly** *adv.*

amaze / अ मेज़् / *verb* चकित या हैरान होना/करना : *He amazed everyone by passing his driving test.* ▸ **amazed**

adj **amazed (at sb/sth)** चकित, भौचक्का : *She looked back at him, amazed at how happy she felt.* **amazement** *noun* आश्चर्य, विस्मय : *He looked at me in amazement.* **amazing** *adj* विस्मयकारी, आश्चर्य-जनक : *an amazing speed* **amazingly** *adv.*

ambassador / ऐम् बैसडर् / *noun* 1 राजदूत 2 आधिकारिक संदेशवाहक, प्रति-निधि।

amber / ऐम्बर् / *noun* 1 कहरुबा, तृण-मणि : *amber beads* 2 कहरुबा रंग : *The traffic lights turned to amber.*

ambience (**ambiance** भी) / ऐम्बि-अन्स् / *noun* वातावरण; परिवेश, माहौल : *The Airport Hotel has an ambience all of its own.*

ambiguity / ऐम्बि ग्यूअटि / *noun* (*pl* **ambiguities**) 1 अनेकार्थता की स्थिति : *A lot of humour depends on ambiguity.* 2 शब्द या वाक्य जिसके दो या अधिक अर्थ निकाले जा सकें 3 अस्पष्टता, संदिग्धता : *the ambiguity of his mother's attitude.*

ambiguous / ऐम् बिग्युअस्/ *adj* 1 अ-नेकार्थक 2 अस्पष्ट, संदिग्ध : *Their position as consultants is ambiguous.* ▸ **ambiguously** *adv.*

ambit / ऐम्बिट् / *noun* [*sing*] (औप) विस्तार; परिधि; (विशेषत: अधिकार या शक्ति की) सीमा : *We aim to bring these buildings within the ambit of local government control.*

ambition / ऐम् बिशन् / *noun* **ambition (to be/to do sth)** 1 महत्त्वाकांक्षा, महत्त्वाभिलाषा : *He felt his son lacked ambition.* 2 विशेष उच्चाकांक्षा : *He finally achieved/fulfilled his boyhood ambition to become a pilot.*

ambitious / ऐम् बिशस् / *adj* **ambitious (to be/to do sth)**; **ambitious**

(for sth) महत्त्वाकांक्षी, उच्चाकांक्षी : *an ambitious attempt* ▸ **ambitiously** *adv.*

ambivalent / ऐम्'बिव़लन्ट् / *adj* ambivalent (about sb/sth) उभयमुखी; द्विधा मनोवृत्ति।

amble / 'ऐम्ब्ल् / *verb* मंथर गति से चलना; धीरे-धीरे चलना, टहलना : *We ambled along for miles.*

ambulance / 'ऐम्ब्यलन्स् / *noun* एम्बु-लेंस, आपातवाहन।

ambush / 'ऐम्बुश्/ *noun* 1 घात; छिपकर अचानक शत्रु पर हमला करने की ताक : *the ambush and shooting of two senior officers* 2 घात लगाकर किया गया अचानक हमला : *killed by/in a terrorist ambush* ▸ **ambush** *verb* घात लगाना; हमला करना : *His car was ambushed by guerrillas.*

ameliorate/ अं'मीलिअरेट्/ *verb* (औप) सुधरना; सुधारना : *Steps have been taken to ameliorate the situation.* ▸ **amelioration** / अ ,मीलिअ'रेश्न् / *noun* सुधार, उन्नति।

amen / आ'मेन्; ए'मेन् / *noun, interj* (प्रार्थना के अंत में कहा गया) 'आमीन' ('ऐसा ही हो', 'तथास्तु')।

amenable / अ'मीनब्ल् / *adj* amenable (to sth) सहज ही अनुकूल हो जाने वाला; विनम्र : *I find him very amenable to reason.*

amend / अ'मेन्ड् / *verb* सुधारना; दोषहीन करना; संशोधन करना : *amend a document/proposal/law* ▸ **amendment** *noun* 1 संशोधन क्रिया, प्रक्रिया 2 amendment (to sth) किसी दस्तावेज़, विधेयक आदि का संशोधन : *Parliament debated several amendments to the bill.*

amends / अ'मेन्ड्ज़् / *noun* [pl]
■ **make amends (to sb) (for sth/ doing sth)** हर्जाना (देना), क्षतिपूर्ति

(करना) : *How can I ever make amends for the things I said to you last night?*

amenity / अ'मीनटि; *US* अं'मेनटि/ *noun* (pl **amenities**) (प्राय: pl) सुख-सुविधाएँ, सुख-साधन, सुविधाएँ : *People who retire to the country often miss the amenities of a town.*

amethyst / 'ऐमथिस्ट् / *noun* जंबुमणि, जामुनी रंग का क़ीमती पत्थर।

amiable / 'एमिअब्ल् / *adj* मैत्रीपूर्ण, सौहार्दपूर्ण; मिलनसार : *Her parents seemed very amiable.* ▸ **amiability** / ,एमिअ'बिलटि / *noun* सौजन्यता, भद्रता **amiably** *adv* उदारता से, सौजन्यता से, भद्रता से।

amicable / 'ऐमिकब्ल् / *adj* सौहार्दपूर्ण; स्नेही : *restore amicable relations between the two sides* ▸ **amicably** *adv* मित्रवत्, मित्रभाव से : *They lived together amicably for several years.*

amid / अ'मिड्/ (**amidst** / अं'मिड्स्ट्/ भी) *prep* बीच में, में; के दौरान : *The firm collapsed amid allegations of fraud.*

amiss / अ'मिस्/ *adj, adv* ग़लत; ख़राब; ग़लत ढंग से : *Something seems to be amiss—can I help?*

amity / 'ऐमटि / *noun* (औप) मित्रतापूर्ण व्यवहार; सौहार्द : *live in amity with sb.*

ammonia / अं'मोनिआ / *noun* अमोनिया गैस।

ammunition/ ,ऐम्यु'निश्न्/ *noun* गोला-बारूद, युद्धोपकरण।

amnesia / ऐम्'नीज़िआ; *US* ऐम्'नीशा / *noun* आंशिक या पूर्ण रूप से याददाश्त खो बैठने की अवस्था : *suffer an attack of amnesia.*

amnesty / 'ऐम्नस्टि / *noun* (pl **amnesties**) 1 amnesty (for sb) (प्राय: राज्य के प्रति किए) अपराधों के लिए

सार्वजनिक क्षमादान, आम माफ़ी : *The rebels returned home under a general amnesty.* 2 अपराध स्वीकरण के लिए दिया गया अभयदान-समय।

amoeba / अ'मीबा / *noun (pl* **amoebas** या **amoebae** अ'मीबी /) अमीबा, जीवाणु।

amok / अ'मॉक् / *adv* ■ **run amok** पागल की तरह दौड़ना और हिंसापूर्ण काम करना : *The soldiers ran amok and set fire to government buildings.*

among / अ'मङ् / (**amongst** अ'मङ्स्ट् / भी) *prep* 1 घिरा हुआ; बीच में : *She works among the poor/the sick.* 2 बहुत-सी चीज़ों या व्यक्तियों में सम्मिलित : *I was among the last to leave.* 3 आपस में : *Politicians are always arguing amongst themselves.*

amoral / ए'मॉरल् / *adj* नैतिक सिद्धांत रहित, सदाचारविहीन : *a totally amoral person.*

amorous / ऐमरस् / *adj (औप)* खुले आम प्रेम प्रदर्शन करने वाला; शृंगार रस से पूर्ण; प्रणयसंबंधी : *amorous looks/letters/poetry* ▸ **amorously** *adv.*

amount / अ'माउन्ट् / *verb* ■ **amount to sth** 1 जोड़ना; योग करना : *The cost amounted to Rs 40,000.* 2 के बराबर होना : *It all amounts to a lot of hard work.* ▸ **amount** *noun* **amount (of sth)** 1 धनराशि : *a bill for the full amount* 2 मात्रा; राशि : *a fair/large amount of work/money/furniture* ■ **any amount of sth** अपार राशि या मात्रा : *There's been any amount of research on the subject.*

amp / ऐम्प् / (**ampere** / ऐम्पअर; *US* ऐम्पिअर / भी) *noun* ऐंपियर, विद्युत धारा की इकाई।

amphibian / ऐम्'फ़िबिअन् / *noun* जल-थल दोनों में रहने वाला प्राणी, जैसे मेंढक ▸ **amphibious** / ऐम्'फ़िबिअस् / *adj*

जल-थल दोनों में कार्यक्षम : *amphibious vehicles.*

amphitheatre (*US* **amphitheater**) / ऐम्फ़िथ़िअटर / *noun* गोलाकार या अंडाकार दीर्घायुक्त रंगमंडल।

ample / ऐम्प्ल् / *adj* (**-r, -st**) 1 लंबा-चौड़ा, विस्तृत 2 पर्याप्त से अधिक; प्रचुर : *ample time to get to the station.*

amplify / ऐम्प्लिफ़ाइ / *verb (pt, pp* **amplified**) 1 (रेडियो संकेतों, विद्युत तरंगों आदि की) शक्ति बढ़ाना : *amplify an electric current/a signal* 2 कथन आदि विस्तार से कहना : *We must ask you to amplify your earlier statement.* ▸ **amplification** / ऐम्प्लिफ़िकेशन् / *noun* प्रवर्धन, विस्तार **amplifier** *noun* (*अनौप* **amp** भी) प्रवर्धक; ध्वनि अथवा विद्युत तरंगों की शक्ति बढ़ाने वाला यंत्र।

amplitude / ऐम्प्लिट्यूड्; *US* ऐम्प्लिटूड् / *noun (तक)* तरंगों की कंपन का अधिकतम आयाम।

amputate / ऐम्प्युटेट् / *verb* (चिकित्सा) ऑपरेशन के दौरान) (हाथ या पैर) काटना : *His arm is so badly injured they will have to amputate (it).* ▸ **amputation** / एम्प्यु'टेशन् / *noun* अंग-विच्छेदन।

amulet / ऐम्युलट् / *noun* ताबीज़।

amuse / अ'म्यूज़् / *verb* 1 जी बहलाना : *These toys will help to keep the baby amused.* 2 हँसाना, मनोरंजन करना : *My funny drawings amused the children.* ▸ **amused** *adj* **amused (at sth)** कोई स्थिति आदि मज़ेदार या विचित्र लगते हुए : *exchange amused glances* **amusement** *noun* 1 मनोरंजन की वस्तु : *The hotel offers its guests a wide variety of amusements.* 2 मनोरंजन, मन बहलाव की स्थिति : *She could not disguise her amusement at his mistake.* **amusing** *adj* मनोरंजक,

हास्यप्रद, विनोदपूर्ण : *an amusing story/ storyteller.*

an / ऐन् / *indef art* → **a** देखिए।

anachronism / अ'नैक्रनिज़म् / *noun* 1 कालदोष, अतीत के वर्णन में वर्तमान को शामिल करना : *It would be an anachronism to talk of King Ashoka watching television.* 2 पुरातनपंथी, दकियानूसी (व्यक्ति, रीति-रिवाज, मनोवृत्ति आदि) : *The monarchy is seen by some as an anachronism in present-day society.* ▸ **anachronistic** / अ,नैक्र'निस्टिक् / *adj.*

anaemia (*US* **anemia**) / अ'नीमिआ / *noun* (चिकि) रक्तहीनता, खून की कमी (की बीमारी) ; रक्तक्षीणता ▸ **anaemic** (*US* **anemic**) / अ'नीमिक् / *adj* 1 रक्तहीन : *She looks anaemic.* 2 शक्तिहीन, दुर्बल : *an anaemic performance.*

anaesthesia (*US* **anesthesia**) / ,ऐनस्'थीज़िआ; *US* ,ऐनस्'थीश़ा / *noun* निश्चेतना, (ऑपरेशन से पहले) बेहोश करने से उत्पन्न संवेदनहीनता ▸ **anaesthetic** (*US* **anesthetic**) / ,ऐनस्'थेटिक् / *noun* चेतनाशून्य कर देने वाला पदार्थ जो प्रायः ऑपरेशन के पहले दिया जाता है : *give sb a general anaesthetic* **anaesthetist** (*US* **anesthetist**) / अ'नीस्थटिस्ट् / *noun* निश्चेतक (व्यक्ति) **anaesthetize, -ise** (*US* **anesthetize**) / अ'नीस्थटाइज़् / *verb* संज्ञाहीन कर देना।

anagram / 'ऐनग्रैम् / *noun* वर्ण विपर्यय, अक्षरों के हेर-फेर से एक शब्द से दूसरा शब्द बनाना : '*Cart-horse' is an anagram of 'orchestra'.*

analgesia / ,ऐनल्'जीज़िआ; *US* ,ऐनल् 'जीश़ा / *noun* (चिकि) पीड़ाशून्यता, दर्द का अनुभव न होना ▸ **analgesic** / ,ऐनल् 'जीज़िक् / *noun* दर्दनाशक दवा : *Aspirin is a mild analgesic.*

analogous / अ'नैलगस् / *adj* analogous (to/with sth) आंशिक रूप से सदृश,

अनुरूप : *The two processes are not analogous.* ○ *Sleep was sometimes held to be analogous to death.*

analogy / अ'नैलजि / *noun* (*pl* **analogies**) 1 analogy (between sth and sth); analogy (with sth) दो वस्तुओं की आंशिक समानता या समरूपता : *The teacher drew an analogy between the human heart and a pump.* 2 सादृश्यता अथवा साधर्म्य के आधार पर तर्कयुक्ति : *My theory applies to you and by analogy to others like you.*

analyse (*US* **analyze**) / 'ऐनलाइज़् / *verb* विश्लेषण करना; किसी तत्त्व के अंशों को पृथक-पृथक करके उसका अध्ययन एवं परीक्षण करना : *analyse the sample and identify it* ○ *By analysing the parts of the sentence we learn more about English grammar.*

analysis / अ'नैलसिस् / *noun* (*pl* **analyses** / अ'नैलसीज़् /) *noun* 1 विश्लेषण : *Close/Careful analysis of the sales figures shows clear regional variations.* 2 विश्लेषण से प्राप्त परिणाम : *present a detailed analysis of the situation* 3 =**psychoanalysis** (मनो-विश्लेषण) ▸ **analytic** / ,ऐन 'लिटिक् / (**analytical** / ,ऐन 'लिटिकल् / भी) *adj* विश्लेषणात्मक, विश्लेषणपरक : *an analytical approach/technique* **analytically** *adv* विश्लेषणात्मक रूप से।

analyst / 'ऐनलिस्ट् / *noun* विश्लेषक, विश्लेषण करने वाला व्यक्ति : *a political analyst.*

anarchy / 'ऐनकि / *noun* 1 अराजकता, शासनहीनता : *The overthrow of the regime was followed by a period of anarchy.* 2 अव्यवस्था; गड़बड़ी : *In the absence of their teacher the class was in a state of anarchy.* ▸ **anarchic** / अ'नार्किक् / (**anarchical** / अ'नार्किकल् / भी) *adj* अराजक **anar-**

chism / ऐनर्किज़म़ / *noun* अराजकतावाद, शासन को अनावश्यक मानने वाला राजनीतिक सिद्धांत **anarchist** / 'ऐनर्किस्ट / *noun* अराजकतावादी; अराजकता फैलाने वाला।

anatomy / अ'नैटमि / *noun* (*pl* **anatomies**) 1 शरीर-रचना विज्ञान, शारीरिकी : *a professor of anatomy* 2 शरीर-संरचना : *the anatomy of the frog* ▶ **anatomical** /ऐन'टॉमिकल् / *adj* शारीरिक; संरचनात्मक **anatomist** /,ए'नैटमिस्ट / *noun* शरीर-संरचना का वैज्ञानिक अध्ययन करने वाला।

ancestor / 'ऐनसेस्टर् / *noun* 1 पूर्वज, पुरखा : *His ancestors had come to England as refugees.* 2 ऐसा जंतु जिससे आधुनिक प्रजाति विकसित हुई हो : *The mammoth was the ancestor of modern-day elephants.* 3 किसी यंत्र का प्रारंभिक रूप जिसे बाद में और विकसित किया गया है ▶ **ancestral** / ऐन'सेस्ट्रल् / *adj* पुश्तैनी, पैतृक : *his ancestral home* **ancestry** / 'ऐनसेस्ट्रि / *noun* वंशावली; कुल-परंपरा : *have a distinguished ancestry.*

anchor / 'ऐङ्कर् / *noun* 1 (जहाज़ का) लंगर 2 सुरक्षा और विश्वास प्रदान करने वाला व्यक्ति/वस्तु : *Without the anchor of family support I would never have survived the ordeal.* ▶ **anchor** *verb* लंगर डालना : *We anchored (our boat) close to the shore.* **anchorage** / 'ऐङ्करिज् / *noun* लंगरगाह।

ancient / 'एन्शन्ट् / *adj* प्राचीन; बहुत पुराना : *ancient civilizations.*

ancillary / ऐन'सिलरि; *US* 'ऐनसलेरि / *adj* **ancillary (to sth)** सहायक : *ancillary staff/duties.*

and / ऐन्ड; अन्ड; अन् / *conj* 1 और : *bread and butter* 2 तब, उसके बाद : *She came in and sat down.* 3 के फलस्वरूप; परिणामत: : *Work hard and you will pass your examinations.*

4 बार-बार; बढ़ते हुए : *He tried and tried but without success.* 5 जुड़कर : *5 and 5 makes 10.*

anecdote / 'ऐनिक्डोट् / *noun* **anecdote (about sb/sth)** चुटकुला, लतीफ़ा : *He's always telling us anecdotes about his childhood in the village.*

anemone / अ'नेमनि / *noun* सफ़ेद, लाल या जामुनी रंग के फूलों वाला एक छोटा पौधा।

anew / अ'न्यू; *US* अ'नू / *adv* (प्राय: *साहि*) फिर से, नए सिरे से : *ponder anew on life's mysteries.*

angel / 'एन्जल् / *noun* 1 (विशेषत: ईसाई मत में) देवदूत, फ़रिश्ता : *An angel appeared to the shepherds.* 2 दयालु, आकर्षक एवं सुंदर व्यक्ति ▶ **angelic** / ऐन 'जेलिक् / *adj* देवदूत-समान : *an angelic smile/voice/face.*

anger / 'ऐङ्गर् / *noun* **anger (at sb/sth)** क्रोध, नाराज़गी : *express/voice one's anger* ▶ **anger** *verb* (किसी को) क्रोधित करना; नाराज़ करना : *The question clearly angered her.*

angle¹ /'ऐङ्गल्/ *noun* 1 (दो रेखाओं के बीच का) कोण : *an angle of 45°* 2 ज़मीन के सापेक्ष एक रेखा या गति की दिशा : *The plane was coming in at a steep angle.* 3 किसी चीज़ को एक कोण से देखने की स्थिति : *Seen from this angle the woman in the picture is smiling.* 4 नज़रिया, दृष्टिकोण : *We're looking for a new angle for our next advertising campaign.* ▶ **angle** *verb* मोड़ देना, घुमाव देना।

angle² /'ऐङ्गल्/ *verb* 1 (प्राय: **go angling**) बंसी से मछली पकड़ना : *angling for trout* 2 **angle for sth** (अनौप) इशारे से कुछ प्राप्त करने का प्रयास करना : *angle for an invitation/a free ticket* ▶ **angler** / 'ऐङ्गलर् / *noun* बंसी से मछली पकड़ने वाला।

Anglican / 'ऐङ्ग्लिकन् / *noun* इंग्लैंड के

चर्च का सदस्य ▶ **Anglican** *adj* : *the Anglican prayer-book.*

Anglicize, -ise / ऐड्ग्लिसाइज़् / *verb* अँग्रेज़ीकरण, अँग्रेज़ीरूप : *'Rome' is the Anglicized form of 'Roma'.*

Anglo- *pref* (*पूर्वपद*) अँग्रेज़ी, आंग्ल : *Anglo-American.*

angry / ऐड्ग्रि / *adj* (**-ier, -iest**) angry (**with sb**) (**at/about sth**) क्रुद्ध, कुपित, ख़फ़ा, नाराज़ : *an angry mob* ▶ **angrily** *adv* क्रोध से, गुस्से में।

anguish / ऐड्ग्विश् / *noun* वेदना; मनोव्यथा : *He groaned in anguish.* ▶ **anguished** *adj* व्यथित; वेदनापूर्ण : *anguished cries.*

angular / ऐड्ग्यलर् / *adj* 1 कोणवाला : *angular blocks of lava* 2 (व्यक्ति) दुबला-पतला, जिसकी हड्डी-हड्डी दिखाई दे : *a gaunt, angular face* 3 टेढ़ा-मेढ़ा : *angular movements* ▶ **angularity** *noun* कोणिकता।

animal / ऐनिम्ल् / *noun* 1 मनुष्य एवं पेड़-पौधों से भिन्न कोई चेतन वस्तु : *the plants and animals of the region* 2 चौपाया जीव : *Animals were grazing near the river.* 3 आदमी सहित सभी जीवधारी : *Man is unique among animals for having developed the power of speech.* ▶ **animal** *adj* पाशविक, पशुवत **animal husbandry** *noun* पशुपालन।

animate[1] / ऐनिमेट् / *verb* 1 सजीव और सक्रिय बनाना, अनुप्राणित करना : *A smile suddenly animated her face.* 2 व्यक्ति अथवा जंतुओं के चित्रों को सजीव चलता हुआ दिखाना ▶ **animated** *adj* 1 सजीव, जोशपूर्ण, फुरतीला : *an animated conversation/discussion* 2 जीवित समान : *animated cartoons/drawings* **animation** / ऐनि मेश्न् / *noun* 1 सजीवता, जोश 2 चित्रों को चलित रूप में दिखाने की तकनीक : *computer animation* **animator** *noun* चलचित्र तैयार करने वाला; प्रोत्साहक।

animate[2] / ऐनिमट् / *adj* जीवित, जीवंत।

animosity / ऐनि मॉसटि / *noun* animosity (**against/towards sb/sth**); animosity (**between A and B**) वैर, विद्वेष, पुरानी दुश्मनी : *He felt/harboured no animosity towards his critics.*

ankle / ऐड्कल् / *noun* टखना ▶ **anklet** / ऐड्क्लट् / *noun* पायल, पाजेब, नूपुर।

annals / ऐनल्ज़् / *noun* [pl] वर्ष वृत्तांत; इतिहास के आलेख; (किसी विद्वत् सभा-समिति का) वार्षिक विवरण : *the Annals of the Society.*

annex / अ नेक्स् / *verb* annex sth (**to sth**) किसी बड़ी वस्तु में मिलाना या जोड़ना, किसी देश को जीतकर अपने में मिलाना : *annex a neighbouring state* ▶ **annexation** / ऐनेक् सेश्न् / *noun* संयोजन, समामेलन; अनुबंध।

annexe (**annex** भी) / ऐनेक्स् / *noun* 1 किसी बड़े भवन से संलग्न या अनुबद्ध छोटा भवन : *The hotel was full so we had to sleep in the annexe.* 2 अनुलग्नक, परिशिष्ट।

annihilate / अ नाइअलेट् / *verb* 1 पूरी तरह नाश करना, अस्तित्व मिटाना : *The enemy was completely annihilated.* 2 करारी हार देना : *She annihilated her opponent, who failed to win a single game.* ▶ **annihilation** / अ नाइअ लेश्न् / *noun* संहार, विध्वंस : *A full-scale nuclear war could lead to the annihilation of the human race.*

anniversary / ऐनि वर्सरि / *noun* वार्षिकोत्सव; वर्षगाँठ, जन्मदिवस, बरसी, वार्षिक पुण्यतिथि : *our wedding anniversary* ○ *the hundredth anniversary of the composer's death.*

annotate / ऐनटेट् / *verb* व्याख्यात्मक टिप्पणियाँ जोड़ना : *an annotated copy/*

edition ▸ **annotation** / ,ऐन 'टेश्न् / *noun* व्याख्या, टीका-टिप्पणी : *The text required extensive annotation.*

announce / अं'नाउन्स् / *verb* 1 घोषणा करना, ऐलान करना : *They announced their engagement in the local paper.* 2 सार्वजनिक स्थान पर सूचना देना : *Has our flight been announced yet?* 3 रेडियो या टी वी प्रोग्राम प्रस्तुत करना या उसकी सूचना देना : *announce the latest news headlines* ▸ **announcement** *noun* 1 घोषणा, अभिज्ञापन, विज्ञप्ति : *Announcements of births, marriages and deaths appear in some newspapers.* 2 आख्यापन, उद्घोषणा : *The announcement of the result has been delayed.* **announcer** *noun* घोषक, उद्घोषक; वाचक।

annoy / अं'नॉइ / *verb* 1 किसी को नाराज़ करने की हद तक चिढ़ाना 2 परेशान करना, तंग करना : *Stop annoying your mother.* ▸ **annoyance** / अं'नॉइअन्स् / *noun* 1 खीझ, चिढ़ 2 परेशानी या खीझ पैदा करने वाली चीज़ **annoyed** *adj* **annoyed (with sb) (at/about sth); annoyed (that.../to do sth)** नाराज़, खीझा हुआ : *He got very annoyed with me about my carelessness.* **annoying** *adj* कष्टकर, खीझ पैदा करने वाला : *This interruption is very annoying.* **annoyingly** *adv.*

annual /'ऐन्युअल् / *adj* 1 वार्षिक, सालाना : *an annual event/meeting/conference* 2 वर्ष भर की अवधि का (हिसाब-किताब) : *an annual income/subscription* ▸ **annual** *noun* 1 एक-वर्षी पौधा 2 वार्षिक प्रकाशन, वार्षिक अंक **annually** *adv* प्रतिवर्ष।

annuity / अं'न्यूअटि / *noun* (*pl* **annuities**) 1 वार्षिकी, वार्षिक भृति : *receive a modest annuity* 2 वार्षिकी प्राप्ति जमा योजना/बीमा आदि : *a mortgage annuity scheme.*

annul / अं'नल् / *verb* (**-ll-**) (किसी क़ानून, संधि, समझौते आदि को) रद्द करना : *annul a contract/a marriage* ▸ **annulment** *noun* निरस्त करना।

anode / 'ऐनोड् / *noun* (*तक*) 1 एनोड, धनाग्र 2 बैट्री का वह सिरा जिससे विद्युत प्रवेश करती है।

anoint / अं'नॉइन्ट् / *verb* **anoint sb (with sth)** (धार्मिक या किसी और संस्कार के रूप में) शरीर या सिर में तेल लगाना : *The high priest anointed him king.*

anomalous / अं'नॉमलस् / *adj* अ-सामान्य, बेमेल : *He is in an anomalous position as the only part-time worker in the firm.* ▸ **anomaly** / अं'नॉमलि / *noun* (*pl* **anomalies**) **anomaly (in sth)** अपसामान्यता, असंगति : *the many anomalies in the tax system.*

anonymity / ऐन'निमटि / *noun* गुमनामी, अनामत्व : *Anyone providing information to the police will be guaranteed anonymity.*

anonymous / अं'नॉनिमस् / *adj* अनाम; अज्ञात (लेखक) : *an anonymous donor/buyer/benefactor* ○ *The author wishes to remain anonymous.* ▸ **anonymously** *adv* नाम न बतलाते हुए; छुपे तौर पर।

anorak / 'ऐनरैक् / *noun* ऐनरक; वर्षा, हवा आदि से सुरक्षा के लिए प्रयुक्त जैकेट जिसके साथ टोपी भी संलग्न होती है।

anorexia / ,ऐन'रेक्सिआ / *noun* भूख की कमी ▸ **anorexic** *noun, adj* क्षुधाहीन व्यक्ति।

another / अं'नदर् / *indef det, indef pron* 1 अन्यतर, उसी प्रकार का दूसरा : *Would you like another cup of tea?* 2 दूसरी प्रकार का : *That's quite another matter.*

answer[1] / आन्सर्; US ऐन्सर् / noun
answer (to sb/sth) 1 उत्तर, जवाब :
The answer he gave was quite surprising. 2 प्रश्न का हल, प्रश्नोत्तर
3 समस्या का समाधान : *This could be the answer to all our difficulties.*

answer[2] / आन्सर्; US ऐन्सर् / verb
1 उत्तर देना : *answer a question/a letter* 2 पर्याप्त और संतोषजनक होना :
answer sb's needs/requirements
■ **answer (sb) back** टोकने पर ढीठ उत्तर
देना : *Don't answer back!* **answer for sb/sth** 1 ज़िम्मेदारी स्वीकार करना/
आरोप स्वीकारना 2 उत्तरदायी होना : *Knowing her well I can certainly answer for her honesty.* ▸ **answerable**
/ आन्सरबल् / adj 1 **answerable to sb (for sth)** जवाबदेह, उत्तरदायी : *I am answerable to the company for the use of this equipment.* 2 उत्तर/
जवाब देने योग्य।

ant / ऐन्ट् / noun चींटी ▸ **ant hill** noun
बॉंबी।

antagonism / ऐन् टैगनिज़म् / noun
antagonism (to/towards sb/sth); antagonism (between A and B)
विरोध, प्रतिरोध : *You could sense the antagonism between them.*

antagonist / ऐन् टैगनिस्ट् / noun
विरोधी, प्रतिद्वंदी।

antagonistic / ऐन् टैग निस्टिक् / adj
विरुद्ध, प्रतिकूल; प्रतिरोधी : *be antagonistic towards new ideas* ▸ **antagonistically** adv.

antagonize, -ise / ऐन् टैगनाइज़/ verb
(किसी को अपना) विरोधी या दुश्मन बनाना;
अत्यधिक नाराज़ करना : *It would be dangerous to antagonize him —
he has a very nasty temper.*

Antarctic / ऐन् टार्क्टिक् / adj दक्षिणी ध्रुव
का प्रदेश : *Antarctic explorers.*

antecedent / ऐन्टि सीड्न्ट् / noun
1 (औप) पूर्व-वृत्तांत : *the antecedent of the current exam system* 2 **antecedents** [pl] पूर्वज; व्यक्ति की पारिवारिक
एवं सामाजिक पृष्ठभूमि ▸ **antecedent**
adj (औप) पूर्ववर्ती : *antecedent events.*

antelope / ऐन्टिलोप् / noun (pl अपरिवर्तित या **antelopes**) एक प्रकार का हिरण।

antenatal / ऐन्टि नेटल् / adj (विशेषत:
US **prenatal** भी) जन्म से पूर्व, उत्पत्ति के
पूर्व का : *Antenatal complications can affect a baby's health.*

antenna / ऐन् टेना / noun 1 (pl
antennae / ऐन् टेनी /) कीड़े के सिर पर
निकले स्पर्शक 2 (pl **antennas** या
antennae) (विशेषत: US) रेडियो अथवा
टी वी का एरियल, ऐंटेना।

anterior / ऐन् टिएरिअर् / adj (औप)
पूर्ववर्ती; अग्रवर्ती।

anthem / ऐन्थ्म् / noun 1 (चर्च में)
धार्मिक समूहगान 2 (**national anthem**
भी) राष्ट्रगान।

anthology / ऐन् थॉलजि / noun (pl
anthologies) 1 (एक ही विषय पर)
विभिन्न लेखकों की रचनाओं का संकलन;
(एक ही लेखक की) विविध कृतियों से चुनी
रचनाओं का समूह, चयनिका : *an anthology of love poetry* 2 गद्यावली/पद्यावली,
गद्य/पद्य संग्रह।

anthropoid / ऐन्थ्रपॉइड्/ adj मानवाकार
का : *anthropoid ancestors of modern humans* ▸ **anthropoid** noun
मानवसदृश जानवर, जैसे गोरिल्ला।

anthropology / ऐन्थ्र पॉलजि / noun
मानव की उत्पत्ति, उसके विश्वासों, प्रथाओं
के प्रारंभ, विकास आदि का वैज्ञानिक अध्ययन,
मानव-विज्ञान ▸ **anthropological** adj
मानवशास्त्रीय **anthropologist** / ऐन्थ्र
पॉलजिस्ट् / noun मानव-विज्ञानी।

anti- pref (उपसर्ग) 1 प्रति, विरोधी :
anti-aircraft (हवामार, विमान-भेदी)

2 विपरीत, उलटा : *anti-hero* ० *anti-clockwise* 3 रोधी, निरोधक : *antiseptic*.

antibiotic / ˌऐन्टिबाइ'ऑटिक / *noun, adj* प्रतिजीव, जीवाणुनाशक : *The doctor has put me on (a course of) antibiotics*.

antibody / 'ऐन्टिबॉडि / *noun (pl* **antibodies)** रोगों से लड़ने की क्षमता के लिए रक्त में तैयार होने वाला पदार्थ।

anticipate / ऐन्'टिसिपेट् / *verb* 1 प्रत्याशा करना, आगे का देखना : *Do you anticipate (meeting) any trouble?* 2 (औप) दूसरे की तुलना में पहले कर लेना 3 किसी घटना के लिए पहले से अनुमान कर लेना/तैयारी कर लेना : *A good general can anticipate what the enemy can do.* 4 किसी पूर्वानुमानित बात के बारे में खुशी और उमंग से सोचना : *We eagerly anticipated the day we would leave school.* ▸ **anticipatory** / ऐन् ˌटिसि 'पेटरि / *adj* (औप) प्रत्याशी, पूर्वाभासी : *a fast anticipatory movement by the goalkeeper.*

anticipation / ऐन्ˌटिसि'पेश्न् / *noun* 1 पूर्वाभास, प्रत्याशा, पूर्वानुमान : *In anticipation of bad weather we took plenty of warm clothes.* 2 किसी आनंदप्रद घटना की अपेक्षा में उत्तेजना : *Her eyes were sparkling with excitement and anticipation.*

anticlimax / ˌऐन्टि'क्लाइमैक्स् / *noun* उच्च, गंभीर या महत्त्वपूर्ण स्थिति का अचानक दुर्बल अथवा निराश अंत : *The trip itself was a bit of an anticlimax after all the excitement of planning it.*

anticlockwise / ˌऐन्टि'क्लॉकवाइज़् / (विशेषत: *US* **counter-clockwise** भी) *adv, adj* घड़ी की सूइयों के घूमने की विपरीत दिशा में : *Turn the key in an anticlockwise direction.*

antics / 'ऐन्टिक्स् / *noun [pl]* मसख़रापन; उछल-कूद : *laughing at the clown's silly antics.*

anticyclone / ˌऐन्टि'साइक्लोन् / *noun* प्रतिचक्रवात; उच्च वायुमंडलीय दबाव वाला क्षेत्र जिससे मौसम साफ़ और शांत हो जाता है।

antidote / 'ऐन्टिडोट / *noun* **antidote (to sth)** 1 विष या बीमारी के हानिकर प्रभाव को रोकने वाली दवाई : *an antidote to snake-bites* 2 किसी भी अप्रिय चीज़ के प्रभाव को समाप्त करने वाली अन्य वस्तु।

antipathy / ऐन्'टिपथ़ि / *noun* **antipathy (to/towards sb/sth); antipathy (between A and B)** 1 प्रतिकूलता की भावना, वैर-भाव : *She made no attempts to hide her feelings of antipathy.* 2 (प्राय: *sing*) विद्वेष का प्रदर्शन/उदाहरण : *He showed a marked antipathy to foreigners.*

antiquated / 'ऐन्टिक्वेटिड् / *adj* (प्राय: अपमा) (वस्तु या विचार) अप्रचलित; पुरातन : *an antiquated bus.*

antique / ऐन्'टीक् / *adj* 1 प्राचीनकाल की और मूल्यवान : *an antique vase* 2 (कभी-कभी अपमा) पौराणिक; अतीत में प्रचलित ▸ **antique** *noun* अतीत की कलाकृति या पुरावशेष : *It appears that the chest is a valuable antique.*

antiquity / ऐन्'टिक्वटि / *noun (pl* **antiquities)** 1 बहुत प्राचीनकाल, विशेषकर मध्यकाल से पहले का इतिहास काल 2 महान युग : *Athens is a city of great antiquity.* 3 (प्राय: *pl*) प्राचीनकालीन कलाकृति : *a museum full of Greek and Roman antiquities.*

antiseptic / ˌऐन्टि'सेप्टिक् / *noun* रोगाणुरोधक पदार्थ : *a bottle of antiseptic* ▸ **antiseptic** *adj* रोगाणुरोधक : *an antiseptic ointment/cream.*

antisocial / ˌऐन्टि'सोश्ल् / *adj* (अपमा) 1 सामाजिक व्यवस्था के विपरीत, असामाजिक : *antisocial behaviour* 2 मैत्री-गोष्ठी से अलग रहने वाला, असामाजिक।

antithesis / ऐन्'टिथिसिस् / noun (pl antitheses / ऐन्'टिथिसीज़ /) (औप) 1 वैपरीत्य, विपरीतता : The style of his speech was in complete antithesis to the previous one. 2 antithesis (of sth/sb) ठीक विपरीत, एकदम उलटा : Slavery is the antithesis of freedom.

antler / ऐन्ट्लर् / noun मृगशृंग।

antonym / 'ऐन्टनिम् / noun विलोम, विपर्याय, विपरीतार्थी शब्द : 'Old' has two possible antonyms — 'young' and 'new'. → synonym देखिए।

anus / एनस् / noun (pl anuses) गुदा, मलद्वार।

anvil / 'ऐन्विल् / noun (लोहार की) निहाई।

anxiety / ऐड् 'ज़ाइअटि / noun (pl anxieties) 1 भय और अनिश्चय की भावना, चिंता 2 घोर चिंता : anxieties about money/job 3 anxiety for sth/ to do sth तीव्र इच्छा : his anxiety to please.

anxious / 'ऐड्क्शस् / adj 1 anxious (about sb/sth) चिंतित, व्याकुल : feel anxious about the future 2 चिंता-जनक : We had a few anxious moments before the plane landed safely. ▸ anxiously adv उत्सुकता से।

any¹ / एनि / indef det 1 कुछ भी/कितनी भी मात्रा : I didn't eat any meat. 2 एक या अधिक : Are there any stamps in that drawer? 3 काफ़ी सारी वस्तुओं में से कोई भी एक : Take any book you like. 4 (नकारात्मक वाक्यों में या संदेह जताते हुए) एक; कोई : I can't see any door in this room. 5 प्रत्येक; कोई भी : Any fool could tell you that.

any² / 'एनि / indef pron 1 कुछ भी मात्रा, कितना भी, थोड़ा : I need some stamps. Have you got any? 2 बहुत-से व्यक्तियों/ वस्तुओं में से एक : If you recognize

any of the people in the photograph, please tell us.

any³ / 'एनि / indef adv (विशेष बल देने के लिए प्रयुक्त) बिलकुल, ज़रा भी, थोड़ा : I can't run any faster. ○ I can't afford to spend any more on food. ▸ **any more** (US anymore) adv 1 अब, अभी : She doesn't live here any more. 2 अब के बाद कभी/फिर कभी : I don't want to see you any more.

anybody / 'एनिबॉडि / (anyone भी) indef pron 1 (नकारात्मक और प्रश्नवाचक वाक्यों में) कोई भी व्यक्ति, कोई भी : Did anybody see you? 2 कोई भी व्यक्ति (चाहे वह कोई भी हो) : The exercises are so simple that anybody can do them.

anyhow / 'एनिहाउ / (anyway भी) indef adv (अनौप) 1 इसके साथ ही; और : It's too expensive and anyhow the colour doesn't suit you. 2 चाहे जैसे भी, जो कुछ भी हो; हर हालत में : The water was cold but I had a bath anyway. 3 (बातचीत का रुख़ बदलते हुए/अंत करते हुए) : Anyhow, let's forget about that for the moment.

anyone / 'एनिवन् / indef pron = anybody.

anyplace / 'एनिप्लेस् / indef adv (US) = anywhere.

anything / 'एनिथिड् / indef pron 1 कुछ भी : Did she tell you anything interesting? 2 कुछ ख़ास/महत्त्वपूर्ण : Is there anything in these rumours? 3 चाहे जो भी हो, कुछ भी : I'm very hungry — I'll eat anything. ■ **anything but** बिलकुल भी नहीं, निश्चित रूप से नहीं : The hotel was anything but cheap. **not for anything** (अनौप) किसी भी क़ीमत पर नहीं : I wouldn't give it up for anything.

anyway / 'ए‌नि‌वे / *indef adv* = **anyhow**.

anywhere / 'ए‌नि‌वेअ‌र् / (*US* **anyplace** भी) *indef adv* 1 कहीं भी, कहीं पर भी : *I can't see it anywhere.* 2 कहीं न कहीं, किसी न किसी जगह : *An accident can happen anywhere.* ▸ **anywhere** *indef pron* कोई जगह : *I haven't anywhere to stay.*

aorta / ए‌'ऑर्टा / *noun* महाधमनी, हृदय के बाँए पार्श्व से रक्त ले जाने वाली धमनी।

apart / अ‌'पार्ट् / *adv part* 1 (व्यक्ति अथवा वस्तुएँ) दूर, अलग : *The two houses stood 500 metres apart.* 2 एक ओर, एक तरफ़ : *She keeps herself apart from other people.* 3 पृथक से, अलग से, भिन्न दिशा में : *She and her husband are living apart.* 4 टुकड़ों में, टुकड़े-टुकड़े : *The bomb ripped the plane apart.* 5 को छोड़ कर : *These considerations apart, the plan seems likely to succeed.*

apartheid / अ‌'पार्टहेट्; अ‌'पार्टहाइट् / *noun* (दक्षिण अफ़्रीका में पूर्व में) यूरोपीयों और ग़ैर-यूरोपीयों के पृथक विकास की नीति; वर्णभेद।

apartment / अ‌'पार्टमन्ट् / *noun* (*US*) एक बड़ी इमारत में एक फ़्लैट।

apathy / 'ऐपथि / *noun* उदासीनता, विराग : *There is a certain apathy about local elections among the public.* ▸ **apathetic** / ऐप'थेटिक् / *adj* उदासीन, विरागी।

ape / एप् / *noun* पूँछरहित बड़ा बंदर (गोरिल्ला, चिंपाजी, गिबन आदि) ▸ **ape** *verb* नक़ल करना : *A number of actors have tried to ape his style.*

aperture / 'ऐपर्चर् / *noun* 1 छेद, छिद्र 2 कैमरे में प्रकाश जाने के लिए छिद्र।

apex / 'एपेक्स् / *noun* (प्राय: *sing*) शिखर; उच्चतम बिंदु; चरमोत्कर्ष : *the apex of a*

triangle ○ (अलं) *At 41, he'd reached the apex of his career.*

apiece / अ‌'पीस्/ *adv* वर्ग के प्रत्येक को, के लिए या द्वारा : *The teams scored one goal apiece.*

apologetic / अ‌,पॉल'जेटिक् / *adj* **apologetic (about sth)** क्षमायाचक, खेदपूर्ण : *He was very apologetic about arriving late.* ▸ **apologetically** *adv* क्षमाशीलता से।

apologize, -ise / अ‌'पॉलजाइज़् / *verb* **apologize (to sb) (for sth)** खेद प्रकट करना, क्षमा-याचना करना : *I must apologize for not being able to meet you.*

apology / अ‌'पॉलजि / *noun* (*pl* **apologies**) 1 **apology (to sb) (for sth)** खेद व्यक्त करते हुए शब्द या विवरण, क्षमायाचना : *a letter of apology* ○ *offer/make/demand/accept an apology* 2 (औप) निर्दोषिता का आश्वासन : *I make no apologies for this decision.*

apoplexy / 'ऐपलेक्सि / *noun* (प्राय: दिमाग़ी चोट के कारण उत्पन्न) मूर्च्छा, चेतनाहीनता।

apostle / अ‌'पॉसल् / *noun* 1 **Apostle** ईसा द्वारा धर्म प्रचार के लिए बारह में से कोई एक पट्ट शिष्य 2 किसी नए विचार, दृष्टिकोण या विश्वास का समर्थक : *an apostle of design/free enterprise.*

apostrophe / अ‌'पॉस्ट्रफ़ि / *noun* वर्णलोप का चिह्न (') जैसे *can't* में।

appal (*US* **appall** भी) / अ‌'पॉल् / *verb* (-ll-) भय या आतंक अनुभव कराना; डरा देना; विस्मित कर देना : *The newspaper report of starving children appalled me.* ▸ **appalled** *adj* **appalled (at sth)** भयभीत; विस्मित; आतंकित **appalling** *adj* (अनौप) भयंकर, भयानक।

apparatus / ऐप'रेटस् / *noun* (*pl* **apparatuses**) 1 (प्राय: *sing*) शारीरिक अंगतंत्र : *the respiratory apparatus*

2 उपकरण, सामग्री : *laboratory apparatus.*

apparel / अं'पैरल् / noun (अप्रया औप्) कपड़े, वेशभूषा, पोशाक : *kings and queens in rich apparel.*

apparent / अं'पैरन्ट् / adj 1 apparent (in/from sth); apparent (to sb) (that ...) स्पष्ट, प्रत्यक्ष, प्रकट : *Certain problems were apparent from the outset.* 2 आभासी, ऊपरी तौर से ही : *Their affluence is more apparent than real.* ▸ apparently adv स्पष्टतया; ऊपरी तौर से ही।

apparition / ऐप'रिश्न् / noun भूत-प्रेत; मृत व्यक्ति की छाया : *You look as though you've seen an apparition.*

appeal / अं'पील् / verb 1 appeal to sb (for sth); appeal for sth अनुरोध करना; निवेदन करना : *Nationalist leaders appealed for calm.* 2 appeal (to sth) (against sth) (क़ानून) किसी प्रश्न या निर्णय पर पुनर्विचार के लिए उच्चतर अधिकारियों/न्यायालय को सौंपना, अपील करना : *She appealed to the high court against her sentence.* 3 appeal (to sb) आकर्षित होना, पसंद आना : *Do these paintings appeal to you?* ▸ appeal noun 1 appeal (for sth) निवेदन, आग्रह, अपील : *make/answer an appeal for help/food/extra staff* 2 आकर्षण, रुचि, पसंद : *Does jazz hold any appeal for you?* 3 appeal (against sth) निर्णय बदलने के लिए अनुरोध 4 (क़ानून) पुनर्वेदन, निर्णय पर पुनर्विचार के लिए न्यायालय/उच्चाधिकारियों से प्रार्थना appealing adj 1 आकर्षक, चित्ताकर्षक 2 हृदयस्पर्शी, संवेदना जगाने वाला appealingly adv संवेदनापूर्ण तरीक़े से।

appear / अं'पिअर् / verb 1 दिखाई पड़ना, प्रकट होना : *A ship appeared on the horizon.* ∘ *A light appeared at the* end of the tunnel. 2 ज़िक्र या चर्चा में आना : *Their names do not appear (on the register).* 3 (पुस्तक, लेख, आदि) प्रकाशित होना : *His new book will be appearing in the spring.* 4 न्यायालय में गवाही/मुक़दमे के लिए उपस्थित होना, पेश होना : *appear as a witness* 5 लगना, प्रतीत होना : *The streets appeared deserted.* 6 पहुँचना।

appearance / अं'पिअरन्स् / noun 1 आविर्भाव, दर्शन : *The sudden appearance of a policeman caused the thief to run away.* 2 (प्राय: sing) प्रकाशन, प्रसारण : *The appearance of these claims in the media is totally unjustified.* 3 (रंगमंच पर अभिनेता के तौर पर या न्यायालय में) पेशी : *His first appearance on stage was at the age of three.* 4 (व्यक्ति/वस्तु) का बाहरी रूप (जो उसका असली रूप नहीं भी हो सकता है) : *She gave every appearance of being extremely rich.*

appease / अं'पीज़् / verb शांत करना; (जो माँग रहा है उसे देकर) संतुष्ट करना : *appease sb's anger/hunger/curiosity* ▸ appeasement noun तुष्टीकरण : *a policy of appeasement.*

append / अं'पेन्ड् / verb append sth (to sth) (औप) साथ लगाना, जोड़ना, संलग्न करना : *append an extra clause to the contract.*

appendicitis / अ‚पेन्ड'साइटिस् / noun बड़ी आंत से जुड़े इस अंश में सूजन आने से उत्पन्न बीमारी।

appendix / अं'पेन्डिक्स् / noun 1 (pl appendices / अं'पेन्डिसीज़ /) परिशिष्ट (प्राय: पुस्तक के अंत में) 2 (pl appendixes) बड़ी आंत से जुड़ा छोटा अंश।

appetite / 'ऐपिटाइट् / noun 1 (प्राय: sing) भूख, क्षुधा, बुभुक्षा : *When I was sick I completely lost my appetite.* 2 appetite (for sth) तीव्र इच्छा, उत्कट

अभिलाषा; प्रवृत्ति : *He has an amazing appetite for hard work.*

appetizer, -iser / ˈऐपिटाइज़र् / *noun* क्षुधा-वर्धक, रुचिवर्धक वस्तु : *Olives make a simple appetizer.*

appetizing, -ising / ˈऐपिटाइज़िङ् / *adj* क्षुधा-वर्धक, स्वादिष्ट; आकर्षक : *an appetizing smell from the kitchen.*

applaud / अˈप्लॉड् / *verb* 1 तालियाँ बजा कर अनुमोदन दिखाना : *The crowd applauded (him/the performance) for five minutes.* 2 किसी की प्रशंसा या अनुमोदन करना : *I applaud your decision.*

applause / अˈप्लॉज़् / *noun* साधुवाद; शाबाशी : *The audience gave her a big round of applause.*

apple / ˈऐपल् / *noun* सेब (फल या पेड़)

■ **the apple of sb's eye** आँख का तारा, अति प्रिय व्यक्ति : *She is the apple of her father's eye.*

appliance / अˈप्लाइअन्स् / *noun* यंत्र; औज़ार या उपकरण : *electrical/kitchen/ surgical appliances.*

applicable / अˈप्लिकबल्; ˈऐप्लिकबल् / *adj* **applicable (to sb/sth)** उपयुक्त, उचित : *This part of the form is not applicable to foreign students.*

applicant / ˈऐप्लिकन्ट् / *noun* **applicant (for sth)** आवेदक; प्रार्थी, उम्मीदवार : *There were over 100 applicants for the marketing manager's post.*

application / ˌऐप्लिˈकेशन् / *noun* 1 **application (to sb)** औपचारिक प्रार्थना, आवेदन करने की क्रिया : *Keys are available on application to the principal.* 2 **application (for sth/to do sth)** आवेदन, आवेदन-पत्र, प्रार्थना-पत्र : *a planning/passport/mort-gage/job application* 3 **application (of sth)** लगाने, प्रयोग करने की

क्रिया : *lotion for external applica-tion* 4 **application (of sth)** विनियोग, लागूकरण।

apply / अˈप्लाइ / *verb* (*pt, pp* **applied**) 1 **apply (to sb) (for sth)** माँगना, आवेदन करना : *You should apply immedi-ately, in person or by letter.* 2 **apply sth (to sth)** लगाना, प्रयोग में लाना : *Apply the ointment spar-ingly.* 3 (क़ानून आदि) लागू करना, विनियोग करना 4 **apply (to sb/sth)** पर प्रयुक्त होना, लागू होना : *What I have said applies to only some of you.* 5 **apply sth (to sth)** (बल) लगाना : *I had to apply the brakes hard.* 6 **apply oneself/sth (to sth/doing sth)** के प्रति प्रयास करना और मन लगाना : *You will pass your exams only if you really apply yourself (to your work).* ▶ **applied** / अˈप्लाइड् / *adj* व्यावहारिक, अनुप्रयुक्त, प्रायोगिक।

appoint / अˈपॉइन्ट् / *verb* 1 **appoint sb (as/to sth); appoint sb (to do sth)** (किसी पद आदि के लिए) किसी का चयन और नियुक्ति करना : *They have ap-pointed Gayatri Ghosh/a new manager.* 2 **appoint sth (for sth)** (औप) (कोई समय अथवा स्थान) निश्चित करना, नियत करना : *appoint a date for a meeting* ▶ **appointee** / अˌपॉइन् ˈटी / *noun* नियुक्त व्यक्ति।

appointment / अˈपॉइन्ट्मन्ट् / *noun* 1 **appointment (with sb)** नियोजित भेंट; नियोजन : *make an appointment with sb* 2 **appointment (as/to sth)** नियुक्तिकरण; पद, नौकरी : *his appoint-ment as Foreign Secretary.*

apposite / ˈऐपज़िट् / *adj* **apposite (to sth)** (औप) परिस्थितियों में उपयुक्त, प्रासंगिक : *an apposite comment/ illustration/example.*

apposition / ˌऐपˈज़िशन् / *noun* (व्या)

समानाधिकरण, एकान्वय : *In 'Paris, the capital of France' 'the capital of France' is in apposition to 'Paris'.*

appraise / अ'प्रेज़् / *verb* कूतना; आँकना : *appraise a student's work* ० *They carefully appraised the situation before deciding.* ▶ **appraisal** / अ'प्रेज़्ल् / *noun* मूल्यांकन : *a staff appraisal scheme.*

appreciable / अ'प्रीशब्ल् / *adj* इंद्रियगोचर, बुद्धिगम्य; पर्याप्त, काफ़ी, अच्छा-ख़ासा : *an appreciable drop in temperature* ० *The change of policy has had no appreciable effect.* ▶ **appreciably** *adv* पर्याप्त मात्रा में।

appreciate / अ'प्रीशिएट् / *verb* 1 समझना, रसास्वादन करना, गुण पहचानना : *You can't fully appreciate foreign literature in translation.* 2 क़दर करना, महत्त्व देना या सहानुभूति दिखाना : *I appreciate your problem, but I don't think I can help you.* 3 (ज़मीन, सामान आदि का) मूल्य बढ़ाना/बढ़ना : *Local property has appreciated greatly since they built the shopping mall nearby.* ▶ **appreciative** / अ'प्रीशटिव् / *adj* 1 गुणग्राही, प्रशंसक 2 **appreciative (of sth)** (किसी चीज़ के लिए) आभार दिखाते हुए **appreciatively** *adv* गुण ग्राहकता से।

appreciation / अ'प्रीशि'एश्न् / *noun* 1 गुण-दोष विवेचन; गुण ग्रहण, समझना : *She shows little appreciation for good music.* 2 आदर, आभार : *Let me express our appreciation for all your hard work.* 3 मूल्यवृद्धि : *The pound's rapid appreciation is creating problems for exporters.*

apprehend / ऐप्रि'हेन्ड् / *verb* 1 (अप्र या साहि) समझना, जानना; आशंका करना, डरना 2 (औप) गिरफ़्तार करना, पकड़ना :

The thief was apprehended in the act of stealing a car.

apprehension / एप्रि'हेन्श्न् / *noun* 1 (भविष्य में कुछ अप्रिय होने की) आशंका, भय : *I feel a certain apprehension about my interview tomorrow.* 2 गिरफ़्तारी, पकड़ : *the apprehension of the robbers/terrorists.*

apprehensive / एप्रि'हेन्सिव् / *adj* **apprehensive (about/of sth); apprehensive (that...)** आशंकित, सशंक ▶ **apprehensively** *adv* आशंका के साथ, सशंक होकर।

apprentice / अ'प्रेन्टिस् / *noun* प्रशिक्षणार्थी, प्रशिक्षु।

approach / अ'प्रोच् / *verb* 1 पास या और अधिक पास आना या पहुँचना : *As you approach the town the first building you see is the church.* 2 **approach sb (about/for sth)** किसी व्यक्ति के पास प्रार्थना या प्रस्ताव के साथ जाना : *They approached their bank manager for a loan.* 3 किसी कार्य या समस्या को किसी विशेष तरीक़े से हल करना शुरू करना : *Before trying to solve the puzzle, let us consider the best way to approach it.* ▶ **approach** *noun* 1 [sing] स्थान या समय में पास आने की क्रिया 2 प्रस्ताव या प्रार्थना प्रस्तुत करने की क्रिया : *The club has made an approach to a local business firm for sponsorship.* 3 **approach (to sth)** कुछ करने का तरीक़ा : *a new approach to language teaching* 4 व्यक्ति अथवा वस्तु के पास पहुँचने का मार्ग : *Police are patrolling the major approach roads to the stadium.*

approbation / ऐप्रॅ'बेश्न् / *noun* (औप) अनुमोदन, मंज़ूरी : *receive official approbation.*

appropriate[1] / अ'प्रोप्रिअट् / *adj* appropriate (for/to sth) उद्देश्य के लिए उपयुक्त; अवसर के अनुकूल : *Jeans are not appropriate for a formal party.* ▶ **appropriately** *adv* उपयुक्त/उचित रीति से **appropriateness** *noun* उपयुक्तता, औचित्य।

appropriate² / अंप्रोप्रिएट् / *verb* 1 स्वयं के उपयोग के लिए लेना, विशेषत: बिना अनुमति के या ग़ैर-क़ानूनी ढंग से; (विचार आदि) चुराना : *appropriate the style of other musicians* 2 **appropriate sth for sth** (विशेष उद्देश्य के लिए) अलग रख छोड़ना : *Rs 20 lakh has been appropriated for the new school buildings.* ▶ **appropriation** / अ प्रोप्रि 'एश्न् / *noun* विनियोग : *a meeting to discuss the appropriation of funds.*

approval / अं'प्रूव्ल् / *noun* संतुष्टि, प्र-दर्शन, स्वीकृति, अनुमोदन : *a nod of approval ○ The crowd showed their approval by cheering loudly. ○ new drug/pesticide approvals.*

approve / अं'प्रूव् / *verb* 1 **approve (of sb/sth)** किसी को अच्छा, स्वीकार्य और संतोषजनक समझना : *I approve of your trying to earn some money, but please don't neglect your studies.* 2 (प्रस्ताव आदि के लिए) सहमति देना; समर्थन करना : *a proposal approved by a majority of shareholders* ▶ **approving** *adj* अच्छा माना हुआ।

approximate¹ / अं'प्रॉक्सिमट् / *adj* लगभग सही : *an approximate price/ figure/amount* ▶ **approximately** *adv* लगभग, क़रीब-क़रीब।

approximate² / अं'प्रॉक्सिमेट् / *verb* 1 **approximate (to) sth** सदृश, लगभग बराबर/समान : *Your story approximates to the facts we already know.* 2 लगभग सही गणना करना ▶ **approximation** / अ प्रॉक्सि'मेश्न् / *noun* 1 लग-

भग सही मोटा अनुमान (गणना में) 2 सा-दृश्यता; नैकट्य; सन्निकटन।

apricot / 'ऐप्रिकॉट् / *noun* 1 ख़ूबानी 2 ख़ूबानी रंग (पीला नारंगी)।

April / 'एप्रल् / *noun* (संक्षि Apr) वर्ष का चौथा महीना, अप्रैल ▶ **April Fool** *noun* पहली अप्रैल को मज़ाक़ में बेवक़ूफ़ बनाया व्यक्ति।

apron / 'एप्रन् / *noun* 1 एप्रन, कपड़ों के ऊपर पहना जाने वाला ढीला कपड़ा ताकि काम करते समय अन्य कपड़े ख़राब न हों 2 हवाई पट्टी का वह क्षेत्र जहाँ पर हवाई जहाज़ वापस घूमते हैं, लादे जाते हैं ■ **(tied to) one's mother's, wife's, etc apron strings** माँ/पत्नी के कुछ अधिक ही प्रभाव और नियंत्रण में होना।

apt / ऐप्ट् / *adj* 1 उपयुक्त, संगत : *an apt quotation* 2 **apt to do sth** प्रवृत्त : *apt to be forgetful/careless* 3 **apt (at doing sth)** मेधावी; सुयोग्य : *very apt at computer programming* ▶ **aptly** *adv* उपयुक्त ढंग से, ठीक ही **aptness** *noun* योग्यता, उपयुक्तता।

aptitude / 'ऐप्टिट्यूड्; US 'ऐप्टिटूड् / *noun* **aptitude (for sth/doing sth)** सहज अभिरुचि, रुझान : *Does she show any aptitude for languages?* ▶ **aptitude test** *noun* अभिरुचि परीक्षा।

aquarium / अ'क्वेअरिअम् / *noun* (*pl* **aquariums** या **aquaria** / अ'क्वेअरि-आ /) मछलीघर, जलजीवशाला।

Aquarius / अ'क्वेअरिअस् / *noun* कुंभ राशि; कुंभ राशि वाला व्यक्ति।

aquatic / अं'क्वैटिक् / *adj* (पौधे या जीव) जल में या जल के पास रहने और बढ़ने वाले।

Arabic / 'ऐरबिक् / *adj* अरब देशवासियों से संबंधित ▶ **Arabic** *noun* अरबी (भाषा)।

arable / 'ऐरब्ल् / *adj* (भूमि) खेती योग्य; ऐसी भूमि पर उगाए जाने वाले अनाज आदि; खेती-संबंधी : *arable fields ○ arable cultivation.*

arbitrary / 'आर्बिट्ररि / *adj* 1 तर्क के

स्थान पर व्यक्तिगत विचारों एवं अनुभवों पर अधिक आधारित, विवेकशून्य : *The choice of players for the team seems completely arbitrary.* 2 मनमाना (निर्णय), दूसरों की परवाह न करते हुए, स्वेच्छाचारी, निरंकुश : *an arbitrary ruler* ○ *arbitrary powers* ▶ **arbitrarily** *adv* मनमाने ढंग से **arbitrariness** *noun* स्वेच्छाचारिता, निरंकुशता, मनमानापन।

arbitrate / 'आर्बिट्रेट् / *verb* मध्यस्थता करना : *arbitrate in a dispute* ○ *arbitrate between management and the unions* ▶ **arbitration** / ‚आर्बि 'ट्रेश्न् / *noun* पंच फ़ैसला, मध्यस्थ निर्णय : *take/refer the matter to arbitration.*

arbitrator / 'आर्बिट्रेटर् / *noun* निर्णायक, पंच।

arc / आर्क् / *noun* 1 वृत्त का एक अंश, वृत्तांश, चाप 2 (कोई भी वस्तु) घुमावदार, वक्राकार : *the arc of a rainbow* ○ *move in a graceful arc.*

arcade / आर् 'केड् / *noun* तोरण पथ, चापों से ढका मार्ग जिसमें दुकानें हों : *a shopping arcade.*

arch / आर्च् / *noun* 1 मेहराब, चाप, तोरण : *a bridge with three arches* 2 (**archway** भी) मेहराबदार, सजा हुआ गलियारा ▶ **arch** *verb* 1 शरीर को मेहराब-नुमा बनाना : *The cat arched its back when it saw the dog.* 2 **arch across/ over sth** आर-पार चाप बनाना : *Tall trees arched across the river.*

arch- *pref* (पूर्वपद) 1 सबसे महत्त्वपूर्ण, मुख्य : *archbishop* 2 घृणित : *archenemy.*

archaeology / ‚आर्कि 'ऑलजि / *noun* पुरातत्त्वविज्ञान ▶ **archaeological** / ‚आर्किअ 'लॉजिकल् / *adj* पुरातत्त्व-विषयक **archaeologist** / ‚आर्कि 'ऑलजिस्ट् / *noun* पुरातत्त्वज्ञ।

archaic / आर् 'केइक् / *adj* 1 (अनौप,

प्राय: *परि*) पुरातनपंथी, पुरातन : *archaic attitudes/views/practices* 2 अ-प्रचलित, पुराना : *'Thou art' is an archaic form of 'you are'.* ▶ **archaism** / 'आर्केइज़म् / *noun* पुराना शब्द या अभिव्यक्ति, पुरातन प्रयोग।

archbishop / आर्च् 'बिशप् / *noun* (ईसाई धर्म में) महाधर्माध्यक्ष : *the Archbishop of Canterbury.*

archer / 'आर्चर् / *noun* तीरंदाज़, धनुर्धर ▶ **archery** / 'आर्चरि / *noun* धनुर्विद्या।

archetype / 'आर्किटाइप् / *noun* (औप) आद्यरूप, आदिरूप ▶ **archetypal** / आर्कि 'टाइप्ल् / *adj* आद्यरूप; आद्य प्रतिरूप।

architect / 'आर्किटेक्ट् / *noun* 1 वास्तु-शिल्पी : *the architect's plan for the new theatre* 2 किसी विशेष घटना या स्थिति की योजना बनाने वाला व्यक्ति : *an architect of economic stability.*

architecture / 'आर्किटेक्चर् / *noun* वास्तु-शास्त्र, वास्तुकला, स्थापत्य ▶ **architectural** / ‚आर्कि 'टेक्चरल् / *adj* वास्तु-शिल्पीय **architecturally** *adv* वास्तुशिल्प की दृष्टि से, संरचना की दृष्टि से।

archives / 'आर्काइव्ज़् / *noun* [*pl*] (**archive** / 'आर्काइव् / भी) पुराने शासकीय, सार्वजनिक या ऐतिहासिक आलेख रखने का स्थान ▶ **archivist** / 'आर्किविस्ट् / *noun* पुरालेखपाल।

Arctic / 'आर्कटिक् / *adj* उत्तरध्रुव प्रदेश, उत्तरध्रुवीय : *Arctic explorers/foxes.*

ardent / 'आर्डन्ट् / *adj* अति उत्साही, उत्कट : *an ardent advocate of free speech* ▶ **ardently** *adv* उत्साह से।

ardour (*US* ardor) / 'आर्डर् / *noun* अत्यधिक उत्साह, जोश : *His revolutionary ardour had inspired a new generation of followers.*

arduous / 'आर्ड्युअस्; 'आर्जुअस् / *adj* श्रमसाध्य, दुष्कर, दु:साध्य : *an arduous journey through the Himalayas* ○ *The work is very arduous.*

area / ˈऐअरिआ / noun 1 क्षेत्रफल, विस्तार : The area of the office is 35 square metres. 2 क्षेत्र, इलाक़ा : desert/mountainous/uninhabited areas of the world 3 विषय क्षेत्र, रुचि विस्तार : the area of finance/training/development ▸ **area code** noun (विशेषत: अमेरिका में) एक विशेष जगह, प्रदेश को इंगित करने वाला फ़ोन-कोड नंबर।

arena / अ'रीना / noun 1 अखाड़ा, रंगभूमि 2 कार्यक्षेत्र, रंगभूमि : the political arena.

argue / ˈआर्ग्यू / verb 1 **argue (with sb) (about/over sth)** तर्क-वितर्क करना 2 **argue (for/against sth)** पक्ष/विपक्ष के मत/तर्क प्रस्तुत करना; बहस करना : He argues convincingly. ▸ **arguable** / ˈआर्ग्युअब्ल् / adj तर्कणीय; विवादास्पद **arguably** adv तार्किक ढंग से।

argument / ˈआर्ग्युमन्ट् / noun 1 **argument (with sb) (about/over sth)** झगड़ा; मतभेद : get into/have an argument with the referee (about his decision) 2 **argument (about sth)** वाद-विवाद, बहस : We agreed without further argument. 3 **argument (for/against sth); argument (that...)** तर्क : There are strong arguments for and against capital punishment.

argumentative / ˌआर्ग्यु'मेन्टटिव् / adj विवादी, विवादप्रिय।

arid / ˈऐरिड् / adj (भूमि) सूखी; बंजर; (मौसम) बिना वर्षा का, शुष्क : the arid deserts of Africa ∘ Nothing grows in these arid conditions. ▸ **aridity** / अ'रिडिट / noun सूखापन, शुष्कता।

Aries / ˈएअरीज़् / noun मेष राशि; मेष राशि वाला व्यक्ति।

arise / अ'राइज़् / verb (pt **arose** / अ'रोज़्/; pp **arisen** / अ'रिज़्न्/) 1 अस्तित्व में आना, प्रकट होना : A new difficulty has arisen. 2 **arise out of/from sth** उत्पन्न होना, के फलस्वरूप पैदा होना : Are there any matters arising from the minutes of the last meeting? 3 (औप या प्रा) उठ खड़ा होना, उठना : They arose before dawn.

aristocracy / ˌऐरि'स्टॉक्रसि / noun (pl **aristocracies**) 1 उच्चवर्गीय व्यक्तियों द्वारा चलाया शासन 2 कुलीन, उच्च वर्ग के व्यक्ति, अभिजात वर्ग।

aristocrat / ˈऐरिस्ट्रैट् / noun कुलीन अथवा उच्च वर्ग का व्यक्ति ▸ **aristocratic** / ˌऐरिस्ट्रै'क्रैटिक् / adj कुलीन, अभिजात वर्ग का।

arithmetic / अ'रिथ्मटिक् / noun अंकगणित : He's not very good at arithmetic.

ark / आर्क् / noun **the ark (Noah's ark** भी) noun [sing] बाइबिल में वर्णित नोह का जहाज़ जिसमें प्रलय से बचने के लिए नोह का परिवार तथा पशु-पक्षी बैठाए गए थे।

arm[1] / आर्म् / noun बाँह, भुजा, बाहु : She held the baby in her arms. ∘ She held the fish at arm's length. (हाथ भर/गज़ भर की दूरी पर) ■ **arm in arm** हाथ में हाथ डाले हुए **the (long) arm of sb/sth** किसी के अधिकार और बल की सीमा; किसी की शक्ति का प्रभाव।

arm[2] / आर्म् / verb 1 **arm oneself/sb (with sth)** शस्त्रास्त्रों से सुसज्जित करना, युद्ध के लिए तैयार होना : a warship armed with nuclear weapons 2 बम आदि को विस्फोट के लिए तैयार करना ▸ **armed** adj हथियारबंद, सशस्त्र।

armada / आर्'मांडा / noun युद्ध संबंधी जहाज़ों का समूह।

armament / ˈआर्ममन्ट् / noun (प्राय: pl) सैन्य शक्तियाँ—जल, थल और वायु सेना; जहाज़, टैंक, तोपें इत्यादि युद्ध सामग्री।

armchair / ˈआर्म्चेअर् / noun हत्थे वाली आरामदेह कुर्सी।

armistice / ˈआर्मिसटिस् / noun (प्राय: sing) युद्ध विराम, युद्ध के बीच कुछ समय

तक लड़ाई न करने की संधि : *ask for/ seek/sign an armistice.*

armour (*US* **armor**) / आर्मर् / *noun* 1 कवच; जहाज़, टैंक आदि की सुरक्षा के लिए धातु (लौह) का आवरण 2 कवच वाली या बकतरबंद गाड़ियाँ : *an attack by infantry and armour* ▸ **armoured** (*US* **armored**) *adj* कवचित, बकतरबंद; बकतरबंद गाड़ियों से सुसज्जित **armoury** (*US* **armory**) / आर्मरि / *noun* (*pl* **armouries**) हथियारघर, शस्त्रागार।

arms / आर्म्ज़् / *noun* [*pl*] आयुध, शस्त्र, हथियार : *arms and ammunition* ■ **take up arms** (**against sb**) युद्ध घोषित करना, लड़ाई करना (**be**) **up in arms** (**about/over sth**) कड़ा विरोध/ प्रतिरोध करना।

army / आर्मि / *noun* (*pl* **armies**) 1 देश की सेना, फ़ौज; **the army** [*sing*] फ़ौजी सेवा : *go into/be in/join/leave the army* 2 बड़ी संख्या, दल, भीड़, समूह : *an army of advisers/officials/ants* 3 संगठित व्यक्तियों का बड़ा दल : *an army of volunteers/workmen.*

aroma / अ'रोमा / *noun* (*pl* **aromas**) सुगंध : *the aroma of coffee/cigars/ hot chestnuts* ▸ **aromatic** / ˌऐरˈमैटिक् / *adj* सुगंधित।

around¹ / अ'राउन्ड् / *adv* 1 (अनौप) लगभग, के आस-पास : *around 100 people* ○ *He arrived (at) around five o'clock.* 2 चारों ओर, चौतरफ़ा : *hear laughter all around.*

around² / अ'राउन्ड् / *adv part* 1 यहाँ-वहाँ, इधर-उधर : *run/drive/walk/look around* 2 जहाँ-तहाँ : *books left around on the floor* 3 कुछ विशेष न करते हुए : *Several young girls were sitting around looking bored.* 4 आस-पास : *I can't see anyone around.*

around³ / अ'राउन्ड् / *prep* (विशेषत:

US) 1 किसी स्थान पर चारों ओर/इधर-उधर : *running around the playground* 2 इधर-उधर, जहाँ-तहाँ : *Chairs were left scattered around the room.* 3 पास में ही कहीं, यहीं-कहीं : *It's around here somewhere.* 4 किसी को/किसी चीज़ को घेरे हुए : *He put his arms around her.* 5 घेरे में चारों ओर घूमते हुए : *The earth moves around the sun.*

arouse / अ'राउज़् / *verb* 1 **arouse sb** (**from sth**) जगाना, सचेत करना : *He was aroused (from his nap) by the doorbell.* 2 भड़काना, उत्तेजित करना : *Her strange behaviour aroused our suspicions.* ○ *He succeeded in arousing the nation's sympathy.*

arrange / अ'रेन्ज् / *verb* 1 व्यवस्थित करना, क़रीने से लगाना, सजाना, संजोना : *arrange the books on the shelves* 2 प्रबंध/इंतज़ाम/व्यवस्था करना : *arrange a dinner to celebrate their anniversary* 3 **arrange with sb about sth**; **arrange with sb** (**to do sth**) निपटाना, समझौता करना : *I've arranged with the neighbours about feeding the cats.*

arrangement / अ'रेन्ज्मन्ट् / *noun* 1 व्यवस्था : *Can I leave the arrangement of the tables to you?* 2 (प्राय: *pl*) इंतज़ाम, प्रबंध; किसी कार्यक्रम की तैयारी : *He's responsible for all the travel arrangements.* 3 **arrangement** (**with sb**) (**about/over sth**) समझौता, बातचीत : *Appointments can be made by arrangement (with my secretary).*

array / अ'रे / *verb* (औप) 1 पंक्तिबद्ध करना; उचित क्रम से रखना : *His soldiers were arrayed along the river bank.* 2 **array sb** (**in sth**) अच्छे-अच्छे कपड़े पहनना/पहनाना : *be arrayed in cer-*

emonial robes ▸ **array** noun प्रभावशाली प्रदर्शन/समूह : *an array of facts/ information/statistics.*

arrears / अ'रिअर्ज़् / noun [pl] बक़ाया, समय पर भुगतान न की हुई राशि : *arrears of salary* ○ *They have fallen into arrears with the rent.*

arrest / अ'रेस्ट् / verb **1 arrest sb (for sth)** क़ानून के अनुसार किसी को गिरफ़्तार करना, बंदी बनाना : *After the match three youths were arrested.* **2** (और) (किसी प्रक्रिया को) रोक देना : *arrest a decline in share prices* **3** (किसी व्यक्ति/वस्तु का) ध्यान आकर्षित करना : *An unusual painting arrested his attention.* ▸ **arrest** noun **1** गिरफ़्तारी, बंदीकरण : *A warrant was issued for his arrest.* **2** रोक, संरोध : *He died after suffering a cardiac arrest.*

arrival / अ'राइवल् / noun **1** आगमन, पहुँच : *Cheers greeted the arrival of the team.* **2** आया हुआ व्यक्ति : *Late arrivals must wait in the foyer.*

arrive / अ'राइव् / verb **1 arrive (at/ in...)** किसी स्थान पर पहुँचना; यात्रा के लक्ष्य तक पहुँचना : *We arrived at the station five minutes late.* **2** (किसी घटना या विशेष समय/क्षण का) आना : *The great day/Spring has arrived.* ■ **arrive at sth** (निर्णय, समझौते आदि पर) पहुँचना : *arrive at an agreement.*

arrogant / ऐरगन्ट् / adj (अपमा) अकड़, घमंडी ▸ **arrogantly** adv अकड़पन से, उद्दंडता से।

arrow / ऐरो / noun **1** तीर : *shoot an arrow* **2** संकेतात्मक निशान (→) : *An arrow pointed the way to the meeting.*

arsenal / आर्सन्ल् / noun शस्त्रों का भंडार/ज़ख़ीरा : (अलं) *The speaker made full use of his arsenal of insulting language.*

arsenic / आर्सनिक् / noun संखिया, एक तीव्र विष।

arson / आर्सन् / noun आगजनी, दंगे-फ़साद में घरों या दुकानों में आग लगाने का अपराध ▸ **arsonist** / आर्सनिस्ट् / noun आगजनी करने वाला।

art / आर्ट् / noun **1** कला, मनुष्य की कृति; कौशल, कलाकारी, निपुणता : *modern art* ○ *Her performance displayed great art.* ○ *This tapestry is a work of art.* **2 the arts** [pl] ललित कलाएँ—चित्रकला, मूर्तिकला, साहित्य, संगीत आदि **3 arts** [pl] विश्वविद्यालयों में पढ़ाई जाने वाली इतिहास, साहित्य, भाषाएँ आदि विधाएँ : *an arts degree with honours in sociology* **4** कोई भी कौशल या योग्यता जो अभ्यास से अर्जित की जा सकती हो : *the art of appearing confident at interviews.*

artery / आर्टरि / noun (pl **arteries**) **1** धमनी, हृदय से खून ले जाने वाली वाहिका **2** मुख्य थल या जल मार्ग, विशेषतः जिससे माल आता जाता है : *arteries of traffic* ▸ **arterial** adj.

artful / आर्ट्फ़ुल् / adj (व्यक्ति) चालाक, हिकमती; धूर्त, चालबाज़ ▸ **artfully** / आर्ट्फ़लि / adv धूर्तता से, चतुराई से।

arthritis / आर्थ्राइटिस् / noun गठिया, संधिवात ▸ **arthritic** / आर्थ्रिटिक् / adj गठियाग्रस्त, गठिया के कारण उत्पन्न।

article / आर्टिकल् / noun **1** वस्तु, सामान, पदार्थ : *articles of clothing* **2** लेख, निबंध : *an interesting article on/ about education* **3** (क़ानून) अनुच्छेद : *the company's articles of association* **4** (व्या) **a/an** या **the** शब्द (अंग्रेज़ी व्याकरण में)।

articulate¹ / आर्टिक्युलट् / adj **1** (व्यक्ति) अपनी बात को व्यक्त करने में स्पष्ट/सक्षम : *She's unusually articulate for a ten-year-old.* **2** (बात/ भाषण) सुस्पष्ट, स्पष्टतः उच्चारित।

articulate² / आर्टिक्युलेट् / verb

1 (शब्द) स्पष्ट उच्चारण करना 2 (बात) सुस्पष्ट रूप से अभिव्यक्त करना : *Children don't always find it easy to articulate their ideas.*

articulation / आर्‌टिक्यु'लेश्न्‌ / noun 1 अभिव्यक्ति : *the articulation of a belief* 2 अभिव्यक्तिकरण, उच्चारण : *As he drank more wine his articulation became worse.*

artificial / आर्‌टि'फ़िश्‌ल्‌ / adj 1 अप्राकृतिक, अवास्तविक, कृत्रिम : *artificial flowers/light/limbs/pearls* 2 नक़ली, बनावटी, छद्म : *The outside of the house gives an artificial impression of wealth.* ▶ **artificiality** noun कृत्रिमता, बनावटीपन **artificially** adv दिखावटी तौर पर, नक़ली **artificial respiration** noun कृत्रिम श्वसन।

artillery / आर्‌'टिलरि / noun पहियों पर चलने वाली बड़ी तोपें, इन्हें इस्तेमाल में लाने वाली सेना की शाखा : *artillery fire.*

artisan / आर्‌टि'ज़ैन्‌ / noun (औप) कारीगर, शिल्पी, शिल्पकार, दस्तकार : *Local artisans displayed handwoven textiles.*

artist / 'आर्‌टिस्ट्‌ / noun 1 कलाकार 2 कौशल्य/निपुणता से किसी कार्य को करने वाला व्यक्ति।

artistic / आर्‌'टिस्टिक् / adj कलात्मक : *She comes from a very artistic family.* ▶ **artistically** adv कलात्मक रूप से।

as / अज़्‌; ऐज़्‌ / prep 1 की तरह, के जैसे, के रूप में : *They entered the building disguised as cleaners.* 2 जब कि, जब : *As a child she was sent to six different schools.* ▶ **as** adv **as ... as** (तुलना करने के लिए प्रयुक्त) समान स्तर का, वैसा ही : *This dress is twice as expensive as the blue one.* **as** conj 1 जब कि, जैसे ही, ज्यों ही : *I watched her as she combed her hair.* 2 चूँकि,

क्योंकि : *As you weren't there, I left a message.* 3 जैसा कि : *Do as I say and sit down.* 4 जैसा कि ज्ञात है : *Cyprus, as you know, is an island in the Mediterranean.* ■ **as against sth** के विपरीत, के उल्टे **as and when** जब; (अनौप) जब भी संभव हो, अंत में **as far as** जहाँ तक कि, एक सीमा तक **as for sb/sth** जहाँ तक उसका/उस वस्तु का प्रश्न है **as if/as though** मानो कि **as it is** वर्तमान स्थिति को देखते हुए।

asbestos / ऐस्‌'बेस्टस्‌ / noun न जलनेवाला एक पदार्थ, अदह।

ascend / अ'सेन्ड्‌ / verb (औप) ऊपर चढ़ना, आरोहण (पर्वतारोहण) : *The path started to ascend more steeply at this point.* ○ *in ascending order* (आरोही क्रम में)।

ascension / अ'सेन्श्न्‌ / noun (औप) 1 बढ़ना, आरोहण 2 **the Ascension** ईसा का पृथ्वी से स्वर्ग की ओर प्रस्थान।

ascent / अ'सेन्ट्‌ / noun 1 चढ़ाव, आरोहण : *the ascent of Mount Everest* 2 चढ़ाई : *The last part of the ascent is very steep.* 3 उन्नति : *the ascent of man.*

ascertain / ऐसर्‌'टेन्‌ / verb (औप) पता लगाना : *ascertain the facts* ○ *The police are trying to ascertain what really happened.*

ascetic / अ'सेटिक् / adj तपस्वी, तपोमय, तापसिक ▶ **ascetic** noun संन्यासी/संन्यासिनी।

ascribe / अ'स्क्राइब् / verb ■ **ascribe sth to sb/sth** श्रेय देना, के लिए उत्तरदायी ठहराना : *He ascribed his failure to bad luck.* ○ *You can't ascribe the same meaning to both words.*

ash / ऐश् / noun राख, भस्म : *volcanic ash* ○ *Don't drop cigarette ash on the carpet.* ▶ **ashtray** noun राखदानी, ऐश्ट्रे।

ashamed / अ'शेम्ड् / *adj* ashamed (of sth/sb/oneself); ashamed (that...); ashamed (to do sth) लज्जित; शर्मिंदा : *She was bitterly/deeply ashamed of her behaviour at the party.*

ashes / 'ऐशिज़् / *noun* [*pl*] 1 राख, भस्म : *the ashes of a camp-fire* 2 मृत शरीर का भस्मावशेष, चिता भस्म : *His ashes were immersed in the river.*

ashore / अ'शॉर् / *adv* तट पर, स्थल पर : *We went ashore when the boat reached the port.*

aside / अ'साइड् / *adv part* 1 एक ओर, किनारे, अलग, दूर : *He took me aside to give me some advice.* 2 बाद में प्रयोग के लिए : *set aside some money for one's retirement* ▸ **aside** *noun* 1 (रंगमंच पर) स्वगत, कलाकार द्वारा एक ओर बोले गए शब्द 2 विषय से हटकर कोई बात : *I mention it only as an aside.*

ask / आस्क़; *US* ऐस्क़ / *verb* (*pt, pp* asked) 1 ask (sb) (about sb/sth) पूछना : *Don't be afraid to ask questions.* 2 ask (sb) for sth; ask sth (of sb) निवेदन करना, माँगना : *Why don't you ask for a pay increase?* 3 कुछ करने के लिए अनुमति माँगना : *I asked my boss whether I could have a day off.* 4 ask (sb) (to sth) बुलाना, निमंत्रण देना : *Ask them to dinner.* ○ *She's asked him to come to the party.* ■ **ask for trouble/it** (*अनौप*) मुसीबत मोल लेना, खुद आफ़त बुलाना **ask after sb** (किसी के स्वास्थ्य के संबंध में) पूछना, हालचाल जानना **ask for sb/sth** किसी से मिलने के लिए पूछना।

askew / अ'स्क्यू / *adj, adv* टेढ़ा-तिरछा : *That picture is askew.*

asleep / अ'स्लीप् / *adj* 1 सोया हुआ : *The baby was asleep upstairs.* 2 (हाथ-पैर) सुन्न हो जाना, जकड़ जाना : *I've been sitting on my leg and now it's asleep.*

asp / ऐस्प् / *noun* उत्तरी अफ़्रीका में पाया जाने वाला एक छोटा विषैला साँप।

asparagus / अ'स्पैरगस् / *noun* शतावर, शतावरी : *asparagus soup.*

aspect / 'ऐस्पेक्ट् / *noun* 1 पहलू, पक्ष : *examine every aspect of the policy* 2 दृष्टिकोण : *Look at the problem from every aspect.*

aspersions / अ'स्पर्श्न्ज़; *US* अ'स्पर्श्न्ज़् / *noun* [*pl*] (*औप या साहि*) निंदा, बदनामी, कलंक : *It is unfair to cast aspersions on his performance at university.*

asphalt / 'ऐस्फ़ैल्ट्; *US* 'ऐस्फ़ॉल्ट् / *noun* डामर (जो सड़कों पर डाला जाता है) ▸ **asphalt** *verb* डामर डालना/लगाना।

asphyxiate / अस्'फ़िक्सिएट् / *verb* साँस रोककर बेहोश कर देना या मार डालना : *He was asphyxiated by the smoke and poisonous fumes.* ▸ **asphyxiation** / अस्'फ़िक्सि'एश्न् / *noun* श्वासावरोध।

aspirate / 'ऐस्परट् / *noun* (*स्वर विद्या*) महाप्राण, ह-कार ध्वनि : *The word 'hour' is pronounced without an initial aspirate.*

aspiration / ऐस्प'रेश्न् / *noun* (*प्राय: pl*) aspiration (for sth); aspiration (to do sth) अभिलाषा, आकांक्षा।

aspire / अ'स्पाइअर् / *verb* aspire to sth; aspire to do sth कुछ पाने की अभिलाषा करना, आकांक्षा करना : *aspire to knowledge/wealth/fame* ▸ **aspirant** / अ'स्पाइअरन्ट् / *noun* महत्त्वाकांक्षी; प्रार्थी।

aspirin / 'ऐस्परिन्; 'ऐस्प्रिन् / *noun* ज्वर/ दर्द-निवारक दवा, पीड़ानाशक औषधि।

ass / ऐस् / *noun* 1 (donkey भी) गधा 2 (*अनौप*) मूर्ख व्यक्ति : *Don't be such an ass!*

assail / अं'सेल् / verb **assail sb (with sth)** (औप) आक्रमण करना, टूट पड़ना : *assailed with fierce blows to the head* ○ (अलं) *assail sb with questions/insults* ▸ **assailant** noun (औप) आक्रमणकारी, हमलावर।

assassin / अं'सैसिन्; अं'सैसन् / noun हत्यारा, वधिक (जो विशेषत: राजनीतिक कारणों या पैसों के लिए किसी महत्त्वपूर्ण व्यक्ति की हत्या करता है)।

assassinate /अं'सैसिनेट्; अं'सैसनेट् / verb (विशेषत: राजनीतिक कारणों या पैसे के लिए) अंतर्राष्ट्रीय/राष्ट्रीय महत्त्व के व्यक्ति की हत्या करना : *The prime minister was assassinated by extremists.* ▸ **assassination** / अ़ सैसि'नेश्न्; US अ़ सैस'नेश्न् / noun महत्त्वपूर्ण व्यक्ति की हत्या।

assault /अं'सॉल्ट् / noun **assault (on/ against sb/sth)** हमला, प्रहार, आक्र- मण : *make an assault on the enemy lines* ○ *an assault on sb's religious beliefs* ▸ **assault** verb हमला करना, आक्रमण करना : *Six women have been sexually assaulted in the area recently.*

assemble / अं'सेम्बल् / verb **1** एकत्र करना, इकट्ठा करना; एकत्र हो जाना, जुट जाना : *assemble evidence/material/ equipment* **2** जोड़ना, पुर्ज़े जोड़ना : *assemble the parts of a watch.*

assembly / अं'सेम्ब्लि / noun (pl **assemblies**) **1** किसी उद्देश्य के लिए जमावड़ा : *deny sb the right of as- sembly* **2** सभा : *The motion was put to the assembly.* **3** किसी यंत्र आदि के भागों को जोड़ने की क्रिया।

assent /अं'सेन्ट् / noun (औप) **assent (to sth)** (औप) सहमति, सम्मति, स्वी- कृति : *give one's assent to a pro- posal* ▸ **assent** verb **assent (to sth)** (औप) (अपनी) सहमति देना, स्वीकृति

देना : *I suggested we share the cost of lunch and he eventually as- sented.*

assert / अं'सर्ट् / verb **1** दावे के साथ कहना, निश्चयपूर्वक/बलपूर्वक कहना : *as- sert one's authority/independence/ rights* **2 assert oneself** दूसरों का ध्यान व आदर पाने के लिए आत्मविश्वासपूर्ण व्यवहार करना।

assertion /अं'सर्शन्/ noun निश्चयपूर्वक कथन, दावा : *the assertion of one's authority* ○ *frequent assertion of power* ○ *I seriously question a number of your assertions.*

assertive / अं'सर्टिव् / adj आग्रही, आत्मविश्वासी।

assess / अं'सेस्/ verb **1 assess sth (at sth)** मूल्य/कीमत निर्धारित करना : *assess sb's taxes* ○ *assess the dam- age at Rs 35,000* **2 assess sth (as sth)** (किसी चीज़ की प्रकृति, गुणवत्ता, महत्त्व, मूल्य आदि) कूतना : *It's difficult to assess the impact of the President's speech.* ▸ **assessment** noun **1** मूल्यांकन **2** सोचा-समझा अभिमत **assessor** noun कर-निर्धारक; मूल्य का अंदाज़ लगाने वाला।

asset / 'ऐसेट्/ noun **asset (to sb/sth)** **1** उपयोगी गुण या कुशलता : *The President's chief/greatest asset is his reputation for honesty.* **2** उपयोगी/ कुशल व्यक्ति या वस्तु : *She's an enor- mous asset to the team.*

assiduous /अं'सिड्युअस्; US अं'सिजु- अस् / adj (औप) परिश्रमी, अध्यवसायी : *be assiduous in one's duties* ○ *The book was the result of ten years' assiduous research.* ▸ **assidu- ously** adv अध्यवसाय से, परिश्रम से।

assign / अं'साइन्/ verb **1 assign sth (to sb)** (किसी को) कोई वस्तु प्रयोग या उपयोग के लिए देना : *The two large* classrooms have been assigned to us. **2 assign sth (to sb)** (किसी का) कार्यभार या अंश निर्धारित करना : I was assigned the task of checking all the equipment. **3 assign sb (to sth/ as sth)** नियुक्त करना, कार्यभार सौंपना **4** स्थान/समय/कारण बताना : It is impossible to assign an exact date to this building. ▶ **assignment** noun कार्यभार, दिया गया कार्य।

assimilate /अ'सिमलेट्/ verb **1** (विचारों को) अपना लेना : Children need to be given time to assimilate what they have been taught. **2** (लोगों को) अन्य सामाजिक वर्ग अथवा स्थिति का अंग बना लेना; सम्मिलित करना : the great American ability to assimilate other cultures ▶ **assimilation** /अ‚सिम्'लेश्न्/ noun आत्मसात्करण; समीकरण।

assist /अ'सिस्ट्/ verb **assist (sb) in/ with sth; assist (sb) in doing sth** (औप) सहायता करना, सहयोग देना : a relief fund to assist families who have lost relatives or property ▶ **assistance**/अ'सिस्टन्स्/ noun **assistance (for/with sth); assistance (in doing sth/to do sth)** (औप) सहायता, सहयोग **assistant** noun सहायक, सहयोगी, मददगार : the assistant manager ○ a senior research assistant.

associate[1] /अ'सोसिएट्/ verb **1 associate sb/sth (with sb/sth)** अपने मस्तिष्क में व्यक्तियों या वस्तुओं में संबंध स्थापित करना, संबद्ध करना : You wouldn't normally associate these two writers — their styles are completely different. ○ I always associate him with fast cars. **2 associate with sb** साहचर्य मानना, संबंध रखना, संपर्क रखना : I don't like you associating with such people.

associate[2] /अ'सोसिअट्/ adj **1** (कार्य, व्यापार, संघ आदि में) सहभागी या साझेदार : an associate company **2** सह, गौण, उप : Associate members have no right to vote. ▶ **associate** noun साझी, साझेदार; सहयोगी।

association /अ‚सोसि'एश्न्/ noun **1** संस्था, सभा, समाज, संघ : Do you belong to any professional associations? **2** [sing] **association (with sb/sth)** संबंध, साहचर्य, संसर्ग : There has always been a close association between these two schools. **3** मानसिक स्तर पर विचारों का संबंध : Does the sea have any strong associations for you?

assorted /अ'सॉर्टिड्/ adj कई प्रकार से छँटे हुए; फुटकर, विविध : a box of assorted chocolates ▶ **assortment** /अ'सॉर्ट्मन्ट्/ noun एक ही वस्तु के विभिन्न प्रकारों अथवा अनेक प्रकार की वस्तुओं का संग्रह; संचय, संकलन।

assuage /अ'स्वेज्/ verb (औप) (पीड़ा, दर्द, भावना, इच्छा आदि) शांत करना, कम करना, बुझाना : assuage one's hunger/grief/longing.

assume /अ'स्यूम्; US अ'सूम्/ verb **1** सत्य प्रमाणित होने से पहले ही किसी बात को सत्य मान लेना, मानना, कल्पना करना : Why do you always assume the worst? **2** (पद भार) ग्रहण करना, उत्तरदायित्व लेना : assume office ○ Rebel forces have assumed control of the capital. **3** स्वाँग भरना, अभिनय करना; (अपना कोई नया नाम आदि) धारण करना : assume ignorance/indifference/an air of concern **4** एक विशेष रूप, गुण या विशेषता धारण करना : The problem is beginning to assume massive proportions. ▶ **assumed** adj कृत्रिम, कल्पित।

assumption /अ'सम्प्श्न्/ noun

1 पूर्वानुमान, पूर्वधारणा : *an implicit/ underlying assumption* ० *The theory is based on a series of false/ wrong assumptions.* 2 (सत्ता) धारण : *her assumption of supreme power.*

assurance / अंशुअरन्स् / *noun* 1 (**self-assurance** भी) आत्मविश्वास : *act with/ display/possess assurance* ० *She shows remarkable assurance on stage for one so young.* 2 विश्वास, आश्वासन, भरोसा : *He gave me his personal assurance that the article would be finished by Friday.*

assure / अंशुअर् / *verb* 1 **assure sb (of sth)** विश्वास के साथ कहना, आश्वासन देना : *We were assured that everything possible was being done.* 2 निश्चित करना, सुनिश्चित करना : *Victory was now assured.* ▸ **assured** *adj* 1 (**self-assured** भी) आत्मविश्वासी 2 आश्वासित; सुनिश्चित।

asterisk / 'ऐस्टरिस्क् / *noun* 1 तारक; तारा चिह्न *; अशुद्ध/अमान्य दर्शाने का चिह्न 2 कंप्यूटर पर बग़ल में * गुणा चिह्न।

asteroid / 'ऐस्ट्रॉइड् / *noun* क्षुद्रग्रह; तारकाभ; तारारूप।

asthma / 'ऐस्म; *US* 'ऐज़्मा / *noun* श्वासरोग, दमा : *a severe asthma attack* ▸ **asthmatic** / ऐस्'मैटिक्; *US* ऐज़्'मैटिक् / *adj* दमा से पीड़ित।

astir / अ 'स्टर् / *adv, adj* गतिशील; उत्तेजित : *The news set the whole town astir.*

astonish / अ'स्टॉनिश् / *verb* विस्मय में डालना, आश्चर्यचकित कर देना : *The news astonished everyone.* ▸ **astonished** *adj* विस्मित, चकित, भौचक्का **astonishing** *adj* आश्चर्यजनक, विस्मय- कारी **astonishingly** *adv* आश्चर्यजनक रूप से, विस्मय से **astonishment** *noun* विस्मय, अचंभा।

astound / अंस्टाउन्ड् / *verb* भौचक्का कर देना, आश्चर्यचकित कर देना : *His arrogance astounded her.* ▸ **astounding** *adj* विस्मयकारक; विस्मयाकुलक।

astray / अं'स्ट्रे / *adv* सही रास्ते से भटका हुआ : *We were led astray by a misleading sign.* ० (अलं) *His friends led him astray and he ended up in prison.* ■ **go astray** (वस्तु का) खो जाना : *Your letter seems to have gone astray.*

astride / अं'स्ट्राइड् / *adv* टाँगें आर-पार फैलाकर।

astrology / अं'स्ट्रॉलजि / *noun* ज्योतिष विद्या, फलित-ज्योतिष : *Do you believe in astrology?* ▸ **astrologer** / अ 'स्ट्रॉलजर् / *noun* ज्योतिषी, दैवज्ञ **astrological** *adj* ज्योतिषीय।

astronaut / 'ऐस्ट्रनॉट् / *noun* अंतरिक्ष यात्री।

astronomy / अं'स्ट्रॉनमि / *noun* खगोल- विद्या, गणित ज्योतिष ▸ **astronomer** / अ 'स्ट्रॉनमर् / *noun* खगोलविद, ज्योतिर्विद् **astronomical** / ऐस्ट्र 'नॉमिक्ल् / *adj* 1 खगोलीय 2 (अनौप) (क़ीमत, मात्रा आदि) अत्यधिक, बहुत ज़्यादा : *The cost will be astronomical.*

astrophysics / ऐस्ट्रो'फ़िज़िक्स् / *noun* खगोल-भौतिकी, तारों/नक्षत्रों की भौतिक/ रासायनिक संरचना से संबंधित विज्ञान।

astute / अं'स्ट्यूट्; *US* अं'स्टूट् / *adj* घाघ, अति होशियार, अपने लाभ को तुरंत देखने वाला; विदग्ध : *an astute lawyer/ businessman/judge of character* ▸ **astutely** *adv* चतुराई से, होशियारी से **astuteness** *noun* चालाकी, होशियारी; विदग्धता।

asylum / अं'साइलम् / *noun* 1 (औप **political asylum** भी) शरणगृह; (किसी राज्य/देश द्वारा) अन्य देश के नागरिक को दी गई शरण (विशेषत: राजनीतिक कारणों के लिए) : *seek asylum in the UK* 2 (अप्र) मानसिक रोगियों की देखभाल के लिए

अस्पताल ▸ **asylum seeker** *noun* शरणार्थी, शरणागत।

asymmetric / ˌ एसि ' मेट्रिक् / (**asymmetrical** भी) *adj* असममित, विषम : *Most people's faces are asymmetrical.*

at / अट्; ऐट् / *prep* 1 (स्थान) में, पर : *at the end of the runway* ○ *at the corner of the street* 2 किसी घटना पर उपस्थिति के संदर्भ में : *at a concert/ conference/match* 3 शिक्षा अथवा व्यवसाय स्थान को संकेत करने में : *I am at the head office.* 4 किसी व्यक्ति के घर या कार्यस्थान को संकेत करने में प्रयुक्त : *They are at Kapoor's.* 5 एक निश्चित समय दर्शाने के लिए : *leave at 2 o'clock* ○ *at the end of the week* 6 वह उम्र दर्शाने के लिए जब व्यक्ति कुछ करता है : *You can retire at 60.* 7 किसी दिशा विशेष की ओर संकेत करने में : *smile/ stare/wave at sb* ○ *aim the ball at the hole* 8 क्रिया के बाद यह दिखाने के लिए प्रयुक्त कि शुरू किया गया काम अधूरा रह गया है : *He clutched wildly at the rope as he fell.* 9 किसी वस्तु से दूरी संकेत करने में : *hold sth at arm's length* 10 एक अवस्था, स्थिति में जारी क्रिया दर्शाने में प्रयुक्त : *put sb at risk* 11 दाम, क़ीमत, दर या गति के लिए प्रयुक्त : *I bought this coat at half-price.* 12 उत्तमावस्था के साथ : *The garden is at its most beautiful in June.*

atheism / ' एश्इज़म् / *noun* नास्तिकवाद, निरीश्वरवाद ▸ **atheist** *noun* नास्तिक **atheistic** *adj.*

athlete / ' ऐथ्लीट् / *noun* 1 खेल-कूद में प्रशिक्षित व्यक्ति; व्यायामी 2 बलिष्ठ/पुष्टकाय व्यक्ति : *She's a natural athlete.*

athletic / ऐथ् ' लेटिक् / *adj* बलिष्ठ, खेल-कूद के लिए उपयुक्त शरीर वाला : *an athletic figure.*

athletics / ऐथ् ' लेटिक्स् / *noun* [*pl*] शारीरिक व्यायाम एवं खेल-कूद प्रतियोगि-ताएँ : *an athletics meeting/squad.*

atlas / ' ऐट्लस् / *noun* मानचित्रावली, एट-लस : *a road atlas of New Delhi.*

atmosphere / ' ऐट्मस्फ़िअर् / *noun* 1 the atmosphere [*sing*] वायुमंडल : *the upper atmosphere* 2 वातावरण, जलवायु : *an atmosphere that supports life* 3 [*sing*] (मानसिक) वातावरण, मन:स्थिति, मनोदशा : *An atmosphere of tension filled the room.*

atmospheric / ˌ ऐट्मस् ' फ़ेरिक् / *adj* 1 वायुमंडलीय 2 एक विशिष्ट मनोदशा पैदा करने वाला ▸ **atmospheric pressure** *noun* वायुदाब।

atom / ' ऐटम् / *noun* 1 परमाणु : *Two atoms of hydrogen combine with one atom of oxygen to form a molecule of water.* 2 अति सूक्ष्म मात्रा या वस्तु : *There isn't an atom of truth in the rumour.*

atomic / अ ' टॉमिक् / *adj* परमाणु-विषयक, परमाण्विक; परमाणु-ऊर्जा संबंधी : *atomic energy/power* ○ *the atomic bomb.*

atone / अ ' टोन् / *verb* **atone (for sth)** (औप) प्रायश्चित करना : *atone for a crime/one's mistakes* ▸ **atonement** *noun* प्रायश्चित।

atrocious / अ ' ट्रोश्स् / *adj* 1 अत्याचारी, क्रूर, नृशंस, पाशविक : *atrocious crimes* 2 (अनौप) घोर, भद्दा, बहुत ही ख़राब : *speak French with an atrocious accent* ▸ **atrociously** *adv* नृशंसता/क्रूरता से।

atrocity / अ ' ट्रॉसिटि / *noun* (*pl* **atroci-ties**) (विशेषत: *pl*) अत्याचार, नृशंसता, क्रूरता, पाशविक कृत्य : *Many atrocities have been committed against innocent people in wartime.*

attach / अ ' टैच् / *verb* 1 **attach sth (to sth)** जोड़ना, लगाना : *attach a label to* each piece of luggage **2 attach oneself to sb/sth** (स्वयं को) संबद्ध कर लेना/सदस्य बन जाना : *I attached myself to a group of tourists entering the museum.* **3 attach sth (to sth)** यक़ीन करना कि कुछ मूल्यवान, महत्त्वपूर्ण या सत्य है : *Do you attach any significance to what he said?* ▸ **attached** *adj* **attached (to sb/sth)** अनुरक्त, आसक्त; लगाव होना : *I have never seen two people so attached (to each other).* **attachment** *noun* 1 लगाव, जुड़ाव : *two centuries of attachment to Britain* 2 संलग्न वस्तु।

attache / अ'टैशे; *US* ऐट'शे / *noun* सहचारी, किसी राजदूत के स्टाफ़ से संलग्न व्यक्ति : *the cultural/military/press attache* ▸ **attache case** *noun* अटैची, छोटा संदूक।

attack / अ'टैक् / *noun* **1 attack (on sb/sth)** हमला, आक्रमण, धावा : *launch/make/mount an attack on the enemy* ○ *a sudden unprovoked attack* **2 attack (on sb/sth)** तीव्र आलोचना, प्रतिकूल बातें, आक्षेप : *a scathing/fierce/powerful attack on the government's policies* **3** दौरा; पीड़ा, रोग आदि का आरंभ : *an attack of asthma/flu/hiccups/nerves* ▸ **attack** *verb* **1** हमला करना : *They decided to attack at night.* **2** आक्रमण करना, हानि पहुँचाना : *a disease that attacks the brain* **3** आक्षेप करना, प्रतिकूल आलोचना करना : *a newspaper article attacking the vice-president* **attacker** *noun* हमलावर, आक्रामक : *a sex attacker.*

attain / अ'टेन् / *verb* **1** करने या पाने में सफलता प्राप्त करना : *attain a position of power* ○ *attain one's goal/ambition* **2** (औप) विशेष आयु या अवस्था तक पहुँचना; पाना : *attain retirement age*

▸ **attainable** *adj* प्राप्य, साध्य, लभ्य
attainment *noun* उपलब्धि, सिद्धि, प्राप्ति।

attempt / अ'टेम्प्ट् / *verb* प्रयत्न करना, प्रयास करना : *The prisoners attempted an escape, but failed.* ▸ **attempt** *noun* **1 attempt (to do sth/at doing sth)** प्रयत्न, कोशिश, यत्न, प्रयास : *a rescue/a coup/an assassination attempt* **2 attempt (at sth)** कुछ नया करने का प्रयास।

attend / अ'टेन्ड् / *verb* **1** (किसी घटना पर) उपस्थित रहना/होना : *I was unable to attend his funeral.* **2** (किसी स्थान पर) नियमित रूप से जाना : *attend school/church* **3 attend to sb/sth** हाथ में लेना, निपटाना, ध्यान देना, सेवा करना : *I have some urgent business to attend to.* ○ *A nurse attends to his needs constantly.* ▸ **attender** *noun* नियमित रूप से किसी स्थान पर जाने वाला।

attendance / अ'टेन्डन्स् / *noun* **1** उपस्थिति, हाज़िरी : *Attendance at these lectures is not compulsory.* **2** उपस्थित व्यक्तियों की बड़ी मात्रा : *They're expecting a large attendance at the meeting.*

attendant / अ'टेन्डन्ट् / *noun* सेवक, नौकर, परिचारक।

attention / अ'टेन्शन् / *noun* **1** ध्यान, अवधान, मनोयोग : *an issue which has become the focus of media/international attention* **2** विशेष ध्यान : *This letter is for the urgent/personal attention of the manager.* ○ *She is in need of medical attention.* **3** (सेना में) सावधान मुद्रा : *come to/stand at attention.*

attentive / अ'टेन्टिव् / *adj* **attentive (to sb/sth)** एकाग्र, सतर्क, सावधान : *an attentive audience* ○ *A good hostess is always attentive to the needs of her guests.* ▸ **attentively** *adv*

ध्यान लगाए हुए, एकाग्रचित्त **attentiveness** *noun* सावधानी; एकाग्रता।

attest / अ'टेस्ट् / *verb* (औप) 1 **attest (to) sth** किसी चीज़ की सत्यता को प्रमाणित करना, तसदीक़ करना : *I can attest to his tremendous energy and initiative.* 2 साक्ष्यांकित करना, किसी चीज़ की गवाही देना : *attest a signature/will.*

attic / 'ऐटिक् / *noun* अटारी : *furniture stored in the attic* ○ *an attic bedroom.*

attire / अ'टाइअर् / *noun* (साहि या औप) कपड़े, वस्त्र, पोशाक : *wearing formal attire.*

attitude / 'ऐटिट्यूड; US 'ऐटिटूड् / *noun* **attitude (to/towards sb/sth)** मनोवृत्ति, रुख, अभिवृत्ति, व्यवहार : *changes in public attitudes.*

attorney / अ'टर्नि / *noun* 1 न्यायवादी 2 वह व्यक्ति जिसे दूसरे की ओर से कार्रवाई अथवा क़ानूनी कार्य करने का क़ानूनी अधिकार है; अटार्नी, प्रतिनिधि ▸ **Attorney-General** *noun* (कुछ देशों में) महान्यायवादी।

attract / अ'ट्रैक्ट् / *verb* 1 **attract sb (to sth)** आकर्षित करना, आकृष्ट करना; मोहित करना : *Her shyness was what attracted me (to her) most.* 2 (किसी कार्य में) रुचि जागृत करना; ध्यान आकर्षित करना, कोई विशेष रुचिकर प्रतिक्रिया उत्पन्न करना : *The new play has attracted considerable criticism.* 3 खींचना : *A magnet attracts steel.*

attraction / अ'ट्रैक्श्न् / *noun* 1 [sing] आकर्षण : *They felt a strong mutual attraction.* 2 आकर्षक व्यक्ति अथवा वस्तु।

attractive / अ'ट्रैक्टिव् / *adj* मनोहर, आकर्षक, मनोहारी ▸ **attractively** *adv* आकर्षक रूप से।

attribute[1] / 'ऐट्रिब्यूट् / *noun* किसी व्यक्ति अथवा वस्तु का लक्षण (गुण, चिह्न या संकेत), विशेषता, गुणधर्म, सहज गुण : *Her*

greatest attribute was her kindness.

attribute[2] / अ'ट्रिब्यूट् / *verb* **attribute sth to (sb/sth)** कारण ठहराना, उत्तरदायी मानना : *She attributes her success to hard work and a bit of luck.*

aubergine / 'ओबर्ज़ीन् / (US **eggplant**) *noun* बैंगन।

auburn / 'ऑर्बन् / *adj* (बालों का) लाल-भूरा रंग।

auction / 'ऑक्श्न् / *noun* नीलामी, सार्वजनिक बिक्री जहाँ सबसे अधिक दाम लगाने वाले को सामान बेचा जाता है : *The house is up for auction/will be sold by auction.* ▸ **auction** *verb* नीलाम करना **auctioneer** *noun* नीलामी का संचालन करने वाला।

audacious / ऑ'डेशस् / *adj* 1 ढीठ, निर्लज्ज : *an audacious remark* 2 साहसी, निर्भीक : *an audacious decision/plan* ▸ **audaciously** *adv* धृष्टता/ढिठाई से; साहसपूर्वक **audacity** / ऑ'डैसिटि / *noun* साहस; (ढिठाई दिखाने की) हिम्मत; ढिठाई।

audible / 'ऑडब्ल् / *adj* श्रव्य, सुनी जा सकने लायक ध्वनि, कर्णगोचर : *Her voice was barely/scarcely audible above the noise of the wind.* ▸ **audibility** / ऑड'बिलटि / *noun* श्रव्यता, श्रवणीयता **audibly** *adv* सुनने में, सुनाई दे सकने लायक।

audience / 'ऑडिअन्स् / *noun* श्रोतागण; दर्शकगण सभा : *She has addressed audiences all over the country.*

audio / 'ऑडिओ / *noun* इलेक्ट्रॉनिक माध्यमों द्वारा अभिलिखित ध्वनि का उत्पादन : *study at home with workbooks, audio and video cassettes.*

audio- *pref* (पूर्वपद) ध्वनि या श्रवणशक्ति से संबंधित : *an audiobook.*

audiovisual / ऑडिओ'विज़ुअल् / *adj* (संक्षि **AV**) ध्वनि एवं चित्र दोनों का प्रयोग

करते हुए : *audiovisual aids for the classroom.*

audit / ऑडिट् / *noun* हिसाब-किताब की जाँच, अंकेक्षण, लेखापरीक्षण : *an annual audit report* ○ *prepare accounts for audit* ▶ **audit** *verb* निर्धारित समय पर हिसाब-किताब की जाँच करना, लेखा-परीक्षण करना, अंकेक्षण **auditor** *noun* लेखापरीक्षक।

audition / ऑडिश्न् / *noun* ध्वनि-परीक्षण; गायक, संगीतकार, कलाकार आदि की आवाज़, संगीत आदि की परीक्षा : *I'm going to the audition but I don't expect I'll get a part.* ▶ **audition** *verb* **audition (for sth)** ध्वनिपरीक्षण देना/करना, कलात्मक गुण दिखाना : *None of the actors we've auditioned is suitable.*

auditorium / ऑडिटॉरिअम् / *noun* (*pl* **auditoriums** या **auditoria** / ऑडि टॉरिआ /) सभाभवन, प्रेक्षागृह; श्रोताकक्ष; ऑडिटोरियम।

augment / ऑग्मेन्ट् / *verb* (औप) (आकार या संख्या) बढ़ना, बढ़ाना : *augment one's income by writing reviews* ▶ **augmentation** / ऑग्मेन् टेश्न् / *noun* वृद्धि, बढ़त; संवर्धन, आवर्धन।

augur / ऑगर् / *verb* आभास या पूर्वसूचना देना : *Does this augur victory or defeat for the government in the election?*

august / ऑ गस्ट् / *adj* भव्य, प्रतापी; महान, सम्मान्य : *an august body of elder statesmen.*

August / ऑगस्ट् / *noun* (*संक्षि* Aug) अगस्त (वर्ष का आठवाँ महीना)।

aunt / आन्ट् / *noun* पिता या माता की बहन; चाचा या मामा की पत्नी (फूफी, बुआ; चाची, काकी; मामी; मौसी, ख़ाला)।

aura / ऑरा / *noun* व्यक्ति/वस्तु के चारों ओर का विशिष्ट वातावरण जो उसी के द्वारा उत्पन्न किया जाता है : *She always has*

an aura of confidence about her.

auspices / ऑस्पिसिज़् / *noun* [*pl*] ■ **under the auspices of sb/sth** के तत्त्वावधान में, की सहायता से : *set up a business under the auspices of a government aid scheme.*

auspicious / ऑ स्पिशस् / *adj* शुभ, मांगलिक; सौभाग्यशाली : *an auspicious date for the wedding.*

austere / ऑ स्टिअर् / *adj* 1 कठोर, नैतिकता पर अत्यधिक बल देते हुए; अति-संयमी : *My father was always a rather distant, austere figure.* 2 अतिसाधारण, सरल और आडंबरहीन ▶ **austerity** / ऑ स्टेरटि / *noun* 1 संयम, तप, तपस्या; कठोरता 2 सरलता, आडंबर-हीनता।

authentic / ऑ थेन्टिक् / *adj* प्रामाणिक, असली; सच्चा : *an authentic document/signature/painting* ▶ **authentically** *adv* प्रामाणिक रूप से **authenticity** / आथेन् टिसटि / *noun* प्रामाणिकता।

authenticate / ऑ थेन्टिकेट् / *verb* प्रामाणिक ठहराना, प्रमाणित करना : *authenticate a claim* ▶ **authentication** / ऑ थेन्टि केश्न् / *noun* प्रमाणी-करण।

author / ऑथर् / *noun* 1 लेखक, रचयि-ता : *Dickens is my favourite author.* 2 कर्ता, प्रवर्तक, स्रष्टा : *As the author of the proposal I can't really comment.* ▶ **authorship** *noun* लेखक की पहचान : *The authorship of the poem is not known.*

authoritarian / ऑ थॉरि टेअरिअन् / *adj* सत्तावादी, अधिकारवादी : *an authoritarian government/regime/doctrine* ▶ **authoritarian** *noun* सत्तावादी व्यक्ति।

authoritative / ऑ थारटेटिव् / *adj* आधिकारिक, साधिकार : *authoritativ* instructions/orders ▸ **authoritatively** adv अधिकार से।

authority / ऑ'श्रॉरटि / noun (pl **authorities**) 1 आदेश देने का अधिकार : The leader must be a person of authority. 2 **authority (to do sth)** अधिकार, सत्ता : Only the treasurer has authority to sign cheques. 3 (प्राय: pl) अधिकारी/अधिकारी वर्ग : The health authorities are investigating the matter. 4 **authority (on sth)** विशेषज्ञ, अधिकारी विद्वान : She is an authority on phonetics.

authorize, -ise / 'ऑश्रराइज़् / verb 1 अधिकार देना : I have authorized him to act for me while I am away. 2 अनुमोदन करना, अनुमति देना : authorize a payment.

auto / 'ऑटो / noun (pl **autos**) (अनौप, विशेषत: US) कार : the auto industry.

auto- pref (पूर्वपद) 1 स्व, अपने बारे में : autobiography ∘ autograph 2 स्वत: अपने आप से : automobile.

autobiography / ऑटबाइ 'ऑग्रफ़ि / noun (pl **autobiographies**) आत्मकथा, आत्मचरित ▸ **autobiographical** adj आत्मकथात्मक, आत्मचरितात्मक : His novels are largely autobiographical.

autocracy / ऑ'टॉक्रसि / noun (pl **autocracies**) एकतंत्र, निरंकुशता; निरंकुश राज्य ▸ **autocrat** / 'ऑटक्रैट् / noun निरंकुश शासक, तानाशाह **autocratic** / ऑट 'क्रैटिक / adj निरंकुश, एकतंत्रीय; स्वेच्छाचारी (व्यक्ति या राज्य) **autocratically** adv निरंकुशता/स्वेच्छाचारिता से।

autograph / 'ऑट्ग्राफ़; US 'ऑटोग्रैफ़ / noun किसी व्यक्ति द्वारा उसी के हाथ से लिखा हुआ पत्र इत्यादि; विशेषकर महान हस्तियों के स्वाक्षर/हस्ताक्षर ▸ **autograph** verb स्वाक्षर/हस्ताक्षर करना।

automate / 'ऑटमेट् / verb व्यक्तियों द्वारा किया जाने वाला कार्य मशीनों की सहायता से करना : Technical advances have enabled most routine tasks to be automated.

automatic / ऑट'मैटिक् / adj 1 स्वयंचालित (मशीन) : an automatic washing-machine 2 बिना पहले से भलीभाँति सोचे किया (कार्य), स्वाभाविक या आदत के कारण (क्रिया) : For most of us breathing is automatic. ▸ **automatically** adv यंत्रवत्; अपने आप से।

automobile / 'ऑटमबील; US 'ऑटोमोबील् / noun (विशेषत: US) मोटर कार।

autonomous / ऑ'टॉनमस् / adj स्वायत्त, अपने आंतरिक मामलों में स्वतंत्र : an alliance of autonomous states ▸ **autonomously** adv स्वतंत्रता/स्वायत्तता से **autonomy** / ऑ'टॉनमि / noun स्वशासन, स्वायत्तता, स्वतंत्रता : a campaign for greater autonomy.

autopsy / 'ऑटॉप्सि / noun (pl **autopsies**) शव-परीक्षा।

autumn / 'ऑटम्/ (US **fall**) noun पतझड़ : The leaves turn brown in autumn. ▸ **autumnal** / ऑ 'टम्नल् / adj पतझड़कालीन।

auxiliary / ऑग्'ज़िलिअरि / adj 1 सहायक; पूरक; अतिरिक्त : auxiliary troops 2 (**auxiliary verb** भी) सहायक क्रिया।

avail / अ'वेल् / verb ■ **avail oneself of sth** (औप) लाभ उठाना, उपयोग में लाना : Guests are encouraged to avail themselves of the full range of hotel facilities. ▸ **avail** noun ■ **of little/no avail** निरर्थक, बेकार : Our protests were of no avail. **to little/ no avail** लाभहीन; असफल/लगभग असफल : The doctors tried everything to keep him alive but to no avail.

available / अ'वेलबल् / adj 1 (वस्तुएँ) प्राप्य/प्राप्त की हुई, उपलब्ध, सुलभ : Tick-

ets are available at the box office.
2 (व्यक्ति, लोग) सुलभ; बातचीत या भेंट के लिए ख़ाली/उपलब्ध : *The director was not available for comment.*
▸ **availability** / अ,वेल'बिलटि / *noun* प्राप्यता, सुलभता।

avalanche / 'ऐवलान्श; US 'ऐवलैन्च् / *noun* हिमस्खलन, (पहाड़ों पर से) गिरती हुई बर्फ़/पत्थर : *Yesterday's avalanche killed a party of skiers and destroyed several trees.* ○ *(अलं) We received an avalanche of letters in reply to our advertisement.*

avant-garde / ऐव्रॉङ्'गार्ड / *adj* नए और असामान्य विचारों (विशेषत: कला और साहित्य) के समर्थन में : *avant-garde writers/artists.*

avarice / 'ऐव्रिस / *noun* (औप) धन-संपत्ति का अत्यधिक लोभ, धन-लोलुपता : *be motivated by greed and avarice* ▸ **avaricious** / ,ऐव'रिशस् / *adj* लालची, धन-लोलुप **avariciously** *adv* लालच से।

avenge / अ'वेन्ज् / *verb* बदला लेना/चुकाना, प्रतिकार करना, प्रतिशोध लेना : *She avenged her father's murder.* ▸ **avenger** *noun* प्रतिशोधी।

avenue / 'ऐव्न्यु; US 'ऐवनू / *noun* 1 (संक्षि Ave) चौड़ी सड़क जिसके दोनों ओर पेड़ या ऊँची इमारतें हों 2 प्रगति/विकास/सफलता का मार्ग : *an avenue to success/fame.*

average / 'ऐव्रिज् / *noun* 1 औसत-संख्या : *They have an average of just over two children per family.* 2 साधारण, औसत दर्जे का, सामान्य : *These marks are well above/below average.* ▸ **average** *adj* सामान्य/साधारण : *children of average intelligence* **average** *verb* औसत निकालना : *Pay rises this year averaged 2%.*

averse / अ'वर्स् / *adj* **averse to sth** (औप या साहि) किसी के प्रति अनिच्छा रखते हुए, प्रतिकूल; रुझान न रखते हुए : *He seems to be averse to hard work.*

aversion / अ'वर्शन् ; US अ'वर्श्न् / *noun* 1 **aversion (to sth/sb)** विमुखता, घृणा, विद्वेष, विरुचि : *I've an aversion to getting up early.* 2 घृणास्पद वस्तु/व्यक्ति : *Smoking is one of my pet aversions.*

avert / अ'वर्ट् / *verb* 1 **avert sth (from sth)** (निगाहें, विचार आदि) फेर लेना : *avert one's eyes/gaze/glance (from the terrible sight)* 2 बचा लेना, रोकना; निवारण करना : *avert an accident/a crisis/a disaster by prompt action.*

aviary / 'एव्रिअरि; US एव्रिएरि / *noun* पक्षीशाला।

aviation / ,एवि'एश्न् / *noun* विमान बनाने और चलाने की कला या विद्या, वैमानिकी : *civil aviation* ▸ **aviator** / 'एविएटर् / *noun* (अप्र) विमानचालक, उड़ाका।

avid / 'ऐविड् / *adj* **avid (for sth)** उत्सुक, उत्कंठ, आतुर ▸ **avidity** / अ'विडिटि / *noun* (औप) उत्कंठा।

avocado / ,ऐव'काडो / (*pl* **avocados**) (**avocado pear** भी) *noun* नाशपाती के सदृश एक फल।

avoid / अ'वॉइड् / *verb* किसी से बचना/दूर रहना, का परिहार करना, बचकर रहना : *Try to avoid (driving in) the rush-hour.* ▸ **avoidable** *adj* परिहार्य, जिससे बचा जा सके **avoidance** *noun* परिहार, बचाव।

await / अ'वेट् / *verb* (औप) 1 किसी व्यक्ति या वस्तु का इंतज़ार करना, प्रतीक्षा करना : *awaiting instructions/results/a reply* 2 तैयार रहना/होना/रखना : *A warm welcome awaits all our customers.*

awake[1] / अ'वेक् / *verb* (*pt* **awoke** / अ'वोक् /; *pp* **awoken** / अ'वोकन् /) 1 जगाना, नींद से उठाना; जगना, नींद से उठना : *His voice awoke the sleep-*

ing child. ○ *She awoke when the nurse entered the room.* 2 किसी को फिर से सक्रिय बनाना : *The letter awoke old fears.*

awake² / अ'वेक् / *adj* 1 जगा हुआ, जागृत, नींद से उठा हुआ : *They aren't awake yet.* 2 **awake to sth** जागरूक, चेतन, सतर्क : *Too few are awake to the danger facing the country.*

awaken / अ'वेकन् / *verb* (औप) 1 जगाना, नींद से उठाना; जगना, नींद से उठना : *We awakened to find the others had gone.* 2 सक्रिय/जागरूक/ सचेत करना; जागरूक होना, सचेत होना : *Her story awakened our interests.* ▶ **awakening** / अ'वेकनिङ् / *noun* उद्बोधन, जागृति।

award / अ'वॉर्ड् / *verb* **award sth (to sb)** (पुरस्कार, वेतन, हर्जाना आदि) देने का आधिकारिक निर्णय करना : *The judges awarded both finalists equal points.* ▶ **award** *noun* 1 पंचनिर्णय, अधिनिर्णय, न्यायालय का निर्णय : *the award of a scholarship* 2 **award (for sth)** पुरस्कार, पारितोषिक।

aware / अ'वेअर् / *adj* **aware of sb/sth; aware that...** अवगत, जानने वाला, भिज्ञ : *be fully aware of the risk/danger/ threat* ▶ **awareness** *noun* [*sing*] जानकारी, ज्ञान, जागृति।

away / अ'वे / *adv part* 1 **away (from sb/sth)** (स्थान, व्यक्ति से) दूर : *The sea is two miles away from the hotel.* 2 किसी दूसरे स्थान पर या अलग दिशा में : *Put your toys away now.* 3 पूरी तरह से ओझल हो जाने तक : *The water boiled away.* ○ *The hut was swept away by the flood.*

awe / ऑ / *noun* भय और आश्चर्य से युक्त आदर, श्रद्धायुक्त विस्मय : *gaze/look with awe at sth* ▶ **awe** *verb* भयभीत कर देना, विस्मित कर देना : *awed by the*

solemnity of the occasion **awesome** / ऑसम् / *adj* विस्मयाकुलक, वि-स्मयकारी **awe-inspiring** *adj* विस्मय-कारी।

awful / 'ऑफ़ल् / *adj* 1 (अनौप) बहुत बुरा, भद्दा, अत्यधिक अरुचिकर : *What awful weather!* 2 भयावह, भयंकर : *an awful accident/shock/experience.*

awhile / अ'वाइल् / *adv* थोड़ी देर के लिए, कुछ समय तक : *Please stay awhile.*

awkward / ऑक्वई / *adj* 1 बेढंगी (बनी हुई वस्तु), अनुपयुक्त : *The handle of this teapot has an awkward shape.* 2 कष्टकर, शर्मनाक : *You've put me in an awkward position.* ▶ **awkwardly** *adv* बेढंगे तरीक़े से, भद्दी तरह से **awkwardness** *noun* भद्दापन, बेढंगापन।

awl / ऑल् / *noun* चमड़े या लकड़ी में छेद करने वाला सूआ, सुतारी।

awry / अ'राइ / *adv* 1 ग़लत ढंग से; गड़बड़, उलटा-पुलटा : *Our plans went awry.* 2 अस्त-व्यस्त।

axe (*US* **ax** भी) / ऐक्स् / *noun* कुल्हाड़ी, कुल्हाड़ा, कुठार ■ **have an axe to grind** किसी बात में मतलबी (आशय से) भाग लेना, प्रधान आशय रखना ▶ **axe** (विशेषत: *US* **ax** भी) *verb* 1 नौकरी से (किसी को) निकाल बाहर करना : *He/His job has been axed.* 2 क़ीमतें, सेवाएँ आदि कम करना/घटाना : *School grants are to be axed next year.*

axiom / 'ऐक्सिअम् / *noun* स्वयंसिद्ध कथन ▶ **axiomatic** / एक्सिअ'मैटिक् / *adj* स्वत:सिद्ध, स्वयंसिद्ध : *It is axiomatic (to say) that a whole is greater than any of its parts.*

axis / 'ऐक्सिस् / *noun* (*pl* **axes** / 'ऐक्सीज़् /) वह काल्पनिक रेखा जिसके चारों ओर एक वस्तु घूमती है, अक्ष, धुरी : *The earth's axis is the line between the North and South Poles.*

axle / ˈऐक्सल् / noun 1 गाड़ी के दो पहियों को जोड़ने वाली कीली/धुरी : *The back axle is broken.* 2 वह कीली जिससे पहिया या पहिए घूमते हैं।

azure / ˈऐश़्ऱ् / adj, noun आसमानी रंग या रंग वाला, नभोनील : *a dress of azure silk* ○ *a lake reflecting the azure of the sky.*

Bb

baa / बा / *noun* भेड़ या मेमने की आवाज़
▸ **baa** *verb* (*pres p* baaing; *pt* baaed
या baa'd / बाड् /) मिमियाना।

babble / 'बैब्ल / *verb* बड़बड़ाना, (बच्चों
की तरह) लगातार बोलते रहना, (अस्पष्ट-
सी) बकबक करना : *What is he bab-
bling (on) about?* ▸ **babble** *noun*
अस्पष्ट और लगातार बकबक, बकवास :
His constant babble irritates me.

babe / बेब् / *noun* 1 (प्रा) छोटा बच्चा,
शिशु 2 (*US, अप*) लड़की या जवान औरत।

babel / 'बेब्ल / *noun* [*sing*] कोलाहल,
शोर-शराबा; कोलाहलपूर्ण स्थान : *a babel
of voices in the busy market.*

baboon / ब'बून् / *noun* कुत्ते जैसे चेहरे
वाला, एक बड़ा अफ़्रीक़ी या अरबी बंदर;
बैबून।

baby / 'बेबि / *noun* (*pl* babies) 1 (चलने
की अवस्था से पहले) छोटा बच्चा, शिशु :
*Both mother and baby are doing
well.* 2 (अपमा) बचकाना व्यक्ति, जो बड़ी
जल्दी डर जाता है : *Stop crying and
don't be such a baby.* 3 (*US, अप*)
लड़की, प्रेमिका/प्रेमी को संबोधित करने के
लिए प्रयुक्त ■ **throw the baby out with
the bath water** किसी महत्त्वपूर्ण एवं
इच्छित वस्तु को बेकार की वस्तु के साथ फेंक
देना ▸ **baby** *verb* (*pt, pp* babied)
किसी के साथ बच्चों जैसा व्यवहार करना;
किसी को अत्यधिक लाड़-प्यार या सम्मान
देना : *Don't baby him—he's old
enough to look after himself.* **ba-
byhood** *noun* बचपन, बाल्यावस्था, शैशव
babysit *verb* किसी बच्चे की देखभाल
करना (उसके माँ-बाप की अनुपस्थिति में)
babysitter (**sitter** भी) *noun* बच्चे की
(उसके माँ-बाप की अनुपस्थिति में) देखभाल
करने वाला/वाली।

bachelor / 'बैचलर् / *noun* 1 अविवाहित
पुरुष : *He remained a bachelor all

his life.* 2 विश्वविद्यालयों की प्रथम स्नातक
उपाधि (प्राप्त व्यक्ति) : *a bachelor's
degree* ○ *Bachelor of Arts/Science*
▸ **bachelorhood** *noun* कुँवारापन,
कौमार्य।

back¹ / बैक् / *noun* 1 पीठ, कमर : *He
lay on his back and looked up at
the sky.* 2 पृष्ठ भाग, पीछे का भाग 3 (कुर्सी
का) वह हिस्सा जिस पर पीठ टिकाते हैं ■ **at
the back of one's mind** अंतर्मन में : *At
the back of his mind was the vague
idea that he had met her before.*
back to front (विशेषत: कपड़े) आगे का
भाग पीछे/पीछे का भाग आगे **behind sb's
back** किसी के पीठ पीछे, बिना किसी की
जानकारी या सहमति के : *They say nasty
things about him behind his back.*
break one's back (to do sth) कठिन
परिश्रम करना **turn one's back on sb**
किसी से अशिष्ट तरीके से मुँह फेर लेना, पीठ
दिखाना ▸ **backache** *noun* पीठ/कमर
दर्द **backbone** *noun* 1 रीढ़ की हड्डी
2 मुख्य समर्थक 3 चरित्र-बल **back-
breaking** *adj* (काम) कमर-तोड़, अति
श्रमसाध्य।

back² / बैक् / *adj* 1 पीछे या पृष्ठ भाग में
स्थित : *the back door* 2 पिछले समय
का/से, पहला : *back issues of a magazine* ■ **by/through the back door**
ग़लत या अप्रत्यक्ष तरीक़े से **on the back
burner** (अनौप) वर्तमान में स्थगित, बाद में
विचारणीय (मुद्दा) ▸ **back-bencher**
noun कक्षा में पीछे की सीट पर बैठने वाला
backlog *noun* (प्राय: *sing*) अधूरा पड़ा
काम **back seat** *noun* (कार में) पिछली
सीट ■ **take a back seat** कम महत्त्वपूर्ण
हो जाना।

back³ / बैक् / *adv* 1 (स्थान की दृष्टि से)
पीछे, पृष्ठ भाग में; पिछली ओर : *I stepped
back to let them pass.* 2 नियंत्रण में,

रोके हुए : *He could no longer hold back his tears.* 3 (समय की दृष्टि से) पहले, पूर्व में : *The village has a history going back to the Mughal times.* ■ **back and forth** एक स्थान से दूसरे स्थान पर और पुन: वहीं वापस।

back⁴ / बैक् / *verb* 1 समर्थन करना, सहारा देना : *Her parents backed her in her choice of career.* 2 (किसी को) आर्थिक सहारा/समर्थन देना : *They persuaded various banks to back the project.* ■ **back away (from sb/sth)** (डर या घृणा से) दूर भागना, पीछे हटना **back down;** *(US)* **back off** दावा छोड़ देना, पीछे हट जाना **back out (of sth)** वादे से मुकरना, पीछे हटना **back sb/ sth up** किसी व्यक्ति/वस्तु का समर्थन करना ▸ **backing** *noun* सहारा, समर्थन, अनु- मोदन।

backbite / बैक्बाइट् / *verb* चुग़ली करना/ खाना, पीठ पीछे निंदा करना ▸ **backbiter** *noun* चुग़लख़ोर, निंदक **backbiting** *noun* निंदा, चुग़ली।

background / 'बैक्ग्राउन्ड् / *noun* 1 [*sing*] पृष्ठ-भूमि, चित्रभूमि : *a photograph with trees in the background* 2 (किसी व्यक्ति का) सामाजिक, पारिवारिक स्तर आदि : *a middle-class family background* 3 किसी चीज़ को समझने में सहायक स्थितियों/परिस्थितियाँ आदि : *These political developments should be seen against a background of increasing civil unrest.* ○ *background information.*

backward / 'बैक्वर्ड् / *adj* 1 पीछे की ओर : *a backward glance* 2 पिछड़ा : *a very backward part of the country, with no paved roads and no electricity* ▸ **backwardness** *noun* पिछड़ापन **backwards (backward** भी) *adv* पीछे (की ओर) : *He looked backwards over his shoulder.*

bacon / बेकन् / *noun* सूअर की पीठ या बग़ल का नमक लगा या भुना हुआ मांस।

bacteria / बैक्'टिअरिआ / *noun* [*pl*] (*sing* **bacterium**) जीवाणु; लघु कीटाणु, बैक्टीरिया ▸ **bacterial** / बैक्'टिअरिअल् / *adj* जीवाणु-विषयक, जीवाण्वीय **bacteriology** / बैक्‚टिअरि'ऑलजि / *noun* जीवाणु विज्ञान **bacteriologist** *noun* जीवाणु विज्ञानी।

bad¹ / बैड् / *adj* (**worse** / वर्स् /; **worst** / वर्स्ट् /) 1 दुष्ट, बुरा 2 (भोजन या पेय आदि) प्रयोग के लिए अनुपयुक्त 3 (मौसम, समाचार आदि) अप्रिय, ख़राब, अरुचिकर : *a bad smell* 4 घटिया, निम्नस्तरीय, निकृष्ट : *a bad lecture/harvest* 5 (व्यक्ति) निकम्मा, अयोग्य : *a bad teacher/poet/hairdresser* 6 **bad for sb/sth** दूषित, नुक़सानदेह : *Smoking is bad for you/your health.* ■ **not bad** (अनौप) अपेक्षित से अच्छा, ठीक- ठाक **too bad** (अनौप) शर्मनाक; दयनीय ▸ **badly** *adv* (अनौप) बुरी तरह से ■ **badly off** ख़स्ता हाल में, कंगाल, ग़रीब : *She's been very badly off since losing her job.* ▸ **bad-tempered** *adj* चिड़चिड़ा, गुस्से-बाज़।

bad² / बैड् / *noun* **the bad** बुरी चीज़ें, लोग या घटनाएँ ■ **take the bad with the good** किसी चीज़ की अच्छाई के साथ ही उसकी ख़राबी भी स्वीकार करना।

badge / बैज् / *noun* पद, वर्ग आदि दर्शाने के लिए (सामान्यत: छोटे कपड़े या धातु का) तमग़ा, पदक; बिल्ला : *a uniform with a badge on it.*

badger¹ / 'बैजर् / *noun* बिल में रहने वाला भूरे रंग का छोटा जंतु, बिज्जू।

badger² / 'बैजर् / *verb* **badger sb (into doing sth)** प्रश्न, अनुरोध आदि से किसी को तंग कर डालना : *Ravi has been badgering us to buy him a camera.*

badminton / 'बैड्मिन्टन् / *noun* रैकेट और शटलकॉक से खेला जाने वाला खेल।

baffle

baffle /'बैफ़ल् / verb चकरा देना, स्तंभित कर देना, बहुत ही कठिन मालूम होना : One of the exam questions baffled me completely. ▸ **bafflement** noun व्यवधान; विस्मय, अचंभा **baffling** adj चकराने वाला।

bag¹ / बैग् / noun 1 थैला, झोला : a shopping bag 2 थैला भर : two bags of coal 3 bags [pl] आँखों के नीचे ढीले स्याह निशान : She had dark bags under her eyes from lack of sleep. 4 एक बार में मारे गए (पक्षी, जानवर आदि) शिकार : We got a good bag today. ■ **bag and baggage** बोरिया बिस्तर के साथ (प्राय: अचानक और चुपके से) : His tenant left, bag and baggage.

bag² /बैग् / verb (-gg-) 1 (शिकारी द्वारा) शिकार मारा या पकड़ा जाना : They bagged nothing except a couple of rabbits. 2 (अनौप) किसी अन्य से पहले ही कोई चीज़ हथिया लेना/हस्तगत करना : She has already bagged the most comfortable chair.

baggage / 'बैगिज् / noun (किसी यात्री का) सामान : excess baggage.

baggy /'बैगि / adj (-ier, -iest) ढीला-ढाला, उभरा/फूला हुआ : baggy shirts.

bail¹ /बेल् / noun 1 ज़मानत (की राशि), प्रतिभूति : Bail was set at Rs 3,00,000. 2 ज़मानत की अनुमति : The judge granted/refused him bail. ■ **go/stand bail (for sb)** ज़मानत देकर छुड़ाना : His father stood bail for him. ▸ **bail** verb ज़मानत पर छोड़ना या छुड़ाना ■ **bail sb out** 1 किसी व्यक्ति को ज़मानत पर छुड़ाना : Her parents bailed her out and took her home. 2 (अनौप) किसी की आर्थिक कष्टों से रक्षा करना : The club faced bankruptcy until a wealthy local businessman bailed them out.

bail² (**bale** भी) / बेल् / verb **bail (sth)** (**out**) नाव आदि में भरे पानी को बालटी आदि से बाहर निकालना, उलीचना : bailing water (out).

bail³ /बेल् / noun (प्राय: pl) (क्रिकेट की) गुल्ली।

bailiff / 'बेलिफ़् / noun 1 (ब्रिटिश न्याय-व्यवस्था में) शेरिफ़ की सहायता करने वाला न्यायाधिकारी 2 ज़मींदार या मकान मालिक का कारिंदा 3 (US) (कचहरी में) पेशकार।

bait / बेट् / noun 1 मछली (या पशु-पक्षी) फँसाने के लिए बंसी के काँटे या जाल में रखा जाने वाला चारा, चुगा 2 किसी को पकड़ने, प्रलोभन देने या ललचाने के लिए प्रयुक्त व्यक्ति या वस्तु : The police used him as bait to trap the killers. ▸ **bait** verb **bait sb (with sth)** चारा/चुगा लगाना : bait a hook with a worm.

bake / बेक् / verb **bake sth (for sb)** भट्ठी या अँगीठी में पकना या पकाना; सेंकना : I'm baking Sujata a birthday cake. ▸ **baker** noun नानबाई, केक/ब्रेड बनाने वाला ■ **a baker's dozen** 13 (तेरह) ▸ **bakery** / 'बेकरि / noun नानबाई की दुकान, ब्रेड/केक बनाने वाले की दुकान।

balance¹ / 'बैलन्स् / noun 1 [sing] **balance (in sth/between A and B)** संतुलन की स्थिति, संतुलन : Try to achieve a proper balance between work and play. 2 संतुलन, सामंजस्य, सुरुचिपूर्ण समन्वय 3 मानसिक समवस्था, स्थिरता; समझदारी 4 (प्राय: sing) (वाणिज्य) बक़ाया, बाक़ी, शेष : check one's bank balance 5 तराज़ू, तुला, काँटा ■ (**be/hang**) **in the balance** (निर्णय, परिणाम, किसी का भविष्य आदि) अभी तक अनिश्चित : The future of the project is hanging in the balance. (**catch/throw sb**) **off balance** किसी को गिरता हुआ पाना या गिराना ▸ **balance sheet** noun पक्का चिट्ठा, तुलन-पत्र।

balance² / 'बैलन्स् / verb 1 संतुलित अवस्था में होना, करना या रखना : a clown *balancing a stick on the end of his nose* 2 (वाणिज्य) (हिसाब-किताब) बराबर करना, तुलना करना, जमा नामे बराबर करना : *balance an account/books* ▸ **balanced** *adj* संतुलित **balancing act** *noun* विरोधी लोगों को नाराज़ किए बग़ैर समझौता करने की कुशलता/निपुणता : *A delicate balancing act is needed in order to satisfy the two sides.*

balcony / 'बैल्कनि / *noun (pl balconies)* 1 छज्जा, बारज़ा 2 (US) रंगभवन, सिनेमा हॉल आदि में दुमंज़िले पर बनी कुर्सियों की पंक्ति, बालकनी।

bald / बॉल्ड् / *adj* 1 गंजा सिर 2 बिना अपेक्षित परत के, अनावृत्त; बिना पत्तों का पेड़ या बिना पंखों की चिड़िया 3 सरल, बिना अलंकरण के, अनलंकृत : *bald facts ∘ a bald statement of the facts* ▸ **baldness** *noun* गंजापन, गंज।

bale[1] / बेल / *noun* गट्ठर, सामान भेजने के लिए बंधी बोरियाँ या गाँठें या बंडल : *The cloth was packed in bales.*

bale[2] / बेल / *verb* ∎ **bale (bail** भी**) out (of sth)** वायुयान से पैराशूट सहित बाहर कूदना।

baleful / 'बेल्फ़ुल् / *adj* बुरा; हानिकारक, अनिष्टकर : *baleful looks/influences.*

ball[1] / बॉल् / *noun* 1 गेंद, कंदुक : *a golf/ tennis/cricket ball/football* 2 गोल वस्तु, गोला : *a meat ball ∘ a ball of wool/string* ∎ **the ball is in one's/ sb's court** वार्ता/बातचीत/समझौते करने के दौरान किसी के अगला क़दम उठाने की बारी **set/start/keep the ball rolling** बातचीत/क्रिया-कलाप शुरू करना या जारी रखना।

ball[2] / बॉल् / *noun* औपचारिक नृत्य के लिए सामाजिक जमाव ▸ **ballroom** *noun* ऐसे नृत्य के लिए विशाल कमरा, बॉल रूम।

ballad / 'बैलड् / *noun* 1 गाथा, कथात्मक गीत अथवा कविता : *a ballad singer* 2 प्रेम-मुहब्बत से अनुप्राणित गीत।

ballast / 'बैलस्ट् / *noun* 1 जहाज़ को स्थिर रखने के लिए रखा भारी सामान 2 रेलवे लाइन या सड़क पर डाली गई गिट्टी, कंकड़, रोड़ी।

ballerina / बैल'रीना / *noun* नर्तकी, नृत्यांगना : *a prima ballerina.*

ballet / 'बैले; *US* बै'ले / *noun* 1 बैले, संगीतात्मक नाटक जो बिना वार्तालाप या गीत के नर्तकों द्वारा सिर्फ़ अभिनीत किया जाता है 2 नृत्यनाटिका, एक कला के रूप में रंगमंचीय नृत्य 3 नर्तक मंडली, नाट्य-नृत्य मंडली।

ballistics / बलिस्टिक्स् / *noun* प्राक्षेपिकी, अस्त्र विज्ञान, हवा में दागे जाने वाले अस्त्रों का अध्ययन शास्त्र : *a ballistics expert.*

balloon / ब'लून / *noun* 1 ग़ुब्बारा : *blow up/burst/pop a balloon* 2 (**hot-air balloon** भी) (विशेषत: आकाश में उड़ाया जाने वाला) गैस का ग़ुब्बारा ▸ **balloon** *verb* ग़ुब्बारे जैसा फूलना।

ballot / 'बैलट् / *noun* 1 गुप्त मतदान : *elected by ballot* 2 मतों की संख्या ▸ **ballot-box** *noun* मतपेटिका **ballot-paper** *noun* मतदान-पत्र, मतपत्र, मतपरची।

balm / बाम् / *noun* 1 (**balsam** भी) सुगंधित मलहम 2 मन को शांति देने वाला : *The gentle music was (a) balm to his ears.* ▸ **balmy** *adj* (**-ier, -iest**) (हवा) गरम एवं सुखदायी, रुचिकर।

bamboo / बैम्'बू / *noun* बाँस; बाँस का पेड़।

ban / बैन् / *verb* (**-nn-**) 1 प्रतिबंध लगाना, आदेश देकर रोक लगाना : *The government has banned the use of chemical weapons.* 2 **ban sb (from sth/ doing sth)** मना करना, (किसी का कोई काम) अवैध घोषित करना : *He's been banned from driving for six months.* ▸ **ban** *noun* **ban (on sth/ sb)** मनाही, प्रतिबंध, रोक, निषेधाज्ञा : *put a ban on the import of alcohol.*

banal / ब'नाल्; *US* ब'नैल् / *adj* सामान्य, साधारण : *banal remarks/thoughts/ sentiments.*

banana / बॅनाना / *noun* (*pl* **bananas**) केला (फल) : *a bunch of bananas.*

band / बैन्ड् / *noun* 1 (प्रायः बाँधने के काम आने वाली) पट्टी, फ़ीता; बंद 2 (किसी विशेष कार्य के लिए) मनुष्यों का समूह, जैसे संगीत का बैंड; दल, टोली, मंडली : *a dance band/a jazz/rock band* 3 (**waveband** भी) रेडियो तरंगों का परास : *a transistor tuned to the FM band* ▸ **bandmaster** *noun* संगीत मंडली का संचालक।

bandage / बैन्डिज् / *noun* (घावों पर बाँधने व लपेटने की) पट्टी ▸ **bandage** *verb* **bandage sth/sb (up) (with sth)** पट्टी बाँधना : *bandage (up) a wound.*

bandit / बैन्डिट् / *noun* दस्यु, (विशेषतः पहाड़ों या जंगलों में) सशस्त्र डाकू।

bandwagon / बैन्ड्वैगन् / *noun* बैंड-वैगन, कोई लोकप्रिय कार्यक्रम ■ **climb/ jump on the bandwagon** (अनौप) सफल लगने वाले कार्यक्रम में दूसरों की देखा-देखी शामिल हो जाना।

bang¹ / बैङ् / *noun* 1 ज़ोरदार प्रहार : *He fell and got a nasty bang on the head.* 2 ज़ोर का स्वर, धमाका, धड़ाका : *The bomb exploded with an enormous bang.*

bang² / बैङ् / *verb* 1 ज़ोर से प्रहार करना; ज़ोर से मारना : *He was banging on the door with his fist.* 2 **bang sth (down, to, etc)** ज़ोर की आवाज़ के साथ बंद करना/होना : *He banged the lid down.* 3 **bang into sb/sth** किसी से/ किसी चीज़ से ज़ोरों से टकरा जाना : *He ran around the corner and banged straight into a lamppost.*

bang³ / बैङ् / *adv* (अनौप) ठीक, एकदम; बिलकुल : *bang in the middle of the performance* ○ *You're bang on time, as usual.*

bangle / बैङ्गल् / *noun* चूड़ी; कड़ा; कंगन।

banish / बैनिश् / *verb* **banish sb (from sth)** दंडस्वरूप देश-निकाला देना निर्वासित कर देना : *He was banished (from his native land) for life.* ▸ **banishment** *noun* निर्वासन, देश-निकाला : *lifelong banishment.*

banister (**bannister** भी) / बैनिस्टर् / *noun* जंगला, जीने के पार्श्व में सहारे के लिए लगे छोटे-छोटे स्तंभ : *hold on to the banister rail* ○ *children sliding down the banister.*

banjo / बैन्जो / *noun* (*pl* **banjos**) बैंजो, एक वाद्ययंत्र।

bank¹ / बैङ्क् / *noun* बाँध, तीर, कूल; नदी का किनारा, तट।

bank² / बैङ्क् / *noun* 1 बैंक जहाँ रुपयों का लेन-देन होता है; अधिकोष; सराफ़ा : *My salary is paid directly into my bank.* 2 ऐसा स्थान जहाँ आवश्यकतानुसार उपयोग के लिए (कुछ भी) जमा करके रखा जाता है : *build up a bank of useful addresses/references/information* ○ *a blood bank/a data bank* ▸ **bank balance** *noun* बैंक में जमा धनराशि **bank book** (**passbook** भी) पासबुक; खाता-पुस्तिका।

bank³ / बैङ्क् / *verb* बैंक में पैसा जमा करना : *bank one's savings/takings* ■ **bank on sb/sth** भरोसा रखना, आश्रित होना : *I'm banking on your help.* ▸ **banker** *noun* बैंकर, साहूकार, महाजन, सर्राफ़ **banking** *noun* साहूकारी, महाजनी, लेन-देन; बैंक में नौकरी (करना)।

bankrupt / बैङ्क्रप्ट् / *noun* (क़ानून) दिवालिया, व्यक्ति जिसे न्यायालय द्वारा ऋण वापस न करने की स्थिति में घोषित करार दिया जाए ▸ **bankrupt** *adj* दिवालिया **bankruptcy** / बैङ्क्रप्ट्सि / *noun* दिवालिया-पन, दिवाला : *moral/political bankruptcy.*

banner / बैनर् / *noun* प्रायः दो डंडो पर लगा ध्वज, झंडा जिस पर कोई नारा, संदेश या

प्रतीक-चिह्न लिखा/छपा होता है ■ under the banner (of sth) 1 एक विशेष विचारधारा के लिए समर्थन की घोषणा करते हुए 2 एक विशेष समूह या संगठन के हिस्से के रूप में।

banquet / बैङ्क्विट् / noun भोज, (किसी विशेष घटना के उपलक्ष में) दावत; प्रीति-भोज : attend a state banquet in honour of the visiting French President.

banter / बैन्टर् / noun हँसी-दिल्लगी, परिहास, ठट्ठा ▸ bantering adj हँसी-दिल्लगी वाला : a bantering remark/ tone of voice.

banyan / बैन्यन् / noun वटवृक्ष; बड़ का पेड़, बरगद।

baptism / बैप्टिज़म् / noun ईसाई चर्च में सदस्य बनाते समय अभिषेक करना (जल छिड़क कर) और फिर नामकरण करना; बपतिस्मा ▸ baptismal adj बपतिस्मा संबंधी।

baptize, -ise / बैप्टाइज़् / verb बपतिस्मा देना, दीक्षित करना; नामकरण करना : She was baptized Mary. ○ I was baptized a Catholic.

bar¹ / बार् / noun 1 शराबख़ाना, मधुशाला 2 ऐसा स्थान जहाँ पर हलके जलपान, चाय, कॉफ़ी बिकता है : a sandwich bar ○ a coffee bar 3 (धातु की) छड़, शलाका, दंड, डंडा : an iron bar 4 ठोस पदार्थ की छड़, टिकिया : a bar of chocolate/ soap 5 दरवाज़े या खिड़की का अर्गल : They fitted bars to their windows to stop burglars getting in. 6 प्रगति में बाधक : Poor health may be a bar to success in life. 7 the Bar [sing] वकालत का पेशा, बैरिस्टरी, वकील समुदाय, विधिज्ञ वर्ग : be called to the Bar ■ behind bars (अनौप) जेल में : The murderer is now safely behind bars. ▸ bar chart noun मात्रा दर्शाने वाली खड़ी रेखाओं का चित्र bar code

noun पुस्तक के आवरण पृष्ठ या अन्य वस्तुओं पर छपा मोटी पतली रेखाओं वाला कूट संकेत जिसे कंप्यूटर समझ सकता है barmaid noun औरत जो काउंटर पर पेय (शराब) प्रस्तुत करती है barman noun काउंटर पर शराब प्रस्तुत करने वाला व्यक्ति

bar² / बार् / verb (-rr-) 1 (दरवाज़े या खिड़की पर) अर्गल या रोक लगाना, बंद करना : barred windows 2 बाधा खड़ी करना, प्रगति रोक देना : (अल) Poverty bars the way to progress. 3 bar sb (from sth/doing sth) कुछ करने पर प्रतिबंध लगाना।

bar³ / बार् / (barring भी) prep को छोड़कर : Meals are available at all times, barring Sunday evenings.

barb / बार्ब् / noun 1 काँटा, पीछे की ओर मुड़ा भाला, तीर या मछली के काटे की नोक 2 चुभती हुई बात जो औरों को आहत कर जाए : Her barbs of sarcasm had clearly struck home. ▸ barbed adj 1 कँटीला, कंटकपूर्ण 2 (कोई बात, टिप्पणी आदि) दंशपूर्ण, कड़वी, कटु barbed wire noun कँटीला तार जो प्राय: बाड़ में लगाया जाता है।

barbarian / बार्बेअरिअन् / noun (प्राय: अपमा) बर्बर, असभ्य और असंस्कृत व्यक्ति; क्रूर, कर्कश।

barbaric / बार्बैरिक् / adj (प्राय: अपमा) बर्बर (आचरण) असभ्य व्यक्ति की भाँति।

barbarism / बार्बरिज़म् / noun 1 असभ्यता, बर्बरता, गँवारूपन, असभ्य रहने की स्थिति 2 क्रूरता, वहशीपन, जंगलीपन।

barbarous / बार्बरस् / adj (अपमा) अतिकठोर, अतिनिर्मम; असभ्य।

barbecue / बार्बिक्यू / noun सींख़, आग पर मांस भूनने के लिए धातु का सीख़चा; बाहर खाना, पार्टी आदि पर इस तरह से खाना बनाना।

barber / बार्बर् / noun नाई, हज्जाम, नापित ▸ barber shop noun नाई की दुकान।

bard / बाई / *noun (प्रा)* कवि; भाट, चारण।

bare¹ / बेअर् / *adj* (-r, -st) 1 नग्न, खुला हुआ, उजाड़, बिना अलंकरण के : *walk around in bare feet* 2 केवल, मात्र, निरा : *the bare necessities/essentials of life* ∎ **lay sth bare** रहस्योद्घाटन करना, भेद खोलना, कोई छुपी हुई बात सामने लाना।

bare² / बेअर् / *verb* उघाड़ना; खोलना, प्रकट करना ∎ **bare one's heart/soul (to sb)** *(साहि या परि)* किसी को अपने दिल की बात कहना, दिल की भावनाएँ व्यक्त करना ▸ **barefoot** *adj* नंगे पाँव **bareheaded** *adj* नंगे सिर, खुले सिर।

barely / बेअर्लि / *adv* 1 मात्र, केवल, सिर्फ़ : *barely perceptible/recognizable* 2 कठिनाई से, मुश्किल से : *He can barely read and write.*

bargain¹ / बार्गन् / *noun* **bargain (with sb)** 1 सौदेबाज़ी; समझौता : *make/strike a bargain with sb* 2 कोई सस्ता सौदा : *You must admit that I'm offering you a bargain.*

bargain² / बार्गन् / *verb* **bargain (with sb) (about/over/for sth)** मोल-तोल करना, सौदेबाज़ी करना, (अपने हित में) व्यापार की शर्तें आदि तय करना ∎ **bargain sth away** कम क़ीमत में (माल) लुटा देना; बलिदान कर देना **bargain for sth** प्रत्याशा करना, तैयार होना।

bargaining / बार्गनिङ् / *noun* सौदाकारी, सौदेबाज़ी।

barge¹ / बार्ज् / *noun* बजरा, नौका।

barge² / बार्ज् / *verb (अनौप)* किसी व्यक्ति/वस्तु से ज़ोर से टकरा जाना; भद्दे तरीक़े से या धक्का-मुक्की करते हुए टकराना, घुसना : *He barged past (me) and went to the front of the line.* ∎ **barge in (on sth)/into sth** ज़बरदस्ती घुसना, घुसपैठ करना, दख़लंदाज़ी करना : *She barged in on our meeting without even knocking.*

bark¹ / बार्क् / *noun* (पेड़ की) छाल, वल्कल।

bark² / बार्क् / *noun* (कुत्ते, लोमड़ी आदि की) भौंक; भौंक से मिलती-जुलती कोई आवाज़, जैसे बंदूक की आवाज़ ∎ **sb's bark is worse than their bite** *(अनौप)* गरजने वाले बरसते नहीं, अमुक व्यक्ति गुस्सेवर है ख़तरनाक नहीं ▸ **bark** *verb* 1 (कुत्ते, लोमड़ी आदि का) भौंकना 2 (लोगों का) खाँसते हुए, बंदूक जैसी आवाज़ करना : *have a barking cough* 3 **bark (at sb)**; **bark sth (out)** कड़वे शब्दों में बोलना, चिड़चिड़ाकर कुछ कहना : *When she's angry, she often barks at the children.*

barley / बार्लि / *noun* जौ, यव।

barn / बार्न् / *noun* खलिहान, भुसौरा; जानवरों (गाय, घोड़े आदि) को रखने के लिए बड़ा कमरा।

barometer / बरॉमिटर् / *noun* 1 वायुदाब को आँकने का यंत्र 2 ऐसी कोई बात/वस्तु जिससे लोगों की भावनाओं, क़ीमतों, जनमत को जाना जा सके : *a reliable barometer of public feeling.*

baron / बैरन् / *noun* 1 (ब्रिटेन में) निम्नतम श्रेणी का संभ्रांत व्यक्ति जो Lord की उपाधि प्रयुक्त करता है, (दूसरे देशों में) संभ्रांत व्यक्ति 2 बड़ा उद्योगपति या व्यापारी : *oil barons.*

baroque (Baroque भी**)** / बरॉक्; *US* ब रोक् / *adj* यूरोप में 17वीं, 18वीं शताब्दियों में प्रचलित अत्यलंकृत कला, विशेष रूप से भवन-निर्माण कला ▸ **baroque churches/palaces** ▸ **baroque (Baroque** भी**)** *noun* इस तरह की कला का नमूना: *paintings representative of the baroque.*

barracks / बैरक्स् / *noun (प्राय: pl)* बैरक, फ़ौजियों के रहने के भवन : *The men marched back to (their) barracks.*

barrage / बैराश्ज़् / *noun* 1 बाँध, बराज़ →**dam** देखिए 2 लगातार ज़ोर की गोलाबारी

3 प्रश्नों, आलोचनाओं, शिकायतों आदि की तेज़ झड़ी, लगातार बौछार : face a barrage of angry complaints.

barrel / 'बैरल् / noun 1 लकड़ी का ढोलनुमा पीपा; पीपाभर (सामान) : barrels of oil 2 बंदूक की नाल, रिवाल्वर की नली।

barren / 'बैरन् / adj 1 (पेड़) निष्फल 2 (भूमि) बंजर 3 (अप्र या औप) (स्त्री) बाँझ, बंध्या 4 (प्रयत्न) व्यर्थ, बेकार, असफल : a barren discussion.

barricade / बैरि'केड् / noun रक्षा या बाधा के लिए निकटतम उपलब्ध वस्तुओं से दीवार-सी संरचना, मोरचा, रोक ▸ **barricade** verb मोरचाबंदी करना, रोक लगाना : They had barricaded all the doors and windows.

barrier / 'बैरिअर् / noun 1 यातायात/ आवागमन रोकने या नियंत्रित करने का साधन 2 **barrier (to/against sth)** प्रगति में बाधा, रोक, अवरोध, व्यवधान : Poor health may be a barrier to success.

barring / 'बारिङ् / prep अपवाद को छोड़कर → **bar** देखिए।

barrister / 'बैरिस्टर् / noun बैरिस्टर; उच्च न्यायालय में बहस करने के अधिकार वाला वकील, विधिवक्ता।

barrow / 'बैरो / noun एक या दो पहियों का हथठेला।

barter / 'बार्टर् / verb **barter sth (for sth); barter sth (away)** वस्तु विनिमय, सामान को किसी सामान के बदले में (न कि रुपये आदि मुद्रा से) ख़रीदना या बेचना, अदला-बदली : barter wheat for machinery○ (अलं) barter away one's rights/honour/freedom.

base¹ / 'बेस् / noun 1 (प्राय: sing) आधार, नींव; पेंदा, तल : the base of a pillar/ column/lamp 2 (ज्यामिति) आधार रेखा : the base of a triangle/pyramid 3 किसी विचार, विश्वास, मत आदि का

आधार बिंदु जहाँ से वह उत्पन्न होता है : She used her family's history as a base for her novel. 4 अड्डा जहाँ अभियान या आक्रमण करते समय स्टोर रखा जाता है : a naval/air base ▸ **baseless** adj आधारहीन, अकारण, निर्मूल।

base² / बेस् / verb **base (sth on sth)** पर आधारित होना, आधार बनाना : What exactly do you base that opinion on?

base³ / बेस् / adj (-r, -st) (औप, अपमा) (व्यक्ति, उनके विचार-व्यवहार) अधम, नीच, पतित : acting from base motives ▸ **base metal** noun सस्ती धातु।

baseball / 'बेस्बॉल् / noun अमेरिका में प्रचलित एक खेल जिसे नौ-नौ खिलाड़ियों की दो टीमें गेंद और बल्ले से खेलती हैं।

basement / 'बेस्मन्ट् / noun इमारत का वह अंश जो पूर्णत: या अंशत: भूमि के नीचे हो, तहख़ाना : a basement flat/car park.

bash / बैश् / verb (अनौप) ज़बरदस्त प्रहार करना : bash sb on the head with a club ■ **bash sb up** (अनौप) ज़ोर से पिटाई करना : He was bashed up in the playground by some older boys. ▸ **bash** noun (अनौप) ज़बरदस्त प्रहार, चोट।

bashful / 'बैश्फ़ल् / adj शर्मीला, संकोची, झेंपू ▸ **bashfully** adv शर्म से, लज्जा सहित।

basic / 'बेसिक् / adj 1 **basic (to sth)** मूल, बुनियादी, आधारभूत 2 मौलिक, मूलभूत : the basic vocabulary of a language ▸ **basically** adv मूलरूप से, साधारण तौर पर **basics** noun [pl] मूलभूत/ आधारभूत तथ्य या सिद्धांत : learn the basics of computer programming.

basil / 'बैज़ल्; US 'बेज़ल् भी / noun तुलसी : flavoured with basil.

basin / 'बेस्न् / noun 1 (**wash-basin** भी) हाथ धोने की चिलमची, कुंडी 2 भूमि का वह क्षेत्र जहाँ की मिट्टी नदी द्वारा बहा ली जाती

है, द्रोणी, नदी थाला, नदी की घाटी : *the Amazon basin* ▸ **basinful** *noun* (*pl* **basinfuls**) कुंडीभर, तसलाभर।

basis / 'बेसिस् / *noun* (*pl* **bases** / 'बेसीज़ /) 1 आधार (तर्क, विचारधारा, विश्वास आदि का) : *The basis of a good marriage is trust.* 2 (विशेषत:) वह तथ्य जिससे बहस उभरती है, जिस पर बहस की जाती है : *a basis for rational debate.*

bask / बास्क; *US* बैस्क / *verb* **bask** (**in** sth) धूप खाना/सेंकना, धूप में आनंद लेना : *basking in the sunshine.*

basket / 'बास्किट् / *noun* 1 डोलची, डलिया, टोकरी : *a shopping basket* 2 बासकेटबॉल में किए गए गोलों की संख्या।

basketball / 'बास्किट्बॉल / *noun* बासकेटबॉल; पाँच-पाँच खिलाड़ियों की दो टीमों का खेल जिसमें ज़मीन से दस फ़ीट ऊँचे खुले जाल में बॉल डालनी होती है।

bastard / 'बैस्टर्ड; बास्टर्ड / *noun* 1 (*अपमान*) अविवाहित माता-पिता की संतान, जारज, हरामी, दोगला 2 (*अप, अपमान*) घटिया क़िस्म का व्यक्ति, क्रूर एवं अप्रिय : *You rotten bastard!* 3 (*अनौप*) कोई चीज़ जो परेशानी एवं कष्ट का कारण बनती है।

bastion / 'बैस्टिअन् / *noun* 1 (व्यक्ति) रक्षक, बचाने वाला : *a bastion of democracy/freedom/socialism* 2 बुर्ज, गढ़ 3 दुश्मन के क्षेत्र के निकट सैनिकों द्वारा रक्षित स्थान, क़िला आदि।

bat¹ / बैट् / *noun* (क्रिकेट का) बल्ला ▸ **bat** *verb* (-tt-) 1 बल्ले को काम में लाना, बल्लेबाज़ी करना : *He bats well.* 2 बल्ले से मारना : *batting a ball* (about) **batsman** *noun* (*pl* **batsmen**) बल्लेबाज़।

bat² / बैट् / *noun* चमगादड़।

bat³ / बैट् / *verb* (-tt-) ■ **not bat an eyelid**; (*US*) **not bat an eye** ज़रा-सा

भी आश्चर्य न प्रकट करना : *She listened to the sad news without batting an eyelid.*

batch / बैच् / *noun* टुकड़ी, दल, समूह : *a new batch of recruits for the army.*

bath / बाथ्; *US* बैथ् / *noun* (*pl* **baths** / बाद्ज़; *US* बैद्ज़ /) 1 स्नान, नहाना, प्रक्षालन 2 (**bathtub** भी) स्नान का टब, नाँद 3 टब में भरा स्नान करने का पानी 4 **baths** [*pl*] स्नानगृह, स्नानागार (विशेषत: जनता के लिए) ▸ **bath** *verb* नहाना; किसी को स्नान कराना : *bath the baby* **bathroom** *noun* स्नानघर, ग़ुस्लख़ाना।

bathe / बेद् / *verb* नहाना, नहलाना, स्नान करना/कराना : *bathe the baby* ▸ **bathed** *adj* **bathed in/with sth** 1 (रोशनी से) पूरा स्थान जगमगा देना 2 पूरी तरह से गीला होना या करना।

batik / ब'टीक्; 'बैटिक् / *noun* कपड़ों पर मोम आदि की सहायता से विभिन्न डिज़ाइन बनाने की विधि : *a batik dress.*

baton / 'बैटॉन्; *US* ब'टॉन् / *noun* 1 सोंटा, डंडा, पुलिस वालों का बेंत : *a baton charge* 2 बैंड या ऑर्केस्ट्रा का संचालन करने वाले की छड़ी।

battalion / ब'टैलिअन् / *noun* (*संक्षि* **Bn**) बटैलियन थलसेना के सिपाहियों की बड़ी टुकड़ी।

batter / 'बैटर् / *noun* (भोजन बनाने में प्रयुक्त) फेंटी हुई मैदे और अंडे की लपसी : *fish fried in batter.*

battery / 'बैटरि; 'बैट्रि / *noun* (*pl* **batteries**) 1 बैटरी, जिसके सेलों में विद्युत धारा बहती है : *a camera battery* 2 तोपख़ाना; तोपख़ाना दल (सैनिक, तोपें, वाहन आदि) : *a battery commander* 3 भ्रमित कर देने वाली समान चीज़ों का बड़ा समूह : (*अलं*) *She faced a battery of tests.*

battle / 'बैट्ल / *noun* 1 (दो सेनाओं के बीच) लड़ाई, युद्ध, संग्राम : *a fierce battle* 2 **battle** (**for/against** sth) कोई भी संघर्ष या प्रतिस्पर्धा; संग्राम : *Their* *whole life was a constant battle against poverty.* ▶ **battle** *verb* **battle (with/against sb/sth) (for sth)** कड़ा संघर्ष करना, कठोर प्रयास करना : *battling against poor health* **battlefield** *noun* रणभूमि, युद्धक्षेत्र।

battlements / बैट्ल्मन्ट्स् / *noun [pl]* किले की दीवारों पर तोपें या तीर चलाने के लिए बने स्थान, फसील, परकोटा, प्राचीर।

bawl / बॉल् / *verb* **bawl (sth) (out)** चीखना, चिल्लाना : *The baby has been bawling for hours.*

bay¹ / बे / *noun* खाड़ी : *the Bay of Bengal* ○ *Hudson Bay.*

bay² / बे / **(bay-tree** भी) *noun* खुशबूदार पत्तों वाली एक झाड़ी, जिसके पत्ते खाने में प्रयोग किए जाते हैं, मसाले के तौर पर ▶ **bay-leaf** *(pl* **bay-leaves)** *noun* तेजपत्र (तेजपत्ता)।

bay³ / बे / *noun* (भवन का) खंड या कक्ष : *a parking/loading bay* ■ **hold/ keep sb/sth at bay** (आक्रमणकारियों, समस्या आदि को) दूर रखना, पास आने से रोकना।

bay⁴ / बे / *adj, noun* (घोड़ा) कुमैत, लाखी रंग का, लाल-भूरे रंग का : *riding a big bay.*

bayonet / बेअनट् / *noun* (राइफल के आगे लगी) संगीन।

bazaar / बˈज़ार् / *noun* बाज़ार; विभिन्न चीज़ें बेचने वाली दुकानें।

BC / बी सी / *abbr* **(before Christ** का संक्षिप्त रूप) ईसापूर्व, ईसवी पूर्व : *in (the year) 2000 BC* → **AD** देखिए।

be¹ / बि; बी / *verb* (*pres t* **am, is, are;** *pres p* **being;** *pt* **was, were;** *pp* **been**) **1** होना, उपस्थित रहना, घटित होना : *There are many such people.* ○ *There are no books on the shelf.* **2** समय बताने के लिए प्रयुक्त : *It's half past two.* ○ *It was late at night when we finally arrived.* **3** कहीं

स्थित होना, किसी स्थान पर होना : *The lamp is on the table.* **4** रहना : *She has been in her room for hours.* **5** कोई स्थिति या गुण प्रकट करने में : *Life is unfair.* **6** परिचय, नाम, रुचि, व्यवसाय आदि व्यक्त करने में : *You are the man I want.* **7** क़ीमत, मात्रा, संख्या आदि की समानता प्रकट करना : *How much is that dress?*

be² / बि; बी / *aux verb* **1** भूत कृदंत के साथ प्रयुक्त : *He was killed in the war.* **2** वर्तमान कृदंत के साथ प्रयुक्त : *They are/ were reading.*

beach / बीच् / *noun* समुद्र तट जो ज्वार-भाटा में जल से भर जाता है, किनारा।

beacon / बीकन् / *noun* **1** संकेत के लिए पहाड़ की चोटी पर जलाई गई आग, संकेत दीप **2** जहाज़ों और विमानों को चेतावनी देने के लिए, (समुद्र या पर्वत पर लगा) प्रकाशस्तंभ, दीपस्तंभ **3** रेडियो स्टेशन या ट्रांसमीटर जिसके संकेत जहाज़ों या विमानों को अपनी स्थिति मालूम करने में सहायक होते हैं।

bead / बीड् / *noun* **1** माला का दाना, मनका, माला : *a string of glass beads* **2** बूँद, बिंदु : *beads of sweat on his forehead.*

beak / बीक् / *noun* चोंच ▶ **beaked** / बीक्ट् / *adj* चोंचदार।

beaker / बीकर् / *noun* **1** चषक, छोटी टोंटी का पात्र **2** बीकर, वैज्ञानिक प्रयोगों में प्रयुक्त होने वाला छोटे मुँह का काँच का खुला पात्र।

beam / बीम् / *noun* **1** शहतीर, धरन (लकड़ी का लंबा मोटा लट्ठा) **2** किरण, किरण पुंज, रश्मिमाला : *the beam of a torch/flashlight* ▶ **beam** *verb* **1** (सूरज का) किरणें बिखेरना, चमकना : *We sat by the pool as the sun beamed down.* **2** दूर से संदेश, टी वी प्रोग्राम आदि प्रसारित करना : *The President's speech was beamed live from Washington to Moscow.*

beaming adj मुसकराता हुआ, चमकता हुआ।

bean / बीन् / noun 1 बीन, सेम : broad beans ० kidney beans 2 अन्य पौधों के इसी प्रकार के बड़े बीज : coffee/cocoa beans ∎ not have a bean (अनौप) धनहीन, पैसे बिना।

bear¹ / बेअर् / noun 1 भालू, रीछ, ऋक्ष : a polar/grizzly bear 2 (वाणिज्य) मूल्यपाती, ऐसा व्यक्ति जो स्टॉक, शेयर आदि इस आशा में बेचता है कि मूल्य गिरने पर फिर से ख़रीद ले ▸ bearish / 'बेअरिश् / adj (वाणिज्य) मूल्यपाती, क़ीमतें गिरने की प्रवृत्ति वाला **bear-hug** noun बाँहों में कसकर पकड़ना।

bear² / बेअर् / verb (pt bore / बॉर् /; pp borne / बॉर्न् /) 1 ढोना, (भार) वहन करना : to bear a heavy load 2 (चिह्न, साक्ष्य, समानता, प्रेम आदि) प्रदर्शित करना : The document bore his signature. 3 भार सहन करना : The ice is too thin to bear your weight. 4 अपने ऊपर ज़िम्मेदारी लेना : You shouldn't have to bear the blame for other people's mistakes. 5 (दुख, पीड़ा, अपमान आदि) सहन करना, बरदाश्त करना 6 **bear sth (against/towards sb)** भाव, विचार आदि दिल/मन में रखना : bear a grudge against sb 7 **bear oneself well, etc** किसी निश्चित/उचित तरीक़े से व्यवहार करना : She bore herself with dignity throughout the funeral. 8 (औप) जन्म देना, उत्पन्न करना : bear a child 9 फलना, उपजाना : trees bearing pink blossom ∎ **bear the brunt of sth** किसी चीज़ का ख़ास प्रभाव, झटका, बल आदि सहन करना **bear fruit** सुखद परिणाम लाना **bear in mind (that)...** यह याद रखना कि... यह ख़याल रखना कि... **bear with sb/sth** किसी व्यक्ति/वस्तु के प्रति धैर्य प्रदर्शित करना।

bearable / 'बेअरब्ल् / adj सहनीय।

beard¹ / बिअई / noun दाढ़ी : a week's growth of beard ▸ **bearded** adj दाढ़ी वाला **beardless** adj बिना दाढ़ी का।

beard² / बिअई / verb किसी को खुलेआम चुनौती देना या विरोध करना ∎ **beard the lion in his den** किसी महत्त्वपूर्ण व्यक्ति को चुनौती देने या उससे अनुग्रह प्राप्त करने के लिए मिलना।

bearer / 'बेअरर् / noun 1 (संदेश या पत्र) वाहक : I'm the bearer of good news. 2 (भार, बोझा आदि) वहन करने वाला 3 बैंक में भुगतान के लिए चेक प्रस्तुत करने वाला : This cheque is payable to the bearer.

bearing / 'बेअरिङ् / noun 1 [sing] (व्यक्ति का) आचरण, बर्ताव, व्यवहार 2 **bearing on sth** (एक वस्तु का दूसरी वस्तु से) संबंध : What he said had little bearing on the problem. 3 (तक) बेयरिंग, मशीन का वह अंग जो अन्य चलनशील अंगों को धारण करता है : ball-bearings.

beast / बीस्ट् / noun 1 (अप्र या औप) पशु, चौपाया, चतुष्पद : wild beasts 2 घृणित व्यक्ति, नरपशु : Alcohol brings out the beast in him. ▸ **beastly** adj 1 पशुवत् 2 (अनौप) जघन्य, घृणित; अरुचिकर **beastliness** noun पशुता, पाशविकता **beast of burden** noun लदू जानवर जैसे गधा, खच्चर आदि।

beat¹ / बीट् / verb (pt beat; pp beaten / 'बीटन् /) 1 (हाथ, डंडे आदि से) पीटना, मारना : Who's beating the drum? 2 **beat against/on sth/sb** (वर्षा, सूर्य, हवा आदि का) टकराना : The waves were beating on the shore. 3 **beat sth (up)** तेज़ी से हिलाकर (चम्मच या काँटे से) फेंटना : beat the flour and the milk together 4 (हृदय का) धड़कना 5 **beat sb (at sth)** किसी को हराना, पराजित करना; किसी के विरुद्ध जीतना : He beats me at chess. 6 किसी चीज़ से

बेहतर होना : *Nothing beats home cooking.* 7 बार-बार आने-जाने या टहनियों को दबाने से रास्ता बनाना : *a well-beaten track* ■ **beat about the bush** घुमा-फिराकर बात करना, मुख्य मुद्दे पर न आना **beat a (hasty) retreat** जल्दी से वापस लौट जाना **beat sb at their own game** किसी को उनके द्वारा चली चालों से ही पराजित करना **beat sth down** (दरवाज़े आदि को) लगातार, खुलने या टूटने तक, पीटना **beat sb up** बुरी तरह से पिटाई करना **off the beaten track** ऐसी जगह में जो परिचित रास्ते से दूर हो ▸ **beating** *noun* 1 पिटाई (विशेषत: दंडस्वरूप) : *give sb/ get a good beating* 2 (अनौप) करारी हार, शिकस्त।

beat² / बीट् / *noun* 1 वार, (नियमित और पुनरावर्ती) आघात : *a single beat on the drum* 2 गश्त, हलक़ा : *a police-woman out on the/her beat.*

beautician / ब्यू'टिश्न् / *adj* सौंदर्य विशेषज्ञ, सौंदर्यकार, ब्यूटी-पार्लर चलाने वाला व्यक्ति।

beautiful /'ब्यूटिफ़ुल् / *adj* सुंदर, खूब-सूरत, रमणीय : *a beautiful face/baby/ view/flower* ▸ **beautifully** *adv* 1 खूबसूरत तरीक़े से, सुंदरता से **beautify** /'ब्यूटिफ़ाइ / *verb* (*pt, pp* **beautified**) सुंदर बनाना, सौंदर्य बढ़ाना, सजाना।

beauty / 'ब्यूटि / *noun* (*pl* **beauties**) 1 सुंदरता, रमणीयता, खूबसूरती 2 सुंदर व्यक्ति या वस्तु ■ **beauty is only skin deep** (कहा) बाहरी सुंदरता आंतरिक गुणों की अपेक्षा कम महत्त्वपूर्ण है ▸ **beauty queen** *noun* सौंदर्य प्रतियोगिता में सर्वोत्कृष्ट सुंदरी **beauty salon (beauty parlour** भी) *noun* सौंदर्य संबंधी समस्याओं एवं सौंदर्य बढ़ाने के लिए व्यावसायिक स्थान।

beaver / 'बीव़र् / *noun* ऐसा जानवर जो पानी और भूमि पर समान रूप से रहता है और अपने नरम भूरे फर के लिए प्रसिद्ध है; इस प्राणी का फर।

because / बि'कॉज़; बिकज़् / *conj* क्योंकि
▸ **because of** *prep* के कारण, के फल-स्वरूप।

beckon / 'बेकन् / *verb* **beckon (to) sb (to do sth)** इशारे से बुलाना : *She beckoned me (to follow).*

become / बि'कम् / *verb* (*pt* **became**; *pp* **become**) 1 होना, बनना : *They soon became angry.* ○ *They became close friends.* 2 होना शुरू हो जाना, बनना शुरू होना : *It's becoming dangerous to go out alone at night.*
▸ **becoming** *adj* (औप) 1 (कपड़े, वस्त्र) शोभनीय; उचित जँचते हुए 2 ठीक, उपयुक्त।

bed¹ / बेड् / *noun* 1 पलंग, चारपाई, शय्या, खाट : *a room with two single beds* 2 बिस्तर में होना; सोना या आराम करना : *It's time for bed.* 3 (नदी, समुद्र, झील आदि का) तल, तलहटी : *explore the ocean bed* 4 फूल/पौधे बोने की क्यारी : *flowerbeds* ■ **a bed of roses** मौज-मस्ती और आराम का जीवन : *Working here isn't exactly a bed of roses.*
▸ **bed and board** *noun* रहने (सोने) और खाने का बंदोबस्त **bed and break-fast** (*संक्षि* B and B; b and b) *noun* सोने और अगली सुबह के खाने की व्यवस्था (होटल आदि में) **bedclothes** *noun* चादर, चद्दर, कंबल आदि **bedroom** *noun* घर में सोने का कमरा, शयनकक्ष **bedtime** *noun* सोने का समय।

bed² / बेड् / *verb* (**-dd-**) बिछौना देना, सोने का प्रबंध करना : *The wounded were bedded in the farmhouse.* ▸ **bed-ding** *noun* बिछौना, बिछावन।

bedlam / बेड्लम् / *noun* कोलाहल की स्थिति; गुलगपाड़ा, गड़बड़ : *When the teacher was called away the class-room was an absolute bedlam.*

bedraggled / बि'डैग्ल्ड् / *adj* बारिश, गारा-मिट्टी आदि में लिथड़ा हुआ, मैला।

bedridden / 'बेड्रिड्न् / *adj* रोग या वृद्धावस्था के कारण शय्याग्रस्त।

bee / बी / *noun* मधुमक्खी, मधुकर ■ **have a bee in one's bonnet (about sth)** (अनौप) किसी बात की धुन/सनक सवार होना : *Our teacher has a bee in his bonnet about punctuation.* ▸ **beehive** *noun* मधुमक्खी का छत्ता; मधुमक्खी पेटिका।

beef / बीफ़ / *noun* 1 गोमांस : *roast beef* 2 (अनौप) मांसपेशियों की ताक़त, शक्ति : *He's got plenty of beef.* ■ **beef sth up** (अनौप, विशेषत: US) किसी चीज़ में शक्ति या बल लगाना : *The company are taking on more staff to beef up production.*

beep / बीप् / *noun* गाड़ी का हॉर्न या विद्युतीय यंत्र की आवाज़; बीप।

beer / बिअर् / *noun* बिअर, माल्ट से तैयार किया जाने वाला एक प्रकार का मादक पेय : *a barrel/bottle/glass of beer.*

beetle / 'बीट्ल् / *noun* एक प्रकार का भौंरा, भृंग।

beetroot / 'बीट्रूट् / *noun* (US **beet** भी) चुकंदर; लाल शलजम।

befall / बि'फ़ॉल् / *verb* (*pt* **befell** / बि 'फ़ेल्/; *pp* **befallen** / बि'फ़ॉल्न्/) (प्रा) घटित होना, आ पड़ना : *A great misfortune befell him.*

befit / बि'फ़िट् / *verb* (**-tt-**) (औप) उपयुक्त एवं उचित होना (किसी के लिए) : *You should dress in a way that befits a woman of your position.* ▸ **befitting** *adj* उपयुक्त, उचित : *a befitting reply.*

before¹ / बि'फ़ॉर् / *adv* (समय की दृष्टि से) पूर्व, भूतकाल में; पहले से ही : *You should have told me so before.*

before² / बि'फ़ॉर् / *prep* 1 किसी व्यक्ति/ वस्तु से पहले : *before lunch* 2 (स्थान/ स्थिति की दृष्टि से) सामने, आगे 3 (क्रम या व्यवस्था की दृष्टि से) किसी से आगे,

पहले : *B comes before C in the alphabet.* 4 (भविष्य की दृष्टि से) किसी के सामने : *The task before us is a daunting one.* 5 किसी के द्वारा विचारणीय या चर्चा योग्य : *The proposal went before the board.*

before³ / बि'फ़ॉर् / *conj* 1 किसी निश्चित समय से पहले : *Do it before you forget.* 2 उस समय तक : *It was sometime before I realized the truth.*

beforehand / बि'फ़ॉर्हैन्ड् / *adv* पूर्व में, पहले से, तैयारी से : *I had made enquiries beforehand.*

befriend / बि'फ़्रेन्ड् / *verb* मित्र के समान आचरण करना; मित्र बनाना : *They befriended the young girl, giving her food and shelter.*

beg / बेग् / *verb* (**-gg-**) 1 **beg (from sb); beg (for) sth (from/of sb)** भीख माँगना 2 **beg sth (of sb)/beg (sb) for sth** बहुत ही भावपूर्वक अनुरोध करना, प्रार्थना करना, याचना करना : *May I beg a favour of you?* ■ **beg sb's pardon** किसी से खेद प्रकट करना ■ **I beg to differ** किसी से शिष्टतापूर्वक असहमति व्यक्त करना ■ **I beg your pardon** कृपया फिर से कहिए।

beget / बि'गेट् / *verb* (**-tt-**; *pt* **begot** / बि'गॉट्/ या (प्रा) **begat** / बि'गैट्/; *pp* **begotten** / बि'गॉट्न्/) 1 (प्रा) (पिता के रूप में) पैदा करना : *Abraham begat Isaac.* 2 (अप्र या औप) का कारण बनना, पैदा करना : *War begets misery and ruin.*

beggar / 'बेगर् / *noun* भिखारी, भिक्षुक, भिखमंगा ■ **beggars can't be choosers** (अनौप, कहा) लाचारी में जो मिले उसी से संतुष्ट हो जाना चाहिए ▸ **beggar** *verb* किसी को निर्धन/कंगाल बना देना, नष्ट कर देना ■ **beggar description** वर्णनातीत होना, वर्णन से परे होना।

begin / बि'गिन् / *verb* (**-nn-**; *pt* **began** / बि'गैन्/; *pp* **begun** / बि'गन्/) 1 आरंभ

करना, शुरू करना : *begin work/a meeting* 2 कोई घटना शुरू होना, प्रारंभ होना : *When does the concert begin?* 3 कुछ बनने या होने से पहले कुछ और होना : *What began as a minor scuffle turned into a full-scale riot.* 4 पहली बार कुछ प्रारंभ/आरंभ होना : *The school began in 1920.* ■ **charity begins at home** (कहा) व्यक्ति की प्रथम ज़िम्मेदारी अपने खुद के परिवार को ठीक रखना है **to begin with** 1 सर्वप्रथम 2 सबसे पहले (तो) ▸ **beginner** *noun* आरंभक, प्रवर्तक; नौसिखिया **beginning** *noun* (समय या स्थान का) प्रारंभ, शुरुआत; पहला भाग/हिस्सा।

beguile / बि'गाइल / *verb* 1 (अप्र या औप) जी बहलाना, मोहित करना : *He beguiled us with many a tale of adventure.* 2 **beguile sb (into doing sth)** बहकाना, फुसलाना, ठगना : *They were beguiled into giving him large sums of money.*

behalf / बि'हाफ़; *US* बि'हैफ़ / *noun* ■ **on behalf of sb/on sb's behalf;** (*US*) **in behalf of sb/in sb's behalf** के पक्ष में, की ओर से; उसकी ओर से, उसके वास्ते; निमित्त : *On behalf of my colleagues and myself I thank you.*

behave / बि'हेव् / *verb* 1 **behave well, badly, etc (towards sb)** आचरण करना, व्यवहार करना : *She behaves (towards me) more like a friend than a mother.* 2 **behave (oneself)** सदाचार करना, अच्छा व्यवहार करना, अच्छे तरीक़े से पेश आना : *Children, please behave (yourselves)!*

behaviour (*US* **behavior**)/ बि'हेव्यर् / *noun* आचरण, व्यवहार : *She was ashamed of her children's (bad) behaviour.*

behead / बि'हेड् / *verb* सिर काट देना :

King Henry VIII had two of his wives beheaded.

behind[1] / बि'हाइन्ड् / *prep* 1 पीछे की ओर, पीछे : *Who's the girl standing behind you?* 2 किसी चीज़ के दूसरी ओर, छिपा हुआ : *hide behind a tree* 3 किसी अन्य व्यक्ति से कम प्रगति पर, पिछड़ा हुआ : *Britain is behind Japan in developing modern technology.*

behind[2] / बि'हाइन्ड् / *adv part* 1 पीछे-पीछे; और पीछे : *The others are a long way behind.* 2 **behind (with/in sth)** भुगतान करने या कार्य पूरा करने में देर का : *He's behind in handing in his homework.*

behold / बि'होल्ड् / *verb* (*pt,pp* **beheld** / बि'हेल्ड् /) (प्रा या *साहि*) देखना (विशेषत: कुछ असामान्य) ▸ **beholder** *noun* दर्शक, प्रेक्षक : *Beauty is in the eye of the beholder.*

beige/ बेश्/ *adj, noun* (रंग) हलका पीला-भूरा : *a beige carpet.*

being / बीइङ् / *noun* 1 सत्ता, अस्तित्व 2 जीवधारी, प्राणी : *the rights of human beings.*

belated / बि'लेटिड् / *adj* विलंब से आया या किया हुआ : *a belated apology* ▸ **belatedly** *adv.*

belch / बेल्च् / *verb* 1 डकार लेना, डकारना 2 **belch sth (out/forth)** (धुआँ, लपटें आदि) बलपूर्वक छोड़ना, वेग से बाहर फेंकना।

belie / बि'लाइ / *verb* (*pres p* **belying;** *pp, pt* **belied**) 1 झुठलाना, किसी चीज़ का मिथ्या रूप प्रस्तुत करना 2 (आशा, वायदा आदि) पूरा न कर पाना, से मुकर जाना, निराश कर देना : *Practical experience belies this theory.*

belief / बि'लीफ़ / *noun* 1 **belief in sth/ sb** विश्वास, आस्था; भरोसा, यक़ीन : *The incident has shaken my belief in the police.* 2 धारणा, विचार, मत 3 धर्म-श्रद्धा, श्रद्धा, धार्मिक विश्वास।

believe / बि'लीव् / verb विश्वास करना, सही मान लेना : *She believed everything he told her.* ■ **believe in sth/sb** 1 किसी व्यक्ति/वस्तु में विश्वास रखना 2 किसी व्यक्ति/वस्तु के मूल्य के प्रति आश्वस्त रहना **make believe (that...)** स्वांग भरना, अभिनय करना : *The boys liked to make believe that they were astronauts.* **not believe one's ears/eyes** आश्चर्य के कारण यक़ीन न कर पाना ▶ **believable** adj विश्वसनीय, यक़ीन के क़ाबिल **believer** noun विश्वासी, आस्तिक।

belittle / बि'लिटल् / verb छोटा करना या समझना; महत्त्व घटाना : *don't belittle yourself.*

bell / बेल् / noun घंटा, घंटी, घड़ियाल : *a hand bell/a bicycle bell.*

belligerent / ब'लिजरन्ट् / adj 1 आक्रामक, लड़ाकू; परियोद्धा : *a belligerent person/manner/speech* 2 युद्ध में संलग्न देश या दल, युद्धरत ▶ **belligerence** noun युद्धकारिता **belligerent** noun युद्धरत देश या दल।

bellow / 'बेलो / noun चीख़, चीत्कार; गरज, गर्जन : *He let out/gave a sudden bellow of rage.*

bellows / 'बेलोज़् / noun धौंकनी, भाथी।

belly / 'बेलि / noun 1 पेट, उदर 2 किसी चीज़ का गोल हिस्सा ▶ **-bellied** /-बे लिड् / (संयुक्त विशेषण बनाने के लिए प्रयुक्त) एक विशेष प्रकार के उदर वाला : *pot-bellied* ○ *big-bellied.*

belong / बि'लॉङ् / verb उचित स्थान होना; का निवासी होना : *I don't feel I belong here.* ■ **belong to sb** की संपत्ति होना : *Who does this pen belong to?* ▶ **belongings** noun [pl] सामान, चल संपत्ति : *The tourists lost all their belongings in the hotel fire.*

beloved adj 1 / बि'लव्ड् / **beloved by/of sb** परमप्रिय 2 / बि'लव्डि / प्रियतम, अति प्रिय; प्रेयसी।

below / बि'लो / prep किसी व्यक्ति अथवा वस्तु से नीचे/निचले स्तर पर ▶ **below** adv part नीचे, निचले स्थान पर : *They live on the floor below.*

belt / बेल्ट् / noun 1 (कमर की) पेटी, कमरबंद, बेल्ट 2 (मशीन का) पट्टा : *conveyor belt.*

bemoan / बि'मोन् / verb (औप) शोक करना, विलाप करना; निराशा व्यक्त करना : *He bemoaned the shortage of funds available for research.*

bench / बेन्च् / noun 1 (लकड़ी या पत्थर की) बेंच, तख़ता 2 **the bench** [sing] न्यायाधीश का आसन; न्यायाधीश; न्यायाधीश समूह; न्यायालय : *The attorney turned to address the bench.*

bend[1] / बेन्ड् / verb (pt, pp bent / बेन्ट् /) 1 मोड़ना, झुकाना, टेढ़ा करना : *bend the wire up/down* 2 (किसी वस्तु का) मोड़ खाना, घुमाव लेना, वक्र बनाना : *The road bends (to the right) after a few yards.* 3 किसी विशेष दिशा में झुकना : *She bent down and picked it up.* ■ **be bent on sth/on doing sth** दृढ़संकल्प, अपने लक्ष्य या उद्देश्य के लिए स्थिर होना।

bend[2] / बेन्ड् / noun मोड़, घुमाव, झुकाव : *a gentle/sharp bend* ■ **round the bend/twist** (अनौप) सनकी; चिड़चिड़ा : *Her behaviour is driving me round the bend.*

beneath / बि'नीथ् / prep (औप) 1 किसी व्यक्ति या वस्तु से निचले स्तर पर, से नीचे 2 किसी चीज़ के अयोग्य : *He considers such jobs beneath him.*

benediction / बेनि'डिक्श्न् / noun (औप) आशीर्वाद, शुभकामना, मंगलकामना।

benefactor / 'बेनिफ़ैक्टर् / noun (fem **benefactress** / 'बेनिफ़ैक्ट्रस् /) दानी, उपकारी, हितकारी (विशेषत: जो स्कूल, अस्पताल जैसी सार्वजनिक संस्थाओं को बड़ी धनराशि दान देता है)।

beneficent / बि'नेफ़िसन्ट् / adj (औप) परोपकारी, उपकारी ▸ **beneficence** / बि 'नेफ़िसन्स् / noun उपकार, परोपकारिता।

beneficial / बेनि'फ़िशल् / adj **beneficial to** (sth/sb) लाभकारी, हितकारी, हितकर : Fresh air is beneficial to one's health.

beneficiary / बेनि'फ़िशरि; US बेनि'फ़ि- शिएरि / noun 1 किसी की मृत्यु के बाद धन या संपत्ति प्राप्त करने वाला व्यक्ति 2 लाभ- भोगी, उपकृत, लाभग्राही।

benefit / 'बेनिफ़िट् / noun 1 लाभ, फ़ायदा, हित, भला 2 (आर्थिक, विशेषत: सरकारी) सहायता : unemployment/ sickness benefit ∎ **for sb's benefit** किसी की सहायतार्थ **give sb the benefit of the doubt** साफ़-साफ़ सबूतों, प्रमाणों के अभाव में किसी को निर्दोष मान लेना ▸ **benefit** verb (pt, pp -fited; US -fitted भी) किसी का हितसाधन करना, किसी का भला करना; लाभ पहुँचाना : The new facilities have benefited the whole town.

benevolent / बे'नेवलन्ट् / adj **benevolent (to/towards sb)** 1 परोपकारी, हित- चिंतक, शुभचिंतक 2 हितैषी, लाभ पहुँचाने वाला : a benevolent society/fund ▸ **benevolence** / बे'नेवलन्स् / noun परोपकार, हितचिंतन, हितैषिता **benevolently** adv दयापूर्वक।

benign / बि'नाइन् / adj 1 (व्यक्ति या उनके कार्य) उदार और सौम्य, भला, हितैषी 2 (शरीर में कोई वृद्धि) हलकी, जो गंभीर अथवा घातक न हो, सुसाध्य : a benign tumour.

bent / बेन्ट् / noun (प्राय: sing) **bent (for sth/doing sth)** रुझान, प्रवृत्ति, झुकाव : He showed a literary bent from a very early age.

bequeath / बि'क्वीद्; बि'क्वीथ् / verb **bequeath sth (to sb)** (औप) वसीयत करना, वसीयत में देना : He bequeathed Rs 50,000 to charity.

bereave / बि'रीव् / verb (औप) वंचित करना (किसी निकट संबंधी या मित्र की मृत्यु द्वारा) : He has recently been be- reaved and is off work. ▸ **bereaved** adj (औप) (किसी प्रियजन की मृत्यु के बाद) शोक संतप्त, शोकाकुल, शोकार्त : the bereaved husband/wife **bereave- ment** noun शोक, ग़मी; वियोग।

bereft / बि'रेफ़्ट् / adj **bereft (of sth)** (औप) से वंचित : bereft of hope/ speech/reason.

berry / 'बेरि / noun (pl berries) बदरी, बेर की तरह के फल, सरस फल : black- berries/gooseberries/strawber- ries.

berth / बर्थ् / noun 1 रेलगाड़ी या जहाज़ में शयन-स्थान, शायिका 2 गोदी, नदी या बंदरगाह में जहाज़ के रुकने का स्थान ▸ **berth** verb रेलगाड़ी या जहाज़ में शयन-स्थान देना/उपलब्ध कराना : Six passengers can be berthed on the lower deck.

beseech / बि'सीच् / verb (pt, pp **besought** / बि'सॉट् / या **beseeched**) (औप) अनुनय करना, विनयपूर्वक माँगना, विनती करना : I beseech you to think seriously about this. ▸ **beseech- ing** adj अनुनय/विनयपूर्ण **beseechingly** adv विनीत भाव से, अनुनयपूर्वक।

beside / बि'साइड् / prep 1 पास में, बग़ल में, पार्श्व में, किसी से अगला 2 की तुलना में : Beside your earlier work this piece seems rather disappointing. ∎ **beside oneself (with sth)** भावुकता या गुस्से में आपे से बाहर।

besides / बि'साइड्ज़् / prep के अतिरिक्त, के साथ-साथ : There will be five of us for dinner, besides the children.

besiege / बि'सीज् / verb 1 (नगर, क़िले आदि का) घेरा डालना 2 घेर लेना : The union spokesman was besieged by reporters.

best[1] / बेस्ट् / adj (**good** की उत्तमावस्था)

उत्तम, सर्वोत्तम, श्रेष्ठ : *The best thing about the party was the food.* ■ **make the best use of sth** समय/अवसर आदि का सर्वाधिक प्रभावी ढंग से प्रयोग करना।

best² / बे़स्ट् / *adv* (well की उत्तमावस्था) 1 सर्वोत्तम/सर्वश्रेष्ठ तरीके़ से : *the best-kept garden in the street* 2 सर्वाधिक, अधिकतम (मात्रा में/स्तर पर) 3 सर्वोत्तम या सर्वाधिक उचित ढंग से : *Do as you think best.* ■ **as best one can** अपनी भरसक कोशिश से जितना जिससे संभव है ▸ **best-seller** *noun* (पुस्तक आदि) सर्वाधिक बिकने वाली।

best³ / बे़स्ट् / *noun* [sing] 1 सर्वश्रेष्ठ; सर्वोच्च गुणों वाला व्यक्ति या वस्तु : *She wants the best of everything.* 2 अपेक्षित या इच्छित वस्तु से यथासंभव समान : *The best we can hope for is that we don't lose money on the deal.* ■ **all the best** (*अनौप*) (विदा लेते समय) शुभकामनाएँ, सर्वमंगलमय हो **at best** अधिक से अधिक **at its/one's best** सर्वोत्तम अवस्था में **do, try, etc one's (level/very) best** भरसक कोशिश करना **to the best of one's belief/knowledge** जहाँ तक किसी को पता है, जहाँ तक कोई जानता है।

bestial / बे़स्टिअल; US बे़स्चल् / *adj* (*अपमा*) पशुवत्, पशुतुल्य; क्रूर ▸ **bestiality** / ‚बे़स्टि'ऐलिटि / *noun* पाशविकता, पशुता : *an act of horrifying bestiality.*

bestow / बि'स्टो / *verb* **bestow sth (on sb)** (*औप*) देना, अर्पित करना, प्रदान करना : *an honour bestowed on her by the king.*

bet / बे़ट् / *verb* (-tt-; *pt, pp* bet या betted) **bet (sth) (on/against sth)** बाज़ी/शर्त लगाना, दाँव लगाना : *He spends all his money betting on horses.* ■ **I bet (that...)** (*अनौप*) मुझे पक्का निश्चय

है : *I bet he arrives late—he always does.* ▸ **bet** *noun* 1 दाँव, बाज़ी, शर्त : *win/lose a bet* 2 दाँव या शर्त पर लगा धन : *put/place a bet on a horse.*

betray / बि'ट्रे / *verb* 1 विश्वासघात करना, धोखा देना : *betray one's country* 2 **betray sb/sth (to sb)** (छल से) शत्रु को देना या दिखा देना : *betray state secrets* 3 **betray oneself** अपना वास्तविक रूप दिखा देना : *He had a good disguise, but as soon as he spoke he betrayed himself.* ▸ **betrayal** / बि'ट्रेअल् / *noun* विश्वासघात, धोखा **betrayer** *noun* विश्वासघाती, धोखेबाज़।

better¹ / बे़टर् / *adj* (good का तुलनात्मक रूप) 1 बेहतर, अधिक अच्छा 2 अधिक कुशल 3 अधिक उपयुक्त, अधिक स्पष्ट : *Having talked to everyone involved I now have a better idea (of) what happened.*

better² / बे़टर् / *adv* (well का तुलनात्मक रूप) 1 बेहतर/अधिक अच्छे/अधिक रुचिपूर्ण ढंग से 2 से अधिक, अधिक (मात्रा में) ■ **be better off** 1 संपन्न, धनी, सुविधाएँ रखने वाला 2 अधिक प्रसन्न या आराम में होना।

better³ / बे़टर् / *noun* वह (व्यक्ति या वस्तु) जो बेहतर है ■ **for better or worse** चाहे जो भी (अच्छा या बुरा) परिणाम हो **get the better of sb/sth** किसी को पराजित करना, मात देना।

better⁴ / बे़टर् / *verb* 1 किसी से बेहतर बना देना, आगे निकल जाना 2 सुधार करना, सुधार लाना : *The government hopes to better the conditions of the workers.* ▸ **betterment** *noun* (*औप*) बेहतरी, सुधार, उन्नति।

between / बि'ट्वीन् / *prep* 1 (प्राय: दो स्थानों, वस्तुओं, विचारों आदि को पृथक करता हुआ) के बीच में 2 समयांतराल (दो दिनों, वर्षों, घटनाओं आदि को पृथक करने वाला) 3 (रेखा) एक स्थान से दूसरे को

पृथक करती हुई 4 (संबंधसूचक) : a clear difference/distinction/contrast between two things 5 दो व्यक्तियों या वस्तुओं में सम्मिलित/साझा : This is just between you and me. ▸ between (in between भी) adv 1 बीच में, मध्यवर्ती 2 दो तारीख़ों या घटनाओं का समयांतराल।

beverage / 'बेवरिज़ / noun (और या परि) पानी के अतिरिक्त कोई भी पेय पदार्थ, जैसे चाय, कॉफ़ी, दूध, शराब आदि।

bevy / 'बेवि / noun बड़ा समूह या समुदाय : a bevy of beautiful girls.

beware / बि'वेअर् / verb beware (of sb/sth) सचेत रहना, सावधान होना या रहना, सतर्क होना : He told us to beware of pickpockets.

bewilder / बि'विल्डर् / verb घबरा देना, चकित कर देना, चकरा देना : I am totally bewildered by these crossword clues. ▸ bewildered adj हक्का-बक्का, किंकर्तव्यविमूढ़, संभ्रांत bewildering adj विस्मयकारी, चकित कर देने वाला bewilderingly adj विस्मय से, व्याकुलता से bewilderment noun घबराहट; संभ्रम।

bewitch / बि'विच् / verb 1 जादू करना/डालना 2 मोहित करना : He was bewitched by her beauty. ▸ bewitching adj मोहिनी, लुभाने वाली, सम्मोहक।

beyond / बि'यॉन्ड् / prep 1 की दूसरी ओर, के परे 2 एक निश्चित समय से बाद में : It won't go on beyond midnight. 3 एक संभावना के बाहर : The bicycle is beyond repair. 4 के अलावा, के अतिरिक्त : He has nothing beyond his pension. ■ be beyond sb (अनौप) किसी की कल्पना या समझ के बाहर : Carrying all the three suitcases was beyond me.

bias / 'बाइअस् / noun (प्राय: sing) पक्षपात, विशेष झुकाव, पूर्वाग्रह ▸ bias verb (-s-, -ss-) bias sb (towards/in favour of/against sb/sth) पक्षपात कराना, तरफ़दारी कराना; दबाव डालना।

bib / बिब् / noun 1 बच्चों के दूध पीते या खाते समय गले में बाँधा जाने वाला कपड़ा, गतिया 2 एप्रन का ऊपरी हिस्सा।

bible / 'बाइबल् / noun 1 (the Bible भी) ईसाइयों का धर्मग्रंथ, बाइबिल 2 कोई भी पुस्तक जिसकी व्यक्ति बहुत क़द्र करता हो।

bibliography / बिब्लि'ऑग्रफ़ि / noun 1 ग्रंथ सूची, पुस्तक सूची 2 पुस्तकों एवं उनके उत्पादन/उत्पत्ति के इतिहास का अध्ययन ▸ bibliographer noun ग्रंथ-सूचीकार, साहित्यिक ग्रंथों का इतिहास लेखक bibliographical adj पुस्तक-सूची विषयक।

bicentenary / बाइसेन्'टीनरि; US बाइसेन्'टे̣नरि / noun द्विशती, द्विशतवार्षिकी।

bicentennial / बाइसेन्'टेनिअल् / adj द्विशतवार्षिक।

bicker / 'बिकर् / verb bicker (with sb) (over/about sth) व्यर्थ की कलह करना, बेकार की बात के लिए झगड़ना।

bicycle / 'बाइसिकल् / noun साइकिल।

bid¹ / बिड् / verb 1 (-dd-; pt, pp bid) bid (sth) (for sth) (नीलामी आदि में) बोली लगाना 2 (pt bade / बेड; बैड्/; pp bidden / 'बिडन्/) (प्रा या औप) आदेश देना; कहना; bid sth to sb (अभिवादन में) कुछ कहना : bid sb good morning ▸ bidder noun बोली लगाने वाला bidding noun 1 (औप) आज्ञा अथवा निवेदन 2 (नीलामी में) बोली।

bid² / बिड् / noun 1 नीलामी में बोली : Any higher/further bids? 2 कुछ करने का प्रयास/पाने की चेष्टा : make a bid for power/popular support.

biennial / बाइ'एनिअल् / adj द्वैवार्षिक, दोसाला, द्विवर्षी : a biennial film festival.

bifocal / बाइ'फ़ोकल् / adj (विशेष रूप से चश्मे) दो हिस्सों वाले लेंस के चश्मे, एक से दूर की वस्तु देखना और दूसरे से पास की वस्तु देखना जिनका उद्देश्य होता है।

bifurcate / 'बाइफ़र्केट् / verb (औप) (सड़क, नदी, पेड़ की शाखा आदि) द्विशाखित होना या द्विभाजित करना ▸ **bifurcated** adj द्विभाजित **bifurcation** noun द्विभाजन।

big / बिग् / adj (-gger, -ggest) 1 (आकार में) बड़ा, विशाल 2 महत्त्वपूर्ण, प्रभाव-शाली : the big match 3 (अनौप) महत्त्वाकांक्षी एवं महान : have big ideas/plans ■ **be/get too big for one's boots** (अनौप) बहुत घमंडी हो जाना, अपने को बहुत ज़्यादा समझना **big deal!** (अनौप) मैं इस (बात) से प्रभावित नहीं हुआ **have a big mouth** बातूनी अथवा शेखी बघारने वाला ▸ **big** adv (अप) बड़े या प्रभावशाली तरीक़े से : We need to think big. ○ He likes to talk big. **big bang** noun (प्राय: sing) वह विस्फोट जिससे, कुछ वैज्ञानिकों का मानना है, कि समस्त ब्रह्मांड की उत्पत्ति हुई **big-hearted** adj दयालु, उदार, विशाल हृदय व्यक्ति।

bigamy / 'बिगमि / noun एक पति/पत्नी से क़ानूनन विवाहित होते हुए किसी दूसरे से विवाह करने का अपराध ▸ **bigamist** noun द्विविवाही, द्विपत्नीक/द्विपतिका **bigamous** adj दो पति/पत्नियाँ रखने का अपराधी (व्यक्ति): a bigamous marriage.

bigot / 'बिगट् / noun कट्टर या धर्मांध व्यक्ति : religious bigots ▸ **bigoted** adj कट्टर विचारों वाला **bigotry** noun धर्मांधता, मताग्रह, कट्टरपन।

bike / बाइक् / noun (अनौप) 1 बाइसिकल 2 मोटरसाइकिल ▸ **bike** verb (अनौप) साइकिल या मोटरसाइकिल की सवारी करना: Let's go biking.

bikini / बि'कीनि / noun स्त्रियों के तैरने के लिए दो अलग-अलग हिस्से वाली पोशाक।

bilateral / बाइ'लैटरल् / adj द्विपक्षी, द्वि-पार्श्व; दुतरफ़ा : a bilateral agreement/treaty ▸ **bilaterally** adv द्विपक्षीय रूप से, दोनों तरफ़ से।

bile / बाइल् / noun 1 पित्त 2 चिड़चिड़ापन, बदमिज़ाजी।

bilingual / बाइ'लिङ्ग्वल् / adj 1 द्विभाषी, दो भाषाएँ जानने वाला 2 द्वैभाषिक 3 दो भाषाओं में व्यक्त अथवा लिखित।

bill¹ / बिल् / noun 1 बिल, सामान या सेवा के एवज़ में प्राप्य धनराशि का हिसाब, प्राप्यक 2 हस्तलिखित अथवा मुद्रित विज्ञप्ति, इश्तहार, विज्ञापन 3 (संसद में प्रस्तुत) विधेयक : propose/pass/throw out/amend a bill 4 (US) बैंक नोट, मुद्रा : a ten-dollar bill ■ **foot the bill** (अनौप) भुगतान के लिए ज़िम्मेदार ▸ **bill** verb 1 **bill sb (for sth)** किसी को किसी वस्तु के लिए बिल भेजना 2 **bill sb/sth as sth** किसी रूप में प्रचार करना, घोषित करना।

bill² / बिल् / noun (पक्षी की) चोंच।

billiards / 'बिलिअर्ड्ज़् / noun बिलियर्ड, क्यू और बॉल की सहायता से दो व्यक्तियों द्वारा मेज़ पर खेला जाने वाला खेल।

billion / 'बिल्यन् / noun (pl अपरिवर्तित या **billions**) एक अरब; 1,000,000,000 या 10^9 का अंक।

billow / 'बिलो / noun 1 (प्रा) समुद्र में विशाल तरंग 2 विशाल तरंग की तरह बढ़ता हुआ धुएँ या भाप का बादल ▸ **billow** verb समुद्री तरंग की तरह उठना और बढ़ना; लहराना।

bin / बिन् / noun आटा, अनाज, कोयला आदि या कूड़ा करकट रखने के लिए बड़ा ढक्कनदार डिब्बा।

binary / 'बाइनरि / adj दोहरा, द्विचर, द्वि-आधारी।

bind / बाइन्ड् / verb (pt, pp **bound** / बाउन्ड् /) 1 **bind A (to B); bind A and B (together)** (रस्सी आदि से) बाँधना; लोगों को एक साथ रखना, लोगों (या वस्तुओं) में एकता बनाकर रखना 2 **bind sth (in sth)** जिल्द बाँधना या चढ़ाना : bind a book 3 **bind sb (to sth)** बाध्य करना, आवश्यक बनाना : bind sb to pay a debt ▸ **bind** noun [sing] (अनौप) परेशानी का कारण बनने वाली स्थिति या बंधन : It's a hell of a bind having to *stay indoors on a nice day like this.* **binder** *noun* 1 काग़ज़ के पन्ने या पत्रिका आदि रखने के लिए कवर 2 जिल्द-साज़, किताबों की जिल्द चढ़ाने वाला व्यक्ति 3 जिल्द बाँधने/चढ़ाने की मशीन **binding** *noun* जिल्द : *books in fine leather bindings.*

binoculars / बि'नॉक्यलर्ज़्/ *noun* [*pl*] दूरबीन।

biochemistry /बाइओ'केमिस्ट्रि/ *noun* जीवरसायन, सजीवों की रासायनिकी का वैज्ञानिक अध्ययन ▸ **biochemist** *noun* जीवरसायनज्ञ।

biodegradable / बाइओडि'ग्रेडब्ल् / *adj* (पदार्थ) जिसे जीवाणुओं द्वारा सड़ाया और नष्ट किया जा सके, जीवाणु द्वारा अप-घटित होने वाला : *biodegradable household cleaning products.*

biography / बाइ'ऑग्रफ़ि / *noun* (*pl* **biographies**) (दूसरे के द्वारा लिखा गया) जीवन-चरित्र, जीवनी; साहित्य की एक विधा ▸ **biographer** /,बाइ'ऑग्रफ़र्/ *noun* जीवनी लेखक।

biological /,बाइअ'लॉजिकल्/ *adj* जीव-विज्ञान विषयक, जैविक।

biology / बाइ'ऑलजि / *noun* प्राणि-विज्ञान, जीव-विज्ञान, पशु और पौधों का विज्ञान ▸ **biologist** / बाइ'ऑलजिस्ट्/ *noun* जीव-विज्ञान का ज्ञाता, जीव-विज्ञानी।

bird / बर्ड / *noun* चिड़िया, पक्षी ■ **a bird in the hand is worth two in the bush** (कहा) आधी छोड़ सारी को धावै, आधी रह न सारी पावै **birds of a feather** (**flock together**) (कहा) चोर-चोर मौसेरे भाई ▸ **bird sanctuary** *noun* पक्षी-विहार, अभयारण्य।

birth / बर्थ / *noun* 1 जन्म : *She gave birth (to a healthy boy) last night.* 2 पैदाइश 3 किसी चीज़ का अस्तित्व में आना, किसी चीज़ की शुरुआत : *the birth of capitalism/socialism* ▸ **birth cer-**

tificate *noun* जन्म प्रमाण-पत्र **birth control** *noun* संतति निग्रह **birth rate** *noun* जन्मदर (प्रतिवर्ष) **birthright** *noun* जन्मसिद्ध अधिकार।

birthday /'बर्थ्डे / *noun* जन्मदिन।

biscuit /'बिस्किट्/ *noun* बिस्कुट।

bisect / बाइ'सेक्ट् / *verb* किसी चीज़ को दो बराबर टुकड़ों में करना, द्विभाजित करना ▸ **bisection** / बाइ'सेक्श्न् / *noun* द्वि-भाजन।

bishop /'बिशप् / *noun* 1 बिशप, चर्च व्यवस्था में नगर या ज़िले का संगठन-पादरी 2 शतरंज का एक मोहरा, ऊँट।

bison /'बाइस्न्/ *noun* (*pl* अपरिवर्तित) जंगली साँड; अमेरिकन जंगली भैंसा।

bit¹ /बिट्/ *noun* छोटा टुकड़ा या मात्रा, अंश, खंड ■ **a bit** 1 थोड़ा-सा, कुछ 2 थोड़ा-सा समय अथवा ज़रा-सी दूरी **bit by bit** थोड़ा-थोड़ा करके, धीरे-धीरे **do one's bit** (अनौप) अपने हिस्से का कार्य करना।

bit² / बिट् / *noun* (घोड़े की) लगाम के मुँह में लगाया जाने वाला धातु का भाग, दहाना।

bit³ / बिट् / *noun* कंप्यूटर द्वारा प्रयुक्त सूचना की सबसे छोटी इकाई।

bitch / बिच् / *noun* 1 कुतिया, कुत्ता जाति की मादा जानवर 2 (अपमा, अप) क्रूर अथवा बुरी औरत, छिनाल।

bite¹ /'बाइट् / *verb* (*pt* **bit** / बिट् /; *pp* **bitten** /'बिट्न्/) 1 **bite (into sth)** दाँतों से काटना 2 (किसी पतंगे या सर्प का) डंक मारना, डसना ■ **bite off more than one can chew** (अनौप) अपने बूते के बाहर काम करने की कोशिश करना **bite the dust** (अनौप) 1 गिरना और मर जाना 2 हार जाना (धूल चाटना) या अस्वीकार किया जाना; बुरी तरह परास्त हो जाना **bite the hand that feeds one** जिस थाली में खाए उसी में छेद करे ▸ **biting** *adj* 1 काटता हुआ, तीखा, तीक्ष्ण; (सर्दी) कड़ाके की 2 (टिप्पणी आदि) चुभती हुई, निर्दय एवं पीड़ादायक, तानेभरी।

bite² / 'बाइट् / noun 1 काट 2 (अनौप्) खाना, भोजन, ग्रास 3 कीट या सर्प के काटने से हुआ घाव : *mosquito bites.*

bitter / 'बिटर् / adj 1 कड़वा, तीखा, कटु, तिक्त 2 दुखदायक, मर्मभेदी : *Failing the exam was a bitter disappointment to him.* 3 क्रोध, ईर्ष्या, द्वेष से उत्पन्न या पूर्ण: *bitter quarrels/enemies/words* ■ **a bitter pill (for sb) (to swallow)** कोई अरुचिकर, दुखदायी, निराशाजनक एवं अस्वीकार्य तथ्य या घटना ▶ **bitterly** adv दुखदायी, कष्टकर ढंग से **bitterness** noun कड़वाहट, कटुता, तीखापन।

bizzare / बि'ज़ार् / adj अनोखा; बेतुका, तर्कहीन : *a bizzare incident/coincidence/situation.*

black¹ / ब्लैक् / adj 1 काला, कृष्ण 2 अंधकारमय, पूर्णत: प्रकाशहीन 3 (चाय या कॉफ़ी) बिना दूध की 4 (**Black** भी) (अपमा) काले रंग वाली मानव जाति : *Many black people emigrated to Britain in the 1950s.* 5 गंदा 6 निराशाजनक 7 दुष्ट, हानिकारक, घिनौना : *a black deed/lie* ■ (**beat sb**) **black and blue** बुरी तरह पीटना ▶ **black belt** noun जूडो/कराटे चैंपियन द्वारा पहनी जाने वाली काली बेल्ट; जूडो/कराटे चैंपियन **blackboard** noun श्यामपट्ट **black box** noun हवाई जहाज़ की उड़ान का पूरा विवरण स्वचालित रूप से रिकॉर्ड करने वाला यंत्र **black magic** noun काला जादू, जादू-टोना **black market** noun [sing] काला बाज़ार, चोर बाज़ार **blackness** noun कालापन, कालिमा **blackout** noun 1 अवधि जिसमें विद्युत ऊर्जा प्राप्त न हो पाए; अवधि जिसमें प्रकाश के स्रोत बुझा दिए जाएँ, विशेषत: हवाई हमले के दौरान 2 कुछ समय के लिए मूर्च्छा।

black² / ब्लैक् / noun 1 काला रंग 2 (प्राय: **Black**) काले रंग के व्यक्ति (जाति, समुदाय) ■ **in black and white** लिखित रूप में, छपा हुआ।

black³ / ब्लैक् / verb काला करना, काला रंग चढ़ाना; काली पॉलिश लगाना।

blacken / 'ब्लैकन् / verb 1 काला करना या होना 2 किसी की इज़्ज़त उछालना, कलंक लगाना।

blacklist / 'ब्लैक्लिस्ट् / noun काली सूची, अपराधियों की सूची।

blackmail / 'ब्लैक्मेल् / noun भयादोहन; कोई रहस्य खोलने की धमकी देकर धन ऐंठने की क्रिया ▶ **blackmail** verb **blackmail sb (into doing sth)** दबाव से या धमकाकर किसी से कुछ करवाना/करने को मजबूर करना।

blacksmith / 'ब्लैक्स्मिथ् / (**smith** भी) noun लोहार।

bladder / 'ब्लैडर् / noun 1 मूत्राशय, शरीर का वह अंग जहाँ मूत्र एकत्र होता है 2 थैलीनुमा कोई चीज़ जिसे हवा (या पानी) से भरा जा सकता है, जैसे फुटबाल का फुकना।

blade / ब्लेड् / noun चाकू, रेज़र आदि का काटने वाला फलक, धार; ब्लेड।

blame / ब्लेम् / verb **blame sb (for sth)/blame sth on sb** दोष देना; ग़लती का ज़िम्मेदार ठहराना ▶ **blame** noun **blame (for sth)** दोष, (ग़लत कार्य का) उत्तरदायित्व **blameless** adj निर्दोष **blamelessly** adv.

bland / ब्लैन्ड् / adj (-er, -est) 1 अनाकर्षक, रोचकता रहित 2 (खाना) कम स्वाद वाला, बेस्वाद-सा।

blandishments / 'ब्लैन्डिश्मन्ट्स् / noun [pl] (औप) चापलूसी, फुसलावा : *He refused to be moved by either threats or blandishments.*

blank / ब्लैंक् / adj (-er, -est) 1 (काग़ज़) कोरा, सादा 2 ख़ाली, शून्य, रिक्त : *a blank wall* ○ *a blank form* 3 भौचक्का, भावशून्य : *She stared at me with a blank expression (on her face).* 4 (नकारात्मक वस्तुओं का) सरासर, पूरा-पूरा : *a blank denial/refusal* ▶ **blank** noun 1 रिक्त स्थान (मुद्रण या लेखन में) : *fill in*

the blanks on the question paper
2 शून्यता, रिक्तता (समय या स्थान की)।
blank cheque (*US* **blank check**)
noun 1 कोरा चेक 2 कुछ करने का पूर्णाधिकार।

blanket / 'ब्लैङ्किट् / *noun* 1 कंबल
2 आवरण, किसी चीज़ को आच्छादित करने
वाली सतह : *a blanket of fog/cloud/
snow* 3 सभी मामलों में लागू होने वाली
बात, अपवादरहित : *a blanket agree-
ment/term/rule* ▶ **blanket** *verb*
blanket sth (in/with sth) किसी चीज़
को मोटी तह से पूर्णत: आच्छादित कर देना/
ढक देना : *The countryside was blan-
keted with snow.*

blare / ब्लेअर् / *verb* 1 **blare (out)** तुरही
की तरह से कर्कश ध्वनि पैदा करना 2 **blare
sth (out)** गरजना; चिल्लाकर पुकारना
▶ **blare** *noun* [*sing*] कर्कश ध्वनि, गर्जन।

blaspheme / ब्लैस्'फ़ीम् / *verb* ईश्वर की
निंदा करना; पवित्र वस्तुओं के संबंध में
अपमानपूर्वक बोलना : *blaspheme
(against) the name of God* ▶ **blas-
phemer** *noun* ईशनिंदक **blasphemous**
/ 'ब्लैस्फ़मस् / *adj* ईशनिंदापूर्ण **blas-
phemy** / 'ब्लैस्फ़मि / *noun* ईशनिंदा।

blast¹ / 'ब्लास्ट्; *US* ब्लैस्ट् / *noun* 1 (हवा
का) भयानक झोंका : *a blast of hot air
from the furnace* 2 विस्फोट, धमाका
3 सीटी, हॉर्न या तुरही की आवाज़ (नाद)
▶ **blast furnace** *noun* धमन-भट्टी, जहाँ
अत्यधिक गर्म हवा के दबाव से कच्चा लोहा
पिघलाया जाता है।

blast² / 'ब्लास्ट्; *US* ब्लैस्ट् / *verb* 1 वि-
स्फोट से उड़ा देना या नष्ट कर देना : *blast
a hole in a mountain* 2 (अनौप) कटु
आलोचना करना; अपशब्द कहना : *The
film was blasted by the critics.*

blatant / 'ब्लेटन्ट् / *adj* खुले-आम, स्पष्ट;
भद्दे ढंग से ध्यान आकर्षित करने वाला :
blatant disregard for the law
▶ **blatantly** *adv*.

blaze¹ / ब्लेज़् / *noun* 1 ज्वाला, धधक :

Five people died in the blaze.
2 ज्वाला की चमक, प्रदीप्ति 3 [*sing*]
blaze (of sth) भावनाओं का अचानक
भड़क उठना : *a blaze of anger/pas-
sion/temper.*

blaze² / ब्लेज़् / *verb* 1 चमकीली ज्वाला
के साथ जलना : *A good fire was
blazing in the fireplace.* 2 **blaze
(with sth)** प्रबल भावनाओं (विशेषत:
क्रोध) के साथ भड़क उठना : *She was
blazing with fury.* ▶ **blazing** *adj*
धधकता हुआ।

blazer / 'ब्लेज़र् / *noun* कोट या जैकेट
जिसपर किसी क्लब, स्कूल या टीम का
बिल्ला लगा होता है।

bleach / ब्लीच् / *verb* रंग उड़ाकर सफ़ेद
करना (या होना) (रासायनिक प्रक्रिया अथवा
धूप के कारण) : *bleach cotton/linen*
▶ **bleach** *noun* रंग उड़ाने वाला रासायनिक
पदार्थ।

bleak / ब्लीक् / *adj* (**-er, -est**) 1 (स्थान)
खुला, हवादार और उजाड़ 2 (स्थिति या
दृष्टिकोण) निराशापूर्ण, उत्साहहीन : *a bleak
outlook/prospect ○ The future looks
bleak.*

bleary / ब्लिअरि / *adj* (आँखें) धुँधली,
थकान के कारण मंद ▶ **blearily** *adv*.

bleat / ब्लीट् / *noun* 1 (प्राय: *sing*) भेड़,
बकरी आदि की आवाज़ 2 कमज़ोर, मूर्खतापूर्ण
अथवा शिकायत भरी चिल्लाहट ▶ **bleat**
verb.

bleed / ब्लीड् / *verb* (*pt, pp* **bled**
/ ब्लेड् /) 1 खून निकलना या निकालना,
रक्तस्राव होना : *bleed to death* 2 खून
निकालना या बहाना ■ **bleed sb white**
किसी का सारा पैसा हड़प लेना।

blemish / 'ब्लेमिश् / *noun* दाग़ या धब्बा
जिससे किसी की पूर्णता या सुंदरता कम हो
जाती है : (अलं) *His character/repu-
tation is without (a) blemish.*
▶ **blemish** *verb* धब्बा लगाना; लांछन
लगाना।

blend / ब्लेन्ड् / verb 1 मिश्रण करना, उचित मात्रा में मिलाना 2 blend (with sth)/ blend (together) अच्छी तरह मिलना, मिश्रण तैयार करना : Oil does not blend with water. ▸ blend noun एक चीज़ के विभिन्न प्रकारों का या विभिन्न प्रकार की चीज़ों का मिश्रण, सम्मिश्रण blender noun भोजन (सब्ज़ी आदि) को काटकर, मिलाकर द्रव में बदलने वाली मशीन।

bless / ब्लेस् / verb (pt, pp blessed / ब्लेस्ट् /) 1 ईश्वर की कृपा चाहना, वरदान माँगना/देना : The priest blessed the harvest. 2 (ईसाई प्रार्थना में) ईश्वर की पूजा करना, प्रशंसा करना ▪ be blessed with sth/sb सौभाग्यशाली होना : We're blessed with five lovely grandchildren.

blessed / ब्लेसिड् / adj 1 पवित्र, आदरणीय 2 (धार्मिक भाषा में) सौभाग्यशाली, धन्य 3 सुखदायी, आनंददायक।

blessing / ब्लेसिङ् / noun 1 ईश्वरकृपा 2 (प्राय: sing) शुभकामना, कृपादान : I cannot give my blessing to such a proposal. ▪ a blessing in disguise अप्रत्यक्ष कृपादान।

blight / ब्लाइट् / noun 1 पौधों में चित्ती पड़ने का रोग, अंगमारी 2 blight (on sb/ sth) अभिशाप : The bad weather cast/put a blight on our holiday.

blind¹ / ब्लाइन्ड् / adj 1 अंधा, नेत्रहीन 2 नेत्रहीन व्यक्तियों के लिए 3 blind (to sth) लापरवाह; समझने में असमर्थ, बेपरवाह 4 तर्कहीन, विवेकशून्य : blind hatred/ obedience/prejudice ▪ turn a blind eye to (sth) न देखने का बहाना करना; जानबूझकर अनदेखा कर देना ▸ blind alley noun 1 बंद गली 2 (अलं) निष्फल प्रयत्न blindly adv blind man's buff noun आँख-मिचौली का खेल blindness noun अंधापन, नेत्रहीनता the blind noun लोग जो अंधे हों।

blind² / ब्लाइन्ड् / verb 1 किसी को अ-स्थायी या स्थायी तौर पर अंधा बनाना : The soldier was blinded in the explosion. 2 blind sb (to sth) विवेकहीन या तर्कहीन बना देना : Her love for him blinded her (to his faults). ▸ blinding adj बहुत तीव्र।

blind³ / ब्लाइन्ड् / noun (US shade, window shade भी) खिड़की का परदा या झिलमिली : draw/lower/raise the blinds.

blindfold / ब्लाइन्ड्फोल्ड् / verb आँखों पर पट्टी बाँधना ▸ blindfold noun आँखों पर पट्टी।

blink / ब्लिङ्क् / verb 1 पलक झपकाना; आँखें मिचकाना 2 (रोशनी का) टिमटिमाना ▪ blink sth away/back पलकें झपकाकर आँसुओं को रोकने का प्रयत्न करना ▸ blink noun झपकी, निमेष ▪ the blink of an eye पलक झपकते ही, ज़रा-सी देर में।

blinkers / ब्लिङ्कर्ज़् / (US blinders भी) noun [pl] घोड़े को इधर-उधर देखने से रोकने के लिए उसकी आँखों पर लगाए जाने वाले चमड़े के टुकड़े, अँधेरी, झापड़े।

bliss / ब्लिस् / noun परमानंद; स्वर्गसुख ▸ blissful adj सुखद, आनंदमय।

blister / ब्लिस्टर् / noun फफोला, छाला ▸ blister verb छाला पड़ जाना, फफोला हो जाना : My feet blister easily. blistered adj छाले पड़ा हुआ blistering adj (गरमी) झुलसा देने वाली।

blitz / ब्लिट्स् / noun अचानक किया गया तूफ़ानी हवाई हमला : carry out a blitz on enemy targets.

blizzard / ब्लिज़र्ड् / noun बर्फ़ानी तूफ़ान; हिम-झंझावात।

bloated / ब्लोटिड् / adj मोटापे, गैस या द्रव से फूला हुआ : (अलं) bloated with pride.

blob / ब्लॉब् / noun (गाढ़े) द्रव की बूँद; एक छोटी गोली, धब्बा या रंग या छींटा : a blob of paint/wax.

bloc / ब्लॉक् / noun गुट, दल; दलबंदी।

block¹ / ब्लॉक् / noun 1 लकड़ी, पत्थर या धातु का बड़ा टुकड़ा, शिलाखंड; (लकड़ी का) कुंदा 2 लकड़ी या प्लास्टिक की खिलौनाईंट: a set of (building) blocks 3 भवन समूह जिसके चारों तरफ सड़कें हों : go for a walk around the block 4 खंडों, प्रखंडों में बँटी हुई विशाल इमारत : blocks of flats 5 (प्राय: sing) (आवागमन या प्रगति में) बाधा, अवरोध : a block in the pipe/gutter.

block² / ब्लॉक् / verb 1 block sth (up) अवरोध या बाधा द्वारा आवागमन में रोक डालना : a drain blocked (up) by mud/dead leaves 2 प्रगति/उन्नति में बाधा डालना/रोड़े अटकाना : The accident blocked downtown traffic. ▸ **blockage** / ब्लॉकिज् / noun अवरोध या बाधा; अवरुद्धता।

blockade / ब्लॉकेड् / noun घेरा, नाकाबंदी।

blockbuster / ब्लॉकबस्टर् / noun (अनौप) अत्यंत सफल पुस्तक या फ़िल्म : a blockbuster movie.

bloke / ब्लोक् / noun (अनौप) आदमी : He's a nice bloke.

blonde / ब्लॉन्ड् / adj (blond भी) 1 (बाल) हलके सुनहरे रंग के 2 (व्यक्ति) ऐसे रंग के बाल वाला ▸ **blonde** noun महिला जिसके बाल हलके सुनहरे रंग के हों।

blood / ब्लड् / noun 1 खून, रक्त 2 (औप) वंश, कुल : He is of noble blood. ■ **be after/out for sb's blood** (अनौप) किसी को घायल करने या दंड देने का इरादा रखना **blood is thicker than water** (कहा) पारिवारिक रिश्ता हमेशा मज़बूत होता है **(have sb's) blood on one's hands** सर पर हत्या का दोष होना; खून से हाथ रँगे होना **make sb's blood boil** (किसी को) अत्यंत क्रोधित कर देना ▸ **blood bank** noun रक्तदान बैंक **blood-brother** noun शपथ से बना हुआ भाई **blood donor** noun रक्तदाता **blood group** noun रक्त समूह जैसे A, B, AB, O **blood poisoning** noun (तक toxaemia भी) noun रक्त विषाक्तता, ख़तरनाक जीवाणुओं से रक्त में संक्रमण **blood pressure** noun रक्तचाप **blood relation (blood relative** भी) noun जन्म से ना कि वैवाहिक संबंध से रक्त-संबंधी **bloodshed** noun रक्तपात, हत्या **blood transfusion** noun व्यक्ति या जानवर के शरीर में नया रक्त डालना **blood vessel** noun शिराएँ, रुधिर-वाहिकाएँ।

bloodhound / ब्लडहाउन्ड् / noun एक बड़ा कुत्ता जो अपनी सूँघने की शक्ति से किसी को ढूँढ निकालता है।

bloodless / ब्लडलस् / adj 1 बिना हत्या किए या खून बहाए 2 (व्यक्ति) रक्तहीन, विवर्ण।

bloodthirsty / ब्लडथर्स्टि / adj रक्त पिपासु, खूँख़्वार।

bloody¹ / ब्लडि / adj (-ier, -iest) 1 खून में लथपथ/लिप्त; खून बहता हुआ 2 रक्तपात-पूर्ण, हत्याओं से पूर्ण : a bloody battle.

bloody² / ब्लडि / adj, adv (अप) 1 अत्यधिक : bloody nonsense/rubbish 2 (क्रोध या चिढ़ की अभिव्यक्ति के लिए प्रयुक्त) : What the bloody hell are you doing?

bloom / ब्लूम् / noun 1 फूल, बहार 2 किसी चीज़ की पूर्ण या सबसे सुंदर अवस्था : be in the bloom of youth ■ **in (full) bloom** (पौधे या बग़ीचा) पूरी तरह खिला हुआ फूल ▸ **bloom** verb 1 फूल खिलना; बौराना 2 बहुत अच्छा स्वास्थ्य होना; पनपना।

blossom / ब्लॉसम् / noun फूल, बौर, मंजरी; फूलों का बड़ा गुच्छा ▸ **blossom** verb 1 (पेड़ या झाड़ी का) पुष्पित होना, खिलना : The cherry tree blossomed early this year. 2 **blossom (out) (into sth)** विकसित होना, फलना-फूलना : a blossoming friendship/career.

blot / ब्लॉट् / noun 1 धब्बा; (काग़ज़ आदि पर) रोशनाई का दाग़ 2 **blot (on sth)**

(चरित्र, सुंदरता आदि पर) कलंक, लांछन : *Their handling of the economic crisis has been a serious blot on the government's record.* ▸ **blot** *verb* (**-tt-**) 1 काग़ज़ पर दाग़ लगाना, धब्बे डालना; मैला करना 2 **blot sth (up)** स्याही-सोख़ते से स्याही के दाग़ सुखाना/सोख़ लेना : *She blotted the ink (up).* **blotting-paper** *noun* स्याही-सोख़ता।

blotch / ब्लॉच् / *noun* छाला, व्रण, दाग़, धब्बा : *His face was covered in ugly red blotches.* ▸ **blotched, blotchy** *adjs* फूला हुआ, धब्बेदार, दग़ीला।

blouse / ब्लाउज़; *US* ब्लाउस् / *noun* ब्लाउज़ (स्त्रियों का ऊपरी वस्त्र)।

blow¹ / ब्लो / *verb* (*pt* **blew** / ब्लू /; *pp* **blown** / ब्लोन् /) 1 (हवा का) बहना; चलना 2 (वस्तुओं का) हवा से उड़ना, बिखरना : *hair blowing (about) in the wind* 3 (सीटी) बजाना; बाजा बजाना 4 शक्तिशाली विद्युत धारा से कुछ पिघलना/पिघलाना : *A fuse has blown.* ■ **blow hot and cold (about sth)** *(अनौप)* किसी बात पर अपना मत बार-बार बदलना **blow one's own trumpet** *(अनौप)* स्वप्रशंसा करना, डींग मारना **blow over** (किसी मुश्किल परिस्थिति का) बिना गंभीर प्रभाव के गुज़र जाना **blow (sb/sth) down, off, over, etc** हवा द्वारा (या फूँक से) किसी दिशा में उड़ना/उड़ाना : *The door blew open.*

blow² / ब्लो / *noun* 1 घूँसा, प्रहार 2 **blow (to sb/sth)** गहरा धक्का, आघात : *His wife's death came as a terrible blow (to him).* ■ **come to blows (over sth)** लड़ना शुरू कर देना/लात-घूँसों पर बात आ जाना।

blower / 'ब्लोअर् / *noun* धौंकनी, फूँकनी।

bludgeon / 'ब्लज्न् / *noun* गदा, सोंटा ▸ **bludgeon** *verb* अंधाधुंध गदा/सोंटा मारना।

blue¹ / ब्लू / *adj* (**-r, -st**) 1 नीला, आसमानी

2 अश्लील : *a blue film/movie/joke* ▸ **blueness** *noun* नीलापन।

blue² / ब्लू / *noun* नीला रंग, नील; नीले कपड़े ■ **a bolt from the blue; out of the blue** अप्रत्याशित रूप से या अकस्मात् किसी घटना का घटित होना।

blueprint / 'ब्लूप्रिन्ट् / *noun* 1 (मकान की योजना की) रूपरेखा, ख़ाका 2 विस्तृत योजना या परियोजना।

bluff / ब्लफ़् / *verb* धोखा देना, झाँसा देना, झूठा रोब गाँठना ■ **bluff sb into doing sth** झाँसा देकर किसी से कुछ करा लेना ▸ **bluff** *noun* झाँसा-पट्टी, धुप्पल; झूठा रोब, धौंस।

blunder / 'ब्लन्डर् / *noun* भद्दी एवं मूर्खतापूर्ण भूल, चूक ▸ **blunder** *verb* भद्दी एवं मूर्खतापूर्ण भूल करना।

blunt / ब्लन्ट् / *adj* (**-er, -est**) 1 (चाकू आदि) कुंद, कुंठित, भोथरा 2 (व्यक्ति अथवा टिप्पणी) रूखा, अतिस्पष्टवादी ▸ **blunt** *verb* 1 (चाकू आदि की) धार ख़त्म करना, कुंठित होना/बनाना 2 किसी वस्तु की शक्ति या प्रभाव कम करना **bluntly** *adv* रुखता से, स्पष्टतया **bluntness** *noun*.

blur / ब्लर् / *noun* अस्पष्ट सुनाई या दिखाई देने वाली चीज़ : *The town was just a blur on the horizon.* ▸ **blur** *verb* (**-rr-**) 1 धुँधला हो जाना या कर देना : *His eyes blurred with tears.* 2 अस्पष्ट कर देना या हो जाना 3 भेद नज़र न आने देना: *She tends to blur the distinction between family and friends.* ▸ **blurred** / ब्लर्ड् / *adj* 1 रूप-आकार में अस्पष्ट 2 अंतर कर पाने में कठिन।

blurt / ब्लर्ट् / *verb* ■ **blurt sth out** बिना सोचे-समझे बोल उठना, (किसी रहस्य को) बिना सोचे अचानक प्रकट कर देना : *He blurted out the bad news before I could stop him.*

blush / ब्लश् / *verb* (लज्जा या झेंप से) मुख पर लाली छा जाना, झेंपना : *She blushed at (the thought of) her* *stupid mistake.* ▶ **blush** *noun* लज्जा की लालिमा; प्रभा।

bluster / 'ब्लस्टर् / *verb* **bluster (on)** **(about sth)** (व्यक्तियों का) घुड़ककर, धमकाकर, गरजकर या डींग मारकर बात करना ▶ **bluster** *noun* घुड़की, डींग, दर्पोक्ति **blustery**/'ब्लस्टरि/ *adj* (मौसम) तूफ़ानी।

boa / 'बोआ / **(boa constrictor** भी) *noun* (दक्षिण अमेरिका में) अजगर।

boar / बॉर् / *noun* (*pl* अपरिवर्तित या **boars**) 1 बनैला सूअर 2 (नर) शूकर, वाराह, सूअर।

board[1] / बॉर्ड / *noun* 1 तख़्ता, पट्टा, पटरा 2 विशेष प्रयोजन के लिए प्रयुक्त लकड़ी आदि का पटल : *a noticeboard* 3 खेलने के लिए विशेष पैटर्न वाला (लकड़ी का) पटल : *a chessboard* 4 समिति, परिषद, मंडल : *attend a board meeting* 5 किराए पर ठहरने के स्थान पर रोज़ के खान-पान, भोजन का मूल्य : *He pays Rs 1000 a week (for) board and lodging.* ■ **(be)** **above board** (विशेषत: सौदा आदि) ईमानदारी से **on board** जहाज़ (या वायुयान) पर सवार।

board[2] / बॉर्ड / *verb* 1 **board sth (up)** तख़्ते लगाना या तख़्तों से ढकना 2 (जहाज़, वायुयान, रेलगाड़ी आदि पर) चढ़ना; सवार होना : *Please board the plane immediately.* ▶ **boarding-school** *noun* ऐसा स्कूल जहाँ कुछ या सभी छात्र सत्र के दौरान रहते हों।

boast / बोस्ट / *verb* **boast (about/of sth)** डींग मारना, शेख़ी बघारना, बढ़-चढ़कर बातें करना : *She boasted of her skill at chess.* ▶ **boast** *noun* 1 **boast (that...)** (*अपमा*) डींग, आत्मप्रशंसा; गर्वोक्ति 2 आत्मतृप्ति का कारण, गौरव या प्रतिष्ठा **boastful** *adj* शेख़ीबाज़, आत्म-श्लाघी **boastfully** *adv* **boastfulness** *noun* आत्मश्लघा।

boat / बोट / *noun* 1 नाव, किश्ती : *a*

rowing-/sailing-boat 2 (*अनौप*)कोई भी जहाज़ ▶ **boating** *noun* नौकाचालन **boatman** *noun* नाविक, केवट।

bob[1] / बॉब् / *verb* (**-bb-**) **bob (sth) (up** **and down)** डूबना-उतराना, ऊभ-चूभ हो जाना ■ **bob up** शीघ्रता से सतह पर आ जाना, अचानक उभर जाना।

bob[2] / बॉब् / *noun* (महिलाओं के) बालों को कंधे तक रखने का फ़ैशन।

bodice /'बॉडिस् / *noun* चोली, अँगिया।

bodily / बॉडिलि / *adj* शरीर-विषयक, शारीरिक ▶ **bodily** *adv* सांगोपांग, पूरा-पूरा, सब मिलाकर।

body / 'बॉडि / *noun* (*pl* **bodies**) 1 (मनुष्य या प्राणी का) शरीर; मृत (व्यक्ति या प्राणी) का शरीर, शव 2 **the body of sth** किसी रचना का मुख्य भाग, ढाँचा : *the body of a motor car* 3 **body of sth** किसी चीज़ की बड़ी मात्रा, (तथ्यों, सूचनाओं आदि का) संकलन : *a body of evidence/information* 4 कोई विशिष्ट पदार्थ 5 दल के रूप में काम कर रहे व्यक्तियों का समूह ■ **body and soul** पूरी तरह, पूरी शक्ति से **keep body and soul together** (जैसे-तैसे) ज़िंदा रहना ▶ **body-building** *noun* कसरत से शारीरिक पुष्टि **body language** *noun* शब्दों के बजाय शरीर की विभिन्न मुद्राओं (जैसे उठना, बैठना, चलना आदि) द्वारा विचार अभिव्यक्ति।

bodyguard /'बॉडिगार्ड/ *noun* अंगरक्षक, विशिष्ट व्यक्ति की रक्षा के लिए नियुक्त रक्षक।

bog / बॉग् / *noun* दलदल, पंक ▶ **bog** *verb* (**-gg-**) ■ **bog (sth/sb) down** 1 दलदल में फँसना या फँसाना 2 प्रगति अवरुद्ध हो जाना/कर देना : *The discussions got bogged down in irrelevant detail.*

bogie /'बोगि/ *noun* (**bogey, bogy** भी) (भारत में) रेल बोगी।

bogus / 'बोगस् / *adj* निस्सार; खोटा, जाली : *a bogus passport/doctor/claim.*

boil[1] / बॉइल् / *verb* 1 (पानी आदि द्रव

उबालना/उबलना 2 boil sth (for sb) (उबाल कर) पकाना या पकना : *Please boil me an egg.* 3 boil (over) उत्तेजित अथवा क्रुद्ध होना : *He was boiling (over) with rage.* ■ boil over 1 (द्रव) उबलकर बहना 2 (अनौप) अत्यधिक क्रुद्ध होना 3 (कोई स्थिति, झगड़ा आदि) विस्फोटक हो जाना, संकटपूर्ण हो जाना boil sth down (to sth) (अनौप) निचोड़ या निष्कर्ष प्रस्तुत करना ▸ boil noun उबालने की प्रक्रिया : *Let it come to the boil slowly.* boiling hot adj (अनौप) खौलता हुआ, गरमागरम boiling-point noun 1 वह तापमान जिस पर कोई द्रव उबलने लगता है 2 उत्तेजक/विस्फोटक स्थिति।

boil² / बॉइल / noun व्रण, फोड़ा।

boiler / 'बॉइलर् / noun 1 क्वथनित्र, जहाँ भाप बनती है 2 घर, भवन गरम रखने के लिए गरम पानी का बरतन।

boisterous / 'बॉइस्टरस् / adj 1 (व्यक्ति और उसका व्यवहार) ऊधमी, उदंड; शोरगुल मचाने वाला किंतु प्रसन्नचित्त 2 (समुद्र, मौसम आदि) विक्षुब्ध, उग्र ▸ boisterously adv boisterousness noun.

bold / बोल्ड् / adj (-er, -est) 1 निर्भीक, निडर; उद्यमितापूर्ण 2 (अप्र) निर्लज्ज, बेशरम 3 साफ-साफ चिह्नों से अंकित, सुस्पष्ट : *bold legible handwriting* ▸ boldly adv boldness noun.

bolt¹ / बोल्ट् / noun 1 दरवाज़े और खिड़कियों की सिटकिनी, चिटखनी 2 बोल्ट, क़ाबला 3 (पुराने समय में) छोटा तीर 4 गाज, वज्रपात, बिजली ▸ bolt verb 1 सिटकिनी द्वारा बंद करना या कसना 2 bolt A to B; bolt A and B (together) क़ाबलों से कसना, बाँधना।

bolt² / बोल्ट् / verb 1 (घोड़े का) अचानक बेक़ाबू होकर भाग जाना; (व्यक्ति का) हड़बड़ाकर/सकपकाकर भाग जाना : *When the police arrived the burglars bolted.* 2 bolt sth (down) गटकना/सटकना, जल्दी-जल्दी खाना निगलना।

bomb / बॉम् / noun 1 बम, गोला 2 किसी वस्तु के साथ जुड़ा विस्फोटक उपकरण : *a letter bomb* ▸ bomb verb बम गिराना/फेंकना : *Terrorists bombed several police stations.* bomber / 'बॉमर् / noun बमवर्षक वायुयान।

bombard / बॉम्'बाई / verb bombard sb/sth (with sth) 1 बमबारी करना, गोलाबारी करना 2 (प्रश्नों आदि की) बौछार करना : *Reporters bombarded the President with questions about his economic policy.* ▸ bombardment noun गोलाबारी।

bona fide / बोना'फ़ाइडि / adj, adv सद्भावना से (क़ानूनन) प्रामाणिक, निष्कपट : *a bona fide agreement/deal/contract* ▸ bona fides / बोना 'फ़ाइडीज़् / noun [pl] (क़ानून) नेकनीयती।

bond / बॉन्ड् / noun 1 बाँधने या जोड़ने वाली शक्ति या भावना : *the bonds of friendship/affection* 2 लिखित अनुबंध-पत्र, इक़रारनामा 3 ऋण-पत्र, रुक्का, बांड ▸ bond verb bond A and B (together) दो चीज़ों को सुरक्षित एक साथ बाँधना, जोड़ना : *You need a strong adhesive to bond wood to metal.*

bondage / 'बॉन्डिज् / noun (अप्र या औप) दासता, गुलामी।

bone / बोन् / noun हड्डी ■ a bone of contention झगड़े की जड़ have a bone to pick with sb किसी से तर्क-वितर्क या झगड़ा करने के लिए कुछ होना ▸ bone china noun हड्डी-चूर्ण मिली हुई चीनी मिट्टी।

bonfire / 'बॉन्फ़ाइअर् / noun अलाव, उत्सवाग्नि; खुले स्थान पर कूड़े-कर्कट के ढेर पर लगाई गई आग।

bonnet / 'बॉनिट् / noun 1 छोटा गोल टोप जो ठुड्डी से बाँधा जाता है और जिसे बच्चे और (पूर्व में) औरतें पहनते हैं 2 (US hood) मोटर गाड़ी के इंजन को ढकने वाला धातु का ढक्कन।

bonny / 'बॉनि / *adj* (-ier, -iest) कमनीय, खूबसूरत; हृष्ट-पुष्ट : *a bonny baby.*

bonsai / 'बॉन्साइ/ *noun* (*pl* अपरिवर्तित) छोटा-सा पेड़, सामान्य बढ़त रोककर गमले में उगाया हुआ पेड़; इस तरह से पेड़ उगाने की जापानी कला।

bonus / 'बोनस् / *noun* (*pl* **bonuses**) बोनस, अधिलाभांश।

bony / 'बोनि/ *adj* 1 दुबला, बहुत कम मांस वाला 2 हड्डियों का या हड्डी जैसा।

book¹ /बुक/ *noun* 1 किताब, पुस्तक, ग्रंथ 2 **books** [*pl*] किसी व्यापार के अर्थप्रबंध का लिखित दस्तावेज़/रिकॉर्ड; बही : *The company's books are audited every year.* ■ **be in sb's good/bad books** (*अनौप*) किसी के कृपापात्र बने/ न बने रहना **bring sb to book (for sth)** (किसी व्यक्ति से उसके आचरण का) स्पष्टीकरण माँगना **by the book** (*अनौप*) सख्ती से नियमानुसार ▶ **book-binder** *noun* जिल्दसाज़ **bookcase** *noun* पुस्तकें रखने की अलमारी **book-keeping** *noun* हिसाब-किताब **bookseller** *noun* पुस्तक-विक्रेता **bookstall** *noun* पुस्तकों की दुकान **bookworm** *noun* किताबी कीड़ा, बहुत पढ़ने वाला विद्यार्थी।

book² /बुक/ *verb* 1 नोटबुक में (बही में) आदेश लिखना/देना या रिकॉर्ड के लिए रखना; (पुलिस रिकॉर्ड में) केस दर्ज करना : *The police booked me for speeding.* 2 जगह/कमरा आरक्षित करा लेना/करना : *book a hotel room* ○ *I'd like to book three seats for tonight's concert.* ▶ **booking** *noun* टिकट सुरक्षित करना या (होटल आदि में) कमरा आदि सुरक्षित करना।

bookish / 'बुकिश् / *adj* 1 किताबों को पढ़ने का चाव रखने वाला 2 किताबी, पंडिताऊ, अव्यवहारिक (ज्ञान)।

boom /बूम् / *noun* गरम बाज़ारी; व्यापार या जनसंख्या में अचानक वृद्धि; समृद्धि और सफलता का काल : *The oil market is enjoying an unprecedented boom.*

boomerang / 'बूमरैङ् / *noun* एक प्रकार का टेढ़ा तीर जो फेंकने पर वापस आ जाता है : (*अलं*) *The plan had a boomerang effect.* (स्वयं को हानि पहुँचाने वाली योजना)।

boon /बून् / *noun* लाभ, वरदान : *Parks are a great boon to people in big cities.*

boost / बूस्ट / *verb* सहायता करना या प्रोत्साहन देना; (शक्ति, मूल्य आदि) बढ़ाना : *boost production* ▶ **booster** *noun* 1 सहायता या प्रोत्साहन प्रदान करने वाली वस्तु 2 विद्युत-धारा की शक्ति बढ़ाने वाला यंत्र।

boot / बूट / *noun* 1 जूता, बूट 2 (*US* **trunk**) कार में सामान रखने का स्थान : *Put the luggage in the boot.*

booth / बूद; *US* बूथ् / *noun* 1 (लकड़ी या कैनवस की) छोटी दुकान 2 विशेष प्रयोजन के लिए छोटा-सा घिरा हुआ स्थान : *a telephone booth/a polling booth.*

booty / 'बूटि / *noun* लूट का माल, लूट।

booze / बूज़् / *verb* (*अनौप*) (अत्यधिक मात्रा में) शराब पीना ▶ **booze** *noun* (*अनौप*) शराब **boozer** *noun* (*अनौप*) शराबी, अंधाधुंध पीने वाला।

border / 'बॉर्डर् / *noun* 1 दो देशों के विभाजक सीमा, सीमांत प्रदेश 2 सजावटी किनारी : *the border of a picture* 3 किनारा; किनारे की भूमि ▶ **border** *verb* 1 **border sth (with sth)** किनारी/गोट लगाना : *a handkerchief bordered with lace* 2 **border on sth** की सीमा होना, समीपवर्ती होना; के लगभग होना : *His reply to the teacher was bordering on rudeness.* **borderline** *noun* सीमारेखा।

bore¹ /बॉर् / *verb* 1 बरमा (एक औज़ार) से या खोदकर छेद करना, बेधना : *This drill can bore through rock.*

2 खोदकर या धकेलकर बढ़ना : *He bored his way to the front of the crowd.*

bore² / बॉर् / *verb* शुष्क, अरुचिकर बातों या कार्यों से व्यक्ति को थका डालना, उबाना ▸ **bore** *noun* (व्यक्ति) कानखाऊ, उबाने वाला; चिढ़ पैदा करने वाली बात/स्थिति **boredom** / बॉरडम् / *noun* एकरसता, उचाट **boring** *adj* ऊबाऊ, नीरस।

born / बॉर्न् / *noun* **be born** जन्म लेना, उत्पन्न होना : *She was born in 1950.* ■ **born with a silver spoon in one's mouth** (कहा) धनी परिवार में जन्म लेना ▸ **born** *adj* जन्मजात, प्राकृतिक गुण संपन्न : *a born leader/writer.*

borrow / बॉरो / *verb* **borrow (sth) (from sb/sth)** 1 उधार लेना/कर्ज़ लेना 2 (विचार) नक़ल करना/अपना बना लेना; उद्धृत करना : *borrow freely from other writers* ▸ **borrower** *noun* ऋणी, कर्ज़दार **borrowing** *noun* 1 ऋण लेना, उधार ग्रहण 2 उधार ली हुई वस्तु (धन, विचार या शब्द) : *French has many borrowings from English.*

bosom / बुज़म् / *noun* 1 छाती, विशेषकर स्त्रियों का वक्षस्थल; स्त्रियों के वक्ष 2 हृदय जहाँ सुख दुख का अनुभव होता है 3 **the bosom of sth** किसी चीज़ का प्यार और सुरक्षा : *live in the bosom of one's family* ▸ **bosom friend** *noun* अंतरंग मित्र।

boss / बॉस् / *noun* (अनौप) कर्मचारियों को आदेश देने वाला अधिकारी; प्रबंधक; मालिक ▸ **boss** *verb* **boss sb (about/around)** (अनौप, अपमा) रोब जमाना, धौंस पेलना, आदेश देना।

botany / बॉटनि / *noun* वनस्पति-विज्ञान (पौधों, वृक्षों आदि का अध्ययन) ▸ **botanical** / बटैनिकल् / *adj* वनस्पति-विज्ञान विषयक **botanist** / बॉटनिस्ट् / *noun* वनस्पति शास्त्री।

both¹ / बोथ् / *adj* दोनों; एक के साथ दूसरा भी : *Both books are expensive.*

▸ **both** *pron* **both (of sb/sth)** दोनों; एक ही नहीं, दूसरा भी : *I like these shirts. I'll take both (of them).*

both² / बोथ् / *adv* **both... and...** न केवल... दोनों ही : *She speaks both Hindi and English.*

bother / बॉदर् / *verb* 1 **bother sb (about/with sth)** परेशान करना/होना, तंग होना/करना : *Does my smoking bother you?* 2 चिंता पैदा करना/होना : *What's bothering you?* 3 **bother about sb/ sth** चिंता करना : *Don't bother about us—we'll join you later.* ▸ **bother** *noun* परेशानी या बतंगड़।

bottle / बॉटल् / *noun* 1 काँच या प्लास्टिक की बोतल, शीशी 2 (प्राय: *sing*) बच्चे को दूध पिलाने वाली बोतल ▸ **bottle** *verb* बोतल में भरना ■ **bottle sth up** भावनाओं को दबाकर/छुपाकर रखना ▸ **bottleneck** *noun* संकीर्ण स्थान, काम में आई बाधा।

bottom / बॉटम् / *noun* 1 सबसे निचला स्तर, तल : *the bottom of a hill/valley* 2 आधार, तली 3 (विशेषत: ब्रिटेन में) नितंब, चूतड़ : *fall on one's bottom* 4 [*sing*] वर्ग या सूची में सबसे निचला स्थान; इस स्थिति पर का व्यक्ति या वस्तु : *He was always bottom of the class in science.* 5 समुद्र, नदी या झील का तल/ तलहटी ■ **at bottom** वास्तव में, सत्य में **be/lie at the bottom of sth** किसी चीज़/बात का मूल कारण/उद्भव होना **get to the bottom of sth** किसी बात का वास्तविक कारण या सत्य का पता लगाना ▸ **bottom** *adj* सबसे निचली स्थिति में : *Put your books on the bottom shelf.* **bottomless** *adj* 1 बहुत गहरा, अथाह 2 (अल) असीम, अगाध।

bough / बाउ / *noun* शाखा, (वृक्ष की) डाल।

boulder / बोल्डर् / *noun* बड़ा पत्थर जो मौसम और वर्षा से लगभग गोल हो गया हो, शिलाखंड।

bounce / 'बाउन्स् / verb 1 (गेंद का) टकरा कर उछलना, उछालना 2 (अनौप) (चेक का) खाते में पर्याप्त धन न होने के कारण बैंक द्वारा बेकार वापस भेज दिया जाना ■ **bounce back** (अनौप) परेशानी, बीमारी या कठिनाइयों के बाद अच्छी तरह स्वास्थ्यलाभ करना/ठीक हो जाना ▸ **bouncing** adj स्वस्थ एवं हृष्ट-पुष्ट।

bound[1] / बाउन्ड् / verb सीमा बनाना, सीमाबद्ध करना : The airfield is bounded by woods on all sides.

bound[2] / बाउन्ड / adj **bound (for...)** (स्थान विशेष) को जाने वाला, के लिए रवाना होने वाला; आरंभ होने जा रहा : We are bound for home.

bound[3] / बाउन्ड / adj 1 **bound (to do sth)** (कुछ करने के लिए) बाध्य होना : They are bound by the contract to deliver the goods on time. 2 **bound to do sth** निश्चित रूप से करना या होना : The weather is bound to get better tomorrow.

boundary / 'बाउन्ड्रि / noun (pl **boundaries**) 1 विभाजक रेखा, सीमारेखा : The fence marks the boundary between our lands. 2 (क्रिकेट में) खेल के क्षेत्र की सीमा से बाहर चली जाने वाली गेंद।

boundless / 'बाउन्ड्लस् / adj असीम, अंतहीन; अति विशाल।

bounds / बाउन्ड्ज़् / noun [pl] सीमा : It is beyond the bounds of human knowledge. ■ **out of bounds (to sb)**; (US) **off limits** (कोई स्थान) अनुमत सीमा के बाहर होना।

bounty / 'बाउन्टि / noun (pl **bounties**) (अप्र) उदारता; वदान्यता ▸ **bountiful** / 'बाउन्टिफ़ुल् / adj (औप या साहि) भरपूर; उदार।

bouquet / बु'के / noun गुलदस्ता, (हाथ में रखने के लिए) पुष्पगुच्छ।

bourgeois / 'बुअश्वा; बुअश्'वा / adj 1 (राज) समाज के मध्य-वर्ग का या .से

संबंधित 2 (अपमा) परिवर्तन का विरोधी, रूढ़िवादी; परंपरावादी ▸ **bourgeois** noun (pl अपरिवर्तित) समाज का मध्यम-वर्गीय व्यक्ति, बुर्जुआ; पूँजीवादी।

bout / बाउट् / noun **bout (of sth/doing sth)** 1 उत्कट क्रियाशीलता का लघु दौर : She has bouts of hard work followed by long periods of inactivity. 2 (बीमारी का) दौरा, हमला : He suffers from frequent bouts of depression.

boutique / बू'टीक् / noun कपड़े या अन्य सामान बेचने की छोटी दुकान।

bow[1] / बो / noun 1 धनुष (तीर फेंकने वाला) 2 (वायलिन आदि बजाने वाला) चाप; गज 3 एक प्रकार की गाँठ, सरक-गाँठ : tie shoelaces in a bow 4 इस प्रकार की गाँठ लगाकर बाँधा हुआ रिबन ▸ **bowed** adj धनुषाकार में मुड़ा/झुका हुआ **bow-tie** noun दोहरे फंदे में टाई बाँधने का तरीका (औपचारिक अवसरों पर प्रयुक्त टाई)।

bow[2] / बाउ / verb 1 **bow (down) (to/ before sb/sth)** (नमस्कार के समय, स्वीकृति में) झुकना : The actors bowed as the audience applauded. 2 (किसी चीज़ को) झुकाना या झुकना : His back was bowed with age. ■ **bow to sth** किसी चीज़ के आगे घुटने टेक देना : bow to sb's opinion.

bowel / 'बाउअल् / noun (प्राय: pl) बड़ी आँत, अँतड़ी।

bowl[1] / बोल् / noun 1 कटोरा, कटोरी : a sugar/fruit/soup bowl 2 कटोरा/कटोरी भर मात्रा : a bowl of sugar/soup.

bowl[2] / बोल् / verb 1 (क्रिकेट में) गेंद फेंकना, गेंदबाज़ी करना : bowl a couple of balls 2 **bowl sb (out)** विकेट पर गेंद मारकर आउट करना ■ **bowl sb over** 1 (किसी को) गिरा देना 2 किसी को घबरा देना/आश्चर्यचकित कर देना।

bowler / 'बोलर् / noun गेंदबाज़।

bowling / 'बोलिङ / noun 1 एक प्रकार का खेल 2 (क्रिकेट में) गेंदबाज़ी: a good piece of bowling.

box[1] / बॉक्स् / noun 1 (लकड़ी, दफ़्ती, धातु आदि का) बक्सा, संदूक; सामान से भरा संदूक: a box of chocolates/matches 2 रंगशाला में पृथक, अनेक लोगों के बैठने या खड़े होने का स्थल; कचहरी में गवाही देने के लिए अलग स्थान: a press box ○ a witness box 3 काग़ज़ पर सीधी रेखाओं से घिरा स्थान: tick the appropriate box ▸ **box number** noun उत्तर लिखने के लिए अख़बार के इश्तहार में दिया गया नंबर **box office** noun (सिनेमा, रंगशाला आदि में) टिकट-घर।

box[2] / बॉक्स् / verb box (against sb) मुक्केबाज़ी का खेल खेलना ■ box sb's ears कान पर घूँसा/मुक्का मारना: He boxed the boy's ears for being rude. ▸ **boxer** noun मुक्केबाज़ **boxing** noun मुक्केबाज़ी।

boy / बॉइ / noun 1 बालक, लड़का 2 लड़का या जवान पुरुष जो कोई कार्य विशेष करता है: the paper-boy ▸ **boyfriend** noun पुरुष साथी; प्रेमी **boyhood** noun लड़कपन, बालपन **boyish** adj लड़के जैसा।

boycott / 'बॉइकॉट् / verb 1 बायकाट करना, बहिष्कार करना: Athletes from several countries boycotted the Olympic Games. 2 विरोध या सज़ा के तौर पर सामान ख़रीदने से मना करना: boycotting foreign imports.

bra / ब्रा / noun=brassière.

brace[1] / ब्रेस् / noun 1 (प्राय: लोहे या लकड़ी का) टेक, पट्टी 2 (US braces [pl]) दाँत सीधे रखने के लिए मुँह के अंदर पहनी जाने वाली धातु की वस्तु 3 braces [pl] (US suspenders) पैंट को सहारा देने के लिए कंधों के ऊपर से पहनी जाने वाली पट्टियाँ 4 धनुकोष्ठक { }।

brace[2] / ब्रेस् / verb 1 सहारा देना, मज़बूत करना 2 brace sth/oneself (against sth) (अपने को) मज़बूती से तैयार करना, दृढ़ करना: He braced himself against the seat of the car as it hit a tree. ▸ **bracing** adj (विशेषत: मौसम) ठंडा और ताज़ा, स्फूर्तिदायक: a bracing wind.

bracelet / 'ब्रेस्लट् / noun (हाथ का आभूषण) कंगन, वलय।

bracket / 'ब्रैकिट् / noun 1 दीवार पर शेल्फ़, लैंप आदि लगाने के लिए लकड़ी या धातु का ब्रैकेट (आधार) 2 (प्राय: pl) कोष्ठक चिह्न (), { }, [ ] 3 निश्चित सीमाओं के अंदर कोई समूह या वर्ग: be in the lower/higher income bracket ▸ **bracket** verb 1 कोष्ठक लगाना 2 bracket A and B (together) समानता या संबंध प्रदर्शित करने के लिए वस्तुओं या व्यक्तियों को एक वर्ग में रखना।

brag / ब्रैग् / verb (-gg-) brag (about/of sth) डींग मारना, शेख़ी बघारना: He has been bragging about his new car.

Braille / ब्रेल / noun नेत्रहीन व्यक्तियों के लिए उभरे अक्षरों की एक लिपि जिसे छूकर पढ़ा जा सकता है, उत्कीर्ण लेख/लिपि।

brain / ब्रेन् / noun 1 मस्तिष्क, दिमाग़; brains [pl] (खाद्य पदार्थ के रूप में प्रयुक्त) भेजा, मग़ज़ 2 (प्राय: pl) बुद्धि, दिमाग़: He hasn't got much brain. ○ You need brains to become a university professor. ▸ **brain drain** noun (प्राय: sing) (अनौप) कुशाग्र-बुद्धि व्यक्तियों का स्वदेश छोड़कर नौकरी के लिए विदेश जाना, मेधापलायन **brainless** adj मूर्ख **brainy** adj (-ier, -iest) अति चतुर; बुद्धिमान।

brainchild / 'ब्रेन्चाइल्ड् / noun [sing] किसी व्यक्ति की अपनी योजना, खोज या विचार।

brainstorming / 'ब्रेन्स्टॉर्मिङ् / noun समस्याओं को सुलझाने का ऐसा तरीक़ा

जिसमें एक समूह के सभी सदस्य उन पर तर्क और सूझ-बूझ से विचार करते हैं।

brainwash / 'ब्रेन्वॉश् / verb brainwash sb (into doing sth) (लगातार प्रयास से) अपने मत का अनुयायी बनाना, मनोमार्जन।

brainwave / 'ब्रेन्वेव् / noun (US brainstorm) (अनौप) अचानक पैदा हुई सूझ।

brake / ब्रेक् / noun चलती हुई वस्तुओं को रोकने के लिए लगाई गई रोक, ब्रेक : put on/ apply/release the brake(s) ▶ brake verb ब्रेक लगाना, गति मंद करना।

bran / ब्रैन् / noun गेहूँ, धान आदि की भूसी या चोकर।

branch / ब्रान्च्; US ब्रैन्च् / noun 1 (पेड़ की) शाखा, टहनी 2 स्थानीय कार्यालय अथवा मुख्य कार्यालय से संचालित और नियंत्रित कार्यालय आदि : The bank has branches in all parts of the country. 3 नदी, सड़क, रेलवे या पर्वत शृंखला का कम महत्त्वपूर्ण भाग (विभाजित) : a branch of the Ganges ▶ branch verb (सड़क का) शाखाओं में विभाजित करना : The road branches in a couple of miles. ■ branch off (वाहन या सड़क का) एक सड़क से दूसरी छोटी सड़क पर मुड़ना branch out (into sth) नई दिशा में सक्रिय होना या रुचि रखना।

brand / ब्रैन्ड् / noun 1 ट्रेडमार्क; मार्का; कंपनी विशेष का उत्पाद : Which brand of toothpaste do you prefer? 2 एक विशेष प्रकार का : a strange brand of humour ▶ brand name noun मार्का, छाप brand new adj नवीनतम।

brandish / 'ब्रैन्डिश् / verb गुस्से से धमकाने या डराने के लिए कुछ घुमाना : brandish a gun/knife/an axe.

brandy / 'ब्रैन्डि / noun ब्रांडी, एक प्रकार की तेज़ शराब।

brash / ब्रैश् / adj (अपमा) ढीठ एवं आक्रामक रूप से उतावला : a brash young salesman.

brass / ब्रास्; US ब्रैस् / noun पीतल (ताँबा और जस्त का मिश्रण); पीतल की बनी वस्तुएँ।
■ get down to brass tacks (अनौप) किसी भी विषय की मूल एवं व्यावहारिक बातों पर विचार शुरू करना।

brassière / 'ब्रेज़िअर्; US ब्रं ज़िअर्/ (bra / ब्रा / भी) noun चोली, अँगिया।

brat / ब्रैट् / noun (अपमा) ढीठ बच्चा।

bravado / ब्रं'वाडो / noun दूसरों को प्रभावित करने के लिए प्रदर्शित अक्खड़पन, डींग।

brave / ब्रेव् / adj (-r, -st) 1 (व्यक्ति) बहादुर, साहसी 2 (कोई कार्य) साहस की आवश्यकता वाला/साहसपूर्ण : a brave act ▶ brave verb साहस/वीरता से सामना करना : We decided to brave the bad weather. **bravely** adv **bravery** / 'ब्रेवरि / noun वीरता, साहस।

bravo / ब्रा 'वो / interj, noun (pl bravos) शाबाश, वाह-वाह।

brawl / ब्रॉल् / noun झड़प/उपद्रव, कोलाहल : a drunken brawl in a bar.

bray / ब्रे / noun गधे की आवाज़, रेंकना; इस तरह की आवाज़ ▶ bray verb (प्राय: अपमा) गधे जैसी आवाज़ निकालना, रेंकना।

breach / ब्रीच् / noun 1 (क़ानून, कर्तव्य, प्रतिज्ञा आदि) भंग करने की क्रिया, उल्लंघन : breach of loyalty/trust/protocol 2 (मित्रवत् संबंधों में) विच्छेद, संबंध-विच्छेद : a breach of diplomatic relations between two countries 3 (दीवार या अवरोध में) दरार : The huge waves made a breach in the sea wall. ▶ breach verb (दीवार या अवरोध में) दरार पैदा करना breach of promise noun (क़ानून) प्रतिज्ञा भंग।

bread / ब्रेड् / noun रोटी, डबलरोटी।

breadth / ब्रेड्थ् / noun 1 चौड़ाई 2 (ज्ञान, परास आदि का) व्यापक विस्तार : Her breadth of experience makes her ideal for the job.

breadwinner / 'ब्रेड्विनर् / noun परिवार का भरण-पोषण करने वाला व्यक्ति।

break¹ / ब्रेक् / *verb* (*pt* broke / ब्रोक्/; *pp* broken/ ब्रोकन्/) 1 break (in/into sth) (तोड़/काट/पीटकर) दो या अधिक टुकड़े करना 2 break sth (in/into sth) (तोड़-फोड़कर) टुकड़े होना/करना : *break a pot/vase/window* 3 (क़ानून, प्रतिज्ञा आदि का) पालन न करना : *break an agreement/a contract* 4 break (off) कुछ क्षण/समय के लिए कुछ करना बंद कर देना : *Let's break for lunch.* 5 किसी बात (चीज़) में व्यवधान डालना : *break sb's concentration* 6 (मात्रा, मौन आदि) भंग करना : *She broke the silence by coughing.* 7 कमज़ोर पड़ जाना या नष्ट हो जाना : *He broke under questioning.* 8 दुख या अन्य तीव्र भावना से अभिभूत हो जाना : *The death of his wife broke him completely.* 9 (आवाज़ का) भावावेश या उत्तेजना से लहजा बदल जाना 10 एक नया कीर्तिमान (रिकॉर्ड) स्थापित करना : *break the Commonwealth/World/Olympic 100 metres record* ■ break away (from sb/sth) 1 क़ैद से भाग जाना 2 कोई पार्टी या राज्य आदि छोड़ना (विशेषत: नया बनाने के लिए) break down 1 (मशीन आदि का) ख़राबी के कारण काम करना बंद कर देना : *The telephone system has broken down.* 2 (व्यक्ति का) मानसिक संतुलन खो बैठना; रो पड़ना : *He broke down and wept.* break into sth बलपूर्वक (घर में) प्रवेश करना break off बोलना बंद कर देना break out (हिंसा की घटना) अचानक शुरू होना break (sth) down (विशेषकर ख़र्च की गई राशि को) विश्लेषण द्वारा अंशों में विभाजित करना break sth down ज़ोर-ज़ोर-से मारकर तोड़ना/चकनाचूर करना break (sth) off बल या तनाव के कारण कुछ अलग कर देना या हो जाना : *The door handle has broken off.* break sth off एकाएक कुछ समाप्त कर देना (संबंध आदि) break (sth) up 1 छोटे-छोटे टुकड़ों में बँटना/बाँटना 2 समाप्त करना या हो जाना : *Their marriage has broken up.* break sth up 1 छोटे हिस्सों में विभाजित करना 2 (कोई कार्य) विविधता लाकर एकरसता ख़त्म करना : *A car radio helps break up the monotony of a long drive.* break through नई और महत्त्वपूर्ण खोज करना break through (sth) भेदन करना; भेदकर रास्ता बनाना break up (समूह के सदस्यों का) भिन्न दिशाओं में चले जाना : *The meeting broke up at eleven o'clock.* break up (with sb); break with sb संबंध समाप्त करना ▸ break-able / ब्रेकब्ल् / *adj* आसानी से टूटने वाला।

break² / ब्रेक् / *noun* 1 break (in sth) तोड़ने से उत्पन्न दरार; टूटा हुआ स्थान 2 अंतराल (काम के समय के बीच), अवकाश : *morning break/lunch break* 3 (अनौप) सौभाग्य, विशेषकर जिससे भविष्य में बड़ी सफलता मिल जाए : *give sb a break.*

breakage / ब्रेकिज् / *noun* 1 टूटने की क्रिया या परिस्थिति : *All breakages must be paid for.* 2 टूट-फूट : *measures to reduce the risk of breakage.*

breakdown / ब्रेकडाउन् / *noun* 1 मशीनी ख़राबी 2 असफलता या भंग 3 (स्वास्थ्य की, विशेषत: मानसिक) ख़राबी, विकार : *She suffered a complete nervous breakdown.*

breaker / ब्रेकर् / *noun* 1 समुद्र की बड़ी लहर जो तट पर टकराकर चूर-चूर होने जा रही है 2 (व्यक्ति या वस्तु) जो कुछ तोड़ता है : *a lawbreaker* ○ *a record-breaker.*

breakfast / ब्रेक्फ़स्ट् / *noun* कलेवा, प्रात: का जलपान।

breakneck / ब्रेक्नेक् / *adj* अत्यधिक तेज़ गति जिससे सहज में दुर्घटना हो सकती है : *drive at breakneck speed.*

breakthrough /ब्रेक्थ्रू/ *noun* महत्त्वपूर्ण खोज (विशेषत: विज्ञान के क्षेत्र में)।

breakup /ब्रेकप्/ *noun* 1 आपसी संबंधों का अंत 2 छोटे-छोटे टुकड़ों में विभाजन।

breast /ब्रेस्ट्/ *noun* 1 (स्त्रियों के) स्तन, वक्ष 2 *(साहि)* मानव शरीर का ऊपरी सामने वाला भाग; छाती।

breath /ब्रेथ्/ *noun* साँस, श्वास; श्वसन, साँस लेना : *take a deep breath* ■ **a breath of fresh air** 1 (घर से बाहर) साफ़ हवा में साँस लेने का अवसर 2 स्वागत योग्य बदलाव (व्यक्ति या वस्तु का) **hold one's breath** (उत्तेजना या घबराहट में) साँस रोक लेना **(be) out of/short of breath** हाँफना **say sth, speak, etc under one's breath** फुसफुसाना **the breath of life (to/for sb)** अत्यावश्यक वस्तु।

breathe /ब्रीद्/ *verb* 1 साँस लेना, श्वसन करना 2 **breathe in/out** ज़ोर-से साँस निकालना/छोड़ना और लेना 3 फुसफुसाकर बोलना ■ **breathe one's last** *(औप)* मृत्यु हो जाना ▶ **breathing** *noun* श्वसन।

breather /ब्रीदर/ *noun* *(अनौप)* 1 लघु अवकाश 2 लघु व्यायाम।

breathless /ब्रेथ्लस्/ *adj* 1 बेदम, हाँफता हुआ : *breathless after running up the stairs* 2 बेदम करने वाला 3 (उत्तेजना या घबराहट में) साँस रोके हुए : *breathless with terror/wonder* ▶ **breathlessly** *adv* **breathlessness** *noun.*

breathtaking /ब्रेथ्टेकिङ्/ *adj* विस्मय-कारक; स्तब्ध कर देने वाला।

breed /ब्रीड्/ *verb* (*pt, pp* **bred** /ब्रेड्/) 1 (पशुओं का) बच्चों को जन्म देना : *How often do lions breed?* 2 (पशुओं या पौधों को) बच्चे/नस्लें पैदा करने के लिए बचाए रखना 3 का कारण होना/ बनना : *Unemployment breeds social unrest.* 4 **breed sb (as sth)** प्रशिक्षण देना, शिक्षा देना : *a well-bred child* ▶ **breed** *noun* 1 (पशुओं या पौधों की) नस्ल, वंश 2 क़िस्म, प्रकार : *a new breed of politician* **breeder reactor** *noun* एक प्रकार की परमाणु भट्टी जो उसमें प्रयुक्त ईंधन से अधिक रेडिओएक्टिव सामग्री उत्पन्न कर देती है **breeding** *noun* 1 प्रजनन के लिए पशुओं को रखना : *a breeding programme* 2 प्रजनन करना : *the breeding season* 3 अच्छा प्रशिक्षण, संस्कार : *a man of good breeding.*

breeze /ब्रीज़्/ *noun* मंद पवन, बयार : *A gentle breeze was blowing.* ▶ **breezily** *adv* **breeziness** *noun* **breezy** *adj.*

brethren /ब्रेद्रन्/ *noun* [*pl*] किसी पुरुष-प्रधान धार्मिक समूह के सदस्य; भाई; ईसाई चर्च या अन्य धार्मिक समूह के सदस्य।

brevity /ब्रेव़िटि/ *noun* संक्षिप्तता, विशेषत: बोलने और लिखने में संक्षेपण : *(कहा) Brevity is the soul of wit.*

brew /ब्रू/ *verb* 1 काढ़ा बनाना; शराब बनाना या खींचना : *He brews his own beer at home.* 2 **brew sth (up)** चाय, कॉफ़ी जैसा गर्म पेय तैयार करना 3 (कुछ अरुचिकर घटना आदि) विकसित होना शुरू हो जाना; षड्यंत्र रचा जाना : *Trouble is brewing in the factory.*

bribe /ब्राइब्/ *noun* घूस, रिश्वत : *take/ accept bribes* ▶ **bribe** *verb* **bribe sb (with sth)** घूस देना, रिश्वत खिलाना : *attempt to bribe a jury with offers of money* **bribery** /ब्राइबरि/ *noun* घूसखोरी।

brick /ब्रिक्/ *noun* 1 ईंट : *a pile of bricks* 2 बच्चों का इमारत बनाने का खिलौना ▶ **bricklayer** *noun* राज, थवई।

brickbat /ब्रिक्बैट्/ *noun* 1 रोड़ा 2 *(अनौप)* कटु टिप्पणी।

bridal /ब्राइडल्/ *adj* विवाह-विषयक; वधू का : *bridal bouquet/gown/suite.*

bride /ब्राइड्/ *noun* वधू; नवविवाहिता, बहू।

bridegroom /'ब्राइड्ग्रूम्/ (groom भी) *noun* दूल्हा, वर।

bridesmaid /'ब्राइड्ज़्मेड्/ *noun* वधू की सहायक या सखी।

bridge¹ /ब्रिज्/ *noun* 1 पुल, सेतु; दो भिन्न वस्तुओं को जोड़ने या संबंध बनाने वाली चीज़ : *Cultural exchanges are a way of building bridges between nations.* 2 नाक का ऊपरी कठोर भाग; चश्मे का वह हिस्सा जो नाक पर ठहरता है
▶ **bridge** *verb* पुल बनाना : *bridge a river/canal* ■ **bridge a/the gap** कोई ख़ाली या अजीब-सा स्थान भरना : *bridge a gap in the conversation.*

bridge² /ब्रिज्/ *noun* ताश के पत्तों का एक खेल।

bridle /'ब्राइड्ल्/ *noun* घोड़े की लगाम, बाग ▶ **bridle** *verb* 1 लगाम लगाना 2 नियंत्रित करना; भावनाओं को क़ाबू में रखना : *bridle one's emotions/temper/rage.*

brief¹ /ब्रीफ़/ *adj* (**-er, -est**) अल्पकालीन, थोड़े समय का; (बात या लेखन) संक्षिप्त : *a brief account/description of the accident* ■ **in brief** संक्षेप में ▶ **briefly** *adv* 1 थोड़े समय के लिए : *He paused briefly before continuing.* 2 संक्षेप में।

brief² /ब्रीफ़/ *noun* 1 अपने कार्य एवं ज़िम्मेदारियों से संबंधित प्राप्त की गई सूचनाएँ या निर्देश, आदेश-पत्र : *I was given the brief of reorganizing the department.* 2 (क़ानून) वकील को बहस के लिए दिया गया केस : *Will you accept this brief?* 3 (क़ानून) वकील के लिए तैयार केस के तथ्यों का संक्षिप्त ब्योरा ▶ **brief** *verb* brief sb (on sth) विस्तृत विवरण या निर्देश देना **briefing** *noun* विवरण या निर्देश देने के लिए बैठक; इस तरह की बैठक में दिया गया विस्तृत विवरण/निर्देश।

briefcase /'ब्रीफ़्केस्/ *noun* काग़ज़-पत्र आदि रखने के लिए छोटा चपटा बैग।

briefs /ब्रीफ़्स्/ *noun* [*pl*] निकर, जाँघिया।

brigade /ब्रि'गेड्/ *noun* 1 ब्रिगेड, दो, तीन या चार बटेलियन की फ़ौज की इकाई 2 सुव्यवस्थित टोली : *the fire brigade*
▶ **brigadier** *noun* सेना में उच्च पद वाला अधिकारी, ब्रिगेडियर।

bright /ब्राइट्/ *adj* (**-er, -est**) 1 चमकीला 2 (रंग) चटकीला, तेज़ 3 चतुर, तीव्र बुद्धि वाला : *He is the brightest (child) in the class.* 4 प्रसन्नचित्त एवं उल्लसित : *She gave me a bright smile.* ■ **look on the bright side** कष्टों और मुसीबतों के बावजूद प्रसन्न एवं प्रफुल्ल रहना
▶ **brighten** *verb* brighten (sth) (up) चमकाना; प्रसन्न/आनंदित हो जाना या करना : *Flowers brighten up (a) room.* **brightly** *adv* **brightness** *noun.*

brilliant /'ब्रिलिअन्ट्/ *adj* 1 अत्यंत प्रतिभावान, कुशाग्रबुद्धि; अति चतुर, प्रभावशाली : *a brilliant achievement/performance* 2 अति प्रकाशमान, चमकता हुआ ▶ **brilliance** /'ब्रिलिअन्स्/ *noun* **brilliantly** *adv.*

brim /ब्रिम्/ *noun* 1 (प्याले, कटोरी, गिलास आदि का) किनारा, ओंठ 2 हैट (एक प्रकार की टोपी) का आगे झुका भाग ▶ **brim** *verb* (**-mm-**) brim (with sth) भरा हुआ होना : *a mug brimming with coffee* ■ **brim over (with sth)** इतना भरा हुआ कि किनारों से बहने लगे।

brine /ब्राइन्/ *noun* 1 नमकीन/खारा पानी विशेषत: खाद्य पदार्थों के परिरक्षण के लिए 2 समुद्र का पानी ▶ **briny** *adj* खारा/नमकीन।

bring /ब्रिङ्/ *verb* (*pt, pp* brought /ब्रॉट्/) 1 लाना, ले आना 2 कुछ होने का कारण बनना, के फलस्वरूप कुछ होना : *Spring brings warm weather and flowers.* 3 लाभ या कमाई के रूप में कुछ पैदा करना : *His writing brings him Rs 1,00,000 a year.* 4 **bring sth (against sb)** अदालत में अभियोग लगाना : *bring a charge/a legal ac-*

tion against sb ▪ **bring A and B together** दो व्यक्तियों का झगड़ा समाप्त करवाना **bring sb/sth forth** (अप्र या औप) जन्म देना; कुछ पैदा करना **bring sth about** कुछ घटित करना : *bring about reforms* **bring sth back** किसी को किसी बात पर पुन: सोचने को प्रेरित करना, याद दिलाना **bring sth down** घटाना; (कीमतों में) कमी लाना **bring sth forward** 1 पूर्वदिनांक या पूर्वसमय में ले आना: *The meeting has been brought forward from 10 May to 3 May.* 2 (खाते में) एक पन्ने से दूसरे पर आगे ले जाना **bring sth off** (अनौप) किसी मुश्किल काम को सफलतापूर्वक कर लेना **bring sth out** 1 स्पष्टतया प्रकट करना 2 दिखने या समझने में आसान बनाना 3 (पुस्तक) प्रकाशित करना **bring sth up** 1 किसी बात की चर्चा चलाना 2 वमन/उल्टी करना।

brink / ब्रिङ्क् / *noun* [sing] 1 भूमि का अंतिम सिरा 2 [sing] **the brink of (do-ing) sth** (अलं) अज्ञात, भयानक या उत्तेजक स्थिति के पास का बिंदु : *on the brink of collapse/war/disaster/success.*

brisk / ब्रिस्क् / *adj* (-er, -est) फुरतीला, तेज़ : *a brisk walk/walker.*

bristle / 'ब्रिस्ल् / *noun* 1 कड़ा छोटा बाल : *a face covered with bristles* 2 ब्रश में एक छोटा बाल : *My toothbrush is losing its bristles.*

brittle / 'ब्रिट्ल् / *adj* कड़ा किंतु सरलता से टूटने वाला (जैसे शीशा, कोयला), भंगुर।

broach / ब्रोच् / *verb* चर्चा चलाना, विषय छेड़ना : *He broached the subject of a loan with his bank manager.*

broad[1] / ब्रॉड् / *adj* (-er, -est) 1 चौड़ा 2 (ज़मीन या समुद्र) बहुत बड़ा क्षेत्र घेरे हुए : *the broad Gangetic plains* 3 सामान्य (विस्तृत नहीं) : *the broad outline of a plan/proposal* 4 (विचार, मत आदि) उदार, खुले विचार वाला: *a man of broad views* ▪ **(in) broad day-**

light दिनदहाड़े ▸ **broaden** / 'ब्रॉड्न् / *verb* **broaden (out)** चौड़ा करना या होना **broadly** *adv* 1 स्पष्ट तौर पर, साफ़-साफ़ 2 सामान्यतया, मोटे तौर पर **broad-minded** *adj* उदारचित्त **broad-mindedness** *noun* **broadness** *noun.*

broadcast / 'ब्रॉड्कास्ट; US 'ब्रॉडकैस्ट् / *verb* (*pt, pp* **broadcast**) प्रसारित करना, विशेषत: रेडियो या टी वी द्वारा : *broadcast the news/a concert/a football game* ▸ **broadcast** *noun* रेडियो या टी वी प्रसारण **broadcaster** *noun* प्रसारक **broadcasting** *noun* प्रसारण।

broadside / 'ब्रॉड्साइड् / *noun* (अलं) (लिखित या बोलने में) उग्र शाब्दिक हमला : *The Prime Minister delivered launched a broadside at his critics.*

broccoli / 'ब्रॉकलि / *noun* फूलगोभी जैसी एक सब्ज़ी।

brochure / 'ब्रोशर; US ब्रो'शुअर् / *noun* विवरण-पुस्तिका, विवरणिका।

broil / ब्रॉइल् / *verb* (विशेषत: US) मांस को लोहे की जाली पर सेंकना ▸ **broiler** *noun* भूनने/सेंकने के लिए पाला गया मुर्गा।

broke / ब्रोक् / *adj* (अनौप) धनरहित, कंगाल : *During the recession thousands of small businesses went broke.*

broken / ब्रोकन् / *adj* 1 टूटा हुआ, क्षतिग्रस्त या घायल; अधूरा या ख़राब पड़ा 2 रुक-रुक के (न कि लगातार), खंडित या बाधाग्रस्त : *broken sleep/sunshine* 3 (समझौता, सहमति) पालन न किया हुआ, वचन झूठा किया हुआ : *a broken promise/marriage* 4 (विदेशी भाषा) टूटी-फूटी, अशुद्ध : *speak in broken English* ▸ **broken-hearted** *adj* शोक-संतप्त, मन का मारा।

broker / 'ब्रोकर् / *noun* 1 आढ़तिया, बिचवैया : *an insurance broker* 2 दलाल

▸ **brokerage** / 'ब्रोकरिज् / *noun* आढ़त, दलाली।

bronchial / 'ब्रॉइकिअल् / *adj* (चिकि) श्वसनी/श्वासनली से संबंधित।

bronchitis / ब्रॉड़्'काइटिस् / *noun* श्वास-नली की सूजन/शोथ।

bronze / ब्रॉन्ज़् / *noun* 1 काँसा (ताँबे और टिन का मिश्रण) : *a statue (cast) in bronze* 2 कांस्य पदक : *win an Olympic bronze* ▸ **the Bronze Age** *noun* कांस्य-युग (पाषाण-काल और लोह-युग के बीच का समय)।

brooch / ब्रोच् / (*US* **pin** / पिन् / भी) जड़ाऊ पिन (पोशाक में लगाने के लिए एक आभूषण)।

brood / ब्रूड् / *noun* घोंसले में पल रहे (एक बार में दिए) बच्चे ▸ **brood** *verb* 1 (पक्षी का) अंडे सेना 2 **brood (on/over sth)** चिंतन करना, काफ़ी समय तक विचारमग्न रहना **brooding** *adj* विचारमग्न, दुखी या अंधकारमय।

brook¹ / ब्रुक् / *noun* छोटी जलधारा, नाला।

brook² / ब्रुक् / *verb* (औप) सहना, बर-दाश्त करना : *a strict teacher who brooks no nonsense from her pupils.*

broom / ब्रूम् / *noun* झाड़, बुहारी ▸ **broomstick** *noun* झाड़ की डंडी।

broth / ब्रॉथ् / *noun* शोरबा ▪ **too many cooks spoil the broth** (कहा) बहुत-से जोगी मठ उजाड़ (एक कार्य में ज़रूरत से ज्यादा लोग लगे हों तो काम ख़राब हो जाता है)।

brothel / 'ब्रॉथ्ल् / *noun* वेश्या-घर।

brother / 'ब्रद्र् / *noun* 1 भाई, सगा भाई 2 उसी व्यवसाय, धर्म-समिति आदि का सदस्य, बंधु ▪ **brothers in arms** साथ-साथ सेवा में (विशेषत: युद्ध में) लगे सैनिक ▸ **brotherhood** *noun* 1 भ्रातृत्व, भाई-चारा, बंधुत्व 2 भ्रातृसंघ **brother-in-law** *noun* (*pl* **brothers-in-law**) बहनोई; साला; साढ़ू; जेठ; देवर **brotherly** *adj*.

brow / ब्राउ / *noun* 1 (प्राय: *pl*) = **eyebrow** 2 माथा, मस्तक।

browbeat / 'ब्राउबीट् / *verb* (*pt* **brow-beat**; *pp* **browbeaten**) **browbeat sb (into doing sth)** धौंस या धमकी से किसी को डराना/धमकाना : *The judge told the lawyer not to browbeat the witness.*

brown / ब्राउन् / *adj* (**-er, -est**) 1 भूरा/चॉकलेटी रंग वाला 2 भूरी त्वचा वाला (प्राकृतिक या सूर्यताप के कारण) ▸ **brown** *noun* 1 भूरा/चॉकलेटी रंग 2 भूरे रंग के कपड़े : *Brown doesn't suit you.*

browse / ब्राउज़् / *verb* 1 पुस्तकों या अन्य वस्तुओं पर सरसरी नज़र डालना : *browse in a library* 2 **browse through sth** पुस्तक या अन्य वस्तु उलट-पलटकर पढ़ना या देखना।

bruise / ब्रूज़् / *noun* चोट (बिना खाल छिले); गुमड़ा ▸ **bruise** *verb* चोट मारना या खाना : *He fell and bruised his leg.*

brunette / ब्रू'नेट् / *noun* काले/भूरे बालों वाली श्वेत जाति की महिला।

brunt / ब्रन्ट् / *noun* → **bear**² देखिए।

brush¹ / ब्रश् / *noun* 1 (खुरचने, रगड़ने, साफ़ करने या चित्रकारी में प्रयुक्त) कूची, तूलिका : *a paintbrush* ○ *a toothbrush* 2 [*sing*] तूलिका/कूची का प्रयोग : *Give one's clothes/teeth/hair a (good) brush.*

brush² / ब्रश् / *verb* ब्रश का प्रयोग करना; ब्रश की सहायता से साफ़, पॉलिश, सुव्यवस्थित या चिकना करना : *brush your clothes/shoes/hair* ▪ **brush sb/sth aside** 1 एक तरफ़ खिसका देना 2 किसी को नकारना/महत्त्व न देना **brush sth away/off** ब्रश या ब्रश जैसी वस्तु की सहायता से किसी वस्तु में से कुछ दूर करना।

brusque / ब्रुस्क्; ब्रस्क्; *US* ब्रस्क् / *adj* अशिष्ट या रूखे व्यवहार से दो बातें करते हुए : *He can be rather brusque at* times. ▶ **brusquely** adv **brusque-ness** noun.

Brussels sprout / 'ब्रसल्ज़ स्प्राउट् / (Brussel sprout, sprout भी) noun (प्राय: pl) बंदगोभी जैसी छोटे आकार की एक सब्ज़ी, चोकीगोभी।

brutal / 'ब्रूटल् / adj क्रूर; अमानवीय; नृशंस ▶ **brutality** / ब्रू'टैलिटि / noun क्रूरता, अमानवीय व्यवहार; नृशंस कार्य/पाशविक क्रिया **brutally** adv क्रूरता से।

brute / ब्रूट् / noun 1 पशु, विशेषकर बड़ा और खूँख्वार 2 (कभी-कभी परि) क्रूर/ निर्दय व्यक्ति ▶ **brute** adj तर्कहीन/पशु-तुल्य; बुद्धि की बजाय बल प्रयोग करते हुए; नीच प्रकृति, कठोर **brutish** adj पशुतुल्य **brutishly** adv.

bubble / 'बबल् / noun 1 बुलबुला, बुदबुदा 2 द्रव या काँच में वायु/गैस का छोटा-सा पिंड ■ the bubble bursts चार दिन की चाँदनी के बाद अंधेरी रात ▶ **bubble** verb 1 (द्रव का) बुलबुलाना, बुदबुदाना : stew bubbling in the pot 2 bubble (over) (with sth) खुशी से भरा होना : be bubbling (over) with high spirits.

bubonic plague / ब्यू बॉनिक् 'प्लेग् / (the plague भी) noun गिलटी वाला प्लेग।

buck[1] / बक् / noun (pl अपरिवर्तित या bucks) मृगछौना, नर-खरगोश।

buck[2] / बक् / noun (US अनौप) अमरीकी डॉलर ■ make a fast/quick buck (अनौप, अक्सर अपमा) (अनुचित तरीके से) तेज़ी से और आराम से पैसा बनाना/ कमाना।

bucket / 'बकिट् / noun बालटी, डोल।

buckle / 'बकल् / noun बकसुआ (बेल्ट/ पेटी बाँधने का बकलस); सजावटी जूतों पर इसी तरह का बकलस।

bud / बड् / noun 1 कली 2 अधखिला फूल ▶ **bud** verb (-dd-) खिलना, विकसित होना : The trees are budding early this year. **budding** adj (अच्छी तरह)

विकसित होता हुआ, उभरता हुआ, उदीयमान।

Buddhism / 'बुद्धिज़्म् / noun गौतम सिद्धार्थ (महात्मा बुद्ध) द्वारा प्रचारित/स्थापित धर्म ▶ **Buddhist** noun, adj बौद्ध।

budge / बज् / verb (प्राय: नकारात्मक और प्रश्नवाचक वाक्यों में) 1 भारी और कड़ी वस्तु/व्यक्ति का मामूली-सा हिलना/हिलाना 2 किसी का अपने विचार या निश्चय से टलना/हटने को प्रेरित करना : Once he's made up his mind, you can never budge him.

budget / 'बजिट् / noun 1 बजट, आय-व्यय पत्र : a family on a tight budget 2 सरकार का वार्षिक बजट 3 किसी कार्य-विशेष के लिए आवश्यक/उपलब्ध धन की मात्रा ▶ **budget** verb **budget** (sth) (for sth) कार्यविशेष/प्रयोजन के लिए धन उपलब्ध करना, बजट बनाना : If we budget carefully, we'll be able to afford a new car. **budgeting** noun.

buffalo / बफ़लो / noun (pl अपरिवर्तित या buffaloes) भैंस/भैंसा : a herd of buffaloes.

buffer / 'बफ़र् / noun 1 बफ़र, ट्रेन आदि में टक्कर का ज़ोर कम करने के लिए स्प्रिंगदार रोक 2 व्यक्ति या वस्तु जो टक्कर/आघात का ज़ोर कम करे या कष्टों से रक्षा करे 3 दो शक्तिशाली राष्ट्रों के बीच का अंतस्थ राज्य जिससे उनके बीच युद्ध की संभावना कम हो जाती है : a buffer state/zone ▶ **buffer** verb बफ़र का काम करना।

buffet / 'बुफ़े; US ब'फ़े / noun 1 (होटल में) किनारे का काउंटर जिस पर भोजन और पेय परोसा जाता है 2 इस तरह की दावत जिसमें मेहमान स्वयं खाना परोसते हैं।

buffoon / ब'फ़ून् / noun भाँड/मसखरा; विदूषक : play the buffoon ▶ **buf-foonery** noun.

bug / बग् / noun 1 (US) कोई भी छोटा-सा (खटमल जैसा) कीट 2 खटमल 3 (प्राय: the bug) [sing] (अनौप) किसी कार्य विशेष में उत्साहपूर्ण रुचि : the travel bug

4 *(अनौप)* दूसरों की बातें छुपकर सुनने के लिए छोटा-सा गुप्त माइक्रोफ़ोन 5 *(अनौप)* मशीन में (विशेषत: कंप्यूटर में) ख़राबी।

bugger / 'बगर् / *noun* *(अप, विशेषत: ब्रिटेन में)* 1 *(अपमा)* परेशान/चिढ़ पैदा करने वाला व्यक्ति; एक क़िस्म विशेष का व्यक्ति (ख़ासकर आदमी) : *He's a clever bugger.* 2 परेशानी/कष्ट देने वाली वस्तु।

bugle / 'ब्यूगल् / *noun* बिगुल ▸ **bugler** / 'ब्यूगलर् / *noun* बिगुल बजाने वाला।

build / बिल्ड् / *verb* *(pt, pp* built / बिल्ट् /) 1 build sth (of/from/out of sth); build sth (for sb) बनाना, निर्माण करना : *build a house/road/railway* 2 मकान बनाना/बनवाना : *The city council intends to build on this site.* ■ build on sth भावी उन्नति के लिए आधार रूप में प्रयोग करना **Rome was not built in a day** *(कहा)* किसी भी कठिन या महत्त्वपूर्ण कार्य के लिए समय एवं कठिन परिश्रम की आवश्यकता होती है ▸ **build** *noun* (मानव शरीर का) गठन, बनावट **builder** *noun* 1 (भवन) निर्माता 2 (यौगिक शब्दों में) (व्यक्ति या वस्तु) विकसित या पैदा करने वाला : *an empire-builder* ○ *a confidence-builder* **built** *(प्रत्यय)* विशेष प्रकार से गठित **built-in (inbuilt** भी) *adj* किसी बड़ी रचना का अंग बनाया हुआ।

building / 'बिल्डिङ् / *noun* 1 भवन, इमारत 2 भवन-निर्माण; भवन-निर्माण कला अथवा व्यवसाय ▸ **building block** *noun* किसी चीज़ का मूलभूत अंग।

bulb / बल्ब् / *noun* 1 कंद, भूमिगत गांठ (जैसे प्याज़, शकरकंद आदि) 2 (light bulb भी) (बिजली का) लट्टू/बल्ब।

bulge / बल्ज् / *noun* 1 उभार : *What's that bulge in your pocket?* 2 *(अनौप)* मात्रा में अस्थायी वृद्धि : *a population bulge* ▸ **bulge** *verb* **bulge (out) (with sth)** उभरना/उभड़ना; फूलना।

bulk / बल्क् / *noun* 1 ढेर, अंबार 2 बड़ा/

वृहत् आकार, शरीर या व्यक्ति 3 [sing] the bulk (of sth) मुख्य भाग, अधिकांश : *The bulk of the work has already been done.* ▸ **bulky** *adj* (-ier, -iest) ज़्यादा जगह घेरने वाला, भारी-भरकम।

bull / बुल् / *noun* 1 साँड़ 2 हाथी, ह्वेल और अन्य कुछ बड़े प्राणियों के नर प्राणी 3 *(वाणिज्य)* तेज़ी आने की आशा में शेयर ख़रीदने वाला : *a bull market* ■ a bull in a china shop ऐसा मनुष्य जो सावधानी बरतने के बदले तोड़-फोड़ करे **take the bull by the horns** आपत्ति/कष्टों का धैर्य और साहस से सामना करना।

bulldog / 'बुलडॉग् / *noun* एक खूँख़्वार क़िस्म का कुत्ता।

bulldoze / 'बुलडोज़् / *verb* 1 बुलडोज़र से धराशायी करना/समतल करना 2 **bulldoze sb (into doing sth)** डरा-धमकाकर कुछ काम कराना ▸ **bulldozer** / 'बुलडोज़र् / *noun* बुलडोज़र, सड़क आदि बनाते समय भूमि समतल करने वाली बड़ी मशीन।

bullet / 'बुलिट् / *noun* (बंदूक़ की) गोली।

bulletin / 'बुलटिन् / *noun* 1 समाचारों का अधिकारिक विवरण, विज्ञप्ति 2 किसी संघ, समूह या समाज की गतिविधियों की जानकारी देती हुई पत्रिका।

bullion / 'बुलिअन् / *noun* (बड़ी मात्रा या सिल के रूप में) सोना-चाँदी।

bullock / 'बुलक् / *noun* बैल।

bull's-eye / 'बुल्ज़आइ / *noun* (bull भी) निशाने का मध्य, चाँद, केंद्र।

bully / 'बुलि / *noun* (pl bullies) धौंस से रोब जमाने वाला, दबंग ▸ **bully** *verb* (pt, pp bullied) अपने से कमज़ोर को धमकाना, धौंस जमाकर रोब गाँठना।

bulwark / 'बुल्वर्क् / *noun* 1 (क़िले आदि का) परकोटा 2 **bulwark (against sth)** (व्यक्ति/वस्तु) रक्षक : *Democracy is a bulwark of freedom.*

bumble-bee / 'बम्बल् 'बी / *noun* भौंरा।

bump / बम्प् / *verb* 1 **bump against/ into sb/sth** टक्कर मारना, धक्का मारना

2 bump sth (against/on sth) टकराना, चोट मारना (खाना) : *Be careful not to bump your head on the low beams.* **3** ऊबड़-खाबड़ सतह पर चलना : *The old bus bumped along the mountain road.* ▶ **bump** noun धक्का, टक्कर **bumpy** *adj* (**-ier, -iest**) **1** ऊबड़-खाबड़ : *a bumpy road/track* **2** अचानक लगने वाले धक्कों/झटकों से पूर्ण।

bumper¹ / 'बम्पर् / noun टक्कर के प्रभाव को कम करने के लिए मोटरकार में आगे और पीछे की तरफ़ लगाए गए भाग, बंपर।

bumper² / 'बम्पर् / adj (फ़सल आदि) भरपूर, ज़ोरदार : *a bumper crop/harvest.*

bun / बन / noun **1** बन, गुलगुला **2** (औरतों का) जूड़ा।

bunch / बन्च् / noun (अंगूर, फूलों, चाबियों आदि का) गुच्छा : *a bunch of grapes/bananas/flowers/keys.*

bundle / बन्डल् / noun बंडल, पोटली/ गठरी : *a bundle of sticks/clothes/newspapers* ▶ **bundle** verb **bundle sth (up)** पोटली बाँधना, बिना किसी क्रम के रखना।

bungalow / 'बङ्गलो / noun बंगला, एक मंज़िला भवन।

bungle / 'बङ्गल् / verb घपला करना; गड़बड़ तरीक़े से काम करना : *He's sure to bungle the job.* ▶ **bungle** noun (प्रायः *sing*) घपला **bungler** / 'बङ्गलर् / noun घपलेबाज़ व्यक्ति, अनाड़ी।

bunk¹ / बङ्क् / noun **1** (जहाज़ या ट्रेन में) दीवार में लगी शायिका **2** (**bunk-bed** भी) (विशेषकर बच्चों के लिए) एक के ऊपर एक जमा कर तैयार शायिका (शयन-स्थान)।

bunk² / बङ्क् / noun ■ **do a bunk** (अनौप) अचानक चुपके से भाग जाना या ग़ायब/रफ़ूचक्कर हो जाना।

bunker / 'बङ्कर् / noun **1** (सेना में) सुरक्षा-गृह, विशेषत: तहख़ाना **2** (जहाज़ पर या घर के बाहर) कोयला-कोठरी।

bunny / 'बनि / (**bunny-rabbit** भी) noun (बच्चों के लिए/द्वारा प्रयुक्त शब्द) ख़रगोश।

bunting¹ / 'बन्टिङ् / noun चिड़िया प्रजाति का कोई भी छोटा पक्षी।

bunting² / 'बन्टिङ् / noun (सजावट के लिए) रंग-बिरंगी झंडियाँ।

buoy / बॉइ; *US* 'बूइ भी / noun **1** पानी में उतराने वाली बंधी वस्तु जो नाविकों के लिए ख़तरनाक जगह का संकेत देती है **2** = **lifebuoy.**

buoyant / 'बॉइअन्ट् / adj **1** (कोई वस्तु) तरणशील, उतरने के योग्य; (कोई द्रव) जो किसी वस्तु को तैराता रहे, उत्प्लावक : *Salt water is more buoyant than fresh water.* **2** (क़ीमतें या व्यापारिक गतिविधि) उच्च स्तर की तरफ़ अग्रसर या बनी हुई; सफलता की ओर ▶ **buoyancy** / 'बॉइअन्सि / noun तरणशीलता, उत्प्लावकता **buoyantly** adv.

burden / 'बर्डन् / noun **1** बोझा, (पीठ पर लादा जाने वाला) वज़न **2** कुछ भी असहनीय एवं अवांछित (उत्तरदायित्व, कर्तव्य, बाध्यता आदि) **3** [*sing*] **the burden of sth** किसी लेख या भाषण का मुख्य सार ▶ **burden** verb **burden sb/oneself (with sth)** बोझा डालना/लादना; किसी को अवांछित ज़िम्मेदारी, कार्य, कर्तव्य या समस्या से लाद कर कष्ट देना **the burden of proof** noun (क़ानून) यह सिद्ध करने की बाध्यता कि जो कहा जा रहा है वह सत्य है।

bureau / 'ब्युअरो / noun (*pl* **bureaux** या **bureaus** / 'ब्युअरोज़् /) सूचनाओं और तथ्यों की जानकारी प्रदान करने वाला कार्यालय : *a travel bureau/an information bureau.*

bureaucracy / ब्युअ 'रॉक्रसि / noun **1** दफ़्तरशाही, नौकरशाही; नौकरशाही पद्धति वाला देश; नौकरशाह/अधिकारी वर्ग **2** (अक्सर अपमा) लालफ़ीताशाही ▶ **bureaucrat** / 'ब्युअर्क्रैट् / noun (अक्सर अपमा) सरकारी अफ़सर, जिस पर सत्ताधारी दल

बदलने से कोई प्रभाव नहीं पड़ता है, लालफ़ीताशाह **bureaucratic** / ˌब्युअर 'क्रैटिक् / *adj* **bureaucratically** *adv.*

burger / 'बर्गर् / *noun* (*अनौप*) = **hamburger** ▸ -**burger** (यौगिक संज्ञाओं में प्रयुक्त) (*अनौप*) हैमबर्गर की तरह बनाया/पकाया गया खाद्य पदार्थ : *a fish-burger.*

burglar / 'बर्ग्लर् / *noun* चोर/सेंधमार ▸ **burglary** / 'बर्ग्लरि / *noun* सेंध मारने का काम; सेंधमारी की घटना।

burgle / 'बर्ग्ल् / *verb* सेंधमारी करना/चोरी करना।

burial / 'बेरिअल् / *noun* दफ़न ▸ **burial-ground** *noun* कब्रगाह।

burn / बर्न् / *verb* (*pt, pp* **burnt** / बर्न्ट् / या **burned** / बर्न्ड् /) 1 अग्नि, गरमी या तेज़ाब से जलाना, नष्ट करना, क्षतिग्रस्त करना : *burn dead leaves/waste paper/rubbish* 2 इस प्रकार से जल जाना, नष्ट हो जाना 3 जलाकर छेद या निशान बनाना : *The cigarette burnt a hole in the carpet.* 4 ज्वलनशील होना : *Paper burns easily.* 5 आग से जलाकर (व्यक्ति या जानवर को) मारना/जलकर मरना : *Joan of Arc was burnt (alive) at the stake.* 6 burn with sth तीव्र भावनाएँ भड़क उठना, मन में सुलगना : *be burning with rage/desire* ■ **burn one's fingers/get one's fingers burnt** भावी परिणाम न सोचकर कार्य करने से हानि उठाना/कटु अनुभव होना **burn oneself out** अत्यधिक कार्य करके अपनी ऊर्जा समाप्त कर लेना या स्वास्थ्य ख़राब कर डालना **burn the midnight oil** देर रात तक पढ़ना या कार्य करना ▸ **burn** *noun* जला, जलने का दाग़ **burning** *adj* 1 (भावनाएँ) प्रचंड, तीव्र 2 बहुत महत्त्वपूर्ण, तुरंत अपेक्षित **burnt** *adj* जलाकर दाग़ा हुआ।

burp / बर्प् / *noun* डकार ▸ **burp** *verb* डकार लेना/लिवाना (बच्चे को)।

burrow / 'बरो / *noun* (ख़रगोश, लोमड़ी आदि का) बिल।

bursar / 'बर्सर् / *noun* (स्कूल या कॉलेज का) कोषाध्यक्ष, ख़ज़ानची ▸ **bursary** *noun* 1 कोषाध्यक्ष का कार्यालय 2 (ब्रिटेन में) छात्रवृत्ति; अनुदान।

burst[1] / बर्स्ट् / *verb* (*pt, pp* **burst**) 1 ज़ोर से फूटकर टुकड़े-टुकड़े हो जाना; विस्फोटित हो जाना 2 **burst (with sth)** (*अलं*) अत्यंत प्रबल भावना से भरा हुआ : *be bursting with happiness/pride/excitement* ■ **burst out** 1 ज़ोर से, प्रबल भाव से अचानक बोलने लगना 2 अचानक कुछ करने लगना : *burst out crying/laughing.*

burst[2] / बर्स्ट् / *noun* 1 फटन, विस्फोट; फटने से उत्पन्न दरार 2 भभक, भड़क या लहर : *a burst of anger/enthusiasm.*

bury / 'बेरि / *verb* (*pt, pp* **buried**) 1 (ज़मीन में) दफ़नाना : *He's been dead and buried for years!* 2 मृत्यु द्वारा किसी को खो देना : *She's eighty-five and has buried three husbands.* 3 खोदकर गाड़ना/छिपाना : *buried treasure* 4 किसी धातु को मिट्टी, पत्थर, पत्तों आदि से ढकना 5 किसी चीज़ का इस तरह ढका जाना कि वह दिखाई न दे : *She buried her face in her hands and wept.* ■ **bury the hatchet** झगड़ा समाप्त करके मित्र बनना।

bus / बस् / *noun* (*pl* **buses**; US **busses** भी) बस, सवारियों के लिए बड़ी मोटरगाड़ी जो निश्चित किराए पर निश्चित मार्ग पर चलती है ▸ **bus stop** *noun* बस अड्डा/पड़ाव।

bush / बुश् / *noun* 1 झाड़ी : *a rose/gooseberry bush* 2 झाड़ी से मिलती-जुलती कोई चीज़ (विशेषत: बाल), झाड़-झंखाड़ ▸ **bushy** *adj* (-**ier, -iest**) 1 झाड़ियों से घिरा/ढका हुआ 2 (बाल) घने : *a bushy moustache.*

business / 'बिज़्नस् / *noun* 1 व्यापार,

कारोबार; व्यापारिक गतिविधि/कार्य 2 पेशा, व्यवसाय ■ **business as usual** परे- शानियों/कठिनाइयों के बावजूद सामान्य गति- विधि जारी **get down to business** गंभीर होना, शुरू होकर मामला हाथ में लेना ▸ **businesslike** *adj* सावधान और सुव्यवस्थित; गंभीर **businessman** *noun* (*fem* **businesswoman**) व्यापारी।

bust / बस्ट / *noun* 1 प्रतिमा (ऊपरी धड़ मात्र, केवल सिर और कंधे) 2 स्त्री का वक्षस्थल (शरीर का ऊपरी भाग); स्त्री की छाती का नाप।

bustle / 'बसल् / *verb* हलचल मचाना, दौड़धूप करना ▸ **bustle** *noun* हलचल, दौड़धूप।

busy / 'बिज़ि / *adj* (-ier, -iest) 1 busy (at/with sth) व्यस्त; काम में लगा हुआ 2 सक्रियता से भरा : *a busy day/life* 3 (फ़ोन) प्रयोग किया जा रहा ■ **(as) busy as a bee** (खुशी-खुशी) अति व्यस्त होना।

but¹ / बट् / *conj* 1 किंतु, परंतु 2 तो भी; के बावजूद 3 और इसके साथ ही; और दूसरी तरफ़ 4 (नकारात्मक वाक्य के बाद वास्त- विकता प्रदर्शित करने के लिए) के बजाय : *It isn't that he tells lies but that he exaggerates.* 5 के अतिरिक्त; अन्यथा : *I had no alternative but to sign the contract.* 6 (कही जाने वाली बात पर खेद व्यक्त करने के लिए) : *I'm sorry but there's nothing we can do to help you.* ■ **but then** 1 पर दूसरी ओर, यद्यपि 2 (कही हुई बात का कारण स्पष्ट करते हुए): *He speaks very good French — but then he did live in Paris for three years.*

but² / बट् / *prep* के अतिरिक्त; को छोड़कर, के अलावा : *The problem is anything but easy.*

but³ / बट् / *adv* (अप्र या औप) केवल, मात्र : *He's but a boy.*

butcher / 'बुचर् / *noun* 1 क़साई 2 हत्यारा, क्रूर क़ातिल ▸ **butcher** *verb* 1 मांस के लिए जानवरों को मारना 2 (अपमा) मार डालना, क्रूरतापूर्ण वध करना **butchery** *noun* 1 क़साई का काम 2 हत्याकांड।

butler / 'बटलर् / *noun* ख़ानसामाँ; भंडारी।

butt¹ / बट् / *verb* 1 किसी को जानबूझकर सिर से टक्कर मारना/सींगों से मारना : *butt sb in the stomach* 2 किसी का सर कहीं टकराना/मारना ■ **butt in (on sb/sth)** (अनौप) किसी चीज़ में/किसी के कार्य में रुकावट डालना या टांग अड़ाना।

butt² / बट् / *noun* हँसी का पात्र व्यक्ति/वस्तु; क्रूर मज़ाक का निशाना : *be the butt of everyone's jokes.*

butt³ / बट् / *noun* औज़ारों/हथियारों का मूठ वाला भाग, कुंदा/दस्ता : *a rifle butt.*

butter / 'बटर् / *noun* 1 मक्खन 2 कुछ विशेष पदार्थों से तैयार समान प्रकार का पदार्थ : *peanut butter* ▸ **butter** *verb* मक्खन लगाना/चुपड़ना : *buttered toast* ■ **butter sb up** (अनौप) चाटुकारी करना; काम निकालने के लिए विनम्रता दिखाना ▸ **buttermilk** *noun* मट्ठा, छाछ।

butterfly / 'बटर्फ़्लाइ / *noun* 1 तितली 2 जीवन के प्रति मूर्खतापूर्ण एवं लापरवाह दृष्टिकोण वाला व्यक्ति।

buttock / 'बटक् / *noun* (विशेषत: pl) चूतड़, नितंब।

button / 'बटन् / *noun* 1 बटन : *sew on a new button* 2 घुंडी (मशीन आदि चलाने के लिए) ▸ **buttonhole** *noun* काज।

buttress / 'बट्रस् / *noun* 1 पुश्ता/टेक/ सहारा (दीवार के लिए) 2 सहारा/समर्थन देने वाला या रक्षा करने वाला व्यक्ति/वस्तु : *The government's tight fiscal policy acts as a buttress against infla- tion.* ▸ **buttress** *verb* किसी चीज़ को सहारा या समर्थन देना : *You need more facts to buttress your argument.*

buy / बाइ / *verb* (*pt, pp* **bought** / बॉट्/) 1 buy sth (for sb) ख़रीदना, मोल लेना 2 (पैसे से) प्राप्त कर सकना : *Money* *can't buy happiness.* **3** घूस/रिश्वत देना : *He can't be bought.* ■ **buy time** किसी घटना/निर्णय आदि में देर लगाने के लिए कुछ करना।

buzz / बज़ / *verb* **1** (शहद की) मक्खियों की भिनभिनाहट या उस तरह की आवाज़ लगातार निकालना : *flies and wasps buzzing round a jar of jam* **2 buzz (with sth)** चहल-पहल, उत्तेजित बात या विचारों से भरा होना : *The office is buzzing with rumours.* ▸ **buzzer** *noun* गूँज की आवाज़ उत्पन्न करने वाली एक वैद्युत युक्ति।

by¹ / बाइ / *prep* **1** समीप, पास, बग़ल में : *a house by the church/railway* **2** द्वारा, के ज़रिये से : *a play (written) by Shakespeare* **3** के साधन से/करके : *May I pay by cheque?* **4** (**the** के बिना) के फलस्वरूप, के कारण, द्वारा : *meet by chance* **5** (यातायात के साधन या मार्ग को इंगित करते हुए) : *travel by boat/ bus/plane* **6** (समय) के पूर्व; निश्चित समय से पहले : *Can you finish the work by five o'clock?* **7** व्यक्ति या वस्तु के पास से : *He walked by me without speaking.* **8** (तय किया गया रास्ता इंगित करते हुए) से गुज़रते हुए : *We travelled to Mumbai by Mathura and Vadodara.* **9** (प्राय: **the** के बिना), के दौरान : *She sleeps by day and works by night.* **10** (व्यक्त मात्रा या सीमा) तक: *The bullet missed him by two inches.* **11** से, के अनुसार : *By my watch it is two o'clock.* **12** के हिसाब से; का पालन करते हुए : *play a game by the rules* **13** (शरीर के अंग या छुए गए कपड़ों को संकेत करते हुए) : *take sb by the hand* **14** (**the** के साथ, निश्चित अवधि या मात्रा संकेत करते हुए) : *sell eggs by the dozen* **15** की दर पर या निश्चित समूह में : *improving day by day/bit by bit* ○ *The children came*

in two by two. **16** (किसी के बारे में अधिक जानकारी देने के लिए) : *be German by birth/a lawyer by profession* **17** (क़सम खाते समय) : *I swear by Almighty God...* **18** (माप प्रदर्शित करने में) : *The room measures fifteen feet by twenty feet.* **19** (गुणा या भाग करने में) : *6 (multiplied) by 2 equals 12.*

by² / बाइ / *adv part* **1** पास से : *drive/ go/walk by* **2** पास में, समीप ही : *He lives close/near by.* **3** एक तरफ़; सुरक्षित : *lay/put/set sth by* ■ **by and by** (अप्र) जल्दी ही, थोड़ी देर में।

by- (**bye-** भी) *pref* (पूर्वपद) (संज्ञाओं और क्रियाओं के साथ प्रयुक्त) **1** कम महत्त्व-पूर्ण : *by-product/bye-law* **2** पास वाला : *bystander* ○ *bypass.*

bye¹ / बाइ / *noun* (खेलों में) **1** (क्रिकेट में) गेंद बल्ले से बिना छुए दूर चले जाने पर लिया गया रन **2** ऐसी स्थिति जिसमें किसी स्पर्धा में कोई खिलाड़ी प्रतिद्वंद्वी न होने के कारण अगले चरण में ऐसे पहुँच जाता है जैसे कि जीत कर गया हो : *She has a bye into the next round.*

bye² / बाइ / (**bye-bye** / बाइ'बाइ / भी) *interj* (अनौप) अलविदा, सलाम।

by-election / 'बाइ इलेक्शन् / *noun* उपचुनाव जो किसी सभासद के इस्तीफ़ा देने या मृत्यु के कारण आवश्यक हो जाता है।

bygone / 'बाइगॉन् / *adj* बीता हुआ : *a bygone age* ○ *in bygone days* ▸ **bygones** *noun* [*pl*] बीती बातें, विगत अप-राध आदि ■ **let bygones be bygones** बीती ताहि बिसार दे, आगे की सुध ले।

by-law / 'बाइ लॉ / *noun* **1** (**bye-law** भी) उपनियम (स्थानीय शासन द्वारा बनाया गया अधिनियम) **2** (*US*) किसी क्लब या कंपनी का नियम, अधिनियम आदि।

bypass / 'बाइपास; *US* 'बाईपैस् / *noun* **1** उपमार्ग, बाह्य-मार्ग (शहर को बचाते हुए बाहर-बाहर जाने वाला मार्ग) **2** (चिकि

हृदय की शल्य-चिकित्सा के दौरान रक्त प्रवाह के लिए भिन्न मार्ग : *bypass surgery*

▶ **bypass** *verb* 1 बचकर/कतराकर उप-मार्ग से निकलना 2 कुछ जल्दी में करने के लिए किसी नियम, प्रक्रिया अथवा आज्ञा प्राप्ति की अवहेलना करना: *She bypassed her colleagues on the board and went ahead with the deal.*

bystander / 'बाइस्टैन्डर् / *noun* दर्शक।

byte / बाइट् / *noun* कंप्यूटर में संग्रहीत सूचनाओं की इकाई।

byword / 'बाइवई / *noun* 1 **byword for sth** वस्तु या व्यक्ति जो किसी विशेषता का प्रतिनिधिक माना जाता हो : *His name has become a byword for cruelty.* 2 कहावत, उक्ति।

Cc

C abbr (संक्षि) सेल्सिअस; सेंटिग्रेड : *Water freezes at 0°C.*

c abbr (संक्षि) शताब्दी : *in the 19th c.*

cab / कैब् / noun टैक्सी ▸ **cab-driver** noun.

cabaret / कैबरे; *US* कैब् 'रे / noun रेस्त्राँ में लोगों के खाते-पीते समय प्रस्तुत मनोरंजन (गाना या नृत्य)।

cabbage / कैबिज् / noun **1** बंदगोभी **2** (*अपमा*) अति सुस्त और उत्साहहीन व्यक्ति **3** (*अपमा*) ऐसा व्यक्ति जो दिमाग के बुरी तरह क्षतिग्रस्त हो जाने से पूर्ण रूप से दूसरों पर निर्भर हो।

cabin / कैबिन् / noun छोटा कमरा (विशेषकर जहाज़ में सोने के लिए); वायुयान में यात्रियों के बैठने का क्षेत्र।

cabinet / कैबिनट् / noun **1** ड्राअर वाली अलमारी : *a filing cabinet ○ a medicine cabinet* **2** (**the cabinet** भी) (राज्य या शासन से संबद्ध) मंत्रिमंडल, मंत्रि-परिषद।

cable / केब्ल् / noun **1** मोटा मज़बूत रस्सा या तार **2** (तार या टेलिफ़ोन संदेश भेजने या विद्युत प्रवाह के लिए) तार; (**cablegram** भी) इस तरह भेजा हुआ संदेश : *send sb/receive a cable* ▸ **cable** verb **1** **cable (to sb) (from...)** केबल द्वारा संदेश भेजना : *She cabled (to her husband) that she would arrive on 15 May.*

cable car noun पर्वतों पर आवागमन के लिए तार के मोटे रस्सों पर चलने वाली गाड़ी

cable television noun रेडियो संकेतों के स्थान पर केबलों से प्राप्त टी वी प्रोग्राम-पद्धति।

cache / कैश् / noun **1** छिपा हुआ भंडार (प्राय: हथियार, धन, खाद्य पदार्थ आदि का) **2** (**cache memory** भी) कंप्यूटर के स्मृति भंडार का एक हिस्सा।

cackle / कैक्ल् / verb **1** (मुर्गी का) कुड़कुड़ाना **2** (व्यक्ति का) ऊँची आवाज़ में बकबक करना/ज़ोर से हँसना।

cacophony / क'कॉफ़नि / noun अप्रिय आवाज़ों का मिला-जुला शोर ▸ **cacophonous** adj.

cactus / कैक्टस् / noun (pl **cactuses** या **cacti** / कैक्टाइ /) नागफनी, सेहुँड़।

cadet / क'डेट् / noun कैडेट, सैन्य छात्र : *army/naval/air force/police cadets.*

cadre / कादर् / noun (उच्च प्रशिक्षण प्राप्त सैनिकों, कर्मचारियों, प्रबंधकों आदि का) छोटा समूह/संवर्ग; इस संवर्ग का सदस्य।

Caesarean / सिज़ेअरिअन् /(**Caesarian, Caesarian section** भी) noun शल्य-क्रिया द्वारा प्रसव कराने की विधि : *The baby was delivered by Caesarean section.*

café / कैफ़े; *US* कैफ़े / noun छोटा रेस्त्राँ/जलपानगृह।

cafeteria / कैफ़'टिअरिआ / noun ऐसा रेस्त्राँ/जलपानगृह जहाँ ग्राहक काउंटर से स्वयं ही जलपान लेते हैं।

caffeine / कैफ़ीन् / noun चाय/कॉफ़ी में पाया जाने वाला मादक द्रव्य।

cage / केज् / noun **1** (पशु-पक्षी का) पिंजरा **2** कोयले या अन्य खान में पिंजरानुमा लिफ़्ट का भाग ▸ **cage** verb पिंजरे में रखना/कैद करना : *caged animals in a zoo.*

cagey / केजि / adj (**cagier, cagiest**) **cagey (about sth)** (*अनौप*) दूसरों को जानकारी देने में अत्यधिक सतर्क; गोपनशील : *He's very cagey about his family.* ▸ **cagily** adv **caginess** noun.

cajole / क'जोल् / verb **1** **cajole sb (into doing sth)** फुसलाना (कुछ काम कराने के लिए) : *She was cajoled into accepting a part in the play.* **2** **cajole sth out of sb** फुसलाकर जानकारी प्राप्त करना : *The confession*

had to be cajoled out of him.
▶ **cajolery** *noun.*

cake / केक् / *noun* **1** केक : *a choco-late/fruit cake* **2** केक के आकार में पकाया खाद्य पदार्थ : *fish cakes ○ potato cakes* **3** टिकिया/टिक्की : *a cake of soap* ■ **get, want a slice/share of the cake** अपने हिस्से का लाभ प्राप्त करना **have one's cake and eat it (too)** *(अनौप)* ऐसी स्थिति में दोहरा लाभ प्राप्त करना जब एक प्रकार से ही संभव हो।

calamity / क'लैमिटि / *noun (pl ca-lamities)* भयावह घटना; विपत्ति : *The earthquake was the worst calam-ity in the country's history.* ▶ **ca-lamitous** / क'लैमिटस् / *adj* विपत्तिपूर्ण।

calcium / 'कैल्सिअम् / *noun* (प्रतीक Ca) एक रासायनिक पदार्थ, चूने का तत्त्व/ सार।

calculate / 'कैल्क्युलेट् / *verb* गणना करना, हिसाब लगाना : *calculate the cost of sth* ▶ **calculated** *adj* सोचा-समझा, सुनियोजित : *a calculated risk/ insult* **calculating** *adj (अपमा)* स्वार्थी, अवसरवादी **calculation** / ,कैल्क्यु 'लेश्न् / *noun* गणना, परिकलन : *math-ematical/political/mental calcula-tion.*

calculator / 'कैल्क्युलेटर् / *noun* परि-कलन यंत्र।

calendar / 'कैलिन्डर् / *noun* **1** कैलेंडर, तिथि-पत्र : *a desk calendar* **2** *(US)* नियोजित भेंटों का दैनिक रिकॉर्ड **3** *(प्राय: sing)* सूची *(विशेष घटनाओं की)* : *The Cup Final is an important date in the sporting calendar.*

calf¹ / काफ़; *US* कैफ़ / *noun (pl calves* / काल्व्ज़; *US* कैव्ज़ /) बछड़ा, बछिया/ बछड़ी; कुछ पशु-जातियों जैसे हाथी, ह्वेल आदि का बच्चा।

calf² / काफ़; *US* कैफ़ / *noun (pl calves* / काल्व्ज़; *US* कैव्ज़ /) टाँग की पिंडली।

calibre *(US* **caliber)** / 'कैलिबर् / *noun* **1** गोली/बंदूक़ की नली या अन्य नली के आंतरिक व्यास का मापन **2** मानसिक क्षमता या चरित्र बल : *His work is of a pretty high/low calibre.*

call¹ / कॉल् / *verb* **1** **call (out) to sb/ (for sth); call (sth) (out)** बुलाना, पुकारना, चिल्लाना : *Why didn't you come when I called (out) (your name)?* **2** *(पक्षी या पशु का)* विशिष्ट प्रकार की ध्वनि करना **3** उपस्थित होने के लिए कहना या ध्यान आकर्षित करना : *Call the children (in).* **4** **call (in/round) (on sb/at...) (for sb/sth)** मिलने जाना, भेंट करना : *Let's call (in) on John/at John's house.* **5** **call at ...** *(ट्रेन आदि का)* किसी स्थान पर रुकना : *The train on platform 1 is for Hyderabad, calling at Bhopal and Nagpur.* **6** फ़ोन करना : *I'll call again later.* **7** बुलावा, घोषणा/आदेश देना : *call a meeting/an election/a strike* **8** किसी को जगाना : *Please call me at 7 o'clock tomorrow morning.* **9** नाम रखना, वर्णन करना : *How dare you call me fat!* ○ *What was the book called?* **10** सोचना, समझना/ मानना : *I call his behaviour mean and selfish.* ■ **bring/call sb/sth to mind** याद दिलाना/रखना **call a spade a spade** अपना मत चाहे दूसरे को बुरा लगे, निस्संकोच व्यक्त करना **call for sth** माँगना, चाहना **call sb's attention to sth** *(औप)* किसी का ध्यान किसी बात पर आकर्षित करना **call sb/sth off** गतिविधि को रोकने के लिए आदेश देना **call sth off** निर्णय आदि रद्द करना : *The meeting was called off without any deci-sion.*

call² / कॉल् / *noun* **1** पुकार, आह्वान : *a call for help* **2** *(पक्षी की)* बोली **3** हॉर्न, बिगुल आदि पर संकेत **4** भेंट/मुलाक़ात

pay a call on a friend 5 फ़ोन पर बात, कॉल 6 बुलावा/आदेश/निमंत्रण।

calligraphy / कॅ'लिग्रफ़ि / *noun* सुलेखन, खुशख़ती ▸ **calligrapher** *noun.*

calling / 'कॉलिङ् / *noun* (औप) व्यवसाय, पेशा।

callous / 'कैलस् / *adj* 1 (चमड़ा) कड़ा 2 दूसरों की भावनाओं की उपेक्षा करने वाला व्यक्ति, बेदर्द : *a callous person/attitude/act* ▸ **callously** *adv* **callousness** *noun.*

calm / काम् / *adj* (-er, -est) शांत ▸ **calm** *noun* शांति; निर्वात ■ **the calm before the storm** तूफ़ान से पहले की शांति ▸ **calm** *verb* **calm (sb) (down)** शांत कर देना या हो जाना **calmly** *adv* **calmness** *noun.*

calorie / 'कैलरि / *noun* (*संक्षि* **cal**) 1 ऊष्मा (गरमी) की इकाई 2 भोजन द्वारा प्राप्त ऊर्जा की इकाई।

camcorder / 'कैम्कॉर्डर् / *noun* यहाँ–वहाँ ले जा सकने लायक वीडियो कैमरा जिससे ध्वनि भी रिकॉर्ड कर सकते हैं।

camel / 'कैमल् / *noun* 1 ऊँट 2 (रंग) हलका भूरा।

camera / कैमरा / *noun* फ़ोटो खींचने का उपकरण, कैमरा ■ **in camera** गुप्त रीति से (न्यायाधीश के) कमरे के भीतर; गुप्त मंत्रणा/बैठक ▸ **cameraman** *noun.*

camouflage / 'कैमफ़्लाश् / *noun* 1 व्यक्ति/वस्तु (विशेषत: युद्ध में तोपों आदि) के स्वरूप को छिपाने या ढकने का तरीक़ा 2 जंतुओं का (स्वरक्षा के लिए) ऐसा रंग या आकार जिससे वे अपने आस–पास के वातावरण में छिपे रहते हैं 3 सत्य को छिपाने का प्रयास : *The minister's reply was described as a pure camouflage.*

camp / कैम्प् / *noun* 1 पड़ाव, शिविर, अस्थायी आवास 2 सैनिकों के रहने या प्रशिक्षण प्राप्त करने का स्थान : *an army camp* 3 समान विचारधारा वाले लोगों का समूह : *the socialist camp* ▸ **camp**

verb 1 पड़ाव डालना; शिविर/कैंप में रहना : *They camped (out) in the woods for a week.* 2 (प्राय: **go camping**) कैंप में रहते हुए छुट्टी बिताना **camper** *noun* कैंप में रहने वाला।

campaign / कैम्'पेन / *noun* 1 (युद्ध) अभियान 2 किसी लक्ष्य को पाने के लिए सुयोजित गतिविधि (विशेषत: राजनीतिक या सामाजिक) : *mount/launch a campaign* 3 आंदोलन : *a campaign against nuclear weapons* ▸ **campaign** *verb* **campaign (for/against sb/sth)** अभियान/आंदोलन में भाग लेना।

campus / 'कैम्पस् / *noun* (*pl* **campuses**) कॉलेज या विश्वविद्यालय का अहाता/परिसर; *(US)* विश्वविद्यालय अथवा विश्वविद्यालय की शाखा : *campus life.*

can¹ / कैन् / *noun* 1 टीन, डिब्बा 2 डिब्बा–बंद खाद्य पदार्थ ▸ **can** *verb* (**-nn-**) खाद्य पदार्थ को सुरक्षित रखने के लिए डिब्बे में बंद करना : *canned fruit.*

can² / कन्; कैन् / *modal verb* (*neg* **cannot** / 'कैनॉट् /; *संक्षि* **can't** / कान्ट्; *US* कैन्ट् /; *pt* **could** / कड्; कुड् /) 1 (सामर्थ्य दर्शाने के लिए) : *I can run fast.* 2 (प्राप्त ज्ञान या कौशल दर्शाने के लिए) : *They can speak French.* 3 (अनुभव/ज्ञान प्रदर्शित करने वाली क्रियाओं के साथ प्रयुक्त): *I can hear music.* ○ *I thought I could smell something burning.* 4 (अनुमति सूचक): *You can take the car, if you want.* 5 (सहायता का अनुरोध सूचक) : *Can you help me with this box?* 6 (संभावना सूचक): *There's someone outside — who can it be?* 7 (संदेह, आश्चर्य या संभ्रांति सूचक) : *What can they be doing?* 8 (विशिष्ट व्यवहार या स्थिति सूचक) : *We can be very tactless sometimes.* 9 (सुझाव देने में प्रयुक्त) : *We can eat in a restaurant, if you like.*

canal / क॑नैल् / noun 1 नहर (सिंचाई या यातायात के लिए) 2 आहार नलिका : the alimentary canal ▸ **canalize, -ise** / केनलाइज़् / verb 1 नहर बनाना 2 नदी को नहर में परिवर्तित करना **canalization, -isation** noun.

canary / क॑नेअरि / noun (pl **canaries**) कनारी चिड़िया जो खूब गाती है।

cancel / केन्स्ल् / verb (-ll-; US -l-) 1 (कार्यक्रम, निर्णय आदि) रद्द करना 2 निशान लगाकर काटना, क्रॉस करना ▸ **cancellation** / केन्स॑लेश्न् / noun.

cancer / केन्सर् / noun 1 कैंसर रोग 2 अति शीघ्र फैलने वाली, ख़तरनाक बुराई : Violence is a cancer in our society. 3 **Cancer** कर्क राशि; कर्क राशि वाला व्यक्ति ▸ **cancerous** / केन्सरस् / adj कैंसर जैसा।

candid / केन्डिड् / adj स्पष्ट, सरल : a candid opinion/remark ▸ **candidly** adv.

candidate / केन्डिडट्; केन्डिडेट् / noun 1 उम्मीदवार : a presidential candidate 2 (किसी पद, परीक्षा आदि के लिए) प्रत्याशी 3 **candidate (for sth)** किसी पद के लिए योग्य व्यक्ति; परीक्षार्थी ▸ **candidature (candidacy** भी) noun (औप) उम्मीदवारी।

candle / केन्ड्ल् / noun मोमबत्ती ▸ **candlelight** noun **candlestick** noun मोमबत्तीदान।

candour (US **candor**) / केन्डर् / noun स्पष्टवादिता का गुण; निष्कपटता।

candy / केन्डि / noun मिश्री; (US) मिठाई या चॉकलेट।

cane / केन् / noun 1 कुछ पौधों का सख़्त, खोखला तना जैसे बाँस 2 बेंत, डंडी, छड़ी ▸ **cane** verb बेंत/छड़ी से मारना : The headmaster caned the boys for disobedience. **cane-sugar** noun गन्ने के रस से बनी शक्कर/चीनी।

canine / केनाइन् / adj कुत्ता-विषयक/कुत्ते से संबंधित ▸ **canine (canine tooth** भी) noun रदनक दंत।

canister / केनिस्टर् / noun टीन का पीपा, कनस्तर।

canker / केङ्कर् / noun 1 पेड़ों का एक विनाशकारी रोग 2 पशुओं, विशेषत: कुत्तों और बिल्लियों, पर चकत्ते पैदा करने वाला रोग 3 पतन की ओर ले जाने वाला कुप्रभाव।

cannibal / केनिबल् / noun 1 नरभक्षी आदमी : a cannibal tribe 2 स्वजाति भक्षी जानवर ▸ **cannibalism** / केनि-बलिज़म् / noun **cannibalistic** adj. **cannibalize, -ise** / केनिबलाइज़् / verb.

cannon / केनन् / noun (pl अपरिवर्तित) 1 (ज़मीन या तोपगाड़ी पर स्थिर) बड़ी तोप 2 हवाई जहाज़ पर लगी तोप ▸ **cannon** verb ■ **cannon against/into/off sb/ sth** (व्यक्ति या वाहन) ज़ोर-से टकराना **cannon-ball** noun तोप का गोला जो पुरानी तोपों से दाग़ा जाता था।

canny / केनि / adj (-ier, -iest) सतर्क, सावधान और चतुर ▸ **cannily** adv **canniness** noun.

canoe / क॑नू / noun लंबी पतली नाव, डोंगी ▸ **canoe** verb (pt, pp **canoed**; pres p **canoeing**) डोंगी से यात्रा करना।

canon / केनन् / noun 1 सामान्य मापदंड जिससे किसी वस्तु का मूल्यांकन होता है 2 प्रामाणिक, स्वीकृत पवित्र पुस्तकों की सूची : the canon of Holy Scripture ▸ **canonical** / क॑नॉनिक्ल् / adj धर्म विधान के अनुकूल; प्रामाणिक, स्वीकृत सूची में शामिल।

canopy / केनपि / noun (pl **canopies**) 1 चँदवा 2 वायु-यान के कॉकपिट का कवर 3 (औप या साहि) ऊपर से किसी स्थान को ढकने का प्रबंध; चाँदनी : the grey canopy of the sky ○ a canopy of leaves.

canteen / केन्टीन् / noun 1 कैंटीन, स्थान जहाँ जलपान, भोजन आदि मिलता है 2 सैनिक या कैंप में रहने वाले का जलपात्र।

cantilever / केन्टिलीवर् / noun बरामदे

या बालकनी का आधार ▶ **cantilever bridge** noun (धातु के) बीमों पर बना पुल।

cantonment / कैन्'टॉन्मन्ट् / noun सैनिक छावनी (स्थायी आवास व्यवस्था)।

canvas /'कैन्वस्/ noun (pl **canvases** /'कैन्वसिज़्/) 1 मोटा भारी कपड़ा जिसके तंबू आदि बनते हैं : canvas bags/chairs/shoes 2 चित्रकारी करने का मोटा कपड़ा; कैन्वस पर की गई चित्रकारी : Turner's canvases.

canvass /'कैन्वस्/ verb 1 **canvass (sb) (for sth)** अपने पक्ष में राजनीतिक समर्थन माँगना : go out canvassing (for votes) 2 लोगों से किसी मुद्दे (या उत्पाद) पर उनकी राय जानना : canvass voters before an election 3 किसी मुद्दे पर खुलकर बहस करना ▶ **canvass** noun **canvasser** noun.

canyon /'कैन्यन्/ noun गहरी संकीर्ण घाटी (जिसमें प्रायः नदी बहती है)।

cap / कैप् / noun 1 टोपी 2 ढक्कन ■ **a feather in one's cap** गौरव देने वाली उपलब्धि।

capability / केप 'बिलिटि / noun (pl **capabilities**) योग्यता, सामर्थ्य/क्षमता।

capable / 'केपबल् / adj 1 **capable of sth/doing sth** कुछ करने की योग्यता/शक्ति रखते हुए 2 होशियार, दक्ष, समर्थ।

capacity / क'पैसटि / noun (pl **capacities**) 1 धारणशक्ति/क्षमता : a hall with a seating capacity of 2000 2 **capacity (for sth)** सीखने, समझने, उत्पन्न करने आदि की क्षमता : She has an enormous capacity for hard work. 3 उत्पादन क्षमता 4 पद, कर्तव्य, हैसियत : acting in her capacity as a manager.

cape¹ / केप् / noun भूमि का नुकीला भाग जो समुद्र में दूर तक चला गया हो : Cape Horn.

cape² / केप् / noun ढीला, बिना बाँहों का कंधों से लटकने वाला ऊपरी वस्त्र, लबादा।

capillary / क'पिलरि; US 'कैपलेरि / noun (pl **capillaries**) केशिका नली, विशेषत: महीन रुधिर-वाहिकाएँ ▶ **capillary attraction (capillary action** भी) noun महीन नलियों द्वारा द्रव आकर्षण।

capital¹ /'कैपिटल्/ noun 1 राजधानी, मुख्य नगरी 2 (**capital letter** भी) स्थूलाक्षर, बड़े अक्षर जैसे A, B, C 3 किसी स्तंभ का ऊपरी भाग; शीर्ष ▶ **capital** adj 1 मृत्युदंड संबंधित : Do you believe in capital punishment? 2 (अप्र) महत्त्वपूर्ण, उत्तम/बहुत अच्छा।

capital² /'कैपिटल्/ noun 1 मूलधन, पूँजी 2 [sing] वाणिज्य/व्यापार शुरू करने के लिए आवश्यक धन की मात्रा 3 किसी व्यक्ति/व्यवसाय की समस्त जमा-पूँजी : capital assets.

capitalism / 'कैपिटलिज़म्/ noun पूँजी-वाद, अर्थव्यवस्था जिसमें उद्योग, व्यापार आदि का नियंत्रण पूँजीवादियों के हाथों में हो ▶ **capitalist** noun पूँजीवादी; बहुत पूँजी रखने वाले व्यक्ति/पूँजीवाद के समर्थक **capitalistic** adj.

capitalize, -ise / 'कैपिटलाइज़् / verb 1 बड़े अक्षरों में लिखना 2 अचल संपत्ति बेचकर पूँजी बनाना 3 कंपनी को पूँजी देना ▶ **capitalization, -isation** noun.

caprice / क'प्रीस् / noun झक, सनक ▶ **capricious** / क'प्रिशस् / adj झक्की/सनकी; मनमौजी **capriciously** adv **capriciousness** noun.

Capricorn / 'कैप्रिकॉर्न् / noun मकर राशि; मकर राशि वाला व्यक्ति।

capsize / कैप्'साइज़; US 'कैप्साइज़् / verb नाव का उलट जाना/डूब जाना; (नाव को) डुबो देना।

capsule/'कैप्स्यूल्/ noun 1 दवा से भरी छोटी संपुटिका जो निगलने पर घुल जाती है; कैप्सूल 2 अंतरिक्षयान का वह भाग जो स्वतंत्र यात्रा के लिए पृथक किया जा सकता है।

captain / 'कैप्टिन् / noun 1 कप्तान, सेना में एक पद 2 (टीम या समूह का) नेता, नायक

3 जहाज़ या वायुयान का अध्यक्ष ▶ **captain** verb टीम आदि का कप्तान बनना : *Who is captaining the side?* **captaincy** / 'कैप्टन्सि / noun.

caption / 'कैप्शन् / noun **1** (चित्र, फ़ोटो आदि का) शीर्षक, अनुशीर्षक **2** (फ़िल्म या टी वी स्क्रीन पर प्रदर्शित) अनुशीर्षक ▶ **caption** verb शीर्षक लगाना।

captivate / 'कैप्टिवेट् / verb मोहित करना; मंत्रमुग्ध कर देना : *He was captivated by her beauty.* ▶ **captivating** adj मोहक/सम्मोहक।

captive / 'कैप्टिव् / adj कैदी, बंदी होना : *They were taken/held captive by masked gunmen.* ▶ **captive** noun कैदी/बंदी **captivity** / कैप्'टिव़टि / noun बंदी होने की स्थिति, दासता/कैद।

captor / 'कैप्टर् / noun बंदी बनाने वाला।

capture / 'कैप्चर/ verb **1** (व्यक्ति या पशु को) क़ैद करना, बंदी बनाना **2** (बल प्रयोग अथवा छल-कपट से) क़ब्ज़ा करना, हथियाना : *capture a town/public support* **3** चित्र या फ़िल्म में कुछ निरूपित करने में सफल होना : *capture a baby's smile in a photograph* ▶ **capture** noun बंदीकरण।

car / कार् / noun **1** (motor car, US automobile भी) मोटरकार **2** (रेलवे ट्रेन में) डिब्बा, यान : *a dining/sleeping-car* **3** गुब्बारे/लिफ़्ट/केबल रेलवे आदि में सवारी डिब्बा।

caramel / 'कैरमेल् / noun खाने में रंग एवं स्वाद लाने में प्रयुक्त जली हुई शक्कर।

carat / 'कैरट् / noun (संक्षि ct) **1** हीरों के तौल की इकाई = 200 mg **2** (US karat) सोने की शुद्धता की इकाई, कैरेट (सबसे ज़्यादा शुद्ध सोना 24 ct का होता है) : *a 20 ct gold ring.*

caravan / 'कैरवैन् / noun **1** कारवाँ, क़ाफ़िला, यात्रियों के दल जो रेगिस्तान आदि भयानक प्रदेश को पार करते समय मिलकर यात्रा करते हैं **2** ढकी हुई गाड़ी जिसमें रहा जा सके **3** (US trailer) एक प्रकार की विशाल गाड़ी जिसमें रहने और सोने का प्रबंध होता है।

carbohydrate / ,कार्बो'हाइड्रेट् / noun **1** कार्बन, हाइड्रोजन और ऑक्सीजन से बना पदार्थ, जैसे शक्कर या स्टार्च **2** **carbohydrates** [pl] कार्बोहाइड्रेट वाले खाद्य पदार्थ।

carbolic / कार्'बॉलिक् / (**carbolic acid** भी) noun तारकोल से बना अम्ल, कीटाणु-नाशक पदार्थ।

carbon / 'कार्बन् / noun **1** (प्रतीक C) रासायनिक तत्त्व जो हीरे, कोयले आदि में होता है **2** (**carbon paper** भी) कार्बन पेपर/मसि-पत्र, जिसे बीच में रखकर काग़ज़ की प्रतियाँ निकालते हैं ▶ **carbon copy** noun **1** कार्बन पेपर रखकर तैयार की गई प्रति **2** किसी दूसरे से हूबहू मिलता व्यक्ति/वस्तु **carbon dioxide** noun कार्बन डाइ-ऑक्साइड **carbon monoxide** noun कार्बन मोनो ऑक्साइड।

carbuncle / 'कार्बङ्कल् / noun **1** बड़ा फोड़ा **2** माणिक्य, लाल।

carburettor / कार्ब'रेटर् / noun इंजिन का वह भाग जहाँ पेट्रोल और हवा मिश्रित होते हैं।

carcass (**carcase** भी) / 'कार्कस् / noun मृत पशु का शरीर।

card / कार्ड / noun **1** कार्ड, मोटा काग़ज़ **2** (**business card, visiting card** भी) छोटा कार्ड जिसमें मिलने वाले का नाम, पता छपा होता है, परिचय कार्ड **3** (**playing-cards** भी) ताश के पत्ते ■ **lay/put one's cards on the table** अपनी स्थिति और योजनाओं को ईमानदारी से स्पष्ट करना **on the cards** (अनौप) संभाव्य/संभव **play one's cards well, right, etc** होशियारी और प्रभावी तरीक़े से काररवाई चलाना।

cardboard / 'कार्डबॉर्ड / noun दफ़्ती, गत्ता।

cardiac / 'कार्डिएक् / adj (चिकि) हृदय संबंधी (रोग, दौरा आदि) : *cardiac patient/arrest.*

cardigan / 'कार्डिगन् / noun बाँहदार सामने से खुली ऊनी जैकेट।

cardinal¹ / 'कार्डिनल् / noun कार्डिनल, पोप को चुनने वाले मुख्य धर्माधिकारियों में से एक।

cardinal² / 'कार्डिनल् / adj सबसे महत्त्व-पूर्ण, मुख्य : a cardinal rule/reason/sin ▶ cardinal (cardinal number भी) noun पूर्ण अंक जैसे 1, 2, 3, 4.

care¹ / केअर / noun 1 परवाह, देखभाल/देख-रेख 2 care (over sth/in doing sth) ध्यान, सावधानी 3 चिंता, परेशानी : free from care 4 चिंता का कारण : weighed down by the cares of a demanding job ■ care of sb (संक्षि c/o) (पत्रों पर पते का एक अंश) उस व्यक्ति के पते पर in the care of sb किसी की देख-रेख में take care of oneself/sb/sth 1 ध्यान रखना, सचेत रहना 2 किसी के लिए उत्तरदायी होना।

care² / केअर / verb 1 care (about sb/sth) किसी व्यक्ति/वस्तु को महत्वपूर्ण समझना; चिंता करना 2 care for sth कुछ करने की इच्छा/पसंद रखना ■ care for sb किसी की देखभाल करना (विशेषतः वृद्ध या अस्वस्थ व्यक्ति की) ▶ caring / 'केअरिड् / adj दूसरों के प्रति चिंता और प्यार दिखाते हुए।

career / क'रिअर / noun 1 जीवन में प्रगति प्रदान करने वाली आजीविका, पेशा : a career in accountancy/journalism 2 जीविका और वृत्ति में बिताया समय ▶ careerist / क'रिअरिस्ट / noun (अक्सर अपमा) व्यक्ति जिसका मुख्य उद्देश्य अपनी आजीविका में कैसे भी प्रगति करना हो।

careful / 'केअरफुल् / adj सावधान, भली-भाँति सोचा हुआ।

careless / 'केअरलस् / adj लापरवाह, बिना अच्छी तरह समझे-बूझे।

caress / क'रेस् / noun प्रेमपूर्ण स्पर्श, दुलार या चुंबन ▶ caress verb प्यार से स्पर्श करना/दुलराना/चूमना।

caretaker / 'केअर्टेकर / noun रखवाला (जब मकान-जायदाद का मालिक दूर हो)।

cargo / 'कार्गो / noun (pl cargoes; US cargos) जहाज़ या हवाई जहाज़ द्वारा ढोया जाने वाला माल : a cargo ship.

caricature / 'कैरिकचुअर / noun व्यंग्य-चित्र; व्यंग्यचित्रकला ▶ caricature verb व्यंग्यचित्र बनाना caricaturist noun.

carnage / 'कार्निज् / noun नरसंहार, सामूहिक हत्याकांड : a scene of carnage.

carnival / 'कार्निवल् / noun आनंदोत्सव, जनोत्सव : a carnival atmosphere.

carnivore / 'कार्निवॉर् / noun मांसभक्षी जानवर ▶ carnivorous / कार्'निव्रस् / adj (जानवर) मांसाहारी।

carol / 'कैरल् / noun भजन, (विशेषतः क्रिसमस के अवसर पर) आनंदगान ▶ carol verb (-ll-; US -l-) 1 खुशी में गाना 2 क्रिसमस में भजन गाना : We often go carolling at Christmas.

carpenter / 'कार्पन्टर / noun बढ़ई ▶ carpentry noun बढ़ईगिरी, काष्ठकला।

carpet / 'कार्पिट् / noun 1 क़ालीन, ग़ालीचा, दरी 2 ज़मीन पर किसी चीज़ की मोटी तह : a carpet of leaves/moss/snow.

carriage / 'कैरिज् / noun 1 (coach भी) (US car) (रेल का) सवारी डिब्बा 2 (coach भी) गाड़ी, विशेषतः चार पहियों की घोड़ों द्वारा चलने वाली 3 वहन, माल ढुलाई; ढोने, ले जाने का किराया/परिवहन व्यय 4 मशीन का चल भाग : a typewriter carriage.

carrier / 'कैरिअर / noun 1 सामान ले जाने वाला व्यक्ति/वस्तु या कंपनी 2 साइकिल आदि के पीछे सामान ले जाने के लिए लगा कैरियर 3 वह व्यक्ति अथवा अन्य प्राणी जो स्वयं प्रभावित हुए बिना कोई बीमारी औरों को दे देता है : Mosquitoes are carriers of malaria.

carrot / 'कैरट् / noun 1 गाजर 2 किसी

को कुछ करने को ललचाने के लिए प्रस्तुत पारितोषिक या वायदा : *hold out/offer a carrot to sb* ■ **the carrot and the stick** किसी से मेहनत कराने के लिए पारितोषिक की आशा और कड़े दंड की धमकी दोनों अपनाना।

carry / कैरि / *verb* (*pt, pp* **carried**) 1 ढोना, वहन करना, (एक स्थान से दूसरे स्थान तक) ले जाना 2 (पाइप, तार आदि का) पानी, बिजली आदि पहुँचाना : *a pipeline carrying oil* 3 अपने पास रखना : *Police in many countries carry guns.* 4 (व्यक्ति, कीट-पतंग आदि) बीमारी फैलाने वाला होना 5 (अप्रय औप) गर्भवती होना : *She was carrying twins.* 6 **carry oneself** विशिष्ट तरीक़े की चाल-ढाल रखना : *She carries herself well.* 7 (आवाज़ों का) दूर तक सुनाई पड़ सकना ■ **carry coals to Newcastle** उलटे बांस बरेली को **carry on** (अनौप) तर्क-वितर्क करना **carry sth out** 1 किसी कार्य को करना (पूर्ण रूप से) 2 प्रयोग करना : *carry out an experiment* 3 कार्यान्वित करना **carry sb through (sth)** कष्टों में किसी की मदद करना **carry sth through** सफलतापूर्वक काम पूरा कर लेना।

cart / कार्ट / *noun* ठेला (दो या चार पहियों की भारवाहक गाड़ी) ; ताँगा : *a horse and a cart* ■ **put the cart before the horse** ग़लत क्रम में रखना, क्रम उलट देना ▶ **cart** *verb* 1 ठेले में/पर ले जाना 2 (अनौप) हाथों से ढोना **carter** *noun* ताँगे वाला/गाड़ी वाला।

cartage / कार्टिज़ / *noun* ढुलाई, किराया।

cartilage / कार्टिलिज़ / *noun* कोमलास्थि, कड़ी लचीली हड्डी।

cartographer / कार् टॉग्रफ़र् / *noun* नक़्शानवीस, मानचित्र और सारणी बनाने वाला।

carton / कार्टन् / *noun* दफ़्ती/गत्ते का डिब्बा।

cartoon / कार्टून् / *noun* 1 (समसामयिक, विशेषत: राजनीतिक, गतिविधि को लेकर) हास्यचित्र, व्यंग्यचित्र 2 (**animated cartoon** भी) अनेक चित्रों की फोटो खींचकर बनाई गई सिनेमा फ़िल्म : *a Walt Disney cartoon* 3 पेंटिंग के लिए प्राथमिक स्केच ▶ **cartoonist** *noun*.

cartridge / कार्ट्रिज़ / *noun* 1 (*US* **shell**) कारतूस, गोली 2 रिकॉर्ड-प्लेअर का वह भाग जिसमें सूई होती है 3 टेप-रिकॉर्डर, कैमरा या पेन आदि के लिए टेप, फ़िल्म या स्याही भरा छोटा-सा डिब्बा।

carve / कार्व् / *verb* 1 **carve (in sth);** **carve sth (out of/from/of/in sth)** काटकर कलाकृति बनाना 2 **carve sth (for sb)** पके मांस को टुकड़ों में काटना : *Please carve me another slice.* ■ **carve sth out (for oneself)** मेहनत से अपना भविष्य बनाना/नाम कमाना ▶ **carver** *noun* 1 मूर्तिकार 2 चाकू **carving** *noun* काटने से बनी कलाकृति, नक़्क़ाशी।

cascade / कैस्केड् / *noun* 1 झरना, जल- प्रपात 2 प्रपात जैसी लगने वाली वस्तु ▶ **cascade** *verb* जलप्रपात होना, (जल- प्रपात की तरह) गिरना।

case[1] / केस / *noun* 1 घटना; उदाहरण 2 **the case** [*sing*] मामला, विषय, परि- स्थिति-विशेष 3 (कचहरी में विचार्य) प्रश्न, समस्या, मुक़दमा 4 रोग; रोगी, मरीज़ : *a case of typhoid* 5 (व्या) कारक : *the nominative/accusative case* ■ **in any case** जो भी हो, किसी भी सूरत में ■ **in that case** उस सूरत/हालत में, अगर ऐसा हो तो ▶ **case history** *noun* व्यक्तिवृत्त **case study** *noun* व्यक्ति/जाति के विकास का विस्तृत अध्ययन।

case[2] / केस / *noun* 1 छोटा बक्सा, संदूक़ची, डिब्बा 2 सूटकेस।

cash / कैश् / *noun* रोकड़, नक़द धन/संपत्ति ■ **cash down** तुरंत नक़द चुकता/हिसाब ▶ **cash** *verb* **cash sth (for sb)** नक़द लेना या देना : *cash a cheque* ■ **cash in**

(on sth) लाभ उठाना/फ़ायदा उठाना ▸ **cash book** noun रोकड़ बही **cash box** noun नक़दी रखने का डिब्बा **cash crop** noun नक़दी फ़सल **cash memo** noun नक़द बिक्री की रसीद **cash register** noun नक़दी का हिसाब रखने की मशीन।

cashier / कै'शिअर् / noun ख़ज़ानची, रोकड़िया।

cashew / 'कैशू, कै'शू / noun (**cashew nut** भी) काजू।

casket / 'कास्किट् / noun 1 आभूषण रत्न आदि की पेटी, मंजूषा 2 (US) शवपेटिका।

casserole / 'कैसरोल् / noun तंदूर-ओवेन में रखे जाने वाला हाँडीनुमा बरतन, हँडिया, ढक्कनदार बर्तन।

cassette / क'सेट् / noun कैसेट : a cassette recorder ○ a video cassette.

cast[1] / कास्ट्; US कैस्ट् / verb (pt, pp **cast**) 1 (दिशा विशेष की ओर) मोड़ना, घुमाना 2 (औप) डालना, ज़ोर से फेंकना : cast a stone 3 (जाल) फेंकना 4 गिरने/उतरने देना : Snakes cast their skins. 5 पिघली हुई धातु साँचे में गिराना/डालना; ढालना : a statue cast in bronze 6 फ़िल्म/नाटक के लिए अभिनेता चुनना ■ **cast one's vote** मतदान करना ▸ **castaway** noun डूबे हुए जहाज़ से बचकर अपरिचित भूमि पर पहुँचा हुआ व्यक्ति **casting** noun 1 भूमिका के लिए अभिनेता चुनने की प्रक्रिया 2 मशीन का ढला हुआ अंग **cast iron** noun ढलवाँ लोहा **cast-off** adj (कपड़े) पुराने, अब काम में न आने वाले।

cast[2] / कास्ट्; US कैस्ट् / noun 1 फ़िल्म/नाटक के समस्त कलाकार : a play with a distinguished cast 2 साँचे में ढाली हुई वस्तु; साँचा 3 फेंकाव : the cast of the dice 4 [sing] (औप) किसी चीज़ का प्रकार, रुझान : He has an unusual cast of mind.

caste / कास्ट्; US कैस्ट् / noun 1 (हिंदुओं में) जाति-व्यवस्था : the caste system 2 वर्ण-व्यवस्था; विशिष्ट सामाजिक वर्ग जो अपने को अलग बनाए रखे।

castle / 'कास्ल्; US 'कैसल् / noun 1 दुर्ग, गढ़ 2 (**rook** भी) (शतरंज में) हाथी, कश्ती ■ (build) **castles in the air/in Spain** हवाई क़िले बनाना, दिवास्वप्न देखना।

castor (**caster** भी) / 'कास्टर्; US 'कैस्टर् / noun खिसकाने के लिए भारी मेज़/कुरसी के नीचे लगे पहिये।

castor oil / कास्टर् 'ऑइल्; US 'कैस्टर् ऑइल् / noun अरंडी का तेल ▸ **castor-seed** noun अरंडी/एरंड का बीज।

castrate / कै'स्ट्रेट्; US 'कैस्ट्रेट् / verb बधिया करना : A bullock is a castrated bull. ▸ **castration** noun.

casual / 'कैशुअल् / adj 1 आकस्मिक : a casual encounter/meeting 2 असावधान; बिना सोचे या बिना उद्देश्य के : a casual remark/invitation 3 अनियमित, अनियत (न कि निरंतर) : a casual labourer ▸ **casually** adv संयोग से, यों ही **casualness** noun **casuals** noun [pl] अनौपचारिक पहनावा (कपड़े, जूते आदि)।

casualty / 'कैशुअल्टि / noun (pl **casualties**) 1 दुर्घटना या युद्ध में घायल या मृत व्यक्ति : Heavy casualties were reported in the fighting. 2 दुर्घटना में नष्ट या खोई गई वस्तु 3 (**casualty ward, casualty department,** US **emergency room** भी) अस्पताल का वह भाग जहाँ गंभीर रूप से घायल व्यक्तियों को तुरंत चिकित्सा के लिए लाया जाता है।

cat / कैट् / noun 1 बिल्ली 2 बिल्ली जाति के वन्य प्राणी जैसे बाघ, शेर, तेंदुआ ■ **curiosity killed the cat** (कहा) अधिक उत्सुकता हानिकर होती है **let the cat out of the bag** किसी रहस्य को अनजाने में या भूल से प्रकट कर देना **play cat and mouse** लगातार रुख बदलकर किसी के साथ क्रूर खेल खेलना **rain cats and dogs**

अतिवृष्टि/मूसलाधार बारिश होना ▸ **cat's eye** *noun* लहसुनिया (एक प्रकार का रत्न) **Cat's-eye** *noun* (*ट्रेडमार्क*) रात में चमकने वाले सड़क पर लगे शीशे **cat-nap** *noun* झपकी।

catalogue (*US* **catalog** भी) / 'कैट-लॉग् / *noun* (स्थान, नाम, सामान आदि का) सूची-पत्र : *a library catalogue* ○ *an exhibition catalogue* ▸ **catalogue** *verb* सूचीबद्ध करना, सारणी बनाना।

catalyst / 'कैटलिस्ट् / *noun* 1 (रासाय-निक) उत्प्रेरक 2 परिवर्तन का कारण बनने वाला व्यक्ति अथवा वस्तु।

cataract / 'कैटरैक्ट् / *noun* 1 बड़ा जल-प्रपात 2 (*चिकि*) मोतिया-बिंद (आँखों की एक बीमारी) ।

catarrh / क'टार् / *noun* जुकाम, नज़ला।

catastrophe / क'टैस्ट्रफ़ि / *noun* तबाही, विभीषिका (जैसे बाढ़, भूचाल, आग) ▸ **catastrophic** / ˌकैट'स्ट्रॉफ़िक् / *adj* **catastrophically** *adv.*

catch¹ / कैच् / *verb* (*pt, pp* **caught** / कॉट् /) 1 (पकड़कर) रोकना; पकड़ना 2 किसी को कुछ करते समय अचानक आकर पकड़ना : *I caught a boy stealing apples from the garden.* 3 समय पर पहुँचना, मिल सकना : *to catch a train/ the post* 4 बीमारी लगना/छूत लगना : *catch flu/pneumonia* 5 (क्रिकेट में) बल्लेबाज़ द्वारा खेली गेंद को ज़मीन पर गिरने से पहले पकड़ना ∎ **catch on (with sb)** (*अनौप*) लोकप्रिय या फ़ैशनेबल हो जाना **catch one's breath** (भय आदि के कारण) साँस रोकना **catch sb red-handed** रँगे हाथों पकड़ना **catch sb's attention/eye** ध्यान आकर्षित करना **catch/take sb's fancy** पसंद आ जाना **catch up on sth** 1 पहले न कर पाने की स्थिति में किसी कार्य में अधिक समय लगाना 2 बीती घटनाओं की जानकारी लेना **catch up (with sb)**; **catch sb up** जा पकड़ना/ बराबर के चरण तक पहुँच जाना ▸ **catchy**

adj (**-ier, -lest**) (कोई लय) मनोहर और सरल।

catch² / कैच् / *noun* 1 (गेंद आदि) पकड़ने की प्रक्रिया, पकड़ : *a difficult catch* 2 पकड़ी हुई वस्तु (की मात्रा) : *a huge catch of fish* 3 (ताले का) वह पुरज़ा जो बंद करता है; (दरवाज़े की) चिटखनी; (बंदूक का) घोड़ा, खटका 4 कुछ गुप्त समस्या अथवा असुविधा : *The house is very cheap. There must be a catch somewhere.* ▸ **catch-22** *noun* (*अप*) कुचक्र।

categorical / ˌकैट'गॉरिक्ल् / *adj* (वक्तव्य) बिना शर्त का, सुस्पष्ट, निश्चित रूप से ▸ **categorically** *adv.*

category / 'कैटगरि; *US* 'कैटगॉरि / *noun* (*pl* **categories**) संवर्ग/वर्ग; विभाजन ▸ **categorize, -ise** / 'कैटगराइज़् / *verb* वर्ग/संवर्ग में रखना; विभाजित करना।

cater / 'केटर् / *verb* 1 **cater (for sth/ sb)** (भोजन, मनोरंजन, सेवाओं आदि का) प्रबंध करना 2 **cater for sb/sth** आवश्य-कता की वस्तु उपलब्ध कराना : *TV must cater for many different tastes.* 3 **cater to sth** किसी विशिष्ट माँग की पूर्ति का प्रयास करना ▸ **caterer** *noun* खान-पान का प्रबंधकर्ता **catering** *noun.*

caterpillar / 'कैटरपिलर् / *noun* सूँडी, इल्ली ▸ **Caterpillar tractor** *noun* (*ट्रेडमार्क*) दाँतों वाले पहियों के ऊपर घूमने वाली पट्टी वाला विशाल वाहन।

catgut / 'कैटगट् / (**gut** भी) *noun* वाय-लिन, गिटार, टेनिस रैकेट आदि की ताँत।

cathedral / क'श्रीड्रल् / *noun* (बिशप का) मुख्य चर्च/बड़ा गिरजा।

cathode / 'कैथ़ोड् / *noun* (तक) 1 बैटरी की बिंदु जहाँ से विद्युत बाहर गुज़रती है 2 ऋणाग्र, कैथोड।

Catholic / 'कैथ़लिक् / *adj* 1 (Roman Catholic भी) रोम का चर्च 2 (catholic भी) सार्वभौम या संपूर्ण ईसाई चर्च ▸ **Catho-lic** *noun* (*संक्षि* Cath) रोमन कैथलिक चर्च का सदस्य **Catholicism** *noun.*

catholic / 'कैथ्लिक् / *adj* उदार, विश्व-जनीन : *have catholic tastes/interests.*

cattle / 'कैट्ल् / *noun* [*pl*] गाय-बैल, मवेशी/ढोर।

cauldron (**caldron** भी) / 'कॉल्ड्रन् / *noun* कड़ाहा, बड़ी कड़ाही।

cauliflower / 'कॉलिफ़्लाउअर् / *noun* फूलगोभी।

cause / कॉज़् / *noun* 1 कारण; हेतु, निमित्त 2 उद्देश्य, सिद्धांत, आंदोलन 3 *(क़ानून)* दावा, पक्ष : *pleading one's cause* ▸ **cause** *verb* **cause sth (for sb)** उत्पन्न करना; कारण/निमित्त बनना : *Smoking can cause lung cancer.*

causeway / 'कॉज़्वे / *noun* गीली भूमि या जलमय क्षेत्र के आर-पार ऊँचा उठा हुआ रास्ता।

caustic / 'कास्टिक् / *adj* 1 दाहक, क्षारक 2 (टिप्पणी आदि) तीखी, व्यंग्यात्मक : *caustic remarks* ▸ **caustically** *adv.*

caution / 'कॉश्न् / *noun* 1 सतर्कता, साव-धानी : *Proceed with caution.* 2 चेता-वनी (विशेषत: भविष्य के लिए) : *let sb off with a caution* ▸ **caution** *verb* **caution (sb) against sth** सावधान/सतर्क होने को कहना; किसी बात के विरुद्ध सावधान करना : *We were cautioned not to drive too fast.* **cautionary** *adj.*

cautious / 'कॉशस् / *adj* सावधान/सतर्क ▸ **cautiously** *adv* **cautiousness** *noun.*

cavalry / 'कैव्ल्रि / *noun* घुड़सवार सेना।

cave / केव् / *noun* गुफा, कंदर ▸ **cave** *verb* ■ **cave in** अंदर गिर जाना/धँस जाना।

cavern / 'कैवर्न् / *noun* बड़ी, अँधेरी गुफा।

cavity / 'कैविटि / *noun* (*pl* **cavities**) बड़ा छेद/खोखला स्थान; दाँत में छिद्र या खोखला स्थान, गुहिका।

CD / सी 'डी / *abbr* (**compact disc** का

संक्षिप्त रूप) कॉम्पैक्ट डिस्क : *a CD player.*

cease / सीस् / *verb* (औप) बंद होना/करना; समाप्त होना/करना : *Hostilities between the two sides ceased at midnight.* ▸ **cease** *noun* ■ **without cease** बेअंत, बिना रुके ▸ **cease-fire** *noun* दो शत्रुओं के बीच अस्थायी शांति-काल **ceaseless** *adj* निरंतर/लगातार **ceaselessly** *adv.*

cedar / 'सीडर् / *noun* देवदार वृक्ष; (**cedar wood** / 'सीडर्वुड् / भी) देवदार की लकड़ी।

cede / सीड् / *verb* **cede sth (to sb)** (औप) सौंपना; (अधिकार, संपत्ति आदि) अक्सर अनिच्छा से अर्पण करना : *cede territory to a neighbouring state.*

ceiling / 'सीलिङ् / *noun* 1 छत का भीतरी भाग 2 सर्वाधिक सीमा : *The government has set a wages and prices ceiling of 5%.*

celebrate / 'सेलिब्रेट् / *verb* (किसी घटना या उत्सव पर) उत्सव मनाना, समारोह करना : *celebrate Christmas/sb's birthday/a wedding anniversary* ▸ **celebrated** *adj* प्रसिद्ध, प्रख्यात **celebration** / सेलि'ब्रेश्न् / *noun* समारोह, उत्सव **celebrity** / स'लेब्रटि / *noun* (*pl* **celebrities**) प्रख्यात व्यक्ति।

celestial / स'लेस्टिअल् / *adj* 1 खगोल विषयक : *celestial bodies* 2 स्वर्गिक : (अलं) *the celestial beauty of her voice.*

celibate / 'सेलिबट् / *adj* अविवाहित (धार्मिक कारणों से) ▸ **celibacy** / 'सेलि-बसि / *noun* अविवाहित रहने की स्थिति, ब्रह्मचर्य **celibate** *noun* अविवाहित व्यक्ति, ब्रह्मचारी।

cell / सेल् / *noun* 1 (प्राय: जेल और मठों में) एक व्यक्ति के रहने लायक कोठरी 2 बड़ी संरचना का एक छोटा एकक : *honeycomb cells* 3 (बैटरी का) सेल, विद्युत उत्पादन की रासायनिक/भौतिक युक्ति

4 (चेतनप्राणी की इकाई-सत्ता) कोशिका/कोशाणु : red blood cells 5 राजनीतिक गतिविधि के केंद्र बने व्यक्तियों का लघु समूह : a terrorist cell.

cellar / 'सेलर / noun 1 (सामग्री जमा करके रखने के लिए) तहख़ाना 2 शराब का तहख़ाना।

Cellophane / 'सेलफ़ेन/ noun (ट्रेडमार्क) पारदर्शी काग़ज़, सेलोफ़ेन : a Cellophane packet.

cellular / 'सेल्यलर/ adj 1 कोशिका निर्मित 2 (कपड़े आदि) ढीले बुने हुए 3 रेडियो तरंगों से काम करने वाला फ़ोन : cellular phone.

Celsius / 'सेल्सिअस/ (centigrade भी) adj (संक्षि C) थर्मामीटर की वह मापनी जिसमें पानी का हिमांक 0° और क्वथनांक 100° पर होता है।

cement / सि'मेन्ट/ noun 1 (मकान आदि बनाने में काम आने वाला) सीमेंट 2 कोई ऐसा चूर्ण जो छेद भरने (जैसे दाँत भरने) या जोड़ने के काम आता हो ▶ cement verb 1 cement sth (over); cement (over) sth सीमेंट लगाना या भरना 2 दृढ़ करना; स्थापित करना : cement a friendship.

cemetery / 'सेमिट्रि/ noun (pl cemeteries) क़ब्रिस्तान।

censor / 'सेन्सर/ noun सेंसर (फ़िल्म, पुस्तक आदि का निरीक्षण-अधिकारी जो अनुचित अंश को प्रकाशन के पहले काट देता है) ▶ censor verb सेंसर के लिए निरीक्षण करना और काटना : the censored version of a film censorship noun सेंसर का कार्य या नीतियाँ।

censure / 'सेन्शर/ verb censure sb (for sth) (औप) नापसंदगी प्रकट करने के लिए कड़ी निंदा करना : Two MPs were censured by the Speaker. ▶ censure noun निंदा, घोर भर्त्सना।

census / 'सेन्सस/ noun (pl censuses) जनगणना, मर्दुमशुमारी।

cent / सेन्ट/ noun डालर, फ़्रैंक आदि मुद्राओं का सौवाँ भाग, शतांश; (संक्षि c) इतनी क़ीमत का एक सिक्का।

centaur / 'सेन्टॉर/ noun (प्राचीन यूनानी कहानियों में) आधा आदमी आधा घोड़ा, (संस्कृत साहित्य में) किन्नर।

centenary / सेन'टीनरि / (US centennial भी) noun (pl centenaries) शताब्दी (समारोह) : centenary year.

centigrade / 'सेन्टिग्रेड / adj = Celsius.

centimetre (US centimeter) / 'सेन्टिमीटर / noun (संक्षि cm) मीटर का शतांश।

centipede / 'सेन्टिपीड / noun कनखजूरा (एक बहुत पैर वाला रेंगने वाला कीड़ा)।

central / 'सेन्ट्रल / adj 1 केंद्रीय 2 मुख्य, सर्वाधिक महत्त्वपूर्ण 3 मुख्य सत्ता या नियंत्रण प्राप्त ▶ central heating noun पूरे भवन को एक ही स्थान से गरम करने की व्यवस्था
centralize, -ise / 'सेन्ट्रलाइज़/ verb केंद्र में लाना; केंद्र के नियंत्रण में आना/रखना।

centre (US center) / 'सेन्टर / noun 1 मध्य भाग या बिंदु, केंद्र : the centre of a circle 2 ध्यान-आकर्षण का केंद्र (व्यक्ति/वस्तु) 3 प्रशासनिक केंद्र : a centre of power 4 ऐसा स्थान जहाँ काफ़ी गतिविधियाँ या सुविधाएँ एकत्रित हों : a centre of industry/commerce ▶ centre verb 1 केंद्र में लाना या रखना 2 centre (around/on sth) केंद्र मानना 3 (फ़ुटबाल, हॉकी में) केंद्र की ओर किक मारना।

century / 'सेन्चरि / noun (pl centuries) 1 सौ साल की अवधि 2 शताब्दी, सदी : the 20th century 3 शतक (जैसे क्रिकेट में 100 रन)।

ceramic / स'रैमिक / adj मिट्टी से बनाकर आग में पकाया हुआ : ceramic tiles/bowls/bricks ▶ ceramic noun मिट्टी के बरतन ceramics noun मिट्टी से सामान या कलाकृति बनाने की कला, मृत्तिकाशिल्प।

cereal / 'सिअरिअल / noun 1 अनाज, अन्न (गेहूँ, चावल आदि) 2 अन्न से बने खाद्य-पदार्थ : breakfast cereals.

cerebral / 'सेरेब्रल् / *adj* मस्तिष्क (ब्रेन) से संबंधित।

ceremonial /,सेरि'मोनिअल्/ *adj* औपचारिक विधान।

ceremony / 'सेरमनि / *noun* (*pl* **ceremonies**) (विवाह, उद्घाटन आदि पर किया जाने वाला) समारोह, अनुष्ठान : *marriage/awards ceremony* ■ **stand on ceremony** शिष्टाचार का बहुत अधिक ध्यान रखना ▸ **ceremonious** *adj* अत्यधिक औपचारिक व्यवहार या कार्य **ceremoniously** *adv*.

certain / 'सर्टन् / *adj* 1 **certain** (that...); **certain** (to do sth) असंदिग्ध, पक्का 2 **certain** (of/about sth; **certain that...**) निश्चित रूप से, संदेह न रखते हुए: *I am not certain (about) what she wants.* 3 वर्णित किंतु अज्ञात : *A certain Mr Bhatt telephoned while you were out.* ■ **for certain** निस्संदेह **make certain (that...)** निश्चित होने के लिए (पूछना) ▸ **certainly** *adv* निस्संदेह, निश्चित रूप से **certainty** / 'सर्टन्टि / *noun* 1 निश्चय 2 निश्चित (तथ्य, वस्तु)।

certificate / सर्'टिफ़िकट् / *noun* लिखित या मुद्रित प्रमाण-पत्र : *marriage/examination certificate* ▸ **certificated** *adj* प्रमाण-पत्र पाने के कारण कुछ करने के लिए अधिकृत : *a certificated teacher/ consultant.*

certify / 'सर्टिफ़ाइ / *verb* (*pt, pp* **certified**) **certify sb/sth as sth** (प्रमाण-पत्र देकर) प्रमाणित करना कि यह सही है, क़ानूनी ढंग से घोषित करना ▸ **certification** *noun* प्रमाणीकरण।

cessation / से'सेश्न् / *noun* (औप) समाप्ति, विराम : *The bombardment continued without cessation.*

chaff / चाफ़्; *US* चैफ़ / *noun* 1 भूसी, चोकर 2 भूसा, कुट्टी ■ **separate the wheat from the chaff** अयोग्य व्यक्तियों/ वस्तुओं से योग्य व्यक्तियों/वस्तुओं को अलग करना।

chagrin / 'शैग्रिन् / *noun* (ग़लती करने पर) नाराज़गी, झेंप, शरमिंदगी : *Much to his chagrin, he came last in the race.*

chain / चेन् / *noun* 1 ज़ंजीर, शृंखला 2 विशेष प्रयोजन के लिए प्रयुक्त ज़ंजीर : *a bicycle chain* 3 संबद्ध वस्तुओं या घटनाओं आदि का सिलसिला : *a chain of events/circumstances* 4 एक ही कंपनी के होटलों या दुकानों का समूह ▸ **chain** *verb* **chain sb/sth (to sb/sth); chain sb/sth (up)** ज़ंजीर से बाँधना **chain reaction** *noun* 1 (तक) ऐसी रासायनिक प्रक्रिया जब उत्पाद स्वयं नए उत्पाद बनाते जाते हैं 2 ऐसी घटनाओं का सिलसिला जिसमें हर घटना नई घटना को जन्म देती जाती है **chain-smoke** *verb* एक के बाद एक सिगरेट या सिगार पीना **chain-smoker** *noun* **chain-store** *noun* ऐसा स्टोर जिसकी बहुत-सी शाखाएँ हों।

chair / चेअर् / *noun* 1 कुरसी 2 (विश्वविद्यालय में प्रोफ़ेसर का) पद 3 **the chair** (किसी सभा का) सभापति या अध्यक्ष : *She takes the chair in all our meetings.* ▸ **chair** *verb* सभापति/अध्यक्ष का कार्य करना।

chairman / 'चेअरमन् / *noun* (*pl* **chairmen**; *fem* **chairwoman**, *pl* **chairwomen**) सभापति, अध्यक्ष (या अध्यक्षा)।

chairperson / 'चेअरपर्सन् / *noun* (*pl* **chairpersons**) अध्यक्ष/अध्यक्षा।

chalk / चॉक् / *noun* 1 खड़िया, चाक मिट्टी 2 चाक स्टिक ▸ **chalk** *verb* **chalk sth (up) (on sth)** चाक से लिखना या चित्र बनाना ■ **chalk sth out** रूपरेखा प्रस्तुत करना।

challenge[1] / 'चैलिन्ज् / *noun* 1 **challenge (to sb) (to do sth)** (किसी खेल या दौड़ के लिए) चुनौती 2 कोई कठिन कार्य जिससे किसी की योग्यता की परख होती है

3 किसी संतरी (पहरेदार) द्वारा आते हुए व्यक्तियों को ललकारना और नाम-पता पूछना।

challenge² / 'चैलिन्ज् / *verb* **challenge sb (to sth)** चुनौती देना : *challenge sb to a game of tennis* ▸ **challenging** *adj* योग्यता परखने वाली (समस्याएँ आदि), चुनौती देने वाली।

chamber / 'चेम्बर / *noun* 1 (पूर्व में) कमरा, शयनकक्ष 2 (यौगिकों में) कोई विशिष्ट प्रकार का कमरा : *a torture/gas/burial chamber* 3 चेंबर, (नियम, क़ानून आदि बनाने की समिति) सदन : *the Upper/Lower Chamber* 4 **chambers** [*pl*] न्यायाधीश का कमरा जहाँ मामलों की सुनवाई हो सकती है ▸ **Chamber of Commerce** *noun* वाणिज्य मंडल, व्यापार बढ़ाने के लिए व्यापारियों की संगठित संस्था।

chambermaid / 'चेम्बरमेड् / (होटल में) शयनकक्ष ठीक-ठाक रखने वाली सेविका।

chameleon / क 'मीलिअन् / *noun* 1 गिरगिट 2 (*अपमा*) अवसर आने पर (लाभ उठाने के लिए) अपना व्यवहार या मत बदलने वाला व्यक्ति।

champion / 'चैम्पिअन् / *noun* 1 (*अनौप* **champ** भी) सर्वश्रेष्ठ विजेता, चैंपियन 2 पक्का हिमायती, घोर समर्थक : *a champion of the poor/of women's rights* ▸ **champion** *verb* समर्थन करना **championship** *noun* 1 (प्राय: *pl*) विजेता चुनने की स्पर्धा 2 चैंपियन का स्थान।

chance¹ / चान्स्; *US* चैन्स् / *noun* 1 **chance of (doing) sth/that...** संभावना 2 **chance (of doing sth/to do sth)** निश्चित सफलता का अवसर/मौका : *This is your big chance.* 3 भाग्य : *Chance plays a big part in many board games.* 4 संयोग; आकस्मिक घटना ■ **take a chance** जानबूझकर कुछ (दाँव वाला/जोखिम वाला काम) करना **take one's chances** अपने अवसरों का सदुपयोग करना।

chance² / चान्स्; *US* चैन्स् / *verb*

1 (*अनौप*) दाँव पर रखना 2 (*औप*) संयोग से होना।

chancellor / 'चान्सलर; *US* 'चैन्सलर् / *noun* 1 (कुछ देशों, जैसे जर्मनी, में) राज्य का प्रधानमंत्री या प्रमुख 2 (कुछ विश्व-विद्यालयों में) प्रमुख अधिकारी, कुलाधिपति 3 वरिष्ठ न्यायाधीश : *Lord Chancellor.*
▸ **Chancellor of the Exchequer** *noun* (ब्रिटेन में) मुख्य वित्त मंत्री।

chandelier / शैन्ड 'लिअर् / *noun* छत से लटके झाड़-फ़ानूस।

change¹ / चेन्ज् / *verb* 1 बदलना, परि-वर्तन करना 2 **change sb/sth (for sb/sth); change sth (to sth)** किसी व्यक्ति/वस्तु के बदले दूसरे को प्रयोग में लाना 3 **change sth (with sb)** (दो व्यक्तियों की) आपस में जगह आदि बदलना : *Can I change seats with you?* 4 **change sth (for/into sth)** (रुपया) भुनाना या तुड़ाना : *Can you change a hundred rupee note?* ○ *I need to change my rupees into dollars.* ■ **change hands** मालिक बदलना **change one's/sb's mind** इरादा बदलना; दूसरा मत मान लेना **change the subject** विषय बदल लेना ▸ **changeable** *adj* परिवर्तन योग्य **change-over** *noun* एक तंत्र या स्थिति से दूसरी में बदलना।

change² / चेन्ज् / *noun* 1 **change (into sth)** परिवर्तन, बदलाव : *There has been a change in the programme.* 2 दूसरे के बदले ली या प्रयुक्त कोई वस्तु 3 रेज़गारी, छुट्टा : *I don't have any small change.* ▸ **changeless** *adj* अपरिवर्तनीय।

channel / 'चैन्ल् / *noun* 1 दो समुद्रों को जोड़ने वाला जलमार्ग या नहर, नदी तल, जलमार्ग 2 प्रसारण के लिए प्रयुक्त तरंग दैर्घ्य : *satellite channels* 3 विचारों, सूचनाओं आदि के आदान-प्रदान का मार्ग : *Your complaint must be made through the proper channels.*

▸ **channel** *verb* (-II-; *US* -I- भी) 1 मार्ग से कुछ ले जाना/प्रवाहित करना 2 मार्ग बनाना।

chant / चान्ट् ; *US* चैन्ट् / *noun* 1 बार-बार एक ही लय में गाए गए या चिल्लाए गए शब्द 2 राग जिसमें अनेक धार्मिक गीत गाए जाते हैं : *a Buddhist chant* ▸ **chant** *verb* 1 एक ही लय-ताल में बार-बार गाना/ चिल्लाना 2 राग से धार्मिक गीत या प्रार्थना गाना।

chaos / 'केऑस् / *noun* पूर्ण अव्यवस्था/ अस्तव्यस्तता; संभ्रांति/उलझन ▸ **chaotic** *adj.*

chap¹ / चैप् / *verb* (-pp-) 1 खाल का फटना या चिटकना : *My skin soon chaps in cold weather.* 2 (मौसम या हवा से) खाल का फटना ▸ **chap** *noun* त्वचा की फटन।

chap² / चैप् / *noun* (अनौप) आदमी, लड़का : *He's a nice chap.*

chapel / 'चैपल् / *noun* 1 ईसाइयों का पूजा स्थल; (घरों, स्कूलों, जेलों आदि में) प्रार्थनालय 2 चर्च में व्यक्तिगत पूजन के लिए बना छोटा स्थान 3 ईसाई चर्च की सदस्यता-रहित लोगों के लिए पूजा स्थल : *a Methodist chapel.*

chaperon (chaperone भी) / 'शैपरोन् / *noun* (पूर्व में) संरक्षिका, विवाहित और प्रौढ़ा स्त्री जो कुमारी कन्या के साथ पार्टी आदि में संरक्षिका के रूप में जाती है ▸ **chaperon (chaperone** भी) *verb* संरक्षिका का कार्य करना।

chaplain / 'चैपलिन् / *noun* सेना से संलग्न पादरी या व्यक्तिगत चैपल का पादरी ▸ **chaplaincy** *noun.*

chapter / 'चैप्टर् / *noun* 1 (*संक्षि* ch, chap) (किसी पुस्तक का) अध्याय 2 किसी व्यक्ति के जीवन का अथवा इतिहास का एक काल : *the most glorious chapter in our country's history* 3 (विशेषतः *US*) किसी क्लब या सभा की स्थानीय शाखा।

char¹ / चार् / *verb* (-rr-) झुलसना/झुलसाना;

जलकर कोयला होना : *the charred remains of the bonfire.*

char² / चार् / *noun* घंटेवार या दैनिक मज़दूरी पर छोटे-मोटे काम करने वाला व्यक्ति ▸ **char** *verb* (-rr-) ऐसा काम करना **charwoman** *noun.*

character / 'कैरक्टर् / *noun* 1 चरित्र; नैतिक बल; विशिष्ट लक्षण 2 नाटक, उपन्यास आदि का पात्र 3 लेखन या मुद्रण में लिपि चिह्न : *Chinese/Greek characters* ▸ **characterless** *adj* रोचक गुण रहित, चरित्रहीन, सामान्य।

characteristic / कैरक्ट 'रिस्टिक् / *noun* विशेष लक्षण, विशेषता।

characterize, -ise / 'कैरक्टराइज़् / *verb* 1 विशिष्टता या लक्षण दिखाना 2 **characterize sb/sth (as sth)** चरित्रांकन करना 3 विशिष्ट लक्षण प्रदान करना : *His work is characterized by its imagery and humour.* 4 किसी विशेष रूप से चिह्नित करना ▸ **characterization, -isation** *noun.*

charade / श 'राड्; *US* श 'रेड् / *noun* **charades** शब्द पहेली।

charcoal / 'चार्कोल् / *noun* 1 लकड़ी का कोयला 2 कोयले का रंग।

charge¹ / चार्ज् / *noun* 1 सामान, की गई सेवा आदि की क़ीमत : *All goods are delivered free of charge.* 2 अभियोग, दोषारोपण : *arrested on a charge of murder* 3 देखरेख या निगरानी का दायित्व; नियंत्रण : *leave a child in a friend's charge* 4 धावा, (शत्रुओं पर) चढ़ाई 5 (ओप) कार्यभार : *His charge was to obtain certain information regarding this.* 6 बैटरी या अन्य पदार्थ में पाई/ डाली/भरी गई विद्युत की मात्रा ▸ **chargesheet** *noun* अभियोग-पत्र।

charge² / चार्ज् / *verb* 1 **charge sb (with sth/doing sth)** आरोप लगाना : *He was charged with murder.* 2 **charge (at) (sb/sth)** धावा बोलना, चढ़ाई

करना 3 **charge (sb/sth) for sth** मूल्य या भुगतान के रूप में माँगना : *How much do you charge for repairing shoes?* 4 बारूद या बिजली की शक्ति भरना: *charge a battery* 5 (औप) आदेश देना; कार्यभार सौंपना : *The judge charged the jury.*

chariot / 'चैरिअट् / *noun* रथ ▸ **charioteer** *noun* रथवान, सारथी।

charisma / कं'रिज़्मा / *noun* आकर्षक एवं मोहक व्यक्तित्व जिससे उत्साह एवं प्रेरणा मिलती है।

charitable / 'चैरटब्ल् / *adj* दानी, परोप-कारी, दयालु।

charity / 'चैरटि / *noun (pl* **charities)** 1 सहायतार्थ संस्था 2 दीन दुखियों की सहायता, परोपकारिता : *raise money for charity* 3 दयालुता; भ्रातृभाव ■ **charity begins at home** (कहा) व्यक्ति का प्रथम कर्तव्य अपने घर और परिवारवालों की देख-भाल करना है।

charm[1] / चार्म / *noun* 1 आकर्षण, मनो-हारित्व; आकर्षक/रोचक गुण 2 मंत्र; ताबीज़: *a charm bracelet* 3 मायाशक्ति (अच्छी या बुरी); जादू।

charm[2] / चार्म / *verb* 1 आकर्षित करना, मोहित करना 2 जादू डालना; माया से प्रभा-वित करना ▸ **charming** *adj* आकर्षक **charmless** *adj* आकर्षण रहित।

chart / चार्ट् / *noun* 1 नाविकों, विमान चालकों द्वारा प्रयुक्त समुद्र का मानचित्र 2 चार्ट, लेखा : *a weather/temperature/sales chart* ▸ **chart** *verb* चार्ट बनाना।

charter / 'चार्टर् / *noun* 1 शासक या शासन द्वारा किसी को प्रदत्त कोई कार्य करने का लिखित अधिकार-पत्र : *the power to grant university charters* 2 किसी संघ या संस्था के सिद्धांतों एवं कार्यों का लिखित दस्तावेज़; संविधान : *the charter of the United Nations* 3 किसी विशेष प्रयोजन या लोगों के लिए जहाज़, वायुयान अथवा बस को किराए पर लेना : *charter flights to Australia* ▸ **charter** *verb*

1 अधिकार-पत्र देना 2 जहाज़, हवाई जहाज़ या बस किराए पर लेना **chartered** *adj.*

chase / चेस् / *verb* 1 **chase (after) sb/sth** (क़ैद करने या भगाने के लिए) पीछा करना, खदेड़ना 2 (अनौप) कुछ पाने या जीतने की कोशिश करना 3 **chase sb (up)** कुछ सूचना प्राप्त करने या कार्य कराने के लिए किसी से पुन: संपर्क करना ▸ **chase** *noun* पीछा करने की क्रिया।

chasm / कैज़्म् / *noun* 1 गहरी खाई 2 (दो वर्गों या राष्ट्रों के विचारों, रुचियों या भावनाओं में) बड़ा अंतर : *the vast chasm separating rich and poor.*

chaste / चेस्ट् / *adj* 1 विचार, कथन और कार्य में शुद्ध/पवित्र 2 (कला शैली) साधा-रण : *chaste designs* 3 दांपत्य से बाहर यौन संबंध/किसी से भी यौन संबंध न रखते हुए ▸ **chastely** *adv.*

chasten / 'चेस्न् / *verb* दंड या ताड़ना से किसी को सुधारना : *chastened by failure.*

chastise / चै'स्टाइज़/ *verb* 1 (अप्र) कठोर दंड देना (या पीटना) 2 ग़लती के लिए कटु आलोचना करना ▸ **chastisement** *noun.*

chastity / 'चैस्टटि / *noun* शुद्धता का गुण, पवित्रता।

chat / चैट् / *noun* **chat (about sb/sth)** गपशप ▸ **chat** *verb* **(-tt-) chat (away); chat (to/with sb) (about sth/sb)** गपशप करना ▸ **chatty** *adj* **(-ier, -iest)** 1 गपशप का शौक़ीन 2 अनौपचारिक, हँसी-मज़ाक़ पसंद करने वाला।

chatter / 'चैटर् / *verb* 1 **chatter (away/on) (to sb) (about sth)** जल्दी में बेवक़ूफ़ी की बातें करना, बकवास करना : *chattering crowds of sightseers* 2 **chatter (away)** (चिड़ियों का) चहचहाना, (बंदर का) किटकिटाना; खड़खड़ाना 3 **chatter (together)** (दंड या डर से) दाँत किटकिटाना ▸ **chatter** *noun* 1 लगातार की बकवास 2 किटकिट की आवाज़ **chatterbox** *noun* बक्की व्यक्ति।

chauffeur / शोफ़र् / *noun* शोफर, निजी कार का चालक ▸ **chauffeur** *verb*.

chauvinism / शोव़िनिज़म् / *noun* 1 अंध देशभक्ति 2 (**male chauvinism** भी) *(अपमा)* कुछ पुरुषों में ऐसी धारणा कि पुरुष वर्ग स्त्री वर्ग से श्रेष्ठ है ▸ **chauvinist** *noun*, *adj* **chauvinistic** *adj* **chauvinistically** *adv*.

cheap / चीप् / *adj* (**-er, -est**) 1 सस्ता, कम दामों में 2 कम क़ीमत वाला; सुलभ : *a cheap hairdresser/restaurant* 3 घटिया (माल) : *cheap furniture/ shoes* 4 (लोगों का व्यवहार, बातें आदि) निम्नस्तरीय, अरुचिकर : *a cheap joke/ remark* ▸ **cheap** *adv* (*अनौप*) कम क़ीमत में : *get sth cheap* **cheaply** *adv* **cheapness** *noun* सस्तापन।

cheapen / चीपन् / *verb* 1 स्वयं को या दूसरों को नीचे गिरा लेना/सम्मान कम कर लेना 2 सस्ता करना; मूल्य कम करना : *cheapen the cost of sth.*

cheat / चीट् / *verb* 1 ठगना, धोखा देना 2 **cheat (at sth)** बेईमानी करना, छल करना ▸ **cheat** *noun* 1 छली, धोखेबाज़ 2 छल-कपट, धोखा।

check¹ / चेक् / *verb* 1 जाँचना, मिलान करना : *check the items against the list* 2 रोकना, रोकथाम करना : *check the enemy's advance* 3 अचानक रोक देना ■ **check in (at...); check into...** हवाई अड्डे पर या होटल में यात्री या अतिथि के रूप में रजिस्टर कराना/नामांकन कराना ▸ **check-up** *noun* पूर्ण जाँच, विशेष रूप से डॉक्टरी जाँच।

check² / चेक् / *noun* 1 **check (on sth)** जाँच की प्रक्रिया अथवा तरीक़ा 2 **check (on sb)** जाँच 3 **check (on sth)** रोक-थाम, नियंत्रण 4 (*US*) रसीद/टोकन 5 (*US*) = **cheque** ■ **keep a check on; hold/ keep sth in check** नियंत्रित करना।

check³ / चेक् / *noun* चौकोर चिह्न; चारख़ाने का कपड़ा।

checkmate / चेकमेट् / *verb* किसी की योजना में बाधा डालना या किसी को हरा देना।

cheek / चीक् / *noun* 1 गाल 2 [*sing*] धृष्टता, गुस्ताख़ी : *He had the cheek to ask me to do his work for him.* ▸ **cheek** *verb* धृष्टता करना, गुस्ताख़ी से बात करना **cheeky** *adj* (**-ier, -iest**) धृष्ट, गुस्ताख़ **cheekily** *adv* **cheekiness** *noun*.

cheer¹ / चिअर् / *verb* 1 ताली बजाकर या जयकार से किसी को आनंदित एवं उत्साहित करना 2 किसी को आशा, दिलासा एवं समर्थन देकर आनंदित करना : *He was greatly cheered by the news.* ■ **cheer (sb) up** उत्साहित होना/करना ▸ **cheering** *adj* उत्साहवर्धक।

cheer² / चिअर् / *noun* 1 वाहवाही, जय-घोष : *Three cheers for the bride and groom!* 2 (*अप्र या औप*) प्रसन्नता की मनोदशा।

cheerful / चिअरफुल् / *adj* 1 प्रसन्न, प्रफुल्ल 2 रोचक एवं चमकदार : *cheerful colours.*

cheerless / चिअरलस् / *adj* उदास एवं खिन्न : *a cold, cheerless day.*

cheese / चीज़् / *noun* पनीर; पनीर से बने पदार्थ : *a selection of French cheeses* ▸ **cheese** *verb* **cheese sb off** किसी को तंग, बोर या निराश करना।

cheetah / चीता / *noun* चीता, चित्तीदार बाघ।

chef / शेफ़् / *noun* (होटल या रेस्त्राँ में) मुख्य रसोइया, महा-सूपकार।

chemical / केमिकल् / *adj* 1 रासाय-निक : *the chemical industry* 2 रासायनिक रूप से उत्पन्न : *a chemical reaction* ▸ **chemical** *noun* रसा-यन विज्ञान में प्रयुक्त पदार्थ **chemically** *adv*.

chemist / केमिस्ट् / *noun* 1 (*US* **druggist**) दवाइयाँ आदि तैयार करने या बेचने वाला 2 रसायन विज्ञान का विद्वान।

chemistry / 'केमिस्ट्रि / *noun* 1 रसायन विज्ञान, तत्त्वों एवं उनके संयोजनों का विज्ञान 2 पदार्थ की रासायनिक संरचना एवं व्यवहार।

cheque (US **check**) / चेक् / *noun* चेक, बैंक को (प्राय: मुद्रित प्रपत्र पर) धन देने का आदेश, धनादेश ▸ **cheque-book** (US **checkbook**) *noun* चेकबुक।

cherish / 'चेरिश् / *verb* 1 स्नेह और संरक्षण देना : *Children feel the need to be cherished.* 2 दिल में (आशा, भावना आदि) संजोए रखना : *cherish the memory of one's dead mother.*

cherry / 'चेरि / *noun* (*pl* **cherries**) 1 चेरी, बेर के जैसा फल जो पकने पर लाल या काला होता है 2 (**cherry red** भी) चमकदार लाल रंग।

chess / चेस् / *noun* शतरंज का खेल ▸ **chessboard** *noun* शतरंज की बिसात **chessman** *noun* (*pl* **chessmen**) शतरंज के मोहरे।

chest / चेस्ट् / *noun* 1 छाती, वक्षस्थल 2 लकड़ी की बड़ी पेटी : *a medicine chest ○ a tool chest* ▸ **chest of drawers** (US **bureau** भी) *noun* कपड़े रखने का बक्स वाला फ़र्नीचर।

chestnut / 'चेस्नट् / *noun* 1 अखरोट प्रजाति का पेड़; इस पेड़ की चमकदार लाल-भूरे रंग की लकड़ी 2 चमकदार लाल-भूरा रंग : *chestnut hair ○ a chestnut mare* 3 इस रंग का घोड़ा।

chew / चू / *verb* **chew** (**at/on/through sth**); **chew sth** (**up**) चबाना : *The dog was chewing at a large bone.* ▸ **chew** *noun* 1 चबाने की क्रिया 2 एक सख्त, चबाने वाली मिठाई **chewing-gum** *noun* एक प्रकार की स्वादिष्ट गोंद जो चबाई जाती है।

chic / शीक् / *noun* फ़ैशनेबल और सुंदर; सुरुचिपूर्ण।

chick / चिक् / *noun* किसी भी पक्षी का छोटा बच्चा।

chicken / 'चिकिन् / *noun* मुर्गी या मुर्गा, मुर्गी या मुर्गा का गोश्त ▸ **chicken** *verb* ■ **chicken out** (**of sth**) (*अनौप*) डरकर कुछ न करने का निर्णय लेना **chicken** *adj* (*अनौप*) डरपोक, दब्बू।

chide / चाइड् / *verb* (*pt* **chided** / 'चाइडिड् / या **chid** / चिड् /; *pp* **chided** या **chidden** / 'चिड्न् /) **chide sb/oneself** (**for sth/doing sth**) डाँटना, डपटना : *She chided him for not telling the truth.*

chief / चीफ़् / *noun* 1 (क़बीलों का) मुखिया 2 संस्था, विभाग आदि में सबसे उच्च पद पर व्यक्ति : *the chief of police* ▸ **chief** *adj* 1 सर्वाधिक महत्त्वपूर्ण 2 मुख्य, सर्वोच्च : *the chief priest* **chiefly** *adv.*

chieftain / 'चीफ़्टन् / *noun* मुखिया, सरदार।

child / चाइल्ड् / *noun* (*pl* **children** / 'चिल्ड्न् /) 1 बच्चा, शिशु 2 पुत्र या पुत्री 3 (*अपमा*) बच्चों की तरह व्यवहार करने वाला व्यक्ति; अनुभवहीन व्यक्ति 4 **child of sth** विशेष काल, स्थान या व्यक्ति से प्रभावित व्यक्ति/वस्तु ▸ **childhood** *noun* बचपन **childlike** *adj* बालोचित; सरल एवं निष्कपट।

childish / 'चाइल्डिश् / *adj* बचकाना; बच्चों जैसा।

chill / चिल् / *noun* 1 सिहरन; ठंड या नमी के कारण ठिठुरन 2 ठंड के कारण बीमार, कँपकँपी एवं बुख़ार 3 [*sing*] उदासी की भावना; सिहरन ▸ **chill** *verb* 1 ठंडा होना या करना : *We were chilled by the icy wind.* 2 ठंडा करके खाद्य पदार्थों को सुरक्षित रखना : *chilled food products* **chilling** *adj* डरावना **chilly** *adj* (**-ier, -iest**) 1 (मौसम) शीतल 2 (व्यवहार) रुष्ट, उत्साहहीन।

chilli (US **chili**) / 'चिलि / *noun* (*pl* **chillies**; US **chilies**) मिर्च।

chime / चाइम् / *noun* घंटियों का गुंजन : *the chime of church bells* ▸ **chime** *verb* 1 घंटियों का बजना/गुंजन करना

2 (समय बताने वाला) घंटा बजना/बजाना ■ **chime in (with sth)** दूसरों की बातचीत में कूद पड़ना।

chimney / 'चिम्नि / *noun* 1 चिमनी (जिससे नीचे का धुआँ ऊपर छत पर निकल जाता है) 2 (*तक*) चट्टान में संकरी दरार जिससे होकर ऊपर चढ़ा जा सकता है ▶ **chimney-sweep (sweep** भी) *noun* चिमनी के अंदर की कालिख साफ़ करने वाला।

chimpanzee / ‚चिम्पैन्'ज़ी / (*अनौप*) (**chimp** भी) *noun* अफ़्रीका में पाया जाने वाला एक तरह का पूँछहीन बंदर।

chin / चिन् / *noun* तुड्डी ▶ **chinless** *adj* बहुत छोटी तुड्डी वाला।

china / 'चाइना / *noun* चीनी मिट्टी जिसके प्लेट, प्याले आदि बनते हैं; चीनी मिट्टी के बर्तन : *household china.*

chink¹ / चिङ्क् / *noun* दरार (जिससे देखा जा सकता है) ■ **a chink in sb's armour** कमज़ोर बिंदु (चरित्र आदि का)।

chink² / चिङ्क् / *noun* chink (of sth) खनखनाहट की आवाज़ (जैसे सिक्कों की आवाज़) ▶ **chink** *verb* **chink (A and B) (together)** (सिक्कों, गिलासों आदि का) खनखनाना।

chip¹ / चिप् / *noun* 1 चिप्पी, (लकड़ी, पत्थर, चीनी मिट्टी आदि का) छोटा टुकड़ा 2 (अक्सर *pl*) आलू, केले आदि के तले हुए गोल पतले टुकड़े 3 (**microchip** भी) माइक्रोचिप ■ **chip off the old block** (*अनौप*) अपने माता-पिता जैसी संतान।

chip² / चिप् / *verb* (**-pp-**) 1 किसी वस्तु को किनारे या ऊपरी सतह से तोड़ना/टूटना या काटना/कट जाना 2 **chip sth from/off sth; chip sth off** चिप काटना 3 **chip off (sth)** छोटे टुकड़ों में निकल आना : *The paint has chipped off where the table touches the wall.* ▶ **chippings** *noun* [*pl*] सड़क बनाने के काम आने वाले छोटे पत्थर के टुकड़े।

chirp / चर्प् / (**chirrup** / 'चिरप् / भी) *noun*

(चिड़ियों की) चींचीं, चहचहाट; झींगुर की झंकार ▶ **chirp (chirrup** भी) *verb* चह- चहाना, झंकारना।

chirpy / 'चर्पि / *adj* (**-ier, -iest**) प्रसन्न एवं प्रफुल्लित ▶ **chirpily** *adv*.

chisel / 'चिज़्ल् / *noun* (लकड़ी, पत्थर काटने की) छेनी ▶ **chisel** *verb* (**-ll-**; *US* **-l-** भी) छेनी से काटना; काटकर आकृति बनाना : *The sculptor chiselled the lump of marble into a fine statue.*

chit / चिट् / *noun* एक छोटी-सी लिखित पर्ची या पत्र।

chit-chat / 'चिट्'चैट् / *noun* (*अनौप*) गपशप।

chivalry / 'शिव्ल्रि / *noun* 1 मध्य युग (यूरोप में) में सामंतों के अपेक्षित आदर्श गुण जैसे साहस, सम्मान और ग़रीबों के प्रति दया आदि; इन गुणों पर आधारित सामंती रीति- विधान : *the age of chivalry* 2 नम्र एवं सहृदयतापूर्ण व्यवहार (विशेषत: स्त्रियों के प्रति) ▶ **chivalrous** / 'शिव्ल्रस् / *adj.*

chlorine / 'क्लोरीन् / *noun* (*प्रतीक* Cl) क्लोरीन।

chloroform / 'क्लॉरफ़ॉर्म् / *noun* क्लोरो- फ़ॉर्म (बेहोश करने के लिए प्रयुक्त रसायन) ▶ **chloroform** *verb* क्लोरोफ़ॉर्म से बेहोश करना।

chlorophyll / 'क्लॉरफ़िल् / *noun* पौधों में पाया जाने वाला हरे रंग का पदार्थ जो पौधों के विकास में सहायक होता है।

chocolate / 'चॉक्लट् / *noun* 1 चाकलेट 2 चाकलेट से बनी मिठाई 3 दूध या गरम पानी में चाकलेट मिलाकर बनाया गया पेय 4 चाकलेटी रंग, गहरा कत्थई ▶ **chocolate** *adj* 1 चाकलेट से बना 2 कत्थई रंग का।

choice / चॉइस् / *noun* 1 **choice (be- tween A and B)** चुनाव, वरण 2 चुनाव का अधिकार/संभावना 3 चुना हुआ व्यक्ति या वस्तु : *I don't like his choice of friends.* ▶ **choice** *adj* (**-er, -est**) 1 (फल, सब्ज़ी आदि) बहुत बढ़िया 2 साव- धानी से चुना हुआ।

choir / क्वाइअर् / noun 1 (विशेषत: चर्च में गाने वाली) गायन-मंडली : *She sings in the school choir.* 2 चर्च में इस मंडली के लिए नियत स्थान ▸ **choirboy** noun **choirmaster** noun.

choke / चोक् / verb 1 **choke (on sth)** दम घुटना 2 **choke (with sth)** गले का रुँधा हुआ होना 3 गला घोंटना, दम घोंटकर मारना 4 **choke sth (up)** खुले मार्ग को अवरुद्ध करना : *dead leaves choking (up) the drains* ▸ **choke** noun 1 अवरुद्धता 2 मोटरकार का एक पुर्ज़ा, चोक **choked** adj **choked (about sth)** (अप) नाराज़, गुस्से में।

cholera / कॉलरा / noun हैज़ा।

cholesterol / क॑लेस्टरॉल् / noun कोशि- काओं एवं रक्त में पाया जाने वाला पदार्थ, जिसकी अधिक मात्रा शरीर के लिए हानिकारक होती है।

choose / चूज़ / verb (pt **chose** / चोज़्/; pp **chosen** / चोज़्न्/) 1 **choose (between A and/or B); choose sb/ sth as sth** दो विकल्पों के बीच में एक का चयन करना या अपनाना 2 पसंद करना।

choosy / चूज़ी / adj (-ier, -iest) (अनौप) चुनने में सतर्क; आसानी से संतुष्ट न होने वाला व्यक्ति।

chop¹ / चॉप् / verb (-pp-) **chop sth (up) (into sth)** (कुल्हाड़ी से) काटना या चीरना।

chop² / चॉप् / noun 1 (कुल्हाड़ी आदि का) वार; हाथ का पार्श्व से वार 2 मांस आदि का टुकड़ा 3 **the chop** [sing] (अप्र) नौकरी से बर्खास्तगी; हत्या या किसी बात का ख़ात्मा ▸ **chopper** noun गँडासा।

choppy / चॉपि / adj (-ier, -iest) छोटी क्षुब्ध लहरों वाला (समुद्र) ▸ **choppiness** noun.

chopsticks / चॉप्स्टिक्स् / noun [pl] दो तीलियाँ जिन्हें चीनी, जापानी लोग मुँह तक भोजन पहुँचाने के लिए काँटे की तरह प्रयुक्त करते हैं।

choral / कॉरल् / adj समवेत (गान) : *Beethoven's Choral Symphony.*

chord / कॉर्ड / noun 1 (संगीत) दो या तीन स्वरों का एक साथ संयोजन 2 (गणित) जीवा, वृत्त के दो बिंदुओं को मिलाने वाली रेखा।

chore / चॉर् / noun 1 आम तौर पर किया जाने वाला कार्य : *doing the household chores* 2 अरुचिकर या शुष्क एकरस कार्य : *She finds shopping a chore.*

choreograph / कॉरिअग्राफ़् ; कॉरि- अग्रैफ़् / verb तालबद्ध नृत्यकला ▸ **chore-ography** / कॉरि'ऑग्रफ़ि / noun तालबद्ध नृत्य।

chorus / कॉरस् / noun 1 समवेत गान, सहगान : *sing in a chorus* 2 (गीत की) टेक 3 कई व्यक्तियों द्वारा एक साथ कही बात : *The proposal was greeted with a chorus of approval.* 4 संगीत- मय हास्य-नाटिका में गाने एवं नृत्य करने वाले कलाकारों का समूह ■ **in chorus** सब साथ मिलकर ▸ **chorus** verb एक साथ गाना या कुछ कहना।

Christ / क्राइस्ट् / noun (**Jesus, Jesus Christ** भी) ईसा मसीह।

christen / क्रिसन् / verb (बच्चे का) नामकरण करना, विशेषत: ईसाइयों में : *The child was christened Mary.* ▸ **christening** noun बपतिस्मा देने की रस्म।

Christian / क्रिस्चन् / adj 1 ईसाई, क्राइस्ट के मतानुयायी 2 ईसा की शिक्षाओं पर आधारित : *a Christian upbringing* 3 ईसाइयों से संबंधित : *the Christian sector of the city* ▸ **Christian** noun ईसाई (व्यक्ति)।

Christianity / क्रिस्टि'ऐनिटि / noun 1 ईसाई धर्म 2 ईसाई होना ▸ **Christian name (first name, forename,** US **given name** भी) noun प्रथम नाम जो बपतिस्मा के साथ रखा जाता है।

Christmas / क्रिस्मस् / (**Christmas**

Day भी) *noun* जीसस क्राइस्ट के जन्म दिवस का समारोह, 25 दिसंबर।

chromosome / 'क्रोमसोम् / *noun* (*जीव विज्ञान*) गुणसूत्र, आनुवंशिक गुणों को एक पीढ़ी से दूसरी में ले जाने वाली कोशिकीय संरचनाएँ।

chronic / 'क्रॉनिक् / *adj* 1 पुरानी, लगातार लंबी अवधि से चली आ रही बीमारी, पीड़ा आदि : *chronic bronchitis/asthma* 2 लंबी अवधि से किसी आदत या रोग से पीड़ित व्यक्ति : *a chronic alcoholic/depressive.*

chronicle / 'क्रॉनिक्ल् / *noun* (अक्सर *pl*) घटनाओं का इतिवृत्त, इतिहास ▸ **chronicle** *verb* इतिवृत्त तैयार करना **chronicler** *noun.*

chronology / क्र 'नॉलजि / *noun* (*pl* **chronologies**) 1 कालक्रम-विज्ञान, तिथि-निर्धारण का विज्ञान 2 घटनाओं का तिथिवार अंकन; ऐसी सूची : *a chronology of Mozart's life* ▸ **chronological** / क्रॉन 'लॉजिकल् / *adj* **chronologically** *adv.*

chubby / 'चबि / *adj* (**-ier, -iest**) गोल-मटोल, थोड़ा मोटा : *a chubby child* ▸ **chubbiness** *noun.*

chuck / चक् / *verb* 1 (*अनौप*) लापरवाही से फेंक देना : *chuck old clothes out* 2 **chuck sb/sth (in/up)** (*अनौप*) छोड़ देना।

chuckle / 'चक्ल् / *verb* मुँह बंद करके हँसना ▸ **chuckle** *noun* दबी हुई हँसी।

chum / चम् / *noun* (*अनौप*) घनिष्ठ मित्र : *an old school chum* ▸ **chum** *verb* (**-mm-**) ■ **chum up (with sb)** घनिष्ठ मित्र बनना **chummy** *adj.*

chunk / चङ्क् / *noun* 1 किसी वस्तु का छोटा, मोटा ठोस हिस्सा : *a chunk of bread/ice* 2 (*अनौप*) किसी चीज़ की ख़ासी बड़ी मात्रा : *I've already written a fair chunk of my article.*

church / चर्च् / *noun* 1 चर्च (ईसाइयों का

पूजा-स्थल); गिरजाघर 2 **the Church** ईसाइयों का संगठन या विभाग जो एक से विश्वास और विधि-विधान मानता है : *The Church has a duty to condemn violence.*

churn / चर्न् / *noun* 1 मथने का मटका; बड़ा मटका 2 मथानी, मथने की मशीन ▸ **churn** *verb* मथना; दही मथकर मक्खन निकालना।

-cide *suff* (*प्रत्यय*) (संज्ञा बनाने में प्रयुक्त) 1 मारने की प्रक्रिया : *genocide* ○ *patricide* 2 मारने वाला पदार्थ या व्यक्ति : *insecticide* ○ *fungicide.*

cider / 'साइडर् / *noun* सेब का आसव/शराब।

cigar / सि'गार् / *noun* सिगार, चुरुट।

cigarette / सिग'रेट्; *US* 'सिगरेट् / *noun* सिगरेट।

cinder / 'सिन्डर् / *noun* (प्राय: *pl*) लकड़ी का अधजला कोयला।

cinema / 'सिनेमा / *noun* 1 सिनेमा हॉल : *our local cinema* 2 **the cinema** [*sing*] (*अनौप* **the pictures**; *US* **the movies** भी) सिनेमा, चलचित्र 3 कला या उद्योग के रूप में फ़िल्में : *He works in the cinema.* ▸ **cinematic** *adj* **cine-camera** *noun* चलचित्र कैमरा।

cinnamon / 'सिनमन् / *noun* दारचीनी।

cipher (**cypher** भी) / 'साइफर् / *noun* 1 कूटलिपि में लिखने की पद्धति; ऐसी पद्धति की विवरणिका 2 सिफ़र, शून्य, ज़ीरो 3 (*अपमा*) नगण्य व्यक्ति, महत्त्वहीन व्यक्ति : *He's a mere cipher.*

circa / 'सर्का / *prep* (*लैटिन*) (*संक्षि* c) (तिथि के साथ प्रयुक्त) के आस-पास : *born circa 150 BC.*

circle / 'सर्कल् / *noun* 1 गोला, वृत्त 2 गोल वस्तु, गोल-सी वस्तु : *a circle of trees/hills* 3 (*US* **balcony**) (रंगशाला, सिनेमा आदि में) दुमंज़िले की सीटें 4 (व्यक्तियों की) मंडली, एक-सी रुचि वाले व्यक्तियों का समूह ▸ **circle** *verb* 1 **circle (about/**

around/round) (above/over sb/sth) (हवा में) चक्कर लगाना 2 किसी के चारों ओर घेरा बनाना या घेरे में चक्कर लगाना 3 वृत्त बनाना।

circuit / 'सर्किट् / noun 1 एक स्थान से प्रारंभ होकर उसी स्थान पर समाप्त होना, परिक्रमा : The earth takes a year to make a circuit of the sun. 2 (विद्युत धारा का) परिपथ : a circuit diagram 3 ऐसे स्थानों की शृंखला जहाँ आयोजन, नुमाइश आदि होते रहते हैं : the lecture/ comedy circuit ▸ circuit-board noun विद्युत यंत्रों के अंदर विद्युत परिपथ बोर्ड।

circular / 'सर्क्युलर् / adj 1 वृत्ताकार, गोल 2 वृत्ताकार में घूमते हुए : a circular tour (एक स्थान से शुरू होकर उसी स्थान पर ख़त्म होने वाली यात्रा) 3 (तर्क-शास्त्र में) जिस तर्क को सिद्ध किया जा रहा हो उसी को निष्कर्ष के लिए प्रमाण मानना : a circular argument 4 बहुत-से व्यक्तियों को भेजा गया (संदेश आदि) : a circular letter ▸ circular noun परिपत्र, गश्ती चिट्ठी।

circulate / 'सर्क्युलेट / verb 1 निरंतर घूमना, चक्कर लगाना : Blood circulates through the body. ○ open a window to allow the air to circulate 2 एक स्थान या व्यक्ति से दूसरे को पहुँचाना : circulate a letter 3 परिपत्र द्वारा किसी को सूचित करना।

circulation / 'सर्क्यु'लेश्न् / noun 1 हृदय से तमाम शरीर को रक्त संचरण 2 एक स्थान या व्यक्ति से दूसरे को कुछ पहुँचाने की क्रिया, संचरण ▸ circulatory adj रक्त संचरण से संबंधित।

circumference / सर्'कम्फ़रन्स् / noun वृत्त की परिधि; परिधि की लंबाई : The circumference of the earth is almost 40,000 kilometres.

circumnavigate / सर्कम्'नैविगेट् / verb (औप) (पृथ्वी की परिक्रमा लगाता

हुआ) नौ-परिचालन ▸ circumnavigation noun.

circumscribe / 'सर्कम्स्क्राइब् / verb 1 (औप) सीमा अंकित करना, सीमा के अंदर रोक देना : a life circumscribed by poverty 2 (तक) चारों ओर वृत्त (या घेरा) खींचना : circumscribe a square.

circumstance / 'सर्कम्स्टन्स्; 'सर्कम्-स्टान्स्; 'सर्कम्स्टैन्स् / noun 1 (प्राय: pl) परिस्थिति या तथ्य 2 circumstances [pl] (औप) किसी व्यक्ति की आर्थिक दशा : What are his circumstances? ■ in/under the circumstances क्योंकि ऐसी परिस्थिति है in/under no circumstances किसी भी हालत में नहीं।

circumstantial / सर्कम्'स्टैन्शल् / adj 1 पूरा विवरण देने वाला 2 परिस्थिति-जन्य।

circumvent / सर्कम्'वेन्ट् / verb (औप) किसी बात से बचने (या रोकने) का उपाय खोजना : circumvent a law/prob-lem/difficulty ▸ circumvention noun.

circus / 'सर्कस् / noun 1 सर्कस; सर्कस के कलाकार 2 (ब्रिटेन में) गोल स्थान जहाँ अनेक मार्ग मिलते हैं; गोल चौक।

cistern / 'सिस्टर्न् / noun टंकी (शौचालय आदि में) पानी भरकर रखने के लिए।

citadel / 'सिटडेल्; 'सिटेडेल् / noun 1 क़िला, दुर्ग 2 दुर्भेद्य एवं सुरक्षित स्थल।

cite / साइट् / verb (औप) 1 उदाहरण-स्वरूप देना; (पुस्तक में से) उद्धृत करना : She cited (a verse from) (a poem by) Keats. 2 (सिपाही के) शौर्य का प्रशंसा-पूर्वक उल्लेख करना 3 (क़ानून) किसी को कचहरी में उपस्थित होने का समन भेजना ▸ citation noun 1 उद्धरण; उद्धृत पद 2 प्रशस्ति-पत्र।

citizen / 'सिटिज़्न् / noun 1 (किसी देश का) नागरिक जिसे जन्म से या ग्रहण करने से उस देश के पूरे अधिकार मिलते हैं : an American citizen 2 नगरवासी (न कि ग्रामवासी) ▸ citizenship noun.

citrus /'सिट्रस्/ noun नींबू के वंश का, जैसे नींबू, संतरा आदि।

city /'सिटि/ noun (pl **cities**) शहर, नगर।

civic /'सिविक्/ adj 1 नगर का या नगर से संबंधित : civic buildings/administration 2 नागरिकों का : civic responsibilities/duties ▸ **civics** /'सिविक्स्/ noun नगर-शासन का अध्ययन, नागरिक-शास्त्र।

civil /'सिव्ल्/ adj 1 मानव समाज-विषयक : civil disorder 2 सामान्य नागरिक-विषयक (न कि फ़ौज या धर्म संस्था विषयक) : civil government 3 नागरिक क़ानून संबंधी (न कि अपराधिक) : civil cases/court ▸ **civil engineering** noun सड़क, पुल, रेलवे, नहर आदि निर्माण एवं प्रारूप अभियंत्रण **civil law** noun व्यक्तिगत अधिकारों का क़ानून **civil marriage** noun बिना धार्मिक संस्कार का विवाह **civil servant** noun सिविल सेवा के अधिकारी **civil war** noun गृह-युद्ध, एक ही देश के भीतर दो दलों का युद्ध **the civil service** noun लोक सेवा, सेना सेवा को छोड़कर सभी सरकारी विभाग सेवा।

civilian /स'विलिअन्/ noun, adj व्यक्ति जो सेना या पुलिस में न हो।

civilization, -isation /,सिव़लाइ 'ज़ेश्न्/ noun 1 सभ्यता 2 मानव जाति 3 विशेष काल में सामाजिक जीवन।

civilize, -ise /'सिव़लाइज़्/ verb 1 सभ्य करना/बनाना 2 व्यवहार और जीवन शैली सुसंस्कृत बनाना/करना ▸ **civilized, -ised** adj 1 सभ्य एवं विकसित 2 उच्च नैतिक मूल्यों वाला 3 सुसंस्कृत : They were brought up to behave in a civilized way in public.

claim¹ /क्लेम्/ verb 1 (कथन की सत्यता का) दावा करना 2 (स्वामित्व या अधिकार का) दावा पेश करना : She claims ownership of the land. 3 नुक़सान के बाद बीमे का दावा पेश करना; हर्जाने की माँग करना : claim a refund.

claim² /क्लेम्/ noun 1 दावा 2 **claim (to sth); (claim on sb/sth)** स्वामित्व या अधिकार का दावा : I make no claim to expertise in such matters. 3 **claim (for sth)** माँग रखने का अधिकार, विशेषत: धन का ■ **lay claim to** किसी चीज़ पर दावा जताना ▸ **claimant** /'क्लेमन्ट्/ noun दावेदार।

clamber /'क्लैम्बर/ verb हाथों और पैरों की सहायता से कठिनाई-पूर्वक चढ़ना : The children clambered over the rocks.

clamour (US **clamor**) /'क्लैमर/ noun 1 होहल्ला, शोर-शराबा : the clamour of the busy market 2 **clamour (for sth)** दुहाई, फ़रियाद : a clamour for revenge ▸ **clamour** verb 1 शोरगुल, होहल्ला करना 2 दुहाई/फ़रियाद करना **clamorous** adj.

clamp /क्लैम्प्/ noun 1 शिकंजा 2 (कसने या दृढ़ करने के लिए) लोहे की पट्टियाँ ▸ **clamp** verb 1 शिकंजे में कसना 2 कसकर वस्तुएँ पकड़ना 3 **clamp A and B (together); clamp A to B** क्लैंप से जोड़ना या दृढ़ करना।

clan /क्लैन्/ noun 1 गोत्र, कुल (जाति से छोटी पारिवारिक इकाई) 2 समान रुचि एवं उद्देश्यों वाले घनिष्ठ लोगों का समूह ▸ **clannish** adj (अक्सर, अपमा) (व्यक्ति) आपस में घनिष्ठ मगर बाहरी लोगों की परवाह न करते हुए।

clandestine /क्लैन'डेस्टिन्; क्लैन'डस्टा-इन्/ adj (औप) छिपाकर किया गया; गुप्त : a clandestine meeting.

clang /क्लैङ्/ noun (घंटों या धातुओं का) टनटनाना : the clang of the school bell ▸ **clang** verb टनटनाने की आवाज़ पैदा करना : The prison gates clanged shut.

clank /क्लैङ्क्/ noun झनझनाने या खड़-खड़ाने की आवाज़ : the clank of heavy chains ▸ **clank** verb (तलवारों का) झनझनाना, (बेड़ियों, ज़ंजीरों को) खड़खड़ाना।

clap / क्लैप् / verb (-pp-) 1 ताली बजाना 2 **clap sb on sth** (हाथों से) थपथपाना : *clap sb on the back* 3 तेज़ी और शक्ति से कुछ रखना : *clap sb in prison* ■ **clap/lay/set eyes on sb/sth** (अनौप) देखना ▶ **clap** noun 1 ताली (हाथ की) 2 **clap on sth** थपकी।

clarify / क्लैरिफ़ाइ / verb (pt, pp **clarified**) 1 स्पष्ट होना या करना : *clarify a remark/statement* 2 गरम करके मक्खन (या चर्बी) शुद्ध करना : *clarified butter* ▶ **clarification** noun स्पष्टीकरण।

clarinet / क्लैरि'नेट् / noun एक प्रकार का बाजा ▶ **clarinettist** noun.

clarity / क्लैरिटि / noun स्पष्टता।

clash¹ / क्लैश् / verb 1 **clash (with sb)** आमने-सामने आना और लड़ना; **clash (with sb) (on/over sth)** गंभीर असहमति प्रकट करना 2 **clash (with sth)** दो (या अधिक) घटनाओं का असुविधाजनक रूप से एक साथ होना : *Your party clashes with a wedding I'm going to.* 3 **clash (with sth)** (रंगों, डिज़ाइनों आदि का) मिलान न होना/साथ अच्छा न लगना।

clash² / क्लैश् / noun 1 **clash (with sb/sth); clash (between A and B)** टक्कर, संघर्ष : *Clashes broke out between police and demonstrators.* 2 तर्कवितर्क, गंभीर असहमति 3 घटनाओं का असुविधाजनक रूप से एक ही समय होना 4 रंगों का मिलान न होना 5 खट-खटाहट की आवाज़।

clasp¹ / क्लास्प्; US क्लैस्प् / noun 1 (दो किनारों को जोड़ने वाला) बकसुआ 2 हाथ की अच्छी पकड़; बाँहों की जकड़/आलिंगन : *He held her hand in a firm clasp.*

clasp² / क्लास्प्; US क्लैस्प् / verb 1 बक-सुए से जोड़ना/बाँधना 2 हाथ में कसकर पकड़ना 3 बाँहों में जकड़ना/आलिंगन करना : *He clasped her to his chest.*

class / क्लास्; US क्लैस् / noun 1 समान सामाजिक या आर्थिक स्तर वालों का वर्ग : *the working/middle/upper class* 2 लोगों को ऐसे वर्गों में विभाजित करने वाली व्यवस्था : *class differences/divisions* 3 इस तरह की व्यवस्था में व्यक्ति की सामाजिक स्थिति 4 (शिक्षार्थियों की) कक्षा; कक्षा पाठ 5 उच्च गुण; उत्कृष्टता 6 परीक्षा परिणाम में दर्जा, श्रेणी ▶ **class** adj उत्कृष्ट; उत्तम **class** verb **class sb/sth (as sth)** वर्गों में विभाजित करना **classless** adj वर्गविहीन (समाज)।

classic / क्लैसिक् / adj 1 अति उत्तम; उत्तम गुण या (उच्चतम) : *a classic novel/comment* 2 विशिष्ट, प्रतिनिधिक 3 रूप और शैली में सहज और सुरुचिपूर्ण; चिरप्रतिष्ठित : *a classic design/dress* ▶ **classic** noun 1 उच्चतम श्रेणी के लेखक, चित्रकार आदि; ऐसे लेखकों/कलाकारों की कृतियाँ : *This novel may well become a classic.* 2 **Classics** चिर-सम्मत उत्कृष्ट ग्रीक एवं लैटिन भाषा एवं साहित्य का अध्ययन।

classical / क्लैसिकल् / adj 1 प्राचीन उच्चस्तरीय ग्रीक एवं लैटिन साहित्य एवं उससे प्रभावित साहित्य : *classical studies* 2 सरल एवं संयत 3 (संगीत, नृत्य आदि) शास्त्रीय शैली का : *the classical music of India* 4 सर्वसम्मत एवं स्थापित : *the classical Darwinian theory of evolution* ▶ **classically** adv.

classify / क्लैसिफ़ाइ / verb (pt, pp **classified**) 1 वर्गीकृत करना : *The books in the library are classified according to subject.* 2 सूचना, दस्तावेज़ आदि गोपनीय घोषित करना ▶ **classifiable** adj **classification** / क्लैसिफ़ि 'केश्न् / noun 1 वर्गीकरण 2 (जीव विज्ञान) जंतुओं एवं पेड़-पौधों को वर्गों में बाँटना।

clause / क्लॉज़् / noun 1 (व्या) उपवाक्य, संयुक्त या मिश्र वाक्य का घटक जिसमें एक उद्देश्य और एक विधेय अंश अवश्य होता है

2 संधि, क़ानून आदि में एक पूरा पैराग्राफ़ : *clause 23 (b) of the treaty.*

claustrophobia / क्लॉस्ट्र्‌फ़ोबिआ / *noun* बंद स्थानों में होने का असमान्य भय।

claw / क्लॉ / *noun* 1 पंजा, चंगुल : *Cats have sharp claws.* 2 पंजानुमा कोई वस्तु या शस्त्र; पंजे के समान काम करने वाली युक्ति ▸ **claw** *verb* **claw (at) sb/sth** पंजे या नाख़ूनों से पकड़ना; पंजे से कठोरता से खींचना।

clay / क्ले / *noun* चिकनी चिपकने वाली मिट्टी जो पकाने पर कड़ी हो जाती है, जिससे मिट्टी के बरतन और ईंटें आदि बनती हैं।

clean[1] / क्लीन् / *adj* (**-er, -est**) 1 साफ़; धुला हुआ; निर्मल 2 अप्रयुक्त, जिसका प्रयोग न हुआ हो : *a clean sheet of paper* 3 सुडौल 4 दाग़रहित; नैतिक रूप से शुद्ध, निर्दोष : *a clean police record* ■ **make a clean breast of sth** सत्य बता देना, क़बूल/स्वीकार कर लेना ▸ **clean** *adv* एकदम और पूर्णत: **clean-cut** *adj* एकदम स्पष्ट रूपरेखा वाला; साफ़-सुथरा (दिखने में)।

clean[2] / क्लीन् / *verb* साफ़ करना; झाड़ना-बुहारना; धोना : *clean the windows* ■ **clean sth out** अंदर से धूल आदि साफ़ करना **clean (sth) up** सुव्यवस्थित करना; सफ़ाई करना ▸ **clean** *noun* सफ़ाई।

cleanliness / 'क्लेन्‌लिनस् / *noun* स्वच्छता।

cleanly / 'क्लीन्‌लि / *adv* सफ़ाईपूर्वक।

cleanse / क्लेन्ज़् / *verb* **cleanse sb/sth (of sth)** पूरी तरह शुद्ध और स्वच्छ करना ▸ **cleanser** *noun.*

clear[1] / क्लिअर् / *adj* (**-er, -est**) 1 देखने, सुनने और समझने में सरल : *a clear voice/speaker/sound* 2 **clear (about/on sth)** संशय या उलझन से रहित : *a clear thinker* 3 **clear (to sb) (that...)** स्पष्ट; सुगम्य 4 निश्चित 5 पारदर्शक 6 बिना बादलों, धुंध या कोहरे वाला आकाश; (त्वचा) उज्ज्वल; (आँखें) चमकदार एवं सतर्क 7 संपूर्ण; पूरे-पूरे : *Allow three clear days for the letter to arrive.* ▸ **clearly** *adv* **clearness** *noun.*

clear[2] / क्लिअर् / *verb* 1 (द्रव का) पारदर्शी हो जाना; (आकाश) बादलों या वर्षा से मुक्त हो जाना 2 **clear A (of B)/clear B (from/off A)** अवांछित वस्तु हटाना 3 बाधा हटाना; कंप्यूटर से विवरण हटाना 4 **clear sb (of sth)** निर्दोष साबित करना 5 जहाज़, वायुयान आदि के लिए प्रवेश या छूटने की अनुमति पाना 6 ऋण से मुक्त होना : *clear one's debts* ■ **clear off** (अनौप) चले जाना, भाग जाना **clear up** 1 (मौसम) साफ़ हो जाना 2 (बीमारी) ठीक हो जाना ▸ **clearing-house** *noun* बैंकों का केंद्रीय कार्यालय।

clearance / 'क्लिअरन्स्/ *noun* 1 सफ़ाई, साफ़ करने की प्रक्रिया : *land clearance* 2 बीच में से निकलने का स्थान : *There is not much clearance for tall vehicles passing under this bridge.* 3 जहाज़/वायुयान के प्रवेश या छूटने का अनुमति-पत्र 4 बैंक के केंद्रीय कार्यालय में चेकों की भुगतान प्रक्रिया।

clearing / 'क्लिअरिंग / *noun* पेड़ साफ़ करने से निकला हुआ खुला स्थान।

clench / क्लेन्च् / *verb* 1 (मुट्ठी) बाँधना, बंद करना, जकड़ना : *clench one's fist/ teeth* 2 **clench sb/sth (in/with)** किसी व्यक्ति/वस्तु को मज़बूती से पकड़ना : *clench the railings (with both hands).*

clergy / 'क्लर्जि / *noun* (प्राय: **the clergy**) ईसाई चर्च का याजक वर्ग ▸ **clergy-man** *noun* पादरी।

clerical / 'क्लेरिकल् / *adj* 1 क्लर्क का कार्य (लिखना और नक़ल करना): *a clerical error* 2 **clergy** से संबद्ध : *a clerical collar.*

clerk / क्लार्क्; *US* क्लर्क् / *noun* 1 क्लर्क, (कार्यालय में) जो पत्र-व्यवहार, हिसाब-किताब आदि करता है : *a bank clerk.*

2 न्यायालय आदि में रिकॉर्ड रखने वाला व्यक्ति : *the Clerk of the Court* ▸ **clerk** *verb*.

clever /'क्लेव़र्/ *adj* (**-er, -est**) 1 सीखने, समझने में होशियार, चतुर; कुशल 2 (वस्तुएँ विचार, कार्य आदि) बुद्धि एवं चातुर्य वाले : *a clever scheme* 3 (*अनौप या अपमा*) चालाकी दिखाने वाला, बोलने में तेज़ : *Do as you're told and don't get clever with me!* ▸ **cleverly** *adv* **cleverness** *noun*.

cliché /'क्लीशे; *US* क्ली'शे / *noun* 1 घिसी-पिटी उक्ति या पद : *a cliché-ridden style* 2 ऐसी उक्तियों का प्रयोग ▸ **clichéd** *adj*.

click /क्लिक्/ *noun* 'खट' की ध्वनि (जैसे चाबी से ताला खोलते समय होती है) : *the click of a switch* ▸ **click** *verb* 1 'खट' की ध्वनि करना/होना : *The door clicked shut.* 2 (*अनौप*) अचानक स्पष्ट होकर समझ में आ जाना : *I puzzled over it for hours before it finally clicked.* 3 **click (with sb)** तुरंत मित्रता हो जाना; तुरंत लोकप्रियता पा जाना : *The TV serials have really clicked (with young audiences).*

client /'क्लाइअन्ट्/ *noun* 1 (वकील का) मुवक्किल 2 ग्राहक।

cliff /'क्लिफ़/ *noun* ऊँची खड़ी चट्टान (विशेषत : समुद्र के किनारे) ▸ **cliff-hanger** *noun* ऐसी रोचक कहानी या परिस्थिति जिसमें 'आगे क्या होगा' इसकी जिज्ञासा लगातार बनी रहती है।

climate /'क्लाइमट्/ *noun* 1 जलवायु; आबोहवा 2 सामान्य भाव/वातावरण : *the present political climate* ▸ **climatic** /क्लाइ'मैटिक/ *adj* जलवायु-विषयक।

climax /'क्लाइमैक्स/ *noun* पराकाष्ठा; सर्वाधिक महत्त्वपूर्ण या रोचक घटना : *the climax of his political career* ▸ **climax** *verb* **climax (sth) (in/with sth)** पराकाष्ठा पर पहुँचना/पहुँचाना।

climb /क्लाइम्/ *verb* 1 (पेड़, पहाड़, सीढ़ी आदि पर) चढ़ना : *climb a wall/a tree* 2 (सामाजिक स्तर पर) ऊँचा उठना : *In a few years he climbed to the top of his profession.* 3 (तापमान, मुद्रा आदि) स्तर में ऊपर उठना : *interest rates began to climb* ■ **climb down (over sth)** (*अनौप*) गलती स्वीकार करना ▸ **climb** *noun* चढ़ने की प्रक्रिया **climber** *noun* चढ़ने वाला व्यक्ति।

clinch /क्लिन्च्/ *verb* (*औप*) अंतत : कुछ पक्का या निश्चित तय करना : *clinch a deal/bargain* ▸ **clinch** *noun* जकड़; (*अनौप*) आलिंगन।

cling /क्लिङ्/ *verb* (*pt, pp* **clung** /क्लङ्/) 1 **cling (on) to sb/sth; cling onto sb/sth; cling on** चिपकना, लिपटना : *The children were clinging on to their mother.* 2 **cling (to sth)** चिपकना; चिपक जाना 3 **cling (on) to sth** कुछ छोड़ने को तैयार न होना; किसी से भावनात्मक रूप से जुड़ जाना (निर्भर रहना) : *cling to a belief/theory* ▸ **clinging** (**clingy** भी) *adj* 1 (कपड़े) बदन से चिपकने वाले 2 (प्राय : *अपमा*) औरों पर अत्यधिक निर्भर।

clinic /'क्लिनिक्/ *noun* 1 क्लीनिक, अस्पताल में रोगियों को देखने और इलाज करने की जगह 2 विशेषज्ञ या प्राइवेट अस्पताल : *He is being treated at a private clinic.*

clinical /'क्लिनिकल्/ *adj* 1 रोगियों को देखने और इलाज करने संबंधी : *clinical training* 2 भावशून्य, हृदयहीनता से 3 (भवन आदि) अति साधारण, बिना सजावट के।

clink /क्लिङ्क्/ *noun* झनझनाहट की आवाज़ ▸ **clink** *verb* (धातु, काँच आदि के टुकड़ों का) झनझनाना : *coins clinking in his pocket.*

clip¹ /क्लिप्/ *noun* 1 (काग़ज़ आदि को इकट्ठा रखने के लिए प्राय : धातु, तार या

प्लास्टिक का) क्लिप 2 क्लिप से कपड़ों पर लगाया गया आभूषण : *a diamond clip*

▸ **clip** *verb* (-pp-) clip (A and B) together; clip (sth) (on) to sth; clip (sth) on साथ-साथ क्लिप में बाँधना या जोड़ना : *clip documents together.*

clip² / क्लिप् / *verb* (-pp-) **1** clip sth (off sth) (कैंची आदि से) काटना, कत- रना : *clip a hedge/one's fingernails* **2** बस या ट्रेन के टिकट में छेद करना, यह चिह्नित करने को कि टिकट प्रयुक्त हो चुका है ▸ **clip** *noun* **1** कतरने की क्रिया **2** फ़िल्म का अलग से दिखाया गया लघु अंश **clippers** *noun* [*pl*] कैंची **clipping** *noun* (विशेषत: *US*) (समाचार-पत्रों से काटी गई) समाचार की कटिंग (अंश)।

clique / क्लीक् / *noun* (कभी-कभी *अपमा*) घनिष्ठ मित्रों का समूह जो साथ रहते हैं और आसानी से अन्यों को मित्र नहीं बनाते हैं : *a small clique of intellectuals.*

cloak / क्लोक् / *noun* **1** बिना बाँहों का ऊपरी कपड़ा; लबादा **2** [*sing*] कोई भी पूरी तरह ढकने या छिपाने वाली वस्तु : *They left under the cloak of darkness.*

▸ **cloak** *verb* cloak sth (in sth) छिपाना, ढकना।

cloakroom / क्लोकरूम् / *noun* स्थान जहाँ थोड़ी देर के लिए सामान रखा जा सके, अमानती सामान घर।

clock¹ / क्लॉक् / *noun* **1** (दीवार या मेज़ की, न कि हाथ की) घड़ी : *The clock struck twelve.* **2** (*अनौप*) समय के अलावा अन्य मापन करने वाला उपकरण, जैसे टैक्सी मीटर ▸ **clockwise** *adj, adv* घड़ी की चलती हुई सूइयों की दिशा में, दाहिना परिक्रमा।

clock² / क्लॉक् / *verb* **1** clock sth (up) एक विशेष समय, दूरी या गति प्राप्त या दर्ज करना : *He clocked 9.6 seconds in the 100 metres.* **2** किसी व्यक्ति/वस्तु के लिए स्टॉप-वॉच से समय रिकार्ड करना ■ clock (sb) out/off आने/जाने के समय

को दर्ज करना : *Workers usually clock off at 5.30.*

clockwork / क्लॉक्वर्क् / *noun* घड़ी जैसे पुर्ज़े रखने वाली मशीन ■ like clockwork नियमित रूप से, बिना किसी परेशानी के।

clog / क्लॉग् / *verb* (-gg-) clog (sth) (up) (with sth) मिट्टी-धूल आदि से किसी चीज़ (मशीन आदि) का अवरुद्ध हो जाना और इस कारण बड़ी कठिनाई से चलना : *a drain clogged (up) with dead leaves.*

cloister / क्लॉइस्टर् / *noun* **1** (प्राय: *pl*) कांवेंट, चर्च या कालेज के भीतरी चौक के चारों तरफ़ का ढका हुआ मार्ग, छत्ता **2** [*sing*] मठ, विहार की ज़िंदगी ▸ **cloistered** *adj* बाहरी दुनिया से कटा हुआ : *a cloistered life* ○ *cloistered academics.*

clone / क्लोन् / *noun* **1** क्लोन, जीनों के प्रयोग से कृत्रिम रूप से पौधा या प्राणी बनाना जो ठीक अपने पूर्वज के समान हो **2** किसी अन्य व्यक्ति या वस्तु का पूर्ण अनुकरण करने वाली वस्तु या प्राणी।

close¹ / क्लोस् / *adj* (-r, -st) **1** close (to sb/sth) समीप का; घनिष्ठ **2** close (to sth) लगभग समान **3** सूक्ष्म, संपूर्ण : *pay close attention to sth* **4** close (about sth) गुप्त; छिपाने वाला : *She's always been a bit close about their relationship.* ■ a close call/shave (*अनौप*) ख़तरे से बाल-बाल बचते हुए ▸ **closely** *adv* **closeness** *noun.*

close² / क्लोस् / *adv* पास में ■ close by (sb/sth) ज़रा सी दूरी पर।

close³ / क्लोज़् / *verb* **1** बंद करना : *close a door/a window* **2** समाप्त करना : *The speaker closed (the meeting) with a word of thanks to the chairman.* ■ a closed book (to sb) अज्ञात विषय **behind closed doors** जनसमुदाय की जानकारी से परे/दूर **close around/round/over sb/sth** घेराव करना **close**

in (on sb/sth) 1 समीप घेरते हुए धावा करना **2** किसी व्यक्ति/वस्तु को घेरना : *Darkness was gradually closing in.* **close/shut one's eyes to sth** जानबूझकर अनदेखी करना **close (sth) down** बंद करना ▸ **closing date** *noun* (कोई कार्य करने की) अंतिम तिथि।

close⁴ / क्लोज़ / *noun* [sing] (औप) समाप्ति : *at the close of the day.*

closed / क्लोज़्ड् / *adj* **1** दूसरों से अप्रभावित **2** (विचारों में) संकीर्ण **3** सीमित (दायरे में)।

closet /'क्लॉज़िट् / *noun* (विशेषत: US) छोटी कोठरी; अलमारी; स्टोर रूम ▸ **closet** *verb* **closet A and B (together)** निजी या गुप्त बात के लिए कमरे में बंद कर देना **closet** *adj* गुप्त।

closure /'क्लोश़र् / *noun* बंद होने या करने की प्रक्रिया : *factory closures* ○ *The threat of closure affected the workers' morale.*

clot / क्लॉट् / *noun* (रक्त का) थक्का ▸ **clot** *verb* (-tt-) थक्का बनना।

cloth / क्लॉथ् / *noun* (pl **cloths** / क्लॉथ्स्; US क्लॉद्ज़ /) **1** (बुना हुआ) कपड़ा (ऊनी, सूती, नायलोन आदि) **2** विशेष प्रयोजन के लिए प्रयुक्त कपड़े का टुकड़ा : *a tablecloth* ○ *a floorcloth.*

clothe / क्लोद् / *verb* **1 clothe sb/ oneself (in sth)** (औप) कपड़े पहनना, कपड़े पहनाना : *They were clothed from head to foot in white.* **2 clothe sth in sth** (औप) वस्त्रों की तरह किसी चीज़ को ढकना : *a landscape clothed in mist.*

clothes / क्लोद्ज़; क्लोज़् / *noun* [pl] वस्त्र, पोशाक, पहनावा ▸ **clothes-line** *noun* कपड़े सुखाने की डोरी, अलगनी **clothes-peg** *noun* अलगनी के क्लिप।

clothing /'क्लोदिङ् / *noun* पोशाक।

cloud¹ / क्लाउड् / *noun* **1** बादल **2** हवा में धुएँ, धूल आदि का गुबार; बहुत सारे कीट-

पतंगों का आकाश में एकसाथ उड़ना : *a cloud of locusts* **3** संशय, दुख आदि उत्पन्न करने वाली चीज़ : *A cloud of suspicion is hanging over him.* ■ **under a cloud** उपेक्षा और तिरस्कार की स्थिति में ▸ **cloudburst** *noun* अचानक मूसलाधार वर्षा **cloudless** *adj* (आकाश) साफ़ **cloudy** *adj* (-ier, -iest) **1** (आकाश) बादलों से ढका हुआ **2** (द्रव) गदला, मटमैला।

cloud² / क्लाउड् / *verb* **1** धुँधला और अस्पष्ट हो जाना : *Tears clouded her eyes.* **2 cloud (over)** दुख, चिंता या क्रोध चेहरे पर उभर आना **3** ख़राब कर देना : *cloud sb's happiness/enjoyment.*

clout / क्लाउट् / *noun* (अनौप) **1** हाथ या कठोर वस्तु का ज़ोरदार प्रहार : *get a clout across the back of the head* **2** शक्ति या प्रभाव : *This union hasn't much clout with the government.*

clove¹ / क्लोव् / *noun* लौंग (मसाला)।

clove² / क्लोव् / *noun* गाँठ वाली कंद जैसे लहसुन आदि : *a clove of garlic.*

clown / क्लाउन् / *noun* **1** विदूषक, जो अपनी मूर्खतापूर्ण हरकतों से औरों को हँसाता है **2** (कभी-कभी अपमा) मूर्ख, गँवार व्यक्ति ▸ **clown** *verb* **clown (about/ around)** (प्राय: अपमा) जोकर की तरह आचरण करना **clownish** *adj.*

club¹ / क्लब् / *noun* क्लब, मंडली : *a working men's club.*

club² / क्लब् / *noun* **1** गदा, मुगदर **2** गोल्फ़ का डंडा ▸ **club** *verb* (-bb-) गदा/डंडे से मारना : *Many of the demonstrators were clubbed to the ground and kicked.*

clubs / क्लब्स् / *noun* ताश के पत्तों में 'चिड़ी' के पत्ते।

cluck / क्लक् / *verb* मुर्गी की तरह आवाज़ करना ▸ **cluck** *noun* मुर्गी की जैसी आवाज़।

clue / क्लू / *noun* **1 clue (to sth)** (किसी समस्या का संभावित उत्तर सुझाने वाला)

संकेत : *We have no clue as to where she went after she left home.* 2 वर्ग-पहेली के उत्तरों के संकेत शब्द ▸ **clue** *verb* ■ **clue sb in (about/on sth)** *(US अनौप)* किसी को ताज़ी जानकारी प्रदान करना ▸ **clueless** *adj (अनौप, अपमा)* मूर्ख, अयोग्य।

clump / क्लम्प् / *noun* वृक्षों, व्यक्तियों या वस्तुओं का झुरमुट : *a clump of specta-tors.*

clumsy / क्लम्ज़ि / *adj* (-ier, -iest) बेडौल, भद्दा; बेढंगा ▸ **clumsily** *adv* **clumsiness** *noun.*

cluster / क्लस्टर् / *noun* 1 गुच्छा : *a cluster of berries/flowers* 2 झुंड, समूह : *a cluster of houses/specta-tors* ▸ **cluster** *verb* ■ **cluster round/around sb/sth** एकत्र होना या करना; झुंड बनाना/बनना।

clutch / क्लच् / *verb* पकड़ लेना; (भय और चिंता के कारण) जकड़ लेना : *clutch a baby in one's arms* ▸ **clutch** *noun* 1 पकड़, चंगुल 2 मशीन में विभिन्न भागों को पकड़ने/छोड़ने का पुर्ज़ा, क्लच 3 **clutches** [pl] शिकंजा, चंगुल : *fall into the clutches of sb/sth ○ escape from sb's clutches.*

clutter / क्लटर् / *noun* (अपमा) अस्त-व्यस्त बिखरी (अनावश्यक) वस्तुएँ; अस्त-व्यस्तता की स्थिति : *My room is always in a clutter.* ▸ **clutter** *verb* **clutter sth (up) (with sth)** अस्त-व्यस्त और बुरे तरीक़े से किसी जगह को वस्तुओं से भर डालना।

co- *pref (पूर्वपद)* साथ-साथ, सह : *co-produced ○ co-author.*

coach[1] / कोच् / *noun* 1 कोच, चार पहियों की घोड़ों द्वारा खींची गई गाड़ी 2 (रेल का) डिब्बा; दूर आने-जाने वाली आरामदेह बस : *travel by overnight coach to Khandala.*

coach[2] / कोच् / *noun* 1 खिलाड़ियों को प्रशिक्षण देने वाला व्यक्ति : *a tennis/ swimming coach* 2 व्यक्तिगत रूप से परीक्षार्थी को परीक्षा के लिए तैयार करने वाला शिक्षक : *a mathematics coach* ▸ **coach** *verb* **coach sb (for/in sth)** प्रशिक्षण देना; सिखाना।

coagulate / कोॲग्युलेट् / *verb* द्रव अवस्था से गाढ़े अर्धठोस में परिवर्तित करना, होना; थक्का बनना : *Blood coagulates in air.* ▸ **coagulation** *noun.*

coal / कोल् / *noun* कोयला, कोयले का टुकड़ा ▸ **coal-black** *adj* एकदम काला रंग **coal-field** *noun* कोयले का खनन प्रदेश **coal-fired** *adj* कोयले की ऊर्जा से चलित **coal-tar** *noun* तारकोल।

coalesce / कोॲलेस् / *verb* (औप) सम्मिलित होना, संलग्न होना : *The views of party leaders coalesced to form a coherent policy.* ▸ **coalescence** *noun.*

coalition / कोॲलिशन् / *noun* 1 राज-नीतिक दलों का विशेष उद्देश्य के लिए अस्थायी सहमिलन : *a coalition gov-ernment* 2 सहमिलन : *the coalition of forces.*

coarse / कॉर्स् / *adj* (-r, -st) 1 मोटा और रूखा; घटिया : *bags made from coarse linen* 2 गँवारू; अपरिष्कृत : *coarse manners/tastes.*

coast / कोस्ट् / *noun* समुद्रतट ▸ **coastal** *adj* तटीय, तट-विषयक **coastguard** *noun* तट-रक्षक **coastline** *noun* समुद्र-तट की बनावट या संरचना।

coat / कोट् / *noun* 1 कोट (वस्त्र) 2 पशुओं की रोएँदार खाल, फ़र 3 रंग, वार्निश का अस्तर, तह : *give the wall a second coat of paint* ■ **cut one's coat ac-cording to one's cloth** (कहा) उतने पैर पसारिये जितनी लंबी सौर ▸ **coat** *verb* **coat sb/sth (in/with sth)** तह/परत चढ़ाना **coating** *noun* (रंग आदि की) परत, आवरण **coat of arms** *noun* (pl **coats**

of arms) अपने कुल, नगर आदि का सूचक चित्रचिह्न; युद्धचिह्न।

coax / कोक्स् / verb coax sb (into/out of (doing) sth) (कुछ कराने के लिए) फुसलाना : coax a child to take its medicine ‣ **coaxing** noun **coaxingly** adv.

cob / कॉब् / noun 1 भुट्टा (मक्का का) : corn on the cob 2 छोटी टाँगों वाला शक्तिशाली घोड़ा, टट्टू 3 नर हंस।

cobble / कॉब्ल् / verb (अप्र) जूते आदि की मरम्मत करना ‣ **cobbler** noun मोची।

cobra / कोब्रा / noun नाग, बड़ा साँप।

cobweb / कॉब्वेब् / noun मकड़ी का जाला।

cocaine / को'केन् / noun एक प्रकार का मादक द्रव्य, उत्तेजक पदार्थ।

cock[1] / कॉक् / noun (US rooster) मुर्गा : The cock crowed. 2 (विशेषतः compounds में) किसी भी पक्षी जाति का नर पक्षी : a cock pheasant/robin ‣ **cock-a-doodle-doo** noun मुर्गों के बोलने की आवाज़, कुकड़ू-कूँ **cock-and-bull story** noun बहानेबाज़ी वाली बात; बेवकूफ़ी वाली मनगढ़ंत कहानी **cock crow** noun उषा, भोर।

cock[2] / कॉक् / verb ऊपर की ओर करना, ऊपर उठाना : The horse cocked (up) its ears when it heard the noise.

cockatoo / कॉक'टू / noun (pl cockatoos) एक प्रकार का तोता जिसके सिर पर काफ़ी बाल (पंख) खड़े रहते हैं।

cock-eyed / कॉक्'आइड् / adj (अनौप) 1 टेढ़ा; तिरछा 2 बेवकूफ़; मूर्खतापूर्ण।

cockney / कॉक्नि / noun (pl cockneys) 1 लंदनिया, विशेषतः पूर्व लंदन (ईस्ट एंड) का निवासी 2 इन निवासियों की उच्चारण शैली : a cockney accent.

cockpit / कॉक्पिट् / noun वायुयान में चालक का स्थान।

cockroach / कॉक्रोच् / noun तिलचट्टा।

cocksure / कॉक्'शुअर् / adj cocksure

(about/of sth) (अनौप) विश्वास के साथ; दंभी।

cocktail / कॉक्टेल् / noun 1 मिश्रित मदिरा (फलों के रस में मिश्रित) : a cocktail bar/lounge 2 भोजन के पहले परोसे जाने वाले खाद्य पदार्थ के छोटे ठंडे टुकड़े : prawn/shrimp cocktail 3 (अनौप) पदार्थों का कोई मिश्रण : a lethal cocktail of drugs.

cocky / कॉकि / adj (-ier, -iest) (अनौप) गर्वीला; दंभी।

cocoa / कोको / noun कोको पाउडर/वृक्ष, चाकलेट पाउडर; कोको पाउडर मिश्रित पेय : a mug of cocoa.

coconut / कोकनट् / noun 1 नारियल : a row of coconut palms 2 नारियल का लच्छा/टुकड़ा : coconut flakes.

cocoon / क'कून् / noun रेशम के कीट का कोष ‣ **cocoon** verb cocoon sb/ sth (in sth) (from sth) आवरण से ढकना।

cod / कॉड् / noun (pl अपरिवर्तित) एक प्रकार की बड़ी समुद्री मछली; इसका मांस ‣ **cod-liver oil** noun कॉड के यकृत से निकाला गया तेल जो दवा के रूप में प्रयोग होता है।

code / कोड् / noun 1 संकेत व्यवस्था, (गुप्त) संदेश भेजने की पद्धति : a letter in code 2 (dialling code भी) फ़ोन कोड 3 नियम सिद्धांत : the penal code 4 आचार-संहिता; नैतिक व्यवस्था : a strict code of conduct ‣ **code** verb संकेत-बद्ध करना (लिखना)।

codify / कोडिफ़ाई / verb (pt, pp codified) आचार-संहिता तैयार करना।

coeducational / कोएजु'केशन्ल् / adj ऐसी शिक्षा-व्यवस्था जहाँ लड़के और लड़कियाँ साथ-साथ पढ़ते हैं।

coerce / को'अर्स् / verb coerce sb (into sth/doing sth) (औप) मजबूर करना, (करने को) बाध्य करना : We were coerced into signing the contract.

▸ **coercion** / को'अर्श्न् / noun ज़बर-दस्ती **coercive** / को'अर्सिव् / adj.

coexist / कोइग्'ज़िस्ट् / verb co-exist **(with sb/sth)** साथ-साथ रहना; (शत्रु देशों या दलों का) बिना लड़े साथ-साथ रहना ▸ **coexistence** noun.

coffee / 'कॉफ़ि / noun 1 कॉफ़ी, **(coffee beans** भी) कहवा (के बीज); कॉफ़ी पाउडर   2 कॉफ़ी पेय : a cup of coffee.

coffer / 'कॉफ़र् / noun 1 तिजोरी; जवाह-रात की भारी संदूकची   2 **coffers** [pl] (औप) ख़ज़ाना, कोषागार : The nation's coffers are empty.

coffin / 'कॉफ़िन् / noun ताबूत (जिसमें शव रखा जाता है)।

cog / कॉग् / noun (पहिये का) दाँता ■ **a cog in the wheel/machine** (अनौप) किसी बड़ी प्रक्रिया में छोटी-सी भूमिका निबाहने वाला व्यक्ति।

cohabit / को'हैबिट् / verb **cohabit (with sb)** (औप) (प्राय: पुरुष और स्त्री का) बिना शादी किए साथ-साथ रहना।

cohere / को'हिअर् / verb 1 संपूर्णता लाने के लिए एक जगह समूह में जुड़े रहना   2 **cohere (with sth)** (विचारों, तर्कों आदि का) सुसंगत होना, तर्कनिष्ठ होना : This view does not cohere with their other beliefs. ▸ **coherence** noun **coherent** adj 1 (विचार, सोच, अभिव्यक्ति) तर्कसंगत   2 (व्यक्ति) स्पष्ट अभिव्यक्ति में सक्षम **coherently** adv.

cohesion / को'हीश्न् / noun 1 संसक्ति, एकसाथ जुटकर रहने की अवस्था   2 (रसा) अणुओं को बाँधकर रखने वाला बल ▸ **cohesive** adj **cohesively** adv **cohesiveness** noun.

coil / कॉइल् / verb **coil (oneself/sth) round sth/up** कुंडलीकृत करना, लपे-टना : The snake coiled (itself) round the branch. ▸ **coil** noun 1 रस्सी आदि की पिंडी   2 (रस्सी का) छल्ला : the thick

coils of a python   3 कुंडल (विद्युत धारा प्रवाहित करने के लिए)।

coin / कॉइन् / noun सिक्का : a handful of coins ■ **the other side of the coin** किसी विषय का दूसरा पहलू, दूसरा दृष्टिकोण ▸ **coin** verb 1 सिक्के बनाना या ढालना   2 नए शब्द या पद का आविष्कार करना।

coincide / कोइन्'साइड् / verb 1 (घट-नाओं का) एक ही समय में पड़ना/होना : His arrival coincided with our depar-ture. 2 आकार या क्षेत्रफल में दो या अधिक वस्तुओं का एक-सा होना : The position of the manor coincides with that of an earlier dwelling. 3 (विचारों आदि का) मेल में होना।

coincidence / को'इन्सिडन्स् / noun 1 (विशेषत: समान घटनाओं का) संयोग वश एक-साथ घटित होना   2 दो या अधिक वस्तुओं की समानता : the coincidence of ideas ▸ **coincidental** adj.

coke / कोक् / noun कोक, कोक से गैस निकलने के बाद बचा हुआ कोयला।

cold[1] / कोल्ड् / adj (-er, -est) 1 ठंडा   2 (व्यक्ति का व्यवहार) उदासीन, तटस्थ : a cold look/stare/reception ■ **give sb/get the cold shoulder** अमित्रतापूर्ण व्यवहार करना/मिलना **in cold blood** बिना ममता या दुख अनुभव किए जानबूझकर कुछ कर देना : kill/murder sb in cold blood **pour/throw cold water on sth** निरुत्साहित करना ▸ **coldly** adv **cold-ness** noun.

cold[2] / कोल्ड् / noun 1 (वायुमंडल की) शीतलता, ठंडक : shiver with cold   2 सर्दी, जुकाम : a bad/slight cold ■ **(leave sb/be) out in the cold** अलग-थलग, उपेक्षित रहना या छोड़ दिया जाना।

colic / 'कॉलिक् / noun आँतों में तेज़ दर्द ▸ **colicky** adj.

collaborate / क'लैबरेट् / verb 1 col-laborate **(with sb) (on sth)** कुछ रचने/उत्पन्न करने में सहयोग देना, साथ काम

करना : *She collaborated with her sister on a biography of their father.* 2 **collaborate (with sb)** (अप्रिय) दुश्मन की फ़ौज से मिल जाना/सहायता करना; ग़द्दारी करना ▶ **collaboration** *noun* 1 **collaboration (with sb) (on sth)** सहयोग 2 **collaboration (with sb)** ग़द्दारी **collaborative** *adj* **collaboratively** *adv* **collaborator** *noun* सहयोगी।

collage / 'कॉलाश्; *US* कं'लाश्/ *noun* 1 कपड़े, काग़ज़, फ़ोटोग्राफ़ आदि के टुकड़ों को एक-साथ चिपकाकर कलाकृति तैयार करने की कला; इस प्रकार का चित्र 2 एक-दूसरे से संबंधित/असंबंधित वस्तुओं का संग्रह।

collapse / कं'लैप्स्/ *verb* 1 ढह जाना, ढेर हो जाना 2 (व्यक्ति का) बेहोशी या बीमारी के कारण गिर पड़ना : *He collapsed (in the street) and died on the way to the hospital.* 3 (क़ीमतें, मुद्रा की क़ीमत) अचानक गिर जाना : *Share prices collapsed after news of poor trading figures.* ▶ **collapse** *noun* 1 विध्वंस 2 विफलता 3 क़ीमतों में अचानक गिरावट **collapsible** *adj* सिमटने वाला, मोड़ा जा सकने वाला : *a collapsible chair.*

collar / 'कॉलर्/ *noun* 1 कालर (शर्ट, कोट आदि का) 2 (कुत्तों आदि के) गले का पट्टा : *Our dog has its name on its collar.* 3 दो नलियों या डंडों को जोड़ने वाली धातु की पट्टी, छल्ला ▶ **collar** *verb* (अनौप) कालर से पकड़ना **collarbone** *noun* जत्रुकास्थि।

collate / कं'लेट्/ *verb* 1 दो या अधिक पुस्तकों अथवा स्रोतों से सूचनाएँ एकत्र करना और जोड़ना, मिलान करना : *collate all the available data* 2 पुस्तक के पृष्ठों को एकत्र करके सही क्रम में रखना ▶ **collation** *noun* मिलान।

collateral / कं'लैटरल्/ *adj* 1 जुड़ा हुआ मगर कम महत्त्वपूर्ण, अतिरिक्त : *collat-*

eral benefits 2 एक ही पूर्वज से मगर दूसरी वंशावली में : *a collateral branch of the family* ▶ **collateral** *noun* गिरवी रखी गई संपत्ति।

colleague / 'कॉलीग्/ *noun* सहकर्मी (विशेषत: व्यवसाय या पेशे में)।

collect / कं'लेक्ट्/ *verb* 1 **collect sth (up/together)** एकत्र करना या होना; जमा करना या होना 2 स्वयं को नियंत्रित एवं संयत रखना : *collect one's thoughts before an interview* ▶ **collect** *adj, adv (US)* फ़ोन की ऐसी व्यवस्था कि जिसे फ़ोन किया जाए वह भुगतान करे : *a collect call* **collected** *adj* अपनी भावनाओं को नियंत्रित रखते हुए; शांत।

collection / कं'लेक्शन्/ *noun* 1 संग्रह क्रिया 2 एकत्र की हुई वस्तुएँ 3 कविताओं, कहानियों आदि का संग्रह : *a collection of critical essays.*

collective / कं'लेक्टिव्/ *adj* सामूहिक।

collector / कं'लेक्टर्/ *noun* संग्रह करने वाला; ज़िलाधीश (कलेक्टर)।

college / 'कॉलिज्/ *noun* 1 उच्च अथवा व्यावसायिक शिक्षा के लिए विद्यालय, कालेज 2 (विश्वविद्यालय से संबद्ध) कालेज ▶ **collegiate** / कं'लीजिअट्/ *adj* कालेज या कालेज के छात्रों से संबंधित।

collide / कं'लाइड्/ *verb* **collide (with sb/sth)** 1 (गतिमान वस्तुओं का) टकराना 2 (व्यक्तियों के मत, उद्देश्य आदि) विपरीत, असहमति में होना : *The interests of the two countries collided.*

colliery / 'कॉलिअरि/ *noun* (*pl* **collieries**) कोयले की खान।

collision / कं'लिश्न्/ *noun* 1 **collision (with sb/sth)** टक्कर 2 असहमति।

colloquial / कं'लोक्विअल्/ *adj* (शब्द आदि) सामान्य बोलचाल में प्रयुक्त (पर औपचारिक भाषण या लेखन में नहीं) ▶ **colloquialism** *noun* **colloquially** *adv.*

collude / कं'लूड्/ *verb* **collude (with**

sb) **(in sth/doing sth)** किसी को ठगने या धोखा देने के लिए साँठ-गाँठ करना।

collusion / क'लूश्न् / noun collusion **(with sb)** (औप) साँठ-गाँठ ▸ **collusive** adj.

colon[1] / 'कोलन् / noun लेखन में या मुद्रण में : का चिह्न।

colon[2] / 'कोलन् / noun बड़ी आँत्र, वृहदाँत्र।

colonel / 'कर्नल् / noun कर्नल, सेना में रेजिमेंट का कमांडर; अमेरिका में समान रैंक का वायुसेना अधिकारी।

colonial / क'लोनिअल् / adj उपनिवेश का, या से संबंधित ▸ **colonial** noun विदेशी व्यक्ति जो उपनिवेश में रहता है **colonialism** noun उपनिवेशवाद **colonialist** noun, adj.

colonist / 'कॉलनिस्ट् / noun उपनिवेश में बसने वाला व्यक्ति।

colonize, -ise / 'कॉलनाइज़् / verb उप-निवेश स्थापित करना/बसाना ▸ **colonization, -isation** noun.

colony / 'कॉलनि / noun (pl **colonies**) 1 उपनिवेश (ऐसा स्थान जो विदेशियों द्वारा विकसित किया गया हो और उन्हीं के देश द्वारा अंशत: या पूर्णत: शासित होता हो) : a former British colony 2 (एक ही व्यवसाय या रुचियों के मनुष्यों की) बस्ती।

color (US) = colour.

colossal / क'लॉस्ल् / adj अति विशाल : a colossal building ▸ **colossally** adv.

colossus / क'लॉसस् / noun (pl **colossi** / फ़'लॉसाइ / या **colossuses** / क 'लॉसिज़् /) विशाल आकार, महत्त्व अथवा योग्यता वाला व्यक्ति या वस्तु।

colour[1] (US color) / 'कलर् / noun 1 (लाल, पीला, नीला आदि) रंग 2 रंगने के काम में प्रयुक्त सामग्री ■ **give/lend colour to sth** किसी बात को सत्य- या संभाव्य-सा बनाना ▸ **colour-blind** adj रंगों में (वि-शेषत: लाल और हरे में) भेद न कर सकने वाला **colourful** (US colorful) adj

1 रंगीन 2 रुचिकर या उत्तेजक **colourless** (US colorless) adj 1 बेरंग 2 मंद, अरुचिकर।

colour[2] (US color) / 'कलर् / verb 1 रँगना, रंग लगाना : colour a picture 2 रंगयुक्त होना, रंग बदलना : It is autumn and the leaves are beginning to colour. ▸ **coloured** (US colored) adj 1 विशिष्ट रंग का 2 (अप्र, अपमा) वे लोग जो श्वेत न हों **colouring** noun 1 रंग लगाने की क्रिया 2 त्वचा का रंग 3 रंग देने वाला पदार्थ।

colt / कोल्ट् / noun बछेड़ा (4-5 वर्ष तक का घोड़े का बच्चा)।

column / 'कॉलम् / noun 1 (भवनों में) खंभा, स्तंभ 2 (संक्षि col) हिसाब-किताब, समाचार-पत्र या पुस्तक के पृष्ठ का ऊर्ध्वाधर विभाजन, स्तंभ 3 समाचार-पत्र/पत्रिका में एक ही पत्रकार द्वारा या एक ही विषय पर नियमित रूप से छपने वाला लेख ▸ **columnist** noun नियमित लेख लिखने वाला पत्रकार।

coma / 'कोमा / noun (pl **comas**) प्रगाढ़ बेहोशी, निश्चेतावस्था : go into a coma.

comb / कोम्ब् / noun 1 कंघा 2 (प्राय: sing) बालों में कंघा करने, बाल सँवारने की क्रिया 3 कंघे के समान मशीन का पुर्ज़ा 4=**honeycomb** ▸ **comb** verb 1 कंघा करना 2 रूई, ऊन आदि को कंघेनुमा चीज़ से साफ़ करके तैयार करना 3 **comb (through) sth (for sb/sth)** (खोजते हुए किसी स्थान को) छान डालना : Police are combing the woods for the missing children. ■ **comb sth out (of sth)** साफ़ करना।

combat / 'कॉम्बैट् / noun लड़ाई, संघर्ष : armed/unarmed combat ▸ **combat** verb 1 लड़ना, संघर्ष करना : combat the enemy 2 कम करने या समाप्त करने का प्रयास करना : combating disease/inflation **combatant** / कॉम्-

बटन्/ *noun* युद्धरत (सैनिक) **combat-ive** *adj.*

combination / ˌकॉम्बि'नेशन् / *noun* 1 संयोजन; सम्मिश्रण 2 एक विशेष ताला खोलने के लिए संख्याओं अथवा अक्षरों की शृंखला।

combine[1] / कम्'बाइन् / *verb* 1 **combine (with sth); combine A and B / A with B** एकसाथ मिलाना, एक कर देना : *Hydrogen combines with oxygen to form water.* 2 **combine A and B / A with B** दो या ज़्यादा चीज़ें एक ही समय में करना; दो या ज़्यादा अलग–अलग विशेषताएँ होना : *combine business with pleasure.*

combine[2] / 'कॉम्बाइन् / *noun* 1 व्यापार संघ 2 (**combine harvester** भी) फ़सल कटाई करने की एक बड़ी मशीन।

combustible / कम्'बस्टब्ल् / *adj* सहज में आग पकड़ने वाला और जलने वाला (पदार्थ), ज्वलनशील : *Petrol is highly combustible.* ▶ **combustible** *noun.*

combustion / कम्'बश्चन् / *noun* 1 आग से जलने की प्रक्रिया 2 पदार्थों के हवा में ऑक्सीजन के साथ मिलकर ऊष्मा और प्रकाश पैदा करने की रासायनिक क्रिया : *an internal combustion engine.*

come / कम् / *verb* (*pt* **came** / केम् /; *pp* **come**) 1 **come (to...) (from...)** आना; पहुँचना 2 स्थान या काल में कुछ होना; घटित होना : *She came first in English.* 3 **come in sth** (वस्तुएँ, उत्पाद आदि) उपलब्ध होना : *This dress comes in three sizes.* ■ **come about (that ...)** घटित होना **come across sb/ sth** (*और* **come on/upon sb/sth** भी) संयोग से पाना या मिल जाना **come by sth** कुछ पाना **come into sth** उत्तराधिकार में (संपत्ति) पाना **come of age** वयस्क होना **come off** (*अनौप*) आशानुकूल फल मिलना; घटित होना **come off (sth)** (वस्तु से) कुछ टूट जाना **come out** (पुस्तक)

प्रकाशित होना; (तथ्यों का) प्रकट होना **come round (come to भी)** होश में आना **come to blows (over sth)** झगड़ा करना।

comedian / क'मीडिअन् / *noun* (*fem* **comedienne** /ˌकमीडि'एन्/) 1 मसख़रा, विदूषक 2 हास्य अभिनेता।

comedown / 'कम्डाउन् / *noun* (प्राय: *sing*) (*अनौप*) सामाजिक स्तर या महत्त्व में गिरावट होना।

comedy / 'कॉमडि / *noun* (*pl* **comedies**) 1 प्रहसन; मनोरंजक नाटक या फ़िल्म : *I prefer comedy to tragedy.* 2 किसी चीज़ का मनोरंजक भाग; हास्य : *He didn't appreciate the comedy of the situation.*

comely / 'कम्लि / *adj* (-**ier**, -**iest**) (*अप्र या औप*) प्रियदर्शन, देखने में सुंदर (व्यक्ति)।

comet / 'कॉमिट् / *noun* धूमकेतु, पुच्छल तारा।

comfort / 'कम्फ़र्ट् / *noun* 1 दुख, कष्ट या चिंता से मुक्त; आराम, चैन 2 (प्राय: *pl*) भौतिक सुख : *The hotel has all modern comforts.* ▶ **comfort** *verb* आराम देना **comforting** *adj* **comfortingly** *adv* **comfortless** *adj.*

comfortable / 'कम्फ़र्टब्ल्; 'कम्फ़र्ट-ब्ल् / *adj* 1 आरामदायक वस्तु : *a comfortable bed* 2 सुखी, आराम से; (*अनौप*) धनवान ▶ **comfortably** *adv.*

comic / 'कॉमिक / *adj* 1 हास्यजनक : *a comic performance* 2 कॉमेडी से संबंधित, मनोरंजक : *a comic actor* ▶ **comic** *noun* 1 हास्य अभिनेता 2 (*US* **comic book**) हास्य पत्रिका **comical** *adj* हास्यकर **comically** *adv.*

comma / 'कॉमा / *noun* लेखन या मुद्रण में , का चिह्न।

command[1] / क'मान्ड; *US* क'मैन्ड् / *verb* 1 आदेश देना, हुक्म देना 2 अधिकार या प्रभुत्व रखना, नियंत्रण रखना 3 स्थान या ऐसी जगह स्थित होना जहाँ से आसपास का

क्षेत्र दिखाई पड़े या उसका नियंत्रण किया जा सके : *The castle commanded the entrance to the valley.* ▸ **commanding** *adj* 1 आदेश देने का अधिकार रखते हुए 2 नियंत्रण या प्रभुत्व स्थापित करने की स्थिति में 3 प्रभावी, अधिकारपूर्ण : *a commanding voice.*

command² / क'मान्ड; *US* क'मैन्ड् / *noun* 1 आदेश, हुक्म 2 नियंत्रण, प्रभुत्व 3 command (of sth) प्रयोग/नियंत्रण के लिए योग्यता : *He has (a) good command of the French language.*

commandant / 'कॉमन्डैन्ट् / *noun* सैनिक लशकर का प्रमुख अधिकारी।

commander / क'मान्डर् / *noun* कमांडर।

commandment / क'मान्ड्मन्ट; *US* क'मैन्ड्मन्ट् / *noun* (बाइबिल में) ईश्वरीय आदेश, विशेषत: दस आदेश जो ईश्वर ने मूसा को दिए थे।

commando / क'मान्डो; *US* क'मैन्डो / *noun (pl* **commandos)** दुश्मन पर तेज़ी से आक्रमण करने में विशेष प्रशिक्षित दल का सदस्य।

commemorate / क'मेमरेट् / *verb* 1 किसी व्यक्ति या घटना के सम्मान में स्मरणोत्सव मनाना : *We commemorate the founding of our nation with a public holiday.* 2 (मूर्ति इत्यादि) किसी की यादगार में : *This memorial commemorates those who died in the war.* ▸ **commemoration** *noun* स्मरणोत्सव **commemorative** *adj.*

commence / क'मेन्स् / *verb* (औप) प्रारंभ होना ▸ **commencement** *noun* (औप) प्रारंभ।

commend / क'मेन्ड् / *verb* 1 **commend sb (on/for sth)** सराहना करना, प्रशंसा करना : *Her work was highly commended.* 2 अनुमोदन करना 3 **commend oneself/itself to sb** (औप) स्वीकार्य होना, पसंद किया जाना ▸ **commendable** *adj* प्रशंसनीय, श्लाघनीय

commendably *adv* **commendation** *noun* श्लाघा, प्रशंसा; शाबाशी।

commensurate / क'मेन्शरट् / *adj* **commensurate (with sth)** (औप) उचित अनुपात में; उपयुक्त।

comment / 'कॉमेन्ट् / *noun* **comment (on sth)** (लिखित) व्याख्या; (घटना आदि पर) टीका-टिप्पणी ▸ **comment** *verb* **comment (on sth)** टीका-टिप्पणी करना; समालोचना करना।

commentary / 'कॉमन्ट्रि / *noun (pl* **commentaries)** 1 किसी घटना का आँखों देखा हाल/वर्णन 2 व्याख्या, टीका।

commentate / 'कॉमन्टेट् / *verb* **commentate (on sth)** (घटना की) समालोचना करना, आँखों देखा वर्णन करना ▸ **commentator** *noun* **commentator (on sth)** समालोचक।

commerce / 'कॉमर्स् / *noun* वाणिज्य (विशेषत: दो देशों के बीच का व्यापार); सामान की ख़रीद-फ़रोख्त और वितरण।

commercial / क'मर्श्ल् / *adj* 1 वाणिज्य संबंधी : *commercial law* 2 (प्राय: *अपमा*) लाभ के उद्देश्य से, गुणवत्ता के आधार पर नहीं ▸ **commercial** *noun* टी वी या रेडियो पर विज्ञापन **commercialize, -ise** *verb* (प्राय: *अपमा*) मात्र पैसा बनाना **commercially** *adv.*

commiserate / क'मिज़रेट् / *verb* **commiserate (with sb)** सहानुभूति व्यक्त करना : *I commiserated with her on the death of her pet dog.*

commission / क'मिश्न् / *noun* 1 **commission (to do sth)** किसी व्यक्ति को दिया गया कार्य, कार्याधिकार : *She has received many commissions to design public buildings.* 2 दलाली, बट्टा, कमीशन : *You get (a) 10% commission on everything you sell.* 3 **commission (of sth)** (औप) आपराधिक या ग़ैर क़ानूनी कार्य : *the commission of a crime* 4 (विशेषत: सेना में अधिकारियों को

दिया गया) नियुक्ति-पत्र 5 (प्राय: **com-mission**) आयोग, कमीशन ▸ **commission** *verb*.

commissioner / क'मिशनर् / *noun* 1 आयोग का सदस्य 2 उच्च शासकीय अधिकारी, आयुक्त, कमिश्नर : *a police commissioner.*

commit / क'मिट् / *verb* (-tt-) 1 कोई अपराध या ग़लत काम करना : *commit murder/theft/suicide* 2 **commit sb to sth** सौंपना, हवाले करना : *commit a man to prison* 3 **commit sb/oneself (to sth/to doing sth)** वचनबद्ध होना, उत्तरदायी बनना : *commit oneself to a course of action* 4 **commit sb for sth** अभियोग के लिए उच्चतर न्यायालय के सुपुर्द करना ▸ **commitment** *noun* 1 वचनबद्धता 2 वादा।

committee / क'मिटि / *noun* कमेटी, समिति।

commodity / क'मॉडिटि / *noun* (*pl* **commodities**) 1 उपयोगी अथवा मूल्यवान वस्तु : *household commodities* 2 (*वाणिज्य*) व्यापार की वस्तु।

common¹ / 'कॉमन् / *adj* (-er, -est) 1 साधारण, सहज, सुलभ 2 **common (to sb/sth)** समाज या वर्ग के अधिकतम सदस्यों द्वारा प्रयुक्त, सर्वसामान्य 3 मामूली : *He's not an officer, but a common soldier.* 4 (*अपमा*) (व्यक्ति अथवा आचरण) गँवारू, अशिष्ट 5 (*गणित*) दो या अधिक मात्राओं में आने वाला : *a common factor/multiple* ■ **be common/public knowledge** अधिकांश लोगों को विदित ज्ञान **make common cause (with sb)** (*औप*) किसी समान उद्देश्य के लिए एकत्र होना/संगठित होना ▸ **commonly** *adv* **common sense** *noun* अनुभवजनित, व्यावहारिक ज्ञान।

common² / 'कॉमन् / *noun* (इंग्लैंड के गाँवों में) घास के मैदान ■ **have sth in common (with sb/sth)** सहभागी होना

in common सभी से प्रयुक्त **out of the common** असाधारण।

commonplace / 'कॉमन्प्लेस् / *adj* साधारण, मामूली ▸ **commonplace** *noun* साधारण/मामूली घटना आदि।

commonwealth / 'कॉमन्वेल्थ् / *noun* 1 राज्यसंघ 2 **the Commonwealth** [*sing*] राष्ट्रमंडल, ब्रिटेन और उसके भूतपूर्व उपनिवेशों का राजनीतिक संगठन।

commotion / क'मोशन् / *noun* शोरगुल, उत्तेजना, हलचल।

communal / 'कॉम्युनल्; क'म्यूनल् / *adj* 1 सर्वसामान्य के लिए : *communal land/ facilities* 2 सामुदायिक, समुदाय-विषयक : *communal life/communal violence.*

commune¹ / क'म्यून / *verb* ■ **commune with sb/sth** (*औप*) घनिष्ठता की भावना रखना; घनिष्ठता से बातचीत करना : *commune with God in prayer.*

commune² / 'कॉम्यून् / *noun* एकसाथ रह रहे, संपत्ति और ज़िम्मेदारियों में समान भागीदारी वाले लोगों का वर्ग, संघ।

communicate / क'म्यूनिकेट् / *verb* 1 **communicate sth (to sb/sth)** जान-कारी देना; (समाचार) दूसरे के पास पहुँचाना या प्रेषित करना : *This poem communicates the author's despair.* 2 (रोग, गरमी आदि) संचारित करना 3 **communicate (with sb)** विचारों या सूचनाओं का आदान-प्रदान करना : *Deaf people communicate by sign language.* 4 **communicate (with sb)** समान विचारधारा और भावना के कारण किसी से अच्छे संबंध रखना।

communication / क'म्यूनि'केश्न् / *noun* 1 संचरण, संप्रेषण 2 (प्राय: औप) संप्रेषित वस्तु (संदेश) 3 (**communications** [*pl*] भी) (रेल, सड़क, तार, टेलिफ़ोन आदि जो एक स्थान को दूसरे स्थान से जोड़ते हैं) संचार-व्यवस्था।

communicative / क'म्यूनिकटिव् / *adj*

बातचीत या विचारों के आदान-प्रदान के लिए तैयार।

communion / क'म्यूनिअन् / *noun* 1 **Communion (Holy Communion** भी) (ईसाई धर्म में) चर्चों में प्रभुभोग का समारोह 2 एक ही धर्म के लोगों का समूह, धर्म समाज 3 **communion (with sb/ sth)** *(औप)* संपर्क, विचारों का आदान-प्रदान।

communiqué / क'म्यूनिके; *US* क'म्यून 'के / *noun* अधिकृत निवेदन, ज्ञापन।

communism / 'कॉम्युनिज़म् / *noun* 1 ऐसी सामाजिक और आर्थिक व्यवस्था मानने वाली विचारधारा कि सारी संपत्ति पर समुदाय का स्वामित्व है और वह सभी सदस्यों के लाभ के लिए है 2 **Communism** साम्यवाद, ऐसी राजनीतिक व्यवस्था जिसमें शासन कम्युनिस्ट पार्टी के उच्चतम सदस्यों के हाथ में हो और पार्टी सारी संपत्ति का तथा उत्पादन-वितरण आदि गतिविधियों का नियंत्रण करती हो ▸ **communist** *noun* 1 साम्य-वाद का समर्थक 2 **Communist** कम्युनिस्ट पार्टी का सदस्य : *a communist coun-try.*

community / क'म्यूनटि / *noun (pl* **communities)** 1 **the community** [*sing*] एक स्थान या ज़िले के निवासी; समुदाय 2 बिरादरी, संप्रदाय : *a commu-nity of monks* 3 सहभागी और सहयोगी होने की स्थिति ▸ **community centre** *noun* सामुदायिक केंद्र।

commute / क'म्यूट / *verb* 1 अपने नगर से दूसरे स्थान को कार्य के लिए प्रतिदिन जाना और वापस आना : *She commutes from Meerut to Delhi every day.* 2 **com-mute sth (to sth)** एक प्रकार के दंड को दूसरे प्रकार के (कम कठोर) दंड में बद-लना : *The judge commuted the death sentence to one of life imprison-ment.*

compact¹ / कम्'पैक्ट् / *adj* 1 भली-भाँति रखा और बाँधा हुआ, सुसंबद्ध : *a compact*

mass of sand 2 (वस्तु) कम जगह लेते हुए : *a compact flat/car* ▸ **compact** *verb* एकसाथ अच्छी तरह दबा देना (भर देना) **compactly** *adv* **compactness** *noun.*

compact² / 'कॉम्पैक्ट् / *noun* 1 कॉम्-पैक्ट, श्रृंगार के लिए प्रयुक्त पाउडर की डिब्बी 2 औपचारिक समझौता : *The two states have made a compact to cooper-ate in fighting terrorism.*

companion / कम्'पैनिअन् / *noun* साथी; मित्र, सहचर; सहायक ▸ **companion-ship** *noun* मैत्री, साहचर्य।

company / 'कम्पनि / *noun (pl* **com-panies)** 1 (प्राय: **Company)** व्यापार हेतु बनाया व्यक्तियों का समूह, कंपनी : *a manufacturing company* 2 दूसरों के साथ रहना : *I enjoy his com-pany.* 3 टोली, मंडली, दल 4 (सेना में) कंपनी (प्राय: कप्तान या मेजर से संचा-लित)।

comparable / 'कॉम्परबल् / *adj* **com-parable (to/with sb/sth)** तुलना योग्य, समान, तुल्य।

comparative / कम्'पैरटिव्/ *adj* 1 तुल-नात्मक, तुलनापरक : *comparative lin-guistics/religion* 2 तुलना करते हुए; आपेक्षिक ▸ **comparatively** *adv.*

compare / कम्'पेअर् / *verb* 1 तुलना करना; कितना समान और कितना असमान, यह पता लगाना : *Compare (the style of) the two poems.* 2 **compare with sb/sth** से तुलना हो सकना : *He cannot compare with Shakespeare as a writer of tragedies.*

comparison / कम्'पैरिसन् / *noun* तुलना; तुलनात्मक कथन ▪ **bear/stand comparison with sb/sth** तुलना योग्य होना **by/in comparison (with sb/sth)** की तुलना में।

compartment / कम'पार्टमन्ट् / *noun* रेलगाड़ी में डिब्बा : *a second-class* *compartment* ▸ **compartmentalize, -ise** *verb* वर्गों में बाँटना/रखना।

compass / 'कम्पस् / *noun* 1 (magnetic compass भी) कुतुबनुमा, दिक् – सूचक (जिसकी सूई सदा उत्तर की ओर रहती है 2 (compasses [pl] भी) (गोला खींचने का) परकार : *a pair of compasses* 3 (प्राय: *sing*) विस्तार, क्षेत्र : *beyond the compass of the human mind.*

compassion / कम्'पैश्न् / *noun* दया-भाव : *The plight of the refugees arouses our compassion.* ▸ **compassionate** *adj* दयालु **compassionately** *adv.*

compatible / कम्'पैटब्ल् / *adj* compatible (with sb/sth) (व्यक्तियों, विचारों, सिद्धांतों की) अनुकूल होने की स्थिति; (कल-पुर्ज़े आदि) एक साथ प्रयुक्त होने लायक ▸ **compatibility** *noun* compatibility (with sb/sth) संगति, अनुरूपता।

compatriot / कम्'पैट्रिअट् / *noun* हम-वतन, देशभाई।

compel / कम्'पेल् / *verb* (-ll-) (औप) 1 बाध्य करना, मजबूर करना 2 बलपूर्वक काम निकालना; तीव्रता से प्रेरित करना ▸ **compelling** *adj* अत्यंत रुचिकर एवं उत्तेजक; सहमति के लायक।

compensate / 'कॉम्पेन्सेट् / *verb* compensate (sb) for sth हर्जाना देना, क्षतिपूर्ति करना (किसी नुक़सान के बदले कुछ अच्छा देना) : *Nothing can compensate for the death of a loved one.* ▸ **compensation** *noun* हर्जाना, क्षतिपूर्ति **compensatory** *adj.*

compère / 'कॉम्पेअर् / *noun* (टी वी अथवा रेडियो पर) कार्यक्रम संचालक ▸ **compère** *verb* कार्यक्रम संचालन करना।

compete / कम्'पीट् / *verb* compete (against/with sb) (in sth) (for sth) (दौड़, प्रतियोगिता) स्पर्धा में भाग लेना।

competent / 'कॉम्पिटन्ट् / *adj* competent (to do sth) योग्य, कार्य करने में सक्षम : *a highly competent driver* ▸ **competence** / 'कॉम्पिटन्स् / *noun* 1 competence (as/in sth); competence (in doing sth/to do sth) क्षमता, योग्यता 2 (क़ानून) किसी मामले में न्यायाधीश या न्यायालय का अधिकार **competently** *adv.*

competition / ,कॉम्प'टिश्न् / *noun* 1 प्रतियोगिता 2 competition (between/ with sb) (for sth) होड़, मुक़ाबला।

competitive / कम्'पेटटिव् / *adj* 1 प्रतियोगितात्मक 2 (competitive with sb/ sth) औरों के समान या औरों से अच्छा।

competitor / कम्'पेटिटर् / *noun* प्रतियोगी (व्यक्ति या संस्था)।

compile / कम्'पाइल् / *verb* 1 (सूचनाएँ) संकलित और सुव्यवस्थित करना 2 संकलित करके पुस्तक या रिपोर्ट तैयार करना ▸ **compilation** *noun* संग्रह, संकलन **compiler** *noun.*

complacent / कम्'प्लेस्न्ट् / *adj* complacent (about sb/sth) (प्राय: अपमा) अपनी उन्नति से संतुष्ट ▸ **complacency** / कम्'प्लेस्न्सि / *noun* आत्मसंतोष **complacently** *adv.*

complain / कम्'प्लेन् / *verb* 1 complain (to sb) (about/of sth) (प्राय: अपमा) शिकायत करना, असंतोष व्यक्त करना 2 complain of sth दर्द आदि के बारे में बताना : *The patient is complaining of acute earache.* ▸ **complainingly** *adv.*

complainant / कम्'प्लेनन्ट् / *noun* (क़ानून) = plaintiff.

complaint / कम्'प्लेन्ट् / *noun* 1 complaint (about sth); complaint (against sb); complaint (that...) शिकायत; असंतोष का कारण : *I have a number of complaints about the service in this hotel.* 2 शिकायत करने की क्रिया (घटना) : *You have no grounds for complaint.* 3 बीमारी

complaisant /कम्'प्लेज़न्ट्/ adj (औप) उपकारी, दूसरों को प्रसन्न करने को सदा तैयार : a complaisant husband ▶ **complaisance** noun.

complement / 'कॉम्प्लिमन्ट् / noun 1 complement (to sth) पूरक (जो पूरा करे) 2 (व्या) पूरक शब्द ▶ **complement** verb सर्वोत्कृष्ट गुण उभारने के लिए कुछ नया जोड़ना : Use herbs that complement each other. **complementary** adj.

complete[1] /कम्'प्लीट्/ adj 1 पूर्ण, अपने सभी अंशों के साथ 2 पूरा किया हुआ, संपन्न ▶ **completely** adv **completeness** noun.

complete[2] / कम्'प्लीट् / verb 1 पूरा करना, समाप्त करना : Fifteen students have completed the course. 2 सर्वथा दोषमुक्त करना; सर्वांगपूर्ण करना।

completion /कम्'प्लीश्न्/ noun 1 पूरा करने/होने की प्रक्रिया 2 पूरा होने की स्थिति : The film is nearing completion.

complex[1] / 'कॉम्प्लेक्स्; US कम्'प्लेक्स् भी / adj 1 बहुत-से भागों से बनी वस्तु : a complex system/network 2 जटिल, समझने-समझाने के तौर पर कठिन : a complex argument/problem ▶ **complexity** noun (pl **complexities**) जटिलता; जटिल वस्तु।

complex[2] / 'कॉम्प्लेक्स् / noun 1 एक स्थान पर समान प्रकार के या समान सुविधाओं वाले भवन : a big industrial complex 2 (मनो) पूर्व उत्पन्न अनुभवों, अतृप्त इच्छाओं से उत्पन्न विकृत मनोवृत्ति : an inferiority complex 3 (अनौप) अत्यंत तीव्र मनोवेग या भय : a weight complex.

complexion / कम्'प्लेक्श्न् / noun 1 (व्यक्ति का) रंग-रूप 2 (प्राय: sing) घटना का सामान्य स्वरूप या लक्षण : the political complexion of Eastern Europe.

compliance / कम्'प्लाइअन्स् / noun

compliance (with sth) 1 (औप) के अनुसार, की आज्ञापूर्ति में 2 (प्राय: अपमा) औरों की आज्ञापालन को तुरंत तैयार : ready compliance with all her wishes ▶ **compliant** /कम्'प्लाइअन्ट्/ adj आज्ञाकारी।

complicate / 'कॉम्प्लिकेट् / verb जटिल कर देना; दुरूह बना देना ▶ **complicated** adj 1 बहुत सारे भागों से पेचीदा तरीक़े से बना हुआ : complicated wiring/machinery 2 जटिल, उलझा हुआ : a very complicated situation/matter.

complication / कॉम्प्लि'केश्न् / noun 1 जटिलता, पेचीदगी 2 complications [pl] (चिकि) बीमारी को गंभीर करने वाले लक्षण, जटिलताएँ : Complications set in after the operation and the patient died.

complicity / कम्'प्लिसिटि / noun **complicity (in sth)** (क़ानून या औप) (किसी ग़लत काम या अपराध में) किसी का साथ देने की क्रिया : He was suspected of complicity in her murder.

compliment / 'कॉम्प्लिमन्ट् / noun 1 प्रशंसा या अनुमोदन की अभिव्यक्ति : pay sb a compliment 2 compliments [pl] (औप) सम्मान, शुभकामनाएँ : compliments of the season ▶ **compliment** / 'कॉम्प्लिमेन्ट् / verb **compliment sb (on sth)** प्रशंसा करना, शुभकामनाएँ अर्पित करना : I complimented him on his success.

complimentary / कॉम्प्लि'मेन्ट्रि / adj 1 सम्मानसूचक 2 सम्मानार्थ मुफ्त भेंट रूप।

comply / कम्'प्लाइ / verb (pt, pp **complied**) **comply (with sth)** आज्ञा, नियम पालन करना, अनुरोध पूरा करना : Certain conditions have to be complied with.

component / कम्'पोनन्ट् / noun घटक, अवयव ▶ **component** adj (एक पूर्ण वस्तु बनाने में) सहायक।

compose / कम्'पोज़् / verb 1 शब्दों, विचारों आदि को साहित्यिक, संगीतात्मक, रागात्मक रूपों में बाँधना : *songs composed by Rahman* 2 (औप) (पत्र, भाषण आदि) ध्यानपूर्वक लिखना : *to compose a letter* 3 **be composed of sth** विशिष्ट अंशों से बना हुआ : *a committee composed largely of lawyers* 4 (मुद्रण में) लेख को मुद्रण के अक्षरों द्वारा संघटित करना, कंपोज़ करना 5 स्वयं को नियंत्रित करना, शांत होना ▸ **composed** adj शांत।

composer / कम्'पोज़र् / noun संगीतकार।

composite / 'कॉम्पज़िट् / adj विभिन्न घटकों से बना हुआ, मिश्रित ▸ **composite** noun.

composition / ,कॉम्प'ज़िश्न् / noun 1 रचना (गीत, कविता आदि) 2 रचना करने की क्रिया।

compositor / कम्'पॉज़िटर् / noun (मुद्रण) प्रेस में कंपोज़ करने वाला।

compost / 'कॉम्पॉस्ट् / noun कूड़ा-खाद ▸ **compost** verb खाद बनाना, ज़मीन में खाद देना : *composting the kitchen waste.*

composure / कम्'पोज़र् / noun मन और आचरण से शांत होने की अवस्था।

compound¹ / 'कॉम्पाउन्ड् / noun 1 दो या अधिक घटकों से बनी वस्तु; (तक) एक से अधिक तत्त्वों से बना पदार्थ 2 (व्या) दो या अधिक शब्दों/शब्दांशों से बनी संज्ञा या विशेषण : *'Travel agent' and 'dark-haired' are compounds.* ▸ **compound** adj **compound interest** noun चक्रवृद्धि ब्याज।

compound² / कम्'पाउन्ड् / verb 1 (औप, तक) मिलाना, दो या अधिक वस्तुओं को मिलाकर कोई भिन्न वस्तु बनाना 2 और अधिक हानि करके स्थिति बिगाड़ देना : *Initial planning errors were compounded by the careless way in which the plan was carried out.*

compound³ / 'कॉम्पाउन्ड् / noun अहाता, हाता : *a prison compound.*

comprehend / ,कॉम्प्रि'हेन्ड् / verb (औप) 1 पूरी तरह समझना : *failing to comprehend the seriousness of the situation* 2 (औप) सम्मिलित करना।

comprehensible / ,कॉम्प्रि'हेन्सब्ल् / adj पूरी तरह समझ में आने योग्य, बोधगम्य : *a book that is comprehensible* ▸ **comprehensibility** noun.

comprehension / ,कॉम्प्रि'हेन्श्न् / noun 1 समझने की शक्ति : *That is beyond my comprehension.* 2 भाषा की समझ की परख करने के लिए प्रयुक्त अभ्यास कार्य : *a French comprehension test.*

comprehensive / ,कॉम्प्रि'हेन्सिव् / adj व्यापक : *the most comprehensive description.*

compress¹ / कम्'प्रेस् / verb **compress sth (into sth)** 1 दबाकर भरना, ठूँसना : *compressing straw into blocks for burning* 2 (लेखन में विचारों को) कम शब्दों में व्यक्त करना : *compress an argument into just a few sentences* ▸ **compression** / कम्'प्रेश्न् / noun दबाव **compressor** noun.

compress² / 'कॉम्प्रेस् / noun कपड़े की मोटी गद्दी जैसी पट्टी (जो रक्तस्राव रोकने या ज्वर कम करने के लिए शरीर पर रखकर दबाई जाती है)।

comprise / कम्'प्राइज़् / verb 1 अपने अंगों के रूप में रखना; बना हुआ होना : *a committee comprising people of widely different views* 2 किसी का अंग या सदस्य हो जाना।

compromise / 'कॉम्'प्रमाइज़् / noun 1 किसी झगड़े में दोनों दलों द्वारा सुलह करने के लिए अपने-अपने दावे छोड़ देना : *There is no prospect of compromise in sight.* 2 **compromise (between A and B)** इस प्रकार का समझौता : *Can the* *two sides ever reach a compromise on this issue?* ▸ **compromise** *verb* compromise (on sth) आपसी विवाद समझौते से सुलझाना।

compulsion / कम्'पल्श्न् / *noun* compulsion (to do sth) 1 दबाव, मजबूरी 2 न रोक सकने लायक तीव्र इच्छा (प्राय: तर्कहीन) ▸ **compulsive** / कम् 'पल्सिव्/ *adj* 1 अत्यंत रुचिकर 2 अनियंत्रित इच्छा के अधीन **compulsively** *adv.*

compulsory / कम्'पल्सरि / *adj* अनिवार्य, आवश्यक ▸ **compulsorily** *adv* अनिवार्यत:।

compunction / कम्'पङ्क्श्न् / *noun* (औप) खेद, अपने किए पर पश्चाताप।

computation / ‚कॉम्प्यु'टेश्न् / *noun* (औप) गणन, अभिकलन ▸ **computational** *adj.*

compute / कम्'प्यूट् / *verb* गणना करना, अभिकलन करना।

computer / कम्'प्यूटर् / *noun* कंप्यूटर, अभिकलन करने का इलेक्ट्रॉनिक उपकरण।

computerize, -ise / कम्'प्यूटराइज़् / *verb* 1 कार्य के लिए कंप्यूटर उपलब्ध कराना 2 कंप्यूटर में सूचना रखना ▸ **computerization, -isation** *noun.*

comrade / कॉम्रेड्; US कॉम्रैड् / *noun* 1 (comrade-in-arms भी) (अप्र) पक्का साथी, विश्वसनीय मित्र 2 समान ट्रेड यूनियन, समाजवादी पार्टी या कम्युनिस्ट पार्टी का सदस्य।

con / कॉन् / *verb* (-nn-) (अनौप) 1 किसी को धोखा देना 2 con sb (into doing sth/out of sth) ग़लत तरीक़े से किसी का विश्वास जीतकर कोई काम करवाना या कुछ लेना।

concave / कॉन्'केव्/ *adj* (रेखा या सतह) अवतल, नतोदर → convex देखिए ▸ **concavity** *noun.*

conceal / कन्'सील् / *verb* conceal sth/sb (from sb/sth) छिपाना, ढकना : *Pictures concealed the cracks in the walls.* ▸ **concealment** *noun* छिपाव।

concede / कन्'सीड् / *verb* 1 concede sth (to sb) कुछ सत्य, सही स्वीकार करना; क़बूल करना : *She grudgingly had to concede defeat.* 2 concede sth (to sb) (अधिकार आदि) देना, प्रदान करना : *We must not concede any of our territory.* 3 हार स्वीकार करना।

conceit / कन्'सीट् / *noun* 1 अहंकार, घमंड 2 (तक) साहित्य में चतुर अभिव्यक्ति या विचार ▸ **conceited** *adj* अहंकारी **conceitedly** *adv.*

conceive / कन्'सीव् / *verb* 1 conceive of sth; conceive sth (as sth) (योजना, विचार आदि की) कल्पना करना 2 (स्त्रियों का) गर्भवती होना : *She was told she couldn't conceive.* ▸ **conceivable** *adj* कल्पनीय, विश्वास योग्य **conceivably** *adv.*

concentrate / 'कॉन्सन्ट्रेट् / *verb* 1 concentrate (sth) (on sth/doing sth) ध्यान, प्रयास आदि एक बिंदु पर आना या करना, केंद्रित करना : *I can't concentrate (on my work) with all that noise going on.* 2 (तक) सांद्रित करना, गाढ़ा करना ▸ **concentrate** *noun* गाढ़ा या सांद्र द्रव **concentrated** *adj* 1 गहन (अध्ययन, प्रयास) 2 सांद्रित, गाढ़ा बनाया हुआ।

concentration / ‚कॉन्सन्'ट्रेश्न् / *noun* 1 concentration (on sth) एकाग्रता : *Stress and tiredness often result in a lack of concentration.* 2 concentration (of sth) केंद्रीभूत होना : *heavy concentrations of enemy troops* ▸ **concentration camp** *noun* नज़र-बंदी शिविर।

concentric / कन्'सेन्ट्रिक् / *adj* concentric (with sth) एक ही केंद्र वाले : *concentric circles/rings.*

concept / 'कॉन्सेप्ट् / *noun* concept

conception (of sth/that...) धारणा, संकल्पना (किसी अमूर्त धारणा का स्वरूप या सिद्धांत) : *The concept of community care is not new.* ▸ **conceptual** *adj.*

conception / कन्'सेप्श्न् / *noun* 1 conception (of sth/that...) धारणा 2 गर्भधारण।

concern¹ / कन्'सर्न् / *verb* 1 से संबंध रखना, के लिए महत्त्वपूर्ण होना : *Don't interfere in what doesn't concern you.* ○ *To whom it may concern...* 2 concern oneself with/in/about sth दिलचस्पी रखना 3 चिंतित होना/करना, उद्विग्न होना : *It concerns me that you no longer seem to care.* ■ be concerned in sth (औप) से संबद्ध होना ▸ **concerned** *adj* concerned (about/for sth) परेशान, उद्विग्न concernedly *adv* concerning *prep* (औप) के विषय में।

concern² / कन्'सर्न् / *noun* 1 concern (about/for/over sth/sb); concern (that...) चिंता, उद्विग्नता : *There is no cause for concern.* 2 किसी के लिए महत्त्व और दिलचस्पी का विषय : *What are your main concerns as a writer?* 3 व्यापारिक संस्था : *a huge industrial concern.*

concert / 'कॉन्सर्ट् / *noun* संगीत समारोह : *give a concert for charity* ■ in concert (with sb/sth) (औप) मेल से, सहमति से : *a plan devised in concert with local business.*

concerted / कन्'सर्टिड् / *adj* दो या अधिक व्यक्तियों के द्वारा आयोजित; संगठित : *a concerted attack/campaign/ effort.*

concession / कन्'सेश्न् / *noun* 1 रियायत, छूट 2 concession (to do sth) मालिक द्वारा किसी को कुछ करने का अधिकार देना या बेचना : *mining/oil concessions* ▸ **concessionary** *adj.*

conciliation / कन्'सिलि'एश्न् / *noun* असहमति का अंत करने या सुलह करने की प्रक्रिया : *She ignored his attempts at conciliation.* ▸ **conciliate** *verb* **conciliatory** / कन्'सिलिअटरि / *adj.*

concise / कन्'साइस् / *adj* थोड़े ही शब्दों में अधिक सूचना देते हुए; (लेखन-शैली आदि) संक्षिप्त ▸ **concisely** *adv* **conciseness** *noun.*

conclude / कन्'क्लूड् / *verb* 1 conclude sth (from sth) निर्णय या निष्कर्ष पर पहुँचना 2 conclude (sth) (with sth) (औप) समाप्त होना या करना 3 conclude sth (with sb) आयोजित या संपन्न करना : *conclude a trade agreement.*

conclusion / कन्'क्लूश्न् / *noun* 1 conclusion (that...) निष्कर्ष, निश्चय 2 समाप्ति, अंत : *bring sth to a speedy conclusion.*

conclusive / कन्'क्लूसिव् / *adj* निश्चायक **conclusively** *adv* अंतिम रूप में।

concoct / कन्'कॉक्ट् / *verb* 1 (अपमा) बहाना बनाना; (कपट) जाल रचना : *She'd concocted some unlikely tale about the train being held up by cows on the line.* 2 विभिन्न वस्तुओं को (प्राय: जो नहीं मिलाए जाते हैं) मिलाकर कुछ बनाना : *He concocted a tasty supper of pasta and vegetables.* ▸ **concoction** *noun* मिश्रण।

concrete¹ / 'कॉङ्क्रीट् / *adj* 1 मूर्त रूप, इंद्रियगोचर : *Physics deals with the forces acting on concrete objects.* 2 निश्चित, सकारात्मक : *concrete proposals/evidence/facts.*

concrete² / 'कॉङ्क्रीट् / *noun* कंक्रीट, सीमेंट, रेत, बजरी आदि मिलाकर तैयार की गई भवन-निर्माण सामग्री ▸ **concrete** *verb* concrete sth (over) कंक्रीट से ढकना : *concrete a road (over).*

concur / कन्'कर् / *verb* (-rr-) concur

(with sb/sth) (in sth/that...) *(औप)* सहमत होना; सहमति प्रकट करना।

concussion /कन्'कशन्/ *noun* मस्तिष्क को क्षति पहुँचाने वाली सिर पर गहरी चोट, जो व्यक्ति को बेहोश कर दे।

condemn /कन्'डेम्/ *verb* 1 condemn sb/sth (for/as sth) निंदा करना : *We all condemn cruelty to children.* 2 condemn sb (to sth/to do sth) *(क़ानून)* अपराधी ठहराकर दंड निर्धारित करना : *condemn sb to death/hard labour* 3 condemn sb to sth/to do sth किसी को ऐसी अवांछित स्थिति में डाल देना जिसे उसे सहना ही पड़े 4 निकम्मा या बेकार साबित करना : *a condemned building* ▸ condemnation /कॉन्डेम् 'नेश्न्/ *noun* भर्त्सना condemned cell *noun* काल कोठरी।

condensation /कॉन्डेन्'सेशन्/ *noun* 1 भाप उड़ते समय बूँदें जम जाना (जैसे बर्फ़ वाले पानी के गिलास के बाहर) 2 संक्षेपण।

condense /कन्'डेन्स्/ *verb* 1 condense (sth) (into/to sth) (गैस, भाप को) द्रवीभूत करना; (द्रव को) गाढ़ा बनाना, सघन करना 2 condense sth (into sth) कम शब्दों में भाव व्यक्त करना।

condescend /कॉन्'डि'सेन्ड्/ *verb* 1 *(प्राय: अपमा)* ऐसा कार्य करना जो अपनी दृष्टि में तुच्छ हो 2 (दूसरों के प्रति व्यवहार) शिष्ट पर स्वयं की वरिष्ठता दिखाते हुए ▸ condescending *adj* condescendingly *adv* condescension /कॉन्'डि'सेन्श्न्/ *noun.*

condiment /'कॉन्डिमन्ट्/ *noun (प्राय: pl)* मसाला।

condition[1] /कन्'डिश्न्/ *noun* 1 स्थिति, अवस्था; स्वास्थ्य की दशा : *be in a good/ excellent/poor condition* 2 conditions [*pl*] परिस्थितियाँ : *under existing conditions* 3 शर्त, प्रतिबंध 4 *(अप्र)* समाज में पद, मर्यादा ■ on condition that... इस शर्त पर, यदि।

condition[2] /कन्'डिश्न्/ *verb* 1 निर्धारण करना, प्रभाव डालना 2 condition sb/ sth (to sth/to do sth) स्थिति/परिस्थिति में किसी को ढालना 3 (स्वास्थ्य आदि) ठीक दशा में रखना।

conditional /कन्'डिश्नल्/ *adj* conditional on/upon sth शर्तों से प्रतिबद्ध, शर्त पर निर्भर।

condolence /कन्'डोलन्स्/ *noun* संवेदना, शोक : *a letter of condolence.*

condom /'कॉन्डॉम्/ *noun* कॉनडम।

condone /कन्'डोन्/ *verb* ग़लत/अनैतिक व्यवहार स्वीकार या नज़रंदाज़ करना : *Foul play can never be condoned.*

conducive /कन्'ड्यूसिव्; *US* कन्'डू- सिव्/ *adj* conducive to sth सहायक, का कारण (बनना) : *The noisy surroundings were hardly conducive to concentrated study.*

conduct[1] /'कॉन्डक्ट्/ *noun* 1 व्यवहार (विशेषत: नैतिक) : *observe the rules of conduct* 2 conduct of sth (व्यापार, मामले आदि का) प्रबंध, परिचालन।

conduct[2] /कन्'डक्ट्/ *verb* 1 निर्देशित करना, प्रबंध करना : *conduct a meeting/business* 2 संचालित एवं नियंत्रित करना : *a concert conducted by Zubin Mehta* 3 नेतृत्व करना, मार्ग दिखाना : *A guide conducted us round the museum.* 4 conduct oneself well, badly, etc *(औप)* व्यवहार करना 5 (पदार्थ का) अपने अंदर से गरमी या विद्युतधारा गुज़रने देना।

conduction /कन्'डक्श्न्/ *noun* (विद्युत/ऊष्मा) प्रवाह।

conductor /कन्'डक्टर्/ *noun* 1 बस या ट्राम का कंडक्टर 2 आर्केस्ट्रा का संचालक 3 *(भौतिकी)* चालक पदार्थ।

cone /कोन्/ *noun* 1 *(ज्यामिति)* शंकु (एक प्रकार की आकृति) 2 शंक्वाकार वस्तु 3 सदाबहार वृक्षों का फल : *pine, fir, cedar cones.*

confectioner / कन्'फ़ेक्श्नर् / *noun* केक, चाकलेट आदि बनाने/बेचने वाला ▸ **confectionery** *noun* केक, चाकलेट आदि।

confederacy / कन्'फ़ेडरसि / *noun* 1 (राज्यों का) संघ, संयुक्त राज्य 2 **the Confederacy** [*sing*] संधि द्वारा स्थापित (राज्य मंडल)।

confederate / कन्'फ़ेडरट् / *adj* संधि-बद्ध : *the Confederate States of America* ▸ **confederate** *noun* 1 अपराध या षड्यंत्र में साथी : *his confederates in the crime* 2 संधिबद्ध राज्यों का समर्थक।

confederation / कन्फ़ेड'रेश्न् / *noun* महासंघ, महासंगठन।

confer / कन्'फ़र् / *verb* (-rr-) 1 **confer sth (on sb)** (अधिकार, पदवी आदि) प्रदान करना 2 **confer (with sb) (on/about sth)** परामर्श करना।

conference / 'कॉन्फ़रन्स् / *noun* सम्मेलन, परामर्श।

confess / कन्'फ़ेस् / *verb* 1 **confess (to sth/doing sth)** अपराध स्वीकार करना; क़बूल करना : *The prisoner refused to confess (his crime).* 2 **confess (sth) (to sb)** (विशेषत: रोमन कैथो-लिकों में) पादरी के सामने अपने पाप या नैतिक अपराध स्वीकार करना; (पादरी द्वारा) पाप-स्वीकार सुनना ▸ **confessedly** *adv.*

confession / कन्'फ़ेश्न् / *noun* 1 अप-राध स्वीकरण 2 पाप स्वीकरण : *The priest will hear confessions in English and French.* ▸ **confessional** *noun* **confessor** *noun* वह पादरी जो पाप-स्वीकरण सुनता है।

confetti / कन्'फ़ेटि / *noun* विवाहित युगल के ऊपर फेंके जाने वाले काग़ज़ के रंगीन टुकड़े।

confidant / 'कॉन्फ़िडैन्ट्; कॉन्फ़ि'डान्ट् / *noun* (*fem* **confidante**) विश्वसनीय व्यक्ति जिसे कोई अपनी व्यक्तिगत गुप्त बातें बता सकता है।

confide / कन्'फ़ाइड् / *verb* **confide sth to sb** किसी को इस विश्वास के साथ रहस्य बताना कि वह औरों को नहीं बताएगा; भरोसे पर बताना : *She confided her troubles to a friend.* ■ **confide in sb** किसी पर विश्वास एवं भरोसा करके कोई रहस्य की बात कहना ▸ **confiding** *adj* **confidingly** *adv.*

confidence / 'कॉन्फ़िडन्स् / *noun* 1 **confidence (in sb/sth)** भरोसा एवं विश्वास : *to have/lose confidence in sb* 2 रहस्य, भेद 3 आत्मविश्वास, स्वयं पर भरोसा ■ **take sb into one's confidence** किसी को अपने रहस्य प्रकट करना।

confident / 'कॉन्फ़िडन्ट् / *adj* 1 विश्वस्त, आत्मविश्वासी 2 निश्चय दिखाते हुए ▸ **confidently** *adv.*

confidential / कॉन्फ़ि'डेन्श्ल् / *adj* 1 गोपनीय : *confidential letters/information* 2 विश्वास से बताई गई बात 3 विश्वासपात्र (व्यक्ति) : *a confidential secretary* ▸ **confidentiality** *noun* **confidentially** *adv.*

configuration / कन्फ़िग'रेश्न् / *noun* (प्राय: तक) किसी वस्तु के विभिन्न भागों की विन्यास व्यवस्था; ऐसे विन्यास से उत्पन्न स्वरूप/संरचना : *the configuration of a computer system.*

confine / कन्'फ़ाइन् / *verb* 1 **confine sb/sth to sth** किसी व्यक्ति/वस्तु को एक सीमा के भीतर निश्चित करके रखना 2 **confine sb/sth (in/to sth)** क़ैद करके रखना : *Isn't it cruel to confine a bird in a cage?* ▸ **confined** *adj* छोटा एवं सीमित **confinement** *noun* 1 सीमित होने या क़ैद की अवस्था 2 समय जिस दौरान माँ बच्चे को जन्म देती है।

confines / 'कॉन्फ़ाइन्ज़् / *noun* [*pl*] (औप) सीमाएँ, सीमांत।

confirm / कन्'फ़र्म् / *verb* 1 किसी कथन

अथवा मत की सत्यता स्थापित करना, पुष्टि करना 2 **confirm sth; confirm sb (in sth)** पक्का विश्वास होना/दिलाना, दृढ़ होना 3 नियुक्ति की संपुष्टि होना, स्थायी होना : *He has been confirmed as captain for the rest of the season.* 4 ईसाई चर्च की पूर्ण सदस्यता पाना ▶ **confirmed** *adj* पक्का; परिवर्तन न करने वाला : *a confirmed bachelor.*

confirmation / ˌकॉन्फ़र्ˈमेश्न् / *noun* 1 पक्का होने या करने की क्रिया 2 चर्च की सदस्यता प्रदान करने का धार्मिक अनुष्ठान।

confiscate / ˈकॉन्फ़िस्केट् / *verb* (दंडस्वरूप किसी की संपत्ति पर) क़ब्ज़ा करना; संपत्ति ज़ब्त करना : *The teacher confiscated Ravi's catapult.* ▶ **confiscation** / ˌकॉन्फ़िˈस्केश्न् / *noun.*

conflict / ˈकॉन्फ़्लिक्ट् / *noun* **conflict between A and B** 1 युद्ध, संघर्ष; गंभीर मतभेद 2 (विचारों का) विरोध, प्रतिकूलता : *a conflict of interests* ▶ **conflict** / कन्ˈफ़्लिक्ट् / *verb* **conflict (with sth)** विरोध होना, मेल न होना : *conflicting evidence.*

conform / कन्ˈफ़ॉर्म् / *verb* 1 **conform (to/with sth)** स्वीकृत नियमों का पालन करना, के अनुकूल होना 2 **conform with/to sth** सहमति में होना : *His ideas do not conform with mine.* ▶ **conformist** *noun* नियमों, स्वीकृत व्यवहार आदि का अनुसरण करने वाला व्यक्ति **conformity** *noun* **conformity (to/with sth)** (औप) अनुरूपता; तत्कालीन व्यवहार शैली के अनुकूल आचरण करने की भावना।

confound / कन्ˈफ़ाउन्ड् / *verb* (औप) 1 उलझन में डालना; गड़बड़ कर देना 2 (शत्रुओं को) हरा देना; (योजनाओं को) छिन्न-भिन्न कर देना : *confound a plan/ an attempt* ▶ **confounded** *adj.*

confront / कन्ˈफ़्रन्ट् / *verb* 1 (मुश्किलों का) सामना करना; आमने-सामने होना 2 **confront sb with sb/sth** किसी का

मुश्किलों या अप्रिय बात से सामना करा देना : *They confronted the prisoner with his accusers.* ▶ **confrontation** *noun* तीव्र विरोध; मुक़ाबला।

confuse / कन्ˈफ़्यूज़् / *verb* 1 गड़बड़ा देना, चकरा देना 2 **confuse A and/with B** एक को दूसरा समझना : *I always confuse the sisters: they look so alike.* 3 अस्त-व्यस्त कर देना ▶ **confused** *adj* 1 चकराया हुआ 2 अस्त-व्यस्त **confusing** *adj.*

confusion / कन्ˈफ़्यूश्न् / *noun* 1 गड़बड़, संभ्रांति 2 अस्तव्यस्तता, गड़बड़घोटाला।

congeal / कन्ˈजील् / *verb* (खून या अन्य द्रव का) ठंडा होकर कड़ा हो जाना या जम जाना।

congenial / कन्ˈजीनिअल् / *adj* 1 (व्यक्ति) समान प्रकृति एवं समान रुचि रखने के कारण प्रिय : *a congenial companion* 2 **congenial (to sb)** (वस्तुएँ) अनुकूल; रुचि के अनुकूल।

congenital / कन्ˈजेनिट्ल् / *adj* 1 (बीमारी) जन्मजात : *congenital defects/blindness* 2 (व्यक्ति) बीमार अवस्था या बीमारी के साथ पैदा हुआ : (अल) *a congenital liar.*

congested / कन्ˈजेस्टिड् / *adj* 1 **congested (with sth)** बेहद भरा हुआ, भीड़ भरा : *streets heavily congested with traffic* 2 (मस्तिष्क, फेफड़ों का) असामान्य रूप से रक्त भरा हुआ; (नाक) रेंट से भरा हुआ।

congestion / कन्ˈजेस्चन् / *noun* भीड़-भाड़।

conglomerate / कन्ˈग्लॉमरट् / *noun* 1 (वाणिज्य) विभिन्न व्यापारिक संस्थाओं को मिलाकर बना विशाल व्यापारिक निगम : *a mining/airline conglomerate* 2 एकसाथ रखी हुई बहुत सारी चीज़ें या हिस्से : *a conglomerate of three different bands* ▶ **conglomeration** / कन्ˈग्लॉमˈरेश्न् / *noun* 1 बहुत-सी

वस्तुओं का घालमेल 2 निगम बनाने की प्रक्रिया।

congratulate / कन्'ग्रैचुलेट् / *verb*
1 **congratulate sb (on sth)** बधाई देना
2 **congratulate oneself (on sth/do-ing sth)** अपने को भाग्यशाली समझना
▶ **congratulation** / कन्‚ग्रैचु'लेश्न् / *noun* 1 अभिनंदन (विजेताओं का)
2 **congratulations** [*pl*] बधाई।

congregate / 'कॉङ्ग्रिगेट् / *verb* इकट्ठा होना या करना : *A crowd quickly congregated (round the speaker).*

congregation / ‚कॉङ्ग्रि'गेश्न् / *noun* (विशेषत: चर्च में) एकत्रित जन-समूह
▶ **congregational** *adj.*

congress / 'कॉङ्ग्रेस्; *US* कॉङ्ग्रस् / *noun* 1 (विचार-विमर्शार्थ) सम्मेलन
2 **Congress** कुछ देशों, जैसे संयुक्त राष्ट्र अमेरिका में विधान-सभा; भारत में राजनीतिक दल 'कांग्रेस' ▶ **congressional** / कन्'ग्रेश्नल् / *adj* कांग्रेस संबंधी।

congruent / 'कॉङ्ग्रुअन्ट् / *adj* 1 (ज्या-मिति) एक ही आकार एवं आकृति वाले : *congruent triangles* 2 **congruent (with sth)** (औप) उपयुक्त, उचित : *meas-ures congruent with the serious-ness of the situation* ▶ **congru-ence** *noun.*

conic / 'कॉनिक् / *adj* (ज्यामिति) शंकु का/वाला ▶ **conical** / 'कॉनिक्ल् / *adj* शंक्वाकार : *a conical hat/shell/hill.*

conifer / 'कॉनिफ़र् / *noun* एक सदाबहार वृक्ष जिसके फल शंक्वाकार के होते हैं : *pines, yews and other conifers* ▶ **coniferous** *adj.*

conjecture / कन्'जेक्चर् / *verb* (औप) अटकलबाज़ी लगाना; बिना प्रामाणिक तथ्यों के राय देना : *It was just as I had conjectured.* ▶ **conjecture** *noun* अटकल।

conjugal / 'कॉन्जगल् / *adj* (औप) विवाहित जीवन के संबंध का; दांपत्य : *conjugal life/bliss/rights.*

conjugate / 'कॉन्जगेट् / *verb* (व्या) क्रिया के रूप देना/होना, जैसे am, is, are, was, were क्रिया 'to be' के रूप हैं ▶ **conjugation** *noun.*

conjunction / कन्'जङ्क्श्न् / *noun* 1 (व्या) शब्दों, उपवाक्यों आदि को जोड़ने वाले शब्द, जैसे and, or, but (समुच्चय बोधक शब्द) 2 (औप) संयुक्त होने की स्थिति; घटनाओं की संयुक्तता : *an unu-sual conjunction of circumstances.*

conjure / कन्'जर् / *verb* जादू का तमाशा करना; हाथ की सफ़ाई दिखाना : *to con-jure a rabbit out of an empty hat* ■ **conjure sth up** मन के सामने चित्र उपस्थित करना, इंद्रजाल बुनना ▶ **conjurer (conjuror** भी**)** *noun* जादूगर **conjur-ing** *noun.*

connect / क'नेक्ट् / *verb* 1 **connect (sth) (up) (to/with sth)** जोड़ना, जुड़ना : *The two towns are connected by bus service.* 2 **connect sb (with sb/sth)** व्यक्तियों/चीज़ों में संबंध स्थापित करना/होना : *We're connected by mar-riage.* 3 **connect sb (with sb)** टेलिफ़ोन द्वारा संबंध स्थापित करना।

connection (connexion भी**)** / क'नेक्श्न् / *noun* 1 **connection be-tween sth and sth; connection with/to sth** संयोजन, संबंध 2 ऐसी बस, ट्रेन, हवाई जहाज़ आदि जो यात्री एक बस, ट्रेन, हवाई जहाज़ से उतरने के बाद ले सके (अपने गंतव्य पर पहुँचने के लिए) 3 (प्राय: *pl*) व्यावसायिक विशेषज्ञ साथी : *I heard about it through one of my busi-ness connections.* ■ **in connection with sb/sth** के संबंध/संदर्भ में।

connective¹ / क'नेक्टिव् / *noun* संयोजक (वस्तु आदि); (व्या) संयोजक शब्द।

connective² / क'नेक्टिव् / *adj* (विशेषत: चिकि) जोड़ने, संयोजन करने वाली।

connive / कं'नाइव् / verb 1 connive at/ in sth (अपमा) ऐसा दिखना कि कुकार्य के संबंध में कुछ जानकारी ही नहीं है, देखी अनदेखी कर देना 2 connive (with sb) (to do sth) किसी से मिलकर कुकार्य करना ▸ **connivance** / कं'नाइवन्स् / noun connivance (at/in sth) कुकर्म में गुप्त सहयोग **conniving** adj धोखेबाज़ (व्यक्ति)।

connoisseur / कॉन'सर् / noun सुरुचि-पूर्ण या (कला) मर्मज्ञ व्यक्ति, गुण ग्राहक : a connoisseur of painting/antiques.

connote / कं'नोट् / verb (शब्दों का) मुख्य अर्थ के अतिरिक्त किसी अर्थ का संकेत देना : a term connoting disapproval ▸ **connotation** / ,कॉन'टेश्न् / noun मुख्य अर्थ के अलावा किसी शब्द से व्यक्त अन्य अर्थ : The word 'hack' means 'journalist' but has derogatory connotations.

conquer / 'कॉङ्कर् / verb 1 जीतना, अधिकार करना 2 (शत्रुओं को) हराना, परास्त करना 3 बाधा दूर करना 4 किसी का प्यार, प्रशंसा पाना : She has conquered the hearts of many men. ▸ **conqueror** noun विजेता।

conquest / 'कॉङ्क्वेस्ट् / noun 1 जीत; हार (अन्य की) 2 जीत से प्राप्त वस्तु : the Spanish conquests in South America.

conscience / 'कॉन्शन्स् / noun अंत:-करण, स्वयं के विचारों/कार्यों के सही या ग़लत होने का विवेक/चेतना : have a clear/guilty conscience.

conscientious / ,कॉन्शि'एन्शस् / adj (व्यक्ति या कार्य) विवेक वाला; कर्तव्यनिष्ठ और ईमानदार ▸ **conscientiously** adv **conscientiousness** noun.

conscious / 'कॉन्शस् / adj 1 (भले-बुरे की) जानकारी रखने वाला; सतर्क; चेतन 2 (कार्य, भावनाएँ आदि) स्वयं नियंत्रित या अनुभूत : I had to make a conscious effort not to be rude to him. ▸ **consciously** adv.

consciousness / 'कॉन्शस्नस् / noun 1 चेतन अवस्था 2 जानकारी होना 3 व्यक्ति के तमाम विचार, भावनाएँ आदि।

conscript / कन्'स्क्रिप्ट् / verb conscript sb (into sth) क़ानून द्वारा सशस्त्र सेना में सेवा अनिवार्य करना ▸ **conscript** / 'कॉन्स्क्रिप्ट् / noun ऐसे भर्ती किया गया व्यक्ति **conscription** / कन्'स्क्रिप्श्न् / noun अनिवार्य सैन्य भर्ती।

consecrate / 'कॉन्सिक्रेट् / verb 1 पवित्र करना, धार्मिक प्रयोग में लाना : The new church was consecrated by the Bishop of Chester. 2 consecrate sth/sb to sb पवित्र कार्य या विशेष उद्देश्य के लिए समर्पित करना : consecrate one's life to the service of God ▸ **consecration** / ,कॉन्सि'क्रेश्न् / noun.

consecutive / कन्'सेक्यटिव् / adj एक के बाद एक निरंतर; क्रम से लगातार : on three consecutive days, Monday, Tuesday and Wednesday ▸ **consecutively** adv.

consensus / कन्'सेन्सस् / noun consensus (on sth/that...) सर्वानुमति, सर्वसम्मति।

consent / कन्'सेन्ट् / verb consent (to sth) सहमति या अनुमति देना : They finally consented to go with us. ▸ **consent** noun consent (to sth) सहमति/अनुमति।

consequence / 'कॉन्सिक्वन्स् / noun 1 (विशेषत: pl) फल या परिणाम : be ready to bear the consequences of one's actions 2 (औप) महत्व : It is of no consequence. ■ in consequence (of sth) (औप) के फलस्वरूप।

consequent / 'कॉन्सिक्वन्ट् / adj consequent (on/upon sth) (औप) परिणाम रूप ▸ **consequently** adv.

conservation / ,कॉन्सर्'वेश्न् / noun

1 ठीक हालत में रखना, ख़राब होने से बचाए रखना : *the conservation of forests* 2 प्राकृतिक वातावरण का संरक्षण ▸ **conservationist** *noun.*

conservatism / कन्'सर्वटिज़म्/ *noun* रूढ़िवाद।

conservative / कन्'सर्वटिव्/ *adj* 1 रूढ़िवादी, तेज़ और आकस्मिक परिवर्तन का विरोधी : *Old people are usually more conservative than young people.* 2 (प्राय: **Conservative**) *noun* ब्रिटेन के एक राजनीतिक दल का, अनुदार दल का 3 (अनुमान) सतर्कतापूर्ण, जानबूझकर कम किया गया ▸ **Conservative** *noun* (प्राय: **Conservative**) ब्रिटेन में Conservative दल का सदस्य।

conservatory / कन्'सर्वट्रि/ *noun* (*pl* **conservatories**) पौधों को ठंड से बचाने के लिए बनाए शीशे की दीवारों और छत वाले भवन, रक्षा गृह।

conserve¹ / कन्'सर्व्/ *verb* नष्ट होने या बदलने से बचाए रखना, सुरक्षित रखना : *conserve one's health/resources.*

conserve² / 'कॉन्सर्व्/ *noun* (प्राय: *pl*) मुरब्बा, जैम।

consider / कन्'सिडर्/ *verb* 1 **consider sb/sth (for/as sth)** किसी के बारे में ध्यान रखना, सोचना 2 **consider sb/sth (as) sth** मानना, समझना : *We consider this (to be) very important.* 3 लिहाज़ करना, (विशेष) ध्यान रखना; विचार करना : *We must consider the feelings of other people.*

considerable / कन्'सिडरबल्/ *adj* महत्त्वपूर्ण, काफ़ी ▸ **considerably** *adv* पर्याप्त, यथेष्ट।

considerate / कन्'सिडरट्/ *adj* **considerate (towards sb)** (दूसरों की आवश्यकता का) ध्यान रखने वाला, लिहाज़ करने वाला।

consideration / कन्'सिड'रेशन्/ *noun* 1 किसी चीज़ पर विचार करने या ध्यान देने

की क्रिया : *Please give the matter your careful consideration.* 2 विचारयोग्य बात; कोई कारण 3 **consideration (for sb/sth)** लिहाज़ 4 (औप) इनाम या भुगतान ■ **in consideration of sth** (औप) के कारण, के बदले में।

considering / कन्'सिडरिङ्/ *prep, conj* ध्यान में रखकर : *She's very active, considering her age.*

consign / कन्'साइन्/ *verb* 1 **consign sb/sth to sb/sth** (औप) सौंपना, छोड़ देना; (अवांछित वस्तु को) दूर हटा देना : *consign a child to its uncle's care* ○ (अल) *The body was consigned to the flames.* 2 **consign sth (to sb)** (किसी व्यक्ति के पास रेल आदि से) सामान भेजना ▸ **consignment** *noun* 1 भेजे गए सामान की मात्रा 2 भेजने की प्रक्रिया।

consist / कन्'सिस्ट्/ *verb* ■ **consist in sth/doing sth** (औप) मुख्य या एकल घटक के रूप में होना या रखना : *The beauty of the poem consists in its imagery.* **consist of sth** का बना हुआ होना : *The committee consists of ten members.*

consistency / कन्'सिस्टन्सि/ *noun* (*pl* **consistencies**) 1 सदैव एक-सा विचार-व्यवहार रखने का गुण 2 गाढ़ेपन की मात्रा : *Mix flour and milk to a firm consistency.*

consistent / कन्'सिस्टन्ट्/ *adj* 1 (व्यक्ति, व्यवहार, विचार आदि) एक नियमित प्रतिमान और शैली के अनुकूल; हमेशा विद्यमान, अपरिवर्तित : *consistent interference/opposition* 2 **consistent (with sth)** सहमति एवं सामंजस्य की स्थिति में : *What you say now is not consistent with what you said last week.* ▸ **consistently** *adv.*

consolation / ,कॉन्स'लेशन्/ *noun* 1 सांत्वना, दिलासा : *a few words of consolation* 2 सांत्वना देने वाली वस्तु

व्यक्ति ▸ **consolation prize** noun प्रति-
योगिता न जीतने वाले को दिया गया पुरस्कार
consolatory adj.

console[1] / कन्'सोल् / verb **console
sb/oneself (with sth)** निराश/दुखी व्यक्ति
को सांत्वना देना, धीरज बँधाना : He con-
soled himself with the thought that
it might have been worse.

console[2] / 'कॉन्सोल् / noun 1 इलेक्ट्रॉ-
निक उपकरणों का स्विच पैनल, नियंत्रक पट
2 रेडियो या टी वी रखने की अलमारी।

consolidate / कन्'सॉलिडेट्/ verb 1 दृढ़
और सबल होना या करना : The time has
come for the firm to consolidate
after several years of rapid expansion. 2 (वाणिज्य) (ऋण, व्यापारिक
संस्थाओं आदि का) एक हो जाना : All the
debts have been consolidated.
▸ **consolidation** / कन्सॉलि'डेशन् /
noun दृढ़ीकरण; (भूमि की) चकबंदी।

consonance / 'कॉन्सनन्स् / noun
1 **consonance (with sth)** (औप)
सहमति, अनुरूपता 2 (तक) (संगीत स्वरों
का) रुचिपूर्ण सामंजस्य।

consonant / 'कॉन्सनन्ट् / noun (व्या)
व्यंजन (स्वर (vowel) नहीं); इन ध्वनियों
को अभिव्यक्त करने वाले अक्षर, जैसे b, c,
d, f आदि।

consort / 'कॉन्सॉर्ट् / noun पति या पत्नी
(विशेषतः शासक के) : the prince consort (शासन करने वाली रानी का पति)
■ **in consort with sb** (औप) किसी के
साथ; से सामंजस्य में।

consortium / कन्'सॉर्टिअम्/ noun (pl
consortiums या **consortia**) समान
उद्देश्य के लिए बहुत-से देशों, कंपनियों या
बैंकों का अस्थायी संघ, मंडल : the Anglo-
French consortium that built the
Channel Tunnel.

conspicuous / कन्'स्पिक्युअस् / adj
1 **conspicuous (for sth)** सहज में
दिखाई पड़ने वाला, ध्यान आकर्षित करने

वाला : make oneself conspicuous
2 उल्लेखनीय ▸ **conspicuously** adv
conspicuousness noun.

conspiracy / कन्'स्पिरसि / noun (pl
conspiracies) षड्यंत्र, दुरभिसंधि : accused of conspiracy to murder.

conspire / कन्'स्पाइअर् / verb 1 **conspire (with sb) (against sb)** षड्यंत्र
रचना, दुरभिसंधि करना : conspire with
others against one's leader 2 **conspire against sb/sth** (घटनाएँ) सम्मि-
लित होकर काम करते प्रतीत होना ▸ **con-
spirator** noun षड्यंत्रकारी।

constable / 'कन्स्टबल्/ noun कान्सटे-
बल, पुलिस का सिपाही ▸ **constabulary**
/ कन्'स्टैबलरी / noun ब्रिटेन में एक स्थान
विशेष का पुलिस दल।

constant / 'कॉन्स्टन्ट्/ adj 1 निरंतर,
अनंत 2 स्थिर, अपरिवर्तित, अटल : a
constant speed/value 3 एकनिष्ठ : a
constant friend/supporter ▸ **constant** noun (गणित या भौतिकी) अचर,
नियतांक **constantly** adv प्रायः, निरंतर,
लगातार।

constellation / कॉन्स्ट'लेशन् / noun
1 नक्षत्रमंडल, तारों का समूह 2 ख्यातिप्राप्त
व्यक्तियों का समूह : a constellation of
Bollywood talent.

consternation / कॉन्स्टर्'नेशन् / noun
अत्यंत विस्मय, उलझन : filled with
consternation.

constipation / कॉन्स्टि'पेशन् / noun
कब्ज ▸ **constipated** adj.

constituency / कन्'स्टिट्युअन्सि / noun
(pl **constituencies**) (राजनीतिक सदनों
का) चुनाव क्षेत्र; चुनाव-क्षेत्र के मतदाता :
constituency opinion.

constituent / कन्'स्टिट्युअन्ट् / adj पूर्ण
बनाने वाला घटक, अवयव : Analyse the
sentence into its constituent parts.
▸ **constituent** noun 1 निर्वाचक
(व्यक्ति) 2 संरचक, घटक : the chemi-

cal constituents of a substance
constituent assembly *noun*
संविधान-सभा।

constitute / 'कॉन्स्टिट्यूट् / *verb* **1** के बराबर होना/बनाना : *My decision does not constitute a precedent.* **2** स्थापित करना; औपचारिक अधिकार देना : *The committee had been improperly constituted.* **3** (औप) हिस्सा होना, पूर्ण करना : *Women constitute more than sixty per cent of the company's workforce.*

constitution / ˌकॉन्स्टि'ट्यूश्न् / *noun* **1** (किसी राज्य का) संविधान **2** (औप) गठन, संरचना; वस्तु की सामान्य रचना : *the constitution of an advisory group* **3** शारीरिक गठन (स्वास्थ्य की दृष्टि से) : *a robust/weak constitution.*

constitutional / ˌकॉन्स्टि'ट्यूशन्ल् / *adj* **1** संवैधानिक : *constitutional government/reform* **2** गठनात्मक; शरीर संरचनात्मक : *a constitutional weakness/robustness* ▸ **constitutionally** *adv.*

constrain / कन्'स्ट्रेन् / *verb* (औप) **1** बाध्य करके कोई काम करवाना : *With some embarrassment she felt constrained to point out his mistake.* **2** किसी का क्षेत्र या दायरा कम कर देना : *constrain sb's potentials/development* ▸ **constrained** *adj* (आवाज़, व्यवहार आदि) अस्वाभाविक; परेशान या उद्विग्न।

constraint / कन्'स्ट्रेन्ट् / *noun* **1** constraint (on sth) नियामक, बाधित करने वाली वस्तु : *constraints of time/ money/space* **2** तीव्र दबाव : *act under constraint* **3** (औप) अस्वाभाविक ढंग।

constrict / कन्'स्ट्रिक्ट् / *verb* (नसों, मांसपेशियों का) सिकुड़ना; सिकोड़ना, छोटा करना : *administering a drug that constricts the blood vessels* ▸ **con-**

stricted *adj* **constriction** / कन् 'स्ट्रिक्शन् / *noun.*

construct / कन्'स्ट्रक्ट् / *verb* **1** construct sth (from/out of/of sth) बनाना; रचना करना : *construct a factory* **2** (ज्यामिति) विशिष्ट निर्देशों के अनुसार आकृति की रचना करना।

construction / कन्'स्ट्रक्शन् / *noun* **1** निर्माण (की प्रक्रिया) **2** निर्मित वस्तु : *The shelter is a brick construction.* **3** (औप) (वाक्य आदि) रचना का तात्पर्य, अर्थ **4** रचना, (वाक्य) विन्यास ▸ **constructive** *adj* निर्माणकारी; रचनात्मक।

construe / कन्'स्ट्रू / *verb* **construe sth (as sth)** (औप) व्याख्या करना, अर्थ निकालना; अनुमान लगाना : *Her remarks were wrongly construed.*

consul / 'कॉन्सल् / *noun* राजदूत ▸ **consular** *adj.*

consulate / 'कान्स्यलट् / *noun* दूता- वास : *the American consulate in Mumbai.*

consult / कन्'सल्ट् / *verb* **1** consult sb/sth (about sth) किसी व्यक्ति से सलाह लेना; किसी पुस्तक को सूचना विशेष पाने के लिए देखना : *consult one's lawyer/a dictionary* **2** consult (with) sb विचार-विमर्श करना : *consult with one's partners.*

consultancy / कन्'सल्टन्सि / *noun* विशेषज्ञ सलाहकार कंपनी।

consultant / कन्'सल्टन्ट् / *noun* **1** consultant (on sth) व्यावसायिक रूप से सलाह देने वाला, परामर्शदाता : *a firm of management consultants* **2** consultant (in sth) विशेषज्ञ सलाह के लिए अस्पताल का वरिष्ठ डॉक्टर : *a consultant surgeon.*

consultation / ˌकॉन्सल्'टेश्न् / *noun* **1** परामर्श **2** परामर्श लेने के लिए मिलना; विचार-विमर्श के लिए गोष्ठी : *a top-level*

consultation on trade matters
▸ **consultative** adj.

consume / कन्'स्यूम्; US कन्'सूम् /
verb 1 ख़र्च कर देना; समाप्ति तक पहुँच
जाना : consume resources/time
2 (आग आदि से) नष्ट करना/होना : The
fire quickly consumed the wooden
hut. ○ (अलं) be consumed with
fury/hatred 3 (औप) खाना-पीना
▸ **consuming** adj सारा समय, शक्ति,
रुचि या ऊर्जा ले जाते हुए।

consumer / कन्'स्यूमर् / noun उपभोक्ता
(व्यक्ति)।

consummate/'कॉन्समेट्/verb (औप)
1 यौन क्रिया करके विवाह को क़ानूनन पूर्ण
बनाना 2 किसी चीज़ को पूर्ण करना ▸ **con-
summation** noun.

consumption / कन्'सम्प्श्न् / noun
1 (भोजन, शक्ति आदि का) उपभोग, खपत :
Gas and oil consumption always
increases in cold weather. 2 उपभोग
की गई वस्तु की मात्रा 3 (अप्र) क्षय की
बीमारी।

contact /'कॉन्टैक्ट् / noun 1 contact
(with sb/sth) स्पर्श, संपर्क 2 contact
(with sb/sth) संचार संपर्क : in constant radio/telephone contact (with
sb) 3 परिचित व्यक्ति : I have a useful
contact in Bangalore. 4 विद्युत
कनेक्शन; विद्युत कनेक्शन की युक्ति : The
switches close the contacts and
complete the circuit. ▸ **contact**
/'कॉन्टैक्ट् / verb संपर्क स्थापित करना
contact lens noun दृष्टि सुधार के लिए
नेत्रों में रखा जाने वाला छोटा प्लास्टिक लेंस।

contagion / कन्'टेजन् / noun 1 निकट
संपर्क से बीमारी का फैलना 2 संक्रामक
रोग।

contagious / कन्'टेजस् / adj 1 (रोग)
संसर्ग से फैलने वाला; (व्यक्ति) संक्रामक
रोग से पीड़ित : Scarlet fever is highly
contagious. 2 आसानी से फैलने वाला :

contagious laughter/enthusiasm
▸ **contagiously** adv.

contain / कन्'टेन् / verb 1 अपने में
रखना : The atlas contains forty
maps. 2 (शत्रुओं, भावनाओं आदि को)
दबाए/नियंत्रित किए रखना : She could
hardly contain her excitement.
▸ **containment** noun.

container / कन्'टेनर् / noun डिब्बा,
बोतल आदि पात्र।

contaminate / कन्'टैमिनेट् / verb गंदा,
अपवित्र या रोगयुक्त करना, संदूषित करना :
Flies contaminate food. ▸ **con-
tamination** / कन्'टैमि'नेश्न् / noun
संदूषण।

contemplate / 'कॉन्टम्प्लेट् / verb
1 संभावनाओं पर सोच-विचार करना : No
one would contemplate such a
thing happening. 2 चिंतन करना; मनन
करना 3 (प्रयोजन विशेष के लिए) दृष्टि में
रखना; ध्यान लगाना ▸ **contemplation**
/ 'कॉन्टम्'प्लेश्न् / noun 1 चिंतन-मनन
2 ध्यान 3 (औप) सोच-विचार **contem-
plative** adj.

contemporary / कन्'टेम्प्ररि / adj
1 contemporary (with sb/sth) सम-
सामयिक, निर्दिष्ट समय का : Dickens
was contemporary with Tha-
ckeray. 2 वर्तमानकालीन, समकालीन,
आधुनिक : contemporary literature
▸ **contemporary** noun (pl **contem-
poraries**) समकालीन व्यक्ति, समवयस्क।

contempt / कन्'टेम्प्ट् / noun 1 contempt (for sb/sth) तिरस्कार, अपमान की
दृष्टि, अवहेलना : opinions which are
generally held in contempt 2 contempt of/for sth अवज्ञा या अपमान की
स्थिति ▸ **contemptible** / कन्'टेम्प्टब्ल् /
adj अनादर के योग्य **contempt of court**
noun न्यायाधीश के आदेश को न मानना
contemptuous / कन्'टेम्प्चुअस् / adj
तिरस्कारपूर्ण **contemptuously** adv.

contend / कन् 'टेन्ड् / verb 1 contend with/against sb/sth; contend for sth संघर्ष करना : *Several teams are contending for the prize.* 2 दावा करना; तर्क प्रस्तुत करना ▸ contender noun दावेदार।

content¹ / कन् 'टेन्ट् / adj content (with sth); content (to do sth) अधिक न चाहते हुए, जो है उसी में संतुष्ट : *Are you content with your present salary?* ▸ content noun संतुष्ट; संतुष्टि content verb 1 content oneself with sth जो भी है उससे संतुष्ट रहना 2 (औप) संतुष्ट करना (औरों को) contented adj संतुष्ट contentedly adv contentment noun संतोष।

content² / 'कॉन्टेन्ट् / noun 1 contents [pl] सामान जो किसी पात्र (डिब्बा, बोतल आदि) में है 2 (पुस्तक, लेख, भाषण आदि की) विषय-वस्तु 3 किसी वस्तु की मात्रा जो किसी अन्य वस्तु/पात्र में है : *the silver content of a coin ○ food with a high fat content.*

contention / कन् 'टेन्शन् / noun 1 contention (for sth/to do sth) संघर्ष; स्पर्धा 2 (औप) झगड़ा; तीव्र असहमति 3 contention (that...) (औप) कथन, दावा, अभिमत : *It is my contention that you are wrong.*

contentious / कन् 'टेन्शस् / adj (औप) 1 असहमति पैदा करने की संभावना होते हुए 2 झगड़ालू, कुतर्की।

contest / कन् 'टेस्ट् / verb 1 विपक्ष में तर्क प्रस्तुत करना : *contest a statement/ point* 2 प्रतियोगिता में भाग लेना : *contest a seat in parliament* ▸ contest / 'कॉन्टेस्ट् / noun 1 contest (for sth) संघर्ष 2 प्रतियोगिता contestant / कन् 'टेस्टन्ट् / noun प्रतियोगी।

context / 'कॉन्टेक्स्ट् / noun 1 (किसी कथन का) संदर्भ, प्रसंग : *Can't you guess the meaning of the word from the context?* 2 घटना घटित होने की परिस्थितियां ▸ contextual adj contextually adv.

continent¹ / 'कॉन्टिनन्ट् / noun 1 महाद्वीप (जैसे यूरोप, एशिया आदि) 2 the Continent [sing] (ब्रिटेन और आयरलैंड को छोड़कर) यूरोप की मुख्य भूमि।

continent² / 'कॉन्टिनन्ट् / adj (चिकि) अपने मूत्राशय एवं आंत को नियंत्रण में रखने में सक्षम 2 (औप) भावनाओं एवं उद्वेगों को वश में रखने वाला, संयमी ▸ continence noun संयम।

continental / 'कॉन्टि'नेन्ट्ल् / adj महाद्वीपीय।

contingency / कन् 'टिन्जन्सि / noun (pl contingencies) आकस्मिकता; संभावना; संभावित घटना : *Be prepared for all contingencies.*

contingent¹ / कन् 'टिन्जन्ट् / adj contingent on/upon sth (औप) संभावित (जो हो भी सकती है और नहीं भी) बात पर निर्भर : *Our success is contingent upon your continued help.*

contingent² / कन् 'टिन्जन्ट् / noun 1 सैन्यदल, सेना की टुकड़ी 2 समान लक्षणों या गुणों (जैसे मूल स्थान) वाले लोगों का बड़ा समूह : *A large contingent from Japan was present at the conference.*

continual / कन् 'टिन्युअल् / adj (विशेषत: अपमा) निरंतर, लगातार : *continual rain/ interference.*

continuation / कन् 'टिन्यु'एशन् / noun 1 निरंतरता 2 वस्तु जो जारी रहती है या किसी को आगे बढ़ाती है।

continue / कन् 'टिन्यु / verb 1 continue (with sth) जारी रखना, बनाए रखना : *Wet weather is likely to continue for a few more days.* 2 आगे बढ़ना, आगे जाना 3 continue (as sth) रहना; बने रहना : *He is to continue as man-*

ager. 4 रुककर फिर शुरू करना ▸ **con-tinued, continuing** *adjs* निरंतर।

continuity /ˌकॉन्टिˈन्युअटि; *US* ˌकॉन्टिˈनूअटि / *noun* 1 निरंतरता : *We must ensure continuity of fuel supply.* 2 किसी चीज़ के अंशों में तर्कयुक्त संबंध : *His article lacks continuity.* 3 (सिनेमा या टी वी में) घटनाओं का सही क्रम।

continuous /कन्ˈटिन्युअस्/ *adj* (समय और स्थान की दृष्टि से) निरंतर, (बीच में बिना कहीं रुके) लगातार।

contort /कन्ˈटॉर्ट्/ *verb* **contort (sth) (with sth)** ऐंठना, मरोड़ना : *His face contorted, then relaxed.* ▸ **con-torted** *adj* ऐंठा हुआ; (अलं) तोड़ा-मरोड़ा हुआ **contortion** *noun* ऐंठन, मरोड़; इस तरह की क्रिया करना **contor-tionist** *noun* बदन ऐंठने में होशियार व्यक्ति।

contour /ˈकॉन्ठुअर्/ *noun* 1 (तट, पर्वत आदि की) परिरेखा, रूपरेखा : *The road follows the natural contours of the coastline.* 2 (**contour line** भी) समोच्च रेखा, नक्शे में वह रेखा जो समुद्रतल से समान ऊँचाई वाले स्थानों को दिखाती है ▸ **contoured** *adj* विशिष्ट रूपरेखा वाला।

contraband /ˈकॉन्ट्राबैन्ड्/ *noun* तस्करी द्वारा निषिद्ध माल देश के भीतर लाना या देश के बाहर ले जाना; तस्करी का सामान : *contraband tobacco.*

contraception /ˌकॉन्ट्राˈसेप्श्न्/ *noun* गर्भनिरोध, संततिनिरोध ▸ **contracep-tive** /ˌकॉन्ट्राˈसेप्टिव्/ *noun* गर्भनिरोधक पदार्थ/युक्ति।

contract¹ /ˈकॉन्ट्रैक्ट्/ *noun* **contract (with sb) (for sth/to do sth)** इकरारनामा, (व्यक्तियों, समूहों एवं राष्ट्रों के बीच) अनु-बंध पत्र; (विशेषत: सामान देने या कार्य करने का) ठेका : *We have a contract with the government for the supply of*

vehicles. ▸ **contractual** *adj* अनुबंध संबंधी।

contract² /कन्ˈट्रैक्ट्/ *verb* 1 इकरारनामा करना; ठेका लेना : *They were con-tracted to do the job.* 2 **contract sth (with sb)** (औप) निश्चित संबंध के लिए क़ानूनी सहमति देना : *She had contracted a most suitable mar-riage.* 3 (औप) बीमारी पकड़ना, ग्रहण करना : *He contracted measles/ AIDS.* 4 (औप) कुछ अप्रिय ग्रहण कर-ना : *debts/bad habits contracted in his youth* 5 **contract sth (to sth)** (व्या) शब्दों के संक्षिप्त रूप बनाना : *'He will' is often contracted to 'He'll'.* 6 छोटा करना या होना; कसना; सिकोड़ना : *Metals contract as they get cooler.* ▸ **contraction** /कन्ˈट्रैक्श्न्/ *noun* 1 सिकुड़न 2 (शब्द का) संक्षिप्त रूप।

contractor /कन्ˈट्रैक्टर्/ *noun* ठेकेदार।

contradict /ˌकॉन्ट्राˈडिक्ट्/ *verb* 1 (किसी तथ्य या कथन का) खंडन करना : *Why do you always contradict everything I say?* 2 (तथ्यों, कथनों का) विपरीत होना : *The two statements contra-dict each other.* ▸ **contradiction** *noun* 1 खंडन 2 **contradiction (be-tween sth and sth)** अंतर्विरोध; परस्पर विरोध : *It's a contradiction to say you love animals and yet wear furs.* ■ **a contradiction in terms** वाक्य जिसमें दो शब्दों के अर्थ एक दूसरे का खंडन करते हों: *'A generous miser' is a contradiction in terms.* ▸ **con-tradictory** *adj.*

contraption /कन्ˈट्रैप्श्न्/ *noun* (अनौप) बहुत असामान्य और जटिल मशीन या उपकरण : *a peculiar contraption for removing the peel from or-anges.*

contrary¹ /ˈकॉन्ट्रेरि; *US* ˈकान्ट्रेरि / *adj* स्वभाव या गुण में विपरीत; प्रतिकूल :

contrary beliefs/ideas/opinions
▸ **contrary to** *prep* के विपरीत : *Contrary to popular belief, the administration is highly centralized.*

contrary² / 'कॉन्ट्रेरि; *US* 'कान्ट्रेरि / *noun* **the contrary** (किसी वस्तु का) उलटा; विपर्यय ∎ **on the contrary** इसके विपरीत।

contrast¹ / कन्'ट्रास्ट; *US* कन्'ट्रैस्ट / *verb* **1 contrast (A and/with B)** एक वस्तु की दूसरी वस्तु के साथ इस प्रकार तुलना करना कि अंतर स्पष्ट हो जाए : *It is interesting to contrast the two writers.* **2 contrast (with sb/sth)** तुलना करके अंतर दिखाना ▸ **contrasting** *adj* शैली, रंग, रूप आदि में भिन्न।

contrast² / 'कॉन्ट्रास्ट; *US* 'कान्ट्रैस्ट / *noun* **1** वैषम्य, सहज अंतर **2** अंतर स्पष्ट करने वाली वस्तु **3 contrast (to/with sb/sth)** दो व्यक्तियों या वस्तुओं के बीच तुलना करके अंतर स्पष्ट करने की प्रक्रिया।

contravene /,कॉन्ट्र'वीन्/ *verb* (औप) (नियम, प्रथा आदि का) उल्लंघन करना; (कथन का) खंडन करना : *You are contravening the Wildlife Protection Act.* ▸ **contravention** /,कॉन्ट्र'वेन्शन्/ *noun* विपरीतता, उल्लंघन।

contribute / कन्'ट्रिब्यूट; 'कॉन्ट्रिब्यूट / *verb* **1 contribute (sth) (to/towards sth)** (चंदा, सहायता, सुझाव आदि) देना; अंशदान करना : *contribute aid for refugees* **2 contribute to sth** में सहायक होना, जोड़ना : *Does smoking contribute to lung cancer?* **3** (समाचार-पत्र, पत्रिका आदि में) लेख लिखकर छपने के लिए भेजना ▸ **contributor** *noun* अंश-दाता; सहभागी; लेखक **contributory** *adj.*

contribution / ,कॉन्ट्रि'ब्यूश्न्/ *noun* **1** चंदा, अंशदान **2** लेख **3** योगदान : *He made a very positive contribution to the project.*

contrivance / कन्'ट्राइव्न्स् / *noun*

(औप) **1** चतुर युक्ति **2** आविष्कार **3** चालाक एवं धोखेबाज़ व्यवहार।

contrive / कन्'ट्राइव् / *verb* (औप) **1** धोखा देने के लिए योजना आदि तैयार करना : *contrive a way of avoiding paying taxes* **2** मुश्किलों के बावजूद कुछ न कुछ उपाय ढूँढ़ निकालना : *contriving to live on a small income* ▸ **contrived** *adj* (अप्रम) पूर्वनियोजित; आविष्कृत (सत्य से हटकर)।

control¹ / कन्'ट्रोल् / *noun* **1 control (of/over sb/sth)** शासन और व्यवस्था बनाए रखने की शक्ति या अधिकार, नियंत्रण : *The pilot lost control of the plane.* **2** शांत रहने और गुस्सा न होने का सामर्थ्य : *He got so angry he lost control.* **3** संचालन और नियंत्रण के नियम एवं साधन : *traffic control* **4** (प्राय: pl) मशीन को नियंत्रित करने वाले स्विच, पुर्ज़े आदि : *the controls of an aircraft* **5** ऐसी जगह जहाँ से आदेश दिए जाते हैं या नियंत्रण रखा जाता है।

control² / कन्'ट्रोल् / *verb* (-ll-) **1** नियंत्रण करना; शासन और व्यवस्था बनाए रखना **2** सीमित या नियंत्रित करना : *control traffic/immigration/prices* ▸ **controllable** *adj* **controlled** *adj* नियंत्रित; सीमित **controller** *noun* व्यवस्था बनाकर रखने वाला (व्यक्ति); नियंत्रक।

controversial /,कॉन्ट्र'वर्शल्/ *adj* विवादित; विवाद का विषय।

controversy / 'कॉन्ट्रवर्सि / *noun* (pl **controversies**) **controversy (about/over/surrounding sth)** वाद; वाद-विवाद : *The appointment of the new director aroused a lot of controversy.*

convalesce /,कॉन्व'लेस्/ *verb* बीमारी के बाद स्वास्थ्य-लाभ करना : *She went to the mountains to convalesce after leaving hospital.* ▸ **convalescence** /,कॉन्व'लेसन्स्/ *noun* स्वास्थ्य-लाभ

convalescent / ˌकॉन्व़'लेस्न्ट् / *noun* बीमारी से अच्छा हो रहा रोगी।

convene / कन्'व़ीन् / *verb* (औप)
1 (किसी समाज, संस्था, समिति आदि के सदस्यों को बैठक के लिए) बुलाना : *convene the members/a conference*
2 बैठक के लिए आना : *The committee will convene at 9.30 tomorrow morning.* ▸ **convener (convenor** भी) *noun* समिति का संयोजक।

convenience / कन्'व़ीनिअन्स् / *noun*
1 सुविधा; उपयुक्तता; मुश्किलों से मुक्त दशा : *a transport system planned for the passengers' convenience*
2 सुविधाजनक दशा या उपकरण; सुविधाएँ : *The house has all the modern conveniences.*

convenient / कन्'व़ीनिअन्ट् / *adj* **convenient (for sb/sth)** 1 सुविधाजनक 2 (स्थान) पास में स्थित 3 उपयुक्त; समय और शक्ति बचाते हुए ▸ **conveniently** *adv.*

convent / 'कॉन्व़न्ट् / *noun* महिला मठ, नन लोगों का आश्रम; उनका समाज : *a convent school.*

convention / कन्'व़ेन्श्न् / *noun*
1 सम्मेलन, सभा : *a teachers'/dentists' convention* 2 परंपरा, रिवाज : *defy convention by wearing outrageous clothes* 3 इकरारनामा, समझौता : *the Geneva Convention.*

conventional / कन्'व़ेन्शन्ल् / *adj*
1 (प्राय: *अपमा*) परंपरागत, रूढ़िवादी : *conventional clothes/behaviour*
2 परंपरा से चला आ रहा : *a conventional design* 3 (हथियार) परमाणविक न होकर परंपरागत ▸ **conventionally** *adv.*

converge / कन्'व़र्ज् / *verb* 1 **converge (on/at...)** (अनेक रेखाओं, वस्तुओं, विचारों का) एक बिंदु की ओर अभिमुख होना : *armies converging on the capital city* 2 समान हो जाना, मिल

जाना : *The policies of the main political parties have started to converge.* ▸ **convergent** *adj* **convergence** *noun.*

conversant / कन्'व़र्सन्ट् / *adj* **conversant (with sth)** (औप) जानकार, किसी चीज़ का ज्ञान रखना या उससे परिचित होना : *You need to be fully conversant with the rules of the game.*

conversation / ˌकॉन्व़'सेश्न् / *noun* **conversation (with sb) (about sth)** बातचीत, वार्तालाप; बातचीत की क्रिया : *He was deep in conversation with his accountant.* ▸ **conversational** *adj.*

converse¹ / कन्'व़र्स् / *verb* **converse (with sb) (about sth)** बातचीत/वार्तालाप करना।

converse² / 'कॉन्व़र्स् / *noun* the **converse** [*sing*] 1 विपरीत, उलटा 2 (विचार, कथन आदि) प्रतिकूल ▸ **converse** *adj* **conversely** *adv.*

conversion / कन्'व़र्श्न् / *noun* **conversion (from sth) (into/to sth)**
1 रूपांतरण, रूप परिवर्तन : *a metric conversion table* 2 धर्म परिवर्तन, मत परिवर्तन : *her conversion to Catholicism.*

convert¹ / कन्'व़र्ट् / *verb* 1 **convert (sth) (from sth) (into/to sth)**
1 रूपांतरित करना (एक स्थिति से दूसरी, भिन्न स्थिति में बदलना) : *convert rags into paper* 2 **convert (sb) (from sth) (to sth)** किसी व्यक्ति के विश्वास या धर्म को बदल लेना; धर्म परिवर्तन करना : *convert sb from Christianity to Islam* ▸ **converter (convertor** भी) *noun* 1 (*भौतिकी*) प्रत्यावर्ती विद्युत धारा को दिष्ट धारा में या दिष्ट धारा को प्रत्यावर्ती धारा में बदलने वाला विद्युत उपकरण 2 रेडियो सिग्नल की तरंग दैर्ध्य बदलने वाला उपकरण।

convert² / 'कॉन्व़र्ट् / noun convert (to sth) धर्म बदला हुआ व्यक्ति।

convertible / कन्'व़र्टबल् / adj परिवर्तित/ रूपांतरित हो सकने योग्य।

convex / 'कॉन्'व़ेक्स् / adj उन्नतोदर, उत्तल : a convex lens/mirror →concave देखिए।

convey / कन्'व़े / verb 1 convey sb/ sth (from ...) (to...) (औप) एक स्थान से दूसरे स्थान ले जाना, ढोना : Pipes convey hot water from the boiler to the radiators. 2 convey sth (to sb) दूसरे व्यक्ति के पास सूचना, विचार, भावनाएँ आदि पहुँचाना; संदेश प्रेषित करना : Please convey my best wishes to your mother. 3 convey sth (to sb) (क़ानून) संपत्ति में पूरा अधिकार देना।

conveyance / कन्'व़ेअन्स् / noun 1 (औप) एक जगह से दूसरी जगह ले जाने की प्रक्रिया : the conveyance of goods by rail 2 (औप) सवारी, वाहन 3 संपत्ति हस्तांतरण; संपत्ति हस्तांतरण का क़ानूनी दस्तावेज़।

convict / कन्'व़िक्ट् / verb 1 convict sb (of sth) न्यायालय द्वारा अपराधी या दोषी ठहराया जाना : a convicted murderer 2 (अपराध का) क़ायल कर देना ▸ convict / 'कॉन्व़िक्ट् / noun अपराधी, क़ैदी : an escaped convict.

conviction / कन्'व़िक्शन् / noun 1 conviction (for sth) दोषी ठहराया जाना 2 क़ायल कर देना 3 conviction (that ...) दृढ़ विश्वास 4 ईमानदार और सही प्रतीत होने की दशा : His arguments are forcefully put, but they lack conviction.

convince / कन्'व़िन्स् / verb 1 convince sb (of sth) क़ायल कर देना : How can I convince you of her honesty? 2 किसी से कुछ करने के लिए मनवा लेना ▸ convinced adj 1 convinced (of sth/that...) क़ायल 2 पक्के तौर से विश्वस्त

convincing adj विश्वास करा देने योग्य ▸ **convincingly** adv.

convocation / कॉन्व़'केशन् / noun 1 (चर्च या विद्यालय में) बड़ी सभा, दीक्षांत समारोह 2 (औप) इस तरह का समारोह आयोजित करने की क्रिया।

convoy / 'कॉन्व़ॉइ / noun सुरक्षा के लिए वाहनों, जहाज़ों आदि का सिपाहियों के साथ, अन्य वाहनों/जहाज़ों के साथ यात्रा करने वाला दल : The convoy was attacked by submarines. ■ in convoy (वाहन, जहाज़ आदि) समूह में, साथ-साथ।

convulsion / कन्'व़ल्शन् / noun 1 (प्राय: pl) (दर्द से) ऐंठन, मरोड़ 2 खलबली : political convulsions 3 convulsions [pl] हँसी जो नियंत्रण में न लाई जा सके।

convulsive / कन्'व़ल्सिव़ / adj 1 मरोड़ पैदा करने वाला 2 अत्यंत खलबली पूर्ण : The French Revolution was a convulsive historical event.

coo / कू / verb (pt, pp cooed / कूड् /; pres p cooing) 1 कूकना, कबूतर के जैसी गुटरगूँ की आवाज़ करना : The baby was cooing happily. 2 प्यार से बहुत ही धीमे स्वर में कुछ कहना ▸ coo noun (pl coos).

cook / कुक् / verb 1 cook sth (for sb) भोजन पकाना 2 (अनौप, अपमा) (हिसाब-किताब आदि में) हेराफेरी करना : cook the account/figures 3 (अनौप) नियोजित होना; एक योजना के तहत घटित होना : What's cooking? ▸ cook noun रसोइया ■ too many cooks spoil the broth (कहा) बहुत से जोगी मठ उजाड़ (एक कार्य में ज़रूरत से ज़्यादा लोग हों तो काम ख़राब हो जाता है) ▸ cooking noun भोजन पकाने की क्रिया, पका हुआ भोजन।

cookbook / 'कुक्बुक् / (cookery book भी) noun व्यंजन पकाने की विधि बताने वाली किताब।

cooker /'कुकर्/ *noun* भोजन पकाने का बरतन : *a gas cooker.*

cookery /'कुकरि/ *noun* पाकशास्त्र।

cookie (cooky भी) /'कुकि/ *noun (pl* **cookies)** मीठा बिस्किट।

cookware /'कुक्वेअर्/ *noun* पकाने के बरतन।

cool¹ /कूल्/ *adj* (-**er, -est**) **1** शीतल, न बहुत ठंडा न बहुत गरम : *a cool breeze* **2** शांत, धैर्यवान : *He has a cool head.* **3** **cool (about sth); cool (towards sb)** उदासीन (व्यवहार) : *a cool reception to sb* ▸ **cool** *noun* **the cool** ठंडी हवा या ठंडा स्थान ∎ **keep/lose one's cool** शांतचित्त रहना/उत्तेजित हो जाना ▸ **coolly** /'कूल्लि/ *adv* उदासीनता से **coolness** *noun.*

cool² /कूल्/ *verb* **cool (sth/sb)(down/ off)** ठंडा करना; शांत करना : *A swim in the sea should cool you (down).* ∎ **cool (sb) down/off** किसी को शांत करना, उतावलापन कम करना।

coolant /'कूलन्ट्/ *noun* इंजन, परमाणु भट्टी आदि में प्रयुक्त शीतलक द्रव।

coolie /'कूलि/ *noun* (*प्रा, अप, अपमा*) कुली, मज़दूर।

coop /कूप्/ *noun* (मुर्गियों का) दरबा ▸ **coop** *verb* ∎ **coop sb/sth up (in sth)** छोटे-से स्थान में बंद रखना, आज़ादी छीन लेना।

cooperate (co-operate भी) /कोऑप्-रेट्/ *verb* **1** **cooperate (with sb) (in doing/to do sth)** सहयोग से कार्य करना : *cooperate with one's friends in raising money* **2** अपने हिस्से का कार्य करके सहायता करना।

cooperation (co-operation भी) /को-ऑप्'रेश्न्/ *noun* **cooperation (with sb) (in doing sth)** सहयोग, सहकारिता।

cooperative (co-operative भी) /को 'ऑपरटिव्/ *adj* सहकारी : *cooperative society* (सहकारी समिति)।

co-opt /को'ऑप्ट्/ *verb* **co-opt sb (onto/into sth)** किसी समिति के सदस्यों का अन्य व्यक्ति को अपनी समिति का सदस्य बनाना, सहयोजित करना : *co-opt a new member (onto the executive).*

coordinate¹ (co-ordinate भी) / को 'ऑर्डिनेट्/ *verb* अनेक व्यक्तियों द्वारा किए जा रहे कार्यों को समन्वित करना; वस्तुओं में समन्वय या सामंजस्य स्थापित करना : *a search coordinated with other police forces* ▸ **coordination (co-ordination** भी) /को 'ऑर्डि'नेश्न्/ *noun* **1** समन्वय **2** समन्वय सामर्थ्य : *have good/poor coordination* **coordinator** *noun* संयोजक, समन्वयकर्ता।

coordinate² (co-ordinate भी) / को 'ऑर्डिनट्/ *noun* **1** ग्राफ़ या नक़्शे में किसी बिंदु की स्थिति नियत करने के लिए प्रयुक्त दो में से कोई भी अंक या अक्षर, निर्देशांक : *the x and y coordinates on a graph* **2 coordinates** [*pl*] स्त्री के कपड़ों के मैचिंग आइटम।

cop /कॉप्/ *noun* (*अनौप*) पुलिस अफ़सर।

cope /कोप्/ *verb* **1** **cope (with sth)** (व्यक्ति द्वारा) नियंत्रण संभालना; सफलता-पूर्वक काम संभालना : *cope with problems/difficulties* **2** **cope with sth** किसी चीज़ से सफलतापूर्वक निपटने का सामर्थ्य रखना : *The roads simply can't cope with all the traffic now using them.*

copious /'कोपिअस्/ *adj* बहुत अधिक मात्रा में (उत्पन्न) : *I took copious notes.* ▸ **copiously** *adv.*

copper /'कॉपर्/ *noun* **1** (प्रतीक Cu) ताँबा, ताम्र **2** ताँबे या काँसे का सिक्का ▸ **copper** *verb* ताँबे का मुलम्मा चढ़ाना।

copy¹ /'कॉपि/ *noun* (*pl* **copies**) **1** नक़ल, प्रतिलिपि **2** (किताब, समाचार-पत्र आदि की) एक प्रति **3** = **photocopy** **4** समाचार-पत्र या विज्ञापन में छपने के लिए

लिखित सामग्री : *prepare copy for a brochure.*

copy² / 'कॉपि / *verb* (*pt, pp* **copied**) **1 copy sth (down/out) (from/off sth) (in/into sth)** नक़ल करना, प्रतिलिपि तैयार करना **2** (मशीन से) प्रतियाँ तैयार करना : *copy documents on a photocopier* **3** किसी व्यक्ति (के व्यवहार आदि) की नक़ल करना; अनुकरण करना : *Do not always copy what others do.* **4 copy (from/off sb)** (परीक्षा में) नक़ल करके धोखा देना।

copybook / 'कॉपिबुक / *noun* कापी।

copycat / 'कॉपिकैट् / *noun* नक़लची व्यक्ति।

copyright / 'कॉपिराइट्/ *noun* प्रतिलिप्य-धिकार, स्वकृत रचना या उत्पाद को छापने, बेचने, प्रसारित अथवा रिकॉर्ड करने का क़ानूनी अधिकार : *Copyright expires fifty years after the death of the author.* ▸ **copyright** *verb* प्रतिलिप्य-धिकार प्राप्त करना **copyright** *adj* प्रति-लिप्यधिकार से सुरक्षित।

coral / 'कॉरल/ *noun* **1** मूँगा **2** मूँगा उत्पन्न करने वाला जीव ▸ **coral** *adj* मूँगिया रंग का (लाल-गुलाबी)।

cord / कॉर्ड/ *noun* **1** डोरी, रस्सी **2** (शरीर में) डोरी जैसी संरचना वाला अंग : *the spinal cord* **3** तार, तंत्री; (गले में) स्वर/ध्वनि तंत्री : *the vocal cords* ▸ **cordless** / 'कॉर्ड्लस् / *adj* बिना डोरी और प्लग वाला यंत्र या टेलिफोन।

cordial¹ / 'कॉर्डिअल् / *adj* (भावनाएँ, शब्द, आचरण, संबंध आदि) मैत्रीपूर्ण या हार्दिक : *a cordial smile/handshake* ▸ **cordiality** / ˌकॉर्डि 'ऐलटि / *noun* **cordially** *adv.*

cordial² / 'कॉर्डिअल् / *noun* मदिरा रहित गाढ़ा, मीठा, फलों का रस : *lime juice cordial.*

cordon / 'कॉर्ड्न् / *noun* पुलिस या सेना द्वारा सुरक्षा के लिए डाला गया घेरा :

Demonstrators tried to break through the police cordon. ▸ **cordon** *verb* ▪ **cordon sth off** किसी स्थान का घेराव करना।

corduroy / 'कॉर्डरॉइ / *noun* **1** मोटा सूती कपड़ा, कार्डराय **2 corduroys** [*pl*] कार्ड-राय की पैंट : *a pair of blue corduroys.*

core / कॉर् / *noun* **1** फलों (जैसे सेब) के बीच का कड़ा भाग **2** किसी वस्तु का केंद्रीय एवं मुख्य भाग : *the earth's core* **3** किसी चीज़ का सर्वाधिक महत्त्वपूर्ण भाग : *Let's get to the core of the argument.* ▪ **to the core** अंदर तक, गहराई तक ▸ **core** *verb* फलों का कड़ा भाग निकालना।

cork / कॉर्क / *noun* **1** कार्क, हलका पदार्थ जो एक पेड़ की छाल होती है एवं प्रायः जिससे बोतलों की डाट बनाई जाती है **2** (बोतल की) डाट ▸ **cork** *verb* **cork sth (up)** डाट लगाना, बंद करना ▪ **cork sth up** (अनौप) भावनाओं को दिल में ही रखना, प्रकट न करना ▸ **corkscrew** *noun* कार्क निकालने का पेंचकस।

corn¹ / कॉर्न् / *noun* **1** अनाज वाले पौधे, जैसे गेहूँ, मक्का, जौ आदि : *a field of corn* **2** अनाज, ग़ल्ला **3** (*US*) मक्का ▸ **corn-cob** *noun* भुट्टा।

corn² / कॉर्न् / *noun* पैर में (विशेषतः अँगूठे पर) घट्टा (कड़ी खाल) बन जाना जो दर्द करता है।

cornea / 'कॉर्निंआ / *noun* (आँख का) पारपटल, बाहरी पारदर्शक रक्षक आवरण ▸ **corneal** *adj* : *a corneal blindness.*

corner¹ / 'कॉर्नर् / *noun* **1** कोना; नुक्कड़; सड़क का तीव्र मोड़ : *The van took the corner too fast.* **2** छिपा हुआ या दूर-दराज़ का क्षेत्र : *He knew every corner of the town.* **3 corner (in/on sth)** (वाणिज्य) मूल्य नियंत्रण या निर्धारण के लिए सारा उपलब्ध माल ख़रीद लेना **4** मुश्किल या पेचीदा स्थिति : *She'll need luck to*

get out of a tight corner like that.
■ **turn the corner** संकट पार करना।

corner² / 'कॉर्नर् / *verb* 1 किसी (व्यक्ति/जानवर) को घेर लेना : *a cornered fox* 2 किसी के पास (बात करने के लिए) दृढ़ निश्चय से जाना 3 (वाहन का) कोने पर से गुज़रना 4 (*वाणिज्य*) (किसी वस्तु पर) नियंत्रण/स्वामित्व पा लेना।

cornerstone / 'कॉर्नर्स्टोन् / *noun* 1 (भवन की) आधारशिला 2 किसी चीज़ की मुख्य एवं अत्यंत महत्त्वपूर्ण बात जिस पर वह आधारित या निर्भर है : *traditions which are the cornerstones of Western civilization.*

corny / 'कॉर्नि / *adj* (-ier, -iest) (*अनौप*) बहुत बार दोहराया हुआ; पुराना : *a corny joke.*

coronary / 'कॉरनरि; US 'कॉरनेरि / *adj* हृदय की या हृदय से संबंधित : *a coronary care unit* ▸ **coronary artery** *noun* हृदय को रक्त संचरण करने वाली धमनी **coronary thrombosis** *noun* (*pl* **thromboses**) (*चिकि*) हृदय को रक्त संचरण करने वाली धमनी में रक्त का थक्का जमना, अवरोध पैदा करना।

coronation / कॉर'नेशन् / *noun* राज्याभिषेक : *the coronation of Elizabeth II.*

coroner / 'कॉरनर् / *noun* अपमृत्यु (संदेहास्पद स्थितियों में मृत्यु) की जाँच करने वाला अधिकारी।

corporal¹ / 'कॉर्परल् / *adj* (*औप*) दैहिक, शारीरिक ▸ **corporal punishment** *noun* शारीरिक दंड (जैसे बेंत लगाना या पीटना)।

corporal² / 'कॉर्परल् / *noun* सेना में सार्जेंट से छोटा पद, नायक।

corporate / 'कॉर्परट् / *adj* 1 पालिका या निगम विषयक : *corporate planning/ finance/borrowing* 2 एक अकेले बड़े समूह में संयुक्त : *a corporate body/ organization* 3 समूह के सभी सदस्यों की भागीदारी वाला : *corporate responsibility/action.*

corporation / कॉर्प'रेशन् / *noun* 1 (*संक्षि* **corp**) महापालिका; निगम (व्यापारिक संघ) 2 नगरपालिका।

corps / कॉर् / *noun* (*pl* अपरिवर्तित / कॉर्ज़् /) 1 थल सेना की एक तकनीकी शाखा, कोर 2 दो या अधिक डिविज़नों से बना सेनादल 3 किसी विशिष्ट कार्य में लगे व्यक्तियों का समूह।

corpse / कॉर्प्स् / *noun* लाश, शव।

correct¹ / क'रेक्ट् / *adj* 1 सही, ठीक; त्रुटिहीन 2 (व्यवहार आदि) उचित ▸ **correctly** *adv* **correctness** *noun.*

correct² / क'रेक्ट् / *verb* 1 ठीक करना, त्रुटिहीन बनाना : *Spectacles correct faulty eyesight.* 2 (अध्यापक का) ग़लतियाँ बताना, ग़लतियाँ ठीक करना।

correction / क'रेक्शन् / *noun* 1 ठीक करने की प्रक्रिया 2 शुद्धि; ठीक करने के निशान 3 (*अप्र*) दंड।

corrective / क'रेक्टिव् / *adj* दोष दूर करने वाले (उपाय)।

correlate / 'कॉरलेट् / *verb* 1 **correlate** (**with sth**) दो या अधिक वस्तुओं में सहसंबंध स्थापित करना : *The data do not seem to correlate.* 2 **correlate A and/with B** सहसंबंध दिखाना ▸ **correlation** *noun* सहसंबंध।

correspond / कॉर'स्पॉन्ड् / *verb* 1 **correspond** (**to/with sth**) बराबर होना, अनुरूप होना 2 **correspond** (**to sth**) समान होना 3 **correspond** (**with sb**) पत्राचार करना ▸ **corresponding** *adj* समान या संबंधित **correspondingly** *adv.*

correspondence / कॉर'स्पॉन्ड्स् / *noun* 1 **correspondence** (**with sth**) (**between sth and sth**) मेल, सादृश्य 2 **correspondence** (**with sb**) पत्राचार; पत्र : *personal/private correspondence.*

correspondent /ˌकॉरˈस्पॉन्डन्ट्/ noun 1 पत्राचार करने वाला 2 (समाचार-पत्र का) संवाददाता : a foreign/war correspondent.

corridor /ˈकॉरिडॉर्/ noun 1 गलियारा 2 एक देश की भूमि का सँकरा भाग जो दूसरे देश की भूमि से गुज़रता है ■ **the corridors of power** (प्राय: परि) शासन का उच्च स्तर जहाँ निर्णय लिए जाते हैं।

corroborate /कˈरॉबरेट्/ verb किसी कथन, विश्वास, सिद्धांत आदि को समर्थन देना या दृढ़ता से मत व्यक्त करना ▸ **corroboration** noun **corroborative** adj.

corrode /कˈरोड्/ verb नष्ट हो जाना/ करना; कुरेदना, (मुख्यत: रासायनिक प्रक्रिया द्वारा) क्षीण हो जाना : Acid corrodes metal. ▸ **corrosion** /कˈरोश्न्/ noun **corrosive** /कˈरोसिव्/ adj.

corrugated /ˈकॉरगेटिड्/ adj नालीदार, लहरदार : corrugated iron (छत के लिए प्रयुक्त नालीदार टीन) ○ corrugated cardboard (पैकिंग में प्रयुक्त लहरदार मोटा काग़ज़)।

corrupt¹ /कˈरप्ट्/ adj 1 भ्रष्ट (व्यक्ति) 2 भ्रष्ट आचरण, दूषित व्यवहार 3 (तक) (भाषा, मूल-पाठ, आदि) अशुद्धियों से पूर्ण और मूल रूप से हटकर ▸ **corruptly** adv.

corrupt² /कˈरप्ट्/ verb (अपमा) 1 भ्रष्ट बनाना; दूषित करना : young people whose morals have been corrupted 2 मूल रूप को बदलकर बिगाड़ देना : corrupted data ▸ **corruptible** adj जिसे (रिश्वत देकर) भ्रष्ट किया जा सके।

corruption /कˈरप्श्न्/ noun 1 भ्रष्टाचार : cases of bribery and corruption 2 दूषित आचरण।

cosmetic /कॉज़ˈमेटिक/ noun (प्राय: pl) चेहरे और केशों को और सुंदर बनाने वाले पदार्थ, सौंदर्य प्रसाधन ▸ **cosmetic** adj (प्राय: अपमा) सिर्फ़ बाहरी दिखावे के लिए, मूल रूप, गुण में उन्नति के लिए नहीं।

cosmic /ˈकॉज़मिक्/ adj 1 ब्रह्मांडीय 2 अति विशाल, महान एवं महत्त्वपूर्ण : a disaster of cosmic proportions ▸ **cosmic rays** noun [pl] अंतरिक्ष से पृथ्वी पर पहुँचने वाली किरणें।

cosmonaut /ˈकॉज़्मनॉट्/ noun अंतरिक्ष यात्री (सोवियत)।

cosmopolitan /ˌकॉज़्मˈपॉलिटन्/ adj 1 संसार के सभी भागों के व्यक्तियों वाला या से प्रभावित : a cosmopolitan city (ऐसी महानगरी जहाँ प्राय: सभी देशों के लोग मिल जाएँ) ○ cosmopolitan views/ interests (संसार के विस्तृत अनुभवों से जनित विचार) 2 राष्ट्रीय पूर्वाग्रहों से मुक्त विचारों वाला व्यक्ति : a cosmopolitan outlook.

cosmos /ˈकॉज़्मॉस्/ noun the cosmos [sing] ब्रह्मांड, अंतरिक्ष।

cost¹ /कॉस्ट्/ verb (pt, pp cost) 1 क़ीमत/दाम होना या चुकाना 2 इस क़ीमत में उपलब्ध होना 3 हानि उठाना : The scandal cost her her career. 4 (pt, pp costed) (वाणिज्य) किसी वस्तु के लिए उपयुक्त क़ीमत निर्धारित करने के लिए धन की मात्रा का अंदाज़ा लगाना : The project has only been roughly costed. ■ **cost sb dear** गंभीर हानि पहुँचना ▸ **costing** noun (वाणिज्य) क़ीमत का अंदाज़ा।

cost² /कॉस्ट्/ noun 1 क़ीमत, मूल्य 2 (प्राय: pl) (व्यापार, वाणिज्य आदि में) कार्य विशेष के लिए आवश्यक ख़र्च 3 costs [pl] (क़ानून) मुक़दमे का ख़र्चा 4 किसी काम में लगा प्रयास, हानि या बलिदान ■ **at all cost/costs** हर क़ीमत पर (चाहे कितना ही ख़र्च करना पड़े या कष्ट उठाना पड़े) **at any cost** किसी भी क़ीमत पर **to one's cost** हानि पर।

co-star /ˈको स्टार्/ verb (-rr-) किसी फ़िल्म में एक स्तर के दो या दो से ज़्यादा मशहूर कलाकारों का आना; **co-star (with sb)** सह-कलाकार के साथ फ़िल्म में काम करना।

costly / 'कॉस्ट्लि / adj (-ier, -iest) बहुमूल्य।

costume / 'कॉस्ट्यूम; US 'कॉस्टूम / noun 1 स्थान विशेष के लोगों का पहनावा या विशिष्ट ऐतिहासिक काल की पोशाक 2 नाटक के लिए पहने जाने वाले कपड़े : five costume changes.

cosy (US cozy) / 'कोज़ि / adj (-ier, -iest) 1 आरामदेह, गरम एवं सुखदायी : a cosy room/chair 2 (प्राय: अपमा) ज़रूरत से ज़्यादा आरामदेह एवं सुविधाजनक और प्राय: ग़लत : a cosy deal/relationship ▸ cosily adv.

cot / कॉट / noun 1 खटिया, चारपाई 2 (US crib) बच्चे के सोने का पालना।

cottage / 'कॉटिज़ / noun झोंपड़ी, कुटीर ▸ cottage industry noun गाँवों में सहज प्राप्त उद्योग; कुटीर-उद्योग।

cotton / 'कॉट्न / noun 1 कपास का पौधा; रूई, सूत 2 सूती कपड़े ▸ cotton wool noun (पट्टी बाँधने आदि के काम आने वाली) डाक्टरी रूई।

couch¹ / काउच् / noun 1 सोफ़ा, गद्देदार पलंग : He slept on the couch. 2 बिस्तर जैसा लंबा फ़र्नीचर, प्राय: डॉक्टर की क्लिनिक में।

couch² / काउच् / verb couch sth (in sth) (औप) कोई विचार एक विशिष्ट शैली में व्यक्त करना : His letter was couched in conciliatory terms.

cough / कॉफ़् / verb 1 खाँसी आना, खाँसना 2 cough sth (up) खाँसकर मुँह से कुछ निकालना : He'd been coughing (up) blood. 3 (मशीन का) घर्र-घर्र करना ■ cough (sth) up ज़बरदस्ती या अनिच्छा से कुछ कहना या करना ▸ cough noun खाँसी; खाँसी की बीमारी : cough medicine/mixture/syrup.

could / कुड् / modal verb (neg could not, संक्षि couldn't / 'कुड्न्ट् /) 1 आज्ञा/ अनुमति प्राप्त करने में प्रयुक्त : Could I use your phone, please? 2 विनम्र निवेदन

प्राप्ति के लिए प्रयुक्त : Could you babysit for us on Friday? 3 संभावना दर्शाने के लिए : You could be right, I suppose. 4 सुझाव देने के लिए प्रयुक्त।

council / 'काउन्स्ल् / noun परिषद; नियुक्त या निर्वाचित व्यक्तियों का समूह, विशेषत: किसी संस्था के संचालन के लिए : a council of elders ▸ councillor (US councilor भी) / काउन्स्लर् / noun परिषद का सदस्य, पार्षद।

counsel¹ / 'काउन्स्ल् / noun 1 (औप) सलाह; विशेषज्ञ की सलाह या सुझाव 2 (pl अपरिवर्तित) counsel (for sb) (क़ानून) मुक़दमा चलाने वाला/वाले वकील : defence counsel.

counsel² / 'काउन्स्ल् / verb (-ll-; US -l- भी) 1 (पेशेवर) सलाह देना, समस्याएँ सुलझाना : a psychiatrist who counsels alcoholics 2 (औप) कोई विशिष्ट कार्यविधि सुझाना या अनुमोदन करना : He counselled them to give up the plan. ▸ counselling noun समस्याओं पर व्यावसायिक सलाहकारी counsellor (US counselor भी) noun सलाहकार, परामर्शदाता; वकील।

count¹ / काउन्ट् / verb 1 count (from sth) (to sth) गिनना, जोड़ना 2 count sth (up) गिनकर हिसाब लगाना : Don't forget to count your change. 3 शामिल करना 4 count (for sth) महत्त्व का होना या महत्त्व रखना : First impressions of people do count. 5 count sb/oneself/sth (as) sb/sth मानना, समझना : I count myself lucky to have a job. ■ count down (to sth) विशिष्ट समय या दिन के आने की सूचना/ संकेत देना count on sb/sth विश्वास के साथ निर्भर होना।

count² / काउन्ट् / noun 1 गिनती की प्रक्रिया : a second count of the votes 2 गिनने से प्राप्त कुल जोड़ : The body count is 62. 3 (क़ानून) अभियोग का

विषय (जिस बात पर अपराधी माना जा रहा हो): *He was found guilty on all counts.* 4 (प्राय: *pl*) वाद-विवाद में रखे गए बिंदु।

count³ / काउन्ट् / *noun* कुछ यूरोपीय देशों में (जैसे फ्रांस और इटली) उच्च कुल के एवं संभ्रांत व्यक्ति की पदवी।

countdown / 'काउन्ट्डाउन् / *noun* **countdown (to sth)** 1 उलटी गिनती गिनने की क्रिया (जैसे अंतरिक्ष यान के रवाना होने से पूर्व उलटे क्रम में गिनती गिनना - 10, 9, 8, 7 आदि) 2 [*sing*] किसी महत्त्वपूर्ण घटना से एकदम पहले की अवधि।

countenance / 'काउन्टनन्स् / *noun* (औप) चेहरा (रूप और भावाभिव्यक्ति की दृष्टि से)।

counter¹ / 'काउन्टर् / *noun* लंबी मेज़ जिस पर दुकानदार सामान रखकर ग्राहकों को दिखाता है; बैंक आदि में ऐसी मेज़; काउंटर: *the ticket reservation counter* ■ **under the counter** (सामान की) गुप्त एवं अवैध बिक्री।

counter² / 'काउन्टर् / *adv* **counter to sth** विरोध में, प्रतिकूलता में : *Economic trends are running counter to the forecasts.*

counter³ / 'काउन्टर् / *verb* **counter (with sth); counter sb/sth (with sth)** विरोध करना; हमला करना ▸ **counter** *noun* **counter (to sb/sth)** (औप) (चुनौतीपूर्ण) विरोधी जवाब।

counter- *pref* (पूर्वपद) 1 विपरीत दिशा या प्रभाव में : *counter-productive* 2 उत्तर में, विरोध में : *counter-attack/ counter-demonstration* 3 समरूप : *counterpart.*

counteract / काउन्टर्'ऐक्ट् / *verb* प्रति-कार करना; (उत्तर में) विरोध करना और विरोधी के कार्य, बल आदि को कम या निष्प्रभाव कर देना, काटना : *counteract a poison.*

counterfeit / 'काउन्टर्फ़िट् / *adj* जाली,

नक़ली (नोट); खोटा (माल) ▸ **counterfeit** *verb* जाली (सिक्का, नोट) बनाना **counterfeiter** *noun* जाली नोट आदि बनाने वाला।

counterfoil / 'काउन्टर्'फ़ॉइल् / *noun* चेक, रसीद आदि का वह अंश जो रिकॉर्ड के लिए रख लिया जाता है, प्रतिपर्ण।

counterpart / 'काउन्टर्पार्ट् / *noun* बिलकुल दूसरी वस्तु या व्यक्ति की तरह की वस्तु या व्यक्ति, प्रतिरूप, प्रतिवस्तु।

countersign / 'काउन्टर्साइन् / *verb* पहले से हस्ताक्षर किए दस्तावेज़ पर किसी अन्य व्यक्ति द्वारा हस्ताक्षर किया जाना, विशेषत: इसकी वैधता सुनिश्चित करने के लिए : *All cheques must be counter-signed by one of the directors.*

countless / 'काउन्ट्लस् / *adj* असीम, असंख्य।

country / 'कन्ट्रि / *noun* (*pl* **countries**) 1 देश (जैसे भारत) 2 **the country** [*sing*] देहात, ग्रामीण क्षेत्र 3 विशिष्ट भौतिक गुणों/लक्षणों वाला भूक्षेत्र : *rough/marshy country.*

countryman / 'कन्ट्रिमन् / *noun* (*fem* **countrywoman**) 1 देहाती, ग्रामवासी (न कि नगरवासी) 2 समदेशवासी, हमवतन।

countryside / 'कन्ट्रिसाइड् / *noun* (प्राय: **the countryside**) नगरों, शहरों के बाहर के ग्रामीण क्षेत्र—खेत, जंगल आदि।

county / 'काउन्टि / *noun* इंग्लैंड में स्थानीय शासन की सबसे बड़ी इकाई।

coup / कू / *noun* (*pl* **coups** / कूज़् /) 1 (सरकार का) तख़्ता पलट, हिंसक एवं ग़ैरक़ानूनी तरीक़े से सत्ता हस्तगत करना : *the army mounted/staged a coup (d' état).* 2 आश्चर्यजनक एवं सफल कार्य।

couple¹ / 'कपल् / *noun* 1 **couple (of sth)** दो व्यक्ति (या वस्तुएँ) जो साथ-साथ देखे जाते हैं, युग्म 2 दंपति, पति-पत्नी : *married couples* 3 कुछेक व्यक्ति या वस्तुएँ : *She jogs a couple of kilo-metres every morning.*

couple² / 'कप्ल् / verb **1 couple A and B (together)** दो वस्तुओं को आपस में जोड़ना : *two computers coupled together* **2 couple sb/sth with sb/ sth** दो वस्तुओं के बीच संबंध जोड़ना ▸ **coupling** / 'कपलिङ् / noun **1** दो वस्तुओं को जोड़ने की प्रक्रिया **2** जोड़ (विशेषत: रेल के डिब्बों को जोड़ने वाला भाग) कप्लिंग।

coupon / 'कूपॉन् / noun **1** कूपन, वह टिकट या पुर्ज़ा जिसे दिखाने से कोई (नियंत्रित) वस्तु मिले **2** किसी प्रतियोगिता आदि में प्रवेश के लिए समाचार-पत्र आदि से काटा गया फ़ॉर्म : *an entry coupon.*

courage / 'करिज् / noun वीरता, साहस ▸ **courageous** / क'रेजस् / adj साहसी।

courier / 'कुरिअर् / noun **1** संदेशवाहक (व्यक्ति) जो पार्सल एवं महत्त्वपूर्ण काग़ज़ात ले जाता है : *We sent the documents by courier.* **2** यात्रा-सहायक।

course¹ / 'कॉर्स् / noun **1** किसी के द्वारा ली गई दिशा, जिस रेखा में कोई वस्तु चल रही है : *The plane was on/off course.* **2 course (of sth)** समय की दृष्टि से अग्र-गति **3 (course of action** भी) कार्रवाई का तरीक़ा या आगे बढ़ना : *The wisest course would be to ignore it.* **4 course (in/on sth)** (शिक्षा में) पाठ्यक्रम, विषय **5 course (of sth)** (चिकि) (इलाज आदि की) मात्रा : *pre-scribe a course of antibiotics* **6** भोजन में पृथक्-पृथक् दौर (विशेषत: पाश्चात्य भोजन शैली में) : *a five-course dinner* **7** गोल्फ़ का मैदान; घुड़दौड़ का मैदान ■ **in course of sth** (औप) दौरान में, उक्त अवधि में **of course 1** अवश्य **2** निस्संदेह।

course² / 'कॉर्स् / verb (साहि) (विशेषत: द्रवों का) मुक्त रूप से बहना : *tears coursed down her cheeks.*

court¹ / कॉर्ट् / noun **1** कचहरी, न्यायालय **2 the court** कचहरी में उपस्थित न्यायाधीश एवं अन्य सभी व्यक्ति : *the court's ruling/decision* **3** (प्राय: **Court**) शासक का आधिकारिक निवास; दरबार **4** खेलने के लिए निश्चित मैदान : *a tennis/squash court* **5** (**courtyard** भी) आँगन, प्रांगण।

court² / कॉर्ट् / verb **1** (अप्र) प्रणय निवेदन करना, प्रेम जताना : *a courting couple* **2** (औप, प्राय: अपमा) किसी का समर्थन/अनुमोदन प्राप्त करने का प्रयत्न करना **3** कुछ ऐसा काम करना जिसका परिणाम अप्रिय हो, ख़तरा उठाना : *Once again he has courted controversy/disap-proval.* ▸ **courtship** noun प्रणय निवेदन।

courteous / 'कर्टिअस् / adj शिष्ट, भद्र ▸ **courteously** adv.

courtesy / 'कर्टिस् / noun (pl **courte-sies**) **1** शिष्ट व्यवहार, सौजन्य **2** (औप) शिष्ट एवं विनम्र टिप्पणी या क्रिया : *ex-change courtesies* ■ **(by) courtesy of sb** के सौजन्य से।

courtier / 'कॉर्टिअर् / noun (पूर्व में) राज दरबार का सदस्य।

court martial / कॉर्ट् 'मार्श्ल् / noun (pl **courts martial**) सैनिक न्यायालय में मुक़दमा ▸ **court-martial** verb (-ll-; US -l-) **court-martial sb (for sth)** सैनिक न्यायालय में मुक़दमा चलाना।

cousin / 'कज़्न् / noun **1** (**first cousin** भी) चाचा, मामा, मौसी, ताऊ या बुआ का लड़का या लड़की **2** (प्राय: pl) किसी और देश में अपने जैसे विचार, प्रथाएँ आदि रखने वाले लोग : *our American cousins.*

cove / कोव् / noun छोटी खाड़ी : *lazing on the sand in a quiet cove.*

cover¹ / कवर् / verb **1 cover sth (up/ over) (with sth)** आवरण/पर्दा सामने करना, ढकना, ढक्कन बंद करना **2** सतह पर फैलाना : *Snow covered the ground.* **3** शामिल करना; निपटना **4** (रुपया) आवश्यकता के लिए पर्याप्त होना **5** (दूरी) पार करना, तय करना : *By sunset we had* *covered thirty kilometres.* 6 cover sb/sth (against/for sth) बचाव करना; बीमा द्वारा सुरक्षित करना : *Are you fully covered against/for fire and theft?* ■ cover sth up (अपमा) दोष, गलतियाँ आदि छुपाने का प्रयास करना ▸ covered adj 1 covered in/with sth लदा-फँदा 2 ढका हुआ covering / 'कव़रिङ् / noun ढकने वाली वस्तु/सतह।

cover² / 'कव़र् / noun 1 आवरण, ढकने वाली वस्तु; ढक्कन 2 (पुस्तक का) आवरण-पृष्ठ 3 the covers [pl] चादरें, कंबल आदि : *She wept under the covers and was soon asleep.* 4 आश्रय, शरण-स्थल : *There was nowhere we could take cover.* 5 cover (for sth) कुछ गैर-क़ानूनी कार्य आदि छुपाने का साधन : *His business was a cover for drug dealing.* 6 cover (for sb) दूसरे के स्थान पर प्रस्तुत होने वाला व्यक्ति 7 cover (against sth) बीमा कवर 8 लिफ़ाफ़ा ▸ cover story noun 1 किसी पत्रिका में मुख्य लेख 2 वास्तविकता छुपाने के लिए गढ़ी गई कहानी।

coverage / 'कव़रिज् / noun coverage (of sth) (समाचार-पत्रादि में) विषयवृत्तांत।

covert / 'कव़र्ट् / adj छिपा हुआ, गुप्त : *a covert glance/threat* ▸ covertly adv.

covet / 'कव़ट् / verb (औप) लालच करना, ललचाना : *covet sb's job* ▸ covetous / 'कव़टस् / adj (प्रायः अपमा) लालची, लोभी covetously adv.

cow¹ / काउ / noun 1 गाय 2 कुछ विशेष जंतुओं, जैसे हाथी, ह्वेल, सील आदि की मादा ▸ cow-pat noun गाय का गोबर।

cow² / काउ / verb cow sb (into sth/doing sth) डराकर काम करवाना : *The men had been cowed into total submission.* ▸ cowed adj डराया-धमकाया हुआ।

coward / 'काउअई / noun (अपमा)

डरपोक, भीरू ▸ cowardice / 'काउअर्डिस् / noun कायरता, भीरूता cowardly adj (अपमा) कायरतापूर्ण।

cowboy / 'काउबॉइ / noun पशुपालक (पश्चिमी अमेरिका के कुछ जनजाति क्षेत्र में)।

cower / 'काउअर् / verb (डर या शर्म के मारे) दुबककर बैठना; सर नीचे कर लेना : *People would cower as he passed.*

coy / कॉइ / adj (-er, -est) (प्रायः अपमा) 1 लज्जालु, संकोची : *a coy smile* 2 सूचना देने या उत्तर देने में अनिच्छुक ▸ coyly adv coyness noun.

crab / क्रैब् / noun 1 केकड़ा; केकड़े का मांस 2 the Crab कर्क राशि

crack¹ / क्रैक् / verb 1 दरार करना; दरकना : *The ice cracked as I stepped onto it.* 2 टुकड़ों में तोड़ना या टूटना : *crack a nut* 3 crack sth (on/against sth) ज़ोर से टकराना : *I cracked my head on the low ceiling.* 4 कड़क की आवाज़ करना या कड़कना (जैसे बंदूक की आवाज़) 5 आवाज़ का भारी होना 6 crack up (अनौप) अत्यधिक परिश्रम के कारण शारीरिक या मानसिक संतुलन खोने लगना 7 (अनौप) समस्या/पहेली का हल खोज निकालना : *crack the enemy's code* 8 चुटकुला सुनाना ▸ crack-down noun crack-down (on sb/sth) अवैध या आपराधिक काररवाई रोकने के कड़े उपाय cracked / क्रैक्ट् / adj 1 दरार वाला, फटा हुआ 2 सनकी।

crack² / क्रैक् / noun 1 crack (in sth) दरार, दरका : *Cracks were beginning to appear in the walls of the house.* 2 कड़क (बंदूक आदि चलने की आवाज़) 3 crack (on sth) 'चट' की आवाज़, चटाका : *give sb/get a crack on the head* 4 crack (about sth) (अनौप) व्यंग्यपूर्ण टिप्पणी; चुटकुला 5 एक नशीली वस्तु : *a crack addict* ▸ crack adj अति चतुर, निपुण, अति उत्तम : *He's a crack shot.* **crack-brained** *adj* *(अनौप)* सनकी; हद दर्जे का बेवकूफ़।

cracker / 'क्रैकर् / *noun* 1 (**cream cracker** भी) पतले कुरकुरे बिस्कुट, क्रैकर 2 पटाखा (आतिशबाज़ी का) : *a box of crackers.*

crackle / 'क्रैकल् / *verb* चट-चट ध्वनि करना।

cradle / 'क्रेडल् / *noun* 1 (बच्चे के सोने के लिए) पालना 2 **cradle of sth** वह स्थान जहाँ किसी चीज़ का उद्भव होता है 3 टेलिफ़ोन का वह भाग जहाँ रिसीवर (चोंगा) रखा जाता है ▸ **cradle** *verb* **cradle sb/sth (in sth)** पालने की तरह रखना या झुलाना : *cradle a baby in one's arms.*

craft / क्राफ़्ट्; US क्रैफ़्ट् / *verb* 1 शिल्प, दस्तकारी 2 *(औप, अपमा)* धूर्तता, चालाकी कपट 3 *(pl अपरिवर्तित)* नाव, जहाज़; वायु-यान ▸ **craft** *verb* दस्तकारी करना; निपुणता से तैयार करना : *a carefully crafted speech* **craftily** *adv* **craftiness** *noun* **crafty** *adj* (-ier, -iest) *(प्रायः अपमा)* धूर्त, मक्कार।

craftsman / 'क्राफ़्ट्स्मन्; US क्रैफ़्ट्स्मन् / *noun* (pl **craftsmen**) 1 शिल्पकार, दस्तकार : *It is clearly the work of a master craftsman.* 2 निपुणता से कार्य करने वाला व्यक्ति ▸ **craftsmanship** *noun* कारीगरी, शिल्पकारी।

crag / क्रैग् / *noun* खड़ी चट्टान।

cram / क्रैम् / *verb* (-mm-) 1 **cram sth** ठूँसना; ठूँस-ठूँसकर भरना : *The car was crammed full.* 2 **cram (for sth)** रटना; रट्टेबाज़ी से पढ़ाना : *cram pupils.*

cramp[1] / क्रैम्प् / *noun* 1 दर्दनाक ऐंठन; ठिठुरन 2 **cramps** [pl] (विशेषतः US) पेट में तीव्र शूल, पीड़ा।

cramp[2] / क्रैम्प् / *verb* (शिकंजे में) जकड़ना; ऐसा अवरोध करना कि वृद्धि रुक जाए : *All these difficulties cramped his progress.* ▸ **cramped** *adj*

1 (स्थान) संकरा एवं सीमित; (व्यक्ति) जगह कम होने के कारण से घुटन महसूस करता हुआ 2 (हस्तलेख) बहुत छोटा व पास-पास लिखा होने से पढ़ने में मुश्किल।

crane[1] / क्रेन् / *noun* 1 सारस 2 भारी वज़न उठाने की शक्तिशाली मशीन।

crane[2] / क्रेन् / *verb* गरदन आगे बढ़ाकर देखना : *craning (forward) to get a better view.*

crank / क्रैंक् / *noun* (अपमा) झक्की, व्यक्ति जिसके किसी विषय पर अजीब और अटल विचार हों : *a health-food crank* ▸ **cranky** *adj* (-ier, -iest) *(अनौप, अपमा)* 1 अजीब, सनकी 2 (मशीन) बे-भरोसे की 3 (US) चिड़चिड़ा, बदमिज़ाज।

cranny / 'क्रैनि / *noun* बहुत छोटा-सा छेद; दरार (विशेषतः दीवार में)।

crash[1] / क्रैश् / *verb* 1 **crash (sth) (into sth)** (गाड़ी आदि का) टकराना (चकनाचूर होना) : *The plane crashed (into the mountains).* 2 तोड़ना (धमाके के साथ), तोड़ते हुए चलना : *an enraged elephant crashing through the undergrowth* 3 टूटकर ढह जाना 4 (व्यापार, सरकार, क़ीमतें आदि) अचानक गिर जाना 5 (**gatecrash** भी) *(अनौप)* किसी पार्टी या सामाजिक कार्यक्रम में बिना निमंत्रण के पहुँच जाना ■ **a crashing bore** अत्यंत बोरिंग व्यक्ति।

crash[2] / क्रैश् / *noun* 1 दुर्घटना जिसमें एक वाहन किसी दूसरी चीज़ (वाहन, पेड़ आदि) से टकराता है और अधिक क्षति एवं लोगों की मृत्यु का कारण बनता है : *a car/plane crash* 2 किसी चीज़ के गिरने या टूटने से उत्पन्न धमाका/ज़ोर की आवाज़ 3 मूल्यों में अचानक गंभीर गिरावट; आर्थिक संकट : *the 1987 stock market crash* ▸ **crash-landing** *noun* दुर्घटनाग्रस्त विमान का धमाके के साथ उतरना।

crass / क्रैस् / *adj* (औप) 1 अत्यंत मूर्ख एवं संवेदनशीलता रहित 2 (ख़राब गुण) अत्यंत; बहुत ही ज़्यादा : *crass stupidity/*

ignorance ▸ **crassly** *adv* **crassness** *noun.*

crate / क्रेट् / *noun* 1 सामान के परिवहन के लिए (या सुरक्षा के लिए) प्रयुक्त लकड़ी का फ़्रेम : *a crate of bananas* 2 बोतलों के परिवहन या इकट्ठा करके रखने के लिए धातु या प्लास्टिक का फ़्रेम (डब्बा) : *a crate of milk/wine* ▸ **crate** *verb* **crate sth (up)** क्रेट में सामान रखना (पैक करना)।

crater / क्रेटर् / *noun* 1 ज्वालामुखी का मुँह 2 ज़मीन में (बम आदि गिरने से) बना विशाल गड्ढा : *a meteorite crater.*

crave / क्रेव् / *verb* 1 **crave (for) sth** लालायित करना 2 *(प्रा)* तरसना, तरसकर माँगना : *crave sb's forgiveness* ▸ **craving** *noun* **craving (for sth)** लालसा : *craving for love.*

crawl / क्रॉल् / *verb* 1 रेंगना, हाथों और घुटनों के बल चलना 2 बहुत धीरे-धीरे चलना : *The traffic crawled over the bridge.* 3 **crawl (to sb)** *(अनौप, अपमा)* किसी की चाटुकारी करना ▸ **crawl** *noun* [*sing*] 1 *(अपमा)* अति धीमी गति 2 एक प्रकार की तैराकी **crawler** *noun (अपमा)* चाटु-कार।

crayon / क्रेअन् / *noun* रंगीन खड़िया या कोयले की बत्ती या पेंसिल : *a crayon drawing* ▸ **crayon** *verb.*

craze / क्रेज़् / *noun* **craze (for sth)** किसी वस्तु के लिए अत्यधिक उत्साह जो कुछ दिनों बाद समाप्त हो जाता है, क्षणोन्माद; वस्तु जिसका उन्माद हो।

crazed / क्रेज़्ड् / *adj* **crazed (with sth)** पागल।

crazy / क्रेज़ि / *adj* (**-ier, -iest**) 1 सनकी, पागल; विक्षिप्त 2 *(अनौप)* परेशान; अत्यंत उत्तेजित या उत्साहित : *The kids went crazy when Shah Rukh Khan appeared.* 3 *(अनौप)* मूर्खतापूर्ण : *a crazy idea/suggestion.*

creak / क्रीक् / *verb* चरमराना, चरचराहट की आवाज़ करना (जैसे किवाड़ करते हैं या नया जूता करता है) ▸ **creak** *noun* चरमराहट **creaky** *adj* ऐसी ध्वनि करने वाली वस्तु; चरमराती हुई : *a creaky old lift.*

cream / क्रीम् / *noun* 1 मलाई; क्रीम 2 क्रीम वाले खाद्य पदार्थ या क्रीम जैसे पदार्थ : *ice cream/chocolate creams* 3 क्रीम जैसे अन्य पदार्थ (जैसे सौंदर्य प्रसाधन क्रीम) : *shaving cream ○ antiseptic cream* 4 **the cream (of sth)** किसी समूह आदि का सर्वोत्तम अंश ▸ **cream** *adj* क्रीम का रंग (हल्का पीला, लगभग सफ़ेद)।

creamy *adj* (**-ier, -iest**) 1 क्रीम वाला या क्रीम की तरह 2 हलका पीला (लगभग सफ़ेद) रंग का।

crease / क्रीस् / *noun* 1 कपड़े में डाली हुई या पड़ी हुई चुन्नट : *iron a crease into one's trousers ○ crease-resistant cloth* 2 त्वचा पर, विशेषत: चेहरे पर, उभरी रेखाएँ 3 (क्रिकेट में) विकेट के पास खींची रेखा ▸ **crease** *verb* चुन्नट डालना या पड़ना; (चेहरे पर) धारियाँ पड़ना।

create / क्रि'एट् / *verb* 1 उत्पन्न करना, सृष्टि करना : *God created the world.* 2 फलस्वरूप कुछ होना; स्थिति या भाव उत्पन्न करना : *create confusion* 3 किसी को विशेष पदवी देना : *create eight new peers.*

creation / क्रि'एश्न् / *noun* 1 उत्पन्न करने की प्रक्रिया : *the creation of the world* 2 रचना; सृष्टि : *a literary/artistic creation* 3 (प्राय: **the Creation**) सृष्टि, विशेषत: ईश्वर द्वारा रचित विश्व; (अक्सर **creation**) संपूर्ण सृष्टि।

creative / क्रि'एटिव् / *adj* 1 सृष्टि-विषयक; सृजनात्मक : *He teaches creative writing.* 2 सृजन करने में समर्थ : *creative energy/ideas* ▸ **creatively** *adv* **creativity** / क्रिए'टिवटि / *noun* सृजनात्मकता, सृजनशीलता।

creator / क्रि'एटर् / *noun* 1 सृजनकर्ता (व्यक्ति) 2 **the Creator** [*sing*] ईश्वर

creature / 'क्रीचर् / noun 1 प्राणी, विशेषत: पशु 2 व्यक्ति (एक विशेष अंदाज़ से देखे जाने पर) : *a poor creature* ■ **sb's creature** (औप, अपमा) किसी अन्य पर निर्भर व्यक्ति।

crèche / क्रेश् / noun माता-पिता की अनुपस्थिति में शिशुओं की देखभाल करने का स्थान।

credentials / क्र'डेन्शल्ज़ / noun [pl] 1 **credentials (for/as sth); credentials (to do sth)** व्यक्ति के गुण, उप-लब्धियाँ, शैक्षिक योग्यता आदि जो उसे किसी योग्य बनाते हैं : *She has the perfect credentials for the job.* 2 व्यक्ति के पद को बताने वाला लिखित पत्र; प्रत्यय-पत्र : *examine sb's credentials.*

credible / 'क्रेडब्ल् / adj विश्वसनीय, जिस पर विश्वास किया जा सके : *His story seems barely credible.* ▶ **credibility** / क्रेड'बिलटि / noun विश्वसनीयता **credibly** adv.

credit[1] / 'क्रेडिट् / noun 1 उधार; उधार की प्रथा : *refuse/grant sb credit* 2 साख, उधार अदा करने या वादा पूरा करने की प्रसिद्धि 3 बैंक द्वारा प्रदत्त ऋण, लोन; बैंक का साखपत्र 4 व्यक्ति के बैंक हिसाब में उसकी ओर जमा धनराशि : *the credit column* 5 (हिसाब-किताब में) किसी व्यक्ति की ओर जमा धनराशि (debit के वैषम्य में) 6 प्रतिष्ठा, प्रसिद्धि 7 **credit to sb** प्रतिष्ठा या यश बढ़ाने में कारण रूप व्यक्ति या वस्तु : *She is a credit to her teachers.* ▶ **credit card** noun **credit-worthy** adj उधार लौटाने में विश्वासयोग्य **creditworthiness** noun.

credit[2] / 'क्रेडिट् / verb 1 **credit sb/sth with doing sth; credit sth to sb/sth** ज़िम्मेदारी के लिए विश्वास करना, आस्था रखना 2 **credit sb/sth with sth; credit sth to sb/sth** किसी व्यक्ति/वस्तु में कुछ विशिष्ट गुण मानना : *Miraculous powers are credited to the relics.*

3 **credit sb/sth with sth; credit sth to sb/sth** जमापक्ष में धनराशि चढ़ाना।

creditable / 'क्रेडिटब्ल् / adj प्रशंसा लाने/ दिलाने वाला : *a creditable attempt.*

creditor / 'क्रेडिटर् / noun लेनदार।

credulity / क्रि'ड्यूलिटि / noun भोलापन।

credulous / 'क्रेड्यलस् / adj भोला-भाला, सहज में विश्वास कर लेने वाला।

creed / क्रीड् / noun धर्म, पंथ।

creek / क्रीक् / noun 1 (नदी या समुद्र की) सँकरी खाड़ी 2 (US) छोटी नदी, धारा।

creep / क्रीप् / verb (pt, pp **crept**) 1 रेंगना, सरककर चलना : *The cat crept silently towards the bird.* 2 धीरे-धीरे खिसकना 3 (पौधों का) दीवार या अन्य वस्तु के सहारे ऊपर चढ़ना ▶ **creep** noun (अनौप, अपमा) चाटुकार व्यक्ति **creeping** adj (कोई बुरी चीज़) धीरे-धीरे और अदृश्य रूप से : *creeping inflation in the housing market.*

creeper / क्रीपर् / noun सहारे से ऊपर चढ़ने वाला पौधा।

creepy / 'क्रीपि / adj (**-ier, -iest**) (अनौप) इस तरह की भावना पैदा करने वाला कि जैसे किसी रेंगने वाले जंतु ने छू लिया हो; रोंगटे खड़े कर देने वाला : *a creepy ghost story.*

cremate / क्र'मेट् / verb दाहकर्म करना, शवदाह करना ▶ **cremation** / क्र'मेश्न् / noun दाह संस्कार **cremation ground** noun श्मशान भूमि **crematorium** / क्रेम 'टॉरिअम् / noun (pl **crematoriums** या **crematoria** / क्रेम'टॉरिआ /) शवदाहगृह।

crepe (**crêpe, crape** भी) / 'क्रेप् / noun 1 एक प्रकार का (मुड़ा तुड़ा-सा लगने वाला) सूती (या रेशमी) कपड़ा 2 एक प्रकार का रबड़ : *crepe-soled shoes.*

crescent / 'क्रेसन्ट; 'क्रेज़न्ट् भी / noun वक्र (चंद्रमा), बालचंद्र; बालचंद्र का आकार : *a crescent moon.*

crest / क्रेस्ट् / noun 1 (पहाड़ की) चोटी; लहरों की उच्चतम सतह 2 (चिड़ियों की)

शिखा, कलगी 3 किसी संस्था, परिवार आदि का प्रतिनिधिक डिज़ाइन : *a cap with the school crest and motto on it* ▸ crest verb 1 चोटी पर पहुँचना 2 कलगी से अलंकृत करना crested *adj.*

crestfallen /'क्रेस्ट्फ़ॉलन्/ *adj* असफलता के कारण निराश; हतोत्साह।

crevice / 'क्रेविस् / *noun* दीवार या चट्टान में छोटी-सी दरार।

crew / क्रू / *noun* 1 जहाज़ पर काम करने वाले सभी कर्मचारी 2 नाव खेने वालों की टीम 3 एकसाथ काम करने वाले लोगों का समूह : *a camera/film crew* ▸ crew *verb* crew (for sb/on sth) जहाज़ पर (या नाव पर) कर्मचारी के तौर पर काम करना।

crib[1] / क्रिब् / *noun* 1 बच्चे का खटोला (झूला) 2 जानवरों के खाना (चारा) रखने की लकड़ी की पेटी, नांद।

crib[2] / क्रिब् / *noun* (*अनौप*) 1 किसी चीज़ को समझने में सहायक अन्य वस्तु जैसे गाइड बुक 2 (परीक्षा में) दूसरों से की गई नक़ल ▸ crib *verb* (-bb-) crib (sth) (from/off sb) परीक्षा में नक़ल करना : *She's always cribbing.*

cricket[1] / 'क्रिकिट् / *noun* झींगुर : *the chirping of crickets.*

cricket[2] / क्रिकिट् / *noun* क्रिकेट का खेल ▸ cricketer *noun* क्रिकेट खिलाड़ी।

crime / क्राइम् / *noun* 1 अपराध जो क़ानूनन दंडनीय है : *commit a (serious) crime* 2 क़ानून तोड़ने वाली हरकत; ग़ैर-क़ानूनी काम : *the spread of organized crime* 3 (प्रायः a crime) बेवक़ूफ़ी वाला ग़लत काम : *It's a crime to waste money like that.*

criminal / 'क्रिमिनल् / *adj* 1 अपराध संबंधी : *criminal offences* 2 दंड संबंधी : *criminal law* 3 नैतिक रूप से ग़लत; अपराधशील : *criminal waste of money* ▸ criminal *noun* अपराधी criminalize, -ise *verb* 1 क़ानून बनाकर दंडनीय घोषित करना 2 किसी के साथ ऐसा व्यवहार करना जैसे वह अपराधी हो; अपराधी-करण करना।

criminology / ,क्रिमि 'नॉलजि / *noun* अपराध विज्ञान; अपराध एवं अपराधियों का वैज्ञानिक अध्ययन।

crimson /'क्रिम्ज़न्/ *adj, noun* क़िरमिज़ी रंग, गहरा लाल।

cringe / क्रिन्ज् / *verb* 1 cringe (at sth) ज़मीन छूते हुए घिसटना (भय के कारण) 2 cringe (to/before sb) (*अपमा*) किसी के आगे गिड़गिड़ाना; चाटुकारी करना।

crinkle / 'क्रिङ्क्ल् / *noun* (काग़ज़) तुड़ामुड़ा होना; (कपड़े की) सिलवट, चुन्नट।

cripple / 'क्रिप्ल् / *noun* (कभी-कभी *अपमा*) अपंग; रीढ़ या टाँग की बीमारी के कारण चलने में असमर्थ : (*अलं*) *a psychological cripple* ▸ cripple *verb* 1 अपंग कर देना : *crippled by polio* 2 किसी व्यक्ति/वस्तु को गंभीर क्षति पहुँचाना : *a ship crippled by a storm.*

crisis / 'क्राइसिस् / *noun* (*pl* crises / 'क्राइसीज़् /) संकट की घड़ी; (बीमारी या जीवन का) परिवर्तन बिंदु : *financial/economical/political crisis.*

crisp / क्रिस्प् / *adj* (-er, -est) 1 (*भोजन*) ख़स्ता, कुरकुरा; (फल एवं सब्ज़ियाँ) ताज़े एवं सख़्त 2 (मौसम) ख़ुश्क और ठंडा : *a crisp winter morning* 3 (कभी-कभी *अपमा*) (शैली, व्यवहार) तुरंत निर्णय-कारी (कभी-कभी रूखा) 4 (बाल) कसे हुए घुँघराले 5 (चित्र) स्पष्ट एवं साफ़ : *in crisp focus* ▸ crisp (potato crisp भी, US potato chip, chip) *noun* आलू के तले हुए चिप crisp *verb* crisp (sth) (up) कुरकुरा एवं ख़स्ता बनाना crisply *adv* crispness *noun.*

criss-cross / 'क्रिस् क्रॉस्/ *adj* एक-दूसरे को काटती हुई रेखाएँ (या सड़कें) : *a criss-cross pattern/design* ▸ criss-cross *verb* एक-दूसरे को काटती हुई रेखाएँ खींचना/पैटर्न बनाना।

criterion / क्राइ 'टिअरिअन् / *noun* (*pl*

criteria / क्राइ'टिअरिआ /) मूल्यांकन की कसौटी, मापदंड : *Success in making money is not always a good criterion of success in life.*

critic /'क्रिटिक्/ noun 1 दोष ढूँढने वाला व्यक्ति 2 साहित्य, कला, संगीत का पारखी आलोचक : *a music/theatre/literary critic.*

critical /'क्रिटिकल्/ adj 1 critical (of sb/sth) दोष निकालते हुए; नापसंदगी दिखाते हुए : *a critical remark/report* 2 आलोचनात्मक, समीक्षात्मक 3 संकटपूर्ण स्थिति में, नाजुक दौर में; अति महत्त्वपूर्ण ▸ critically adv.

criticism /'क्रिटिसिज़म्/ noun 1 निंदा, दोषान्वेषण 2 समीक्षा, आलोचना : *literary criticism.*

criticize, -ise /'क्रिटिसाइज़्/ verb 1 criticize sb/sth (for sth) दोष निकालना 2 आलोचना/समीक्षा करना।

critique / क्रि'टीक्/ noun विवेचनात्मक टीका, समालोचना।

croak / क्रोक्/ noun (मेंढक की) टर्र-टर्र की आवाज़; (कौए की) काँव-काँव ▸ croak verb 1 मेंढक का टर्र-टर्र करना; कौए का काँव-काँव करना 2 (व्यक्ति का) फटी हुई बेसुरी आवाज़ में कुछ कहना/बोलना : *He croaked (out) a few words.*

crochet /'क्रोशे; US क्रो'शे / noun क्रोशिए से बुनाई करने का तरीका, इस तरह बुना हुआ कपड़ा : *a beige crochet sweater.*

crockery /'क्रॉकरि / noun (crocks [pl] भी) कप, प्लेट आदि चीनी मिट्टी के बरतन; क्रॉकरी।

crocodile /'क्रॉकडाइल् / noun मगर, घड़ियाल ■ crocodile tears घड़ियाली आँसू; झूठे आँसू।

crony /'क्रोनि / noun (अनौप, प्रायः अपमा) घनिष्ठ मित्र, यार।

crook / क्रुक्/ noun 1 (अनौप) धूर्त, अपराधी, बेईमानी से जीविका चलाने वाला : *That used-car salesman is a real*

crook. 2 मुड़ी हुई लठिया, विशेषतः गड़ेरियों द्वारा प्रयुक्त 3 किसी वस्तु में मोड़, जैसे घुटने या कोहनी का मोड़ ▸ crook verb मोड़ना, विशेषतः अँगुली या भुजा।

crooked /'क्रुकिड् / adj 1 (अनौप) (व्यक्ति या क्रिया) कपटी, बेईमान : *All the officials are crooked.* 2 मुड़ा-तुड़ा, असरल : *a crooked lane/branch* ▸ crookedly adv crookedness noun.

crop¹ / क्रॉप्/ noun 1 पैदावार (अन्न आदि की), फ़सल 2 crops [pl] फ़सलें (खेत में खड़ी) 3 [sing] crop of sth एक समय पर उपस्थित (व्यक्तियों) या एक समय में उत्पादित (वस्तुओं) चीज़ों का समूह : *a crop of complaints* 4 पक्षियों के गले में थैलीनुमा संरचना जहाँ वे भोजन इकट्ठा कर लेते हैं ▸ crop verb (-pp-) 1 बहुत छोटा काटना; चित्र, फ़ोटो आदि के किनारे काटना 2 (पशुओं का) घास चरना : *Sheep had cropped the grass (short).* 3 (पौधों, खेतों का) फ़सल पैदा करना; फ़सल (काटकर) इकट्ठा करना; (ज़मीन को) खेती के काम में लाना ■ crop up (कठिनाइयों आदि का) अचानक प्रकट होना, उत्पन्न होना।

cross¹ / क्रॉस्/ noun 1 (+, x,† आदि) चिह्न जहाँ एक रेखा पर दूसरी रेखा काटती है 2 सूली; the Cross [sing] सूली जिस पर ईसा मसीह चढ़ाए गए थे; ईसाई धर्म : *the Cross and the Crescent* 3 cross (between A and B) विभिन्न प्रकार के दो पशुओं की संतान या पौधों की उपज, संकर प्रजाति : *A mule is a cross between a horse and a donkey.* 4 प्रतिकूल परिस्थिति, कष्ट आदि।

cross² / क्रॉस्/ verb 1 cross (over) (from/to sb/sth) आर-पार जाना, दूसरी तरफ़ जाना : *cross a river/a road/a desert/the sea* 2 (विपरीत दिशा में जाते हुए) पास से गुज़रना 3 काटना, आर-पार रेखा खींचना : *cross a cheque* (चेक पर

दो रेखाएँ खींच देना जिसके कारण चेक बैंक खाते में ही जमा होगा। 4 (किसी की इच्छाओं, योजनाओं में) बाधा डालना : *to be crossed in love* 5 **cross (sth with sth)** जानवरों या पौधों की संकर प्रजाति तैयार करना ■ **cross one's fingers** योजनाओं की सफलता की आशा करना **cross one's mind** विचार सूझना **cross over** एक संस्कृति, राजनीतिक पार्टी आदि से दूसरे में चले जाना।

cross³ / क्रॉस् / *adj* (-er, -est) 1 **cross (with sb) (about sth)** बदमिजाज और किसी पर क्रोधित : *I was cross with him for being late.* 2 (पवन) प्रतिकूल ■ **at cross purposes** (लोगों में) ग़लतफ़हमी ▸ **crossly** *adv.*

crossbar / क्रॉस्बार् / *noun* दो खड़े दंडों पर लगा क्षैतिज दंड (साइकिल, फुटबाल गोल आदि में)।

cross-breed / क्रॉस् ब्रीड् / *noun* जानवरों या पौधों की दो अलग जातियों के समागम से उत्पन्न जानवर या पौधा, संकर प्रजाति ▸ **cross-breed** *verb* (*pt, pp* **cross-bred**) संकर प्रजाति तैयार करना : *improve crops by cross-breeding.*

cross-check / क्रॉस् चेक् / *verb* **cross-check sth (against sth)** जाँचने की भिन्न पद्धति द्वारा जाँचकर सूचनाओं, संख्याओं आदि की सत्यता की पुष्टि करना : *Cross-check your answer by using a calculator.* ▸ **cross-check** *noun.*

cross-country / क्रॉस् कन्ट्रि / *adj, adv* (सड़कों का) मुख्य रास्तों से न होकर खुले मैदानों और ग्रामीण इलाकों से होते हुए : *a cross-country run/race/route* ▸ **cross-country** *noun.*

cross-examine / क्रॉस् इग् ज़ैमिन् / *verb* (विशेषत: क़ानून) बारीकी से सवाल पूछना; विस्तार से प्रश्न पूछना ▸ **cross-examination** *noun.*

cross-eyed / क्रॉस् आइड् / *adj* भैंगा व्यक्ति।

crossfire / क्रॉस्फ़ाइअर् / *noun* 1 दो या अधिक तरफ़ों से जवाबी गोलीबारी 2 दो समूहों के वाद-विवाद या झगड़े में किसी तीसरे का इच्छाविरुद्ध ही उलझ जाना।

crossing / क्रॉसिङ् / *noun* 1 दो सड़कों या रेल पटरियों के मिलने की जगह 2 एक देश से दूसरे देश को जाने के लिए स्थान 3 सड़क पार करने का सुरक्षित स्थान 4 समुद्र (या चौड़ी नदी) पार की यात्रा।

cross-legged / क्रॉस् लेग्ड्; क्रॉस् लेगिड् / *adv* पालथी मारकर बैठना; एक पैर के ऊपर दूसरा पैर रखकर बैठना।

cross-reference / क्रॉस् रेफ़्रन्स् / *noun* पुस्तक के एक अंश का दूसरे अंश में संदर्भ ▸ **cross-reference** *verb.*

crossroads / क्रॉस्रोड्ज़ / *noun* (*pl* अपरिवर्तित) [*sing*] चौराहा ■ **at a/the crossroads** जीवन में किसी महत्त्वपूर्ण निर्णायक मोड़ पर।

cross-section / क्रॉस् सेक्शन् / *noun* 1 पदार्थ का आड़ा-तिरछा समकोण में कटाव : *examining a cross-section of the kidney under the microscope* 2 कोई विशिष्ट या प्रतिनिधि नमूना : *a cross-section of the population.*

crossword / क्रॉस्वई / (**crossword puzzle** भी) *noun* वर्ग पहेली।

crouch / क्राउच् / *verb* 1 दुबककर बैठना 2 **crouch over sb/sth** किसी व्यक्ति या वस्तु के ऊपर झुककर बहुत पास आ जाना ▸ **crouch** *noun* **crouched** *adj.*

crow¹ / क्रो / *noun* कौआ।

crow² / क्रो / *verb* 1 (मुर्गे का) बाँग देना 2 (बच्चे का) किलकारी मारना 3 **crow (about/over sb/sth)** (अक्सर *अपमा*) विजय की प्रसन्नता में हर्षध्वनि करना ▸ **crow** *noun* बाँग।

crowbar / क्रोबार् / *noun* सब्बल (भारी वस्तुओं को हिलाने के लिए प्रयुक्त लोहे का डंडा)।

crowd¹ / क्राउड् / noun 1 भीड़; जनसमूह; (अनौप, अक्सर अपमा) विशिष्ट प्रकार के लोगों का समूह : the media crowd 2 the crowd [sing] (कभी-कभी अपमा) जनसाधारण, आम जनता : move with/ follow the crowd.

crowd² / क्राउड् / verb 1 crowd about/ around/round (sb/sth) भीड़ में आना, बहुत पास-पास जमा होना 2 (स्थान में) भीड़ कर देना : Tourists crowded the pavement. 3 (अनौप) किसी के पास जमा होकर (मानसिक) दबाव पैदा करना ▸ crowded adj crowded (with sth) 1 भीड़ भरा 2 पूर्ण रूपेण भरा हुआ।

crown¹ / क्राउन् / noun 1 राजा-रानियों का सोने-चांदी का मुकुट 2 (प्राय: the Crown) [sing] सम्राट की शक्ति एवं सत्ता का प्रतीक 3 पुरस्कार या जीत के प्रतीक के रूप में सिर पर बाँधा हुआ फूलों/पत्तियों का घेरा 4 टोपी का सर्वोच्च सिरा; किसी भी वस्तु का सर्वोच्च बिंदु : the crown of a hill 5 कोई भी मुकुट जैसी वस्तु।

crown² / क्राउन् / verb 1 मुकुट पहनाना (सत्ता सौंपना) : She was crowned (queen) in 1953. 2 crown sth (with sth) कुछ पूर्ण या सर्वांगपूर्ण बनाना; (साहि) किसी वस्तु का सर्वोच्च सिरा बनाना या ढकना 3 (cap भी) दाँत पर कृत्रिम परत चढ़ाना ▸ crowning adj सर्वांगपूर्ण बनाने वाला : Her crowning glory is her hair.

crucial / क्रूशल् / adj crucial (to/for sth) अत्यंत महत्त्वपूर्ण; निर्णायक स्थिति में : a crucial decision/issue/factor ▸ crucially adv.

crucible / क्रूसिबल् / noun कुल्हिया (पात्र जिसमें धातु गलाते हैं)।

crucifix / क्रूसफ़िक्स् / noun सूली पर चढ़े ईसा की छोटी मूर्ति।

crucifixion / क्रूस'फ़िक्श्न् / noun सूली पर चढ़ाकर मारना : the Crucifixion (i.e. of Christ).

crucify / क्रूसिफ़ाइ / verb सूली पर कीलें ठोंककर हत्या करना।

crude / क्रूड् / adj (-r, -st) 1 कच्चा माल, अपरिष्कृत, जिससे अभी वस्तुएँ बनानी हैं : crude oil/ore 2 अनगढ़ कारीगरी; औसत अंदाज़ा : a crude sketch/method/ approximation 3 (व्यक्ति और व्यवहार) रूखा, अभद्र ▸ crudely adv crude- ness noun crudity / 'क्रूडटि / noun.

cruel / क्रूअल् / adj (-ller, -llest) 1 cruel (to sb/sth) (अपमा) क्रूर, निर्दय 2 पीड़ा- कारक ▸ cruelly adv.

cruelty / क्रूअल्टि / noun (pl cruelties) 1 क्रूरता 2 (प्राय: pl) पीड़ादायक कार्य : cruelties of life.

cruise / क्रूज़ / verb 1 पर्यटन के लिए समुद्री यात्रा या, (युद्ध में) शत्रुओं के जहाजों का पता लगाने के लिए परिभ्रमण 2 ईंधन के दक्ष प्रयोग के लिए (गाड़ी या वायुयान का) मंथर गति से चलना 3 बिना अधिक प्रयास के ही आसानी से उद्देश्य पा लेना : cruise to a victory ▸ cruise noun समुद्री पर्यटन; समुद्री गश्त cruise missile noun कंप्यूटर नियंत्रित नीची उड़ान वाली आण्विक मिसाइल cruiser / 'क्रूज़र् / noun 1 लड़ाकू जहाज़ 2 (cabin cruiser भी) पर्यटन नौका जिसमें सोने की व्यवस्था होती है।

crumb / क्रम् / noun 1 (रोटी, केक आदि का) छोटा-सा टुकड़ा, टूटा हुआ अंश 2 बहुत ज़रा-सी वस्तु या टुकड़ा : a few crumbs of information 3 ब्रेड का अंदर वाला मुलायम भाग।

crumble / क्रम्बल् / verb 1 crumble (sth) (into/to sth); crumble (sth) (up) टुकड़े-टुकड़े हो जाना या कर देना : crumble one's bread (up) 2 crum- ble (into/to sth) शक्ति खोना शुरू करना, धीरे-धीरे समाप्त हो जाना : The great empire began to crumble. ▸ crum- bly adj.

crumple / 'क्रम्पल् / verb 1 crumple

(sth) (into sth); crumple (sth) (up) सिलवटों में कुचल जाना/देना : *The front of the car crumpled on impact.* 2 अचानक अति कमज़ोर हो जाना; (टूट कर) गिर जाना; मुड़ जाना ▶ crumpled *adj* : *a crumpled suit.*

crunch / क्रन्च् / *verb* 1 crunch sth (up) आवाज़ करते हुए (दाँतों से खाते समय) कुचलना : *crunch peanuts/biscuits* 2 कुचलने की तीक्ष्ण आवाज़ करना ▶ crunch *noun* 1 कुचलने की क्रिया और उससे उत्पन्न आवाज़ 2 the crunch [*sing*] कुछ महत्त्वपूर्ण और प्राय: अप्रिय बात या मुद्दा।

crusade / क्रू'सेड् / *noun* 1 (प्राय: *pl*) धर्मयुद्ध, जिहाद (मध्य युग में यूरोप में मुसलमानों से ईसा मसीह की भूमि वापस लेने के लिए ईसाई राज्यों द्वारा छेड़े युद्ध) 2 crusade (for/against sth); crusade (to do sth) किसी भी अच्छे लक्ष्य की प्राप्ति के लिए छेड़ा संघर्ष : *a crusade against corruption* ▶ crusade *verb* crusader *noun.*

crush¹ / क्रश् / *verb* 1 कुचलना; पैरों तले रौंदना : *Wine is made by crushing grapes.* 2 crush sth (up) कठोर वस्तु को छोटे टुकड़ों में तोड़ना या चूर्ण बनाना 3 दबाकर सिलवटें डालना या पड़ जाना : *The clothes were badly crushed in the suitcase.* 4 नष्ट करना या करारी हार देना 5 (गन्ना आदि) पेरना ▶ crushing *adj* 1 पूरा, बुरी तरह : *crushing defeat* 2 किसी को नीचा दिखाने के इरादे से crushingly *adv.*

crush² / क्रश् / *noun* 1 तंग स्थान में अत्यधिक व्यक्तियों का होना 2 crush (on sb) (*अनौप*) प्यार का क्षणिक तीव्र आकर्षण 3 फलों के रस से बना पेय।

crust / क्रस्ट् / *noun* 1 डबलरोटी का ऊपरी कड़ा भाग, पपड़ी 2 (विशेषत: *साहि*) पपड़ी का भाग, सूखी पतली डबलरोटी 3 किसी मुलायम वस्तु या द्रव के ऊपर का कड़ा भाग,

पपड़ी ▶ crusted *adj* crusted (with sth) पपड़ीदार होना crusty / 'क्रस्टि / *adj* 1 पपड़ीदार एवं कुरकरा 2 (अनौप) (विशेषत: वयस्क व्यक्ति) जल्दी भड़क जाने वाला : *a crusty old soldier.*

crutch / क्रच् / *noun* 1 (चलने में मुश्किल अनुभव करने वाले व्यक्ति की) बैसाखी : *a pair of crutches* 2 किसी के लिए सहारा बनने वाला व्यक्ति या वस्तु।

crux / क्रक्स् / *noun* किसी समस्या का सबसे महत्त्वपूर्ण अंश, जिसे सुलझाना सबसे कठिन हो, मर्म : *Now we come to the crux of the matter.*

cry¹ / क्राइ / *verb* (*pt, pp* cried) 1 cry (for/over sth/sb) रोना, विलाप करना : *cry with pain/hunger* 2 cry (out) (व्यक्ति या जानवर का) ज़ोर से चिल्लाना/पुकारना 3 cry (out) (for sth) चीख़ मारना, चिल्लाना (क्रोध, पीड़ा, भय, आश्चर्य आदि की अभिव्यक्ति ■ cry over spilt milk किसी ऐसी घटना पर दुख अनुभव करना जिसे बदला न जा सके cry wolf झूठ-मूठ के ख़तरे के लिए सहायता को पुकारना।

cry² / क्राई / *noun* (*pl* cries) 1 (क्रोध, भय, पीड़ा, आश्चर्य आदि के कारण) चीख़ चिल्लाहट : *a cry of terror* 2 पुकार; पक्षियों की बोली 3 cry (for sth) बहुत ज़रूरी या महत्त्वपूर्ण माँग (निवेदन) : *a cry for freedom* 4 सैद्धांतिक नारा : *a war cry.*

crypt / क्रिप्ट् / *noun* चर्च के तहख़ाने का कमरा।

cryptic / 'क्रिप्टिक् / *adj* गुप्त अर्थ वाला, रहस्यमय : *cryptic crossword clues* ▶ cryptically *adv.*

crystal / 'क्रिस्टल् / *noun* 1 बिल्लौर, स्फटिक पत्थर की तरह एक साफ़ पारदर्शी पदार्थ; आभूषण रूप में उसका टुकड़ा : *a crystal bracelet* 2 उत्तम कोटि का काँच 3 साफ़ सतहों वाला छोटा ठोस टुकड़ा : *sugar/salt crystals* 4 मणिभ; (रसा) रवा।

crystalline /'क्रिस्टलाइन्/ *adj* 1 क्रिस्टल जैसी, क्रिस्टलीय 2 साफ़, पारदर्शी।

crystallize, -ise /'क्रिस्टलाइज़्/ *verb* 1 (विचारों, योजनाओं आदि का) स्पष्ट हो जाना 2 किसी पदार्थ के क्रिस्टल बनाना ▸ **crystallization, -isation** *noun*.

cub /कब्/ *noun* शेर, भालू, लोमड़ी आदि का बच्चा।

cube /क्यूब्/ *noun* 1 (ज्यामिति) छह समान पृष्ठ वाला ठोस पिंड 2 छह सतहों वाली कोई वस्तु, विशेषत: खाद्य पदार्थ का टुकड़ा : *an ice cube* 3 (गणित) एक संख्या को आपस में दो बार गुणा करने से प्राप्त फल, घन : *The cube of 5 (5^3) is 125 ($5 \times 5 \times 5 = 125$).* ▸ **cube** *verb* 1 घन निकालना 2 क्यूब आकार में वस्तु काटना।

cubic /'क्यूबिक्/ *adj* 1 घनाकार 2 घन में व्यक्त (संख्या) 3 घन का आयतन/मात्रा।

cubicle /'क्यूबिकल्/ *noun* बड़े कमरे का छोटे भागों में बाँटा हुआ हिस्सा, कोठरी।

cuckoo /'कुकू/ *noun* (*pl* **cuckoos**) कोयल।

cucumber /'क्यूकम्बर्/ *noun* ककड़ी; खीरा।

cud /कड्/ *noun* गाय-बैल की जुगाली।

cuddle /'कडल्/ *verb* (प्यार में) गले से लिपट जाना : *The child cuddled her doll (to her chest).* ■ **cuddle up (to/ against sb/sth)** पास-पास आराम से बैठना या लेटना ▸ **cuddle** *noun*.

cudgel /'कजल्/ *noun* छोटा-मोटा डंडा या मुद्गर ■ **take up (the) cudgels for/ on behalf of sb/sth** किसी (चीज़) की सुरक्षा या समर्थन करना ▸ **cudgel** *verb* (-ll-; *US* -l- भी) डंडे या मुद्गर से पीटना।

cue¹ /क्यू/ *noun* 1 **cue (for sth/to do sth)** संकेत, इशारा 2 दूसरे को इस बात का इशारा देना कि वह क्या करे, क्या बोले; व्यवहार, कार्य आदि के लिए उदाहरण ▸ **cue** *verb* (*pres p* **cueing**) **cue sb (in)** इशारा करना।

cue² /क्यू/ *noun* स्नूकर, बिलियर्ड्स आदि खेलों में गेंद को मारने के लिए लकड़ी का लंबा डंडा।

cuff¹ /कफ़/ *noun* 1 (कमीज़ आदि की बाँहों का) कफ़ 2 **cuffs** [*pl*] (**hand- cuffs** भी) (अप) हथकड़ी।

cuff² /कफ़/ *verb* थप्पड़ मारना ▸ **cuff** *noun* तमाचा, थप्पड़।

cuisine /क्वि'ज़ीन्/ *noun* (फ़्रेंच) भोजन पकाने की शैली : *a restaurant where the cuisine is excellent.*

cul-de-sac /'कल् ड सैक्/ *noun* (*pl* **cul-de-sacs**) (फ़्रेंच) बंद गली : (अल) *This brand of socialism has en- tered a cul-de-sac.*

culinary /'कलिनरि; *US* 'कलिनेरि/ *adj* (औप) भोजन पकाने संबंधी, पाक कला- विषयक : *culinary skills/implements.*

cull /कल्/ *verb* **cull sth (from sth)** विभिन्न सूत्रों से जानकारी, सूचना आदि ग्रहण करना या चुनना : *information culled from a number of reference books.*

culminate /'कल्मिनेट्/ *verb* ■ **culmi- nate in sth** (औप) (प्रयत्नों, उन्नति की) पराकाष्ठा पर पहुँचना; विशेष परिणाम पा लेना : *a long struggle that culmi- nated in success* ▸ **culmination** /,कल्मि'नेश्न्/ *noun* पराकाष्ठा।

culpable /'कल्पबल्/ *adj* (औप) दोषा- स्पद, ग़लत काम के लिए ज़िम्मेदार एवं दोष लगाने योग्य : *culpable officials* ▸ **cul- pability** *noun*.

culprit /'कल्प्रिट्/ *noun* 1 दोषी, अप- राधी 2 समस्या के लिए ज़िम्मेदार व्यक्ति या वस्तु : *A faulty light switch was the culprit.*

cult /कल्ट्/ *noun* 1 पूजा-पद्धति 2 **cult (of sb/sth)** (कभी-कभी अपमा) किसी व्यक्ति या वस्तु के लिए अत्यधिक प्रशंसा या प्यार 3 लोकप्रिय फ़ैशन या क्षणोन्माद।

cultivable /'कल्टिवेब्ल्/ *adj* खेती योग्य।

cultivate /'कल्टिवेट्/ *verb* 1 (खेत)

जोतना, खेती करना; फ़सल उगाना 2 *(कभी-कभी अपमा)* किसी वस्तु को ध्यान या समय देकर बढ़ाना : *cultivating the friendship of influential people* ▸ **cultivated** *adj* (व्यक्ति) शिक्षित एवं भद्र **cultivation** /कल्टि'वेश्न्/ *noun* जुताई, खेती **cultivator** / 'कल्टिवेटर्/ *noun* 1 किसान 2 जुताई की मशीन।

cultural /'कल्चरल्/ *adj* सांस्कृतिक : *cultural differences/activities.*

culture /'कल्चर/ *noun* 1 किसी राष्ट्र के बौद्धिक विकास का साक्ष्य (साहित्य, कला संगीत एवं अन्य बौद्धिक उपलब्धियाँ), संस्कृति 2 प्रशिक्षण एवं अनुभव से मन, शरीर, बुद्धि एवं मानसिक शक्तियों का विकास 3 प्रजाति बढ़ाने के लिए पौधों एवं जंतुओं का प्रजनन एवं विकास 4 *(जीव विज्ञान)* अध्ययन के लिए विकसित जीवाणुओं का समूह : *a culture of cholera germs* ▸ **cultured** *adj* (व्यक्ति) सुसंस्कृत।

culvert /'कल्वर्ट्/ *noun* नाला, पुलिया।

cum / कम्/ *prep* (दो सदृश संज्ञाओं को जोड़ने के लिए प्रयुक्त) और यह भी; साथ में : *bedroom-cum-sitting-room.*

cumbersome /'कम्बर्सम्/ *adj* 1 भद्दा और भारी, हिलाने और ले जाने में कठिन 2 धीमा एवं अकुशल : *the university's cumbersome administrative procedures.*

cumulative / 'क्यूम्यलटिव्; US 'क्यू-म्यलेटिव्/ *adj* एक के बाद एक जुड़ने से मात्रा या बल में क्रमिक रूप से बढ़ता हुआ, संचित : *the cumulative effect of several illnesses* ▸ **cumulatively** *adv.*

cunning /'कनिङ्/ *adj* 1 (प्राय: *अपमा*) धूर्त एवं चालाक (व्यक्ति) 2 (कोई युक्ति, खोज, समस्या आदि) चतुर; चतुराईपूर्ण : *a cunning device for cracking nuts* ▸ **cunning** *noun* (प्राय: *अपमा*) धूर्त आचरण या व्यवहार **cunningly** *adv.*

cup¹ /कप्/ *noun* 1 (चाय आदि पीने का)

प्याला; कपभर : *a cup of coffee* 2 इनाम में मिलने वाला सोने-चाँदी का कप 3 कप के आकार की कोई वस्तु : *an egg-cup* ■ **(not) sb's cup of tea** अपनी रुचि का विषय होना/न होना ▸ **cupful** *noun* (*pl* **cupfuls**) प्यालाभर।

cup² / कप्/ *verb* (-pp-) हाथों को प्याले की तरह मिलाकर मोड़ना; **cup sth (in/with sth)** इस तरह मोड़ी हुई हथेलियों में कुछ लेना/पकड़ना : *cup one's chin in one's hands.*

cupboard / 'कबई/ *noun* (कपड़े, क्रॉकरी आदि रखने की) अलमारी।

curable / 'क्युअरब्ल्/ *adj* (बीमारी आदि) साध्य, जिसकी चिकित्सा संभव है।

curate /'क्युअर्ट्/ *noun* (इंग्लैंड के चर्च में) मठ के पादरी का सहायक।

curator / क्युअ'रेटर्/ *noun* अजायबघर (संग्रहालय) का अध्यक्ष।

curb / कर्ब्/ *noun* 1 घोड़े के मुँह में लगी जंजीर या पट्टी, दहाना 2 कोई भी वस्तु जो नियंत्रित करे : *put/keep a curb on one's anger* ▸ **curb** *verb* नियंत्रित करना : *curb spending/waste.*

curd / कई/ *noun* (**curds** [*pl*] भी) दही।

curdle /'कईल्/ *verb* द्रव (विशेषत: दूध) का फटना : *The milk has curdled.* ∘ *(अल) His screams were enough to curdle one's blood.*

cure¹ /क्युअर्/ *verb* 1 **cure sb (of sth)** इलाज करना, स्वस्थ करना : *The doctors cured her (of cancer).* 2 किसी चीज़ का हल ढूँढ लेना, बुराई को दूर करना (अंत कर देना) 3 मांस आदि को नमक लगाकर रखना ताकि काफ़ी दिनों तक ख़राब न हो : *well-cured bacon.*

cure² /क्युअर्/ *noun* 1 इलाज, चिकित्सा 2 **cure (for sth)** उपचार।

curfew / 'कर्फ़्यू / *noun* यह सरकारी आदेश कि लोग घरों के भीतर रहें, बाहर न निकलें।

curio /'क्युअरिओ/ *noun* (*pl* **curios**)

कला की छोटी अद्भुत एवं असाधारण कृति जिसका मूल्य उसके अजीब होने के कारण है : *a collection of curios.*

curiosity / क्युअरि ऑसटि / *noun (pl* **curiosities)** 1 कुतूहल 2 कुतूहलजनक वस्तु ■ **curiosity killed the cat** *(कहा)* अधिक उत्सुकता हानिकर होती है।

curious / क्युअरिअस / *adj* 1 **curious (about sth/to do sth)** जानने-समझने या पढ़ने को उत्सुक 2 *(अपमा)* दूसरों के मामलों में आवश्यकता से अधिक रुचि लेते हुए 3 अद्भुत, अजीब : *Isn't he a curious-looking little man?* ▸ **curiously** *adv.*

curl¹ / कर्ल / *noun* छल्ला; विशेषत: घुँघराले बाल ▸ **curly** *adj* (**-ier, -iest)** घुँघराला : *curly hair.*

curl² / कर्ल / *verb* 1 मोड़ना, जिससे किनारे गोलाई में उठ जाएँ : *She has curled (up) her hair.* 2 छल्ले के आकार का होना या करना।

currant / करन्ट / *noun* 1 किशमिश 2 छोटी झाड़ी जिसमें अंगूर जैसे छोटे फल गुच्छों में लगते हैं; इसका फल : *black currants.*

currency / करन्सि / *noun* 1 प्रचलित सिक्कों की व्यवस्था (मुद्रा) 2 सामान्य व्यवहार या प्रयोग में होने की स्थिति : *The rumour soon gained currency.*

current¹ / करन्ट / *adj* 1 वर्तमान कालीन : *current issues/events* 2 प्रचलित : *current opinion/beliefs* ▸ **currently** *adv* वर्तमान समय में।

current² / करन्ट / *noun* 1 पानी की धारा, हवा का प्रवाह : *The swimmer was swept away by the current.* 2 विद्युत धारा 3 (घटनाओं, विचारों, जीवन की) गति।

curriculum / क रिक्यलम् / *noun (pl* **curricula** / क रिक्यला /) स्कूल/कॉलेजों में अध्ययन का पाठ्यक्रम ▸ **curriculum vitae** / क रिक्यलम् वीटाइ / *(संक्षि* cv; *US* **résumé** भी) *noun* व्यक्ति वृत्त, बायो डेटा।

curry¹ / करि / *noun (pl* **curries)** रसेदार डिश; सब्ज़ियों, मीट, आदि का सालन; शोरबेदार पकवान ▸ **curried** *adj* सालन बनाया हुआ **curry** *verb (pt, pp* **curried)** सालन बनाना।

curry² / करि / *verb (pt, pp* **curried)** ■ **curry favour (with sb)** *(अपमा)* खुशामद करना।

curse¹ / कर्स / *noun* 1 अपशब्द, दुर्वचन 2 [*sing*] शाप 3 अभिशाप; आपत्ति या नाश का कारण : *the curse of poverty.*

curse² / कर्स / *verb* अपशब्द बोलना, दुर्वचन कहना; शाप देना : *He cursed his bad luck.* ■ **be cursed with sth** के कारण दुख उठाना ▸ **cursed** / कर्सिड् / *adj (अनौप)* घृणित।

cursor / कर्सर / *noun* कंप्यूटर के स्क्रीन पर गतिमान बिंदु जो स्थिति-विशेष दर्शाता है।

cursory / कर्सरि / *adj (प्राय: अपमा)* जल्दी में और लापरवाही से किया गया : *give sth a cursory glance/look* ▸ **cursorily** *adv.*

curt / कर्ट / *adj (अपमा)* (वक्ता के लिए प्रयुक्त) रूखा, अभद्र एवं संक्षिप्त : *a curt answer* ▸ **curtly** *adv* **curtness** *noun.*

curtail / कर टेल् / *verb* (जो पहले सोचा था उससे) कम करना; घटाना : *curtail a speech* ▸ **curtailment** *noun* कमी, कटौती।

curtain / कर्टन् / *noun* 1 (*US* **drape)** (दरवाज़े या खिड़कियों का) परदा 2 [*sing*] (रंगमंच का) परदा, यवनिका 3 (विशेषत: *sing*) कोई भी ढकने, छिपाने वाली वस्तु : *a curtain of fog/mist* ▸ **curtain** *verb* परदा लगाना।

curtsy (curtesy भी) / कर्टसि / *noun (pl* **curtsies)** आदर एवं अभिवादन अभिव्यक्त करने की महिलाओं द्वारा प्रयुक्त विशेष क्रिया।

curve / कर्व / *noun* वक्र रेखा जो कहीं भी सीधी न हो, जैसे ∩; मोड़ या घुमाव

▶ **curve** *verb* वक्राकार मुड़ना या मोड़ना; वक्र रेखा में गति करना **curvy** *adj.*

cushion /'कुशन्/ *noun* 1 (कुर्सी आदि की) गद्दी, गद्दा 2 बहुत नर्म मुलायम वस्तु का ढेर : *a cushion of moss on the rock*

▶ **cushion** *verb* 1 गद्दी लगाना 2 किसी चीज़ का प्रभाव कम करना 3 **cushion sb/ sth (against/from sth)** हानि से बचाना, सुरक्षा करना।

cushy /'कुशि/ *adj* (-ier, -iest) (*अनौप, प्राय: अपमा*) (नौकरी, काम) आराम वाला, कम मेहनत की ज़रूरत वाला: *It's a cushy life for the rich.*

custard /'कस्टर्ड/ *noun* दूध और अंडे या कार्नफ्लाउर के मिश्रण से बना मीठा पकवान।

custodian /क'स्टोडिअन्/ *noun* देख-भाल करने वाला, ज़िम्मेदार परिरक्षक : *a self-appointed custodian of public morals.*

custody /'कस्टडि/ *noun* 1 अभिरक्षा : *The court gave the mother custody of the child.* 2 हिरासत : *be held in custody* ▶ **custodial** *adj.*

custom /'कस्टम्/ *noun* 1 प्रथा या प्रचलित रिवाज :*the custom of giving presents at Diwali.*

customary /'कस्टमरि/ *adj* परंपरागत ▶ **customarily** *adv.*

customer /'कस्टमर्/ *noun* 1 (दुकान-दार का) ग्राहक 2 (*अनौप*) व्यक्ति विशेष : *a queer/awkward/tough customer.*

customs /'कस्टम्ज़/ *noun* [pl] चुंगी, आयात शुल्क; (**the Customs** भी) चुंगी विभाग।

cut¹ /'कट्/ *verb* (-tt-; *pt, pp* cut) 1 (चाकू, कैंची आदि से) काटना, कतरना 2 **cut sth (from sth)** काटकर अलग करना : *cut some flowers* 3 **cut sth (in/into sth)** काटकर छोटा करना 4 (*ज्यामिति*) (एक लाइन का) दूसरी लाइन को क्रास करना 5 (*अनौप*) कक्षा, बैठक

आदि से अनुपस्थित रहना : *cut a class/ lecture* 6 किसी को शारीरिक या मानसिक कष्ट पहुँचाना : *His cruel remarks cut her deeply.* 7 फ़िल्म, नाटक, किताब आदि का संपादन के समय कोई अंश निकालना/ हटा देना ■ **cut sb down:** (*औप*) (काट-कर) मार डालना **cut sth down** 1 काटकर गिराना 2 आकार या मात्रा में कम करना **cut sth up** चाकू से छोटे-छोटे टुकड़े करना

▶ **cut and dried** *adj* (निर्णय) निश्चित और तैयार।

cut² /कट्/ *noun* 1 घाव 2 काटने की प्रक्रिया 3 **cut (in sth)** आकार, लंबाई, मात्रा आदि में कटौती : *announce a cut in unemployment benefit* 4 **cut (in sth)** फ़िल्म, नाटक, क़िताब आदि में संपादन के समय काट दिया गया अंश 5 (*अनौप*) बेईमानी के लाभ में हिस्सा 6 (कपड़े या बाल) काटने का ■ **a cut above sb/sth** (*अनौप*) औरों/अन्य वस्तुओं से थोड़ा अधिक अच्छा।

cute /क्यूट्/ *adj* (-r, -st) (कभी-कभी *अपमा*) 1 आकर्षक, सुंदर : *a cute baby* 2 (*अनौप* विशेषत: *US*) हाज़िर-जवाब, तुरंत सोचकर निर्णय करने वाला; चालाक और चिढ़ पैदा करने वाला ▶ **cutely** *adv* **cuteness** *noun.*

cutlery /'कट्लरि/ *noun* खाने की मेज़ के काँटे, छुरी, चम्मच, चाकू आदि।

cutlet /'कट्लट्/ *noun* 1 मांस का मोटा पका हुआ टुकड़ा 2 कटलेट के आकार का आलू, सब्ज़ी आदि का तला हुआ टुकड़ा, टिक्की।

cutter /'कटर्/ *noun* काटने वाला (व्यक्ति/ वस्तु) : *a pair of wire cutters.*

cut-throat /'कट् थ्रोट्/ *adj* (प्रतिस्पर्धा) अत्यंत तीव्र एवं तीखी।

cutting¹ /'कटिङ्/ *noun* 1 (*US* clip-ping) समाचार-पत्र या पत्रिका से काटी कतरन 2 (पौधे की) कलम 3 (**cut** भी) खुदाई।

cutting² /'कटिङ्/ *adj* 1 कड़कड़ाती सर्दी

2 भावनाओं को चोट पहुँचाने वाला कथन या कार्य।

cyanide / 'साइअनाइड् / *noun* एक अत्यंत विषैला रासायनिक पदार्थ।

cycle / 'साइक्ल् / *noun* 1 नियमित रूप से, क्रमश: घटित होने वाली घटनाओं का चक्र, घटनाचक्र : the cycle of the seasons 2 एक पूरी शृंखला 3 बाइसिकिल का संक्षिप्त रूप, साइकिल ▶ **cycle** *verb* साइकिल की सवारी करना **cycling** *noun*.

cyclone / 'साइक्लोन् / *noun* बवंडर, चक्रवात।

cygnet / 'सिग्नट् / *noun* हंस-शावक।

cylinder / 'सिलिन्डर्/ *noun* 1 (*ज्यामिति*) बेलनाकार पिंड 2 बेलनाकार वस्तु : a gas cylinder 3 इंजिन का सिलिंडर जिसमें पिस्टन चलता है : a six-cylinder engine ▶ **cylindrical** / स 'लिन्ड्रिक्ल् /

adj बेलनाकार : cylindrical columns.

cymbal / 'सिम्ब्ल् / *noun* (प्राय: *pl*) झांझ, मंजीरा।

cynic / 'सिनिक् / *noun* (प्राय: *अपमा*) 1 मानवद्वेषी, दोषदर्शी 2 जिसे भविष्य की घटनाओं पर, उनके महत्त्व आदि पर हमेशा संदेह बना रहता है 3 व्यक्ति जिसे मानव सदाशयता और शुभ-भावना में विश्वास न हो ▶ **cynical** / 'सिनिक्ल् / *adj* **cynically** *adv* **cynicism** / 'सिनिसिज़म् / *noun* दोषदर्शिता।

cypress / 'साइप्रस् / *noun* एक सदाबहार ऊँचा पेड़, देवदार।

cyst / सिस्ट् / *noun* शरीर के अंदर बन जाने वाली एक खोखली गाँठ जिसमें द्रव पदार्थ जमा हो जाता है।

cystitis / सि 'स्टाइटिस् / *noun* मूत्राशय की सूजन, मूत्राशय दाह।

Dd

dab / डैब् / *verb* (-bb-) **1** dab (at) sth (with sth) बार-बार हलके दबाव से कुछ लगाना : *She stopped crying and dabbed her eyes (with a tissue).* **2** dab sth on/off (sth) पेंट, पाउडर आदि थप-थपाकर लगाना या हटाना : *dab paint on a picture* ▶ **dab** *noun* **1** पेंट, पाउडर की थोड़ी-सी मात्रा जो कहीं पर थप-थपा दी जाए **2** हलकी-सी थपकी।

dabble / डैब्ल् / *verb* **1** dabble sth (in sth) (पानी में हाथ या पैर से) थप-थप करना, छींटे उछालना **2** dabble (in/at/ with) किसी चीज़ में हलकी-फुलकी (न कि गंभीर) रुचि रखना : *He just dabbles in music/politics.*

dad / डैड् / *noun* (अनौप) पिता (विशेषत: संबोधन रूप में प्रयुक्त)।

daddy / डैडि / *noun* (बच्चों द्वारा प्रयुक्त शब्द) पिता।

daffodil / डैफ़डिल् / *noun* लंबी-सी डंडी वाला एक पीले रंग का फूल।

daft / डाफ़्ट्; US डैफ़्ट् / *adj* (-er, -est) (अनौप) मूर्ख, बुद्धू ▶ **daftness** *noun*.

dagger / डैगर् / *noun* छुरा, कटार (दो धार वाला बड़ा चाकू) ■ **at daggers drawn** (with sb) (किसी के प्रति) अत्यंत नफ़रत से पेश आना : *He and his partners are at daggers drawn.*

daily / डेलि / *adj, adv* प्रतिदिन, दैनिक ▶ **daily** *noun* **1** दैनिक समाचार-पत्र **2** (daily help भी) (अनौप) घर की सफ़ाई आदि काम के लिए प्रतिदिन आने वाला नौकर।

dainty / डेन्टि / *adj* (-ier, -iest) **1** छोटी व देखने में उत्तम : *dainty porcelain/ lace* **2** (व्यक्ति) साफ़-सुथरा एवं नाज़ुक मिज़ाज; सुरुचिपूर्ण, कठिनाई से प्रसन्न होने वाला (विशेषत: खाने से) : *a dainty eater* ▶ **daintily** *adv* **daintiness** *noun*.

dairy / डेअरि / *noun* (*pl* **dairies**) **1** डेरी, जहाँ दूध इकट्ठा किया जाता है और दुग्ध उत्पाद जैसे मक्खन, दही आदि बनाए जाते हैं **2** दूध-मक्खन की दुकान ▶ **dairy** *adj* **1** दूध से बना : *dairy products* **2** दुग्ध उत्पादन से संबंधित : *the dairy indus-try.*

dais / डेइस् / *noun* मंच, चबूतरा (भाषण आदि के लिए)।

daisy / डेज़ि / *noun* (*pl* **daisies**) सामान्यत: अपने आप उगने वाला छोटा-सा सफ़ेद फूल।

dale / डेल् / *noun* बड़ी घाटी।

dally / डैलि / *verb* (*pt, pp* **dallied**) धीरे-धीरे चलना; समय गँवाना ■ **dally with sb/sth** खिलवाड़ करना : *She was merely dallying with my affections.*

dam[1] / डैम् / *noun* बाँध (पानी रोकने के लिए नदी पर बनाया गया) ▶ **dam** *verb* (-mm-) dam sth (up) बाँध बनाना, (बाँध बनाकर बहाव) रोकना।

dam[2] / डैम् / *noun* (पशुओं में) बच्चे वाली मादा।

damage / डैमिज़् / *noun* **1** damage (to sth) हानि; क्षति : *brain damage* **2** damages [*pl*] हरजाना, किसी को नुक़सान होने पर क़ानूनन दिया जाने वाला धन ▶ **damage** *verb* हानि पहुँचाना, नुक़सान करना : *damage a car/fence* **damag-ing** *adj* damaging (to sth) हानिकर (प्रभाव वाला)।

dame / डेम् / *noun* **1** (US अप) (पुरुषों द्वारा प्रयुक्त शब्द) स्त्री **2** Dame 'सर' की पदवी के अनुरूप पदवी पाने वाली स्त्री।

damn[1] / डैम् / *verb* **1** (ईश्वर द्वारा) नरक भोगने का दंड दिया जाना, चिरदंड **2** कटु निंदा करना : *The play was damned by the reviewers.* ▶ **damning** *adj* अत्यंत प्रतिकूल, घृणित।

damn[2] / डैम् / (**dammit** / डैमिट् /; damn

it भी) *interj* (अनौप) झुँझलाहट व्यक्त करने वाला शब्द : *Damn (it)! I've lost my pen.*

damn³/डैम्/(damned भी) *adj* (अनौप) गुस्सा या खीझ व्यक्त करने के लिए प्रयुक्त शब्द : *Where's that damn book.*

damnable /'डैम्नबल्/ *adj* निंदनीय।

damnation / डैम्'नेश्न् / *noun* तबाही; तबाह होना।

damp¹/डैम्प्/ *adj* (-er, -est) नम (न पूरी तरह गीला, न सूखा); सीलनभरा : *damp, dark corridors* ∎ **a damp squib** (अनौप) अपेक्षित रूप से प्रभावी न साबित होने वाली घटना ▸ **damp** *noun* सीलन; नमी **damply** *adj* **dampness** *noun*.

damp²/डैम्प्/ *verb* 1 नम करना 2 **damp sth down** शोर, आग आदि कम करना।

dampen /'डैम्पन्/ *verb* 1 नम करना 2 **dampen sth down** (शोर, आग आदि की) शक्ति क्षीण करना : *dampen down sb's spirits/enthusiasm.*

damper /'डैम्पर्/ *noun* 1 (स्टोव आदि में) आग को कम करने वाला पुर्जा 2 शोर या झटके कम करने की युक्ति।

dance¹/डान्स; *US* डैन्स/ *noun* 1 नाच, नृत्य : *learn new dance steps* 2 नृत्य-संगीत : *a dance band* 3 नृत्य-कला : *a student of modern dance.*

dance²/डान्स; *US* डैन्स/ *verb* 1 नाचना, नृत्य करना 2 (खुशी में) नाचने जैसा चलना/गति : *leaves dancing in the wind* ▸ **dancer** *noun* नर्तक/नृत्यांगना **dancing** *noun*.

dandelion /'डैन्डिलाइअन्/ *noun* एक प्रकार का छोटा पीले रंग का फूल।

dandruff /'डैन्ड्रफ़्/ *noun* सिर में सूखी मृत त्वचा के छोटे-छोटे कण, बालों में रूसी।

danger /'डेन्जर्/ *noun* 1 **danger (of sth)** ख़तरा, संकट 2 **danger (to sb/sth)** ख़तरे/परेशानी या हानि पहुँचाने वाली वस्तु : *Smoking is recognized as a serious danger to health.*

dangerous /'डेन्जरस्/ *adj* **dangerous (for sb/sth)** ख़तरनाक, संकटपूर्ण ▸ **dangerously** *adv*.

dangle /'डैङ्गल्/ *verb* झूलना, लटकना; झूलने वाली वस्तु लटकाए चलना : *He dangled his watch in front of the baby.*

dare¹ / डेअर् / *verb* 1 साहस करना 2 (किसी व्यक्ति को किसी बात की) चुनौती देना : *Somebody dared me to jump off the bridge into the river.* ∎ **don't you dare (do sth)** किसी को धमकाना, कुछ करने से रोकना **how dare you, he, she, etc** रोष व्यक्त करते हुए चुनौती देना।

dare² / डेअर् / *noun* (जोखिमपूर्ण काम के लिए) चुनौती।

daredevil / 'डेअर्डेव्ल् / *noun, adj* दुस्साहसी, (मूर्खता के कारण) निडर व्यक्ति।

daring / 'डेअरिङ्/ *noun* साहस ▸ **daring** *adj* साहसी और निडर **daringly** *adv*.

dark¹ / डार्क् / *adj* (-er, -est) 1 अँधेरा, प्रकाश का बहुत कम या न होना 2 (रंग) काला; (बाल, आँखों, त्वचा का रंग) गहरा भूरा या काला : *a dark complexion* 3 छुपा हुआ, रहस्यमय : *a dark secret/mystery* 4 दुखी, आशाहीन : *dark predictions about the future* 5 बुरा : *dark powers/influence* ▸ **darkly** *adv* **darkness** *noun*.

dark² / डार्क् / *noun* **the dark** [*sing*] अँधेरा ∎ **in the dark (about sth)** किसी बात की जानकारी न होना।

darken /'डार्कन्/ *verb* अँधेरा (काला) करना या हो जाना।

darling / 'डार्लिङ् / *noun* परम प्रिय (व्यक्ति); घनिष्ठ मित्रता या प्यार का संबोधन ▸ **darling** *adj* परम प्रिय; (अनौप) आकर्षक, सुंदर।

darn / डार्न्/ *verb* (कपड़े में हुए छेदों को) रफू करना ▸ **darn** *noun* रफू किया स्थान

darning noun रफ़ू क्रिया; रफ़ू होने वाले कपड़े।

dart¹ / डार्ट् / noun 1 छोटा-सा तीर जो darts के खेल में हाथ से फेंका जाता है 2 अचानक और तेज़ गति : *She made a dart for the exit.* 3 **darts** डार्ट का खेल।

dart² / डार्ट् / verb 1 (तीर की तरह) झपटना 2 तेज़ी से और अचानक कुछ बाहर जाना या भेजना।

dash¹ / डैश् / verb 1 कसकर फेंकना या चोट करना; झपटना; (आशाएँ) भग्न करना 2 तेज़ी से चले जाना : *She dashed into the shop.* ▶ **dashing** adj आकर्षक और जोशीला **dashingly** adv.

dash² / डैश् / noun 1 **dash (for sth)** झपट, झपटना 2 (विशेषत: US) छोटी-सी दौड़ : *the 100-metre dash* 3 **a dash (of sth)** चुटकी भर कोई वस्तु (किसी अन्य वस्तु में मिलाने के लिए) 4 **dash (of sth)** पानी में कुछ टकराने से 'छपाक' की ध्वनि 5 लेखन या मुद्रण में — चिह्न 6 ज़ोरदार कार्य करने के लिए जोश, उत्साह।

dashboard / 'डैशबॉर्ड / noun डैशबोर्ड, ड्राइवर के ठीक सामने लगा बोर्ड जिसमें अनेक प्रकार के स्विच आदि लगे होते हैं।

data / 'डेटा; 'डाटा; US 'डैटा भी / noun 1 [pl] ज्ञात, आंकड़े और तथ्य (जिनसे कोई परिणाम या निष्कर्ष निकाला जाता है) : *very little data is available* 2 कंप्यूटर में संग्रहीत (या द्वारा तैयार) सूचना, तथ्य सामग्री : *data analysis.*

database / 'डेटबेस् / (**data bank** भी) noun कंप्यूटर में संग्रहीत विशाल तथ्य सामग्री।

date¹ / डेट् / noun 1 तिथि, दिनांक 2 विशिष्ट ऐतिहासिक काल जिसका किसी वस्तु से संबंध है : *This vase is of an earlier date than that one.* 3 (अनौप) मित्र के साथ बाहर घूमने जाने का कार्यक्रम; प्रेमी/प्रेमिका से मिलने का कार्यक्रम; (विशेषत: US) प्रेमी/प्रेमिका जिससे मिलना है : *My date is meeting me at seven.* ■ (**be/**

go) **out of date** अप्रचलित **to date** अब तक **up to date** नवीन सूचनाएँ रखने या प्रयुक्त करने वाला; आधुनिक, फ़ैशनेबल।

date² / डेट् / verb 1 तिथि या दिनांक लिखना : *His last letter was dated 24 May.* 2 उम्र अथवा काल निर्धारित करना : *modern methods of dating rocks/fossils* 3 **date back to.../ from...** उस तिथि से चला आ रहा : *Our partnership dates back to 1960.* 4 (अनौप, विशेषत: US) मित्र के साथ मिलने का कार्यक्रम तय करना/घूमना ▶ **dated** adj अप्रचलित।

date³ / डेट् / noun खजूर; छुहारा।

daub / डॉब् / verb 1 **daub A on (B); daub B (with A)** लीपना, पोतना; गंदे निशान लगाना : *trousers daubed with mud* 2 बिना कौशल के चित्र रँगना ▶ **daub** noun 1 लीपने/पोतने में प्रयुक्त सामग्री (जैसे मिट्टी) 2 भद्दा रंगा हुआ चित्र।

daughter / 'डॉटर् / noun पुत्री, लड़की ▶ **daughter-in-law** noun (pl **daughters-in-law**) पुत्रवधू, बहू।

daunt / डॉन्ट् / verb निरुत्साहित करना; डराना ▶ **daunting** adj : *a daunting task* **dauntingly** adv **dauntless** adj निर्भीक, निडर।

dawdle / 'डॉड्ल् / verb 1 सुस्ती से काम करना; समय गँवाना : *We dawdled over our meal for two hours.* 2 सुस्ती से धीरे-धीरे चलना।

dawn¹ / डॉन् / noun 1 ऊषा-काल, प्रात: काल : *He works from dawn till dusk.* 2 **dawn (of sth)** प्रारंभ, या पहले संकेत : *the dawn of a new age.*

dawn² / डॉन् / verb 1 दिन निकलना 2 **dawn (on/upon sb)** (विचार) सूझना, अचानक कुछ बात स्पष्ट हो जाना : *The truth began to dawn on him.*

day / डे / noun 1 दिन, सूर्योदय से सूर्यास्त तक का समय; 24 घंटे का समय 2 (प्राय: pl) समय की कोई विशेष अवधि : *in his* *younger days* ■ **a nine days' wonder** क्षणिक आकर्षण पैदा करने वाली वस्तु/व्यक्ति **carry/win the day** विरोधियों पर सफलता प्राप्त करना **one day** किसी दिन (भविष्य में) **pass the time of day (with sb)** बातचीत करना **some day** किसी दिन (भविष्य में) **to this day** अब भी ▸ **daybreak** *noun* सूर्योदय **day-dream** *noun, verb* दिवास्वप्न (देखना); मन में उज्ज्वल भविष्य की कल्पना करते हुए समय गँवाना **daylong** *adj* सारे दिन का।

daylight / 'डेलाइट् / *noun* दिन के समय का प्रकाश।

daze / डेज़् / *verb* चकाचौंध कर देना या चकाचौंध में पड़ जाना; सुन्न या जड़ हो जाना : *He was dazed for a moment by the blow to his head.* ▸ **daze** *noun* ■ **in a daze** चकित-भ्रमित; जड़ ▸ **dazed** *adj* : *a dazed expression.*

dazzle / 'डैज़ल् / *verb* 1 अत्यधिक प्रकाश या तड़क-भड़क के कारण व्यक्ति को स्पष्ट देखने या स्वाभाविक रूप से कार्य करने में असमर्थ कर देना 2 सुंदरता, ज्ञान या निपुणता से किसी को अत्यंत प्रभावित कर देना : *She was dazzled by her first sight of the ancient city.* ▸ **dazzle** *noun* 1 चमकदार चकाचौंध प्रकाश 2 प्रभावोत्पादक दृश्य।

dead / डेड् / *adj* 1 मृत; निर्जीव; जिसका अब अस्तित्व न हो 2 (अनौप) बुरी तरह थका हुआ; बीमार 3 (अनौप) निश्चेष्ट; निष्क्रिय 4 प्रयोग के कारण समाप्त; जो अब प्रयोग में नहीं है : *a dead language* 5 पूर्ण; बिलकुल : *dead calm/silence* 6 (अनौप) रुचिहीन 7 (ध्वनि) नीरस : *a dead voice* 8 (रंग) भद्दा ■ **the dead hand of sth** कोई नियंत्रित करने वाली चीज़ या प्रभाव ▸ **dead** *adv* 1 पूर्णतया : *dead tired/drunk* 2 (अनौप) बहुत : *The instructions are dead easy to follow.* **dead** *noun* **the dead** [*pl*] मृत व्यक्ति : *We carried the dead and*

(the) wounded off the battlefield. ■ **in the/at dead of night** रात के सन्नाटे में ▸ **dead-beat** *noun* (अनौप) 1 बेरोज़गार और निराश व्यक्ति 2 (US) बोर करने वाला **dead heat** *noun* दौड़ में ऐसा परिणाम जब दो प्रतियोगी एक साथ विजयस्तंभ पर पहुँच गए हों **dead letter** *noun* 1 ऐसा नियम जिसका परिपालन न हो रहा हो 2 ऐसा पत्र जो संबंधित व्यक्ति न मिलने से डाकघर में जमा कर लिया गया हो **dead stock** *noun* बेकार माल **dead wood** *noun* (अलं) बेकार, अनावश्यक व्यक्ति।

deaden / 'डेडन् / *verb* बल या भावना कम या समाप्त कर देना : *drugs to deaden the pain.*

deadline / 'डेडलाइन् / *noun* अंतिम तिथि जिसके पहले ही कार्य समाप्त कर लेना है।

deadlock / 'डेडलॉक् / *noun* समझौते पर पहुँचने में असफलता, गतिरोध : *The negotiations have reached deadlock.*

deadly / 'डेडलि / *adj* (-ier, -iest) 1 घातक, प्राणघाती : *deadly poison* 2 अत्यंत; पूर्ण : *deadly seriousness* 3 अत्यंत प्रभावी 4 मौत के जैसा : *deadly paleness/coldness* 5 (अनौप) अत्यंत बोरिंग; घृणापूर्ण।

deaf / डेफ़् / *adj* (-er, -est) 1 बहरा, बधिर 2 **deaf to sth** सुनने को तैयार न होने वाला, ध्यान न देने वाला : *be deaf to all advice/requests* ■ **fall on deaf ears** दूसरों द्वारा उपेक्षित कर दिया जाना **turn a deaf ear (to sb/sth)** ध्यान न देना ▸ **deaf** *noun* **the deaf** बहरे व्यक्ति **deafness** *noun.*

deafen / 'डेफ़न् / *verb* सुनना कठिन या असंभव कर देना; बहरा कर देना ▸ **deafening** *adj* बहुत ऊँची आवाज़।

deal¹ / डील् / *verb* (pt, pp **dealt** / डेल्ट् /) **deal sth (out); deal sth (to sb)** ताश के खेल में पत्ते बाँटना : *Deal out ten cards each.* ■ **deal in sth** व्यापार करना, लेन-देन करना : *We deal in* *computer software.* **deal with sb** (किसी से) निपट लेना; (विशेष स्थिति में) बात करना **deal with sb/sth** संबंध रखना **deal with sth** किसी कार्य को निपटाना, समस्या को सुलझाना : *You dealt with an awkward situation very tactfully.*

deal² / डील / *noun* 1 व्यापारिक समझौता : *to make/conclude/finalize a deal* 2 ताश के खेल में पत्तों की बँटाई ■ a **fair/square deal** उचित व्यवहार **a good/ great deal (of sth)** अत्यधिक **a raw/ rough deal** (*अनौप*) अनुचित व्यवहार या शर्तें।

dealer / डीलर् / *noun* 1 **dealer (in sth)** व्यापारी 2 ताश के पत्ते बाँटने वाला।

dealing / डीलिङ् / *noun* 1 **dealings** [*pl*] व्यापारिक संबंध 2 व्यवहार (विशेषत: व्यापार में)।

dean / डीन् / *noun* 1 चर्च में कैथेड्रल का अध्यक्ष 2 विश्वविद्यालय में विभाग या संकाय का अध्यक्ष : *dean of the faculty of law.*

dear / डिअर् / *adj* (-er, -est) 1 **dear (to sb)** प्रिय, प्यारा 2 पत्राचार में शिष्ट संबोधन : *Dear Sir/Madam* 3 (प्राय: **dearest**) दिल से, सच्ची भावनाओं से 4 महँगा ▶ **dear** *adv* महँगे दामों पर **dear** *noun* प्रिय व्यक्ति **dearly** *adv* 1 अत्यधिक 2 हानि से; महँगा **dearness allowance** *noun* महँगाई भत्ता।

dearth / डर्थ् / *noun* [*sing*] **dearth (of sth)** कमी, दुर्लभता (विशेषत: भोज्य पदार्थों की)।

death / डेथ् / *noun* 1 मौत : *a sudden death* 2 मृत्यु, शरीरांत, निधन 3 **death of sth** समाप्ति या विनाश : *the death of one's plans/hopes* 4 (**Death** भी) काल जो सब कुछ ग्रस लेता है ■ **put sb to death** मार डालना ▶ **deathbed** *noun* मृत्युशय्या **deathless** *adj* (*औप*) कभी न मरने वाला; कभी न भुलाया जा सकने वाला **death rate** *noun* मृत्यु दर, प्रतिवर्ष 1,000

व्यक्तियों में मरने वालों की औसत संख्या **death sentence** *noun* मृत्यु दंड **death-toll** *noun* (दुर्घटना आदि में) मरने वालों की संख्या।

deathly / डेथ्लि / *adj* (-lier, -liest) मृत्यु समान : *deathly silence/ stillness.*

debacle / डे'बाक्ल् / *noun* अचानक और पूर्ण असफलता, हार; घोर असफलता : *a political debacle.*

debar / डि'बार् / *verb* (-rr-) **debar sb (from sth/doing sth)** 1 कुछ करने से क़ानूनन मना किया जाना : *Convicted criminals are debarred from voting in elections.* 2 बाहर निकाल देना : *People in jeans were debarred (from the club).*

debase / डि'बेस् / *verb* 1 घटिया कर देना, अपना (या दूसरों का) स्तर गिरा लेना 2 सिक्कों में खोट मिलाकर मूल्य गिरा देना : *debase the currency* ▶ **debasement** *noun.*

debate / डि'बेट् / *noun* 1 वाद-विवाद (सार्वजनिक सभा, संसद आदि में) : *a debate on abortion/capital punishment* 2 सामान्य चर्चा/परिचर्चा ▶ **debate** *verb* 1 **debate (about sth)** वाद-विवाद करना, वाद-विवाद में भाग लेना : *They debated closing the factory.* 2 निर्णय लेने से पहले सोच-विचार करना **debatable** *adj* विवाद योग्य (विषय); मतभेद का विषय **debater** *noun* वाद-विवाद करने वाला।

debauch / डि'बॉच् / *verb* चरित्र बिगाड़ना, कुमार्ग पर ले जाना (विशेषत: यौन व्यभिचार से) : *He debauched many innocent girls.* ▶ **debauch** *noun* व्यभिचार कर्म **debauched** *adj* **debauchee** *noun* कुमार्गोन्मुख व्यक्ति **debauchery** *noun* विलासिता, व्यभिचार : *a life of debauchery.*

debenture / डि'बेन्चर् / *noun* ऋण-पत्र : *debenture shares.*

debilitate / डि'बिलिटेट् / verb व्यक्ति को अशक्त/क्षीण बना देना : a debilitating illness/climate.

debility / डि'बिलटि / noun (pl debilities) (बीमारी से उत्पन्न) क्षीणता।

debit / 'डेबिट् / noun (वाणिज्य) 1 हिसाब की किताब में ख़र्च का कॉलम : on the debit side of an account 2 खाते में से निकाली गई रक़म ▶ debit verb debit sth (against/to sb/sth) रक़म ख़र्चे में डालना : Debit Rs 200 against my account.

debris / 'डेब्रि; US डं'ब्री / noun मलबा, बिखरे हुए टूटे-फूटे टुकड़े : After the crash, debris from the plane was spread over a large area.

debt / डेट् / noun 1 क़र्ज़, ऋण, उधार, विशेषत: जो चुकता न हो सकता हो : third world debt 2 सहायता, दया आदि के लिए कृतज्ञता : owe sb a debt of gratitude ■ be in sb's debt (औप) आभारी/कृतज्ञ रहना ▶ debtor noun क़र्ज़दार, ऋणी।

debunk / डी'बङ्क् / verb यह सिद्ध करना कि किसी व्यक्ति, विचार या संस्था का सम्मान झूठा और अनपेक्षित है : debunking the myths that have come to be regarded as historical facts.

debut (début भी) / 'डे'ब्यू; US डे'ब्यू / noun किसी व्यक्ति का रंगमंच पर जनता के सामने प्रथम कार्यक्रम/प्रदर्शन।

decade / 'डेकेड; डि'केड् / noun दशक, दस वर्ष का समय।

decadence / 'डैकडन्स् / noun (अपमा) अवनति, ह्रास : the decadence of modern society/of late Victorian art ▶ decadent / 'डैकडन्ट् / adj (व्यक्ति, राष्ट्र, साहित्य, कला) पतनशील, ह्रासोन्मुख।

decant / डि'कैन्ट् / verb (शराब आदि द्रव) एक बोतल से दूसरी में इस सावधानी से डालना कि अशुद्धियाँ तली में रह जाएँ, छानना ▶ decanter noun साफ़ बोतल जिसमें शराब सावधानी से उँड़ेलते हैं।

decapitate / डि'कैपिटेट् / verb (व्यक्ति या जानवर का) सिर धड़ से अलग कर देना ▶ decapitation / डिकैपि'टेश्न् / noun.

decay / डि'के / verb 1 ख़राब होना, सड़ना, ख़राब करना : decaying teeth/vegetables 2 शक्ति, प्रभाव या स्वास्थ्य खोना : a decaying culture/society ▶ decay noun ख़राबी की प्रक्रिया, क्षय।

deceased / डि'सीस्ट् / adj (क़ानून या औप) मृत; दिवंगत (व्यक्ति) ▶ the deceased noun (pl अपरिवर्तित) (क़ानून या औप) मृत व्यक्ति।

deceit / डि'सीट् / noun धोखा, बेईमानी का कार्य या कथन ▶ deceitful adj deceitfulness noun.

deceive / डि'सीव् / verb 1 deceive sb/ oneself (into doing sth) धोखा देना, छलना 2 deceive sb (with sb) दांपत्य से बाहर यौन संबंध रखना।

December / डि'सेम्बर् / noun (संक्षि Dec) दिसंबर (महीना)।

decency / 'डीसन्सि / noun 1 उचित होना, शिष्टाचार 2 the decencies [pl] समाज में भद्र व्यवहार के सिद्धांत।

decent / 'डीसन्ट् / adj 1 उचित और उपयुक्त 2 शिष्ट; दूसरों को लज्जित न करने वाला : That dress isn't decent. 3 संतोषजनक, काफ़ी अच्छा : That was quite a decent lunch. ▶ decently adv शिष्टता पूर्वक।

deception / डि'सेप्श्न् / noun 1 धोखा देने की क्रिया 2 धोखेबाज़ी की चाल।

deceptive / डि'सेप्टिव् / adj भ्रामक, धोखा देने वाला ▶ deceptively adv.

decibel / 'डेसिबेल् / noun (भौतिकी) ध्वनि तीव्रता की मापन इकाई, डेसिबल।

decide / डि'साइड् / verb 1 decide (between sth/sb); decide (on/ against sth/sb) सोच-विचारकर निष्कर्ष पर पहुँचना; निश्चय करना : It's difficult to decide between the two. 2 विवाद के विषय पर निर्णय देना : The judge will *decide (the case) tomorrow.* 3 (घट-नाएँ, कार्य आदि) किसी चीज पर महत्त्वपूर्ण एवं निश्चित प्रभाव रखना : *A chance meeting decided my career.* ▷ **decided** *adj* 1 स्पष्ट, निश्चित : *a person of decided views* 2 **decided (about sth)** दृढ़निश्चयी **decidedly** *adv* निस्संदेह, निश्चित ही।

deciduous / डि'सिजुअस्; डि'सिड्युअस् भी / *adj* (पेड़) जिसमें वार्षिक रूप से पतझड़ आता है।

decimal / 'डेसिम्ल् / *adj* दशमलव से संबद्ध : *the decimal system* (मुद्रा, भार, दूरी आदि की दशमलव पद्धति, जिसमें निकटतम इकाई दस गुणा या दसवाँ अंश होती है) ▷ **decimal point** *noun* दशम-लव बिंदु (जैसे 15.62 में 15 के बाद का बिंदु)।

decimate / 'डेसिमेट्/ *verb* 1 (जनसंख्या आदि का) एक बहुत बड़ा हिस्सा मौत का ग्रास बना दिया जाना या नष्ट हो जाना : *Disease has decimated the population.* 2 (अनौप) मात्रा या संख्या में कमी करना/होना : *Student numbers have been decimated by cuts in grants.* ▷ **decimation** *noun* विनष्टीकरण।

decipher / डि'साइफ़र् / *verb* लिखे हुए को पढ़ना तथा अर्थ निकालना; गुप्त संकेत में लिखे हुए को पढ़ना : *I can't decipher the inscription on the pillar.*

decision / डि'सिश्न् / *noun* 1 **decision (on/against sth)**; **decision (to do sth)** निर्णय; निश्चय : *arrive at/come to/take a decision* 2 निर्णय करने और दृढ़ता से उसे पूरा करने की योग्यता/शक्ति।

decisive / डि'साइसिव् / *adj* 1 निर्णा-यक : *a decisive victory/moment* 2 निर्णयात्मक : *a decisive person/manner/answers* ▷ **decisively** *adv* **decisiveness** *noun.*

deck¹ / डेक् / *noun* 1 जहाज़ का फ़र्श;

(जहाज़ में) कोई-सी भी मंज़िल (मुख्यत: सबसे ऊपर वाला फ़र्श); उसी के समान कोई अन्य स्थान : *the top deck of a double-decker bus* 2 (*US*) ताश के पत्ते 3 म्यूज़िक सिस्टम आदि उपकरणों में कैसेट, टेप आदि चलाने की युक्ति ■ **clear the decks** (अनचाही वस्तुएँ हटाकर) किसी कार्य के लिए तैयार होना।

deck² / डेक् / *verb* **deck sb/sth (out) (in/with sth)** सजाना, सजावट करना : *streets decked with flags.*

declaim / डि'क्लेम् / *verb* (कभी-कभी अपमा) बातचीत में भाषण की तरह ज़ोर-ज़ोर से बोलना : *declaim poetry.*

declamation / डेक्ल'मेश्न् / *noun* 1 भाषण (देने की कला); वक्तृता 2 भाषण (भावपूर्ण) ▷ **declamatory** *adj.*

declaration / डेक्ल'रेश्न् / *noun* 1 घोषणा : *the Declaration of Human Rights* 2 घोषणा-पत्र : *a declaration of income.*

declare / डि'क्लेअर् / *verb* 1 घोषित करना; निस्संदेह दृढ़ता से कहना 2 **declare for/against sth/sb** (औप) अपना पक्ष स्पष्ट करना : *The commission declared against the proposed scheme.* 3 कस्टम्स या टैक्स अधिकारियों के सामने आयात-शुल्क या टैक्स लगने वाली वस्तुएँ/आय का विवरण देना : *You must declare all you have earned in the last year.* ▷ **declared** *adj* घोषित।

decline¹ / डि'क्लाइन्/ *verb* 1 'न' कहना, अस्वीकार करना : *He declined to comment on the proposal.* 2 छोटा, कम-ज़ोर और मात्रा में कम होते जाना, क्षीण हो जाना : *Her influence declined after she lost the elections.*

decline² / डि'क्लाइन् / *noun* **decline (in sth)** क्रमिक क्षय, अवनति : *a decline in population/prices/popularity.*

decode / डी'कोड् / *verb* 1 संकेत लिपि (कूट लिपि) का अर्थ समझना; भावाथ

करना : *decode the symbolism of her paintings* 2 इलेक्ट्रॉनिक संकेतों को ग्रहण करना और अर्थ समझना।

decompose / ˌडीकम्ˈपोज़् / *verb* 1 सड़ना, गलना : *a decomposing corpse* 2 टुकड़े-टुकड़े हो जाना ▸ **decomposition** / ˌडीकॉम्प्ˈज़िश्न् / *noun.*

deconstruct / ˌडीकन्ˈस्ट्रक्ट् / *verb* (तक) साहित्य की भाषा का विश्लेषणात्मक अध्ययन करना, विशेषत: यह तर्क करने के लिए कि साहित्य के विभिन्न अंशों का आपस में कोई तालमेल नहीं है : *deconstruct Shakespeare* ▸ **deconstruction** *noun* **deconstructionism** *noun* **deconstructionist** *noun, adj* : *a deconstructionist critic/approach to literature.*

decor / ˈडेकॉर्; *US* डेˈकॉर् / *noun* किसी कमरे या मंच का फ़र्नीचर एवं साज-सज्जा : *a stylish modern decor.*

decorate / ˈडेकरेट् / *verb* 1 **decorate sth (with sth)** आभूषण पहनना/पहनाना; सजाना : *The building was decorated with flags.* 2 (भवन को) रंग से पोतना; पेंट करना 3 **decorate sb (for sth)** (सम्मानार्थ) पदक देना; पुरस्कार से विभूषित करना : *Several soldiers were decorated.* ▸ **decorator** *noun* सजाने वाला, रंगने वाला।

decoration / ˌडेकˈरेश्न् / *noun* 1 सजावट 2 सजावट की वस्तु 3 पदक, पुरस्कार आदि।

decorative / ˈडेकरटिव् / *adj* सजावटी।

decorum / डिˈकॉरम् / *noun* शिष्टाचार, मर्यादापूर्ण व्यवहार।

decoy / ˈडीकॉइ / *noun* 1 कोई भी पशु या पक्षी जिसका प्रयोग किसी अन्य पशु या पक्षी को फँसाने हेतु किया जाता है 2 कोई व्यक्ति या वस्तु जिसके द्वारा अन्य को गुमराह किया जाता है ▸ **decoy** / डिˈकॉइ / *verb* फँसाने वाली वस्तु या व्यक्ति प्रयुक्त करके गुमराह करना : *The thieves had decoyed*

customers by means of a false fire alarm.

decrease / डिˈक्रीस् / *verb* घटना या घटाना ▸ **decrease** / ˈडीक्रीस् / *noun* **decrease (in sth)** 1 कमी/घटने की प्रक्रिया : *decrease in the birthrate* 2 घटी हुई मात्रा, कमी : *a decrease of 3% in the rate of inflation.*

decree / डिˈक्री / *noun* 1 (वादी को संपत्ति आदि पर) अधिकार दिलाने वाला आदेश 2 क़ानून का दर्जा रखने वाला शासक या अधिकारी का आदेश : *issue a decree* ▸ **decree** *verb* (*pt, pp* **decreed**) (न्यायालय द्वारा) अधिकार संपन्न आदेश दिया जाना : *The governor decreed a day of mourning.*

decrepit / डिˈक्रेपिट् / *adj* बुढ़ापे या अत्यधिक व्यवहार से जर्जर ▸ **decrepitude** / डिˈक्रेपिट्यूड् / *noun* (औप) जरा, जर्जर अवस्था : *The house had a forlorn air of decrepitude.*

dedicate / ˈडेडिकेट् / *verb* 1 **dedicate oneself/sth to sth/doing sth** (अपना जीवन, सब कुछ किसी उद्देश्य के लिए) अर्पित करना : *She dedicated her life to helping the poor.* 2 **dedicate sth to sb** (पुस्तक के प्रारंभ में लेखक द्वारा) समर्पण की अभिव्यक्ति 3 **dedicate (to sb/sth)** विशेष धार्मिक संस्कार में अपने को अर्पित करना ▸ **dedicated** *adj* समर्पित (भाव से)।

dedication / ˌडेडिˈकेश्न् / *noun* 1 **dedication (to sth)** किसी उद्देश्य के लिए समर्पण 2 अर्पण समारोह।

deduce / डिˈड्यूस्; *US* डिˈडूस् / *verb* **deduce sth (from sth)** तार्किक विश्लेषण द्वारा किसी निष्कर्ष, तथ्य या सिद्धांत पर पहुँचना : *Forensic scientists can deduce a great deal from the victim's remains.* ▸ **deducible** *adj.*

deduct / डिˈडक्ट् / *verb* **deduct sth (from sth)** (किसी अंश या राशि को)

काटना, निकालकर अलग रखना : *Tax is deducted from your salary.* ▶ **deductible** / डि'डक्टबल् / *adj.*

deduction / डि'डक्शन् / *noun* **deduction (from sth)** 1 तार्किक निगमन; अनुमान 2 तर्क से प्राप्त निष्कर्ष : *a reasonable deduction from the known facts* 3 कमी; कटौती : *deductions from pay for insurance and pension* ▶ **deductive** *adj.*

deed / डीड् / *noun* 1 (विशेषत: औप) कार्य, जानबूझकर किया हुआ काम : *deeds of heroism* 2 (प्राय: *pl*) (क़ानून) स्वामित्व अथवा अधिकार संबंधी लिखित और हस्ताक्षरयुक्त अनुबंध।

deem / डीम् / *verb* (औप) समझना; मानना : *He was deemed (to be) the winner.*

deep[1] / डीप् / *adj* (-er, -est) 1 गहरा : *a deep well/river* 2 (सतह या किनारे से) नीचे या अंदर की तरफ़ : *a deep wound/ shelf* 3 पीछे या धँसा हुआ; नीचे या अंदर की ओर : *water six feet deep* 4 (श्वास) काफ़ी हवा अंदर लेते हुए 5 (ध्वनि) धीमी, भारी 6 (रंग) गहरा, गाढ़ा : *a deep red* 7 (निद्रा) गहन 8 **deep in sth** (विचारों की) गंभीरता, एकाग्रता : *deep in thought/ study* ▶ **-deep** *suff* (प्रत्यय) (संयुक्त विशेषण बनाने में प्रयुक्त) गहराई तक : *knee-deep/ankle-deep* **deepen** / 'डीपन् / *verb* गहरा होना या गहरा बनाना : *The mystery deepens.* ○ *The lake deepened after the dam was built.* **deeply** *adv* अत्यधिक; गहराई तक : *dig deeply* **deepness** *noun.*

deep[2] / डीप् / *adv* (-er, -est) नीचे गहराई तक या अंदर : *We had to dig deep to find water.* ▶ **deep-rooted** *adj* (विचार, विश्वास, भाव) गहराई से जमा हुआ।

deep[3] / डीप् / *noun* **the deep** (औप या अप्र) समुद्र।

deer / डिअर् / *noun (pl* अपरिवर्तित) हरिण, हिरन।

deface / डि'फ़ेस् / *verb* लिखकर या चिह्न आदि लगाकर वस्तु का रूप-रंग गंदा करना : *The wall had been defaced with slogans.* ▶ **defacement** *noun.*

defame / डि'फ़ेम् / *verb* बदनाम करना ▶ **defamation** *noun* बदनामी ।

default[1] / डि'फ़ॉल्ट् / *noun* (क़ानून) कर्तव्य अपूर्णता या समय पर अनुपस्थिति या क़र्ज़ की अदायगी न हो पाने की स्थिति : *win a case by default.*

default[2] / डि'फ़ॉल्ट् / *verb* 1 कर्तव्य पालन न करना, समय पर (कचहरी में) उपस्थित न होना : *A party to the contract defaulted.* 2 **default (on sth)** क़र्ज़ अदा न करना : *default on a loan* ▶ **defaulter** *noun* व्यक्ति (विशेषत: सैनिक) जिसने अपना कर्तव्य पूरा नहीं किया है।

default[3] / डि'फ़ॉल्ट् / *noun* कंप्यूटर में पहले से पड़ा हुआ विकल्प जो तब तक उसी प्रकार कार्य करता रहेगा जब तक कोई उसे न बदले।

defeat / डि'फ़ीट् / *verb* 1 हरा देना, जीतना 2 (अनौप) समझे जाने में असमर्थ होना : *I've tried to solve the problem, but it defeats me.* 3 (आशाएँ, उद्देश्य आदि) व्यर्थ करना या होना : *By not working hard enough you defeat your own purpose.* 4 प्रयास या प्रस्ताव सफल न होने देना ▶ **defeat** *noun* हार, असफलता **defeatism** *noun* निराशावादी दृष्टिकोण (असफलता के बारे में सोचना) **defeatist** *noun, adj.*

defecate / 'डेफ़केट्; 'डीफ़केट् / *verb* (औप) मल त्याग करना।

defect[1] / डि'फ़ेक्ट्; 'डीफ़ेक्ट् / *noun* दोष, ख़राबी : *defects in the education system* ▶ **defective** / डि'फ़ेक्टिव् / *adj* ख़राब, अपूर्ण या बिगड़ा हुआ : *a defective machine/method* **defectively** *adv.*

defect² / डिˈफ़ेक्ट् / *verb* **defect (from sth) (to sth)** दल या स्वदेश छोड़कर दूसरे दल या परदेश में चले जाना; दलबदल/देश-बदल करना ▸ **defection** *noun* **defection (from sth)** : *Some dissidents are considering defection.* **defector** *noun* दलबदलू।

defence (*US* **defense**) / डिˈफ़ेन्स् / *noun* **1 defence (against sth)** (आक्रमण से) रक्षा; रक्षा करने वाली वस्तु; देश की रक्षा के लिए सैनिक उपाय/कार्र-वाई : *The country's defences are weak.* **2** (*क़ानून*) **defence (against sth)** प्रतिवादी की ओर से प्रस्तुत तर्क, प्रमाण आदि; **the defence** प्रतिवादी का वकील, बचाव पक्ष का वकील **3** गोल की रक्षा; (प्राय: **the defence**) गोल की रक्षा करने वाले खिलाड़ी ▸ **defenceless** *adj* बिना रक्षा का, अरक्षित **defencelessness** *noun*.

defend / डिˈफ़ेन्ड् / *verb* **1 defend sb/sth (from/against sb/sth)** (आक्रमण से) रक्षा करना : *defend sb from attack/injury* **2** किसी व्यक्ति/वस्तु के समर्थन में लिखना, बोलना, कार्य करना : *defend a lawsuit* **3** (खेल में) गोल बचाना; (पूर्व विजेता द्वारा) अपनी स्थिति बचाने के लिए स्पर्धा में भाग लेना : *the defending champion* ▸ **defender** *noun*.

defendant / डिˈफ़ेन्डन्ट् / *noun* प्रतिवादी, जिसके ख़िलाफ़ मुकदमा चलाया गया है।

defensible / डिˈफ़ेन्सब्ल् / *adj* रक्षणीय, समर्थनीय।

defensive / डिˈफ़ेन्सिव् / *adj* **1** रक्षात्मक, प्रतिरक्षात्मक : *defensive warfare/measures* **2 defensive (about sb/sth)** आलोचना या आक्रमण से बचाव में तत्पर ▸ **defensive** *noun* ■ **on the defensive** आक्रमण की आशंका से रक्षा में संलग्न **defensiveness** *noun*.

defer¹ / डिˈफ़र् / *verb* (**-rr-**) **defer sth (to sth)** स्थगित करना : *defer one's departure to a later date* ○ *defer*

making a decision ▸ **deferment** **deferral** / डिˈफ़रल् / *noun* आस्थगन।

defer² / डिˈफ़र् / *verb* (**-rr-**) **defer to sb/sth** झुकना, दूसरे की राय को आदर के लिए मान लेना : *I defer to your greater experience in such things.*

deference / 'डेफ़रन्स् / *noun* सम्मान, सम्मानार्थ सहमति : *show deference to a judge* ▸ **deferential** / डेफ़ˈरेन्शल् / *adj* श्रद्धापूर्वक।

defiance / डिˈफ़ाइअन्स् / *noun* (शासक या अधिकारी के आदेश की) अवज्ञा, आदेश मानने से खुला इनकार; विरोध।

defiant / डिˈफ़ाइअन्ट् / *adj* अवज्ञा करते हुए ▸ **defiantly** *adv*.

deficiency / डिˈफ़िशन्सि / *noun* **deficiency (in/of sth)** **1** कमी **2** आवश्यक गुण की अपर्याप्त मात्रा।

deficient / डिˈफ़िशन्ट् / *adj* **1 deficient (in sth)** आवश्यक वस्तु का अभाव : *be deficient in skill/experience* **2** (औप) अपर्याप्त : *deficient funds.*

deficit / 'डेफ़िसिट् / *noun* धनराशि की कमी, घाटा; आय से व्यय का अधिक होना : *a budget deficit.*

defile / डिˈफ़ाइल् / *verb* (औप या साहि) **1** गंदा या दूषित करना : *rivers defiled by pollution* **2** जानबूझकर धार्मिक-स्थल को क्षति पहुँचाना : *The altar had been defiled by vandals.* ▸ **defilement** *noun*.

define / डिˈफ़ाइन् / *verb* **1 define sth (as sth)** परिभाषा देना **2** व्याख्या देना, स्पष्टतया समझाना : *The powers of a judge are defined by law.* **3** आकार, रूपरेखा या सीमाएँ निर्धारित करना : *The mountain was sharply defined against the eastern sky.* ▸ **definable** *adj*.

definite / 'डेफ़िनट् / *adj* **1** स्पष्ट, संदेह-रहित **2 definite (about sth/that...)** निश्चित, पक्का ▸ **definitely** *adv*.

definition / ˌडेफ़िˈनिश्न् / noun 1 परि-
भाषा; परिभाषा देने की प्रक्रिया 2 स्पष्टता
(आकार, रूप या सीमा की) 3 व्याख्या।

definitive / डिˈफ़िनिटिव् / adj 1 अंतिम
और निश्चित : a definitive answer/
solution 2 सर्वोत्कृष्ट एवं अपरिवर्तनीय :
the definitive biography of Nehru.

deflate / डिˈफ़्लेट् / verb 1 (टायर आदि
में से) हवा निकाल देना; हवा निकला हुआ
2 किसी को उसकी आशा के विपरीत कम
महत्त्वपूर्ण या कम आत्मविश्वासी महसूस
करा देना : Nothing could deflate his
ego. 3 / ˌडीˈफ़्लेट् / देश में उपलब्ध धन की
मात्रा में कमी करना जिससे क़ीमतें कम हो
जाएँ : The government were forced
to deflate (the economy). ▸ **defla-
tion** noun **deflationary** adj.

deflect / डिˈफ़्लेक्ट् / verb 1 रास्ता बद-
लना/बदल देना : The bullet deflected
from the wall. 2 **deflect sb (from
sth)** मार्ग से किसी को हटाना; विचलित
करना ▸ **deflection** noun विचलन।

deforestation / ˌडीˈफ़ॉरिˈस्टेश्न् / noun
वनोन्मूलन (एक बड़े क्षेत्र से सभी पेड़ों को
काट डालना)।

deform / डिˈफ़ॉर्म् / verb रूप या आकृति
ख़राब करना या बिगाड़ना : A crippling
disease had deformed his hands.
▸ **deformation** noun **deformed** adj
(व्यक्ति या शरीर का अंग) कुरूप **deform-
ity** noun (pl **deformities**) कुरूपता।

defraud / डिˈफ़्रॉड् / verb **defraud sb
(of sth)** ठगना, धोखा देना।

defrost / ˌडीˈफ़्रॉस्ट् / verb 1 (रेफ़्रिजरेटर
में जमे) बर्फ़ीले कणों को पिघलाना 2 जमे
हुए खाद्य पदार्थ को सामान्य अवस्था में
लाना : How long will it take to
defrost this meat?

deft / डेफ़्ट् / adj चतुर; (हस्तकला में)
दक्ष : music played with deft strokes
▸ **deftly** adv **deftness** noun दक्षता।

defunct / डिˈफ़ङ्क्ट् / adj (औप)

अस्तित्वहीन, अप्रयुक्त या अप्रभावी : a
largely defunct railway network.

defuse / ˌडीˈफ़्यूज़् / verb 1 (बम आदि
को) नाकाम करना, फ़्यूज़ निकाल देना
2 किसी मुश्किल परिस्थिति में तनाव या ख़तरा
कम या समाप्त करना : defuse a crisis.

defy / डिˈफ़ाई / verb (pp, pt **defied**)
1 कहना मानने या सम्मान करने से इनकार
करना : She defied her parents and
got married. 2 तीव्र विरोध करना
3 किसी व्यक्ति से ऐसा काम करने को कहना
जो वह जानता है कि नहीं कर सकता है या
कदापि नहीं करेगा : I defy you to prove
I have cheated.

degenerate / डिˈजेनरेट् / verb ख़राब हो
जाना, पतित होना : His health is de-
generating rapidly. ▸ **degenerate**
adj (शारीरिक, मानसिक या नैतिक गुण)
ख़राब हो गए, पतित **degenerate** / डि
ˈजेनरट् / noun पतित व्यक्ति **degenera-
tion** noun पतन।

degrade / डिˈग्रेड् / verb 1 (दंड रूप)
पद-अवनति करना : degrade oneself
by cheating and telling lies 2 भ्रष्ट
करना, बिगाड़ना : Pollution is degrad-
ing the environment. 3 अवकर्षण
करना; पदार्थ को उसके मूल तत्त्वों तक
पहुँचाना ▸ **degradable** adj **degrada-
tion** noun पदावनति, अधोगति।

degree / डिˈग्री / noun 1 डिग्री, कोण का
अंश : an angle of ninety degrees
2 (संक्षि **deg**) तापमान को मापने की इकाई
3 किसी प्रक्रिया में मात्रा, सीमा, प्रगति आदि
को सूचित करने वाली स्थिति : She shows
a high degree of skill in her work.
4 विश्व-विद्यालय द्वारा प्रदत्त उपाधि : a
degree in law/a law degree 5 समाज
में पद, प्रतिष्ठा; कोटि ∎ **by degrees**
क्रमश:, सोपान क्रम से।

dehydrate / ˌडीˈहाइड्रेट् / verb 1 (खाद्य
पदार्थों में से) पानी निकालना : dehydrated milk in powdered form

2 (शरीर एवं ऊतकों का) अधिक मात्रा में पानी खो देना : *Her body had dehydrated dangerously in extreme heat.* ▶ **dehydration** *noun*.

deign / डेन् / *verb* (कभी-कभी *अप्रिय*) कोई ऐसा काम करना जिससे दूसरे को लगे कि विशेष मेहरबानी दिखा रहे हैं।

deity / डेअटि; डीअटि / *noun* (*pl* deities) 1 देवी, देवता : *Roman deities* 2 the Deity ईश्वर।

dejected / डि'जेक्टिड् / *adj* निराश, मायूस : *Repeated failures had left him feeling very dejected.* ▶ **dejectedly** *adv* **dejection** *noun* हताशा/ निराशा।

delay / डिले / *verb* 1 देरी करना/करवाना; धीमे-धीमे कार्य करना : *Don't delay! Book your trip today.* 2 आगे के लिए टालना : *Why have they delayed opening the school?* ▶ **delay** *noun* 1 देरी 2 देरी में लगा समय।

delectable / डि'लेक्टब्ल् / *adj* (*औप*) चित्ताकर्षक, अति सुंदर : *a delectable meal.*

delegate¹ / डेलिगेट् / *verb* 1 (किसी को प्रतिनिधि के रूप में किसी बैठक में) भेजना; कार्य सौंपना : *The new manager was delegated to reorganize the department.* 2 **delegate sth (to sb)** अपने से निम्न स्तर के व्यक्ति को) ज़िम्मेदारी सौंपना : *A boss must know how to delegate (work).*

delegate² / डेलिगट् / *noun* प्रतिनिधि (व्यक्ति)।

delegation / डेलि'गेश्न् / *noun* 1 प्रतिनिधिमंडल 2 कार्य सौंपने की प्रक्रिया।

delete / डि'लीट् / *verb* **delete sth (from sth)** (लिखित या मुद्रित पंक्ति से) कुछ या पूरा अंश काट देना, हटा देना : *The editor deleted the last paragraph from my article.* ▶ **deletion** / डि 'लीश्न् / *noun* विलोप।

deliberate¹ / डि'लिबरट् / *adj* 1 जान-बूझकर किया हुआ : *the deliberate killing of unarmed civilians* 2 सतर्क और सावधान ▶ **deliberately** *adv*.

deliberate² / डि'लिबरेट् / *verb* **deliberate (about/on/over sth)** (*औप*) सावधानी से सोचना और विचार-विमर्श करना : *deliberate what action to take.*

deliberation / डि,लिब'रेश्न् / *noun* 1 (*प्राय: pl*) सावधानीपूर्वक किया गया विचार-विमर्श 2 बोलने में या कार्य करने में सतर्कता और धीमापन : *take aim with great deliberation.*

delicacy / डेलिकसि / *noun* (*pl* delicacies) 1 नाज़ुकता : *the delicacy of her features* 2 स्वादिष्ट भोज्य पदार्थ।

delicate / डेलिकट् / *adj* 1 सूक्ष्म और महीन (सामग्री); मुलायम और कोमल : *a baby's delicate skin* 2 नाज़ुक; सुकुमार : *a delicate child/constitution* 3 (ज्ञानेंद्रिय अथवा यंत्र) मामूली अंतर को भी ग्रहण करने वाले या स्पष्ट करने वाले; संवेदनशील : *a delicate sense of smell/ touch* 4 (रंग) हलका, न कि तेज़ 5 (भोजन एवं स्वाद) सुरुचिपूर्ण एवं स्वा-दिष्ट : *the delicate flavour of salmon* 6 भद्र व्यक्ति, औरों की भावनाओं का समादर करने वाला : *I admired your delicate handling of the situation.* ▶ **delicately** *adv*.

delicious / डि'लिशस् / *adj* 1 स्वादिष्ट और सुगंधिपूर्ण, सुखद : *a delicious meal* 2 मनोहर, रमणीय : *a delicious thrill* ▶ **deliciously** *adv*.

delight¹ / डि'लाइट्/ *verb* किसी को प्रसन्न करना : *Her singing delighted every-one.* ■ **delight in sth/doing sth** प्रसन्नता पाना/प्रसन होना : *He delights in shocking people.* ▶ **delighted** *adj* **delightedly** *adv*.

delight² / डि'लाइट् / *noun* 1 अत्यंत

प्रसन्नता 2 प्रसन्नता का कारण/वस्तु : *the delights of living in the country* ▸ **delightful** *adj* **delightful (to sb)** आकर्षक, प्रसन्नता देने वाली वस्तु।

delinquent / डि 'लिङ्क्वन्ट् / *adj* (किशोरों का) अपराध करने की प्रवृत्ति दिखाते हुए; (*तक*) अपचारी।

delineate / डि'लिनिएट् / *verb* (*औप*) विस्तार से वर्णन करके या चित्र बनाकर समझाना : *delineate one's plans* ▸ **delineation** *noun.*

delirious / डि'लिरिअस; डि'लिअरिअस / *adj* 1 (ज्वर में) प्रमाद से पीड़ित 2 अत्यंत उत्तेजित एवं प्रसन्न ▸ **deliriously** *adv.*

delirium / डि'लिरिअम्; डि'लिअरिअम् / *noun* 1 (ज्वर में) प्रमाद अवस्था, सरसाम 2 अत्यंत उत्तेजना और प्रसन्नता।

deliver / डि'लिव़र् / *verb* 1 **deliver (sth) (to sb/sth)** (पत्र, सामान आदि) व्यक्ति के घर पर जाकर देना : *A courier delivered the parcels to our office.* 2 (भाषण, उपदेश आदि) देना 3 बच्चे को जन्म देने में माँ की सहायता करना 4 **deliver sb (from sth)** (*प्रा*) (संकट, लालच आदि से) मुक्त करना; रक्षा करना ▸ **deliverance** / डि'लिव़रन्स् / *noun* मुक्ति।

delivery / डि'लिव़रि / *noun* (*pl* **deliveries**) 1 पत्र, सामान आदि देने/पहुँचाने की क्रिया 2 पत्र, सामान आदि जो दिया गया है 3 [*sing*] भाषण, उपदेश आदि में बोलने की शैली 4 शिशु-जन्म : *a difficult/easy delivery.*

delta / 'डेल्टा / *noun* 1 नदी का मुहाना जहाँ नदी कई भागों में बँट जाती है : *the Ganga Delta* 2 ग्रीक वर्णमाला का चौथा अक्षर (Δ, δ)।

delude / डि'लूड् / *verb* **delude sb/ oneself (with sth/into doing sth)** धोखा देना, बहकाना : *delude sb with empty promises* ▸ **delusion** / डि'लूश़न् / *noun* 1 धोखा, भ्रांति 2 विभ्रांति

(का रोग) जो पागलपन का लक्षण हो सकती है **delusive** *adj* भ्रांतिमय।

deluge / 'डेल्यूज़् / *noun* 1 मूसलाधार वर्षा; बाढ़ 2 एकदम किसी वस्तु की अत्यधिक मात्रा : *a deluge of complaints/criticism/inquiries* ▸ **deluge** *verb* 1 **deluge sth (with sth)** बाढ़ से डुबो देना 2 **deluge sb/sth (with sth)** बाढ़ की भाँति कोई वस्तु अत्यधिक मात्रा में किसी को भेजना/देना : *I was deluged with phone calls.*

de luxe / ड 'लक्स़; ड 'लुक्स़् / *adj* उच्च श्रेणी का और सुखपूर्वक।

delve / डेल्व़् / *verb* **delve in/into sth** बारीकी से गहरी खोज करना।

demand¹ / डि'मान्ड् / *verb* 1 अधिकार के साथ कोई वस्तु माँगना : *The workers are demanding higher pay.* 2 आवश्यक होना : *This sort of work demands great patience.*

demand² / डि'मान्ड् / *noun* 1 (अधिकार या दृढ़ता के साथ) माँग : *It is impossible to satisfy all their demands.* 2 **demand (for sth/sb)** (ख़रीदारों की ओर से) सामान, सेवा आदि की माँग; आवश्यकता : *a sudden upsurge in consumer demand.*

demanding / डि'मान्डिङ् / *adj* 1 (कार्य) कुशलता, प्रयास और धैर्य की आवश्यकता वाला 2 (व्यक्ति) दूसरों से कठिन श्रम की अपेक्षा रखने वाला : *a demanding boss/ father.*

demarcate / 'डीमार्केट् / *verb* (*औप*) सीमा निर्धारित या अंकित करना : *The playing area is demarcated by a white line.* ▸ **demarcation** / ,डीमार् 'केश़न् / *noun* सीमा रेखा : *a line of demarcation.*

demean / डि'मीन् / *verb* 1 **demean oneself** अपनी प्रतिष्ठा गिराना 2 किसी को प्रदत्त सम्मान कम करना : *images which are considered to demean women*

▸ **demeaning** *adj* प्रतिष्ठा गिराने वाला (कार्य या व्यवहार)।

demeanour (*US* **demeanor**) / डि 'मीनर् / *noun* (औप) बरताव, व्यवहार : *maintain a professional demeanour.*

demented / डि'मेन्टिड् / *adj* 1 पागल : *a poor, demented creature* 2 क्रोध, चिंता आदि के कारण अत्यंत उत्तेजित एवं पागल जैसा : *When her child was two hours late, she became quite demented.* ▸ **dementedly** *adv.*

demerit / डी'मेरिट् / *noun* (प्राय: *pl*) (औप) दोष, अवगुण।

demilitarize, -ise / डी'मिलिटराइज़् / *verb* समझौते के द्वारा सेनाएँ हटाना : *a demilitarized zone* ▸ **demilitarization, -isation** *noun.*

demise / डि'माइज़् / *noun* [*sing*] 1 (औप अथवा परि) देहांत, मृत्यु 2 किसी विचार, संस्था अथवा उद्यम की समाप्ति/खात्मा।

demobilize, -ise / डि'मोबलाइज़् / *verb* अनिवार्य सैनिक सेवा के बाद किसी को मुक्त करना ▸ **demobilization, -isation** *noun.*

democracy / डि'मॉक्रिस / *noun* (*pl* **democracies**) 1 लोकतंत्र, जनतंत्र; किसी देश में लोकतंत्र 2 किसी संस्था का उसके सदस्यों के हाथों में नियंत्रण (जो नीति-निर्णय में भाग लेते हैं): *industrial democracy* 3 नागरिकों द्वारा एक दूसरे का बराबर सम्मान।

democrat / 'डेम्क्रैट् / *noun* 1 लोकतंत्री (व्यक्ति) 2 **Democrat** संयुक्त राष्ट्र अमेरिका के एक प्रमुख राजनीतिक दल का सदस्य।

democratic / डेम्'क्रैटिक / *adj* 1 प्रजातंत्रीय : *democratic rights/elections* 2 संस्था का नियंत्रण सदस्यों के हाथों में होने का समर्थक 3 जाति अथवा धन संपत्ति पर आधारित वर्ग-विभाजनों की उपेक्षा करने वाला : *a democratic society* ▸ **democratically** *adv.*

demolish / डि'मॉलिश् / *verb* 1 (किसी भवन, इमारत आदि को) गिरा देना, नष्ट करना 2 किसी सिद्धांत की धज्जियाँ उड़ा देना : *Her article brilliantly demolished his whole argument.* 3 (परि) कुछ लोलुपता से खाना ▸ **demolition** / डेम'लिशन् / *noun* विध्वंस।

demon / 'डीमन् / *noun* 1 दुष्टात्मा; दैत्य, राक्षस 2 (अनौप) अनिष्टकारी समझा जाने वाला व्यक्ति, दुष्ट : *Your son's a little demon.* 3 **demon** (**for sth**) अति उद्यमी व्यक्ति ▸ **demonic** *adj.*

demonstrate / 'डेमन्स्ट्रेट् / *verb* 1 **demonstrate sth** (**to sb**) प्रमाण, उदाहरण आदि से प्रदर्शन एवं सिद्ध करना; अपने कार्य द्वारा कुछ व्यक्त करना 2 **demonstrate sth** (**to sb**) किसी वस्तु की कार्यविधि या कुछ करने का तरीका समझाना 3 **demonstrate** (**against/in favour of sb/sth**) विरोध अथवा समर्थन जुलूस आदि में भाग लेना।

demonstration / डेमन्'स्ट्रेशन् / *noun* 1 प्रदर्शन, प्रमाण सहित कार्य करके दिखाने की क्रिया 2 किसी बात का उदाहरण या संकेत : *They gave a clear demonstration of their intentions.* 3 (अनौप **demo** भी) सार्वजनिक सभा अथवा जुलूस : *take part in/go on a student demonstration.*

demonstrative / डि'मॉन्स्ट्रटिव् / *adj* (व्यक्ति) आसानी से भावनाएँ, प्यार प्रदर्शन करने वाला।

demonstrator / 'डेमन्स्ट्रेटर् / *noun* जुलूस या सार्वजनिक प्रदर्शन में भाग लेने वाला व्यक्ति।

demoralize, -ise / डि'मॉरलाइज़् / *verb* मनोबल गिराना या उत्साह भंग करना : *The teams were not demoralized by their defeat.* ▸ **demoralization, -isation** *noun* मनोबल ह्रास **demoralized, -ised** *adj* **demoralizing, -ising** *adj.*

demote / डी'मोट् / verb demote sb (from sth) (to sth) व्यक्ति को उसके पद से नीचे वाले पद पर कर देना, पदावनति : He was demoted (from sergeant to corporal). ▶ **demotion** noun पदाव-नति।

demure / डी'म्युअर् / adj शांत, गंभीर एवं नम्र : a demure young lady.

den / डेन् / noun 1 (शेर आदि की) माँद, गुफा 2 (अपमा) दुष्टों का गुप्त अड्डा : a den of thieves 3 (अनौप) अध्ययन के लिए एकांत कमरा।

denationalize, -ise / डी'नैशनलाइज़् / verb राष्ट्रीयकृत उद्योगों को (शेयर बेचकर) व्यक्तिगत संस्था के अधिकार में दे देना ▶ **denationalization, -isation** noun.

denial / डिनाइअल् / noun 1 denial (of sth/that ...) खंडन 2 (अधिकार, निवेदन आदि का) अस्वीकार : the denial of basic human rights.

denigrate / डेनिग्रेट् / verb किसी की अनुचित निंदा करना, किसी (व्यक्ति/वस्तु) को बेकार, निम्न श्रेणी का सिद्ध करना; बदनामी करना : denigrate sb's char-acter/achievements ▶ **denigration** noun.

denim / डेनिम् / noun 1 मज़बूत मोटा सूती कपड़ा 2 denims [pl] (अनौप) डेनिम के वस्त्र।

denomination / डिनॉमि'नेशन् / noun 1 ईसाई धार्मिक संस्था/समुदाय 2 मापन इकाईयों का वर्ग (विशेषत: मुद्रा का) ▶ **de-nominational** adj.

denominator / डि'नॉमिनेटर् / noun (गणित) भिन्न वाली संख्या में हर; भाजक संख्या, जैसे $\frac{3}{4}$ में 4.

denote / डि'नोट् / verb 1 किसी चीज़ का द्योतक होना, द्योतित करना : In algebra, the sign x usually denotes an un-known quantity. 2 नाम होना; कुछ अर्थ रखना : What does the term 'organic' denote?

denounce / डि'नाउन्स् / verb de-nounce sb/sth (as sth) सार्वजनिक रूप से विरोध करना, तीव्र निंदा करना : She denounced the government's han-dling of the crisis.

dense / डेन्स् / adj (-r, -st) 1 (द्रव या वाष्प) गाढ़ा, ऐसा घना होना कि आर-पार दिखाई न दे : dense fog/smoke 2 (व्यक्तियों या वस्तुओं का) ठसाठस भरा होना : a dense crowd/forest 3 (अनौप) मूर्ख ▶ **densely** adv.

density / डेन्सटि / noun (pl densities) 1 गाढ़ा या घना होने का स्तर; घनत्व : population density 2 (भौतिकी) भार का आयतन से संबंध।

dent / डेन्ट् / noun चोट या दबाव से पिचकने का निशान; (अलं) नुकसान ▶ **dent** verb कड़ी, समान सतह को चोट या दबाव से पिचका देना।

dental / डेन्ट्ल् / adj दाँत संबंधी : dental decay/care/treatment.

dentist / डेन्टिस्ट् / noun दाँत का डॉक्टर, दंत-चिकित्सक।

denture / डेन्चर / noun (प्राय: pl) दंतावली; नकली दाँतों की प्लेट।

denude / डि'न्यूड् / verb denude sth (of sth) नंगा करना; अनावृत करना।

denunciation / डि'नन्सि'एशन् / noun किसी व्यक्ति या नीति के सार्वजनिक विरोध या निंदा की घटना : her fierce denun-ciation of her enemies.

deny / डि'नाइ / verb (pt, pp denied) 1 (किसी तथ्य का) खंडन करना, सत्यता को नकारना : deny a statement/claim 2 deny sth (to sb) कुछ देने से इनकार करना, प्रार्थना अस्वीकार करना 3 जानकारी होने से मना करना; अस्वीकार करना : The government denies responsibility for the disaster.

deodorant / डि'ओडरन्ट् / noun किसी व्यक्ति अथवा वस्तु से दुर्गंध दूर करने वाला पदार्थ; दुर्गंधनाशक।

depart / डि'पार्ट् / verb **depart (for...)
(from...)** (औप) प्रस्थान करना; से हट
जाना : *We departed for Athens at
10 am.*

departed / डि'पार्टिड् / adj मृत ▸ **the
departed** noun (pl अपरिवर्तित) मृत
व्यक्ति।

department / डि'पार्टमन्ट् / noun
1 (सरकार, व्यापार, विश्वविद्यालय आदि
का) विभाग 2 ज़िम्मेदारी का क्षेत्र।

departure / डि'पार्चर् / noun 1 प्रस्थान
2 सामान्य काररवाई से हटने की क्रिया : *a
departure from tradition/the
standard procedure.*

depend / डि'पेन्ड् / verb ■ **depend on/
upon sb/sth** विश्वास, निश्चित भरोसा
होना : *You can never depend on his
arriving on time.* **depend on sb/
sth (for sth)** किसी विशेष उद्देश्य के लिए
(किसी अन्य पर) निर्भर होना : *We depend on the radio for news.* **depend on sth** अन्य द्वारा निश्चित होना : *A
lot will depend on how she re-
sponds to the challenge.* **that depends; it (all) depends** अन्य पर निर्भर
है, अन्य पर भी विचार करना है ▸ **depend-
able** adj भरोसेमंद, विश्वसनीय **depend-
ability** noun विश्वसनीयता।

dependant (*US* **dependent** भी) / डि
'पेन्डन्ट् / noun आश्रित व्यक्ति।

dependence / डि'पेन्डन्स् / noun **dependence (on/upon sb/sth)**
1 निर्भरता, आश्रित रहने की स्थिति : *his
dependence on his parents* 2 किसी
वस्तु की नियमित आवश्यकता होने की
स्थिति : *medical treatment for drug/
alcohol dependence.*

dependency / डि'पेन्डन्सि / noun (pl
dependencies) 1 किसी अन्य द्वारा
शासित देश : *The Hawaian Islands
are no longer a dependency of the
USA.* 2 अन्य पर निर्भरता 3 नियमित
आवश्यकता : *drug/chemical dependency.*

dependent / डि'पेन्डन्ट् / adj **dependent (on/upon sb/sth)** पराए पर अपनी
आवश्यकता पूर्ति के लिए आश्रित; परनिर्भर।

depict / डि'पिक्ट् / verb चित्रित करना;
शब्दों में वर्णन करना/शब्द चित्र खींचना :
*The painting depicts her lying on
a bed.* ▸ **depiction** noun चित्रण।

deplete / डि'प्लीट् / verb मात्रा, आकार,
शक्ति या महत्त्व से खाली करना/हो जाना :
*The election has severely depleted
the party's funds.* ▸ **depletion** / डि
'प्लीशन् / noun : *the depletion of the
ozone layer.*

deplore / डि'प्लॉर् / verb शोचनीय बात या
अवस्था की निंदा करना : *I deplore the
fact that there are so few women in
top jobs.* ▸ **deplorable** adj शोचनीय,
निंदनीय।

deploy / डि'प्लॉइ / verb 1 सैनिक कार-
रवाई के लिए सेना तैनात करना 2 कुछ प्रभावी
ढंग से इस्तेमाल करना : *deploy one's
arguments/resources* ▸ **deploy-
ment** noun.

depopulate / डी'पॉप्युलेट् / verb स्थान
के निवासियों की संख्या को कम करना : *an
island depopulated by disease*
▸ **depopulation** noun.

deport / डि'पॉर्ट् / verb **deport sb
(from ...)** देश निकाला देना ▸ **deportation** noun : *illegal immigrants facing deportation.*

depose / डि'पोज़् / verb गद्दी से (विशेषत:
शासक को) उतारना : *The king was
deposed in a military coup.*

deposit[1] / डि'पॉज़िट् / verb 1 निर्धारित
स्थान पर कुछ रखना : *The bus depos-
ited them near the station.* 2 (द्रव,
नदी आदि का) रेत-मिट्टी आदि जमा करना
3 बैंक आदि में सुरक्षा एवं ब्याज के लिए पैसा
रखना; **deposit sth (in sth/with sth)**

क़ीमती धरोहर को सुरक्षित स्थान पर रखना
4 बड़ी रक़म का छोटा अंश भुगतान करना;
प्रतिभूति के तौर पर पहले से ही धन का
भुगतान करना जो कि वापिस मिल जाएगा।

deposit² / डि'पॉज़िट् / noun 1 बैंक में
जमा की गई धनराशि 2 **deposit (on sth)**
रक़म का भुगतान किया गया एक अंश
3 प्रतिभूति धनराशि 4 द्रवों, नदियों द्वारा जमा
रेत-मिट्टी; भूमि के नीचे प्राकृतिक जमा-
भंडार : *rich mineral deposits.*

depot / 'डेपो / US 'डीपो / noun 1 डिपो,
गोदाम; बस डिपो 2 (US) रेलवे/बस स्टेशन।

deprave / डि'प्रेव् / verb (किसी का)
नैतिक चरित्र ख़राब करना : *a film likely
to deprave and corrupt young peo-
ple* ▸ **depraved** / डि'प्रेव्ड् / adj चरित्र-
हीन, पतित।

depravity / डि'प्रैविटि / noun चरित्रहीनता,
दुष्टता : *a life of depravity.*

depreciate / डि'प्रोशिएट् / verb 1 मूल्य
घटना या घटाना : *New cars depreciate
quickly.* 2 (औप) यह कहना कि अमुक
वस्तु मूल्यवान/महत्त्वपूर्ण नहीं है ▸ **depreciation** / डि,प्रोशि'एश्न् / noun : *currency depreciation.*

depress / डि'प्रेस् / verb 1 उदास करना;
दुखी करना 2 (औप) नीचे दबाना, ढकेलना
या खींचना : *depress the clutch*
3 सक्रियता कम करना; (मूल्यों का) नीचे
गिरना : *The rise in oil prices will
depress the car market.* ▸ **depressed** adj उदास एवं खिन्न **depress-
ing** adj उदास करने वाला **depressingly**
adv.

depression / डि'प्रेश्न् / noun 1 उदासी,
खिन्नता : *He committed suicide during a fit of depression.* 2 (व्यापार में)
मंदी का समय 3 दबाने से बना गड्ढा
4 मौसम की स्थिति जिसमें वायुदाब कम हो
जाता है और प्राय: वर्षा होती है : *a
depression over Iceland* ▸ **depres-
sive** adj, noun.

deprive / डि'प्राइव् / verb ■ **deprive sb/
sth of sth** (कोई वस्तु किसी से) छीन
लेना; प्रयोग और उपभोग करने से वंचित
करना : *be deprived of one's civil
rights* ▸ **deprivation** / ,डेप्रि'वेश्न् /
noun 1 वंचना : *sleep deprivation*
2 सामान्य वस्तुओं से वंचित होने की स्थिति
3 छीनी गई वस्तु **deprived** adj.

depth / डेप्थ् / noun 1 (ऊपर से नीचे की
या आगे से पीछे तक की) गहराई, जैसे कुएँ
की गहराई 2 (प्राय: pl) किसी वस्तु/विषय
का सबसे गंभीर, सबसे गूढ़ पक्ष; गंभीरता
3 (रंगों की) तीव्रता 4 (भावनाओं की)
तीव्रता एवं शक्ति 5 गूढ़ विचारों को समझने
एवं समझाने की योग्यता ■ **in depth**
पूर्णतया **out of one's depth** 1 अपनी
ऊँचाई से भी गहरे पानी में होना 2 अपनी बुद्धि
से परे की सोचना; समझने में असमर्थ।

deputation / ,डेप्यु'टेश्न् / noun प्रति-
निधि-मंडल।

depute / डि'प्यूट् / verb (औप) 1 **depute sth to sb** किसी स्थानापन्न को अपना
अधिकार या कार्य देना 2 किसी को यह
अधिकार देना कि वह उसके प्रतिनिधि के रूप
में कार्य करे : *They were deputed to
put our views to the assembly.*

deputize, -ise / 'डेप्युटाइज़् / verb
deputize (for sb) प्रतिनियुक्त व्यक्ति के
रूप में कार्य करना।

deputy / 'डेप्युटि / noun (pl **deputies**)
सहायक, उप- : *I am acting as a
deputy till the manager returns.*

derail / डि'रेल् / verb रेलगाड़ी का पटरियों
से उतर जाना ▸ **derailment** noun.

deranged / डि'रेन्ज्ड् / adj विशेषत:
मानसिक बीमारी के कारण सामान्य रूप से
काम में असमर्थ ▸ **derangement** noun.

derelict / 'डेरलिक्ट् / adj अप्रयुक्त एवं
उपेक्षित और ख़राब स्थिति में : *a derelict
building/ship* ▸ **derelict** noun घर-
बार, नौकरी और संपत्ति विहीन व्यक्ति।

dereliction / ,डेर'लिक्श्न् / noun

1 उपेक्षित एवं ख़राब 2 *(औप)* कुछ करने में जानबूझकर असफल : *Police officers were found guilty of a serious dereliction of duty.*

deride / डिˈराइड् / *verb* **deride sb/sth (as sth)** घृणापूर्ण उपहास करना : *They derided his efforts (as childish).* ▸ **derision** *noun* उपहास **derisive** *adj.*

derivation / डेरिˈवेश्न् / *noun* किसी शब्द की उत्पत्ति और विकास, व्युत्पत्ति।

derivative / डिˈरिवटिव् / *adj* दूसरे से व्युत्पन्न (शब्द, वस्तु आदि) ▸ **derivative** *noun.*

derive / डीˈराइव् / *verb* **derive sth from sth** 1 व्युत्पत्ति के रूप में कुछ पाना 2 *(औप)* पाना, लाभ मिलना : *derive great pleasure from art.*

derogatory / डिˈरॉग्टरि; *US* डिˈराग्-टॉरि / *adj* प्रतिष्ठा या साख को गिराने वाला; अपमानजनक।

descend / डिˈसेन्ड / *verb* 1 *(औप)* उतरना, नीचे आना; (पहाड़ी का) नीचे की ओर ढलाव होना 2 *(औप)* (रात्रि या अंधकार) छा जाना ∎ **be descended from sb** 1 के वंशज होना, पुत्र-पौत्रादि होना 2 (संपत्ति का) पिता से पुत्र को मिलना **descend on/upon sb/sth** अचानक धावा मारना, टूट पड़ना ▸ **descendant** / डिˈसेन्डन्ट् / *noun* वंशज, उक्त व्यक्ति के पुत्र-पौत्रादि।

descent / डिˈसेन्ट् / *noun* 1 उतरने की प्रक्रिया; ढलान : *Here there is a gradual descent to the sea.* 2 **descent (from sb)** वंशक्रम, पीढ़ी।

describe / डिˈस्क्राइब् / *verb* 1 **describe sb/sth (to/for sb); describe sth as sth** (किसी व्यक्ति या वस्तु का) वर्णन करना : *Words cannot describe the beauty of the scene.* 2 **describe sb/oneself as sth** बताना; कहना 3 *(औप या तक)* खींचना : *describe a circle on the ice.*

description / डिˈस्क्रिप्श्न् / *noun* 1 वर्णन 2 शब्दचित्र।

descriptive / डिˈस्क्रिपटिव् / *adj* वर्णनात्मक।

desecrate / ˈडेसिक्रेट् / *verb* (किसी पवित्र वस्तु या स्थान को) दुष्प्रयोग द्वारा अपवित्र करना : *desecrate a temple/church* ▸ **desecration** / डेसिˈक्रेश्न् / *noun.*

desert[1] / डिˈज़र्ट् / *verb* 1 किसी व्यक्ति को बिना सहायता या सहारे के अकेला छोड़ देना : *He deserted his wife and children and went abroad.* 2 अधिकारियों की अनुमति के बिना सेना-सेवा छोड़ देना; भाग जाना 3 किसी स्थान को त्याग देना 4 (कोई गुण) ज़रूरत के समय साथ छोड़ देना ▸ **deserted** *adj* त्यक्त; अकेला छोड़ा हुआ; वीरान, सुनसान **deserter** *noun* विशेषत: भगोड़ा सिपाही **desertion** *noun.*

desert[2] / ˈडेज़र्ट् / *noun* रेगिस्तान ।

deserve / डिˈज़र्व् / *verb* अपने आचरण, गुण आदि के कारण पुरस्कार, विशिष्ट व्यवहार, दंड आदि पाने के योग्य होना : *She deserves some reward for her efforts.* ▸ **deservedly** / डिˈज़र्विड्लि / *adv* ठीक, योग्यता के अनुकूल।

deserving / डिˈज़र्विंग् / *adj* योग्य, सु-पात्र।

design / डिˈज़ाइन् / *noun* 1 **design (for sth)** ख़ाका, रूपरेखा : *designs for a dress/an aircraft* 2 (किसी मशीन, चित्र आदि का) योजना विन्यास : *special new design features* 3 पैटर्न, कला-कार्य : *floral/abstract designs* 4 योजना, इरादा : *We don't know if it was done by accident or by design.* ▸ **design** *verb* 1 रूपरेखा बनाना : *design a car* 2 विशेष उद्देश्य या प्रयोग के लिए इरादा करना।

designate / ˈडेज़िग्नेट् / *verb* 1 सीमा आदि का स्पष्ट अंकन करना, निर्दिष्ट

करना : *designate the boundaries of sth* **2 designate sb/sth (as) sth** (और) किसी पद या स्थान पर नियुक्त किया जाना।

designation /ˌडेज़िग्'नेश्न्/ *noun* **1** पद पर नियुक्ति **2** पद-नाम।

designer / डिˈज़ाइनर् / *noun* **1** रूपरेखा खींचने वाला **2** (कपड़े) सुंदर दिखाई पड़े ऐसा डिज़ाइन तैयार करने वाला; वेशभूषाकार।

desirable / डिˈज़ाइअरब्ल् / *adj* **1** अभीष्ट, वांछनीय **2** कामासक्ति उत्पन्न करने वाला ▸ **desirability** / डिˌज़ाइअर'बिलटि / *noun* वांछनीयता।

desire¹ / डिˈज़ाइअर् / *noun* **1 desire (for sth/to do sth)** अभिलाषा, विकट इच्छा **2** तीव्र कामेच्छा : *passionate/ burning desires* **3** (प्राय: *sing*) इच्छित/ अभीष्ट वस्तु/व्यक्ति।

desire² / डिˈज़ाइअर् / *verb* **1** (और) अभिलाषा रखना, इच्छा करना : *We all desire happiness and health.* **2** किसी के प्रति आसक्त होना।

desirous / डिˈज़ाइअरस् / *adj* इच्छा रखने वाला।

desist / डिˈज़िस्ट् / *verb* **desist (from sth/doing sth)** (और या साहि) कुछ रोक देना/करना छोड़ देना।

desk / डेस्क् / *noun* **1** डेस्क, मेज़ **2** कार्य-पटल ▸ **desktop** /ˈडेस्क्टॉप्/ *noun* मेज़ का ऊपरी भाग **desktop publishing** *noun* (संक्षि **DTP**) कंप्यूटर एवं प्रिंटर की सहायता से उच्च कोटि की मुद्रित सामग्री तैयार करने के लिए प्रयोग।

desolate /ˈडेसलट्/ *adj* **1** (स्थान) जहाँ कोई न रहता हो और न रहने लायक हो, निर्जन **2** (व्यक्ति) एकाकी, उपेक्षित एवं उदास ▸ **desolate** *verb* **1** (स्थान) निर्जन एवं उजाड़ छोड़ देना **2** व्यक्ति को एकाकी एवं उदास छोड़ देना।

desolation /ˌडेस'लेश्न्/ *noun* **1** निर्जनता; उजाड़ **2** एकाकीपन एवं उपेक्षा।

despair / डिˈस्पेअर् / *noun* निराशा

(पूर्ण) : *a cry of despair* ▸ **despair** *verb* **despair (of sth/doing sth)** पूर्णत: निराश हो जाना **despairing** *adj* निराश **despairingly** *adv*.

despatch → **dispatch** देखिए।

desperate /ˈडेस्परट् / *adj* **1** अत्यधिक निराशा के कारण प्रबल, उद्दंड और न्याय व्यवस्था की उपेक्षा करने वाला **2 desperate (for sth/to do sth)** अत्यधिक आवश्यकता में (व्यग्र) : *I was absolutely desperate to see her.* **3** अति गंभीर एवं ख़तरनाक **4** आशारहित : *a desperate bid for freedom* ▸ **desperately** *adv* **desperation** /ˌडेस्प 'रेश्न् / *noun*.

despicable / डिˈस्मिकब्ल् / *adj* (और) घृणास्पद, तिरस्कार योग्य : *a despicable crime.*

despise / डिˈस्पाइज़् / *verb* घृणा करना, तिरस्कार करना : *despise sb's hypocrisy.*

despite / डिˈस्पाइट् / *prep* के होते हुए भी : *They had a wonderful holiday, despite the bad weather.*

despondent / डिˈस्पॉन्डन्ट् / *adj* **despondent (about sth/doing sth)** निराश, हतोत्साह ▸ **despondency** *noun* उदासी, निराशा **despondently** *adv*.

despot /ˈडेस्पॉट् / *noun* निरंकुश शासक जो अपनी निस्सीम शक्ति से अत्याचार करता है ▸ **despotic** / डिˈस्पॉटिक् / *adj* : *despotic rule* **despotism** /ˈडेस्पटिज़म् / *noun* तानाशाही, निरंकुशता।

dessert / डिˈज़र्ट् / *noun* किसी भी भोजन की समाप्ति पर परोसी गई मीठी वस्तु : *a pineapple dessert.*

destination /ˌडेस्टिˈनेश्न्/ *noun* गंतव्य स्थान : *arrive at/reach one's destination.*

destined /ˈडेस्टिन्ड् / *adj* (और) **1 destined for sth/to do sth** निर्दिष्ट; (ईश्वर, भाग्य अथवा व्यक्ति द्वारा) नियत

2 destined for ... किसी स्थान के लिए निर्धारित : *food aid destined for Central Africa.*

destiny / 'डेस्टनि / noun (pl destinies) 1 भाग्य, नियति 2 (व्यक्ति विशेष के साथ) घटित होने वाली घटनाएँ।

destitute / 'डेस्टिट्यूट / adj 1 जीवन की आवश्यकताओं (भोजन, धन, वस्त्र आदि) से रहित 2 destitute of sth (औप) से रहित, हीन : *They seem destitute of ordinary human feelings.* ▸ **destitution** noun गरीबी; अभाव।

destroy / डि'स्ट्रॉइ / verb 1 नष्ट करना, तोड़-फोड़ करना : *They've destroyed all the evidence.* 2 बीमार या अवांछित जानवर को मार देना ▸ **destroyer** noun 1 छोटा तेज़ लड़ाकू जहाज़ 2 (औप) नष्ट करने वाला व्यक्ति/वस्तु।

destruction / डि'स्ट्रक्शन् / noun 1 विनाश, विध्वंस 2 (औप) विनाशकारी वस्तु/आदत : *Gambling was his destruction.*

destructive / डि'स्ट्रक्टिव् / adj 1 विनाशकारी : *the destructive force of the storm* 2 तोड़-फोड़ की प्रवृत्ति वाला : *destructive urges* ▸ **destructively** adv.

detach / डि'टैच् / verb 1 detach sth/itself (from sth) किसी बड़ी या लंबी वस्तु से कोई भाग खोलकर अलग करना : *detach a wagon from a train* 2 detach oneself from sb/sth स्वयं को औरों से अलग/असंबद्ध करना 3 (सेना में) मुख्य टोली से कुछ लोगों को अलग भेज देना ▸ **detachable** adj **detached** adj 1 दूसरों से प्रभावित न होने वाला; विरक्त व्यक्ति 2 किसी अन्य से न लगा हुआ मकान, असंबद्ध।

detachment / डि'टैच्मन्ट् / noun 1 विरक्ति; उदासीनता या तटस्थता 2 (सेना में) टुकड़ी 3 अलग होने की प्रक्रिया।

detail¹ / 'डीटेल / noun 1 विवरण, ब्योरा आदि का कोई छोटा अंश 2 विशिष्ट पहलू 3 (सेना में) विशेष काम के लिए नियुक्त सैनिक टुकड़ी।

detail² / 'डीटेल / verb 1 विवरण देना, पूरी तरह वर्णन करना : *an inventory detailing all the goods in a shop* 2 detail sb (for sth) विशेष सेवा के लिए (विशेषत: सैनिकों को) नियुक्त करना ▸ **detailed** adj ब्योरेवार, संपूर्ण।

detain / डि'टेन् / verb 1 किसी को अधिकारिक स्थान (जैसे हवालात) में रखना : *The police detained him for questioning.* 2 (औप) रोक लेना; प्रतीक्षा कराते रहना ▸ **detainee** / डीटे'नी / noun हवालात में बंद व्यक्ति : *political detainees.*

detect / डि'टेक्ट् / verb (किसी वस्तु/व्यक्ति की उपस्थिति या सत्ता का) पता लगा लेना : *Opticians can detect various cancers.* ▸ **detectable** adj **detection** / डि'टेक्शन् / noun खोज निकालने/खोज निकाले जाने की प्रक्रिया : *detection of radioactivity* **detector** noun धातु, विस्फोटक आदि का पता लगाने वाला उपकरण : *a metal detector.*

detective / डि'टेक्टिव् / noun जासूस (विशेषत: पुलिस अफ़सर)।

détente / डे'टान्ट / noun (फ्रेंच) (औप) (विशेषत: दो देशों के बीच) तनाव शैथिल्य, नरमी।

detention / डि'टेन्शन् / noun 1 नज़रबंदी, क़ैद 2 दंड के रूप में स्कूल में रोक रखना (छुट्टी के बाद) : *be given two hours' detention.*

deter / डि'टर् / verb (-rr-) deter sb (from doing sth) (किसी को कोई कार्य करने से) रोकना; बाधा डालना : *Stiff penalties are needed to deter crimes.*

detergent / डि'टर्जन्ट् / noun कपड़ों आदि से धोते समय मैल निकालने वाला पदार्थ, प्रक्षालक।

deteriorate / डि'टिअरिअरेट् / verb deteriorate (into sth) (स्थिति) बिगड़ती जाना, बदतर होते जाना ▸ **deterioration** / डि,टिअरिअ'रेश्न् / noun गिरावट, अधोगति।

determination / डि,टर्मि'नेश्न् / noun 1 determination (to do sth) दृढ़ निश्चय; संकल्प 2 ठीक-ठीक पता लगाने की प्रक्रिया 3 गणना करना या पता लगाना।

determine / डि'टर्मिन् / verb (औप) 1 निर्धारण करना 2 निर्णायक स्थिति में लाना : The exam results could determine your career. 3 निश्चय करना 4 ठीक-ठीक पता लगाना ▸ **determined** adj determined (to do sth) दृढ़ निश्चयी (व्यक्ति)।

determiner / डि'टर्मिनर् / noun (व्या) निर्धारक।

deterrent / डि'टेरन्ट् / noun बाधा डालने वाली वस्तु, निवारक उपाय ▸ **deterrent** adj.

detest / डि'टेस्ट् / verb घृणा करना : I detest people complaining. ▸ **detestable** adj घृणित, घृणा के योग्य **detestation** noun.

dethrone / ,डी'थ्रोन् / verb राजा को राजगद्दी से उतारना; सत्ताच्युत करना।

detonate / 'डेटनेट् / verb विस्फोट करना, दागना : The bomb failed to detonate. ▸ **detonation** / डेट'नेश्न् / noun विस्फोट; दागने की प्रक्रिया **detonator** noun विस्फोटक उपकरण।

detour / 'डीटुअर् / noun चक्करदार रास्ता; समस्या (जैसे बंद सड़क आदि) से बचने के लिए अपनाया गया अन्य रास्ता : We had to make a detour round the floods.

detract / डि'ट्रैक्ट् / verb detract from sth (मूल्य आदि) घटाना, कम करना : detract from the merit/excellence of sth ▸ **detractor** noun निंदक।

detriment / 'डेट्रिमन्ट् / noun हानि ∎ to the detriment of sb/sth; without

the detriment to sb/sth (औप) हानि पहुँचाते/न पहुँचाते हुए ▸ **detrimental** adj detrimental (to sb/sth) हानिकर : The recession had a detrimental effect on business. ▸ **detrimentally** adv.

deuce / ड्यूस् ; US डूस् / noun (टेनिस में) 40-40 का स्कोर।

devalue / ,डी'वैल्यू / verb 1 devalue sth (against sth) मुद्रा का दूसरे देश की मुद्रा के सापेक्ष मूल्य घटाना : devalue the dollar/pound 2 किसी चीज़ का मूल्य या महत्त्व घटाना; मूल्य कम आँकना ▸ **devaluation** / डी,वैल्यु'एश्न् / noun (मुद्रा का) अवमूल्यन।

devastate / 'डेवस्टेट् / verb 1 सर्वनाश करना; तबाह करना : a country devastated by war 2 दुख या मानसिक झटके से किसी को अति क्लेश पहुँचना/ पहुँचाना ▸ **devastating** / 'डेवस्टेटिङ् / adj 1 विनाशकारी 2 क्लेशकर 3 (अनौप) अत्यंत प्रभावी या प्रभावोत्पादक : devastating wit **devastation** / ,डेव'स्टेश्न् / noun सर्वनाश।

develop / डि'वेलप् / verb 1 develop (sth) (from sth) (into sth) बढ़ाना, विकसित करना; अधिक पूर्ण करना : The child is developing well. 2 कुछ शुरू होकर (समस्या, बीमारी आदि) वृद्धि करना 3 फ़ोटो फ़िल्म में चित्र उभारना; डेवलप करना 4 ज़मीन पर की संपत्ति (भवन आदि) को फ़ायदे के लिए विकसित करना, निर्माण कार्य करना ▸ **developed** adj 1 विकसित अवस्था में; परिपक्व : a highly developed system of agriculture 2 (देश) उन्नत **developer** noun 1 निर्माणकर्ता (व्यक्ति) 2 फ़ोटो फ़िल्म डेवलप करने वाला पदार्थ **developing** adj (देश) विकासशील।

development / डि'वेलप्मन्ट् / noun 1 विकास (प्रक्रिया) 2 नई अवस्था या घटना 3 नई खोज या आविष्कार 4 नया भवन-

निर्मित क्षेत्र : *a commercial development* ▸ **developmental** *adj* 1 विकासशील अवस्था में 2 विकास से संबंधित।

deviant /'डीव़िअन्ट् / *noun, adj* (प्राय: *अपमा*) उचित या उपयुक्त सामाजिक व्यवहार से अलग हटकर चलने वाला व्यक्ति ▸ **deviance** *noun.*

deviate / 'डीव़िएट् / *verb* **deviate (from sth)** (उचित या उपयुक्त व्यवहार से) हट जाना : *He never deviated from what he believed to be right.* ▸ **deviation** /,डीव़ि'एश्न् / *noun* 1 विचलन; विपथन 2 *(राज)* दल की सामान्य नीतियों से अलगाव।

device / डिव़ाइस् / *noun* 1 युक्ति; विशेष प्रयोजन के लिए निर्मित वस्तु : *a device for measuring pressure* 2 योजना; चाल; युक्ति ■ **leave sb to their own devices** किसी को बिना सहायता या नियंत्रण के छोड़ देना।

devil / 'ड़ेव़ल् / *noun* 1 **the Devil** शैतान 2 दुष्ट आत्मा (भूत-प्रेत) 3 *(अनौप)* दुष्ट स्वभाव का व्यक्ति ■ **between the devil and the deep blue sea** एक तरफ़ कुआँ दूसरी तरफ़ खाई ▸ **devilish** *adj* दुष्ट, क्रूर **devilishly** *adv.*

devious / 'डीव़िअस् / *adj* 1 बेईमान, छलपूर्ण 2 (रास्ता, सड़क आदि) चक्करदार ▸ **deviously** *adv* **deviousness** *noun.*

devise /डि'व़ाइज़/ *verb* आविष्कार करना; सावधानीपूर्वक विचार करके युक्ति खोज लेना; अभिकल्पना करना : *devise a scheme for redeveloping the city centre.*

devoid / डि'व़ॉइड् / *adj* **devoid of sth** से ख़ाली, रहित : *an argument devoid of logic.*

devolution / ,डीव़'लूश्न् / *noun* शक्ति अथवा अधिकारों का निचले स्तर पर हस्तांतरण।

devote / डि'व़ोट् / *verb* ■ **devote oneself/sth to sb/sth** अपनी शक्ति या समय किसी व्यक्ति या कार्य के लिए ख़र्च करना, अर्पित करना : *She devoted herself to her career.* ▸ **devoted** *adj* **devoted (to sb/sth)** सेवा में रुचि रखने वाला, ईमानदार एवं स्वामिभक्त; प्यार करने वाला **devotion** / डि'व़ोश्न् / *noun* 1 **devotion (to sb/sth)** निष्ठा एवं स्नेह : *a mother's devotion to her children* 2 **devotion (to sb/sth)** समय या शक्ति समर्पित करने की क्रिया 3 भक्ति भाव : *a life of devotion* 4 **devotions** [*pl*] प्रार्थनाएँ **devotional** *adj.*

devour /डि'व़ाउअर्/ *verb* 1 (भूख में बड़े चाव से) सब कुछ तेज़ी से खा जाना, भक्षण करना : *an animal devouring its prey* 2 उत्सुकता एवं ध्यान से देखना, सुनना या पढ़ना 3 नष्ट करना ■ **be devoured by sth** तीव्र भाव से भर जाना।

devout / डि'व़ाउट् / *adj* 1 धर्मनिष्ठ, श्रद्धालु : *a devout Muslim* 2 सेवानिष्ठ; दिल से : *a devout hope/wish* ▸ **devoutly** *adv* **devoutness** *noun.*

dew / ड्यू / *noun* ओस : *The grass was wet with dew.* ▸ **dewy** *adj* **dewy-eyed** *adj* 1 भोला-भाला एवं विश्वसनीय 2 भावुक।

dexterity /डेक्'स्टेरटि/ *noun* 1 निपुणता, दक्षता : *mental/verbal dexterity* 2 हाथों को कुशलता से प्रयोग करने की चतुराई : *A juggler needs great dexterity.*

dexterous (dextrous भी) / 'डेक्स्ट्रस्/ *adj* हस्तकला में दक्ष; कुशलता से किया गया : *a dexterous flick of the wrist* ▸ **dexterously** *adv.*

diabetes /,डाइअ'बीटीज़् / *noun* मधुमेह (की बीमारी) ▸ **diabetic** *adj* **diabetic** *noun* मधुमेह का रोगी।

diabolic /,डाइअ'बॉलिक् / *adj* शैतान के जैसा; दुष्टतापूर्ण : *a diabolic plan/trick* ▸ **diabolical** /,डाइअ'बॉलिकल् *adj* अत्यंत दुष्टतापूर्ण।

diagnose / 'डाइअग्नोज़् / *verb* 1 **diagnose sth (as sth)** समस्या (विशेषत: रोग का) पता लगाना : *The doctor diagnosed measles.* 2 रोग का पता लगाकर निदान करना : *be diagnosed as a diabetic* ▸ **diagnosis** / ‚डाइअग् 'नोसिस् / *noun* (*pl* **diagnoses** / ‚डाइअग् 'नोसीज़् /) रोग के पता लगाने की क्रिया, निदान **diagnostic** *adj* बीमारी का लक्षण-सूचक।

diagonal / डाइ'ऐगन्ल् / *adj* (सीधी रेखा) एक कोने से दूसरे कोने तक : *diagonal stripes* ▸ **diagonal** *noun* एक कोने से दूसरे कोने तक खींची गई सीधी रेखा; विकर्ण **diagonally** *adv*.

diagram / 'डाइअग्रैम् / *noun* आरेख, डायाग्राम ▸ **diagrammatic** *adj* आरेखीय **diagrammatically** *adv*.

dial[1] / 'डाइअल् / *noun* 1 घड़ी का डायल जिस पर घंटों के निशान बने होते हैं 2 (भार, दबाव आदि) मापक यंत्रों का वह पृष्ठ जिस पर मापन के अंक पड़े होते हैं 3 प्रोग्राम चुनने के लिए प्रयुक्त रेडियो या टी वी की प्लेट 4 टेलिफ़ोन का वह भाग जिस पर नंबर पड़े होते हैं।

dial[2] / 'डाइअल् / *verb* (**-ll-**; *US* **-l-**) टेलिफ़ोन द्वारा बात करने के लिए घुमाकर या दबाकर नंबर मिलाना।

dialect / 'डाइअलेक्ट् / *noun* किसी प्रदेश-विशेष या वर्ग-विशेष की बोली : *the local dialect.*

dialogue (*US* **dialog** भी) / 'डाइअलॉग् / *noun* 1 वार्तालाप (प्राय: दो व्यक्तियों के बीच) 2 लोगों के बीच चर्चा जिसमें मत व्यक्त किए जाते हैं।

diameter / डाइ'ऐमिटर / *noun* 1 (*ज्यामिति*) वृत्त के केंद्र से जाने वाली रेखा की लंबाई, व्यास 2 (*तक*) किसी यंत्र से देखने पर प्रतीत होती चौड़ाई या मोटाई : *a lens that magnifies 20 diameters.*

diametrically / ‚डाइअ'मेट्रिकलि / *adv* पूरी तरह।

diamond / 'डाइअमन्ड् / *noun* 1 हीरा (एक प्रकार का रत्न) 2 (*ज्यामिति*) सम-चतुर्भुज 3 **diamonds** ताश के पत्तों में ईंट के पत्ते : *play a diamond* ▸ **diamond jubilee** *noun* 60वाँ वार्षिक समारोह।

diaper / 'डाइअपर; *US* 'डाइपर् / *noun* (*US*) = **nappy.**

diaphragm / 'डाइअफ्रैम् / *noun* वक्ष और पेट के बीच की मांसपेशियों की दीवार, मध्यपटल।

diarrhoea (*US* **diarrhea**) / ‚डाइअ'रिआ; *US* ‚डाइअ'रीआ / *noun* दस्त, अतिसार।

diary / 'डाइअरि / *noun* (*pl* **diaries**) 1 डायरी, दैनिकी 2 (*US* **calendar**) भेंट, भावी कार्यक्रम आदि लिखने के लिए प्रयुक्त डायरी : *a desk diary* ▸ **diarist** *noun*.

dice / डाइस् / *noun* (*pl* अपरिवर्तित) पासा ▸ **dice** *verb* किसी वस्तु (जैसे सब्ज़ी, मांस आदि) को छोटे-छोटे वर्गों में काटना : *diced cucumber.*

dictate / डिक्'टेट् / *verb* **dictate sth (to sb)** 1 लिखाना, एक का बोलना और दूसरे का लिखना या टाइप करना : *dictate a letter to one's secretary* 2 आदेश देना, हुक्म चलाना : *dictate terms to a defeated enemy* ▸ **dictate** *noun* (प्राय: *pl*) आदेश या हुक्म।

dictation / डिक्'टेशन् / *noun* 1 बोलकर लिखवाने की क्रिया 2 श्रुतलेख (परीक्षा)।

dictator / डिक्'टेटर; *US* 'डिकटेटर् / *noun* तानाशाह शासक, जो शक्ति अथवा अनियमित विधि से सत्ता हथियाकर निरंकुश होकर शासन करता है ▸ **dictatorial** *adj* तानाशाह की भाँति **dictatorship** *noun* तानाशाही।

diction / 'डिक्शन् / *noun* बोलने की शैली; बोलने या लिखने में शब्दों का चयन एवं प्रयोग।

dictionary / 'डिक्शनरि / *noun* (*pl* **dictionaries**) शब्दकोश।

die[1] / डाइ / *verb* (*pt, pp* **died**; *pres p* **dying**) 1 मरना, जीवन समाप्त हो जाना :

die of cancer/hunger 2 अस्तित्व समाप्त हो जाना, लुप्त हो जाना : *dying traditions/customs* ■ **be dying for sth/to do sth** *(अनौप)* उत्कट अभिलाषा रखना, लालसा रखना।

die² / डाइ / *noun* लकड़ी का या धातु का साँचा या ठप्पा, डाइ ▸ **die** *noun (प्रा)* = **dice** ■ **the die is cast** निर्णय ले लिया गया है और बदला नहीं जा सकता।

diesel / डीज़ल / *noun* 1 (**diesel engine** भी) डीज़ल इंजिन; भारी तेल (न कि पेट्रोल) से चलने वाला इंजिन 2 (**diesel fuel, diesel oil** भी) एक भारी खनिज तेल।

diet / डाइअट् / *noun* 1 पथ्य (डाक्टर द्वारा बताया भोजन) 2 सामान्य भोजन, आहार : *eat a balanced diet* ▸ **diet** *verb* (वज़न कम करने के लिए) पथ्य पर रहना **dietary** *adj* **dieter** *noun* **dietician** *noun*.

differ / डिफ़र् / *verb* 1 **differ (from sb/ sth)** भिन्न/अलग होना 2 **differ (with/ from sb) (about/on/over sth)** मतभेद रखना : *We differ over many things.*

difference / डिफ़रन्स् / *noun* 1 **difference (in sth) (between A and B)** अंतर 2 **difference (between A and B)** असमानता, भिन्नता 3 **difference (between A and B) (over sth)** झगड़ा, मनमुटाव।

different / डिफ़रन्ट् / *adj* 1 **different (from/to sb/sth)** भिन्न, अलग 2 विभिन्न प्रकार का 3 असामान्य; नया : *The flavour was really different.*

differentiate / डिफ़ रेन्शिएट् / *verb* 1 **differentiate between A and B** भेद दिखाना 2 **differentiate sth (from sth)** अंतर स्पष्ट करना : *Can you differenti- ate between the two varieties?* 3 **differentiate between A and B** व्यक्तियों में अनुचित अंतर करना, भिन्न व्यवहार करना : *It is wrong to differ- entiate between people according*

to their family background. ▸ **dif- ferentiation** *noun*.

difficult / डिफ़िकल्ट् / *adj* 1 **difficult (to do sth)** (समस्या, कार्य आदि) कठिन, मुश्किल 2 कठिनाई, मुश्किलें पैदा करने वाला 3 (व्यक्ति) सहयोग न देने वाला; मुश्किल से प्रसन्न होने वाला : *a difficult child/boss.*

difficulty / डिफ़िकल्टि / *noun (pl difficulties)* 1 (प्राय: pl) कठिन समस्या, गूढ़ : *the difficulties of English syn- tax* 2 **difficulty (in sth/doing sth)** कठिनाई; (किसी कार्य में आई) बाधा या अड़चन : *do sth with/without diffi- culty.*

diffident / डिफ़िडन्ट् / *adj* **diffident (about sth)** आत्मविश्वास न रखने वाला ▸ **diffidence** *noun* आत्मविश्वास की कमी **diffidently** *adv*.

diffuse¹ / डि'फ़्यूज़् / *verb* 1 (चारों ओर) फैलाना, बिखेरना : *On a cloudy day, sunlight is diffused and shadows are paler.* 2 (तक) (गैसों या द्रवों का) धीरे-धीरे अन्य वस्तुओं में मिल जाना : *The milk diffused in the water, making it cloudy.* ▸ **diffusion** / डि'फ़्यूश्न् / *noun* फैलाव, विस्तार।

diffuse² / डि'फ़्यूस् / *adj* 1 विकीर्ण, चारों ओर फैला हुआ : *diffuse light* 2 बहुत अधिक शब्दों का प्रयोग करने वाली कथन शैली, समझने में मुश्किल ▸ **diffusely** *adv* **diffuseness** *noun*.

dig / डिग् / *verb* (**-gg-**; *pt, pp* **dug** / डग् /) 1 खोदना, गड्ढा करना; फावड़े से खोदना : *dig a pit/tunnel/shaft* 2 **dig for sth** खोदकर कुछ ढूँढ निकालना : *dig for mineral deposits* ■ **dig sb/sth out (of sth)** 1 खोदकर बाहर निकालना 2 ढूँढकर, पढ़कर खोज निकालना : *dig out the truth* ▸ **dig** *noun* 1 अँगुली से कोंचना, घोंपना : *give sb a dig in the ribs* 2 किसी को चिढ़ाने या गुस्सा दिलाने

वाली टिप्पणी 3 पुरातात्विक उद्देश्य से की गई खुदाई।

digest¹ / डाइ'जेस्ट्; डि'जेस्ट् / verb 1 (आहार का) पाचन, पचाना : *Some foods take longer to digest.* 2 मन में रखना, आत्मसात करना : *Have you digested the report yet?* ▶ **digestible** adj सुपाच्य, सुग्राह्य।

digest² / डाइजेस्ट् / noun (समाचार आदि का) सारांश।

digestion / डाइ'जेस्चन्; डि'जेस्चन् / noun पाचनक्रिया; पाचनशक्ति ▶ **digestive** adj पाचन-संबंधी।

digit / 'डिजिट् / noun 1 (गणित) 0 से 9 तक के अंक 2 (हाथ या पैर की) अँगुलियाँ ▶ **digital** adj 1 अंकों द्वारा संख्या/मात्रा व्यक्त करना 2 अँगुलियों संबंधी।

dignify / 'डिग्निफाइ / verb (pt, pp dignified) (औप) 1 सम्मानित करना, प्रतिष्ठा-युक्त करना : *The ceremony was dignified by the presence of the ambassador.* 2 (किसी ऐसे व्यक्ति/वस्तु को जो इस योग्य भी नहीं है) सम्मानित नाम देना, प्रतिष्ठित नामकरण करना ▶ **dignified** adj प्रतिष्ठा/मान-मर्यादा-पूर्ण।

dignitary / 'डिग्निटरि; US 'डिग्निटेरि / noun (pl dignitaries) (औप) उच्च पद पर प्रतिष्ठित व्यक्ति।

dignity / 'डिग्नटि / noun 1 शांत और गंभीर आचरण 2 सच्ची योग्यता, प्रतिष्ठा एवं मान-मर्यादा 3 (औप) उच्चपद।

digress / डाइ'ग्रेस् / verb **digress (from sth)** (बोलने या लिखने में) अपने विषय से हट जाना, विषयांतर होना ▶ **digression** noun विषयांतर।

dilapidated / डि'लैपिडेटिड् / adj (भवन, फर्नीचर आदि) टूटी-फूटी अवस्था में ▶ **dilapidation** / डि‚लैपि'डेश्न् / noun जीर्ण-शीर्ण स्थिति।

dilate / डाइ'लेट् / verb विस्तृत करना, फैलाना (जैसे नथुने या आँखें) : *The*

pupils of your eyes dilate when you enter a dark room.

dilemma / डि'लेमा; डाइ'लेमा / noun दुविधा/असमंजस की स्थिति; धर्मसंकट : *a moral/ethical dilemma.*

diligence / 'डिलिजन्स् / noun सतत परिश्रम।

diligent / 'डिलिजन्ट् / adj परिश्रमी, सावधानी और प्रयत्न से कार्य करने वाला।

dilly-dally / 'डिलि डैलि / verb (pt, pp dilly-dallied) (अनौप) हिचकिचाना; आगा-पीछा करना।

dilute / डाइ'ल्यूट्; डाइ'लूट् / verb 1 **dilute sth (with sth)** (पानी या कोई अन्य द्रव मिलाकर) किसी द्रव या रंग को पतला या हलका करना : *Dilute the wine (with a little water).* 2 किसी चीज़ की शक्ति या प्रभाव कम करना ▶ **dilute** adj तनु : *dilute sulphuric acid* **dilution** noun पतला, हलका या फीका करना या होना।

dim / डिम् / adj (-mmer, -mmest) 1 (प्रकाश या वस्तु) धुँधला, अस्पष्ट 2 (स्थान) जहाँ अच्छी तरह दिखाई न दे : *a dim corridor with no windows* 3 (आँखें) अच्छी तरह देख पाने में असमर्थ 4 (याददाश्त) कमज़ोर, धुँधली पड़ गई : *a dim memory/recollection* 5 (अनौप) (व्यक्ति) मूर्ख ▶ **dim** verb (-mm-) धुँधला या अस्पष्ट कर देना **dimly** adv **dimness** noun.

dime / डाइम् / noun दस सेंट के बराबर का अमेरिका और कनाडा में प्रचलित सिक्का।

dimension / डाइ'मेन्श्न्, डि'मेन्श्न् / noun 1 लंबाई, क्षेत्र आदि का मापन, आयाम 2 **dimensions** [pl] परिमाण, लंबाई-चौड़ाई 3 किसी परिस्थिति, समस्या आदि का पहलू : *There is a further dimension to this issue.* ▶ **-dimensional** suff (प्रत्यय): *two-dimensional, three-dimensional.*

diminish / डि'मिनिश् / verb 1 कम करना या होना : *His strength had dimin-*

ished over the years. **2** किसी व्यक्ति/ वस्तु का महत्त्व घटाना : *The opposition is trying to diminish our achievements.*

diminutive / डि'मिन्यटिव़् / *adj* अत्यंत या असामान्य रूप से छोटा ▸ **diminutive** *noun* **1** ऐसा शब्द या शब्द का अंतिम अक्षर जिससे वस्तु के छोटे होने का पता लगता है **2** शब्द, विशेषतः नाम, का लघु रूप : *'Jo' is a diminutive of 'Joanna'.*

dimple / 'डिम्प्ल् / *noun* (किसी के मुसकुराते समय) गाल या तुड्डी पर बने गड्ढे ▸ **dimpled** *adj.*

din / डिन् / *noun* [sing] शोरगुल ▸ **din** *verb* (-nn-) ■ **din sth into sb/sth** ज़ोर-ज़ोर से दुहराकर किसी को कुछ समझाना : *These rules were dinned into me/my head when I was at school.*

dine / डाइन् / *verb* **dine (on sth)** भोजन (विशेषतः दिन का मुख्य भोजन) करना ▸ **dining-room** *noun* भोजन-कक्ष।

dinghy / 'डिंडि; डिंडगि / *noun* छोटी खुली नाव, डोंगी; हवा-भरी रबर की नाव।

dingy / 'डिन्जि / *adj* (-ier, -iest) (स्थान) गंदा एवं अंधेरा, मैला-कुचैला : *a dingy room in a cheap hotel* ▸ **dinginess** *noun.*

dinner / 'डिनर् / *noun* **1** दिन का मुख्य भोजन (दोपहर या शाम को) **2** बड़ा सामाजिक भोज; रात्रिभोज।

dinosaur / 'डाइनसॉर् / *noun* **1** एक विशालकाय जानवर, अब विलुप्त **2** (*अपमा*) पुरातनपंथी एवं अपरिवर्तनशील व्यक्ति या वस्तु।

dint / डिन्ट् / *noun* ■ **by dint of sth** की शक्ति से; के द्वारा : *He succeeded by dint of hard work.*

dip / डिप् / *verb* (-pp-) **1 dip sth (into sth); dip sth (in)** डुबोना, द्रव में रखना : *Dip your pen into the ink.* **2** तल या स्तर के नीचे जाना : *Profits dipped again this year.* **3** भूमि का ढालू होना

▸ **dip** *noun* **1** (*अनौप*) डुबकी; समुद्र आदि में स्नान : *have/take/go for a dip* **2** ढाल (जैसे सड़क का) : *a dip in the road.*

diphtheria / डिफ़्'थ्रिअरिआ / *noun* गले की एक गंभीर बीमारी जिसके कारण साँस लेने में तकलीफ़ होती है।

diphthong / 'डिफ़्थॉङ् / *noun* दो स्वर ध्वनियों का एक स्वर ध्वनि बनना, जैसे **pipe** / paɪp (पाइप) / में / aɪ (आइ) / ध्वनि।

diploma / डि'प्लोमा / *noun* डिप्लोमा, शैक्षिक प्रमाण-पत्र।

diplomacy / डि'प्लोमसि / *noun* **1** राज-नय, अंतर्राष्ट्रीय कूटनीति **2** व्यवहार कौशल।

diplomat / 'डिप्लमैट् / *noun* राजनयिक (व्यक्ति); व्यवहार कुशल व्यक्ति ▸ **diplomatic** / ¸डिप्ल'मैटिक् / *adj* **1** कूटनीतिक **2** व्यवहार कुशल : *be diplomatic in dealing with people* **diplomatically** *adv.*

dire / 'डाइअर् / *adj* **1** (*औप*) भयानक, भयंकर **2** (*अनौप*) अत्यंत : *We are in dire need of your help.*

direct¹ / ड'रेक्ट्; डि'रेक्ट्; डाइ'रेक्ट् / *adj* **1** सीधे, बिना मुड़े; ऋजु, बिना मोड़ और घुमाव के : *follow a direct course/ route* **2** सीधा, स्पष्ट; सरल रीति से **3** (पारिवारिक रिश्ता) माता-पिता से सीधा संतान को **4** पूर्ण, बिलकुल ▸ **direct** *adv* **1** सीधा रास्ता तय करके, बिना यात्रा का क्रम भंग किए **2** बिना किसी अन्य के बीच में रहे; व्यक्तिगत रूप से **direct current** *noun* विद्युत की दिष्ट धारा **directly** *adv* **1** सीधी दिशा में या सीधे तरीक़े से **2** एकदम, तुरंत; जल्दी ही **directly** *conj* ज्यों ही **direct-ness** *noun* **direct speech** *noun* साक्षात् कथन, वक्ता द्वारा कहे हुए शब्द।

direct² / ड'रेक्ट्; डि'रेक्ट्; डाइ'रेक्ट् / *verb* **1** (फ़िल्म आदि) निर्देशित करना, निर्देश देना : *She directed the planning of the festival.* **2 direct sb (to...)** मार्गदर्शन करना **3 direct sth at/to sb** (*औप*)

किसी का ध्यान किसी ओर आकर्षित करना 4 direct sth to... (औप) पत्र में पता लिखना 5 (औप) किसी व्यक्ति को टिप्पणी आदि बोलकर या लिखकर देना; आदेश देना।

direction / ड'रेक्शन; डि'रेक्शन; डाइ 'रेक्शन / noun 1 गति-दिशा; (गति में) लक्ष्यबिंदु 2 मार्गदर्शन या प्रबंध 3 (प्राय:pl) निर्देश, आदेश ▸ **directional** adj.

director / ड'रेक्टर, डि'रेक्टर, डाइ'रेक्टर / noun 1 निदेशक, निर्देशक (व्यक्ति) 2 व्यापारिक कंपनी के प्रबंधकों में से एक : the managing director 3 फ़िल्म या नाटक का निर्देशक ▸ **directorial** adj.

directory / ड'रेक्टरि; डि'रेक्टरि; डाइ 'रेक्टरि/ noun (pl **directories**) सामान्यत: वर्ण क्रम में नामों (और प्राय: पतों) की सूची : a telephone directory.

dirt / डर्ट / noun 1 मैल, गंदगी 2 धूल 3 (अनौप) नीचतापूर्ण और गंदी बात 4 (अनौप) टट्टी।

dirty¹ / 'डर्टि / adj (-ier, -iest) 1 मैला, गंदा 2 (मौसम) तूफ़ानी और अप्रिय 3 (अनौप) बोलचाल और विचारों में नीच, घृणित; बेईमान : That's a dirty lie!

dirty² / डर्टि / verb (pt, pp **dirtied**) गंदा होना या करना।

disability / डिस'बिलटि / noun (pl **disabilities**) 1 शारीरिक असमर्थता, विकलांगता 2 असमर्थ बनाने वाली चीज़ या गुण-धर्म; किसी आवश्यक वस्तु की कमी आदि : disabilities of sight, hearing and speech.

disable / डिस'एब्ल / verb 1 अयोग्य या बेकार कर देना (विशेषत: हाथ-पाँव के प्रयोग में) : He was disabled after a car accident. 2 disable sb/sth (from sth/doing sth) किसी को कुछ करने या ठीक तरह से करने में असमर्थ बना देना : This choice disables you from pursuing a career in medicine. ▸ **disabled** adj विकलांग, बेकार the disabled noun विकलांग व्यक्ति।

disadvantage / डिसड् 'व्रान्टिज; US डिसड् 'वैन्टिज् / noun प्रतिकूल अवस्था, सफलता या उन्नति में बाधक ▸ **disadvantaged** adj **disadvantageous** / डिसैड्वैन् 'टेजस / adj अहितकर : in a disadvantageous position.

disaffected / डिस'फ़ेक्टिड् / adj अपनी स्थिति, मित्रों आदि से) असंतुष्ट और इसलिए अनिष्ठावान ▸ **disaffection** noun.

disagree / डिस'ग्री / verb 1 disagree (with sth) मेल न रखना, असहमति होना 2 disagree (with sb/sth) (about/on/ over sth) दूसरा दृष्टिकोण रखना; हलका-सा विवाद होना ■ disagree with sb (मौसम, भोजन आदि) अनुपयुक्त या प्रतिकूल होना।

disagreeable / डिस'ग्रीअब्ल / adj अप्रिय; झगड़ालू ▸ **disagreeably** adv.

disagreement / डिस'ग्रीमन्ट् / noun 1 disagreement (about/on/over sth) मतभेद 2 वाद-विवाद; झगड़ा : a silly disagreement with our neighbours.

disappear / डिस'पिअर/ verb 1 अदृश्य हो जाना : The plane disappeared behind a cloud. 2 लुप्त हो जाना 3 खो जाना या मिल न पाना ▸ **disappearance** noun.

disappoint / डिस'पॉइन्ट् / verb 1 आशा, रुचि या अपेक्षा के अनुसार कुछ होने में/करने में असफल रहना : His decision to cancel the concert will disappoint his fans. 2 निराश होना : My expectations were not disappointed. ▸ **disappointed** adj **disappointed (by/ about/at sth); disappointed (with sb/sth)** adj निराश, हताश **disappointing** adj निराश करने वाली वस्तु।

disappointment / डिस'पॉइन्ट्मन्ट् / noun 1 निराश 2 disappointment (to sb) निराश करने वाला व्यक्ति या वस्तु।

disapprove / डिस'प्रूव् / verb **disapprove (of sb/sth)** किसी व्यक्ति/वस्तु को

बुरा, ग़लत या मूर्ख समझना ▸ **disapproval** *noun* **disapproving** *adj* : *a disapproving look/frown* **disapprovingly** *adv.*

disarm / डिस्'आर्म् / *verb* 1 निरस्त्र करना, अस्त्रहीन करना : *Most of the rebels were captured and disarmed.* 2 (देश की) सैनिक शक्ति कम करना 3 ऐसा करना कि व्यक्ति का क्रोध या संदेह कम हो जाए ▸ **disarmament** / डिस्'आर्ममन्ट् / *noun* निरस्त्रीकरण : *nuclear disarmament.*

disarray / डिस'रे / *noun* वस्तुओं या व्यक्तियों की घोर अव्यवस्था की दशा : *With three teachers off sick the timetable has been thrown into complete disarray.*

disaster / डि'ज़ास्टर; US डि'ज़ैस्टर / *noun* 1 बहुत बुरी दुर्घटना : *Thousands died in the disaster.* 2 आफ़त, घोर संकट 3 (अनौप) पूर्णतः असफल व्यक्ति या वस्तु : *As a teacher, he's a disaster.* ▸ **disastrous** / डि'ज़ास्ट्रस; US डि'ज़ैस्ट्रस / *adj* संकटजनक **disastrously** *adv.*

disband / डिस्'बैन्ड् / *verb* (सेना को) विसंघटित कर देना, सेना की टुकड़ी को भंग कर देना : *The regiment (was) disbanded soon after the war.*

disbelieve / डिस्बि'लीव् / *verb* 1 विश्वास न करना : *He says it's true, and I have no reason to disbelieve him.* 2 **disbelieve in sth** अस्तित्व में विश्वास न करना, श्रद्धा न रखना ▸ **disbelief** *noun* अविश्वास; शंका।

disc (विशेषतः US **disk** भी) / डिस्क् / *noun* 1 पतली गोल चपटी वस्तु; गोल सतह जो चपटी प्रतीत होती है : *the moon's disc* 2 रिकॉर्ड डिस्क : *recordings on disc and cassette* 3 रीढ़ की हड्डियों के बीच की कोमलास्थि : *a slipped disc* ▸ **disc jockey** *noun* (संक्षि **DJ**) (रेडियो या टी वी पर) लोकप्रिय संगीत बजाने एवं संगीत के बारे में बात करने वाला व्यक्ति।

discard / डिस्'कार्ड / *verb* 1 (बेकार समझ कर) फेंक देना, अलग कर देना 2 (वस्तु) प्रयोग करना बंद कर देना : *discard one's winter clothes in spring* ० (अलं) *discard outdated beliefs.*

discern / डि'सर्न् / *verb* (औप) 1 जानना, मालूम करना : *discern sb's true intentions* 2 प्रयत्न करके ही देख या पहचान पाना : *In the gloom I could just discern the outline of a building.* ▸ **discerning** *adj* विवेकशील **discernment** *noun* पहचान, विवेक।

discharge / डिस्'चार्ज् / *verb* 1 (कर्तव्यपूर्ति के बाद) जाने की अनुमति देना; छुट्टी देना : *discharge a patient from hospital* 2 (जेल से) मुक्त करना; (सेवा से) हटा देना 3 (औप) ऋण चुका देना; कर्तव्य पालन करना : *She discharged her responsibility with great efficiency.* 4 (किसी द्रव, गैस या धारा को) छोड़ना या निकालना 5 (बंदूक) दाग़ना; (तीर) छोड़ना ▸ **discharge** / 'डिस्चार्ज् / *noun* 1 सेवानिवृत्ति 2 छोड़ा/निकाला हुआ पदार्थ (द्रव, गैस आदि)।

disciple / डि'साइप्ल् / *noun* 1 (किसी मत का) अनुयायी; (किसी धार्मिक संप्रदाय का) चेला, शिष्य 2 ईसा के बारह घनिष्ठ अनुयायियों में से कोई एक।

discipline / 'डिसिप्लिन् / *noun* 1 मन या स्वभाव पर नियंत्रण 2 आत्मसंयम, भद्र व्यवहार 3 अनुशासन 4 ज्ञान-विज्ञान की शाखा; विषय : *scientific disciplines* ▸ **disciplinary** / 'डिसिप्लिनरि; US 'डिसप्लेनेरि / *adj* अनुशासनात्मक **discipline** *verb* 1 अनुशासन में रहना/करना; आत्मनियंत्रण करना 2 किसी को दंड देना **disciplined** *adj* अनुशासित।

disclaim / डिस्'क्लेम् / *verb* किसी कार्य को करने या वस्तु आदि रखने से इनकार

करना : *They disclaimed all responsibility for the explosion.* ▸ **disclaimer** noun परित्याग, अस्वीकरण।

disclose / डिस्'क्लोज़् / verb **disclose sth (to sb)** (औप) 1 प्रकट करना : *refuse to disclose one's name and address* 2 कुछ देखने देना ▸ **disclosure** / डिस्'क्लोश्र / noun प्रकट करने की क्रिया; प्रकट की गई बात (रहस्य आदि) : *startling disclosures about the minister's life.*

disco / 'डिस्को / (pl discos) (**discotheque** / 'डिस्कटेक् / भी) noun डिस्को।

discolour (US **discolor**)/ डिस्'कलर् / verb 1 रंग बिगाड़ना 2 धब्बे पड़ना, रंग बदलना या फीका पड़ना : *Smoking discolours the teeth.* ▸ **discolouration** noun.

discomfort / डिस्'कम्फ़र्ट् / noun 1 आराम की कमी, असुविधा; थोड़ा कष्ट 2 असुविधा पैदा करने वाली वस्तु : *the discomforts of travel* 3 थोड़ी चिंता या शर्म : *His presence caused her considerable discomfort.* ▸ **discomfort** verb असुविधा/चिंता पैदा करना।

disconcert / ‚डिस्कन्'सर्ट् / verb 1 (किसी की योजना आदि को) गड़बड़ा देना 2 चित्त को क्षुब्ध कर देना : *He was disconcerted to find other guests formally dressed.* ▸ **disconcerting** adj **disconcertingly** adv.

disconnect / ‚डिस्क'नेक्ट् / verb **disconnect A (from B)** अलग कर देना; संबंध तोड़ देना : *disconnect a TV from power supply* ▸ **disconnected** adj (भाषण अथवा लेख) असंबद्ध : *the disconnected ramblings of an old man.*

disconsolate / डिस्'कॉन्सलट् / adj निराश, मायूस, उदास ▸ **disconsolately** adv.

discontent / ‚डिस्कन्'टेन्ट् / (**discon-**

tentment / डिस्कन्'टेन्ट्मन्ट् / भी) noun

discontent (with sth) असंतुष्टि : *The strikes are a sign of growing discontent (with government policies).* ▸ **discontented** adj **discontented (with sth)** असंतुष्टि **discontentedly** adv.

discontinue / ‚डिस्कन्'टिन्यू / verb (औप) (नियमित पूर्ति आदि) बंद कर देना; छोड़ देना ▸ **discontinuity** noun **discontinuous** adj अनियमित।

discord / 'डिस्कॉर्ड् / noun (औप) 1 असहमति; अनबन या झगड़ा : *A note of discord crept into their relationship.* 2 (संगीत) बेसुरी ध्वनि ▸ **discordant** / डिस्'कॉर्डन्ट् / adj 1 असहमत, बेमेल : *discordant views* 2 बेसुरी, कर्कश ध्वनि।

discount¹ / 'डिस्काउन्ट् / noun (दाम में) छूट, कटौती; (ब्याज में) मिती-काटा : *The shop was selling everything off at a discount.*

discount² / डिस्'काउन्ट् / verb 1 छूट देना, कटौती करना 2 किसी चीज़ को महत्त्वहीन या असत्य मानना।

discourage / डिस्'करिज् / verb 1 **discourage sb (from doing sth)** हतोत्साहित करना, उत्साह भंग करना 2 (बाधा डालकर या नकारात्मक रुख़ अपनाकर) किसी को कुछ करने से रोकना : *Parents should discourage smoking.* ▸ **discouraged** adj हतोत्साहित **discouragement** noun.

discourse / 'डिस्कॉर्स् / noun 1 (औप) भाषण, प्रवचन आदि 2 (भाषा विज्ञान) लिखित या बोली जाने वाली भाषा : *analyse the structure of discourse* ▸ **discourse** / डिस्'कॉर्स् / verb **discourse on/upon sth** (औप) भाषण या प्रवचन करना; किसी विषय पर विस्तार से बोलना या लिखना।

discourteous / डिस्'कर्टिअस् / adj

(औप) अभद्र, अशिष्ट ▸ **discourte-ously** *adv* **discourtesy** *noun* अभद्रता, अशिष्टता।

discover / डिं'स्कव़र् / *verb* 1 पहली बार/ कुछ नया खोज निकालना (स्थान, वस्तु आदि) : *Columbus discovered America.* 2 (कोई बात) पता लगाना : *He was later discovered to have been a spy.* 3 किसी (व्यक्ति के) गुण, प्रतिभा आदि का पता लगना/लगाना : *Who discovered Marilyn Monroe?* ▸ **discoverer** *noun.*

discovery / डिं'स्कव़रि / *noun (pl* **discoveries)** 1 खोज : *an acciden-tal/unexpected discovery* 2 खोजी गई वस्तु या व्यक्ति।

discredit / डिस्'क्रेडिट् / *verb* 1 किसी वस्तु के मूल्य या व्यक्ति की साख में संदेह उत्पन्न कर देना; किसी का सम्मान गिरा देना : *an attempt to discredit the President* 2 अविश्वास उत्पन्न कर देना; विश्वास करने से मना करना : *His theories were largely discredited by other scientists.* ▸ **discredit** *noun* साख/सम्मान की क्षति **discreditable** *adj.*

discreet / डिं'स्क्रीट् / *adj* (बातचीत करने में) सावधान और सतर्क; विवेकशील ▸ **dis-creetly** *adv* सावधानी से : *I saw him glance discreetly at his watch.*

discrepancy / डिस्'क्रे़पन्सि / *noun (pl* **discrepancies) discrepancy (in sth/ between A and B)** (विवरण, हिसाब आदि में) अंतर; (कथन में) असंगति : *There were many serious discrep-ancies between the witnesses' ac-counts.*

discretion / डिं'स्क्रे़शन् / *noun* 1 विवेक, सूझ-बूझ : *She acted with consider-able discretion.* 2 अपने आप निर्णय लेने की स्वतंत्रता ▸ **discretionary** *adj.*

discriminate / डिं'स्क्रिमिनेट् / *verb* 1 **discriminate (between A and B)**

भेदभाव करना या रखना 2 भेद करना, अंतर करना 3 **discriminate (against sb/in favour of sb)** भेदभावपूर्ण व्यवहार करना : *Society still discriminates against women.* ▸ **discriminating** *adj* **discrimination** / डिं,स्क्रिमि'नेशन् / *noun* 1 **discrimination (against/in favour of sb)** 1 भेदभावपूर्ण व्यवहार 2 अच्छी निर्णय शक्ति : *show discrimi-nation in one's choice of friends.* 3 *(औप)* अंतर करने की योग्यता; अंतर **discriminatory** *adj.*

discus / 'डिस्कस् / *noun* डिस्कस, खेल के तौर पर प्रयुक्त डिस्क (चक्का); **the discus** चक्का फेंकने का खेल।

discuss / डिं'स्कस् / *verb* **discuss sth (with sb)** (किसी समस्या आदि पर) विचार-विमर्श करना : *discuss the im-plication/merits of sth* ▸ **discus-sion** / डिं'स्कशन् / *noun* विचार-विमर्श की प्रक्रिया; वाद-विवाद।

disdain / डिस्'डेन् / *noun* **disdain (for sb/sth)** तिरस्कार, घृणा ▸ **disdain** *verb (औप)* तिरस्कार (से देखना), घृणा करना : *He disdains to sit with people like us.* **disdainful** *adj* **disdainfully** *adv.*

disease / डिं'ज़ीज़् / *noun* (शरीर, मन, पौधों आदि का) रोग, बीमारी; बीमारी का प्रकार या दशा : *serious/infectious/ curable diseases* ▸ **diseased** *adj* बीमार; रुग्ण : *(अलं) diseased society.*

disembark / ,डिसिम्'बार्क् / *verb* 1 **disembark (from sth)** (लोगों का) जहाज़ या वायुयान से उतरना : *Passen-gers may disembark (from the plane) by the front or rear doors.* 2 **disembark sb/sth (from sth)** व्यक्तियों या वस्तुओं को जहाज़ अथवा वायुयान से उतारना/उतरने को कहना ▸ **dis-embarkation** *noun.*

disenchanted / ,डिसिन्'चान्टिड्; *US* डिसिन् 'चैन्टिड् / *adj* **disenchanted**

(with sb/sth) किसी व्यक्ति या वस्तु के बारे में अपनी अच्छी धारणा खो देना : *disenchanted Communists* ▸ **disenchantment** *noun*.

disengage / ˌडिसिन्'गेज् / *verb* 1 **disengage sth/sb (from sth/sb)** *(औप)* किसी व्यक्ति या वस्तु को किसी की पकड़ से मुक्त करना, छुड़ाना : *disengage the clutch* 2 **disengage (sb/sth) (from sth)** *(सेना)* युद्ध रोक देना/रुकवा देना : *We must disengage our troops.* ▸ **disengagement** *noun*.

disentangle / ˌडिसिन्'टैङ्ग्ल / *verb* 1 **disentangle sth/sb (from sth)** किसी लिपटी हुई वस्तु से व्यक्ति या वस्तु को मुक्त करना/कराना : *He tried to disentangle himself (from the bushes into which he had fallen).* 2 ऊन, बाल, धागों आदि की गाँठें सुलझाना।

disfigure / डिस्'फ़िगर् / *verb* आकार या आकृति बिगाड़ना : *The accident disfigured him for life.* ▸ **disfigurement** *noun* कुरूपता, विकृति : *She suffered permanent physical disfigurement.*

disgorge / डिस्'गॉर्ज् / *verb* बहुत बड़ी मात्रा में वस्तुओं या व्यक्तियों को बाहर निकालना : *The pipe is disgorging sewage (into the river).*

disgrace / डिस्'ग्रेस् / *noun* 1 बदनामी, सार्वजनिक कलंक; उच्च पद/प्रतिष्ठा से गिरने की अवस्था : *His behaviour has brought disgrace on himself.* 2 **a disgrace (to sb/sth)** बदनामी लाने वाला व्यक्ति या वस्तु : *Corrupt lawyers are a disgrace to the legal profession.* ▸ **disgrace** *verb* 1 बदनामी करना या लाना 2 **be disgraced** कलंकित होना; कलंक लगाकर पद से हटाया जाना **disgraceful** *adj*.

disgruntled / डिस्'ग्रन्ट्ल्ड् / *adj* **disgruntled (at/about sth); disgrun-**

tled (with sb) नाराज़, असंतुष्ट : *a disgruntled look.*

disguise / डिस्'गाइज़् / *verb* 1 **disguise sb/sth (with sth); disguise sb/sth (as sb/sth)** धोखा देने के लिए वेशभूषा (या शकल) में परिवर्तन करना : *The thieves disguised themselves as security guards.* 2 अपना वास्तविक उद्देश्य या भाव छिपाना ▸ **disguise** *noun* 1 छद्मवेश : *grow a beard as a disguise* 2 छद्मवेश धारण की कला।

disgust / डिस्'गस्ट् / *noun* **disgust (at sth); disgust (for/with sb)** जुगुप्सा, प्रबल अनिच्छा ▸ **disgust** *verb* जुगुप्सा उत्पन्न करना **disgusted** *adj* **disgusting** *adj* घृणाजनक।

dish¹ / डिश् / *noun* 1 डिश, रकाबी 2 **the dishes** *[pl]* प्लेट, प्याले आदि जिनमें भोजन परोसा जाता है 3 **(dishful** भी) डिश में परोसा हुआ भोजन 4 खाने के लिए विशिष्ट प्रकार से तैयार व्यंजन : *a restaurant specializing in vegetarian dishes* 5 कोई भी रकाबी की आकृति की वस्तु।

dish² / डिश् / *verb* ■ **dish sth out** 1 *(अनौप)* रकाबी में भोजन परोसना 2 कोई वस्तु किसी को अत्यधिक मात्रा में देना : *dish out compliments/abuse.*

dishearten / डिस्'हार्ट्न् / *verb* हताश होना या करना ▸ **disheartened** *adj* हताश **disheartening** *adj* हताश करने वाला : *disheartening news.*

dishevelled *(US* **disheveled)** / डि'शेव्ल्ड् / *adj* (कपड़े, बाल, शकल) अस्त-व्यस्त, बिखरे हुए।

dishonest / डिस्'ऑनिस्ट् / *adj* 1 बेईमान, धोखेबाज़ व्यक्ति : *a dishonest trader/partner* 2 (पैसा) बेईमानी से कमाया हुआ ▸ **dishonestly** *adv* **dishonesty** *noun* बेईमानी।

dishonour *(US* **dishonor)** / डिस्'ऑनर् / *noun* *(औप)* बदनामी, कलंक : *bring dishonour on one's family/*

regiment ▸ **dishonour** *verb* (औप) कलंक या बदनामी लाना **dishonourable** *adj* बदनाम, कलंकित **dishonourably** *adv.*

disillusion /ˌdɪsɪˈluːʃn/ *verb* मिथ्या मोह से छूट जाना; भ्रम दूर हो जाना ▸ **disillusioned** *adj* **disillusioned (with sb/sth)** किसी व्यक्ति/वस्तु पर विश्वास टूट जाने के कारण निराशाग्रस्त : *She's disillusioned with life in general.* **disillusionment** *noun.*

disinclined /ˌdɪsɪnˈklaɪnd/ *adj* **disinclined (to do sth)** अनिच्छुक : *I am disinclined to believe his story.* ▸ **disinclination** /ˌdɪsˌɪnklɪˈneɪʃn/ *noun* **disinclination (to do sth)** (औप) अनिच्छा, अरुचि : *a strong disinclination to travel at night.*

disinfect /ˌdɪsɪnˈfekt/ *verb* रोगाणुओं से मुक्त करना/होना : *disinfect a wound* ▸ **disinfectant** *noun* रोगाणुरोधक पदार्थ : *a strong smell of disinfectant.*

disinherit /ˌdɪsɪnˈherɪt/ *verb* उत्तराधिकार से वंचित करना : *He disinherited his eldest son.*

disintegrate / dɪsˈɪntɪgreɪt / *verb* 1 विघटित करना या होना : *The plane flew into a mountain and disintegrated on impact.* 2 कम शक्तिशाली होना या एकता खोना : *The family is starting to disintegrate.* ▸ **disintegration** *noun* विघटन, टुकड़े-टुकड़े होना।

disinterest / dɪsˈɪntrəst / *noun* अरुचि, अनिच्छा ▸ **disinterested** / dɪsˈɪntrɪstɪd / *adj* 1 अपनी भावनाओं और रुचियों से प्रभावित हुए बिना : *a disinterested act of kindness* 2 (अनौप) निष्काम **disinterestedly** *adv.*

disjointed / dɪsˈdʒɔɪntɪd / *adj* (बातचीत या लेख) असंबद्ध और इस कारण समझने में मुश्किल : *The film was so*

disjointed that I couldn't tell you what the story was about. ▸ **disjointedly** *adv.*

disk / dɪsk / *noun* 1 (विशेषत: *US*) = **disc** 2 (**floppy disk** भी) गोलाकार प्लेट (चकती) जिस पर तथ्य और आँकड़े कंप्यूटर के प्रयोग के लिए रिकॉर्ड किए जा सकते हैं ▸ **disk drive** *noun* कंप्यूटर से डिस्क पर और डिस्क से कंप्यूटर पर तथ्य आदि प्रतिरोपित करने वाला उपकरण जो कंप्यूटर में लगा होता है **diskette** / dɪsˈket / *noun* =**floppy disk.**

dislike / dɪsˈlaɪk / *verb* नापसंद करना, अप्रिय समझना : *I like cats but dislike dogs.* ▸ **dislike** *noun* 1 **dislike (of/ for sb/sth)** नापसंदगी : *I have a strong dislike of modern music.* 2 (प्राय: *pl*) अप्रिय वस्तु : *likes and dislikes.*

dislocate / dɪsˈlokeɪt/ *verb* 1 (हड्डी का) अपने स्थान से हट जाना/हटा दिया जाना : *a dislocated shoulder* 2 (औप) (यातायात में या अन्य योजना में) व्यवस्था भंग होना : *Flights have been dislocated by the fog.* ▸ **dislocation** *noun.*

dislodge / dɪsˈlɒdʒ / *verb* **dislodge sb/sth (from sth)** (किसी को किसी स्थान से) बलपूर्वक हटा देना, निकाल देना : *The wind dislodged some tiles from the roof.*

disloyal / dɪsˈlɔɪəl / *adj* **disloyal (to sb/sth)** (संबद्ध सत्ता से) द्रोह करने वाला, नमकहराम : *disloyal to one's country* ▸ **disloyalty** *noun* नमक-हरामी।

dismal / ˈdɪzməl / *adj* 1 निराशाजनक; दुख-पूर्ण 2 (अनौप) प्रत्याशित से कम अच्छा : *The team gave a dismal performance.* ▸ **dismally** *adv.*

dismantle / dɪsˈmæntl / *verb* 1 (किसी मशीन या अन्य वस्तु के) पुर्ज़े खोल देना : *dismantle and repair a faulty mo-*

tor 2 क्रमिक एवं नियोजित तरीक़े के किसी संघ या तंत्र को समाप्त करना : *We should dismantle our inefficient tax system.* ▸ **dismantling** *noun.*

dismay / डिस्'मे / *noun* भय और उत्साहहीनता की भावना ▸ **dismay** *verb* भय और उत्साहहीनता से भर देना।

dismember / डिस्'मेम्बर् / *verb* 1 (व्यक्ति अथवा जानवर के) हाथ-पैर काट देना या उखाड़ देना : *The victim's dismembered body was found in a trunk.* 2 देश का विभाजन करना, टुकड़े कर देना ▸ **dismemberment** *noun.*

dismiss / डिस्'मिस् / *verb* 1 **dismiss sb (from sth)** (पद या नौकरी से) मुक्त करना; बरख़ास्त करना 2 **dismiss sth (from sth)** (मन से चिंता आदि) निकाल देना : *He tried to dismiss the suspicions from his mind.* 3 **dismiss sb/ sth (as sth)** किसी व्यक्ति या वस्तु को सोचने/बातचीत के लायक न समझना 4 (क़ानून) कोई मामला अस्वीकार/निरस्त करना : *The court dismissed his appeal.* ▸ **dismissal** / डिस्'मिसल् / *noun* बरख़ास्तगी; सेवामुक्ति **dismissive** *adj.*

dismount / डिस्'माउन्ट् / *verb* **dismount (from sth)** घोड़े, साइकिल आदि से उतरना : *He helped Sara dismount (from her pony).*

disobedient / ‚डिस्'बीडिअन्ट् / *adj* आज्ञा न मानने वाला; अवज्ञा करने वाला : *a disobedient child* ▸ **disobedience** *noun* **disobediently** *adv.*

disobey / ‚डिस्'बे / *verb* आज्ञा, आदेश आदि को न मानना।

disorder / डिस्'ऑर्डर् / *noun* 1 अव्यवस्था, गड़बड़ी 2 दंगा, उपद्रव 3 बीमारी, विकार ▸ **disordered** *adj* **disorderly** *adj* 1 अस्त-व्यस्त : *a disorderly heap of clothes* 2 (व्यक्ति अथवा व्यवहार) उपद्रवी;

अनियंत्रित : *a disorderly demonstration.*

disorganize, -ise / डिस्'ऑर्गनाइज़् / *verb* क्रम या व्यवस्था को बिगाड़ना, विसंगठित करना ▸ **disorganization, -isation** *noun* **disorganized, -ised** *adj* अव्यवस्थित।

disown / डिस्'ओन् / *verb* अपना मानने से इनकार करना; (किसी व्यक्ति से) संबंध तोड़ लेना।

disparage / डि'स्पैरिज् / *verb* (अनुचित रूप से) तुच्छ समझना, महत्त्वहीन मानना : *disparage sb's achievements/ character* ▸ **disparagement** *noun* **disaparaging** *adj* : *disparaging remarks/comments.*

disparate / 'डिस्परट् / *adj* (औप) (दो या अधिक वस्तुओं का) इतना अधिक भिन्न होना कि तुलना न की जा सके।

disparity / डि'स्पैरिटि / *noun* (*pl* **disparities**) असमानता, अत्यधिक विभिन्नता।

dispassionate / डिस्'पैशनट् / *adj* भावनाओं से अप्रभावित, निर्विकार; निष्पक्ष : *a dispassionate view/observer* ▸ **dispassionately** *adv.*

dispatch[1] (**despatch** भी) / डि'स्पैच् / *verb* 1 **dispatch sb/sth (to...)** (औप) (विशेष उद्देश्य से) किसी व्यक्ति/वस्तु को कहीं भेजना; पत्र या संदेश भेजना 2 (औप) किसी समस्या उत्पन्न करने वाले या ख़तरा बन जाने वाले व्यक्ति से निपटना।

dispatch[2] (**despatch** भी) / डि'स्पैच् / *noun* 1 (औप) भेजे जाने की क्रिया 2 तत्परता से भेजा हुआ आधिकारिक संदेश 3 समाचार-पत्र के लिए संवाददाता द्वारा भेजी गई विशेष रिपोर्ट।

dispel / डि'स्पेल् / *verb* (-ll-) भगा देना, (शंकाओं, बादलों आदि को) तितर-बितर कर देना : *dispel sb's doubts/fears/ worries.*

dispensable / डि'स्पेन्सबल् / *adj* अनावश्यक।

dispensary / डिस्पेन्सरि / noun (pl **dispensaries**) डिस्पेंसरी, दवाख़ाना।

dispensation / ‚डिस्पेन्'सेश्न् / noun 1 (औप) वितरण (की विधि) 2 किसी नियम या अपेक्षा को पूरा न कर पाने की अनुमति।

dispense / डि'स्पेन्स / verb 1 **dispense sth (to sb)** देना, वितरित करना : a machine dispensing paper towels 2 दवा तैयार करना और लोगों को देना ■ **dispense with sb/sth** किसी व्यक्ति/ वस्तु के बिना काम चला लेना; से मुक्ति पा लेना।

disperse / डि'स्पर्स् / verb छितरा देना, छिन्न-भिन्न कर देना : The wind dispersed the clouds. ▶ **dispersal** noun **dispersion** noun (औप) छितराने की प्रक्रिया।

dispirited / डि'स्पिरिटिड् / adj निरुत्साहित; उदास ▶ **dispiriting** adj खिन्न करने वाला : a rather dispiriting account of office life.

displace / डिस्'प्लेस् / verb 1 किसी का स्थान ले लेना, छीन लेना : Moderates have displaced the extremists on the committee. 2 उपयुक्त एवं सामान्य स्थान से हटा देना 3 विस्थापित करना, ज़बरदस्ती घर से दूसरे स्थान पर भेजना : families displaced by the fighting ▶ **displacement** noun 1 (एक स्थान से दूसरे स्थान पर) विस्थापन 2 (भौतिकी) विस्थापन (किसी ठोस पिंड द्वारा हटाई गई जल की उतनी ही मात्रा)।

display[1] / डि'स्प्ले / verb **display sth (to sb)** 1 प्रदर्शन करना, दिखाना : Alok proudly displayed his tattoo to his friends. 2 गुण या भाव का प्रदर्शन करना : display one's ignorance/fear.

display[2] / डि'स्प्ले / noun 1 प्रदर्शन, दिखावा : a spectacular firework display 2 प्रदर्शित वस्तु 3 कंप्यूटर की स्क्रीन पर प्रदर्शित शब्द, चित्र आदि।

displease / डिस्'प्लीज़् / verb किसी को अप्रसन्न करना, नाराज़ करना : Her insolence greatly displeased the judge. ▶ **displeased** adj **displeased (with sb/sth)** नाराज़, अप्रसन्न **displeasing** adj **displeasing (to sb/sth)** अरुचिकर, अप्रिय : The overall effect is not displeasing to the eye.

displeasure / डिस्'प्लेश़र् / noun नाराज़गी, अप्रसन्नता।

disposable / डि'स्पोज़ब्ल् / adj 1 प्रयोग के बाद फेंकने योग्य : disposable razors/syringes 2 (वाणिज्य) उपयोग के लिए उपलब्ध : disposable assets/ resources.

disposal / डि'स्पोज़ल् / noun 1 (किसी वस्तु से) छुट्टी, मुक्ति पाने की क्रिया : a bomb disposal squad 2 (वाणिज्य) जायदाद, व्यापार आदि के हिस्से की बिक्री ■ **at one's/sb's disposal** उपभोगार्थ अपने वश और अधिकार में।

dispose / डि'स्पोज़् / verb (औप) व्यक्तियों अथवा वस्तुओं को ठीक क्रम से लगाना : Various objects were disposed on the desk in front of her. ■ **dispose of sb/sth** 1 निपटना, निपटाना; कार्य पूरा करना : Their objections were easily disposed of. 2 बेकार/ काम में न आने वाली वस्तु को फेंक देना।

disposition / ‚डिस्प'ज़िश्न् / noun (प्राय: sing) 1 मन और चरित्र के विशेष गुण, चित्तवृत्ति : have a cheerful disposition 2 **disposition to sth/to do sth** (औप) प्रवृत्ति 3 (औप) व्यवस्था।

dispossess / ‚डिस्प'ज़ेस् / verb **dispossess sb (of sth)** किसी की संपत्ति (विशेषत: भूमि) छीन लेना; (मकान से) बेदख़ल कर देना, निकाल देना ▶ **dispossession** noun **the dispossessed** noun बेदख़ल किए गए लोग।

disproportionate / ‚डिस्प्र'पॉर्शनट् /

adj असंगत, असमानुपाती ▶ **disproportionately** *adv*.

disprove / डिस्'प्रूव् / *verb* किसी बात को ग़लत या असत्य सिद्ध करना : *The allegations have been completely disproved.*

dispute¹ / डि'स्प्यूट; 'डिस्प्यूट / *noun* 1 वाद-विवाद 2 **dispute (about/over sth)** झगड़ा; मत-भेद : *a dispute over fishing rights.*

dispute² / डि'स्प्यूट / *verb* 1 किसी बात पर वाद-विवाद करना 2 सत्यता या औचित्य को चुनौती देना 3 **dispute (with sb)** झगड़ा करना; मतभेद करना : *dispute a statement/decision* ▶ **disputable** *adj*.

disqualify / डिस्'क्वालिफ़ाइ / *verb* (*pt, pp* disqualified) **disqualify sb (from sth/doing sth)** किसी व्यक्ति को किसी कार्य के अयोग्य या अनुपयुक्त ठहराना (विशेषतः नियम का उल्लंघन करने के लिए): *Two players were disqualified for cheating.* ▶ **disqualification** *noun*.

disquiet / डिस्'क्वाइअट् / *noun* अशांति, बेचैनी : *There is considerable public disquiet about the safety of the new trains.* ▶ **disquiet** *verb* (औप) अशांत या बेचैन कर देना **disquieting** *adj*.

disregard / डिसरि'गार्ड / *verb* ध्यान न देना, उपेक्षा करना : *disregard a warning* ▶ **disregard** *noun* **disregard (for/of sb/sth)** उपेक्षा : *She shows a total disregard for other people's feelings.*

disrepair / डिसरि'पेअर् / *noun* असावधानी के कारण ख़राब स्थिति में/मरम्मत करने की स्थिति में होना : *The building was in a state of disrepair.*

disreputable / डिस्'रेप्युटब्ल् / *adj* बदनाम; अशोभनीय, आदर के अयोग्य : *a disreputable appearance.*

disrepute / डिसरि'प्यूट / *noun* बदनामी, अशोभनीय स्थिति।

disrespect / डिसरि'स्पेक्ट् / *noun* **disrespect (to/towards sb/sth)** अनादर, अशिष्टता ▶ **disrespectful** *adj* **disrespectfully** *adv*.

disrupt / डिस्'रप्ट् / *verb* भंग करना, संचार, यातायात व्यवस्था आदि को बलपूर्वक भंग करना : *Demonstrators succeeded in disrupting the meeting.* ▶ **disruption** *noun* **disruptive** / डिस्'रप्टिव् / *adj* व्यवस्था भंग करने वाला : *A few disruptive students can easily ruin a class.*

dissatisfaction / डिस्ˌसैटिस्'फ़ैक्शन् / *noun* **dissatisfaction (with/at sb/sth)** नाराज़गी, असंतुष्टि।

dissatisfied / डिस्'सैटिस्फ़ाइड् / *adj* **dissatisfied (with sb/sth)** असंतुष्ट, नाराज़ : *a dissatisfied customer.*

dissect / डि'सेक्ट; डाइ'सेक्ट् / *verb* 1 (किसी पौधे या प्राणी का शरीर) संरचना का अध्ययन करने के लिए काटना 2 किसी विषय पर विस्तार से बहस करना; परीक्षण करना ▶ **dissection** / डि'सेक्शन्; डाइ'सेक्शन् / *noun* विच्छेदन : *anatomical dissection.*

disseminate / डि'सेमिनेट् / *verb* विश्वास, मत आदि व्यापक रूप से फैला देना : *The mass media are used to disseminate information.* ▶ **dissemination** *noun*.

dissent¹ / डि'सेन्ट् / *verb* **dissent (from sth)** (औप) असहमत होना, असहमति व्यक्त करना ▶ **dissenter** *noun* असहमति व्यक्त करने वाला।

dissent² / डि'सेन्ट् / *noun* असहमति, विरोध।

dissertation / डिसर'टेशन् / *noun* **dissertation (on sth)** किसी विषय पर लंबा निबंध, विशेषतः शोध-प्रबंध : *a doctoral dissertation on Arabic dialects.*

dissident / 'डिसिडन्ट् / noun आधिकारिक मत एवं नीतियों का तीव्र विरोधी व्यक्ति
▸ **dissidence** noun.

dissimilar / डि'सिमिलर् / adj **dissimilar (from/to sb/sth)** असमान, एक जैसा नहीं ▸ **dissimilarity** noun.

dissipate / 'डिसिपेट् / verb 1 (भय, अज्ञानता, बादल आदि) दूर हट जाना/हटा देना; छितरा देना 2 (समय, शक्ति) व्यर्थ, मूर्खतापूर्ण बरबाद करना ▸ **dissipated** adj (अपमा) बरबाद; मूर्खतापूर्ण और प्राय: हानिकर भोग-विलास से पूर्ण : a dissipated life **dissipation** noun 1 हानिकर भोग-विलास का जीवन 2 (औप) विघटन, विहरण।

dissociate / डि'सोसिएट् / verb 1(**disassociation** भी) **dissociate oneself from sb/sth** असहमति व्यक्त करना; किसी को समर्थन देने/संबंध रखने से मना करना : I wish to dissociate myself from the views expressed by my colleagues. 2 **dissociate sb/sth from sth** अलग करना, संबंध-विच्छेद कर देना ▸ **dissociation** noun.

dissolution / डिस'लूश्न् / noun **dissolution (of sth)** (विवाह, साझेदारी, संसद आदि का) विच्छेदन, भंग : the dissolution of a marriage.

dissolve / डि'ज़ॉल्व् / verb 1 घुलना : Water dissolves salt. ○ Salt dissolves in water. 2 **dissolve sth (in sth)** घोलना : Dissolve the salt in water. 3 दूर करना या समाप्त करना : a washing powder that dissolves stains 4 विच्छेद करना/भंग करना : dissolve a marriage/partnership 5 **dissolve in/into sth** पिघलना; अचानक भावनाओं का फूट पड़ना : dissolve in (to) tears/laughter.

dissuade / डि'स्वेड् / verb **dissuade sb (from sth/doing sth)** किसी व्यक्ति को कोई कार्य-विशेष करने से रोकना, मना करना : He tried to dissuade me from going to live abroad.

distance[1] / 'डिस्टन्स् / noun 1 (दो वस्तुओं, दो स्थानों के बीच) दूरी : a distance of 20 kilometres 2 समय एवं स्थान का अंतर 3 व्यक्तिगत संबंधों में प्यार का अभाव : There was a growing distance between them.

distance[2] / 'डिस्टन्स् / verb **distance oneself/sb (from sb/sth)** (अपने आप को या अन्य को किसी से) अलग या दूर कर लेना।

distant / 'डिस्टन्ट् / adj 1 बहुत दूर : travel to distant parts of the world 2 (व्यक्ति) दूर के रिश्ते का 3 मित्रतारहित 4 किसी विषय पर विचार करता हुआ, खोया हुआ ▸ **distantly** adv.

distaste / डिस्'टेस्ट् / noun **distaste (for sb/sth)** (किसी के प्रति) अरुचि; नापसंदगी : have a distaste for violent sports ▸ **distasteful** adj अरुचिकर।

distemper / डि'स्टेम्पर् / noun डिस्टेंपर, गोंद के साथ पानी में घोलकर दीवारों पर प्रयोग किया जाने वाला रंग ▸ **distemper** verb दीवारों पर डिस्टेंपर करना।

distend / डि'स्टेन्ड् / verb फुलाना/ फूलना : starving children with huge distended bellies ▸ **distension** / डि'स्टेन्श्न् / noun.

distil (US **distill**) / डि'स्टिल् / verb (-ll-) 1 आसवन करना, द्रव को भाप बनाकर, ठंडा करके फिर से द्रव बनाना : distil fresh water from sea water 2 द्रव का आसवन करके शुद्ध करना; आसव, मादक द्रव आदि बनाना : whisky distilled in Scotland 3 **distil sth (from/into sth)** (किसी द्रव या ठोस का) सार निकालना; अत्यंत महत्त्वपूर्ण अर्थ या सारांश निकालना ▸ **distillation** noun.

distillery / डि'स्टिलरि / noun (pl **distilleries**) स्थान जहाँ मादक द्रव आदि बनते हैं।

distinct / डि'स्टिङ्क्ट् / adj 1 निश्चित; स्पष्ट रूप से सुनाई, दिखाई पड़ने या समझ में आने वाला : distinct footprints in the snow 2 distinct (from sth) भिन्न, पृथक ▸ **distinctly** adv.

distinction / डि'स्टिङ्क्शन् / noun 1 distinction (between A and B) भिन्नता, पृथक-पृथक मालूम होना 2 एक को दूसरे से पृथक करने वाला गुण 3 श्रेष्ठता का गुण, उत्कर्ष : a writer of distinction 4 सम्मान या पुरस्कार का चिह्न : win the highest distinction for bravery.

distinctive/ डिस्टिङ्क्टिव्/ adj भेदकारी।

distinguish / डि'स्टिङ्ग्विश् / verb 1 distinguish (between) A and B अंतर को भली-भाँति सुन, देख या समझ सकना 2 distinguish A (from B) अंतर, तादात्म्य या चरित्र का चिह्न बनना 3 distinguish oneself अपने को प्रसिद्ध बनाना, सम्मानित या पुरस्कृत होना : She distinguished herself by her coolness and bravery. ▸ **distinguishable** adj **distinguished** adj 1 सम्मानित, प्रख्यात 2 व्यवहार में गौरव एवं प्रतिष्ठा युक्त।

distort / डि'स्टॉर्ट् / verb 1 विकृत करना, सामान्य आकृति को खींच-तानकर या तोड़-मरोड़कर बिगाड़ना : a face distorted by pain 2 अज़ीब या असामान्य बना देना 3 तथ्यों को तोड़-मरोड़कर ग़लत धारणा बनाने के लिए प्रस्तुत करना : Newspapers often distort facts. ▸ **distortion** noun.

distract / डि'स्ट्रैक्ट् / verb distract sb/sth (from sth) ध्यान हटाना ▸ **distracted** adj distracted (with/by sth) जिसका ध्यान विभिन्न दिशाओं में बँटा हो; व्याकुल : She looked distracted. **distracting** adj ध्यान विचलित करने वाला।

distraction/ डि'स्ट्रैक्शन्/ noun 1 ध्यान विचलित करने वाली चीज़ 2 घबराहट या चिंता से ध्यान हटाने वाली चीज़ 3 भ्रांति, व्याकुलता।

distraught / डि'स्ट्रॉट् / adj व्याकुल; विक्षिप्त : His mother's death left him distraught.

distress[1] / डि'स्ट्रेस् / noun 1 अत्यधिक पीड़ा, कष्ट; धन या अन्य आवश्यक वस्तुओं के अभाव का कष्ट 2 गंभीर संकट में और सहायता की आवश्यकता में होना : a ship in distress.

distress[2] / डि'स्ट्रेस् / verb संकट/कष्ट उत्पन्न करना ▸ **distressing** adj.

distribute / डि'स्ट्रिब्यूट्; 'डिस्ट्रिब्यूट् / verb 1 distribute sth (to/among sb/sth) बाँटना या वस्तुएँ बेचना : goods distributed and sold worldwide 2 (एक विशाल क्षेत्र में) फैलाना ▸ **distribution**/ डिस्ट्रि'ब्यूशन्/ noun 1 वितरण, बँटवारा 2 विभिन्न भागों को सामान की आपूर्ति : a distribution company/system ▸ **distributor** noun 1 वितरक 2 इंजिन में एक उपकरण **distributive** adj.

district / 'डिस्ट्रिक्ट् / noun 1 विशिष्टता वाला क्षेत्र : mountainous/agricultural districts 2 ज़िला : rural/urban districts.

distrust / डिस्'ट्रस्ट् / noun शंका, अविश्वास : have a distrust of strangers ▸ **distrust** verb अविश्वास या शंका करना **distrustful** adj.

disturb / डि'स्टर्ब् / verb 1 गड़बड़ करना, शांति भंग करना : 'Exam in Progress—Do Not Disturb.' 2 सामान्य स्थान या अवस्था से हटा देना : Don't disturb the papers on my desk. 3 आंदोलित करना; चिंता पैदा करना ▸ **disturbed** adj (मनो) (मानसिक रूप से) बीमार **disturbing** adj चिंता या घबराहट पैदा करने वाला **disturbingly** adv.

disturbance/ डि'स्टर्बन्स्/ noun 1 गड़बड़ी, अशांति 2 [sing] गड़बड़ी उत्पन्न करने वाला व्यक्ति या वस्तु 3 सामाजिक या राजनीतिक अव्यवस्था, उपद्रव।

disunite / ˌडिस्यु'नाइट् / *verb* एकता भंग करना ▸ **disunity** / ˌडिस्'यूनटि / *noun* फूट, मतभेद : *growing signs of disunity within the party.*

disuse / डिस्'यूस् / *noun* (वस्तु) अप्रचलित होने की अवस्था ▸ **disused** / ˌडिस्'यूझ़्ड् / *adj* अप्रचलित।

ditch / डिच् / *noun* खाई ▸ **ditch** *verb* 1 (अनौप) किसी से मुक्ति पा लेना या (धोखा देकर) छोड़ देना 2 संकट के समय वायुयान को समुद्र में उतार लेना।

dither / 'डिदर् / *verb* **dither** (**about**) किंकर्तव्यविमूढ़ होना; निश्चय न कर पाना : *Stop dithering (about) or we'll be late!*

ditto / 'डिटो / *noun* (संक्षि **do**) जैसा ऊपर दिया गया है वैसा ही।

divan / डि'वैन्, US 'डाइवैन् भी / *noun* दीवान; लंबा, नीचा, बिना पीठ का सोफ़ा जो सोने के भी काम आ सकता है।

dive¹ / डाइव् / *verb* (*pt, pp* **dived**; *US pt* **dove** / डोव् / भी) 1 **dive** (**from/off sth**) (**into sth**) सिर के बल पानी में ग़ोता लगाना 2 **dive** (**down**) (**for sth**) (पानी के) निचले स्तर पर जाना, पानी के अंदर जाना : *dive for pearls* 3 (पक्षी या वायुयान का) तेज़ी से नीचे की तरफ़ जाना; गहरे पैठना 4 **dive into, under, etc sth** तेज़ी से कहीं घुस जाना, छलाँग लगा देना : *dive under the bed* ▸ **diver** *noun* ग़ोताख़ोर जो विशेष पोशाक पहनकर गहरे पानी के अंदर कार्य करता है **diving** / 'डाइविड़् / *noun* ग़ोताख़ोरी **diving-board** *noun* ग़ोता लगाने का मंच।

dive² / डाइव् / *noun* 1 ग़ोता 2 (अनौप) गंदा-सा रेस्त्राँ।

diverge / डाइ'वर्ज् / *verb* 1 **diverge** (**from sth**) (रेखाओं, मार्गों आदि का) एक दूसरे से अलग होना; भिन्न दिशाओं में जाना; (औप) (विचारों का) भिन्न होना 2 **diverge from sth** (योजना, सामान्य आदि से) हट जाना : *diverge from the truth*

▸ **divergence** *noun* अलगाव **divergent** *adj* : *divergent paths/opinions.*

diverse / डाइ'वर्स् / *adj* विभिन्न गुण-स्वभाव वाला; विविध : *people from diverse cultures.*

diversify / डाइ'वर्सिफ़ाई / *verb* (*pt, pp* **diversified**) विविधता उत्पन्न करना ▸ **diversification** *noun.*

diversion / डाइ'वर्श्न् / *noun* 1 मार्ग/ दिशा बदलने की क्रिया : *the diversion of a stream* 2 (*US* detour) सामान्य रास्ता बंद होने पर कोई अन्य रास्ता प्रयुक्त होना 3 आराम देने वाली या जी बहलाने वाली वस्तु : *the diversions of city life.*

diversity / डाइ'वर्सटि / *noun* (*pl* **diversities**) विविधता, अंतर।

divert / डाइ'वर्ट् / *verb* 1 **divert sb/sth** (**from sth**) (**to sth**) दूसरी तरफ़ मोड़ देना/ फेर देना; किसी ओर से ध्यान हटा लेना; किसी को विचलित करना : *divert attention from the real issues* 2 जी बहलाना : *Children are easily diverted.* ▸ **diverting** *adj* मनोरंजक।

divest / डाइ'वेस्ट् / *verb* (औप)1 **divest sb/sth of sth** (शक्ति, अधिकारों आदि से) वंचित करना : *Many feel that local councils should be divested of their public health responsibilities.* 2 **divest oneself of sth** छोड़ देना, छुटकारा पाना।

divide / डि'वाइड् / *verb* 1 **divide** (**sth**) (**up**) (**into sth**) विभाजन करना : *Cells multiply by dividing.* 2 **divide sth** (**out/up**) (**between/among sb**) हिस्से करके वितरित करना : *divide (out/up) the money* 3 **divide A from B** दो व्यक्तियों या वस्तुओं को अलग करना : *divide a mother from her baby* 4 लोगों को असहमति में डालना 5 (गणित) किसी संख्या को विभाजित करना : *30 divided by 6 is 5.* ▸ **divide** *noun*

1 divide (between A and B) विभाजन या अलगाव; मतभेद 2 विभाजक रेखा **divider** noun 1 विभाजक 2 **dividers** [pl] (ज्यामिति में) रेखा दूरी मापने का उपकरण।

dividend / 'डिविडेन्ड् / noun 1 (गणित) विभाज्य संख्या 2 (वाणिज्य) लाभांश, भागीदारों को समय-समय पर दिए ब्याज का भुगतान।

divination / ,डिवि 'नेश्न् / noun सगुन विचारकर भविष्यवाणी करने की योग्यता।

divine¹ / डि 'वाइन् / adj 1 दैवी, ईश्वरीय : divine wisdom/justice 2 (अप्र या अनौप) बढ़िया, अति सुंदर ▶ **divinely** adv.

divine² / डि 'वाइन् / verb 1 (औप) अनुमान लगाना : divine sb's thoughts/intentions 2 सगुन विचारना।

divinity / डि 'विनिटि / noun 1 दैवी होने का गुण : the divinity of Christ 2 देवी, देवता : the Roman/Greek divinity 3 धर्म-विज्ञान।

divisible / डि 'विज़ब्ल् / adj (गणित) विभाज्य।

division / डि 'विश्न् / noun 1 विभाजन या विभाजित होने की क्रिया : the division of labour 2 (गणित) एक संख्या को दूसरी संख्या से विभाजित करना 3 विभाजित अंश; विभाजन से प्राप्त संख्या : a fair/unfair division of money 4 किसी संस्था का मुख्य विभाग 5 विभाजक रेखा; सीमा रेखा 6 असहमति, जीवनचर्या में अंतर 7 (संसद में बहस के बाद) मत-विभाजन : The Bill was read without a division. ▶ **division sign** noun अंकगणित में + चिह्न।

divisive / डि 'वाइसिव् / adj विभाजक, मतभेद उत्पन्न करने वाला : a divisive influence/policy ▶ **divisiveness** noun.

divorce¹ / डि 'वॉर्स् / noun 1 **divorce** (from sb) तलाक़, विवाह-विच्छेद 2 di-

vorce (between A and B) संबंध-विच्छेद।

divorce² / डि 'वॉर्स् / verb 1 तलाक़ देना : They are divorcing each other. 2 **divorce** sb/sth from sth एक (व्यक्ति/वस्तु) को दूसरे (व्यक्ति/वस्तु) से पृथक करना : You can't divorce science from ethical questions. ▶ **divorcee** / डि ,वॉर्'सी / noun तलाक़शुदा व्यक्ति (विशेषतः महिला)।

divulge / डाइ 'वल्ज् / verb **divulge** sth (to sb) (रहस्य) खोल देना : divulge a confidential report/sb's identity.

dizzy / 'डिज़ि / adj (-ier, -iest) 1 (व्यक्ति) जिसे चक्कर आ रहे हों, चकराया हुआ : dizzy with happiness/exhaustion 2 इस तरह की भावना उत्पन्न करने का कारण : a dizzy height/speed ▶ **dizzily** adv **dizziness** noun **dizzying** adj चकराने वाला : the dizzying pace of events.

do¹ / डू / verb (3rd pers sing pres t **does** / डज़ /; pt **did** / डिड् /; pp **done** / डन् /) 1 (विशेषतः what, anything, nothing और something के साथ प्रयुक्त, अब तक अनिश्चित क्रियाएँ दर्शाने के लिए : What are you doing this evening? 2 (कुछ कार्य) करना; व्यवहार करना : Do as you wish/please. 3 कोई काम करना, कार्य संपन्न करना : I have a number of important things to do today. 4 (the + संज्ञा या my, his, etc के साथ प्रयुक्त) कार्य विशेष करना : do the dishes ∘ do the ironing/cooking/washing 5 (US अनौप) व्यवस्था करना या हिस्सा लेना; 6 सीखना या कुछ पढ़ना : do accountancy/engineering 7 उत्तर खोजना, हल ढूँढ़ना : I can't do the sum. 8 do sth (for sb) कुछ बनाना या उत्पन्न करना : do a drawing/painting 9 नाटक आदि संचालित करना 10 (कोई चरित्र) अभिनय करना 11 कुछ संपन्न करना।

पूरा करना ■ **do away with oneself/sb** (अनौप) स्वयं को/किसी और को मारना **do away with sth** (अनौप) समाप्त करना, कुछ रोक देना।

do² / डू / *aux verb* **1** (नकारात्मक एवं प्रश्नवाचक वाक्यों में प्रयुक्त) : *I don't like fish.* ○ *Does she speak French?* **2** (tag questions बनाने में) : *You live in London, don't you?* **3** (पूरे verb को दोहराने से बचने के लिए प्रयुक्त) : *She works harder than he does.* **4** (क्रियाविशेषण अथवा क्रियाविशेषण उपवाक्य को वाक्य के शुरू में लाने पर subject और verb का क्रम बदलने के लिए) : *Only rarely did he visit us.* **5** किसी अन्य सहायक क्रिया की अनुपस्थिति में, यह ज़ोर देने के लिए कि क्रिया सकारात्मक है : *He does look tired.* ○ *Do shut up!*

do³ / डू / *noun* (*pl* dos या do's / डूज़् /) (अनौप) दावत : *I hear the Madans are having a big do tonight* ■ **do's and don'ts** नियम।

docile / डोसाइल् / *adj* (व्यक्ति या जानवर) सरलता से नियंत्रण में होने वाला, जो आसानी से साधा जा सके ▸ **docility** / डो 'सिलटि / *noun*.

dock¹ / डॉक् / *noun* **1** गोदी, बंदरगाह में वह स्थान जहाँ जहाज़ का माल उतारा-चढ़ाया जाता है **2** docks [*pl*] गोदी, बाड़ा : *He works at the docks.*

dock² / डॉक् / *verb* **1** जहाज़ों का गोदी में आना **2** (दो या अधिक अंतरिक्ष विमानों का) आकाश में जोड़ा जाना : *docking manoeuvres/procedures.*

dock³ / डॉक् / *noun* कचहरी में अभियुक्त का कठघरा।

dock⁴ / डॉक् / *verb* **1** जानवर की पूँछ काटकर छोटा कर देना **2 dock sth (from/ off sth)** कुछ हिस्सा (विशेषत: धन का) ले लेना, काट लेना : *They have docked my salary.*

doctor / 'डॉक्टर् / *noun* (संक्षि Dr) **1** डाक्टर, चिकित्सक **2** विश्वविद्यालय से डाक्टर की उपाधि प्राप्त व्यक्ति : *Doctor of Philosophy* ▸ **doctor** *verb* (अनौप) धोखा देने के लिए कुछ बदलना : *doctor evidence/accounts* **doctoral** *adj* 'डॉक्टर' की उपाधि से संबंधित : *a doctoral thesis.*

doctrine / 'डॉक्ट्रिन् / *noun* (चर्च, राज-नीतिक दल या वैज्ञानिकों द्वारा प्रतिपादित) सिद्धांत, मत ▸ **doctrinal** *adj.*

document / 'डॉक्युमन्ट् / *noun* लिखित या मुद्रित सामग्री जो प्रमाण या प्रलेख के रूप में प्रयुक्त होनी है, काग़ज़ात, दस्तावेज़ ▸ **document** / 'डॉक्युमेन्ट् / *verb* **1** दस्तावेज़ में लिखना/तैयार करना **2** दस्तावेज़ की सहायता से किसी बात को सिद्ध करना, समर्थन देना : *Can you document these claims?* **documentation** *noun.*

documentary / ,डॉक्यु'मेन्ट्रि / *adj* **1** दस्तावेज़ सहित : *documentary evidence/proof* **2 documentary film** वृत्त-चित्र।

dodge / डॉज् / *verb* **1** दाएँ-बाएँ या इधर-उधर होकर बच जाना; वार बचाना : *They managed to dodge the bullets and escape unhurt.* **2** किसी व्यक्ति से कतरा जाना; किसी काम से बच जाना; (अनौप) चकमा दे देना : *dodge military service* ○ *dodge paying one's taxes* ▸ **dodge** *noun* **1** वार बचाने की क्रिया **2** (अनौप) चकमा : *a tax dodge* **dodger** *noun* (अनौप) चकमा देने वाला : *a fare dodger* (बसों में किराया न देने वाला)।

doe / डो / *noun* हरिणी; रेनडिअर, ख़रगोश या खरहा की मादा।

dog¹ / डॉग् / *noun* **1** कुत्ता प्रजाति; कुत्ता, भेड़िया या लोमड़ी का नर जानवर **2** (अनौप) दुष्ट एवं अप्रिय आदमी ■ **a dog's life** मुसीबतों भरा जीवन **go to the dogs** (अनौप) बदतर स्थिति में पहुँच जाना ▸ **dog-**

eared *adj* (पुस्तक के) प्रयोग के कारण पृष्ठों के कोने मुड़े हुए होना।

dog² / डॉग् / *verb* (-gg-) 1 किसी का निरंतर पास से ही पीछा करना : *dog sb's footsteps* 2 (किसी अप्रिय स्थिति को) निरंतर पास-पास रहकर घेरे रखना : *Her career was dogged by misfortune.*

dogged / डॉगिड् / *adj* 1 धैर्ययुक्त, अडिग व्यवहार वाला : *their dogged defence of the city* 2 ज़िद्दी : *dogged persist-ence/refusal* ▸ **doggedly** *adv* **dog-gedness** *noun.*

dogma / डॉग्मा / *noun* संस्था आदि से प्रस्तुत सिद्धांत जिन्हें बिना प्रश्न किए स्वीकारना होता है : *political/social dogma* ▸ **dogmatically** *adv* **dogmatism** *noun* हठधर्मिता।

dogmatic / डॉग्'मैटिक् / *adj* (अपमा) मताग्रही, हठधर्मी (व्यक्ति) : *You can't be dogmatic in matters of taste.*

doldrums / डॉल्ड्रम्ज़् / *noun* the doldrums [*pl*] भूमध्य रेखा के आस-पास के समुद्र का भाग जहाँ न के बराबर (या नहीं) हवा होती है और पतवार वाले जहाज़ नहीं चलते हैं ■ **in the doldrums** 1 खिन्न; उदास 2 कार्य या विकास थमे हुए।

dole¹ / डोल् / *verb* ■ **dole sth out (to sb)** कुछ बाँटना, विवरण करना।

dole² / डोल् / *noun* the dole (अनौप) ख़ैरात; (ब्रिटेन में) बेरोज़गारी भत्ता : *length-ening dole queues.*

doleful / डोल्फ़ुल् / *adj* दुखी, उदास : *a doleful face* ▸ **dolefully** *adv.*

doll / डॉल् / *noun* 1 गुड़िया 2 (अप्र, अप, विशेषत: *US*) आकर्षक स्त्री।

dollar / डॉलर् / *noun* 1 (प्रतीक $) अमेरिका, कनाडा, ऑस्ट्रेलिया एवं कुछ अन्य देशों में प्रचलित मुद्रा 2 the dollar [*sing*] (वाणिज्य) अंतर्राष्ट्रीय मुद्रा बाज़ार में अमेरिकी डॉलर की क़ीमत।

dollop / डॉलप् / *noun* (अनौप) मुलायम वस्तु का (विशेषत: खाद्य पदार्थ का) बेडौल पिंड : *a dollop of cream/mashed potatoes.*

dolphin / डॉल्फ़िन् / *noun* बहुत छोटा व्हेल की तरह का समुद्री जीव।

domain / ड'मेन्; डो'मेन् / *noun* 1 राज्य क्षेत्र, रियासत 2 (ज्ञान, विचार आदि का) क्षेत्र।

dome / डोम् / *noun* 1 गुंबद : *the dome of St Paul's Cathedral* 2 गुंबद के आकार की वस्तु : *the dome of a hill* ▸ **domed** *adj.*

domestic / ड'मेस्टिक् / *adj* 1 घर-परिवार आदि का, घरेलू : *domestic gas/elec-tric supply* 2 अपने देश का : *domestic trade/imports* 3 (जानवर) पालतू।

domesticate / ड'मेस्टिकेट् / *verb* 1 (जानवरों को) पालतू बनाना 2 (व्यक्तियों को) घरेलू जीवन की आदतों, कार्यों में ढालना ▸ **domesticated** *adj.*

dominant / डॉमिनन्ट् / *adj* प्रबल, प्रभुत्वपूर्ण : *the dominant personality in a group* ▸ **dominance** *noun.*

dominate / डॉमिनेट् / *verb* 1 शासन, प्रभाव या अधिकार में रखना 2 सबसे महत्त्व-पूर्ण या प्रकट व्यक्ति या वस्तु होना 3 (भवन या स्थान आदि) बड़ा, प्रभावशाली एवं औरों से ऊपर स्थित होना ▸ **domination** / डॉमि'नेश्न् / *noun* प्रभुत्व।

domineering / डॉमि'निअरिङ् / *adj* धाक जमाने वाला : *a domineering hus-band.*

dominion / ड'मिनिअन् / *noun* 1 do-minion (over sb/sth) (औप) प्रभुत्व, स्वामित्व : *under foreign dominion* 2 अधिकार क्षेत्र, राज्य 3 (प्राय: Domin-ion) ब्रिटिश कामनवेल्थ आफ़ नेशंस के कुछ स्वतंत्र क्षेत्र।

donate / डो'नेट्; *US* डोनेट् / *verb* **donate sth (to sb/sth)** दान देना : *donate large sums to relief or-ganizations* ▸ **donation** / डो'नेश्न् / *noun* दान।

done / डन् / *adj* 1 (भोजन आदि) पर्याप्त पका हुआ : *a well-done steak* 2 (अनौप) सामाजिक रूप से स्वीकृत, विशेषत: कड़े क़ायदे वाले लोगों में 3 **done (with)** ख़त्म, पूर्ण, समाप्त : *Let's get the washing-up done with and then we can relax.*

donkey / 'डॉङ्कि / *noun* (*pl* **donkeys**) गधा ▸ **donkey-work** *noun* अत्यधिक शारीरिक थकान उत्पन्न करने वाला नीरस कार्य।

donor / 'डोनर् / *noun* 1 दाता 2 (चिकि) रक्त या शरीर का अंग दान करने वाला व्यक्ति : *a blood donor.*

doodle / 'डूडल् / *verb* कुछ अन्य बात पर सोचते हुए या बोर होकर यूँ ही रेखाएँ खींचना, चित्र बनाना, आकृतियाँ आदि बनाना : *doodling in the margin of his note-book* ▸ **doodle** *noun* ऐसी आकृतियाँ।

doom / डूम / *noun* सर्वनाश; मृत्यु; दुर्भाग्य : *send a man to his doom* ▸ **doom** *verb* **doom sb/sth (to sth)** सर्वनाश करना, (किसी के लिए) दुर्भाग्य लाना **doomed** *adj* जिसकी मृत्यु या असफलता निश्चित है।

doomsday / 'डूम्ज़्डे / *noun* क़यामत का दिन ■ **till doomsday** क़यामत तक (हमेशा)।

door / डॉर् / *noun* दरवाज़ा, द्वार ■ **out of doors** बाहर खुले में ▸ **doorstep** *noun* देहरी **doorway** *noun* दीवार में दरवाज़े की जगह।

dope / डोप् / *noun* 1 (अप) (ग़ैर-क़ानूनी) मादक द्रव्य : *peddle dope* 2 (अप) खिलाड़ियों द्वारा अपना प्रदर्शन बेहतर बनाने के लिए लिया गया मादक द्रव्य : *fail a dope test* 3 (अनौप) मूर्ख व्यक्ति ▸ **dope** *verb* मादक द्रव्य लेना या देना (व्यक्ति को या पशु को); बेहोश करने के लिए खाने या पीने की चीज़ में नशीली दवा मिलाना **dopey** / 'डोपि / *adj* 1 (अनौप) निद्रामग्न (मादक द्रव्य/दवा लेने के कारण) 2 (अप्र) मूर्ख।

dormant / 'डॉर्मन्ट् / *adj* निष्क्रिय, यद्यपि भावी सक्रियता अथवा विकास की प्रतीक्षा की स्थिति में।

dormitory / 'डॉर्मट्रि / *noun* (*pl* **dormitories**) शयनशाला जिसमें कई लोगों के सोने के लिए पलंग होते हैं (जैसे बोर्डिंग स्कूल में)।

dosage / 'डोसिज् / *noun* (प्राय: *sing*) दवा की एक बार में ली जाने वाली मात्रा, ख़ुराक।

dose / डोस् / *noun* 1 (दवा की) ख़ुराक; एक समय में दी जाने वाली दवा की मात्रा 2 किसी (विशेषत: अप्रिय) चीज़ की मात्रा अथवा अवधि : *a lethal dose of radiation* ▸ **dose** *verb* **dose sb/oneself (up) (with sth)** दवा की ख़ुराक देना/लेना।

dossier / 'डॉसिए / *noun* **dossier (on sb/sth)** किसी व्यक्ति, घटना या विषय के बारे में एकत्रित सूचनाओं/तथ्यों का संग्रह; फ़ाइल।

dot / डॉट् / *noun* 1 बिंदी; लिखने में प्रयुक्त इस प्रकार का चिह्न (जैसे i एवं j के ऊपर) 2 कोई बहुत छोटी दूरस्थ वस्तु : *The island was just a dot on the horizon.* ▸ **dot** *verb* (**-tt-**) 1 बिंदी लगाना (किसी स्थान पर); बिंदुदार बनाना 2 व्यक्तियों या वस्तुओं को विभिन्न स्थानों पर फैलाना/फैला हुआ होना : *The sky was dotted with stars.* **dot matrix printer** *noun* डॉट मैट्रिक्स, एक आधुनिक मुद्रण मशीन जो बिंदुओं के समूहन से अक्षर बनाती है **dotted line** *noun* बिंदुदार रेखा।

dotage / 'डोटिज् / *noun* ■ **in one's dotage** बूढ़ा एवं (उम्र के कारण) दिमाग़ से कमज़ोर, सठियापा।

dote / डोट् / *verb* ■ **dote on/upon sb/sth** किसी व्यक्ति/वस्तु के प्रति अत्यधिक अनुराग अनुभव करना या दिखाना ▸ **doting** *adj* दुलार करने वाला।

dotty / 'डॉटि / *adj* (**-ier, -iest**) 1 (अनौप) अजीबो-ग़रीब, सनकी; बेवक़ूफ़ : *He's getting a bit dotty in his old age.*

2 dotty about sb/sth किसी व्यक्ति या वस्तु को बहुत चाहने वाला।

double¹ / 'डब्ल् / adj 1 (लंबाई, चौड़ाई, मात्रा या आकार में) दुगुना 2 एक जैसे दो अंश या वस्तुओं का होना : double doors 3 दो व्यक्तियों या वस्तुओं के लिए बना : a double bed/room 4 दो वस्तुओं या गुणों के संयोजन से : a double meaning/ purpose/aim ▸ double agent noun दोहरा जासूस (जो दो शत्रु देशों की जासूसी करता है) double dealer noun (अपमा) कपटी, (व्यापार में) धोखेबाज़ double life noun दोहरी ज़िंदगी (एक खुली, एक छुपी हुई)।

double² / 'डब्ल् / adv 1 दो अंशों या हिस्सों में; दोहरा : fold a blanket double 2 दो-दो में या दो-दो करके double-cross verb धोखा देना।

double³ / 'डब्ल् / noun 1 दोगुना (मात्रा में) : He gets paid double for doing the same job I do. 2 बिलकुल दूसरे के जैसा व्यक्ति या वस्तु 3 युग्म, जोड़ा 4 doubles [pl] जोड़ों में खेले जाने वाला खेल : mixed doubles ■ at the double; (US) on the double (अनौप) तेज़ी से, उतावलेपन से।

double⁴ / 'डब्ल् / verb 1 दुगुना होना या करना 2 दोहरा मोड़ना या तहाना : double a blanket for extra warmth 3 double as sth दूसरा या गौण कार्य भी करना : When we have guests, the sofa doubles as a bed.

doubly / 'डब्लि / adv 1 मात्रा में दुगुना करना 2 दो तरीकों या कारणों से।

doubt¹ / डाउट् / noun 1 doubt (about/ as to sth); doubt (as to) whether... संदेह, अनिश्चय 2 doubt about sth/ that... अविश्वास का कारण ■ in doubt अनिश्चित no doubt लगभग निश्चित।

doubt² / डाउट् / verb संदेह करना या रखना : We have no reason to doubt her story.

doubtful / 'डाउट्फ़ुल् / adj 1 संदेहपूर्ण, संदिग्ध 2 doubtful (whether/if/that...) असंभावित 3 अनिश्चित, संदेहास्पद 4 संभवतः बेईमान या असत्य : a witness of doubtful character ▸ doubtfully adv.

doubtless / 'डाउट्ल्स् / adv प्रायः निश्चित, संदेहरहित।

dough / डो / noun 1 गूँधा हुआ आटा, लोई 2 (अप) पैसा ▸ doughnut (विशेषतः US donut भी) / 'डोनट् / noun तला हुआ छोटा गोल केक, गुलगुला।

dour / 'डाउअर; डोर् / adj कठोर और धमकाने वाला; उदास : a dour expression.

douse / डाउस् / verb douse sb/sth (in/with sth) भिगो देना, सराबोर कर देना : As a joke, they doused him with a bucket of water.

dove / डव् / noun 1 फ़ाख़्ता, कबूतर प्रजाति का पक्षी; सफ़ेद रंग का ऐसा पक्षी जो शांति का प्रतीक माना जाता है 2 शांति का हिमायती राजनयिक।

dowdy / 'डाउडि / adj (-ier, -iest) (अपमा) 1 (पोशाक) अनाकर्षक, फ़ैशन के बाहर 2 (व्यक्ति) अनाकर्षक पोशाक पहने हुए।

down¹ / डाउन् / adv 1 ऊँचे से नीचे की ओर (गति) : fall/climb/jump down 2 खड़े से लेटने की (गति) : go and lie down 3 कम होने या घटने का सूचक 4 काग़ज़ पर (लिखने के संबंध में) : write it down 5 down (to sb/sth) किसी शृंखला की ऊपरी और निचली सीमा।

down² / डाउन् / prep 1 ऊँचे से निचले स्तर पर : The stone rolled down the hill. 2 नदी, जलधारा के निचले भाग पर या समुद्र के नज़दीक : There's a bridge a mile down the river from here. 3 (सपाट सतह के) साथ-साथ, व्यक्ति के सामने की दिशा में : He lives just down the street. 4 एक संपूर्ण कालावधि के दौरान :

an exhibition of costumes down the ages.

down³ / डाउन् / *verb* (*अनौप*) 1 पेय को जल्दी से गटक जाना : *We downed our beer and left.* 2 (वायुयान आदि को) मार गिराना ∎ **down tools** अचानक काम करने से मना कर देना।

down⁴ / डाउन् / *adj* 1 (*अनौप*) दुखी, उदास एवं खिन्न 2 (कंप्यूटर) काम न कर पाने की अवस्था में।

down⁵ / डाउन् / *noun* मुलायम रोएँ या (चिड़ियों के अंदरूनी) पंख : *pillows filled with down.*

downcast / 'डाउन्कास्ट् / *adj* उदास; (आँखों का) नीचे की ओर देखते हुए।

downfall / डाउन्फ़ॉल् / *noun* [*sing*] अध:पतन; इसका कारण : *Greed led to his downfall.*

downgrade / डाउन्'ग्रेड् / *verb* **downgrade sb/sth (from sth) (to sth)** पदावनत करना।

downhill / डाउन्'हिल् / *adv* ढाल या उतार की ओर : *run downhill.*

down-market / डाउन्'मार्किट् / *adj* (*प्राय: अपमा*) (निम्न सामाजिक वर्ग से सहज स्वीकार्य) बाज़ारी माल या सेवा।

downpour / 'डाउन्पॉर् / *noun* मूसलाधार वर्षा।

downright / 'डाउन्राइट् / *adj* पूर्णतया (अहितकारी)।

downs / डाउन्ज़् / *noun* [*pl*] खाली पठारी भूमि (दक्षिण इंगलैंड में)।

downstairs / डाउन्'स्टेअर्ज़् / *adv* निचली मंज़िल पर।

downstream / डाउन्'स्ट्रीम् / *adj* (नदी के) प्रवाह के साथ-साथ; अनुप्रवाह।

downtrodden / 'डाउन्ट्रॉड्न् / *adj* पद-दलित और पीड़ित।

downward / 'डाउन्वई् / *adj* निचले स्तर की ओर गमनशील ▸ **downwards** *adv* नीचे की ओर।

dowry / 'डाउरि / *noun* दहेज : *the dowry system.*

doze / डोज़् / *verb* झपकी लेना; ऊँघना : *dozing fitfully* ▸ **doze** *noun* झपकी।

dozen / 'डज़्न् / *noun* (*pl* **dozens** या अपरिवर्तित) (*संक्षि* **doz**) दर्जन, बारह का समुच्चय : *Eggs are sold by the dozen.*

drab / ड्रैब् / *adj* (**-bber,-bbest**) 1 नीरस, एकरस 2 हलका भूरा या मटमैला : *dressed in drab clothes* ▸ **drabness** *noun.*

draft¹ / ड्राफ़्ट; *US* ड्रैफ़्ट् / *noun* 1 किसी कार्य या कृति (भाषण, पत्र, नक़्शा आदि) की रूपरेखा 2 (*वाणिज्य*) ड्राफ़्ट, बैंक के लिए धनादेश 3 (विशेषत: *US*) विशेष कार्य के लिए बड़े समूह से कुछ लोगों, विशेषकर सिपाहियों, का चयन।

draft² / ड्राफ़्ट्; *US* ड्रैफ़्ट् / *verb* 1 रूपरेखा तैयार करना : *draft a contract* 2 लोगों को चयन करके भेजना 3 **draft sb (into sth)** (*US*) किसी को सेना में कार्य करने का आदेश देना ▸ **draftee** *noun.*

draftsman / 'ड्राफ़्ट्स्मन् / *noun* = **draughtsman.**

drag¹ / ड्रैग् / *verb* (**-gg-**) 1 (प्रयल और कठिनाई के साथ) घसीटना : *They dragged him from his bed.* 2 (स्वयं को) घसीटते जाना, धीरे–धीरे सुस्त क़दमों से चलना : *She always drags behind.* 3 किसी को उसकी अनिच्छा से कहीं जाने को तैयार करना 4 किसी वस्तु का घिसटना 5 **drag (on)** (समय का) नीरसता और सुस्ती से बीतना; कार्यक्रम का लंबा खिंचना : *The film dragged terribly.*

drag² / ड्रैग् / *noun* 1 **drag on sb/sth** प्रगति में बाधक वस्तु या व्यक्ति 2 (*अप*) बोरिंग आदमी या वस्तु 3 (*अप*) सिगरेट का कश।

dragon / 'ड्रैगन् / *noun* 1 (पुरानी कहानियों में) आग उगलने वाला एक बड़ा पंखदार छिपकली जैसा जीव; परदार साँप 2 (*अपमा*) गुस्सैल और उग्र व्यक्ति, विशेषत: महिला।

drain¹ / ड्रेन् / *noun* 1 (मकान, सड़क

आदि की) नाली 2 [*sing*] drain on sb/
sth शक्ति, धन और समय का निरंतर अपव्यय
करने वाली वस्तु : *Military spending
is a huge drain on the country's
resources.* ■ (go) down the drain
(*अनौप*) बरबाद हो जाना, अपव्यय हो जाना।

drain² /ड्रेन्/ *verb* 1 drain (sth) (from
sth); drain (sth) (away/off) बह जाना
या द्रव को बहने देना : *The bathwater
slowly drained away.* 2 द्रव निकल
जाने से सूखा हो जाना; सूखा कर देना :
good, well-drained soil 3 पीना;
(प्याला आदि) खाली कर देना 4 drain sb/
sth (of sth) किसी व्यक्ति को धीरे-धीरे
धन, शक्ति आदि से क्षीण कर देना : *feel
drained of energy.*

drainage /'ड्रेनिज़/ *noun* 1 बहकर
खाली होने या करने की प्रक्रिया 2 निकास-
व्यवस्था।

drama /'ड्रामा/ *noun* 1 नाटक : *a
historical drama* 2 नाट्यकला 3 उत्ते-
जक घटनाओं की शृंखला ■ make a
drama out of sth ज़रा-सी बात को
अतिशय कर देना, नाटकीय बना देना।

dramatic /ड्रमैटिक्/ *adj* 1 नाट्य विष-
यक : *a dramatic representation of
a real event* 2 (घटना या बदलाव) नाट-
कीय; अचानक एवं उत्तेजक : *dramatic
results/developments* 3 विशेष प्रभाव
के लिए अतिशयोक्तिपूर्ण ▸ **dramatically**
adv dramatics *noun* 1 नाट्यकला का
अध्ययन 2 (*अपमा*) नाटकीय अतिशयोक्तिपूर्ण
व्यवहार।

dramatist /'ड्रैमटिस्ट्/ *noun* नाटककार।

dramatize, -ise /'ड्रैमटाइज़/ *verb*
1 (किसी कहानी आदि को) नाटक की विधा
में प्रस्तुत करना 2 घटनाओं को नाटकीय रूप
दे देना ▸ **dramatization, -isation**
noun.

drape /ड्रेप/ *verb* 1 drape sth round/
over sth लपेटकर किसी चीज़ पर कपड़े
लटकाना 2 drape sb/sth in/with sth

कपड़े से कुछ ढकना या सजाना 3 drape
sth around/round/over sth कोई चीज़
कहीं पर ढीले-ढाले लटकने देना : *She
draped her arms round his neck.*
▸ drape *noun* (प्राय: *pl*) (*US*) लंबा
परदा।

draper /'ड्रेपर्/ *noun* (विशेषत: पूर्व में)
कपड़ा बेचने वाला, बज़्ज़ाज़ ▸ **drapery**
noun 1 बज़्ज़ाज़ द्वारा बेचा जाने वाला कपड़ा
2 (draperies [*pl*] भी) ढीले-ढाले लटकते
कपड़े, शाल, पर्दे आदि।

drastic /'ड्रैस्टिक्;'ड्रास्टिक्/ *adj* 1 उग्र,
प्रचंड : *drastic measures* 2 सशक्त;
अति गंभीर : *a drastic shortage of
food* ▸ **drastically** *adv.*

draught /ड्राफ़्ट्/ (*US* draft /ड्रैफ़्ट्/)
noun 1 किसी बंद स्थान या कमरे या चिमनी
आदि में हवा की धारा, झोंका 2 (पेय का)
एक घूँट : *He emptied his glass in
one long draught.* 3 draughts (*US*
checkers) ड्राफ़्ट्स का खेल जो मेज़ पर दो
खिलाड़ियों द्वारा खेला जाता है ▸ **draughty**
adj हवादार (स्थान) : *draughty corridors.*

draughtsman /'ड्राफ़्ट्समन्/ (*US*
draftsman /'ड्रैफ़्ट्समन्/) *noun* नक़्शा-
नवीस (विशेषत: इंजिनियरिंग या वास्तुकला
में)।

draw¹ /ड्रॉ/ *verb* (*pt*, drew /डू/; *pp*
drawn /ड्रॉन्/) 1 (क़लम, पेंसिल, चाक
आदि से) खींचना; ख़ाका, रेखाचित्र आदि
बनाना 2 (आगे, समीप) आना, बढ़ना
3 खींचना, खींचकर निकालना : *draw the
cork out of a bottle* 4 घसीटना 5 (परदे
आदि) खींचकर बढ़ाना : *The blinds
were drawn.* 6 (आक्रमण करने को)
तलवार, बंदूक़ आदि निकालना : *She drew
a revolver on me.* 7 draw sth from
sth/sb कुछ लेना या पाना : *draw information from many different
sources* 8 draw sth (from sth);
draw sth out (of sth) खाते से पैसे

निकालना : *Can I draw Rs 800 from my account?* 9 साँस लेकर कुछ अंदर खींचना; चिमनी से हवा आने देना 10 **draw sb (to sth)** आकर्षित करना 11 **draw (with/ against sb)** (दो खिलाड़ियों या खिलाड़ी दलों का) बराबर का खेल खेलना अर्थात किसी की हार–जीत न होना 12 **draw sth (from sth)** (निष्कर्ष) निकालना 13 (तुलना) करना : *draw an analogy/a comparison.* ■ **draw a blank** कोई उत्तर या परिणाम न पाना।

draw² / ड्रॉ / *noun* 1 **draw (for sth)** (लाटरी, पुरस्कार, विजेता आदि का) यादृच्छिक रूप से निर्णय करने की क्रिया 2 बिना हार–जीत का खेल, बराबरी का खेल 3 (प्राय: *sing*) कोई व्यक्ति या वस्तु जो बहुत लोगों को आकर्षित करे।

drawback / ड्रॉबैक / *noun* कमी; अ-सुविधा।

drawer *noun* 1 / ड्रॉर् / (मेज़ आदि की) दराज़ 2 / 'ड्रॉअर् / चेक काटने वाला।

drawing / 'ड्रॉइङ् / *noun* आरेखन कला; चित्र, आरेख।

drawing-room / 'ड्रॉइङ् रूम् / *noun* (प्रा या औप) बैठक, ड्राइंग-रूम।

drawl / ड्रॉल् / *verb* लंबी स्वरध्वनियों में सुस्त तरीके से बोलना : *'Well, hi there!' he drawled.* ▸ **drawl** *noun* [*sing*] इस प्रकार की बोलने की शैली।

drawn / ड्रॉन् / *adj* अत्यंत थका हुआ या चिंतित प्रतीत होता हुआ।

dread / ड्रेड् / *noun* भय (भावी घटना का); वह वस्तु या व्यक्ति जिससे भय या आतंक उत्पन्न होता है ▸ **dread** *verb* भयभीत और आशंकित होना : *dread illness* **dreaded** (औप **dread** भी) *adj* भयप्रद : *a dreaded criminal.*

dreadful / ड्रेड्फ़ुल् / *adj* कष्ट, भय और आशंका उत्पन्न करने वाला; (अनौप) अप्रिय ▸ **dreadfully** *adv* 1 बहुत-बहुत 2 अप्रिय और बुरी तरह से : *They suffered dreadfully during the war.*

dream¹ / ड्रीम् / *noun* 1 सपना, स्वप्न 2 ऐसी मानसिक दशा जब आसपास की वस्तुएँ अवास्तविक प्रतीत होती हैं 3 कोई अवास्तविक-सा आदर्श या महत्त्वाकांक्षा : *achieve/realize one's lifelong dream* 4 [*sing*] (अनौप) अति सुंदर या आश्चर्यजनक व्यक्ति या वस्तु।

dream² / ड्रीम् / *verb* (*pt, pp* **dreamt** / ड्रेट् / या **dreamed** / ड्रीम्ड् /) 1 सपने देखना 2 **dream (of/about sth/doing sth)** (किसी बात की) कल्पना करना 3 **dream (of sth/doing sth); dream about sb/sth/doing sth** सपने में किसी को देखना, अनुभव करना ▸ **dreamer** *noun* 1 सपने देखने वाला व्यक्ति 2 (प्राय: अपमा) अवास्तविक योजनाओं और विचारों वाला व्यक्ति; हमेशा कल्पनाओं में खोया रहने वाला व्यक्ति।

dreamland / 'ड्रीमलैन्ड् / *noun* (अपमा) आनंददायक परंतु अवास्तविक काल्पनिक स्थिति।

dreamlike / 'ड्रीमलाइक् / *adj* स्वप्न-सा।

dreamy / 'ड्रीमि / *adj* (-ier, -iest) 1 (व्यक्ति) विचारों में खोया हुआ, स्वप्निल 2 अस्पष्ट 3 (अनौप) सुखदायक, मनो-हारी : *dreamy music* ▸ **dreamily** *adv* **dreaminess** *noun*.

dreary / 'ड्रिअरि / *adj* (-ier, -iest) 1 उदास और खिन्न करने वाला : *a dreary winter day* 2 (अनौप) नीरस ▸ **drearily** *adv* **dreariness** *noun* नीरसता : *the dreariness of the landscape.*

dredge / ड्रेज् / *verb* 1 नदी, नाले या नहर के तले से मशीन द्वारा कीचड़-मिट्टी आदि साफ़ करना : *They have to dredge the canal so that ships can use it.* 2 **dredge sth (up) (from sth)** इस तरह की मशीन या नाव से कुछ ऊपर लाना ■ **dredge sth up** (अपमा) गड़े मुर्दे उखाड़ना ▸ **dredger** *noun* नदी-तल से कीचड़-मिट्टी निकालने वाला यंत्र/नाव।

dregs / ड्रेग्ज़ / *noun* [*pl*] 1 तलछट;

गिलास, बोतल आदि में द्रव का कूड़ा–करकट भरा शेष भाग : He drank it to the dregs. 2 किसी चीज़ का अंतिम भाग; सबसे ख़राब और सबसे बेकार भाग : the dregs of society.

drench / ड्रेन्च् / verb (पानी में) पूरी तरह भिगो देना : We were caught in the storm and got drenched to the skin.

dress¹ / ड्रेस् / noun 1 स्त्रियों और लड़कियों द्वारा पहनी पोशाक 2 पोशाक; पहनावा : traditional Scottish dress.

dress² / ड्रेस् / verb 1 वस्त्र पहनना/ पहनाना; औपचारिक अवसर के लिए पोशाक पहनना 2 किसी वस्तु को सजाना : dress a shop window ○ dress a street with flags 3 घाव की मरहम-पट्टी करना 4 खाने को पकाने या खाने के लिए तैयार करना : dress a chicken/salad.

dresser / ड्रेसर् / noun 1 (ब्रिटेन में) रसोई का एक फ़र्नीचर जिसमें तश्तरी आदि रखते हैं 2 (US) शीशा लगी शृंगार मेज़।

dressing / ड्रेसिड् / noun 1 कपड़े, वस्त्र आदि पहनने की क्रिया : Dressing always takes her such a long time. 2 मरहम, पट्टी आदि चीज़ें 3 सलाद में डालने वाला तेल, सॉस आदि 4 **dressing gown** noun [sing] रात के कपड़ों पर पहनने वाली ढीली पोशाक।

dribble / 'ड्रिब्ल् / verb 1 मुँह से लार गिरना : Take care the baby doesn't dribble over your suit. 2 बूँद-बूँद करके (कुछ द्रव) गिरना 3 बूँद-बूँद करके गिराना 4 (फ़ुटबाल, हॉकी, बास्कटबाल में) गेंद को हलके स्पर्शों या टप्पों द्वारा आगे ले जाना ▸ **dribble** noun 1 बूँद या पतली धार 2 noun (मुँह से) लार।

drift¹ / ड्रिफ़्ट् / noun 1 बहाव या (हवा का) लगातार झोंका; हवा के बहाव के कारण जहाज़ का पथ से विचलन 2 (विशेषकर ग़लत चीज़ की तरफ़) प्रवृत्ति या झुकाव : a slow drift into debt/war/crisis

3 भाषण, वार्ता या लेख का सामान्य अर्थ, सारांश : My German isn't very good, but I got the drift of what she said.

drift² / ड्रिफ़्ट् / verb 1 हवा या जल की धारा से बह जाना/बहाकर ले जाया जाना : The boat drifted down the river. 2 (व्यक्ति का) बिना खास उद्देश्य या प्रयोजन के जीवन बिताना 3 (बर्फ़, रेत आदि का) हवा द्वारा ढेर लगा दिया जाना : drifting snow.

drill¹ / ड्रिल् / noun 1 ड्रिल मशीन, बरमा (लकड़ी, पत्थर आदि में छेद करने का यंत्र) 2 सैनिक (शारीरिक) प्रशिक्षण; क़वायद 3 (शिक्षण में) अभ्यास ▸ **drill** verb 1 (ड्रिल मशीन या बरमे से) छेद करना : drill for oil 2 लगातार अभ्यास द्वारा प्रशिक्षित करना या होना।

drill² / ड्रिल् / noun बीज बोने की सीधी पंक्ति; बोए हुए बीजों की पंक्ति; इस प्रकार बीज बोने की मशीन।

drink¹ / ड्रिड्क् / noun 1 पेय पदार्थ : food and drink 2 शराब 3 शराब की आदत।

drink² / ड्रिड्क् / verb (pt **drank** / ड्रैड्क्/; pp **drunk** / ड्रड्क्/) 1 पेय पदार्थ पीना 2 शराब पीना : He never drinks. 3 **drink sth (in/up)** (पौधों या मिट्टी का) पानी सोखना ▸ **drinkable** adj पीने योग्य (पानी) **drinker** noun 1 मद्यप, शराबी 2 पेय विशेष पीने का आदी : a coffee drinker **drinking** noun शराब पीने की क्रिया **drinking-water** noun पीने का पानी।

drip / ड्रिप् / verb (-pp-) बूँद-बूँद कर टपकना; टपकना : Is that roof still dripping? ▸ **drip** noun 1 बूँद (द्रव की) 2 यंत्र जिसके द्वारा नस में दवाई, रक्त आदि पहुँचाया जाता है : put sb on a drip **dripping** adj **dripping (with sth)** बिलकुल भीगा हुआ।

drive / ड्राइव् / verb (pt **drove** / ड्रोव् /; pp **driven** / 'ड्रिव्न् /) 1 गाड़ी चलाना; गाड़ी चलाकर कहीं पहुँचना/किसी को कहीं ले जाना : Could you drive me home/

to the airport? 2 (पशु, व्यक्ति आदि को) चलाना, हाँकना : *drive sheep into a field* 3 (जल या वायु द्वारा) बहाकर ले जाना : *dead leaves driven along by the wind* 4 (वर्षा, पानी आदि का) हवा के दबाव से तेज़ी से एक ओर बहना 5 किसी वस्तु को किसी विशेष दिशा/अवस्था में बल- पूर्वक लाना (जैसे कील ठोंकना), (सुरंग आदि) खोदना : *They drove a tunnel through the solid rock.* 6 चलाने वाली शक्ति बनना : *a steam-driven locomo- tive* 7 प्रेरक तत्त्व बनना; अत्यंत कठिन काम करना 8 अरुचिकर स्थिति में पहुँचना/पहुँचा दिया जाना : *drive sb crazy/out of their mind.*

drive² / ड्राइव् / noun 1 कार या वैन में सैर 2 (**driveway** भी) घर का (व्यक्तिगत) प्रवेश मार्ग 3 गेंद पर किया प्रहार : *a forehand/backhand drive* 4 प्रेरक शक्ति; ऊर्जा; इच्छा संतुष्ट करने की कामना।

driver / ड्राइवर् / noun चालक; पशुओं को हाँकने वाला।

driving¹ / ड्राइविङ् / noun चालन योग्यता।

driving² / ड्राइविङ् / adj 1 महान प्रभाव रखते हुए 2 महान शक्ति रखते हुए।

drizzle / ड्रिज़्ल् / verb रिम-झिम बरसना ▸ **drizzle** noun हलकी फुहार।

drone / ड्रोन् / verb 1 (मक्खियों का) भिनभिनाना; भिनभिनाहट जैसी आवाज़ करना : *An aircraft droned over- head.* 2 भिनभिनाहट जैसी नीरस आवाज़ में गाना या बात करना : *a droning voice* ▸ **drone** noun 1 नर मधुमक्खी 2 भिन- भिनाहट 3 लगातार नीरस बातचीत।

drool / ड्रूल् / verb 1 लार टपकना 2 **drool (over sb/sth)** (अनौप, अपमा) ख़ूब अच्छा लग रहा है ऐसा बेतुकापन दिखाना।

droop / ड्रूप् / verb (दुर्बलता या थकावट से) झुक जाना : *flowers drooping for lack of water* ▸ **droop** noun [sing] **droopy** adj.

drop¹ / ड्रॉप् / noun 1 बूँद : *drops of rain/dew* 2 द्रव की ज़रा-सी मात्रा; बूँद के आकार की कोई वस्तु 3 **drops** [pl] दवा (की बूँदें) 4 पतन, गिरावट : *a drop in prices/temperature* 5 ऊँचाई से सीधी नीचे दूरी 6 हवाई जहाज़ आदि से कुछ गिराया जाना।

drop² / ड्रॉप् / verb (-pp-) 1 गिरना या गिराना : *The bottle dropped and broke.* 2 (पशु या व्यक्ति) थके होने से गिर पड़ना 3 दुर्बल या पतनशील होने देना 4 कुछ वस्तु कहीं पहुँचाना; पत्र डालना ■ **a drop in the bucket/ocean** समुद्र में एक बूँद के समान विशाल समूह में कोई अकेला **drop a line** पत्रोत्तर देना **drop behind (sb)** पिछड़ जाना **drop dead** 1 मरना (अचानक) 2 (अप्र) किसी को गुस्से में चुप होने को कहना **drop in (on sb)** अनौपचारिक रूप से मुलाक़ात करना ▸ **drop-out** noun पढ़ाई छोड़ देने वाला व्यक्ति **droppings** noun [pl] बीट, गोबर।

dross / ड्रॉस् / noun धातु या लोहे का मैल जो पिघलने पर ऊपर आ जाता है।

drought / ड्राउट् / noun सूखा, अनावृष्टि।

drown / ड्राउन् / verb 1 डूब कर मरना; डुबो कर मारना 2 **drown sth (in sth)** भिगोना, गीला करना।

drowsy / ड्राउज़ि / adj (-ier, -iest) 1 अर्धनिद्रा में; ऊँघता हुआ 2 नींद लाने वाली ▸ **drowsily** adv.

drudge / ड्रज् / noun अरुचिकर कार्यों को परिश्रम से लंबे समय तक करने वाला व्यक्ति ▸ **drudgery** noun नीरस कठिन कार्य।

drug / ड्रग् / noun 1 दवा, औषधि : *a pain-killing drug* 2 ज्ञानेंद्रियों को प्रभावित करने वाला पदार्थ : *be on drugs* ▸ **drug** verb (-gg-) 1 दवा देना 2 भोजन या पेय में चेतनाहर मादक पदार्थ मिला देना : *in a drugged state* **drug addict** noun नशेबाज़, मादक सेवी **druggist** / ड्रगिस्ट् / noun (US) = chemist ▸ **drugstore** noun (US) दवा आदि बेचने वाली दुकान।

drum / ड्रम् / noun 1 (संगीत) ढोल, मृदंग 2 ढोलनुमा पीपा, ड्रम 3 कान का परदा ▸ drum verb (-mm-) 1 ढोल/मृदंग बजाना 2 drum (sth) on sth अँगुलियों से थपथपाना : drum on the table **drummer** noun ढोल आदि बजाने वाला।

drunk / ड्रंक् / adj 1 शराब के नशे में मदहोश/चूर 2 drunk with sth उत्तेजना के कारण अजीब व्यवहार करते हुए : drunk with power/success ▸ drunkard / ड्रंकर्ड / noun पियक्कड़।

drunken / ड्रंकन् / adj 1 पिए हुए/नशे में चूर : a drunken reveller 2 बहुत अधिक शराब पीने का प्रभाव दिखाने वाला : a drunken argument/laughter.

dry[1] / ड्राइ / adj (drier, driest) 1 सूखा, शुष्क 2 वर्षा रहित मौसम 3 भावनाहीन, सूखे स्वभाव वाला व्यक्ति 4 (भाषण, पुस्तक आदि) नीरस 5 (अनौप) प्यासा (बनाने वाला) 6 (रोटी) बिना मक्खन के 7 ऐसा देश या क्षेत्र जहाँ शराब बेचना/ख़रीदना अवैध है ▸ drily (dryly भी) adv dryness noun.

dry[2] / ड्राइ / verb (pt, pp dried) शुष्क होना; सुखाना : Leave the dishes to dry (off). ■ dry up 1 (नदी, नाले आदि) सूख जाना 2 किसी स्रोत आदि का बंद हो जाना ▸ drier (dryer भी) noun सुखाने वाला यंत्र।

dual / ड्यूअल्; US ड्ूअल् / adj दो का विशेषण; द्वैत; दुहरा ▸ dual carriage-way noun बीच में विभाजित सड़क जो आने और जाने वाले वाहनों को अलग रखती है dualism noun (दर्शन) द्वैतवाद।

dub / डब् / verb (-bb-) 1 किसी को विशिष्ट नाम देना 2 dub sth (into sth) एक भाषा की फ़िल्म के संवाद दूसरी भाषा में रूपांतरित करना : an English film dubbed into Hindi.

dubious / ड्यूबिअस्; US ड्ूबिअस् / adj 1 dubious (about sth/doing sth) (व्यक्ति) अनिश्चित एवं संदेहपूर्ण 2 (अपमा) संभवत: बेईमान या संदेहास्पद : a rather dubious character 3 संदिग्ध महत्त्व वाला ▸ dubiously adv.

duchess / डचस् / noun 1 ड्यूक की पत्नी या विधवा : the Duchess of Kent 2 ड्यूक के अधिकार रखने वाली महिला।

duck[1] / डक् / noun (pl अपरिवर्तित या ducks) 1 बतख़ 2 (क्रिकेट में) बल्लेबाज़ का शून्य स्कोर : be out for a duck ▸ duckling noun बतख़ का चूज़ा।

duck[2] / डक् / verb 1 (आक्रमण से/देखे जाने से बचने के लिए) तुरंत नीचे झुक जाना 2 वार से बचना : duck a punch 3 किसी को पानी में ढकेल देना या स्वयं पानी में डुबकी लगा जाना : Her sisters ducked her in the river. 4 duck (out of) sth (अनौप) ज़िम्मेदारी से बचना, कन्नी काटना।

duct / डक्ट् / noun 1 द्रव, गैस, विद्युत/टेलिफ़ोन के तार आदि ले जाने वाली नली 2 पौधों में या प्राणी के शरीर में द्रव पदार्थ वहन करने वाली नलिका : the bile duct.

dud / डड् / noun निरुपयोगी वस्तु; ठीक से काम न करने वाली वस्तु ▸ dud adj बेकार, ख़राब : a dud cheque.

due[1] / ड्यू; US ड्ू / adj 1 due (for sth) प्राप्य 2 देय (धन) 3 due (to do sth) अपेक्षित; व्यवस्था किया हुआ 4 due to sth/sb के कारण, के फलस्वरूप : absent due to illness 5 उपयुक्त, समुचित : after due consideration 6 due (to sb) ऋण या कृतज्ञता के रूप में ■ in due course उपयुक्त समय पर।

due[2] / ड्यू; US ड्ू / noun 1 one's/sb's due प्राप्य वस्तु 2 dues[pl] शुल्क (सदस्यता आदि के लिए); चुंगी।

due[3] / ड्यू; US ड्ू / adv (north, south, east या west से पहले प्रयुक्त) ठीक, बिलकुल : walk three miles due north.

duel / ड्यूअल्; US ड्ूअल् / noun 1 (पूर्व में) तलवार या पिस्तौल का द्वंद्वयुद्ध 2 दो

व्यक्तियों या वर्गों में स्पर्धा, प्रतियोगिता : *a complex legal duel* ▸ **duel** *verb* (-ll-) द्वंद्वयुद्ध लड़ना **duelling** *noun*.

duet / ड्यु'एट् ; *US* डु'एट्/ (duo भी) *noun* युगल (गान, वादन) : *a duet for violin and piano*.

duke / ड्यूक ; *US* डूक / *noun* 1 ड्यूक, उच्च पद के संभ्रांत व्यक्ति 2 (कुछ यूरोप के देशों में) किसी छोटे-से स्वतंत्र राज्य का पुरुष शासक।

dull / डल् / *adj* (-er, -est) 1 मंद, सुस्त; स्फूर्तिहीन 2 अस्पष्ट, फीका (रंग) : *a dull colour* 3 बुद्धि से मंद, मूर्ख 4 (दर्द आदि) धीमा-धीमा : *a dull ache* 5 (व्यापार) मंद, सुस्त ▸ **dull** *verb* मंद या सुस्त करना; चमक खोना **dullness** *noun* **dully** *adj*.

duly / 'ड्यूलि; *US* 'डूलि / *adv* (औप) 1 उपयुक्त या उचित रीति से 2 अपेक्षित और उचित समय पर।

dumb / डम् / *adj* (-er, -est) 1 गूँगा; बोलने में असमर्थ 2 मौन : *He stood looking around him, baffled and dumb.* 3 (अनौप) मूर्ख ▸ **dumbly** *adv* **dumbness** *noun*.

dumbfounded / डम्'फ़ाउन्डिड् / *adj* (**dumbstruck** भी) भौंचक्का, हक्का-बक्का : *We were completely dumbfounded by her rudeness.*

dummy / 'डमि / *noun* (pl **dummies**) 1 मानव आकृति का मॉडल : *a tailor's dummy* 2 वास्त-विक प्रतीत होने वाली नक़ली वस्तु : *The bottles of whisky on display are all dummies.* 3 (अनौप) मूर्ख व्यक्ति।

dump / डम्प् / *verb* 1 लापरवाही से (कूड़े की तरह) फेंकना या रखना : *Just dump it over there —I'll sort it out later.* 2 कूड़ा-कचरा फेंकना/डालना 3 (अनौप, प्राय: अपमा) किसी को बेपरवाही से छोड़ देना 4 (वाणिज्य, अपमा) अपने देश के बाज़ार में न बिकने वाला माल दूसरे देश में कम क़ीमत पर बेच डालना ▸ **dump** *noun*

1 कूड़ाघर; हानिकर पदार्थ डालने का स्थान : *a toxic nuclear waste dump* 2 अस्थायी गोदाम 3 (अनौप) गंदा, अरुचिकर स्थान।

dumper (**dumper truck** भी) *noun* कूड़ा ढोने वाला ट्रक **dumping** *noun*.

dumpling / 'डम्प्लिङ् /*noun* 1 मैदे का छोटा पिंड जो शोरबेदार व्यंजनों के साथ पकाया जाता है 2 मीठा व्यंजन जो लोई में फलों का गूदा भरकर बनाया जाता है।

dumps / डम्प्स् / *noun* [pl] ■ **down in the dumps** (अनौप) खिन्न, उदास।

dune / ड्यून् ; *US* डून् / (**sand-dune** भी) *noun* (तेज़ हवा के झोंकों से बना) बालू का टीला/टिब्बा (समुद्र के पास या रेगिस्तान में)।

dung / डङ् / *noun* गोबर, लीद (जो खाद के काम आए) : *cow dung.*

dungeon / 'डन्जन् / *noun* अंधकारपूर्ण तहख़ाना जो पहले कारागार के रूप में काम आता था।

duo / 'ड्यूओ; *US* 'डूओ / *noun* (pl **duos**) 1 कलाकारों की जोड़ी/युगल : *a comedy duo* 2 युगलगान/वादन।

dupe / ड्यूप् ; *US* डूप् / *verb* **dupe sb (into doing sth)** किसी को धोखा देकर कुछ काम करा लेना ▸ **dupe** *noun* आसानी से धोखे में आने वाला भोला आदमी।

duplex / 'ड्यूप्लेक्स् ; *US* 'डूप्लेक्स् /*noun* (विशेषत: *US*) 1 दो घरों में विभाजित भवन 2 दुमंज़िली इमारत या फ़्लैट : *a duplex apartment.*

duplicate¹ / 'ड्यूप्लिकट् ; *US* 'डूप्लि-कट्/ *adj* 1 प्रतिकृति, किसी वस्तु की ठीक वैसी ही नक़ल : *a duplicate set of keys* 2 दो अंश जो बिलकुल एक जैसे हों : *a duplicate receipt/form* ▸ **duplicate** *noun* (पत्र आदि की) ठीक उसी प्रकार की नक़ल ■ **in duplicate** (काग़ज़ात आदि) दो प्रतियों में।

duplicate² / 'ड्यूप्लिकेट् ; *US* 'डूप्लि-केट्/ *verb* 1 नक़ल या प्रति तैयार करना 2 कुछ (अनावश्यक रूप से) दोबारा करना, दोहराना : *This research merely* *duplicates work already done elsewhere.* ▸ **duplication** noun.

duplicity / इ़यु'प्लिसटि / noun छल, कपट।

durable /'डयुअरब्ल; US 'डुरब्ल्/ adj टिकाऊ (वस्तु) ▸ **durability** /,इयुअर 'बिलटि; US,डुर 'बिलटि / noun.

duration /इयु'रेशन्; US डु'रेशन्/ noun (समय की) अवधि, मियाद : *of three years' duration.*

duress /इयु'रेस; US डु'रेस / noun किसी से काम कराने के लिए प्रयुक्त धमकी अथवा बल प्रयोग : *sign a confession under duress.*

during /'डयुअरिङ्; US 'डुरिङ्/ prep 1 किसी समय की संपूर्ण अवधि में 2 एक निर्धारित कालावधि में : *They met only twice during the whole time they were neighbours.* 3 किसी कार्य की प्रगति के विशेष समय के दौरान : *The phone rang during the meal.*

dusk /डस्क/ noun शाम का झुटपुटा; संध्या समय (सायंकाल)।

dusky /'डस्कि / adj (-ier, -iest) 1 मंद (प्रकाश) 2 गहरा रंग : *dusky blue* 3 (व्यक्ति) काले रंग का।

dust¹ /डस्ट/ noun धूल; किसी भी धातु का चूरा ▸ **dustbin** noun कूड़ेदान।

dust² /डस्ट/ verb 1 धूल साफ करना या झाड़ना/पोंछना 2 **dust sb/oneself down/ off** अपनी या औरों की धूल झाड़ना : *Dust yourself down—you're covered in chalk.* ▸ **duster** noun झाड़न (कपड़ा); ब्लैकबोर्ड डस्टर।

dusty /'डस्टि / adj (-ier, -iest) धूल-धूसरित, धूलभरा; (रंग) मटमैला : *a dusty pink.*

dutiful /'डयुटिफ्ल; US 'डूटिफ्ल / adj कर्तव्यनिष्ठ, निष्ठावान।

duty /'डयुटि; US 'डूटि / noun (pl **duties**) 1 कर्तव्य, फ़र्ज़ 2 कार्य, कर्म : *routine administrative duties*

3 **duty (on sth)** शुल्क, कर (आयातित, निर्यातित या उत्पादित वस्तुओं पर) : *customs/excise duties* ▸ **duty-free** adj, adv करमुक्त (सामान)।

dwarf /ड्वॉर्फ़् / noun (pl **dwarfs** या **dwarves**) 1 (व्यक्ति, पशु या पौधा) बौना 2 (किस्से-कहानियों में) जादुई शक्तियों वाला (बौना व्यक्ति) ▸ **dwarf** verb दूरी या तुलना में बहुत छोटा दिखना या दिखलाना; सामान्य आकार तक बढ़ने से रोकना।

dwell /ड्वेल् / verb (pt, pp **dwelt** /ड्वेल्ट्/; US **dwelled**) **dwell in, at, etc...** (प्रा या औप) रहना ■ **dwell upon/ on sth** विस्तार से किसी विषय पर बोलना या सोचना ▸ **dweller** noun (विशेषत: यौगिक शब्दों में) स्थान विशेष में रहने वाला : *town/city dweller* **dwelling** noun (औप या परि) निवास स्थान।

dwindle /'डविन्ड्ल् / verb **dwindle (away) (to sth)** क्रमिक रूप से कम या क्षीण होते जाना : *Their savings have dwindled (away) to almost nothing.*

dye¹ / डाइ / verb (3rd pers sing pres t **dyes**; pt, pp **dyed**; pres p **dyeing**) रँगना, विशेषत: द्रव में घुले रंग में डुबोकर : *dye a white dress blue.*

dye² /डाइ/ noun किसी वस्तु को रँगने वाला रंग : *blue dye.*

dying /'डाइइङ् / adj मरते समय; मरते हुए।

dyke (dike भी) / डाइक् / noun 1 बाँध 2 नहर।

dynamic / डाइ'नैमिक् / adj 1 (भौतिक बल, शक्ति) गति उत्पन्न करने वाला 2 (व्यक्ति या संस्था) चरित्रबल एवं शक्ति वाला : *a dynamic personality* ▸ **dynamic** noun गतिदायक बल **dynamically** adv.

dynamics /डाइ'नैमिक्स् / noun गति और बल के अध्ययन से संबंधित भौतिकी की शाखा।

dynamite /'डाइनमाइट् / noun 1 बड़ी शक्ति का विस्फोटक पदार्थ 2 उग्र प्रतिक्रिया

की संभावना वाली चीज़ : *The abortion issue is political dynamite.* 3 *(अनौप)* अत्यंत प्रभावशाली व्यक्ति या वस्तु ▸ **dynamite** *verb* डाइनमाइट से विस्फोट करके उड़ा देना।

dynamo / 'डाइनमो / *noun (pl* **dynamos)** 1 बिजली उत्पन्न करने वाला यंत्र, डाइनमो 2 *(अनौप)* कार्य करने की असामान्य क्षमता वाला व्यक्ति; कर्मठ व्यक्ति : *a human dynamo.*

dynasty / 'डिनस्टि; *US* 'डाइनस्टि / *noun (pl* **dynasties)** वंशपरंपरा, राजवंश; एक राजवंश का राज्यकाल : *during the Mughal dynasty* ▸ **dynastic** *adj.*

dysentery / 'डिसन्ट्रि; *US* 'डिसन्टेरि / *noun* पेचिश (का रोग)।

dyslexia / डिस्'लेक्सिआ / *noun (चिकि)* एक हलका मानसिक विकार जिसके कारण पढ़ने एवं वर्तनी ठीक से लिखने में कठिनाई होती है ▸ **dyslexic** *adj.*

Ee

each/ ईच् / *indef det* (दो या अधिक में)
प्रत्येक व्यक्ति, वस्तु या समूह आदि को
अलग-अलग देखने पर : *in each corner
of the room* ▸ *each indef pron* वर्ग
या समूह का प्रत्येक सदस्य : *each of the
boys/books/buildings* **each** *indef
adv* अलग-अलग हर एक : *The cakes
are Rs 10 each*. **each other** *pron*
एक दूसरे को/से।

eager/ ईगर् / *adj* **eager** (for sth/to do
sth) आतुर, उत्सुक : *eager for success*
▸ **eagerly** *adv* **eagerness** *noun*
[*sing*].

eagle/ ईग्ल् / *noun* एक तीव्र दृष्टि वाला
शिकारी पक्षी, बाज़ ▸ **eaglet** *noun* बाज़
का बच्चा।

ear¹ / इअर् / *noun* 1 कान 2 [*sing*] **an
ear** (for sth) संगीत या भाषा में स्वर की
पहचान करने का सामर्थ्य 3 किसी के द्वारा
कही जाने वाली बात को सुनने और ध्यान देने
की इच्छा ▸ **eardrum** *noun* कान का परदा
earshot *noun* ■ **(be) within/out of
earshot** श्रवण सीमा के अंदर/बाहर, वह
क्षेत्र जहाँ से बोला हुआ सुनाई पड़ता/नहीं
पड़ता है ▸ **earsplitting** *adj* (आवाज़)
बहुत तेज़।

ear² / इअर् / *noun* अनाज की बाली जिसमें
दाने लगते हैं।

earl / अर्ल् / *noun* (ब्रिटेन में) उच्च स्तर के
संभ्रांत व्यक्ति का पद, अर्ल।

early / अर्लि / *adj* (-ier, -iest)
1 प्रारंभिक; (औरों की या सामान्य स्थिति
की तुलना में) जल्दी : *an early breakfast* 2 दिन के प्रारंभ में या किसी अन्य समय
के प्रारंभ में : *in the early days of
space exploration* ▸ **earliness**
noun **early** *adv* 1 सामान्य अथवा अपेक्षित
समय से पहले : *The bus arrived five
minutes early.* 2 किसी कालावधि के
प्रारंभ में ■ **early on** प्रारंभिक स्थिति में

▸ **early warning** *noun* समयपूर्व
चेतावनी।

earmark / इअरमार्क् / *verb* **earmark
sb/sth** (for sth/sb) (व्यक्ति या वस्तु को)
विशेष प्रयोजन के लिए अलग कर देना :
*earmark a sum of money for re-
search.*

earn / अर्न् / *verb* 1 (धन) अर्जित करना,
कमाना : *She earned her living by
singing in a nightclub.* 2 लाभ कमाना,
निवेश पर ब्याज कमाना : *Money earns
more in a high interest account.*
3 अपनी उपलब्धियों या व्यवहार से कुछ प्राप्त
करना : *His honesty earned him
great respect.* ▸ **earner** *noun* कमाने
वाला व्यक्ति; लाभकारी व्यवसाय **earnings**
noun [*pl*] अर्जित धन।

earnest / अर्निस्ट् / *adj* निष्ठावान, गंभीरता
और लगन से काम करने वाला : *a terribly
earnest young woman* ▸ **earnest**
noun ■ **in (deadly) earnest** 1 बहुत हद
तक; दृढ़ संकल्प और शक्ति से 2 गंभीरता के
साथ, न कि मज़ाक में ▸ **earnestly** *adv.*

earth / अर्थ् / *noun* 1 (**Earth** भी) [*sing*]
संसार; पृथ्वी (ग्रह जिस पर हम रहते हैं)
2 [*sing*] स्थल, ज़मीन (न कि जलमय स्थान
या आकाश) 3 मिट्टी : *fill a hole with
earth* 4 जंगली जानवरों (जैसे लोमड़ी) की
माँद 5 (प्राय: *sing*) विद्युत परिपथ को ज़मीन
से जोड़कर पूरा करने वाला तार ▸ **earth**
verb विद्युत उपकरण का ज़मीन से संपर्क
करना **earthy** *adj* (-ier, -iest) 1 मिट्टी
जैसा : *earthy colours/smells* 2 (व्यक्ति
या चुटकुले आदि) मूल भौतिक कार्यों से जुड़े,
न कि बौद्धिक : *an earthy sense of
humour.*

earthenware / अर्थ्न्वेअर् / *noun* मिट्टी
के बरतन, प्याले-तश्तरी, घड़े आदि।

earthly / अर्थ्लि / *adj* 1 सांसारिक (न कि
पारलौकिक) 2 संभव।

earthquake / 'अर्थक्वेक् / (quake भी) *noun* भूकंप।

earthworm / 'अर्थवर्म् / *noun* केंचुआ ।

ease¹ / ईज़् / *noun* 1 आराम, आसानी : *He passed the exam with ease.* 2 चैन; काम, दर्द या चिंता से मुक्ति : *The injection brought him immediate ease.* ■ **ill at ease** परेशान नज़र आना (**stand) at ease** (सेना में आदेश के रूप मे प्रयुक्त) आराम की स्थिति में पैर फैलाकर खड़े होना।

ease² / ईज़् / *verb* 1 आसान और कम गंभीर बना देना : *ease the burden of debt* 2 (मन या शरीर को) आराम पहुँचाना : *The aspirins eased my headache.* 3 ढीला कर देना, (गति या प्रयत्नों को) धीमा कर देना 4 क़ीमत या महत्त्व में कम कर देना या हो जाना : *Interest rates have eased since December.*

easel / 'ईज़्ल् / *noun* ईज़ल, लकड़ी का फ़्रेम जिस पर ब्लैकबोर्ड को या बन रहे चित्र को रखते हैं।

east / ईस्ट् / *noun* [*sing*] (संक्षि E) 1 (प्राय: the east) पूर्व दिशा, पूरब 2 **the East** एशिया के देश, विशेषत: चीन और जापान ▸ **east** *adj* 1 पूर्व में या पूर्व की तरफ़ : *East Africa* 2 पूर्व दिशा से आया : *an east wind* **east** *adv* पूर्व की तरफ़ : *two kilometres east of here* **eastward/eastwards** *adj, adv* पूर्वाभिमुख (गमन)।

Easter / 'ईस्टर् / *noun* (प्राय: *sing*) ईस्टर, ईसा मसीह के पुनरुत्थान की जयंती जो मार्च या अप्रैल के किसी रविवार को मनाई जाती है।

eastern / 'ईस्टर्न् / (**Eastern** भी) *adj* पूर्व में स्थित, पूर्व विषयक : *eastern customs/religions.*

easy¹ / 'ईज़ि / *adj* (**-ier, -iest**) 1 आसान, सरल 2 आरामदेह; शारीरिक कष्ट या मानसिक झंझट से मुक्त : *lead an easy life* 3 प्रिय एवं मित्रवत्, सख्त या रूक्ष नहीं : *have an easy manner* 4 आक्रमण या दुर्व्यवहार के लिए खुला : *become easy prey* ■ **take the easy way out** किसी कठिन स्थिति से बचने के लिए सरल उपाय अपनाना ▸ **easily** *adv* 1 आसानी से 2 संदेहरहित 3 बहुत संभव, हर संभव 4 जल्दी ही, सामान्य से शीघ्र : *I get bored easily.* **easygoing** *adj* (व्यक्ति) आराम तलब, न कष्ट देने वाला न कष्ट उठाने वाला।

easy² / 'ईज़ि / *adv* (**-ier, -iest**) (आदेश के रूप में) सावधान ■ **easier said than done** कहने में सरल पर करने में कठिन।

eat / ईट् / *verb* (*pt* **ate** / एट्; *US* एट् /; *pp* **eaten** / ईट्न् /) 1 **eat (up)/eat sth (up)** खाना : *He was too ill to eat.* 2 (अनौप) चिंता या कुढ़न पैदा करना ■ **eat one's words** दीनता से अपनी बात वापिस लेना **eat away at sth/eat into sth** नष्ट करना ▸ **eatable** *adj* खाने योग्य, खाने के लिए अच्छा **eats** *noun* [*pl*] (अनौप) भोजन, विशेषत: पार्टी के लिए।

eau-de-Cologne / ओ ड क'लोन् / *noun* (**cologne** भी) कोलोन (जर्मनी) में बना एक प्रसिद्ध इत्र।

eaves / ईव़्ज़् / *noun* [*pl*] छत का वह भाग जो मकान की दीवारों के बाहर होता है।

eavesdrop / 'ईव़्ज़्ड्रॉप् / *verb* (**-pp-**) किसी की निजी बातचीत को चुपके से छिपकर सुनना : *He admitted eavesdropping on his wife's phone calls.*

ebb / एब् / *noun* (प्राय: **the ebb**) (ज्वार-भाटा का) उतार, ह्रास : *The tide is on the ebb.* ■ **the ebb and flow (of sth/sb)** दिशा, शैली आदि में लगातार होता बदलाव; तीव्रता या संख्या में लगातार घटत-बढ़त ▸ **ebb** *verb* 1 (ज्वार का) पानी उतरना 2 **ebb (away)** धीरे-धीरे कम और क्षीण हो जाना : *Our enthusiasm soon began to ebb.*

ebony / 'एबनि / *noun* आबनूस; आबनूस की लकड़ी।

eccentric / इक्'सेन्ट्रिक् / *adj* 1 (व्यक्ति अथवा व्यवहार) असामान्य या अजीब; सनकी,

झक्की 2 (वृत्त) जिनका केंद्र एक न हो ▸ **eccentric** *noun* **eccentricity** /एक्सेन्'ट्रिसिटि/ *noun* (*pl* **eccentricities**) 1 झक्की व्यवहार 2 सनक : *One of his eccentricities is sleeping under the bed instead of on it.*

ecclesiastic / इ‚क्लीज़ि'ऐस्टिक् / *noun* पादरी या ईसाई चर्च का याजक वर्ग ▸ **ecclesiastical** / इ‚क्लीज़ि'ऐस्टिक्ल् / *adj* चर्च विषयक; पादरी विषयक।

echo /'एको/ *noun* (*pl* **echoes**) 1 प्रतिध्वनि, गूँज : *The cave has a wonderful echo.* 2 एक से मिलती-जुलती दूसरी चीज़ जिसे देखकर पहली की याद आए : *Her speech evoked echoes of the past.* ▸ **echo** *verb* 1 (आवाज़ का) प्रतिध्वनित होना : *His footsteps echoed in the empty hall.* 2 दुहराना; हाँ में हाँ मिलाना : *They echoed their leader's every word.* 3 किसी चीज़ का अन्य से समानता रखना।

éclair / इ 'क्लेअर् / *noun* एक प्रकार का केक जो चॉकलेट से ढका होता है और जिसके अंदर क्रीम भरी होती है।

eclipse / इ'क्लिप्स् / *noun* 1 (सूर्य- या चंद्र-) ग्रहण : *a total/partial eclipse of the sun* 2 महत्त्व, प्रसिद्धि या शक्ति में हानि : *His reputation as a writer has suffered something of an eclipse in recent years.* ▸ **eclipse** *verb* 1 ग्रहण करना; प्रकाश किरणों को बीच में रोक लेना 2 तुलना द्वारा किसी व्यक्ति या वस्तु को फीका या श्रीहीन कर देना।

ecology / इ'कॉलजि / *noun* पर्यावरण विज्ञान, पौधों एवं जंतुओं का एक दूसरे से एवं उनके वातावरण से संबंध (का अध्ययन) ▸ **ecological** *adj* **ecologically** *adv* **ecologist** *noun.*

economic /‚ईक'नॉमिक्/ *adj* 1 व्यापार, उद्योग और संपदा के विकास से संबंधित, अर्थशास्त्र विषयक : *the government's economic policy* 2 लाभदायक : *It is*

not always economic for buses to run on Sundays.

economical / ‚ईक 'नॉमिकल्; ‚एक 'नॉमिकल् / *adj* 1 खर्च किए धन के अनुसार अच्छी सेवा या क़ीमत प्रदान करने वाला 2 आवश्यकता से अधिक प्रयोग न करने वाला : *an economical style of writing.*

economics / ‚ईक 'नॉमिक्स; ‚एक 'नॉमिक्स / *noun* अर्थशास्त्र, धन और माल के वितरण की व्यवस्था और उत्पादन का विज्ञान।

economist / इ 'कॉनमिस्ट् / *noun* अर्थशास्त्री।

economize, -ise / इ'कॉनमाइज़् / *verb* **economize (on sth)** पहले की तुलना में कम (शक्ति, धन, समय आदि) खर्च करना : *economize on fuel/manpower.*

economy /इ'कॉनमि/ *noun* (*pl* **economies**) 1 (प्रायः **the economy**) (समाज, राष्ट्र आदि की) अर्थव्यवस्था 2 किफ़ायत; बिना बेकार खर्च किए धन, शक्ति आदि का प्रयोग।

ecstasy /'एक्स्टसि / *noun* (*pl* **ecstasies**) 1 परम हर्ष और आनंद की भावना 2 आनंद प्राप्ति के लिए ली जाने वाली एक मादक वस्तु ▸ **ecstatic** / इक्'स्टैटिक् / *adj* आनंदित, समाधिमग्न : *ecstatic praise/applause* **ecstatically** *adv.*

eczema /'एक्सिमा/ *US* इग्'ज़ीमा/ *noun* एक्ज़ीमा, एक चर्म रोग।

eddy /'एडि / *noun* (*pl* **eddies**) जल, वायु, धूल आदि का भँवर जो वृत्ताकार में घूमता है।

edge¹ / एज् / *noun* 1 किसी समतल भूमि की बाहरी सीमा, कोर; किनारा 2 चाकू- तलवार आदि की धार; गोल चपटी वस्तु का किनारा : *stand the coin on its edge* 3 किसी व्यक्ति या वस्तु की तुलना में अच्छी स्थिति 4 तीव्रता एवं प्रायः उत्तेजक गुण ▸ **-edged** /एज्ड्/ *suff* (प्रत्यय) (यौगिक विशेषण बनाने में प्रयुक्त) धार विशेष वाला : *a blunt-edged razor.*

edge² / एज् / verb 1 **edge sth (with sth)** किनारा बनाना : *a road edged with grass* 2 धीरे-धीरे आगे की ओर बढ़ना या बढ़ाना : *The climber edged carefully along the narrow rock ledge.* 3 क्रमिक रूप से बढ़ना या घटना : *Share prices edged up by 1.5% over the year.* ▸ **edging** noun किनारा।

edgeways / 'एज्वेज़् / (US **edgewise** / 'एज्वाइज़्/) adv धार या किनारे को बाहर की ओर किए हुए।

edgy / 'एजि / adj (-ier, -iest) (अनौप) चिड़चिड़ा; व्याकुल।

edible / 'एडब्ल् / adj खाने योग्य : *edible fungi/snails.*

edict / 'ईडिक्ट् / noun राजाज्ञा, फ़रमान।

edifice / 'एडिफ़िस् / noun (औप या परि) बड़ा भवन, प्रासाद।

edit / 'एडिट् / verb 1 समाचार-पत्र, पत्रिका या पुस्तक का संपादन करना 2 (किसी अन्य के) लेख को प्रकाशन योग्य बनाना (काट-छाँटकर); विभिन्न अंशों को समुचित क्रम में व्यवस्थित करके किसी कार्यक्रम को रेडियो, टी वी या फ़िल्म के लिए तैयार करना।

edition / इडिश्न् / noun 1 (पुस्तक का) संस्करण : *a paperback/hardback edition* 2 कोई विशिष्ट पत्रिका, या रेडियो/टी वी कार्यक्रम 3 पुस्तक या पत्र-पत्रिका की मुद्रण संख्या : *a limited edition of 500.*

editor / 'एडिटर / noun संपादक; पुस्तक या फ़िल्म का संपादन करने वाला।

editorial / एडि'टॉरिअल् / adj संपादक से संबंधित ▸ **editorial** noun संपादकीय लेख।

educate / 'एजुकेट् / verb 1 शिक्षा देना, शिक्षित करना : *She was educated in France.* 2 **educate sb (in sth)** कार्य-विधि समझाना, प्रशिक्षण देना ▸ **educated** adj शिक्षित; अच्छी शिक्षा के फलस्वरूप : *an educated voice.*

education / एजु'केश्न् / noun 1 [sing] शिक्षा 2 शिक्षाशास्त्र का क्षेत्र : *a college of*

education 3 किसी कार्य विशेष की जान-कारी देने की प्रक्रिया : *an AIDS education programme* ▸ **educational** adj **educationist** noun.

eel / ईल् / noun साँपनुमा लंबी मछली।

eerie / 'इअरि / adj रहस्य, रोमांच एवं भय उत्पन्न करने वाला : *a strange and eerie silence* ▸ **eerily** adv.

efface / इ'फ़ेस् / verb (औप) (रगड़कर) मिटा देना : (अलं) *Time alone will efface those unpleasant memories.*

effect / इ'फ़ेक्ट् / noun 1 प्रभाव, असर 2 **effect (on sb/sth)** परिणाम, नतीजा : *the effect of heat on metal* 3 **effects** [pl] (औप) चल संपत्ति, धरोहर : *The army sent her his personal effects.* ■ **bring/put sth into effect** व्यवहार में लाना, चालू करना **in effect** 1 वास्तव में; व्यावहारिक उद्देश्य के लिए 2 (क़ानून, नियम आदि) व्यवहार में (होना) **take effect** 1 कार्यरूप में परिणत होना 2 लागू होना **to the effect that ...** (इस) अभिप्राय से... **with immediate effect/with effect from...** (औप) अब से आरंभ/से आरंभ ▸ **effect** verb (औप) (कुछ) उत्पन्न करना, कुछ प्राप्त करना : *effect a cure/change.*

effective / इ'फ़ेक्टिव् / adj 1 कारगर, परिणामकारी; प्रभावोत्पादक : *a very effective colour scheme* 2 व्यवहार में लागू ▸ **effectively** adv.

effectual / इ'फ़ेक्चुअल् / adj (औप) सफल प्रभावोत्पादक।

effeminate / इ'फ़ेमिनट् / adj (अपमा) (पुरुष एवं उसका व्यवहार) ज़नाना, स्त्रियों जैसा : *an effeminate manner/voice/walk* ▸ **effeminacy** noun.

effervescent / एफ़र'वेसन्ट् / adj 1 (व्यक्ति और व्यवहार) उत्तेजित एवं उत्साहपूर्ण 2 (द्रव) गैस से बुलबुले छोड़ते हुए ▸ **effervescence** / एफ़र'वेसन्स् / noun बद-बुदाहट।

efficacious / एफ़ि'केशस् / adj (औप)

अभीष्ट परिणाम उत्पन्न करने में समर्थ (वस्तु) ▶ **efficacy**/ 'एफ़िकसि / *noun* इस प्रकार की क्षमता : *prove the efficacy of a new drug.*

efficient / इ'फ़िश्न्ट् / *adj* 1 (व्यक्ति) कार्य-कुशल : *an efficient secretary/ administrator* 2 (उपकरण, मशीन आदि) अभीष्ट परिणाम लाने में पूर्णत: सक्षम : *efficient database software* ▶ **efficiency** / इ'फ़िश्न्सि / *noun.*

effigy / 'एफ़िजि / *noun (pl* **effigies)** (लकड़ी, पत्थर आदि की) किसी व्यक्ति की मूर्ति, पुतला : *They burnt a crude effigy of the Minister.*

effort / 'एफ़र्ट् / *noun* 1 प्रयत्न, मानसिक या शारीरिक प्रयास 2 प्रयास का परिणाम ▶ **effortless** *adj* आसान, सरल **effortlessly** *adv.*

effrontery / इ'फ़्रन्टरि / *noun* धृष्टता, ढिठाई।

effusion / इ'फ़्यूश्न् / *noun* 1 (तक) (द्रव का) बाहर निकलकर अधिक मात्रा में बहना : *an effusion of blood* 2 (औप) उद्गार (भावनाओं का)।

effusive / इ'फ़्यूसिव् / *adj* (अक्सर अपमा) सहज में भावनाओं का उद्गार करने वाला, भावपूर्ण।

egalitarian / इ,गैलि'टेअरिअन् / *adj* समतावादी; सभी को समान अधिकार, अवसर आदि मिलें ऐसा मानने वाला।

egg[1] / एग् / *noun* 1 अंडा 2 (मादा स्तनधारियों में) अंडकोशिका, जिससे जीव की उत्पत्ति होती है : *The male sperm fertilizes the female egg.*

egg[2] / एग् / *verb* ■ **egg sb on (to do sth)** किसी को उकसाना या लगातार विनती करना।

ego / 'ईगो, 'एगो / *noun (pl* **egos)** व्यक्ति का स्वयं के बारे में भाव, अहंभाव : *It was a blow to her ego when she lost the job.*

egocentric/'ईगो'सेन्ट्रिक्/ *adj* अहंकारी, स्वार्थी।

egotism / 'एगोटिज़म्,'ईगोटिज़म् / (**egoism** / 'ईगोइज़म्,'एगोइज़म् / भी) *noun* अपनी ही प्रशंसा करना, अहंमन्यता ▶ **egotist** / 'एगोटिस्ट् / (**egoist** भी) *noun* अहंकारी, स्वार्थी **egotistic, egotistical** *adjs* **egotistically** *adv* आत्मश्लाघा से।

eh/ ए / *interj* (*US* **huh** भी) (अनौप) (आश्चर्य, शंका, सहमति व्यक्त करने के लिए प्रयुक्त; कोई बात दोहराने के लिए कहना)।

eiderdown/'आइडर्डाउन्/ *noun* पलंग पर बिछाने के लिए मुलायम पंखों आदि से बनी रज़ाई।

eight / एट् / *noun, pron, det* आठ (का अंक) ▶ **eighth** / एट्थ् / *pron, det* आठवाँ।

eighteen / ,ए'टीन् / *noun, pron, det* अठारह (का अंक) ▶ **eighteenth** / ,ए 'टीन्थ् / *noun pron, det* अठारहवाँ।

eighty/'एटि/ 1 *noun, pron, det* अस्सी (का अंक) 2 **the eighties** *noun [pl]* अंकों, वर्षों या तापमान की 80 से 89 तक का परास ▶ **eightieth** / 'एटिअथ् / *noun, pron, det* अस्सीवाँ; 1/80.

either / 'आइद्र; 'ईद्र् / *indef det, indef pron* 1 दोनों में से कोई एक : *You can park on either side of the street.* 2 (*det*) दोनों में से प्रत्येक : *The offices on either side were empty.* ▶ **either** *indef adv* 1 दोनों ही (समान रूप से) 2 **either... or...** या ये या वो : *She's either French or Spanish.*

ejaculate / इ'जैक्युलेट्/ *verb* (पुरुष का) वीर्य स्खलन करना ▶ **ejaculation** *noun* 1 वीर्य स्खलन 2 (औप) अचानक बोल उठना या गुस्सा हो जाना; विस्मय प्रदर्शन।

eject / इ 'जेक्ट् / *verb* 1 **eject sb/sth (from sth)** (औप) (किसी व्यक्ति को किसी स्थान से) निकाल बाहर करना : *eject an invading army* 2 **eject sth (from sth)** (किसी द्रव आदि का) बाहर निकल

पड़ना या निकाल देना : *lava ejected from a volcano* 3 संकट काल में वायुयान से बाहर स्वयं को गिरा लेना : *The pilot had to eject.* ▸ **ejection** / इ'जेक्शन् / *noun* **ejector seat** *noun* आपातकाल में झटके से बाहर आ जाने वाली विमान सीट।

eke / ईक् / *verb* ■ **eke sth out** 1 किसी विशेष उद्देश्य के लिए आवश्यकतानुसार थोड़ा-थोड़ा करके धन, भोजन आदि इकट्ठा करना : *eke out a student grant* 2 इस तरह से जीविका चलाना : *eking out a meagre existence on the barren soil.*

elaborate / इ'लैबरट् / *adj* विस्तारपूर्वक आयोजित; विस्तृत : *devise an elaborate plan* ▸ **elaborate** / इ'लैबरेट् / *verb* (औप) 1 **elaborate (on sth)** विस्तार से वर्णन करना 2 विस्तृत एवं दुरूह योजना बनाना : *She greatly elaborated the simple plot of the original comic poem.* **elaborately** *adv* **elaboration** *noun*.

elapse / इ'लैप्स् / *verb* (औप) (समय का) बीतना, गुज़रना : *Three years elapsed before they met again.*

elastic / इ'लैस्टिक् / *adj* 1 लचीला, खींचकर या दबाकर छोड़ने से पुन: अपनी पूर्व अवस्था पर आ जाने वाला: *elastic straps/strings* 2 लचकदार, जिसे परिवर्तित किया जा सके : *Our plans are fairly elastic.* ▸ **elastic** *noun* लचीला फ़ीता या अन्य सामान **elasticity** *noun*.

elated / इ'लेटिड् / *adj* **elated (at/by sth)** उल्लसित, गौरवान्वित (होना) ▸ **elatedly** *adv* **elation** / इ'लेश्न् / *noun* उल्लास, गौरव।

elbow / 'एल्बो / *noun* 1 कोहनी : *He sat with his elbow on the table.* 2 शर्ट, कोट आदि की बाँह में कोहनी वाला भाग 3 पाइप, चिमनी आदि में मोड़ ▸ **elbow** *verb* ■ **elbow one's way in, through, etc** कोहनी से ढकेलते हुए भीड़ में आगे बढ़ना **elbow sb out, aside, etc** किसी को कोहनी मारना।

elder / 'एल्डर् / *adj* 1 (दो व्यक्तियों में आयु में) बड़ा, ज्येष्ठ : *my elder brother* 2 **the elder** (औप) समान नामों वाले व्यक्तियों में अंतर करने के लिए प्रयुक्त : *Pitt the elder* ▸ **elder** *noun* 1 **my, etc elder** [*sing*] बड़ा, ज्येष्ठ : *He is her elder by several years.* 2 **elders** [*pl*] गुरुजन, सम्माननीय व्यक्ति : *the village elders.*

elderly / 'एल्डर्लि / *adj* अधेड़, वयोवृद्ध।

eldest / 'एल्डिस्ट् / *adj* आयु में सबसे बड़ा, अग्रज : *Megha is the eldest of my three children.*

elect / इ'लेक्ट् / *verb* 1 **elect sb (to sth)**; **elect sb (as sth)** (मतदान द्वारा) किसी (व्यक्ति) को चुनना : *an elected representative/assembly* 2 (औप) किसी वस्तु या कार्य को चुनना : *She elected to work overtime on Mondays.* ▸ **elect** *adj* चुना हुआ (पर अभी नियुक्त नहीं) : *the president elect* **the elect** *noun* (औप) सर्वश्रेष्ठ चुने गए व्यक्ति।

election / इ'लेक्श्न् / *noun* निर्वाचन, विशेषत: मतदान द्वारा (जैसे लोकसभा चुनाव)।

elective / इ'लेक्टिव् / *adj* 1 निर्वाचन करने की शक्ति प्राप्त : *an elective assembly* 2 निर्वाचित : *an elective office* ▸ **elective** *noun* चुना जा सकने वाला अध्ययन का विषय।

elector / इ'लेक्टर् / *noun* मतदाता ▸ **electoral** *adj* चुनाव संबंधी **electorate** / इ'लेक्टरट् / *noun* चुनाव क्षेत्र के सभी मतदाता (एक समूह के रूप में)।

electric / इ'लेक्ट्रिक् / *adj* 1 बिजली से चलने वाला (उपकरण); विद्युत उत्पन्न करने वाला; विद्युत वहन करने वाला; विद्युत उत्पन्न : *an electric oven ○ an electric plug/socket ○ an electric generator* 2 अचानक उत्तेजना उत्पन्न करने

वाला : *The atmosphere was electric.*

electrical / इ'लेक्ट्रिकल् / *adj* विद्युत विषयक।

electrician / इ‚लेक्ट्रिशन्/ *noun* बिजली वाला मिस्त्री; विद्युत विशेषज्ञ।

electricity / इ‚लेक्'ट्रिसटि / *noun* बिजली, विद्युत धारा।

electrify / इ'लेक्ट्रिफ़ाइ / *verb (pt, pp* **electrified)** 1किसी स्थान से विद्युत प्रवाहित करना : *an electrified fence* 2 (रेलवे लाइन आदि का) विद्युतीकरण करना 3 किसी को बिजली जैसा धक्का लगाना, चौंकाना : *Her speech electrified the audience.* ▸ **electrification** *noun* विद्युती-करण।

electrocute/इ'लेक्ट्रक्यूट्/ *verb* बिजली के झटके से मारना या चोट पहुँचाना; बिजली द्वारा प्राणदंड देना।

electrode / इ'लेक्ट्रोड्/ *noun* (प्राय: *pl*) विद्युत बैटरी में विद्युत आने या जाने देने वाले दो बिंदु, विद्युताग्र।

electron / इ'लेक्ट्रॉन्/ *noun* (भौतिकी) परमाणु में उपस्थित ऋण विद्युत आवेश युक्त द्रव्य।

electronic / इ‚लेक'ट्रॉनिक् / *adj* 1 विद्युत प्रवाह को नियंत्रित एवं निर्देशित करने वाले छोटे-छोटे हिस्सों-पुरज़ों से बना या संचा-लित : *an electronic calculator* 2 इस तरह के हिस्सों-पुरज़ों से संबंधित : *an electronic engineer* ▸ **electroni-cally** *adv* **electronic mail (e-mail, email** भी) *noun* कंप्यूटर आदि के माध्यम से लिखित सामग्री का आदान-प्रदान।

electronics / इलेक्'ट्रॉनिक्स् / *noun* 1 इलेक्ट्रॉन सिद्धांतों का रेडियो, टी वी, कंप्यूटर आदि में प्रयोग; इस विषय के अध्य-यन के लिए विज्ञान की शाखा 2 [*pl*] इलेक्ट्रॉ-निक उपकरणों में प्रयुक्त पुरज़े एवं परिपथ।

elegant / 'एलिगन्ट् / *adj* 1 ललित, सुरुचिपूर्ण : *an elegant woman/style* 2 (योजना, विधि आदि) चतुराईपूर्ण एवं

▸ समुपयुक्त ▸ **elegance** *noun* लालित्य **el-egantly** *adv.*

elegy / 'एलिजि / *noun* शोक कविता, शोक-गीत।

element / 'एलिमन्ट्/ *noun* 1 **element (in/of sth)** तत्त्व 2 (प्राय: *sing*) ele-ment of sth किसी चीज़ की थोड़ी-सी मात्रा; संकेत : *There's an element of truth in his story.* 3 (रसा) मूल तत्त्व 4 **the elements** [*pl*] मौसम, आँधी-तूफ़ान 5 **elements** [*pl*] किसी विषय के मूलभूत तथ्य; सबसे पहले सीखे जाने वाले अंश ∎ **in/out of one's element** स्वाभाविक और प्रियकर वातावरण में/के बाहर ▸ **elemental** *adj* 1 (और) शक्ति-शाली एवं अनियंत्रित (प्रकृति की शक्ति जैसा) : *the elemental fury of the storm* 2 प्रारंभिक एवं मूलभूत : *an el-emental truth/concept.*

elementary / ‚एलि'मेन्ट्रि / *adj* प्रारंभिक (विकास की) स्थिति वाला : *an elemen-tary class.*

elephant / 'एलिफ़न्ट्/ *noun* (*pl* अपरि-वर्तित या **elephants)** हाथी ▸ **elephan-tine**/एलि'फ़ैन्टाइन्; *US* एलि'फ़ैन्टीन्/ *adj* (अपमा या परि) हाथी जैसा विशालकाय एवं बेडौल।

elevate / 'एलिवेट् / *verb* **elevate sb/ sth (to sth)** (और) 1 ऊपर उठाना, उच्च स्तर पर पहुँचाना : *She's been elevated to the post of trade minister.* 2 (मन को) उन्नत बनाना ▸ **elevated** *adj* 1 (और) उच्चस्तरीय; प्रतिष्ठित 2 आस-पास के क्षेत्र से ऊँचा : *an elevated road* **elevating** *adj* (और या परि) मन की उन्नति करने वाला।

elevation / ‚एलि'वेश्न्/ *noun* 1 (और) ऊँचा उठने या उठाने की प्रक्रिया, उन्नयन : *his elevation to the peerage* 2 (समुद्र तल से) ऊँचाई; पहाड़ी या ऊँचा स्थल 3 भवन के एक पक्ष का चित्र या ख़ाका : *the front/ rear/side elevation of a house.*

elevator / 'एलिवेटर् / noun 1 (विशेषत: US) लिफ़्ट 2 वायुयान के पृष्ठभाग में एक गतिशील हिस्सा जो उसे ऊपर चढ़ाने या ग़ोता लगाने में प्रयोग होता है 3 सामान ऊपर उठाने का यंत्र।

eleven / इ'लेवन् / noun, pron, det 1 ग्यारह (का अंक) 2 ग्यारह सदस्यों की टीम ▸ **eleventh** / इ'लेवन्थ् / noun, pron, det ग्यारहवाँ; 1/11.

elf / एल्फ़् / noun (pl **elves** / एल्ज़् /) एक छोटी शरारती परी।

elicit / इ'लिसिट् / verb **elicit sth (from sb)** (औप) (उत्तर, सत्यता, तथ्य आदि किसी व्यक्ति से) निकलवाना : *elicit a reply.*

eligible / 'एलिजबल् / adj **eligible (for sth/to do sth)** योग्य, उपयुक्त : *eligible for promotion/membership* ▸ **eligibility** / ‚एलिज‚'बिलटि / noun योग्यता।

eliminate / इ'लिमिनेट् / verb 1 **eliminate sb/sth (from sth)** (अवांछित होने के कारण) हटा देना; छुटकारा पाना : *eliminate drug trafficking* 2 (अनौप) मार देना (विशेषत: भावी शत्रु या प्रतिपक्षी को) 3 **eliminate sb (from sth)** प्रतियोगिता से (हराकर) बाहर कर देना : *He was eliminated in the fourth round.* ▸ **elimination** noun.

elite (**elite** भी) / ए'लीट्; इ'लीट् / noun (प्राय: *अपमा*) अपनी सत्ता, प्रतिभा, संपत्ति आदि के कारण समाज में सर्वश्रेष्ठ समझा जाने वाला वर्ग, अभिजात वर्ग : *a member of the ruling/intellectual elite* ▸ **elitism** noun 1 अभिजात वर्ग का व्यवहार या दृष्टिकोण 2 यह विश्वास कि सामाजिक विकास का उद्देश्य अभिजात दशा की ओर बढ़ना है : *Many people believe that private education encourages elitism.* **elitist** noun, adj.

ellipse / इ'लिप्स् / noun दीर्घवृत्त, अंडाकार आकृति ▸ **elliptic** (**elliptical** भी) adj लंबवर्तुलाकार।

elm / एल्म् / noun बड़े-बड़े पत्तों वाला एक ऊँचा पेड़, चिराबेल; इस पेड़ की सख्त लकड़ी।

elocution / ‚एल'क्यूशन् / noun वक्तृत्व, सार्वजनिक भाषण की कला।

elongate / 'ईलॉङ्गेट् / verb बढ़ाना, लंबा करना ▸ **elongated** adj लंबा और पतला; खींचा हुआ **elongation** noun.

elope / इ'लोप् / verb **elope (with sb)** विवाह करने के लिए चुपचाप घर से भाग जाना ▸ **elopement** noun.

eloquence / 'एलक्वन्स् / noun किसी को प्रभावित करने या बात मनवा लेने में भाषा का चतुर प्रयोग; वाक्-पटुता ▸ **eloquent** adj (औप) वाक्-पटु, वाग्मी **eloquently** adv.

else / एल्स् / adv 1 (प्रश्नवाचक वाक्य बनाने के लिए how या why आदि के बाद, या nothing, nobody, something, anything, little, much आदि शब्दों के बाद प्रयुक्त) के अतिरिक्त, इसके साथ, अन्य ■ **or else** 1 अन्यथा, नहीं तो : *He must be joking, or else he's crazy.* 2 (अनौप) (धमकी या चेतावनी के लिए प्रयुक्त) नहीं तो! : *Give me the money or else!*

elsewhere / ‚एल्स्'वेअर् / adv अन्यत्र, और कहीं।

elucidate / इ'लूसिडेट् / verb (औप) व्याख्या करना; स्पष्ट करना : *The notes help to elucidate the difficult parts of the text.* ▸ **elucidation** noun.

elude / इ'लूड् / verb 1 (चालाकी से) बच निकलना : *He eluded capture for weeks by hiding underground.* 2 भुला दिया जाना या समझा न जाना : *I recognize her face, but her name eludes me.*

elusive / इ'लूसिव् / adj 1 आसानी से पकड़ में न आने वाला : *a most elusive criminal* 2 याद रखने में कठिन।

emaciated / इ'मेसिएटिड् / adj क्षीण-काय, जर्जर शरीर वाला : *He looks very* *emaciated after his illness.* ▶ **emaciation** *noun.*

emanate / 'एमनेट् / *verb (अ)*
1 **emanate from sth/sb** निकलना, उत्पन्न होना : *Delicious smells were emanating from the kitchen.* 2 निस्सारित करना, निकालना : *His whole body seemed to emanate energy and confidence.* ▶ **emanation** *noun.*

emancipate / इ'मैन्सिपेट्/ *verb (अ)* **emancipate sb (from sth)** (राजनीतिक, क़ानूनी अथवा सामाजिक) बंधनों से मुक्त करना : *be emancipated from colonialist rule* ▶ **emancipation** *noun* : *the emancipation of women.*

embalm / इम्'बाम् / *verb* मसाला या रसायन लगाकर शव को सुरक्षित रखना : *The Egyptians used to embalm the bodies of their dead kings and queens.* ▶ **embalmer** *noun.*

embankment / इम्'बैङ्क्मन्ट् / *noun* बाँध, सड़क या रेल को सहारा देने के लिए या बढ़ते पानी को रोकने के लिए मिट्टी, पत्थर की दीवार, तटबंध।

embargo / इम्'बार्गो / *noun (pl* **embargoes)** (व्यापार, जहाज़ों के आवागमन आदि पर लगाई) रोक, निषेधाज्ञा : *a trade/economic embargo against another country* ▶ **embargoed** *adj.*

embark / इम्'बार्क् / *verb* **embark (for...)** जहाज़ अथवा वायुयान पर चढ़ना, सवार होना ■ **embark on/upon sth** प्रारंभ करना, कार्य में भाग लेना : *embark on a long journey/new career.*

embarrass / इम्'बैरस् / *verb* 1 उलझन, परेशानी, घबराहट या शर्म-संकोच में डाल देना : *I was embarrassed by his comments about my clothes.* 2 अड़चन या बाधा डालना : *embarrassed by lack of money* ▶ **embarrassed** *adj*

व्याकुल, लज्जित **embarrassing** *adj* परेशानी या उलझन में डालने वाला **embarrassingly** *adv* **embarrassment** *noun* शर्म, घबराहट या परेशानी; इस तरह का भाव उत्पन्न करने वाला व्यक्ति या वस्तु : *He's an embarrassment to his family.*

embassy / 'एम्बसि / *noun (pl* **embassies)** राजदूत एवं दूतावास के कर्मचारी; राजदूत का आवास, दूतावास : *outside the Russian Embassy.*

embed / इम्'बेड् / *verb* **(-dd-) embed sth (in sth)** जड़ना, मज़बूती से बैठा देना (जैसे अँगूठी में नग को) : *stones embedded in concrete.*

embellish / इम्'बेलिश् / *verb* **embellish sth (with sth)** 1 सजाना, अलंकृत करना : *a dress embellished with lace and ribbons* 2 नई बातें जोड़कर कोई कहानी या कविता अलंकारपूर्ण बनाना ▶ **embellishment** *noun.*

ember / 'एम्बर / *noun* (प्राय: *pl*) अंगारे, बुझती आग में कोयले के दहकते टुकड़े।

embezzle / इम्'बेज़ल् / *verb* ग़बन करना : *embezzle the company's pension fund* ▶ **embezzlement** *noun* ग़बन **embezzler** *noun.*

embitter / इम्'बिटर् / *verb* कटुता एवं निराशा पैदा करना : *She became embittered by repeated failures.* ▶ **embittered** *adj.*

emblem / 'एम्ब्लम्/ *noun* किसी वस्तु या व्यक्ति का सूचक चिह्न, प्रतीक : *The dove is an emblem of peace.* ▶ **emblematic** *adj* प्रतीकात्मक।

embody / इम्'बॉडि / *verb (pt, pp* **embodied)** *(अ)* 1 (विचारों, भावनाओं को) मूर्तरूप देना 2 सम्मिलित करना, रखना : *The latest computer model embodies many new features.* ▶ **embodiment** *noun.*

emboss / इम्'बॉस्/ *verb* नक़्क़ाशी करना;

सतह से उभरे हुए अक्षर लिखना ▸ **em-bossed** / इम्'बॉस्ट् / *adj.*

embrace / इम्'ब्रेस् / *verb* 1 (प्यार से) आलिंगन करना, गले लगाना 2 *(और)* स्वीकार करना, ग्रहण करना : *embrace Christianity* 3 सम्मिलित या समाविष्ट करना : *The term 'mankind' embraces all men, women and children.* ▸ **embrace** *noun* आलिंगन।

embroider / इम्'ब्रॉइडर् / *verb* 1 **embroider A (on B) / embroider B (with A)** बेलबूटे काढ़ना : *She embroidered the cushion with flowers.* 2 कहानी में (प्राय: असत्य) अलंकरण जोड़ना : *He's inclined to embroider the facts.* ▸ **embroidery** *noun* 1 कशीदा, कशीदाकारी; फुलकारी, कढ़ाई 2 (कहानी में) अलंकरण।

embryo / 'एम्ब्रिओ / *noun* (*pl* **embryos**) भ्रूण, पैदा होने से पहले गर्भ में स्थित बच्चा या जीव; अंडे से बाहर न निकले पक्षी का बच्चा ▸ **embryologist** *noun* **embryology** / एम्ब्रि'ऑलजि / *noun* भ्रूण के निर्माण एवं विकास का वैज्ञानिक अध्ययन **embryonic** / एम्ब्रि'ऑनिक् / *adj* विकास की अवस्था में।

emerald / 'एमरल्ड् / *noun* चमकीले हरे रंग का रत्न, मरकत ▸ **emerald (emerald green** भी) *adj* चमकीले हरे रंग का : *cream and emerald tiles.*

emerge / इ'मर्ज् / *verb* 1 **emerge (from sth)** दृष्टिगोचर होना; (विशेषत: जल के ऊपर) उभरना : *The moon emerged from behind the clouds.* 2 **emerge (as sth)** विकसित होना एवं महत्त्वपूर्ण अथवा मुख्य बन जाना : *He emerged as leader at the age of thirty.* 3 (विचारों, तथ्यों का) प्रकट होना 4 **emerge (from sth)** एक निश्चित परिणाम के साथ मुश्किल परिस्थितियों से निकल जाना : *He emerged from the accident unscathed.*

▸ **emergence** / इ'मर्जन्स् / *noun* उन्मज्जन, आविर्भाव **emergent** *adj.*

emergency / इ'मर्जन्सि / *noun* (*pl* **emergencies**) 1 आकस्मिक संकट, आपातकाल : *This door should only be used in an emergency.* 2 (*US*) = **casualty** : *the emergency ward.*

emigrate / 'एमिग्रेट् / *verb* **emigrate (from...) (to...)** अपने देश से दूसरे देश में बसने के लिए जाना : *emigrate from India to Australia to find work* ▸ **emigrant** / 'एमिग्रन्ट् / *noun* प्रवासी व्यक्ति **emigration** / एमि'ग्रेश्न् / *noun* प्रवास।

eminence / 'एमिनन्स् / *noun* 1 (और) प्रतिष्ठा, उत्कर्ष : *reach eminence as a doctor* 2 (अप्र या और) ऊँचा स्थान, पहाड़ी 3 **Eminence** रोमन कैथोलिक कार्डिनल का पद : *His/Your Eminence.*

eminent / 'एमिनन्ट् / *adj* 1 (व्यक्ति) प्रतिष्ठाप्राप्त : *an eminent architect* 2 (और) (गुण) उल्लेखनीय एवं मान्य : *a man of eminent good sense* ▸ **eminently** *adv* उत्कृष्ट रूप में।

emission / इ'मिश्न् / *noun* 1 (और) प्रकाश, गरमी, गैस आदि का निस्सरण 2 निस्सारित वस्तु : *clean up emissions from power stations.*

emit / इ'मिट् / *verb* (-tt-) (प्रकाश, द्रव, ध्वनि आदि को) निस्सारित करना या बाहर भेजना : *The cheese was emitting a strong smell.*

emolument / इ'मॉल्युमन्ट् / *noun* (प्राय: *pl*) (और या साहि) धन या सुविधा प्राप्ति; आय : *Her emoluments amounted to very little.*

emotion / इ'मोश्न् / *noun* 1 मनोभाव : *Love, joy, hate, fear and jealousy are all emotions.* 2 भावावेश अथवा उत्तेजना की स्थिति : *overcome by/with emotion* ▸ **emotional** *adj* 1 भावा-

तमक : *emotional problems* 2 भावुक emotionally *adv.*

emotive / इ 'मोटिव् / *adj* (शब्द आदि) मनोभाव उभारने वाले : *Capital punishment is a highly emotive issue.*

empathy / 'एम्पथि / *noun* empathy (with sb/sth) समानुभूति (किसी अन्य की भावनाओं, अनुभवों आदि को समझने का सामर्थ्य)।

emperor / 'एम्परर् / *noun* (*fem* empress / 'एम्प्रस् /) सम्राट/सम्राज्ञी।

emphasis / 'एम्फ़सिस् / *noun* (*pl* emphases / 'एम्फ़सीज़् /) 1 बलाघात 2 emphasis (on sth) विशेष अर्थ या महत्त्व : *The emphasis is on hard work, not enjoyment.*

emphasize, -ise / 'एम्फ़साइज़् / *verb* महत्त्व देने के लिए शब्द या शब्दों पर बलाघात देना; किसी वस्तु पर विशेष बल डालना : *He emphasized the importance of careful driving.*

emphatic / इम् 'फ़ैटिक् / *adj* ज़ोरदार, स्पष्ट एवं निश्चित ▶ emphatically *adv.*

empire / 'एम्पाइअर् / *noun* 1 साम्राज्य : *the Roman Empire* 2 (*अप्र या औप*) साम्राज्य शक्ति 3 एक व्यक्ति या समूह द्वारा नियंत्रित विशाल वाणिज्य संघ : *a publishing empire.*

empirical / इम् 'पिरिक्ल् / *adj* (सिद्धांतों के बजाय) अनुभव एवं प्रयोग पर आधारित (ज्ञान) : *empirical evidence/knowledge* ▶ empiricism *noun.*

employ / इम् 'प्लॉइ / *verb* 1 employ sb (as sth)काम में लगाना, नौकरी पर रखना : *She's employed as a shop assistant.* 2 employ sth (as sth) (*औप*) प्रयुक्त करना; ध्यान या समय लगाना : *He employed his knife as a lever.* ▶ employ *noun* (*औप*) सेवा या कार्य

employee / इम् 'प्लॉई / *noun* वेतनभोगी कर्मचारी employer *noun* नियोक्ता (व्यक्ति या कंपनी)।

employment / इम् 'प्लॉइमन्ट् / *noun* 1 नियोजन, रोज़गार : *be in regular employment* 2 काम, विशेषत: नौकरी : *give employment to sb.*

empower / इम् 'पाउअर् / *verb* (*औप*) (कोई कार्य विशेष करने का किसी को) अधिकार देना : *The lawyer was empowered to pay all her client's bills.* ▶ empowerment *noun.*

empress / 'एम्प्रस् / *noun* सम्राट की पत्नी या विधवा; सम्राज्ञी।

empty[1] / 'एम्प्टि / *adj* (-ier, -iest) 1 ख़ाली : *an empty box/house* 2 बिना महत्व, ज्ञान या उद्देश्य के : *empty threats/ words/dreams* 3 (*अनौप*) भूखा ▶ empties *noun* [*pl*] (*अनौप*) ख़ाली बोतलें, डिब्बे आदि emptiness *noun* [*sing*] ख़ालीपन।

empty[2] / 'एम्प्टि / *verb* (*pt, pp* emptied*) 1 empty (sth out); empty sth (of sth) ख़ाली होना या करना : *The streets soon emptied (of people) when the rain started.* 2 empty sth (out) (into/onto sth) किसी एक वस्तु को एक पात्र से दूसरे में डालकर ख़ाली कर देना : *She emptied the milk into the pan.*

emulate / 'एम्युलेट् / *verb* (*औप*) उत्साह से (किसी के) बराबर होने या आगे बढ़ने की चेष्टा करना : *She is keen to emulate her sister's sporting achievements.* ▶ emulation *noun.*

emulsion / इ 'मल्श्न् / *noun* 1 (emulsion paint भी) एक प्रकार का रंग जो बिना चमकदार सतह छोड़े सूख जाता है 2 फ़ोटो-ग्राफ़िक फ़िल्म की सतह पर प्रकाश-संवेदी पदार्थ 3 तेल या वसा की छोटी-छोटी बूँदों वाला कोई गाढ़ा द्रव।

enable / इ 'नेब्ल् / *verb* 1 (किसी कार्य को करने के) योग्य बनाना, समुचित साधन एवं अधिकार देना : *This pass enables me to travel half-price on trains.*

2 कुछ संभव बनाना : *enable greater international cooperation.*

enact / इ'नैक्ट् / *verb* 1 *(औप)* अभिनय द्वारा प्रस्तुत करना : *a one-act drama enacted by children* 2 *(औप या क़ानून)* विधि/क़ानून बनाना या पास करना : *a bill enacted by Parliament* ▸ **enactment** *noun* 1 *(क़ानून या औप)* क़ानून, अधिनियम निर्माण की प्रक्रिया; अभिनय 2 क़ानून।

enamel / इ'नैम्ल् / *noun* 1 एनैमल, ताम-चीनी : *enamel paint* (सूख कर चमकीला और चिकना हो जाने वाला रंग) 2 दाँत की बाहरी सतह ▸ **enamel** *verb* (-ll-; *US* -l- भी) एनैमल से ढकना/चमकाना।

enchant / इन्'चान्ट् / *verb* मोहित एवं प्रसन्न करना, मंत्रमुग्ध करना : *be enchanted by the singing of the choir* ▸ **enchanted** *adj* मोहित, मंत्रमुग्ध **enchanting** *adj* मंत्रमुग्ध कर देने वाला **enchantment** *noun* 1 हर्षित/मोहित करने वाली वस्तु 2 सम्मोहक; सम्मोहन, वशीकरण **enchantress** / इन्'चान्ट्रस् / *noun* अत्यंत आकर्षक स्त्री; जादूगरनी।

encircle / इन्'सर्क्ल् / *verb* चारों ओर घेरा बनाना; घेरना : *a lake encircled by trees.*

enclose / इन्'क्लोज़् / *verb* 1 घेरना, बाड़ा लगाना; चारों ओर से बंद करना 2 **enclose sth (with sth)** (किसी वस्तु को लिफ़ाफ़े, पार्सल आदि में, पत्र के साथ) रखना : *I'll enclose your application with mine.* ▸ **enclosed** *adj* बंद एवं बाह्य प्रभाव से कटा हुआ : *an enclosed order of monks.*

enclosure / इन्'क्लोश्र् / *noun* 1 (in-closure भी) घेरे या बाड़े में घिरी ज़मीन 2 संलग्न, अनुलग्न वस्तु : *There were several enclosures in the envelope.*

encore / 'ऑङ्कॉर् / *interj* (श्रोताओं/ दर्शकों द्वारा पुकारा जाना) फिर से, फिर से कहिए (या कीजिए) ! मुकरर ! ▸ **encore** *noun* गीत या कला प्रदर्शन को फिर से करने के लिए माँग : *The group got/took three encores.*

encounter / इन्'काउन्टर् / *verb* (औप) 1 मुठभेड़ होना, अकस्मात् किसी से संकटपूर्ण स्थिति में सामना होना : *He encountered many problems when he first started this job.* 2 किसी से अकस्मात् मिलना ▸ **encounter** *noun* **encounter (between A and B); encounter (with sb/sth)** मुठभेड़; अकस्मात् मिलन।

encourage / इन्'करिज् / *verb* 1 हिम्मत बढ़ाना, प्रोत्साहित करना : *Her parents always encouraged her in her studies.* 2 विकसित करने में मदद करना : *encourage exports* ▸ **encouragement** *noun* **encouragement (to sb) (to do sth)** प्रोत्साहन, बढ़ावा; प्रोत्साहित करने वाली वस्तु **encouraging** *adj* **encouragingly** *adv*.

encroach / इन्'क्रोच् / *verb* **encroach (on/upon sth)** अनधिकार हस्तक्षेप करना; अतिक्रमण करना : *encroach on sb's property* ▸ **encroachment** *noun*.

encumber / इन्'कम्बर् / *verb* **encumber sb/sth (with sth)** (निर्बाध एवं आसान गति में) बाधा डालना; बोझा या भार डालना ▸ **encumbrance** / इन्'कम्ब्रन्स् / *noun* (औप) भार; बाधा।

encyclopedia (encyclopaedia भी) / इन्साइक्ल'पीडिआ / *noun* विश्वकोश, ज्ञानकोश, एक या अनेक पुस्तकों की शृंखला जिसमें अकारादि क्रम से ज्ञान के सभी विषयों की अथवा किसी एक ही विषय से संबद्ध सूचनाएँ दी जाती हैं : *an encyclopedia of music* ▸ **encyclopedic (encyclopaedic भी)** *adj*.

end¹ / एन्ड् / *noun* 1 सिरा, छोर : *the end of a road/line* 2 अंत, समाप्ति; निष्कर्ष : *see a film from beginning to end* 3 किसी चीज़ को प्रयोग करने के बाद बचा

छोटा टुकड़ा : *a cigarette-end* 4 उद्देश्य, प्रयोजन 5 (व्यापारिक गतिविधि आदि का) हिस्सा : *We need someone to handle the marketing end.* 6 (प्राय: sing) मृत्यु : *He's nearing his end.* ■ **make (both) ends meet** खर्च लायक किसी प्रकार कमा लेना **on end** निरंतर, बिना बीच में रुकावट के : *It lasted for weeks on end.* **put an end/a stop to sth** नष्ट कर देना, सदा के लिए रोक देना।

end² /एन्ड्/ *verb* समाप्त कर देना या होना, समाप्ति पर पहुँचना : *They ended the play with a song.* ○ *How does the story end?* ■ **end up** ऐसी जगह/स्थिति में होना जहाँ जाने/पहुँचने के लिए नहीं सोचा हो।

endanger / इन्'डेन्जर् / *verb* खतरे या संकट में डालना : *Smoking endangers your health.* ▶ **endangered** *adj* संकटग्रस्त : *The giant panda is an endangered species.*

endear / इन्'डिअर् / *verb* **endear sb/oneself to sb** (औप) प्रिय बनाना : *He managed to endear himself to everybody.* ▶ **endearment** *noun* प्रेमालाप।

endeavour (*US* **endeavor**) / इन्'डे-वर् / *noun* (औप) प्रयत्न, प्रयास : *His endeavours should be fairly rewarded.* ▶ **endeavour** *verb* (औप) प्रयास करना।

endemic / एन्'डेमिक् / *adj* किसी देश या क्षेत्र विशेष में या एक वर्ग विशेष के लोगों में नियमित रूप से पाया जाने वाला/फैला हुआ : *Malaria is endemic in/to many countries.* ○ *plants endemic to Madagascar.*

ending / 'एन्डिङ्/ *noun* शब्द, कथा, नाटक आदि का अंतिम अंश।

endless / 'एन्ड्लस् / *adj* अंतहीन : *endless opportunities for making money* ▶ **endlessly** *adv.*

endorse /इन्'डॉर्स्/ *verb* 1 (किसी कथन का) समर्थन करना : *The proposal was endorsed by the committee.* 2 (चेक आदि के पीछे) अपने हस्ताक्षर करना 3 किसी कंपनी उत्पाद की (विज्ञापन में) हिमायत करना ▶ **endorsement** *noun.*

endow / इन्'डाउ / *verb* **endow sb/sth (with sth)** (किसी विद्यालय आदि सार्व-जनिक संस्था को धन-संपत्ति आदि) दान में देना : *endow the hospital with a bed* 2 **endow sb/sth with sth** स्वाभाविक अथवा सहजात प्रतिभा से युक्त होना : *She's endowed with intelligence as well as good looks.* ▶ **endowment** *noun* 1 वृत्तिदान, धर्मदान 2 (प्राय: pl) आय प्रदान करने के लिए दिया गया पैसा, संपत्ति 3 (प्राय: pl) जन्मजात प्रतिभा।

endurance / इन्'ड्युअरन्स् / *noun* सहनशक्ति, धैर्य; स्थायित्व : *He showed remarkable endurance during his illness.*

endure / इन्'ड्युअर् / *verb* 1 (दुख, दर्द कष्ट आदि) धैर्य से झेलना : *He endured three years in prison for his reli-gious beliefs.* 2 सहन करना, सहना : *He can't endure to be left alone.* 3 बने रहना, टिकना : *fame that will endure forever* ▶ **endurable** *adj* टिकने वाला।

enemy / 'एनमि / *noun* (pl **enemies**) 1 शत्रु, दुश्मन 2 **the enemy** (युद्ध के समय) शत्रु देश की सेना/सैनिक 3 कोई भी हानिकारक या कमज़ोर बनाने वाली चीज़ : *Poverty and ignorance are the enemies of progress.*

energetic / एनर्'जेटिक् / *adj* उत्साही कर्मठ; ओजस्वी : *an energetic child* ▶ **energetically** *adv.*

energize, -ise /एनर्जाइज़्/ *verb* ऊर्जा प्रदान करना, उत्साह बढ़ाना; उपकरण में विद्युत प्रवाहित करना।

energy / 'एनर्जि / *noun* (pl **energies**) 1 शक्ति/योग्यता; कार्य करने की शक्ति : *His*

work seemed to lack energy.
2 (भौतिकी) ऊर्जा 3 ईंधन एवं अन्य शक्ति
के साधन : *nuclear/electrical/solar
energy.*

enfold / इन्'फ़ोल्ड् / *verb* **enfold sb/sth
(in/with sth)** अपनी बाँहों में भरना; लपेटना।

enforce / इन्'फ़ॉर्स / *verb* **1 enforce
sth (on/against sb)** क़ानून मानने के
लिए बाध्य करना; प्रभावी बनाना : *enforce
sanctions on/against a country*
2 (किसी व्यक्ति से कोई कार्य) बलपूर्वक
कराना : *enforced silence/discipline*
▸ **enforceable** *adj* **enforcement**
noun.

enfranchise / इन्'फ़्रैन्चाइज़् / *verb*
राजनीतिक अधिकार देना : *In Britain
women were enfranchised in 1918.*

engage / इन्'गेज् / *verb* **1** (औप) (टैक्सी
आदि सवारी के लिए) किराए पर लेना;
नौकरी पर रखना : *engage a new secretary* **2** (औप) व्यस्त रखना : *Nothing
engages his attention for long.*
3 (औप) झगड़ा शुरू करना **4 engage
(with sth)** समझने के प्रयास में संबंध
स्थापित करना।

engaged / इन्'गेज्ड् / *adj* **1 engaged
(on/upon sth); engaged (with sb/
sth)** व्यस्त **2** (*US* **busy**) (टेलिफ़ोन लाइन)
प्रयोग की जा रही **3 engaged (to sb)**
वाग्दत्त/वाग्दत्ता, जिसकी सगाई हो चुकी है
▸ **engaging** *adj* ध्यान खींचने वाला।

engagement / इन्'गेज्मन्ट् / *noun*
1 सगाई **2** निर्धारित समय पर किसी से मिलने
या कहीं जाने का वादा : *I have very few
engagements (for) next week.*
3 (औप) युद्ध; मुठभेड़ **4** जानने के प्रयास
में संबंध की स्थापना : *his engagement
with theology.*

engender / इन्'जेन्डर् / *verb* (औप)
उत्पन्न करना, किसी स्थिति या दशा का कारण
बनना : *Some people believe that
poverty engenders crime.*

engine / 'एन्जिन् / *noun* **1** इंजिन, यंत्र जो
ऊर्जा को गति में परिवर्तित करता है **2** (**locomotive** भी) रेलवे इंजिन ▸ **engine-driver**
noun (रेलवे) इंजिन का ड्राइवर।

engineer / एन्जि'निअर् / *noun* **1** इंजी-
नियर, अभियंता; मशीन, पुल, रेल, जहाज़,
यंत्र आदि का डिज़ाइन करने वाला व्यक्ति
2 जहाज़ अथवा वायुयान के इंजिन का
नियंत्रक व्यक्ति : *a flight engineer*
3 सैनिक प्रयोग की संरचनाएँ डिज़ाइन करने
एवं बनाने वाला सैनिक ▸ **engineer** *verb*
1 इंजीनियर के रूप में निर्माण करना/
नियंत्रित करना **2** (अपमा) षड्यंत्र रचना :
engineer a plot/scheme **engineering** *noun* वैज्ञानिक ज्ञान का व्याव-
हारिक अनुप्रयोग; इंजीनियर का कार्य,
व्यवसाय, विज्ञान आदि : *an engineering
degree.*

English / 'इंग्लिश् / *noun* **1** इंग्लैंड के
लोग **2** अंग्रेज़ी भाषा ▸ **English** *adj*
1 इंग्लैंड के लोगों से संबंधित **2** अंग्रेज़ी भाषा
संबंधी।

engrave / इन्'ग्रेव् / *verb* **1 engrave B
on A/engrave A (with B)** पत्थर, धातु
की प्लेट आदि पर शब्द लिखना या चित्र आदि
बनाना : *His name was engraved on
the trophy.* **2 engrave sth on sth**
याददाश्त अथवा मस्तिष्क पर गहरी छाप
छोड़ना : *Memories of that terrible
day are forever engraved on my
mind.* ▸ **engraver** *noun* **engraving**
noun **1** इस प्रकार की नक्क़ाशी कला
2 नक्क़ाशी, चित्र।

engross / इन्'ग्रोस् / *verb* किसी काम में
तल्लीन हो जाना : *be engrossed in
one's work/a book.*

engulf / इन्'गल्फ़् / *verb* **engulf sb/sth
(in sth)** घेर लेना, पूरी तरह ढक लेना : *a
boat engulfed in the waves.*

enhance / इन्'हान्स्; *US* इन्'हैन्स् / *verb*
(आकर्षण, शक्ति, मूल्य, गुणवत्ता आदि)
बढ़ाना : *enhance the reputation/*

position of sb ▸ **enhancement** *noun.*

enigma / इ'निग्मा / *noun (pl* enigmas) पहेली, बुझौवल; न समझ में आने वाला रहस्य : *I've known him for many years, but he remains a complete enigma to me.* ▸ **enigmatic** /,एनिग् 'मैटिक्/ *adj* रहस्यमय, पेचीदा।

enjoin / इन्'जॉइन्/ *verb* (औप) आदेश देना; (क़ानून) लागू करना : *We were enjoined not to betray the trust placed in us.*

enjoy / इन्'जॉइ / *verb* 1 आनंद लेना 2 भोगना, उपभोग में लाना; लाभ उठाना : *Men and women should enjoy equal rights.* ■ **enjoy oneself** आनंद अनुभव करना, प्रसन्न होना ▸ **enjoyable** *adj* आनंददायक **enjoyment** *noun* 1 आनंद, संतुष्टि 2 (औप) आनंददायक वस्तु 3 (औप) स्वामित्व एवं उपभोग।

enlarge / इन्'लार्ज्/ *verb* 1 बढ़ाना; बढ़ना; काग़ज़ात, फ़ोटो आदि बड़ा करना : *The police had the photograph of the missing girl enlarged.* 2 **enlarge (on sth)** विस्तार के साथ कहना या लिखना ▸ **enlargement** *noun* 1 किसी वस्तु को आकार में बड़ा करने की प्रक्रिया, किसी वस्तु का आकार में बड़ा होना 2 बड़ी की गई वस्तु, विशेषत: फ़ोटोग्राफ़।

enlighten / इन्'लाइट्न् / *verb* और अधिक ज्ञान देना; अज्ञानता दूर करना एवं प्रबुद्ध बनाना : *The report makes enlightening reading.* ▸ **enlightened** *adj* पूर्वाग्रहों, अंधविश्वासों आदि से मुक्त, प्रबुद्ध **enlightenment** *noun* (औप) प्रबोधन।

enlist / इन्'लिस्ट्/ *verb* 1 **enlist (sb) (in/into/for sth); enlist (sb) (as sth)** फ़ौज में भरती होना या करना : *He enlisted at the age of 17.* 2 **enlist sth/sb (in sth/doing sth)** (किसी का) सहयोग, सहारा या समर्थन प्राप्त करना : *a demon-*

stration designed to enlist public sympathy ▸ **enlistment** *noun.*

enliven / इन्'लाइव्न् / *verb* किसी चीज़ को सजीव, रुचिकर या प्रफुल्लित बना देना : *His jokes enlivened an otherwise dull evening.*

en masse / ऑन्'मैस् / *adv* (फ़्रेंच) सामूहिक रूप में : *The guests arrived en masse.*

enmity / 'एन्मटि / *noun (pl* enmities) शत्रुता, वैर/बैर : *traditional enmities between tribes.*

enormity / इ'नॉर्मटि / *noun (pl* enormities) 1 किसी चीज़ का विशाल आकार, विस्तार या पैमाना 2 (प्राय: *pl*) (औप) महापातक, महापराध : *the enormities of the Hitler regime.*

enormous / इ'नॉर्मस् / *adj* बहुत बड़ा, अत्यधिक विशाल : *an enormous amount of money/effort* ▸ **enormously** *adv* विशाल मात्रा में।

enough[1] / इ'नफ़् / *indef det* **enough sth (for sth/sb); enough sth (for sb) to do sth** पर्याप्त, काफ़ी : *Have you made enough copies?* ▸ **enough** *indef pron* यथेष्ट, जितना चाहिए।

enough[2] / इ'नफ़् / *adv* (verbs, adjs एवं advs के बाद प्रयुक्त) 1 **enough (for/sth) (to do sth)** पर्याप्त मात्रा में 2 कुछ मगर काफ़ी मात्रा में नहीं : *He's nice enough but he doesn't particularly impress me.*

enrage / इन्'रेज्/ *verb* गुस्सा दिलाना/ होना; क्रुद्ध होना/करना : *His arrogance enraged her.*

enrapture / इन्'रैप्चर्/ *verb* (औप) मोहित करना, आनंद विभोर करना : *We were enraptured by the view.*

enrich / इन्'रिच्/ *verb* 1 धनी बनाना; समृद्ध करना : *a nation enriched by oil revenues* 2 किसी चीज़ का महत्त्व, गुणवत्ता, स्वाद आदि बढ़ाना : *soil en-*

riched with fertilizer ▸ **enrichment** *noun*.

enrol (*US* **enroll** भी) / इन्'रोल् / *verb* (-ll-) **enrol** (**sb**) (**in/on sth**); **enrol** (**sb**) (**as sth**) सदस्य बनना; सूची या रजिस्टर में नाम लिखना/लिखवाना : *enrol in evening classes* ▸ **enrollee** *noun* **enrolment** (विशेषत: *US* **enrollment** भी) *noun* नामांकन; नामांकन संख्या।

en route / ,ऑन् 'रूट् / *adv* (फ़्रेंच) **en route** (**from...**) (**to...**) मार्ग में : *We stopped at Paris en route from Rome to London.*

ensemble / ऑन्'सॉम्बल् / *noun* **1** एक साथ कार्यक्रम पेश करने वाले संगीतकारों, नर्तकों या अभिनेताओं का छोटा-सा समूह : *a woodwind ensemble* **2** एक साथ पहने जाने वाले कपड़ों का सेट : *A pair of pink shoes completed her striking ensemble.* **3** एक पूर्णता में देखी जाने वाली अनेक वस्तुएँ : *The arrangement of the furniture formed a pleasing ensemble.*

ensign / एन्'सन् / *noun* झंडा (विशेषत: जहाज़ का) : *the white ensign.*

ensue / इन्'स्यू / *verb* परिणाम रूप घटित होना : *Chaos/Panic ensued.* ▸ **ensuing** / इन्'स्यू-इङ् / *adj* आगामी, अनुवर्ती : *in the ensuing years.*

ensure / इन्'शुअर् / *verb* निश्चित कर लेना : *The book ensured his success.*

entail / इन्'टेल् / *verb* के लिए आवश्यक होना, आवश्यक भाग के रूप में सम्मिलित करना : *This job entails a lot of hard work.*

entangle / इन्'टैङ्ग्ल् / *verb* **1** **entangle sb/sth/oneself** (**in/with sth**) जाल में फँसाना/फँस जाना; बाधाओं में अटका देना या अटक जाना : *The bird was entangled in the wire netting.* **2** **entangle sb/oneself in sth/with sb** किसी

को परेशानी में डाल देना/उलझा देना; स्वयं परेशानी में उलझ जाना : *become entangled in money problems* ▸ **entanglement** *noun* **1** उलझन, उलझाव **2** (प्राय: *pl*) उलझा हुआ या मुश्किल संबंध या परिस्थिति : *entanglements with the police.*

enter / 'एन्टर् / *verb* **1** घुसना, प्रवेश करना : *Don't enter without knocking.* **2** (संस्था या व्यवसाय का) सदस्य बनना : *enter a school/college* **3** किसी प्रक्रिया या परिस्थिति में पड़ जाना या उलझ जाना : *enter a relationship/conflict/ war* **4 enter** (**for sth**); **enter sb** (**in/ for sth**) भाग लेना : *Several new firms have now entered the market.*

enterprise / 'एन्टर्प्राइज़् / *noun* **1** उद्यम या कार्य जिसमें साहस की आवश्यकता हो या जोखिमों का सामना करना पड़े **2** (नए उद्यमों को प्रारंभ करने का) साहस, उत्सुकता, योग्यता **3** अकेले व्यक्ति/कुछ व्यक्तियों द्वारा विकसित एवं नियंत्रित (न कि राज्य द्वारा) व्यापार कार्य; व्यापारिक कंपनी या फ़र्म ▸ **enterprising** *adj* उत्साही, उद्यमी।

entertain / ,एन्टर्'टेन् / *verb* **1 entertain sb** (**to sth**) लोगों का अतिथि के रूप में सत्कार करना; भोजन आदि से सम्मान करना **2 entertain sb** (**with sth**) जी बहलाना, रिझाना **3** (औप) विचार करना; ध्यान में रखना ▸ **entertainer** *noun* **entertaining** *adj* मनोरंजक।

entertainment / ,एन्टर्'टेन्मेन्ट् / *noun* **1** मनोरंजन/सत्कार **2** मनोरंजन की वस्तु।

enthral (विशेषत: *US* **enthrall** भी) / इन्'थ्रॉल् / *verb* (-ll-) पूरा-पूरा ध्यान खींच लेना, मंत्रमुग्ध कर देना ▸ **enthralling** *adj*.

enthusiasm / इन्'थ्यूज़िऐज़म्; *US* इन्'थूज़िऐज़म् / *noun* **1 enthusiam** (**for/ about sth**) उमंग, उत्साह **2** उमंग/उत्साह पैदा करने वाली वस्तु ▸ **enthusiast** / इन्'थ्यूज़िऐस्ट्; *US* इन्'थूज़िऐस्ट् / *noun* उमंगी, उत्साही व्यक्ति **enthusiastic** *adj* **en-**

-thusiastic (about sb/sth/doing sth) उत्साहपूर्ण **enthusiastically** adv.

entice / इन् 'टाइस् / verb **entice sb (away) (from sth) (to sth); entice sb (into sth/doing sth)** किसी व्यक्ति को (कोई कार्य करने या न करने के लिए) फुस-लाना ▸ **enticement** noun **enticing** adj आकर्षक, मोहक **enticingly** adv.

entire / इन् 'टाइअर् / adj संपूर्ण, अखंड ▸ **entirely** adv पूरी तरह से **entirety** / इन् 'टाइअरटि / noun (औप) संपूर्णता; अखंडता।

entitle / इन् 'टाइट्ल् / verb 1 (किसी पुस्तक आदि का) शीर्षक देना : She read a poem entitled 'The Apple Tree'. 2 **entitle sb to sth/to do sth** किसी व्यक्ति को (किसी चीज़ पर या कुछ करने का) अधिकार देना ▸ **entitlement** noun.

entity / 'एन्टटि / noun (pl **entities**) अलग एवं स्वतंत्र अस्तित्व वाली वस्तु : a separate legal entity.

entrails / 'एन्ट्रेल्ज़् / noun [pl] किसी जंतु के अंतरंग, विशेषत: आँत।

entrance[1] / 'एन्ट्रन्स् / noun 1 **entrance (to sth)** प्रवेश, प्रवेश द्वार 2 **entrance (into/onto sth)** (प्राय: sing) प्रवेश करने या (किसी कार्य में) भागीदारी लेने की क्रिया 3 **entrance (to sth)** प्रवेश का अधिकार या अवसर : They refused entrance to the club.

entrance[2] / इन् 'ट्रान्स्; US इन् 'ट्रैन्स् / verb सम्मोहित/मंत्रमुग्ध कर देना : They were completely entranced by the music. ▸ **entrancing** adj.

entrant / 'एन्ट्रन्ट् / noun 1 **entrant (to sth)** किसी व्यवसाय, संस्था या प्रतियोगिता में भाग (प्रवेश) लेने वाला व्यक्ति 2 किसी दौड़, प्रतियोगिता या परीक्षा में भाग लेने वाला व्यक्ति या पशु : There were fifty entrants for the dog show.

entreat / इन् 'ट्रीट् / verb (औप) अनुनय-विनय करना, चिरौरी करना : He en-

treated the king to grant him one wish.

entreaty / इन् 'ट्रीटि / noun (pl **entreaties**) (औप) अनुनय, चिरौरी।

entrepreneur / ,ऑन्ट्रप्रनर् / noun नवीन व्यावसायिक उद्यम (विशेषत: वित्तीय ख़तरे वाला) शुरू करने वाला व्यक्ति ▸ **entrepreneurial** adj **entrepreneurship** noun.

entrust / इन् 'ट्रस्ट् / verb **entrust A to B/entrust B with A** कर्तव्य या उत्तरदायित्व के रूप में किसी को कुछ सौंपना; विश्वास करना : entrust an assistant with the task.

entry / 'एन्ट्रि / noun (pl **entries**) 1 (प्राय: sing) **entry (into sth)** प्रवेश की क्रिया : The thieves had forced an entry into the building. 2 **entry (to/into sth)** प्रवेश का अधिकार, साधन या अव-सर : museums that charge for entry 3 **entry (in sth)** शब्दकोश या किसी सूची में दर्ज सूचना आदि, प्रविष्टि : entries in a dictionary 4 **entry (for sth)** किसी प्रतियोगिता, स्पर्धा आदि में भाग लेने वाला व्यक्ति या वस्तु; प्रतियोगिता आदि में भाग लेने की क्रिया; भाग लेने वालों की कुल संख्या : fifty entries for the 800 metres ○ Entry is open to anyone over the age of 18.

enumerate / इ 'न्यूमरेट् / verb (औप) गिनना, नाम ले-लेकर किसी सूची में दी वस्तुओं की गिनती करना ▸ **enumeration** noun.

enunciate / इ 'नन्सिएट् / verb 1 (शब्दों का) स्पष्ट उच्चारण करना 2 (औप) (किसी सिद्धांत या विचार को) स्पष्ट रूप से व्यक्त करना ▸ **enunciation** / इ ,नन्सि 'एश्न् / noun.

envelop / इन् 'वेलप् / verb **envelop sth/sb (in sth)** चारों ओर से ढकना, लपेटना : a baby enveloped in a blanket.

envelope / 'एन्व्रलोप्; 'ऑन्व्रलोप् / noun लिफ़ाफ़ा (विशेषत: पत्र का) : *an airmail envelope.*

enviable /'एन्विअब्ल्/ *adj* ईर्ष्या उत्पन्न करने वाला तथा स्पृहा ▸ **enviably** *adv.*

envious /'एन्विअस्/ *adj* envious (of sb/sth) ईर्ष्या करने वाला; जलने वाला व्यक्ति।

environment / इन्'वाइरन्मन्ट् / noun 1 वातावरण जनित परिस्थितियाँ; पर्यावरण, परिस्थितियाँ, माहौल 2 the environment [sing] वातावरण : *measures to protect the environment* ▸ **environmental** *adj* **environmentalist** *noun.*

envisage / इन्'विज़िज़् / (विशेषत: US **envision** / इन्'विश़्न्/ भी) *verb* भविष्य में हो सकने वाली बात की कल्पना करना, अंदाज़ लगाना।

envoy / 'एन्वॉइ / noun राजदूत; विशेष दूत : *a special envoy of the Swedish government.*

envy¹ /'एन्वि / *verb* (pt, pp envied) ईर्ष्या करना; जलन रखना।

envy² /'एन्वि / noun 1 envy (of sb); envy (at/of sth) ईर्ष्या, जलन : *He couldn't conceal his envy of me.* 2 the envy [sing] the envy of sb/sth जलन उत्पन्न करने वाला व्यक्ति या वस्तु : *a garden which is the envy of all our neighbours.*

enzyme /'एन्ज़ाइम्/ noun (जीव विज्ञान या रसा) जीवधारियों के शरीर में प्राकृतिक रूप से उत्पन्न रसायन जो शरीर में रासायनिक क्रियाएँ संपन्न करता है।

ephemeral / इ'फ़ेमरल् / *adj* क्षण-भंगुर; क्षणिका।

epic /'एपिक् / noun 1 किसी राष्ट्र के इतिहास या वीर व्यक्तियों की गाथा; महाकाव्य : *Homer's 'Iliad' is a famous epic.* 2 वीरता के कारनामों या उत्तेजक साहसिक अभियानों को चित्रित करने वाली फ़िल्म या लंबी कहानी ▸ **epic** *adj* अविस्मरणीय; महान।

epicure /'एपिक्युअर् / noun स्वादलोलुप एवं भोगवादी व्यक्ति ▸ **epicurean** *adj.*

epidemic /'एपि'डेमिक् / noun 1 महामारी : *a cholera/flu epidemic* 2 महामारी की तरह फैलती कोई बुराई ▸ **epidemic** *adj* महामारी जैसा व्यापक।

epigram /'एपिग्रैम्/ noun सूक्ति, सुभाषित वचन ▸ **epigrammatic** *adj.*

epilepsy / 'एपिलेप्सि / noun मिरगी (रोग), अपस्मार ▸ **epileptic** *adj* : *an epileptic fit* **epileptic** noun मिरगी का रोगी।

epilogue (US **epilog**)/'एपिलॉग्/ noun पुस्तक, नाटक, फ़िल्म या टी वी कार्यक्रम के अंत में टीका-टिप्पणी के साथ जोड़ा गया भाग; उपसंहार।

episode / 'एपिसोड् / noun 1 घटना चक्र में किसी एक घटना का वर्णन, वृत्तांत 2 नियमित रूप से प्रकाशित या प्रसारित कहानी का एक अंश : *the final episode of a TV series* ▸ **episodic** *adj.*

epistle / इ'पिस्ल् / noun 1 **Epistle** (बाइबल में) धर्मपत्र, काव्यपत्र 2 (प्राय: परि) पत्र : *Her mother sends her a long epistle every week.* ▸ **epistolary** / इ 'पिस्टलरि / *adj (औप)* पत्र रूप में व्यक्त अथवा लिखित : *an epistolary novel.*

epitaph /'एपिटाफ़् / noun समाधि-लेख।

epithet /'एपिथेट्/ noun कोई विशेषता या महत्त्वपूर्ण गुण वर्णन करने वाला विशेषण, उपाधि, जैसे Akbar *the Great.*

epitome / इ'पिटमि /noun the epitome of sth 1 किसी गुण या प्रकार का आदर्श उदाहरण, नमूना : *She's the epitome of kindness.* 2 किसी बड़ी वस्तु को संक्षेप में प्रस्तुत करती अन्य वस्तु ▸ **epitomize, -ise** / इ 'पिटमाइज़् / *verb* आदर्श नमूना होना; सार संक्षेप लिखना।

epoch / 'ईपॉक्; US 'एपक्/ noun युग,

काल : *Einstein's theories marked a new epoch in mathematics.* ▸ **epoch-making** *adj.*

equable / एक्वब्ल् / *adj* हमेशा शांत और तर्कसंगत : *an equable temperament* ▸ **equably** *adv.*

equal / 'ईक्वल् / *adj* 1 equal (to sb/ sth) आकार, मात्रा, संख्या, गुण आदि में समान, बराबर 2 equal to sth के योग्य; के बराबर : *He proved equal to the occasion.* ▸ **equal** *noun* किसी के बराबर या बराबरी वाला व्यक्ति या वस्तु **equal** *verb* (-II-; *US* -I-) 1 मात्रा या संख्या में बराबर करना या होना 2 equal sb/ sth (as/in sth) बराबरी करना या समान स्तर पर पहुँचना : *Few politicians can equal her as a public speaker.* **equally** *adv* 1 समान रूप से/स्तर पर 2 समान हिस्सों या मात्रा में : *The money was equally divided among her four children.* 3 अतिरिक्त और समान महत्त्व वाला।

equality / इ'क्वॉलटि / *noun* समानता, बराबरी।

equalize, -ise / 'ईक्वलाइज़् / *verb* बराबर करना, एकरूप करना ▸ **equalization, -isation** *noun.*

equanimity / एक्व'निमटि / *noun* धैर्य, समबुद्धि : *She is facing the prospect of her operation with cheerful equanimity.*

equate / इ'क्वेट् / *verb* 1 equate sth (with sth) किसी वस्तु को दूसरे के बराबर मानना या करना 2 equate to sth किसी अन्य के बराबर होना/समतुल्य होना।

equation / इ'क्वेश्न् / *noun* (*गणित*) समीकरण, जैसे $2x + 5 = 11$.

equator / इ'क्वेटर् / *noun* भूमध्य रेखा, विषुवद्रेखा ▸ **equatorial** *adj* भूमध्यवर्ती, विषुवद् रेखा विषयक।

equestrian / इ'क्वेस्ट्रिअन् / *adj* घुड़सवारी से संबंधित : *equestrian skill.*

equidistant / ईक्वि'डिस्टन्ट् / *adj* दो या ज़्यादा स्थानों से समान दूरी पर स्थित, सम-दूरस्थ : *Our house is equidistant from the two shops in the village.*

equilateral / ईक्वि'लैटरल् / *adj* (*ज्यामिति*) समभुज : *an equilateral triangle.*

equilibrium / ईक्वि'लिब्रिअम् / *noun* साम्य या संतुलन की स्थिति : *the need to keep supply and demand in equilibrium.*

equinox / 'ईक्विनॉक्स् / *noun* वर्ष का वह समय जब दिन और रात दोनों बराबर होते हैं।

equip / इ'क्विप् / *verb* (-pp-) 1 equip oneself/sb/sth (with sth) सज्जित करना, लैस करना 2 किसी को किसी ख़ास कार्य के लिए मानसिक रूप से तैयार करना ▸ **equipment** *noun* साज-सामान, उप-करण।

equitable / 'एक्विटब्ल् / *adj* (*औप*) न्यायसंगत, उचित : *an equitable distribution of wealth.*

equivalent / इ'क्विवलन्ट् / *adj* equivalent (to sth) समतुल्य, बराबर; समानार्थी : *250 grams or an equivalent amount in ounces* ▸ **equivalent** *noun.*

equivocal / इ'क्विवकल् / *adj* (*औप*) अर्थ या अभिप्राय में अस्पष्ट, जिसके एक से अधिक अर्थ निकाले जा सकते हैं ▸ **equivocate** / इ'क्विवकेट् / *verb* (*औप*) गुमराह करने या छिपाने के लिए अस्पष्ट तरीक़े से बात करना **equivocation** *noun.*

era / 'इअरा / *noun* (इतिहास में) संवत्, युग : *the postwar era.*

eradicate / इ'रैडिकेट् / *verb* पूर्णतः नष्ट कर देना, जड़ से उखाड़ देना : *Smallpox has now been eradicated.* ▸ **eradication** *noun.*

erase / इ'रेज़् / *verb* 1 erase sth (from sth) पूरी तरह मिटा देना : *erase sb's anxieties/doubts* 2 रबड़ से मिटा देना

▶ **eraser** / इ'रेज़र्; *US* इ'रेसर्/ *noun* रबड़ **erasure** / इ'रेश़र्/ *noun* (औप) मिटाने की क्रिया।

erect¹ / इ'रेक्ट्/ *adj* सीधा खड़ा : *hold oneself erect.*

erect² / इ'रेक्ट्/ *verb* निर्माण करना, स्थापित करना ▶ **erection** / इ'रेक्श्न्/ *noun* (औप) निर्माण, स्थापना।

erode / इ'रोड्/ *verb* (पानी की धारा, वर्षा, वायु, तेज़ाब आदि से) कटाव होना, खाया जाना या क्षय हो जाना : *Metals are eroded by acids.* ▶ **erosion** / इ'रोश्न्/ *noun* कटाव।

erotic / इ'रॉटिक्/ *adj* काम-वासना उत्तेजित करने वाला; शृंगारिक : *The photographs are profoundly erotic.* ▶ **erotica** / इ'रॉटिका/ *noun* कामोद्दीपक पुस्तक, चित्र या अन्य सामग्री **eroticism** *noun.*

err / अर्/ *verb* भूल करना, ग़लती कर बैठना।

errand / 'एरन्ड्/ *noun* किसी वस्तु को पाने या लाने (जैसे कोई ख़रीदारी) के लिए की गई छोटी यात्रा; ऐसी यात्रा का उद्देश्य या प्रयोजन : *He was tired of running errands for his sister.*

erratic / इ'रैटिक्/ *adj* (प्राय: अपमा) मौजी, अनिश्चित व्यवहार अथवा मत वाला : *a gifted but erratic player* ▶ **erratically** *adv.*

erratum / ए'राटम्/ *noun* (*pl* **errata** /ए'राटा/)(प्राय: *pl*) (औप) लिखने या मुद्रण की त्रुटियाँ, अशुद्धि : *a list of errata.*

erroneous / इ'रोनिअस्/ *adj* (औप) ग़लत, भ्रांतिपूर्ण : *erroneous ideas.*

error / 'एरर्/ *noun* ग़लती, त्रुटि।

erstwhile / 'अर्स्ट्वाइल्/ *adj* (औप) पूर्व, पहले का : *His erstwhile friends turned against him.*

erudite / 'एरुडाइट्/ *adj* (औप) पांडित्यपूर्ण, पंडित : *an erudite lecture* ▶ **erudition** / एरु'डिश्न्/ *noun* विद्वत्ता।

erupt / इ'रप्ट्/ *verb* 1 (ज्वालामुखी का) फट पड़ना 2 **erupt (into sth)** अचानक फूट पड़ना या घटित होना : *The scandal erupted only days before the election.* 3 **erupt (in sth)** (ज़ोर-से चिल्लाकर) तीव्र भावनाएँ व्यक्त करना : *erupt in tears/fits of laughter* 4 फोड़े-फुंसी उभर आना ▶ **eruption** / इ'रप्श्न्/ *noun* फूटकर बाहर आना, उद्गार; फोड़ा-फुंसी।

escalate / 'एस्कलेट्/ *verb* बढ़ाना, तीव्र करना ▶ **escalation** *noun.*

escalator / 'एस्कलेटर्/ *noun* चलती सीढ़ी।

escapade / एस्क'पेड, 'एस्कपेड/ *noun* दुःसाहसिक घटना : *a foolish escapade.*

escape¹ / इ'स्केप्/ *verb* 1 **escape (from sb/sth)** बचना, निकल भागना 2 (गैसों, द्रवों आदि का) निकल जाना : *heat escaping through a window* 3 **escape (with sth)** (होने वाली हानि से) बाल-बाल बचना 4 ध्यान से हट जाना।

escape² / इ'स्केप्/ *noun* **escape (from sth)** 1 पलायन, भागने की क्रिया 2 भागने का साधन : *our escape route.*

escapism / इ'स्केपिज़म्/ *noun* (प्राय: अपमा) पलायनवादी प्रवृत्ति।

escort / 'एस्कॉर्ट्/ *noun* 1 किसी व्यक्ति (या जहाज़) की सुरक्षा के लिए या सम्मान के लिए साथ-साथ जाने वाला व्यक्ति (या जहाज़), अनुरक्षक 2 (अप्र या औप) विशिष्ट अवसर पर किसी के साथ-साथ जाने वाला व्यक्ति ▶ **escort** / इ'स्कॉर्ट्/ *verb* अनुरक्षक के रूप में जाना।

especial / इ'स्पेश्ल्/ *adj* 1 विशिष्ट, असाधारण : *a matter of especial interest* 2 ख़ास, एक व्यक्ति या वस्तु विशेष से संबद्ध : *for your especial entertainment* ▶ **especially** *adv* विशेष रूप से।

espionage / 'एस्पिअनाश्/ *noun* जासूसी, गुप्तचरी : *found guilty of espionage.*

essay / 'एसे/ *noun* 1 **essay (on sth)**

निबंध 2 **essay (in sth)** *(औप)* प्रयास
▶ **essayist** *noun* निबंधकार।

essence / 'एस्न्स् / *noun* 1 तत्त्व, सार
तत्त्व 2 किसी पौधे या द्रव का (उबालकर)
निकाला हुआ सार, आसव : *vanilla essence* 3 सुगंध।

essential / इ'सेन्श्ल् / *adj* 1 **essential
(to/for sth)** अत्यावश्यक, अनिवार्य 2 मूल,
किसी चीज़ की मूल प्रकृति से संबंधित
▶ **essential** *noun* (प्राय:*pl*) आवश्यक
मूल तत्त्व : *learn the essentials of
English grammar* **essentially** *adv*
अनिवार्यत: मूलत:।

establish / इ'स्टैब्लिश् / *verb* 1 पक्की
नींव पर स्थापित करना : *establish a
close relationship with sb* 2 कुछ
बात निश्चित या सत्य सिद्ध करना : *We've
established his innocence.* ▶ **established** *adj* प्रतिष्ठित; (धर्म) मान्य।

establishment / इ'स्टैब्लिश्मन्ट् / *noun*
1 स्थापना (करना) 2 (औप या परि) संग-
ठन या प्रतिष्ठान 3 **the Establishment**
(अक्सर अपमा) विचारों, नीतियों आदि को
नियंत्रित या प्रभावित करने वाले सत्ता संपन्न
लोगों का समूह : *the military/political
Establishment.*

estate / इ'स्टेट् / *noun* 1 एक व्यक्ति के
स्वामित्व वाली भू-संपत्ति, जागीर 2 विशिष्ट
प्रयोजन (जैसे निर्माण कार्य) के लिए विकसित
विशेष भूक्षेत्र : *an industrial estate*
3 (क़ानून) जायदाद ▶ **estate agent**
noun जायदाद का दलाल।

esteem / इ'स्टीम् / *noun* (औप) सम्मान
एवं श्रद्धा ▶ **esteem** *verb* (औप)
1 सम्मान व श्रद्धा से देखना : *two highly
esteemed professional scientists*
2 विशिष्टता से विचार करना : *I esteem it
a privilege to address such a distinguished audience.*

estimate¹ / 'एस्टिमेट् / *verb* **estimate
sth (at sth)** मूल्यांकन करना; (क़ीमत
आदि का) अंदाज़ा लगाना, आँकना।

estimate² / 'एस्टिमट् / *noun* 1 (क़ीमत
आदि का) अनुमान, आकलन 2 विचार या
राय।

estimation / ,एस्टि'मेश्न् / *noun* (औप)
विचार या राय : *In my estimation, he's
the more suitable candidate.*

estrange / इ'स्ट्रेन्ज् / *verb* किसी व्यक्ति
को (किसी अन्य से) विमुख या अलग कर
देना ▶ **estranged** *adj* **estranged
(from sb)** 1 (पति या पत्नी) एक-दूसरे से
अलग रहते हुए : *an attempt at reconciliation with her estranged husband* 2 (व्यक्तियों या समूहों का) मनमुटाव
▶ **estrangement** *noun* अलगाव, मनमुटाव।

estuary / 'एस्चुअरि / *noun* (*pl* **estuar-
ies**) नदी का मुहाना।

etch / एच् / *verb* 1 धातु की पतली प्लेट पर
सूई और अम्ल की सहायता से चित्र आदि
बनाना जिससे अन्य प्रतियाँ मुद्रित की जा
सकती हैं 2 **etch A (in/on/onto B)**;
etch B (with A) किसी चीज़ पर पक्का
स्पष्ट निशान बनाना ▶ **etching** *noun* इस
प्रकार की कला (का नमूना)।

eternal / इ'टर्न्ल् / *adj* 1 नित्य, अनादि और
अनंत : *eternal life* 2 कभी ख़त्म न होता
हुआ प्रतीत होने वाला ▶ **eternally** *adv.*

eternity / इ'टर्नटि / *noun* 1 अनंतकाल;
पारलौकिक जीवन 2 **an eternity** [*sing*]
(अनौप) अनंत प्रतीत होता बहुत लंबा समय।

ether / 'ईथर् / *noun* 1 एलकोहल से बना
एक रंगहीन द्रव, ईथर 2 **the ether** हवा
जिसके माध्यम से रेडियो और इलेक्ट्रॉनिक
संचार होता है।

ethereal / ई'थ्रिअरिअल् / *adj* वायवीय,
लोकोत्तर : *ethereal beauty.*

ethic / 'एथ्रिक् / *noun* 1 नीतिशास्त्र, आच-
रणशास्त्र 2 **ethics** [*pl*] नीति या आचारशास्त्र;
दर्शनशास्त्र की नीति संबंधी शाखा ▶ **ethical**
adj 1 नीतिशास्त्र संबंधी : *rules which
govern ethical standards* 2 नैतिक
ethically *adv.*

ethnic / 'एथ्निक् / *adj* 1 जातीय, मानव

जातीय : *ethnic minorities* 2 (व्यक्ति) किसी विशिष्ट देश या क्षेत्र का निवासी (जन्म से या कुल परंपरा से) : *ethnic Turks* 3 गैर-यूरोपीय/-अमरीकी: *ethnic clothes.*

etiquette / 'एटिकेट, 'एटिकट् / *noun* शिष्टाचार।

etymology / एटि'मॉलजि / *noun* शब्दों की व्युत्पत्ति एवं अर्थ के अध्ययन का विज्ञान; शब्द विशेष की उत्पत्ति एवं इतिहास ▶ **etymological** *adj.*

eulogize, -ise / 'यूलजाइज़् / *verb* eulogize (on/over sb/sth) (औप्) प्रशस्ति वाचन या लेखन।

eulogy / 'यूलजि / *noun* (*pl* **eulogies**) eulogy (on/of/for/to sb/sth) (विशेषत: औप्) प्रशस्ति, प्रशंसा भरा भाषण या लेख।

euphemism / 'यूफ़मिज़म् / *noun* euphemism (for sth) कटु सत्य को कम अप्रिय शब्दों द्वारा कहने वाली अभिव्यक्ति: *'Pass away'* is a euphemism for *'die'.* ▶ **euphemistic** *adj* euphemistically *adv.*

euphoria / यू'फ़ॉरिआ / *noun* अत्यंत प्रसन्नता एवं उत्तेजित उल्लास की तीव्र भावना: *the euphoria of recent independence* ▶ **euphoric** *adj.*

evacuate / इ'वैक्युएट् / *verb* 1 evacuate sth; evacuate sb (from...) लोगों को ख़तरनाक स्थान से हटा कर अन्यत्र ले जाना : *Police evacuated a nearby cinema.* 2 किसी स्थान को लोगों से (ख़तरे के कारण) ख़ाली करवाना : *Families in the area were urged to evacuate their homes immediately.* ▶ **evacuation** *noun.*

evade / इ'वेड् / *verb* 1 (किसी से) बचना या जी चुराना : *evade capture by the police* 2 टालमटोल करना; ज़िम्मेदारी से बचना : *evade military service/ taxes.*

evaluate / इ'वैल्युएट् / *verb* मूल्यांकन करना : *evaluate the possibility of*

sth ▶ **evaluation** / इवैल्यु'एशन् / *noun* मूल्यांकन।

evaporate / इ'वैपरेट् / *verb* 1 भाप में परिवर्तित करना, भाप बनाकर उड़ा देना 2 अस्तित्व समाप्त हो जाना या खो जाना : *His hopes evaporated into thin air.* ▶ **evaporation** *noun* वाष्पन।

evasion / इ'वेश़न् / *noun* 1 बचाव, टाल-मटोल : *He's been charged with tax evasion.* 2 बहाना।

evasive / इ'रेसिव् / *adj* 1 जानबूझकर अनिश्चित एवं अस्पष्ट : *an evasive answer* 2 कपटपूर्ण ▶ **evasiveness** *noun.*

eve / ईव़् / *noun* पूर्वसंध्या, किसी विशेष दिवस के पहले की संध्या या पूरा दिन : *a New Year's Eve party.*

even¹ / 'ईव़न् / *adv* 1 भी : *He never even opened the letter.* 2 (तुलना के लिए प्रयुक्त) फिर भी, अब भी : *You know even less about it than I do.* 3 यहाँ तक कि ■ **even if/though** यद्यपि : *I will get there, even if I have to walk all the way.* **even now/then/so** के बावजूद : *Even then he would not admit his mistake.*

even² / 'ईव़न् / *adj* 1 समतल, चौरस : *The footpath is not very even.* 2 एक-सा, एकरूप : *Our scores are now even.* 3 (संख्याएँ) सम; 2, 4, 6, 8, आदि संख्याएँ जो 2 से विभाजित हो जाती हैं 4 (चरित्र, व्यवहार) शांत : *of an even disposition* ■ **on an even keel** (कठिन परिस्थितियों से गुज़रने के बाद) स्वभाविक जीवन बिताते हुए ▶ **evenly** *adv* **evenness** *noun.*

even³ / 'ईव़न् / *verb* बराबर करना : *Sanjay evened the score just after half-time.*

evening / 'ईव़निङ् / *noun* 1 शाम, सायं-काल 2 सायंकाल की कोई विशिष्ट घटना।

event / इ'व़ेन्ट् / *noun* 1 घटना, विशेषत: महत्त्वपूर्ण 2 कोई आयोजित सामाजिक समा-

रोह; खेलकूद कार्यक्रम में कोई एक स्पर्धा (दौड़ आदि) : *The 800 metres is the fourth event of the afternoon.* ∎ **at all events/in any event** चाहे जो कुछ भी हो, हर स्थिति में **in that event** उस स्थिति में, यदि वैसा हो तो ▸ **eventful** *adj* महत्त्वपूर्ण घटना वाला।

eventual / इ'वेन्चुअल / *adj* (परिणाम रूप) अंत में घटित ▸ **eventuality** / इ,वेन्चु'ऐलटि / *noun* (औप) संभावित घटना या परिणाम **eventually** / इ'वेन्चुअलि / *adv* अंत में।

ever / 'एवर्/ *adv* 1 (नकारात्मक या प्रश्न–वाचक वाक्यों में अथवा संदेह या शर्त व्यक्त करने वाले वाक्यों में) किसी भी समय, कभी 2 अब तक कभी भी : *Have you ever been in a helicopter?* 3 हमेशा : *Her novels are as popular as ever.* 4 **ever-**(यौगिकों में) लगातार : *the ever-growing problem* ∎ **ever more** और अधिक **ever since** (...) तब से हमेशा।

evergreen / 'एवर्ग्रीन् / *noun, adj* सदाबहार (वृक्ष)।

everlasting / ,एवर् 'लास्टिङ्; *US* ,एवर् 'लैस्टिङ् / *adj* 1 स्थायी, सदा बना रहने वाला : *everlasting fame* 2 (अनौप, अपमा) बारंबार दोहराया जाने वाला।

every / 'एव्रि / *indef det* 1 समूह में से प्रत्येक, हर एक : *Every child in the class passed the examination.* 2 सभी संभव : *He tried every conceivable combination of numbers.* 3 प्रत्येक में एक बार : *The buses go every 10 minutes.* ∎ **every other** 1 अन्य सभी लोग या चीज़ें 2 हर दूसरा ▸ **everybody** (**everyone** भी) *pron* प्रत्येक और सभी व्यक्ति **everyday** *adj* हर रोज़ (का); साधारण **everything** *pron* 1 प्रत्येक और सभी वस्तुएँ 2 सर्वाधिक महत्त्वपूर्ण वस्तु : *Money isn't everything.* **everywhere** (*US* अनौप**every-**

place भी) *adv* सर्वत्र, सब जगह : *He follows me everywhere.*

evict / इ'विक्ट् / *verb* **evict sb (from sth)** बेदख़ल करना, किसी व्यक्ति को (मकान, भूमि आदि किसी स्थान से) क़ानूनन निकाल देना : *The tenants were evicted for not paying the rent.* ▸ **eviction** *noun.*

evidence / 'एविडन्स् / *noun* 1 **evidence (for sth/to do sth/that...)** गवाही; प्रमाण (तथ्य और कथन) 2 साक्ष्य; लक्षण : *The room bore evidence of a struggle.* ∎ **(be) in evidence** स्पष्ट रूप से दिखाई पड़ने वाला ▸ **evidence** *verb* (औप) प्रमाण से सिद्ध करना; साक्ष्य देना।

evident / 'एविडन्ट् / *adj* **evident (to sb) (that...); evident (in/from sth)** स्पष्ट, प्रकट एवं प्रत्यक्ष ▸ **evidently** *adv.*

evil / 'ईव्ल् / *adj* 1 दुष्ट; पापी : *evil thoughts/deeds* 2 अत्यंत अप्रिय अथवा हानिकर : *an evil smell* ▸ **evil** *noun* 1 (औप) दुष्टता, बुराई, पाप 2 (प्राय: *pl*) ख़राब वस्तु या हानिकारक वस्तु : *social evils* **evilly** *adv* दुष्ट तरीक़े से **the evil eye** *noun* नज़र लगाने की जादुई शक्ति।

evince / इ'विन्स् / *verb* (औप) (अपनी भावना या गुण) दिखाना, प्रदर्शित करना : *He evinced a strong desire to be reconciled with his family.*

evocative / इ'वॉकटिव्/ *adj* **evocative (of sth)** मस्तिष्क पर यादें, भावनाएँ, चित्र आदि तीव्र रूप से लाने वाला : *an evocative account of his life as a coal-miner.*

evoke / इ'वोक् / *verb* (पुरानी यादों, भावनाओं आदि को) मस्तिष्क पर प्रकट करना, लाना : *The music evoked memories of her youth.* ▸ **evocation** *noun.*

evolution / ,ईव'लूश्न्; ,एव'लूश्न् / *noun* 1 (*जीव विज्ञान*) विकास; पौधों एवं जंतुओं

का क्रमिक विकास 2 क्रमिक विकास की प्रक्रिया : the evolution of farming methods 3 योजना के अनुसार (नर्तकों, सैनिकों आदि की) चाल ▸ **evolutionary** adj विकासशील।

evolve / इ'वॉल्व्/ verb 1 **evolve (from sth) (into sth)** क्रमिक रूप से विकसित होना या करना : He has evolved a new theory. 2 (जीव विज्ञान) पौधों एवं जंतुओं का क्रमिक विकास होना।

ewe / यू / noun मादा भेड़।

ex¹ / एक्स / noun (pl **exes, ex's**) (अनौप) भूतपूर्व (पति, पत्नी या अन्य संबंध में भागीदार)।

ex² / एक्स/ prep किसी चीज़ को न मिला- कर, से अलग : prices quoted are ex sales tax.

ex- pref (पूर्वपद) भूतपूर्व : ex-wife ○ ex-president.

exacerbate /इग्'ज़ैसर्बेट्/ verb (औप) बीमारी, दर्द या स्थिति को और ख़राब कर देना, बढ़ा देना : Scratching exacerbates a skin rash.

exact¹ / इग्'ज़ैक्ट्/ adj 1 पूरी तरह ठीक, त्रुटिहीन : an exact copy/replica of the painting 2 त्रुटिहीन होने में समर्थ; (विज्ञान) माप और निर्धारित नियमों पर आधारित ▸ **exactly** adv 1 पूरी तरह से, बिलकुल सही-सही 2 हर दृष्टि से : Your answer is exactly right. 3 (उत्तर में) तुम एकदम सही हो **exactness** noun.

exact² / इग्'ज़ैक्ट्/ verb **exact sth (from sb)** (बलपूर्वक) माँगना और ले लेना : The kidnappers exacted a ransom of Rs 1,00,000 from the family. ▸ **exacting** adj बड़ी माँगें रखने वाला; श्रमसाध्य, कठोर **exaction** noun.

exaggerate / इग्'ज़ैजरेट् / verb बढ़ा-चढ़ाकर कहना : You're exaggerating the difficulties. ▸ **exaggerated** adj बढ़ा-चढ़ाकर कहा या दिखाया हुआ; अति-शयोक्तिपूर्ण एवं झूठ : an exaggerated

laugh **exaggeratedly** adv **exaggeration** / इग्'ज़ैज'रेशन् / noun अति-शयोक्ति।

exalt / इग्'ज़ॉल्ट्/ verb (औप) 1 पद में ऊँचा करना, शक्ति बढ़ाना 2 अत्यधिक प्रशंसा करना : He was exalted as a pillar of the community. ▸ **exaltation** noun 1 अत्यंत आध्यात्मिक प्रसन्नता की अवस्था 2 पदवर्धन **exalted** adj.

examination / इग्ज़ैमि'नेशन् / noun 1 (औप) (**exam** भी) परीक्षा 2 जाँच, जाँच करने की क्रिया : undergo a medical examination.

examine /इग्'ज़ैमिन्/ verb 1 **examine sth/sb (for sth)** परखना, जाँचना : The team examined the wreckage thoroughly. 2 **examine sb (in/on sth)** (औप) परीक्षा लेना, प्रश्नों के उत्तरों से जाँचना 3 (क़ानून) जिरह करना ▸ **examiner** / इग्'ज़ैमिनर् / noun परीक्षक।

example / इग्'ज़ाम्प्ल्; US इग्'ज़ैम्प्ल् / noun 1 उदाहरण 2 नमूना 3 **example (to sb)** (व्यक्ति का चरित्र, व्यवहार आदि) अनुकरण करने योग्य : Her bravery should be an example to us all. ■ **make an example of sb** चेतावनी के रूप में किसी को दंडित करना।

exasperate /इग्'ज़ैस्परेट्/ verb उत्तेजित करना, क्रुद्ध करना ▸ **exasperated** adj **exasperated (at/with sb/sth)** क्रोधित **exasperating** adj क्रुद्ध करने वाला **exasperation** noun.

excavate / 'एक्स्कवेट्/ verb 1 खोदकर निकालना, प्रकट करना : excavate a buried city 2 (औप) ज़मीन खोदकर सुरंग (या नहर) बनाना : excavate a trench ▸ **excavation** noun खुदाई **excavator** noun खोदने वाला व्यक्ति; खुदाई की मशीन।

exceed / इक्'सीड्/ verb 1 (संख्या या मात्रा में) से अधिक होना, से बढ़कर होना : Births far exceed deaths at the *moment.* **2** आवश्यकता या मर्यादा से परे जाना ▸ **exceedingly** *adv* अत्यधिक।

excel / इक्'सेल् / *verb* (-ll-) **excel (in/ at sth/at doing sth)** से बढ़कर होना; किसी कार्य में श्रेष्ठ होना : *The firm excels at producing radios.*

excellence / 'एक्सलन्स् / *noun* श्रेष्ठता, उत्कर्ष : *the university's reputation for academic excellence.*

Excellency / 'एक्सलन्सि / *noun* महा-महिम (राज्यपाल, राजदूत आदि के लिए प्रयुक्त सम्मान शब्द)।

excellent / 'एक्सलन्ट् / *adj* **1** अति उत्तम **2** प्रसन्नता या स्वीकृति जताने के लिए प्रयुक्त : *You can all come? Excellent!*

except¹ / इक्'सेप्ट् / *prep* **except (for sb/sth); except (that...)** को छोड़कर, के अतिरिक्त।

except² / इक्'सेप्ट् / *verb* **except sb/ sth (from sth)** *(औप)* छोड़ देना (ताकि सम्मिलित न हो) : *Children under five are excepted from the survey.*

exception / इक्'सेप्श्न् / *noun* **1** अप-वाद, जो सामान्य से भिन्न हो; अपवादस्वरूप छोड़ने, सम्मिलित न करने की क्रिया **2** अप-वाद, जिस पर नियम लागू न होता हो : *an exception to a rule of grammar* ▸ **exceptionable** *adj* *(औप)* (संभा-वित) आपत्तिजनक।

exceptional / इक्'सेप्श्नल् / *adj* अप-वाद-स्वरूप, असाधारण रीति से ▸ **excep-tionally** *adv* : *an exceptionally beautiful child.*

excerpt / 'एक्सर्प्ट् / *noun* **excerpt (from sth)** पुस्तक से लिया गया उद्धरण; फ़िल्म, संगीत आदि से लिया गया एक हिस्सा : *excerpts from a novel.*

excess¹ / इक्'सेस् / *noun* **1** **an excess of sth** *(अप/मा)* अधिकता, ज़रूरत से ज़्यादा : *an excess of enthusiasm/ anger* **2** ज़्यादती, असंयम : *He's drink-*

ing to excess. **3** **excesses** [*pl*] *(औप)* अतिक्रमण ▸ **excessive** / इक्'सेसिव् / *adj* बहुत अधिक, बहुत बड़ा **exces-sively** *adv.*

excess² / 'एक्सेस् / *adj* अतिरिक्त, आव-श्यकता से अधिक : *pay an excess fare.*

exchange¹ / इक्स्'चेन्ज् / *noun* **1** विनि-मय, अदला-बदली **2** तर्क-वितर्क या वि-वाद : *bitter exchanges between MPs in Parliament* **3** एक देश की मुद्रा का दूसरे देश की मुद्रा से विनिमय **4** *(प्राय: Exchange)* स्थान जहाँ पूँजीपति या व्यापारी व्यापार के लिए जमा होते हैं **5** (**telephone exchange** भी) केंद्रीय कार्यालय जहाँ टेलीफ़ोन की लाइनें मिलाई जाती हैं।

exchange² / इक्स्'चेन्ज् / *verb* **1** **ex-change A for B; exchange sth (with sb)** आदान-प्रदान करना, एक वस्तु के बदले दूसरी वस्तु लेना : *He exchanged the blue sweater for a red one.* **2** विनि-मय करना : *exchange blows* ▸ **ex-changeable** *adj.*

exchequer / इक्स्'चेकर् / *noun* **1** **the Exchequer** सरकार का अर्थ विभाग, राजकोष **2** धन की राष्ट्रीय आपूर्ति; नक़दी संपत्ति : *This resulted in a consider-able loss to the exchequer.*

excise¹ / 'एक्साइज़् / *noun* उत्पादन शुल्क ■ **excise department** *noun* आबकारी विभाग।

excise² / इक्'साइज़् / *verb* **excise sth (from sth)** *(औप)* पूर्णत: हटा देना : *excise all references to the USSR.*

excitable / इक्'साइटब्ल् / *adj* सहज में उत्तेजित होने वाला।

excite / इक्'साइट् / *verb* **1** उत्तेजित करना; भड़काना **2** **excite sth (in sb)** उकसाना, उद्दीप्त करना : *excite public suspicion* **3** *(औप)* (शरीर के अंगों को) जाग्रत करना : *drugs that excite the nerv-ous system* ▸ **excited** *adj* उत्तेजित **exciting** *adj* उत्तेजना पैदा करने वाला।

excitement / इक्'साइट्मन्ट् / *noun*
1 उत्तेजना : *The excitement soon wore off.* 2 (औप) उत्तेजक वस्तु या घटना 3 विक्षुब्धी।

exclaim / इक्'स्क्लेम् / *verb* अचानक (विस्मय से) ज़ोर से कुछ कहना।

exclamation / एक्स्क्ल'मेश्न् / *noun* चिल्लाहट; (विस्मयादि बोधक) चीत्कार : *Mrs Davis gave an exclamation of disgust.* ▶ **exclamation mark** *noun* ! का चिह्न।

exclude / इक्'स्क्लूड् / *verb* 1 **exclude sb/sth (from sth)** किसी व्यक्ति को कहीं जाने से या कहीं सम्मिलित होने से रोकना 2 संभावना से इनकार करना : *The police have excluded robbery as a motive for the murder.* 3 कुछ छोड़ देना, सम्मिलित न करना।

exclusion / इक्'स्क्लूश्न् / *noun* 1 **exclusion (of sb/sth) (from sth)** अलग करना या होना 2 अलग की गई वस्तु या व्यक्ति : *exclusions on account of age.*

exclusive / इक्'स्क्लूसिव् / *adj* 1 ग़ैर-मिलनसार (व्यक्ति), नए व्यक्तियों को अपने में शामिल न करने वाला (वर्ग) : *He belongs to an exclusive club.* 2 **exclusive of sb/sth** को छोड़कर, के अतिरिक्त : *The price of the excursion is exclusive of accommodation.* ▶ **exclusive** *noun* **exclusively** *adv* **exclusiveness** *noun.*

excommunicate / एक्स्क'म्यूनिकेट् / *verb* बहिष्कार कर देना, (धर्म या जाति-बिरादरी के) बाहर कर देना ▶ **excommunication** / एक्स्क'म्यूनि'केश्न् / *noun.*

excrement / 'एक्स्क्रिमन्ट् / *noun* (औप) मल, विष्ठा।

excrete / इक्'स्क्रीट् / *verb* (औप) मल त्याग करना ▶ **excretion** *noun.*

excruciating / इक्'स्क्रूशिएटिङ् / *adj* (शारीरिक या मानसिक पीड़ा) तीक्ष्ण,

संतप्त : *Backache can be excruciating.* ▶ **excruciatingly** *adv.*

excursion / इक्'स्कर्श्न् / *noun* सैर-सपाटा, पर्यटन : *All the excursions had been arranged by the travel company.*

excuse[1] / इक्'स्क्यूज़् / *verb* 1 **excuse sb (for sth/doing sth); excuse sth** माफ़ करना, दोष पर ध्यान न देना 2 **excuse sb/oneself for sth/doing sth; excuse sth** किसी अन्य या स्वयं के कार्यों/आचरणों को उचित ठहराने हेतु कारण बताना; बहाना बनाना : *Nothing can excuse such rudeness.* 3 **excuse sb (from sth)** किसी कर्तव्य, दंड आदि से बचाना ■ **excuse me** 1 (किसी का ध्यान आकर्षित करने में प्रयुक्त) : *Excuse me, do you have the right time?* 2 (शिष्टाचार के लिए प्रयुक्त) : *Excuse me, but I don't think that's quite true.* 3 **excuse me?** (विशेषत: *US*) कृपया अपनी बात दोहराइए ▶ **excusable** *adj* क्षम्य।

excuse[2] / इक्'स्क्यूस् / *noun* **excuse (for sth/for doing sth)** बहाना, माफ़ी; सफ़ाई।

execute / 'एक्सिक्यूट् / *verb* 1 (औप) (दिया गया कार्य) पूरा करना : *execute sb's commands* 2 (क़ानून) अमल में लाना, लागू करना : *execute a legal document* 3 क़ानूनन बाध्य करना 4 फाँसी पर चढ़ाना (या मृत्युदंड देना) : *execute suspected rebels* 5 (औप) अभिनय करना, गा-बजाकर प्रस्तुत करना : *execute a dance step.*

execution / एक्सि'क्यूश्न् / *noun* 1 फाँसी (या मृत्युदंड) 2 अमल, लागूकरण ▶ **executioner** / एक्सि'क्यूशनर् / *noun* फाँसी देने वाला, जल्लाद।

executive / इग्'ज़ेक्यटिव् / *adj* 1 प्रबंधक, व्यवस्थापक : *a woman of considerable executive ability* 2 महत्त्वपूर्ण निर्णय, क़ानून आदि लागू करने की शक्ति-

संपन्न, कार्यकारिणी (समिति) ▸ **execu-tive** *noun* 1 प्रबंधक (व्यक्ति या वर्ग) : *a sales executive* 2 **the executive** कार्यपालिका।

executor / इग्'ज़ेक्यटर् / *noun* वसी-यतनामे के निर्देशों को अमल में लाने वाला, प्रबंधक।

exemplary / इग्'ज़ेम्प्लरि / *adj* 1 अनुकरणीय 2 (क़ानूनया और) उदाहरण-रूप, निवारक : *exemplary punishment.*

exemplify / इग्'ज़ेम्प्लिफ़ाइ / *verb* (*pt, pp* exemplified) 1 उदाहरण या दृष्टांत द्वारा समझाना 2 विशिष्ट उदाहरण होना : *Her style exemplified modern Indian cooking at its best.* ▸ **exemplification** *noun.*

exempt / इग्'ज़ेम्प्ट् / *adj* **exempt (from sth)** किसी कार्य, कर्तव्य या कर से मुक्त : *exempt from working overtime* ▸ **exempt** *verb* **exempt sb/sth (from sth)** (और) किसी कार्य या कर से छूट देना।

exemption / इग्'ज़ेम्प्श्न् / *noun* **exemption (from sth)** छूट, माफ़ी।

exercise[1] / 'एक्सरसाइज़/ *noun* 1 (शरीर या मन का) व्यायाम, कसरत 2 **exercise of sth** प्रयोग : *the exercise of one's civil rights* 3 **exercise (in sth)** अभ्यास।

exercise[2] / 'एक्सरसाइज़/ *verb* 1 व्या-याम/कसरत करना 2 प्रशिक्षण देना 3 कुछ प्रयोग करना : *exercise patience* 4 (और) चिंता में डालना।

exert / इग्'ज़र्ट् / *verb* 1 **exert sth (on sb/sth)** (अपने अधिकार, प्रभाव, गुण आदि का) प्रयोग करना 2 **exert oneself** प्रयास करना : *You'll have to exert yourself more if you want to pass your exam.* ▸ **exertion** *noun.*

exhale / एक्स्'हेल् / *verb* श्वास निकालना; (गैस या भाप) छोड़ना : *exhale air from the lungs* ▸ **exhalation** / ,एक्सह 'लेश्न् / *noun.*

exhaust[1] / इग्'ज़ॉस्ट् / *verb* 1 (प्रयोग करके) ख़ाली कर देना, पूरा-पूरा समाप्त कर डालना : *exhaust a money supply* 2 थका देना 3 किसी विषय पर सब कुछ पढ़/कह/लिख डालना ▸ **exhausted** *adj* थककर चूर **exhausting** *adj* थकाने वाला।

exhaust[2] / इग्'ज़ॉस्ट् / *noun* 1 गाड़ियों आदि से निकलने वाला बेकार पदार्थ, धुआँ आदि : *exhaust fumes* 2 (**exhaust-pipe** भी) (इंजिन में भाप, धुआँ आदि निकलने की) निकास नली।

exhaustion/ इग्'ज़ॉस्चन् / *noun* 1 थकान 2 (और) समाप्ति।

exhaustive / इग्'ज़ॉस्टिव् / *adj* संपूर्ण।

exhibit[1] / इग्'ज़िबिट् / *verb* 1 प्रदर्शित करना 2 **exhibit (at/in...)** (चित्रों आदि) का प्रदर्शन करना 3 कोई गुण या भाव दिखाना ▸ **exhibitor** *noun* वस्तुएँ प्रदर्शित करने वाला।

exhibit[2] / इग्'ज़िबिट् / *noun* 1 प्रदर्शित वस्तु 2 कचहरी में प्रमाण रूप प्रस्तुत दस्ता-वेज़।

exhibition /,एक्सि'बिश्न् / *noun* 1 प्र-दर्शनी, नुमाइश 2 **exhibition of sth** प्रदर्शन; कला प्रदर्शन : *a dancing exhibition.*

exhilarate / इग्'ज़िलरेट् / *verb* आनंदित करना, उल्लासपूर्ण बना देना : *exhilarated by the news* ▸ **exhilarating** *adj* आनंदकारी, आह्लादी **exhilaration** *noun* उल्लास।

exhort / इग्'ज़ॉर्ट् / *verb* **exhort sb (to sth/to do sth)** (और) प्रोत्साहित करना; उपदेश देना ▸ **exhortation** /,एग्ज़ॉर्'टे-श्न् / *noun* उपदेश, प्रबोधन।

exile / 'एक्साइल्; 'एग्ज़ाइल् / *noun* 1 देश निकाला, निर्वासन : *live in exile* 2 अपने देश से लंबे समय तक दूर रहना 3 निर्वासित व्यक्ति : *a tax exile* ▸ **exile** *verb* **exile**

sb (from) देश-निकाला देना, निर्वासित करना : *be exiled for life.*

exist / इग्'ज़िस्ट् / *verb* 1 होना, अस्तित्व होना : *laws that have existed for hundreds of years* 2 **exist (on sth)** (कठिनाई के साथ) रहना, गुज़ारा करना ▸ **existent** *adj* (औप) अस्तित्व में (वर्तमान) **existing** *adj* वर्तमान समय के, अब उपलब्ध : *existing rates of pay.*

existence / इग्'ज़िस्टन्स् / *noun* 1 अस्तित्व, सत्ता 2 रहन-सहन; गुज़ारा करते जाना।

exit / 'एक्सिट्; 'एग्ज़िट् / *noun* 1 प्रस्थान, बाहर निकलने, जाने की क्रिया : *The heroine makes her exit (from the stage).* 2 बाहर निकलने का मार्ग; निकास द्वार 3 मुख्य सड़क या गोल चक्कर से हटने के लिए मोड़ या स्थान : *At the roundabout take the third exit.* ▸ **exit** *verb* बाहर निकलना या हो जाना **exit poll** *noun* मतदान के तुरंत बाद मतदाताओं से हुई बातचीत पर आधारित चुनाव (परिणाम)।

exodus / 'एक्सडस् / *noun* **exodus (from...) (to...)** (औप या परि) बहुत-से लोगों का एक साथ निकलना।

exonerate / इग्'ज़ॉनरेट् / *verb* **exonerate sb (from sth)** दोषमुक्त घोषित करना : *A commission of inquiry exonerated him (from all responsibility for the accident).*

exorbitant / इग्'ज़ॉर्बिटन्ट् / *adj* (औप) (क़ीमत, मूल्य, माँग आदि) अत्यधिक, बहुत ऊँची : *The price of food here is exorbitant.* ▸ **exorbitantly** *adv.*

exorcize, -ise / 'एक्सॉर्साइज़् / *verb* **exorcize sth (from sb/sth)** अपदूत भगाना, झाड़-फूँक करना (भूत उतारना) ▸ **exorcism** *noun* झाड़-फूँक, भूत-अपसरण **exorcist** *noun* ओझा।

exotic / इग्'ज़ॉटिक् / *adj* 1 अन्य स्थान से आई वस्तु, विदेशी 2 असामान्य (या विदेशी) होने के कारण आकर्षक : *exotic plumage/clothes.*

exotica / इग्'ज़ॉटिका / *noun* [*pl*] असामान्य एवं उत्कृष्ट वस्तुएँ।

expand / इक्'स्पैन्ड् / *verb* **expand (sth) (into sth)** (संख्या, महत्त्व या आकार में) बढ़ना या बढ़ाना, फैलना/फैलाना।

expanse / इक्'स्पैन्स् / *noun* विस्तार, फैलाव।

expansion / इक्'स्पैन्शन् / *noun* फैलाव, विस्तार, प्रसार ▸ **expansionism** *noun* विस्तारवाद (देश की सीमा, व्यापार आदि का)।

expansive / इक्'स्पैन्सिव् / *adj* 1 प्र-सरणशील, विस्तार योग्य 2 मित्रतापूर्ण।

expatriate / एक्स्'पैट्रिअट् / *noun* स्वदेश से बाहर रहने वाला व्यक्ति, विदेशवासी।

expect / इक्'स्पेक्ट् / *verb* 1 **expect sth (from sb/sth)** आशा करना, प्रत्याशा करना 2 **expect sth (from sb)** किसी से कुछ पाने की आशा रखना 3 **expect sth (from sb)** किसी से (अधिकार, कर्तव्य आदि की) अपेक्षा रखना 4 (अनौप) विश्वास करना, मानना ■ **be expecting (a baby/child)** (अनौप) (महिला का) गर्भवती होना ▸ **expectancy** *noun* प्रत्याशा, संभावना **expectant** *adj* 1 आशापूर्ण 2 शिशु-जन्म की आशा में।

expectation / एक्स्पेक्'टेश्न् / *noun* 1 **expectation (of sth)** प्रत्याशा, आशा : *He has little expectation of winning a prize.* 2 (प्रायः *pl*) अपेक्षा, विश्वासपूर्ण उम्मीद।

expedient / इक्'स्पीडिअन्ट् / *adj* (योजना या कार्य) हितकर, कार्यसाधक ▸ **expedience (expediency** भी) *noun* कार्यसिद्धि (करने की क्षमता) **expedient** *noun* कार्यसिद्धि के साधन (अच्छे या बुरे)।

expedite / 'एक्स्पडाइट् / *verb* (औप) जल्दी पूरा करने में सहायता करना, शीघ्र निबटाना।

expedition / एक्स्प'डिश्न् / *noun* 1 खोज यात्रा, अभियान : *go on an expedition to the North Pole* 2 अभियान पर जाने

वाले व्यक्ति और गाड़ियाँ आदि, अभियान दल ▸ **expeditionary** adj.

expel / इक्'स्पेल् / verb (-ll-) **expel sb (from sth)** 1 निकाल बाहर करना 2 बल-पूर्वक भगा देना, निकाल देना : expel air from the lungs.

expend / इक्'स्पेन्ड् / verb **expend sth (in/on sth/doing sth)** (औप) (संसाधन या धन) ख़र्च करना : expend time, effort and money ▸ **expendable** adj व्ययकरणीय।

expenditure / इक्'स्पेन्डिचर् / noun 1 ख़र्चा, व्यय; ख़र्च करने की क्रिया : Limit your expenditure to what is essential. 2 संसाधनों का उपयोग (करना)।

expense / इक्'स्पेन्स् / noun 1 व्यय करना, ख़र्च करना 2 **expenses**[pl] लागत ख़र्च : travelling expenses.

expensive / इक्'स्पेन्सिव् / adj महँगा, क़ीमती ▸ **expensively** adv.

experience / इक्'स्पिअरिअन्स् / noun 1 अनुभव, प्रत्यक्ष कार्य या दर्शन से प्राप्त ज्ञान 2 घटना आदि जिससे अनुभव प्राप्त होता है : an unpleasant experience ▸ **experience** verb अनुभव प्राप्त करना या होना : experience pleasure/pain **experienced** adj अनुभव प्राप्त/अनुभवी (व्यक्ति) **experiential** adj (औप) अनुभव-जन्य या अनुभव पर आधारित।

experiment / इक्'स्पेरिमन्ट् / noun 1 (वैज्ञानिक) प्रयोग, परीक्षण 2 **experiment (in sth)** किसी बात का प्रभाव देखने के लिए नया कार्य (करना) : an experiment in communal living ▸ **experiment** verb experiment (on sb/sth); experiment (with sth) प्रयोग/परीक्षण करना **experimentation** noun (औप) प्रयोग करने की प्रक्रिया।

experimental / इक्'स्पेरि'मेन्ट्ल् / adj प्रयोगात्मक : an experimental farm **experimentally** adv.

expert / 'एक्स्पर्ट् / noun expert (at/in/

on sth/doing sth) विशेषज्ञ व्यक्ति : an expert in psychology ▸ **expert** adj expert (at/in sth/doing sth) निपुण, कुशल; निपुणता/कुशलता से किया गया : take expert advice **expertly** adv.

expertise / एक्स्पर्'टीज़् / noun expertise (in sth/doing sth) विशेषज्ञ ज्ञान।

expire / इक्'स्पाइअर् / verb 1 (समयावधि का) समाप्त हो जाना; अवैध हो जाना : When does your driving licence expire? 2 (विशेषत: चिकि) सांस बाहर निकलना/निकालना 3 (अप्रया औप) मरना ▸ **expiration** / एक्स्प'रेशन् / noun.

expiry / इक्'स्पाइअरि / noun समाप्ति/ कालावधि पूरी हो जाना; (क़ानून) अब लागू न रहना।

explain / इक्'स्प्लेन् / verb 1 **explain sth (to sb)** अर्थ समझाना, व्याख्या करना : He explained his plan to us. 2 **explain sth (to sb)** सफ़ाई देना, कारण बताना ∎ **explain oneself** 1 अपनी बात का अर्थ स्पष्ट करना 2 (औप) अपनी सफ़ाई पेश करना।

explanation / एक्स्प्ल'नेशन् / noun 1 व्याख्या करने/देने की क्रिया : He left the room without (further) explanation. 2 स्पष्टीकरण।

explanatory / इक्'स्प्लैनट्रि / adj व्याख्या-त्मक।

explicable / इक्'स्प्लिकबल्; 'एक्स्प्लि-कब्ल् / adj (औप) व्याख्या/स्पष्टीकरण योग्य।

explicit / इक्'स्प्लिसिट् / adj 1 (कथन आदि) सुस्पष्ट, भली-भाँति व्यक्त : He gave me explicit directions (on) how to get there. 2 (व्यक्ति) स्पष्टवादी, साफ़-साफ़ कहने वाला ▸ **explicitly** adv **explicitness** noun.

explode / इक्'स्प्लोड् / verb 1 विस्फोट करना या होना : The firework exploded in his hand. 2 **explode (with/into sth)** (व्यक्ति का) अचानक

भड़क उठना; (भावों का) अचानक उत्तेजित हो जाना : At last his anger exploded. 3 explode (into sth) अचानक बदल जाना या विकसित हो जाना : The protest march exploded into a riot. 4 (जन-संख्या की) अचानक वृद्धि 5 (किसी मत सिद्धांत आदि का) खंडन करना : explode a superstition ▸ exploded adj.

exploit¹ / 'एक्स्प्लॉइट् / noun (प्राय: pl) कारनामे, साहसिक कार्य : He describes his exploits as a war correspondent in his new autobiography.

exploit² / इक्'स्प्लॉइट् / verb 1 (खानों, जल शक्ति और अन्य प्राकृतिक संसाधनों को) काम में लाना, उपयोग करना : exploit oil resources 2 (अपमा) अपने लाभ के लिए किसी का शोषण करना, अनुचित लाभ उठाना : child labour exploited in factories ▸ exploitation / एक्स्प्लॉइ टेश्न्/ noun (कभी-कभी अपमा) उपयोग; शोषण exploitative adj (अपमा) शोषणपूर्ण exploiter noun.

explore / इक्'स्प्लॉर् / verb 1 खोज के लिए स्थान-स्थान या देश में घूमना : explore the Arctic regions 2 (समस्या आदि पर) पूरी तरह ग़ौर करना ▸ exploration / एक्स्प्ल' रेश्न्/ noun खोज यात्रा, छान-बीन; गवेषणा exploratory adj explorer noun.

explosion / इक्'स्प्लोश्न् / noun 1 विस्फोट; भावों की अचानक तीव्र अभिव्यक्ति 2 अचानक तीव्र वृद्धि : a population explosion.

explosive / इक्'स्प्लोसिव्/ adj 1 वि-स्फोटक : an explosive mixture of chemicals 2 भावनाओं (क्रोध, घृणा आदि) को भड़काने वाला; हिंसात्मक बनाने वाला : an explosive situation/issue ▸ explosive noun विस्फोटक सामग्री।

exponent / इक्'स्पोनन्ट् / noun 1 मत, सिद्धांत, वाद आदि का समर्थक : a leading exponent of free trade 2 किसी कार्य में कुशल व्यक्ति 3 (गणित) घात : In a³, the figure ³ is the exponent. ▸ exponential adj (गणित) घात से संबंधित।

export¹ / इक्'स्पॉर्ट् / verb 1 export (sth) (to...) माल निर्यात करना, देश के बाहर भेजना 2 मत या सिद्धांत आदि दूसरे देश या क्षेत्र में फैलाना ▸ exportation noun माल निर्यात करना exporter noun निर्यातक (देश या व्यक्ति)।

export² / एक्स्पॉर्ट् / noun 1 निर्यात व्या-पार : launch an export drive 2 (प्राय: pl) निर्यातित माल।

expose / इक्'स्पोज़् / verb 1 प्रदर्शित करना, दिखाना 2 expose sth/sb/one-self (to sth) खुला छोड़ देना, अरक्षित छोड़ देना 3 रहस्य खोलना, भंडा फोड़ देना : expose a plot/a fraud 4 (कैमरा फ़िल्म पर) प्रकाश पड़ने देना ▸ exposed adj 1 (स्थान) खुला, अरक्षित 2 (आक्रमण या आलोचना के लिए) खुला एवं समर्थन रहित।

exposition / एक्स्प 'ज़िश्न् / noun (औप) 1 किसी सिद्धांत अथवा योजना की व्याख्या : a brilliant exposition of the advantages of nuclear power 2 वस्तुओं या कलाकृतियों की प्रदर्शनी।

exposure / इक्'स्पोश़र् / noun 1 expo-sure (to sth) प्रदर्शित करने/होने की क्रिया; खुला/अरक्षित रहने की क्रिया या अवस्था : brief exposure to radiation 2 टी वी या समाचार-पत्रों में प्रचार 3 फ़ोटोग्राफ़।

expound / इक् 'स्पाउन्ड् / verb ex-pound sth (to sb); expound on sth (औप) उदाहरण आदि देकर व्याख्या करना, समझाना : He expounded his views on education to me at great length.

express¹ / इक्'स्प्रेस् / verb 1 शब्दों, संकेतों, कार्यों द्वारा अपने विचारों को दूसरों पर प्रकट करना, अभिव्यक्ति करना : express one's doubts/fears about sth 2 express oneself बोल कर, लिख कर या किसी अन्य तरीक़े से अपने भाव व्यक्त करना 3 express sth as/in sth (विशेषत:

गणित) विशिष्ट ढंग से (जैसे चिह्नों द्वारा) कुछ दर्शाना : *The figures are expressed as percentages.*

express² / इक्'स्प्रेस् / *adj* 1 कम समय लेने वाली (विशिष्ट डाक या यातायात सेवा) : *express bus/train* 2 साफ़-साफ़ बताया हुआ, निश्चित ▸ **expressly** *adv* 1 स्पष्ट/ निश्चित रूप से 2 विशेष उद्देश्य से।

express³ / इक्'स्प्रेस् / *noun* 1 (**express train** भी) एक्सप्रेस (रेलगाड़ी) 2 (विशेषत: *US* **special delivery** भी) तुरंत सेवा व्यवस्था।

expression / इक्'स्प्रेश्न् / *noun* 1 (चेहरे, हावभाव की) मुद्रा, रुख़ 2 शब्द या पद-बंध : *'Shut up' is not a polite expression.* 3 अपने भाव, विचार, मत आदि व्यक्त करने की प्रक्रिया ▸ **expression-less** *adj* भावरहित।

expressive / इक्'स्प्रेसिव् / *adj* 1 अभि-व्यक्ति सक्षम 2 **expressive (of sth)** (औप) द्योतक, सूचक।

expulsion / इक्'स्पल्श्न् / *noun* **expulsion (from...)** निष्कासन, निकालने की क्रिया।

exquisite / इक्'स्क्विज़िट्; 'एक्सक्वि-ज़िट् / *adj* 1 अति उत्तम, उत्कृष्ट रूप से सुंदर : *an exquisite little painting* 2 (औप) अति संवेदनशील, सूक्ष्मग्राही : *an exquisite sense of timing* ▸ **exqui-sitely** *adv*.

extend / इक्'स्टेन्ड् / *verb* 1 (समय या स्थान में) फैलाना, बढ़ाना : *extend a fence/garden* 2 व्यापार, विचार या प्रभाव का विस्तार करना 3 **extend sth to sb** (औप) उपलब्ध कराना; प्रस्ताव करना : *extend hospitality to overseas students* 4 पसारना, (हाथ-पैर) फैलाना : *He extended his hand to the new employee.* ▸ **extendable** *adj* **extended** *adj*.

extension / इक्'स्टेन्श्न् / *noun* 1 वि-स्तार, प्रसार 2 **extension (to sth)**

(मुख्य भवन आदि में) जोड़ा गया भाग : *build a 160-bed extension to a hospital* 3 **extension (of sth)** अतिरिक्त (दिया गया) समय 4 मुख्य टेलिफोन लाइन से किसी अन्य कमरे आदि को गई हुई लाइन।

extensive / इक्'स्टेन्सिव् / *adj* 1 व्यापक, विस्तीर्ण 2 मात्रा में बहुत ज़्यादा : *cause extensive damage* ▸ **extensively** *adv*.

extent / इक्'स्टेन्ट् / *noun* लंबाई, क्षेत्र; परास ■ **to some, what, such an, a certain, etc extent** की मात्रा/सीमा तक।

extenuate / इक्'स्टेन्युएट् / *verb* कोई बहाना ढूँढ़कर किसी अपराध को हलका करना, लघु बनाना ▸ **extenuating** *adj* अपराध कम आँकने के लिए आधार बनाते हुए।

exterior / इक्'स्टिअरिअर् / *adj* बाहरी, बाहर का ▸ **exterior** *noun* 1 किसी व्यक्ति की बाह्य प्रतीति 2 किसी स्थान (भवन आदि) का बाह्य भाग : *The house has a Georgian exterior.*

exterminate / इक्'स्टर्मिनेट् / *verb* (मनुष्य या पशु की जाति आदि) पूर्णत: नष्ट करना; अंत करना : *The indigenous population was virtually exterminated by the settlers.* ▸ **extermina-tion** *noun* विध्वंस, विनाश।

external / इक्'स्टर्नल् / *adj* 1 बाह्य, बाहर स्थित : *the external walls of the building* 2 बाहरी, बाहर से आने वाला : *a tribe hardly affected by external influences ○ an external examina-tion* ▸ **externally** *adv* **externals** *noun* [*pl*] (औप) बाहरी प्रतीति/दृष्टि।

extinct / इक्'स्टिङ्क्ट् / *adj* 1 (पौधों या पशुओं की प्रजाति) लुप्त, अविद्यमान : *The red squirrel is now virtually extinct in England.* 2 (ज्वालामुखी) मृत ▸ **extinction** *noun*.

extinguish / इक्'स्टिङ्ग्विश् / *verb* (औप) 1 (रोशनी या आग) बुझाना : *They*

tried to extinguish the flames.
2 (आशा या भाव का) अंत कर देना
▸ **extinguisher** *noun* (fire extinguisher भी) अग्निशामक यंत्र।

extol / इक्'स्टोल् / *verb* (-ll-) **extol sb**
(as sth) (औप) बहुत प्रशंसा करना, गुणगान
करना : *He was extolled as a hero.*

extort / इक्'स्टॉर्ट् / *verb* **extort sth**
(from sb) धमकाकर या बलात् कुछ (पैसा,
वायदा आदि) ले लेना : *extort money/*
bribes from sb ▸ **extortion** *noun.*

extortionate / इक्'स्टॉर्शनट् / *adj*
(अप्रा) (माँग, क़ीमत आदि) बहुत ऊँची।

extra / 'एक्स्ट्रा / *adj* सामान्य से अधिक;
अतिरिक्त : *demand extra pay for*
extra work ▸ **extra** *adv* अतिरिक्त
extra *noun* 1 अतिरिक्त वस्तु 2 (फ़िल्म
में) बहुत छोटी भूमिका करने वाला व्यक्ति।

extract / इक्'स्ट्रैक्ट् / *verb* **extract sth**
(from sb/sth) 1 (प्रयत्न या बल से) कुछ
निकाल लेना या खींचना : *manage to*
extract a cork from a bottle 2 (किसी
व्यक्ति से उसकी अनिच्छा के बावजूद) सूचना
(या पैसा) प्राप्त कर लेना 3 किसी विशेष
प्रक्रिया से किसी वस्तु से कुछ निकालना/
खींचना : *extract juice from oranges*
4 पुस्तक, कविता आदि से उद्धरण छाँटना
और उतारना ▸ **extract** / 'एक्स्ट्रैक्ट् /
noun 1 निचोड़, सार : *herbal extracts*
2 **extract (from sth)** पुस्तक आदि से
उद्धरण **extraction** / इक्'स्ट्रैक्श्न् / *noun*
1 निकालने या खींचने की प्रक्रिया 2 (औप)
व्यक्ति की वंशावली का उद्भव।

extracurricular / एक्स्ट्राक्'रिक्यलर् /
adj (स्कूल/कॉलेज में) नियमित पाठ्यक्रम
से बाहर का : *She's involved in many*
extracurricular activities, includ-
ing music, sports and drama.

extradite / 'एक्स्ट्रडाइट् / *verb* **extra-**
dite sb (to...) (from...) किसी अपराधी
को उसी देश में वापिस भेज देना जहाँ उसने
अपराध किया था।

extraordinary / इक्'स्ट्रॉईनरि; इक्
'स्ट्रॉर्डिनरि / *adj* 1 असाधारण; उल्लेखनीय :
a most extraordinary story 2 (तक)
(अधिकारी आदि) विशेष रूप से नियुक्त :
an ambassador extraordinary
▸ **extraordinarily** *adv.*

extrapolate / इक्'स्ट्रैपलेट् / *verb* **ex-**
trapolate (sth) (from sth) (औप)
उपलब्ध तथ्यों या आँकड़ों के आधार पर
तथ्यों का पूर्व आकलन या अनुमान करना
▸ **extrapolation** *noun.*

extravagant / इक्'स्ट्रैव्गन्ट् / *adj*
1 फ़िज़ूलख़र्च, अपव्ययी 2 (विचार, व्यवहार,
भाषण आदि) अनावश्यक एवं तर्क से परे
▸ **extravagance** *noun* **extrava-**
gantly *adv* उच्छृंखलता पूर्ण।

extreme / इक्'स्ट्रीम् / *adj* 1 चरम
(संभव), अत्यधिक : *suffering from*
extreme anxiety 2 (अक्सर अप्रा)
(स्वभाव, विचार) उग्र, तीव्र : *hold ex-*
treme left-wing/right-wing views
3 दूर तम सिरे का ▸ **extreme** *noun*
1 (प्राय: *pl*) पराकाष्ठा के गुण 2 अंतिम
(स्थिति, अंश); सिरा, छोर ■ **go to ex-**
tremes उग्र उपाय करना ▸ **extremely**
adv (अत्यंत) उच्चस्तरीय।

extremist / इक्'स्ट्रीमिस्ट् / *noun* (प्राय:
अप्रा) उग्रवादी (विचारों का व्यक्ति)।

extremity / इक्'स्ट्रेमटि / *noun* (औप)
1 सिरा या छोर; **extremities** [*pl*] हाथ और
पैर 2 (दुख, आपत्ति, निराशा आदि की)
पराकाष्ठा।

extricate / 'एक्स्ट्रिकेट् / *verb* **extricate**
oneself/sb/sth (from sth) (औप)
(मुसीबतों आदि से) छुड़ा लेना, मुक्त
करना : *The bird had to be extri-*
cated from the netting.

extrovert / 'एक्स्ट्रवर्ट् / *noun* बहिर्मुखी।

exuberant / इग्'ज़्यूबरन्ट् / *adj* 1 उल्लास-
पूर्ण 2 (पेड़-पौधे) तेज़ी से उग रहे : *exu-*
berant foliage ▸ **exuberance** *noun*
exuberantly *adv.*

exude / इग्'ज़्यूड़; *US* इग्'जूड़ / *verb*
1 (कोई द्रव या गंध) धीरे-धीरे बाहर
निकलना, रिसना या नि:स्रावित होना
2 मनोभावों को खुले तौर पर और तीव्रता से
व्यक्त करना : *She exudes confidence.*

exult / इग्'ज़ल्ट् / *verb* **exult (at/in sth)**
(औप) फूले न समाना : *The nation
exulted at the team's success.*
▶ **exultant** *adj* **exultant (at sth)**
उल्लासित **exultation** / ,एग्ज़ल्'टेश्न् /
noun उल्लास, जयकार।

eye[1] / आइ / *noun* 1 आँख, नेत्र; आँख का
दिखाई देने वाला रंगीन भाग 2 (प्राय: *pl*)
देखने की शक्ति/सामर्थ्य; (प्राय: *sing*)
अच्छे निर्णय लेने की शक्ति : *She has a
good eye for a bargain.* 3 आँख के
समान वस्तु (छेद) : *the eye of a needle*
○ *the eye of a potato* ■ **clap/lay/set**
eyes on sb/sth (अनौप) देखना **close/
shut your eyes to sth** जानबूझ कर
अनदेखी करना **(not) see eye to eye**
सहमत (न) होना **with an eye to** (इस)
आशा से ▶ **eyeball** / 'आइबॉल् / *noun*
आँख की पुतली, तारा **eyebrow** / 'आइ-
ब्राउ / *noun* भौंहें **eye-catching** *adj*
आकर्षक **eyelash** / 'आइलैश् / *noun*
(lash भी) पलकें **eyesight** / 'आइसाइट् /
noun दृष्टि **eyesore** / 'आइसॉर् / *noun*
कुरूप वस्तु **eyewitness** / 'आइविट्नस्/
noun चश्मदीद गवाह, प्रत्यक्षदर्शी : *an
eyewitness account of a crime.*

eye[2] / आइ / *verb* (*pres p* **eyeing** या
eying) देखना, दृष्टि डालना (उत्सुकता,
संदेह या वासना से) : *The children
were eyeing the sweets hungrily.*

eyewash / 'आइवॉश् / *noun* (अनौप)
छल-छद्म वाली बात; बकवास।

Ff

fable / फ़ेबल् / noun नीतिकथा, लघुकथा जिसमें कोई उपदेश होता है : *Aesop's fables.*

fabric / फ़ैब्रिक् / noun 1 कपड़ा (मुख्यत: बुना हुआ) 2 [sing] the fabric (of sth) ढाँचा; बनावट।

fabricate / फ़ैब्रिकेट् / verb 1 जालसाज़ी करना : *fabricate evidence* 2 विभिन्न पदार्थों से कोई वस्तु तैयार करना ▸ **fabrication** noun.

fabulous / फ़ैब्यलस् / adj 1 आश्चर्यजनक एवं काल्पनिक 2 (अनौप) जो सिर्फ़ नीति-कथाओं में ही मिलता/होता है 3 (अनौप) अत्यधिक अच्छा : *a fabulous performance.*

facade / फ़साड / noun 1 (औप) इमारत का सामने वाला भाग 2 बाहरी दिखावा, विशेषत: जिससे अवास्तविकता झलकती है।

face¹ / फ़ेस् / noun 1 चेहरा, मुख 2 किसी के सामने का भाग, अग्रभाग : *the face of a clock* 3 किसी चीज़ का कोई पहलू; किसी चीज़ की प्रकृति ∎ **face to face (with sb/sth)** आमने-सामने **in the face of sth** 1 के बावजूद : *succeed in the face of danger* 2 किसी के विरोध करने पर **make/pull a face at (sb)** मुँह बिचकाना **on the face of it** (अनौप) ऊपरी तौर से ▸ **face value** noun सिक्के, नोट आदि पर अंकित मूल्य।

face² / फ़ेस् / verb 1 सामने होना, अभिमुख होना 2 कठिन या अप्रिय परिस्थिति का सामना करना : *The directors face charges of fraud.* ∎ **face the music** (अनौप) (किए का) परिणाम भुगतना ▸ **-faced** suff (प्रत्यय) (यौगिक विशेषणों में प्रयुक्त) चेहरा-विशेष : *red-faced* o *baby-faced.*

facet / फ़ैसिट् / noun 1 पहलू, पक्ष 2 तराशे हुए पत्थर या नग का पार्श्व।

facetious / फ़सीशस् / adj (प्राय: अपमा) अनुपयुक्त ढंग से या अनुचित समय पर विनोदी/हँसमुख होने का प्रयास करने वाला ▸ **facetiously** adv.

facial / फ़ेशल् / adj मौखिक (मुद्रा आदि) ▸ **facial** noun चेहरे का सौंदर्य-उपचार।

facile / फ़ैसाइल् / adj (प्राय: अपमा) 1 आसान 2 कुशल; सरलता से मामूली कार्य संपन्न करने वाला 3 (भाषण, लेखन आदि) सुसाध्य एवं अनायास : *a facile remark.*

facilitate / फ़सिलिटेट् / verb (औप) सरल एवं सुसाध्य बनाना : *It would facilitate matters if you were co-operative.* ▸ **facilitation** noun.

facility / फ़सिलिटि / noun (pl **facilities**) 1 सुविधा, सीखने या कुछ करने की योग्यता 2 (प्राय: pl) सुविधाएँ, सहूलियतें : *sports facilities* 3 मशीन, सेवा आदि का अतिरिक्त गुण।

facsimile / फ़ैक्सिमिलि / noun 1 (चित्र, आलेख आदि की) सच्ची प्रतिकृति 2 = **fax** : *Send a letter by facsimile.*

fact / फ़ैक्ट् / noun 1 तथ्य; 2 सूचना आदि जिस पर कोई मत या तर्क आधारित हो 3 सत्य, वास्तविकता : *The story is founded on fact.* ∎ **as a matter of fact; in fact** वस्तुत:, वास्तव में; सचमुच।

faction / फ़ैक्शन् / noun दल या गुट; दलबंदी।

factitious / फ़ैक्टिशस् / adj (औप) कृत्रिम।

factor / फ़ैक्टर् / noun 1 घटक या कारक जो कार्य संपन्न करने में सहायक होता है : *environmental factors* 2 (गणित) गुणक, (1 को छोड़कर) वह पूर्ण संख्या जिससे एक पूर्ण बड़ी संख्या पूर्णत: विभाजित हो सकती है (जैसे 12 के गुणक 2, 3, 4, 6, 12 हैं) 3 किसी वस्तु में वृद्धि या कमी की मात्रा; मापन में एक स्तर।

factory / फ़ैक्ट्रि; फ़ैक्टरि / noun (pl **factories**) फ़ैक्टरी, कारख़ाना।

faculty /फ़ैकल्टि/ noun (pl **faculties**) 1 मानसिक योग्यता; ज्ञानेंद्रियों की शक्ति 2 **faculty of/for doing sth** विशिष्ट योग्यता/क्षमता 3 (विश्वविद्यालयों में) संकाय; प्राध्यापक वर्ग : the Engineering Faculty.

fad /फ़ैड्/ noun झक, फ़ैशन; क्षणिक प्रचलन ▸ **faddy** adj झक्की।

fade /फ़ेड्/ verb 1 मुरझाना, कुम्हलाना; रंग फीका पड़ना 2 **fade (away)** (याददाश्त, दृष्टि आदि से) लुप्त हो जाना, मंद पड़ना : All memory of her childhood had faded from her mind.

faeces (US **feces**) /फ़ीसीज़/ noun [pl] (ओप) मल।

fag /फ़ैग्/ noun 1 (अनौप) सिगरेट 2 (अनौप) कठोर परिश्रमसाध्य काम ■ **fag-end** noun 1 सिगरेट का बचा हुआ टुकड़ा 2 किसी चीज़ का अंतिम या निकृष्ट भाग : the fag-end of the day.

Fahrenheit /फ़ैरन्हाइट्/ adj (संक्षि F) थर्मामीटर की वह मापनी जिसमें हिमांक 32° और क्वथनांक 212° पर होता है।

fail /फ़ेल्/ verb 1 **fail (in sth/to do sth)** असफल होना; अनुत्तीर्ण होना, परीक्षा में असफल होना या करना : The examiners failed over half the candidates. 2 कुछ करना भूल जाना 3 कम या अपर्याप्त होना 4 (वस्तु) आवश्यकतानुसार विकसित न होना या समाप्त हो जाना : The crops have failed again. 5 (स्वास्थ्य, दृष्टिशक्ति आदि) दुर्बल/क्षीण होना : Her eyesight is failing. 6 (व्यापार) ठप्प हो जाना, दिवालिया हो जाना ▸ **fail** noun (परीक्षा में) असफलता ■ **without fail** निश्चयपूर्वक।

failing[1] /फ़ेलिङ्/ noun (चरित्र की) दुर्बलता या अशक्तता।

failing[2] /फ़ेलिङ्/ prep अगर ऐसा न हो तो; के बिना : Ask a friend to recommend a doctor or, failing that look up the telephone directory.

failure /फ़ेल्यर/ noun 1 असफलता 2 असफल व्यक्ति या प्रयास : He was a failure as a teacher. 3 अपेक्षाकृत कार्य न कर पाने की स्थिति 4 **failure to do sth** चूक : failure to comply with the regulations.

faint /फ़ेन्ट्/ adj (-er, -est) 1 अस्पष्ट, धुँधला 2 (शारीरिक क्षमता) दुर्बल; (व्यक्ति) मूर्छित-सा होने को : in a faint voice 3 (विचार आदि) संभव लेकिन अनिश्चित; (क्रिया) परिणाम में अनिश्चित ▸ **faint** verb मूर्छित या बेहोश होना : He fainted from hunger. **faint** noun बेहोशी की दशा, मूर्छा **faint-hearted** adj बुज़दिल, कायर **faintly** adv **faintness** noun.

fair[1] /फ़ेअर/ adj 1 **fair (to sb)** उचित और सम्मानजनक; **fair (to/on sb)** न्याय-संगत और नियमानुकूल 2 मध्यम श्रेणी का 3 (वर्ण या बालों का रंग) गोरा या हलका : a fair complexion 4 (मौसम) साफ़ और सुहावना; (पवन) अनुकूल ■ **by fair means or foul** जिस किसी भी तरीके से होने की स्थिति ▸ **fair copy** noun साफ़ और स्पष्ट प्रति **fair dealing** noun छलहीन व्यवहार **fairness** noun उचित और न्याय-संगत **fair play** noun ईमानदारी का व्यवहार **fair-weather friend** noun सिर्फ़ सुख का साथी।

fair[2] /फ़ेअर/ adv नियमानुसार; ईमानदारी से ■ **fair enough** (अनौप) (कभी-कभी अनिच्छुक रूप से सहमति व्यक्त करने के लिए) ठीक है।

fair[3] /फ़ेअर/ noun 1 मेला; पशुमेला 2 बड़ी प्रदर्शनी : a world trade fair.

fairly /फ़ेअर्लि/ adv 1 न्याय से, उचित रूप से 2 साधारण ढंग से 3 पूर्णत:; वास्तव में।

fairy /फ़ेअरि/ noun (pl **fairies**) 1 परी 2 (अप, अपमा) समलिंगी व्यक्ति (विशेषत: पुरुष) ▸ **fairy tale** (**fairy story** भी) noun 1 परियों की कथा 2 मनगढ़ंत किस्सा।

faith /फ़ेथ्/ noun 1 **faith (in sb/sth)**

पूर्ण विश्वास; श्रद्धा 2 धार्मिक आस्था 3 धर्म ■ in bad faith बदनीयती से in good faith नेकनीयती से।

faithful / 'फ़ेथ्फ़्ल् / *adj* 1 faithful (to sb/sth) सच्चा और वफ़ादार 2 विश्वसनीय 3 ठीक, तथ्य के अनुसार : *a faithful account* ▸ **faithfully** *adv* **faithfulness** *noun.*

faithless / 'फ़ेथ्लस् / *adj* झूठा; विश्वास-घाती।

fake / फ़ेक् / *noun* (वस्तु) जाली, नक़ली; (व्यक्ति) अपना नक़ली रूप प्रयोग करके ठगने वाला ▸ **fake** *adj* नक़ली : *fake jewellery* **fake** *verb* 1 नक़ली चीज़ बनाना : *He faked his father's signature.* 2 किसी भाव/स्थिति का झूठा प्रदर्शन करना : *fake surprise/illness.*

falcon / 'फ़ॉल्कन्; US 'फ़ैल्कन् / *noun* बाज़।

fall / फ़ॉल् / *verb* (*pt* **fell** / फ़ेल् /; *pp* **fallen** / 'फ़ॉलन्/) 1 गिरना; ढलना या ज़मीन की ओर आना, उतरना 3 (संख्या या श्रेणी में) कम होना : *The temperature fell sharply in the night.* 4 शक्ति या सत्ता खो देना 5 होना, पड़ना, घटित होना : *Christmas Day falls on a Monday.* 6 fall (away/off) नीचे की ओर फिसलना या खिसकना 7 fall (into sth) किसी स्थिति विशेष में जाना : *He fell silent.* ○ *The house fell into decay.* 8 fall (on sb/sth) अचानक कुछ होना : *An expectant hush fell on the guests.* 9 किसी विशेष श्रेणी, समूह या ज़िम्मेदारी के क्षेत्र में होना : *This case falls outside my jurisdiction.* ■ **fall back** पीछे हटना या मुड़ना **fall back on sb/sth** (अन्य उपायों के असफल होने पर) किसी पर निर्भर होना **fall behind (sb/sth)** पीछे छूट जाना **fall into sth** जाल में फँस जाना **fall in with sb/sth** (किसी व्यक्ति की योजना से) सहमत हो जाना **fall off** संख्या या मात्रा में कम हो जाना **fall on/upon sb/sth**

आक्रमण करना **fall out (with sb)** झगड़ना **fall through** असफल होना **fall to (do-ing sth)** प्रारंभ करना ▸ **fall** / फ़ॉल् / *noun* 1 गिरने की प्रक्रिया 2 fall (of sth) गिरी हुई वस्तु की मात्रा (जैसे वर्षा की) 3 fall (in sth) मात्रा, संख्या या क़ीमत में गिरावट, कमी 4 (US) शरद ऋतु; पतझड़ : *in the fall of 1970* 5 **falls** [*pl*] जलप्रपात : *Niagara Falls.*

fallacy / 'फ़ैलसि / *noun* (*pl* **fallacies**) 1 भ्रामकता, भ्रांति 2 (तर्कशास्त्र में) हेत्वा-भास : *a statement based on fallacy* ▸ **fallacious** / फ़'लेशस् / *adj* भ्रामक।

fallible / 'फ़ैलब्ल् / *adj* जिसके द्वारा या जिसमें ग़लतियों की गुंजाइश हो ▸ **fallibil-ity** *noun.*

fallow / 'फ़ैलो / *adj* 1 (कृषि भूमि) ख़ाली, जिसकी खुदाई हो चुकी हो किंतु जिसमें बुवाई न हुई हो; बंजर 2 (समयांतराल) अक्रियात्मक या बेकार।

false / फ़ॉल्स् / *adj* 1 ग़लत 2 भ्रामक; कपटपूर्ण या कृत्रिम, झूठ; मिथ्या : *false hair/teeth* ○ *false tears* ▸ **false** *adv* ■ **play sb false** (किसी व्यक्ति के साथ) कपटपूर्ण व्यवहार करना ▸ **falsely** *adv.*

falsehood / 'फ़ॉल्स्हुड् / *noun* 1 मिथ्या कथन; झूठ 2 ग़लत/झूठे होने की अवस्था।

falsify / 'फ़ॉल्सिफ़ाइ / *verb* 1 मिथ्याकरण, हिसाब, विवरण आदि में गोलमाल कर सच्चाई छिपाना : *falsify the records* 2 कपटता-पूर्वक कुछ कहना या वर्णित करना ▸ **falsi-fication** *noun.*

falter / 'फ़ॉल्टर / *verb* 1 लड़खड़ाना 2 हिचकिचाना : *Jagat walked boldly up to the platform without falter-ing.* 3 आवाज़ का लड़खड़ाना ▸ **falter-ing** *adj.*

fame / फ़ेम् / *noun* यश, कीर्ति; प्रसिद्धि ▸ **famed** *adj* famed (for sth) प्रसिद्ध।

familiar / फ़'मिलिअर् / *adj* 1 familiar (to sb) परिचित; प्रायः देखा या सुना हुआ 2 familiar with sth से परिचित, की

अच्छी जानकारी रखने वाला 3 **familiar (with sb)** घनिष्ठ, अंतरंग : *familiar friends* ▶ **familiarity** / फ़ॅ‚मिलि'ऐरिटि / *noun* 1 अच्छी जानकारी 2 अंतरंगता **familiarize, -ise** / फ़ॅ'मिलिअराइज़ / *verb* ■ **familiarize sb/oneself with sth** किसी चीज़ की पूरी जानकारी पाना या देना।

family / फ़ॅमलि / *noun* (*pl* **families**) 1 माता-पिता और बच्चे, परिवार 2 कुटुंब, कुल (पति-पत्नी, बच्चे और बच्चों के बच्चे आदि) 3 वंश (सभी रक्त-संबंधी) 4 (पौधों एवं पशुओं का) वर्ग, जाति : *Lions belong to the cat family.* 5 एक ही स्रोत की भाषाएँ (भाषा-परिवार)।

famine / फ़ॅमिन् / *noun* अकाल, दुर्भिक्ष : *raise money for famine relief.*

famished / 'फ़ॅमिश्ट् / *adj (अनौप)* भूखों मरता हुआ।

famous / 'फ़ेमस् / *adj* **famous (for sth)** प्रसिद्ध।

fan¹ / फ़ॅन् / *noun* उत्साही प्रशंसक : *visiting football fans.*

fan² / फ़ॅन् / *noun* 1 हाथ का पंखा 2 बिजली का पंखा ▶ **fan** *verb* (**-nn-**) 1 पंखा करना 2 किसी भाव या अफ़वाह को और तेज़ करना : *Public anxiety is being fanned by the media.*

fanatic / फ़ॅ'नैटिक् / *noun (प्राय: अपमान)* कट्टर, दुराग्रही ▶ **fanatical** *adj* **fanatically** *adv* **fanaticism** *noun* कट्टरपन, मतांधता : *religious fanaticism.*

fanciful / 'फ़ॅन्सिफ़ुल् / *adj* 1 काल्पनिक 2 (वस्तुएँ) अजीब परंतु रचनात्मक शैली में।

fancy¹ / 'फ़ॅन्सि / *adj* (**-ier, -lest**) 1 अ-सामान्य एवं विचित्र (वस्तुएँ) 2 रंगबिरंगी एवं आकर्षक (वस्तुएँ); नेत्रों को मनोरम लगने वाली (वस्तुएँ) ▶ **fancy dress** *noun* विचित्र एवं अति असामान्य पोशाक।

fancy² / 'फ़ॅन्सि / *verb* (*pt, pp* **fancied**) 1 *(अनौप)* (किसी व्यक्ति को) बहुत पसंद करना : *I think she fancies me.* 2 कल्पना करना; सोचना/मानना 3 किसी

व्यक्ति/वस्तु की जीत या सफलता की आशा करना/ विश्वास रखना 4 *(अनौप)* रुचि रखना/मोह करना : *I fancy a cup of tea.* ■ **fancy oneself** *(अनौप, प्राय: अपमान)* घमंड करना, अपने बारे में ऊँची सम्मति रखना।

fancy³ / 'फ़ॅन्सि / *noun* 1 कल्पित वस्तु 2 कल्पना शक्ति, आधारहीन कल्पना।

fanfare / 'फ़ॅन्फ़ेअर् / *noun* 1 तुरहीनाद 2 धूमधाम से स्वागत।

fang / फ़ॅङ् / *noun* लंबा नुकीला दाँत; सर्प का विषदंत।

fantastic / फ़ॅन्'टैस्टिक्/ *adj* 1 *(अनौप)* अत्युत्तम : *a fantastic opportunity* 2 *(अनौप)* बहुत बड़ा, असामान्य 3 (**fantastical** भी) अजीब, विलक्षण 4 (योजना, विचार आदि) बेतुके; काल्पनिक: *fantastic proposals* ▶ **fantastically** *adv.*

fantasy / 'फ़ॅन्टसि / *noun* (*pl* **fantasies**) 1 कल्पना, विशेषत: वास्तविकता से कोसों दूर की बात 2 अजीब एवं अवास्तविक विचार : *She has written a romantic escapist fantasy.* ▶ **fantasize, -ise** *verb* **fantasize (about sth)** कल्पना करना।

far¹ / फ़ार् / *adv* (**farther** / 'फ़ार्दर् / या **further** / 'फ़र्दर् /; **farthest** / 'फ़ार्दिस्ट् / या **furthest** / 'फ़र्दिस्ट् /) 1 (स्थान या दूरी में) दूर, दूरवर्ती 2 बहुत हद (सीमा) तक : *live far beyond one's means* ■ **as/so far as** उस सीमा तक **as/so far as sb/ sth is concerned** प्रासंगिक सीमा तक **carry/take sth too far** समुचित सीमा के परे भी कुछ करते जाना **far and away** अत्यधिक **far and near/wide** सर्वत्र, व्यापक तौर से **in so far as** जहाँ तक : *That's the truth, in so far as I know it.* **so far; thus far** अब तक : *The results have been encouraging, so far* **so far, so good** *(कहा)* अब तक सभी कुछ सफल हुआ है ▶ **far-away** *adj* दूर तक **Far East** *noun* सुदूरपूर्व, पूर्वी

एशिया के देश **far-fetched** adj (प्राय: अपमा) ज़बरदस्ती की तुलना; (अनौप) अस्वाभाविक एवं अतिशयोक्तिपूर्ण **far-flung** adj दूर तक व्याप्त **far-off** adj दूर **far-sighted** adj 1(**far-seeing** भी) बुद्धिमान 2 दूरदर्शी।

far² / फ़ार् / adj (farther/further, farthest/furthest) 1 और अधिक दूर : at the far end of the street 2 (अप्र या औप) सुदूर ∎ **a far cry from sth/doing sth** (अनौप) किसी से/कुछ करने से एकदम अलग अनुभव।

farce / फ़ार्स् / noun 1 प्रहसन, स्वाँग 2 तमाशे की तरह का घटना-चक्र, बेकार या बेढंगे तरीक़े से नियोजित घटना : The trial was a complete farce. ▶ **farcical** / फ़ार्सिकल् / adj हास्यजनक।

fare¹ / फ़ेअर् / noun (जहाज़, रेल, बस आदि का) भाड़ा, किराया।

fare² / फ़ेअर् / verb (औप) प्रगति करना; सफल होना।

fare³ / फ़ेअर् / noun (अप्र या औप) खाना-पीना।

farewell / ,फ़ेअर्'वेल् / interj (प्रा या औप) अलविदा ▶ **farewell** noun विदाई।

farm¹ / फ़ार्म् / noun 1 खेत, कृषिकार्य 2 (**farmhouse**) (आजकल) फ़ार्म में स्थित भव्य आधुनिक सुविधापूर्ण मकान 3 स्थान जहाँ पर मछलियों या अन्य जंतुओं का पालन किया जाता है : a trout farm ○ a dairy farm.

farm² / फ़ार्म् / verb खेती करना; ज़मीन को फ़ार्म के रूप में प्रयोग करना ▶ **farmer** noun किसान **farming** noun कृषि।

fascinate / 'फ़ैसिनेट् / verb अति-आकर्षित करना; मोहित कर लेना ▶ **fascinating** adj अति-आकर्षक, सम्मोहक **fascination** / ,फ़ैसि'नेश्न् / noun 1 सम्मोहन 2 **fascination (for/in/with sb/sth)** सम्मोहित हो जाने की अवस्था।

fascism (**Fascism** भी) / 'फ़ैशिज़म् /

noun समाजवाद-विरोधी राजनीतिक व्यवस्था या दृष्टिकोण।

fashion / फ़ैश्न् / noun (कपड़ों, विचार, व्यवहार आदि का) फ़ैशन, लोकप्रिय शैली ∎ **after a fashion** कुछ हद तक लेकिन बहुत अच्छा नहीं ▶ **fashion** verb **fashion A from/out of B** कुछ तैयार करना, आकृति या शैली प्रदान करना : fashion a doll.

fashionable / 'फ़ैश्नब्ल् / adj 1 लोकप्रिय शैली अपनाने वाला, शौक़ीन 2 शौक़ीनों या उच्च वर्ग के लोगों द्वारा प्रयुक्त (वस्तु या स्थान) : a fashionable hotel ▶ **fashionably** adv.

fast¹ / फ़ास्ट्; US फ़ैस्ट् / adj (-er, -est) 1 तेज़, द्रुतगामी 2 (सतह आदि) तेज़ गति प्रदान करने वाली 3 घड़ी का तेज़ चलते हुए : That clock is ten minutes fast. ∎ **fast and furious** (खेल, पार्टी आदि) तेज़ एवं उल्लासपूर्ण ▶ **fast** adv तेज़ी से **fast food** noun जल्दी से तैयार हो जाने वाला भोजन।

fast² / फ़ास्ट्; US फ़ैस्ट् / adj 1 स्थिर, दृढ़ : make a boat fast 2 (रंग) पक्का 3 घनिष्ठ : fast friends ▶ **fast** adv दृढ़ता से, मज़बूती से : be fast asleep (गहरी नींद में)।

fast³ / फ़ास्ट्; US फ़ैस्ट् / verb उपवास रखना; अनशन करना : Muslims fast during Ramadan. ▶ **fast** noun उपवास, उपवास-काल।

fasten / 'फ़ास्न्; US 'फ़ैस्न् / verb 1 **fasten sth (down)** जकड़ना, कसना या बाँधना : fasten down the lid of a box 2 बँध जाना, जकड़ा जाना 3 **fasten sth (on/to sth)** एक चीज़ को दूसरी से मज़बूती से जोड़ना 4 **fasten sth (up)** दृढ़ करना या जोड़ना : Fasten up your coat. ▶ **fastener** (**fastening** भी) noun जकड़ने, बाँधने या कसने वाली वस्तु।

fastidious / फ़ै'स्टिडिअस् / adj 1 सावधानी से चुनने वाला 2 तुनक मिज़ाजी, सहज

में संतुष्ट न होने वाला ▸ **fastidiously** *adv* **fastidiousness** *noun*.

fat¹ /फ़ैट् / *noun* 1 चरबी; खाना पकाने योग्य चरबी 2 तेल; वसा : *Fried potatoes are cooked in deep fat.*

fat² /फ़ैट् / *adj* (**-tter, -ttest**) 1 (शरीर) मोटा, मांसल 2 चरबीदार 3 आकृति में बड़ा (भरा हुआ); (अनौप) मात्रा में ज़्यादा : *a fat sum/profit* ▸ **fatness** *noun*.

fatal /फ़ेटल् / *adj* 1 **fatal (to sb/sth)** घातक, जिससे अंत में मौत हो जाए : *a fatal accident* 2 विध्वंसकारी : *a fatal mistake* ▸ **fatally** *adv*.

fatalism /फ़ैटलिज़म् / *noun* भाग्यवाद, दैववाद (यह धारणा कि जो होना है वह होकर ही रहेगा) ▸ **fatalist** *noun* भाग्यवादी।

fatality /फ़टैलटि / *noun* (*pl* **fatalities**) 1 दुर्घटना/युद्ध आदि में मृत्यु संख्या 2 भाग्यवाद।

fate /फ़ेट् / *noun* 1 भाग्य, नियति 2 होने वाली या हो चुकीं (विशेषत: बुरी) घटनाएँ : *abandon sb to their fate* 3 मृत्यु; विनाश।

fated /फ़ेटिड् / *adj* **fated (to do sth)** नियत, बदा।

fateful /फ़ेट्फ़ुल् / *adj* भाग्य का निर्णायक, महत्त्वपूर्ण : *a fateful decision.*

father¹ /फ़ादर् / *noun* 1 पिता, बाप; (पशुओं में) नर जनक 2 प्रवर्तक, संस्थापक 3 **Father** ईश्वर 4 पुरोहित, पादरी (विशेषत: रोमन कैथोलिक चर्च में) ▸ **fatherhood** *noun* पितृत्व **father-in-law** *noun* ससुर **fatherly** *adj* पितृवत्।

father² /फ़ादर् / *verb* 1 पिता/बाप बनना 2 कुछ उत्पन्न या नियोजित करना : *father a plan.*

fathom /फ़ैदम् / *noun* फ़ैदम, (पानी की गहराई नापने में प्रयुक्त) 1.8 मीटर की नाप ▸ **fathom** *verb* **fathom sb/sth (out)** समझना, किसी बात की तह तक पहुँचना।

fatigue / फ़टीग् / *noun* 1 (औप) थकावट 2 बार-बार के तनाव से धातु में उत्पन्न कमज़ोरी : *The plane's wing showed signs of metal fatigue.* ▸ **fatigue** *verb* थकाना, थकान उत्पन्न करना **fatigued** *adj*.

fatten /फ़ैटन् / *verb* मोटा होना या करना।

fatty /फ़ैटि / *adj* (**-ier, -iest**) तेल/चरबी वाला : *fatty foods* ▸ **fatty** *noun* (अनौप, अपमा) मोटा व्यक्ति।

faucet /फ़ॉसिट् / *noun* (विशेषत: US) नल, पानी की टोंटी।

fault /फ़ॉल्ट् / *noun* 1 त्रुटि, कमी, ग़लती 2 अपराध, दोष : *The fault really lies with the leadership of the movement.* ■ **at fault** दोषी ▸ **fault** *verb* किसी व्यक्ति/वस्तु में ग़लती/दोष ढूँढ निकालना **faultless** *adj* दोषहीन **faultlessly** *adv* **faulty** *adj* अपूर्ण, दोषयुक्त।

fauna / फ़ॉना / *noun* किसी काल विशेष या स्थान विशेष में पाए जाने वाले सभी पशु : *the unique fauna of East Africa.*

faux pas /फ़ो 'पा / (*pl* **faux pas** /फ़ो 'पाज़ /) *noun* झेंप या शर्म पैदा करने वाला विवेकहीन कार्य या कथन।

favour¹ (*US* **favor**) /फ़ेवर् / *noun* 1 अनुग्रह या समर्थन : *win sb's favour* ○ *The scheme found favour with the town planners.* 2 पक्षपातपूर्ण व्यवहार 3 सहायता 4 **favours** [*pl*] प्रेम प्रदर्शन करने देने की कृपा (करना) ■ **in favour of sb/sth** 1 के पक्ष में 2 किसी (व्यक्ति या वस्तु) के स्थान पर अन्य को रखना।

favour² (*US* **favor**) /फ़ेवर् / *verb* पक्षपात करना, पक्ष में समर्थन करना : *favour a candidate* ▸ **favoured** *adj*.

favourable (*US* **favorable**) /फ़ेवरबल् / *adj* 1 अनुकूल 2 **favourable (to/toward sb/sth)** सहायतापूर्ण; सुखद ▸ **favourably** *adv*.

favourite (*US* **favorite**) /फ़ेवरिट् / *adj* सबसे ज़्यादा पसंद (वस्तु या व्यक्ति) ▸ **favourite** (*US* **favorite**) *noun* अन्य

से ज्यादा पसंद (व्यक्ति या वस्तु) : *This record is my all-time favourite.*

favouritism (*US* favoritism) /'फ़ेव़रि-टिज़म/ *noun* (*अप्रा*) पक्षपात, तरफ़दारी।

fawn¹ /फ़ॉन/ *noun* 1 मृगछौना, एक वर्ष से कम उम्र का हिरन 2 हलका पीला भूरा रंग ▸ **fawn** *adj* हलके पीले भूरे रंग का।

fawn² /फ़ॉन/ *verb* **fawn (on/upon sb)** (*अप्रा*) चापलूसी करना : *a fawning aide.*

fax /फ़ैक्स/ *verb* **fax sth (through) (to sb)** इलेक्ट्रॉनिक तंत्र द्वारा टेलिफ़ोन लाइन से संदेश भेजना, प्रतिकृति भेजना ▸ **fax** *noun* फ़ैक्स तंत्र; (facsimile भी) फ़ैक्स द्वारा प्रेषित संदेश।

fear¹ /फ़िअर/ *noun* 1 डर, भय : *overcome by fear* 2 आशंका, अंदेशा ▸ **fearful** *adj* 1 **fearful (of sth/of doing sth)** डरा हुआ, भयभीत 2 डरावना, भयानक 3 (*अनौप*) अतिविशाल, बहुत बुरा **fearless** *adj* निर्भय, निडर **fearsome** /'फ़िअर्सम/ *adj* देखने में भयानक/भयंकर।

fear² /फ़िअर/ *verb* 1 डर जाना, भयभीत होना : *fear death/illness* 2 बुरा होने की आशंका रखना; चिंतित होना।

feasible /'फ़ीज़बल/ *adj* संभाव्य एवं व्यावहारिक, जिसका किया जाना संभव हो : *a feasible idea/suggestion* ▸ **feasibility** /फ़ीज़'बिलटि/ *noun* संभाव्यता।

feast /फ़ीस्ट/ *noun* 1 (*औप*) पर्व, त्योहार 2 दावत, प्रीतिभोज : *a wedding feast* 3 मन या इंद्रियों को प्रिय लगने वाली वस्तु : *a feast of sounds* ▸ **feast** *verb* **feast (on/off sth)** दावत में शामिल होना ■ **feast one's eyes (on sb/sth)** सौंदर्य निहारना।

feat /फ़ीट्/ *noun* करतब, असाधारण कार्य; कमाल : *perform feats of daring.*

feather¹ /'फ़ेदर/ *noun* पंख, पर ▸ **feathered** *adj* परदार **feathery** *adj* हलका व मुलायम; परों से ढका।

feather² /'फ़ेदर/ *verb* पंखों/परों से ढकना

■ **feather one's (own) nest** (*प्राय: अप्रा*) औरों के खर्च पर आरामदायक/सुखद जीवन बिताना।

feature /'फ़ीचर/ *noun* 1 चेहरे का कोई एक भाग जैसे आँख, नाक, आदि; [*pl*] नाक-नक्शा, आकृति : *a woman of handsome features* 2 लक्षण, विशेषता 3 **feature (on sb/sth)** किसी पर (अख़बार या टी वी पर) एक विशेष लेख या कार्यक्रम; सिनेमा प्रोग्राम में मुख्य फ़िल्म : *a feature film* ▸ **feature** *verb* 1 (प्रदर्शन या विज्ञापन के लिए) किसी को मुख्य भाग देना 2 **feature in sth** कहीं पर मुख्य भाग के रूप में आना 3 का लक्षण/विशेषता होना **featureless** *adj* साधारण, नीरस : *a featureless landscape.*

February /'फ़ेब्रूअरि/ *noun* (*संक्षि* Feb) फ़रवरी (का महीना)।

federal /'फ़ेडरल/ *adj* 1 संघ का, संघीय 2 (संघीय तंत्र के अंतर्गत) केंद्र से संबंधित, न कि स्थानीय सरकार से : *a federal law* ▸ **federalism** *noun* संघवाद।

federation /फ़ेड'रेशन/ *noun* 1 (राज) संघ शासन (ऐसी शासन व्यवस्था जिसमें राज्य अपने मामलों में स्वतंत्र हैं किंतु विदेशनीति, रक्षा आदि केंद्रीय सरकार के अधीन होते हैं) 2 राज्य संघ; कर्मचारी संघ, श्रम संघ आदि 3 संघबद्ध होने की क्रिया।

fed up /,फ़ेड 'अप/ *adj* **fed up (about/with sb/sth)** (*अनौप*) जी ऊबे हुए।

fee /फ़ी/ *noun* 1 (*प्राय: pl*) फ़ीस, शुल्क; (क्लब का) सदस्यता शुल्क, (परीक्षा की) फ़ीस 2 मेहनताना, पारिश्रमिक।

feeble /'फ़ीबल/ *adj* (-r /'फ़ीबलर/ -st /'फ़ीब्लिस्ट/) कमज़ोर, दुर्बल; (*अप्रा*) शक्तिहीन, अप्रभावी : *a feeble argument/joke* ▸ **feeble-minded** *adj* मूर्ख, बुद्धिहीन **feebleness** *noun* **feebly** *adv.*

feed¹ /फ़ीड/ *verb* (*pt, pp* fed /फ़ेड्/) 1 **feed sb/sth (on sth)**; **feed sth to sb/sth** खिलाना, भोजन देना; (पशुओं को) दाना-चारा देना 2 **feed (on/off sth)**

(पशुओं का) चारा खाना : *The cows were feeding on hay in the barn.* 3 feed A (with B)/feed B into A कुछ देकर किसी वस्तु की आपूर्ति करना : *feed the fire (with wood)* 4 नियमित रूप से सूचना या सलाह प्रदान करना ■ feed (on/ off sth) किसी चीज़ द्वारा तीव्रता/उग्रता बढ़ना।

feed² / फ़ीड् / noun 1 (पशुओं का) चारा; (बच्चे का) आहार 2 किसी मशीन के लिए आपूर्ति किया गया पदार्थ 3 पदार्थ वहन के लिए पाईप आदि : *The petrol feed is blocked.*

feedback / फ़ीड्बैक / noun प्रत्युत्तर प्राप्ति, पुनर्धरण; *(तक)* फ़ीडबैक।

feel¹ / फ़ील् / verb (pt, pp felt / फ़ेल्ट् /) 1 हाथ से छूना; छूकर जानना 2 अनुभव करना, महसूस करना 3 feel (to sb) (like sth/sb) लगना, प्रतीत होना : *The water feels warm.* 4 शारीरिक या मानसिक भाव-विशेष रखना, संवेदना पाना : *feel cold/hungry/sad/happy* ■ feel (it) in one's bones (that...) बिना बाहरी प्रमाण के किसी तथ्य को निश्चित मानते रहना feel like sth/doing sth कुछ होने/करने की इच्छा होना. feel one's way सावधानी से टटोल-टटोलकर चलना feel up to (doing) sth अपने को (कार्य विशेष के लिए) सक्षम मानना ▸ feelingly adv अति गहन भावुकता से।

feel² / फ़ील् / noun [sing] 1 अनुभव/ प्रतीत (करना) 2 the feel स्पर्शज्ञान : *rough/smooth to the feel* 3 the feel स्थिति, स्थान आदि का प्रभाव : *the feel of the place.*

feeler / फ़ीलर् / noun कुछ कीटों में टोह लेने वाला भाग, शृंगिका।

feeling / फ़ीलिङ् / noun 1 feeling (of sth) भावना : *a feeling of hunger* 2 मनोभाव; दृष्टिकोण, मत : *My own feeling is that we should buy it.* 3 feelings [pl] व्यक्ति के मनोवेग, न कि

विचार : *deep religious feelings* ○ *You've hurt my feelings.* 4 feeling for sb/sth संवेदनात्मक बोध; सहानुभूति।

feign / फ़ेन् / verb किसी से प्रभावित होने का ढोंग करना; झूठा अभिनय करना।

feline / फ़ीलाइन् / adj, noun बिल्ली (प्र-जाति) संबंधी/के समान।

fell / फ़ेल् / verb 1 (पेड़) काट डालना 2 (व्यक्ति को) नीचे गिरा देना : *He felled his opponent with a single blow.*

fellow / फ़ेलो / noun 1 (अनौप) आदमी, व्यक्ति 2 (प्रायः pl) सहभागी, साथी : *fellows in good fortune/misery* 3 (अनौप) महिला का पुरुष साथी, प्रेमी 4 (विशेषत: ब्रिटेन में) विद्वत् परिषद् या व्यावसायिक परिषद् का सदस्य: *Fellow of the Royal Academy* 5 विश्वविद्यालय/ कालेजों की शासी परिषद् का सदस्य 6 (विशेषत: US) फेलोशिप पाया हुआ विद्यार्थी ▸ fellow adj समान श्रेणी/प्रकार का : *fellow members/citizens* fel-low-feeling noun सहानुभूति।

fellowship / फ़ेलोशिप् / noun 1 मैत्रीपूर्ण साहचर्य 2 समानधर्मी/सहभागी व्यक्तियों का समाज 3 (किसी समिति आदि की) सदस्यता 4 विद्यार्थियों को पढ़ाई या शोध-कार्य के लिए प्रदान आर्थिक सहायता, छात्रवृत्ति।

felony / फ़ेलनि / noun बहुत बड़ा अपराध ▸ felon / फ़ेलन् / noun महापराधी।

felt / फ़ेल्ट् / noun फ़ेल्ट, नमदा : *felt hats/ slippers.*

female / फ़ीमेल् / adj 1 मादा, नारी 2 स्त्री विषयक 3 (पौधे, फूल) फल उत्पन्न करने वाले ▸ female noun 1 मादा पशु या पौधा 2 स्त्री।

feminine / फ़ेमनिन् / adj 1 स्त्रियों के योग्य, स्त्री सदृश; स्त्री सुलभ, स्त्री-विष-यक : *a feminine voice* 2 *(व्या)* स्त्रीलिंग (शब्द)।

feminism / फ़ेमनिज़म् / noun ऐसा सिद्धांत एवं विचार कि स्त्री को पुरुष के समान

ही अधिकार एवं विकास के अवसर प्राप्त हों ▸ **feminist** noun.

fence[1] / फ़ेन्स् / noun बाड़ा या घेरा; तार, खंभे आदि से बनाई सुरक्षात्मक संरचना ▸ **fence** verb बाड़ा लगाना,(अहाता आदि) घेरना **fencing** noun बाड़ा बनाने में प्रयुक्त सामान।

fence[2] / फ़ेन्स् / verb 1 तलवार चलाने का अभ्यास करना, पटेबाज़ी करना 2 **fence (with sb)** सीधा उत्तर न देना, (शब्दों की चालाकी से) टालना : *We were fencing with each other, both refusing to come to the point.* ▸ **fencer** noun **fencing** noun तलवारबाज़ी (का खेल)।

fend / फ़ेन्ड् / verb ■ **fend for oneself** स्वयं का पालन-पोषण करना, स्वयं के लिए भोजन आदि का प्रबंध करना **fend sth/sb off** वार बचाना, वार रोकना : *fend off a blow.*

fender / फ़ेन्डर् / noun 1 जलते कोयले नीचे गिरने से रोकने के लिए प्रयुक्त अँगीठी की जाली 2 नाव की बग़ल में लगाई गई मुलायम वस्तु (रस्सी, रबर टायर आदि) जो उसे टक्कर में हानि से बचाती है; जहाज़, मोटर आदि में समान प्रकार के भाग 2 (*US*) साइकिल का मडगार्ड।

ferment / फ़र्‌मेन्ट् / verb ख़मीर उठना या उठाना : *Fruit juices ferment if they are kept a long time.* ▸ **ferment** / फ़मेन्ट् / noun (राजनीतिक या सामाजिक) उत्तेजना एवं अनिश्चितता : *The country was in (a state of) ferment.* **fermentation** / फ़र्मेन्‌टेश्न् / noun ख़मीर उठाने की प्रक्रिया।

fern / फ़र्न् / noun हरी कोमल पत्तियों वाला पौधा जिसमें फूल नहीं खिलते।

ferocious / फ़'रोशस् / adj क्रूर; खूँख़्वार या उग्र ▸ **ferociously** adv.

ferocity / फ़'रॉसटि / noun उग्र या क्रूर व्यवहार; हिंसा।

ferret / फ़ेरिट् / noun नेवले जैसा दिखने वाला एक हिंस्र जंतु ▸ **ferret** verb **ferret (about) (for sth)** (अनौप) कोई छिपी हुई या खोई हुई वस्तु ढूँढ़ निकालना।

ferry / फ़ेरि / noun (pl **ferries**) व्यक्तियों और सामान के वहन के लिए प्रयुक्त नाव; घाट जहाँ नदी या जलमार्ग से व्यक्ति एवं सामान दूसरी पार ले जाए जाते हैं ▸ **ferry** verb (pt, pp **ferried**) नाव या हवाई जहाज़ द्वारा छोटी दूरी के लिए व्यक्तियों या सामान को ले जाना/लाना : *ferry goods to the mainland.*

fertile / फ़र्टाइल; *US* फ़र्ट्ल् / adj 1 (भूमि या मिट्टी) उपजाऊ 2 (पौधे या पशु) खूब फलने-फूलने वाले; बच्चे पैदा करने की शक्ति वाले 3 जो अच्छा परिणाम ला सकता है : *a fertile partnership* 4 (व्यक्ति का मस्तिष्क) योजनाओं, विचारों से भरा-पूरा : *have a fertile imagination* ▸ **fertility** / फ़र्‌टिलिटि / noun उर्वरता, जनन क्षमता।

fertilize, -ise / फ़र्टलाइज़् / verb 1 निषेचन करना; गर्भाधान करना : *a fertilized egg/cell* 2 भूमि की उर्वरता बढ़ाना ▸ **fertilization, -isation** / फ़र्टलाइ ज़ेश्न् / noun **fertilizer, -iser** noun खाद, उर्वरक।

fervent / फ़र्वन्ट् / (औप **fervid** / फ़र्विड्/भी) adj जोशीला, उत्साहपूर्ण; गरम : *a fervent admirer/believer* ▸ **fervently** adv.

fervour (*US* **fervor**) / फ़र्वर् / noun गहरी भावना, जोश; उत्साह : *speak with great fervour.*

fester / फ़ेस्टर् / verb 1 (घाव का) पक जाना, मवाद पड़ना : *a festering sore* 2 (बुरे विचार, भाव आदि) मन पर विष की तरह प्रभाव करना; कड़वाहट पैदा करना।

festival / फ़ेस्टिव्ल् / noun 1 उत्सव, त्योहार 2 नियमित रूप से (विशेषतः वर्ष में एक बार) संगीत, नाटक, फ़िल्मों आदि का श्रृंखलाबद्ध आयोजन : *the International Film Festival.*

festive / 'फ़ेस्टिव् / adj उत्सव-विषयक, उल्लासपूर्ण।

festivity / फ़ें'स्टिव़्टि / noun (pl festivities) 1 उत्सव की खुशियाँ 2 festivities [pl] आनंदोत्सव, खुशियों भरी घटनाएँ (किसी के सम्मान में आयोजित) : wedding festivities.

festoon / फ़ेंस्टून् / noun (फूल-पत्तियों, रंगीन काग़ज़ आदि की) बंदनवार ▸ **festoon** verb **festoon sb/sth (with sth)** बंदनवार से सजाना : a room festooned with paper streamers.

fetch / फ़ेच् / verb 1 **fetch sb/sth (for sb)** जाकर (किसी व्यक्ति या वस्तु को) लाना : Fetch a doctor at once. 2 (सामान) मूल्य पर बिकना : Those old books won't fetch (you) much. 3 (अनौप) हाथ से आघात करना।

fetching / 'फ़ेचिङ् / adj (अनौप) आकर्षक, मोहक : a fetching smile.

fête / फ़ेट् / noun (प्राय: खुले मैदान में) उत्सव, मेला : the school fête ▸ **fête** verb किसी का विशिष्ट तरीक़े से सम्मान करना/मनोरंजन करना।

fetish / 'फ़ेटिश् / noun 1 (प्राय: अपमा) कोई वस्तु जिसको मूर्खता के कारण अत्यधिक आदर दिया जाए : He makes a fetish of his work. 2 जड़ वस्तु जिसकी पूजा की जाए ▸ **fetishism** noun **fetishist** noun.

fetter / 'फ़ेटर् / noun (प्राय: pl) 1 (पैरों की) बेड़ियाँ; ज़ंजीरें 2 (अल) बाधाएँ या अड़चनें : freed from the fetters of ignorance ▸ **fetter** verb 1 बेड़ियों में बाँधना 2 बाधा या अड़चनें डालना।

feud / फ़्यूड् / noun **feud (between A and B); feud (with sb)** पुश्तैनी दुश्मनी, कुल-वैर ▸ **feud** verb **feud (with sb/sth)** झगड़े में शामिल होना।

feudal / 'फ़्यूडल् / adj सामंती प्रथा, यूरोप में मध्ययुग में भूमि वितरण की प्रथा : the feudal system ▸ **feudalism** noun सामंतवाद, सामंतशाही।

fever / 'फ़ीवर् / noun 1 बुख़ार, ज्वर 2 उत्तेजित अवस्था; (अनौप) अत्यधिक उत्साह : election fever ▸ **fevered** adj 1 ज्वरग्रस्त 2 उत्तेजनाग्रस्त **feverish** / 'फ़ीवरिश् / adj ज्वर से त्रस्त; उत्तेजित : feverish activity.

few¹ / फ़्यू / indef det, adj (-er, -est) कुछ, थोड़े से : The few houses we have seen are in terrible condition. ■ **few and far between** छितरे हुए और लंबे अंतराल पर ▸ **few** indef pron अधिक नहीं, इने-गिने (लोग, वस्तुएँ) स्थान आदि) : Of the 150 passengers, few escaped injury. **fewer** indef pron **the few** noun व्यक्तियों का छोटा-सा वर्ग : Real power belongs to the few.

few² / फ़्यू / **a few** indef det थोड़े से, कुछ : a few letters ▸ **a few** indef pron वस्तुओं, व्यक्तियों, स्थानों आदि की थोड़ी-सी संख्या, कुछ : A few of the seats were empty. **a few** adv थोड़ी परंतु महत्त्वपूर्ण संख्या : a few too many mistakes.

fez / फ़ेज़् / noun (pl **fezzes**) लाल रंग की टोपी, तुर्की टोपी।

fiancé (fem **fiancée**) / फ़ि'ऑन्से; US फ़ीआन्'से / noun वह आदमी या औरत जिससे विवाह होने जा रहा है।

fiasco / फ़ि'ऐस्को / noun (pl **fiascos**; US **fiascoes**) घोर एवं पूर्ण असफलता : The party turned into a complete fiasco.

fib / फ़िब् / noun (अनौप) झूठ, असत्य ▸ **fib** verb झूठ बोलना।

fibre (US **fiber**) / 'फ़ाइबर् / noun 1 रेशा, तंतु 2 तंतुओं से बनी वस्तु 3 खाने का वह भाग जो पचाया नहीं जा सकता परंतु पेट साफ़ रखता है 4 (औप) सशक्त चरित्र : a woman of strong moral fibre ▸ fi-

brous / 'फ़ाइब्रस् / *adj* रेशेदार : *fibrous tissue.*

fibreglass (*US* fiberglass) / 'फ़ाइबर्-ग्लास; *US* 'फ़ाइबर्ग्लैस् / (glass fiber भी) *noun* काँच के महीन रेशों एवं प्लास्टिक से बना मज़बूत पदार्थ जो कार, नाव आदि बनाने के काम आता है।

fickle / 'फ़िकुल् / *adj* (*प्रायः अप्रम*) 1 अस्थिर : *The weather here is notoriously fickle.* 2 (व्यक्ति) चंचलचित्त, निष्ठाहीन ▸ **fickleness** *noun.*

fiction / 'फ़िक्शन् / *noun* 1 काल्पनिक घटनाओं और व्यक्तियों को लेकर रचा गया साहित्य; कथा-साहित्य (उपन्यास, कहानियाँ आदि) : *Truth is often stranger than fiction.* 2 ('सत्य' के विपरीत में) काल्पनिक वस्तु ▸ **fictional** *adj* काल्पनिक **fictionalize, -ise** *verb* सत्य घटना को काल्पनिक घटना की तरह लिखना।

fictitious / फ़िक्'टिशस् / *adj* काल्पनिक; फ़रज़ी।

fiddle / 'फ़िडुल् / *noun* 1 (अनौप) बेला, वायलिन 2 (अप) बेईमानी : *tax fiddles* ▸ **fiddle** *verb* 1 **fiddle** (about/around) with sth अँगुलियों को किसी वस्तु पर चलाते रहना; कुछ (स्विच आदि) अदल-बदलकर कुछ कार्य करने की कोशिश करते रहना : *He was fiddling with the remote control.* 2 बेईमानी करके कुछ (लाभ) प्राप्त करना 3 **fiddle about/around** इधर-उधर घूमकर बेकार समय गँवाना।

fidelity / फ़ि'डेलटि / *noun* **fidelity (to sb/sth)** ईमानदारी, स्वामिभक्ति, आपसी संबंधों में निष्ठा : *fidelity to one's principles.*

fidget / 'फ़िजिट् / *verb* **fidget (with sth)** बेचैन होकर हिलते-डुलते रहना, कुछ करते रहना, जिससे दूसरे परेशान हों ▸ **fidget** *noun* **fidgety** *adj* सदैव चंचल व चलायमान।

field[1] / फ़ील्ड् / *noun* 1 खेत; मैदान 2 (प्रायः समास में) क्षेत्र जहाँ से खनिज आदि मिलता है : *coalfields/goldfields* 3 विस्तार, खुली जगह : *an ice-field* 4 अध्ययन क्षेत्र 5 कार्य क्षेत्र : *in the field of politics* 6 वह क्षेत्र जहाँ कोई विशेष शक्ति अनुभव की जा सकती है : *a strong magnetic field* ■ **hold the field (against sb/sth)** प्रभावी रहना **take the field** खेल के मैदान में जाना ▸ **field events** *noun* [*pl*] खेल-कूद की स्पर्धाएँ (दौड़ को छोड़कर)।

field[2] / फ़ील्ड् / *verb* 1 (क्रिकेट में) फ़ील्डिंग करना 2 खेल के लिए खिलाड़ियों का चुनाव करना : *They are fielding a very strong side this season.* 3 (राजनीतिक दल का) प्रत्याशी को मैदान में उतारना/समर्थन देना ▸ **fielder** *noun.*

fiend / फ़ीन्ड् / *noun* 1 शैतान, नरकदूत 2 दुष्ट/बदमाश व्यक्ति ▸ **fiendish** *adj* 1 क्रूर : *a fiendish temper* 2 (अनौप) दुष्टतापूर्ण; चालाकी भरा।

fierce / फ़िअर्स् / *adj* (**-r, -st**) 1 उग्र, क्रूर 2 तीव्र : *fierce hatred* 3 (गरमी, हवा आदि) प्रचंड, घोर : *fierce heat* ▸ **fiercely** *adv.*

fiery / 'फ़ाइअरि / *adj* 1 आग की तरह, लपटों से पूर्ण; (गले में) जलन पैदा करने वाला : *fiery liquor* 2 सहज में क्रोधित हो जाने वाला व्यक्ति; (शब्द) ओज भरे : *a fiery speech.*

fifteen / फ़िफ़्'टीन् / *noun, pron, det* पंद्रह (का अंक) ▸ **fifteenth** / फ़िफ़्'टीन्श् / *noun, pron, det* पंद्रहवाँ, 1/15.

fifth / फ़िफ़्थ् / *pron, det, adv* पाँचवाँ : *Today is the fifth (of March).* ▸ **fifth** *noun* पाँचवाँ हिस्सा, 1/5.

fifty / 'फ़िफ़्टि / *noun, pron, det* 1 पचास (का अंक) 2 **the fifties** [*pl*] 50 से 59 तक की संख्याएँ, वर्ष या तापमान की डिग्रियाँ ▸ **fiftieth** *noun, pron, det* पचासवाँ, 1/50.

fig / फ़िग् / *noun* अंजीर।

fight[1] / फ़ाइट् / *verb* (*pt, pp* **fought**

/फ़ाट् /) 1 हाथ या हथियारों से लड़ना; संघर्ष करना 2 fight (against sth) कुछ रोकने, नष्ट करने या विजय पाने का प्रयत्न करना : *fight (against) disease/oppression* 3 fight (about/over sth) झगड़ा या वाद-विवाद करना ■ fight shy of sth कुछ करने को अनिच्छुक होना fight sth out लड़कर किसी विवाद को सुलझाना ▸ fighter noun 1 (युद्ध या खेल में) लड़ने वाला 2 जो आसानी से हार स्वीकार नहीं करता है 3 लड़ाकू हवाई जहाज़।

fight² /फ़ाइट्/ noun 1 संघर्ष, लड़ने की प्रक्रिया 2 संघर्ष-शक्ति, धैर्य : *In spite of many defeats, they still had plenty of fight left in them.*

figment /फ़िग्मन्ट्/ noun ■ a figment of sb's imagination मनगढ़ंत कथा, कल्पित वस्तु या बात।

figurative /फ़िगरटिव्/ adj 1 शब्दों का आलंकारिक प्रयोग, प्रतीकात्मक प्रयोग (इस कोश में ऐसे प्रयोगों से पूर्व इसका संक्षिप्त रूप 'अलं' दिया गया है) 2 कला में व्यक्तियों/ जानवरों/वस्तुओं का ज्यों का त्यों निरूपण : *a figurative animal sculpture* ▸ figuratively adv.

figure¹ /फ़िगर; US फ़िग्यर/ noun 1 संख्याओं के अंक, 0,1,...9 2 (विशेषत: pl) निर्धारित/विशिष्ट मात्रा : *the latest unemployment figures* 3 figures [pl] (अनौप) अंक-गणित 4 मनुष्य का रूप, चेहरा-मोहरा, आकृति : *She's always had a good figure.* 5 व्यक्ति-विशेष, प्रसिद्ध और महत्त्वपूर्ण व्यक्ति : *a cult figure* 6 आरेख, किताब में दिए गए डायग्राम ▸ figure of speech noun काव्य-लंकार।

figure² /फ़िगर; US फ़िग्यर/ verb 1 figure (in/on sth) (किसी घटना आदि में) भाग लेना या उल्लेख किया जाना 2 सोचना, अनुमान लगाना : *I figured (that) you wouldn't come.* ■ figure sb/sth out 1 हिसाब लगाना, गणना करना

2 किसी व्यक्ति के व्यवहार को सोच-विचार के बाद समझना।

figurehead /फ़िगरहेड्/ noun उच्च स्थान पर किंतु अधिकारहीन व्यक्ति; नाममात्र का शासक : *The elected head of state is a figurehead only—the real power lies elsewhere.*

filament /फ़िलमन्ट्/ noun 1 महीन रेशे जैसा तंतु 2 महीन तार जो बल्बों में प्रयुक्त होता है।

file¹ /फ़ाइल/ noun 1 (काग़ज़ात रखने की) फ़ाइल; फ़ाइल एवं उसके काग़ज़ात : *top secret police files* 2 कंप्यूटर में एकत्रित संगठित सूचना सामग्री ▸ file verb 1 file sth (away) फ़ाइल में क्रम से रखना 2 आधिकारिक रिकॉर्ड के लिए कुछ भेजना : *file a complaint.*

file² /फ़ाइल/ noun व्यक्तियों या वस्तुओं की एक के पीछे एक क़तार ■ (in) Indian/single file एक ही पंक्ति में, एक के पीछे एक : *walking in single file along the narrow path* ▸ file verb file in, out, off, past, etc पंक्ति बनाकर निर्धारित दिशा में जाना।

file³ /फ़ाइल/ noun लोहे की रेती (कड़ी वस्तु को काटने या चिकना या तेज़ करने के लिए) ▸ file verb रेती से रेतकर काटना, चिकना या तेज़ बनाना : *file one's fingernails* filings /फ़ाइलिङ्ज़/ noun [pl] कटे हुए या रेते हुए कण, चूरा।

filial /फ़िलिअल्/ adj संतान-विषयक, संतान से अपेक्षित : *filial affection.*

fill¹ /फ़िल/ verb 1 fill sth (with sth); fill sth (for sb) भरना, पूरा करना या हो जाना; fill (with sth) पूरा भर जाना : *The hall soon filled.* 2 fill sth (with sth) भरकर (ख़ाली जगह) बंद करना : *The dentist filled two of my teeth.* 3 कोई पद धारण करना; किसी को पद पर नियुक्त करना : *The vacancy has already been filled.* ■ fill out गोल-मटोल होना fill sth in 1 (US fill sth out भी) (पूछी

गई) आवश्यक जानकारी देकर कुछ पूरा करना : *fill in an application form* 2 पूर्णत: भर देना ▸ **filler** noun कुछ भरने के लिए प्रयुक्त पदार्थ।

fill² /फ़िल्/ noun 1 भरने के लिए आवश्यक मात्रा : *a fill of tobacco/oil* 2 **one's fill (of sth/sb)** (औप) जितना कोई खा सकता है; जितना कोई सहन कर सकता है।

fillet /'फ़िलिट; US फ़ि'ले/ noun मछली या गोश्त का मोटा टुकड़ा जिसमें काँटा या हड्डी न हो।

filling /'फ़िलिङ्/ noun 1 दाँतों में भरा जाने वाला सीमेंट 2 व्यंजन (जैसे सैंडविच, केक आदि) के अंदर भरा जाने वाला खाद्य पदार्थ।

filly /'फ़िलि/ noun बछेड़ी, घोड़े का मादा बच्चा।

film¹ /फ़िल्म्/ noun 1 सिनेमा फ़िल्म : *my favourite horror film* 2 फ़ोटो फ़िल्म 3 (प्राय: sing) **film (of sth)** (धूल, धुंध आदि की) परत : *a film of oil on water.* ▸ **filmy** adj महीन और लगभग पारदर्शी।

film² /फ़िल्म्/ verb 1 फ़िल्माना, कहानी आदि पर फ़िल्म बनाना 2 परत से ढक जाना।

filter /'फ़िल्टर/ noun 1 फ़िल्टर, छन्नी (द्रव छानने के लिए) 2 ऐसा परदा जो एक विशिष्ट प्रकाश को ही पार गुज़रने देता है ▸ **filter** verb 1 छानना 2 **filter in, out, through, etc** धीरे-धीरे निर्धारित दिशा में (द्रव या प्रकाश आदि) गुज़रना; धीरे-धीरे पहचान बना लेना।

filth /फ़िल्थ्/ noun 1 गंदगी, मैल : *the stench and filth of the prison* 2 गंदा एवं अश्लील साहित्य, पत्रिका, शब्द आदि ▸ **filthy** adj (-ier, -iest) 1 गंदगी भरा; अश्लील 2 (अनौप) (मौसम) अत्यंत अरुचिकर।

fin /फ़िन्/ noun 1 मछली के पंख जैसा अंग जिनके सहारे वह तैरती है 2 पंखनुमा वस्तु, जैसे हवाई जहाज़ या कार में : *tail fins.*

final /'फ़ाइनल्/ adj 1 अंतिम 2 (निर्णय आदि) जिस पर और बहस नहीं हो सकती है और जो बदला नहीं जा सकता है : *The*

referee's ruling is final. ▸ **final** noun 1 (pl भी) अंतिम परीक्षा, दौड़, प्रतियोगिता आदि : *the tennis finals* 2 (प्राय: pl) विश्वविद्यालय की अंतिम परीक्षाएँ **finally** adv 1 अंत में 2 आख़िर में 3 आख़िरकार, अंतत:।

finale /फ़ि'नालि/ noun (नाटक या संगीत का) अंतिम चरण, समापन।

finance /'फ़ाइनैन्स; फ़ाइ'नैन्स; फ़'नैन्स्/ noun 1 **finance (for sth)** किसी कार्य-विशेष के लिए आवश्यक धन 2 विशेषत: सार्वजनिक धन का प्रबंध-संचालन (का विज्ञान) : *the Minister of Finance* 3 **finances** [pl] सरकार, व्यापारिक प्रतिष्ठान या व्यक्ति को उपलब्ध धन, वित्त ▸ **finance** verb किसी कार्य में धन (पूँजी) लगाना : *publicly financed services* **financial** /फ़ाइ'नैन्श्ल्/ adj वित्तीय।

financier /फ़ाइ'नैन्सिअर; US फ़िनन्'सिअर्/ noun वित्त विशेषज्ञ; पूँजी लगाने वाला।

find¹ /फ़ाइन्ड्/ verb (pt, pp **found** /फ़ाउन्ड्/) 1 (अचानक/संयोग से) पा जाना 2 **find sth/sb (for sb)** ढूँढ निकालना; पता लगाना 3 अनुभव से पाना/जानना : *He finds his new job rather boring.* 4 प्राकृतिक रूप से जाना, पहुँचना : *Water will always find its own level.* 5 **find sth/sb (for sb)** (कोई खोई हुई वस्तु या व्यक्ति) मिलना, पाना 6 (क़ानून) निर्णय करना; (दोषी) ठहराना या क़रार देना : *The jury found him guilty (of manslaughter).* ■ **find fault (with sb/sth)** ग़लती निकालना, दोष ढूँढना **find one's feet** अपनी शक्ति पहचानना और भली-भाँति कार्य करने लग जाना **find sb out** दोषी या अपराधी का पता लगाना **find sth out** पूछ-ताछकर जानना, सीखना, समझना; पता लगाना ▸ **finding** noun (प्राय: pl) 1 जाँच के परिणाम, निष्कर्ष 2 (क़ानून) निर्णय।

find² /फ़ाइन्ड्/ noun ढूँढने से पाई गई वस्तु

या व्यक्ति (विशेषत: जो रुचिकर एवं महत्त्वपूर्ण हो)।

fine¹ / फ़ाइन् / *adj* (-r, -st) 1 श्रेष्ठ, उत्तम; निपुणता एवं कुशलता से तैयार की गई (वस्तु) : *fine silk/china* 2 बहुत अच्छा; सुंदर या प्रियकर; (व्यक्ति) स्वस्थ, ठीक-ठाक 3 (मौसम) बढ़िया, सुहावना; (धातु) शुद्ध, परिष्कृत : *fine gold* 4 बहुत बारीक कणों से बना 5 सूक्ष्म : *a pencil with a fine point* 6 गूढ़, समझ में आने में मुश्किल : *You are making very fine distinctions.* 7 (भाषण या लेख) महान, लेकिन दिखावटी रूप में 8 (अनौप) 'हाँ', 'संतोषजनक है' ▸ **fine art** *noun* (**the fine arts** [*pl*] भी) ललित कला **finely** *adv* 1 बढ़िया; श्रेष्ठ ढंग से 2 सूक्ष्म कणों के रूप में 3 बहुत सूक्ष्म एवं कुशल ढंग से।

fine² / फ़ाइन् / *noun* अर्थदंड, जुरमाना ▸ **fine** *verb* **fine sb (for sth/doing sth)** जुरमाना करना : *She was fined for dangerous driving.*

fine³ / फ़ाइन् / *adv* 1 (अनौप) बहुत बढ़िया 2 (समास में) पता लगाने या समझने में मुश्किल : *fine-drawn distinctions* 3 निपुण/सूक्ष्म ढंग से : *fine-spun cloth* ■ **cut it/things fine** मुश्किल से पर्याप्त समय देना।

finery / फ़ाइनरि / *noun* सुंदर अच्छे सिले कपड़े, चमकीले आभूषण आदि, ठाट-बाट।

finesse / फ़ि'नेस् / *noun* युक्ति या चतुरता से व्यक्तियों या स्थिति से निपटने की कुश-लता : *a politician of great skill and finesse.*

finger¹ / फ़िङ्गर् / *noun* 1 अँगुली, उँगली 2 दस्ताने का अँगुली वाला भाग ▸ **finger-print** *noun* (प्राय: *pl*) अँगुलियों की छाप (जो अपराधी को पहचानने में काम आती है)।

finger² / फ़िङ्गर् / *verb* अँगुली से छूना या महसूस करना : *She fingered the knife hidden in her pocket.*

finish¹ / फ़िनिश् / *verb* 1 समाप्त होना या करना 2 **finish sth (off)** पूरा करना : *Could you finish this typing off for me?* 3 **finish sth (off/up)** बचा-खुचा समाप्त करना 4 **finish sb (off)** (अनौप) किसी को पूर्णत: थका देना ■ **finish sb/sth off** (अनौप) मार देना/ख़त्म कर देना।

finish² / फ़िनिश् / *noun* 1 (प्राय: *sing*) अंतिम बिंदु या अंत : *an exciting finish to the race* 2 पूर्णता की अवस्था; परि-सज्जा, पॉलिश आदि : *a gloss/matt finish.*

finished / फ़िनिश्ट् / *adj* सुसज्जित।

finite / फ़ाइनाइट् / *adj* 1 सीमित 2 (व्या) पूर्ण क्रिया : *finite verbs.*

fiord (fjord भी) / फ़्यॉर्ड् / *noun* दो खड़ी चट्टानों के बीच समुद्र का संकरा भाग (विशेषत: नॉर्वे में)।

fir / फ़र् / (**fir-tree** भी) *noun* देवदारु (वृक्ष)।

fire¹ / फ़ाइअर् / *noun* 1 आग, अग्नि : *Are you afraid of fire?* 2 आग लगना, जलने लगना : *The house in on fire.* 3 ईंधन, लकड़ी-कोयला (गरमाने या खाना पकाने के लिए) : *light a fire in the grate* 4 बंदूक की गोलीबारी : *Troops came under heavy fire.* ■ **by/come under fire** कड़ी निंदा/आलोचना का पात्र/विषय होना : *The government in under fire from all sides for its economic policy.* ▸ **fire-alarm** *noun* आग लगने पर बजने वाला अलार्म **firearm** *noun* राईफल या रिवॉल्वर **fire brigade** *noun* [*sing*] आग बुझाने वालों का दल **fire-engine** *noun* दमकल, आग बुझाने का इंजन **fire-escape** *noun* जलते हुए मकान से लोगों को बाहर निकालने वाली सीढ़ी **fireman** *noun* आग बुझाने वाला व्यक्ति **fireplace** *noun* अँगीठी **fireproof** *adj* अदाह्य, अज्वलनशील।

fire² / फ़ाइअर् / *verb* 1 **fire (sth) (at sb/ sth); fire (sth) into sth; fire (on sb/**

sth) गोली दाग़ना, कमान से तीर छोड़ना; बंदूक़ छूटना, तीर छूटना 2 **fire sth at sb** तेज़ी से कुछ (अपशब्द आदि) बोलना, बौछार करना : *fire insults at sb* 3 **fire sb (for sth/doing sth)** (अनौप) नौकरी से निकाल देना 4 आग लगाना; जलने लगना 5 **fire sb (with sth)** (भावना) भड़काना, (कल्पना को) उत्तेजित करना 6 आँवे में (ईंट, बरतन आदि) पकाना : *fire pottery in a kiln* ▸ **firing** / 'फ़ाइअरिङ् / *noun* गोलीबारी; गोलीकांड।

firework / 'फ़ाइअरवर्क् / *noun* आतिश-बाज़ी।

firm¹ / फ़र्म् / *adj* (-er, -est) 1 पक्का, दृढ़; मज़बूत 2 सरलता से प्रभावित या परिवर्तित न होने वाला : *a firm belief* 3 **firm (with sb)** व्यवहार एवं दृष्टिकोण में दृढ़; निर्णायक : *Parents must be firm with their children.* 4 **firm (against sth)** (मुद्रा) अन्य मुद्रा के मुक़ाबले क़ीमत में कम नहीं और संभवत: चढ़ती क़ीमत वाली ▸ **firm** *verb* दृढ़ करना या बनाना या होना **firmly** *adv* दृढ़ता से **firmness** *noun*.

firm² / फ़र्म् / *noun* फ़र्म, व्यापार के लिए दो या अधिक व्यक्तियों का संघ।

firmament / 'फ़र्ममन्ट् / *noun* the fir-mament (प्रा) आकाश।

first¹ / फ़र्स्ट् / *det* 1 प्रथम; सबसे पहले 2 सर्वप्रथम घटित और अनुभव किया हुआ : *his first real taste of success* ▸ **first aid** *noun* प्राथमिक चिकित्सा **first class** *noun* प्रथम श्रेणी **first lady** *noun* the First Lady [*sing*] (US) राष्ट्रपति की पत्नी **firstly** *adv* प्रथमत:, पहले **first-rate** *adj* सर्वोत्तम; उत्कृष्ट।

first² / फ़र्स्ट् / *adv* 1 किसी अन्य से पहले; प्रारंभ में 2 किसी अन्य घटना या समय से पहले 3 (किसी सूची को प्रस्तुत करने में) शुरुआत में ▸ **first-born** *noun, adj* (अप्र) पहली (सबसे बड़ी) संतान।

first³ / फ़र्स्ट् / *noun* 1 the first (*pl* अपरिवर्तित) प्रथम उल्लिखित या आने वाला

व्यक्ति या वस्तु 2 (अनौप) पहले न कभी घटित या अनुभूत घटना 3 **first (in sth)** प्रथम श्रेणी : *She got a first in philosophy at JNU.*

firsthand / फ़र्स्ट् हैन्ड् / *adj, adv* प्रत्यक्ष अनुभवों से प्राप्त, न कि किताबों से प्राप्त ज्ञान।

fiscal / 'फ़िस्कल् / *adj* वित्तीय, विशेषत: कर संबंधी : *the government's fiscal policy.*

fish¹ / फ़िश् / *noun* (*pl* अपरिवर्तित या fishes) मछली; मछली का मांस ▸ **fish-monger** / 'फ़िशमङ्गर् / *noun* मछली बेचने वाला **fishy** *adj* (-ier, -iest) 1 स्वाद या गंध में मछली जैसा : *a fishy smell* 2 (अनौप) संदेहजनक : *There's something fishy going on here.*

fish² / फ़िश् / *verb* **fish (for sth)** 1 मछली पकड़ना 2 कुछ ढूँढना, विशेषत: किसी अंधेरे एवं छुपे हुए स्थान में : *She fished (around) in her bag for the keys.* ■ **fish sth out (of sth)** पाना, खोज निकालना ▸ **fishing** *noun* मछली पकड़ना **fishing-line** *noun* मछली पकड़ने की लगी (डोरी)।

fisherman / 'फ़िशरमन् / *noun* मछुआरा।

fissure / 'फ़िशर् / *noun* (चट्टान या भूमि में) गहरी दरार; फटना ▸ **fissured** *adj*.

fist / फ़िस्ट् / *noun* मुट्ठी : *He clenched his fists.* ▸ **fistful** *noun*.

fit¹ / फ़िट् / *adj* (-tter, -ttest) 1 **fit (for sth/to do sth)** अच्छे स्वास्थ्य या स्थिति में 2 **fit for sb/sth; fit to do sth** उपयुक्त, उचित : *beaches fit for swimming* 3 (औप) ठीक, उपयुक्त : *a fit subject for discussion* ■ **fit as a fiddle** (अनौप) पूरी तरह स्वस्थ ▸ **fitness** *noun*.

fit² / फ़िट् / *verb* (-tt-; *pt, pp* fitted; US fit भी) 1 उचित आकार और आकृति का होना : *These shoes don't fit (me).* 2 **fit sb oneself/sth for sth** किसी व्यक्ति को, वस्तु या अपने आप को किसी कार्य के लिए उपयुक्त बनाना 3 **fit A (on/**

to B); fit B with A (कोई वस्तु) किसी स्थान पर लगाना : *fit handles on the cupboard* 4 बनवाए गए कपड़े पहनकर देखना और आवश्यकता अनुसार ठीक करना ■ fit in (with sb/sth) मेल और अनुरूपता से रहना fit sb/sth out/up (with sth) तैयार करना, सज्जित करना fit sth/sb in कुछ करने या किसी से मिलने का समय निकालना ▶ fitter *noun* मिस्त्री, (विशेषत:) मशीन को ठीक बैठाने वाला कारीगर।

fit³ / फ़िट् / *noun* [sing] उपयुक्त या ठीक होने की रीति का परिणाम।

fit⁴ / फ़िट् / *noun* 1 दौरा, मूर्छा : *an epileptic fit* 2 (क्रोध, हँसी आदि की) लहर, मौज : *get a fit of hysterics/ (the) giggles* ■ by/in fits and starts ऐसे प्रयत्न जो शुरू होते हैं, ठप हो जाते हैं और फिर शुरू हो जाते हैं ▶ fitful *adj* अनियमित fitfully *adv.*

fitting¹ / 'फ़िटिङ् / *adj* उपयुक्त, उद्देश्य के अनुकूल।

fitting² / 'फ़िटिङ् / *noun* 1 माप के अनुकूल कपड़े बनवाने की प्रक्रिया/बने होने का अवसर 2 (प्राय: pl) मकान में स्थायी रूप से लगी वस्तुएँ : *electrical fittings.*

five / फ़ाइव् / *noun, pron, det* पाँच (का अंक) ▶ five-pref (पूर्वपद) (समास में) पंच : *a five-day week/a five-year contract.*

fix¹ / फ़िक्स् / *verb* 1 स्थिर करना, टिकाना 2 निर्धारित या निश्चित करना : *Has (the date of) the next meeting been fixed?* 3 fix sth on sb/sth (नेत्र, ध्यान) किसी एक ओर लगाना 4 (रंग) पक्का करना, (फ़ोटोग्राफ़ आदि को) ऐसा करना कि रंग फीका न हो 5 fix sth (up) व्यवस्थित करना; निश्चित करना : *You have to fix visits up in advance with the museum.* ■ fix sth up मरम्मत करना; सजाना : *He fixed up the flat before they moved in.* ▶ fixed

/ फ़िक्स्ट् / *adj* 1 निर्धारित, निश्चित 2 स्थिर अचल (विचार आदि) 3 (अभिव्यक्ति) न बदलने वाली, कृत्रिम fixedly / 'फ़िक्सिड्लि / *adv* अत्यधिक रुचि से; अपलक दृष्टि से : *look fixedly at sth.*

fix² / फ़िक्स् / *noun* 1 (प्राय: sing) (अनौप) मुसीबत या उलझन : *get oneself into a fix* 2 (अनौप) बेईमानी से व्यवस्थित कार्य 3 जहाज़, वायुयान आदि की स्थिति (का पता लगाना)।

fixation / फ़िक्'सेशन् / *noun* fixation (on/with sb/sth) किसी व्यक्ति/वस्तु में अस्वाभाविक/असामान्य रुचि।

fixture / 'फ़िक्स्चर् / *noun* 1 दौड़ आदि की नियत तिथि 2 (प्राय: pl) जड़ी हुई वस्तु जैसे कमरे में अलमारी आदि।

fizz / फ़िज़् / *verb* 1 (द्रव से) सी-सी की आवाज़ से गैस निकलना 2 जलती हुई लकड़ी के जैसे आवाज़ करना ▶ fizz noun 1 द्रव में गैस के बुलबुले 2 सी-सी की आवाज़।

fizzle / 'फ़िज़्ल् / *verb* (हलकी-सी) सी-सी की आवाज़ करना ■ fizzle out निराशा-जनक रूप से असफल हो जाना।

fizzy / 'फ़िज़ि / *adj* (-ier, -iest) (द्रव) बुदबुदाने वाला।

flab / फ़्लैब् / *noun* (अनौप, अपमा) (मोटे व्यक्ति के शरीर का) ढीला-ढाला मांस ▶ flabby / 'फ़्लैबि / *adj* (-ier, -iest) (अपमा) 1 ढीला-ढाला; थुलथुल 2 कम-ज़ोर; अप्रभावी : *a flabby argument/ speech.*

flabbergasted / 'फ़्लैबर्गास्टिड् / *adj* (अनौप) आश्चर्यचकित, भौंचक्का।

flag¹ / फ़्लैग् / *noun* झंडा, ध्वजा; पताका ▶ flag verb (-gg-) झंडा लगाना; झंडों से कोई स्थान सजाना ▶ flagstaff (flag-pole भी) noun ध्वजदंड।

flag² / फ़्लैग् / *verb* (-gg-) थक जाना, ढीला पड़ जाना : *My enthusiasm is flag-ging.*

flagrant / 'फ़्लेग्रन्ट् / *adj* (प्राय: कोई ख़राब कार्य) जघन्य, लज्जाजनक : *flagrant violations of human rights* ▸ **fla-grantly** adv.

flail / 'फ्लेल् / verb हाथ-पैर मारना; ज़ोर-ज़ोर से हाथ-पैर हिलाना : *flail one's arms above one's head.*

flair / फ़्लेअर् / noun 1 flair for sth जन्म-जात कौशल : *She has a real flair for languages.* 2 मौलिक एवं आकर्षक गुण; शैली, कल्पना आदि : *theatrical flair* ○ *She dresses with real flair.*

flake / फ़्लेक् / noun बर्फ के रूई जैसे टुकड़े; पतली परत; पतले छोटे टुकड़े : *dried onion flakes* ▸ **flake** verb **flake (off)** टुकड़े-टुकड़े करके झड़ना; पपड़ी जमना **flaky** adj (-ier, -iest) पपड़ीदार।

flamboyant / फ़्लैम्'बॉइअन्ट् / adj 1 (व्यक्ति, व्यवहार) आकर्षक, सहज ही में आकर्षित करने वाला 2 (रंग) चमकदार एवं चित्ताकर्षक ▸ **flamboyance** noun.

flame¹ / फ़्लेम् / noun 1 लपट, ज्वाला 2 (रंग की) चमक (प्राय: लाल रंग की) 3 (अलं) तीव्र भाव, विशेषत: प्यार का : *the flame of passion* 4 (प्राय: old flame) (अनौप) पूर्व प्रेमी अथवा प्रेमिका।

flame² / फ़्लेम् / verb 1 धधकना, लौ की तरह चमकना 2 flame (out/up) क्रोध आदि से तमतमाना : *Hatred flamed (up) within him.* ▸ **flaming** adj प्रज्वलित; तमतमाया हुआ।

flammable / फ़्लैमब्ल् / adj ज्वलनशील।

flank / फ़्लैङ्क् / noun 1 (व्यक्ति या जान-वर के शरीर का) पार्श्व भाग 2 पहाड़ या भवन का पार्श्व भाग 3 सेना या (खेल की) टीम का बायाँ या दायाँ भाग/पार्श्व ▸ **flank** verb व्यक्ति या वस्तु के एक या दोनों तरफ़ होना।

flannel / 'फ़्लैन्ल् / noun 1 फ़लालेन, नर्म ऊनी कपड़ा 2 flannels [pl] फ़लालेन की पतलून 3 (US wash-cloth भी) फ़लालेन का टुकड़ा।

flap¹ / फ़्लैप् / noun 1 पल्ला (जैसे जेब का पल्ला) : *the flap of an envelope* 2 फड़फड़ाहट; थपथपाहट : *With a flap*

of the wings, the bird was gone. 3 [sing] (अनौप) मानसिक उत्तेजना।

flap² / फ़्लैप् / verb (-pp-) 1 पंख फड़-फड़ाना; फड़फड़ाहट जैसी आवाज़ करना; थपथपाना : *The sails were flapping gently in the wind.* 2 (अनौप) उत्तेजित हो जाना।

flare / फ़्लेअर् / verb 1 धधकना; भभकना 2 (अचानक) भड़कना : *Tempers flared at the conference.* ■ **flare up** 1 अचानक ज़ोर की ज्वाला धधक उठना 2 अचानक क्रोधोन्माद में पहुँच जाना ▸ **flare** noun 1 लपट, लौ 2 लौ उत्पन्न करने की युक्ति।

flared / फ़्लेअर्ड् / adj (वस्त्रों का) नीचे से ज़्यादा चौड़ा होना : *flared trousers.*

flash¹ / फ़्लैश् / noun 1 कौंध, (अचानक) चमक; अचानक आने वाला भाव 2 (कैमरे के साथ प्रयुक्त) फ़्लैश ■ **in/like a flash** पलभर में ▸ **flashlight** noun छोटी टॉर्च; कैमरे के फ़्लैश की बत्ती।

flash² / फ़्लैश् / verb 1 कौंधना 2 अचानक दृष्टि के सामने या मन में आ जाना 3 तत्काल ही कोई समाचार रेडियो/टी वी द्वारा प्रसारित करना : *News of the tragedy was flashed across the country.* 4 ज़रा-सी देर के लिए कुछ दिखाना।

flashy / फ़्लैशी / adj (-ier, -iest) भड़कीला।

flask / फ़्लास्क्; US फ़्लैस्क् / noun 1 फ़्लास्क, छोटे मुँह की बोतल 2 (hip flask भी) जेब में आ सकने वाली शराब की छोटी बोतल 3 (vacuum flask भी) फ़्लास्क, गरम को गरम और ठंडे को ठंडा बनाए रखने वाली बोतल।

flat¹ / फ़्लैट् / adj (-tter, -ttest) 1 समतल; चिकना तल 2 बिल्कुल, साफ़-साफ़; पूर्ण रूप से निश्चित : *give sb a flat denial/refusal* 3 नीरस, फीका-फीका 4 (बिअर आदि) स्वादहीन, उतरी हुई 5 (संगीत) बेसुरा 6 सभी वस्तुओं या सेवाओं की एक ही क़ीमत (वाला) : *The firm charges a flat fee for their services.* 7 (बैटरी)

विद्युतविहीन 8 (पैर) सपाट 9 पंचर के कारण टायर में पर्याप्त हवा न होना ▶ **flat-footed** adj सपाट पैर वाला व्यक्ति **flatly** adv 1 नीरसता से, अरुचि से 2 साफ़-साफ़ तरीके से।

flat² / फ़्लैट् / noun 1 (विशेषत: US apartment भी) फ़्लैट, एक ही मंज़िल में कमरों का सेट 2 **the flat (of sth)** (चाकू, तलवार आदि का) बिना धार वाला भाग 3 सपाट भूमि, विशेषत: जल के पास : salt flats 4 (अनौप, विशेषत: US) वायुरहित टायर।

flat³ / फ़्लैट् / adv 1 सपाट, एकसार फैला हुआ/लेटा हुआ : She lay flat on her back. 2 निश्चित रूप से, बिल्कुल 3 (संगीत) सुर से नीचे।

flatter / फ़्लैटर् / verb 1 चापलूसी करना, खुशामद करना 2 किसी को जैसा वह है उससे अच्छा दिखाना : You need a hairstyle that flatters the shape of your face. 3 **flatter oneself (that...)** अपने बारे में उच्च ख़याल रखना : He flatters himself that he speaks French well. ▶ **flatterer** noun चापलूस **flattering** adj **flattery** noun चापलूसी, खुशामद।

flaunt / फ़्लॉन्ट् / verb (प्राय: अपमा) इठलाना, इतराना; गुस्ताख़ी से प्रदर्शन करना : He's always flaunting his wealth.

flautist / फ़्लॉटिस्ट् / noun बाँसुरी-वादक।

flavour (US flavor) / फ़्लेवर् / noun 1 (खाने की) सुगंध, स्वाद; विशिष्ट स्वाद 2 विशिष्ट गुण, लक्षण या वातावरण : a room with a definite French flavour ▶ **flavour** (US flavour) verb **flavour sth (with sth)** सुगंधित/स्वादिष्ट बनाना -**flavoured** suff (प्रत्यय) (समास में) विशिष्ट प्रकार के स्वाद या सुगंध वाला : lemon-flavoured sweets **flavourless** adj.

flaw / फ़्लॉ / noun **flaw (in sb/sth)** 1 दरार; ऐब 2 दोष; त्रुटि 3 चरित्र की कम-

ज़ोरी ▶ **flaw** verb दोषपूर्ण करना; कमज़ोर बनाना **flawless** adj परिपूर्ण, अनिंद्य।

flax / फ़्लैक्स् / noun 1 एक प्रकार का पौधा जिसके तंतुओं से कपड़ा बनता है, फ़्लैक्स 2 फ़्लैक्स तंतु ▶ **flaxen** / फ़्लैक्सन् / adj हलके पीले रंग के (बाल)।

flay / फ़्ले / verb 1 चमड़ा उतारना 2 कोड़े लगाना 3 कटु आलोचना करना : Paul flayed her with reproaches.

flea / फ़्ली / noun पिस्सू।

fleck / फ़्लेक् / noun (प्राय: pl) **fleck (of sth)** 1 (रंग का) धब्बा, दाग़ 2 (धूल के) कण : flecks of dust/foam/dandruff ▶ **fleck** verb **fleck sth (with sth)** दाग़-धब्बे डालना।

fledged / फ़्लेज्ड् / adj (चिड़ियों का) पूरे बड़े पंखवाला बनना, उड़ने योग्य बनना।

fledgling (fledgeling भी) / फ़्लेज्-लिङ् / noun 1 चिड़िया का बच्चा जिसने अभी-अभी उड़ना सीखा है 2 अनुभवहीन (व्यक्ति, संस्था), अनाड़ी।

flee / फ़्ली / verb (pt, pp fled / फ़्लेड् /) **flee (from sb/sth)** भाग जाना, बचकर निकल भागना; डर के कारण घर या देश छोड़ देना : flee in search of a better life.

fleece / फ़्लीस् / noun 1 (भेड़ या बकरी की) ऊन 2 ऊन की तरह का एक कपड़ा ▶ **fleece** verb (अनौप) पैसा ऐंठना/लूटना **fleecy** / फ़्लीसि / adj (बादलों या आकाश का, कपड़े आदि का) ऊन जैसा लगना।

fleet¹ / फ़्लीट् / noun 1 नौसेना; जहाज़ी बेड़ा 2 जहाज़, हवाई जहाज़ या बसों का बेड़ा जो एक व्यक्ति के अधीन हो।

fleet² / फ़्लीट् / adj (अप्र) फुरतीला; क्षण-भंगुर : fleet-footed.

fleeting / फ़्लीटिङ् / क्षणिक; क्षणभंगुर ▶ **fleetingly** adv.

flesh / फ़्लेश् / noun 1 मांस, गोश्त 2 **the flesh** [sing] मानव शरीर एवं उसकी इच्छाएँ/ज़रूरतें : the pleasures/sins of the *flesh* 3 फलों, सब्ज़ियों का गूदा ■ **flesh and blood** भौतिक शरीर एवं भावनाएँ; सामान्य मानव प्रकृति **one's (own) flesh and blood** अपने निकट संबंधी ▸ **fleshy** *adj* मांसल; गूदेदार।

flex / फ़्लेक्स् / *verb* हाथों, जोड़ों या पेशियों को कसरत के लिए मोड़ना, घुमाना ■ **flex one's muscles** (घमंड से या चेतावनी के लिए) बाहुबल का प्रदर्शन करना।

flexible / फ़्लेक्सबल् / *adj* 1 लचीला : *flexible plastic tubing* 2 (व्यक्ति) नई परिस्थितियों के अनुसार स्वयं को ढाल लेने वाला; परिवर्तनीय : *You need to be more flexible and imaginative in your approach.* ○ *Our plans are quite flexible.* ▸ **flexibility** *noun* लचीलापन।

flick / फ़्लिक् / *noun* 1 अचानक हलका प्रहार : *We have electricity at the flick of a switch.* 2 पुस्तक आदि को सरसरी नज़र से देखना ▸ **flick** *verb* 1 अचानक हलका प्रहार करना, विशेषत: अँगुलियों से : *flicked dust off his collar* 2 अचानक तेज़ी से हिलना/हिलाना : *The cow's tail flicked from side to side.* 3 **flick sth (on/off)** मशीन आदि चालू बंद करने के लिए जल्दी से बटन दबाना।

flicker / फ़्लिकर् / *verb* 1 (प्रकाश या ज्योति) टिमटिमाना, झिलमिलाना; (किसी भावना को) ज़रा-सी देर के लिए अनुभव करना : *A suspicion flickered through her mind.* 2 हलके-से आगे-पीछे घुमाना/गति करना : *Shadows flickered across the garden.* ▸ **flicker** *noun* 1 टिम-टिमाने वाली रोशनी 2 (भावना की) क्षणिक अनुभूति।

flight[1] / फ़्लाइट् / *noun* 1 उड़ना; उड़ान; उड़ानपथ : *the flight of an arrow* 2 (हवाई जहाज़ की) उड़ान 3 **flight of sth** चिड़ियों या उड़ने वाली वस्तुओं का झुंड 4 सीढ़ियों की कतार 5 **flight of sth**

कल्पनाशील परंतु अव्यावहारिक विचार : *wild flights of fancy/imagination* ▸ **flightless** *adj* उड़ने में असमर्थ (कीट या पक्षी)।

flight[2] / फ़्लाइट् / *noun* [*sing*] भागना, पलायन ■ **put sb to flight** भगा देना **take (to) flight** भाग जाना।

flimsy / फ़्लिम्ज़ि / *adj* (-ier, -iest) 1 (कपड़ा) पतला और हलका; (सामग्री या पदार्थ) शीघ्र टूटने या नष्ट होने वाला : *a flimsy cardboard box* 2 कमज़ोर; न जँचने वाला : *a flimsy excuse.*

flinch / फ़्लिन्च् / *verb* 1 **flinch (at sth)** दर्द, डर या घबराहट से अचानक पीछे हटना : *She flinched away from the dog.* 2 **flinch from sth/from doing sth** किसी (अप्रिय) बात से पीछे हटना/बचना/के बारे में न सोचना।

fling / फ़्लिङ् / *verb* (*pt, pp* **flung** / फ़्लङ् /) 1 (गुस्से से) फेंकना, दे मारना 2 (किसी वस्तु या व्यक्ति को) जल्दी से कहीं ज़ोर से पटक देना 3 हाथ पैर इधर-उधर अचानक पटकना 4 **fling sth (at sb)** (गुस्से में) कुछ कहना ▸ **fling** *noun* (अनौप) थोड़े समय की रंगरलियाँ; हलका-फुलका इश्क़।

flint / फ़्लिन्ट् / *noun* चकमक पत्थर, जिस पर लोहा रगड़ने से चिनगारियाँ निकलती हैं; सिगरेट-लाईटर में लगा ऐसा पत्थर।

flip / फ़्लिप् / *verb* (-pp-) 1 **flip (over)** अचानक पलट जाना या पलटा देना : *The plane crashed and flipped over.* 2 तेज़ी से स्विच खोलना या बंद करना 3 (सिक्का आदि) उछालना 4 (अप) अचानक गुस्सा होना या उत्तेजित एवं उत्साहित होना ■ **flip through sth** तेज़ी से (पुस्तक के) पृष्ठ पलटना।

flippant / फ़्लिपन्ट् / *adj* ढीठ; चंचल; शोख़ ▸ **flippancy** *noun*।

flipper / फ़्लिपर् / *noun* 1 कुछ समुद्री जीवों (जैसे पेंग्विन) का वह अंग जिसकी सहायता से वे तैरते हैं 2 गहरे समुद्र में तैरने

के लिए रबर या प्लास्टिक का उपकरण जो पैरों में पहना जाता है।

flirt / फ़्लर्ट् / verb 1 flirt (with sb) इश्कबाज़ी करना, प्रेम का खिलवाड़ करना 2 flirt (with sth) (किसी योजना के बारे में) चलताऊ ढंग से सोचना; ख़तरा मोल लेना : *flirt with danger/death* ▶ flirt noun बहुतों से प्रेम का खिलवाड़ करने वाला व्यक्ति **flirtation** noun **flirtatious** adj.

flit / फ़्लिट् / verb (-tt-) flit (from A to B) फुदकना; (उड़कर) जल्दी-जल्दी स्थान बदलना।

float¹ / फ़्लोट् / verb 1 उतराना, तिरना 2 उतरते रहना,(हवा में) बहना : *A balloon floated across the sky.* 3 विचार के लिए सुझाना : *float a couple of ideas* 4 (वाणिज्य) नई कंपनी खोलना/ खोलने के लिए शेयर बेचना ▶ floating adj अस्थिर।

float² / फ़्लोट् / noun 1 कॉर्क का टुकड़ा जो मछली पकड़ने की लग्गी को डूबने नहीं देता है 2 (वाणिज्य) कंपनी के शेयर पहली बार बेचने की प्रक्रिया।

flock / फ़्लॉक् / noun 1 flock (of sth) चिड़ियों या पशुओं का झुंड 2 व्यक्तियों का बहुत बड़ा जत्था/झुंड ▶ flock verb झुंड में होना/एकत्र होना।

flog / फ़्लॉग् / verb (-gg-) कोड़े से पीटना।

flood¹ / फ़्लड् / noun 1 बाढ़ 2 flood (of sth) किसी वस्तु की बहुत बड़ी मात्रा या संख्या; मूसलाधार वर्षा।

flood² / फ़्लड् / verb 1 बाढ़ आ जाना; जल से भर जाना या भर देना 2 बड़ी संख्या या मात्रा में भेजना/आ जाना 3 (विचार या भावना) अचानक बहुत तीव्रता से आना : *A great sense of relief flooded over him.*

floodlight / फ़्लडलाइट् / noun बहुत तेज़ प्रकाश जो इमारतों या क्रीड़ा क्षेत्रों को सुप्रकाशित करता है ▶ floodlight verb (pt, pp **floodlighted** या **floodlit** / फ़्लडलिट् /) तेज़ रोशनी से किसी बड़े क्षेत्र को प्रकाशित करना।

floor¹ / फ़्लॉर् / noun 1 फ़र्श 2 समुद्र, भू क्षेत्र या गुफा की सतह 3 मंज़िल, एक ही सतह पर के सभी कमरे आदि : *Her office is on the second floor.* 4 the floor संसद में सदस्यों के बैठने का स्थान; संसद, मीटिंग आदि में बोलने का अधिकार : *speak from the floor* ○ *The floor is yours—present the proposal.* 5 क़ीमतों या वेतन का निम्नतम स्तर ■ hold the floor लंबे समय तक भाषण देना ▶ flooring noun फ़र्श बनाने का सामान।

floor² / फ़्लॉर् / verb 1 (अनौप) पराजित करना या गड़बड़ा देना 2 धक्का मारकर नीचे गिरा देना 3 कमरे में फ़र्श लगाना : *The room is floored with pine.*

flop / फ़्लॉप् / verb (-pp-) 1 असहाय होकर गिरना या डगमगाते हुए चलना 2 थककर चूर होने से बैठ जाना या गिर पड़ना 3 (अनौप) बुरी तरह असफल हो जाना : *His first record flopped.* ▶ flop noun 1 डगमगाती चाल 2 (अनौप) पूर्ण विफलता **floppy** adj ढीले-ढाले लटकना **floppy** noun (ओप **floppy disk** भी) कंप्यूटर फ़्लॉपी।

flora / फ़्लॉरा / noun (किसी समय या स्थान विशेष के) सभी पेड़-पौधे → **fauna** देखिए।

floral / फ़्लॉरल् / adj फूलों से बना हुआ; फूलों के डिज़ाइन से सज्जित : *floral wallpaper.*

florid / फ़्लॉरिड् / adj 1 गुलाबी लाल (चेहरा) 2 (प्राय: अपमा) अत्यधिक अलंकृत : *a florid style of writing.*

florist / फ़्लॉरिस्ट् / noun फूल बेचने वाला; फूलों का उत्पादन करने वाला।

flotilla / फ़्लटिला; US फ़्लो'टिला / noun (विशेषत: नौसेना का) बेड़ा।

flounder / फ़्लाउन्डर् / verb 1 (पानी में डूबते हुए या कीचड़, बर्फ़ आदि में फँसकर) छटपटाना 2 कुछ कहते हुए (या करते हुए) हिचकिचाकर या आश्चर्यचकित होकर भूल कर बैठना : *The question took him by* *surprise and he floundered for a while.*

flour / फ़्लाउअर् / *noun* आटा ▸ **flour** *verb* किसी वस्तु पर आटा बुरकना।

flourish / फ़्लरिश् / *verb* 1 फलना-फूलना; समृद्ध होना 2 ध्यान आकर्षित करने को कुछ लहराना ▸ **flourish** *noun* 1 ध्यान आकर्षित करने के लिए घुमाव 2 कुछ करने का प्रभावी ढंग : *The exhibition opened with a flourish—a huge firework display.*

flout / फ़्लाउट् / *verb* आज्ञापालन से इनकार करना; क़ानून का उल्लंघन करना।

flow / फ़्लो / *verb* 1 (द्रव आदि) बहना; (रक्त आदि) संचरण होना 2 (बालों, पोशाक का) लटकना : *long flowing robes* 3 किसी चीज़ का स्वाभाविक रूप से बहना : *Conversation flowed freely throughout the meal.* 4 ज्वार का बढ़ना : *The tide began to flow, covering our footprints.* ▸ **flow** *noun* 1 **flow (of sth/sb)** बहने की गति 2 **flow (of sth)** (किसी वस्तु का) निरंतर उत्पादन एवं आपूर्ति : *the constant flow of information* 3 अंदर आता हुआ ज्वार : *the ebb and flow of the sea.*

flower / फ़्लाउअर् / *noun* 1 फूल 2 **the flower of sth** (साहि) किसी चीज़ का सर्वश्रेष्ठ भाग : *the flower of the nation's youth* ▸ **flower** *verb* फूल उत्पन्न करना/होना; पूर्ण विकसित होना **flowered** *adj* **flowery** *adj.*

flu / फ़्लू / (और **influenza** भी) *noun* फ़्लू, ज़ुकाम के साथ बुखार।

fluctuate / फ़्लक्चुएट् / *verb* **fluctuate (between sth and sth)** (आकार, क़ीमतों आदि का) ऊँचा-नीचा होना; बार-बार बदलना; (भावनाओं, दृष्टिकोण आदि का) अनियमितता से बार-बार बदलना ▸ **fluctuation** / फ़्लक्चुएश्न् / *noun* उतार-चढ़ाव : *fluctuations of temperature.*

fluent / फ़्लूअन्ट् / *adj* 1 **fluent (in sth)** (भाषा, विशेषत: विदेशी भाषा) धाराप्रवाह बोलने वाला (व्यक्ति) 2 कार्य आसानी और कुशलता से करने वाला : *a fluent dancer/musician* ▸ **fluency** / फ़्लूअन्सि / *noun* धाराप्रवाह बोलने का गुण **fluently** *adv.*

fluff / फ़्लफ़् / *noun* रोयाँ; मुलायम ऊनी कंबल के रोयें; जानवरों या पक्षियों का मुलायम फ़र ▸ **fluffy** *adj.*

fluid / फ़्लूइड / *noun* तरल पदार्थ (जैसे द्रव और गैस) ▸ **fluid** *adj* सरलता से बहने वाला पदार्थ, तरल; *(औप)* (विचार) अनिश्चित परिवर्तनशील; (गति) सरल प्रवाहयुक्त।

fluke / फ़्लूक् / *noun* (प्राय: *sing*) सुखद संयोग एवं भाग्य से प्राप्त (न कि परिश्रम आदि से) : *Passing the exam was a real fluke — he did no work at all.*

fluorescent / फ़्लॉ रेसन्ट्; फ़्लूअ रेसन्ट्/ *adj* प्रतिदीप्त : *a fluorescent lamp.*

flurry / फ़्लरि / *noun* 1 (पानी या हवा का) झोंका 2 **flurry (of sth)** हलचल; एक साथ घटित बहुत-सी घटनाएँ।

flush[1] / फ़्लश् / *verb* 1 (व्यक्ति का चेहरा) स्वास्थ्य, बीमारी, नशे या भावना के कारण लाल हो जाना 2 **flush sth (out)** (शौचालय या नाली को) पानी के बहाव से साफ़ करना; हो जाना : *Please flush the toilet after you've used it.* 3 **flush sth away, down, through, etc (sth)** पानी के बहाव से कोई चीज़ नष्ट, ख़त्म या साफ़ करना : *He tore up the letter and flushed it down the lavatory.* ▸ **flushed** *adj* **flushed (with sth)** भावावेग से उत्तेजित।

flush[2] / फ़्लश् / *noun* 1 चेहरे की लालिमा 2 भावावेग 3 पानी का बहाव या प्रवाह 4 (पौधों की) ताज़ी उपज या विकास।

fluster / फ़्लस्टर् / *verb* घबरा जाना; व्याकुल हो जाना ▸ **fluster** *noun* घबराहट; व्याकुलता।

flute /फ़्लूट/ *noun* बाँसुरी, मुरली ▸ **flutist** *noun (US)* = flautist.

flutter /'फ़्लटर्/ *verb* 1 (पंखों का) फड़फड़ाना 2 (कीट, पक्षी आदि का) मँडराना 3 (हृदय का) तेज़ी से धक-धक करना : *His heart fluttered with excitement.* ▸ **flutter** *noun* 1 (प्राय: *sing*) फड़फड़ाहट 2 व्याकुलता; भावावेग : *feel a flutter of panic* 3 दिल की धक-धक 4 हलचल : *to be in a flutter.*

flux /फ़्लक्स्/ *noun* 1 निरंतर परिवर्तन; अस्थिरता की स्थिति 2 **flux (of sth)** (विशेषत: तक) बहाव, प्रवाह की प्रक्रिया : *a flux of neutrons.*

fly¹ /फ़्लाइ/ *verb (pt flew* /फ़्लू/; *pp flown* /फ़्लोन्/) 1 (चिड़िया, कीट-पतंग या हवाई जहाज़ का) उड़ना 2 हवाई जहाज़ को उड़ाना; हवाई जहाज़ से सफ़र करना : *I'm flying to Hong Kong tomorrow.* 3 तेज़ी से दौड़ना या चलना; तेज़ गति से जाना : *The train was flying along.* 4 (समय का) तेज़ी से गुज़रना : *Doesn't time fly?* 5 (ध्वजा का) ऊँचाई पर उड़ना ताकि सभी देख सकें 6 मुक्त रूप से घूमना/ उड़ना : *hair flying (about) in the wind* 7 (साहि) कहीं से/किसी से बच निकलना : *Both suspects have flown the country.* ■ **fly high** सफलता प्राप्त करना **fly into a rage, passion, temper, etc** सहसा क्रुद्ध हो जाना **let fly (at sb/sth) (with sth)** (किसी को अपने क्रोध का) निशाना बनाना, हमला करना (शब्दों या हाथों से)।

fly² /फ़्लाइ/ (*pl flies*) *noun* मक्खी।

fly³ /फ़्लाइ/ *noun* पैंट का सामने का खुला भाग जो ज़िप या बटन से बंद होता है।

flyer (flier भी) /'फ़्लाइअर्/ *noun* 1 विमानचालक; विमानयात्री 2 पतंगबाज़ 3 (किसी विशेष तरीक़े से) उड़ने वाली वस्तु 4 सूचना-पत्र : *to hand out flyers for a new café* 5 तेज़ी से चलने वाली वस्तु/ व्यक्ति।

flying /'फ़्लाइइङ्/ *adj* उड़ने वाली (वस्तु); उड़ने में सक्षम ■ **get off to/have a flying start** बहुत अच्छी शुरुआत करना **with flying colours** बहुत अच्छी तरह/ अच्छे अंकों से (सफल होना) ▸ **flying visit** *noun* एक संक्षिप्त भेंट।

flyover /'फ़्लाइओवर्/ (*US* **overpass**) *noun* रास्ते के ऊपर से जाने वाला पुल।

foal /फ़ोल्/ *noun* घोड़े या गधे का बच्चा, बछेड़ा ▸ **foal** *verb* बछेड़े को जन्म देना।

foam /फ़ोम्/ *noun* 1 झाग, फेन 2 झाग उत्पन्न करने वाला पदार्थ : *shaving foam* 3 स्पंज जैसा हलका रबर या प्लास्टिक : *foam rubber* ▸ **foam** *verb* झाग छोड़ना, फेनदार बनाना **foamy** *adj.*

focus /'फ़ोकस्/ *noun (pl* **focuses** या **foci** /'फ़ोसाइ /) 1 **focus (for/on sth)** क्रियाविधि, रुचि आदि का केंद्र बिंदु : *an intellectual focus* 2 फ़ोकस, किरणकेंद्र 3 (कैमरे से देखने पर) वस्तु की स्पष्ट रूपरेखा दिखाने वाला बिंदु : *The focus on my camera is faulty.* ▸ **focus** *verb* (-s- या -ss-) 1 **focus (sth) (on sb/ sth)** ध्यान, भाव, प्रयास आदि केंद्रित करना 2 **focus sth (on sth)** (कैमरे को) फ़ोकस करना; प्रकाश के अनुसार (आँखों को) अनुकूल बनाना **focused** *adj.*

fodder /'फ़ॉडर्/ *noun* (पशुओं का) चारा, सूखी घास आदि।

foe /फ़ो/ *noun* (अप्र या औप) शत्रु।

foetus (*US* **fetus**) /'फ़ीटस्/ *noun* भ्रूण, गर्भ में विकसित होता बच्चा ▸ **foetal** *adj.*

fog /फ़ॉग्/ *noun* कोहरा ▸ **fog** *verb* (-gg-) 1 कोहरे से ढक जाना या ढक देना 2 चकित/भ्रमित कर देना; मुश्किल बना देना : *obscure arguments that only fog (up) the real issues* **foggy** *adj* (-ier, -iest) 1 कोहरे के कारण अस्पष्ट 2 (विचार आदि) भ्रमपूर्ण/अस्पष्ट।

foil¹ /फ़ॉइल्/ *noun* 1 (धातु को पीटकर बनाई हुई काग़ज़ जैसी पतली) पन्नी 2 वस्तु या व्यक्ति जो वैषम्य से दूसरे के गुण को

प्रदर्शित करता है : *The pale walls provide a perfect foil for the brightly painted dishes and jars.*

foil² / फ़ॉइल / *verb* (किसी षड्यंत्र को) विफल कर देना, व्यक्ति को योजना पूरी न करने देना : *His attempt to deceive us was foiled.*

foist / फ़ॉइस्ट / *verb* ■ foist sth on/ upon sb चालाकी से कोई वस्तु किसी व्यक्ति के गले मढ़ देना (कभी-कभी बल-पूर्वक)।

fold¹ / फ़ोल्ड / *verb* 1 fold sth (up); fold sth (back, down, over, etc) मोड़ना, तहाना : *fold the sheet down* 2 fold A in B/fold B round A किसी चीज़ को दूसरी वस्तु में लपेटना/ढकना : *Fold the glass bowl in newspaper.* 3 fold (up) मोड़ना; मुड़ सकना (ताकि आसानी से उठाया या रखा जा सके) : *The garden table folds (up) flat.* ■ fold sb/sth in one's arms बाँहों में भरना, लिपटा लेना : *The father folded the child in his arms.* ▸ fold *noun* 1 (कपड़े की) तह; तहाने से बनी रेखा 2 पहाड़ी में ख़ाली स्थान।

fold² / फ़ोल्ड / *noun* 1 भेड़शाला, बाड़ा 2 the fold [*sing*] रक्षात्मक या एक ही मत वाले लोगों का समूह : *leave the party fold.*

-fold *suff* (प्रत्यय) गुणा : *tenfold* ∘ *two-fold.*

folder / फ़ोल्डर / *noun* काग़ज़ आदि रखने के लिए गत्ते या प्लास्टिक का आवरण।

foliage / फ़ोलिइज़ / *noun* (पेड़ों की) पत्तियाँ आदि।

folk / फ़ोक् / *noun* 1 (*US* folks भी) लोग, जनसाधारण; किसी क्षेत्र विशेष या परंपरा से आए लोग/रीति-रिवाज़/संगीत आदि : *country folk* ∘ *a folk concert* 2 folks [*pl*] (अनौप) अपने संबंधी, परिवार के सदस्य : *How are your folks?* ▸ folk *adj* (कला, संस्कृति आदि) लोक, जनसाधारण

से उत्पन्न : *folk music* **folk-dance/ -song** *noun* लोकनृत्य, लोकगीत **folk-lore** / फ़ोक्लॉर / *noun* लोक साहित्य, लोकवार्ता।

follicle / फ़ॉलिकल् / *noun* रोमछिद्र, त्वचा में छिद्र जहाँ से बाल उगते हैं।

follow / फ़ॉलो / *verb* 1 follow sth (by/ with sth) किसी के पीछे-पीछे जाना या रहना 2 (सड़क के साथ-साथ) चलते रहना 3 अनुसरण करना, पालन करना : *follow the instructions* 4 (किसी व्यवसाय आदि में) लगना : *follow a legal career* 5 (किसी विषय को) समझना, ध्यान से सुनना 6 follow (on/from sth); follow (on from sth) परिणाम निकलना : *Disease often follows (on from) star-vation.* 7 (पुस्तक, फ़िल्म आदि) किसी के जीवन/घटनाओं पर आधारित : *The novel follows the fortunes of a village community in Scotland.* ■ as follows निम्नलिखित, जैसा कि अब दिया जा रहा है **follow sth up** 1 अनुवर्तन करना; काम को आगे बढ़ाना 2 गहराई से छानबीन करना ▸ follower *noun* समर्थक; अनुयायी।

following / फ़ॉलोइङ् / *adj* 1 (समय के अनुसार) अगला, आगे आने वाला 2 निम्न-लिखित या कथित : *Answer the follow-ing questions.* ▸ following *noun* 1 शिष्यसमुदाय; अनुयायीगण 2 the fol-lowing निम्नलिखित (कथित) **follow-ing** *prep* परिणामस्वरूप : *Following his arrest there were demonstra-tions in many parts of the country.*

folly / फ़ॉलि / *noun* (*pl* follies) मूर्खता; मूर्खतापूर्ण काम।

foment / फ़ोमेन्ट / *verb* 1 (असंतोष, अ-व्यवस्था आदि) भड़काना, उकसाना 2 (प्रा) (दर्द कम करने के लिए शरीर को गरम पानी या कपड़े से) सेंकना ▸ fomentation *noun* प्रोत्साहन; सेंक; सिंकाई का कपड़ा आदि।

fond / फ़ॉन्ड / *adj* (-er, -est) 1 स्नेहशील;

प्रिय : *fond memories* 2 fond of sb/ (doing) sth बहुत पसंद करना; में आनंद लेना : *fond of music* 3 (आशाओं/ आकांक्षाओं को) बनाए रखने वाला, यद्यपि उनके पूरे होने की आशा बहुत कम है : *fond hopes of success* ▸ fondly *adv* fondness *noun*.

fondle / 'फ़ॉन्ड्ल् / *verb* दुलारना, प्यार से थपथपाना।

food / फ़ूड् / *noun* 1 भोजन, आहार 2 आहार/भोजन विशेष : *baby/health food* ■ food for thought विचारणीय विषय ▸ foodstuff *noun* (प्राय: *pl*) खाद्य पदार्थ।

fool / फ़ूल् / *noun* 1 (*अपमा*) मूर्ख, बेव- कूफ़ 2 (पूर्व में) विदूषक, मसखरा ■ act/ play the fool बेवकूफ़ी की हँसी-दिल्लगी करना make a fool of sb मूर्ख बना देना ▸ fool *verb* 1 fool (about/around) मूर्ख की तरह आचरण करना; बहाना बनाना, मज़ाक़ करना 2 fool sb (into doing sth) मूर्ख बनाना : *You can't fool me!*

foolhardy / फ़ूल्हार्डी / *adj* दुस्साहसी।

foolish / 'फ़ूलिश् / *adj* 1 (व्यक्ति) मूर्ख; (कार्य) मूर्खतापूर्ण 2 नासमझ।

foolproof / 'फ़ूल्प्रूफ़् / *adj* इतना सरल कि मूर्ख भी बिना ग़लती किए काम पूरा कर सके : *a foolproof security system.*

foolscap / 'फ़ूल्स्कैप्/ *noun* (17x13.5 इंच का काग़ज़) फुलिस्केप काग़ज़।

foot¹ / फ़ुट् / *noun* (*pl* feet / फ़ीट् /) 1 पैर, पाँव 2 (*pl* feet या मापन में foot; *संक्षि* ft) 12 इंच का माप, फुट 3 the foot of sth बिस्तर का आखिरी किनारा; किसी वस्तु का निचला भाग : *at the foot of the stairs/ the page* 4 (कविता में) पद 5 (*प्रा* या *औप*) पैदल सेना ■ my foot! (*अनौप*) बकवास! बेकार! on foot पैदल put one's foot down किसी चीज़ का दृढ़ता से विरोध करना ▸ footprint *noun* पदचिह्न, पैरों की छाप footstep *noun* क़दम; पदचिह्न।

foot² / फ़ुट् / *verb* ■ foot the bill (*अनौप*) बिल के भुगतान के लिए तैयार/ ज़िम्मेदार होना।

football / 'फ़ुट्बॉल् / *noun* फुटबाल का खेल।

footfall / 'फ़ुट्फ़ॉल् / *noun* (*औप*) पद- चाप, पैरों की आहट।

foothills / 'फ़ुट्हिल्स् / *noun* [*pl*] पर्वत के नीचे की छोटी पहाड़ियाँ।

foothold / 'फ़ुट्होल्ड्/ *noun* 1 पैर जमाने की जगह 2 आधार।

footing / 'फ़ुटिंग् / *noun* 1 पाँव की मज़बूत पकड़ 2 लोगों से संबंध, सामाजिक प्रतिष्ठा 3 आधार, नींव।

footlights / 'फ़ुट्लाइट्स् / *noun* [*pl*] (रंगमंच पर) सामने से लगे लैंप।

footman / 'फ़ुट्मन्/ *noun* (*pl* footmen / 'फ़ुट्मेन् /) अतिथियों को प्रवेश देने वाला व्यक्ति, द्वारपाल।

footnote / 'फ़ुट्नोट् / *noun* पृष्ठ के नीचे मुद्रित अंश, पाद-टिप्पणी।

footpath / 'फ़ुट्पाथ् / *noun* सड़क के किनारे की पटरी, पगडंडी।

for¹ / फ़र्; फ़ॉर् / *prep* 1 (व्यक्ति/वस्तु या समय) के लिए : *There's a letter for you.* ○ *I'm going away for a few days.* 2 के पक्ष में : *Are you for or against the proposal?* 3 के बदले में (पाने के लिए) : *exchange one's car for a new one* 4 के कारण : *The town is famous for its cathedral.* 5 की ओर से, किसी के प्रतिनिधि के रूप में 6 (कोई कार्य या उद्देश्य दर्शाने के लिए) : *go for a walk* 7 किसी को सहायता या लाभ पहुँचाने के लिए : *What can I do for you?* 8 (गंतव्य या लक्ष्य दर्शाने के लिए) : *Is this the bus for Agra?* 9 किसी व्यक्ति/वस्तु से संबंधित : *anxious for sb's safety.*

for² / फ़र्; फ़ॉर् / *conj* (*अप्र* या *औप*) चूँकि, क्योंकि : *We listened eagerly, for he brought news of our fami- lies.*

forbear / फ़ॉर्'बेअर् / verb (pt **forbore** / फ़ॉर्'बॉर् /; pp **forborne** / फ़ॉर्'बॉर्न् /) **forbear (from sth/doing sth)** (औप) (किसी काम से) बचे रहना, दूर रहना; अपना व्यवहार और भावनाएँ नियंत्रण में रखना ▸ **forbearance** / फ़ॉर्'बेअरन्स् / noun (औप) धैर्य; सहिष्णुता **forbearing** adj धैर्यवान, सहिष्णु।

forbid / फ़र्'बिड् / verb (pt **forbade** / फ़र्'बैड्; फ़र्'बेड्; pp **forbidden** / फ़र् 'बिड्न् /) 1 (किसी को कोई काम–विशेष करने से) मना करना, रोकना : I can't forbid you from seeing him again. 2 (औप) कुछ मुश्किल या असंभव बना देना ▸ **forbidding** adj कठोर; धमकाने वाला : a forbidding appearance.

force¹ / फ़ॉर्स् / noun 1 शक्ति, बल; हिंसक बल प्रयोग 2 ताकत या प्रभाव : the full force of her argument 3 (व्यक्ति, वस्तु आदि की) परिवर्तनकारी शक्तियाँ : the forces of evil 4 (भौतिकी) बल : the force of gravity 5 **the forces** [pl] सेना (थल, जल या वायु सेना) : join the forces ■ **bring sth/come into force** (क़ानून, नियम आदि) लागू होना, प्रयुक्त होना **in force** 1 (व्यक्ति) बड़ी संख्या में 2 (क़ानून, नियम आदि का) लागू होना।

force² / फ़ॉर्स् / verb 1 (किसी को/अपने आप को) बाध्य करना : force a confession out of sb 2 बल प्रयोग करना (कुछ पाने के लिए) 3 शक्ति लगाकर कुछ तोड़ना : force (open) a door ▸ **forced** adj 1 कृत्रिम 2 इच्छा के विरुद्ध **forced labour** noun बाध्य होकर किया गया कठिन श्रम, बेगार।

forceful / फ़ॉर्स्फ़ुल् / adj शक्तियुक्त, प्रभावशाली।

forceps / फ़ॉर्सेप्स् / noun [pl] (डॉक्टरों द्वारा प्रयुक्त) चिमटी।

forcible / फ़ॉर्सब्ल् / adj बल प्रयोग द्वारा (किया कार्य); बलप्रयोग का प्रदर्शन ▸ **forcibly** adv : be forcibly restrained.

fore / फ़ॉर् / adj अगला भाग ▸ **fore** noun ■ **be/come to the fore** प्रमुखता से सामने होना/आना ▸ **fore** adv (वाहन के) अग्रभाग में स्थित : in the fore of the ship.

fore- pref (पूर्वपद) 1 (स्थान में) सामने वाला या पहला : foreground 2 (समय में) पहले या पूर्ववर्ती : forefather/foretell.

forearm¹ / फ़ॉर्आर्म् / verb (किसी ख़तरे, हमले आदि के लिए) पहले से तैयार रहना।

forearm² / फ़ॉर्आर्म् / noun कोहनी से कलाई तक का भाग।

forebode / फ़ॉर्'बोड् / verb (प्रा या साहि) संकेत देना या चेतावनी देना कि कोई संकट आ रहा है ▸ **foreboding** noun आने वाले संकट का पूर्वाभास, पूर्वज्ञान।

forecast / फ़ॉर्कास्ट्; US फ़ॉर्कैस्ट् / verb (pt, pp **forecast** या **forecasted**) पूर्वानुमान लगाना; (मौसम की) पूर्वसूचना देना ▸ **forecast** noun पूर्वसूचना; पूर्वानुमान।

forecourt / फ़ॉर्कॉर्ट् / noun भवन के सामने का खुला क्षेत्र।

forefather / फ़ॉर्फ़ादर् / noun (प्रायः pl) पूर्वज, पुरखा।

forefinger / फ़ॉर्फ़िङ्गर् / (**index finger** भी) noun तर्जनी (अँगूठे के बग़ल वाली) अँगुली।

forefront / फ़ॉर्फ़्रन्ट् / noun **the forefront (of sth)** सबसे आगे का या सबसे महत्त्वपूर्ण भाग : in/at the forefront of my mind.

foregone / फ़ॉर्गॉन् / adj ■ **a foregone conclusion** पूर्वनिश्चित निष्कर्ष।

foreground / फ़ॉर्ग्राउन्ड् / noun **the foreground** सबसे महत्त्वपूर्ण या सबसे मुख्य स्थिति; अग्र भाग, सबसे सामने दिखने वाला अंश : The figure in the foreground is the artist's mother.

forehand / फ़ॉर्हैन्ड् / noun [sing] (टेनिस में) हथेली को बाहर की तरफ़ करके बॉल मारने का तरीक़ा।

forehead / 'फ़ॉर्हेड्; 'फ़ॉरिड्; *US* 'फ़ॉरुड् / *noun* ललाट, मस्तक, माथा।

foreign / 'फ़ॉरन् / *adj* 1 विदेशी; विदेश से संबंधित : *foreign affairs* 2 **foreign to sb/sth** (औप) अस्वाभाविक, असंबद्ध 3 (औप) बाहरी, बाहर से आने वाली (वस्तु) : *a foreign body in the eye* ▸ **foreigner** *noun* 1 विदेशी व्यक्ति 2 अनजान व्यक्ति या बाहरी व्यक्ति।

foreman / 'फ़ॉर्मन् / *noun* (*pl* **foremen** / 'फ़ॉर्मेन् /) 1 फ़ोरमैन (मैकेनिक) 2 जूरी का अध्यक्ष (मुखिया)।

foremost / 'फ़ॉर्मोस्ट / *adj* सर्वप्रथम; सबसे महत्त्वपूर्ण : *the foremost painter of his time* ▸ **foremost** *adv* मुख्यतः, सबसे पहले।

forename / 'फ़ॉर्नेम् / *noun* (औप) प्रथम नाम, वंशनाम से पहले का नाम।

forensic / फ़'रेनसिक; फ़'रेनज़िक् / *adj* पुलिस छानबीन और क़ानूनी समस्याओं में सहायक वैज्ञानिक परीक्षण : *forensic medicine/science.*

forerunner / 'फ़ॉर्रनर् / *noun* **forerunner (of sb/sth)** पहले आने वाला व्यक्ति/ वस्तु जो अन्य को प्रभावित करती है; कुछ घटित होने का संकेत : *forerunners of modern diesel engine.*

foresee / फ़ॉर्'सी / *verb* (*pt* **foresaw** / फ़ॉर्'सॉ /; *pp* **foreseen** / फ़ॉर्'सीन् /) पहले से जान लेना, दूरदर्शिता रखना ▸ **foreseeable** *adj.*

foreshadow /फ़ॉर्'शैडो/ *verb* पूर्वाभास, पूर्वलक्षण देना : *The increase in taxes had been foreshadowed in the minister's speech.*

foresight / 'फ़ॉर्साइट् / *noun* दूरदर्शिता, भविष्य की आवश्यकताओं के लिए तैयारी : *a lack of foresight.*

forest / 'फ़ॉरिस्ट / *noun* जंगल, वन ▸ **forested** *adj* जंगल से ढका हुआ **forestry** *noun* जंगल उगाने एवं पालने की विद्या।

forestall / फ़ॉर्'स्टॉल / *verb* पहले से ही रोकने का प्रबंध करना; पहले से ही रोकथाम करना : *forestall a rival.*

foretell / फ़ॉर्'टेल् / *verb* (*pt, pp* **foretold**/फ़ॉर्'टोल्ड्/) (औप) भविष्यवाणी करना : *It is impossible to foretell how the game will end.*

forethought/'फ़ॉर्थॉट्/*noun* दूरदर्शिता, पूर्वविचार।

forever / फ़र्'एवर् / *adv* 1 सदा के लिए, सर्वदा : *I'll love you forever!* 2 हमेशा।

forewarn / फ़ॉर्'वॉर्न् / *verb* **forewarn sb (of sth)** पहले से चेतावनी देना।

foreword / 'फ़ॉर्वर्ड् / *noun* प्राक्कथन, प्रस्तावना।

forfeit / 'फ़ॉर्फ़िट् / *verb* ज़ब्त हो जाना, अधिकार से वंचित हो जाना ▸ **forfeit** *noun* ज़ब्त वस्तु **forfeiture** /'फ़ॉर्फ़िचर्/ *noun* **forfeiture (of sth)** ज़ब्ती।

forge¹ / फ़ॉर्ज् / *noun* 1 भट्टी, लोहारख़ाना जहाँ तपाकर लोहा गढ़ा जाता है 2 (फ़ैक्ट्री में) ढलाईघर।

forge² / फ़ॉर्ज् / *verb* धीरे–धीरे या क्रमशः आगे बढ़ना : *forge steadily onwards* ■ **forge ahead** प्रयास करके आगे निकल जाना, दौड़ आदि में आगे हो जाना।

forge³ / फ़ॉर्ज् / *verb* 1 नक़ल बनाकर धोखा देना, जालसाज़ी करना : *forge a banknote* 2 लोहा (या धातु) गढ़कर आकार में लाना : *forge a sword* 3 कठिन श्रम से संबंध मज़बूत बनाना : *a friendship forged in adversity* ▸ **forger** *noun* जालसाज़ **forgery** / 'फ़ॉर्जरि / *noun* 1 जालसाज़ी 2 जाली वस्तु।

forget / फ़र्'गेट् / *verb* (*pt* **forgot** / फ़र् 'गॉट् /; *pp* **forgotten** / फ़र् 'गॉट्न् /) 1 **forget (about) sth** भूलना, याद न आना/रहना : *I've forgotten her name.* 2 कुछ (कार्य करना) याद न रहना 3 **forget (about) sb/sth** भुला देना, बारे में न सोचना ▸ **forgetful** *adj* 1 भुलक्कड़

2 forgetful of sb/sth लापरवाह forgetfulness noun.

forgive / फ़र्'गिव् / verb (pt forgave / फ़र्'गेव् /; pp forgiven / फ़र्'गिव्न् /) 1 forgive sth; forgive sb (for sth/ doing sth) क्षमा करना 2 forgive sb (for doing sth) (नम्र व्यवहार के लिए प्रयुक्त) माफ़ करना : Please forgive me for interrupting, but... 3 ऋण माफ़ करना ▶ forgivable adj क्षम्य (अपराध आदि) forgiveness noun क्षमाशीलता; क्षमा forgiving adj क्षमाशील।

forgo / फ़ॉर्'गो / verb (pt forwent; pp forgone) विशेषत: किसी प्रिय वस्तु के बिना काम चला लेना, छोड़ देना : The workers agreed to forgo their pay increase for the sake of greater job security.

fork / फ़ॉर्क् / noun 1 काँटा (छुरी) 2 घास आदि हटाने वाला खेती का औज़ार, पाँचा 3 पेड़ या सड़क का वह स्थान जहाँ से एक या अधिक शाखाएँ फूट रही हों : Go on to the fork and turn left. 4 (प्राय: pl) साइकिल या मोटरसाइकिल का फ़ॉर्क ▶ fork verb 1 काँटे (या पाँचे से) से उठाना, खींचना या खोदना 2 (सड़क) शाखाओं में बँटना forked adj.

forlorn / फ़र्'लॉर्न् / adj 1 (व्यक्ति) उदास/ निराश; परित्यक्त 2 (स्थान) उजाड़ एवं निर्जन 3 सफलता की संभावना रहित : make a forlorn attempt to lose weight.

form¹ / फ़ॉर्म् / noun 1 रूप, बाह्य आकृति 2 विशेष गठन : different literary forms 3 विविधता; प्रकार 4 [sing] प्रचलन, रीति 5 छपा हुआ प्रपत्र, फ़ार्म 6 शारीरिक/मानसिक दशा (विशेषत: घोड़ों या खिलाड़ियों की): These exercises will keep you in form. 7 कक्षा, दर्जा : He's in the sixth form. ▶ formless adj रूपहीन, निराकार।

form² / फ़ॉर्म् / verb 1 रूप या आकार देना : Using your hands, form the dough into balls. 2 (शब्दों के) सही

रूप बनाना 3 विशिष्ट संरचना बनाना : form a queue/circle 4 होना, अस्तित्व में आना : Ice forms at 0° Celsius.

formal / 'फ़ॉर्म्ल् / adj 1 (वस्त्र, बोलचाल, लिखने या व्यवहार की शैली) औपचारिक, बाह्याचार के अनुकूल : She always has a very formal manner. 2 (बाग़ या घर की सजावट आदि) नियमित या ज्यामितीय डिज़ाइन में 3 रूढ़ि और नियम के अनुकूल 4 बाह्य आकार विषयक (न कि भीतरी यथार्थ या तत्त्वों से संबद्ध) : There is a formal resemblance between the two political systems.

formality / फ़ॉर्'मैलटि / noun (pl formalities) 1 औपचारिकता 2 (प्राय: pl) शिष्टाचार 3 औपचारिक प्रक्रिया : go through all the formalities to get a gun licence.

format / 'फ़ॉर्मैट् / noun 1 किसी चीज़ की साधारण/सामान्य व्यवस्था, रूपरेखा आदि : The talk show format is popular with viewers. 2 किताब या पत्रिका का आकार, रूप आदि : change the format of the newspaper 3 (कंप्यूटर में रखने के लिए) जानकारी एवं आँकड़ों का निर्धारण/ संगठन ▶ format verb (-tt-) 1 आँकड़े जमा करने के लिए कंप्यूटर डिस्क को तैयार करना 2 (तक) मूल-पाठ को पृष्ठ पर विशेष तरीके से सजाना/व्यवस्थित करना।

formation / फ़ॉर्'मेशन् / noun निर्माण; गठन।

formative / 'फ़ॉर्मटिव् / adj किसी चीज़ के विकास या किसी के चरित्र को महत्त्वपूर्ण रूप से प्रभावित करने वाला : a child's formative years.

former / 'फ़ॉर्मर् / adj 1 पहले समय का 2 the former दो में से पहला : The former option would be much more sensible. ▶ formerly adv पहले समय में the former pron दो में से पहला।

formidable / 'फ़ॉर्मिडब्ल् / adj 1 आकार, शक्ति या मुश्किलों के कारण भयानक,

डर पैदा करने वाला : *A formidable task lies ahead of us.* 2 दुर्जेय, विकट ▸ **formidably** *adv.*

formula / 'फ़ॉर्म्यला / *noun* (*pl* **formulas** या, वैज्ञानिक प्रयोगों में, **formulae** / 'फ़ॉर्म्यली /) 1 (गणित, भौतिकी) सूत्र रूप में नियम का कथन, फार्मूला 2 रासायनिक यौगिकों की संरचना प्रदर्शित करने वाले संकेत : H_2O *is the formula for water.* 3 **formula (for sth)** कुछ (प्राप्त) करने का ढंग या प्रक्रिया : *There's no magic formula for a perfect marriage.* 4 निर्धारित परिस्थितियों में प्रयुक्त शब्दों का निर्धारित स्वरूप : *They have been using the same legal formulae in English law courts for centuries.* ▸ **formulaic** / फ़ॉर्म्यु'लेइक / *adj* निर्धारित शब्द विन्यास से बना/अभिव्यक्त।

formulate / 'फ़ॉर्म्युलेट् / *verb* 1 प्रतिपादन करना : *formulate a rule* 2 स्पष्टतया कहना ▸ **formulation** *noun* प्रतिपादन।

forsake / फ़र्'सेक् / *verb* (*pt* **forsook** / फ़र्'सुक् /; *pp* **forsaken**/ फ़र्'सेकन् /) 1 (औप) छोड़ देना, त्याग देना 2 छोड़कर चले जाना, परित्याग कर देना : *forsake one's family and friends.*

fort / फ़ॉर्ट् / *noun* क़िला, दुर्ग; गढ़।

forth / फ़ॉर्थ् / *adv part* (कुछ idioms एवं phrasal verbs के अतिरिक्त सामान्यत: प्रा) 1 बाहर, किसी स्थान से दूर : *They set forth at dawn.* 2 आगे (गतिमान) : *Water gushed forth from a hole in the rock.* 3 (समय में) से आगे : *From that day forth he was never seen again.*

forthcoming / फ़ॉर्थ्'कमिङ् / *adj* 1 आगामी 2 ज़रूरत पड़ने पर तैयार 3 सहायता करने को तत्पर, तैयार : *The secretary at the reception desk was not very forthcoming.*

forthright / 'फ़ॉर्थ्राइट् / *adj* स्पष्टवादी, खरा (बोलने वाला)।

forthwith / ,फ़ॉर्थ्'विथ्; ,फ़ॉर्थ्'विद् / *adv* तुरंत, फ़ौरन।

fortify / 'फ़ॉर्टिफ़ाइ / *verb* (*pt, pp* **fortified**) 1 **fortify sth (against sth/sb)** किसी स्थान को रक्षा के लिए मज़बूत करना; क़िलाबंदी करना; अपना साहस बढ़ाना 2 **fortify sth (with sth)** खाद्य पदार्थ की शक्ति एवं गुण (कुछ मिलाकर) बढ़ाना : *cereal fortified with extra vitamins* ▸ **fortification** / ,फ़ॉर्टिफ़ि'केशन् / *noun* 1 क़िला/दुर्ग 2 क़िलाबंदी।

fortitude / 'फ़ॉर्टिट्यूड् ; *US* 'फ़ॉर्टिटूड् / *noun* धैर्य; साहस।

fortnight / 'फ़ॉर्ट्नाइट् / *noun* दो सप्ताह की अवधि; पखवाड़ा ▸ **fortnightly** *adj, adv* पखवाड़े में एक बार : *a fortnightly magazine.*

fortress / 'फ़ॉर्ट्रिस् / *noun* क़िला, गढ़ी।

fortunate / 'फ़ॉर्चनट् / *adj* सौभाग्यशाली।

fortune / 'फ़ॉर्चून् / *noun* 1 भाग्य, नियति; संयोग 2 (प्राय: *pl*) दैवयोग 3 भविष्य (व्यक्ति का) : *She tells your fortune by looking at the lines on your hand.* 4 समृद्धि; बड़ी संपत्ति ▸ **fortune-teller** *noun* ज्योतिषी।

forty / 'फ़ॉर्टि / *noun, pron, det* 1 चालीस (का अंक) 2 **the forties** [*pl*] 40 से 49 तक की संख्याएँ, वर्ष आदि ▸ **fortieth** / 'फ़ॉर्टिअथ् / *noun pron, det* चालीसवाँ, चालीसवाँ अंश (1/40)।

forum / 'फ़ॉरम् / *noun* (*pl* **forums**) 1 **forum (for sth)** ऐसी जगह जहाँ किसी विशेष मुद्दे पर लोग अपने विचार/मत व्यक्त कर सकते हैं 2 इस उद्देश्य के लिए संगठित/आयोजित सभा।

forward[1] / 'फ़ॉर्वर्ड् / *adj* 1 अग्रवर्ती; अग्रगतिमान 2 (आशा से अधिक) प्रगतिशील : *She's very forward for her age.* 3 भविष्य संबंधी : *forward planning*

4 ढीठ, अत्यंत उत्सुक ▸ **forwardness** *noun.*

forward² /'फ़ॉर्वई/ *adv* 1 (**forwards** भी) आगे की दिशा में, की तरफ़ 2 सफल निष्कर्ष की ओर : *an important step forward* 3 भविष्य की ओर; (समय में) आगे।

forward³ /'फ़ॉर्वई/ *verb* 1 **forward sth (to sb)** नए पते पर पत्र भेजना; (और) (सामान या सूचना) भेजना : *forward a shipment of spare parts* 2 विकास या उन्नति में सहायता करना : *forward sb's plans/career.*

forward⁴ /'फ़ॉर्वई/ *noun* अग्रवर्ती खिलाड़ी (फ़ुटबाल, हॉकी आदि में)।

fossil /'फ़ॉस्ल्/ *noun* 1 जीवाश्म, पौधों और जंतुओं के प्रागैतिहासिक कालीन अवशेष जिनसे उनकी आकृति आदि का अध्ययन किया जा सकता है 2 (*अनौप, अपमा*) अपरिवर्तनशील व्यक्ति।

foster /'फ़ॉस्टर्/ *verb* 1 विकास करना, उन्नति में प्रोत्साहन देना : *foster an interest* 2 पालन पोषण/देखभाल करना (ऐसे बच्चे की जो अपना न हो) ▸ **foster-pref** (*पूर्वपद*) (समास में प्रयुक्त) : *foster-parent* [पालक माता-पिता, धात्री (माँ)] **foster-brother/-sister** *noun* दूध-भाई/दूध-बहन, माता-पिता द्वारा पोषित होने के कारण बना भाई/बहन।

foul¹ /फ़ाउल्/ *adj* 1 (*अनौप*) वीभत्स, घिनौना : *His boss has a foul temper.* 2 गंदा, बदबूदार : *foul water* 3 दुष्ट, कपटपूर्ण 4 अशोभनीय भाषा : *use foul language* 5 ख़राब मौसम (आँधी-तूफ़ान वाला) ▸ **foul play** *noun* (खेल-कूद में) नियम विरुद्ध; बड़ा अपराध, जैसे हत्या।

foul² /फ़ाउल्/ *verb* 1 गंदा करना, घिनौना बनाना 2 **foul (sth) (up)** लिपट जाना या लिपटा लेना : *The rope fouled the propeller.* 3 (खेल में) नियम विरुद्ध खेलना।

found /फ़ाउन्ड्/ *verb* 1 **found sth on** sth नींव डालना; आधार बनाना 2 स्थापित करना (संघ, संस्था आदि) : *found a research institute* 3 नगर बसाना।

foundation /फ़ाउन्'डेश्न्/ *noun* 1 स्थापना 2 निधि (धनराशि जो किसी स्थापित कार्य के लिए प्रयुक्त हो) : *the Ford Foundation* 3 (*प्राय: pl*) नींव, बुनियाद 4 आधार (सिद्धांत, तथ्य आदि)।

founder¹ /'फ़ाउन्डर्/ *noun* संस्थापक व्यक्ति।

founder² /'फ़ाउन्डर्/ *verb* **founder (on sth)** 1 (योजना आदि) असफल हो जाना : *The project foundered as a result of lack of finance.* 2 जहाज़ का पानी भर जाने से डूबना।

foundry /'फ़ाउन्ड्रि/ *noun* ढलाई का कारख़ाना जहाँ लोहे या शीशे को पिघलाकर वस्तुएँ गढ़ी जाती हैं।

fountain /'फ़ाउन्टन्; *US* 'फ़ाउन्ट्न्/ *noun* 1 (कृत्रिम या सजावटी) फ़व्वारा 2 (*साहि*) झरना ▸ **fountain-pen** *noun* फ़ाउंटेनपेन, क़लम।

four /फ़ॉर्/ *noun, pron, det* 1 चार (का अंक) 2 चार का समूह : *make up a four at tennis* 3 (क्रिकेट में) चौका ■ **on all fours** (व्यक्ति) हाथों और घुटनों के बल ▸ **fourth** /फ़ॉर्थ्/ *pron, det* चौथा।

fourteen /फ़ॉर्'टीन्/ *noun, pron, det* चौदह (का अंक) ▸ **fourteenth** /फ़ॉर् 'टीन्थ्/ *noun, pron, det* चौदहवाँ, 1/14.

fowl /फ़ाउल्/ *noun* 1 (*pl* अपरिवर्तित या **fowls**) मुर्गा, मुर्गी 2 (*प्रा*) (कोई भी) पक्षी : *the fowls of the air.*

fox /फ़ॉक्स्/ *noun* 1 (*fem* **vixen** /'विक्स्न्/) लोमड़ी 2 (*अनौप, विशेषत: अपमा*) चालाक एवं धूर्त व्यक्ति : *He's a sly old fox.* ▸ **foxy** *adj.*

foyer /'फ़ॉइए; *US* 'फ़ॉइअर्/ *noun* होटल, थिएटर आदि में अंदर जाते ही विशाल खुला क्षेत्र जहाँ लोग मिल या प्रतीक्षा कर सकते हैं।

fraction / फ़्रैक्शन् / noun 1 अंश, ज़रा-सा हिस्सा 2 *(गणित)* भिन्न, जैसे 1/3, 1/4, 0.76 आदि ▸ **fractional** adj.

fracture / 'फ़्रैक्चर् / noun हड्डी का टूटना, अस्थिभंग; टूटना : *a fracture of the leg* ▸ **fracture** verb टूट जाना, दरार पड़ना : *He fractured his pelvis in the accident.*

fragile / फ़्रैजाइल / adj 1 भंगुर (सहज में टूटने वाला) 2 *(अनौप)* नाज़ुक; कमज़ोर ▸ **fragility** / फ़्र'जिलटि / noun.

fragment / फ़्रैग्मन्ट् / noun 1 टुकड़ा, खंड 2 अधूरा अंश, अपूर्ण : *I heard only a fragment of their conversation.* ▸ **fragment** /फ़्रैग्'मेन्ट् / verb खंड-खंड कर देना/हो जाना **fragmentary** adj अपूर्ण टुकड़ों से बना; आंशिक **fragmentation** noun.

fragrance / फ़्रेग्रन्स् / noun खुशबू, सुगंध ▸ **fragrant** / 'फ़्रेग्रन्ट्/ adj सुगंधित : *fragrant herbs/flowers.*

frail / फ़्रेल् / adj (-er, -est) 1 (व्यक्ति) सुकुमार, शरीर से दुर्बल 2 भंगुर, शीघ्र टूटने वाला : *a frail vessel* 3 चरित्र से कम-ज़ोर : *frail human nature* ▸ **frailty** / 'फ़्रेल्टि/noun 1 दुर्बलता 2 नैतिक/चारित्रिक दुर्बलता।

frame[1] / फ़्रेम् / noun 1 (द्वार, ऐनक आदि का) फ्रेम; चौखटा 2 (जहाज़, भवन आदि का) ढाँचा 3 (प्राय: sing) मनुष्य या पशु का) शरीर : *Sobs shook her slender frame.* 4 कोई पृष्ठभूमि तैयार करने वाला सामान्य तंत्र : *the frame of contemporary society* ▸ **frame of mind** noun मनोदशा।

frame[2] / फ़्रेम् / verb 1 चौखटा बनाना या लगाना 2 रचना करना, बनाना : *frame a question/an argument* 3 गढ़ना, रूप-आकार देना 4 *(अनौप)* निर्दोष व्यक्ति के विरुद्ध झूठे साक्ष्य गढ़ना।

framework / फ़्रेम्वर्क् / noun 1 ढाँचा 2 सामाजिक व्यवस्था : *the framework*

of society 3 निर्णय या निश्चय के आधार-भूत सिद्धांत आदि।

franc / फ़्रैङ्क् / noun फ़्रैंक; फ़्रांस, बेल्जियम आदि देशों की मुद्रा।

franchise / फ़्रैन्चाइज़् / noun 1 आम चुनावों में मत देने का अधिकार 2 किसी कंपनी का सामान क्षेत्र विशेष में बेचने की औपचारिक अनुमति : *grant a franchise.*

frank / फ़्रैङ्क् / adj (-er, -est) निष्कपट, स्पष्टवादी ▸ **frankly** adv.

frantic / 'फ़्रैन्टिक् / adj 1 (कष्ट या चिंता के मारे) उन्मत्त 2 (जल्दी के कारण) उत्तेजित, व्यग्र : *make frantic attempts to rescue sb* ▸ **frantically** adv.

fraternal / फ़्र'टर्नल् / adj भ्रातृ-, भ्रातृ-विषयक : *fraternal feelings.*

fraternity / फ़्र'टर्निटि / noun 1 भ्रातृ-संघ (एक ही व्यवसाय के लोगों का) 2 बंधुत्व, भाईचारा : *believe in liberty, equality and fraternity.*

fraud / फ़्रॉड् / noun 1 छल, कपट 2 कपटी, धोखेबाज़ व्यक्ति; धोखे वाली वस्तु ▸ **fraudster** noun ठग (व्यक्ति) **fraudulence** noun धोखेबाज़ी **fraudulent** / 'फ़्रॉड्युलन्ट् / adj 1 धोखे से प्राप्त 2 कपटपूर्ण।

fraught / फ़्रॉट् / adj 1 **fraught with sth** (कुछ अरुचिकर परिणामों से) परिपूर्ण, संबद्ध : *a situation fraught with danger* 2 तनाव या व्यग्रता उत्पन्न करने वाला।

fray[1] / फ़्रे / noun **the fray** (अक्सर *परि*) संघर्ष, स्पर्धा, प्रतियोगिता, वाद-विवाद आदि; उत्तेजक या साहसिक कार्य : *stand above the political fray.*

fray[2] / फ़्रे / verb 1 (कपड़े, रस्सी आदि का) अत्यधिक प्रयोग से घिस जाना 2 तनाव या थकान के लक्षण दिखाना : *Tempers began to fray in the heat.*

freak[1] / फ़्रीक् / noun 1 विलक्षण (कुछ हद तक बेतुका) विचार या कार्य 2 *(अनौप)* सनकी व्यक्ति : *health-food freaks*

3 (freak of nature भी) रूप-आकार में विलक्षण व्यक्ति, पशु या पौधा ▸ **freakish** *adj* अप-सामान्य, विचित्र।

freak² / फ़्रीक् / *verb* **freak (out)** *(अनौप)* तीव्र प्रतिक्रिया करना जिससे किसी को आश्चर्य, हर्ष, दुख या भय हो जाए; उत्तेजित या व्यग्र व्यवहार करना।

freckle / फ़्रेकल् / *noun* (प्राय: *pl*) (धूप के कारण शरीर पर पड़ा) चकत्ता ▸ **freckle** *verb* चकत्तों से ढक जाना **freckled** *adj* : *a freckled face.*

free¹ / फ़्री / *adj* (-r, -st) 1 (व्यक्ति) स्वतंत्र (न कि दास या कैदी) 2 (पशु/पक्षी) आज़ाद, पिंजरे या बंधन से मुक्त 3 अनियंत्रित : *free speech/press* 4 साफ़, अन-वरुद्ध : *a free flow of water* 5 free from/of sth किसी अवांछित या हानिकर पदार्थ से मुक्त : *free of typographical errors* 6 मुफ़्त, नि:शुल्क : *a free sample* 7 मुक्त; ख़ाली : *the free end of the rope ॰ Is that seat free? ॰ Are you free for lunch?* ■ **get, have, give sb a free hand** बेरोक-टोक काम करना/करने देना ▸ **freehand** *adj, adv* बिना रूलर या कंपस के (रेखाचित्र आदि) बनाया गया **freehold** *adj* ज़मीन का पूर्ण स्वामित्व **freely** / फ़्रीलि / *adv* स्वतंत्र रीति से, मुक्त भाव से; उदारता से **freetrade** *noun* अंतर्राष्ट्रीय करमुक्त व्यापार **free will** *noun* स्वेच्छा।

free² / फ़्री / *verb* (*pt, pp* **freed** / फ़्रीड्/) 1 free sb/sth (from sth) मुक्त करना, स्वतंत्र करना 2 free sb/sth of sth (किसी को) अवांछित वस्तु से मुक्ति दिलाना 3 किसी को कुछ करने की स्वतंत्रता प्रदान करना।

freedom / फ़्रीडम् / *noun* 1 स्वतंत्रता; दासता से मुक्ति 2 freedom (of sth) अभिव्यक्ति, कार्य आदि की स्वतंत्रता; free-dom (to do sth) (कुछ) प्रयोग करने की अनुमति 3 freedom from sth किसी अवांछित पदार्थ/प्रभाव से मुक्ति : *freedom*

from pain/hunger/fear ▸ **freedom fighter** स्वतंत्रता सेनानी।

freelance / फ़्रीलान्स; US फ़्रीलैन्स / *adj, adv* अपनी सेवाएँ या रचनाएँ कई संस्थाओं को बेचकर/प्रदान करके जीवनयापन करना : *a freelance designer.*

freeze / फ़्रीज़ / *verb* (*pt* **froze** / फ़्रोज़ / *pp* **frozen** / फ़्रोज़न् /) 1 अत्यधिक सर्दी के कारण पानी जम जाना 2 (व्यक्ति का) मारे ठंड के अकड़ जाना; अत्यधिक ठंड लगना 3 (खाद्य पदार्थ) ठंडा करना, जमा देना 4 क़ीमतें या वेतन एक निर्धारित समय के लिए अपरिवर्तनीय/नियत कर देना : *Salaries have been frozen for the current year.* ▸ **freezing** *adj* *(अनौप)* अति ठंडा **freezing point** *noun* हिमांक, ताप-मान का वह बिंदु जहाँ द्रव जम जाता है।

freezer / फ़्रीज़र् / (**deep freezer** भी) *noun* एक ऐसा विद्युत उपकरण जिसमें खाद्य पदार्थ को ठंड में रखकर बासी होने से बचाया जा सकता है।

freight / फ़्रेट् / *noun* (माल का) भाड़ा, किराया; ढोया हुआ माल, भार ▸ **freight** *verb* माल के रूप में कुछ भेजना **freighter** *noun* माल जहाज़/वायुयान।

French / फ़्रेन्च् / *noun* 1 the French फ़्रांसीसी 2 फ़्रेंच भाषा ■ **take French leave** बिना अनुमति के काम छोड़कर चले जाना या छुट्टी मनाना ▸ **French window** (US **French door** भी) *noun* बग़ीचे या बालकनी में खुलने वाली खिड़की जो द्वार का भी काम करे।

frenzy / फ़्रेन्ज़ि / *noun* (प्राय: *sing*) उन्माद, पागलपन : *The news threw him into a frenzy.* ▸ **frenzied** / फ़्रेन्ज़िड् / *adj* उन्मादग्रस्त।

frequency / फ़्रीक्वन्सि / *noun* 1 बारं-बारता; बार-बार घटित होने की प्रक्रिया 2 *(तक)* आवृत्ति।

frequent¹ / फ़्रीक्वन्ट् / *adj* प्राय: घटित होने वाला, बहुत बार होने वाला, सामान्य ▸ **frequently** *adv* प्राय:, अक्सर।

frequent² / फ़्रि'क्वेन्ट् / verb (औप) किसी स्थान पर बार-बार जाना : He used to frequent the town's bars and nightclubs.

fresh / फ़्रेश् / adj (-er, -est) 1 नया, भिन्न : fresh evidence 2 हाल ही में प्राप्त या बना हुआ 3 (भोजन, फल, सब्ज़ी आदि) ताज़ा, न कि टिन में बंद; (पानी) मीठा, खारा नहीं 4 (मौसम) शीतल; (हवा) ठंडी एवं तेज़ 5 साफ़, चमकदार एवं आकर्षक रंगत वाला : The new paint makes the kitchen look fresh and clean. ▸ **freshly** adv.

freshen / फ़्रेश्न् / verb 1 **freshen (sth up)** किसी चीज़ को साफ़-सुथरा करके उसे और मनोहर एवं आकर्षक बनाना : The kitchen walls were freshened up with a new coat of paint. 2 हवा का और ठंडा एवं तेज़ होना ■ **freshen (oneself) up** यात्रा के बाद हाथ-मुँह धोकर साफ़ होना ▸ **freshener** / फ़्रेश्नर् / noun ठंडी एवं ताज़ा करने वाली वस्तु : breath freshener.

fresher / फ़्रेशर् / noun (अनौप) कालेज या विश्वविद्यालय में पहले वर्ष का छात्र।

fret / फ़्रेट् / verb (-tt-) 1 **fret (oneself); fret (about/over sth)** चिंतित या असंतुष्ट होना; चिड़चिड़ा हो जाना 2 कुतरना, काटना ▸ **fret** noun [sing] चिंता : be in a fret **fretful** adj चिड़चिड़ा।

friction / फ़्रिक्शन् / noun 1 रगड़; (भौतिकी) घर्षण : The force of friction slows the spacecraft down as it re-enters the earth's atmosphere. 2 **friction (between A and B)** संघर्ष, मन-मुटाव, वैमनस्य।

Friday / फ़्राइडे / noun (संक्षि Fri) शुक्रवार।

fridge / फ़्रिज् / noun (अनौप) रेफ्रीजरेटर।

friend / फ़्रेन्ड् / noun मित्र, दोस्त।

friendly / फ़्रेन्ड्लि / adj (-ier, -iest) 1 **friendly (to sb)** मित्र के समान आचरण (करना) 2 मृदु एवं प्रिय व्यवहार दिखाते हुए 3 मैत्रीपूर्ण; गंभीरता या प्रतियोगिता रहित : a friendly game of football ▸ **friendliness** noun मैत्रीभाव।

friendship / फ़्रेन्ड्शिप् / noun दोस्ती।

fright / फ़्राइट् / noun 1 अत्यधिक एवं आकस्मिक भय : trembling with fright 2 (प्राय: sing) (अनौप) बेहूदा या कुरूप व्यक्ति या वस्तु।

frighten / फ़्राइट्न् / verb भय उत्पन्न करना/भय युक्त होना ▸ **frightened** adj भयभीत **frightening** adj.

frightful / फ़्राइट्फुल् / adj 1 अप्रियकर, अरुचिकर, डरावना 2 (अनौप) अत्यंत अत्यंत ख़राब ▸ **frightfully** adv.

frigid / फ़्रिजिड् / adj 1 बहुत ठंडा : the frigid zones 2 मित्रता, दया आदि न दिखाते हुए : a frigid look/voice.

frill / फ़्रिल् / noun 1 झालर 2 **frills** [pl] अतिरिक्त वस्तु (सजावटी) : a simple meal with no frills ▸ **frilled** adj झालरदार।

fringe / फ़्रिन्ज् / noun 1 (US bangs [pl]) माथे पर लटकते हुए काटे गए बाल; लटें : She has a fringe and glasses. 2 (शाल आदि के) झब्बे 3 (प्राय: pl) किनारा, सीमांत : the fringe of the forest ▸ **fringe** verb **fringe sth (with sth)** झब्बे लगाना; झब्बे बनाना **fringe benefit** noun कर्मचारियों को वेतन के अतिरिक्त दिया गया लाभ **fringed** adj झब्बेदार।

frisk / फ़्रिस्क् / verb 1 (अनौप) तलाशी के लिए शरीर के अंगों पर हाथ फेरना : Everyone was frisked before getting on the plane. 2 (पशुओं का) कलोल मचाना, उछल-कूद करना ▸ **frisky** adj उछल-कूद करने वाला; सजीव एवं उल्लासित : a frisky puppy.

frivolous / फ़्रिवलस् / adj 1 (व्यक्ति, उनका व्यवहार) चंचल, ओछा एवं छिछोरा 2 अमहत्त्वपूर्ण, व्यर्थ समय ख़राब करने

वाला : *frivolous objections/complaints* ▸ frivolity / फ़्रि'व़ॉलटि / *noun* छिछोरापन; ओछी हरकत।

frock / फ़्रॉक़ / *noun* 1 फ़्रॉक़; बच्चों या महिलाओं का वस्त्र 2 भिक्षुओं/पादरियों का लबादा।

frog / फ़्रॉग़ / *noun* मेंढक ▸ frogman *noun* गोताखोर।

frolic / फ़्रॉलिक़ / *verb* (*pt, pp* frolicked) frolic (about) आमोद-प्रमोद करना, मस्ती में समय काटना ▸ frolic *noun* उल्लासपूर्ण खेल आदि frolicsome *adj* (औप) उल्लसित, ज़िंदादिल : *a frolicsome kitten.*

from / फ़्रम़; फ़्रॉम़ / *prep* 1 से, स्थान/समय का प्रारंभ बिंदु : *go from Kolkata to Mumbai* 2 से, समय का आरंभ बिंदु : *I'm on leave from June 30.* 3 से (व्यक्ति से संबंधित) : *a letter from my brother* 4 अलग होना, बचाव; मुक्त होना : *release sb from prison* 5 (स्थान) से, दृष्टिकोण से : *From this angle this looks crooked.* 6 दो स्थानों के बीच की दूरी : *50 metres from the scene of accident* 7 उत्पन्न, स्रोत, उद्गम स्थान : *I'm from Chennai.* 8 from sth (to sth) निर्धारित, सीमांतर्गत : *write from 10 to 15 letters daily* 9 अंतर, विषमता : *Is Portuguese very different from Spanish?*

front / फ़्रन्ट / *noun* 1 the front (प्राय: *sing*) अगला भाग, सर्वाधिक महत्त्वपूर्ण पक्ष, [*sing*] (व्यक्ति/वस्तु के ठीक) सामने : *The front of the car was badly damaged. ○ There's a garden at the front of the house.* 2 the front समुद्र या झील के किनारे का क्षेत्र या सड़क 3 (युद्ध में) अग्रिम मोर्चा जहाँ लड़ाई हो रही है : *serve at the front* 4 कार्य का क्षेत्रविशेष : *on the domestic/economic front* 5 बाहरी दिखावा : *put on a bold front* ■ put on, show etc a bold/

brave front भय ना दिखाना ▸ front *adj* अगले भाग पर (या में)।

frontal / फ़्रन्ट्ल / *adj* 1 सामने वाले भाग का : *a frontal view* 2 (चिकि) मस्तक (का)।

frontier / फ़्रन्टिअर / *noun* 1 frontier (between sth and sth); frontier (with sth) सीमांत प्रदेश 2 the frontiers [*pl*] ज्ञान या क्रिया की सीमा, हदें : *advance the frontiers of science.*

frost / फ़्रॉस्ट / *noun* 1 सरदी, हिमांक के नीचे के तापमान वाली ठंड 2 पाला ▸ frost *verb* frost (sth) (over/up) 1 तुषार/ पाले से ढकना 2 (विशेषत: *US*) केक को चीनी की तह से ढकना frostbite *noun* पाले के कारण शरीर के किसी भाग पर आहत frosted *adj*.

frosty / फ़्रॉस्टि / *adj* 1 (मौसम) बहुत ठंडा; (वस्तु) तुषार से ढकी हुई 2 (व्यवहार) रूखा एवं अमित्रवत्।

froth / फ़्रॉथ़ / *noun* 1 झाग, फेन 2 (अपमा) बेकार की बकवास या काम ▸ froth *verb* झाग छोड़ना frothy *adj* 1 झागदार, झाग से आच्छादित 2 (अपमा) मज़ेदार एवं मनोरंजक परंतु व्यर्थ।

frown / फ़्राउऩ / *verb* frown (at sb/sth) त्योरी चढ़ाना (अप्रसन्नता प्रकट करना) ■ frown on/upon sb/sth नाराज़गी दिखाना ▸ frown *noun* त्योरी; तेवर।

frugal / फ़्रूग्ल / *adj* 1 (खानपान या ख़र्च में) नियमित, मिताहारी/मितव्ययी : *a frugal existence* 2 साधारण एवं सस्ता ▸ frugality / फ़्रु'गैलटि / *noun* मिताहारिता/ मितव्ययिता frugally *adv.*

fruit / फ़्रूट / *noun* 1 फल; (वनस्पति विज्ञान) फूल झड़ने के बाद पौधे पर लगा भाग जिसमें बीज बनते हैं 2 the fruits [*pl*] लाभ, परिणाम, फल : *enjoy the fruits of one's labours* ▸ fruit *verb* (पेड़-पौधों का) फलना।

fruitful / फ़्रूट्फ़ल / *adj* 1 (पेड़) फलदार, उपजाऊ 2 लाभदायक, सफल।

fruition / फ़्रु'इश्न् / *noun* आशाओं/ आकांक्षाओं का फलीभूत होना, सफलता प्राप्ति।

fruitless /'फ़्रूट्लस्/ *adj* निष्फल, व्यर्थ।

fruity /'फ़्रूटि/ *adj* (-ier, -iest) (स्वाद एवं गंध में) फल जैसा।

frustrate / फ़्र'स्ट्रेट्; *US* 'फ़्रस्ट्रेट् / *verb* 1 (किसी को कार्य विशेष करने से) रोक देना, योजना निष्फल कर देना 2 निरुत्साहित एवं निराश करना : *She was frustrated by the lack of appreciation shown of her work.* ▸ **frustrated** *adj* **frustration** / फ़्र'स्ट्रेश्न् / *noun* 1 आशाभंग, कुंठा 2 (प्राय: *pl*) कुंठा उत्पन्न करने वाली वस्तु या स्थिति : *Every job has its frustrations.*

fry / फ़्राइ / *verb* (*pt, pp* fried / फ़्राइड् /) (घी या तेल में) तलना, भूनना ■ **out of the frying pan into the fire** बद से बदतर स्थिति में जाना।

fuel / 'फ़्यूअल् / *noun* ईंधन (कोयला, लकड़ी, गैस आदि); परमाणु ऊर्जा उत्पन्न करने वाले पदार्थ ▸ **fuel** *verb* (-ll-; *US* -l-) 1 ईंधन डालना/भरना 2 किसी वस्तु की मात्रा या प्रभाव तेज़ कर देना : *inflation fuelled by big wage increases.*

fugitive / 'फ़्यूजटिव् / *noun* **fugitive (from sb/sth)** भगोड़ा, फ़रारी (संकट या न्याय से बचने के लिए भागा हुआ) ▸ **fugitive** *adj* 1 फ़रार (अपराधी) 2 (औप) क्षणभंगुर : *fugitive thoughts.*

fulfil (fulfill भी) / फ़ुल्'फ़िल्/ *verb* (-ll-) 1 (कार्य, कर्तव्य) पूरा करना : *fulfil a duty* 2 (नियम, प्रतिबंध आदि का) पालन करना; कार्य को पूरा करना 3 आशाओं/ आकांक्षाओं पर खरा उतरना : *fulfil sb's dreams* 4 **fulfil oneself** अपनी योग्यता और चरित्र का पूर्णत: विकास करना। 5 विशिष्ट ज़रूरतें/माँगें पूरी करना : *fulfil the conditions of entry to a university* ▸ **fulfilment** *noun.*

full / फ़ुल् / *adj* (-er, -est) 1 **full (of sth/ sb)** पूर्णतया भरा हुआ : *My cup is full.* 2 भीड़ भरा 3 **full of sth** (कोई विशेष गुण से) पूर्ण; व्यस्त (विचार आदि में) 4 खूब, विस्तार से : *give full information/ details* ■ (at) **full pelt/tilt/speed** सर्वाधिक तेज़ गति से **in full** पूरे विस्तार के साथ **to the full** सीमा तक ▸ **full** *adv* 1 बिलकुल, ठीक-ठीक 2 बहुत; पूर्णतया : *as you know full well* **full-length** *adj* सामान्य लंबाई की वस्तु **full stop** *noun* पूर्णविराम **full-time** *adj* पूर्ण कालिक **fully** *adv* 1 पूर्णतया, पूरी तरह से 2 (औप) सब का सब, सारा **fully-fledged** (*US* **full-fledged**) *adj* पूर्णत: विकसित या स्थापित।

fumble /'फ़म्बल्/ *verb* 1 **fumble (for/ with sth)** टटोलना; गड़बड़ाना : *fumble for the light switch;* **fumble about/ around** कुछ ढूँढते हुए/करते हुए बेढंगे तरीक़े से चलना 2 किसी वस्तु को अच्छी तरह न पकड़ पाना ▸ **fumble** *noun* (**fumbling** भी) गड़बड़ी **fumbling** *adj.*

fume /फ़्यूम्/ *verb* 1 **fume (at/over sb/ sth)** असंतोष या क्रोध प्रकट करना 2 धुआँ छोड़ना।

fumes / फ़्यूम्ज़् / *noun* [*pl*] धुआँ; भाप; भभक : *sulphur fumes.*

fumigate /'फ़्यूमिगेट् / *verb* धुआँरना; धुआँ छोड़कर कीटाणुरहित करना : *The hospital wards were fumigated after the outbreak of typhus.*

fun /फ़न्/ *noun* 1 मनोरंजन, आमोद-प्रमोद 2 हँसी-मज़ाक ■ **in fun** खेल-खेल में **make fun of sb/sth** मज़ाक उड़ाना, हँसी उड़ाना।

function /'फ़ङ्क्श्न् /*noun* 1 कार्य, प्र-कार्य : *bodily functions* 2 समारोह, उत्सव ▸ **function** *verb* 1 कार्य करना 2 **function as sth** का कार्य या कर्तव्य करना; के रूप में कार्य करना : *The sofa can also function as a bed.* **functional** *adj* 1 व्यावहारिक एवं उपयोगी

functional furniture 2 कार्य संबंधी : *a functional disorder* 3 कार्यशील, कार्यक्षम।

fund / फ़न्ड / *noun* 1 किसी विशेष कार्य/ योजना के लिए जमा की हुई या उपलब्ध धन-राशि : *a disaster relief fund* 2 [*sing*] **fund (of sth)** भंडार : *a fund of experience* 3 **funds** [*pl*] निधि, कोष : *The hospital is trying to raise funds for a new kidney machine.* ▸ **fund** *verb* 1 धन उपलब्ध कराना (कार्य या संस्थान के लिए) 2 (*वाणिज्य*) ऋण प्रदान करना **funding** *noun*.

fundamental / फ़न्ड 'मेन्ट्ल् / *adj* 1 मूलभूत; आधारभूत 2 अति महत्त्वपूर्ण या गंभीर : *fundamental differences* 3 (*भौतिकी*) मौलिक, जिसको और विभाजित नहीं किया जा सकता है : *fundamental particles* ▸ **fundamental** *noun* (प्राय: *pl*) आधारभूत सिद्धांत और नियम।

fundamentalism / फ़न्ड 'मेन्ट्लिज़म् / *noun* धार्मिक कट्टरपन, रूढ़िवाद।

funeral / फ़्यूनरल् / *noun* अंत्येष्टि संस्कार; दफ़नाने की क्रिया ▸ **funereal** / फ़्यु 'निअरि-अल् / *adj* अंत्येष्टि के उपयुक्त; दुखदायी/ दुखपूर्ण।

fungus / फ़ङ्गस् / *noun* (*pl* fungi / फ़ङ्गी; फ़ङ्गाइ; फ़न्जाइ /) फफूँदी।

funnel / फ़न्ल् / *noun* 1 कीप (छोटे मुँह के बरतन में द्रव डालने के लिए प्रयुक्त) 2 चिमनी, धुआँ निकलने का मार्ग ▸ **funnel** *verb* (-ll-; *US* -l-) कीप द्वारा कोई द्रव डालना : *funnel petrol into a can* ○ (*अलं*) *The money is being funnelled through a secret bank account.*

funny / फ़नि / *adj* (-ier, -iest) 1 हास्य-जनक : *funny stories* 2 विचित्र, अज़ीब 3 (*अनौप*) थोड़ा-सा बीमार।

fur / फ़र् / *noun* 1 फर, कुछ पशुओं की रोएँदार खाल 2 फ़र से बनी पोशाक : *a fur coat* ▸ **furred** *adj* फ़र (या मैल) चढ़ा

हुआ **furry** *adj* (-ier, -iest) 1 रोएँदार खाल वाला (जंतु) 2 फ़र जैसा।

furious / फ़्युअरिअस् / *adj* 1 **furious (with sb)**; **furious (at sb/sth)** क्रोधित 2 प्रचंड, उग्र : *a furious storm/debate* ▸ **furiously** *adv*.

furlong / फ़र्लॉङ् / *noun* फर्लांग = 220 गज़।

furnace / फ़र्निस् / *noun* 1 भट्ठी 2 अँगीठी।

furnish / फ़र्निश् / *verb* 1 **furnish sth (with sth)** फ़र्नीचर रखना 2 **furnish sb/ sth with sth**; **furnish sth (to sb/sth)** (*औप*) सामान जुटाना/उपलब्ध कराना : *furnish all the equipment for a major expedition* ▸ **furnishings** *noun* [*pl*] फ़र्नीचर, फ़िटिंग, परदे आदि।

furniture / फ़र्निचर् / *noun* मेज़, कुरसी आदि फ़र्नीचर।

furrow / फ़रो / *noun* 1 हल से बनी रेखा : *furrow ready for planting* 2 झुर्री, शिकन : *Deep furrows lined his brow.* ▸ **furrow** *verb* (हल से) रेखा डालना।

further / फ़र्द्र् / *adv* 1 (समय की दृष्टि से) और आगे, और दूर 2 और अधिक सीमा तक/स्तर तक 3 के अतिरिक्त; भी ▸ **further** *adj* अतिरिक्त, और अधिक : *Have you any further questions?* **further** *verb* (*औप*) (योजना को) आगे बढ़ाना, प्रोत्साहन देना **furthermore** *adv* इसके अति-रिक्त।

furthest / फ़र्दिस्ट् / *adv, adj* →**far** देखिए।

furtive / फ़र्टिव् / *adj* 1 गुप्त, नज़र बचा-कर किया गया : *a furtive glance* 2 (व्यक्ति) लुक-छिपकर आने वाले, संदेहास्पद।

fury / फ़्युअरि / *noun* 1 उन्माद, क्रोध का पागलपन; क्रोध/उन्माद की दशा 2 (मौसम या अन्य क्रिया की) शक्ति, विध्वंस : *the fury of the storm.*

fuse¹ / फ़्यूज़ / noun 1 बिजली का फ़्यूज़ 2 बारूद उड़ाने का पलीता।

fuse² / फ़्यूज़ / verb 1 fuse (sth) with sth; fuse (A and B) (together) जोड़ना, जोड़कर एक करना 2 गरमी से पिघलाकर जोड़ना/जुड़ना : *fuse two pieces of wire together.*

fuselage / फ़्यूज़लाश़् / noun हवाई जहाज़ का धड़।

fusion / फ़्यूश़न् / noun 1 दो वस्तुओं का मिश्रण, विलयन 2 *(भौतिकी)* नाभिकीय संलयन : *nuclear fusion* 3 मिश्रित संगीत।

fuss / फ़स् / noun 1 (बेकार की) घबराहट 2 बात का बतंगड़ : *She's making an awful fuss about the high rent.* ▸ **fuss** verb 1 **fuss (about); fuss about/over/with sth** संभ्रम में पड़ना, चिंता करना (विशेषत: छोटी-छोटी और महत्त्वहीन बातों को लेकर) 2 किसी को नाराज़ या परेशान करना।

fussy / फ़सि / adj (-ier, -iest) 1 (प्राय: *अपमा*) छोटी-छोटी बातों पर चिंता करने वाला या उत्तेजित होने वाल 2 **fussy (about sth)** आसानी से प्रसन्न न होने वाला।

futile / फ़्यूटाइल; US फ़्यूटल् / adj व्यर्थ; सारहीन, तुच्छ : *a futile attempt* ▸ **futility** / फ़्यू'टिलटि / noun व्यर्थता : *the futility of war.*

future / फ़्यूचर् / noun 1 **the future** भविष्य, भावी 2 **futures** [pl] *(वाणिज्य)* उधार ख़रीदा गया सामान या शेयर : *buy oil/ coffee futures* ▸ **future** adj भविष्य में घटित होने वाला, भविष्य का।

fuzzy / फ़ज़ि / adj (-ier, -iest) 1 (बाल) बहुत घुँघराले 2 (आकार या आवाज़) अस्पष्ट 3 (विचार आदि) अस्पष्ट रूप से व्यक्त : *fuzzy ideas/thinking.*

Gg

gabardine (gaberdine भी)/ˈगैबरडीन्/ noun (कोट आदि बनाने में प्रयुक्त) मज़बूत कपड़ा : *a gabardine jacket.*

gabble /ˈगैब्ल्/ verb **gabble (on/ away); gabble sth (out)** बड़बड़ाना ▸ **gabble** noun बड़बड़ : *the gabble of children.*

gadget /ˈगैजिट्/ noun छोटा उपकरण, औज़ार ▸ **gadgetry** noun.

gag /गैग्/ noun किसी को बोलने से रोकने के लिए मुँह में ठूँसी गई वस्तु (कपड़ा आदि); दाँतों के डॉक्टर द्वारा मुँह खुला रखने के लिए मुँह में रखी वस्तु; अभिव्यक्ति की स्वतंत्रता का हनन करने वाली कोई भी चीज़ : *a gag rule* ▸ **gag** verb (-gg-) गैग का प्रयोग करना; अभिव्यक्ति की स्वतंत्रता छीनना : *The hostages were bound and gagged.*

gaiety /ˈगेअटि/ noun उल्लास/प्रसन्नता; [pl] (अप्र) आमोद-प्रमोद।

gain[1] /गेन्/ noun 1 लाभ : *One man's loss is another man's gain.* 2 प्राप्ति; (शक्ति आदि में) बढ़ोतरी ▸ **gainful** adj लाभदायक; समृद्धि कारक : *gainful employment.*

gain[2] /गेन्/ verb 1 **gain sth (for sb)** प्राप्त करना, पाना : *gain possession of sth* 2 **gain by/from (doing) sth** लाभ प्राप्त करना : *You can gain by watching how she works.* 3 (औप) प्रयास करके पहुँचना ■ **gain in sth** प्रगति करना, विकसित होना **gain time** जानबूझकर विलंब करके अपनी स्थिति को दृढ़ करना।

gait /गेट्/ noun चाल : *walk with an unsteady gait.*

gala /ˈगाला; US ˈगेला/ noun सार्वजनिक आमोद-प्रमोद, आनंदोत्सव : *a gala dinner.*

galaxy /ˈगैलक्सि/ noun (pl **galaxies**) 1 आकाश में तारों का समूह 2 **the galaxy (the Milky Way** भी) [sing] आकाश गंगा 3 (अलं) प्रसिद्ध एवं प्रतिष्ठित व्यक्तियों का समूह।

gale /गेल्/ noun 1 झंझावात, तूफान 2 शोर का विस्फोट, विशेषत: हँसी का।

gall /गॉल्/ noun 1 (अनौप) दुस्साहसपूर्ण रुक्ष व्यवहार; आदरहीनता 2 घृणा; कड़वाहट : *words full of venom and gall* ▸ **gall-bladder** noun पित्ताशय।

gallant /ˈगैलन्ट्/ adj 1 (औप या साहि) वीर, बहादुर 2 भव्य, रमणीक : *a gallant ship* ▸ **gallant** /गˈलैन्ट्; ˈगैलन्ट्/ noun (अप्र) फ़ैशनेबल पुरुष जो स्त्रियों को ज्यादा ध्यान एवं सम्मान देता है, छैला **gallantry** /ˈगैलन्ट्रि/ noun 1 वीरता, बहादुरी : *a medal for gallantry* 2 पुरुषों का स्त्रियों के प्रति नम्र व्यवहार।

gallery /ˈगैलरि/ noun (pl **galleries**) 1 कला प्रदर्शन का कमरा, कला वीथिका 2 थियेटर में ऊँची और सस्ते टिकट की सीटें 3 गैलरी, दीर्घा : *a shooting gallery* 4 चर्च या हॉल में ढका हुआ गलियारा।

galley /ˈगैलि/ noun 1 (प्राचीन समय में) नीचा समतल जहाज जिसे दास या कैदी चलाते थे 2 जहाज/वायुयान का रसोईघर।

gallivant /ˈगैलिवैन्ट्/ verb (अनौप, अपमा) मौज-मज़े की तलाश में इधर-उधर घूमना।

gallon /ˈगैलन्/ noun (संक्षि **gal; gall**) गैलन, द्रव की एक नाप, लगभग 4.5 लीटर (US में 3.8 लीटर)।

gallop /ˈगैलप्/ noun 1 (घोड़े की) सरपट चाल 2 असामान्य तीव्र गति : *to work at a gallop* ▸ **gallop** verb सरपट दौड़ना; घोड़े को सरपट दौड़ाना।

gallows /ˈगैलोज़्/ (**the gallows** भी) noun (pl अपरिवर्तित) फाँसी देने का लकड़ी का ढाँचा।

galore /गˈलॉर्/ adv प्रचुर मात्रा में : *have books/money galore.*

galvanic /गैल्ˈवैनिक्/ adj 1 रासायनिक

क्रिया द्वारा विद्युत उत्पन्न करना : *a galvanic battery* 2 अचानक और नाटकीय।

galvanize, -ise / 'गैल्वनाइज़ / *verb* 1 लोहे आदि पर जिंक की पॉलिश (कलई) चढ़ाना 2 **galvanize sb (into sth/doing sth)** किसी व्यक्ति को कोई कार्य करने के लिए प्रेरित/उत्तेजित करना।

gambit / गैम्बिट् / *noun* 1 चाल, शतरंज में पहली चाल 2 किसी भी स्थिति में बढ़त हासिल करने के लिए पहली चाल : *a conversational gambit.*

gamble / 'गैम्ब्ल् / *verb* **gamble sth (on sth)** जुआ खेलना; दाँव पर लगाना ▸ **gamble** *noun* दाँव; जुआबाज़ी **gambler** / 'गैम्ब्लर् / *noun* जुआरी **gambling** *noun.*

gambol / 'गैम्ब्ल् / *verb* (-ll-; *US* -l- भी) उछल-कूद मचाना।

game¹ / गेम् / *noun* 1 खेल जिसके अपने नियम होते हैं, जैसे फुटबाल 2 **games** [*pl*] खेल-प्रतियोगिता : *the Olympic Games* 3 (*अनौप*) चाल, छल-योजना : *I want none of your games!* ■ **play the game** नियमों का पालन करना; सम्मानपूर्वक आचरण करना।

game² / गेम् / *adj* **game (for sth/to do sth)** उत्साही, साहसी कार्य करने को उद्यत : *He's always game for an adventure.* ▸ **gamely** *adv.*

game³ / गेम् / *noun* (सामूहिक रूप से) शिकार किए गए पशु-पक्षी ▸ **gamekeeper** *noun* शिकार-रक्षक, आखेट-रक्षक।

gander / 'गैन्डर् / *noun* नर हंस।

gang / गैङ् / *noun* 1 गिरोह : *a gang of robbers* 2 तोड़-फोड़ करने वाले युवकों का दल : *a street gang* 3 मज़दूरों का संगठित दल : *a gang of builders* ▸ **gang** *verb* ■ **gang up (on/against sb)** किसी के ख़िलाफ़ गिरोहबंदी करना।

gangrene / 'गैङ्ग्रीन् / *noun* रक्त संचारण रुक जाने से शरीर के किसी अंग का सड़ जाना।

gangster / 'गैङ्स्टर् / *noun* डाकू, अपराधी गिरोह का सदस्य।

gangway / 'गैङ्वे / *noun* 1 जहाज़ के बग़ल का खुला स्थान; जहाज़ से भूमि तक जाने वाली चल-सीढ़ी 2 थिएटर या वायुयान में सीटों के बीच का रास्ता।

gaol / जेल् / *noun* = **jail**.

gaoler / 'जेलर् / *noun* = **jailer**.

gap / गैप् / *noun* **gap (in/between sth)** 1 दरार, छेद 2 ख़ाली स्थान; पर्याप्त दूरी; समयांतराल, बीच का समय : *After a gap of 30 years the custom was reintroduced.* 3 मतभेद, अंतर : *a widening gap between the rich and poor* 4 कमी।

gape / गेप् / *verb* 1 **gape (at sb/sth)** (*अक्सर अपमा*) मुँह खोलकर टकटकी लगाकर देखना; मुँह बाए रह जाना, (आश्चर्य से) जंभाई लेना 2 पूरी तरह खुल जाना/खुला हुआ होना ▸ **gape** *noun.*

garage / 'गैराश्; 'गैराज्; 'गैरिज्; *US* ग राज् / *noun* 1 गैराज जहाँ मोटर-कार आदि रखी जाती है 2 स्थान जहाँ वाहनों की मरम्मत की जाती है : *a garage mechanic.*

garb / गार्ब् / *noun* पहनावा, पोशाक (विशेषत: अपने विशिष्ट व्यवसाय के लिए पहनी जाने वाली) : *military/prison garb.*

garbage / 'गार्बिज् / *noun* 1 कूड़ा-कर-कट, कचरा; कूड़े का ढेर 2 (*अनौप*) बेकार की बकवास : *You do talk a load of garbage!*

garble / 'गार्ब्ल् / *verb* (तथ्यों या कथनों को) तोड़-मरोड़कर पेश करना ताकि ग़लत धारणा बने ▸ **garbled** *adj* : *a garbled account of the accident.*

garden / 'गार्ड्न् / *noun* 1 बग़ीचा, उपवन 2 **gardens** [*pl*] सार्वजनिक उद्यान 3 फूल-सब्ज़ी आदि उगाने के लिए उपयुक्त स्थान ▸ **gardener** *noun* माली **gardening** *noun* बाग़वानी।

gargle / 'गार्ग्ल् / *verb* **gargle (with**

sth) कुल्ला या ग़रारा करना ▸ **gargle** noun 1 ग़रारा (करना) 2 ग़रारे के लिए प्रयुक्त द्रव : use a gargle of salt water.

garish / 'गेअरिश् / adj (अपमा) चटकीला; भड़कीला : garish clothes/lights ▸ **garishly** adv.

garland / 'गार्लन्ड् / noun माला ▸ **garland** verb garland sb (with sth) माला पहनाना/डालना।

garlic / 'गार्लिक् / noun लहसुन ▸ **garlicky** adj लहसुन जैसी गंध वाला या लहसुन जैसे स्वाद वाला।

garment / 'गार्मन्ट् / noun (औप) कपड़े, वस्त्र : woollen/winter garments.

garnish / 'गार्निश् / verb garnish sth (with sth) भोजन को अन्य खाद्य पदार्थों से सजाना ▸ **garnish** noun भोजन की सजावट के लिए प्रयुक्त खाद्य पदार्थ : a garnish of mixed herbs.

garret / 'गैरट् / noun दुछत्ती, अटारी।

garrison / 'गैरिसन् / noun गैरिसन, शहर या क़िले में स्थित सेना ▸ **garrison** verb 1 गैरिसन से युक्त करना : Two regiments are being sent to garrison the town. 2 garrison sb in ... सैनिकों को ऐसे कार्य के लिए लगाना।

garrulous / 'गैर्युलस्; 'गैरलस् / adj बातूनी, वाचाल : becoming garrulous after a few glasses of wine ▸ **garrulity** noun **garrulously** adv.

garter / 'गार्टर् / noun मोज़े की गेटिस।

gas / गैस् / noun (pl gases) 1 गैस 2 जलाने के काम आने वाली गैस (कोयला गैस) : butane/coal gas 3 (US) पेट्रोल 4 (अनौप; अपमा) डींग भरी बात, गप्प : Don't believe a word he says—it's all gas! ▸ **gas** verb (-ss-) 1 (व्यक्ति या पशु को) ज़हरीली गैस सुँघाना 2 gas (about sth) (अनौप, अपमा) देर तक व्यर्थ बात करना।

gaseous / 'गैसिअस्; 'गेसिअस् / adj गैसीय : a gaseous mixture.

gash / गैश् / noun gash (in/on sth) गहरा घाव ▸ **gash** verb घाव करना।

gasoline (**gasolene** भी) / 'गैसलीन् / noun (US) पेट्रोल।

gasp / गास्प्; US गैस्प् / verb 1 gasp (at sth); gasp (for sth) जल्दी-जल्दी छोटी साँसें लेना; हाँफना : The runner was gasping for air. 2 gasp sth (out) हाँफते हुए कुछ कहना : She managed to gasp (out) a few words. 3 gasp (for sth) (अनौप) किसी चीज़ (सिगरेट, शराब आदि) की तीव्र इच्छा होना, तलब लगना ▸ **gasp** noun (तकलीफ़/आश्चर्य से) हाँफना ■ at one's last gasp बुरी तरह थका हुआ।

gastric / 'गैस्ट्रिक् / adj (चिकि) आमाशय संबंधी ▸ **gastritis** / गै'स्ट्राइटिस् / noun (चिकि) आमाशय की एक बीमारी।

gastro-enteritis / ,गैस्ट्रो,एन्ट'राइटिस् / noun (चिकि) आमाशय एवं आँत की एक बीमारी।

gate / गेट् / noun 1 फाटक, मुख्य द्वार 2 हवाई अड्डे या स्टेडियम आदि का प्रवेश द्वार ▸ **gatecrash** verb बिना निमंत्रण के किसी पार्टी या समारोह में, प्रायः समूह में, पहुँच जाना **gatekeeper** noun द्वारपाल **gate-pass** noun प्रवेश-पत्र **gateway** noun प्रवेश द्वार, मुख्य द्वार।

gather / 'गैदर् / verb 1 gather sb/sth round (sb/sth); gather (round sb/ sth) इकट्ठा करना या होना 2 gather sth (from sth) (फूल) तोड़ना; (पौधे, फल आदि) व्यापक क्षेत्र से एकत्र करना : gather wild flowers/nuts 3 gather sth (from sb/sth) समझना; निष्कर्ष निकालना 4 gather sth (in) (कपड़े में) तह डालना; चुनट डालना 5 कुछ करने/प्रयास करने के लिए स्वयं को मानसिक/शारीरिक रूप से तैयार करना : He gathered all his strength and swung the axe. 6 gather sth (in) फ़सल काटकर इकट्ठा

करना ▶ **gathering** noun लोगों का जमाव/मिलन।

gaudy /'गॉडि/ adj (-ier, -iest) (अपमा) भड़कीला; सस्ती तड़क-भड़क वाला : gaudy jewellery ▶ **gaudily** adv **gaudiness** noun.

gauge (US **gage** भी) /गेज्/ noun 1 मानक माप, गेज; आकार या विस्तार 2 रेल की पटरियों के बीच की दूरी (**metre-gauge** छोटी लाइन = दूरी एक मीटर; **broad-gauge** बड़ी लाइन = दूरी 1.69 मीटर या 4' 8 $\frac{1}{2}$ ") 3 वर्षा, हवा, दबाव आदि नापने का यंत्र; चद्दर या तार की मोटाई नापने का यंत्र : a petrol/pressure/speed gauge 4 कुछ निर्णय करने के लिए उपलब्ध तथ्य या परिस्थिति ▶ **gauge** verb 1 ठीक-ठीक नापना/मापना; अंदाज़ा लगाना 2 राय बनाना, आँकना : try to gauge sb's reactions.

gaunt /गॉन्ट्/ adj 1 (व्यक्ति) भूख या कष्ट आदि के कारण अत्यंत दुबला-पतला : the gaunt face of a starving man 2 (इमारत) बिना किसी सजावट के, अनाकर्षक।

gauntlet /'गॉन्ट्लट्/ noun 1 दस्ताना 2 (मध्य युगों में) कवच के साथ सैनिकों द्वारा पहना जाने वाला लोहे का दस्ताना ■ **run the gauntlet** ख़तरे, क्रोध या आलोचना का सामना करना **take up/throw down the gauntlet** चुनौती लेना/देना।

gauze /गॉज़्/ noun महीन पारदर्शी सूती या रेशमी कपड़ा (जाली); महीन तार की जाली : a gauze curtain ▶ **gauzy** adj.

gay /गे/ adj 1 समलिंगी (व्यक्ति) 2 चिंता-मुक्त : spending money with gay abandon ▶ **gay** noun समलिंगी व्यक्ति **gaily** adv.

gaze /गेज़्/ verb टकटकी लगाकर देखना ▶ **gaze** noun टकटकी वाली नज़र।

gazette /ग'ज़ेट्/ noun गज़ट, सरकारी सूचना-पत्र जिसमें अधिकारी लोगों की नियुक्तियाँ और सार्वजनिक घोषणाएँ आदि प्रकाशित होती हैं।

gazetteer /ˌगैज़'टिअर्/ noun स्थानों के नामों की अकारादि क्रमबद्ध सूची : a world gazetteer.

gear /गिअर्/ noun 1 (विशेषत: समासों में) विशेष प्रयोजन की मशीन : winding-gear for lifting heavy loads 2 गियर, दाँत वाले पहियों का सेट जिससे मोटर की शक्ति को गति में परिवर्तन किया जाता है : Careless use of the clutch may damage the gears. 3 गति या सामर्थ्य का स्तर ■ **in/out of gear** इंजिन के साथ मेल/बेमेल में ▶ **gear** verb ■ **gear sb/sth up** (for/to sth); **gear up** (for/to sth) किसी को किसी चीज़ के लिए तैयार करना या खुद तैयार होना।

gel /जेल्/ noun (यौगिक शब्दों में प्रयुक्त) जेली जैसा दिखने वाला एक गाढ़ा पदार्थ (बालों एवं त्वचा पर लगाया जाने वाला) : bath/shower gel.

gem /जेम्/ noun 1 मणि, रत्न 2 अत्यधिक सौंदर्य के कारण मूल्यवान कोई वस्तु; गुणों के कारण महत्त्व प्राप्त व्यक्ति : She's a real gem!

Gemini /'जेमिनाइ; 'जेमिनि/ noun मिथुन राशि; मिथुन राशि वाला व्यक्ति।

gender /'जेन्डर्/ noun 1 (व्या) लिंग, अँग्रेज़ी में तीन लिंग हैं—masculine, feminine और neuter 2 पुरुष या स्त्री होना : gender issues.

gene /जीन्/ noun (जीव विज्ञान) जीव-कोशिका में एक तत्त्व जो माता-पिता के विशेष गुण उनके बच्चों तक पहुँचाता है।

genealogy /ˌजीनि'ऐलजि/ noun 1 वंशावली, वंशक्रम बताने वाली सारणी/तालिका 2 वंशक्रम इतिहास का अध्ययन ▶ **genealogical** adj.

general /'जेन्रल्/ adj 1 सामान्य/साधारण, आम : a matter of general interest 2 एक भाग या पहलू तक सीमित नहीं; व्यापक 3 विस्तारसहित; विषय में विशेषता

प्राप्त नहीं : *general knowledge/science* 4 (सरकारी पद के पश्चात प्रयुक्त) प्रमुख : *Attorney/Inspector/Governor General* ■ **in general** 1 मुख्यतया; सामान्यतया 2 पूरा, संपूर्ण रूप से।

General / 'जेन्रल् / noun (संक्षि Gen) सेना में सर्वोच्च अधिकारी का पद, जनरल।

generality /,जेन्'रैलटि/ noun 1 सामान्य नियम या कथन 2 सामान्यता : *An account of such generality is of little value.* 3 **the generality** [pl] (औप) बहुमत, अधिकांश।

generalize, -ise /'जेन्रलाइज्/ verb 1 सामान्य निष्कर्ष निकालना 2 **generalize (about sth)** सामान्य कथन प्रस्तुत करना।

generally / 'जेन्रलि / adv 1 सामान्यतया 2 व्यापक रूप में : *He is generally popular.*

generate / 'जेनरेट् / verb उत्पन्न करना, पैदा करना : *generate heat/electricity.*

generation /,जेन्'रेश्न्/ noun 1 उत्पत्ति : *nuclear power generation* 2 पीढ़ी : *Three generations were present — myself, my mother and my grandmother.* 3 लगभग एक ही समय के पैदा सभी व्यक्ति, पीढ़ी ▶ **the generation gap** noun [sing] बुजुर्गों और युवकों के दृष्टिकोण एवं समझ में अंतर।

generator / 'जेनरेटर् / noun विद्युत उत्पन्न करने वाली मशीन, डाइनेमो।

generosity /,जेन्'रॉसटि / noun **generosity (to/towards sb)** उदारता।

generous / 'जेनरस् / adj 1 उदार, देने में मुक्तहस्त; स्वभाव से उदात्त 2 उदारता से दिया गया; प्रचुर मात्रा में : *a generous gift* 3 दयालु स्वभाव ▶ **generously** adv.

genesis / 'जेनसिस् / noun (pl **geneses** /जेनसीज्/) (औप) प्रारंभ, आरंभ-बिंदु : *the genesis of civilization.*

genetics / ज'नेटिक्स् / noun विभिन्न

लक्षणों का एक पीढ़ी से दूसरे पीढ़ी तक पहुँचाने का वैज्ञानिक अध्ययन।

genial / 'जीनिअल् / adj 1 सहानुभूतिपूर्ण, मिलनसार 2 (मौसम) अनुकूल ▶ **geniality** / जीनि'ऐलटि / noun **genially** adv.

genie / 'जीनि / noun (pl **genies** या **genii** / 'जीनिआइ /) (अरबी कथाओं में) अद्वितीय शक्ति वाला भूत, जिन्न।

genitals / 'जेनिटल्ज़् / (**genitalia** /,जेनि 'टेलिआ / भी) noun [pl] जननेंद्रियाँ।

genitive / 'जेनिटिव् / noun (व्या) षष्ठी विभक्ति ▶ **genitive** adj (व्या) संबंध-कारक रूप।

genius / 'जीनिअस् / noun (pl **geniuses**) 1 प्रतिभा; प्रतिभाशाली व्यक्ति 2 **a genius for sth** कुछ करने की विशिष्ट योग्यता : *have a genius for languages.*

genocide / 'जेनसाइड् / noun जाति-संहार, पूरी जाति को मार डालने का प्रयत्न।

genteel / जेन्'टील् / adj 1 (अक्सर अपमा) सामान्य से कहीं अधिक भद्र, संभ्रांत (व्यक्ति) 2 (अप्र) उच्च कुलीनों का अनुकरण करने वाला : *living in genteel poverty* ▶ **genteelly** adv.

gentile (**Gentile** भी) / 'जेन्टाइल् / adj, noun ग़ैर-यहूदी।

gentility / जेन् 'टिलटि / noun भद्रता, कुलीनता।

gentle / 'जेन्ट्ल् / adj (-r / 'जेन्ट्लर् /; -st / 'जेन्ट्लिस्ट् /) 1 दयालु; शांत : *a gentle person/manner* 2 (ढलाव) हलका : *a gentle slope* 3 (मौसम) शांत : *a gentle breeze* ▶ **gentleness** noun सज्जनता **gently** / 'जेन्ट्लि/ adv सज्जनता से; धीरे/हलके-से।

gentleman / 'जेन्ट्ल्मन् / noun (pl **gentlemen**) सज्जन, भद्र पुरुष ▶ **gentlemanly** adj.

gentry / 'जेन्ट्रि / noun (प्राय: **the gentry**) कुलीन वर्ग : *the landed gentry* (ज़मींदार)।

genuine /'जेन्युइन्/ adj 1 असली; यथार्थ 2 ईमानदार, प्रामाणिक : a genuine offer of help ▸ **genuinely** adv **genuineness** noun.

genus /'जीनस्/ noun (pl **genera** /'जेनरा/) 1 (जीव विज्ञान) परिवार के भीतर पशुओं और पौधों का उपविभाजन 2 (अनौप) व्यक्ति/वस्तु का प्रकार, वर्ग।

geocentric /,जीओ'सेन्ट्रिक/ adj भू-केंद्रीय : a geocentric view of the universe.

geography /जि'ऑग्रफ़ि/ noun 1 भूगोल 2 **the geography (of sth)** (अनौप) किसी स्थान के (धरातल आदि के) लक्षण ▸ **geographer** noun भूगोलवेत्ता **geographical** adj.

geology /जि'ऑलजि/ noun भूविज्ञान (पृथ्वी के पत्थरों, चट्टानों और भूमि का अध्ययन) ▸ **geological** /जीअ'लॉजिकल्/ adj भूविज्ञान-विषयक **geologist** /जि'ऑलजिस्ट्/ noun भूविज्ञानी।

geometry /जि'ऑमट्रि/ noun ज्यामिति, रेखागणित ▸ **geometric** /जीअ'मेट्रिक्/ (**geometrical** /जीअ'मेट्रिकल्/ भी) adj ज्यामितीय।

geophysics /,जीओ'फ़िज़िक्स्/ noun भू-भौतिकी।

geriatrics /,जेरि'ऐट्रिक्स्/ noun वृद्धों के रोगों एवं उनकी देखभाल का चिकित्सा-विज्ञान।

germ /जर्म्/ noun 1 जीवाणु; रोगाणु 2 जीवधारियों का अणु रूप हिस्सा जो विकसित होने में समर्थ हो; बीज का भ्रूण 3 **germ of sth** (विचार आदि का) आरंभ-बिंदु : the germ of an idea.

germinate /'जर्मिनेट्/ verb (बीजों में) अंकुर निकलना; वृद्धि करना ▸ **germination** noun अंकुरण।

gerund /'जेरन्ड्/ noun (व्या) क्रिया-वाचक संज्ञा।

gestation /जे'स्टेशन्/ noun 1 गर्भधारण एवं भ्रूण की विकास प्रक्रिया; गर्भावस्था का कुल समय : Gestation in humans lasts about nine months. 2 किसी विचार अथवा योजना की विकास प्रक्रिया।

gesticulate /जे'स्टिक्युलेट्/ verb हाथ-पैर या सिर हिलाकर संकेत करना, इशारा करना; बोलने के साथ-साथ शरीर हिलाना ▸ **gesticulation** /जे,स्टिक्यु'लेश्न्/ noun अंग-संचालन : wild/frantic gesticulations.

gesture /'जेस्चर्/ noun 1 किसी विचार/भावना को प्रदर्शित करने में हाथों या सिर का हिलाना 2 भाव प्रदर्शित करने के लिए की गई क्रिया; इंगित चेष्टा : The invitation was meant as a friendly gesture. ▸ **gesture** verb भाव प्रदर्शन के लिए विशेष इंगित चेष्टा करना।

get /गेट्/ verb (-tt-; pt **got** /गॉट्/; pp **got**; US **gotten** /'गॉट्न्/) 1 प्राप्त करना, पाना; खरीदना; कमाना; जीतना; लाना; मिलना; समझना 2 घटित करना; पहुँचना या भेजना : get dressed/get the children ready for school 3 कष्ट झेलना; बीमार होना : I have got a cold. 4 अनुभव करना : get angry/bored/better ■ **get about/around** (लोगों का) चलना-फिरना; (समाचार, अफ़वाह का) फैलना **get along** 1 कोई स्थान छोड़ देना 2 (get on भी) प्रगति करना 3 (get on भी) प्रबंध कर लेना **get along with sb** मित्रता-पूर्वक किसी के साथ रहना **get at sb/sth** पता लगा लेना, पहुँचना **get at sth** सीखना **get away with sth** अपराध करने पर भी पकड़ में न आना या समुचित दंड न पाना **get back to sb** (किसी से) पुन: मौखिक या लिखित चर्चा करना **get down to sth/doing sth** किसी कार्य पर लग या जुट जाना **get in** (गाड़ी आदि) पहुँचना **get in/into sth** चुन लिया जाना **get off** यात्रा आरंभ करना **get (oneself/sb) into sth** स्वयं अथवा किसी को विशिष्ट मानसिक या शारीरिक दशा में पहुँचाना **get on with sb** मित्रतापूर्वक रहना **get out of sth/doing sth** (कोई

आदत) छोड़ देना **get over sth** (कठिनाइयों पर) पार पा जाना **get over sb/sth** (बीमारी से) ठीक हो जाना; (किसी कार्य को) पूरा कर देना **get round/around sb** (अनौप) किसी व्यक्ति को किसी कार्य के लिए मना/फुसला लेना **get round/around sth** 1 सफलतापूर्वक किसी बात से निपट लेना 2 (किसी नियम/क़ानून को) टाल-टूल जाना **get (sb) through (sth)** (परीक्षा) उत्तीर्ण करना **get (sth) across (to sb)** किसी को कुछ समझाना या अपनी बात मनवाना **get sth in** 1 इकट्ठा करना 2 कुछ ख़रीदना **get through sth** (कार्य) समाप्त करना/होना **get through to sb** किसी के पास प्रत्यक्षत: या संपर्क साधन से पहुँचना **get through with sth** (किसी कार्य को) पूरा कर डालना **get to sb** (अनौप) किसी की मनोदशा पर बुरा प्रभाव डालना ▶ **get-together** noun (अनौप) सामाजिक मिलन/उत्सव **get-up** noun वस्त्र, विशेषत: असामान्य; रूप-सज्जा, सजावट।

getaway / 'गेटअवे / noun अपराध करके भाग जाना, रफ़ू-चक्कर : make a quick getaway.

geyser / 'गीज़र; US 'गाइज़र / noun 1 गरम पानी का प्राकृतिक स्रोत/चश्मा 2 पानी गरम करने का यंत्र।

ghastly / 'गास्ट्लि; US 'गैस्ट्लि / adj (-ier, -iest) 1 डरावना, भयावह 2 (अनौप) बहुत ख़राब/अरुचिकर : a ghastly error/mistake 3 (औप) मृत्यु-सदृश, पीला, विवर्ण : His face was a ghastly white.

ghost / गोस्ट / noun प्रेतात्मा, भूत ▶ **ghostly** adj (-ier, -iest) प्रेत समान, भूत-जैसा।

giant / 'जाइअन्ट / noun (fem **giantess** / 'जाइअन्टेस् /) 1 दैत्य 2 भीमकाय मनुष्य, पशु या पौधा 3 असामान्य सामर्थ्य या प्रतिभा-संपन्न व्यक्ति : Shakespeare is a giant among poets. ▶ **giant** adj असामान्य रूप से विशाल।

gibber / 'जिबर् / verb (डर के कारण) जल्दी-जल्दी अस्पष्ट-से शब्द बोलना : a gibbering idiot.

gibberish / 'जिबरिश् / noun अस्पष्ट एवं समझ में न आने वाले शब्द; बकवास।

gibe (jibe भी) / जाइब् / noun gibe (about/at sb/sth) ताना, उपहास ▶ **gibe** (jibe भी) verb.

giddy / 'गिडि / adj (-ier, -iest) 1 सिर में चक्कर देने वाला/चक्कर आ रहा हो इस प्रकार की वेदना वाला : have a giddy feeling 2 मस्ती में ▶ **giddily** adv : stagger giddily round the room **giddiness** noun : overcome by nausea and giddiness.

gift / गिफ़्ट / noun 1 उपहार, भेंट 2 **gift** (for sth/doing sth) प्रतिभा, सहज योग्यता ▶ **gifted** adj प्रतिभाशाली।

gigantic / जाइ'गैनटिक् / adj भीमकाय : a problem of gigantic proportions.

giggle / 'गिग्ल् / verb giggle (at sb/sth) हलके-से हीं-हीं करते हुए हँसना ▶ **giggle** noun 1 इस प्रकार की हँसी 2 the giggles [pl] न थमने वाली इस प्रकार की हँसी : get the giggles.

gild / गिल्ड / verb 1 सोना चढ़ाना, मुलम्मा चढ़ाना 2 (अल) किसी चीज़ को ऐसे चमकाना जैसे सोना हो ▶ **gilded** adj अति समृद्ध, धनवान।

gill / गिल् / noun (प्राय: pl) गिल, मछली का वह अंग जिससे वह साँस लेती है।

gilt / गिल्ट् / adj सोना चढ़ी हुई वस्तु; सुनहरे रंग का ▶ **gilt** noun मुलम्मा चढ़ाने की सामग्री।

gimlet / 'गिम्लट् / noun लकड़ी में छेद करने वाला यंत्र, बरमा।

gimmick / 'गिमिक् / noun (अप्रा) ध्यान आकृष्ट करने का विचित्र उपाय : a publicity/marketing gimmick ▶ **gimmickry** noun.

gin / जिन् / noun एक प्रकार की शराब, जिन।

ginger /'जिन्जर्/ *noun* 1 अदरक 2 अद-
रक के रंग का (हलका नारंगी)।

gingerly /'जिन्जर्लि/ *adv* सावधानी-से,
डरते-डरते : *She gingerly tested the
water with her toe.*

gipsy, gypsy /'जिप्सि/ *noun* जिप्सी,
एक ख़ानाबदोश जाति, कंजर।

giraffe /ज'राफ़/ *US* ज'रैफ़/ *noun* (*pl*
अपरिवर्तित या **giraffes**) जिराफ़।

girder /'गर्डर्/ *noun* गर्डर, लोहे, लकड़ी
आदि की शहतीर।

girdle /'गर्ड्ल/ *noun* 1 करधनी; कमर की
पेटी 2 (*अलं*) घेरा ▸ **girdle** *verb* (*अलं*)
घेरना।

girl /गर्ल्/ *noun* 1 लड़की, कन्या; पुत्री
2 नवयुवती; प्रेमिका ▸ **girlhood** *noun*
कन्यावस्था **girlish** /'गर्लिश्/ *adj* कन्या-
सुलभ।

girth /गर्थ्/ *noun* 1 घेरा; घेरे की माप : *a
tree one metre in girth* 2 घोड़े की
कमर की पेटी।

gist /जिस्ट्/ *noun* **the gist** (किसी कथन
का) सारांश या तात्पर्य : *get the gist of an
argument.*

give¹ /गिव्/ *verb* (*pt* **gave** /गेव्/; *pp*
given /'गिव्न् /) 1 देना; कुछ बदले में
लेकर देना : *I gave each of the boys an
apple.* 2 समय देना, विचार करना : *I've
given the matter a lot of thought.*
3 बहाना बनाना या सफ़ाई पेश करना 4 पार्टी/
भोज आदि देना 5 शब्द-विशिष्ट पैदा
करना : *give a groan/laugh* 6 कुछ
भाव-विशेष किसी के अंदर पैदा करना : *All
that heavy lifting has given me a
pain in the back.* ■ **give in** (**to sb/
sth**) हार मानना, कुछ करने या पाने के प्रयत्न
से रुक जाना **give oneself/sb up** (**to
sb**) आत्म-समर्पण/समर्पण कर देना **give
out** 1 (सामान का) चुक जाना, ख़त्म हो
जाना 2 (इंजिन) काम करना बंद कर देना
give over (**doing sth**) (*अनौप*) किसी
कार्य को पूरा किए बिना छोड़ देना (प्राय:

आदेश या सुझाव रूप में): *Give over
complaining!* **give sb away** (विवाह
के अवसर पर) कन्यादान करना **give sb to
understand that** किसी को किसी बात
का विश्वास दिलाना **give sth away**
1 मुफ़्त में कुछ देना 2 कुछ वितरित करना
3 मौक़ा गँवा देना **give sth in** किसी को
कुछ हस्तांतरित करना **give sth out**
1 बाँटना 2 घोषणा करना 3 कुछ बाहर
निकालना/फेंकना **give sth/sb away**
रहस्योद्घाटन कर देना **give sth up** कोई
आदत त्याग देना **give up** किसी कार्य को
निराश होकर छोड़ देना।

give² /गिव्/ *noun* लचक, लोच ■ **give
and take** 1 (शब्दों, विचारों का) आदान-
प्रदान 2 संबंधों में समझौता करने की तत्परता
एवं इच्छा।

given /'गिव्न्/ *adj* पूर्व निश्चित; उल्लिखित
▸ **given** *prep* को ध्यान में रखते हुए :
*Given that she is interested in chil-
dren, I am sure that teaching is the
right career for her.* **given name**
noun (अमेरिकी अंग्रेज़ी में) व्यक्ति का
प्रथम नाम।

glacial /'ग्लेसिअल; 'ग्लेश्ल्/ *adj* 1 (भू-
विज्ञान) हिम-युग संबंधी; ग्लेस्यर (हिमानी)-
विषयक 2 बहुत ठंडा, बर्फ़ जैसा।

glacier /'ग्लैसिअर्; *US* 'ग्लेशर्/ *noun*
हिमनदी, हिमानी, बर्फ़ का टीला जो पहाड़ों
से घाटियों की ओर फिसलता रहता है।

glad /ग्लैड्/ *adj* (**-dder, -ddest**) 1 **glad**
(**about sth/to do sth/that...**) प्रसन्न;
संतुष्ट 2 **glad of sth** आभारी, कृतज्ञ
▸ **gladden** *verb* प्रसन्न करना **gladly**
adv **gladness** *noun*.

glade /ग्लेड्/ *noun* जंगल या वन में खुला
क्षेत्र/ख़ाली जगह।

glamour (*US* **glamor** भी) /'ग्लैमर्/
noun 1 मोहकता; आकर्षकता : *Now
that she's an air hostess, foreign
travel has lost its glamour for her.*
2 कामुक रूप से सुंदर, मोहक ▸ **glamor-**

ize, -ise *verb* किसी चीज़ को वास्त-विकता से अधिक आकर्षक प्रदर्शित करना : *Television tends to glamorize acts of violence.* **glamorous** / 'ग्लैमरस् / *adj* लुभावना।

glance / ग्लान्स्; *US* ग्लैन्स् / *verb* 1 दृष्टि डालना, एक नज़र डालना 2 **glance at/ down/over/through sth** जल्दी से कुछ पढ़ना : *glance at the newspaper* 3 (चमकीली वस्तुओं का) चमकना 4 वार का अपने लक्ष्य से तिरछे फिसल जाना ■ **at first glance** प्रथम दृष्टि में ▸ **glance** *noun* झलक **glancing** *adj.*

gland / ग्लैन्ड् / *noun* (शरीर की) ग्रंथि : *a snake's poison glands ○ thyroid glands* ▸ **glandular** / 'ग्लैन्ड्युलर; *US* 'ग्लैन्जलर् / *adj* ग्रंथि-विषयक।

glare / ग्लेअर् / *noun* 1 चकाचौंध करने वाला प्रकाश : *the glare of the sun* 2 आँखें तरेरकर देखने वाली दृष्टि, क्रोधित दृष्टि : *give sb a hostile glare* ▸ **glare** *verb* 1 चकाचौंध होना/करना 2 **glare (at sb/sth)** आँखें तरेरना; क्रुद्ध दृष्टि डालना **glaring** *adj* 1 चकाचौंध 2 क्रोधित 3 सहज ही में दिखाई पड़ने वाली (त्रुटि आदि)।

glass / ग्लास्; *US* ग्लैस् / *noun* 1 काँच, पारदर्शी शीशा, (अप्र) दर्पण 2 (प्राय: समास में) पानी आदि पीने का बरतन : *a beer/brandy/whisky glass* 3 शीशे के बरतन या अन्य सामान 4 **glasses (spec-tacles,** *अनौप* **specs** भी) [*pl*] ऐनक, चश्मा 5 **glasses (field-glasses** भी) दूरबीन ▸ **glass-blower** *noun* कारीगर जो पिघले काँच से वस्तुएँ बनाता है **glass-house** *noun* (पौधों को उगाने/बढ़ाने के लिए) शीशे की दीवारों और छत वाला मकान **glassy** *adj* (-ier, -iest) 1 शीशे जैसा 2 (आँखें) मंद, स्थिर, भावशून्य।

glaze / ग्लेज़् / *verb* 1 (खिड़कियों आदि में) काँच/शीशा लगाना 2 **glaze sth (with sth); glaze sth (over)** (बरतनों पर)

शीशे जैसी पालिश चढ़ाना ■ **glaze over** (आँखों का) भावशून्य हो जाना, पथरा जाना ▸ **glaze** *noun* बरतनों पर काँच चढ़ाने का सामान **glazed** *adj* (विशेषत: आँखें) पथराई हुई।

glazier / 'ग्लेज़िअर् / *noun* खिड़कियों में शीशे लगाने वाला कारीगर।

gleam / ग्लीम् / *noun* 1 झिलमिल रोशनी : *the sudden gleam of a match in the darkness* 2 [*sing*] किसी भाव की हलकी-सी झलक : *a gleam of hope in an apparently hopeless situa-tion* ▸ **gleam** *verb* 1 झिलमिलाना 2 (चिकनी सतह का) चमकना 3 **gleam with sth** (चेहरे और आँखों का) भाव प्रदर्शित करना : *eyes gleaming with anticipation/excitement.*

glean / ग्लीन् / *verb* 1 **glean sth (from sb/sth)** प्रयास से थोड़ा–थोड़ा करके किसी से कुछ समाचार, तथ्य या सूचना प्राप्त करना 2 खेत में बचे अनाज को बीनना : *glean wheat.*

glee / ग्ली / *noun* **glee (at sth)** सफलता का उल्लास ▸ **gleeful** *adj* **gleefully** *adv.*

glen / ग्लेन् / *noun* (विशेषत: स्कॉटलैंड् और आइरलैंड् से) संकरी घाटी।

glib / ग्लिब् / *adj* (अपमा) (वक्ता या वक्तव्य) मीठा परंतु कपटपूर्ण : *a glib talker/salesman* ▸ **glibly** *adv.*

glide / ग्लाइड् / *verb* 1 फिसलना, सर-कना : *birds gliding overhead* 2 बिना इंजिन शक्ति के उड़ान जैसे वायुयान में (इंजिन ख़राब होने से) या ग्लाइडर में ▸ **glide** *noun* इस प्रकार की गति; (स्वर विद्या) मुँह की एक स्थिति से दूसरी स्थिति में गति से उत्पन्न ध्वनि (शब्द) **glider** / 'ग्लाइडर् / *noun* एक प्रकार का हवाई जहाज़ जो बिना इंजिन के उड़ता है।

glimmer / 'ग्लिमर् / *verb* टिमटिमाना : *lights glimmering in the distance* ▸ **glimmer** *noun* 1 टिमटिमाती रोशनी

glimpse 2 किसी चीज़ का हलका-सा लक्षण/झलक : *a glimmer of hope* **glimmering** *noun.*

glimpse /'ग्लिम्प्स्/ *noun* **glimpse (at sb/sth); glimpse (into sth)** (किसी व्यक्ति/वस्तु की) अस्पष्ट सी झलक ▸ **glimpse** *verb* एक झलक देख लेना : *She glimpsed him between the half-drawn curtains.*

glint / ग्लिन्ट् / *verb* **1** (रोशनी का) चमकना, झिलमिलाना **2** (व्यक्ति की आँखों का) भाव-विशेष दिखाना : *eyes glinting with mischief.*

glisten /'ग्लिस्न्/ *verb* **glisten (with sth)** (किसी गीली या पालिशदार सतह का) चमकना : *grass glistening with dew.*

glitter /'ग्लिटर्/ *verb* **glitter (with sth)** जगमगाना; चमकना ▸ **glitter** *noun* **1** जगमग रोशनी **2** आकर्षक एवं मोहक परंतु झूठा प्रदर्शन : *the superficial glamour and glitter of the show business* **glitterati** *noun* [*pl*] (अक्सर *अपमा*) फ़ैशनेबल लोग **glittering** *adj.*

gloat / ग्लोट् / *verb* **gloat (about/over sth)** अपनी सफलता या दूसरे की विफलता से आनंदित होना ▸ **gloating** *adj.*

global / ग्लोबल् / *adj* विश्व-संबंधी, संपूर्ण विश्व को प्रभावित करने वाला : *global issues/problems* ▸ **global warming** *noun* कुछ गैसों की वायुमंडल में अधिक मात्रा में उपस्थिति के कारण सूर्य की गरमी रुक जाने से पृथ्वी के तापमान में वृद्धि।

globe / ग्लोब् / *noun* **1** ग्लोब, पृथ्वी का गोलाकार मानचित्र **2 the globe** पृथ्वी : *travel (all) around the globe* **3** गेंद जैसी गोलाकार वस्तु।

globule /'ग्लॉब्यूल्/ *noun* (औप) बहुत छोटी बूंद या गोलाकार वस्तु (विशेषत: द्रव या पिघला ठोस पदार्थ)।

gloom / ग्लूम् / *noun* **1** धुँधलापन; गहरी छाया **2** [*sing*] उदासी, निराशा ▸ **gloomy** *adj* (-ier, -iest) **gloomily** *adv.*

glorify /'ग्लॉरिफ़ाइ/ *verb* (*pt, pp* **glorified**) **1** (प्राय: *अपमा*) वास्तविकता से बढ़कर गुणगान करना; जरूरत से ज्यादा प्रशंसा करना **2** महिमागान करना; स्तुति पूजन करना ▸ **glorification** *noun.*

glorious / ग्लॉरिअस् / *adj* **1** यशप्रद **2** सुंदर; महान **3** (*अनौप*) भोग्य : *have a glorious time.*

glory / ग्लॉरि / *noun* **1** यश, कीर्ति **2** (भगवान का) महिमागान, प्रशंसा **3** सुंदर और महान होने का गुण : *the glory of a sunset* **4** यश और आदर के योग्य वस्तु; प्रशंसापात्र : *the glories of nature* ▸ **glory** *verb* (*pt, pp* **gloried**) ■ **glory in sth** पर गर्व/गौरव करना।

gloss¹ / ग्लॉस् / *noun* **1** चिकनी सतह पर चमक; चिकनी चमकदार वस्तु : *varnishes available in gloss and matt* **2** आकर्षक रूप जो सिर्फ़ बाहरी दिखावा हो : *the gloss and glitter of Hollywood* ▸ **gloss** *verb* ■ **gloss over sth** किसी अप्रिय बात को छुपा जाना या बहुत कम ज़िक्र करना ▸ **glossy** *adj* (-ier, -iest) **1** चमकदार **2** झूठी चमक-दमक वाला : *a glossy image.*

gloss² / ग्लॉस् / *noun* **gloss (on sth)** कठिन शब्दों या पदबंधों की (फ़ुटनोट या पुस्तक के अंत में दी गई) व्याख्या; अर्थ स्पष्ट करने/निकालने का तरीक़ा; व्याख्या ▸ **gloss** *verb* व्याख्या जोड़ना/लिखना : *a difficult word that needs to be glossed.*

glossary /'ग्लॉसरि/ *noun* (*pl* **glossaries**) शब्दार्थ सूची।

glove / ग्लव् / *noun* दस्ताना।

glow / ग्लो / *verb* **1** बिना ज्वाला के चमक और गरमी बिखेरना : *glowing embers* **2 glow (with sth)** चेहरे का तमतमाना **3 glow (with sth)** तेज़ और चटक रंगों की छटा : *The countryside glowed with autumn colours.* ▸ **glow** *noun* [*sing*] **1** मंद प्रकाश **2** तमतमाहट **3** प्रसन्नता एवं संतोष की अनुभूति : *She felt* *a glow of pride in her achievement.* **glowing** *adj* **glow-worm** *noun* जुगनू।

glower / 'ग्लाउअर् / *verb* **glower (at sb/sth)** आँखें तरेरना।

glucose / 'ग्लूकोस्; ग्लूकोज़् / *noun* फलों में पाई जाने वाली प्राकृतिक शक्कर (जिसे शरीर आसानी से ऊर्जा में बदल सकता है)।

glue / ग्लू / *noun* सरेस ▸ **glue** *verb* **glue A (to/onto B)** सरेस से जोड़ना, चिपकाना : *glue the leg (back) onto the chair.*

glum / ग्लम् / *adj* (अनौप) उदास; अप्रसन्न : *glum expressions* ▸ **glumly** *adv.*

glut / ग्लट् / *verb* (-tt-) **glut sb/sth (with sth)** अत्यधिक आपूर्ति कर देना, भरमार कर देना; छककर खाना ▸ **glut** *noun* (प्राय: *sing*) अतितृप्ति, भरमार।

glutton / 'ग्लटन् / *noun* 1 (अपमा) पेटू 2 **glutton for sth** (अनौप) कुछ भी (कठिन या अरुचिकर काम) करने को सदैव तत्पर ▸ **gluttonous** / 'ग्लटनस् / *adj* खाऊ **gluttony** / 'ग्लटनि / *noun* पेटूपन।

glycerine (*US* **glycerin**) / 'ग्लिसरीन् / *noun* ग्लिसरीन।

gnarled / नार्ल्ड् / *adj* (पेड़ का तना) मुड़ा-तुड़ा एवं गाँठदार, (व्यक्ति के हाथ और अँगुलियाँ) (वृद्धावस्था या कठिन श्रम के कारण) टेढ़े एवं गठीले; खुरदरे : *hands gnarled with age.*

gnash / नैश् / *noun* दाँत कटकटाना; दाँत पीसना ▸ **gnashing** *noun.*

gnat / नैट् / *noun* डाँस, एक प्रकार का बड़ा मच्छर जो काटता है।

gnaw / नॉ / *verb* 1 **gnaw (at) sth** कड़ी वस्तु को कुतरना : *a dog gnawing (at) a bone* 2 **gnaw (at) sb/sth** चिंता आदि से लगातार सताना/सताया जाना : *fear gnawing (at) one's heart.*

gnome / नोम् / *noun* 1 (कहानियों में) बौना जो भूमि के भीतर रहता है और ख़ज़ाने की रक्षा करता है 2 (अनौप, प्राय: अपमा) आर्थिक मामलों में प्रभावशाली व्यक्ति : *the gnomes of Zürich.*

go¹ / गो / *verb* (3rd *person sing pres t* **goes** / गोज़् /; *pt* **went** / वेन्ट् /; *pp* **gone** / गॉन् /) 1 जाना; चलना; चला जाना; प्रस्थान करना 2 बेकार हो जाना, टूट जाना : *My sweater has gone at the elbows.* 3 स्थिति में परिवर्तन आना : *This milk has gone sour.* 4 समाप्त या लुप्त हो जाना : *I've washed it repeatedly, but the stain won't go.* 5 शेष रह जाना : *two more exams to go* ○ *There are only two days to go before the final examination.* ▪ **go about sth/doing sth** (एक निश्चित तरीक़े से) किसी काम पर लग जाना **go after sb** किसी का पीछा करना **go after sb/sth** पाने का प्रयास करना **go ahead 1** आगे-आगे जाना और औरों से पहले पहुँचना 2 आरंभ करना, घटित होना; प्रगति करना **go away** घर छोड़ना, दूर चले जाना **go back (on sth)** वादे से पीछे हट जाना **go back (to sth)** कुछ पहले कहे कथन पर पुनर्विचार करना **go by** (समय) गुज़रना **go by sth 1** के द्वारा निर्देशित होना 2 कोई राय या मत/निर्णय बनाना **go by the name of** कहलाना **go down** नीचे गिरना, पहुँचना या जाना; कम हो जाना **go halves (with sb)** बराबर-बराबर बाँट लेना **go in 1** प्रवेश करना 2 (सूर्य या चाँद) बादल के पीछे चला जाना/छुप जाना **go in for sth** (परीक्षा, प्रतियोगिता आदि में) भाग लेना; (शौक़ या व्यवसाय के रूप में) ग्रहण करना : *She doesn't go in for team games.* **go into sth 1** (वाहन का) टकरा जाना 2 (किसी व्यवसाय में) प्रवेश करना 3 किसी चीज़ की जाँच करना : *I don't want to go into the minor details now.* **go off 1** स्थान छोड़ देना 2 (बंदूक़, विस्फोट आदि का) धमाके के साथ दाग़ा जाना 3 (बिजली, प्रकाश आदि) गुल हो जाना : *Suddenly* the lights went off. 4 (भोजन का) बासी हो जाना, सड़ना : *This milk has gone off.* (दूध खट्टा हो गया है।) **go off well/badly** (किसी समारोह, योजना आदि का) योजनानुसार सफल होना : *The performance went off well.* **go on** जारी रखना, होना **go on doing sth** बिना रुके कोई कार्य करते रहना **go out** घर छोड़ना (कहीं जाने के लिए) **go over sth** सावधानी से जाँचना या पढ़ना **go round** (सामान) सभी के लिए पूरा होना: *Is there enough food to go round?* **go round/around/about** 1 एक स्थान से दूसरे स्थान पर जाना : *She often goes about barefoot.* 2 एक से दूसरे के पास पहुँचना **go through (sth)** 1 तकलीफ़ उठाना 2 सावधानीपूर्वक जाँच करना/पढ़ना **go through with sth** (कोई कार्य) पूरा करना **go together; go with sth** साथ रहने पर संतुष्ट रहना; मेल खाना; (रंगों का) मेल में रहना **go to law** (किसी के विरुद्ध) क़ानूनी कार्रवाई करना **go to pieces** चूर-चूर हो जाना; अत्यधिक परेशानी में पड़ जाना **go to sea** नाविक बनना **go without (sth)** अभाव को सह लेना।

go² /गो/ *noun* (*pl* goes /गोज़/) 1 (खेल आदि में) किसी की बारी, अवसर : *Whose ga is it?* 2 (अनौप) शक्ति, उत्साह : *She's full of go.* ■ **at one go** एक ही प्रयास में **be on the go** (अनौप) व्यस्त होना **have a go (at sth/doing sth)** (अनौप) प्रयत्न करना।

goad / गोड् / *noun* 1 अंकुश 2 प्रेरक तत्त्व : *offer economic help as a goad to political reform* ▸ **goad** *verb* **goad sb/sth (into sth/doing sth)** किसी व्यक्ति या पशु को लगातार परेशान किए या भड़काए जाना।

goal / गोल् / *noun* 1 लक्ष्य;/उद्देश्य : *pursue/achieve one's goal in life* 2 (फ़ुटबाल, हॉकी आदि का) वह स्थान जहाँ गोल किया जाता है; दौड़ का अंतिम

बिंदु ▸ **goalkeeper** *noun* गोलरक्षक, गेंद को गोल में जाने से रोकने वाला खिलाड़ी।

goat / गोट् / *noun* 1 बकरा, बकरी 2 (अप) अप्रिय वृद्ध व्यक्ति।

gobble /'गॉब्ल्/ *verb* **gobble sth (up/down)** निगल जाना, शीघ्रता से गटक जाना : *gobble up all the cakes.*

go-between / 'गो बि'ट्वीन् / *noun* बिचौलिया, मध्यस्थ, दो व्यक्तियों की मुलाक़ात कराने वाला।

goblet / 'गॉब्लट् / *noun* शराब पीने का प्याला।

goblin / 'गॉब्लिन् / *noun* बैताल।

god / गॉड् / *noun* 1 देवता; देवमूर्ति 2 **God** ईश्वर, परमात्मा ▸ **godless** *adj* नास्तिक; दुष्ट **godly** / 'गॉड्लि / *adj* (-ier, -iest) धर्मपरायण।

goddess / गॉडिस् / *noun* 1 देवी 2 पूजित स्त्री।

godforsaken / 'गॉड्फ़र्सेकन् / *adj* (स्थान) निराशाजनक; दुखी; सुनसान।

godsend / 'गॉड्सेन्ड् / *noun* **godsend (to sb)** ईश्वरीय वरदान; अचानक मिली संपत्ति; सौभाग्य।

goggle / 'गॉग्ल् / *verb* **goggle (at sb/ sth)** आँखें घुमाना; आँखें फाड़कर देखना : *He goggled at the magnificent display of goods.*

goggles / 'गॉग्ल्ज़् / *noun* [*pl*] धूप का चश्मा।

going / 'गोइङ् / *noun* 1 [*sing*] स्थान छोड़कर जाने की क्रिया; प्रस्थान : *We were all sad at her going.* 2 भूमि, मार्ग आदि की स्थिति/दिशा (यात्रा के लिए) : *The path was rough going.* 3 प्रगति, मात्रा आदि की गति/दर : *It was good going to reach Dehradun by midday.* ▸ **going** *adj* ■ **the going rate (for sth)** (सेवाओं आदि के लिए दी जाने वाली) साधारण राशि/मूल्य; चालू दर।

-going *suff* (प्रत्यय) (यौगिक विशेषणों में

प्रयुक्त) नियमित रूप से किसी स्थान विशेष पर जाने वाला : *the film-going public.*

goings-on / 'गोइङ्स ऑन् / *noun* [pl] (अनौप, प्राय: *अपमा*) आश्चर्यजनक व्यवहार या घटना।

goitre (*US* goiter) / 'गॉइटर् / *noun* घेंघा रोग।

gold / गोल्ड् / *noun* 1 सोना 2 (*साहि*) बड़ी मात्रा में धन; विशाल संपत्ति : *a miser and his gold* 3 स्वर्ण-वर्ण 4 स्वर्ण-पदक (खेलों में) : *an Olympic gold* ▸ **gold foil** (**gold leaf** भी) *noun* सोने का पत्तर, सोने का वरक़ **gold standard** *noun* (प्राय: the gold standard) स्वर्ण-मान, सोने का भाव जिससे विभिन्न देशों की संपत्ति की तुलना की जाती है।

golden / 'गोल्डन् / *adj* 1 सोने का बना हुआ; स्वर्ण-समान, सुनहरे रंग का 2 स्वर्णिम; सुनहरा (मौक़ा) : *golden memories/ days.*

goldfish / 'गोल्ड्फ़िश् / *noun* (pl अपरिवर्तित) नारंगी या लाल रंग की छोटी मछली जो अक्सर पाली जाती है।

goldsmith / 'गोल्ड्स्मिथ् / *noun* सुनार।

golf / गॉल्फ़् / *noun* एक खेल, गॉल्फ़ ▸ **golfing** *noun* गॉल्फ़ खेलना।

gong[1] / गॉङ् / *noun* घंटा-घड़ियाल।

good[1] / गुड् / *adj* (**better** / 'बेटर् /; **best** / बेस्ट् /) 1 अच्छा; उत्तम; तृप्तिदायक : *a good lecture/meal* 2 उच्च सामाजिक प्रतिष्ठा वाला : *from a good family* 3 **good** (**at sth/doing sth**) कुछ अच्छी तरह करने में समर्थ : *good at mathematics/languages* 4 नैतिक रूप से उचित; अच्छे व्यवहार वाला, विनम्र : *a good deed* 5 **good for sth** के योग्य, समर्थ : *This car's good for many more miles.* ■ **as good as** समान, लगभग वही : *The matter is as good as settled.* **good for you/sb/them/ etc** (अनौप) (प्रशंसा के लिए प्रयुक्त) : *She's passed the exam? Good for*

her! **make** (**sth**) **good** ख़र्चा देना; (वादा) निभाना; काम पूरा करना; क्षतिपूर्ति करना ▸ **good-for-nothing** *noun, adj* बेकार (व्यक्ति) **Good Friday** *noun* ईस्टर से पहले का शुक्रवार।

good[2] / गुड् / *noun* 1 नैतिक दृष्टि से उचित/स्वीकृत : *the difference between good and evil* 2 हित, लाभ; फ़ायदा : *work for the good of one's country* 3 **the good** महान व्यक्ति; प्रतिष्ठित ■ **do** (**sb**) **good** लाभ पहुँचाना **for good** (**and all**) सदा के लिए : *She's leaving the country for good.*

goodbye / ˌगुड्'बाइ / *interj, noun* अल- विदा।

goodness / 'गुड्नस् / *noun* 1 अच्छाई, साधुता 2 (आश्चर्य प्रकट करते हुए) : *My goodness/Goodness me!*

goods / गुड्ज़् / *noun* [pl] चल संपत्ति; ख़रीदने/बेचने वाला सामान : *stolen goods.*

goodwill / ˌगुड्'विल् / *noun* सद्भावना, मैत्री भाव।

googly / 'गूग्लि / *noun* (क्रिकेट में) इस तरह से फेंकी गई गेंद जो एक दिशा में मुड़ती हुई प्रतीत होती हो परंतु वास्तव में उसके ठीक विपरीत दिशा में मुड़े।

goose / गूस् / *noun* (pl **geese** / गीस् /) 1 (*masc* **gander** / 'गैन्डर् /) हंसनी 2 (अप्र) मूर्ख व्यक्ति।

gore / गॉर् / *verb* सींग भोंककर व्यक्ति या पशु को घायल करना ▸ **gore** *noun* घाव से निकला हुआ गाढ़ा रक्त।

gorge[1] / गॉर्ज् / *noun* पहाड़ियों के बीच तंग द्वार; घाटी मार्ग।

gorge[2] / गॉर्ज् / *verb* **gorge** (**oneself**) (**on/with sth**) भकोसना; ठूँस-ठूँसकर खाना/ भर लेना।

gorgeous / 'गॉर्जस् / *adj* 1 (अनौप) शानदार; विस्मयकारक : *gorgeous weather* 2 (अनौप) अति सुंदर 3 भड़- कीला (रंग) ▸ **gorgeously** *adv.*

gorilla / ग'रिला / *noun* (pl **gorillas**)

गोरिला, आदमी की शकल वाला विशाल बंदर।

gory / 'गॉरि / *adj* खून से सना; खूनी : *a gory battle/film.*

gospel / 'गॉस्पल्/ *noun* 1 (बाईबल में) (प्राय: the Gospel) ईसा मसीह का जीवनवृत्त और उपदेश; प्रवचन : *preach the Gospel* 2 (बाईबल के) सुसमाचार।

gossip / 'गॉसिप्/ *noun* 1 (अपमा) गपशप; गप 2 (प्राय: अपमा) अख़बारों आदि में किसी व्यक्ति या घटना पर अनौपचारिक लेख : *gossip column* 3 (अपमा या परि) दूसरों के बारे में निरर्थक बातें करने वाला ▸ **gossip** *verb* **gossip (with sb) (about sth)** गप मारना।

gouge / गाउज्/ *noun* (तक) गोल रूखानी (बढ़ई का एक औज़ार) ▸ **gouge** *verb* **gouge sth (in sth)** रूखानी से छेद करना/ खाँचा काटना।

gourd / गुअर्ड; गॉर्ड/ *noun* 1 कद्दू, पेठा, लौकी, तुरई आदि तरकारी 2 तूँबा।

gourmet / 'गुअर्मे/ *noun* अच्छे खान-पान के बारे में ज्ञान रखने वाला एवं स्वादिष्ट भोजन आदि का आनंद लेने वाला व्यक्ति।

gout / गाउट्/ *noun* गठिया-वात, संधि-वात (जोड़ों का दर्द)।

govern / 'गवर्न्/ *verb* 1 (देश आदि पर) शासन करना 2 नियंत्रण रखना 3 (व्या) संज्ञा या सर्वनाम का क्रिया या पूर्वसर्ग पर निर्भर होना ▸ **governance** *noun* प्रशासन **governing** *adj.*

governess / 'गवर्नस्/ *noun* (पूर्व में) बच्चों को घर पर ही पढ़ाने के लिए रखी अध्यापिका।

government / 'गवर्न्मन्ट्/ *noun* 1 (प्राय: the Government) सरकार, प्रशासन; शासक-मंडल 2 प्रशासन-तंत्र : *communist/liberal government.*

governor / 'गवर्नर्/ *noun* 1 गवर्नर; राज्यपाल 2 मशीन में गति-नियंत्रक पुर्जा।

gown / गाउन्/ *noun* 1 गाउन, स्त्रियों की एक पोशाक : *a wedding gown* 2 चोगा,

विश्वविद्यालय के सदस्यों या न्यायाधीशों द्वारा पहना जाने वाला लबादा 3 अन्य कपड़ों की सुरक्षा के लिए ऊपर से पहना जाने वाला चोगा : *a surgeon's gown.*

grab / ग्रैब्/ *verb* (-bb-) 1 **grab sth (from sb/sth)** झपटकर पकड़ना; अवसर का तत्परता से लाभ उठाना : *When I gave him the chance, he grabbed it at once.* 2 **grab at sb/sth** हथियाना/छीनना 3 (अनौप, परि) जल्दी से कुछ लेने का प्रयास करना : *grab a seat* ▸ **grab** *noun* (प्राय: *sing*) छीना-झपटी।

grace / ग्रेस्/ *noun* 1 लालित्य, मनोहरता 2 (ईश्वर की) कृपादृष्टि 3 किसी कार्य के लिए प्रदत्त अतिरिक्त समय 4 विशेष कृपा; सद्भावना ▪ **be in sb's good graces** (किसी का) कृपा-पात्र बने रहना **with (a) bad/good grace** अनिच्छा से/खुशी से ▸ **grace** *verb* (औप) 1 शोभा बढ़ाना 2 **grace sb/sth (with sth)** सम्मानित करना।

graceful / 'ग्रेस्फुल्/ *adj* 1 लालित्यपूर्ण; मनोरम 2 प्रिय तरीके से ▸ **gracefully** *adv.*

graceless / 'ग्रेस्लस्/ *adj* 1 शोभारहित 2 निर्लज्ज, अशिष्ट : *graceless behaviour.*

gracious / 'ग्रेशस्/ *adj* 1 **gracious (to sb)** उदार; अनुकूल/कृपापूर्ण 2 भव्य, शानदार : *a gracious old mansion* 3 **gracious (to sb)** (ईश्वर) दयालु, कृपाल ▸ **graciously** *adv* **graciousness** *noun.*

gradation / ग्रेडेश्न्/ *noun* 1 क्रम, कोटि 2 एक से दूसरी अवस्था में क्रमिक परिवर्तन।

grade¹ / ग्रेड्/ *noun* 1 श्रेणी, वर्ग/कोटि : *high/low grade materials* 2 परीक्षा में दिए गए अंक/प्राप्त अंक 3 (*US*) कक्षा-स्तर : *Tom is in the third grade.*

grade² / ग्रेड्/ *verb* 1 श्रेणी/वर्ग में रखना 2 परीक्षा में ग्रेड/श्रेणी देना 3 (सड़क आदि के लिए) भूमि को लगभग समतल करना।

gradient / 'ग्रेडिअन्ट / noun 1 (सड़क आदि की) ढलान की मात्रा 2 एक क्षेत्र से दूसरे क्षेत्र के बीच तापमान, वायुदाब, प्रकाश आदि के परिवर्तन की दर।

gradual / 'ग्रैजुअल / adj 1 क्रमिक : a gradual increase/decrease 2 (ढलान) बहुत ढालू न होना : a gradual incline ▸ **gradually** adv क्रमश:, धीरे-धीरे : Things gradually improved.

graduate[1] / 'ग्रैजुअट / noun 1 graduate (in sth) (विश्वविद्यालय का) स्नातक 2 (US) स्कूली शिक्षा पूर्ण करने वाला व्यक्ति : a high-school graduate.

graduate[2] / 'ग्रैजुएट / verb 1 graduate (in sth) (at/from sth) विश्वविद्यालय की उपाधि (विशेषत: पहली उपाधि) पाना : graduate in history 2 graduate (from sth) to sth प्रगति/उन्नति करना 3 नापने के लिए अंशों से अंकित करना ▸ **graduation** noun उपाधि पाने की प्रक्रिया (एवं समारोह); अंकन।

graffiti / ग्र'फ़ीटि / noun [pl] सार्वजनिक स्थानों में दीवारों पर लेखन या चित्र (विशेषत: अभद्र, राजनीतिक या हास्यक) : The mall was covered wth graffiti.

graft / ग्राफ़्ट; US ग्रैफ़्ट / noun 1 क़लम (पौधे का एक टुकड़ा दूसरे पर लगाना) 2 (चिकि) अंग-प्रत्यारोपण : a skin graft ▸ **graft** verb क़लम लगाना, क़लम बाँधना; अंग-प्रत्यारोपण करना।

grain / ग्रेन् / noun 1 अनाज का दाना; एक दाना : a few grains of rice 2 कुछ पदार्थों (जैसे सोने-चाँदी आदि) का छोटा कण, रवा : a grain of salt/sugar 3 भार मापने की लघुतम ब्रिटिश इकाई, ग्रेन (पाउंड का 0.00143 वाँ, या ग्राम का 0.065 वाँ भाग) 4 (लकड़ी में) तंतु-रचना ■ (be/go) against the grain स्वभाव/प्रकृति के विपरीत ▸ **grainy** adj दानेदार; (फ़ोटो) धब्बेदार।

gram / ग्रैम् / noun 1 (gramme भी)

(संक्षि g) भार की मीट्रिक इकाई (एक हज़ार ग्राम का एक किलोग्राम होता है) 2 चना।

-gram comb form 1 भार की इकाई : milligram/kilogram 2 लिखित या चित्रित वस्तु : telegram/hologram.

grammar / 'ग्रैमर् / noun 1 व्याकरण 2 व्यक्ति का भाषा ज्ञान एवं अनुप्रयोग : use bad grammar ▸ **grammarian** / ग्र 'मेअरिअन् / noun वैयाकरण।

grammatical /ग्र'मैटिकल्/ adj व्याकरण के अनुकूल; व्याकरण-विषयक ▸ **grammatically** adv.

gramophone /'ग्रैमफ़ोन्/ noun (अप्र) = record-player.

granary / 'ग्रेनरि / noun (pl granaries) अनाज-घर, अन्न-भंडार।

grand / ग्रैन्ड् / adj (-er, -est) 1 शानदार, भव्य 2 व्यापक; विस्तृत : a grand design/plan 3 (अनौप) अभिमानी 4 प्रधान; सर्वाधिक महत्त्वपूर्ण : a grand occasion ▸ **grand** noun (pl अपरिवर्तित) (प्राय: pl) $ 1,000; £ 1,000 : It'll cost you six grand. **grandchild** noun नाती/नातिन/पोता/पोती **grandfather** noun दादा/नाना **grandly** adv **grand master** noun सर्वश्रेष्ठ शतरंज खिलाड़ी **grandmother** noun दादी/नानी **grandparent** noun नाना/नानी/दादा/दादी **grand total** noun कुल योग।

grandeur / 'ग्रेन्जर् / noun शान, वैभव; श्रेष्ठता।

grandstand / 'ग्रैन्स्टैन्ड् / noun घुड़-दौड़ आदि में दर्शकों के बैठने के लिए छतदार स्थान।

granite /'ग्रैनिट/ noun ग्रेनाइट, कड़ा पत्थर जो मकान बनाने में उपयोग किया जाता है।

granny (**grannie** भी) /'ग्रैनि / noun (pl grannies) (अनौप) दादी, नानी।

grant / ग्रान्ट्; US ग्रैन्ट् / verb 1 अनुमति देना : grant a favour 2 प्रदान करना : These lands were granted to our *family.* ■ **take sb/sth for granted** किसी व्यक्ति/वस्तु से इतना अधिक परिचित होना कि उसका महत्त्व कम मानने लगे **take sth for granted** किसी तथ्य को सत्य मानकर चलना ▸ **grant** *noun* grant (to do sth/towards sth) *(कानून)* प्रदान की हुई वस्तु; *(आर्थिक)* अनुदान।

granular / 'ग्रैन्यलर् / *adj* 1 दानेदार 2 खुरदरा : *a granular surface.*

granulated sugar / ग्रैन्युलेटिड् 'शुगर् / *noun* दानेदार चीनी।

granule / 'ग्रैन्यूल् / *noun* किसी पदार्थ के छोटे दाने; छोटा कण; रवा : *instant-coffee granules.*

grape / ग्रेप् / *noun* अंगूर।

grapefruit / 'ग्रेप्फ्रूट् / *noun (pl* अपरि-वर्तित) छोटा चकोतरा।

graph / ग्राफ़; ग्रैफ़् / *noun (गणित)* ग्राफ़; लेखाचित्र ▸ **graph paper** *noun* लेखाचित्र काग़ज़।

-graph *suff (प्रत्यय)* 1 शैली विशेष में लिखित या चित्रित वस्तु : *autograph/ monograph/photograph* 2 लिखने या रिकॉर्ड करने वाला यंत्र (उपकरण) : *seismograph.*

graphic / 'ग्रैफ़िक् / *adj* 1 लिखने, खींचने या रँगने से संबद्ध : *graphic displays* 2 मन में पूरा चित्र खींचने वाला वर्णन, सजीव चित्रण : *a graphic account of a battle* ▸ **graphically** *adv* **graphics** *noun [pl]* (व्यापारिक प्रयोग के लिए) डिज़ाइन, चित्र, कलाकृति आदि : *computer graphics.*

grapple / 'ग्रैप्ल् / *verb* 1 grapple (with sb/sth) (विरोधी को) कसकर पकड़ना; आमने-सामने लड़ना 2 grapple (with sth) समस्या सुलझाने के लिए प्रयास करना : *He has been grappling with the problem for a long time.*

grasp / ग्रास्प्; *US* ग्रैस्प् / *verb* 1 हाथों या बाँहों से कसकर पकड़ लेना 2 आतुरता से स्वीकार करना : *grasp an opportunity*

3 *(मन से)* पूर्णत: समझ लेना ■ **grasp at sth** पकड़ने का प्रयत्न करना ▸ **grasp** *noun (प्राय: sing)* 1 पकड़; पकड़ने की शक्ति; नियंत्रण 2 समझ।

grasping / 'ग्रास्पिङ्; *US* ग्रैस्पिङ् / *adj (अपमा)* लोभी, लालची।

grass / ग्रास्; *US* ग्रैस् / *noun* 1 घास 2 the grass घास का मैदान; लॉन 3 *(अप्र, प्राय: अपमा)* पुलिस का मुख़बिर/भेदिया ■ **the grass is greener on the other side (of the fence)** *(कहा)* उन लोगों के लिए कहा जाता है जो हमेशा असंतुष्ट होते हैं और यह सोचते हैं कि दूसरों की परिस्थिति उनसे बेहतर है ▸ **grass-roots** *adj* (केवल संज्ञाओं से पहले प्रयुक्त) (समाज या किसी संस्था में) जन-साधारण से संबंधित, न कि नेताओं आदि से : *We need to win support at the grass-roots level.* **grassy** *adj.*

grasshopper / 'ग्रास्हॉपर्; *US* ग्रैस्-हॉपर् / *noun* टिड्डा।

grate[1] / ग्रेट् / *verb* 1 grate sth (into sth) घिसना; कद्दूकस में कसना : *Grate the carrot finely.* 2 किरकिराना 3 grate (on sb/sth) चिड़चिड़ा प्रभाव उत्पन्न करना : *His whining voice grates on my ears/nerves.* ▸ **grater** *noun (*कद्दूकस आदि) घिसने/कसने वाला साधन **grating** *adj.*

grate[2] / ग्रेट् / *noun (*अँगीठी की) जाली, झंझरी।

grateful / 'ग्रेट्फ़ुल् / *adj* grateful (to sb) (for sth); grateful (to do sth); grateful (that...) कृतज्ञ, एहसानमंद ▸ **gratefully** *adv.*

gratify / 'ग्रैटिफ़ाइ / *verb (pt, pp* grati-fied) *(औप)* 1 प्रसन्न करना, संतुष्ट करना 2 किसी को उसकी इच्छित वस्तु देकर संतुष्ट करना : *gratify a person's whims* ▸ **gratification** *noun* 1 संतुष्टि, तृप्ति 2 तृप्तिदायक वस्तु **gratifying** *adj* संतोष-प्रद।

grating / ग्रेटिङ् / noun (खिड़की की) जाली।

gratis / ग्रैटिस; ग्रेटिस् / adj, adv मुफ़्त : a gratis copy of a book.

gratitude / ग्रैटिट्यूड; US ग्रैटिटूड् / noun gratitude (to sb) (for sth) कृतज्ञता, एहसानमंदी।

gratuitous / ग्र ट्यूइटस; US ग्र टूइटस् / adj (औप, अपमा) औचित्य रहित; निराधार/ अकारण : a gratuitous insult/lie ▸ gratuitously adv.

gratuity / ग्र ट्यूअटि; US ग्र टूअटि / noun (pl gratuities) 1 (औप) इनाम, सेवा के बदले धन का उपहार 2 सेवानिवृत्ति पर मिलने वाली धन-राशि।

grave¹ / ग्रेव् / noun 1 क़ब्र, समाधि 2 (प्रायः the grave) (साहि) मौत; मृत्यु हो जाना : He took his secret to the grave. ▸ **gravestone** noun क़ब्र का पत्थर जिस पर व्यक्ति का नाम आदि लिखा रहता है **graveyard** noun क़ब्रिस्तान।

grave² / ग्रेव् / adj (-r, -st) 1 (औप) (स्थिति आदि) गंभीर, संगीन; विचारणीय 2 (व्यक्ति, व्यवहार) गंभीर, शांतचित्त ▸ **gravely** adv.

gravel / ग्रैव्ल् / noun कंकड़, बजरी ▸ **gravelled** adj.

gravitate / ग्रैविटेट् / verb ■ **gravitate to/towards sb/sth** आकर्षित होना; धीरे–धीरे किसी की ओर गति करना : Many young people gravitate to the city. ▸ **gravitation** / ग्रैवि टेशन् / noun गुरुत्वाकर्षण (बल) **gravitational** adj.

gravity / ग्रैवटि / noun 1 दो वस्तुओं के बीच का भौतिकीय आकर्षण, भार के कारण वस्तु का पृथ्वी के केंद्र की ओर खींचा जाना : the law of gravity 2 (औप) गंभीरता (स्थिति की); गंभीर चेहरा, आवाज़ या व्यवहार 3 भार।

gravy / ग्रेवि / noun 1 शोरबा, सब्ज़ी या मांस पकाने पर उससे निकला रस; उस रस से बना सालन 2 (अप, विशेषतः US) आराम से या अप्रत्याशित रूप से प्राप्त धन/लाभ।

graze¹ / ग्रेज् / verb 1 (जानवरों का) घास चरना 2 पशुओं को चरागाह में चराना; चरागाह के लिए ज़मीन छोड़ना : That field's being grazed this year. ▸ **grazing** noun.

graze² / ग्रेज् / verb 1 **graze sth (against/on sth)** शरीर पर खरोंच लगना 2 खरोंचना, खुरच जाना ▸ **graze** noun खरोंच (शरीर पर)।

grease / ग्रीस् / noun 1 चरबी 2 ग्रीस, एक प्रकार की गाढ़ी चिकनाई जो मशीनों में चिकनाई के लिए प्रयुक्त होती है ▸ **grease** verb ग्रीस लगाना/रगड़ना ■ **grease sb's palm** (अनौप) रिश्वत देना।

greasy / ग्रीसि; ग्रीज़ि / adj (-ier, -iest) 1 ग्रीस से लिप्त; फिसलन भरा; (खाना) अत्यधिक चिकनाई युक्त 2 (अनौप, अपमा) (व्यक्ति या व्यवहार) चापलूसी भरा/खुशामदी।

great / ग्रेट् / adj (-er, -est) 1 बड़ा, विशाल, महान 2 महत्त्वपूर्ण, उल्लेखनीय ▸ **greatness** noun महानता; बड़प्पन : achieve greatness in one's lifetime.

greed / ग्रीड् / noun greed (for sth) (अपमा) 1 लोभ, लालच 2 भोजन की लोलुपता (विशेषकर, भूख न रहते हुए भी) ▸ **greedy** adj (-ier, -iest) लोभी, लोलुप/ लालची **greedily** adv **greediness** noun धनलिप्सा।

green¹ / ग्रीन् / adj (-er, -est) 1 हरा (रंग); घास से ढका हुआ या पेड़ों से आच्छादित 2 (फल) कच्चा, न पका हुआ; (लकड़ी) कच्ची : green banana 3 (अनौप) (व्यक्ति) अनुभवहीन, अनाड़ी ▸ **green** verb 1 हरा रँगना/हो जाना 2 पर्यावरण विषयक जागरूकता लाना।

green² / ग्रीन् / noun 1 हरा रंग 2 हरे वस्त्र : dressed in green 3 चरागाह, घास का मैदान 4 **greens** [pl] सब्ज़ियाँ, तरकारियाँ।

greengrocer / 'ग्रीन्ग्रोसर् / noun कुँजड़ा, सब्ज़ी बेचने वाला।

greenhouse / 'ग्रीन्हाउस् / noun शीशे का मकान जिसमें फल-सब्ज़ी/पौधे उगाए जाते हैं ▸ **greenhouse effect** noun पृथ्वी के वायुमंडल में प्रदूषण के कारण तापवृद्धि।

green room / 'ग्रीन् रूम् / noun नेपथ्य-शाला।

Greenwich Mean Time / ग्रेनिच् 'मीन् टाइम् / (संक्षि GMT) (**Universal Time** भी) noun ग्रेनिच (इंग्लैंड) से गुज़रने वाली 0° देशांतर रेखा पर का समय जो संपूर्ण विश्व में समय-गणना के लिए आधार माना जाता है।

greet / ग्रीट् / verb 1 **greet sb (with sth)** मिलने पर अभिवादन करना 2 **greet sth with sth** समाचार मिलने पर प्रतिक्रिया व्यक्त करना : *The appointment was greeted with widespread approval.* ▸ **greeting** noun पत्र का सिरानामा (जैसे Dear Sir, Dear John); मिलने पर अभिवादन के शब्द जैसे नमस्कार।

gregarious / ग्रि'गेअरिअस् / adj 1 (व्यक्ति) मिलनसार 2 (जीव विज्ञान) (पशु-पक्षी) साथ-साथ मिलकर समूह में चलने वाले ▸ **gregariously** adv **gregariousness** noun.

Gregorian / ग्रि'गॉरिअन् / adj ▸ **the Gregorian calendar** noun पोप ग्रिगोरी XIII (1502-85) द्वारा प्रचलित वर्ष को महीनों और महीनों को दिनों में व्यवस्थित करने की कैलेंडर योजना जो इस समय प्रचलन में है।

grenade / ग्रे'नेड् / noun हथगोला, हाथ से फेंकने वाला छोटा बम।

grey (विशेषत: US **gray** भी) / ग्रे / adj 1 धूसर/राख जैसा रंग; धूसर रंग के बाल वाला 2 उत्साहरहित; शोकपूर्ण : *a grey existence* ▸ **grey** (विशेषत: US **gray** भी) noun 1 धूसर/भूरा रंग 2 राख जैसे रंग के वस्त्र **grey** (विशेषत: US **gray** भी) verb (बालों का) धूसर होना/करना।

greyhound / 'ग्रेहाउन्ड् / noun कुत्ते की नसल (ये कुत्ते बहुत तेज़ दौड़ सकते हैं)।

grid / ग्रिड् / noun 1 बिजली के ऊपरी तारों की व्यवस्था, ग्रिड 2 मानचित्रों में वर्ग बनाने एवं उन्हें नंबर देने की व्यवस्था 3 जाली, (लकड़ी या लोहे का) फ़्रेम 4 एक-दूसरे को काटकर वर्ग बनाती लाइनों का पैटर्न।

grief / ग्रीफ़् / noun 1 **grief (over/at sth)** व्यथा, संताप 2 व्यथा/संताप देने वाली वस्तु : *His marriage to someone outside their faith was a great grief to his parents.* ■ **come to grief** (अनौप) 1 पूर्णत: असफल होना 2 दुर्घटना घटित होना, गिर पड़ना/नष्ट होना ▸ **grief-stricken** adj शोक संतप्त।

grievance / 'ग्रीव्न्स् / noun **grievance (against sb)** वास्तविक या काल्पनिक शिकायत का कारण।

grieve / ग्रीव् / verb 1 **grieve (for sb); grieve (at/over/about sb/sth)** व्यथित होना, दुख अनुभव करना 2 किसी को दुख पहुँचाना : *The loss of such a close friend grieved her deeply.*

grill / ग्रिल् / noun 1 कुकर का वह भाग जहाँ मांस या अन्य खाद्य पदार्थ भूना जा सकता है 2 भुनने के लिए झंझरी, जाली 3 भुना मांस या अन्य खाद्य पदार्थ ▸ **grill** verb 1 ग्रिल में आँच के नीचे पकाना 2 (अनौप) सीधे आँच के सामने बैठना; अत्यंत गरमी सहन करना 3 (अनौप) (अप्रिय तरीक़े से) लंबे समय तक सवाल पूछना : *The police grilled him for five hours.*

grille (**grill** भी) / ग्रिल् / noun दरवाज़े, खिड़की आदि के लिए लोहे की जाली।

grim / ग्रिम् / adj (-mmer, -mmest) 1 अत्यंत गंभीर (चेहरा), अप्रसन्न 2 अप्रिय, मनहूस : *grim news* 3 कठोर; निर्दयी 4 (स्थान) डरावना; कष्टप्रद : *the grim walls of the prison* 5 अत्यंत ख़राब, निकृष्ट।

grimace / ग्रि'मेस् / noun कष्ट, शोक, घृणा आदि दिखाने या हँसी उत्पन्न करने के

लिए बनाई भद्दी मुखाकृति : *give a grimace of pain* ▸ **grimace** *verb* grimace (at sb/sth) तरह-तरह के मुँह बनाना।

grime / ग्राइम् / *noun* धूल की मोटी परत; कालिख ▸ **grimy** / 'ग्राइमि / *adj* (-ier, -iest) धूल चढ़ा/कालिख पुता हुआ : *grimy hands/windows.*

grin / ग्रिन् / *verb* (-nn-) grin (at sb); grin (with sth) खीसें काढ़ना/निपोड़ना; दाँत निकालना ▸ **grin** *noun.*

grind / ग्राइन्ड् / *verb* (pt, pp ground / ग्राउन्ड् /) 1 पीसना; दलना 2 grind sth (on/with sth) रगड़कर चमकाना/तेज़ करना : *grind a knife/lens* 3 grind sth (together); grind sth in/into sth परस्पर रगड़ना; (दाँत) पीसना : *He grinds his teeth when he's asleep.* 4 grind (away) रगड़ने से शोर उत्पन्न करना : *grinding brakes.*

grinder / 'ग्राइन्डर / *noun* पीसने वाला उपकरण/व्यक्ति।

grindstone / 'ग्राइन्ड्स्टोन् / *noun* सान (का पत्थर)।

grip / ग्रिप् / *verb* (-pp-) 1 कसकर पकड़ना 2 (अलं) पूरा ध्यान आकृष्ट करना या किसी की भावना को प्रभावित करना : *Terror has gripped the city.* ▸ **grip** *noun* 1 grip (on sth/sb) पकड़; पकड़ने का ढंग 2 अधिकार, नियंत्रण शक्ति : *a ruler with a powerful grip on the people* 3 समझ 4 पकड़ा जाने वाला भाग (हत्था आदि) ■ come/get to grips with sb किसी को पकड़कर लड़ना शुरू करना come/get to grips with sth किसी समस्या पर गंभीरता से कार्य करना ▸ **gripping** *adj* उत्तेजक/चित्ताकर्षक।

grisly / 'ग्रिज़्लि / *adj* (-ier, -iest) डरावना, आतंक/भय उत्पन्न करने वाला : *a grisly account of the murder.*

grit / ग्रिट् / *noun* 1 छोटी कंकड़ी, कण 2 साहस एवं धैर्य ▸ **grit** *verb* (-tt-) (सड़क पर) कंकड़ बिछाना ■ grit one's

teeth 1 (तकलीफ़ में) दाँत भींचना 2 साहस दिखाना ▸ **gritty** *adj* (-ier, -iest) 1 कंकड़ भरा, कण समान 2 साहसी/धैर्यवान 3 अप्रिय स्थिति का वास्तविक चित्रण/वर्णन करते हुए।

groan / ग्रोन् / *verb* 1 groan (at sb/sth); groan (with sth) कराहना; काँखना 2 (वस्तुओं का) भार से दबकर आवाज़ उत्पन्न करना 3 groan (about/over sth) (अपमा) शिकायत करना : *stop moaning and groaning* ■ groan with sth भार से दब जाना ▸ **groan** *noun* कराहट; शिकायत।

grocer / 'ग्रोसर् / *noun* पंसारी, चाय-चीनी आदि बेचने वाला ▸ **groceries** *noun* [pl] पंसारी का सामान **grocery** *noun* 1 पंसारी का व्यापार 2 (विशेषत: US) पंसारी की दुकान।

groggy / 'ग्रॉगि / *adj* (-ier, -iest) (किसी रुग्णता या नींद की कमी के कारण) लड़खड़ाता और डगमगाता हुआ।

groin / ग्रॉइन् / *noun* शरीर का वह भाग जहाँ टाँग मिलती हैं।

groom / ग्रूम् / *noun* 1 साईस 2 = bridegroom (दूल्हा, वर) ▸ **groom** *verb* 1 घोड़ों की देखभाल और सफ़ाई करना; (पशु का) अपने या दूसरे के शरीर की सफ़ाई करना 2 groom sb (for/as sth) किसी व्यवसाय के लिए युवा व्यक्ति का चयन करना एवं उसे तैयार करना **groomed** *adj.*

groove / ग्रूव् / *noun* 1 (लकड़ी आदि में बनाया हुआ) खाँचा, नाली 2 लीक ■ get into/be stuck in a groove रूढ़िवादी जीवन बिताना ▸ **groove** *verb* खाँचा/नाली बनाना **grooved** *adj.*

grope / ग्रोप् / *verb* 1 grope (about/around) (for sth) टटोलना; मन में हल सोचना 2 अंधे की तरह खोजना।

gross[1] / ग्रोस् / *adj* (-er, -est) 1 सुस्त; स्थूलकाय एवं कुरूप 2 गँवार 3 (विशेषत: क़ानून, औप) बहुत स्पष्ट एवं बहुत बुरा (ग़लती) : *gross negligence/errors*

4 कुल (योग); जोड़ : *sb's gross income* ▸ **grossly** *adv* 1 अत्यंत रूप से : *grossly unfair* 2 गँवार ढंग से।

gross² /ग्रोस्/ *noun* (*pl* अपरिवर्तित) 12 दर्जन (144)।

grotesque / ग्रो'टेस्क् / *adj* 1 बेतुका, भोंडा/कुरूप 2 ऊटपटांग, हास्यजनक।

ground¹ /ग्राउन्ड/ *noun* 1 **the ground** भूमि, ज़मीन, भूक्षेत्र 2 विशेष प्रयोजन के लिए प्रयुक्त भूक्षेत्र : *a parade-ground/playground* 3 **grounds** [*pl*] मकान के अहाते वाली ख़ाली भूमि/बग़ीचा आदि : *the school grounds* 4 (विशेषत: *pl*) **grounds (for sth/doing sth)** (कुछ कहने/करने का) आधार : *You have no grounds for complaint.* ■ **hold/keep/stand one's grounds** डटे रहना, पीछे न हटना।

ground² / ग्राउन्ड् / *verb* 1 **ground (sth) (in/on sth)** (जहाज़ का) तल छूना; तल छुआना : *Our ship was grounded in shallow water.* 2 वायुयानों को ज़मीन पर ही रहने देना/रहने को बाध्य करना।

groundless /'ग्राउन्ड्लस्/ *adj* निराधार, अकारण।

groundnut /'ग्राउन्ड्नट्/ *noun* मूँगफली।

groundwork / 'ग्राउन्ड्वर्क्/ *noun* **groundwork (for sth)** प्रारंभिक अध्ययन आदि।

group /ग्रूप्/ *noun* 1 समूह 2 एकाधिक में कंपनियाँ ▸ **group** *verb* **group (sb/sth) (round/around sb/sth); group (sb/sth) (together)** समूह में लाना/करना : *group together in fours* **grouping** *noun*.

grove / ग्रोव् / *noun* बग़ीचा, वृक्षों का समूह : *a mango grove.*

grovel /'ग्रॉव्ल् / *verb* (-ll-; *US* -l-) **grovel (to sb) (for sth)** (अपमा) औंधे मुँह लेटना, किसी के आगे नाक रगड़ना ▸ **grovelling** *adj.*

grow / ग्रो / *verb* (*pt* grew / ग्रू /; *pp*

grown /ग्रोन्/) 1 बढ़ना, उगना 2 **grow sth (from sth)** बढ़ने देना/बढ़ाना; उगाना (फ़सलें आदि): *grow roses* 3 (एक समयांतराल में) होना : *grow old/richer/weak* 4 कुछ करने के लिए एक स्थिति विशेष में पहुँचना : *He grew increasingly to rely on her.* ■ **grow up** वयस्क (होना) ▸ **grower** *noun* 1 उत्पादक/उगाने वाला : *rose growers* 2 बढ़ने वाला पौधा : *a quick grower* **growing** *adj* **grown-up** *noun* वयस्क व्यक्ति।

growl /ग्राउल्/ *verb* 1 **growl (at sb/sth)** (जानवरों का) गुर्राना 2 **growl sth (out)** गुर्राकर कुछ कहना : *He growled (out) a warning.* ▸ **growl** *noun* गुर्राहट, धमकी।

growth / ग्रोथ् / *noun* 1 वृद्धि; विकास 2 आर्थिक क्रियाकलापों, लाभ आदि में वृद्धि; बढ़ने की प्रक्रिया, उपज/पैदावार 3 बढ़ने वाली वस्तु; शरीर में कहीं पर असामान्य वृद्धि (बीमारी से) : *a malignant growth.*

grub / ग्रब् / *noun* 1 लार्वा 2 (अनौप) खाना, भोजन।

grubby / 'ग्रबि/ *adj* (-ier, -iest) 1 गंदा, मैला 2 नैतिक दृष्टि से नीच या निकृष्ट व्यवहार : *a grubby affair/scandal* ▸ **grubbiness** *noun.*

grudge / ग्रज्/ *verb* अनिच्छा से देना या करना : *He grudges every penny he has to spend.* ▸ **grudge** *noun* **grudge (against sb)** किसी के प्रति घृणा, वैमनस्य, ईर्ष्या या दुर्भावना (किसी दुर्व्यवहार के कारण) **grudging** *adj* अनिच्छुक **grudgingly** *adv* अनिच्छा से।

gruel /'ग्रूअल् / *noun* (दूध या पानी में पकाया) दलिया, काँजी।

gruelling (*US* grueling) /'ग्रूअलिङ्/ *adj* बहुत कठिन और थका देने वाला : *a gruelling climb/race/trail.*

gruesome /'ग्रूसम्/ *adj* वीभत्स; डरा-

वना : *gruesome pictures of dead bodies.*

gruff / ग्रफ़ / *adj* (व्यक्ति, व्यवहार या कथन) रूखा और मित्रतारहित : *a gruff reply* ▶ **gruffly** *adv.*

grumble / ग्रम्बॅल् / *verb* 1 **grumble(at/to sb) (about/at/over sth)** बदमिज़ाजी से शिकायत करना; भुनभुनाना 2 गरजना ▶ **grumble** *noun* 1 **grumble (about/at/over sth)** शिकायत 2 गर्जन शब्द **grumbler** *noun* शिकायत करने वाला व्यक्ति।

grumpy / ग्रम्पि / *adj* (-ier, -iest) (अनौप) बदमिज़ाज।

grunt / ग्रन्ट् / *verb* 1 (पशुओं का, विशेषत: सूअर का) घुरघुराना; (व्यक्ति का) दर्द या नाराज़गी के कारण ऐसी ही आवाज़ करना 2 सूअर की तरह गुर्राना ▶ **grunt** *noun* घुरघुराहट की आवाज़।

guarantee / गैरन्टी / *noun* 1 गारंटी; आश्वासन 2 ज़मानत ▶ **guarantee** *verb* 1 गारंटी/आश्वासन देना 2 निश्चित रूप से कुछ होना या घटित होना 3 **guarantee sth (against sth)** ज़मानत देना 4 ज़िम्मेदारी उठाना : *guarantee (to pay) sb's debts.*

guarantor / गैरन्टॉर् / *noun* (औप या क़ानून) ज़ामिन, ज़मानत देने वाला व्यक्ति।

guard[1] / गाई / *noun* 1 पहरा, रखवाली 2 पहरेदार, संतरी, रक्षक : *a security guard* 3 (रेल का) गार्ड 4 (समास में) रक्षक; चोट या नुक़सान से बचाने वाला : *fireguard/mudguard* ■ **on guard/off (one's) guard** (आत्म-) रक्षा के लिए तैयार/तैयार नहीं **stand guard (over sb/sth)** संतरी बनना, पहरेदारी करना।

guard[2] / गाई / *verb* 1 रक्षा करना; पहरा देना 2 **guard against sth/doing sth** से बचाव रखना : *guard against disease* ▶ **guarded** *adj* सतर्क (टिप्पणी आदि)।

guardian / गार्डिअन् / *noun* 1 रक्षक

2 संरक्षक; अभिभावक ▶ **guardianship** *noun* संरक्षण।

guava / ग्वावा / *noun* अमरूद।

guerrilla (**guerilla** भी) / गरिला; गेरिला / *noun* छापामार ■ **guerrilla war** *noun* छापामार युद्ध।

guess / गेस् / *verb* 1 **guess (at sth)** अटकल/अंदाज़ा लगाना 2 संभावना के बारे में सोचना; अनुमान करना/लगाना ▶ **guess** *noun* 1 **guess (at sth); guess (that...)** अटकल; अंदाज़ा 2 अनुमान।

guest / गेस्ट् / *noun* मेहमान, अतिथि।

guidance / गाइडन्स् / *noun* 1 सहायता या उपदेश (विशेषत: बड़ों या अनुभवी लोगों द्वारा दिया जाने वाला) 2 किसी गतिशील वस्तु का दिशा-नियंत्रण : *a missile guidance system.*

guide[1] / गाइड / *noun* 1 मार्गदर्शक, गाइड 2 मत बनाने या निर्णय लेने में सहायक वस्तु 3 व्यवहार को प्रभावित अथवा नियंत्रित करने वाला व्यक्ति 4 **guide (to sth) (guide book** भी) संदर्शिका (पुस्तक); कुंजी ▶ **guideline** *noun* साधारण/सामान्य नियम, निर्देश या उपदेश।

guide[2] / गाइड / *verb* 1 पथ प्रदर्शन करना 2 व्यवहार को नियंत्रित/प्रभावित करना : *Be guided by your sense of what is right and just.* ▶ **guided** *adj* निर्देशित।

guild / गिल्ड् / *noun* गिल्ड, शिल्पियों (कारीगरों) का संघ, व्यावसायिक हितों को बढ़ाने वाला संघ : *the guild of carpenters.*

guile / गाइल् / *noun* छल-कपट ▶ **guileful** *adj* **guileless** *adj.*

guillotine / गिलटीन् / *noun* 1 [*sing*] गिलटिन, (अपराधी का) सिर काटने का यंत्र 2 काग़ज़ काटने का एक यंत्र ▶ **guillotine** *verb* सिर (गिलोटिन से) काटना।

guilt / गिल्ट् / *noun* 1 (क़ानून) अपराध 2 दोष 3 दोष-भावना/अपराध भाव : *a guilt complex* ▶ **guiltless** *adj* निरपराध **guilty** *adj* (-ier, -iest) 1 **guilty (of**

sth) *(क़ानून)* अपराधी 2 दोषी : *have a guilty conscience.*

guinea / 'गिनि / *noun* (पूर्व में प्रचलित) 21 शिलिंग का एक सिक्का; सोने का सिक्का, गिन्नी।

guinea-pig / 'गिनिपिग्/ *noun* 1 बड़े चूहे जैसा जानवर 2 चिकित्सकीय या अन्य शोध में प्रयुक्त प्राणी या वस्तु।

guise / गाइज़ / *noun* बहाना; रूप : *racialist sentiments expressed under the guise of nationalism.*

guitar / गि'टार्/ *noun* गिटार, एक वाद्य-यंत्र।

gulf / गल्फ़/ *noun* 1 खाड़ी, समुद्र का वह भाग जो भूमि से लगभग घिरा हुआ हो 2 **the Gulf** फ़ारस की खाड़ी : *the Gulf War/ the Gulf states* 3 **gulf (between A and B)** विचारों की खाई/बड़ा अंतर 4 खाई, गहरा गड्ढा।

gullet / 'गलिट् / *noun* (गले में) आहार-नली।

gullible / 'गलब्ल्/ *adj* भोला-भाला जिसे आसानी से छला जा सके ▸ **gullibility** *noun.*

gully / 'गलि / *noun* नाली; गहरी संकरी खाई।

gulp / गल्प्/ *verb* **gulp sth (down)** गटकना, निगलना; लीलना ▸ **gulp** *noun* 1 निगलने/गटकने की प्रक्रिया 2 कौर, ग्रास, घूँट।

gum[1] / गम् / *noun* (प्रायः *pl*) मसूड़ा ▸ **gumboil** *noun* मसूड़े का फोड़ा/व्रण।

gum[2] / गम्/ *noun* 1 गोंद 2 =**chewing-gum** ▸ **gum** *verb* (-mm-) **gum A to/ onto B; gum A and B together** गोंद फैलाना/गोंद से चिपकाना **gummy** *adj* चिपचिपा।

gun / गन्/ *noun* बंदूक़; तोप ▸ **gun** *verb* (-nn-) ■ **gun sb down** *(अनौप)* गोली मारना : *He was gunned down as he left his home.* ▸ **gunpowder** *noun* बारूद **gunshot** *noun* तोप या बंदूक़ की

मार की सीमा : *be out of/within gun-shot.*

gurgle / 'गर्गल्/ *noun, verb* गड़गड़ करने की ध्वनि (जैसे कि छोटे मुँह की बोतल से पानी निकलते समय शब्द होता है); गड़गड़ करना।

gush / गश् / *verb* 1 **gush (out) (of/ from sth)** धार के साथ बाहर बह निकलना 2 *(अपमा)* बढ़ा-चढ़ाकर प्रशंसा करना या लिखना ▸ **gush** *noun* 1 (द्रव की) धारा 2 अत्यधिक प्रशंसा **gushing** *adj* : *gushing compliments/letters.*

gust / गस्ट्/ *noun* 1 (हवा या वर्षा का) झोंका 2 (क्रोध आदि भावना का) अचानक तीव्र उद्गार : *a gust of laughter/ anger* ▸ **gust** *verb* (वायु का) झोंकों में बहना **gusty** *adj.*

gusto / 'गस्टो / *noun* मज़ा; उत्साह।

gut / गट्/ *noun* 1 *(अनौप* **guts** [*pl*] भी) उदर एवं आँतें 2 **guts** [*pl*] *(अनौप)* साहस और धैर्य 3 **guts** [*pl*] *(अनौप)* अत्यावश्यक या सर्वाधिक महत्त्वपूर्ण भाग 4 ताँत ▸ **gut** *verb* (-tt-) 1 किसी इमारत या कमरे के अंदर की सब चीजें नष्ट करना : *gut the kitchen and install new units* 2 (मछली या अन्य जंतु की) आँतें निकालना **gutless** *adj* डरपोक **gutted** *adj.*

gutter[1] / 'गटर्/ *noun* 1 नाली; नाला 2 **the gutter** *(प्रायः अपमा)* ग़रीबी, गंदगी और अनैतिकता से भरी ज़िंदगी : *She rose from the gutter to become a great star.*

gutter[2] / 'गटर्/ *verb* (मोमबत्ती का) ऐसी लौ के साथ जलना जैसे बस बुझने को ही हो।

guttural / 'गटरल्/ *adj* कंठ्य ध्वनियाँ।

guy / गाइ / *noun* 1 *(अनौप)* जवान, आदमी : *a big/tough guy* 2 **guys** [*pl*] *(US)* (किसी भी लिंग के) दोस्तों का समूह, विशेषत: सहकर्मी : *the guys at the office.*

guzzle / 'गज़ल्/ *verb* *(अनौप, प्रायः अपमा)* जल्दी-जल्दी या बहुत अधिक मात्रा

में खाना या पीना : *guzzle soft drinks/ cakes.*

gymnasium / जिम्'नेज़िअम् / *noun (pl* **gymnasiums** या **gymnasia** / जिम् 'नेज़िआ /) व्यायामशाला।

gymnastics / जिम्'नैस्टिक्स् / *noun* [*pl*] व्यायाम, कसरतें ▶ **gymnastic** *adj* शारीरिक व्यायाम संबंधी।

gynaecology (*US* **gynecology**) / गाइन'कॉलजि / *noun (चिकि)* स्त्रियों के रोग (एवं उनकी जाँच) का चिकित्सा विज्ञान ▶ **gynaecologist** (*US* **gynecologist**) *noun.*

gypsum / जिप्सम् / *noun* चाक की तरह दिखने वाला एक खनिज पदार्थ, प्लास्टर ऑफ़ पैरिस बनाने में प्रयुक्त।

gyrate / जाइ'रेट् / *verb* चक्कर काटना ▶ **gyrations** *noun* [*pl*].

Hh

habeas corpus / ˌहेबिअस्ˈकॉर्पस् / *noun* (क़ानून) बंदी प्रत्यक्षीकरण (याचिका), बंदी को न्यायाधीश के सामने अदालत में प्रस्तुत किए जाने की याचिका, विशेषत: उसकी रिहाई का निर्धारण करने के लिए।

habit / ˈहैबिट् / *noun* आदत; सामान्य व्यवहार।

habitable / ˈहैबिटबुल् / *adj* रहने योग्य।

habitat / ˈहैबिटैट् / *noun* (पशुओं, पौधों का) प्राकृतिक आवास-स्थान।

habitation / ˌहैबिˈटेशन् / *noun* 1 रहने की प्रक्रिया : *houses unfit for human habitation* 2 (औप) रहने का स्थान; घर।

habitual / हˈबिचुअल् / *adj* नियमित, जिसका अभ्यास पड़ा हुआ है : *habitual drunkard/liar* ▸ **habitually** *adv* प्राय:; आदतन।

habituated / हंˈबिचुएटिड् / *adj* **habituated (to sth)** (औप) अभ्यास या आदत के कारण परिचित।

hack¹ / हैक् / *verb* 1 काटना, टुकड़े कर देना 2 जंगली/असभ्य तरीक़े से ठोकर मारना : *hack the ball (away)/sb's legs* ▸ **hack** *noun* 1 काटने की क्रिया 2 बूट की नोक की ठोकर।

hack² / हैक् / *noun* 1 कठिन एवं नीरस काम करने के लिए नियुक्त व्यक्ति (विशेषत: लेखक) : *a publisher's hack* 2 लद्दू घोड़ा या जिसको किराए पर सवारी के लिए लिया जा सकता है।

hackneyed / ˈहैक्निड् / *adj* (कहावत, मुहावरा) घिसा-पिटा; अत्यंत सामान्य और इसलिए नीरस।

hacksaw / ˈहैक्सॉ / *noun* धातुओं को काटने वाली आरी।

haddock / ˈहैडक् / *noun* (*pl* अपरिवर्तित) एक समुद्री मछली जिसे अक्सर धुँआकर खाया जाता है।

haemoglobin / ˌहीम्ˈग्लोबिन् / *noun* रक्त का वह लाल पदार्थ जो ऑक्सीजन का वहन करता है।

haemophilia / ˌहीम्ˈफ़िलिआ / *noun* एक बीमारी जिसके कारण रक्त का थक्का नहीं जमता और कहीं कट जाने पर बिना रुके रक्त बहता रहता है ▸ **haemophiliac** *noun*.

haemorrhage / ˈहेमरिज् / *noun* 1 (अत्यधिक एवं अचानक) रक्तस्राव : *suffer a massive brain haemorrhage* 2 देश में धन-जन की गंभीर क्षति ▸ **haemorrhage** *verb* रक्तस्राव होना।

hag / हैग् / *noun* (अपमा) बूढ़ी या बदसूरत महिला; चुड़ैल।

haggard / ˈहैगई / *adj* दुबला-पतला, मरियल; चिंता से क्षीण : *a haggard face.*

haggle / ˈहैग्ल / *verb* **haggle (with sb) (about/over sth)** मोल-भाव करना, मूल्य के लिए झगड़ा करना : *haggling over a few pennies.*

hail¹ / हेल् / *noun* 1 ओले (वर्षा में कभी-कभी गिरने वाले बर्फ़ के गोले) 2 (हानि पहुँचाने के लिए) एक साथ बहुत सारी चीज़ें बलात् आ जाना ▸ **hail** *verb* ओले गिरना **hailstone** *noun* ओला **hailstorm** *noun* ओलावृष्टि।

hail² / हेल् / *verb* 1 स्वागत के लिए अभिवादन करना; किसी का ध्यान आकर्षित करने के लिए पुकारना : *hail a waiter* 2 **hail sb/sth (as) sth** उत्साहपूर्वक स्वीकार करना, मानना ■ **hail from...** उस स्थान का रहने वाला होना : *She hails from Kashmir.*

hair / हेअर् / *noun* बाल, रोएँ; सिर पर उगे हुए बाल ■ **make one's hair stand on end** मारे डर के रोंगटे खड़े हो जाना **split hairs** बाल की खाल निकालना ▸ **hairdo** *noun* (*pl* **hairdos**) केश-प्रसाधन-विन्यास की शैली **hairdresser** *noun* बालों के प्रसाधन करने वाला व्यक्ति, नाई **hairpin**

noun हेयरपिन, बालों की चिमटी **hair-raising** adj अत्यधिक डरावना **hair-splitting** noun बाल की खाल निकालना **hairy** adj (-ier, -iest) बालों भरा; बालों जैसा।

hale / हेल / adj (प्राय: वृद्ध व्यक्तियों के लिए प्रयुक्त) स्वस्थ : *At over 90, he's still hale and hearty.*

half¹ / हाफ़; US हैफ़ / noun (pl halves / हाव्ज़; US हैव्ज़ /) 1 आधा; आधा भाग 2 (खेल में) विभाजित समय का एक भाग : *No goals were scored in the first half.* 3 (बच्चों के लिए) आधा टिकट ■ **go half and half/go halves (with sb)** (क़ीमत आदि) बराबर-बराबर हिस्सा करना/बाँटना **too clever by half** अत्यंत चालाक।

half² / हाफ़; US हैफ़ / indef det आधा ▶ **half-baked** adj (अनौप) (योजना आदि) अधकचरा, अनियोजित **half-brother/-sister** noun सौतेला भाई/बहन **half-day** noun तीसरे पहर की छुट्टी वाला दिन **half-time** noun मध्यांतर (प्राय: खेलों के मैचों में) **half-truth** noun (प्राय: अपमा) अर्ध-सत्य, पूरे सच को छिपाने के लिए कहा कथन।

half³ / हाफ़; US हैफ़ / adv 1 आधी मात्रा में : *The jug was half full.* 2 आंशिक रूप से : *half cooked* ▶ **half-hearted** adj बेमन से किया (कार्य)।

hall / हॉल / noun 1 (hallway भी) मुख्य द्वार से अंदर आने पर मिलने वाली खाली जगह 2 हॉल; सभा-भवन; (कालेज में) भोजन-कक्ष 3 (विश्वविद्यालय आदि में छात्रों के लिए) निवास-भवन।

hallo (hello, hullo भी) / ह'लो / interj हलो, ध्यानाकर्षक पुकार।

hallowed / हैलोड़ / adj 1 पवित्र किया हुआ : *be buried in hallowed ground* 2 श्रद्धा से देखी जाने वाली (विशेषत: कोई पुरानी चीज़)।

hallucinate / ह'लूसिनेट् / verb दृष्टिभ्रम/मतिभ्रम होना/करना।

hallucination / ह ़लूसि'नेशन् / noun 1 दृष्टिभ्रम/मतिभ्रम, वस्तु सामने न होने पर ऐसा लगना कि दिखाई दे रही है 2 छलावा, दृष्टिभ्रम के कारण दिखाई पड़ने वाली वस्तु ▶ **hallucinatory** adj.

halo / 'हेलो / noun (pl haloes या halos) (aureole भी) 1 चित्रों में महापुरुषों के चेहरे के चारों ओर दिखाई पड़ने वाला प्रभामंडल 2 सूर्य और चंद्रमा के चारों ओर दिखाई देने वाला प्रभामंडल।

halt / हॉल्ट / noun 1 अस्थायी रुकावट, प्रगति में बाधा : *The car skidded to a halt.* 2 पड़ाव; यात्रा में रुकना 3 रेलवे लाइन पर छोटा स्थान जहाँ स्थानीय गाड़ियाँ रुकती हैं ▶ **halt** verb अस्थायी तौर पर कार्य आदि रोक देना/रुकावट डालना।

halting / 'हॉल्टिङ् / adj हिचकिचाते हुए बोलना या कुछ करना : *speak in a halting voice* ▶ **haltingly** adv.

halve / हाव् / verb 1 आधा-आधा बाँटना 2 अधियाना, आधा कम कर देना : *Supersonic planes halved the time needed for crossing the Atlantic.*

ham / हैम् / noun 1 सूअर की टाँगों का ऊपरी भाग जो सुखाकर या भूनकर खाने के लिए रख लिया जाता है 2 घुटने से ऊपर की टाँग का भाग ▶ **ham** verb (-mm-) **ham (it/sth up)** (अप) जानबूझकर कृत्रिम या अतिशयोक्तिपूर्ण ढंग से काम करना।

hamburger / 'हैम्बर्गर् / noun हैमबर्गर, पावरोटी के बीच में मांस का पका हुआ टुकड़ा भरकर बनाया खाद्य पदार्थ।

hamlet / 'हैम्लट् / noun छोटा-सा गाँव, पुरवा।

hammer¹ / 'हैमर् / noun 1 हथौड़ा 2 किसी उपकरण का वह भाग जो कहीं टकराता है, जैसे पियानो में तारों से टकराने वाला हथौड़ा ■ **be/go at it/each other hammer and tongs** खूब ज़ोर-शोर से लड़ना या बहस करना।

hammer² / 'हैमर् / verb 1 हथौड़े से ठोकना या तोड़ना : *He hammered the* *sheet of copper (flat).* **2** ज़ोर से प्रहार करना : *hammer at the door* **3** (अनौप) किसी को बुरी तरह परास्त करना; कटु आलोचना करना या आक्रमण करना ■ **hammer away at sth** कड़ा श्रम करना।

hammock /'हैमक्/ *noun* झूला-बिछौना; रस्सी से बना झूला या गद्दा जिसके दोनों किनारे दीवार, पेड़ या खंभे से बंधे हों।

hamper¹ /'हैम्पर्/ *verb* बाधा डालना, उलझाना : *Our progress was hampered by the bad weather.*

hamper² /'हैम्पर्/ *noun* **1** ढक्कन सहित डलिया **2** उपहार-स्वरूप भेजी डलिया : *a Christmas hamper.*

hand¹ /हैन्ड्/ *noun* **1** हाथ (कलाई के नीचे का भाग) **2 a hand** [*sing*] (अनौप) सक्रिय सहायता : *Do you want/need a hand?* **3** (समास में) घड़ी की सूई : *the hour-/minute-/second-hand of a watch* **4** फ़ैक्टरी, खेत आदि में कर्मचारी; जहाज़ का कर्मचारी; कार्यकर्ता **5** (समास में) व्यक्ति द्वारा कृत, न कि मशीन से : *hand-built/-crafted* **6** [*sing*] हस्तलिपि : *have a legible hand* ■ **at first, second, etc hand** प्रत्यक्ष/अप्रत्यक्ष रूप से **(be) hand in glove (with sb)** घनिष्ठ रूप से मिलकर कोई कार्य करना **(close/ near) at hand** पास में, पहुँच के भीतर **have one's hands full** अत्यधिक व्यस्त होना **live from hand to mouth** कमाए धन का आवश्यकताओं में पूर्ण रूप से खर्च हो जाना **on hand** उपलब्ध **out of hand** नियंत्रण से बाहर ▸ **handbag** (*US* **purse**) *noun* औरतों का बटुआ, पर्स **handful** *noun* **1 a handful (of sth)** मुट्ठीभर **2** थोड़ी मात्रा/संख्या में **handwriting** *noun* हस्त-लेख, हस्तलिपि।

hand² /हैन्ड्/ *verb* **hand sth (to sb)** देना; दूसरे के हाथ में सौंपना : *Please hand me that book.*

handbill /'हैन्ड्बिल्/ *noun* इश्तहार, हाथों से बँटने वाला विज्ञापन।

handbook /'हैन्ड्बुक्/ *noun* पुस्तिका (किसी एक विषय पर आवश्यक सूचनायुक्त छोटी पुस्तक)।

handbrake /'हैन्ड्ब्रेक्/ *noun* (गाड़ी में) हाथ से इस्तेमाल किया जाने वाला ब्रेक (विशेषत: जब गाड़ी रुकी हुई हो)।

handcart /'हैन्ड्कार्ट्/ *noun* हाथ का ठेला।

handcuffs /'हैन्ड्कफ्स्/ *noun* [*pl*] हथकड़ियाँ ▸ **handcuff** *verb* **handcuff sb/oneself (to sb/sth)** हथकड़ी लगाना।

handicap /'हैन्डिकैप्/ *noun* **1** अड़चन; असुविधा **2** शारीरिक विकलांगता : *Deafness can be a serious handicap.* ▸ **handicap** *verb* (-**pp**-) अड़चन/बाधा डालना **handicapped** *adj* विकलांग : *a mentally/visually handicapped child.*

handicraft /'हैन्डिक्राफ़्ट्; *US* 'हैन्डिक्रैफ़्ट्/ *noun* दस्तकारी।

handiwork /'हैन्डिवर्क्/ *noun* व्यक्ति की कृति।

handkerchief /'हैङ्कर्चिफ़्; 'हैङ्कर्चीफ़्/ *noun* रूमाल, रुमाल।

handle /'हैन्ड्ल्/ *noun* **1** मूठ, दस्ता (दरवाज़े, खिड़की आदि का); (बैग आदि का) हत्था **2** ऐसा तथ्य जिससे लाभ उठाया जा सकता हो ▸ **handle** *verb* **1** हाथ से छूना या प्रयोग में लाना **2** (व्यक्ति, वस्तु, परिस्थिति, कार्यभार आदि) से निपटना, को नियंत्रण में रखना : *He doesn't know how to handle old people.* **handlebars** *noun* [*pl*] (साइकिल आदि का) हैंडिल।

handloom /'हैन्ड्लूम्/ *noun* हथ-करघा (हाथ से कपड़ा बुनना)।

handsome /'हैन्सम्/ *adj* **1** (व्यक्ति) देखने में सुंदर **2** (भेंट आदि) उदार : *a handsome gift* **3** मात्रा में विशाल : *make a handsome profit.*

handy /'हैन्डि/ *adj* (-**ier**, -**iest**) **1** लाभ-

दायक, सुविधाजनक 2 handy (for sth/ doing sth) सुविधाजनक स्थान पर स्थित, पास में स्थित।

hang¹ / हैङ् / verb (pt, pp hung / हङ्/ या hanged) 1 लटकाना/टाँगना; लटकना/ टँगना 2 hang (sth with sth) (चित्र आदि) टाँगना; सजावट के लिए लटकाना 3 फाँसी देना, फाँसी पर लटकाना/फाँसी पर लटकना : He was hanged (for murder). ■ be/get hung up (about/on sb/sth) (अनौप) चिंतित या व्याकुल होना hang about/around (अनौप) प्रतीक्षा करते हुए पास में ही रहना hang back (from sth) झिझकना hang fire (घटनाओं/ योजनाओं का) बहुत धीरे-धीरे विकसित/ फलीभूत होना : The project had hung fire for several years. hang on to sth पकड़े रहना, छोड़ने को तैयार न होना ▶ hanger-on noun (अपमा) पिछलग्गू, लाभ उठाने वाला समर्थक hanging noun 1 फाँसी 2 hangings [pl] सजावट के लिए दीवार पर लटकाने वाली वस्तुएँ hangman noun जल्लाद।

hang² / हैङ् / noun [sing] (कपड़े आदि के) लटकने का ढंग : the hang of a coat ■ get the hang of sth (अनौप) किसी चीज़ को काम में लाने की विधि जानना।

hangar / हैङर् / noun हवाई जहाज़ रखने का स्थल, विमानशाला।

hanger / हैङर् / (clothes-hanger भी) noun कपड़े टाँगने का हैंगर।

hangover / हैङ्ओवर् / noun अत्यधिक शराब पीने से (अगले दिन) उत्पन्न सरदर्द या बीमार होने की स्थिति।

hanker / हैङकर् / verb ■ hanker after/for sth ललचना, लालायित रहना : hanker for big city life ▶ hankering noun.

haphazard / हैप्हैज़र्ड् / adj बिना योजना के, अव्यवस्थित ▶ haphazardly adv.

hapless / हैप्लस् / adj (औप) क़िस्मत के मारे, दुर्भाग्य के सताए हुए।

happen / हैपन् / verb 1 होना, घटित होना 2 संयोग से कुछ होना/करना : He happens to be a friend of mine. ■ it (just) so happened that... संयोग से : It just so happened they'd been invited too. happen to sb/sth (किसी घटना आदि के) परिणामस्वरूप होना/प्रभावित करना ▶ happening / हैपनिङ् / noun (प्राय:pl)घटना; अनौपचारिक कार्यक्रम आदि।

happy / हैपि / adj (-ier, -iest) 1 प्रसन्न, खुश; प्रसन्नतादायक : a happy day 2 happy (about/with sb/sth) संतुष्ट; तृप्त 3 happy to do sth (औप) (कुछ करने का) इच्छुक 4 भाग्यवान ▶ happily adv happiness / हैपिनस् / noun happy-go-lucky adj निश्चिंत भाव से; संतुष्ट रहने वाला व्यक्ति; भविष्य के बारे में चिंतित न होने वाला व्यक्ति।

harangue / हरैङ् / noun लंबा-चौड़ा उग्र भाषण।

harass / हैरस्, हरैस् / verb 1 तंग करना, सताना 2 दुश्मन पर बार-बार हमला करना ▶ harassed adj परेशान harassment noun.

harbinger / हार्बिन्जर् / noun harbinger (of sb/sth) (औप या साहि) अग्र- दूत : harbinger of peace.

harbour (US harbor) / हार्बर् / noun बंदरगाह ▶ harbour (US harbor) verb 1 (अपराधियों को) छिपाकर एवं सुरक्षित रखना 2 दुर्भावना बनाए रखना : harbour a grudge 3 विकसित होने देना।

hard¹ / हार्ड् / adj (-er, -est) 1 कठोर, कड़ा; ठोस, पक्का 2 hard (for sb) (to do sth) कठिन; (समझने, उत्तर देने में) मुश्किल : a hard task 3 अधिक शारीरिक या मानसिक शक्ति की आवश्यकता वाला 4 मुश्किल भरा : have a hard life 5 सत्य एवं अखंडनीय : the hard facts of life ■ be hard on sb कटु निंदा करना; किसी से भेदभाव करना give sb a hard time अप्रिय और कठिन परिस्थिति पैदा करना

hard and fast (नियम-क़ानून) अपरि-वर्तनीय, अनुल्लंघनीय **hard of hearing** लगभग बहरा **no hard feelings** अप्रिय भावना न रखना ▸ **hardcash** noun नक़द, रोकड़ **hard core** noun, adj दृढ़ विश्वासी **hard disk** noun (कंप्यूटर) हार्ड डिस्क **hard-headed** adj व्यावहारिक; भावना से न बहकने वाला **hard-hearted** adj भावना-शून्य, निर्दयी **hard-labour** noun सपरिश्रम क़ैद **hard-line** adj कट्टर विश्वास रखने वाला।

hard² / हार्ड / adv परिश्रम से; कठिन प्रयास से ∎ **be hard put (to it) (to do sth)** (कुछ करना) बहुत मुश्किल पाना **be hard up for sth** (अनौप) तंगहाल, धनाभाव से परेशान ▸ **hard-boiled** adj (अंडे का) उबलने पर पूर्ण रूप से कठोर हो जाना **hard by** prep, adv पास में **hard-earned** adj बड़े प्रयास से अर्जित **hard-hitting** adj सीधे प्रभाव करने वाला (कथन) **hard-pressed** adj **hard-pressed (to do sth)** कठिन परिस्थितियों में (रहना) **hard-working** adj सावधानी से कड़ा परिश्रम करने वाला।

harden / हार्ड्न / verb कठोर होना या बनाना; भावनाशून्य होना या बनना : *a hardened criminal* ▸ **hardening** noun.

hardly / हार्ड्लि / adv 1 मुश्किल से; ठीक अभी 2 कठिनाई से 3 शायद ही कोई; लगभग नहीं।

hardship / हार्ड्शिप् / noun धन, भोजन आदि के अभाव से उत्पन्न कठिन परिस्थिति।

hardware / हार्डवेअर् / noun 1 धातु का सामान 2 कंप्यूटर मशीनरी (सॉफ़्टवेयर अर्थात् प्रोग्रामों के वैषम्य में)।

hardy / हार्डि / adj (-ier, -iest) 1 कष्टों को सहने में समर्थ 2 (पौधा) जो सर्दी में बाहर भी ठीक प्रकार रह सकता है ▸ **hardiness** noun.

hare / हेअर् / noun खरहा, ख़रगोश से बिलकुल मिलता-जुलता एक जीव।

harem / हारीम्; US हैरम् / noun हरम/ज़नान-ख़ाना।

harm / हार्म् / noun शारीरिक, मानसिक या नैतिक हानि, नुक़सान : *He meant no harm.* ▸ **harm** verb हानि/नुक़सान पहुँचाना **harmful** adj **harmful (to sb/sth)** हानिकारक **harmless** adj हानिरहित; किसी को नाराज न करने वाला।

harmonious / हार्'मोनिअस् / adj 1 मेल में, सुमेल में 2 संगति में व्यवस्थित : *harmonious colour combinations* 3 मधुर स्वर वाला।

harmonize, -ise / हार्मनाइज़् / verb 1 मेल में लाना; संगत में लाना/करना/होना 2 (संगीत) संगति करना।

harmony / हार्मनि / noun (pl **harmonies**) 1 (भावना, विचार, रुचि आदि में) मेल/सहमति 2 संबद्ध वस्तुओं का रुचिकर मेल/मिश्रण : *the harmony of colour in nature* 3 (संगीत) स्वर-संगति; (चित्रकला में) वर्ण-संगति।

harness / हार्निस् / noun 1 घोड़े का साज़ 2 पैराशूट आदि से व्यक्ति को बाँधने वाली डोरियाँ ▸ **harness** verb 1 **harness sth (to sth)** (घोड़े को) जोतना 2 नदी-जल को विद्युत उत्पादन में लगाना; प्राकृतिक शक्ति पर नियंत्रण करना एवं प्रयोग में लाना : *harness the sun's rays as a source of energy.*

harp / हार्प् / noun एक प्रकार का तार वाला वाद्य यंत्र ▸ **harp** verb ∎ **harp on/about sth** एक ही बात निरंतर दोहराते रहना।

harpoon / हार्'पून् / noun हार्पून, काँटेदार बर्छी जिससे व्हेल मछली को पकड़ते हैं।

harrow / हैरो / noun जोतने के बाद बड़े ढेले तोड़ने एवं भूमि समतल करने का कृषि यंत्र ▸ **harrow** verb : *The field had been ploughed and harrowed.*

harrowing / हैरोइङ् / adj अति संकटपूर्ण।

harsh / हार्श् / adj (-er, -est) 1 कर्कश, रूखा 2 कठोर, निर्दय; सहानुभूतिरहित

harsh criticism **3** (मौसम) अप्रिय
▸ **harshly** *adv* **harshness** *noun.*

harvest / 'हार्विस्ट् / *noun* **1** फ़सल
काटने और जमा करने की क्रिया; फ़सल
काटने का मौसम; फ़सल : *Farmers are
very busy during (the) harvest.* ○ *a
succession of good harvests* **2** परि-
णाम ▸ **harvest** *verb* फ़सल काटना और
जमा करना **harvester** *noun* **1** फ़सल
काटने वाला व्यक्ति **2** फ़सल काटने की
मशीन।

hash / हैश् / *noun* **1** क़ीमा **2** पुराने सामान
का पुन: प्रयुक्त किया मिश्रण ▪ **make a
hash of sth** (अनौप) काम गड़बड़ कर
देना।

hashish / 'हैशीश्; हे'शीश् / (**hash** भी)
noun गाँजा।

hasp / हास्प; *US* हैस्प् / *noun* (दरवाज़े
का) कुंडा।

hassle / 'हैसल् / *noun* (अनौप) परेशानी
या कुछ मुश्किल काम करने से उत्पन्न चिढ़;
तर्क-वितर्क ▸ **hassle** *verb* **hassle
(with sb)** (अनौप) लगातार कुछ माँग करके
किसी को परेशान/नाराज़ करना : *Don't
keep hassling me! I'll do it later.*

haste / हेस्ट् / *noun* जल्दी, शीघ्रता ▪ **in
haste** जल्दी में, हड़बड़ी में।

hasten / 'हेसन् / *verb* **1** जल्दी चलना या
जल्दी काम करना **2** कोई काम जल्दी पूरा
करवाना।

hasty / 'हेस्टि / *adj* (**-ier, -iest**) जल्दी में
किया हुआ, बहुत जल्द; **hasty (in doing
sth/to do sth)** (व्यक्ति) जल्दबाज़
▸ **hastily** *adv* जल्दबाज़ी से **hastiness**
noun.

hat / हैट् / *noun* **1** हैट, टोप **2** (अनौप)
आधिकारिक या व्यावसायिक पदभार : *wear
two hats* ▸ **hat trick** *noun* **1** खेल में
एक खिलाड़ी द्वारा तीन बार सफलता प्राप्त
करना : *score a hat trick of goals*
2 क्रिकेट में किसी गेंदबाज़ का लगातार एक
के बाद एक तीन विकेट लेना।

hatch^1 / हैच् / *noun* दरवाज़े, फ़र्श या छत
में प्रवेश मार्ग; (**hatchway** भी) जहाज़ के
डेक या हवाई जहाज़ के तली में दरवाज़ा
जिसके द्वारा माल चढ़ाया जाता है; दो कमरों
के बीच में प्रवेश मार्ग (विशेषत: कमरे और
रसोई के बीच छोटी-सी खिड़की); हवाई
जहाज़ में दरवाज़ा : *an escape hatch.*

hatch^2 / हैच् / *verb* **1** **hatch (out)** छोटे
पक्षी या मछली का अंडे में से बाहर निकलना
2 अंडे सेना : *The hen hatches her
young by sitting on the eggs.*
3 **hatch sth (up)** गुप्त योजना बनाना,
षड्यंत्र रचना : *hatch (up) a scheme.*

hatchet / 'हैचिट् / *noun* छोटी कुल्हाड़ी।

hate / हेट् / *verb* **1** (व्यक्तियों से) घृणा
करना, (वस्तुओं को) नापसंद करना **2** द्वेष
रखना : *I hate fried food.* ▸ **hate**
noun घृणा, द्वेष।

hateful / 'हेट्फ़ुल् / *adj* घृणास्पद, घृणित।

hatred / 'हेट्रिड् / *noun* घृणा, नाप-
संदगी : *feel hatred for the enemy.*

haughty / 'हॉटि / *adj* (**-ier, -iest**)
(व्यक्ति, व्यवहार) घमंडी, औरों को छोटा
समझने वाला ▸ **haughtily** *adv.*

haul / हॉल् / *verb* घसीटना, खींचना :
elephants hauling logs ▸ **haul**
noun एक बार में पकड़ी गई मछलियों की
मात्रा; प्रयास से प्राप्त सामान।

haunt / हॉन्ट् / *verb* **1** (भूत-प्रेत आदि)
किसी स्थान पर बार-बार आना **2** (कोई
अप्रिय बात) बार-बार याद आना, भुलाए न
भूलना, मरे हुए व्यक्ति की याद (डर के साथ)
आना : *The memory of it still haunts
me.* ▸ **haunt** *noun* स्थान जहाँ कोई
व्यक्ति-विशेष बार-बार जाता हो **haunted**
adj (व्यक्ति) चिंतित।

have^1 / हैव् / *verb* (*perfect tense* बनाने
के लिए *past participle* के साथ प्रयुक्त) :
I have finished my work.

have^2 / हैव् / *aux verb* **1** रखना, पास
रखना : *He has a house in Boston
and a beach house on the coast.*

2 सहन करना : *We can't have students arriving late all the time.* 3 किसी से कोई काम कराना : *Why don't you have your hair cut?* 4 रोग आदि से पीड़ित होना : *He says he has a headache.* 5 कुछ समय के लिए कोई कार्य करना : *I had to swim to cool down.* 6 कोई गुण-विशेष दिखाना, प्रदर्शित करना : *She had the confidence to take a risk.* 7 किसी को आमंत्रित करना : *We have guests to stay for the weekend.* 8 खाना, पीना आदि : *have breakfast/lunch/dinner* 9 जन्म देना : *My wife's having a baby.* 10 कोई मानसिक या शारीरिक गुण होना/प्रदर्शित करना : *She has a good memory.* 11 दिमाग़ में रखना : *I have no doubt that you're right.* 12 कोई कार्य करने की आवश्यकता की स्थिति में होना : *I must go, I have a bus to catch.* 13 कुछ अनुभव करना : *We're having a wonderful time.* 14 (कार्य-क्रम आदि) आयोजित करना : *Let's have a party.* ■ **have it out with sb** आपसी झगड़ा बातचीत द्वारा सुलझाना **have something/nothing to do with** संबद्ध/असंबद्ध होना **have sth against sb/sth** किसी कारण किसी वस्तु/व्यक्ति से घृणा/द्वेष करना।

haven / 'हेव्न् / *noun* सुरक्षित स्थान, आश्रय : *Terrorists will find a safe haven here.*

haversack / 'हैव्रसैक् / *noun* (सिपाहियों, घुमक्कड़ों आदि का) मज़बूत झोला।

havoc / 'हैव्क् / *noun* बरबादी, तबाही : *The floods created havoc throughout the area.*

hawk[1] / हॉक् / *noun* 1 बाज़ 2 (राजनीति में) उग्र नीतियों का समर्थक ▸ **hawkish** *adj* (राजनीति में) उग्रवादी दृष्टिकोण।

hawk[2] / हॉक् / *verb* **hawk sth (about/around)** घर-घर जाकर सामान बेचना, फेरी

लगाना ▸ **hawker** / 'हॉक्र् / *noun* फेरी वाला।

hay / हे / *noun* सूखी घास ■ **make hay while the sun shines** (कहा) अवसर का सदुपयोग कर लेना ▸ **hay fever** *noun* एक प्रकार की बीमारी जिसमें नाक से पानी बहता है।

haywire / 'हेवाइअर् / *adj* ■ **go haywire** (अनौप) नियंत्रण खो देना/गड़बड़ा जाना; अनियंत्रित हो जाना।

hazard / 'हैज़र्ड् / *noun* **hazard (to sb/ sth)** ख़तरा, संभावित संकट : *Smoking is a serious health hazard.* ▸ **hazard** *verb* 1 ख़तरा उठाना, जोखिम में रहना 2 ग़लत हो सकता है जानते हुए भी उत्तर या सुझाव देना : *hazard a guess* **hazardous** *adj* जोखिमभरा।

haze / हेज़् / *noun* 1 हलकी-सी धुंध 2 ऐसी मानसिक स्थिति जब स्पष्ट न सोचा जा सके।

hazel / 'हेज़्ल् / *noun* पहाड़ी बादाम ▸ **hazel** *adj* हलका भूरा रंग : *hazel eyes.*

hazy / 'हेज़ि / *adj* (-ier, -iest) 1 धुंध से ढका/भरा हुआ 2 अस्पष्ट, धूमिल 3 (व्यक्ति) उलझन/दुविधा में : *I'm a little hazy about what to do next.*

he / ही / *pers pron* (पुरुष) वह ▸ **he-man** *noun* शक्तिमान, शक्तिशाली व्यक्ति।

head[1] / हेड् / *noun* 1 सिर 2 मस्तिष्क, दिमाग़ 3 **heads** [*pl*] सिक्के का वह पक्ष जिस पर व्यक्ति का चेहरा आदि बना होता है : *We tossed a coin and it came down heads.* 4 **head** [*pl*] प्रत्येक व्यक्ति या पशु : *50 head of cattle* 5 हथौड़े, कुल्हाड़ी आदि की चोट करने वाला भाग (सिर के समान दिखने वाला या स्थिति वाला भाग) 6 निबंध, भाषण आदि में विषय का मुख्य विभाजन : *a speech arranged under five heads* 7 (समूह या संस्था का) प्रधान; उच्चतम व्यक्ति : *heads of department* ■ **above/over sb's**

head समझने में मुश्किल, गूढ़ a/per head प्रति व्यक्ति bang one's head against a brick wall (अनौप) असफलता के बावजूद कुछ असंभव करने का प्रयल करते रहना head over heels पूर्णतया make head or tail of sth (किसी तथ्य को) समझ पाना off one's head (अनौप) पागल take it into one's head अचानक ठान लेना ▸ head-dress noun (विशेषत: अलंकृत) पगड़ी; टोपी head-on adj, adv आमने-सामने की (टक्कर आदि) headphones noun [pl] सिर में लगाने वाला फ़ोन/उपकरण headquarters noun प्रधान कार्यालय headway noun अग्रगति; प्रगति : We are making little headway with the negotiations. headwind noun प्रतिकूल पवन।

head² / हेड् / verb 1 किसी चीज़ के आगे या ऊपर होना : head a procession 2 मुखिया/अध्यक्ष/नेता होना 3 निर्दिष्ट दिशा में गति करना/जाना : head towards the town centre 4 निबंध आदि को शीर्षकांकित करना 5 सिर से मारना : head the ball (into the goal).

headache / हेडेक् / noun 1 सरदर्द 2 परेशानी/चिंता पैदा करने वाला व्यक्ति/वस्तु।

heading / हेडिङ् / noun शीर्षक।

headland / हेड्लैन्ड् / noun समुद्र में प्रविष्ट ज़मीन, अंतरीप।

headlight / हेड्लाइट् / (headlamp भी) noun कार आदि के आगे की बत्ती/रोशनी।

headline / हेड्लाइन् / noun 1 किसी लेख/पृष्ठ के ऊपर मोटे अक्षरों में छपी पंक्ति 2 the headlines [pl] (समाचारों आदि के) मुख्यांश, ख़ास ख़बरें।

headlong / हेड्लॉङ् / adj, adv 1 सिर की ओर से : fall headlong 2 बिना सोचे-विचारे हड़बड़ी में : rush headlong into danger.

headstrong / हेड्स्ट्रॉङ् / adj ज़िद्दी।

headword / हेड्वर्ड् / noun शब्दकोश में मुख्य प्रविष्टि।

heal / हील् / verb 1 heal (up) स्वस्थ होना या करना; बीमारी ठीक करना 2 (कुछ अप्रिय बात) समाप्त करना; सहने योग्य बनाना : Time heals all sorrows.

health / हेल्थ् / noun 1 स्वास्थ्य 2 शारीरिक एवं मानसिक अवस्था : have poor health 3 किसी चीज़ का सुरक्षात्मक ढंग से एवं सफलतापूर्वक कार्य करना : the health of one's marriage/finances.

healthy / हेल्थि / adj (-ier, -iest) 1 स्वस्थ 2 स्वस्थकर।

heap / हीप् / noun 1 ढेर, राशि 2 heaps [pl] heaps (of sth) (अनौप) बहुत अधिक : There's no hurry — we've heaps of time. ▸ heap verb 1 heap sth (up) ढेर लगाना, राशि में रखना 2 heap sth on sb/sth; heap sth with sth भरना, लादना : heap food on one's plate.

hear / हिअर् / verb (pt, pp heard / हर्ड् /) 1 सुनना : I heard someone laughing. 2 ध्यान देना 3 hear (about sb/sth) बताया जाना या सूचित किया जाना : You sing very well, I hear. 4 (न्यायाधीश का) मुक़दमे की सुनवाई करना ■ hear! hear! अनुमोदन की अभिव्यक्ति ▸ hearing / हिअरिङ् / noun 1 सुन सकने की योग्यता 2 सुनाई पड़ने की सीमा 3 (मुक़दमे की) सुनवाई; अपनी स्थिति या मत स्पष्ट करने का अवसर।

hearsay / हिअर्से / noun साधारण चर्चा; अफ़वाह।

hearse / हर्स् / noun कफ़न की गाड़ी; लाश की गाड़ी।

heart / हार्ट् / noun 1 दिल, हृदय 2 प्रेम और भावनाओं का केंद्र : have everything my heart desires 3 किसी चीज़ का केंद्र या सर्वाधिक महत्त्वपूर्ण भाग : in the heart of the forest/city 4 हृदय की आकृति की वस्तु (विशेषत: ताश के पत्ते में, जिसे हिंदी में पान का पत्ता कहते हैं ■ after one's own heart अपनी रुचि का/पसंद का break

sb's heart किसी का दिल दुखाना/दुख पहुँचाना **by heart** अच्छी तरह याद कर लेना **change of heart** दृष्टिकोण या भावनाओं में बदलाव **one's heart bleeds (for sb)** (अक्सर व्यंग्यपूर्वक प्रयोग में) किसी के प्रति दया, करुणा रखना (परंतु वास्तव में इसके विपरीत होना) **take/lose heart** हिम्मत बाँधना/खो देना **take sth to heart** किसी बात का बहुत बुरा मानना ▸ **heart-beat** noun दिल की धड़कन **heart-breaking** adj दिल तोड़ने वाला, हृदय-विदारक **heartless** adj निर्दय, कठोर **heart-rending** adj हृदय-विदारक **heart-to-heart** noun मैत्रीपूर्ण, खुले दिल से।

hearten /'हार्टन् / verb उत्साहित करना : *We were much heartened by the news.*

hearth /हार्थ् / noun चूल्हा; भट्टी : *a fire burning in the hearth.*

hearty /'हार्टि / adj (-ier, -iest) 1 सच्ची निष्कपट भावनाएँ; हार्दिक 2 स्वस्थ और सबल 3 (भोजन, भूख) पर्याप्त, तीव्र ▸ **heartily** adv.

heat[1] /हीट् / noun 1 गरमी, ऊष्मा; गरमी का स्रोत 2 उत्तेजना, जोश; (क्रोध का) आवेश 3 प्रारंभिक दौड़ जिसमें जीतने वाले अंतिम दौड़ में भाग लेते हैं।

heat[2] /हीट् / verb **heat (sth) up** गरम करना/होना ▸ **heated** adj (व्यक्ति, वाद-विवाद) क्रुद्ध **heatedly** adv क्रोध से **heater** /'हीटर् / noun हीटर, गरम करने वाला उपकरण।

heath /हीथ् / noun झाड़-झंखाड़; बंजर भूमि।

heathen /'हीदन् / noun (अपमा) 1 प्रचलित/प्रसिद्ध धर्मों से भिन्न धर्म का अनुयायी 2 (अप्र, अनौप) जंगली, अभद्र।

heather /'हेदर् / noun जामुनी/गुलाबी रंग के फूलों वाली एक झाड़ी।

heatwave /'हीटवेव् / noun अत्यंत गरमी की लहर।

heave /हीव् / verb (pt, pp **heaved** या कुछ अर्थों में **hove** /होव् /) 1 कोई भारी चीज़ ऊपर उठाना, खींचना 2 **heave (at/on sth)** रस्सी को ऊपर खींचना : *heave at the anchor* 3 भारी चीज़ उठाकर फेंक देना 4 लगातार ऊपर उठना-गिरना : *his heaving chest* 5 लहराना; हाँफना; प्रयास करके शब्द निकालना : *heave a sigh of relief* ▸ **heave** noun.

heaven /'हेवन् / noun 1 स्वर्ग 2 आनंद; सुख-शांति का स्थान 3 (**Heaven** भी) ईश्वर; भाग्य 4 **the heavens** [pl] आकाश, आसमान ▸ **heavenly** /'हेवन्लि / adj 1 स्वर्ग-समान 2 स्वर्गिक : *a heavenly angel/vision* 3 आनंदप्रद।

heavy /'हेवि / adj (-ier, -iest) 1 भारी; वज़नी, जो आसानी से हिलाया या उठाया न जा सके 2 सामान्य से ज़्यादा : *heavy traffic/rain/seas* 3 व्यस्त, गतिविधिपूर्ण ▸ **heavily** adv **heavyweight** / 'हेवि-वेट् / noun मुक्केबाज़ जिसका वज़न 79.5 किलोग्राम या उससे अधिक हो।

heck /हेक् / interj, noun ■ **for the heck of it** (अनौप) केवल आनंद/खुशी के लिए किया गया न कि किसी कारणवश **what the heck** (अनौप) कोई निषिद्ध कार्य करने के समय कहा गया।

heckle /'हेकल् / verb सार्वजनिक सभा में किसी को प्रश्न पूछ-पूछकर तंग करना : *He was heckled continuously during his speech.* ▸ **heckler** / हेकलर् / noun तंग करने वाला व्यक्ति।

hectare /'हेक्टेअर् / noun 10,000 वर्ग-मीटर (2.5 एकड़)।

hectic /'हेक्टिक् / adj अत्यंत व्यस्त; गतिविधि एवं उत्तेजना से पूर्ण : *lead a hectic life.*

hect(o)- pref (पूर्वपद) = 100 : *hectare ○ hectogram.*

hedge /हेज् / noun 1 (साफ़, कटी झाड़ियों का) घेरा, बाड़ा 2 **hedge (against sth)** संभावित हानि से सुरक्षित रखने का

साधन : *by gold on a hedge against inflation* ▶ **hedge** *verb* 1 बाड़/घेरा लगाना 2 सीधा-सीधा उत्तर देने से कतराना : *Answer 'yes' or 'no'— stop hedging!* 3 **hedge sb/sth (about/round) (with sth)** चारों ओर से सीमित करना, बाधाएँ लगाना : *His belief was hedged with doubt.* **hedgerow** *noun* बाड़ा/घेरा।

hedgehog / 'हेज्हॉग् / *noun* काँटों वाला चूहा; साही।

heed / हीड् / *verb* (औप) ध्यान देना : *heed sb's advice/warning* ▶ **heed** *noun* (औप) ध्यान **heedful** *adj* **heedful (of sb/sth)** (औप) सावधान, सतर्क **heedless** *adj* **heedless (of sb/sth)** (औप) असावधान, लापरवाह : *be heedless of danger* **heedlessly** *adv.*

heel[1] / हील् / *noun* 1 एड़ी 2 आकृति या स्थान में एड़ीनुमा वस्तु : *the heel of the hand* 3 जूते की एड़ी/मोज़े की एड़ी ■ **bring sb/sth to heel** बलपूर्वक किसी को अपनी आज्ञा मनवाना **come to heel** (व्यक्ति का) आज्ञाकारी बनना; आज्ञा का पालन करने को राज़ी होना **take to one's heels** भाग जाना, पलायन कर जाना ▶ **heel** *verb* जूते पर नई एड़ी लगाना।

heel[2] / हील् / *verb* ■ **heel over (keel over** भी) (जहाज़ का) एक ओर झुकना।

hefty / 'हेफ्टि / *adj* (-ier, -iest) 1 (व्यक्ति/वस्तु) भारी-भरकम 2 (धन-राशि) सामान्य से बहुत ज़्यादा : *She earns a hefty salary.* 3 बलपूर्वक : *give sb a hefty kick* ▶ **heftily** *adv.*

heifer / हेफ़र् / *noun* बछिया, गाय जिसके अभी बच्चा नहीं हुआ हो।

height / हाइट् / *noun* 1 ऊँचाई, समुद्रतल से ऊँचाई 2 ऊँचा स्थान, चोटी 3 पराकाष्ठा : *in the height of summer.*

heighten / 'हाइट्न् / *verb* और अधिक ऊँचा करना/उठाना, बढ़ाना।

heinous / 'हेनस् / *adj* घृणित, जघन्य/घोर : *a heinous crime.*

heir / एअर् / *noun* **heir (to sth)** वारिस, उत्तराधिकारी ▶ **heiress** / 'एअरेस् / *noun* महिला वारिस।

heirloom / 'एअर्लूम् / *noun* पुरखों से आई वस्तु/संपत्ति।

helicopter / 'हेलिकॉप्टर / (अनौप **chopper** भी) *noun* हेलिकॉप्टर।

hell / हेल् / *noun* 1 नरक 2 यातना देने वाला स्थान; यातनापूर्ण अनुभव ▶ **hellish** *adj* नरक-समान।

hello / ह'लो / *interj* = **hallo.**

helm / हेल्म् / *noun* पतवार, कर्ण : (अलं) *the helm of state.*

helmet / 'हेल्मिट् / *noun* (सिर को चोट से बचाने के लिए प्रयुक्त) प्रायः लोहे का टोप।

help[1] / हेल्प् / *verb* 1 **help (sb) (with sth)** सहायता करना; सहारा देना; समय पर मदद देना 2 स्थिति में सुधार लाना या कुछ घटित करना 3 **help oneself/sb (to sth)** (स्वयं को) परसना, परोसना : *May I help you to some more meat?* ▶ **helper** *noun* सहायक, मददगार **helping** *noun* प्लेट पर परसा हुआ भोजन।

help[2] / हेल्प् / *noun* 1 सहायता/मदद 2 **a help (to sb)** सहायक व्यक्ति/वस्तु ▶ **helpful** *adj* सहायक, उपयोगी **helpless** *adj* बेबस, लाचार; निस्सहाय।

hem / हेम् / *noun* (कपड़े का) किनारा, गोट ▶ **hem** *verb* (-mm-) किनारा बनाना, गोट लगाना : *hem a skirt/handkerchief* ■ **hem sb in** घेरना।

hemisphere / 'हेमिस्फ़िअर् / *noun* 1 अर्धवृत्त, आधा गोला 2 पृथ्वी का आधा भाग : *the northern/southern hemisphere* 3 मस्तिष्क का आधा भाग : *the left cerebral hemisphere.*

hemp / हेम्प् / *noun* 1 सन, जिससे रस्सी बनती है 2 गाँजा।

hen / हेन् / *noun* 1 मुर्गी 2 कोई भी मादा पक्षी : *a guinea-hen/a hen pheasant*

▶ **henpecked** adj (अनौप) पत्नी द्वारा शासित (पुरुष)।

hence / हेन्स् / adv 1 यहाँ से, अब से : *a week hence* 2 इस कारण से ▶ **henceforth (henceforward** भी) adv आज/अब से प्रारंभ कर।

henchman / हेन्च्मन् / noun (pl **henchmen**) (प्राय: अपमा) अनुचर।

hepatitis / हेप'टाइटिस् / noun यकृत की एक गंभीर बीमारी; पीलिया रोग।

her¹ / हर् / pers pron **she** शब्द का कर्मकारक रूप; उस, उसे।

her² / हर् / possess det उस (स्त्री) का/की ▶ **hers** / हर्ज़् / possess pron उस (स्त्री) का/की।

herald / हेरल्ड / noun 1 (पूर्व में) अग्रदूत; किसी व्यक्ति/वस्तु के आगमन की पूर्वसूचना देने वाला व्यक्ति/वस्तु: *I think of primroses as the heralds of spring.* 2 शासक की ओर से मुख्य सार्वजनिक घोषणाएँ करने वाला ▶ **herald** verb आगमन की सूचना देना।

herb / हर्ब्; US अर्ब् / noun जड़ी-बूटी; छोटे-छोटे कोमल पौधे ▶ **herbal** adj.

herbivore / हर्बिवॉर्; US अर्बिवॉर् / noun तृणभोजी पशु, घास खाने वाले पशु।

herd / हर्ड /noun 1 पशुओं का झुंड 2 **the herd** [sing] (प्राय: अपमा) व्यक्तियों का बड़ा समूह, भीड़ : *the common herd* ▶ **herd** verb 1 झुंड के रूप में आगे बढ़ना/बढ़ाया जाना 2 पशुओं के झुंड की देखभाल करना **herdsman** noun (pl **herdsmen**) चरवाहा।

here / हिअर् / adv यहाँ ■ **here and there** यत्र-तत्र, जहाँ-तहाँ **here, there and everywhere** चारों तरफ़, सर्वत्र **neither here nor there** असंगत, अप्रासंगिक ▶ **hereabouts** adv आस-पास; पास में ही (औप) **hereafter** / हिअर'आफ़्टर् / adv (औप) 1 अब से, इसके बाद से 2 भविष्य में **hereby** adv (औप) इस साधन से, इसके परिणामस्वरूप।

hereditary / ह'रेडिट्रि / adj 1 माता-पिता से बच्चों में पहुँचे (लक्षण आदि), वंशानुगत 2 पुश्तैनी, पूर्वजों से आई हुई : *a hereditary ruler.*

heredity / ह'रेडिटि / noun अपने लक्षण बच्चों में पहुँचा देने की प्रवृत्ति, वंशानुक्रमता।

heresy / हेरसि / noun (धार्मिक मामलों में) अधिकांश जनों द्वारा स्वीकृत मत के विपरीत मत (रखना), विधर्म ▶ **heretic** noun प्रचलित मत को न मानने वाला, विधर्मी **heretical** adj विधर्म-/विधर्मी-विषयक।

heritage / हेरिटिज् / noun पैतृक संपत्ति, दायभाग; विरासत : *our literary heritage.*

hermit / हर्मिट् / noun सामाजिक जीवन से दूर एकांत में रहने वाला (ऋषि, यति) ▶ **hermitage** noun ऋषि कुटी।

hernia / हर्निआ / noun (चिकि) हर्निया, शरीर के किसी भीतरी अंग (विशेषत: आँतों) का सूजना और बाहर की तरफ़ आ जाना।

hero / हिअरो / noun (pl **heroes**) 1 वीर, बहादुर : *receive a hero's welcome* 2 कथा-साहित्य, नाटक या कविता का नायक ▶ **heroism** / हेरोइज़म् / noun वीरता, बहादुरी।

heroic / ह'रोइक् / adj वीरोचित; वीर-/वीरता-विषयक : *heroic myths.*

heroine / हेरोइन् / noun नायिका।

heron / हेरन् / noun बगुला।

herring / हेरिङ् / noun एक समुद्री मछली जो खाने में बहुत प्रयुक्त होती है।

herself / हर'सेल्फ़् / pron (स्त्री के लिए प्रयुक्त) 1 (reflex) स्वयं को : *She hurt herself.* 2 (emph) स्वयमेव, खुद ही : *She told me the news herself.*

hesitant / हेज़िटन्ट् / adj हिचकिचाने वाला ▶ **hesitantly** adv हिचकिचाते/झिझकते हुए।

hesitate / हेज़िटेट् / verb 1 **hesitate (at/about/over sth)** हिचकिचाना, आगा-पीछा करना 2 कुछ करने को चिंतित होना या

शर्म मानना ▸ **hesitation** / हेज़ि'टेश्न् / noun.

heterodox / हेटरडॉक्स् / adj (औप) जो सनातनी नहीं है; स्वीकृत/स्थापित धर्म, विचार, मत आदि को न मानने वाला ▸ **heterodoxy** noun.

heterogeneous / हेटर'जीनिअस् / adj (औप) विभिन्न तत्त्वों से बना, विषमांग; विषमरूप, पंचमेल : the heterogeneous population of the USA ▸ **heterogeneity** / हेटरज'नीअटि / noun.

hew / ह्यू / verb (pt **hewed** या **hewn** / ह्यून् /) 1 कुल्हाड़ी या तलवार से काटना/चीरना 2 **hew sth (down)** काटकर गिराना 3 काटकर कुछ बनाना या आकृति देना : They hewed a path through the forest.

hexagon / हेक्सगन्; US हेक्सगॉन् / noun (ज्यामिति) षट्कोण ▸ **hexagonal** adj.

hey / हे / interj ध्यान आकर्षित करने के लिए प्रयुक्त शब्द : Hey, come and look at this!

heyday / हेडे / noun सर्वाधिक सफलता, प्रभुत्व या प्रभाव का समय, बहार का समय।

hi / हाइ / interj (अनौप) हलो।

hibernate / हाइबर्नेट् / verb (कुछ पशुओं/जंतुओं का) शीतकाल सोकर बिताना ▸ **hibernation** / हाइबर्'नेश्न् / noun.

hiccup (hiccough भी) / हिकप् / noun 1 हिचकी 2 (अनौप) कोई अस्थायी रुकावट या देरी : There's been a slight hiccup in our mailing system. ▸ **hiccup (hiccough** भी) verb हिचकी लेना।

hide¹ / हाइड् / verb (pt **hid** / हिड् /; pp **hidden** / हिड्न् /) 1 छिपना/छिपाना 2 **hide sth (from sb)** किसी से कोई बात गुप्त रखना/जानकारी न देना ▸ **hide** noun गुप्त/छिपने का स्थान **hidden** adj गुप्त, छिपा हुआ **hidden agenda** noun (अपमा) गुप्त योजना; षड्यंत्र।

hide² / हाइड् / noun (पशुओं की) खाल (जिससे चमड़े का सामान बनता है)।

hideous / हिडिअस् / adj घृणित; जघन्य।

hiding¹ / हाइडिङ् / noun छिपाव ■ **be in/go into hiding** गुप्त स्थान पर छिप जाना।

hiding² / हाइडिङ् / noun (अनौप) चपत लगाना : His dad gave him a good hiding.

hierarchy / हाइअराकि / noun सोपानक्रम, पदानुक्रम; उच्च-नीच क्रम, श्रेणीबद्ध समाज संगठन ▸ **hierarchical** adj.

hieroglyphics / हाइअरग्लिफ़िक्स् / noun ऐसी लेखन प्रणाली जिसमें शब्द आदि के लिए विशेष चित्र/प्रतीक आदि का प्रयोग किया जाता है (जैसे पुरातन मिस्र और अन्य पुरातन सभ्यताओं में)।

hi-fi / हाइ फ़ाइ / adj (अनौप) (**high fidelty** भी) उच्च क्षमता संपन्न।

high¹ / हाइ / adj (**-er, -est**) 1 (वस्तु) ऊँची/ऊँचा, उच्च 2 महत्त्व या गुणों में अन्य से उच्च : a high official 3 सामान्य से ऊपर; अधिक महत्त्व वाला; (इरादे, विचार आदि) नैतिक दृष्टि से अच्छे, श्रेष्ठ : have high ideals 4 (मांस-मछली) सड़ने लगना ■ **high and dry** कठिन स्थिति में **run high** भावनाओं का उत्तेजित होना ▸ **high-born** adj उच्च कुलीन **higher education** noun उच्च-शिक्षा **high-handed** adj निरंकुश, स्वेच्छाचारी **high-land** noun पर्वतीय प्रदेश **high-level** adj उच्चस्तरीय **high-minded** adj उच्चाशय वाला, मनस्वी **high-pitched** adj कर्णभेदी (स्वर), उच्च सुर **high-rise** adj (भवनों के लिए) अत्युच्च **high-tech** adj उच्च-तकनीकी प्रविधि वाला।

high² / हाइ / noun 1 ऊँचा स्तर/संख्या, उच्च बिंदु : Profits reached an all-time high last year. 2 उच्च वायुदाब का क्षेत्र।

high³ / हाइ / adv 1 उच्च स्तर पर/से, ऊँचे 2 (स्वर) ऊँचा।

highbrow / 'हाइब्राउ / adj उच्चभ्रू, केवल बौद्धिक अथवा सांस्कृतिक दृष्टि से विचार करने वाला (व्यक्ति); अभिजात्य।

highlight / 'हाइलाइट् / noun किसी कार्यक्रम, मैच आदि का सबसे दिलचस्प भाग : The highlights of the match will be shown at 10.25 tonight.

highly / 'हाइलि / adv 1 अत्यधिक 2 बहुत तरफ़दारी से, प्रशंसा से : speak highly of sb ▸ **highly-strung** adj (व्यक्ति) उत्तेजनशील, सहजकोपी।

highness / हाइ 'नस् / noun (**Highness**) राजकुमार/राजकुमारी के लिए प्रयुक्त संबोधन: His/Her/Your Royal Highness.

highway / 'हाइवे / noun (विशेषत: US) मुख्यमार्ग, राजमार्ग।

hijack / 'हाइजैक् / verb (विमान) अप- हरण : The plane was hijacked while on a flight to Delhi. ▸ **hijack** noun **hijacker** noun (विमान) अपहर्ता।

hike / हाइक् / noun 1 लंबी पैदल यात्रा (विशेषत: ग्रामीण/पहाड़ी क्षेत्र में) 2 (अनौप) क़ीमतों, दरों आदि में तीव्र वृद्धि : the latest hike in the interest rates ▸ **hike** verb 1(प्राय: go hiking) लंबी पैदल यात्रा के लिए जाना 2 hike sth (up) (अनौप) क़ीमतें आदि अचानक बढ़ा देना।

hilarious / हि 'लेअरिअस् / adj अत्यधिक हास्यजनक; उल्लासपूर्ण ▸ **hilariously** adv **hilarity** noun.

hill / हिल् / noun 1 पहाड़ी 2 (सड़क का) ढाल ▸ **hilly** adj पहाड़ी-पठारी (क्षेत्र) **hillside** noun.

hillock / 'हिलक् / noun छोटी पहाड़ी, टीला।

hilt / हिल्ट् / noun (तलवार या बर्छी का) हत्था, मूठ ■ (up) to the hilt पूरी तरह से : We're mortgaged up to the hilt.

him / इम्; हिम् / pers pron he का कर्मकारक रूप : When did you see him?

himself / हिम् 'सेल्फ़ / pron (पुरुष के लिए प्रयुक्त) 1 (reflex) स्वयं को : He cut/ killed himself. 2 (emph) स्वयमेव, ख़ुद ही : The doctor said so himself.

hind / हाइन्ड् / adj शरीर के पीछे का एक अंग, विशेषत: जानवरों में : The horse reared up on its hind legs. ▸ **hind-most** adj सबसे पिछला।

hinder / 'हिन्डर् / verb hinder sb/sth (from sth/doing sth) बाधा/अड़चन डालना।

hindrance / 'हिन्ड्रन्स् / noun बाधा, अड़चन।

hindsight / 'हाइन्ड्साइट् / noun कुछ घटित होने के बाद ही उसके बारे में आने वाली समझ (कि वह कार्य किसी अन्य तरीक़े से भी किया जा सकता था) : With hindsight it is easy to say they should not have released him.

hinge / हिन्ज् / noun दरवाज़े, ढक्कन आदि के क़ब्ज़े ▸ **hinge** verb क़ब्ज़ों से जोड़ना ■ **hinge on sth** पर निर्भर होना : Every-thing hinges on the outcome of these talks.

hint / हिन्ट् / noun 1 संकेत/इशारा 2 ज़रा-सी मात्रा या लक्षण 3 व्यावहारिक सूचना या सलाह (थोड़ी-सी) : handy hints for home decorators ▸ **hint** verb hint (at sth) संकेत करना/देना।

hip[1] / हिप् / noun कूल्हा, पुट्ठा।

hip[2] / हिप् / interj ■ hip, hip, hooray/hurrah/hurray! प्रसन्नता व्यक्त करने की अभिव्यक्ति।

hippopotamus / हिप 'पॉटमस् / noun (pl **hippopotamuses** / हिप 'पॉटम-सिज़् / या **hippopotami** / हिप 'पॉट-माइ /) (अनौप **hippo** भी) दरियाई घोड़ा।

hire / 'हाइअर् / verb 1 किराए या भाड़े पर लेना 2 (विशेषत: US) किसी को नौकरी देना; थोड़े समय के लिए या विशेष प्रयोजन के लिए नौकरी पर रखना : hire a lawyer 3 hire sth (out) (to sb) कोई वस्तु भाड़े

किराए पर देना ▸ **hire** noun किराया/भाड़ा

hire purchase (US **instalment plan** भी) noun ऐसी पद्धति जिसमें निश्चित भुगतानों के बाद किराए वाली वस्तु ख़रीद ली जाती है **hirer** noun किराएदार।

his / इज़; हिज़् / possess det उस (पुरुष) का/की ▸ **his** possess pron : It's not mine, it's his.

hiss / हिस् / verb **hiss** (at sb/sth) (साँप का) विरोध प्रदर्शित करने के लिए फुफकारना, सी-सी की आवाज़ करना ▸ **hiss** noun इस प्रकार की आवाज़।

historian / हिस्टॉरिअन् / noun इतिहास-कार, इतिहासज्ञ।

historic / हिस्टॉरिक् / adj 1 महत्त्वपूर्ण; इतिहास-प्रसिद्ध 2 ऐतिहासिक : in historic times.

historical / हिस्टॉरिकल् / adj 1 ऐतिहासिक; अतीत में वस्तुत: घटित (न कि काल्पनिक या दंतकथाओं से आगत) 2 (पुस्तक या फ़िल्म) वास्तविक इतिहास पर आधारित : a historical novel.

history / हिस्ट्रि / noun [pl] 1 इतिहास, घटनावृत्त 2 भूतकाल (एक संपूर्णता के रूप में देखा गया) : a people with no sense of history.

hit¹ / हिट् / verb (-tt-; pt, pp hit) 1 आघात करना; चोट मारना/पहुँचाना 2 टक्कर हो जाना/लग जाना : the lorry hit the lamp post 3 किसी पर बुरा प्रभाव डालना/बुरी तरह प्रभावित करना 4 आक्रमण करना 5 (अनौप) कुछ अप्रिय अनुभव करना : hit a snag/problem 6 **hit** sth (on sth) शरीर के किसी अंग का किसी चीज़ से टकराना : He hit his head on the low ceiling. ■ **hit on/upon** (sth) संयोग से पाना या सूझना।

hit² / हिट् / noun 1 आघात/टक्कर 2 बहुत लोकप्रिय व्यक्ति या वस्तु ■ **make a hit (with sb)** सामान्य अनुमोदन पाना, किसी पर अच्छा प्रभाव डालना।

hitch / हिच् / verb 1 (औरों के वाहन पर) मुफ़्त सवारी करना 2 **hitch** sth (up) (कपड़े) झटके से ऊपर खींचना : She hitched (up) her skirt so as not to get it wet. 3 रस्सी या काँटे से बाँधना : hitch a horse to a fence ▸ **hitch** noun 1 कोई मुश्किल या समस्या जिसके कारण देरी हो रही हो : The ceremony went off without any hitch. 2 (नाविकों की) गाँठ।

hitch-hike / हिच्हाइक् / verb लोगों से मुफ़्त सवारी माँग-माँगकर सैर करना।

hither / हिदर् / adv (प्रा) यहाँ।

hitherto / हिदर्'टू / adv (औप) अभी तक : a hitherto unknown species of moth.

HIV / एच् आइ 'वी / abbr (**human immunodeficiency virus**) एड्स (AIDS) पैदा करने वाला वायरस।

hive / हाइव् / noun 1 (**beehive** भी) मधु-मक्खियों का छत्ता या बक्सा 2 व्यस्त लोगों से भरा स्थान : The office is a hive of activity.

hoard / हॉर्ड / noun खाद्य-पदार्थों या रुपये-पैसों का जमा किया भंडार; तथ्यों का समूह ▸ **hoard** verb **hoard** (sth) (up) जमा करना।

hoarding / हॉर्डिङ् / noun 1 (US **billboard**) विज्ञापनों के लिए प्रयुक्त बड़ा-सा तख़्ता 2 निर्माण-स्थल को घेरने के लिए प्रयुक्त तख़्तों का घेरा 3 जमाखोरी।

hoarse / हॉर्स / adj 1 फटा-फटा स्वर; कर्कश ध्वनि 2 ऐसे स्वर वाला (व्यक्ति) ▸ **hoarsely** adv **hoarseness** noun.

hoax / होक्स् / noun मज़ाक में किया गया धोखा/छल : play a hoax on sb ▸ **hoax** verb ऐसे धोखा करना **hoaxer** noun.

hobble / हॉबल् / verb 1 लड़खड़ाना, लंगड़ाना : The old man hobbled along (the road). 2 घोड़े की पिछाड़ी बाँधना ▸ **hobble** noun लड़खड़ाहट (चाल में)।

hobby / हॉबि / noun (pl **hobbies**) शौक़ ▸ **hobby-horse** noun किसी का

प्रिय विषय, जिसे वह उत्सुकता से बातों के लिए चुनता है।

hobnob / 'हॉब्नॉब् / *verb* (-bb-) hobnob (with sb); hobnob (together) (कभी-कभी *अपमा*) किसी व्यक्ति के साथ ज्यादा समय गुज़ारना/मेल-जोल बढ़ाना; मित्रतापूर्ण बातों में समय बिताना/गँवाना।

hockey / 'हॉकि / *noun* 1 (*US* field hockey) हॉकी (का खेल) 2 (*US* ice hockey) बर्फ़ पर खेला जाने वाला हॉकी का खेल।

hoe / हो / *noun* कुदाली ▸ hoe *verb* (*pres p* hoeing; *pt, pp* hoed) कुदाली प्रयोग करना : *do some hoeing.*

hog / हॉग् / *noun* 1 ख़स्सी सूअर 2 (*अनौप, अपमा*) (भोजन, पेय आदि के लिए) अत्यधिक लालची व्यक्ति ■ go the whole hog किसी काम को पूरा-पूरा कर डालना ▸ hog *verb* (-gg-) (*अनौप*) अपने हिस्से से अधिक हथिया लेना : *hog the limelight.*

hoist / हॉइस्ट् / *verb* ऊपर उठाना; (झंडा) फहराना : *hoist a flag/the sails* ▸ hoist *noun* (भार) ऊपर उठाने का उपकरण/यंत्र।

hold¹ / होल्ड् / *verb* (*pt, pp* held / हेल्ड् /) 1 कसकर पकड़ना, थामना 2 भार वहन/सहन करना : *Is that branch strong enough to hold your weight?* 3 रोके रखना, नियंत्रण में रखना : *The dam could not hold the flood waters.* 4 रखना/ स्थिति विशेष बनाए रखना : *Hold your head up.* 5 का अधिकारी होना, के पद पर होना : *How long has he held offfice?* 6 (कोई बैठक, परीक्षा आदि) आयोजित करना 7 किसी को रोककर रखना, जाने न देना : *The terrorists are holding three men hostage.* 8 कोई मत या विचार रखना : *He holds strange views on religion.* ■ hold back (from doing sth) संकोचवश न कहना या करना, हिचकिचाना hold forth भाषण देना hold good सत्य होना, घटित होना; अब भी चालू रहना hold off (sth/doing sth) टाल

देना, (कार्य) लटका देना hold on (to sb/ sth) कसकर पकड़े रहना hold one's tongue/peace चुप रहना hold onto sth अपने क़ब्ज़े में ही रखना hold out अपनी स्थिति मज़बूत बनाए रखना hold sb/ sth back आगे बढ़ने से रोकना hold sb/ sth up बाधित करना, विलंबित करना hold sth back 1 छिपाए रखना 2 भावनाओं को नियंत्रण में रखना hold sth/sb off दूर रखना hold sth over स्थगित करना hold sth together (किसी चीज़ को) बाँधे रखना; एकता बनाए रखना hold together एक साथ बने रहना hold with sth अनुमोदन करना।

hold² / होल्ड् / *noun* 1 पकड़े रहने/थामने की प्रक्रिया 2 hold (on/over sb/sth) प्रभुत्व/दबाव।

hold³ / होल्ड् / *noun* वायुयान/जहाज़ में डेक के नीचे का भाग जिसमें माल रहता है।

holdall / 'होल्डॉल् / *noun* होल्डाल, यात्रा के लिए बड़ा बैग।

holder / 'होल्डर् / *noun* 1 (समास में) किसी वस्तु-विशेष का अधिकार/स्वामित्व वाला व्यक्ति : *a licence holder* 2 रोक रखने वाली वस्तु : *a pen-holder.*

holding / 'होल्डिङ् / *noun* 1 (प्राय: *pl*) स्वामित्व वाली वस्तु, जैसे जोत-क्षेत्र, शेयर, निजी संपत्ति आदि 2 संपत्ति; किसान के पास भूमि का पट्टा।

hole / होल् / *noun* 1 छेद, सूराख़ 2 (जान-वर का) बिल ■ pick holes in sth दोष ढूँढ़ना ▸ hole *verb* 1 छेद करना 2 hole (out) (गोल्फ़ आदि खेलों में) छेद में गेंद डालना।

holiday / 'हॉलिडे / *noun* 1 (विशेषत: *US* vacation) (प्राय: *pl*) छुट्टियों के दिन 2 छुट्टी : *a public holiday.*

holiness / 'होलिनिस् / *noun* 1 पवित्र (होना), पवित्रता 2 His/Your Holiness पोप के लिए प्रयुक्त सम्बोधन।

hollow / 'हॉलो / *adj* 1 खोखला, पोला : *a hollow tree/ball* 2 ख़ाली; (आवाज़)

खोखले में से निकली हुई-सी 3 अवास्तविक; (व्यक्ति) बेईमान; (वस्तु) महत्त्वहीन, बेकार : She gave a hollow laugh. ○ hollow threats 4 पिचका हुआ (बीमारी या भूख से) सूखा हुआ : hollow cheeks ▸ hollow noun खोखला स्थान, छेद; (पहाड़ी में) घाटी hollow verb ■ hollow sth out 1 छेद करना 2 छेद करके कुछ बनाना : hollow out a nest.

holly / 'होलि / noun (pl hollies) चमकदार एवं कॉंटेदार पत्तों वाला एक छोटा पेड़ जो क्रिसमस पर सजावट के लिए प्रयुक्त किया जाता है।

holocaust /'हॉलकॉस्ट/ noun 1 (अग्नि-कांड आदि से) धन-जन की गंभीर हानि, विध्वंस 2 the Holocaust [sing] द्वितीय विश्वयुद्ध के दौरान जर्मन नात्सियों द्वारा किया गया यहूदियों का नर-संहार।

holster /'होल्स्ट्र / noun पिस्तौल रखने का चमड़े का खोल।

holy /'होलि / adj (-ier, -iest) 1 ईश्वरीय, पवित्र, धार्मिक : the Holy Bible/Scriptures ○ holy ground 2 धर्मपरायण : a holy man ▸ the Holy City noun जेरुसलम।

homage /'हॉमिज्/ noun homage (to sb/sth) श्रद्धांजलि।

home¹ / होम् / noun 1 घर, जहाँ व्यक्ति परिवार के साथ रहता है 2 स्थान या देश जहाँ व्यक्ति पैदा हुआ हो और जहाँ से वह भावनात्मक रूप से जुड़ा हो : my home town 3 बूढ़ों/मरीज़ों के लिए आवास-गृह : an old people's home ■ at home 1 घर पर/में 2 स्वदेश में 3 आराम से, चैन से : They always make us feel very much at home. ▸ homeless adj बेघर home-made adj घर का बना हुआ homesick adj जिसे घर-परिवार की याद आ रही हो homeward adj, adv घर की ओर homework noun गृहकार्य the homeless noun बेघर लोग।

home² / होम् / adv 1 स्वदेश में/घर में/

पर : She's on her way home. 2 निशाने पर; उचित स्थिति पर : drive a nail home ■ bring sth home to sb किसी को सच्चाई का पूरा आभास करा देना।

home³ / होम् / adj 1 घर से संबंधित : have a happy home life 2 घर में बना या प्रयुक्त : home cooking 3 अपने देश से संबंधित : home news/affairs.

homely / 'होम्लि / adj (-ier, -iest) 1 सादा-सरल; अनाकर्षक, साधारण 2 घर जैसा लगने वाला या घर की याद दिलाने वाला।

homeopathy (homoeopathy भी) / होमि'ऑपथि / noun होमियोपैथी (एक चिकित्सा पद्धति)।

homespun /'होम्स्पन् / adj साधारण, सरल, सादा : homespun remedies for minor ailments.

homicide /'हॉमिसाइड् / noun नरहत्या ▸ homicidal adj नरहत्या-विषयक।

homily /'हॉमिलि / noun (प्राय: अपमा) लंबा, उबाऊ प्रवचन; धर्मोपदेश।

homogeneous / होम'जीनिअस् / adj (औप) एक जैसे तत्त्वों/अंगों से बना, समांगी; एकरूप : a homogeneous group/society ▸ homogeneity noun.

homonym /'हॉमनिम् / noun एक जैसी वर्तनी एवं उच्चारण वाले परंतु भिन्न अर्थ वाले शब्द, जैसे bark¹, bark².

homophone / 'होमफोन् / noun एक जैसे उच्चारण वाले परंतु भिन्न वर्तनी एवं अर्थ वाले शब्द, जैसे some, sum/knew, new.

homosexual / होम'सेक्शुअल् / adj समलैंगिक (व्यक्ति) ▸ homosexuality noun समलैंगिकता।

hone / होन् / verb 1 hone sth (to sth) विशिष्ट प्रयोजन के लिए विकसित/परिवर्धित करना, परिमार्जन करना : a finely honed judgement 2 चाकू/छुरी आदि तेज़ करना ▸ hone noun सान (पत्थर)।

honest /'ऑनिस्ट् / adj 1 (व्यक्ति) ईमान-दार, सच्चा; निष्कपट 2 (मज़दूरी आदि)

मेहनत से कमाई हुई : *make an honest living* ▸ **honestly** *adv.*

honesty / 'ऑनिस्ट / *noun* ईमानदारी।

honey / 'हनि / *noun* 1 शहद, मधु 2(*अनौप, विशेषत: US*) (संबोधन में प्रयुक्त) प्रिय ▸ **honeycomb** *noun* शहद का छत्ता।

honeymoon / 'हनिमून् / *noun* नव-विवाहितों द्वारा आमोद-प्रमोद के लिए ली गई छुट्टी ▸ **honeymoon** *verb.*

honk / हॉङ्क् / *noun* गाड़ी के हॉर्न की आवाज़ ▸ **honk** *verb* गाड़ी का हॉर्न बजाना, ऐसी आवाज़ करना।

honorarium / ऑन' रेअरिअम् / *noun* (*pl* **honoraria,** ऑन' रेअरिआ /) मानदेय, कार्यशुल्क।

honorary / 'ऑनररि / *adj* 1 अवैतनिक पद : *the honorary (post of) Presi-dent* 2 सम्मानार्थ (दी गई उपाधि) : *be awarded an honorary doctorate.*

honour[1] (*US* honor) / 'ऑनर् / *noun* 1 सम्मान, आदर; [*sing*] सम्मान एवं गौरव की भावना : *It is a great honour to be invited.* 2 प्रतिष्ठा; मान-मर्यादा : *a man of honour* 3 **an honour to sth/sb** गौरव प्रदान करने वाला व्यक्ति/वस्तु 4 **His/Her/Your Honour** न्यायाधीश के लिए प्रयुक्त आदरसूचक संबोधन 5 **honours** [*pl*] (कुछ विश्वविद्यालयों द्वारा प्रदत्त) ऑनर्स की उपाधि ▪ **have the honour (of sth/doing sth)** (*औप*) कोई कार्य करने का विशेषाधिकार।

honour[2] (*US* honor) / 'ऑनर् / *verb* 1 सम्मान करना/देना 2 **honour sb (with sth) (for sth)** सार्वजनिक प्रतिष्ठा/सम्मान देना 3 समझौता/वायदा पूरा करना 4 (*वाणिज्य*) भुगतान करने का उत्तरदायित्व लेना (चेक आदि का)।

honourable (*US* honorable) / 'ऑन-रब्ल् / *adj* 1 आदर के योग्य, आदरणीय; आदर प्रदान करने वाला (कार्य) 2 (the Honourable, *संक्षि* Hon) प्राय: न्यायाधीश

के नाम के साथ लगने वाला आदर-सूचक शब्द ▸ **honourably** *adv.*

hood / हुड् / *noun* 1 सिर और गरदन को ढकने वाली टोपी 2 विश्वविद्यालय के गाउन के साथ पहनी जाने वाली टोपी 3 छिपने/चेहरा ढकने के लिए लपेटा गया कपड़ा : *The robbers all wore hoods to hide their faces.* 4 मोटरकार का हुड, टप; हुड के आकार की कोई वस्तु ▸ **hooded** *adj.*

hoodwink / 'हुड्विङ्क् / *verb* **hood-wink sb (into doing sth)** ठगना, छल लेना।

hoof / हूफ् / *noun* (*pl* **hoofs** या **hooves** / हूव्ज़् /) (घोड़े या अन्य पशुओं के) खुरा।

hook[1] / हुक् / *noun* 1 हुक, काँटा; खूँटी 2 हँसिया (काटने वाली) 3 (बॉक्सिंग में) मुक्के का प्रहार ▪ **by hook or by crook** किसी भी तरीक़े से, जैसे भी हो सके काम सिद्ध करना।

hook[2] / हुक् / *verb* हुक से बाँधना, फँसाना; हुक से कुछ पकड़ना : *hook a large fish* ▸ **hooked** *adj* 1 हुक से बना हुआ/हुक लगा हुआ 2 हुक की आकृति में मुड़ा हुआ।

hookworm / 'हुक्वर्म् / *noun* आँतों का एक कृमि।

hooligan / 'हूलिगन् / *noun* गुंडा, सार्व-जनिक उपद्रवी भीड़ का सदस्य ▸ **hooli-ganism** *noun* गुंडागर्दी।

hoop / हूप् / *noun* 1 लोहे या लकड़ी का (वस्तु के चारों ओर, जैसे पीपे के) छल्ला 2 (खेल में या सर्कस में प्रयुक्त) बड़ा घेरा; छल्ला ▸ **hooped** *adj* छल्ले जैसा।

hoot / हूट् / *noun* 1 ज़ोर की हँसी 2 (दर्शकों या श्रोताओं का) शोरगुल मचाना, सीटी बजाना, ठहाका 3 मोटरकार के हॉर्न की आवाज़ 4 उल्लू की आवाज़ ▸ **hoot** *verb* 1 ज़ोरों से हँसना 2 शोरगुल करके स्टेज से भगा देना 3 गाड़ी का हॉर्न बजाना 4 उल्लू के जैसे आवाज़ करना : *the eerie sound of an owl hooting* **hooter** *noun* 1 (मिल-फ़ैक्टरी का) भोंपू 2 कार का हॉर्न।

hop[1] / हॉप् / *verb* (-pp-) 1 (व्यक्ति का)

एक पैर से कूदना; (चिड़ियों का) फुदकना 2 hop across/over (to...) (अनौप) छोटी दूरी की यात्रा जल्दी में करना 3 एक विषय से दूसरे पर जाना : *hop from channel to channel on the TV* ▸ hop *noun* 1 छोटी कूद (एक पैर पर) 2 बड़ी उड़ानों से संबद्ध करने वाले हवाई जहाज़ की छोटी उड़ान।

hop² / हॉप् / *noun* गुच्छेदार फूलों वाली एक लता; hops [*pl*] इस लता के सूखे फूल जो बीयर में तीखा स्वाद लाने में प्रयुक्त होते हैं।

hope / होप् / *noun* 1 hope (of/for sth); hope (of doing sth/that...) आशा, अभिलाषा 2 (प्राय: *sing*) आशा पूरी करने वाला व्यक्ति/वस्तु या स्थिति ▸ hope *verb* hope (for sth) आशा करना, विश्वास रखना।

hopeful / होप्फ़ुल् / *adj* hopeful (of/ about sth) आशाप्रद ▸ hopefully *adv.*

hopeless / होप्लस् / *adj* 1 आशारहित; निराशापूर्ण : *a hopeless situation* 2 hopeless (at sth) (अनौप) (व्यक्ति) पूर्णत:योग्यताहीन/अयोग्य, बेकार : *a hopeless cook/teacher* ▸ hopelessly *adv.*

horde / हॉर्ड / *noun* (कभी-कभी अपमा) व्यक्तियों का बड़ा समूह; गिरोह, जत्था : *hordes of tourists/football supporters.*

horizon / ह 'राइज़न् / *noun* 1 the horizon क्षितिज रेखा, जहाँ पृथ्वी-आकाश मिले हुए दिखाई देते है 2 (प्राय: *pl*) व्यक्ति के ज्ञान, अनुभव, रुचि आदि की सीमा।

horizontal / हॉरिज़ॉन्टल् / *adj* क्षितिज के समानांतर, समतल/सपाट।

hormone / 'हॉर्मोन् / *noun* हॉर्मोन (शरीर या पेड़-पौधों से उत्पन्न) एक रासा- निक पदार्थ जो विकास में सहायक होता है एवं कोशिकाओं और ऊतकों की क्रिया को प्रभावित करता है; ऐसा ही एक कृत्रिम (रासायनिक) पदार्थ।

horn / हॉर्न् / *noun* 1 (पशुओं के) सींग

2 तुरही; भोंपू : *a hunting horn* ▸ horned *adj* सींगयुक्त horny *adj* सींग जैसा; खुरदरा : *horny hands.*

hornet / 'हॉर्निट् / *noun* हाड़ा, एक प्रकार का डंक मारने वाला कीड़ा ■ a hornet's nest बहुत सारे लोगों को क्रुद्ध करने वाली बात।

horoscope / 'हॉरस्कोप् / *noun* जन्म- कुंडली, जन्मपत्री।

horrendous / हॉ उेन्डस् / *adj* (अनौप) 1 अत्यधिक वीभत्स या भयानक : *horrendous injuries* 2 अत्यंत अप्रिय/अस्वीकार्य।

horrible / 'हॉर्बल् / *adj* भयावह, डरावना; (अनौप) अत्यंत अरुचिकर।

horrid / 'हॉरिड् / *adj* (प्राय: अनौप) बहुत बुरा/अरुचिकर।

horrific / ह 'रिफ़िक् / *adj* भयानक।

horrify / 'हॉरिफ़ाइ / *verb* (pt, pp horri- fied) भयभीत करना ▸ horrifying *adj.*

horror / 'हॉरर् / *noun* 1 संत्रास, जुगुप्सा, भय का भाव 2 तीव्र घृणा का भाव 3 संत्रास/ घृणा उत्पन्न करने वाला व्यक्ति या वस्तु ▸ horror-stricken (horror-struck भी) *adj* भय से अभिभूत; संत्रस्त।

horse / हॉर्स् / *noun* घोड़ा ▸ horseman *noun* (fem horsewoman) घुड़सवार horseshoe *noun* घोड़े की नाल।

horsepower / 'हार्स्पाउर् / *noun* (संक्षि hp) अश्वशक्ति (इंजिन की पावर की इकाई)।

horticulture / 'हॉर्टिकलचर् / *noun* बाग़वानी ▸ horticultural *adj.*

hose / होज़् / (hose-pipe भी) *noun* पानी छिड़कने का रबड़, प्लास्टिक आदि का पाइप ▸ hose *verb* hose sth/sb (down) होज़पाइप से पानी छिड़कना/कुछ धोना : *hose the flower beds* ○ *hose down the car.*

hospitable / 'हॉस्पिटब्ल् / *adj* 1 hos- pitable (to/towards sb) (व्यक्ति) मेहमानों की आवभगत करने को तत्पर/प्रसन्न 2 (स्थान) रहने के लिए/भ्रमण के लिए अच्छा : *a hospitable climate/place.*

hospital / 'हॉस्पिटल् / *noun* अस्पताल
  ▸ **hospitalize, -ise** *verb* अस्पताल में
  भर्ती करना/भेजना।

hospitality / ˌहॉस्पि'टैलिटि / *noun*
  (अतिथियों का) आदर-सत्कार; आवभगत :
  generous acts of hospitality.

host¹ / होस्ट / *noun* 1 अतिथियों का
  सत्कार करने वाला, मेज़बान, मेहमानदार
  2 किसी कार्यक्रम को आयोजित एवं तमाम
  प्रबंध करने वाला व्यक्ति/स्थान/देश 3 टी वी/
  रेडियो पर कार्यक्रम प्रस्तुत करने वाला ▸ **host**
  verb 1 मेज़बानी करना 2 टी वी या रेडियो
  कार्यक्रम प्रस्तुत करना।

host² / होस्ट / *noun* host of sb/sth बड़ी
  संख्या : *a host of possibilities.*

hostage / 'हॉस्टिज् / *noun* बंधक व्यक्ति,
  वह व्यक्ति जिसे तब तक पकड़कर रखा जाता
  है जब तक कि माँगें पूरी न हों : *The
  hijackers kept the pilot as (a) hostage on board the plane.*

hostel / 'हॉस्टल् / *noun* होस्टल, छात्रावास।

hostess / 'होस्टस्; 'होस्टेस् / *noun* महिला
  मेज़बान।

hostile / 'हॉस्टाइल् / *adj* 1 hostile (to/
  towards sb/sth) शत्रुतापूर्ण; द्वेषभावपूर्ण
  2 शत्रु सेना से संबद्ध : *hostile aircraft.*

hostility / हॉ 'स्टिलिटि / *noun* 1 hostility (to/towards sb/sth) शत्रुता की भावना
  2 hostilities [*pl*] युद्ध : *at the outbreak of hostilities.*

hot / हॉट / *adj* (-tter, -ttest) 1 गरम; उच्च
  तापमान वाला; (व्यक्ति) जिसे गरमी लग रही
  हो 2 (भोजन पदार्थ) चरपरा, मिर्च-मसाले
  वाला; तीता (स्वाद) 3 (स्थिति) विस्फोटक
  एवं ख़तरनाक : *When things got too
  hot the reporters left the area.*
  3 (भावनाएँ) उग्र : *a hot temper* ■ **be
  in/get into hot water** (अनौप) मुसीबत
  में होना/पड़ना **go/sell like hot cakes**
  बहुत लोकप्रिय (बिक्री में) **hot on sb's/
  sth's tracks/trail** (अनौप) लगभग पकड़
  की स्थिति में **in hot pursuit (of sb)**

पकड़ने के दृढ़ निश्चय से पीछा करना ▸ **hot
line** *noun* विशेष जानकारी आदि प्राप्त
करने के लिए विशेष टेलिफ़ोन लाइन **hot-
tempered** *adj* जल्दी क्रोधित हो जाने
वाला।

hotchpotch / 'हॉच्पॉच् / (*US* **hodge-
podge** भी) *noun* गड़बड़-झाला : *a
hotchpotch of ideas.*

hotel / हो 'टेल् / *noun* होटल ▸ **hotelier**
  / हो 'टेलिअर् / *noun* होटल मालिक।

hothead / 'हॉट्हेड् / *noun* उतावला
  व्यक्ति, बिना सोचे काम करने वाला (उत्तेजित)
  व्यक्ति ▸ **hotheaded** *adj* क्रोधी, उतावला।

hothouse / 'हॉट्हाउस् / *noun* गरम-घर
  (प्रायः काँच का)।

hound / हाउन्ड् / *noun* शिकारी कुत्ता
  ▸ **hound** *verb* किसी का लगातार पीछा
  करना ■ **hound sb out (of sth)** (किसी
  का जीना दूभर बनाकर) जगह छोड़ने को
  मज़बूर कर देना : *He was hounded out
  of the area by rival traders.*

hour / 'आउअर् / *noun* 1 घंटा (साठ मिनट
  का) 2 **hours** [*pl*] कार्यालय आदि का
  निश्चित समय : *hours of business*
  3 समय का कोई बिंदु : *Who can be
  ringing us at this hour?* 4 (औप)
  महत्त्वपूर्ण घटना का समय : *She helped
  me in my hour of need.* ■ **at the
  eleventh hour** अंतिम क्षण में/पर **keep
  late hours** रात में देर तक काम करना
  ▸ **hourly** *adv* प्रत्येक घंटे में **hourly** *adj*
  घंटावार : *an hourly bus service.*

house¹ / हाउस् / *noun* (*pl* **houses**
  / 'हाउज़िज़्/) 1 मकान; मकान में रहने वाले
  लोग 2 (समास में) रेस्राँ : *a coffee-
  house* 3 थिएटर के श्रोतागण : *play to
  packed houses* 4 (प्रायः **the House
  of sb/sth**) विख्यात परिवार : *the House
  of Windsor* 5 व्यापारिक फ़र्म : *a pub-
  lishing/banking house* ▸ **house-
  agent** *noun* मकान बेचने/किराए पर उठाने
  का व्यवसाय करने वाला **houseboat** *noun*

शिकारा, बजरा **housebreaker** *noun* सेंधमार **housekeeper** *noun* गृह-व्यवस्था करने वाला नौकर/नौकरानी **housekeeping** *noun* घर संभालने/चलाने का कार्य **housewife** *noun* गृहिणी; गृह-स्वामिनी **the Houses of Parliament** *noun* संसद-सदन।

house² / हाउज़् / *verb* **1** निवास की व्यवस्था करना : *The council should house homeless people.* **2** सुरक्षा के लिए किसी स्थान पर रखना : *books housed in glass-fronted cases.*

household / हाउसहोल्ड् / *noun* घर में रहने वाले सभी लोग; घरेलू (सामान आदि)।

housing / हाउज़िङ् / *noun* **1** आवास; इससे जुड़ी क़ीमत, उपलब्धियाँ, आकार आदि : *public/private housing ○ poor housing conditions* **2** लोगों को घर आदि उपलब्ध कराने का कार्य : *a housing committee.*

hovel / हॉव़्ल्; *US* 'हव़्ल् / *noun* (*अपमा*) छोटा गंदा घर, झोंपड़ी।

hover / हॉव़्र; *US* 'हव़्र / *verb* **1** (चिड़ियों का) मँडराना **2** (व्यक्ति का) शर्म के मारे अनिश्चित ढंग से घूमना/प्रतीक्षा करना **3** अनिश्चित-सा रहना : *hovering between life and death.*

hovercraft / हॉव़्रक्राफ़्ट् / *noun* (*pl* अपरिवर्तित) पानी और भूमि पर चलने वाली एक विशेष प्रकार की नाव।

how / हाउ / *interrog adv* **1** कैसे, किस तरह : *How do you spell your name?* **2** (स्थिति/दशा पूछने के लिए) : *How is your job?* **3** (आयु, सीमा, मात्रा आदि पूछने के लिए) : *How old is she?* ▸ **how** *conj* (*अनौप*) उस तरीक़े से; जिस तरीक़े से : *I'll dress how I like in my house!*

however / हाउ 'एव़्र / *adv* **1** किसी भी तरह; किसी भी सीमा तक **2** यद्यपि; तो भी ▸ **however** *conj* किसी भी तरह; फिर भी।

howl / हाउल् / *noun* **1** (कुत्ते का) हू-हू

कर चिल्लाना : *a mournful howl* **2** दर्द, क्रोध आदि से चीख़ना **3** वायु से उत्पन्न ज़ोर का शोर ▸ **howl** *verb* **1** (कुत्ते का) ज़ोर-ज़ोर से चिल्लाना **2** (व्यक्ति का) गुस्से में ज़ोर से कुछ कहना : *'I hate you all!' she howled.*

hub / हब् / *noun* **1** पहिए का केंद्र **2** (*प्रायः sing*) महत्त्व/गतिविधि का केंद्र : *the financial hub of the city.*

hubbub / 'हबब् / *noun* कोलाहल; शोरगुल भरी व्यस्त स्थिति।

huddle / हड्ल् / *verb* अव्यवस्थित रूप से भीड़ इकट्ठा करना; डर या ठंड से थोड़े-से स्थान में सिमटना ■ **huddle up (against/ to sb/sth)** सिमटकर बैठना (ताकि शरीर गरम बना रहे) ▸ **huddle** *noun* थोड़े-से व्यक्ति/वस्तुएँ एक जगह सघन/एकत्रित।

hue¹ / ह्यू / *noun* (*औप*) रंग; रंग का शेड : *birds of many different hues.*

hue² / ह्यू / *noun* ■ **hue and cry** शोरगुल, हो-हल्ला।

huff / हफ़् / *noun* ■ **in a huff** (*अनौप*) नाराज़/क्रोधित होकर : *She walked out in a huff.*

hug / हग् / *verb* (**-gg-**) **1** गले लगाना; आलिंगन करना **2** कसकर/तंग रूप से फिट होना : *a figure-hugging dress* ▸ **hug** *noun* आलिंगन।

huge / ह्यूज़ / *adj* विशाल, बहुत बड़ा ▸ **hugely** *adv* अत्यंत, बहुत अधिक।

hull / हल् / *noun* जहाज़ का ढाँचा।

hullo / ह 'लो / *interj* = **hallo.**

hum / हम् / *verb* (**-mm-**) **1 hum sth (to sb)** (गीत/लय) गुनगुनाना **2** मक्खियों का भिनभिनाना **3** (*अनौप*) अत्यधिक क्रियाशील होना ▸ **hum** *noun* गुनगुनाहट/भिनभिनाहट।

human / 'ह्यूमन् / *adj* **1** मानव (जाति) का, मानवीय (न कि ईश्वरीय, मशीनी या पाशविक) : *human activity/behaviour* **2** मानवोचित, दयालु/अच्छा ▸ **human (human being** भी) *noun* मनुष्य, मानव **humanly** *adv* मनुष्य की दृष्टि या शक्ति से।

humane / ह्यू'मेन् / *adj* 1 दयामय, सहानुभूतिपूर्ण : *a humane prison system* 2 उदारतापूर्ण; कम से कम दर्द पैदा करते हुए : *the humane killing of animals.*

humanism / ह्यूमनिज़म् / *noun* मानवतावाद, व्यक्ति/मानव के कल्याण पर ज़ोर देने वाली और मानव जाति से जुड़ी समस्याओं को तर्क से सुलझाने वाली व्यवस्था।

humanitarian / ह्यू, मैनि'टेअरिअन् / *adj* मानवतावादी, लोकोपकारी ▶ **humanitarian** *noun* मानवतावादी व्यक्ति।

humanity / ह्यू'मैनटि / *noun* 1 मानव-जाति : *crimes against humanity* 2 मानव स्वभाव : *the humanity of Jesus* 3 मानवता का गुण, उदारता 4 **the humanities** [*pl*] साहित्य, भाषा, इतिहास, दर्शन आदि शिक्षा-विषय।

humble / 'हम्ब्ल् / *adj* (**humbler** / 'हम्ब्लर् /; **humblest** / 'हम्ब्लिस्ट् /) 1 विनम्र 2 निर्धन; प्रतिष्ठा में निम्न : *men of humble birth/origin* 3 (वस्तु) महत्त्वहीन ▶ **humble** *verb* 1 विनम्र बनाना; प्रतिष्ठा घटाना 2 (खेल में) हराना **humbly** *adv.*

humbug / 'हम्बग् / *noun* बेईमानी या कपटपूर्ण आचरण, व्यवहार या व्यक्ति।

humdrum / 'हम्ड्रम् / *adj* नीरस/फीका; अति साधारण : *the humdrum business of making money.*

humid / 'ह्यूमिड् / *adj* (हवा, मौसम) सीलनभरा ▶ **humidity** / ह्यू'मिडटि / *noun* सीलन; (भौतिकी) आर्द्रता : *75 per cent humidity.*

humiliate / ह्यू'मिलिएट् / *verb* नीचा दिखाना, अवमानना करना : *The party was publicly humiliated in October's elections.* ▶ **humiliation** *noun* अपमान।

humility / ह्यू'मिलटि / *noun* विनम्रता; दीनता : *His greatest quality was his humility.*

humorous / 'ह्यूमरस् / *adj* हास्यकर, हास्यजनक।

humour (*US* **humor**) / 'ह्यूमर् / *noun* 1 परिहास, विनोद 2 वस्तुओं/व्यक्तियों या स्थिति को विनोदी रूप से देखने का स्वभाव; ऐसी मनोदशा ▶ **humour** (*US* **humor**) *verb* किसी का मन रखना; संतुष्ट करना।

hump / हम्प् / *noun* 1 कूबड़ (जैसे ऊँट की पीठ पर होता है) 2 मिट्टी आदि का ऊँचा टीला ▶ **humpback** *noun* कुबड़ा।

humus / 'ह्यूमस् / *noun* पत्तियों, गोबर आदि के सड़ने के बाद बना गहरे रंग का पदार्थ जो भूमि की उर्वरा शक्ति बढ़ाता है।

hunch[1] / हन्च् / *noun* प्रमाण की बजाय स्वयं की तीव्र भावना पर आधारित विचार : *My hunch is that he's already left the country.*

hunch[2] / हन्च् / *verb* झुककर चलना या बैठना, कूबड़ निकालकर चलना या बैठना ▶ **hunchback** *noun* कुबड़ा व्यक्ति।

hundred / 'हन्ड्रड् / *noun, pron, det* (*pl* अपरिवर्तित या **hundreds**) 1 सौ (का अंक) 2 **hundreds** [*pl*] (अनौप) बहुत बड़ी संख्या : *for hundreds of years* ▶ **hundredth** / 'हन्ड्रड्थ् / *noun, pron, det* सौवां, सौवां अंश, 1/100 **hundredweight** *noun* (*pl* अपरिवर्तित) (संक्षि **cwt**) टन का बीसवाँ भाग; 50.8 kg (*US* 45.4 kg).

hung / हङ् / *adj* (संसद) बहुमत न मिलने से अनिश्चय की स्थिति में।

hunger / 'हङ्गर् / *noun* 1 भूख; भोजन की इच्छा 2 **hunger** (**for sth**) (औप) तीव्र इच्छा/अभिलाषा : *have an insatiable hunger for adventure* ▶ **hunger** *verb* ■ **hunger for/after sth/sb** कामना रखना।

hungry / 'हङ्ग्रि / *adj* (**-ier, -iest**) 1 भूखा 2 **hungry for sth** किसी चीज़ के लिए उत्सुक ▶ **hungrily** *adv.*

hunt[1] / हन्ट् / *verb* 1 शिकार करना, शिकार पर जाना 2 **hunt** (**for sth/sb**) खोजना

ढूँढ़ना : *hunt for a lost book* ○ *Police are hunting an escaped criminal.* ■ **hunt sb/sth down** पीछा करना जब तक पकड़ में न आ जाए ▸ **hunter** *noun* शिकारी **hunting** *noun* शिकार **huntsman** *noun* शिकारी।

hunt² / हन्ट् / *noun* **1 hunt (for sb/sth)** खोज **2** शिकार, मृगया।

hurdle / 'हर्डल / *noun* **1** (घुड़दौड़ में) बाड़ा; बाधा-दौड़ में लगाया जाने वाला ढाँचा **2** बाधा/अड़चन **3 hurdles** [*pl*] बाधा दौड़ : *win the 400 metres hurdles* ▸ **hurdle** *verb* **hurdle (over) sth** दौड़ते हुए किसी वस्तु के ऊपर से कूद जाना **hurdler** *noun* बाधा-दौड़ का धावक/घोड़ा।

hurl / हर्ल् / *verb* **1** ज़ोर-से फेंकना **2 hurl sth (at sth/sb)** ज़ोर-से चिल्लाकर कुछ कहना : *He stood there hurling insults/abuse (at me).*

hurrah / ह 'रा / (**hurray, hooray** भी / हु 'रे /) *interj* प्रसन्नता, विजय आदि का जयघोष : *Hurrah for the weekend!*

hurricane / 'हरिकन् / *noun* आँधी-तूफ़ान।

hurry / 'हरि / *noun* जल्दी; आतुरता; जल्दी/आतुरता करने की इच्छा ■ **in a hurry 1** जल्दी में, शीघ्रता से **2** समयाभाव में **3** उत्सुक ▸ **hurry** *verb* (*pt, pp* **hurried**) जल्दी करना/कराना ■ **hurry up** (अनौप) जल्दी करना ▸ **hurried** *adj* शीघ्रता से किया हुआ **hurriedly** *adv.*

hurt / हर्ट् / *verb* (*pt, pp* **hurt**) **1** चोट पहुँचाना; दर्द पैदा करना **2** किसी को मानसिक आघात/संताप पहुँचाना : *These criticisms have hurt him deeply.* **3** बुरा प्रभाव डालना; हानि पहुँचाना ▸ **hurt** *adj* दुखित/व्यथित **hurt** *noun* [*sing*] मनोव्यथा **hurtful** *adj.*

hurtle / 'हर्टल् / *verb* दिशा विशेष में तेज़ी से या ख़तरनाक रूप से बढ़ना : *The van hurtled round the corner.*

husband / 'हज़्बन्ड् / *noun* पति।

husbandry / 'हज़्बन्ड्रि/ *noun* (औप) **1** खेती या कृषि कर्म (करना) **2** संसाधनों का कुशल प्रबंध।

hush / हश् / *verb* चुप होना/करना; (आज्ञार्थक) चुप हो जाओ : *He hushed her and told her not to be foolish.* ■ **hush sth up** (प्राय: अपमा) लज्जाजनक मामले को गुपचुप रफ़ा-दफ़ा कर देना/दबा देना ▸ **hush** *noun* [*sing*] शांति; (शोर के बाद) सन्नाटा : *There was a sudden deathly hush.*

husk / हस्क् / *noun* भूसा; कुछ सूखे फलों का बाहरी आवरण/छिलका ▸ **husk** *verb* भूसा/छिलका निकालना।

husky / 'हस्कि / *adj* (**-ier, -lest**) **1** (आवाज़) सूखी एवं भारी **2** (अनौप) (व्यक्ति) आकर्षक : *a husky young truck driver* ▸ **huskily** *adv.*

hustle / 'हस्ल् / *verb* **1** धकेलना/धक्का देकर बढ़ना **2 hustle sb (into sth/doing sth)** किसी को सोचने का समय दिए बग़ौर जल्दी कराना ▸ **hustle** *noun* हलचल; धकमधक्का : *I love all the hustle and bustle of the market.*

hut / हट् / *noun* झोंपड़ी/कुटिया।

hutch / हच् / *noun* ख़रगोशों का बकसा।

hybrid / 'हाइब्रिड् / *noun* **1** (पशु या पौधे की नसल) संकर : *A mule is a hybrid of a male donkey and a female horse.* **2** दो भिन्न वस्तुओं के संयोग से बनी कोई वस्तु; दोग़ला ▸ **hybrid** *adj* संकर/दोग़ला।

hydrant / 'हाइड्रन्ट् / *noun* (सड़क के किनारे) नल जिसमें होज़ पाइप लगाकर आग बुझाई जा सकती है या सड़क साफ़ की जा सकती है।

hydraulic / हाइ 'ड्रॉलिक् / *adj* **1** (पानी, तेल आदि) दाब के कारण पाइप से बहता हुआ : *hydraulic fluid* **2** (यंत्रशक्ति) बहते पानी से संबद्ध; जलशक्ति से चालित : *a hydraulic pump/lift.*

hydro- *pref (पूर्वपद)* 1 जल-विषयक : *hydroelectricity* 2 हाइड्रोजन से संयुक्त/ विषयक : *hydrochloric.*

hydrogen / 'हाइड्रजन् / *noun* हाइड्रोजन गैस।

hyena (hyaena भी) / हाइ'ईना / *noun* लकड़बग्घा।

hygiene /'हाइजीन् / *noun* सफ़ाई ▸ **hygienic** / हाइ'जीनिक् / *adj* साफ़; कीटाणु आदि से रहित; स्वास्थ्यकर **hygienically** *adv.*

hymn / हिम् / *noun* स्तोत्र, स्तुति; सूक्ति ▸ **hymn** *verb* स्तुति गाना **hymn-book** *noun* भजन संग्रह।

hyper- *pref (पूर्वपद)* अत्यधिक मात्रा तक; सामान्य से अधिक/ऊँचा : *hyper-critical* ∘ *hyperactive.*

hyperbole / हाइ'पर्बलि / *noun* अति-शयोक्ति (भाषा या लेखन में)।

hypersensitive / ‚हाइपर् 'सेन्सटिव् / *adj* 1 आसानी से नाराज़ हो जाने वाला; नाजुक-मिज़ाज 2 **hypersensitive (to sth)** (कोई विशेष पदार्थ, दवा आदि के प्रति) अति संवेदनशील : *Her skin is hypersensitive to make-up.*

hypertension / ‚हाइपर् 'टेन्श्न् / *noun* (चिकि) रक्तचाप (असामान्य रूप से ऊँचा)।

hyphen / 'हाइफ़्न् / *noun* दो शब्दों को संयुक्त करने के लिए प्रयुक्त एक छोटी-सी रेखा, हाइफ़न, जैसे *Indo-American* में लगा चिह्न।

hypnosis / हिप्'नोसिस् / *noun* सम्मोहन ▸ **hypnotism** /. 'हिप्नटिज़्म् / *noun* सम्मोहन **hypnotize, -ise** /'हिप्नटाइज़् / *verb* 1 सम्मोहित करना 2 गहराई से प्रभावित करना।

hypochondria /‚हाइप'कॉन्ड्रिआ/ *noun* (व्यक्ति की) अपने स्वास्थ्य को लेकर असाधारण एवं अत्यधिक व्याकुलता/चिंता; बीमार न होते हुए भी अपने आप को बीमार मानना ▸ **hypochondriac** *noun* ऐसा सोचने वाला व्यक्ति।

hypocrisy / हि'पॉक्रसि / *noun* (*pl* **hypocrisies**) पाखंड, ढोंग ▸ **hypocrite** /'हिपक्रिट् / *noun* (अपमा) पाखंडी/ढोंगी **hypocritical** *adj* पाखंड-विषयक।

hypodermic / ‚हाइप 'डर्मिक् / *adj* (चिकि) त्वचा के नीचे इंजेक्शन देने के लिए प्रयुक्त (यंत्र): *hypodermic syringe.*

hypothesis / हाइ'पॉथ़सिस् / *noun* (*pl* **hypotheses** / हाइ'पॉथ़सीज़्/) प्राक्कल्पना ▸ **hypothetical** *adj* प्राक्कल्पना पर (न कि निश्चित ज्ञान पर) आधारित।

hysteria / हि'स्टिअरिआ / *noun* 1 हि-स्टीरिया (एक बीमारी) 2 (अपमा) उन्माद; अत्यधिक उत्तेजित एवं अतिशयोक्तिपूर्ण प्रति-क्रिया : *public hysteria about AIDS* ▸ **hysterical** / हि'स्टेरिक्ल / *adj* 1 हि-स्टीरिया ग्रस्त या से उत्पन्न 2 (अनौप) अत्यंत हास्यजनक **hysterics** *noun* [*pl*] 1 हिस्टीरिया के दौरे : *She was in hysterics.* 2 (अनौप) उन्मुक्त हँसी।

Ii

I / आइ / *pers pron* मैं → **me** देखिए।

ice¹ / आइस् / *noun* 1 बर्फ़ 2 *(अप्र)* आइसक्रीम ▸ **iceberg** / आइस्बर्ग / *noun* समुद्र में बहती हुई बर्फ़ की बहुत बड़ी चट्टान **ice-bound** *adj* (बंदरगाहों आदि का) बर्फ़ के कारण बंद हो जाना।

ice² / आइस् / *verb* (केक पर) डिज़ाइन बनाने के लिए घिसी गीली चीनी आदि का मिश्रण डालना ■ **ice sth over/up** बर्फ़ से ढकना या ढक जाना : *The pond (was) iced over during the cold spell.*

ice-cream / आइस्क्रीम् / *noun* जमाई हुई क्रीम से बना एक मीठा व्यंजन; आइसक्रीम।

icicle / आइसिकल् / *noun* लटकती हुई नुकीली बर्फ़।

icing / आइसिङ् / *noun* केक पर डिज़ाइन बनाने के लिए घिसी गीली चीनी का मिश्रण।

icy / आइसि / *adj* 1 अत्यधिक ठंडा (बर्फ़ के समान) 2 (व्यक्ति का व्यवहार आदि) रूखा, उदासीन : *an icy glare* ▸ **icily** / आइसिलि / *adv* (व्यक्ति का) रूखता/उदासीनता से पेश आना : *'I have nothing to say to you,' she said icily.*

idea / आइडिआ / *noun* 1 [*sing*] विचार, भाव, धारणा 2 योजना, सुझाव 3 मत, विश्वास।

ideal / आइडीअल / *adj* 1 आदर्शपूर्ण; सर्वांगपूर्ण : *ideal weather for a swim* 2 मानसिक मात्र; काल्पनिक : *ideal plans for reform* ▸ **ideal** *noun* 1 आदर्श 2 (प्राय: *pl*) आदर्श का मापदंड **ideally** *adv*.

idealism / आइडीअलिज़म् / *noun* आदर्शवाद ▸ **idealist** *noun* आदर्शवादी (व्यक्ति)।

idealize,-ise / आइडीअलाइज़ / *verb* आदर्श बनाना; आदर्श के रूप में सोचना/प्रदर्शित करना।

identical / आइडेन्टिकल् / *adj* 1 एक-रूप; अभिन्न 2 identical (to/with sb/sth) सर्वसम, बिलकुल एक जैसा।

identify / आइडेन्टिफ़ाइ / *verb* (*pt, pp* **identified**) 1 identify sb/sth as sb/sth पहचानना, पहचान करना 2 identify sth with sth समान समझना/समानता प्रदर्शित करना : *One should not identify wealth with happiness.* ■ **identify (oneself) with sb/sth** अपना पूरा समर्थन देना; तादात्म्य स्थापित करना ▸ **identification** / आइडेन्टिफ़िकेशन् / *noun* पहचान, अभिज्ञान।

identity / आइडेन्टटि / *noun* (*pl* **identities**) 1 परिचय; व्यक्तित्व 2 **identity (between A and B)** तादात्म्य, अभिन्नता : *a feeling of identity between managers and staff.*

ideology / आइडिऑलजि / *noun* (*pl* **ideologies**) विचारधारा, सिद्धांत (विशेषत: आर्थिक और राजनीतिक व्यवस्था-विषयक) ▸ **ideological** *adj* सैद्धांतिक, वैचारिक।

idiom / इडिअम् / *noun* 1 मुहावरा 2 किसी विशेष काल, समूह या व्यक्ति से संबंधित भाषा/कला शैली ▸ **idiomatic** / इडिअमैटिक् / *adj* मुहावरेदार **idiomatically** *adv*.

idiosyncrasy / इडिअसिङ्क्रसि / *noun* (व्यक्ति की) स्वभाव-विशेषता; वैशिष्ट्य ▸ **idiosyncratic** *adj*.

idiot / इडिअट् / *noun* 1 *(अनौप)* मूर्ख, जड़बुद्धि 2 मंदबुद्धि : *an idiot since birth* ▸ **idiotic** / इडिऑटिक् / *adj* मूर्खतापूर्ण **idiotically** *adv*.

idle / आइड्ल् / *adj* 1 बेकार, जो चालू/प्रयोग में नहीं है; बेरोज़गार 2 (व्यक्ति) आलसी, कामचोर : *an idle student* 3 व्यर्थ, तुच्छ ▸ **idle** *verb* 1 आलसी बनना 2 (इंजन) चलते हुए भी काम न करना **idleness** *noun* आलस्य **idler** *noun* **idly** *adv*.

idol / आइडल् / *noun* 1 (किसी देवी-देवता की) मूर्ति 2 भक्ति और श्रद्धा के योग्य

व्यक्ति या वस्तु : *He is still the idol of countless teenagers.*

idolater / आइ 'डॉलटर् / *noun* (प्राय: अपमान) मूर्तिपूजक ▸ **idolatry** / आइ 'डॉलट्रि / *noun* मूर्तिपूजा; अतिशय श्रद्धा/भक्ति।

idolize, -ise /'आइडलाइज़्/ *verb* अत्यधिक श्रद्धा रखना : *idolize a pop group.*

idyll /'इडिल्; *US* 'आइडल्/ *noun* प्रियकर एवं शांतिपूर्ण घटना, अनुभव, स्थान आदि (विशेषत:ग्राम-संबंधी); ऐसी स्थिति प्रदर्शित करता हुआ काव्य/लेख : *a rural idyll* ▸ **idyllic** / इ 'डिलिक् / *adj* प्रियकर एवं शांतिपूर्ण : *an idyllic setting/cottage.*

ie /,आइ 'ई/ *abbr* (संक्षि) (लैटिन **id est**) अर्थात्; दूसरे शब्दों में : *Hot drinks, ie tea and coffee, are also available.*

if / इफ़् / *conj* 1 यदि, अगर : *If you have finished eating you may leave the table.* 2 (औप) (**will** और **would** के साथ नम्रतासूचक प्रयोग में) : *If you will sit down for a few moments I'll tell the manager you are here.* 3 कि : *Do you know if he's married?*

igloo / 'इग्लू / *noun* एस्कीमों का बर्फ़ से बना घर।

ignite / इग् 'नाइट् / *verb* सुलगाना, आग लगाना; आग पकड़ना : *Petrol ignites very easily.* ▸ **ignition** / इग् 'निश्न् / *noun* दहन; प्रज्वलन।

ignominy / 'इग्नमिनि / *noun* शर्मिंदगी, अपयश, बदनामी ▸ **ignominious** *adj.*

ignorance / 'इग्नरन्स् / *noun* **ignorance (of sth)** अज्ञान, अनभिज्ञता : *Their fear arises out of ignorance.*

ignorant / 'इग्नरन्ट् / *adj* 1 **ignorant (of sth)** अनभिज्ञ, अनजान 2 अज्ञानी, (एवं उस कारण से) अभद्र : *ignorant behaviour.*

ignore / इग् 'नॉर् / *verb* 1 उपेक्षा करना, (जान-बूझकर) ध्यान न देना : *ignore advice/criticism* 2 किसी के अभिवादन

को (या किसी को पहचानने से)जानबूझकर मना करना।

il- *pref* (उपसर्ग) अ-, अन- (नकार, उलटा/विपरीत अर्थ) : *illegal, illogical, etc.*

ill¹ / इल् / *adj* 1 बीमार, अस्वस्थ 2 बुरा, ख़राब : *resign on grounds of ill health* 3 हानिप्रद/नुक़सानदेह : दुष्टतापूर्ण 4 प्रतिकूल : *ill luck* ◼ **ill at ease** बेचैन, परेशान नज़र आना ▸ **ill** *noun* (औप) 1 हानि, बुराई 2 (प्राय: *pl*) विपत्ति, समस्या।

ill² / इल् / *adv* 1 बुरी तरह से; ग़लत ढंग से : *ill-advised* 2 प्रतिकूलता से 3 मुश्किल से/कठिनाई के साथ : *We can ill afford the time or money for a holiday.* ▸ **ill-bred** *adj* अशिष्ट; असंस्कृत **ill-disposed** *adj* अमैत्रीपूर्ण **ill-timed** *adj* अनुपयुक्त समय पर **ill-treat** *verb* दुर्व्यवहार करना **ill-will** *noun* द्वेष भाव; दुर्भावना।

illegal / इ'लीगल् / *adj* ग़ैर-क़ानूनी, अवैध।

illegible / इ'लेजब्ल् / (**unreadable** भी) *adj* (हाथ से लिखा) जो पढ़ा न जा सके, अपाठ्य।

illegitimate /इल'जिटमट् / *adj* 1 (संतान) अवैध, अविवाहित माता-पिता से उत्पन्न 2 ग़ैर-क़ानूनी ▸ **illegitimacy** *noun.*

illicit / इ 'लिसिट् / *adj* 1 ग़ैर-क़ानूनी, अनधिकृत : *illicit alcohol/drugs* 2 सामाजिक नियमों के प्रतिकूल ▸ **illicitly** *adv.*

illiterate / इ'लिटरट् / *noun, adj* 1 जिसे लिखना-पढ़ना नहीं आता; निरक्षर 2 क्षेत्र-विशेष से अनभिज्ञ/अनजान : *be scientifically illiterate* ▸ **illiteracy** *noun* निरक्षरता।

illness /'इल्नस् / *noun* 1 बीमारी, रोगग्रस्त होना 2 बीमारी का प्रकार या अवधि : *serious illness.*

illogical / इ'लॉजिकल् / *adj* तर्कसंगत न होना ▸ **illogically** *adv.*

illuminate / इ'लूमिनेट् / *verb* 1 प्रकाश डालना, प्रकाशित करना 2 दीपों से (मकानों/सड़कों को) सजाना : *illuminate a* *building* 3 (औप) स्पष्ट करना, व्याख्या करना : *illuminate a difficult passage in a book* ▸ **illumination** / इ,लूमि'नेश्न् / noun 1 प्रकाश स्रोत 2 दीप सज्जा 3 जलाना या जलने की क्रिया/प्रक्रिया।

illusion / इ'लूश्न् / noun 1 भ्रांति, धोखा; मिथ्या विश्वास 2 माया, छलावा : *an illusion of happiness* ▸ **Illusory** adj मिथ्या।

illustrate / 'इलस्ट्रेट् / verb 1 illustrate sth (with sth) उदाहरणों, चित्रों आदि द्वारा समझाना, स्पष्ट करना 2 पुस्तक में उदाहरण, चित्र आदि देना ▸ **illustration** / ,इल 'स्ट्रेश्न् / noun 1 चित्रों आदि द्वारा समझाने की प्रक्रिया, उदाहरण 2 चित्र-आरेख आदि।

illustrious / इ'लस्ट्रिअस् / adj प्रख्यात, सुप्रसिद्ध।

im- pref (उपसर्ग) (नकार, विपरीत/उलटा अर्थ): *immoral, impossible, impure, etc.*

image / 'इमिज् / noun 1 बिंब; धारणा; छवि 2 मूर्ति, प्रतिमा; प्रतिरूप 3 प्रतिबिंब (दर्पण में)।

imaginable / इ'मैजिनब्ल् / adj कल्पनीय।

imaginary / इ'मैजिनरि / adj काल्पनिक, अयथार्थ।

imagination / इ,मैजि'नेश्न् / noun 1 कल्पना शक्ति 2 कल्पना की वस्तु ▸ **imaginative** adj कल्पनाशील (व्यक्ति); काल्पनिक (वस्तु)।

imagine / इ'मैजिन् / verb 1 कल्पना करना; मन में कोई चित्र खींचना 2 संभावना/ संभाव्यता पर विचार करना।

Imam / इ'माम् / noun इमाम, मुस्लिम धर्मगुरु की एक पदवी; imam मस्जिद में नमाज़ पढ़ने वाला धर्मगुरु।

imbalance / इम्'बैलन्स् / noun imbalance (between A and B); imbalance (in sth) असंतुलन।

imbecile / 'इम्बसील् / noun अल्पबुद्धि, मूर्ख व्यक्ति ▸ **imbecile** adj मूर्खतापूर्ण **imbecility** noun.

imbibe / इम्'बाइब् / verb 1 आत्मसात् करना, (विचारों को) जीवन में उतार लेना : *imbibe fresh air/knowledge* 2 (औप या परि) (शराब) पीना।

imbue / इम्'ब्यू / verb imbue sb/sth (with sth) (औप) ओतप्रोत करना, (देशभक्ति, श्रद्धा आदि भावनाओं से) पूरी तरह भर देना : *imbued with patriotism.*

imitate / 'इमिटेट् / verb 1 नकल उतारना; अनुकरण करना 2 के समान बनना ▸ **imitator** noun नक्क़ाल।

imitation / ,इमि'टेश्न् / noun 1 नकल, प्रतिलिपि 2 अनुकरण 3 व्यवहार या बोल-चाल की नकल।

imitative / 'इमिटटिव्; US 'इमिटेटिव् / adj नकली, अनुकरण किया हुआ।

immaculate / इ'मैक्यलट् / adj 1 पूरी तरह साफ़-सुथरा 2 त्रुटिहीन ▸ **immaculately** adv.

immaterial / इम्'टिअरिअल् / adj 1 immaterial (to sb/sth) अप्रासंगिक; महत्त्व-हीन 2 (औप) अमूर्त।

immature / ,इम्'ट्युअर् / adj 1 (व्यक्ति) अपरिपक्व 2 (पेड़-पौधे, फल आदि) जो पूर्ण रूप से विकसित न हुए हों।

immediate / इ'मीडिअट् / adj 1 निकट-तम, आसन्न; प्रत्यक्ष 2 तात्कालिक, तुरंत (किया हुआ) ▸ **immediately** adv 1 तुरंत, तत्काल; अविलंब 2 (समय या स्थान में) निकटतम।

immemorial / ,इम्'मॉरिअल् / adj (औप या साहि) स्मरणातीत; अति प्राचीन : *Farmers have been tilling these fields since time immemorial.*

immense / इ'मेन्स् / adj अति विशाल ▸ **immensely** adv **immensity** / इ 'मेन्सटि / noun विशालता; अनंतता : *the immensity of the universe.*

immerse / इ'मर्स् / verb 1 immerse sth (in sth) डुबोना 2 immerse one-self (in sth) स्वयं को तल्लीनता से लगाना,

ध्यानमग्न करना ▸ **immersion** / इ'मर्शन् / noun 1 डुबकी, निमज्जन 2 तल्लीनता

immersion heater noun पानी गरम करने का एक प्रकार का यंत्र।

immigrant / 'इमिग्रन्ट् / noun आप्रवासी (व्यक्ति)।

immigration / इमि'ग्रेश्न् / noun आप्रवास।

imminent / 'इमिनन्ट् / adj निकट भविष्य में ही होने वाला : The system is in imminent danger of collapse. ▸ **imminence** / 'इमिनन्स् / noun (घटना की) समीपता **imminently** adv.

immobile / इ'मोबाइल; US इ'मोबल् / adj 1 हिलने-डुलने/चलने-फिरने में असमर्थ 2 अचल : He sat immobile, like a statue.

immoral / इ'मॉरल् / adj 1 अनैतिक, दुष्ट: It's immoral to steal. 2 व्यभिचारी, भ्रष्ट ▸ **immorality** / इम'रैलटि / noun अनैतिकता; दुराचार **immorally** adv.

immortal / इ'मॉर्टल् / adj 1 अमर 2 अविस्मरणीय : the immortal Shakespeare ▸ **immortality** / इमॉर्'टैलटि / noun अमरत्व; (जीवन या यश की) अविनाशिता **immortalize, -ise** / इ'मॉर्टलाइज़् / verb अमर कर देना; अविस्मरणीय बना देना।

immune / इ'म्यून् / adj 1 immune (to sth) (किसी अनिष्ट अथवा बीमारी से) प्रतिरक्षित, मुक्त 2 immune (to sth) किसी से अप्रभावित : immune to criticism/flattery 3 immune (from sth) रक्षित/मुक्त ▸ **immunity** / इ'म्यूनटि / noun (रोग, नियम आदि से) प्रतिरक्षा; उन्मुक्ति **immunize, -ise** / 'इम्युनाइज़् / verb **immunize sb (against sth)** प्रतिरक्षित करना **immunization, -isation** noun.

imp / इम्प् / noun 1 छोटे आकार का शैतान 2 (प्यार/दुलार में) नटखट बच्चा।

impact / 'इम्पैक्ट् / noun 1 (प्राय: sing) **impact (on sb/sth)** (विचारों आदि का) प्रभाव : the impact of technology on

modern industry 2 टक्कर; संघात ▸ **impact** / इम्'पैक्ट् / verb कुछ दृढ़ता से दबा/जमा देना।

impair / इम्'पेअर् / verb क्षीण या दुर्बल करना; हानि पहुँचाना : Too much alcohol impairs your ability to drive. ▸ **impairment** noun.

impalpable / इम्'पैल्पबल् / adj (औप) 1 जिसे शारीरिक रूप से छुआ या अनुभव न किया जा सके : impalpable darkness/horror 2 समझने में कठिन, दुर्जेय।

impart / इम्'पार्ट् / verb (औप) 1 **impart sth (to sth)** कोई गुण किसी वस्तु को देना : Her presence imparted an air of gaiety to the occasion. 2 **impart sth (to sb)** (कोई समाचार, ज्ञान, रहस्य आदि) दूसरे को बताना/देना।

impartial / इम्'पार्शल् / adj निष्पक्ष; (निर्णय देने में) पक्षपात रहित ▸ **impartiality** noun **impartially** adv.

impasse / 'ऐम्पास; US 'इम्पैस् / noun (प्राय: sing) ऐसी मुश्किल स्थिति जिससे बच निकलना असंभव हो : resolve the impasse.

impassive / इम्'पैसिव् / adj भावशून्य; दूसरों की भावनाओं से विचलित न होने वाला, शांत : an impassive expression ▸ **impassively** adv.

impatient / इम्'पेश्न्ट् / adj 1 **impatient (with/at sb/sth)** आतुर; अधीर 2 **impatient (to do sth); impatient (for sth)** उतावला, अत्यंत उत्सुक : impatient for change/success/power 3 **impatient (of sth)** (औप) असहनशील : impatient of criticism/delay ▸ **impatience** noun अधीरता; आतुरता **impatiently** adv.

impeach / इम्'पीच् / verb 1 **impeach sb (for sth/doing sth)** राजनीतिक नेता आदि पर (राज्य के विरुद्ध अपराध करने का) आरोप/अभियोग लगाना 2 (औप) किसी पर संदेह करना, उत्तर माँगना : impeach sb's

motives ▸ **impeachment** *noun*
महाभियोग।

impeccable / इम्'पेकब्ल् / *adj* त्रुटिहीन;
निर्दोष : *His written English is impeccable.* ▸ **impeccably** *adv.*

impede / इम्'पीड् / *verb* बाधा/अड़चन
डालना : *regulations which impede
imports.*

impediment / इम्'पेडिमन्ट् / *noun*
1 impediment (to sb/sth) बाधा/अड़चन
2 उच्चारण दोष : *a speech impediment.*

impel / इम्'पेल् / *verb* (-ll-) impel sb (to
sth) (विचार, भाव आदि) प्रेरित करना;
उकसाना; ठेलना : *I felt impelled to
investigate the matter further.*

impending / इम्'पेन्डिङ् / *adj* निकट
भविष्य में घटित होने वाला; आसन्न :
warnings of impending disaster.

imperative / इम्'पेरटिव् / *adj* (और)
अत्यावश्यक, जिसकी अवहेलना न की जा
सके ▸ **imperative** *noun* 1 अत्यावश्यक
वस्तु 2 (व्या) आज्ञार्थक वृत्ति।

imperfect / इम्'परफ़िक्ट् / *adj* 1 त्रुटिपूर्ण
2 (व्या) (क्रिया) अपूर्ण, अधूरा ▸ **imperfect** *noun* (the imperfect) अपूर्णकाल
imperfection *noun* त्रुटि, दोष।

imperial / इम्'पिअरिअल् / *adj* साम्राज्य-
विषयक; सम्राट-योग्य : *the imperial
palace/army/power.*

imperialism / इम्'पिअरिअलिज़म् /
noun (प्राय: अपमा) साम्राज्यवाद।

imperious / इम्'पिअरिअस् / *adj* (और)
उद्धत, दबंग : *an imperious look/
gesture* ▸ **imperiously** *adv.*

impersonal / इम्'परसन्ल् / *adj* 1 (प्राय:
अपमा) मानवीय भावनाओं से प्रभावित न
होने वाला/अप्रभावित रहने वाला : *a cold
impersonal stare* 2 व्यक्तिगत भावनाओं
से प्रभावित न होने वाला : *give an
impersonal opinion* 3 किसी एक
व्यक्ति को निर्दिष्ट न करने वाला; अव्यक्तिक।

impersonate / इम्'परसनेट् / *verb*
1 (नाटक आदि में) अभिनय करना, दूसरे
व्यक्ति के हाव-भाव की नक़ल करना : *He
can impersonate many well-known
politicians.* 2 दूसरा व्यक्ति बनकर धोखा
देना ▸ **impersonation** *noun* **impersonator** *noun* दूसरे व्यक्तियों को नक़ल
करने वाला, विशेषत: मनोरंजन के लिए।

impertinent / इम्'परटिनन्ट् / *adj* impertinent (to sb) उद्धत; ढीठ/गुस्ताख़
▸ **impertinence** / इम्'परटिनन्स् / *noun*
ढिठाई।

imperturbable / इम्पर्'टर्बब्ल् / *adj*
धीर, शांत/अविचलित।

impervious / इम्'परविअस् / *adj* impervious (to sth) 1 (ऐसा पदार्थ)
जिसमें से पानी, वायु आदि न निकल सके,
अभेद्य : *impervious to water* 2 दूसरों
के द्वारा प्रभावित न होने वाला : *impervious to fear/argument.*

impetuous / इम्'पेचुअस् / *adj* जल्दबाज़;
अविवेकी/उतावला : *impetuous behaviour* ▸ **impetuosity** / इम्'पेचु ऑसिटि /
noun जल्दबाज़ी।

impetus / 'इम्पिटस् / *noun* impetus
(to sth/to do sth) प्रेरणा/प्रोत्साहन; प्रेरक
शक्ति : *The treaty gave fresh impetus to trade.*

impious / 'इम्पिअस्; इम्'पाइअस् / *adj*
नास्तिक/अधर्मी; दुष्ट ▸ **impiety** *noun.*

implement[1] / 'इम्प्लिमन्ट् / *noun* औज़ार/
उपकरण : *farm implements.*

implement[2] / 'इम्प्लिमेन्ट् / *verb* कार्या-
न्वित करना, अमल में लाना : *implement
changes/policies* ▸ **implementation** / इम्प्लिमेन्'टेश्न् / *noun* कार्यान्वयन।

implicate / 'इम्प्लिकेट् / *verb* implicate sb (in sth) (किसी अपराध के आरोप
में) किसी को फँसाना।

implication / इम्प्लि'केश्न् / *noun*
1 implication (for sb/sth) आशय,
तात्पर्य; निहितार्थ; भविष्य में पड़ने वाल

प्रभाव : *They failed to consider the wider implications of their actions.* 2 (किसी अपराध में) सम्मिलित होने/करने की क्रिया।

implicit / इम्'प्लिसिट् / *adj* 1 implicit (in sth) अव्यक्त, अंतर्निहित : *implicit assumptions* 2 असंदिग्ध, परम : *I have implicit faith in your abilities.* ▸ **implicitly** *adv*.

implore / इम्'प्लॉर् / *verb* प्रार्थना/याचना करना : *They implored her to stay.*

imply / इम्'प्लाइ / *verb* (*pt, pp* implied) 1 अप्रत्यक्ष रूप से कुछ सुझाना/व्यक्त करना : *implied criticism/threats* 2 तर्कसंगत निष्कर्ष/परिणाम के रूप में कुछ सुझाना ▸ **implied** / इम्'प्लाइड् / *adj* ध्वनित, लक्षित; अंतर्निहित।

import¹ / इम्'पॉर्ट् / *verb* import sth (from/into) देश के बाहर से भीतर माल या सेवा लाना ▸ **importer** *noun* आयात-कर्ता (व्यक्ति, कंपनी या देश)।

import² / 'इम्पॉर्ट् / *noun* 1 (प्राय: *pl*) आयात में आया सामान : *a sharp rise in foreign imports* 2 आयात : *import duties* 3 (औप) महत्त्व 4 the import [*sing*] the import (of sth) (औप) अर्थ, तात्पर्य : *It is difficult to understand the full import of this statement.*

important / इम्'पॉर्ट्न्ट् / *adj* 1 important (to sb/sth) महत्त्वपूर्ण/गंभीर : *an important decision* 2 (व्यक्ति) प्रभाव-शाली ▸ **importance** / इम्'पॉर्ट्न्स् / *noun* importance (to/for sb/sth) महत्त्व/प्रभाव।

impose / इम्'पोज़् / *verb* 1 impose sth (on sb) (विचार, मत आदि) थोपना, आरोपित करना : *She imposed her ideas on the group.* 2 impose sth (on sb/sth) (कर आदि) लगाना/लाद देना 3 impose (oneself) (on sb/sth) (किसी की सज्जनता आदि का) दुरुपयोग करना

▸ **imposing** *adj* शानदार, भव्य **imposition** / इम्प'ज़िशन् / *noun* 1 imposition (on sb/sth) (कर, क़ानून आदि को) लागू करने/थोपने की क्रिया 2 (प्राय: *sing*) अनुचित माँग।

impossible / इम्'पॉसब्ल् / *adj* 1 असंभव 2 असाध्य, कठिन : *The decision places me in an impossible position.* ▸ **impossibility** *noun*.

impostor (imposter भी) / इम्'पॉस्-टर् / *noun* ढोंगी, पाखंडी; धोखेबाज़।

impotent / 'इम्पटन्ट् / *adj* 1 (औप) बेबस, असमर्थ : *Without the chairman's support, the committee is impotent.* 2 (पुरुष) नपुंसक ▸ **impotence** *noun*.

impoverish / इम्'पॉवरिश् / *verb* 1 दरिद्र कर देना 2 गुणों को कम/बेकार कर देना : *Intensive cultivation has impoverished the soil.* ▸ **impoverishment** *noun*.

impracticable / इम्'प्रैक्टिकब्ल् / *adj* 1 अव्यावहारिक; दु:साध्य 2 (मार्ग) दुर्गम ▸ **impracticability** *noun*.

impractical / इम्'प्रैक्टिक्ल् / *adj* अव्या-वहारिक, दुष्कर।

impregnable / इम्'प्रेग्नब्ल् / *adj* 1 अ-प्रवेश्य, अभेद्य : *an impregnable fortress* 2 अजेय, अटल।

impress / इम्'प्रेस् / *verb* 1 impress sb (with sth) (किसी के मन पर) गहरी छाप छोड़ना, अत्यंत प्रभावित करना 2 impress sth/itself on/upon sb छाप लगाना, भारी प्रभाव रखना : *His words impressed themselves on my memory.*

impression / इम्'प्रेशन् / *noun* 1 impression (of sb/sth/of doing sth/that...) (किसी के बारे में) विश्वास, भाव या धारणा : *What were your first impressions of the new headmaster?* 2 impression (on sb) (मन या भावनाओं पर) गहरा प्रभाव 3 छाप,

अंकन : *the impression of a leaf in a fossil* 4 (पुस्तक आदि का) पुनर्मुद्रण : *fifth impression 2002.*

impressionable / इम्'प्रेशनबल् / *adj* सहज में प्रभावित होने वाला।

impressive / इम्'प्रेसिव् / *adj* प्रभावोत्पादक; भव्य।

imprint / इम्'प्रिन्ट् / *verb* ■ **imprint sth/ itself in/on sth** 1 छापना, मुहर या चिह्न लगाना 2 मन पर छाप छोड़ना ▶ **imprint** / 'इम्प्रिन्ट् / *noun* 1 छाप 2 प्रभाव 3 प्रकाशक का नाम।

imprison / इम्'प्रिज़्न् / *verb* **imprison sb (in sth)** क़ैद करना, बंदी बनाना ▶ **imprisonment** *noun*.

improbable / इम्'प्रॉबबल् / *adj* असंभावित ▶ **improbability** *noun*.

impromptu / इम्'प्रॉम्प्ट्यू; US इम्'प्रॉम्प्टू / *adj, adv* बिना तैयारी के, तात्कालिक : *an impromptu speech/performance.*

improper / इम्'प्रॉपर् / *adj* 1 अनुचित, अशोभनीय 2 असंगत, अनुपयुक्त 3 ग़लत : *improper use of drugs* ▶ **improperly** *adv*.

improve / इम्'प्रूव् / *verb* सुधारना, बेहतर करना : *His work is improving.* ■ **improve on/upon sth** (पूर्वोल्लिखित से) बेहतर बनाना ▶ **improvement** *noun* 1 **improvement (on/in sth)** सुधार, बेहतरी 2 उन्नति।

improvise / 'इम्प्रवाइज़् / *verb* 1 तत्काल रचना करना (गाते हुए गीत की, कविता सुनाते हुए कविता की रचना करना) 2 काम-चलाऊ प्रबंध करना, तत्काल जो मिला उसी को ठीक-ठाक कर प्रयुक्त करना : *a hastily improvised meal* ▶ **improvisation** *noun*.

imprudent / इम्'प्रूडन्ट् / *adj (औप)* अविवेकी, असावधान ▶ **imprudence** *noun*.

impudent / 'इम्प्यडन्ट् / *adj* निर्लज्ज, ढीठ

▶ **impudence** *noun* **impudently** *adv*.

impulse / 'इम्पल्स् / *noun* 1 **impulse (to do sth)** अंत:प्रेरणा, आदेश : *He felt an irresistible impulse to giggle.* 2 धक्का; आवेग 3 प्रतिक्रिया करने के लिए तंत्रिका में गति।

impulsive / इम्'पल्सिव् / *adj* आवेशपूर्ण, आवेशजन्य : *an impulsive decision* ▶ **impulsiveness** *noun*.

impure / इम्'प्युअर् / *adj* 1 अशुद्ध (या गंदा) : *impure water* 2 (*अप्र*) अपवित्र : *impure thoughts* ▶ **impurity** *noun* 1 अशुद्धि 2 अशुद्ध करने वाली वस्तु।

in¹ / इन् / *prep* 1 (स्थिति) में : *a country in Africa* 2 (समयावधि) में : *in 2001* ○ *in spring/summer* 3 (कुछ पहने हुए, पोशाक) में : *boys dressed in their best clothes* 4 (भौतिक पर्यावरण) में : *go out in the rain* 5 (अवस्था या दशा) में : *I'm in love!* ○ *The house is in good repair.* 6 (मात्रा या सीमा सूचक) में : *She learnt to drive in three weeks.* 7 (रीति/शैली वाचक) में : *Speak in English.* 8 (नौकरी/पेशा) में : *She's in business/journalism.* 9 (दर या अनुपात सूचक) में से : *One in ten said they preferred their old brand of butter.* 10 के संदर्भ/संबंध में : *a country rich in minerals.*

in² / इन् / *adv part* 1 (किसी वस्तु जगह या पदार्थ के) भीतर, अंदर (**out** के वैषम्य में) : *The top drawer is the one with the cutlery in.* ○ *She opened the door and went in.* 2 (**be** क्रिया के साथ) (किसी व्यक्ति/वस्तु का ऑफिस/घर या किसी अन्य स्थान पर) उपस्थित होना : *Nobody was in when we called.* ○ *Is the train in yet?* 3 फ़ैशनेबल या लोकप्रिय होना : *Long skirts are (coming) in again.* ■ **be in for sth** (किसी अप्रिय घटना की) संभावना होना, अनुभव करना :

He's in for a nasty shock. **in and out (of sth)** किसी स्थान पर प्रायः नियमित रूप से जाना : *He's been in and out of hospital all year.* ▸ **in** *adj* (अनौप) लोकप्रिय एवं फ़ैशन में : *It's the in thing to do at the moment.*

in- *pref* (उपसर्ग) (नकार, उलटे अर्थ में) : *inaccurate, insincere, etc.*

inability / इन्'बिलिटि / *noun* [*sing*] **inability (to do sth)** असमर्थता।

inaccessible / इनैक्'सेसबल् / *adj* **inaccessible (to sb)** (किसी की) पहुँच के बाहर; अगम्य।

inaccurate / इन्'ऐक्यरट् / *adj* त्रुटिपूर्ण, ग़लत : *an inaccurate statement* ▸ **inaccuracy** *noun.*

inadequate / इन्'ऐडिक्वट् / *adj* 1 अपर्याप्त, आवश्यकता से कम 2 (व्यक्ति) कोई कार्यभार या परिस्थिति सँभालने में असमर्थ ▸ **inadequacy** *noun* 1 अपर्याप्त होने की स्थिति 2 **inadequacy in/of sth** कमज़ोरी : *inadequacies of the present voting system.*

inadvertent / इनड्'व़र्टन्ट् / *adj* (कोई कार्य) अनजाने में किया गया : *an inadvertent omission* ▸ **inadvertently** *adv.*

inadvisable / इनड्'व़ाइज़बल् / *adj* विवेकहीन; मूर्खतापूर्ण (कार्य आदि)।

inane / इ'नेन् / *adj* बिना किसी मतलब/अर्थ के; महत्त्वहीन/तुच्छ।

inappropriate / इन्'प्रोप्रिअट् / *adj* **inappropriate (to/for sb/sth)** (किसी व्यक्ति/वस्तु के लिए) अनुचित, अनुपयुक्त, असंगत : *an inappropriate name/ moment.*

inasmuch as / इनज़्'मच् अज़् / *conj* (औप) क्योंकि, चूँकि : *He shows an interest in other people only inasmuch as they can be useful to him.*

inaugurate / इ'नॉग्यरेट् / *verb* 1 समारोह का उद्घाटन करना या कोई कार्य प्रारंभ करना

2 **inaugurate sb (as sth)** विशेष समारोह में किसी नेता या जन–अधिकारी का परिचय कराना : *inaugurate the President* 3 किसी चीज़ की शुरुआत होना ▸ **inauguration** / इनॉग्य'रेश्न् / *noun* उद्घाटन।

inborn / इन्'बॉर्न् / *adj* (गुण, योग्यता आदि) जन्मजात, सहजात : *an inborn talent for music.*

incapable / इन्'केपबल् / *adj* **incapable of sth/doing sth** कोई कार्य करने में असमर्थ।

incapacitate / इनक'पैसिटेट् / *verb* (औप) अक्षम कर देना, पंगु बना देना।

incarnate / इन्'कार्नट् / *adj* मूर्त मानव रूप में : *virtue incarnate.*

incarnation / इनकार'नेश्न् / *noun* 1 अवतार (देवी–देवताओं का) 2 (गुण आदि का) साक्षात् मूर्ति।

incendiary / इन्'सेनडिअरि / *adj* 1 भवन आदि में आग लगाने वाला : *an incendiary bomb/device* 2 आगजनी करने, हिंसा करने या जनता में उपद्रव फैलाने वाला : *incendiary words* ▸ **incendiary** *noun* आग लगाने वाला बम।

incense[1] / इन्'सेन्स् / *verb* अतिक्रुद्ध करना : *I feel deeply incensed by the way I have been treated.*

incense[2] / 'इन्सेन्स् / *noun* महकदार धुआँ, जैसे अगरबत्ती या धूप का।

incentive / इन्'सेन्टिव़् / *noun* **incentive (to do sth)** 1 प्रोत्साहन देने वाली वस्तु : *an incentive scheme* 2 प्रोत्साहन, उत्प्रेरणा।

inception / इन्'सेप्श्न् / *noun* (औप) किसी चीज़ का प्रारंभ/शुरुआत।

incessant / इन्'सेसन्ट् / *adj* निरंतर, अविच्छिन्न : *a week of almost incessant rain* ▸ **incessantly** *adv* लगातार।

inch / इन्च् / *noun* 1 (संक्षि **in**) इंच, लंबाई की एक इकाई 2 ज़रा–सी मात्रा या दूरी : *He escaped death by an inch.* 3 वर्षा/ बर्फ़ की मात्रा मापने की एक इकाई : *three* *inches of rain* ▸ **inch** *verb* ■ **inch (sth) forward, past, through, etc** किसी चीज़ को निर्धारित दिशा में धीरे-धीरे सावधानीपूर्वक बढ़ाना : *inch the car forward.*

incidence / 'इन्सिडन्स् / *noun* [*sing*] **incidence of sth** 1 कुछ घटित होने की सीमा; प्रभाव-सीमा : *high incidence of crime/unemployment* 2 (तक) सतह पर रोशनी का पड़ने का तरीका।

incident / 'इन्सिडन्ट् / *noun* 1 घटना 2 जन-उपद्रव या हिंसा की घटना : *The demonstration proceeded without incident.*

incidental / इन्सि'डेन्ट्ल् / *adj* 1 साथ में परंतु छोटा और अपेक्षाकृत कम महत्त्व का : *incidental expenses* 2 **incidental (to sth)** किसी अन्य चीज़ के साथ आकस्मिक रूप से घटित : *findings incidental to the main research* ▸ **incidentally** *adv* प्रसंगवश, अकस्मात्।

incise / इन्'साइज़् / *verb* किसी सतह पर शब्द, कलाकृति आदि काटना : *an incised letter/pattern* ▸ **incision** / इन्'सिश्न् / *noun* चीरा; चीरा देने की क्रिया (विशेषत: शल्य-क्रिया के दौरान)।

incite / इन्'साइट् / *verb* 1 **incite sb (to sth)** भड़काना, उभारना : *incite the workers to violence* 2 हिंसा या संघर्ष पैदा करना : *incite a riot* ▸ **incitement** *noun.*

inclination / इन्क्लि'नेश्न् / *noun* 1 **inclination (to/for/towards sth); inclination (to do sth)** झुकाव, अभिरुचि 2 प्रवृत्ति : *He has an inclination to overdramatize.* 3 ढाल; झुकाव।

incline[1] / इन्'क्लाइन् / *verb* 1 झुकाना, ढलाव/मोड़ देना 2 शरीर का अंग, विशेषत: सिर, आगे झुकाना : *She inclined her head in prayer.* 3 (औप) **incline sb towards sth** प्रभावित/प्रवृत्त करना; **incline to/towards sth** भौतिक या मानसिक

प्रवृत्ति रखना : *He inclines towards laziness.* ▸ **inclined** *adj* **inclined (to do sth)** कुछ करने को प्रवृत्त/उद्यत।

incline[2] / 'इन्क्लाइन् / *noun* ढलान।

include / इन्'क्लूड् / *verb* 1 अंतर्विष्ट करना, अंतर्गत करना : *Does the price include tax?* 2 **include sb/sth (in/among sth)** सम्मिलित करना, हिस्सा बनाना/होना ▸ **inclusion** / इन्'क्लूश्न् / *noun* **inclusion (in sth)** सम्मिलित करना; सम्मिलित व्यक्ति/वस्तु।

inclusive / इन्'क्लूसिव् / *adj* 1 **inclusive (of sth)** सब को सम्मिलित करने वाला 2 निर्दिष्ट सीमाएँ मिलाकर : *pages 7 to 26 inclusive.*

incognito / ,इन्कॉग्'नीटो / *adj, adv* नक़ली (छद्म) नाम से, छद्म वेश से : *He didn't want to be recognized, so he travelled incognito.*

incoherent / इन्को'हिअरन्ट् / *adj* असंगत, असंबद्ध; (बातचीत) अस्पष्ट : *incoherent rambling.*

income / 'इन्कम् / *noun* आय, आमदनी।

incoming / 'इन्कमिङ् / *adj* 1 अंदर (की तरफ़) आने वाला : *the incoming tide* ○ *incoming telephone calls* 2 हाल ही में चुना गया : *the incoming president.*

incomparable / इन्'कॉम्प्रब्ल् / *adj* अतुलनीय, अद्वितीय ▸ **incomparably** *adv.*

incompetent / इन्'कॉम्पिटन्ट् / *adj* अक्षम ▸ **incompetently** *adv.*

incomplete / ,इन्कम्'प्लीट् / *adj* अधूरा ▸ **incompletely** *adv.*

incongruous / इन्'कॉङ्ग्रुअस् / *adj* बेमेल/असंगत होने के कारण अजीब; अनुप-युक्त : *Such traditional methods seem incongruous in this modern age.* ▸ **incongruity** / ,इन्कॉन्'ग्रूअटि / *noun* असंगति।

inconsiderate / ,इन्कन्'सिडरट् / *adj*

(अपमा) दूसरों की सुविधा आदि का ध्यान न रखने वाला, बेमुरौवत।

inconsistent / इन्कन्'सिस्टन्ट् / *adj* 1 **inconsistent (with sth)** बेमेल; (तथ्यों आदि का) असंगत होना 2 परिवर्तनशील : *inconsistent weather.*

inconspicuous / इन्कन्'स्पिक्युअस् / *adj* सरलता से ध्यान में न आने वाला; बिना महत्त्व का, नगण्य।

inconvenience / इन्कन् 'वीनिअन्स्/ *noun* असुविधा, कष्ट; असुविधाजनक वस्तु/ व्यक्ति : *put up with minor inconveniences* ▶ **inconvenience** *verb* असुविधा/कष्ट पहुँचाना।

inconvenient / इन्कन्'वीनिअन्ट् / *adj* असुविधाजनक : *They arrived at an inconvenient time.*

incorporate / इन्'कॉर्परेट् / *verb* 1 **incorporate sth (in/into sth)** समाविष्ट करना, हिस्सा बनाना : *Many of our suggestions have been incorporated (in the new plan).* 2 (किसी संस्था, वर्ग या संघ में) सम्मिलित कर लेना ▶ **incorporated** *adj* (संक्षि **Inc**) (कंपनी) क़ानूनी तौर पर संगठित : *Nelson Products Inc* **incorporation** / इन्कॉर्प'रेश्न् / *noun* स्वांगीकरण।

incorrect / इन्क'रेक्ट् / *adj* ग़लत : *an incorrect answer.*

incorrigible/इन्'कॉरिजब्ल्/*adj* (*अपमा या परि*) बुरी आदतों वाला (व्यक्ति) जिसे सुधारा न जा सके : *an incorrigible liar.*

increase[1] / इन्'क्रीस् / *verb* **increase (sth) (from A) (to B)** बढ़ावा देना/बढ़ाना, वृद्धि करना : *He increased his speed to overtake the bus.*

increase[2] / इङ्क्रीस्/ *noun* **increase (in sth)** वृद्धि, बढ़त : *a wage increase.*

incredible/इन्'क्रेडब्ल्/*adj* 1 अविश्वसनीय 2 (*अनौप*) आश्चर्यजनक।

incredulous / इन् 'क्रेड्यलस्; *US* इन् 'क्रेजलस्/ *adj* शक्की; शंका दिखाते हुए।

increment/इङ्क्रमन्ट्/*noun* 1 वेतनवृद्धि 2 बढ़ती।

incriminate / इन्'क्रिमिनेट्/ *verb* अभियोग लगाना, अभियोग में फँसाना : *incriminating evidence* ▶ **incrimination** *noun.*

incubate / 'इङ्क्युबेट्/ *verb* 1 (अंडे) सेना 2 (*चिकि या जीव विज्ञान*)(जीवाणु/ कीटाणु आदि को) उचित दशा में विकसित करना : *incubate germs in a laboratory* ▶ **incubation** / इङ्क्यु'बेश्न् / *noun* 1 अंडे सेने की क्रिया 2 (जीवाणुओं आदि का) विकास; विकासकाल **incubator** *noun* एक प्रकार का गरमी बनाए रखने वाला उपकरण।

incumbent / इन्'कम्बन्ट्/ *adj* 1 **incumbent on/upon sb** (*औप*) (किसी व्यक्ति के) कर्तव्य या कार्यभार के रूप में आवश्यक होना 2 वर्तमान पद पर : *the incumbent president* ▶ **incumbent** *noun* सरकारी/अधिकारी पद पर व्यक्ति : *the present incumbent at the Rashtrapati Bhavan.*

incur / इन्'कर्/ *verb* (-rr-) अपने ऊपर (ऋण, किसी व्यक्ति का रोष, कष्ट आदि) लेना : *incur debts/great expense.*

incursion / इन्'कर्श्न् / *noun* **incursion (into sth)** (*औप*) 1 अचानक आक्रमण या घुसपैठ 2 किसी के समय या व्यक्तिगत जीवन में बाधा या गड़बड़ी : *I resent these incursions into my leisure time.*

indebted / इन्'डेटिड्/ *adj* **indebted (to sb) (for sth)** ऋणी; आभारी।

indecent / इन्'डीसन्ट्/ *adj* 1 (व्यवहार, बातचीत आदि) अश्लील, अभद्र 2 अशोभनीय : *leave a party in indecent haste* ▶ **indecency** *noun.*

indecision / इन्डि'सिश्न् / *noun* अस्थिरता/अनिश्चित होने की स्थिति; हिचकिचाहट।

indecisive / इन्डि'साइसिव्/ *adj* 1 अ-

निश्चित, निर्णय लेने में असमर्थ 2 अपूर्ण,
बिना किसी परिणाम के : *an indecisive
meeting.*

indeed / इन्'डीड्/ *adv* वस्तुत:, वास्तव में,
सच।

indefinite / इन्'डेफ़िनट्/ *adj* 1 अनि-
श्चित : *an indefinite strike* 2 अस्पष्ट
▸ **indefinite article** *noun (व्या)* अँग्रेज़ी
में *a, an* **indefinitely** *adv*.

indelible / इन्'डेलब्ल्/ *adj* (निशान,
रोशनाई आदि) अमिट, स्थायी।

indemnify / इन्'डेम्निफ़ाइ / *verb* (*pt,
pp* **indemnified**) 1 **indemnify sb
(against sth)** (*क़ानून* या *वाणिज्य*)
हर्जाना या क्षतिपूर्ति देना : *indemnify sb
against damage* 2 **indemnify sb
(for sth)** (किसी ख़र्च का) पैसा वापिस
करना : *I undertook to indemnify
them for expenses incurred on my
behalf.*

indemnity / इन्'डेम्नटि / *noun* (*pl*
indemnities) 1 **indemnity (against
sth)** क्षति आदि से सुरक्षा 2 क्षतिपूर्ति।

indent / इन्'डेन्ट् / *verb* 1 (छापने में)
हाशिये से हटकर पंक्ति आरंभ करना
2 (किनारा) दातेंदार काटना।

independence /,इन्डि'पेन्डन्स्/ *noun*
independence (from sb/sth) स्व-
तंत्रता।

independent /,इन्डि'पेन्डन्ट् / *adj*
1 **independent (of sb/sth)** स्वतंत्र,
आज़ाद 2 पृथक, असंलग्न : *independent
investigations* 3 जो जीविकार्जन में
पराश्रित न हो; आर्थिक रूप से स्वतंत्र (सरकारी
धन पर आश्रित नहीं) : *independent
school* 4 निष्पक्ष; मुक्तचिंतक, अपने मन
की करने वाला ▸ **independently** *adv*.

indestructible /,इन्डि'स्ट्रक्टब्ल्/ *adj*
अविनाशी, अनश्वर।

index / 'इन्डेक्स्/ *noun* (*pl* **indexes** या
indices / 'इन्डिसीज़्/) 1 **index (of sth)**
सूचक/लक्षण 2 (प्राय: पुस्तक के अंत में दी)

अकारादि क्रम से सूची, अनुक्रमणिका ▸ **index** *verb* सूची बनाना, निर्देशिका तैयार
करना **index finger** *noun* तर्जनी अँगुली।

indicate / 'इन्डिकेट्/ *verb* 1 **indicate
sth (to sb)** बताना, दिखाना 2 लक्षण होना
3 उल्लेख करना, संक्षेप में कहना 4 संकेत
करना, सूचित करना : *a diagnosis of
cancer indicating an emergency
operation* ▸ **indication** / ,इन्डि
'केश्न्/ *noun* 1 **indication (of sth/
doing sth)**; **indication (that...)** सूचक,
संकेत 2 संकेत करना।

indicative / इन्'डिकटिव्/ *adj* **indicative (of sth)** संकेतात्मक, सांकेतिक।

indicator / 'इन्डिकेटर्/ *noun* लक्षण/
संकेत; संकेतक (यंत्र)।

indictment / इन्'डाइट्मन्ट् / *noun*
अभियोग/आरोप लगाने की क्रिया; अभियोग-
पत्र।

indifference / इन्'डिफ़्रन्स्/ *noun*
उदासीनता/तटस्थता।

indifferent / इन्'डिफ़्रन्ट्/ *adj* 1 **indifferent (to sb/sth)** उदासीन; विरक्त
तटस्थ 2 मामूली, तुच्छ : *an indifferent
meal/performance* ▸ **indifferently**
adv.

indigenous / इन्'डिजनस्/ *adj* **indig-
enous (to sth)** (*औप*) देशी, देशज :
*The kangaroo is indigenous to
Australia.*

indigestible /,इन्डि'जेस्टब्ल् / *adj*
अपचनीय, खाने/हज़म करने में कठिन : *a
lumpy indigestible pudding.*

indigestion /,इन्डि'जेस्चन् / *noun*
बदहज़मी, अजीर्ण।

indignant / इन्'डिग्नन्ट् / *adj* **indignant (at/over/about sth)** रोषपूर्ण,
(अन्याय, अपनिंदा आदि पर) क्रुद्ध : *Strik-
ers are indignant at what they
regard as false accusations.* ▸ **in-
dignantly** *adv* **indignation** /,इन्डिग्
'नेश्न् / *noun* **indignation (against**

sb) (at/over/about sth) रोष, क्रोध : *arouse sb's indignation.*

indignity / इन्'डिग्नटि / *noun* अनादर, अपमान; तिरस्कारपूर्ण कार्य : *The hijackers subjected their captives to all kinds of indignities.*

indigo / 'इन्डिगो / *noun* नील, नीला रंग।

indirect / इन्ड'रेक्ट्; इन्डाइ'रेक्ट् / *adj* 1 अप्रत्यक्ष, परोक्ष : *an indirect cause/ result* 2 सीधी रेखा में नहीं, ऋजुरेखीय : *an indirect route* ▸ **indirectly** *adv.*

indiscipline / इन्'डिसिप्लिन् / *noun* अनुशासन-हीनता।

indiscreet / इन्डि'स्क्रीट् / *adj* अविवेकी, असावधान।

indiscretion / इन्डि'स्क्रेश्न् / *noun* अविवेक, असावधानी; अविवेकपूर्ण कार्य/ टिप्पणी : *political/sexual indiscretions.*

indiscriminate / इन्डि'स्क्रिमिनट् / *adj* जो सुविचारित न हो; मनमाना।

indispensible / इन्डि'स्पेन्सब्ल् / *adj* **indispensible** (to sb/sth) (for sth/ doing sth) अपरिहार्य, जिसके बिना काम न चल सके : *A good dictionary is indispensible for learning a foreign language.*

indisposed / इन्डि'स्पोज़्ड् / *adj* 1 (औप) अस्वस्थ 2 अनिच्छुक ▸ **indisposition** / इन्डिस्प'ज़िश्न् / *noun* (औप) अस्व-स्थता।

individual / इन्डि'विजुअल् / *adj* 1 अकेला/अलग, पृथक 2 (general के विपरीत) व्यक्तिगत, वैयक्तिक : *giving individual attention* 3 एक व्यक्ति/ वस्तु के लिए विशिष्ट ▸ **individual** *noun* कोई एक व्यक्ति : *a talented individual* **individually** *adv* एक-एक कर।

individuality / इन्डिविजु'ऐलटि / *noun* विशिष्टता, पृथकता का भाव, वैयक्तिकता।

indivisible / इन्डि'विज़ब्ल् / *adj* अविभाज्य।

indolent / 'इन्डलन्ट् / *adj* (औप) सुस्त, आलसी : *an indolent husband* ▸ **indolence** *noun* सुस्ती/आलस्य।

indomitable / इन्'डॉमिटब्ल् / *adj* (औप) अदम्य, जिसे दबाया न जा सके : *indomitable courage/will* ▸ **indomitably** *adv.*

indoor / 'इन्डॉर् / *adj* घर के भीतर स्थित, घर के भीतर किया जाने वाला (कार्य) : *indoor games/photography.*

indoors / इन्'डॉर्ज़् / *adv* घर के अंदर।

induce / इन्'ड्यूस्; *US* इन्'डूस् / *verb* 1 फुसलाना, राज़ी करना 2 कुछ उत्पन्न करना : *drugs which induce sleep* 3 (चिकि) (दवाई की सहायता से) शिशु-जन्म प्रेरित करना : *an induced labour* ▸ **inducement** *noun* **inducement** (to do sth) प्रलोभन; प्रोत्साहन।

indulge / इन्'डल्ज् / *verb* 1 **indulge in sth** आनंद लूटना, भोग भोगना : *indulge in gossip* 2 किसी (अवैध) कार्य में लिप्त होना : *indulge in profiteering* 3 **indulge oneself/sb (with sth)** इच्छित वस्तु पाना/इच्छापूर्ति करना ▸ **indulgence** / इन्'डल्जन्स् / *noun* 1 अति-भोग, अतिसेवन 2 अतिसेवित/लिप्त करने वाली वस्तु **indulgent** *adj* 1 खुश रखना, किसी को मनमानी करने देना 2 ग़लती अनदेखी करना/करने को तैयार : *take an indulgent view of the play.*

industrial / इन्'डस्ट्रिअल् / *adj* 1 उद्योगविषयक; उद्योगों में प्रयुक्त : *industrial alcohol* 2 औद्योगिक : *an industrial society* ▸ **industrialize, -ise** *verb* (देश या क्षेत्र का) उद्योगीकरण करना।

industrious / इन्'डस्ट्रिअस् / *adj* परि-श्रमी, अध्यवसायी।

industry / 'इन्डस्ट्रि / *noun* (pl **indus-tries**) 1 उद्योग : *the car industry* 2 **industries** [pl] उद्योग-धंधे 3 (औप) कठोर परिश्रम करने की शक्ति, अध्यवसाय : *praise sb for his industry.*

inebriated / इ'नीब्रिएटिड् / adj (औपया परि) नशे में चूर।

inedible / इन्'ऐडब्ल / adj (औप) अखाद्य, खाने के लायक़ नहीं।

ineffective /इनि'फ़ेक्टिव् / adj अप्रभावी, निष्फल।

inefficient /इनि'फ़िश्न्ट् / adj कुशलता-पूर्वक कार्य करने में असमर्थ; अयोग्य ▸ in-efficiency noun.

inept / इ'नेप्ट् / adj inept (at sth/doing sth) अयोग्य, असंगत।

inequality / इनि'क्वॉलटि / noun (pl inequalities) असमानता।

inert / इ'नर्ट् / adj 1 हिलने-डुलने में असमर्थ, सुस्त; शक्तिहीन 2 (तक) सक्रिय रासायनिक गुणरहित : an inert gas.

inertia / इ'नर्शा / noun 1 (प्राय: अपमा) निष्क्रियता, शक्तिहीनता 2 (भौतिकी) जड़त्व; जड़ता ▸ inertial adj.

inevitable / इन्'एविटब्ल् / adj 1 अ-परिहार्य (जिससे बचा न जा सके); अवश्य होने वाला, अवश्यंभावी : Defeat looks inevitable. 2 (प्राय: परि) बहुत जाना-पहचाना एवं अपेक्षित : tourists with their inevitable cameras ▸ inevi-tably adv.

inexpensive / इनिक्'स्पेन्सिव् / adj सस्ता।

inexperience / इनिक्'स्पिअरिअन्स् / noun अनुभवहीनता ▸ inexperienced adj.

inexplicable / इनिक्'स्प्लिकब्ल् / adj जो समझा न जा सके; अस्पष्ट।

infallible / इन्'फ़ैलब्ल् / adj 1 कभी ग़लत न होने वाला : None of us is infallible. 2 प्रभावशाली : infallible remedy.

infamous / 'इन्फ़मस् / adj 1 infa-mous (for sth) बदनाम 2 (औप) दुष्ट।

infamy / 'इन्फ़मि / noun (pl infamies) (औप) बदनामी; अनैतिक व्यवहार : the infamies of the slave trade.

infancy / 'इन्फ़न्सि / noun 1 शैशव,

बचपन 2 विकास की आरंभिक स्थिति : a science still in its infancy.

infant / 'इन्फ़न्ट् / noun बच्चा, शिशु।

infantile /'इन्फ़न्टाइल् / adj 1 छोटे बच्चों के बारे में, बच्चों को होने वाला (रोग आदि) 2 (अपमा) (व्यवहार) बचकाना : infan-tile behaviour/jokes.

infantry / 'इन्फ़न्ट्रि / noun पैदल सेना।

infatuated / इन्'फ़ैचुएटिड् / adj infatu-ated (with sb/sth) प्रेम में अंधा हो जाना ▸ infatuation / इन्,फ़ैचु'एश्न् / noun infatuation (with/for sb/sth) सम्मोहन, आसक्ति : develop an infatuation for sb.

infect / इन्'फ़ेक्ट् / verb infect sb/sth (with sth) 1 छूत लगाना; बीमारी के कीटाणु संक्रमित करना 2 (भोजन, पानी आदि) प्रदूषित/संदूषित करना : an in-fected reservoir 3 भावनाओं, विचारों को फैलाना/प्रभावित करना : Her enthu-siasm and laughter infected the whole class.

infection / इन्'फ़ेक्श्न् / noun 1 संक्र-मण, दूषण क्रिया 2 संक्रमणशील रोग : pass on an infection.

infectious /इन्'फ़ेक्शस् / adj 1 (बीमारी) छुतहा 2 दूसरों को भी तुरंत प्रभावित करने वाला : Panic is infectious.

infer / इन्'फ़र् / verb (-rr-) 1 infer sth (from sth) (तथ्यों और तर्कों से) निष्कर्ष निकालना, परिणाम पर पहुँचना : infer a connection between smoking and heart disease 2 (अनौप) अप्रत्यक्ष रूप से कुछ सत्य मानना ▸ inference / 'इन्फ़-रन्स् / noun 1 परिणाम, निष्कर्ष 2 निष्कर्ष निकालने की प्रक्रिया।

inferior / इन्'फ़िअरिअर् / adj inferior (to sb/sth) सामाजिक प्रतिष्ठा, पद, महत्त्व, गुण आदि में निम्न या घटिया : make sb feel inferior ▸ inferior noun अधीनस्थ कर्मचारी inferiority / इन्,फ़िअरि'ऑरिटि / noun हीनता की स्थिति।

infernal / इन्'फ़र्न्ल् / adj (औप) नार-
कीय : the infernal regions.

infertile / इन्'फ़र्टाइल् / adj अनुपजाऊ;
बाँझ।

infest / इन्'फ़ेस्ट् / verb infest sth (with
sth) (चूहों, कीड़ों आदि का) बड़ी संख्या में
उपस्थित होकर उपद्रव मचाना : a cat
infested with fleas.

infidel / 'इन्फ़िडल् / noun (प्रा, अपमा)
अविश्वासी; नास्तिक।

infidelity / इन्फ़ि'डेलटि / noun (pl infidelities) दांपत्य जीवन में विश्वासघात :
She tolerated her husband's frequent infidelities.

infiltrate / 'इन्फ़िल्ट्रेट् / verb 1 infiltrate (into sth) गुप्त रूप से घुसपैठ करना/
कराना : infiltrate a drugs ring 2 (द्रव
या गैस) छन-छनकर प्रवेश करना, रिसना
▶ Infiltration / इन्फ़िल्'ट्रेश्न् / noun
(शत्रुओं की) घुसपैठ Infiltrator noun
घुसपैठिया।

infinite / 'इन्फ़िनट् / adj 1 विशालता के
कारण नापने, गणना करने या कल्पना करने के
लिए असंभव, अत्यंत विशाल 2 असीमित,
अनंत : Space is infinite. ▶ Infinitely
adv the Infinite noun (साहि) ईश्वर।

infinitesimal / इन्फ़िनि'टेसिम्ल् / adj
अत्यणु, इतना सूक्ष्म कि नापा न जा सके।

infinity / इन्'फ़िनटि / noun (pl Infini-
ties) 1 (गणित) असंख्य संख्या 2 निस्सीमता;
अनंत बिंदु : gaze into infinity.

infirm / इन्'फ़र्म् / adj अशक्त, दुर्बल
▶ Infirmity noun कमज़ोरी, दौर्बल्य the
Infirm noun दुर्बल जन।

inflame / इन्'फ़्लेम् / verb 1 भावनाएँ
भड़काना/उत्तेजित करना : inflame public opinion 2 क्रुद्ध करना, हिंसा भड़काना
▶ Inflamed adj 1 (शरीर का अंग)
(संक्रमण आदि से) तप्त और लाल 2 क्रुद्ध
एवं हिंसा पर उतारू।

inflammable / इन्'फ़्लैमब्ल् / adj
1 (flammable भी) ज्वलनशील, तुरंत आग

पकड़ने वाला 2 हिंसा उत्पन्न करने की
संभावना : a highly inflammable situation.

inflammation / इन्फ़्ल'मेश्न् / noun
सूजन, जलन।

inflammatory / इन्'फ़्लैमट्रि / adj
1 (अपमा) भड़काने वाला, उत्तेजित करने
वाला (भाषण आदि) 2 सूजन/जलन उत्पन्न
करने वाला, दाहक : an inflammatory
condition of the liver.

inflate / इन्'फ़्लेट् / verb 1 inflate sth
(with sth) हवा या गैस भरकर फुलाना
2 अतिशयोक्ति करना, गुण बखानना : in-
flated egos 3 क़ीमत आदि अत्यधिक बढ़ा
देना ▶ inflatable adj.

inflation / इन्'फ़्लेश्न् / noun 1 मुद्रा-
स्फीति (ऐसी आर्थिक दशा जहाँ बहुत पैसों
से बहुत थोड़ा सामान ख़रीदा जा सके) 2 हवा
या गैस से कुछ भरने/फुलाने की क्रिया।

inflection (inflexion भी) / इन्'फ़्लेक्-
श्न् / noun 1 (व्या) विभक्ति 2 व्यक्ति
की आवाज़ का उतार-चढ़ाव।

inflexible / इन्'फ़्लेक्सब्ल् / adj 1 (अपमा)
कठोर, परिवर्तित न होने वाल 2 मोड़ा न जाने
वाला; कड़ा।

inflict / इन्'फ़्लिक्ट् / verb 1 inflict sth
(on/upon sb/sth) कष्ट या पीड़ा पहुँचाना;
दंड देना : inflict injuries/pain/suf-
fering on sb 2 inflict oneself on sb
(परि) किसी के साथ ज़बरदस्ती लग जाना
▶ Infliction noun कष्ट/पीड़ा।

inflight / इन्'फ़्लाइट् / adj हवाई जहाज़
में यात्रा के दौरान (घटित होने वाल) : inflight entertainment.

influence / 'इन्फ़्लुअन्स् / noun
1 influence (on/over sb/sth) दूसरों के
चरित्र, मान्यताओं, कार्यों को प्रभावित करने
की शक्ति : exert a powerful influence on sb/sth 2 Influence (on sb/
sth) ऐसा प्रभाव डालने वाला व्यक्ति या कार्य
3 Influence (on sth) (भौतिक शक्तियों
का) प्रभाव, असर : the influence of the

moon on the tides **4 influence (with sb)** दूसरों के ऊपर (चारित्रिक गुणों आदि के कारण) प्रभाव : *use one's influence (with sb) to obtain a job* ▸ **influence** *verb* प्रभाव डालना।

influential / इन्फ़्लु'एन्श्ल् / *adj* प्रभाव-शाली।

influenza / इन्फ़्लु'एन्ज़ा / *noun* (औप) (*अनौप* flu) फ़्लू, ज़ुकाम के साथ बुख़ार।

influx / 'इन्फ़्लक्स् / *noun* **influx (in-to...)** (आने वालों, धन, नए विचारों आदि की) बाढ़, आगमन।

inform / इन्'फ़ॉर्म् / *verb* **1 inform sb (of/about sth)** सूचना देना, सूचित करना **2 inform against/on sb** किसी के ख़िलाफ़ आरोप लगाना या गवाही/साक्ष्य देना ▸ **informant** *noun* **1** (शोध कार्य आदि में) जानकारी देने वाला **2** पुलिस का मुख़बिर **informer** *noun*.

informal / इन्'फ़ॉर्म्ल् / *adj* **1** अनौप-चारिक; मित्रवत् : *an informal manner* **2** (कपड़े) सादे एवं घरेलू **3** (भाषा) सामान्य बोलचाल में प्रयुक्त : *an informal expression/letter* ▸ **informality** / इन्फ़ॉर्'मैलिटि / *noun* अनौपचारिकता **informally** *adv*.

information / इन्फ़र्'मेश्न् / (*अनौप* **info** भी) *noun* **information (on/about sb/sth)** सूचना, ख़बर; जानकारी : *an information bureau/desk* ▸ **information technology** *noun* (*संक्षि* **IT**) इलेक्ट्रॉनिक उपकरण (विशेषत: कंप्यूटर) संबंधी प्रौद्योगिकी; कंप्यूटर का अध्ययन एवं उसके प्रयोग की जानकारी।

informative / इन्'फ़ॉर्मटिव् / *adj* उपयोगी/ लाभदायक जानकारी देने वाल : *an informative account of her visit.*

infrastructure / 'इन्फ़्रस्ट्रक्चर् / *noun* बुनियादी संरचना; आवश्यक आधाररूप घटक।

infringe / इन्'फ़्रिन्ज् / *verb* **1** क़ानून, नियम आदि तोड़ना **2 infringe (on/ upon) sth** (किसी के अधिकार का) हनन

या अतिक्रमण करना : *infringe sb's liberty* ▸ **infringement** *noun*.

infuriate / इन्'फ़्युअरिएट् / *verb* क्रोध में पागल कर देना : *Their constant criticism infuriated him.* ▸ **infuriating** *adj*.

infuse / इन्'फ़्यूज़् / *verb* **1 infuse sth into sb/sth** (गुणों से) भर देना; अनुप्राणित करना : *infuse new life into the debate* **2** (चाय की पत्ती आदि पर) पानी उँडेलना : *leave the tea to infuse* ▸ **infusion** / इन्'फ़्यूश्न् / *noun*.

ingenious / इन्'जीनिअस् / *adj* **1** (वस्तु) नई, मौलिक शैली की एवं उद्देश्य के लिए उपयुक्त : *an ingenious device* **2** (विचार) चतुराईपूर्ण एवं मौलिक **3** (व्यक्ति) नई वस्तु बनाने या आविष्कार करने में कुशल ▸ **ingenuity** / इन्जे'न्युअटि / *noun* पटुता, प्रवीणता।

ingenuous / इन्'जेन्युअस् / *adj* (औप) सच्चा; निष्कपट : *an ingenuous smile.*

ingot / 'इङ्गट् / *noun* (सोने-चाँदी आदि की) सिल्ली।

ingrained / इन्'ग्रेन्ड् / *adj* **1 ingrained (in sb)** (आदतें, दृष्टिकोण आदि) गहराई से जमी हुई, बहुत पुरानी : *ingrained prejudices* **2** (दाग़, धब्बा आदि) पक्का, न छूटने वाला।

ingratiate / इन्'ग्रेशिएट् / *verb* **ingratiate oneself (with sb)** (औप, अपमा) किसी का कृपापात्र बन जाना (विशेषत: अपने निजी लाभ के लिए) ▸ **ingratiating** *adj* (*अपमा*) : *an ingratiating smile* **ingratiatingly** *adv*.

ingratitude / इन्'ग्रैटिट्यूड् / *noun* कृतघ्नता, नमकहरामी।

ingredient / इन्'ग्रीडिअन्ट् / *noun* **ingredient (for/of sth) 1** मिश्रण के अनेक उपादानों में से एक **2** उन बहुत-सी चीज़ों या गुणों में से एक जिनसे कोई वस्तु बनी है : *the basic ingredients of a good mystery story.*

inhabit / इन्'हैबिट् / verb बसना, रहना :
an island inhabited only by birds
▶ **inhabitant** / इन्'हैबिटन्ट् / noun
निवासी।

inhale / इन्'हेल् / verb **inhale sth (into
sth)** साँस लेना; **inhale (on sth)** (सिगरेट
आदि का) कश लेना।

inherent / इन्'हिअरन्ट् / adj **inherent
(in sb/sth)** जन्मजात, स्वाभाविक और
स्थायी अवयव के रूप में होना/रहना ▶ **in-
herently** adv.

inherit / इन्'हेरिट् / verb **inherit sth
(from sb)** 1 (धन-संपत्ति, पद, अधिकार
आदि को) उत्तराधिकार में पाना 2 पूर्वजों से
गुण आदि विरासत के रूप में पाना : *She
inherited her mother's good looks
and her father's bad temper.* ▶ **in-
heritance** noun 1 बपौती, विरासत
2 विरासत में पाई संपत्ति/गुण आदि **inheri-
tor** noun.

inhibit / इन्'हिबिट् / verb 1 **inhibit sb
(from sth/doing sth)** किसी को
(आशंकित या शर्मिंदा करके) कुछ करने से
रोकना/बाधा डालना : *Shyness inhibited him (from speaking).* 2 किसी
कार्य की प्रगति में अवरोध पैदा करना
▶ **inhibited** adj (व्यक्ति/व्यवहार)
नैसर्गिक अभिव्यक्ति में असमर्थ/अवरुद्ध **in-
hibition** noun.

inhospitable / ,इन्हॉ'स्पिटब्ल् / adj
1 (व्यक्ति) अतिथि सत्कार न करने वाला;
रूखा 2 (स्थान) अप्रिय।

inhuman / इन्'ह्यूमन् / adj 1 अमानुषिक,
क्रूर 2 अमानवीय : *the inhuman logic
of the machine* ▶ **inhumanity** noun
अमानुषिक/क्रूर व्यवहार।

inhumane / इन्ह्यू'मेन् / adj निर्दय, दूसरों
के कष्टों से अप्रभावित।

inimical / इ'निमिक्ल् / adj **inimical (to
sb/sth)** (औप) 1 द्वेषपूर्ण; हानिकारक
2 शत्रुतापूर्ण : *politicians inimical to
federalism.*

inimitable / इ'निमिटब्ल् / adj अद्वितीय,
इतना सुंदर या कुशलता से बनाया हुआ कि
नक़ल न की जा सके।

initial / इ'निश्ल् / adj आरंभिक ▶ **initial**
noun (प्राय: pl) व्यक्ति के नाम के आद्य-
क्षर : *John Fitzgerald Kennedy was
well-known by his initials JFK.*
initial verb (-ll-; US -l-) संक्षिप्त हस्ताक्षर
करना **initially** adv प्रारंभ में।

initiate / इ'निशिएट् / verb 1 (औप)
आरंभ करना; (किसी योजना को) प्रवर्तित
करना 2 **initiate sb (into sth)** दीक्षित
करना, (किसी को किसी धर्म/समाज या गुप्त
समिति आदि का) सदस्य बनाना : *initiate
sb into a secret society* ▶ **initiate**
/ इ'निशिअट् / noun दीक्षित व्यक्ति **initiation** noun.

initiative / इ'निशटिव् / noun 1 उपक्रम,
(समस्या सुलझाने का) प्रयास 2 **the initiative** पहल करने का अधिकार/अवसर : *The
company took the initiative in
opening up markets in Eastern
Europe.* 3 कोई कार्य आदि प्रवर्तित करने
की योग्यता/कल्पनाशक्ति (बिना किसी की
सहायता के) : *He lacks the necessary
initiative to be a leader.*

inject / इन्'जेक्ट् / verb 1 **inject sth
(into oneself/sb/sth); inject one-
self/sb/sth (with sth)** सूई (सिरिंज)
द्वारा कोई द्रव शरीर के अंदर पहुँचाना
2 **inject sth (into sth)** किसी चीज़ में नया
गुण/तत्त्व लाना : *inject some fresh
ideas into the project* ▶ **injection**
/ इन्'जेक्श्न् / noun इंजेक्शन; सूई लगाना;
सूई द्वारा डाली जाने वाली दवाई।

injunction / इन्'जङ्क्श्न् / noun **injunction (against sb)** (औप) निषेधाज्ञा;
आधिकारिक आदेश : *be granted an
injunction against sb.*

injure / 'इन्जर् / verb 1 चोट पहुँचाना,
शारीरिक क्षति करना/होना 2 नुक़सान पहुँचाना,
और अधिक ख़राब कर देना : *Such mali-*

cious gossip could seriously in-jure his reputation. ▶ **injured** *adj* 1 घायल; क्षतिग्रस्त 2 दुर्व्यवहार किया हुआ; ठेस पहुँचाया हुआ।

injurious / इन्'जुअरिअस् / *adj* **injurious to (sb/sth)** (औ) हानिकर/हानि-कारक।

injury / 'इन्जरि / *noun* **injury (to sb/sth)** चोट; चोट खाया शरीर का अंग; हानि।

injustice / इन्'जस्टिस् / *noun* 1 अ-न्याय : *victim of injustice* 2 अनुचित कार्य, अन्यायपूर्ण कृत्य ■ **do oneself/sb an injustice** किसी के साथ अन्याय करना।

ink / इङ्क् / *noun* स्याही, रोशनाई ▶ **ink** *verb* रोशनाई से चिह्न बनाना, रोशनाई से गंदा करना/छपाई के लिए रोशनाई लगाना **inky** / 'इङ्कि / *adj* 1 स्याही जैसा काला 2 स्याही से गंदा : *inky fingers.*

inkling / 'इङ्क्लिङ् / *noun* **inkling (of sth/that...)** संकेत, आभास : *He had no inkling of what was going on.*

inland / 'इन्लैन्ड् / *adj* 1 देश का भीतरी भाग/बीच में स्थित भाग : *inland water-ways* 2 देश के अंदर प्रयुक्त होने वाला : *inland letter* ▶ **inland** / इन्'लैन्ड् / *adv* समुद्र-तट से दूर का भूभाग : *move further inland.*

in-laws / 'इन्लॉज़् / *noun* [pl] (अनौप) विवाह-संबंध से बने रिश्तेदार।

inlay / इन्'ले / *verb* (*pt, pp* **inlaid** / इन्'लेड् /) **inlay A (with B)/inlay B (in/into A)** लकड़ी या धातु के डिज़ाइन किसी अन्य वस्तु में जड़ना : *ivory inlaid with gold* ▶ **inlaid** *adj* ऐसे डिज़ाइन से सजाया हुआ **inlay** / 'इन्ले / *noun* जड़ाऊ काम : *a wooden box with gold inlay.*

inlet / 'इन्लेट् / *noun* 1 छोटी खाड़ी : *a sheltered inlet* 2 प्रवेश मार्ग (गैस या द्रव के लिए) : *an inlet pipe.*

inmate / 'इन्मेट् / *noun* साथ बसने/रहने वाला (जैसे जेल, अस्पताल, हॉस्टल आदि का संवासी)।

inn / इन् / *noun* सराय।

innate / इ'नेट् / *adj* (गुण, भावनाएँ आदि) जन्मजात, स्वाभाविक ▶ **innately** *adv* स्वाभाविक रूप से : *innately dishonest.*

inner / 'इनर् / *adj* 1 भीतरी, अंदर की तरफ़ 2 (भावनाएँ) व्यक्तिगत या अव्यक्त : *inner conflict/doubts.*

innermost / 'इनर्मोस्ट् / *adj* 1 सबसे भीतरी भाग में स्थित 2 (**inmost** भी) व्यक्तिगत या गुप्त।

innings / 'इनिङ्ज़् / *noun* (pl अपरिवर्तित) क्रिकेट की पारी ■ **have had a good innings** (अनौप) लंबा और सफल शासन काल/प्रभाव काल/जीवन होना : *She's had a good innings but now it's time she retired.*

innocent / 'इनस्न्ट् / *adj* 1 **innocent (of sth)** निरपराध, बेगुनाह 2 निरपराध होते हुए भी कष्ट सहने वाला : *an innocent bystander* 3 निरीह, अहानिकर 4 धोखे-बाज़ी या अन्य ग़लत कार्यों से अनभिज्ञ : *her innocent young niece* ▶ **innocence** / 'इनस्न्स् / *noun.*

innovate / 'इनवेट् / *verb* नई प्रक्रिया आदि को कार्य में लाना ▶ **innovation** / इन'वेश्न् / *noun* **innovation (in sth)** नवीन प्रक्रिया/प्रथा आदि, नई तकनीक/विचार आदि।

innuendo / इन्यु'एन्डो / *noun* (pl **innuendos** या **innuendoes**) (अपमा) व्यंग्य/छुपा हुआ संकेत : *The play is full of sexual innuendo.*

innumerable / इ'न्यूमरब्ल् / *adj* असंख्य, गणनातीत।

inoculate / इ'नॉक्युलेट् / *verb* **inoculate sb (with sth) (against sth)** बीमारी से बचने के लिए) टीका लगवाना : *inoculate sb against cholera* ▶ **inocula-tion** / इ‚नॉक्यु'लेश्न् / *noun* टीका।

inordinate / इन्'ऑर्डिनट् / *adj* (औ) अत्यधिक; सामान्य से अधिक : *inordi-nate delays.*

in-patient / 'इन्'पेशन्ट् / noun अस्पताल में भर्ती बीमार → out-patient देखिए।

input / 'इन्पुट् / noun 1 input (into/to/sth) किसी वस्तु में कुछ लगाने/डालने की क्रिया; किसी योजना आदि में लगाया गया समय/शक्ति/धन आदि : the input of additional resources into the scheme 2 (कंप्यूटर में) जानकारी/तथ्य आदि रखना/डालना; कंप्यूटर में रखी गई जानकारी → output देखिए।

inquest / 'इङ्क्वेस्ट् / noun inquest (on/into sth) 1 (विशेषत: मृत्यु संबंधी) तथ्य पता लगाने की सरकारी जाँच : a coroner's inquest 2 (अनौप) किसी असंतोषजनक बात पर चर्चा : hold an inquest on the team's miserable performance.

inquire (enquire भी) / इन्'क्वाइअर / verb (औप) 1 जाँच-पड़ताल करना, पूछताछ करना : inquire where to go 2 inquire (about sb/sth) पूछना, जानकारी प्राप्त करना : inquire about flights to Amsterdam ■ inquire after sb हाल-चाल पूछना inquire into sth तथ्य पता लगाना ▸ inquirer (enquirer भी) / इन्'क्वाइअर / noun पूछताछ/जाँच-पड़ताल करने वाला।

inquiry (enquiry भी) / इन्'क्वाइअरि / noun (pl inquiries; enquiries भी) 1 inquiry (about/concerning sb/sth) जानकारी के लिए पूछताछ 2 inquiry (into sth) जाँच-पड़ताल : hold an official inquiry.

inquisition / ,इन्क्वि'ज़िशन् / noun inquisition (into sth) (औप या परि) जिज्ञासा; कुतूहल।

inquisitive / इन्'क्विज़टिव् / adj (अक्सर अपमा) जिज्ञासु; दूसरों के मामलों में कुतूहल रखने वाला ▸ inquisitiveness noun.

insane / इन्'सेन / adj विक्षिप्त, पागल।

insatiable / इन्'सेशब्ल् / adj 1 (लालसा आदि) जो संतुष्ट न की जा सके: an insa-tiable appetite/curiosity 2 (व्यक्ति) अतिलोभी।

inscribe / इन्'स्क्राइब् / verb inscribe (A on/in B); inscribe B (with A) (नाम या शब्द) अंकित करना, खोदना : inscribe one's name in a book ▸ inscription / इन्'स्क्रिप्शन् / noun धातु, पत्थर आदि पर अंकित शब्द/नाम।

inscrutable / इन्'स्क्रूटब्ल् / adj रहस्यमय; अज्ञेय : an inscrutable expression.

insect / 'इन्सेक्ट् / noun 1 कीट-पतंग, कीड़ा 2 (चींटी, मक्खी आदि) कीड़े-मकोड़े ▸ insecticide / इन्'सेक्टिसाइड् / noun कीटनाशक/कृमिनाशक पदार्थ।

insecure / ,इन्सि'क्युअर / adj असुरक्षित।

insensible / इन्'सेन्सब्ल् / adj (औप) 1 वेदनाशून्य, (किसी बीमारी या चोट के कारण) बेहोश 2 insensible (to sth) भावहीन, दूसरों की भावनाओं से अनभिज्ञ : He seemed insensible to her needs. ▸ insensibly adv.

insensitive / इन्'सेन्सटिव् / adj insensitive (to sth) 1 दूसरों की भावनाओं/प्रतिक्रियाओं पर विचार न करने वाला/संवेदनाहीन : an insensitive person 2 अनुभव करने में असमर्थ : insensitive to pain/cold ▸ insensitivity noun.

insert / इन्'सर्ट् / verb insert sth (in/into/between sth) घुसेड़ना; शामिल करना; बीच में रखना ▸ insert / 'इनसर्ट् / noun बीच में रखी/घुसेड़ी गई वस्तु inser-tion / इन्'सर्शन् / noun 1 सन्निवेश : the insertion of a coin into a slot 2 बीच में रखी वस्तु।

inshore / इन्'शॉर् / adj समुद्र-तट के नज़दीक : an inshore breeze.

inside¹ / इन्'साइड् / noun 1 (प्राय: the inside) भीतरी भाग या सतह : the inside of the box 2 (प्राय: the inside) फुटपाथ, (सड़क की पटरी) के पास का सड़क का भाग : Walk on the inside to avoid the traffic fumes. 3 [sing] (insides

/ इन्'साइड्ज़् / [pl] भी) (अनौप) पेट और आँतें ∎ **inside out** अंदर के हिस्से को बाहर करके: *wearing his socks inside out* ▸ **inside** adj 1 भीतरी, अंदरूनी: *the inside pages of a newspaper* 2 किसी समूह/संस्था के सदस्य द्वारा किया गया/को ज्ञात (कार्य आदि): *The robbery appeared to be an inside job.*

inside² / इन्'साइड् / prep 1 भीतरी भाग में: *go inside the house* 2 (समय) से कम में: *The job is unlikely to be finished inside (of) a year.* ▸ **inside** adv 1 अंदर की तरफ़/पर: *The coat has a detachable lining inside.* 2 (अप) जेल में।

insidious / इन्'सिडिअस् / adj (औप, अपमा) चुपचाप हानि पहुँचाने वाला (व्यक्ति/ वस्तु), कपटी (व्यक्ति): *Jealousy is insidious.* ▸ **insidiously** adv.

insight / इन्साइट् / noun **insight (into sth)** 1 अंतर्दृष्टि: *show insight into human character* 2 पैठ, गहरी पहुँच; समझ।

insignificant / ,इनसिग्'निफ़िकन्ट् / adj उपेक्षणीय, नगण्य।

insincere / ,इन्सिन्'सिअर् / adj झूठा, कपटी, पाखंडी।

insinuate / इन्'सिन्युएट् / verb 1 परोक्ष रूप से अप्रियकर संकेत देना: *insinuate base motives* 2 **insinuate sth/oneself into sth** (अपमा) (किसी पद अथवा लाभ की स्थिति में) चुपचाप युक्तिपूर्वक प्रवेश कर जाना: *He insinuated himself into my confidence.* ▸ **insinuation** / इन्,सिन्यु'एश्न् / noun परोक्ष रूप से दोषारोपण करना; परोक्ष दोष।

insipid / इन्'सिपिड् / adj (अपमा) 1 स्वादहीन, फीका 2 रुचिहीन, उत्साह-रहित: *an insipid performance.*

insist / इन्'सिस्ट् / verb **insist (on sth)** 1 आग्रह करना, हठ करना 2 ज़ोरदार ढंग से घोषित करना: *She kept insisting on*

her innocence. ▸ **insistence** / इन् 'सिस्टन्स् / noun **insistence (on/upon sth)** आग्रह, हठ: *their insistence on strict standards of behaviour* **insistent** adj 1 **insistent (about/on/ upon sth)** आग्रही, हठी 2 बार-बार दोहराया जाने वाला एवं ध्यानाकर्षक: *insistent demands for higher wages.*

insolent / 'इन्सलन्ट् / adj अपमानजनक, अक्खड़/बदतमीज़ ▸ **insolence** noun बदतमीज़ी: *dumb insolence* **insolently** adv.

insoluble / इन्'सॉल्यबल् / adj 1 (पदार्थ) जो घोला न जा सके 2 जो सुलझाया न जा सके।

insomnia / इन्'सॉम्निआ / noun अनिद्रा रोग ▸ **insomniac** / इन् 'सॉम्निऐक् / noun.

inspect / इन्'स्पेक्ट् / verb 1 सावधानी से परखना/देखना 2 निरीक्षण करना, मुआयना करना: *inspect a school/regiment* ▸ **inspection** noun.

inspector / इन्'स्पेक्टर् / noun निरीक्षण अधिकारी; पुलिस अधिकारी।

inspiration / ,इन्स्प'रेश्न् / noun 1 **inspiration (to do sth); inspiration (for sth)** प्रेरणा, प्रेरित होने की क्रिया 2 (प्राय: sing) (अनौप) अचानक मन में आया विचार, अंत:प्रेरणा 3 प्रेरक व्यक्ति/ वस्तु।

inspire / इन्'स्पाइर् / verb 1 **inspire sb (to sth)** उच्च लक्ष्यों, विचारों, भावनाओं आदि से किसी को कुछ करने के लिए प्रेरित करना 2 **inspire sb (with sth); inspire sth (in sb)** विचारों/भावनाओं से किसी को भर देना/अनुप्राणित कर देना: *inspire affection/enthusiasm* ▸ **inspired** adj 1 अति उत्तम गुण/योग्यता/सृजनशक्ति वाला: *an inspired poet* 2 भावनाओं/ विचारों से प्रेरित: *an inspired guess/ choice.*

instability / ˌइन्स्'बिलिटि / *noun (pl* **instabilities)** अस्थिरता।

install (*US* **instal** भी) / इन्'स्टॉल् / *verb* 1 **install sth (in sth)** (भवन में उपकरण आदि) लगाना : *I'm having a shower installed.* 2 पद पर स्थापित करना 3 किसी स्थान पर बसना/किसी को बसाना : *be comfortably installed in a new home* ▸ **installation** / ˌइन्स्ट'लेश्न् / *noun* 1 घर/भवन में यंत्र आदि लगाने की क्रिया; लगाया गया यंत्र : *a heating installation* 2 स्थान जहाँ विशिष्ट प्रयोग के लिए उपकरण/सामान रखा जाता है : *a military installation.*

instalment (*US* प्राय: **installment)** / इन्'स्टॉल्मन्ट् / 1 **instalment (on sth)** (भुगतान या लेन-देन की) क़िस्त : *pay for a car in 24 monthly instalments* 2 एक अवधि में किसी कहानी का एक प्रस्तुत अंश।

instance / 'इन्स्टन्स् / *noun* **instance (of sth)** उदाहरण, दृष्टांत ∎ **for instance** उदाहरणार्थ, उदाहरण के लिए ▸ **instance** *verb* उदाहरण के रूप में देना/प्रस्तुत करना।

instant[1] / 'इन्स्टन्ट् / *adj* 1 तुरंत, तात्का-लिक : *instant relief from pain* 2 (भोजन का तैयार होना) अतिशीघ्र और आसानी से : *instant coffee* ▸ **instantly** *adv* तुरंत।

instant[2] / 'इन्स्टन्ट् / *noun* (विशेषत: *sing*) 1 समय का एक बिंदु : *Come here this instant.* 2 क्षण : *I'll be back in an instant.*

instantaneous / ˌइन्स्टन्'टेनिअस् / *adj* तात्कालिक/तुरंत ▸ **instantaneously** *adv.*

instead / इन्'स्टेड् / *adv* के स्थान पर, बदले में : *I've no coffee. Would you like tea instead?* ▸ **instead of** *prep* के स्थान पर : *drink tea instead of coffee.*

instep / 'इन्स्टेप् / *noun* पैर के अँगूठे से टखने तक का ऊपरी भाग।

instigate / 'इन्स्टिगेट् / *verb* भड़काना, उकसाना : *instigate a strike* ▸ **instigation** *noun* उकसाने की क्रिया **instigator** *noun* उकसाने वाला।

instil (*US* **instill)** / इन्'स्टिल् / *verb* (-ll-) **instill sth (in/into sb)** मन में विचार आदि धीरे-धीरे बैठाना : *instilling a sense of responsibility (in/into one's children).*

instinct / 'इन्स्टिङ्क्ट् / *noun* **instinct (for sth/doing sth); instinct (to do sth)** स्वाभाविक प्रवृत्ति; बिना तर्क के विशेष प्रकार से आचरण करने की प्रवृत्ति ▸ **instinctive** / इन्'स्टिङ्क्टिव् / (**instinctual** भी) *adj* नैसर्गिक प्रवृत्ति पर आधारित **instinctively** *adv.*

institute[1] / 'इन्स्टिट्यूट्; *US* 'इन्स्टिटूट् / *noun* (प्राय: सामाजिक और शैक्षिक) संस्थान, प्रतिष्ठान; संस्थान भवन।

institute[2] / 'इन्स्टिट्यूट्; *US* 'इन्स्टि-टूट् / *verb* (औप) (जाँच-पड़ताल या नियम आदि का) प्रारंभ करना : *institute legal proceedings against sb.*

institution / ˌइन्स्टि'ट्यूश्न् / *noun* 1 प्रथा; संस्था 2 संस्था भवन 3 प्रथा/संस्था प्रारंभ करने की क्रिया/प्रक्रिया : *the institution of new safety procedures* ▸ **institutional** *adj* संस्था-संबंधी **institutionalize, -ise** *verb.*

instruct / इन्'स्ट्रक्ट् / *verb* 1 **instruct sb (in sth)** सिखाना 2 आदेश देना/ निर्देश देना 3 (विशेषत: क़ानून) किसी को सूचना देना ▸ **instructor** *noun* सिखाने वाला/प्रशिक्षक; *(US)* विश्वविद्यालय शिक्षक।

instruction / इन्'स्ट्रक्श्न् / *noun* 1 **instruction (in sth)** शिक्षण/प्रशिक्षण 2 **instruction (to do sth/that...)** आदेश, निर्देश : *give detailed instructions* 3 **instructions** [*pl*] **instructions (to**

do sth/ that...) निर्देशन (इस बात के
संकेत कि कोई चीज़ कैसे की जाए)।

instructive / इन्'स्ट्रक्टिव् / *adj* शिक्षाप्रद,
ज्ञानप्रद।

instrument / 'इन्स्ट्रमन्ट् / *noun* 1 यंत्र
2 गति/दूरी आदि मापने/रिकॉर्ड करने का यंत्र/
उपकरण 3 (musical instrument भी)
वाद्य यंत्र 4 instrument for/of sth कुछ
करने में साधन व्यक्ति/वस्तु : *an instrument of change.*

instrumental / इन्स्ट्र'मेन्ट्ल् / *adj*
1 *(संगीत)* वाद्य संगीत-संबंधी 2 यंत्रीय
3 instrumental in sth/doing sth
सहायक कारण।

insubordinate / इन्स'बॉर्डिनट् / *adj*
(औप) आज्ञा न मानने वाला, दुर्विनीत
▸ **insubordination** / इन्स बॉर्डि
'नेश्न् / *noun.*

insufferable / इन्'सफ़्रब्ल् / *adj* अ-
सहनीय; (व्यक्ति) परेशान या खीज उत्पन्न
करने वाला।

insufficient / इन्स'फ़िश्न्ट् / *adj*
insufficient (for sth/ to do sth)
अपर्याप्त।

insular / 'इन्स्यलर् / *adj (अपमा)*
संकुचित मन वाला, अनुदार : *insular
views* ▸ **insularity** / इन्स्यु'लैरिटि / *noun.*

insulate / 'इन्स्युलेट् / *verb* 1 **insulate
(sth) (from/against sth)** गरमी या
बिजली को रोकने के लिए अ-चालक से
ढकना या पृथक् करना 2 **insulate sb/sth
from/against sth** किसी को अप्रिय प्रभाव
से बचाने के लिए रक्षा करना : *children
carefully insulated from harmful
experiences* ▸ **insulated** *adj* अ-
चालक वस्तु से ढका हुआ (ताकि गरमी,
बिजली, आवाज़ आदि बाहर न जा सके) **in-
sulation**/इन्स्युलेश्न्/*noun* पृथक्करण;
रोधन।

insult / इन्'सल्ट् / *verb* अपमान/अनादर
करना ▸ **insult** / 'इन्सल्ट् / *noun* **insult**

(to sb/sth) अपमान/अनादर **insulting**
adj.

insuperable/इन्'सूपरब्ल्/*adj (औप)*
जिस पर कठिनाई से पार पाया जा सके,
दुर्लंघ्य : *insuperable obstacles.*

insurance / इन्'शुअरन्स् / *noun*
1 **insurance (against sth)** बीमा
2 बीमा व्यापार 3 बीमा राशि 4 **insurance
(against sth)** किसी संभावित संकट को
ध्यान में रखकर उठाया गया क़दम : *have
a large family as (an) insurance
against old age.*

insure / इन्'शुअर् / *verb* **insure one-
self/sb/sth (against sth)** बीमा करना/
बीमा कराना : *insure one's house
against fire.*

insurgent / इन्'सर्जन्ट् / *noun* विद्रोही,
अपने देश की सरकार के ख़िलाफ़ लड़ने
वाला।

insurrection / इन्स'रेक्श्न् / *noun*
विद्रोह, (शासन के प्रति) बग़ावत।

intact / इन्'टैक्ट् / *adj* समूचा, बिना किसी
क्षति के : *He can scarcely survive
this scandal with his reputation
intact.*

intake/'इन्टेक्/*noun* 1 (शरीर या मशीन
में) ग्रहण प्रक्रिया, अंतर्ग्रहण : *restrict
one's salt intake* 2 (एक निश्चित
अवधि में) किसी संस्थान में प्रवेश करने वालों
की संख्या : *the annual student intake*
3 यंत्र आदि का वह स्थान जहाँ से द्रव, गैस
आदि अंदर जाती है।

intangible / इन्'टैन्जब्ल् / *adj* 1 जो
आसानी से या स्पष्ट रूप से समझा न जा सके;
वर्णनातीत 2 *(वाणिज्य)* अमूर्त : *intangible assets.*

integral/'इन्टिग्रल्/*adj* 1 **integral (to
sth)** संपूर्णता के लिए आवश्यक 2 संपूर्ण :
an integral design 3 संपूर्णता के भाग
के रूप में शामिल, न कि अलग से प्रदत्त : *a
machine with an integral power
source.*

integrate /'इन्टिग्रेट/ *verb* 1 integrate sth (into/with sth) दो वस्तुओं को मिलाकर एक करना, एकीकृत करना 2 integrate (sb) (into/with sth) किसी को समूह/समुदाय का अभिन्न अंग बनाना/बनना : *immigrants who try hard to integrate* ▸ integrated *adj* एकीकृत, समन्वित integration *noun*.

integrity /इन्टेग्रटि/ *noun* 1 ईमानदारी, सत्य-निष्ठा 2 संपूर्णता, एकता : *preserve a nation's territorial integrity.*

intellect /'इन्टलेक्ट/ *noun* 1 बुद्धि, तर्क-शक्ति 2 बुद्धिमान व्यक्ति।

intellectual /इन्ट 'लेक्चुअल/ *adj* 1 बौद्धिक, बुद्धि-विषयक 2 तर्कशक्ति से संबंधित/को प्रभावित करने वाला; बुद्धिमत्ता-पूर्ण ▸ intellectual *noun* बुद्धिजीवी (व्यक्ति)।

intelligence / इन् 'टेलिजन्स् / *noun* 1 बुद्धि, समझने की शक्ति 2 सूचना (विशेषत: सेना-संबंधी), (गुप्त) समाचार (किसी अन्य देश के बारे में) : *intelligence-gathering agency* ▸ intelligent / इन्टेलिजन्ट्/ *adj* बुद्धिमान, समझदार।

intelligible / इन्टेलिजबल्/ *adj* बोधगम्य : *His lecture was barely intelligible to most of the students.* ▸ intelligibility / इन्टेलिज 'बिलटि / *noun* बोधगम्यता।

intend /इन्टेन्ड्/ *verb* 1 intend sth (as sth) इरादा करना, मन में योजना रखना 2 intend sth (by sth) (विशिष्ट) अर्थ/अभिप्राय रखना : *No criticism was intended.* ▸ intended *adj* 1 योजना किया हुआ; (अर्थ) अभिप्रेत 2 intended for sb/sth के लिए नियोजित/तैयार किया गया : *a programme intended for children.*

intense / इन्टेन्स्/ *adj* 1 (गुण) तीव्र, उत्कट 2 (भावनाएँ) तीव्र, उत्तेजित 3 गंभीर एवं केंद्रित : *an intense discussion/debate* 4 (व्यक्ति) प्रबलता से महसूस करने वाला ▸ intensely *adv* intensify / इन्'टेन्सिफ़ाइ / *verb* (*pt, pp* intensified) उत्कट/तीव्र बनाना/होना : *Her anger intensified.* intensity / इन्'टेन्सटि / *noun* (*pl* intensities) 1 तीव्रता (का भाव) 2 भाव-प्रबलता।

intensive /इन्'टेन्सिव्/ *adj* 1 तीव्र, गहन 2 ध्यानपूर्वक एवं पूर्ण रूप से।

intent¹ / इन्'टेन्ट / *adj* 1 उत्सुक, आतुर 2 intent on/upon sth/doing sth दृढ़ इरादे सहित : *be intent on promotion* 3 तल्लीन/एकाग्र ▸ intently *adv*.

intent² / इन्'टेन्ट / *noun* intent (to do sth) (औप या क़ानून) उद्देश्य : *arrest sb for loitering with intent* ■ to all intents and purposes सभी आवश्यक तत्त्वों की दृष्टि से।

intention /इन्टेन्श्न्/ *noun* intention (to do sth/of doing sth/that...) अभिप्राय, इरादा।

intentional / इन् 'टेन्शन्ल् / *adj* इरादा करके किया गया (आकस्मिक नहीं) ▸ intentionally *adv* जान-बूझकर, साभिप्राय : *I would never intentionally hurt your feelings.*

inter- *pref* (पूर्वपद) 1 बीच में, एक से दूसरे तक : *interface* ○ *international* 2 पारस्परिक, अन्योन्य : *interconnect/interlink.*

interact /इन्टर्'ऐक्ट/ *verb* 1 interact (with sth) एक-दूसरे को प्रभावित करना 2 interact (with sb) (लोगों का) आपसी मेल-जोल; मिलकर कार्य करना ▸ interaction *noun*.

intercede /इन्टर्'सीड्/ *verb* intercede (with sb) (for/on behalf of sb) (औप) मध्यस्थता करना; अनुनय करना ▸ intercession / इन्टर्'सेश्न् / *noun*.

intercept /इन्टर्'सेप्ट्/ *verb* बीच में रोक देना; (कार्य में) बाधा डालना : *intercept a missile* ▸ interception *noun*.

interchange / इन्टर्'चेन्ज / *verb*

1 (विचारों का) आदान-प्रदान करना 2 interchange sth/sb (with sth/sb) परस्पर (स्थान) बदल देना : *interchange the front and rear tyres of a car* ▸ interchange / इन्ट्रचेन्ज् / noun आदान-प्रदान interchangeable / इन्ट्र 'चेन्ज-बल्/ adj interchangeable (with sth) परस्पर बदला जा सकने वाला (अन्य के कार्य को प्रभावित न करते हुए)।

intercom / इन्ट्रकॉम् / noun एक ही स्थान के कार्यालयों आदि के बीच/अंदर टेलिफ़ोन या रेडियो संपर्क, अंतरकार्यालीय टेलिफ़ोन/दूरभाष।

interconnect / इन्ट्रक 'नेक्ट् / verb सदृश वस्तुओं को आपस में जोड़ना/संबंध स्थापित करना; सदृश वस्तुओं का एक-दूसरे से संबद्ध होना : *interconnected computers.*

intercontinental / इन्ट्र कॉन्टि 'नेन्ट्ल्/ adj दो महाद्वीपों के बीच : *intercontinental travel.*

intercourse / इन्ट्रकॉर्स् / noun intercourse (with sb); intercourse (between sb and sb) *(औप)* 1 (दो व्यक्तियों/राष्ट्रों के बीच विचारों, व्यापार आदि का) पारस्परिक व्यवहार 2 स्त्री-पुरुष समागम।

interdependent / इन्ट्रडि'पेन्डन्ट्/ adj एक-दूसरे पर निर्भर।

interest¹ / इन्ट्रस्ट; इन्ट्रेस्ट् / noun 1 interest (in sb/sth) रुचि, दिलचस्पी 2 कुतूहल : *The subject holds no interest for me.* 3 *(प्राय: pl)* लाभ, हित : *look after one's own interests* 4 interest (on sth) *(वाणिज्य)* ब्याज, सूद : *make interest payments on a loan* 5 अभिरुचि : *a person of wide interests.*

interest² / इन्ट्रस्; इन्ट्रेस् / verb interest sb/oneself (in sth) रुचि जाग्रत करना/चिंता उत्पन्न करना : *a topic that interests me greatly* ▸ interested adj 1 interested in (sb/sth); inter-

ested (in doing sth) रुचि दिखाने वाला 2 अपना हित देखने वाला interesting adj रोचक, दिलचस्प interestingly adv.

interfere / इन्ट्र 'फ़िअर् / verb interfere (in sth) (दूसरों के मामलों में) दख़ल देना/हस्तक्षेप करना ■ interfere with sb किसी के कार्य में बाधा डालना interfere with sth 1 गड़बड़ कर देना/बाधा डालना 2 बिना अनुमति छेड़-छाड़ करना : *Who's been interfering with the clock?* ▸ interference / इन्ट्र 'फ़िअरन्स् / noun 1 interference (in/with sth) हस्तक्षेप 2 रेडियो संकेतों में गड़बड़ी।

interim / 'इन्टरिम् / noun ■ in the interim इसी अवधि में ▸ interim adj अंतरिम : *an interim government/ report.*

interior / इन्'टिअरिअर्/ noun 1 भीतरी भाग 2 the interior [sing] समुद्र तट से दूर का भू-भाग/ग्रामीण क्षेत्र।

interjection / इन्ट्र 'जेक्शन् / noun *(व्या)* विस्मयादि बोधक शब्द जैसे *Oh!, Hurray!* और *Damn!*

interlock / इन्ट्र लॉक् / verb interlock (sth) (with sth) गूँथना, गूँथ जाना, जकड़ना/ जकड़ा जाना : *interlocking pipes/ tubes.*

interloper / 'इन्ट्रलोपर् / noun बिना अधिकार के दख़ल डालने वाला व्यक्ति : *She felt an interloper in her own family.*

interlude / 'इन्ट्रलूड्/ noun 1 मध्यांतर/ मध्यावकाश 2 दो घटनाओं के बीच की समयावधि : *a brief interlude of peace between two wars.*

intermediary / इन्ट्र 'मीडिअरि / noun (pl intermediaries) intermediary (between sb and sb) मध्यवर्ती (वस्तु), मध्यस्थ (व्यक्ति) ▸ intermediary adj मध्यस्थ/बिचवई (व्यक्ति) : *play an intermediary role in a dispute.*

intermediate / ˌइन्टर् 'मीडिअट् / *adj* **intermediate between A and B** 1 (समय, स्थान, मात्रा आदि की दृष्टि से) मध्यवर्ती 2 मध्यम; माध्यमिक : *intermediate skiers/students.*

interminable / इन् 'टर्मिनब्ल् / *adj* (प्राय: *अपमा*) अनंत; अत्यधिक लंबा होने के कारण ऊबाऊ : *an interminable lecture* ▶ **interminably** *adv.*

intermission / ˌइन्टर् 'मिश्न् / *noun* मध्यांतर (फ़िल्म, नाटक आदि में); समयांत-राल।

intermittent / ˌइन्टर् 'मिटन्ट् / *adj* रुक-रुक कर होने वाला/आने-जाने वाला : *intermittent rain/flashes of lightning* ▶ **intermittently** *adv.*

intern / इन्'टर्न् / *verb* **intern sb (in sth)** नज़रबंद करना (युद्ध आदि में विशेष कैंप या सीमित सीमा में रहने को बाध्य करना) ▶ **internee** *noun* नज़रबंद व्यक्ति **internment** / इन्'टर्न्मन्ट् / *noun.*

internal / इन्'टर्नल् / *adj* 1 आंतरिक 2 शरीर के भीतर (का) : *internal bleeding* 3 मन में आने वाला (परंतु अव्यक्त) 4 देश/संस्था के भीतर होने वाले विषयों से संबद्ध : *internal affairs/trade* 5 स्वयं उसी वस्तु से उत्पन्न : *a theory which lacks internal consistency* ▶ **internally** *adv.*

international / ˌइन्टर् 'नैश्नल् / *adj* अंतर्राष्ट्रीय : *an international conference.*

interpret / इन्'टर्प्रिट् / *verb* 1 अर्थ स्पष्ट करना, व्याख्या करना 2 **interpret sth as sth** अर्थ लगाना/मतलब लगाना : *Am I to interpret your silence as acceptance or refusal?* 3 **interpret (for sb)** दुभाषिये का काम करना ▶ **interpretation** / इन्टर्प्रि 'टेश्न् / *noun* व्याख्या करना; व्याख्या **interpreter** *noun* दुभाषिया।

interrelate / ˌइन्टर्रि 'लेट् / *verb* (दों या अधिक वस्तुओं का) एक-दूसरे से संबंध होना एवं प्रभावित करना।

interrogate / इन् 'टेरगेट् / *verb* पूछताछ करना; प्रश्न करना ▶ **interrogation** *noun* पूछ-ताछ : *The prisoner gave way under interrogation.*

interrogative / ˌइन्टर् 'रॉगटिव् / *adj* 1 (औप) प्रश्न-विषयक 2 (व्या) प्रश्नवाची।

interrupt / ˌइन्टर्रप्ट् / *verb* 1 (कुछ समय के लिए) रोक देना; बाधा डालना : *Trade between the two countries was interrupted by the war.* 2 **interrupt (sb/sth) (with sth)** (*अपमा*) टोकना, बीच में बोल पड़ना 3 सीधी रेखा/सतह को तोड़ना : *a vast flat plain interrupted only by a few trees* 4 किसी के रास्ते में आना/पड़ना ▶ **interruption** *noun.*

intersect / ˌइन्टर् 'सेक्ट् / *verb* 1 **intersect sth (with sth)** (आर-पार कुछ होने से) विभाजित होना/करना : *a landscape of small fields intersected by hedges and streams* 2 (रेखाओं का/ सड़क का) एक-दूसरे को काटना ▶ **intersection** *noun* बिंदु/स्थान जहाँ रेखाएँ, सड़कें आदि एक-दूसरे को काटती हैं।

intersperse / ˌइन्टर् 'स्पर्स् / *verb* **intersperse A with B; intersperse B among/between/throughout A** एक चीज़ को दूसरे के बीच में बिखेरना, छितराना।

interval / 'इन्टर्वल् / *noun* 1 मध्यांतर 2 समयांतराल ■ **at intervals** 1 रुक-रुक कर; समयांतराल से : *Buses to the city leave at regular intervals.* 2 बीच-बीच में जगह छोड़कर : *The trees were planted at 6 metre intervals.*

intervene / ˌइन्टर् 'वीन् / *verb* (औप) 1 **intervene (in sth/between A and B)** (व्यक्तियों का) बीच-बचाव करना, हस्त-क्षेप करना : *intervene between two people who are quarrelling* 2 (घट-नाओं का) बीच में घटित होकर अड़चन डालना 3 (समय का) बीच में पड़ना

आना : *during the intervening years*
▸ **intervention** / इन्_ट्र्'वेन्शन् / *noun* हस्तक्षेप।

interview / 'इन्टर्व्यू / *noun* **interview (with sb) 1** साक्षात्कार, इंटरव्यू **2** भेंट/ मुलाक़ात ▸ **interview** *verb* **interview sb (for sth)** साक्षात्कार लेना; भेंट करना **interviewee** *noun* साक्षात्कार का प्रत्याशी **interviewer** *noun* साक्षात्कार लेने वाला व्यक्ति।

intestine / इन्'टेस्टिन् / *noun* (प्राय: *pl*) आँत ▸ **intestinal** *adj.*

intimate[1] / 'इन्टिमट् / *adj* **1** (व्यक्ति) घनिष्ठ और परिचित; (संबंध) अंतरंग, आत्मीय **2** व्यक्तिगत : *an intimate conversation* ▸ **intimacy** / 'इन्टि- मसि / *noun* आत्मीयता, अंतरंगता।

intimate[2] / 'इन्टिमेट् / *verb* **intimate sth (to sb)** (औप) (अपना अनुमोदन) सूचित करना ▸ **intimation** / इन्टि'मेशन् / *noun* (औप) सूचना।

intimidate / इन्'टिमिडेट् / *verb* **intimidate sb (into sth/ doing sth)** (किसी विशेष कार्य के लिए) धमकाना, डराना : *intimidate a witness (into silence)* ▸ **intimidating** *adj* **intimidation** *noun.*

into / 'इन्टु; इन्टू / *prep* **1** के भीतर : *Come into the house.* **2** में; परिणाम में : *cut the paper into strips* ○ *frighten sb into submission* **3** के बारे में : *an inquiry into safety pro- cedures* ■ **be into sth** (अनौप) में रुचि रखना, में शामिल रहना।

intolerable / इन्'टॉलरब्ल् / *adj* असहनीय।

intolerant / इन्'टॉलरन्ट् / *adj* असहनशील।

intonation / इन्ट'नेशन् / *noun* अनुतान, बोलने में उतार-चढ़ाव।

intone / इन्'टोन् / *verb* लय से (भजन) पढ़ना; लय से बोलना : *intone a prayer.*

intoxicated / इन्'टॉक्सिकेटिड् / *adj* **1** नशे में धुत्त/मतवाला **2 intoxicated (by/**

with sth) उत्तेजित : *intoxicated by success* ▸ **intoxicating** *adj* **intoxi- cation** / इन्_टॉक्सि'केशन् / *noun* नशा, मस्ती।

intransitive / इन्'ट्रैन्सटिव् / *adj* (व्या) अकर्मक क्रिया।

intrepid / इन्'ट्रेपिड् / *adj* (विशेषत: *साहि*) निर्भीक, साहसी : *an intrepid explorer.*

intricate / 'इन्ट्रिकट् / *adj* जटिल, पेचीदा; उलझा हुआ : *an intricate pattern* ▸ **intricacy** / 'इन्ट्रिकसि / *noun* जटि- लता।

intrigue / इन्'ट्रीग् / *verb* **1** किसी की रुचि या उत्सुकता जगाना : *The children were intrigued by the new toy.* **2 intrigue (with sb)** षड्यंत्र रचना, कुचक्र तैयार करना ▸ **intrigue** *noun* षड्यंत्र, कुचक्र।

intrinsic / इन्'ट्रिन्सिक्; इन्'ट्रिन्ज़िक् / *adj* **intrinsic (to sth)** (गुण आदि) आंतरिक (न कि बाहरी कारणों से उत्पन्न) : *an intrinsic part of the plan* ▸ **intrin- sically** *adv.*

introduce / इन्ट्र'ड्यूस् / *verb* **1 intro- duce sth (into/to sth)** प्रस्तुत करना; पहली बार प्रयोग में लाने लगना **2 intro- duce oneself/sb (to sb)** स्वयं को/ किसी व्यक्ति को औपचारिक रूप से दूसरे से परिचित कराना : *Allow me to intro- duce my wife.* **3 introduce sb to sth** किसी को विषय के मूलभूत तत्त्वों की जानकारी देना; कुछ नया अनुभव कराना : *The first lecture introduces stu- dents to the main topics of the course.*

introduction / इन्ट्र'डक्शन् / *noun* **1** प्रस्तुति, प्रथम प्रयोग **2** परिचय **3** (पुस्तक आदि की) प्रस्तावना : *a general intro- duction.*

introductory / इन्ट्र'डक्टरि / *adj* परि- चयात्मक; प्रारंभिक।

introvert / 'इन्ट्रवर्ट् / noun अंतर्मुखी (व्यक्ति)।

intrude / इन्'ट्रूड् / verb intrude (into/on/upon sth/sb) अनुचित रूप से घुस आना; intrude (in/into/on sth) अरुचिकर प्रभाव छोड़ना ▶ intruder noun घुस-पैठिया।

intrusion / इन्'ट्रूश्न् / noun intrusion (on/upon/into sth) अनधिकार प्रवेश; अनुचित हस्तक्षेप : the unwelcome intrusion of politics into sport.

intuition / ,इन्ट्यु'इश्न्; US ,इन्टु'इश्न् / noun अंत:प्रज्ञा, सहजबुद्धि (तर्कशक्ति लगाए बिना ही तुरंत समझने की विशेष शक्ति); intuition (that...) सहजबुद्धि से ज्ञात विचार/ज्ञान ▶ intuitive adj.

inundate / 'इनन्डेट् / verb 1 inundate sb (with sth) अत्यधिक मात्रा में वस्तुएँ देना/भेजना : We were inundated with enquiries. 2 बाढ़ से पानी भर जाना ▶ inundation / ,इनन्'डेश्न् / noun बाढ़; भरमार।

invade / इन्'वेड् / verb 1 (किसी देश पर) आक्रमण/हमला करना 2 हस्तक्षेप करना, गड़बड़ करना : invade sb's privacy/rights ▶ invader noun हमलावर।

invalid¹ / इन्'वैलिड् / adj 1 अमान्य, अप्रामाणिक : an invalid passport 2 असत्य, तर्करहित : an invalid assumption ▶ invalidate verb अमान्य करना।

invalid² / 'इन्वलिड्; 'इन्वलीड् / noun अपंग/असमर्थ व्यक्ति, रोगी ▶ invalid verb invalid sb (out of sth) अपंगता/रोग के कारण नौकरी छोड़ने की अनुमति देना।

invaluable / इन्'वैल्युअब्ल् / adj invaluable (to/for sb/sth); invaluable (in sth) अमूल्य : invaluable help/information.

invariable / इन्'वेअरिअब्ल् / adj (औप) कभी न बदलने वाला; स्थायी, स्थिर ▶ invariably adv हमेशा।

invasion / इन्'वेश्न् / noun 1 हमला/आक्रमण 2 हस्तक्षेप।

invent / इन्'वेन्ट् / verb 1 आविष्कार करना, नई चीज़ बनाना 2 (अक्सर अपमा) बहाना बनाना; कहानी गढ़ना : All the characters in the book are invented. ▶ inventor noun आविष्कारक (व्यक्ति)।

invention / इन्'वेन्श्न् / noun 1 खोज, आविष्कार प्रक्रिया 2 आविष्कृत वस्तु : the scientific inventions of the 20th century 3 बहानेबाज़ी।

inventory / 'इन्वन्ट्रि / noun (सामान की) विस्तृत सूची।

inverse / ,इन्'वर्स् / adj विपरीत स्थिति/दिशा में : The number of copies the paper sells seems to be in inverse proportion to the amount of news it contains. (उलटे अनुपात में, अर्थात् यदि एक वस्तु बढ़ती है तो दूसरी घटती है) ▶ inverse / 'इन्वर्स् / noun the inverse ठीक विपरीत।

inversion / इन्'वर्श्न् / noun उलटा होने/करने की क्रिया/अवस्था, प्रतिलोमन : (an) inversion of normal word order.

invert / इन्'वर्ट् / verb उलटा करना, औंधा करना, विपरीत करना।

invest / इन्'वेस्ट् / verb 1 invest (sth) (in sth/with sb) (व्यापार आदि में) पूँजी लगाना 2 invest sth (in sth/ doing sth) अच्छे परिणाम की आशा में किसी काम में समय, प्रयास या शक्ति खर्च करना : invest a few hours a week in learning a new language ▶ investment noun 1 investment (in sth) (पूँजी) निवेश 2 निवेश करने योग्य वस्तु : A burglar alarm is always a good investment. investor noun पूँजी लगाने वाला, निवेशकर्ता।

investigate / इन्'वेस्टिगेट् / verb छान-बीन करना; खोज करना : investigate allegations/complaints ▶ investigation / इन्‌वेस्टिं'गेशन् / noun **investigation** (into sth) जाँच-पड़ताल : *The matter is under investigation.* **investigative** *adj* **investigator** *noun* छानबीन करने वाला; अन्वेषक।

invigilate / इन्‌'विजिलेट् / *verb* निरीक्षण करना।

invigorate / इन्‌'विगरेट् / *verb* शक्ति या पुष्टि देना ▸ **invigorating** *adj* शक्ति-दायक : *an invigorating climate.*

invincible / इन्‌'विन्सबल् / *adj* अपराजेय।

invisible / इन्‌'विज़िबल् / *adj* **invisible** (to sb/sth) अदृश्य।

invite / इन्‌'वाइट् / *verb* 1 **invite sb** (to/ for sth) आमंत्रित करना, निमंत्रण देना 2 **invite sth** (from sb) विचार/सुझाव आदि माँगना : *After his speech he invited questions (from the audience).* 3 किसी चीज़ (विशेषतः अप्रियकर) को आकर्षित करना/का कारण बनना : *behaviour that is sure to invite criticism* ▸ **invitation** / इन्‌वि'टेशन् / *noun* 1 निमंत्रण 2 **invitation** (to sb) (to sth/to do sth) न्योता 3 (प्रायः *sing*) **invitation to sb/sth** (to do sth) प्रलोभन; प्रोत्साहन **inviting** *adj* मोहक, आकर्षक।

invoice / इन्‌वॉइस् / *noun* **invoice** (for sth) (*वाणिज्य*) बिल/बीजक : *send an invoice for the goods* ▸ **invoice** *verb* **invoice sb** (for sth)/**invoice sth** (to sb) (*वाणिज्य*) बीजक/बिल बनाना या भेजना।

invoke / इन्‌वोक् / *verb* (*औप*) 1 सहा-यता-सुरक्षा की याचना करना 2 **invoke sth** (against sb) कुछ करने हेतु किसी नियम, क़ानून आदि का प्रयोग करना 3 प्रेरणा के लिए किसी का उल्लेख/संदर्भ देना 4 (भगवान को) गुहारना; जादू के ज़रिए कुछ उपस्थित करना/बुलाना : *invoke evil spirits* ▸ **invocation** *noun.*

involuntary / इन्‌'वॉलन्ट्रि / *adj* 1 बिना

अभिप्राय के अनजाने में किया गया 2 इच्छा-विरुद्ध, बलात्/हठात् किया/कराया गया : *the involuntary repatriation of immigrants* ▸ **involuntarily** *adv.*

involve / इन्‌'वाल्व् / *verb* 1 (स्थिति या घटना में) कुछ भाग के रूप में शामिल रहना/करना 2 **involve sb** (in sth/doing sth) किसी को कुछ अनुभव कराना या कार्य में लगाना : *The strike involved many people.* 3 **involve sb** (in sth) उलझा देना; (अपराध आदि में) फँसा देना : *The witness's statement involves you in the robbery.* ▸ **involved** *adj* 1 **involved** (in sth) शामिल; **involved** (with sb) संबद्ध 2 जटिल, उलझा हुआ।

inward / 'इन्‌वर्ड / *adj* 1 भीतरी : *an inward curve* 2 अंतर्मुखी : *inward joy* ▸ **inward** (**inwards** भी) *adv* 1 भीतर की ओर : *toes turned inwards* 2 अंतर्मन में **inwardly** *adv* मन ही मन।

iodine / 'आइअडीन् / *noun* (*प्रतीक* I) (*रसा*) आयोडीन।

IOU / आइ ओ 'यू / *noun* (*अनौप*) (I owe you का लघु रूप) लिखित/हस्ताक्षर किया पत्र कि मैंने अमुक से इतनी धनराशि ऋण के रूप में ली है : *Give sb an IOU for Rs 20,000.*

irate / आइ'रेट् / *adj* अति क्रुद्ध : *irate customers demanding their money back.*

ire / 'आइअर् / *noun* (*औप*) क्रोध।

iris / 'आइरिस् / *noun* आँख की पुतली।

irksome / 'अर्कसम् / *adj* क्लेशकर; नाराज़ करने वाला; (कार्य) थकाने वाला : *irksome delays.*

iron¹ / 'आइरन् *US* 'आइअरन् / *noun* 1 (*प्रतीक* Fe) लोहा 2 **irons** [*pl*] क़ैदियों की बेड़ियाँ, ज़ंजीरें 3 दवा के रूप में उपयुक्त लौह तत्त्व : *iron tablets* ▪ **have too many irons in the fire** एक ही समय में बहुत सारे काम हाथ में ले लेना।

iron² / 'आइरन्; *US* 'आइअरन् / *noun*

इस्तरी ▸ **iron** *verb* कपड़ों पर इस्तरी करना **ironing** *noun*.

ironic / आइ'रॉनिक / (**ironical** आइ 'रॉनिकल्/ भी) *adj* विडंबनापूर्ण; व्यंग्यपूर्ण, व्यंग्योक्ति।

ironmonger / 'आइरन्मङ्गर् / *noun* घर में प्रयुक्त होने वाले औज़ार आदि बेचने वाला।

irony / 'आइरनि / *noun* (*pl* **ironies**) 1 व्यंग्य, व्यंग्योक्ति 2 (घटना की) विडंबना (ऐसी घटना जो मनचाही थी किंतु तब घटित हुई जब परिस्थितियों के कारण वह व्यर्थ हो गई हो): *the irony of fate.*

irrational / इ'रैशन्ल् / *adj* अतार्किक, विवेकहीन।

irreconcilable / इ'रेकन्साइलब्ल्/ *adj* **irreconcilable (with sb/sth)** (और) 1 इतना अधिक मतभेद होना कि मेल न कराया जा सके 2 (लोगों का) एक दूसरे से पूर्णत: असहमत होना 3 (तथ्यों, विचारों आदि का) अन्य से बेमेल/असंगत होना।

irregular / इ'रेग्युलर् / *adj* अनियमित, असाधारण ▸ **irregularity** *noun*.

irrelevant / इ'रेलव्न्ट् / *adj* **irrelevant (to sth)** अप्रासंगिक, असंगत ▸ **irrelevance** *noun* असंगत होने की स्थिति।

irreparable / इ'रेपरब्ल् / *adj* (क्षति/ हानि) जिसकी पूर्ति न की जा सके; (चोट/ घाव) जिसे ठीक न किया जा सके।

irresistible / इरि'ज़िस्टब्ल् / *adj* अत्य-धिक आकर्षक; जिसका प्रतिरोध करना बहुत ही कठिन हो : *His arguments were irresistible.* ▸ **irresistibly** *adv*.

irrespective / इरि'स्पेक्टिव्/ **irrespective of** *prep* पर बिना विचार किए; बिना किसी चीज़ से प्रभावित हुए : *Candidates are assessed on merit, irrespective of race, creed or colour.*

irresponsible / इरि'स्पॉन्सब्ल् / *adj* (व्यक्ति, कार्य) ग़ैर-ज़िम्मेदार ▸ **irrespon-sibility** *noun*.

irreverent / इ'रेवर्न्ट् / *adj* साधारणतया सम्मानित व्यक्ति/वस्तु का अनादर करते/ दिखाते हुए (व्यक्ति) ▸ **irreverence** *noun*.

irreversible /इरि'वर्सब्ल्/ *adj* जो बदल न जा सके; जिसे पुन: मूल रूप में न लाया जा सके।

irrigate /'इरिगेट्/ *verb* (नहर आदि द्वारा) सिंचाई करना : *irrigate desert areas to make them fertile* ▸ **irrigation** /इरि'गेश्न्/ *noun* सिंचाई।

irritable /'इरिटब्ल्/ *adj* चिड़चिड़ा।

irritate /'इरिटेट्/ *verb* 1 चिढ़ाना, गुस्सा दिलाना 2 (त्वचा में) जलन/खुजली उत्पन्न करना : *Acid irritates the stomach lining.* ▸ **irritation** /इरि'टेश्न्/ *noun*.

is / इज़्/ *verb* → **be** देखिए।

Islam / 'इज़्लाम्; इज़्'लाम् / *noun* इस्लाम (मुस्लिम धर्म); [*sing*] विश्व के सभी मुस्लिम लोग व देश ▸ **Islamic** *adj*.

island / 'आइलन्ड् / *noun* द्वीप, टापू।

isle /'आइल्/ *noun* छोटा द्वीप/टापू।

isolate /'आइसलेट्/ *verb* 1 **isolate oneself/sb/sth (from sb/sth)** स्वयं को/किसी को दूसरों से अलग-थलग कर लेना 2 **isolate sth (from sth)** (रसा) अलग करना, पृथक करना ▸ **isolated** *adj* पृथक; अलग-थलग; अकेला **isolation** / आइस 'लेश्न्/ *noun* **isolation (from sb/sth)** पृथक्करण; अलगाव : *feelings of isola-tion in a new community.*

issue / 'इशू; 'इस्यू; इश्यू / *noun* 1 चर्चा/ विवाद का महत्त्वपूर्ण विषय 2 (पत्रिका आदि के) प्रकाशन का क्रम 3 (टिकट, नोट, सिक्के आदि का) प्रचालन : *buy a set of new stamps on the day of issue* 4 [*sing*] (और) फल, परिणाम 5 [*sing*] स्राव, निकास : *an issue of blood from a wound* 6 (क़ानून) संतान : *die without issue* ▸ **issue** *verb* 1 **issue sth (to sb)** औपचारिक रूप से जानकारी देना 2 **issue sth (to sb)/sb with sth** बाँटना 3 प्रकाशित करना ■ **issue from sth**

(औप) आना; जाना; स्राव होना; बहना : *smoke issuing from a chimney.*

isthmus / 'इस्मस् / *noun* (*pl* **isthmuses**) भूडमरूमध्य।

it[1] / इट् / *pron* (*pl* **they, them**) **1** पूर्वोल्लिखित जंतु या वस्तु आदि के लिए प्रयुक्त : *Fill a glass with water and dissolve this tablet in it.* **2** बहुत छोटा बच्चा **3** व्यक्ति का परिचय/पहचान बताने के लिए प्रयुक्त : *It's the postman.* ▸ **its** *possess det* उस का/की : *The dog had hurt its paw.*

it[2] / इट् / *pron* **1** बाद के पदबंध/उपवाक्य के लिए प्रयुक्त : *It's no use shouting.* **2** *be* आदि क्रिया के कर्ता के रूप में : *It's quite warm at the moment.*

italic / इ' टैलिक् / *adj* तिरछे छपे/लिखे (अक्षर) ▸ **italicize, -ise** *verb* **italics** *noun* [*pl*] तिरछे अक्षर।

itch / इच् / *noun* **1** (प्राय: *sing*) खुजली/ खाज **2** [*sing*] **itch (for sth/to do sth)** *(अनौप)* उत्कंठा ▸ **itch** *verb* **1** खुजलाना **2** **itch for sth/to do sth** *(अनौप)* उत्कंठा रखना : *students itching for the lesson to end* **itchy** *adj.*

item / 'आइटम् / *noun* **1** सूची का एक पद : *check the items in a catalogue* **2** समाचार।

itinerary / आइ'टिनररि / *noun* (*pl* **itineraries**) यात्रा क्रम, यात्रा विवरण।

itself / इट्'सेल्फ् / *reflex, emph pron* **1** (reflex) स्वयं : *The cat was washing itself.* **2** (emph) स्वत: ही : *The village itself is pretty, but the surrounding countryside is rather dull.*

ivory / 'आइवरि / *noun* (*pl* **ivories**) **1** हाथी-दाँत **2** हाथी-दाँत की बनी वस्तुएँ।

ivy / 'आइवि / *noun* एक प्रकार की लता : *ivy-covered walls.*

Jj

jab / जैब् / *verb* (-bb-) jab (at sb/sth); jab sb/sth (with sth) कोंचना, चुभोना; धक्का मारना ▸ **jab** *noun* 1 धक्का 2 *(अनौप)* टीका (दवाई का)।

jabber / जैबर् / *verb* jabber (away) बक-बक करना ▸ **jabber** *noun* बकवास।

jack¹ / जैक् / *noun* (पहिए निकालते समय) भारी वाहनों को उठाने का उपकरण ■ **a jack of all trades** हरफ़नमौला, कई विभिन्न कौशलों को जानने वाला।

jack² / जैक् / *verb* jack sth up 1 जैक से वाहन ऊपर उठाना 2 कुछ अचानक बहुत ऊपर उठा देना : *jack up the prices.*

jackal / जैकॉल; जैक्ल् / *noun* सियार, गीदड़।

jacket / जैकिट् / *noun* 1 जैकेट, मिरजई (एक प्रकार का छोटा कोट) 2 (dust jacket भी) पुस्तक का आवरण 3 पके हुए आलू का छिलका 4 टैंक, पाइप आदि का आवरण।

jackpot / जैक्पॉट् / *noun* सबसे बड़ा दाँव या इनाम राशि।

jade / जेड् / *noun* एक प्रकार का (प्राय: हरा) रत्न।

jaded / जेडिड् / *adj* थका-माँदा; घिसा-घिसाया : *feeling jaded with city life.*

jagged / जैगिड् / *adj* दाँतेदार; कटा-फटा : *a piece of glass with a jagged edge.*

jaguar / जैग्युअर् / *noun* मध्य अमेरिका में मिलने वाली चित्तीदार बड़ी बिल्ली।

jail (gaol भी) / जेल् / *noun* जेल ▸ **jail (gaol भी)** *verb* jail sb (for sth) बंदी बनाना, क़ैद करना।

jailer (gaoler भी) / जेलर् / *noun* जेलर, कारापाल।

jam¹ / जैम् / *verb* (-mm-) 1 jam sb/sth In, Into, under, between, etc sth दो (कड़ी) वस्तुओं के बीच जकड़ या कस जाना : *sitting on a bus, jammed between two fat men* 2 मशीन के पुर्ज़ों का ऐसा फँस जाना कि चलें ही नहीं : *There is something jamming (up) the photocopier.* 3 jam sth (with sth) ठूँस देना, ठसाठस भर देना कि चलने-फिरने की जगह न रहे ▸ **jam** *noun* 1 बहुत-सी वस्तुओं का एक साथ ऐसा इकट्ठा हो जाना कि चलना-फिरना कठिन हो जाए : *a traffic jam* 2 *(अनौप)* मुश्किल/अजीब परिस्थिति।

jam² / जैम् / *noun* (फलों का) जैम।

jamboree / जैम्ब'री / *noun* बड़ी पार्टी; स्काउटों/गाइडों की खुशी मनाने वाली रैली।

jangle / जैङ्ग्ल् / *verb* 1 (धातु टकराने जैसी) खड़खड़ाहट करना 2 किसी को नाराज़ करना : *The slow pace jangled her nerves.* ▸ **jangle** *noun* खड़खड़ाहट।

January / जैन्युअरि / *noun* *(संक्षि Jan)* जनवरी (महीना)।

jar¹ / जार् / *verb* (-rr-) 1 jar (on sth) अप्रिय प्रभाव डालना/होना 2 jar (with sth) खड़खड़ाना, अप्रिय या कष्टप्रद रूप से भिन्न होना; अप्रिय व्यवहार करना 3 शारीरिक या मानसिक धक्का देना/लगना : *He jarred his back badly when he fell.* ▸ **jar** *noun* [*sing*] अचानक शारीरिक/मानसिक धक्का।

jar² / जार् / *noun* जार, मर्तबान (एक प्रकार का, प्राय: काँच का, बरतन)।

jargon / जार्गन् / *noun* *(प्राय: अपमा)* (व्यावसायिक अथवा तकनीकी शब्दों से भरी) भाषा, विशिष्ट बोली : *banking/legal jargon.*

jaundice / जॉन्डिस् / *noun* पीलिया रोग ▸ **jaundiced** *adj* ईर्ष्यालु।

jaunt / जॉन्ट् / *noun* सैर, (आनंद के लिए की गई) छोटी यात्रा : *She's gone on a jaunt to town.*

jaunty / जॉन्टि / *adj* (-ier, -iest) ज़िंदादिल, प्रफुल्लित : *a jaunty tune* ▸ **jauntily** *adv.*

javelin / जैव्लिन् / *noun* प्राय: खेलों के

लिए प्रयुक्त हलका भाला; **the javelin** [*sing*] भाला-फेंक प्रतियोगिता।

jaw / जॉ / *noun* 1 (प्राय: *pl*) जबड़ा : *the upper/lower jaw* 2 **jaws** [*pl*] (दाँतों समेत) मुँह की हड्डियाँ 3 **jaws** [*pl*] (भयानक स्थान का) मुखद्वार; किसी मशीन या उपकरण का कसने/दबाने वाला (दाँतेदार) भाग : *the jaws of a vice* ▶ **jaw** *verb* (अनौप) बातचीत करना।

jazz / जैज़् / *noun* अफ़्रीकी-अमेरिकी उद्भव का एक पश्चिमी संगीत।

jealous / 'जेलस् / *adj* 1 **jealous (of sth/sb)** ईर्ष्यापूर्ण, डाह से भरा हुआ 2 **jealous (of sth)** (अपनी प्रतिष्ठा आदि की ओर) सतर्क : *keep a jealous eye on one's property* ▶ **jealously** *adv* **jealousy** / 'जेलसि / *noun* (*pl* **jealousies**) ईर्ष्या।

jeans / जीन्ज़् / *noun* [*pl*] मज़बूत सूती कपड़े की पतलून; जींस।

Jeep / जीप् / *noun* (ट्रेडमार्क) जीप (एक प्रकार की मोटरगाड़ी)।

jeer / जिअर् / *verb* **jeer (at sb/sth)** मज़ाक़ उड़ाना, ताना मारना : *jeer at a speaker* ▶ **jeer** *noun* ताना।

jelly / 'जेलि / *noun* 1 जेली (एक प्रकार का फलों का पारदर्शक अवलेह) 2 जेली जैसा कोई पदार्थ : *petroleum jelly.*

jellyfish / 'जेलिफ़िश् / *noun* (*pl* अपरिवर्तित) एक प्रकार का जलचर।

jeopardize, -ise / 'जेपर्डाइज़् / *verb* क्षतिग्रस्त करना; ऐसा करने से संकट में डाल देना।

jeopardy / 'जेपर्डि / *noun* ■ **in jeopardy** संकट में : *Thousands of jobs are now in jeopardy.*

jerk / जर्क् / *noun* 1 झटका, ऐंठन 2 (अनौप, अपमा) मूर्ख व्यक्ति ▶ **jerk** *verb* 1 झटका देना 2 झटका दे-देकर खींचना/धकेलना : *The train jerked to a halt.* **jerky** *adj* (**-ier, -iest**) झटके देकर चलने/रुकने वाला।

jersey / 'जर्ज़ि / (**sweater/jumper/ pullover** भी) *noun* (*pl* **jerseys**) जर्सी, ऊनी बाँहदार पोशाक।

jest / जेस्ट् / *noun* (औप) हँसी-दिल्लगी ■ **in jest** हँसी में, बिना गंभीरता के ▶ **jest** *verb* (औप) हँसी-दिल्लगी करना : *One should not jest about such important matters!* **jester** *noun* विदूषक।

Jesus / 'जीजस् / = Christ.

jet / जेट् / *noun* 1 एक पतले छेद से तेज़ी से निकलती हुई भाप, हवा, द्रव आदि की धारा 2 जेट इंजिन वाला वायुयान : *a jet fighter/ airliner.*

jettison / 'जेटिसन् / *verb* 1 जहाज़/वायुयान आदि को हलका करने के लिए अनावश्यक वस्तुएँ बाहर फेंकना : *tankers jettisoning crude oil* 2 अनावश्यक/फ़ालतू समझकर कुछ त्याग देना।

jetty / 'जेटि / *noun* (*pl* **jetties**) घाट (नदी/ समुद्र में)।

Jew / जू / *noun* यहूदी।

jewel / 'जूअल् / *noun* 1 रत्न, जवाहर; **jewels** [*pl*] रत्न जड़ित आभूषण 2 अमूल्य समझा जाने वाला व्यक्ति/वस्तु : *a jewel of an idea* ▶ **jeweller** (*US* **jeweler**) *noun* जौहरी **jewellery** (*US* **jewelry**) / 'जूअल्रि / *noun* जवाहरात, गहने।

jib / जिब् / *verb* (**-bb-**) 1 कुछ करने/स्वीकार करने को अनिच्छुक होना; अड़ जाना 2 **jib (at sth/doing sth)** करने से मना करना/अनिच्छा प्रकट करना : *She jibbed at investing any more money in the scheme.*

jig / जिग् / *noun* एक प्रकार का नाच ▶ **jig** *verb* (**-gg-**) जिग नाचना; (बच्चे को) हलके से उछालना (खेल-खेल में) : *to jig a baby (up and down) on one's knees.*

jigsaw / 'जिग्सॉ / (**jigsaw puzzle** भी) *noun* चित्र आदि के बेतरतीब कटे हुए टुकड़े जिन्हें जोड़कर पूरी तस्वीर बनानी होती है।

jilt / जिल्ट् / *verb* कोई भावनात्मक संबंध

अचानक और क्रूर ढंग से तोड़ देना, अस्वीकार कर देना : *a jilted lover.*

jingle / 'जिङ्ग्ल् / *noun* 1 छनछनाहट की आवाज़ 2 आकर्षित करने के लिए बनाई गई छोटी, सहज कविता, विशेषत: विज्ञापनों में ▸ **jingle** *verb* छनछनाना : *jingling bracelets and bangles.*

jinx / जिङ्क्स् / *noun* (प्राय: *sing*) (अनौप) **jinx (on sb/sth)** अभिशाप; अशुभ व्यक्ति या वस्तु।

jittery / 'जिटरि / *adj* (अनौप) घबराया हुआ; अनिश्चयी।

job / जॉब् / *noun* 1 नौकरी, काम : *He's been out of a job for six months.* 2 (प्राय: *sing*) ज़िम्मेदारी, कर्तव्य 3 संपन्न वस्तु, उत्पाद : *That car's a neat little job.* ■ **a good job** सौभाग्य का विषय, स्थिति **make a bad, good, excellent, etc job of sth** बहुत बुरी/अच्छी तरह करना।

jockey / 'जॉकि / *noun* (*pl* **jockeys**) (प्राय: पेशेवर) घुड़सवार (घुड़दौड़ में)।

jocular / 'जॉक्यलर् / *adj* विनोदप्रिय; विनोदपूर्ण : *jocular remarks/fellow* ▸ **jocularity** *noun* **jocularly** *adv.*

jog / जॉग् / *verb* (**-gg-**) 1 (प्राय: **go jogging**) लगातार देर तक धीरे-धीरे दौड़ना 2 हलका-सा धक्का लगाना : *He jogged my arm and made me spill my tea.* 3 झूमते हुए चलना ■ **jog along/on** शांत एवं मंथर गति से बढ़ना **jog sb's memory** (अल) याद दिलवाना ▸ **jog** *noun* 1 हलकी दौड़ 2 हलका-सा धक्का।

join / जॉइन् / *verb* 1 **join sth onto sth/on; join A to B; join A and B (together/up)** जोड़ना 2 साथी या सदस्य बनना : *join a union/choir* 3 (पद विशेष पर) सेवारंभ करना : *join the army* 4 (समारोह आदि में) साथ देना : *join a demonstration* ▸ **join** *noun* जोड़।

joiner / 'जॉइनर् / *noun* बढ़ई, मिस्तरी ▸ **joinery** *noun* बढ़ईगिरी।

joint[1] / जॉइन्ट् / *noun* 1 जोड़/संधि, गाँठ 2 शरीर में हड्डियों को जोड़ने वाली संरचना : *ankle/knee/elbow joints* 3 (गोश्त का) बड़ा टुकड़ा ▸ **joint** *verb* गोश्त का पारचा काटना।

joint[2] / जॉइन्ट् / *adj* अनेक व्यक्तियों का; संयुक्त : *joint ownership/authors.*

joke / जोक् / *noun* 1 चुटकुला, लतीफ़ा : *tell (sb) a joke* 2 मज़ाक, परिहास; परिहासजनक परिस्थिति : *play a joke on sb* ▸ **joke** *verb* **joke (with sb) (about sth)** चुटकुला सुनाना; मज़ाक करना **jokingly** *adv* मज़ाक में।

joker / 'जोकर् / *noun* 1 (अनौप) विदूषक 2 (ताश के पत्तों में) जोकर।

jolly / 'जॉलि / *adj* (**-ier, -iest**) आनंदित, प्रसन्न; आमोदप्रिय : *a jolly face* ▸ **jollity** / 'जॉलटि / *noun* (अप्र) प्रफुल्लित मन:स्थिति **jolly** *adv* (अनौप) अत्यधिक : *She's a jolly good teacher.*

jolt / जोल्ट् / *verb* 1 (किसी को) अचानक झटका देना : *An earthquake jolted Australia's tallest building.* 2 (वाहन का) झटके के साथ चलना : *jolt along a rough track* ▸ **jolt** *noun* झटका; अप्रत्याशित आश्चर्य/शोक।

jostle / 'जॉस्ल् / *verb* 1 धक्कम-धक्का करना : *The youths jostled (against) her.* 2 **jostle (for sth)** कुछ पाने के लिए धक्का-मुक्की करना।

jot[1] / जॉट् / *noun* ■ **not a jot** रत्ती भर नहीं: *There's not a jot of truth in his story.*

jot[2] / जॉट् / *verb* (**-tt-**) ■ **jot sth down** जल्दी से (संक्षेप में) कुछ लिख लेना : *I'll just jot down their phone number before I forget it.* ▸ **jotter** *noun* **jottings** *noun* [*pl*] संक्षिप्त टिप्पणियाँ।

journal / जर्नल् / *noun* 1 जर्नल; समाचारपत्र; पत्रिकाएँ : *a medical/scientific journal* 2 रोज़ के समाचार/घटना आदि का रिकॉर्ड, रोज़नामचा ▸ **journalism** / 'जर्नलिज़म् / *noun* पत्रकारिता : *a*

career in journalism **journalist**
/ˈजर्नलिस्ट् / *noun* पत्रकार।

journey / ˈजर्नि / *noun* (*pl* **journeys**)
1 सफ़र, (विशेषत: दूर की) यात्रा 2 यात्रा में
लगने वाला समय : *It's a day's journey
by car.* ▸ **journey** *verb* यात्रा करना।

jovial / ˈजोविअल् / *adj* प्रसन्नचित्त,
आमोदप्रिय : *in a jovial mood* ▸ **joviality** *noun* **jovially** *adv.*

joy / जॉइ / *noun* 1 खुशी, हर्ष 2 हर्षित करने
वाला व्यक्ति/वस्तु : *The match was a
joy to watch.* ▸ **joyful** / ˈजॉइफ़ुल् / *adj*
हर्षपूर्ण **joyfully** *adv* **joyless** *adj* उदास,
नीरस **joylessly** *adv* **joyous** / ˈजॉइ-
अस् / *adj* (*औप*) हर्षपूर्ण, हर्ष–कारक : *a
joyous occasion.*

joystick / जॉइस्टिक् / *noun* वायुयान,
कंप्यूटर आदि की गति नियंत्रक हैंडिल।

jubilant / ˈजूबिलन्ट् / *adj* (*औप*) उल्लास-
पूर्ण, उल्लासित : *jubilant crowds*
▸ **jubilation** / जूबिˈलेशन् / *noun* उल्लास,
आनंदोत्सव : *scenes of jubilation.*

jubilee / ˈजूबिली / *noun* जयंती, किसी
घटना का आनंदोत्सव : *silver jubilee*
(रजत जयंती : 25 वर्ष पर); *golden
jubilee* (स्वर्ण जयंती : 50 वर्ष पर);
diamond jubilee (हीरक जयंती : 60
वर्ष पर)।

judge / जज् / *noun* 1 (न्यायालय में)
न्यायाधीश 2 (प्रतियोगिता आदि में) निर्णा-
यक : *The judge's decision is final.*
3 पारखी, समीक्षक : *a good judge of
art* ▸ **judge** *verb* 1 **judge (sb/sth)
by/from/on sth** आँकना; विचार करके
सम्मति देना; राय बनाना 2 न्यायाधीश या
निर्णायक के रूप में निर्णय देना।

judgement (judgment भी**)** / ˈजज्मन्ट् /
noun 1 निर्णयशक्ति; विवेक/परख : *show
a lack of judgement* 2 न्यायालय का
निर्णय, फ़ैसला 3 **judgement (on sb)**
(*औप या परि*) ईश्वरीय दंड के रूप में
विपत्ति।

judicial / जुˈडिशल् / *adj* न्यायपरक;
अदालती : *a judicial inquiry.*

judiciary / जुˈडिशिअरि /; *US* जुˈडिशिअरि /
(*प्राय:* **the judiciary**) *noun* न्यायपालिका,
न्यायाधिकारी।

judicious / जुˈडिशस् / *adj* विवेकशील
(व्यक्ति); विवेकपूर्ण (कार्य) : *a judicious choice* ▸ **judiciously** *adv.*

judo / ˈजूडो / *noun* आत्मरक्षा की जापानी
पद्धति, जूडो।

jug / जग् / *noun* सुराही, घड़ा।

juggle / ˈजग्ल् / *verb* 1 **juggle (with
sth)** बाज़ीगरी करना 2 **juggle (sth)(with
sth)** सफलता/संतोषजनक परिणाम के लिए
किसी चीज़ की व्यवस्था लगातार बदलना :
juggle one's family responsibilities with the demands of one's job
▸ **juggler** *noun* बाज़ीगर।

juice / जूस् / *noun* 1 रस 2 (*प्राय: pl*)
अमाशय में उत्पन्न पाचक रस : *gastric/
digestive juices.*

juicy / ˈजूसि / *adj* (**-ier, -iest**) 1 रसदार
2 उत्तेजक होने के कारण रुचिकर, प्रिय :
juicy gossip.

July / जुˈलाइ / *noun* (*संक्षि* **Jul**) जुलाई
(वर्ष का सातवाँ महीना)।

jumble / ˈजम्बल् / *verb* **jumble sth
(up)** गड़बड़ कर देना, अव्यवस्थित कर
देना : *The details of the accident
were all jumbled up in his mind.*
▸ **jumble** *noun* **jumble (of sth)**
गड़बड़झाला, अव्यवस्था **jumble sale** (*US*
rummage sale) *noun* गड़बड़झाला
बाज़ार की बिक्री।

jumbo / ˈजम्बो / *adj* (*अनौप*) बहुत
बड़ा : *a jumbo(-sized) packet of
washing powder.*

jump¹ / जम्प् / *verb* 1 कूदना, उछलना
2 लाँघना, फाँदना : *The horses jumped
all the fences.* 3 (डर, आश्चर्य या
उत्तेजना से) चौंकना : *The loud bang
made me jump.* 4 **jump (by) sth**

अचानक बहुत अधिक बढ़ जाना : *Prices jumped by 60% last year.* ■ **jump at sth** आतुरता से स्वीकार करना।

jump² / जम्प् / *noun* **1** कूदने की क्रिया **2** (मूल्यों में) अचानक वृद्धि ▸ **jumpy** *adj* (अनौप) अशांत; आशंकित।

jumper / जम्पर् / *noun* **1** = **jersy 2** कूदने/छलाँगने वाला।

junction / जङ्क्शन् / *noun* रेलवे जंक्शन (दो लाइनों का संधिस्थान); दो या अधिक वस्तुओं का संधिस्थान : *the junction of two electric cables.*

juncture / जङ्क्चर् / *noun* ■ **at this, etc juncture** (औप) घटनाचक्र में किसी (विशेष, महत्त्वपूर्ण) अवस्था में : *be at a critical juncture.*

June / जून् / *noun* (संक्षि **Jun**) जून (वर्ष का छठा महीना)।

jungle / जङ्गल् / *noun* **1** जंगल **2** अ- व्यवस्थित, अस्तव्यस्त वस्तुओं की भरमार : *the concrete jungle.*

junior / जुनिअर् / *adj* **1** पद, आयु आदि की दृष्टि से छोटा, अवर : *junior doctor* **2** (खेलों में) 16-18 साल तक के बच्चों के लिए : *the national junior swimming championships.*

junk / जङ्क् / *noun* कूड़ा-करकट ▸ **junk** *verb* अमान्य कर देना; अस्वीकार करना : *Plans for new offices were uncer-emoniously junked.* **junk food** *noun* (अनौप) सेहत के लिए बेकार परंतु तुरंत तैयार होने वाला आहारा।

Jupiter / जूपिटर् / *noun* (खगोल) बृहस्पति ग्रह।

jurisdiction / जुअरिस्'डिक्शन् / *noun* **1** न्यायाधिकार : *The court has no jurisdiction over foreign diplomats.* **2** क्षेत्राधिकार (सीमा) : *come within sb's jurisdiction.*

jury / जुअरि / *noun* (*pl* **juries**) **1** जूरी, पंच **2** (प्रतियोगिता में) निर्णायक मंडल।

just¹ / जस्ट् / *adv* **1** ठीक-ठीक, बिलकुल **2** अभी-अभी, तुरंत **3 just (for sth/to do sth)** केवल : *There's just one way of saving him.* ■ **just like that** अचानक, बिना कोई कारण **just now 1** अभी **2** थोड़ी देर पहले।

just² / जस्ट् / *adj* **1** न्यायसंगत, वैध : *a just decision* **2** उचित, यथोचित ▸ **justly** *adv* न्यायसंगत/यथोचित रूप से।

justice / जस्टिस् / *noun* **1** औचित्य, इंसाफ़ : *laws based on the princi-ples of justice* **2** न्याय : *the Euro-pean Court of Justice* **3 Justice** न्यायमूर्ति, न्यायाधीश ■ **bring sb to justice** अपराध के लिए क़ैद करके क़ानूनी कारर्वाई करना **do justice to sb/sth; do sb/sth justice 1** के साथ न्याय करना **2** की क़दर करना ▸ **Justice of the Peace** *noun* मैजिस्ट्रेट।

justify / जस्टिफ़ाइ / *verb* (*pt, pp* **justified**) **1** औचित्य सिद्ध करना **2** आधार (या कारण) प्रस्तुत करना; स्पष्टीकरण देना : *seek to justify a massive jump in prices* ▸ **justifiable** / जस्टिफ़ाइ-अबल् / *adj* जिसका औचित्य सिद्ध किया जा सके; समर्थनीय : *justifiable behav-iour* **justification** / जस्टिफ़ि'केश्न् / *noun*.

jut / जट् / *verb* (**-tt-**) **jut (out) (into, over, etc sth)** बाहर उभरा हुआ, बाहर को निकला हुआ : *a balcony that juts out over the garden.*

jute / जूट् / *noun* जूट, पटसन (जिसकी रस्सी, बोरे आदि बनते हैं)।

juvenile / जूवनाइल् / *noun* (औप या क़ानून) तरुण, किशोर ▸ **juvenile** *adj* **1** तरुण से संबद्ध; तरुण-विषयक : *juve-nile crime* **2** (अपमा) मूर्ख/अपरिपक्व।

juxtapose / जक्स्ट'पोज़् / *verb* **juxta-pose A and/with B** (औप) पास-पास रखना : *juxtapose light and shade.*

Kk

kaleidoscope / कं'लाइडस्कोप् / *noun*
काँच के टुकड़ों से भरी नली का खिलौना जिसे
घुमाने से विभिन्न प्रकार की रंग-बिरंगी
आकृतियाँ दिखाई देती हैं।

kangaroo / ˌकैङ्ग्'रू / *noun (pl kan-*
garoos) कंगारू।

karate / कं'राटि / *noun* बिना शस्त्र के
आत्मरक्षा की जापानी पद्धति, कराटे।

keel / कील् / *noun* जहाज के ढाँचे का
लकड़ी-लोहे का आधार ▸ **keel** *verb*
■ **keel over** 1 जहाज का उलट जाना
2 *(अनौप)* गिर पड़ना।

keen / कीन् / *adj* (**-er, -est**) 1 *(अनौप)*
keen on sb/sth में रुचि रखने वाला,
शौकीन : *keen on (playing) tennis*
2 **keen (to do sth/that...)** उत्साही,
उत्सुक (व्यक्ति) : *keen to develop new*
trade links 3 (भावनाएँ आदि) उत्कट,
गंभीर 4 (ज्ञानेंद्रियाँ) संवेदनशील, प्रखर-
बुद्धि 5 तीक्ष्ण, पैना; नुकीला : *a keen*
blade ▸ **keenly** *adv* **keenness**
noun.

keep¹ / कीप् / *verb* (*pt, pp* **kept**
/ केप्ट् /) 1 रखना, पास रखना 2 (नियमों
का) पालन करना; (व्रत-उपवास) रखना;
(वादा) निभाना : *keep an appointment/*
a promise 3 भरण-पोषण करना : *He*
scarcely earns enough to keep him-
self and his family. 4 देख-रेख करना,
पालन करना : *keep bees/goats* 5 रिकार्ड/
हिसाब-किताब रखना : *keeping an ac-*
count of one's expenses 6 छिपाना,
गुप्त रखना : *keep a secret* 7 (स्थिति/
दिशा/स्थान विशेष को) बनाए रखना : *keep*
calm in an emergency 8 कोई प्रक्रिया
करते/होते रहना : *keep smiling/walk-*
ing ■ **keep hold of** न जाने देना **keep**
house गृहस्थी चलाना **keep in mind**
याद रखना **keep off sth** दूर रखना, परहेज़
करना; (पूछने पर भी) उस विषय को टाल

देना **keep one's feet (balance)** संतुलन
बनाए रखना; न गिरना **keep one's**
temper शांत रहना **keep (sb) at sth**
निरंतर करते रहना **keep (sb/sth) away**
(from sb/sth) दूर रहना, अलग रहना
keep up with (sb/sth) उसी तरह से कार्य
करते रहना **keep watch (for sb/sth)**
सतर्क रहना।

keep² / कीप् / *noun* भरण-पोषण, गुज़ारा :
It's time you got a job to earn your
keep. ■ **for keeps** *(अनौप)* स्थायी रूप
से : *Can I have it for keeps or do*
you want it back?

keeper / 'कीपर् / *noun* 1 रक्षक, पालक
2 (समास में) प्रबंधक : *a shopkeeper*
○ *a gamekeeper.*

keeping / 'कीपिङ् / *noun* ■ **in/out of**
keeping (with sth) मेल बेमेल से रहना।

keepsake / 'कीप्सेक् / *noun* यादगार,
स्मृतिचिह्न।

kennel / 'केन्ल् / (*US* **doghouse** भी)
noun कुत्ताघर।

kerb (*US* **curb**) / कर्ब् / *noun* सड़क के
किनारे पर उठा हुआ पत्थर या पटरी का
किनारा।

kernel / 'कर्न्ल् / *noun* 1 (अखरोट,
बादाम आदि की) गरी, मींगी 2 समस्या या
विषय का केंद्र : *the kernel of her*
argument.

kerosene (**kerosine** भी) / 'केरसीन् /
noun मिट्टी का तेल।

ketchup / 'केचप् / (विशेषत: *US* **catsup**
/ 'कैट्सप् / भी) *noun* कैचप, टमाटरों से
बनी एक तरह की स्वादिष्ट चटनी।

kettle / 'केट्ल् / *noun* केतली : *an*
electric kettle.

key¹ / की / *noun* 1 चाबी, ताली; घड़ी
कूकने की घुंडी 2 (संगीत) सुर, स्वर : *a*
sonata in the key of E flat major
3 कुंजी (पियानो, टाइपराइटर आदि की) :

function keys on a computer key-board.

key² / की / *adj* अत्यावश्यक, अति महत्त्व-पूर्ण : *a key figure in the dispute.*

keyboard / 'कीबॉर्ड / *noun* (टाइपराइटर या कंप्यूटर का) कुंजी-पटल।

keynote / 'कीनोट् / *noun* (संगीत में) मूल स्वर; (भाषण या पुस्तक की) केंद्रीय विषय वस्तु : *a keynote speech.*

kick¹ / किक् / *verb* 1 ठोकर मारना, लात मारना 2 (फुटबाल में) अंक अर्जित करना ■ **kick off** (फुटबाल के खेल में) खेल का प्रारंभ करना **kick sth off** (ठोकर मारकर) फेंक देना **kick the bucket** (अप) मृत्यु हो जाना **kick up a row** (अनौप) उपद्रव मचाना।

kick² / किक् / *noun* 1 ठोकर/लात मारने की प्रक्रिया 2 (अनौप) अत्यंत प्रसन्नता/ उत्तेजना का भाव 3 बंदूक के फ़ायर होने पर लगने वाला झटका।

kid¹ / किड् / *noun* 1 (अनौप) बच्चा 2 मेमना; मेमने का चमड़ा : *kid gloves.*

kid² / किड् / *verb* (-dd-) (अनौप) मज़ाक़ में धोखा देना, चिढ़ाना : *No kidding! It's the honest truth.*

kidnap / 'किड्नैप / *verb* (-pp-; *US* -p-) अपहरण करना, किसी को ज़बरदस्ती भगा ले जाना : *Two businessmen have been kidnapped by terrorists.* ▸ **kidnap** *noun* अपहरण **kidnapping** *noun.*

kidney / 'किड्नि / *noun* (*pl* kidneys) गुरदा, वृक्क; भोजन के रूप में भेड़, बैल का गुरदा।

kill / किल् / *verb* 1 मारना/मरवाना 2 नष्ट करना; ख़त्म करना : *kill sb's affection/ interest* 3 (अनौप) असफल करवाना/ अस्वीकार कराना : *kill an idea/pro-posal* ■ **kill time** प्रतीक्षा करते समय कुछ करना **kill two birds with one stone** एक तीर से दो शिकार; एक पंथ, दो काज ▸ **kill** *noun* 1 मारने की क्रिया 2 शिकार :

lions feeding on their kill **killing** *noun, adj.*

kiln / किल्न् / *noun* भट्ठी, आवाँ : *lime kiln ○ brick kiln.*

kilo- *pref* (पूर्वपद) = 1000 : *kilogram ○ kilometre.*

kilt / किल्ट् / *noun* किल्ट, घुटनों तक लटकता चुनट वाला स्कर्ट जैसा वस्त्र जिसे पारंपरिक उत्सवों में स्कॉटलैंड के पुरुष पहनते हैं।

kin / किन् / *noun* (अप्र या औप) रिश्तेदार, सगे-संबंधी ■ **next of kin** निकटतम संबंधी।

kind¹ / काइन्ड् / *noun* 1 प्रकार; जाति : *fruits of various kinds* 2 वर्ग; भाँति : *They differ in size but not in kind.* ■ **in kind** (भुगतान) वस्तुओं द्वारा, न कि रुपये से।

kind² / काइन्ड् / *adj* (-er, -est) 1 **kind (to sb/sth)** कृपालु, दयालु 2 कृपापूर्ण (नम्र निवेदन में प्रयुक्त) ▸ **kindliness** *noun* **kindly** *adv* 1 कृपा/दयापूर्वक : *treat sb kindly* 2 (नम्र निवेदन में) कृपया : *Kindly leave me alone!* **kindly** *adj* (-ier, -iest) संवेदना/अनु-ग्रह के साथ : *give sb some kindly advice.*

kindergarten / 'किन्डर्गार्टन् / *noun* बहुत छोटे बच्चों के लिए स्कूल।

kindle / 'किन्डल् / *verb* 1 (भावनाएँ, आशाएँ) उभारना, उकसाना : *kindle hopes/ anger* 2 आग सुलगाना, जलाना ▸ **kin-dling** *noun* जलाऊ लकड़ी।

kindness / 'काइन्ड्नस् / *noun* दया, दयालुता।

kindred / किन्ड्रड् / *noun* (अप्र या औप) परिवार संबंधी/संबंध; सभी कुटुंबी/परिवार के सदस्य : *Most of his kindred still live in Ireland.* ▸ **kindred** *adj* (औप) 1 (अप्र) संबंधित, एक ही उद्भव वाले : *kindred families* 2 सदृश।

king / किङ् / *noun* 1 राजा 2 (समास में)

जाति का सबसे बड़ा प्रकार : *a king cobra*
▸ **kingly** *adj* भव्य, राजोचित।

kingdom / 'किङ्डम् / *noun* 1 (राजा या रानी से शासित) राज्य 2 भौतिक जगत के तीन बड़े विभाजन : *the animal, plant/ vegetable and mineral kingdoms.*

kink / किङ्क् / *noun* 1 धागे, रस्सी आदि में पड़ने वाला बल (ऐंठन) 2 (प्राय: *अपमा*) सनक, झक : *straighten out the kinks in one's psyche* ▸ **kink** *verb* ऐंठन पड़ना/डालना।

kinship / 'किन्शिप् / *noun* पारिवारिक संबंध, रिश्तेदारी 2 समान उद्भव के कारण निकट संबंध की भावना।

kiosk / 'कीऑस्क् / *noun* सार्वजनिक टेलिफ़ोन गृह; सड़क या स्टेशन पर अख़बार, सिगरेट आदि बेचने के लिए छोटी दुकान।

kiss / किस् / *verb* चुंबन करना, चूमना
▸ **kiss** *noun* चुंबन।

kit / किट् / *noun* 1 (सिपाही, नाविक या यात्री का) पूरा सामान 2 कारीगर के सभी उपयोगी औज़ार 3 विशेष कार्य में प्रयुक्त औज़ार और उपकरण : *a first-aid kit.*

kitchen / 'किचिन् / *noun* रसोई (घर)
▸ **kitchenware** *noun* रसोई के उपकरण/ बरतन।

kite / काइट् / *noun* 1 चील 2 पतंग, कनकौआ।

kith / किथ् / *noun* ∎ **kith and kin** बंधु-बांधव, मित्र-संबंधी।

kitten / 'किटन् / *noun* बिल्ली का बच्चा, बिलौटा।

kiwi / 'कीवी / *noun* न्यूज़ीलैन्ड में पाया जाने वाला एक तरह का पक्षी जो उड़ नहीं सकता।

knack / नैक् / *noun* 1 **knack (for sth/ doing sth)** कौशल, दक्षता, (अनुभवों से अर्जित) निपुणता 2 **knack of doing sth** कुछ करने की आदत या कला : *He has this unfortunate knack of always saying the wrong thing.*

knapsack / 'नैपसैक् / *noun* झोला, थैला।

knave / नैव् / *noun* (प्रा॰) बेईमान, धोखेबाज़।

knead / नीड् / *verb* 1 आटा गूँधना/मींड़ना 2 मालिश करना (दर्द आदि से मुक्ति के लिए)।

knee / नी / *noun* घुटना; वस्त्र का घुटने वाला भाग ▸ **kneecap** *noun* घुटने की हड्डी।

kneel / नील् / *verb* (*pt, pp* **knelt** / नेल्ट् / या, विशेषत: *US,* **kneeled**) **kneel (down)** घुटने टेकना; घुटनों के बल बैठना : *They knelt (down) to pray.*

knell / नेल् / *noun* (गिरजे से) धीरे-धीरे घंटे बजने की ध्वनि (किसी के मरण के समय)।

knick-knack (**nick-nack** भी) / 'निक् नैक् / *noun* (प्राय: *pl*) दिखाऊ गहना; नुमाइशी (न कि उपयोगी) वस्तु : *a collection of knick-knacks.*

knife / नाइफ़् / *noun* (*pl* **knives** / ना-इव्ज़् /) 1 चाकू, छुरा 2 मशीन या उपकरण का काटने वाला भाग।

knight / नाइट् / *noun* 1 (यूरोप में मध्ययुग में) सामंत 2 'सर' की उपाधि वाला व्यक्ति, नाइट 3 शतरंज का एक मोहरा ▸ **knight** *verb* 'सर' बनाना : *He was knighted by the Queen (for his services to the industry).* **knighthood** *noun.*

knit / निट् / *verb* (**-tt-**) 1 (ऊन आदि का) बुनना 2 **knit (sth) (together)** पक्के तौर से पास-पास लाकर जोड़ना : *The broken bones have knit (together) well.* ∎ **knit one's brow(s)** भौंहें टेढ़ी करना, नाराज़ होना।

knob / नॉब् / *noun* 1 (दरवाज़े, लाठी आदि का) गोल दस्ता, मूठ; रेडियो, टी वी आदि को समंजित करने वाला बटन, घुंडी 2 (पेड़ के तने आदि पर) गोल उभार, गुमठा 3 कोयले, मक्खन आदि का डला।

knobbly / 'नॉब्लि / (*US* **knobby** / 'नॉबि भी) *adj* गाँठदार : *knobbly trees/carrots.*

knock[1] / नॉक् / *noun* 1 (दरवाज़े पर) खटखटाहट 2 मारने/गिरने से लगी चोट : *She fell off her bike and got a nasty* *knock on the head.* 3 (इंजिन में) खड़-खड़ाहट।

knock² / नॉक् / *verb* 1 (दरवाज़ा) खट-खटाना 2 **knock sth (against/on sth)** टक्कर मारना; ठोकर से गिरा देना; अनजाने में चोट खा लेना : *His hand knocked against the glass.* 3 (इंजिन का) खड़खड़ाहट करना 4 (डर के मारे) (दिल का) ज़ोर से धड़कना या घुटनों का काँपना ■ **knock off (sth)** (अनौप) काम करना बंद कर देना **knock sb down** किसी को मार कर/धक्का देकर नीचे गिरा देना **knock sb out** (मुक्केबाज़ी में) पछाड़ देना, हरा देना **knock sb up** (अनौप) खटखटा कर जगा देना ▸ **knockout** *noun* पछाड़ देने वाला प्रहार।

knocker / नॉकर् / *noun* दरवाज़े की कुंडी (जिससे खटखटाया जा सके)।

knoll / नोल् / *noun* गोल टीला।

knot¹ / नॉट् / *noun* 1 गाँठ 2 आभूषण की तरह प्रयुक्त रिबन की गाँठ; जूड़ा 3 (पेड़ के तने में) गाँठ जहाँ से शाखा निकलती है 4 (व्यक्तियों का) समूह ■ **tie oneself/sb (up) into/in knots** किसी विषय में बुरी तरह स्वयं उलझ जाना / किसी को उलझा देना ▸ **knot** *verb* (-tt-) 1 गाँठ बाँधना; गाँठ बनाना : *knot one's tie* 2 (पेशियों का) सख्त पड़ जाना **knotty** *adj* (-ier, -iest) 1 गाँठदार 2 उलझन पैदा करने वाला।

knot² / नॉट् / *noun* जहाज़ों की गति नापने की इकाई, समुद्री मील = 6,080 फीट।

know / नो / *verb* (*pt* knew / न्यू; *US* नू /; *pp* known / नोन् /) 1 जानना, समझना 2 परिचित होना, पहचानना : *I know Jaipur well.* 3 सुनिश्चित होना; व्यक्तिगत अनुभव रखना ■ **be known to sb** परिचित होना/जानकारी रखना या होना **know sb/ sth inside out; know sb/sth like the back of one's hand** बहुत अच्छी तरह एवं पूर्ण रूप से जानना/परिचित होना **know which side one's bread is buttered** (अनौप) अपने लाभ की बात जानना **let sb know** सूचित करना/जानकारी देना ▸ **know-how** *noun* (अनौप) कौशलपरक जानकारी।

knowing / नोइङ् / *adj* जानकार, चतुर ▸ **knowingly** *adv* जान बूझकर।

knowledge / नॉलिज् / *noun* 1 ज्ञान, बोध 2 ज्ञात विषय, जानकारी ▸ **knowledgeable** *adj*.

knuckle / नकल् / *noun* पोर (अँगुली की गाँठ); (जानवर का) टखना/घुटना ▸ **knuckle** *verb* ■ **knuckle down to sth** (अनौप) कठिन परिश्रम करना **knuckle under (to sb/sth)** (अनौप) अधीर होना, झुकना : *knuckle under to threats.*

koala / को'आला / (**koala bear** भी) *noun* ऑस्ट्रेलिया में पाया जाने वाला (भालू की तरह दिखने वाला) एक छोटा जंतु जो पेड़ों पर रहता है।

Koran (Qur'an भी) / क'रान् / *noun* **the Koran** [*sing*] कुरान शरीफ़ ▸ **Koranic** *adj*.

Ll

label / 'लेबल् / noun 1 लेबल, किसी वस्तु पर चिपका/लगा काग़ज़ या धातु का टुकड़ा जिस पर वस्तु का नाम/दाम आदि लिखा हो 2 किसी व्यक्ति/समूह के लिए प्रयुक्त शब्द या पदबंध : apply a label to sb/sth ▸ label verb (-ll-; US -l-) लेबल लगाना।

laboratory / ल'बॉरट्रि; US 'लैब्रटॉरी / noun (pl laboratories) (प्राय:वैज्ञानिक अध्ययन के लिए) प्रयोगशाला।

laborious / ल'बॉरिअस् / adj 1 (कार्य) परिश्रम की आवश्यकता वाला 2 (व्यक्ति) अध्यवसायी; गंभीरता से प्रयत्न करने वाला; श्रमपूर्ण : a laborious style of writing.

labour¹ (US labor) / 'लेबर / noun 1 श्रम, मेहनत 2 (प्राय: pl) (औप) कार्य; कार्यकृति : see the fruits of one's labours 3 श्रमिक, मज़दूर वर्ग 4 [sing] प्रसव 5 Labour (संक्षि Lab) ब्रिटेन में लेबर पार्टी (समाजवादी पार्टी)।

labour² (US labor) / 'लेबर / verb 1 मेहनत करना 2 कठोर प्रयत्न करना ■ labour under sth (मिथ्या कल्पना अथवा धारणा से) कष्ट झेलना ▸ labourer (US laborer) noun मज़दूर, श्रमिक।

labyrinth / 'लैबरिन्श् / noun भूल-भुलैया ▸ labyrinthine adj.

lace / लेस् / noun 1 लेस, जाली 2 फ़ीता, डोरी; किनारी ▸ lace verb lace (sth) up डोरी या फ़ीता बाँधना : lace one's shoes up lacy adj लेस का या लेस जैसा।

lack / लैक् / verb के बिना रहना; पर्याप्त से कम होना : lack ambition ■ be lacking अभाव होना : Money for the project is still lacking. ▸ lack noun आवश्यकता, कमी : a lack of confidence.

laconic / ल'कॉनिक् / adj संक्षिप्त रूप में : a laconic remark ▸ laconically adv.

lacquer / 'लैकर / noun रोग़न, एक प्रकार की वार्निश ▸ lacquer verb रोग़न/वार्निश लगाना : a lacquered table.

lad / लैड् / noun लड़का, किशोर; छोकरा।

ladder / 'लैडर / noun 1 (बाँस आदि की) सीढ़ी 2 प्रगति के सोपान/अवस्थाएँ : climbing the ladder of success 3 (स्त्रियों के) मोज़ों में उघड़ा हुआ अंश ▸ ladder verb (मोज़े) उघड़ जाना।

laden / 'लेड्न् / adj laden (with sth) से लदा हुआ : trees laden with apples.

ladle / 'लेड्ल् / noun करछी; बड़ा चमचा : a soup ladle ▸ ladle verb चमचे से परोसना।

lady / 'लेडि / noun (pl ladies) 1 महिला 2 Lady संभ्रांत; अँग्रेज़ी महिलाओं के नाम से पूर्व लगने वाला शब्द : Lady Asquith ▸ ladylike adj महिलोचित; विनम्र।

ladybird / 'लेडिबर्ड / (US ladybug) noun एक छोटा उड़ने वाला कीट (प्राय: लाल के ऊपर काले धब्बों वाला)।

lag / लैग् / verb (-gg-) lag (behind sb/sth); lag (behind) मंथर गति से चलना; औरों से पिछड़ जाना; कछुवे की चाल चलना ▸ lag (time-lag भी) noun देरी; दो घटनाओं के बीच समयांतराल : a lag of several seconds between lightning and thunder.

laggard / 'लैगर्ड / noun फिसड्डी।

lagoon / ल'गून / noun 1 समुद्री पानी की झील 2 झील या नदी के किनारे घिरा हुआ पानी : go swimming in the lagoon.

laid-back / ,लेड् 'बैक् / adj (अनौप) चिंतामुक्त, बेफ़िक्र।

lair / लेअर / noun 1 (जंगली पशु की) माँद 2 (व्यक्ति के) छुपने का स्थान।

laissez-faire / ,लेसे 'फ़ेअर / noun (फ़्रेंच) सरकार द्वारा वाणिज्य/व्यापार के क्षेत्र में हस्तक्षेप न करने की नीति।

laity /'लेअटि/ *noun* **the laity** जनसाधारण (पुरोहित वर्ग के वैषम्य में)।

lake / लेक् / *noun* झील, सरोवर।

lamb / लैम् / *noun* 1 मेमना; मेमने का गोश्त 2 (अनौप) (व्यक्ति) निरीह, दया का पात्र : *You poor lamb!*

lame / लेम् / *adj* 1 लँगड़ा, पंगु 2 (दलील, तर्क/बहाना आदि) कमज़ोर एवं अविश्वस- नीय : *That was a pretty lame ex- cuse.* ▸ **lamely** *adv* **lameness** *noun.*

lament / ल'मेन्ट् / *verb* (औप) विलाप करना, शोक प्रकट करना : *He lamented the decline in standards.* ▸ **lament** *noun* 1 विलाप, शोक 2 शोकगीत : *a funeral lament* **lamentation** *noun* विलाप; शोक प्रकट करना।

laminated /'लैमिनेटिड्/ *adj* 1 (लकड़ी, प्लास्टिक आदि की) पतली तहें जोड़कर बनाई गई : *a laminated table top* 2 (वस्तु) पारदर्शी पन्नी चढ़ाई हुई।

lamp / लैम्प् / *noun* 1 लैंप, दीया/चिराग़ : *a street/table lamp* 2 विकिरण उत्पन्न करने वाला विद्युत उपकरण : *an infrared/ ultraviolet lamp* ▸ **lamppost** *noun* बत्ती का खंभा।

lampoon / लैम्'पून् / *verb* सार्वजनिक निंदा करके किसी का मज़ाक़ उड़ाना ▸ **lam- poon** *noun* मज़ाक़िया लेख जो निंदापूर्ण हो।

lance¹ / लान्स; *US* लैन्स् / *noun* बल्लम (घुड़सवारों द्वारा प्रयुक्त लंबा भाला)।

lance² / लान्स; *US* लैन्स् / *verb* सर्जरी में सूई या चाकू से चीरना या काटना।

land¹ / लैन्ड् / *noun* 1 स्थल 2 (**lands** [*pl*] भी) ज़मीन, भूमि: *disputed land(s)* 3 (साहि) देश : *my native land* 4 (**lands** [*pl*] भी) विशेष प्रकार की भूमि; विशेष उद्देश्य के लिए प्रयुक्त भूमि: *waste/ derelict land* ○ *arable/grazing land* 5 भूसंपत्ति : *land for sale* ▸ **landed** *adj* भूसंपत्ति वाला **landslide** *noun* 1 भू-स्खलन, पहाड़/चट्टान का लुढ़क

जाना 2 अत्यधिक बहुमत : *win a land- slide victory.*

land² / लैन्ड् / *verb* 1 (**land sb/sth**) (**at...**) जहाज़ से भूमि पर आ जाना, उतर- ना : *We landed at Boston.* 2 वायुयान को भूमि पर उतारना 3 गिरकर/कूदकर ज़मीन पर आना।

landing /'लैन्डिङ् / *noun* 1 अवतरण, भूमि पर पहुँचने की प्रक्रिया 2 जहाज़ से उतरने का पटरा या चौकी 3 ज़ीने के अंत में समतल चौड़ी जगह : *a first-floor land- ing.*

landlady /'लैन्ड्लेडि / *noun* मकान- मालकिन।

landlord /'लैन्ड्लॉर्ड् / *noun* ज़मींदार, मकान-मालिक।

landmark /'लैन्ड्मार्क् / *noun* 1 **land- mark** (**in sth**) सीमाचिह्न (महत्त्वपूर्ण घटना, खोज आदि) : *a political/cultural landmark* 2 ऐसा निशान जो दूर से ही देखा और पहचाना जा सके।

landscape /'लैन्ड्स्केप् / *noun* स्थल- प्रकृति; स्थल-प्रकृति का चित्र : *oil land- scapes by local artists.*

lane / लेन् / *noun* 1 गली 2 यातायात नियंत्रण के लिए किया गया सड़क का विभाजन : *Don't change lanes with- out indicating.* 3 जहाज़ों, वायुयानों द्वारा नियमित प्रयुक्त मार्ग।

language /'लैङ्ग्विज् / *noun* 1 भाषा; भाषा शैली 2 किसी विशेष वर्ग द्वारा प्रयुक्त भाषा (शैली): *the language of sci- ence/courtroom* 3 भाषा-विशेष : *the English language* 4 (कंप्यूटर) प्रोग्राम लिखने के लिए प्रयुक्त शब्द, चिह्न, नियम आदि : *a new programming lan- guage.*

languid /'लैङ्ग्विड् / *adj* शिथिल, नि- रुत्साह : *a languid wave of the hand.*

languish /'लैङ्ग्विश् / *verb* (औप) 1 शिथिल/कमज़ोर होना 2 **languish** (**in sth**) किसी को लंबे समय तक दुख में रहने/

दिन काटने के लिए बाध्य करना : *lan-guishing in a foreign jail.*

languor / 'लैङ्गर् / *noun* उदासीनता, दुर्बलता, क्लांति ▸ **languorously** *adv.*

lank / लैङ्क् / *adj* (प्राय: *अप्रमा*) (बाल) लंबे और सीधे, न कि घुंघराले (अनाकर्षक)
▸ **lanky** *adj* (-ier, -iest) (व्यक्ति) लंबा एवं दुबला, छरहरा : *a lanky teenager.*

lantern / 'लैन्टर्न् / *noun* लालटेन।

lap¹ / लैप् / *noun* गोद।

lap² / लैप् / *noun* 1 दौड़ में ट्रैक का एक चक्कर 2 यात्रा का एक भाग : *The next lap takes us into the mountains.*

lap³ / लैप् / *verb* (-pp-) 1 **lap sth (up)** (विशेषत: पशुओं का) लप-लप कर पानी पीना (जैसे बिल्ली करती है) 2 (पानी की लहरों का) छप-छप करते हुए किनारे से टकराना : *waves lapping on the beach* ■ **lap sth up** (अनौप) आतुरता से स्वीकारना/लेना।

lapel / ल'पेल् / *noun* कोट, जैकिट आदि के गरेबान का सामने का मुड़ा हुआ भाग।

lapse / लैप्स् / *noun* 1 चूक, मामूली भूल 2 **lapse (from sth) (into sth)** उचित से हटकर ग़लत व्यवहार : *the inevitable lapse into petty crime* 3 समय का बीतना; (समय का) अंतराल : *after a lapse of six months* ▸ **lapse** *verb* 1 (संधि/समझौता) अवैध हो जाना 2 **lapse into sth** अपनी स्थिति को न बनाए रखना, अवनति होना : *lapse into silence* ○ *The building has lapsed into decay.*

larceny / 'लार्सनि / *noun* (क़ानून) (पूर्व में) चोरी।

lard / लाई / *noun* सूअर की चरबी।

larder / 'लार्डर् / *noun* (पूर्व में) खाने का भंडार : *stock the larder.*

large / लार्ज / *adj* (-r, -st) 1 बड़ा, विशाल 2 व्यापक, विस्तृत ■ **by and large** सामान्यतया; अधिकांशतया **larger than life** (आकार, व्यवहार आदि) अतिशयोक्तिपूर्ण ▸ **large** *noun* ■ **at large** 1 सामान्यत:; कुल मिलाकर : *the opinion of students at large* 2 (अपराधी, ख़तरनाक जानवर) स्वतंत्र, मुक्त ▸ **largely** *adv* अधिकांश: **largeness** *noun* **large-scale** *adj* बड़े पैमाने पर, बड़ी मात्रा/संख्या में।

lark / लार्क् / *noun* एक छोटी गाने वाली चिड़िया।

larva / 'लार्वा / *noun* (*pl* **larvae** / 'लार्वी /) अंडे से तुरंत निकला हुआ कीड़ा, लार्वा।

laryngitis / लैरिन्'जाइटिस् / *noun* (चिकि) स्वर-यंत्र का सूजन।

laser / 'लेज़र् / *noun* लेज़र, तीव्र एवं नियंत्रित प्रकाश किरणे उत्पन्न करने वाला यंत्र।

lash¹ / लैश् / *verb* 1 (व्यक्ति अथवा पशु को) कोड़े लगाना 2 (लहरें, वर्षा आदि को) थपेड़े मारना, ज़ोर से मारना/टकराना : *rain lashing (down) on the roof* 3 (क्रोध से) उत्तेजित होकर हिलना या हिलाना : *a tiger lashing its tail angrily* 4 **lash A to B** कसकर रस्सी से बाँधना ■ **lash out (at sb/sth)** किसी पर अचानक उग्र रूप से हमला करना (शारीरिक रूप से अथवा शब्दों से)।

lash² / लैश् / *noun* 1 (eyelash) बरौनी 2 चाबुक, कोड़ा।

lass / लैस् / (**lassie** / 'लैसि / भी) *noun* (विशेषत:स्कॉटलैंड, उत्तरी इंग्लैंड में) लड़की, किशोरी; प्रेयसी।

lasso / लै'सू; *US* 'लैसो भी / *noun* (*pl* **lassos** या **lassoes**) कमंद, रस्सी का फंदा जिसे फेंककर पशुओं को फँसाते हैं ▸ **lasso** *verb* कमंद से पशु को पकड़ना।

last¹ / लास्ट; *US* लैस्ट् / *noun* **the last** (*pl* अपरिवर्तित) 1 अंतिम (व्यक्ति या वस्तु) 2 अंत में उल्लिखित व्यक्ति या वस्तु ■ **at (long) last** अंत में, बहुत प्रतीक्षा के बाद, आखिरी बचा हुआ।

last² / लास्ट; *US* लैस्ट् / *adj* 1 अंतिम, आख़िरी/पिछला 2 हाल का ही; सबसे अभि-नव : *last night/week* 3 आख़िरी बचा

हुआ ■ **be on one's/its last legs** लगभग बेकार और क्षीणशक्ति **the day, week, month, etc, before last** पिछले दिन इत्यादि से तुरंत पहले वाला दिन आदि ▸ **lastly** adv अंत में, आख़िरकार।

last³ /लास्ट्; US लैस्ट्/ verb 1 **last (for) sth** बने रहना : The war lasted (for) five years. 2 **last (out); last (for) sth** पर्याप्त होना 3 **last sth (out)** कुछ सहन करके बने/बचे रहना : He's very ill and probably won't last (out) the night. ▸ **lasting** adj टिकाऊ; स्थायी।

last⁴ /लास्ट्; US लैस्ट्/ adv अन्य सब के बाद : He came last in the race.

latch / लैच् / noun 1 (दरवाज़े की) सिटकिनी 2 खटकेदार ताला, लैच ▸ **latch** verb सिटकिनी से बंद करना।

late¹ / लेट् / adj (-r, -st) 1 निर्धारित या सामान्य समय के बाद, देर का 2 (समय) परवर्ती, समयावधि के अंत में : in the late afternoon 3 (superlative में) (सबसे) हाल का : the latest craze/fashion 4 भूतपूर्व, मृत ■ **at (the) latest** निर्धारित समय या तिथि तक।

late² / लेट् / adv 1 देर से : get up late 2 समयावधि के अंत में ■ **of late** हाल में ▸ **later (later on** भी) adv बाद में।

lately / लेट्लि / adv हाल में : Have you seen her lately?

latent / लेटन्ट् / adj निहित, प्रच्छन्न (जो है तो किंतु सक्रिय न होने के कारण प्रकट नहीं है) : latent abilities/talent/energy.

lathe / लेद् / noun ख़राद मशीन।

lather / लादर्; US लैदर् / noun झाग, फेन ▸ **lather** verb झाग बनाना; झाग से ढकना : Soap will not lather in sea water.

Latin / लैटिन्; US लैटन् / noun प्राचीन रोम की भाषा, लैटिन ▸ **Latin** adj लैटिन-विषयक; लैटिन से निकली भाषाएँ बोलने वाले लोग, जैसे फ्रेंच, इतालवी, पुर्तगाली आदि।

latitude / लैटिट्यूड्; US लैटिटूड्/ noun 1 (भूगोल) अक्षांश (भूमध्यरेखा के समांतर उत्तर या दक्षिण की रेखाएँ) 2 **latitude (in sth/to do sth)** कार्य करने या सम्मति देने की स्वतंत्रता/छूट; उदारता : They allow their children for too much latitude.

latrine / ल'ट्रीन् / noun प्रायः कैंप या सार्वजनिक स्थानों पर भूमि में गड्ढा खोदकर बनाया गया शौचालय, पाख़ाना।

latter / लैटर् / adj (औप) अवधि के अंत से संबद्ध ▸ **the latter** noun, adj दो उल्लेखों में परवर्ती।

lattice / लैटिस् / (**lattice-work** भी) noun जाली, झँझरी।

laugh / लाफ़्; US लैफ़् / verb हँसना ■ **laugh in sb's face** खुलकर किसी के प्रति अवज्ञा दिखाना **laugh sth off** हँसकर किसी तथ्य की महत्ता अस्वीकार करना ▸ **laugh** noun 1 हँसी 2 (अनौप) हँसी का पात्र व्यक्ति या हास्यजनक घटना **laughable** / लाफ़्बुल् / adj हास्यजनक, उपहास के योग्य **laughing** adj प्रसन्नता व्यक्त करता हुआ; हँसमुख **laughing-stock** noun (विशेषतः sing) हँसी/उपहास का पात्र।

laughter / लाफ़्टर् / noun हँसी : roar with laughter.

launch¹ / लॉन्च् / verb 1 (किसी नए कार्य का) प्रारंभ करना 2 नए जहाज़ को जल में उतारना 3 (आक्रमण/योजना) आरंभ करना : launch a campaign/an appeal 4 आक्रमण/प्रहार करना; (प्रक्षेपास्त्र आदि) छोड़ना : launch a missile/rocket ▸ **launch** noun नई वस्तु का लाया जाना : a book launch.

launch² / लॉन्च् / noun लाँच, मुसाफ़िरों को ले जाने वाली पेट्रोल आदि से चलित बड़ी नौका।

launder / लॉन्डर्/ verb 1 (औप) कपड़े धोना और इस्त्री करना 2 काले धन को विदेशी बैंक में अवैध रूप से हस्तांतरित करना।

launderette (**laundrette** भी) / 'लॉन्
'ड्रेट् / noun स्थान/दुकान जहाँ लोग पैसे देकर
स्वयं मशीन में कपड़े धो सकते हैं।

laundry / 'लॉन्ड्रि/ noun 1 धोए जाने वाले
कपड़े 2 कपड़ों आदि की धुलाई का
व्यवसाय।

laurel / 'लॉरल् / noun 1 एक सदाबहार
झाड़ी 2 **laurels** [pl] (युद्ध, कला, साहित्य
में) विशेष सम्मान : She won laurels
for her first novel.

lava / 'लावा / noun लावा, ज्वालामुखी से
बहा पिघला हुआ द्रव; चट्टान के रूप में जमा
हुआ लावा।

lavatory / 'लैवट्रि; US 'लैवटॉरि / noun
(pl **lavatories**) शौचालय।

lavender / 'लैवन्डर्/ noun 1 खुशबूदार
फूलों वाली एक झाड़ी; इसके सुखाए गए फूल
एवं उनकी खुशबू 2 हलका बैंगनी रंग।

lavish / 'लैविश्/ adj 1 **lavish (in/with
sth)** मुक्तहस्त, उदार 2 (विस्तार में) बहुत
बड़ा; (गुण में) अत्यधिक; फ़जूलखर्च ▸ **lavish** verb ■ **lavish sth on/upon sb/
sth** उदारतापूर्वक देना, खुले हाथ से खर्च
करना : lavish gifts on sb ▸ **lavishly**
adv.

law / लॉ / noun 1 (**the law** भी) विधि
व्यवस्था 2 क़ानून, विधि 3 विधि-संहिता
4 सिद्धांत; (प्राकृतिक विज्ञानों में) नियम :
the law of gravity ▸ **law-abiding**
adj नियमों/क़ानूनों का पालन करने वाला
lawcourt (**court of law** भी) noun
न्यायालय **lawful** adj वैध, क़ानूनी; क़ानून-
सम्मत **lawless** adj 1 विधिविरुद्ध :
lawless youth 2 (स्थान या देश) जहाँ
क़ानून न हों या उनका पालन/सम्मान न किया
जाता हो **lawsuit** noun मुक़दमा।

lawn / लॉन् / noun लॉन, दूब का मैदान
▸ **lawnmower** noun लॉन की घास काटने
की मशीन।

lawyer / 'लॉयर्/ noun वकील।

lax / लैक्स्/ adj (प्राय: अपमा) लापरवाह,
असावधान; (नियमों का पालन करने-कराने

में) शिथिल : a lax attitude to health
and safety regulations ▸ **laxity**
/ 'लैक्सटि / noun शिथिलता/ढीलापन।

lay¹ / ले / verb (pt, pp **laid** / लेड् /)
1 किसी सतह पर रखना/बिछाना; रखना
2 **lay sth (on/over sth)** बिछाना; किसी
चीज़ से ढकना : lay newspaper/straw
everywhere 3 अंडे देना 4 मेज़ पर
आवश्यक वस्तुएँ रखना : lay the table/
the supper ■ **lay sth aside** (औप)
1 कुछ त्याग/छोड़ देना 2 (**lay sth by** भी)
भविष्य के लिए रखना/बचाना; बचाकर रखना
lay sth down 1 (**lay it down that...** भी)
निर्धारित करना (विशेषत: नियम या व्यवस्था
का) : You can't lay down hard and
fast rules. 2 (आगे प्रयोग न करने के
लिए) रख देना : lay down one's pen/
tools **lay sth out** योजना तैयार करना।

lay² / ले / adj 1 अविशेषज्ञ (विशेषत: क़ानून
और चिकित्सा के) : speaking as a lay
person 2 गैर-पुरोहितों द्वारा पुरोहितों वाला
कार्य किया जाना : a lay preacher
▸ **layman** / 'लेमन् / noun साधारण
व्यक्ति, अविशेषज्ञ।

layer / 'लेअर/ noun (किसी वस्तु की)
तह, परत/स्तर ▸ **layer** verb तह लगाना/
परत जमाना।

layout / 'लेआउट्/ noun प्रबंध; सामान्य
योजना प्रारूप आदि।

laze / लेज़/ verb **laze (about/around)**
आलसी बने रहना।

lazy / 'लेज़ि / adj (-ier, -iest) (अपमा)
कामचोर; कम काम करने वाला/प्रयास न
करने वाला; आलसी ▸ **lazily** adv **laziness** noun.

lead¹ / लेड्/ noun 1 (प्रतीक Pb) सीसा,
लेड 2 ग्रेफ़ाइट, पेंसिल में प्रयुक्त लिखिज
▸ **leaden** / 'लेड्न् / adj 1 सीसे के रंग
वाला (धूसर/ग्रे) 2 सीसे की तरह भारी/
धीमा : a leaden heart ○ moving at a
leaden pace.

lead² / लीड् / verb (pt, pp **led**

/ लेड् / 1 नेतृत्व करना 2 मार्गदर्शन करना; आगे-आगे चलना 3 **lead (sb to sth)** किसी कार्य में अन्य से आगे होना 4 **lead sb (to sth)** प्रलोभन या उदाहरण देकर कार्य का संचालन-निर्देशन करना 5 (पथ का) किसी विशेष दिशा/गंतव्य तक लाना; रास्ता होना : *A path led up the hill.* 6 (कार्यों का) परिणाम : *Excessive drinking can lead to health problems.* 7 एक विशेष जीवन शैली रखना/होना : *lead a life of luxury.*

lead³ / लीड् / *noun* 1 (व्यवहार का) उदाहरण जो अनुकरणीय हो 2 **lead (over sb/sth)** प्रतिस्पर्धा या दौड़ में आगे वाले प्रतियोगी द्वारा प्राप्त बढ़त 3 **the lead** [*sing*] **the lead (over sb/sth)** प्रथम स्थान; सबसे आगे होने की स्थिति 4 सुराग़, सूत्र 5 विद्युत धारा प्रवाह के लिए प्रयुक्त (प्लास्टिक चढ़ा) तार 6 (नाटक आदि में) मुख्य भूमिका; मुख्य भूमिका निभाने वाला व्यक्ति।

leader / 'लीडर् / *noun* नेता; नेतृत्व करने वाला ▶ **leadership** *noun* 1 नेता होना : *leadership problems* 2 नेतृत्व।

leading / 'लीडिङ् / *adj* महत्त्वपूर्ण; मुख्य।

leaf / लीफ़् / *noun* (*pl* **leaves** / ली-व़्ज़् /) 1 पत्ती, पत्तियाँ 2 किताब का पन्ना (पृष्ठ); धातु की पतली पन्नी (विशेषत: सोने/चाँदी की) ∎ **take a leaf out of sb's book** नक़ल करना, किसी के व्यवहार की नक़ल करना **turn over a new leaf** नए सिरे से बेहतर एवं ज़िम्मेदारी से व्यवहार करना ▶ **leafless** *adj* पत्तों से रहित **leafy** *adj* (-ier, -iest) 1 पत्तीदार 2 पत्तियों की तरह; पत्तों से बनाया गया : *a leafy shade.*

leaflet / 'लीफ़्लट् / *noun* 1 छोटी हरी पत्ती 2 छोटी सीमित पन्नों वाली पुस्तिका/परिचायिका : *an explanatory leaflet.*

league / लीग् / *noun* 1 लीग, संघ 2 खेलों के लिए बनाया गया खेल-क्लबों का संघ : *the local darts league.*

leak / लीक् / *noun* 1 छेद या दरार जिससे पानी/द्रव या गैस चूता है/रिसती है : *a leak in the roof* 2 गुप्त सूचना प्रकट करने का काम : *a security leak* ▶ **leak** *verb* 1 (द्रव/गैस का) चूना, रिसना/टपकना 2 **leak sth (to sb)** गुप्त समाचार या रहस्य प्रकट कर देना ∎ **leak out** रहस्य प्रकट हो जाना : *The details were supposed to be secret but they leaked out somehow.* ▶ **leakage** / 'लीकिज़् / *noun* 1 गैस/द्रव चूना/रिसना 2 रहस्योद्घाटन **leaky** *adj* (-ier, -iest) दरार वाला।

lean¹ / लीन् / *adj* (-er, -est) 1 (व्यक्ति) दुबला-पतला 2 (गोश्त) बिना चरबी का 3 मात्रा में कम; (समयावधि) महत्त्वहीन, अनुत्पादक : *lean years* ▶ **lean** *noun* बिना चरबी का गोश्त **leanness** *noun.*

lean² / लीन् / *verb* (*pt, pp* **leant** / लेन्ट् / या **leaned** / लीन्ड् /) 1 झुकना 2 **lean against/on/upon sth** टेकना, सहारा लेना 3 **lean sth against/on sth** टिकाना, सहारा देना ∎ **lean on/upon sb/ sth (for sth)** निर्भर रहना **lean to/towards sth** के प्रति रुझान रखना ▶ **leaning** *noun* झुकाव; प्रवृत्ति **lean-to** / 'लीन टू / (*pl* **lean-tos**) *noun* सायबान, टेकदार छत।

leap / लीप् / *verb* (*pt, pp* **leapt** / लेप्ट् / या **leaped** / लीप्ट् /) 1 कूदना; छलाँग लगाना 2 (क़ीमतों, मात्रा/संख्या आदि का) अचानक और बड़ी मात्रा में बढ़ना ▶ **leap** *noun* 1 छलाँग 2 अचानक वृद्धि **leap year** *noun* फ़रवरी में एक अतिरिक्त दिन (29 February) वाला हर चौथे वर्ष पड़ने वाला वर्ष।

learn / लर्न् / *verb* (*pt, pp* **learnt** / लर्न्ट् / या **learned** / लर्न्ड् /) 1 **learn (sth) (from sb/sth)** सीखना 2 **learn (of/about) sth** मालूम कर लेना, जान लेना : *learn what it means to be poor* ▶ **learned** / 'लर्निड् / *adj* विद्वान, पंडित (व्यक्ति) **learner** *noun* सीखने

जानने वाला **learning** / 'लर्निङ् / noun अध्ययन से प्राप्त ज्ञान; जानकारी।

lease / 'लीस् / noun पट्टा, इजारा (भूमि या भवन को काम में लाने का वैधानिक अधिकार) ▶ **lease** verb **lease sth (to/from sb); lease sth out** पट्टे पर लेना या देना।

least[1] / लीस्ट् / det, indef pron (**little** की उत्तमावस्था के रूप में प्रयुक्त) कम से कम, न्यूनतम : (det) He's the best teacher, even though he has the least experience. ० (pron) That's the least of my worries.

least[2] / लीस्ट् / adv लघुतम/न्यूनतम ■ **at least 1** कम से कम; से कम नहीं : at least 3 months **2** ख़ैर **3** किसी तरह तो।

leather / 'लेदर् / noun चमड़ा; **leathers** [sing] चमड़े के कपड़े एवं अन्य सामान।

leave[1] / लीव् / verb (pt, pp **left** / लेफ़्ट् /) **1** चले जाना; स्थान/संघ आदि छोड़ देना **2** शेष रह जाना/शेष छोड़ देना : Red wine leaves a stain. **3** (गणित) शेष बच जाना : Ten minus seven leaves three. **4 leave sth/sb (behind)** लाने/ लेने को भूल जाना **5** मृत्यु के बाद परिवार रहना; **leave sth to sb** वसीयत में मृत्यु के बाद धनराशि छोड़ जाना **6** किसी स्थिति-/ स्थान-विशेष में छोड़ देना : Leave the door open, please. ■ **leave sb/sth off (sth)** छोड़ देना **leave sb/ sth out (of sth)** सम्मिलित न करना; (बाहर) छोड़ देना : Leave me out of this quarrel, please! **leave sth aside** किसी पर विशेष ध्यान न देना।

leave[2] / लीव् / noun **1** छुट्टी, अवकाश; छुट्टी/अवकाश की अनुमति : take a month's leave **2 leave to do sth** (औप) कुछ करने की आधिकारिक अनुमति ■ **by/with your leave** (औप) आपकी अनुज्ञा से **take (one's) leave (of sb)** (औप) विदाई लेना।

leaven / 'लेव़न् / noun **1** ख़मीर **2** गंभीर वातावरण को परिवर्तित करके प्रफुल्लित बनानेवाला प्रभाव ▶ **leaven** verb **leaven sth (with sth)** और अधिक प्रफुल्लित बनाना **leavening** noun.

lecture / 'लेक्चर् / noun **1 lecture (to sb) (on sth)** व्याख्यान **2** डाँट/आलोचना ▶ **lecture** verb **1 lecture (in/on sth)** (शिक्षा के लिए कक्षा में) व्याख्यान देना **2 lecture sb (about/on sth/doing sth)** डाँट लगाना, आलोचना करना : lecture one's children about smoking **lecturer** noun व्याख्याता (शिक्षक)।

ledge / लेज् / noun दीवार या चट्टान से आगे को निकला भाग।

ledger / 'लेजर् / noun बही-खाता।

lee / ली / noun [sing] हवा के झोंके से बचने का सुरक्षित स्थान : shelter in the lee of a hedge.

leek / लीक् / noun प्याज़ की तरह की एक सब्ज़ी।

leer / लिअर् / noun बुरी नज़र ▶ **leer** verb **leer (at sb/sth)** बुरी नज़र से देखना।

leeway / 'लीवे / noun व्यक्ति को कोई कार्य आदि करने के लिए दी गई छूट/स्वतंत्रता : Most people have considerable leeway in how they spend their money.

left / लेफ़्ट् / adj, adv बायाँ ■ **left, right and centre (right, left and centre)** भी) हर दिशा में; चारों ओर ▶ **left** noun **1** बाईं ओर का किनारा/छोर या क्षेत्र **2** (राज) **the Left** समाजवाद के समर्थक (वामपंथी) **left-handed** adj बाएँ हाथ से काम करने वाला **leftist** noun वामपंथी।

leftovers / 'लेफ़्टओवर्ज़् / noun [pl] बचा हुआ भोजन।

leg / लेग् / noun **1** पैर, टाँग **2** कुर्सी, मेज़ आदि की टाँग **3** क्रिकेट में दाएँ हाथ से खेलने वाले बल्लेबाज़ के पीछे बाईं ओर का मैदान ▶ **leg** verb (-gg-) ■ **leg it** (अनौप) दौड़ लगाना : leg it to the nearest telephone.

legacy / 'लेगसि / noun (pl **legacies**)

1 पैतृक संपत्ति 2 पहले रह चुके व्यक्तियों से आने वालों को प्राप्त वस्तु।

legal / 'लीगल् / adj 1 न्यायसंगत, वैध 2 क़ानूनन आवश्यक/ज़रूरी ▸ **legality** / ली'गैलिटि / noun वैधता : *challenge the legality of sth in the courts* **legalize, -ise** / 'लीगलाइज़् / verb वैध या न्यायसंगत बनाना : *legalize abortion* **legally** adv क़ानूनन।

legend / 'लेजन्ड् / noun 1 पुराणकथा, आख्यान, दंत-कथा 2 (अनौप) अत्यधिक प्रसिद्ध व्यक्ति (क्षेत्र-विशेष में) : *a cinema legend* 3 नक़्शे की कुंजी ▸ **legendary** adj 1 (अनौप) सुप्रसिद्ध/विख्यात 2 कथाओं में होने के कारण प्रसिद्ध : *legendary heroes.*

leggings / 'लेगिङ्ज़् / noun [pl] महिलाओं की तंग/चुस्त पतलून।

legible / 'लेजबल् / adj सुवाच्य; (लिखा या छपा) सुपाठ्य ▸ **legibility** noun **legibly** / 'लेजिब्लि / adv.

legion / 'लीजन् / noun 1 दूसरे देश की सेना में भर्ती स्वैच्छिक सैनिकों की टुकड़ी : *the French Foreign Legion* 2 प्राचीन रोमन सेना में 3000 से 6000 की टुकड़ी ▸ **legion** adj (साहि) बहुत अधिक।

legislate / 'लेजिस्लेट् / verb **legislate (for/against/on sth)** विधि या क़ानून बनाना : *legislate against discrimination in the workplace* ▸ **legislation** / लेजिस्'लेश्न् / noun विधान; विधान तैयार करने की प्रक्रिया **legislative** / 'लेजिस्लटिव् / adj विधायी : *a legislative assembly/council* **legislator** / 'लेजिस्लेटर् / noun विधान सभा का सदस्य, विधायक **legislature** / 'लेजिस्ले-चर् / noun (औप) विधान-मंडल : *the U.P. legislature.*

legitimate / लि'जिटिमट् / adj 1 युक्ति-संगत; औचित्यपूर्ण 2 वैध, न्यायसंगत 3 (संतान) औरस ▸ **legitimacy** noun **le-gitimize, -ise** verb वैध बनाना।

leisure / 'लेश़र् / noun फुरसत, ख़ाली समय ∎ **at leisure** 1 (औप) ख़ाली 2 इत्मीनान से ▸ **leisurely** adj, adv धीरे-धीरे, इतमीनान/आराम से।

lemon / 'लेमन् / noun 1 नींबू 2 हलका पीला रंग।

lemonade / लेम'नेड् / noun नींबू का पेय (शर्बत)।

lend / लेन्ड् / verb (pt, pp lent / लेन्ट् /) 1 **lend sth (to sb)** उधार देना; किराए पर देना; बैंक का धनराशि ब्याज पर उधार देना 2 **lend sth (to sth)** किसी (वस्तु) में कुछ अतिरिक्त जोड़ देना, बढ़ा देना ∎ **lend itself to sth** उपयोगी और सहायक होना **lend one's name to sth** (औप) किसी दूसरे के कार्य में समर्थन देना **lend (sb) a (helping) hand (with sth)** सहायता करना ▸ **lender** noun उधार देने वाला **lending** noun वित्तीय (वाणिज्य) व्यवस्था के लिए ऋण प्रदान।

length / लेङ्थ् / noun 1 लंबाई; (समय और स्थान की) दूरी 2 माप की इकाई के रूप में प्रयुक्त वस्तु का आकार : *I can swim 50 lengths of the school pool.* 3 एक खास लंबाई का कपड़ा; किसी वस्तु का टुकड़ा : *a length of wire* ∎ **at length** 1 (औप) अंत में, बहुत देर के बाद 2 बहुत लंबा समय लेने वाला, विस्तार से **go to any, some, great, etc lengths (to do sth)** कुछ प्राप्त करने के लिए कुछ/बहुत करने को तैयार होना **the length and breadth of sth** किसी चीज़ (या क्षेत्र) के पूरे हिस्से में ▸ **lengthen** verb लंबा करना, खींचना : *lengthen a skirt* **lengthways (lengthwise** भी) adv लंबाई में।

lengthy / 'लेङ्थि / adj (-ier, -iest) लंबा : *lengthy discussions.*

lenient / 'लीनिअन्ट् / adj उदार : *a lenient view* ▸ **leniency** / 'लीनि-अन्सि / noun उदारता **leniently** adv.

lens / लेन्ज़् / noun 1 लेंस; (भौतिकी) ताल

2 (आँख में) पुतली के पीछे पारदर्शी अंग जिससे प्रकाश समंजित होता है।

lentil / 'लेन्ट्ल् / *noun* मसूर (की दाल)।

Leo / 'लीओ / *noun* सिंह राशि; इस राशि का व्यक्ति।

leopard / 'लेपर्ड् / *noun* तेंदुआ।

leper / 'लेपर् / *noun* 1 कोढ़ी, कुष्ठरोग से पीड़ित व्यक्ति 2 दूसरों के द्वारा त्यक्त व्यक्ति।

leprosy / 'लेप्रसि / *noun* कोढ़।

lesbian / 'लेज़्बिअन् / *noun* समलिंगी स्त्री।

less¹ / लेस् / *indef det, indef pron* 1 कम 2 less (sth) (than...) तुलना में कम।

less² / लेस् / *adv* less (than...) कम; निर्धारित से कम : *less colourful.*

lessen / 'लेस्न् / *verb* कम करना/होना।

lesser / 'लेसर् / *adj* किसी अन्य से कम महत्त्वपूर्ण या महान : *a lesser offence.*

lesson / 'लेस्न् / *noun* 1 पाठ; पाठ की अवधि 2 lesson (to sb) सबक, शिक्षा; चेतावनी।

lest / लेस्ट् / *conj* (औप) 1 ऐसा न हो कि, कहीं ऐसा न हो जाए 2 (be afraid, fear, be anxious आदि के बाद प्रयुक्त) कि : *She was afraid lest he might drown.*

let / लेट् / *verb* (-tt-; *pt, pp* let) 1 होने देना, अनुमति देना 2 अंदर आने/बाहर जाने देना 3 let sth (out) (to sb) किराए पर भवन आदि देना 4 सुझाव या आदेश देने के लिए प्रयुक्त : *Let's go to the beach.* 5 किसी बात पर ज़ोर देने के लिए प्रयुक्त : *Let the boy speak for himself.* ■ **let oneself go** अपनी भावनाओं को मुक्त छोड़ देना **let sb down** आवश्यकता के समय सहायता न करना **let sb/sth go; let go of sb/sth** छोड़ देना, पकड़े न रहना; किसी को मुक्त कर देना **let sb in on/into sth** (अनौप) राज़ या भेद का हिस्सा बँटाना **let sb off (with sth)** बिना दंड दिए अपराधी को जाने देना **let sth down** नीचे की ओर

करना **let up** (अनौप) तीव्रता/शक्ति कम हो जाना।

lethal / 'लीथ्ल् / *adj* 1 प्राणघातक : *a lethal dose of poison* 2 हानिकारक ▶ **lethally** *adv.*

lethargy / 'लेथर्जि / *noun* अकर्मण्यता, आलस ▶ **lethargic** / ल'थार्जिक् / *adj* तंद्रापूर्ण; आलसी।

letter / 'लेटर् / *noun* 1 वर्ण, अक्षर जैसे *A, B* 2 पत्र, ख़त 3 **letters** [*pl*] साहित्य; किताबें; साहित्यकार : *a man of letters* ▶ **letter-box** (*US* **mailbox**) *noun* घर/भवन के बाहर लगा डिब्बा/बक्स जिसमें चिट्ठियाँ आदि छोड़ी जाती हैं; पत्रादि डालने का डिब्बा।

lettuce / 'लेटिस् / *noun* सलाद पत्ता।

leukaemia (*US* **leukemia**) / लू'की-मिआ / *noun* एक ऐसा रोग जिसमें रक्त में श्वेत कोशिकाएँ अत्यधिक मात्रा में उत्पन्न होती हैं।

level¹ / 'लेव्ल् / *noun* 1 तल/स्तर 2 अधि-कार आदि की आपेक्षिक स्थिति/स्तर/अवस्था या मात्रा : *discussions at district/national level* 3 ऊँचाई 4 मंज़िल : *a multi-level parking lot* ■ **on the level** (अनौप) ईमानदार; वैध।

level² / 'लेव्ल् / *adj* 1 समतल 2 समान स्तर/अवस्था वाला 3 समान, बराबर ■ **do your level best** यथाशक्ति सब कुछ करना ▶ **level crossing** *noun* वह स्थान जहाँ रेल की पटरी और सड़क एक-दूसरे को समान तल पर काटती हैं **level-headed** *adj* संतुलित/समझदार व्यक्ति।

level³ / 'लेव्ल् / *verb* (-ll-; *US* -l-) 1 समतल करना/बनाना 2 समान करना; सामाजिक वर्गों को समान/बराबर करना : *level social differences* 3 भवन को पूर्णत: गिराना 4 level sth (at sb) बंदूक का निशाना लगाना ■ **level sth against/at sb** दोषारोपण करना।

lever / 'लीवर्; *US* 'लेवर् / *noun* 1 लीवर; उत्तोलक, डंडा या छड़ जिसे किसी चीज़ पर

टेककर कोई भारी चीज़ उठाई/खोली जाए 2 किसी मशीन को चलाने या नियंत्रित करने के लिए प्रयुक्त हत्था/मूठ : *the gear lever* ▸ **lever** *verb* लीवर से कुछ उठाना/चलाना।

levity / ˈलेवटि / *noun* (औप) छिछोरापन, आचरण का हलकापन; गंभीर समस्या को हलके-फुलके ढंग से निपटाने की प्रवृत्ति।

levy / ˈलेवि / *verb* (*pt, pp* levied) **levy sth (on sb)** कर (टैक्स) आदि की माँग करना और उगाहना : *levy interest charges* ▸ **levy** *noun* कर उगाहने की प्रक्रिया; उगाहा गया धन।

liability / ˌलाइअˈबिलिटि / *noun* (*pl* liabilities) 1 उत्तरदायी होना, ज़िम्मेदारी 2 (प्राय: *pl*) ऋण और अन्य व्यक्तिगत उत्तरदायित्व : *minimize one's tax liabilities* 3 (अनौप) क्षति या समस्या उत्पन्न करने वाला व्यक्ति या वस्तु।

liable / ˈलाइअब्ल् / *adj* 1 **liable (for sth)** नियम के अनुसार उत्तरदायी 2 **liable to sth** (अप्रिय अनुभव आदि मिलने की) संभावना होना; (कर, दंड आदि का) पात्र बनना 3 **liable to do sth** कुछ करने की प्रवृत्ति होना/रखना।

liaise / लिˈएज़् / *verb* 1 **liaise (with sb)** किसी के साथ बहुत निकट रूप से कार्य करना/ सूचना आदि का आदान-प्रदान करना 2 **liaise (between A and B)** दो या अधिक व्यक्तियों/समुदायों के बीच कड़ी होना।

liaison / लिˈएज़न्; US लिˈएज़ॉन् / *noun* 1 **liaison (between A and B)** संपर्क : *a liaison officer* 2 **liaison (with sb)** (कभी-कभी अपमा) गुप्त यौन संबंध।

liar / ˈलाइअर् / *noun* झूठा; झूठ बोलने वाला।

libel / ˈलाइब्ल् / *noun* 1 किसी की प्रतिष्ठा पर चोट पहुँचाने वाला कथन या लिखित बात 2 (क़ानून) इस तरह के कथन का प्रकाशन : *sue a newspaper for libel* 3 (अनौप) कोई भी अपमानजनक वस्तु या कथन ▸ **libel** *verb* (-ll-; US -l-) अपमानजनक कथन छापना; किसी व्यक्ति के संबंध में बुरी धारणा देना/फैलाना : *She alleged that the magazine had libelled her.*

libellous (*US* libelous) / ˈलाइबलस् / *adj.*

liberal / ˈलिबरल् / *adj* 1 उदार; खुले विचारों वाला 2 उदारहृदय, दानी 3 (शिक्षा) तकनीकी एवं व्यावसायिक न होकर सामान्य ज्ञान एवं अनुभव से संबद्ध 4 (राज) उदारवाद का समर्थन करने वाला ▸ **liberal** *noun* 1 उदारवादी विचारों वाला व्यक्ति 2 उदारवादी पार्टी का सदस्य **liberalism** *noun* उदारवाद, उदारतावाद **liberally** *adv* उदारता से।

liberate / ˈलिबरेट् / *verb* **liberate sb/ sth (from sth)** आज़ाद/मुक्त करना ▸ **liberated** *adj* मुक्त **liberation** / ˌलिबˈरेश्न् / *noun* [*sing*] मुक्ति : *animal liberation.*

liberty / ˈलिबर्टि / *noun* (*pl* liberties) 1 स्वतंत्रता 2 स्वेच्छाचारिता, अपनी इच्छा से करने, रहने, बोलने आदि की छूट 3 स्वच्छंदतापूर्ण कृत्य जिससे कोई नाराज़ हो सकता है।

Libra / ˈलीब्रा / *noun* तुला राशि; इस राशि का व्यक्ति।

library / ˈलाइब्ररि; US ˈलाइब्रेरि / *noun* (*pl* libraries) पुस्तकालय ▸ **librarian** / लाइˈब्रेअरिअन् / *noun* पुस्तकालय का प्रभारी, पुस्तकालयाध्यक्ष/पुस्तकाध्यक्ष।

licence (*US* license) / ˈलाइस्न्स् / *noun* 1 लाइसेंस, अनुज्ञापत्र 2 स्वतंत्रता का दुरुपयोग; नियमों, प्रथाओं की अवहेलना 3 शब्दों/प्रतीकों को बदलने या अतिशयोक्ति की स्वतंत्रता : *artistic/poetic licence.*

license (licence भी) / ˈलाइस्न्स् / *verb* लाइसेंस देना, अनुमति प्रदान करना : *shops licensed to sell tobacco* ▸ **licensee** *noun* लाइसेंसधारी व्यक्ति।

lichee (lychee भी) / ˌलाइˈची / *noun* लीची (फल)।

lick / लिक् / *verb* 1 चाटना 2 (लहरों/ ज्वाला का) धीरे-से छूना 3 (अप) आराम से हरा देना ▸ **lick** *noun* चाटने की क्रिया।

lid / लिड् / *noun* 1 (डिब्बे आदि का) ढक्कन 2 पलक।

lie¹ / लाइ / *verb* (*pt, pp* **lied**; *pres p* **lying**) 1 **lie** (**to sb**) (**about sth**) झूठ बोलना 2 झूठी धारणा देना; गुमराह करना ■ **lie through one's teeth** (*अनौप*) पूर्ण रूप से एवं अत्यधिक झूठ बोलना ► **lie** *noun* झूठ **lie-detector** *noun* ऐसा यंत्र जिससे यह पता लगाया जा सकता है कि कोई व्यक्ति झूठ बोल रहा है या नहीं।

lie² / लाइ / *verb* (*pt* **lay** / ले /; *pp* **lain** / लेन्/; *pres p* **lying**) 1 लेटना 2 लेटकर आराम करना 3 (वस्तुओं का) पड़ा रहना 4 होना; (स्थिति-विशेष में) रहना 5 किसी प्रतियोगिता में एक स्थिति-विशेष पर रहना ■ **lie in wait** (**for sb**) छुपकर प्रतीक्षा करना ► **lie** *noun* (लेटने की) स्थिति; रूप, बनावट ■ **the lie of the land**; (*US*) **the lay of the land** 1 क्षेत्र विशेष की संरचना 2 (*अनौप*) वर्तमान स्थिति **lie-in** *noun* (प्राय: *sing*) (*अनौप*) समय के बाद भी बिस्तर पर पड़े रहने की क्रिया।

lieu / लू/ल्यू / *noun* ■ **in lieu** (**of sth**) के बदले में।

lieutenant / लेफ़्टेनन्ट्; *US* लू टेनन्ट् / *noun* 1 लेफ़्टिनेंट (सेना का एक पद) 2 (समास में) दिए गए पद से ठीक नीचे वाला पद: *lieutenant-general/lieutenant-colonel.*

life / लाइफ़ / *noun* (*pl* **lives** / लाइ-व्ज़्/) 1 प्राण, चेतना जो पशु-पौधों को जड़ पदार्थों (चट्टान, पृथ्वी आदि) से पृथक करता है 2 प्राणी : *animal and plant life* 3 मानव के रूप में अस्तित्व 4 मानव जीवन की घटनाएँ, अनुभव आदि 5 व्यक्ति का जीवन; रहने का ढंग 6 जीवन, आयु (अस्ति-त्व की कालावधि) 7 जीवन चरित 8 स्फूर्ति; ज़िंदादिली : *Children are always so full of life.* ■ **full of beans/life** अति प्रसन्न, उत्साहपूर्ण **lay down one's life** (**for sb/sth**) (*साहि*) आत्म-त्याग करना ► **lifebelt** *noun* रक्षा-पेटी **lifeboat** *noun* समुद्र में डूबने से बचाने वाली नौका **life cycle** *noun* (*जीव विज्ञान*) प्राणियों तथा वनस्पतियों का जीवन चक्र **life imprisonment** *noun* आजीवन कारावास **life-jacket** *noun* डूबने से बचाने वाली जैकेट **lifeless** *adj* 1 अरुचिकर 2 निर्जीव; मृत **lifelong** *adj* आजीवन **life sciences** *noun* जैविक-विज्ञान **life sentence** *noun* आजीवन दंड **lifestyle** *noun* जीवन शैली **lifetime** *noun* आजीवन।

lift / लिफ़्ट् / *verb* 1 **lift sb/sth** (**up**) ऊपर उठाना 2 **lift sth** (**from sb/sth**) (*अनौप*) चोरी करना; किसी के विचार आदि बिना अनुमति के प्रयोग करना 3 नियंत्रण/प्रतिबंध आदि उठा लेना : *lift a ban/curfew* 4 एक जगह से उठाकर दूसरी जगह रखना : *lift a suitcase down from the rack* ► **lift** *noun* 1 (*US* **elevator**) लिफ़्ट 2 (कार आदि में) मुफ़्त सवारी 3 उत्थान; उत्थान की प्रक्रिया।

ligament / 'लिगमन्ट् / *noun* स्नायु; ऊतक जो शरीर की हड्डियों को आपस में जोड़ते हैं।

light¹ / लाइट् / *noun* 1 प्रकाश, रोशनी 2 प्रकाश स्रोत/पुंज : *switch the light on/off* 3 (नया) व्याख्यात्मक ज्ञान 4 (कला में) रंग का आपेक्षिक हलकापन : *light and shade* ■ **come** (**or bring**) **to light** (जाँच-पड़ताल के परिणामस्वरूप) विदित होना, प्रकाश में आना ► **light** *adj* (**-er, -est**) 1 उज्ज्वल, प्रकाश से पूर्ण 2 (रंग) हलका **lighthouse** *noun* प्रकाश स्तंभ, आकाशदीप।

light² / लाइट् / *verb* (*pt, pp* **lit** / लिट् / या **lighted**) 1 जलना/जलाना, सुलगाना 2 प्रकाशमय करना : *a single bulb lit the corridor* 3 (*औप*) प्रकाश दिखाकर मार्गदर्शन करना ■ **light sth up** 1 (व्यक्ति का चेहरा) चमकना, प्रफुल्लित होना 2 चम-काना, उज्ज्वलित करना।

light³ / लाइट् / *adj* (**-er, -est**) 1 हलका 2 औसत वज़न से कम 3 नाज़ुक : *light footsteps* 4 करने में आसान, (कसरत)

न थकाने वाली 5 मनोरंजन के लिए (खेल, किताबें आदि) 6 (भोजन) मात्रा में कम; सुपाच्य : *a light snack/supper* 7 (पेय, शराब आदि) हलका, कम अलकोहल वाला 8 प्रसन्न, चिंतामुक्त : *with a light heart* 9 तीव्रता में कम : *light rain* ▸ **light** *adv* कम सामान के साथ : *I always travel light.* **light-headed** *adj* चंचल, अवि-वेकी **light-hearted** *adj* प्रफुल्ल, चिंतामुक्त **lightly** *adv* 1 हलके से, नज़ाकत-से 2 बिना गंभीर विचार के : *Involvement in the conflict is not to be taken lightly.* 3 चिंतामुक्त ढंग से **lightness** *noun*.

lighten¹ /'लाइट्न्/ *verb* आलोकित करके और अधिक प्रकाशमय बनाना।

lighten² /'लाइट्न्/ *verb* 1 वज़न में हलका करना 2 कम गंभीर बना देना।

lighter /'लाइटर्/ *noun* जहाज़ से बंदरगाह तक माल ढोने की नौका।

lightning /'लाइट्निङ्/ *noun* (आकाश की) बिजली, तड़ित ▸ **lightning rod/lightning conductor** *noun* तड़ित चालक।

lightship /'लाइट्शिप्/ *noun* दीपनौका (दीपस्तंभ का काम करने वाली नौका)।

like¹ /लाइक्/ *verb* 1 पसंद करना; में रुचि रखना; से आनंद उठाना 2 (नकारात्मक वाक्यों में) नापसंद होना, करने में अनिच्छा होना : *He doesn't like asking for help.* 3 (**would, should** के साथ) इच्छा प्रकट करना : *Would you like something to eat?* ▸ **likeable** (**likable** भी) /'लाइकबुल्/ *adj* रुचिकर, रमणीय।

like² /लाइक्/ *adj* समान, सदृश/तुल्य ▸ **like** *adv* (अनौपचारिक बातचीत में यूँ ही प्रयुक्त)।

like³ /लाइक्/ *prep* 1 किसी की तरह/से मिलता-जुलता 2 किसी की शैली में; समान मात्रा में/स्तर पर : *You're behaving like children.* 3 उदाहरणार्थ : *I'm fond of modern playwrights like Pinter*

and Ayckbourn. ▸ **like** *conj* (अनौप) समान तरह से/शैली में।

likelihood /'लाइकलिहुड्/ *noun* संभावना की मात्रा/अवसर।

likely /'लाइकलि/ *adj* (-ier, -iest) 1 **likely** (**to do sth/that...**) संभावित, अपेक्षित : *a likely cause/result* 2 उचित, उपयुक्त : *a likely candidate for the job.*

liken /'लाइकन्/ *verb* ▪ **liken sth/sb to sth/sb** (औप) समानता दर्शाना।

likeness /'लाइकनस्/ *noun* समानता, सादृश्य।

likes /लाइक्स्/ *noun* [pl] पसंद की चीज़ें, रुचि : *He has so many likes and dislikes that it's impossible to please him.*

likewise /'लाइक्वाइज्/ *adv* (औप) 1 वैसा ही, वही; उसी ढंग से 2 भी : *The food was excellent, (and) likewise the wine.*

liking /'लाइकिङ्/ *noun* पसंद, रुचि ▪ **have a liking for sth** बहुत पसंद करना **to sb's liking** (औप) किसी की रुचि/पसंद के अनुसार; तृप्ति के साथ।

lilac /'लाइलक्/ *noun* 1 सफ़ेद या बैंगनी रंग के फूलों वाली एक छोटी झाड़ी 2 हलका बैंगनी रंग।

lily /'लिलि/ *noun* (pl **lilies**) कुमुदिनी, लिली।

limb /लिम्/ *noun* 1 हाथ-पैर; पंख 2 पेड़ की विशाल शाखा।

lime¹ /लाइम्/ (**quicklime** भी) *noun* चूना ▸ **lime** *verb* मिट्टी या लकड़ी का चूने से उपचार करना **limestone** *noun* चूना पत्थर।

lime² /लाइम्/ *noun* 1 काग़ज़ी नींबू 2 (**lime-green** भी) हलका हरा रंग।

limelight /'लाइम्लाइट्/ (प्राय: the **limelight**) *noun* ध्यान का केंद्र; प्रसिद्धि।

limit¹ /'लिमिट्/ *noun* 1 सीमा (स्थान या बिंदु जिसे पार न किया जा सके) 2 अधिकतम

संभव मात्रा, राशि, संख्या आदि : *a speed limit of 70 kph* ▶ **limitless** *adj* असीम, निस्सीम।

limit² / 'लिमिट् / *verb* limit oneself/sb/ sth (to sth) सीमा बाँधना/बनाना ▶ **limited** *adj* सीमित; (दृष्टिकोण) संकुचित; संकीर्ण **limited company** *noun* कंपनी जिसके मालिकों को (दिवाला निकलने पर) ऋण का एक सीमित अंश चुकाना पड़ता है।

limitation / लिमि'टेश्न् / *noun* 1 सीमा-निर्धारण 2 प्रतिबंध, बंधन : *impose limitations on imports* 3 (योग्यता की) कमी; सीमाबद्धता : *I know my limitations.*

limousine / 'लिमज़ीन्; लिम्'ज़ीन् / *noun* एक बड़ी आरामदेह महँगी गाड़ी।

limp¹ / लिम्प् / *adj* 1 ढीला, शिथिल 2 ऊर्जा/शक्ति रहित : *a limp handshake.*

limp² / लिम्प् / *verb* लँगड़ाते हुए चलना ▶ **limp** *noun* लँगड़ी चाल : *walk with a slight limp.*

line¹ / लाइन् / *noun* 1 रेखा 2 कला में रेखा प्रयोग 3 सैन्य रक्षा पंक्ति : *the front line* 4 कतार, (व्यक्तियों की) पंक्ति : *a line of people waiting at the Post Office* 5 वंशावली : *a line of kings* 6 लिखी/छपी हुई पंक्ति 7 lines [pl] अभिनेता के संवाद शब्द 8 (विशेष प्रयोजन के लिए प्रयुक्त) तार, डोरी : *a fishing line* 9 रेलवे लाइन; पटरी 10 यातायात की संगठित व्यवस्था : *an airline/a shipping line* ■ all along the line प्रत्येक चरण-सोपान पर : *He's created problems all along the line.* bring sth, come, fall, get, move, etc into line (with sb/sth) सहमत होना drop sb a line (चाहे संक्षेप में ही) पत्र लिखना in line for sth (किसी उपलब्धि) की आशा में read between the lines जो व्यक्त किया गया है उससे अधिक अर्थ निकालना; अंतर्निहित आशय निकालना।

line² / लाइन् / *verb* 1 रेखाओं से चिह्नित

करना/होना : *a lined paper* 2 रेखा बनाना।

line³ / लाइन् / *verb* अस्तर लगाना : *an overcoat lined with silk.*

linear / 'लिनिअर् / *adj* 1 रेखीय 2 लंबाई में : *linear measurement.*

linen / 'लिनिन् / *noun* 1 सूती कपड़ा 2 कपड़े से बनी चादर आदि।

liner / 'लाइनर् / *noun* जहाज़, हवाई जहाज़।

linesman / 'लाइन्ज़मन् / *noun* (खेल-कूद में) खेल के मैदान की रेखाओं का ध्यान रखने वाला निर्णायक।

linger / 'लिङ्गर् / *verb* 1 देर तक रुके रहना (जब कि और लोग चले गए हों) 2 धीरे-धीरे काम करना; धीमा होना : *linger (long) over one's meal* 3 जीर्ण-शीर्ण हो जाना ▶ **lingering** *adj.*

lingerie / 'लैन्शरि; लान्ज़'रे /*noun* अधो-वस्त्र।

linguist / 'लिङ्ग्विस्ट् / *noun* भाषाविद्, भाषाविज्ञानी; जो कई विदेशी भाषाओं का ज्ञाता हो ▶ **linguistic** *adj* **linguistics** *noun* भाषा-विज्ञान।

liniment / 'लिनमन्ट् / *noun* लेप (चोट आदि पर लगाने के लिए)।

lining / 'लाइनिङ् / *noun* 1 अस्तर 2 शरीर के अंतरंगों के ऊतक : *the stomach lining.*

link / लिङ्क् / *noun* 1 **link (between A and B)** दो वस्तुओं या व्यक्तियों को जोड़ने वाला बंध, संपर्क : *a rail link between two towns* 2 (ज़ंजीर की) कड़ी, छल्ला ▶ **link** *verb* **link A to/with B; link A and B (together)** जोड़ना; संपर्क स्थापित करना।

linoleum / लि'नोलिअम् / (*अनौप* **lino** भी) *noun* फ़र्श पर बिछाने वाला मज़बूत कपड़ा, लिनोलियम।

lint / लिन्ट् / *noun* घाव को ढकने के लिए एक प्रकार की रूई, फाहा।

lintel / 'लिन्टल् / *noun* द्वार या खिड़कियों के ऊपर लगा पत्थर, लिंटल।

lion / लाइअन् / *noun* (*fem* **lioness** / 'लाइअनेस् /) सिंह, शेर ■ **the lion's share (of sth)** सबसे बड़ा या अच्छा हिस्सा।

lip / लिप् / *noun* 1 ओंठ 2 (प्याले आदि का) किनारा : *the lip of a cup/saucer/ crater* 3 ओंठनुमा भाग ▶ **lip-service** *noun* ■ **give/pay lip-service to sth** दिखावटी अनुमोदन/आदर/प्रेम आदि ▶ **lip-stick** *noun* लिपस्टिक।

liquefy / 'लिक्विफ़ाइ / *verb* (*pt, pp* **liquefied**) द्रव में बदलना या बदल जाना : *liquefied gas.*

liqueur / लि'क्युअर् / *noun* तेज़, प्राय: मीठी, शराब जो विशेषत: भोजन के बाद ली जाती है।

liquid / 'लिक्विड् / *noun* द्रव, तरल पदार्थ ▶ **liquid** *adj* 1 द्रव रूप में : *liquid food/fertilizer* 2 स्वच्छ, उज्ज्वल 3 (*वाणिज्य*) आसानी से मुद्रा में बदला जा सकने वाला : *liquid assets.*

liquidate / 'लिक्विडेट् / *verb* 1 दिवाला निकाल देना 2 कर्ज़ा चुकाना 3 हत्या कर देना/करवा देना : *He retained power by liquidating his opponents.* ▶ **liquidation** / ˌलिक्वि'डेशन् / *noun* दिवाला।

liquidize, -ise / 'लिक्विडाइज़् / *verb* सब्ज़ी, फल आदि को पीसकर गाढ़े द्रव जैसा बनाना।

liquor / 'लिकर् / *noun* 1 शराब; मद्य 2 रस।

lisp / लिस्प् / *noun* तुतलाहट ▶ **lisp** *verb* तुतलाना, s और z का सही उच्चारण न कर पाना।

list / लिस्ट् / *noun* सूची, तालिका ▶ **list** *verb* सूची बनाना; सूची में शामिल करना : *The books are listed alphabetically.*

listen / 'लिसन् / *verb* 1 **listen (to sb/ sth)** (ध्यान से) सुनना; कान लगाकर सुनना 2 **listen (to sb/sth)** किसी की बात पर ध्यान देना : *Why won't you listen to reason?* ■ **listen in (on/to sth)**

1 रेडियो प्रोग्राम सुनना 2 (गुप्त) वार्तालाप सुनना ▶ **listener** *noun.*

listless / 'लिस्ट्लस् / *adj* निरुत्साह/ निर्जीव, इतना अधिक थका हुआ कि काम करने की इच्छा न हो ▶ **listlessness** *noun.*

literacy / 'लिटरसि / *noun* साक्षरता, पढ़ने-लिखने की जानकारी/क्षमता।

literal / 'लिटरल् / *adj* 1 शाब्दिक; (अनुवाद) शब्दश: 2 शब्द के मूल अर्थ से संबंधित 3 (*प्राय: अप्रमा*) कल्पनारहित, साधारण ▶ **literally** *adv* 1 अक्षरश: 2 (*अनौप*) पूर्णत:।

literary / 'लिटररि / *adj* साहित्यिक, साहित्य अथवा साहित्यकारों से संबद्ध।

literate / 'लिटरट् / *adj* साक्षर, पढ़-लिख सकने वाला ▶ **literate** *noun* साक्षर व्यक्ति।

literature / 'लिटरचर् / *noun* 1 साहित्य 2 **literature (on sth)** वाङ्मय, विशिष्ट साहित्य।

lithe / लाइद् / *adj* लचीला (बदन)।

litigate / 'लिटिगेट् / *verb* (*क़ानून*) मुक़दमा लड़ना ▶ **litigation** / ˌलिटि'गेशन् / *noun* (*क़ानून*) मुक़दमेबाज़ी : *run the risk of litigation.*

litre (*US* **liter**) / 'लीटर् / *noun* (*संक्षि* l) लिटर, द्रव मापने की इकाई।

litter / 'लिटर् / *noun* 1 कूड़ा-करकट 2 (पशुओं के लेटने के लिए) घास-फूस 3 पालतू जानवर (विशेषत: बिल्लियों) के लिए घर के अंदर बनाए गए शौचघर में इस्तेमाल पदार्थ 4 पशुओं के नवजात बच्चे : *a litter of puppies* ▶ **litter** *verb* कूड़े-करकट की तरह फैला रहना; **litter sth (with sth)** कूड़ा फैलाना/बिछाना, डालना।

little[1] / 'लिटल् / *adj* 1 छोटा, छोटे आकार का 2 अन्य की अपेक्षा छोटा 3 तुच्छ (न कि महत्त्वपूर्ण); हलका (न कि गंभीर) : *a little mistake/problem* 4 आयु में छोटा : *I had curly hair when I was little.*

little² /'लिट्ल् / indef det (वस्तु की) थोड़ी-सी मात्रा, अपर्याप्त : *I have little time for reading.* ▸ **little** indef pron थोड़ी-सी मात्रा : *I understood little of what he said.* **little** adv अपर्याप्त, अधिक नहीं; बस थोड़ा-सा : *He is little known as an artist.* ■ **little by little** धीरे-धीरे।

little³ /'लिट्ल् / a little indef det थोड़ी-सी मात्रा, कुछ लेकिन काफ़ी नहीं : *a little milk/sugar* ▸ **a little** indef pron 1 थोड़ी-सी मात्रा 2 (समय या दूरी) थोड़ी-सी **a little** (a little bit भी) adv कुछ हद तक।

live¹ /लिव् / verb 1 जीना, जीवित रहना 2 निवास करना : *live in Lucknow* 3 एक रीति-विशेष से रहना : *live and die a bachelor* 4 (अमूर्त वस्तुओं का) अस्तित्व में बने रहना ■ **live and let live** (कहा) सहिष्णु बनना (जीओ और जीने दो) **live on sth** 1 भोजन के रूप में लेना 2 किसी पर निर्भर रहना।

live² /लाइव् / adj 1 जीवित, ज़िंदा : *live fish* 2 चमकते/जलते हुए : *live coals* 3 सक्रिय, क्रियाशील; विस्फोट के योग्य : *several rounds of live ammunition* 4 (विद्युत तार) स्रोत से जुड़ा हुआ 5 (संगीत कार्यक्रम आदि) कार्यक्रम के दौरान ही प्रसारित (स्टूडियो में तैयार करके नहीं)।

livelihood /'लाइव्लिहुड् / noun जीविका, वृत्ति : *deprive sb of his livelihood.*

lively /'लाइव्लि / adj (-ier, -iest) 1 (व्यक्ति) प्रफुल्ल एवं सक्रिय; उत्साह से भरा 2 (स्थान या घटना आदि) आनंददायक, रुचिकर 3 फुरतीला; एक विषय से दूसरे विषय पर शीघ्रता से जाने वाला : *a lively wit/discussion* ▸ **liveliness** noun.

liven /'लाइव्न् / verb ■ **liven** (sb/sth) up सजीव/प्रफुल्लित बनना/बनाना : *Put on some music to liven things up.*

liver /'लिव़र् / noun 1 कलेजा, यकृत/जिगर (जो खून को साफ़ करता है) 2 (गोश्त के रूप में पशुओं की) कलेजी : *chicken livers.*

livery /'लिव़रि / noun 1 राजमहल आदि में नौकरों की विशेष पोशाक, वरदी 2 किसी कंपनी विशेष से जुड़े रंग, डिज़ाइन आदि।

livestock /'लाइव्स्टॉक् / noun पशुधन, लाभ के लिए पाले जाने वाले पशु।

livid /'लिविड् / adj 1 (अनौप) अत्यंत क्रोधित : *livid with rage* 2 सुरमई रंग का।

living¹ /'लिविङ् / adj 1 जीवित, वर्तमान 2 प्रयुक्त; सक्रिय : *living languages.*

living² /'लिविङ् / noun 1 जीविका : *make a good living* 2 रहन-सहन, जीवन शैली : *plain/healthy living* ▸ **living-room** noun बैठक, सामान्य कमरा **living wage** noun निर्वाह योग्य मज़दूरी।

lizard /'लिज़र्ड् / noun छिपकली।

load¹ /लोड् / noun 1 भार, बोझा 2 लदान, खेप 3 व्यक्ति/मशीन द्वारा किए जाने वाले कार्य की मात्रा 4 ज़िम्मेदारी/दुख/चिंता का बोझ : *a heavy load of guilt* 5 विद्युत जनित्र द्वारा आपूर्ति की जाने वाली विद्युत की मात्रा।

load² /लोड् / verb 1 load (up); load (up with sth); load sth/sb (up)(with sth); load sth (into/onto sth/sb) बोझा लादना; सामान लादना : *load a lorry (up) with bricks* 2 load B(into A) बंदूक में गोली, कैमरे में रील आदि भरना।

loaf¹ /लोफ़् / noun (pl loaves /लो-व्ज़् /) एक बार में पकाया जाने वाला डबल रोटी/पाव रोटी का आकार (जिससे स्लाइस काटे जाते हैं)।

loaf² /लोफ़् / verb (अनौप) समय व्यर्थ बरबाद करना, आवारागर्दी करना : *loaf around (the house all day)* ▸ **loafer** noun आवारा।

loam /लोम् / noun दोमट मिट्टी जो उपजाऊ होती है।

loan /लोन् / noun 1 ऋण, कर्ज़ 2 (औप) ऋण देना, ऋण में दी वस्तु ▸ **loan** verb

(और) loan sth (to sb) ऋण (में कुछ) देना।

loath (loth भी) / लोथ् / *adj* loath to do sth *(और)* अनिच्छुक।

loathe / लोद् / *verb* घृणा करना, नापसंद करना : *loathe the smell of fried fish* ▸ **loathing** *noun* **loathing for (sb/ sth)** घृणा **loathsome** *adj (और)* घृणित : *a loathsome disease.*

lobby / 'लॉबि / *noun* (*pl* **lobbies**) 1 प्रवेशकक्ष : *the lobby of a hotel* 2 लोगों का एक समूह जो किसी विशेष मुद्दे पर राजनीतिज्ञों को अपने प्रभाव में लाने का प्रयत्न करता है, लॉबि : *the anti-nuclear lobby* ▸ **lobby** *verb* (*pt, pp* **lobbied**) lobby (sb) (for sth) लॉबि करना **lobbyist** *noun.*

lobe / लोब् / *noun* 1 (कान की) लौ, पाली 2 शरीरांग का गोल चपटा हिस्सा जैसे फेफड़े या मस्तिष्क का।

lobster / 'लॉब्स्टर / *noun* समुद्री झींगा; गोश्त के रूप में प्रयुक्त झींगा।

local / 'लोकल् / *adj* 1 स्थानीय 2 (विशेषतः *चिकि*) (दवा) एक अंश को (न कि पूरे को) प्रभावित करती हुई, आंशिक : *a local anaesthetic* ▸ **local** *noun* (प्रायः *pl*) स्थानीय निवासी **locally** *adv.*

locality / लो'कैलटि / *noun* (*pl* **localities**) 1 इलाक़ा; मुहल्ला 2 स्थान; संस्थिति : *trying to pinpoint the ship's exact locality.*

locate / लो'केट् / *verb* *(और)* 1 स्थान पता लगाना 2 स्थान में बिठाना, स्थापित करना; स्थित करना।

location / लो'केशन् / *noun* 1 स्थान; अवस्थिति 2 फ़िल्म चित्रण का स्थान।

loch / लॉक् / *noun* (स्कॉटलैंड में) 1 पतली खाड़ी 2 झील : *Loch Ness.*

lock¹ / लॉक् / *noun* 1 ताला 2 नहर का बाँध 3 जकड़ जाने की स्थिति।

lock² / लॉक् / *verb* 1 ताला बंद करना 2 lock (sth/sb) (in/into sth); lock (sb/sth) (together) जकड़ देना; जकड़ जाना, फँस/अटक जाना, न खुल पाना : *The brakes locked, causing the car to skid.* ■ lock oneself/sb out (of sth)/ in अपने आप को/किसी को बाहर/भीतर बंद कर देना lock sth away (lock sth up भी) ताले में सुरक्षित स्थान पर रखना lock (sth) up अच्छी तरह मकान को बंद कर देना ▸ **lock-up** *noun* हवालात।

lock³ / लॉक् / *noun* (प्रायः *pl*) (बालों की) लटें, ज़ुल्फ़ें।

locker / 'लॉकर / *noun* लॉकर, बैंक आदि में सुरक्षित डिब्बा।

locket / 'लॉकिट् / *noun* लॉकेट, लटकन।

lockout / 'लॉक्आउट् / *noun* तालाबंदी।

locksmith / 'लॉक्स्मिथ् / *noun* तालासाज़।

locomotion / लोक'मोशन् / *noun (और)* गति, एक स्थान से दूसरे स्थान तक जाने की शक्ति ▸ **locomotive** / लोक'मोटिव् / *adj* गति-मान/गति संबंधी **locomotive** *noun* रेलवे इंजिन।

locust / 'लोकस्ट् / *noun* टिड्डी।

lodge¹ / लॉज् / *noun* 1 भवन के मुख्य द्वार के पास कर्मचारी के लिए बना मकान, लॉज 2 मौसम-विशेष के लिए देहात में बना मकान : *a hunting/fishing lodge.*

lodge² / लॉज् / *verb* 1 lodge sth (with sb) (against sb) ध्यानाकर्षण के लिए तथ्य, कथन आदि प्रस्तुत करना : *lodge an appeal/a protest/an objection.* 2 lodge sth (in sth) गढ़ना, जड़ना 3 किसी को रहने के लिए कमरे देना 4 lodge sth with sb/in sth (पैसा आदि) सुरक्षित स्थान पर रखना 5 lodge (with sb/at...) किराएदार के रूप में रहना ▸ **lodger** / 'लॉजर / *noun* किराएदार।

lodging / 'लॉजिङ् / *noun* 1 अस्थायी आवास 2 **lodgings** [*pl*] किराए का आवास/ स्थान : *It's cheaper to live in lodgings than in a hotel.*

loft / लॉफ़्ट् / *noun* 1 अटारी 2 चर्च में गैलरी।

lofty / 'लॉफ़्टि / *adj* (-ier, -iest) 1 *(और)*

ऊँचा एवं प्रभावशाली 2 (विचारों, उद्देश्यों आदि से) उदात्त, उच्चमना : *lofty ideals/ principles* 3 (*अपमा*) (व्यक्ति) अत्यंत घमंडी ▶ **loftiness** noun

log¹ / लॉग / noun लकड़ी का लट्ठा; कुंदा ▶ **log** verb लकड़ी के लिए पेड़ काटना : *The whole area had been logged.* **logging** noun.

log² / लॉग / (**logbook** भी) noun जहाज़ की यात्रा का वृत्तांत/हवाई जहाज़ की उड़ान का रिकॉर्ड ▶ **log** verb (**-gg-**) 1 आधिकारिक रिकॉर्ड (कार्यपंजिका) में सूचना प्रविष्ट करना : *The phone call had been logged at the police station.* 2 जहाज़ या हवाई जहाज़ यात्रा में एक निर्धारित दूरी तय करना या निर्धारित घंटे काम करना : *The pilot had logged over 200 hours in the air.*

logarithm / लॉगरिद्म् / noun (*गणित*) लघुगणक, लॉगरिथ्म्।

loggerheads / लॉगरहैड्ज़् / noun ■ **at loggerheads (with sb)** एक-दूसरे के प्रतिकूल; असहमत; संघर्षरत।

logic / लॉजिक् / noun 1 तर्कशास्त्र 2 तर्क की एक शैली विशेष : *Aristotelian logic* 3 तर्कसंगत ढंग से विचार रखना : *I fail to see the logic of his argument.* ▶ **logical** adj 1 तर्कसंगत 2 (कार्य या घटना) नैसर्गिक, तर्कयुक्त : *the logical outcome* 3 तर्कसंगत रूप से विचार करने में समर्थ **logically** adv **logician** / ल 'जिश्न् / noun तार्किक (व्यक्ति)।

logo / लोगो / noun (pl **logos**) किसी कंपनी, संघ आदि का प्रतीक-चिह्न।

loin / लॉइन् / noun 1 कमर का गोश्त 2 **loins** [pl] कमर से नीचे और जाँघों से ऊपर का हिस्सा, कटिभाग ▶ **loincloth** noun लंगोटा।

loiter / लॉइटर् / verb **loiter (about/ around)** मटरगश्ती करना; आवारागर्दी करना।

loll / लॉल् / verb 1 **loll (about/around)** आराम से लेटे रहना 2 (सिर या हाथ-पैरों

का) ढीले-ढाले अनियंत्रित लटकना ■ **loll out** (जीभ को) बाहर निकालना, लटकाना।

lollipop / लॉलिपॉप् / noun छोटी-सी डंडी पर लगी चपटी गोल मिठाई जिसे चूसा जाता है।

lone / लोन् / adj (विशेषत: *साहि*) अकेला, बिना संगी-साथी के।

lonely / लोन्लि / adj 1 अकेला, बिना साथी का 2 (स्थान) सूना, निर्जन 3 साथियों के न होने से उदास ▶ **loneliness** noun 1 अकेलापन 2 एकांत।

lonesome / लोन्सम् / adj (विशेषत: US) 1 (व्यक्ति) अकेला और उदास 2 (स्थान) सूना।

long¹ / लॉङ् / adj (**-er, -est**) 1 लंबा 2 दीर्घ 3 लंबे समय तक चलने वाला : *a long book/film* 4 (यादाश्त) अधिक ■ **cut a long story short** सीधे अपनी बात पर आना **go a long way** (किसी वस्तु का) पर्याप्त समय तक बने रहना **have come a long way** पर्याप्त प्रगति करना **in the long run** दूर के भविष्य से संबंधित ▶ **long-sighted** adj समीप की वस्तु न देख पाने वाला **long-term** adj दीर्घकालिक।

long² / लॉङ् / adv (**-er, -est**) 1 लंबे समय तक : *Long live the king!* 2 काफ़ी समय (वर्तमान से पूर्व या पश्चात) : *long ago* 3 सारा समय : *wait all day long* ■ **as/so long as** 1 इस शर्त पर 2 जब तक ▶ **long-lasting** adj दीर्घ समय तक चलने रहने वाली (वस्तु) **long-standing** adj दीर्घ समय से चलने वाली (समस्या आदि)।

long³ / लॉङ् / verb **long for sth/long (for sb) to do sth** लालायित रहना/होना ▶ **longing** noun लालसा **longingly** adv.

longhand / लॉङ्हैन्ड् / noun सामान्य लिपि (**shorthand** के विपरीत)।

longitude / लॉन्जिट्यूड्, 'लॉङ्गिट्यूड्, US 'लान्जटूड् / noun (*भूगोल*) देशांतर रेखांश, लंदन (ग्रीनिच) से पूर्व या पश्चिम में

स्थित ध्रुवीय रेखा का अंश ▸ **longitudinal** *adj* 1 देशांतर रेखीय 2 नीचे की ओर (न कि आर-पार) : *longitudinal section/strips.*

loo / लू / *noun* (*pl* **loos**) *(अनौप)* शौचालय।

look / लुक् / *verb* 1 look (at sb/sth) (ध्यान से) देखना, की ओर देखना/निगाह डालना 2 look (for sb/sth) खोजना 3 look (to sb) like sb/sth; look (to sb) as if.../as though... के समान होना, के समान लगना : *It looks like rain.* 4 दिशा विशेष को अभिमुख होना/दिखना; दिखाई देना/पड़ना : *look healthy/pale/sad* ■ look after (sb) पालन-पोषण करना look after sth रखवाली करना look ahead (to sth) भविष्य में होने वाली घटना के बारे में सोचना look down on sb/sth तुच्छ/हेय दृष्टि से देखना look forward to sth/doing sth भविष्य की किसी घटना का सुखमय चिंतन (करना); (उत्सुकता से) प्रतीक्षा करना look in (on sb/at ...) मिलते जाना : *The doctor will look in again this evening.* look into sth वास्तविकता जानने का प्रयास करना look on दर्शक मात्र बनना look out सतर्क रहना look out for sb/sth 1 ताक में रहना 2 व्यक्ति/वस्तु को खोज निकालने का प्रयत्न करना look sth over निरीक्षण करना look sth up (शब्दकोश आदि से) कुछ ढूँढ़ निकालना look through sb उपेक्षा करना look through sth दृष्टि डालना, पढ़ना look up to sb आदर करना ▸ **looking-glass** *noun* दर्पण।

look² / लुक् / *noun* 1 देखने की प्रक्रिया 2 देखने का तरीका; अभिव्यक्ति : *a look of pleasure/fear* 3 रूप-रंग; शैली 4 looks [*pl*] व्यक्ति का चेहरा और रूप-रंग : *good looks* ▸ **looker-on** *noun* (*pl* **lookers-on**) दर्शक।

lookout / लुक्आउट् / *noun* 1 पहरा देने का स्थान, चौकी 2 पहरेदार ■ be sb's

lookout *(अनौप)* उत्तरदायित्व होना : *If you want to waste your money, that's your lookout.*

loom¹ / लूम् / *noun* (कपड़ा बुनने का) करघा।

loom² / लूम् / *verb* धुँधली डरावनी छाया के रूप में दिखना; (भविष्य की घटनाओं की) धुँधली छाया प्रतीत होना : *the looming threat of a strike.*

loony / लूनि / *adj* *(अप)* पागल, सनकी।

loop / लूप् / *noun* 1 फंदा, छल्ला 2 कुंडली; विद्युत प्रवाह का पूर्ण परिपथ ▸ **loop** *verb* 1 फंदा/छल्ला बनाना 2 फंदे से बाँधना : *loop the rope round the post.*

loophole / लूपहोल् / *noun* बचने का उपाय (विशेषतः नियम/क़ानून के शब्दों के ठीक-ठीक न होने के कारण)।

loose¹ / लूस् / *adj* (-r, -st) 1 स्वच्छंद, बंधनहीन/मुक्त 2 ढीला, बहुत कसा हुआ नहीं 3 (भाषण, आचरण आदि) अपर्याप्त रूप से नियंत्रित : *a loose alliance* 4 अनिश्चित; अस्पष्ट : *a loose translation.* ▸ **loosely** *adv* ढीले-ढाले तरीक़े से; अस्पष्ट रूप से।

loose² / लूस् / *verb* 1 मुक्त करना, नियंत्रण हटा लेना 2 ढीला करना; खोल देना : *She loosed her belt.*

loosen / लूसन् / *verb* मुक्त करना/ढीला करना।

loot / लूट् / *noun* 1 लूट (का माल) 2 *(अनौप)* धन, संपत्ति ▸ **loot** *verb* लूटना : *The mob looted many shops in the area.*

lop / लॉप् / *verb* (-pp-) पेड़ की टहनियाँ छाँटना; शाखा काटना।

lopsided / लॉप्साइडिड् / *adj* असंतुलित, एकतरफ़ा : *have a lopsided view of things.*

lord / लॉर्ड / *noun* 1 पुरुष शासक; अधिपति/स्वामी 2 the Lord प्रभु; ईश्वर; ईसा मसीह 3 लॉर्ड, सामंत : *She has married a lord.* 4 Lord (ब्रिटेन में)

कुछ उच्च पदाधिकारी; कई सामंतों के नाम के आगे प्रयुक्त ▸ **lord** *verb* ■ **lord it over sb** (*अपमा*) स्वामी की तरह शासित करना; दूसरों को तुच्छ मानना।

lordship /'लॉ:ड्शिप्/ *noun* लॉर्ड या हाई-कोर्ट के जज को संबोधित करते समय प्रयुक्त शब्द।

lorry / 'लॉरि / (*US* **truck** भी) *noun* (*pl* **lorries**) लारी (वाहन)।

lose / लूज़ / *verb* (*pt, pp* **lost** / लॉ-स्ट्/) 1 खो देना, न पाना 2 दुर्घटना या मृत्यु आदि से किसी को खो देना : *He lost both his sons in the war.* 3 (भावनाओं आदि को) नियंत्रण में न रख पाना : *lose one's confidence/interest/balance* 4 **lose sth (to sb/sth)** किसी चीज़ से वंचित हो जाना; कुछ हाथ से निकल जाना 5 (घड़ी का) अत्यधिक धीरे चलना : *This clock loses two minutes a day.* 6 **lose (sth) (to sb)** (प्रतियोगिता, मुक़दमा आदि) हार जाना ■ **a losing battle** ऐसा संघर्ष जिसमें हार निश्चित दिखाई दे रही हो **lose face** सम्मान खो बैठना, अपमानित होना **lose heart** आत्मविश्वास खो बैठना **lose one's bear-ings** अपनी स्थिति के बारे में सशंकित होना; भ्रमित होना **lose one's head** अति उत्तेजित होना **lose one's mind** मानसिक रोगी हो जाना **lose one's way** मार्ग से भटक जाना **lose touch with sb/sth** संपर्क टूट जाना ▸ **loser** *noun* हार जाने वाला व्यक्ति।

loss / लॉस् / *noun* 1 कुछ खो देने की प्रक्रिया; न रख पाना 2 खोया हुआ व्यक्ति/वस्तु : *The enemy suffered heavy losses.* 3 हानि/क्षति; धनहानि; अभाव ■ **at a loss** किंकर्तव्यविमूढ़।

lost / लॉस्ट् / *adj* 1 खोया हुआ, रास्ता पाने में असमर्थ 2 चकराया हुआ/मुश्किल में 3 जिसको पुन: प्राप्त नहीं किया जा सकता : *recalling her lost youth.*

lot[1] / लॉट् / *noun* **the lot, the whole lot** (*अनौप*) सभी; प्रत्येक।

lot[2] / लॉट् / **a lot, lots** *pron* (*अनौप*) बड़ी संख्या या मात्रा ▸ **a lot of** *det* (*अनौप* **lots of** भी) बड़ी मात्रा में : *What a lot of presents!*

lot[3] / लॉट् / *noun* 1 व्यक्तियों/वस्तुओं का समूह विशेष 2 विशेष प्रयोजन के लिए पृथक क्षेत्र : *a parking lot* 3 (व्यक्ति का) भाग्य, दैवगत 4 (नीलाम आदि में) बेची गई वस्तुएँ और वस्तुओं की संख्या ■ **cast/draw lots (for sth/to do sth)** पर्ची डालकर या किसी अन्य आकस्मिकता पर निर्भर पद्धति से कोई निर्णय करना।

lotion /'लोश्न्/ *noun* शरीर पर चिकित्सार्थ या सुंदरता के लिए लगाया जाने वाला द्रव, लोशन।

lottery / 'लॉटरि / *noun* (*pl* **lotteries**) 1 लॉटरी 2 (प्राय: *अपमा*) भाग्य का खेल : *Some people think that marriage is a lottery.*

lotus / 'लोटस् / *noun* (*pl* **lotuses**) कमल का फूल।

loud / लाउड् / *adj* (**-er, -est**) 1 शोर भरा; आसानी से सुना जा सकने वाला 2 (*अपमा*) (रंग, व्यक्ति या व्यवहार) ज़ोरदार, बलपूर्वक आकर्षित करने वाले ▸ **loud** *adv* (**-er, -est**) ज़ोर-से : *Speak louder—I can't hear you.* **loudly** *adv* **loudspeaker** *noun* लाउडस्पीकर।

lounge / 'लाउन्ज् / *verb* आराम से बैठना या किसी वस्तु को टेककर खड़ा होना ▸ **lounge** *noun* आरामदेह कुर्सियों से युक्त विश्राम-कक्ष (विशेषत: होटलों आदि में)।

louse / लाउस् / *noun* 1 (*pl* **lice** / ला-इस् /) जूँ, चीलर 2 (*pl* **louses**) (*अप*) घृणास्पद व्यक्ति।

lousy / 'लाउज़ि / *adj* (**-ier, -iest**) (*अनौप*) अत्यधिक बुरा, भद्दा; घृणा/तिरस्कार व्यक्त करने के लिए प्रयुक्त : *a lousy day/ hotel.*

lout / 'लाउट् / *noun* बुरे आचरण/व्यवहार वाला व्यक्ति (विशेषत: पुरुष)।

lovable / 'लव़बल़ / *adj* प्यारा/आकर्षक; प्यार करने योग्य : *a lovable character.*

love¹ / लव़ / *noun* 1 प्रेम, प्यार 2 यौन-कर्षण, आसक्ति : *a love song/story* 3 अत्यधिक चाहत : *a love of learning* 4 (टेनिस में) शून्य अंक ■ **be in love (with sb)** आसक्त होना **fall in love** प्रेम करने लगना **make love (to sb)** प्रेम करना; संभोग करना ▸ **loveless** *adj* प्रेमहीन; निर्मोही।

love² / लव़ / *verb* 1 प्रेम/प्यार करना 2 अत्यधिक पसंद करना/आनंद उठाना।

lovely / 'लव़लि / *adj* (-ier, -iest) 1 सुंदर; आकर्षक 2 (*अनौप*) रुचिकर, प्रसन्न करने वाला : *a lovely dinner* ▸ **loveliness** *noun.*

lover / 'लव़ऱ / *noun* 1 प्रेमी 2 **lovers** [*pl*] प्रेमी-प्रेमिका 3 (समास में) शौक़ीन : *a lover of music ○ art-lovers.*

lovesick / 'लव़सिक़ / *adj* प्रेमातुर; विरही।

loving / 'लव़िङ़ / *adj* स्नेही, प्रेममय : *loving care/words.*

low¹ / लो / *adj* (-er, -est) 1 नीचा, निम्न 2 तीव्रता में नीचा/धीमा; स्तर या मात्रा में कम : *low wages/prices* 3 धीमा, कठिनाई से सुना जाने वाला : *a low rumble of thunder* 4 जो उच्च स्तर पर संगठित नहीं है; निम्न स्तरीय 5 दुर्बल, शक्ति-हीन; उदास : *in a low state of health ○ feel low* 6 ग्राम्य; सामान्य जनोचित : *low tastes* 7 (मत, किसी के बारे में विचार) निम्न, प्रतिकूल : *have a low opinion of sb* ■ **be/run low (on sth)** (आपूर्ति/सामान का) लगभग चुक जाना **lay sb low** बीमार और दुर्बल करना।

low² / लो / *adv* (-er, -est) 1 निचले स्तर या स्थिति पर/में 2 धीरे-से : *Speak lower or she'll hear you!* ▸ **low-lying** *adj* (भूमि) निचली (या समुद्रतल से कम ऊँचाई की) और समतल।

lowbrow / 'लोब्राउ / *adj* (प्राय: *अपमा*) असंस्कृत (रुचि या व्यक्ति)।

low-down / 'लोडाउऩ / *noun* **low-down (on sb/sth)** (*अनौप*) किसी से संबद्ध सूचना या उसकी वास्तविकता/सच्चाई।

lower / 'लोअऱ / *verb* 1 नीचे करना/लाना 2 कम ऊँचा करना/होना : *lower (the height of) the ceiling* 3 मात्रा/तीव्रता/स्तर में कम करना 4 **lower oneself (by doing sth)** (*अनौप*) अपनी प्रतिष्ठा गिरा देना/सम्मान कम कर देना।

lowly / 'लोलि / *adj* (-ier, -iest) विनम्र; दीन : *a lowly shop assistant.*

loyal / 'लॉइअल़ / *adj* **loyal (to sb/sth)** स्वामिभक्त, ईमानदार; निष्ठावान : *remain loyal to one's principles* ▸ **loyalist** *noun* राजभक्त (विशेष रूप से क्रांति के समय) **loyally** *adv* **loyalty** / 'लॉइ-अल़्टि / *noun* वफ़ादारी, निष्ठा; (प्राय: *pl*) अटूट स्वामिभक्ति।

lozenge / 'लॉज़िन्ज़् / *noun* एक तरह की मीठी गोली, विशेषत: दवाई युक्त : *throat lozenges.*

lubricate / 'लूब्रिकेट़ / *verb* मशीन आदि में घर्षण कम करने के लिए तेल/ग्रीस डालना ▸ **lubricant** *noun* तेल, ग्रीस आदि।

lucid / 'लूसिड़ / *adj* सुबोध; साफ़/सरल शब्दों में : *a lucid explanation* ▸ **lucidity** *noun* **lucidly** *adv.*

luck / लक़ / *noun* 1 सौभाग्य, दैवयोग से प्राप्त सफलता 2 भाग्य, नियति ■ **be in/out of luck** सौभाग्यशाली/दुर्भाग्यशाली होना **the best of/good luck (to sb) (with sth)** किसी को, जो कोई महत्त्वपूर्ण कार्य संपन्न करने जा रहा हो, शुभकामना ▸ **luckless** *adj* दुर्भाग्यपूर्ण।

lucky / 'लकि / *adj* (-ier, -iest) भाग्यशाली, शुभ : *a lucky guess/escape* ▸ **luckily** *adv* सौभाग्य से।

lucrative / 'लूक्रटिव़ / *adj* लाभदायक, फ़ायदेमंद।

ludicrous / 'लुडिक्रस़ / *adj* हास्यजनक; बेतुका : *a ludicrous idea/situation.*

lug / लग़ / *noun* (-gg-) बहुत परिश्रम और

कठिनाई से कुछ ढोना या घसीटना : *lug a heavy suitcase up the stairs.*

luggage / 'लगिज् / (*US* **baggage** भी) *noun* (यात्रा का) सामान, असबाब।

lukewarm / ˌलूक्'वॉर्म् / *adj* 1 (द्रव) गुनगुना 2 lukewarm (about sb/sth) मंद उत्साह वाला; (प्रतिक्रिया) न तो समर्थन में और न ही विरोध में : *a lukewarm reception/response.*

lull / लल् / *verb* 1 lull sb/sth (to sth) व्यक्ति/पशु को शांत/अक्रिय कर देना : *lull a baby to sleep* 2 (तूफ़ान आदि का) अक्रिय या शांत हो जाना ▶ lull *noun* शांति/ अक्रियता/मंदी की अवधि : *a lull before the storm.*

lullaby / 'ललबाइ / *noun* लोरी।

lumber[1] / 'लम्बर् / *noun* (विशेषत: ब्रिटेन में) काठ-कबाड़।

lumber[2] / 'लम्बर् / *verb* धीरे-धीरे एवं बेढंगे तरीक़े से चलना/गति करना : *A huge lorry lumbered by.*

luminous / 'लूमिनस् / *adj* उज्ज्वल, प्रकाशमान/चमकीला : *luminous paint.*

lump / लम्प् / *noun* 1 ढेला, पिंड : *a lump of clay* 2 सूजन, गुमड़ा 3 (अनौप) थुलथुल, बेढंगा या मूर्ख व्यक्ति ▶ lump *verb* lump sb/sth together (with sb/sth) (as sth) वस्तुओं अथवा व्यक्तियों को एक जैसा समझना/के साथ एक जैसा व्यवहार करना : *Can we lump all these items together as 'incidental expenses'?* ■ lump it (अनौप) कोई अन्य उपाय न होने के कारण किसी अप्रिय बात को स्वीकार कर लेना या मान लेना ▶ lump sum *noun* एकमुश्त (भुगतान) **lumpy** *adj.*

lunacy / 'लूनसि / *noun* 1 पागलपन, उन्माद 2 मूर्खतापूर्ण व्यवहार।

lunar / 'लूनर् / *adj* चंद्रमा-संबंधी : *a lunar eclipse* ▶ lunar month *noun* चंद्र-मास।

lunatic / 'लूनटिक् / *noun* 1 अत्यंत मूर्ख,

वहशी 2 (अप्र) पागल ▶ lunatic asylum *noun* (अप्र) मानसिक चिकित्सालय; पागलखाना।

lunch / लन्च् / *noun* दोपहर का भोजन ▶ lunch *verb* दोपहर का भोजन लेना।

luncheon / 'लन्चन् / *noun* (अनौप) दोपहर का भोजन।

lung / लङ् / *noun* फेफड़ा।

lunge / लन्ज् / *noun* झपट्टा; (तलवार आदि का) अचानक किया वार ▶ lunge *verb* झपट्टा मारना; वार करना।

lurch[1] / लर्च् / *noun* ■ leave sb in the lurch मुसीबत में अकेला छोड़ देना।

lurch[2] / लर्च् / *noun* एक ओर लुढ़क जाना, लुढ़कना : *The ship gave a lurch to starboard.* ▶ lurch *verb* लुढ़कना।

lure / लुअर्; ल्युअर् / *noun* 1 प्रलोभन; चारा 2 (प्राय: *sing*) किसी चीज़ के आकर्षक गुण : *the lure of adventure* ▶ lure *verb* प्रलोभन/चारा देना : *lure sb into a trap.*

lurid / 'लुअरिड्; 'ल्युअरिड् / *adj* 1 चमकदार रंगों के मिश्रण वाला : *dressed in a lurid orange and green blouse* 2 हिंसात्मक एवं डरावना; सनसनीख़ेज़ : *The paper described the killings in lurid details.* ▶ luridly *adv.*

lurk / लर्क् / *verb* 1 (हमला करने के लिए) छिपकर बैठना, घात लगाकर बैठना 2 मन या किसी कोने में रहना : *a lurking doubt/ suspicion.*

luscious / 'लशस् / *adj* 1 ज़्यादा मीठा, सुमधुर 2 (कपड़े, कलाकृति) चित्ताकर्षक : *luscious silks and velvets* 3 कामोत्तेजक रूप से आकर्षक : *a luscious young girl.*

lush / लश् / *adj* 1 प्रचुर; अधिक मात्रा में उत्पन्न होने वाला 2 धन-दौलत की प्रचुरता और समृद्धि दर्शाने वाला : *lush decor.*

lust / लस्ट् / *noun* (प्राय: अपमा) 1 lust (for sb) कामुकता 2 lust (for/of sth) लालसा : *a lust for power/gold* ▶ lust *verb* ■ **lust after/for sb/sth** लालायित होना; कामातुर होना; प्रबल इच्छा रखना : *He lusted for revenge.*

lustre (*US* **luster**) / 'लस्टर् /. *noun* 1 अत्यंत चिकना होने के कारण चमक : *the deep lustre of pearls* 2 कीर्ति, यश ▶ **lustrous** *adj.*

lute / लूट् / *noun* वीणा जैसा एक वाद्ययंत्र ▶ **lutenist** (**lutanist** भी) *noun* उस वाद्य का वादक।

luxuriant / लग्'श़ुअरिअन्ट् / *adj* प्रचुर, बहुत पैदा होने वाला; अधिक मात्रा में : *luxuriant vegetation* ▶ **luxuriance** *noun* **luxuriantly** *adv.*

luxurious/लग्'श़ुअरिअस्/*adj*विलसिता पूर्ण, आरामदेह।

luxury / 'लक्शरि / *noun* (*pl* **luxuries**) 1 भोग-विलास : *live in luxury* 2 विलास की वस्तुएँ (जो रुचिकर हैं किंतु आवश्यक नहीं हैं)।

lynch / लिन्च् / *verb* (किसी तथाकथित अपराधी को बिना मुक़दमा चलाए) जनता द्वारा ही मार दिया जाना : *innocent men lynched by the angry mob.*

lynx/ लिङ्क्स्/ *noun* बन बिलाव (अपनी तीक्ष्ण दृष्टि के लिए प्रसिद्ध)।

lyre /'लाइअर् / *noun* उँगलियों से बजाया जाने वाला प्राचीन यूरोपीय वाद्ययंत्र।

lyric /'लिरिक् / *adj* 1 (कविता) गीतात्मक एवं कवि की भावनाओं को व्यक्त करने वाली 2 गेय पद ▶ **lyric** *noun* 1 गीतिकाव्य 2 **lyrics** [*pl*] गीत, पद : *a song with happy lyrics* ▶ **lyrical** /'लिरिक़्ल् / *adj* 1 भावनाओं को गीत अथवा पद्य रूप में व्यक्त करते हुए 2 उत्साहपूर्ण **lyricism** *noun* **lyricist** *noun* गीतकार कवि।

Mm

ma /मा/ *noun* (*pl* **mas**) (अनौप) माँ; मम्मी।

ma'am /मैम्/ *noun* **madam** का संक्षिप्त रूप।

macabre /म'काब्र/ *adj* मृत्यु से संबंधित एवं वीभत्स, भयानक।

macaroni /मैक'रोनि/ *noun* मैदे और पानी से बना एक प्रकार का इटालियन खाद्य पदार्थ।

mace /मेस्/ *noun* **1** राजदंड **2** गदा।

machine /म'शीन्/ *noun* **1** मशीन, यंत्र : *a sewing/washing machine* **2** किसी संस्था/राजनीतिक वर्ग को नियंत्रित करने के लिए संगठित व्यक्ति-संगठन : *the well-built party machine* ▶ **machine** *verb* मशीन की सहायता से कुछ तैयार करना : *The edge of the disc had been machined flat/smooth.* **machinery** /म'शीनरि/ *noun* **1** मशीनरी; मशीन के कल-पुर्जे़ **2** **machinery (of sth/for doing sth)** कार्यतंत्र, शासनतंत्र : *reform the machinery of government.*

mackerel /मैकरल्/ *noun* (*pl* अपरिवर्तित) समुद्री मछली जो भोजन के काम आती है।

mackintosh /मैकिन्टॉश्/ (अनौप **mack, mac** भी) *noun* रबड़ की बरसाती।

mad /मैड्/ *adj* (**-dder, -ddest**) **1** पागल, विक्षिप्त **2** बिलकुल/निपट मूर्ख **3** **mad about/on sth/sb** (अनौप) अत्यंत उत्साहित/उत्तेजित : *be mad on football* **4** **mad (at/with sb)** (अनौप) अत्यंत क्रुद्ध **5** (कुत्ता) रेबीज़ से पागल ▶ **madly** *adv* **madness** *noun* विक्षिप्तता; निपट मूर्ख व्यवहार।

madam (**Madam** भी) /मैडम्/ *noun* (औप) महिलाओं को संबोधित करने में प्रयुक्त शब्द।

Madame /म'डाम्; US म'डैम्/ *noun* (संक्षि **Mme**)(*pl* **Mesdames** /मे'डाम्/ संक्षि **Mmes**) विवाहित या बड़ी उम्र की महिलाओं अथवा उन महिलाओं के लिए, जो ब्रिटिश या अमेरिकी न हों, प्रयुक्त फ्रांसीसी शब्द।

madden /मैड्न्/ *verb* पागल बना देना; अत्यंत क्रुद्ध कर देना।

Mademoiselle /मैडम्व'ज़ेल्/ *noun* (संक्षि **Mlle**) अविवाहित महिलाओं (कन्याओं) के नाम के पूर्व प्रयुक्त फ्रेंच शब्द।

madonna /म'डॉना/ *noun* **1** **the Madonna** कुँवारी मरियम (ईसा की माता) **2** माता मरियम की मूर्ति या चित्र।

maestro /माइस्ट्रो/ *noun* (*pl* **maestros**) संगीताचार्य।

magazine¹ /मैग'ज़ीन्/ *noun* **1** बारूद-ख़ाना **2** बंदूक आदि में गोली रखने का स्थान, मैगज़ीन।

magazine² /मैग'ज़ीन्/ *noun* **1** (अनौप **mag** भी) पत्रिका : *women's magazines/a literary magazine* **2** रेडियो या टी वी पर नियमित प्रसारित कार्यक्रम : *an arts/a news magazine.*

maggot /मैगट्/ *noun* लार्वा।

magic /मैजिक्/ *noun* **1** जादू **2** जादूगरी **3** बाज़ीगरी के करिश्मे, इंद्रजाल **4** आकर्षक एवं आश्चर्यजनक गुण : *the magic of Shakespeare's poetry* ▶ **magic** *adj* **1** जादू में प्रयुक्त; जादूभरा **2** विशिष्ट एवं महत्त्वपूर्ण **3** आश्चर्यजनक **magical** *adj* **magician** /म'जिश्न्/ *noun* जादूगर, बाज़ीगर।

magistrate /मैजिस्ट्रेट्/ *noun* मैजिस्ट्रेट, दंडाधिकारी।

magnanimous /मैग्'नैनिमस्/ *adj* (औप) उदारचित्त, विशाल हृदय ▶ **magnanimity** /मैग्न'निमिटि/ *noun.*

magnate /मैग्नेट्/ *noun* संपन्न एवं प्रभावशाली व्यक्ति : *an oil magnate.*

magnet /मैग्नट्/ *noun* **1** चुंबक

2 **magnet (for sb/sth)** चुंबकीय आकर्षण वाला व्यक्ति/वस्तु/स्थान ▸ **magnetic** adj 1 चुंबकीय 2 अत्यंत आकर्षक **magnetism** noun **magnetize, -ise** / 'मैग्नटाइज़् / verb चुंबकीय करना; चुंबक की तरह आकर्षित करना।

magnificent / मैग्'निफ़िस्न्ट् / adj शानदार, भव्य, अत्यधिक सुंदर।

magnify / 'मैग्निफ़ाइ / verb (pt, pp **magnified**) 1 (लेंस की सहायता से) बड़ा करके दिखाना 2 बढ़ा-चढ़ाकर बताना, अतिशयोक्ति करना ▸ **magnification** noun.

magnitude / ' मैग्निट्यूड् ; US 'मैग्निट्रूड् / noun 1 (औप) (आकार की) विशालता 2 महत्ता 3 (खगोल) किसी तारे की चमक की तीव्रता : a star of the first magnitude.

magpie / ' मैग्पाइ / noun एक प्रकार की चिड़िया जो बहुत शोर मचाती है (और चमकदार चीज़ों से आकर्षित होकर उन्हें उठा ले जाती है)।

mahogany / म'हॉगनि / noun 1 महोगनी, एक वृक्ष जिसकी लकड़ी फ़र्नीचर बनाने के काम आती है 2 लाल-भूरा रंग।

maid / मेड् / noun 1 (प्रा) अविवाहिता स्त्री 2 (समास में) घर की नौकरानी : housemaid/nursemaid 3 (साहि) कुमारी।

maiden / 'मेड्न् / noun 1 (प्राच साहि) कुमारी, अविवाहिता युवती 2 (**maiden over** भी) (क्रिकेट में) ऐसा ओवर जिसमें एक भी रन न बन सका हो ▸ **maiden** adj अपने तरह की सर्वप्रथम घटना या कार्य : a maiden speech/maiden voyage **maiden name** noun कुमारी नाम, स्त्री का विवाहपूर्व का नाम।

mail¹ / मेल् / noun कवच : a coat of mail.

mail² / मेल् / noun 1 डाक व्यवस्था 2 डाक से भेजे गए पत्र, पार्सल आदि; एक बार में प्राप्त पत्र आदि ▸ **mail** verb **mail sth (to sb)** डाक द्वारा भेजना **mail order** noun डाक से सामान मँगाने का आदेश।

maim / मेम् / verb ऐसी चोट मारना कि व्यक्ति अपंग हो जाए, अशक्त बना देना : killing and maiming innocent civilians.

main¹ / मेन् / adj मुख्य, सर्वाधिक महत्त्वपूर्ण ■ **in the main** अधिकांशत: ▸ **mainly** adv मुख्यत:, मुख्यतया।

main² / मेन् / noun 1 बिजली, पानी, गैस आदि का मुख्य तार, नल, पाइप आदि 2 मुख्य बड़ा नाला जिससे घरों की नालियाँ जुड़ी हों।

mainland / 'मेन्लैन्ड् / noun मुख्य भूभाग।

mainstay / 'मेन्स्टे / noun (अलं) मुख्य आधार।

mainstream / 'मेन्स्ट्रीम् / noun [sing] सामान्य/प्रचलित विचारधारा, मत आदि।

maintain / मेन्'टेन् / verb 1 बनाए/चालू/ क़ायम रखना : maintain friendly relations with sb 2 (किसी कथन को सच्चा ही) मानना : maintain one's innocence 3 आर्थिक सहारा देना : This school is maintained by a charity.

maintenance / 'मेन्टनन्स् / noun 1 क़ायम रखने की स्थिति/प्रक्रिया 2 निर्वाह राशि जो किसी को क़ानूनन देय हो : He has to pay maintenance to his ex-wife.

maize / मेज़् / noun मक्का।

majestic / म'ज़ेस्टिक् / adj तेजस्वी, प्रतापी, भव्य।

majesty / 'मैजिस्टि / noun 1 प्रभावशाली मान-मर्यादा अथवा सुंदरता : the sheer majesty of the mountain scenery 2 राजसत्ता; सम्राटोचित आचरण/ऐश्वर्य 3 **Majesty** सम्राट/सम्राज्ञी को संबोधित करने का रूप : Thank you, Your Majesty.

major¹ / 'मेजर् / adj दो अंशों में से बड़ा या महत्त्वपूर्ण अंश; मुख्य : play a major role in sth.

major² / 'मेजर् / noun मेजर (सैन्य अधि-

कारी का पद) ‣ **major general** *noun* (सेना में) उच्च अधिकारी का पद, मेजर-जनरल।

majority / म'जॉरटि /*noun* 1 **the majority** बहुमत; बहुलांश : *The majority of people prefer TV to radio.* 2 **majority (over sb)** (वोटों का) बहुमत 3 वयस्क होने की क़ानूनी आयु।

make¹ / मेक् / *verb* (*pt, pp* **made** / मेड् /) 1 **make sth (from/(out) of sth); make sth (for sb)** बनाना; निर्माण करना, अस्तित्व में लाना; तैयार करना; उत्पन्न/ पैदा करना : *make a desk/a dress/a cake* 2 मजबूर करना : *They made me repeat the whole story.* 3 करना/ कराना : *make a noise/disturbance* 4 पहुँचना; कार्य संपन्न करना : *Do you think we'll make Chennai by midday?* 5 मानना/समझना 6 बन जाना, बना देना : *He'll never make an actor.* 7 जीतना/बढ़त हासिल करना; (लाभ) प्राप्त करना : *make a profit* ∎ **make for sth** 1 की ओर जाना 2 कुछ संभव करना (में मदद करना) **make fun of sb** मज़ाक़ बनाना/ उड़ाना, उपहास करना **make light of sth** गंभीरता से न लेना **make off** (*अनौप*) भाग जाना **make sb/sth out** देख/पढ़/समझ लेना **make sth out** चेक लिखना अथवा फ़ॉर्म भरना **make sth up** 1 (कहानी/ बहाना) गढ़ना 2 (पूर्ति के लिए) आवश्यक वस्तुएँ देना 3 (दवाइयाँ) तैयार करना 4 बिस्तर लगाना/तैयार करना **make the most of sth/sb** अधिक से अधिक लाभ उठाना **make up; make oneself/sb up** किसी अभिनेता को रंगमंच के लिए सजाना/श्रृंगार करना/तैयार करना; चेहरे पर क्रीम, पाउडर आदि लगाना ‣ **make-believe** *noun* बहाना, ढोंग **make-up** *noun* 1 शृंगार का सामान (पाउडर, क्रीम आदि) 2 संरचना, विन्यास 3 (परीक्षा) पूरक।

make² / मेक् / *noun* 1 **make (of sth)**

(कंपनी का) निर्माण, उत्पाद : *cars of all makes* 2 गठन, बनावट।

maker / 'मेकर् / *noun* 1 (समास में) उत्पादक व्यक्ति/कंपनी : *decision/policy/ programme makers* 2 **the/our Maker** ईश्वर, सर्जनहार।

makeshift / मेकशिफ़्ट् / *adj* कामचलाऊ (वस्तु या व्यवस्था)।

making / 'मेकिङ् / *noun* बनाने/उत्पन्न करने की प्रक्रिया : *film-making* ∎ **be the making of sb** क्षेम कल्याण करना **have the makings of sth** निर्माण योग्य गुण रखना।

mal- *pref* (*उपसर्ग*) 1 बुरा/बुरी तरह : *maltreat/maladjusted* 2 नकारात्मक : *malcontent.*

malady / 'मैलडि / *noun* (*pl* **maladies**) (*औप*) बीमारी, रोग; (*अलं*) बुराई।

malaise / म'लेज़् / *noun* (*औप*) (बिना किसी स्पष्ट लक्षण के) बीमारी का आमतौर पर अनुभव/भाव; सामान्य असंतोष या शक्तिहीनता जिसका ठीक-ठीक कारण मालूम न किया जा सके : *the current malaise in our society.*

malaria / म'लेअरिअ / *noun* मलेरिया (रोग) ‣ **malarial** *adj* : *malarial patients.*

male / मेल् / *adj* 1 नर, पुंजातीय 2 (पौधा) जो फल उत्पन्न नहीं करता, केवल परागकणों वाले फूल उत्पन्न करता है ‣ **male** *noun* नर व्यक्ति, पशु आदि।

malformation / मैलफ़ॉर'मेश्न् / *noun* कु-रचना; कु-गठित भाग : *a malformation of the spine* ‣ **malformed** *adj.*

malice / 'मैलिस् / *noun* **malice (towards sb)** द्वेष, दुर्भावना, दूसरे को हानि पहुँचाने की अभिलाषा : *She certainly bears you no malice.* ‣ **malicious** / म'लिशस् / *adj* द्वेषपूर्ण **maliciously** *adv.*

malign / म'लाइन् / *verb* निंदा करना, बुराई करना : *malign an innocent person*

▸ **malign** adj (औप) हानिकारक, अ-शुभ : a malign influence.

malignant / म'लिग्नन्ट् / adj 1 द्वेषी, अहितकर (व्यक्ति) 2 (रोग, फोड़ा) सांघातिक, घातक : The growth is not malignant. ▸ **malignancy** noun.

mall / मॉल; मैल / (**shopping mall** भी) noun (विशेषत: बड़े शहरों में) विशाल ढका हुआ स्थान या भवन जहाँ बहुत सारी दुकानें हों (कपड़े इत्यादि की)।

malleable / मैलिअब्ल् / adj 1 (धातु एवं अन्य पदार्थ) जिसे पीटकर बढ़ाया जा सके और उससे पात्र आदि बनाए जा सकें 2 (व्यक्ति, विचार आदि) जिसे आसानी से प्रभावित/परिवर्तित किया जा सके : The young are more malleable than the old. ▸ **malleability** noun.

mallet / मैलिट् / noun 1 लकड़ी की मुंगरी 2 पोलो स्टिक।

malnutrition / मैल्न्यू'ट्रिश्न् / noun (औप) कुपोषण, पुष्ट भोजन न मिलने के कारण उत्पन्न स्थिति।

malt / मॉल्ट् / noun बिअर बनाने में प्रयुक्त जौ आदि, माल्ट।

maltreat / मैल्'ट्रीट् / verb दुर्व्यवहार करना; अत्याचार करना : maltreated children ▸ **maltreatment** noun.

mammal / मैम्ल् / noun स्तनपायी प्राणी ▸ **mammalian** adj.

mammoth / मैमश् / noun रोएँदार बड़ा हाथी (अब विलुप्त) ▸ **mammoth** adj विशाल; विशालकाय : a mammoth project/task.

man¹ / मैन् / noun (pl **men** / मेन् /) 1 मनुष्य, आदमी; पुरुष 2 मानव; मानवजाति ■ **a man of the world** बहुत अनुभवी व्यक्ति **the man in the street** जन-साधारण।

man² / मैन् / verb (-nn-) **man sth (with sb)** (जहाज़ आदि के संचालन के लिए) आवश्यक व्यक्तियों को तैनात करना।

manacle / मैनकृल् / noun (प्राय: pl) हथकड़ी-बेड़ी ▸ **manacle** verb बेड़ी डालना : His hands were manacled behind his back.

manage / मैनिज् / verb 1 (व्यापार आदि का) संचालन करना, व्यवस्था करना 2 व्यवस्थाबद्ध बनाए रखना, क़ाबू में रखना : manage a difficult horse 3 **manage (with/without sb/sth)** काम चला लेना, क़ायम रखना ▸ **manageable** adj नियंत्रण/संचालन-योग्य; जिसकी व्यवस्था/प्रबंध किया जा सके।

management / मैनिज्मन्ट् / noun 1 संचालन; प्रबंध/व्यवस्था 2 संचालक/प्रबंधक; व्यवस्थापक : The management is/are considering closing the factory.

manager / मैनिजर् / noun (fem **manageress** / मैनिज'रेस् /) संचालक/संचालिका।

mandate / मैन्डेट् / noun 1 **mandate for sth/to do sth** (कुछ करने का) अधिकार; (औप) अधिकारियों का आदेश, आदेश : Our election victory has given us a clear mandate for our policies. 2 शासनादेश ▸ **mandate** verb (औप) आदेश देना/निर्देश देना **mandated** adj शासनादेश से अधिकृत प्रदेश

mandatory adj **mandatory (for sb)** (औप) क़ानूनन आवश्यक : a mandatory life sentence for murder.

mane / मेन् / noun सिंह के गले के बड़े बाल, केसर; घोड़े के गले के बाल।

mange / मेन्ज् / noun कुत्तों एवं अन्य रोएँ वाले जंतुओं की खाज ▸ **mangy** adj (-ier, -iest) 1 खाज वाला; गंदा 2 उपेक्षित (कुत्ता)।

manger / मेन्जर् / noun नाँद (गाय, घोड़े आदि को चारा डालने की)।

mangle / मैङ्ग्ल् / verb 1 बुरी तरह काट-पीट या फाड़-फूड़ देना 2 (लेखक, अभिनेता आदि का) रचना या अभिनय का

बुरा प्रदर्शन करना : *a mangled translation.*

mango / 'मैङ्गो / *noun* (*pl* **mangoes**) आम।

manhandle / 'मैन्हैन्ड्ल / *verb* 1 (व्यक्ति के साथ) बुरी तरह पेश आना, धक्का देना/ थप्पड़ मारना 2 बड़ी कठिनाई एवं प्रयास से सरकाना/ले जाना : *We manhandled the piano up the stairs.*

manhole / 'मैन्होल् / *noun* नाली/नाले में प्रवेश करने का मुख्य मार्ग; नाले का मेन होल जो ढका होता है।

manhood / 'मैन्हुड् / *noun* पुरुषत्व; पुरुषोचित गुण, पुरुषार्थ।

mania / 'मेनिआ / *noun* 1 (*मनो*) उन्माद, पागलपन 2 **mania** (**for sth**) सनक, झक : *have a mania for cleanliness.*

-mania *suff* (*प्रत्यय*) मानसिक रोग अथवा विशिष्ट प्रकार का असामान्य व्यवहार : *kleptomania/nymphomania.*

maniac / 'मेनिऐक् / *noun* 1 विक्षिप्त, पागल 2 (*अपमा या परि*) सनकी/झक्की; अति उत्साही : *a football maniac.*

manicure / 'मैनिक्युअर् / *noun* हाथों एवं नाख़ूनों की देखभाल; नख-प्रसाधन ▸ **manicure** *verb* नख-प्रसाधन करना : *beautifully manicured nails* **manicurist** *noun.*

manifest / 'मैनिफ़ेस्ट् / *adj* **manifest** (**to sb**) (**in sth**) (*औप*) सुस्पष्ट, प्रत्यक्ष रूप से स्पष्ट : *a manifest truth* ▸ **manifest** *verb* **manifest sth** (**in sth**) (*औप*) 1 स्पष्टतया दिखाना; संकेत करना 2 **manifest itself** (**in sth**) प्रकाश में आना; आविर्भूत होना : *The symptoms manifested themselves ten days later.* **manifestation** / ˌमैनिफ़े'स्टेश्न् / *noun.*

manifesto / ˌमैनि'फ़ेस्टो / *noun* (*pl* **manifestos** या **manifestoes**) राजनीतिक दल द्वारा अपने उद्देश्यों और योजनाओं का लिखित विवरण।

manifold / 'मैनिफ़ोल्ड् / *adj* (*औप*)

अनेक प्रतियों वाला; विविध/नानारूप : *a person with manifold interests.*

manipulate / म'निप्युलेट् / *verb* 1 (यंत्र आदि को) कुशलता से काम में लाना; कार्य का चतुरतापूर्वक संचालन करना 2 (*अपमा*) चालाकी से काम निकालना : *She uses her charm to manipulate people.* ▸ **manipulation** *noun* चालाकी; व्यवहार-कौशल **manipulative** *adj.*

mankind / मैन्'काइन्ड् / *noun* मानव जाति।

manly / 'मैन्लि / *adj* (**-ier, -iest**) 1 (पुरुष का) पौरुष, साहसादि पुरुषोचित गुणों से संपन्न होना 2 (*अपमा*) (स्त्री) पुरुष जैसे लक्षणों वाली।

man-made / ˌमैन्'मेड् / *adj* मनुष्य द्वारा बनाया गया, न कि प्राकृतिक; कृत्रिम।

mannequin / 'मैनिकिन् / *noun* 1 (विज्ञापनों अथवा दुकानों पर कपड़ों के प्रदर्शन के लिए प्रयुक्त) मानव शरीर का मॉडल 2 मॉडल (व्यक्ति)।

manner / 'मैनर् / *noun* 1 [*sing*] (*औप*) कार्य किए जाने का ढंग, रीति 2 [*sing*] (व्यक्ति का दूसरे व्यक्ति के साथ किया) व्यवहार, आचरण : *have an aggressive manner* 3 **manners** [*pl*] नम्र सामाजिक व्यवहार/आचरण : *good/bad manners* 4 **manners** [*pl*] रीति-रिवाज : *18th century aristocratic manners* 5 (*औप या साहि*) व्यक्ति/वस्तु की प्रकृति, प्रकार : *What manner of man is he?*

mannerism / 'मैनरिज़्म् / *noun* 1 व्यवहार में विचित्रता, विचित्र आदत 2 कला या साहित्य में विशिष्ट शैली का अत्यधिक प्रयोग : *painting that is not free of mannerism.*

manoeuvre (*US* **maneuver**) / म'नू-वर् / *noun* 1 सुनियोजित निपुण चाल/गति; (किसी को धोखा देने के लिए प्रयुक्त) योजना, चालबाज़ी/दाँव : *a skilful political manoeuvre* 2 सेना की सुनियोजित चाल; **manoeuvres** [*pl*] सैनिक

अभ्यास/युद्धाभ्यास ▸ **manoeuvre** (*US* **maneuver**) *verb* निपुणता से चलना/गति करना; युक्ति से काम निकालना, चाल चलना : *manoeuvre the conversation round to money.*

manor / मैनर् / *noun* (**manor-house** भी) जागीर, ज़मींदारी।

manpower / 'मैनपाउअर् / *noun* किसी काम के लिए उपलब्ध व्यक्तियों की संख्या; श्रमशक्ति।

mansion / 'मैन्श्न् / *noun* हवेली, कोठी।

manslaughter / 'मैन्स्लॉटर् / *noun* नरवध, मानवहत्या।

mantelpiece / 'मैन्ट्ल्पीस् / *noun* कमरे में चिमनी वाली अँगीठी पर बनी कॉर्निस।

mantis / 'मैनटिस् / (**praying mantis** भी) *noun* एक प्रकार का कीट।

mantle / 'मैन्ट्ल् / *noun* **1** the mantle of sb/sth (*साहि*) महत्त्वपूर्ण व्यक्ति अथवा नौकरी की ज़िम्मेदारियों एवं भूमिका : *inherit the mantle of supreme power* **2** (बिना बाँह का) लबादा **3** (*साहि*) आवरण : *hills with a mantle of snow* **4** गैस मैंटल।

manual[1] / 'मैन्युअल् / *adj* हाथ से किया (कार्य आदि), हस्त- : *manual labour* ▸ **manually** *adv.*

manual[2] / 'मैन्युअल् / *noun* **1** नियम-पुस्तिका/विवरणिका **2** (संगीत में) हाथ से चलाया जाने वाला की-बोर्ड।

manufacture / ,मैन्यु'फ़ैक्चर् / *verb* **1** उत्पादन करना (बड़ी मात्रा में मशीनों द्वारा चीज़ें बनाना) **2** (प्राय: *अप्रम*) बहाना, झूठा प्रमाण आदि तैयार करना, गढ़ना : *a news story manufactured by an unscrupulous journalist* ▸ **manufacture** *noun* **1** उत्पादन **2** manufactures [*pl*] निर्मित माल **manufacturer** *noun* निर्माता/उत्पादक।

manure / म'न्युअर् / *noun* (गोबर की) खाद ▸ **manure** *verb* खाद डालना : *well-manured soil.*

manuscript / 'मैन्युस्क्रिप्ट् / *noun* **1** छपने/टाइप होने से पूर्व का लेखक की हाथ की लिखी मूल प्रति **2** पाँडुलिपि, हस्तलिखित पुराना ग्रंथ।

many / 'मेनि / *indef det, indef pron* **1** व्यक्तियों/वस्तुओं की बड़ी संख्या **2** many a (*औप*) बहुत-से/सी : *I've been there many a time.*

map / मैप् / *noun* नक्शा, मानचित्र (भौगोलिक चित्र) ▸ **map** *verb* (**-pp-**) मानचित्र बनाना ▪ **map sth out** योजना बनाना, प्रबंध करना।

mar / मार् / *verb* (**-rr-**) बिगाड़ना, चौपट करना।

marathon / 'मैरथ्न् / *noun* **1** लगभग 42 किलोमीटर (26 मील) की लंबी दौड़ **2** प्रयास और सहनशक्ति का परीक्षण करने वाला कोई कार्य या घटना : *a marathon legal battle.*

marble / 'मार्ब्ल् / *noun* **1** संगमरमर **2** (बच्चों के खेलने वाली) काँच की गोली, कंचा।

March / मार्च् / *noun* (संक्षि **Mar**) मार्च (महीना)।

march[1] / मार्च् / *verb* **1** (सैनिकों द्वारा) मार्च करना, क़दम से क़दम मिलाकर चलना **2** दृढ़ निश्चय के साथ तेज़ी से चलना : *She marched into my office and demanded an apology.* **3** (प्रदर्शन/विरोध के लिए) रास्तों पर जुलूस बनाकर चलना : *march for peace.*

march[2] / मार्च् / *noun* **1** मार्च, प्रयाण **2** जुलूस **3** (प्रयाण) गीत : *a funeral march* **4** [*sing*] the march of sth नियमित प्रगति, अग्रगति।

mare / मेअर् / *noun* घोड़ी/गदही।

margarine / ,मार्ज'रीन् / *noun* मार्जरीन, वनस्पति तेलों या चरबी से बना मक्खन।

margin / 'मार्जिन् / *noun* **1** मार्जिन, हाशिया **2** (झील, तालाब आदि का) किनारा **3** मार्जिन, पहले से सोचे समय, क़ीमत आदि से अधिक मात्रा; अतिरिक्त राशि; गुंजाइश : *a* *good safety margin* 4 *(वाणिज्य)* नफ़ा, मुनाफ़ा ▸ **marginal** *adj* 1 हाशिए पर : *marginal notes/comments* 2 बहुत थोड़ा, ज़रा-सा; बहुत कम महत्त्व-पूर्ण : *petty rivalry between marginal groups* **marginally** *adv*.

marine¹ / म'रीन् / *adj* 1 समुद्री, समुद्र में/ के पास पाया जाने वाला/उत्पन्न होने वाला : *marine mammals/organisms* 2 जहाज़-विषयक; नौसेना-विषयक।

marine² / म'रीन् / *noun* नौसैनिक।

mariner / 'मैरिनर् / *noun (अप्र या औप)* नाविक।

marionette / मैरिअ'नेट् / *noun* कठ-पुतली।

marital / 'मैरिट्ल् / *adj* विवाह-संबंधी; पति-पत्नी के बीच : *marital harmony.*

maritime / 'मैरिटाइम् / *adj* समुद्री; समुद्रतटीय।

mark¹ / मार्क् / *noun* 1 निशान, चिह्न 2 (शरीर का) उल्लेखनीय लक्षण 3 परीक्षा में प्राप्त अंक : *give sb high/low marks (for sth)* 4 *(औप)* लक्ष्य : *The arrow missed its mark.* ■ **make one's mark** प्रसिद्ध होना **upto the mark** अपेक्षित स्तर का।

mark² / मार्क् / *verb* 1 **mark A (with B)/ mark B on A** निशान/चिह्न लगाना; गंदा करना/होना 2 स्थिति या स्थान दर्शाना 3 (महत्त्वपूर्ण घटना को) सम्मानित करना 4 परीक्षा में अंक देना, परीक्षण करना : *mark examination papers* 5 ध्यान देना ■ **mark sth off** सीमा लगाकर पृथक करना **mark sth out** रेखाएँ डालकर सीमांकित करना **mark time** 1 पैरों को ऊपर-नीचे उठाना किंतु एक क़दम भी न चलना 2 शांति से उचित समय की प्रतीक्षा करना ▸ **marked** / मार्क्ड् / *adj* स्पष्ट, सहज ही दिखाई पड़ने योग्य : *a marked difference/improvement.*

market¹ / 'मार्किट् / *noun* 1 बाज़ार, हाट/ मंडी 2 व्यापार की स्थिति : *a dull market*

(in coffee) 3 **market (for sth)** माँग (वस्तुओं की खपत) 4 ख़रीद-फ़रोख़्त 5 देश या प्रदेश जहाँ माल की खपत होती है या हो सकती है : *find new markets* ▸ **market-place** *noun* सब्ज़ी, फल आदि का बाज़ार।

market² / 'मार्किट् / *verb* **market sth (as sth); market sth (to sb)** बाज़ार में ले जाना या भेजना/ख़रीदना या बेचना; विज्ञापन करना और बेचना : *market sth imaginatively/aggressively* ▸ **marketing** *noun*.

marksman / 'मार्क्स्मन् / *noun* निशाने-बाज़।

marmalade / 'मार्मलेड् / *noun* संतरे का जैम या मुरब्बा, मार्मलेड।

maroon¹ / म'रून् / *verb* किसी को निर्जन द्वीप या समुद्र में अकेला छोड़ देना; असहाय अवस्था में निर्जन प्रदेश में छूट जाना : *marooned sailors.*

maroon² / म'रून् / *noun* गहरा लाल-भूरा रंग।

marquee / मार्'की / *noun* शामियाना; *(US)* थिएटर, सिनेमा आदि का ढका हुआ प्रवेश द्वार।

marriage / 'मैरिज् / *noun* 1 शादी/विवाह 2 विवाह समारोह ▸ **marriageable** *adj* विवाह-योग्य।

marrow¹ / 'मैरो / *noun* (हड्डी के भीतर की) मज्जा : *a bone marrow transplant.*

marrow² / 'मैरो / *noun* (**vegetable marrow,** *US* **squash** भी) कुम्हड़ा/लौकी जैसी तरकारियाँ।

marry / 'मैरि / *verb* (*pt, pp* **married**) 1 शादी/विवाह करना 2 (बेटी/बेटे का) विवाह करना।

Mars / मार्ज़् / *noun* मंगल ग्रह।

marsh / मार्श् / *noun* दलदल, कछार प्रदेश ▸ **marshy** *adj* कछारी।

marshal / 'मार्शल् / *noun* 1 मार्शल (सेना में उच्चतम पद) : *Field Marshal* (थल

सेना में) ○ *Air Marshal* (वायु सेना में) 2 कुछ विशिष्ट स्थानों पर भीड़ को नियंत्रित करने वाला अधिकारी।

martial / 'मार्शल् / *adj* 1 *(औप)* युद्ध संबंधी, सामरिक : *martial music* 2 युद्धप्रिय; लड़ाका ▸ **martial law** *noun* मार्शल लॉ, सैनिक शासन।

martyr / 'मार्टर् / *noun* 1 शहीद; आत्म-बलिदान करने वाला 2 **martyr to sth** *(अनौप)* (किसी भयंकर बीमारी आदि से) यातना भोगने वाला ▸ **martyr** *verb* शहीद बनाना/कर देना **martyrdom** *noun* शहादत, बलिदान।

marvel / 'मार्वल् / *noun* 1 चमत्कार (प्रियकर आश्चर्य); चमत्कारिक व्यक्ति/वस्तु 2 **marvels** [*pl*] आश्चर्यजनक परिणाम अथवा उपलब्धियाँ ▸ **marvel** *verb* (-**ll**-; *US* **-l-**) **marvel (at sth)** अत्यंत आश्चर्य-चकित होना **marvellous** (*US* **marvelous**) / 'मार्वलस् / *adj* चमत्कारिक; आश्चर्यजनक : *a marvellous idea/writer.*

mascara / मै'स्कारा / *noun* (आँखों/बरौनी का) अंजन, जिससे आँखें सुंदर दिखती हैं।

mascot / 'मैस्कट् / *noun* शुभजनक वस्तु/व्यक्ति/पशु; शुभंकर।

masculine / 'मैस्क्युलिन् / *adj* 1 पुरुषो-चित, मरदाना 2 *(व्या)* पुल्लिंग।

mash / मैश् / *noun* 1 (जानवरों को खिलाने का) पकाया हुआ दलिया, भरता/भुरता 2 कोई भी दलिये की तरह कुचलकर बनाया पदार्थ : *a mash of wet paper and paste* 3 *(अनौप)* कुचले हुए उबले आलू ▸ **mash** *verb* **mash (sth up)** कुचल देना और दलिये जैसा बना देना।

mask / मास्क़; *US* मैस्क् / *noun* 1 नक़ाब, मुखौटा 2 गैस, धुएँ आदि से बचाव के लिए लगाया आवरण 3 वास्तविक भावनाएँ/चरित्र छिपाने को प्रयुक्त अभिव्यक्ति/रीति : *She conceals her worries behind a mask of cheerfulness.* ▸ **mask** *verb*

1 मास्क/नक़ाब पहनना 2 भावनाएँ/चरित्र आदि छिपाना : *mask an unpleasant smell.*

mason / 'मेसन् / *noun* राजमिस्त्री (ईंट, पत्थर का काम करने वाला) ▸ **masonry** / 'मेसनरि / *noun* पत्थर या ईंट का बना इमारती अंश : *brick and masonry walls.*

masquerade / मैस्क'रेड् / *noun* 1 *(प्रा)* मुखौटा लगाकर नाचने का उत्सव 2 छद्म कार्य, शैली या रीति : *Her sorrow is just a masquerade.* ▸ **masquerade** *verb* **masquerade (as sth)** छद्मवेश में आना।

Mass (**mass** भी) / मैस् / *noun* रोमन कैथोलिक चर्च द्वारा आयोजित धर्म-समारोह; इसके विभिन्न भागों के लिए संगीत का आयोजन : *Beethoven's Mass in D.*

mass / मैस् / *noun* 1 **mass (of sth)** ढेर, राशि (बहुत अधिक मात्रा किंतु कोई नियमित आकार नहीं); एक साथ ढेर सारे व्यक्ति/वस्तुएँ 2 **masses** [*pl*] *(अनौप)* बहुत बड़ी मात्रा 3 **the masses** [*pl*] जनसाधारण 4 *(भौतिकी)* द्रव्यमान, संहति ▸ **mass** *adj* बहुत सारे व्यक्तियों/वस्तुओं को प्रभावित करने वाला : *mass education/unemployment* **mass** *verb* ढेर में इकट्ठा होना या करना **mass media** *noun* लोकमाध्यम, जनमाध्यम **mass production** *noun* बड़ी मात्रा में एक-सी चीज़ का उत्पादन।

massacre / 'मैसकर् / *noun* 1 क़त्ले-आम, बड़ी संख्या में निरपराध निहत्थे लोगों की हत्या 2 *(अनौप)* टीम या पार्टी की भारी पराजय ▸ **massacre** *verb* 1 सामूहिक हत्या करना 2 भारी शिकस्त देना।

massage / 'मैसाझ़; *US* म'साझ़् / *noun* (शरीर की) मालिश ▸ **massage** *verb* 1 मालिश करना 2 हिसाब-किताब में हेरा-फेरी करना : *massage the accounts.*

masseur / मै'सर् / *noun* (*fem* **mas-**

seuse / मैं'सर्ज़् /) मालिश को व्यवसाय के रूप में अपनाने वाला व्यक्ति।

massive / 'मैसिव् / adj महाकाय/स्थूल; प्रभावकारी : a massive building.

mast / मास्ट् / noun 1 (जहाज़ का) मस्तूल 2 रेडियो/टी वी स्टेशन का मस्तूल।

master¹ / 'मास्टर; US 'मैस्टर् / noun 1 (अप्र) मालिक, स्वामी 2 घोड़े, कुत्ते आदि का मालिक; जहाज़ का कप्तान; गृहपति 3 विशेषज्ञ, आचार्य : a master craftsman 4 महान कलाकार, प्रायः चित्रकार : a painting by an old Dutch master 5 Master विश्वविद्यालय की स्नातकोत्तर उपाधि : a Master of Arts/Sciences 6 पुरुष अध्यापक 7 लड़कों के नाम के पूर्व प्रयुक्त : Master Charles Smith 8 फ़िल्म या टेप की वह स्थायी प्रति जिससे प्रतिलिपियाँ बनाई जाती हैं 9 master (of sth) किसी चीज़ पर नियंत्रण रखने वाला व्यक्ति।

master² / 'मास्टर; US 'मैस्टर् / verb 1 किसी कार्य में विशेषज्ञता प्राप्त करना : master a foreign language 2 वश में करना; अधीन बनाना/करना।

masterly / 'मास्टर्लि; US 'मैस्टर्लि / adj उत्कृष्ट; चतुरतापूर्ण : their masterly handling of a difficult situation.

mastermind / 'मास्टर्माइन्ड्; US 'मैस्टर्माइन्ड् / noun अतिशय बुद्धिमत्ता वाला व्यक्ति जो महत्त्वपूर्ण कार्य की योजना बनाता है ▶ **mastermind** verb परियोजना को कुशलतापूर्वक संपन्न कराना।

masterpiece / 'मास्टर्पीस् / noun श्रेष्ठ रचना/कृति।

mastery / 'मास्टरि; US 'मैस्टरि / noun 1 mastery (of sth) पूर्ण विशेषज्ञता 2 mastery (of/over sb/sth) पूर्ण नियंत्रण : finally gain mastery over a long illness.

mat / मैट् / noun 1 चटाई 2 मोटे रबड़ या कपड़े का पायदान 3 घना, गुँथा हुआ ढेर/ पुंज : a mat of weeds/hair ▶ **mat**

seuse *verb* (-tt-) गूँथ देना या उलझा देना : matted hair (उलझे हुए बाल)।

match¹ / मैच् / noun दियासलाई, माचिस : strike a match.

match² / मैच् / noun 1 मैच, प्रतियोगिता-खेल : a tennis/football match 2 match for sb; sb's match बराबरी का जोड़ा; जोड़ीदार 3 (प्रा) विवाह; वर-वधू 4 [sing] match (for sb/sth) अनुरूप, सदृश (व्यक्ति/वस्तु) : The new curtains are a perfect match for the carpet. ▶ **matchless** adj अद्वितीय, अनुपम।

match³ / मैच् / verb 1 match (with sth) अनुरूप होना 2 match sb/sth (to/ with sb/sth) बराबर का होना : The two players are well-matched.

mate¹ / मेट् / noun (अनौप) (समास में प्रयुक्त) साथी, साथ काम करने वाला सहायक : her teammates/classmates.

mate² / मेट् / verb mate sth (with/to sth) (पशु-पक्षियों का) संतानोत्पत्ति के लिए जोड़ा बनाना : We mated the grey mare (with a champion stallion).

material¹ / मटिअरिअल् / noun 1 सामान/ माल; कच्चा माल/उपादान जिससे वस्तुएँ बनती हैं; सामग्री 2 कपड़ा : cotton/ woollen material 3 पुस्तक आदि लिखने, सलाह देने के लिए तथ्य, सूचनाएँ आदि।

material² / म'टिअरिअल् / adj 1 भौतिक (न कि आध्यात्मिक) : the material world 2 शारीरिक, पार्थिव; आर्थिक : our material needs 3 material (to sth) (औप या क़ानून) महत्त्वपूर्ण, सारतत्त्व।

materialism / म'टिअरिअलिज़म् / noun 1 (प्रायः अपमा) भौतिकवाद, भौतिक संसार में रुचि की प्रवृत्ति 2 (दर्शन) यह मत कि सिर्फ़ भौतिक संसार का ही अस्तित्व है ▶ **materialist** noun भौतिकवादी व्यक्ति।

materialize, -ise / म'टिअरिअलाइज़् / verb 1 सत्य होना, घटित होना : Our *plans did not materialize.* 2 शारीरिक रूप में दिखाई पड़ना; प्रकट होना।

maternal / म'टर्नल् / *adj* 1 मातृ-सुलभ : *maternal instincts/love* 2 माता से संबद्ध : *maternal aunt* (मौसी); *maternal uncle* (मामा)।

maternity / मटर्नटि / *noun* मातृत्व, माता बनना/होना ▸ **maternity home** *noun* प्रसूति निकेतन (गृह) **maternity leave** *noun* प्रसूति अवकाश।

mathematics / मैथ'मैटिक्स् / *noun* (**maths** / मैथ्स्/भी) गणित-शास्त्र ▸ **mathematical** *adj* गणित-विषयक; सुनिश्चित **mathematician** / मैथम'टिश्न् / *noun* गणितज्ञ।

matinee / मैटिने / *noun* मैटिनी, थिएटर का/सिनेमा का तीसरे पहर का शो/खेल।

matriculate / मट्रिक्युलेट् / *verb* (परीक्षा उत्तीर्ण करने के बाद) विश्वविद्यालय में प्रवेश के योग्य बनाना/होना ▸ **matriculation** *noun.*

matrimony / 'मैट्रिमनि; *US* 'मैट्रिमोनि / *noun* (औप) वैवाहिक जीवन ▸ **matrimonial** / मैट्रि'मोनिअल् / *adj* वैवाहिक; विवाह-विषयक : *matrimonial bliss.*

matron / 'मेट्रन् / *noun* 1 मैट्रन, स्कूल या अन्य संस्था में आवासादि व्यवस्था का प्रबंध करने वाली महिला 2 (पूर्व में) अस्पताल में नर्सों की अध्यक्षा महिला, मैट्रन, अध्यक्षा।

matter¹ / 'मैटर् / *noun* 1 विषय/बात; मामला 2 भौतिक पदार्थ (चित्त और चेतना के विपरीत) 3 प्रकार विशेष की सामग्री : *decaying vegetable matter* ∘ *printed matter* 4 (औप) किसी पुस्तक/भाषण की विषय-वस्तु/विचार आदि (भाषा-शैली के विपरीत) : *interesting subject matter* ■ **a matter of life and death** अत्यंत महत्त्वपूर्ण बात; जीवन-मृत्यु का प्रश्न **(as) a matter of course** स्वाभाविक, जिसकी सहज संभावना हो **as a matter of fact** वस्तुत:, वास्तविक स्थिति (चाहे आप अपने मन में कुछ भी सोचते हों) **no matter**

when/where/how/who/what/etc यह महत्त्वपूर्ण नहीं कि कब/कहाँ/कैसे/किसने/क्या किया ▸ **matter-of-fact** *adj* तथ्यात्मक (कल्पनाशील/भावुक न होना) : *a very matter-of-fact way.*

matter² / 'मैटर् / *verb* **matter (to sb)** महत्त्वपूर्ण होना : *Some things matter more than others.*

mattress / 'मैट्रस् / *noun* (बिछाने का) गद्दा।

mature¹ / म'चुअर; म'ट्युअर् / *adj* 1 परिपक्व, प्रौढ़ (व्यक्ति) 2 (शराब, पनीर) प्रयोग योग्य तैयार 3 (विचार, योजना आदि) सुविचारित : *after mature reflection* 4 (फल आदि) पका हुआ, पूर्ण विकसित 5 (*वाणिज्य*) (बीमा पॉलिसी आदि) भुगतान के लिए तैयार ▸ **maturity** *noun* प्रौढ़ता।

mature² / म'चुअर; म'ट्युअर् / *verb* 1 पूर्ण विकसित/परिपक्व होना; प्रौढ़ होना, बनाना : *Experience has matured him greatly.* 2 (*वाणिज्य*) (बीमा पॉलिसी आदि) भुगतान को तैयार होना।

maul / मॉल् / *verb* 1 **maul sb/sth (about)** दुर्व्यवहार से बुरी तरह बिगाड़ देना 2 मांस फाड़कर व्यक्ति/पशु को घायल कर देना; क्षत-विक्षत कर देना : *He died after being mauled by a tiger.*

mauve / मोव् / *adj, noun* हलका बैंगनी (रंग का)।

maxim / 'मैक्सिम् / *noun* नीतिवचन/सूक्ति; सिद्धांत वाक्य/सूत्र।

maximize, -ise / 'मैक्सिमाइज़् / *verb* अधिकतम सीमा तक बढ़ाना : *We must maximize profits.*

maximum / 'मैक्सिमम् / *noun* अधिकतम (स्थिति) : *develop one's skills to the maximum* ▸ **maximum** *adj* अधिकतम संभव।

May / मे / *noun* मई (महीना)।

may / मे / *modal verb* (*pt* **might**) (संभावना/अनुमति आदि का सूचक) : *You* *may come if you wish.* ○ *Passengers may cross by the footbridge.*

maybe / 'मेबी / *adv* शायद, कदाचित : *Maybe he'll come.*

mayonnaise / ‚मेअ'नेज़; *US* 'मेअनेज़/ *noun* अंडे, तेल, सिरके आदि से बना एक तरह का सॉस।

mayor / मेअर् / *noun* मेयर, नगर प्रमुख ▸ **mayoress** /मेअ'रेस्/ *noun* 1 महिला मेयर 2 मेयर की पत्नी।

maze / मेज़/ *noun* 1 भूल–भुलैयाँ 2 जटिल (तथ्य, सूचना आदि) : *finding one's way through the maze of rules and regulations.*

me / मी / *pers pron* मुझे : *Give it to me.→* I देखिए।

meadow / 'मेडो/ *noun* घास का मैदान।

meagre (*US* **meager**) / 'मीगर् / *adj* अपर्याप्त, अल्पमात्रा; दुबला–पतला।

meal¹ / मील् / *noun* भोजन।

meal² / मील् / *noun* (समास में) आटा : *oatmeal.*

mean¹ / मीन् / *verb* (*pt, pp* **meant** /मेन्ट्/) 1 mean sth (to sb) अर्थ निकालना, किसी शब्द का अर्थ होना 2 mean sth for sb; mean sth (as sth); mean sth (to sb) इरादा होना; चाहना : *He means what he says.* 3 mean sth to sb के लिए महत्त्वपूर्ण होना : *Your friendship means a great deal to me.* ■ **mean business** (अनौप) इरादे में गंभीर होना।

mean² / मीन्/ *adj* (**-er, -est**) 1 स्वार्थी, कंजूस 2 mean (to sb) (व्यक्ति, उनका व्यवहार) संकुचित मनोवृत्ति वाला, घटिया; नीच ▸ **meanness** *noun.*

mean³ / मीन् / *noun* 1 औसत, मध्यम 2 (*गणित*) मध्यमान, माध्य; औसत : *The mean of 13, 5 and 27 is found by adding them together and dividing them by 3.* ▸ **mean** *adj* औसत।

meander /मि'ऐन्डर्/ *verb* 1 (नदी आदि

का) टेढ़े–मेढ़े मार्ग से धीमी गति से बहना 2 (व्यक्ति का) बिना किसी उद्देश्य के इधर–उधर घूमना।

meaning /'मीनिङ् / *noun* 1 अर्थ 2 तात्पर्य, प्रयोजन ▸ **meaningless** *adj.*

means / मीन्ज़ / *noun* (*pl* अपरिवर्तित) 1 (किसी कार्य पूर्ति के) उपाय, साधन : *The passport was obtained by illegal means.* 2 संपत्ति, आय : *be a man of means* ■ **by all means** (औप) निश्चय ही **by no means** कदापि नहीं।

meantime /'मीन्टाइम्/ *noun* ■ **in the meantime** बीच के समय (में)।

meanwhile /'मीन्वाइल् / *adv* इतने में, इसी बीच।

measles / 'मीज़ल्ज़/ *noun* खसरा, एक प्रकार की चेचक (छोटी माता)।

measly / 'मीज़्लि/ *adj* (अनौप, अपमा) (आकार, मूल्य या मात्रा में) बहुत छोटा या कम : *They're paid a measly Rs 75 per day.*

measure¹ / 'मेश़र्/ *noun* 1 कार्रवाई, उपाय : *safety measures* 2 इकाई, एकक ■ **beyond measure** (औप) अत्यंत, अत्यधिक **give full/short measure** पूरी/अधूरी राशि देना **made to measure** नाप से (कपड़े आदि) बनाना।

measure² /'मेश़र्/ *verb* measure sth (in sth); measure sb/sth (up) (for sth) माप, मात्रा आदि मालूम करना : *measure the width of a door* ■ **measure sth out** नापकर निश्चित करना, नापना ▸ **measurement** *noun* 1 नाप–तौल की प्रक्रिया 2 (प्राय: *pl*) किसी वस्तु या आकृति की लंबाई/चौड़ाई/ऊँचाई आदि का वर्णन।

meat / मीट् / *noun* गोश्त, मांस।

mechanic / म'कैनिक् / *noun* मैकेनिक, मिस्त्री।

mechanical / म'कैनिकल्/ *adj* यांत्रिकीय।

mechanics /म'कैनिक्स्/ *noun* 1 (भौ–

तिकी) गतिविज्ञान/यांत्रिकी 2 मशीनरी का व्यावहारिक ज्ञान/अध्ययन : *a course in car mechanics* 3 the mechanics [*pl*] कुछ करने/संचालित होने की रीति।

mechanism / 'मे़कनिज़म् / *noun* मशीन के कल-पुर्ज़े।

mechanize, -ise / 'मे़कनाइज़् / *verb* मशीनों को प्रयोग में लाना; किसी कार्य में मशीनों का प्रयोग करना : *highly mechanized factories.*

medal / 'मे़ड्ल् / *noun* पदक, (पुरस्कार या घटना के स्मारक के रूप में) तमग़ा।

meddle / 'मे़ड्ल् / *verb* (*अपमा*) 1 **meddle (in sth)** (किसी के कार्य में बिना बुलाए) हस्तक्षेप करना 2 **meddle (with sth)** बिना जानकारी के (किसी यंत्र आदि से) छेड़-छाड़ करना : *It's dangerous to meddle with the electrical wiring.* ▸ **meddlesome** / 'मे़ड्लसम् / *adj* हस्तक्षेप करने के स्वभाव वाला।

media / 'मीडिआ / *noun* **the media** [*pl*] संचार माध्यम जैसे टी वी, रेडियो, दैनिक आदि।

mediate / 'मीडिएट् / *verb* 1 **mediate (between sb and sb)** बीच-बचाव करना, मध्यस्थता करना : *mediate a peace settlement* 2 (*औप*) संपर्क माध्यम स्थापित करना ▸ **mediation** *noun* मध्यस्थता **mediator** *noun* मध्यस्थ (व्यक्ति/संघ/वस्तु)।

medical / 'मे़डिकल् / *adj* चिकित्सा-शास्त्र से संबद्ध, डॉक्टरी : *medical treatment/ knowledge.*

medicated / 'मे़डिकेटिड् / *adj* औषधियुक्त (पदार्थ) : *medicated shampoo.*

medication / मे़डि'केश्न् / *noun* (विशेषत: *pl*) रोग-चिकित्सा औषधि।

medicine / 'मे़डिसन्; 'मे़ड्स्न् / *noun* 1 चिकित्सा-शास्त्र : *study medicine* 2 दवाई, औषध ▸ **medicine man** *noun* ओझा।

medieval (mediaeval भी) / मे़डि'ईवल् /

adj मध्यकालीन; यूरोप में 1100-1400 ईसवी का काल, (*अनौप, अपमा*) पुरातन-पंथी।

mediocre / मीडि'ओकर् / *adj* (*अपमा*) मामूली; दूसरी श्रेणी का : *a mediocre actor* ▸ **mediocrity** / मीडि'ऑक्रिटि / *noun* 1 (*अपमा*) साधारण योग्यता 2 साधारण योग्यता का व्यक्ति : *a government of mediocrities.*

meditate / 'मे़डिटेट् / *verb* 1 **meditate (on/upon sth)** चिंतन/मनन करना; ध्यान लगाना 2 (*औप*) मन में विचार करना/योजना बनाना : *meditate revenge* ▸ **meditation** / मे़डि'टेश्न् / *noun* 1 ध्यान : *seek peace through yoga and meditation* 2 (प्राय: *pl*) **meditation (on sth)** (*औप*) गहन/गंभीर विचारों की अभिव्यक्ति।

medium[1] / 'मीडिअम् / *noun* (*pl* **media** / 'मीडिया / या **mediums**) माध्यम, साधन (जिससे कोई कार्य पूरा होता है)।

medium[2] / 'मीडिअम् / *adj* मध्यम/मँझला, बीच का : *a man of medium height* ▸ **medium wave** (*संक्षि* **MW**) *noun* रेडियो में मध्यम तरंगें।

medley / 'मे़ड्लि / *noun* 1 खिचड़ी की तरह विविध वस्तुओं (रंगों/ध्वनियों आदि) का मिश्रण, घाल-मेल 2 अन्य गीतों के घाल-मेल से तैयार गीत-संगीत।

meek / मीक् / *adj* (**-er, -est**) विनम्र; दब्बू ▸ **meekly** *adv* **meekness** *noun.*

meet[1] / मीट् / *verb* (*pt, pp* **met** / मे़ट् /) 1 मिलना (कई दिशाओं या स्थानों से एक स्थान पर आना/पहुँचना); औपचारिक रूप से बातचीत के लिए मिलना 2 किसी स्थान पर जाकर किसी के आगमन की प्रतीक्षा करना 3 अनुभव करना, (बुरा मौसम आदि) झेलना; (दुर्घटना आदि) घटित होना।

meet[2] / मीट् / *noun* खेल प्रतियोगिता : *an athletics meet.*

meeting / 'मीटिङ् / *noun* 1 बैठक, सभा (विचार-विमर्श के लिए) 2 खेलों के लिए लोगों का जमाव।

megaphone / 'मेगफ़ोन् / noun मेगाफ़ोन, भोंपू।

melancholy / 'मेलन्कलि / noun (औप) उदासी ▸ **melancholy** (**melancholic** भी) adj 1 उदास : a melancholy mood 2 उदासी लाने वाला।

mellow / 'मेलो / adj (-er, -est) 1 मुलायम, पूर्णत: पका हुआ, रसीला और स्वादिष्ट; (वर्ण या ध्वनि) शुद्ध, मृदु और मनोरम 2 आयु एवं अनुभवों के कारण सहानुभूतिपूर्ण और सौम्य ▸ **mellow** verb मृदु/मनोरम बनना या बनाना।

melodrama / 'मेलड्रामा / noun सुखांत भावुकतापूर्ण नाटक; वास्तविक जीवन में इस प्रकार की घटनाएँ/व्यवहार/भाषा आदि ▸ **melodramatic** adj (अपमा) नाटकीय; सनसनीख़ेज़।

melody / 'मेलडि / noun (pl **melodies**) 1 सहज धुन का मधुर गीत 2 गीत की धुन (शब्दों के वैषम्य में) ▸ **melodic** adj **melodious** / म'लोडिअस् / adj संगीतात्मक : melodious voices.

melon / 'मेलन् / noun ख़रबूज़ा (फल)।

melt / मेल्ट् / verb 1 पिघलाना (गरमी से) 2 (खाना) मुलायम पड़ना, पसीजना; घुल जाना : a sweet that melts in the mouth 3 (किसी की भावनाएँ) नर्म/नम्र हो जाना/कर देना : Her anger quickly melted. ■ **melt** (**sth**) **away** गलना, विघटित होना, विलीन हो जाना।

member / 'मेम्बर् / noun (किसी सभा, समिति, समूह, वर्ग आदि का) सदस्य ▸ **membership** noun 1 सदस्यता 2 सदस्यों की संख्या : large membership.

membrane / 'मेम्ब्रेन् / noun झिल्ली; पन्नी।

memento / म'मेन्टो / noun (pl **mementoes** या **mementos**) यादगार, निशानी, स्मारक।

memo / 'मेमो / noun (pl **memos**) (अनौप) = memorandum.

memoir / 'मेमवार् / noun 1 लघु जीवनवृत्त 2 **memoirs** [pl] आत्म-कथा; संस्मरण।

memorable / 'मेमरबल् / adj स्मरणीय : a memorable occasion.

memorandum / मेम'रैनडम् / noun (संक्षि **memo**) (pl **memoranda** / मेम'रैन्डा /) 1 **memorandum** (**to sb**) ज्ञापन-पत्र, ज्ञापिका 2 (क़ानून) भविष्य में काम आने के लिए लिखा नोट/रिकॉर्ड, स्मरण-पत्र।

memorial / म'मॉरिअल् / noun **memorial** (**to sb/sth**) स्मारक।

memorize, -ise / 'मेमराइज़् / verb कंठस्थ करना, भली-भाँति याद करना : memorize passages from Shakespeare.

memory / 'मेमरि / noun (pl **memories**) 1 **memory** (**for sth**) स्मरणशक्ति, याददाश्त 2 याद, स्मृति।

menace / 'मेनस् / noun 1 **menace** (**to sb/sth**) (व्यक्ति/वस्तु) संकट, हानिकर : Plastic bags are a menace to the environment. 2 धमकी ▸ **menace** verb धमकाना।

menagerie / म'नैजरि / noun पशुओं की चलती-फिरती प्रदर्शनी।

mend / मेन्ड् / verb 1 मरम्मत करना/ठीक करना; पैबंद लगाना/रफ़ू करना 2 सुधारना/संशोधित करना : They tried to mend their broken marriage. ■ **mend** one's ways बुरी आदतें सुधारना।

menial / 'मीनिअल् / adj (प्राय: अपमा) (कार्य) बिना कौशल की आवश्यकता के ▸ **menial** noun (अप्र, प्राय: अपमा) घरेलू नौकर।

mental / 'मेन्ट्ल् / adj 1 मानसिक, मनोगत : an enormous mental effort 2 मानसिक बीमारी संबंधी; विक्षिप्त : a mental hospital ▸ **mentally** adv.

mentality / मेन्'टैलिटि / noun (pl **mentalities**) मनोवृत्ति।

mention / 'मेन्शन् / verb **mention sth**/

sb (as sth); mention sth/sb (to sb) उल्लेख करना (लिखने/बोलने में); नाम लेना ▸ **mention** noun (प्राय: sing) उल्लेख, चर्चा।

menu / 'मे्न्यू / noun 1 भोजन-सूची, व्यंजन-सूची 2 कंप्यूटर पर कार्य करने के लिए उपलब्ध कार्यों की सूची।

mercantile / 'मर्कन्टाइल् / adj व्यापार और परिणामों से संबंधित : mercantile law.

mercenary / 'मर्सनरि / adj (अपमा) केवल धन या पुरस्कार के लिए किया गया कार्य; धन-लोलुपता पर आधारित ▸ **mercenary** noun (pl **mercenaries**) विदेशी सेना में भाड़े का सैनिक।

merchandise / 'मर्चन्डाइज़् / noun सौदा/माल ▸ **merchandise** verb.

merchant / 'मर्चन्ट् / noun 1 व्यापारी/ सौदागर 2 (अनौप, अपमा) क्रिया विशेष का शौकीन : a speed merchant ▸ **merchant navy** noun (**merchant marine** भी) देश की व्यापारिक जहाज़रानी।

Mercury / 'मर्क्युरि / noun बुध ग्रह।

mercury / 'मर्क्युरि / noun (प्रतीक Hg) पारा (जो थर्मामीटर के भीतर होता है)।

mercy / 'मर्सि / noun (pl **mercies**) 1 दया, रहम 2 (अनौप) सौभाग्य ■ **at the mercy of sb/sth** के पूरे आधीन : be at the mercy of a moneylender ▸ **merciful** adj दयालु/रहमदिल **mercifully** adv **merciless** adj निर्दय; कठोर **mercilessly** adv.

mere / मिअर् / adj (**merest**) (कोई तुल-नात्मक रूप नहीं) केवल; एकमात्र : The interview lasted a mere five minutes. ▸ **merely** adv केवल।

merge / मर्ज़् / verb 1 **merge (with/ into sth); merge together; merge A and B (together)** (विशेषत: वाणिज्य) दो वस्तुओं को एक में मिलाना; दो व्यापारिक संस्थाओं का एक हो जाना : The bank merged with its major rival. ○ We

can merge the two businesses into a larger one. 2 **merge (into sth)** (दूसरे में) विलीन हो जाना ▸ **merger** noun विलय।

meridian / म'रिडिअन् / noun (भूगोल) याम्योत्तर रेखा, उत्तरी और दक्षिणी ध्रुवों को जोड़ने वाली किसी एक स्थान के ऊपर से जा रही रेखा : the Greenwich meridian.

merit / 'मेरिट् / noun 1 (प्राय: pl) गुण, खूबी 2 गुणवान होने की स्थिति; प्रशंसा, पुरस्कार आदि पाने की योग्यता रखना ▸ **merit** verb (औप) के योग्य होना : Her suggestion merits consideration.

meritorious / ़मेरि'टॉरिअस् / adj (औप) सराहनीय, प्रशंसनीय : a merito-rious conduct.

mermaid / 'मर्मेड् / noun जल-परी (कथाओं में जलसुंदरी जिसके पैरों के स्थान पर मछली की पूँछ है)।

merry / 'मेरि / adj (**-ier, -iest**) 1 खुश, आनंदित/प्रमुदित 2 (अनौप) हलकी-सी पिए हुए ■ **make merry** (अप्र) आमोद-पार्टी में सम्मिलित होना ▸ **merrily** adv **merriment** noun (औप) आमोद, मौज **merrymaking** noun मौज उड़ाना।

mesh / मेश् / noun 1 जाल, जाली; (प्राय: pl) जाल का छेद 2 गूढ़ तंत्र या पैटर्न; (अल) कपट-जाल; फंदा ▸ **mesh** verb **mesh (sth) (with sth/together)** 1 सामंजस्य में होना/लाना 2 मशीन के पुर्ज़ों का फँस/ जकड़ जाना।

mesmerize -ise / 'मेज़्मराइज़् / verb पूर्ण रूप से किसी का ध्यान आकर्षित करना; मंत्रमुग्ध होना।

mess¹ / मेस् / noun 1 (प्राय: sing) गंदी अव्यवस्थित स्थिति : This kitchen is a mess! 2 मुश्किल या चकरा देने वाली समस्या; अव्यवस्था ▸ **mess** verb (US अनौप) गंदा/अव्यवस्थित करना ■ **mess sth up** ख़राब कर देना ▸ **messy** adj (**-ier, -iest**) 1 गंदा, मैला-कुचैला 2 गंदगी फैलाने वाला।

mess² /मेस्/ *noun* मेस, स्थान जहाँ किसी विशिष्ट वर्ग के सदस्य भोजन करते हैं।

message /'मेसिज्/ *noun* message (from sb) (to sb) 1 संदेश 2 राजनीतिक/ नैतिक/धार्मिक अथवा सामाजिक महत्त्व का कथन/विचार ■ get the message *(अनौप)* प्रत्यक्ष कथन, संकेत आदि समझ जाना।

messenger /'मेसिन्जर/ *noun* संदेश-वाहक, दूत।

Messiah / म'साइआ / *noun* 1 (messiah भी) मसीहा, समाज का उद्धारकर्ता 2 the Messiah ईसा मसीह।

Messrs /'मेसर्ज्/ *abbr* (Mr का बहुवचन) *(फ्रेंच Messieurs)* (व्यापारिक साझेदारों के) नामों के पूर्व प्रयुक्त पद; सर्वश्री : *Messrs Smith, Brown and Robinson.*

metabolism /म'टैबलिज़म्/*noun [sing] (जीव-विज्ञान)* पेड़-पौधों एवं जंतुओं में ऐसी रासायनिक प्रक्रिया जिससे ऊर्जा उत्पन्न होती है।

metal /'मेटल्/ *noun* 1 धातु (जैसे लोहा आदि) 2 (road metal भी) सड़क बनाने में प्रयुक्त रोड़ी ▶ metallic / म'टैलिक / *adj* धातु-विषयक, धातु-सदृश।

metamorphosis / मेट'मॉर्फ़सिस् / *noun (pl metamorphoses* /मेट'मॉर्फ़-सीज़ /) *(औप)* पूर्ण रूप से (प्राकृतिक कारणों से) आकृति में परिवर्तन : *the metamorphosis of a larva into a butterfly.*

metaphor /'मेटफ़र/ *noun* रूपक; रूपक अलंकार : *She has a heart of stone.* (यहाँ *stone* रूपक अलंकार का उदाहरण है जिसका अर्थ 'कठोरता' है, न कि 'पत्थर') ▶ metaphorical *adj* metaphorically *adv.*

meteor /'मीटिअर; 'मीटिऑर / *noun* उल्का (आकाशीय पिंड जो बाहरी अंतरिक्ष से पृथ्वी के वातावरण में आने से जल जाते हैं)।

meteorology /मीटिअ'रॉलजि / *noun*

मौसम विज्ञान ▶ meteorological *adj* meteorologist *noun* मौसम विज्ञानी।

meter / 'मीटर/ *noun* (समास में) मीटर, बिजली, पानी आदि नापने का यंत्र।

method / 'मेथड्/ *noun* 1 करने का ढंग/ तरीका 2 व्यवस्था, क्रमबद्धता ▶ methodical / म'थॉडिकल् / *adj.*

methylated spirit /मेथलेटिड् 'स्पि-रिट्/ *noun* (जलने वाली) स्पिरिट।

meticulous / म'टिक्यलस् / *adj* meticulous (about sth/doing sth) अत्यंत ध्यानपूर्वक एवं सावधानी से कोई कार्य करते हुए; सूक्ष्म ▶ meticulously *adv.*

metre¹ (*US* meter) / 'मीटर् / *noun (संक्षि* m) लंबाई की इकाई (39.37 इंच)।

metre² (*US* meter) / 'मीटर् / *noun* (कविता में) छंद।

metric /'मेट्रिक्/ *adj* दशमलव प्रणाली पर आधारित ▶ the metric system *noun [sing]* दशमलव प्रणाली।

metrical / 'मेट्रिकल् / *adj* (कविता) छंदोबद्ध।

metropolis / म'ट्रॉपलिस् / *noun* महा-नगर, राजधानी ▶ metropolitan / मेट्र 'पॉलिटन् / *adj* महानगर-विषयक; महानगर में।

mettle /'मेटल्/ *noun* दिलेरी/साहस ■ on one's mettle अतिशय दिलेरी/साहस दिखाने की स्थिति में।

microbe /'माइक्रोब्/ *noun* जीवाणु, रोगाणु।

microphone /'माइक्रफ़ोन् / *noun* (*अनौप* mike भी) माइक, ध्वनि तीव्र करने का एक प्रकार का यंत्र।

microscope /'माइक्रस्कोप् / *noun* सूक्ष्मदर्शी, बहुत छोटी समीपवर्ती वस्तु को बड़ा दिखाने वाला यंत्र ▶ microscopic *adj* 1 अति सूक्ष्म 2 सूक्ष्मदर्शी के प्रयोग संबंधी।

microwave /'माइक्रवेव्/ *noun* एक प्रकार का विद्युत यंत्र जिसमें बहुत कम समय में खाना पकाया व गरम किया जा सकता है।

mid / मिड् / *adj* मध्य, मध्य में : *from mid July to mid August.*

mid- *pref* (*पूर्वपद*) बीच या मध्य में : *a mid-air collision.*

midday / मिड्'डे / *noun* दोपहर।

middle / मिड्ल् / *noun* **1** the middle [*sing*] बीच, मध्य (दो या अनेक बिंदुओं से समान दूरी का बिंदु या स्थान) : *the middle of the room* **2** प्रारंभ और अंत के बीच का स्थान : *in the middle of dinner* **3** (प्राय: *sing*) (*अनौप*) (व्यक्ति की) कमर ▸ **middle** *adj* बीच में, मध्यस्थ **middle age** *noun* मध्यावस्था, प्रौढ़ावस्था **middle class** *noun* समाज का मध्यम वर्ग **the Middle Ages** *noun* (यूरोपीय इतिहास में) 1100-1400 ईसवी के बीच का काल **the Middle East** *noun* पश्चिम एशिया, ईरान, तुर्की, जोर्डन, मिस्र आदि देश।

middleman / मिड्लमैन् / *noun* (व्यापार में) दलाल; उत्पादक और उपभोक्ता के बीच का व्यापारी।

middling / मिड्लिङ् / *adj* **1** मध्यम, मँझला **2** मामूली ढंग से।

midget / मिजिट् / *noun* बौना/नाटा ▸ **midget** *adj* लघु रूप : *a midget submarine.*

midnight / मिड्नाइट् / *noun* ठीक आधी-रात।

midst / मिड्स्ट्; मिट्स्ट् / *noun* बीच में ▪ **in the midst of** के बीच, के दौरान **in our/your/their midst** हम/तुम/उन लोगों के बीच।

midsummer / मिड्समर् / *noun* ग्रीष्म ऋतु का मध्य।

midway / मिड्'वे / *adj, adv* **midway between sth and sth** आधे रास्ते पर।

midwife / मिड्वाइफ् / *noun* (*pl* **midwives**) प्रसवकारिणी दाई (बच्चा पैदा होने में सहायता देने वाली स्त्री), नर्स; धात्री ▸ **midwifery** *noun* धात्री कर्म।

might / माइट् / *noun* (*औप*) बल/शक्ति; महाबल/महाआकार।

mighty / माइटि / *adj* (-ier, -iest) **1** (विशेषत: *साहि*) महाबली **2** महान, प्रभावशाली।

migrate / माइ'ग्रेट् / *verb* **migrate (from...) (to...)** **1** एक स्थान से दूसरे स्थान पर बसने के लिए जाना **2** (पशु-पक्षियों का) मौसम के अनुसार नियमित रूप से कहीं जाना और फिर लौटना : *These birds migrate to North Africa in winter.* ▸ **migrant** / माइग्रन्ट् / *noun* प्रवासी (व्यक्ति), प्रवासी (पक्षी) **migration** / माइ'ग्रेश्न् / *noun* देशांतरण; स्थानांतरण : *a period of mass migration.*

mild / माइल्ड् / *adj* (-er, -est) **1** मुलायम; सौम्य : *a mild punishment* **2** (व्यक्ति) सौम्य एवं दयालु **3** मध्यम, स्वाद में तेज़/तीखा नहीं : *a mild cigar/curry* **4** (मौसम) अधिक ठंडा नहीं ▸ **mildly** *adv.*

mile / माइल् / *noun* **1** मील (=1.6 किमी) **2** (प्राय: *pl*) (*अनौप*) बहुत अधिक; लंबा रास्ता ▸ **milestone** *noun* **1** सड़क के किनारे लगा मील का पत्थर **2** महत्त्वपूर्ण घटना : *His election victory was an important milestone in the country's history.*

mileage (**milage** भी) / माइलिज् / *noun* **1** मील में दूरी **2** **mileage** (**in sb/sth**) (*अनौप*) लाभ, फ़ायदा।

militant / मिलिटन्ट् / *adj* लड़ाकू/लड़ाका; युद्धरत ▸ **militancy** *noun* **militant** *noun* राजनीतिक लाभ के लिए बल प्रयोग को उद्धत व्यक्ति।

military / मिलटरि; *US* मिलटेरि / *adj* सैनिक का/सैनिक के लिए; सेना-विषयक ▸ **the military** *noun* फ़ौज (विशेषत: थल-सेना)।

militia / म'लिशा / *noun* नागरिक सेना : *local militia units.*

milk / मिल्क् / *noun* **1** दूध **2** कुछ पेड़ों और पौधों का दूधिया रस, जैसे नारियल का रस ▸ **milk** *verb* **1** दूध दुहना **2** **milk sb/sth**

(of sth); milk sth (out of/from sb/ sth) किसी से चालाकी से सूचना/धन आदि प्राप्त करना : *milk the benefits system* **milkmaid** *noun* ग्वालिन **milkman** *noun* ग्वाला **milk tooth** *noun* (बच्चों के) दूध वाले दाँत **milky** *adj* (-ier, -iest) 1 दूध युक्त 2 दूध की तरह।

mill¹ / मिल् / *noun* 1 (विशेषत: समास में) कारखाना, मिल : *a cotton/paper mill* 2 चक्की, आटा-चक्की 3 (समास में) पीसने की छोटी मशीन : *a pepper mill.*

mill² / मिल् / *verb* पीसना : *freshly milled pepper.*

millennium / मि'लेनिअम् / *noun* (*pl* **millennia**) सहस्राब्दी।

miller / 'मिलर् / *noun* आटा-चक्की का मालिक या काम करने वाला।

millet / 'मिलिट् / *noun* बाजरा।

milli- *pref* (पूर्वपद) एक हज़ारवाँ भाग : *milligram/millimetre.*

milliner / 'मिलिनर् / *noun* स्त्रियों के हैट बनाने व बेचने वाला ▶ **millinery** *noun* स्त्रियों के हैट बनाने/बेचने का व्यापार।

million / 'मिलयन् / *noun* 1 दस लाख या 1,000,000 2 **millions** [*pl*] अत्यधिक विशाल मात्रा : *an audience of millions.*

millionaire / मिलय'नेअर् / *noun* लखपति, अत्यधिक अमीर व्यक्ति।

mime / माइम् / *noun* स्वांग; शब्दों के प्रयोग के बिना केवल मुद्राओं एवं अभिव्यक्तियों द्वारा कहानी कहने की प्रणाली : *a play acted entirely in mime* ▶ **mime** *verb* स्वांग भरना, बिना बोले इशारों में ही कहानी कहना।

mimic / 'मिमिक् / *verb* (*pt, pp* **mimicked**) 1 (हँसी-मज़ाक में) दूसरों की नक़ल उतारना : *mimic sb's accent* 2 (जीवों, वस्तुओं का) सदृश होना : *insects that mimic dead leaves to avoid being eaten by birds* ▶ **mimic** *noun* नक़लची, नक़ल उतारने वाला **mimicry** *noun* नक़ल।

minaret / मिन'रेट् / *noun* मीनार।

mince / मिन्स् / *verb* क़ीमा करना, काट-काटकर टुकड़े करना।

mind¹ / माइन्ड् / *noun* 1 चित्त, मन; तर्क-शक्ति : *have a brilliant mind* 2 मनोदशा; प्रयोजन, राय : *The tragedy affected his mind.* 3 (प्राय: *sing*) स्मृति, याददाश्त ■ **be in two minds about sth/doing sth** दुविधा में होना **be of one/the same mind (about sb/sth)** सहमति में होना **be/go out of one's mind** (अनौप) पागल हो जाना **bring/call sb/sth to mind** याद दिलाना/रखना **change one's/sb's mind** इरादा बदल देना **have a (good) mind to do sth** कुछ करने की तीव्र इच्छा होना **keep/bear sth in mind** याद रखना **make up one's mind** निश्चय कर लेना **(not) in one's right mind** पागल, सनकी **put sb in mind of sb/sth** याद दिलाना **take one's/ sb's mind off (sth)** किसी वस्तु से ध्यान हटा लेना।

mind² / माइन्ड् / *verb* 1 आपत्ति (उज्र) करना; कष्ट उठाना : *Do you mind the noise? ○ Do you mind if I smoke?* 2 देखभाल करना : *mind the baby* 3 ध्यान रखना; सावधानी बरतना : *Mind your manners!* ■ **mind one's own business** अपने काम से काम रखना और दूसरों के मामले में टाँग न अड़ाना **mind out (for sb/sth)** सावधान होना : *Mind out for falling rocks.*

minded / 'माइन्डिड् / *adj* (यौगिक शब्दों में प्रयुक्त) 1 विशेष प्रकार की मनोदशा बताते हुए : *a strong-minded/narrow-minded person* 2 किसी चीज़ में अधिक रुचि रखते हुए : *money-minded.*

mindful / 'माइन्ड्फ़ुल् / *adj* **mindful of sb/sth** (औप) सावधान; ध्यान रखते हुए।

mindless / 'माइन्ड्लस् / *adj* 1 **mindless of sb/sth** (औप) बिना परवाह किए

2 बिना विचारे, निरुद्देश्य 3 तर्कहीन : *mindless hooligans.*

mine¹ / माइन् / *possess pron* मेरी/मेरा : *That book is mine.*

mine² / माइन् / *noun* 1 खान, (कोयले आदि की) खदान : *a silver mine* 2 (बारूदी) सुरंग जिसे विस्फोट से उड़ाया जा सकता है : *clear the coastal waters of mines* ▸ **minefield** *noun* भूमि या समुद्र का वह स्थल जहाँ सुरंगें बिछी हों।

mine³ / माइन् / *verb* 1 mine for sth खान/खदान से कोयला आदि निकालना 2 समुद्र, भूमि आदि में बारूदी सुरंग बिछाना; सुरंगों द्वारा कुछ नष्ट करना : *The cruiser was mined, and sank in five minutes.* 3 सुरंग खोदना।

miner / माइनर् / *noun* खान में काम करने वाला मज़दूर, खनिक।

mineral / मिनरल् / *noun* खनिज पदार्थ ▸ **mineral water** *noun* झरनों आदि का खनिज लवणों युक्त पानी; बोतलबंद पीने का ऐसा पानी।

mingle / मिङ्गल् / *verb* 1 mingle with sth/mingle (together) मिश्रण करना, मिलाना : *allow the flavours to mingle (together)* 2 mingle with sb/sth; mingle (together) घूम-फिरकर लोगों से मिलना/संपर्क करना।

mini- *pref* (पूर्वपद) आकार, लंबाई आदि में बहुत ही छोटा : *minibus ० mini-bar.*

miniature / मिनचर् / *noun* लघुरूप; किसी की बहुत छोटे पैमाने पर खींची आकृति ▸ **miniature** *adj* लघु : *a miniature railway.*

minimize, -ise / मिनिमाइज़् / *verb* न्यूनतम करना।

minimum / मिनिमम् / *noun* (pl minima / मिनिमा /) न्यूनतम, लघुतम मात्रा; राशि आदि : *reduce sth to the minimum* ▸ **minimum** *adj* लघुतम, निम्नतम : *a minimum charge.*

minister¹ / मिनिस्टर् / *noun* 1 (US

secretary) (राज्य शासन में) मंत्री : *the Minister of Education* (शिक्षा मंत्री) 2 पुरोहित, (चर्च में) अनुष्ठाता।

minister² / मिनिस्टर् / *verb* ■ minister to sb/sth (औप) सहायता करना : *nurses ministering to the sick.*

ministry / मिनिस्ट्रि / *noun* (pl ministries) 1 (US department) मंत्रालय : *the Ministry of Defence* (रक्षा मंत्रालय) 2 मंत्रिमंडल 3 the ministry [sing] धर्मसेवा : *enter/take up the ministry.*

minor / माइनर् / *adj* गौण, कम महत्त्वपूर्ण : *minor repairs/alterations* ▸ **minor** *noun* (क़ानून) 18 वर्ष से कम का व्यक्ति, नाबालिग़, अवयस्क।

minority / माइ'नॉरिटि / *noun* (pl minorities) 1 अल्पसंख्यक वर्ग : *the rights of ethnic minorities* 2 अल्पांश; मतदान में अल्पमत 3 (क़ानून) नाबालिग़ होने की स्थिति।

minster / मिन्स्टर् / *noun* बड़ा या महत्त्वपूर्ण चर्च, विशेषत: मठ से संबंधित।

mint¹ / मिन्ट् / *noun* 1 टकसाल (जहाँ सिक्के आदि ढलते हैं) 2 [sing] (अनौप) अत्यधिक धन का भंडार ▸ **mint** *verb* सिक्के ढालना।

mint² / मिन्ट् / *noun* 1 पुदीना (पौधा) 2 पेपरमिंट (की गोलियाँ)।

minus / माइनस् / *prep* 1 (गणित) ऋण, कम : *Seven minus three equals four (7–3 = 4).* 2 शून्य से कम/नीचे : *a temperature of minus ten degrees centigrade (-10°C)* ▸ **minus** *adj* (गणित) ऋण संख्या, शून्य से कम, जैसे–*15* **minus** *noun* 1 (minus sign भी) '-' चिह्न 2 (अनौप) हानि, नुक़सान।

minute¹ / मिनिट् / *noun* 1 (संक्षि min) मिनट (घंटे का 60वाँ अंश) 2 कोण में अंश का 60वाँ अंश 3 किसी साक्षात्कार आदि का (टिप्पणी आदि सहित) सरकारी विवरण : *make a minute of sth* 4 minutes

[pl] कार्यवृत्त विवरण : *We read the minutes of the last meeting.* ▶ **minute** *verb* कार्यवृत्त विवरण तैयार करना।

minute² / माइ'न्यूट् / *adj* (-r, -st) 1 बहुत सूक्ष्म 2 छोटे-छोटे विवरण के साथ एवं सटीक : *a minute examination/inspection.*

miracle / 'मिरकल् / *noun* 1 चमत्कार : *perform/work miracles* 2 [*sing*] (अनौप) उल्लेखनीय घटना : *an economic miracle* 3 **miracle of sth** अनुपम उदाहरण ▶ **miraculous** / मि'रैक्यलस् / *adj* चमत्कारिक; अनुपम।

mirage / 'मिराश् / *noun* 1 मृगमरीचिका (रेगिस्तान में हवा में बना मिथ्या-दर्शन) 2 मृगतृष्णा; न पूरी होने वाली आशाएँ : *a mirage of equality.*

mire / 'माइअर् / *noun* कीचड़; दलदल ▶ **mire** *verb* **mire sb/sth in sth** उन्नति रोक देना।

mirror / 'मिरर् / *noun* 1 दर्पण; शीशा 2 प्रतिबिंबित करने वाली वस्तु; प्रतिनिधित्व करने वाली वस्तु : *Dickens's novels are a mirror of his times.* ▶ **mirror** *verb* **mirror sth (in sth)** प्रतिबिंब देना; प्रतिनिधित्व करना।

mirth / मर्थ् / *noun* (औप) उल्लास, हँसी-ठिठोली ▶ **mirthless** *adj.*

mis- *pref* (पूर्वपद) (बुरा, ग़लत आदि सांकेतिक करते हुए) हिंदी में प्रयुक्त बु-, दुर- आदि उपसर्ग : *misdirect ○ misconduct.*

misanthrope / 'मिसन्थ्रोप् / *noun* (औप) मानव-द्वेषी ▶ **misanthropic** / मिसन् 'थ्रोपिक् / *adj* **misanthropy** *noun.*

misbehave / मिसबि'हेव् / *verb* **misbehave (oneself)** अनुचित/अशिष्ट आचरण करना : *Harry and Tom misbehaved themselves.* ▶ **misbehaviour** (*US* **misbehavior**) / मिसबि 'हेव्यर् / *noun.*

miscarriage / मिस्'कैरिज् / *noun* 1 गर्भपात 2 (औप) योजना की असफलता ▶ **miscarriage of justice** *noun* (क़ानून) दंड देने या निर्णय करने में ग़लती, न्याय-हत्या : *Sending an innocent man to prison is a clear miscarriage of justice.*

miscarry / मिस्'कैरि / *verb* (*pt, pp* **miscarried**) 1 गर्भपात होना 2 योजनाओं का असफल हो जाना; आशा से भिन्न परिणाम हो जाना।

miscellaneous / मिस'लेनिअस् / *adj* फुटकर; विविध : *miscellaneous items.*

mischance / मिस्'चान्स् / *US* मिस्'चैन्स् / *noun* (औप) दुर्भाग्य : *By pure mischance our secret was discovered.*

mischief / 'मिस्चिफ् / *noun* 1 शरारत; नटखटपन : *do sth out of mischief* 2 जानबूझकर हानि (पहुँचाना) या अनिष्ट (करना)।

mischievous / 'मिस्चिवस् / *adj* 1 शरारती, शरारत में लीन 2 (औप) हानिकर/ अनिष्टकारक वस्तु।

misconception / मिसकन् 'सेप्श्न् / *noun* **misconception about sth** ग़लत धारणा।

misconduct / मिस्'कॉन्डक्ट् / *noun* (औप) 1 ग़लत या बुरा व्यवहार; दुराचार 2 बहुत ख़राब प्रबंध : *misconduct of the company's affairs.*

misconstrue / मिसकन् 'स्ट्रू / *verb* **misconstrue sth (as sth)** (औप) ग़लत धारणा बना लेना; किसी को ग़लत समझना : *I don't want my remarks to be misconstrued.*

miscreant / 'मिस्क्रिअन्त् / *noun* (औप) बदमाश या अपराधी (व्यक्ति)।

misdeed / मिस्'डीड् / *noun* (प्रायः *pl*) (औप) दुष्कर्म; अपराध।

misdirect / मिसड 'रेक्ट्; मिसडाइ 'रेक्ट् / *verb* 1 **misdirect sb/sth (to sth)** ग़लत रास्ता बताना, बहकाना 2 (क़ानून)

(न्यायाधीश द्वारा) जूरी को ग़लत सूचना देना/ गुमराह करना 3 किसी चीज़ का ग़लत प्रयोग करना : *misdirected energies/abilities.*

miser / 'माइज़र् / *noun (अपमा)* कंजूस, कृपण ▸ **miserly** *adj* 1 कृपण समान 2 मुश्किल से पर्याप्त, बहुत कम : *a miserly amount/helping.*

miserable / 'मिज़्रब्ल् / *adj* 1 (स्थिति) दयनीय, दुखद : *He makes her life miserable.* 2 (गुणवत्ता) घटिया 3 अति निराशाजनक : *The plan was a miserable failure.* ▸ **miserably** / 'मिज़्- रब्लि / *adv* बुरी तरह से।

misery / 'मिज़रि / *noun (pl miseries)* 1 दुर्दशा, विपत्ति; कंगाली   2 *(अनौप)* फटेहाल एवं दुर्दशाग्रस्त व्यक्ति : *My father's a real old misery!*

misfire / ˌमिस्'फ़ाइअर् / *verb* 1 (बंदूक का निशाने पर) गोली न दागना 2 (मोटरकार के इंजन का) न चलना 3 अपेक्षित प्रभाव न उत्पन्न कर पाना : *The joke misfired completely.* ▸ **misfire** *noun.*

misfit / 'मिस्फ़िट् / *noun* अनुपयुक्त : *a social misfit.*

misfortune / ˌमिस्'फ़ॉर्चून् / *noun* दुर्भाग्य; विपत्ति।

misgiving / ˌमिस्'गिविङ् / *noun* **misgiving (about sth/doing sth)** *(औप)* संदेह; अविश्वास : *I've serious misgivings about (taking) the job.*

misguided / ˌमिस्'गाइडिड् / *adj* बहकाया हुआ, ग़लत अनुमानित।

mishap / 'मिस्हैप् / *noun* अनिष्ट, *(प्रायः* मामूली) दुर्घटना : *Our journey ended without (further) mishap.*

mislay / ˌमिस्'ले / *verb (pt, pp mislaid* / ˌमिस्'लेड् /) किसी वस्तु को किसी स्थान पर रखकर भूल जाना कि कहाँ रख दी है।

mislead / ˌमिस्'लीड् / *verb (pt, pp misled)* **mislead sb (about sth)**; **mislead sb (into doing sth)** पथभ्रष्ट करना;

ग़लत धारणा देना : *Don't be misled by the brochure—it's not a very nice place.* ▸ **misleading** *adj.*

misplace / ˌमिस्'प्लेस् / *verb (औप)* ग़लत जगह पर रख देना ▸ **misplaced** *adj* 1 (प्रेम, स्नेह आदि) अपात्र को दिया गया : *misplaced admiration* 2 स्थिति के अनुसार सही नहीं/अनुचित : *misplaced optimism.*

misprint / 'मिस्प्रिन्ट् / *noun* मुद्रण में ग़लती : *The book is full of misprints.*

misrepresent / ˌमिस्ˌरेप्रि'ज़ेन्ट् / *verb* **misrepresent sb/sth (as sth)** ग़लत विवरण देना ▸ **misrepresentation** *noun.*

misrule / ˌमिस्'रूल् / *noun* कुशासन।

Miss / मिस् / *noun* 1 कुमारियों के लिए प्रयुक्त संबोधन : *Miss Jyoti Luthra* 2 युवतियों के लिए प्रयुक्त संबोधन।

miss¹ / मिस् / *verb* 1 (मारने, पकड़ने, पढ़ने, देखने, सुनने आदि में) चूकना; हाथ से जाने देना : *miss the target/goal* 2 कहीं पर न पहुँच पाना, देर से पहुँचना : *miss a meeting* 3 किसी वस्तु या व्यक्ति के अभाव का अनुभव करना : *We seem to be missing two chairs.* ■ **miss sb/sth out** कहने से रह जाना/छोड़ देना **miss the boat/bus** अवसर चूक जाना ▸ **missing** *adj* 1 अपने स्थान पर अप्राप्त : *The book had two pages missing.* 2 लापता; ग़ायब : *Our cat's been missing for a week.*

miss² / मिस् / *noun* चूक; भूल; अभाव।

misshapen / ˌमिस्'शेपन् / *adj* विकृत (अंग), कुरूप।

missile / 'मिसाइल् / *noun* मिसाइल; प्रक्षेपास्त्र : *ballistic/nuclear missiles.*

mission / 'मिशन् / *noun* 1 मिशन, विशेष कार्य के लिए (विशेषतः विदेश में) भेजा हुआ शिष्टमंडल : *a British trade mission to China* 2 ईसाई धर्म की शिक्षा एवं प्रचार के लिए समर्पित लोगों का समूह; ऐसे

व्यक्तियों द्वारा किया कार्य, उनके भवन, संगठन आदि 3 विशिष्ट कार्य जिनके लिए व्यक्ति अपना जीवन समर्पित करने को तैयार रहता है : *Her mission in life is to help AIDS victims.*

missionary / 'मिश्नरि / *noun* (*pl* **missionaries**) मिशनरी, धर्म प्रचारक।

mist¹ /मिस्ट् / *noun* कुहासा (कोहरे से कम घना) : *hills hidden in mist* ▶ **misty** / 'मिस्टि/ *adj* (**-ier, -iest**) 1 कुहासे से पूर्ण 2 धुँधला।

mist² / मिस्ट् / *verb* ■ **mist** (**sth**) (**up**) कुहासे से ढक जाना/देना।

mistake¹ / मि'स्टेक् / *noun* 1 भूल; मूर्खतापूर्ण कार्य 2 ग़लती, त्रुटि : *spelling mistakes.*

mistake² /मि'स्टेक् / *verb* (*pt* **mistook** / मि'स्तुक् /; *pp* **mistaken** / मि'स्टे- कन् /) ग़लत समझना : *She is often mistaken for her twin sister.* ▶ **mistaken** *adj.*

mistress / 'मिस्ट्रस् / *noun* 1 मालकिन, अधिकारिणी 2 गृहिणी; गृहस्वामिनी 3 स्कूल अध्यापिका : *the French mistress.*

mistrust /मिस्'ट्रस्ट् / *verb* 1 किसी वस्तु/ व्यक्ति में विश्वास न रखना 2 (किसी के प्रति) संदेह/अविश्वास करना : *mistrust sb's motives* ▶ **mistrust** *noun* **mistrust** (**of sb/sth**) अविश्वास, संदेह **mistrustful** *adj* **mistrustful** (**of sb/sth**) शक्की, शंकालु।

misunderstand /मिसन्डर्'स्टैन्ड् / *verb* (*pt, pp* **misunderstood**) (कहे या लिखे का) ग़लत अर्थ लगाना; किसी व्यक्ति/ वस्तु के संबंध में ग़लत धारणा बनाना ▶ **misunderstanding** *noun* 1 ग़लतफ़हमी 2 भ्रम से उत्पन्न वैमनस्य : *We had a slight misunderstanding over the bill.*

misuse /मिस्'यूज़् / *verb* 1 ग़लत उद्देश्य के लिए प्रयोग करना, दुरुपयोग करना 2 क्रूरतापूर्ण व्यवहार करना ▶ **misuse**

/मिस्'यूस्/ *noun* दुरुपयोग : *the misuse of power/authority.*

mitigate / 'मिटिगेट् / *verb* (औप) (कष्ट आदि को) कम करना : *mitigate sb's suffering/anger* ▶ **mitigation** /,मिटि 'गेश्न् / *noun.*

mitten / 'मिट्न् / (**mitt** भी) *noun* एक प्रकार का दस्ताना जो चारों उँगलियों को एक साथ और अँगूठे को अलग ढकता है।

mix / मिक्स् / *verb* 1 **mix A with B/mix A and B** (**together**) मिश्रण करना, मिलाना : *mix the sugar with the flour* 2 मिश्रण करके कुछ तैयार करना 3 **mix** (**with sb/sth**) (लोगों का) मिलना- जुलना : *I mix with all sorts of people.* ▶ **mix** *noun* मिश्रण।

mixed / 'मिक्स्ट् / *adj* मिश्रित, विविध प्रकार का; मिला-जुला : *a mixed school.*

mixer / 'मिक्सर् / *noun* विभिन्न वस्तुओं को मिश्रित करने का यंत्र : *a food mixer.*

mixture / 'मिक्स्चर् / *noun* 1 मिश्रण 2 घाल-मेल : *The city is a mixture of old and new buildings.* 3 मिश्रण करने की प्रक्रिया।

moan / मोन् / *noun* 1 कराहट : *the moans of the wounded* 2 (अनौप) शिकायत ▶ **moan** *verb* 1 कराहना 2 **moan** (**about sth**) शिकायत करना।

moat /मोट् / *noun* क़िले के चारों ओर बनी खाई, खंदक ▶ **moated** *adj.*

mob / मॉब् / *noun* 1 भीड़, विशेषत: उग्र भीड़; जनसाधारण 2 (अनौप) आपराधिक प्रवृत्ति के लोगों का समूह, गिरोह ▶ **mob** *verb* (**-bb-**) भीड़ करना; मिलकर घेर लेना : *a pop singer mobbed by fans.*

mobile / 'मोबाइल् / *adj* 1 गतिशील; चलता-फिरता : *mobile library* 2 (व्यक्ति) वर्ग, जीविका या स्थान आसानी से बदल सकने वाले : *a mobile work- force* ▶ **mobile** (**mobile phone, cel- lular phone, cell phone** भी) *noun*

मोबाइल फ़ोन **mobility** / मो'बिलटि / *noun* गतिशीलता।

mobilize, -ise /'मोबलाइज़् / *verb* 1 शक्ति, सामग्री आदि को कार्य और प्रयोग (विशेषत: युद्ध) के लिए इकट्ठा करना 2 विशेष उद्देश्य के लिए लोगों/वस्तुओं को संगठित करना : *mobilize local residents to oppose the new development* ▸ **mobilization, -isation** / मोबिलाइ'ज़ेशन् / *noun* लामबंदी।

mock[1] / मॉक् / *verb* 1 mock (at sb/sth) हँसी उड़ाना; नक़ल उतारकर मज़ाक़ बनाना 2 (औप) किसी व्यक्ति/वस्तु का सम्मान या भय न करना।

mock[2] / मॉक् / *adj* नक़ली; अवास्तविक : *a mock battle/exam* ▸ **mockingly** *adv.*

mockery / 'मॉकरि / *noun* 1 उपहास, हँसी उड़ाने की क्रिया 2 **mockery (of sth)** बुरा अथवा निंदनीय उदाहरण : *a political system that is a mockery of democracy* 3 उपहास का पात्र व्यक्ति/वस्तु।

mode / मोड् / *noun* 1 **mode (of sth)** (औप) ढंग, रीति 2 (कपड़ों आदि का) फ़ैशन; प्रथा 3 (तक) (उपकरण आदि से) कार्य करने का तरीक़ा : *manual or automatic mode.*

model[1] /'मॉडल् / *noun* 1 किसी वस्तु का लघुरूप; नमूना 2 **model (of sth)** आदर्श प्रतिमान (वस्तु या व्यक्ति) : *a model student/teacher* 3 मॉडल, डिज़ाइन; विज्ञापन आदि के प्रदर्शन के लिए प्रयुक्त युवती/युवक 4 व्याख्या आदि के लिए प्रयुक्त किसी वस्तु का प्रतिरूप : *a model of a molecule.*

model[2] / मॉडल् / *verb* (-ll-; *US* -l-) 1 **model oneself/sth on sb/sth** आदर्श या प्रतिमान के रूप में लेना, स्वयं को तदनुरूप ढालना 2 मॉडल के रूप में कार्य करना : *She models swimwear in her spare time.* 3 (मूर्ति) गढ़ना ▸ **modelling** (*US* **modeling**) *noun.*

modem / मोडेम् / *noun* एक उपकरण जो टेलिफ़ोन लाइन के माध्यम से दो या अधिक कंप्यूटरों को जोड़ता है।

moderate[1] /'मॉडरट् / *adj* 1 माध्यम, सामान्य 2 (राज) उदारवादी : *a man with moderate views* ▸ **moderate** *noun* उदारवादी व्यक्ति **moderately** *adv* साधारण (रूप से)।

moderate[2] /'मॉडरेट् / *verb* संयत होना/ करना, कम या मंद होना : *He must learn to moderate his temper.*

moderation /मॉड'रेशन् / *noun* नियमन।

moderator /'मॉडरेटर् / *noun* नियामक व्यक्ति।

modern / 'मॉडर्न् / *adj* 1 आधुनिक : *modern European history* 2 नवीन और अधुनातन : *modern marketing techniques* 3 वर्तमान फ़ैशन वाला ▸ **modernism** *noun* आधुनिकतावाद **modernity** *noun* (औप) आधुनिकता।

modernize, -ise / 'मॉडर्नाइज़् / *verb* 1 आधुनिक स्थितियों के अनुकूल बनाना 2 आधुनिक बनाना : *a fully modernized office.*

modest / 'मॉडिस्ट् / *adj* 1 साधारण (न कि बहुत बड़ा) : *live on a modest income* 2 विनम्र, सुशील 3 **modest (about sth)** संकोची, निरंहकारी : *a quiet and modest man* ▸ **modestly** *adv* **modesty** / 'मॉडिस्टि / *noun* विनम्रता।

modify /'मॉडिफ़ाइ / *noun* (*pt, pp* **modified**) 1 मामूली परिवर्तन करना 2 (व्या) दूसरे शब्द का अर्थ सीमित करना ▸ **modification** /मॉडिफ़ि'केशन्/ *noun.*

module / 'मॉड्यूल् / *noun* 1 किसी भवन या फ़र्नीचर के अलग-अलग जोड़े गए हिस्सों में से एक 2 अंतरिक्ष यान का स्वतंत्र रूप से कार्य कर सकने वाला भाग : *the command module* 3 पाठ्यक्रम का एक स्वतंत्र भाग 4 बड़ी संरचना की एक छोटी, किंतु स्वतंत्र सत्ता वाली, इकाई।

moist / 'मॉइस्ट् / *adj* नम, गीला ▸ **mois-**

ten / 'मॉइस्न् / *verb* नम/गीला होना/ करना : *a cloth moistened with water.*

moisture /'मॉइस्चर्/*noun* नमी, आर्द्रता; सील।

molar / 'मोलर् / *noun* चर्वण-दंत, दाढ़।

mole[1] / मोल् / *noun* छछूँदर ▸ **molehill** *noun* छछूँदर की बाँबी।

mole[2] / मोल् / *noun* (त्वचा पर) तिल, मस्सा।

molecule /'मॉलिक्यूल् / *noun* अणु ▸ **molecular** / म'लेक्यलर् / *adj* आण्विक।

molest / म'लेस्ट् / *verb* 1 उग्र रूप से छेड़छाड़ करना, दुर्व्यवहार करना : *an old man molested and robbed by a gang of youths* 2 (महिला के साथ) शारीरिक छेड़-छाड़ करना ▸ **molestation** *noun* **molester** *noun.*

molten /'मोल्टन्/ *adj* पिघला हुआ : *molten rock/lava.*

moment / 'मोमन्ट् / *noun* 1 क्षण 2 [*sing*] समय का यथार्थ बिंदु : *the moment of birth* 3 कुछ करने का अवसर : *wait for the right moment* ▪ **in a moment** तुरंत **the moment/minute (that...)** जैसे ही।

momentary /'मोमन्टरि / *adj* क्षणिक ▸ **momentarily** *adv.*

momentous / म'मेन्टस् / *adj* अति महत्त्वपूर्ण : *a momentous decision.*

momentum / म'मेन्टम्; मो'मेन्टम् / *noun* संवेग, गति-मात्रा।

monarch /'मॉनर्क् / *noun* राजा ▸ **monarchical** *adj* **monarchy** / 'मॉनर्कि / *noun* (*pl* **monarchies**) 1 the monarchy राजशाही 2 राजा द्वारा शासित देश।

monastery /'मॉनस्ट्रि / *noun* (*pl* **monasteries**) मठ।

monastic /म'नैस्टिक्/ *adj* 1 मठ-विषयक 2 साधारण और शांत, मठ की ज़िंदगी जैसा : *lead a monastic life.*

Monday /'मन्डे / *noun* (*संक्षि* **Mon**) सोमवार।

monetary /'मनिट्रि; *US* 'मनिटेरि / *adj* मुद्रा संबंधी, आर्थिक।

money / 'मनि / *noun* (*pl* कुछ अर्थों में **moneys** या **monies**) 1 रुपया-पैसा, मुद्रा 2 धन-संपत्ति 3 [*pl*] (*प्रा* या *क़ानून*) धनराशि।

mongrel / 'मङ्ग्रल् / *noun* दोगला कुत्ता।

monitor / 'मॉनिटर् / *noun* 1 निरीक्षण, परीक्षण या रिकॉर्ड करने के लिए प्रयुक्त उपकरण : *a heat monitor* 2 (*fem* **monitress**) कक्षा-नायक, मानिटर 3 कंप्यूटर का उपकरण जिसके स्क्रीन पर सूचना प्रकट होती है ▸ **monitor** *verb* निरीक्षण एवं नियंत्रण करना : *monitor sb's performance.*

monk / मङ्क् / *noun* मठवासी, भिक्षु।

monkey /'मङ्कि / *noun* बंदर ▸ **monkey** *verb* ▪ **monkey about/around** (*अनौप*) शैतानी/शरारत करना।

mono /'मॉनो / *adj* एक ही चैनल से उत्पन्न या रिकॉर्ड की गई ध्वनि : *a mono recording.*

mon(o)- *pref* (*पूर्वपद*) एक : *monorail* ∘ *monoplane.*

monogamy / म'नॉगमि /*noun* एक समय पर केवल एक पत्नी या पति रखने की प्रथा ▸ **monogamous** *adj.*

monologue (*US* **monolog** भी) /'मॉनलॉग् / *noun* एकालाप (नाटक का ऐसा दृश्य जिसमें केवल एक अकेला व्यक्ति बोलता है)।

monopolize, -ise /म'नॉपलाइज़्/*verb* एकाधिकार करना/पाना/रखना ▸ **monopolization, -isation** *noun.*

monopoly / म'नॉपलि / *noun* (*pl* **monopolies**) 1 monopoly (**in/on** **sth**) (*वाणिज्य*) किसी वस्तु के उत्पादन या वितरण का एकाधिकार 2 monopoly (**in/** **of/on sth**) (व्यापार आदि का) एकाधिकार : *A good education should not*

be the monopoly of the rich.
▸ **monopolist** / म॒'नॉप'लिस्ट् / *noun* एकाधिकार रखने वाला व्यक्ति/कंपनी।

monosyllable / 'मॉन्‌सिलबल् / *noun* एकाक्षरी शब्द, जैसे *'it'* या *'no'* ▸ **monosyllabic** / ‚मॉनसि'लैबिक् / *adj* एकाक्षरी।

monotone / 'मॉनटोन् / *noun* (गाने में) एक स्वर, बोलने का एकसुरा नीरस ढंग ▸ **monotone** *adj* एकसुर : *monotone utterances.*

monotonous / म॒'नॉटनस् / *adj* एकसुरा; नीरस, उबाऊ ▸ **monotony** / म॒'नॉटनि / *noun* एकरसता/नीरसता; ऊब : *relieve the monotony of everyday life.*

Monsieur / म॒'स्यर् / *noun* (*pl* **Messieurs** / मे'स्यर् /) (*संक्षि* M) (उन देशों में जहाँ फ्रेंच बोली जाती है) पुरुष के लिए प्रयुक्त शिष्ट संबोधन, श्रीमान।

monsoon / ‚मॉन'सून् / *noun* 1 मानसून (हिंद महासागर में गरमी में दक्षिण-पश्चिम और सर्दी में उत्तर-पूर्व से हवा का बहना) 2 वर्षाकाल।

monster / 'मॉन्स्टर् / *noun* 1 विरूप (प्राय: महाकाय) जंतु या पौधा 2 (कथाओं में) दैत्य, राक्षस (काल्पनिक प्राणी) 3 अति निर्दयी व्यक्ति : *He was described as an unfeeling, treacherous monster.*

monstrous / 'मॉन्स्ट्रस् / *adj* 1 दैत्याकार, महाकाय 2 दैत्यविषयक 3 बेतुका, निरर्थक एवं अविश्वसनीय : *a monstrous lie.*

month / मन्थ् / *noun* महीना, मास ▸ **monthly** *adj* , *adv* मासिक, महीना-वार; महीने में एक बार घटित।

monument / 'मॉन्युमन्ट् / *noun* 1 monument (to sb/sth) स्मारक; कीर्तिस्तंभ 2 monument to sth यादगार का नमूना/ उदाहरण।

monumental / ‚मॉन्यु'मेन्ट्ल् / *adj* विलक्षण रूप से महान; यादगार स्वरूप।

mood / मूड् / *noun* 1 मनोदशा,

मन:स्थिति : *She's in a good mood.* 2 क्रोध, नाराज़गी आदि का समय ▸ **moody** / 'मूडि / *adj* (**-ier, -iest**) मनमौजी, अस्थिर-चित्त; बदमिज़ाज **moodily** *adv* उदासी से **moodiness** *noun.*

moon / मून् / *noun* 1 (प्राय: the moon) चंद्रमा 2 उपग्रह : *How many moons does Jupiter have?* ▸ **moonlight** *noun* चंद्रकिरण **moonstruck** *adj* (थोड़ा-सा) पागल।

moor¹ / मुअर् / *noun* (प्राय: pl) खुला भूक्षेत्र जहाँ खेती न हो रही हो।

moor² / मुअर् / *verb* moor sth (to sth) (जहाज़, नाव आदि को) तार-रस्सों से बाँधना : *The boat was moored to the river bank.* ▸ **mooring** *noun* 1 **moorings** [*pl*] तार-रस्से आदि जिनसे नाव आदि बाँधी जाए 2 लंगर स्थल।

mop / मॉप् / *noun* फ़र्श साफ़ करने का साधन; उलझे हुए बाल ▸ **mop** *verb* (**-pp-**) झाड़न से झाड़ना/पोंछना।

moral¹ / 'मॉरल् / *adj* 1 नैतिक 2 सदाचारी, सदाचारपूर्ण : *lead a moral life* 3 सदाचार की शिक्षा देने वाला : *a moral drama/tale* ▸ **morally** *adv.*

moral² / मॉरल् / *noun* 1 morals [*pl*] आचार; नीतिशास्त्र 2 (किसी घटना, कथा या अनुभव से) शिक्षा, सीख।

morale / म॒'राल्; *US* म॒'रैल् / *noun* मनोबल, हौसला; संघर्ष करने का उत्साह : *Morale among the troops was low.*

morality / म॒'रैलटि / *noun* 1 नैतिकता : *matters of public morality* 2 सदाचार 3 विशिष्ट नैतिक मूल्य : *Muslim/Hindu/ Christian morality.*

moralize, -ise / 'मॉरलाइज़् / *verb* (अक्सर *अपमा*) नैतिक प्रश्नों का विवेचन करना; (दूसरों पर) नैतिकता थोपना।

morass / म॒'रैस् / *noun* (प्राय: sing) 1 दलदल जैसी भूमि 2 morass (of sth) उलझी हुई स्थिति।

morbid / 'मॉर्बिड् / *adj* (किसी का चित्त

या विचार) रुग्ण; रोगी ▶ **morbidity** / मॉर्
'बिडिटि / *noun* रुग्णता **morbidly** *adv.*

more¹ / मॉर् / *indef det, indef pron*
more (sth) (than...) और, अधिक :
(det) Would you like some more
coffee? ○ *(pron) I couldn't possi-*
bly eat any more. ■ **more and more**
अधिकाधिक।

more² / मॉर् / *adv* 1 *adjs* एवं *advs* के
तुलनात्मक रूपों के साथ प्रयुक्त : *She was*
more intelligent than her sister.
2 अधिक मात्रा/सीमा में : *a course for*
more advanced students ■ **more or**
less लगभग, न्यूनाधिक।

moreover / मॉर्'ओव्र् / *adv* इसके अति-
रिक्त/अलावा।

morgue / मॉर्ग् / *noun* शव-गृह।

morning / 'मॉर्निङ् / *noun* प्रात: काल,
सवेरा; अर्धरात्रि से दोपहर के पूर्व तक का
समय : *He died in the early hours of*
Sunday morning.

moron / 'मॉरॉन् / *noun* (अनौप, अपमा)
मंदबुद्धि व्यक्ति, बुद्धू।

morose / म'रोस् / *adj* चिड़चिड़ा; उदास
▶ **morosely** *adv.*

morphine / 'मॉर्फ़ीन् / *noun* मार्फ़िया,
दर्दनिवारक दवा।

Morse code / मॉर्स् 'कोड् / *noun*
मॉर्स-कोड; तार आदि भेजने की डॉट (.)
डैश (-) व्यवस्था।

morsel / 'मॉर्सल् / *noun* **morsel (of**
sth) (भोजन का) कौर, ग्रास : *a tiny*
morsel of food.

mortal / 'मॉर्टल् / *adj* 1 मरणशील, नश्वर
2 सांघातिक; प्राणघातक : *a mortal*
wound/injury 3 मरण-पर्यंत : *mortal*
enemies 4 अत्यंत : *live in mortal*
fear ▶ **mortal** *noun* मनुष्य **mortally**
adv 1 मृत्युकारक; सांघातिक : *mortally*
wounded 2 अत्यंत रूप से : *mortally*
afraid.

mortality / मॉर्'टैलिटि / *noun* (*pl*

mortalities) 1 नश्वरता 2 मृत्यु-संख्या
(बीमारी आदि से मरने वालों की संख्या)
3 मृत्यु : *traffic mortalities.*

mortar¹ / 'मॉर्टर् / *noun* 1 मकान बनाने
का (सीमेंट, चूना, रेत आदि का) गारा
2 खरल।

mortar² / 'मॉर्टर् / *noun* हलकी तोप :
under mortar fire.

mortgage / 'मॉर्गिज्/ *noun* रेहन, गिरवी;
बंधक-पत्र ▶ **mortgage** *verb* **mort-**
gage sth (to sb) बंधक या रेहन रखना :
He mortgaged his house in order
to start a business. **mortgagee**
/ मॉर्गि'जी / *noun* देनदार **mortgagor**
/ 'मॉर्गिजॉर् / *noun* लेनदार।

mortify / 'मॉर्टिफाइ / *verb* (*pt, pp*
mortified) 1 (किसी का) मान-मर्दन
करना, अपमानित करना 2 (इच्छाओं का)
दमन करना 3 (घाव आदि का) सड़ना-
गलना ▶ **mortification** / मॉर्टिफ़ि'के-
शन् / *noun.*

mortuary / 'मॉर्चरि; *US* 'मॉर्चुअरि /
noun (*pl* **mortuaries**) शव-गृह; मुरदाघर
▶ **mortuary** *adj* (औप) मृत्यु/दाहकर्म
संबंधी : *mortuary rites.*

mosaic / मो'ज़ेइक् / *noun* **mosaic (of**
sth) मोज़ेक, पत्थर आदि के छोटे-छोटे
टुकड़ों से पच्चीकारी; इस तरह का डिज़ाइन।

mosque / मॉस्क् / *noun* मसजिद।

mosquito / मस्'कीटो / *noun* (*pl* **mos-**
quitoes) मच्छर ▶ **mosquito-net**
noun मच्छरदानी।

moss / मॉस् / *noun* काई ▶ **mossy** *adj*
1 काईयुक्त 2 काई जैसा।

most¹ / मोस्ट् / *indef det, indef pron*
(**many, much** के उत्तमावस्था के रूप में
प्रयुक्त) 1 अधिकतम, सबसे अधिक :
Sanjay made the most mistakes of
all the class. 2 अधिकांश : *Most*
European countries are democra-
cies. ■ **at (the) most** अधिक से अधिक
for the most part लगभग सभी **make**

the most of sth पूरा लाभ उठाना ▸ **mostly** *adv* मुख्यत: ; सामान्यतया।

most² / मोस्ट् / *adv* 1 सबसे अधिक : *most boring/beautiful* 2 अत्यधिक, बहुत ज्यादा; पूर्णत:।

moth / मॉथ् / *noun* पतंगा (रात में रोशनी के पास आने वाला कीड़ा)।

mother / मद्र् / *noun* 1 माँ, माता 2 (विशेषत: संबोधन रूप में प्रयुक्त शब्द) धार्मिक समुदाय की अध्यक्षा ▸ **mother** *verb* 1 माँ के समान बच्चों का पालन-पोषण करना 2 लाड़-प्यार और अत्यधिक देखभाल करना **motherhood** / मद्रहुड् / *noun* मातृत्व **mother-in-law** *noun* सास (पत्नी या पति की माँ) **motherland** *noun* मातृभूमि, स्वदेश **motherly** *adj* माता-सदृश, मातृ-सुलभ : *motherly love/ affection* **mother tongue** *noun* मातृभाषा, अपनी स्वयं की भाषा।

motif / मो'टीफ़् / *noun* सजावटी डिज़ाइन या आकृति।

motion / मोश्न् / *noun* 1 गति 2 चाल, इंगित इशारा : *At a single motion of his hand the room fell silent.* 3 (सभा/ समिति में विचारार्थ प्रस्तुत) प्रस्ताव 4 (औप) शौच क्रिया ▸ **motion** *verb* इशारे से (किसी को) आदेश देना : *He motioned to the waiter.* **motionless** *adj* गति-हीन, अचल।

motivate / मोटिव़ेट् / *verb* 1 का कारण बनना, प्रेरित करना : *be motivated by fear/greed* 2 किसी की रुचि जागृत करना ▸ **motivation** / मोटि 'व़ेश्न् / *noun* प्रेरणा।

motive / मोटिव़् / *noun* **motive (for sth)** उद्देश्य, अभिप्राय; प्रेरणा : *be suspicious of sb's motives* ▸ **motive** *adj* गतिकारक : *motive power.*

motley / मॉट्लि / *adj* (अपमा) रंग-बिरंगा, विविध प्रकार का : *wearing a motley collection of old clothes.*

motor / मोट्र् / *noun* मोटर (वाहन आदि को गतिशील बनाने वाला यंत्र) जो पेट्रोल, बिजली आदि से चलता है ▸ **motor** *adj* (संज्ञाओं के साथ) मोटर-चालित (साइकिल, कार आदि) **motor** *verb* (किसी व्यक्ति को) मोटर-कार से घुमाना।

motto / मॉटो / *noun* (*pl* **mottoes** या **mottos**) आचरण-विषयक आदर्श वाक्य : *'Live each day as it comes.' That's my motto.*

mould¹ (*US* **mold**) / मोल्ड् / *noun* 1 साँचा 2 (व्यक्ति का) सामान्य या अपेक्षित प्रकार : *She doesn't fit (into) the traditional mould of a university professor.* ▸ **mould** *verb* 1 आकृति देना, साँचे में ढालना 2 **mould sb/sth (into sb/sth)** नियंत्रित या प्रभावित करके तदनुरूप ढाल देना : *mould sb's character.*

mould² (*US* **mold**) / मोल्ड् / *noun* (नम पदार्थों पर उगने वाली) फफूँदी ▸ **mouldy** (*US* **moldy**) *adj* 1 फफूँदी भरा, फफूँदी की गंध वाला 2 (अनौप, अपमा) पुराना एवं सड़ा-गला : *Let's get rid of this mouldy old furniture.*

moult (*US* **molt**) / मोल्ट् / *verb* (पक्षियों के) पंख/पर झड़ना (बाद में नए निकलने के लिए); (कुत्ते, बिल्ली के) बाल गिरना/ झड़ना : *a dog that moults all over the house.*

mound / माउन्ड् / *noun* 1 मिट्टी का टीला; एक छोटी-सी पहाड़ी 2 ढेर : *a mound of mashed potato.*

mount¹ / माउन्ट् / *verb* 1 कुछ व्यवस्था करना, शुरू करना : *mount an exhibition* 2 **mount (up) (to sth)** राशि या मात्रा का बहुत बढ़ जाना 3 (औप) (सीढ़ी, पहाड़ आदि) ऊपर चढ़ना 4 **mount sb (on sth)** घोड़े पर चढ़ना/चढ़ाना : *She mounted the boy on the horse.* 5 **mount sth (on/onto/in sth)** विशेष दिशा में निश्चित करना : *mount specimens on slides* ■ **mount guard (at/**

over sb/sth) रक्षक या गार्ड की ड्यूटी करना; निगरानी करना ▸ **mount** *noun* 1 घोड़ा 2 (कार्ड) जिस पर चित्र आदि चिपकाए जाते हैं।

mount² / माउन्ट् / *noun* (*संक्षि* Mt) (*अप्र*) (अब केवल व्यक्तिवाचक संज्ञाओं के साथ प्रयुक्त) पर्वत : *Mount (Mt) Everest.*

mountain / 'माउन्टन् / *noun* 1 पर्वत/ पहाड़ 2 (*प्राय: pl*) mountains of sth बहुत बड़ी राशि, अंबार : *mountains of food/paperwork* ▸ **mountaineer** / माउन्ट'निअर् / *noun* पर्वतारोही, पर्वता- रोहण में निपुण व्यक्ति **mountaineering** *noun* पर्वतारोहण **mountainous** / 'मा- उन्टनस्/ *adj* 1 पहाड़ी (प्रदेश) 2 पर्वताकार, बहुत बड़े आकार वाला : *mountainous waves.*

mourn / मॉर्न् / *verb* mourn (for/over sb/sth) मृत्यु या हानि पर दुख/शोक मना- ना : *Few will mourn his passing.* ▸ **mourner** / 'मॉर्नर् / *noun* मातम करने वाला **mournful** *adj* दुखपूर्ण; दुखित, शोकग्रस्त **mournfully** *adv* **mourning** *noun* 1 शोक, मातम 2 मातमी (विशेषत:) काला लिबास : *His widow was dressed in mourning.*

mouse / माउस् / *noun* (*pl* mice / मा- इस् /) 1 चुहिया 2 कंप्यूटर का चलशील नियंत्रक उपकरण।

moustache / मॅस्टाश् / (*US* mustache / 'मस्टैश् /) *noun* मूँछ।

mouth¹ / माउथ् / *noun* (*pl* mouths / माउद्ज़्/) 1 मुँह 2 किसी वस्तु का मुँह/ मुख (प्रवेश मार्ग) : *the mouth of a cave* 3 नदी का मुहाना (जहाँ वह समुद्र में गिरती है) ▸ **mouthful** *noun* (*pl* mouthfuls) कौर **mouth-organ** (harmonica भी) *noun* मुँह से बजाया जाने वाला एक बाजा, माउथऑर्गन् **mouthpiece** *noun* 1 बाजे का वह भाग जो मुँह से लगाया जाता है 2 समाचार-पत्र, व्यक्ति आदि जिसे कोई विशिष्ट दल अपने विचार जनता में प्रस्तुत करने का माध्यम बनाता है।

mouth² / माउद्ज़् / *verb* 1 बिना आवाज़ के कुछ कहना : *silently mouthing curses* 2 (*अपमा*) ऐसे कुछ कहना कि समझ में ना आए : *mouthing slogans.*

movable (**moveable** भी) / 'मूव़बल् / *adj* चलनशील।

move¹ / मूव़ / *verb* 1 move (sb/sth) (about/around) हिलाना/हिलना; खिस- कना/खिसकाना, हटाना 2 move (ahead/ on) निर्धारित दिशा में प्रगति करना : *Time is moving on.* 3 move sb (to sth) (किसी की भावनाओं को) प्रभावित करना : *We were deeply moved (by her plight).* 4 सभा-समिति में विचार और निर्णय के लिए प्रस्ताव प्रस्तुत करना 5 (शत- रंज आदि खेलों में) चाल चलना 6 move (from...) (to...) एक स्थान छोड़कर दूसरे स्थान पर जाना, कार्यस्थान बदलना 7 निर्णय, व्यवहार आदि बदलना/बदलवाना : *The government will not move on this issue.* ■ **move on (to sth)** जगह, विषय आदि बदलना **move out** घर छोड़ना।

move² / मूव़ / *noun* 1 स्थान या स्थिति में परिवर्तन 2 move (towards sth/to do sth) उद्देश्यपूर्ति के लिए उठाया चरण, चाल : *Diplomatic moves are afoot to reduce the tension in the area.* 3 (शतरंज आदि में) चली गई चाल ■ **on the move** चलना-फिरना; प्रगतिशील।

movement / 'मूव़मन्ट् / *noun* 1 चलना- फिरना, गतिविधि 2 movement (in sth) मात्रा में परिवर्तन : *not much movement in oil prices* 3 movement (to do sth) (जनता का) आंदोलन : *the Quit India Movement* 4 समान विचार वाले व्यक्तियों का वर्ग 5 (*US औप*) शौच क्रिया।

movie / 'मूव़ि / *noun* (विशेषत: *US*) चल- चित्र, सिनेमा।

mow / मो / *verb* (*pt* mowed; *pp* mown / मोन् /) घास काटना ▸ **mower**

noun (समास में) घास काटने की मशीन : *an electric mower.*

Mr / 'मिस्टर् / *abbr* 1 पुरुषों को संबोधित करने का शब्द 2 कुछ अधिकारियों को संबोधन के लिए प्रयुक्त शब्द : *Mr Chairman.*

Mrs / 'मिसिज़ / *abbr* विवाहित महिलाओं के लिए प्रयुक्त संबोधन : *Mrs Bhatt.*

Ms / मिज़् / *abbr* (विवाहित या अविवाहित) महिलाओं के लिए प्रयुक्त संबोधन : *Ms (Mary) Green.*

much¹ / मच् / *indef det, indef pron* बहुत : (*det*) *I don't have much money with me.* ○ (*pron*) *She never eats much for breakfast.*

much² / मच् / *adv* बहुत/काफ़ी हद तक : *I didn't enjoy the book much.* ■ **as much** उतना ही।

mucus / 'म्यूकस् / *noun* श्लेष्मा, बलग़म।

mud / मड् / *noun* कीचड़ ▶ **muddy** / 'मडि / *adj* (**-ier, -iest**) 1 कीचड़ से भरा 2 (द्रव या रंग) मटमैला **muddy** *verb* गंदा बनाना/करना।

muddle / 'मड्ल् / *verb* 1 **muddle sth (up)** गड़बड़ी/अव्यवस्थित करना; काम बिगाड़ना 2 **muddle sb (up)** किसी को (मानसिक रूप से) चकरा देना : *Don't try and explain it again or you'll muddle me (up) completely.* ▶ **muddle** *noun* **muddle (about/over sth)** 1 गड़बड़ी : *My desk is in a real muddle.* 2 भ्रांति **muddled** *adj* संभ्रांति की दशा में, चकराया हुआ।

muffle / 'मफ्ल् / *verb* 1 **muffle sb/sth (up) (in sth)** (गरमाने के लिए) ओढ़ाना/ओढ़ना 2 (कपड़े से ढककर) आवाज़ को कम करना या दबाना ▶ **muffled** *adj* (आवाज़) अस्पष्ट।

muffler / 'मफ़्लर् / *noun* मफलर, गरमाहट के लिए प्रयुक्त गुलुबंद।

mug¹ / मग् / *noun* मग, एक प्रकार का चौड़े मुँह का बड़ा प्याला।

mug² / मग् / *verb* (**-gg-**) (अनौप) किसी को सार्वजनिक स्थान पर हमला बोलकर लूट लेना : *An old lady was mugged by a gang of youths in the park.* ▶ **mugger** *noun* **mugging** *noun.*

mule / म्यूल् / *noun* ख़च्चर ▶ **mulish** *adj* अड़ियल, ज़िद्दी।

mull / मल् / *verb* ■ **mull sth over** किसी चीज़ के बारे में देर तक और ध्यानपूर्वक सोचना : *Thank you for your suggestion — I'd like to mull it over for a few days.*

multi- *pref* (पूर्वपद) अनेक-, बहु- : *multicoloured/multifaceted/multipurpose.*

multinational / मल्टि'नैश्नल् / *adj* बहुराष्ट्रीय ▶ **multinational** *noun* बहुराष्ट्रीय कंपनी।

multiple / 'मल्टिप्ल् / *adj* अनेक एवं विविध (व्यक्ति, प्रकार, वस्तु आदि) : *suffer multiple injuries* ▶ **multiple** *noun* (गणित) खंड, गुणज : *14, 21 and 28 are multiples of 7.*

multiplication / मल्टिप्लि'केश्न् / *noun* गुणा करना, गुणन : *children learning to do multiplication and division* ▶ **multiplication sign** *noun* गुणन चिह्न (x).

multiply / 'मल्टिप्लाइ / *verb* (*pt, pp* **multiplied**) 1 **multiply A by B/multiply A and B (together)** गुणा करना : *2 multiplied by 4 is 8 (2 × 4 = 8).* 2 (जीव विज्ञान) बड़ी संख्या में उत्पन्न होना या उत्पादन करना : *Rabbits multiply rapidly.* 3 संख्या या मात्रा बढ़ जाना या बढ़ाना।

multitude / 'मल्टिट्यूड्; *US* 'मल्टिट्रूड् / *noun* (औप) **multitude (of sb/ sth)** भीड़, बहुत भारी संख्या में (एकत्र व्यक्ति); **the multitude (the multitudes** [*pl*] भी) जनसाधारण, आम जनता

▸ **multitudinous** adj (औप) भारी संख्या में।

mumble / 'मम्बल् / verb mumble (about sth); mumble sth (to sb) कुछ बुदबुदाते हुए या फुसफुसाते हुए (अस्पष्ट) कहना : speak in a mumbling voice ▸ **mumble** noun बुदबुदाए शब्द **mumbling** noun.

mummy[1] / 'ममि / (US प्राय: mommy / 'मॉमि /) noun (अनौप) बच्चों द्वारा माँ को संबोधित करने का शब्द, मम्मी।

mummy[2] / 'ममि / noun (pl mummies) ममी, (मिस्र में) पुराने संभालकर रखे गए शव ▸ **mummify** / 'ममिफ़ाइ / verb ममी के रूप में शव रखना।

munch / मन्च् / verb munch (on sth) चबा-चबाकर खाना : munch (on) an apple.

mundane / मन्'डेन् / adj (अक्सर अपमा) साधारण एवं मामूली, उत्साहहीन : a mundane film/job.

municipal / म्यू'निसिप्ल् / adj नगर-पालिका का : municipal buildings ▸ **municipality** / म्यू‌निसि'पैलटि / noun (pl municipalities) (औप) नगरपालिका, नगर का स्थानीय स्वशासन।

munitions / म्यू'निश्न्ज़् / noun [pl] गोला बारूद, युद्धसामग्री ▸ **munition** adj : munition workers/factories.

mural / 'म्यूअरल् / noun भित्ति-चित्र, दीवार पर की गई चित्रकारी ▸ **mural** adj दीवार-विषयक।

murder / 'मर्डर / noun 1 खून, हत्या 2 (अनौप) बहुत मुश्किल या अत्यंत अरुचि-कर कार्य/अनुभव : That exam was murder! ▸ **murder** verb 1 murder sb (with sth) हत्या करना 2 (अनौप) अकुशलता से कुछ ख़राब कर देना : murder a piece of music **murderer** noun (fem **murderess**) हत्यारा (या हत्यारिन) **murderous** / 'मर्डरस् / adj 1 हिंसक, हत्या के लिए आयोजित 2 (अनौप) अत्यंत कठोर/अरुचिकर।

murk / मर्क् / noun अंधेरा; मंद प्रकाश : peering through the murk ▸ **murky** / 'मर्कि / adj (-ier, -iest) 1 अंधकारमय; विषादमय 2 (पानी) गंदला; (अपमा या परि) (व्यक्ति) संदेहास्पद चरित्र वाला।

murmur / 'मर्मर / noun 1 भिनभिना-हट : the murmur of bees in the garden 2 बुदबुदाहट, फुसफुसाहट : a murmur of agreement ▸ **murmur** verb 1 भिनभिनाना : a murmuring brook 2 बुदबुदाकर/फुसफुसाकर कुछ कहना।

muscle / 'मस्ल् / noun 1 मांस-पेशी 2 शारीरिक बल 3 इच्छानुसार आज्ञापालन कराने की शक्ति : legal/political muscle ▸ **muscle** verb ■ **muscle in** (on sb/sth) (अनौप, अपमा) अपने लाभ के लिए बलात हस्तक्षेप करना।

muscular / 'मस्क्यलर् / adj 1 मांसपेशीय 2 (अनौप **muscly** / 'मसलि / भी) हट्टा-कट्टा (व्यक्ति)।

muse / 'म्यूज़् / verb 1 muse (about/on/over/upon sth) ध्यानमग्न होना, एकाग्रचित्त चिंतन करना 2 ध्यानमग्न स्वयं से ही कुछ कहना।

museum / म्यु'ज़ीअम् / noun संग्रहालय, अजायबघर।

mushroom / 'मश्रूम् / noun कुकुरमुत्ता; छत्रक ▸ **mushroom** verb 1 (प्राय: go mushrooming) कुकुरमुत्ते इकट्ठा करना 2 कुकुरमुत्ते की तरह बड़ी संख्या में उत्पन्न होना/फैलना : new housing mushrooming all over the city.

music / 'म्यूज़िक् / noun संगीत ■ face the music साहसपूर्वक संभावित कटु आलोचना का सामना करना ▸ **musical** / 'म्यूज़िक्ल् / adj 1 संगीत-विषयक 2 संगीत में निपुण, संगीत पसंद करने वाला 3 संगीतमय : have a musical voice.

musician / म्यु'ज़िशन् / *noun* संगीतज्ञ; संगीतकार।

Muslim / 'मुज़्लिम् / (**Moslem** / 'मॉज़्-लम् / भी) *noun* मुसलमान ▸ **Muslim (Moslem** भी) *adj* मुसलमानों या इस्लाम विषयक।

muslin / 'मज़्लिन् / *noun* मलमल (एक प्रकार का कपड़ा)।

mussel / 'मस्ल् / *noun* सीपी।

must / मस्ट् / *modal verb* (*neg* **must not**; *संक्षि* **mustn't** / 'मस्न्ट् /) 1 अवश्य : *I must go to the bank to get some money.* 2 अधिक संभावना : *You must be hungry after your long walk.* 3 (सलाह/सुझाव के लिए) : *I must ask you not to do that again.* ▸ **must** *noun* (अनौप) आवश्यकता (नितांत)।

mustard / 'मस्टर्ड / *noun* 1 राई; सरसों 2 गहरा पीला रंग ▸ **mustard gas** *noun* त्वचा जलाने वाली एक ज़हरीली गैस।

muster / 'मस्टर् / *noun* निरीक्षण, विशेषत: सिपाहियों की हाज़िरी, के लिए इकट्ठा होना ▸ **muster** *verb* 1 इकट्ठा होना या कर-ना : *muster the troops* 2 **muster sth (up)** कुछ (भाव आदि) जुटाना : *muster public support for sth.*

musty / 'मस्टि / *adj* (**-ier, -iest**) बासी; सीलन भरी : *a musty attic.*

mute / म्यूट् / *adj* 1 चुप; कुछ न बोलने वाला 2 (*अप्र*) गूँगा, बोलने में असमर्थ ▸ **mute** *noun* (*अप्र*) गूँगा **mute** *verb* स्वर धीमा या मंद कर देना।

mutilate / 'म्यूटिलेट् / *verb* कोई अंश तोड़, फाड़ या काटकर हानि पहुँचाना, विकृत करना ▸ **mutilation** / म्यूटि'लेशन् / *noun* विकृति।

mutiny / 'म्यूटनि / *noun* (*pl* **mutinies**) ग़दर, सैनिक-विद्रोह ▸ **mutineer** / म्यूट 'निअर् / *noun* बाग़ी, विद्रोही **mutiny** *verb* (*pt, pp* **mutinied**) mutiny

(against sb/sth) विद्रोह करना ▸ **muti-nous** *adj* विद्रोहपूर्ण, बाग़ी।

mutter / 'मटर् / *verb* 1 **mutter (sth) (to sb/oneself) (about sth)** बुदबुदाना, बहुत धीरे से कहना 2 **mutter (about/against/at sb/sth)** फुसफुसाकर शिकायत करना जो सुनाई न दे।

mutton / 'मटन् / *noun* भेड़ का मांस ■ **mutton dressed as lamb** (*अनौप, अपमा*) बूढ़ी घोड़ी लाल लगाम।

mutual / 'म्यूचुअल् / *adj* 1 पारस्परिक, आपसी : *mutual affection* 2 (*अनौप*) दो या अधिक में सामान्य ▸ **mutuality** *noun* **mutually** *adv.*

muzzle / 'मज़्ल् / *noun* 1 कुत्ते, लोमड़ी आदि की थूथन; कुत्ते आदि की थूथन पर बाँधा जाने वाला मुसका (जिससे वह काट न सके) 2 बंदूक की नली का मुँह ▸ **muzzle** *verb* 1 पशुओं को मुसका चढ़ाना 2 (*अपमा*) (किसी व्यक्ति या समाचार-पत्र को) स्वतंत्रतापूर्वक विचार न प्रकट करने देना : *accuse the government of muz-zling the press.*

my / माइ / *possess det* 1 मेरा/मेरी : *Where's my hat?* 2 (विस्मयबोधक अभिव्यक्तियों में प्रयुक्त) : *My goodness, what a surprise!*

myself / माइ 'सेल्फ़् / *pron* 1 (re-flex) : *I cut myself with a knife.* 2 (emph) : *I myself will present the prizes.*

mysterious / मि'स्टिअरिअस् / *adj* 1 रहस्यमय 2 गुप्त ▸ **mysteriously** *adv.*

mystery / 'मिस्टरि / *noun* (*pl* **myster-ies**) 1 रहस्य 2 मर्म, धार्मिक सत्य जो सामान्यतया नहीं समझा जा सकता है : *the mystery of the incarnation.*

mystic / 'मिस्टिक् / *noun* रहस्यवादी (संत)।

mystical / 'मिस्टिकल् / *adj* (**mystic** / 'मिस्टिक् / भी) 1 रहस्यवादी : *mystical* *rites/forces* 2 आध्यात्मिक शक्ति संपन्न; रहस्यवादी अध्यात्म पर आधारित।

mysticism / 'मिस्टिसिज़म् / *noun* रहस्यवाद : *Christian mysticism.*

mystify / मिस्टिफ़ाइ / *verb (pt, pp* **mystified)** रहस्यमय बना देना; उलझा देना ▸ **mystification** *noun.*

myth / मिथ् / *noun* 1 मिथक, पौराणिक कथा 2 मनगढ़ंत बात, काल्पनिक

किस्सा : *the myth of a classless society* ▸ **mythical** / 'मिथ्रिकल् / *adj* 1 मिथक-विषयक 2 काल्पनिक, अयथार्थ।

mythology / मि'थ़ॉलजि / *noun (pl* **mythologies)** पुराण-शास्त्र; मिथक-शास्त्र : *study Greek mythology* ▸ **mythological** /ˌमिथ़'लॉजिकल्/ *adj* पौराणिक।

Nn

nab / नैब् / *verb* (-bb-) (अनौप) अपराध करते हुए पकड़ना : *He was nabbed (by the police) for speeding.*

nadir / नेडिअर् / *noun* [sing] 1 निम्नतम स्थिति : *Company losses reached their nadir in 1992.* 2 अधोबिंदु।

nag / नैग् / *verb* (-gg-) 1 nag (at sb) लगातार शिकायत करना या किसी की आलोचना करते रहना : *He nagged (at) her all day long.* 2 लगातार पीड़ित करना : *a nagging pain/doubt/worry.*

nail / नेल् / *noun* 1 नाखून 2 कील ■ **a nail in sb's/sth's coffin** किसी योजना, व्यापार आदि का अंत करने वाली कोई चीज़ या क्रिया **fight tooth and nail** कसकर लड़ना **hit the nail on the head** ठीक बात कहना या करना ▶ **nail** *verb* 1 (अनौप) गिरफ़्तार करना 2 कील ठोंकना।

naive (**naïve** भी) / नाईईव् / *adj* 1 (विशेषत: अपमा) अनुभवहीन : *a naive person/remark* 2 भोला-भाला, निष्कपट (व्यक्ति) ▶ **naively** (**naïvely** भी) *adv* **naivety** (**naïvety** भी) / नाई ईव़टि / *noun* भोलापन/अनुभवहीनता।

naked / नेकिड् / *adj* 1 नंगा; खुला हुआ 2 छिपाव रहित : *the naked truth* ▶ **nakedness** *noun* नंगापन; नग्नता।

name[1] / नेम् / *noun* (व्यक्ति, वस्तु, स्थान आदि का) नाम ■ **call sb names** भला-बुरा कहना **in the name of sb/sth** के द्वारा दिए अधिकार से; के नाम पर ▶ **namesake** *noun* नाम-रासी।

name[2] / नेम् / *verb* 1 **name sb/sth (after sb)** किसी के अनुकरण पर नाम रखना 2 नाम बताना : *Can you name all these plants?*

nameless / नेम्लस् / *adj* 1 बिना नाम का 2 जिसका नाम सुर्ख़ियों में न आया हो 3 अ-वर्णनीय।

namely / नेम्लि / *adv* अर्थात, यानी।

nanny / नैनि / *noun* (pl **nannies**) 1 बच्चे की नर्स 2 (**nan**/ नैन् भी) (अनौप) बच्चे द्वारा नानी/दादी के लिए प्रयुक्त शब्द; नानी/दादी।

nap / नैप् / *noun* झपकी (विशेषत: दिन में) ▶ **nap** *verb* (-pp-) झपकी लेना ■ **catch sb napping** किसी को असावधान स्थिति में पाकर उसका फ़ायदा उठाना।

napalm / नेपाम् / *noun* पेट्रोल से तैयार एक ज्वलनशील पदार्थ (प्राय: बम बनाने में प्रयुक्त)।

nape / नेप् / *noun* (प्राय: sing) गुद्दी (गरदन के पीछे का भाग)।

naphthalene / नैफ़्थलीन् / *noun* पेट्रोलियम से बना पदार्थ (जिसकी गोलियाँ कपड़ों को कीड़ों से बचाने में प्रयोग की जाती हैं)।

napkin / नैप्किन् / (table napkin भी) *noun* भोजन के समय कपड़ों को ख़राब होने से बचाने के लिए प्रयुक्त कपड़ा (या काग़ज़)।

nappy / नैपि / (US diaper) *noun* (pl **nappies**) छोटे बच्चों का डाइपर/लँगोट; नैप्पी।

narcissism / नार्सिसिज़म् / *noun* (मनो) आत्म-मोह (स्वयं को अत्यधिक सुंदर, गुणी आदि मानना); एक रुग्ण मनोदशा।

narcissus / नार्'सिसस् / *noun* (pl **narcissuses** or **narcissi** / नार्'सिसाइ /) नरगिस (का फूल)।

narcotic / नार्'कॉटिक् / *noun* 1 नींद या बेहोशी लाने वाला पदार्थ 2 (प्राय: pl) नशेवाली हानिकारक दवा ▶ **narcotic** *adj* संवेदनमंदक।

narrate / न'रेट्; US नैरेट् / *verb* (किसी घटना/कथा का) वर्णन करना ▶ **narration** *noun* विवरण, कथन **narrative** / नैरटिव़ / *adj, noun* कथनात्मक/विवरणात्मक वर्णन **narrator** *noun* कथावाचक; वर्णन करने वाला।

narrow / 'नैरो / adj (-er, -est) 1 संकीर्ण 2 सीमित 3 बहुत कम मार्जिन वाला; बाल-बाल (बचना) : *have a narrow escape from death* ▸ **narrow** *verb* संकीर्ण होना या बनाना ∎ **narrow sth down** संभावनाओं को कम करना ▸ **narrowly** *adv* 1 बड़ी कठिनाई से 2 अत्यधिक सावधानी/सूक्ष्मता से **narrow-minded** *adj* संकीर्ण मानसिकता वाला।

nasal / 'नेज़ल / adj नासिका-विषयक; (स्वर) नास्य, जैसे म, न, ङ आदि।

nasty / 'नास्टि; US 'नैस्टि / adj (-ier, -iest) 1 गंदा, क्षोभ उत्पन्न करने वाला : *a nasty smell ○ She has a nasty temper.* 2 ख़तरनाक; धमकी भरा : *He had a nasty look in his eye.* ▸ **nastily** *adv* **nastiness** *noun.*

nation / 'नेशन / *noun* राष्ट्र, कौम।

national / 'नैशनल / adj राष्ट्रीय ▸ **national** *noun* राष्ट्रीयता विशेष का व्यक्ति।

nationalism / 'नैशनलिज़म / *noun* राष्ट्रीयतावाद; स्वतंत्रता आंदोलन ▸ **nationalist** *noun, adj* राष्ट्रीयतावादी।

nationality /,नैश 'नैलटि / *noun* नागरिकता; राष्ट्रिकता।

nationalize, -ise / 'नैशनलाइज़ / *verb* (भूमि, व्यापार आदि को) निजी क्षेत्र से सरकारी स्वामित्व में रखना; राष्ट्रीयकरण करना ▸ **nationalization, -isation** /,नैशनलाइ 'ज़ेशन / *noun* राष्ट्रीयकरण, सरकार द्वारा निजी कंपनी या संस्था का नियंत्रण लेना।

native / 'नेटिव् / *noun* 1 निवासी (व्यक्ति): *a native of the north-east* 2 (पेड़-पौधे, पशु-पक्षी) मूल-स्थानीय : *The kangaroo is a native of Australia.* ▸ **native** *adj* 1 अपने जन्म के स्थान, परिस्थिति आदि का : *Her native language is Tamil.* 2 जन्मजात गुण (न कि शिक्षा आदि से प्राप्त) 3 **native to...** (पेड़-पौधे, पशु-पक्षी) किसी स्थान के जन्मत: निवासी।

nativity / न'टिवटि / *noun* 1 जन्म 2 **the**

Nativity [*sing*] ईसा मसीह का जन्म 3 **Nativity** ईसा मसीह के जन्म का चित्र ▸ **nativity play** *noun* ईसा के जन्म से संबंधित नाटक।

natural / 'नैचरल / adj 1 प्राकृतिक (न कि मानव द्वारा निर्मित), जन्मजात 2 सामान्य; आशानुकूल: *It's only natural to worry about your children.*

naturalist / 'नैचरलिस्ट / *noun* प्रकृति विज्ञानी।

naturalize, -ise / 'नैचरलाइज़ / *verb* 1 (किसी विदेशी को) नागरिकता देना 2 (किसी पौधे या जंतु को) पराए परिवेश में रखना ▸ **naturalization, -isation** /,नैचरलाइ 'ज़ेशन / *noun.*

naturally / 'नैचरलि / *adv* 1 स्वाभाविक रीति से 2 सहज ही, स्वभावत:।

nature / 'नेचर / *noun* 1 सृष्टि (संपूर्ण विश्व और उसकी वस्तुएँ): *the wonders of nature* 2 (प्राय: Nature) प्रकृति : *contrary to the laws of Nature* 3 (व्यक्ति या पशु का) स्वभाव 4 प्रकार : *Things of that nature do not interest me.* ∎ **(go, etc) back to nature** (सभ्यता की कृत्रिमताओं से दूर) सहज सरल जीवन : *man's yearning to get back to nature* ▸ **nature cure** *noun* प्राकृतिक चिकित्सा।

naughty / 'नॉटि / adj (-ier, -iest) 1 नटखट, शरारती (बच्चा) 2 कहना न मानने वाला ▸ **naughtily** *adv* **naughtiness** *noun.*

nausea / 'नॉज़िआ; 'नॉसिआ / *noun* 1 मचली, मतली 2 घृणा ▸ **nauseate** / 'नॉज़िएट्; 'नॉसिएट् / *verb* जी मचलाना **nauseating** *adj.*

nautical / 'नॉटिकल् / adj नाविक संबंधी; समुद्री : *nautical mile.*

naval / 'नेवल् / adj नौसेना-विषयक : *a naval officer/uniform/battle.*

nave / नेव् / *noun* चर्च का मध्य भाग (जहाँ लोग बैठते हैं)।

navel / 'नेवल् / noun नाभि।

navigable / 'नैविगब्ल् / adj 1 नदी आदि जहाँ जहाज़ जा सके 2 समुद्री यात्रा के योग्य (जहाज़)।

navigate / 'नैविगेट् / verb 1 किसी यान का मानचित्र, यंत्र आदि की सहायता से निपुणतापूर्वक संचालन करना : navigate a ship through coastal waters 2 नाव या जहाज़ चलाना ▸ **navigation** / नैवि 'गेश्न् / noun 1 (नौ या विमान) संचालन विज्ञान 2 नौ या विमान संचालन।

navy / 'नेवि / noun 1 नौसेना 2 (**navy blue** भी) गहरा नीला रंग।

near¹ / निअर् / adj (-er, -est) 1 समीप, पास में 2 अगला; निकटतम 3 संबंध या मित्रता की दृष्टि से घनिष्ठ 4 (विशेषत: **nearest**) (आकार, मात्रा, गुण आदि में) लगभग बराबर; प्रकृति में लगभग बराबर ■ **one's nearest and dearest** (परि) सगे संबंधी ▸ **nearness** noun निकटता।

near² / निअर् / adv 1 (समय या स्थान की दृष्टि से) समीप, निकट 2 लगभग : a near-perfect performance ▸ **nearby** adj, adv पास में ही।

near³ / निअर् / (**near to** भी) prep 1 बगल में; निकट 2 (संख्या से पहले) लगभग बराबर; (आकार, मात्रा आदि में) समान : report profits near to Rs 10 crore 3 मित्रवत् या भावात्मक रूप से जुड़ा : It's very difficult to get near him.

near⁴ / निअर् / verb (समय या स्थान में) पास आना।

nearly / 'निअर्लि / adv प्राय:, लगभग ■ **not nearly** (पर्याप्त से) बहुत दूर।

neat / नीट् / adj (-er, -est) 1 (वस्तुएँ) सुव्यवस्थित; (व्यक्ति) साफ़-सुथरा एवं व्यवस्था पसंद 2 (वस्त्र) सादा एवं रुचि-कर : a neat uniform 3 निपुणता से कहा या किया हुआ, कुशल 4 (US प्राय: **straight**) (शराब) पानी न मिलाई हुई ▸ **neatly** adv **neatness** noun.

nebula / 'नेब्युला / noun (pl **nebulae** / 'नेब्युली / या **nebulas**) आकाश में तारों की नीहारिका, गैस या धूल का आकाश में चमकता हुआ पुंज ▸ **nebulous** / 'नेब्यु-लस् / adj अस्पष्ट, धुँधला।

necessarily / नेस'सेरलि / adv अनिवार्य रूप से।

necessary / 'नेससरि; US 'नेससेरि / adj 1 आवश्यक, ज़रूरी 2 अनिवार्य, तर्कयुक्त : accept the necessary consequences of one's actions ▸ **necessaries** noun [pl] जीने के लिए आवश्यक पदार्थ।

necessitate / न'सेसिटेट् / verb (औप) अनिवार्य बना देना : Increased traffic necessitated widening the road.

necessity / न'सेसिटि / noun (pl **necessities**) 1 **necessity** (**of/for sth**) आवश्यकता 2 आवश्यक वस्तु।

neck / नेक् / noun 1 गरदन; वस्त्र का गरदन वाला भाग 2 गरदन-नुमा वस्तु (जैसे बोतल में) : the neck of a bottle/violin ■ **neck and neck** (**with sb/sth**) बिलकुल पास-पास, बराबरी से : The leading runners are neck and neck.

necklace / 'नेक्लस् / noun नेकलेस, कंठी।

nectar / 'नेक्टर् / noun मधुमक्खियों द्वारा शहद बनाने के लिए फूलों से एकत्रित मीठा द्रव, मकरंद।

need¹ / नीड् / verb 1 की आवश्यकता होना : Do you need any help? 2 बाध्यता होना : Will we need to show our passports?

need² / नीड् / modal verb (neg **need not**; संक्षि **needn't** / 'नीड्न्ट् /) (केवल नकारात्मक वाक्यों और प्रश्नों के साथ) बाध्यता प्रदर्शित करना : You needn't finish that work today.

need³ / नीड् / noun 1 [sing] **need** (**for sth**); **need** (**for sb**) **to do sth** आवश्यकता; अभाव की परिस्थिति : He *stressed the need for a cautious approach.* **2 needs** [pl] आवश्यक वस्तुएँ ▸ **needful** adj (अप्र) आवश्यक **needless** adj निरर्थक।

needle / 'नीड्ल् / noun **1** सूई (कपड़ा सिलने की) **2** सलाई (जैसे ऊन बुनने की) **3** (घड़ी या सूचक यंत्रों की) सूई **4** इंजेक्शन की सूई; सूई के आकार की वस्तु ▸ **needle-work** noun सिलाई-कढ़ाई का काम।

needy / 'नीडि / adj (-ier, -iest) जीवन की आवश्यक वस्तुओं से हीन : *a needy family.*

negative / 'नेगटिव् / adj **1** (शब्द या वाक्य) नकारात्मक; 'न', 'नहीं' के अर्थ वाले शब्द या उत्तर **2** (गणित) ऋण संख्या (शून्य से कम अंक) **3** नकारात्मक दृष्टिकोण : *He has a very negative approach to his work.* ▸ **negative** noun **1** नकारात्मक शब्द या उत्तर **2** (फ़ोटोग्राफ़ी में) निगेटिव (फ़िल्म) **3** बैटरी का ऋणाग्र **negatively** adv.

neglect / नि'ग्लेक्ट् / verb **1** (औप) ध्यान न देना; उपेक्षा करना (जो करना था वह न करना) **2** ख़याल न रखना, भली-भाँति (बच्चों का) पालन-पोषण न करना : *accuse sb of neglecting their studies/ children/health* ▸ **neglect** noun उपेक्षा : *The garden was in a state of total neglect.* **neglected** adj उपेक्षित।

negligence / 'नेग्लिजन्स् / noun लापरवाही, असावधानी : *The accident was the result of negligence.*

negligent / 'नेग्लिजन्ट् / adj लापरवाह, असावधान ▸ **negligently** adv लापरवाही से।

negligible / 'नेग्लिजब्ल् / adj नगण्य, उपेक्षणीय।

negotiable / नि'गोशिअब्ल् / adj निर्णयपूर्व बातचीत के लिए खुला (विषय); (तक) (चेक आदि) विनिमय।

negotiate / नि'गोशिएट् / verb **1 nego-tiate (with sb) (for/about sth)** (किसी सहमति पर पहुँचने के लिए) बातचीत करना,

वार्ता करना **2 negotiate sth (with sb)** सौदे के संबंध में समझौता या मोल-तोल करना **3** किसी बाधा को पार करना : *The climbers had to negotiate a steep rock face.*

negotiation / नि'गोशि'एश्न् / noun वार्ता।

Negro / 'नीग्रो / noun (pl **Negroes** / 'नीग्रोज़् /) (अप्र, अक्सर अपमा) नीग्रो, हबशी ▸ **Negress** / 'नीग्रेस् / noun (अप्र, अक्सर अपमा) नीग्रो महिला।

neigh / ने / noun हिनहिनाहट की आवाज़ ▸ **neigh** verb (घोड़े का) हिनहिनाना।

neighbour (US **neighbor**) / 'नेबर् / noun **1** पड़ोसी **2** पड़ोसी देश या क्षेत्र ▸ **neighbourhood** (US **neigh-borhood**) noun **1** घर के आस-पास, समीपता की स्थिति **2** आस-पास के क्षेत्र के निवासी **neighbouring** (US **neigh-boring**) adj समीपवर्ती **neighbourly** (US **neighborly**) adj मैत्रीपूर्ण, मिलनसार।

neither / 'नाइद्रर्; 'नीद्रर् / det, pron दोनों में से कोई भी नहीं : *Neither team liked the arrangement.* ○ *I chose neither of them.* ▸ **neither** adv **1** ...और न... **2 neither... nor...** न...न... : *The hotel is neither spacious nor comfortable.*

nemesis / 'नेमसिस्/ noun [sing] (औप) दंड या पतन जिससे बच नहीं सकते : *He met his nemesis.*

neon / 'नीऑन् / noun एक रासायनिक तत्त्व; एक रंगहीन गैस जिसमें से विद्युत प्रवाहित करने पर चमकीला प्रकाश उत्पन्न होता है।

nephew / 'नेफ्यू; 'नेव्यू / noun भतीजा; भाँजा।

nepotism / 'नेपटिज़म् / noun भाई-भतीजा-वाद, स्वजन पक्षपात : *achieve promotion through nepotism.*

Neptune / 'नेप्ट्यून; US 'नेप्टून् / noun सूर्य से आठवाँ ग्रह, वरुण।

nerve / नर्व्/ *noun* 1 स्नायु, नस 2 **nerves** [*pl*] (*अनौप*) सहज उत्तेजित एवं चिंतित होने की स्थिति 3 धैर्य, साहस एवं आत्मविश्वास ■ **get on sb's nerves** (*अनौप*) किसी को परेशान कर देना।

nervous / 'नर्वस्/ *adj* 1 उत्तेजित, आशंकित : *Interviews always make me nervous.* 2 स्नायु संबंधी।

nest / नेस्ट्/ *noun* 1 (पक्षियों का) घोंसला 2 चींटी, बर्र आदि के अंडे रखने का स्थान : *a wasps' nest* 3 छिपा हुआ या सुरक्षित स्थान : *a nest of thieves* ▸ **nest** *verb* घोंसला बनाना, घोंसले में पालना।

nestle / 'नेस्ल्/ *verb* 1 गरमाहट में सुख से बस जाना 2 चिपटकर बैठ जाना, बैठाना : *She nestled the baby in her arms.* 3 **nestle sth against, on, etc sth** (प्यार से) सर या कंधा कहीं पर रखना : *She nestled her head on his shoulder.*

nestling / 'नेस्ट्लिङ्/ *noun* घोंसले में रह रहा चिड़िया का छोटा बच्चा।

net[1] / नेट् / *noun* जाल : *a piece of nylon net* ▸ **net** *verb* (-tt-) 1 फँसाना, जाल में पकड़ना 2 पौधों आदि को जाल से ढकना 3 (खेलों में) बॉल को गोल में पहुँचाना।

net[2] (**nett** भी) / नेट् / *adj* (धन) शेष, जिसके बाद अब कुछ निकालना नहीं है; (क़ीमत) कुल, संपूर्ण; (वज़न, भार, आदि) डिब्बे या पैकिंग को छोड़कर (सिर्फ़ सामान का भार)।

nether / 'नेद्र्/ *adj* (प्रा) निचला, निम्न-स्थ : *the nether world* (नरक)।

netting / 'नेटिङ्/ *noun* जाल बनाने का सामान, जाल : *wire netting.*

nettle / 'नेट्ल्/ *noun* बिच्छू पौधा (जिसकी पत्ती छूने से बिच्छू काटे जैसी जलन होती है) ▸ **nettle** *verb* किसी को थोड़ा नाराज़ या उत्तेजित कर देना।

network / 'नेट्वर्क् / *noun* 1 जाल तंत्र (जैसे एक-दूसरे को काटती हुई सड़कों, नहरों का) 2 एक-दूसरे से घनिष्ठता से जुड़े लोगों, कंपनियों, आदि का समूह 3 एक ही कार्यक्रम को एक ही साथ प्रसारित करने वाले एक-दूसरे से जुड़े प्रसारण केंद्र : *the three big US television networks* ▸ **networked** *adj* नेटवर्क से जुड़े।

neurology / न्युऽ'रॉलजि; *US* नुऽ'रॉ-लजि / *noun* तंत्रिका विज्ञान ▸ **neurologist** *noun.*

neurosis / न्युऽ'रोसिस; *US* नुऽ'रोसिस् / *noun* (*pl* **neuroses** / न्युऽ'रोसीज़्; *US* नुऽ'रोसीज़् /) 1 (चिकि) स्नायुरोग जिससे अवसाद एवं अन्य लक्षण उत्पन्न होते हैं 2 तीव्र भय या चिंता।

neurotic / न्युऽ'रॉटिक; *US* नुऽ'रॉटिक् / *adj* स्नायुरोग से पीड़ित ▸ **neurotic** *noun* स्नायुरोगी।

neuter / 'न्यूटर्; *US* 'नूटर् / *adj* 1 (व्या) नपुंसकलिंग 2 (पौधे या जंतु) नपुंसक।

neutral / 'न्यूट्रल्; *US* 'नूट्रल् / *adj* 1 युद्ध या झगड़े में किसी भी पक्ष का साथ न देने वाला, तटस्थ; तटस्थ देश का 2 कोई विशिष्ट या सकारात्मक लक्षण न रखने वाला; (रंग) हलका, चमकीला नहीं : *a neutral background for a display* 3 (रसा) न अम्लीय, न क्षारीय ▸ **neutral** *noun* 1 तटस्थ (देश या व्यक्ति); हलका रंग 2 इंजिन के अन्य भागों से असंबद्ध होने वाली गियर की स्थिति **neutrality** / न्यू'ट्रैलटि; *US* नू'ट्रै-लटि / *noun* तटस्थता, उदासीनता **neutralize, -ise** *verb* (किसी क्रिया को) प्रभावहीन या निष्फल कर देना; तटस्थ घोषित करना : *neutralize a poison/threat* **neutrally** *adv.*

neutron / 'न्यूट्रॉन्; *US* 'नूट्रॉन् / *noun* (भौतिकी) परमाणु के नाभिक में पाया जाने वाला विद्युत आवेश रहित कण।

never / 'नेवर्/ *adv* कभी नहीं; कदापि नहीं ■ **never mind!** चिंता न करें।

nevertheless / ,नेवर्द'लेस् / *adv* ऐसा होने पर भी; तथापि : *The old system had its flaws, but nevertheless it was preferable to the new one.*

new / न्यू; *US* नू / *adj* (**-er, -est**) **1** नया (जो पहले नहीं था); सबसे पहली बार अनुभव किया या बनाया हुआ **2 new (to sb)** पहले से विद्यमान लेकिन देखा या अनुभव न किया गया : *learn new words in a foreign language* **3** फिर से प्रारंभ हुआ : *start a new life* **4 new (to sth)** (व्यक्ति) अपरिचित : *I am new to this town.* **5** पुराने से परिवर्तित एवं अलग : *a new job/teacher* **6** ताज़ा उत्पन्न : *new potatoes/carrots* ► **newborn** *adj* नवजात (शिशु) **newcomer** *noun* नवागत **new deal** *noun* नई (एवं पहले से बेहतर) योजना या व्यवस्था **newly** *adv* हाल ही में **new year (New Year** भी)*noun* नव वर्ष।

news / न्यूज़; *US* नूज़ / *noun* **1** समाचार; **the news** रेडियो या टी वी पर प्रसारित समाचार **2** सुर्ख़ियों में आया व्यक्ति, वस्तु या घटना ■ **break the news (to sb)** किसी को दु:खद समाचार प्रथम सुनाना **no news is good news** (कहा) बुरी ख़बर सुनने में आ ही जाती है, यदि कोई ख़बर न मिले तो संभव यही है कि कुछ बुरा नहीं घटा है ► **news agency** *noun* समाचार एजेंसी **newsagent (US newsdealer)** *noun* समाचार पत्र-पत्रिकाएँ आदि बेचने वाला **newscaster (newsreader** भी) *noun* रेडियो, टी वी आदि पर समाचार पढ़ने वाला **newsletter** *noun* किसी क्लब, संघ या समाज की लघु पत्रिका।

newspaper / न्यूज़पेपर्; *US* नूज़पेपर् / *noun* समाचार-पत्र, अख़बार।

newt / न्यूट्; *US* नूट्/ *noun* छिपकली जैसा एक जंतु जो जल एवं स्थल दोनों पर वास करता है।

next¹ / नेक्स्ट् / *adj* next (to sb/sth) **1** (समय या स्थान की दृष्टि से) अगला **2** (बिना the के प्रयुक्त) तुरंत आने वाला ► **next door** *adv* साथ वाले मकान या कमरे में **next-door** *adj* **next of kin** *noun* (*pl* अपरिवर्तित) (औप) नज़दीकी नाते-रिश्तेदार, निकटतम संबंधी।

next² / नेक्स्ट् / *adv* **1** किसी के बाद; तब : *What did you do next?* **2** उसके बाद वाला, समीपवर्ती : *The next oldest building is the church.* ► **next to** *prep* **1** के पास, के निकट; बग़ल में **2** लगभग : *Painting the ceiling proved next to impossible without a ladder.* **3** क्रम से बाद में।

nexus / नेक्सस् / *noun* [*sing*] गूढ़ संबंधों की शृंखला; अंतर्बंधन : *the nexus between industry and political power.*

nib / निब् / *noun* (क़लम की) निब।

nibble / निब्ल् / *verb* nibble (at sth) **1** कुतरना : *fish nibbling the bait* **2** किसी प्रस्ताव में सावधानी रखते हुए रुचि दिखाना ► **nibble** *noun.*

nice / नाइस् / *adj* (**-r, -st**) **1** रुचिकर, सुखदायी **2 nice (to sb)** मित्रतापूर्ण; कृपापूर्ण **3** सूक्ष्म, बारीक : *a nice distinction* ► **nicely** *adv* **1** रुचिकर शैली में **2** (अनौप) बहुत अच्छा।

nicety / नाइसटि / *noun* (*pl* niceties) **1** (प्राय: *pl*) सूक्ष्मता **2** (औप) यथार्थता, त्रुटिहीनता।

niche / निच्; नीश् / *noun* **1** ताक़ या आला : *Two small candles and some flowers were placed in a niche.* **2** उपयुक्त एवं संतुष्टिपरक भूमिका, नौकरी या जीवन शैली **3** व्यापार में अवसर।

nick / निक् / *noun* ख़ाँच या काट : *Make a nick in the cloth with the scissors.* ► **nick** *verb* ख़ाँच लगना या छोटी-सी काट लगाना ■ **in the nick of time** ऐन मौक़े पर।

nickel / निक्ल् / *noun* **1** (प्रतीक Ni) सफ़ेद चाँदी जैसी धातु, निकल **2** अमेरिका या कनाडा में 5 सेंट का सिक्का।

nickname / निक्नेम् / *noun* उपनाम ► **nickname** *verb* उपनाम डालना : *She was nicknamed 'Madonna'.*

nicotine / निकटीन् / *noun* निकोटिन (तंबाकू में पाया जाने वाला विषैला पदार्थ)।

niece / नीस् / noun भतीजी, भाँजी।

niggardly / 'निगर्ईलि / adj (व्यक्ति) नीच; कंजूस।

nigger / 'निगर् / noun (अप, अपमा) हबशी (नीग्रो)।

niggle / 'निगल् / verb 1 niggle (at sb) (about/over sth) किसी की निंदा करना, तुच्छ बातों को लेकर समय ख़राब करना : *Stop niggling about every penny we spend.* 2 किसी को थोड़ा नाराज़ या चिंतित करना ▸ niggling adj लगातार चिंता या संदेह उत्पन्न करने वाला : *a niggling pain* ∘ *niggling doubt.*

night / नाइट् / noun रात; शाम ■ an early/a late night वह रात जब कोई अपने सामान्य समय से पहले या बाद में सोता है ▸ nightdress (nightgown, अनौप nightie भी) noun लंबा ढीला लबादा जो स्त्रियाँ या बच्चे रात में पहनते हैं nightly adj, adv हर रात को होने वाला, रात्रिकालीन।

nightclub / 'नाइट्क्लब् / noun नाच-गाने आदि के लिए देर रात तक खुला रहने वाला क्लब।

nightfall / 'नाइट्फ़ॉल् / noun संध्या, शाम का झुटपुटा।

nightingale / 'नाइटिङ्गेल् / noun बुलबुल।

nightmare / 'नाइट्मेअर् / noun 1 डरावना सपना 2 (अनौप) भयानक अनुभव।

nihilism / 'नाइइलिज़म् / noun 1 मानव व्यवहार के आधार रूप में धार्मिक एवं नैतिक सिद्धांतों का पूर्ण अस्वीकार 2 शून्यवाद या नाशवाद ▸ nihilist noun शून्यवादी।

nil / निल् / noun शून्य, कुछ नहीं।

nimble / 'निम्बल् / adj (-r, -st) 1 फुर्तीला एवं दक्ष 2 (दिमाग़) कुशाग्रबुद्धि; तुरंत समझने वाला ▸ nimbly adv.

nimbus / 'निम्बस् / noun (pl nimbuses / 'निम्बसिज़् / या nimbi / 'निम्बाइ /) वर्षास्तरी विशाल बादल।

nine / नाइन् / noun, pron, det नौ (का अंक), 9 ▸ ninth noun, pron, det नौवां; 1/9.

nineteen / नाइन्'टीन् / noun, pron, det उन्नीस (का अंक), 19 ▸ nineteenth noun, pron, det उन्नीसवाँ; 1/19.

ninety / 'नाइन्टि / noun, pron, det नब्बे (का अंक), 90 ▸ ninetieth noun, pron, det नब्बेवाँ, 1/90.

nip / निप् / verb (-pp-) 1 चुटकी, चिकोटी काटना : *A crab nipped my toe while I was paddling.* 2 (कोहरा, शीत लहर आदि) हानि पहुँचाना, विशेषत: पौधों को ■ nip sth in the bud (किसी अवांछित तत्त्व को) बढ़ने से पूर्व ही रोक देना या नष्ट कर देना nip sth off (sth) किसी चीज़ का एक भाग अँगुलियों से पकड़कर हटाना, तोड़ना ▸ nip / निप् / noun 1 चुटकी या चिकोटी 2 तेज़ सर्दी : *There's a distinct nip in the air.*

nipple / 'निपल् / noun 1 स्तन का अग्रभाग जिससे बच्चा दूध पीता है 2 इस तरह की अन्य संरचना (जैसे तेल की कुप्पी)।

nitrogen / 'नाइट्रजन् / noun (प्रतीक N) रंगहीन, गंधहीन गैस, नाइट्रोजन।

nitroglycerine / नाइट्रो'ग्लिसरीन्, नाइट्रो 'ग्लिसरिन् / noun एक शक्तिशाली विस्फोटक द्रव।

nitty-gritty / निटि'ग्रिटि / noun the nitty-gritty [sing] (अनौप) किसी कार्य, परिस्थिति आदि के सबसे महत्त्वपूर्ण पहलू।

nitwit / 'निट्विट् / (nit भी) noun (अनौप) मूर्ख, बुद्धू : *He's a complete nitwit.*

no / नो / det 1 नहीं, कोई नहीं, एक भी नहीं 2 (असहमति या नकार प्रकट करने का शब्द): *No smoking.* 3 (विशेषण से पहले) कथन का विपरीत अर्थ व्यक्त करने को प्रयुक्त : *It was no easy matter.* ▸ no interj (नकारात्मक उत्तर देने में प्रयुक्त) no adv (तुलनात्मक विशेषणों एवं क्रियाविशेषणों के पहले प्रयुक्त) नहीं : *This book is no more exciting than his others.*

nobility / नो'बिलटि / noun 1 श्रेष्ठता का गुण, कुलीनता 2 the nobility अभिजात वर्ग।

noble / 'नोब्ल् / adj (-r, -st) 1 उच्च गुणों और योग्यताओं वाला 2 उच्चकुल का : a family of noble descent 3 श्रेष्ठ, आदरणीय; आकार या रूप में प्रभावी ▶ noble noun अभिजात वर्ग का व्यक्ति **nobleman** (pl noblemen; fem noblewoman, pl noblewomen) noun उच्चकुल या अभिजात वर्ग का व्यक्ति **nobly** adv.

nobody / 'नोबडि / (no one / 'नो वन्/ भी) pron कोई भी नहीं, कोई व्यक्ति नहीं ▶ nobody noun (pl nobodies) नगण्य व्यक्ति, महत्त्वहीन व्यक्ति : a bunch of nobodies.

nocturnal / नॉक्'टर्नल् / adj 1 रात में ही सक्रिय (रात्रिचर) : nocturnal animals 2 रात्रि संबंधी।

nod / नॉड् / verb (-dd-) 1 सहमति जताने के लिए सिर हिलाना; nod sth (at/to sb) परिचितों से अभिवादन के समय सिर हिलाना : nod a greeting 2 ऊँघने पर सिर का आगे झुक जाना 3 (फूलों का) हवा में झूमना ▶ nod noun सिर की ऐसी गति।

node / नोड् / noun 1 (वनस्पति विज्ञान) तने या जड़ में गाँठ; तने का वह स्थान जहाँ से शाखा या पत्ती निकलती है 2 मानव शरीर में (जोड़ों आदि पर) ऊतकों की छोटी गाँठ : lymph nodes 3 (तक) ऐसा स्थान जहाँ दो रेखाएँ या तंत्र एक-दूसरे से मिलते हैं या काटते हैं ▶ nodal / 'नोडल् / adj पातिक; ग्रंथिल।

nodule / 'नॉड्यूल्; US 'नॉजूल् / noun छोटा-सा गोलाकार पिंड या सूजन, विशेषत: पौधों पर।

noise / नॉइज़् / noun 1 शोर-गुल, हो-हल्ला 2 (रेडियो) शोर (प्रसारित कथन के विद्युत विक्षोभों के कारण साफ़-साफ़ न सुनना) 3 noises [pl] तरह-तरह की टिप्पणियाँ ▶ noiseless adj नीरव, मौन।

noisy / 'नॉइज़ि / adj (-ier, -lest) शोर मचाने वाला; कोलाहल-पूर्ण ▶ noisily / 'नॉइज़िलि / adv.

nomad / 'नोमैड् / noun 1 ख़ानाबदोश जनजाति के लोग 2 आवारा घूमने वाला व्यक्ति ▶ nomadic / नो'मैडिक / adj.

nomenclature / न'मेन्क्लचर्; US 'नोमन्क्लेचर् / noun (औप) नामपद्धति, नामतंत्र : botanical nomenclature.

nominal / 'नॉमिनल् / adj 1 नाम मात्र का (न कि वास्तव में) : the nominal value of the shares 2 (धन आदि की मात्रा) बहुत मामूली ▶ nominally adv.

nominate / 'नॉमिनेट् / verb 1 nominate sb (for/as sth) किसी व्यक्ति का नाम किसी पद के चुनाव के लिए प्रस्तुत करना; किसी पद के लिए नियुक्त करना; नामांकित करना 2 nominate sth (as sth) किसी घटना के लिए स्थान या तारीख़ निश्चित करना : 1 December has been nominated as the day of the election.

nomination / ,नॉमि'नेशन् / noun 1 नामांकित करने की क्रिया या नामांकित होने की स्थिति 2 नामांकन।

nominee / ,नॉमि'नी / noun 1 नामज़द, मनोनीत 2 (वाणिज्य) जिसके नाम से कंपनी में निवेश किया गया हो।

non- pref (उपसर्ग) ग़ैर-, इसे जोड़ने से विलोम शब्द बनता है : nonsense ○ non-alcoholic.

non-aligned / नान्अ'लाइन्ड् / adj (देश) किसी महाशक्ति को समर्थन न देने या उससे समर्थन न लेने वाला, निर्गुट ▶ non-alignment noun निर्गुटता, निर्गुट रहना।

nonchalant / 'नॉन्शलन्ट् / adj उदासीन, लापरवाह या भावहीन : try to sound nonchalant.

noncommittal / ,नॉन्क'मिटल् / adj अपने विचार व्यक्त न करते हुए; तटस्थ।

nonconformist / ,नॉन्कन्'फॉर्मिस्ट्/ noun, adj 1 (व्यक्ति) जो सामान्य स्वीकृत सामाजिक मर्यादा को अस्वीकृत करता है 2 Nonconformist प्रोटेस्टेंट चर्च का सदस्य, जो स्थापित चर्च के विधि-विधान को नहीं मानता।

non-cooperation /ˌnɑːn kəʊ ˌɒpəˈreɪʃn̩/ *noun* असहयोग।

nondescript /ˈnɒndɪskrɪpt/ *adj* (अपमा) (व्यक्ति या वस्तु) कोई विशेष या उल्लेखनीय गुण/लक्षण रहित; नीरस।

none /nʌn/ *indef pron* 1 none (of sb/sth) एक भी नहीं; कोई भी नहीं : *None of these pens works/work.* 2 none of (sth) बिलकुल भी नहीं : *I wanted some string but there was none in the house.* ■ none but केवल none other than के अतिरिक्त कोई नहीं ▶ none *adv* 1 (तुलनात्मक शब्द और the के साथ) बिलकुल नहीं : *He's none the worse for falling into the river.* 2 (too एवं विशेषण या क्रियाविशेषणों के साथ) अत्यधिक नहीं : *She's none too well this morning.*

nonentity /nɒˈnentəti/ *noun* 1 (अपमा) नगण्य/महत्त्वहीन व्यक्ति 2 काल्पनिक अस्तित्व वाली वस्तु।

non-existent /ˌnɒn ɪɡˈzɪstənt/ *adj* जिसका (इस समय) अस्तित्व न हो।

nonplus /ˌnɒnˈplʌs/ *verb* (-ss-; US -s-) किसी को ऐसा चकित कर देना कि वह किंकर्तव्यविमूढ़ हो जाए : *I was completely nonplussed by his reply.*

nonsense /ˈnɒnsns; US ˈnɒnsens/ *noun* 1 अनाप-शनाप, अंड-बंड 2 मूर्खतापूर्ण विचार या व्यवहार ▶ **nonsensical** *adj* मूर्खतापूर्ण : *nonsensical argument.*

non-smoker /ˌnɒn ˈsməʊkə/ *noun* धूम्रपान न करने वाला व्यक्ति ▶ **non-smoking** *adj.*

non-stick /ˌnɒn ˈstɪk/ *adj* (बरतन या सतह आदि) ऐसे पदार्थ की परत चढ़ा हुआ जो भोजन को चिपकने नहीं देता है : *a non-stick frying-pan.*

non-stop /ˌnɒn ˈstɒp/ *adj, adv* 1 (ट्रेन या यात्रा) न रुकने वाली (बीच के किसी स्टेशन, हवाई अड्डे आदि पर) 2 (कार्य) बिना रुके किया गया : *He chattered non-stop all the way.*

non-violence /ˌnɒn ˈvaɪələns/ *noun* अहिंसा (की नीति) ▶ **non-violent** *adj* अहिंसात्मक : *a non-violent demonstration.*

noodle /ˈnuːdl̩/ *noun* (प्राय: pl) नूडल, एक प्रकार का चीनी खाद्य पदार्थ।

nook /nʊk/ *noun* कोना, एकांत स्थान : *a shady nook in the garden.*

noon /nuːn/ *noun* [sing] 12 बजे दोपहर।

noose /nuːs/ *noun* फंदा (जो रस्सी खींचने से कसा जा सकता है); फाँसी का फंदा।

nor /nɔː/ *conj, adv* 1 (neither के बाद दूसरा विकल्प दर्शाने को प्रयुक्त) और न (ही) : *I have neither the time nor the patience to listen to his complaints.* 2 (नकारात्मक कथन के बाद प्रयुक्त) : *My parents don't like him, and nor do I.*

norm /nɔːm/ *noun* 1 (प्राय: the के साथ) मानक, (सामाजिक व्यवहार का) मानदंड : *cultural/social norms* 2 किसी चीज़ का अभीष्ट प्रतिमान, मात्रा, स्तर आदि।

normal /ˈnɔːml̩/ *adj* 1 सामान्य, बदस्तूर 2 मानसिक बीमारी से मुक्त : *People who commit such crimes aren't normal.* ▶ **normal** *noun* सामान्य (अवस्था, स्तर, मानदंड आदि) **normality** (US **normalcy**) *noun* सामान्य होने की स्थिति **normalize, -ise** *verb* सामान्य होना या करना **normally** *adv* सामान्यतया।

north /nɔːθ/ *noun* [sing] (संक्षि N) (प्राय: the north) उत्तर दिशा; देश का अपेक्षाकृत उत्तरी भाग ▶ **north** *adj* उत्तर दिशा (में, का, की तरफ़) : *a north wind* **north** *adv* उत्तर की ओर : *sail/drive (due) north* **northerly** /ˈnɔːðəli/ *adj* 1 उत्तर को/की ओर 2 (हवा) उत्तर दिशा से आने वाली **northward (northwards** भी) *adv* उत्तर दिशा की ओर।

northern /ˈnɔːðn̩/ *adj* उत्तरी।

nose¹ / नोज़ / noun [pl] 1 नाक 2 किसी वस्तु के आगे का निकला अंश 3 **nose for sth** (अनौप) पता लगाने/खोज निकालने की योग्यता ■ **keep one's nose to the grindstone** (अनौप) बहुत अधिक परिश्रम करते रहना (लंबे समय तक) **pay through the nose** बहुत ऊँची क़ीमत देना ▸ **nosedive** / 'नोज़्डाइव़् / noun (हवाई जहाज़ का) नाक की सीध में नीचे पृथ्वी की ओर गिरावट; (वाणिज्य) (व्यापार में) अचानक गिरावट **nosedive** verb.

nose² / नोज़् / verb 1 सावधानी से आगे बढ़ना : The taxi nosed its way into the middle lane. 2 (जानवर का) सूँघना, सूँघकर ढूँढ़ना : a dog nosing into an old rucksack.

nostalgia / नॉस्टैल्जा / noun अतीत में खो जाने से उत्पन्न दुख और प्रसन्नता की मिली-जुली भावना ▸ **nostalgic** adj.

nostril / 'नॉस्ट्रल् / noun नथुना।

nosy (nosey भी) / 'नोज़ि / adj (-ier, -iest) (अनौप, प्राय: अपमा) (दूसरों के मामलों में) कुतूहल रखने वाला।

not / नॉट् / adv (नकारात्मक वाक्य बनाने में प्रयुक्त) नहीं ■ **not at all** 1 धन्यवाद/ कृतज्ञता स्वीकारने या सहमति जताने के लिए प्रयुक्त 2 बिलकुल नहीं।

nota bene / नोटा 'बेने / noun (लैटिन) (संक्षि NB, nb) ध्यान दें।

notable / 'नोटब्ल् / adj **notable (for sth)** उल्लेखनीय : a notable discovery ▸ **notable** noun बहुत महत्त्वपूर्ण व्यक्ति **notably** adv विशेषत:।

notary / 'नोटरि / (pl **notaries**) (**notary public** भी) noun कचहरी में वह अधिकारी जो क़ानूनी काग़ज़ात और उन पर किए हस्ताक्षरों का साक्षी होता है, नोटरी।

notation / नो'टेश्न् / noun संख्या, मात्रा, संगीत स्वरों आदि की अंकनपद्धति : musical/scientific notation.

notch / नॉच् / noun 1 **notch (in/on sth)** खाँच, खाँचा 2 (गुण, उपलब्धि आदि का) स्तर, दर्जा।

note¹ / नोट् / noun 1 (याद रखने के लिए) तथ्यों का संक्षिप्त विवरण, नोट्स 2 छोटा अनौपचारिक पत्र : a note of thanks 3 (पुस्तक में) टीका-टिप्पणी : a new edition of 'Hamlet' with copious notes 4 (**bank note** भी, US प्राय: **bill**) नोट (करेंसी) 5 रुक्का 6 संगीत के स्वर; स्वर चिह्न 7 **note (of sth)** चिह्न, स्थिति, भाव : The book ended on an optimistic note. 8 ध्यान : Take note of what he says. ■ **of note** प्रतिष्ठा या महत्त्व वाला, रुचिकर : a writer of some note ▸ **notebook** नोटबुक **note pad** noun नोट पैड।

note² / नोट् / verb (औप) ध्यान देना ■ **note sth down** लिख लेना ▸ **noted** adj **noted (for/as sth)** प्रख्यात, प्रसिद्ध **noteworthy** adj ध्यान देने योग्य, विचारणीय।

nothing / 'नथिङ् / neg pron कुछ नहीं, शून्य ■ **come to nothing** निष्फल, व्यर्थ **for nothing** 1 मुफ़्त में 2 निष्फल, बेकार में **make nothing of** समझने में असमर्थ, लाभ उठाने में असफल ▸ **nothingness** noun.

notice / 'नोटिस् / noun 1 ध्यान : Take no notice of what you read in the papers. 2 नोटिस, (लिखित या मुद्रित) सूचना : a notice saying 'Keep off the Grass'. 3 अधिसूचना या चेतावनी : You must give proper notice of changes in the arrangements. ■ **at short/at a moment's notice** थोड़ी-सी पूर्व सूचना पर **bring sth to the notice of sb** ध्यान में लाना ▸ **notice** verb 1 जानकार होना, देखना 2 किसी पर ध्यान देना **noticeable** adj **noticeable (in sth)** सहज में ही दिखाई पड़ने वाला **noticeboard** noun ज्ञापन/अधिसूचना टाँगने का तख्ता/बोर्ड।

notify / 'नोटिफ़ाइ / *verb* (*pt, pp* **notified**) **notify sb (of sth); notify sth to sb** अधिसूचना देना, सूचित करना ▸ **notifiable** *adj* **notification** / ,नोटिफ़ि'केशन् / *noun* (औप) अधिसूचना।

notion / 'नोशन् / *noun* 1 **notion (that...)** विचार, धारणा 2 **notion (of sth)** जानकारी या समझ : *She has no notion of the difficulty of this problem.*

notorious / नो'टॉरिअस् / *adj* **notorious (for/as sth)** (अपमा) बदनाम : *a notorious criminal* ▸ **notoriety** / ,नोट'राइअटि / *noun* बदनामी।

notwithstanding / ,नॉट्विथ्'स्टैन्डिङ् / *prep* **notwithstanding (that...)** (औप) के होते हुए भी, से प्रभावित न होते हुए : *Notwithstanding a steady decline in numbers, the school has had a very successful year.* ▸ **notwithstanding** *adv* (औप) यद्यपि, हालाँकि।

nought / नॉट् / *noun* 1 शून्य, 0 2 (**naught** भी) (प्रा) कुछ नहीं।

noun / नाउन् / *noun* (व्या) संज्ञा।

nourish / 'नरिश् / *verb* 1 पोषण करना, भोजन आदि से पुष्ट/बली बनाना 2 (औप) (आशा, द्वेष आदि भाव) बनाए रखना ▸ **nourishing** *adj* पुष्टिकर (भोजन) **nourishment** *noun* आहार; पोषण की शक्ति।

novel[1] / 'नॉव्ल् / *adj* अद्भुत एवं नए प्रकार का : *a novel idea* ▸ **novelty** / 'नॉव्ल्टि / *noun* (*pl* **novelties**) 1 नवीनता; अनूठापन 2 पहले से अज्ञात विचार, पदार्थ, अनुभव आदि 3 विविध प्रकार के प्रायः कम क़ीमत वाले सामान, आभूषण आदि।

novel[2] / 'नॉव्ल् / *noun* उपन्यास ▸ **novelist** *noun* उपन्यासकार।

November / नो'व़ेम्बर् / *noun* (संक्षि **Nov**) नवंबर (महीना)।

novice / 'नॉविस् / *noun* 1 नौसिखिया

2 ऐसा घोड़ा जिसने अभी कोई ख़ास दौड़ नहीं जीती है 3 हाल ही में कोई धर्म-संप्रदाय ग्रहण करने वाला व्यक्ति (जो अभी नन या मंक नहीं बना है)।

now / नाउ / *adv* अब, इस समय ■ (**every**) **now and again/then** कभी-कभी; समय-समय पर (**it's**) **now or never** अभी या कभी नहीं।

nowadays / 'नाउअडेज़् / *adv* आजकल।

nowhere / 'नोव़ेअर् / *adv* कहीं भी नहीं।

noxious / 'नॉक्शस् / *adj* (औप) हानिकर, विषैला या अत्यंत अप्रिय : *noxious substances/fumes.*

nozzle / 'नॉज़्ल् / *noun* पाइप की टोंटी।

nuance / 'न्यूआन्स्; *US* 'नूआन्स् / *noun* अर्थ, रंग या भावों की बारीकियाँ, सूक्ष्म भेद : *appreciate delicate nuances of language* ▸ **nuanced** *adj.*

nuclear / 'न्यूक्लिअर्; *US* 'नूक्लिअर् / *adj* 1 नाभिकीय (ऊर्जा से); परमाणु अस्त्र संबंधित : *a nuclear weapon/missile* 2 (भौतिकी) परमाणविक ▸ **nuclear disarmament** *noun* परमाणु-अस्त्र परित्याग (संधि)।

nucleus / 'न्यूक्लिअस्; *US* 'नूक्लिअस् / *noun* (*pl* **nuclei** / 'न्यूक्लिआइ /) 1 (जीव विज्ञान) जीवकोशिका का केंद्रक; (भौतिकी) परमाणु का नाभिक जो धनावेशित होता है 2 किसी वस्तु का केंद्रीय भाग : *The fortress was the nucleus of the ancient city.*

nude / न्यूड़ ; *US* नूड़ / *adj* नंगा, वस्त्रविहीन ▸ **nude** *noun* (कलाकृति या फ़ोटोग्राफ़) निर्वस्त्ररूप **nudity** *noun* नग्नता।

nudge / नज् / *verb* 1 कोहनी मारकर ध्यान आकर्षित करना 2 हलके-से धक्का देना 3 **nudge sb into/towards (doing) sth** हलके दबाव या प्रोत्साहन से किसी को कुछ करने को प्रेरित करना ▸ **nudge** *noun* कोहनी का हलका-सा धक्का।

nugget / 'नगिट् / *noun* 1 ढेला (विशेषतः मूल्यवान धातु जैसे सोने का) 2 मूल्यवान छोटी वस्तु (विचार या तथ्य आदि)।

nuisance / 'न्यूसन्स; US 'नूसन्स् / noun (विशेषत: sing) **nuisance (to sb)** उपद्रवी; परेशानी पैदा करने वाला व्यक्ति या पदार्थ।

null / नल् / adj ∎ **null and void** (क़ानून) रद्द, अमान्य : The contract has been declared null and void. ▶ **nullify** / 'नलिफ़ाइ / verb (pt, pp **nullified**) 1 रद्द या अमान्य करना 2 (औप) प्रभाव समाप्त करना।

numb / नम् / adj (शरीर का अंग) सुन्न या जड़ हो जाना ▶ **numb** verb सुन्न कर देना, मानसिक आघात से संज्ञाशून्य हो जाना : She was completely numbed by her father's death.

number / 'नम्बर् / noun 1 संख्या (जैसे 1, 2, ...) 2 संख्या या राशि या मात्रा : A large number of people have applied. 3 किसी पत्रिका का अंक 4 (व्या) वचन (एकवचन, बहुवचन आदि) : 'Men' is plural in number. 5 क्रमांक : the passenger in seat number 32 ∎ **any number of sth/sb** बहुत सारी वस्तुएँ/ बहुत सारे लोग ▶ **number** verb 1 कोई संख्या देना/लगाना : The doors were numbered 2, 4, 6 and 8. 2 (संख्या तक) जोड़ना ∎ **number (sb/sth) among sth** सम्मिलित करना ▶ **numberless** adj असंख्य।

numeral / 'न्यूमरल्; US 'नूमरल् / noun अंक (जैसे 1, 2, 3...)।

numerator / 'न्यूमरेटर्; US 'नूमरेटर् / noun (गणित) भिन्न में रेखा के ऊपर वाला अंक, जैसे 3/4 में 3.

numerical / न्यु 'मेरिक्ल्; US नू 'मेरिक्ल् / (**numeric** भी) adj संख्या- त्मक।

numerous / 'न्यूमरस; US 'नूमरस् / adj बहुत-से, बहुसंख्यक।

nun / नन् / noun मठ में रहने वाली उपा- सिका, मठवासिनी ▶ **nunnery** / 'ननरि / noun (अप्र) मठ।

nuptial / 'नप्श्ल् / adj (औप) विवाह- विषयक : the nuptial ceremony ▶ **nuptials** noun [pl] (औप या साहि) विवाह-समारोह।

nurse[1] / नर्स् / noun 1 नर्स (अस्पताल आदि में) 2 (**nursemaid** भी) धाय; आया।

nurse[2] / नर्स् / verb 1 नर्स का कार्य करना 2 (माँ द्वारा) बच्चे को अपना दूध पिलाना 3 गोद में लेना, संभालकर पकड़ना : nurse a child/puppy 4 ध्यानपूर्वक पालन- पोषण करना; (नए व्यवसाय आदि को) बढ़ने देना : nurse young plants ▶ **nursing** noun.

nursery / 'नर्सरि / noun (pl **nurseries**) 1 नर्सरी जहाँ बच्चे पढ़ते हैं या जहाँ उनकी देखभाल की जाती है 2 पेड़-पौधों की नर्सरी; पौधशाला।

nurture / 'नर्चर् / verb (औप) 1 पालन- पोषण करना; प्रशिक्षित एवं विकसित कर- ना : children nurtured by loving parents ∘ nurture a friendship/new project 2 लंबे समय तक भाव बनाए रखना : nurture an ambition ▶ **nurture** noun देख-भाल; पालन-पोषण; विकसित करने की क्रिया।

nut / नट् / noun 1 अखरोट, बादाम आदि कड़े छिलके वाला मेवा : nuts and raisins 2 (बोल्ट में लगाने वाला) नट, ढिबरी या क़ाबला 3 (अप) व्यक्ति का सिर; (अप, अपमा) मूर्ख व्यक्ति ∎ **the nuts and bolts of sth** (अनौप) किसी विषय आदि की प्रारंभिक बातें, मूलभूत चीज़ें ▶ **nutcrackers** noun [pl] अखरोट आदि तोड़ने वाला सरौता **nutshell** / 'नट्शेल् / noun मेवे का छिलका ∎ **(put sth) in a nutshell** अति संक्षेप में (कहना) ▶ **nutty** adj (**-ier, -lest**) 1 बादाम; बादाम, अखरोट आदि मेवे वाला 2 (अप) सनकी।

nutmeg / 'नट्मेग् / noun जायफल (एक प्रकार का कड़ा मसाला)।

nutrition / न्यु 'ट्रिश्न्; US नु 'ट्रिश्न् / noun

आहार, पोषण ▶ **nutritious** / न्यु'ट्रिशस्; US नु'ट्रिशस् / adj (और) आहार के रूप में महत्त्वपूर्ण, पोषक गुणों से युक्त : a nutritious meal.

nuzzle / 'नज़्ल् / verb (किसी वस्तु से)

नाक या थूथन रगड़ना : The cow licked and nuzzled its calf.

nylon /नाइलॉन्/ noun नाइलोन (कपड़ा)।

nymph / निम्फ़ / noun (कथाओं में) अप्सरा।

Oo

O, oh / ओ / interj आश्चर्य, भय आदि का उद्गार : *O God, not another bill!*

oak / ओक् / noun बलूत (अपनी कठोर लकड़ी के कारण महत्त्वपूर्ण); बलूत की लकड़ी।

oar / ऑर् / noun नाव खेने का चप्पू ▸ **oarsman** / ऑर्ज़्मन् / noun खेवैया।

oasis / ओएसिस् / noun (pl **oases** / ओ 'एसीज़्/) 1 नख़लिस्तान, मरूद्यान; रेगिस्तान में पानी-पेड़ का प्रदेश 2 अरुचिकर चीज़ों के बीच रुचिकर स्थान या समय।

oath / ओथ् / noun 1 शपथ (पदग्रहण आदि के लिए) 2 क़सम, सौगंध 3 अशिष्ट वचन।

oats / ओट्स् / noun [pl] जई (विशेषत: घोड़ों के खाने के लिए) ▸ **oatmeal** / 'ओट्मील् / noun जई का दलिया (पॉरिज आदि में प्रयुक्त)।

obedient / अ'बीडिअन्ट् / adj **obedient (to sb/sth)** आज्ञाकारी ▸ **obedience** / अ'बीडिअन्स् / noun आज्ञाकारिता **obediently** adv.

obese / ओ'बीस् / adj (औप या चिकि) (व्यक्ति) बहुत मोटा, स्थूलकाय ▸ **obesity** / ओ'बीसटि / noun मोटापा : *Obesity can increase the risk of heart disease.*

obey / अ'बे / verb आज्ञा मानना, कहे के अनुसार चलना : *Soldiers are trained to obey without question.*

obituary / अ'बिचुअरि; US ओ'बिचुएरि / noun (pl **obituaries**) (किसी व्यक्ति की) निधन-सूचना (प्राय: संक्षिप्त जीवन चरित के साथ)।

object¹ / 'ऑब्जिक्ट; US 'ऑब्जेक्ट् / noun 1 मूर्त पदार्थ, वस्तु (जिसे देखा या छुआ जा सके) : *a distant object* ○ *inanimate object* 2 उद्देश्य, लक्ष्य : *She left college with the object of going into business.* 3 (व्या) कर्म : *'He*

took the money' में *'the money'* object है ▸ **object-lesson** noun प्रदर्शन-पाठ।

object² / अब्'जेक्ट् / verb 1 **object (to sb/sth)**; **object (to doing sth)** आपत्ति या एतराज़ उठाना 2 विरोध का कारण देना : *'But he is too young,'* I objected.

objection / अब्'जेक्श्न् / noun **objection (to sth/doing sth)** आपत्ति/एतराज़ ▸ **objectionable** / अब्'जेक्शनब्ल् / adj (औप) आपत्तिजनक; अप्रियकर : *highly objectionable remarks.*

objective / अब्'जेक्टिव् / noun ध्येय; उद्देश्य; (सेना में) लक्ष्य ▸ **objective** adj 1 निष्पक्ष : *an objective report/assessment of sth* 2 (प्रश्न आदि) वस्तुनिष्ठ 3 (दर्शन) विचारों/मन से अलग वास्तविक वस्तु (जिसे देखा और प्रमाणित किया जा सके): *objective knowledge.*

obligation / ऑब्लि'गेश्न् / noun 1 (क़ानून) बाध्यता 2 कर्तव्य, दायित्व; कर्तव्यबोध : *They attended the party more out of a sense of obligation than anything else.* ■ **be under an obligation to sb** प्रतिबद्ध होना ▸ **obligatory** / अ'ब्लिगट्रि / adj (औप) (नियम, विधि या प्रथानुसार) अनिवार्य, आवश्यक।

oblige / अ'ब्लाइज् / verb 1 प्रतिज्ञा आदि द्वारा किसी को किसी कार्य के लिए प्रतिबद्ध करना : *The law obliges parents to send their children to school.* 2 **oblige sb (with sth/by doing sth)** एहसान करना, अनुग्रह करना ▸ **obliged** adj अनुगृहीत, आभारी **obliging** adj उपकारी, अनुग्रह करने वाला **obligingly** adv.

oblique / अ'ब्लीक् / adj 1 (रेखा) तिरछी; टेढ़ा 2 अप्रत्यक्ष रूप से व्यक्त : *an oblique*

comment/hint ▶ **oblique (slash** भी)
noun / चिह्न।

obliterate / अ 'ब्लिटरेट् / *verb* 1 मिटाना,
सभी चिह्न लुप्त कर देना 2 किसी चीज़ का
दृश्य, स्वर आदि दबा/ढक देना : *The view
was totally obliterated by the fog.*
▶ **obliteration** / अ 'ब्लिट रेश्न् / *noun.*

oblivion / अॅ'ब्लिव़िअन् / *noun* 1 विस्म-
रण; अचेतन जैसी स्थिति : *drink oneself
into oblivion* 2 भुला दिया जाना।

oblivious / अॅ'ब्लिव़िअस् / *adj* **oblivious (of/to sth)** भुलक्कड़; जानकारी/चेतना
न रखने वाला : *oblivious to what was
happening* ▶ **obliviousness** *noun.*

oblong / 'ऑब्लॉङ् / *noun* आयत ▶ **oblong** *adj* आयताकार : *an oblong mirror.*

obnoxious / अब्'नॉक्सस् / *adj* अप्रीतिकर;
हानिकारक या ठेस पहुँचाने वाला ▶ **ob-
noxiously** *adv.*

oboe / 'ओबो / *noun* शहनाई जैसा बाजा
▶ **oboist** *noun* इस बाजे का वादक।

obscene / अब्'सीन् / *adj* (शब्द या आच-
रण) अश्लील; कुत्सित ▶ **obscenely**
adv **obscenity** / अब्'सेनटि / *noun* (*pl*
obscenities) अश्लील/कुत्सित आचरण;
अश्लील शब्द या कार्य : *scribble obscenities on the wall.*

obscure / अब्'स्क्युअर् / *adj* 1 अंधकार-
मय; गुप्त, दुर्बोध : *I found the lecture
very obscure.* 2 अप्रसिद्ध : *an obscure German poet* ▶ **obscure** *verb*
गुप्त बनाना; अज्ञात बना देना : *Mist ob-
scured the view.* **obscurity** / अब्
'स्क्युअरटि / *noun* (*pl* **obscurities**)
1 अंधकार 2 अज्ञात होने की स्थिति; अज्ञात/
दुर्बोध वस्तु : *a philosophical essay
full of obscurities.*

observance / अब्'ज़र्वन्स् / *noun*
1 क़ानून/नियम का अनुपालन 2 धार्मिक
अनुष्ठान क्रिया : *religious observ-
ances.*

observant / अब्'ज़र्वन्ट् / *adj* 1 ध्यानपूर्वक
एवं तेज़ी से निरीक्षण करने वाला 2 (और)
नियमों का सावधानीपूर्वक पालन करने
वाला : *She's a Catholic, but not
particularly observant.*

observation / ˌऑब्ज़र्'वेश्न् / *noun*
1 सावधानी से देखने की क्रिया, प्रेक्षण : *his
astonishing powers of observa-
tion* 2 कथन, टिप्पणी : *record scientific observations.*

observatory / अब्'ज़र्वट्रि / *noun* (*pl*
observatories) वेधशाला (वह भवन
जहाँ नक्षत्रों-तारों को देखने के लिए दूरदर्शक
आदि यंत्र लगे हों)।

observe / अब्'ज़र्व़ / *verb* 1 (ध्यानपूर्वक)
देखना; अवलोकन करना; पर्यवेक्षण करना :
He observes keenly but says little.
2 (नियमों का) अनुपालन करना; नियम
मानना/ मनाना 3 उत्सव/त्योहार आदि
मनाना : *Do they observe Christmas?*
4 (और) कहना, टिप्पणी करना ▶ **observer** *noun.*

obsess / अब्'सेस् / *verb* धुन सवार होना
▶ **obsession** *noun* **obsession
(with/about sth/sb)** धुन; सम्मोह; व्यक्ति/
वस्तु जिसकी धुन हो **obsessive** *adj.*

obsolete / 'ऑब्सलीट् / *adj* अप्रचलित :
obsolete words found in old texts.

obstacle / 'ऑब्स्टकल् / *noun* अवरोध;
प्रगति के मार्ग में आई अड़चन/बाधा।

obstetrics / अब्'स्टेट्रिक्स् / *noun* (चिकि)
प्रसव-संबंधी चिकित्सा विज्ञान ▶ **obste-
trician** / ˌअब्स्ट 'ट्रिश्न् / *noun* प्रसूति-
विज्ञान चिकित्सक।

obstinate / 'ऑब्स्टिनट् / *adj* 1 ज़िद्दी,
दुराग्रही 2 जो आसानी से क़ाबू में न आ
सके : *obstinate resistance* ▶ **obstinacy** *noun* ज़िद, दुराग्रह **obstinately**
adv.

obstruct / अब्'स्ट्रक्ट् / *verb* 1 बाधा
डालना या बनना; रुकावट डालना 2 प्रगति के
मार्ग में अड़चनें और विघ्न डालना ▶ **ob-**

structive / अब् 'स्ट्रक्टिव् / adj बाधा डालने वाला; अड़चनें डालने वाला।

obstruction / अब् 'स्ट्रक्शन् / noun 1 अवरोध/अवरुद्ध होने की प्रक्रिया 2 बाधा, विघ्न।

obtain / अब् 'टेन् / verb 1 (अक्सर औप) प्राप्त करना, पाना; प्रयास से स्वामित्व पाना : *obtain permission/approval* 2 (औप) (प्रथा, नियमों आदि का) स्थापित अथवा प्रचलित होना ▸ **obtainable** adj लभ्य, सुलभ।

obtrude / अब् 'ट्रूड् / verb (औप) 1 obtrude (sth/oneself) (on/upon sb) (अवांछित तरीक़े से) ख़ुद को दिखाना या दिखाई पड़ना : *obtrude one's opinion on others* 2 बाहर को निकलना/ निकला हुआ होना ▸ **obtrusive** / अब् 'ट्रू-सिव् / adj अप्रियकर ढंग से नज़र आने वाला; आशांति पैदा करने वाला : *Try to wear less obtrusive colours.* **obtrusively** adv.

obtuse / अब् 'ट्यूस् / adj (अपमा) मंदबुद्धि, कुंद ▸ **obtuse angle** noun (ज्यामिति) 90° से अधिक किंतु 180° से कम का कोण **obtuseness** noun.

obvious / 'ऑब्विअस् / adj सुस्पष्ट, प्रकट ▸ **obviously** adv स्पष्ट रूप से : *He was obviously drunk.* **obviousness** noun.

occasion / अ 'केश्न् / noun 1 अवसर (घटना विशेष होने का); सुअवसर 2 occasion (for sth) सुअवसर; उचित/ उपयुक्त समय 3 विशेष महत्त्व की घटना/ समारोह : *a great/memorable/happy occasion* 4 (औप) कारण; आवश्यकता ▸ **occasion** verb (औप) का कारण बनना : *The decision occasioned us much anxiety.* **occasional** / अ 'के-श्न्ल् / adj 1 यदा-कदा घटित होने वाला 2 (औप) विशेष अवसर के लिए रचित (साहित्य रचना) : *occasional verses* **occasionally** adv कभी-कभी, बीच-

बीच में समय छोड़कर : *He visits me occasionally.*

occult / अ 'कल्ट्; US आ 'कल्ट् / adj 1 रहस्यमय; तंत्र-मंत्रात्मक : *occult powers* 2 गुप्त, छिपा हुआ ▸ **the occult** noun तंत्र-मंत्र।

occupant / 'ऑक्युपन्ट् / noun घर/कमरे में रहने वाला व्यक्ति; किसी वाहन (कार आदि) में बैठा हुआ व्यक्ति।

occupation / ,ऑक्यु 'पेश्न् / noun 1 (औप) जीविका, वृत्ति 2 समय बिताने का ढंग 3 व्यवसाय ▸ **occupational** adj व्यक्ति की नौकरी/जीविका से संबंधित।

occupy / 'ऑक्युपाइ / verb (pt, pp occupied) 1 (मकान में) रहना, निवास करना 2 (भूमि, खेत आदि पर) अधिकार रखना; (युद्ध में किसी शहर आदि को) क़ब्ज़े में करना : *The army occupied the enemy's capital.* 3 जगह भरना 4 occupy sb/oneself (in doing sth / with sth) व्यस्त रहना/ रखना; समय बिताना : *She needs something to occupy her mind.* ▸ **occupied** adj 1 प्रयुक्त; भरा हुआ : *The toilet was occupied.* 2 occupied (in doing sth/with sth) व्यस्त।

occur / अ 'कर् / verb (-rr-) 1 घटित होना : *When did the accident occur?* 2 होना, पाया जाना : *Child abuse occurs in all classes of society.* 3 occur to sb सूझना, मन में आना : *An idea has occurred to me.*

occurrence / अ 'करन्स् / noun 1 घटना 2 (औप) घटना का होना अथवा आवृत्ति।

ocean / 'ओश्न् / noun (प्रायः the ocean) महासागर : *the Atlantic/Pacific/Indian Ocean.*

o'clock / अ 'क्लॉक् / adv (1 से 12 तक की संख्या के साथ समय बताने के लिए प्रयुक्त) : *go to bed at 11 o'clock.*

octagon / 'ऑक्टगन् / noun (ज्यामिति)

अष्टभुज आकृति ▶ **octagonal** adj अष्ट-
भुजाकार : an octagonal table.

octave / 'ऑक्टिव् / noun (संगीत)
अष्टक, आठ चरणों का पद्य, बाजे का परदा।

October / ऑक् 'टोबर् / noun (संक्षि
Oct) अक्टूबर (महीना)।

octopus / 'ऑक्टपस् / noun (pl **octo-
puses**) आठ बड़ी भुजाओं वाला समुद्री
जीव (जिसे समुद्री हाथी भी कहा जाता है)।

odd / ऑड् / adj 1 (-er, -est) विचित्र,
अनूठा : an odd tale 2 विषम संख्या (जैसे
1, 3, 5, 7,....) 3 कुछ अतिरिक्त : five
hundred odd (पाँच सौ से कुछ अधिक)
4 किसी वस्तु का सेट या जोड़ी से बचा
होना : an odd shoe/glove ∘ two odd
volumes of an encyclopedia
5 अनियमित रूप से घटित, लगातार नहीं,
अनियमित अवसरों पर : weed the garden at odd times 6 (प्राय: the odd)
ख़ाली (समय आदि); अतिरिक्त ▶ **odd
jobs** noun [pl] फुटकर कार्य **oddly** adv
अजीब ढंग से।

oddity / 'ऑडिटि / noun (pl **oddities**)
1 विचित्रता 2 विचित्र मनुष्य, आचरण, वस्तु
आदि।

odds / ऑड्ज़् / noun [pl] 1 किसी घटना
के होने/न होने की संभावनाएँ : The odds
are in your favour. 2 प्रबल विरोध :
Against all the odds she achieved
her dreams. 3 **be at odds (with sb)
(over/on sth)** झगड़ा करना, अनबन होना,
■ **odds and ends** [pl] (अनौप) छुट-
पुट, फुटकर सामान।

ode / ओड् / noun ओड (उदात्त भावनाओं
की एक कविता) : Keats's 'Ode to
Autumn'.

odious / 'ओडिअस् / adj (औप) घृणित,
अरुचिकर : I find this flattery odious.

odour (US **odor**) / 'ओडर् / noun
(औप) गंध; महक, सुगंध ▶ **odourless**
adj.

odyssey / 'ऑडिसि / noun अनुभवों से
भरी एक लंबी यात्रा।

o'er / ऑर् / adv, prep (प्रा) कविता में
over के लिए प्रयुक्त।

of / ऑव् / prep 1 का, के, की; से संबद्ध,
के (द्वारा) स्वामित्व में : that house of
theirs in the country 2 किसी की
भूमिका, पद या स्थिति से संबंधित : the role
of a teacher 3 के द्वारा रचित : the
works of Milton 4 से बना हुआ : a
dress of blue silk 5 (वर्णनात्मक) : a
woman of great beauty 6 के विषय
में; दर्शाते हुए : stories of crime and
adventure 7 कारण : die of pneumonia 8 (व्यक्ति की) उत्पत्ति/निवास स्थान
आदि के बारे में बताते हुए : the inhabitants of the area.

off¹ / ऑफ़् / prep 1 से अलग, कुछ दूरी पर;
नीचे की ओर : The rain ran off the
roof. 2 समीप में, थोड़ी दूर पर : a big
house off the main street
3 (सड़क आदि) से निकला हुआ : a
narrow lane off the main road
4 (अनौप) (कुछ लेने को) अनिच्छुक : I
am off alcohol for a week.

off² / ऑफ़् / adv 1 दूर, दूरी पर, 2 (से
अलग; से पृथक) : take one's coat/tie
off 3 शुरू करना (यात्रा आदि) : I must
be off soon. 4 (अनौप) रद्द; घटित न होने
वाला : The engagement is off.
5 (किसी विद्युत उपकरण का) काम न
करना, बंद होना 6 कार्य आदि से छुट्टी पर
होना : She's off today. 7 (क़ीमत पर)
छूट होना : All shirts have 10% off.
■ **off and on/on and off** समय-समय
पर, यदा-कदा : It rained off and on all
day.

off³ / ऑफ़् / adj 1 **off (with sb)** (अनौप)
(विशेषत: rather, very slightly आदि
के बाद प्रयुक्त) मित्रवत् नहीं, विनम्र नहीं :
She sounded rather off on the
phone. 2 अस्वीकार्य 3 अस्वस्थ : You

look a bit off this morning, Sapna.
4 जीर्ण; सड़ा हुआ : *That meat is off.*
‣ **off chance** *noun* [*sing*] बहुत ही कम संभावना।

off- *pref* (*पूर्वपद*) पर नहीं; दूर, दूरी पर : *off-stage* ○ *off-peak.*

offal / ऑफ़्ल् / *noun* पशुओं का भीतरी मांस जो खाने के काम आता है, जैसे कलेजी, मग़ज़ आदि।

offence (*US* **offense**) / अ'फ़ेन्स् / *noun* 1 **offence** (**against sth**) अपराध, नियम का उल्लंघन : *commit an offence* 2 **offence** (**to sb/sth**) तिरस्कार, दुर्व्यवहार 3 **offence** (**to sb/sth**) (*औप*) किसी की भावनाओं को चोट/ठेस पहुँचाने वाली बात।

offend / अ'फ़ेन्ड् / *verb* 1 **offend** (**against sb/sth**) अपराध करना; नियमोल्लंघन करना 2 आघात/ठेस पहुँचाना : *She was offended by his sexist remarks.* 3 नाराज़ करना ‣ **offender** / अ'फ़ेन्डर् / *noun* नियम तोड़ने वाला, अपराधी।

offensive / अ'फ़ेन्सिव् / *adj* 1 अपमानजनक; आघात और ठेस पहुँचाने वाला : *offensive language* 2 (*औप*) आक्रामक, हमलावर : *offensive weapons/ operations* ■ **go on (to)/take the offensive** आक्रमण या हमला करना ‣ **offensively** *adv.*

offer / ऑफ़र् / *verb* 1 **offer sth** (**to sb**) (**for sth**) अर्पित करना, सामने रखना 2 **offer sth** (**to sb**) कुछ देने/करने की इच्छा ज़ाहिर करना : *We offered to leave.* 3 (*औप*) अवसर प्रदान करना 4 **offer sth/sb** (**up**) (**to sb**) (**for sth**) (*औप*) (ईश्वर के आगे) अर्पित करना, चढ़ाना : *She offered (up) a prayer (to God).* ‣ **offer** *noun* 1 **offer** (**to sb/to do sth**) प्रस्ताव 2 **offer** (**for sth**) प्रस्तावित धनराशि; अर्पण; भेंट : *I've had an offer of Rs 22,000 for the car.* **offering** / ऑफ़रिङ् / *noun* भेंट/ चढ़ावा।

offhand / ऑफ़्'हैन्ड् / *adj* (*अपमा*) (व्यवहार, भाषण आदि) रूखा, असम्मानजनक : *He was rather offhand with me.* ‣ **offhand** *adv* बिना तैयारी के, तत्काल : *Offhand, I can't think of anyone who could help you.*

office / ऑफ़िस् / *noun* 1 कार्यालय, दफ़्तर 2 **office** (समास में) सरकारी विभाग : *work in the Foreign Office* 3 कार्यभार, पद : *hold the office of mayor* ■ **through sb's good offices** (*औप*) (किसी व्यक्ति की) सहायता से।

officer / ऑफ़िसर् / *noun* 1 (सेना, पुलिस आदि में) अफ़सर 2 (प्राय: समास में) सरकारी अधिकारी : *executive and clerical officers* 3 (किसी समिति आदि का) सचिव, पदाधिकारी।

official / अ'फ़िश्ल् / *adj* 1 अधिकारी; सरकारी/शासकीय : *official powers* 2 अधिकार से कहा/किया गया : *an official announcement* 3 पदाधिकारी उच्चाधिकारी के योग्य/उपयुक्त : *an official reception* ‣ **official** *noun* उच्चाधिकारी **officially** *adv* 1 आधिकारिक रूप से 2 सरकारी तौर पर।

officiate / अ'फ़िशिएट् / *verb* **officiate** (**at sth**) किसी पद पर काम करना।

officious / अ'फ़िशस् / *adj* (*अपमा*) बिना माँगे सहायता/सलाह/हुक्म देने वाला, हस्तक्षेप करने वाला।

offing / ऑफ़िङ् / *noun* ■ **in the offing** (*अनौप*) निकट भविष्य में घटित होने वाला : *I've heard there are more staff changes in the offing.*

offload / ऑफ़्'लोड् / *verb* **offload sb/ sth** (**on/onto sb**) अवांछित व्यक्ति/वस्तु से छुटकारा पाना (विशेषत: किसी अन्य को सौंपकर)।

off-peak / ऑफ़्'पीक् / *adj* ऐसे समय में प्रयुक्त या ऐसा समय जब माँग (विद्युत, रेल सेवा आदि) कम हो : *off-peak holiday prices.*

off-putting /ऑफ़ 'पुटिङ/ *adj* (अनौप) अप्रियकर, चिंताजनक।

offset /'ऑफ़्सेट्/ *verb* (-tt-; *pt, pp* offset) offset sth (against sth) क्षतिपूर्ति करना; संतुलित कर देना।

offshoot /'ऑफ़्शूट/ *noun* शाखा, प्र-शाखा : *an offshoot of the parent company.*

offshore /ˌऑफ़्'शॉर्/ *adj* 1 (तट के समीप) समुद्र में : *offshore oil rig* 2 (पवन) समुद्र की ओर बहती हुई।

offside /ˌऑफ़्'साइड्/ *adj* दूर वाला सिरा, (यातायात की दृष्टि से, भारत और ब्रिटेन में) दाहिनी ओर।

offspring /'ऑफ़्स्प्रिङ्/ *noun* (*pl* अपरिवर्तित) (औप या *परि*) 1 संतान 2 पशुओं के बच्चे : *How many offspring does a cat usually have?*

off-white /ˌऑफ़ 'वाइट्/ *noun, adj* कुछ पीलापन/मटमैलापन लिए सफ़ेद।

often /'ऑफ़्न्; 'ऑफ़्टन्/ *adv* (-er, -est) 1 प्राय:, अक्सर/बहुधा : *We often go there.* 2 सामान्यतया, बहुत-सी बातों में : *Old houses are often damp.*

ogre /'ओगर्/ *noun* (*fem* ogress /'ओ-ग्रेस्/) 1 (बच्चों की कहानियों में) नरभक्षी दानव, दैत्य 2 एक डरावना व्यक्ति : *My boss is a real ogre.*

oil /ऑइल्/ *noun* 1 तेल 2 खनिज तेल : *drilling for oil in the desert* ▸ **oil** *verb* चिकनाई के लिए तेल डालना/लगाना **oil colours** *noun* [pl] तेल वाले रंग **oily** /'ऑइलि/ *adj* (-ier, -iest) 1 तैलीय 2 तेल जैसा; तेल-चुपड़ा।

oilskin /'ऑइल्स्किन्/ *noun* मोमजामा।

ointment /'ऑइन्ट्मन्ट्/ *noun* मरहम।

OK (okay भी) /ओ 'के/ *adj, adv* (अनौप) ठीक है, अच्छा (है) ▸ **okay** (ok भी) *interj* ठीक है! अच्छा!

old /ओल्ड्/ *adj* (-er, -est) 1 (आयु में) बड़ा; (किसी ख़ास) उम्र का : *He's forty years old.* 2 बूढ़ा, वृद्ध 3 लंबे समय से अस्तित्व में होना; बहुत पुराना : *old customs/beliefs* 4 पिछला/पूर्व समय का : *in my old job* 5 अतीत काल का ▸ **old age** *noun* वृद्धावस्था **old-fashioned** *adj* पुराना; पुरानी रूढ़ियों/प्रथाओं को मानने वाला **the old** *noun* वृद्ध लोग।

olive /'ऑलिव्/ *noun* 1 जैतून (वृक्ष व फल) 2 (olive-green भी) पीला-हरा (रंग) ▸ **olive** *adj* 1 पीला-हरा 2 (त्वचा) पीली-भूरी **olive branch** *noun* शांति/प्रेम का प्रतीक।

Olympic /अ'लिम्पिक/ *adj* ऑलिम्पिक खेलों से संबंधित ▸ **the Olympic Games** (**Olympics** भी) *noun* [pl] हर चार साल बाद आयोजित अंतरराष्ट्रीय खेल प्रतियोगिता।

ombudsman /'ऑम्बुड्ज़्मन्; 'ऑम्बु-ड्ज़्मैन्/ *noun* सरकारी अधिकारियों के विरुद्ध शिकायत सुनने के लिए नियुक्त लोकपाल।

omelette (omelet भी) /'ऑम्लट्/ *noun* ऑमलेट (अंडों से बना हुआ)।

omen /'ओमन्/ *noun* omen (of sth) सगुन, शकुन : *a good/bad omen.*

ominous /'ऑमिनस्/ *adj* अपशकुन, अनिष्ट की सूचना वाला; धमकी भरा : *an ominous silence* ▸ **ominously** *adv*.

omission /अ'मिशन्/ *noun* 1 छोड़ना, भूल 2 छोड़ी हुई वस्तु।

omit /अ'मिट्/ *verb* (-tt-) 1 (कुछ शामिल करने में) भूल जाना; कुछ करने में असमर्थ रहना 2 छोड़ देना, शामिल न करना : *This chapter may be omitted.*

omnipotent /ऑम्'निपटन्ट्/ *adj* (औप) सर्वशक्ति संपन्न : *an omnipotent deity* ▸ **omnipotence** *noun*.

omnipresent /ˌऑम्नि'प्रेज़्न्ट्/ *adj* (औप) सर्वव्यापी, सब जगह विराजमान/उपस्थित : *the omnipresent squalor/dread.*

omniscient /ऑम्'निसिअन्ट्/ *adj* (औप) सर्वज्ञ, सब जानने वाला ▸ **omniscience** *noun* सर्वज्ञता।

omnivorous /ऑम्'निव्रस्/ adj (औप) 1 सर्वभक्षी 2 सब उपस्थित/प्राप्य वस्तुओं का उपयोग करने वाला : an omnivorous reader.

on /ऑन्/ prep 1 (और upon भी) पर, के ऊपर; समीप : a picture on the wall 2 (घटित होने के समय पर) : on Sunday 3 के बारे में, विषय में : speak/write on Shakespeare 4 की ओर : march on the capital 5 पर (आश्रित) : live on bread and water 6 किसी के पास उपलब्ध होना : Have you got any money on you? 7 (और upon भी) (कारण या आधार दर्शाते हुए) परिणामस्वरूप होना : a story based on fact 8 (किसी साधन) के द्वारा; के प्रयोग से : play a tune on the flute 9 (व्यक्ति/वस्तु) के संबंध/ संदर्भ में; को प्रभावित करते हुए : a ban on imports 10 कोई कार्य, उद्देश्य, स्थिति आदि दर्शाते हुए : go on an errand ▸ **on** adv part 1 (स्थिति, प्रगति या कार्य की निरंतरता) : He worked on without a break. 2 (समय या स्थान में गति) : hurry on to the end of the lane 3 (कपड़े) पहनना : Put your coat on. 4 घटित हो रहा 5 (विद्युत उपकरण आदि) चालू, प्रयोग में 6 भविष्य में घटित होने के लिए नियो- जित : Is the match on at 2 pm or 3 pm? 7 वाहन के भीतर; अंदर : Four people got on.

once /वन्स्/ adv 1 एक बार (केवल) : He cleans his car once a week. 2 अतीत में किसी समय : I once met your mother. 3 (नकारात्मक वाक्यों या प्रश्नों में) कभी; बिलकुल : He never once offered to help. ■ **all at once** अचानक **at once** 1 तुरंत, तत्काल 2 एक ही समय : Don't speak all at once! **once and for all** अभी और अंतिम बार **once bitten twice shy** (कहा) दूध का जला छाछ भी फूँककर पीता है **once in a blue moon** यदा-कदा; बहुत कम **once**

in a while कभी-कभी **once upon a time** बहुत पहले ▸ **once** conj ज्यों ही, जैसे ही : Once you learn the basic rules, it's easy to play.

oncoming /'आन्कमिङ्/ adj (केवल संज्ञा से पहले) आप की तरफ़ आता हुआ : oncoming traffic.

one¹ / वन्/ noun, pron, det 1 संख्या एक, 1 2 (सौ, हज़ार, दर्जन आदि के साथ 'एक' के अर्थ में 'a' की जगह प्रयुक्त) : one hundred and fifty pounds 3 केवल एक; एक ही : There's only one piece of cake left. 4 किसी समूह में कोई एक व्यक्ति/वस्तु : One of my friends lives in Chennai. 5 व्यक्ति या वस्तु विशेष, केवल वही : The one way to success is hard work. 6 (भूत या भविष्य में) किसी समय : one morning/afternoon last week 7 वही, एक समान : They all went off in one direction. ■ **one by one** एक के बाद एक, एक-एक करके ▸ **one-sided** adj 1 (विशेषत: तर्क के) किसी एक ही पक्ष पर ध्यान रखने वाला, एकांगी 2 (मत, विचार) दुराग्रह पूर्ण, पक्षपात पूर्ण **one-way** adj (किसी मार्ग पर) एकतरफ़ा यातायात; (यात्रा के लिए) एक तरफ़ का टिकट (बिना रिटर्न टिकट)।

one² / वन्/ pers pron (और) कोई व्यक्ति, आम व्यक्ति : One must be sure of one's facts before making a public accusation.

one³ / वन्/ noun 1 (एक व्यक्ति या व्यक्तियों के समूह के लिए प्रयुक्त जिसका उल्लेख पहले न किया गया हो) : It's time the little ones were in bed. 2 (this, that, which अथवा विशेषण के बाद प्रयुक्त) : I prefer that one. 3 **the one(s)** किसी व्यक्ति/वस्तु की पहचान कराने के लिए प्रयुक्त : Our hotel is the one nearest to the beach. ▸ **one** pron (और) किसी विशेष स्वभाव/चरित्र वाला व्यक्ति : She was never one to gossip.

oneself / वन्'सेल्फ़ / *pron* **1** (reflex) स्वयं को, ख़ुद को : *one's ability to wash and dress oneself* **2** (emph) स्वयं/ख़ुद ही : *One could easily arrange it all oneself.*

ongoing / 'ऑन्गोइङ् / *adj* (केवल संज्ञा के पहले) इस समय भी चालू : *ongoing problems.*

onion / अन्यन् / *noun* प्याज़।

online / ऑन्'लाइन् / *adj* (उपकरण एवं प्रक्रिया) किसी केंद्रीय कंप्यूटर से जुड़ा हुआ एवं उसके द्वारा नियंत्रित : *an on-line ticket booking system.*

onlooker / 'ऑन्लुकर् / *noun* दर्शक; प्रेक्षक : *A crowd of onlookers gathered there.*

only[1] / 'ओन्लि / *adj* **1** केवल, एकमात्र अकेला : *His only answer was a grunt.* **2** सर्वश्रेष्ठ : *She's the only woman for the job.*

only[2] / ओन्लि / *adv* **1** अकेला, एकमात्र : *I only saw Mary.* **2** केवल (कुछ समय पहले ही) : *I saw him only yesterday.* **3** के पूर्व नहीं : *They arrive only on Thursday.*

only[3] / 'ओन्लि / *conj* (अनौप) को छोड़ कर; किंतु : *He's always making promises, only he never keeps them.*

onset / 'ऑन्सेद् / *noun* ज़ोरदार (विशेषत: अरुचिकर) आरंभ; आक्रमण : *the onset of winter/old age.*

onslaught / 'ऑन्स्लॉद् / *noun* **onslaught (against/on sb/sth)** चढ़ाई, आक्रमण।

onto (on to भी) / 'ऑन्टु / *prep* सतह के ऊपर किसी स्थान पर/की ओर : *step out of the train onto the platform.*

onus / 'ओनस् / *noun* (प्राय: **the onus**) (औप) दायित्व, कुछ करने की ज़िम्मेदारी।

onward / 'ऑन्वई / *adj* आगे : *an*

onward journey ▶ **onward** (**onwards** / 'ऑन्वईज़् / भी) *adv* से लेकर, से आगे : *from the 1980s onwards.*

ooze / ऊज़् / *verb* **ooze from/out of sth** टपकना, रिसना; **ooze (with) sth** (अलं) ओत-प्रोत होकर रिसना/टपकना, भर जाना :(अलं) *They oozed confidence.* ▶ **ooze** *noun* **1** पतला मुलायम कीचड़ (विशेषत: झील, नदी के तल में) **2** टपकाव, रिसाव : *a steady ooze of blood from a wound.*

opal / ओपल् / *noun* दूधिया रत्न जिसमें रंग बदलते दिखाई देते हैं ▶ **opalescent** / ओप 'लेसन्ट् / *adj* रंग बदलने वाला : *an opalescent sky.*

opaque / ओ'पेक् / *adj* **1** अपारदर्शी **2** (कथन, लेख आदि) अस्पष्ट, समझने में मुश्किल : *use opaque language.*

open[1] / 'ओपन् / *adj* **1** खुला हुआ; अनावृत **2** घिरा हुआ नहीं, अनवरुद्ध : *open country* **3** व्यापार आदि कामकाज के लिए तैयार : *The banks aren't open yet.* **4** खुला हुआ (मुड़ा हुआ नहीं) **5** **open (to sb/ sth)** सार्वजनिक, जिसमें सभी भाग/प्रवेश ले सकते हैं : *an open debate/competition* **6** अनिर्णीत (प्रश्न आदि) **7** सबको ज्ञात, गुप्त नहीं : *an open quarrel/scandal* ■ **have/keep an open mind (about/on sth)** उदारमति, नए विचार ग्रहण करने को तैयार **open to sth** सुनने/ बातचीत को तैयार **with open arms** उत्साह के साथ, हार्दिक स्वागत ▶ **open-air** *adj* भवन आदि के बाहर खुले मैदान में : *open-air concert* **open-handed** *adj* मुक्तहस्त, उदार **open-hearted** *adj* निष्कपट **openly** *adv* खुले तौर पर; ईमानदारी से **Open University** *noun* [sing] विश्वविद्यालय जिसके छात्र दूर अपने घर बैठे शिक्षा ग्रहण करते हैं और पाठ्यक्रम पूरा करते हैं : *Indira Gandhi National Open University* **the open** *noun* [sing]

खुला मैदान **the open sea** *noun* थल से बहुत दूर का समुद्र।

open² / 'ओपन्/ *verb* 1 खोलना/ खुलना 2 छेद करना; (काटकर) द्वार बनाना : *open a mine/tunnel* 3 **open (sth) (out)** (लिपटी हुई वस्तु को) खोलकर फैलाना : *open a map on the table* 4 शुरू करना; प्रयोग हेतु तैयार करना : *open an account* ■ **open (sth) up** विकास हेतु खोल देना, उपलब्ध कराना **open up** 1 दिल खोल कर बात करना 2 गोलियाँ चलाना शुरू करना।

opening / 'ओप्निङ्/ *noun* 1 प्रवेश मार्ग, खुला स्थान : *an opening in a hedge/ fence ○ an opening in the clouds* 2 (विशेषत: *pl*) आरंभ : *the opening of a book/film* 3 (व्यापारिक प्रतिष्ठानों आदि में) नौकरी का रिक्त स्थान/अवसर ▸ **opening** *adj* प्रथम/पहला।

opera / 'ऑप्रा/ *noun* ओपेरा; गीति-नाट्य ▸ **operatic** *adj*.

operate / 'ऑपरेट्/ *verb* 1 (औप) परि-चालित करना, चलाना (मशीन आदि), लागू होना, चालू करना 2 कार्य में होना, प्रभावी होना : *A new timetable is now operating.* 3 **operate (on sb) (for sth)** शल्य क्रिया (ऑपरेशन) करना : *The doctors decided to operate (on her) immediately.*

operation /ऑप'रेश्न्/ *noun* 1 **operation (on sb/sth) (for sth)** (चिकि) शल्य क्रिया, ऑपरेशन 2 व्यापारिक कंपनी 3 (प्राय: *pl*) व्यापारिक या औद्योगिक कारखाई : *operations research* 4 प्रक्रिया, संचालन-पद्धति 5 (प्राय: *pl*) सैनिक कारखाई, गतिविधि : *Operation Vijaya* ▸ **operational** *adj* (औप) 1 संचालन पद्धति/गतिशील-संबंधी : *operational costs* 2 प्रयोग के लिए तैयार।

operative / 'ऑपरटिव्/ *adj* (औप) चालू; लागू, प्रभावकारी।

operator / 'ऑपरेटर् / *noun* 1 मशीन (यंत्र) आदि को चलाने वाला 2 टेलिफ़ोन स्विचबोर्ड को नियंत्रित करने वाला : *Dial 1 and ask for the operator.*

opinion / अ'पिन्यन्/ *noun* 1 **opinion (of/about sb/sth)** राय, विचार 2 (आम) धारणा, मत : *Opinion is shifting in favour of the new scheme.*

opium / 'ओपिअम्/ *noun* अफ़ीम।

opponent / अ'पोनन्ट्/ *noun* 1 **opponent (at /in sth)** प्रतिद्वंद्री : *a political opponent* 2 **opponent (of sth)** विरोधी : *opponent of reforms.*

opportune / 'ऑपर्ट्यून; *US* ,ऑपर्टून् / *adj* 1 (समय) उपयुक्त 2 (घटना या कार्य) समयोचित : *an opportune remark* ▸ **opportunely** *adv*.

opportunism /,ऑपर्'ट्यूनिज़म्/ *noun* अवसरवाद, मौक़ापरस्ती ▸ **opportunist** /,ऑपर्'ट्यूनिस्ट् / *noun, adj* (विशेषत: *अपमा*) अवसरवादी : *He is an opportunist.*

opportunity /,ऑपर्'ट्यूनटि / *noun (pl* **opportunities) opportunity (for/of doing sth); opportunity (to do sth)** सुअवसर, मौक़ा : *create an opportunity.*

oppose / अ'पोज़्/ *verb* विरोध करना : *oppose the motion in a debate* ▸ **opposed** *adj* **opposed (to sth)** 1 विरुद्ध में (तीव्र रूप से) 2 किसी से एकदम भिन्न : *Our views are diametrically opposed on this issue.* **opposing** *adj* विरोधी/विरुद्ध।

opposite / 'ऑपज़िट्; 'ऑपसिट् / *adj* 1 **opposite (to sb/sth)** सामने, विपरीत दिशा में : *on the opposite page* 2 पूर्ण-तया भिन्न, विरोध में; उलटा : *Their opinions are entirely opposite.* ▸ **opposite** *noun*.

opposition / ऑप'ज़िश्न् / *noun* 1 **opposition (to sb/sth)** विरोध : *The army met (with) fierce opposition.*

2 the opposition प्रतिद्वंद्वी/दुश्मन 3 the Opposition विरोधी राजनीतिक दल ।

oppress / अ'प्रेस् / verb 1 अत्याचार करना, दमनपूर्वक शासन करना 2 सताना, परेशान करना : *The heat oppressed him and made him ill.* ▸ **oppressed** adj सताया हुआ : *an oppressed people* **oppression** noun अत्याचार **oppressive** / अ'प्रेसिव् / adj 1 अत्याचारी, कठोर : *oppressive laws/rules* 2 असहनीय **oppressively** adv **oppressor** noun अत्याचारी व्यक्ति।

opt / ऑप्ट् / verb कुछ करने का निर्णय लेना; कुछ करना पसंद करना ■ **opt for sth** किसी चीज़ के बारे में निर्णय लेना; चुनना : *Very few students are opting for science courses.*

optic / ऑप्टिक् / adj दृष्टि-संबंधी, नेत्र-विषयक ▸ **optics** noun दृष्टि-विज्ञान।

optical / ऑप्टिकल् / adj 1 दृष्टि/नेत्र-विषयक : *optical effects* 2 दृष्टि-शक्ति बढ़ाने से संबंधित : *optical instruments* ▸ **optically** adv.

optician / ऑप्'टिशन् / noun 1 चश्मा बनाने व बेचने वाला 2 (ophthalmic optician भी) नेत्रों की जाँच करके निर्धारित प्रकार का चश्मा सुझाने वाला।

optimism / ऑप्टिमिज़म् / noun सफलता में विश्वास; आशावादिता ▸ **optimist** / ऑप्टिमिस्ट् / noun आशावादी व्यक्ति **optimistic** / ऑप्टि'मिस्टिक् / adj आशापूर्ण; सुपरिणामों के प्रति आश्वस्त : *an optimistic view of events.*

option / ऑप्शन् / noun 1 विकल्प, दो या अनेक में से किसी एक को चुनने की सामर्थ्य : *I have no option but to go.* 2 पसंद, चुनी हुई वस्तु ▸ **optional** / ऑप्शन्ल् / adj वैकल्पिक : *optional subjects at school.*

opulent / ऑप्युलन्ट् / adj (औप) 1 महँगी वस्तुओं से बना या सजा हुआ : *opulent furnishings* 2 धनी/समृद्ध;

भरपूर : *opulent vegetation* ▸ **opulence** / ऑप्युलन्स् / noun.

or / ऑर् / conj 1 (दो विकल्पों में से एक) : *Are you coming or not?* 2 नहीं तो; अन्यथा : *Turn the heat down or the cake will burn.* 3 (नकारात्मक के बाद) न ही : *He can't read or write.* 4 (दो वस्तुएँ या विचार जो पूर्णत: समान हों) : *geology, or the science of the earth's crust.*

oral / ऑरल् / adj 1 मौखिक, ज़बानी : *an oral examination* 2 मुँह से/विषयक : *oral hygiene* ▸ **oral** noun मौखिक परीक्षा **orally** adv.

orange / ऑरिन्ज् / noun 1 संतरा, नारंगी 2 नारंगी रंग ▸ **orange** adj नारंगी रंगीन : *an orange hat.*

oration / ऑ'रेशन् / noun (औप) भाषण, वक्तृता।

orator / ऑरटर् / noun वक्ता ▸ **oratorical** / ऑर'टॉरिकल् / adj (औप, कभी-कभी अपमा) भाषण-विषयक, वक्ता-विषयक : *oratorical skills.*

oratory / ऑरटरि/ noun (pl **oratories**) जनता में भाषण देने की कला।

orbit / ऑर्बिट् / noun 1 परिक्रमा-पथ; ग्रह/उपग्रह का परिक्रमा-पथ, ग्रह/उपग्रह के चारों ओर किसी अंतरिक्ष यान आदि का परिक्रमा-पथ : *a space station in orbit round the moon* 2 शक्ति/प्रभाव आदि का क्षेत्र ▸ **orbit** verb परिक्रमा करना।

orchard / ऑर्चर्ड् / noun फलवाटिका।

orchestra / ऑर्कुिस्ट्रा / noun वाद्य-वृंद; वाद्यमंडल; रंगमंडल में वाद्यमंडल का स्थान : *a dance symphony orchestra* ▸ **orchestral** adj.

orchestrate / ऑर्किस्ट्रेट् / verb 1 वाद्य-वृंद के लिए संगीत रचना करना 2 (कभी-कभी अपमा) इच्छित परिणाम के लिए कुछ सावधानीपूर्वक व्यवस्थित करना।

orchid / ऑर्किड् / noun ऑर्किड (एक प्रकार का फूलों वाला पौधा)।

ordain / ऑर्'डेन / verb 1 किसी को पुरोहित/पादरी बनाना : He was ordained (as) a priest last year. 2 (औप) (ईश्वर, भाग्य या क़ानून द्वारा) निर्णय लिया जाना; नियुक्त करना : Fate had ordained that they would never meet again.

ordeal / ऑर्'डील;'ऑर्डील / noun सत्य-परीक्षा/अग्निपरीक्षा; चरित्र और धैर्य की कठिन परीक्षा : The hostages went through a terrible ordeal.

order¹ / 'ऑर्डर् / noun 1 क्रम 2 व्यवस्था; कार्ययोग्य दशा : set one's affairs in order 3 शांति व्यवस्था : The police are trying to restore public order. 4 order (for sb to do sth) आदेश 5 order (for sth) सामान मँगाने का आदेश; माँग पत्र : fill an order 6 मँगवाया गया सामान 7 (पोस्ट-ऑफ़िस आदि को) रुपया देने का लिखित आदेश 8 सार्वजनिक बैठक के नियम : bring/call a meeting to order 9 (विशेषत: pl) (अपमा या परि) सामाजिक श्रेणी/वर्ग; 10 (जीव विज्ञान) गण : the order of primates ■ in order that ताकि, के अभिप्राय से in order to (do sth) कुछ करने के लिए made to order विशेष/व्यक्तिगत अपेक्षाओं के अनुसार बनी वस्तु on order जिसकी माँग आ चुकी है पर जो वस्तु अभी आई नहीं है take holy orders पुरोहित बनना।

order² / 'ऑर्डर् / verb 1 आदेश देना, 2 order sth (for sb/oneself) सामान मँगाने के लिए अनुरोध करना/भेजना 3 (औप) व्यवस्थित करना, क्रम में रखना : I need time to order my thoughts.

orderly¹ / 'ऑर्डर्लि / adj 1 सुव्यवस्थित, अच्छी दशा में 2 शांतिपूर्ण; भली-भाँति आचरित : an orderly football crowd.

orderly² /'ऑर्डर्लि / noun (pl orderlies) 1 अर्दली (सेना में दूत या अन्य सेवा करने वाला कर्मचारी) 2 अस्पताल में सेवक।

ordinal /'ऑर्डिन्ल् / (ordinal number भी) noun क्रमसूचक संख्या जैसे first, second, third.

ordinance /'ऑर्डिनन्स् / noun (औप) अध्यादेश (राष्ट्रपति, राज्यपाल आदि द्वारा जारी विशेष आदेश)।

ordinary /'ऑर्डनरि / adj सामान्य/ साधारण; औसत : ordinary people like you and me ■ in the ordinary way अगर परिस्थितियाँ सामान्य रहें out of the ordinary असाधारण ▸ ordinarily adv 1 साधारण ढंग से 2 सामान्यतया।

ordination /,ऑर्डि'नेश्न् / noun चर्च में पुरोहित बनाते समय आयोजित (अभिषेक) समारोह।

ordnance /'ऑर्डनन्स् / noun युद्ध सामग्री : an ordnance depot.

ore / ऑर् / noun कच्ची धातु (खनिज पदार्थ): iron ore.

organ¹ /'ऑर्गन् / noun 1 प्राणी का अवयव/अंग : The heart is a vital organ. 2 (औप) कार्य साधन, आधिकारिक संगठन।

organ² /'ऑर्गन् / (US pipe-organ भी) noun आर्गन, संगीत का वाद्ययंत्र ▸ organist noun आर्गन वाद्ययंत्र बजाने वाला।

organic / ऑर्'गैनिक् / adj 1 (औप) आंगिक, अंगों को प्रभावित करने वाला : organic diseases 2 जैविक 3 (भोजन, कृषि के तरीक़े आदि) बाह्य रसायनों के बिना उत्पन्न: organic horticulture 4 (औप) संबद्ध अंगों से बना, तंत्र जैसा व्यवस्थित : an organic society.

organism /'ऑर्गनिज़म् / noun (औप) 1 जीव, अवयवी 2 अंतरसंबद्ध अंगों से बना तंत्र।

organization, -isation /,ऑर्गनाइ-'ज़ेश्न् / noun 1 संगठित करने की क्रिया; संगठन/व्यवस्था 2 (व्यक्तियों का) संगठन : the World Health Organization.

organize, -ise /'ऑर्गनाइज़् / verb 1 organize sb/sth (into sth) कार्ययोग्य दशा में व्यवस्थित करना; लोगों, अंगों आदि

को व्यवस्था में लाना : *organize a political party* 2 व्यवस्थाबद्ध करना, तैयारी करना 3 **organize sb (into sth)** कर्मचारियों को कर्मचारी संघ बनाकर संगठित करना ▸ **organized, -ised** *adj* 1 संगठित 2 सुव्यवस्थित **organizer, -iser** *noun* संगठन कर्ता ।

orgy / 'ऑर्जि / *noun* 1 (प्राय: *अपमा*) रंगरेलियाँ 2 **orgy(of sth)** (*अनौप*) किसी कार्य/क्रिया की अति : *an orgy of killing and destruction.*

Orient / 'ऑरिएन्ट / *noun* **the Orient** (*औप* या *साहि*) यूरोपीय साहित्य में, भूमध्यसागर से पूर्व एशिया में स्थित देश।

orient / 'ऑरिएन्ट / (**orientate** भी) *verb* **orient sb/sth (to/towards sb/sth)** किसी की रुचि/रुझान आदि को निश्चित दिशा प्रदान करना : *Our students are oriented towards the science subjects.*

oriental / ऑरि'एन्ट्ल् / *adj* पूर्व एशिया के क्षेत्र एवं देशों से संबद्ध ▸ **Oriental** *noun* (अक्सर *अपमा*) इन देशों का वासी (विशेषत: चीन या जापान का)।

origin / 'ऑरिजिन् / *noun* 1 उद्गम-बिंदु; स्रोत 2 (प्राय: *pl*) वंश, कुल (व्यक्ति का) : *ethnic origins.*

original / अ'रिजन्ल् / *adj* 1 प्रथम या आदिम : *Most of the original inhabitants have left for the mainland.* 2 नवरचित/नवसृष्ट; मौलिक (नक़ली नहीं) : *an original idea* 3 मूल (प्रति आदि) : *the original manuscript* ▸ **original** *noun* 1 **the original** मूल (जिससे प्रतिलिपि या अनुकृति तैयार की जाती है) 2 **the original** लेखक द्वारा प्रयुक्त मूल भाषा : *Read Homer in the original.* **originality** / अ,रिज'नैलटि / *noun* मौलिकता; सृष्टि की योग्यता : *show originality* **originally** *adv* मौलिक ढंग से; प्रारंभ से।

originate / अ'रिजिनेट् / *verb* (*औप*)

1 प्रारंभ या उत्पन्न होना : *That style of architecture originated with the ancient Greeks.* 2 अन्वेषण करना; नया उत्पन्न/आरंभ करना : *originate a new style of dancing.*

ornament / 'ऑर्नमन्ट् / *noun* 1 आभूषण, गहना 2 (*औप*) अलंकार, सजावट ▸ **ornament** / 'ऑर्नमेन्ट् / *verb* **ornament sth (with sth)** सुंदर बनाना; अलंकृत करना/ होना : *a dress elaborately ornamented with lace* **ornamental** / ,ऑर्न'मेन्ट्ल् / *adj* अलंकारिक; सजावटी/ शोभाकारी।

ornate / ऑर्'नेट् / *adj* 1 अलंकृत 2 (भाषा, शब्द) बनावटी, कृत्रिम।

ornithology / ,ऑर्नि'थॉलजि / *noun* पक्षियों का वैज्ञानिक अध्ययन ▸ **ornithologist** *noun*.

orphan / 'ऑर्फ़न् / *noun* अनाथ बच्चा (जिसके माता-पिता मर चुके हों) ▸ **orphan** *verb* अनाथ कर देना/हो जाना, **orphanage** / 'ऑर्फ़निज् / *noun* अनाथालय ।

orthodox / 'ऑर्थडॉक्स् / *adj* 1 (व्यवहार, विश्वास आदि) रूढ़िवादी 2 (धर्म) सनातनी : *orthodox Jews* ▸ **orthodoxy** / 'ऑर्थडॉक्सि / *noun* 1 परंपरानिष्ठा 2 रूढ़िवादी विचारधारा, मत आदि।

oscillate / 'ऑसिलेट् / *verb* 1 **oscillate (between sth and sth)** (एहसास, मत, व्यवहार की चरम सीमाओं के बीच अनिश्चय में) डोलना 2 झूलना/डोलना 3 (भौतिकी) (विद्युत/रेडियो तरंगों का) लगातार शक्ति/ दिशा बदलना ▸ **oscillation** *noun* डोलन।

ostensible / ऑ'स्टेन्सब्ल् / *adj* सत्य लगने वाला मगर दिखावटी : *The ostensible reason for his absence was illness.* ▸ **ostensibly** *adv*.

ostentation / ,ऑस्टेन्'टेशन् / *noun* (*अपमा*) (धन, संपत्ति या ज्ञान का) आडंबर; पाखंड, पांडित्य-प्रदर्शन ▸ **ostentatious** / ,ऑस्टेन्'टेशस् / *adj* दिखावटी, आडंबर-

पूर्ण : *her ostentatious concern for the poor.*

ostracize, -ise /'ऑस्ट्रसाइज़ / *verb* समाज से निकाल देना, बहिष्कृत कर देना ▸ **ostracism** / 'ऑस्ट्रसिज़म् / *noun* बहिष्कार : *social ostracism.*

ostrich /'ऑस्ट्रिच् / *noun* शुतुरमुर्ग।

other /'अद्र् / *det, pron* **1** अतिरिक्त, अन्य/भिन्न : *Are there any other questions?* **2** (**the, my, your, his** आदि के बाद singular noun के साथ प्रयुक्त) दो व्यक्तियों/वस्तुओं में से दूसरा (एक का ज़िक्र पहले हो चुका हो) : *My other sister is a doctor.* **3** (समूह में) बाक़ी : *The other books belong to Ravi.* ■ **the other day** कुछ दिन पूर्व; हाल ही में **other than** से भिन्न ▸ **other** *adv* ■ **other than 1** अलावा, के अतिरिक्त : *He never speaks to me other than to ask for something.* **2** दूसरी/भिन्न प्रकार से; नहीं : *She seldom appears other than happy.* ▸ **otherness** *noun* भिन्नता।

otherwise /'अद्र्वाइज़् / *adv* **1** भिन्न/विपरीत दशा/परिस्थिति में **2** इसके अलावा; दूसरी दृष्टि से **3** भिन्न प्रकार से ▸ **otherwise** *conj* नहीं तो; अन्यथा; अथवा।

otter /'ऑटर् / *noun* ऊदबिलाव (जो नदी में रहते हैं और मछली खाते हैं)।

ouch /आउच् / *interj* (आकस्मिक पीड़ा/दर्द व्यक्त करने के लिए प्रयुक्त) : *Ouch! That hurt!*

ought to / ऑट् टु / *modal verb* (neg **ought not to**) **1** चाहिए सूचक : *Children ought to respect their parents.* **2** संभावना सूचक : *There ought to be more buses during the rush hour.* **3** (सुझाव देने/सलाह-मशविरा देने में प्रयुक्त) : *This cake is delicious, you ought to try some.*

ounce / आउन्स् / *noun* **1** (*संक्षि* **oz**) (पाउंड का 1/16 भाग) वज़न की एक इकाई (28.35 ग्राम के बराबर) **2 ounce (of sth)** (*अनौप*) कुछ; ज़रा-सी मात्रा : *There's not an ounce of truth in his story.*

our / आर्; 'आउअर् / *det* **1** हमारा/हमारी, हम से संबंधित **2 Our** (ईश्वर या श्रद्धेय व्यक्ति को संबोधन में प्रयुक्त) : *Our Father* (ईश्वर) ▸ **ours** / आर्ज़्; 'आउर्ज़् / *pron* हमारा : *Their house is similar to ours.*

ourselves / आर्'सेल्व्ज़्, आउर्'सेल्व्ज़् / *pron* : (reflex) *We shouldn't blame ourselves for what happened.* ○ (emph) *The only people there were ourselves.*

oust / आउस्ट् / *verb* **oust sb (from sth/as sth)** बेदख़ल करना; स्थान से बलात् हटा देना : *He was ousted (from his position) as chairman.*

out / आउट् / *adv* **1** बाहर, दूर **2** (पुस्तक आदि) पुस्तकालय में नहीं : *The book you wanted is out (on loan).* **3** (सूर्य) प्रकट अवस्था में **4** (पुस्तक) प्रकाशित : *Her new book is out.* **5** किनारे से दूरी पर : *The boy dashed out on the road.* **6** (*अनौप*) लोकप्रिय/फ़ैशनेबल नहीं **7** (क्रिकेट में) बल्लेबाज़ का आउट होना : *The captain/The whole side was out for 106.* **8** अंत तक, पूर्णत: *work out a plan* **9** आग, बल्ब आदि जलती हुई चीज़ों का जलना बंद हो जाना/बुझ जाना : *The candle has gone out.* ▸ **out of** / 'आउट् अव् / *prep* **1** किसी स्थान/जगह से दूर हटते हुए; निर्धारित स्थान पर नहीं : *Jump out of bed* ○ *Mr Patel is out of town.* **2** के कारण : *do sth out of malice* **3** से; के प्रयोग से **4** समूह या अनेक में से (चुनना) : *choose one out of six.* **5** के बिना; की कमी होना : *be out of sugar* **6** के बाहर होना; से संबद्ध न होना : *We are out of the championships.*

outbid /आउट्'बिड्/ *verb* (**-dd**; *pt, pp* **outbid**) **outbid sb (for sth)** नीलाम में अन्य से बढ़कर बोली लगाना : *She outbid me (for the vase).*

outbreak/ 'आउट्ब्रेक् / *noun* (युद्ध, बीमारी आदि का) प्रकोप, प्रादुर्भाव ।

outburst / 'आउट्बर्स्ट् / *noun* (क्रोध, उत्तेजना आदि की) सहसा अभिव्यक्ति : *an outburst of laughter/anger.*

outcast / 'आउट्कास्ट् / *noun* बहिष्कृत व्यक्ति, निर्वासित : *an outcast from society* ▸ **outcast** *adj.*

outclass /,आउट् 'क्लास्; US ,आउट् 'क्लैस् / *verb* बढ़कर होना : *In design and quality of manufacture the cars were totally outclassed by their Italian competitors.*

outcome / 'आउट्कम् / *noun* परिणाम, नतीजा ।

outcrop / 'आउट्क्रॉप् / *noun* नंगी चट्टान : *perched on a rocky outcrop.*

outcry / 'आउट्क्राइ / *noun* **outcry (over/against sth)** सार्वजनिक विरोध, आक्रोश ।

outdated /,आउट् 'डेटिड्/ *adj* अप्रचलित; लोकप्रिय नहीं।

outdo /,आउट् 'डू/ *verb* (*3rd pers sing pres t* **outdoes** /,आउट् 'डज़्/; *pt* **outdid**; *pp* **outdone**) अन्य से बढ़कर होना या करना।

outdoor / 'आउट्डॉर् / *adj* खुले मैदान में, घर के बाहर : *outdoor clothing* ▸ **outdoors** *adv* घर/भवन के बाहर **the outdoors** *noun* देहात एवं खुली जगह।

outer / 'आउट्र् / *adj* बाहरी; केंद्र/बीच/भीतर से दूर : *the outer suburbs of the city* ▸ **outermost** *adj* बीच/भीतर से अधिकतम दूर।

outfit / 'आउट्फ़िट् / *noun* **1** विशेषत: किसी विशेष उद्देश्य या अवसर के लिए उपयुक्त कपड़े : *a skiing outfit* **2** किसी

विशेष उद्देश्य के लिए प्रयुक्त सामान/उपकरण : *a bicycle repair outfit* **3** (*अनौप*) एक साथ काम करने वाले लोगों का समूह, संघ।

outgrow /,आउट् 'ग्रो / *verb* (*pt* **outgrew**/आउट् 'ग्रू,/ *pp* **outgrown** /आउट् 'ग्रोन्,/) **1** कपड़ों की दृष्टि से अधिक मोटा या लंबा हो जाना **2** अन्य व्यक्ति की तुलना में अधिक बढ़ना : *He's already outgrown his older brother.* **3** बड़ा होने पर पुरानी आदतें छोड़ते जाना : *outgrow childish interests.*

outing / 'आउटिङ् / *noun* **1 outing (to...)** सैर-सपाटा **2** (*अनौप*) आउटडॉर खेलों में प्रदर्शन।

outlandish /आउट् 'लैन्डिश्/ *adj* (प्राय: *अपमा*) अजीब या अद्भुत (प्रतीत होने वाला) : *outlandish clothes.*

outlast /,आउट् 'लास्ट्/ *verb* अधिक समय तक टिकना या ज़िंदा रहना।

outlaw / 'आउट्लॉ / *noun* (पुराने समय में) ग़ैर-क़ानूनी घोषित व्यक्ति; निर्वासित, अपराधी/भगोड़ा ▸ **outlaw** *verb* ग़ैर-क़ानूनी घोषित करना।

outlay/ 'आउट्ले / *noun* **outlay (on sth)** (*वाणिज्य*) लागत; व्यय : *an outlay of Rs 100,000 on new machinery.*

outlet / 'आउट्लेट् / *noun* **1 outlet (for sth)** भावनाओं की अभिव्यक्ति का साधन या अवसर **2** (*वाणिज्य*) कोई उत्पाद विशेष बेचे जाने का स्थान **3** (जल, भाप आदि का) निकास : *a sewage outlet.*

outline / 'आउट्लाइन् / *noun* **1** ख़ाका, रेखाचित्र **2** मुख्य तथ्यों का साररूप कथन, रूपरेखा : *an outline of Roman history* ▸ **outline** *verb* **1 outline sth (to sb)** रूपरेखा प्रस्तुत करना : *We outlined our proposals and how we intended to proceed.* **2** ख़ाका खींचना, रेखाचित्र बनाना।

outlive / ,आउट् 'लिव् / *verb* (किसी

व्यक्ति) से अधिक समय तक जीवित रहना : *He outlived his wife by three years.*

outlook / 'आउट्लुक् / *noun* 1 **outlook (on sth)** दृष्टिकोण, नज़रिया : *a tolerant outlook* 2 **outlook (for sth)** (प्राय: *sing*) संभावना, संभावित मौसम 3 दृश्य : *The house has a pleasant outlook over the valley.*

outlying / 'आउट्लाइइङ् / *adj* दूरवर्ती; सुदूरवर्ती : *outlying villages.*

outnumber / ,आउट्'नम्बर् / *verb* संख्या में अधिक होना।

out-of-date / ,आउट् अव् 'डेट् / *adj* 1 पुरानी शैली वाला, अप्रचलित : *an out-of-date dictionary* 2 अवैध (समय बीत जाने के कारण) : *an out-of-date driving licence.*

outpace / ,आउट्'पेस् / *verb* तेज़ चलकर किसी से आगे निकल जाना : *He easily outpaced the other runners.*

out-patient / 'आउट् पेशन्ट् / *noun* अस्पताल में आने वाले बाह्य रोगी जो केवल मर्ज़ दिखाने आते हैं, भर्ती नहीं होते हैं : *the out-patient department.*

outpost / 'आउट्पोस्ट् / *noun* 1 सेना की सीमा चौकी 2 गाँव से दूर स्थित कुछ भवन; नाका।

output / 'आउट्पुट् / *noun* 1 (खेत की) पैदावार; (व्यक्ति, मशीन या संघ का) उत्पादन मात्रा : *The average output of the factory is 20 cars a day.* 2 (तक) कंप्यूटर द्वारा संपादित एवं प्रस्तुत सूचना-सामग्री 3 किसी यंत्र/उपकरण द्वारा उत्पादित ऊर्जा/शक्ति : *an output of 100 watts.*

outrage / 'आउट्रेज् / *noun* 1 गुस्से एवं दुख की तीव्र भावना : *There has been public outrage over the recent terrorist attacks.* 2 अत्याचार, कठोर अन्यायपूर्ण कार्य ▸ **outrage** *verb* गुस्सा एवं दुख की तीव्र भावना पैदा करना।

outrageous / आउट्'रेजस् / *adj*

1 घृणित/निंदनीय : *outrageous behaviour* 2 अनैतिक एवं असामान्य; विचित्र : *wear outrageous clothes* ▸ **outrageously** *adv.*

outright / आउट्'राइट् / *adv* 1 साफ़-साफ़, बिलकुल स्पष्ट रूप से 2 तत्काल, पूर्णतया; एकदम : *Most of the crash victims were killed outright.* ▸ **outright** *adj* सुस्पष्ट; पूर्णतया पक्का : *She was the outright winner.*

outset / 'आउट्सेट् / *noun* ■ **at/from the (very) outset (of sth)** किसी चीज़ के प्रारंभ से : *His innocence was clear from the very outset.*

outside¹ / आउट्'साइड् / *noun* 1 (प्राय: **the outside**) (प्राय: *sing*) बाहरी या ऊपरी सतह : *The outside of the house needs painting.* 2 सड़क का बाहरी किनारा 3 किसी विशेष समूह, संघ या संस्था से बाहर की दुनिया : *get help from outside* ■ **at the outside** अधिक से अधिक ▸ **outside** / 'आउट्साइड् / *adj* 1 बाहर की दिशा में, बहिर्मुख 2 बाह्य, मुख्य भवन में नहीं : *an outside toilet* 3 (संभावना/पसंद आदि) बहुत कम : *have an outside chance of winning.*

outside² / ,आउट्'साइड् / (**outside of** भी) *prep* 1 बाहरी सतह/भाग पर : *Leave your muddy boots outside the door.* 2 किसी स्थान से दूर : *It's the biggest theme park outside the USA.* 3 किसी स्थान के समीप : *a small village just outside Delhi* ▸ **outside** *adv* 1 बाहर : *Please wait outside.* 2 भवन से बाहर : *It's pleasant enough to eat outside.*

outsider / ,आउट्'साइडर् / *noun* 1 बाहरी व्यक्ति (जो अंतरंग नहीं है) 2 किसी प्रति-स्पर्धा में भाग लेने वाला मगर जीतने की अपेक्षा न रखने वाला व्यक्ति/पशु : *It was won by a complete outsider.*

outskirts / 'आउट्स्कर्ट्स् / *noun* [*pl*]

नगर के बाहरी भाग : *They live on the outskirts of Allahabad.*

outspoken / आउट्'स्पोकन / *adj* **outspoken (in sth)** खरा बोलने वाला ▸ **outspokenly** *adv* : *outspokenly critical* **outspokenness** *noun*.

outstanding / आउट्'स्टैन्डिङ् / *adj* 1 अत्यंत अच्छा; विशिष्ट, उल्लेखनीय 2 सुस्पष्ट : *an issue of outstanding importance* 3 (भुगतान, कार्य, समस्या) बक़ाया/शेष ▸ **outstandingly** *adv* विशिष्टता से।

outstrip / आउट्'स्ट्रिप् / *verb* (-pp-) 1 किसी से बड़ा, अधिक महत्त्वपूर्ण आदि हो जाना 2 (दौड़ में) पीछे छोड़ देना : *He soon outstripped the slower runners.*

outward / आउट्वर्ड् / *adj* 1 (यात्रा) बहिर्गामी, जाने की दिशा की ओर : *Our luggage got lost on the outward journey.* 2 बाहरी छोर पर स्थित, बाहरी ओर का 3 (भावना) सत्य भावना के विपरीत अभिव्यक्ति : *An outward show of confidence concealed his nervousness.* ▸ **outwardly** *adv* बाहर की ओर से; प्रतीत रूप में **outwards** / आउट्वर्ड्ज़् / *adv* बाहर की ओर; केंद्र से दूर : *The door opens outwards.*

outweigh / आउट्'वे / *verb* भार, मूल्य या महत्त्व में अधिक होना।

outwit / आउट्'विट् / *verb* (-tt-) चालाकी से मात देना।

oval / ओवल् / *adj* अंडाकार : *an oval mirror* ▸ **oval** *noun*.

ovation / ओ'वेश्न् / *noun* जय-जयकार : *The team was given an enthusiastic ovation.*

oven / अवन् / *noun* बक्सनुमा भट्ठी : *a gas/ electric oven.*

over¹ / ओवर् / *adv part* 1 ऊपर से नीचे की ओर व बाहर की ओर : *Don't knock that vase over.* 2 एक तरफ़ से दूसरी

तरफ़ : *Turn over the page.* 3 सड़क या मैदान के आर-पार 4 पूरी तरह ढकते हुए : *Cover her over with a blanket.* 5 शेष, अप्रयुक्त : *food left over* 6 ऊपर, अधिक 7 समाप्त : *Their relationship is over.* ■ **(all) over again** दोबारा आरंभ करना **over and over again** बहुत बार; बारंबार।

over² / ओवर् / *prep* 1 सतह के ऊपर एवं ढकते हुए : *Spread a cloth over the table.* 2 के/से ऊपर (न छूते हुए) 3 एक तरफ़ से दूसरी तरफ़; आर-पार : *a bridge over the river* 4 अधिकांश भागों में 5 निर्धारित समय, मात्रा या क़ीमत से अधिक : *He's over two metres tall.* 6 के कारण; के बारे में : *an argument over money* ■ **over and above** इसके अलावा; के अतिरिक्त।

over³ / ओवर् / *noun* (क्रिकेट में) ओवर; एक सिरे से एक ही गेंदबाज़ द्वारा डाली गई छह गेंदें।

over- *pref* (पूर्वपद) 1 ऊपर/बाहर/आर-पार से : *overhang ○ over-arching* 2 अति-, बहुत अधिक : *overwork ○ overemphasis ○ overambitious.*

overall / ओवर् 'ऑल् / *adj* 1 कुल मिलाकर, सब मिलाकर : *an overall increase of Rs 1.3 million* 2 सब कुछ दृष्टि में रखते हुए; सामान्य : *an overall improvement* ▸ **overall** *adv*.

overalls / ओवरऑल्ज़् / (*US* **coveralls**) *noun* [*pl*] ढीला-ढाला लबादा जो सामान्य कपड़ों पर पहना जाता है ताकि वे ख़राब न हों : *The mechanic was wearing a pair of blue overalls.*

overawe / ओवर् 'ऑ / *verb* मंत्रमुग्ध कर देना; अत्यधिक प्रभावित करना।

overbalance / ओवर् 'बैलन्स् / *verb* 1 संतुलन खो देना (और गिर जाना) 2 (संतुलन बिगाड़कर) किसी को गिरा देना।

overbearing / ओवर् 'बेअरिङ् / *adj* (*अपमा*) दबंग एवं उद्धत; रोबीला (दूसरों

को दबाकर रखने वाला) : *an overbear-ing manner/father.*

overboard / ओव्र्बॉर्ड / *adv* जहाज़ पर से पानी में : *fall/jump overboard.*

overcast / ओव्र्'कास्ट / *adj* (आकाश) बादलों से घिरा हुआ : *a dark, overcast day.*

overcoat / ओव्र्कोट् / *noun* ओवरकोट (सब कपड़ों के ऊपर पहना जाने वाला बड़ा कोट)।

overcome / ओव्र्'कम् / *verb* (*pt* **overcame**; *pp* **overcome**) 1 (मुश्किलों पर) पार पाना; किसी चीज़ पर नियंत्रण पाना : *overcome an obstacle/a dif-ficulty* 2 (औप) हरा देना ■ **be over-come by/with sth** अभिभूत हो जाना : *She was overcome by embarrass-ment/grief.*

overcrowded / ओव्र्'क्राउडिड् / *adj* (स्थान) व्यक्ति/वस्तुओं से ठसा-ठस भरा हुआ।

overdo / ओव्र्'डू / *verb* (*pt* **overdid**; *pp* **overdone**) 1 बहुत बढ़ा-चढ़ाकर करना 2 किसी चीज़ को हद से ज़्यादा प्रयोग करना : *Don't overdo the salt in the food.* 3 अधिक देर तक पकाना।

overdose / ओव्र्डोस् / *noun* (दवा आदि की) सामान्य से अधिक मात्रा (जो हानिकारक हो सकती है)।

overdraft / ओव्र्ड्राफ़्ट् / *noun* जमाराशि से अधिक निकाली गई धनराशि, ओव्र्-ड्राफ़्ट : *run up a large overdraft.*

overdraw / ओव्र्'ड्रॉ / *verb* (*pt* **overdrew** / ओव्र्'ड्रू /; *pp* **overdrawn** / ओव्र्'ड्रॉन् /) बैंक में जमा राशि से अधिक निकालना।

overdue / ओव्र्'ड्यू / *adj* (भुगतान, आगमन आदि) जिसका नियम/समय समाप्त हो चुका है : *These forms were long overdue.*

overestimate / ओव्र्'एस्टिमेट् / *verb* किसी चीज़ का वास्तविकता से अधिक बड़ा,

बेहतर या महत्त्वपूर्ण होने का अनुमान लगाना।

overflow / ओव्र्'फ़्लो / *verb* 1 पूरा भर जाने के कारण बहने लगना 2 **overflow with sth** (भावना से) ओत-प्रोत होना : *overflowing with happiness* ▶ **overflow** / ओव्र्फ़्लो / *noun* पात्र से बाहर बहने की क्रिया; इस प्रकार बहते हुए द्रव (की मात्रा)।

overgrown / ओव्र्'ग्रोन् / *adj* 1 **over-grown (with sth)** घास, पेड़-पौधों आदि से ढका हुआ : *wall overgrown with ivy* 2 (प्रायः *अपमा*) बहुत जल्दी बढ़ा हुआ : *an overgrown village* ▶ **overgrowth** *noun* अतिवृद्धि।

overhang / ओव्र्'हैङ् / *verb* (*pt*, *pp* **overhung** / ओव्र्'हङ् /) ऊपर से लट-कना : *The road is dark with over-hanging trees.*

overhaul / ओव्र्'हॉल् / *verb* 1 पूर्णतः मरम्मत करना / सही दशा में करना 2 पीछे से आकर आगे निकल जाना : *He over-hauled the leader in the final lap.* ▶ **overhaul** / ओव्र्हॉल् / *noun* पूरी जाँच एवं मरम्मत।

overhead / ओव्र्हेड् / *adj* 1 पृथ्वी (एवं व्यक्ति के सिर) के ऊपर से जाने वाले : *overhead lighting/cables/power lines* 2 (व्यापार में) (उत्पादन-लागत के अलावा) उपरिव्यय-संबंधी : *increasing overhead costs* ▶ **overhead** / ओव्र्-हेड् / *adv* ऊपर; आकाश में : *birds flying overhead* **overhead** *noun* (*US*) = **overheads.**

overheads / ओव्र्हेड्ज़् / *noun* [*pl*] (*US* **overhead**) (व्यापार में) बँधे खर्चे; उपरिव्यय (उत्पादन-लागत के अलावा)।

overhear / ओव्र्'हिअर् / *verb* (*pt*, *pp* **overheard** / ओव्र्'हर्ड् /) छिपकर सुन लेना; जो न सुनना था संयोग से सुन लेना : *I overheard them quarrelling.*

overjoyed / ओव्र्'जॉइड् / *adj* **over-**

joyed (at sth/to do sth) अति आनंदित/ प्रफुल्लित।

overland / 'ओवर्लैन्ड् / adj, adv भूमि/ स्थल से, न कि जल या वायु द्वारा : an overland journey.

overlap /,ओवर्'लैप् / verb (-pp-) 1 कुछ अंश तक ढकना : The wooden planks overlap (one another). 2 एक साथ ही घटित होना 3 कुछ हद तक एक समान रुचि/ज़िम्मेदारी निबाहना ▶ overlap /'ओ-वर्लैप्/ noun 1 ऐसा समय जब दो घटनाएँ एक साथ हों 2 overlap (between sth and sth) एक तरह की रुचि/रुझान आदि।

overleaf /,ओवर्'लीफ़् / adv (किताब आदि के) पृष्ठ के दूसरी तरफ़ : See picture overleaf.

overload /,ओवर्'लोड्/ verb 1 अत्यधिक वज़न/भार डाल देना/हो जाना 2 overload sb (with sth) किसी को अत्यधिक कार्यभार/ काम आदि दे देना; कंप्यूटर/विद्युत प्रणाली पर अतिभार डालना, जिसके परिणामस्वरूप यह बंद/ख़राब हो जाए।

overlook /,ओवर्'लुक् / verb 1 ऊपर से पूरा दृश्य देखना, विहंगम दृष्टि से देखना : a flat overlooking Central Park 2 देखकर भी ध्यान न देना, उपेक्षा करना : Despite her qualifications she has been repeatedly overlooked for the job.

overnight /,ओवर्'नाइट्/ adv 1 पूर्वरात्रि में; रातभर के लिए : stay overnight at a friend's house 2 अचानक और बड़ी तीव्रता से : She became famous overnight. ▶ overnight adj 1 रात्रि-कालीन 2 (अनौप) अचानक; अत्यंत तेज़ी से।

overpower /,ओवर्'पाउअर् / verb 1 पराजित करना; नियंत्रण में कर लेना 2 इतना तीव्र या शक्तिशाली होना कि प्रभावित या परेशान कर दे : He was overpowered by the cigarette smoke. ▶ over-powering adj अत्यंत शक्तिशाली, प्रबल।

overrate /,ओवर्'रेट् / verb ज़रूरत से ज़्यादा उच्च विचार/मत/राय रखना/होना; किसी चीज़ का ज़रूरत से ज़्यादा मूल्य रखना।

overreach /,ओवर्'रीच् / verb over-reach oneself (विशेषत: अपमा) अधिक आकांक्षा के कारण विफल होना और अपने हित की हानि करना : In making these promises, the government clearly overreached itself.

override /,ओवर्'राइड् / verb (pt over-rode; pp overridden) 1 किसी के निर्णय या दावे को अपने उच्चाधिकार से रद्द कर देना : override sb's decisions 2 किसी अन्य वस्तु से अधिक महत्त्वपूर्ण होना ▶ over-riding adj अधिक महत्त्वपूर्ण।

overrule /,ओवर्'रूल् / verb किसी दावे को अपने अधिकार से रद्द करना/अस्वीकार करना।

overrun /,ओवर्'रन्/ verb (pt overran /,ओवर्'रैन्/; pp overrun) 1 (किसी अवांछनीय चीज़ का) फैल जाना और अधिकार कर लेना : a warehouse overrun by rats 2 (समय या क़ीमत की) सीमा के बाहर चले जाना : The lecturer overran by ten minutes. ▶ overrun /'ओवर्रन्/ noun.

overseas /,ओवर्'सीज़् / adj, adv समुद्रपार (विदेश में) : overseas trade.

oversee /,ओवर्'सी/ verb (pt over-saw /,ओवर्'सॉ/; pp overseen /,ओवर्'सीन्/) निरीक्षण करना : oversee sb's work ▶ overseer /'ओवर्सिअर्/ noun (अप्र) निरीक्षक, सर्वेक्षक।

overshadow /,ओवर्'शैडो / verb 1 अन्य का महत्त्व कमकर देना; अन्य से अधिक प्रबल होना; छा जाना 2 किसी अवसर की प्रसन्नता को कम कर देना 3 किसी पर छाया होना/पड़ना : The garden is over-shadowed by trees.

oversight /'ओवर्साइट्/ noun 1 कुछ करने या ध्यान देने में भूल/चूक 2 निरीक्षण/ सर्वेक्षण करने की ज़िम्मेदारी : give sb/

have oversight of broadcasting standards.

oversleep /ओवर्'स्लीप्/ *verb* (*pt, pp* **overslept** /ओवर्'स्लेप्ट्/) देर तक सोते रहना; निश्चित अवधि से ज़्यादा सोना।

overstep /ओवर्'स्टेप्/ *verb* (**-pp-**) अतिक्रमण करना, कार्य सीमा के बाहर जाना : *overstep the boundaries of one's authority.*

overt /'ओवर्ट्/ *adj* खुले रूप से किया हुआ (न कि गुप्त रूप से) : *an overt display of jealousy/hostility* ▶ **overtly** *adv.*

overtake /ओवर्'टेक्/ *verb* (*pt* **overtook** /ओवर्'टुक्/; *pp* **overtaken** /ओवर्'टेकन्/) 1 (वाहन या व्यक्ति के) पीछे से आकर आगे निकल जाना : *overtake a tractor* 2 संख्या अथवा राशि में इतना बढ़ना कि अन्य से अधिक हो जाए 3 (आँधी/तूफ़ान अथवा अन्य अप्रिय घटना का) अचानक आ जाना : *The same fate overtook France several years later.*

overthrow /ओवर्'थ्रो/ *verb* (*pt* **overthrew** /ओवर्'थ्रू/; *pp* **overthrown** /ओवर्'थ्रोन्/) किसी को बलप्रयोग से सत्ता से हटा देना; पराजित कर देना : *The rebels tried to overthrow the government.*
▶ **overthrow** /'ओवर्थ्रो/ *noun* (प्राय: *sing*) बलात् सत्ताच्युति, पतन।

overtime /'ओवर्टाइम्/ *noun* 1 (सामान्य कार्यघंटों के बाद) काम में लगा अतिरिक्त समय, अधिसमय : *do 2 hours overtime* 2 (खेलों में) दिया गया अतिरिक्त समय ▶ **overtime** *adv.*

overtone /'ओवर्टोन्/ *noun* (प्राय: *pl*) इंगित, व्यंजना।

overture /'ओवर्चर्/ *noun* 1 प्रस्तावना संगीत, पूर्वरंग 2 (प्राय: *pl*) **overtures** (**to sb**) बातचीत आरंभ करने का इशारा/ इंगित : *All overtures of peace were rejected.*

overturn /ओवर्'टर्न्/ *verb* 1 उलट जाना या उलटा देना : *The car overturned and burst into flames.* 2 क़ानूनी निर्णय या परिणाम को उलट देना : *The court overturned the ruling.*

overweight /ओवर्'वेट्/ *adj* 1 (व्यक्ति) मोटा 2 (सामान आदि का) औसत से ज़्यादा वज़न होना।

overwhelm /ओवर्'वेल्म्/ *verb* 1 पूर्णत: पराजित कर देना, (श्रेष्ठ शक्ति/निपुणता या अधिक संख्या के बल पर) पूरी तरह हरा देना 2 (पानी आदि का) जल्दी ही फैलकर सब कुछ ढक लेना : *The skiers were overwhelmed by an avalanche.* 3 दबा देना; तीव्र भावनात्मक प्रभाव होना : *overwhelmed by despair* ▶ **overwhelming** *adj* 1 अत्यंत विशाल/महान, तीव्र 2 पूर्ण, संपूर्ण।

overwrought /ओवर्'रॉट्/ *adj* बहुत अधिक कार्यभार या उत्तेजना से थका हुआ।

owe /ओ/ *verb* 1 **owe (sb) for sth owe sth (to sb)** ऋणी होना 2 **owe sth to sb/sth** किसी व्यक्ति/वस्तु को कारण या आधार के रूप में स्वीकार करना : *He owes his success more to his contacts than to his ability.* 3 **owe sth to sb** आभारी होना; नैतिक ज़िम्मेदारी मानना : *owe one's parents respect.*

owing /'ओइङ्/ *adj* बाक़ी (ऋण)
▶ **owing to** *prep* के कारण : *Owing to torrential rain, the game was cancelled.*

owl /आउल्/ *noun* उल्लू।

own¹ /ओन्/ *adj, pron* 1 अपना, निजी : *It was her own idea.* 2 स्वयं किया हुआ या अपने आप बनाया हुआ : *She makes all her own clothes.* ■ **hold one's own (against sb/sth) (in sth)** डटकर सामना करना **on one's own** अकेले, स्वतंत्र रूप से।

own²/ओन्/ *verb* 1 (किसी वस्तु का) स्वामी होना 2 (औप) सहमत होना, सत्य मानना; स्वीकार करना : *I own (that) it* *was entirely my fault.* **3 own (to sth/doing sth)** (दोष) स्वीकार करना।

owner /'ओनर्/ *noun* मालिक, स्वामी : *boat owners* ▸ **ownership** *noun* स्वामित्व।

ox / ऑक्स् / *noun* (*pl* **oxen** /'ऑक् - सन् /) **1** बैल जो प्राय: गाड़ी या खेतों में काम आता है **2** (विशेषत: *pl*) (अप्र) गाय-बैल।

oxygen /'ऑक्सिजन् / *noun* ऑक्सीजन (गैस) ▸ **oxygenate** *verb* ऑक्सीजन देना।

oyster / 'ऑइस्टर् / *noun* शुक्ति, सीपी।

oz *abbr* (*pl* अपरिवर्तित या **ozs**) **ounce** (आउन्स) का संक्षिप्त रूप।

ozone /'ओज़ोन् / *noun* (*रसा*) एक प्रकार की रंजकहीन गैस ▸ **ozone layer** *noun* [*sing*] पृथ्वी की सतह से ऊपर इस गैस की परत जो पृथ्वी को सूर्य की हानिकारक किरणों से बचाती है।

Pp

pa / पा / *noun* (अनौप) (बच्चे की बोली में) पिता।

pace¹ / पेस् / *noun* 1 क़दम, पग 2 गति, वेग : *at a good pace* 3 विकास/बदलाव आदि की गति/दर; तीव्र गति : *He gave up his job in advertising because he couldn't stand the pace.* ■ **keep pace (with sb/sth)** उसी गति से बढ़ना/विकसित होना **put sb through their/its paces** किसी की योग्यता को परखना।

pace² / पेस् / *verb* 1 टहलना, क़दम-क़दम चलना 2 घटना या विकास की दर/गति निर्धारित करना : *The play was badly paced.* ■ **pace sth off/out** क़दमों से नापना : *She paced out the length of the room.*

pacific / पंसिफ़िक् / *adj* (औप) शांतिपूर्ण, शांतिप्रिय : *Their intentions are purely pacific.*

pacifism / 'पैसिफ़िज़म् / *noun* शांतिवाद (यह धारणा कि युद्ध और हिंसा के बजाए शांतिपूर्ण साधनों से सभी विवाद निपटाए जा सकते हैं) ▶ **pacifist** *noun* शांतिवादी।

pacify / 'पैसिफ़ाइ / *verb* (*pt, pp* **pacified**) 1 शांत करना 2 युद्ध क्षेत्र में शांति लाना ▶ **pacification** *noun* **pacifier** *noun*.

pack¹ / पैक् / *noun* 1 काग़ज़ या गत्ते का डिब्बा; पैकेट : *a pack of Christmas cards* 2 गठरी/गट्टर; बंडल/पोटली : *donkeys carrying packs of wool* 3 **pack (of sb/sth)** (अक्सर *अपमा*) वस्तुओं/व्यक्तियों का समूह, अक्सर ख़राब/बुरे : *a pack of reporters* 4 (शिकारी कुत्तों/भेड़ियों आदि का) झुंड 5 (*US* **deck**) ताश की गड्डी।

pack² / पैक् / *verb* 1 **pack (sth) (in/into sth)** डिब्बे, बंडल, बैग आदि में रखना; बक्से को चीज़ों से भरना : *Haven't you packed (your suitcase) yet?* 2 **pack sth (in sth)** सुरक्षा के लिए किसी मुलायम चीज़ से चारों ओर लपेटना : *pack china in newspaper* 3 **pack sth (with sth/sb)** ठसाठस भरना; अत्यधिक भीड़ करना : *The stadium was packed with chanting fans.* ■ **pack sb off (to...)** किसी को कहीं दूर भेज देना **pack sth away** अनावश्यक चीज़ों को बक्से, अलमारी में डाल देना **pack (sth) up** 1 जगह छोड़ने से पहले अपनी वस्तुओं को बक्सों आदि में डालना 2 (*अनौप*) कुछ करना छोड़ देना : *Business is terrible—I might as well pack up and go home.* **pack up** (*अनौप*) (मशीन, इंजन आदि का) काम करना बंद होना।

package / 'पैकिज् / *noun* 1 पार्सल, पुलिंदा/बंडल 2 डिब्बा या बक्सा 3 (**package deal** भी) प्रस्तावों/सुझावों का एक समुच्चय : *an economic package* ▶ **package** *verb* 1 बिक्री के लिए कुछ बैग/डिब्बे में डालना : *They are packaged in 2 kg and 5 kg bags.* 2 किसी को विशेष तरीक़े से प्रस्तुत करना **packaging** *noun* बिक्री या भेजने से पहले चीज़ों को लपेटने के लिए प्रयुक्त सामान।

packet / 'पैकिट् / *noun* 1 काग़ज़ या गत्ते का डिब्बा/बंडल 2 [*sing*] (*अनौप*) बड़ी धनराशि।

packing / 'पैकिङ् / *noun* 1 पैक करने की प्रक्रिया 2 पैक करने में प्रयुक्त सामान।

pact / पैक्ट् / *noun* समझौता; संधि : *sign a non-aggression pact.*

pad¹ / पैड् / *noun* 1 पैड, गद्दी 2 (प्रायः *pl*) सुरक्षा के लिए कुछ खेलों में प्रयुक्त गद्देदार वस्तु 3 अंतरिक्ष यान या हेलिकॉप्टर के उड़ान भरने के लिए समतल जगह 4 लेटर-पैड 5 कुछ जंतुओं के गद्देदार पंजे, जैसे कुत्ते/लोमड़ी के।

pad² / पैड् / *verb* (**-dd-**) सुरक्षा के लिए गद्देदार चीज़ें लगाना : *a padded envelope* ○ *All the sharp edges were* *padded with foam.* ▸ **padding** noun.

paddle¹ / 'पैड्ल् / noun 1 छोटा चप्पू 2 किसी उपकरण या मशीन में ऐसा भाग जो चप्पू के आकार का हो 3 चप्पू से नाव खेने की प्रक्रिया/अवधि ▸ **paddle** verb चप्पू से छोटी नाव खेना : *paddle across the river.*

paddle² / 'पैड्ल् / verb नंगे पैर पानी में चलना; पानी में हाथ चलाना।

paddock / 'पैडक् / noun 1 घोड़ों को रखने का बाड़ा 2 बाड़ा जहाँ रेस से पहले घोड़ों/कारों को एकत्र किया जाता है।

paddy / 'पैडि / noun 1 धान (जिससे चावल का दाना निकलता है) 2 (**paddy field** भी) धान का खेत।

padlock / 'पैड्लॉक् / noun ताला ▸ **padlock** verb ताला लगाना : *The gate was securely padlocked.*

paediatrician (US **pediatrician**) / पीडिअ'ट्रिशन् / noun बालरोग-विशेषज्ञ।

pagan / 'पेगन् / noun (कभी-कभी अपमा) 1 विधर्मी, किसी मुख्य प्रचलित धर्म को न मानने वाला 2 (पूर्व में) ईसाई धर्म को न मानने वाला ▸ **pagan** adj.

page¹ / पेज् / noun 1 (किताब, समाचार-पत्र आदि का) पृष्ठ 2 (साहि) इतिहास का एक काल या घटना चक्र : *a glorious page of Indian history.*

page² / पेज् / verb 1 किसी सार्वजनिक स्थान (जैसे हवाई अड्डा) से किसी को संदेश देने के लिए नाम पुकारना 2 रेडियो संकेत भेजकर (किसी उपकरण के माध्यम से, जो आवाज़ उत्पन्न करता है) किसी से संपर्क स्थापित करना : *country-wide radio paging services* ▸ **pager** noun रेडियो संकेत ग्रहण करने वाला उपकरण।

page³ / पेज् / (**page-boy** भी) noun (क्लब, होटल में) परिचालक।

pageant / 'पैजन्ट् / noun 1 जुलूस जिसमें झाँकियाँ भी निकाली जा रही हों 2 विशेष समारोहों पर शोभायात्रा ▸ **pageantry** / 'पैजन्ट्रि / noun भव्य/शानदार प्रदर्शन या समारोह : *all the pageantry of a coronation.*

pail / पेल् / noun बालटी, डोल : *a pail of water.*

pain / पेन् / noun 1 दुख/दर्द; तकलीफ़; पीड़ा 2 (अनौप) कोई परेशान करने/चिढ़ पैदा करने वाला व्यक्ति/वस्तु ■ **a pain in the neck** गुस्सा दिलाने वाला/रुचिहीन व्यक्ति **on/under pain of sth** (औप) आज्ञा उल्लंघन करने पर निर्धारित दंड की धमकी ▸ **pain** verb दुख/पीड़ा पहुँचाना, तकलीफ़ देना **painful** adj पीड़ादायी **painfully** adv **painless** adj पीड़ारहित **painlessly** adv.

pains / पेन्ज़् / noun [pl] ■ **be at (great) pains to do sth** बहुत परिश्रम/मेहनत करना : *She was at great pains to stress the advantages of the new system.* ▸ **painstaking** / 'पेन्ज़्टेकिङ् / adj परिश्रमी; परिश्रम से किया गया : *with painstaking attention to details.*

paint¹ / पेन्ट् / noun 1 तेल या अन्य तरल पदार्थ में घुला रंग, पेंट; पेंट की सूखी परत : *The paint is starting to peel off.* 2 **paints** [pl] पेंट का सेट।

paint² / पेन्ट् / verb 1 रँगना, पेंट लगाना : *paint a door* 2 चित्र बनाना, रंग भरना।

painter / 'पेन्टर् / noun 1 दीवारों/भवन आदि पर रंग करने वाला 2 चित्रकार : *a landscape painter.*

painting / 'पेन्टिङ् / noun 1 रँगाई 2 चित्रकारी, चित्रकला 3 चित्र : *a famous painting by Tagore.*

pair / पेअर् / noun 1 जोड़ी/जोड़ा : *a pair of gloves/shoes* 2 दो भागों वाली जुड़ी हुई वस्तु : *a pair of binoculars/tights* 3 एक साथ रहने/काम करने वाले दो व्यक्ति 4 पशुओं का नर-मादा का जोड़ा ■ **in pairs** जोड़े में; एक बार में दो : *These earrings are only sold in pairs.* ▸ **pair** verb 1 **pair A with B; pair A and B (to-**

gether) जोड़ा बनाना; जोड़े में व्यवस्थित करना/होना 2 (पशुओं का) संतानोत्पत्ति के लिए जोड़ा बनाना ■ pair (sb/sth) off (with sb) जोड़ा/जोड़े बनाना pair up (with sb) खेल/कार्य के लिए जोड़ी बनाना।

pal / पैल / noun (अनौप, अप्र) 1 साथी, मित्र 2 (अनौप) (किसी को धमकाते हुए संबोधन) दोस्त : Now look here, pal, you're asking for trouble! ▶ pally / 'पैलि / adj pally (with sb) (अनौप) स्नेही, मैत्रीपूर्ण।

palace / 'पैलस् / noun 1 राजा/महाराजा का महल 2 बहुत बड़ा शानदार भवन।

palatable / 'पैलटब्ल् / adj 1 स्वादिष्ट 2 मन को रुचिकर/प्रिय।

palate / 'पैलट् / noun 1 मुँह का तालु : the hard/soft palate 2 (प्राय: sing) स्वाद की अनुभूति।

palatial / प'लेश्ल् / adj महल जैसा; अत्य-धिक विशाल या भव्य/शानदार।

pale¹ / पेल् / adj (-r, -st) 1 (व्यक्ति, चेहरा) विवर्ण, निस्तेज; पीला चेहरा : have a pale complexion 2 (रंग) फीका/धुँधला; (प्रकाश) मंद/धीमा : the pale light of dawn ▶ pale verb pale (at sth) (चेहरे का) रंग उड़ जाना, विवर्ण हो जाना : He paled visibly (at the news).

pale² / पेल् / noun 1 खूँटा, बाड़े की नुकीली लकड़ी 2 (अलं) सीमा ■ beyond the pale आम धारणा में आचरण की सीमा के बाहर; अस्वीकार्य : His remarks were clearly beyond the pale.

palette / 'पैलट् / noun रंग-पट्टिका, बोर्ड जिस पर चित्रकार रंग मिलाते हैं।

pall¹ / पॉल् / verb बहुत बार अनुभव होने के कारण अरुचिकर हो जाना।

pall² / पॉल् / noun 1 कफ़न का मोटा कपड़ा 2 (प्राय: sing) कोई भारी काला आवरण : A pall of smoke hung over the town.

pallid / 'पैलिड् / adj 1 (व्यक्ति, चेहरा)

बीमारी के कारण पीला/विवर्ण 2 हलका या मंद : a pallid sun.

pallor / 'पैलर् / noun (बीमारी या भय के कारण) चेहरे का पीलापन।

palm¹ / पाम् / noun हथेली ▶ palm verb हाथ की सफ़ाई दिखाते समय सिक्का आदि हथेली में छुपा कर रखना ■ palm sb off (with sth) (अनौप) झूठ बोल कर किसी को कुछ स्वीकार करने के लिए राज़ी करना palm sb/sth off (on/onto sb) स्वयं को नापसंद वस्तु किसी और के गले मढ़ देना।

palm² / पाम् / (palm tree भी) noun ताड़, खजूर आदि का पेड़ : a date palm ○ a coconut palm.

palmist / 'पामिस्ट् / noun हस्तरेखा विशे-षज्ञ।

palpable / 'पैल्पब्ल् / adj 1 जिसे देखा या महसूस किया जा सके : a palpable sense of loss 2 सुस्पष्ट।

palpitate / 'पैल्पिटेट् / verb 1 दिल की धड़कनों का बढ़ जाना 2 palpitate (with sth) (व्यक्ति के शरीर या अंगों का) कँपकँपाना (जैसे डर के कारण) : palpitating with terror ▶ palpitation / ,पैल्पि 'टेश्न् / noun.

palsy / 'पॉल्ज़ि / noun एक ऐसा रोग जिसमें चल पाना मुश्किल हो और जोड़ों में दर्द हो।

paltry / 'पॉल्ट्रि / adj (प्राय: अपमा) 1 तुच्छ, नगण्य : a paltry amount 2 बेकार; अस्वीकार्य, उपेक्षणीय : a paltry excuse.

pamper / 'पैम्पर् / verb (प्राय: अपमा) बहुत अधिक लाड़-प्यार करना : a pampered child of rich parents.

pamphlet / 'पैम्फ़्लट् / noun पैम्फ़्लेट, पुस्तिका ▶ pamphleteer noun पुस्तिका लेखक।

pan / पैन् / noun 1 कड़ाहा, कड़ाही, तसला 2 तराज़ू के पलड़े ▶ pan verb (-nn-) 1 pan (for sth) सोना या अन्य मूल्यवान खनिज पदार्थ अलग करने के लिए तश्तरी में

पत्थर धोना 2 (अनौप) अत्यधिक निंदा करना।

pan- *pref* (उपसर्ग) अखिल-, सर्व-: *pan-African.*

panacea /ˌपैन्ˈसीआ/ *noun* **panacea (for sth)** सब रोगों या मुश्किलों को दूर करने वाली दवाई, रामबाण : *There is no single panacea for the country's economic ills.*

pancake /ˈपैन्केक्/ *noun* मैदे, अंडे और दूध से बना एक प्रकार का तला हुआ पकवान।

panda /ˈपैन्डा/ *noun* **(giant panda** भी) भालू जैसा एक सफ़ेद और काले रंग का जानवर।

pandemonium /ˌपैन्ड्ˈमोनिअम्/ *noun* हुल्लड़ या कोलाहल का दृश्य।

pander /ˈपैन्डर्/ *verb* ■ **pander to sth/sb** (अपमा) (पाप कर्म, तुच्छ इच्छा में) सहायता करना/प्रोत्साहन देना : *newspapers pandering to the public love of scandal.*

pane /पेन्/ *noun* खिड़की का एक शीशा : *a pane of glass.*

panel /ˈपैन्ल्/ *noun* 1 दरवाज़े का दिल्ला 2 वस्त्रों में लगाई गई पट्टी आदि : *The sleeves had lace panels.* 3 वायुयान, कार आदि के नियंत्रक उपकरणों वाला समतल पट्टा : *a control panel* 4 नामिका, व्यक्तियों की विशेष कार्य के लिए बनाई सूची : *a panel of experts* ▸ **panel** *verb* (**-ll-**; *US* **-l-**) पैनल से सजाना या ढकना **panelling** (*US* **paneling**) *noun* 1 दीवार आदि पर (अलंकृत) पट्टिका श्रेणी 2 पैनल के लिए प्रयुक्त लकड़ी : *oak panelling.*

pang /पैङ्/ *noun* **pang (of sth)** 1 दर्द की कसक, टीस 2 दर्दीली भावनाओं की टीस : *feel a pang of jealousy/remorse.*

panic /ˈपैनिक्/ *noun* भगदड़; आतंक, तहलका : *There was (an) immediate panic when the alarm sounded.*

▸ **panic** *verb* **(-ck-)** आतंक मचाना या आतंकित होना **panicky** /ˈपैनिकि/ *adj* (अनौप) आतंकित : *a panicky voice.*

panorama /ˌपैन्ˈरामा; *US* पैन्ˈरैमा/ *noun* 1 किसी बड़े क्षेत्र का दृश्य 2 निरंतर बदलता हुआ परिदृश्य : *The book presents a panorama of social history since the Middle Ages.*

▸ **panoramic** /ˌपैन्ˈरैमिक्/ *adj* : *a panoramic view from the top of the tower.*

pansy /ˈपैन्ज़ि/ *noun* (*pl* **pansies**) पैंज़ी; एक प्रकार का पौधा।

pant /पैन्ट्/ *verb* हाँफना ■ **pant for sth** हाँफते हुए दर्शाना कि पानी, हवा आदि की ज़रूरत है **pant sth out** हाँफते हुए कहना : *He panted out the message.* ▸ **pant** *noun.*

panther /ˈपैन्थर्/ *noun* (विशेषत: काला) तेंदुआ (एक प्रकार का चीता)।

panties /ˈपैन्टिज़/ *noun* [*pl*] (अनौप) स्त्रियों की जांघिया।

pantomime /ˈपैन्टमाइम्/ *noun* 1 परी-कथाओं पर आधारित बच्चों का क्रिसमस नाटक 2 मूक-अभिनय 3 (प्राय: *sing*) बहुत सारी गड़बड़-भरी हास्यप्रद घटना।

pantry /ˈपैन्ट्रि/ *noun* (*pl* **pantries**) रसोई-भंडार।

pants /पैन्ट्स्/ *noun* [*pl*] 1 पैंट, पतलून 2 निकर।

papa /पˈपा; *US* ˈपापा/ *noun* (अप्र, अनौप) बच्चे द्वारा पिता के लिए प्रयुक्त शब्द।

papaya /पˈपाइआ/ (**pawpaw** /ˈपॉपॉ/ भी) *noun* पपीता।

paper /ˈपेपर्/ *noun* 1 काग़ज़ 2 समाचार-पत्र 3 **papers** [*pl*] काग़ज़ात, दस्तावेज़ : *Immigration officials will ask to see your papers.* 4 प्रश्न-पत्र 5 विशेषज्ञों के लिए किसी विषय पर लिखा निबंध : *reading a paper at the conference* ■ **on paper** 1 लिखित रूप में 2 केवल लिखित/सैद्धांतिक सूचना पर आधारित,

व्यावहारिक नहीं ▶ **paperback** *noun* काग़ज़ के जिल्द की किताब **paperwork** *noun* फ़ार्म आदि में विवरण आदि लिखने का कार्य; मामूली लेखनप्रधान प्रशासनिक कार्य।

par / पार् / *noun* ■ **below/under par** (अनौप) सामान्य/आपेक्षित से कम अच्छा **on a par with sb/sth** सममूल्य/समस्तर पर : *As a writer she was on a par with the great novelists.*

parable / 'पैरब्ल् / *noun* नीतिकथा; दृष्टांत : *the parable of the prodigal son.*

parachute / 'पैरशूट् / *noun* पैराशूट, हवाईछतरी ▶ **parachute** *verb* पैराशूट से नीचे उतरना/उतारना **parachutist** *noun.*

parade / प'रेड् / *noun* 1 जुलूस 2 सैन्य बलों की परेड 3 (प्रायः *अपमा*) किसी को प्रभावित करने के लिए प्रदर्शन : *He is always making a parade of his wealth.* ▶ **parade** *verb* 1 जुलूस निकालना 2 (प्रभावित या ध्यान आकर्षित करने के लिए) प्रदर्शन करना 3 निरीक्षण आदि के लिए जमा होना : *The colonel paraded his troops.* **parade-ground** *noun* परेड-भूमि।

paradise / 'पैरडाइस् / *noun* 1 Para-dise [*sing*] ईडन की वाटिका 2 [*sing*] स्वर्ग 3 पूर्ण शांति का स्थान; पूर्ण प्रसन्नता की अवस्था।

paradox / 'पैरडॉक्स् / *noun* 1 दो विरोधी गुणों वाला व्यक्ति/वस्तु/परिस्थिति और इस कारण विचित्र 2 विरोधी विचारों वाला असंगत कथन, और इस कारण बेतुका, विरोधाभास: *'More haste, less speed' is a well-known paradox.* ▶ **para-doxical** *adj* विरोधाभासी; विरोधाभास-पूर्ण।

paraffin / 'पैरफ़िन् / (**paraffin oil** भी; *US* **kerosene**) *noun* पैराफ़िन, कोयले आदि से प्राप्त तेल।

paragon / 'पैरगन्; *US* 'पैरगॉन् / *noun*

paragon of sth आदर्श (व्यक्ति/वस्तु) : *be seen as a paragon of virtue.*

paragraph / 'पैरग्राफ़्; *US* 'पैरग्रैफ़ / *noun* 1 पैराग्राफ़, अनुच्छेद 2 समाचार-पत्र में एक छोटी रिपोर्ट : *There's a para-graph on the accident in the local paper.*

parallel / 'पैरलेल् / *adj* 1 **parallel to/with sth** (रेखाएँ) समानांतर 2 समकक्ष, सदृश/तुल्य : *a parallel case/devel-opment* ▶ **parallel** *noun* 1 सदृश व्यक्ति/वस्तु/घटना 2 तुलना : *It is possi-ble to draw a parallel between their experience and ours.* 3 (**par-allel of latitude** भी) अक्षांश रेखा **paral-lel** *verb* (**-l-**) 1 समकक्ष/तुल्य होना : *His performance has never been par-alleled.* 2 एक ही समय पर घटित होना।

parallelogram / ‚पैर 'लेल्ग्रैम् / *noun* (ज्यामिति) समांतर चतुर्भुज।

paralyse (*US* **paralyze**) / 'पैरलाइज़् / *verb* 1 शरीर/शरीर के अंग का लक़वे से प्रभावित होना 2 **paralyse sb/sth** (**with sth**) किसी को सामान्य रूप/गति से काम करने में बाधा डालना : *a country para-lysed by industrial disputes.*

paralysis / प'रैलसिस् / *noun* (*pl* **paralyses** / प'रैलसीज़ /) 1 फ़ालिज, (शरीर के किसी अंग का) पक्षाघात, लक़वा 2 कार्य करने, प्रगति करने आदि की नितांत असमर्थता : *the growing paralysis of Europe's air traffic control sys-tem* ▶ **paralytic** *adj.*

paramilitary / ‚पैर 'मिलट्रि; *US* ‚पैर 'मिलटेरि / *adj* अर्धसैनिक।

paramount / 'पैरमाउन्ट् / *adj* (औप) 1 अधिक/अत्यंत महत्त्व का; सर्वोच्च 2 सर्वोच्च अधिकार रखने वाला : *a para-mount chief/leader.*

paranoia / ‚पैर 'नॉइआ / *noun* 1 मानसिक रोग जिसमें रोगी को भ्रांति होती है कि उसके साथ दुर्व्यवहार किया जाता है 2 दूसरे पर

विश्वास न करने की असामान्य प्रवृत्ति ▸ **paranoid** / 'पैरनॉइड् / (**paranoiac** भी) *adj, noun* इस रोग से ग्रस्त व्यक्ति।

parapet / 'पैरपिट्; 'पैरपेट् / *noun* 1 (छत की) मुंडेर; (पुल की) दोनों ओर की नीची दीवार; प्राकार 2 (युद्ध में) खाई के साथ सामने लगी मिट्टी/पत्थर की रक्षक दीवार।

paraphernalia / पैरफ़र्'नेलिआ / *noun* साज-सामान; सामग्री/उपकरण : *surrounded by all the paraphernalia of family life.*

paraphrase / 'पैरफ़्रेज़् / *verb* किसी कथन को दूसरे शब्दों में कहना : *paraphrase a speech in colloquial English* ▸ **paraphrase** *noun* पदान्वय।

parasite / 'पैरसाइट् / *noun* 1 परजीवी (जीव या पौधा जो दूसरों पर आश्रित रह कर उससे अपना भोजन ग्रहण करता है) 2 (*अपमा*) अति स्वार्थी एवं दूसरों पर आश्रित व्यक्ति : *live as a parasite on society* ▸ **parasitic** / पैर'सिटिक् / *adj* (**parasitical** भी) परजीवी रूप; परजीवी द्वारा उत्पन्न : *a parasitic disease.*

paratroops / 'पैरट्रूप्स् / *noun [pl]* वायुयान से पैराशूट से कूदने के लिए प्रशिक्षित सैनिक ▸ **paratrooper** / 'पैरट्रूपर् / *noun* छतरी-सैनिक, पैराशूट से कूदने वाला सैनिक।

parcel / 'पार्सल् / *noun* 1 (*US* **package** भी) पार्सल (डाक घर, रेल आदि द्वारा भेजा जाने वाला सामान का पैकेट) 2 ज़मीन का छोटा टुकड़ा ▸ **parcel** *verb* (**-ll-**; *US* **-l-**) ■ **parcel sth out** विभाजन करना; बाँटना : *He parcelled out the land into small plots.*

parch / पार्च् / *verb* 1 (गरमी से ज़मीन का) सूखना, झुलसना 2 (भट्टी आदि में) आग से भूनना ▸ **parched** / पार्च्ट् / *adj* 1 झुलसा हुआ; गरम एवं शुष्क 2 बहुत प्यासा।

parchment / 'पार्च्मन्ट् / *noun* 1 पार्चमेंट, एक तरह का काग़ज़ 2 चर्म-पत्र (पूर्व समय में लिखने में प्रयुक्त)।

pardon¹ / 'पाड्न् / *noun* (*औप*) क्षमा, माफ़ी ■ **beg sb's pardon** (शिष्ट प्रयोग) किसी के प्रति किए अशिष्ट अथवा असुविधाजनक व्यवहार के लिए खेद प्रकट करना; क्षमाप्रार्थी बनना।

pardon² / 'पाड्न् / *verb* **pardon sb (for sth/doing sth)** (प्राय: *औप*) क्षमा करना, माफ़ करना : *pardon an offence/a fault* ▸ **pardon** (**pardon me** भी) *interj* कृपया फिर से कहिए / मैं सुन नहीं पाया या समझ नहीं पाया; कृपया क्षमा कर दें **pardonable** *adj* क्षमा योग्य।

parent / 'पेअरन्ट् / *noun* 1 (प्राय: *pl*) माता/पिता; माता-पिता 2 वह पेड़/पौधा या पशु/पक्षी जिससे अन्य उत्पन्न हुआ हो : *the parent tree* ▸ **parentage** / 'पेअर्न्टिज् / *noun* माता/पिता का निर्धारण; उत्पत्ति : *of humble parentage* **parental** *adj* माता-पिता विषयक।

parenthesis / प'रेन्थ्सिस् / *noun (pl* **parentheses** / प'रेन्थ्सीज़् /) 1 वाक्य के भीतर कोष्ठक या कॉमा चिह्न द्वारा चिह्नित वाक्य या वाक्यांश 2 (प्राय: *pl*) कोष्ठक ▸ **parenthetic** (**parenthetical** भी) *adj* कोष्ठक में सन्निविष्ट।

pariah / प'राइआ / *noun* अछूत; चांडाल।

parish / 'पैरिश् / *noun* 1 क्षेत्र जिसका अपना चर्च और पादरी हो : *a parish church* 2 (इंग्लैंड में) स्थानीय स्वशासन वाला गाँव : *the parish council.*

parity / 'पैरिटि / *noun (pl* **parities**) 1 (*औप*) समानता : *parity of treatment* 2 (*वाणिज्य*) मुद्रा की सममूल्यता।

park¹ / पार्क् / *noun* 1 सार्वजनिक उद्यान, पार्क 2 देहात-स्थित मकान से संलग्न भूमि, प्राय: खेतों और पेड़ों से भरी 3 उद्देश्य विशेष के लिए प्रयुक्त भूखंड : *an industrial park.*

park² / पार्क् / *verb* 1 वाहन पार्क करना 2 (*अनौप*) किसी चीज़ को कहीं कुछ देर के लिए छोड़ देना : *Park your luggage here while you buy a ticket.*

parka / 'पार्का / *noun* एक गरम जैकिट, प्राय: टोपी सहित।

parking / 'पार्किङ् / *noun* वाहन पार्क करना; पार्क करने का स्थान ▸ **parking lot** *noun (US)* गाड़ी पार्क करने का स्थान (विशेषत: भवन आदि के सामने)।

parley / 'पार्लि / *noun (pl* **parleys)** *(अप्र)* विरोधियों के बीच संधिवार्ता के लिए बैठक ▸ **parley** *verb* **parley (with sb)** *(अप्र)* संधिवार्ता करना।

parliament / 'पार्लमन्ट / *noun* 1 **Parliament** संसद 2 देश के लिए क़ानून बनाने वाले लोगों का समूह 3 संसद-भवन ▸ **parliamentarian** *noun* सांसद **parliamentary** *adj* संसदीय।

parlour *(US* **parlor)** / 'पार्लर् / *noun* 1 *(अप्र)* बैठक (ख़ाना) 2 (समास में) सेवा या सामान विशेष प्रदान करने वाली दुकान : *a beauty/an ice-cream parlour.*

parochial / प'रोकिअल् / *adj* 1 *(औप)* पैरिश विषयक 2 *(अपमा)* सीमित, संकुचित : *a parochial attitude/outlook* ▸ **parochialism** *noun.*

parody / 'पैरडि / *noun (pl* **parodies) parody (of sth)** 1 पैरोडी, किसी कृति की नक़ल (विद्रूपिका) 2 बहुत ख़राब ढंग से किया गया कार्य : *The trial was a parody of justice.* ▸ **parody** *verb (pt, pp* **parodied)** पैरोडी करना।

parole / प'रोल् / *noun* पैरोल, क़ैदी को (अच्छे व्यवहार आदि के लिए) सज़ा समाप्त होने से पहले थोड़े समय के लिए रिहा करना : *release sb on parole.*

parrot / 'पैरट् / *noun* 1 तोता 2 *(अपमा)* किसी की बात को बिना सोचे तोते की तरह दोहराने वाला व्यक्ति ▸ **parrot** *verb (अपमा)* नक़ल करना; बिना सोचे-समझे किसी की बात दोहराना।

parsimony / 'पार्सि'मनि / *noun (औप, प्राय: अपमा)* किफ़ायत, मितव्ययता ▸ **parsimonious** / पार्सि'मोनिअस् / *adj (औप, प्राय: अपमा)* कंजूस; मितव्ययी।

parsley / 'पार्स्लि / *noun* एक प्रकार का पुदीने जैसा पौधा जिसके पत्ते खाने में प्रयोग होते हैं।

parsnip / 'पार्स्निप् / *noun* चुकंदर-गाजर जैसी तरकारी : *roast parsnips.*

parson / 'पार्स्न् / *noun (अनौप)* (ईसाई धर्म में) पैरिश का पुरोहित; पादरी ▸ **parsonage** / 'पार्स्निज् / *noun* पुरोहित/पादरी का घर/आश्रम।

part¹ / पार्ट् / *noun* 1 **part (of sth)** अंश, हिस्सा (न कि पूर्ण/पूरा) 2 **part (of sth)** मानव/जीव/पौधे का कोई निश्चित अंग : *Which part of your leg hurts?* 3 किसी देश, प्रदेश या शहर का हिस्सा : *Which part of Goa do you come from?* 4 **parts** [*pl*] *(अनौप)* प्रदेश 5 **part (in sth)** किसी कार्य-विशेष में व्यक्ति की भूमिका : *He had no part in the decision.* 6 नाटक, फ़िल्म आदि में अभिनेता की भूमिका : *He played the part of Hamlet.* 7 बराबर विभाजन का कोई भाग : *a sixtieth part of a minute* 8 (सामान्यत: *sing*) सदस्यता : *work as part of a team* ∎ **for my, his, their, etc part** जहाँ तक मेरा (उसका) संबंध है **for the most part** ज़्यादातर; सामान्यत: **in part** कुछ हद तक : *His success was due in part to luck.* **on the part of sb/on sb's part** किसी के द्वारा किया या बनाया गया : *It was an error on my part.* **part and parcel of sth** अभिन्न अंग **take sb's part** समर्थन देना/करना **take sth in good part** बुरा न मानना **best/better part of sth** अधिकाधिक; आधे से ज़्यादा : *I spent the best part of an hour trying to find my car keys.* ▸ **partly** *adv* अंशत:; कुछ अंश/हद तक **part-time** *adj, adv* अंशकालिक : *a part-time job.*

part² / पार्ट् / *verb* 1 *(औप)* **part (from sb)** किसी से अलग होना, साथ छोड़ कर जाना : *She has parted from her* *husband.* **2 part sb (from sb)** किसी को अन्य व्यक्ति से अलग कर देना **3** विभाजित करना/होना : *Her lips parted in a smile.* **4** सिर में माँग निकालना ■ **part company (with sb/sth)** संबंध तोड़ लेना **part with sth** छोड़ देना, दे देना।

partial / 'पार्शल् / *adj* **1** आंशिक (न कि पूर्ण) : *a partial recovery* **2 partial to sb/sth** किसी व्यक्ति/वस्तु को अधिक पसंद करने वाला : *He's partial to a glass of brandy after dinner.* **3 partial (towards sb/sth)** (प्राय: *अपमा*) पक्षपाती ▸ **partiality** / ,पार्शि'ऐलटि / *noun* **1** (*अपमा*) तरफ़दारी, पक्षपात : *He judged the case without partiality.* **2 partiality for sb/sth** (*औप*) किसी व्यक्ति/वस्तु के प्रति विशेष आग्रह होना **partially** *adv*.

participate / पार्'टिसिपेट् / *verb* **participate (in sth)** भाग लेना, भागी बनना : *participate in a competition/discussion* ▸ **participant** / पार्'टिसिपन्ट् / *noun* **participant (in sth)** सहभागी : *All the participants in the debate had an opportunity to speak.* **participation** *noun* **participation (in sth)** सहयोग, सहभागिता।

participle / 'पार्टिसिपल् / *noun* (*व्या*) कृदंत रूप (जैसे *'write'* धातु का *present participle* रूप *'writing'* और *past participle* रूप *'written'* है) ▸ **participial** / ,पार्टि'सिपिअल् / *adj* कृदंती।

particle / 'पार्टिकल् / *noun* **1** कण, बहुत छोटा-सा अंश : *particles of dust* **2** (*भौतिकी*) पदार्थ का मूल कण जिससे परमाणु बनता है : *particle physics.*

particular / पर्'टिक्यलर् / *adj* **1** किसी एक व्यक्ति/वस्तु विशेष से संबद्ध, न कि सबसे; व्यक्तिगत : *his particular problems* **2** विशिष्ट; सामान्य से अधिक : *a matter of particular importance* **3 particular (about/over sth)** सख़्त,

बहुत सावधान : *She's very particular about what she wears.* ■ **in particular** विशेषकर, ख़ासकर : *The whole meal was good but the fish in particular was excellent.* ▸ **particular** *noun* (प्राय: *pl*) (*औप*) विवरण, ब्योरा : *The police officer took down all the particulars about the missing child.* **particularly** *adv* विशेष रूप से।

parting / 'पार्टिङ् / *noun* **1** अलग होने/ साथ छोड़ने की क्रिया **2** विभाजन करने की क्रिया **3** सिर में बालों की माँग।

partisan / ,पार्टि'ज़ैन्; 'पार्टिज़ैन्; *US* 'पार्टज़्न् / *noun* **1** किसी दल, वर्ग या हित का अंधभक्त/पक्का हिमायती **2** देश के दुश्मनों से गुप्त रूप से लड़ने वाली सशस्त्र सेना का सदस्य ▸ **partisan** *adj* (प्राय: *अपमा*) अत्यधिक अंधभक्ति वाला।

partition / पार्'टिश्न् / *noun* **1** (एक देश का) अंशों या टुकड़ों में विभाजन **2** विभाजक (जैसे पतली विभाजक दीवार) ▸ **partition** *verb* विभाजन करना : *India was partitioned in 1947.*

partner / 'पार्टनर् / *noun* **1** भागीदार, साथी, संगी : *business partners* **2** नृत्य या खेल में हिस्सेदार : *be sb's partner at bridge/badminton* **3** पति या पत्नी ▸ **partner** *verb* (खेल, नृत्य आदि में) भागीदार/साथी बनना/बनाना **partnership** / 'पार्टनरशिप् / *noun* **partnership (with sb)** भागीदारी/हिस्सेदारी।

partridge / 'पार्ट्रिज् / *noun* (*pl* अपरिवर्तित या **partridges**) तीतर; तीतर का मांस।

party / 'पार्टि / *noun* (*pl* **parties**) **1** पार्टी, प्रीतिभोज **2** पार्टी, (विशेषत:) राजनीतिक दल **3** (यात्रा या कार्य के लिए) टोली : *a party of school children* **4** (*औप*) मुक़दमें आदि में एक पक्ष : *the guilty party* ■ **be (a) party to sth** किसी कार्य, योजना का समर्थक होना/में भागीदार होना

be party to an agreement/a dispute ▸ **party** *verb* (*pt, pp* **partied**) (अनौप) पार्टी (प्रीतिभोज) में आनंद उठाना : *partying all night long.*

pass¹ / पास् / *US* पैस् / *verb* 1 गुज़रना; आगे बढ़ना; (स्थान या व्यक्ति को) पार कर जाना : *pass a barrier/sentry* 2 **pass sth (to sb)** किसी को कुछ देना, हाथों-हाथ देना : *Pass (me) the salt, please.* 3 **pass to sb** एक व्यक्ति से दूसरे को हस्तगत/हस्तांतरित हो जाना : *On his death, the title passed to his eldest son.* 4 **pass (sth) (to sb)** (खेलों में) गेंद को दूसरे खिलाड़ी की तरफ़ बढ़ाना 5 **pass from sth to/into sth** एक दशा से दूसरी में बदलना : *pass from boyhood to manhood* 6 (समय) गुज़रना, बीतना/ बिताना : *The holidays passed far too quickly.* 7 समाप्त हो जाना : *The dizziness will soon pass.* 8 (परीक्षा में) एक निश्चित स्तर पाना; परख कर स्वीकार किया जाना या स्वीकार करना : *She hasn't passed her driving test yet.* 9 (क़ानून, प्रस्ताव आदि का) अनुमोदन करना 10 **pass sth (on sb/sth)** निर्णय देना : *pass sentence (on sb found guilty of a crime)* 11 **pass (between A and B)** घटित होना, दो व्यक्तियों के बीच निर्णीत होना : *after all that has passed between them* 12 की सीमा से गुज़र जाना 13 मंजूर करना, सहना : *I don't like it, but I'll let it pass.* 14 (मल-मूत्र आदि का) विसर्जन करना ■ **pass away** मर जाना **pass by (sb/sth)** गुज़-रना : *I saw the procession pass by.* **pass for/as sb/sth** किसी रूप में स्वीकार होना **pass off** घटनाओं का (शांतिपूर्वक) घटित हो जाना **pass out** बेहोश हो जाना **pass sb/oneself/sth as sb/sth** किसी व्यक्ति/वस्तु को ग़लत रूप में कुछ और प्रदर्शित करना : *He escaped by passing himself off as a guard.* **pass sb/**

sth by बिना प्रभाव डाले घटित होना **pass sb over** किसी व्यक्ति की उपेक्षा करना **pass sth down** एक पीढ़ी से दूसरी को देना/जाना ▸ **passer-by** / ˌपासर'बाइ; *US* ˌपैसर'बाइ / *noun* (*pl* **passers-by**) राह-चलता व्यक्ति।

pass² / पास्; *US* पैस् / *noun* 1 **pass (to sb)** (फ़ुटबाल आदि खेलों में) गेंद दूसरे खिलाड़ी की तरफ़ बढ़ाने की क्रिया 2 (किसी स्थान पर आने-जाने का) अनुज्ञा-पत्र, पास 3 परीक्षा में सफलता; उत्तीर्ण होना 4 (पहाड़ों में) दर्रा, पहाड़ों के बीच में से निकला मार्ग : *The pass was blocked by snow.* 5 गुज़रने की क्रिया ■ **come to such a pass** (अप्र या परि) कठिन परिस्थिति में पहुँच जाना।

passable / ˈपासबल्; *US* ˈपैसबल् / *adj* 1 जिसे पार किया जा सके; (नदी) जो पार की जा सके 2 जो पर्याप्त अच्छा होने के कारण स्वीकार किया जा सके : *have a passable knowledge of German* ▸ **passably** *adv.*

passage / ˈपैसिज् / *noun* 1 गुज़रने की प्रक्रिया; पार-गमन : *the passage of time* 2 (प्राय: *sing*) पार-गमन मार्ग 3 (जहाज़ या हवाई जहाज़ में) यात्रा 4 गलि-यारा, कॉरीडोर 5 उद्धरण, लेखांश : *a passage from the Bible* 6 संसद में बिल का पारित होना।

passbook / ˈपासबुक; *US* ˈपैसबुक् / *noun* पास बुक, (बैंक, डाकघर आदि की) लेखा-पुस्तिका।

passenger / ˈपैसिन्जर् / *noun* 1 (बस, रेल, जहाज़ आदि का) यात्री 2 (अनौप, अपमा) दल में कामचोर व्यक्ति।

passing / ˈपासिङ्; *US* ˈपैसिङ् / *adj* बहुत कम समय के लिए : *a passing thought/ fancy* ▸ **passing** *noun* 1 गुज़रने की प्रक्रिया (समय आदि की) : *the passing of time* 2 (औप) अंत : *the passing of the old year* ■ **in passing** बिना गंभीरता के, यों ही।

passion / 'पैशन् / *noun* 1 ज़ोरदार मनोभाव, भावावेश : *a man of violent passions* 2 **passion (for sb)** तीव्र यौनाकर्षण 3 [*sing*] **passion.for sth** अत्यधिक उत्साह/उल्लास : *have a passion for chocolates.*

passionate / 'पैशनट् / *adj* 1 कामुकता से उत्पन्न या कामुकतापूर्ण 2 भावावेशपूर्ण : *a passionate plea for mercy* 3 सहज में ही तीव्र मनोभावों से विक्षुब्ध होने वाला; क्रोधी ▸ **passionately** *adv.*

passive / 'पैसिव् / *adj* 1 निष्क्रिय, नि-श्चेष्ट : *a passive observer of events* 2 (*व्या*) कर्मवाच्य, जैसे '*Her leg was broken.*' कर्मवाच्य वाक्य है ▸ **passively** *adv.*

passport /'पास्पॉर्ट; US 'पैस्पॉर्ट/ *noun* 1 पासपोर्ट (विदेशी यात्री का पार-पत्र जिसमें यात्री का विवरण दिया होता है) 2 **passport to sth** कुछ प्राप्त करने में सहायक वस्तु : *The only passport to success is hard work.*

password /'पास्वर्ड् / *noun* गुप्त शब्द (विशेषतः किसी स्थान में प्रवेश पाने या कंप्यूटर को चलाने के लिए)।

past¹ / 'पास्ट; US पैस्ट् / *adj* 1 अतीत/ भूतकाल का, पिछला 2 (*व्या*) क्रिया का वह रूप जिससे भूतकाल का पता चलता है : *The past tense of 'take' is 'took'.* ▸ **past** *noun* 1 **the past** [*sing*] अतीतकाल; बीती हुई घटनाएँ 2 व्यक्ति का बीता हुआ जीवन/घटनाएँ 3 (**past tense** भी, *संक्षि* **pt**) [*sing*] (*व्या*) क्रिया का भूतकाल रूप।

past² /पास्ट; US पैस्ट् / *prep* 1 (समय) बाद में : *half past two* 2 दूसरे छोर पर, (स्थान में) आगे/परे; के पार : *She walked past the shop.* 3 सीमा के परे, आगे : *I'm past caring.* ▸ **past** *adv* एक सिरे से दूसरे सिरे तक : *walk/march past.*

pasta / 'पैस्ट; US 'पास्य/ *noun* मैदे, अंडे और पानी के मिश्रण से बना एक खाद्य पदार्थ जो विभिन्न तरीकों से पकाया जाता है।

paste¹ /'पेस्ट् / *noun* 1 लेई 2 गीला आटा 3 मांस-मछली का लेईनुमा मिश्रण।

paste² /'पेस्ट् / *verb* 1 लेई से चिपकाना : *paste posters on the wall* 2 काट-चिपका कर कुछ तैयार करना।

pasteboard / 'पेस्ट्बॉर्ड / *noun* कार्ड बोर्ड, दफ़्ती।

pastel / 'पैस्ट्ल; US पै'स्टेल् / *noun* 1 चित्रकारी में प्रयुक्त मुलायम रंगीन चाक-स्टिक 2 हलका कोमल रंग।

pasteurize, -ise /'पास्चराइज़; US 'पैस्चराइज़/ *verb* गरम करके जीवाणु रहित करना ▸ **pasteurization, -isation** *noun.*

pastime /'पास्टाइम; US 'पैस्टाइम् / *noun* मनबहलाव के लिए क्रिया; आमोद-प्रमोद : *Photography is her favourite pastime.*

pastor / 'पास्टर / *noun* ईसाई पुरोहित।

pastoral / 'पास्टरल; US 'पैस्टरल् / *adj* 1 ग्रामीण जीवन या किसानों, ग्वाले-गड़ेरियों से संबद्ध जीवन; ऐसे जीवन का साहित्यिक, अलंकारिक चित्रण : *a pastoral scene/ poem/painting* 2 (ईसाई) पुरोहित या गुरु का कार्य या प्रदत्त सलाह : *pastoral care.*

pastry / 'पेस्ट्रि / *noun* (*pl* **pastries**) पेस्ट्री; एक प्रकार की मिठाई।

pasture / 'पास्चर; US 'पैस्चर / *noun* 1 चारागाह 2 **pastures** [*pl*] जीवन, काम आदि की परिस्थितियाँ : *greener/richer pastures* ▸ **pasture** *verb* 1 पशुओं को चराना 2 (पशुओं का) घास चरना।

pasty /'पेस्टि/ *adj* 1 लेईदार; गिलगिला 2 विवर्ण और बीमार जैसा (दिखने में) : *a pasty-faced youth.*

pat¹ / पैट् / *verb* (**-tt-**) 1 थपथपाना : *pat a dog* 2 थपथपा कर कुछ ठीक स्थान पर जमाना : *She patted her hair into shape.* ■ **pat sb/oneself on the back** किसी की प्रशंसा करना, सफलता पर बधाई देना ▸ **pat** *noun* 1 थपकी 2 **pat (of**

sth) थपथपाने से बनी टिकिया (जैसे मक्खन की टिकिया) ■ **a pat on the back (for sth/doing sth)** प्रशंसा या अनुमोदन : *She deserves a pat on the back for all the hard work she's done.*

pat² / पैट् / *adv* ■ **have/know sth off pat** पूरी तरह जानना ताकि कभी भी दोहराया जा सके ▸ **pat** *adj* 1 एकदम ठीक, सटीक 2 *(अपमा)* अति तीव्र, रटा-रटाया (जवाब आदि)।

patch¹ / पैच् / *noun* 1 पैवंद (फटे कपड़े के छेद पर लगाया कपड़े का टुकड़ा); मज़बूती के लिए कपड़े पर लगाई चकती : *a jacket with leather patches on the elbows* 2 घायल आँख की सुरक्षा के लिए पहनी पट्टी 3 किसी सतह पर आस-पास के क्षेत्र से भिन्न रंग, बनावट आदि वाला हिस्सा; धब्बा : *damp patches on a wall* 4 सब्ज़ी-भाजी आदि उगाने के लिए प्रयुक्त ज़मीन का टुकड़ा 5 *(अनौप)* विशेष प्रकार की (विशेषत: मुश्किलों से पूर्ण या अप्रिय) अवधि : *Their marriage has been going through a bad patch.* ■ **not be a patch on sb/sth** *(अनौप)* किसी और से काफ़ी कम अच्छा, सफल, रुचिकर आदि होना।

patch² / पैच् / *verb* 1 पैवंद लगाना 2 **patch sth (up)** फटे-पुराने कपड़ों की मरम्मत करना ■ **patch sth/sb up** 1 घाव आदि का तीव्रता से इलाज करना 2 झगड़ों/ मनमुटाव आदि का निपटारा करना।

patchwork / 'पैचवर्क् / *noun* जोड़-जाड़ से बना हुआ काम; भिन्न-भिन्न छोटे टुकड़ों से बना हुआ।

patchy / 'पैचि / *adj* (**-ier, -iest**) 1 पैवंद लगा हुआ 2 असमान गुण/स्तर वाला कार्य आदि : *a patchy essay/performance.*

patent¹ / 'पेटन्ट्; US 'पैटन्ट् / *adj* स्पष्ट, साफ़ : *a patent lie* ▸ **patently** *adv.*

patent² / 'पेटन्ट्; US 'पैटन्ट् / *noun* 1 पेटेंट, एकस्व अधिकार (क़ानून द्वारा किसी अन्वेषण को उसकी नक़ल से बचाने का

संरक्षण) 2 पेटेंट द्वारा रक्षित कोई खोज या प्रक्रिया : *It's my patent.* ▸ **patent** *verb* पेटेंट कराना **patentee** *noun* पेटेंट-धारक **patent leather** / 'पेटन्ट् 'लेदर् / *noun* कड़े चिकने चमकीले सतह का चमड़ा।

paternal / प'टर्न्ल् / *adj* 1 पितासदृश, पितृसुलभ : *paternal affection* 2 पिता से संबंधित : *her paternal grand-mother.*

paternity / प'टर्नटि / *noun* पितृत्व।

path / पाथ्; US पैथ् / *noun* (*pl* **paths** / पाद्ज़्; US पैद्ज़् /) 1 (**pathway, footpath** भी) पगडंडी; रास्ता 2 पथ, वह रेखा जिस पर कोई व्यक्ति/वस्तु चले : *the path of a tornado* 3 कार्रवाई का ढंग 4 *(सामान्यत: sing)* **path to sth** कुछ प्राप्त करने का तरीक़ा : *the path to victory/ruin.*

pathetic / प'थेटिक् / *adj* 1 दयनीय, करुणाजनक 2 *(अनौप)* बिलकुल बेकार/ अपर्याप्त; महत्वहीन : *a pathetic attempt* ▸ **pathetically** *adv.*

pathological / पैथ'लॉजिक्ल् / *adj* 1 *(अनौप)* अविवेकपूर्ण या आधारहीन : *a pathological fear* 2 शारीरिक या मानसिक बीमारी से उत्पन्न : *a pathological depression* 3 रोग विज्ञान-विषयक : *pathological laboratory.*

pathology / प'थॉलजि / *noun* रोग विज्ञान ▸ **pathologist** / प'थॉलजिस्ट् / *noun* रोग विज्ञानी।

pathos / 'पेथॉस् / *noun* दयनीयता, कारुणिकता (विशेषकर साहित्य में)।

patience / 'पेशन्स् / *noun* 1 **patience (with sb/sth)** सहनशक्ति; धैर्य : *People have lost patience with the slow pace of reform.* 2 **patience (for sth/ to do sth)** धैर्य (विशेषत: कठिन कार्य के लिए) 3 *(US* solitaire) ताश का एक खेल जो अकेले खेला जाता है।

patient¹ / 'पेशन्ट् / *adj* **patient (with**

sb/sth) धैर्यवान, सहनशील : *patient determination* ▸ **patiently** *adv.*

patient² / 'पेश्न्ट् / *noun* मरीज़/रोगी जिसका इलाज हो रहा हो।

patriarch / 'पेट्रिआर्क् / *noun* 1 परिवार अथवा क़बीले का पुरुष मुखिया 2 आदरणीय वयोवृद्ध पुरुष 3 **Patriarch** (पूर्वी सनातनी एवं रोमन कैथलिक चर्च में) उच्च पद वाला बिशप ▸ **patriarchal** *adj* 1 वयोवृद्ध समान/विषयक 2 पुरुष-प्रधान या पुरुषों द्वारा शासित : *a patriarchal society* **patriarchy** *noun.*

patriot / 'पेट्रिअट्, 'पैट्रिअट् / *noun* देश-भक्त ▸ **patriotism** *noun* देशभक्ति : *an upsurge of patriotism.*

patriotic / ,पेट्रि'ऑटिक् / *adj* देशभक्ति पूर्ण।

patrol / प'ट्रोल् / *verb* (-ll-) गश्त लगाना ▸ **patrol** *noun* 1 गश्त : *Security guards make hourly patrols of the site.* 2 गश्ती कार्य पर व्यक्ति, जहाज़ या वायुयान।

patron / 'पेट्रन् / *noun* (*fem* **patroness** / ,पेट्रन्'एस् /) 1 संरक्षक (सभा-समिति या कलाकार का धन आदि से संरक्षण करने वाला व्यक्ति) : *a wealthy patron of the arts* 2 (औप) संरक्षक, (किसी दुकान, रेस्त्राँ आदि का) नियमित ग्राहक ▸ **patron saint** *noun* संरक्षक संत।

patronage / 'पैट्रनिज् / *noun* 1 संरक्षण एवं समर्थन 2 संरक्षणात्मक व्यवहार; किसी उच्च पद पर नियुक्ति या सिफारिश करने का अधिकार/शक्ति : *dependent on patronage to advance their careers.*

patronize, -ise / 'पैट्रनाइज़; *US* 'पेट्रना-इज़् / *verb* 1 (अपमा) किसी अन्य व्यक्ति को अपने से छोटा समझ कर कृपादृष्टि दिखाना 2 (औप) संरक्षक/नियमित ग्राहक बनना ▸ **patronizing, -ising** *adj* (अपमा) स्वयं को श्रेष्ठ मानना/दिखाना।

patter / 'पैट्र् / *noun* 1 [*sing*] पट-पट

ध्वनि (पदचाप या टीन पर बूँदों जैसी ध्वनि) 2 लगातार चुटकुले सुनाते/कुछ करतब दिखाते/कुछ बेचते हुए व्यक्ति की लगातार की बात ▸ **patter** *verb* पट-पट ध्वनि करना।

pattern / 'पैट्न् / *noun* 1 कुछ घटित होने, विकास करने या व्यवस्थित किए जाने का ढंग : *patterns of behaviour* 2 अत्युत्तम उदाहरण, आदर्श नमूना 3 पैटर्न, प्रतिकृति (प्राय: वस्त्र बनाते समय) 4 अलंकृत रचना और आकृति : *a checked/flowery pattern* ▸ **pattern** *verb* 1 नमूना/प्रतिकृति तैयार करना/बनाना 2 **pattern sth on sth** उदाहरण/नमूने के तौर पर प्रयुक्त करना; अनुसरण करना : *a new approach patterned on Japanese ideas.*

paucity / 'पॉसिटि / *noun* [*sing*] (औप) **paucity (of sth)** कमी; अभाव : *a paucity of funds.*

paunch / पॉन्च् / *noun* मोटा पेट, तोंद (विशेषत: पुरुष की)।

pauper / 'पॉपर् / *noun* कंगाल, मुफ़्लिस (केवल पाए हुए दान से पलने वाला)।

pause / पॉज़् / *noun* **pause (in sth)** क्रिया या बातचीत में विराम : *He slipped out during a pause in the conversation.* ▸ **pause** *verb* **pause (for sth)** रुकना, विराम देना : *He paused for a moment before continuing.*

pave / पेव् / *verb* **pave sth (with sth)** रास्ते में (ईंट, पत्थर आदि का) फ़र्श लगाना ■ **pave the way (for sb/sth)** कुछ करने/होने के लिए स्थिति आसान बनाना : *economic policies that will pave the way for industrial expansion* ▸ **paving** *noun* समतल पत्थरों की सतह; इस हेतु प्रयुक्त पत्थर आदि।

pavement / 'पेव्मन्ट् / *noun* 1 सड़क के किनारे की पटरी (पैदल चलने वालों के लिए) 2 समतल पत्थरों से बना क्षेत्र/पट्टी।

pavilion / प'विलिअन् / *noun* 1 खेल के मैदान के पास बना खिलाड़ियों/दर्शकों के लिए भवन : *a cricket pavilion* 2 मंडप

शरणगृह 3 नृत्य-गान आदि के लिए बना शोभामंडप 4 बड़ा तंबू, शिविर।

paw / पॉ / *noun* (जानवरों का) पंजा; (परि) व्यक्ति का हाथ ▸ **paw** *verb* **paw (at) sth** पंजे से खोदना/खुरचना।

pawn[1] / पॉन / *noun* 1 शतरंज के मोहरों में प्यादा (पैदल) 2 दूसरों के द्वारा अपनी स्वार्थ-सिद्धि के लिए प्रयुक्त व्यक्ति : *They are being used as political pawns in the struggle for power.*

pawn[2] / पॉन / *verb* (कोई वस्तु) बंधक या रेहन रखना : *He pawned his gold watch to pay the rent.* ▸ **pawn** *noun* ■ **in pawn** रेहन रखी वस्तु ▸ **pawnbroker** *noun* वह व्यक्ति जो बंधक रखने/रेहन रखने का व्यवसाय करता है **pawnshop** *noun.*

pay[1] / पे / *verb* (*pt, pp* **paid** / पेड् /) 1 **pay (sb) (for sth); pay sth (to sb) (for sth)** अदा करना, भुगतान करना : *Have you paid the milkman this week?* 2 लाभप्रद होना : *Crime doesn't pay.* 3 **pay (for sth)** कुपरिणाम भोगना, दंड भुगतना : *Many paid with their lives.* 4 (ध्यान) देना; (भेंट आदि) करना; (भेंट आदि) देना : *She paid no heed to our warning.* ■ **pay one's respects (to sb)** (औप) आदरपूर्वक किसी से भेंट करना **pay sb back (for sth)** पलटकर वैसा ही कु-आचरण करना या दंडित करना **pay sb off** 1 वेतन देकर नौकरी से बाहर निकाल देना 2 रिश्वत देना **pay sth back** वापस लौटाना **pay sth off** ऋण चुकाना **pay the price for sth** पर्याप्त हानि उठाकर कुछ पाना **pay through the nose (for sth)** (अनौप) किसी वस्तु आदि के लिए अत्यधिक भुगतान करना : *You'll pay through the nose for a house in that area.* ▸ **payable** / 'पेअबल् / *adj* देय **payee** *noun* प्राप्तकर्ता, प्रापी।

pay[2] / पे / *noun* वेतन/मज़दूरी।

payment / 'पेमन्ट् / *noun* **payment**

(for sth) 1 भुगतान क्रिया, अदायगी 2 भुगतान की राशि 3 [*sing*] पुरस्कार।

pea / पी / *noun* मटर।

peace / पीस् / *noun* 1 शांति : *peace negotiations* 2 नीरवता : *disturb the peace* 3 सामंजस्य एवं मित्रतापूर्ण वातावरण : *be at peace with the world.*

peaceable / 'पीसबल् / *adj* 1 शांतिपूर्ण 2 शांतिप्रिय : *a peaceable temperament.*

peaceful / 'पीस्फ़ुल् / *adj* 1 शांतिप्रिय 2 शांत, नीरव, शांतिपूर्ण : *peaceful aims.*

peach / पीच् / *noun* 1 आड़ू 2 गुलाबी-नारंगी रंग।

peacock / 'पीकॉक् / *noun* मोर।

peak[1] / पीक् / *noun* 1 चोटी (विशेषत: पहाड़ की) 2 (प्राय: *sing*) तीव्रता, महत्त्व या प्राप्ति का सर्वोच्च शिखर : *She's at the peak of her career.* 3 चोटी की तरह संरचना।

peak[2] / पीक् / *verb* शीर्ष स्थिति/पराकाष्ठा पर पहुँचना : *Demand for electricity peaks in the early evening.*

peal / पील् / *noun* 1 **peal (of sth)** एकदम से होने वाली ज़ोरों की आवाज़ : *a peal of thunder/laughter* 2 घंटानाद, घनघनाहट : *A peal of bells rang out.* ▸ **peal** *verb* **peal (out)** ज़ोर की आवाज़ होना/करना; घंटानाद करना।

peanut / 'पीनट् / *noun* 1 (**groundnut** भी) मूँगफली 2 **peanuts** [*pl*] (अनौप) बहुत ही कम धनराशि : *work for peanuts.*

pear / पेअर् / *noun* नाशपाती (फल/पेड़)।

pearl / पर्ल् / *noun* 1 मोती, मुक्ता 2 मोती के रंग/आकृति की वस्तु : *pearls of dew on the grass* 3 अत्यंत बहुमूल्य वस्तु : *pearls of wisdom.*

peasant / 'पेज़न्ट् / *noun* 1 (पूर्व समय में) ग़रीब किसान, खेतिहर 2 (अनौप) अभद्र या अज्ञानी व्यक्ति ▸ **peasantry** *noun* किसान-वर्ग।

peat / पीट् / noun सड़े-गले पौधों से बना काला/भूरा मुलायम पदार्थ जो जलाने या ज़मीन को उपजाऊ बनाने के काम आता है।

pebble / पेब्ल् / noun (समुद्र या नदी के किनारे का) चिकना और कुछ गोलाकार कंकड़।

peck / पेक् / verb 1 peck (at sth) (चिड़ियों का) चोंच मारना; चुगना; चोंच मार कर छेद करना : The birds have pecked a hole in the sack. 2 peck sb (on sth) (अनौप) हलके-से जल्दी चुंबन करना ■ peck at sth (अनौप) भूख न होने पर बहुत थोड़ा-थोड़ा खाना, टूँगना ▸ peck noun 1 चोंच का प्रहार 2 (अनौप) जल्दी में हलका-सा चुंबन।

peculiar / पि'क्यूलिअर् / adj 1 अद्भुत, विशेषकर अप्रिय ढंग से; सामान्य से भिन्न/ अनोखा : a peculiar taste 2 (अप्र या औप) विशिष्ट/विशेष : his own peculiar way of doing things 3 peculiar to sb/sth विलक्षण, व्यक्तिगत विशेषता से संबद्ध : an accent peculiar to this region ▸ peculiarity / पि,क्यूलि'ऐर-टि / noun (pl peculiarities) 1 विशेषता 2 अनूठापन 3 विलक्षणता : a peculiarity of this disease peculiarly adv 1 अद्भुत तरीक़े से 2 सामान्य से ज़्यादा, विशेषत:।

pedagogue / पेडगॉग् / noun (अप्र या औप) शिक्षक ▸ pedagogy / पेडगॉजि / noun शिक्षण की विधि एवं शैली का अध्ययन pedagogic (pedagogical भी) adj.

pedal / पेड्ल् / noun 1 (साइकिल/कार का) पेडल जिस पर पैर रखकर चलाते हैं 2 वाद्ययंत्रों (जैसे पियानो, आर्गन आदि) के स्वर को नियंत्रित करने का पेडल ▸ pedal verb (-ll-; US -l-) भी) पेडल चलाना; पेडल से मशीन चलाना/नियंत्रित करना।

pedantic / पि'डैन्टिक् / adj (अपमा) अति पांडित्यपूर्ण, पंडिताऊ : a pedantic insistence on the rules.

peddle / पेड्ल् / verb peddle sth (to sb) 1 फेरी लगाना, घर-घर जा कर पुकारते हुए सामान बेचना : peddle one's wares 2 कोई विचार/अफ़वाह फैलाना : peddle malicious gossip ▸ peddler / पेड-लर् / noun 1 अवैध नशीली दवा बेचने वाला व्यक्ति 2 (US) फेरी वाला।

pedestal / पेडिस्ट्ल् / noun खंभे का आधार, मंचिका; मूर्ति की मंचिका।

pedestrian / पडेस्ट्रिअन् / noun (सड़क पर) पैदल चलने वाला ▸ pedestrian adj 1 पैदल चलने वालों का/के लिए : a pedestrian walkway 2 सुस्त; उत्साह-/कल्पना-रहित : a pedestrian description of events.

pedigree / पेडिग्री / noun 1 पशुओं की नसल का आधिकारिक लेखा-जोखा 2 (व्यक्ति की) वंशावली : proud of his long pedigree ▸ pedigree adj (पशु की) चुनिंदा नसल से।

pedlar (US peddler) / पेड्लर् / noun (विशेषत: पूर्व समय में) फेरी वाला।

pee / पी / verb (pt, pp peed) (अनौप) पेशाब करना।

peek / पीक् / verb peek (at sth) झाँकना : peek over the fence ▸ peek noun [sing] peek (at sb/sth) ताक-झाँक।

peel / पील् / verb 1 peel sth (for sb) फल आदि छीलना 2 peel (sth) away/off सतह पर से कुछ उतर जाना/उतार देना : peel away the outer layer 3 peel (off) (ऊपरी परत आदि का) छोटे टुकड़ों में झड़ना 4 किसी सतह का छोटी पट्टियों में उतरना : The walls have begun to peel. ▸ peel noun फल/तरकारी का छिलका peeler noun छीलने वाला चाकू आदि peelings / पीलिङ्ज़् / noun [pl] छीलन : potato/orange peelings.

peep / पीप् / verb 1 peep (at sth) चुपके से झाँकना : peep at a secret document 2 (प्रकाश का) छोटे-से झरोखे में से

आना 3 धीरे-धीरे उभरना/निकलना : *green shoots peeping through the soil.* ▸ **peep** *noun* [*sing*] चुपके-से ताक-झाँक।

peer¹ / पिअर् / *noun* 1 (प्रायः *pl*) समान वर्ग, पद या योग्यता का व्यक्ति; समान उम्र का व्यक्ति : *gain the respect of one's peers* 2 (*fem* **peeress** / 'पिअरेस् /) (ग्रेट ब्रिटेन में) हाउस ऑफ़ लॉर्ड्स में बैठने के अधिकार वाला व्यक्ति, पिअर ▸ **peerage** / 'पिअरिज् / *noun* 1 पिअर (एक वर्ग रूप में) 2 पिअर का पद **peerless** *adj* अद्वितीय, अनुपम : *a peerless performance.*

peer² / पिअर् / *verb* peer (at sth/sb) आँखें गड़ा कर देखना : *peer into the mist.*

peeved / पीव्ड् / *adj* peeved (about sth) (*अनौप*) नाराज़, परेशान ▸ **peevish** / 'पीविश् / *adj* चिड़चिड़ा, बद-मिज़ाज।

peg¹ / पेग् / *noun* खूँटी; (कपड़ों की) चिमटी ■ **a peg to hang sth on** कुछ करने के लिए कारण, बहाना या अवसर **a square peg (in a round hole)** अपने पद पर असंगत व्यक्ति।

peg² / पेग् / *verb* (-gg-) 1 खूँटियों से जकड़ना 2 peg sth (at sth) मूल्यों को एक निश्चित स्तर पर स्थिर करना, मूल्यवृद्धि रोकना : *pay increases were pegged at five per cent* 3 peg sb (as sth) (*US अनौप*) किसी को कोई नाम-विशेष देना/वर्ग में रख देना ■ **peg sth out** खूँटियों द्वारा भूमि पर चिह्न लगाना।

pelican / 'पेलिकन् / *noun* पेलिकन (जल में रहने वाला पक्षी जिसकी चोंच के नीचे भोजन-संग्रह के लिए एक थैली लटकती रहती है)।

pellet / 'पेलिट् / *noun* 1 छर्रा, गोली 2 काग़ज़ या अन्य वस्तु का गोला।

pell-mell / पेल् 'मेल् / *adv* हड़बड़ी के कारण अव्यवस्थित रूप से : *The children rushed pell-mell down the stairs.*

pelt / पेल्ट् / *verb* 1 **pelt sb (with sth)** (ईंट-पत्थरों की बौछार से) हमला करना : *pelt sb with snowballs/stones* 2 **pelt (down)** (बारिश आदि का मूसलाधार) बरसना 3 किसी एक दिशा में तेज़ी से दौड़ना : *pelting down the hill.*

pelvis / 'पेल्विस् / *noun* मेरुदंड के निचले सिरे पर चौड़ा वक्राकार अस्थि-ढाँचा (श्रोणि स्थल) ▸ **pelvic** *adj* श्रोणीय।

pen¹ / पेन् / *noun* 1 पेन, क़लम 2 [*sing*] (साहि) लेखन कार्य : *He lives by his pen.* ▸ **pen** *verb* (-nn-) (*औप*) (पत्र आदि) लिखना **penfriend** / 'पेन्फ्रेन्ड् / (**pen pal** भी) *noun* बिना आमना-सामना हुए केवल पत्रों के आदान-प्रदान से बना मित्र।

pen² / पेन् / *noun* जानवरों का बाड़ा : *a sheep pen* ▸ **pen** *verb* (-nn-) pen sb/sth (in/up) जानवर/व्यक्ति को (बाड़े में) बंद करना।

penal / 'पीनल् / *adj* 1 विशेषकर क़ानूनी दंड या सज़ा से संबद्ध : *penal laws/ reforms* 2 अति कठोर दंड दिया जाना : *penal taxation* 3 जिसके लिए क़ानून में सज़ा का प्रावधान है : *penal offence.*

penalize, -ise / 'पीनलाइज़् / *verb* 1 **penalize sb (for sth)** किसी को क़ानूनन सज़ा देना/कार्य को दंडनीय बनाना 2 किसी खिलाड़ी को नियमभंग का दंड देना (कुछ अंक काट कर या अन्य ढंग से) : *Persistent foul play will be severely penalized.* 3 किसी को ग़लत ढंग से विपरीत परिस्थितियों में ला खड़ा करना।

penalty / 'पेनल्टि / *noun* (*pl* **penalties**) 1 penalty (for sth) दंड/सज़ा 2 क्रिया या स्थिति के कारण उत्पन्न हानि या असुविधा 3 खेल-कूद में पेनल्टी : *The referee awarded a penalty (kick) to the home team.*

penance / 'पेनन्स् / *noun* penance (for sth) प्रायश्चित; तपस्या : *do penance for one's sins.*

pence / पेन्स् / *noun* **penny** का बहुवचन।

pencil / ˈपेन्स्ल् / noun पेंसिल; पेंसिल की लिखाई : *Pencil rubs out easily.* ▸ **pencil** verb (-II-; US -I-) पेंसिल से लिखना/चित्र बनाना **pencil-case** noun पेंसिल आदि रखने का डिब्बा **pencil-sharpener** noun पेंसिल तेज़ करने का उपकरण।

pendant / ˈपेन्डन्ट् / noun गले की चेन में लटकने वाला छोटा आभूषण, पेंडेंट।

pending / ˈपेन्डिङ् / adj (औप) 1 विचाराधीन, निर्णयाधीन 2 शीघ्र घटित होने वाला : *A decision on this matter is pending.* ▸ **pending** prep (औप) तक, के समय : *She was held in custody pending trial.*

pendulum / ˈपेन्ड्यलम् / noun 1 पेंडुलम, घड़ी का लोलक 2 एक स्थिति से उसकी विपरीत स्थिति में लगातार बदलाव : *The pendulum of public opinion has swung dramatically.*

penetrate / ˈपेनिट्रेट् / verb 1 **penetrate (into/through)** sth प्रवेश करना, घुसना 2 किसी चीज़ के आर-पार/अंदर देखना : *Our eyes could not penetrate the darkness.* 3 अति कठिन या छिपी हुई बात का रहस्य या मर्म समझना : *He seemed to be able to penetrate my thoughts.* ▸ **penetrating** adj 1 तुरंत स्पष्टतया मर्म समझने वाला, तीक्ष्णबुद्धि : *a penetrating mind* 2 (आवाज़ या ध्वनि) कर्णभेदी, बेधने वाली **penetration** / ˈपेनिˈट्रेश्न् / noun 1 प्रवेश करना 2 रहस्य या मर्म समझना।

penguin / ˈपेङ्ग्विन् / noun पेंग्विन, दक्षिणी ध्रुवप्रदेश में पाया जाने वाला जल-पक्षी जो उड़ नहीं पाता है।

penicillin / ˈपेनिˈसिलिन् / noun पेनिसिलीन, एक विशेष औषधि।

peninsula / पˈनिन्स्यला / noun (भूगोल) प्रायद्वीप (जैसे इटली/भारत का दक्षिणी प्रदेश जो तीन तरफ़ से जल से घिरा हुआ है) ▸ **peninsular** adj.

penitent / ˈपेनिटन्ट् / adj (औप) पश्चाताप पूर्ण : *a penitent sinner* ▸ **penitent** noun पश्चाताप करने वाला व्यक्ति।

penitentiary / ˈपेनिˈटेन्शरि / noun (pl **penitentiaries**) (US) कारागार।

penknife / ˈपेन्नाइफ़् / noun (pl **penknives**) छोटा जेब का चाकू।

penniless / ˈपेनिलस् / adj अति निर्धन, कंगाल।

penny / ˈपेनि / noun (pl **pennies** / ˈपेनिज़् / या **pence** / पेन्स् /) 1 (संक्षि p) ब्रिटिश सिक्का जो एक पाउंड में सौ की मात्रा में होता है 2 (संक्षि d) पूर्व समय का ब्रिटिश सिक्का जो एक शिलिंग में 12 की मात्रा में होता था।

pension / ˈपेन्श्न् / noun पेंशन, नौकरी समाप्ति के बाद का विशेष वेतन।

pensive / ˈपेन्सिव् / adj विचार-मग्न, विशेषकर दुखी या गंभीर ढंग से : *a pensive expression* ▸ **pensively** adv.

pentagon / ˈपेन्टग्न्; US ˈपेन्टगॉन् / noun (ज्यामिति) पंचभुज ▸ **pentagonal** adj.

penthouse / ˈपेन्ट्हाउस् / noun बहु-मंज़िला भवन का सबसे ऊपर वाला मकान जो सबसे अच्छा माना जाता है।

pent up / ˌपेन्ट् ˈअप् / adj (भाव, आवेश आदि) बंद, जो व्यक्त न किए जा सकें : *pent up anger/energy.*

penultimate / पेन् ˈअल्टिमट् / adj आख़िरी से पहले वाला, उपांत्य।

penury / ˈपेन्यरि / noun (औप) ग़रीबी, दरिद्रता : *living in penury.*

people / ˈपीप्ल् / noun 1 [pl] आम लोग, पुरुष और स्त्रियाँ : *streets crowded with people* 2 प्रजाति, राष्ट्र : *the English-speaking peoples* 3 [pl] किसी जाति या राष्ट्र के सभी लोग : *the French/Russian people* 4 **the people** [pl] देश के नागरिक (शासकों के विपरीत); आम जनता 5 [pl] (अनौप) व्यक्ति के अपने सगे-संबंधी : *She's spending Christmas with her people.*

▶ **people** *verb* people sth (with sth) लोगों से कोई क्षेत्र भरना; लोगों को क्षेत्र में रखना/बसाना : *a village peopled by hardy seafolk.*

pepper / 'पेपर् / *noun* 1 गोल या काली मिर्च 2 शिमला मिर्च ▶ **pepper** *verb* 1 (खाने में) मिर्च डालना 2 pepper sb/ sth with sth बौछार करना : *The wall had been peppered with bullets.* **peppery** *adj* 1 मिर्च के कारण तीखा 2 चिड़चिड़ा, क्रोधी।

peppermint / 'पेपरमिन्ट् / *noun* एक प्रकार का पुदीना; इससे बनी मीठी गोली, पेपरमिंट।

pep talk / 'पेप् टॉक / *noun* (अनौप) प्रोत्साहन/उत्साह/मनोबल बढ़ाने वाला भाषण।

per / पर् / *prep* (क़ीमत, दर आदि व्यक्त करने में) प्रत्येक के लिए; प्रत्येक में : *Rs 60 per day ○ Rs 10 per person* ■ **as per** sth (अनौप) के अनुसार : *work done as per instructions.*

perceive / पर्'सीव् / *verb* 1 (औप) अनुभव करना, देखना : *I perceived a change in his behaviour.* 2 **perceive sth (as sth)** किसी ख़ास ढंग से समझना/अर्थ निकालना : *I perceived his comment as a challenge.*

per cent (*US* **percent**) / पर्'सेन्ट् / *adj, adv, noun* प्रतिशत % : *a fifty per cent increase in price ○ working twenty per cent harder ○ Over sixty per cent of all families own/owns a television.*

percentage / पर्'सेन्टिज् / *noun* प्रति-शतता।

perceptible / पर्'सेप्टब्ल् / *adj* **perceptible (to sb)** (औप) 1 इंद्रियगोचर : *perceptible smell* 2 इतना बड़ा कि स्पष्ट नज़र आए ▶ **perceptibly** *adv.*

perception / पर्'सेप्श्न् / *noun* (औप) 1 देखने, सोचने, समझने की योग्यता, प्रत्यक्ष ज्ञान/बोध 2 सामान्य से अधिक गहराई से जानने की क्षमता 3 देखने, समझने का ढंग; दृष्टिकोण : *Our perceptions of the world around us are constantly changing.*

perceptive / पर्'सेप्टिव् / *adj* 1 सूक्ष्म दृष्टि/समझ वाला 2 समझने/परखने में तेज़।

perch / पर्च् / *noun* 1 चिड़ियों का अड्डा; डंडा जिस पर चिड़िया बैठती है 2 (अनौप) उच्च स्थिति/ऊँची जगह ▶ **perch** *verb* **perch (on sth)** 1 (चिड़िया का) शाखा आदि पर बैठना 2 **perch (on sth)** (व्यक्ति का) ऊँची/संकरी जगह टिकना/बैठना।

percolate / 'पर्कलेट् / *verb* **percolate (through sth)/percolate (through)** (गैस, तरल पदार्थ का) धीरे–धीरे रिसना या छनना : *Water has percolated through the rocks.* ▶ **percolator** *noun* स्रावकयंत्र।

percussion / पर्'कश्न् / *noun* वाद्य-यंत्र जो छड़ी मार कर, पीट कर बजाए जाते हैं।

peremptory / प'रेम्प्टरि / *adj* (औप, विशेषत: *अपमा*) (व्यक्ति का व्यवहार आदि) तुरंत ध्यान एवं आदेश का पालन करने की अपेक्षा रखने वाला : *a peremptory summons/tone of voice.*

perennial / प'रेनिअल् / *adj* लगातार/बार-बार होने वाला; चिरस्थायी।

perfect¹ / 'पर्फ़िक्ट् / *adj* 1 परिपूर्ण, दोषरहित : *an absolutely perfect set of teeth* 2 सबसे अच्छा; अति उत्तम : *That was a perfect evening.* 3 **perfect (for sb/sth)** सर्वथा उचित, सर्वो-त्तम 4 (अनौप) पूरा-पूरा : *perfect nonsense* ▶ **perfect** *noun* the per-fect [*sing*] (व्या) पूर्ण काल **perfectly** *adv* 1 दोषरहित ढंग से, सर्वथा उचित रीति से 2 पूर्णत:।

perfect² / पर्'फ़ेक्ट् / *verb* सर्वांगपूर्ण/पूर्ण बनाना : *perfect an art.*

perfection / पर्'फ़ेक्श्न् / *noun* 1 पूर्णता; उच्चतम संभव स्थिति/गुण : *Her* *singing was perfection itself.* 2 पूर्ण बनाने के लिए सुधार की प्रक्रिया ▶ **perfectionist** *noun* पूर्णतावादी।

perforate / 'परफ़रेट् / *verb* छोटे-छोटे छेद करना : *perforated bricks* ▶ **perforation** *noun* छोटे-छोटे छेद (काग़ज़ आदि में)।

perform / परˈफ़ॉर्म / *verb* 1 कुछ कार्य करना; निर्देशित या नियत कार्य करना : *perform a miracle/a remarkable feat* 2 आधिकारिक रूप से काम करना, संचालन करना : *perform a ceremony/ rite* 3 (नाटक का) अभिनय करना, संगीत का प्रदर्शन करना, तमाशा दिखाना : *perform somersaults* 4 काम करना, क्रियाशील होना : *How is the new car performing?* ▶ **performer** *noun* प्रदर्शन/तमाशा/कार्य करने वाला।

performance / परˈफ़ॉर्मन्स / *noun* 1 किसी कार्य का निष्पादन 2 अभिनय/प्रदर्शन (का ढंग/तरीक़ा) 3 ठीक प्रकार से कार्य करने आदि की योग्यता : *high performance cables.*

perfume / 'परफ़्यूम; *US* परˈफ़्यूम / *noun* 1 इत्र, सुगंधित द्रव 2 सुगंध : *the fragrant perfume of the flowers* ▶ **perfume** *verb* 1 इत्र लगाना 2 सुगंध देना/ सुगंधित बनाना : *Roses perfumed the air.*

perhaps / परˈहैप्स; प्रैप्स / *adv* 1 संभवत: : *Perhaps the weather will change tomorrow.* 2 कदाचित्; शायद : *It is, perhaps, the best known of his works.* 3 (शिष्ट अनुरोध के लिए प्रयुक्त) : *Perhaps you'd like some tea.*

peril / 'पेरल् / *noun* (साहि या औप) 1 गंभीर संकट/ख़तरा : *be in dire peril* 2 (प्राय: *pl*) ख़तरनाक परिस्थिति : *a book warning of the perils of drug abuse* ▶ **perilous** *adj.*

perimeter / पˈरिमिटर् / *noun* 1 परिधि,

परिमिति 2 *(ज्यामिति)* किसी आकृति की बाहरी सीमा की लंबाई।

period / 'पिअरिअड् / *noun* 1 समय की अवधि; मियाद : *This offer is available for a limited period only.* 2 युग, काल : *during the period of the French Revolution* 3 (स्कूल में) पाठ समय 4 स्त्रियों का मासिक रज: स्राव : *period pains* 5 पूर्ण विराम।

periodic / 'पिअरिˈऑडिक् / (**periodical** भी) *adj* नियमित अवधि के बाद पुन: आने/ होने वाला, आवर्ती (साप्ताहिक, मासिक आदि)।

periodical / ,पिअरिˈऑडिकल् / *noun* (औप) साप्ताहिक/मासिक पत्रिका।

periphery / पˈरिफ़रि / *noun* (*pl* **peripheries**) (औप) (प्राय: *sing*) 1 किसी क्षेत्र की सीमा, किनारा : *industrial development on the northern periphery of the town* 2 किसी सामाजिक, राजनीतिक आदि गुट की सीमा के बाहरी किनारे का स्थान : *minor poets on the periphery of the movement* ▶ **peripheral** / पˈरिफ़रल् / *adj* 1 peripheral (to sth) कम महत्त्वपूर्ण : *Fundraising is peripheral to their main activities.* 2 सीमा/किनारे पर : *peripheral zones* 3 (यंत्र, उपकरण आदि) कंप्यूटर से जुड़ा हुआ और इस्तेमाल किया जाने वाला परंतु अनिवार्य भाग नहीं।

periscope / 'पेरिस्कोप् / *noun* पेरिस्कोप, पनडुब्बी में लगा यंत्र जिससे जल के नीचे रह कर भी समुद्र तल देखा जा सकता है।

perish / 'पेरिश् / *verb* 1 (औप या साहि) नष्ट होना या कर दिया जाना : *Thousands of people perished in the earthquake.* 2 (रबर का) गल जाना, लचीलापन खो देना : *The seal on the bottle has perished.* ▶ **perishable** *adj* आसानी से सड़ने या ख़राब होने वाला (सामान)।

perjure / 'परजर् / *verb* **perjure oneself** *(क़ानून)* (विशेषत: कचहरी में) सच

बोलने की क़सम खा कर भी झूठा बयान देना : *Several witnesses perjured themselves in order to protect the accused.*

perjury / 'परजरि / *noun* (क़ानून) (विशेषत: कचहरी में) सच बोलने की क़सम खा कर भी झूठ बोलने का अपराध।

perk¹ / पर्क / *noun* (अनौप) (प्राय: pl) 1 कर्मचारी को धन या सामान के रूप में मिलने वाला भत्ता 2 किसी नौकरी से जुड़े अतिरिक्त लाभ (→ perquisite देखिए)।

perk² / पर्क / *verb* ■ **perk up** (अनौप) (बीमारी या शोकग्रस्तता के बाद) प्रसन्न एवं प्रफुल्लित होना **perk sb/sth up** (अनौप) 1 किसी को और प्रफुल्लित कर देना : *A cup of coffee will perk you up.* 2 कपड़ों, कमरे या वाटिका को दिखने में और अच्छा बना देना ▸ **perky** *adj* (-ier, -iest) (अनौप) 1 प्रफुल्लित 2 अकड़ कर चलने वाला, बाँका **perkiness** *noun.*

perm / पर्म् / (और permanent wave भी) *noun* केश को लहरदार बनाने की कृत्रिम रीति ▸ **perm** *verb.*

permanence / 'पर्मनन्स् / (permanency भी) *noun* स्थायित्व, पक्कापन।

permanent / 'पर्मनन्ट् / *adj* स्थायी/चिर स्थायी : *the permanent members of the UN Security Council* ▸ **permanently** *adv.*

permeate / 'पर्मिएट् / *verb* (औप) सर्वत्र फैल जाना, व्याप्त हो जाना : *The smell of cooking permeated (through) the house.* ▸ **permeable** *adj* (तक) पारगम्य पदार्थ जिसमें से द्रव और गैस आर-पार चले जाएँ।

permissible / पर्'मिसब्ल् / *adj* (औप) अनुमतियोग्य, जिसकी अनुमति दी जाए।

permission / पर्'मिश्न् / *noun* **permission (to do sth)** अनुमति/इजाज़त : *They were refused permission to leave the country.*

permissive / पर्'मिसिव् / *adj* (प्राय: अपमा) 1 अत्यधिक स्वतंत्रता (व्यवहार की) प्रदान करने वाला : *permissive parents* 2 उच्छृंखल व्यवहार ▸ **permissiveness** *noun.*

permit / पर्'मिट् / *verb* (-tt-) (औप) 1 अनुमति देना, कुछ करने देना : *We do not permit smoking in the office.* 2 कुछ संभव बनाना : *These vents permit air to enter.* ■ **permit of sth** (औप) (विशेषकर नकारात्मक वाक्यों में) कुछ संभव स्वीकार करना/सहन करना : *The situation does not permit of any delay.* ▸ **permit** / 'पर्मिट् / *noun* परमिट, अनुज्ञापत्र।

perpendicular / ‚पर्पन्'डिक्यलर् / *adj* 1 (ज्यामिति) **perpendicular (to sth)** लंब (रेखा), दूसरी रेखा से 90° पर बनी रेखा 2 भूमि से 90° के कोण पर, सीधा खड़ा ▸ **perpendicular** *noun* 1 लंब रेखा 2 सीधी स्थिति में।

perpetrate / 'पर्पट्रेट् / *verb* (औप) अपराध या ग़लती करना ▸ **perpetration** *noun* **perpetrator** *noun* अपराधी; ग़लत काम करने वाला : *the perpetrator of a hoax.*

perpetual / पर्'पेचुअल् / *adj* 1 कभी समाप्त न होने वाला, अनंत : *live in a state of perpetual fear* 2 (अनौप) अक्सर, बार-बार घटित होने वाला : *How can I work with these perpetual interruptions?* 3 जीवनभर स्थायी ▸ **perpetually** *adv.*

perpetuate / पर्'पेचुएट् / *verb* (औप) क़ायम/बनाए रखना : *perpetuate a myth/belief* ▸ **perpetuation** *noun.*

perplex / पर्'प्लेक्स् / *verb* हैरान कर देना, चकरा देना; घबरा देना ▸ **perplexed** *adj* चकित; भ्रमित : *The audience looked perplexed.* **perplexity** / पर्'प्लेक्सटि / *noun* 1 जटिलता; भ्रम 2 जटिल वस्तु : *try to cope with the perplexities of life.*

perquisite / 'पर्क्विज़िट् / *noun* 1 (अनौप

perk भी) (विशेषत: *pl*) नियमित वेतन के अतिरिक्त मिलने वाली सुविधाएँ/लाभ : *Perquisites include the use of the company car.* 2 अपने पद के कारण मिलने वाली विशेष सुविधा/लाभ।

persecute / 'परसिक्यूट् / *verb* 1 **persecute sb (for sth)** सताना (विशेषत: जाति व धार्मिक विश्वासों के कारण) 2 (प्रश्नों आदि से) लगातार परेशान करना : *He accused the media of persecuting him and his family.* ▸ **persecution** / ˌपर्सि'क्यूश्न् / *noun* अत्याचार, उत्पीड़न **persecutor** *noun.*

persevere / ˌपर्सि'विअर् / *verb* **persevere (at/in/with sth); persevere (with sb)** कठिनाइयों के बावजूद जारी रखना/बनाए रखना : *She persevered in her efforts to win the championship.* ▸ **perseverance** / ˌपर्सि'विअरन्स् / *noun* दृढ़ता, अध्यवसाय : *show great perseverance in the face of extreme hardship* **persevering** *adj.*

persist / पर्'सिस्ट् / *verb* 1 **persist (in sth/in doing sth/with sth)** असफलता या विरोध के होते हुए भी निरंतर (कार्य) करते रहना या (विश्वास) बनाए रखना : *If you persist, you will annoy them even more.* 2 अस्तित्व बनाए रखना ▸ **persistence** *noun* 1 दृढ़ता/आग्रह 2 लगातार बना अस्तित्व **persistent** *adj* 1 आग्रही 2 लगातार बिना रुके; बार-बार घटित।

person / 'पर्सन् / *noun* (*pl* **people** या, औप प्रयोग में, **persons**) 1 व्यक्ति (पुरुष, महिला या बच्चा) : *He's just the person we need for the job.* 2 (औप या अपमा) कोई भी (अपरिचित) व्यक्ति 3 (व्या) पुरुष : *first person* (उत्तम पुरुष) ○ *second person* (मध्यम पुरुष) ○ *third person* (अन्य पुरुष) ▪ **in person** स्वयं उपस्थित (रहना)।

personal / 'पर्सन्ल् / *adj* 1 व्यक्ति विशेष से संबद्ध : *personal affairs* 2 व्यक्तिगत, वैयक्तिक : *a letter marked 'Personal'* 3 स्वयंकृत, निजी : *The President made a personal appearance at the event.* 4 व्यक्ति के निजी गुण; व्यक्तिगत जीवन से जुड़ी बात 5 शरीर-संबंधी : *personal hygiene* ▸ **personally** / 'पर्सन्लि / *adv* 1 स्वयं के द्वारा, न कि अन्य द्वारा : *All letters will be answered personally.* 2 व्यक्ति रूप में : *I don't know him personally, but I've read his books.* 3 अपनी ओर से (न कि समूह की ओर से) : *Personally speaking, I'm in favour of the scheme.* ▪ **take sth personally** किसी चीज़ से नाराज़ होना ▸ **personal pronoun** *noun* (व्या) पुरुषवाचक सर्वनाम।

personality / ˌपर्स'नैलटि / *noun* (*pl* **personalities**) 1 व्यक्तित्व : *have an artistic personality* 2 व्यक्तिगत गुण जो किसी को विशेष और रोचक बनाते हैं 3 प्रसिद्ध व्यक्ति : *a sports personality.*

personalize, -ise / 'पर्सनलाइज़् / *verb* 1 व्यक्तिगत संबद्धता दिखाने के लिए वस्तु पर चिह्न लगाना : *handkerchiefs personalized with her initials* 2 मामले को व्यक्तिगत तूल देना : *We don't want to personalize the argument.*

personify / पर्'सॉनिफ़ाइ / *verb* (*pt, pp* **personified**) 1 (कविता आदि में) बेजान वस्तुओं को जानदार व्यक्ति की तरह व्यवहार में लाना/मनुष्य के गुण का आरोपण करना : *The sun and the moon are often personified in poetry.* 2 व्यक्ति रूप में गुण या विशेषता का उदाहरण होना : *He is kindness personified.* ▸ **personification** *noun.*

personnel / ˌपर्स'नेल् / *noun* 1 [*pl*] स्टाफ़, कार्यकर्ता-वर्ग 2 कर्मचारियों की भर्ती, कल्याण आदि से संबंधित विभाग : *work in the personnel department.*

perspective / पर्'स्पेक्टिव् / noun 1 रेखाचित्र में ऐसी चित्रण कला कि सपाट सतह पर ठोस वस्तुओं की ऊँचाई, चौड़ाई, गहराई आदि सही-सही दिखाई पड़े; परिदृश्य 2 परिप्रेक्ष्य (किसी बड़े फैले हुए क्षेत्र का दृश्य) : get a perspective of the whole valley 3 दृष्टिकोण विशेष : see things from a global perspective ■ in/into/out of perspective 1 दृश्य वस्तुओं के बीच सही/ग़लत संबंध दिखाते हुए : draw the buildings in perspective 2 संदर्भानुकूल दृष्टिकोण।

perspire / पर्'स्पाइअर् / verb (औप) पसीना आना ▸ **perspiration** / ˌपर्स्प'रेश्न् / noun पसीना।

persuade / पर्'स्वेड् / verb 1 persuade sb (into sth/doing sth) तर्क द्वारा राज़ी करना, मना लेना 2 persuade sb (of sth) (औप) क़ायल करना, विश्वास मनवा लेना : She finally persuaded us that she was telling the truth.

persuasion / पर्'स्वेश्न् / noun 1 राज़ी होने या करने की क्रिया 2 विश्वास; आस्था : people of all persuasions.

persuasive / पर्'स्वेसिव् / adj विश्वास दिलाने में समर्थ; ऐसा कि विश्वास किया जा सके।

pert / पर्ट् / adj (विशेषत: लड़की अथवा युवती) ढीठ, उद्धत : her pretty, pert face.

pertain / पर्'टेन् / verb pertain (to sth) (औप) 1 किसी से संबंधित या प्रासंगिक होना : evidence pertaining to the case 2 (विशेषत: क़ानून) किसी का हिस्सा होना : the manor and the land pertaining to it.

pertinent / 'पर्टिनन्ट् / adj pertinent (to sth) (औप) संगत, उपयुक्त ▸ **pertinence** noun.

perturb / पर्'टर्ब् / verb (औप) घबरा देना, व्याकुल कर देना ▸ **perturbation** noun.

peruse / प'रूज़् / verb (औप या परि) ध्यानपूर्वक पढ़ना : peruse a document ▸ **perusal** / प'रूज़ल् / noun : a brief perusal of the agenda.

pervade / पर्'वेड् / verb सर्वत्र फैल जाना/व्याप्त होना : The smell of flowers pervaded the house.

pervasive / पर्'वेसिव् / adj व्याप्त।

perverse / पर्'वर्स् / adj 1 (व्यक्ति, इरादा या कार्य) जानबूझ कर दुष्कर्म की तरफ़ जाने वाला/करते रहने वाला : a perverse child 2 तर्कविरुद्ध ▸ **perversity** noun.

perversion / पर्'वर्श्न्; US पर्'वर्ज़्न् / noun 1 (विशेषत: यौन-संबंधी) अस्वाभाविक और अस्वीकार्य आचरण या इच्छाएँ 2 विकार-विमुख होना (सदाचार या सुविचार से) : the perversion of innocence.

pervert / पर्'वर्ट् / verb 1 नैसर्गिक प्रकृति या प्रयोग से हटा देना : pervert the truth 2 (व्यक्ति, विचार को) सदाचार या सुविचार से विमुख करना : pervert (the mind of) a child ▸ **pervert** / 'पर्वर्ट् / noun (अपमा) दुराचारी व्यक्ति।

pessimism / 'पेसिमिज़म् / noun निराशावादिता (हमेशा इसी आशंका से चिंतित रहना कि बहुत बुरा होगा) ▸ **pessimist** / 'पेसिमिस्ट् / noun निराशावादी व्यक्ति : It's easy to sell insurance to a pessimist. **pessimistic** adj.

pest / पेस्ट् / noun 1 फ़सलों, पौधों, खाद्य पदार्थों को हानि पहुँचाने वाले कीड़े-मकोड़े/पशु-पक्षी 2 (अनौप) चिढ़ पैदा करने वाला व्यक्ति।

pester / 'पेस्टर् / verb pester sb (for sth); pester sb (with sth) सताना; बार-बार के अनुरोध आदि से परेशान करना : Beggars pestered him for money.

pesticide / 'पेस्टिसाइड् / noun कीटनाशक दवा।

pestilence / 'पेस्टिलन्स् / noun (प्रा) महामारी, छूत का रोग।

pet / पेट् / noun 1 पालतू (प्राणी) : pet dog 2 (प्राय: अपमा) दुलारा व्यक्ति : She's teacher's pet. 3 विशेष ध्यान दी जाने वाली वस्तु या विषय : Once he starts talking about censorship you can't stop him—it's his pet subject. ▶ pet verb (-tt-) दुलार करना; प्यार करना pet name noun प्यार का (घरेलू) नाम।

petal / 'पेटल् / noun फूल की पँखड़ी/ दल : a flower with five petals.

peter / 'पीटर् / verb ■ peter out शनै:-शनै: समाप्त हो जाना : The path petered out at the edge of the wood.

petite / प'टीट् / adj (लड़की या स्त्री) कद में छोटी व आकर्षक देह यष्टि।

petition / पि'टिशन् / noun petition (to sb) 1 औपचारिक अर्जी : a petition for tighter safety standards 2 (क़ानून) न्यायालय में प्रस्तुत याचिका; प्रार्थना ▶ petition verb petition for/against sth; petition sb (for sth) अर्जी/याचिका प्रस्तुत करना; प्रार्थना करना।

petrify / 'पेट्रिफ़ाइ / verb (pt, pp petrified) 1 (भयभीत होकर) स्तब्ध हो जाना/ कर देना 2 पथरा जाना/देना : petrified trees.

petrol / 'पेट्रल् / (US gasoline, gas) noun पेट्रोल ▶ petrol station (filling station, US gas station भी) noun स्थान जहाँ गाड़ियों के लिए पेट्रोल मिलता है एवं उनकी मरम्मत भी की जाती है।

petroleum / पं'ट्रोलिअम् / noun पेट्रोलियम (खनिज तेल)।

petticoat / 'पेटिकोट् / noun पेटीकोट (औरतों का अधोवस्त्र) : white lacy petticoats.

petty / 'पेटि / adj (-ier, -iest) (अपमा) 1 नगण्य, तुच्छ : petty squabbles 2 संकीर्ण विचार वाला; दुष्ट/क्रूर : a petty

desire for revenge ▶ **pettiness** noun **petty cash** noun छोटे भुगतानों के लिए धन।

pew / प्यू / noun गिरजाघर में बैठने के लिए लकड़ी की लंबी बेंच।

pewter / 'प्यूटर् / noun प्यूटर, सीसा/टिन की मिश्र धातु; इससे बने बरतन।

phantom / 'फ़ैन्टम् / noun 1 भूत-प्रेत 2 भ्रांति, कोई छलावा; काल्पनिक/अवास्तविक वस्तु (मानो सपने में देखा हो) : phantom visions created by a tormented mind.

pharmaceutical / फ़ार्म 'सूटिकल्; फ़ार्म 'स्यूटिक्ल् / adj दवाई/औषधि बनाने एवं वितरण से संबंधित ▶ **pharmaceutical** noun (प्राय: pl) (तक) दवा या औषधि।

pharmacy / 'फ़ार्मसि / noun (pl pharmacies) 1 (US drug store भी) औषधालय, दवा की दुकान 2 वह स्थान जहाँ दवाइयाँ तैयार की जाती हैं 3 दवाइयाँ एवं उनके तैयार करने की विधि का अध्ययन : be trained in pharmacy ▶ **pharmacist** noun.

phase / फ़ेज़ / noun 1 (विकास या बदलाव की) अवस्था, चरण : a phase of history 2 चंद्रमा की कला ■ in/out of phase एक समय पर एक-सी अवस्था में होना/न होना : The two sets of traffic lights were out of phase and several accidents occurred. ▶ **phase** verb क्रमिक रूप से कार्य करना/योजना बनाना : a phased withdrawal of troops ■ phase sth out धीरे-धीरे इस्तेमाल करना बंद कर देना।

pheasant / 'फ़ेज़न्ट् / noun (pl अपरिवर्तित या pheasants) चेड़, लंबी पूँछ वाला एक पक्षी जिसका किसी-किसी देश में शिकार किया जाता है।

phenomenal / फ़'नॉमिनल् / adj असाधारण; चमत्कारिक; अति उल्लेखनीय : the phenomenal success of her books

▸ **phenomenally** *adv* असाधारण रूप से/स्तर तक।

phenomenon / फ़'नॉमिनन् / *noun* (*pl* **phenomena** / फ़'नॉमिना /) 1 इंद्रियगोचर, दृश्यघटना : *natural phenomenon* 2 उल्लेखनीय व्यक्ति/वस्तु/घटना : *the phenomenon of their rapid rise to power.*

phew / प्यू / *interj* अचानक साँस छोड़ने या अंदर लेने से उत्पन्न आवाज़, विशेषत: राहत/आराम या आश्चर्य व्यक्त करने के लिए प्रयुक्त।

phial / 'फ़ाइअल / (**vial** / 'वाइअल /भी) *noun* छोटी-सी काँच की शीशी।

philanthropy / फ़ि'लैन्थ्रपि / *noun* लोकोपकार/मानव प्रेम से प्रेरित कार्य ▸ **philanthropic** *adj* : *philanthropic organizations* **philanthropist** *noun* लोकोपकारी व्यक्ति।

philately / फ़ि'लैटलि / *noun* डाक-टिकटों का संग्रह एवं उनका अध्ययन ▸ **philatelic** *adj* **philatelist** /फ़ि'लैट-लिस्ट/ *noun* डाक-टिकट संग्रह का शौक़ीन।

philology / फ़ि'लॉलजि / *noun* भाषा के विकास का अध्ययन।

philosopher / फ़'लॉसफ़र् / *noun* 1 दार्शनिक 2 दर्शनशास्त्र का अध्येता 3 (*अनौप*) व्यक्ति जो गंभीरता से सोचता हो।

philosophy / फ़'लॉसफ़ि / *noun* 1 दर्शन शास्त्र 2 सत्य/ज्ञान की खोज से जुड़े विभिन्न दर्शन : *the philosophy of the Vedantas* 3 नैतिकता/व्यवहार का निर्धारण करने वाली जीवन-दृष्टि : *free-market philosophies* ▸ **philosophical** /फ़िल 'सॉफ़िक्ल / (**philosophic** भी) *adj* 1 दर्शन-विषयक : *philosophical speculations* 2 (व्यक्ति) शांतचित्त; स्थिरबुद्धि; निस्पृह।

phlegm / फ़्लेम् / *noun* कफ़, बलग़म।

phlegmatic /फ़्लेग्'मैटिक्/ *adj* शांतचित्त, आसानी से गुस्सा न होने वाला : *a phlegmatic temperament.*

phobia / 'फ़ोबिअ / *noun* किसी चीज़ के प्रति अत्यधिक एवं अस्वाभाविक भय तथा अरुचि : *learn to control one's phobia about flying.*

phone / फ़ोन् / *noun* टेलिफ़ोन ▸ **phone** *verb* **phone** (sb) (up) फ़ोन करना **phone call** *noun* = **call²** ▸ **phone card** *noun* फ़ोन कार्ड **phone number** (**telephone number** भी) *noun* टेलि-फ़ोन नंबर।

phonetic / फ़ 'नेटिक् / *adj* 1 (भाषा ध्वनियों को लिखने की विधि संबंधित) प्रत्येक ध्वनि के लिए चिह्न प्रयोग करते हुए : *a phonetic symbol* 2 (वर्तनी) उच्चारण के अनुसार : *Spanish spelling is phonetic.* 3 मानव बोली की ध्वनियों से संबंधित ▸ **phonetics** *noun* ध्वनि विज्ञान।

phoney (**phony** भी) / 'फ़ोनि / *adj* (-ier, -iest) (*अनौप, अपमा*) 1 बहु-रूपिया (व्यक्ति) 2 (वस्तु) नक़ली (न कि असली) : *a phoney American accent.*

phosphorescent / ,फ़ॉस्फ़' रेस्न्ट् / *adj* बिना गरम किए प्रकाश उत्पन्न करने वाला (पदार्थ) ; हलका प्रकाश उत्पन्न करने वाला ▸ **phosphorescence** / ,फ़ॉस्फ़ 'रेस्न्स् / *noun.*

phosphorus / 'फ़ॉस्फ़रस् / *noun* (*प्रतीक* P) (*रसा*) फ़ासफ़ोरस (एक पीला पदार्थ जो सहज ही जलने लगता है और अंधेरे में हलका प्रकाश देता है)।

photocopy / 'फ़ोटोकॉपि / *noun* (*pl* **photocopies**) फ़ोटोकॉपी, छायाचित्र प्रति ▸ **photocopy** *verb* (*pt, pp* **photocopied**) फ़ोटोग्राफ़ी प्रक्रिया से छायाप्रति निकालना।

photograph / 'फ़ोट्ग्राफ़; *US* 'फ़ोट्ग्रैफ़ / (*अनौप* **photo** भी) *noun* फ़ोटो, छायाचित्र ▸ **photograph** *verb* छायाचित्र लेना **photographer** /फ़'टॉग्रफ़र्/ *noun* फ़ोटो-ग्राफ़र **photographic** / ,फ़ोट 'ग्रैफ़िक् / *adj* **photography** / फ़'टॉग्रफ़ि / *noun*

छायाचित्रकारी, फ़ोटोग्राफ़ी : *colour/flash/aerial photography*.

phrase / फ़्रेज़ / *noun (व्या)* पदबंध, कई शब्दों का अर्थपूर्ण समूह जो वाक्य का अंश बनता है : *'The green car' and 'at half past four' are phrases*. ▸ **phrasal verb** *noun* क्रिया पदबंध जैसे 'blow up' **phrase** *verb* शब्दों में व्यक्त करना : *phrase one's criticism carefully*.

physical / फ़िज़िकल / *adj* 1 भौतिक (आध्यात्मिक या नैतिक के वैषम्य में) : *the physical world* 2 शारीरिक : *physical strength* 3 विश्व की भौतिक रचना संबंधी : *a physical map* 4 अजीव प्राकृतिक शक्तियों/वस्तुओं से संबंधित ▸ **physically** *adv* 1 शरीर या शारीरिक गुणों से संबंधित 2 प्रकृति के नियमानुसार।

physician / फ़िज़िशन् / *noun (अप्र या औप)* डॉक्टर (विशेषत: वह जो सर्जरी नहीं करता है)।

physics / फ़िज़िक्स् / *noun* भौतिकी, भौतिक-विज्ञान ▸ **physicist** / फ़िज़िसिस्ट् / *noun* भौतिक-शास्त्री।

physiognomy / फ़िज़िऑनमि / *noun (औप)* (व्यक्ति के) चेहरे के नयन-नक्श।

physiology / फ़िज़िऑलजि / *noun* 1 शरीरक्रिया-विज्ञान (चेतन वस्तु के सामान्य प्रकार्यों का विज्ञान) 2 जीवधारियों की सामान्य प्रक्रियाओं का ढंग : *plant physiology* ▸ **physiological** *adj* शरीरक्रिया-विज्ञान-विषयक **physiologist** *noun* शरीरक्रिया विज्ञानी।

physiotherapy / फ़िज़िओ थेरपि / *noun* मालिश/व्यायाम/सेंक आदि से इलाज ▸ **physiotherapist** *noun*.

physique / फ़िज़ीक् / *noun* शरीर का गठन; डील-डौल : *a muscular physique*.

piano / पि ऐनो / *noun (pl pianos* / पि ऐनोज़ /) पियानो (वाद्ययंत्र) ▸ **pianist** / पिअनिस्ट् / *noun* पियानो-वादक।

pick[1] / पिक् / *verb* 1 छाँटना, चयन करना : *He picked his words carefully*. 2 (फूल/फल) चुनना, बीनना (वहाँ से जहाँ वे उगाए जा रहें हों) 3 **pick sth (from/off sth)** अँगुली या नाखून से कुरेदना : *pick the nuts off the top of the cake* 4 बिना चाबी के किसी अन्य तरीक़े से ताला खोल लेना (सेंधमारी करना) : *The burglars had picked the lock on the back door*. ■ **pick a fight/quarrel (with sb)** जानबूझ कर झगड़ा खड़ा कर लेना/झगड़ा मोल लेना **pick oneself up** गिर कर उठना **pick sb/sth out** औरों से विशेष रूप से चुनना **pick sb's pocket** जेब से चुपके से चुरा लेना (जेब काटना) **pick sb up** किसी को निर्धारित स्थान से (गाड़ी में) लेना : *I'll pick you up at 7 p.m.* **pick sb/sth up** (व्यक्ति/वस्तु को) पकड़ कर (नीचे से) उठाना : *He picked her child up in his arms*. **pick sth up** 1 (सुन कर या देख कर) कुछ सहज रूप से सीखना/जानना : *pick up bad habits* 2 कोई समाचार आदि अकस्मात् जानना/जान लेना **pick up** 1 बेहतर होना, सुधरना 2 पुन: आरंभ करना ▸ **pickpocket** / पिक्पॉकिट् / *noun* जेबकतरा।

pick[2] / पिक् / *noun [sing]* 1 चुनी हुई, छाँटी हुई वस्तु 2 **the pick of sth** किसी चीज़ का सर्वश्रेष्ठ नमूना/उदाहरण, चुनिंदा।

pick[3] / पिक् / (**pickaxe**, *US* **pickax** भी) *noun* गैंती, खोदनी; कुरेदने वाली वस्तु।

picket / पिकिट् / *noun* 1 निगरानी के लिए छोटी-सी टोली; हड़ताल के दौरान धरना देने और दूसरों को प्रोत्साहित करने वाले कार्यकर्ता : *men on picket duty* 2 खूँटा ▸ **picket** *verb* 1 खूँटा गाड़ना; अवरोध के लिए खूँटे खड़े करना 2 पिकेटिंग करना, धरना देना : *Some of the members did not want to picket*. **picketing** *noun*.

pickle / पिकल् / *noun* अचार : *a lime pickle* ▸ **pickle** *verb* अचार डालना : *onions pickled in vinegar*.

picnic / 'पिक्निक् / noun 1 छोटी आमोद यात्रा के दौरान खाने के लिए डिब्बे आदि में भरा भोजन 2 मौज-मस्ती के लिए छोटी यात्रा, जिसमें पैक किया हुआ भोजन साथ ले जाया जाए ▶ **picnic** verb (-ck-) पिकनिक में शामिल होना/मनाना : *They were picnicking in the woods.* **picknicker** noun.

pictorial / पिक्'टॉरिअल् / adj सचित्र; चित्रमय; चित्रों का प्रयोग करते हुए : *a pictorial account of the expedition* ▶ **pictorially** adv.

picture / 'पिक्चर् / noun 1 चित्र, तस्वीर; छायाचित्र (फ़ोटो) 2 टी वी स्क्रीन पर उभरे चित्र 3 चलचित्र, सिनेमा : *a low-budget picture* 4 यथावत् वर्णन जिससे किसी चीज़ की मन में छवि बनाई जा सके : *Her book gives a good picture of everyday life in ancient Rome.* 5 the **picture** [sing] परिदृश्य/सामान्य स्थिति : *The overall picture is unchanged.* ■ **be the picture of health, happiness, etc** (अनौप) बहुत स्वस्थ, खुश आदि दिखाई पड़ना **get the picture** (अनौप) (विशेषत: वर्णित) स्थिति को समझना ▶ **picture** verb 1 कल्पना करना; मन में छवि बनाना 2 **picture sb/sth as sth** व्यक्ति/वस्तु को किसी विशेष दृष्टि से प्रस्तुत करना 3 चित्र बनाना।

picturesque / ‚पिक्च'रेस्क् / adj 1 (स्थान/दृश्य आदि) देखने में मनोरम एवं आकर्षक 2 (भाषा) विशद् एवं सशक्त; मनोहर ▶ **picturesqueness** noun.

pie / पाइ / noun मांस या फल से बना केक, पाइ।

piece¹ / पीस् / noun 1 **piece (of sth)** ठोस पदार्थ का टुकड़ा, अंश : *a piece of chalk* 2 (प्राय: pl) हिस्से, पुरज़ें : *He took the clock to pieces.* 3 **piece of sth** एक पृथक उदाहरण : *a piece of advice/luck* 4 **piece (of sth)** (कला, कविता, संगीत आदि की) एक रचना : *a*

piece of music/poetry 5 खंड : *The vase broke into a thousand pieces.* 6 सेट (समुच्चय) में से अकेली वस्तु : *a piece of furniture/jewellery* 7 सिक्का : *a five-cent piece* ■ **a piece of cake** (अनौप) बहुत आसान चीज़ **give sb a piece of one's mind** (अनौप) किसी के अनुचित लग रहे व्यवहार पर अपने विचार सही-सही व्यक्त करना **go to pieces** (अनौप) (व्यक्ति) घबरा कर स्वयं पर संयम खो बैठना : *He went completely to pieces when they told him she was dead.* **in one piece** (अनौप) (व्यक्ति या वस्तु) सही-सलामत; विशेषत: किसी ख़तरनाक अनुभव के बाद **pick/pull/tear sb to pieces** कड़ी आलोचना करना।

piece² / पीस् / verb ■ **piece sth together** 1 जोड़ना/हिस्से मिलाना 2 बिखरे तथ्यों को एकत्र करके कहानी तैयार करना।

piecemeal / 'पीस्मील् / adv खंड-खंड करके किया गया कार्य।

pier / पिअर् / noun 1 समुद्र तट पर निकला घाट 2 लकड़ी या लोहे की ज़मीन से समुद्र में बनी संरचना जहाँ नावें रुकती है : *take the river bus from the pier* 3 (तक) खंभा/स्तंभ।

pierce / पिअर्स् / verb 1 (नुकीले औज़ार से) छेद करना, बेधना/भेदना : *The arrow pierced his shoulder.* 2 बलपूर्वक कहीं घुसना; (प्रकाश, ध्वनि आदि) जल्दी से और अचानक आर-पार होना : *Her shrieks pierced the air.* ▶ **piercing** adj 1 (ध्वनि) कर्णभेदी, कर्कश 2 (आँखें) बहुत तेज़ और गहराई तक देखने वाली, (नज़र) तीखी व सीधी : *the cold, piercing gaze of the lawyer* 3 (विचार, भाव आदि) अति तीव्र और सीधा 4 (वायु, सर्दी आदि) अति तीखी।

piety / 'पाइअटि / noun धर्मपरायणता, धार्मिकता/श्रद्धा : *put on a show of piety.*

pig / पिग् / *noun* 1 सूअर 2 *(अनौप, अपमा)* अत्यंत स्वार्थी एवं लालची व्यक्ति ▸ **piggery** *noun* सूअर का बाड़ा **pigsty** / 'पिग्स्टाइ / *noun* सूअर-बाड़ा।

pigeon / 'पिजिन् / *noun* कबूतर ▸ **pigeon-hole** *noun* पत्र आदि डालने या काग़ज़ात रखने के लिए छोटे-छोटे ख़ाने।

piggy bank / 'पिगि बैङ्क् / *noun* बच्चों की ग़ोलक।

pigheaded / ,पिग् 'हेडिड् / *adj* ज़िद्दी, अड़ियल।

piglet / 'पिग्लट् / *noun* सूअर का बच्चा।

pigment / 'पिग्मन्ट् / *noun* रंग; रंजक पदार्थ ▸ **pigmentation** *noun*.

pigtail / 'पिग्टेल् / *noun* (US **braid** भी) केश विन्यास की शैली जिसमें बाल खुले गुच्छे के रूप में बाँधे जाते हैं।

pile¹ / पाइल् / *noun* 1 ढेर/राशि, अंबार : *a pile of books* 2 *(प्रायः pl)* **piles of sth** *(अनौप)* बड़ी मात्रा या राशि ■ **make a pile** *(अनौप)* बहुत-सा धन कमाना।

pile² / पाइल् / *verb* 1 **pile sth (up)** ढेर रखना/लगाना, चीज़ों को एक के ऊपर एक डाल देना : *She piled furniture into the spare room.* 2 **pile A in (to)/ on (to) B; pile B with A** बोझ लाद देना ■ **pile it on** *(अनौप)* बढ़ा-चढ़ा कर बोलना **pile up** मात्रा में बढ़ना, जमा हो जाना : *Her debts are piling up.*

pile³ / पाइल् / *noun* बल्ली आदि जो नींव के लिए या पुल को सहारा देने के लिए ज़मीन में गाड़ी जाती है : *pile moorings.*

piles / पाइल्ज़् / **(haemorrhoids** भी) *noun* [pl] बवासीर (रोग)।

pilgrim / 'पिल्ग्रिम् / *noun* तीर्थयात्री ▸ **pilgrimage** / 'पिल्ग्रिमिज़् / *noun* तीर्थयात्रा : *make an annual pilgrimage to Benares.*

pill / पिल् / *noun* 1 दवाई की छोटी गोली 2 **the pill** *(अनौप)* महिलाओं द्वारा प्रयुक्त गर्भ-निरोधक गोली : *She's on the pill.*

■ **sugar/sweeten the pill** कम अप्रिय बनाना।

pillage / 'पिलिज़् / *noun* (औप) (विशेषतः युद्ध में सैनिकों द्वारा) लूटमार ▸ **pillage** *verb* लूटमार करना : *The town was pillaged by the invading army.*

pillar / 'पिलर् / *noun* 1 खंभा 2 **pillar of sth** प्रबल समर्थक/पक्का सदस्य; किसी तंत्र, संघ का मूल तत्त्व : *dismantling the pillars of apartheid* ■ **(go, be driven, etc) from pillar to post** बिना कुछ हासिल किए एक व्यक्ति/वस्तु से दूसरे की ओर जाना।

pillion / 'पिलिअन् / *noun* मोटर-साइकिल पर पीछे की सीट ▸ **pillion** *adv* : *ride pillion.*

pillow / 'पिलो / *noun* तकिया ▸ **pillow case** *noun* तकिए का आवरण।

pilot / 'पाइलट् / *noun* 1 पायलट, विमान-चालक 2 जहाज़ का मार्गदर्शक ▸ **pilot** *adj* प्रयोग के लिए छोटे पैमाने पर कृत (कार्य) : *a pilot project* **pilot** *verb* 1 **pilot sb/ sth (through sth)** पायलट का कार्य करना 2 योजना को प्रयोग से परखना।

pimple / 'पिम्प्ल् / *noun* त्वचा पर छोटी फुंसी।

pin¹ / पिन् / *noun* 1 पिन (आलपिन, सेफ़्टीपिन आदि) 2 लकड़ी या धातु का बहुउद्देशीय पिन, मेख : *a 2-pin electric plug* 3 हथगोले का पिन जो उसे विस्फोट से रोकता है ▸ **pins and needles** *noun* प्रायः हाथ पैर में, काफ़ी समय तक दबे रहने के कारण, झनझनाहट।

pin² / पिन् / *verb* (-nn-) **pin sth (on/to sth/sb); pin sth (together)** चीज़ों को पिन से नत्थी करना; जकड़ देना : *Pin the bills together so you don't lose them.* ■ **pin sb down** 1 पकड़ कर जकड़े रखना 2 किसी से साफ़-साफ़ इरादा व्यक्त करवाना **pin sb down (to sth/ doing sth)** किसी को कुछ करने के लिए राज़ी करना **pin sb/sth against/to/un-**

der sth हिलने-डुलने में असमर्थ कर देना
pin sth down यथार्थ निरूपण करना :
*There's something wrong with the
colour scheme but I can't quite
pin it down.* pin sth on sb किसी को
जवाबदेह बनाना ▶ pin-up noun (अनौप)
दीवार पर लगाने के लिए अभिनेता, मॉडल
आदि का चित्र।

pinafore / 'पिनफ़ॉर् / noun कपड़ों के
ऊपर पहने जाने वाला बिना बाँहों का ढीला-
ढाला वस्त्र (कपड़ों को ख़राब होने से बचाने
के लिए)।

pincer / 'पिन्सर् / noun 1 (प्राय: pl)
चिमटा/चिमटी, सँड़सी 2 केकड़े आदि के
नाखून जैसे मुड़े हुए अंग।

pinch / पिन्च् / verb 1 चुटकी से पकड़ना;
दो कड़ी वस्तुओं के बीच से पकड़ना;
चिकोटी काटना : *The door pinched
my finger as it shut.* ○ *He pinched
the child's cheek playfully.* 2 कस
कर पकड़ना 3 (जूता) कठोर या सख्त होने
के कारण दर्द करना/काटना : *These new
shoes pinch.* ▶ pinch noun 1 चुटकी,
चिकोटी 2 चुटकी भर : *Add a pinch of
salt.* ■ at a pinch (अनौप) यदि आवश्यक
है और कोई दूसरा उपाय नहीं है।

pine¹ / पाइन् / noun 1 (pine tree भी)
चीड़ का पेड़ 2 चीड़ की लकड़ी।

pine² / पाइन् / verb 1 दुख से घुलना,
विशेषत: किसी के मरने या कहीं चले जाने के
कारण 2 pine (for sb/sth) ललकना,
लालायित रहना; किसी की बहुत याद
आना : *a dog pining for its master*
■ pine away ग़म के कारण बीमार/कमज़ोर
हो जाना (मरने तक ऐसे ही रहना)।

pineapple / 'पाइन्एप्ल् / noun अनन्नास।

ping-pong / 'पिङ् पौङ् / (table tennis
भी) noun (अनौप) टेबल टेनिस का खेल।

pink / पिङ्क् / adj 1 गुलाबी 2 (अनौप)
वामपंथी राजनीतिक विचारधारा वाला ▶ pink
noun 1 गुलाबी रंग 2 एक प्रकार का फूल
■ in the pink (अनौप, परि) बहुत स्वस्थ;

बहुत अच्छा ▶ pinkish adj हलका गुलाबी
(रंग) : *pinkish tint.*

pinnacle / 'पिनक्ल् / noun 1 परा-
काष्ठा : *reach the pinnacle of one's
career* 2 भवन का शिखर/चोटी; छत पर
बनाया गया सजावटी नुकीला शिखर 3 नु-
कीली ऊँची चट्टान।

pinpoint / 'पिन्पॉइन्ट् / noun बहुत ही
छोटा क्षेत्र (पिन की नोक के बराबर)
▶ pinpoint verb लक्ष्य, कारण आदि का
ठीक-ठीक पता लगाना।

pinprick / 'पिन्प्रिक् / noun 1 पिन की
चुभन 2 छोटी या अनावश्यक किंतु परेशान
करने वाली चीज़।

pint / पाइन्ट् / noun (संक्षि pt) पिंट (नापने
का एक माप = गैलन का आठवाँ भाग—0.568
लिटर)।

pioneer / पाइअ'निअर् / noun 1 (ज्ञान,
संस्कृति के नए क्षेत्र में) अग्रणी, अगुआ :
*They were pioneers in the field of
microsurgery.* 2 किसी नई जगह का
खोजकर्ता; अन्वेषक ▶ pioneer verb
अग्रणी/अन्वेषक बनना : *She pioneered
the use of the drug.* pioneering adj
अग्रणी : *pioneering research.*

pious / 'पाइअस् / adj 1 भक्त, धर्मपरायण
2 (अपमा) पाखंडी/कर्मकांडी ▶ piously
adv.

pip¹ / पिप् / noun 1 (US seed भी) (नींबू/
सेब आदि के) छोटे बीज 2 (प्राय: pl) रेडियो
पर समय संकेत के लिए ध्वनि : *The news
will follow the pips at six o'clock.*

pip² / पिप् / verb (-pp-) (थोड़े-से बहुमत
से) पराजित करना; असफल होना : *We
didn't win the contract : we were
pipped at the post by another firm.*

pipe¹ / पाइप् / noun 1 नली/नल 2 तंबाकू
पीने वाला पाइप : *smoke a pipe* 3 वंशी,
मुरली आदि वाद्ययंत्र।

pipe² / पाइप् / verb 1 नली/नल द्वारा पानी/
गैस आदि पहुँचाना 2 तार या केबल द्वारा
संगीत प्रसारित करना 3 (चिड़िया का) गाना।

pipeline / 'पाइप्लाइन् / noun पाइपलाइन, नल तक द्रव-गैस को ले जाने वाली नलिका
■ **in the pipeline** (क़ानून, प्रस्ताव, बदलाव) बनाए जा रहे और विचाराधीन; जल्द ही अस्तित्व में आने वाले।

piper / 'पाइपर् / noun बैगपाइप को बजाने वाला।

piping / 'पाइपिङ् / noun 1 नल विशेष या नल की लंबाई : ten metres of lead piping 2 वंशी/मुरली आदि बजाना 3 वस्त्र आदि को सजाने के लिए कपड़े की मुड़ी हुई पट्टी ▸ **piping** adj सीटी जैसी ध्वनि
■ **piping hot** (द्रव पदार्थ या भोजन) बहुत गरम, उबलता हुआ।

pirate / 'पाइरट् / noun 1 (पूर्व समय में) समुद्री डाकू/जल-दस्यु 2 अवैध रूप से कुछ नक़ल करके बेचने वाला : a pirate video/tape 3 लाइसेंस के बग़ैर कार्यक्रम प्रसारित करने वाला : pirate radio stations ▸ **pirate** verb चुराना/अवैध ढंग से नक़ल करना **piracy** / 'पाइरसि / noun 1 समुद्री डकैती 2 अवैध नक़ल।

Pisces / 'पाइसीज़् / noun मीन राशि; इस राशि का व्यक्ति।

pistol / 'पिस्ट्ल् / noun पिस्तौल, तमंचा।

piston / 'पिस्टन् / noun पिस्टन (इंजन में अन्य भागों को गतिमान करने वाला भाग)।

pit¹ / पिट् / noun 1 गड्ढा : dig/ excavate a pit 2 कोयले/खनिजों आदि की खदान।

pit² / पिट् / verb (-tt-) **pit sth (with sth)** किसी सतह पर छोटे-छोटे गड्ढे बनाना : Acid has pitted the surface of the silver. ■ **pit sb/sth against sb/sth** मुक़ाबले पर खड़ा करना : pit oneself against the reigning champion.

pitch¹ / पिच् / noun 1 खेल के लिए तैयार मैदान : a football/cricket pitch 2 [sing] स्वर की ऊँचाई का स्तर : A train whistle seems to have a higher pitch as the train approaches. 3 [sing] किसी चीज़ की तीव्रता/मात्रा : a

frenetic pitch of activity 4 [sing]
pitch of sth पराकाष्ठा : This dancer's talents have reached a/the pitch of perfection. 5 ऐसा स्थान जहाँ कोई व्यापारी अपना व्यापार करता है (विशेषत: सड़क पर या बाज़ार में) 6 (तक) जहाज़ का डूबना-उतरना; हवाई-जहाज़ का ऊपर-नीचे होना 7 (तक) (विशेषत: छत की) ढाल।

pitch² / पिच् / verb 1 किसी चीज़ को निश्चित स्तर पर स्थित कर देना : pitch one's hopes high 2 (संगीत) तारत्व/ सुर पर बजाना/गाना : a low-pitched voice 3 (गेंद आदि) फेंकना 4 आगे या बाहर की तरफ़ गिरना : He suddenly pitched forward out of his seat. 5 (जहाज़ या वायुयान का) हिचकोले मारना 6 तंबू लगाना ■ **pitch for sth** (अनौप) कुछ पाने के लिए कोशिश करना : Several firms are pitching for the contract. **pitch in (with sth)** समर्थन या सहायता प्रस्तुत करना : They pitched in with contributions of money. **pitch in; pitch into sth** (अनौप) किसी कार्य/ गतिविधि में सम्मिलित हो जाना।

pitch³ / पिच् / noun कोलतार (डामर) ▸ **pitch-black** adj बहुत ही काला **pitch-dark** adj घुप्प अँधेरा।

pitcher / 'पिचर् / noun सुराही/घड़ा; जग।

pitchfork / 'पिच्फ़ॉर्क् / noun पाँचा (जिससे घास एकत्र की जाती है)।

piteous / 'पिटिअस् / adj (औप) दयनीय, करुणाजनक : a piteous cry/sight.

pitfall / 'पिट्फ़ॉल् / noun pitfall (for sb) संकट या मुश्किल, विशेषत: अनपेक्षित।

pith / पिथ् / noun 1 फल का गूदा 2 [sing] सबसे महत्त्वपूर्ण अंश : the pith of her argument ▸ **pithy** adj लघु मगर सारगर्भित।

pitiable / 'पिटिअबल् / adj 1 दयनीय, करुणाजनक 2 (अपमा) तुच्छ, अवहेलना/ घृणा का पात्र : a pitiable lack of talent.

pitiful / 'पिटिफ़्ल् / adj 1 दया उत्पन्न करने वाला : a pitiful sight 2 (अपमा) तुच्छ : pitiful excuses.

pitiless / 'पिटिलस् / adj क्रूर, निर्दय।

pittance / 'पिट्न्स् / noun (प्राय: sing) (अपमा) किसी काम के लिए बहुत थोड़ा पैसा (देना) : work all day for a pittance.

pity / 'पिटि / noun 1 pity (for sb/sth) दया/करुणा, तरस : be full of pity for starving animals 2 [sing] pity (that...) दुर्भाग्य; हलके खेद या नाराज़गी का विषय/कारण : What a pity (that) you can't come with us tonight. ▸ pity verb (pt, pp pitied) दया करना/तरस खाना।

pivot / 'पिव़ट् / noun 1 पहिये की धुरी/कीली 2 केंद्र बिंदु या सबसे महत्त्वपूर्ण व्यक्ति/वस्तु : His sculpture provides the pivot of the whole exhibition. ▸ pivot verb 1 pivot (on sth) धुरी के आधार पर घुमाना/घूमना 2 धुरी पर रखना **pivotal** adj अत्यंत महत्त्वपूर्ण, क्योंकि बाकी उस पर पूर्णत: निर्भर हैं।

pixie / 'पिक्सि / (pixy भी) noun (pl pixies) परिकथाओं में नुकीले कान वाली छोटी परी।

pizza / 'पीट्सा / noun पिज़्ज़ा, ओवन में पकी मोटी रोटी जैसी खाद्य सामग्री जिस पर टमाटर आदि लगे होते हैं।

placard / 'प्लैकाई / noun सार्वजनिक प्रदर्शन के लिए लिखी/छपी हुई सूचना (दीवार या ऊँचे स्थान पर चिपकाई हुई या डंडी पर लगाई हुई) : They carried placards saying : 'Stop racist murders!'

placate / प्ल'केट् / verb शांत करना; संतुष्ट करना : These concessions are unlikely to placate extremists. ▸ placatory adj.

place¹ / प्लेस् / noun 1 विशेष स्थान; क्षेत्र; पद 2 शहर/क़सबा/गाँव : Paris is a big place. 3 कोई विशेष भवन, कमरा आदि;

विशेष उद्देश्य के लिए प्रयुक्त भवन : We are looking for a place to eat. ○ a place of worship 4 किताब, नाटक आदि का कोई विशेष अंश 5 विशेषत: सुरक्षित स्थान (व्यक्ति/वाहन के लिए) : Four places were laid at the table. 6 (व्यक्ति का) घर, रहने की जगह : I'm looking for a place of my own. 7 (प्राय: sing) खेल-कूद/स्पर्धा आदि में स्थान : He finished in third place. 8 [sing] place (in sth) दूसरों के संबंध में किसी का स्तर, कर्तव्य या भूमिका; समाज में व्यक्ति का स्तर, कर्तव्य 9 place (for sth) किसी वस्तु का स्वाभाविक या उचित स्थान ■ in place उचित/अनुकूल स्थान पर in place of sb/sth के स्थान पर, बदले में out of place 1 उचित स्थान पर नहीं 2 किसी विशेष परिस्थिति में अनुचित/अस्वीकार्य; अस्वीकार्य : Her criticisms were quite out of place. put oneself in sb else's/sb's place अपने आप को दूसरे की परिस्थिति में देखना/सोचना take place (घटना का) घटित होना take sb's/sth's place; take the place of sb/sth बदले में जगह लेना।

place² / प्लेस् / verb 1 विशिष्ट स्थान पर कोई वस्तु (विशेषत: सावधानी से और जानबूझ कर) रखना : He placed the money on the counter. 2 place sth on sth किसी विषय पर कोई मत/विचारधारा रखना/विशेष तरीक़े से सोचना : place a high value on honesty 3 किसी के बारे में मत बनाना/निर्णय करना; वर्गीकृत करना : I would place her among the world's greatest singers. 4 (सामान मँगाने का) आदेश देना 5 place sb(in sth); place sb (with sb/sth) किसी के लिए घर, नौकरी आदि का प्रबंध करना : The agency places about 2000 secretaries a year. 6 (विशेषत: खेलों में) मुक़ाबले में विशेष स्थान आना ■ be well-placed for sth/to do sth 1 कुछ करने

के लिए अच्छी स्थिति में होना/अच्छा अवसर मिलना 2 अच्छे स्थान पर स्थित होना ▸ **placement** noun स्थापन, नियोजन।

placid / 'प्लैसिड् / adj 1 (व्यक्ति/पशु) जल्दी उत्तेजित न होने वाला 2 शांत/धीर-गंभीर : the placid waters of the lake ▸ **placidity** noun **placidly** adv.

plagiarize, -ise / 'प्लेजराइज़् / verb plagiarize sth (from sb/sth) किसी और के विचारों या शब्दों को अपना बना कर प्रयोग करना : Whole passages of the book are plagiarized. ▸ **plagiarism** noun.

plague / प्लेग् / noun 1 (the plague भी) प्लेग (महामारी) 2 plague of sth विपत्ति/कीड़े-मकोड़ों या जानवरों का बड़ी मात्रा में आना और मुसीबत खड़ी करना : a plague of locusts ▸ **plague** verb plague sb/sth (with sth) 1 किसी के लिए परेशानी खड़ी करना 2 बार-बार किसी चीज़ के लिए आग्रह करके किसी को परेशान करना : plague sb with requests for money.

plain¹ / प्लेन् / adj (-er, -est) 1 देखने, सुनने, समझने में स्पष्ट/साफ़ 2 (शब्द) सच (धोखे वाले नहीं), सीधे : The plain truth is I don't want to go. 3 सरल, साधारण, बिना फ़ैशन के : a plain but very elegant dress 4 बिना डिज़ाइन या निशान के : write on plain paper 5 साधारण, बुनियादी : You don't need any special skills for this job, just plain common sense. 6 (अपमा) (प्राय: महिला की रूप-आकृति) सादी, बहुत सुंदर नहीं ▸ **plain** adv (अनौप) स्पष्टतया; पूर्णत: : That is just plain stupid. **plain clothes** noun [pl] (विशेषत: पुलिस अधिकारियों के प्रसंग में) सामान्य लोगों के कपड़े, न कि वरदी **plainly** adv 1 स्पष्ट रूप से : He plainly ignored my advice. 2 आसानी से **plainness** noun.

plain² / प्लेन् / noun समतल भूमि (न कि ऊँची-नीची या पहाड़ी/पठारी) : the Gangetic plains.

plaintiff / 'प्लेन्टिफ़् / (complainant भी) noun (क़ानून) न्यायालय में वादी, जिसने मुक़दमा दायर किया है।

plaintive / 'प्लेन्टिव् / adj दुखपूर्ण, विशेषत: कातर, शिकायती लहजे में : a plaintive cry/voice.

plait / प्लैट् / (US braid) noun बालों की चोटी : wear one's hair in plaits ▸ **plait** verb 1 चोटी बनाना/वेणी गूँथना 2 (कपड़े में) चुनट डालना।

plan / प्लैन् / noun 1 plan (for sth/doing sth); plan (to do sth) भावी कार्यक्रम की योजना; कार्यप्रणाली : a plan to produce/for producing energy from waste material ○ a development plan 2 (मकान आदि का) नक़्शा 3 plan (for sth) (प्राय: pl) मकान/मशीन आदि का ख़ाका, नक़्शा 4 कुछ व्यवस्थित करने का ढंग : a seating plan 5 आर्थिक व्यवस्था की योजना : a pension plan ▸ **plan** verb (-nn-) 1 योजना बनाना 2 plan (for/on sth) भविष्य के लिए तैयारी करके रखना; plan (on doing sth) इरादा बनाना/रखना ◼ plan sth out पहले से ही विस्तार से सोच-विचार करना : plan out one's annual expenditure ▸ **planning** noun योजना निर्माण (की क्रिया), नियोजन।

plane¹ / प्लेन् / noun 1 हवाई जहाज़ 2 (ज्यामिति) समतल सतह 3 (विचार, अस्तित्व या विकास का) स्तर : reach a higher plane of achievement ▸ **plane** adj पूरी तरह समतल : a plane surface.

plane² / प्लेन् / noun बढ़ई का औज़ार रंदा ▸ **plane** verb रंदा करना : plane the edge of a plank.

planet / 'प्लैनिट् / noun ग्रह (मंगल, शुक्र आदि) जो सूर्य की परिक्रमा करते हैं ▸ **plan-**

etarium / ˌप्लैनि'टेअरिअम् / noun (pl **planetariums** या **planetaria**) तारा-गृह **planetary** adj.

plank / प्लैङ्क् / noun तख़्ता; पटरा।

plant[1] / प्लान्ट; US प्लैन्ट् / noun 1 पौधा 2 प्लांट, किसी औद्योगिक प्रक्रिया में प्रयुक्त मशीन आदि; संयंत्र : The firm has made a huge investment in its new plant. 3 स्थान जहाँ औद्योगिक या उत्पादन प्रणाली प्रयोग में लाई जाती है : a chemical plant.

plant[2] / प्लान्ट; US प्लैन्ट् / verb 1 plant sth (with sth) (बाग़ीचे में) पौधे लगाना 2 खेत/क्यारियों में उगने के लिए बीज बोना : plant flowers around the pool 3 किसी वस्तु को किसी स्थिति में पक्की तरह लगाना 4 plant sth (in sth) किसी के दिमाग़ में कोई विचार डाल देना/घुसा देना : plant doubts/rumours ▶ **planter** noun बाग़ान-मालिक।

plantation / प्लान्'टेश्न्; US प्लैन्'टेश्न् / noun 1 बाग़, बाग़ीचा : forestry plantations 2 चाय-बाग़ान आदि।

plaque[1] / प्लैक्; प्लाक् / noun किसी व्यक्ति/घटना की स्मृति में, उसका नाम एवं तिथि व्यक्त करती हुई प्रस्तर या धातु पट्टिका।

plaque[2] / प्लैक्; प्लैक् / noun दाँतों पर जमी हानिकार परत, जो जीवाणु को उत्पन्न होने में मदद करती है।

plaster / 'प्लास्टर; US 'प्लैस्टर / noun 1 दीवार, छत आदि पर लगाने के लिए प्लास्टर 2 (plaster of Paris भी) (शरीर की) टूटी हुई हड्डियों को जोड़ने के लिए या मूर्तियाँ बनाने में प्रयुक्त प्लास्टर 3 (sticking plaster, US Bandaid भी) छोटी चोट पर चिपकाने के लिए कपड़े, प्लास्टिक आदि की औषधि-पट्टिका ▶ **plaster** verb 1 दीवार पर प्लास्टर करना 2 plaster A with B/plaster B on(to) A गाढ़ा-गाढ़ा पोतना : hair plastered with oil.

plastic / 'प्लैस्टिक् / noun 1 (प्राय: pl) प्लास्टिक 2 **plastics** प्लास्टिक बनाने का विज्ञान 3 (अनौप) उधार पर माल आदि ख़रीदने और नियमित अंतरालों पर भुगतान कर सकने के लिए एक छोटा प्लास्टिक का कार्ड ▶ **plastic** adj 1 (वस्तुएँ) प्लास्टिक की बनी हुई : a plastic bag 2 (पदार्थ/सामान) जिसे आसानी से मोड़ा जा सके एवं आकृति दी जा सके **plastic surgery** noun जली या चोट खाई त्वचा को शल्य-क्रिया द्वारा ठीक करना या बदलना या व्यक्ति के चेहरे अथवा शरीर को शल्य-क्रिया द्वारा सुडौल एवं सुंदर बनाना।

plate[1] / प्लेट् / noun 1 प्लेट, तश्तरी; भोजन की परोसी हुई थाली/प्लेट 2 सोने या चाँदी के भोजन वाले बरतन : display the family plate 3 किसी धातु की चद्दर या पत्र : The ship's hull is made of welded steel plates. 4 (भूविज्ञान) भूसतह बनाने वाली बड़ी चट्टान की परत : the Oceanic plate 5 नाम अथवा संख्या से अंकित प्राय: लघु धातु-पट्टिका : a brass plate 6 (denture भी) नक़ली दाँत की प्लेट 7 किताब में उदाहरण के तौर पर इस्तेमाल की गई फ़ोटोग्राफ़/चित्र 8 शब्द/चित्र छापने के लिए एक विशेष धातु या प्लास्टिक की चादर।

plate[2] / प्लेट् / verb 1 plate sth (with sth) धातु की चद्दर से मढ़ना; एक धातु पर दूसरी की परत/मुलम्मा चढ़ाना : a copper tray plated with silver 2 वाहन को धातु की चद्दर से ढकना ▶ **plating** noun धातु आदि की पतली परत।

plateau / 'प्लैटो; US प्लै'टो / noun (pl **plateaux** या **plateaus** / 'प्लैटोज़ /) 1 (भूगोल) पठार 2 विकास/वृद्धि की अवधि के बाद बदलाव थम या बहुत कम हो जाने की अवस्था : Prices have now reached a plateau after a period of rapid inflation.

platform / 'प्लैट्फ़ॉर्म् / noun 1 रेलवे स्टेशन का प्लेटफ़ार्म 2 सभा-मंडप का ऊँचा चबूतरा : appear on the same platform 3 (प्राय: sing) (राज) राजनीतिक

दल का कार्यक्रम, मोरचा, घोषणा-पत्र आदि 4 (जूतों का) मोटा तलुवा : *platform soles.*

platinum / 'प्लैटिनम् / *noun* (*प्रतीक* Pt) एक रासायनिक तत्त्व जो उद्योग एवं गहने बनाने में प्रयुक्त होता है।

platonic / प्ल'टॉनिक् / *adj* दो व्यक्तियों के बीच वासनारहित प्रेम एवं मैत्री।

platoon / प्ल'टून् / *noun* सेना की छोटी टुकड़ी।

plausible / 'प्लॉज़ब्ल् / *adj* 1 (कथन, बहाना आदि) देखने में तर्कसंगत/उपयुक्त, विश्वास करने योग्य : *His story sounded perfectly plausible.* 2 (*अपमा*) (व्यक्ति) (विशेषत: धोखा देने के लिए) प्रभावकारी तर्क देने में कुशल : *a plausible liar* ▸ **plausibility** *noun.*

play[1] / प्ले / *verb* 1 **play (with sb/sth)** खेलना : *play with a toy/dog* 2 **play (sth) (on sth); play sth (to sb)** (वाद्य-यंत्र) बजाना : *play a tune on the guitar* 3 अभिनय करना 4 लहराना 5 पानी/रोशनी डालना : *play the torch beam over the walls* 6 **play sth (on sb)** मज़ाक़ करना : *play a joke/trick (on sb)* ■ **play along (with sb/sth)** किसी से सहमत होने का ढोंग करना **play on/upon sth** किसी की भावनाओं का अनुचित लाभ उठाना **play sth down** किसी चीज़ का महत्त्व कम करना।

play[2] / प्ले / *noun* 1 खेल, क्रीड़ा; खेल-कूद 2 हिलने-डुलने की गुंजाइश : *We need more play on the rope.* 3 प्रभाव : *the free play of market forces* ■ **bring sth into play** काम में लाने लगना **come into play** प्रयोग में आना शुरू हो जाना **in play** बिना गंभीरता के **play on words** श्लेष-कथन ▸ **playground** / 'प्लेग्रा-उन्ड् / *noun* क्रीड़ा-स्थल; खेल का मैदान।

play[3] / प्ले / *noun* ड्रामा, नाटक : *a radio play* ▸ **playgoer** *noun* नाटक देखने का

शौक़ीन **playwright** / 'प्लेराइट् / *noun* नाटककार।

player / 'प्लेअर् / *noun* 1 खिलाड़ी 2 (वाद्ययंत्र का) वादक 3 (*अप्र या औप*) अभिनेता।

playful / 'प्लेफ़ुल् / *adj* 1 मज़ाकिया; विनोदपूर्ण : *a playful mood* 2 खेल-खेल में किया ▸ **playfully** *adv.*

playmate / 'प्लेमेट् / *noun* खेल का साथी।

plaything / 'प्लेथ्रिड् / *noun* खिलौना।

plea / प्ली / *noun* 1 (*औप*) **plea (for sth)** निवेदन; अपील : *plea for forgiveness* 2 (*क़ानून*) न्यायालय में सफ़ाई/ दलील।

plead / प्लीड् / *verb* (*pt, pp* **pleaded**; *US* **pled** / प्ल्ड् /) 1 **plead (with sb) (for sth)** चिरौरी करना, याचना करना : *plead for mercy* 2 सफ़ाई देना या बहाना करना : *He apologized for not coming to the party, pleading pressure of work.* 3 (*क़ानून*) न्यायालय में वकालत करना; सफ़ाई प्रस्तुत करना 4 **plead (for) sth** समर्थन में तर्क/दलील देना : *plead the cause of political prisoners* ▸ **pleadingly** *adv* भावुक-तापूर्ण और विनयपूर्वक।

pleasant / 'प्लेज़न्ट् / *adj* (**-er, -est**) 1 **pleasant (to sth)** रमणीय; सुखकर 2 **pleasant (to sb)** मैत्रीपूर्ण एवं शिष्ट : *a pleasant smile* ▸ **pleasantly** *adv* **pleasantness** *noun.*

please / प्लीज़ / *verb* 1 किसी को ख़ुश प्रसन्न करना : *It's difficult to please everybody.* 2 (*औप*) चुनना; पसंद करना; चाहना : *You may stay as long as you please.* ■ **if you please** (*औप* या *अप्र*) (शिष्टाचार के लिए प्रयुक्त) : *Come this way, if you please.* ▸ **please** *interj* 1 (शिष्टाचार में अनुरोध या आदेश के लिए प्रयुक्त) : *Please come in.* 2 (*अनौप*) (कोई प्रस्ताव स्वीकार करते समय) हाँ : *'Do you want some*

help?' 'Please!' **pleasing** adj
pleasing (to sb/sth) सुखकर; रोचक :
music that is pleasing to the ear.

pleasure / 'प्लेश़र् / noun 1 सुख, संतोष
आनंद 2 सुख देने वाली वस्तु; आराम : the
pleasures of living in the country
3 (अप्र, औप) इच्छाएँ, कामना : You are
free to come and go at your pleasure. ■ **have the pleasure of sth/
doing sth** (शिष्ट अनुरोध करने, निमंत्रण
देने आदि में प्रयुक्त) : May I have the
pleasure of this dance? **with pleasure** (औप) 'आप की बात मानने में खुशी
होगी' इसकी अभिव्यक्ति में प्रयुक्त : 'May
I borrow your car?' 'Yes, with
pleasure.' ▸ **pleasurable** / 'प्लेश़र-
बल् / adj खुशी प्रदान करने वाला।

pleat / प्लीट् / noun कपड़े की चुनट
(स्थायी रूप से सिली गई) ▸ **pleat** verb
चुनट डालना **pleated** adj : a pleated
skirt.

plebiscite / 'प्लेबिसिट; 'प्लेबिसाइट् /
noun (राज) जनमत-संग्रह, (राजनीतिक
प्रश्न का) जनमत से निर्णय : hold a
plebiscite.

pledge / प्लेज् / noun 1 **pledge (to do
sth)** प्रतिज्ञा, वचन : a pledge of support 2 प्रेम, समर्थन आदि के रूप में दी वस्तु
3 बंधक; रेहन रखी वस्तु ▸ **pledge** verb
1 **pledge sth (to sb/sth); pledge sb/
oneself (to sth/do sth); pledge to
do sth/that...** कुछ देने/करने के लिए
औपचारिक रूप से वचन देना : pledge a
donation ○ The government has
pledged itself to reduce bureaucracy. 2 रेहन/घरोहर रखना : He pledged
his mother's wedding ring.

plenty / 'प्लेन्टि / pron प्रचुरता : plenty
of eggs/time ▸ **plenty** noun पर्याप्त
से अधिक, प्रचुरता की स्थिति : in times of
plenty **plentiful** / 'प्लेन्टिफ़ुल् / adj बहुत
मात्रा में।

pliable / 'प्लाइअबल् / adj 1 जो आसानी
से मुड़ या घूम सके या आकृति में ढाला जा
सके; लचीला : Cane is pliable when
wet. 2 (व्यक्ति का मस्तिष्क) आसानी से
प्रभावित होने वाला।

pliant / 'प्लाइअन्ट् / adj 1 बिना टूटे आसानी
से मुड़ने वाला : the pliant twigs of
young trees 2 (कभी-कभी अप्रिय)
आसानी से प्रभावित : a pliant husband.

pliers / 'प्लाइअर्ज़् / noun [pl] प्लायर जो
तार आदि मोड़ने, काटने के काम आता है।

plight / प्लाइट् / noun गंभीर और दुखद
दशा/स्थिति : the plight of the homeless.

plinth / प्लिन्थ् / noun पत्थर जिस पर खंभा
या मूर्ति खड़ी हो।

plod / प्लॉड् / verb (-dd-) **plod (along/
on)** भारी कदमों या कठिनाई के साथ धीरे-
धीरे चलना : Labourers plodded home
through the muddy fields. ▸ **plod-
der** noun (प्रायः अप्रिय) कोल्हू का बैल
plodding adj.

plonk / प्लॉङ्क् / verb ■ **plonk one-
self/sth (down) in/on sth** (अनौप)
ज़ोरों से पटकते हुए और अव्यवस्थित ढंग से
गिराना/रखना : He plonked the groceries on the kitchen floor and ran
upstairs.

plop / प्लॉप् / noun (प्रायः sing) छपछप
(ध्वनि)।

plot¹ / प्लॉट् / noun किसी विशेष उपयोग
के लिए अंकित छोटा भूमिखंड : a building plot ▸ **plot** verb (-tt-) **plot sth
(on sth)** चार्ट या ग्राफ़ पर कोई स्थिति
अंकित करना।

plot² / प्लॉट् / noun 1 नाटक या उपन्यास
का कथानक, कथा-वस्तु 2 **plot (to do
sth)** षड्यंत्र, कुचक्र : devise a plot to
overthrow the government ▸ **plot**
verb (-tt-) **plot (with sb) (against
sb); plot (to do sth)** षड्यंत्र/कुचक्र
रचना **plotter** noun.

plough (*US* **plow**) / प्लाउ / *noun*
1 हल, लाँगल (किसान के औज़ार) 2 **the
Plough** (*US* **the Big Dipper** भी)
[*sing*] सप्तर्षि मंडल (सात तारों का समूह
जो हलाकृति में व्यवस्थित रहते हैं) ▸ **plough**
(*US* **plow**) *verb* **plough sth (up)** हल
चलाना, जोतना ■ **plough (one's way)
through sth** 1 शक्ति लगा कर रास्ता
बनाना/आगे बढ़ना 2 मुश्किल से उन्नति
करना।

ploy / प्लॉइ / *noun* किसी का लाभ उठाने
के लिए सुनियोजित कथन या कार्य : *a
marketing ploy.*

pluck¹ / प्लक् / *verb* 1 **pluck sth (off/
out)** फल/फूल बीनना या चुनना; उखाड़ना,
नोचना : *pluck a rose from the garden ○ pluck out a grey hair* 2 पक्षी
के पंख नोचना 3 **pluck sth (from sth);
pluck (at sth)** अँगुली से पकड़ कर
खींचना : *He plucked a handkerchief
from his pocket.* 4 **pluck sb from
sth** किसी को कठिन स्थिति से बचाना
■ **pluck sth up** साहस बटोरना : *I finally
plucked up the courage to tell her.*

pluck² / प्लक् / *noun* (अनौप) साहस/
हिम्मत : *She showed a lot of pluck in
dealing with the burglars.* ▸ **plucky**
adj (-ier, -iest) साहसी।

plug / प्लग् / *noun* 1 रबड़ या धातु की छेद
बंद करने वाली डाट, प्लग 2 बिजली का प्लग
3 स्पार्क-प्लग ▸ **plug** *verb* (-gg-) प्लग
लगा कर छेद बंद करना : *plug a leak in
the roof* ■ **plug sth in** बिजली का प्लग
लगाना।

plum / प्लम् / *noun* आलूचा, आलू बुखारा
▸ **plum cake, plum pudding** *nouns.*

plumage / प्लूमिज् / *noun* चिड़ियों के
पंख।

plumb¹ / प्लम् / *verb* 1 साहुल-सूत्र प्रयोग
करके कुछ जाँचना 2 (औप या अल) कुछ
पूरी तरह समझने का प्रयास करना : *plumb
the mysteries of the universe*

■ **plumb the depths of sth** अति
गहराई/सबसे निचले हिस्से में पहुँचना : *The
film plumbs new depths of bad
taste.*

plumb² / प्लम् / *adv* बिलकुल : *plumb
in the middle.*

plumber / प्लम्बर् / *noun* नल आदि लगाने
वाला/ठीक करने वाला कारीगर।

plumbing / प्लमिङ् / *noun* 1 पानी जमा
रखने व पहुँचाने वाले नल, पाइप, टैंक आदि
2 नल के कारीगर का कार्य।

plumb-line / प्लम्लाइन / *noun* साहुल-
सूत्र, डोरी से बँधा सीसे का टुकड़ा जिससे
पानी की गहराई या दीवार की सिधाई नापी
जाती है।

plume / प्लूम / *noun* 1 पक्षी का विशेषत:
बड़ा (सजावट के लिए) पंख 2 पंखनुमा
वस्तु : *a plume of smoke* 3 सजावट के
लिए (बालों में या टोपी पर) लगाया पंख या
पंख जैसी चीज़ ▸ **plumed** *adj.*

plummet / प्लमिट् / *noun* रस्सी के छोर
पर लगाया गया वज़न ▸ **plummet** *verb*
बहुत तेज़ी से गिरना : *House prices
have plummeted in this area.*

plump¹ / प्लम्प् / *adj* 1 गोल-मटोल
(व्यक्ति या पशु) 2 मोटा (किंतु देखने में
प्रिय)।

plump² / प्लम्प् / *verb* **plump sth (up/
out)** गोल-मटोल होना या बनाना : *plump
(up) the cushions* ■ **plump (one-
self/sb/sth) down** अचानक ज़ोरों से
गिरना या गिरा देना : *plump down the
bags* **plump for sb/sth** 1 किसी के पक्ष
में निर्णय देना 2 उत्साहपूर्वक समर्थन देना।

plunder / प्लन्डर् / *verb* लूटना; (दंगों या
युद्ध में) लूटपाट करना : *plunder a
palace of its treasures* ▸ **plunder**
noun 1 लूटपाट 2 लूट का सामान : *They
loaded the carts with plunder.*

plunge / प्लन्ज् / *verb* 1 **plunge sth
in(to sth)** ताक़त के साथ कहीं कुछ
घुसाना : *plunge a rod into a blocked*

drain **2 plunge in (to sth)** छलाँग लगा कर कूदना; डुबकी लगाना : *plunge into the icy water* **3** अचानक ज़ोरों से आगे की ओर गिरना या ढकेलना : *The car plunged over the cliff.* **4** किसी विशेष स्थिति/दशा में जाना/भेजना : *The country (was) plunged into civil war after the death of its President.* ▸ **plunge** *noun* **1** (विशेषत: *sing*) अचानक तीव्र गति या गिरावट : *a plunge into debt* **2** छलाँग, गोता ■ **take the plunge** सोच-विचार के बाद साहसी एवं महत्त्वपूर्ण कदम उठाना।

plural / 'प्लुअरल् / *noun* (संक्षि pl) (व्या) बहुवचन ▸ **plural** *adj* **1** (व्या) बहुवचन **2** एक से अधिक : *a plural society.*

plus /प्लस्/ *prep* **1** और; मिला कर : *Two plus five is seven.* **2** (अनौप) और साथ ही : *We've to fit five people plus all their luggage in the car.* ▸ **plus** *adj* **1** इंगित संख्या या मात्रा से अधिक : *The work will cost Rs 10,000 plus.* **2** शून्य से अधिक : *The temperature is plus four degrees.* **plus** *noun* (pl **pluses** / 'प्लसिज़्/) **1** (गणित में प्रयुक्त) + चिह्न **2** (अनौप) अच्छा गुण; लाभ : *Knowledge of French is a plus in her job.*

plush /प्लश्/ *noun* मख़मल ▸ **plush (plushy** भी) *adj* (अनौप) अत्यंत आरामदेह और महँगा : *a plush hotel.*

Pluto / 'प्लूटो / *noun* प्लूटो ग्रह (जो सूर्य से सबसे दूर है)।

plutonium /प्लूं'टोनिअम्/ *noun* (प्रतीक **Pu**) (रसा) प्लूटोनियम, परमाणु अभिक्रिया में प्रयुक्त किरणें विकीर्ण करने वाला तत्त्व।

ply[1] /प्लाइ/ *noun* **1** लकड़ी की परत, प्लाई; कपड़े की मोटाई : *three-ply wood* **2** धागे, ऊन आदि की लड़ : *four-ply knitting wool.*

ply[2] /प्लाइ/ *verb* (pt, pp **plied** /प्ला-इड्/) **1** जहाज़, बस आदि का नियमित रूप से आना-जाना : *ferries that ply between Mumbai and Goa* **2** (औप) किसी औज़ार को काम में लाना ■ **ply one's trade** व्यापार करना, अपना काम करना **ply sb with sth 1** खाद्य पदार्थ आदि बार-बार देते रहना **2** सवालों की झड़ी लगाना।

plywood / 'प्लाइवुड् / *noun* प्लाईवुड।

p.m. /'पी'एम् / (US **P.M.**) *abbr* (लैटिन **post meridiem**) दोपहर के 12 बजे से रात के 12 बजे तक का समय।

pneumatic / न्यू'मैटिक्; US नू'मैटिक् / *adj* **1** हवा से भरा हुआ : *a pneumatic tyre* **2** दबाव के साथ भरी हवा से काम करने वाला : *a pneumatic drill.*

pneumonia / न्यू'मोनिआ; US नू'मो-निआ / *noun* निमोनिया (फेफड़ों में सूजन का रोग)।

poach[1] /पोच्/ *verb* **1** अंडे का छिलका उतार कर लगभग उबलते हुए पानी में पकाना **2** मछली, फलों आदि को थोड़े द्रव के साथ हलके ताप से पकाना।

poach[2] /पोच्/ *verb* **1** किसी की भूमि में जा कर पशु-पक्षी, मछली आदि चुरा लाना **2 poach (on sth)** किसी के क्षेत्र में अतिक्रमण करके कार्य करना; किसी के विचार, कर्मचारी आदि अपने बना लेना : *A rival computer firm poached our best programmers.* ▸ **poacher** *noun* ऐसा करने वाला व्यक्ति; शिकार-चोर।

pocket / 'पॉकिट् / *noun* **1** जेब; बक्से, कार आदि में छोटा सामान रखने के लिए जेब जैसा पात्र **2** (प्राय: *sing*) उपयोग/खर्च के लिए उपलब्ध धन **3** कोई पृथक क्षेत्र या समूह ▸ **pocket** *verb* **1** जेब में रखना **2** बेई-मानी से कुछ अपने पास रख लेना : *He was given Rs 2,000 for expenses, but pocketed most of it.* **pocketbook** *noun* **1** छोटी-सी डायरी जैसी पुस्तिका जो जेब में आ जाए **2** नोट आदि रखने के लिए बटुआ **pocket money** *noun* जेब-ख़र्च।

pod / पॉड् / noun (मटर आदि की) फली।

podium / 'पोडिअम् / noun मंच, चबूतरा।

poem / 'पोइम् / noun कविता।

poet / 'पोइट् / noun कवि।

poetic / पो'एटिक् / (**poetical** / पो'एटि-क्ल् / भी) adj काव्यात्मक; कविता-विषयक : the poetical works of Keats.

poetry /'पोअट्रि / noun काव्य; कवित्व; काव्यात्मकता : a ballet dancer with poetry in every movement.

poignant / 'पॉइन्यन्ट् / adj भावनाओं को गहराई से प्रभावित करने वाला हृदय-विदारक : a poignant scene ▸ **poignancy** noun **poignantly** adv.

point¹ / पॉइन्ट् / noun 1 नोक : the point of a pin 2 बिंदु, डॉट : a decimal point 3 (ज्यामिति) नक्शे, चित्र, ग्राफ़ आदि पर अंकित स्थिति : Lines AB and CD intersect at the point P. 4 कोई विशेष स्थान या क्षेत्र : Guards had been posted at several points around the perimeter. 5 विशेष समय या क्षण : At one point I thought she was going to refuse. 6 बदलाव या विकास की प्रक्रिया में कोई विशेष चरण : reach danger/crisis point 7 दिशासूचक कंपास के 32 बिंदु : the cardinal points 8 माप या क़ीमत की इकाई : a point on a scale 9 एक पृथक अंक जिसे दूसरे अंकों में जोड़ कर संपूर्ण स्कोर बनाया जाता है : We needed one more point to win the game. 10 कोई विशिष्ट विवरण या व्याख्या बिंदु : explain a theory point by point 11 चर्चा के दौरान कही गई विशेष बात; कोई प्रभावशाली तर्क : 'But she might not agree.' 'You've got a point there.' 12 (प्रायः **the point**) [sing] विचार बिंदु; मौलिक बात : Let's stop discussing trivial details and come/get to the point. 13 [sing] किसी चीज़ का मूल भाव, उद्देश्य, गुण आदि 14 **points** [pl] (US **switch**) रेल की

पटरी के प्वाइंट (काँटा) जिनकी स्थिति बदल कर गाड़ी का ट्रैक बदला जाता है ■ **beside the point** अप्रासंगिक, विषय से असंबद्ध **if/when it comes to the point** यदि कोई मुश्किल क़दम उठाने या निर्णय लेने का समय आएगा **make a point of doing sth** कोई कार्य महत्त्वपूर्ण या ज़रूरी होने के कारण सावधानी से करना : I make a point of checking that all the windows are shut whenever I go out. **make one's point** अपने विचार या भावनाएँ प्रस्तुत करना **the point of no return** ऐसी स्थिति कि पूर्वनिश्चित कार्य को करना ही पड़ता है और उससे पीछे नहीं हटा जा सकता **to the point** उचित एवं संबद्ध ▸ **point of view** noun (pl **points of view**) विचार, मत, दृष्टिकोण।

point² / पॉइन्ट् / verb 1 **point (at/to sb/sth)** अँगुली से इशारा करके किसी की ओर लोगों का ध्यान आकर्षित करना : It's rude to point. 2 उपकरण पर स्थिति, दशा, समय, स्तर आदि को सूचित करना : A compass needle points north. 3 **point sth (at/towards sb/sth)** निशाना लगाना/बनाना 4 किसी दिशा-विशेष की ओर होना या करना : A hedgehog's spines point backwards. ■ **point a/ the finger (at sb)** (अनौप) किसी को खुले-आम दोषी ठहराना **point sth out (to sb)** किसी चीज़ पर ध्यान केंद्रित करना : point out a mistake **point the way (to/towards sth)** भविष्य में होने वाली घटना की संभावना दर्शाना **point to sth** कुछ इंगित करना ▸ **pointed** adj 1 नुकीला 2 किसी के आचरण की ओर स्पष्ट संकेत करते हुए : a pointed comment.

point-blank / 'पॉइन्ट् 'ब्लैङ्क् / adj बहुत समीप से (गोली का निशाना बनाना); (कुछ कही हुई बात) सीधे-सीधे (प्रायः अभद्रता से) : a point-blank refusal ▸ **point-blank** adv सीधे-सीधे ढंग से; सीधे निशाना लगाते हुए।

pointer / 'पॉइन्टर् / *noun* 1 मानचित्र, रेखाचित्र आदि पर चर्चित तथ्यों को इंगित करने के लिए पतली छड़ी; डायल, स्केल आदि पर अंकों, स्थितियों को इंगित करने के लिए धातु, प्लास्टिक आदि का लंबा, पतला टुकड़ा 2 **pointer (to sth)** भविष्य में होने वाली घटनाओं को दर्शाने वाली वस्तु/बात।

pointless / 'पॉइन्ट्ल्स् / *adj* व्यर्थ, निरर्थक : *a pointless remark* ▸ **pointlessly** *adv* **pointlessness** *noun.*

poise / पॉइज़् / *verb* संतुलित या लटके रहना या रखना : *He poised the javelin in his hand before throwing it.* ▸ **poise** *noun* 1 लालित्य संतुलन 2 आत्म-विश्वास एवं लालित्यपूर्ण स्थिति : *a woman of great poise* **poised** *adj* 1 **poised (in, on, above, etc sth)** संतुलित स्थिति में 2 **poised (in/on/ above/for sth); poised (to do sth)** (व्यक्ति, पशु आदि) क्रिया के लिए तैयार : *(अलं) The party is poised to return to power.* 3 आत्म-विश्वास दिखाते हुए।

poison / 'पॉइज़न् / *noun* 1 ज़हर, विष 2 अत्यंत हानिकारक वस्तु या व्यक्ति : *the poison of racial hatred* ▸ **poison** *verb* **poison sb/sth (with sth)** 1 ज़हर देना; विष दे कर मारना 2 (नैतिक रूप से) भ्रष्ट करना; घृणा फैलाना **poisoner** *noun* **poisonous** *adj* विषाक्त।

poke / पोक् / *verb* 1 **poke sb/sth (with sth)** छड़ी या अँगुली से कोंचना, कुरेदना 2 **poke sth in sth** घोंपना, चुभाना : *Poke two holes in the sack so you can see through.* 3 **poke at sth** बार-बार धकेलना, ठेलना 4 ज़ोर से धक्का देना ■ **poke fun at sb/sth** मज़ाक़ उड़ाना।

poker[1] / 'पोकर् / *noun* धातु की कुरेदनी। **poker**[2] / 'पोकर् / *noun* ताश का एक खेल।

poky / 'पोकि / *adj* (अनौप, अपमा) (कमरा) छोटा, (कोठरी) तंग : *a poky little room.*

polar / 'पोलर् / *adj* 1 ध्रुव प्रदेशीय 2 ध्रुवीय : *polar attraction* 3 (औप या तक) बिलकुल विपरीत।

Polaroid / 'पोलरॉइड् / *noun* (ट्रेडमार्क) 1 (**Polaroid camera** भी) एक प्रकार का कैमरा जिससे खींची गई फ़ोटोग्राफ़ कुछ ही पलों में तैयार मिलती है; ऐसे कैमरे से खींची गई फ़ोटोग्राफ़ 2 धूप की चमक कम करने के लिए चश्मे, खिड़की आदि पर लगाई गई पतली पारदर्शी फ़िल्म।

pole[1] / पोल् / *noun* 1 पृथ्वी के उत्तरी एवं दक्षिणी ध्रुव 2 (भौतिकी) चुंबक के दोनों सिरे; बिजली की बैटरी के दोनों अंत्यबिंदु 3 विपरीत या एकदम भिन्न बातें : *Our points of view are at opposite poles.* ▸ **polestar** *noun* ध्रुव तारा।

pole[2] / पोल् / *noun* डंडा/लट्ठा; खंभा ▸ **pole** *verb* डंडे से (नाव आदि) धकेलना।

police / प 'लीस् / *noun* (प्राय: **the police**) पुलिस, आरक्षी ▸ **police** *verb* पुलिस द्वारा या पुलिस की तरह नियंत्रण करना, व्यवस्था बनाए रखना : *community policing* **policeman** / प 'लीस्मन् / (*pl* **policemen**; *fem* **policewoman** / प 'लीसवुमन् / *pl* **policewomen**) *noun* पुलिसमैन, पुलिस का सिपाही **police station** *noun* थाना।

policy / 'पॉलिसि / *noun* (*pl* **policies**) 1 **policy (on sth)** नीति (विशेषत: सरकार की) 2 पॉलिसी, बीमा की शर्तें एवं नियम : *a fire-insurance policy.*

polio / 'पोलिओ / (औप **poliomyelitis** / ˌपोलिओमाइ 'लाइटिस् / भी) *noun* पोलियो रोग; एक ऐसा रोग जिसमें अक्सर बच्चों के हाथ या पाँव काम करना बंद कर देते हैं/बेकार हो जाते हैं।

polish / 'पॉलिश् / *verb* 1 **polish sth (up) (with sth)** पॉलिश करना, चमकाना 2 **polish sth (up)** ठीक करके या बदल कर सुधार करना/अच्छा बनाना : *polish (up) a speech/an article* ▸ **polish** *noun* 1 पॉलिश, चमकाने वाला पदार्थ :

furniture/shoe polish 2 (पॉलिश के कारण) चिकनी सतह 3 सुरुचिपूर्ण एवं परिष्कृत आचरण शैली : *He is still young and lacks polish.* **polished** *adj* 1 चिकना, चमकदार 2 सुसंस्कृत, परिष्कृत।

polite / प'लाइट् / *adj* (-er, -est) 1 नम्र, शिष्ट 2 (औप) परिमार्जित : *a rude word not used in polite society* ▸ **politely** *adv* **politeness** *noun.*

political / प'लिटिकल् / *adj* 1 राजनीतिक; शासनिक/सरकारी : *political rights* 2 (कार्य) सरकार या राज्य के लिए हानिकर समझे जाने वाले : *a political crime* 3 (व्यक्ति) राजनीति में रुचि रखने वाला 4 (अपमा) गुट में सत्ता, प्रतिष्ठा आदि, न कि नैतिकता, से संबंधित : *I suspect that he was dismissed for political reasons.* ▸ **politically** *adv.*

politician / पॉल'टिश्न् / *noun* राज-नीतिज्ञ।

politics / 'पॉलटिक्स् / *noun* 1 राजनीति; राजनीतिक प्रश्न, समस्याएँ आदि; राजनीतिक दलों के बीच प्रतिपक्षी स्पर्धा 2 (**political science** भी) राजनीति शास्त्र : *She's reading politics at university.* 3 (अपमा) गुट या संघ में सत्ता और अधिकार से संबंधित मामले : *get involved in office politics.*

poll[1] / पोल् / *noun* 1 (**the polls** भी) चुनाव में मतदान; मत-गणना 2 जनमत सर्वेक्षण : *a public opinion poll* ▸ **poll tax** *noun* व्यक्ति कर (प्रत्येक व्यक्ति पर बराबर-बराबर लगने वाला कर)।

poll[2] / पोल् / *verb* 1 (चुनाव प्रत्याशी द्वारा) मत प्राप्त करना 2 सर्वेक्षण द्वारा लोगों की राय जानना ▸ **polling** *noun* मतदान प्रक्रिया **polling-booth** *noun* मतदान-कक्ष **polling-station** *noun* मतदान-केंद्र।

pollen / 'पॉलन् / *noun* पराग कण (फूल का)।

pollute / प'लूट् / *verb* **pollute sth** (with sth) दूषित करना, गंदा करना ▸ **pollutant** *noun* प्रदूषक पदार्थ **pollution** / प'लूश्न् / *noun* प्रदूषण; दूषित करने वाला सामान/पदार्थ : *the pollution of our beaches with oil* ○ *beaches covered with pollution.*

polo / 'पोलो / *noun* चौगान का खेल।

poly- *pref* (पूर्वपद) बहु-।

polyandry / पॉलि'ऐन्ड्रि / *noun* किसी स्त्री के एक समय पर एक से ज्यादा पति होने की प्रथा।

polyester / पॉलि'एस्टर् / *noun* कपड़े आदि बनाने के लिए एक कृत्रिम पदार्थ।

polygamy / प'लिगमि / *noun* किसी पुरुष की एक समय पर एक से ज्यादा पत्नियाँ होने की प्रथा।

polygon / 'पॉलिगन; US 'पॉलिगॉन् / *noun* (ज्यामिति) पाँच या पाँच से अधिक भुजाओं एवं कोणों वाली आकृति।

polytechnic / पॉलि'टेक्निक् / *noun* ऐसा कॉलेज जहाँ अनेक वैज्ञानिक तथा तकनीकी विषय पढ़ाए जाते हैं।

polythene / 'पॉलिथीन् / *noun* एक प्रकार का पतला प्लास्टिक।

pomp / पॉम्प् / *noun* तड़क-भड़क, ठाट-बाट/आडंबर से भरपूर प्रदर्शन।

pompous / 'पॉम्पस् / *adj* (अपमा) आडंबरपूर्ण; स्वयं को दूसरों से कहीं ज्यादा महत्त्वपूर्ण समझते हुए : *pompous language* ▸ **pomposity** *noun* आडंबर, आडंबर प्रियता : *prick sb's pomposity.*

pond / पॉन्ड् / *noun* तालाब, ताल-तलैया।

ponder / 'पॉन्डर् / *verb* **ponder (on/over sth)** विचार करना, गंभीरतापूर्वक देर तक चिंतन करना : *I am pondering how to respond.*

ponderous / 'पॉन्डरस् / *adj* 1 अधिक वज़न के कारण बहुत धीमा 2 (अपमा) (भाषण, लेखन आदि) नीरस, ऊबाऊ ▸ **ponderousness** *noun.*

pony / 'पोनि / *noun* (*pl* **ponies**) टट्टू (एक प्रकार का छोटी जाति का घोड़ा)।

pooh /पू/ *interj* ऊँह ! (तिरस्कार/अवहेलना सूचक उद्गार)।

pool[1] /पूल/ *noun* 1 पोखरा, ताल-तलैया 2 किसी सतह पर जमा पानी या अन्य द्रव पदार्थ : *After the rainstorm, there were pools on the road.* 3 (**swimming pool**) तरण ताल।

pool[2] /पूल/ *noun* 1 बहुत-से लोगों से एकत्र की गई धनराशि जैसे व्यापार, जुए आदि में 2 एकत्रित धन या संसाधन जो संबंधित लोगों को आवश्यकता के समय उपलब्ध हो जाए; आवश्यकता के समय उपलब्ध कार्य करने वाले लोगों का समूह : *a pool of doctors available for emergency work* 3 स्नूकर जैसा एक खेल ▸ **pool** *verb* (धन, संसाधन आदि) किसी सामान्य लाभ के लिए एकत्रित करना : *They pooled their savings for a holiday abroad.*

poor /पुअर/ *adj* (**-er, -est**) 1 ग़रीब, निर्धन 2 **poor in sth** गुणवत्ता या मात्रा में कम : *a country poor in minerals* 3 (अनौप) बेचारा, सहायता या सहानुभूति का पात्र : *Poor fellow, his wife has just died.* 4 (व्यक्ति) अकुशल, कम जानकारी वाला 5 सामान्य की तुलना में निम्नस्तरीय; घटिया ▸ **poor-spirited** *adj* कायर, साहसहीन।

poorly[1] /पुअर्लि/ *adv* बुरी तरह से।

poorly[2] /पुअर्लि/ *adj* (अनौप) बीमार : *You look rather poorly to me.*

pop[1] /पॉप/ *verb* (**-pp-**) 1 तड़ाक या फट्-सी आवाज़ करना (जैसे बोतल से कॉर्क निकालते समय होती है); ऐसी आवाज़ के साथ कुछ फोड़ना : *The children were popping balloons.* 2 (अनौप) आदतन (नशीली) दवा लेना : *popping pills*
■ **pop across, down, out** etc किसी विशेष दिशा में अचानक और जल्दी से आना या जाना **pop in** थोड़ी देर के लिए मिलने आना/जाना **pop off** (अनौप) मर जाना **pop up** (अनौप) अप्रत्याशित प्रकट होना :

He seems to pop up in the most unlikely places.

pop[2] /पॉप/ *noun* 1 तड़ाक या फट् जैसी ध्वनि 2 (अनौप) पॉप-संगीत और गायन।

popcorn /'पॉप्कॉर्न्/ *noun* मक्का का लावा।

pope /पोप/ *noun* पोप (रोमन कैथोलिक चर्च के सर्वोच्च धर्मगुरु)।

poplin /'पॉप्लिन्/ *noun* चमकदार सूती कपड़ा; पापलीन।

poppy /'पॉपि/ *noun* (*pl* **poppies**) खसखस।

populace /'पॉप्यलस्/ (प्राय: **the populace**) *noun* (औप) जन-साधारण।

popular /'पॉप्यलर/ *adj* 1 लोकप्रिय; **popular with sb** व्यक्ति या वर्ग विशेष में प्रशंसित : *I'm not very popular with the boss.* 2 (कभी-कभी *अपमा*) साधारण जनता की रुचि एवं शिक्षा के अनुकूल : *novels with popular appeal* 3 (धारणाएँ आदि) आम जनता द्वारा मानी हुई : *a popular misconception* 4 जनता का या जनता के लिए : *a popular uprising* ▸ **popularity** /'पॉप्यु'लैरिटि/ *noun* लोकप्रियता : *enjoy widespread popularity with the voters* **popularize, -ise** /'पॉप्यलराइज्/ *verb* लोकप्रिय बनाना; सर्वसाधारण को बताना या उपलब्ध कराना **popularly** *adv*.

populate /'पॉप्युलेट्/ *verb* 1 स्थान आबाद करना 2 बस्ती बसाना : *The islands were gradually populated by settlers from Europe.*

population /'पॉप्यु'लेशन्/ *noun* 1 जन-संख्या, आबादी 2 जनसंख्या घनत्व : *areas of dense/sparse population.*

porcelain /'पॉर्सलिन्/ *noun* पोर्सिलन, चीनी-मिट्टी; चीनी-मिट्टी की वस्तुएँ।

porch /पॉर्च/ *noun* 1 पोर्च (ढका हुआ प्रवेश द्वार) 2 *US* = **veranda**

porcupine /'पॉर्क्युपाइन्/ *noun* साही।

pore¹

pore¹ / पॉर् / noun रोमकूप, रोएँ का छेद।

pore² / पॉर् / verb ∎ pore over sth (पुस्तक आदि का) बड़े ध्यान से अध्ययन और परीक्षण करना : *She was poring over an old map of the area.*

pork / पॉर्क / noun सूअर का मांस।

pornography / पॉर्'नॉग्रफ़ि /noun काम-वासना उत्तेजित करने वाली फ़िल्म, चित्र, साहित्य आदि।

porous / पॉरस् / adj छिद्रिल, ऐसा कि द्रव या हवा रिस सके (जैसे बालू की भूमि होती है) ▶ **porosity** / पॉ'रॉसटि / noun.

porpoise / पॉर्पस् / noun डॉल्फ़िन से मिलता-जुलता एक समुद्री जीव।

porridge / पॉरिज् / (US oatmeal भी) noun दलिया (पानी या दूध में पकाया)।

port¹ / पॉर्ट / noun 1 बंदरगाह से लगा शहर 2 बंदरगाह : *The ship spent four days in port.*

port² / पॉर्ट / noun जहाज़/वायुयान के बग़ल का द्वार-मार्ग (जो सामने मुँह करने पर बाईं ओर होता है)।

port³ / पॉर्ट / noun पुर्तगाल में बनी मीठी लाल शराब जो विशेषत: खाने के अंत में ली जाती है।

portable / पॉर्टबल् / adj जिसे हाथ में उठाए घूमा जा सके अथवा आसानी से एक स्थान से दूसरे स्थान ले जाया जा सके : *a portable heater/phone/computer* ▶ **portability** noun.

porter / पॉर्टर् / noun 1 रेलवे स्टेशन, होटल आदि में सामान ले जाने वाला कुली 2 (US doorman) द्वारपाल : *the night porter.*

portfolio / पॉर्ट'फ़ोलिओ /noun 1 (प्राय: चमड़े का) पोर्टफ़ोलियो, काग़ज़ात रखने का बस्ता 2 व्यक्ति/बैंक के निवेश (सेट) : *My stockbroker manages my portfolio for me.* 3 (औप) (सरकार में) मंत्री का विशेष कार्य एवं कर्तव्य : *the defence portfolio.*

porthole / पॉर्टहोल् / noun छोटी गोल शीशे की खिड़की जो जहाज़/वायुयान के बग़ल में होती है।

portion / पॉर्श्न् / noun 1 (बाँटने पर दिया जाने वाला) हिस्सा/भाग/अंश 2 एक व्यक्ति के लिए पर्याप्त खाना : *a generous portion of roast duck* ▶ **portion** verb ∎ **portion sth out (among/between sb)** हिस्सों में बाँटना : *She portioned out the money equally between both children.*

portly / पॉर्टलि / adj (विशेषत: प्रौढ़ व्यक्ति) स्थूलकाय : *portly members of the city council.*

portrait / पॉर्ट्रेट्, पॉर्ट्रट् / noun 1 किसी व्यक्ति का (विशेषत: केवल चेहरे का) चित्र, रेखाचित्र या फ़ोटोग्राफ़ 2 शब्द चित्र (वर्णन) : *The book paints a fascinating portrait of life at the court of Akbar.*

portray / पॉर्ट्रे / verb **portray sb/sth (as sb/sth)** 1 किसी को चित्र में दर्शाना, चित्र खींचना 2 विशेषत: आंशिक वर्णन द्वारा किसी के बारे में कुछ प्रभाव/धारणा छोड़ना ▶ **portrayal** / पॉर्ट्रेअल् / noun 1 वर्णन 2 वर्णन क्रिया।

pose / पोज़् / verb 1 एक कठिन समस्या या प्रश्न उत्पन्न या प्रस्तुत करना : *Pollution poses a serious threat to the environment.* 2 **pose (for sb/sth)** रुख से बैठना, चित्र बनवाते समय विशेष रीति से खड़ा होना या बैठना : *The artist asked her to pose for him.* 3 **pose as sb/sth** ऐसे होने या बनने का ढोंग रचना; आडंबर दिखा कर प्रभावित करना ▶ **pose** noun 1 (चित्र के लिए) मुद्रा : *a relaxed pose for the camera* 2 (अपमा) ढोंग/ आडंबर : *His concern for the poor is only a pose.* **poser** / पोज़र् / noun 1 (अनौप) पहेली, कठिन समस्या 2 (po-seur / पो'ज़र् / भी) ढोंगी।

posh / पॉश् / adj (-er, -est) (अनौप) 1 उत्कृष्ट एवं महँगा : *a posh hotel/*

2 (कभी-कभी *अपमा*) समाज के उच्चवर्गीय लोगों से संबंधित : *They live in the posh part of town.*

position / प'ज़िश्न् / *noun* 1 स्थिति, जगह; (विशेषत: *pl*) *(तक)* फ़ौजी ठिकाने जहाँ वे लड़ने के लिए तैयार हों : *attack the enemy positions* 2 उपयुक्त स्थान : *The runners got into position on the starting-line.* 3 अंगस्थिति, टिकने की रीति : *lie in a comfortable position* 4 (विशेषत: *sing*) परिस्थितियाँ, ख़ासकर वे जो अधिकार या सामर्थ्य को प्रभावित करती हों : *The company's financial position is not very sound.* 5 (समाज में) प्रतिष्ठा, स्थान; *(औप)* (नौकरी में) पद : *discuss the position of women in society* 6 **position (on sth)** मत या धारणा : *He stated the government's official position on the issue.* ▸ **position** *verb* स्थिति विशेष में होना/करना : *She positioned herself near the door.*

positive / 'पॉज़टिव् / *adj* 1 निश्चित/ असंदिग्ध : *positive instructions/order* 2 रचनात्मक : *make positive proposals/suggestions* 3 आनंददायक बढ़ोतरी या विकास दिखाते हुए : *a positive growth rate* 4 **positive (about sth/ that...)** सुनिश्चित विचार वाला, पक्का : *She was quite positive about the amount of money involved.* 5 (अनौप) पूर्ण; बिलकुल 6 (*गणित*) धनात्मक संख्या, 0 से अधिक संख्या 7 (*तक*) धन-विद्युत : *a positive charge* 8 (चिकित्सीय या वैज्ञानिक परीक्षण का परिणाम) किसी पदार्थ/जीवाणु की मौजूदगी दिखाते हुए : *be HIV-positive* ▸ **positive** *noun* 1 रचनात्मक गुण 2 0 से अधिक संख्या 3 निगेटिव से तैयार फ़ोटोग्राफ़ **positively** *adv* रचनात्मक, निश्चित रूप से, पक्के तौर पर : *Her attacker has now been positively identified.*

possess / प'ज़ेस् / *verb* 1 (*औप*) स्वामी होना; अधिकार में रखना; गुण रखना : *She admitted possessing illegal drugs.* ○ *The new prime minister possesses a strong will.* 2 नियंत्रण में रखना (विशेषत: किसी के मन-मस्तिष्क को वश में कर लेना) : *She seemed to be possessed (by the devil).*

possession / प'ज़ेश्न् / *noun* 1 स्वा-मित्व 2 (विशेषत: *pl*) संपत्ति, जायदाद 3 अन्य द्वारा शासित देश।

possessive / प'ज़ेसिव् / *adj* 1 **possessive (about sth/sb)** क़ब्जे में रखने को आतुर और बाँटने को अनिच्छुक; अधिकार जताने वाला; पूर्ण ध्यान या स्नेह माँगने वाला : *Lalita's very possessive about her toys.* ○ **possessive parents** 2 (व्या) संबंधवाचक : *the possessive case* ▸ **possessively** *adv.*

possibility / ˌपॉस'बिलिटि / *noun* (*pl* **possibilities**) 1 **possibility (of sth/ doing sth); possibility (that.....)** संभावना : *within the bounds of possibility* 2 अस्तित्व में संभव वस्तु 3 अवसर : *new export possibilities.*

possible / 'पॉसब्ल् / *adj* 1 संभव, जो हो सकता है; जो अस्तित्व में हो सकता है : *a possible future leader* 2 उद्देश्य के लिए उपयुक्त; स्वीकार्य : *a possible solution to the dispute* ▸ **possibly** / 'पॉसब्लि / *adv* संभवत:, शायद।

post¹ / पोस्ट् / *noun* 1 (समास में) खूँटा, खंभा : *a rusty old post* 2 [*sing*] वह स्थान जहाँ से दौड़ शुरू या जहाँ पर समाप्त होती है 3 (*अनौप*) गोल पोस्ट ▸ **post** *verb* **post sth (up)** सार्वजनिक रूप से प्रदर्शित करना, सूचना-पट लगाना : *Have the election results been posted yet?*

post² / पोस्ट् / *noun* 1 (नौकरी में) पद, स्थान : *fill a post* 2 व्यक्ति का कार्य-स्थल, विशेषत: सैनिक या अधिकारी का : *a* *customs post* ▸ **post** *verb* **1 post sb (to sth)** पद पर रखना, नियुक्त करना **2 post sb (at/on sth)** तैनात करना : *We posted sentries (at the gates).* **posting** *noun* पद पर नियुक्ति।

post³ / पोस्ट् / (*US* mail भी) *noun* **1** डाक, पत्र आदि **2** डाक व्यवस्था (विभाग) ▸ **postcard** *noun* पोस्टकार्ड **postman** *noun* डाकिया **postmark** *noun* डाक-मुहर **post office** *noun* डाक-ख़ाना।

post⁴ / पोस्ट् / (*US* mail भी) *verb* **1** पत्र डाक में डालना : *Could you post this letter for me?* **2 post sth (to sb)** डाक से पत्र आदि भेजना ■ **keep sb posted** किसी को नवीनतम सूचना बताते रहना।

post- *pref* (*पूर्वपद*) (समय में) उत्तर-; (स्थान में) पश्च-।

postage / पोस्टिज् / *noun* डाक-व्यय, डाक-शुल्क : *What is the postage on this parcel?*

postal / पोस्ट्ल् / *adj* डाक-विषयक; डाक से ▸ **postal order** *noun* पोस्टल-ऑर्डर।

postdate / पोस्ट्'डेट् / *verb* पत्र, चेक आदि में वास्तविक दिनांक से बाद की दिनांक डालना।

poster / पोस्टर् / *noun* सार्वजनिक स्थान पर प्रदर्शन के लिए बड़ा नोटिस; बड़ा छपा हुआ चित्र, पोस्टर।

posterity / पॉ'स्टेरटि / *noun* **1** भावी-पीढ़ियाँ : *plant trees for the benefit of posterity* **2** वंशज।

postgraduate / पोस्ट्'ग्रैजुअट् / *noun, adj* स्नातकोत्तर।

posthumous / पॉस्ट्युमस्; *US* पॉस्-चमस् / *adj* मरणोपरांत : *posthumous fame.*

post-mortem / पोस्ट् 'मॉर्टम् / *noun* **post-mortem (on sb/sth)** शव-परीक्षा।

postpone / प'स्पोन् / *verb* **postpone sth (to/until sth)** स्थगित करना, मुलतवी

करना : *The match was postponed to the following Saturday because of bad weather.* ▸ **postponement** *noun.*

postscript / पोस्ट्स्क्रिप्ट् / *noun* (संक्षि PS) **postscript (to sth)** पुनश्च; पत्र आदि समाप्त करने के बाद उसी पत्र में जोड़ा गया अंश।

postulate / पॉस्ट्युलेट्; *US* पॉस्च-लेट् / *verb* (औप) आवश्यक तथ्य के रूप में पहले से ही मान लेना, अभिधारणा करना ▸ **postulate** / पॉस्ट्युलट्; *US* पॉस्च-लट् / *noun* (औप) अभिधारणा।

posture / पॉस्चर् / *noun* **1** (प्राय: *sing*) शरीर की संस्थिति/भंगिमा, मुद्रा : *an awkward posture* **2** रुख; मन: स्थिति; दृष्टिकोण : *The government has adopted a defensive posture on immigration.* ▸ **posture** *verb* झूठी मुद्रा धारण करना; ढोंग रचना : *He postured as a political activist.*

pot¹ / पॉट् / *noun* **1** हँडिया; बरतन : *a coffee pot* **2** गमला (फूल-पौधों का) **3 the pot** (विशेषत: *US*) एक समूह के लोगों द्वारा एकत्र किया गया (विशेष काम के लिए) सारा धन ■ **the pot calling the kettle black** (कहा) अपने अवगुण न देख कर दूसरों पर अँगुली उठाना।

pot² / पॉट् / *verb* (-tt-) **1 pot sth (up)** गमले में पौधा लगाना/खाद-मिट्टी डालना **2** गोली दाग़ कर मारना : *They potted dozens of rabbits.*

potable / पोट्बल् / *adj* (औप या परि) पीने योग्य।

potato / प'टेटो / *noun* (*pl* potatoes) आलू।

potent / पोटन्ट् / *adj* **1** शक्तिशाली; प्रभावकारी : *a potent drink/drug* **2** (पुरुष) पुंसत्व संपन्न ▸ **potency** / पोट्न्सि / *noun* (*pl* potencies) शक्ति।

potential / प'टेन्शल् / *adj* **1** संभाव्य : *a potential source of energy* ○ *po-*

tential customers 2 विकास और प्रयोग की संभावना से पूर्ण : *a device with many potential applications* ▸ **potential** *noun* **1 potential (for sth)** होने या विकसित होने की संभावना **2** (अस्तित्व में और विकसित होने योग्य) गुण : *seek to fulfil one's potential.*

pothole / 'पॉटहोल् / *noun* सड़क पर गड्ढा; चट्टान में यातायात/बारिश/पानी से बना गड्ढा।

potter[1] / 'पॉटर् / *noun* कुम्हार ▸ **pottery** / 'पॉटरि / *noun* (*pl* **potteries**) **1** मिट्टी के बरतन : *a valuable collection of Japanese pottery* **2** मिट्टी के बरतनों को बनाने की कला **3** कुम्हार की कार्यशाला।

potter[2] / 'पॉटर् / (*US* **putter** / 'पटर् /) *verb* **potter (about/around (sth))** भटकना/व्यर्थ घूमना; समय गँवाना : *potter about at the exhibition.*

potty / 'पॉटि / *noun* (*pl* **potties**) (*अनौप*) छोटे बच्चों का पाख़ाना।

pouch / पाउच् / *noun* **1** (प्राय: समास में) थैली : *a key/tobacco pouch* **2** कंगारू की थैली जिसमें वह बच्चा रख लेती है **3** बीमार की आँखों के नीचे लटकती त्वचा।

poultry / 'पोल्ट्रि / *noun* [*pl*] मुरगियाँ, बत्तख़ आदि ▸ **poultry farming** *noun* मुरगी पालन।

pounce / पाउन्स् / *verb* **pounce (on/upon sb/sth)** **1** झपट्टा मारना **2** ग़लती, टिप्पणी आदि तीव्रता से पकड़ कर उससे फ़ायदा उठाना : *They pounced on the only word they could understand.*

pound[1] / पाउन्ड् / *noun* **1** (*प्रतीक* £) (**pound sterling** भी) पाउंड, ब्रिटिश मुद्रा **2** (*संक्षि* **lb**) 16 आउंस का पाउंड = 0.454 kg.

pound[2] / पाउन्ड् / *verb* **1** किसी चीज़ को ज़ोर-ज़ोर से मारना **2 pound sth (to sth)** कूटना/पीसना; चूर-चूर कर देना **3 pound (with sth)** हृदय का ज़ोरों से धड़कना।

pour / पॉर् / *verb* **1** (विशेषत: द्रव का) उँड़ेलना, धारा में बहाना : *pour milk into a jug* ○ *Blood was pouring from the wound.* **2** (बारिश) मूसलाधार बरसना : *The rain was pouring down.* **3** (किसी वस्तु या व्यक्तियों का) बड़ी संख्या में आना-जाना : *Letters of complaint have poured in (to the office).* ■ **pour sth out** भावनाएँ व्यक्त करना; पूर्ण और बिना संकोच के विवरण देना : *She poured out her troubles to me over a cup of coffee.*

pout / पाउट् / *verb* थूथुन (विशेषत: निचला होंठ) निकालना; (खीझ के कारण) मुँह फुलाना : *a child that always pouts when teased* ▸ **pout** *noun* ऐसी मुख-मुद्रा।

poverty / 'पॉवर्टि / *noun* **1** ग़रीबी, निर्धनता **2** निकृष्ट कोटि का होना : *the poverty of the soil* **3** [*sing*] कमी ▸ **poverty-stricken** *adj* बहुत ग़रीब, अकिंचन।

powder / 'पाउडर् / *noun* **1** पाउडर, चूर्ण, चूरा **2** बारूद ▸ **powder** *verb* पाउडर (मुँह आदि पर) लगाना : *powder one's face/nose.*

power / 'पाउअर् / *noun* **1** (लोगों में कुछ करने की) योग्यता, शक्ति, अवसर **2** (*pl* **powers** भी) शारीरिक या मानसिक शक्ति-विशेष : *He has lost the power of speech.* **3** ऊर्जा, शक्ति : *The ship was helpless against the power of the storm.* **4** नियंत्रण, शासन **5** (विशेषत: *pl*) अधिकार : *legal powers* **6** परिवर्धन की शक्ति/सामर्थ्य : *the power of a microscope* **7** (*गणित*) घात : *4 to the power of 3 is* 4^3 (i.e. 4x4x4=64). **8** प्रभावशाली व्यक्ति, समूह, राज्य : *world powers* ▸ **power** *verb* **1** यंत्र आदि को ऊर्जा प्रदान कर चलने में समर्थ बनाना : *aircraft powered by jet engines* **2** तीव्र गति से और ताक़त के साथ चलना

power station (*US* **power plant**) *noun* बिजलीघर।

powerful / 'पाउअरफ़ुल् / *adj* शक्तिशाली; प्रभावशाली।

powerless / 'पाउअरलस् / *adj* 1 शक्तिहीन 2 **powerless to do sth** कुछ करने में पूर्णत: असमर्थ : *I feel powerless to help.*

practicable / 'प्रैक्टिकबल् / *adj* जिसे उपयोग में लाया जा सके, व्यावहारिक : *a practicable solution.*

practical / 'प्रैक्टिकल् / *adj* 1 व्यावहारिक (न कि सैद्धांतिक) : *practical experiences/skills* 2 उपयोगी 3 प्रयोगात्मक (परीक्षा आदि) 4 (व्यक्ति) व्यवहार कुशल, सक्रिय, विवेकी, यथार्थवादी 5 व्यवहारोचित; वास्तविक : *a practical certainty* ▸ **practical** *noun* (अनौप) विज्ञान में प्रयोग द्वारा किसी सिद्धांत का अध्ययन **practically** *adv* 1 लगभग 2 वस्तुत: 3 व्यावहारिक रीति से।

practice / 'प्रैक्टिस् / *noun* 1 व्यवहार, प्रयोग : *put a plan into practice* 2 अभ्यास : *an hour's practice every day* 3 रिवाज, प्रथा; आदत 4 कार्य या पेशा जैसे वकालत, चिकित्सा : *a doctor working in general practice* 5 कुछ करने का प्रचलित ढंग/तरीक़ा : *Are such methods common practice in this country?* ■ **in practice** अभ्यस्त, सधा हुआ **out of practice** हाल में अभ्यास न करने वाला, जिसका अभ्यास छूट गया है।

practise (*US* **practice**) / 'प्रैक्टिस् / *verb* 1 अभ्यास करना : *I haven't been practising enough.* 2 आदत/स्वभाव के अनुसार नियमित रूप से कुछ करना 3 **practise (as sth)** वकील, डॉक्टर आदि जैसे व्यावसायिक रूप में कार्य करना ■ **practise what one preaches** जैसा औरों को उपदेश दो वैसा ही स्वयं करो ▸ **practised** (*US* **practiced**) *adj*

practised in sth अभ्यास या अनुभव के फलस्वरूप विशेषज्ञ, माहिर।

practitioner / प्रैक्'टिशनर् / *noun* व्यवसायी, विशेषत: चिकित्सा के क्षेत्र में।

pragmatic / प्रैग्'मैटिक् / *adj* व्यावहारिक, यथार्थवादी, वास्तविकता से संबंधित : *a politician with a pragmatic approach.*

prairie / 'प्रेअरि / *noun* घास के बड़े-बड़े मैदान (जहाँ पेड़ न हों, उत्तरी अमेरिका में), प्रेअरी।

praise[1] / प्रेज़् / *verb* 1 **praise sb/sth** (**for sth**); **praise sb/sth as sth** प्रशंसा करना, सराहना : *She praised his cooking.* 2 ईश्वर स्तुति या गुणगान करना : *praise the Lord.*

praise[2] / प्रेज़् / *noun* 1 प्रशंसा/सराहना 2 ईश्वर स्तुति/गुणगान ▸ **praiseworthy** *adj* प्रशंसनीय; श्लाघनीय **praiseworthiness** *noun.*

pram / प्रैम् / (*औप* **perambulator** भी) *noun* चार पहियों की बच्चा गाड़ी।

prance / प्रान्स्; *US* प्रैन्स् / *verb* 1 (व्यक्ति का) इठलाते हुए या उत्तेजनापूर्ण चलना : *She was prancing along in her new outfit.* 2 (घोड़े का) ऊँचे क़दमों से, पिछले पैरों को कुदाते हुए चलना।

prank / प्रैङ्क् / *noun* शरारत/मूर्खतापूर्ण नटखटी : *play a prank on sb.*

prattle / 'प्रैट्ल् / *verb* **prattle (on/ away) (about sb/sth)** (बच्चों का) बड़बड़ाना; बच्चों की तरह बड़-बड़ करके बेकार की बात करना ▸ **prattle** *noun* बड़-बड़ एवं व्यर्थ की बकवास : *full of idle prattle.*

prawn / प्रॉन् / *noun* झींगा।

pray / प्रे / *verb* 1 **pray (to sb) (for sb/ sth)** (भगवान से) प्रार्थना करना : *They knelt down and prayed.* 2 **pray (for sth)** अत्यधिक आशा करना : *I was praying that nobody would notice my mistake.*

prayer / प्रेअर / noun 1 prayer (for sth) प्रार्थना; स्तोत्र; पूजा-प्रार्थना 2 (प्राय: sing) प्रार्थना में माँगी वस्तु; अत्यंत अपेक्षित वस्तु : *My one prayer is that he will walk again.*

pre- pref (उपसर्ग) पूर्व- : *pre-heat* ○ *pre-war* ○ *prehistoric.*

preach / प्रीच् / verb 1 preach (to sb) (about/against/on sth) प्रवचन अथवा उपदेश देना; नैतिक उपदेश देना : *preach a sermon every Sunday* 2 लोगों को कोई मत/विधि स्वीकार करने को प्रेरित करना : *He always preached the virtues of capitalism.* 3 preach (at/ to sb) (प्राय: *अपमा*) नैतिकता/व्यवहार पर भाषण झाड़ना ▸ **preacher** noun उपदेशक।

preamble / प्रि'ऐम्ब्ल्; 'प्रीऐम्ब्ल् / noun preamble (to sth) प्रस्तावना, आमुख।

precarious / प्रि'केअरिअस् / adj 1 अ-सुरक्षित; ख़तरनाक : *He was unable to get down from his precarious position on the rocks.* 2 अनिश्चित; भाग्याधीन ▸ **precariously** adv : *balance precariously on top of a rock.*

precaution / प्रि'कॉश्न् / noun precaution (against sth) एहतियात, पूर्वोपाय, सावधानी : *precautions against fire* ▸ **precautionary** adj (उपाय आदि) एहतियाती।

precede / प्रि'सीड् / verb (स्थान, समय या क्रम में) पूर्ववर्ती होना : *the events that preceded this.*

precedence / 'प्रेसिडन्स् / noun precedence (over sb/sth) पूर्ववर्तिता; वरीयता, प्राथमिकता : *a list of the guests in order of precedence.*

precedent / 'प्रेसिडन्ट् / noun 1 कोई पहले लिया निर्णय जो उदाहरण/पूर्वनियम का काम करे, नज़ीर/पूर्विका : *a ruling that set a precedent for future cases* 2 पूर्व में घटी घटना के समान कोई घटना, काररवाई : *historical precedents.*

precept / 'प्रीसेप्ट् / noun (औप) नीति-वचन; नियम (व्यवहार के लिए)।

precinct / 'प्रीसिङ्क्ट् / noun 1 निर्धारित विशेष प्रयोग के लिए क्षेत्र 2 किसी स्थान के आस-पास का क्षेत्र : *within the city precincts* 3 precincts [pl] सीमा : *No parking is allowed within the hospital precincts.* 4 दीवार आदि से घिरा क्षेत्र, विशेषत: कालेज, मंदिर आदि में।

precious / 'प्रेशस् / adj 1 कीमती, बहु-मूल्य 2 precious (to sb) किसी के लिए बहुत महत्त्वपूर्ण/प्यारा : *Each life is precious.* 3 (*अपमा*) शिष्ट भाषा या व्यवहार को अति महत्त्व देने वाला ▸ **precious-ness** noun.

precipice / 'प्रेसपिस् / noun खड़ी चट्टान।

precipitate / प्रि'सिपिटेट् / verb (औप) 1 किसी घटना को अचानक या समय से पूर्व घटित करना/होने देना : *events that precipitated his fall from power* 2 precipitate sb/sth into sth किसी व्यक्ति/वस्तु को अचानक किसी विशेष दशा में डाल देना/फेंक देना ▸ **precipitate** / प्रि'सिपिटट् / adj (औप) बिना सोचे-समझे किया कार्य।

précis / 'प्रेसी / noun (pl अपरिवर्तित / 'प्रेसीज़्/) किसी भाषण, लेख या कथन का सारांश ▸ **précis** verb (pp **précised** / 'प्रेसीड् /; pres p **précising** / 'प्रेसी-इङ्/) कथन/लेख आदि का सारांश प्रस्तुत करना : *precising a scientific report.*

precise / प्रि'साइस् / adj 1 ठीक-ठीक, त्रुटिहीन; सही ढंग से कहा हुआ : *give precise details* 2 यथार्थता के लिए सावधानी बरतने वाला : *a precise worker* 3 यथार्थ; विशिष्ट : *at that precise moment* ▸ **precisely** adv 1 ठीक-ठीक; बिलकुल 2 सावधानीपूर्वक 3 (कथन से सहमति की अभिव्यक्ति) हाँ : *'He was drunk again?' 'Precisely.'*

precision / प्रि'सिश्न् / noun यथार्थता।

precocious / प्रि'कोशस् / adj 1 (कभी-कभी अपमा) (बच्चा) सामान्य से पूर्व किसी योग्यता को अर्जित करने वाला 2 (गुण, व्यवहार, ज्ञान) समय के पूर्व ही अर्जित/विकसित : display a precocious talent for computing ▸ **precociousness, precocity** nouns.

preconceived /प्रीकन्'सीव्ड् / adj (विचार, मत आदि) पूर्व-अवधारित : preconceived notions.

preconception /प्रीकन्'सेप्श्न्/ noun (प्राय: pl) पूर्व-धारणा (न कि पर्याप्त जानकारी या अनुभव पर आधारित)।

predator / 'प्रेडटर् / noun परजीवभक्षी, हिंस्र जानवर।

predecessor / 'प्रीडिसेसर् / noun 1 पूर्वाधिकारी (जो इसके पूर्व इसी पद पर रह चुका है) 2 पूर्व प्रचलित वस्तु : The latest car phones are much more efficient than their predecessors.

predicament / प्रि'डिकमन्ट् / noun (औप) दुखद या अप्रिय परिस्थिति, विशेषत: जो दुविधा में डाल दे : a financial predicament.

predicate[1] / 'प्रेडिकट् / noun (व्या) विधेय ('उद्देश्य' के वैषम्य में)।

predicate[2] / 'प्रेडिकेट् / verb (औप) 1 predicate sth on/upon sth किसी पर आधारित करना; फलस्वरूप निर्णय लेना : The project was predicated on the assumption that the economy was expanding. 2 कुछ होने की घोषणा करना।

predicative / प्रि'डिकटिव् / adj (व्या) (विशेषण) विधेय के रूप में प्रयुक्त, क्रिया के बाद आने वाला, जैसे 'He is asleep' में 'asleep'.

predict / प्रि'डिक्ट् / verb भविष्यवाणी करना : accurately predict the outcome of sth ▸ **predictable** adj 1 भविष्यवाणी किए जाने योग्य 2 (व्यक्ति) जिसके व्यवहार के बारे में पहले से बताया जा

सके **prediction** / प्रि'डिक्श्न्/ noun 1 भविष्यवाणी : the UN's predictions of famine 2 भविष्यवाणी करने की क्रिया : set up a new centre for the prediction of climate change.

predominant / प्रि'डॉमिनन्ट् / adj 1 प्रबल; अधिकार या प्रभाव में दूसरों से ज्यादा : the predominant opinion 2 सर्वाधिक उल्लेखनीय/महत्त्वपूर्ण ▸ **predominance** noun **predominance (of sth)** प्राधान्य **predominate** / प्रि'डॉमिनेट्/ verb 1 **predominate (over sb/sth)** नियंत्रण या प्रभाव रखना 2 संख्या अथवा मात्रा में अधिक होना : Sal trees predominate in this forest.

pre-eminent /प्रि'एमिनन्ट्/ adj सर्वश्रेष्ठ ▸ **pre-eminence** noun **pre-eminence (in sth)** : awards for those who achieve pre-eminence in public life.

preen / प्रीन् / verb **preen (oneself/itself)** 1 (प्राय: अपमा) (व्यक्ति का) सजने-सँवरने में समय लगाना और स्वयं के रंगरूप की प्रशंसा करना; अत्यधिक आत्मसंतुष्ट होना 2 (पक्षी का) चोंच द्वारा खुद को साफ करना या पंख बराबर करना।

preface / 'प्रेफस्/ noun पुस्तक की भूमिका/प्रस्तावना/आमुख ▸ **preface** verb 1 **preface sth with sth** पुस्तक की भूमिका तैयार करना 2 **preface sth by sth/with sth/by doing sth** प्रारंभ करना, भूमिका स्वरूप कहना : She prefaced her talk with an apology.

prefect / 'प्रीफ़ेक्ट् / noun 1 कई स्कूलों में व्यवस्था बनाए रखने का उत्तरदायी छात्र 2 (**Prefect** भी) कुछ देशों, जैसे फ्रांस और जापान, में मुख्य प्रशासनिक अधिकारी (क्षेत्र विशेष का)।

prefer / प्रि'फ़र् / verb (-rr-) **prefer sth (to sth)** (तुलना में) अधिक पसंद करना : I prefer chocolate to ice-cream. ▸ **preferable** / 'प्रेफ़रब्ल्/ adj prefer-

able (to sth/doing sth) अधिक आकांक्षित या उपयुक्त **preferably** *adv*.

preference / 'प्रेफ़्रन्स् / *noun* 1 [*sing*] **preference (for sth)** अधिमान, पसंद; पसंद की वस्तु 2 किसी एक व्यक्ति/गुट के प्रति दिखाई गई कृपा दृष्टि : *Employees who have worked here for many years will be given preference in the allocation of parking spaces.* ▪ **in preference to sb/sth** उसकी उपेक्षा।

preferential / प्रेफ़्'रेन्श्ल् / *adj* पसंदीदा, प्राथमिकता, अधिमान्य।

prefix / 'प्रीफ़िक्स् / *noun* 1 (व्या) उपसर्ग 2 (अग्र) नाम के पूर्व जोड़े गए *Mr, Dr* आदि शब्द ▸ **prefix** *verb* **prefix A to B/prefix B with A** उपसर्ग जोड़ना; प्रारंभ में कुछ जोड़ना।

pregnant / 'प्रेग्नन्ट् / *adj* (स्त्री) गर्भवती ▸ **pregnancy** *noun*.

prehistoric /प्रीहिं'स्टॉरिक्/ *adj* प्रागैति- हासिक; इतिहासपूर्व समय का : *prehis- toric cave paintings.*

prejudice /'प्रेजुडिस्/ *noun* **prejudice (about/against sb/sth)** पूर्वाग्रह, बिना पर्याप्त जानकारी या अनुभव के पसंदगी/ नापसंदगी की राय बनाना; ऐसी राय : *He was a tireless opponent of racial prejudice.* ▸ **prejudice** *verb* 1 मन में पूर्वाग्रह उत्पन्न करना, प्रभाव डालना 2 किसी के हित को हानि पहुँचाना : *The judge said the chances of a fair trial had been prejudiced by the press cov- erage.* **prejudiced** *adj* **prejudiced (against/in favour of sb/sth)** (प्रायः अपमा) पूर्वाग्रहग्रस्त **prejudicial** / प्रेजु 'डिश्ल्/ *adj* **prejudicial (to sth)** (औप) अधिकार, लाभ/हित आदि के लिए हानिकर।

preliminary / प्रि'लिमिनरि / *adj* प्रा- रंभिक : *the preliminary results of the survey* ▸ **preliminary** *noun* (*pl* **preliminaries**) (प्रायः *pl*) **preliminary (to sth)** प्रारंभिक उपाय या चरण।

prelude / 'प्रेल्यूड् / *noun* 1 **prelude (to sth)** घटना जो किसी अधिक महत्त्वपूर्ण भावी घटना की प्रस्तावना के रूप में घटित होती है 2 (संगीत) पूर्वरंग।

premature / 'प्रेमचर; *US* प्रीम 'चुर् / *adj* 1 उचित, प्रत्याशित एवं सामान्य समय से पूर्व : *premature baldness* 2 **prema- ture (in doing sth)** (अपमा) बहुत जल्दी घटित या किया गया : *a premature conclusion* ▸ **prematurely** *adv*.

premeditated / प्री 'मेडिटेटिड् / *adj* योजनाबद्ध, पहले से सोचा हुआ : *a pre- meditated decision/murder.*

premier / 'प्रेमिअर; *US* प्रि 'मिर् / *adj* प्रमुख, महत्त्व में सर्वप्रथम ▸ **premier** *noun* प्रधान मंत्री **premiership** *noun*.

premiere / 'प्रेमिएअर; *US* प्रि 'मिर् / *noun* नाटक या फ़िल्म आदि का पहला सार्वजनिक प्रदर्शन।

premise (premiss भी) / 'प्रेमिस् / *noun* (औप) कथन या विचार जिस पर तर्क आधारित हो : *I am working on the premise that we shall have very little support.*

premises / 'प्रेमिसिज़् / *noun* [*pl*] भवन, अहाता : *The firm is looking for larger premises.*

premium / 'प्रीमिअम् / *noun* 1 बीमे की क़िस्त 2 अतिरिक्त राशि जैसे प्रिमियम, लाभांश/बोनस : *A premium of 2% is paid on long-term investments.* ▪ **at a premium** 1 कम होने या मुश्किल से मिलने के कारण महँगा 2 (वाणिज्य) शेयर स्टॉक का अधिमूल्य पर होना : *Shares are selling at a premium.*

premonition / प्रेम'निश्न्; प्रेम'निश्न्/ *noun* **premonition (of sth/that...)** पूर्वाभास, आगामी संकट की मन ही मन अनुभूति : *a premonition of disaster* ▸ **premonitory** *adj*.

preoccupation / प्रि ऑक्यु'पेश्न् / *noun* 1 कोई विचार/विषय जिसके बारे में

व्यक्ति काफ़ी सोचता है : *His main preoccupation at that time was getting enough to eat.* **2 preoccupation with sth** किसी विषय पर हमेशा सोचने या चिंतित रहने की अवस्था : *She found his preoccupation with money irritating.* **3** मानसिक दशा जिसमें व्यक्ति अपने ही ख़यालों में खोया रहता है।

preoccupy / प्रि'ऑक्युपाइ / *verb (pt, pp preoccupied)* किसी कार्य में इतना तल्लीन होना या करना कि कुछ और न सोचा जा सके : *Health worries preoccupied him constantly.*

preparation / प्रेप'रेशन् / *noun* **1 preparation (for sth)** तैयारी; आयोजन **2** विशेष रूप से तैयार किया गया पदार्थ (दवाई आदि)।

preparatory / प्रि'पैरटरि / *adj* आरंभिक; तैयारी के लिए किया गया : *preparatory investigations.*

prepare / प्रि'पेअर् / *verb* **1 prepare (sth/sb/oneself) (for sb/sth)** तैयार करना, बनाना; तैयार होना **2** खाना तैयार करना **3 prepare sth (from sth)** (रस) एक पदार्थ से दूसरा पदार्थ बनाना : *prepare penicillin in the laboratory* ■ **prepare the ground (for sth)** किसी का विकसित/उत्पन्न होना संभव/आसान बनाना : *Early experiments with rockets prepared the ground for space travel.* ▸ **prepared** *adj* **1 prepared (for sth)** निपटने में समर्थ **2 prepared to do sth** किसी कार्य के लिए तैयार, इच्छुक होना : *They seem prepared to compromise.* **3** पहले से लिखा, किया या बनाया गया : *I often buy prepared meals at the supermarket.*

prepay / प्री'पे / *verb (pt, pp prepaid)* पहले से भुगतान करना ▸ **prepaid** *adj* : *a prepaid envelope* **prepayment** *noun.*

preposition / प्रेप'ज़िशन् / *noun* (व्या) पूर्वसर्ग जैसे *in, from, to, out, of, on behalf of* ▸ **prepositional** *adj* : *a prepositional phrase* (जैसे *at night*).

preposterous / प्रि'पॉस्टरस् / *adj* (औप) पूर्णत: तर्कहीन; अस्वाभाविक एवं मूर्खतापूर्ण : *The accusation is preposterous.* ▸ **preposterously** *adv.*

prerequisite / ‚प्री'रेक्विज़िट् / *noun* **prerequisite (for/of/to sth)** (औप) कुछ होने/करने के लिए आवश्यक वस्तु : *A degree is a prerequisite for employment at this level.*

prerogative / प्रि'रॉगटिव् / *noun* किसी व्यक्ति या समूह (वर्ग) को प्राप्त विशेष अधिकार : *the royal prerogative.*

prescribe / प्रि'स्क्राइब् / *verb* **prescribe sth (for sb/sth)** **1** (डॉक्टर का) दवा नियत करना : *The optician prescribed tinted lenses.* **2** साधिकार कुछ करने या नियम पालन के लिए आदेश देना : *You can't prescribe fixed standards for art.*

prescription / प्रि'स्क्रिप्शन् / *noun* **1 prescription (for sth)** दवाई का पर्चा; नुसख़ा **2 prescription (for sth)** निर्धारित काररवाई : *a prescription for sustainable development.*

presence / प्रेज़न्स् / *noun* **1** उपस्थिति **2** उपस्थित व्यक्तियों की संख्या **3** (प्राय: *sing*) उपस्थित व्यक्ति/वस्तु ■ **make one's presence felt** दूसरों को अपने अस्तित्व के बारे में अवगत कराना, विशेषत: अपने व्यक्तित्व या श्रेष्ठ अधिकारों के आधार पर ▸ **presence of mind** *noun* प्रत्युत्पन्न-मति, तत्काल बुद्धि।

present[1] / प्रेज़न्ट् / *adj* **1 present (at sth)** (व्यक्ति) उपस्थित **2 present (in sth)** (वस्तु) विद्यमान : *The threat of war is still present.* **3** वर्तमान (काल का समय) में हो रहा (न कि भूत या भविष्य में) : *the present situation* ▸ **present**

noun (प्राय: the present) [*sing*] वर्तमान समय; (व्या) वर्तमान काल ■ **at present** अब; अभी **for the present** इस समय के लिए।

present² / 'प्रेज़न्ट् / *noun* भेंट, उपहार : *birthday/Christmas presents.*

present³ / प्रि'ज़ेन्ट् / *verb* 1 **present sb with sth; present sth (to sb)** पेश करना, भेंट देना, प्रस्तुत करना : *A local celebrity presented the prizes.* 2 **present sth (for sth); present sth (to sb)** देखने के लिए प्रस्तुत करना : *present one's passport at the border* 3 **present sth/sb/oneself as sth** किसी विशेष दृष्टिकोण से दिखाना 4 **present sb with sth; present sth (to sth)** कुछ उत्पन्न/अनुभव कराना : *Army life presents many difficulties to the new recruit.* 5 रेडियो/टी.वी पर कार्यक्रम प्रस्तुत करना; किसी कार्यक्रम का निर्माण करना 6 **present sb (to sb)** (औप) (किसी व्यक्ति को उससे उच्च पदस्थ के सामने उपस्थित कर) मिलाना, परिचित कराना 7 **present oneself at, for, in etc sth** (औप) औपचारिक अवसर पर उपस्थित होना : *I have to present myself in court on 20 May.* 8 **present sth (to sb)** (औप) भाषण या लेख के माध्यम से व्यक्त करना : *present apologies (to sb)* ▸ **presenter** *noun* रेडियो या टी.वी कार्यक्रम का प्रस्तुतकर्ता।

presentable / प्रि'ज़ेन्टब्ल् / *adj* सामने लाने या आने योग्य; प्रस्तुति योग्य।

presentation / ‚प्रेज़न्'टेश्न् / *noun* 1 प्रस्तुतीकरण : *I admire the clear, logical presentation of her argument.* 2 (सार्वजनिक समारोह में) उपहार समर्पण, समर्पण समारोह 3 नाटक का मंचन 4 (विशेषत: वाणिज्य) सभा जिसमें नया उत्पाद या विचार प्रस्तुत किया जाए : *I gave a presentation to local teachers on our new range of textbooks.*

presently / 'प्रेज़न्ट्लि / *adv* 1 जल्दी ही, बस थोड़ी ही देर में : *I'll be with you presently.* 2 (विशेषत: US) अभी, तुरंत : *The book is presently unavailable.*

preservation / ‚प्रेज़'वेश्न् / *noun* 1 संरक्षित करने की प्रक्रिया : *the preservation and conservation of wildlife* 2 संरक्षित रहने की स्थिति/स्तर।

preservative / प्रि'ज़र्वटिव् / *noun* सुरक्षित रखने के लिए प्रयुक्त पदार्थ ▸ **preservative** *adj* परिरक्षक।

preserve¹ / प्रि'ज़र्व् / *verb* 1 सुरक्षित रखना, ख़राब होने से बचाना : *Wax polish preserves wood and leather.* 2 **preserve sb/sth (from sth)** नष्ट होने से बचाना; भूमि, नदी, पशु-पक्षी आदि को संरक्षित करना : *preserve endangered species* 3 कोई गुण/रूप आदि सतत बनाए रखना : *preserve one's sense of humour.*

preserve² / प्रि'ज़र्व् / *noun* 1 कोई कार्य, रुचि आदि जो व्यक्ति या वर्ग विशेष की धरोहर मानी जाती हो : *Fishing is a traditionally male preserve.* 2 (औप) जैम, मुरब्बा।

preside / प्रि'ज़ाइड् / *verb* **preside (at/over sth)** सभा की अध्यक्षता करना; व्यापारिक अनुष्ठान का संचालन करना : *The Prime Minister presides at/over meetings of the Cabinet.* ■ **preside over sth** किसी परिस्थिति के लिए उत्तरदायी होना/प्रभारी होना : *The President's wife will personally preside over the health reforms.*

presidency / 'प्रेज़िडन्सि / *noun* (*pl* **presidencies**) राष्ट्रपतित्व; अध्यक्षता।

president / 'प्रेज़िडन्ट् / *noun* 1 **President** राष्ट्रपति 2 सभा, समिति, कंपनी आदि का अध्यक्ष या संचालक : *He was made president of the cricket club.*

▸ **presidential** / प्रेज़िं'डेन्श्ल् / *adj* राष्ट्रपति/अध्यक्ष के कार्य से संबंधित।

press¹/प्रेस्/ *noun* 1 (प्राय: the Press) समाचार-पत्र, पत्रिकाओं एवं रेडियो और टी वी का समाचार विभाग; इनमें काम करने वाले पत्रकार : *The incident was widely reported in the press.* 2 (printing-press भी) प्रेस, छापे की मशीन (मुद्रणयंत्र) 3 पुस्तक आदि छापने की प्रक्रिया; प्रकाशन व्यवसाय : *prepare a book for press* ○ *Oxford University Press* 4 दबाने/ निचोड़ने आदि का यंत्र : *a trouser-press/a wine-press* 5 (प्राय: *sing*) दबाने/निचोड़ने की क्रिया।

press²/प्रेस्/ *verb* 1 press (sth/sb/ oneself) against sth; press sth to sth; press sth together दबना, दबाना 2 press sb (for sth) आग्रह करना, बार-बार निवेदन करना : *The bank is pressing us for repayment of the loan.* 3 अपनी बात आग्रह के साथ पेश करना : *She is still pressing her claim for compensation.* 4 दबाव डालते हुए सपाट बनाना; इस्तरी करना : *press the soil flat with the back of a spade* ◼ **press sth on sb** (भोजन, धन आदि ग्रहण करने के लिए) बार-बार आग्रह करना ▸ **pressed** *adj* 1 pressed (for sth) (विशेषत: धन, समय आदि) पर्याप्त न होना 2 pressed (to do sth) कुछ करने/अर्जित करने में असमर्थ या कष्ट की स्थिति में **pressing** *adj* तुरंत ध्यान देने योग्य (कार्य आदि); अत्यावश्यक : *He left the meeting early, saying he had a pressing engagement.* **pressing** *noun* दबाकर बनाई हुई वस्तु : *The second pressing was of much higher quality than the first.*

pressure /प्रेशर/ *noun* 1 दबाव, दाब; दाब की मात्रा : *reduce the tyre pressure* 2 वायुमंडलीय दाब 3 pressure (of sth); pressure (to do sth) कुछ करने या अर्जित करने की प्रबल आवश्यकता : *pressure of work* ◼ **bring pressure to bear on sb (to do sth)** प्रभाव और ज़ोर-दबाव डाल कर किसी से कोई कार्य करवाना **put pressure on sb (to do sth)** (कार्य के लिए) दबाव डालना **under pressure** 1 (द्रव या गैस) पात्र में दाब के अधीन 2 अत्यावश्यक ज़रूरत या मजबूरी से प्रभावित : *work under pressure* 3 तनाव-ग्रस्त ▸ **pressure cooker** *noun* प्रेशर-कुकर (दाब से भोजन पकाने का बरतन)।

pressurize, -ise / प्रेशराइज़् / *verb* (pressure भी) pressurize sb (into sth/doing sth) कुछ काम कराने के लिए किसी पर ज़ोर-दबाव या प्रभाव का प्रयोग करना ▸ **pressurized, -ised** / प्रेशराइ-ज़्ड्/ *adj* वायुयान या पनडुब्बी के भीतरी भाग को एक सहनीय वायु-दाब के भीतर रखना : *The compartments are all fully pressurized.* **pressurization, -isation** *noun*.

prestige / प्रे'स्टीश्/ *noun* 1 प्रतिष्ठा, ख्याति : *social/academic prestige* 2 प्रतिष्ठा/ख्याति से उत्पन्न प्रभाव और शक्ति ▸ **prestigious** / प्रे'स्टिजस्/ *adj* लब्ध-प्रतिष्ठ।

presumably / प्रि'ज़्यूमब्लि / *adv* संभा-व्यत:, अनुमानत:।

presume / प्रि'ज़्यूम/ *verb* 1 पहले से ही मान कर चलना; सच मान कर आरंभ करना : *Twelve passengers are missing, presumed dead.* 2 (औप) साहस करना : *I wouldn't presume to argue with you.*

presumption / प्रि'ज़म्प्श्न् / *noun* 1 presumption (of sth) परिकल्पना, धारणा; सत्य मानी गई धारणा 2 (औप) दु:साहस/ढिठाई।

presumptuous / प्रि'ज़म्प्चुअस्/ *adj* (व्यक्ति/आचरण) ज़रूरत से ज़्यादा निर्भीक या आत्मविश्वासपूर्ण।

presuppose /प्रीस'पोज़/ verb 1 बिना साबित हुए पहले से ही (सत्य) मान लेना 2 शर्त के रूप में आवश्यक होना : *Solutions presuppose problems, as answers presuppose questions.*
▸ **presupposition** /प्रीसप'ज़िश्न्/ noun पूर्वधारणा, पूर्वकल्पना।

pretence (*US* **pretense**) /प्रि'टेन्स्/ noun 1 बहानेबाज़ी, छल/कपट : *Their friendliness was only pretence.* 2 [sing] **pretence of sth** ढोंग, अभिनय : *make a pretence of grief* 3 **pretence to sth/doing sth** गुण होने का दावा।

pretend /प्रि'टेन्ड्/ verb 1 स्वाँग भरना; धोखा देना : *She pretended (that) she was not at home when we rang the bell.* 2 ढोंग रचना, अभिनय मात्र करना; बहाना बनाना : *She pretended illness as an excuse.* ■ **pretend to sth** (औप) दावा करना : *I don't pretend to any great understanding of music.*

pretension /प्रि'टेन्श्न्/ noun 1 (प्राय: pl) **pretension (to sth/doing sth)** दावा 2 मिथ्याभिमानी व्यवहार।

pretentious /प्रि'टेन्शस्/ adj (अपमा) मिथ्याभिमानी; महत्त्वाकांक्षी : *expressed in pretentious language.*

pretext /'प्रीटेक्स्ट्/ noun **pretext (for sth/doing sth)** बहाना : *He came to see me on/under the pretext of wanting to borrow a book.*

pretty¹ /'प्रिटि/ adj (-ier, -iest) मनोरम और आकर्षक : *a pretty girl* ▸ **prettily** adv अच्छी तरह, आकर्षक ढंग से : *She decorated the room very prettily.*

pretty² /'प्रिटि/ adv (अ,नौप) बहुत कुछ, काफ़ी : *The situation seems pretty hopeless.*

prevail /प्रि'वेल्/ verb 1 **prevail (in sth)** सामान्यत: पाया जाना, व्याप्त रहना; प्रचलित होना : *The use of animals for ploughing still prevails in many countries.* 2 **prevail (against/over sb/sth)** (औप) सफलतापूर्वक सामना करना, जीतना : *Virtue will prevail (against evil).* ■ **prevail on/upon sb to do sth** (औप) किसी को राज़ी कर लेना ▸ **prevailing** adj.

prevalent /'प्रेव्ल्न्ट्/ adj (औप) **prevalent (in/among sb/sth)** (औप) प्रचलित; सामान्यत: हो रहा : *an attitude prevalent among university students* ▸ **prevalence** noun.

prevent /प्रि'वेन्ट्/ verb 1 **prevent sb/sth (from doing sth)** घटित होने से रोकना : *prevent the spread of a disease* 2 न करने देना ▸ **preventable** adj निवारण योग्य।

prevention /प्रि'वेन्श्न्/ noun रोकथाम, निवारण : *the prevention of cruelty to animals.*

preventive /प्रि'वेन्टिव्/ adj निवारक।

preview /'प्रीव्यू/ noun पूर्वदर्शन, पूर्वसमीक्षा ▸ **preview** verb पूर्वदर्शन, पूर्वसमीक्षा करना/करवाना।

previous /'प्रीविअस्/ adj (समय या क्रम से) पूर्ववर्ती : *We had met on two previous occasions.* ▸ **previously** adv पहले, पूर्व।

prey /प्रे/ noun 1 शिकार 2 ऐसा व्यक्ति जिसे कोई अपने लाभ का निशाना बना सके या हानि पहुँचा सके : *She was easy prey for dishonest salesmen.* ■ **be/fall prey to sth** (औप) 1 निशाना/शिकार बन जाना 2 (व्यक्ति का) किसी चीज़ से अत्यधिक परेशान होना : *She was prey to irrational fears.* ▸ **prey** verb ■ **prey on/upon sb/sth** 1 शिकार करना 2 निशाना बनाना; लाभ उठाना।

price /प्राइस्/ noun 1 क़ीमत/मूल्य 2 वस्तु को पाने या बनाए रखने के लिए चुकाया दाम : *Loss of independence was a high price to pay for peace.* ■ **at a**

price बहुत ऊँची क़ीमत पर **at any price** किसी भी क़ीमत पर ▸ **price** verb **1** **price sth (at sth)** क़ीमत नियुक्त करना : *The agent priced the house at the right level for the market.* **2** क़ीमत पूछना/जानना **3** वस्तुओं पर क़ीमत की छाप लगाना : *The assistant priced the garments before putting them on display.* **priceless** adj बहुत क़ीमती, बहुमूल्य **pricey** adj (**-ier, -iest**) महँगा।

prick¹ / प्रिक् / verb **1** **prick sth (with sth)** (नुकीली वस्तु से) छेद करना : *prick holes in paper with a pin* **2** **prick sth (on/with sth)** चुभाना : *She pricked her finger on a needle.* **3** दुखाना, मानसिक असुविधा, कसक पैदा करना; दुखना/कसकना : *His conscience is pricking him now.* ■ **prick up one's ears 1** (घोड़े या कुत्ते का) कान खड़े करना **2** (व्यक्ति का) अचानक कुछ ध्यान से सुनने लगना।

prick² / प्रिक् / noun **1** छिद्रित करने/चुभाने की क्रिया **2** (चुभाने से उत्पन्न) दर्द : *(अलं) the pricks of conscience.*

prickle / 'प्रिक्ल् / noun **1** (पौधे का) काँटा; (कुछ जानवरों के शरीर पर) काँटेनुमा बाल : *a hedgehog's prickles* **2** त्वचा पर चुभन की अनुभूति ▸ **prickle** verb गोदना/चुभाना **prickly** adj **1** काँटेदार; चुभन पैदा करने वाला **2** (अनौप) (व्यक्ति) जल्दी क्रोधित हो जाने वाला, भड़क जाने वाला।

pride / प्राइड् / noun **1** **pride (in sb/sth)** गर्व, अभिमान **2** [sing] **the pride of sth** गौरव : *The new sports centre was the pride of the town.* **3** (अपना) घमंड; अभिमान **4** ख़ुद की योग्यता की जानकारी; आत्मसम्मान, आत्मगौरव **5** शेरों का झुंड ■ **pride of place** सर्वाधिक अच्छा या पसंदीदा होने के कारण सबसे महत्त्वपूर्ण या प्रसिद्ध स्थान **take(a) pride in sth** किए गए कार्य पर गर्व महसूस करना ▸ **pride**

verb ■ **pride oneself on sth/doing sth** (अपने कार्य) पर गर्व करना।

priest / प्रीस्ट् / noun **1** ईसाई धर्म का प्रीस्ट, पुरोहित **2** (fem **priestess**) पुरोहित, पुजारी।

prim / प्रिम् / adj (प्राय: अपमा) **1** (व्यक्ति) (कुछ ज़्यादा ही) ठीक व्यवहार करने वाला एवं अनुचित बातों/कार्यों को नापसंद करने वाला : *You can't tell that joke to her—she's much too prim and proper.* **2** व्यवहार, दर्शन एवं बातचीत में अधिक ही औपचारिक ▸ **primly** adv.

prima facie / ‚प्राइमा 'फ़ेशि / adj, adv (विशेषत: क़ानूनी) प्रथम दृष्टि में, बिना अतिरिक्त छान-बीन के, सही या सत्य लगने वाले तथ्य पर आधारित : *Prima facie, there is a strong case against him.*

primary / 'प्राइमरि; US 'प्राइमेरि / adj **1** समय, क्रम या विकास में प्राथमिक, अग्रिम, आरंभिक : *in the primary stages of development* **2** सर्वाधिक महत्त्वपूर्ण; मूलभूत **3** प्रारंभिक शिक्षा विषयक : *primary teachers/school* ▸ **primarily** adv मुख्यत: **primary colour** (US **color**) noun मूलवर्ण, लाल, पीला एवं नीला रंग (जिन्हें मिलाने से अन्य रंग बनाए जा सकते हैं)।

prime¹ / प्राइम् / adj **1** मुख्य, मूलभूत; सर्वाधिक महत्त्वपूर्ण : *My prime concern is to protect my property.* **2** सर्वोत्तम गुणों वाला, उत्कृष्ट : *a prime site for development* **3** सर्वगुण संपन्न ▸ **prime number** (गणित) रूढ़ या अभाज्य संख्या जैसे 7, 17, 41.

prime² / प्राइम् / noun [sing] संपूर्णता की स्थिति/अवस्था; सर्वोत्तम अंश : *in the prime of life/youth.*

prime³ / प्राइम् / verb **1** कार्य या प्रयोग के लिए तैयार होना/करना : *The bomb was primed, ready to explode.* **2** लकड़ी, धातु आदि को पेंटिंग के लिए तैयार करना

3 prime sb (with sth) घटना से पहले प्रतिक्रिया के लिए जानकारी प्राप्त करवाना।

primer¹ / 'प्राइमर / noun रंजक, रँगने से पहले धातु/लकड़ी पर परत लगाने के लिए प्रयुक्त पदार्थ।

primer² / 'प्राइमर; US 'प्रिमर / noun (अप्र) नौसिखियों के लिए प्रारंभिक पाठ्य-पुस्तक।

primitive / 'प्रिमिटिव् / adj 1 आदिम, सामाजिक विकास की आदिकालीन अवस्था में : primitive culture/rituals 2 (अक्सर अप्रय) साधारण एवं अविकसित, असुविधाजनक : The cave provided a primitive shelter from the storm.

primrose / 'प्रिम्रोज् / noun 1 एक पीले रंग का जंगली फूल 2 हलका पीला रंग।

prince / प्रिन्स् / noun 1 राजकुमार 2 छोटे राज्य का शासक 3 **prince of/among sth** क्षेत्र विशेष में सर्वश्रेष्ठ व्यक्ति: Kapoor, a prince among chefs ▸ **princely** adj 1 राजोचित : princely states 2 भव्य, उदार **princess** / प्रिन्'सेस् / noun राजकुमारी।

principal / 'प्रिन्सपल् / adj मुख्य, प्रधान ▸ **principal** noun 1 प्रिंसिपल, स्कूल/कॉलेज का प्राचार्य 2 नाटक/ओपेरा का नेतृत्व करने वाला : a principal actor 3 (प्राय: sing) (वाणिज्य) (व्यापार में) मूलधन जिस पर ब्याज लगता है 4 (व्यापार, क़ानून आदि में) वह व्यक्ति जिसकी ओर से कोई दूसरा व्यक्ति (अभिकर्ता) कार्य कर रहा है, मालिक **principally** adv मुख्यतया।

principle / 'प्रिन्सपल् / noun 1 मूलतत्त्व, आधारभूत तथ्य/कारण : the basic principles of geometry 2 (प्राय: pl) आचरण का नियम/सिद्धांत : live according to one's principles 3 [sing] (विज्ञान का) सामान्य सिद्धांत ◼ **in principle** 1 आधारभूत तथ्यों के अनुसार 2 सामान्यतया (पर विस्तार से नहीं) **on principle** सिद्धांत के कारण (न कि निजी स्वार्थ के

लिए) : Many people are opposed to abortion on principle. ▸ **principled** adj आचरण के (विशेषत:) अच्छे सिद्धांतों पर आधारित/अच्छे सिद्धांत रखने वाला।

print¹ / प्रिन्ट् / noun 1 मुद्रण, टाइप : Headlines are written in large print. 2 चिह्न, निशान/छाप : The lion left its prints in the sand. 3 मुद्रित चित्र, आरेख आदि; निगेटिव से तैयार किया गया छायाचित्र 4 छपा हुआ कपड़ा, प्रिंट : a print dress ◼ **in print** 1 (पुस्तक) मुद्रित और बिक्री के लिए उपलब्ध 2 (व्यक्ति की रचना) पुस्तक/समाचार-पत्र में प्रकाशित **out of print** मुद्रित पुस्तक जिसकी सभी प्रतियाँ बिक चुकी हैं।

print² / प्रिन्ट् / verb 1 **print sth (in/on sth)** (पुस्तक आदि) छापना; मुद्रित करना 2 मुद्रण के समान अक्षर बिना जोड़े लिखना 3 सतह पर/कपड़ों की छपाई करना : print a design on a T-shirt 4 **print sth (off)** (फ़ोटोग्राफ़ी में) निगेटिव से छायाचित्र बनाना ▸ **printable** adj मुद्रण/प्रकाशन योग्य **printer** noun 1 मुद्रक यंत्र 2 मुद्रित करने वाला व्यक्ति; छापाखाने का मालिक **printing** noun 1 मुद्रण की क्रिया 2 एक समय पर एक किताब की छपने वाली प्रतियों की संख्या 3 बिना जोड़े लिखे गए अक्षर **printing-press** noun मुद्रण यंत्र, छापा-ख़ाना **printout** / 'प्रिन्टआउट् / noun कंप्यूटर में स्थित सामग्री का मुद्रण।

prior / 'प्राइअर / adj समय, क्रम या महत्त्व में पूर्व, पूर्ववर्ती : They have a prior claim to the property. ▸ **prior to** prep (औप) किसी से पहले : We received no notification prior to the event.

priority / प्राइ'ऑरिटि / noun (pl priorities) 1 अग्रता, अधिक महत्त्वपूर्ण 2 **priority (over sth)** प्राथमिकता।

prise / प्राइज़ / (विशेषत: US prize / प्राइज़् / या pry / प्राइ / भी) verb बल के

प्रयोग से दो व्यक्तियों/वस्तुओं को अलग करना।

prism / 'प्रिज़म / noun 1 (ज्यामिति) समपार्श्व ठोस आकृति 2 पारदर्शी समपार्श्व जिससे सूर्यकिरण अनेक रंगों में बँट जाती है।

prison / 'प्रिज़्न / noun 1 जेलख़ाना, क़ैद-ख़ाना; (अपमा) ऐसी जगह जहाँ से बच निकलना असंभव हो 2 जेलख़ाने में रहने की स्थिति : *He was sent to prison for five years.*

prisoner / 'प्रिज़्नर / noun 1 क़ैदी 2 (prisoner of war) युद्धबंदी 3 पकड़ कर रखा गया व्यक्ति अथवा पशु : *He was taken prisoner by rebel soldiers.*

pristine / 'प्रिस्टीन / adj 1 आदि/मूल दशा में 2 नए जैसा साफ़ और ताज़ा : *a pristine layer of snow.*

privacy / 'प्रिवसि; US 'प्राइवसि / noun 1 एकांतता की स्थिति : *He preferred to read in the privacy of his study.* 2 अवस्था जिसमें कोई बाहरी हस्तक्षेप न हो।

private / 'प्राइवट / adj 1 निजी, व्यक्तिगत (public के वैषम्य में) : *private property* 2 गुप्त 3 (व्यक्ति) अपने विचार/भाव दूसरों को न बताने वाला 4 (बातचीत, सभा आदि) बहुत थोड़े लोगों के मध्य 5 (स्थान) एकांत 6 ग़ैरसरकारी, आधिकारिक पद के बाहर : *The President is making a private visit to Canada.* 7 व्यक्तिगत रूप से प्रबंधित (सरकारी प्रबंध में नहीं) : *private industry* ○ *private education* ▸ **private** noun 1 सामान्य सैनिक (सबसे नीचे पद का) 2 **privates** [pl] (अनौप) गुप्तांग ■ **in private** एकांत में ▸ **privately** adv एकांत में, अकेले (में)।

privation / प्राइ'वेश्न / noun (औप) 1 (प्राय: pl) तंगी, जीवन की आवश्यकताओं से रहित रहना : *a life of privation and misery* 2 (प्राय: sing) किसी वस्तु से वंचित रहने की स्थिति।

privatize, -ise / 'प्राइवटाइज़ / verb सरकारी संस्थाओं का प्रबंध सरकार से

हटाकर निजी व्यक्तियों/संस्थाओं के हाथ में सौंपना ▸ **privatization, -isation** noun.

privilege / 'प्रिविलिज़ / noun 1 किसी व्यक्ति या वर्ग के लिए विशेष अधिकार/विशेष सुविधा 2 (अपमा) समाज के धनी एवं शक्तिशाली वर्ग को प्राप्त अधिकार/लाभ : *She had led a life of luxury and privilege.* ▸ **privileged** adj 1 (कभी-कभी अपमा) विशेष सुविधा प्राप्त व्यक्ति/वर्ग 2 सार्वजनिक होने से बचाने के लिए क़ानूनन रक्षित : *privileged information.*

privy¹ / 'प्रिवि / adj **privy to sth** (औप) किसी गोपनीय बात की जानकारी होना : *I wasn't privy to the negotiations.*

privy² / 'प्रिवि / noun ▸ **the Privy Council** noun ब्रिटेन में राजा/रानी द्वारा नियुक्त अनुभवी राजनीतिज्ञ **the privy purse** noun [sing] ब्रिटेन में सरकार द्वारा राजा/रानी के व्यक्तिगत ख़र्च के लिए दी गई धन-राशि।

prize / प्राइज़ / noun 1 पुरस्कार, इनाम 2 कोई वस्तु जिसे प्राप्त करने में किया परिश्रम सार्थक लगे ▸ **prize** adj 1 पुरस्कार जीतने वाला या जीतने की आशा वाला : *prize cattle* 2 अपनी क़िस्म का सर्वोत्तम **prize** verb अत्यधिक महत्त्व/सम्मान देना : *I prize my independence too much to get married.* **prize-fight** noun धन के लिए मुक्केबाज़ी।

pro¹ / प्रो / (pl **pros**) noun (अनौप) पेशेवर व्यक्ति (विशेषत: खिलाड़ी) : *a tennis pro.*

pro² / प्रो / noun ■ **the pros and cons** किसी चीज़ के लाभ और हानि।

pro- pref (उपसर्ग) समर्थन में, के पक्ष में : *pro-government forces/pro-abortion.*

probability / प्रॉब'बिलिटि / noun (pl **probabilities**) 1 संभावना : *What's the probability of its success?* 2 संभावित वस्तु, घटना या परिणाम 3 (गणित) संभाव्यता अनुपात।

probable / 'प्रॉबबल् / *adj* संभावित : *the most probable explanation* ▶ **probable** *noun* probable (for sth) खेल या ईनाम के लिए चुने जाने की सर्वोच्च संभावना वाला व्यक्ति : *All four players are probables for the national team, to be announced tomorrow.* **probably** *adv.*

probation / प्र'बेशन्; *US* प्रो'बेशन् / *noun* 1 (क़ानून) अपराधियों की परिवीक्षा-पद्धति जिसमें अपराधी को कारागार नहीं भेजा जाता, परंतु उसे एक निश्चित अवधि के लिए अधिकारी विशेष के सम्मुख नियमित रूप से पेश होना पड़ता है 2 परिवीक्षा काल (वह अवधि जिसमें नियुक्त व्यक्ति की योग्यताओं की परख की जाती है) : *a three-month period of probation* ▶ **probationary** *adj.*

probe / प्रोब् / *noun* 1 मरीज़ की जाँच के लिए एक सलाईनुमा डॉक्टरी उपकरण 2 (space probe भी) मानव रहित अंतरिक्ष-यान जो सूचना संग्रह के लिए छोड़ा जाता है 3 probe (into sth) (समाचार-पत्र में) किसी मामले की पूरी-पूरी एवं सावधानीपूर्वक जाँच : *set up a probe into the disappearance of government funds* ▶ **probe** *verb* 1 जाँच-परख करना 2 probe (into sth) गहराई से खोजबीन करना 3 गुप्त या व्यक्तिगत बातें जानने के लिए सवाल पूछना **probing** *adj* खोजी।

problem / 'प्रॉब्लम् / *noun* 1 समस्या : *pressing economic problems* 2 प्रश्न जिसका हल या उत्तर विशेषत: तर्क या हिसाब द्वारा निकाला जाए : *a mathematical problem* ▶ **problematic** / ,प्रॉब्ल'मैटिक् / (**problematical** भी) *adj* समस्याग्रस्त एवं कठिन।

procedure / प्र'सीजर् / *noun* 1 (क़ानूनी, राजनीतिक या व्यापारिक मामलों में) कार्य-पद्धति, कार्य करने का औपचारिक तरीक़ा : *follow the standard procedure(s)* 2 procedure (for sth) प्रक्रिया : *proce-dure for making a complaint* ▶ **procedural** *adj.*

proceed / प्र'सीड्; प्रो'सीड् / *verb* (औप) 1 (अगले स्थान/चरण की ओर) जाना, बढ़ना : *Work is proceeding slowly.* 2 proceed (with sth) कुछ आरंभ करना या जारी रखना ■ proceed against sth (क़ानून) किसी के विरुद्ध क़ानूनी कार्रवाई शुरू करना proceed from sth (औप) उत्पन्न होना, निकलना : *the evils that proceed from human greed.*

proceedings / प्र'सीडिंग्ज़ / *noun* [pl] 1 proceedings (against sb/for sth) क़ानूनी कार्रवाई : *institute divorce proceedings* 2 सभा, समारोह आदि की कार्रवाई 3 proceedings (of sth) सभा-समिति आदि की प्रकाशित रिपोर्ट।

proceeds / 'प्रोसीड्ज़ / *noun* [pl] proceeds (of/from sth) किसी कार्य से कमाई गई राशि, लाभ/आय प्राप्ति : *They gave a concert and donated the proceeds to charity.*

process / 'प्रोसेस; *US* 'प्रॉसेस् / *noun* 1 प्रक्रम, क्रिया और परिवर्तन का संबद्ध कार्य : *Unloading the cargo was a slow process.* 2 (विशेषत: स्वाभाविक रूप से होने वाले) परिवर्तनों की शृंखला : *a normal part of the ageing process* 3 (विशेषत: उद्योगों में) प्रक्रिया, विधि ▶ **process** *verb* 1 (उद्योगों में) कच्चे माल को विशेष औद्योगिक/उत्पादक प्रक्रिया द्वारा तैयार, परिरक्षित आदि करना 2 काग़ज़ात/निवेदन आदि पर कार्रवाई करना **processor** *noun* संसाधक।

procession / प्र'सेशन् / *noun* 1 जुलूस; जुलूस निकालना : *The choir entered the church in procession.* 2 एक के बाद एक आते लोगों की विशाल संख्या।

proclaim / प्र'क्लेम् / *verb* 1 घोषणा करना : *proclaim a public holiday* 2 (औप) स्पष्ट दिखाना, पता लगना : *His accent proclaimed him a Scot.*

▶ **proclamation** / ˌprɒklə'meɪʃn / noun
घोषणा।

procrastinate / prə'kræstɪneɪt / verb
(औप, अपमा) कार्रवाई करने में देर लगाना,
टालना ▶ **procrastination** noun (औप,
अपमा) टाल-मटोल, दीर्घसूत्रिता : She
condemned the government's procrastination.

procure / prə'kjʊər / verb (औप)
1 **procure sth (for sb)** सावधानी और
यत्नपूर्वक पाना, प्राप्त करना : procure the
services of a lawyer 2 ग्राहकों के लिए
वेश्या लाना ▶ **procurement** noun
(औप) अधिप्राप्ति, सरकारी ख़रीद **pro-
curer** noun (fem **procuress**) वेश्याओं
का दलाल।

prod / prɒd / verb (-dd-) 1 **prod (at sb/
sth)** कोंचना, छेड़ना : He prodded me
in the ribs with his rifle. 2 **prod sb
(into sth/doing sth)** (अनौप) आलसी/
अनिच्छुक व्यक्ति को कुछ करने को प्रेरित
करना ▶ **prod** noun 1 कोंचना, छेड़-छाड़
2 (अनौप) किसी को कार्रवाई करने के लिए
याद दिलाने की क्रिया।

prodigal / 'prɒdɪgl / adj (औप, अपमा)
अपव्ययी, फ़िज़ूलख़र्च : a prodigal administration.

prodigious / prə'dɪdʒəs / adj (औप)
अनोखे/आश्चर्यजनक रूप से अतिविशाल :
their prodigious achievement
▶ **prodigiously** adv.

prodigy / 'prɒdɪdʒi / noun (pl **prodi-
gies**) विलक्षण प्रतिभा का (विशेषतः कम
उम्र का) व्यक्ति : a child/an infant
prodigy.

produce / prə'djuːs; US prə'duːs / verb
1 पैदा करना, उत्पन्न करना; उत्पादन करना :
This soil produces good tomatoes.
2 निपुणता द्वारा सृजन/रचना करना 3 प्रा-
कृतिक प्रक्रिया द्वारा उत्पन्न करना; उगाना;
जन्म देना : The plant is producing
new leaves. ○ His cow has pro-

duced a calf. 4 स्थिति विशेष का कारण
बनना : A phone call to the manager
soon produced results. 5 **produce
sth (from/out of sth)** (परीक्षणार्थ) पेश/
प्रस्तुत करना : produce a ticket for
inspection 6 नाटक, फ़िल्म आदि को
अभिनयार्थ प्रस्तुत करना ▶ **produce** / 'prɒd-
juːs; US 'prɒduːs / noun उपज/फ़सल।

producer / prə'djuːsər; US prə'duːsər / noun
1 उत्पादक (व्यक्ति, कंपनी, देश आदि)
2 (फ़िल्म आदि का) प्रस्तुतकर्ता, निर्माता।

product / 'prɒdʌkt / noun 1 उत्पादन,
उपज 2 **product of sth** किसी चीज़ का
परिणाम; किसी बात से अत्यंत प्रभावित व्यक्ति
3 (गणित) गुणनफल : The product of
4 and 10 is 40.

production / prə'dʌkʃn / noun 1 उत्पा-
दन प्रक्रिया 2 उत्पादित मात्रा : increase in
production 3 (विशेषतः नाटक, फ़िल्म)
निर्मिति, निर्माण ■ **on production of sth**
(औप) कुछ दिखाने पर/से : On production of your membership card, you
will receive a discount on all your
purchases.

productive / prə'dʌktɪv / adj 1 उत्पादन
योग्य, उपजाऊ 2 लाभकारी : a productive meeting 3 **productive of sth**
(औप) परिणति लाने वाला।

productivity / ˌprɒdʌk'tɪvɪti / noun
उत्पादकता, उपजाऊपन; उत्पादनशक्ति।

profane / prə'feɪn / adj (औप) 1 ईश्वर
और धार्मिक वस्तुओं को अपमानित करने
वाला, अधर्मी 2 इहलौकिक, सांसारिक :
songs of sacred and profane
love ▶ **profane** verb (औप) धार्मिक
स्थान एवं वस्तुओं को अपमानित करना
profanity / prə'fænɪti; US prə'fænɪti /
noun (pl **profanities**) (औप) अपमान-
पूर्ण व्यवहार एवं वचन; (प्रायः pl) गाली।

profess / prə'fes / verb (औप) 1 दावा
करना (प्रायः झूठा) 2 अपने विचार, विश्वास,
भाव आदि को खुले-आम कहना, घोषित

करना 3 किसी धर्म-विशेष का होना : *profess Islam* ▸ **professed** *adj* 1 दावा (कभी-कभी झूठा) किया हुआ 2 घोषित।

profession /प्रं'फ़ेशन्/ *noun* 1 जीविका, पेशा (जिसमें विशेषत: उच्च शिक्षा या दीर्घ प्रशिक्षण आवश्यक होता है, जैसे वक्कालत, डॉक्टरी, स्थापत्य कला आदि) : *She is a lawyer by profession.* 2 **profession of sth** दावा, घोषणा : *a profession of belief.*

professional /प्रं'फ़ेशन्ल्/ *adj* 1 व्यावसायिक : *a distinguished professional career* 2 व्यावसायिक निपुणता वाला : *a very professional piece of work* 3 पेशेवर, पैसा लेकर कौशल दिखाने वाला : *a professional boxer/tennis player* 4 (खेल आदि) पेशे के रूप में अपनाया गया, न कि शौक के लिए : *professional football* ▸ **professional** *noun* 1 व्यवसायी 2 पेशेवर (खिलाड़ी या अन्य कलाकार) 3 अत्यंत निपुण या अनुभवी व्यक्ति **professionally** *adv* व्यावसायिक रूप से; (कार्य आदि) व्यावसायिक निपुणता से (किया गया); अनुभवी एवं निपुण व्यक्ति द्वारा किया गया।

professor /प्रं'फ़ेसर्/ *noun* (*संक्षि* **Prof**) 1 विश्वविद्यालय में उच्चतम पद का अध्यापक, प्रोफ़ेसर 2 (*US*) विश्वविद्यालय/कॉलेज अध्यापक ▸ **professorship** *noun.*

proficient /प्रं'फ़िशन्ट्/ *adj* **proficient (in/at sth/doing sth)** कुशल, दक्ष ▸ **proficiency** /प्रं'फ़िशन्सि/ *noun* **proficiency (in sth/doing sth)** निपुणता, प्रवीणता : *increase proficiency.*

profile /'प्रोफ़ाइल्/ *noun* 1 मानव चेहरे का एक बग़ल का चित्र, पार्श्वदृश्य 2 पृष्ठभूमि पर किसी वस्तु की रूपरेखा 3 समाचार-पत्र आदि के लेख में किसी व्यक्ति/वस्तु का वर्णन : *The magazine publishes a profile of a leading sports personality each month.* 4 स्वयं की सार्वजनिक

छवि : *raise one's profile* ■ **a high/ low profile** सुस्पष्ट/अस्पष्ट व्यवहार, सार्वजनिक ध्यान आकर्षित करने/दूर रखने के लिए : *high profile politicians* ▸ **profile** *verb* वर्णन करना/लिखना।

profit¹ /'प्रॉफ़िट्/ *noun* 1 (व्यापार में) लाभ, नफ़ा 2 (औप) फ़ायदा, किसी वस्तु से मिलने वाला लाभ।

profit² /'प्रॉफ़िट्/ *verb* ■ **profit by/ from sth** लाभ पाना/फ़ायदा मिलना : *profit by one's experience/mistakes.*

profitable /'प्रॉफ़िटब्ल्/ *adj* लाभदायक ▸ **profitability** *noun* **profitably** *adv.*

profound /प्रं'फ़ाउन्ड्/ *adj* 1 (औप) (कोई स्थिति या गुण) गहरा, महान : *a profound silence/shock* 2 अत्यधिक ज्ञान या समझ से पूर्ण : *a profound awareness of the problem* 3 विचार और अध्ययन की ज़रूरत वाला: *the profound mystery of life* ▸ **profoundly** *adv* गंभीरता से, काफ़ी हद तक : *She was profoundly shaken by the news.*

profundity /प्रं'फ़न्डटि/ *noun* (*pl* **profundities**) (औप) 1 ज्ञान/विचारों की गहराई 2 (विशेषत: *pl*) गंभीर उक्ति/ कथन।

profuse /प्रं'फ़्यूस्/ *adj* प्रचुर; अत्यधिक मात्रा में : *profuse apologies* ▸ **profusely** *adv* **profusion** /प्रं'फ़्यूश्न्/ *noun* [*sing*] **profusion of sth** (औप) बाहुल्य, प्रचुरता : *a profusion of colours/flowers.*

progeny /'प्रॉजनि/ *noun* [*pl*] (औप या परि) मानव/पशुओं के बच्चे/संतान।

program /'प्रोग्रैम्/ *noun* (कंप्यूटर में) विशिष्ट उद्देश्य से क्रमबद्ध अनुदेशों का समुच्चय ▸ **program** *verb* (-mm-; *US* -m-) कंप्यूटर को कुछ करने का आदेश देना **programmer** *noun* कंप्यूटर के लिए प्रोग्रैम लिखने वाला व्यक्ति; प्रोग्रैमर।

programme (*US* **program**) /'प्रोग्रैम्/

noun 1 टी वी, रेडियो आदि पर प्रसारित कार्यक्रम (फ़िल्म, नाटक आदि) 2 (भविष्य की) योजना : *draw up a training programme for new staff* 3 अध्ययन, संगीत आदि का कार्यक्रम ▸ **programme** (*US* **program**) *verb* (-mm-; *US* -m-) 1 **programme sth (for sth)** प्रोग्रैम तैयार करना; योजना बनाना 2 विशिष्ट रूप से कार्य करने को प्रेरित करना (विशेषत: स्वचालित रूप से)।

progress / 'प्रोग्रेस; *US* 'प्राॅग्रेस / *noun* 1 प्रगति : *The walkers were making slow progress up the rocky path.* 2 विकास; उन्नति/सुधार : *evolutionary progress* ∎ **in progress** (औप) (कोई कार्य) चल/हो रहा ▸ **progress** / प्रॅ'ग्रेस / *verb* 1 प्रगति करना; उन्नति करना 2 (काल क्रम में) आगे बढ़ना।

progression / प्रॅ'ग्रेशन् / *noun* (औप) 1 **progression (from sth) (to sth)** आगे बढ़ने या विकसित होने की प्रक्रिया, विशेषत: चरणों में 2 क्रम, शृंखला।

progressive / प्रॅ'ग्रेसिव् / *adj* 1 प्रगतिशील 2 क्रमिक, उत्तरोत्तर बढ़ने वाला 3 पुरोगामी; प्रगति की ओर अग्रसर : *a progressive nation/school.*

prohibit / प्रॅ'हिबिट्; *US* प्रो'हिबिट् / *verb* (औप) 1 **prohibit sth; prohibit sb (from doing sth)** क़ानून, नियम आदि से निषेध करना या रोकना/मना करना : *Parking without a permit is prohibited.* 2 कुछ असंभव बना देना, रोक देना : *The high cost prohibits the widespread use of the drug.*

prohibition / ,प्रोइ'बिशन्; *US* ,प्रोअं'बि-शन् / *noun* 1 निषेध; प्रतिबंध 2 **prohibition (against sth)** निषेधाज्ञा : *a prohibition against shops opening on Sunday.*

prohibitive / प्रॅ'हिबिटिव्; *US* प्रो'हिब-टिव्/ *adj* 1 निषेधकारी 2 (क़ीमतें आदि) इतनी ऊँची होना कि वस्तु ख़रीदी न जा

सके : *The cost of property in the city is prohibitive.*

project[1] / 'प्राॅ'जेक्ट्/ *noun* 1 परियोजना; योजनाबद्ध कार्य : *a research project* 2 स्कूल/कॉलेजों में विद्यार्थियों द्वारा किया गया लघु शोध कार्य : *a history project.*

project[2] / प्रॅ'जेक्ट् / *verb* 1 परियोजना बनाना; कार्य-योजना तैयार करना; आँकना : *The unemployment rate is projected to fall by 7%.* 2 **project sth (into sth)** प्रक्षेप करना : *project missiles into space* 3 **project sth (on/onto sth)** प्रकाश, छाया, छवि आदि किसी सतह पर डालना 4 आस-पास की सतह से बाहर की तरफ़ उठा हुआ होना : *a balcony that projects over the street* 5 इस तरह पेश आना/करना कि अच्छा प्रभाव पड़े।

projectile/प्रॅ'जेक्टाइल/ *noun* (औप या तक) प्रक्षेपास्त्र।

projection/प्रॅ'जेक्शन्/ *noun* 1 वर्तमान के अध्ययन पर आधारित भावी स्थिति/प्रवृत्ति का आकलन : *sales projections for the next year* 2 छवि उत्पन्न करने की क्रिया; इस तरह डाली गई छवि 3 सतह से बाहर निकली हुई वस्तु : *a projection of rock.*

projector / प्रॅ'जेक्टर् / *noun* प्रक्षेपक, प्रोजेक्टर, फ़िल्म बड़ी करके परदे पर फेंकने वाला यंत्र।

proletariat / ,प्रोल'टेअरिअट्/ *noun* **the proletariat** (अप्र या अपमा) श्रमजीवी वर्ग, पूर्ण प्रशिक्षित तथा अर्धप्रशिक्षित मज़दूरों का वर्ग, सर्वहारा वर्ग।

proliferate / प्रॅ'लिफ़रेट्/ *verb* (औप) (पौधों, पशुओं, कोशिकाओं आदि का) तीव्रता से प्रजनन एवं वृद्धि करना; संख्या में तीव्र वृद्धि करना : *a pond in which minute organisms proliferate* ▸ **proliferation** / प्र,लिफ़'रेशन्/ *noun* [*sing*] संख्या में तेज़ी से बढ़ोतरी; वस्तु-विशेष की विशाल संख्या।

prolific/प्रॅ'लिफ़िक्/ *adj* 1 (पौधे, पशु-

पक्षी आदि) काफ़ी पैदावार देने वाले, उर्वर : *prolific milk yields* 2 (साहित्यकार, कलाकार) प्रचुर मात्रा में रचनाएँ सृजन करने वाला : *a prolific author.*

prologue (*US* **prolog** भी) / 'प्रोलॉग् / *noun* prologue (to sth) 1 कविता या नाटक का मंगलाचरण/प्रस्तावना : *the 'Prologue' to the 'Canterbury Tales'* 2 घटनाचक्र की भूमिका बाँधने वाली/आरंभिक घटना।

prolong / प्र'लॉङ् / *verb* लंबा करना; अवधि बढ़ाना : *drugs that help to prolong life* ▸ **prolongation** *noun* (औप) दीर्घकालिकता लाने की क्रिया **prolonged** *adj* लंबी अवधि वाला।

prominent / 'प्रॉमिनन्ट् / *adj* 1 महत्त्वपूर्ण; प्रमुख/प्रसिद्ध : *play a prominent part in sth* 2 सुस्पष्ट, साफ़ दिखाई देने वाला : *the most prominent feature in the landscape* 3 बाहर निकला या उठा हुआ : *prominent cheek-bones/teeth* ▸ **prominence** / 'प्रॉमिनन्स् / *noun* [*sing*] प्रमुख होने की अवस्था।

promiscuous / प्र'मिस्क्युअस् / *adj* (अपमा) व्यभिचारी (व्यक्ति)।

promise¹ / 'प्रॉमिस् / *noun* 1 promise (of sth) वादा/वचन; प्रतिज्ञा : *go back on a promise* 2 सफलता या सुपरिणाम की आशा या संकेत : *She shows great promise.* 3 [*sing*] promise of sth कुछ होने की संभावना/आशा।

promise² / 'प्रॉमिस् / *verb* 1 promise sth (to sb) वादा करना, वचन देना : *I can't promise, but I'll do my best.* 2 (औप) आशा या विश्वास दिलाना ▸ **promising** *adj* भविष्य में सफलता या सुपरिणाम होने का संकेत देने वाला; आशा–वान : *The weather doesn't look too promising.*

promote / प्र'मोट् / *verb* 1 प्रगति के लिए सहायता/बढ़ावा देना, समर्थन देना 2 विक्रय में वृद्धि के लिए प्रचार करना : *We're*

promoting it worldwide. 3 **promote sb (from sth) (to sth)** पदोन्नति करना, तरक्क़ी देना ▸ **promoter** *noun* 1 नया व्यापार चलाने और बढ़ाने में सहायता करने वाला व्यक्ति/कंपनी 2 **promoter (of sth)** समर्थक।

promotion / प्र'मोशन् / *noun* 1 पदोन्नति 2 प्रचार–प्रसार।

prompt¹ / प्रॉम्प्ट् / *adj* 1 बिना विलंब किया कार्य, तुरंत : *a prompt reply* 2 **prompt (in doing sth)** (व्यक्ति) तत्पर, मुस्तैद : *We are always prompt in paying our bills.* ▸ **prompt** *adv* (एक निर्धारित समय के संबंध में) बिलकुल, ठीक : *at 6 o'clock prompt* **promptly** *adv* 1 बिना विलंब के 2 ठीक निर्धारित समय पर **promptness** *noun* तत्परता, मुस्तैदी।

prompt² / प्रॉम्प्ट् / *verb* 1 (कोई कार्य या भावना) प्रेरित और प्रोत्साहित करना : *The ban on smoking was prompted by complaints from members of staff.* 2 कुछ करने का कारण बनना : *What prompted him to be so generous?* 3 रंगमंच में अभिनेता को नेपथ्य से संभाषण की याद दिलाते जाना ▸ **prompt** *noun* (संभाषण आदि में) याद दिलाए जाने की क्रिया **prompter** *noun* पार्श्वसूचक (व्यक्ति)।

promulgate / 'प्रॉमल्गेट् / *verb* (औप) 1 दूर-दूर तक परिचित कराना : *promulgate a belief/an idea* 2 औपचारिक रूप से नए क़ानून, नियम आदि की घोषणा करना ▸ **promulgation** *noun.*

prone / प्रोन् / *adj* 1 **prone to sth/to do sth** किसी चीज़ से पीड़ित होने या कुछ करने या कुछ पाने की संभावना रखना : *land prone to flooding* 2 औंधे मुँह लेटा हुआ : *lying prone* ▸ **proneness** *noun.*

prong / प्रॉङ् / *noun* काँटा, शूल (जैसे त्रिशूल का)।

pronoun / 'प्रोनाउन् / noun (व्या) सर्व-नाम जैसे he, she, hers, me.

pronounce / प्र'नाउन्स् / verb 1 किसी शब्द या अक्षर को उच्चारित करना 2 घोषणा करना, विशेषत: औपचारिक या आधिकारिक रूप से : pronounce an opinion/a judgement ■ pronounce (sth) for/against sb/sth (क़ानून) अदालत में निर्णय घोषित करना : pronounce (sentence) against the accused ▶ pronounced adj 1 सुस्पष्ट 2 (मत आदि) निश्चित।

pronunciation / प्र.नन्सि'एश्न् / noun 1 उच्चारण-रीति 2 व्यक्ति की उच्चारण शैली : His pronunciation of English is still not good, but it is improving.

proof¹ / प्रूफ़ / noun 1 प्रमाण, सबूत : ask sb for proof of identity 2 (विशेषत: pl) मुद्रण के पहले की प्रति जिसमें कुछ सुधार किया जा सकता है, प्रूफ़ 3 जाँच, परख : Is the claim capable of proof? 4 अल-कॉहल वाले द्रवों की तीव्रता की माप जिसमें सर्वाधिक तीव्रता 100% होती है : This whisky is 70% proof.

proof² / प्रूफ़ / adj 1 proof against sth (औप) सुरक्षा देने वाला; जो मुक़ाबला कर सके या झेल सके : Their clothing was not proof against the bitter weather. 2 (समासों में) वस्तु-विशेष से सुरक्षा देने वाला : rainproof/windproof clothing.

prop¹ / प्रॉप् / noun 1 सहारा देने (खड़ा करने का) लकड़ी, धातु आदि से बना टेक : Props were used to prevent the roof collapsing. 2 सहारा देने वाला व्यक्ति/वस्तु ▶ prop verb (-pp-) 1 सहारा देना, टिकाए रखना 2 prop sb/sth (up) against sth किसी वस्तु का सहारा लेकर टिकाना : a bicycle propped against the wall.

prop² / प्रॉप् / noun (प्राय: pl) रंगमंच या फ़िल्मसेट में प्रयुक्त परदे, फ़र्नीचर, पोशाक आदि : stage props.

propaganda / प्रॉप'गैन्डा / noun (प्राय: अपमा) किसी आंदोलन में विचार आदि (प्राय: अतिशयोक्तिपूर्ण या झूठे) को प्रचारित करने के उपाय, दुष्प्रचार : a propaganda campaign ▶ propagandist noun propagandize, -ise verb.

propagate / 'प्रॉपगेट् / verb 1 (औप) (समाचार, विचार आदि) और अधिक व्यापक क्षेत्र में फैलाना, प्रसारित करना : religious leaders who travelled overseas to propagate their faith 2 पौधों को उगा कर संख्या में वृद्धि करना; (पौधों का) प्रजनन करना : Plants won't propagate in these conditions. ▶ propagation / प्रॉप'गेश्न् / noun.

propel / प्र'पेल् / verb (-ll-) 1 आगे की ओर धकेलना/चलाना/धक्का देना 2 किसी को आगे धक्का देना या (विकट) परिस्थिति में डाल देना : His addiction to drugs propelled him towards a life of crime. ▶ propellant (propellent भी) noun आगे भेजने या प्रेरित करने वाली वस्तु propeller noun जहाज़ आदि में लगा पंखनुमा यंत्र, प्रोपेलर।

propensity / प्र'पेन्सटि / noun (pl propensities) propensity (for/to sth); propensity (for doing/to do sth) (औप) कुछ (विशेषत: कुछ अनुचित) करने की प्रवृत्ति : show a propensity for violence.

proper / 'प्रॉपर् / adj 1 यथार्थ, जैसा कहा जा रहा है, ठीक वैसे ही, असली रूप में : She hadn't had a proper holiday for years. 2 उचित, उपयुक्त : use the proper tool for the job 3 समाज द्वारा स्वीकृत, मर्यादा के भीतर : He always behaves in a formal and proper way. 4 (अनौप) पूर्ण, पूरा-पूरा : give this room a proper clean ▶ properly adv उचित/उपयुक्त ढंग से proper

noun (proper name भी**)** noun (व्या) व्यक्तिवाचक संज्ञा।

property /'प्रॉपर्टि / noun (pl **properties) 1** संपत्ति, जायदाद; भूमि, भवन आदि **2** (विशेषत: pl) (तक) गुणधर्म, विशेषता : compare the physical properties of two substances ▸ **propertied** adj (औप) संपत्ति और जायदाद (विशेषत: भूमि) का स्वामी।

prophecy /'प्रॉफ़सि / noun (pl **prophecies)** भविष्यवाणी; भविष्यवाणी करने की शक्ति।

prophesy /'प्रॉफ़साइ / verb (pt, pp **prophesied)** भविष्यवाणी करना।

prophet /'प्रॉफ़िट् / noun **1** (विशेषत: ईसाई, यहूदी एवं इस्लाम धर्मों में) पैगंबर (धर्मोपदेशक जो यह दावा करता है कि उसे यह ज्ञान सीधे ईश्वर से मिला है) : Hebrew prophets **2 the Prophet** [sing] इस्लाम के संस्थापक पैगंबर मुहम्मद **3** भविष्यवक्ता, नबी **4 prophet (of sth)** नए विचार, सिद्धांत आदि प्रतिपादित-प्रसारित करने वाला : the early prophets of socialism ▸ **prophetic** / प्र'फ़ेटिक / adj (औप) **1** भविष्यसूचक : prophetic remarks **2** पैगंबरी।

propitiate / प्र'पिशिएट् / verb (औप) क्रोध शांत करके (संतुष्ट करके) कृपा और अनुग्रह प्राप्त करना : They offered sacrifices to propitiate the gods. ▸ **propitiation** noun.

proponent / प्र'पोनन्ट् / noun **proponent of sth** (औप) किसी सिद्धांत, उद्देश्य आदि का समर्थक व्यक्ति : one of the leading proponents of aromatherapy.

proportion / प्र'पॉर्शन् / noun **1** भाग, अंश **2 proportion (of sth to sth)** एक वस्तु का दूसरी वस्तु के आकार, मात्रा आदि से संबंध, अनुपात : The proportion of men to women in the college has changed dramatically over the years. **3** (प्राय: pl) दो वस्तुओं का या किसी वस्तु के अनेक भागों का परस्पर उपयुक्त अनुपात में होना **4 proportions** [pl] आकार, मापन : a room of modest proportions **5** (गणित) अनुपात, समानुपात ■ **in proportion** दूसरी वस्तुओं से सही संबंध में **in proportion to sth** किसी के सापेक्ष में **out of proportion (to sth)** एक वस्तु का दूसरी वस्तुओं से ग़लत संबंध में होना : a severe punishment that was out of proportion to other crimes ▸ **proportioned** adj (समास में) निर्धारित अनुपात/आकार वाला।

proportional / प्र'पॉर्शन्ल् / adj **proportional (to sth)** (औप) उचित अनुपात में।

proportionate / प्र'पॉर्शनट् / adj **proportionate (to sth)** (औप) से समानुपाती।

proposal / प्र'पोज़्ल् / noun **1 proposal (for sth/doing sth); proposal (to do sth)** प्रस्ताव **2** प्रस्ताव प्रस्तुतीकरण क्रिया **3** विवाह प्रस्ताव।

propose / प्र'पोज़् / verb **1** योजना, सुझाव आदि विचारार्थ प्रस्तुत करना, प्रस्ताव रखना **2 propose (sth) (to sb)** विवाह के लिए (औपचारिक रूप से) प्रस्ताव रखना **3 propose sb for sth; propose sb as sth** किसी पद के लिए किसी व्यक्ति का नाम प्रस्तुत करना : I propose Maya Rao for membership of the committee.

proposition / प्रॉप'ज़िशन् / noun **1** सुझाव **2** (अनौप) कठिन कार्य या समस्या : a tricky proposition **3 proposition (that...)** कथन जो निर्णय या मत व्यक्त करे।

propound / प्र'पाउन्ड् / verb (औप) विचार या समाधान के लिए कोई सिद्धांत आदि प्रस्तुत करना : propound an idea/a policy.

proprietor / प्र'प्राइअटर् / noun (fem **proprietress)** भूमि/संपत्ति, होटल/दुकान

आदि का मालिक, स्वामी ▶ **proprietorial** *adj.*

propriety / प्र'प्राइअटि / *noun* (औप) 1 व्यवहार का औचित्य, मर्यादा : *have no sense of propriety* 2 propriety (of sth) उपयुक्तता, न्यायोचित होने की स्थिति : *The social worker questioned the propriety of separating children from their parents.*

propulsion / प्र'पल्शन् / *noun* प्रणोदन बल ▶ **propulsive** *adj* : *propulsive power/forces.*

prosaic / प्र'ज़ेइक् / *adj* (प्राय: अपमा) 1 घिसा-पिटा, कल्पना रहित : *a prosaic style/writer* 2 नीरस, उबाऊ : *a prosaic job* ▶ **prosaically** *adv.*

prose / प्रोज़् / *noun* गद्य ('पद्य' का विलोम): *a prose writer.*

prosecute / 'प्रॉसिक्यूट् / *verb* 1 prosecute sb (for sth/doing sth) किसी के विरुद्ध क़ानूनी कार्रवाई चलाना, अभियोग चलाना : *Trespassers will be prosecuted.* 2 (औप) (व्यापार, अध्ययन आदि को) जारी रखना : *prosecute a war* ▶ **prosecutor** *noun.*

prosecution / प्रॉसि'क्यूश्न् / *noun* 1 अदालत में अभियोग प्रक्रिया 2 the prosecution अभियोग चलाने वाला व्यक्ति/ संस्था एवं उसके वकील आदि : *The prosecution lack(s) sufficient evidence.*

prospect¹ / 'प्रॉस्पेक्ट; *US* 'प्रास्पेक्ट / *noun* 1 prospect (of sth/doing sth) संभावना, प्रत्याशा : *There is no immediate prospect of a peace settlement.* 2 prospects [*pl*] सफलता की संभावना/आशा : *Further training would improve your job prospects.* 3 [*sing*] मन या कल्पना में आया परिदृश्य 4 सफलता की आशा वाला प्रत्याशी 5 (अप्र) भूमि/समुद्र का बड़ा परिदृश्य।

prospect² / प्र'स्पेक्ट; *US* 'प्रास्पेक्ट / *verb* prospect (for sth) सोना, खनिज, तेल आदि के लिए भूमिगत खोज करना ▶ **prospector** *noun* सोना, खनिज, तेल आदि की खोज करने वाला।

prospective / प्र'स्पेक्टिव् / *adj* भविष्य-विषयक, भावी : *show the house to a prospective buyer.*

prospectus / प्र'स्पेक्टस् / *noun* विद्यालय, व्यापारिक अनुष्ठान आदि की विवरणिका (मुद्रित पुस्तिका जिसमें आवश्यक सूचनाएँ, नियम, विज्ञापन आदि होते हैं)।

prosper / 'प्रॉस्पर / *verb* समृद्ध होना, फलना-फूलना : *The business is prospering.*

prosperity / प्रॉ'स्पेरटि / *noun* समृद्धि/ वैभव; सफलता : *material prosperity.*

prosperous / 'प्रॉस्परस् / *adj* समृद्ध, सफल।

prostitute /'प्रॉस्टिट्यूट; *US* 'प्रास्टट्यूट / *noun* वेश्या ▶ **prostitute** *verb* prostitute (oneself) (अपमा) अपनी योग्यता/ प्रतिभा का दुरुपयोग करना; वेश्यावृत्ति करना।

prostrate / 'प्रॉस्ट्रेट् / *adj* 1 साष्टांग दंडवत् प्रणाम करता हुआ : *fall prostrate in worship* 2 prostrate (with sth) अत्यंत दुखी, असहाय : *She was prostrate with grief after his death.* ▶ **prostrate** *verb* 1 prostrate oneself दंडवत् हो जाना 2 (बीमारी आदि के कारण) असहाय हो जाना **prostration** / प्रॉ'स्ट्रेश्न् / *noun* 1 दंडवत् की स्थिति 2 अत्यधिक शारीरिक दुर्बलता।

protagonist / प्र'टैगनिस्ट् / *noun* 1 (औप) नाटक का मुख्य पात्र; किसी कहानी या सत्य घटना का मुख्य पात्र/व्यक्ति 2 protagonist (of sth) आंदोलन या कार्रवाई का नेतृत्व करने वाला : *a leading protagonist of the conservation movement.*

protect / प्र'टेक्ट् / *verb* 1 protect sb/ sth (against/from sth) (सं)रक्षा कर-ना : *protect the environment* 2 आ-

यातित सामग्री पर शुल्क लगाकर घरेलू उद्योगों को प्रोत्साहन देना : *a heavily protected industry* **3 protect sb/ sth (against sth)** *(तक)* (बीमा पॉलिसि द्वारा) नुक्सान होने पर कीमत अदा करने का वचन दिया जाना।

protection / प्र'टेक्शन् / *noun* **1 protection (for sb) (against sth)** (सं)रक्षण प्रक्रिया/की स्थिति; (सं)रक्षण देने वाली वस्तु : *The union is campaigning for greater protection against unfair dismissal.* ○ *legal protections for unions* **2** उद्योगों के (सं)रक्षण की व्यवस्था **3** अपराधियों को अपने व्यापार पर हमला करने से रोकने के लिए धन आदि देने की व्यवस्था : *paying protection money.*

protective / प्र'टेक्टिव् / *adj* (सं)रक्षा देने वाला; **protective (of sth/towards sb)** रक्षा को तत्पर।

protector / प्र'टेक्टर् / *noun* (सं)रक्षा करने वाला व्यक्ति या संघ; (सं)रक्षा देने वाली वस्तु।

protégé (*fem* **protégee**) / 'प्रॉटेश्; *US* 'प्रोटेश्ो / *noun* व्यक्ति जिसके हित, व्यवसाय आदि की देखभाल कोई प्रभावशाली या अधिकारपूर्ण व्यक्ति करे।

protein / 'प्रोटीन् / *noun* मांस, मछली, कई सब्ज़ियों आदि में पाया जाने वाला एक पौष्टिक तत्त्व; प्रोटीन।

protest¹ / प्र'टेस्ट् / *verb* **protest (about/against/at sth)** विरोध प्रकट करना; आपत्ति उठाना; प्रतिवाद करना : *Demonstrators protested against the new legislation.*

protest² / 'प्रोटेस्ट् / *noun* प्रतिवाद; अ-सहमति; विरोध : *The minister resigned in protest.* ■ **under protest** अनिच्छा और विरोध प्रकट करते हुए (कुछ काम करना)।

Protestant / 'प्रोटिस्टन्ट् / *noun, adj* ईसाई धर्म के प्रोटेस्टेंट चर्च के (अनुयायी)।

protestation / ,प्रॉट'स्टेश्न् / *noun* (औप) प्रतिज्ञापन, प्रबल घोषणा : *protestations of love.*

protocol / 'प्रोटकॉल् / *noun* **1** औपचारिक अवसरों के लिए नियमों की व्यवस्था **2** (औप) किसी संधि का पहला या मूल (लिखित) रूप।

prototype / 'प्रोटटाइप् / *noun* आदि रूप, पहला नमूना जो कृति का आधार हो : *the prototype for future school buildings.*

protracted / प्र'ट्रैक्टिड्; *US* प्रो'ट्रैक्टिड् / *adj* (प्राय: अपमा) दीर्घकालिक : *protracted delays/disputes/negotiations.*

protrude / प्र'ट्रूड्; *US* प्रो'ट्रूड् / *verb* **protrude (from sth)** बाहर की ओर निकलना/निकालना : *Several pens protruded from his top pocket.*

proud / प्राउड् / *adj* (**-er, -est**) **1 proud (of sb/sth); proud (to do sth/that...)** गर्व का अनुभव करने वाला, गौरवान्वित : *a proud father* **2** गर्व का कारण; आत्माभिमान **3** (अपमा) घमंडी : *She was too proud to admit that she was wrong.* **4** (औप) शानदार, वैभवशाली : *The statue stands tall and proud in the main square.* ▸ **proudly** *adv* गर्व से : *She proudly displayed her prize.*

prove / प्रूव् / *verb* (*pp* **proved;** *US* **proven** / 'प्रूव्न्/) **1 prove sth (to sb)** प्रमाण देकर सिद्ध करना : *prove sb's guilt* **2 prove (oneself) sth** परीक्षण आदि होने पर सिद्ध/स्थापित होना : *The old methods proved best after all.* ▸ **provable** *adj* सिद्ध किया जा सकने लायक।

proven / 'प्रूव्न्; 'प्रोव्न् / *adj* प्रयोग/जाँच द्वारा सिद्ध किया गया: *a man of proven ability.*

proverb / 'प्रॉवर्ब् / *noun* कहावत, लोकोक्ति ▸ **proverbial** / प्र'वर्बिअल् / *adj* **1** कहा-

वत/लोकोक्ति संबंधी 2 लोक प्रसिद्ध एवं सर्वमान्य : His obstinacy is proverbial.

provide /प्र'व्राइड्/ verb 1 provide sb (with sth); provide sth (for sb) उत्तर, उदाहरण, अवसर आदि प्रदान करना; अनिवार्य आवश्यकता की पूर्ति कर देना; प्रयोग के लिए उपलब्ध करवाना : provide evidence ○ Can you provide accommodation for thirty people? 2 (औप) आवश्यकता के रूप में व्यक्त करना ■ provide against sth (औप) किसी आकस्मिक घटना के लिए तैयारी करना provide for sb जीवन-यापन की वस्तुएँ प्रदान करना/आर्थिक सहायता करना ▶ provider noun पूर्तिकर्ता।

provided /प्र'व्राइडिड्/(provided that, providing, providing that भी) conj इस शर्त पर, यदि : I will agree to go provided (that) my expenses are paid.

providence/'प्रॉव्रिडन्स्/noun (Providence भी) ईश्वर, विधाता; परमात्मा का विधान : trust in divine providence

provident /'प्रॉव्रिडन्ट्/ adj (औप) भविष्य की आवश्यकताओं की पूर्ति के लिए जागरूक।

providential /,प्रॉव्रि'डेन्श्ल/ adj (औप) सही समय पर होने के कारण सौभाग्यपूर्ण : their providential departure just before the floods.

province /'प्रॉव्रिन्स्/ noun 1 प्रशासन के लिए देश के विभाजित प्रांत/प्रदेश 2 the provinces [pl] राजधानी से भिन्न प्रांतीय राज्य : He found the life in the provinces boring. 3 [sing] (औप) ज्ञान, कार्य भार या विशेषज्ञता का क्षेत्र : The matter is out of my province.

provincial/प्र'व्रिन्श्ल/adj 1 प्रादेशिक, प्रदेशीय : provincial taxes 2 (अपमा) बोलने, आचरण आदि में प्रदेशीय विशेषता; देहातीपना; संकीर्ण दृष्टिकोण दिखाते हुए

▶ **provincial** noun (प्राय: अपमा) (राजधानी से दूर) देहात से आया हुआ व्यक्ति **provincialism** noun (अपमा) क्षेत्रवाद।

provision /प्र'व्रिश्न्/ noun 1 provision of sth प्रदान करना या उधार देना; (प्राय: sing) प्रदत्त/उधार दी हुई मात्रा : The provision of specialist teachers is being increased. 2 provision for sth/sb; provision against sth भविष्य की आवश्यकताओं के लिए प्रबंध और तैयारी 3 provisions [pl] यात्रा आदि के लिए आहार-वस्तुएँ; रसद 4 क़ानूनी काग़ज़ात में व्यक्त शर्त/व्यवस्था : under the provisions of the agreement ▶ **provision** verb provision sb/sth (with sth) (औप) आवश्यक वस्तुएँ (भोजन आदि) उपलब्ध कराना।

provisional /प्र'व्रिश्न्ल्/ adj कामचलाऊ/स्थायी नहीं; अंतरकालीन : a provisional government ▶ **provisionally** adv.

proviso /प्र'व्राइज़ो/ noun (pl provisos) प्रतिबंध, शर्त : I agreed to go, with the proviso that my family should come with me.

provocation /,प्रॉव्र'केश्न्/ noun 1 उत्तेजित करने/छेड़छाड़ की प्रक्रिया 2 उत्तेजक वस्तु, उत्तेजनाजनक कार्य : The police remained calm in the face of repeated provocations.

provocative /प्र'व्रॉकटिव्/ adj 1 क्रोधोत्तेजक 2 कामोत्तेजक।

provoke /प्र'व्रोक्/ verb 1 (व्यक्ति/पशु को) नाराज़ करना; चिढ़ाना, भड़काना 2 provoke sb into doing sth/to do sth उकसा कर कुछ करवाना : His selfish behaviour finally provoked her into leaving him. 3 कोई प्रतिक्रिया उत्पन्न करना : provoke laughter/riots ▶ **provoking** adj (अप्र या औप) उत्तेजक; नाराज़ करने वाला।

prow / प्राउ / *noun (औप)* जहाज़ का नुकीला अग्रभाग।

prowess / 'प्राउअस् / *noun (औप)* पराक्रम; उत्कृष्ट निपुणता/योग्यता : *academic prowess.*

prowl / प्राउल् / *verb* 1 (पशुओं का) शिकार या भोजन ढूँढ़ने के लिए निकलना; चुपचाप, गोपनीय रीति से किसी कार्य के लिए विचरणा : *thieves prowling the streets at night* 2 (बेचैनी से) इधर-उधर घूमना ▸ **prowl** *noun* ■ **(be/go) on the prowl** विचरण की प्रक्रिया में ▸ **prowler** *noun* विचरण करता हुआ व्यक्ति या पशु।

proximity / प्राॅक्'सिमटि / *noun* **proximity (to sth)** *(औप)* समय/स्थान में समीपता, निकटता : *in the proximity of the building.*

proxy / 'प्राॅक्सि / *noun (pl* **proxies)** 1 किसी और का प्रतिनिधित्व करने का अधिकार 2 मुख्तार व्यक्ति : *He made his wife his proxy.*

prude / प्रूड् / *noun (अपमा)* छद्म लज्जालु; बहुत विनम्र/शर्मीला ▸ **prudery** *noun.*

prudent / 'प्रूडन्ट् / *adj* सावधान; अति विवेकपूर्ण : *make a prudent investment* ▸ **prudence** / 'प्रूडन्स् / *noun (औप)* : *exercise prudence in balancing expenditure against income* **prudently** *adv.*

prune[1] / प्रून् / *noun* सुखाया हुआ आलू-बुख़ारा।

prune[2] / प्रून् / *verb* 1 **prune sth (from/ off sth)** पेड़-झाड़ियों को छाँटना : *She has been pruning the roses.* 2 **prune sth (of sth); prune sth (down)** काट-छाँट कर सही परिमाण में लाना : *prune expenditure* ▸ **pruning** *noun.*

pry[1] / प्राइ / *verb (pt, pp* **pried** / प्राइड् /) **pry (into sth)** दूसरों के व्यक्तिगत मामलों में रुचि लेकर हस्तक्षेप करना, ताक-झाँक करना : *I don't want them prying into my affairs.*

pry[2] / प्राइ / *verb (pt, pp* **pried)** अलग करना; खोलना : *pry the lid off (a can).*

psalm / साम् / *noun* भजन, स्तोत्र ▸ **psalmist** *noun* भजनकार, भजन लिखने वाला।

pseudo / 'स्यूडो; *US* 'सूडो/ *adj (अनौप)* आभासी, छद्म : *pseudo poetry.*

pseud(o)- *pref (पूर्वपद)* मिथ्या, छद्म : *pseudo-intellectual ○ pseudonym.*

pseudonym / 'स्यूडनिम्; *US* 'सूडनिम्/ *noun* छद्मनाम, उपनाम : *Mark Twain was the pseudonym of Samuel Langhorne Clemens.*

psych / साइक् / *verb* **psych sb (out/ out of sth)** *(अनौप)* अत्यंत आत्म-विश्वास या आक्रमणशीलता दिखाते हुए प्रतिद्वंद्वी का विश्वास कम करना।

psyche / 'साइकि / *noun* मानस, चित्त।

psychiatry / साइ'काइअट्रि / *noun* मनो-रोग अध्ययन एवं चिकित्सा ▸ **psychiatric** *adj* **psychiatrist** *noun* मनो-चिकित्सक/विशेषज्ञ; मनोवैज्ञानिक।

psychic / 'साइकिक् / *adj* 1 (**psychical** भी) पारलौकिक प्रतीत होने वाली घटना या प्रक्रिया : *psychic energy* 2 पारलौकिक शक्ति संबंधी या शक्ति संपन्न : *psychic healing* 3 (**psychical** भी) आत्मिक, मानसिक : *psychical disorders.*

psychoanalysis / ‚साइकोअ'नैलिसिस् / *noun* मनो-विश्लेषण ▸ **psychoanalyse** *verb* **psychoanalyst** *noun.*

psychology / साइ'काॅलजि / *noun* 1 मनोविज्ञान 2 [*sing*] *(अनौप)* व्यक्ति/वर्ग के मानसिक लक्षण : *the psychology of the teenager* ▸ **psychological** / ‚साइक'लाॅजिक्ल् / *adj* 1 मानसिक 2 मनो-विज्ञान संबंधी।

psychopath / 'साइकोपैथ् / *noun* मानसिक तनाव/रोग से पीड़ित व्यक्ति जो उग्र एवं हिंसात्मक रूप से व्यवहार करता है।

psychotherapy / साइकोथेरपि / noun मनोरोग चिकित्सा।

pub / पब् / (और **public house** भी) noun मधुशाला, मै-खाना।

puberty / प्यूबर्टि / noun यौवनारंभ।

public / पब्लिक् / adj 1 सामान्य जनता-विषयक : a danger to public health 2 सार्वजनिक (**private** के वैषम्य में), आम/लोक : public services/education 3 आम जनता के लिए (खुला या ज्ञात) : a public apology ▸ **public** noun 1 the public आम जनता, जनसाधारण 2 एक जैसी रुचि या बातों वाले लोगों का वर्ग : the theatre-going public ▪ in public खुले आम ▸ **publicly** adv खुले आम **public relations** noun (संक्षि PR) 1 आम जनता के सामने किसी संस्था की अच्छी छवि प्रस्तुत करने संबंधी कार्य 2 आम जनता और संस्था के बीच के संबंधों की अवस्था **public transport** noun जनसाधारण के लिए यातायात व्यवस्था।

publication / पब्लिकेशन् / noun 1 पुस्तक, पत्रिका आदि का प्रकाशन 2 पुस्तक, पत्रिका आदि प्रकाशित ग्रंथ : specialist publications 3 किसी बात को सार्वजनिक करने की क्रिया : publication of the exam results.

publicity / पब्लिसिटि / noun 1 प्रसिद्धि; प्रत्येक के द्वारा जानने या देखे जाने की स्थिति : seek publicity 2 ध्यान आकर्षित करने की क्रिया; विज्ञापन।

publicize, -ise / पब्लिसाइज़ / verb किसी वस्तु के प्रति जनता के ध्यान को आकर्षित करना और उस संबंध में सूचना देना : an advertising campaign to publicize the new film.

publish / पब्लिश् / verb 1 पुस्तक आदि प्रकाशित करना; समाचार/लेख छापना; (लेखक आदि का) लेखन कार्य प्रकाशित होना : This book was published by Oxford University Press. ○ She has just published her first novel.

○ Her letter was published in the Times of India. 2 जनता में प्रचारित करना ▸ **publisher** noun (पुस्तक/पत्रिका आदि का) प्रकाशक **publishing** noun पुस्तक/पत्रिका आदि प्रकाशन का व्यवसाय।

pucker / पकर् / verb pucker (sth) (up) सिकुड़ना/सिकोड़ना; शिकन पड़ना/डालना : pucker one's lips.

pudding / पुडिङ् / noun 1 पुडिंग (भोजन के बाद दिया जाने वाला मीठा पकवान) 2 मैदे, चावल या डबल रोटी और अंडे, घी आदि के मिश्रण को पका कर बनाया मीठा पकवान।

puddle / पड्ल् / noun बारिश के पानी या अन्य द्रव का गड्ढे में (विशेषत: सड़क पर) रुक जाना।

puff¹ / पफ् / noun 1 झोंका; धुएँ/भाप आदि की फूँक : a puff of smoke 2 (समास में) क्रीम/जैम आदि से भरी खोखली पेस्ट्री : a cream puff 3 (अनौप) श्वास ▸ **puffy** adj मुलायम और फूला/सूजा हुआ।

puff² / पफ् / verb 1 हवा के झोंके चलना 2 puff (at/on) sth सिगरेट आदि के कश लेना 3 (अनौप) हाँफना ▪ puff sth out विशेषत: हवा भर कर फुलाना/फूल जाना : puff out one's cheeks puff (sth) up फुलाना/फूलना।

puffin / पफिन् / noun उत्तरी एटलांटिक में पाया जाने वाला एक सफेद और काले रंग का पक्षी जिसकी चोंच बड़ी एवं रंग-बिरंगी होती है।

puke / प्यूक् / verb puke (sth) (up) (अप) वमन/उलटी करना।

pull¹ / पुल् / verb 1 खींचना, घसीटना; बाहर निकालना : Pull the plug out. 2 परदे आदि खींचना (खोलने या बंद करने को) 3 मांसपेशी में बल आ जाना : pull a ligament/muscle/tendon 4 उपकरण, यंत्र को चलाने के लिए झटके से स्विच आदि को खींचना : Pull the lever to start the motor. 5 pull sb/sth (In) किसी का ध्यान/समर्थन पाना : a campaign to pull *in the voters* ■ **pull oneself together** अपनी भावनाओं को नियंत्रण में रखना **pull one's socks up** (अनौप) स्वयं कार्य, निष्पादन, व्यवहार को बेहतर बनाना **pull one's weight** औरों के साथ अपने हिस्से का कार्य पूरा करना **pull sb's leg** (अनौप) किसी मिथ्या तथ्य पर किसी को विश्वास दिलाने का मज़ाक में प्रयत्न करना **pull (sb) through (sth)** 1 बीमारी या संकट से निकल आना/निकलने में सहायता करना 2 कुछ कठिन करने में सफल होना/ किसी की सहायता करना **pull (sb/sth) out (of sth)** किसी स्थिति से निकलना/ निकालना **pull sb up** ग़लती पर खिंचाई करना **pull sth down** इमारत, ढाँचे आदि को गिराना **pull up** (वाहन या उसके चालक का) रुक जाना।

pull² / पुल् / *noun* 1 pull (at/on sth) खींचने की प्रक्रिया : *a pull on the rope* 2 [sing] the pull (of sth) खींचने की शक्ति; भावनाओं/व्यवहार को प्रभावित करने वाली शक्ति 3 (अनौप) दूसरों पर प्रभाव और अधिकार : *She has a lot of pull with the board of directors.*

pulley / 'पुलि / *noun* गरारी, घिरनी, पुली (सामान ऊपर उठाने का यंत्र)।

pullover / 'पुल्ओवर् / *noun* ऊनी स्वेटर, पुलोवर।

pulp / पल्प / *noun* 1 फल का गूदा; कूटने- पीटने से बनी गूदे जैसी चीज़ : *tomato pulp* 2 लकड़ी, काग़ज़ आदि की लुगदी 3 (अपमा) निकृष्ट कोटि की पुस्तकें/ पत्रिकाएँ : *pulp fiction* ▶ **pulp** *verb* लुगदी बनाना : *Unsold copies of the book were pulped.* **pulpy** *adj* 1 गूदे- दार; लुगदी जैसा 2 निकृष्ट (साहित्य)।

pulpit / 'पुल्पिट् / *noun* चर्च में बना मंच जहाँ पादरी खड़े होते हैं।

pulsate / पल् 'सेट् / *verb* 1 (pulse भी) नियमित गति के साथ/अंतराल से फैलना और सिकुड़ना : *A vein was pulsating on his forehead.* 2 नियमित गति से काँपना/

ध्वनि या तरंग उत्पन्न करना 3 pulsate (with sth) स्फूर्ति और उत्तेजना से भरपूर होना : *The streets were pulsating with life.*

pulse¹ / पल्स / *noun* 1 (प्राय: sing) नाड़ी, नब्ज़ : *The doctor took my pulse.* 2 संगीत की लय 3 ध्वनि, प्रकाश, विद्युत-धारा आदि की एक कंपन/तरंग; तरंगों की शृंखला : *The machine emits sound pulses.* ▶ **pulse** *verb* 1 pulse (through sth) धड़कना 2 pulse (with sth) उत्तेजना, उत्साह, ऊर्जा आदि से भरा हुआ होना।

pulse² / पल्स / *noun* (प्राय: pl) दाल।

pulverize, -ise / 'पल्वराइज़ / *verb* 1 (औप) चूर-चूर कर देना, पीस देना 2 (अनौप) करारी हार देना या पूरी तरह नष्ट कर देना : *We absolutely pulverized the opposition.*

pump / पम्प् / *noun* 1 (समासों में) गैस, द्रव या हवा बलपूर्वक निकालने या भरने का यंत्र : *a petrol/bicycle pump* 2 पंप करने की क्रिया ▶ **pump** *verb* 1 पानी, हवा, गैस आदि पंप से निकालना 2 ज़ोर से धड़कना 3 किसी चीज़ से भरना : *He was pumped full of drugs.* 4 pump sb (for sth) किसी से बहुत-से प्रश्न पूछ कर सूचना पाने की कोशिश करना : *We tried to pump him for more details.* ■ **pump sth in/into sth** किसी कार्य, वस्तु आदि में बहुत-सा धन, प्रयास आदि लगाना **pump sth out** (अनौप) बड़ी मात्रा में उत्पादन करना।

pumpkin / 'पम्प्किन् / *noun* कद्दू, सीता- फल।

pun / पन् / *noun* pun (on sth) दो अर्थों वाले या एक-समान उच्चारण परंतु भिन्न अर्थों वाले शब्दों का विनोदी प्रयोग; श्लेष (अलंकार) ▶ **pun** *verb* (-nn-) श्लेष बनाना।

punch¹ / पन्च् / *verb* 1 punch sb (in/ on sth) ज़ोरों से घूँसा/मुक्का मारना : *punch sb in the face/stomach*

2 कंप्यूटर, टेलिफ़ोन आदि के बटन दबाना : *She punched the wrong number.* ▸ **punch** *noun* 1 घूँसा/मुक्का 2 किसी में रुचि या उत्तेजना जगाने की शक्ति : *a speech with plenty of punch.*

punch² / पन्च् / *noun* पंच (छेद) करने की मशीन ▸ **punch** *verb* **punch sth (in sth)** पंच से किसी चीज़ में छेद करना : *punch a train ticket.*

punctual / 'पङ्क्चुअल् / *adj* ठीक/निश्चित समय पर; ठीक/निश्चित समय पर आने या काम करने वाला ▸ **punctuality** / ,पङ्क्चु 'ऐलिटि / *noun* समय की पाबंदी **punctually** *adv*.

punctuate / 'पङ्क्चुएट् / *verb* 1 **punctuate sth (with sth)** बीच-बीच में बाधित कर देना/रोक देना : *Her speech was punctuated by bursts of applause from the crowd.* 2 लेखन में विराम आदि चिह्न लगाना ▸ **punctuation** / ,पङ्क्चु 'एश्न् / *noun* **punctuation mark** *noun* लिखने में प्रयुक्त विराम आदि चिह्न।

puncture / 'पङ्क्चर् / *noun* साइकिल/मोटर साइकिल के टायर/ट्यूब में किसी नुकीली चीज़ से हुआ छोटा छेद; ऐसा ही कोई और छोटा छेद ▸ **puncture** *verb* 1 छेद करना/होना 2 किसी का गर्व, आत्मविश्वास आदि कम करना : *puncture sb's illusions.*

pungent / 'पन्जन्ट् / *adj* 1 स्वाद या गंध में तीखा, तिक्त 2 तीव्र, सीधी एवं प्रायः निंदापूर्ण (टिप्पणी आदि) : *pungent remarks/criticism* ▸ **pungency** *noun*.

punish / 'पनिश् / *verb* **punish sb (for sth/doing sth) (by/with sth)** किसी ग़लत काम के लिए सज़ा/दंड देना ▸ **punishable** *adj* **punishable (by sth)** (क़ानूनन) दंडनीय (अपराध आदि) **punishing** *adj* थका देने वाला या कमज़ोर कर देने वाला : *a punishing routine* **punishment** / 'पनिश्मन्ट् / *noun* 1 सज़ा देने/

पाने की क्रिया; सज़ा (का तरीक़ा) : *The punishment should fit the crime.* 2 ख़राब/सख़्त व्यवहार।

punitive / 'प्यूनिटिव् / *adj* (औप) दंड-विषयक; रूखा/कठोर।

punk / पङ्क् / *noun* 1 (**punk rock** भी) एक प्रकार का ज़ोरदार संगीत 2 (अनौप, अपमा) अशिष्ट आचरण या महत्त्वहीन होने के कारण तिरस्कार से देखा जाने वाला व्यक्ति।

puny / 'प्यूनि / *adj* (-ier, -iest) (प्रायः अपमा) 1 छोटा और दुर्बल 2 योग्यता, गुण, मात्रा या आकार में निकृष्ट।

pup / पप् / *noun* = **puppy**.

pupil¹ / 'प्यूप्ल् / *noun* शिष्य, विद्यार्थी।

pupil² / 'प्यूप्ल् / *noun* आँखों की पुतली।

puppet / 'पपिट् / *noun* 1 कठपुतली 2 (प्रायः अपमा) दूसरों के इशारों पर काम करने/नाचने वाला व्यक्ति/वर्ग : *a puppet government* ○ *The union representative was accused of being a puppet of the management.* ▸ **puppeteer** *noun* कठपुतली का खेल/नाच दिखाने वाला **puppetry** *noun* कठपुतली नर्तन की कला।

puppy / 'पपि / *noun* (*pl* **puppies**) (**pup** भी) 1 (कुत्ते का) पिल्ला 2 (अप्र, अनौप, अपमा) घमंडी अभद्र युवक।

purchase¹ / 'पर्चस् / *noun* (औप) 1 ख़रीदारी; ख़रीदी हुई वस्तु : *loans for the purchase of equipment* ○ *He laid his purchases out on the table.* 2 पक्की पकड़ : *The climbers had difficulty getting any purchase on the rock face.*

purchase² / 'पर्चस् / *verb* (औप) **purchase sth (from sb/with sth)** (औप) ख़रीदना ▸ **purchaser** *noun* (औप) ख़रीदार **purchasing** *noun* (वाणिज्य) वस्तुएँ (विशेषतः व्यावसायिक संस्था में) ख़रीदने की प्रक्रिया **purchasing power** *noun* वस्तुएँ ख़रीदने के लिए उपलब्ध धन : *Inflation reduces the* *purchasing power of people living on fixed incomes.*

pure / प्युअर् / *adj* (-r / 'प्युअरर् /; -st / 'प्युअरिस्ट् /) 1 शुद्ध, बिना किसी मिलावट का (पदार्थ) : *pure gold/silk* 2 साफ़, प्रदूषित-पदार्थ रहित : *pure water* 3 पवित्र, निरपराध/निष्पाप : *pure thoughts* 4 (ध्वनि) साफ़ एवं स्पष्ट 5 पूर्ण, निरा : *pure folly/nonsense* 6 (पाठ्य विषय) सिर्फ़ सिद्धांत के लिए पढ़ा जाने वाला : *pure mathematics/science* ▸ **purely** *adv* केवल; पूरी तरह/समग्रतया।

purée / 'प्युरे / *US* प्यु 'रे / *noun* गाढ़े द्रव के रूप में तैयार खाद्य-पदार्थ।

purge / पर्ज् / *verb* 1 **purge oneself/ sb/sth (of sth); purge sth from sth** ख़राब या अवांछित वस्तु को बाहर निकाल कर स्वयं/औरों को शुद्ध करना/स्वस्थ बनाना : *She wanted to purge her mind of these unhappy memories.* 2 **purge sth (of sb); purge sb (from sth)** किसी संघ/दल से अवांछित व्यक्तियों को बाहर निकालना : *purge the party of extremists* ▸ **purge** *noun* शुद्धी-करण।

purify / 'प्युअरिफ़ाइ / *verb* (*pt,pp* puri-fied) **purify sth (of sth)** शुद्ध/साफ़ करना; (पापों आदि से मुक्ति दिला कर) पवित्र बनाना : *Hindus purify themselves by bathing in the river Ganges.* ▸ **purification** / 'प्युअरिफ़ि'केशन् / *noun* शोधन; शुद्धीकरण।

puritan / 'प्युअरिटन् / *noun* 1 (प्रायः अपमा) नैतिकता पर बहुत बल डालने वाला व्यक्ति 2 **Puritan** (16वीं एवं 17वीं शताब्दियों में) इंग्लिश प्रोटैस्टेंट वर्ग का सदस्य ▸ **puritan** *adj* (प्रायः अपमा) अति नैतिकतावादी।

purity / 'प्युअरिटि / *noun* शुद्धता/पवित्रता।

purl / पर्ल् / (**purl stitch** भी) *noun* बुनाई में उलटी सिलाई।

purple / 'पर्पल् / *adj* 1 बैंगनी रंग का

2 (औप) (लेखन या भाषण शैली) अतिशयो-क्तिपूर्ण ▸ **purple** *noun* बैंगनी रंग ।

purpose / 'पर्पस् / *noun* 1 प्रयोजन, इरादा, उद्देश्य 2 **purposes** [*pl*] स्थिति विशेष की आवश्यकताएँ : *These gifts count as income for tax purposes.* 3 अर्थ, संतुष्टि; (औप) योजना बनाने और तदनुसार कार्य करने की शक्ति/सामर्थ्य : *Her approach to the job lacks purpose.* ■ **on purpose** जानबूझ कर (न कि संयोग से) **to little/no/some purpose** बिना/थोड़े ही लाभदायक परिणाम के ▸ **purposeful** *adj* 1 कुछ करने के लिए दृढ़ता दिखाते हुए 2 (औप) अर्थपूर्ण उद्देश्य वाला **purposeless** *adj* बिना उद्देश्य के **purposely** *adv* जानबूझकर।

purr / पर् / *verb* 1 बिल्ली का घुरघुराना 2 (मशीन का) घरघर की आवाज़ करना/ करते हुए चलना 3 हलकी आवाज़ में बोलना (विशेषतः प्रसन्नता और संतुष्टि से) : *purr with delight* ▸ **purr** *noun* घरघर की आवाज़।

purse¹ / पर्स् / *noun* 1 पर्स, बटुआ 2 [*sing*] ख़र्च के लिए उपलब्ध धन : *excursions to suit every purse* 3 (खेलों में) इनाम के रूप में दी गई धनराशि।

purse² / पर्स् / *verb* (ओंठ) सिकोड़ना।

purser / 'पर्सर् / *noun* जहाज़/वायुयान का हिसाब-किताब रखने वाला और यात्रियों की देखभाल करने वाला अफ़सरा।

pursue / पर 'स्यू; *US* पर 'सू / *verb* 1 (पकड़ने या मार डालने के लिए) पीछा करना : *bank robbers closely pursued by the police* 2 (औप) कुछ करना/रखना या किसी चीज़ में भाग लेना : *pursue a goal* 3 (औप) (अध्ययन आदि में) लगे रहना, जारी रखना, रुचि रखना : *pursue her studies* ▸ **pursuer** *noun* किसी का पीछा करने वाला व्यक्ति।

pursuit / पर 'स्यूट्; *US* पर 'सूट् / *noun* 1 **pursuit of sth** खोज 2 पीछा करने की

क्रिया (पकड़ने के लिए) 3 (प्राय:*pl*) लक्ष्य, व्यवसाय/धंधा : *outdoor/scientific pursuits.*

purview /'पर्व्यू/ *noun* (औप) प्रभाव या गतिविधियों का विस्तार-क्षेत्र, सीमा : *These questions lie outside the purview of the present inquiry.*

pus / पस्/ *noun* मवाद, पीप।

push[1] / पुश्/ *verb* 1 धकेलना, ठेलना; दबाव डालकर आगे की ओर बढ़ाना : *He was pushing a pram.* ○ *The dog pushed the door open.* 2 भीड़ में धक्का-मुक्की करके आगे बढ़ना : *The crowd pushed past (us).* 3 स्विच या बटन दबाना : *Push the doorbell.* 4 **push sb (into sth/doing sth)**; **push sb (for sth/to do sth)** (अनौप) विनती या दबाव डाल कर किसी से कुछ कराना : *push sb for payment* 5 (अनौप) लोगों को विचार मानने/चीज़ें ख़रीदने आदि के लिए राज़ी करने का प्रयत्न करना : *We shall be pushing the new model hard.* ■ **push ahead/forward/on (with sth)** दृढ़ता से कोई कार्य जारी रखना **push along** (अनौप) किसी स्थान से जाना : *It's late—I'd better be pushing along now.* **push for sth** बार-बार अनुरोध करना **push sb about/around** (अनौप) अप्रिय ढंग से निर्देश/आज्ञा देना : *She left because she didn't like being pushed around by her manager.* **push (sth) through sth** आधिकारिक रूप से स्वीकार करवाना या शीघ्रता से कार्य संपन्न करवाना **push sth up** मूल्य आदि में बढ़ोतरी होना : *A shortage of building land will push property values up.*
▸ **pushed** *adj* (अनौप) **pushed for sth** किसी चीज़ का आवश्यकता से कम होना, अपर्याप्त होना : *be very pushed for money/time.*

push[2] / पुश्/ *noun* 1 धक्का, ठेल 2 बड़ा फ़ौजी आक्रमण; अभियान 3 (अनौप)

सफलता के लिए धैर्य/दृढ़ता ■ **at a push** (अनौप) दबाव से, केवल मुश्किल से : *We can provide accommodation for six people at a push.* **give sb/get the push** 1 किसी को नौकरी से निकालना 2 संबंध समाप्त करना।

pushy /'पुशि/ *adj* (अनौप, अपमा) ख़ुद की तरफ़ ध्यान आकर्षित करने का लगातार प्रयत्न करते हुए; खुले तौर पर महत्त्वाकांक्षी : *a pushy wife.*

puss / पुस्/ *noun* बिल्ली ▸ **pussy** /'पुसि/ *noun* (**pussy-cat** भी) बच्चों की बोली में 'बिल्ली'।

put / पुट्/ *verb* (**-tt-**; *pt, pp* **put**) 1 किसी स्थान पर रखना, किसी स्थिति में लाना/रखना : *She put the book on the table.* 2 ज़ोर से मारना/रखना : *She put a knife between his ribs.* 3 लिखना या निशान बनाना : *Put your name here.* 4 **put sth on sth** किसी चीज़ में विशेष महत्त्व, भरोसा या क़ीमत रखना : *Our company puts the emphasis on quality.* 5 किसी विशेष स्तर पर क्रमित या वर्गीकरण करना 6 कुछ ढंग विशेष से व्यक्त करना : *She put it very tactfully.* 7 **put sth on/onto/to sth** किसी को कुछ महसूस कराना/किसी चीज़ से प्रभावित होना : *His new job has put a great strain on him.* ■ **put in for sth** (किसी पद के लिए) अभ्यर्थी होना **put oneself/sth across/over (to sb)** किसी से अपनी भावनाएँ, विचार आदि सफलतापूर्वक व्यक्त करना : *She's not very good at putting her views across in meetings.* **put sb down** (अनौप) दूसरों के सामने नीचा दिखाना **put sb down as sb** किसी को कुछ समझना **put sb off** 1 (वाहन या चालक का) किसी को रास्ता देने के लिए रुकना 2 पूर्व नियोजित साक्षात्कार रद्द कर देना 3 किसी में चिढ़ पैदा करना **put sb through sth** कुछ अप्रिय अनुभव कराना **put sb up** किसी के लिए भोजन-आवास आदि की

व्यवस्था करना **put sth aside** भूल जाना/ उपेक्षा या नज़रंदाज़ करना : *They decided to put aside their differences.* **put sth aside/by** भविष्य के लिए बचाकर रखना **put sth at sth** किसी की उम्र, मात्रा आदि आँकना/होने का अनुमान लगाना : *I would put his age at about 55.* **put sth away** (इस्तेमाल के बाद) उचित स्थान पर रखना **put sth back 1** उचित स्थान पर वापस रख देना **2** सही समय दिखाने के लिए घड़ी की सूइयों को पीछे घुमाना **3** कुछ स्थगित कर देना **put sth before/above sth** प्राथमिकता देना : *He puts his children's welfare before all other considerations.* **put sth down 1** लिख लेना **2** दबा देना; बलात् कुछ रोक देना **3** मेज़ आदि पर रखना : *Put that knife down on the table.* **put sth forward 1** घड़ी की सूइयों को आगे बढ़ाना **2** तिथि या समय की पूर्व में लाना **3** विचार के लिए प्रस्ताव रखना **put sth in 1** फ़िट करना **2** पत्र, कहानी में सम्मिलित करना **3** औपचारिक रूप से (दावा आदि) प्रस्तुत करना : *put in a claim for damages/ higher wages* **put sth in; put sth into sth/doing sth 1** किसी कार्य में समय, प्रयास आदि लगाना **2** पूँजी लगाना/धन देना **put sth off; put off doing sth** स्थगित करना; (समय) आगे बढ़ाना **put sth on 1** पहन लेना, वेश धारण करना **2** और अधिक का प्रबंध करना **3** (वेग, भार आदि) बढ़ाना **4** कोई विशेष भाव, गुण होने का झूठा दावा करना **put sth out** किसी जलती हुई वस्तु को बुझा देना **put sth through** योजना, कार्यक्रम आदि को आगे बढ़ाना और सफलतापूर्वक संपन्न करना **put sth together** कुछ एकत्र करना/(पुर्जे आदि) जोड़ना **put sth up 1** ऊपर की ओर उठाना **2** निर्माण करना **3** प्रदर्शन के लिए

लगाना **4** किसी चीज़ में बढ़ोतरी करना **5** विचार आदि चर्चा/वाद-विवाद के लिए प्रस्तुत करना **put up with sb/sth** चुपचाप सहन करना।

putrefy / 'प्यूट्रिफ़ाइ / *verb* (*pt, pp* **putrefied**) सड़ना/सड़ाना ▸ **putrefaction** / प्यूट्रि'फ़ैक्शन् / *noun* सड़न : *the stink of putrefaction.*

putty / 'पटि / *noun* पुटीन (खिड़कियों के शीशों को मज़बूती से टिका कर रखने के लिए किनारे पर लगाई जाने वाली वस्तु)।

puzzle / 'पज़ल् / *noun* **1** पहेली **2** (प्राय: *sing*) कठिन समस्या, दुरूह प्रश्न : *The reason for his actions remains a puzzle to historians.* ▸ **puzzle** *verb* (समझ न पाने के कारण) किसी को चकरा डालना, परेशान कर डालना ◼ **puzzle sth out** गंभीर चिंतन के बाद समस्या का समाधान ढूँढ़ निकालना : *puzzle out a riddle* ▸ **puzzled** *adj* समझने में असमर्थ, गड़बड़ाया हुआ : *We are puzzled about what to do next.*

pygmy (**pigmy** भी) / 'पिग्मि / *noun* **1** Pigmy पिग्मी (अफ़्रीका की एक बौनी मानव जाति) **2** बौना (व्यक्ति/पशु/ पौधा)।

pyjamas (*US* **pajamas**) / प'जामज़् / *noun* [*pl*] पायजामा; सलवार।

pylon / 'पाइलन् / *noun* ऊँचा तोरणनुमा खंभा (जो विद्युत ले जाने के लिए बनाया जाता है)।

pyramid / 'पिरमिड् / *noun* **1** पिरैमिड; सूचीस्तंभ **2** ऐसी रचना का संघ/अवस्था जिसमें जितना ऊपर का स्तर हो, उसमें उतने ही कम व्यक्ति/वस्तुएँ समाई हों : *the social pyramid* ▸ **pyramidal** *adj.*

pyre / 'पाइअर् / *noun* शव जलाने की चिता।

python / 'पाइथ्न; *US* 'पाइथॉन् / *noun* अजगर।

Qq

quack¹ / क्वैक् / *verb* बत्तख़ का कॉं-कॉं करना ▸ **quack** *noun* बत्तख़ की आवाज़।

quack² / क्वैक् / *noun* (अनौप, अपमा) नीम-हकीम; डॉक्टरी का पक्का ज्ञान न रखने वाला मगर उसका दावा करने वाला, तथाकथित डॉक्टर ▸ **quackery** *noun.*

quadrangle / 'क्वॉड्रैङ्ग्ल् / *noun* 1 चतुर्भुज, चौकोर आकृति 2 तीन या चार ओर से घिरा प्रांगण, चौक (विशेषत: स्कूल/ कालेज में)।

quadrant / 'क्वॉड्रन्ट् / *noun* 1 वृत्त का चौथाई भाग; चतुर्थांश 2 ज्योतिष अथवा नौ- चालन में प्रयुक्त कोण-मापी यंत्र, क्वाड्रैंट।

quadrilateral / क्वॉड्रि'लैटरल् / *adj, noun* (ज्यामिति) चतुर्भुज।

quadruped / 'क्वॉड्रुपेड् / *noun* (तक) 1 चौपाया 2 चतुष्पाद।

quadruplet / 'क्वॉड्रुप्लट् / (अनौप **quad** भी) *noun* [pl] एक ही माँ के एक ही समय जन्मे चार बच्चों में से एक।

quaff / क्वाफ़; US क्वैफ़् / *verb* (अप्रचा साहि) (शराब) पीना।

quagmire / 'क्वैग्माइअर् / *noun* 1 दल- दल 2 मुश्किल और ख़तरनाक स्थिति जिससे बच निकलना बहुत मुश्किल हो : *He got bogged down in the political quagmire.*

quail¹ / क्वेल् / *noun* (pl अपरिवर्तित या **quails**) बटेर।

quail² / क्वेल् / *verb* **quail (at/before sb/sth)** घबराना, हिम्मत हारना।

quaint / क्वेन्ट् / *adj* अनूठा या निराला होने के कारण प्रियकर ▸ **quaintly** *adv.*

quake / क्वेक् / *verb* 1 (ज़मीन का) हिलना, कंप करना : *They felt the ground quake as the bomb exploded.* 2 **quake (with sth) (at sth)** (व्यक्ति का) काँपना, सिहरना ▸ **quake** *noun* (अनौप) = **earthquake.**

qualification / क्वॉलिफ़ि'केश्न् / *noun*

1 योग्यता; योग्यता प्रमाण-पत्र आदि 2 प्रति- बंध, सीमाकारक : *She gave her ap- proval to the scheme but not with- out several qualifications.* 3 सीमित करने की क्रिया।

qualify / 'क्वॉलिफ़ाइ / *verb* (pt, pp **qualified**) 1 **qualify (as sth)** किसी कार्य के लिए योग्यता या प्रशिक्षण सफलतापूर्वक पूरा करना : *She won't qualify (as a doctor).* 2 **qualify sb (for sth)** (किसी को) कुछ करने का अधिकार देना/पाना 3 (अर्थ आदि) सीमित कर देना; क्षेत्र कम कर देना; (व्या) किसी शब्द द्वारा अन्य शब्द को एक अर्थ-विशेष देना : *In 'the open door', 'open' is an adjective qualifying 'door'.* ▸ **qualified** *adj* 1 **qualified (for sth)** प्रशिक्षित/योग्यता प्राप्त 2 सीमित।

quality / 'क्वॉलटि / *noun* (pl **qualities**) 1 गुण, योग्यता : *goods of the highest quality* 2 उच्च स्तर 3 विशेषता, लक्षण; धर्म/स्वभाव : *His voice has a rich melodic quality.* ▸ **qualitative** *adj.*

qualm / क्वाम् / *noun* (प्राय: pl) **qualm (about sth)** संशय, आशंका (विशेषत: उस कार्य के संबंध में जो किया जा रहा है या किया जा चुका है) : *He had no qualms about cheating his employer.*

quandary / 'क्वॉन्डरि / *noun* उलझन : *leave sb in a quandary.*

quantity / 'क्वॉन्टिटि / *noun* (pl **quan- tities**) 1 मात्रा, गुण-धर्म जो नापा जा सके 2 एक निश्चित राशि या संख्या : *a huge quantity of food* 3 बड़ी राशि या संख्या : *buy goods in quantity.*

quarantine / 'क्वॉरन्टीन् / *noun* (प्राय: sing) बीमार व्यक्ति/पशु को औरों से अलग रखने की अवधि ताकि उसकी बीमारी अन्य को न लगे : *The dog was kept in* *quarantine for six weeks.* ▶ **quarantine** *verb.*

quarrel / 'क्वॉरल् / *noun* 1 quarrel (with sb) झगड़ा (बातचीत का) : *a family quarrel* 2 quarrel with sth क्रोध का विषय, शिकायत का कारण : *I have no quarrel with his methods.* ▶ **quarrel** *verb* (-ll-; *US* -l-) quarrel (with sb) (about/over sth) झगड़ना, झगड़े में भाग लेना **quarrelsome** / 'क्वॉरल्सम् / *adj* झगड़ालू, कलहप्रिय।

quarry[1] / 'क्वॉरि / *noun* (*pl* quarries) खुली खान, खदान ▶ **quarry** *verb* (*pt, pp* quarried) खान से पत्थर निकालना : *quarrying the hillside for granite.*

quarry[2] / 'क्वॉरि / *noun* शिकार किया जाने वाला पशु-पक्षी; पीछा किया जाने वाला व्यक्ति।

quart / क्वॉर्ट् / *noun* (*संक्षि* qt) क्वार्ट; 2 पिंट या 1.14 लिटर का माप।

quarter / 'क्वॉर्टर् / *noun* 1 चौथाई भाग; 1/4 : *a quarter of a mile* 2 एक घंटे से 15 मिनट पहले या बाद में : *I'll meet you at quarter past ten.* 3 तिमाही, तीन महीने की अवधि 4 अंश, दिशा : *Her travels had taken her to all quarters of the globe.* 5 नगर का इलाका : *a residential quarter* 6 (अमेरिका में) 25 सेंट का सिक्का 7 चांद्र मास का चतुर्थांश, अष्टमी की चंद्रकला 8 भार का एक माप, क्वार्टर (UK में 28 पाउंड और US में 25 पाउंड) 9 quarters [*pl*] आवासभवन, विशेषतः सैनिकों के लिए प्रयुक्त 10 (अप्र) पराजित शत्रु के लिए दयादान : *no quarter from such a ruthless adversary* ■ at/from close quarters घनिष्ठता के साथ ▶ **quarter** *verb* 1 चतुर्थांशों में बाँटना : *peel and quarter an apple* 2 आवास स्थान देना **quarter day** *noun* वह दिन जिसके एक दिन पूर्व लेन-देन का तिमाही हिसाब तैयार कर लिया जाता है।

quarterly / 'क्वॉर्टर्लि / *adj, adv* तिमाही,

त्रैमासिक : *pay the rent quarterly* ▶ **quarterly** *noun* वर्ष में चार बार प्रकाशित होने वाली पत्रिका।

quartet / क्वॉर्टेट् / *noun* 1 चार वादकों या चार गायकों का सहगान; इस प्रकार के समूह के लिए संगीत 2 चार व्यक्तियों/वस्तुओं का समूह : *the last in a quartet of novels.*

quartz / क्वॉर्ट्स् / *noun* स्फटिक, कंचनमणि।

quash / क्वाश् / *verb* (औप) सरकारी निर्णय अवैध घोषित करना, न्यायिक निर्णय निरस्त करना।

quaver / 'क्वेवर् / *verb* 1 (आवाज या लय का) काँपना 2 थरथराती आवाज में बोलना या गाना : *His voice quavered with emotion.* ▶ **quaver** *noun* काँपती आवाज।

quay / की / *noun* (जहाज़ी) घाट।

queen / क्वीन् / *noun* 1 रानी (किसी देश की शासिका) 2 राजा की पत्नी, रानी 3 (अलं) सर्वश्रेष्ठ मानी जाने वाली स्त्री, जगह या वस्तु : *Venice, the queen of the Adriatic* 4 अंडे देने वाली मधुमक्खी ▶ **queen** *verb* ■ queen it (over sb) (अपमा) (स्त्री द्वारा) अत्यधिक अभिमानपूर्वक व्यवहार किया जाना **queenly** *adj* रानी-विषयक/के जैसा।

queer / क्विअर् / *adj* 1 अजीब, अद्भुत, असाधारण : *a queer mood/feeling* 2 (अप्र) बीमार 3 संदिग्ध, संदेह उत्पन्न करने वाला ▶ **queerly** *adv* **queerness** *noun.*

quell / क्वेल् / *verb* 1 विद्रोह दबाना/शांत करना 2 भावनाएँ दबा लेना : *quell sb's fears/doubts.*

quench / क्वेन्च् / *verb* 1 प्यास बुझाना 2 (आग की लपटें) बुझाना : *quench the flames.*

query / 'क्विअरि / *noun* (*pl* queries) 1 प्रश्न, विशेषतः किसी वस्तु की सत्यता के संबंध में संदेह उत्पन्न करने वाला प्रश्न : *raise a query about sth* 2 प्रश्न चिह्न

(?) ▸ **query** *verb* (*pt, pp* **queried**) 1 किसी बारे में संदेह व्यक्त करना 2 प्रश्न पूछना।

quest / क्वेस्ट् / *noun* (औप या अल) **quest (for sth)** खोज, तलाश : *He set off in quest of adventure.* ▸ **quest** *verb* (औप या अल) खोजना, तलाश करना।

question¹ / क्वेस्चन् / *noun* 1 प्रश्न, सवाल 2 **question (of sth)** विचार और निर्णय करने योग्य समस्या 3 संदेह या अनिश्चितता : *His sincerity is beyond question.* ▪ **out of the question** असंभव (**the man,** etc) **in question** व्यक्ति जिसके संबंध में विचार किया जा रहा है ▸ **question mark** *noun* 1 प्रश्न चिह्न (?) 2 संदेह।

question² / क्वेस्चन् / *verb* 1 **question sb (about/on sth)** सवाल पूछना, प्रश्न करना 2 संदेह व्यक्त करना : *He also questioned whether it was solely the lorry driver's fault.* ▸ **questionable** *adj* 1 विवादास्पद 2 संदिग्ध, संदेहपूर्ण।

questionnaire / क्वेस्च'नेअर् / *noun* प्रश्नावली।

queue / क्यू / *noun* क्यू, पंक्तिबद्ध (व्यक्ति, वाहन आदि प्रतीक्षा में) ▸ **queue** *verb* **queue (up) (for sth)** पंक्ति में खड़े होना (प्रतीक्षा करते हुए) : *Queue here for taxis.*

quick¹ / क्विक् / *adj* (**-er, -est**) 1 तेज़, शीघ्रगामी; तीव्रता से किया गया : *have a quick bath* 2 सजीव, फुरतीला; संवेदनशील : *Her quick thinking saved the boy's life.* 3 **quick (at sth)** कुशाग्र बुद्धि ▸ **quickly** *adv.*

quick² / क्विक् / *noun* मांस का संवेदनशील भाग, विशेषतः नाखूनों के नीचे ▪ **cut sb to the quick** भावनाओं को ठेस पहुँचाना।

quicken / 'क्विकन् / *verb* 1 जल्दी करना

2 और अधिक क्रियाशील होना/करना : *a play that quickened her interest in drama.*

quicksand / क्विक्सैन्ड् / *noun* दलदल, बलुआ दलदल।

quicksilver / 'क्विक्सिल्वर् / *noun* पारा।

quiet¹ / 'क्वाइअट् / *adj* (**-er, -est**) 1 बिना शोरगुल या किसी प्रकार की हलचल किए : *Be quiet!* 2 शांत; अधिक लोगों या क्रियाशीलता रहित : *lead a quiet life* 3 (व्यक्ति) शांतचित्त, सौम्य; चिंतारहित ▸ **quiet (quieten** भी) *verb* **quiet (sb/ sth) (down)** शांत होना या करना; निश्चेष्ट/ नीरव होना : *quiet a frightened horse* **quietly** *adv.*

quiet² / 'क्वाइअट् / *noun* शांति।

quill / क्विल् / *noun* 1 (**quill-feather** भी) पक्षी का बड़ा पंख 2 (**quill pen** भी) इस तरह के पंख से बनाई गई लेखनी।

quilt / क्विल्ट् / *noun* रज़ाई, लिहाफ़।

quinine / क्वि 'नीन्; US 'क्वाइनाइन् / *noun* मलेरिया की दवाई, कुनैन।

quintuplet / 'क्विन्ट्यूप्लट् / *noun* (अनौप **quin,** US **quint** भी) एक ही माँ के एक साथ पैदा हुए पाँच बच्चों में से एक।

quirk / क्वर्क् / *noun* 1 अजीब आदत या व्यवहार 2 विचित्र आकस्मिक घटना।

quit / क्विट् / *verb* (**-tt-**; *pt, pp* **quit** या **quitted**) 1 छोड़ना, त्यागना 2 (अनौप) कुछ करने से रुक जाना : *I've quit smoking.* ▪ **be quit of sb/sth** और अधिक परेशान न होना, कुछ छोड़कर निश्चिंत होना ▸ **quitter** *noun* कार्य बीच में ही छोड़ देने वाला।

quite / क्वाइट् / *adv* 1 किसी हद तक; काफ़ी : *They had to wait quite a long time.* 2 पूर्णतया, पूरी तरह : *He's quite happy at his new school.* 3 बेशक, निश्चय ही : *quite empty/ perfect* 4 (औप **quite so** भी) (उत्तर में प्रयुक्त) निश्चय ही : '*He's bound to*

*feel shaken after his accident.'
'Quite so.'* ■ **not quite 1** लगभग
2 पूरी तरह नहीं।

quiver¹ / 'क्विव़र् / *verb* थरथराना, काँपना:
His voice quivered with emotion.
▸ **quiver** *noun* थरथराहट, कँपन।

quiver² / 'क्विव़र् / *noun* तरकश।

quixotic / क्विक्'सॉटिक् / *adj* काल्पनिक
विचार या योजना, न कि वास्तविकता, पर
आधारित।

quiz / क्विज़ / *noun* (*pl* **quizzes**) ज्ञान-
परीक्षण के लिए प्रश्न प्रतियोगिता ▸ **quiz**
verb (**-zz-**) **quiz sb (about sb/sth)**
ज्ञान-परीक्षा के लिए प्रश्न पूछना।

quizzical / 'क्विज़िक्ल् / *adj* दुविधा या
अस्पष्टता दर्शाते हुए (विशेषत: विनोदपूर्ण
रूप में) : *a quizzical smile* ▸ **quiz-**
zically *adv.*

quota / 'क्वोटा / *noun* **1** कोटा, सामग्री
वितरण का नियत अंश **2** व्यक्तियों/वस्तुओं
की एक सीमित निर्धारित संख्या/मात्रा :
*introduce a strict import quota on
grain.*

quotation / क्वो 'टेश्न् / *noun* **1** उद्धरण
2 उद्धरण देने की क्रिया **3** (*अनौप* **quote**
भी) क़ीमत/भाव ▸ **quotation marks**
(*अनौप* **quotes, inverted commas**
भी) *noun* [*pl*] ' ' या " " चिह्न जो उद्धरण
के पहले और बाद में रखे जाते हैं।

quote / क्वोट् / *verb* **1 quote sth (from
sb/sth)** दूसरे के शब्दों को उद्धृत करना : *to
quote Keats* **2** अपने कथन की पुष्टि में
दूसरे के मत का उद्धरण देना **3** भाव/क़ीमत
बताना **4 quote sth (at sth)** (*वाणिज्य*)
शेयर आदि की क़ीमत देना ▸ **quote** *noun*
(*अनौप*) उद्धरण **quotable** *adj.*

Rr

rabbi / 'रैबाइ / *noun* (*pl* **rabbis**)यहूदियों का धर्मगुरु; यहूदी विद्वान।

rabbit / 'रैबिट् / *noun* ख़रगोश, शशक।

rabble / 'रैबल् / *noun* 1 (असंगठित) भीड़ 2 **the rabble** (*अपमा*) निचले तबक़े के लोग : *speeches appealing to the rabble.*

rabid /'रैबिड्/ *adj* रेबीज़ग्रस्त : *a rabid dog* 2 उग्र, प्रचंड (भावनाएँ) : *rabid hate.*

rabies /'रेबीज़/ *noun* रेबीज़, कुत्ते एवं उस प्रजाति के अन्य जंतुओं को होने वाला रोग जिससे वे पागल होकर मर जाते हैं; जलांतक।

race[1] / रेस् / *noun* 1 **race (against/ with sb/sth)**; **race (between A and B)** दौड़-प्रतियोगिता 2 लोगों में प्रचंड प्रति-योगिता/आपा-धापी : *join the race for the presidency* ▸ **racecourse** *noun* घुड़दौड़ का मैदान।

race[2] / रेस् / *verb* 1 **race (against) sb/ sth** दौड़-प्रतियोगिता में भाग लेना 2 तेज़ चलना : *He raced along the road.* 3 घुड़दौड़ में घोड़ा दौड़ाना 4 (हृदय का) ज़ोर से धड़कना ▸ **racing** *noun* (घुड़) दौड़।

race[3] / रेस् / *noun* 1 जाति (मानव); प्रजाति 2 समान संस्कृति, भाषा एवं इतिहास वाले लोगों का वर्ग : *the Spanish/Ger-manic races* 3 जीवित प्राणियों का वंश-विभाजन, नसल 4 (औप) वंश, पारिवारिक उद्भव।

racial / 'रेशल् / *adj* जातीय, जातिगत; अंतर्जातीय : *racial pride/discrimi-nation* ▸ **racialism** *noun* = **racism racialist** *noun, adj* = **racist**.

racism / 'रेसिज़म् / *noun* (**racialism** भी) (*अपमा*) जातिवाद, यह धारणा कि कुछ मानव जातियाँ अन्य से उत्कृष्ट हैं : *victims of racism* ▸ **racist** (**racialist** भी) *noun, adj.*

rack[1] / रैक् / *noun* 1 (प्राय: समास में) लकड़ी आदि का रैक, टाँड़ : *a vegetable/ wine rack* 2 (मशीन में) चारा रखने की चरही 3 (प्राय: **the rack**) (पूर्व समय में) अत्याचार में प्रयुक्त शिकंजा : *put sb on the rack.*

rack[2] / रैक् / (**wrack** भी) *verb* सताना; अत्यधिक पीड़ा पहुँचाना ■ **rack one's brain(s)** किसी बात को सोचने/याद करने के लिए अत्यधिक मानसिक प्रयास करना : *We racked our brains for an an-swer.*

rack[3] / रैक् / *noun* ■ **go to rack and ruin** लापरवाही के कारण तबाह होना।

racket[1] / 'रैकिट् / *noun* (अनौप) 1 हल्ला, शोरगुल 2 धन प्राप्त करने का अवैध या बेईमानी भरा ढंग : *be involved in the smuggling racket.*

racket[2] (**racquet** भी) / 'रैकिट् / *noun* 1 टेनिस आदि खेलों का बल्ला, रैकेट 2 **rac-kets** (**racquets** भी) [*pl*] रैकेट की सहायता से खेला जाने वाला एक खेल।

radar / 'रेडार् / *noun* रडार (एक उपकरण जिसके द्वारा कोहरे या अंधकार में भी उसके क्षेत्र में दूर से आने वाली ठोस वस्तुओं की सूचना रेडियो तरंगों द्वारा मिल जाती है)।

radial / 'रेडिअल् / *adj* केंद्र बिंदु से निकलने वाली त्रिज्याओं की तरह व्यवस्थित : *radial spokes* ▸ **radially** *adv* त्रिज्यीय।

radiant / 'रेडिअन्ट् / *adj* 1 विकिरण करने वाला, चमकदार 2 **radiant (with sth)** उल्लसित, प्रसन्न 3 तरंगों के रूप में वि-किरित : *radiant heat/energy* ▸ **radi-ance** *noun* चमक।

radiate / 'रेडिएट् / *verb* 1 (व्यक्ति का) भावनाओं की स्पष्ट एवं तीव्र अभिव्यक्ति करना, (हर्षोल्लास से) चमकना : *radiate charm/confidence* 2 **radiate from sth** (प्रकाश या ताप की तरंगें) बिखेरना, विकिरण करना; किरणें निकलना : *warmth* *radiating from the stove* **3 radiate (from/out from sth)** (रेखाओं का) केंद्र से वृत्त की त्रिज्याओं की तरह चारों ओर फैलाना।

radiation /रेडि'एश्न्/ *noun* 1 विकिरण; विकिरित ताप/ऊर्जा आदि 2 रेडियो-एक्टिव पदार्थों से विकिरित हानिकारक तरंगें 3 (**radiation therapy** भी) विकिरण से कैंसर आदि गंभीर रोगों की चिकित्सा।

radiator /'रेडिएटर्/ *noun* 1 मोटरकार आदि का रेडिएटर 2 (कमरा गरम रखने के लिए) ताप विकिरक उपकरण।

radical /'रैडिकल्/ *adj* 1 जड़ या आधार से, आमूल; मूलभूत : *a radical flaw in the system* 2 संपूर्ण, पूरा-पूरा : *radical reforms* 3 उग्र, राजनीतिक सिद्धांतों में अतिवादी; आमूल परिवर्तन चाहने वाला ▸ **radical** *noun* उग्र सुधारवादी **radicalize, -ise** *verb* और अधिक उग्र बना देना **radically** *adv*.

radio /'रेडिओ / *noun* (*pl* **radios**) 1 रेडियो तरंगों द्वारा संदेश भेजने/प्राप्त करने की प्रक्रिया 2 (प्राय: **the radio**) बेतार की संचार सेवा : *I heard it on the radio.* 3 रेडियो सेट (उपकरण) ▸ **radio** *verb* (*pt, pp* **radioed**) रेडियो तरंगों द्वारा संदेश भेजना : *radio sb for help.*

radio- *pref* (पूर्वपद) विकिरण संबंधी या किरण संबंधी : *radioactive/radiotherapy.*

radioactive /रेडिओ'ऐक्टिव्/ *adj* परमाणुओं के विघटन पर शक्तिशाली और हानिकारक किरणों का निकलना : *Radium and uranium are radioactive elements.* ▸ **radioactivity** *noun*.

radiography /रेडि'ऑग्रफ़ि/ *noun* एक्स-रे चित्र लेने की प्रक्रिया ▸ **radiographer** *noun* व्यक्ति जो एक्स-रे चित्र लेता है या एक्स-रे का प्रयोग कैंसर आदि रोगों के उपचार के लिए करता है।

radish /'रेडिश्/ *noun* मूली।

radium /'रेडिअम्/ *noun* (*प्रतीक* **Ra**) रेडियम (धातु)।

radius /'रेडिअस्/ *noun* (*pl* **radii** /'रे-डिआइ /) 1 वृत्त की त्रिज्या; त्रिज्या की लंबाई 2 त्रिज्या द्वारा मापा जाने वाला गोलाकार क्षेत्र : *Police searched all the woods within a six-mile radius.* 3 मानव हाथ की कलाई से कोहनी तक की छोटी हड्डी।

raffle /'रैफ़ुल्/ *noun* लॉटरी की तरह टिकटें बेचकर अच्छे कार्य के लिए धन इकट्ठा करना ▸ **raffle** *verb* **raffle sth (off)** रैफ़ल में इनाम देना/वस्तुएँ बेचना।

raft /राफ़्ट्; *US* रैफ़्ट्/ *noun* लकड़ी के लट्ठों को जोड़कर बनाया बेड़ा, नाव आदि; रबड़ या प्लास्टिक की हवा-भरी छोटी नाव : *an inflatable raft* ▸ **rafting** *noun*.

rafter /'राफ़्टर्; *US* रैफ़्टर्/ *noun* छत की ढलुवाँ कड़ी; शहतीर।

rag¹ /रैग्/ *noun* 1 चिथड़ा, लत्ता : *Wipe off the excess dirt with an old rag.* 2 (अप्र) अख़बार ■ **be in rags** फटे-पुराने कपड़े पहने हुए : *be dressed in rags* **(from) rags to riches** अत्यंत ग़रीबी से अमीरी।

rag² /रैग्/ *verb* (**-gg-**) **rag sb (about/ for sth)** (अप्र, अनौप) मज़ाक़ आदि से तंग करना।

rage /रेज्/ *noun* क्रोधोन्माद; हिंसा : *be crimson with rage* ▸ **rage** *verb* 1 **rage (at/against sb/sth)** क्रोध में क्षुब्ध होना 2 (आँधी, तूफ़ान आदि) ज़ोरों से चलना, प्रचंड बनना; (बीमारी) तेज़ी से फैलना **raging** *adj* बहुत ज़ोरदार : *a raging hunger/passion.*

ragged /'रैगिड्/ *adj* 1 फटा पुराना उधड़ा हुआ (कपड़ा) 2 ख़ुरदरा, कर्कश; उलझा हुआ, कटा-पिटा : *a ragged edge to the lawn* ○ *The choir gave a rather ragged performance.*

raid /रेड्/ *noun* **raid (on sth)** 1 दुश्मन पर अचानक धावा (बोलना) : *make a bombing raid on enemy bases*

2 (अपराध करने के लिए) अचानक किसी भवन पर हमला : *an armed bank raid* 3 (पुलिस द्वारा) छापा : *Police seized drugs in a dawn raid on the house.* ▸ **raid** *verb* हमला बोलना/छापा मारना **raider** *noun* हमला या धावा करने वाला (व्यक्ति, जहाज़ या हवाई जहाज़)।

rail¹ / रेल / *noun* 1 जंगला, रेलिंग; छड़; (विशेषत: *pl*) रेल या ट्राम की पटरी 2 रेलवे (यातायात का साधन) ▸ **rail** *verb* ◼ **rail sth in/off** घेरना, रेलिंग लगाना।

rail² / रेल / *verb* ◼ **rail at/against sb/ sth** (औप) आक्रोश प्रकट करना; गाली देना : *He railed against fate.*

railing / रेलिङ्ग / *noun* (प्राय: *pl*) जंगला, रेलिंग, घेरा : *park railings.*

railway / रेल्वे / (US **railroad**) *noun* 1 (प्राय: *pl*) रेलवे यातायात व्यवस्था 2 (**railway line** भी) ट्रेन के लिए बनी पटरी।

rain¹ / रेन / *noun* 1 [*sing*] वर्षा, बारिश 2 **the rains** [*pl*] बरसात (का मौसम) 3 [*sing*] **rain of sth** बौछार : *a rain of arrows/bullets* ▸ **raindrop** *noun* बारिश की एक बूँद **rainfall** *noun* किसी स्थान पर एक विशेष अवधि में वर्षा की मात्रा : *an average annual rainfall of 10 cm.*

rain² / रेन / *verb* 1 बरसात होना, बर- सना : *It's still raining.* 2 **rain on sb/ sth** बौछार करना, बौछार पड़ना।

rainbow / रेनबो / *noun* इंद्रधनुष।

rainy / रेनि / *adj* (-ier, -iest) बरसाती, अत्यधिक वर्षा वाला : *a rainy after- noon/day* ◼ **save, keep etc sth for a rainy day** ज़रूरत के समय के लिए धन आदि बचा कर रखना।

raise¹ / रेज़ / *verb* 1 उठाना, ऊपर उठाना : *raise one's hand;* सीधा खड़ा करना : *We raised the fence and fixed it in position.* 2 **raise sth (to sth)** मात्रा या स्तर बढ़ाना : *raise salaries*

3 उभारना, ऊपर करना 4 एकत्र करना; पाना : *raise money* 5 कोई तथ्य विचार के लिए सम्मुख रखना : *The book raises many important issues.* 6 घटित करना, सामने लाना : *raise doubts/fears* 7 (फ़सल) उगाना; (पशु-पक्षियों की) संख्या बढ़ाना; (बच्चों को) पालन करके बड़ा करना : *My parents died when I was very young, so I was raised by my aunt.* 8 प्रतिबंध आदि समाप्त करना, उठा लेना : *raise a blockade/ban* ◼ **raise hell** (अनौप) क्रोधित होकर विरोध करना; उपद्रव खड़ा करना **raise one's eye- brows** किसी बात पर अप्रसन्नता या आश्चर्य दिखाना : *Eyebrows were raised when he arrived at the party with- out his wife.* **raise one's voice** ऊँची आवाज़ में बात करना, विशेषत: क्रोध आने के कारण **raise sb's spirits** किसी को प्रसन्नचित्त या साहसी अनुभव करवाना : *The sunny weather raised my spir- its a little.* **raise the temperature** तनाव, वैमनस्य आदि बढ़ाना : *Her sud- den outburst raised the tempera- ture of the discussion.*

raise² / रेज़ / *noun* (US) बढ़ोतरी।

raisin / रेज़्न् / *noun* किशमिश।

rake / रेक / *noun* (खेत में काम आने वाला) पाँचा ▸ **rake** *verb* पाँचा प्रयोग में लाना; पाँचे से समतल बनाना : *rake the soil (smooth)* ◼ **rake sth up** (अनौप) गड़े मुर्दे उखाड़ना : *rake up old quarrels/ grievances.*

rally / रैलि / *verb* (*pt, pp* **rallied**) 1 **rally (round/behind/to sb/sth); rally (round)** (लोगों का) संकट/आपत्ति के समय एक होकर समर्थन करना : *Her colleagues rallied to her defence when she was accused of stealing.* 2 **rally sb/sth (round sb)** (लोगों को) इकट्ठा करना/इकट्ठा होना 3 स्वास्थ्य-लाभ करना : (अल) *The team rallied after* *a poor first half.* **4** *(वाणिज्य)* (शेयरों की क़ीमतों का) गिरकर चढ़ना ▸ **rally** *noun (pl* **rallies**) **1** सार्वजनिक सभा, रैली : *stage a peace rally* **2** [*sing*] स्वास्थ्य, शक्ति आदि का पुन:लाभ **3** कार आदि की रैली : *rally driving.*

ram¹ /रैम्/ *noun* **1** मेढ़ा, भेड़ा **2** (**battering ram** भी) टक्कर मारने या कूटने का उपकरण, थापी/दुरमुट **3** मशीन में थापी जैसा उपकरण।

ram² /रैम्/ *verb* (**-mm-**) **1 ram into sth** टक्कर मारना, कूटना : *The ice skater rammed into the barrier.* **2** (वाहन का) जानबूझकर टकराना : *The police van was rammed by a stolen car.* **3 ram sth in, down, into, on, etc** कूटकर ठूँसना, ज़ोर डालना : *He rammed his foot down on the accelerator .*

ramble /ˈरैम्बल्/ *verb* **1** सैर/भ्रमण करना **2 ramble (on) (about sb/sth)** (बोलते-बोलते) विषय से बहक जाना; अनर्गल ढंग से बोलना/लिखना : *The old man rambled (on) happily about the past.* **3** (पौधों का) दूसरे पेड़-पौधों आदि पर चढ़कर उगना : *roses rambling over an old stone wall* ▸ **ramble** *noun* सैर/भ्रमण **rambling** *adj* **1** (विशेषत: सड़कों या मकानों का) बेतरतीबी से बने रहना **2** *(अपमा)* (बातचीत, लेख आदि) बहकी-बहकी, प्राय: विषयांतर के साथ : *a long rambling letter/speech.*

ramification /ˌरैमिफ़िˈकेश्न्/ *noun* (प्राय: *pl*) किसी निर्णय या कार्य के बाद उत्पन्न होने वाली जटिलताएँ, विषमताएँ, अप्रत्याशित परिणाम आदि।

ramp /रैम्प्/ *noun* **1** दो सड़कों, भवनों आदि को जोड़ती हुई ढाल, ढलान : *push a wheelchair up a ramp* **2** सड़क के आर-पार बनाया गया बाँध या अवरोध।

rampage /रैम्ˈपेज; ˈरैम्पेज्/ *verb* क्रोधावेश में भागना, गुस्से से उबलना, क्रोधोन्माद : *mobs rampaging (about)*

through the streets ▸ **rampage** *noun.*

rampant /ˈरैम्पन्ट्/ *adj* **1** (बीमारी, अपराध) अनियंत्रित रूप से फैलती हुई, उच्छृंखल : *rampant corruption* **2** (पौधे) बेतरतीबी एवं तेज़ी से उगते हुए।

rampart /ˈरैम्पार्ट्/ *noun* (प्राय: *pl*) सुरक्षा के लिए निर्मित परकोटा, फ़सील : *Visitors can walk along the castle ramparts.*

ramshackle /ˈरैम्शैक्ल्/ *adj* **1** (मकान, वाहन आदि) टूटा-फूटा, जर्जर **2** (संघ/ संस्था आदि) असंगठित, ग़लत ढंग से संगठित : *ramshackle government policies.*

ranch /रान्च्; *US* रैन्च्/ *noun* (विशेषत: उत्तरी अमेरिका या ऑस्ट्रेलिया में) खेती का बड़ा फ़ार्म ▸ **rancher** *noun* **ranching** *noun.*

rancid /ˈरैन्सिड्/ *adj* **1** (मक्खन, घी, दूध आदि) बासी/खट्टा : *The butter has gone/turned rancid.* **2** विकृत गंध : *There was a rancid smell in the kitchen.*

rancour (*US* **rancor**) /ˈरैङ्कर/ *noun* गहरा वैमनस्य; बहुत पुरानी घृणा ▸ **rancorous** *adj* : *rancorous debate.*

random /ˈरैन्डम्/ *adj* बिना किसी पूर्व-नियोजन के किया गया (कार्य/चयन), याद्दृच्छिक : *books in random order* ▸ **random** *noun* ∎ **at random** बिना पूर्वनियोजन या विशिष्ट क्रम के : *The terrorists fired into the crowd at random.* ▸ **randomly** *adv.*

range¹ /रेन्ज्/ *noun* **1** एक ही प्रकार की विभिन्न वस्तुएँ : *a whole range of goods* **2** दो सीमाओं के बीच का क्षेत्र : *people with a broad range of experience* **3** (गोली आदि का) परास, मार; देखने या सुनने की अधिकतम दूरी : *It is outside my range of vision.* **4** चाँद-मारी का क्षेत्र : *an army range* **5** पर्वतों

की पंक्ति/शृंखला 6 अंगीठी, पुराने तरह का चूल्हा।

range² / रेन्ज् / *verb* 1 range between A and B/range from A to B सीमाओं के बीच बदलते रहना : *Prices range between Rs 70 and Rs 100.* 2 पंक्तिबद्ध होना/करना : *flowerpots ranged in rows on the window sill*; range sb/oneself with/against sb/sth किसी विशेष वर्ग में शामिल होना : *On this issue, she has ranged herself with the Opposition.* 3 स्वतंत्र रूप से किसी क्षेत्र में घूमना : *At this stage, the young animals do not range far from the family.* 4 बहुत सारे विषयों को एक साथ (लेख, भाषण आदि में) समेटना : *a discussion ranging over many different topics.*

rangefinder / रेन्ज़्फ़ाइन्डर् / *noun* (गोली आदि की) मार/परास पता लगाने वाला यंत्र।

rank¹ / रैङ्क् / *noun* 1 ज़िम्मेदारी, गुण या सामाजिक स्तर के मापदंड में स्थिति/श्रेणी : *a painter of the top rank* 2 पुलिस/सेना में पद : *be promoted to the rank of captain* 3 सैनिकों/पुलिस अफ़सरों आदि की पंक्ति 4 the ranks [*pl*] साधारण सैनिक 5 व्यक्तियों/वस्तुओं की पंक्ति ▸ rank *verb* 1 पद, श्रेणी, क्रमस्थिति के अनुसार स्थिति-विशेष में रखना 2 स्थान या पद रखना ■ break ranks किसी दल को छोड़ना, विशेषतः असमर्थन दिखाने के लिए: *Large number of MPs felt compelled to break ranks over the issue.* the rank and file संस्था, संघ के आम सदस्य: *rank and file workers/members/supporters.*

rank² / रैङ्क् / *adj* 1 बहुत बदबूदार : *the rank smell of rotting vegetation* 2 (विशेषतः अप्रमा) पूर्ण एवं बिलकुल : *a rank beginner/outsider* 3 (पौधा) बहुत अधिक फैलने वाला : *rank grass.*

rankle / रैङ्कल् / *verb* rankle (with sb) अपमान, क्रोध आदि कड़वे भावों का मन में कसकना : *The insult still rankled with him.*

ransack / रैन्सैक् / *verb* 1 ransack sth (for sth) किसी स्थान की बारीकी से छानबीन करना, ढूँढ़ना : *I've ransacked the house for those papers, but I can't find them.* 2 लूट-खसोट करना : *The apartment had been ransacked and all her valuables stolen.*

ransom / रैन्सम् / *noun* अपहृत व्यक्ति को छुड़ाने के लिए दिया गया धन, फिरौती; मुक्तिमूल्य : *The kidnappers demanded a ransom of Rs 50,000 from his family.* ■ hold sb to ransom 1 अपहृत बनाकर फिरौती माँगना 2 (अप्रमा) धमकी-भरी चेतावनी द्वारा किसी से मनमानी बात करवाना : *By threatening strike action the unions are holding the country to ransom.* ▸ ransom *verb* फिरौती देकर छुड़ाना।

rant / रैन्ट् / *verb* (अप्रमा) बकना, प्रलाप करना ■ rant and rave गुस्से में बकना : *You can rant and rave all you like, but you'll still have to pay the fine.*

rap / रैप् / *verb* (-pp-) 1 खटखटाना : *rap at/on the door*; अचानक ज़ोर से मारना : *She rapped on my knuckles.* 2 (अप US) तेज़ी से लगातार बात करना ▸ rap *noun* 1 खटखटाहट : *a sharp rap on the elbow* 2 एक प्रकार का तेज़ संगीत ■ give sb/get a rap on/over the knuckles (अनौप) आलोचना करना/पाना; दोषारोपण करना/दोषारोपित होना : *get a rap over the knuckles for being late.*

rapacious / रपेशस् / *adj* (औप) अति लोभी, धन का लालची ▸ rapacity / र पैसटि / *noun* लालच, लोभ।

rape / रेप् / *verb* बलात्कार करना ▸ rape *noun* बलात्कार।

rapid /'रैपिड्/ adj 1 तेज़, कम समय में घटित होने वाला : *rapid growth* 2 तेज़, शीघ्रगामी, तेज़ चलने वाला : *ask several questions in rapid succession* ▸ **rapidity** noun **rapidly** adv.

rapids /'रैपिड्ज़/ noun [pl] नदी का वह भाग जहाँ ढलान सीधी होने के कारण पानी तेज़ी से बहता है।

rapport /रै'पॉर्/ noun [sing] rapport (with sb/between A and B) घनिष्ठ संबंध जिसमें दो या ज़्यादा व्यक्ति एक दूसरे को बहुत अच्छी तरह समझ पाते हैं : *He has a very good rapport with his pupils.*

rapt /रैप्ट्/ adj लगभग सम्मोहित अवस्था में, तन्मय, तल्लीन : *a rapt audience.*

rapture /'रैप्चर्/ noun सम्मोहन, आनंद-विह्वलता : *gazing with rapture at the beautiful image* ■ **be in, go into, etc raptures (about/over sb/sth)** अत्यंत हर्ष या उत्साह अनुभव/व्यक्त करना : *The critics went into raptures about her last film.* ▸ **rapturous** /'रैप्चरस्/ adj.

rare /रेअर्/ adj (-r, -st) 1 विरल, बहुत कम घटित होने/पाया जाने वाला : *a rare book/bird* 2 असाधारण रीति से, अ-सामान्य : *It is extremely rare for the weather in April to be this hot.* ▸ **rarely** adv विरले ही।

rarefied /'रेअरिफ़ाइड्/ adj 1 (वायु) विरल, कम ऑक्सीजन युक्त : *the rarefied air of the Andes* 2 (प्राय: अपमा) सामान्य जीवन से कटे हुए, केवल उच्च (विशेषत: शैक्षिक) स्तर से संबद्ध।

raring /'रेअरिङ्/ adj raring to do sth (अनौप) कुछ करने को अति उत्सुक/आतुर ■ **raring to go** कुछ आरंभ करने को उत्सुक।

rarity /'रेअरिटि/ noun (pl rarities) 1 विरलता, कमी 2 दुर्लभ वस्तु : *Rain is a rarity in this country.*

rascal /'रास्कल्; US 'रैस्कल्/ noun 1 (परि) नटखट, चंचल (बच्चा) 2 (अप्र) धूर्त, बेईमान।

rash¹ /रैश्/ noun 1 (प्राय: sing) छोटे-छोटे दाने जो शरीर में निकल आते हैं 2 [sing] rash of sth एक के बाद एक घटित होने वाली दुर्भाग्यपूर्ण घटनाएँ : *There has been a rash of burglaries in the area over the last month.*

rash² /रैश्/ adj (व्यक्ति/कार्य) बहुत शीघ्रता करने वाला, जल्दबाज़ एवं अवि-वेकी : *It would be rash of them to make up their minds before they've heard all the evidence.* ▸ **rashly** adv **rashness** noun.

rasher /'रैशर्/ noun सूअर के मांस का कतला।

rasp /रास्प्; US रैस्प्/ noun 1 [sing] किरकिराहट; कर्कश, अप्रिय ध्वनि : *the rasp of a saw on wood* 2 रेती (एक औज़ार) ▸ **rasp** verb 1 rasp sth (out) अप्रिय ढंग से कुछ कहना; किरकिराना 2 रेती से रेतना : *rasp the surface (smooth).*

raspberry /'राज़्बरि; US 'रैज़्बेरि/ noun (pl raspberries) रसभरी।

rat /रैट्/ noun 1 चूहा 2 (अनौप या अपमा) धोखेबाज़ व्यक्ति; दब्बू एवं अप्रिय।

rate¹ /रेट्/ noun 1 दर, अनुपात-दर : *walk at a rate of 5 kilometres an hour* 2 निर्धारित क़ीमत, भुगतान आदि : *insurance rates* 3 गति, परिवर्तन आदि की चाल : *At the rate you work, you'll never finish!* 4 (प्राय: pl) उपकर, उपशुल्क ■ **at any rate** 1 चाहे जो भी हो या हुआ हो, हर स्थिति में 2 (अपना पूर्व कथन ठीक तरह से कहने में प्रयुक्त) : *He said he'll be coming tomorrow. At any rate, I think that's what he said.* **at this/that rate** अगर ऐसे ही चलता रहा तो : *At this rate, we'll soon be bankrupt.*

rate² /रेट्/ verb 1 rate sth at sth; rate

sb/sth as sth मूल्यांकन करना : *He is widely rated as one of the best players in the world.* 2 मानना/समझना : *Do you rate Tina among your friends?* 3 योग्य, अधिकार होना : *The incident didn't even rate a mention in the local paper.*

rather / ' रादर ; *US* 'रैदर / *adv* 1 (थोड़ी निंदा, निराशा या आश्चर्य व्यक्त करने में प्रयुक्त) किसी हद तक; काफ़ी : *The instructions were rather complicated.* 2 काफ़ी हद तक, बहुत : *It seems rather a good idea.* 3 बल्कि; और यथार्थत: : *The walls were not white, but rather a sort of dirty grey.* ▶ **rather than** *prep* की तुलना में अधिक पसंद; के स्थान पर।

ratify / ' रैटिफ़ाइ / *verb* (*pt, pp* **ratified**) (औप) किसी संधिपत्र को हस्ताक्षर अथवा अन्य औपचारिकता से संपुष्ट करना : *ratify the treaty* ▶ **ratification** *noun* संपुष्टि।

rating / ' रेटिङ् / *noun* 1 गुणवत्ता आदि के अनुसार वर्ग विभाजन, श्रेणी : *poor ratings in the opinion polls* 2 (प्राय: *pl*) टी वी/रेडियो कार्यक्रम की लोकप्रियता का माप 3 (विशेषत: ब्रिटेन में) साधारण नौसैनिक (जो अफ़सर नहीं है)।

ratio / ' रेशिओ / *noun* (*pl* **ratios**) (गणित) अनुपात : *a student/teacher ratio of 20:1.*

ration / ' रैश्न् / *noun* 1 राशन, प्रति व्यक्ति खाद्य पदार्थ के वितरण में नियतांश 2 **rations** [*pl*] सैनिक को मिलने वाली नियत खाद्य पदार्थ की मात्रा ▶ **ration** *verb* **ration sb/sth (to sth)** राशन करना, राशन व्यवस्था लागू करना।

rational / ' रैश्न्ल् / *adj* 1 (व्यक्ति) समझदार, विवेकी 2 (विचार और कार्य) तर्क पर आधारित, तर्कसंगत : *a rational argument* 3 स्पष्ट रूप से सोचने/समझने में समर्थ : *No rational person would*

behave like that. ▶ **rationality** *noun* **rationally** *adv.*

rationalism / ' रैश्नलिज़म् / *noun* बुद्धिवाद, तर्कणावाद।

rationalize, -ise / ' रैश्नलाइज़् / *verb* 1 कार्य, भाव आदि को तर्क द्वारा समझाने की कोशिश करना : *She rationalized her decision to buy a car by saying it would save her money on bus fares.* 2 किसी व्यवसाय को और अधिक वैज्ञानिक रीति से सुसंगठित करना ▶ **rationalization, -isation** *noun.*

rattle / ' रैट्ल् / *verb* 1 खड़खड़ाना : *The windows were rattling in the wind.* 2 (अनौप) किसी को चिंतित या भयाक्रांत कर देना : *She was clearly rattled by the question.* ■ **rattle along, off, past, etc** खड़खड़ाते हुए चलना : *The old bus rattled along the stony road.* **rattle away/on** जल्दी-जल्दी लंबे समय के लिए बोलते जाना, विशेषकर अनावश्यक या रुचिहीन विषय पर : *He rattled on for hours about his job.* **rattle sth off** जल्दी-जल्दी बोलना या दोहराना : *The child rattled off the poem he had learnt.* ▶ **rattle** *noun* 1 खड़खड़ाहट की आवाज़ 2 बच्चों का झुनझुना।

raucous / ' रॉकस् / *adj* (ध्वनि) कर्कश, कर्णकटु।

ravage / ' रैविज़् / *verb* उजाड़ना, विध्वंस करना/होना; लूटमार करना : *Rebel forces are ravaging the countryside.* ▶ **the ravages** *noun* [*pl*] **the ravages of sth** बरबादी, विनाशकारी प्रभाव : *the ravages of war.*

rave / रेव् / *verb* 1 **rave (at/against/ about sb/sth)** क्रोध में प्रलाप करना, पागलों की तरह बेसिर-पैर की बातें करना 2 **rave (about sb/sth)** (अनौप) किसी के बारे में अत्यधिक प्रशंसापूर्ण बात करना या लिखना : *Everyone is raving about* *her latest film.* ▶ **rave** *noun (अनौप)* युवकों की मस्त पार्टी **rave** *adj (अनौप)* अत्यंत उत्साहित **raving** *adj* 1 प्रलाप करने वाला 2 पूर्ण, पूरा-पूरा : *Their daughters were all raving beauties.* **ravings** *noun [pl]* प्रलाप।

raven / 'रेव्न् / *noun* एक प्रकार का चमकीला कौआ ▶ **raven** *adj* (बाल) काले और चमकदार।

ravenous / 'रैवनस् / *adj* 1 मरभुखा 2 (भूख) बहुत तीव्र : *a ravenous appetite.*

ravine / रं'व़ीन् / *noun* गहरी संकरी घाटी, खड्ड।

ravishing / 'रैविशिङ् / *adj* अत्यंत आनंद देने वाला; अति सुंदर, मनमोहक : *a ravishing smile.*

raw / रॉ / *adj* 1 कच्चा ('पक्का' के वैषम्य में) : *raw vegetables* 2 प्राकृतिक अवस्था में; कच्ची स्थिति में, प्रयोग किए जाने से पूर्व : *raw silk/sugar* 3 अपरिष्कृत, अविश्लेषित : *feed raw data into a computer* 4 (घाव) हरा, (शरीर की) कच्ची खाल या त्वचा : *There is a nasty raw patch on my arm where I burned it on the cooker.* 5 (व्यक्ति) अप्रशिक्षित, अनुभवहीन : *raw recruits* 6 (मौसम) ठंडा एवं नम 7 ईमानदार एवं सत्य; यथार्थ : *a raw portrayal of working-class life* ▶ **raw** *noun* ■ **in the raw** 1 यथार्थ; अच्छा या प्रियकर दिखाने जैसा न बनाया हुआ : *The documentary shows life in the raw.* 2 (अनौप) वस्त्रहीन।

ray / रे / *noun* 1 किरण, रश्मि : *the rays of the sun* 2 **ray of sth** प्रत्याशित बात या अच्छी चीज़ की ज़रा-सी मात्रा : *a few rays of hope* 3 केंद्र से निकली हुई कोई एक रेखा।

rayon / 'रेऑन् / *noun* एक रेशमी कपड़ा, रेयान।

raze / रेज़् / *verb* नगर, भवन आदि को मिटा या ढा देना : *During the war, whole villages were razed to the ground.*

razor / 'रेज़र् / *noun* (दाढ़ी बनाने का) रेज़र, उस्तरा।

re- *pref (उपसर्ग)* 1 फिर से : *reapply* ○ *redecoration* 2 फिर किसी भिन्न रीति से : *regroup* ○ *redistribution.*

reach / रीच् / *verb* 1 पहुँचना : *reach the end of the book* 2 पाना, प्राप्त करना : *reach a conclusion/decision* 3 **reach for sth; reach out (to sb/ sth)** हाथ फैलाना (छूने या लेने के लिए) : *He reached for a pencil.* 4 **reach sth (down) for sb** (अनौप) हाथ पसारना और वस्तु ले लेना; (हाथ) बढ़ाकर छू लेना 5 किसी से संपर्क (बातचीत) स्थापित करना : *We could reach more people by advertising.* ▶ **reach** *noun* 1 [sing] पहुँच, फैलने की सीमा 2 (प्राय: pl) दो घुमावों के बीच नदी का सतत प्रवाह : *the upper/lower reaches of the Ganga* ■ **beyond/out of reach** पहुँच के बाहर **within reach** पहुँच के भीतर।

react / रि'ऐक्ट् / *verb* 1 **react (to sb/ sth)** प्रतिक्रिया स्वरूप विशेष रीति से व्यवहार करना : *react positively to a suggestion* 2 **react (against sb/ sth)** शत्रुता या प्रतिशोध के साथ प्रतिक्रिया करना : *react strongly against tax increases* 3 **react with sth; react (together)** (रसा) रासायनिक तत्त्वों का आपस में क्रिया करना : *Iron reacts with water and air to produce rust.*

reaction / रि'ऐक्शन् / *noun* 1 **reaction (to sb/sth)** प्रतिक्रिया; शारीरिक व्यवहार : *an allergic reaction to sth* 2 [sing] **reaction (against sth)** भाव, दृष्टिकोण आदि में विपरीत के लिए बदलाव 3 विरोध, विशेषकर राजनीतिक उन्नति या सुधार के लिए : *The forces made change difficult.* 4 रासायनिक क्रिया,

अभिक्रिया ▸ **reactionary** / रि'ऐक्शनरि / noun, adj प्रतिक्रियावादी व्यक्ति, प्रगति में बाधक (व्यक्ति/वस्तु)।

reactor / रि'ऐक्टर् / noun (nuclear reactor भी) विशाल मशीन जो परमाणु (नाभिकीय) ऊर्जा उत्पन्न करती है।

read / रीड् / verb (pt, pp read / रेड् /) 1 पढ़ना; पढ़कर सुनाना; पढ़कर जान लेना : I read about her death in today's paper. 2 read (for) sth अध्ययन करना : read for a physics degree 3 (किसी मापक उपकरण का) माप प्रदर्शित करना : What does the thermometer read? 4 अर्थ समझ लेना : Doctors must be able to read symptoms correctly. 5 पढ़ने पर ऐसा प्रभाव देना : The story reads well/badly. ■ read between the lines वह अर्थ ढूँढ़ना जो स्पष्ट वर्णित न हो read on पढ़ना जारी रखना : That's the story so far. Now read on. read sb like a book (अनौप) किसी के मनोभाव आदि को अच्छी तरह समझ पाना : I can read you like a book : you're not sorry at all. read sb/sth up; read up on sb/sth किसी विषय का गहराई से अध्ययन करना read sth into sth वास्तविकता से अधिक अर्थ जोड़ना : You have read too much into what she said. I'm sure she didn't mean it! ▸ **read** / रीड् / noun [sing] 1 पढ़ने की अवधि : have a long read 2 पढ़ने लायक पुस्तक read / रेड् / adj पढ़ा हुआ/विद्वान : a well-read person **readable** / 'रीडब्ल् / adj 1 पठनीय; पढ़ने में अच्छा लगने वाला 2 पढ़ने में सरल।

reader / 'रीडर् / noun 1 पाठक, पढ़ने वाला : an avid reader 2 भाषा सिखाने की पाठ्यपुस्तक : graded English readers 3 Reader (in sth) विश्वविद्यालय में प्रोफ़ेसर और लेक्चरर के बीच का पद, रीडर ▸ **readership** noun 1 (अख़बार, पत्रिका

आदि के) पाठक; पाठकों की संख्या 2 रीडर की पदवी।

reading / 'रीडिङ् / noun 1 पठन क्रिया; पुस्तकें आदि : be fond of reading ○ Her articles make interesting reading. 2 माप : a thermometer reading 3 किसी विशेष ढंग/तरह से समझना : a feminist/Marxist reading 4 संसद में किसी बिल का वाचन।

ready / 'रेडि / adj (-ier, -iest) 1 ready (for sth/ to do sth) (व्यक्ति) कुछ करने को पूर्णत: तैयार; तैयार और उपयोग में लाने को उपलब्ध : Come on, dinner's ready! 2 ready (for sth/to do sth) कुछ करने को स्वेच्छा से राज़ी और उत्सुक : He's always ready to help his friends. 3 तेज़ और समझदार : have a ready wit 4 आसानी से उपलब्ध/प्राप्य : The account provides you with a ready source of income. ▸ **readily** adv 1 सहर्ष, स्वेच्छा से, बेझिझक : She readily agreed to help. 2 आसानी से : Spare parts are readily available. **readiness** noun 1 readiness (for sth) के लिए तैयार 2 readiness (to do sth) स्वेच्छा, उत्कंठा 3 शीघ्रता : readiness of wit **readymade** adj (विशेषत: कपड़े) बने-बनाए; (खाद्य पदार्थ) पहले से तैयार किए हुए **ready money** (ready cash भी) noun (अनौप) नक़द पैसा।

real / 'रिअल ; 'रीअल् / adj 1 वास्तविक (न कि काल्पनिक); यथार्थ सत्य : real and imagined fears 2 असली (न कि कृत्रिम) : real silk/gold 3 पूर्ण; संपूर्ण; गंभीर : The camping trip was a real disaster. ▸ **real** adv (US) बहुत; वास्तव में : have a real fine time **real estate** noun (क़ानून) अचल संपत्ति (भूमि, भवन आदि)।

realism / 'रीअलिज़म् / noun 1 वास्त– विकता को स्वीकार करने और उसका सामना

करने की मनोवृत्ति 2 वर्णित व्यक्ति/वस्तु/
स्थिति के स्वरूप होने का गुण 3 (साहित्य
और कला में) चिर-परिचित वस्तुओं/घटनाओं
को यथार्थ रूप में प्रस्तुतीकरण. ▶ **realist**
noun **realistic** /रीअ'लिस्टिक्/ *adj*
1 किए/पाए जा सकने की सक्रिय धारणा
दिखाते हुए : *Is this a realistic salary
for such a responsible job?*
2 (साहित्य और कला में) वास्तविकता
दिखाते हुए।

reality /रि'ऐलिटि/ *noun (pl* **realities)**
1 वास्तविकता, यथार्थता 2 व्यक्ति की यथार्थ
स्थिति, जीवन की समस्याएँ आदि 3 (प्राय:
pl) वास्तव में अनुभूत या दृष्ट वस्तु : *the
harsh realities of poverty* ■ **in reality** वस्तुत:।

realize, -ise /'रिअलाइज़्;'रीअलाइज़्/
verb 1 स्पष्ट रूप से समझना; यथार्थ को
समझना/स्वीकार करना शुरू करना : *realize one's mistakes* 2 (आशा या योजना
को) वास्तविकता में लाना, कार्यान्वित
करना : *realize one's hopes/ambi-
tions* 3 संपत्ति को बेचकर धनराशि पाना;
(संपत्ति का) विशेष लाभ पर बिकना; बेचकर
धन पाना : *How much did you realize
(on those paintings)?* ▶ **realization, -isation** /रिअलाइ'ज़ेशन्/ *noun*
वसूली/उगाही; अनुभूति; (कार्य) सिद्धि :
*the realization of his greatest am-
bition.*

really /'रिअलि; 'रीअलि/ *adv* 1 वस्तुत:,
सच में : *What do you really think
about it?* 2 निस्संदेह : *a really long
journey* 3 विस्मयद्योतक : *'We are
going to Japan next month.' 'Oh,
really?'*

realm /रेल्म्/ *noun* 1 (ओप या साहि)
राज्य (प्राय: राजतांत्रिक) 2 रुचि या कार्य का
क्षेत्र : *in the realm of science.*

ream /रीम्/ *noun* 1 (तक) काग़ज़ का रीम
(480/500 पन्ने) 2 **reams** [*pl*] (अनौप)
काग़ज़ या लिखित सामग्री की बहुत बड़ी

मात्रा : *write reams (and reams) of
bad verse.*

reap /रीप्/ *verb* 1 फ़सल काटना 2 अपने
कार्य या कर्म का फल पाना : *reap the
rewards of years of study* ▶ **reaper**
noun फ़सल काटने वाला व्यक्ति।

reappear /रीअ'पिअर्/ *verb* फिर से
दिखाई पड़ना/दृष्टिगत होना।

rear[1] /रिअर्/ *noun* [*sing*] 1 (प्राय: **the
rear**) पिछवाड़ा; पिछला हिस्सा 2 शरीर का
हिस्सा जिस पर बैठते हैं ■ **bring up the
rear** सबसे पीछे होना या आना ▶ **rear-
most** *adj* सबसे पीछे का।

rear[2] /रिअर्/ *verb* 1 पालन-पोषण करना,
पालना; पशु-पक्षियों का प्रजनन कराकर
संख्या बढ़ाना : *rear cattle/poultry*
2 **rear (up)** (घोड़े का) पिछले पैरों पर
खड़ा होना 3 सिर ऊपर उठाना : *The snake
reared its head.*

rearrange /रीअ'रेन्ज्/ *verb* 1 स्थान
या क्रम बदलना : *rearrange the furni-
ture/one's books* 2 बनी हुई योजना
आदि में परिवर्तन करना : *Can we rearrange the meeting (for next week)?*
▶ **rearrangement** *noun.*

reason[1] /'रीज़न्/ *noun* 1 **reason (for
sth/doing sth); reason (to do sth);
reason (why.../that...)** कारण, हेतु :
*We have good reason to believe
that he is lying.* 2 तर्क-शक्ति, विवेक
3 ग़लत/ठीक की निर्णय-शक्ति, व्यावहारिक
ज्ञान : *be open to reason.*

reason[2] /'रीज़न्/ *verb* 1 सोच-विचार
करना 2 तर्क करना, तर्करूप प्रस्तुत करना :
*He reasoned that if we started at
6 a.m. we would be there at midday.* ▶ **reasoning** *noun* तर्क।

reasonable /'रीज़नबल्/ *adj* 1 (व्यक्ति)
विवेकी, तर्क मानने वाला : *No reasonable person could refuse.* 2 (विचार,
मत, विश्वास आदि) तर्कयुक्त, युक्तिसंगत : *a
reasonable belief* 3 यथोचित, पर्याप्त

4 (क़ीमत आदि) उचित, स्वीकार्य ▶ **reasonably** adv 1 तर्कयुक्त रूप से : *discuss the matter calmly and reasonably* 2 कुछ/काफ़ी हद तक (उचित/ पर्याप्त) : *reasonably good/cheap*.

reassure /रीअ'शुअर्/ verb **reassure sb (about sth)** आश्वासन देना : *The police reassured her about her safety.* ▶ **reassurance** noun आश्वासन **reassuring** adj भय/शंका मिटाने वाला : *a reassuring glance/ word.*

rebate /'रीबेट्/ noun ऋण, कर आदि पर दी गई छूट : *qualify for tax rebate.*

rebel /'रेबल्/ noun बाग़ी; विद्रोही ▶ **rebel** /रि'बेल्/ verb (-II-) **rebel (against sb/ sth)** 1 विद्रोह करना; बग़ावत करना 2 अधिकारियों से प्रतिरोध प्रदर्शित करना; किसी बात के विरुद्ध कड़ा विरोध व्यक्त करना : *He finally rebelled against his strict upbringing.* **rebellion** /रि'बेल्यन्/ noun **rebellion (against sb/sth)** 1 बग़ावत, सशस्त्र विद्रोह : *stage a rebellion against the military rulers* 2 प्रतिरोध **rebellious** adj विद्रोह की आकांक्षा दिखाने वाला; आसानी से नियंत्रण में न रहने वाला : *rebellious tribe.*

rebound /रि'बाउन्ड्/ verb 1 **rebound (from/off sth)** टकराकर लौटना 2 **rebound (on sb)** किसी व्यक्ति पर प्रतिकूल प्रभाव होना : *The scheme rebounded (on her) in a way she had not expected.* ▶ **rebound** /'रीबाउन्ड् / noun (वाणिज्य) नकारात्मक के बाद सकारात्मक प्रतिक्रिया : *a rebound in oil exports* ■ **on the rebound** टकरा कर लौटते समय।

rebuff /रि'बफ़्/ noun दो टूक जवाब; अक्खड़ ढंग से प्रस्ताव आदि की अस्वीकृति : *Her kindness to him was met with a cruel rebuff.* ▶ **rebuff** verb.

rebuild /'रीबिल्ड्/ verb (pt, pp **rebuilt** /'रीबिल्ट्/) 1 फिर से निर्माण करना 2 पुरानी स्थिति में लाना।

rebuke /रि'ब्यूक्/ verb **rebuke sb (for sth/doing sth)** (औप) डाँटना-फटकारना ▶ **rebuke** noun डाँट-डपट, फटकार : *administer a stern rebuke (to sb).*

recall /रि'कॉल्/ verb 1 याद करना या कराना : *I can't recall his name.* 2 **recall sb (from ....) (to ...)** वापस बुलाना : *recall an ambassador (from his post)* 3 कुछ वापस करने का आदेश देना ▶ **recall** /रि'कॉल्; 'रीकॉल्/ noun 1 [sing] वापसी का आदेश 2 स्मरण करने की शक्ति।

recapitulate /रीक'पिचुलेट्/ verb (अनौप **recap** भी) 1 (तर्क आदि के) मुख्य बिंदुओं को दोहराना : *Let me just recapitulate (on) what we've agreed so far.* 2 टी वी धारावाहिक आदि में पिछली बार के कुछ प्रमुख दृश्यों को दोहराना ▶ **recapitulation** (अनौप **recap** भी) noun.

recede /रि'सीड्/ verb 1 **recede (from sth)** पीछे हटना; वापस लौट जाना : *As the tide receded (from the shore) we were able to look for shells.* ○ (अल) *The prospect of bankruptcy has now receded.* 2 पीछे की ओर झुका हुआ होना : *a receding chin/ hairline.*

receipt /रि'सीट्/ noun 1 **receipt (of sth)** (औप) प्राप्ति, पाने की क्रिया : *acknowledge receipt of a letter* 2 **receipt (for sth)** रसीद (पाए हुए धन/ वस्तु की लिखित प्राप्ति-स्वीकृति) 3 **receipts** [pl] (व्यापार में) प्राप्त धन : *net/ gross receipts.*

receive /रि'सीव्/ verb 1 **receive sth (from sb/sth)** पाना, प्राप्त करना 2 अनुभव करना : *receive a good education* 3 **receive sb (with sth) (as sth)** (औप) औपचारिक रूप से स्वागत करना :

She was received with warm applause. **4 receive sb (with sth)** प्रवेश देना : *He has been received into the Church.* **5** ध्यान दिया जाना/ आकर्षित करना : *He said the idea would receive serious consideration.* ■ **be at/on the receiving end (of sth)** *(अनौप)* कुछ अप्रिय भुगतने वाला बनना/होना : *The party in power soon learns what it's like to be on the receiving end of political satire.* ▸ **received** *adj* लोगों द्वारा सही माना हुआ (यद्यपि सही नहीं भी हो सकता है) : *received opinion.*

receiver / रि'सीव़र् / *noun* **1** टेलिफ़ोन का वह भाग जहाँ से सुनाई देता है **2** रेडियो/ टी वी का रिसीवर **3** प्राप्तकर्ता व्यक्ति।

recent / 'रीसन्ट् / *adj* हाल का, अभिनव : *a recent event* ▸ **recently** *adv* हाल ही में, अधिक पहले नहीं।

receptacle / रि'सेप्टक्ल् / *noun* **receptacle (for sth)** *(औप)* थैला; संदूक या पात्र।

reception / रि'सेप्श्न् / *noun* **1** ग्रहण (करना); स्वीकृति **2** [*sing*] लोगों की प्रतिक्रिया का ढंग : *The play was given an enthusiastic reception by the critics.* **3** स्वागत-कक्ष (होटल आदि में) **4** औपचारिक स्वागत-समारोह : *hold a wedding reception* **5** रेडियो या टी वी प्रसारण सिगनल की स्पष्टता का स्तर ▸ **receptionist** *noun* स्वागत हेतु उपस्थित व्यक्ति।

receptive / रि'सेप्टिव़् / *adj* **receptive (to sth)** सुझाव आदि का स्वागत करने वाला, ग्रहणशील।

recess / रि'सेस्; 'रीसेस् / *noun* **1** मध्या- वकाश, दो कार्य अवधियों के बीच का ख़ाली समय; मध्यांतर (स्कूलों में) **2** कमरे का वह भाग जो दीवार पीछे हटाकर बनाने से बना है : *put a book case in the recess* **3** (प्राय: *pl*) *(साहि)* गुप्त एकांत स्थान :

the dark recesses of a cave ▸ **re- cess** *verb* अवकाश लेना/अवकाश लेने का आदेश देना।

recession / रि'सेश्न् / *noun* देश की अर्थ-व्यवस्था में अवनति; व्यापार, उद्योग आदि मंद पड़ जाना एवं बेरोज़गारी बढ़ जाना।

recipe / 'रेसिपि / *noun* **1 recipe (for sth)** भोजन आदि बनाने के निर्देश : *recipe book* **2 recipe for sth** नुस्ख़ा; पाने का तरीक़ा : *his recipe for success.*

recipient / रि'सिपिअन्ट् / *noun* **recipi- ent (of sth)** *(औप)* पाने वाला व्यक्ति : *recipients of awards.*

reciprocal / रि'सिप्रक्ल् /*adj* पारस्प- रिक : *reciprocal trade deals* ▸ **re- ciprocally** *adv.*

reciprocate/रि'सिप्रकेट्/*verb* **1** *(औप)* (दो व्यक्तियों का) परस्पर आदान-प्रदान करना : *reciprocate greetings* **2** (एक व्यक्ति का बदले में) भावनाएँ, मुद्रा, अभि- वादन आदि लौटाना : *His smile was not reciprocated.* ▸ **reciprocation** *noun.*

recital / रि'साइट्ल् / *noun* **1** संगीत समारोह; कविता पाठ : *give a piano recital* **2** तथ्यों का वर्णन; यात्रा का विवरण।

recitation / रेसि'टेश्न् / *noun* कविता वाचन, कथा साहित्य से उद्धरण सुनाना।

recite / रि'साइट्/ *verb* **1 recite sth (to sb)** कविता पाठ करना, कविता सुनाना : *recite a speech from 'Hamlet' to the class* **2 recite sth (to sb)** तथ्यों/ नामों आदि को सूची रूप में एक के बाद एक गिनना।

reckless / 'रेक्लस् / *adj* **reckless (of sth)** (व्यक्ति एवं उनके कार्य) दु:साहसी; लापरवाह; उतावला : *cause death by reckless driving* ▸ **recklessly** *adv* **recklessness** *noun.*

reckon/ 'रेकन्/*verb* **1** मानना; इस विचार का होना : *I reckon (that) he's too old for the job.* **2** *(अनौप)* आशा करना :

We reckon to finish by midday.
3 गिनती करना, हिसाब लगाना : *reckon the total volume of imports* ■ **reckon sth up** (हिसाब) जोड़ना **reckon with sb/sth** 1 ध्यान में रखना, संभावना मानना 2 सामना करना 3 महत्त्वपूर्ण मानना।

reckoning / रेकनिङ् / *noun* गिनती; हिसाब : *the reckoning of debts* ■ **out of the reckoning** (खेलों में) संभावित विजेताओं में से नहीं।

reclaim / रिक्लेम् / *verb* 1 **reclaim sth (from sb/sth)** दिया हुआ/खोया हुआ सामान वापस पाना : *reclaim lost property* 2 **reclaim sth (from sth)** भूमि को कृषि या अन्य उद्योग के योग्य बनाना : *reclaimed marshlands* 3 **reclaim sth (from sth)** रद्दी से या बेकार बचे उत्पादों से कच्चा माल तैयार करना जिसे पुन: प्रयोग में लाया जा सकता है : *reclaim glass (from old bottles)* ▶ **reclamation** / रेक्ल'मेश्न् / *noun* सुधार, उद्धार।

recline / रिक्लाइन् / *verb* 1 लेट जाना, आराम करने के लिए टेक लगा लेना : *recline on a sofa* 2 सीट के पिछले भाग को ढलान में झुकाना।

recluse / रिक्लूस् / *noun* एकांतवासी : *lead the life of a recluse.*

recognition / रेकग्'निश्न् / *noun* पहचानने की प्रक्रिया/पहचान; क़द्र; मान्यता : *international recognition in the field of tropical medicine.*

recognize, -ise / रेकग्नाइज़् / *verb* 1 **recognize sb/sth (by/from sth)** पहचानना 2 **recognise sb/sth (as sth)** मान्यता देना, स्वीकार करना : *recognize sb's claim to ownership* 3 योग्यता, उपलब्धि आदि की क़द्र करना : *The Queen recognized his services by awarding him a knighthood.*

recoil / रिकॉइल् / *verb* 1 **recoil (from**

sb/sth); recoil (at sth) पीछे हटना (घबरा कर या घृणा से) : *He recoiled in horror at the sight of the corpse.* 2 तोप/बंदूक का पीछे की ओर धक्का देना ▶ **recoil** / ' रीकॉइल् / *noun.*

recollect / रेक'लेक्ट् / *verb* (औप) याद करना, स्मरण करना : *recollect sb's name.*

recollection / रेक'लेक्श्न् / *noun* 1 अनुस्मरण, संस्मृति 2 घटना आदि का संस्मरण : *recollections of her youth.*

recommend / रेक'मेन्ड् / *verb* 1 **recommend sb/sth (to sb) (for sth/as sth)** सिफ़ारिश करना : *recommend a good restaurant/book* 2 सलाह देना : *My doctor has recommended a long period of rest.* 3 **recommend sb/sth (to sb)** (गुण आदि को) प्रियकर अथवा आकर्षक बनाना ▶ **recommendation** / रेक'मेन्'डेश्न् / *noun* 1 सिफ़ारिश प्रक्रिया : *I stayed there on your recommendation.* 2 सिफ़ारिश पत्र/कथन; संस्तुति-पत्र 3 सलाह 4 गुणवत्ता।

recompense / ' रेकम्पेन्स् / *verb* **recompense sb (for sth)** (औप) पुरस्कार देना; हानि की क्षतिपूर्ति करना, हर्जाना देना : *recompense employees for working overtime* ▶ **recompense** *noun* [*sing*] **recompense (for sth)** (औप) पुरस्कार, हर्जाना भुगतान : *receive adequate recompense for one's efforts.*

reconcile / ' रेकन्साइल् / *verb* 1 **reconcile sth (with sth)** विपरीत विचारों/स्थितियों का सामंजस्य करा देना : *reconcile different political views* 2 **reconcile sb (with sb)** मेल-मिलाप करा देना; (झगड़े का) निपटारा करना/कराना : *They are unable to reconcile their differences.* 3 **reconcile sb/oneself to sth** अपनी नापसंदगी को

दबा देना; समझौता कर लेना : He cannot reconcile himself to a lifetime of unemployment. ▸ **reconciliation** /ˌरेकन्सिलि'एश्न् / noun.

recondition /ˌरीकन्'डिश्न् / verb मरम्मत करना, फिर से कार्य योग्य बनाना : a reconditioned engine.

reconnaissance / रि'कॉनिस्न्स् / noun (अनौप recon भी) टोह।

reconnoitre (US **reconnoiter**) /ˌरेक्'नॉइटर् / verb शत्रुओं की स्थिति, संख्या आदि की टोह लगाना।

reconsider /ˌरीकन्'सिडर् / verb किसी विषय पर पुन: विचार करना, विशेषत: अपना विचार या निर्णय बदलने के लिए।

reconstruct / रीकन्'स्ट्रक्ट् / verb 1 reconstruct sth (from sth) पुनर्निर्माण करना 2 किसी घटना का सही-सही विवरण देना; घटनाक्रम निर्धारित करना।

record[1] /'रेकॉर्ड / noun 1 तथ्य, घटना आदि का अभिलेख, विवरण : medical records ० The airline has an impressive safety record. 2 (disc, अग्र gramophone record भी) ग्रामोफ़ोन का रिकॉर्ड 3 प्राप्त अंकों का उच्च मान; खेलों में कीर्तिमान : beat/break a record ■ (just) for the record मात्र संदर्भ हेतु : Just for the record, I would like to clarify something my colleague said earlier. off the record वर्णन, बयान आदि प्रकाशन के लिए नहीं : The vice-president admitted, (strictly) off the record, that the talks had failed. on (the) record (वक्तव्य) सार्वजनिक रूप से जाना हुआ : put one's views/objections on (the) record put/set the record straight पहले ग़लत वर्णित किए गए तथ्यों, घटनाओं का सही विवरण देना : To put the record straight, I do not support that idea and never have done.

record[2] / रि'कॉर्ड / verb 1 दर्ज करना,

भविष्य के संदर्भ के लिए रखना : record the proceedings of a meeting 2 record (sth) (from sth) (on sth) टेप या फ़िल्म पर प्रतिलिपि बना कर भविष्य के लिए सुरक्षित करना : record (a programme) from the radio 3 (किसी यंत्र का) मात्रा आदि अंकित करना; माप दिखाना : The thermometer recorded temperature of 40°C.

recorder / रि'कॉर्डर् / noun 1 रिकॉर्डर यंत्र 2 संगीत यंत्र 3 लेखा, वृत्त आदि लिखने व रखने वाला।

recording / रि'कॉर्डिङ् / noun ध्वनि, चित्र आदि को टेप, फ़िल्म आदि पर रिकॉर्ड करने की प्रक्रिया; रिकॉर्ड किया गया चित्र या ध्वनि।

recount / रि'काउन्ट् / verb recount sth (to sb) वर्णन करना, बताना।

recoup / रि'कूप् / verb ख़र्च किए/खोए धन को वापस पाना; क्षतिपूर्ति प्राप्त करना : We hope to recoup our initial investment in the first year.

recourse / रि'कॉर्स् / noun (औप) मुश्किल समय में सहायता का स्रोत ■ have recourse to sb/sth (औप) शरण लेना, सहारा लेना।

recover / रि'कवर् / verb 1 recover (from sb/sth) स्वास्थ्य-लाभ करना; खोई हुई शक्ति पाना : recover one's sight/ hearing 2 पुन: शांत होना, संभल जाना : She recovered her posture and smiled. 3 recover sth (from sb/sth) (खोई हुई) वस्तु को वापस पाना; खोया समय/धन वापस पाना।

recovery / रि'कवरि / noun 1 (प्राय: sing) recovery (from/in sth) स्वास्थ्य-लाभ 2 recovery (of sth/sb) पुन: प्राप्ति; वसूली; पुनर्लाभ : recovery of the missing diamonds.

recreation /ˌरेक्रि'एश्न् / noun मनोरंजन, मन-बहलाव : funds for leisure and recreation.

recruit / रि'क्रूट् / noun 1 सेना में/पुलिस में नया भरती हुआ अप्रशिक्षित व्यक्ति, रंगरूट 2 recruit (to sth) किसी समिति, सभा या समाज में शामिल हुआ नया व्यक्ति ▸ recruit verb 1 recruit (sb) (to sth); recruit sb (as sth) रंगरूट भरती करना 2 समर्थकों द्वारा दल या सेना बनाना recruitment noun.

rectangle / 'रेक्टैङ्ग्ल् / noun (ज्यामिति) आयत ▸ rectangular / रेक्'टैङ्ग्यलर् / adj आयताकार।

rectify / 'रेक्टिफ़ाइ / verb (pt, pp rectified) सुधारना; ठीक करना : rectify an error/omission ▸ rectification noun परिशोधन, सुधार।

rector / 'रेक्टर् / noun 1 (इंग्लैंड के चर्च में) पुरोहित 2 विश्वविद्यालयों और महाविद्यालयों का अध्यक्ष, रेक्टर ▸ rectory noun रेक्टर का आवास।

rectum / 'रेक्टम् / noun (pl rectums या recta) मलाशय।

recuperate / रि'कूपरेट् / verb 1 recuperate (from sth) (औप) बीमारी के बाद स्वास्थ्य-लाभ करना 2 खर्च किया/ खोया धन वापस पाना : He hoped to recuperate at least part of his investment. ▸ recuperation noun.

recur / रि'कर् / verb (-rr-) दोबारा घटित होना, बार-बार घटित होना : The symptoms tend to recur. ▸ recurrence / रि'करन्स् / noun पुनरावृत्ति recurrent adj.

recycle / री'साइक्ल् / verb इस्तेमाल की जा चुकी वस्तु का पुनर्निर्माण करना : recycle newspaper/packaging.

red / रेड् / adj (-dder, -ddest) 1 लाल रंग का 2 (आँखें) लाल होना 3 (बाल या जानवर का फ़र) ललौहा-भूरा ▸ red-letter day noun महत्त्वपूर्ण/खुशी का दिन red tape noun (अपमा) (सार्वजनिक मामलों में) नियमों पर अत्यधिक ध्यान देना; लालफ़ीता(शाही) ▸ red noun लाल रंग;

लाल रंग के कपड़े ■ see red (अनौप) क्रोध से संतुलन खो देना।

redden / रेड्न् / verb 1 लाल होना या करना 2 (व्यक्ति का चेहरा) शर्म से गुलाबी या क्रोध से लाल हो जाना : She stared at him and he reddened.

redeem / रि'डीम् / verb 1 (गुण की कमी या त्रुटि की) क्षतिपूर्ति करना : The sole redeeming feature of this job is the good salary. 2 redeem oneself क्षतिपूर्ति के लिए कुछ करना 3 redeem sth (from sb/sth) किसी वस्तु का दाम चुका कर छुड़ाना; ऋण चुकता करना : I redeemed my watch (from the pawn shop). 4 redeem sb (from sth) (ईसाई धर्म में) पाप मुक्त करना; मुक्त करना, निस्तार करना ▸ the Redeemer noun ईसा मसीह।

redemption / रि'डेम्प्श्न् / noun (औप) दुष्कर्म या पाप से उद्धार : the redemption of the world from sin.

red-handed / रेड् हैन्डिड् / adj ■ catch sb red-handed रंगे हाथ पकड़ना, अपराध करते हुए पकड़ना।

redistribute / रीडि'स्ट्रिब्यूट् / verb भिन्न तरीके से बाँटना ▸ redistribution noun [sing] पुनर्वितरण।

redouble / री'डब्ल् / verb शक्ति या तीव्रता और अधिक बढ़ा देना : We must redouble our efforts if we want to succeed.

redress / रि'ड्रेस् / verb (औप) ग़लत को ठीक कर देना; अपराध या कमी की क्षतिपूर्ति कर देना; सुधारना : redress an injustice ▸ redress noun redress (for/against sth) (औप) किसी ग़लत बात से हुई तकलीफ़ की क्षतिपूर्ति (माँगने का अधिकार) : seek legal redress for unfair dismissal.

reduce / रि'ड्यूस्; US रि'डूस् / verb 1 reduce sth (from sth) (to sth); reduce sth (by sth) आकार, मात्रा,

संख्या, स्तर आदि घटाना, छोटा करना : *reduce pressure/speed* 2 (अनौप, विशेषत: *US*) विशेष खुराक लेकर वज़न घटाना ■ **reduce sb/sth (from sth) to sth/doing sth** स्थिति-विशेष में, प्राय: बदतर, ला देना : *reduce sb to tears/ poverty.*

reduction / रि'डक्शन् / *noun* 1 कमी, कटौती 2 कमी की मात्रा 3 मूल प्रति की छोटी की गई प्रति (मानचित्र आदि की)।

redundant / रि'डन्डन्ट् / *adj* 1 फ़ालतू, अतिरिक्त : *The picture has too much redundant detail.* 2 काम न होने के कारण निकाले जाने से बेरोज़गार (कर्मचारी) 3 अनावश्यक, निरर्थक : *redundant factories* ▸ **redundancy** *noun* (pl **redundancies**) 1 बेरोज़गारी : *a high level of redundancy among unskilled workers* 2 बेरोज़गार कर्मचारी : *The factory closure will result in 200 redundancies.*

reed / रीड् / *noun* 1 नरकुल, सरकंडा (जो पानी में उगता है) 2 बाँसुरी ▸ **reedy** *adj* 1 नरकुल से भरा 2 (अपमा) बाँसुरी जैसी तीखी पतली (कर्कश) ध्वनि।

reef¹ / रीफ़् / *noun* (जहाज़ के) पाल का एक भाग-विशेष ▸ **reef** *verb* पाल समेटना **reef-knot** (*US* **square knot**) *noun* साधारण दोहरी गाँठ जो आसानी से खुलती नहीं है।

reef² / रीफ़् / *noun* समुद्री चट्टान, शैल-भित्ति : *a coral reef.*

reek / रीक् / *noun* [sing] तीव्र दुर्गंध ▸ **reek** *verb* **reek (of sth)** 1 किसी चीज़ की दुर्गंध आना : *His breath reeked of tobacco.* 2 कोई अप्रिय या संदेहास्पद संकेत देना : *Their actions reek of corruption.*

reel¹ / रील् / *noun* (*US* **spool** भी) रील, चरखी; रील पर लपेटा हुआ धागा, फ़िल्म आदि : *a reel of cotton/film* ▸ **reel** *verb* ■ **reel sth in/out** रील पर लपेटना/

पर से उतारना **reel sth off** धड़ाधड़ बोलना : *reel off a poem/a list of names.*

reel² / रील् / *verb* 1 डगमगाते हुए चलना : *They reeled out of the pub.* 2 चकरा जाना, ऐसा लगना कि चीज़ें चारों ओर घूम रही हैं : *His mind reeled at the news.*

refectory / रि'फ़ेक्टरि / *noun* (pl **refectories**) कॉन्वेंट, कॉलेज आदि में भोजनालय : *refectory table.*

refer / रि'फ़र् / *verb* (-rr-) ■ **refer to sb/sth** 1 ज़िक्र करना, उल्लेख करना 2 किसी से संबंध बताना, वर्णन करना : *This paragraph refers to the events of last year.* 3 सूचनार्थ देखना, संदर्भ देना : *refer to a dictionary* **refer to sb/sth as sth** किसी का वर्णन करना **refer sb/ sth to sb/sth** किसी के पास आवश्यक कार्रवाई या निर्णयार्थ भेजना/देना/सौंपना : *The doctor referred me to a psychiatrist.*

referee / रेफ़'री / *noun* 1 (खेलकूद में) रेफ़री, निर्णायक 2 झगड़े आदि का निर्णायक 3 किसी की सिफ़ारिश में संदर्भ देने वाला व्यक्ति : *The principal often acts as (a) referee for his students.* ▸ **referee** *verb* निर्णायक के रूप में कार्य करना।

reference / रेफ़्रन्स् / *noun* 1 **reference (to sb/sth)** ज़िक्र/उल्लेख : *Try to avoid making any reference to his illness.* 2 संदर्भ कथन : *The book is full of references to places I know.* 3 संदर्भ के लिए कुछ देखने की क्रिया : *Keep this list of numbers near the phone for easy reference.* 4 पुस्तक आदि में संदर्भ-सूची (ग्रंथों की) : *There is a list of references at the end of each chapter.* 5 किसी व्यक्ति के चरित्र, योग्यता आदि पर कथन देने को तैयार व्यक्ति 6 (संक्षि **ref**) (वाणिज्य) पत्र का स्रोत/ फ़ाइल संख्या आदि पहचानने का तरीक़ा : *Please quote our reference when* *applying.* ■ **in/with reference to** *(और)* के संबंध में, के उत्तर में।

referendum / रेफ़'रेन्डम्/ *noun* (*pl* **referendums** या **referenda**) किसी विशिष्ट राजनीतिक मुद्दे पर जनमत संग्रह।

refill / री'फ़िल्/ *verb* फिर से भरना ▸ **refill** / 'रीफ़िल्/ *noun* (पात्र में) फिर से भरने के लिए पदार्थ की मात्रा : *a packet of refills for a cartridge pen.*

refine / रि'फ़ाइन्/ *verb* 1 शुद्ध करना; मिलावट दूर करना : *refine sugar/oil* 2 थोड़ा-बहुत परिवर्तन करके सुधार लाना; (व्यवहार) परिष्कृत करना : *We need to refine our process of selection.* ▸ **refined** *adj* (कभी-कभी *अपमा*) परिष्कृत/सुसंस्कृत **refinery** / रि'फ़ाइनरि / *noun* (*pl* **refineries**) शोधन-कार्य-शाला : *oil refinery.*

refinement / रि'फ़ाइनमन्ट् / *noun* 1 सुधार के लिए थोड़ा-सा परिवर्तन : *all the refinements of modern computer technology* 2 परिष्कार, शोधन : *the refinement of oil* 3 सुरुचि : *The house has an atmosphere of elegant refinement.*

refit / री'फ़िट्/ *verb* (-tt-) **refit sth (with sth)** मरम्मत करना; जहाज़ को आगे की यात्राओं के लिए ठीक करना : *refit a car/kitchen* ▸ **refit** /'रीफ़िट्/ *noun* मरम्मत।

reflect / रि'फ़्लेक्ट्/ *verb* 1 (किसी सतह का) प्रकाश, ताप या ध्वनि परावर्तित करना; दर्पण में प्रतिबिंब दिखाना : *The white houses reflect the glare of the sun.* 2 व्यक्त करना; स्वभाव प्रकट करना 3 **reflect (on/upon sth)** समझना, विचार करना : *reflect on a problem* ■ **reflect well, badly, etc on sb/sth** कार्यों, परिणामों आदि की प्रतिष्ठा बढ़ाना/घटाना : *This scandal is bound to reflect badly on the police as a whole.*

reflection (**reflexion** भी) / रि'फ़्लेक्-शन् / *noun* 1 प्रतिबिंब 2 परावर्तन 3 किसी चीज़ का आभास, सूचना : *Your clothes are often a reflection of your personality.* 4 सावधानीपूर्वक किया गया विचार, अनुचिंतन 5 विचारों की भाषा द्वारा अभिव्यक्ति।

reflective / रि'फ़्लेक्टिव्/ *adj* 1 विचार-शील : *in a reflective mood* 2 परावर्तन-शील : *reflective car number plates.*

reflex /'रीफ़्लेक्स/ *noun* अनैच्छिक अथवा सहज क्रिया (जिसे नियंत्रित नहीं किया जा सकता है, जैसे छींकना) : *a reflex movement/response* ▸ **reflex angle** *noun* 180° से अधिक का कोण।

reform / रि'फ़ॉर्म्/ *verb* सुधारना, में सुधार लाना : *reform one's ways/habits* ▸ **reform** *noun* 1 सुधार (प्रक्रिया) : *demands for electoral reform* 2 परिवर्तन (तरीक़े आदि) : *carry out reforms in education* **reformer** *noun* (समाज) सुधारक।

reformation / ‚रेफ़र'मेशन् / *noun* 1 सुधार प्रक्रिया : *the reformation of criminals* 2 **the Reformation** [*sing*] यूरोप में 16वीं सदी में प्रोटेस्टेंट आंदोलन।

refrain¹ / रि'फ़्रेन्/ *verb* **refrain (from sth/doing sth)** अपने को रोकना (विशेषत: उस चीज़ से जो स्वयं को पसंद हो) : *refrain from comments/criticism.*

refrain² / रि'फ़्रेन्/ *noun* 1 कविता या गीत में टेक 2 बार-बार दोहराई जाने वाली शिकायत या टिप्पणी : *a familiar refrain.*

refresh / रि'फ़्रेश्/ *verb* ताज़ा करना, नई शक्ति प्रदान करना : *The long sleep refreshed her.* ■ **refresh one's/sb's memory (about sb/sth)** याद दिलाना, विशेषत: किसी दिखाई या सुनाई देने वाली वस्तु से : *Perhaps this photo will refresh your memory.* ▸ **refreshing** *adj* 1 स्फूर्तिदायक, तरोताज़ा बनाने वाला : *a nice refreshing shower* 2 प्रियकर

रूप से नया या भिन्न : *It's refreshing to see some new faces in the company.* **refreshingly** *adv.*

refreshment / रि'फ्रेश्मन्ट् / *noun* 1 *(और या परि)* खाना-पीना 2 **refreshments** [*pl*] जलपान, अल्पाहार 3 ताज़ा होना।

refrigerate / रि'फ्रिज़रेट् / *verb* खाना आदि सुरक्षित रखने के लिए ठंडा करना ▶ **refrigerator** / रि'फ्रिज़रेटर् / *noun* (*अनौप* **fridge** / फ्रिज्/) फ्रिज, रिफ्रिजरेटर।

refuge / रेफ्यूज़् / *noun* 1 **refuge (from sb/sth)** मुसीबत में भागे हुए को शरण, आश्रय 2 शरणस्थल : *a refuge for rare birds.*

refugee / रेफ्यु'जी / *noun* शरणार्थी : *set up refugee camps.*

refund / रि'फ़न्ड् / *verb* **refund sth (to sb)** (धन) वापस करना, लौटाना : *refund a deposit* ▶ **refund** / 'रीफ़न्ड् / *noun* वापस किया हुआ धन।

refusal / रि'फ़्यूज़ल् / *noun* इनकार, अस्वीकृति : *a blunt refusal.*

refuse[1] / रि'फ़्यूज़् / *verb* इनकार करना, 'न' कहना : *refuse one's consent/ help.*

refuse[2] / रेफ्यूस् / *noun* कूड़ा-करकट : *kitchen/household refuse.*

refute / रि'फ़्यूट् / *verb* 1 किसी को ग़लत साबित करना : *refute a claim* 2 किसी बात/तथ्य का खंडन करना ▶ **refutable** *adj* **refutation** *noun* खंडन-मंडन।

regain / रि'गेन् / *verb* 1 दोबारा प्राप्त करना, (खोई हुई वस्तु) पुन: पाना : *regain one's freedom* 2 किसी स्थान/पद पर पुन: पहुँचना : *regain one's balance.*

regal / 'रीगल् / *adj* राजोचित, राजसी : *regal splendour* ▶ **regally** *adv.*

regale / रि'गेल् / *verb* ■ **regale sb with sth** कहानी, चुटकुलों आदि से मनोरंजन करना।

regard[1] / रि'गार्ड् / *verb* 1 *(औप)* ध्यान-

पूर्वक देखना : *She regarded him closely.* 2 **regard sb/sth (with sth); regard sb/sth as sth** मानना, समझना : *She is very highly regarded.* 3 सम्मान देना ■ **as regards sb/sth** *(औप)* से संबद्ध; के संबंध में : *I have little information as regards his past.* ▶ **regarding** *prep* के संबंध में : *She said nothing regarding your request.*

regard[2] / रि'गार्ड् / *noun* *(औप)* 1 **regard to/for sb/sth** ध्यान; चिंता : *show little regard for the feelings of others* 2 **regard (for sb/sth)** सम्मान, आदर; कोमल भावनाएँ 3 **regards** [*pl*] (प्राय: पत्र के अंत में) शुभकामनाएँ ■ **in/with regard to sb/sth** *(औप)* किसी के संबंध में : *a country's laws in regard to human rights* **in this/ that regard** *(औप)* पहले उल्लिखित विषय से संबंधित : *I have nothing further to say in this regard.* ▶ **regardless** *adv* **regardless of** *prep* की परवाह न करते हुए।

regency / 'रीजन्सि / *noun* (*pl* **regencies**) रीजेंट (संरक्षक) का पद, अधिकार आदि।

regenerate / रि'जेनरेट् / *verb* 1 पुनरुज्जीवित करना, पुन: शक्ति संचार करना : *regenerate the economy* 2 *(जीव विज्ञान)* पुनर्जीवित होना/करना, फिर से उगना : *Once destroyed, brain cells do not regenerate.* ▶ **regeneration** / रि'जेन'रेश्न् / *noun.*

regent / 'रीजन्ट् / (प्राय: **Regent**) *noun* रीजेंट (बहुत वृद्ध, बालक, बीमार या अनुपस्थित राजा के स्थान पर शासन संभालने वाला व्यक्ति, संरक्षक) : *act as regent* ▶ **regent** (प्राय: **Regent**) *adj* : *the Prince Regent.*

regime / रे'श्रीम् / *noun* शासन प्रणाली; शासन : *a socialist/fascist regime.*

regimen / 'रेजिमन् / *noun* (*चिकि या*

औप) स्वास्थ्य-लाभ हेतु आहार, व्यायाम, आचरण आदि पर हिदायतें।

regiment / 'रेजिमन्ट् / noun 1 रेजिमेंट, सैन्यदल : an infantry regiment 2 regiment of sth/sb बहुसंख्या ▶ **regiment** verb संगठित करना, अनुशासन में रखना।

region / 'रीजन् / noun 1 क्षेत्र 2 (देश का) प्रशासनिक विभाग 3 **the regions** [pl] राजधानी को छोड़कर बाक़ी सारा देश : develop new rail services to the regions ■ **in the region of sth** (संख्या, क़ीमत, वज़न आदि) के समीप/आसपास ▶ **regional** / 'रीजन्ल् / adj क्षेत्रीय।

register¹ / 'रेजिस्टर् / noun 1 रजिस्टर, पंजिका : the register of voters 2 रिकॉर्ड रखने का यंत्र : a cash register 3 मानव आवाज़ या वाद्ययंत्र की परास (का एक भाग) : notes in the upper/middle register.

register² / 'रेजिस्टर् / verb 1 register (at/for/with sth); register sth (in sth); register (sb) as sth सूचीबद्ध करना, पंजीकरण करना; रजिस्टर में नाम चढ़ाना : register a birth/death 2 किसी मापक यंत्र जैसे थर्मामीटर द्वारा अंकित किया जाना 3 (अनौप) भावनाएँ व्यक्त करना : Her face registered dismay. 4 पत्र आदि पंजीकृत डाक से भेजना।

registrar / रेजि'स्ट्रार; 'रेजिस्ट्रार् / noun 1 पंजीकरण-अधिकारी 2 विश्वविद्यालय में मुख्य प्रशासन अधिकारी।

registration / ‚रेजि'स्ट्रेश्न् / noun पंजीकरण।

registry / 'रेजिस्ट्रि / noun (pl registries) रजिस्टर रखने का स्थान।

regret¹ / रि'ग्रेट् / verb (-tt-) 1 दुखी होना, निराश या कुंठित होना : His death was regretted by all. ○ I don't regret what I said. 2 खेद व्यक्त करना : We regret any inconvenience caused.
▶ **regrettable** / रि'ग्रेटब्ल् / adj खेद-

जनक, शोचनीय : a regrettable failure.

regret² / रि'ग्रेट् / noun खेद, अनुताप ▶ **regretful** adj उदास, खिन्न : She sounded regretful. **regretfully** adv.

regular / 'रेग्युलर् / adj 1 सुव्यवस्थित : regular teeth/features 2 नियमित, बराबर-बराबर अवधि के बाद घटित होने वाला : a regular pulse/heartbeat 3 (व्यक्ति) प्रायः एक ही काम बार-बार करने वाला; सामान्य, नियमित : our regular listeners ○ my regular doctor 4 यथोचित : Those without regular visas were refused entry. 5 प्रशिक्षण-प्राप्त, पूर्णकालिक या व्यावसायिक : a regular soldier/army 6 शुद्धता के मानक के अनुसार 7 (विशेषतः US) सामान्य, विशेष नहीं : He's just a regular guy. ▶ **regular** noun 1 नियमित सेना का सैनिक 2 (अनौप) (किसी दुकान का) नियमित ग्राहक **regularly** adv 1 नियमित रूप से; नियमित समय पर 2 प्रायः : He regularly appears on television.

regularize, -ise / 'रेग्युलराइज़् / verb वैध और नियमानुकूल बनाना : Illegal immigrants are being given the opportunity to regularize their position.

regulate / 'रेग्युलेट् / verb 1 व्यवस्था और नियमों द्वारा नियंत्रित करना : regulate one's expenditure 2 किसी यंत्र को ठीक और समंजित करना ▶ **regulator** noun 1 (व्यापार या उद्योग का) नियंत्रक व्यक्ति 2 समंजित।

regulation / ‚रेग्यु'लेश्न् / noun 1 (प्रायः pl) नियम-क़ानून; व्यवस्था : building regulations 2 नियंत्रित करना या होना ▶ **regulation** adj नियमानुकूल : in regulation uniform.

rehabilitate / ‚रीअ 'बिलिटेट् / verb 1 लंबी अस्वस्थता या क़ैद के बाद सामान्य

जीवन बिताने में सहायता करना 2 भवन आदि की मरम्मत करके पुन: अच्छी स्थिति में लाना।

rehearse / रि'हर्स् / verb 1 **rehearse (for sth)** (नाटक आदि का) अभ्यास (रिहर्सल) करना; **rehearse sb (for sth)** ऐसे अभ्यास का मार्ग निर्देशन करना : *rehearse the actors for the fight scene* 2 मन में तैयारी करके रखना : *He rehearsed the interview in his mind beforehand.* 3 (प्राय: *अपमा, औप*) फिर से कहना, दोहराना : *rehearse one's grievances* ▸ **rehearsal** / रि'हर्सल् / noun.

reign / रेन् / noun राज्यकाल ▸ **reign** verb 1 **reign (over sb/sth)** राज/शासन करना : *the reigning monarch* 2 (कोई विचार, भाव या वातावरण) अधिक प्रभावशाली होना : *Silence reigned.*

reimburse / रीइम्'बर्स् / verb **reimburse sth (to sb); reimburse sb (for sth)** (सामान्यत: *औप*) प्रतिपूर्ति करना, किसी को वह राशि देना जो उसने अपनी ओर से पहले खर्च की है: *We will reimburse the customer for any loss or damage.* ▸ **reimbursement** noun : *receive reimbursement of medical expenses.*

rein / रेन् / noun 1 (प्राय: *pl*) लगाम/रास, बागडोर 2 **reins** [*pl*] **the reins (of sth)** (विशेषत: *साहि*) नियंत्रण करना, नेतृत्व संभालना ▸ **rein** verb ■ **rein sth in; rein sb/sth back** 1 नियंत्रित करना : *The leader wants to rein back the extremists in his party.* 2 घोड़े को लगाम से नियंत्रित करना।

reindeer / 'रेन्डिअर् / noun (*pl* अपरिवर्तित) रेनडियर, उत्तरी ठंडे प्रदेशों में पाया जाने वाला एक बड़ा हिरन।

reinforce / ,रीइन्'फ़ॉर्स् / verb 1 सुदृढ़ या मज़बूत करना; तीव्र करना 2 किसी का स्तर या पद बढ़ाना 3 कुमक भेजना : *The garrison must be reinforced against attack.* 4 किसी संरचना को अन्य पदार्थ मिलाकर सुदृढ़ बनाना : *reinforce a wall/bridge* ▸ **reinforcement** noun 1 **reinforcements** [*pl*] कुमक (अतिरिक्त सेना, रसद आदि) 2 दृढ़ीकरण, मज़बूती प्रदान करना।

reinstate / ,रीइन्'स्टेट् / verb **reinstate sb/sth (in/as sth)** 1 किसी को उसके पूर्व पद (प्राय: महत्त्वपूर्ण) पर आसीन करना : *reinstate sb as manager* 2 पूर्व अवस्था या स्थिति में करना ▸ **reinstatement** noun.

reiterate / री'इटरेट् / verb (औप) बार-बार दोहराना : *reiterate a demand* ▸ **reiteration** noun (सामान्यत: *sing*).

reject / रि'जेक्ट् / verb 1 अस्वीकार करना : *reject a decision* 2 एक तरफ़ रख देना या प्रयोग न करना; अलग निकाल देना : *Imperfect articles are rejected by our quality control.* 3 उचित देखभाल न किया जाना/न करना : *The lioness rejected the smallest cub.* ▸ **reject** / 'रीजेक्ट् / noun अस्वीकृत वस्तु/व्यक्ति **rejection** / रि'जेक्शन् / noun.

rejoice / रि'जॉइस् / verb **rejoice (at/in/over sth)** (अप्र या औप) हर्ष मनाना, उल्लास मनाना : *rejoice over a victory* ▸ **rejoicing** noun.

rejuvenate / रि'जूवनेट् / verb फिर से तरुण होना या बनाना : *feel rejuvenated after a long holiday* ▸ **rejuvenation** noun : *the rejuvenation of a flagging career.*

relapse / रि'लैप्स् / verb **relapse (into sth/doing sth)** सुधार के बाद पुन: उसी स्थिति में हो जाना; अच्छा होकर फिर से बीमार हो जाना : *relapse into bad habits○ relapse into unconsciousness* ▸ **relapse** noun पुन: पतन।

relate / रि'लेट् / verb 1 **relate sth (to/with sth)** विचारों, घटनाओं, स्थितियों,

अर्थों आदि में संबंध स्थापित करना : *I found it difficult to relate the two concepts in my mind.* **2 relate sth (to sb)** (औप) वर्णन करना, तथ्यों का विवरण देना : *relate one's experiences* ■ **relate to sth/sb 1** किसी से संबंधित होना; किसी का ज़िक्र करना : *statements relating to economic policy* **2** (अनौप) किसी से सहानुभूति, हमदर्दी अनुभव कर पाना : *Some adults can't relate to children.* ▸ **related** *adj* **related (to sth/sb) 1** से संबद्ध : *crime related to drug abuse* **2** एक ही परिवार, समूह आदि का सदस्य होना : *related species/languages* **relatedness** *noun.*

relation / रि'लेशन् / *noun* **1 relations** [*pl*] **relations (between sb/sth and sb/sth); relations (with sb/sth)** संबंध; परस्पर-संबंध **2 relation (between sth and sth); relation (to sth)** आपस की सह-संबद्धता : *the relation of cause and effect* **3** नातेदार, संबंधी व्यक्ति : *a close relation of mine* **4 relation (to sb)** पारिवारिक संबंध **5** तथ्य-कथन ■ **in relation to sb/sth 1** के विषय में : *his comments in relation to this affair* **2** के अनुपात में; मात्रा, आकार आदि के संदर्भ में : *Temperature varies in relation to pressure.* ▸ **relational** *adj.*

relationship / रि'लेश्न्शिप् / *noun* संबंध।

relative¹ / 'रेलटिव् / *adj* **1 relative (to sth)** से संबद्ध **2** अन्य की तुलना में उच्च स्तरीय : *in relative comfort* **3 relative to sth** (औप) के संबंध में, के संदर्भ में : *the facts/papers relative to the case* **4** सापेक्षिक, तुलनात्मक ▸ **relatively** *adv* अपेक्षाकृत; के अनुपात में।

relative² / 'रेलटिव् / *noun* नातेदार, रिश्तेदार : *friends and relatives.*

relax / रि'लैक्स् / *verb* **1** काम या प्रयास के बाद विश्राम करना; उत्कंठा, चिंता आदि कम करना/होना **2** शिथिल करना/होना : *Let your muscles relax slowly.* **3** नियमों, क़ायदे-क़ानूनों में शिथिलता लाना, नरमी बरतना : *relax the entry requirements* **4** दुर्बल करना ▸ **relaxation** / रीलैक्'सेशन् / *noun* ढील; विश्राम।

relay¹ / 'रीले / *noun* **1** (**relay race** भी) रिले दौड़ **2** काम से थके हुए व्यक्ति, पशु आदि का अन्य ताज़ादम व्यक्ति, पशु द्वारा स्थान लिया जाना : *work in relay* **3** रेडियो सिगनल ग्रहण करके उन्हें उच्च शक्ति से पुन: भेजने वाला उपकरण; इस तरह प्रसारित कार्यक्रम।

relay² / रि'ले; 'रीले / *verb* (*pt, pp* **relayed**) **1** संदेश लेकर आगे भेजना **2** रिले कार्यक्रम प्रसारित करना : *a concert relayed (live) from the Nehru Stadium.*

release / रि'लीस् / *verb* **1 release oneself/sb/sth (from sth)** छोड़ना, जाने देना; मुक्त करना/खोल देना : *release a prisoner (from captivity)* **2** किसी आवश्यकता/कर्तव्य से मुक्त करना **3 release sth (to sb/sth)** समाचार, सूचना आदि प्रकाशित होने देना **4** सार्वजनिक प्रयोग/प्रदर्शन के लिए उपलब्ध कराना : *new products released into the market* **5** शिथिल करना, बंधन ढीले करना; छोड़ना : *release one's grip on sth* ▸ **release** *noun* **1 release (from sth)** मुक्ति, खोलना **2** सार्वजनिक रूप से प्रस्तुत फ़िल्म, सूचना आदि : *the latest new releases.*

relegate / 'रेलिगेट् / *verb* **relegate sb/ sth (to sth)** किसी (व्यक्ति/वस्तु) को कम महत्त्वपूर्ण पद, कार्य या स्थान देना/पर पहुँचाना।

relent / रि'लेन्ट् / *verb* **1 relent (in sth)** नरम पड़ जाना, दया दिखाने लगना : *The police will not relent in their fight* *against crime.* 2 कम तीव्र होना : *The pressure of this job never relents.* 3 (ख़राब मौसम) अच्छा होने लगना ▸ **relentless** *adj* 1 लगातार, अनवरत : *relentless criticism* 2 निर्दय, कठोर : *be relentless in punishing offenders* **relentlessly** *adv.*

relevant / 'रेलवन्ट् / *adj* **relevant (to sth/sb)** (विचार किए जा रहे विषय से) संबद्ध; प्रासंगिक, संगत : *a highly relevant point* ▸ **relevance** *noun.*

reliable / रि'लाइअब्ल् / *adj* विश्वसनीय, भरोसेमंद : *a reliable goalkeeper* ▸ **reliability** *noun* भरोसा, विश्वसनीयता **reliably** *adv.*

reliance / रि'लाइअन्स् / *noun* **reliance (on/upon sth/sb)** विश्वास/यक़ीन/सहारा, निर्भरता : *the country's reliance on imported oil* ▸ **reliant** / रि'लाइअन्ट् / *adj* विश्वस्त; विश्वासी; निर्भर : *He's heavily reliant on bank loans.*

relic / 'रेलिक् / *noun* 1 **relic (of/from sth)** स्मृतिशेष, अतीत का अवशेष जो स्मृति जागृत करता है : *relics of ancient civilizations* 2 **relics** [*pl*] महान व्यक्ति की मृत्यु के बाद रखे उसके अवशेष।

relief¹ / रि'लीफ़् / *noun* 1 [*sing*] **relief (from sth)** कष्ट, चिंता आदि से राहत, आराम 2 मुसीबत में घिरे लोगों को दी गई राहत सामग्री, खाना-कपड़े आदि 3 विशेष ज़रूरत या कठिनाई के समय सरकार द्वारा प्रदत्त धन : *temporary financial relief for those adversely affected by the new law* 4 **relief (from sth)** एकरसता के स्थान पर विविधता का बदलाव : *comic relief* 5 पुलिस अफ़सरों या सैनिकों का ऐसा दल जो दूसरे दल का स्थान ले : *'B' Relief come(s) on duty at 9 o'clock.*

relief² / रि'लीफ़् / *noun* 1 (कला में) नक़्क़ाशी आदि में उभार 2 किसी चीज़ को और अधिक मुखर बनाने के लिए रंगों,

विपरीत मिश्रणों आदि का प्रयोग 3 उच्चावच ▸ **relief map** *noun* उभारदार नक़्शा।

relieve / रि'लीव् / *verb* 1 कष्ट/चिंता आदि में राहत पहुँचाना/लाना : *drugs to relieve the pain* 2 कम मुश्किल या कम गंभीर बनाना; तीव्रता कम करना : *efforts to relieve famine in Africa* 3 भिन्नता लाना : *relieve the boredom of waiting* 4 किसी व्यक्ति को उसके कार्यभार से निवृत्त करना : *relieve a driver* ■ **relieve sb of sth** 1 (प्रायः *परि*) कुछ पकड़ने में किसी की सहायता करना : *Let me relieve you of your coat and hat.* 2 (औप) किसी और का कर्तव्य निभाना, काम करना : *The new secretary will relieve us of some of the paperwork.* 3 कार्यपद से हटाना : *The general was relieved of his command/duties.* ▸ **relieved** *adj* चिंतामुक्त अनुभव करना : *We were very relieved to hear you were safe.*

religion / रि'लिजन् / *noun* 1 ईश्वर/ देवताओं के अस्तित्व में विश्वास 2 धर्म : *the Christian/Jewish/Hindu religion.*

religious / रि'लिजस् / *adj* 1 धार्मिक : *a religious service* 2 (व्यक्ति) धर्मपरायण 3 धर्मसेवा में लगे लोग, भिक्षुक आदि ▸ **religiously** *adv.*

relinquish / रि'लिङ्क्विश् / *verb* **relinquish sth (to sb)** (औप) त्याग देना, अधिकार छोड़ देना : *relinquish one's position as Governor.*

relish / 'रेलिश् / *noun* 1 **relish (for sth)** स्वाद, रस; अत्यंत आनंद : *eat with great relish* 2 मसालेदार सब्ज़ियाँ : *cucumber/sweetcorn relish* ▸ **relish** *verb* स्वाद लेना, रस लूटना/भोगना।

relive / री'लिव् / *verb* किसी अनुभव को फिर से दोहराना/जीना, विशेषतः मन में।

reluctant / रि'लकटन्ट् / *adj* **reluctant (to do sth)** कोई कार्य करने को अनि-

च्छुक : *a reluctant helper* ▸ **reluctance** *noun* **reluctantly** *adv*.

rely / रि'लाइ / *verb* (*pt, pp* **relied**)
■ **rely on/upon sb/sth (to do sth)**
1 निर्भर होना, किसी की ओर सहायता के लिए देखना 2 किसी पर भरोसा करना, विश्वास करना : *You can rely on me to keep your secret.*

remain / रि'मेन् / *verb* 1 शेष या बाक़ी रहना : *Very little of the house remained after the fire.* 2 बने रहना, उसी स्थिति में रहना : *remain standing/ seated* 3 (और) कुछ करना/कहना बाक़ी रह जाना : *Much remains to be done.*

remainder / रि'मेन्डर् / *noun* 1 (प्रायः **the remainder**) बचे हुए व्यक्ति/वस्तुएँ आदि : *She kept a few of his books but gave away the remainder.* 2 (प्रायः *sing*) (*गणित*) शेष 3 पुस्तक की बिना बिकी प्रतियाँ

remains / रि'मेन्ज़् / *noun* [*pl*] 1 बाक़ी बचा हुआ भाग : *the remains of a meal* 2 पुराने अवशेष (भवन आदि) : *the remains of ancient Rome* 3 (और) मृत शरीर।

remand / रि'मान्ड् / *verb* (अपराधी को) मुक़दमा होने तक हवालात में भेजना या ज़मानत पर छोड़ना : *The accused was remanded in custody for a week.*
▸ **remand** *noun*.

remark / रि'मार्क् / *verb* **remark on/ upon sth/sb** कुछ कहना/टिप्पणी करना; ध्यान से देखना : *Critics remarked that the play was not original.* ▸ **remark** *noun* 1 कथन/टिप्पणी : *make pointed/cutting/rude remarks* 2 (अप्र या और) ध्यानपूर्वक देखना **remarkable** *adj* **remarkable (for sth)** उल्लेखनीय; असाधारण **remarkably** *adv*.

remedy / 'रेमडि / *noun* (*pl* **remedies**) **remedy (for sth)** 1 (और) दवा, इलाज; चिकित्सा : *a popular remedy for flu/*

toothache/cramp 2 उपाय, प्रतिकार : *seek a remedy for injustice* ▸ **remedial** / रि'मीडिअल् / *adj* **remedy** *verb* (*pt, pp* **remedied**) कुछ अनिश्चित को बदलना, सुधारना; (अवांछित को) ठीक कर देना।

remember / रि'मेम्बर् / *verb* 1 याद रखना, स्मरण करना; कुछ करना न भूलना : *Do you remember where you put the key?* ○ *Remember to ring your father.* 2 नमस्कार पहुँचाना; इज़्ज़त देना : *a church service to remember the war dead.*

remembrance / रि'मेम्ब्रन्स् / *noun* (और) 1 स्मरण, याद 2 स्मृतिचिह्न, यादगार/निशानी।

remind / रि'माइन्ड् / *verb* **remind sb (of/about sth)** याद दिलाना/स्मरण कराना : *Remind me to answer that letter.* ▸ **reminder** *noun* 1 याद दिलाने वाली वस्तु 2 स्मरण-पत्र : *I've received another reminder from the electricity board.*

reminisce / ‚रेमि'निस् / *verb* **reminisce (about sb/sth)** पूर्व घटनाओं, अनुभवों आदि को याद करना, प्रायः खुशी के साथ।

reminiscence / ‚रेमि'निस्न्स् / *noun* 1 अतीत की यादें, अनुभवों का स्मरण : *reminiscence of childhood* 2 **reminiscences** [*pl*] संस्मरण : *the writer's reminiscences of his life abroad.*

reminiscent / ‚रेमि'निस्न्ट् / *adj* 1 **reminiscent of sb/sth** स्मरण कराने वाला : *His style is faintly reminiscent of Picasso's.* 2 अतीत के स्मरण से संबंधित।

remiss / रि'मिस् / *adj* **remiss (in sth)** (और) लापरवाह, काहिल; अपने काम में ढीला : *I have been very remiss in my duty.*

remission / रि'मिश्न् / *noun* 1 अच्छे

व्यवहार के कारण जेल सज़ा में कमी; ऋण, भुगतान, दंड आदि का निरस्तीकरण, माफ़ी/ क्षमा : *partial remission of exam fees* 2 कष्ट या बीमारी की तीव्रता में कमी : *The drug produced dramatic remissions in some patients.* 3 ईश्वर द्वारा पापक्षमा।

remit / रि'मिट् / *verb* (-tt-) *(औप)* 1 remit sth (to sb) डाक द्वारा धन भेजना : *remit a fee/cheque* 2 (ऋण, सज़ा आदि) माफ़ करना : *remit a prison sentence* ■ remit sth to sb *(क़ानून)* किसी मामले को निर्णयार्थ अधिकारी के पास भेजना : *The case has been remitted for rehearing before another judge.*

remittance / रि'मिट्न्स् / *noun* 1 अदायगी के लिए रुपया (भेजना) 2 रुपया भेजने की क्रिया।

remnant / 'रेम्नन्ट् / *noun* 1 *(प्रायः pl)* शेष, अवशेष : *the remnants of a meal*; बाक़ी बची हुई, (अस्तित्व में) वस्तु का ज़रा-सा अंश : *the last remnants of a traditional way of life* 2 बिक्री के बाद बचे हुए कपड़े/क़ालीन आदि का टुकड़ा जिसे कम दामों पर बेचा जाता है : *cushions made from remnants.*

remonstrate / 'रेमन्स्ट्रेट् / *verb* remonstrate (with sb) (about sth) *(औप)* विरोध करना; प्रतिवाद करना : *We remonstrated with the neighbours about the noise.*

remorse / रि'मॉर्स् / *noun* remorse (for sth/doing sth) पश्चाताप ▸ remorseful *adj* remorseless *adj* 1 निर्दय, पश्चाताप रहित 2 तीव्र और निरंतर जिसे रोका न जा सके : *the remorseless rise of inflation.*

remote / रि'मोट् / *adj* (-r, -st) 1 (समय, स्थान या संबंध की दृष्टि से) बहुत दूर 2 remote (from sth) दूरस्थ, अलग-थलग 3 थोड़ा, कम : *a remote possi-*

bility 4 *(व्यक्ति या व्यवहार)* अमित्रवत्, रुचिहीन : *a remote expression* ▸ remotely *adv* remote control *noun* व्यवस्था जिससे दूर से ही किसी मशीन को नियंत्रित किया जा सके।

remove / रि'मूव् / *verb* 1 remove sth/ sb (from sth) हटाना, ले जाना; (कपड़े आदि) उतारना : *remove one's hat* 2 remove sth (from sth) किसी चीज़ को ग़ायब कर देना/छुट्टी पा लेना : *remove doubts/fears from sb's mind* 3 remove sb (from sth) किसी को उसके पद से हटा देना ▸ removable *adj* removal *noun.*

remunerate / रि'म्यूनरेट् / *verb* remunerate sb (for sth) कार्य या सेवा के बदले में पारिश्रमिक (मेहनताना) देना ▸ remuneration / रि,म्यून'रेश्न् / *noun* पारिश्रमिक।

renaissance / रि'नेसन्स्; *US* 'रेनसान्स् / *noun* 1 the Renaissance [*sing*] 14वीं, 15वीं और 16वीं शताब्दियों की अवधि जिसमें प्राचीन यूनानी विचारों के अध्ययन से प्रेरित हो कला, साहित्य आदि में एक ताज़ी रुचि पैदा हुई थी 2 आम लोगों में ऐसी ही कुछ ताज़ी रुचि का जागना; पुनर्जागरण : *Folk music is currently enjoying a renaissance.*

render / 'रेन्डर् / *verb* (औप) 1 किसी स्थिति में करना या होना : *render sth harmless/useless* 2 render sth (for sth); render sth (to sb) बदले में देना (जो अपेक्षित है) : *render homage/ obedience* 3 भुगतान के लिए हिसाब भेजना 4 संगीत, नाटक आदि प्रस्तुत करना; चित्रकारी में कुछ प्रदर्शित करना : *The artist had rendered her gentle smile perfectly.* ▸ rendering *noun.*

rendezvous / 'रॉन्डिव़ू / *noun* (pl अपरिवर्तित 'रॉन्डिव़ूज़्/) 1 rendezvous (with sb) पूर्वनिश्चित स्थान एवं समय पर

किसी से मिलना : *a secret rendezvous* 2 ऐसी जगह जहाँ एक वर्ग विशेष के लोग प्राय: मिलते हैं ▸ **rendezvous** *verb* (*pt* **rendezvoused**).

renew /रि'न्यू/ *verb* 1 फिर से करना (शुरू करना) : *renew peace talks* 2 एक अंतराल के बाद फिर से कुछ बनाना; फिर से कहना, देना, पाना आदि : *renew a friendship/a request* 3 नवीनीकरण करना/ कराना; नए के समान करना : *renew a passport* 4 किसी पुरानी वस्तु के स्थान पर नई वस्तु लगा देना : *renew worn tyres* 5 नई शक्ति का संचार करना ▸ **renewable** *adj* **renewal** /रि'न्यूअल्/ *noun* नवीनी-करण।

renounce /रि'नाउन्स्/ *verb* (औप) 1 दावा/स्वामित्व छोड़ देना : *renounce a claim/title* 2 कोई आदत छोड़ देना, त्याग करना 3 संबंध त्याग देना; सांसारिक वस्तुओं का त्याग कर देना (संन्यास लेना) ▸ **renouncement** *noun* = **renunciation**.

renovate /'रेनवेट्/ *verb* पुराने मकान आदि को अच्छी, सुदृढ़ स्थिति में लाना, पुन-रुद्धार करना : *The house has been completely renovated and modernized.* ▸ **renovation** /रेन्'वेश्न्/ *noun* पुनरुद्धार।

renown /रि'नाउन्/ *noun* (औप) यश, कीर्ति ▸ **renowned** *adj* **renowned** (**as/for sth**) यशस्वी, प्रसिद्ध : *renowned as an actress/for her acting.*

rent /रेन्ट्/ *noun* (मकान आदि का) किराया : *Rents are going up again.* ▸ **rent** *verb* 1 **rent sth** (**from sb**) किराया देना, किराए पर लेना : *rent a holiday cottage from an agency* 2 **rent sth** (**out**) (**to sb**) किराए पर देना **rental** *noun* 1 किराए की राशि 2 किराए पर देने की प्रक्रिया : *a car rental company.*

renunciation /रि'नन्सि'एश्न्/ (re-

nouncement भी) *noun* किसी वस्तु का औपचारिक रूप से त्याग कर देना : *a/the renunciation of nuclear weapons/ a sinful life.*

reorganize, -ise /रि'ऑर्गनाइज़्/ *verb* पुन: संगठित या व्यवस्थाबद्ध करना; भिन्न रीति से संगठित करना।

repair /रि'पेअर्/ *verb* 1 मरम्मत करना 2 ठीक करना; सुधारना : *repair an error* ▸ **repair** *noun* 1 (प्राय: *pl*) मरम्मत कार्य 2 मरम्मत में : *a road under repair* **repairer** *noun* मरम्मत कार्य करने वाला : *a watch repairer.*

repartee /रेपार्'टी/ *noun* निपुण और प्राय: व्यंग्यपूर्ण चतुर उत्तर/वार्ता : *indulge in brilliant repartee.*

repast /रि'पास्ट्/ *noun* (औप या साहि) दावत, भोज : *enjoy a light repast.*

repatriate /री'पैट्रिएट्/ *verb* **repatri-ate sb** (**to sth**) किसी को उसके देश वापस भेजना या लौटाना : *repatriate refugees* ▸ **repatriation** *noun*.

repay /रि'पे/ *verb* (*pt, pp* **repaid** /रि'पेड्/) 1 **repay sth** (**to sb**) धन लौटाना : *repay a loan* 2 **repay sb** (**for sth**); **repay sth** (**with sth**) सहायता, दया आदि के बदले में कुछ लौटाना/ देना ▸ **repayable** *adj* **repayment** *noun*.

repeal /रि'पील्/ *verb* (क़ानून आदि को) अधिकारिक रूप से रद्द करना ▸ **repeal** *noun*.

repeat /रि'पीट्/ *verb* 1 दोबारा कहना या लिखना; किसी काम को बार-बार करना : *repeat an action*; **repeat** (**itself**) एक से ज़्यादा बार होना 2 किसी के कहे को या पहले से याद किए को सुनाना या दोह-राना : *Repeat each sentence after me.* ▸ **repeat** *noun* 1 दोहराने की क्रिया : *a repeat order* 2 पुन: प्रसारित कार्यक्रम **repeated** *adj* **repeatedly** *adv* बार-बार।

repel / रि'पेल् / *verb* (-ll-) 1 मार भगाना, पीछे धकेल देना : *repel an attacker* 2 वितृष्णा या घृणा उत्पन्न करना : *Gratuitous violence repels most people.* ▸ **repellent** *adj.*

repent / रि'पेन्ट् / *verb* **repent (of sth)** पछताना, पश्चाताप करना, यह सोचना कि काश ऐसा न किया होता : *He soon repented his actions.* ▸ **repentance** / रि'पेन्टन्स् / *noun* पछतावा **repentant** *adj.*

repercussion / ‚रीपर'कशन् / *noun* (प्राय: *pl*) किसी घटना के (प्राय: अप्रिय) दूरगामी और अप्रत्यक्ष प्रभाव : *the social repercussions of the case.*

repertoire / 'रेपर्टवार् / (और **repertory** भी) *noun* 1 नाटकों, गानों आदि का संपूर्ण संग्रह जिसे नाटक मंडली अभिनीत करने या गाने में सक्षम रहती है; रंगपटल : *extend one's repertoire* 2 किसी व्यक्ति की संपूर्ण निपुणता जिसे वह उपयोग में ला सकता है।

repetition / ‚रेप'टिशन् / *noun* 1 पुनरावृत्ति : *learn by repetition* 2 दोहराई हुई वस्तु, प्रतिकृति ▸ **repetitious, repetitive** *adjs.*

replace / रि'प्लेस् / *verb* 1 किसी व्यक्ति/ वस्तु का स्थान ले लेना : *Machines have replaced people in many areas of industry.* 2 वापस स्थान पर रख देना : *replace the book on the shelf* 3 **replace sb/sth with sb/sth** किसी वस्तु/व्यक्ति के स्थान पर बेहतर या नई वस्तु/ व्यक्ति को बदल देना ▸ **replacement** *noun* 1 बदलना, बदला जाना 2 **replacement (for sb/sth)** अन्य के स्थान पर रखा जाने वाला/आने वाला वस्तु या व्यक्ति।

replay / ‚री'प्ले / *verb* 1 अनिर्णीत खेल को फिर से खेलना 2 खेल आदि का टेप/ विडियो दुबारा से चलाना ▸ **replay** / 'रीप्ले / *noun.*

replenish / रि'प्लेनिश् / *verb* (और

1 **replenish sth (with sth)** फिर से पूर्ण कर देना, भरा-पूरा कर देना 2 किसी वस्तु की और आपूर्ति प्राप्त करना : *replenish one's stocks of pet food* ▸ **replenishment** *noun.*

replete / रि'प्लीट् / *adj* **replete (with sth)** (औप) 1 परिपूर्ण, भरा-पूरा : *a game replete with drama and high tension* 2 खाने से ठसाठस भरा : *replete with turkey and plum pudding after Christmas lunch.*

replica / 'रेप्लिका / *noun* 1 प्रतिकृति, ठीक-ठीक नक़ल : *make a replica of the Taj* 2 बिलकुल मिलता-जुलता व्यक्ति/ वस्तु ▸ **replicate** *verb* (औप) प्रतिकृति बनाना : *The virus replicates itself a number of times in the computer.*

reply / रि'प्लाइ / *verb* (*pt, pp* **replied**) **reply (to sb/sth) (with sth)** बोलकर या लिखकर उत्तर देना; क्रिया करके उत्तर देना : *He replied with a nod.* ▸ **reply** *noun* 1 उत्तर क्रिया : *She made no reply.* 2 लिखित या कथन में उत्तर : *receive several replies to an advertisement.*

report[1] / रि'पोर्ट् / *verb* 1 **report (on sb/ sth) (to sb/sth); report sth (to sb)** रिपोर्ट देना, विवरण देना : *report a debate* 2 घोषणा करना, प्रकाशित या प्रसारित करके जानकारी देना; **report (on sth)** पत्रकार के रूप में सूचना भेजना 3 **report (to sb/sth) for sth** अपनी उपस्थिति की सूचना देना 4 **report sb (for sth); report sb/sth (to sb)** औपचारिक रूप से शिकायत करना/दर्ज कराना : *report a burglary (to the police)* 5 **report to sb/sth** अधीक्षक को जवाबदेह होना : *All representatives report (directly) to the sales manager.* ■ **report back (from sth)** वापस आना : *The officer reported back from leave on Sunday night.* **report back (to**

sb/sth) की गई छानबीन का मौखिक या लिखित विवरण देना : *He was requested to report back to the committee about/on his findings.* ▸ **reporter** *noun* समाचार पत्रों का संवाददाता।

report² / रि'पॉर्ट् / *noun* 1 report (on sth) रिपोर्ट, विवरण 2 साधारण सूचना, उड़ती ख़बर : *reports of UFO sightings* 3 विद्यार्थी या कर्मचारी के व्यवहार की सूचना 4 धमाके की आवाज़।

repose / रि'पोज़् / *verb* (औप) 1 आराम करना, लेटना; सहारे के लिए (बाजू) टिकाना : *repose one's head on a cushion* 2 किसी स्थान पर रखा जाना ■ **repose sth in sth/sb** (औप) विश्वास/आस्था रखना : *He reposed too much confidence in her.* ▸ **repose** *noun* (औप या साहि) 1 आराम, निद्रा 2 विश्राम/शांति।

represent / ˌरेप्रि'ज़ेन्ट् / *verb* 1 प्रतिनिधित्व करना : *MPs representing the UP constituencies* 2 होना, बनाना; परिणाम होना; उदाहरण देना/होना : *Those comments do not represent all our views.* 3 **represent sth (to sb)** वर्णन करना; प्रतिवेदन प्रस्तुत करना : *represent your grievances to the Governor* 4 प्रतीक होना; अनुरूप होना : *Phonetic symbols represent sounds.* ▸ **representation** / ˌरेप्रिज़ेन'टेश्न् / *noun* 1 प्रतिनिधित्व 2 **representations** [*pl*] **representations (to sb)** (औप) प्रतिवेदन 3 (औप) निरूपण, चित्रण : *plastic representations of dinosaurs.*

representative / ˌरेप्रि'ज़ेन्टटिव् / *adj* 1 **representative (of sb/sth)** वर्ग या समूह का प्रतिनिधि रूप; कई प्रकारों के उदाहरण वाला 2 प्रतिनिधिक (शासन/संस्था आदि) ▸ **representative** *noun* **representative (of sb/sth)** 1 वर्ग या समूह का विशिष्ट उदाहरण/प्रतिनिधि 2 (अनौप

rep भी) (वाणिज्य) कंपनी आदि का एजेंट/ प्रतिनिधि 3 किसी व्यक्ति या संस्था का प्रतिनिधि।

repress / रि'प्रेस् / *verb* 1 भावना को दबा देना, दमन करना : *repress an urge to scream* 2 विरोध, चर्चा आदि को बलात् कुचल देना : *All opposition is brutally repressed by the regime.* ▸ **repressed** *adj* दमन के कारण दुखी **repression** *noun* **repressive** *adj* दमनकारी।

reprieve / रि'प्रीव् / *verb* 1 (फाँसी की) सज़ा रोकना या निरस्त करना : *reprieve a condemned prisoner* 2 परेशानी, ख़तरे आदि से कुछ देर के लिए आराम देना ▸ **reprieve** *noun* (प्रायः sing) 1 फाँसी की सज़ा पर रोक या निरस्तीकरण 2 अस्थायी आराम (परेशानी से)।

reprimand / ˈरेप्रिमान्ड; US ˈरेप्रिमैन्ड् / *verb* **reprimand sb (for sth)** फटकारना, भर्त्सना करना : *The company was reprimanded and fined Rs 1,00,000 for failing to submit accounts.* ▸ **reprimand** *noun* फटकार, भर्त्सना : *a letter of reprimand.*

reprisal / रि'प्राइज़्ल् / *noun* प्रतिशोध, बदला : *They shot 10 hostages in reprisal.*

reproach / रि'प्रोच् / *verb* (औप) 1 **reproach sb/oneself (for sth)** असफलता या कुछ भूल जाने के लिए धिक्कारना : *She reproached him gently for forgetting their anniversary.* 2 **reproach sb/oneself with sth** ग़लती पर किसी को/स्वयं को फटकारना/डाँटना ▸ **reproach** *noun* 1 दोष, निंदा; शब्द या टिप्पणी जो निंदात्मक हो : *Her manners are above reproach.* ○ *heap reproaches on sb* 2 (औप) बदनामी; उलहाना : *bring reproach upon oneself;* [*sing*] **reproach (to sb/sth)** लज्जा, खेद आदि लाने वाला व्यक्ति/वस्तु : *Poverty is a*

constant reproach to our society.
reproachful *adj* उलाहनाभरा, निंदात्मक।
reproduce /रीप्र'ड्यूस्/ *verb* **1 reproduce sth (as sth)** दोबारा करना/बनाना; नक़ल करना : *Can this effect be reproduced in a laboratory?* **2** चित्र आदि की प्रति तैयार करना : *This copier can reproduce colour photographs.* **3** (व्यक्ति/पशु-पौधे आदि का) प्रजनन करना, बच्चे पैदा करना ▶ **reproduction** /रीप्रडक्शन्/ *noun* **1** पुनरुत्पादन प्रक्रिया : *Compact disc recordings give excellent sound reproduction.* **2** प्रजनन **3** पुनरुत्पादित वस्तु, प्रतिकृति : *reproduction furniture* **reproductive** *adj* प्रजनन संबंधी।

reproof /रि'प्रूफ्/ *noun* (औप) भर्त्सना; दोष, निंदा; निंदात्मक कथन, टिप्पणी आदि : *receive a mild reproof from the teacher.*

reprove /रि'प्रूव्/ *verb* **reprove sb (for sth/doing sth)** (औप) कड़ी निंदा करना : *The priest reproved people for not attending church more often.*

reptile /'रेप्टाइल्/ *noun* सरीसृप, रेंगने वाले जीव (जैसे साँप, छिपकली आदि) ▶ **reptilian** *adj.*

republic /रि'पब्लिक्/ *noun* गणतंत्र; गणतांत्रिक राज्य : *the Republic of Ireland.*

republican /रि'पब्लिकन्/ *adj* गणराज्यीय ▶ **republican** *noun* गणतंत्र समर्थक।

repudiate /रि'प्यूडिएट्/ *verb* (औप) **1** (किसी के अधिकार आदि को) नकारना; अस्वीकार करना : *repudiate a treaty* **2** (मित्रता) अस्वीकार करना, संबंध-विच्छेद करना : *repudiate one's son/lover* ▶ **repudiation** *noun.*

repugnant /रि'पग्नन्ट्/ *adj* **repugnant (to sb)** (औप) अत्यधिक अरुचिकर : *The idea of eating meat is repugnant to me.* ▶ **repugnance** *noun* **repugnance (at/for/towards sth/sb)** (औप) अरुचि, जुगुप्सा : *the moral repugnance felt by many at this brutal massacre.*

repulse /रि'पल्स्/ *verb* (औप) **1** शत्रुओं को (पीछे) ढकेल देना, हमले को निष्फल कर देना **2** किसी का प्रस्ताव, सहायता आदि अस्वीकार करना : *repulse sb's kindness* **3** घृणा या तीव्र जुगुप्सा उत्पन्न करना : *repulsed by the horrible smell.*

repulsion /रि'पल्श्न्/ *noun* **1** अत्यधिक घृणा, अरुचि **2** (भौतिकी) प्रतिकर्षण बल : *There are forces of attraction and repulsion between atoms.*

repulsive /रि'पल्सिव्/ *adj* **1** अरुचिकर, घृणास्पद **2** (भौतिकी) प्रतिकर्षक।

reputable /'रेप्यटब्ल्/ *adj* प्रतिष्ठित; ख्याति प्राप्त (व्यक्ति)।

reputation /रेप्यु'टेश्न्/ *noun* **reputation (for sth/doing sth)** प्रतिष्ठा, ख्याति : *a school with an excellent reputation.*

repute /रि'प्यूट्/ *noun* (औप) ख्याति, नाम : *a player of international repute* ▶ **reputed** /रि'प्यूटिड्/ *adj* **reputed (to be sth/to have done sth)** प्रख्यात, लब्धप्रतिष्ठ, माना हुआ : *He is reputed to be the best surgeon in Delhi.* **reputedly** *adv.*

request /रि'क्वेस्ट्/ *noun* **request (for sth/that...)** अनुरोध/निवेदन; प्रार्थना; प्रार्थित वस्तु : *make an official request for more money* ○ *Her request was granted.* ▶ **request** *verb* **request sth (from/of sb)** (औप) अनुरोध करना : *He requested a loan from the bank.*

require /रि'क्वाइअर्/ *verb* **1** आवश्यक होना; निर्भरता होना : *All cars require* *servicing regularly.* **2 require sth (of sb)** *(औप)* आदेश देना : *I have done all that is required by law.* **3** *(औप)* माँगना, इच्छा रखना : *Is that all you require sir?* ▸ **requirement** *noun* (विशेषत: *pl*) आवश्यकता, ज़रूरत।

requisite / ˈ रेक्विज़िट् / *adj* *(औप)* ज़रूरी, आवश्यक : *have/lack the requisite experience for the job* ▸ **requisite** *noun* **requisite (for/of sth)** *(औप)* किसी काम के लिए आवश्यक वस्तु।

requisition / ˌ रेक्वि ज़िशन् / *noun* **requisition (on sb) (for sth)** संपत्ति या सामान प्रयोग करने के लिए आधिकारिक, प्राय: लिखित में, माँग : *a requisition form/order* ▸ **requisition** *verb* : *requisition ships (from the merchant navy).*

rescue / ˈ रेस्क्यू / *verb* **rescue sb/sth (from sth/sb)** (मुसीबत से) छुड़ाना; मुक्त कराना (शत्रुओं से) : *rescue sb from drowning* ▸ **rescue** *noun* बचाव, उद्धार : *a rescue operation* **rescuer** *noun*.

research / रि सर्च; ˈ रीसर्च / *noun* **research (into/on sth); research (on sb)** अनुसंधानात्मक अध्ययन : *scientific/ clinical research* ▸ **research** *verb* **research (into/on sth); research (on sb)** अनुसंधान करना **researcher** *noun*.

resemble / रि ज़ेम्बल् / *verb* **resemble sb/sth (in sth)** सदृश होना, के समान होना : *She resembles her mother.* ▸ **resemblance** *noun* **resemblance (to sb/sth); resemblance (between A and B)** सादृश्य, समानता : *There is a degree of resemblance between the two boys.*

resent / रि ज़ेन्ट् / *verb* बुरा मानना, नाराज़/ क्रोधित होना : *I bitterly resent your criticism.* ▸ **resentful** *adj* नाराज़, द्वेषपूर्ण : *She felt angry and resentful*

at what had happened. **resentment** *noun* नाराज़गी, मनोमालिन्य/कुढ़न : *bear no resentment against anyone.*

reservation / ˌ रेज़र् वेशन् / *noun* **1** आरक्षण (जैसे रेलवे बर्थ या सीट का) **2** (विशेषत: *pl*) योजना, विचार आदि अस्वीकार करने का कारण : *express minor reservation about the offer.*

reserve¹ / रि ज़र्व् / *verb* **reserve sth (for sb/sth) 1** भविष्य में काम आने या विशेष प्रयोग में लाने के लिए बचाकर रखना : *seats reserved for special guests* **2** कुछ शक्ति/अधिकार विशेष रखना : *The management reserves the right to refuse admission.* **3** विशेष व्यक्ति/प्रयोजन के लिए कुछ सुरक्षित रखना।

reserve² / रि ज़र्व् / *noun* **1** (प्राय: *pl*) भविष्य में प्रयोग के लिए बचाकर/सुरक्षित रखी वस्तु; निधि/संचय **2** आरक्षित क्षेत्र (वन्य पशुओं आदि के लिए सुरक्षित क्षेत्र) : *a wildlife reserve* **3 reserves** [*pl*] रिज़र्व सेना **4** सहमत न होने के कारण आदि : *We accept your statement without reserve (i.e. fully).* **5** (**reserve price** भी) न्यूनतम मूल्य **6** (व्यक्ति की प्रकृति) संकोची; अल्पभाषी होना : *For once, she lost/dropped her customary reserve and became quite lively.*

reserved / रि ज़र्व्ड् / *adj* (व्यक्ति) अल्पभाषी; ग़ैर-मिलनसार; (क्षेत्र) आरक्षित।

reservoir / ˈ रेज़र्व्वार् / *noun* **1** प्राकृतिक या कृत्रिम जलाशय; पानी की टंकी/हौज़ **2 reservoir of sth** किसी वस्तु की बड़ी आपूर्ति या संग्रह : *a reservoir of knowledge.*

reshuffle / ˌ री शफ़ल् / *verb* समूह में व्यक्तियों के कार्यों में फेर-बदल करना ▸ **reshuffle** *noun*.

reside / रि ज़ाइड् / *verb* **reside in/at ...** *(औप)* **1** रहना, निवास करना : *reside* abroad 2 अस्तित्व में रहना या किसी स्थान पर रखा/पाया जाना : *exhibits currently residing at the museum* ■ **reside in/ with sb/sth** *(औप)* (गुण या अधिकार) किसी व्यक्ति/वस्तु में होना : *Supreme authority resides with the President.*

residence / 'रेज़िडन्स् / *noun (औप)* निवासस्थान।

resident / 'रेज़िडन्ट् / *noun* 1 निवासी (आगंतुक के वैषम्य में) : *a (local) residents' association* 2 होटल में ठहरा व्यक्ति : *The hotel is open to non-residents.*

residential /,रेज़ि'डेन्शल्/ *adj* 1 आवासी, रिहायशी : *a residential area/ district* 2 किसी स्थान पर रहने से संबंधित।

residue / 'रेज़िड्यू / *noun* **residue (of sth)** 1 अवशेष, बचा हुआ भाग : *pesticide residues in food* 2 *(क़ानून)* मृत व्यक्ति की संपत्ति में से क़र्ज़ आदि चुकाने के बाद बचा भाग : *The residue was left to Cancer Research.* ▶ **residual** *adj.*

resign / रि'ज़ाइन् / *verb* **resign (from sth)** इस्तीफ़ा देना, पद-त्याग करना : *I resigned (my post) as chairman.* ■ **resign oneself to sth/doing sth** अपरिहार्य मानकर कुछ सहने को तैयार होना : *They had clearly resigned themselves to defeat.* ▶ **resigned** / रि'ज़ाइन्ड् / *adj* संतोषी, सब्र करने वाला : *She seems resigned to not having a holiday this year.*

resignation /,रेज़िग्'नेशन्/ *noun* 1 **resignation (from sth)** त्याग-पत्र 2 कुछ स्वीकार या सहन करने को तैयार : *accept failure with resignation.*

resilient / रि'ज़िलिअन्ट् / *adj* 1 (व्यक्ति) शोक/चोट आदि से संभलने में समर्थ : *She is very resilient to change.* 2 (वस्तु) लचकदार : *made of a tough*

resilient fabric ▶ **resilience** / रि'ज़िलिअन्स् / **(resiliency** भी) *noun* 1 शोक/चोट आदि से अतिशीघ्र उबर पाने का सामर्थ्य; टूट-फूट/चोट आदि से जल्दी ही ठीक हो जाने की पेड़-पौधों/पशुओं आदि की क्षमता : *Her natural resilience helped her to overcome the crisis.* 2 लोच, लचक : *an alloy combining strength and resilience.*

resist / रि'ज़िस्ट् / *verb* 1 विचार, योजना आदि का विरोध या प्रतिरोध करना; बल द्वारा कुछ होने से रोकना 2 नुक़सान आदि से अप्रभावित रहना : *resist disease* 3 अपने को रोकना, बचा लेना : *resist temptation.*

resistance / रि'ज़िस्टन्स् / *noun* 1 **resistance (to sth/sb)** प्रतिरोध; प्रतिरोध करने की शक्ति : *armed resistance* 2 *[sing]* **resistance (to sth)** प्रतिरोधी शक्ति : *a low wind resistance.* 3 *[sing]* **resistance (to sth)** योजना आदि के प्रति नापसंदगी या विरोध : *There is a resistance to allocation of resources.* 4 *[sing]* **resistance (to sth)** बिना क्षति या चोट के सहने की शक्ति : *the body's natural resistance to disease* 5 *(भौतिकी)* गरमी अथवा बिजली का प्रतिरोध करने की शक्ति/ ऐसी शक्ति का माप।

resistant / रि'ज़िस्टन्ट् / *adj* **resistant (to sth)** प्रतिरोध करने वाला (व्यक्ति/ वस्तु): *be resistant to change.*

resolute / 'रेज़ॅल्यूट / *adj* **resolute (in sth)** कृतसंकल्प, दृढ़संकल्प : *be resolute in one's demands for peace* ▶ **resolutely** *adv* : *remain resolutely independent.*

resolution /,रेज़ॅ'लूशन्/ *noun* 1 दृढ़ता, संकल्पबद्धता : *show great resolution* 2 कुछ करने/न करने का पक्का निर्णय : *her resolution never to marry* 3 सभा या समिति द्वारा स्वीकार किया गया प्रस्ताव : *pass/reject a resolution* 4 *(औप)*

(विवादों का) निपटारा करने की क्रिया : *the resolution of a dispute* 5 [sing] विभेदन शक्ति; भागों में अलग-अलग करने की प्रक्रिया : *a computer screen/ printer with a high resolution.*

resolve / रि'ज़ॉल्व् / *verb* (औप)
1 resolve on/upon/against sth/do-ing sth पक्का निश्चित या निर्धारित करना : *resolve never to give up* 2 (सभा या समिति द्वारा) प्रस्ताव पास करना, निर्णय करना 3 संशय/शंका/समस्या का समाधान करना : *resolve an argument/ a dispute* 4 resolve sth (in sth) भागों या अंशों में विभाजित करना : *resolve a complex argument into its basic elements* ▸ resolve *noun* (औप) 1 संकल्प; प्रस्ताव 2 संकल्प शक्ति।

resonant / 'रेज़नन्ट् / *adj* (औप)
1 (ध्वनि) स्पष्ट एवं अनुनाद करने वाली 2 resonant (with sth) (स्थान) किसी ध्वनि से भरा हुआ 3 प्रतिध्वनित करने-कराने वाला 4 किसी के दिमाग़ में चित्रों, विचारों और यादों को लाने का सामर्थ्य : *The house was still resonant with memories of his childhood.* ▸ resonance / 'रेज़नन्स् / *noun* (औप) 1 अनुनाद, गूँज 2 (लेख, संगीत आदि में) भाव प्रतिध्वनित करने की शक्ति।

resort / रि'ज़ॉर्ट् / *verb* ■ resort to sth का सहारा या आश्रय लेना (विशेषत: किसी अप्रिय चीज़ का) : *resort to violence/ terrorism* ▸ resort *noun* 1 सैर-गाह : *seaside/mountain resort* 2 [sing] सहारा या आश्रय प्रदान करने वाली वस्तु या व्यक्ति : *The judge has an-nounced his decision, and our only resort is an appeal to higher court.* 3 resort to sth आश्रय लेना : *talk calmly, without resort to threats* ■ in the last resort (सभी प्रयासों के असफल होने पर) अंतिम प्रयास के रूप में।

resound / रि'ज़ाउन्ड् / *verb* 1 resound (through sth); resound (with/to sth) (ध्वनि, आवाज़ आदि का) गूँजना; प्रतिध्वनित होना : *Church bells resounded (through the valley).* ○ *The hall resounded with applause.* 2 re-sound through, around, etc sth (औप) (प्रसिद्धि, घटना की चर्चा आदि) फैल जाना : *Her name resounded throughout Europe.* ▸ resounding *adj* 1 किसी स्थान को ध्वनित करना : *resounding applause* 2 (घटना आदि) उल्लेखनीय, असाधारण : *The party was a resounding success.* resound-ingly *adv.*

resource / रि'सॉर्स् / *noun* 1 (प्राय: pl) संसाधन, देश या व्यक्ति की संपदा/धन : *mineral/agricultural resources* 2 (प्राय: pl) आवश्यकता के समय सहायता, सहारा या आराम देने वाली वस्तु 3 (औप) युक्ति, उपाय ▸ resource *verb* धन/संपदा से युक्त करना : *The scheme must be properly resourced.* resourceful *adj* उपाय-कुशल, चतुर।

respect¹ / रि'स्पेक्ट् / *noun* 1 respect (for sb/sth) आदर-भावना 2 respect (for sb/sth) ध्यान, लिहाज़ : *have respect for sb's feelings* 3 पक्ष, पहलू-विशेष : *in this respect* ■ in respect of sth (औप या वाणिज्य) के बारे में, के संबंध में : *price rise in respect of gas and water costs* with respect to sth (औप या वाणिज्य) के संबंध में : *I am writing with re-spect to your recent enquiry.* ▸ re-spects *noun* [pl] प्रणाम।

respect² / रि'स्पेक्ट् / *verb* 1 respect sb/sth (for sth) आदर करना 2 ध्यान रखना, लिहाज़ रखना/करना; हस्तक्षेप न करना, मान्यता देना : *respect sb's rights* ▸ respecting *prep* (औप) के विषय में : *laws respecting property.*

respectable / रि'स्पेक्टब्ल् / *adj* 1 व्य-

वहार, पोशाक आदि की दृष्टि से उचित; आदरणीय, सम्मान-योग्य : *a respectable middle-class background* 2 काफ़ी मात्रा या राशि में ▸ **respectably** *adv.*

respectful / रि'स्पेक्टफ़ल / *adj* respectful (to/towards sb); respectful (of sth) आदरपूर्ण : *respectful of other people's opinions* ▸ **respectfully** *adv.*

respective / रि'स्पेक्टिव् / *adj* अपना-अपना : *well-known in their respective fields* ▸ **respectively** *adv* क्रमश:।

respiration / ‚रेस्प'रेशन् / *noun* (औप) श्वास लेने की क्रिया।

respire / रि'स्पाइअर् / *verb* (औप) साँस लेना।

respite / 'रेस्पाइट् / *noun* 1 [sing] respite (from sth) राहत, आराम : *a temporary respite from pain* 2 विश्राम; कुछ अप्रिय या कठिन काम करने से पहले थोड़ी देरी या राहत : *We are prepared to grant him temporary respite, after which the debt must be repaid in full.*

resplendent / रि'स्प्लेन्डन्ट् / *adj* resplendent (in sth) (औप) चमकता-दमकता हुआ; भव्य : *the resplendent tail feathers of the male peacock* ▸ **resplendently** *adv.*

respond / रि'स्पॉन्ड् / *verb* 1 respond (to sb/sth) (with sth) (औप) उत्तर देना, जवाब देना : *I asked where he'd been but he didn't respond.* 2 respond (to sth) (with sth/by doing sth) उत्तर स्वरूप कुछ करना, प्रतिक्रिया दिखाना : *He kicked the dog, which responded by growling.* 3 respond (to sth) तुरंत (पक्ष में) प्रतिक्रिया करना : *Animals respond to kindness.*

response / रि'स्पॉन्स् / *noun* re-sponse (to sb/sth) 1 उत्तर 2 प्रति-क्रिया; अनुक्रिया।

responsibility / रि‚स्पॉन्स'बिलटि / *noun (pl* responsibilities) 1 responsibility (for sb/sth) उत्तरदायित्व/ज़िम्मेदारी 2 responsibility (to sb) जवाब-देही : *It's my responsibility to lock the doors.*

responsible / रि'स्पॉन्सबल् / *adj* 1 responsible (for sb/sth); responsible (for doing sth) (व्यक्ति) किसी बात के लिए उत्तरदायी/ज़िम्मेदार : *The driver is responsible for the safety of his passengers.* 2 responsible (for sth) उत्तरदायी, किसी कारण का ज़िम्मेदार : *Who's responsible for this mess?* 3 (व्यक्ति/व्यवहार) विश्वसनीय 4 (पद) उत्तरदायी व्यक्ति की आवश्यकता वाला : *a highly responsible position* 5 responsible to sb/sth जवाबदेह : *be directly responsible to the President* ▸ **responsibly** *adv* विश्वसनीय या समझदार ढंग से : *act/behave responsibly.*

responsive / रि'स्पॉन्सिव् / *adj* responsive (to sb/sth) 1 रुचि एवं उत्साह-पूर्वक उत्तर देने वाला; अनुकूल : *a responsive class/audience* 2 तुरंत (और पक्ष में) उत्तर देने वाला/प्रतिक्रिया करने वाला : *Managers should be more responsive to the needs of their staff.*

rest¹ / रेस्ट् / *verb* 1 आराम करना, सुस्ताना या सो जाना, क्रियाशील स्थिति से मुक्त रहना या रखना 2 rest (sth) on/against sth टिकाना, टेकना : *Rest the ladder against the wall.* 3 (औप) (चर्चा का विषय) बिना आगे चर्चा किए छोड़ देना : *Let the matter rest.* ■ **rest assured (that...)** (औप) निश्चित होना कि... : *You may be rest assured that everything possible is being done.* **rest on sb/sth** 1 निर्भर होना : *The* team's hopes of a medal now rest on Gopichand. **2** (नज़र आदि) कुछ समय तक एक वस्तु/व्यक्ति पर टिके रहना : *Her eyes travelled slowly around the room and finally rested on me.* **rest with sb (to do sth)** (औप) किसी की ज़िम्मेदारी होना : *The decision rests entirely with you.*

rest² / रेस्ट् / *noun* **1 rest (from sth)** आराम की स्थिति; विश्राम : *Sunday is a day of rest.* **2** सहारा, टेक ■ **at rest 1** गतिहीन **2** बिना तकलीफ़ या चिंता के **come to rest** (चलती हुई वस्तु) रुक जाना : *The car crashed through the barrier and came to rest in a field.* **give sth/it a rest** (अनौप) थोड़ी देर के लिए काम रोक देना : *If you've hurt your ankle you should give sport a rest for a few weeks.* **lay/put sth to rest** कुछ ग़लत/झूठ प्रमाणित करना : *An official announcement finally laid speculation to rest.* ▸ **restful** *adj* **restful (to sb/sth)** आरामदेह, सुखप्रद : *restful sleep.*

rest³ / रेस्ट् / *noun* **the rest (of sth) 1** बाक़ी बचा हुआ, शेष : *the rest of my life* **2** अन्य लोग/वस्तुएँ आदि।

restaurant / ' रेस्ट्रॉन्ट्; US ' रेस्ट्रान्ट् / *noun* रेस्तराँ, भोजनालय।

restitution / , रेस्टि'ट्यूश्न् / *noun* **restitution (of sth) (to sb/sth) 1** (औप) खोई हुई या चुराई हुई वस्तु की मालिक को वापसी : *the restitution of property to owner* **2** (क़ानून) चोट आदि के लिए मुआवज़ा : *restitution claims.*

restive / ' रेस्टिव् / *adj* बेचैन; नियंत्रण के बाहर जाता हुआ : *Another hour passed and the crowd grew/became increasingly restive.*

restless / ' रेस्ट्लस् / *adj* **1** बेचैन, अधीर : *The audience was becoming restless.* **2** अशांत, बेआराम; निद्रा-

हीन : *a restless night* ▸ **restlessly** *adv* **restlessness** *noun.*

restoration / , रेस्ट'रेश्न् / *noun* **1** मरम्मत कार्य, पुनर्रचना **2 restoration (to sb/sth)** वस्तु की वापसी **3** पुनः प्रयोग में लाना : *the restoration of old customs* **4 the Restoration** [*sing*] ब्रिटेन में 1660 में राजशाही की वापसी के बाद का काल (विशेषतः साहित्य में) : *Restoration comedy.*

restore / रि'स्टॉर् / *verb* **1 restore sb (to sth); restore sth (to sb)** पुरानी स्थिति में लाना **2 restore sb/sth to sth** फिर से पूर्व पद पर आसीन कर देना : *restore laid-off workers to their old jobs* **3 restore sth (to sb)** फिर से काम में लाना **4 restore sth (to sth)** मरम्मत करना; कलाकृति आदि की पुनर्रचना करना : *restore a Mughal fort* **5 restore sth (to sb/sth)** (औप) खोई/ चुराई हुई वस्तु का लौटाना, वापस करना : *restore the water supply.*

restrain / रि'स्ट्रेन् / *verb* **restrain oneself/sb/sth (from sth/doing sth)** नियंत्रण में रखना, कुछ करने से रोकना : *restrain one's anger/laughter* ▸ **restrained** *adj* **1** शांत; भावहीन : *a restrained discussion* **2** ज़्यादा सज़ावटी नहीं **restraint** / रि'स्ट्रेन्ट् / *noun* **1** (प्रायः *pl*) **restraint (on sb/sth)** नियंत्रण, रोक; प्रतिबंध **2** शांत व्यवहार/ बर्ताव।

restrict / रि'स्ट्रिक्ट् / *verb* **restrict oneself/sb/sth (to sth/doing sth)** सीमा में रखना; सीमित कर लेना/देना : *restrict the number of students in a class* ▸ **restricted** *adj* **1** नियंत्रित **2** प्रतिबंधित (भूमि, क्षेत्र) **restriction** / रि 'स्ट्रिक्श्न् / *noun* **1** रोक, प्रतिबंध **2** (प्रायः *pl*) **restriction (on sth)** प्रतिबंधात्मक क़ानून : *speed restrictions.*

result / रि'ज़ल्ट् / *noun* **1 result (of**

sth) परिणाम/नतीजा 2 **results** [*pl*] सफल परिणाम : *begin to show/produce/achieve results* 3 (विशेषत: *pl*) **result (of sth)** खेलकूद/प्रतियोगिता/परीक्षा के विजेता का नाम, प्राप्त अंक आदि का विवरण : *announce the election results* वैज्ञानिक या चिकित्सीय जाँच के परिणाम का विवरण: *When will you get the result of your X-ray?* 4 गणित के प्रश्न का हल ▶ **result** *verb* **result (from sth)** परिणाम होना या निकलना; परिणामस्वरूप घटित होना : *injuries resulting from a fall* ■ **result in sth** परिणामस्वरूप कुछ प्राप्त करना : *Our efforts resulted in success/failure.*

resume / रि'ज़्यूम / *verb* (औप) 1 (कुछ रुकने के बाद) पुन: कार्य जारी करना, दोबारा करना : *resume production* 2 पुन: ग्रहण करना : *resume one's seat* ▶ **resumption** / रि'ज़म्प्श्न् / *noun.*

resumé / 'रेज़्युमे; *US* 'रेज़मे / *noun* 1 सारांश : *a resumé of the evidence* 2 (*US*) = **curriculum vitae** व्यक्ति का जीवन वृत्त।

resurgent / रि'सर्जन्ट् / *adj* (औप) शिथिलता की अवधि के बाद प्रसिद्धि, भावनाओं आदि का दोबारा सक्रिय होना : *resurgent hope/nationalism* ▶ **resurgence** *noun.*

resurrect / रेज़'रेक्ट् / *verb* 1 स्मृति में या प्रयोग में फिर से लाना : *resurrect old customs* 2 पुनर्जीवित करना ▶ **resurrection** *noun* 1 **the Resurrection** [*sing*] (ईसाई विश्वास के अनुसार) ईसा का क़ब्र से पुनर्जीवित हो उठना 2 [*sing*] (औप) पुनर्जीवन, नया आरंभ।

resuscitate / रि'ससिटेट् / *verb* (औप) किसी को (जैसे डूबे हुए को) चेतना में लाना ▶ **resuscitation** *noun.*

retail / 'रीटेल् / *noun* खुदरा, फुटकर : *retail traders* ▶ **retail** *verb* 1 खुदरा में बेचना/बिकना 2 **retail sth (to sb)**

(औप) किस्सा या वृत्तांत किसी को वर्णन करना **retailer** *noun* परचूनी, खुदरा में वस्तुएँ बेचने वाला।

retain / रि'टेन् / *verb* (औप) 1 रखना, अधिकार में बनाये रखना : *retain one's freedom* ○ *The police retained control of the situation.* 2 पकड़ कर रखना : *Clay soil retains water.* 3 (तक) नियमित राशि देकर किसी की सेवाएँ, विशेषत: वकील की, लेना : *retain a barrister/consultant.*

retaliate / रि'टैलिएट् / *verb* **retaliate (against sb/sth) (by doing sth/with sth)** बदला लेना, प्रतिकार करना : *They are likely to retaliate.* ▶ **retaliation** / रि,टैलि'एश्न् / *noun* बदले की कार्रवाई, प्रतिकार : *the danger of retaliation against UN aid workers* **retaliatory** *adj.*

retard / रि'टाई / *verb* (औप) प्रगति या विकास में बाधा पहुँचाना; रोकना : *Lack of sun retards plant growth.* ▶ **retardation** *noun* **retarded** *adj* मंदबुद्धि।

retention / रि'टेन्श्न् / *noun* [*sing*] (औप) 1 किसी वस्तु आदि पर लगातार स्वामित्व, अधिकार होना; लगातार अस्तित्व होना : *retention of one's rights/privileges* 2 याद रखने का सामर्थ्य : *show an amazing retention of facts/details* 3 किसी वस्तु को उसके स्थान पर ही रोके रखना, बाहर न आने देना : *the retention of flood waters.*

rethink / री'थ्रिङ्क् / *verb* (*pt, pp* **rethought** / री'थॉट् /) किसी योजना आदि पर पुनर्विचार करना, विशेषत: उसे बदलने के उद्देश्य से।

reticent / 'रेटिसन्ट् / *adj* **reticent (about sth)** अल्पभाषी, अपने भाव या योजना आसानी से न व्यक्त करने वाला : *be reticent about one's plans* ▶ **reticence** *noun* (औप) मौन, चुप्पी।

retina / 'रेटिना; *US* 'रेटना; / *noun* (*pl*

retinas या **retinae**) (विशेषत: *sing*) दृष्टिपटल।

retinue / 'रेटिन्यू / *noun* परिजन (किसी उच्च पदाधिकारी के साथ चलने वाले अधिकारी, नौकर आदि)।

retire / रि'टाइअर / *verb* 1 **retire (from sth)** पदनिवृत्त या सेवानिवृत्त होना, रिटायर होना : *He will retire from the army next year.* 2 **retire (from) (to ...)** (औप) (सेना के) पुनर्गठन आदि के लिए वापस मुड़ना : *The battalion retired to prepared positions.* 3 (औप) सोने जाना 4 **retire (from...) (to ...)** एकांत-वास को चले जाना : *The jury retired (from the courtroom) to consider their verdict.* 5 **retire (from sth)** (खेलों में) चोट लगने के कारण खेल बीच में छोड़ देना : *The batsman retired hurt.* ▶ **retired** *adj* सेवानिवृत्त, अवकाश प्राप्त **retiring** *adj* एकांतसेवी।

retirement / रि'टाइअर्मन्ट / *noun* 1 सेवानिवृत्ति, अवकाशग्रहण : *the age of retirement* 2 सेवानिवृत्ति के बाद का जीवन।

retort / रि'टॉर्ट / *verb* मुँहतोड़ जवाब देना : *He retorted that it was my fault as much as his.* ▶ **retort** *noun* किसी दोषारोपण आदि का मुँहतोड़ जवाब।

retouch / री'टच् / *verb* फोटो, चित्र आदि में छोटे-मोटे संशोधन करना।

retrace / रि'ट्रेस् / *verb* 1 (ठीक उसी रास्ते) लौटना : *We retraced our steps to the car.* 2 किसी अन्य के रास्ते की खोज करना और उस पर चलना : *retrace the explorer's original route.*

retract / रि'ट्रैक्ट् / *verb* (औप) 1 मुकर जाना, कथन वापस ले लेना : *He made a false confession which he later retracted.* 2 किसी समझौते को मानने से इनकार करना : *retract a promise* 3 सिकोड़ना, समेटना ▶ **retractable** *adj*

समेटने योग्य : *a knife with a retract-able blade.*

retreat / रि'ट्रीट् / *verb* 1 (ख़तरे या कठिनाई में) वापस मुड़ जाना, पीछे हटना : *force the enemy to retreat* 2 लोगों की निंदा या धमकी के कारण निर्णय या दृष्टिकोण बदलना : *retreat from a demand* 3 ऐसे स्थान पर जाना जहाँ कोई परेशान न करे 4 आकार या व्यापकता में घटना : *The flood water slowly retreated.* ▶ **retreat** *noun* 1 (प्राय: *sing*) वापसी की कार्रवाई 2 **the retreat** [*sing*] सेना को वापसी का संकेत 3 शांत/एकांत स्थान : *spend the weekends at a country retreat.*

retrench / रि'ट्रेन्च् / *verb* (औप) (खर्च आदि) कम कर देना, कर्मचारी कम कर देना : *Inflation has forced the company to retrench.* ▶ **retrenchment** *noun* कटौती, छंटनी।

retribution / रेट्रि'ब्यूश्न् / *noun* **retribution (for sth)** (औप) प्रतिफल, दंड प्रतिशोध, बदला, प्रतिकार।

retrieve / रि'ट्रीव् / *verb* 1 **retrieve sth (from sb/sth)** (विशेषत: औप) दोबारा पाना 2 कंप्यूटर की मेमरी से एकत्रित सूचना प्राप्त करना : *retrieve data (from a disk)* 3 (औप) त्रुटि सुधारना; संपत्ति बचाना : *retrieve one's losses* ▶ **retrievable** *adj* **retrieval** *noun*.

retrograde / 'रेट्रग्रेड् / *adj* (औप) पश्चगामी, अवनति की ओर जाता हुआ : *Closing small village schools is a retrograde step.*

retrospect / 'रेट्रस्पेक्ट् / *noun* ■ **in retrospect** सिंहावलोकन (पुरानी घटनाओं का पश्चदर्शन) करना : *In retrospect, it's easy to see where we went wrong.* ▶ **retrospection** *noun* **retrospective** / रेट्र 'स्पेक्टिव् / *adj* 1 (औप) अनुभव के आधार पर पीछे मुड़ कर देखने की प्रक्रिया 2 क़ानून, भुगतान आदि पुरानी तिथि

से ही लागू हो जाना : *The legislation was made retrospective.*

return¹ / रि'टर्न् / *verb* **1** return (to...) (from ...) लौटना, वापस आना : *return (home) from a trip* **2** return sth (to sth/sb) वापस लौटना/भेजना; स्थान पर वापस रखना : *I returned the letter unopened.* **3** return (to sth) किसी विषय, आदत या अवस्था में वापस जाना : *The bus service has returned to normal.* **4** उत्तर में कुछ कहना, प्रति-क्रिया में वैसा ही कुछ करना, कहना, अनु-भव करना : *return an invitation/ stare* **5** कुछ लाभ देना, कुछ प्राप्ति होना : *Our investment accounts return a high rate of interest.* ▸ **returnable** *adj* लौटाने योग्य : *returnable bottles.*

return² / रि'टर्न् / *noun* **1** [*sing*] return (to...) (from...) वापस लौटने की क्रिया **2** (return ticket भी; *US* round-trip ticket) जाने और आने दोनों का टिकट **3** [*sing*] return (to sth) पहले जैसी स्थिति, अवस्था में वापसी : *his return to consciousness* **4** आधिकारिक विवरण, विशेषत: किसी औपचारिक माँग के उत्तर में **5** (प्राय: *pl*) return (on sth) पूँजी लगाने से प्राप्त आय ■ in return (for sth) बदले में भुगतान या इनाम : *I bought him a drink in return for his help.*

reunion / री'यूनिअन् / *noun* **1** (लंबे वियोग के बाद हुआ) पुनर्मिलन : *an emotional reunion between the two sisters* **2** किसी संघ या समूह का एकीकरण होना।

reunite / रीयू'नाइट्/ *verb* **1** reunite sb/ sth (with sb/sth) दो या ज़्यादा व्यक्तियों का फिर से मिलना, एक हो जाना : *Parents were reunited with their lost children.* **2** अलग-अलग क्षेत्रों या समूहों को जोड़ना।

revalue / री'वैल्यू/ *verb* फिर से मूल्यांकन

करना ▸ **revaluation** / ‚रीवैल्यू'एशन् / *noun.*

reveal / रि'वील्/ *verb* **1** reveal sth (to sb) कुछ प्रकट करना, रहस्य खोलना : *reveal secrets/details* **2** कुछ दिखाना; प्रदर्शित होने देना : *A closer examination revealed a crack in the vase.* ▸ **revealing** *adj.*

revel¹ / 'रेवल्/ *verb* (-ll-; *US* -l-) ■ revel in sth/doing sth मौज मनाना, आमोद-प्रमोद करना।

revel² / 'रेवल्/ *noun* (प्राय: *pl*) (अप्र) आमोद-प्रमोद, शोरगुल भरा समारोह ▸ **revelry** / 'रेवल्रि/ *noun* (प्राय: *pl*) रंग-रलियाँ, गुलछर्रे : *sounds of drunken revelry.*

revelation / ‚रेवल्'लेशन्/ *noun* **1** प्रकटन; रहस्य खुलना : *She was stunned by the revelation that he was already married.* **2** रहस्य खुली बात : *revelations about her private life in the press.*

revenge / रि'वेन्ज्/ *noun* **1** बदला, प्रतिशोध **2** बदला लेने की भावना, जानबूझ कर हानि पहुँचाने की इच्छा : *an act of revenge* ▸ **revenge** *verb* ■ revenge oneself on sb; be revenged on sb प्रतिकार करना, प्रतिशोध लेना ▸ **revengeful** *adj* प्रतिशोध की भावना से पूर्ण।

revenue / 'रेवन्यू / *noun* (revenues [*pl*] भी) राजस्व, राज्य या संघ की पूर्ण वार्षिक आय।

reverberate / रि'वर्बरेट् / *verb* **1** (ध्वनि) गूँजना **2** reverberate (with sth) (वातावरण या स्थान) गुँजायमान होना; तीव्र ध्वनि से अशांत हो जाना : *The room reverberated with the noise of the shot.* **3** तीव्र और चिंताजनक प्रभाव होना : *Repercussions of the case continue to reverberate (in/ through the financial world).*

revere / रि'विअर् / *verb* (औप) आदर

करना, श्रद्धा रखना : *a teacher revered by generations of students.*

reverence / ' रेव़रन्स् / *noun* **reverence (for sb/sth)** श्रद्धा : *The crowd knelt in reverence and worship.*

reverend / ' रेव़रन्ड् / *adj* **the Reverend** (*संक्षि* Rev; Revd) ईसाई पादरियों की पदवी : *the Reverend Charles Dodgson.*

reverent / रेव़रन्ट् / *adj* श्रद्धालु।

reverie / ' रेव़रि / *noun* (*औप*) दिवास्वप्न, प्रियकर कल्पनापूर्ण विचारों में मग्न रहने की स्थिति।

reversal / रिव़र्स्ल् / *noun* 1 विपरीत के लिए बदलाव 2 दो व्यक्तियों के बीच पद, कार्यभार आदि में अदला-बदली।

reverse¹ / रिव़र्स् / *adj* **reverse (of/to sth)** उलटा, विपरीत : *go in the reverse direction.*

reverse² / रिव़र्स् / *noun* 1 **the reverse (of sth)** [*sing*] उलटा/विपरीत 2 (*औप*) सफल प्रगति में विपरीत के लिए बदलाव 3 पृष्ठ भाग : *the reverse of a painting* 4 विपत्ति, पराजय।

reverse³ / रिव़र्स् / *verb* 1 (वाहन आदि को) पीछे की ओर चलाना 2 उलटी स्थिति में रखना : *reverse a procedure* 3 पहले किए का उलटा/विपरीत करना 4 (निर्णय आदि) रद्द करना : *reverse the decision of a lower court* ▶ **reversible** *adj* जिसे उलटा/विपरीत किया जा सके।

revert / रिव़र्ट् / *verb* ■ **revert to sth** 1 पूर्व स्थिति/दशा में लौट जाना; पुरानी आदत पर आ जाना : *revert to smoking when under stress* 2 (*औप*) पुराने विषय पर वापस आना : *To revert to your earlier question,...*

review / रिव़्यू / *noun* 1 पुन: परीक्षण (बदलाव की संभावना के साथ) : *a rent review* 2 पूर्व घटनाओं का सर्वेक्षण : *present a review of the year's sport*

3 पत्रिका में घटनाओं पर लेख, पुस्तकों की समीक्षा आदि ▶ **review** / रिव़्यू / *verb* 1 पुन: परीक्षण करना; मन में दोहराना : *review one's successes and failures* 2 नई पुस्तक आदि की समीक्षा लिखना : *The play was (well/favourably) reviewed in 'India Today'.* 3 सैन्यदल आदि का औपचारिक निरीक्षण करना **reviewer** *noun* समीक्षक।

revile / रिव़ाइल् / *verb* **revile sb (for sth/doing sth)** (*औप*) गाली देना, कटु शब्दों में निंदा करना।

revise / रिव़ाइज़् / *verb* 1 शुद्ध करने या सुधारने के लिए (लेख आदि को) ध्यानपूर्वक पढ़ना, संशोधन करना : *revise a manuscript before publication* 2 **revise sth (for sth)** पढ़े हुए को परीक्षा के पूर्व दोहराना ▶ **revision** / रिव़िश्न् / *noun* संशोधन; संशोधन विवरण : *They made some hasty revisions to the schedule.*

revival / रिव़ाइव़्ल् / *noun* 1 पुनर्जीवन, पुनरुत्थान; नव जागरण : *the revival of hope* 2 पुन: प्रचलन : *the revival of old customs.*

revive / रिव़ाइव़् / *verb* 1 पुनर्जीवित करना; पहले जैसी शक्ति, स्वास्थ्य या स्थिति पाना : *The flowers will revive in water.* 2 (अप्रचलित प्रथा आदि को) फिर से प्रचलित करना : *revive old practices* 3 नाटक आदि पुन: प्रदर्शित करना।

revoke / रिव़ोक् / *verb* (*औप*) (क़ानून आदि को) रद्द करना; डिग्री, लाइसेंस आदि वापस लेना : *revoke planning permission.*

revolt / रिव़ोल्ट् / *verb* 1 **revolt (against sb/sth)** विद्रोह करना; तीव्र विरोध करना : *revolting against a military dictatorship* 2 घृणा या ग्लानि से भर जाना; जुगुप्सा से भर जाना : *I was revolted by the smell of whisky on his breath.* ▶ **revolt** *noun* विद्रोह;

तीव्र प्रतिरोध : *stir militant party members to revolt.*

revolting / रि'वोल्टिङ् / *adj* घृणा/जुगुप्सा उत्पन्न करने वाला; अत्यंत अरुचिकर।

revolution / रेव्'लूश्न् / *noun* **1** क्रांति (शासन व्यवस्था आदि का आमूल परिवर्तन): *the French Revolution of 1789* **2 revolution (in sth)** कायाकल्प, आमूल परिवर्तन: *revolution in printing techniques* **3 revolution (on/round sth)** परिक्रमण (किसी वस्तु के चारों ओर का चक्कर); (पहिए आदि का) एक पूरा चक्र घूमना ▸ **revolutionary** / रेव्'लूश्नरि / *adj* **1** क्रांतिकारी **2** काया-पलट करने वाला: *a revolutionary idea* **revolutionary** *noun* क्रांतिकारी (व्यक्ति) **revolutionize, -ise** *verb* क्रांति लाना; आमूल परिवर्तन करना: *This chip could revolutionize the design of computers.*

revolve / रि'वोल्व् / *verb* **1 revolve (around/round sth)** (ग्रह/उपग्रह का) घूमना, परिक्रमा करना; चक्कर खाना **2** किसी वृत्ताकार में घूमना ■ **revolve around sb/sth** कोई व्यक्ति/वस्तु मुख्य केंद्र होना : *My life revolves around my job.* ▸ **revolving** *adj.*

revolver / रि'वोल्व्र् / *noun* रिवॉल्वर, तमंचा।

revulsion / रि'वल्श्न् / *noun* [*sing*] **revulsion (against/at/over/from sth)** घृणा या जुगुप्सा का भाव : *feel a sense of revulsion at the bloodshed.*

reward / रि'वॉर्ड् / *noun* **1** पुरस्कार, इनाम **2** पुलिस की सहायता करने के बदले में प्राप्त पारितोषिक (धन) ▸ **reward** *verb* **reward sb (for sth/doing sth) (with sth)** पुरस्कार/इनाम देना **rewarding** *adj* (कार्य आदि) संतोषजनक।

rewind / री'वाइन्ड् / *verb* (*pt*, *pp* **rewound** / री'वाउन्ड् /) सुने गए शब्दों को फिर से सुनने के लिए कैसेट को पीछे करना।

rewrite / री'राइट् / *verb* (*pt* **rewrote**

/ री'रोट् /; *pp* **rewritten** / री'रिट्न् /) **rewrite sth (for sth); rewrite sth (as sth)** दोबारा, बेहतर करके या भिन्न रूप से, लिखना।

rhapsody / 'रैप्सडि / *noun* (*pl* **rhapsodies**) (प्राय: *pl*) प्रशंसा और आह्लाद से भरा गीत-संगीत : *rhapsodies of praise* ▸ **rhapsodic** *adj.*

rhetoric / 'रेटरिक् / *noun* **1** शब्दों को प्रभावपूर्ण रीति से प्रयोग करने की कला, वाक्पटुता **2** (प्राय: *अपमा*) शब्दों का आडंबरपूर्ण प्रयोग : *the empty rhetoric of politicians* ▸ **rhetorical** / रि'टॉरिक्ल् / *adj* **1** शब्दांबर कला-विषयक **2** केवल शब्दांबर के लिए किया गया प्रश्न (न कि उत्तर पाने के लिए) : *rhetorical question.*

rheumatic / रु'मैटिक् / *adj* गठिया संबंधी; गठिया से पीड़ित : *rheumatic pain.*

rheumatism / 'रूमटिज़म् / *noun* गठिया (रोग)।

rhinoceros / राइ'नॉसरस् / *noun* (*pl* अपरिवर्तित या **rhinoceroses**) गैंडा।

rhombus / 'रॉम्बस् / *noun* (*pl* **rhombuses**) (*ज्यामिति*) समचतुर्भुज, भुजाएँ समान लेकिन कोण 90° अंश के नहीं।

rhyme / राइम् / *noun* **1** तुक, अंत्यानुप्रास **2** तुकांत कविता **3 rhyme (for sth)** वह शब्द जो किसी दूसरे से तुक में मिलता हो : *Can you think of a rhyme for yellow?* ■ **rhyme or reason** (प्राय: नकारात्मक वाक्यों में) तर्क या अर्थ : *a decision without rhyme or reason* ▸ **rhyme** *verb* **1 rhyme (with sth)** (शब्दों, पंक्तियों की) तुक मिलना : *'Gift' rhymes with 'lift'.* **2** तुकांत कविता करना।

rhythm / 'रिद्म् / *noun* **1** लय; संगीत, भाषण, नृत्य आदि में ताल **2** बारंबार दोहराती हुई घटनाओं या प्रक्रियाओं का क्रम : *rhythm of the tides/seasons* ▸ **rhy-**

thmic /'रिद्मिक् / (rhythmical भी) adj
लयात्मक, तालबद्ध।

rib / रिब् / noun 1 पसली की हड्डी
2 पसली के समान मुड़ी हुई या वैसा काम
करने वाली वस्तु ▶ **rib** verb (-bb-) **rib
sb (about/for/over sth)** किसी को
चिढ़ाना/मज़ाक उड़ाना : *She was ribbed
mercilessly (about her accent).*

ribbon / 'रिबन् / noun 1 रेशम, नाइलॉन
आदि का रिबन (फ़ीता) 2 टाइपराइटर/कुछ
कंप्यूटर प्रिंटरों में प्रयुक्त रिबन, फ़ीता : *a
typewriter ribbon.*

rice / राइस् / noun धान, चावल : *grains
of rice.*

rich / रिच् / adj (-er, -est) 1 अमीर,
धनवान 2 **rich (in sth)** भरपूर, बहुलतापूर्ण;
(भूमि) उपजाऊ : *Oranges are rich in
vitamin C.* 3 बड़ी मात्रा में; मिश्रित और
रोचक 4 (भोजन) स्वादिष्ट, बढ़िया : *a rich
creamy sauce* 5 मूल्यवान एवं सुंदर
वस्तु : *rich fabrics* 6 (रंग) भड़कीला,
चटकदार : *the rich colours of autumn leaves* ▶ **the rich** noun दौल-
मंद लोग **richly** adv 1 शानदार रीति से
2 भरपूर, पूर्णता के साथ : *She was richly
rewarded for her trouble.* **rich-
ness** noun.

riches /'रिचिज़् / noun [pl] धनदौलत।

rickety /'रिकटि / adj (अनौप) दुर्बल
(विशेषत: जोड़ों पर); डाँवाँडोल, जर्जर :
rickety wooden stairs.

ricochet / 'रिकशे / verb (pt, pp **rico-
cheted** /'रिकशेड् /) **ricochet (off sth)**
(गोली का) सतह से टकरा कर वापस आना।

rid / रिड् / verb (-dd-; pt, pp **rid**) ■ **be/
get rid of sb/sth** पीछा छुड़ाना; पिंड
छुड़ाना, छुटकारा पाना : *get rid of dry
skin* **rid oneself/sb/sth of sth**
मुक्त कर लेना : *rid the house of mice.*

riddance /'रिड्न्स् / noun ■ **good riddance (to sb/sth)** छुटकारा और राहत
(की साँस)।

ridden / 'रिड्न् / adj (समासों में) के द्वारा
पीड़ित, वशीभूत : *be guilt-ridden.*

riddle[1] /'रिड्ल् / noun 1 पहेली, बुझौ-
वल : *solve a riddle* 2 ऐसा व्यक्ति या
घटना जो समझ में न आए/चकरा दे : *the
riddle of how the universe originated.*

riddle[2] /'रिड्ल् / verb **riddle sb/sth
(with sth)** छलनी कर देना, छेद-छेद कर
देना : *Sniper fire riddled the building.* ■ **be riddled with sth** बेकार या
अवांछित बातों/वस्तुओं से भरा होना : *His
essay is riddled with mistakes.*

ride[1] /राइड् / noun 1 घुड़सवारी 2 (वाहन
में) सवारी : *Can I hitch a ride with
you?* 3 झूला (मेले आदि में) ■ **take
sb for a ride** (अनौप) ठगना, धोखा
देना।

ride[2] / राइड् / verb (pt **rode** / रोड् /; pp
ridden / 'रिड्न् /) 1 घोड़े आदि पर चढ़कर
यात्रा करना; घुड़सवारी करना 2 साइकिल,
घोड़े आदि की सवारी करना 3 **ride (in/on
sth)** (बस आदि में) सवारी करना : *ride
in a bus/on a train* 4 तैरना, तिरना
▶ **rider** noun 1 सवार, घुड़सवार 2 **rider
(to sth)** वक्तव्य आदि के बाद अतिरिक्त
कथन : *We should like to add a rider
to the previous remark.*

ridge / रिज् / noun 1 शीर्ष का वह भाग जहाँ
दो ढालू सतहें मिलती हैं; खेत की मेंड़ : *the
ridge of a roof* ○ *series of ridges in
a ploughed field* 2 पहाड़ का ऊपरी
चपटा भाग; पर्वतश्रेणी ▶ **ridge** verb मेंड़
बनाना/से भरना : *a slightly ridged
surface.*

ridicule /'रिडिक्यूल् / noun खिल्ली उड़ाने
वाली बात या भाषा ▶ **ridicule** verb मज़ाक
बनाना, उपहास करना, खिल्ली उड़ाना : *The
opposition ridiculed the government's attempt to explain the mistake.* **ridiculous** / रि 'डिकुलस् / adj
उपहास योग्य, बेतुका : *You look ridicu-*

lous in those tight trousers. **ridiculously** *adv.*

rife / राइफ़् / *adj (औप)* 1 (विशेषत: बुरी बात/चीज़) फैला हुआ : *area where crime is rife* 2 **rife with sth** (बुरी बातों/चीज़ों) से पूर्ण/भरा हुआ।

rifle¹ / राइफ़्ल् / *noun* राइफ़ल (लंबी नली की बंदूक)।

rifle² / राइफ़्ल् / *verb* **rifle (through) sth** चोरी करने की दृष्टि से चप्पा-चप्पा ढूँढ़ लेना; बारीकी से तलाशी ले लेना : *The safe had been rifled through.*

rift / रिफ़्ट् / *noun* 1 दरार : *a rift in the clouds* 2 मित्रों, संगठनों के बीच गंभीर मतभेद : *a growing rift between the two factions.*

rig¹ / रिग् / *verb* (-gg-) **rig sth (with sth)** जहाज़/नाव को मस्तूल-पाल आदि से सज्जित करना ■ **rig oneself/sb out (in/ with sth)** आवश्यक कपड़े और साज-सामान से युक्त करना : *a cavalry regiment rigged out in green and gold* **rig sth up** जो भी सामान उपलब्ध हो उसी से जल्दी-जल्दी कोई रचना तैयार करना : *rig up a shelter for the night* ▸ **rig** *noun* 1 मस्तूल और पाल की व्यवस्था/ सजावट 2 विशेष प्रयोजन के लिए ज़रूरत के उपकरण : *an oil drilling rig* **rigging** *noun* मस्तूल-पाल बाँधने वाली रस्सियाँ आदि।

rig² / रिग् / *verb* (-gg-) (प्राय: *अपमा*) स्वयं के लाभ के लिए व्यवस्थित/नियंत्रित करना : *He claimed that the election had been rigged.* ▸ **rigging** *noun.*

right¹ / राइट् / *adj* 1 (व्यवहार, कार्य आदि) नैतिक रूप से उचित; न्यायोचित : *Is it ever right to kill?* 2 यथार्थ रूप से सत्य : *Did you get the answer right?* 3 मत या परख में सही : *They were right about her being lazy.* 4 **right (for sth/sb)** सर्वोचित, सबसे अच्छा : *He is the right man for the job.* 5 (**all**

right भी) ठीक, सही 6 (कपड़ों का) सीधा हिस्सा ■ **get sth right/straight** (कभी-कभी धमकी जैसे प्रयोग) स्पष्ट रूप से समझ लेना : *Let's get this right once and for all.* **put/set sth right** ठीक, सुधार करना : *put one's watch right* ▸ **right angle** *noun* (*गणित*) 90° का कोण **rightly** *adv* 1 ठीक ही, उचित ही : *act rightly* 2 सही कारण से : *She has been sacked, and rightly so.* 3 ठीक-ठीक।

right² / राइट् / *adv* 1 बिलकुल ठीक; सीधे/ प्रत्यक्ष : *sitting right beside you* 2 पूर्णत:, पूरा-पूरा : *Go right to the end of the road.* 3 सही तरह से; संतोषजनक ढंग से : *Have I guessed right or wrong?* ○ *Nothing seems to be going right for me today.* 4 तुरंत ■ **right/straight away/off** बिना विलंब के; तुरंत **right now** तुरंत, अभी।

right³ / राइट् / *noun* 1 (**wrong** के वैषम्य में) उचित, सही : *know the difference between right and wrong* 2 **right (to sth/to do sth)** विधि-विधान के अनुसार अधिकार : *exercise one's legal rights* 3 **rights** [*pl*] (संविधानिक) अधिकार, दावे : *all rights reserved* ■ **be in the right** न्याय के पक्ष में; विधि-सम्मत कर्तव्य/ अधिकार **by right of sth** (*औप*) के कारण **by rights** अगर न्याय किया गया होता; न्यायसंगत रूप से : *By rights, half the reward should be mine.* **in one's own right** स्वयं की योग्यता, अधिकार, प्रयास के कारण, न कि किसी के परिचय से **the rights and wrongs of sth** सच्चे तथ्य।

right⁴ / राइट् / *verb* 1 सीधी, उचित या सही स्थिति में होना/करना या खड़ा होना : *I righted some chairs and we sat down.* 2 स्वयं को/अन्य को ठीक करना, ग़लती सुधारना : *right a wrong.*

right⁵ / राइट् / *adj* (**left** के वैषम्य में) दाहिना; दाहिने : *my right eye* ▸ **right**

noun 1 दाहिनी दिशा 2 **the Right** (राज) दक्षिण-पंथ ▸ **right-hand man** *noun* विश्वस्त सहायक व्यक्ति **right** *adv* दाहिनी दिशा में : *Turn right at the end of the street.* ■ **right and left** हर तरफ़ : *She owes money right and left.*

righteous / 'राइचस् / *adj* 1 नैतिक रूप से उचित : *righteous indignation* 2 (औप) धर्मपरायण; नियमों का पालन करने वाला: *righteous people* ▸ **righteously** *adv* **righteousness** *noun.*

rightful / 'राइटफ़ुल् / *adj* न्यायोचित : *a rightful claim* ▸ **rightfully** *adv* ठीक ही, उचित ही : *They must have what is rightfully theirs.*

rigid / 'रिजिड् / *adj* 1 कड़ा, न मुड़ने वाला; आकार न बदलने वाला: *a rigid support for the tent* 2 दृढ़, नियमों का पालन करने-कराने में दृढ़ : *a man of rigid principles* ▸ **rigidity** / रि'जिडटि / *noun* कठोरता; दृढ़ता **rigidly** *adv.*

rigmarole / 'रिग्मरोल् / *noun* (प्रायः *sing*) (अपमा) 1 प्रायः अनावश्यक, उलझी हुई प्रक्रिया : *go through the whole rigmarole of filling out forms* 2 लंबी, उलझी हुई कहानी या अनाप-शनाप कथन।

rigour (*US* **rigor**) / 'रिगर् / *noun* (औप) 1 कड़ाई, संयम : *be treated with the utmost rigour of the law* 2 **rigours** [*pl*] कठोर परिस्थितियाँ : *face the rigours of prison life* ▸ **rigorous** / 'रिगरस् / *adj* (औप) 1 कड़ा, सख्त : *rigorous discipline* 2 कष्ट-साध्य, श्रमसाध्य : *rigorous attention to detail* 3 (मौसम आदि) कठोर **rigorously** *adv.*

rim / रिम् / *noun* 1 गोलाकार वस्तु का किनारा : *the rim of a cup* 2 पहिये का घेरा, नेमि जिस पर टायर चढ़ाया जाता है ▸ **rim** *verb* (-mm-) किनारा बनना; किनारे

से युक्त होना : *a huge lake rimmed by glaciers.*

rind / राइन्ड् / *noun* फल आदि का छिलका; छाल : *grated lemon rind.*

ring¹ / रिङ् / *noun* 1 अँगूठी 2 (विशेषतः समासों में) छल्ला, घेरा : *a key-ring* 3 घेरा 4 सर्कस का अखाड़ा/घेरा; कुश्ती का अखाड़ा : *knock sb out of the ring* ▸ **ring** *verb* (*pt, pp* **ringed**) 1 **ring sb/sth** (**with sth**) घेरना, घेरा डालना : *The area was ringed by/with police.* 2 किसी चीज़ के चारों ओर वृत्ताकार निशान बनाना : *Ring the correct answer (with your pencil).* 3 (बैल को) नाथना; पक्षी के पैर में छल्ला डालना **ring-leader** *noun* गुट का नेता।

ring² / रिङ् / *verb* (*pt* **rang** / रैङ् /; *pp* **rung** / रङ् /) 1 (*US* **call** भी) **ring sb/sth** (**up**) टेलिफ़ोन से बात करना 2 बजना, बजाना : *ring the fire-alarm* 3 **ring** (**for sb/sth**) घंटी बजाकर या किसी और आवाज़ से किसी को देखभाल के लिए बुलाना : *ring for the maid* 4 (घड़ी या घंटी) बजाकर समय बताना : *This clock only rings the hours.* 5 **ring** (**with sth**) गूँजना, प्रतिध्वनित होना : *The playground rang with children's shouts.* 6 सुने जाने पर प्रभाव विशेष उत्पन्न करना : *Her words rang hollow.* ■ **ring a bell** (अनौप) अस्पष्ट रूप से याद दिलाना; कुछ परिचित लगना : *His name rings a bell; perhaps we've met at a conference.* ▸ **ring** *noun* 1 (अनौप) (*US* **call**) फ़ोन पर बात 2 (घंटी) बजाना, बजना : *There was a ring at the door.* 3 [*sing*] बजने की ध्वनि : *the ring of the hooves on the cobblestones.*

rinse / रिन्स् / *verb* 1 साफ़ पानी से धोना, शीघ्रता से कुछ धोना : *rinse one's hands before eating* 2 साफ़ पानी से साबुन छुड़ाना (धोने के बाद); खँगालना : *Rinse* *your hair thoroughly after shampooing it.* ■ **rinse sth off/out** पानी से धोकर गंदगी, साबुन आदि दूर करना, खँगालना ▶ **rinse** *noun* 1 धोने, खँगालने की क्रिया 2 बालों को अस्थायी तौर पर रँगने का रंग : *a blue rinse.*

riot / 'राइअट्/ *noun* 1 दंगा, बलवा/हंगामा 2 [*sing*] **riot of sth** बड़ा एवं भव्य प्रदर्शन : *The flower-beds were a riot of colour.* ◘ **run riot** क़ाबू के बाहर होना ▶ **riot** *verb* दंगा करना, दंगे में भाग लेना : *They are rioting against food prices.* **rioter** *noun* **rioting** *noun*

rip / रिप्/ *verb* (-pp-) 1 चीरना, काटना : *rip a piece of cloth in two* 2 **rip sth open** उखाड़ना, चीर कर खोलना : *rip open a letter* ■ **rip sb off** (*अनौप*) ठगना : *Tourists complain of being ripped off by local taxi drivers.* **rip sth off** चुराना : *Somebody's ripped off my wallet.* **rip sth off (sth)/out** जल्दी और रूखेपन से उखाड़ना : *rip the cover off a book* **rip sth up** छोटे टुकड़ों में फाड़ना/चीरना : *He ripped up the report and threw it in the bin.* ▶ **rip** *noun* चीरा, कटा हुआ।

ripe / राइप्/ *adj* 1 (फल, अनाज) पका हुआ 2 पूर्ण विकसित 3 (व्यक्ति) प्रौढ़, वृद्ध 4 **ripe (for sth)** तैयार, उपयुक्त : *a nation ripe for revolution* ▶ **ripen** / 'राइपन्/ *verb* पकाना; तैयार करना : *ripening corn* **ripeness** *noun.*

ripple / 'रिप्ल्/ *noun* 1 छोटी-सी लहर या लहरों की शृंखला 2 लहर जैसी कोई वस्तु : *slight ripples on the surface of the metal* 3 (प्राय: *sing*) ध्वनि/ आवाज़ का हलका उतार-चढ़ाव : *a ripple of laughter* ▶ **ripple** *verb* लहराना, लहरें बनाना।

rise¹ / राइज़्/ *noun* 1 चढ़ाव; ऊर्ध्वगति या उन्नति 2 **rise (in sth)** मात्रा, संख्या, तीव्रता आदि में वृद्धि : *a rise in the price of*

meat 3 ऊपर को चढ़ाव, छोटी पहाड़ी ■ **give rise to sth** (*औप*) उत्पन्न करना।

rise² / राइज़्/ *verb* (*pt* **rose** / रोज़्/; *pp* **risen** / 'रिज़्न्/) 1 उठना/उठाना; ऊपर की ओर जाना/उठना : *smoke rising from the chimney* 2 (*औप*) खड़ा होना, बिस्तर से उठना/उठाना, जगना 3 (*औप*) (संसद आदि की बैठक का) समाप्त होना 4 संख्या/मात्रा बढ़ना 5 (ध्वनि) तेज़ हो जाना : *His vioce rose in anger.* 6 (पवन) और ज़ोर से चलना 7 (*औप*) **rise (up) (against sb/sth)** विद्रोह करना 8 समाज, लोकप्रियता, पद आदि में ऊपर उठना/उन्नति करना : *a rising young politician* 9 (नदी) बहना आरंभ होना, स्रोत होना : *The Ganga rises in the Himalayas.* 10 खुश होना/आनंदित होना : *Her spirits rose (at the news).* ■ **rise above sth** मुश्किलों से सामना करने की और उन्हें प्रगति में बाधा बनने से रोकने की योग्यता दिखाना : *She had the courage and determination to rise above her physical disability.* **rise to sth** अप्रत्याशित स्थिति से सामना करने की सामर्थ्य दिखाना ▶ **rising** *noun* विद्रोह।

risk / रिस्क्/ *noun* 1 **risk (of sth/ that...)** जोखिम या हानि का खतरा; दाँव : *a calculated risk* 2 खतरे/जोखिम का कारण व्यक्ति या वस्तु : *Many people see it as a major health/security risk.* ■ **at one's own risk** अपनी सुरक्षा, संपत्ति आदि के लिए खुद ज़िम्मेदार होना **at risk** खतरे में : *put one's life at risk* **at the risk of (doing sth)** हालांकि कुछ होने/ करने की संभावना है **run the risk (of doing sth); run risks** खतरे में डालने वाला कार्य करना ▶ **risk** *verb* 1 जोखिम में होना/रखना; दाँव पर रखना 2 हानि की संभावना होते हुए भी कार्य करना : *risk failure* **risky** *adj* (-ier, -iest) हानि की संभावना से युक्त : *a risky undertaking.*

rite / राइट् / noun संस्कार, धार्मिक कृत्य या अनुष्ठान : initiation rites.

ritual / 'रिचुअल् / noun 1 अनुष्ठान, कर्म-कांड 2 (विशेषत: परि) हर बार एक ही तरह से की जाने वाली क्रिया/प्रक्रिया : He went through the ritual of filling and lighting the pipe. ▸ ritual adj अनुष्ठान विषयक : a ritual dance.

rival / 'राइवल् / noun rival (to sb/sth) (for/in sth) प्रतिद्वंद्वी : business rivals ▸ rival verb (-ll-; US -l- भी) rival sb/sth (for/in sth) प्रतिद्वंद्वी बनना; किसी अन्य के बराबर होने का दावा करना : Golf cannot rival football in excitement. **rivalry** / 'राइवल्रि / noun (pl rivalries) rivalry (with sb/sth); rivalry (between A and B) प्रतिद्वंद्विता; प्रतिस्पर्धा।

river / 'रिवर् / noun 1 नदी 2 नदी की तरह विशाल प्रवाह वाला द्रव : a river of lava.

rivet / 'रिविट् / noun रिवेट (एक प्रकार की कील) ▸ rivet verb 1 रिवेट की सहायता से जोड़ना : riveted steel plates 2 किसी वस्तु को एक स्थान पर जड़ देना : We stood riveted (to the spot). 3 आँखें गड़ाना; किसी का सारा ध्यान आकर्षित कर लेना : I was absolutely riveted by her story.

rivulet / 'रिव्यलट् / noun छोटी धारा।

road / रोड् / noun 1 सड़क 2 प्राप्ति-मार्ग, प्राप्त करने का उपाय : take the road of privatization ■ on the road 1 सफ़र में 2 (वाहन) प्रयोग में 3 घुमंतु, स्थायी निवास न होना ▸ roadblock noun सड़क के आर-पार खड़ी की गई रुकावट road-side noun सड़क का किनारा।

roam / रोम् / verb बिना स्पष्ट उद्देश्य, लक्ष्य के घूमना, भ्रमण करना : just roaming about/around.

roar / रॉर् / noun (शेर आदि की) गर्जन, दहाड़ ▸ roar verb 1 दहाड़ना, गर्जन करना : tigers roaring in their cages 2 roar sth (out) गरजते हुए कहना : roar out an order **roaring** adj.

roast / रोस्ट् / verb 1 भूनना : roast coffee beans/peanuts 2 (अनौप) तेज़ आँच/ताप सहन करना : roast one's toes in front of the fire 3 (अनौप या परि) कड़ी आलोचना करना : The critics really roasted her new play. ▸ roast adj भुना हुआ **roasting** adj.

rob / रॉब् / verb (-bb-) rob sb/sth (of sth) 1 लूटना, डाका डालना 2 किसी को किसी आवश्यक वस्तु से वंचित करना/छीन लेना : be robbed of sleep by noisy neighbours ▸ robber noun डाकू, डकैत, लुटेरा **robbery** / 'रॉबरि / noun (pl robberies) डकैती, लूटमार : three robberies in one week.

robe / रोब् / noun 1 (समासों में) ढीला बाहरी वस्त्र : a beach-robe 2 (प्राय: pl) (विशेषत: उच्च राजकर्मचारियों की) पोशाक : coronation robes ▸ robe verb robe sb/oneself (in sth) (औप) पोशाक पहनना/पहनाना।

robin / 'रॉबिन् / noun भूरे रंग की छोटी चिड़िया जिसकी छाती लाल रंग की होती है।

robot / 'रोबॉट् / noun 1 मनुष्य की तरह काम करने वाली मशीन; रोबोट 2 (विशेषत: अपमा) व्यक्ति जो बिना सोचे यंत्र की तरह काम करता है।

robust / रो'बस्ट् / adj 1 हृष्ट-पुष्ट, तगड़ा व्यक्ति 2 मज़बूत : a robust chair 3 दृढ़ और उत्साहपूर्ण : a robust speech ○ take a more robust view 4 (अपमा) सुरुचिपूर्ण नहीं : a rather robust sense of humour.

rock[1] / रॉक् / noun 1 पत्थर की चट्टान; समुद्र तल से निकला भूखंड : the ship hit some rocks and sank 2 चट्टान; बड़ा ढेला ■ as solid/steady as a rock ठोस, मज़बूत और दृढ़; अत्यंत विश्वसनीय **on the rocks** 1 (जहाज़) पत्थरों/चट्टानों से ठोकर खाकर टूट जाना 2 (अनौप) (विवाह, व्यापार आदि) असफल होने के गहरे ख़तरे में ▸ rocky adj (-ier, -iest)

1 चट्टान से भरा हुआ : *a rocky coastline* 2 चट्टान के समान कड़ा 3 अस्थिर, हिलने वाला : *This chair is a bit rocky.*

rock² / 'रॉक् / *verb* 1 आगे-पीछे या दाएँ-बाएँ हिलाना : *rock a baby to sleep* 2 हिलना या ज़ोर से हिलाना : *The town was rocked by an earthquake.* 3 परेशानी या आघात पहुँचाना : *The scandal rocked the government.*

rock³ / 'रॉक् / (rock music भी) *noun* एक प्रकार का तेज़ आधुनिक संगीत जिसे विद्युतीय गिटार आदि पर बजाते हैं।

rocket / 'रॉकिट् / *noun* 1 रॉकेट, अग्नि बाण 2 अंतरिक्ष यान/मिसाइल दाग़ने में प्रयुक्त रॉकेट ▸ **rocket** *verb* 1 बहुत तेज़ी से बढ़ना : *House prices are rocketing.* 2 अत्यंत तीव्रता से गति करना 3 रॉकेटों से हमला करना।

rod / रॉड् / *noun* 1 (प्राय: समासों में) धातु या लकड़ी की छड़ : *a measuring rod* 2 दंड देने के लिए प्रयुक्त छड़ी 3 मछली पकड़ने की वंशी।

rodent / 'रोडन्ट् / *noun* कुतरने वाला जीव जैसे चूहा, गिलहरी, ख़रगोश।

roe¹ / रो / *noun* मत्स्यांड (hard roe) या मत्स्यशुंक्र (soft roe)।

roe² / रो / *noun* (*pl* अपरिवर्तित या roes) हरिणी।

rogue / रोग् / *noun* 1 (अप्र) दुर्जन, दुष्ट व्यक्ति 2 (परि) नटखट, शैतान 3 झुंड से अलग रहने वाला, प्राय: ख़तरनाक, पशु : *a rogue elephant*; व्यक्ति या वस्तु, सामान्य से भिन्न आचार वाला और प्राय: परेशानी उत्पन्न करने वाला ▸ **roguish** / 'रोगिश् / *adj* नटखट, शैतान।

role / रोल् / *noun* 1 नाटक या फ़िल्म में अभिनेता की भूमिका 2 भूमिका, कार्य : *play a significant role.*

roll¹ / रोल् / *noun* 1 बेलनाकार बनी हुई वस्तु, लपेटी हुई वस्तु 2 लंबी या गोलाकार ब्रेड (प्राय: भरवाँ) : *a cheese roll* 3 गोल-गोल घूमने, डगमगाने की क्रिया

4 लगातार आती हुई आवाज़ : *the distant roll of thunder* 5 नाम सूची : *the electoral roll.*

roll² / रोल् / *verb* 1 लुढ़कना/लुढ़काना : *The ball rolled down the hill.* 2 घूमना, घुमाना : *rolling a pencil between his fingers* 3 लपेटना, किसी वस्तु को गेंद या बेलन की आकृति में मोड़ना : *roll wool (up) into a ball* 4 बेलना, बेलनाकार वस्तु की सहायता से कुछ समतल करना : *roll out the pastry* 5 डगमगाना : *walk with a rolling gait* 6 गरजना, गड़गड़ाना : *rolling drums* ■ **roll in** (अनौप) बड़ी संख्या में आना **rolled into one** एक ही व्यक्ति, वस्तु में संयोजित : *He's an artist, a scientist and a businessman all rolled into one.* **roll sth back** 1 पीछे हटाना या घूमाना 2 क़ीमतें आदि घटाना।

roller / 'रोलर् / *noun* 1 बेलन, रोलर : *a garden roller* 2 लंबी उठती हुई तरंग/लहर : *rollers crashing on the beach.*

Roman / 'रोमन् / *adj* 1 रोम का : *the Roman dialect* 2 रोम-विषयक : *Roman temple/villa* 3 रोम के ईसाई चर्च विषयक; रोमन कैथोलिक ▸ **roman numeral** *noun* रोमन अंक जैसे I, II, III .... आदि।

romance / रो'मैन्स् / *noun* 1 रोमांचक प्रेम का अनुभव : *a teenage romance* 2 रोमांचक अनुभव एवं भाव : *the romance of travel* 3 प्रेम कथा, रोमांचकारी घटना आदि, प्राय: पूर्व समय की : *a medieval romance* ▸ **romance** *verb* रोमांचक किस्से सुनाना।

romantic / रो'मैनिटक् / *adj* 1 प्रेम-विषयक, रूमानी : *a romantic attachment* 2 भावुकतापूर्ण; (व्यक्ति) भावुक एवं कल्पनाशील 3 (Romantic भी) (विशेषत: 19वीं शताब्दी का) रोमांस साहित्य/संगीत आदि।

romp / रॉम्प् / *verb* (बच्चों या पशुओं का)

खिलवाड़ करना, कूदना-फाँदना : *puppies romping around in the garden* ▶ romp *noun* खिलवाड़, कूद-फाँद।

roof / रूफ़ / *noun* (*pl* **roofs**) छत ∎ **go through the roof** (*अनौप*) 1 अत्यंत क्रोधित हो जाना 2 (क़ीमतें आदि) तीव्रता से बढ़ना **have a roof over one's head** निवास के लिए स्थान होना **under one/the same roof** एक ही/उसी घर या इमारत में : *Although divorced, they continued to live under the same roof.* ▶ roof *verb* **roof sth (over/in); roof sth (with sth)** छत डालना; छप्पर डालना/बनाना : *a garage roofed with tiles.*

rook¹ / रूक़ / *noun* कौवे की तरह बड़ी काली चिड़िया।

rook² / रूक़ / *noun* हाथी (शतरंज का एक मोहरा)।

room / रूम् / *noun* 1 कमरा; होटल में शयनकक्ष 2 **rooms** [*pl*] निवास, फ़्लैट 3 **room (for sb/sth); room (to do sth)** स्थान, रिक्त स्थान (जिसका प्रयोग उपयोग किया जा सके) : *This table takes up too much room.* 4 **room (for sth)** कुछ घटित होने/अस्तित्व में आने की संभावना : *There's no room for doubt.* ▶ **roomful** *noun* कमरे में समा सकने योग्य संख्या या मात्रा **roomy** *adj* (**-ier, -iest**) लंबा-चौड़ा।

roost / रूस्ट् / *noun* ऊँचे स्थान पर चिड़ियों का बसेरा ▶ **roost** *verb* (चिड़ियों का) बसेरा लेना, अड्डे पर बैठना : *a roosting place for pigeons.*

rooster / रूस्टर् / *noun* (विशेषत: अमेरिकी अँग्रेज़ी में) मुर्ग़ा।

root¹ / रूट् / *noun* 1 (पेड़-पौधों की) जड़ 2 बालों, दाँतों, नाख़ूनों आदि की जड़ 3 किसी बात की उत्पत्ति या आधार : *We need to tackle the root (cause) of the trouble.* 4 **roots** [*pl*] वंश उत्पत्ति, मूल स्थान से लगाव 5 (*व्या*) धातु, शब्दों का वह रूप जिससे बहुत से शब्द बनते हैं 6 (*गणित*)

मूल : *4 is the square root of 16 and cube root of 64.* ∎ **take root** (पौधों का) 1 उगना प्रारंभ करना, जड़ें निकलना 2 स्थिति मज़बूत करना, स्थापित हो जाना

root² / रूट् / *verb* (पौधों का) जड़ पकड़ना, जड़ें जमाना; **root sth/sb out** जड़ उखाड़ना, मिटा देना/उखाड़ फेंकना : *root out corruption* ∎ **root (about/around) for sth** अव्यवस्थित ढंग से चीज़ों के बीच कुछ ढूँढना **root for sb/sth** (*अनौप*) उत्साहपूर्वक समर्थन देना : *We are rooting for the college baseball team.* ▶ **rooted** *adj* 1 एक स्थान पर जड़ें होना 2 मज़बूती से स्थापित होना 3 किसी चीज़ में/से आरंभ होना।

rope / रोप् / *noun* 1 रस्सी 2 रस्सी की तरह गूँथी हुई वस्तु : *a rope of pearls* 3 **the rope** [*sing*] (*अनौप या साहि*) फाँसी का फंदा ▶ **rope** *verb* रस्सी से बाँधना; रस्सी से घेरना ∎ **rope sb in (to do sth)** किसी को भाग लेने के लिए मनाना।

rosary / 'रोज़रि / *noun* (*pl* **rosaries**) सुमिरनी, जपमाला।

rose / रोज़् / *noun* 1 गुलाब का फूल 2 गुलाबी रंग।

rostrum / 'रॉस्ट्रम् / *noun* (*pl* **rostrums** या **rostra** / 'रॉस्ट्रा /) भाषण आदि देने के लिए मंच, चबूतरा।

rosy / 'रोज़ि / *adj* (**-ier, -iest**) 1 (त्वचा) गुलाबी एवं स्वस्थ; चमकीला 2 संतोषजनक होने की आशा वाला : *She painted a rosy picture of the firm's future.*

rot / रॉट् / *verb* (**-tt-**) 1 सड़ना, ख़राब होना; गलना : *a heap of rotting leaves* 2 सड़ाना, गलाना : *Eating too much sugar can rot your teeth away.* ▶ **rot** *noun* 1 सड़न, गलन; मवाद पड़ना (पकना) 2 (*अप्र*) बकवास।

rota / 'रोटा / *noun* (*pl* **rotas**) किसी कार्य को करने वालों की क्रम सूची : *work on a rota system.*

rotate / रो'टेट् / *verb* 1 धुरी पर घूमना

घुमाना; चक्कर काटना : *rotate through 360 degrees* 2 घटना का चक्र-क्रम से होना या करना : *the technique of rotating crops* ▸ rotation / रो'टेश्न्/ noun 1 घूर्णन 2 चक्र-क्रम आवर्तन।

rote / रोट्/ *noun* रटना, रट्टा : *learn sth by rote.*

rotor / 'रोटर्/ *noun* मशीन का भाग जो एक केंद्र/धुरी के गिर्द घूमता है : *rotor blades on a helicopter.*

rotten / 'रॉट्न्/ *adj* 1 (खाद्य पदार्थ या अन्य वस्तु) सड़ा-गला : *rotten eggs* 2 (अनौप) बेकार, रद्दी 3 (अनौप) बीमार, अस्वस्थ : *feel rotten.*

rotund / रो'टन्ड्/ *adj* (औप या परि) (व्यक्ति) गोलमटोल ▸ rotundity *noun.*

rouble (ruble भी) / 'रूबल्/ *noun* रूस की मुद्रा।

rouge / रूश्/ *noun* (अप्र) रूज़, गालों पर लगाने वाली लाली।

rough¹ / रफ़्/ *adj* (-er, -est) 1 (सतह) खुरदरा : *rough ground* 2 (समुद्र) अशांत, विक्षुब्ध 3 तेज़, उग्र, अशिष्ट : *rough behaviour* 4 आरंभिक, कच्चा (कार्य); जल्दी और अविस्तृत ढंग से किया गया : *a rough sketch/outline* 5 रूखा/ कठोर, असुविधाजनक, अशांत 6 (ध्वनि) कर्णकटु; (स्वाद) तीखा : *a rough wine/ voice* 7 (अनौप) अस्वस्थ; अप्रसन्न ■ **be rough (on sb)** 1 (अनौप) किसी के लिए अप्रिय या अशुभ होना : *Losing his job was rough on him.* 2 अत्यंत क्रोधित या सख़्त होना : *I'm so sorry I was so rough on you.* **have/give sb a rough ride** काफ़ी आलोचना या विरोध सहन करना/करवाना ▸ roughly *adv* 1 रुक्ष व्यवहार से 2 लगभग।

rough² / रफ़्/ *noun* 1 (the rough भी) गोल्फ़ कोर्स का खुरदरा भाग जहाँ घास भी ज़्यादा हो 2 कच्चा काम 3 (अनौप) उग्र अपराधी : *beaten up by a gang of roughs* ■ **in rough** आरंभिक कच्ची

स्थिति में **take the rough with the smooth** प्रिय-अप्रिय को एक समान स्वीकार करना।

rough³ / रफ़्/ *adv* रूखे/उग्र ढंग से : *playing rough.*

rough⁴ / रफ़्/ *verb* ■ **rough it** (अनौप) कष्ट सहकर रहना **rough sb up** (अनौप) हमला करना **rough sth out** कच्चे तौर पर चित्र बनाना या वर्णन करना।

roughage / 'रफ़िज्/ *noun* भोजन का वह भाग जो पचाया नहीं जा सकता परंतु पेट साफ़ रखता है।

roughen / रफ़्न्/ *verb* खुरदरा/रूखा बनना/बनाना : *a face roughened by the sun and wind.*

roulette / रू'लेट्/ *noun* खेल जिसमें गेंद को संख्यांकित घूमते हुए पहिए पर डाला जाता है और पहिए के रुकने की संख्या पर बाज़ी लगाई जाती है।

round¹ / राउन्ड्/ *adj* 1 गोलाकार, गोल 2 (शरीर के अंग) पूर्ण विकसित एवं उभार-दार : *round cheeks* 3 पूर्ण : *a round sum of money* ■ **in round figures/ numbers** मोटे तौर से, मोटी संख्या में, जैसे 10, 20, 30, 100 आदि।

round² / राउन्ड् / *adv* (around भी) 1 गोल चक्कर में घूमते हुए, घूर्णन में : *children spinning round and round* 2 एक चक्र पूरा करते हुए 3 चारों ओर घेरा नापते हुए; चारों ओर, सभी ओर : *People stood round waiting for something to happen.* 4 सीधे की बजाय लंबे रास्ते से 5 एक के बाद दूसरे को, बारी-बारी से प्रत्येक को : *Pass the biscuits round.* 6 विपरीत दिशा में/की ओर : *She looked round at the sound of his voice.* ■ **round about** 1 आस-पास : *the villages round about* 2 लगभग : *We're leaving round about midday.* **the other way round** विपरीत तरीक़े या क्रम से।

round³ / राउन्ड्/ *noun* 1 फेरा, गश्त, बारी;

दौर, दौरा 2 (सभा या चर्चा आदि की) बैठक : *the next round of the peace talks* 3 (खेलों में) पाली, फेरा : *a qualifying round* 4 गोल टुकड़ा : *Cut the pastry into small rounds, one for each pie.* 5 गोली (दाग़ना) : *They fired several rounds.* 6 बहुत-से लोगों द्वारा एक साथ किया अनुमोदन/प्रशंसा : *She got a big round of applause.*

round⁴ / राउन्ड् / *prep* (विशेषत: *US* **around** भी) 1 चारों ओर (कुछ केंद्र बिंदु मानते हुए) : *sail round the world* 2 दूसरी ओर के बिंदु तक 3 सभी ओर; गोल घेरे में : *look round the room.*

round⁵ / राउन्ड् / *verb* 1 गोल बनाना या बनना : *round the lips* 2 घेरे में या चक्कर में घूमना : *We rounded the corner at high speed.* ■ **round sb/sth up** (व्यक्तियों को) इकट्ठा करना; (पशुओं को) हाँकना **round sth off** 1 संतोषजनक ढंग से पूरा करना, समाप्त करना 2 किनारे घिसना; परिष्कृत रूप देना।

roundabout¹ / राउन्डबाउट् / *adj* घुमाव-फिराव वाला, चक्करदार : *a roundabout route.*

roundabout² / 'राउन्डबाउट् / *noun* 1 (*US* **traffic circle** भी) चौराहे का गोल चक्कर 2 (**merry-go-round** भी; *US* **carousel, whirligig**) चरखी झूला।

rouse / राउज़् / *verb* 1 **rouse sb (from sth)** जगाना, नींद से उठाना 2 किसी कार्य के लिए प्रेरित/क्रियाशील करना : *rouse sb to action* 3 कोई भाव उत्पन्न करना 4 किसी को क्रोध दिला देना।

rout / राउट् / *noun* बुरी/पूर्ण हार ▶ **rout** *verb* बुरी तरह हरा देना : *He resigned after his party was routed in the election.*

route / रूट् / *noun* एक स्थान से दूसरे स्थान तक जाने का मार्ग, रास्ता ▶ **route** *verb* (*pres p* **routing**; *pp* **routed**) मार्ग-

विशेष से भेजना : *routing data via satellite.*

routine / रू'टीन् / *noun* 1 दिनचर्या, नित्यक्रम 2 (नृत्य आदि में) गति की निश्चित प्रक्रिया ▶ **routine** *adj* 1 सामान्य, नियमित : *routine tasks* 2 (*अपमा*) (सामान्य होने के कारण) अरुचिकर।

rove / रोव़् / *verb* (विशेषत: *साहि*) घूमना, मटरगश्ती करना : *a roving reporter.*

row¹ / रो / *noun* (व्यक्तियों या वस्तुओं की) पंक्ति : *a row of books* ■ **in a row** लगातार, बिना अंतराल के।

row² / रो / *verb* (नाव) खेना; खेते हुए नाव में सैर करना/कराना : *He rowed us across the river.* ▶ **row** *noun* (प्राय: *sing*) नौका-विहार : *go for a row.*

row³ / राउ / *noun* (*अनौप*) 1 (बहस) झगड़ा 2 [*sing*] उपद्रव, अप्रिय शोर : *What a row they're making!* ▶ **row** *verb* **row (with sb)** झगड़ा करना।

rowdy / 'राउडि / *adj* (**-ier, -iest**) (*अपमा*) झगड़ालू; शोर और उपद्रव मचाने वाला (व्यक्ति) : *a group of rowdy teenagers.*

royal / 'रॉइअल् / *adj* 1 राजकीय; राजोचित 2 राजा या रानी के परिवार से संबंधित : *the royal palaces* 3 राजकीय सेवा में; भव्य, शानदार ▶ **royalist** *noun* राजभक्त **royally** *adv* भव्य रूप में।

royalty / 'रॉइअल्टि / *noun* (*pl* **royalties**) 1 राजा, राजवंशी (व्यक्ति) 2 रॉयल्टी, स्वत्व-शुल्क (लेखक, आविष्कारक आदि को अपनी कृति बिकने पर मिलने वाला प्रतिशत लाभ)।

rub / रब् / *verb* (**-bb-**) 1 **rub sth (with sth)** रगड़ना : *He rubbed his eyes.* 2 रगड़ कर स्थिति-विशेष में पहुँचाना : *rub the surface smooth* 3 **rub sth (in/ into/on/over sth)** मलना : *Rub the lotion into your skin.* ■ **rub salt into the wound/sb's wound** जले पर नमक छिड़काना **rub sb the wrong way**

(अनौप) किसी को *(जानबूझ कर)* क्रोधित करना **rub (sth) off (sth)** रगड़ कर या छील कर निशान मिटा देना **rub sth out** रबड़ से पेंसिल आदि के लिखे को मिटाना ▸ **rub** *noun* 1 *(प्राय: sing)* रगड़ 2 **the rub** *[sing]* *(अप्र या साहि)* समस्या, कठिनाई : *There lies the rub.*

rubber /'रबर् / *noun* 1 रबड़ 2 *(US* **eraser** भी) पेंसिल के लिखे को मिटाने वाला रबड़ ▸ **rubber band** *noun* चीज़ों को पकड़े रखने के लिए पतला गोल रबड़ का टुकड़ा **rubber stamp** *noun* 1 किसी दस्तावेज़ पर लगाई जाने वाली रबड़ की मोहर जिस पर नाम, पता, तिथि आदि अंकित हों 2 *(अपमा)* व्यक्ति या गुट जो दूसरों के कार्यों का बिना सोचे-समझे हमेशा अनुमोदन करे।

rubbish /'रबिश् / *noun* 1 *(US* **garbage** भी) कूड़ा-करकट; रद्दी माल; बेकार, गुणवत्ता में निकृष्ट : *The film is (a load of) rubbish.* 2 *(अनौप)* अंड-बंड, बकवास।

rubble /'रब्ल् / *noun* ईंट-पत्थर की रोड़ी; मलबा : *dig people out of the rubble.*

ruby /'रूबि / *noun (pl* **rubies)** 1 माणिक्य (लाल रत्न) 2 गहरा लाल रंग : *ruby red lips.*

rucksack /'रक्सैक् / *(US* **backpack** भी) *noun* रकसैक, पीठ का थैला।

rudder /'रडर् / *noun* पतवार, कर्ण।

ruddy /'रडि / *adj* 1 (व्यक्ति का चेहरा) स्वास्थ्य से लाल 2 *(औप)* लालिमा : *a ruddy glow in the sky* ▸ **ruddiness** *noun.*

rude / रूड् / *adj (-r, -st)* 1 (व्यक्ति/ व्यवहार) रूखा, कठोरतापूर्ण; उग्र : *a rude remark* 2 अशिष्ट : *a rude joke* 3 अचानक, अप्रिय और अप्रत्याशित 4 *(अप्र या औप)* आदिम; अपरिष्कृत; अनगढ़ : *a rude shelter of branches and leaves* ▸ **rudely** *adv* **rudeness** *noun.*

rudiments /'रूडिमन्ट्स् / *noun [pl]* **the rudiments (of sth)** प्रारंभिक ज्ञान, किसी विषय पर ज्ञान आदि की प्रारंभिक स्थिति; आधारभूत सिद्धांत : *learn the rudiments of economics* ▸ **rudimentary** /ˌरूडि'मेन्ट्रि / *adj* प्रारंभिक, अविकसित; सिर्फ़ मूल सिद्धांतों के विषय में : *He received only a rudimentary education.*

ruffian /'रफ़िअन् / *noun* *(अप्र)* गुंडा, बदमाश।

ruffle /'रफ़ल् / *verb* 1 **ruffle sth (up)** शांत सतह को बिगाड़ना, क्षुब्ध करना : *a breeze ruffling the calm surface of the lake* 2 किसी को क्रोधित, चिंतित या भ्रमित कर देना : *He never gets ruffled, even under pressure.* ▸ **ruffle** *noun* झालर (कपड़े आदि की)।

rug / रग् / *noun* 1 क़ालीन, ग़लीचा 2 कंबल : *a travelling rug.*

Rugby /'रग्बि / **(Rugby football** भी) *noun* रगबी फ़ुटबॉल (दोनों ओर 13 या 15 खिलाड़ी होते हैं, गेंद अंडाकार होती है जिसे पैर से खेलने के साथ हाथों से उठा कर भी खेल सकते हैं)।

rugged /'रगिड् / *adj* 1 ऊबड़-खाबड़ (भूमि) : *a rugged coastline* 2 (व्यक्ति का चेहरा) तीखे नाक-नक्श वाला : *a rugged face* 3 मज़बूत, जल्दी ख़राब न होने वाला 4 (व्यक्ति) देखने में कठोर और दृढ़निश्चयी परंतु बिना अच्छे सामाजिक व्यवहार के : *a rugged individualist.*

ruin /'रूइन् / *verb* 1 तबाह करना, बरबाद करना : *The mistake ruined his chances of ever becoming President.* 2 धन और पद छिन जाना/छीन लेना, खो देना : *a ruined man* ▸ **ruin** *noun* 1 बरबादी, तबाही : *a city reduced to a state of ruin by war* 2 आर्थिक एवं सामाजिक बरबादी की स्थिति 3 *(प्राय: pl)* खंडहर, भग्नावशेष ■ **in ruins** बुरी तरह क्षतिग्रस्त ▸ **ruinous** /'रूइनस् / *adj* 1 तबाह करने वाला 2 बरबाद : *ruinous castle.*

rule / रूल् / *noun* 1 नियम, क़ायदा : *observe/follow the rules* 2 (प्राय: *sing*) सामान्य प्रथा या आदत : *As a (general) rule I'm~home by six.* 3 शासन, अधिकार : *democratic majority rule* 4 पैमाना (बढ़ई द्वारा प्रयुक्त) 5 सीधी खींची रेखा a rule of thumb अनुभव (न कि यथार्थ माप) पर आधारित कच्चा सक्रिय जाँचने का तरीक़ा bend stretch the rules सुविधानुसार नियमों को बदलना/नियमों का अर्थ निकालना ▶ **rule** *verb* 1 rule (over sb/sth) शासन करना 2 नियम निर्धारित करना, निर्णय देना 3 पटरी से सीधी रेखा खींचना 4 किसी के भावों, विचारों आदि पर नियंत्रण, प्रभाव होना : *She let her heart rule her head.*

ruler / रूलर् / *noun* 1 शासक (व्यक्ति) 2 पटरी, पैमाना।

ruling¹ / रूलिङ् / *noun* आधिकारिक आदेश या निर्णय।

ruling² / रूलिङ् / *adj* शासन करने वाला; सबसे अधिक प्रभावशाली : *the ruling class.*

rum¹ / रम् / *noun* रम (गन्ने की शराब)।

rum² / रम् / *adj* (अप्र या अनौप) अजीब, अनोखा : *He's a rum character.*

rumble / रम्ब्ल् / *verb* 1 गड़गड़ाना, धड़धड़ाना : *thunder rumbling in the distance* 2 धड़धड़ाते हुए गुज़रना/चलना : *tanks rumbling through the streets* ▶ **rumble** *noun* 1 गड़गड़ाहट/धड़धड़ाहट की ध्वनि 2 (*US*, अप) गली में लड़ाई-झगड़ा।

ruminate / रूमिनेट् / *verb* ruminate (about/on/over sth) चिंतन करना।

rummage / रमिज् / *verb* rummage (among/in/through sth) (for sth); rummage (about/around) कुछ ढूँढ़ते हुए चीज़ें इधर-उधर फैलाना।

rumour (*US* rumor) / रूमर् / *noun* अफ़वाह, जनश्रुति ▶ **rumoured** *adj* अफ़वाह रूप में कथित, जनश्रुत।

run¹ / रन् / *verb* (-nn-; *pt* ran / रैन् /; *pp* run) 1 दौड़ना 2 run (in sth) दौड़ में भाग लेना : *run the marathon* 3 (बस, ट्रेन का) चलना, यात्रा करना 4 (मशीन आदि का) चलना, चालू करना 5 (सड़कों, रेखाओं आदि का) दिशा-विशेष की ओर जाना, दूरी तक पहुँचना : *A fence runs round the whole field.* 6 run (for sth) कुछ समय तक अस्तित्व में बिना रुकावट के होना, हो जाना : *Her last musical ran for six months.* 7 (द्रव का) बहना; बहाना : *Tears ran down her cheeks.* 8 (रंग आदि का) घुलना और फैल जाना : *I am afraid the colour ran when I washed your new skirt.* 9 (ठोस पदार्थ का) पिघलना : *It was so hot that the butter ran.* 10 किसी स्थिति में पहुँच जाना : *The river ran dry during the drought.* 11 नियंत्रित करना, (व्यापार आदि का) संचालन करना : *run a hotel* 12 व्यवस्था करना; उपलब्ध कराना 13 run (for sth/sb); run (in sth) चुनाव में प्रत्याशी बनना/खड़ा होना ■ run across (sb/sth) संयोग से मिलना या पाना run after sb दौड़कर किसी को पकड़ने की कोशिश करना run away (from sb) अचानक कोई जगह छोड़ देना; भाग निकलना run away from sth झेंप, झिझक के कारण किसी से बचना run away with sb; run away (together) (अनौप run with sb, run off (together) भी) किसी से संबंध बनाने के लिए घर छोड़ देना run away with sth आसानी से या स्पष्टतया जीत जाना run sb/sth down 1 (वाहन या वाहक) ठोकर मार कर गिराना 2 निर्दयी ढंग से आलोचना करना run into sb अचानक मिल जाना run into sth 1 मुश्किलों, तकलीफ़ों का सामना करना : *The project is running into financial difficulties.* 2 स्थिति/दिशा-विशेष में पहुँचना run on बिना रुके जारी रहना/रखना; आवश्यकता से ज़्यादा देर तक जारी रखना run out (समझौता,

काग़ज़ात आदि का) वैध न रहना : *The lease on our apartment runs out in a few months.* **run out (of sth)** संभरण आदि समाप्त होना : *We ran out of fuel.* **run over sb; run sb over** (वाहन/वाहक) व्यक्ति या पशु को ठोकर मार कर उस पर/उसके किसी अंग पर से गुज़र जाना : *I ran over a cat last night.* **run over sth** जल्दी से कुछ पढ़ना या अभ्यास करना : *I always run over my lines before going on stage.* ▸ **runaway** / 'रनअवे / *adj* 1 (व्यक्ति) भागा हुआ, भगोड़ा 2 (पशु या वाहन) अनियंत्रित, क़ाबू से बाहर : *a runaway horse* 3 बहुत आसानी/तेज़ी से घटित : *a runaway victory.* **runaway** *noun* भगोड़ा व्यक्ति **rundown** *adj* 1 जीर्ण-शीर्ण अवस्था में 2 (व्यक्ति) बुरी तरह थका हुआ; बीमार **run-up** *noun* 1 **run-up (to sth)** घटना से पूर्व समय की अवधि : *during the run-up to the elections* 2 गेंद फेंकने/कूदने से पहले वेग बढ़ाने के लिए भागने का फ़ासला।

run² / रन् / *noun* 1 दौड़ 2 यात्रा (कार, ट्रेन आदि से) 3 अवधि, दौर : *a run of bad luck* 4 (प्राय: समासों में) प्राय: घिरा हुआ स्थान जिसमें पालतू पशु-पक्षी घूम-फिर सकते हैं : *a chicken-run* 5 क्रिकेट में रन, गणना की इकाई : *Our team won by 87 runs.* ■ **in the long run** अंत में, अंततोगत्वा।

rung / रङ् / *noun* 1 सीढ़ी का डंडा 2 समाज, संस्था आदि में पद या स्तर : *start on the bottom rung of the salary scale.*

runner / 'रनर् / *noun* 1 दौड़ने वाला, धावक 2 (समासों में) वस्तुओं का अवैध धंधा करने वाला व्यक्ति : *gun-runners* 3 (मशीनरी की) पटरी 4 रेंगने वाला पौधा ▸ **runner-up** *noun* (*pl* **runners-up**) प्रतियोगिता में विजेता दल या व्यक्ति के बाद का दल या व्यक्ति : *They finished runners-up behind Sweden.*

running / 'रनिङ् / *noun* 1 भागने की प्रक्रिया; दौड़ 2 संचालन की प्रक्रिया : *the day-to-day running of a shop/business/country* ■ **in/out of the running (for sth)** (अनौप) सफलता, कार्य सिद्धि की संभावना होना/न होना ▸ **running** *adj* 1 लगातार; क्रम से : *She has now won the championship three times running.* 2 (पानी) बहता हुआ 3 (घाव) मवाद बहता हुआ : *an animal covered in running sores* ■ **in/out of the running (for sth)** (अनौप) दौड़ या अन्य किसी कार्य में सफलता की संभावना होना/न होना ▸ **running commentary** *noun* आँखो देखा हाल, चल वर्णन।

runny / 'रनि / *adj* (अनौप) 1 (आँखों से या नाक से) ज़ुकाम के कारण पानी बहता हुआ 2 (कभी-कभी *अपमा*) (द्रव या व्यंजन) अत्यधिक तरल।

runway / 'रन्वे / *noun* हवाई जहाज़ के लिए उतरते या उड़ते समय दौड़ने के लिए बना पथ।

rupee / रू'पी / *noun* रूपया (भारत, पाकिस्तान की मुद्रा)।

rupture / 'रप्चर् / *noun* 1 (औप) संबंध-विच्छेद; अलग होना 2 (चिकि) (शरीर के अंगों में) फटन : *the rupture of a blood-vessel* ▸ **rupture** *verb* 1 शरीर के अंगों का टूटना/भंग होना 2 (औप) संबंध तोड़ना/समाप्त करना 3 पात्र में दरार पड़ना।

rural / 'रुअरल् / *adj* ग्राम-विषयक, ग्रामीण परिवेश से संबंधित : *rural communities.*

ruse / रूज़् / *noun* धोखा, छल : *think up a ruse for getting into the cinema without paying.*

rush¹ / रश् / *verb* 1 झपटना, वेगपूर्वक बढ़ना 2 **rush (sb) (into sth/doing sth)** किसी को बिना सोचे-समझे कार्य करने को विवश करना/स्वयं ऐसा करना : *I'm afraid she rushed into marriage.*

3 अचानक धावा बोलने, चढ़ाई करने की कोशिश करना।

rush² / रश् / *noun* 1 [*sing*] हड़बड़ी; दौड़ 2 [*sing*] अचानक वृद्धि 3 **rush on/for** sth वस्तुओं की अचानक बढ़ी माँग।

rush³ / रश् / *noun* तालाब आदि के पास उगने वाला एक प्रकार का पौधा।

russet / 'रसिट् / *adj* गेरुए रंग का ▸ **russet** *noun* गेरुआ रंग।

rust / रस्ट् / *noun* 1 जंग, (लोहे आदि पर लगा हुआ) मोरचा : *patches of rust* 2 लाल-भूरा-सा रंग ▸ **rust** *verb* जंग लगना **rusty** *adj* (-**ier, -iest**) 1 जंग लगा हुआ 2 (*अनौप*) अभ्यास के आभाव में निकृष्ट : *My tennis is pretty rusty.*

rustic / 'रस्टिक् / *adj* 1 देहाती, ग्राम्य : *rustic simplicity* 2 खुरदरी लकड़ी का बना हुआ, अपरिष्कृत : *a rustic bench*

▸ **rustic** *noun* (प्रायः *अपमा*) गँवार व्यक्ति।

rustle / 'रस्ल् / *verb* सरसराना (जैसे हवा चलने पर पत्तों की आवाज़) ▸ **rustle** *noun* सरसराहट : *the rustle of papers/leaves.*

rut / रट् / *noun* 1 (मुलायम भूमि पर) पहियों की लीक 2 नियत एवं निराश जीवन पद्धति : *I feel as though I'm stuck in a rut—I need a new job.* ■ **get into a rut** रूढ़िग्रस्त हो जाना।

ruthless / 'रूथ्लस् / *adj* (व्यक्ति या व्यवहार) निर्दय; क्रूर : *a ruthless dictator* ▸ **ruthlessly** *adv.*

rye / राई / *noun* राई (एक पौधा जिसका दाना पशुओं के आहार अथवा आटा या शराब बनाने में प्रयुक्त होता है) : *rye grass* ○ *rye bread.*

Ss

sabbath / 'सैबथ् / *noun* (प्रायः the Sabbath) [*sing*] (औप) विश्राम दिवस, जिस दिन विशेष प्रार्थना करते हैं (यहूदियों में शनिवार, ईसाइयों में रविवार)।

sable / 'सेब्ल् / *noun* एक छोटे से पशु की रोएँदार खाल जिससे कोट, ब्रश आदि बनाते है।

sabotage / 'सैबटाश् / *noun* तोड़-फोड़; जानबूझकर वाहन, मशीनरी, उपकरण आदि को पहुँचाई गई क्षति : *industrial sabotage* ▶ **sabotage** *verb* जानबूझकर क्षतिग्रस्त करना।

sabre (*US* **saber**) / 'सेबर् / *noun* तेग़, एक प्रकार की तलवार।

saccharin / 'सैकरिन् / *noun* एक अत्यंत मीठा पदार्थ जो कभी-कभी चीनी के बजाय प्रयोग किया जाता है।

sachet / 'सैशे; *US* सै'शे / *noun* प्लास्टिक या काग़ज़ का बंद छोटा लिफ़ाफ़ा जिसमें किसी वस्तु की थोड़ी मात्रा भरी हो : *a sachet of sugar/sauce/shampoo.*

sack[1] / सैक / *noun* 1 बोरा, बोरी : *plastic rubbish sacks* 2 (*US*) कोई भी थैला।

sack[2] / सैक् / *verb* (अनौप) किसी को नौकरी से निकाल देना : *be sacked for incompetence* ▶ **the sack** *noun* [*sing*] (अनौप) नौकरी से निकाले जाने का आदेश : *give sb/get the sack.*

sacrament / 'सैक्रमन्ट् / *noun* 1 ईसाई-चर्च का संस्कार-विशेष : *the sacrament of baptism* 2 **the sacrament** (**the Holy Sacrament** भी) [*sing*] (ईसाई धर्म में) यूकेरिस्ट की ब्रेड एवं शराब : *receive the sacrament* ▶ **sacramental** *adj.*

sacred / 'सेक्रिड् / *adj* 1 ईश्वर विषयक; धर्म संबंधी 2 **sacred** (**to sb**) पवित्र, पावन : *Her marriage is sacred to her.* 3 (औप) बहुत महत्त्वपूर्ण समझा जाने वाला : *regard sth as a sacred duty* ▶ **sacredness** *noun.*

sacrifice / 'सैक्रिफ़ाइस् / *noun* 1 त्याग, उत्सर्ग; बलिदान की गई वस्तु : *financial sacrifices* 2 **sacrifice** (**to sb**) बलिदान, यज्ञ; बलि चढ़ाई गई वस्तु; चढ़ावा : *kill a sheep as a sacrifice* ▶ **sacrifice** *verb* 1 **sacrifice sth** (**to/for sth**) त्याग/उत्सर्ग करना 2 **sacrifice to sb**; **sacrifice sth** (**to sb**) बलिदान करना, चढ़ाना : *They sacrificed a lamb (to the gods).*

sacrilege / 'सैक्रलिज् / *noun* (प्रायः *sing*) पवित्र (स्थान या वस्तु) का अपमान करना; अपवित्रीकरण ▶ **sacrilegious** / ˌसैक्र'लिजस् / *adj* : *Harming these animals is considered sacrilegious.*

sad / सैड् / *adj* (-dder, -ddest) 1 उदास, खिन्न मन : *a sad look* 2 बुरा, ख़राब; निंदनीय : *a sad state of affairs* ▶ **sadden** / 'सैड्न् / *verb* उदास कर देना **sadly** *adv* **sadness** *noun* 1 उदासी/खिन्नता 2 उदास करने वाली वस्तु।

saddle / 'सैड्ल् / *noun* 1 घुड़सवार की काठी, जीन 2 साइकिल/मोटर साइकिल की सीट ▶ **saddle** *verb* **saddle up; saddle sth** (**up**) घोड़े की जीन बाँधना/कसना ■ **saddle sb with sth** किसी को कोई भारी कार्य या उत्तरदायित्व, उसकी इच्छा के विपरीत, सौंप देना।

sadism / 'सेडिज़म् / *noun* किसी को मानसिक या शारीरिक पीड़ा पहुँचाने में या किसी को पीड़ा में देख कर आनंदित होने की प्रवृत्ति : *accusations of sadism in the treatment of prisoners* ▶ **sadist** / 'सेडिस्ट् / *noun* (व्यक्ति) जो किसी की पीड़ा देख खुश होता हो **sadistic** / स'डिस्-टिक् / *adj* परपीड़क, परपीड़नशील।

safari / स'फ़ारि / *noun* (*pl* **safaris**)

(विशेषत: पूर्वी अफ़्रीका में) वन्य पशुओं को देखने या उनका शिकार करने के लिए थल का लंबा सफ़र : be on a safari ▸ safari park noun वन्य पशुओं को देखने का स्थल जहाँ पर्यटक गाड़ियों के अंदर से उन्हें देखते हैं।

safe¹ / सेफ़ / adj (-r, -st) 1 safe (from sth/sb) सुरक्षित, निरापद 2 सही-सला-मत : The missing child was found safe. 3 भयरहित, निरापद 4 (व्यक्ति) सावधान, सुरक्षित काम करने वाला : a safe driver ▸ safely adv.

safe² / सेफ़ / noun सेफ़, तिजोरी।

safeguard / 'सेफ़गाई / noun safeguard (against sb/sth) बचाव, सुरक्षा : We made copies of our computer disks as a safeguard against accidents. ▸ safeguard verb सुरक्षा करना/बचाना।

safe keeping / सेफ़ 'कीपिङ् / noun देख-भाल, संरक्षण।

safety / 'सेफ़्टि / noun सुरक्षा : I'm worried about the safety of the children. ▸ safety pin noun सेफ़्टिपिन, बकसुआ।

saffron / 'सैफ़्रन् / noun केसर, जाफ़रान ▸ saffron adj नारंगी-पीला : saffron robes.

sag / सैग् / verb (-gg-) 1 बीच से झुक जाना; दबाव के कारण लटक जाना, झोल पड़ जाना : a sagging roof 2 धसक जाना, कमज़ोर पड़ जाना : morale began to sag ▸ saggy adj.

saga / 'सागा / noun 1 लंबी वीरगाथा 2 लंबी, घटनाओं से भरपूर कहानी; आ-ख्यान : Do you want to hear the latest episode in our house-hunt-ing saga?

sage / सेज् / noun मुनि; बुद्धिमान व्यक्ति ▸ sage adj (औप) बुद्धिमान/मनीषी।

Sagittarius / सैजि'टेअरिअस् / noun राशिचक्र की नौवीं राशि; धनु राशि; इस राशि का व्यक्ति।

sail¹ / सेल् / noun 1 नौका का पाल 2 समुद्री सैर : go for a sail 3 पवनचक्की के फट्टे जो हवा चलने पर चक्की को घुमाते हैं ■ set sail (from/to/for...) यात्रा प्रारंभ करना।

sail² / सेल् / verb 1 पाल के सहारे (या इंजिन शक्ति से) पानी में आगे बढ़ना 2 समुद्री यात्रा करना 3 किसी दिशा में आसानी और विश्वास के साथ आगे बढ़ना : clouds sailing across the sky.

sailor / 'सेलर / noun नाविक ■ a good/bad sailor तूफ़ानी समुद्र में भी बीमार न पड़ने वाला (या विपरीत) व्यक्ति।

saint / सेन्ट् / noun 1 (संक्षि St) ईसाई चर्च द्वारा घोषित महान एवं पवित्र व्यक्ति, संत : the gospel of St John 2 संत, धर्मात्मा/पवित्रात्मा ▸ sainthood noun saintly adj संत जैसा; साधु saintliness noun.

sake / सेक् / noun ■ for the sake of sb/sth; for sb's/sth's sake के लिए, के हित के लिए for the sake of sth/doing sth कुछ रखने या पाने हेतु : We made concessions for the sake of peace.

salad / 'सैलड् / noun सलाद।

salary / 'सैलरि / noun (pl salaries) वेतन, तनख्वाह।

sale / सेल् / noun 1 बिक्री, बेचना : the sale of cars 2 sales [pl] बिक्री की मात्रा : increased sales of ice-cream 3 सस्ते दामों पर बिक्री, सेल : hold an end-of-season sale 4 नीलामी ▸ sale-able / 'सेलब्ल् / adj बिकाऊ; बिक्री योग्य : not in a saleable condition

salesman noun (fem **saleswoman**) (pl **salesmen; saleswomen**) (दुकान पर) बेचने वाला कार्यकर्ता; बिक्री बढ़ाने के लिए नियुक्त व्यक्ति, विक्रय कला में कुशल **salesmanship** noun विक्रय कला, बेचने की कुशलता।

salient / 'सेलिअन्ट / *adj* प्रमुख, सहज में ही दिखाई पड़ जाने वाला : *all the salient features of the new design.*

saline / 'सेलाइन; US 'सेलीन / *adj* (औप) रासायनिक नमक से भरा हुआ; नमकीन : *a saline lake ○ use a saline solution for cleaning contact lenses* ▸ **salinity** / स 'लिनिटि / *noun.*

saliva / स 'लाइवा / *noun* थूक, लार ▸ **salivary** / स 'लाइव़रि, 'सैलिव़रि; US 'सैलव़ेरि / *adj* : *the salivary glands*

salivate / 'सेलिवेट् / *verb* (औप) थूक बनना/उत्पन्न करना, टपकाना : *The smell of food cooking made him salivate.*

sallow / 'सैलो / *adj* (व्यक्ति की त्वचा या चेहरा) पीला और अस्वस्थ ▸ **sallowness** *noun.*

salmon / 'सैमन् / *noun* (*pl* अपरिवर्तित) एक बड़ी, चमकीली मछली।

saloon / स 'लून् / *noun* 1 जहाज़ आदि का बड़ा कमरा, बैठक 2 (**saloon car** भी) चार दरवाज़ों वाली बड़ी गाड़ी 3 प्रयोजन विशेष के लिए सार्वजनिक स्थान : *a billiard-saloon* 4 बार, शराबख़ाना।

salt / सॉल्ट् / *noun* 1 (**common salt** भी) नमक 2 (*रसा*) लवण, साल्ट : *mineral salts* 3 **salts** [*pl*] स्वाद या रूप में नमक जैसी वस्तु ▸ **salt** *verb* 1 खाने में नमक डालना 2 नमक डाल कर सुरक्षित रखना : *salted beef/pork* **salty** *adj* (**-ier, -iest**) 1 नमकीन, लवणयुक्त 2 (बातचीत) लच्छेदार।

salubrious / स 'लूब्रिअस्/ *adj* (औप) (आसपास का वातावरण) स्वास्थ्यवर्धक; स्वच्छ : *the less salubrious parts of town.*

salutary / 'सैल्यट्रि; US 'सैल्यटेरि / *adj* (शरीर और मन पर) अच्छा प्रभाव डालने वाला, हितकर : *a salutary lesson/experience.*

salute / स 'लूट / *noun* सलाम, अभि- वादन : *fire a ten-gun salute* ▸ **salute** *verb* 1 सलाम करना, अभिवादन करना 2 (औप) किसी व्यक्ति या उसकी उपलब्धियों की प्रशंसा करना : *salute sb's courage.*

salvage / 'सैल्व़िज्/ *noun* नष्ट हुए जहाज़ एवं उसके सामान को समुद्र से हटाना; (आग या अन्य तबाही से) नष्ट होने से बचाना; इस प्रकार बचाई गई संपत्ति : *Salvage of the wreck was delayed by bad weather.* ▸ **salvage** *verb* **salvage sth (from sth)** 1 आग आदि से संपत्ति को बचाना 2 किसी को संकट से बचाना।

salvation / सैल् 'व़ेश्न्/ *noun* 1 (धर्म) मुक्ति, मोक्ष : *pray for the salvation of the world* 2 रक्षा, बचाव : *Music is my salvation.*

same¹ / सेम्/ *adj* 1 **the same sb/sth (as sb/sth/that...)** वही, वैसा ही : *We have lived in the same house for twenty years.* 2 **the same sb/sth (as sb/sth/that...)** पूर्व उल्लिखित के बिलकुल समान : *I saw the same shoes last week.* ■ **amount to/come to/be the same thing** एक समान परिणाम/अर्थ आदि रखना/होना **at the same time** 1 एक ही समय 2 फिर भी **be all in the same boat** एक-सी परिस्थिति में होना; एक-से ख़तरों का सामना करना : *She and I are in the same boat—we both failed the exam.* **in the same breath** कुछ बात कहने के तुरंत बाद ही उसके ठीक विपरीत बात कहना : *He praised my work and in the same breath told me I would have to leave.*

same² / सेम् / *pron* वही (बातें, चीज़ें, रंग, आकार आदि) : *He and I said the same.* ■ **all the same** फिर भी।

sample / 'साम्प्ल्; US 'सैम्प्ल् / *noun* 1 नमूना 2 नमूने के तौर पर दी गई वस्तु : *a sample sachet* ▸ **sample** *verb* नमूना लेना/परीक्षण करना।

sanatorium /सैन्'टॉरिअम्/ noun (pl **sanatoriums** या **sanatoria**) (US **sanitarium, sanatarium** /सैन्'टेअरि-अम्; सैन्'टेरिअम्/) लंबी बीमारी से पीड़ित रोगियों के उपचार या स्वास्थ्य-लाभ के लिए अस्पताल जैसी जगह।

sanctify /'सैङ्क्टिफ़ाइ/ verb (pt, pp **sanctified**) 1 पवित्र करना, पापमुक्त करना 2 किसी चीज़ को नियमानुकूल, वैध सिद्ध करना, औचित्य सिद्ध करना : a practice sanctified by tradition ▸ **sanctification** noun.

sanctimonious /सैङ्क्टि'मोनिअस्/ adj (अपमा) जो खुद को नैतिकता में दूसरों से श्रेष्ठ समझे; पाखंडी : a sanctimonious smile/voice/newspaper editorial ▸ **sanctimoniously** adv **sanctimoniousness** noun.

sanction /'सैङ्क्श्न्/ noun 1 (औप) अधिकारियों द्वारा कार्यविशेष करने की अनुज्ञा या अनुमति, अनुज्ञप्ति : The book was translated without the sanction of the author. 2 **sanction (against** sth) दंड, सज़ा 3 (प्रायः pl) **sanctions (against sb)** किसी देश को अंतर्राष्ट्रीय क़ानून मानने को बाध्य करना : lift economic sanctions ▸ **sanction** verb मंजूरी देना, समर्थन करना।

sanctity /'सैङ्क्टटि/ noun पवित्रता, पुनीतता : believe in the sanctity of life.

sanctuary /'सैङ्क्चुअरी; US'सैङ्क्चु-एरि/ noun (pl **sanctuaries**) 1 मंदिर, पुण्य स्थान 2 शरण स्थान 3 पशु-पक्षियों का निर्भय घूमने का स्थान; अभयारण्य : a bird sanctuary.

sand /सैन्ड्/ noun 1 बालू, रेत 2 (प्रायः pl) समुद्र की रेतीली भूमि, बालूतट ▸ **sand** verb 1 **sand** sth **(down)** रेगमाल आदि से लकड़ी को चिकना करना 2 किसी सतह पर रेत डालना **sandpaper** noun रेगमाल **sandstone** noun बलुआ पत्थर **sandy**

adj (-ier, -iest) 1 बालुकामय, रेतीला 2 बालों की ललाई।

sandal /'सैन्ड्ल्/ noun सैंडल, चप्पल।

sandwich /'सैन्विज़्; 'सैन्विच्/ noun सैंडविच ▸ **sandwich** verb ▪ **sandwich** sb/sth **between** sb/sth दो व्यक्तियों या वस्तुओं के बीच किसी को दबाना/रखना ।

sane /सेन्/ adj (-r, -st) 1 स्वस्थचित्त, प्रकृतिस्थ 2 समझदार, विवेकी : a sane person/decision ▸ **sanely** adv.

sanguine /'सैङ्ग्विन्/ adj **sanguine (about** sth) (औप) आशापूर्ण, आश्वस्त : She remained sanguine about our chances of success.

sanitary /'सैन्टरि; US'सैन्टेरि/ adj 1 रोगजनक धूलि से रहित; स्वास्थ्यकर 2 स्वास्थ्य रक्षा, सफ़ाई आदि से संबंधित : sanitary ware/regulations.

sanitation /सैनि'टेश्न्/ noun सफ़ाई व्यवस्था ।

sanity /'सैनटि/ noun 1 मानसिक संतुलन 2 समझदारी : try to restore some sanity to a ridiculous situation.

sap¹ /सैप्/ noun पेड़-पौधों का रस ▸ **sappy** adj.

sap² /सैप्/ verb (-pp-) **sap** sb/ sth **(of** sth) धीरे-धीरे नष्ट करना या दुर्बल करना : The long trek sapped our energy.

sapling /'सैपलिङ्/ noun पौधा।

sapphire /'सैफ़ाइअर्/ noun नीलम, नील-मणि ▸ **sapphire** adj चमकदार नीला।

sarcasm /'सार्कैज़म्/ noun ताना, व्यंग्यपूर्ण टिप्पणी, कटाक्ष : bitter sarcasm ▸ **sarcastic** /सार्'कैस्टिक्/ adj व्यंग्यपूर्ण : sarcastic comments.

sardine /सार्'डीन्/ noun सार्डीन (छोटी मछली)।

sash /सैश्/ noun कंधे से कमर तक पहुँचने वाला लंबे कपड़े का टुकड़ा, कमरबंद।

Satan / 'सेटन् / noun शैतान ▸ **satanic** adj शैतानी; दुष्टतापूर्ण।

satchel / 'सैचल् / noun बच्चों की किताबें रखने का बस्ता।

satellite / 'सैटलाइट् / noun 1 उपग्रह : a weather satellite 2 प्राकृतिक उपग्रह : The moon is the Earth's satellite. 3 अनुचर देश या संघ; अन्य (अधिक शक्तिशाली) देश/संघ द्वारा नियंत्रित देश/संघ।

satiate / 'सेशिएट् / verb (औप) तृप्त करना, अघाना; छकना/छकाना : feel satiated after Christmas dinner ▸ **satiation** noun.

satin / 'सैटिन्; US 'सैटन् / noun साटन (एक रेशम जैसा चिकना चमकदार कपड़ा)।

satire / 'सैटाइअर् / noun 1 व्यंग्य करने की कला : political satire 2 satire (on sb/sth) व्यंग्य रचना, प्रहसन ▸ **satirical** (satiric भी) adj व्यंग्यपूर्ण, व्यंग्यात्मक **satirize, -ise** verb उपहास करना, व्यंग्य करना : famous personalities satirized in comedy shows.

satisfaction / ,सैटिस् 'फ़ैक्शन् / noun 1 **satisfaction (at/with sth)** संतोष, संतुष्टि : She can look back on her career with great satisfaction. 2 **satisfaction of sth** संतुष्ट करना; तृप्त करना : the satisfaction of one's goals.

satisfactory / सैटिस् 'फ़ैक्टरि / adj प्रियकर, संतोषजनक; यथेष्ट : a satisfactory meal.

satisfy / 'सैटिस्फ़ाइ / verb (pt, pp **satisfied**) 1 संतुष्ट करना, तृप्त करना : Nothing satisfies him. 2 आवश्यकताओं, इच्छाओं की पूर्ति करना; आवश्यकता के लिए पर्याप्त होना : satisfy sb's hunger 3 क़ायल करना, संदेह दूर कर देना ▸ **satisfied** adj संतुष्ट।

saturate / 'सैचरेट् / verb 1 तर करना, संतृप्त करना : The continuous heavy rain had saturated the fields.

2 **saturate sth/sb (with/in sth)** सराबोर करना ▸ **saturated** adj संतृप्त/सराबोर।

Saturday / 'सैटर्डे / noun (संक्षि Sat) शनिवार।

Saturn / 'सैटर्न् / noun शनि-ग्रह।

satyr / 'सैटर् / noun (ग्रीक और रोमन कथाओं में) आधा मानव आधा पशु रूप वन देवता।

sauce / सॉस् / noun 1 सॉस, चटनी 2 (अनौप) रूखा/अभद्र व्यवहार ▸ **saucy** / 'सॉसि / adj (-ier, -iest) अविनीत, अभद्र : a saucy comedian/answer.

saucepan / 'सॉस्पन्; US 'सॉस्पैन् / noun डेगची (भोजन बनाने का एक बरतन)।

saucer / 'सॉसर् / noun 1 तश्तरी जिस पर प्रायः प्याला रखा जाता है 2 तश्तरीनुमा वस्तु, डिश।

sauna / 'सॉना; US 'साउना / noun भापस्नान; इसके लिए बना स्नानघर : have a sauna ○ sit in the sauna.

saunter / 'सॉन्टर् / verb टहलना, चहलक़दमी करना : saunter down the road ▸ **saunter** noun चहलक़दमी।

sausage / 'सॉसिज् / noun गुलमा, लंगोचा।

savage / 'सैविज् / adj 1 असभ्य, जंगली/बर्बर : savage criticism/fight 2 उग्र, प्रचंड; क्रूर ▸ **savage** noun 1 क्रूर व्यक्ति, 2 (अप्र) असभ्य/जंगली जाति।

save / सेव् / verb 1 **save sb/sth (from sth/doing sth)** सुरक्षा करना, बचाना : save sb's life 2 **save sth (for sb/sth)** भविष्य के लिए बचाकर रखना, सुरक्षित रखना 3 **save (on) sth** बचाना, परिहार करना; अनावश्यक वस्तु पर ख़र्च न करना : save money on decorating by doing it yourself 4 **save (sth) (up) (for sth)** भविष्य में प्रयोग के लिए धन जमा करना, विशेषतः कुछ ख़रीदने के लिए : save money for a house 5 (कंप्यूटर में) प्रोग्राम को सुरक्षित रखने का निर्देश देना

6 **save sb (from sth)** मोक्ष दिलाना, पापमुक्त करना।

saving / 'सेविङ् / noun (विशेषत: pl) बचत : achieve big savings on fuel through greater efficiency.

saviour (US **savior**) / 'सेव्यर् / noun 1 बचाने वाला, मुक्तिदाता; परित्राता : hailed as the saviour of the club 2 **the Saviour, Our Saviour** ईसा मसीह।

savour (US **savor**) / 'सेवर् / noun (प्राय: sing) स्वाद-सुगंध; मज़ा, रस : soup with a slight savour of garlic ▸ **savour** verb 1 स्वाद/मज़ा लेना 2 किसी अनुभव का आनंद उठाना ■ **savour of sth** इंगित करना, सुझाव देना : Her attitude savours of hypocrisy.

savoury (US **savory**) / 'सेवरि / adj 1 (खाना) नमकीन या तीखे, न कि मीठे, स्वाद का : a savoury sauce 2 सुगंधित, स्वादिष्ट 3 नैतिकता के आधार पर स्वीकार्य या आदरणीय : not a very savoury topic for discussion.

saw / सॉ / noun (प्राय: समासों में) आरा/ आरी, करौंत : cutting logs with a power saw ▸ **saw** verb (pt **sawed**; pp **sawn**) आरी से काटना/चीरना **sawdust** noun लकड़ी का बुरादा **sawmill** noun आरा घरा।

saxophone / 'सैक्सफ़ोन् / noun (अनौप sax भी) सैक्सोफ़ोन, एक प्रकार का बाजा।

say[1] / से / verb (3rd pers sing pres t **says** / सेज़्/; pt, pp **said** / सेड्/) 1 **say sth (to sb)** कहना, बोलना 2 दोहराना (सीखी हुई बात को) : say a short prayer 3 विचार व्यक्त करना : say what you like 4 कोई सूचना या निर्देश देना : a notice saying 'Keep Out' ■ **go without saying** स्पष्ट होना : It goes without saying that I'll help you. **let us say** हमें कहने दो **never say die** (कहा) कभी आशा न छोड़ना **that is to**

say अर्थात्, दूसरे शब्दों में **to say the least** बिना अतिशयोक्ति किए।

say[2] / से / noun [sing] **say (in sth)** मत व्यक्त करने या भाग लेने का अधिकार : have no say (in a matter) ■ **have one's say** अपना मत स्पष्ट रूप से व्यक्त करना : Thank you for your comments. Now let somebody else have their say.

saying / 'सेइङ् / noun सामान्य कथन; लोकोक्ति/कहावत।

scab / स्कैब् / noun 1 भरते हुए घाव पर जमने वाली पपड़ी, खुरंड 2 पामा 3 (अपमा) हड़ताल में भाग न लेने वाला कर्मचारी : scab labour ▸ **scabby** adj खुजली/ खुरंड से पूर्ण, पपड़ीदार : scabby hands.

scabbard / 'स्कैबई / noun तलवार आदि की म्यान।

scabies / 'स्केबीज़ / noun खाज, खुजली।

scaffold / 'स्कैफ़ोल्ड् / noun 1 फाँसी का तख़्ता : die on the scaffold 2 टिकटी; मंच, पाड़ : a scaffold bridge ▸ **scaffolding** noun टिकटी/मंच आदि।

scald / स्कॉल्ड् / verb 1 (गरम द्रव या भाप से) शरीर के किसी अंग का जल जाना : scald one's hand (with hot fat) 2 दूध को लगभग उबलने तक गरम करना ▸ **scald** noun गरम द्रव या भाप से जलने से उत्पन्न दाह **scalding** adj.

scale[1] / स्केल् / noun 1 (प्राय: sing) अनुमाप, सापेक्षिक आकार/व्यापकता आदि : Here was corruption on a grand scale. 2 माप, मापक्रम : a scale of fees/ charges 3 स्केल, पैमाना; माप के निश्चित चिह्न : This ruler has one scale in centimetres and another in inches. 4 अनुपात (जैसे मानचित्र में) : a scale of ten kilometres to the centimetre 5 (संगीत) सरगम, स्वरक्रम ▸ **scale** verb ■ **scale sth down/up** विशेष अनुपात से घटाना/बढ़ाना : the scaling down of military forces.

scale² / स्केल् / *verb* खड़ी चीज़ (जैसे दीवार या चट्टान) पर चढ़ना।

scale³ / स्केल् / *noun* 1 कवच, शल्क : *scrape the scales from a mackerel* 2 बरतनों पर या पाइप में जमी पपड़ी, परत 3 दाँतों पर जम जाने वाली सख़्त पपड़ी ▸ **scaly** *adj*.

scale⁴ / स्केल् / *noun* 1 [*pl*] तुला, तराज़ू 2 तराज़ू के पल्ले।

scalp / स्कैल्प् / *noun* 1 सिर की खाल 2 सिर की खाल एवं बाल ▸ **scalp** *verb* सिर की खाल उतारना : (अलं, अनौप) *He'll scalp me if he finds me here!*

scalpel / 'स्कैल्पल् / *noun* सर्जन का चाकू।

scam / स्कैम् / *noun* (अनौप) घोटाला : *a currency scam.*

scamp / स्कैम्प् / *noun* शरारती बच्चा।

scamper / 'स्कैम्पर् / *verb* (अक्सर बच्चे या छोटे जानवर के लिए प्रयुक्त) (डर या उत्तेजना से) दौड़ना, चौकड़ी भरना : *The rabbit scampered away in fright.*

scan / स्कैन् / *verb* (-nn-) 1 ध्यानपूर्वक देखना, ध्यान से परीक्षण करना : *He scanned the horizon for any sign of land.* 2 किसी काग़ज़-पत्र आदि को सरसरी तौर पर देखना 3 (चिकि) परीक्षण के लिए शरीर के अंगों के चित्रों को देखना (कंप्यूटर या अल्ट्रा-साउंड तकनीक द्वारा) ▸ **scan** *noun* निरीक्षण/परीक्षण का कार्य।

scandal / 'स्कैन्ड्ल् / *noun* 1 कलंक, बुरा उदाहरण : *attempts to hush up the scandal* 2 बदनामी, लोकनिंदा : *spread scandal* ▸ **scandalize, -ise** / 'स्कैन्ड-लाइज़्/ *verb* बुरा काम करके विक्षुब्ध करना **scandalous** *adj* 1 विक्षोभकारी, आघात पहुँचाने वाला : *scandalous behaviour* 2 निंदात्मक।

scant / स्कैन्ट् / *adj* (औप) अत्यल्प, अ-पर्याप्त : *pay scant attention to sb's advice.*

scanty / 'स्कैन्टि / *adj* अल्पमात्रा में, थोड़ा ▸ **scantily** *adv* : *scantily dressed.*

scapegoat / 'स्केप्गोट् / *noun* बलि का बकरा, दूसरों की ग़लतियों और अपराध का दंड भुगतने वाला।

scar / स्कार् / *noun* 1 दाग़, चोट का निशान 2 किसी अप्रिय घटना के बाद की शोकग्रस्तता या अपराध-भावना : *the scars of war* 3 पहाड़ी पर ऐसी जगह जहाँ सिर्फ़ नंगी चट्टान हो, घास आदि न हो ▸ **scar** *verb* (-rr-) दाग़/निशान छोड़ देना; निशान से अंकित करना : *a face scarred by acne.*

scarce / स्केअर्स् / *adj* (-er, -est) 1 विरला, सामान्यतया अप्राप्त : *Food soon became scarcer and more expensive.* 2 दुर्लभ : *scarce resources* ▸ **scarcity** / 'स्केअर्सटि / *noun* कमी, अभाव; दुर्लभता : *frequent scarcities of raw materials.*

scarcely / 'स्केअर्सलि / *adv* 1 बहुत ही कम, नहीं के बराबर : *I scarcely know him.* 2 बस थोड़ी देर पहले ही 3 निश्चित रूप से नहीं।

scare / स्केअर् / *verb* 1 डराना, भयभीत करना : *That noise scared me.* 2 भय-भीत हो जाना : *He scares easily.* ▸ **scare** *noun* आतंक, संत्रास **scare-crow** *noun* बिजूका, डरावा, खेत में कपड़े से लिपटा डंडा जिसे आदमी समझ कर पक्षी खेत में नहीं आते हैं **scared** *adj* **scared (of sb/sth); scared (of doing sth/to do sth)** भयभीत।

scarf / स्कार्फ़् / *noun* (*pl* **scarfs** या **scarves** / स्कार्व्ज़् /) स्कार्फ़, दुपट्टा।

scarlet / 'स्कार्लट् / *adj, noun* लाल, सिंदूरी : *scarlet flowers.*

scathing / 'स्केदिड्ग् / *adj* **scathing (about sb/sth)** (आलोचना आदि) कठोर, सख़्त; तिरस्कार या उपहास से भरा हुआ : *The report was scathing about the lack of safety precautions.*

scatter / 'स्कैटर् / *verb* 1 तितर-बितर

करना : *The crowd scattered.* 2 छित-
राना, इधर-उधर बिखेरना/बिखर जाना :
scatter seed (over the ground)
▶ **scatter (scattering** भी) *noun* बिखरा
हुआ सामान **scattered** *adj* बिखरा पड़ा,
असंबद्ध : *a few scattered settle-
ments.*

scavenge /'स्कैविन्ज़्/ *verb* 1 **scavenge (for sth)** (पशु या पक्षी का) खाने के
लिए (सड़ा हुआ) मांस ढूँढ़ना : *a crow
scavenging for carrion* 2 **scavenge (for) sth** किसी व्यक्ति का कूड़ा-
कबार से व्यवहार करने के लिए सामान
निकालना : *tramps scavenging
through dustbins.*

scenario / स'नारिओ; *US* स'नैरिओ /
noun (*pl* **scenarios**) 1 **scenario
(for sb/sth)** भावी घटनाओं का कल्पित
क्रम : *The worst scenario would be
closure of the factory.* 2 पटकथा,
फ़िल्म का दृश्यविधान।

scene / सीन् / *noun* 1 (प्राय: *sing*)
घटनास्थल : *the scene of the accident*
2 वास्तविक घटना, दृश्य, देखी हुई वस्तु :
*the horrific scenes after the earth-
quake* 3 दृश्य, चित्र 4 (प्राय: *sing*)
रंगमंच पर सचित्र परदा/मंचसज्जा : *The
scene is set in Normandy.* 5 (प्राय:
sing) भावनाओं या क्रोध का प्रदर्शन :
make a scene 6 फ़िल्म या नाटक में
घटनाक्रम : *a love scene* ■ **behind the
scenes** 1 नेपथ्य में, परदे के पीछे 2 गुप्त
रूप से : *political deals done behind
the scenes.*

scenery /'सीनरि / *noun* 1 प्राकृतिक
दृश्य : *mountain scenery* 2 मंचसज्जा।

scenic /'सीनिक् / *adj* प्राकृतिक सुंदरता;
सुरम्य : *the scenic splendours of the
Himalayas* ▶ **scenically** *adv* प्राकृतिक
रूप से।

scent / सेन्ट् / *noun* 1 गंध, सुगंध; गंध-
विशेष : *a delicate scent of lavender*

2 (प्राय: *द्रव*) इत्र 3 (प्राय: *sing*) गंध जिसे
कुत्ता अपनी प्राणशक्ति से सूंघकर पीछा करता
है : *Hounds hunt by scent.* 4 **scent
of sth** सुराग़, सूत्र : *a scent of danger/
fear* ▶ **scent** *verb* 1 गंध से पहचान
लेना, खोज लेना : *The dog scented a
rat.* 2 भाँप लेना, ताड़ जाना : *scent a
crime* 3 **scent sth (with sth)** सुगंधित
करना।

sceptic (*US* **skeptic**) /'स्केप्टिक् /
noun 1 संशयवादी, विशेषत: धार्मिक
धारणाओं को असत्य मानने वाला व्यक्ति
2 जो किसी कथन, दावे आदि की सत्यता
पर संदेह करता है ▶ **sceptical** (*US*
skeptical) *adj* संशय में : *I'm rather
sceptical about his chances of winning.* **scepticism** *noun* संशयवाद।

sceptre (*US* **scepter**) /'सेप्ट्र् / *noun*
राजदंड, अधिकार का प्रतीक चिह्न।

schedule /'शेड्यूल्; *US* 'स्केजूल् /
noun 1 योजना-कार्यसूची; समयसारणी
2 समझौते के बिंदुओं की सूची : *Schedule
4 of the Companies Act* ▶ **schedule** *verb* **schedule sth (for sth)**
कार्यसूची में शामिल करना, किसी चीज़ का
समय-विशेष पर आयोजन करना : *a sched-
uled flight.*

scheme /स्कीम्/ *noun* 1 **scheme (for
sth/to do sth)** कार्ययोजना 2 विन्यास,
सुनियोजित व्यवस्था : *a coordinated
lighting scheme* ▶ **scheme** *verb*
षड्यंत्र रचना : *rebels scheming against
their leader.*

schizophrenia / स्किट्स'फ़्रीनिआ /
noun (*चिकि*) मानसिक बीमारी जिसमें
रोगी अपने व्यक्तित्व के बारे में भ्रमित होकर
काल्पनिक दुनिया में खो जाता है ▶ **schizophrenic** /स्किट्स'फ़्रेनिक् / *noun, adj*
इस रोग से पीड़ित : *a schizophrenic
personality* ○ *She was diagnosed
a schizophrenic while at university.*

scholar / 'स्कॉलर् / noun 1 छात्रवृत्ति पाने वाला विद्यार्थी 2 विद्वान, पंडित : *a Greek/ history scholar* ▶ **scholarly** adj 1 विद्याध्ययन से संबंधित 2 पांडित्यपूर्ण, विद्वत्पूर्ण।

scholarship / 'स्कॉलरशिप् / noun 1 छात्रवृत्ति 2 विद्वता, पांडित्य।

scholastic/ स्कॅ'लैस्टिक्/adj 1 (औप) शैक्षिक : *one's scholastic achievements* 2 शास्त्रीय, पंडिताऊ।

school[1] / स्कूल / noun 1 स्कूल, पाठ- शाला; स्कूल भवन 2 विषय-विशेष का अध्ययन केंद्र : *art/drama school* 3 अध्ययन करने/शिक्षा प्राप्त करने की प्रक्रिया 4 समान विचारधारा, सिद्धांतों वाले लेखकों, कलाकारों का वर्ग : *the Mathura school of painting* ■ **a school of thought** विचारधारा-विशेष मानने वाला वर्ग ▶ **school** verb **school sb/oneself/sth (in sth)** प्रशिक्षित करना, दीक्षित करना **schoolfellow, school friend, schoolmate** nouns सहपाठी, स्कूल का मित्र।

school[2] / स्कूल / noun मछलियों का झुंड।

science / 'साइअन्स् / noun 1 विज्ञान 2 विज्ञान की शाखा-विशेष : *medical science ○ computer science* ▶ **scientist** noun वैज्ञानिक।

scientific/साइअन्'टिफ़िक्/adj 1 विज्ञान संबंधी, वैज्ञानिक : *a scientific discovery* 2 विज्ञान-सम्मत : *scientific farming.*

scissors / 'सिज़र्ज़ / noun [pl] कैंची : *a pair of scissors.*

scoff / स्कॉफ़् / verb **scoff (at sb/sth)** ताना मारना, उपहास करना : *scoff at other people's beliefs* ▶ **scoffer** noun.

scold / स्कोल्ड / verb **scold sb (for sth/doing sth)** डाँटना, झिड़कना।

scone / स्कॉन्; स्कोन् / noun छोटा केक, प्रायः मक्खन या क्रीम और जैम के साथ खाने के लिए।

scoop / स्कूप् / noun 1 बेलचा; कलछी 2 अख़बारों द्वारा उछाली गई महत्त्वपूर्ण या उत्तेजक ख़बर : *a royal scoop* 3 विशाल धनराशि या लाभ ▶ **scoop** verb 1 कलछी से उठाना या निकालना 2 **scoop sth (out)** बेलचे से गड्ढा करना : *scoop a hole in the sand* 3 शत्रु/प्रतिद्वंद्वी से पहले ही ख़बर सार्वजनिक करना 4 विशाल लाभ/राशि कमाना/पाना।

scooter / 'स्कूटर् / noun 1 स्कूटर (एक प्रकार की मोटर साइकिल) 2 बच्चे की L आकार की गाड़ी।

scope / स्कोप् / noun 1 **scope (for sth/ to do sth)** कुछ करने/प्राप्त करने का अवसर, गुंजाइश 2 कार्यक्षेत्र, व्याप्ति/ विस्तार : *Their powers are rather limited in scope.*

scorch / स्कॉर्च / verb 1 झुलसाना : *scorch one's fingers* 2 झुलस जाना।

score[1] /स्कॉर्/ noun 1 खिलाड़ी आदि के प्राप्तांकों का लेखा : *a high/low score* 2 परीक्षा के प्राप्तांक : *a score of 120 in the IQ test* 3 (pl अपरिवर्तित) 20 का समूह/सेट : *a score of people* 4 **scores** [pl] बहुत सारे : *Scores of people were fainting in the heat.* ■ **on that/ this score** उस/इस बात पर : *You don't have to worry on that score.*

score[2] / स्कॉर् / verb 1 (खेल में) उतने अंक पाना : *Joginder scored two goals before half-time.* 2 अंकों का लेखा-जोखा रखना 3 परीक्षा में अंक प्राप्त करना 4 सफलता पाना : *The movie scored an instant success.*

scorn / स्कॉर्न् / noun **scorn (for sth/ sb)** घृणा, अवज्ञा, अपमान ▶ **scorn** verb 1 तिरस्कार करना, अनादरपूर्वक आचरण करना : *scorn sb's efforts* 2 कहा ठुक- राना, (करने से) मना करना : *scorn sb's invitation/advice* **scornful** adj घृणा/ अवज्ञा भरा **scornfully** adv.

Scorpio / 'स्कॉर्पिओ / noun राशिचक्र

की आठवीं राशि; वृश्चिक; इस राशि में पैदा हुआ व्यक्ति।

scorpion / 'स्कॉर्पिअन् / noun बिच्छू।

scot-free / ‚स्कॉट्'फ़्री / adv बिना कोई दंड पाए : They escaped scot-free because of lack of evidence.

scoundrel / 'स्काउन्ड्रल् / noun (अप्र) दुष्ट, बदमाश।

scour / 'स्काउअर् / verb 1 scour sth (out) माँजना, रगड़ कर चमकाना : scour the pots and pans 2 (पानी, नदी आदि के) बहते रहने से गहरी खाई का बनना ▸ scourer noun माँजने में प्रयुक्त नायलॉन आदि का टुकड़ा।

scourge / स्कर्ज् / noun 1 (पूर्व में) दंड देने के लिए प्रयुक्त कोड़ा 2 (प्राय: sing) महाविपत्ति, अनर्थ का कारण व्यक्ति/ वस्तु : the scourge of war/disease ▸ scourge verb (अप्र) कोड़े मारना।

scout / स्काउट् / noun 1 स्काउट, बालचर 2 गुप्तचर, भेदिया (व्यक्ति/वायुयान आदि) ▸ scout verb (अनौप) ▪ scout around/about (for sb/sth) कुछ खोजने के लिए इधर-उधर देखना।

scowl / स्काउल् / noun त्योरी ▸ scowl verb scowl (at sb/sth) त्योरी चढ़ाना, नाक-भौं सिकोड़ना : The receptionist scowled at me.

Scrabble / 'स्क्रैबल् / noun (ट्रेडमार्क) अक्षरों को जोड़कर शब्द बनाने का एक खेल।

scrabble / 'स्क्रैबल् / verb 1 scrabble (about) (for sth) अव्यवस्थित ढंग से अँगुलियों से किसी ऐसी चीज़ को ढूँढ़ना जो दिखाई न पड़ रही हो : She scrabbled in her bag for her spectacles. 2 आवाज़ करते हुए खरोंचना : mice scrabbling behind the skirting board 3 ज़मीन को संतुलन बनाए रखने के लिए खरोंचना : The children were scrabbling up the slope.

scraggy / 'स्क्रैगि / adj (अपमा) इतना पतला कि हड्डियाँ दिखाई पड़ें; मरियल : a scraggy neck.

scramble / 'स्क्रैम्बल् / verb 1 जल्दी से हाथ-पैर के बल चढ़ना, रेंगना : The girl scrambled over the wall. 2 scramble (for sth) छीना-झपटी करना 3 वस्तुओं को मिला देना, क्रम ख़राब कर देना 4 अंडे को तोड़ कर सफ़ेद एवं पीला भाग एक साथ मिलाकर पकाना : scrambled eggs on toast ▸ scramble noun [sing] 1 रेंगना 2 scramble (for sth) छीना-झपटी।

scrap¹ / स्क्रैप् / noun 1 कतरन, टुकड़ा : scraps of paper/cloth 2 scraps [pl] खाने की बची जूठन 3 रद्दी माल, कूड़ा-करकट 4 ज़रा-सी मात्रा : There's not a scrap of truth in the claim. ▸ scrap verb (-pp-) रद्दी करके फेंक देना scrap iron noun लोहा और इस्पात की रद्दी चीज़ें (गलाने के लिए)।

scrap² / स्क्रैप् / noun scrap (with sb) (अनौप) झगड़ा : get into a scrap ▸ scrap verb (-pp-) scrap (with sb) झगड़ा करना।

scrape¹ / स्क्रेप् / verb 1 रगड़ या घिस कर बराबर करना/चिकना करना 2 scrape sth from/off sth रगड़ कर मिट्टी या पेंट खरोंचना : scrape away the top layer 3 scrape sth (against/on/along sth) खरोंचना, खरोंच कर चोट पहुँचाना 4 scrape sth (out) खोदना : scrape a hole in the ground 5 scrape sth from/off sth; scrape sth away/ off रगड़ खाते हुए निकल जाना 6 बड़ी मुश्किल से कुछ पाना/प्राप्त करना : scrape a living ▪ scrape through (sth) किसी भाँति बस उत्तीर्ण हो जाना ▸ scraper noun छीलने का औज़ार।

scrape² / स्क्रेप् / noun 1 (विशेषत: sing) खरोंच, रगड़ की ध्वनि 2 खरोंच से लगी चोट : a nasty scrape on the *elbow* 3 *(अनौप)* (मूर्खतापूर्ण आचरण के कारण) उलझन की स्थिति।

scratch¹ / स्क्रैच् / *verb* 1 खरोंचना, चाकू आदि से खुरचना; कुरेदना : *The dog is scratching at the door.* 2 नोचना; नाखूनों से त्वचा खुजलाना : *Stop scratching (yourself).* 3 खरोंच कर कर्कश शब्द उत्पन्न करना 4 **scratch (sb/sth) (from sth)** प्रतियोगिता आदि से हट जाना : *I had to scratch (from the marathon) because of illness.*

scratch² / स्क्रैच् / *noun* खरोंच, खुजलाना ▸ **scratch** *adj* कामचलाऊ वस्तु : *a scratch meal/team* **scratchy** *adj* (-ier, -iest) खुजलाहट भरा।

scrawl / स्क्रॉल् / *verb* लापरवाही से जल्दी-जल्दी लिखना या चित्र खींचना ▸ **scrawl** *noun* घसीट मार कर लिखा हुआ या खींचा हुआ; इस प्रकार से लिखी हुई लंबी टिप्पणी : *Her signature was an illegible scrawl.*

scream / स्क्रीम् / *verb* 1 (डर या दर्द से) चीखना, चिल्लाना 2 चीख़ कर ऊँचे स्वर में कुछ कहना : *demonstrators screaming obscenities* 3 (वायु या मशीन का) चीत्कार, शोर ▸ **scream** *noun* 1 चीख़, चीत्कार 2 *(अनौप)* हँसी उत्पन्न करने वाला व्यक्ति या वस्तु : *He's an absolute scream.*

screech / स्क्रीच् / *verb* 1 उत्तेजना, दर्द या भय से चीख़ मारना : *screech out in pain* 2 चीख़ कर कुछ कहना; कर्कश ध्वनि निकालना : *The brakes screeched as the car stopped.* ▸ **screech** *noun* [sing] चीख़ या कर्कश ध्वनि।

screen / स्क्रीन् / *noun* 1 परदा, ओट, आड़ : *a screen of trees* 2 जालीदार दरवाज़ा 3 सिनेमा आदि का परदा; कंप्यूटर, टी वी आदि की स्क्रीन 4 चलनी, छलनी : *a window screen* ▸ **screen** *verb* 1 **screen sth/sb (off) (from sb/sth)** आड़ में करना, छिपाना : *The trees screen the house from view.* 2 किसी को दोष, दंड आदि से बचाना 3 **screen sb/sth (for sth)** ग़लती, कमी आदि का पता लगाने के लिए परीक्षण करना 4 टी वी, सिनेमा आदि पर फ़िल्म दिखाना।

screw / स्क्रू / *noun* 1 पेंच, स्क्रू 2 पेंच कसने की क्रिया 3 जहाज़ या हवाई जहाज़ के प्रोपेलर : *a twin-screw cruiser* ▸ **screw** *verb* 1 पेंच (से) कसना : *screw a bracket to the wall* 2 ऐंठना, मरोड़ना ■ **screw sth up** 1 पेंच से कुछ कसना 2 बोतल आदि का ढक्कन बंद करना 3 आँखें सिकोड़ना (बहुत अधिक रोशनी या दर्द के कारण) 4 *(अप)* किसी स्थिति को संभाल न पाना ▸ **screw driver** *noun* पेंचकस।

scribble / 'स्क्रिब्ल् / *verb* 1 लापरवाही या शीघ्रता से कुछ लिख डालना : *some scribbled notes* 2 निरर्थक चिह्न बनाते रहना : *a child scribbling all over a book* ▸ **scribble** *noun* 1 लापरवाही की लिखावट 2 निरर्थक निशान।

scribe / स्क्राइब् / *noun* लिपिक; मुंशी।

scrip / स्क्रिप् / *noun (तक)* पावती पत्र : *a scrip issue.*

script / स्क्रिप्ट् / *noun* 1 नाटक, फ़िल्म आदि की पटकथा 2 लिखावट : *his neat script* 3 लिपि; मुद्रण-टाइप 4 उत्तर (पुस्तिका) : *The examiner had to mark 150 scripts.*

scripture / 'स्क्रिप्चर् / *noun* 1 **Scripture (the scriptures** [pl]**)** भी) बाइबिल 2 **scriptures** [pl] धर्मग्रंथ : *Vedic scriptures.*

scroll / स्क्रोल् / *noun* 1 लिखने के लिए काग़ज़ का खर्रा, चीरक : *Chinese scroll paintings* 2 खर्रे पर लिखी पुस्तक; प्राचीन ग्रंथ ▸ **scroll** *verb* कंप्यूटर स्क्रीन पर किसी भी पाठ को धीरे-धीरे ऊपर-नीचे घुमाना जिससे इसके हर भाग को प्रदर्शित किया जा सके।

scrub¹ / स्क्रब् / *verb* (-bb-) **1 scrub sth (down/out)** ब्रुश, साबुन और पानी से साफ़ करना : *scrub the floor* **2** (अनौप) कोई योजना आदि रद्द करना ▸ **scrub** *noun* [sing] सफ़ाई **scrubbing-brush** *noun* साफ़ करने का ब्रुश।

scrub² / स्क्रब् / *noun* झाड़-झंखाड़ (वाला स्थान) ▸ **scrubby** *adj*.

scruff / स्क्रफ़् / *noun* ▪ **by the scruff of the/one's neck** किसी पशु या व्यक्ति की गरदन के पिछले भाग पर पकड़ : *She grabbed him by the scruff of his neck and threw him out.*

scruffy / स्क्रफ़ि / *adj* (-ier, -iest) (अनौप) मैला, अस्त-व्यस्त : *You can't go to a job interview looking so scruffy!*

scruple / स्क्रूपल् / *noun* (प्राय: pl) नैतिक संकोच, धर्मभीरुता : *moral/religious scruples.*

scrupulous / स्क्रूप्यलस् / *adj* **1** अति-सावधान, ईमानदार, नियमनिष्ठ : *behave with scrupulous honesty* **2** धर्मभीरु, अति संकोची (नैतिकता में)।

scrutinize, -ise / स्क्रूटनाइज़ /*verb* पूर्णत: जाँच करना : *He scrutinized minutely all the documents relating to the trial.*

scrutiny / स्क्रूटनि / *noun* (औप) पूरी तरह से की गई जाँच।

scuffle / स्कफ़ल् / *noun* **scuffle (with sb)** हाथापाई : *Scuffles broke out between police and demonstrators.* ▸ **scuffle** *verb* **scuffle (with sb)** हाथापाई करना।

scull / स्कल् / *noun* **1** (प्राय: pl) नाव का छोटा चप्पू **2 sculls** [pl] छोटी नौकाओं की दौड़ : *single/double sculls.*

scullery / स्कलरि / *noun* रसोईघर के साथ जुड़ा बरतन माँजने का स्थान, विशेषत: बड़े घरों में।

sculptor / स्कल्प्टर् / *noun* (fem

sculptress / स्कल्प्ट्रस् /) बुत-तराश, मूर्तिकार।

sculpture / स्कल्पचर् / *noun* **1** मूर्ति-कला **2** मूर्ति : *a bronze sculpture of Venus* ▸ **sculpture (sculpt** भी) *verb* मूर्ति बनाना।

scum / स्कम् / *noun* **1** (प्राय: sing) (तालाब आदि के पानी का) झाग, फेन : *stinking water covered by a thick green scum* **2** समाज का निम्नवर्ग; घृणास्पद व्यक्ति।

scurrilous / स्करलस् / *adj* बहुत अभद्र और अपमानजनक, प्राय: किसी का नाम नष्ट करने के इरादे से : *He wrote a scurrilous piece about me in the local press.* ▸ **scurrilously** *adv* अश्लीलता के साथ।

scurry /स्करि/ *verb* (pt, pp **scurried**) छोटे-छोटे तेज़ क़दमों से दौड़ना : *mice scurrying across the floor* ▸ **scurry** *noun*.

scurvy / स्कर्वि / *noun* विटामिन C की कमी से होने वाला रोग, स्कर्वी।

scuttle¹ /स्कटल्/ *noun* (**coal scuttle** भी) कोयले का टोकरा।

scuttle² / स्कटल् / *verb* **1** जहाज़ में छेद कर डुबो देना **2** किसी चीज़ को जानबूझकर असफल कर देना/बनाना : *scuttle a peace plan.*

scuttle³ / स्कटल् / *verb* छोटे तेज़ क़दमों से भाग जाना : *The rain sent people scuttling for shelter.*

scythe / साइद् / *noun* हँसिया, दराँती ▸ **scythe** *verb* हँसिया से घास काटना।

sea / सी / *noun* **1** (प्राय: **the sea**, विशेषत: *साहि* **seas** [pl] भी) समुद्र **2** [sing] **sea of sth** किसी बड़े क्षेत्र को घेरते हुए किसी वस्तु की अत्यंत विशाल मात्रा : *I stood amid a sea of corn.* ▪ **at sea** उलझन में, परेशान : *She tried to follow the instructions, but was completely at sea.* **go to sea** नाविक बनना

▶ **seafaring** adj समुद्री यात्रा पर; समुद्री यात्रा (कार्य) से संबद्ध **seafood** noun खाने लायक समुद्री मछली आदि **seagull** noun बड़े पंखों वाली साधारण समुद्री चिड़िया **sea level** noun समुद्र तल **sea-man** / 'सी- मन् / noun (नौसेना में) नाविक (न कि अफ़सर) **seasick** adj जहाज़ी मतली से बीमार **seaside** noun, adj समुद्र तट **seaweed** noun समुद्री शैवाल।

seal¹ / सील / noun 1 सील, मोहर 2 पीतल या अन्य धातु की मोहर (जिससे सील करते हैं) 3 छेद, दरार आदि बंद करने के लिए प्रयुक्त पदार्थ : *a rubber seal in the lid of a jar* ▶ **seal** verb 1 सील करना, मोहर लगाना 2 **seal sth (up)** पत्र, पार्सल आदि चिपकाना/बंद करना 3 **seal sth (up)** कस कर बंद करना : *The jar must be properly sealed.* 4 (क़ानून) क़ानूनी/ आधिकारिक सील लगाना; किसी स्थान पर आने-जाने पर रोक लगाना : *The army sealed the country's borders.* 5 (औप) कुछ निश्चित होना/करना : *in the weeks before the GATT deal was sealed* **sealing wax** noun लाख।

seal² / सील / noun सील, एक समुद्री पशु।

seam / सीम / noun 1 कपड़े की सिलाई की सीवन : *the seams down the side of the trousers* 2 एक रेखा जहाँ दो किनारे मिलते हों 3 परत (जैसे कोयले की परत) : *a rich seam of iron ore* ▶ **seam** verb सीवन सिलना **seamless** adj सीवन रहित।

search / सर्च / verb 1 **search (sth) (for sth/sb); search through/among sth (for sth/sb)** खोजना, ढूँढना, तलाश करना 2 **search sb (for sth)** किसी व्यक्ति की तलाशी लेना 3 **search for sth; search sth (for sth)** गहराई से सोचना/ चिंतन करना, विशेषतः कोई समस्या हल करने के लिए ▶ **search** noun खोज, तलाश।

searchlight / 'सर्चलाइट् / noun शक्ति-

शाली विद्युत लैंप जो प्रायः खोजने में प्रयुक्त किया जाता है।

season¹ / 'सीज़्न् / noun 1 मौसम, ऋतु : *the rainy season* 2 मौसम, उपयुक्त समय : *the football season* 3 किसी एक विषय/प्रसंग पर आधारित फ़िल्म, नाटक या संगीत-समारोह की शृंखला : *a short season of silent film classics* ▶ **season ticket** noun निश्चित अवधि में मनचाहा प्रवेश देने वाला टिकट, मौसमी टिकट।

season² / 'सीज़्न् / verb 1 **season sth (with sth)** मसाले, मिर्च आदि डालकर भोजन को छौंकना/बघारना 2 (लकड़ी को) प्रयोग योग्य बनाना या होना।

seasonal / 'सीज़न्ल् / adj मौसमी : *seasonal work.*

seasoned / 'सीज़न्ड् / adj किसी कार्यक्षेत्र में अनुभवी : *a seasoned traveller/ political campaigner.*

seasoning / 'सीज़निङ् / noun नमक, काली मिर्च, मसाले।

seat¹ / सीट् / noun 1 बैठने का आसन/ स्थान : *take a seat* 2 सार्वजनिक परिवहन, थिएटर आदि में जगह जहाँ बैठने के लिए भुगतान करना पड़ता है : *There are no seats left on the flight.* 3 समिति, सभा, असेंबली आदि में सदस्य के रूप में स्थान : *a seat on the city council* 4 अधिष्ठान, कार्य स्थान : *a seat of learning.*

seat² / सीट् / verb 1 (औप) किसी को बैठाना/स्वयं बैठना 2 (स्थान में) बैठने की जगह होना : *a hall that seats 500 (people)* ▶ **seating** noun बैठने की जगह; कुर्सियाँ।

secede / सि'सीड् / verb **secede (from sth)** (औप) से अलग या स्वतंत्र हो जाना : *Latvia seceded from the Soviet Union in 1991.* ▶ **secession** noun.

seclude / सि'क्लूड् / verb **seclude oneself/sb (from sb/sth)** स्वयं को/

किसी को दूसरों से अलग कर लेना : *seclude oneself from the world* ▸ **secluded** *adj* (स्थान) एकांत, निर्जन; औरों से अलग **seclusion** / सि'क्लूश्न् / *noun* अकेले या एकांत स्थान पर होने की स्थिति : *in the seclusion of one's own home.*

second¹ / 'से कन्ड् / *pron, det* **1 second (to sb/sth)** क्रम से दूसरा, समय या महत्त्व में दूसरा : *the second month of the year* **2** दूसरा, अतिरिक्त : *a second helping of soup* **3** पहले जैसे समान स्तर का : *The press are calling him a second Tendulkar.* ▸ **second-best** *adj* सर्वश्रेष्ठ से द्वितीय **second-class** *adj* द्वितीय श्रेणी का **second-hand** *adj, adv* **1** पुराना, पूर्व प्रयुक्त : *a second-hand car* **2** सुनी-सुनाई/न कि आँखों देखी : *second-hand gossip* **second nature** *noun* स्वभाव, आदत **second lieutenant** *noun* सेकिंड लेफ्टिनेंट **second-rate** *adj* मामूली, घटिया : *a second-rate restaurant.*

second² / 'से कन्ड् / *noun* **1** विद्यालय/विश्वविद्यालय की द्वितीय श्रेणी **2** (प्राय: *pl*) द्वितीय कोटि का उत्पाद (जिसमें कुछ कमी होती है) : *These plates are seconds.* **3** सहायक, साथी।

second³ / 'से कन्ड् / *verb* **1** समर्थन करना, प्रस्ताव का अनुमोदन करना : *Mr Raghavan proposed the motion and Mr Palekar seconded (it).* **2** सहायता देना।

second⁴ / 'से कन्ड् / *noun* **1** सेकिंड (एक मिनट या डिग्री का 60 वाँ अंश) **2** (अनौप) क्षण; पल भर का समय : *I'll be ready in a second.*

secondary / 'से कन्ड्रि / *adj* **1 secondary (to sth)** गौण, न कि मुख्य; कम महत्त्वपूर्ण : *a secondary issue/role* **2** द्वितीयक, मूल से उत्पन्न : *a secondary effect/infection* **3** प्राथमिक और विश्व-विद्यालय शिक्षा के बीच की शिक्षा, माध्यमिक शिक्षा : *secondary teachers.*

secrecy / 'सीक्रसि / *noun* गोपनीयता; छिपाव-दुराव : *The meeting was held in great secrecy.*

secret / 'सीक्रट् / *adj* **1 secret (from sb)** गुप्त, गोपनीय : *a secret meeting* **2** अन्य लोगों से अज्ञात/छुपा हुआ : *a secret drinker* **3** रहस्यमय ▸ **secret** *noun* **1** भेद, रहस्य : *keep a secret* **2** कुछ उपलब्धि का रहस्य : *What is the secret of your success?* **3** गूढ़, समझने में मुश्किल : *the secrets of creation* ■ **in secret** चुपचाप, गुप्त तौर पर ▸ **secretly** *adv* चुपचाप, गुप्त रीति से।

secretary / 'सेक्रट्रि; US 'सेक्रटेरि / *noun* (*pl* **secretaries**) **1** सचिव, सेक्रेटरी **2** क्लब, समाज आदि का सेक्रेटरी **3** मंत्री का मुख्य सचिव ▸ **secretarial** / सेक्र'टेअरिअल् / *adj* सचिव-विषयक : *secretarial staff* **Secretary of State** *noun* **1** (ब्रिटेन में) मंत्री **2** (अमेरिका में) विदेश मंत्री।

secrete / सि'क्रीट् / *verb* (औप) पौधे, जंतु या मनुष्य के किसी अंग से किसी विशेष प्रकार के द्रव का निकलना : *Saliva is secreted by glands in the mouth.*

secretive / 'सीक्रटिव् / *adj* गोपनशील, छिपाने के स्वभाव वाला।

sect / सेक्ट् / *noun* संप्रदाय, पंथ/मत : *a minor Christian sect.*

sectarian / सेक्'टेअरिअन् / *adj* **1** किसी पंथ से जुड़ा : *sectarian violence* **2** (अपमा) दूसरे पंथों आदि के लिए आदर भावना न होना; संकुचित विचारों का : *sectarian prejudices/views* ▸ **sectarianism** *noun.*

section / 'सेक्श्न् / *noun* **1** कटा अंश, टुकड़ा : *This section of the road is closed.* **2** अंश, खंड **3** भाग, विभाग, अनुभाग : *head of the finance section* **4** पुस्तक, काग़ज़ात आदि के खंड, परिच्छेद (प्रकरण, कांड) **5** (चिकि) काट कर अलग

करने की प्रक्रिया : *the section of a diseased organ* ▸ **sectional** *adj* अनुभागीय ।

sector / 'सेक्टर् / *noun* 1 *(ज्यामिति)* त्रिज्य-खंड, वृत्तखंड 2 क्षेत्र, अंचल : *the manufacturing sector* ○ *the service sector* 3 युद्धक्षेत्र का हिस्सा/खंड।

secular / 'सेक्यलर् / *adj* 1 लौकिक (न कि धार्मिक या आध्यात्मिक) : *secular education* 2 धर्मनिरपेक्ष।

secure / सि'क्युअर् / *adj* 1 **secure (about sth)** सुरक्षित, चिंतामुक्त 2 निश्चित, पक्का : *make a secure investment* 3 **secure (against/from sth)** रक्षित, सुरक्षित : *secure from attack* 4 दृढ़, मज़बूती से जमा हुआ ▸ **secure** *verb* 1 **secure sth (for sb/sth)** *(औप)* पाना, (कठिनाई से) प्राप्त करना : *secure a bank loan* 2 जकड़ना, कस कर बाँधना, 3 **secure sth (against/from sth)** सुरक्षित करना : *secure a building (from collapse).*

security / सि'क्युअरिटि / *noun* (*pl* **securities**) 1 सुरक्षा, चिंतामुक्ति 2 सुरक्षात्मक उपाय : *national security* 3 प्रतिभूति, ज़मानत 4 (प्राय: *pl*) ऋण पत्र, स्वामित्व पत्र : *government securities.*

sedate[1] / सि'डेट् / *adj* प्रशांत, गंभीर एवं सौम्य।

sedate[2] / सि'डेट् / *verb* किसी को शांत करने के लिए नींद की गोली देना : *She is heavily sedated.* ▸ **sedation** / सि 'डेश्न् / *noun* नींद की गोली लेने के कारण आराम या नींद की अवस्था : *The patient is under heavy sedation.*

sedative / 'सेडटिव् / *noun* नींद की गोली, शामक औषधि।

sediment / 'सेडिमन्ट् / *noun* 1 तलछट, (द्रव के) नीचे जमा कूड़ा-करकट 2 हवा या पानी द्वारा बहाकर लाया गया रेत, पत्थर, गारा आदि जो नदियों, झीलों की तली में जमा हो जाता है ▸ **sedimentary** *adj.*

sedition / सि'डिश्न् / *noun* राजद्रोह ▸ **seditious** / सि'डिशस् / *adj* : *seditious activities/speech.*

seduce / सि'ड्यूस; *US* सि'डूस् / *verb* 1 **seduce sb (from sth); seduce sb (into sth/doing sth)** *(औप)* प्रलोभन देना : *Higher salaries are seducing many teachers into industry.* 2 संभोग के लिए राज़ी करना : *She claimed that he had seduced her.* ▸ **seducer** *noun.*

seduction / सि'डक्श्न् / *noun* संभोग के लिए राज़ी करने/होने की क्रिया ▸ **seductive** / सि'डक्टिव् / *adj* प्रलोभनीय, आकर्षक : *a seductive smile/look* **seductively** *adv* **seductiveness** *noun.*

see / सी / *verb* (*pt* **saw** / सॉ /; *pp* **seen** / सीन् /) 1 देखना : *I looked out of the window but saw nothing.* 2 समझना : *Do you see what I mean?* 3 किसी से मिलना : *Come and see us again.* ■ **see about sth/doing sth** प्रबंध करना : *I must see about lunch soon.* **see sb off** यात्रा करने वाले को विदाई देना : *We all went to the airport to see her off.* **see sb through (sth)** यथासंभव सहायता करना **see through sb/sth** भाँपना, धोखे में न आना **see to it that...** निश्चय करना **see to sth** ध्यान देना : *Will you see to the arrangements for the next committee meeting?* **see which way the wind is blowing** कोई क़दम उठाने से पहले भविष्य की संभावनाएँ विचार लेना : *I'd like to see which way the wind is blowing before applying for another job.*

seed / सीड् / *noun* 1 बीज : *a tiny poppy seed* 2 (प्राय: *pl*) **seed (of sth)** कारण, उद्गम : *Are the seeds of criminal behaviour sown early in* *life ?* 3 (विशेषत:टेनिस में) सर्वश्रेष्ठ समझे जाने वाले खिलाड़ी ▶ **seedling** / 'सीड्‌लिङ्‌ / *noun* छोटा नया पौधा, नवोद्भिद्‌।

seedy / 'सीडि / *adj* (-ier, -iest) 1 मैला, (देखने में) अशोभनीय : *a cheap hotel in a seedy part of town* 2 (अनौप) अस्वस्थ, बीमार : *feeling seedy.*

seek / सीक् / *verb* (pt, pp sought / सॉट्‌/) (औप) 1 seek (after/for) sth ढूँढ़ना, खोजना : *seek happiness/comfort* 2 seek sth (from sb) अनुरोध करना/लेना : *seek help/advice* 3 प्रयास करना, करने का प्रयत्न करना : *They sought to mislead us.*

seem / सीम् / *verb* seem (to sb)(to be) sth प्रतीत होना, लगना/जान पड़ना : *Do whatever seems best.* ▶ **seeming** *adj* (औप) प्रतीत होता हुआ।

seemly / 'सीम्‌लि / *adj* (अप्र या औप) अवसर पर उपयुक्त; भद्र समाज में उपयुक्त : *Try and behave in a more seemly manner.* ▶ **seemliness** *noun*.

seep / सीप् / *verb* seep through (sth)/ into sth/out (of sth)/away (द्रव) टपकना, रिसना, चूना : *water seeping through the roof of the tunnel* ▶ **seepage** *noun*.

seer / सिअर् / *noun* (अप्र या साहि) भविष्य में देखने वाला, भविष्य द्रष्टा, मनीषी।

see-saw / 'सीसॉ / *noun* 1 (US teetertotter भी) बच्चों का सीसॉ-झूला, ढेंकी, 2 उतार-चढ़ाव का क्रम : *a see-saw in prices/trading* ▶ **see-saw** *verb* 1 ढेंकी पर झूलना/खेलना 2 उतार-चढ़ाव आना।

seethe / सीद् / *verb* 1 (द्रवों का) उबल कर खौलना, बुदबुदाना 2 seethe (with sth) क्रोध से उबलना : *She was seething at his remarks.*

segment / 'सेग्मन्‌ / *noun* 1 खंड, हिस्सा, 2 संतरे, नींबू आदि की फाँक 3 वृत्त का खंड; रेखा का खंड : *Lines divided*

the area into segments. ▶ **segment** *verb* खंडों में विभाजित करना।

segregate / 'सेग्रिगेट् / *verb* segregate sb/sth (from sb/sth) 1 पृथक करना, दूसरों से अलग करना : *segregate cholera patients* 2 (जाति के कारण) एक समूह के लोगों को अन्य से अलग करना ▶ **segregation** / सेग्रि 'गेशन् / *noun* पृथक्करण, अलग-अलग करना : *a policy of social segregation.*

seismic / 'साइज़्मिक् / *adj* भूकंप से संबंधित या भूकंप द्वारा उत्पन्न : *seismic activity/tremors/data.*

seize / सीज़् / *verb* 1 छीनना, झपट लेना : *He seized my bag and ran off with it.* 2 क़ब्ज़ा करना : *The army has seized power.* 3 ज़ब्त करना : *All the company's assets were seized.* 4 अवसर का तुरंत लाभ उठाना 5 अचानक ग्रस्त हो जाना/प्रभावित होना : *Panic seized us.* ▶ **seizure** / 'सीझर् / *noun* 1 झपट, ज़ब्ती, 2 दिल/दिमाग़ का दौरा : *epileptic seizures.*

seldom / 'सेल्डम् / *adv* बिरले ही, यदा-कदा : *Seldom have I seen such brutality.*

select / सि 'लेक्ट् / *verb* select sb/sth (as sth) चुनना/छाँटना; पसंद करना : *select a gift/candidate/wine* ▶ **select** *adj* 1 सावधानी से चुना हुआ, चुनिंदा : *a select bibliography* 2 (क्लब, समाज, संघ आदि) केवल चुनिंदा लोगों के लिए : *a documentary shown to a select audience.*

selection / सि 'लेक्शन् / *noun* 1 चयन, चुनाव : *the selection process* 2 चयनित व्यक्ति/वस्तुएँ : *read selections from 18th century English poetry* 3 चयनिका, संकलन; समूह जिसमें से चुनाव करना है : *a shop with a huge selection of paperbacks.*

selective / सि 'लेक्टिव् / *adj* 1 केवल कुछ

विशिष्ट व्यक्तियों/वस्तुओं के लिए : *a selective pesticide* **2 selective (about sb/sth)** चयनात्मक, सोच-समझ कर चयन करने वाला : *I am very selective about the books I read.* ▶ **selectively** *adv* : *The document had been selectively leaked to the press.*

self / सेल्फ़ / *noun (pl* **selves** / सेल्व्ज़् /) **1 (the self** [*sing*] भी) *(औप)* स्वत्व : *the conscious self* **2** व्यक्ति का स्वभाव; विशेषगुण **3** स्वार्थ : *You always put self first.* **4** व्यक्तित्व ■ **one's better self** स्वभाव का अच्छा पक्ष।

self- *pref (पूर्वपद)* स्वयं-, स्वत:-, स्व-।

self-centred (*US* **self-centered**) / सेल्फ़ 'सेन्टर्ड् / *adj (अपमा)* केवल अपने बारे में सोचने वाला : *her self-centred attitude.*

self-conscious / सेल्फ़ 'कॉन्शस् / *adj* संकोची; आत्मचेतन।

self-control / सेल्फ़ कन् 'ट्रोल् / *noun* आत्मनियंत्रण।

self-defence (*US* **self-defense** भी) / सेल्फ़ डि'फ़ेन्स् / *noun* आत्मरक्षा।

selfish / 'सेल्फ़िश् / *adj (अपमा)* स्वार्थी, केवल अपना हित देखने वाला : *selfish behaviour* ▶ **selfishly** *adv* **selfishness** *noun* : *act out of pure selfishness.*

selfless / 'सेल्फ़्लस् / *adj* नि:स्वार्थ ▶ **selflessly** *adv* **selflessness** *noun.*

self-made / सेल्फ़ 'मेड् / *adj* अपने प्रयासों के कारण सफल होना तथा धन अर्जन करना।

self-respect / सेल्फ़ रि 'स्पेक्ट् / *noun* आत्मगौरव।

self-sufficient / सेल्फ़ स'फ़िशन्ट् / *adj* आत्मनिर्भर।

self-willed / सेल्फ़ 'विल्ड् / *adj (अपमा)* हठी : *a troublesome self-willed child.*

sell / सेल् / *verb (pt, pp* **sold** / सोल्ड्/) **1 sell (sth) (to sb) (at/for sth)** बेचना : *sell (sth) at a high price* **2 sell (at/for sth)** बिकाऊ होना, बिकना **3 sell oneself (to sb)** कुछ ग़लत काम के लिए पैसे ले लेना, स्वयं को बेच देना ■ **sell sth off** सस्ता बेचना **sell out (of sth)** बेच कर माल समाप्त कर देना : *We've sold out (of bread) but we'll be getting some more later.*

seller / 'सेलर् / *noun* **1** (प्राय: समासों में) विक्रेता : *a bookseller* **2** बिकने वाली वस्तु : *The book has been a steady seller for years.*

selvage (**selvedge** भी) / 'सेल्व़िज् / *noun* कपड़े या साड़ी का किनारा (इस तरह से बुना हुआ कि धागे न निकलें)।

semantic / सि'मैन्टिक् / *adj* शब्दों और वाक्यों के अर्थ से संबंधित : *semantic analysis* ▶ **semantics** *noun* शब्दों के अर्थों का अध्ययन।

semblance / 'सेम्ब्लन्स् / *noun* [*sing*] **semblance of sth** सादृश्य, एक-सा दिखाई पड़ना : *put on a semblance of cheerfulness.*

semi- *pref (उपसर्ग)* **1** अर्ध : *semicircular* (अर्धवृत्तीय) **2** आंशिक; अंशत: : *semi-detached ∘ semicivilized.*

semicolon / 'सेमि 'कोलन् / *noun* लिखने और मुद्रण का चिह्न (;)।

semi-final / 'सेमि 'फ़ाइनल् / *noun* उपांत।

seminar / 'सेमिनार् / *noun* विचार-गोष्ठी : *a one-day business management seminar.*

senate / 'सेनट् / *noun* **1** (प्राय: **the Senate**) सीनेट; फ़्रांस, अमेरिका, ऑस्ट्रेलिया आदि में उच्च सदन : *a Senate committee* **2** विश्वविद्यालय आदि की शासी-परिषद्, सीनेट **3** (प्राचीन रोम में) उच्चतम सभा ▶ **senator** / 'सेनटर् / *noun* (प्राय: **Senator**) सीनेट सदस्य।

send / सेन्ड् / *verb (pt, pp* **sent**

/ सेन्ड् /) **1 send sb/sth (to sb/sth)** भेजना **2 send sth (out)** संकेत (रेडियो तरंगों द्वारा) भेजना **3** बना देना/कर देना : *send sb mad/crazy* ■ **send for sb (to do sth); send for sth** बुलाना, मँगा भेजना **send sth in** (प्रतियोगिता, पद आदि के लिए) अपना नाम दर्ज कराना : *Have you sent in your application for the job?* **send sth off** (पत्र, सामान आदि) भेजना **send sth out 1** बिखेरना, विकीर्ण करना **2** (परिपत्र आदि) वितरित करना : *The trees send out new leaves in spring.* ▸ **send-off** *noun* विदाई, विदाई के समय हितैषियों का मिलन।

senile / सीनाइल् / *adj* बड़ी उम्र में शारीरिक और मानसिक असमर्थता से कुछ-कुछ पीड़ित : *senile decay* ▸ **senility** / स 'निलटि / *noun*.

senior / सीनिअर / *adj* **1 senior (to sb)** पद में वरिष्ठ : *a senior staff meeting* **2** आयु में ज्येष्ठ; (खेलों में) 18 वर्ष से अधिक **3** (प्राय: Senior, *संक्षि* Snr) वरिष्ठ (अक्सर एक समान नाम होने पर पिता के नाम के साथ लगाया जाने वाला) : *Pataudi Senior* ▸ **senior** *noun* आयु में हमसे बड़ा व्यक्ति **senior citizen** *noun* वरिष्ठ नागरिक (60 वर्ष से अधिक के पुरुष व महिलाएँ) जिन्हें राज्य से कुछ विशिष्ट सुविधाएँ मिलती हैं **seniority** / सीनि 'ऑरटि / *noun* वरिष्ठता, ज्येष्ठता, प्रवरता।

sensation / सेन्सेशन् / *noun* **1** संवेदन, अनुभूति : *a sensation of dizziness* **2** सनसनी; सनसनी उत्पन्न करने वाला व्यक्ति/वस्तु/घटना : *The news caused a great sensation.* ▸ **sensational** *adj* **1** सनसनीखेज़; जानबूझ कर सनसनी फैलाने वाला : *a sensational crime* **2** (अनौप) बहुत अच्छा, आश्चर्यजनक।

sense / सेन्स् / *noun* **1** इंद्रिय, ज्ञानेंद्रियाँ : *sense of smell* **2** किसी चीज़ के मूल्य की समझ : *a strong sense of purpose* **3** बोध, बुद्धि : *There's no sense in*

going alone. **4** ज्ञानेंद्रियजनित अनुभूति, संवेदन **5 senses** *[pl]* होश, चेतना : *come to one's senses* **6** अर्थ, तात्पर्य : *a word with several senses* ▸ **sense** *verb* **1** कुछ जान लेना, भाँपना **2** (किसी मशीन/उपकरण का) पता लगा लेना : *an apparatus that senses the presence of toxic gases.*

senseless / सेन्सलस् / *adj* **1** (अपमा) मूर्खतापूर्ण : *a senseless idea/action* **2** अचेत, बेहोश : *knock sb senseless.*

sensibility / सेन्स 'बिलटि / *noun* (*pl* **sensibilities**) **1** संवेदनशीलता (विशेषत: कला, संगीत आदि के प्रति) **2 sensibilities** *[pl]* भावुकता, संवेदनशीलता : *offend readers' sensibilities.*

sensible / सेन्सबल् / *adj* **1** समझदार, विवेकी : *It was sensible of you to lock the door.* **2** (कपड़े आदि) व्यावहारिक, न कि फ़ैशन वाले : *wear sensible shoes* **3 sensible of sth** (अप्र) किसी चीज़ से परिचित।

sensitive / सेन्सटिव् / *adj* **1 sensitive (to/about sth)** भावुक (निंदा आदि का तीक्ष्ण अनुभव करने वाला) : *a frail and sensitive child* **2 sensitive (to sth)** (यंत्र आदि) सूक्ष्मग्राही, ज़रा-से भी परिवर्तन को महसूस (अंकित) करने वाला **3** अति-संवेदनशील : *the sensitive skin of a baby* **4** सावधानी से व्यवहार किया जाने वाला : *sensitive military information.*

sensual / सेन्शुअल् / *adj* भोगविलास में लगा हुआ/से पूर्ण।

sensuous / सेन्शुअस् / *adj* इंद्रियसंबंधी (सुख) : *a sensuous gesture.*

sentence / सेन्टन्स् / *noun* **1** (व्या) वाक्य **2** (क़ानून) न्यायाधीश द्वारा दिया गया दंड का आदेश : *a jail sentence* ▸ **sentence** *verb* **sentence sb (to sth)** फैसला सुनाना, दंड का आदेश देना : *sentence a thief to imprisonment.*

sentiment / सेन्टिमन्ट् / noun 1 (कभी-कभी *अपमा*) भावुकता; दया, प्यार आदि के नाज़ुक भाव : *love story full of cloying sentiment* 2 (*औप*) मनोभाव, सामान्य भाव : *Public sentiment is against any change to the law.* 3 राय, विचार; भावाभिव्यक्ति : *a speech full of noble sentiment.*

sentimental / सेन्टि'मेन्ट्ल् / adj 1 भावुकतापूर्ण 2 (कभी-कभी *अपमा*) भावाभिव्यक्तिपूर्ण (जैसे दया, प्यार आदि) : *a sloppy sentimental love story* ▸ **sentimentality** noun.

sentinel / सेन्टिन्ल् / noun (*अप्र* या *औप*) पहरेदार सैनिक।

sentry / सेन्ट्रि / noun संतरी, पहरेदार।

separable / सेपरब्ल् / adj वियोज्य, पृथक करने या होने योग्य।

separate¹ / सेपरट् / adj 1 **separate (from sth/sb)** अलग, पृथक; न जुड़ा हुआ : *They lead separate lives.* 2 भिन्न : *That is a separate issue and irrelevant to our discussion.*

separate² / सेपरेट् / verb 1 **separate (sb/sth) (from sb/sth)** अलग होना/रखना/करना : *separate two dogs fighting* 2 **separate (from sb)** (लोगों का) अलग हो जाना; अलग-अलग जाना : *She has separated from her husband.* ○ *We talked for an hour before separating.* 3 भिन्न होना/करना।

separation / सेप'रेश्न् / noun 1 **separation (from sb/sth)** अलग-अलग होना, पार्थक्य : *the separation between church and state* 2 वियोग की अवधि 3 [*sing*] शादी-शुदा लोगों का (मन-मुटाव के कारण) अलग रहना : *decide on (a) separation.*

September / सेप्'टेम्बर् / noun (*संक्षि* Sept) सितंबर (महीना)।

septic / सेप्टिक् / adj (घाव) पका हुआ; विषाक्त, सेप्टिक।

sepulchre (*US* **sepulcher**) / सेपल्कर् / noun (*अप्र*) क़ब्र, समाधि/मक़बरा : *the Holy Sepulchre* ▸ **sepulchral** adj.

sequel / सीक्वल् / noun **sequel (to sth)** 1 परिणाम : *Famine is often the sequel to war.* 2 उत्तरकथा : *He is writing a sequel to his recent best-seller.*

sequence / सीक्वन्स् / noun 1 क्रमबद्ध विचार या घटनाएँ, जो एक-दूसरे से संबद्ध हो; अनुक्रम : *describe the sequence of events* 2 फ़िल्म का एक सीन दिखाने वाला भाग।

seraph / सेरफ़् / noun (pl **seraphim** या **seraphs**) स्वर्गदूत ▸ **seraphic** adj.

serene / स'रीन् / adj शांतिपूर्ण एवं अविक्षुब्ध : *a serene sky* ○ *Throughout the crisis she remained serene and in control.* ▸ **serenely** adv **serenity** / स'रेनटि / noun : *An atmosphere of serenity pervades the place.*

serf / सर्फ़् / noun 1 (पूर्व में) यूरोप में कृषिदास 2 दास की तरह बर्ताव किया गया मज़दूर ▸ **serfdom** noun 1 सामाजिक व्यवस्था जिसमें खेती दास करते थे 2 दासता का जीवन : *released from his serf-dom.*

sergeant / सार्जन्ट् / noun सार्जेंट (सेना और ब्रिटिश पुलिस में एक पद)।

serial / सिअरिअल् / adj 1 क्रमबद्ध, क्रमिक 2 (कथा आदि) धारावाहिक ▸ **serial** noun धारावाहिक कथा : *a detective serial* **serially** adv.

series / सिअरीज़् / noun (pl अपरिवर्तित) 1 वस्तुओं की शृंखला; घटनाओं का सिल-सिला : *a series of lectures* 2 श्रेणीबद्ध विद्युत धारा : *batteries connected to series.*

serious / सिअरिअस् / adj 1 गंभीर, विचारशील : *a serious person* 2 संभा-वित संकट के कारण महत्त्वपूर्ण : *a serious* *illness* **3 serious (about sb/sth); serious (about doing sth)** गंभीरता से, न कि मज़ाक़ में : *Is she serious about wanting to be a pilot?* ▸ **seriously** *adv* **seriousness** *noun*.

sermon / 'सर्मन् / *noun* **1** प्रवचन : *preach a sermon* **2** *(अनौप या परि)* नैतिकता या ग़लतियों पर भाषण ▸ **sermonize, -ise** *verb (अपमा)* नैतिकता पर भाषण झाड़ना।

serpent / 'सर्पन्ट् / *noun* साँप ▸ **serpentine** *adj* सर्प जैसा कुंडलीनुमा।

serrated / स'रेटिड् / *adj* दंदानेदार; आरे के समान किनारे पर दाँत होना; दंतुर : *a knife with a serrated blade* ○ *serrated leaves.*

servant / 'सर्वन्ट् / *noun* **1** नौकर **2 servant (of sth/sb)** कर्मचारी।

serve / सर्व् / *verb* **1 serve (sb) (as sth)** किसी की नौकरी करना : *serve as (a) gardener and chauffeur* **2** कर्मचारी के रूप में कार्य करना : *serve (a year) in the army* **3 serve sb (with sth)** (खाना) परोसना **4 serve sb (with sth); serve sth (to sb)** (दुकान में) ग्राहकों को देखना; (माल) देना-लेना : *serve in a supermarket* **5 serve (for/as sth)** *(औप)* आवश्यकता पूरी करना; पर्याप्त होना : *This room can serve for a study.* **6 serve sth (on sb); serve sb with sth** *(क़ानून)* तामील करना : *serve notice* ○ *serve a warrant* **7 serve (sth) (to sb)** (टेनिस में) रैकट से विरोधी खिलाड़ी को गेंद फेंकना : *It's your turn to serve (to me).* ■ **serve sb right** उपयुक्त ही होना (जो दंड उसे मिला है, ठीक ही मिला है)।

service / 'सर्विस् / *noun* **1 service (to sth)** नौकरी, सेवा : *ten years' service in the navy* **2** वाहन/मशीन आदि द्वारा किया कार्य : *My car has given me excellent service.* **3** सेवा विभाग : *the*

Civil Service **4 service (to sb/sth)** सहायता, सेवा : *They need the services of a good lawyer.* **5** सार्वजनिक आवश्यकताओं की सेवाएँ : *a bus/train service* **6** परिचर्या, ख़िदमत : *a quick-service restaurant* **7** (ईसाई धर्म में) धार्मिक अनुष्ठान : *three services every Sunday* **8** भोजन परोसने का सेट : *a 30-piece dinner service* **9** (टेनिस में) विरोधी खिलाड़ी को गेंद फेंकने की प्रक्रिया : *Whose service is it?* ▸ **service** *verb* **1** वाहन/ मशीन आदि की मरम्मत करना : *Has this heater been regularly serviced?* **2** सेवा आपूर्ति करना **3** उधार पर ब्याज देना **serviceable** *adj* **1** प्रयोग योग्य **2** टिकाऊ और दृढ़।

serviette / सर्वि'एट् / *noun* खाने के समय प्रयुक्त नैपकिन।

servile / 'सर्वाइल् / *adj (अपमा)* दास सदृश, दासोचित : *servile flattery* ▸ **servility** / सर्'विलटि / *noun.*

sesame / 'सेसमि / *noun* तिल का पेड़, तिल।

session / 'सेश्न् / *noun* **1** (न्यायालय, संसद आदि का) सत्र : *an emergency session of the State Legislature* **2** कार्य विशेष में लगी समयावधि : *a recording session* **3** (विशेषत: स्काटलैंड में) कालेज/स्कूल का वार्षिक सत्र।

set¹ / सेट् / *verb* (-tt-; *pt, pp* **set**) **1** (स्थिति-विशेष में) रखना; गाड़ना; स्थापित करना : *She set a tray down on the table.* **2** नाटक, उपन्यास आदि की कहानी स्थान- या समय-विशेष में स्थापित करना : *The novel is set in pre-war London.* **3** एक निश्चित स्थिति में रखना/ पहुँचाना : *The revolution set the country on the road to democracy.* **4 set sth (for oneself/sb)** कोई कार्य आदि करना/करवाना; समस्या का हल निकलवाना आदि : *She's set herself a difficult task.* **5** हड्डी जोड़ना : *The*

surgeon set her broken arm.
6 (घड़ी, मशीन, आदि को) प्रयोग के लिए तैयार करना : *set the controls of a machine ० set a trap ० She set the alarm for 7 o'clock.* 7 आदर्श के रूप में स्थापित करना : *I rely on you to set a good example.* 8 कुछ निश्चित या निर्धारित करना : *They haven't set a date for their wedding yet.* 9 (तक) (किताब आदि) मुद्रण के लिए तैयार करना 10 (सूर्य या चंद्रमा का) अस्त होना ■ **set about sth/doing sth** (कोई कार्य) आरंभ करना **set forth** (औप) यात्रा आरंभ करना **set off** यात्रा आरंभ करना **set sb/sth on sb** व्यक्ति या जानवर को किसी पर आक्रमण के लिए प्रेरित करना **set sth forth** (औप) (विचार आदि) स्पष्टतया प्रकट करना **set sth off** 1 आतिशबाज़ी आदि आरंभ करना 2 घटनाचक्र आरंभ करना **set sth up** 1 विशेष स्थान पर रखना; निर्माण करना, बनाना : *set up a monument/statue* 2 (कोई मशीन, उपकरण आदि) प्रयोग के लिए तैयार करना, चालू करना 3 स्थापित करना : *set up (a) business* ▸ **set-back** *noun* प्रगति में बाधा या अड़चन; रुकावट, गतिरोध : *Defeat in the by-election is a major set-back for the ruling party.* **set book** (**set text** भी) *noun* परीक्षा में अध्ययन के लिए निर्धारित पुस्तक।

set² / सेट् / *noun* 1 **set (of sth)** सेट, समूह, समुच्चय : *a set of cutlery/golf clubs* 2 (रेडियो या टी वी) उपकरण 3 नाटक, फ़िल्म आदि का दृश्य 4 (गणित) समुच्चय।

settee / से'टी / *noun* एक प्रकार का लंबा, मुलायम सोफ़ा।

setting / 'सेटिङ् / *noun* 1 वातावरण 2 मंच-सज्जा 3 उपकरणों का पूरा सेट।

settle / 'सेट्ल् / *verb* 1 **settle sth (with sb)** निश्चय करना, समझौते पर पहुँचना : *settle a dispute* 2 (नए स्थान पर)

बसना : *She married and settled close to her parents' home.* 3 **settle (on/over sth)** (धूल आदि का) बैठ जाना, तह में जम जाना : *Dust had settled on everything.* 4 **settle (back)** बैठ जाना; टिक जाना : *settle (back) in one's armchair* 5 शांत होना/करना : *The baby wouldn't settle.* 6 **settle (up) (with sb)** (ऋण का) भुगतान करना 7 (भूमि या नींव का) धँसना ■ **settle a score (with sb); settle an old score** बदला लेना, प्रतिशोध लेना **settle down** 1 आरामदायक स्थिति में बैठना या लेटना 2 नए जीवन या नए व्यवसाय से अभ्यस्त हो जाना : *She is settling down well in her new job.*

settlement / 'सेट्ल्मन्ट् / *noun* 1 समझौता, निपटारा : *an out-of-court settlement* 2 (क़ानून) समझौते की शर्तें आदि : *a divorce settlement* 3 बस्ती, उपनिवेश।

settler / 'सेट्लर् / *noun* उपनिवेशी, बसने वाला।

seven / 'सेव्न् / *noun, pron, det* सात (का अंक) ▸ **seventh** / 'सेव्न्थ् / *pron, det* सातवाँ।

seventeen / ,सेव्न्'टीन् / *noun, pron, det* सत्रह (का अंक)।

seventy / 'सेव्न्टि / *noun, pron, det* सत्तर (का अंक) ▸ **seventieth** / 'सेव्न्टि-अथ् / *noun, pron, det* सत्तरवाँ; सत्तरवाँ अंश 1/70 .

sever / 'सेवर् / *verb* (औप) 1 **sever sth (from sth)** किसी चीज़ को दो भागों में काट देना : *sever a rope* 2 संबंध तोड़ लेना : *sever all ties/links* ▸ **severance** *noun* (औप) संबंध-विच्छेद; काटना।

several / 'सेव्रल् / *indef det, pron* तीन से अधिक; कुछ : (*det*) *Several letters arrived this morning.* ० (*pron*) *Several of the paintings were destroyed in the fire.* ▸ **sev-**

erally / 'सेव्‌रलि / adv (क़ानून या औप) अलग-अलग।

severe / सि'विअर् / adj (-r, -st) 1 severe (on/with sb/sth) (व्यक्ति/ व्यवहार) कठोर, सख़्त (नियम पालन करने- कराने में) : a severe look ○ be severe with one's children 2 उग्र, प्रचंड : a severe shortage 3 अधिक मेहनत, निपुणता या कारीगरी की आवश्यकता वाला : severe competition for uni- versity places 4 (शैली आदि) सरल, अलंकार रहित : She wore a severe suit of plain grey with a white blouse. ▸ **severely** adv **severity** noun.

sew / सो / verb (pt sewed; pp sewn / सोन् / या sewed) सीना, सिलाई करना; सिलाई करके जोड़ देना : sew a skirt/ dress ▸ **sewing** / 'सोइङ् / noun कपड़ों का सिला जाना; सिले गए/जाने वाले कपड़े **sewing-machine** noun सिलाई मशीन।

sewage / 'सूइज्; स्यूइज् / noun नालियों (विशेषतः भूमिगत) में बहता हुआ मल।

sewer / 'सूअर्; स्यूअर् / noun बड़ा भूमि- गत नाला।

sex / सेक्स् / noun 1 लिंग (पुरुष या स्त्री होने की स्थिति) : Anyone can apply, regardless of age, race or sex. 2 sex (with sb) स्त्री-पुरुष सहवास, संभोग, सेक्स।

sexism / 'सेक्सिज़म् / noun लोगों, वि- शेषकर महिलाओं, के प्रति उनके लिंग के कारण अनुचित बर्ताव; ऐसा बर्ताव करने वाली मनोवृत्ति : blatant sexism in the se- lection of staff ▸ **sexist** / 'सेक्सि- स्ट् / adj : sexist language.

sexual / 'सेक्शुअल् / adj सेक्स से संबंधित; यौनाकर्षण विषयक।

shabby / 'शैबि / adj (-ier, -iest) 1 (वस्तुएँ) जीर्ण-शीर्ण दशा में 2 (व्यक्ति) फटेहाल; फटे-पुराने गंदे कपड़े पहनने वाला : You look pretty shabby in those clothes. 3 (व्यवहार) नीच,

कमीना : play a shabby trick ▸ **shab- bily** adv.

shack / शैक् / noun झोंपड़ी, कुटीर।

shackle / 'शैकल् / noun 1 (प्रायः pl) हथकड़ी, बेड़ी 2 shackles [pl] the shackles of sth बंधन, बाधा (स्वतंत्र अभिव्यक्ति आदि में) : the shackles of convention ▸ **shackle** verb 1 हथकड़ी डालना 2 बाधा डालना।

shade / शेड् / noun 1 shade (from sth) छाया 2 शेड (बल्ब आदि के ऊपर लगा ढक्कन) : a new shade for the lamp 3 रंग की मात्रा या गहराई : material in several shades of blue 4 चित्र का धुँधला भाग : There is not enough light and shade in your drawing. 5 shade of sth ज़रा-सा अंतर : people with all shades of opinion ▸ **shade** verb 1 shade sb/sth (from sth) ढकना, आड़ करना : shaded terraces 2 shade sth (in) चित्र को छायित करना, शेड देना : shade in a drawing 3 shade from sth into sth; shade (off) into sth धीरे-धीरे बदलना : scarlet shading (off) into pink.

shadow / 'शैडो / noun 1 छाया, परछाई : The chair cast a shadow on the wall. 2 गहरा धब्बा : have shadows under the eyes 3 लगातार पीछे-पीछे घूमने वाला व्यक्ति या पशु : The dog became his shadow and never left his side. 4 लगातार चुपचाप पीछा करने वाला व्यक्ति 5 आभासी वस्तु ▸ **shadow** verb 1 परछाई डालना; धुँधला करना 2 चुपचाप पीछा करना : He was shad- owed for a week by the secret police. **shadowy** adj 1 छायादार 2 छाया-सदृश 3 रहस्यमय।

shady / 'शेडि / adj (-ier, -iest) 1 छाया- दार : a shady corner of the garden 2 (अनौप, अपमा) बेईमानी वाला, अवैध : a shady deal.

shaft / शाफ़्ट; *US* शैफ़्ट / *noun* 1 तीर या भाले का डंडा; कुल्हाड़ी, हथौड़े आदि का डंडा 2 मोटर या मशीन आदि का डंडा, शाफ़्ट 3 गाड़ी का बम (जिनके बीच घोड़ा/बैल गाड़ी में जोता जाता है) 4 **shaft of sth** (प्रकाश का) किरण-पुंज : *a shaft of sth/sun- light* 5 खान आदि में वायु संचार या लिफ़्ट के आने जाने के लिए ऊर्ध्वाधर मार्ग : *a mine shaft.*

shaggy / 'शैगि / *adj* (बाल, रोएँ आदि) लंबे, घने, उलझे और मैले-कुचैले : *shaggy hair/eyebrows.*

shake / शेक् / *verb* (*pt* **shook**/ शुक् /; *pp* **shaken** / 'शेकन् /) 1 हिलना/ हिलाना : *Shake the bottle well be- fore pouring.* 2 **shake (with sth)** काँपना, लड़खड़ाना 3 **shake sb (up)** झँझोड़ना : *They were badly shaken (up) in the accident.* 4 (आवाज़ का) थरथराना, काँपना।

shaky / 'शेकि / *adj* (**-ier, -iest**) 1 हिलता हुआ; काँपता हुआ, कमज़ोर : *a shaky voice* 2 अस्थिर।

shall / शैल् / *modal verb* (*neg* **shall not;** *pt* **should** / शुड् /; *neg* **should not**) 1 भविष्य काल बनाने की सहायक क्रिया : *This time next week I shall be on holiday.* 2 (औप) निश्चयसूचक क्रिया : *I shall write to you again.* 3 सुझाव या प्रस्ताव सूचक : *Shall I do the washing-up?* 4 (औप) आदेश या निर्देश सूचक : *Candidates shall remain in their seats until all the papers have been collected.*

shallow / 'शैलो / *adj* (**-er, -est**) 1 छिछला : *shallow water* 2 (अपमा) (व्यक्ति) स्वभाव से ओछा, छिछोरा/ छिछला : *a shallow expression of emotion* ▸ **shallowly** *adv* **shallow- ness** *noun.*

sham / शैम् / *verb* (**-mm-**) स्वाँग भरना, नाटक करना : *sham illness/sleep*

▸ **sham** *noun* (प्राय: *अपमा*) 1 ढोंगी, नाटकबाज़ 2 ढोंग, दिखावा **sham** *adj* (प्राय: *अपमा*) बनावटी, जाली/मिथ्या : *a sham marriage ∘ sham jewellery.*

shambles / 'शैम्ब्ल्ज़् / *noun* (अनौप) पूर्ण अव्यवस्था की दशा : *Your room is (in) a shambles. Tidy it up!*

shame / शेम् / *noun* 1 लज्जा, शर्म : *feel shame at having told a lie* 2 कलंक, बदनामी 3 **a shame** [*sing*] (*अपमा, अनौप*) खेद की बात : *What a shame you didn't win.* ▸ **shame** *verb* 1 बदनाम करना, लज्जित करना : *You've shamed your family.* 2 शर्मिंदा करना; बाध्य करना : *shame sb into apologiz- ing* **shamefaced** *adj* झेंपू, संकोची : *a shamefaced expression* **shameful** *adj* शर्मनाक, लज्जाजनक **shameless** *adj* बेशरम, निर्लज्ज।

shampoo / शैम्'पू / *noun* 1 शैंपू 2 बालों में शैंपू लगाने की क्रिया; कालीन आदि को शैंपू से साफ़ करने के क्रिया : *give sb/sth a shampoo* ▸ **shampoo** *verb* शैंपू से केश, कालीन आदि मार्जन करना।

shape[1] / शेप / *noun* 1 शकल, आकृति : *a round/square shape* 2 (अनौप) स्थिति, दशा : *She's in good shape.* 3 किसी वस्तु की प्रकृति, गुण आदि ■ **in any shape (or form)** किसी भी प्रकार का : *I can't eat eggs in any shape or form.* ▸ **shapeless** *adj* बेडौल, भद्दा : *a shapeless dress* **shapely** *adj* अच्छी आकृति वाला : *a shapely figure.*

shape[2] / शेप / *verb* 1 **shape sth (into sth)** शकल/आकृति देना : *shape the clay into a ball* 2 किसी पर प्रभाव डालना, प्रकृति निर्धारित करना : *shape sb's future* ■ **shape (up)** (अनौप) विकास करना।

share / शेअर् / *noun* 1 **share (in sth/ sth of sth)** भाग / हिस्सा, अंश 2 **share (in/of sth)** किसी कार्य में या प्राप्ति में व्यक्ति

का हिस्सा : *She must take her share of the blame.* 3 *(वाणिज्य)* शेयर, अंश-दान ▸ **share** *verb* 1 **share sth (out) (among/between sb)** हिस्सा देना 2 **share (sth) (with sb)** बाँटना 3 **share (sth) (with sb)** साथ काम में लाना 4 **share (sth with sb)** किसी को कुछ बताना : *She won't share her secret (with us).*

shark / शार्क / *noun* 1 शार्क मछली 2 *(अनौप, अपमा)* बेईमान व्यक्ति या सूद-ख़ोर : *a loan shark.*

sharp / शार्प / *adj* (-er, -est) 1 तेज़ धार वाला : *a sharp knife/needle* 2 (मोड़, ढाल आदि) अचानक या जल्दी-जल्दी बदलने वाला : *a sharp bend in the road* 3 (चेहरा या नक्श) सुस्पष्ट, तीखा : *a sharp photographic image* 4 (ध्वनि) तीक्ष्ण, कर्णभेदी 5 (भोजन) खट्टा, तीखा या तीव्र गंध वाला 6 (वेदना) तीव्र, तेज़ : *a sharp frost/wind* 7 (निगाह) तुरंत पकड़ने वाली; कुशाग्र बुद्धि, तेज़ : *have sharp eyes* 8 **sharp (with sb)** *(अपमा)* कठोर, उग्र : *sharp criticism* 9 (अक्सर *अपमा*) तेज़, फुर्तीला, अवसर का या दूसरों के लाभ उठाने वाला : *a sharp lawyer* 10 *(संगीत)* सामान्य स्वर से ऊँचा स्वर : *That note sounded sharp.* ▸ **sharp** *noun* *(प्रतीक #)* संगीत में उच्च स्वर (तार स्वर) **sharp** *adv* 1 *(अनौप)* बिलकुल ठीक : *Please be here at seven sharp.* 2 *(अनौप)* अचानक : *stopped sharp* 3 *(संगीत)* उच्च स्वर में : *sing sharp* **sharpen** *verb* **sharpen (sth) (up)** तेज़ या पैना करना; बाढ़ पर चढ़ाना : *sharpen a pencil* **sharpener** / 'शॉर्पनर् / *noun* (वस्तुएँ) तेज़ करने का उपकरण : *a pencil-sharpener* **sharply** *adv*.

shatter / शैटर् / *verb* 1 चूर-चूर कर देना, टुकड़े-टुकड़े कर देना : *The explosion shattered all the windows.* 2 *(अनौप)*

आशाएँ तोड़ देना; मन को धक्का पहुँचाना : *We were shattered by the news.* 3 *(अनौप)* पूर्णत: नष्ट कर देना : *shatter sb's hope* ▸ **shattering** *adj*.

shave / शेव् / *verb* 1 **shave sth (off)** हजामत/दाढ़ी बनाना 2 **shave sth (off/ from sth)** पतली-पतली छीलन काटना 3 **shave sth (off sth)** थोड़ी मात्रा में कम करना : *shave half a second off the world record* ▸ **shave** *noun* हजामत **shavings** *noun* [*pl*] (लकड़ी की) छीलन, कतरन।

shawl / शॉल् / *noun* ओढ़ने की चादर (प्राय: ऊनी)।

she / शी / *pron* 1 स्त्रीवाचक 'वह', 'यह' : *Doesn't she look like her mother?* 2 स्त्रीवाचक अन्य संज्ञाएँ जैसे देश, जहाज़ आदि : *Nice car—how much did she cost?* ▸ **she** *noun* [*sing*] मादा।

sheaf / शीफ़् / *noun* (*pl* **sheaves** / शीव्ज़् /) 1 धान आदि का पूला, गट्ठर 2 काग़ज़ों का बंडल, पुलिंदा : *a sheaf of notes.*

shear / शिअर् / *verb* (*pt* **sheared**; *pp* **shorn** / शॉर्न् / या **sheared**) 1 भेड़ की ऊन काटना 2 **shear sth (off)** बाल काटना 3 **shear (off)** ऐंठ जाना या दबाव से टूट जाना : *The bolt sheared (off) and the wheel came off.* ■ **be shorn of sth** कुछ छिन जाना/छीन लिया जाना।

shears / शिअर्ज़् / *noun* [*pl*] घास, पौधे आदि काटने की बड़ी कैंची, कैंचा।

sheath / शीथ् / *noun* (*pl* **sheaths** / शीद्ज़् /) 1 (तलवार आदि की) म्यान 2 कोष आवरण, निरोध।

sheathe / शीद् / *verb* 1 (औप) म्यान में तलवार आदि रखना 2 **sheathe sth (in/ with sth)** आवरण चढ़ाना : *electric wire sheathed with plastic.*

shed¹ / शेड् / *noun* (प्राय: समासों में) शेड, सायबान : *a tool-shed/cattle-shed.*

shed² / शेड् / *verb* (**-dd-**; *pt, pp* **shed**)
1 गिराना, गिरने देना : *Many trees shed
their leaves in autumn.* 2 (औप)
बहाना, बहने देना : *shed tears* 3 उतारना,
फेंकना; छुटकारा पाना 4 **shed sth (on/
over sb/sth)** फैलाना : *The candle
shed a soft glow over the room.*

sheen / शीन् / *noun* [*sing*] चमक;
तड़क-भड़क : *the sheen of silk.*

sheep / शीप् / *noun* (*pl* अपरिवर्तित)
भेड़।

sheepish / 'शीपिश् / *adj* बेवकूफ़ी या
ग़लती के कारण शर्म-संकोच भरा : *a
sheepish grin.*

sheer / शिअर् / *adj* 1 एकदम, पूरा-पूरा :
sheer nonsense 2 (कपड़ा) बारीक,
हलका और लगभग पारदर्शी : *sheer nylon* 3 ऊर्ध्वाधर खड़ा : *a sheer rock
face.*

sheet / शीट् / *noun* 1 (कपड़े की) चादर
2 किसी भी पदार्थ की चदर; काग़ज़, शीशे
आदि का पत्तर : *a sheet of glass.*

sheikh (**shaikh, sheik** भी)/ शेख़/ शेक़ /
noun 1 शेख़ (अरबी मुखिया) 2 मुस्लिम
धार्मिक नेता ▸ **sheikhdom** *noun.*

shelf / शेल्फ़ / *noun* (*pl* **shelves**
/ शेल्व्ज़्/) 1 (अलमारी आदि का) ख़ाना;
टाँड़ : *the book on the top shelf*
2 कगार : *the continental shelf.*

shell / शेल् / *noun* 1 बाहरी कड़ा आवरण,
छिलका; कोष; सीप, सीपी : *collect shells
on the beach* 2 खंडहर वाले भवन की
बाहरी दीवार 3 तोप के गोले का बाहरी खोल;
कारतूस : *shell, mortar and sniper
fire* ▸ **shell** *verb* 1 बाहरी आवरण उतारना,
छिलका उतारना : *shell peas/peanuts*
2 गोले फेंकना/गोलीबारी करना : *shell the
enemy positions.*

shelter / 'शेल्टर / *noun* 1 **shelter
(from sth)** शरण, आश्रय 2 शरणस्थल,
पनाह की जगह : *They built a rough
shelter from old pieces of wood*
and cardboard. ▸ **shelter** *verb*
1 **shelter sb/sth (from sth/sb)** शरण
देना, सुरक्षा करना : *shelter an escaped
prisoner* 2 **shelter (from sth)** आश्रय
ढूँढ़ना; पनाह लेना : *shelter under the
trees ○ shelter from the rain.*

shelve / शेल्व् / *verb* 1 ताक / टाँड़ पर
रखना 2 योजना को स्थगित करना : *Plans
for a new theatre have had to be
shelved because of lack of money.*

shepherd /'शेपर्ड/ *noun* (*fem* **shep-
herdess**/ शेपर्'डेस्/) गडेरिया ▸ **shepherd** *verb* (लोगों का भेड़ों की तरह से)
मार्गदर्शन करना; नेतृत्व करना : *A guide
shepherded us into the museum.*

sheriff /'शेरिफ़/ *noun* एक शासनाधिकारी।

shield / शील्ड / *noun* 1 (विशेषत: पूर्व
समय में) कवच, ढाल 2 खेलों में पुरस्कार
के रूप में दी जाने वाली शील्ड 3 **shield
(against sth)** परिरक्षक, ओट : *This car
polish is an effective shield against
rust.* ▸ **shield** *verb* 1 **shield sb/sth
(against/from sth/sb)** रक्षा करना,
बचाना : *shield one's eyes (from the
sun) with one's hand* 2 **shield sb
(against/from sb/sth)** किसी को हानि
या ग़लत प्रभाव से बचाना : *I tried to
shield him against prying journalists.*

shift¹ / शिफ़्ट् / *verb* 1 **shift (sth)
(from...) (to...)** खिसकाना, खिसकना;
परिवर्तन, विचलन करना : *shift our priorities to another project* 2 घबराहट
या बेचैनी के कारण पहलू बदलना।

shift² / शिफ़्ट / *noun* 1 स्थान, दिशा या
प्रवृत्ति में बदलाव : *shifts in public
opinion* 2 (कर्मचारियों की) पाली; कार्य-
समय : *be on the night shift at the
factory.*

shifty / 'शिफ़्टि / *adj* (अनौप, अपमा)
अविश्वसनीय और बेईमान : *He looks
rather a shifty character.*

shilling / 'शिलिङ् / noun एक ब्रिटिश सिक्का (1971 तक प्रयुक्त)।

shimmer / 'शिमर् / verb झिलमिलाना : *moonlight shimmering on the lake* ▸ **shimmer** noun झिलमिल।

shin / शिन् / noun घुटने से नीचे टखने तक पैर का अग्रभाग।

shine / शाइन् / verb (pt, pp **shone** / शॉन्/) 1 चमकना, चमकाना : *I polished the glasses until they shone.* 2 **shine (at / in sth)** श्रेष्ठ होना, यशस्वी होना : *He didn't shine at games.* ▸ **shine** noun [sing] चमक, दीप्ति **shiny** / 'शा- इनि / adj (-ier, -iest) चमकदार।

shingle / 'शिङ्ग्ल् / noun (समुद्र तट पर) कंकड़ का ढेर : *a shingle beach.*

ship¹ / शिप् / noun जहाज़, पोत : *on board ship* ▸ **shipmate** noun सह- नाविक **shipyard** noun जहाज़ बनाने का कारख़ाना।

ship² / शिप् / verb (-pp-) जहाज़ द्वारा माल भेजना : *We ship goods to any part of the world.* ▸ **shipment** / 'शिप्मन्ट् / noun 1 जहाज़ पर सामान का लदान : *a shipment of grain for West Africa* 2 भेजा गया सामान, विशेषत: जहाज़ से **shipper** noun पोतवाणिक।

shipshape / 'शिप्शेप् / adj ठीक-ठाक; सुव्यवस्थित।

shipwreck / 'शिप्रेक् / noun तूफ़ान में जहाज़ का डूबना/टकरा कर विध्वंस होना : *suffer shipwreck* ▸ **shipwreck** verb जहाज़ को ध्वंस करना/डुबो देना।

shirk / शर्क् / verb (अपमा) काम से जी चुराना; भाग जाना : *He never shirks responsibility.* ▸ **shirker** noun कर्तव्य-त्यागी; कामचोर।

shirt / शर्ट् / noun कमीज़ ■ **in (one's) shirt sleeves** सिर्फ़ क़मीज़ में, बिना जैकेट के।

shiver / 'शिवर् / verb **shiver (with sth)** ठिठुरना, काँपना : *shivering with cold* ▸ **shiver** noun ठिठुरन, कँपकँपी।

shoal / शोल् / noun 1 मछलियों का झुंड 2 बड़ी संख्या में व्यक्ति/वस्तुएँ : *shoals of tourists.*

shock¹ / शॉक् / noun 1 आघात, सदमा 2 (चिकि) चोट से उत्पन्न अत्यंत कम- ज़ोरी : *suffer from shock after an accident* 3 (बिजली का) धक्का; तीव्र झटका : *If you touch this live wire, you'll get a shock.* 4 दहशत, जड़ता।

shock² / शॉक् / verb 1 धक्का/आघात पहुँचाना : *I was shocked by the news of her death.* 2 चकित करना, जड़ कर देना/हो जाना ▸ **shocking** adj.

shoddy / 'शॉडि / adj (-ier, -iest) (अपमा) घटिया, रद्दी : *shoddy work- manship* ▸ **shoddily** adv **shoddi- ness** noun.

shoe / शू/ noun 1 जूता 2 (**horseshoe** भी) घोड़े की नाल ■ **be in/put yourself in sb's shoes** अपने को किसी और की स्थिति में होने की कल्पना करना **if I was/ were in your shoes** (किसी सलाह के पूर्व प्रयुक्त) : *If I were in your shoes he'd soon know what I thought of him.* ▸ **shoe** verb (pt, pp **shod** / शॉड्/) घोड़े के नाल लगाना **shoestring (shoelace)** noun जूते का फ़ीता।

shoot¹ / शूट् / verb (pt, pp **shot** / शॉट् /) 1 **shoot (sth) (at sb/sth)**; **shoot sth (from sth)**; **shoot sth (off)** (राइफ़ल आदि से) गोली मारना, गोली चलाना 2 निपुणता से गोली चलाना : *Can you shoot (well)?* 3 बहुत ही तेज़ी से निकलना, जाना या भेजना : *The sports car shot past us.* 4 (दर्द का) टीसना, हूक उठना : *have a shooting pain in the back* 5 फ़िल्म की फ़ोटोग्राफ़ी करना ▸ **shooting** noun 1 गोली मारना 2 फ़िल्म की फ़ोटोग्राफ़ी **shooting star** noun उल्का (पिंड)।

shoot² / शूट् / noun 1 अंकुर : *healthy green shoots* 2 शिकार।

shop / शॉप् / noun 1 (*US* **store** भी) दुकान 2 (**workshop** भी) कारख़ाना, वर्कशॉप : *a machine shop* ■ **set up shop** अपना व्यवसाय शुरू करना ‣ **shop** verb (**-pp-**) **shop** (**for sth**) ख़रीदारी करना ■ **go shopping** बाज़ार जाना (ख़रीदारी के लिए) **shop around** (**for sth**) (*अनौप*) ख़रीदने से पहले अलग-अलग दुकानों में किसी वस्तु की क़ीमत, गुण आदि को ध्यानपूर्वक परखना ‣ **shop-keeper** noun दुकानदार **shoplift** / शॉप्-लिफ्ट् / verb दुकान से बिना दाम दिए वस्तु उठा लाना (एक प्रकार से चोरी करना) : *He started to shoplift as a fifteen-year-old.* **shoplifter** noun **shop-per** noun ख़रीदार **shopping** noun ख़रीदारी की क्रिया।

shore / शॉर् / noun समुद्र या झील का तट, पुलिन : *go on shore* (थल पर पहुँचना)।

short¹ / शॉर्ट् / adj (**-er, -est**) 1 छोटा; ठिगना, नाटा : *a short person* 2 संक्षिप्त; अधिक समय तक न रहने वाला : *a short speech* 3 **short** (**of sth**) सामान्य या अपेक्षित से कम होना; कम पड़ जाना; अपर्याप्त : *be short of time* 4 **short on sth** (*अनौप*) अपेक्षित गुण न होना : *He's short on tact.* 5 **short for sth** नाम, शब्द आदि का संक्षिप्त रूप होना 6 (पेस्ट्री, केक आदि) भुरभुरा ■ **in short** संक्षेप में ‣ **shortcoming** noun (प्राय: pl) त्रुटि; कमी/कसर **short cut** noun सुगम मार्ग, सरल उपाय **shorthand** noun आशु-लिपि (बोले हुए को विशेष चिह्नों से जल्दी-जल्दी लिखना) **short-handed** adj कार्यकर्ताओं की कमी वाला **short-sighted** adj 1 दूरवर्ती वस्तुओं को ठीक से न देख सकने वाला 2 (*अलं*) अदूरदर्शी **short-tempered** adj चिड़चिड़ा, बद-मिज़ाज।

short² / शॉर्ट् / adv अचानक, अकस्मात् : *She stopped short when she saw the accident.* ■ **fall short of** अपेक्षित पाने में असफल।

shortage / 'शॉर्टिज् / noun अभाव, अ-पर्याप्तता : *food/fuel shortages.*

shorten / 'शॉर्टन् / verb छोटा/संक्षिप्त करना : *shorten one's journey by several miles.*

shortly / 'शॉर्ट्लि / adv 1 तुरंत, अविलंब 2 **shortly after.../before...** निकट भविष्य/अतीत में।

shorts / शॉर्ट्स् / noun [pl] 1 हाफ़पैंट, 2 निकर, जाँघिया।

shot / शॉट् / noun 1 **shot** (**at sb/sth**) बंदूक से दाग़ी गई गोली या इस प्रक्रिया से उत्पन्न आवाज़ : *take a shot at the enemy* 2 (**lead shot** भी) छर्रे 3 (pl अपरिवर्तित) तोप का गोला 4 फ़ोटोग्राफ़ : *a close-up shot* 5 खेल में बॉल को तेज़ी से मारना ■ **a shot in the arm** नई ताज़गी, स्फूर्ति और उत्साह से भर देने वाली बात या चीज़।

should / शुड् / modal verb (neg **should not**) 1 (कर्तव्य, ज़रूरत या औचित्य व्यक्त करने के लिए प्रयुक्त) : *You shouldn't drink and drive.* 2 (सुझाव माँगने/देने में प्रयुक्त) : *Should I phone him and apologize?* 3 (संभावना व्यक्त करने में प्रयुक्त) 4 (किसी के कहे को दोह-राने के लिए **shall** के भूतकाल रूप में प्रयुक्त)।

shoulder / 'शोल्डर् / noun 1 कंधा 2 **shoulders** [pl] स्कंध; कंधे : *a person with broad shoulders* 3 किसी वस्तु का कंधेनुमा भाग, जैसे बोतल या पर्वत का ‣ **shoulder** verb 1 कंधे पर रखना; कंधा देना : *She shouldered her backpack and set off along the road.* 2 ज़िम्मेदारी/दोष लेना : *shoulder the burdens of high office* 3 कंधा मारकर रास्ते से हटाना **shoulder-blade** noun कंधे की हड्डी।

shout / शाउट् / noun चीख़-पुकार; शोर-गुल : *shouts of joy* ▸ **shout** *verb* 1 **shout sth (at/to sb); shout sth (out)** चीख़ कर कुछ कहना 2 **shout (out)** शोर मचाना/चीख़कर बुलाना ■ **shout sb down** कोलाहल मचाकर किसी को बोलने से रोकना : *The crowd kept shouting the speaker down.*

shove / शव् / verb 1 रूखेपन से ठेलना, धकेलना : *He shoved her out of the way.* 2 (अनौप) लापरवाही से कहीं कुछ रख/पटक देना : *shove papers (away) in a drawer* ▸ **shove** noun (प्राय: sing) धक्का।

shovel / शव़्ल् / noun 1 बेलचा 2 बड़ी मशीन का मिट्टी उठाने वाला भाग ▸ **shovel** verb (-ll-; US -l-) बेलचे से उठाना/हटाना : *spend hours shovelling snow.*

show¹ / शो / noun 1 कार्यक्रम, प्रदर्शन; प्रदर्शनी आदि : *a comedy show* 2 प्र-दर्शन, दिखावा : *put on a show of strength* 3 (अनौप) किसी घटना, संस्थान या व्यवसाय का प्रदर्शन : *She runs the whole show.* ■ **for show** केवल प्रभाव जमाने के लिए, न कि इस्तेमाल करने के लिए : *These books are just for show—she never reads them.* **on show** ऐसे स्थान पर रखा हुआ जहाँ आम लोग देख सकें : *The collection is on show at the National Museum.* ▸ **show-business** (अनौप **showbiz** भी) noun कौतुक-व्यवसाय, व्यावसायिक मनोरंजन, विशेषरूप से रंगमंच से जुड़ा **showcase** noun प्रदर्शन-मंजूषा **show-down** noun किसी विवाद के अंत में निर्णायक बहस, झगड़ा या बलपरीक्षा : *Management are seeking a show-down with the unions.* **showy** adj (-ier, -iest) भड़कीला, दिखाऊ।

show² / शो / verb (pt **showed**; pp **shown**/शोन्/या, बहुत कम ही, **showed**)

1 **show sth (to sb)** दिखाना, दिखा देना प्रदर्शित करना : *She showed the technique to her students.* 2 इंगित करके दिखाना : *I showed him the way out.* 3 **show sth (at...)** (फ़िल्म आदि) प्रदर्शित करना, चलाना : *The film is being shown at the local cinema.* 4 प्रमाण आदि प्रस्तुत करना; अपनी योग्यता सिद्ध करना : *a soldier who showed great courage* 5 कोई माप, अंकन आदि दिखाना : *The town hall clock showed midnight.* 6 सामने आना; प्रकट होना : *His annoyance showed itself in his face.* ■ **show sb/sth off** लोगों को जतलाने का प्रयल करना, क्योंकि उसे इस पर नाज़ है : *a dress that shows off her figure* **show up** (अनौप) पहुँचना, विशेषकर जब कोई प्रतीक्षा कर रहा हो : *We were hoping for a full team today but only five players showed up.* ▸ **show-off** noun (अपमा) दूसरों को प्रभावित करने का प्रयास करने वाला व्यक्ति।

shower / ˈशाउअर् / noun 1 बौछार (बारिश आदि की) : *snow showers* 2 शावर, फुहारा-स्नान : *an electric shower* ○ *have a quick shower* 3 (छोटी) वस्तुओं का गुच्छा : *a shower of sparks* ○ (अलं) *a shower of insults* ▸ **shower** verb 1 बौछार करना, छिड़कना; बरसना 2 शावर के नीचे नहाना : *He showered, changed and went out.*

shred / श्रेड् / noun 1 (प्राय: pl) धज्जी : *His jacket was torn to shreds by the barbed wire.* 2 **shred of sth** (प्राय: sing, नकारात्मक वाक्यों में) ज़रा-सी मात्रा : *There is not a shred of evidence to support what he says.* ▸ **shred** verb (-dd-) धज्जियाँ करना (छोटे-छोटे टुकड़े करना) : *shredded cabbage.*

shrewd / श्रूड् / *adj* (**-er, -est**) समझदार, चतुर, सयाना : *make a shrewd guess.*

shriek / श्रीक् / *verb* **1** shriek (with sth); shriek (out) अचानक चीख़ मारना **2** shriek sth (out) चीख़ मारकर कुछ कहना ▸ **shriek** *noun* चीख़।

shrill / श्रिल् / *adj* **1** (**-er, -est**) (ध्वनि, आवाज़ आदि) तीक्ष्ण, कर्णभेदी : *a shrill cry/whistle* **2** (कभी-कभी *अपमा*) (विरोध, माँग आदि) तीख़ा एवं शक्ति-शाली : *shrill complaints.*

shrimp / श्रिम्प् / *noun* **1** झींगा मछली **2** (*परि* या *अपमा*) छोटा-सा आदमी।

shrine / श्राइन् / *noun* shrine (to sb/ sth); shrine (for sb) मक़बरा, रौज़ा, समाधि : *make a pilgrimage to local shrines.*

shrink / श्रिङ्क् / *verb* (*pt* **shrank** / श्रैङ्क् / या **shrunk** / श्रङ्क् /; *pp* **shrunk**) **1** (कपड़े का) धुलने पर सिकुड़ जाना : *Will this shirt shrink in the wash?* **2** आकार या मात्रा में कम होना : *the shrinking countryside* **3** डर या घृणा से पीछे हटना : *shrink back in horror* ■ **shrink from sth/doing sth** कुछ करने को अनिच्छुक होना : *There's no point in shrinking from the truth.* ▸ **shrunken** *adj* सिकुड़ा हुआ।

shrivel / 'श्रिवल् / *verb* (**-ll-**; *US* **-l-**) shrivel (up) झुर्री या शिकन पड़ना; कुम्ह-लाना : *The leaves had shrivelled (up) in the sun.*

shroud / श्राउड् / *noun* **1** (**winding-sheet** भी) कफ़न **2** shroud of sth ढकने, छुपाने वाली वस्तु : *shrouds of fog/smoke* ▸ **shroud** *verb* shroud sth in sth ढकना, छुपाना : *shrouded in darkness/mystery.*

shrub / श्रब् / *noun* झाड़ी, झाड़-झंखाड़ ▸ **shrubbery** *noun.*

shrug / श्रग् / *verb* (**-gg-**) (उपेक्षा या अरुचि जताने के लिए) कंधे उचकाना : *He shrugged his shoulders and walked away.* ■ **shrug (sth) off** टालना, उपेक्षा करना, ध्यान नहीं देना : *The government is trying to shrug off blame for the economic crisis.* ▸ **shrug** *noun* (प्राय: *sing*) कंधे उचकाना : *give a resigned shrug (of the shoulders).*

shudder / 'शडर् / *verb* **1** shudder (with sth) काँप उठना, थरथराना : *shudder with disgust* **2** (वाहन, मशीन, भवन आदि का) हिलना, काँपना : *The whole house shuddered as the bomb exploded.* ▸ **shudder** *noun.*

shuffle / 'शफ़्ल् / *verb* **1** घिसटते हुए चलना : *The queue shuffled forward slowly.* **2** बैठे हुए या खड़े हुए (बोर होकर) पैरों की स्थिति बदलना : *The audience began to shuffle (their feet) impatiently.* **3** ताश के पत्तों को बाँटने से पहले फेंटना; काग़ज़ात अस्त-व्यस्त करना ▸ **shuffle** *noun.*

shun / शन् / *verb* (**-nn-**) किसी व्यक्ति/ वस्तु से दूर रहना, बचना : *shun public-ity/other people.*

shunt / शन्ट् / *verb* **1** रेल के डिब्बे को बग़ल की पटरी पर ले जाना (शंट करना) **2** (*अनौप*) किसी को कहीं (कम महत्त्वपूर्ण स्थान पर) भेज देना, स्थानांतरित करना : *She's been shunted off to a re-gional office.*

shut / शट् / *verb* (**-tt-**; *pt, pp* **shut**) **1** (द्वार, खिड़की आदि) बंद करना; (किसी चीज़ को) बंद कर देना : *The window won't shut.* **2** खुली चीज़ (जैसे आँखें, पुस्तक, पर्स आदि) बंद करना : *shut a book/wallet* **3** दुकान बंद करना ■ **shut sb/oneself in (sth)** (किसी व्यक्ति का) भीतर बंद हो जाना shut (sb) up (*अनौप*) बोलना बंद करना/करवाना shut (sth) down फ़ैक्टरी बंद हो जाना shut sth off (गैस, पानी आदि का) बंद हो जाना या करना; (रेडियो या टी वी आदि को) बंद कर देना

shut sth up (सुरक्षा के लिए) द्वार-खिड़की आदि बंद कर लेना।

shutter / 'शटर्/ noun 1 शटर, (खिड़की की) झिलमिली। दुकानों आदि का शटर 2 कैमरे का शटर : *hear the shutter click.*

shuttle / 'शट्ल्/ noun 1 शटल (सिलाई मशीन की भरनी, फिरकी) 2 दो स्थानों के मध्य नियमित यात्रा करने वाला वायुयान अथवा बस सेवा : *There's a shuttle service between Delhi and Meerut.* 3 बेडमिंटन खेल में प्रयुक्त शटल कॉक (चिड़िया) ▸ **shuttle** *verb* दो बिंदुओं के मध्य नियमित गति करना।

shy / शाइ / adj (shyer, shyest) 1 (व्यक्ति) संकोची, झेंपू 2 संकोच दिखाने वाला : *a shy smile* 3 **shy of sth/ doing sth** किसी बात से/कहीं हिस्सा लेने से डरने वाला : *be shy of publicity* 4 (पशुओं का) बहुत जल्दी घबरा/भड़क जाना, भड़कैल; बिदकने वाला ▸ **shy** *verb* (*pt, pp* shied / शाइड् /) **shy (at sth)** (विशेषतः घोड़े का) भड़क जाना : *The colt shied at a paper bag blowing in the wind.* **shyly** *adv* **shyness** *noun.*

sibling / सिब्लिङ्/ noun (औप) सहोदर भाई और/या बहन।

sick / सिक्/ adj (-er, -est) 1 मानसिक या शारीरिक रूप से बीमार, अस्वस्थ : *She's been sick for weeks.* 2 उलटी करने की इच्छा होना, वमन/कै होना : *feeling sick* 3 **sick of sth/sb/doing sth** (अनौप) ऊबा हुआ : *I'm sick of waiting around like this.* 4 **sick (at/about sth/doing sth)** अत्यंत ऊबा या झुंझलाया हुआ, निराश : *We were pretty sick about losing the match.*

sicken / 'सिकन्/ verb 1 किसी को ऊबा देना, वितृष्णा पैदा कर देना : *Cruelty sickens me.* 2 **sicken (for sth)** बीमार होना शुरू होना (बीमारी की पहली अवस्था

में) : *He slowly sickened and died.* ▸ **sickening** *adj* **sickeningly** *adv.*

sickle / 'सिकुल्/ noun हँसिया, घास काटने वाली दराँती।

sickly / 'सिकुलि / adj 1 दुर्बल, प्रायः अस्वस्थ रहने वाला : *a sickly child* 2 जी मतलाने वाला : *a sickly smell/ taste.*

sickness / 'सिकनस् / noun बीमारी, अस्वास्थ्यकर; बीमारी-विशेष : *sleeping sickness.*

side[1] / साइड्/ noun 1 (विशेषतः *sing*) बग़ल, पार्श्व : *drive along the left side of the street* 2 (गणित) ठोस के पार्श्व तल : *the six sides of a cube* 3 समतल की भुजाएँ : *the four sides of a square* 4 झगड़े/प्रतिस्पर्धा आदि में दल/पक्ष : *the two sides in the strike (ie employ- ers and workers)* 5 (तर्क-वितर्क में) पक्ष : *You must hear his side of things now.* 6 खिलाड़ियों का दल/पक्ष, टीम : *the winning/losing side* ■ **on every side** हर तरफ़ **put sth on one side** रख लेना, बचाना **side by side** पास-पास, बग़ल-बग़ल **take sides (with sb); take sb's side** समर्थन करना, विवाद में पक्ष लेना ▸ **side-car** *noun* मोटर साइकिल के बग़ल में लगी एक पहिये की साइड-कार **sidewalk** *noun* (*US*) सड़क के किनारे की पटरी, फुटपाथ **sideways** *adj, adv* तिरछा।

side[2] / साइड् / verb ■ **side with (against sb)** विवाद में समर्थन करना।

sideboard / 'साइड्बॉर्ड् / noun भोज- नालयों की ख़ानों वाली मेज़।

sideline / 'साइड्लाइन् / noun 1 मुख्य जीविका-कार्य से अतिरिक्त (गौण) कार्य 2 **sidelines** [*pl*] फुटबॉल पिच या टेनिस कोर्ट की लंबाई की तरफ़ की दो रेखाएं; इन रेखाओं के ठीक बाहर की जगह ■ **on the sidelines** किसी चीज़ का आवलोकन करना पर उसमें सम्मिलित न होना ▸ **side-**

line *verb* किसी को मैच, टीम आदि से बाहर करना; निष्क्रिय करना।

sidetrack / 'साइड्ट्रैक् / *verb* मुख्य विषय या मुद्दे से हटकर बातें करना।

siding / 'साइडिङ् / *noun* रेलवे स्टेशन पर मुख्य लाइन के बग़ल की छोटी लंबाई की लाइन।

sidle / 'साइड्ल् / *verb* **sidle up/over (to sb/sth); sidle along, past, away,** etc झिझकते हुए दब कर चलना : *He apologized and sidled out of the room.*

siege / सीज् / *noun* 1 (युद्ध में क़िले आदि की) घेराबंदी : *the siege of Troy* 2 पुलिस द्वारा किसी भवन की घेराबंदी : *The siege was finally brought to an end when the terrorists surrendered.* ■ **lay siege to sth** घेरा डालना : *Crowds of journalists laid seige to the star's flat.*

sieve / सिव् / *noun* चलनी/छलनी; छन्नी ■ **have a memory/mind like a sieve** बहुत कमज़ोर स्मरणशक्ति होना; आसानी से भूल जाना ▸ **sieve** *verb* छानना (छलनी से) : *sieve the flour into a bowl.*

sift / सिफ़्ट् / *verb* 1 चालना, छानना : *sift the flour/sugar*; **sift sth (out) from sth; sift sth out** छलनी में डाल कर अलग करना 2 **sift (through) sth** अत्यंत सावधानी से परीक्षण/जाँच करना : *sift the evidence.*

sigh / साइ / *verb* **sigh (with sth)** आह भरना, ठंडी साँस खींचना/लेना : *He sighed with relief on finding the key in his pocket.* ■ **sigh for sth/sb** (औप) ललकना, लालायित रहना ▸ **sigh** *noun* आह (भरने की ध्वनि या प्रक्रिया)।

sight¹ / साइट् / *noun* 1 दृष्टि : *lose one's sight* 2 **sight of sb/sth** देखना, दिखाई पड़ना : *faint at the sight of blood* 3 जहाँ तक दृष्टि जा सकती है वह क्षेत्र : *He ate everything in sight.*

4 **sights** [*pl*] दर्शनीय स्थल, दृश्य 5 (प्राय: *pl*) राइफ़ल में निशाना ठीक लगाने वाली युक्ति, दीदबान : *the sights of a rifle* ■ **at/on sight** जैसे ही कुछ/कोई दिखे : *Soldiers were ordered to shoot on sight anybody trying to enter the building.* **hate, be sick of, etc the sight of sb/sth** (अनौप) किसी से अत्यंत घृणा करना : *My car breaks down so often that I'm beginning to hate the sight of it.* **out of sight, out of mind** (कहा) न दिखाई देने वाले व्यक्ति/ वस्तु को हम अक्सर भूल जाते हैं ▸ **sighted** *adj* देखने में समर्थ **-sighted** (समासों में) इस तरह से देखने का सामर्थ्य : *short-/ long-/far-sighted* **sightseeing** *noun* सैर-सपाटा, पर्यटन।

sight² / साइट् / *verb* (समीप आने पर) देख पाना : *After twelve days at sea, we sighted land.*

sign¹ / साइन् / *noun* 1 चिह्न, प्रतीक : *mathematical signs* (जैसे +, x और ÷) 2 सार्वजनिक सूचना देने वाले संकेत : *traffic signs* 3 बिना बोले (उत्तर में या निर्देश देने के लिए) किया गया इशारा : *She gave me a sign to sit down.* 4 **sign (of sth)** इंगित, लक्षण : *signs of suffering on his face* 5 (**sign of the zodiac** भी) बारह राशियों और प्रतीक चिह्नों में से कोई भी एक ▸ **signboard/signpost** *noun* सार्वजनिक सूचना पट्ट।

sign² / साइन् / *verb* 1 हस्ताक्षर करना : *sign a letter/cheque/contract* 2 इशारों से कहना : *The police officer signed (for) them to stop.* 3 **sign (sb) (for/with/to sb/sth)** किसी खिलाड़ी, संगीतकार आदि के साथ समझौते पर हस्ताक्षर करना : *The band signed to/with Venus Records.* ■ **sign off** 1 पत्र की समाप्ति करना : *She signed off with 'Yours ever, Rajni'.* 2 किसी प्रसारण को विशेष प्रकार से समाप्त करना : *This is* *your resident DJ signing off and wishing you a pleasant weekend.* **sign (sb) in/out** किसी स्थान (जैसे होटल) पर पहुँचने/से प्रस्थान करने पर अपना नाम लिखना : *You must sign guests in when they enter the club.* **sign (sb) on/up (for sth)** कार्य करने के लिए अनुबंध पर हस्ताक्षर करना।

signal / 'सिग्नल् / 1 चेतावनी, सूचना आदि के लिए प्रयुक्त संकेत : *She flashed the torch as a signal.* 2 यातायात को संकेत देने के लिए उपकरण : *traffic signal* ० *The signal (i.e. light) was at red, so the train stopped.* 3 किसी बात का संकेत; ऐसी घटना या कार्य जिससे अन्य कार्रवाई शुरू होती हो : *The President's arrival was the signal for an outburst of cheering.* ▶ **signal** *verb* (-II-; *US* -I-) 1 **signal (to sb/sth) (for sth)** संकेत करना; सांकेतिक यंत्र काम में लाना; सूचना देना : *signal a message* **signal-box** *noun* रेलवे सिगनल-घर।

signature / 'सिग्नचर् / *noun* 1 हस्ताक्षर; हस्ताक्षर करना 2 अद्वितीय गुण : *The film bears the signature of the director.*

significance / सिग् 'निफ़िकन्स् / *noun* 1 तात्पर्य, अर्थ : *I didn't understand the significance of his remark until later.* 2 महत्त्व : *a speech of great significance.*

significant / सिग् 'निफ़िकन्ट् / *adj* महत्त्वपूर्ण; अर्थपूर्ण : *a significant remark* ० *make a significant saving.*

signify / 'सिग्निफ़ाइ / *verb* 1 अर्थ होना, अर्थ रखना : *Do the dark clouds signify rain?* 2 संकेत करना, संकेत द्वारा बताना, व्यक्त करना : *She signifed her approval with a smile.* 3 महत्त्व रखना।

silence / 'साइलन्स् / *noun* 1 मौन, ख़ामोशी : *A scream shattered the silence.* 2 चुप्पी : *They listened to*

him in silence. ० *I can't understand his silence on the matter.* ▶ **silence** *verb* चुप करना/कराना, मौन कर देना : *His look of disapproval silenced her.*

silent / 'साइलन्ट् / *adj* 1 चुप, ख़ामोश; नीरव; बिना आवाज़ किए : *with silent footsteps* 2 मूक; अल्पभाषी : *There were several questions I wanted to ask but I kept/remained silent.* 3 (अक्षर) लिखा जाने वाला लेकिन उच्चारित न किया जाने वाला : *The 'b' in 'doubt' is silent.*

silhouette / सिल्‌'उएट् / *noun* 1 सफ़ेद पर्दे पर काली परछाई जिसमें पूरी आकृति साफ़ दिखाई पड़ जाती है, छायाचित्र 2 हलकी पृष्ठभूमि में किसी व्यक्ति या वस्तु की काली आकृति : *the silhouettes of the trees against the evening sky* ▶ **silhouette** *verb* **silhouette sb/sth (against sth)** छायाचित्र के रूप में दिखाना।

silicon / 'सिलिकन् / *noun* (प्रतीक Si) एक रासायनिक पदार्थ जो रेत और कई तरह के पत्थरों में पाया जाता है और जिसका प्रयोग काँच, कंप्यूटर और अन्य विद्युत यंत्र बनाने में होता है ▶ **silicon chip** / 'सिलिकन् 'चिप् / *noun* सिलिकॉन का एक बहुत छोटा टुकड़ा जिसमें जटिल इलेक्ट्रॉनिक परिपथ होता है।

silk / सिल्क् / *noun* 1 रेशम; रेशमी वस्त्र : *dressed in silk* 2 **silks** [*pl*] (*अप्र*) रेशमी कपड़ा।

silky / 'सिल्कि / *adj* (-ier, -iest) रेशम जैसा, रेशमी।

sill / सिल् / *noun* खिड़की या दरवाज़े के नीचे का कुछ आगे निकला पत्थर या पटरा, दासा।

silly / 'सिलि / *adj* (-ier, -iest) 1 बेवकूफ़ी भरा, मूर्खतापूर्ण : *silly mistakes* 2 अल्प-बुद्धि; लापरवाह; बच्चों जैसा : *play silly games.*

silt / सिल्ट् / *noun* नदी द्वारा मुहाने पर छोड़ा रेत, कीचड़, गाद ▶ **silt** *verb* ■ **silt (sth)**

up (बंदरगाह आदि का) गाद से भर जाना : *The harbour has silted up.*

silver / 'सिल्वर् / *noun* 1 चाँदी 2 चाँदी का सामान, सिक्के आदि 3 रजत पदक : *Puja won the silver for India.*
▶ **silver** *verb* 1 चाँदी की परत चढ़ाना 2 चाँदी जैसा चमकना : *The years have silvered her hair.* **silver** *adj* रुपहला; चाँदी से बना या चाँदी जैसा : *a silver plate/dish/watch* **silver jubilee** / सिल्वर् जूबिली / *noun* (प्राय: *sing*) पच्चीसवीं सालगिरह/वर्षगाँठ **silvery** *adj* 1 रुपहला, चाँदी सदृश : *silvery grey hair* 2 (ध्वनि) सुमधुर, स्पष्ट।

similar / 'सिमलर् / *adj* **similar (to sb/sth); similar (in sth)** समान, समतुल्य, मिलता-जुलता : *We have similar tastes in music.* ▶ **similarly** *adv* वैसा ही, उस जैसा : *The two boys dress similarly.* **similarity** / सिम्'लैरटि / *noun* (*pl* **similarities**) **similarity (to sb/sth); similarity (between A and B)** समानता, सादृश्य : *points of similarity between the two proposals.*

simile / 'सिमिलि / *noun* उपमा-अलंकार, जैसे 'brave as a lion'.

simmer / 'सिमर् / *verb* 1 (भोजन बनाते समय) किसी पात्र या भोजन को लगभग उबलती हुई स्थिति में बनाए रखना : *Leave the soup to simmer.* 2 **simmer (with sth)** अंदर ही अंदर (क्रोध आदि से) उबलना : *simmer with rage/annoyance* ▶ **simmer** *noun*.

simple / 'सिम्प्ल् / *adj* (-r, -st) 1 साधारण, सहज में किया या समझा जा सकने वाला : *a simple task/sum* 2 सादा : *simple food* 3 रचना एवं कार्य में सरल, अत्यंत विकसित स्थिति में नहीं : *simple forms of life* 4 निष्कपट, सरल, सच्चा : *behave in a simple, open way* 5 बुद्धू, अनुभवहीन : *He's not as simple as he looks.* 6 इससे ज्यादा नहीं, इसके अलावा

कुछ नहीं : *give a simple unbiased account of the events* 7 (व्या) वर्तमान या भूतकाल में क्रिया के लिए उपयुक्त जब कर्तृवाच्य क्रिया बिना किसी सहायक क्रिया से बने ▶ **simply** / 'सिम्प्लि / *adv* 1 आसान रीति से : *solved quite simply* 2 साधारण ढंग से : *be dressed simply* 3 बिल्कुल, एकदम : *I simply refuse to go!* 4 केवल, मात्र : *I bought the picture simply because I liked it.*

simplicity / सिम्'प्लिसटि / *noun* सरलता, निष्कपटता; साधारणता, सहजता : *the simplicity of the problem.*

simplify / 'सिम्प्लिफ़ाइ / *verb* (*pt, pp* **simplified**) सरल करना, आसान बनाना : *simplify the instructions* ▶ **simplification** / सिम्प्लिफ़ि'केशन् / *noun* 1 [*sing*] सहज, सरल बनाने की प्रक्रिया : *simplification of the rules* 2 कथन, स्थिति आदि जो किसी चीज़ को ज्यादा सरल बनाने से उत्पन्न हो : *That's a simplification—the reality is more complex.*

simplistic / सिम्'प्लिस्टिक् / *adj* (प्राय: *अपमा*) परिस्थितियों, विषयों आदि को वास्तविकता से कम जटिल दिखाते/समझते हुए : *a rather simplistic assessment of the situation.*

simulate / 'सिम्युलेट् / *verb* 1 कोई मनोभाव महसूस करने का स्वांग भरना : *simulate anger/joy/interest* 2 किसी प्रतिमान या ढाँचे के द्वारा कोई परिस्थिति उत्पन्न करना : *simulate a battle* ○ *The computer simulates conditions on the sea bed.* 3 किसी व्यक्ति/वस्तु की शकल या आकार लेना : *insects that simulate dead leaves.*

simultaneous / सिम्ल्'टेनिअस; *US* साइमल्'टेनिअस / *adj* **simultaneous (with sth)** एककालिक, एक ही समय घटित होने वाला : *simultaneous demonstrations in New Delhi and*

Bangalore ▸ **simultaneously** *adv* साथ-साथ, युगपत् : *All the eggs hatch simultaneously.*

sin / सिन् / *noun* 1 पाप (कर्म) 2 गंभीर अपराध/ग़लती ▸ **sin** *verb* (-nn-) **sin** (**against sth**) पाप करना; अपराध करना : *He had sinned and repented.* **sinful** *adj* पापपूर्ण; पापी; बुरा **sinfully** *adv* **sinfulness** *noun* **sinner** / 'सिनर् / *noun* पापी।

since / सिन्स् / *prep* के बाद से : *She's been ill since Sunday.* ∘ *Since the party he had only spoken to her once.* ▸ **since** *adv* (भूतकाल की) किसी तिथि-विशेष के बाद से; वर्तमान से पूर्व : *The original building has long since been demolished.* **since** *conj* 1 के बाद से : *Rekha hasn't phoned since she went to Lucknow.* 2 क्योंकि, चूँकि : *Since I haven't got her address I can't write to her.*

sincere / सिन्'सिअर् / *adj* (-r, -st) 1 (भाव, व्यवहार) सच्चा, न कि दिखावटी : *sincere affection* 2 (व्यक्ति) निष्कपट; सच्चा : *a sincere well-wisher* ▸ **sincerely** *adv* : *thank somebody sincerely* **sincerity** / सिन्'सेरटि / *noun* सच्चाई, निष्कपटता; ईमानदारी : *the warmth and sincerity of his welcome.*

sing / सिङ्/ *verb* (*pt* **sang** / सैङ्/; *pp* **sung** / सङ्/) 1 **sing** (**sth**) (**for/to sb**) गाना, गीत गाना; (चिड़ियों का) चहचहाना, चहकना : *She always sings in the bath.* 2 गूँजना : *The kettle was singing (away) on the cooker.* ■ **sing along** (**with sb/sth**); **sing along** (**to sth**) किसी व्यक्ति, बाजे, रिकॉर्ड आदि के साथ गाना **sing sb's/sth's praises** किसी व्यक्ति या चीज़ की खूब प्रशंसा करना ▸ **singer** *noun* गायक/गायिका **singing** *noun* गायन **sing-song**

adj (भाषण में उबा देने वाला) आरोही-अवरोही (स्वर)।

singe / सिन्ज्/ *verb* (*pres p* **singeing**) (प्राय: ग़लती से) झुलसना/झुलसाना : *He leaned over the candle and singed his jacket.*

single / 'सिङ्ग्ल् / *adj* 1 अकेला, न कि समूह में; अलग, पृथक : *a single red rose* ∘ *the single most important event in the history of the world* 2 अविवाहित : *single men and women* 3 एक ही व्यक्ति द्वारा किया/प्रयोग में लाया जाने वाला : *a single bed* 4 (*US* **one-way**) एक तरफ़ा टिकट (न कि वापसी टिकट) : *a single fare/ticket* ▸ **single** *noun* 1 (अनौप) एक तरफ़ा टिकट 2 **singles** [*pl*] (विशेषत: *US*) अविवाहित लोग 3 **singles** खेल जिसमें दोनों ओर केवल एक-एक खिलाड़ी हो : *the men's/women's singles in the golf tournament* **single** *verb* ■ **single sb/sth out** (**for sth**) समूह में से किसी एक को छाँटना, चुनना : *He was singled out for punishment.* ▸ **single-handed** *adj, adv* बिना दूसरे की सहायता के : *do sth single-handed* **single-handedly** *adv* **singly** *adv* एक-एक करके; अकेले।

singular / 'सिङ्ग्यलर् / *adj* 1 (व्या) एकवचन : *a singular verb/noun* 2 (औप) असाधारण, अनोखा : *a singular achievement* ▸ **singular** *noun* (व्या) एकवचन रूप : *The word 'clothes' has no singular.* **singularly** *adv*.

sinister / 'सिनिस्टर् / *adj* अमंगल; अनर्थकारी : *a sinister motive/conspiracy.*

sink¹ / सिङ्क् / *verb* (*pt* **sank** / सैङ्क्/; *pp* **sunk** / सङ्क् /) 1 डूबना; जहाज़ को डुबोना या डूबने देना : *The ship sank.* 2 (अनौप) किसी योजना, व्यक्ति आदि को असफल कर देना : *The press want to sink his bid for the presidency.* 3 ढलवाँ होना; क्षीण होना; धँसना

घट जाना : *Share prices are sinking.*
4 खोदना : *sink a post (into the ground)* 5 (द्रवों का) गहरे जाना; (व्यक्ति की आवाज़) शांत होते जाना।

sink² / सिङ्क् / *noun* (**wash-basin** भी) बरतन धोने की पत्थर, चीनी-मिट्टी आदि की हौज़; हाथ धोने का स्थान।

sinus / साइनस् / *noun* (*pl* **sinuses**) हड्डी में ख़ाली जगह, विशेषतः सिर की हड्डियों में ख़ाली जगह जो नाक के अंदरूनी हिस्सों से जुड़ी हों।

sip / सिप् / *verb* (**-pp-**) **sip (at)** sth चुस्की ले कर पीना, घूँट-घूँट पीना : *She sipped at her mineral water.* ▸ **sip** *noun* घूँट/चुस्की : *He took a sip of brandy from the glass.*

siphon / साइफ़न् / *noun* 1 साइफ़न, एक प्रकार की निकास नली 2 सोडा वाटर की एक विशेष प्रकार की बोतल ▸ **siphon** *verb* **siphon** sth **into/out of** sth; **siphon** sth **off/out** तरल पदार्थ को साइफ़न द्वारा एक पात्र से दूसरे पात्र में डालना : *siphon petrol out of a car into a can.*

sir / सर् / *noun* 1 श्रीमान, महोदय, (आदर-वाची संबोधक शब्द) सर 2 **Sir** इंग्लैंड में **Knight** या **Baronet** के नाम से पूर्व लगा पद : *Sir John Jackson has arrived.*

siren / साइरन् / *noun* 1 साइरन, भोंपू : *The factory siren signalled the end of the night shift.* 2 (ग्रीक पौराणिक कथाओं में) आधा स्त्री आधा पक्षी के शरीर वाला जीव; आकर्षक एवं ख़तरनाक समझी जाने वाली स्त्री।

sissy / सिसि / *noun* (*अनौप, अपमा*) मेहरा, ज़नख़ा : *The other boys call me a sissy because I don't like games.*

sister / सिस्टर् / *noun* 1 बहन 2 (**Sister**) (अस्पताल में) वरिष्ठ नर्स 3 **Sister** (चर्च में) सिस्टर 4 (महिला संघ की सदस्या के संबोधन में प्रयुक्त शब्द) : *They supported their sisters in the dispute.* 5 समान गठन/प्रकार वाली वस्तु :

our sister company in India ▸ **sisterhood** *noun* **sister-in-law** *noun* (*pl* **sisters-in-law**) साली; भौजाई; सलहज; ननद; देवरानी; जेठानी **sisterly** *adj.*

sit / सिट् / *verb* (**-tt-**; *pt, pp* **sat** / सैट् /) 1 बैठना 2 (संसद, सभा, कचहरी आदि का) बैठना, अधिवेशन में होना : *The Lok Sabha was still sitting at 11 pm.* 3 **sit (for** sth**)** परीक्षा में बैठना/सम्मिलित होना 4 **sit (on** sb**)** (कपड़ों का) (ठीक) फिट बैठना : *a jacket that sits well on* sb ■ **sit around** (*अनौप*) बिना कोई कार्य किए बैठे रहना, अक्सर गप्पें लड़ाने के लिए **sit back** आराम से बैठना जब और लोग किसी काम पर लगे हों **sit on the fence** निर्णय लेने के प्रति अनिच्छुक होना **sit through** sth अपनी जगह पर बैठे रहना जब तक कार्यक्रम ख़त्म न हो जाए, विशेषतः जी ऊब जाने के बाद भी **sit up (and do** sth**)** (*अनौप*) किसी घटना, बात आदि पर ध्यान देना आरंभ करना **sit up (for** sb**)** देर तक जागते रहना, देर से सोना, विशेषतः किसी की प्रतीक्षा में ▸ **sitting-room** *noun* बैठने का कमरा।

site / साइट् / *noun* 1 भवन निर्माण आदि का स्थान, स्थल : *a site for a new school* 2 घटना स्थल : *the site of the battle* ▸ **site** *verb* स्थल पर निर्माण कार्य करना : *Is it safe to site a power station here?*

sitting / सिटिङ् / *noun* 1 न्यायालय या संसद की बैठक 2 वह समय जब बहुत लोगों को एक साथ खाना परोसा जाता है जैसे होटल में।

situate / सिचुएट् / *verb* 1 (*औप*) स्थित होना/करना : *The village is situated in a valley.* 2 (*औप*) स्थिति बताना/वर्णन करना : *Let me try and situate the assassination historically.* ▸ **situated** *adj* (कमरा, नगर, भवन आदि की) स्थिति; (*औप*) (व्यक्ति) स्थिति-विशेष में

पड़ा हुआ : *Having six children and no income, I was badly situated.*

situation /ˌसिचुˈएश्न्/ *noun* 1 स्थिति, हालत : *the worsening diplomatic/ financial situation* 2 स्थल, स्थान : *The house is in a beautiful situation overlooking the lake.* 3 (औप) नौकरी, जगह : *find a new situation.*

six / सिक्स् / *noun, pron, det* छह (का अंक) ▸ **sixth** / सिक्स्थ् / *pron, det* छठा; छठा अंश 1/6.

sixteen /ˌसिक्स्ˈटीन्/ *noun, pron, det* सोलह (का अंक)।

sixty / सिक्स्टि / *noun, pron, det* साठ (का अंक) ▸ **sixtieth** / सिक्स्टिअथ् / *noun, pron, det* साठवाँ; साठवाँ भाग 1/60.

size / साइज़् / *noun* 1 परिमाण, आकार : *What's the size of your garden?* 2 [*sing*] विशाल आकार या मात्रा : *The sheer size of the place is impressive ○ I couldn't believe the size of his debts.* 3 माप : *It's the right size for me.* ▸ **size** *verb* ■ **size sb/sth up** (अनौप) किसी व्यक्ति/स्थिति को आँकना : *He sized up the situation very quickly.* ▸ **sizeable** (**sizable** भी) *adj* काफ़ी बड़ा : *a sizeable town ○ Coming first in the race was, for him, a sizeable achievement.*

sizzle / सिज़्ल् / *verb* तलते समय कड़कड़ की आवाज़ होना : *sausages sizzling (away) in the pan* ▸ **sizzling** *adj* काफ़ी उत्तेजना, सनसनी पैदा करने वाला।

skate / स्केट् / *noun* 1 (**ice-skate** भी) बर्फ़ पर स्केटिंग करने के लिए जूतों पर लगाए जाने वाले ब्लेड, स्केट 2 (**roller-skate** भी) जूता जिसमें छोटे पहिये लगे हों ▸ **skate** *verb* स्केट पर चलना।

skeleton / स्केलिट्न् / *noun* 1 कंकाल, अस्थिपंजर 2 (प्रायः *sing*) रूपरेखा, ढाँचा, ख़ाका : *a skeleton of girders*

3 आवश्यकता के लिए लोगों/वाहनों आदि की कम-से-कम संख्या : *a skeleton staff* ▸ **skeleton key** *noun* चोर-कुंजी जो तरह-तरह के ताले खोल सके।

sketch / स्केच् / *noun* 1 रूपरेखा, कच्चा नक्शा; ख़ाका : *a pencil sketch* 2 संक्षिप्त वर्णन : *give a quick sketch of how the changes will affect staff* 3 छोटा प्रहसन : *She writes satirical sketches for a magazine.* ▸ **sketch** *verb* रूपरेखा/ख़ाका बनाना ■ **sketch sth out** रूपरेखा बनाना : *sketch out proposals for a new road* ▸ **sketchy** *adj* (**-ier, -iest**) अधूरा; पूरा विवरण न देने वाला : *I have only a sketchy knowledge of British history.* ▸ **sketchily** *adv.*

skewer / स्क्यूअर् / *noun* सीख़ (जिसमें गोश्त आदि के टुकड़े फँसाकर भूने जाते हैं, जैसे सीख़ की क़बाब बनाने में प्रयत्न ▸ **skewer** *verb* सीख़ या किसी लंबी, नुकीली चीज़ पर फँसाना।

ski / स्की / *noun* (*pl* **skis**) स्की, बर्फ़ पर चलने के लिए जूतों में बाँधी जाने वाली लकड़ी, प्लास्टिक आदि की पट्टियाँ : *a pair of skis* ▸ **ski** *verb* (*pres t* **skis**; *pt, pp* **ski'd** या **skied**; *pres p* **skiing**) बर्फ़ पर स्की बाँध कर चलना।

skid / स्किड् / *verb* (**-dd-**) वाहन आदि का फिसल जाना : *The car skidded off the road.* ▸ **skid** *noun* मोटर आदि के पहियों का गीली सड़क पर फिसलना।

skill / स्किल् / *noun* 1 **skill (at/in sth/ doing sth)** निपुणता, हुनर : *his skill in marketing* 2 हुनर-विशेष : *technical skills* ▸ **skilled** *adj* 1 प्रशिक्षित, कुशल : *a skilled negotiator* 2 (कार्य) कुशलता की अपेक्षा रखने वाला : *Furniture-making is a skilled job.* **skilful** *adj* कुशलता दिखाने/रखने वाला **skilfully** *adv.*

skim / स्किम् / *verb* (**-mm-**) 1 द्रव के सतह पर से कोई ठोस पदार्थ हटाना या दूध से क्रीम निकालना : *skim milk* 2 किसी सतह के

ऊपर से तीव्र गति से बिना छुए या ज़रा-सा छूते हुए निकल जाना : *swallows skimming over the water* **3 skim (through/ over) sth** सरसरी नज़र से पढ़ना : *His eyes skimmed the front page for her name.*

skimp / स्किम्प् / *verb* **skimp (on sth)** ज़रूरत से कम प्रयोग करना/प्रबंध करना; बचत करने के लिए कम खर्च करना : *Don't skimp by using margarine instead of butter.* ▸ **skimpy** *adj* (**-ier, -iest**) (*अप्रमा*) ज़रूरत से कम परिमाण में : *a rather skimpy meal.*

skin / स्किन् / *noun* **1** त्वचा, चर्म **2** चमड़ा, चाम **3** कुछ फलों का छिलका : *a banana skin* ▸ **skin** *verb* (**-nn-**) चमड़ा उतारना/ निकालना : *skin a rabbit* **skin-deep** *adj* सतही **skinny** *adj* (**-ier, -iest**) **1** (*अनौप, प्रायः अप्रमा*) (*व्यक्ति*) अति दुबला-पतला **2** (*कपड़े*) एकदम तंग : *a skinny black jumper.*

skip / स्किप् / *verb* (**-pp-**) **1** उछलना- कूदना : *A child was skipping along (the road).* **2** रस्सी कूदना/फाँदना : *children skipping in the playground* **3** (*अनौप*) स्थान/विषय जल्दी- जल्दी बदलते रहना **4** क्लास आदि में उपस्थित न होना, किसी कार्य में चूकना : *skip a lecture/an appointment/a class* **5** किताब के कुछ हिस्सों को छोड़- छोड़ कर पढ़ना : *skip the second chap- ter* ▸ **skip** *noun* उछलने-कूदने जैसी गति।

skipper / स्किपर / *noun* **1** छोटे व्या- पारिक जहाज़ का कप्तान **2** (*अनौप*) टीम का कप्तान।

skirmish / स्करमिश् / *noun* **1** (सेनाओं/ युद्धपोतों की) भिड़ंत, मामूली मुठभेड़ : *a brief skirmish on the frontier* **2** कटु वाद-विवाद : *a skirmish between the two party leaders* ▸ **skirmish** *verb* मुठभेड़ में भाग लेना।

skirt / स्कर्ट / *noun* **1** स्कर्ट, घाघरा **2** किसी मशीन या वाहन के आधार का रक्षक आवरण : *the rubber skirt around the bottom of a hovercraft* ▸ **skirt** *verb* **1** सीमांत पर चलना : *We skirted (round) the field and crossed the bridge.* **2 skirt (around/ round sth)** किसी मुश्किल या उलझन वाली बात को कहने से बचने की कोशिश करना।

skit / स्किट् / *noun* **skit (on sth)** व्यंग्य रचना, प्रहसन।

skittles / स्किट्ल्स् / *noun* एक खेल- विशेष।

skulk / स्कल्क् / *verb* (*अप्रमा*) छुपना या गुप्त रूप से इधर-उधर चलना, विशेषत: बुरी या दुष्ट योजना के इरादे से : *I don't want reporters skulking around (my house).*

skull / स्कल् / *noun* **1** खोपड़ी, कपाल **2** (*अनौप*) सिर या व्यक्ति का मस्तिष्क।

sky / स्काइ / *noun* (*प्रायः* **the sky**) (*pl* **skies**) आसमान, आकाश ▸ **skylight** / स्काइलाइट् / *noun* (छत पर) ऊपरी रोशनदान **skyline** / स्काइलाइन् / *noun* आकाश की पृष्ठभूमि में क्षितिज पर स्थित वस्तुओं की रूपरेखा : *the New York skyline* **skyscraper** / स्काइस्क्रेपर् / *noun* गगनचुंबी भवन।

slab / स्लैब् / *noun* पत्थर आदि की पटरी, पटिया : *a slab of marble.*

slack[1] / स्लैक् / *adj* (**-er, -est**) **1** ढीला, न कि कसा हुआ : *a slack rope* **2** (*व्या- पार*) मंदा : *times of slack demand* **3** (*व्यक्ति*) अपने काम में लापरवाह, सुस्त : *be slack in one's work* ▸ **slack** *verb* सुस्त/लापरवाह होना, काम से बचना **slackly** *adv.*

slack[2] / स्लैक् / *noun* **1** बंधी रस्सी का ढीला लटकता भाग **2** मंदी का दौर : *slack in the economy.*

slacken / स्लैकन् / *verb* ढीला/मंद/सुस्त

होना या कर देना : *He slackened his grip.*

slacks / स्लैक्स् / *noun* [*pl*] *(अप्र)* अनौपचारिक पतलून : *a pair of slacks.*

slake / स्लेक् / *verb* 1 प्यास बुझाना : *We slaked our thirst in a stream.* 2 *(तक)* चूने और पानी को रासायनिक प्रक्रिया से मिलाना : *slaked lime.*

slam / स्लैम् / *verb* (-mm-) 1 धम से (द्वार) बंद कर देना : *The door slammed (shut).* 2 ज़ोर से फेंकना या रखना : *She slammed the books on the table.*
▸ **slam** *noun* (प्राय: *sing*) बंद करने का धमाका (धम की आवाज़) : *the slam of a car door.*

slander / 'स्लान्डर; *US* 'स्लैन्डर / *noun* झूठी निंदा : *a vicious slander* ▸ **slander** *verb* झूठी निंदा करना/दोष लगाना **slanderous** *adj* : *a slanderous attack.*

slang / स्लैङ् / *noun* अत्यधिक अनौपचारिक व्यवहार में प्रयुक्त शब्द, मुहावरे आदि जो सिर्फ़ बोलचाल की भाषा में प्रयुक्त होते हैं, औपचारिक भाषा व्यवहार के उपयुक्त नहीं माने जाते ▸ **slang** *verb* *(अनौप)* गंदी भाषा का प्रयोग करना : *The two drivers were slanging each other in the middle of the road.*

slant / स्लान्ट्; *US* स्लैन्ट् / *verb* 1 तिरछा होना/करना: *slanting eyes* 2 सूचना को तोड़ मरोड़ कर पेश करना : *The report was slanted.* ▸ **slant** *noun* 1 तिरछा : *Her hat was set at a slant.* 2 **slant (on sth/sb)** दृष्टिकोण-विशेष : *They have decided to give the programme a more youthful slant.*

slap / स्लैप् / *verb* (-pp-) 1 थप्पड़ मारना 2 कोई वस्तु धम से पटक देना : *slap the money on the counter* ∎ **slap sb/ sth down** *(अनौप)* व्यावसायिक कंपनी में किसी को बोलने से, सुझाव देने से रोकना : *All his ideas were slapped down at*

the publicity meeting. **slap sth on sb/sth** कुछ माँगने या निषेध करने के लिए आदेश देना : *slap visa restrictions on tourists* **slap sth on sth** *(अनौप)* क़ीमत बढ़ाना : *They've slapped 50 paise on the price of a packet of cigarettes.* ▸ **slap** *noun* थप्पड़/तमाचा या चाँटा ∎ **a slap in the face** अस्वीकृति या अपमान : *It was a real slap in the face when she refused to see me.* **a slap on the wrist** चेतावनी, हलकी-सी सज़ा : *I got a slap on the wrist for turning up late.*

slapdash / 'स्लैपडैश् / *adj* बहुत जल्दी में और लापरवाह ढंग से किया गया काम : *slapdash work* ∘ *a slapdash approach/method.*

slapstick / 'स्लैप्स्टिक् / *noun* दोहरी पट्टी, भड़ैती : *slapstick comedy.*

slash / स्लैश् / *verb* 1 ज़ोर के झटके से एक ही बार में काटना, चीरना : *The tyres of my car had been slashed.* 2 बड़ी मात्रा में कम करना/घटा देना : *slash costs/ prices* ▸ **slash** *noun* 1 (चाकू आदि का) गहरा या लंबा चीरा : *a razor slash* 2 तिरछी लकीर (/)।

slat / स्लैट् / *noun* (प्राय: *pl*) लकड़ी या धातु की पट्टी ▸ **slatted** *adj.*

slate / स्लेट् / *noun* 1 स्लेट पत्थर; स्लेट के चौकोर या आयताकार टुकड़े (छत पाटने में प्रयुक्त) : *slate tiles* 2 स्लेट की तख़्ती (लिखने के लिए) ▸ **slate** *verb* 1 **slate sb/sth (for sth)** कड़ी निंदा करना : *They were slated for their poor performance.* 2 स्लेट से छत पाटना 3 **slate sth (for....)** किसी विशेष समय पर कुछ घटित होने की योजना बनाना : *a conference slated for next July.*

slaughter / 'स्लॉटर / *verb* 1 पशु को सामान्यत: आहार के लिए काटना/मारना 2 बड़ी संख्या में नरहत्या करना : *Men, women and children were slaugh-*

tered and whole villages destroyed. 3 (अनौप) खेल या प्रतियोगिता में करारी हार देना ▸ **slaughter** *noun* 1 पशुवध 2 क़त्ले-आम : *slaughter of innocent civilians* **slaughterhouse** *noun* (**abattoir** भी) बूचड़ख़ाना।

slave / स्लेव़ / *noun* 1 ग़ुलाम, दास 2 **slave of/to sth** पूर्णत: किसी प्रभाव के अंतर्गत : *a slave to fashion/drink* ▸ **slave** *verb* **slave (away) (at sth)** बहुत मेहनत से काम करना : *slaving (away) at the housework for hours*

slavery / 'स्लेव़रि / *noun* 1 दासत्व, ग़ुलामी 2 दास-प्रथा : *abolish slavery.*

slavish / 'स्लेव़िश् / *adj* (अपमा) मौलिकता रहित (नक़ल) : *a slavish imitation of another writer's work.*

slay / स्ले / *verb* (*pt* **slew** / स्लू /; *pp* **slain** / स्लेन् /) (अप्र या औप) मार डालना, हत्या करना : *soldiers slain in battle.*

sleazy / 'स्लीज़ि / *adj* (**-ier, -iest**) (अनौप) (विशेषत: जगह) साफ़-सुथरी और सम्मानपूर्ण न होना : *a sleazy club/hotel* ○ *a rather sleazy atmosphere.*

sledge / स्लेज़ / (*US* **sled** / स्लेड् / भी) *noun* स्लेज (बर्फ़ पर फिसलने वाली गाड़ी) ▸ **sledge** *verb* (*US* **sled** भी; **-dd-**) स्लेज पर सवारी करना।

sledge-hammer / 'स्लेज़ैहैमर् / *noun* लोहार का घन।

sleek / स्लीक़ / *adj* (**-er, -est**) चिकना-चुपड़ा : *sleek hair/fur* 2 (कभी-कभी अपमा) (व्यक्ति) धनवान एवं चिकना-चुपड़ा लगने वाला : *sleek yuppies in their city suits* 3 उत्तम आकार वाला : *a sleek car* ▸ **sleekly** *adv* **sleekness** *noun.*

sleep[1] / स्लीप् / *noun* 1 निद्रा, नींद 2 [*sing*] नींद की अवधि : *a good sleep* ▸ **sleepless** *adj* निद्रा-रहित : *have a*

sleepless night **sleeplessness** *noun.*

sleep[2] / स्लीप् / *verb* (*pt, pp* **slept** / स्लेप्ट् /) 1 सोना : *We slept (for) eight hours.* 2 (होटल आदि में) पर्याप्त बिछौने रखना : *The hotel sleeps 300 guests.* ■ **sleep like a log** (अनौप) गहरी नींद में सोना **sleep on sth** (अनौप) किसी विषय आदि पर निर्णय लेने में देर करना : *Don't say now if you'll take the job— sleep on it first.* ▸ **sleeping-pill** *noun* नींद लाने वाली दवा।

sleeper / 'स्लीपर् / *noun* (रेलगाड़ी में) शायिता।

sleepy / 'स्लीपि / *adj* (**-ier, -iest**) 1 निद्रालु, उनींदा : *look/feel sleepy* 2 (स्थान) निष्क्रिय; व्यापार रहित : *a sleepy little village.* ▸ **sleepily** *adv.*

sleet / स्लीट् / *noun* बर्फ़ मिली वर्षा : *heavy rain, turning to sleet and snow* ▸ **sleet** *verb* : *It is sleeting.*

sleeve / स्लीव़ / *noun* (क़मीज़ आदि की) आस्तीन, बाँह : *He rolled up his sleeves and washed his hands.* ■ **laugh up one's sleeve** मन ही मन ख़ुश होना ▸ **sleeveless** *adj* बिना बाँह का : *a sleeveless sweater.*

sleigh / स्ले / *noun* घोड़े द्वारा खींची जाने वाली बर्फ़गाड़ी।

sleight / स्लाइट् / *noun* ■ **sleight of hand** 1 हाथों के इस्तेमाल में निपुणता, विशेषत: जादू के करतब दिखाने में 2 हाथ की सफ़ाई, छल-कपट : *Last year's profits were more the result of financial sleight of hand than genuine growth.*

slender / 'स्लेन्डर् / *adj* 1 (व्यक्ति) पतला, छरहरा : *a slender figure/waist* 2 थोड़ा-सा (मात्रा या आकार में) : *slender resources/hopes* ▸ **slenderness** *noun.*

slice / स्लाइस् / *noun* 1 फाँक, कतला : *a slice of bread/cheese* 2 *(अनौप)* हिस्सा, अंश : *capture a large slice of the market* ▸ **slice** *verb* 1 **slice sth (up)** फाँक काटना : *slice up the meat* 2 **slice sth off (sth)** काटना, तराशना।

slick / स्लिक् / *adj* (-er, -est) 1 *(कभी-कभी अपमा)* दक्षता, निपुणता से किया गया, विशेषत: बिना ज़्यादा प्रयत्न के, *(व्यक्ति)* जो इस प्रकार से काम करे : *slick advertising/designs/presentation ∘ a slick performer* 2 चिकना, फिसलाऊ : *The roads were slick with wet mud.* ▸ **slick** *verb* **slick sth (back/down)** बालों को तेल आदि लगा कर चपटा करना : *His hair was slicked across his forehead.*

slide¹ / स्लाइड् / *verb* (pt, pp **slid** / स्लिड् /) 1 फिसलना, खिसकना : *The ship slid into the water.* 2 धीरे-धीरे चुपचाप चलना, निर्बाध व शांत गति से सरकना, बिना किसी का ध्यान आकृष्ट किए : *He lifted the mat and slid the key under it.* 3 **slide (into sth)** क्रमश: नीचे या बुरी स्थिति की ओर खिसकना : *He got depressed and began to let things slide.*

slide² / स्लाइड् / *noun* 1 [sing] *(बर्फ़ आदि पर)* फिसलने, सरकने की क्रिया : *Let's go for a slide on the frozen pond.* 2 एक ढाँचा जिस पर फिसला जा सकता है 3 *(प्राय: sing)* निकृष्ट या बुरी स्थिति में परिवर्तन : *a slide in his fortunes* 4 स्लाइड जिसे प्रोजेक्टर में लगा कर पर्दे पर चित्र दिखाते हैं 5 काँच की पट्टी जिस पर वस्तु रखकर सूक्ष्मदर्शी से देखते हैं।

slight¹ / स्लाइट् / *adj* (-er, -est) 1 दुबला-पतला, छरहरा : *a slight figure/girl* 2 हलका, मामूली; कम महत्त्वपूर्ण : *a slight error/change* ▪ **not in the slightest** बिलकुल ही नहीं : *You didn't embarrass me in the slightest*

▸ **slightly** *adv* 1 थोड़ा-सा : *a slightly bigger house* 2 मामूली रीति से।

slight² / स्लाइट् / *verb* उपेक्षा की दृष्टि से देखना; नम्रता न दिखाना : *She felt slighted because no one spoke to her.* ▸ **slight** *noun* **slight (on sb/sth)** उपेक्षा, अवज्ञा/तिरस्कार : *My comment was not meant as a slight (on you/your achievements).*

slim / स्लिम् / *adj* (-mmer, -mmest) 1 दुबला-पतला, छरहरा : *a slim person* 2 अपेक्षित या इच्छित से कम : *only a slim hope* ▸ **slim** *verb* (-mm-) 1 छरहरा बनने के लिए व्यायाम करना और कम खाना : *I'm trying to slim.* 2 **slim sth (down) (to sth)** संख्या, आकार या स्तर में कम कर देना।

slime / स्लाइम् / *noun* कीचड़, चहला : *There was a coating of slime on the unwashed sink.* ▸ **slimy** *adj* (-ier, -iest) 1 कीचड़ से लिप्त : *The stones were slimy with weed.* 2 *(अनौप)* बेईमान मगर बहुत ही नम्र/शिष्ट : *You slimy little creep!*

sling¹ / स्लिङ् / *noun* 1 ज़ख्मी हाथ आदि को सहारा देने के लिए प्रयुक्त पट्टी : *have one's arm in a sling* 2 लूप के आकार की पट्टी, बेल्ट या रस्सी जिससे किसी वस्तु को ऊपर उठाया जा सके या नीचे लाया जा सके; बच्चों को लटका कर ले जाने की ऐसी ही झोली 3 *(पूर्व समय में)* पत्थर फेंकने के लिए प्रयुक्त *(चमड़े की)* गुलेल।

sling² / स्लिङ् / *verb* (pt, pp **slung** / स्लङ् /) 1 *(अनौप)* लापरवाही से या ज़ोर से फेंक देना : *slinging stones (at birds)* 2 ढीले-ढाले लटका देना/सहारा देना : *with her bag slung over her shoulder.*

slink / स्लिङ्क् / *verb* (pt, pp **slunk** / स्लङ्क् /) लुक-छिप कर आना, जाना : *The dog slunk away with its tail between its legs.* ▸ **slinky** *adj.*

slip¹ / स्लिप् / *verb* (-pp-) **1** slip (over) (on sth) फिसल जाना, फिसल कर गिर पड़ना **2** slip from/out of/through sth चुपके से या जल्दी से खिसक जाना; हाथों से सरक जाना या फिसल कर निकल जाना : *The fish/vase slipped out of my hand.* **3** slip (into sth); slip (from sth) to sth क्रमश: निकृष्ट या बुरी स्थिति में पहुँच जाना/बदल जाना : *His popularity has slipped a lot.* **4** slip into/out of sth; slip sth on/off (कपड़े) जल्दी से पहन लेना या उतार देना ■ let sth slip **1** अवसर चूक जाना : *She let slip a chance to work abroad.* **2** भूल से या जानबूझ कर लापरवाही से कोई बात उगल देना : *I didn't let a word slip.* slip away (अवसर आदि) कम होते या गुम होते हुए दिखाई पड़ना : *She could see her chances of victory slipping away.* slip up (on sth) (अनौप) लापरवाह भूल होना slip your mind याद न रहना ▸ slip-knot *noun* सरक-गाँठ।

slip² / स्लिप् / *noun* **1** (प्राय: *sing*) फिसलना; फिसलन **2** छोटी भूल या ग़लती : *One slip and you could lose the game.* **3** काग़ज़ की चिट, परची : *write a phone number on a slip of paper* **4** नीचे पहनने वाला ढीला-ढाला वस्त्र ■ give sb the slip (अनौप) पीछा करते व्यक्ति से/छिप कर भाग जाना : *I managed to give him the slip by hiding behind the wall.*

slipper / स्लिपर / *noun* स्लीपर, पैर में पहनने वाली चट्टी।

slippery / स्लिपरि / *adj* **1** (अनौप slippy भी) फिसलन भरा : *a slippery road* **2** (अनौप) अविश्वसनीय (व्यक्ति) **3** (अनौप) (स्थिति) जिसे संभाला न जा सके : *the slippery subject of race relations.*

slipshod / स्लिप्शॉड् / *adj* फूहड़, अव्यवस्थित : *a slipshod worker/ writer.*

slit / स्लिट् / *noun* दरार, चीरा : *a long slit in her skirt* ▸ slit *verb* (-tt-; *pt, pp* slit) दरार बनाना, चीरा देना : *slit sb's throat.*

slither / 'स्लिदर् / *verb* फिसल जाना; फिसलते हुए चलना : *The snake slithered off (into the grass) as we approached.* ▸ slithery *adj.*

slob / स्लॉब् / *noun* (अनौप, अपमा) आलसी या अशिष्ट व्यक्ति; जो लापरवाही से तैयार होता हो : *Get out of bed, you fat slob!*

slog / स्लॉग् / *verb* (-gg-) (अनौप) **1** (खेल में) गेंद को ज़ोर से, पर बिना निपुणता या शुद्धता के, मारना : *slog the ball all around the ground* **2** घोर परिश्रम के साथ विशेषत: लंबा ऊबाने वाला काम करना : *a teacher slogging away at/slogging through a pile of marking* **3** बहुत प्रयत्न या कठिनाई के साथ निर्धारित दिशा में चलना : *slogging through the snow with heavy shopping bags.*

slogan / 'स्लोगन् / *noun* नारा, स्लोगन : *political slogans.*

slop / स्लॉप् / *verb* (-pp-) **1** (द्रव का) छलक जाना, विशेषकर लापरवाही की वजह से : *The tea slopped into the saucer.* **2** इस प्रकार से छलकाना : *You've slopped food all down your shirt!* ▸ slop *noun* (प्राय: *pl*) **1** सूअरों के लिए खाद्य पदार्थ (अक्सर बचा हुआ भोजन आदि) **2** रसोई, स्नानघर आदि का गंदा पानी : *a slop-bucket* **3** (अप्र) मरीज़ आदि के लिए बनाया तरल खाद्य पदार्थ, सूप आदि।

slope / स्लोप् / *noun* **1** ढाल; ऊँची-नीची पहाड़ी भूमि : *the lower slopes of Mt Everest* **2** ढाल की मात्रा : *a 40° slope*

▶ **slope** verb ढालू करना, ढाल बनाना : the ceiling/floor slopes.

sloppy / स्लॉपि / adj 1 गीला; बहुत अधिक द्रव की मात्रा का होना : sloppy porridge 2 (अनौप, अपमा) अति भावुक : I hate sloppy romantic films. 3 गंदा, बेढंगा और लापरवाह : sloppy work/typing/thinking ▶ **sloppily** adv **sloppiness** noun.

slosh / स्लॉश / verb (अनौप) **slosh (sth) (around/about)** (अनौप) (द्रव का काफ़ी मात्रा में) पात्र में आवाज़ करते हुए घूमना : water sloshing against the sides of the bath; द्रव को शोर करते हुए या लापरवाही के साथ घुमाना : He sloshes water all over the floor whenever he has a bath.

slot / स्लॉट् / noun 1 झिरी, खाँचा : put a coin in the slot 2 सूची, कार्यक्रम आदि में स्थिति, समय या अवसर : fill the night current affairs slot on BBC 2 ▶ **slot** verb (-tt-) **slot (sth/sb) in; slot (sb/sth) in (to sth)** किसी को कार्यक्रम सूची में फिट कर देना; झिरी में ठीक बैठ जाना : The bolt slotted smoothly into place. **slot-machine** noun मशीन जिसमें सिक्का डाल कर कुछ पाया जा सके।

sloth / स्लोथ् / noun (औप) सुस्ती/ आलस्य, काहिली ▶ **slothful** adj (औप) काहिल।

slouch / स्लाउच् / verb सुस्ती से बैठना, खड़ा होना या चलना : slouching about all day doing nothing.

slovenly / स्लव्न्लि / adj (अपमा) लापरवाह, (पोशाक आदि के संबंध में) अव्यवस्थित अथवा गंदा : a slovenly waiter.

slow¹ / स्लो / adj (-er, -est) 1 धीमे-धीमे काम करने वाला; ढीला/सुस्त : make slow progress 2 मंदबुद्धि : a slow learner 3 **slow to sth/to do sth; slow (in/ about) doing sth** कुछ करने, बोलने में

हिचकिचाने वाला : They were very slow (about) paying me. 4 (घड़ी का) सुस्त चलना 5 रुचिहीन एवं उत्साह- हीन : Business is rather slow today. ▶ **slowly** adv **slow-motion** noun (फ़िल्म आदि में) किसी गतिविधि को इस प्रकार दिखाने का तरीक़ा कि वह वास्तविक गति से बहुत कम हो : a slow motion replay **slowness** noun.

slow² / स्लो / adv (-er, -est) धीरे : Please walk a bit slower. ■ **go slow** सामान्य से कम गति/सुस्ती से काम करना **go slow on sth** कुछ पाने के लिए कम उत्साह दिखाना : going slow on European integration.

slow³ / स्लो / verb **slow (sth/sb) (down/up)** पहले से कम गति से चलना/ चलाना : The train slowed down (to a crawl). ■ **slow down/up** कम परिश्रम से काम करना : You must slow up a bit, or you'll make yourself ill.

sludge / स्लज् / noun 1 गाढ़ा कीचड़ या इस तरह दिखने वाला कोई तरल पदार्थ 2 फैक्ट्रियों आदि से निकला गंदा गाढ़ा तरल : chemical sludge.

slug / स्लग् / noun बिना शंख का घोंघा जो धीरे-धीरे चलता है।

sluggish / स्लगिश् / adj सुस्त, मंद, धीमी गति से चलने/कार्य करने वाला; चौकस या फुरतीला न रहने वाला : sluggish traffic/ conversation.

slum / स्लम् / noun ग़रीबों की घनी गंदी बस्ती; ऐसी बस्ती में मकान/घर।

slumber / स्लम्बर् / verb (औप, विशेषत: अलं) सोना : slumbering peacefully ▶ **slumber** noun निद्रा : fall into a deep slumber.

slump / स्लम्प् / verb 1 ज़ोर से बैठना या गिर पड़ना : Tired from her walk she slumped (down) onto the sofa. 2 (मूल्यों, व्यापार आदि में) भारी गिरावट आना, मंदी आना : Sales have slumped.

▸ **slump** *noun* slump (in sth) 1 व्यापार में मंदी, गिरावट 2 (खेलों आदि में) असफलता, बुरे परिणामों का दौर : *a slump in her career.*

slur / स्लर् / *verb* (-rr-) 1 ध्वनियों को मिलाकर बोलना जिससे उच्चारण अस्पष्ट हो जाता है : *He was drunk and kept slurring his words.* 2 दोषारोपण करके किसी की प्रतिष्ठा ख़राब करना ▸ **slur** *noun* 1 slur (on sb/sth) लांछन, निंदा जिससे किसी की प्रतिष्ठा ख़राब हो : *cast a slur on sb* 2 अस्पष्ट उच्चारण।

slurp /स्लर्प/ *verb* (अनौप) कुछ खाते या पीते समय होंठों से आवाज़ करना; ऐसी आवाज़ निकालना : *He slurped (down) his soup greedily.* ▸ **slurp** *noun* (प्राय: sing) (अनौप) ऐसी आवाज़।

slush /स्लश्/ *noun* 1 पिघलती हुई (प्राय: गंदी) बर्फ़ 2 (अनौप, अपमा) भावुकतापूर्ण भाषण या लेख : *a romantic novel full of slush* ▸ **slushy** *adj*.

slut / स्लट् / *noun* (अपमा) दुश्चरित्र की स्त्री।

sly / स्लाइ / *adj* 1 (प्राय: अपमा) गुप्त रूप से छल-कपटपूर्ण : *a sly political move* 2 गोपनशील, छिपाऊ : *a sly glance/ grin* ■ **on the sly** चोरी-छिपे ▸ **slyly** *adv* **slyness** *noun*.

smack¹ / स्मैक् / *verb* 1 थप्पड़ मारना 2 कुछ ज़ोर से दे मारना/पटक देना : *He smacked the report on my desk.* ■ **lick/smack one's lips** स्वादिष्ट वस्तु देखकर चटकारे मारना ▸ **smack** *noun* 1 थप्पड़, तमाचा : *give sb a smack in the face* 2 (अनौप) ज़ोर की आवाज़ के साथ चुंबन; ज़ोर की आवाज़।

smack² / स्मैक् / *verb* ■ **smack of sth** विशेषत: कुछ अप्रिय का संकेत या पहचान होना : *behaviour that smacks of guilt/dishonesty.*

smack³ /स्मैक्/ *noun* (अप्र) एक नशीला पदार्थ।

small / स्मॉल् / *adj* (-er, -est) 1 (large के वैषम्य में) छोटा : *a small house* 2 बच्चा, कम उम्र का : *I lived in the country when I was small.* 3 उतना बड़ा नहीं जितना उसी प्रकार की कोई और वस्तु हो; (अक्षर) छोटे (capital के वैषम्य में) 4 कम महत्त्वपूर्ण, मामूली : *make a few small changes to the report* 5 थोड़ा-सा या लगभग नहीं ■ **look/feel small** लज्जित होना, अपमानित-सा महसूस करना ▸ **small change** *noun* रेज़गारी, छोटे सिक्के **small hours** *noun* [*pl*] रात के 12 बजे के बाद का समय।

smallpox / 'स्मॉल्पॉक्स् / *noun* चेचक (का रोग), शीतला/बड़ी माता।

smart¹ / स्मार्ट् / *adj* (-er, -est) 1 (व्यक्ति) साफ़-सुथरा, बना-ठना/आकर्षक 2 (व्यक्ति) चतुर, हाज़िर जवाब/प्रत्युत्पन्नमति : *a smart answer* 3 फ़ैशनेबल (कपड़े) 4 फुरतीला, तीक्ष्ण : *a smart rebuke from the teacher* ▸ **smarten** *verb* ■ **smarten (sb/sth/oneself) up** आकर्षक बनाना/बनना **smartly** *adv*.

smart² / स्मार्ट् / *verb* 1 smart (from sth) टीस मारना/सालना, अखरना : *His eyes were smarting from the dust.* 2 smart (from/over/under sth) निंदा, पराजय आदि अखरना : *They're still smarting from their defeat in the final.*

smash / स्मैश् / *verb* 1 smash sth (up); smash sth open तोड़ना, टुकड़े-टुकड़े कर देना : *smash a window* 2 ज़ोर-से टक्कर मारना/भिड़ना; टकराना : *smash sb in the face* 3 smash sth (up) कुचल देना : *She's smashed (up) her new car.* 4 (अनौप) हरा देना; ख़त्म कर देना : *We are determined to smash terrorism.* ▸ **smash** *noun* 1 [*sing*] टूटना या टूटने की ध्वनि 2 भिड़ंत, टक्कर 3 (टेनिस आदि में) गेंद को ज़ोर-से नीचे की तरफ़ नेट के उस पार फेंकना

4 (smash hit भी) अत्यंत लोकप्रिय व क़ामयाब गाना, फ़िल्म आदि **smashing** *adj* (अनौप) श्रेष्ठ, उत्तम।

smattering / 'स्मैटरिङ् / *noun* [*sing*] **smattering (of sth)** ऊपरी जानकारी, अल्पज्ञान।

smear / स्मिअर / *verb* 1 **smear sth on/ over sb/sth; smear sth/sb with sth** तेल या चिकनाई पोतना/लगाना 2 लांछन लगाना, झूठी निंदा करना 3 लिखावट, चित्र आदि को रगड़ कर धुँधला कर देना : *I accidentally smeared the ink before it was dry.* ▶ **smear** *noun* 1 तेल आदि का धब्बा : *a smear of lipstick* 2 झूठी निंदा/लांछन।

smell¹ / स्मेल् / *noun* 1 [*sing*] गंध 2 गंध की गुणवत्ता; सूँघना ▶ **smelly** *adj* (-ler, -lest) दुर्गंध देने वाला।

smell² / स्मेल् / *verb* (*pt, pp* **smelt** / स्मेल्ट् / या **smelled**) 1 सूँघना, सूँघ कर पता लगाना : *The dog had smelt a rabbit.* 2 सूँघ सकना : *Can birds smell?* 3 **smell (of sth)** गंध आना, इंगित देना 4 सहज ज्ञान द्वारा पता लगाना : *He smelt danger.* ■ **smell a rat** (अनौप) कुछ अनुचित होने का संदेह होना : *I smelt a rat when he started being so helpful.* **smell sb/sth out** गंध के कारण ज्ञात होना : *The dogs are trained to smell out drugs.*

smelt / स्मेल्ट् / *verb* (कच्ची धातुएँ) पिघलाना, गलाना; धातुएँ साफ़ या पृथक करना ▶ **smelter** *noun* धातुएँ पिघलाने का संयंत्र।

smile / स्माइल् / *noun* मुस्कुराहट : *give sb a broad smile* ▶ **smile** *verb* 1 **smile at sb/sth** मुस्कुराना 2 मुस्कुराहट के द्वारा व्यक्त करना : *She smiled her approval.* ■ **smile on sb/sth** (औप) किसी को अनुग्रहपूर्वक देखना : *Fortune smiled on us.* ▶ **smilingly** *adv.*

smirk / स्मर्क् / *noun* व्यंग्यात्मक हँसी : *Wipe that smirk off your face!*

smith / स्मिथ् / *noun* धातुकार; लोहार ▶ **smithy** *noun* लोहार की दुकान, लोहाख़ाना।

smoek / स्मॉक् / *noun* ढीला व आरामदेह क़मीज़ की तरह पहना जाने वाला वस्त्र : *a shapeless cotton smock.*

smog / स्मॉग् / *noun* धुएँ और कोहरे का सम्मिश्रण।

smoke¹ / स्मोक् / *noun* 1 धुआँ 2 (अनौप) तंबाकू पीना : *They stopped work to have a smoke.* ■ **go up in smoke** 1 पूरा जल जाना : *The whole row of houses went up in smoke.* 2 असफल होना; महत्त्व योग्य कुछ न छोड़ना : *Hopes of an early end to the dispute have clearly gone up in smoke.* **(there is) no smoke without fire** (कहा) बिना आग के धुआँ नहीं होता।

smoke² / स्मोक् / *verb* 1 धुआँ निका- लना : *a smoking volcano/factory/ chimney* 2 सिगरेट, बीड़ी आदि पीना 3 धुआँरना (मांस, मछली आदि को धुआँ देना) ■ **smoke sb/sth out** 1 धुआँ देकर भगाना 2 किसी को वह स्थान छोड़ने के लिए बाध्य करना जहाँ वह छुपा हो या गुप्त बात को सार्वजनिक करना ▶ **smoker** *noun* धूम्रपान करने वाला व्यक्ति : *a heavy smoker* **smoky** / 'स्मोकि / *adj* (-ler, -lest) 1 बहुत अधिक धुआँ देने वाला; धुएँ से भरा हुआ : *the smoky atmosphere of a room* 2 धुएँ जैसी गंध/स्वाद वाला।

smooth¹ / स्मूद् / *adj* (-er, -est) 1 चिकनी सतह वाला : *Marble is smooth to touch.* 2 महीन पिसा हुआ/चिकना; (द्रव आदि) अच्छी तरह मिला हुआ : *smooth custard* 3 स्वाद में मधुर, कटु या तिक्त नहीं 4 दुविधाओं से मुक्त : *as smooth a journey as possible* 5 मधुर, प्रवाहमय (भाषा/भाषण) : *a smooth voice* 6 (प्रायः अपमा) (व्यक्ति) चापलूस, चाटुकार : *a* smooth manner ▸ **smoothly** adv **smoothness** noun.

smooth² / स्मूद् / verb **smooth sth (away, back, down, out, etc)** चिकना बना देना : smooth wood (with sandpaper) ■ **smooth over** समस्याओं पर परदा डालना, उनके महत्त्व को घटा देना : An attempt was made to smooth over the disagreement between the two leaders.

smother / 'स्मदर् / verb 1 **smother sb (with sth)** दम घोंट कर मारना : He smothered the baby with a pillow. 2 आग को रेत, राख आदि डाल कर बुझाना : She smothered the flames from the burning pan with a wet towel. 3 (किसी का) विकास रोक देना : smother a yawn/smile 4 **smother sth/sb with/in sth** पूरी तरह ढक लेना : a pudding smothered in cream.

smoulder (US **smolder**) / 'स्मोल्डर् / verb आग (बिना ज्वाला के) सुलगना।

smudge / स्मज् / noun कुछ रगड़े जाने से बना धब्बा/गंदा दाग़ : You've got a smudge of dust/paint on your cheek. ▸ **smudge** verb 1 रगड़ कर धब्बे लगा देना : smudged lipstick 2 (रोशनाई) फैल जाना।

smug / स्मग् / adj (अपमा) दंभी, आत्म-संतुष्ट; अपनी उपलब्धियों पर स्वयं ही बहुत खुश होने वाला : smile with smug satisfaction.

smuggle / 'स्मगल् / verb **smuggle sth/sb (into/out of/across/through sth)** 1 चोरी से/ग़ैर-क़ानूनी ढंग से माल देश में लाना या देश से बाहर ले जाना; तस्करी करना : smuggle Swiss watches 2 चुपके से छिपा कर कोई वस्तु ले आना/भेज देना : smuggle a letter into prison ▸ **smuggler** noun तस्कर-व्यापारी **smuggling** noun.

snack / स्नैक् / noun हलका नाश्ता (प्रायः जल्दी में किया गया) : a snack lunch.

snag / स्नैग् / noun 1 छिपा हुआ या अप्रत्याशित संकट : come across a snag 2 कहीं उलझ जाने से कपड़े में हो जाने वाला छेद फटना या धागा बाहर निकल आना : I've got a snag in my tights.

snail / स्नेल् / noun घोंघा।

snake / स्नेक् / noun 1 साँप, सर्प 2 धोखे-बाज़ व्यक्ति ■ **snake in the grass** धोखेबाज़ व्यक्ति जो मित्र होने का ढोंग करता है।

snap¹ / स्नैप् / verb (-pp-) 1 किसी वस्तु का अचानक, तीक्ष्ण आवाज़ करते हुए टूट जाना : He stretched the rubber band till it snapped. 2 **snap (at sb/sth)** (पशु का) अचानक आवाज़ करते हुए काटना 3 (अनौप) जल्दी से फ़ोटो खींचना : I snapped you on the beach. 4 **snap (at sb)** किसी से तीखे, क्रोधित स्वर में बोलना ■ **snap one's fingers** चुटकी बजाना **snap sth up** किसी को जल्दी उत्सुकतापूर्वक पकड़ लेना/ख़रीद लेना।

snap² / स्नैप् / noun 1 चटकने/तड़कने की आवाज़ : The lid shut with a snap. 2 (**snapshot** भी) फ़ोटोग्राफ़ 3 [sing] (US अनौप) आसान कार्य : This job's a snap. ▸ **snap** adj (अनौप) जल्दी में, बिना चेतावनी के किया गया : a snap election/decision **snappy** adj (-ier, -iest) 1 (अनौप) फुरतीला, ज़िंदादिल, तेज़ : a snappy dancer 2 (अनौप) फ़ैशनप्रिय, लोकप्रिय, प्रचलित : a snappy outfit 3 तीखे स्वर में पेश आने वाला : She's always snappy in the morning.

snare / स्नेअर् / noun 1 (चिड़ियों या छोटे पशुओं को फँसाने के लिए) जाल, फंदा 2 (औप) चोट पहुँचाने या फँसाने की संभावना वाली वस्तु : He fell victim to the sensual lures and snares of city life. ▸ **snare** verb फंदा डालना।

snarl / स्नार्ल् / *verb* 1 snarl (at sb/sth) (कुत्ते आदि का) गुर्राना 2 snarl (sth) (at sb) (व्यक्ति का) क्रोध में बदमिज़ाजी से कुछ कहना : *snarl abuse (at strangers).*

snatch / स्नैच् / *verb* 1 झपटना, लपककर छीनना : *He snatched up the gun and fired.* 2 चुराना : *Somebody snatched my wallet.* 3 अवसर पाते ही प्राप्त करना : *snatch an hour's sleep* ▸ **snatch** *noun* 1 (प्रायः *pl*) किसी चीज़ का एक छोटा-सा भाग जिसे देखा या सुना जा सके : *short snatches of song* 2 (प्रायः *pl*) छोटी-सी अवधि : *sleep in snatches* 3 जल्दी-से कुछ छीनने की कोशिश : *make a snatch at sth* **snatcher** *noun* चोर/उचक्का : *a handbag snatcher.*

sneak / स्नीक् / *verb* 1 sneak (on sb)(to sb) (अनौप) बच्चों द्वारा अपने साथियों की ग़लतियों/बुरी बातों को बड़ों को बताना : *She sneaked on her best friend to the teacher.* 2 (अनौप) चोरी करके ले जाना/कुछ करना : *sneak a chocolate from the box* 3 आँख बचाकर चले जाना : *He sneaked out of the restaurant without paying.* ■ **sneak up (on sb/sth)** दबे पाँव किसी के पास जाना, विशेषत: उसे चौंकाने के लिए : *He enjoys sneaking up on his sister to frighten her.* ▸ **sneak** *noun* (अनौप) कायर और धोखेबाज़ व्यक्ति।

sneer / स्निअर् / *verb* sneer (at sb/sth) हँसी उड़ाना, मुँह बिचका कर उपहास करना : *He's always sneering at people less clever than he is.* ▸ **sneer** *noun* तिरस्कार भरे शब्द, हँसी आदि : *endure the jeers and sneers of one's enemies.*

sneeze / स्नीज़ / *noun* छींक : *coughs and sneezes* ▸ **sneeze** *verb* छींकना।

snide / स्नाइड् / *adj* (अपमा) अप्रत्यक्ष और अप्रिय ढंग से आलोचक होना : *He's always making snide comments about her appearance.*

sniff / स्निफ़् / *verb* 1 नाक से साँस खींचते समय सूँ-सूँ करना (बहता नाक रोकने के लिए या घृणा से) 2 sniff (at) sth सूँघना 3 शिकायती लहज़े में कुछ कहना ▸ **sniff** *noun* **snifferdog** *noun* प्रशिक्षित सूँघने वाला कुत्ता।

sniffle / 'स्निफ़्ल् / *verb* नाक से साँस खींचना, सूँ-सूँ करना : *I wish you wouldn't keep sniffling.* ▸ **sniffle** *noun* नाक सुड़कना।

snigger / 'स्निगर् / *noun* धीमी अप्रिय हँसी, विशेषत: खिल्ली उड़ाने के लिए : *His bad jokes brought embarrassed sniggers from the audience.* ▸ **snigger** *verb* snigger (at sb/sth) इस प्रकार हँसना : *What are you sniggering at?*

snip / स्निप् / *verb* (-pp-) snip (at) sth कैंची से काटना : *snip a stray lock of hair.*

snipe / स्नाइप् / *verb* 1 snipe (at sb/sth) अँधेरे में से या छिपे-छिपे (किसी पर) गोली चलाना; इस प्रकार से गोली चलाकर मार डालना या घायल करना 2 किसी पर अप्रिय कटाक्ष या निंदाभरा हमला करना : *politicians sniping at each other* ▸ **sniper** *noun* छिप कर गोली चलाने वाला व्यक्ति।

snippet / 'स्निपिट् / *noun* snippet (of sth) किसी सूचना/जानकारी का छोटा-सा अंश; संक्षिप्त सार : *hear odd snippets of conversation.*

snivel / 'स्निव्ल् / *verb* (-ll-; *US* -l- भी) (अपमा) झींखना, खीजना, दयनीय रूप से सूँ-सूँ करते हुए खीजना : *Don't keep snivelling about how poor we are.*

snob / स्नॉब् / *noun* (अपमा) सामाजिक प्रतिष्ठा, धन-संपत्ति आदि को अत्यधिक सम्मान देने वाला व्यक्ति, दंभी; अपने को

अत्यधिक सुसंस्कृत समझने वाला व्यक्ति : *intellectual/cultural snobs* ▶ **snobbery** / 'स्नॉबरि / *noun* (अपमान) दंभ **snobbish** (अनौप **snobby** भी) *adj.*

snooker / 'स्नूकर / *noun* स्नूकर; 15 लाल व 7 अन्य रंगों की गेंदों के साथ एक विशेष तरह की मेज़ पर खेला जाने वाला खेल।

snoop / स्नूप् / *verb* **snoop (around sth); snoop (around)** (अनौप, प्राय: अपमान) गोपनीय, विशेषत: ग़ैर-क़ानूनी, ढंग से खोजना, ताक-झाँक करना, किसी पर निगाह रखना : *Someone was snooping around (outside) your house last night.* ○ *journalists snooping into people's private affairs.*

snooty / 'स्नूटि / *adj* (अनौप, अपमान) दंभी; दूसरों (विशेषत: अपने से नीचे सामाजिक स्तर के व्यक्तियों) के लिए नापसंदी और तिरस्कार की भावना दिखाते हुए : *a snooty letter refusing the invitation* ▶ **snootiness** *noun.*

snooze / स्नूज़ / *verb* (अनौप) झपकी लेना, विशेषकर दिन के समय और बिस्तर में नहीं : *Dad was snoozing by the fire.* ▶ **snooze** *noun* [sing] झपकी।

snore / स्नॉर् / *verb* सोते में खर्राटे भरना ▶ **snore** *noun* खर्राटा (की ध्वनि)।

snorkel / 'स्नॉर्कल् / *noun* ग़ोता लगाते समय साँस लेने की नली।

snort / स्नॉर्ट / *verb* 1 (जानवरों का) फुफ्कारना; **snort (at sth)** (व्यक्ति का) क्रोध, चिढ़ आदि में ऐसी ही आवाज़ करना : *snort with rage/laughter* 2 नाक से नशीली दवा लेना ▶ **snort** *noun* फुफ्कार।

snot / स्नॉट् / *noun* (अनौप) रेंट, नाक से निकलने वाला गाढ़ा द्रव ▶ **snotty** *adj* (अनौप) 1 (प्राय: अपमान) रेंट भरा : *washing his snotty handkerchief* 2 (**snotty-nosed** भी) (अपमान) घमंडी।

snout / स्नाउट् / *noun* 1 (पशुओं का) थूथन 2 किसी वस्तु का उभरा हुआ अगला

भाग : *I found myself staring into the snout of a pistol.* 3 (परि) (व्यक्ति का) नाक।

snow¹ / स्नो / *noun* 1 हिम, बर्फ़ 2 **snows** [pl] गिरती हुई या गिरी हुई बर्फ़ ▶ **snowy** *adj* (-ier, -iest) 1 हिमाच्छादित; बर्फ़ गिरती हुई : *a snowy night* 2 बर्फ़ के समान (सफ़ेद, ठंडा)।

snow² / स्नो / *verb* 1 बर्फ़ गिरना, हिमपात होना 2 (US, अनौप) किसी को धोखा देने या बहकाने की कोशिश करना ■ **snow sb in/up** बर्फ़ के कारण आना-जाना रुक जाना।

snub / स्नब् / *verb* (-bb-) 1 अवज्ञापूर्ण व्यवहार करना : *I tried to be friendly but she snubbed me completely.* 2 किसी के सुझाव को दुरदुराना, ठुकराना ▶ **snub** *noun* **snub (to sb)** ऐसे शब्द या व्यवहार : *His remarks in a radio interview are being interpreted as a deliberate snub to the minister.*

snuff¹ / स्नफ़् / *noun* सूँघनी (तंबाकू)।

snuff² / स्नफ़् / *verb* **snuff sth (out)** गुल (मोमबत्ती की बत्ती) काटना; रोशनी बुझाना।

snug / स्नग् / *adj* 1 सुखद आश्रय; सुरक्षित : *a snug little house* 2 (कपड़े) ठीक-ठीक बैठना : *a snug fitting coat.*

snuggle / 'स्नगल् / *verb* **snuggle (up to sb/sth); snuggle (up/down)** सटकर, छाती लगा कर लेटना, गरमी, आराम या स्नेह के लिए : *Snuggle down and go to sleep.*

so¹ / सो / *adv* 1 इस सीमा तक, इतना : *Don't look so angry.* 2 बहुत, अत्यधिक : *I'm so glad to see you.* 3 उस हद तक नहीं : *It wasn't so bad as we expected.* 4 इतना : *The fish was about so big.* 5 ऐसा; सत्य : *'She is very unreliable.' 'Is that so?'* 6 यही/वही तो : *George is going to help me, or so he says.* 7 भी; और भी : *He is divorced and so am I.* 8 इस प्रकार, ऐसे : *As you treat me, so*

shall I treat you. ■ and so forth;
and so on (and so forth) इत्यादि : We
discussed everything : when to go,
what to see and so on (and so
forth). not so much sth as sth एक
चीज़ नही, बल्कि कुछ और : She is not
so much poor as careless with
money. or so लगभग इतना : There
were twenty or so people there. so
as to do sth कुछ करने के इरादे से : He
disconnected the phone so as not
to be disturbed. so be it ऐसा ही हो :
If he doesn't want to be involved,
then so be it. so much for sb/sth इस
पर और कुछ कहने या करने की ज़रूरत
नही : So much for our new secretary—she left after three days. so
much sth बहुत सारा, विशेषत: बेकार :
His promises were just so much
meaningless nonsense. ▸ so-and-
so noun अमुक, फलाँ so-called adj
तथाकथित so-so adj (अनौप) जैसे-तैसे,
किसी प्रकार, न बुरा न अच्छा।

so²/सो/conj 1 इसलिए, इस कारण : The
shop was closed so I couldn't get
any milk. 2 इस इरादे से : I gave you
a map so you wouldn't get lost.
3 तो क्या : 'You've been drinking
again.' 'So?'

soak/सोक्/verb 1 soak sth (in sth)
भीगना, भिगोना 2 soak into/through
sth; soak in (द्रवों का) तरबतर कर देना :
The rain had soaked through his
coat. 3 (अनौप) अत्यधिक कर लगाकर
धन ऐंठ लेना : soak the rich.

soap/सोप्/noun 1 साबुन 2 (अनौप)
= soap opera ▸ soap verb साबुन
लगाना, साबुन से साफ़ करना : She soaped
her skin and hair. soap opera noun
टी वी या रेडियो के सीरियल जिनमें वर्ग-
विशेष के जीवन की समस्याओं पर प्रकाश
डाला जाता है soap suds noun [pl]

साबुन के झाग **soapy** adj (-ier, -iest)
साबुन जैसा/साबुन वाला : warm soapy
water.

soar/सॉर्/verb 1 soar into sth ऊँचे
मँडराना; ऊँचे चढ़ना या उड़ना : The
rocket soared (up) into the air.
2 अचानक ऊँचे चले जाना : soaring
prices 3 सामान्य से बहुत अधिक ऊँचे
बढ़ना; बहुत ऊँचा होना : a city of soaring skyscrapers.

sob/सॉब्/verb (-bb-) 1 सिसकना : The
child began to sob loudly. 2 रो-
रोकर कुछ कहना : She sobbed out her
story. ▸ **sob** noun सिसकी (की ध्वनि)।

sober/'सोबर्/adj 1 अमत्त, न पिए
हुए : Were you completely sober
when you said that? 2 संयत, गंभीर/
संतुलित : a sober and hardworking
young man 3 (रंग) सौम्य ▸ **sober**
verb गंभीर/संयत करना या होना।

sobriety/स'ब्राइअटि/noun (औप)
संयत एवं गंभीर होना : a man noted for
his sobriety.

soccer/'सॉकर्/noun फुटबाल का खेल।

sociable/'सोशब्ल्/adj मिलनसार,
मैत्रीपूर्ण : He has never really been
the sociable type.

social/'सोश्ल्/adj 1 सामाजिक,
समाज-विषयक : social problems
2 समाज में रहने वालों का/से संबंधित :
social class/background 3 झुंड/
समुदाय में रहने वाला : Most bees and
wasps are social insects. 4 मिलन-
सार : He's not a very social person.
▸ **social** noun मैत्री-गोष्ठी : a church
social.

socialism/'सोशलिज़म्/noun समाजवाद
▸ **socialist** noun समाजवादी।

society/स'साइअटि/noun (pl socie-
ties) 1 समाज/समुदाय; सामाजिक संगठन
2 उद्देश्य-विशेष के लिए गठित संघ/संग-
ठन : a co-operative society 3 उच्च-

वर्ग : *high society* 4 *(औप)* साहचर्य, संगति : *avoid the society of other people.*

sociology /सोसिऑलजि/ *noun* समाज-शास्त्र, समाज की प्रकृति और विकास का अध्ययन करने वाला विज्ञान ▸ **sociological** *adj.*

sock / सॉक् / *noun* मोज़ा।

socket / सॉकिट् / *noun (US outlet* भी) 1 सॉकेट (छेददार पुरज़ा जिसमें कोई प्लग जैसा अन्य पुरज़ा फ़िट किया जा सके) : *a socket at the back of a TV for the aerial* 2 छोटा-सा ख़ाली स्थान जहाँ कुछ स्थिर हो या किया जा सके : *the eye socket.*

soda / सोडा / *noun* 1 सोडा, क्षार : *washing soda* 2 सोडा वॉटर।

sofa / सोफ़ा / *noun* सोफ़ा ▸ **sofa bed** *noun.*

soft / सॉफ़्ट् / *adj* (-er, -est) 1 (**hard** के वैषम्य में) मुलायम, नरम : *a soft pencil/ cheese* 2 (सतह) चिकनी; (कपड़ा) चिकना; नाज़ुक : *as soft as velvet* 3 (रंग) हलका, सौम्य; सादा : *lamp-shades that give a soft light* 4 (ध्वनि) धीमी/मंद : *soft music in the background* 5 *(अनौप)* (भाषा) प्रियकर, सौम्य : *His reply was soft and calm.* 6 **soft** (**on sb/sth**); **soft** (**with sb**) (व्यक्ति) बहुत अधिक सहानुभूतिपूर्ण एवं दयापूर्ण, बिना किसी सख़्ती के : *He's a bit too soft to keep his class under control.* 7 *(अनौप, अपमा)* अति भावुक; संकल्प में कमज़ोर : *Don't be so soft—there is nothing to be afraid of.* ■ **have a soft spot for sb/sth** *(अनौप)* किसी के लिए ख़ास स्नेह होना : *He's a strange man, but I've always had a soft spot for him.* ▸ **soft drink** *noun* पेय जिसमें अल्कोहल नहीं होता है **soft-hearted** *adj* कोमल-हृदय; क्षमाशील **softly** *adv.*

soften / सॉफ़्न् / *verb* 1 नरम बनाना/ करना: *a lotion to soften the skin* 2 कम कठोर बनाना।

software / सॉफ़्ट्वेअर् / *noun* प्रोग्राम जिनसे कंप्यूटर पर काम किया जाता है।

softy (**softie** भी) / सॉफ़्टि / *noun (अनौप)* 1 *(अपमा)* डरपोक , कमज़ोर 2 सहानुभूतिपूर्ण एवं भावुक व्यक्ति।

soggy / सॉगि / *adj* (-ier, -iest) (प्रायः अपमा) गीला व नरम; दलदली भूमि।

soil / सॉइल् / *noun* 1 मिट्टी, धरती 2 *(औप)* देश, ज़मीन : *one's native soil* ▸ **soil** *verb (औप)* मैला करना, धब्बे डालना : *a basket for soiled sheets.*

sojourn /सॉज़र्न; *US* सोज़र्न / *verb (औप)* कुछ समय के लिए ठहरना, टिकना ▸ **sojourn** *noun (औप)* (घर से बाहर) अस्थायी ठहराव/रुकना : *a brief sojourn in the mountains.*

solace / सॉलस् / *noun (औप)* तसल्ली, राहत; सांत्वना देने वाली वस्तु ▸ **solace** *verb (औप)* तसल्ली/सांत्वना देना।

solar / सोलर् / *adj* 1 सूर्यसंबंधी : *the solar system* 2 सौर ऊर्जा प्रयोग करने संबंधी : *solar heating/solar powered.*

solder / सोल्डर; *US* साड्र / *noun* टाँका लगाने में प्रयुक्त राँगा ▸ **solder** *verb* टाँका लगाना, टाँका लगा कर जोड़ना : *solder the two pieces together.*

soldier / सोल्जर् / *noun* सैनिक, सिपाही।

sole[1] / सोल् / *noun* 1 पैर का तलुआ 2 जूते का तल्ला : *leather/rubber soles* ▸ **sole** *verb* नया तल्ला लगवाना/लगाना : *have a pair of shoes soled.*

sole[2] / सोल् / *noun* (*pl* अपरिवर्तित या **soles**) कुकुरजीभी (एक प्रकार की समुद्री मछली)।

sole[3] /सोल्/ *adj* 1 एकमात्र, अकेला : *the sole survivor of the crash* 2 अनन्य, सिर्फ़ एक से संबंधित : *the sole owner/ distributor* ▸ **solely** *adv* अकेले;

केवल : *be solely responsible for the accident.*

solemn / 'सॉलम् / *adj* 1 गंभीर मुद्रा में, प्रसन्नवदन या मुस्कुराते हुए नहीं : *solemn faces* 2 गंभीर एवं सौम्य ढंग से कहा या किया गया : *a solemn promise* 3 समारोह के साथ संपन्न, विधिवत् : *a solemn procession/ritual* ▸ **solemnly** *adv.*

solemnity / स'लेम्नटि / *noun* (औप) 1 गंभीरता/सौम्यता : *He was buried with great solemnity.* 2 (प्राय: *pl*) विधिवत् समारोह, उत्सव : *observe the solemnities of the occasion.*

solemnize, -ise / 'सॉलम्नाइज़् / *verb* (औप) विधिवत् संस्कार संपन्न करना : *solemnize a marriage.*

solicit / स'लिसिट् / *verb* 1 solicit (sb) (for sth); solicit (sth) (from sb) (औप) माँगना, याचना करना : *solicit (sb) for money* 2 (वेश्या द्वारा) स्वयं को प्रस्तुत करना।

solicitor / स'लिसिटर / *noun* वसीयत जैसे क़ानूनी काग़ज़ात बनाने वाला और क़ानूनी मामलों में राय देने वाला वकील, सॉलिसिटर।

solicitous / स'लिसिटस् / *adj* (औप) किसी और के कल्याण के लिए चिंतित, व्याकुल; उत्कंठित : *be solicitous about sb's health.*

solicitude / स'लिसिट्यूड्; *US* स'लिसिटूड् / *noun* solicitude (for/about sb/ sth) (औप) (विशेषकर औरों के कल्याण के लिए) उत्कंठा, उत्सुकता।

solid / 'सॉलिड् / *adj* 1 ठोस (न तो द्रव, न गैस) 2 ठोस, घनीभूत (छिद्रिल नहीं) : *a solid wall of rock* 3 पक्का एवं मज़बूत; पुष्ट : *solid buildings* 4 विश्वसनीय, भरोसेमंद : *solid evidence* 5 लगातार, नियमित : *The essay represents a solid week's work.* 6 (ज्यामिति) घनाकार : *a solid figure/ solid geometry* 7 ख़ालिस, खरा : *solid gold* ▸ **solid** *noun* 1 ठोस पदार्थ

2 (ज्यामिति) पिंड, घनाकार **solidity** (**solidness** भी) *noun* **solidly** *adv.*

solidarity / ,सॉलि'डैरटि / *noun* सामान्य हित और भावना से उत्पन्न एकता, एकात्मकता : *show solidarity in the face of opposition.*

solidify / स'लिडिफ़ाइ / *verb* (*pt, pp* solidified) solidify (into sth) 1 ठोस बनना या करना/बनाना : *The paint had solidified in the tin.* 2 (विचारों का) स्थायी हो जाना, बदलने की संभावना न रहना : *Vague objections solidified into firm opposition.*

soliloquy / स'लिलक्वि / *noun* (*pl* soliloquies) स्वगत कथन (नाटक में) : *Hamlet's famous soliloquy.*

solitary / 'सॉलिट्रि; *US* 'सॉलटेरि / *adj* 1 अकेला, बिना साथी के : *a solitary kind of person* 2 केवल-मात्र एक 3 सुनसान, ग़ैर-आबाद : *a solitary island/valley* ▸ **solitary confinement** (अनौप **solitary** भी) *noun* एक सज़ा जिसके तहत क़ैदी को अलग कक्ष में रखा जाता है।

solitude / 'सॉलिट्यूड् / *noun* अकेलापन : *enjoy/seek solitude.*

solo / 'सोलो / *noun* (*pl* solos) 1 एकल (वादन, गायन, संगीत रचना आदि) : *a violin solo* 2 पायलट द्वारा बिना प्रशिक्षक के उड़ान : *fly one's first solo* ▸ **solo** *adj, adv* अकेले **soloist** *noun* एकल वादक/गायक।

soluble / 'सॉल्यबल् / *adj* 1 soluble (in sth) घुलनशील : *Glucose is soluble in water.* 2 (औप) (समस्या) जिसका हल निकाला जा सके।

solution / स'लूश्न् / *noun* 1 solution (to sth) (समस्या का) हल, समाधान 2 विलयन, घोल : *a solution of salt in water* 3 घोल बनाने की प्रक्रिया।

solve / सॉल्व् / *verb* 1 समस्या का हल/ समाधान निकालना : *solve a crossword* *puzzle/mathematical equation* 2 मुश्किल स्थिति से निपटने का रास्ता ढूँढना : *solve the problem of environmental pollution* ▸ **solvable** *adj.*

sombre (*US* **somber**) / 'सॉम्बर् / *adj* 1 गहरा रंग वाला; धुँधला, निराशाजनक : *sombre clothes* 2 उदास, खिन्न : *be in a sombre mood* ▸ **sombrely** *adv.*

some[1] /सम्/ *indef det* 1 कुछ (अनिश्चित मात्रा या राशि) : *There's some ice in the fridge.* 2 (**one, an, a** का *pl*) कुछ : *Some children were playing in the park.* 3 कोई अनिश्चित स्थान/समय आदि : *See you again some time.* 4 कुछ थोड़ी-सी मात्रा/संख्या, लेकिन अधिक नहीं : *There is some hope, I suppose.*

some[2] / सम् / *indef pron* व्यक्तियों/ वस्तुओं की कुछ मात्रा/संख्या : *Some disapprove of the idea.*

somebody (**someone** भी) / 'सम्-बडि / *indef pron* कोई; महत्त्वपूर्ण व्यक्ति : *He thinks he's really somebody.*

someday (**some day** भी) / 'सम्डे / *indef adv* भविष्य में कभी : *Some day he will be famous.*

somehow / 'सम्हाउ / (*US* **someway** भी) *indef adv* 1 किसी तरह से : *We must stop him from seeing her somehow.* 2 किसी अज्ञात या अस्पष्ट कारण से : *Somehow, I don't feel I can trust him.*

somersault / 'समर्सॉल्ट् / *noun* कलाबाज़ी, कलैया (सिर के ऊपर से एड़ियाँ निकालते हुए कूदना) ▸ **somersault** *verb* कलाबाज़ी/कलैया खाना।

something / 'सम्थ्भिङ्ग् / *indef pron* 1 अज्ञात या अस्पष्ट वस्तु; कुछ : *I want something to eat.* ○ *I wish there*

was something I could do to help. 2 कुछ महत्त्वपूर्ण या ध्यान देने योग्य : *There's something in what she says.* ■ **or something** (अनौप) वैसा ही कुछ : *She's writing a dictionary or something.* **something else** (अनौप) असाधारण व्यक्ति, वस्तु, घटना आदि : *I've seen some fine players, but she's something else.* **something like sb/ sth** 1 कुछ पहलुओं में मिलता-जुलता : *It tastes something like melon.* 2 लगभग : *It costs something like Rs 350.* **something of a sth** किसी विशेष चीज़ से कुछ हद तक समानता : *I'm something of an expert on antiques.* **something or other** (अनौप) अपरिचित या भूला हुआ : *He's a professor of something or other at Allahabad University.*

sometime (**some time** भी) / 'सम्टा-इम् / *indef adv* समय जो निर्धारित न किया गया हो : *I saw him sometime last summer.*

somewhat / 'सम्वॉट् / *adv* कुछ-कुछ : *I was somewhat surprised to see him.*

somewhere / 'सम्वेअर् / (*US* **someplace** भी) *indef adv* कहीं : *I have seen him somewhere before.* ■ **or somewhere** वैसी ही कोई और जगह **somewhere around, about, between, etc sth** निर्धारित मूल्य, अंक के लगभग।

somnolent / 'सॉम्नलन्ट् / *adj* (औप) 1 निंदासा, निद्रालु, लगभग सोया हुआ : *feel rather somnolent after a large lunch* 2 नींद लाने वाला : *The noise of the stream had a pleasantly somnolent effect.*

son / सन् / *noun* 1 पुत्र, लड़का : *I have a son and two daughters.* 2 (साहि) परिवार, देश आदि का पुरुष सदस्य : *one of*

India's most famous sons ▸ **son-in-law** *noun* (*pl* **sons-in-law**) दामाद।

sonata / सं'नाटा / *noun* एक या दो वाद्य यंत्रों (पिआनो सामान्यत: उसमें से एक है) के लिए तैयार संगीत।

song / सॉङ् / *noun* **1** गीत, गाना : *a popular song* **2** गायन **3** पक्षियों की संगीतमय आवाज़ : *the song of the bulbul.*

sonic / 'सॉनिक् / *adj* ध्वनिसंबंधी : *sonic waves;* → **supersonic** भी देखिए।

sonnet / 'सॉनिट् / *noun* 14 पंक्तियों की एक प्रकार की कविता, सॉनेट : *Shake-spearean sonnets.*

soon / सून् / *adv* (**-er, -est**) **1** अविलंब, तत्काल : *We'll soon be home.* **2 the sooner... the sooner...** जल्दी, तुरंत ही : *The sooner you begin, the sooner you'll finish.* ■ **as soon as** ज्यों ही **no sooner... than** तुरंत तभी या बाद में : *No sooner had I shut the door than I realized I'd left my purse inside.* **sooner or later** कभी न कभी : *You should tell her, because she'll find out sooner or later.* **sooner rather than later** लंबे अंतराल के बजाए थोड़े समय मे : *I hope we can sort it out sooner rather than latter.* **the sooner the better** जितनी जल्दी हो सके : *'When shall I tell him?' 'The sooner the better.'*

soot / सुट् / *noun* कालिख, काजल ▸ **sooty** *adj* **1** कालिख लगा हुआ/चढ़ा हुआ : *a sooty chimney* **2** काला : *a sooty coat.*

soothe / सूद्र / *verb* **1** किसी परेशान व्यक्ति को शांत करना : *soothe a crying baby* **2 soothe sth (away)** दर्द आदि कम करना : *soothe sb's backache by rubbing it* ▸ **soothing** *adj* : *soothing music* **soothingly** *adv.*

sop / सॉप् / *noun* **sop (to sb/sth)** (प्राय: *अपमा*) मुँहभराई, घूस (ताकि व्यक्ति झंझट न पैदा करे) : *The change of policy is seen as a sop to the moderates in the party.*

sophisticated / सं'फ़िस्टिकेटिड् / *adj* **1** अनुभवी एवं परिष्कृत, कृत्रिम व्यवहार : *a sophisticated young woman* **2** जटिल, काफ़ी सुधार के पश्चात, विस्तृत : *a sophisticated computer system* **3** जटिल बातों को समझने में समर्थ; जो अब सरल/साधारण नहीं रह गया है : *Voters are much more sophisticated nowadays.* ▸ **sophistication** *noun.*

soppy / 'सॉपि / *adj* (*अनौप, अपमा*) मूर्खतापूर्ण अति भावुक : *a soppy film/love story.*

soprano / सं'प्रानो; *US* सं'प्रैनो / *noun* (*pl* **sopranos** / सं'प्रानोज़् /) (संगीत) उच्चतम स्वर; ऐसे स्वर में गाने वाला : *The sopranos sang beautifully.*

sorcerer / 'सॉर्सरर् / *noun* (*fem* **sorceress** / 'सॉर्सरस् /) ओझा, झाड़-फूँक करने वाला; जादूगर(तांत्रिक) ▸ **sorcery** *noun* जादू-टोना।

sordid / 'सॉर्डिड् / *adj* **1** (दशा, स्थान) फटेहाल, गंदा : *living in sordid poverty* **2** (व्यक्ति, व्यवहार आदि) नीच, स्वार्थपूर्ण, कुटिल : *a sordid affair/person* ▸ **sordidly** *adv.*

sore / सॉर् / *adj* (**-r, -st**) **1** (शरीर का अंग) दुखने वाला, दर्दीला : *have a sore finger/throat* **2** (औपया अप्र) अप्रिय, अरुचिकर; गंभीर : *be in sore need of help* **3** (अनौप) उदास, क्रोधित : *She is sore about not being invited to the party.* ■ **a sore point** किसी को क्रोधित या निराश करने वाला विषय **stand/stick out like a sore thumb** स्पष्ट और प्राय: कुरूप होना ▸ **sore** *noun* सूजा हुआ या कटा-फटा **sorely** *adv* (औप) गंभीरता से; अत्यधिक : *Your financial help is sorely needed.*

sorrow / 'सॉरो / *noun* **sorrow (at/for/ over sth)** दुख, व्यथा/उदासी; दुख का कारण विशेष : *the joys and sorrows of life* ▸ **sorrow** *verb* **sorrow (at/for/ over sth)** (औप) दुखी होना या दुख दिखाना : *sorrowing over his child's death* **sorrowful** *adj* (औप) उदास, दुख-भरा : *a sorrowful voice/face.*

sorry / 'सॉरि / *adj* (-ier, -iest) **1 sorry (to do sth/that ...)** अभाव और निराशा के कारण दुख/कष्ट का अनुभव : *I'm sorry that you're leaving.* **2 sorry (for/ about sth)** शर्म और खेद से भरा, विशेषकर किसी पिछली घटना के लिए : *Aren't you sorry for/about what you've done?* **3** (खेद की अभिव्यक्ति के लिए प्रयुक्त) : *I'm sorry, but I don't agree.* **4** (प्राय: अपमा) दयनीय (अवस्था में) : *a sorry sight/state* ▪ **be/feel sorry for sb** किसी पर दया आना : *I feel sorry for anyone who has to drive in this weather.* ▸ **sorry** *interj* माफ़ कीजिए ...।

sort¹ / सॉर्ट / *noun* **1** समान प्रकार के व्यक्तियों/वस्तुओं का समूह, वर्ग : *There is some sort of spice in it.* **2** (प्राय: *sing*) (अनौप) एक प्रकार; व्यक्ति विशेष ▪ **of a sort/of sorts** (अनौप, अपमा) तुच्छ प्रकार का : *It was a holiday of sorts but we weren't able to relax much.* **it takes all sorts (to make a world)** (कहा) लोगों की योग्यताओं और आचरण में विभिन्नता है (और यह अच्छी बात है) **out of sorts** (अनौप) **1** अस्वस्थ; कुछ-कुछ बीमार : *She's been out of sorts lately.* **2** गुस्से में।

sort² / सॉर्ट / *verb* **sort sth (out) (into sth); sort sth (out) from sth** (आकार आदि के अनुसार) छाँटकर अलग करना, वर्ग बनाना : *sort out the dirty washing.*

SOS / एस ओ एस / *noun* **1** जहाज़, हवाई जहाज़ आदि द्वारा रेडियो से भेजा संकटकालीन सहायता का संदेश (**save our souls** का संक्षिप्त रूप) : *send an SOS to the coastguard* **2** संकट की स्थिति में किसी के भी द्वारा सहायता माँगने का संदेश।

soul / सोल् / *noun* **1** आत्मा : *Do you believe in the immortality of the soul?* **2** अंत:करण; तीव्र भावनाएँ : *a man with no soul* **3** [*sing*] **the soul of sth** आदर्श व्यक्तित्व : *He is the soul of honour.* **4** (विशेषकर नकारात्मक वाक्यों में) मानव प्राणी : *There wasn't a soul to be seen.* **5** (दया, करुणा आदि दिखाते हुए विशेषणों के साथ प्रयुक्त) व्यक्ति : *She's lost all her money, poor soul.* ▸ **soulful** *adj* भावपूर्ण; भावनाओं को झकझोरने वाला।

sound¹ / साउन्ड / *noun* **1** ध्वनि, आवाज़ : *Sound travels slower than light.* **2** ध्वनि उत्पन्न करने वाली वस्तु : *the sound of the wind* **3** ध्वनि श्रवण की दूरी : *Their house is within (the) sound of the sea.* ▪ **by the sound of it** किसी के द्वारा प्रयोग किए गए शब्दों, दृष्टिकोण आदि के आधार पर परखना : *They had a wonderful time by the sound of it.* ▸ **soundproof** *adj* ध्वनि-रोधक, जहाँ बाहर की ध्वनि भीतर और भीतर की ध्वनि बाहर न जा सके : *a soundproof studio.*

sound² / साउन्ड / *verb* **1** ध्वनि उत्पन्न करना; सुने जाने पर विशेष प्रभाव होना : *That music sounds beautiful.* **2 sound (to sb) as if.../as though.../ like...** यह प्रभाव डालना कि : *I hope I don't sound as if I am criticizing you.* **3** ध्वनि उत्पन्न करना (किसी वस्तु/ उपकरण की सहायता से) : *sound a trumpet* **4** ध्वनि से संदेश भेजना : *sound the alarm.*

sound³ / साउन्ड / *noun* (भूगोल में, प्राय: स्थानों के नामों में) जल संयोजी : *Plymouth Sound.*

sound⁴ /साउन्ड्/ *adj* (**-er, -est**) **1** अच्छी दशा में, स्वस्थ : *house built on sound foundations* **2** तर्कसंगत, विवेकपूर्ण : *a sound argument* ○ *sound advice* **3** पूरा-पूरा, समग्र : *give sb a sound thrashing* **4** सावधान, सही; योग्य : *a very sound tennis player* **5** (निद्रा) गहन : *a sound night's sleep* ▸ **sound** *adv* : *fall sound asleep* **soundly** *adv* भली भाँति; विवेक के साथ : *a soundly based argument* **soundness** *noun*.

soup / सूप / *noun* शोरबा, झोल : *chicken/tomato/vegetable soup.*

sour /साउअर्/ *adj* **1** खट्टा (नींबू या कच्चे आम की तरह) : *This apple is really sour.* **2** (दूध) फटा हुआ **3** असंतुष्ट, बदमिज़ाज, चिड़चिड़ा : *a sour and disillusioned man* ■ **go/turn sour** अप्रिय या प्रतिकूल हो जाना : *Their relationship went sour.* **sour grapes** (कहा) अंगूर खट्टे हैं : *He says he didn't want to marry her anyway, but that's just sour grapes.* ▸ **sour** *verb* खट्टा होना या करना : *soured cream* **sourly** *adv*.

source /सॉर्स्/ *noun* **1** (नदी का) स्रोत; प्रारंभ बिंदु **2** उद्गम स्थान; सूचना का स्रोत : *He cited many sources for his book.*

south / साउथ् / *noun, adj, adv* दक्षिण दिशा ▸ **southwards** *adv* दक्षिण की ओर।

southern (**Southern** भी) / 'सदर्न्/ *adj* दक्षिणी; दक्षिण-विषयक : *the southern hemisphere.*

souvenir /सूव़'निअर्/ *noun* स्मारिका, (पुस्तक के रूप में) स्मृतिचिह्न, निशानी : *buy a souvenir programme of the concert.*

sovereign /सॉव़्रिन्/ *noun* **1** (औप) शासक (विशेषत: राजा या रानी) **2** पहले प्रचलित एक पाउंड का ब्रिटिश सिक्का,

अशरफ़ी ▸ **sovereign** *adj* (औप) प्रधान या परम शक्ति; संप्रभु (व्यक्ति) : *a sovereign ruler* **2** (राज्य) प्रभुसत्ता संपन्न; पूर्णत: स्वतंत्र : *become a sovereign state* **3** उत्तम एवं प्रभावी : *Education was seen as a sovereign remedy for all ills.* **sovereignty** /'सॉव़्रन्-टि / *noun* **1** प्रभुसत्ता (संपन्न) : *economic sovereignty* **2** प्रभुसत्ता (आधिपत्य)।

soviet / 'सोव़िअट्/ *noun* (अप्र) **1** सोविएट संघ में कर्मचारियों की एक विशेष परिषद्; (सोविएट संघ में) सर्वोच्च परिषद् **2** the Soviets [pl] सोविएट संघ के लोग ▸ **Soviet** *adj* (अप्र) सोविएट संघ से संबंधित।

sow¹ /सो/ *verb* (pt **sowed**; pp **sown** / सोन् / या **sowed**) **1** बीज बोना; पौधा रोपना : *sow seeds in pots* **2** sow sth (in sth) भावनाएँ, विचार आदि फैलाना : *sow the seeds of hatred* ▸ **sower** *noun*.

sow² / साउ / *noun* मादा सूअर।

soya bean / 'सॉइ बीन्/ (US **soybean** भी) *noun* सोया बीन।

spa / स्पा / *noun* पानी का झरना, जिसमें स्वास्थ्यवर्धक तत्त्व हों; वह जगह जहाँ ऐसा झरना हो।

space¹ / स्पेस्/ *noun* **1** दो या अधिक वस्तुओं के बीच की दूरी (अवकाश की मात्रा) : *a narrow space* **2** रिक्त स्थान, ख़ाली जगह : *office space* **3** ख़ाली भूभाग जिस पर मकान आदि नहीं बना है : *the freedom and space of the country side* **4** लंबाई, चौड़ाई, ऊँचाई का आयाम जिसमें सब कुछ अस्तित्व में है **5** (**outer space** भी) अंतरिक्ष, आकाश : *journey through space* **6** (प्राय: sing) समय की अवधि : *(within) the space of two hours* ▸ **spacecraft** *noun* अंतरिक्ष यान **spaceman** (*fem* **spacewoman**) *noun* अंतरिक्ष यात्री।

space² / स्पेस् / verb space sth (out) वस्तुओं को नियत दूरी पर क्रम से लगाना : space out the posts three metres apart.

spacious / 'स्पेशस् / adj लंबा-चौड़ा; पर्याप्त ख़ाली स्थान वाला : a very spacious kitchen.

spade / स्पेड् / noun 1 फावड़ा (खोदने का उपकरण) 2 spades [pl] ताश के पत्तों में 'हुकुम' के पत्ते।

spadework / 'स्पेड्वर्क् / noun कठिन प्रारंभिक कार्य : I have to do all the spadework for the committee meeting.

spaghetti / स्प'गेटि / noun एक प्रकार का इतालवी भोजन (पास्ता) जिसे लंबे पतले कतलों में बनाया जाता है।

span / स्पैन् / noun 1 समय की अवधि : average life span 2 एक सिरे से दूसरे सिरे तक की दूरी, पहुँच की दूरी 3 पुल आदि के दो खंभों के बीच का विस्तार, पाट/चौड़ाई : The arch has a span of 60 metres. ▸ span verb (-nn-) 1 पुल या मेहराब बनाना 2 आर-पार फैलाना : a career spanning over 30 years.

spank / स्पैङ्क् / verb विशेषत: बच्चे को चूतड़ पर थप्पड़ मारना : We never spank our children. ▸ spank noun थप्पड़।

spanner / स्पैनर् / noun स्पैनर, पाना (क़ाबले खींचने का एक उपकरण)।

spare¹ / स्पेअर् / adj 1 अतिरिक्त; किसी कार्य विशेष के लिए निकाली गई धनराशि, समय इत्यादि : a spare room 2 (समय) ख़ाली : Since starting my new job, I've had very little spare time. 3 (विशेषकर औप) (व्यक्ति) दुबला-पतला : a tall spare figure 4 साधारण, सादा ▸ spare noun मशीन आदि के अतिरिक्त कल-पुर्ज़े।

spare² / स्पेअर् / verb 1 spare sb/sth (from sth) नष्ट या क्षत होने से बचाना, दया

दिखाना : spare sb's life 2 spare sth (for sb/sth) समय, धन आदि कार्य-विशेष के लिए निकालना : Can you spare old clothes for the homeless? ∎ to spare जिसके बिना काम चल सके; आवश्यकता से ज़्यादा; बचा हुआ : Do you have any milk to spare? ▸ sparing adj sparing (with/of/in sth) (औप) सावधानी से काम में लाना; किफ़ायत से काम करना : be sparing with the sugar sparingly adv किफ़ायत से : Add garlic sparingly.

spark / स्पार्क् / noun 1 (आग की) चिंगारी : Sparks from the fire were flying up the chimney. 2 [sing] spark of sth गुण की थोड़ी-सी मात्रा : without a spark of enthusiasm ▸ spark verb 1 चिंगारी उत्पन्न करना : I tried to restart the engine, but it wouldn't spark. 2 spark sth off तात्कालिक कारण बनना, विशेषत: किसी अप्रिय चीज़ का : an increase in consumer spending sparked off by tax cuts.

sparkle / 'स्पार्क्ल् / verb 1 sparkle (with sth) झिलमिलाना : Her diamonds sparkled in the candlelight. 2 उत्साह और हँसी-मज़ाक से पूर्ण : She always sparkles at parties. ▸ sparkle noun झिलमिल; उल्लास; ज़िंदादिल मौलिक गुण sparkling / 'स्पार्क्लिङ् / adj 1 (अनौप sparkly भी) चमकते हुए : the sparkling blue waters of the Mediterranean. 2 सजीव, ज़िंदादिल, प्रतिभाशाली, हास्यकर : sparkling conversation ○ The champion was in sparkling form.

sparrow / 'स्पैरो / noun गौरैया, घरेलू छोटी चिड़िया।

sparse / स्पार्स् / adj (-r, -st) छितरा, बिखरा हुआ (न कि घना) : a sparse population ▸ sparsely adv

विरलतया : *a sparsely furnished room* **sparseness** *noun*.

spartan / 'स्पार्टन् / *adj* *(अनौप)*(स्थिति या अवस्था) सादी और कठोर; बिना सुख–साधनों के : *the spartan life of a refugee camp*.

spasm / 'स्पैज़म् / *noun* 1 (कार्य का) छोटा–सा तीव्र दौर : *spasm of energy* 2 ऐंठन, मरोड़, दौरा : *muscular spasms*.

spastic / 'स्पैस्टिक / *adj* *(चिकि)* मस्तिष्क-संस्तंभ से पीड़ित : *spastic children*.

spate / स्पेट् / *noun* [*sing*] (घटनाओं की) बाढ़, अचानक वृद्धि : *a spate of orders for our products*.

spatial (**spacial** भी) / 'स्पेश्ल् / *adj* *(औप या तक)* स्थानिक : *the spatial arrangement of atoms within the molecule ∘ exercises to develop a child's spatial awareness*.

spatter / 'स्पैटर् / *verb* **spatter sth (on/over sb/sth); spatter sb/sth (with sth)** बूँदें छिड़कना, छींटें डालना; बूँदों का आवाज़ करते हुए स्थल पर गिरना : *We heard the rain spattering (down) on the roof of the hut*.

spawn / स्पॉन् / *verb* 1 (मेंढक, मछली आदि का) अंडे देना 2 *(अपमा)* कुछ अत्यधिक मात्रा/संख्या में उत्पन्न करना : *departments which spawn committees and sub-committees* ▷ **spawn** *noun* मछली, मेंढक आदि के अंडे।

speak / स्पीक् / *verb* (*pt* **spoke** / स्पोक् /; *pp* **spoken** / 'स्पोकन् /) 1 बोलना, कहना : *He can't speak because of a throat infection*. 2 **speak of/about sth** किसी का ज़िक्र करना/के बारे में बात करना : *She spoke about her plans for the future*. 3 **speak (on/about sth); speak (against sth)** भाषण देना 4 बातचीत

करना; भाषा बोल सकना : *He speaks several languages*. ■ **be on speaking terms (with sb)** मैत्रीपूर्ण संबंध होना; बातचीत के लिए, विशेषकर बहस के बाद, तैयार होना : *She has not been on speaking terms with her parents for years*. **nothing to speak of** उल्लेखनीय न होना **so to speak** कहा जा सकता है कि : *Teachers need to learn from their students, so to speak*. **speak for itself** अपने में स्पष्ट होना; अतिरिक्त व्याख्या की ज़रूरत न होना : *Recent events speak for themselves*. **speak for sb** दूसरों की तरफ़ से बोलना : *Our party speaks for the poor and unemployed*. **speak one's mind** साफ़-साफ़ कहना **speak out/up** स्पष्टतया कहना ▷ **speaker** / 'स्पीकर् / *noun* 1 वक्ता (भाषण आदि में) 2 भाषा बोल सकने वाला : *French speaker* 3 लाउडस्पीकर 4 **the Speaker** स्पीकर, संसद का अध्यक्ष।

spear / स्पिअर् / *noun* भाला, बरछी।

spearhead / 'स्पिअर्हेड् / *noun* (प्रायः *sing*) व्यक्ति या समूह जो अभियान आदि का नेतृत्व या आरंभ करे : *The new party was the spearhead of popular discontent*. ▷ **spearhead** *verb* अभियान आदि का आरंभ या नेतृत्व करना।

special / 'स्पेश्ल् / *adj* 1 विशेष (न कि साधारण); असाधारण, विशिष्ट (सामान्य से अलग) : *goods on special offer* 2 अन्य से अधिक महत्त्वपूर्ण; विशिष्ट : *a very special friend* 3 विशिष्ट प्रयोजन/व्यक्ति के लिए तैयार किया गया 4 मात्रा, स्तर या गुण में अतिविशेष (सामान्यतया न मिलने वाला) : *Why should we give you special treatment?* ▷ **specialist** / 'स्पेशलिस्ट् / *noun* (चिकित्सा आदि में) विशेषज्ञ : *an eye specialist* **specially** / 'स्पेशलि / *adv* 1 किसी विशेष उद्देश्य के लिए : *I made this specially for your* *birthday.* 2 (**especially** भी) असाधारण/ विशेष रूप से : *I enjoyed the evening, but the meal wasn't especially good.*

speciality /ˌस्पेशिˈऐलटि/(**US speciality** भी) *noun* (*pl* **specialities**) 1 कोई सेवा या उत्पादन जिसके लिए कोई व्यक्ति, जगह, कंपनी आदि प्रसिद्ध हो : *Wood carvings are a speciality of this village.* 2 रुचि/गतिविध/कौशल जिसमें व्यक्ति को विशेषज्ञता/प्रसिद्धि प्राप्त है : *Her speciality is medieval literature.*

specialize, -ise /ˈस्पेशलाइज़्/ *verb* **specialize** (**in sth**) विशेषज्ञ बनना, विशेष योग्यता प्राप्त करना : *specialize in oriental history* ▸ **specialization, -isation** *noun.*

species /ˈस्पीशीज़्/ *noun* (*pl* अपरि- वर्तित) 1 जाति (प्राणि-विज्ञान में **genus** का उप-विभाजन) 2 (*अनौप*) प्रकार, क़िस्म : *an odd species of writer.*

specific /स्पˈसिफ़िक़्/ *adj* 1 विस्तार और सूक्ष्मता के साथ निश्चित या निर्धारित : *specific instructions* 2 विशिष्ट, विशेष : *move from the general to the specific* ▸ **specific gravity** *noun* (*तक*) आपेक्षिक घनत्व।

specification /ˌस्पेसिफ़िˈकेशन्/ *noun* विस्तृत सूचना (किसी के बारे में) कि वह कैसे बना।

specify /ˈस्पेसिफ़ाइ/ *verb* (*pt, pp* **specified**) (*औप*) निश्चित रूप से उल्लेख करना; विस्तार आदि देना : *The contract specifies red tiles for the roof.*

specimen /ˈस्पेसिमन्/ *noun* 1 नमूना (वर्ग में से एक उदाहरण स्वरूप) : *There were some five specimens of fossils in the museum.* 2 चिकित्सीय परीक्षण के लिए पेशाब आदि का नमूना 3 (*अनौप*) व्यक्ति जो किसी प्रकार से असाधारण हो : *a fine physical specimen.*

speck /स्पेक्/ *noun* धूल-कण : *specks of dust.*

spectacle /ˈस्पेकटक्ल्/ *noun* 1 प्र- दर्शन, तमाशा; भव्य और स्मरणीय दृश्य : *The carnival parade was a magnificent spectacle.* 2 (*प्राय: अपमा*) ध्यान आकृष्ट करने वाली वस्तु, विशेषत: जो असामान्य या बेतुकी हो: *The poor fellow was a sad spectacle.* ∎ **make a spectacle of oneself** सार्वजनिक स्थानों पर बेतुकी हरकतों द्वारा ध्यान आकृष्ट करना : *make a spectacle of oneself by arguing with the waiter.*

spectacles /ˈस्पेकटक्ल्ज़्/ *noun* [*pl*] (*अप्र या औप*) चश्मा, ऐनक।

spectacular /स्पेकˈटैक्यलर/ *adj* (*प्रदर्शन*) शानदार एवं प्रभावी : *a spectacular display of fireworks* ▸ **spectacularly** *adv.*

spectator /स्पेकˈटेटर/ *noun* दर्शक : *noisy spectators.*

spectre (*US* **specter**) /ˈस्पेक्टर/ *noun* (*औप*) 1 भूत-प्रेत, काली छाया 2 आगामी संकट का भय : *the spectre of unemployment/war.*

spectrum /ˈस्पेक्ट्रम्/ *noun* (*pl* **spectra** /ˈस्पेक्ट्रा/) 1 वर्णक्रम; इंद्रधनुष में दिखने वाले सात रंगों की पट्टी का प्रतिबिंब : *A spectrum is formed by a ray of light passing through a prism.* 2 आवाज़ की स्तरों की शृंखला : *the saund spectrum* 3 (*प्राय: sing*) संबंधित गुण, विचारों आदि की विस्तृत शृंखला : *views from across the political spectrum.*

speculate /ˈस्पेक्युलेट/ *verb* 1 **speculate** (**about/on/upon sth**) पूरी जानकारी या सबूत के बिना राय बनाना, अटकल लगाना : *speculate upon the future* 2 **speculate** (**in sth**) (*वाणिज्य*) सट्टा लगाना : *speculate in oil shares.*

speculation /ˌस्पेक्यूˈलेशन्/ *noun* 1 **speculation** (**over/about/upon/on**

sth) अटकलबाज़ी, ऐसे बना मत : *There was much speculation over the cause of the crash/his resignation.* ○ *Our speculations proved totally wrong.* **2 speculation (in sth)** सट्टेबाज़ी।

speech / स्पीच / *noun* **1** बोलने की शक्ति; बोलने की रीति **2 speech (on/about sth)** औपचारिक भाषण : *a very boring after-dinner speech* ▸ **speechless** *adj* आश्चर्य या क्रोध के कारण भौंचक्का, अवाक् : *speechless with rage.*

speed / स्पीड् / *noun* **1** चाल, रफ़्तार : *move at a very slow speed* **2** तेज़ी, जल्दी : *act with speed and decisiveness* ▸ **speed** *verb* (*pt, pp* **sped** / स्पेड् /) **1** तेज़ी से चलना/चलाना : *cars speeding past the school* **2** जल्दी-जल्दी करना/कराना : *The drugs will help speed her recovery.* ■ **speed (sth) up** रफ़्तार बढ़ाना : *They have speeded up production of the new car.* ▸ **speeding** *noun* ग़ैर-क़ानूनी ढंग से या बहुत तेज़ी से वाहन चलाने के लिए यातायात अपराध **speedily** *adv* **speedy** *adj* (**-ier, -iest**) **1** तेज़, द्रुतगामी **2** अ-विलंब होने या आने वाला : *wish sb a speedy recovery from illness.*

spell¹ / स्पेल् / *verb* (*pt, pp* **spelt** / स्पेल्ट् / या **spelled** / स्पेल्ड् /) **1** शब्दों को (लिखित रूप की) वर्तनी में लिखना या बोलना **2** (अक्षरों को) विशेष क्रम में जोड़कर शब्द बनाना : *C-A-T spells cat.* ठीक हिज्जे करना : *How do you spell your name?* **3** परिणाम निकलना; अर्थ होना : *The failure of their crops spelt disaster for the farmers.* ■ **spell sth out 1** समझने में आसान व साफ़ बनाना : *My instructions were simple enough—do I have to spell them out again?* **2** शब्दों के अक्षरों को ठीक क्रम में लिखना या बोलना : *Could*

you spell that word out for me again? ▸ **spelling** *noun* वर्तनी, वर्ण-विन्यास; अक्षरी।

spell² / स्पेल् / *noun* **1** मंत्र, जादू : *The wizard recited a spell.* **2** मंत्रमुग्ध, मोहित करने वाला गुण : *the spell of her beauty.*

spell³ / स्पेल् / *noun* **1** समय, कर्तव्यकाल या गतिविधि की अवधि : *a long spell of warm weather* **2 spell (at/on sth)** दो या अधिक व्यक्तियों की सहभागिता में कोई कार्य या कर्तव्य : *have a spell on the typewriter.*

spellbinding / 'स्पेल्बाइन्डिङ् / *adj* मुग्ध करने वाला ▸ **spellbound** *adj* मोहित, मंत्रमुग्ध : *listen spellbound.*

spend / स्पेन्ड् / *verb* (*pt, pp* **spent** / स्पेन्ट् /) **1 spend sth (on sth)** खर्च करना, व्यय करना : *She's spent all her money.* **2** समय बिताना : *spend a weekend in Paris* **3 spend sth (on sth/(in) doing sth)** काम में समय लगाना; पूरी तरह व्यय करना, गँवा देना : *They went on firing until they had spent all their ammunition.* ▸ **spending** *noun* ख़र्च की गई या ख़र्च के लिए उपलब्ध राशि : *spending cuts.*

spendthrift / 'स्पेन्ड्थ्रिफ़्ट् / *noun* फ़िज़ूलख़र्च करने वाला व्यक्ति।

spew / स्प्यू / *verb* **1 spew (sth) (up)** (विशेषकर *अनौप*) वमन करना, उलटी करना **2** धारा से बाहर निकल जाना या निकाल देना : *Water spewed out of the hole.*

sphere / स्फ़िअर / *noun* **1** (*ज्यामिति*) गोला; गोलाकार वस्तु, जैसे गेंद **2** व्यक्ति का कार्यक्षेत्र : *be distinguished in many different spheres* ▸ **spherical** / 'स्फ़े-रिक्ल् / *adj* गोलीय, गेंदाकार।

sphinx / स्फ़िङ्क्स् / *noun* (विशेषत: **the Sphinx**) मिस्र देश में सिंह के धड़ और स्त्री के मुँह-सिर वाली पत्थर की प्रतिमा;

(अलं) रहस्यमय, अपने विचारों और योजनाओं को गुप्त रखने वाला : *a sphinx-like smile.*

spice / स्पाइस् / *noun* 1 मसाले (मिर्च, हल्दी आदि) 2 अतिरिक्त रुचि या उत्तेजना : *a story that lacks spice* ▶ **spice** *verb* **spice sth (up) (with sth)** 1 छौंकना, बघारना : *He spiced up the soup with some chilli powder.* 2 अतिरिक्त तत्त्व जोड़कर रुचि बढ़ा देना : *a horror movie spiced with dark humour.*

spick / स्पिक् / *adj* ■ **spick and span** साफ़-सुथरा और चमकदार : *They always keep their kitchen spick and span.*

spider / स्पाइडर् / *noun* मकड़ी/मकड़ा।

spike / स्पाइक् / *noun* 1 नोक, छड़ का नुकीला भाग 2 जूतों को फिसलने से बचाने के लिए लगाई कीलें 3 जौ, गेहूँ आदि अनाज की बाली ▶ **spike** *verb* छेद या कील लगाना; कील से घायल हो जाना : *spike oneself on a nail.*

spill / स्पिल् / *verb (pt, pp spilt* / स्पिल्ट् / या **spilled)** द्रव का छलक जाना, गिर जाना ■ **spill blood** *(औप)* लोगों को मारना, घायल करना : *Much innocent blood is spilt in war.* **spill over** एक जगह के भर जाने पर दूसरी जगह पर जाना; बहने लगना : *The meeting spilt over from the hall into the corridor.* **spill the beans** *(अनौप)* अनचाहे गुप्त सूचना को प्रकट करना ▶ **spill** *noun* 1 घोड़े या साइकिल से गिर जाना 2 छलकाव : *an acid spill.*

spin / स्पिन् / *verb (-nn-; pt* **spun** / स्पन्/;*pp* **spun)** 1 **spin sth (round)** घुमाना, चक्कर खिलाना : *spin the ball* 2 **spin (round/around)** जल्दी से घूम जाना : *She spun round to face him.* 3 कातना : *spin goat's hair into wool* 4 बुनना : *spiders spinning their webs* ▶ **spin** *noun* 1 चक्कर, घुमाव

2 *(अनौप)* मौज-मज़े के लिए कार आदि की सवारी।

spinach / स्पिनिच्; स्पिनिज् / *noun* पालक।

spinal / स्पाइनल् / *adj* रीढ़-विषयक : *a spinal injury.*

spindle / स्पिन्ड्ल् / *noun* तकली; धुरी।

spine / स्पाइन् / *noun* 1 रीढ़ की हड्डी 2 पौधों या जंतुओं का काँटा, शूल : *Hedgehogs and porcupines have spines, and so do some cactuses.* 3 किताब का वह भाग जहाँ पन्ने जुड़े रहते हैं (विशेषत: आवरण वाला भाग) ▶ **spineless** *adj* 1 रीढ़-विहीन प्राणी 2 *(अपमा)* (व्यक्ति) कमज़ोर, दब्बू एवं डरपोक **spiny** *adj* काँटेदार।

spinster / स्पिन्स्टर् / *noun* (कभी-कभी *अपमा)* अविवाहित बड़ी उम्र की महिला : *an elderly spinster.*

spiral / स्पाइरल् / *noun* 1 सर्पिल, कुंडली 2 लगातार उतार/चढ़ाव : *the vicious spiral of rising wages and prices* ▶ **spiral** *adj* सर्पिलाकार, कुंडलाकार : *a spiral staircase* **spiral** *verb* **(-ll-;** US **-l-)** 1 सर्पिल गति से चढ़ना : *The smoke spiralled upwards.* 2 उत्तरोत्तर बढ़ना : *Spiralling costs are facing some businesses to cut staff.*

spire / स्पाइअर् / *noun* (चर्च की) मीनार।

spirit / स्पिरिट् / *noun* 1 आत्मा; चित्त 2 प्रेतात्मा, भूत 3 *(अप्र)* परी, बैताल, वन-देवता 4 मिज़ाज, मनोदशा : *a brave/proud spirit* 5 हिम्मत, धैर्य; उत्साह : *show a fighting spirit* 6 [*sing*] समूह, दल आदि के लिए निष्ठा की भावना 7 **spirits** [*pl*] मनोदशा, भाव : *in high spirits (i.e. cheerful)* 8 मनोवृत्ति, आवश्यक गुण, अर्थ : *obey the spirit, not the letter of the law* 9 (प्राय: *pl*) तेज़ शराब 10 स्पिरिट : *insects preserved in spirit* ▶ **spirit** *verb* ■ **spirit sb/sth away/off** चुपके से उड़ा

ले जाना **spirited** *adj* साहसी, उत्साह-पूर्ण : *a spirited conversation* **spiritless** *adj* मायूस, हतोत्साह।

spiritual / 'स्पिरिचुअल् / *adj* 1 धार्मिक (न कि भौतिक), आध्यात्मिक : *concerned about sb's spiritual welfare* 2 धर्म से संबंधित।

spit / स्पिट् / *verb* (-tt; *pt, pp* **spat** / स्पैट् / या विशेषत: *US* **spit**) 1 **spit sth (out)** थूकना 2 **spit sth (out)** क्रोध में ज़ोर-ज़ोर से कुछ कहना : *She spat (out) curses at me.* ▶ **spit** *noun* थूक, पीक, लार।

spite / स्पाइट् / *noun* द्वेष भावना, हानि पहुँचाने की भावना; दुर्भावना ■ **in spite of sth** के होते हुए भी, बावजूद : *They went out in spite of the rain.* ▶ **spite** *verb* परेशान/तंग करना : *The neighbours play loud music every evening just to spite us.* **spiteful** *adj* द्वेषी **spitefully** *adv*.

splash / स्प्लैश् / *verb* 1 **splash sth (about); splash sth (on/onto/over sb/sth); splash sb/sth (with sth)** छिड़कना, छींटें डालना : *She splashed her face with cold water.* 2 छिड़क कर भिगोना; (द्रव के) छींटें उड़ाना 3 छप-छपाना; छपछपाते हुए पानी में से गुज़रना : *splash through puddles* 4 **splash sth (with sth)** रंग, पेंट आदि के धब्बों से सजाना : *a bath towel splashed with blue and green* ▶ **splash** *noun* 1 छपछपाने की आवाज़ या क्रिया : *He fell into the pool with a splash.* 2 छींटा, धब्बा : *There are some splashes of mud on your skirt.* 3 रंग का चमकदार धब्बा।

splashdown / 'स्प्लैश्डाउन् / *noun* (अंतरिक्ष यान का) समुद्र पर उतर जाना।

splatter / 'स्प्लैटर् / *verb* 1 (द्रव की बड़ी बूंदों का) गिरना : *rain splattering on the roof* 2 **splatter sb/sth (with sth)**

छिड़कना : *overalls splattered with paint.*

splay / स्प्ले / *verb* **splay (sth) (out)** एक सिरे को चौड़ा फैलाना : *His legs were splayed out at an awkward angle.*

spleen / स्प्लीन् / *noun* तिल्ली।

splendid / 'स्प्लेन्डिड् / *adj* 1 भव्य, शानदार : *a splendid sunset/house* 2 (अनौप) बहुत अच्छा, अत्युत्तम : *a splendid dinner/idea* ▶ **splendidly** *adv*.

splendour (*US* **splendor**) / 'स्प्लेन्डर् / *noun* शान/वैभव : *the splendour of the stained glass windows.*

splice / स्प्लाइस् / *verb* 1 (रस्सी के दो सिरों को) गूँथ कर जोड़ना 2 लकड़ी, फ़ीता, फ़िल्म आदि के टुकड़ों को एक-दूसरे पर रख कर जोड़ना ▶ **splice** *noun* लकड़ी, फ़ीते, फ़िल्म आदि में जोड़।

splint / स्प्लिन्ट् / *noun* (टूटी हड्डी को सीधा रखने के लिए प्रयुक्त) (लकड़ी की) खपची : *put a leg in splints.*

splinter / 'स्प्लिन्टर् / *noun* किरच, लकड़ी की पट्टी, शीशे आदि के छोटे नुकीले टुकड़े : *splinters of ice* ▶ **splinter** *verb* 1 **splinter (sth) (into/to sth)** टुकड़ों/किरचों में तोड़ना/टूट जाना : *The mirror cracked but did not splinter.* 2 **splinter (off)** बड़े वर्ग से अलग करना, तोड़ना : *extremists who splintered off from the army of liberation.*

split / स्प्लिट् / *verb* (-tt-; *pt, pp* **split**) 1 **split (sth) (up) (into sth)** विभाजित करना, लोगों के दल को अलग-अलग तोड़ना : *This issue has split the party (from top to bottom).* 2 तोड़ना, चीरना, फाड़ना : *She split the log (in two) with an axe.* 3 **split (sth) (open)** फोड़ना ■ **split one's sides (laughing/with laughter)** हँसते-हँसते

लोट-पोट हो जाना ▸ split *noun* 1 split (between A and B) विभाजन 2 दरार, फटन : *mend a split in a skirt* 3 फूट।

spoil/ स्पॉइल् / *verb* (*pt, pp* spoilt / स्पॉइल्ट्/ या spoiled / स्पॉइल्ड्/) 1 बि-गाड़ देना, बेकार/ख़राब कर देना : *The bad news has spoilt my day.* 2 (विशेषत: बच्चों को) गुस्ताख़ बना देना, सिर चढ़ाना/ अधिक दुलार करना 3 (भोजन का) बिगड़ जाना, खाने योग्य न रहना : *It will spoil if you don't put it in the fridge.* ▸ spoil *noun* (प्राय: the spoils [*pl*]) 1 लूट-खसोट का माल 2 लाभ : *the spoils of high office.*

spoke / स्पोक् / *noun* (पहिये का) आरा; तीली।

spokesman / स्पोक्स्मन् / *noun* (*pl* spokesmen; *fem* spokeswoman, *pl* spokeswomen) spokesman (for sb/sth) समूह की ओर से प्रवक्ता : *a spokesman for the government.*

sponge / स्पन्ज् / *noun* 1 स्पंज (एक समुद्री जीव) 2 तरल पदार्थ सोखने के लिए रबड़ आदि का स्पंज 3 एक प्रकार का केक ▸ sponge *verb* 1 sponge sb/one-self/sth (down) स्पंज से धोना, साफ़ करना; sponge sth (off/out/up) स्पंज द्वारा कुछ हटाना : *sponge (out) a stain in the carpet* 2 sponge (sth) (from/ off sb); sponge (on sb) (अनौप, अपमा) किसी और के ख़र्चे पर रहना, न देने के इरादे से पैसा आदि ले लेना : *She sponges (meals) all the time.* spongy *adj* स्पंज के समान मुलायम, छिद्रिल एवं रसीला : *spongy moss.*

sponsor / स्पॉन्सर् / *noun* 1 प्रवर्तक, समर्थक : *We need more sponsors for next week's charity walk.* 2 किसी के प्रशिक्षण का ख़र्च वहन करने वाला व्यक्ति/कंपनी : *an athlete in need of a sponsor* 3 प्रतिभू, ज़ामिनदार : *act*

as sb's sponsor ▸ sponsor *verb* प्रवर्तक या प्रतिभू के रूप में कार्य करना sponsorship *noun.*

spontaneous / स्पॉन् टेनिअस् / *adj* स्वाभाविक रूप से घटित, स्वत: प्रवर्तित; सहज; प्राकृतिक : *a spontaneous offer of help* ▸ spontaneously *adv* अपने आप से, अनायास/सहज ही : *react spontaneously* spontaneity *noun.*

spooky / स्पूकि / *adj* (-ier, -iest) ऐसा अजीब कि डर पैदा हो : *a spooky old house.*

spool / स्पूल् / *noun* कैमरा, फ़िल्म आदि की रील; फिरकी/चरख़ी ▸ spool *verb* रील/फिरकी पर (धागा आदि) चढ़ाना/उतारना।

spoon / स्पून् / *noun* चम्मच, चमचा ▸ spoon *verb* चम्मच भर कर उठाना : *spoon sugar from the packet into a bowl* spoonful *noun* चम्मचभर।

sporadic / स्प रैडिक् / *adj* केवल कभी-कभी या कहीं-कहीं ही होने या दिखने वाला; अनियमित अंतरालों में होने वाला : *sporadic raids/gunfire/fighting.*

sport / स्पॉर्ट् / *noun* 1 (US प्राय: sports [*pl*]) खेल-कूद, बाहरी मैदान की क्रीड़ाएँ 2 तैराकी, फुटबाल आदि खेल-कूद, प्रकार-विशेष का खेल : *team sports* 3 (औप) मज़ाक़ या हँसी में (कहा गया) : *say sth in sport* 4 व्यक्ति जो मुश्किल स्थिति में भी उदारचित्त या प्रिय रहता है ▸ sport *verb* 1 खेलना/जी बहलाना 2 गर्व से कुछ पहनना या रखना : *sport a moustache/a dia-mond ring* sporting *adj* 1 खेल-कूद का/विषयक : *sporting event/occa-sion* 2 निष्पक्ष तथा उदार; दूसरों के साथ अच्छा व्यवहार करने वाला : *It's very sporting of you to change your plans because of me.* sportsman *noun* 1 (*fem* sportswoman) खिलाड़ी 2 हार जाने पर भी प्रसन्नचित्त, खेल की भावना से खेलने वाला sportsmanlike *adj* निष्पक्ष, स्वाभिमानी, नियमों का पालन करने

वाला : *a sportsmanlike attitude*
sportsmanship *noun.*

sporty / 'स्पॉर्टि / *adj (अनौप)* 1 खेल-कूद पसंद करने वाला या खेल-कूद में निपुण : *She's very sporty.* 2 (विशेषत: कपड़े) आकर्षक : *a sporty shirt.*

spot¹ / स्पॉट् / *noun* 1 चित्ती, धब्बा, दाग : *a white skirt with red spots* 2 (त्वचा पर बीमारी के कारण) चकत्ते, फुंसी 3 स्थान-विशेष, जगह : *a nice picnic spot* 4 विशिष्ट गुण वाली बात/भाग : *weak spots in sb's argument* 5 द्रव की छोटी बूँद : *Did you feel a few spots of rain?* 6 किसी चीज़ की थोड़ी-सी मात्रा 7 क्रम में स्थिति; पद : *the number one spot in the top charts* ■ **in a (tight) spot** *(अनौप)* मुश्किल स्थिति में : *I'm in a bit of tight spot financially.* **on the spot** 1 एकदम, वहीं : *He was hit by a falling tree and killed on the spot.* 2 वारदात की जगह पर : *The police were on the spot within a few minutes of my telephone call.* 3 मुश्किल परिस्थिति में जहाँ कोई विशेष प्रतिक्रिया दिखानी हो : *The interviewer's questions about her private life really put her on the spot.* ▸ **spotless** *adj* 1 साफ़-सुथरा, बेदाग : *a spotless uniform* 2 (औप) निर्दोष, निष्कलंक : *a spotless reputation* **spotty** *adj* 1 धब्बेदार 2 गुण में असमान : *a spotty performance.*

spot² / स्पॉट् / *verb* (-tt-) 1 **spot sb/sth (as sth)** बहुतों में से किसी एक (व्यक्ति/वस्तु) को देख, पहचान या छाँट लेना : *She spotted her friend in the crowd.* 2 **spot sth (with sth)** धब्बे डालना, चिह्नित करना/होना।

spotlight / 'स्पॉट्लाइट् / *noun* 1 (spot भी) लैंप जो सीधे किसी वस्तु या व्यक्ति पर रोशनी की शक्तिशाली किरण डाले 2 **the spotlight** [*sing*] वृहद सार्वजनिक अव-धान : *This week the spotlight is on the world of fashion.*

spouse / स्पाउस, स्पाउज़् / *noun* (औप या क़ानून) पति या पत्नी : *Fill in your spouse's name here.*

spout / स्पाउट् / *noun* 1 टोंटी (नल या चायदानी की) 2 द्रव की वेगवान धारा ▸ **spout** *verb* 1 **spout (from sth/out)** द्रव का धारा में बहुत शक्ति के साथ गिरना; द्रव की तेज़ धार छोड़ना/डालना : *volcanoes spouting ash and lava* 2 (अनौप, प्राय: अपमा) काफ़ी समय तक या आत्मविश्वास के साथ बोलना।

sprain / स्प्रेन् / *verb* मोच आ जाना : *sprain one's wrist* ▸ **sprain** *noun* मोच।

sprawl / स्प्रॉल् / *verb* (प्राय: अपमा) 1 पसर कर बैठना या लेटना 2 अव्यवस्थित रूप से फैलना : *sprawling handwriting* ▸ **sprawl** *noun* (प्राय: *sing*) 1 अव्यवस्थित फैले भवनों वाला विशाल क्षेत्र : *the city's suburban sprawl* 2 पसरी हुई दशा में।

spray / स्प्रे / *noun* 1 फुहारा, स्प्रे; फुहारे से छिड़का गया द्रव : *spray paint/perfume* 2 (फूल या पत्ती सहित) पेड़ की छोटी टहनी 3 (बैठक में सजाने के लिए) काटे हुए फूल/पत्तियाँ आदि ▸ **spray** *verb* **spray sth (on onto/over sb/sth); spray sb/sth (with sth)** फुहारे (स्प्रेअर) से पानी या द्रव छिड़कना : *farmer spraying his crops (with pesticides).*

spread / स्प्रेड् / *verb* (*pt, pp* **spread**) 1 फैलना/फैलाना; बिछाना : *spread butter on bread* 2 **spread sth (out) (on/over sth)** बिछाना/खोलना : *The bird spread its wings.* 3 (बीमारी आदि) व्यापक रूप से फैलना : *The disease is spreading fast.* 4 **spread sth (over sth)** एक समयावधि में बाँटना : *a course of study spread over three years* ■ **spread (sb/oneself) out** समूह

दूसरों से अलग होना ताकि ज़्यादा जगह में फैला जा सके : *The search party spread out over the moor.* ▸ **spread** *noun* 1 (प्राय: *sing*) **spread (of sth)** व्यापकता, विस्तार; चौड़ाई : *the spread of a bird's wings* 2 फैलाव (क्रिया); प्रचार 3 (पत्र-पत्रिका आदि का) लेख, विज्ञापन आदि जो एक कॉलम से ज़्यादा पर छपे हों 4 रोटी, डबल-रोटी आदि पर लगाने वाला मक्खन, पनीर जैसा पदार्थ : *cheese spread.*

spree / स्त्री / *noun* (अनौप) रंगरेलियों/ आमोद-प्रमोद का समय : *on a spending/shopping spree.*

sprightly / स्प्राइट्लि / *adj* ज़िंदादिल और शक्ति से भरपूर : *a sprightly 72-year-old* ▸ **sprightliness** *noun.*

spring[1] / स्प्रिङ् / *noun* 1 स्प्रिंग, कमानी 2 झरना, (पानी का) सोता, चश्मा : *a cool mountain spring* 3 लोच, लचक : *The old bed has lost most of its spring.* 4 उछाल, झपट्टा : *With an easy spring the cat reached the branch.* ▸ **springy** *adj* (-ier, -iest) 1 लचीला, लोचदार : *a spring bed* 2 हलका एवं आत्मविश्वासी : *a youthful springy step* **spring tide** *noun* अमावस्या/ पूर्णमासी का उच्च ज्वार।

spring[2] / स्प्रिङ् / *noun* वसंत ऋतु ▸ **spring-time** *noun* (साहि) वसंत ऋतु।

spring[3] / स्प्रिङ् / *verb* (*pt* **sprang** / स्त्रैङ्/; *pp* **sprung** / स्प्रङ्/) 1 उछलना, झपटना; लपकना : *A cat sprang out of the bushes.* 2 अचानक झटके से बंद होना, खुलना या गति करना : *The box sprang open.* ■ **spring from sth** 1 किसी चीज़ से आरंभ होना; कोई स्रोत होना : *Hatred often springs from fear.* 2 (अनौप) अचानक प्रकट होना **spring sth (on sb)** (अनौप) बिना चेतावनी प्रस्तुत करना : *spring bad news/a surprise on sb* **spring up** उत्पन्न होना,

विकास करना; उगना : *weeds springing up everywhere.*

sprinkle / स्प्रिङ्क्ल् / *verb* **sprinkle A (on/onto/over B); sprinkle B (with A)** छिड़कना, छितराना : *sprinkle water on a dusty path* ▸ **sprinkle** *noun* (प्राय: *sing*) छिड़काव; ज़रा-सी छितरी हुई वस्तु।

sprint / स्प्रिन्ट् / *verb* (थोड़ी दूरी) अतिवेग से दौड़ना : *He had to sprint to catch the bus.* ▸ **sprint** *noun* थोड़ी दूरी की तेज़ दौड़ : *a 100-metre sprint.*

sprout / स्प्राउट् / *verb* 1 **sprout (up) (from sth)** अंकुरित होना; बढ़ना या बढ़ाना : *new buds sprouting from the trees* 2 बढ़ना/विकसित होना प्रारंभ करना : *When do deer first sprout horns?* ▸ **sprout** *noun* 1 = **Brussels sprout** 2 अंकुर, कल्ला; अँखुआ।

spruce / स्प्रूस् / *adj* देखने में साफ़-सुथरा ▸ **spruce** *verb* ■ **spruce (sb/oneself) up** स्वयं को साफ़-सुथरा रखना/ करना।

spur / स्प्र् / *noun* 1 घोड़े को ऐड़ लगाने के लिए प्रयुक्त (जूतों में लगे) महमेज 2 (प्राय: *sing*) **spur (to sth)** उत्प्रेरक, प्रेरणा : *a spur to greater efficiency* 3 उच्च भूमि का क्षेत्र जो पहाड़ी फैलाव से बना हो ■ **on the spur of the moment** तत्काल, अकस्मात् : *I bought the house on the spur of the moment.* ○ *a spur-of-the-moment idea* ▸ **spur** *verb* (**-rr-**) **spur sb/sth (to/on to sth); spur sb/sth on** प्रोत्साहन देना, प्रेरित करना : *Failure spurred her to try harder.*

spurious / स्प्युअरिअस् / *adj* 1 नक़ली, जाली : *spurious claims/documents/ evidence* 2 ग़लत तर्कों पर आधारित : *a spurious argument* ▸ **spuriously** *adv.*

spurn / स्प्र्न् / *verb* तिरस्कार करना, ठुकराना : *spurn sb's offer of help.*

spurt / स्पर्ट / verb 1 spurt (out) (from sth) (द्रव, लपट आदि का) अचानक फूट निकलना, फुहारा छोड़ना : Blood spurted out from the wound. 2 अचानक थोड़ी देर के लिए बड़ी तेज़ी से काम करना : He spurted (past the others) as they approached the line. ‣ spurt noun 1 तेज़ धार, झोंक 2 तेज़ दौड़।

spy / स्पाइ / noun (pl spies) जासूस/ भेदिया; गुप्तचर : suspected of being a spy ‣ spy verb (pt, pp spied) जासूसी करना ∎ spy on sb/sth चुपचाप देखरेख में रखना।

squabble / 'स्क्वॉब्ल् / verb squabble (with sb) (about/over sth) तू-तू, मैं-मैं करना : They spent the whole evening squabbling (over what to watch on TV). ‣ squabble noun बेकार की तू-तू, मैं-मैं।

squad / स्क्वॉड / noun स्क्वैड/दस्ता; (पुलिस की) टुकड़ी : an anti-terrorist squad.

squadron / 'स्क्वॉड्रन् / noun 1 स्क्वाड्न, हवाई जहाज़ों या जहाज़ों का दल (वायु या नौ सेना में) 2 100-200 घुड़सवारों का दल।

squalid / 'स्क्वॉलिड् / adj (अपमा) 1 गंदा-मैला, घिनौना (विशेषत: ग़रीबी के कारण) : live in squalid conditions 2 नैतिक रूप से पतित, कुत्सित : a squalid tale of greed and corruption.

squall / स्क्वॉल् / noun 1 झंझावात; पानी या बर्फ़ के साथ आँधी 2 (बच्चे का) डर या दर्द से ज़ोर से चिल्लाना ‣ squalling adj : a squalling baby.

squalor / 'स्क्वॉलर् / noun गंदगी : live in squalor.

squander / 'स्क्वॉन्डर् / verb squander sth (on sb/sth) अपव्यय करना, धन या समय गँवाना : He squandered all his money on gambling.

square¹ / स्क्वेअर् / adj 1 वर्गाकार : a square room 2 (माप की इकाई) वर्ग : a carpet six metres square 3 आकृति में चौड़ा, ठोस : a woman of square frame/build 4 ईमानदार, निष्कपट : square dealings 5 सुव्यवस्थित; (हिसाब-किताब) चुकता, बेबाक़ : get one's accounts square ∎ a square meal संतोषप्रद भोजन : He looks as though he hasn't had a square meal for months. ‣ squarely adv 1 सीधे, न कि तिरछे 2 निष्पक्षता और ईमानदारी से : act squarely 3 सीधा : Economists have put the blame for the crisis squarely on the government. square root noun वर्गमूल : The square root of 16 is 4.

square² / स्क्वेअर् / noun 1 (ज्यामिति) वर्ग 2 वर्गाकार (क्षेत्रफल आदि) 3 (शहरों में) चौक : a market square 4 वर्ग-फल : The square of 7 is 49. 5 (तक) T या L के आकार का समकोण नापने का उपकरण : use a T-square.

square³ / स्क्वेअर् / verb 1 square sth (off) चौकोर बनाना, चौरस करना : square off some wooden planks 2 वर्गाकार बनाना : squared paper 3 वर्ग करना : 3 squared is 9. 4 हिसाब चुकता करना।

squash¹ / स्क्वॉश् / verb 1 कुचलना, भुरता बनाना : squashed tomatoes 2 ठूँसना, छोटी-सी जगह में ज़बरदस्ती भरना : They managed to squash forty people into the bus. 3 व्यक्ति का आत्मविश्वास ख़त्म कर देना, चुप करा देना : I felt completely squashed by her sarcastic comments. 4 समाप्त कर देना; कोई प्रस्ताव, योजना आदि अस्वीकार कर देना : My plan was firmly squashed by the committee.

squash² / स्क्वॉश् / noun 1 कुचला हुआ 2 एक प्रकार का शरबत।

squash³ / स्क्वॉश् / noun रैकेट और रबड़ की गेंद से खेला जाने वाला एक खेल।

squat¹ / स्क्वॉट / verb (-tt-) 1 squat

(down) उकड़ूँ बैठना : *The children squatted (down) by the fire.* 2 बिना अनुमति के कोई ख़ाली मकान या जगह क़ब्ज़ा लेना : *homeless people squatting in a derelict house* ▸ **squat** *noun* 1 उकड़ूँ 2 क़ब्ज़ाया हुआ मकान : *live in a squat* **squatter** *noun* कोई ख़ाली मकान या ज़मीन पर नाजायज़ क़ब्ज़ा करने वाला व्यक्ति।

squat² / स्क्वॉट् / *adj* छोटा/नाटा व्यक्ति, ठिगना; (भवन) ऊँचाई के अनुपात में अधिक चौड़ा।

squawk / स्क्वॉक् / *verb* 1 (पक्षी का) चीख़-भरा कलरव करना : *The parrot squawked loudly.* 2 (अनौप, विशेषत: परि) तेज़ आवाज़ में शिकायत करना।

squeak / स्क्वीक् / *noun* चरमराहट, चूँ-चूँ की ध्वनि : *The door opened with a squeak.* ▸ **squeak** *verb* 1 चरमराना, चूँ-चूँ करना : *These new shoes squeak.* 2 **squeak sth (out)** उत्तेजना या आशंका के कारण चूँ-चूँ जैसी आवाज़ में बोलना **squeaky** *adj.*

squeal / स्क्वील् / *verb* 1 **squeal (with sth)** किलकारी मारना : *The pigs were squealing.* 2 किलकारी मार कर कुछ कहना ▸ **squeal** *noun* किलकारी।

squeeze / स्क्वीज़ / *verb* 1 निचोड़ना; ऐंठना : *squeeze a tube of toothpaste* 2 **squeeze sth (from/out of sth); squeeze sth (out)** निचोड़ कर (पानी, रस आदि) निकालना 3 **squeeze (sb/sth) into, through, etc sth** ठूँसना, घुसेड़ना : *squeeze (one's way) into a crowded bus* 4 **squeeze sth (out of sb)** धमकी से/बलात् पैसा लेना, सूचना प्राप्त करना आदि ▸ **squeeze** *noun* 1 निचोड़, दबाव 2 दबा कर निकाली गई थोड़ी-सी मात्रा 3 (प्राय: *sing*) पैसा या साधनों की कमी से होने वाली मुश्किलें : *a credit squeeze* 4 [*sing*] छोटी-सी जगह में ठूसे रहने की अवस्था।

squib / स्क्विब् / *noun* फुलझड़ी, पलीता।

squid / स्क्विड् / *noun* (*pl* अपरिवर्तित या **squids**) एक लंबा दस छोटी बाँहों वाला समुद्री प्राणी।

squiggle / ˈस्क्विग्ल् / *noun* टेढ़ी-मेढ़ी रेखा : *Is this squiggle supposed to be a signature?* ▸ **squiggly** *adj.*

squint / स्क्विन्ट् / *verb* 1 अधखुली आँखों से देखना; कनखी से देखना : *squinting through the key hole* 2 भेंगा होना ▸ **squint** *noun* 1 भेंगापन 2 (अनौप) सरसरी नज़र : *Take a squint at this.*

squire / ˈस्क्वाइअर् / *noun* (उपाधि में **Squire**) (पूर्व में) उच्च सामाजिक स्तर का ज़मींदार।

squirm / स्क्वर्म् / *verb* 1 छटपटाना, तड़पना : *He was squirming around on the floor in agony.* 2 झेंपना : *It made him squirm to think how he'd messed up the interview.*

squirrel / ˈस्क्विरल्; US ˈस्क्वर्रल् / *noun* गिलहरी।

squirt / स्क्वर्ट् / *verb* 1 फुहारा छोड़ना, पिचकारी मारना; (द्रव का) फुहार के रूप में बाहर निकलना 2 **squirt sb/sth (with sth)** फुहार छोड़ कर या पिचकारी मार कर भिगो देना : *The little girl squirted us with (water from) her water-pistol.* ▸ **squirt** *noun* फुहार, पिचकारी (द्रव की)।

stab / स्टैब् / *verb* (**-bb-**) 1 कटार, छुरा या चाकू भोंकना : *He had been stabbed to death.* 2 **stab (at) sb/sth (with sth)** उँगली या नुकीली चीज़ से कोंचना, गोदना : *She stabbed angrily at the lift button.* ■ **stab sb in the back** (अनौप) विश्वासघात करना ▸ **stab** *noun* 1 चाकू या छुरे का प्रहार/वार 2 अचानक उठा तेज़ दर्द **stabbing** *adj* (विशेषत: दर्द) तीखा और अचानक **stabbing** *noun* छुरा भोंकने की वारदात।

stable¹ / ˈस्टेबल् / *adj* 1 स्थिर, दृढ़;

अचल : *a stable relationship* 2 (व्यक्ति) स्थिर मनोभावों वाला, संतुलित चित्त वाला : *Mentally, she's not very stable.* ▸ **stability** / स्ट'बिलिटि / *noun* स्थिरता : *economic stability* **stabilize, -ise** / 'स्टेबलाइज़् / *verb* स्थिर/दृढ़ करना/होना **stabilization, -isation** *noun.*

stable² / 'स्टेब्ल् / *noun* 1 अस्तबल, घुड़साल 2 सभी को समान स्तर का प्रशिक्षण प्रदान करने वाला स्कूल, क्लब या संघ : *actors from the same stable* ▸ **stable** *verb* (घोड़े) अस्तबल में रखना।

stack / स्टैक् / *noun* 1 सुव्यवस्थित रूप से लगाया गया ढेर, अंबार : *a stack of books/plates* 2 (प्रायः *pl*) **stack of sth** (अनौप) बहुत परिमाण या संख्या में चीज़ें : *stacks of money* 3 ऊँची चिमनी (धुआँ निकलने के लिए), विशेषतः कारख़ाने में ▸ **stack** *verb* 1 **stack sth (up)** सुव्यवस्थित रूप से ढेर लगाना या ढेर में रखना 2 **stack sth (with sth)** किसी स्थान पर वस्तुएँ इकट्ठी करना : *The floor was stacked with books.*

stadium / 'स्टेडिअम् / *noun* (*pl* **stadiums** या **stadia**) खेल का खुला मैदान जिसके चारों तरफ़ दर्शकों के बैठने के लिए जगह हो : *a football stadium.*

staff / स्टाफ़ / *noun* 1 कर्मचारीगण, स्टाफ़ : *the hotel staff* 2 स्कूल के अध्यापकगण : *a staff room/meeting* 3 वरिष्ठ सैनिक अधिकारी, स्टाफ़ : *a staff officer* 4 (औप या अप्र) लंबा डंडा/ छड़ी : *The old man leant on a long wooden staff.* ▸ **staff** *verb* स्टाफ़ के रूप में काम करना; स्टाफ़ देना : *The school is staffed entirely by graduates.*

stag / स्टैग् / *noun* 1 हिरन 2 नए स्टॉक और शेयरों को लाभ से बेचने की आशा में ख़रीदने वाला।

stage¹ / स्टेज् / *noun* 1 मंच, रंगमंच

2 **the stage** [*sing*] नाट्यकला : *be on the stage* 3 [*sing*] महत्वपूर्ण घटनाओं का स्थान : *the political stage* ▸ **stage** *verb* 1 नाटक का मंचन करना; अभिनय करना 2 किसी घटना में भाग लेना, कुछ घटित करना : *stage a protest rally.*

stage² / स्टेज् / *noun* 1 विकास की अवस्था, चरण 2 मंज़िल, पड़ाव।

stagger / स्टैगर् / *verb* 1 लड़खड़ाना, डगमगाना : *He staggered to his feet.* 2 आश्चर्यचकित/विचलित कर देना; धक्का पहुँचाना : *I was staggered to hear of his death.* 3 (कार्यालयों के समय आदि को) ऐसे व्यवस्थित करना कि अलग-अलग समय खुल और बंद हो सकें : *staggered office hours* ▸ **staggering** / 'स्टैग- रिङ् / *adj* आश्चर्यजनक।

stagnant / 'स्टैग्नन्ट् / *adj* 1 (पानी) ठहरा हुआ, रुका हुआ (और बदबूदार) : *stagnant pools* 2 गतिहीन, विकास- रुद्ध : *a period of stagnant growth.*

stagnate / स्टैग्'नेट् / *verb* 1 (पानी) ठहर जाना 2 विकास और उन्नति रोक देना/ रुक जाना : *Profits have stagnated.* ▸ **stagnation** *noun.*

staid / स्टेड् / *adj* (प्रायः *अप्रमा*) नीरस, उबाने वाला, रुचिहीन।

stain / स्टेन् / *verb* 1 **stain sth (with sth)** धब्बा लगाना, दाग़ पड़ना/डालना : *fingers stained with nicotine* 2 लकड़ी या कपड़े का रंग बदलना, रँगना : *He stained the wood dark brown.* 3 किसी की इज़्ज़त ख़राब करना, कलंक लगाना ▸ **stain** *noun* 1 धब्बा, दाग़ 2 रँगाई का द्रव 3 **stain (on sth)** कलंक : *He left the court without a stain on his character.* **stainless steel** *noun* स्टील जिसमें ज़ंग नहीं लगता।

stair / स्टेअर् / *noun* 1 **stairs** [*pl*] सीढ़ियाँ, ज़ीना : *He came rushing down the stairs to greet her.* 2 सीढ़ी का तख़्ता : *The child was sitting on* *the bottom stair.* ▸ **staircase** (**stairway** भी) *noun* सीढ़ियाँ, जीना।

stake / स्टेक् / *noun* 1 खूँटा 2 **the stake** [*sing*] (पूर्व समय में) खंभा जिससे अपराधी को बाँध कर ज़िंदा जलाया जाता था : *be burnt at the stake* 3 (प्राय: *pl*) दाँव (पर लगाई धनराशि आदि) : *The stakes are high—if we don't win this contract, we go out of business.* 4 कहीं नियोजित धन ■ **at stake** दाँव पर (जहाँ हार-जीत कुछ भी संभव है) : *The future of this company is at stake.* ▸ **stake** *verb* 1 खूँटे से बाँधना/सहारा देना : *stake newly planted trees* 2 **stake sth (on sth)** (धन आदि) दाँव पर लगाना : *stake Rs 2,500 on the favourite* ■ **stake (out) a/one's claim (to sb/sth)** किसी में विशेष रुचि प्रकट करना; किसी पर अधिकार जताना : *In his speech the minister clearly staked a/his claim to the leadership of the party.* **stake sth out** खूँटों से घेरना, सीमा चिह्नित करना।

stale / स्टेल् / *adj* 1 (भोजन) बासी 2 घिसा-पिटा, रुचिहीन, उबाने वाला : *Their marriage has gone stale.* ▸ **staleness** *noun.*

stalemate / 'स्टेल्मेट् / *noun* (प्राय: *sing*) 1 गतिरोध (विवाद के हल में रुकावट) : *Negotiations have reached (a) stalemate.* 2 (शतरंज में) ऐसी स्थिति जिसमें हार/जीत का फ़ैसला न हो पाए।

stalk¹ / स्टॉक् / *noun* 1 डंठल, डंडी (फल/फूल/पत्ती आदि की) 2 (कुछ जंतुओं में) किसी अंग को सहारा देने वाली पतली रचना : *The crab's eyes are at the end of short stalks.*

stalk² / स्टॉक् / *verb* 1 लुक-छिप कर शिकार का पीछा करना : *hunters stalking deer* 2 अकड़ कर चलना : *He stalked out of the room.*

stall¹ / स्टॉल् / *noun* 1 छोटी दुकान, मेज़ आदि जिस पर व्यापारी सामान रखते हैं : *set up a stall* 2 कोई छोटा कमरा, प्राय: एक व्यक्ति के लिए : *stalls for changing in at the swimming-pool* 3 एक पशु के लिए धान का हिस्सा 4 **stalls** [*pl*] रंगमंच के समीप की सीटें।

stall² / स्टॉल् / *verb* 1 (मोटर आदि का) अचानक रुक जाना : *The car stalled at the traffic lights.* 2 सवाल का निश्चित उत्तर न देना, ढुलमुल नीति अपनाना 3 किसी घटना की प्रगति रोक देना/रुक जाना : *Peace talks have stalled.*

stallion / 'स्टैलिअन् / *noun* वयस्क घोड़ा, विशेषत: जो नसल बढ़ाने के काम आए।

stalwart / 'स्टॉल्वर्ट् / *adj* 1 वफ़ादार और विश्वस्त : *one of the team's most stalwart supporters* 2 (ओप) हट्टा-कट्टा ▸ **stalwart** *noun* पक्का समर्थक (राजनीतिक दल आदि का)।

stamina / 'स्टैमिना / *noun* दम-ख़म, सहनशक्ति : *Marathon runners need plenty of stamina.*

stammer / 'स्टैमर् / *verb* हकलाना : *'I'm s-s-sorry,'* she stammered. ▸ **stammer** *noun* (प्राय: *sing*) हकलाने की प्रवृत्ति।

stamp¹ / स्टैम्प् / *verb* 1 पैर पटकना/ज़ोर से ज़मीन पर मारना : *Rekha stamped her foot in annoyance.* 2 पैर पटकते हुए चलना : *She stamped out of the room.* 3 छापना, काग़ज़ या कपड़े पर मुद्रण करना; मोहर लगाना : *They didn't stamp my passport.* 4 लिफ़ाफ़े पर मोहर या टिकट लगाना 5 **stamp sb as sth** किसी पर एक गुण विशेष की छाप लगाना/लग जाना : *This latest novel stamps her as a genius.* ■ **stamp on sth** कुचल देना; दबा देना : *She stamped on the burning paper to put it out.* ○ *The rebellion was soon stamped on by the army.* **stamp sth on sth** किसी पर पक्का प्रभाव छोड़ना : *stamp* *one's personality on a game* **stamp out sth** शक्ति द्वारा कुचल, दबा या हटा देना।

stamp² / स्टैम्प् / *noun* 1 (और post-age stamp भी) डाक-टिकट 2 छाप, मोहर/मुद्रा : *a date stamp* 3 पटकना : *give a childish stamp of impatience.* 4 (प्राय: sing) (और) छाप (गुणवत्ता की) : *Her work carries the unmistakable stamp of authority.*

stampede / स्टैम्'पीड् / *noun* 1 डर के कारण पशुओं की भगदड़ 2 भगदड़ : *There was a stampede towards the stage when the singer appeared.* ▸ **stampede** *verb* भगदड़ मचना/मचाना।

stance / स्टैन्स; स्टान्स भी / *noun* (प्राय: sing) 1 मुद्रा; खड़े होने का अंदाज़ 2 **stance (on sth)** किसी विषय आदि पर नैतिक या बौद्धिक दृष्टिकोण : *take/adopt an uncompromising stance on immigration.*

stand¹ / स्टैन्ड् / *verb* (*pt, pp* **stood** / स्टुड् /) 1 खड़ा होना; सीधा खड़ा रहना : *She was too weak to stand.* ◦ *After the bombing only a few houses were left standing.* 2 **stand (up)** किसी और अवस्था से पाँव पर खड़े हो जाना : *We stood up in order to see better.* 3 सीधा खड़ा कर देना : *Stand the ladder up against the wall.* 4 ऊँचाई-विशेष होना : *The tower stands 60 metres high.* 5 एक/किसी जगह पर होना : *A tall poplar tree once stood here.* 6 (वाहन आदि) उसी जगह पर रहना : *the train standing at platform 3* 7 (द्रव, मिश्रण आदि) निश्चल, अचल रहना : *Mix the batter and let it stand for twenty minutes.* 8 पहले जैसा रहना, वैध रहना : *The agreement must stand.* 9 किसी विशेष अवस्था या स्थिति में रहना : *The house stood empty for months.* 10 **stand at sth** किसी विशेष, निर्देशित स्तर आदि पर होना :

Interest rates stand at an attractive 9%. 11 कुछ करने की दशा में होना : *You stand to make a lot of money from this deal.* 12 कोई विशेष दृष्टिकोण, मत रखना 13 (विशेषत: नकारात्मक और **can/could** और प्रश्नात्मक वाक्यों में) सहन करना : *He can't stand hot weather!* 14 (*US* run भी) **stand (for sth)** चुनाव में खड़े होना ■ **it stands to reason** तर्कसंगत होना **stand a good chance** अच्छी संभावना होना **stand aside** 1 एक तरफ़ हो जाना : *She stood aside to let us pass.* 2 कुछ न करना; भाग न लेना : *Don't stand aside and let others do all the work.* **stand back (from sth)** 1 किसी स्थान से पीछे हटना : *The police ordered the crowd to stand back (from the building).* 2 किसी से दूर स्थित होना : *The house stands back a little (from the road).* **stand by** किसी बुरी घटना का मात्र दर्शक होना; अगले कार्य के लिए तैयार रहना **stand by sb** पक्ष लेना या साथ देना : *I'll stand by you whatever happens.* **stand by sth** वचन, निर्णय आदि पर क़ायम रहना : *She still stands by every word she said.* **stand down** पद छोड़ देना, पीछे हट जाना **stand for sth** 1 संक्षिप्त रूप होना : *What does BBC stand for?* 2 समर्थन देना : *a party that stands for racial tolerance* 3 प्रतिनिधित्व करना : *I reject fascism and all that it stands for.* **stand in (for sb)** किसी और के स्थान पर काम करना : *My assistant will stand in for me while I'm away.* **stand out (from/against) sth** आसानी से दिखाई पड़ना **stand out (from sb/sth)** दूसरों से अच्छा या ज़्यादा महत्त्वपूर्ण होना : *In a long career, certain memories stand out from the rest.* **stand over sb** निगरानी करना : *I don't like you standing over me while I am cooking.*

stand up for sb/oneself/sth पक्ष लेकर बोलना; समर्थन देना stand up to sb किसी का विरोध करना : It was brave of her to stand up to those bullies. stand up to sth (पदार्थ आदि) अच्छी अवस्था में रहना ▸ stand-alone adj स्वतंत्र रूप से कार्य करने वाला : a stand-alone computer stand-by noun (pl stand-bys) (व्यक्ति या वस्तु) एवज़ी stand-in noun (व्यक्ति) किसी और का स्थान लेने वाला stand-off noun समझौते पर पहुँचने में असफलता।

stand² /स्टैन्ड् / noun 1 [sing] दृष्टिकोण, मत; (तर्क में) पक्ष : She has always taken a firm stand on nuclear disarmament. 2 (प्राय: sing) हमला रोकने का धैर्यशाली प्रयास; विरोध के बावजूद अपना पक्ष सामने रखने का प्रयास : The time has come to make a stand on the issue of environmental pollution. 3 टेकने-टिकाने का साधन, स्टैंड : an umbrella stand 4 (प्राय: pl) खेल देख रहे दर्शकों के बैठने का स्थान 5 वाहनों का सवारियों के लिए इंतज़ार करने की जगह : a taxi stand.

standard /स्टैन्डर्ड/ noun 1 (प्राय: pl) गुण का मानक (जिससे अन्य का गुण, परिमाण आदि मापा जाए) : maintain safety standards 2 गुण का स्तर-विशेष : His work does not reach the required standard. 3 झंडा, ध्वजा : the royal standard 4 [pl] नैतिक सिद्धांत व आचरण : People's standards are not what they used to be. ▸ standard adj सामान्य, औसत, मान्य, नियमित : pay the standard rate of tax ∘ It is standard procedure in museums to register objects as they are acquired. standard of living noun जीवन-स्तर : They enjoy a high standard of living.

standardize, -ise /स्टैन्डर्डाइज़/ verb आकार, संख्या आदि में मानक बनाना : an attempt to standardize spelling ▸ standardization, -isation /स्टैन्डर्डाइ'ज़ेश्न्/ noun मानकीकरण।

standing /स्टैन्डिङ्/ noun 1 स्थिति या इज़्ज़त; समाज में स्तर : a scientist of high standing 2 किसी वस्तु के अस्तित्व की अवधि : a friendship of long standing ▸ standing adj स्थायी : a standing army.

standpoint /स्टैन्ड्पाइन्ट्/ noun (प्राय: sing) आधार रूप दृष्टिकोण।

standstill /स्टैन्ड्स्टिल्/ noun [sing] गतिरोध, रुकावट : Work is grinding to a standstill. ∘ bring sth to a standstill.

stanza /स्टैन्ज़ा/ noun (pl stanzas) (तक) कविता में पंक्तियों की इकाई; छंद : a ten-line stanza.

staple¹ /स्टेप्ल्/ noun स्टेपल, काग़ज़ों को बाँधने का ⊔ आकार का तार ▸ staple verb स्टेपल से काग़ज़ आदि जोड़ना/बाँधना : staple papers together.

staple² /स्टेप्ल्/ adj मुख्य : the staple products/industries of a country ▸ staple noun (प्राय: pl) 1 उत्पादन या व्यापार की मुख्य क़िस्म की वस्तु : Cotton is one of Egypt's staples. 2 आहार/खाने की मुख्य वस्तु : Bread, potatoes and other staples continue to rise in price.

star /स्टार्/ noun 1 तारा, नक्षत्र 2 तारे की आकृति की सजावटी वस्तु; सर्वश्रेष्ठ के लिए तारा चिह्न : Put a star by his name. 3 सर्वश्रेष्ठ अभिनेता, गायक, खिलाड़ी आदि : a tennis star 4 भाग्य का नक्षत्र : born under a lucky star 5 समूह में सबसे अच्छा : She is my star pupil. ▸ star verb (-rr-) 1 ताराचिह्न (*) लगाना 2 star (in sth) सर्वश्रेष्ठ अभिनेता या गायक बनना; star sb (in sth) (फ़िल्म आदि में) अभिनेताओं द्वारा कार्य किया

जाना : *a film starring Anthony Hopkins and Emma Thompson*

starry *adj* (-ier, -iest) 1 तारों भरा 2 तारों की तरह चमकने वाला : *starry eyes*

starry-eyed *adj* (अनौप, प्राय: अपमा) उत्साही किंतु अनुभवहीन।

starboard /स्टार्बई / *noun* सामने से देखने पर जहाज़ का दाहिना भाग, दायाँ।

starch / स्टार्च / *noun* 1 स्टार्च, माँड़ी/ कलफ़ 2 आहार पदार्थ का एक तत्त्व; स्टार्च वाले खाद्य पदार्थ : *cut down on starch*
▸ **starch** *verb* कलफ़ लगाना।

stardom /स्टार्डम/ *noun* प्रसिद्ध अभि-नेता, कलाकार आदि होने का दर्जा : *her rapid rise to stardom.*

stare /स्टेअर/ *verb* 1 stare (at sb/sth) घूरना; टकटकी लगा कर देखना : *It's rude to stare.* 2 (आँखें) फाड़े हुए एवं स्थिर : *Her lifeless eyes stared at me.*
▸ **stare** *noun* टकटकी।

stark / स्टार्क् / *adj* (-er, -est) 1 कड़ा, कठोर एवं बेआराम, ख़ाली : *stark prison conditions* 2 स्पष्ट, सरासर साफ़ : *Her wealth is in stark contrast to the poverty all around her.* 3 पूर्ण, बिल-कुल : *stark madness/terror* ▸ **stark** *adv* ■ **stark naked** बिलकुल नंगा।

starling /स्टार्लिङ् / *noun* चमकदार पंखों वाली एक छोटी चिड़िया।

start¹ / स्टार्ट् / *verb* 1 start (out) यात्रा आरंभ करना, रवाना होना : *We plan to start at 6 o'clock.* 2 कोई कार्य शुरू करना, घटित होना शुरू होना : *I arrived after the play had started.* 3 (यंत्र आदि) चालू होना/करना : *The car won't start.* 4 कुछ अस्तित्व में लाना; कुछ संभव बनाना : *start a fire* 5 start (up) (औप) चौंक उठना, (भय, आश्चर्य आदि से) उछल पड़ना : *She started at the sound of my voice.* 6 (औप) जानवर को हकारना, हाँकना 7 (अनौप) शिकायत या आलोचना करना : *Don't you start—*

it's not my fault. ■ **start back** 1 वापसी शुरू करना : *Isn't it time we started back?* 2 डर, हैरानी आदि से उछल पड़ना : *He started back in alarm.* **start for** एक जगह छोड़कर दूसरी पर जाना : *What time do you start for work?* **start off** चलना शुरू करना **start off on the right/wrong foot (with sb)** (अनौप) अच्छे/ख़राब ढंग से संबंध बनाना शुरू करना : *He started off on the wrong foot by being rude to his new boss.* **start over** फिर से शुरू करना : *She wasn't satisfied with our work and made us start all over again.* **start something** (अनौप) लड़ाई, बहस आदि शुरू करना **start (sth) from scratch** बिना किसी विशेष तैयारी या अनुकूल परिस्थिति के शुरुआत से शुरू करना : *He lost all his money and had to start again from scratch.* **start (sth) up** काम करना, भागना, होना शुरू करना : *start up a new company* ○ *We couldn't start the car.* **to start with** 1 प्रथम : *To start with we don't have enough money, and secondly, we are too busy.* 2 शुरुआत में : *I'll have melon to start with.*

start² / स्टार्ट् / *noun* 1 यात्रा आदि का आरंभ : *We won't finish the job today but we can make a start (on it).* 2 the start [sing] दौड़ की शुरुआत का स्थान 3 (प्राय: sing) प्रतियोगिता आरंभ होने के पूर्व समय या दूरी की (लाभ के लिए) दी गई मात्रा : *The smaller boys were given a start of 10 seconds in the race.* 4 (प्राय: sing) चौंकना/उछ-लना ■ **by/in fits and starts** अनियमित तौर से, रुक-रुक कर, तरंग/मौज आने पर।

starter / स्टार्ट् / *noun* 1 व्यक्ति, घोड़ा आदि जो दौड़ के शुरुआत में भाग लेता हो : *Of the ten starters in the race, only three finished.* 2 व्यक्ति जो दौड़ शुरू

करने का संकेत देता हो : *waiting for the starter's gun to fire* 3 व्यक्ति या चीज़ जो कोई कार्य शुरू करे : *He was a late starter as a child.* 4 चालू करने का यंत्र 5 भोजन का पहला दौर।

startle / स्टार्टल् / *verb* आश्चर्य, भय आदि से चौंक जाना/चौंका देना : *The sudden noise in the bushes startled her horse.* ▶ **startled** *adj* : *a startled expression* **startling** *adj.*

starve / स्टार्व् / *verb* 1 भूखों मरना : *starve to death* 2 (अनौप) बहुत तेज़ भूख लगी होना : *What's for dinner? I'm starving!* ■ **be starved of sth** पर्याप्त न मिलने के कारण कष्ट भोगना : *children starved of affection* ▶ **starvation** / स्टार्वेश्न् / *noun* भुखमरी।

state¹ / स्टेट् / *noun* 1 दशा, अवस्था : *a confused state of mind* 2 (**State** भी) शासन, राज्य; (राज्य में) प्रदेश : *How many States are there in the United States of America?* 3 समारोह, प्रतिष्ठा : *The Queen was in her robes of state.* 4 देश की सरकार : *free education provided by the state* ■ **in/into a state** (अनौप) चिंतित व उत्तेजित मानसिक अवस्था में : *She got herself into a state about her exams.* **lie in state** मृत शरीर का दर्शनार्थ रखा जाना **state of affairs** परिस्थिति : *What a shocking state of affairs!* **state of mind** मनोदशा ▶ **state** (**State** भी) *adj* 1 राज्य द्वारा प्रदत्त या राज्य से संबंधित : *state education* 2 राजकीय समारोह आदि **state of-the-art** *adj* बहुत ही आधुनिक व उन्नत तरीकों से बना : *a state-of-the-art computer program.*

state² / स्टेट् / *verb* 1 व्यक्त करना; सावधानी से स्पष्ट शब्दों में कहना : *state one's views* 2 पहले से ही प्रबंध करके रखना, निर्धारित करना : *at stated times.*

stately / स्टेट्लि / *adj* भव्य, वैभवशाली, राजसी, शानदार ठाट-बाट वाला।

statement / स्टेट्मन्ट् / *noun* 1 कथन, उक्ति 2 तथ्यों, समाचारों, समस्याओं आदि का औपचारिक ब्यौरा : *an official statement.*

stateroom / स्टेट्रूम् / *noun* 1 जहाज़ में सोने का निजी कमरा 2 राजसी परिवार, प्रमुख सरकारी अधिकारियों के लिए कमरा।

statesman / स्टेट्स्मन् / *noun* (*pl* **statesmen**; *fem* **stateswoman**, *pl* **stateswomen**) राजनीतिज्ञ, राजनेता : *an elder statesman of the party.*

static / स्टैटिक् / *adj* 1 थमा हुआ; निष्क्रिय : *a static society* ○ *House prices, which have been static for several months, are now rising again.* 2 (भौतिकी) (बल) वज़न द्वारा, बिना चाल के : *static pressure* ▶ **static** *noun* 1 वातावरण में ऐसी स्थिति जिसके कारण प्रसारण का स्तर ख़राब हो 2 (**static electricity** भी) विद्युत जो ऐसी वस्तु के आस-पास जमा हो जाए जो विद्युत का चालन नहीं कर सकती : *My hair gets full of static in very dry weather.*

station / स्टेश्न् / *noun* 1 रेलवे स्टेशन 2 (पुलिस) चौकी; भवन जहाँ कोई विशेष सेवा मुहैया कराई जाए, केंद्र : *a radar station* 3 रेडियो/टी वी प्रसारण केंद्र : *satellite TV stations* 4 (अप्र या औप) सामाजिक पद-मर्यादा ▶ **station** *verb* उद्देश्य विशेष के लिए किसी को/स्वयं को नियत स्थान पर तैनात करना : *Their regiment is stationed in Cyprus.*

stationary / स्टेशनरि; *US* स्टेशनेरि / *adj* 1 स्थावर, स्थिर, अचल : *hit a stationary vehicle* 2 दशा या मात्रा में न बदलने वाला : *a stationary population.*

stationer / स्टेशनर् / *noun* लेखन-सामग्री बेचने वाला, काग़ज़ी।

stationery / स्टेशनरि; *US* स्टेशनेरि / *noun* लेखन-सामग्री।

statistics / स्टʼटिस्टिक्स् / noun 1 [pl] तुलना के लिए क्रमबद्ध और संग्रहीत संख्यात्मक तथ्य, आँकड़े : *crime/unemployment statistics* 2 सांख्यिकी : *She is studying statistics at university.*
▸ **statistical** adj.

statue / 'स्टैच्यू / noun मूर्ति, प्रतिमा : *erect a bronze statue of the Buddha.*

stature / 'स्टैचर् / noun 1 व्यक्ति का कद, लंबाई : *be small in stature* 2 योग्यता से अर्जित महत्त्व एवं प्रतिष्ठा : *a scientist of international stature.*

status / 'स्टेटस् / noun 1 सामाजिक स्थिति, प्रतिष्ठा : *be given equal status with other members of staff* 2 उच्च पद अथवा सामाजिक स्थिति : *seek status and security* ▸ **status symbol** noun वैभव, उच्च सामाजिक दर्जा, दौलत आदि का स्वामित्व का प्रतीक।

status quo / स्टेटस् 'क्वो / noun the status quo [sing] स्थिति जैसी अभी है या जिस हाल में बदलाव के पहले थी : *upset/restore/preserve the status quo.*

statute / 'स्टैच्यूट / noun 1 संसद अथवा अन्य विधान-सभाओं से पारित क़ानून या अधिनियम : *a parliamentary statute* 2 संविधि, किसी संस्था के नियम ▸ **statutory** / 'स्टैचटरि; US 'स्टैचटॉरि / adj क़ानून द्वारा निर्धारित या अपेक्षित : *statutory control of prices and incomes.*

staunch / स्टॉन्च् / adj (-er, -est) निष्ठावान, विशेषत: मुश्किल परिस्थितियों में : *one of our staunchest allies.*

stave / स्टेव् / verb (pt, pp staved या stove / स्टोव् /) ■ **stave sth off** (pt, pp staved) कुछ बुरा होने से रोकना; कुछ देर के लिए स्थगित करना : *stave off disaster/danger.*

stay / स्टे / verb 1 ठहरना, रहना : *stay (at) home* 2 स्थिति-विशेष में रहना :

stay awake 3 (अतिथि के रूप में) रहना, टिकना : *We stayed in a hotel.* ■ **be here to stay/have come to stay** (अनौप) आमतौर पर स्वीकार कर लिया गया : *I hope that (the idea of) equality of opportunity for men and women has come to/is here stay.* **stay behind** दूसरों के घर चले जाने के बाद भी वहीं रहना : *They stayed behind after the party to help clean up.* **stay in** घर के अंदर ही रहना **stay out** घर के बाहर रहना, विशेषत: शाम के बाद **stay out of sth** एक जगह पर बने रहना जहाँ न कोई पहुँच सके और न किसी द्वारा प्रभावित किया जा सके **stay put** (अनौप) जहाँ हैं वहीं रहना : *We had thought of moving house, but we've decided to stay put for a while.* **stay up** जागते रहना; देर से सोना ▸ **stay** noun टिकने की अवधि, वासअवधि : *an overnight stay in Karachi* **staying power** noun सहनशक्ति; ताक़त।

stead / स्टेड् / noun ■ **in sb's/sth's stead** (औप) किसी के स्थान पर : *The old church was demolished and a modern office built in its stead.* **stand sb in good stead** ज़रूरत पड़ने पर उपयोगी, मददगार होना।

steadfast / 'स्टेड्फ़ास्ट; US 'स्टेड्फ़ैस्ट / adj steadfast (in sth/to sth) (औप) अटल, पक्का/अपरिवर्तनीय : *remain steadfast in one's beliefs/to one's principles* ▸ **steadfastly** adv **steadfastness** noun.

steady / 'स्टेडि / adj (-ier, -iest) 1 स्थिर, अटल/संतुलित : *hold the camera steady* 2 नियमित रूप से बिना रुकावट के विकसित होता हुआ : *steady progress* 3 स्थिर/नियमित/एकसमान : *move at a steady pace* 4 (व्यवहार, आचरण, आदत आदि में) सुस्थिर, संयमी : *a steady worker* ▸ **steady** verb (pt, pp steadied) स्थिर बनना/बनाना : *Prices are steadying.* **steadily** *adv.*

steak / स्टेक् / *noun* मांस या मछली का मोटा टुकड़ा, टिक्का।

steal / स्टील् / *verb* (*pt* stole / स्टोल्/; *pp* stolen / 'स्टोलन्/) 1 steal sth (from sb/sth) चुराना, चोरी करना : *Someone has stolen my watch.* ○ *steal sb's ideas* 2 अचानक (चोरी से) पा लेना, चालाकी से प्राप्त करना : *steal a glance at oneself in the mirror* 3 चुपचाप आना-जाना : *He stole into the room.* ▪ **steal a march (on sb)** गुप्त रूप से कुछ करके किसी व्यक्ति पर लाभ लेना **steal the show** ध्यान और प्रशंसा आकर्षित करना।

stealth / स्टेल्थ् / *noun* गुप्त रूप से करने की क्रिया : *The terrorists operate by stealth.* ▸ **stealthy** *adj* (-ier, -iest) गुप्त रूप से किया जा रहा : *stealthy movements* **stealthily** *adv.*

steam / स्टीम् / *noun* भाप; भाप शक्ति : *a steam brake* ▸ **steam** *verb* 1 भाप निकालना : *steaming hot coffee* 2 भाप से (खाना) पकाना : *Steam the fish for 10 minutes.* 3 भाप शक्ति से चलाना : *a boat steaming up the Nile* **steamer** *noun* 1 भाप से चलने वाला जहाज़ 2 भाप से खाना पकाने वाला छेददार बरतन **steamy** *adj* 1 भाप के समान 2 भापयुक्त/भाप-विषयक 3 कामुकतापूर्ण : *steamy love scenes.*

steel / स्टील् / *noun* 1 स्टील, इस्पात/फ़ौलाद 2 इस्पात उद्योग/उत्पादन : *deserted steel mills* 3 (प्रा या साहि) हथियार ▪ **of steel** शक्ति और साहस से भरा : *a man of steel* ▸ **steel** *verb* (अलं) **steel oneself (for/against sth)** **steel oneself (to do sth)** किसी अप्रिय से निपटने के लिए मन और दिमाग़ को दृढ़ बनाना।

steep¹ / स्टीप् / *adj* (-er, -est) 1 (चढ़ाई,

जीना आदि) खड़ा, (ढलुवाँ नहीं) 2 (मात्रा में उतार या चढ़ाव) अचानक और बड़ा : *a steep increase in prices* 3 (अनौप) (मूल्य, माँग आदि) बहुत अधिक, अनुचित।

steep² / स्टीप् / *verb* ▪ **steep sb/oneself/sth in sth** पूर्णत: भर देना, पूरा ज्ञान पाना : *He steeped himself in the literature of ancient Greece and Rome.* **steep sth in sth** भिगोना, घोलना : *plums steeped in brandy.*

steeple / 'स्टीप्ल् / *noun* चर्च की ऊँची मीनार।

steer¹ / स्टिअर् / *verb* 1 नाव, वाहन आदि का परिचालन करना, चलाना : *steer a boat (into the harbour)* 2 किसी के विचारों/गतिविधियों आदि का निर्देशन करना, नियंत्रण करना : *He managed to steer the discussion away from the subject of money.* ▸ **steering** *noun* **steering wheel** (wheel भी) *noun* वाहन को परिचालित करने वाला पहिया।

steer² / स्टिअर् / *noun* जवान बैल।

stem¹ / स्टेम् / *noun* 1 (पेड़-पौधों का) तना 2 (प्याले की) डंडी 3 डंठल, डंडी 4 (व्या) शब्द का मुख्यांश, प्रतिपादक : *'Writ' is the stem of the forms 'writes', 'writing' and 'written'.* ▸ **stem** *verb* (-mm-) ▪ **stem from sth** किसी से उत्पन्न होना; कारण होना : *discontent stemming from low pay and poor working conditions.*

stem² / स्टेम् / *verb* (-mm-) रोकना, रोकथाम करना; बाँध बनाना : *bandage a cut to stem the bleeding.*

stench / स्टेन्च् / *noun* (प्राय: *sing*) बदबू, सड़ाँध : *the stench of rotting meat.*

stencil / 'स्टेन्स्ल् / *noun* गत्ते/धातु का पतरा जिस पर चित्र/डिज़ाइन/अक्षर उभरे/कटे होते है और उन्हें स्याही/पेंट की सहायता से किसी अन्य वस्तु पर उतारा जाता है; इस

तरह बनाया गया डिज़ाइन आदि : *decorate a wall with flower stencils.*

stenographer / स्ट'नॉग्रफ़र् / *noun* स्टेनोग्राफ़र, टाइपिस्ट जो शॉर्टहैंड भी जानता हो ▸ **stenography** *noun.*

step¹ / स्टेप् / *verb* (**-pp-**) क़दम रखना, डग भरना : *step across a stream* ■ **step aside/down** कोई महत्त्वपूर्ण पद किसी और के लिए छोड़ना : *It's time for me to step aside/down as chief executive and let a younger person take over.* **step in** किसी मुश्किल परिस्थिति को सुलझाने के लिए उसमें सम्मिलित हो जाना **step into sb's shoes** किसी और का कार्यभार संभालना : *She stepped into her father's shoes when he retired.* **step sth up** किसी चीज़ का मूल्य, गति, उत्पादन आदि बढ़ाना : *step up production* ▸ **stepping stone** *noun* पैर रखने का पत्थर; उन्नति की सीढ़ी।

step² / स्टेप् / *noun* 1 क़दम, डग 2 क़दमों की आहट : *We heard steps outside.* 3 उपाय, चरण : *the first step on the road to recovery* 4 प्रक्रिया का चरण; सोपान; पैमाने पर चिह्न-विशेष : *When do you get your next step up?* 5 (प्राय: pl) नाचने में क़दमों की गति/मेल : *I don't know the steps for this dance.* 6 सीढ़ी : *a flight of steps* ■ **in/out of step (with sb/sth)** मार्च/नाच में क़दम का मेल/बेमेल होना **mind/watch one's step** 1 ध्यान से चलना 2 सोच-समझकर काम/व्यवहार करना : *You'll be in trouble if you don't watch your step.* **step by step** क्रमश:।

step- *pref* (पूर्वपद) सौतेला : *step-son/ step-daughter/step-father/step-mother.*

stereo / 'स्टेरिओ / *noun* (*pl* **stereos**) (**stereo system** भी) रेडियो, टेप रिकार्डर आदि यंत्र जो दो स्पीकरों से जुड़े हुए हों।

stereotype / 'स्टेरिअटाइप् / *noun* किसी व्यक्ति, चीज़ के बारे में आम धारणा जो प्राय: वास्तविकता में सच नहीं होती है; रूढ़, परंपराबद्ध रूप : *He doesn't conform to the usual stereotype of the city businessman with a dark suit and briefcase.* ▸ **stereotyped** *adj* : *a play full of stereotyped characters* **stereotypical** *adj.*

sterile / 'स्टेराइल्; *US* स्टेर्ल् / *adj* 1 (मानव या पशु) प्रजनन में अक्षम/अ-समर्थ : *Medical tests showed that he was sterile.* 2 जीवाणु-रहित : *sterile bandages* 3 (भूमि) बंजर, अनुर्वर/ अनुपजाऊ 4 (चर्चा, वार्ता आदि) अर्थहीन, परिणाम रहित : *a sterile debate* 5 (पेड़-पौधे) फलहीन, फलोत्पादन में अक्षम ▸ **sterility** / स्ट'रिलटि / *noun* बंध्यता : *The disease can cause sterility in men/women.* **sterilize, -ise** / 'स्टेर-लाइज़/ *verb* 1 जीवाणुरहित करना 2 बंध्या बनाना **sterilization, -isation** *noun.*

sterling / 'स्टर्लिङ् / *noun* ब्रिटिश मुद्रा (पाउंड) : *payable in sterling* ▸ **sterling** *adj* 1 खरा, असली, भरोसेमंद 2 मानक गुणवत्ता वाली चाँदी।

stern¹ / स्टर्न् / *adj* (**-er, -est**) 1 गंभीर, निर्दय, आज्ञापालन की अपेक्षा रखने वाला : *a stern warning/message* 2 सख्त, कठोर : *sterner measures to combat crime* ■ **be made of sterner stuff** दृढ़ व्यक्तित्व का होना; मुश्किलों का सामना करने के लिए दूसरे से ज्यादा दृढ़ होना : *Many would have given up, but Ravi was made of sterner stuff.* ▸ **sternly** *adv.*

stern² / स्टर्न् / *noun* जहाज़ या नाव का पश्च भाग : *walk towards the stern.*

stethoscope / 'स्टेथस्कोप् / *noun* डॉक्टर द्वारा दिल की धड़कन, फेफड़ों की जाँच के लिए प्रयोग किया जाने वाला एक उपकरण।

stew / स्ट्यू; *US* स्टू / *noun* सीझा हुआ

गोश्त/सब्ज़ी आदि ▸ **stew** *verb* सींझना : *The meat needs to stew for several hours ○ stewed apple and custard.*

steward /'स्ट्यूअर्ड; *US* स्टूअर्ड/ *noun* 1 (*fem* **stewardess**) जहाज़ या हवाई जहाज़ में परिचारक : *an air stewardess* 2 (भू-संपत्ति आदि का) प्रबंधक, कारिंदा 3 (सार्वजनिक सभा का) प्रबंधक 4 कॉलेज, क्लब आदि का भंडारी ▸ **stewardship** *noun* (औप)।

stick¹ / स्टिक / *noun* 1 पतली सूखी लकड़ी का टुकड़ा, छड़ी : *walking stick* 2 हॉकी/पोलो स्टिक आदि 3 (समासों में) छड़नुमा वस्तु : *sticks of chalk/charcoal.*

stick² / स्टिक / *verb* (*pt, pp* **stuck** / स्टक /) 1 **stick sth in/into/through sth; stick sth in/through** चुभाना, घुसेड़ना : *stick a fork into the meat* 2 चिपक जाना/चिपकाना, चुभा रह जाना : *stick a stamp on an envelope* 3 लापरवाही से चिपका देना 4 **stick (in sth)** अटक जाना : *The key has stuck in the lock.* 5 (अनौप) स्थापित हो जाना : *They couldn't make the changes stick.* ■ **stick around** (अनौप) किसी स्थान पर रहना, प्रतीक्षा करना : *Stick around, we may need you.* **stick at sth** (अनौप) दृढ़ता से काम जारी रखना **stick by sb/sth** (अनौप) समर्थन देते रहना, निष्ठावान बने रहना, विशेषत: मुश्किल स्थितियों में **stick out** (अनौप) बाहर निकालना या निकाले रखना : *She stuck her tongue out at me.* **stick out for sth** (अनौप) माँग पर डटे रहना **stick to one's guns** (अनौप) अपने विचार आदि पर दृढ़ रहना, आलोचना के बावजूद भी **stick to sth** काम जारी रखना, साथ न छोड़ना : *stick to a job until it is finished* **stick up for sb/oneself/sth** पक्ष लेना, समर्थन देना।

sticker / स्टिकर् / *noun* 1 चिपकने वाला

लेबल 2 (अनौप) व्यक्ति जो मुश्किलों के बावजूद भी डटा रहता है।

stickler / स्टिक्लर् / *noun* **stickler for sth** व्यक्ति जो किसी गुण, व्यवहार को अत्यधिक महत्त्व देता हो और दूसरों से भी यही अपेक्षा करता हो : *a stickler for accuracy/punctuality/discipline.*

sticky / स्टिकि / *adj* (**-ier, -iest**) 1 चिपकने वाला/चिपचिपा : *sticky toffee* 2 (अनौप) (मौसम) ख़राब/गंदा; (व्यक्ति) पसीने से तरबतर 3 (अनौप) मुश्किल, अप्रिय : *a sticky situation* ▸ **stickily** *adv* **stickiness** *noun.*

stiff / स्टिफ़् / *adj* (**-er, -est**) 1 सख़्त, न झुकने/मुड़ने वाला : *a stiff cardboard* 2 गाढ़ा (लगभग ठोस) : *a stiff dough* 3 दुस्साध्य : *a stiff climb/exam* 4 (व्यवहार) औपचारिक एवं रूखा 5 (अनौप) (मूल्य) बहुत ज़्यादा 6 (वायु) तेज़ 7 (शराब) अधिक अलकोहल वाली ▸ **stiffly** *adv* **stiffness** *noun.*

stiffen / 'स्टिफ़न् / *verb* **stiffen (sth) (up) (with sth)** सख़्त होना या करना : *He stiffened with fear.*

stifle / 'स्टाइफ़ुल् / *verb* 1 (विद्रोह आदि) दमन करना/नियंत्रण में लाना : *The rebellion was quickly stifled.* 2 दम घोंटना/घुटना 3 आग को जलने से रोकना, बुझाना : *stifle the flames with a blanket* ▸ **stifling** *adj.*

stigma / 'स्टिग्मा / *noun* (प्राय: *sing*) कलंक, लांछन : *There is still (a) social stigma attached to being unemployed.*

still¹ / स्टिल् / *adj* (**-er, -est**) 1 निस्तब्ध, निश्चेष्ट : *Please keep still while I take your photograph.* 2 वायुरहित : *a still summer day* ▸ **still** *verb* (औप) निश्चेष्ट होना या करना : *The wind stilled.* **stillness** *noun.*

still² / स्टिल् / *adv* 1 अब तक : *It's still raining.* 2 तो भी, तिस पर भी : *Al-*

though she felt ill, she still went to work. 3 अधिक : *Tarun is tall, but Megha is taller still.* 4 और अधिक : *He came up with still more stories.*

stillborn / 'स्टिल्बॉर्न् / *adj* (शिशु) मृत पैदा हुआ।

stilt / स्टिल्ट् / *noun* 1 बाँसों के सहारे चलने वाले व्यक्ति के लंबे बाँस : *walk on stilts* 2 ज़मीन के ऊपर इमारत को सहारा देने वाले खंभे : *a house built on stilts at the edge of a lake.*

stilted / 'स्टिल्टिड् / *adj* (अप्रमा) (व्यवहार, बातचीत) कृत्रिम, अति औपचारिक।

stimulant / 'स्टिम्यलन्ट् / *noun* 1 प्रेरक या उत्तेजक पेय; उद्दीपक (भेषज) : *Coffee and tea are mild stimulants.* 2 **stimulant (to sth)** अन्य बड़ी घटना को उत्प्रेरित करने वाली घटना या क्रिया।

stimulate / 'स्टिम्युलेट् / *verb* 1 **stimulate sb/sth (to sth)** प्रेरित करना, उत्तेजित करना : *This success stimulated him to even greater effort.* 2 किसी वस्तु को कार्यशील बना देना 3 अधिक रोचक एवं उत्तेजक बना देना : *The lecture failed to stimulate me.* ▸ **stimulating** *adj* **stimulation** *noun.*

stimulus / 'स्टिम्यलस् / *noun* (*pl* **stimuli** / 'स्टिम्यलाइ /) **stimulus (to/for sth)**; **stimulus (to do sth)** 1 उद्दीपन, प्रेरणा : *the stimulus of competition in business* 2 (जीवधारियों में) प्रतिक्रिया का उद्दीपन : *produce a response to a stimulus.*

sting¹ / स्टिङ् / *noun* 1 डंक (जैसे बिच्छू का) : *the sting of a bee/wasp* 2 कुछ पौधों की पत्तियों में शूल जैसी रचना : *Nettles have a nasty sting.* 3 डंक मारने/लगने से उत्पन्न टीस : *That bee gave me a nasty sting.* 4 टीसना (शरीर या मन का कोई दर्द) : *the sting of remorse/jealousy.*

sting² / स्टिङ् / *verb* (*pt, pp* **stung**

/ स्टङ् /) 1 डंक मारना : *A bee stung me on the cheek.* 2 दुखना, जलना 3 **sting sb (to/into sth/doing sth)** किसी को क्रोधित करके/वेदना पहुँचा कर कुछ करने को उकसाना : *Their taunts stung me to action.*

stingy / 'स्टिन्जि / *adj* (अनौप) अनिच्छा से ख़र्च, प्रयोग या दान करने वाला : *He's very stingy about lending money.*

stink / स्टिङ्क् / *verb* (*pt* **stank** / स्टैङ्क् / या **stunk** / स्टङ्क् /; *pp* **stunk**) (अनौप) **stink (of sth)** 1 बदबू उठना : *Her breath stank of garlic.* 2 दुर्भाव वाला, बेईमान या बुरा प्रतीत होना : *The whole business stinks (of corruption)!* ▸ **stink** *noun* (अनौप) बदबू, दुर्गंध।

stint / स्टिन्ट् / *noun* व्यक्ति की निर्धारित मात्रा या काम की अवधि : *I've done my stint in the kitchen for today.*

stipend / 'स्टाइपेन्ड् / *noun* निर्धारित राशि जो नियमित रूप से अदा की जाती है; वेतन।

stipulate / 'स्टिप्युलेट् / *verb* (औप) आवश्यक शर्त के रूप में प्रस्तुत करना : *agree to the terms stipulated in the contract* ▸ **stipulation** / ‚स्टिप्यु 'ले-श्न् / *noun.*

stir / स्टर् / *verb* (-rr-) 1 **stir sth (with sth)** चम्मच आदि से चलाना, विलोड़ना : *Stir continuously until the mixture thickens.* 2 **stir sth into sth; stir sth in** एक पदार्थ को दूसरे में इस प्रकार मिलाना 3 हिलना/हिलाना : *A gentle breeze stirred the leaves.* 4 **stir sb (to sth)** तीव्र भावनाएँ भड़काना, उत्तेजित करना : *a story that stirs the imagination* ■ **stir sb up** उकसाना **stir sth up** 1 मुसीबत खड़ी करना, विशेषतः दूसरों के लिए : *stir up trouble/unrest/ discontent* 2 अच्छी तरह हिलाना : *stir up the mud at the bottom of the pond* **stir the blood** उत्तेजित या उत्साहित

करना ▸ **stir** noun 1 चलाने/विलोडन की क्रिया 2 [sing] सामान्य उत्तेजना या धक्का; भड़काना।

stirrup / 'स्टिरप् / noun घुड़सवार की रक़ाब।

stitch / स्टिच् / noun 1 (सिलाई का) टाँका; (बुनाई में) फंदा, घर 2 टाँका/फंदा : make long stitches 3 सिलाई/बुनाई का पैटर्न विशेष : an embroidery stitch ▸ **stitch** verb सिलना, टाँके लगाना।

stock[1] / स्टॉक् / noun 1 बिक्री के लिए माल, स्टॉक : Your order can be supplied from stock. 2 stock (of sth) प्रयोग के लिए उपलब्ध सामान या आपूर्ति : have a good stock of logs for the winter 3 पशुधन : buy some more breeding stock 4 व्यक्ति का वंश : She comes from Welsh farming stock. 5 सरकारी ऋण : government stock 6 (बंदूक का) कुंदा 7 पौधा जिस/पर क़लम लगाई जाती है ▪ **in/out of stock** दुकान आदि के भंडार में माल होना/न होना **take stock (of sb/sth)** सर्वेक्षण करना; विचार के बाद किसी स्थिति/किसी की योग्यता के बारे में निर्णय लेना : After a year in the job, she decided it was time to take stock (of her career). ▸ **stock** adj 1 भंडार में होना और आसानी से उपलब्ध होना : one of our stock items 2 बहुत ज़्यादा प्रयोग में होना, और इसलिए रुचिहीन, प्रभावहीन हो जाना : stock characters in soap opera **stock exchange (stock market** भी) वह स्थल जहाँ स्टॉक और शेयर बेचे व ख़रीदे जाते हैं।

stock[2] / स्टॉक् / verb 1 सामान/माल रखना : We stock all sizes. 2 stock sth (with sth) माल जुटाना/आपूर्ति करना।

stockbroker / 'स्टॉक्ब्रोकर् / (**broker** भी) noun शेयर-दलाल।

stocking / 'स्टॉकिङ् / noun लंबा मोज़ा,

विशेषत: लड़कियों और महिलाओं द्वारा पहना जाने वाला।

stocky / 'स्टॉकि / adj (**-ier, -iest**) (अनौप, सामान्यत: अपमा) देखने में नाटा, तगड़ा और ठोस : a stocky little man ▸ **stockily** adv.

stoke / स्टोक् / verb 1 **stoke sth (up) (with sth)** (इंजन, भट्ठी आदि में) कोयला झोंकना 2 **stoke sth (up)** (किसी प्रवृत्ति, भाव आदि को) बढ़ावा देना : stoke fears of a property slump ▸ **stoker** noun भट्ठी में कोयला झोंकने वाला।

stolid / 'स्टॉलिड् / adj (प्राय: अपमा) भावशून्य; सहज में उत्तेजित न होने वाला : a stolid character/manner ▸ **stolidly** adv **stolidity** noun.

stomach / स्टमक् / noun 1 पेट 2 आमाशय 3 भूख (खाने की इच्छा); किसी चीज़ के लिए इच्छा या उत्सुकता ▸ **stomach** verb 1 सहन करना 2 बिना बीमार पड़े खाना : I can't stomach seafood.

stomp / स्टॉम्प् / verb (अनौप) भारी क़दमों से दिशा-विशेष में जाना/चलना : She slammed the door and stomped out of the house.

stone / स्टोन् / noun 1 पत्थर : stone walls/buildings 2 पत्थर का टुकड़ा 3 (**precious stone** भी) रत्न, मणि-माणिक्य : a sapphire ring with six small stones 4 (US **pit** भी) गुठली (आम/आड़ आदि की) 5 (गुर्दे आदि की) पथरी 6 (pl अपरिवर्तित) (सांक्षिst) स्टोन, 6.4 किलोग्राम का भार : He weighs over 10 stone. ▪ **a stone's throw** पत्थर फेंकने की दूरी, थोड़ी दूरी : We live a stone's throw from here. **leave no stone unturned** हर मुमकिन कोशिश करना ▸ **stone** verb 1 पत्थर फेंकना/मारना : be stoned to death 2 गुठली निकालना : stoned date/olives **stone-deaf** adj निपट बहरा।

stonemason / 'स्टोन्मेस्न् / noun संगतराश (मिस्त्री)।

stony / 'स्टोनि / adj (-ier, -iest) 1 पथरीला: stony ground/soil 2 संगदिल, कठोर स्वभाव का।

stool / स्टूल / noun 1 तिपाई, स्टूल 2 (औप, चिकि) मल (डॉक्टरी परीक्षण के लिए)।

stoop / स्टूप / verb stoop (down) 1 झुकना 2 कुबड़ों की तरह आगे झुके होना ■ **stoop so low (as to do sth)** (अलं) नैतिक दृष्टि से स्वयं को गिराना: I never thought he'd stoop so low as to cheat on his best friend. ‣ **stoop** noun (प्रायः sing) झुकाव: walk with a slight stoop.

stop[1] / स्टॉप / verb (-pp-) 1 रोकना; करने से मना करना; रुक जाना; चालू कार्य को बंद कर देना: stop work/talking 2 **stop sth (up) (with sth)** छेद भरना, छेद बंद करना: stop a leak in a pipe 3 (भुगतान) बंद करना, देने से मना करना: stop a cheque/sb's wages 4 (थोड़ी देर के लिए) अंदर रहना, बंद रहना: We stopped at a campsite for a week. ■ **stop by/round** भेंट के लिए थोड़ी देर किसी के घर रुकना **stop over (at/in)** यात्रा रोक कर कहीं थोड़ी देर के लिए रुकना **stop (sb) short** अचानक रुकना या किसी को कुछ करने से रोकना: I stopped him short before he could see anything more. **stop short of sth/doing sth** एक सीमा के बाहर कुछ करने को तैयार न होना: He suspected his boss of acting dishonestly but stopped short of accusing him of anything. ‣ **stopgap** noun कामचलाऊ (प्रबंध) **stoppage** / 'स्टॉपिज् / noun 1 विराम, रोक/ बाधा: a 24-hour stoppage at the local car plant 2 रुकावट: a stoppage in the pipe **stop press** noun नवीनतम समाचार जो मुद्रित होते समय समाचार-पत्र में जोड़ा गया हो।

stop[2] / स्टॉप / noun 1 रोक, ठहराव: make a short stop on a journey 2 बस/ट्रेन का स्टॉप 3 (लेखन में) विराम चिह्न।

stopper / 'स्टॉपर् / noun (US **plug**) (बोतल की) डाट, काग।

stopwatch / 'स्टॉप्वाच् / noun दौड़ आदि का समय नापने के लिए घड़ी, विराम-घड़ी।

storage / 'स्टोरिज् / noun 1 संग्रहण 2 गोदाम 3 संग्रहण शुल्क: pay storage.

store / स्टॉर् / noun 1 सामान भंडार: have a good store of food in the house 2 नाना प्रकार का सामान बेचने वाली दुकान: a big department store 3 **stores** [pl] विशेष उद्देश्य के लिए या विशेष प्रकार का माल: medical/military stores 4 गोदाम, भंडारगृह: available from stores ■ **in store (for sb/sth)** 1 प्रयोग के लिए तैयार 2 आने वाला; होने वाला: I can see trouble in store. **set great store by sth** महत्त्व देना ‣ **store** verb 1 **store sth (up/away)** संचित करना, जमा करना/भरना: store information on computer 2 गोदाम में सुरक्षित रखना 3 **store sth (with sth)** भर देना, समाना: a mind well stored with facts.

storey (US **story**) / 'स्टोरि / noun (pl **storeys**; US **stories**) मंज़िल, तल्ला: an office block twenty storeys high.

stork / स्टॉर्क् / noun लक्कलक्क, एक प्रकार का सारसनुमा जलपक्षी।

storm / स्टॉर्म् / noun 1 आँधी-तूफ़ान: a thunderstorm 2 **storm (of sth)** तीव्र भावनाओं का आकस्मिक उद्गार: a storm of abuse/protest ■ **a storm in a teacup**; (US) **a tempest in a teapot** किसी बेकार की बात पर ग़ुस्सा होना/चिंता

करना **take sth/sb by storm** धावा बोलकर या हमला करके पकड़ लेना ▸ **storm** *verb* 1 **storm (at sb)** क्रोध में गरजना, आग-बबूला हो जाना 2 धावा बोलकर क़ब्ज़ा कर लेना, हमला करके पकड़ लेना : *Troops stormed (their way) into the city.* **stormy** *adj* (-ier, -iest) 1 तूफ़ानी : *a stormy night* 2 तीव्र भावनाओं से युक्त।

story¹ / 'स्टॉरि / *noun* (*pl* **stories**) 1 **story (about/of sb/sth)** क़िस्सा-कहानी : *stories of ancient Greece* 2 बीती घटनाओं का वर्णन 3 (**story-line** भी) नाटक, पुस्तक आदि की कथावस्तु : *Her novels always have the same basic story (-line).* 4 (अनौप) झूठ-मूठ की बातें : *Don't tell stories, Rina.* 5 समाचार लेख; ऐसे लेख के लिए उपयुक्त घटना/विषय।

story² / स्टॉरि / *noun* (*US*) = **storey**

stout / स्टाउट् / *adj* (-er, -est) 1 पक्का, मज़बूत : *stout walking shoes* 2 थोड़ा मोटा (व्यक्ति) 3 (औप) दृढ़ निश्चय और दिलेर : *a stout effort/defence* ▸ **stoutly** *adv* दृढ़ता से।

stove / स्टोव् / *noun* (मिट्टी या बिजली आदि का) स्टोव, अँगीठी।

stow / स्टो / *verb* **stow sth (away) (in sth)** सावधानी से सजा कर माल भरना : *stow clothes (away) in a trunk* ■ **stow away** जहाज़ में छिप कर बिना किराया दिए यात्रा करना : *stow away on a ship bound for New York* ▸ **stow-away** / 'स्टोअवे / *noun* छिप कर, बिना किराया दिए, यात्रा करने वाला व्यक्ति।

strafe / स्ट्राफ़्; *US* स्ट्रेफ़् / *verb* वायुयान द्वारा गोलियों या बमों से लगातार हमला करना : *strafe a beach.*

straggle / 'स्ट्रैगल् / *verb* 1 सहयात्रियों से पिछड़ जाना या अलग हो जाना, भटक जाना : *a few young children straggling along (behind their parents)*

2 अस्त-व्यस्त उगना, फैलना : *straggling hair/hedges.*

straight¹ / स्ट्रेट् / *adj* (-er, -est) 1 सीधी दिशा में, सरल रेखा में, बिना मोड़ का : *a straight line* 2 सीधा ('उलटा' के वैषम्य में) 3 व्यवस्थित; ठीक, साफ़-सुथरा : *It took hours to get the house straight.* 4 ईमानदार, सच्चा/निष्कपट : *give a straight answer to a straight question* 5 केवल दो स्पष्ट विकल्पों वाला, साधारण 6 एक के बाद एक; लगातार ▸ **straighten** / 'स्ट्रेट्न् / *verb* **straighten(sth) (up/out)** सीधा करना या होना : *straighten one's tie/skirt.*

straight² / स्ट्रेट् / *adv* 1 सीधी रेखा में; सीधा : *sit up straight* 2 सीधे मार्ग से : *come straight home* 3 ईमानदारी से, प्रत्यक्ष रूप से 4 लगातार, बिना रुके ■ **play straight (with sb)** ईमानदारी से पेश आना **straight away/off** तुरंत **straight on/in/out** बिना घुमाव-फिराव के : *I didn't ask him to tell me—he just came straight out with it.*

straightforward / स्ट्रेट्फ़ॉर्वई / *adj* 1 स्पष्टवादी, ईमानदार एवं सीधा-सादा : *be straightforward in one's business dealings* 2 आसान, सरल : *a straightforward question.*

strain¹ / स्ट्रेन् / *verb* 1 पूरी शक्ति लगा कर काम करना : *She spoke very quietly and I had to strain my ears to hear her.* 2 पूरी शक्ति लगा कर स्वयं को थका डालना; अत्यधिक प्रयास या कार्य से स्वयं को चोट पहुँचा लेना : *strain a muscle/one's heart* 3 स्वीकार्य या संभावना की सीमा तक या सीमा से बाहर ले जाना/होना : *The dispute has severely strained relations between the two countries.* 4 (द्रव को) कपड़े या जाली से छानना : *strain vegetables/tea* ■ **strain every nerve (to do sth)** यथासंभव सर्वाधिक प्रयास करना ▸ **strained** *adj*

1 (स्थिति) तनावपूर्ण, असामान्य : *Relations between the two families are rather strained.* 2 थका हुआ, चिंतित या उत्सुक 3 अस्वाभाविक/आयासजन्य : *a strained laugh* **strainer** *noun* चलनी/ छलनी।

strain² /स्ट्रेन्/ *noun* 1 घोर परिश्रम, थकान देने वाला प्रयास : *the stresses and strains of modern life* 2 तनाव, खिंचाव; चोट : *a groin strain* 3 मोच, क्षति 4 (प्राय: *pl*) राग/तान या लय : *hear the strains of church organ* 5 बोलने या लिखने का लहज़ा या शैली : *in a cheerful strain* 6 कस कर तने या खिंचे होने की अवस्था।

strain³ /स्ट्रेन्/ *noun* (प्राय: *sing*) **strain (of sth)** प्रवृत्ति : *There's a strain of madness in the family.*

strait /स्ट्रेट्/ *noun* 1 (प्राय: *pl*) (भूगोल में) जल संयोजी : *the Straits of Gibraltar* 2 **straits** [*pl*] मुसीबत/परेशानी: *be in serious financial straits.*

straitened / 'स्ट्रेट्न्ड् / *adj* तंगहाली/ ग़रीबी : *live in straitened circumstances.*

strait-jacket (straight jacket भी) / 'स्ट्रेट्जैकिट् / *noun* 1 जैकेट जैसा वस्त्र जिसकी लंबी बाँहें उग्र हो रहे व्यक्ति को नियंत्रण में लाने के लिए बाँध दी जाती हैं 2 (*अपमा*) वस्तु आदि जो किसी के विकास या बढ़त को रोके : *the strait-jacket of repressive taxation.*

strand¹ /स्ट्रैन्ड् / *verb* 1 जहाज़ का समुद्र तल से अड़ जाना, भूग्रस्त हो जाना; मछली, ह्वेल आदि का तट पर छूट जाना और समुद्र में न जा पाना : *The ship was stranded on a sandbank.* 2 किसी का असहाय स्थिति में छूट जाना/छोड़ दिया जाना : *I was stranded in a foreign country without a passport.* ▶ **stranded** *adj* असहाय, बेसवारी : *stranded tourists.*

strand² /स्ट्रैन्ड् / *noun* 1 धागे या तार की लड़ी/लड़ 2 एक अकेला बाल 3 किसी चीज़ के विभिन्न भाग या पहलू जिनसे संपूर्ण वस्तु बनती है : *drawing together the strands of the narrative.*

strange /स्ट्रेन्ज्/ *adj* (**-r, -st**) 1 अनोखा, निराला; समझने में मुश्किल : *He wears the strangest clothes.* 2 **strange (to sb)** जिसे पहले देखा/सुना/जाना न हो 3 थोड़ा बीमार/अस्वस्थ : *It was terribly hot and I started to feel strange.* 4 अजनबी महसूस करना : *She felt very strange among these people she had never met before.* ▶ **strangely** *adv* **strangeness** *noun.*

stranger / 'स्ट्रेन्जर् / *noun* अजनबी; बाहरी व्यक्ति : *Our dog barks at strangers.*

strangle / 'स्ट्रैङ्ग्ल् / *verb* 1 गला घोंट कर मार डालना, दम घोंटना : *He strangled her with her own scarf.* 2 विकास या कार्रवाई रोक देना : *The government's monetary policy is slowly strangling the economy.*

strangulation / ,स्ट्रैङ्ग्यु'लेश्न् / *noun* गला घोंटना/दम घुटना : *die of strangulation.*

strap / स्ट्रैप् / *noun* 1 पट्टा/फ़ीता : *an adjustable watch-strap* 2 **the strap** [*sing*] (पूर्व में) दंड देने के लिए पिटाई करने को प्रयुक्त चमड़े का फ़ीता ▶ **strap** *verb* 1 फ़ीता बाँधना 2 घाव आदि पर पट्टी बाँधना : *His injured arm was tightly strapped (up).*

strategic / स्ट्र 'टीजिक् / *adj* (**strategical** भी) 1 विशेष उद्देश्य के लिए तैयार योजना का हिस्सा : *a strategic approach/argument* 2 सामरिक महत्त्व का : *strategic forces* ▶ **strategically** *adv.*

strategy / 'स्ट्रैटिजि / *noun* (*pl* **strategies**) 1 विशेष उद्देश्य के लिए तैयार योजना : *devise economic strategies*

2 युद्धनीति, रण योजना : *defence strategies.*

straw / स्ट्रॉ / *noun* 1 पुआल 2 तिनका 3 ठंडे पेय पीने के लिए प्रयुक्त काग़ज़ या प्लास्टिक की पतली नलिका।

strawberry / 'स्ट्रॉबॅरि; US 'स्ट्रॉबेरि / *noun* (*pl* **strawberries**) स्ट्राबेरी।

stray / स्ट्रे / *verb* 1 पथ से विचलित हो जाना : *We strayed off the route because I didn't read the map correctly.* 2 विषय से हट जाना, विषयांतर करना : *My mind kept straying from the discussion (to other subjects).*
▸ **stray** *adj* 1 (घरेलू पशु) खोए हुए, बेघर 2 आकस्मिक, छुट-पुट, बिरला : *killed by a stray bullet.*

streak / स्ट्रीक / *noun* **streak (of sth)** 1 धारी, परत : *streaks of grey in her hair* 2 झुकाव (चरित्र में), पुट : *a streak of jealousy/cruelty* 3 सफलता या असफलता की लगातार चलती अवधि : *a streak of good luck* ▸ **streak** *verb* 1 **streak sth (with sth)** धारियों से अंकित करना 2 (अनौप) तीव्रता से गति करना : *She streaked away (from the rest) to win by several metres.*
streaky *adj* धारीदार।

stream / स्ट्रीम / *noun* 1 छोटी संकरी नदी 2 **stream (of sth/sb)** व्यक्तियों/वस्तुओं का तांता, प्रवाह : *a steady stream of traffic entering the city* ○ *a stream of telephone calls* 3 धारा, प्रवाह/बहने की दिशा : *drift along with the stream* ▸ **stream** *verb* 1 (द्रव की) धारा बह निकलना : *Sweat was streaming down his face.* 2 धारा/वायु में हिलना/हिलाना; मुक्त रूप से बहना।

streamline / 'स्ट्रीमलाइन / *verb* 1 किसी वस्तु को इस प्रकार से धारा-रेखित करना कि पानी या हवा के बहाव से कम प्रतिरोध उत्पन्न हो : *streamlined racing cars* 2 संबंधित कार्यप्रणालियों को सुधार कर

व्यवस्था/संस्था को अधिक प्रभावशाली बनाना।

street / स्ट्रीट / *noun* सड़क।

strength / स्ट्रेइथ् / *noun* 1 ताक़त, बल 2 भाव या मत की शक्ति : *the strength of public opinion/anger* 3 उपस्थित या उपलब्ध व्यक्तियों की संख्या : *What is the strength of the workforce?* 4 किसी व्यक्ति/चीज़ के गुण : *His strength as a manager lies in his ability to communicate.* ○ *the strengths and weaknesses of an argument* ■ **be at full/be below strength** ज़रूरत/ज़रूरत से कम संख्या में विशेषकर अनुभवी व्यक्ति उपलब्ध होना : *The team will be back at full strength for the next match.* **on the strength of sth** किसी के आधार पर, किसी के प्रभाव के कारण : *I got the job on the strength of your recommendation.* ▸ **strengthen** / 'स्ट्रेइ-थ्न् / *verb* और अधिक बलशाली बनाना/बनना : *take up swimming to strengthen your muscles.*

strenuous / 'स्ट्रे‌न्युअस् / *adj* 1 (कार्य) श्रमसाध्य : *strenuous work/exercise* 2 (व्यक्ति) भरपूर कोशिश के साथ; चुस्त : *a strenuous defender of government policies.*

stress / स्ट्रेस् / *noun* 1 दबाव, तनाव/ चिंता, तकलीफ़; इन सबका कारण : *suffer from stress* 2 **stress (on sth)** विशेष ज़ोर या महत्त्व : *She lays great stress on punctuality.* 3 बलाघात, स्वराघात (बोलते समय दिया गया बल) : *primary/ secondary stress* 4 **stress (on sth)** भौतिक बल जो किसी को तोड़/मोड़ दे : *a stress fracture of a bone* ▸ **stress** *verb* 1 विशेष ज़ोर या महत्त्व देना : *He stressed the importance of treating customers politely.* 2 स्वराघात डालना : *You stress the first syllable in 'happiness'.* **stressed** *adj*

stressed (out) मानसिक तनाव से ग्रस्त : *She has a heavy workload at the moment and is very stressed.*
stressful *adj* तनाव पैदा करने वाला : *She finds her new job very stressful.*

stretch¹ /स्ट्रेच्/ *verb* 1 खींच कर बढ़ाना, तानना या फैलाना; खिंच कर बढ़ना : *stretch a pair of gloves* 2 कसना, तानना : *The mooring rope was stretched tight.* 3 हाथ-पैर पसार कर लेटना; अँगड़ाई लेना : *He woke up, yawned and stretched.* 4 व्यापक रूप से फैलाना/फैलना 5 **stretch sth (out) (to sth)** किसी को प्रत्याशा से ज़्यादा देर तक काम में लाना, विशेषतः उसे सावधानी से प्रयोग में लाकर 6 स्वीकार्य सीमाओं या तर्कसंगत कारणों से अधिक किसी बात को ले जाना : *stretch the truth* ■ **stretch a point** विशिष्ट परिस्थितियों के कारण कुछ असामान्य होने देना/करना : *She was hoping they would stretch a point and allow her to stay in the hostel an extra week.* **stretch one's legs** व्यायाम या सैर के लिए जाना : *We stopped and got out of the car to stretch our legs.* **stretch (oneself) out** लेट कर आराम करना : *He stretched (himself) out on the sofa and fell asleep.*

stretch² /स्ट्रेच्/ *noun* 1 **stretch (of sth)** ज़मीन या पानी का क्षेत्र : *a beautiful stretch of countryside* 2 समय या दूरी का अविच्छिन्न फ़ासला, अवधि : *work in long stretches* 3 तनाव, खिंचाव/ अँगड़ाई : *stretch jeans* ■ **at a stretch** बिना रुके, निरंतर।

stretcher /स्ट्रैचर्/ *noun* स्ट्रैचर जिस पर मरीज़ को लिटाते हैं।

strew /स्ट्रू/ *verb* (*pt* **strewed**; *pp* **strewed** या **strewn** /स्ट्रून्/) 1 बिखेरना, छितराना : *strew papers over the floor* 2 बिखरा हुआ/छितरा हुआ होना : *Papers strewed the floor.*

stricken /'स्ट्रिकन्/ *adj* **stricken(by/with sth)** से आक्रांत या पीड़ित : *grief-/panic-/poverty-/terror-stricken.*

strict /स्ट्रिक्ट्/ *adj* (**-er, -est**) 1 सख़्त, अतिनियमनिष्ठ; तुरंत आज्ञाकारिता चाहने वाला : *a strict teacher* 2 जिसका पालन किया जाए; नियम/विश्वास का पालन करने वाला : *a strict Catholic* 3 सुपरिभाषित अथवा सीमित : *a strict interpretation* ▶ **strictly** *adv* 1 सख़्ती से : *be strictly brought up* 2 बिलकुल; हर परिस्थिति में : *Smoking is strictly forbidden.* 3 **strictly for sb/sth** केवल किसी वस्तु/व्यक्ति के लिए : *an area reserved strictly for members* 4 बिलकुल, पूर्णतया : *do only work that is strictly necessary* ■ **strictly speaking** एकदम सही होना : *Strictly speaking, he's not qualified for the job.*

stride /स्ट्राइड्/ *verb* (*pt* **strode**) 1 लंबे डग भरना : *stride along the road* 2 **stride across/over sth** लाँघना : *stride over a ditch* ▶ **stride** *noun* 1 एक लंबा क़दम, डग : *He reached the door in three strides.* 2 प्रगति की ओर अग्रसर करने वाली वस्तु : *Great strides have recently been made towards world peace.* ■ **make great strides** तीव्र प्रगति करना **take sth in one's stride** किसी नई/मुश्किल परिस्थिति का आसानी से या चिंतामुक्त होकर सामना करना : *Some people find retirement stressful, but he has taken it all in his stride.*

strife /स्ट्राइफ़्/ *noun* अनबन; संघर्ष : *a nation torn by political strife.*

strike¹ /स्ट्राइक्/ *noun* 1 हड़ताल : *a miners' strike* 2 अचानक का हमला : *air/nuclear strikes.*

strike² /स्ट्राइक्/ *verb* (*pt, pp* **struck**

/ स्ट्रक् /) 1 मारना, प्रहार करना 2 **strike at sb/sth** किसी को प्रहार का निशाना बनाना 3 अचानक हमला करना : *The lion crouched ready to strike.* 4 (विचार) सूझना, अचानक मन में आना : *An awful thought has just struck me.* 5 (विपत्ति, बीमारी) अचानक आना और हानि पहुँचाना: *The area was struck by an outbreak of cholera.* 6 **strike sb as sth** किसी विशेष तरह का प्रभाव छोड़ना : *The plan strikes me as ridiculous.* 7 (कर्मचारियों का) हड़ताल करना, काम छोड़ देना : *The union has voted to strike for a pay increase of 10%.* 8 (माचिस की तीली) रगड़ कर जलाना 9 समय बताने के लिए घड़ी का बजना : *The clock struck ten.* 10 कुंजी/लीवर आदि बजाकर संगीतमय ध्वनि उत्पन्न करना 11 पता लगाना; पाना : *strike a rich vein of ore* 12 सिक्के ढालना ■ **strike a balance (between A and B)** दो परम स्थितियों के बीच का मार्ग ढूढना : *It was difficult to strike the right balance between justice and expediency.* **strike a bargain (with sb)** समझौता करना **strike fear etc into sb's heart** मन में डर आदि की भावना पैदा करना **strike out (for/towards sth)** दृढ़तापूर्वक और तेज़ी से चलना **strike sth off/ out** रेखा खींच कर काट देना **strike up sth (with sb)** बातचीत, संबंध शुरू करना।

striker / 'स्ट्राइकर् / *noun* 1 हड़ताली कार्यकर्ता 2 (फुटबाल में) गोल करने वाला खिलाड़ी।

striking / 'स्ट्राइकिङ् / *adj* असाधारण, प्रभावशाली/आकर्षक : *striking colours/ images* ▸ **strikingly** *adv.*

string¹ / स्ट्रिङ् / *noun* 1 डोरी, फीता 2 लड़ी, माला; पंक्ति, शृंखला : *a string of beads/small lakes* 3 तंत्री, तार (जैसे वायलिन या गिटार का तार) 4 धनुष की प्रत्यंचा; रैकेट की डोरी : *break a string*

■ **with no strings attached** (अनौप) बिना किसी शर्तों या नियमों के : *an offer of Rs 250 crore in aid with no strings attached* ▸ **stringy** *adj* डोरी के समान : *lank stringy hair.*

string² / स्ट्रिङ् / *verb* (*pt, pp* **strung** / स्ट्रङ् /) 1 **string sth (up)** रस्सी या डोरी से लटकाना या बाँधना 2 **string sth (together)** माला पिरोना : (अल) *carbon atoms strung together to form giant molecules* 3 धनुष की प्रत्यंचा चढ़ाना, रैकेट में डोरी लगाना : *a loosely/ tightly strung squash racket.*

stringent / 'स्ट्रिन्जन्ट् / *adj* (औप) 1 (क़ानून, नियम आदि) सख्त, कड़ा, जिसका पालन करना ज़रूरी हो : *stringent controls/standards/regulations* 2 (वित्तीय अवस्था) तंगी के कारण मुश्किल : *a stringent economic climate* ▸ **stringency** *noun* : *in these days of financial stringency* **stringently** *adv.*

strip¹ / स्ट्रिप् / *verb* (-pp-) 1 **strip sth (from/off sth/sb); strip sth/sb (of sth); strip sth (away)** आवरण उतारना, निरावृत करना : *strip paint off an old pine chest* 2 किसी स्थान से सब चीज़ें हटा लेना और ख़ाली छोड़ देना : *Thieves stripped the house bare.* 3 **strip (down) (to sth); strip (off)** कपड़े उतारना 4 **strip sb of sth** किसी को उसकी संपत्ति आदि से वंचित करना, छीनना/ पदच्युत करना : *The general was stripped of his rank.* ▸ **strip** *noun* (अक्सर *sing*) कपड़े उतारने की क्रिया, विशेषत: दर्शकों के सामने : *do a strip.*

strip² / स्ट्रिप् / *noun* पट्टी, धज्जी।

stripe / स्ट्राइप् / *noun* 1 धारी : *the tiger's stripes* 2 (सैनिकों/पुलिस अफ़सरों के पद का सूचक) प्राय: V-आकार का चिह्न : *How many stripes are there on a sergeant's sleeve?*

strive / स्ट्राइव् / verb (pt **strove** / स्ट्रोव्/ या **strived**; pp **striven** / 'स्ट्रि-ल्/) (और) 1 strive (for/after sth) प्रयास करना, पाने के लिए संघर्ष करना : strive for success 2 strive (against sb/sth) किसी के विरुद्ध संघर्ष करना : strive against oppression ▸ **striv-ing** noun.

stroke[1]/स्ट्रोक्/noun 1 (खेल में) (रैकेट, बल्ले आदि की) मार : play a forehand stroke 2 कलम, ब्रश आदि के प्रयोग से बना निशान : paint with bold strokes 3 घंटी या घड़ी की टनटन की ध्वनि : on the stroke of three 4 नियमित, बार-बार होने वाला (हाथ का) संचालन, जैसे तैरने या नाव खेने में : long, powerful strokes 5 a stroke (of sth) एक सफल और प्रभावशाली घटना/क्रिया 6 प्रहार, आघात : six strokes of the cane 7 थपथपाना, थपकी : give the cat a stroke 8 (चिकि॰) पक्षाघात, फ़ालिज का दौरा।

stroke[2] / स्ट्रोक् / verb 1 थपथपाना : stroke a pet 2 (गेंद आदि को) मारना।

stroll / स्ट्रोल् / verb टहलना, सैर करना : strolling around (in) the park ▸ **stroll** noun सैर।

strong /स्ट्रॉङ्/ adj (-er, -est) 1 (व्यक्ति या पशु) हष्ट-पुष्ट, सुस्वस्थ, बलवान : He's strong enough to lift a piano on his own. 2 शक्तिशाली : a strong push 3 मज़बूत, पक्का/टिकाऊ : a strong stick/rope 4 तीव्र; अच्छी मात्रा से युक्त : a strong smell of gas 5 (भावनाएँ, विचार या मत) तीव्र रूप से अनुभव या व्यक्त : I had a strong impression that someone was following me. 6 मन और ज्ञानेंद्रियों पर पर्याप्त प्रभाव डालने वाला; प्रभावशाली : a strong leader/personality 7 (संबंध) प्रगाढ़, घनिष्ठ : a strong marriage 8 काफ़ी संख्या में : A strong turnout is expected at the election. 9 (अंकों के बाद प्रयुक्त) व्यक्तियों की विशेष संख्या का होना : a five thousand strong army ■ be strong on sth 1 किसी कार्य में अच्छा होना : I'm not very strong on dates. 2 किसी विषय पर अनेक विचार होना; किसी चीज़ पर केंद्रित होना : The report is strong on criticism but short on practical suggestions. **going strong** (अनौप॰) किसी कार्य को उत्साहपूर्वक जारी रखना; स्वस्थ बने रहना : The Kenyan runner is still going strong on the last lap. ▸ **strongly** adv.

stronghold /'स्ट्रॉङ्होल्ड्/ noun क़िला, केंद्र; प्रभाव क्षेत्र : guerrilla strong-holds in the mountains.

structure /'स्ट्रक्चर्/ noun 1 बनावट, रचना : the structure of the human body 2 भवन; ढाँचा या प्रमुख अवयव : a single-storey structure ▸ **structure** verb रचना करना; योजना बनाना : an intelligently structured essay **structural** adj ढाँचा-विषयक, संरचना-त्मक : structural alterations to a building.

struggle / 'स्ट्रग्ल् / verb 1 struggle (for sth); struggle (to do sth) कुछ पाने के लिए संघर्ष करना, कोशिश करना : struggle for political recognition 2 हाथ-पैर मारना, मुश्किल से रास्ता बनाना : He struggled up the hill with his heavy shopping-bags. 3 struggle (against/with sth/sb) अप्रिय घटना को रोकना, समस्या से जूझना : struggle against corruption within the party ▸ **struggle** noun 1 संघर्ष, कड़ा मुक़ाबला 2 हाथापाई, लड़ाई 3 कठिन काम।

strum / स्ट्रम् / verb (-mm-) strum (on sth) सहज रूप से कोई वाद्ययंत्र बजाना : strumming (on) my guitar.

strut[1] / स्ट्रट् / noun लकड़ी या धातु की टेक।

strut² / स्ट्रट् / verb (-tt-) (प्राय: अप्रा) अकड़ कर चलना : *She strutted past us, ignoring our greeting.*

stub / स्टब् / noun 1 पेंसिल, सिगरेट आदि का अंतिम बहुत छोटा अंश (जो काम में न आने के कारण फेंक दिया जाता है) 2 चेक, टिकट आदि का वह छोटा हिस्सा जो किसी के पास रह जाता है, बड़ा हिस्सा दे देने के बाद ▸ **stub** verb (-bb-) **stub sth (against/on sth)** ठोकर खाना (विशेषत: पैर के अँगूठे में) : *I've stubbed my toe (on a rock).*

stubble / स्टब्ल / noun 1 फ़सल काट लिए जाने पर खेत में खड़ी नीचे की खूँटी : *a ban on burning stubble* 2 दाढ़ी के कड़े छोटे बाल : *three day's stubble on his chin* ▸ **stubbly** adj.

stubborn / स्टब़र्न् / adj 1 (प्राय: अप्रा) ज़िद्दी, अड़ियल : *be too stubborn to apologize* 2 दूर करने, बदलने, हटाने में मुश्किल : *a stubborn cough that has lasted for weeks* ▸ **stubbornly** adv **stubbornness** noun.

stubby / स्टबि / adj (-ier, -iest) छोटा और मोटा, ठूँठ जैसा : *stubby fingers.*

stud / स्टड् / noun 1 नाक/कान की कील (एक आभूषण) : *diamond studs in her ears;* दुहरे सिरे का बटन 2 बेल्ट आदि में लगाने की जड़ाऊ कील; जूतों के तले में लगाए जाने वाले चौड़े काँटे : *screw-in studs for football boots* ▸ **stud** verb (-dd-) ▪ **stud sth (with sth)** मूल्यवान नगों आदि से सतह को सजाना : *a studded leather belt.*

student / स्ट्यूड्न्ट; US स्टूड्न्ट् / noun 1 छात्र, विद्यार्थी 2 **student of sth** (औप) किसी विषय आदि का विश्लेषण करने वाला या उसमें गहन रुचि रखने वाला : *a keen student of current affairs.*

studio / स्ट्यूडिओ; US स्टूडिओ / noun (pl **studios**) 1 रेडियो, टी वी कार्यक्रम रिकॉर्ड करने या प्रसारित करने का कमरा 2 फ़िल्म बनाने का स्थान, स्टूडिओ 3 चित्रकार, फ़ोटोग्राफ़र आदि की कार्यशाला 4 संगीत या ध्वनि कार्यक्रम रिकॉर्ड करने के सभी उपकरणों से सज्जित कमरा : *a recording studio.*

studious / स्ट्यूडिअस; US स्टूडिअस / adj अध्ययनशील, मेहनती : *a studious child.*

study¹ / स्टडि / noun (pl **studies**) 1 अध्ययन करना, कुछ सीखने या नई बात पता लगाने के लिए पढ़ना : *devote one's spare time to study* 2 **studies** [pl] कॉलेज या विश्वविद्यालय में औपचारिक अध्ययन : *return to one's studies after illness* 3 परीक्षण, जाँच : *The proposals deserve careful study.* 4 घर में पढ़ने-लिखने का कमरा।

study² / स्टडि / verb (pt, pp **studied**) 1 अध्ययन करना : *study at Delhi University* 2 जाँच करना, परीक्षण करना : *study the map/menu/proposal.*

stuff¹ / स्टफ़् / noun 1 (अनौप) पदार्थ, सामान, सामग्री; वस्तुएँ; क्रियाएँ आदि : *What's that brown stuff on your jacket? ○ Leave your stuff in the hall. ○ I like canoeing, wind surfing and stuff like that.* 2 (औप) किसी वस्तु का सर्वाधिक महत्त्वपूर्ण लक्षण या गुण : *We must find out what (kind of) stuff he is made of.*

stuff² / स्टफ़् / verb 1 **stuff A (up) (with B)** ठूस कर भरना : *stuff envelopes* 2 **stuff oneself/sb (with sth)** (अनौप) ठूस-ठूस कर खाना/खिलाना 3 **stuff sth (with sth)** चिकन या सब्ज़ी आदि में मसाला भरना 4 पशु-पक्षी की खाल में सामान/पदार्थ आदि भरना (संग्रहालय में रखने के लिए) : *a stuffed tiger/owl* ▸ **stuffing** / स्टफ़िङ् / noun 1 चिकन, सब्ज़ी आदि में भरा गया मसाला 2 तकिया, खिलौने आदि में भरने का सामान।

stuffy / स्टफ़ि / adj (-ier, -iest) 1 (कमरा

आदि) घुटन भरा : *a stuffy room/ atmosphere* 2 (अनौप, अपमा) अति औपचारिक एवं रुचिहीन : *a stuffy news-paper.*

stumble / 'स्टम्बल् / *verb* 1 stumble (over sth) ठोकर खाना (और लगभग गिरना) : *stumbled over a tree root* 2 stumble (over sth/through sth) बोलने या संगीत बजाने आदि में ग़लतियाँ करना 3 लड़खड़ाना : *stumbling around in the dark* ■ stumble across/on/ upon sb/sth संयोग से, सहसा ही कुछ ढूँढ़ लेना, मिल जाना : *Police investigating tax fraud stumbled across a drugs ring.* ▸ stumbling-block *noun* stumbling-block (to sth) अड़ँगा, ठोकर; बाधा।

stump¹ / स्टम्प् / *noun* 1 पेड़ का ठूँठ 2 मुख्य भाग के कट जाने/टूट जाने के बाद बचा गौण अंश : *the stump of a pencil/ tooth* 3 (क्रिकेट में) डंडा, स्टंप।

stump² / स्टम्प् / *verb* 1 (अनौप) चकरा देना, बहुत कठिन होना : *Everybody was stumped by the problem.* 2 अकड़ कर या आवाज़ करते हुए चलना : *He stumped out (of the room) in fury.* 3 (क्रिकेट में) खिलाड़ी को स्टंप पर गेंद लगा कर (जब वह क्रीज़ से बाहर हो) आउट कर देना।

stumpy / 'स्टम्पि / *adj* छोटा और मोटा।

stun / स्टन् / *verb* (-nn-) 1 बेहोश कर देना, सिर पर मारकर या सिर पर आघात लगने से : *The fall stunned me for a moment.* 2 हक्का-बक्का कर देना/हो जाना : *be stunned into silence* 3 किसी को अत्यंत प्रभावित करना : *stunned by her beauty* ▸ stunning *adj* अति आकर्षक; सुंदर; प्रभावशाली; चकित कर देने वाला : *You look stunning in that dress.* ○ *a stunning achievement.*

stunt¹ / स्टन्ट् / *noun* 1 (कभी-कभी अपमा) (ध्यानाकर्षण के लिए किया)

असामान्य कार्य, करतब : *It was just a publicity stunt.* 2 ख़तरनाक या कठिन काम, कमाल : *a stunt pilot.*

stunt² / स्टन्ट् / *verb* विकास या वृद्धि रोक देना : *stunted trees.*

stupefy / 'स्ट्यूपिफ़ाइ; *US* स्टूपिफ़ाइ / *verb* (*pt, pp* stupefied) stupefy sb (with sth) 1 जड़ कर देना, स्तंभित/विस्मित कर देना : *I was stupefied by what I read.* 2 सोचने में असमर्थ कर देना, सुन्न कर देना : *be stupefied with drink* ▸ stupefaction / स्ट्यूपि फ़ैक्शन्; *US* स्टूपि फ़ैक्शन्; / *noun.*

stupendous / स्ट्यू पेन्डस; *US* स्टू पेन्डस् / *adj* अत्यधिक विस्मयकारक; अति महान या विशाल : *a stupendous mis-take/appetite* ▸ stupendously *adv.*

stupid / 'स्ट्यूपिड; *US* 'स्टूपिड / *adj* (-er, -est) 1 नासमझ, अल्पबुद्धि; मूर्ख 2 (अनौप) बेकार; (किसी की महत्त्वहीनता दिखाने के लिए प्रयुक्त) : *This stupid car won't start.* ▸ stupidity *noun* मूर्खता; मूर्खता-पूर्ण काम/ग़लती stupidly *adv.*

stupor / 'स्ट्यूपर; *US* 'स्टूपर / *noun* [*sing*] आघात, मादक द्रव्य आदि से लगभग चेतना-शून्यता; जड़ता/व्यामोह : *in a drunken stupor.*

sturdy / 'स्टर्डि / *adj* (-ier, -iest) 1 मज़बूत, ठोस : *a sturdy chair/frame* 2 स्वस्थ, तंदरुस्त : *a sturdy child* 3 सु-निश्चित, दृढ़, टिकाऊ : *sturdy resist-ance to the plan* ▸ sturdiness *noun.*

stutter / 'स्टटर् / *verb* 1 हकलाना 2 (गाड़ी/ इंजिन का) मुश्किल से चालू होना।

sty / स्टाइ / *noun* (*pl* sties या styes) 1 सूअर-बाड़ा, गंदी जगह 2 (stye भी) पलक पर निकली फुंसी, अंजनहारी।

style / स्टाइल् / *noun* 1 विशिष्ट ढंग : *a comedian with his own very per-sonal style* 2 बनावट, आकृति (कपड़ों आदि की); फ़ैशन : *the latest styles in* *dresses, shoes, swimwear* 3 प्रचलित या सुरुचिपूर्ण विशेषता : *Her house is furnished in the latest style.* 4 लेखन-शैली : *make a study of Dickens's style* 5 *(औप)* व्यक्ति को संबोधित करने की शैली (शीर्षक या पद नाम) ▸ **style** *verb* 1 विशेष शैली, आकृति में बनाना : *have one's hair styled* 2 *(औप)* विशेष नाम या शीर्षक से वर्णन करना : *The country styles itself 'People's Democratic Republic'.*

stylish / 'स्टाइलिश् / *adj* सुरुचिपूर्ण, फ़ैशनेबल : *stylish clothes/furniture.*

stylus / 'स्टाइलस् / *noun (pl* **styluses)** ग्रामोफ़ोन से साथ जुड़ी सख़्त, नुकीली सूई।

suave / स्वाव् / *adj* (कभी-कभी *अपमा)* (सामान्यत: पुरुषों के लिए) देखने या व्यवहार में आत्मविश्वासपूर्ण और शिष्ट ▸ **suavely** *adv* **suavity** *noun.*

sub- *pref (उपसर्ग)* 1 (पद या संगठन के पूर्व) उप-, अनु-, अवर/कनिष्ठ : *sub-lieutenant/sub post office* 2 (कुछ-कुछ) अल्प, लगभग : *subtropical* ○ *substandard* ○ *subnormal* 3 से नीचे, अव- : *subzero.*

subconscious / ,सब्'कॉन्शस् / *adj* अवचेतन, ऐसी मानसिक क्रियाएँ जिनकी पूरी जानकारी नहीं हो पाती है : *subconscious desires/urges/fears.*

subcontinent / ,सब्'कॉन्टिनन्ट् / *noun* उपमहाद्वीप, महाद्वीप का भाग : *the Indian subcontinent.*

subdivide / 'सब्डिवाइड्; ,सब्डि'व्राइड् / *verb* **subdivide (sth) (into sth)** और आगे विभाजन करना, उपविभाजन करना : *The religious group subdivided into a number of smaller sects.* ▸ **subdivision** *noun.*

subdue / सब्'ड्यू; *US* सब्'डू / *verb* 1 हराना, नियंत्रण में लाना : *subdue the rebels* 2 (भावनाएँ आदि) शांत करना, मंद

करना : *unable to subdue a mounting sense of excitement.*

subject¹ / 'सब्जिक्ट्; 'सब्जेक्ट् / *noun* 1 चर्चा/वर्णन का विषय (व्यक्ति या वस्तु) : *an unpleasant subject of conversation* 2 अध्ययन का विषय : *Physics and chemistry are my favourite subjects.* 3 चित्र या फ़ोटोग्राफ़ का मुख्य या विशेष मद : *Focus the camera on the subject.* 4 *(व्या)* कर्ता 5 प्रजा : *a British/French subject* ▸ **subject-matter** *noun* कोई विषय, मामला आदि जिस पर कोई पुस्तक, फ़िल्म आदि आधारित हो : *the controversial subject-matter of his latest film.*

subject² / 'सब्जेक्ट्; 'सब्जिक्ट् / *adj* 1 **subject to sth** जिसके होने या प्रभावित होने की संभावना हो : *The timetable is subject to alteration.* 2 **subject to sth** शर्त पर, निर्भर : *sold subject to contract* 3 **subject to sth/sb** अधीन : *We are all subject to the law of the land.* 4 पराधीन, परतंत्र (राज्य या राष्ट्र)।

subject³ / सब्'जेक्ट् / *verb* 1 **subject sb/sth to sth** अनुभव कराना, भुक्तभोगी बनाना : *subject sb to ridicule/torture* 2 अपने अधीन करना ▸ **subjection** *noun* अधीनीकरण; पराधीनता : *the city's frequent subjection to bombing raids.*

subjective / सब्'जेक्टिव् / *adj* 1 (कभी-कभी *अपमा)* व्यक्तिगत पसंद या विचारों पर आधारित : *a highly subjective comment/description* 2 (विचार, भाव या अनुभव) मन या चित्त में बसा हुआ, न कि बाहरी कारणों से उत्पन्न : *Our perception of things is often influenced by subjective factors, such as tiredness.* ▸ **subjectively** *adv.*

sub judice / ,सब्'जूडिस; ,सब्'जूडसे / *adj (लैटिन)* (क़ानूनी मुक़दमा) न्यायालय

में विचाराधीन, इसलिए सार्वजनिक चर्चा के दायरे से बाहर।

subjugate / 'सब्जुगेट् / verb (औप) किसी पर क़ाबू पाना; किसी को हराना, नियंत्रण में लाना ▸ **subjugation** noun.

sublet / सब्'लेट् / verb (-tt-; pt, pp **sublet**) किरायेदार द्वारा मकान आदि का भाग किसी अन्य व्यक्ति को किराए पर देना : *sublet a room to a friend.*

sublime / स'ब्लाइम् / adj 1 (प्राय: साहि) महान, उदात्त; लोकोत्तर : *sublime beauty* 2 (प्राय: अपमा) अत्यधिक आत्मविश्वास दिखाते हुए और परिणामों की चिंता न करते हुए; परम : *He shows sublime indifference to the sufferings of others.*

submarine/ सब्मं'रीन्; 'सब्मरीन्/ noun पनडुब्बी (जहाज़) ▸ **submarine** adj (औप या तक) समुद्र की सतह के नीचे (स्थित अथवा कार्य करने वाला) : *a submarine cable.*

submerge / सब्'मर्ज् / verb 1 पानी की सतह के नीचे जाना; पानी के भीतर डालना : *a road submerged by flood water* 2 आँखों से ओझल हो जाना; पूरी तरह छिपना/छुपाना : *The main argument was submerged in a mass of tedious detail.*

submission / सब्'मिश्न् / noun **submission (to sb/sth)** 1 प्रस्तुतीकरण : *the submission of a claim* 2 हार की स्वीकृति, समर्पण : *a gesture of submission.*

submissive / सब्'मिसिव् / adj **submissive (to sb)** दब्बू; विनम्र; अति आज्ञाकारी : *a submissive daughter.*

submit / सब्'मिट् / verb (-tt-) 1 **submit sth (to sb/ sth) (for sth)** विचारार्थ प्रस्तुत करना : *submit an application* 2 (क़ानून) सुझाव देना/तर्क देना : *Counsel for the defence submitted that his client was clearly innocent.* 3 **submit (oneself) (to sb/sth)** दूसरे

की अधीनता स्वीकार कर लेना, आत्मसमर्पण कर देना, झुक जाना : *submit to one's opponent.*

subnormal / सब्'नॉर्म्ल् / adj सामान्य स्तर से कम बुद्धि, ज्ञानशक्ति का।

subordinate / स'बॉर्डिनट् / adj 1 **subordinate (to sb)** मातहत, अधीनस्थ (कर्मचारी) 2 **subordinate (to sth)** गौण, कम महत्त्वपूर्ण : *All other issues are subordinate to this one.* ▸ **subordinate** noun मातहत (व्यक्ति) : *delegate work to one's subordinates* **subordinate** verb **subordinate sth (to sth)** अधीनस्थ करना, कम महत्त्व का मानना : *fears that safety considerations were being subordinated to commercial interests.*

subscribe / सब्'स्क्राइब् / verb 1 **subscribe (to sth)** अग्रिम राशि का भुगतान कर पत्र-पत्रिकाओं का नियमित ग्राहक बनना 2 **subscribe (for) sth** (वाणिज्य) शेयर ख़रीदने के लिए आवेदन करना 3 **subscribe (sth) (to sth)** चंदा देना : *subscribe to a charity* ■ **subscribe to sth** (औप) समर्थन करना, (विचार/सिद्धांत का) अनुमोदन करना : *Do you subscribe to her pessimistic view of the state of the economy?* ▸ **subscriber** noun **subscription** / सब्'स्क्रिप्श्न् / noun 1 चंदा 2 ग्राहक चंदा।

subsequent / 'सब्सिक्वन्ट् / adj परवर्ती, बाद का : *Subsequent events proved me wrong.* ▸ **subsequently** adv बाद में : *They subsequently heard he had left the country.* **subsequent to** prep (औप) के बाद : *There have been further developments subsequent to our meeting.*

subservient / सब्'सर्विअन्ट् / adj **subservient (to sb/sth)** 1 (प्राय: अपमा) अत्यधिक सम्मान देते हुए 2 कम महत्त्वपूर्ण ▸ **subservience** noun.

subside / सब्'साइड़ / *verb* 1 (क्रोध आदि) शांत हो जाना, घट जाना, तेज़ हवा मंद पड़ जाना : *The storm began to subside.* 2 (पानी) उतर जाना 3 (भूमि का) धँस जाना; (भवन का) ज़मीन में धँस जाना : *Weak foundations caused the house to subside.* 4 (अनौप, परि) (कुर्सी पर) गिर जाना ▸ **subsidence** *noun.*

subsidiary / सब्'सिडिअरि; US सब् 'सिडिएरि / *adj* 1 **subsidiary (to sth)** सहायक, पूरक : *a subsidiary question/subject* 2 (व्यापारिक कंपनी) किसी अन्य से नियंत्रित ▸ **subsidiary** *noun (pl* **subsidiaries)** व्यापारिक कंपनी जो किसी अन्य कंपनी द्वारा नियंत्रित हो : *our Italian subsidiary.*

subsidy / 'सब्सडि / *noun (pl* **subsidies)** आर्थिक सहायता (उन संगठनों को जो आत्मनिर्भर नहीं हो पाए हैं) : *agricultural subsidies* ▸ **subsidize, -ise** / 'सब्सिडाइज़् / *verb* आर्थिक सहायता देना : *Lunch for employees is subsidized by the Company.*

subsist / सब्'सिस्ट् / *verb* 1 **subsist (on sth)** (औप) जीवित रहना, विशेषत: बहुत कम पूँजी या खाद्य पदार्थ के साथ : *He subsisted mainly on vegetables and fruit.* 2 (औप) जीवित रहना जारी रहना, अस्तित्व बनाए रखना : *This pattern of industry still subsists in certain countries.* ▸ **subsistence** / सब्'सिस्टन्स् / *noun* जीविका, जीविकोपार्जन/जीवित रहने का साधन : *subsistence farming.*

substance / 'सब्स्टन्स् / *noun* 1 पदार्थ, तत्त्व : *a poisonous substance* 2 वास्तविक भौतिक तत्त्व : *They maintained that ghosts had no substance.* 3 अर्थ, सारतत्त्व : *the substance of the speech* 4 अहमियत;

महत्त्व 5 (औप) धन-संपत्ति : *a man/woman of substance.*

substandard / ,सब्'स्टैन्डड़् / *adj* सामान्य या आवश्यक मान्य या मापदंड से नीचे होना : *substandard goods.*

substantial / सब्'स्टैन्श्ल् / *adj* 1 मात्रा या क़ीमत में बड़ा/विशाल : *a substantial improvement* 2 मज़बूत, ठोस एवं बड़ा : *a substantial house* 3 वास्तविक; महत्त्वपूर्ण विषयों के सारतत्त्व से संबंधित : *We are in substantial agreement.* ▸ **substantially** *adv.*

substantiate / सब्'स्टैन्शिएट् / *verb* (औप) दावे, वक्तव्य आदि को प्रमाणित या सिद्ध करना : *Can you substantiate your accusations against him?*

substitute / 'सब्स्टिट्यूट्; US 'सब्स्टि टूट् / *noun* **substitute (for sb/sth)** एवज़ी, स्थानापन्न : *a substitute teacher/player* ▸ **substitute** *verb* **substitute for sb/sth** स्थानापन्न करना : *Can you substitute for me at the meeting?* **substitution** / सब्स्टि'ट्यूश्न्; US ,सब्स्टि'टूश्न् / *noun* प्रतिस्थापन, स्थानापत्ति; बदलाव।

subterranean / ,सब्ट'रेनिअन् / *adj* भूमिगत, भूगर्भगत : *a subterranean passage.*

subtitle / 'सब्टाइट्ल् / *noun* 1 किताब का गौण या अतिरिक्त शीर्षक 2 (प्राय: *pl*) लिखित शब्द जो फ़िल्म के संवाद को दूसरी भाषा में अनूदित करते हैं और चित्रपट के निचले भाग पर प्रकट होते हैं।

subtle / 'सट्ल् / *adj* (-**r**, -**st**) 1 सूक्ष्म, महीन; रहस्यमय : *a subtle charm/flavour* 2 चतुर रूप से व्यवस्थित, जटिल/दुर्बोध : *a subtle argument/design* 3 कुशाग्रबुद्धि : *a subtle observer/critic* ▸ **subtlety** / 'सट्ल्टि / *noun* **subtly** *adv.*

subtract / सब्'ट्रैक्ट् / *verb* **subtract**

sth (from sth) संख्या घटाना : *subtract 6 from 9* ▶ **subtraction** *noun*.

suburb / 'सबर्ब / *noun* उपनगर (नगर की बाहरी बस्तियाँ आदि) ▶ **suburban** / स 'बर्बन् / *adj* उपनगरीय, उपनगर विषयक : *suburban street/shop.*

subversive / सब्'वर्सिव् / *adj* उच्छेदक, विनाशक : *subversive activities/ propaganda* ▶ **subversively** *adv* **subversiveness** *noun*.

subvert / सब्'वर्ट / *verb* 1 राजनीतिक व्यवस्था, धर्म आदि के प्राधिकरण को नष्ट करना/समाप्त करने की कोशिश करना : *punish attempts to subvert public order* 2 किसी को उसकी निष्ठा/नैतिक मूल्यों से विश्वासघात कराना : *a diplomat subverted by a foreign power* ▶ **subversion** *noun*.

subway / 'सब्वे / *noun* 1 सुरंग-पथ 2 (US) भूमिगत रेलवे : *a subway train/ station.*

succeed / सक्'सीड् / *verb* 1 **succeed (in sth/doing sth)** कुछ करने में/प्राप्त करने में सफल होना : *Our plan succeeded.* 2 परवर्ती होना : *Who succeeded Kennedy?* 3 **succeed (to sth)** उत्तराधिकारी होना 4 कामयाब होना, अच्छा परिणाम पाना ■ **nothing succeeds like success** (कहा) सफलता अतिरिक्त सफलताओं का मार्ग बनती है।

success / सक्'सेस् / *noun* 1 सफलता, कामयाबी : *He's hoping to make a success of the business.* 2 सफल व्यक्ति : *be a success as a teacher* ▶ **successful** *adj*.

succession / सक्'सेशन् / *noun* 1 अनु-क्रमण : *a succession of poor leaders* 2 अनुक्रम, सिलसिला : *the succession of the seasons* 3 उत्तराधिकार ■ **in succession** लगातार, उत्तरोत्तर, क्रमश:।

successive / सक्'सेसिव् / *adj* क्रमिक :

successive governments ▶ **successively** *adv*.

successor / सक्'सेसर् / *noun* **successor (to sb/sth)** उत्तराधिकारी : *appoint a successor to the presidency.*

succinct / सक्'सिङ्क्ट् / *adj* संक्षिप्त और स्पष्ट रूप से व्यक्त किया गया : *His speech was short and succinct.* ▶ **succinctly** *adv* **succinctness** *noun*.

succumb / स'कम् / *verb* **succumb (to sth)** (औप) (प्रलोभन के सामने) झुक जाना; (बीमारी से) हार मान लेना, मर जाना : *The driver later succumbed to his injuries.*

such / सच् / *det* 1 ऐसा, इस प्रकार का : *Such a disaster as this had never happened before.* 2 इतना अधिक : *She's got such talent.* ▶ **such** *pron* ऐसा व्यक्ति/वस्तु : *Cricket was boring. Such was her opinion before meeting Ravi.* ■ **as such** यथार्थ : *The new job is not a promotion as such but it has good prospects.* **such as** जैसे, उदाहरण के लिए : *Wild flowers such as orchids and primroses are becoming rare.*

suck / सक् / *verb* 1 चूसना 2 द्रव की चुसकी लेना : *suck the juice from an orange* 3 किसी व्यक्ति/वस्तु को दिशा-विशेष में बलपूर्वक खींचना ▶ **suck** *noun*.

suction / 'सक्शन् / *noun* चूषण; चूषण से उत्पन्न बल : *a suction pump/pad.*

sudden / 'सड्न् / *adj* अचानक होने वाला : *a sudden decision/change* ■ **all of a sudden** अचानक ▶ **suddenly** *adv*.

suds / सड्ज़् / *noun* [*pl*] 1 (**soap suds** भी) साबुन का झाग, फेन 2 (अनौप) बियर।

sue / सू/ स्यू / *verb* 1 **sue (sb) (for sth)** मुक़दमा दायर करना : *sue sb for dam-*

ages **2 sue for sth** (और) चिरौरी करना, विनय-अनुनय करना।

suede / स्वेड् / *noun* एक प्रकार का मुलायम चमड़ा : *brown suede shoes.*

suffer / 'सफ़र् / *verb* **1 suffer (from/ with/for sth)** कष्ट उठाना, भुगतना; भोगना : *She's suffering from loss of memory.* **2** कुछ अप्रिय सहन करना : *suffer pain/torture/defeat* **3** बदतर स्थिति में पहुँच जाना : *Your studies will suffer if you play too much sport.* ▸ **suffering** *noun* **1** पीड़ा, कष्ट/वेदना **2 sufferings** [*pl*] पीड़ा की अनुभूति : *the physical and mental sufferings of the refugees.*

suffice / स'फ़ाइस् / *verb* **suffice (for sb/sth)** (और) पर्याप्त होना : *one coat of paint should suffice.*

sufficient / स'फ़िश्न्ट् / *adj* **sufficient (for sth/sb); sufficient (to do sth)** पर्याप्त : *sufficient money/time* ▸ **sufficiency** / स'फ़िश्न्सि / *noun* **sufficiency (of sth)** (और) पर्याप्त मात्रा : *a sufficiency of nursing skills.*

suffix / 'सफ़िक्स् / *noun* (व्या) प्रत्यय, जैसे *rusty* में *y.*

suffocate / 'सफ़केट्/ *verb* **1** दम घुटना, गला घुटने से मरना/मारना : *Many passengers suffocated in the burning aircraft.* **2** साँस लेने में कष्ट अनुभव करना : *I'm suffocating here—can we open a window?* ▸ **suffocation** *noun.*

suffrage / 'सफ़्रिज् / *noun* राजनीतिक चुनाव में मतदान का अधिकार : *universal suffrage.*

sugar / 'शुगर् / *noun* **1** चीनी, शक्कर **2** फलों में पाए जाने वाले विभिन्न मीठे पदार्थ जैसे ग्लूकोस या सुक्रोस ▸ **sugar** *verb* मीठा करना : *Is this tea sugared?* **sugary** *adj* **1** मीठा, चीनी जैसा **2** (अपमा) अत्यधिक भावुक; अति आकर्षक।

suggest / स'जेस्ट्; *US* सग्'जेस्ट् / *verb* **1 suggest sb (for sth); suggest sth (to sb); suggest sb/sth (as sth)** सुझाव देना, मत या प्रत्याशी को विचारार्थ प्रस्तुत करना : *I suggested a tour of the museum.* ○ *Is there anyone you'd like to suggest for the job?* **2 suggest sth (to sb)** सुझाना, मन में आना, व्यंजित करना : *What do these symptoms suggest (to you)?* ▸ **suggestive** *adj* **suggestive (of sth)** विचारोत्तेजक : *suggestive symbolism.*

suggestion / स'जेस्चन्; *US* सग्'जेस्-चन्/ *noun* **1** सुझाव **2** सुझाव देना : *On/ At your suggestion I bought the more expensive model.* **3** संकेत, व्यंजना : *speak English with the suggestion of a French accent.*

suicide / 'सूइसाइड; स्यूइसाइड् / *noun* **1** आत्महत्या; आत्महत्या की घटना : *three suicides in one week* **2** स्वयं के लिए हानिकर सिद्ध होने वाली घटना, कार्य ▸ **suicidal** *adj* **1** आत्महत्या-विषयक, आत्म-हत्याकारी **2** (व्यक्ति) संभवत: आत्महत्या करने वाला : *I was desperately unhappy, almost suicidal.*

suit¹ / सूट; स्यूट / *noun* **1** सूट (कोट-पैंट आदि) **2** (**lawsuit** भी) मुकदमा, नालिश : *file a suit against sb* **3** याचना, (शासक को) दरख़ास्त।

suit² / सूट; स्यूट् / *verb* **1** (विशेषत: कपड़ों का) ठीक बैठना, शोभा देना : *That colour doesn't suit your complexion.* **2** उपयुक्त/सुविधाजनक होना : *The seven o'clock train will suit you very well.* **3** अनुकूल होना; संतुष्ट करना ▸ **suited** *adj* **suited (for/to sb/sth)** उचित/उपयुक्त होना, फ़िट बैठना।

suitable / 'सूटब्ल; 'स्यूटब्ल् / *adj* **suitable (for/to sth/sb)** अनुकूल, उपयुक्त/उचित : *a suitable candidate* ▸ **suitability** *noun* **suitably** *adv.*

suitcase / 'सूट्केस्; 'स्यूट्केस् / *noun* सूटकेस।

suite / स्वीट् / *noun* साज-सज्जा के साथ कमरों का सेट : *The luxury suite consists of a bedroom, a bathroom and a sitting-room.*

suitor / 'सूटर्; 'स्यूटर् / *noun* (*अप्र*) विवाहार्थी : *She had rejected all her many suitors.*

sulk / सल्क् / *verb* (*अपमा*) रूठना, खीजना : *sulking teenagers* ▸ **sulky** *adj* रूठने वाला, चिड़चिड़ा : *a sulky mood* **sulkily** *adv*.

sullen / 'सलन् / *adj* 1 चिड़चिड़ा, उदास एवं घुना : *a sullen person* 2 विषण्ण; मनहूस/अमंगल : *a sullen sky.*

sulphur (*US* **sulfur**) / 'सल्फ़र् / *noun* (*प्रतीक* S) गंधक ▸ **sulphurous** *adj* गंधक का या गंधक जैसा।

sultry / 'सल्ट्रि / *adj* उमस भरा (मौसम) : *a sultry summer afternoon.*

sum / सम् / *noun* 1 **sum** (**of sth**) धनराशि : *He was fined the sum of Rs 2000.* 2 (*प्राय: sing*) **sum** (**of sth**) संख्याओं का जोड़, योगफल : *The sum of 5 and 3 is 8.* 3 (*प्राय: pl*) अंक-गणित का प्रश्न : *be good at sums* ▸ **sum** *verb* (**-mm-**) ■ **sum sb/sth up** विचार/ मत बनाना या व्यक्त करना : *He summed up the situation immediately* **sum (sth) up** संक्षेप में मुख्य तथ्यों को व्यक्त करना : *Before we end the meeting, perhaps I can sum up (what we have agreed).*

summary / 'समरि / *noun* (*pl* **summaries**) संक्षिप्त, सारांश : *a news summary* ▸ **summary** *adj* 1 संक्षिप्त : *a summary account of a long debate* 2 (*कभी-कभी अपमा*) बिना औपचारिक तरीक़ा अपनाए किया गया (काम आदि) : *summary justice/dismissal/execution* **summarily** *adv* **summarize,**

-ise *verb* संक्षेप करना, सारांश प्रस्तुत करना।

summer / 'समर् / *noun* ग्रीष्म ऋतु।

summit / 'समिट् / *noun* 1 चोटी, शीर्ष; उच्चतम बिंदु : *climb to the summit* 2 दो या अधिक देशों के सरकारी शीर्षस्थ अधिकारियों की बैठक : *a summit talk.*

summon / 'समन् / *verb* 1 **summon sb** (**to sth**) (*औप*) बुला भेजना, इकट्ठा करना : *We had to summon the doctor (to look at her).* 2 (*औप*) न्यायालय में उपस्थित होने का आदेश : *I was summoned to appear before the magistrates.* 3 (*औप*) सभा के लिए इकट्ठा होने का आदेश देना : *summon a conference* 4 **summon sth** (**up**) (अपनी सभी) शक्तियाँ प्रयुक्त करना : *I had to summon (up) all my courage to face him.*

summons / 'समन्ज़् / *noun* (*pl* **summonses** / 'समन्ज़िज़्/) न्यायालय से जारी किया गया बुलावा, सम्मन : *issue a summons* ▸ **summons** *verb* **summons sb** (**for sth**) सम्मन देना/जारी करना।

sumptuous / 'सम्प्चुअस् / *adj* क़ीमती, भव्य : *sumptuous food/ meals.*

sun / सन् / *noun* 1 (**the sun** भी) [*sing*] सूर्य, सूरज 2 (*प्राय:* **the sun**) [*sing*] धूप, घाम ■ **under the sun** दुनिया में कहीं भी : *the best food under the sun* ▸ **sun** *verb* (**-nn-**) **sun oneself** धूप सेंकना **sunny** *adj* (**-ier, -iest**) 1 धूप वाला, चमकदार : *a sunny day* 2 प्रसन्न-चित्त, खुश : *a sunny disposition* **sunblind** *noun* खिड़की की झिलमिली **sunburn** *noun* धूप में जलकर ताँबे जैसा वर्ण हो जाना **sundown** *noun* सूर्यास्त **sunlit** *adj* (मकान) धूप भरा **sunrise** *noun* सूर्योदय **sunshade** *noun* छतरी **sunstroke** *noun* धूप या लू लगने से बीमार पड़ जाना।

Sunday /'सन्डे / *noun* (*संक्षि* Sun) रविवार, इतवार।

sundry /'सन्ड्रि / *adj* विविध : *sundry items of food* ■ **all and sundry** (*अनौप*) सभी, हर प्रकार के लोग ▸ **sundries** /'सन्ड्रिज़् / *noun* [*pl*] फुटकर वस्तुएँ, प्रकीर्णक।

super- *pref* (*उपसर्ग*) 1 असाधारण, असामान्य : *superhuman/supernatural* 2 अत्यंत उच्च मात्रा में, अत्यधिक : *super-intelligent/super-rich* 3 ऊपर, शीर्षस्थ : *superstructure.*

superannuated /'सूपर् 'ऐन्युएटिड् / *adj* (*अनौप*, विशेषत: *परि*) (व्यक्ति या वस्तु) काफ़ी वृद्ध; किसी कार्य के लिए उचित या मुनासिब न रहना : *superannuated pop stars* ▸ **superannuation** /'सूपर् ऐन्यु 'एश्न् / *noun* सेवा-निवृत्ति उपरांत पेंशन के रूप में भुगतान की गई राशि : *a superannuation fund/scheme.*

superb / सू'पर्ब्; स्यू'पर्ब् / *adj* श्रेष्ठ, बढ़िया, आलीशान : *The weather was absolutely superb.*

supercilious /'सूपर् 'सिलिअस्; स्यूपर् 'सिलिअस् / *adj* (*अपमा*) दंभी, मग़रूर, दूसरों की अवमानना करने वाला : *a supercilious attitude* ▸ **superciliously** *adv* **superciliousness** *noun.*

superficial /'सूपर् 'फ़िश्ल्; स्यूपर् 'फ़िश्ल् / *adj* 1 सतही, गहरा नहीं : *a superficial wound* 2 (*ज्ञान*) छिछला : *have only a superficial knowledge of history* ▸ **superficiality** *noun* **superficially** *adv.*

superfluity /'सूपर् 'फ़्लूअटि; स्यूपर् 'फ़्लुअटि / *noun* **superfluity (of sth)** बहुत अधिक मात्रा में : *a superfluity of helpers.*

superfluous / सू'पर्फ़्लुअस्; स्यू'पर्-फ़्लुअस् / *adj* फ़ज़ूल, अतिरिक्त/फ़ालतू : *a superfluous remark* ▸ **superfluously** *adv.*

superimpose /'सूपरिम्'पोज़् / *verb* **superimpose sth (on sth)** किसी वस्तु को दूसरी वस्तु पर रखना, ताकि नीचे की वस्तु भी देखी, सुनी जा सके : *a diagram of the new road layout superimposed on a map of the city.*

superintend /'सूपरिन्'टेन्ड्; स्यूपरिन्'टेन्ड्/ *verb* (*औप*) प्रबंध, नियंत्रण, निरीक्षण करना, (कार्य की) देख-रेख करना : *superintend the building work* ▸ **superintendence** *noun* **superintendent** /'सूपरिन्'टेन्डन्ट्/ *noun* 1 अधीक्षक, संचालक 2 पुलिस अधीक्षक।

superior / सू'पिअरिअर्; स्यू'पिअरिअर् / *adj* 1 **superior (to sb/sth)** से बेहतर; उच्च पद पर; वरिष्ठ : *a superior court/ position* 2 औसत से अधिक अच्छा, श्रेष्ठ : *superior accommodation* 3 (*अपमा*) स्वयं को श्रेष्ठ समझने वाला : *a superior look* ▸ **superior** *noun* 1 (प्राय: *pl*) वरिष्ठ, उच्चतर पद पर; ज्येष्ठ 2 (उपाधियों में) धार्मिक समुदाय का अध्यक्ष : *the Father/Mother Superior* **superiority** / सू 'पिअरि'ऑरटि; स्यू 'पिअरि'ऑरटि / *noun* **superiority (in sth); superiority (to/over sth/sb)** उच्चता/श्रेष्ठता : *military superiority.*

superlative / सू'पर्लटिव्; स्यू'पर्लटिव्/ *adj* 1 उच्चतम मात्रा या गुण का : *a superlative performance* 2 (*व्या*) उत्तमतासूचक जैसे *best, worst, slowest, most difficult* ▸ **superlative** *noun* विशेषण या विशेषज्ञ का उत्तमतासूचक रूप : *It's hard to find enough superlatives to describe him!*

supermarket /'सूपरमार्किट्; 'स्यूपर-मार्किट् / *noun* एक ही भवन में बड़ा बाज़ार जिसमें लगभग सभी प्रकार का सामान मिलता हो।

supernatural /'सूपर् 'नैचरल्; स्यूपर् 'नैचरल् / *adj* अलौकिक, लोकोत्तर,

जिसकी भौतिक नियमों से व्याख्या न की जा सके : *supernatural forces.*

supersede / ˌसूपर्'सीड्; ˌस्यूपर्'सीड् / *verb* किसी को हटा कर उसका स्थान ले लेना : *Steam locomotives have been superseded by diesel or electric trains.*

supersonic / ˌसूपर्'सॉनिक्; ˌस्यूपर्'सॉ-निक् / *adj* ध्वनि के वेग से अधिक वेग-शाली : *a supersonic aircraft.*

superstar / 'सूपर्स्टार्; 'स्यूपर्स्टार् / *noun* (*अनौप*) अतिप्रसिद्ध अभिनेता, गायक, खिलाड़ी आदि।

superstition / ˌसूपर् 'स्टिश्न्; ˌस्यूपर् 'स्टिश्न् / *noun* 1 (प्राय: *अपमा*) अंध-विश्वास : *behaviour based on fear and superstition* 2 अंधविश्वास मूलक प्रथाएँ ▸ **superstitious** *adj* (प्राय: *अपमा*) अंधविश्वासी; अंधविश्वास पर आधारित: *superstitious beliefs/practices.*

supervise / 'सूपर्वाइज़्; 'स्यूपर्वाइज़् / *verb* देख-रेख करना, निगरानी करना : *supervise the building work* ▸ **supervision** *noun* निरीक्षण **supervisor** *noun* निरीक्षक।

supper / 'सपर् / *noun* दिन का आख़िरी भोजन।

supplant / स'प्लान्ट् / *verb* (*औप*) किसी का स्थान ले लेना : *Computers will never completely supplant books.*

supple / 'सप्ल् / *adj* लचीला, सुनम्य : *have a supple body.*

supplement / 'सप्लिमन्ट् / *noun* 1 **supplement (to sth)** पूरक; अतिरिक्त जोड़ी वस्तु : *vitamin supplements* 2 परिशिष्ट : *I read it in the Sunday colour supplement.* ▸ **supplement** / 'सप्लिमेन्ट् / *verb* **supplement sth (with sth)** पूरित करना, जोड़ना/बढ़ाना : *a diet supplemented with vitamin tablets.*

supplementary / ˌसप्लि'मेन्टरि / *adj* **supplementary (to sth)** अतिरिक्त : *a supplementary payment/pension.*

supply / स'प्लाइ / *verb* (*pt, pp* **supplied**) 1 **supply sth (to sb)**; **supply sb (with sth)** ज़रूरत की माँगी हुई वस्तु को देना, आपूर्ति करना : *supply sb with food/fuel* 2 आवश्यकता के लिए पर्याप्त देना/पूर्ति करना ▸ **supply** *noun* 1 आ-पूर्ति : *the supply of blood to the heart* 2 (प्राय: *pl*) पूर्ति की गई वस्तु : *the gas-/water-supply.*

support / स'पॉर्ट् / *verb* 1 **support sb/sth (in sth)** सहायता करना, समर्थन देना : *support a cause/political party* 2 थाम रखना, संभालना : *The chair wasn't strong enough to support his weight.* 3 पुष्टि करना 4 भरण-पोषण करना, रोटी-कपड़ा देना : *She earns enough to support herself.* ▸ **support** *noun* 1 **support (for sth)** प्रोत्साहन, समर्थन : *He has the full support of his colleagues.* 2 थामने की प्रक्रिया; संभालने वाली वस्तु: *She held on to his arm for support.* 3 भरण-पोषण करने वाला या सहानुभूति दिखाने वाला व्यक्ति **supporter** *noun* समर्थक।

supportive / स'पॉर्टिव् / *adj* सहायता, प्रोत्साहन या समर्थन देते हुए : *She was very supportive during my father's illness.*

suppose / स'पोज़् / *verb* 1 मानना, कल्पना करना; संभव मानना : *Suppose (that) the news is true : what then?* 2 समझना, अटकल लगाना : *What do you suppose he wanted?* 3 (सुझाव के लिए प्रयुक्त) : *Suppose we don't tell anybody else about this.* ■ **be supposed to do/be sth** आशा किया जाना : *You are supposed to pay the bill by Friday.* ▸ **supposed** *adj* कल्पित; माना हुआ परंतु सच नहीं : *His*

supposed confession was forged.
supposing (supposing that भी) *conj*
यदि, अगर : *Supposing (that) you are wrong, what will you do then?*

supposition / सप्'ज़िश्न् / *noun* अप्रमाणित, परंतु सच माना गया, विचार, अनुमान : *I am proceeding on the supposition that...* ○ *a newspaper article based entirely on supposition.*

suppress / स'प्रेस् / *verb* 1 दमन करना, कुचलना, दबाना : *suppress an uprising* 2 (प्राय: *अपमा*) छिपाना, गुप्त कर देना : *suppress the truth about sth*
▸ **suppression** *noun*.

supreme / सू'प्रीम्; स्यू'प्रीम् / *adj* 1 पद या अधिकार में सर्वोच्च : *the Supreme Commander of NATO* 2 सर्वाधिक महत्त्वपूर्ण, महान : *a supreme achievement* ▸ **supremacy** / सू'प्रेमसि; स्यू'प्रेमसि / *noun* **supremacy (over sb/ sth)** उच्चता **the Supreme Being** *noun* [sing] (और) ईश्वर।

surcharge / 'सर्चार्ज् / *noun* **surcharge (on sth)** सामान्य क़ीमत के अलावा भुगतान की अतिरिक्त राशि : *a 10% surcharge on imported goods.*

sure / शुअर्; शॉर् / *adj* (-r, -st) 1 **sure (of/about sth); sure that....** निश्चित, संशयहीन : *I'm not sure when I saw her last.* 2 **sure of sth/doing sth** सफलता आदि के प्रति आश्वस्त : *India must win this game to be sure of qualifying for the World Cup.* 3 संशयरहित सत्य : *in the sure and certain knowledge that one is right* 4 विश्वस्त, अचूक/अमोघ : *a sure sign of economic recovery* ■ **be sure to do sth** निश्चित रूप से करना : *Be sure to write and tell me all your news.* **make sure (of sth/that ...)** कुछ पाने के लिए आवश्यक उपाय कर लेना; निश्चित रूप

से कुछ होने का पता लगाना **sure of oneself** (कभी-कभी *अपमा*) स्वयं के विचारों, सामर्थ्य पर बहुत भरोसा होना : *He seems very sure of himself.* ▸ **sure** *adv* निश्चित रूप से : *It sure was cold!* ■ **sure enough** निश्चित रूप से, आशानुसार।

surely / 'शुअर्लि; 'शॉर्लि / *adv* 1 निश्चित रूप से : *This will surely cause problems.* 2 सर्वाधिक संभावना के साथ : *This is surely her best play.*

surety / 'शुअरटि; 'शॉरटि / *noun* (*pl* **sureties**) 1 ज़मानत (राशि) 2 ज़मानती (व्यक्ति) : *stand surety for sb.*

surf / सर्फ़ / *noun* चट्टानों से या तट से टकराने पर समुद्री लहरों का फेन : *splashing about in the surf* ▸ **surf** *verb* (**go surfing** भी) पटरे पर खड़े होकर लहरों पर खेलना।

surface / 'सर्फ़िस् / *noun* 1 बाहरी सतह, ऊपरी परत : *the earth's surface* 2 (प्राय: *sing*) वस्तु का पृष्ठ, सतह 3 [*sing*] बाह्य रूप, ऊपरी रंग-रूप : *Look beyond the surface before you judge someone.* ▸ **surface** 1 **surface sth (with sth)** ऊपरी परत चढ़ाना : *surfacing the area with concrete* 2 पानी के सतह पर आना/लाना : *The ducks dived and surfaced again several metres away.* 3 कुछ समय तक छिपे रहने के बाद फिर से प्रकट होना : *Doubts/Fears/Problems began to surface.*

surfeit / 'सर्फ़िट् / *noun* (प्राय: *sing*) **surfeit (of sth)** वस्तु की अत्यधिकता, भरपेट (से अधिक) भोजन और पेय : *a surfeit of programmes containing violence on TV.*

surge / सर्ज / *verb* 1 लहराना, लहरों की तरह आगे बढ़ना : *a surging river* ▸ *surging crowds* 2 **surge (up)** अचानक तीव्रता से बढ़ना : *surging*

property prices ▸ **surge** *noun*
surge (of/in sth) 1 हिलोरा 2 तीव्र
आवेग/बढ़त : *feel a surge of anger.*

surgeon /'सर्जन्/ *noun* शल्य चिकित्सक,
सर्जन।

surgery /'सर्जरि/ *noun (pl* **surgeries)**
1 शल्य चिकित्सा, ऑपरेशन द्वारा चिकि-
त्सा : *need major surgery* 2 डॉक्टर का
कमरा ▸ **surgical** /'सर्जिकल्/ *adj*
शल्यक्रिया संबंधी।

surly /'सर्लि/ *adj* **(-ier, -iest)** बदमिज़ाज
और उजड्ड : *a surly child* ▸ **surli-
ness** *noun.*

surmise /सर्'माइज़्/ *verb* (औप)
अनुमान लगाना, अंदाज़ा करना : *We can
only surmise (that) he must have
had an accident.* ▸ **surmise** /'सर्मा-
इज़्/ (प्राय: *sing*) (औप) *noun* अनु-
मान : *This is pure surmise on my
part.*

surmount /सर्'माउन्ट्/ *verb* 1 कठिना-
इयाँ पार करना, बाधाएँ जीत लेना : *She has
had to surmount immense physi-
cal disabilities.* 2 किसी ऊँची जगह पर
स्थित होना/करना : *The spire is sur-
mounted by a weather-vane.* ▸ **sur-
mountable** *adj.*

surname /'सर्नेम्/ *noun* कुलनाम,
उपनाम : *Smith is a common English
surname.*

surpass /सर्'पास; *US* सर्'पैस्/ *verb*
surpass sb/sth (in sth) (औप) बढ़-
कर निकलना, मात देना : *He set standards that are unlikely to be sur-
passed.*

surplus /'सर्प्लस्/ *noun* बचत; ज़रूरत
से अतिरिक्त मात्रा : *food surpluses* ∘ *a
trade surplus of Rs 400 million*
▸ **surplus** *adj* **surplus (to sth)** ज़रूरत
से ज़्यादा : *surplus staff/labour.*

surprise /सर्'प्राइज़्/ *noun* आश्चर्य; आ-
श्चर्यजनक वस्तु/घटना : *Her letter came*
as a complete surprise (to me).
■ **take sb by surprise** अचानक प्रकट
आदि होकर किसी को चौंका देना : *Her
sudden resignation took us all by
surprise.* **take sb/sth by surprise**
बिना चेतावनी अचानक किसी पर हमला
आदि करना : *The town was well
defended so there was little chance
of taking it by surprise.* ▸ **surprise**
verb 1 आश्चर्यचकित करना/होना : *She
was rather surprised by his rude
behaviour.* 2 अचानक हमला करना :
surprise the opposition **surprised**
adj **surprised (at/by sth/sb)** आश्चर्य-
चकित : *We were very surprised at
the news.* **surprising** *adj* आश्चर्य-
जनक : *A surprising number of people came.*

surrender /स'रेन्डर्/ *verb* 1 **surrender (oneself) (to sb)** आत्मसमर्पण करना,
लड़ना बंद करना : *We shall never
surrender.* 2 **surrender sth/sb (to
sb)** (औप) किसी को कुछ सौंप देना; किसी
की अधीनता स्वीकार कर लेना; झुक जाना :
*They surrendered their guns to
the police.* ■ **surrender to sth** (साहि
या औप) (भावनाओं के) वश में हो जाना,
भावनाओं में बह जाना : *He finally
surrendered to his craving for
drugs.* ▸ **surrender** *noun* **surrender (to sth/sb)** आत्मसमर्पण, परित्याग।

surreptitious /ˌसरप्'टिशस्/ *adj* गुप्त
तरीके से किया गया ताकि दूसरों को पता न
चले; प्रच्छन्न : *He started making
surreptitious visits to the club on
his way home.* ▸ **surreptitiously**
adv.

surrogate /'सरगट्/ *noun* **surrogate
(for sb/sth)** (औप) व्यक्ति या वस्तु जो
किसी और के स्थान पर प्रयोग की जाए;
एवज़ी : *She looked upon them as a
surrogate family when her real*

parents were killed. ○ *a surrogate mother.*

surround / सर्'राउन्ड् / *verb* **surround sb/sth (with sb/sth)** चारों ओर से घेर लेना, चारों ओर होना : *They have surrounded the area with police.* ○ (अलं) *Uncertainty still surrounds the appointment of a new director.*

▸ **surrounding** *adj* आस-पास : *From the church tower, you can get a splendid view of the village and the surrounding countryside.* **surroundings** *noun* [pl] पास-पड़ोस; परिवेश/वातावरण : *live in pleasant surroundings.*

surveillance / सर्'वेलन्स् / *noun* निगरानी : *The police are keeping the suspects under constant surveillance.*

survey / सर्वे / *verb* **1** किसी को पूर्ण रूप से ध्यानपूर्वक देखना, विशेषतः कुछ दूरी से : *survey the countryside from the top of a hill* **2** सामान्य दशाओं का अध्ययन एवं वर्णन करना : *a speech in which she surveyed the whole state of the economy* **3** स्थिति आदि माप कर अंकित करना, सर्वे करना : *survey a plot of land for building* **4** भवन आदि की सुदृढ़ता का सर्वेक्षण करना : *have a house surveyed before deciding to buy it* ▸ **survey** / 'सर्वे / *noun* **1** सर्वेक्षण : *a comprehensive survey of modern music* **2** सर्वेक्षण का नक्शा : *an aerial survey* **3** लोगों के मत, व्यवहार आदि की छानबीन : *a public opinion survey* **surveyor** *noun* सर्वेक्षक।

survival / सर्'वाइव्ल् / *noun* **1** जीवित या अस्तित्व में रहने की स्थिति : *the miraculous survival of some people in the air crash* **2** **survival (from sth)** (प्राणी) अवशेष; रूढ़ि : *The*

ceremony is a survival from pre-Christian times.

survive / सर्'वाइव् / *verb* **1** **survive (from sth); survive (on sth)** जीवित या अस्तित्व में बने रहना : *Of the six people in the plane when it crashed, only one survived.* **2** लगभग मृत्यु या विनष्ट होने के बाद भी जीवित बचे रहना; (भूकंप आदि) संकटों से बच जाना : *survive an earthquake/shipwreck* **3** किसी की मृत्यु के बाद जीवित रहना : *The old lady has survived all her children.* ▸ **survivor** *noun* दुर्घटना से बचा व्यक्ति : *send help to the survivors of the earthquake.*

susceptible / स'सेप्टब्ल् / *adj* **1** **susceptible to sth** सरलता से (रोग, चाटुकारी आदि से) प्रभावित होने वाला : *highly susceptible to flattery* ○ *Children are more susceptible to some diseases than adults.* **2** भावुक **3** **susceptible (of sth)** (औप) योग्य; को अनुमति देने वाला : *The facts are susceptible of various interpretations.* ▸ **susceptibility** *noun.*

suspect / स'स्पेक्ट् / *verb* **1** ऐसा लगना कि...., विश्वास करना : *He suspected an ambush.* **2** संदेह करना : *suspect sb's motives* **3** **suspect sb (of sth/ doing sth)** किसी को अपराधी समझना : *He is suspected of drug dealing.* ▸ **suspect** / 'सस्पेक्ट् / *noun* (अपराध के संबंध में) संदिग्ध व्यक्ति : *a prime suspect in the murder case.* **suspect** / 'सस्पेक्ट् / *adj* अविश्वसनीय; संभवतः ग़लत : *His reasoning is suspect.*

suspend / स'स्पेन्ड् / *verb* **1** **suspend sth (from sth)** (औप) लटकाना : *A lamp was suspended from the ceiling above us.* **2** स्थगित करना, कुछ समय के लिए होने से रोक देना : *suspend* *a rule* **3 suspend sb (from sth)** निलंबित करना/मुअत्तल करना, (पद, सदस्यता आदि से) सस्पेंड करना : *She was suspended from school for stealing.*

▶ **suspended** *adj* लटकता हुआ : *particles suspended in water.*

suspense / स'स्पेन्स् / *noun* असमंजस, अनिश्चय/दुविधा, (आने वाले समाचार, घटना आदि की प्रतीक्षा में) चिंता : *a story of mystery and suspense* ○ *Don't keep us in suspense any longer— tell us what happened.*

suspension/सं स्पेन्शन्/*noun* लटकना/ झूलना; निलंबन, स्थगन ▶ **suspension-bridge** *noun* झूला पुल (जैसे लक्ष्मण झूला, ऋषिकेश)।

suspicion / स'स्पिशन् / *noun* **1** संदेह, शक : *He was arrested on the suspicion of having stolen the money.* **2** [*sing*] **suspicion (of sth)** पुट, ज़रा-सी मात्रा : *not the slightest suspicion of jealousy in her voice* ■ **above suspicion** संदेह से परे : *Nobody who was near the scene of crime is above suspicion.* **under suspicion** जिसपर ग़लत करने के लिए संदेह किया जा रहा हो।

suspicious / स'स्पिशस् / *adj* **1 suspicious (about/of sth/sb)** संदेह करने वाला, शक्की : *a suspicious look* **2** संदेहास्पद : *suspicious behaviour* ▶ **suspiciously** *adv.*

sustain / स'स्टेन् / *verb* **1** सँभालना, जीवित रखना, अस्तित्व में बनाए रखना : *not enough oxygen to sustain life* **2** (औप) भुगतना, हानि उठाना : *sustain a defeat/loss* **2** (क़ानून) दावे की वैधता का निर्णय देना : *Objection sustained!*

sustenance / 'सस्टनन्स् / *noun* पोषक आहार : *weak from lack of sustenance.*

swab /स्वॉब्/ *noun* चिकित्सा में घाव साफ़ करने आदि के लिए प्रयुक्त मुलायम कपड़ा ▶ **swab** *verb* **(-bb-)** **1** मुलायम कपड़े से साफ़ करना : *swab the blood off sb's face* **2** कपड़े द्वारा पानी से साफ़ करना : *swab the decks.*

swagger / 'स्वैगर् / *verb* (प्राय: अपमा) अकड़कर चलना, इठलाना/इतराना : *He swaggered into the room looking very pleased with himself.* ▶ **swagger** *noun* (कभी-कभी अपमा) अकड़ : *walk with a swagger.*

swallow[1] / 'स्वॉलो / *verb* **1** निगलना : *Chew your food properly before swallowing it.* **2** (अनौप) बहुत जल्दी यक़ीन कर लेना; बिना विरोध के अपमान बरदाश्त कर लेना: *He swallowed all the criticism without saying a thing.* **3 swallow sb/sth (up)** ग्रहण करना; समा लेना; समाप्त करना : *The aircraft was swallowed (up) in the clouds.* **4** कोई भावना छुपा या दबा लेना : *She swallowed her anger and carried on.* ▶ **swallow** *noun* निगलना; निगली हुई वस्तु की मात्रा।

swallow[2] / 'स्वॉलो / *noun* अबाबील (पक्षी)।

swamp[1]/ स्वॉम्प्/*noun* दलदल ▶ **swampy** *adj* दलदली : *swampy ground.*

swamp[2]/स्वॉम्प्/ *verb* **1** पानी से भर देना/ भर जाना : *The sink overflowed and swamped the kitchen.* ○ *A huge wave swamped the boat.* **2 swamp sb/sth (with sth)** (अल) भरमार कर देना, परेशान कर देना : *I've been swamped by work this year.*

swan /स्वॉन्/ *noun* हंस (पक्षी)।

swap (**swop** भी) / स्वॉप् / *verb* **(-pp-)** **swap (sth) (with sb); swap (sb) sth for sth; swap sth (over/round)** (अनौप) अदला-बदली करना : *swap jokes/stories/information* ▶ **swap** *noun* (प्राय: *sing*) अदला-बदली करने

की प्रक्रिया, अदला-बदली की गई वस्तु : *Shall we do a swap—your fishing rod for my tennis racket?*

swarm / स्वॉर्म / *noun* 1 कीड़ों, चिड़ियों आदि का झुंड : *a swarm of ants/ locusts/starlings* 2 (प्रायः *pl*) व्यक्तियों का बड़ा झुंड, भीड़ : *She's always surrounded by swarms of photographers.* ▶ **swarm** *verb* 1 (मधु-मक्खियों का) झुंड बना कर उड़ना 2 बड़ी संख्या/हुजूम बना कर निर्धारित दिशा में चलना ■ **swarm with sb/sth** भरा हुआ होना, बड़ी संख्या में एकत्रित होना : *The capital is swarming with police.*

swat / स्वॉट / *verb* (-tt-) चपटी, ठोस चीज़ से मारना : *swat a fly.*

swathe / स्वेद् / *verb* **swathe sb/sth (in sth)** लपेटना, पट्टी बाँधना : *Thick bandages swathed his head.*

sway / स्वे / *verb* 1 झूलना, डोलना : *trees swaying in the wind* 2 नियंत्रित करना, किसी का मत या कार्यविधि प्रभावित करना : *a speech that swayed many voters* ▶ **sway** *noun* 1 झूलना 2 (साहि) नियंत्रण, शासन : *The country fell under the sway of powerful invaders.* ■ **hold sway (over sb/sth)** (प्रायः साहि) काफी अधिकार या प्रभाव होना : *areas of the country where the Congress Party holds sway.*

swear / स्वेअर / *verb* (*pt* **swore** / स्वॉर् /; *pp* **sworn** / स्वॉर्न् /) 1 **swear (at sb/sth)** गाली बकना, कोसना : *The foreman is always swearing at the workers.* 2 क़सम खाना, शपथ लेना : *She swore that she'd never seen him.* 3 शपथ दिलाना (जैसे गोपनीयता एवं पद की) ■ **swear by sb/sth** 1 किसी को साक्षी मानना : *I swear by almighty God that I will tell the truth.* 2 (अनौप) किसी के महत्त्व में विश्वास रखना : *Most of my friends use word*

processors but I still swear by my old typewriter. **swear sb in** गोपनीयता, पद आदि की शपथ दिलाना **swear to sth** (अनौप) विश्वास के साथ किसी की सत्यता का दावा करना : *I think I've met him before but I wouldn't/couldn't swear to it.* ▶ **swear-word** *noun* गाली, अपशब्द।

sweat / स्वेट् / *noun* 1 पसीना 2 **a sweat** [*sing*] पसीना आना; व्याकुलता/परेशानी की हालत 3 (अनौप) घोर परिश्रम : *Climbing all these stairs is a real sweat!* ▶ **sweat** *verb* 1 पसीना निकलना/बहाना : *He was sweating heavily.* 2 (अनौप) व्याकुल/उत्सुक/परेशान रहना 3 **sweat (over sth)** घोर परिश्रम करना : *I really sweated over that essay.* ■ **sweat it out** (अनौप) व्याकुलता से कुछ होने की प्रतीक्षा करना : *We just had to sit and sweat it out until the results were announced.* ▶ **sweaty** *adj* 1 पसीना भरा, पसीने से तरबतर 2 पसीना लाने वाला : *a hot sweaty day.*

sweater / स्वेटर् / *noun* जर्सी।

sweep¹ / स्वीप् / *verb* (*pt, pp* **swept** / स्वेप्ट् /) 1 **sweep sth (from, off, into, etc sth); sweep sth (away, up, etc)** झाड़ू देना, बुहारना : *Have you swept in here?* 2 किसी क्षेत्र में तेज़ी से और बलपूर्वक चलना : *A huge wave swept over the deck.* 3 फैला हुआ होना : *The road sweeps round the lake.* 4 जाँचने, तलाश करने के लिए ऊपर से घुमाना : *Search lights swept the sky.* ■ **sweep sb off their feet** किसी को अत्यंत भावुक कर देना : *I was swept off my feet by her beauty and charm.* **sweep sth under the carpet** दोषारोपण से बचने के लिए तथ्य आदि छुपाना : *The government are trying to sweep the affair under the carpet.*

sweep² / स्वीप् / noun 1 (सामान्यत: sing) झाड़ू-बुहारी, सफ़ाई 2 (सामान्यत: sing) फैलाव, विस्तार; नदी, सड़क, तट आदि का लंबा क्षेत्र : the broad sweep of white cliffs round the bay 3 चिमनी साफ़ करने वाला।

sweeper / 'स्वीपर् / noun सफ़ाई-कर्मचारी, मेहतर : a road sweeper.

sweeping / 'स्वीपिङ् / adj 1 व्यापक : sweeping reforms 2 पूरा; ज़बरदस्त : a sweeping victory 3 (अपमा)(कथन) अति सामान्य, विशिष्ट मामले या अपवादों की परवाह न करने वाला : make a sweeping generalization.

sweet¹ / स्वीट् / adj (-er, -est) 1 मीठा : sweet apples 2 रुचिकर, रोचक गंध वाला : The air was sweet with the scent of lilies. 3 सुनने में रुचिकर : the sweet song of a nightingale 4 ताज़ा और शुद्ध : the sweet air of the country-side 5 संतोष या आनंद देने वाला : the sweet feeling of freedom/success 6 (अनौप) आकर्षक, मुग्ध करने वाला : a sweet face/gesture/smile 7 प्रिय स्वभाव होना : a sweet child/old lady

■ **have a sweeth tooth** (अनौप) मीठी चीज़ें खाना अत्यंत पसंद होना **in one's own sweet time/way** अपनी इच्छा अनुसार करना/कुछ करने के लिए समय लेना, न कि निर्देश के अनुसार : It's no use getting impatient with him—he'll do it in his own sweet time.

▸ **sweetheart** / 'स्वीट्हार्ट् / noun 1 पति, पत्नी, दुलारे बच्चे के लिए प्रयुक्त संबोधन 2 (अप्र) प्रेमी, प्रेमिका : They were childhood sweethearts. **sweetly** adv **sweetness** noun.

sweet² / स्वीट् / noun 1 (प्राय: pl) मिठाई 2 खीर, पुडिंग।

sweeten / 'स्वीट्न् / verb 1 मीठा करना या होना : tea sweetened with a little sugar 2 रुचिकर या स्वीकार्य बनाना :

Bonus shares will be thrown in to sweeten the deal. 3 **sweeten sb (up)** (अनौप) किसी को (उपहार आदि देकर) मना लेना ▸ **sweetener** noun मीठा बनाने का पदार्थ, विशेषकर चीनी/गुड़ के अभाव में।

swell / स्वेल् / verb (pt swelled / स्वेल्ड् /; pp swollen / स्वोलन् / या swelled) 1 **swell (sth) (up) (with sth)** फूलना/फुलाना : Wood often swells when wet. 2 **swell (into/to sth); swell sth (to sth) (with sth)** तीव्रता, संख्या, मात्रा या आयतन में अधिक हो जाना/करना : The murmur swelled into a roar. 3 **swell (sth) (with sth)** तीव्र भावनाओं से अभिभूत हो जाना : His heart swelled with pride at his achievement. ▸ **swell** noun 1 [sing] फूलना 2 समुद्र तल का क्रमश: घटना-बढ़ना 3 (संगीत में) ध्वनि का क्रमश: बढ़ना।

swelling / 'स्वेलिङ् / noun सूजन।

swelter / 'स्वेल्टर् / verb (अनौप) उमस होना, कड़ी गरमी पड़ना ▸ **sweltering** adj.

swerve / स्वर्व् / verb अचानक दिशा बदल देना या मुड़ जाना : The ball swerved to the left. ▸ **swerve** noun ऐसी गति : make a sudden swerve.

swift / स्विफ्ट् / adj (-er, -est) 1 **swift (to do sth)** तेज़, शीघ्र : a swift response 2 द्रुतगामी : a swift runner/horse ▸ **swiftly** adv **swiftness** noun.

swig / स्विग् / verb (-gg-) **swig sth (down)** (अनौप) जल्दी, तेज़ी से (विशेषत: शराब का) घूँट भरना, पीना : swigging beer (from a bottle).

swill / स्विल् / verb 1 **swill sth (out/down)** साफ़ करने के लिए काफ़ी मात्रा में पानी आदि डालना; निर्धारित दिशा में डालना, बहाना : swill down the front steps

2 (अनौप, अपमा) बड़ी मात्रा में पीना : *swill beer/tea.*

swim / स्विम् / *verb* (-mm-; *pt* **swam** / स्वैम् /; *pp* **swum** / स्वम् /) 1 तैरना : *I can't swim.* 2 **swim (with sth)**; **swim in sth** द्रव से भर जाना; तैरना, उत-रना : *Her eyes were swimming (with tears).* ○ *meat swimming in gravy* 3 चक्कर काटना, घूमना : *The room swam before his eyes.* ▸ **swim** *noun* तैरना : *have a swim* **swimmer** *noun* **swimming-pool** *noun*.

swindle / 'स्विन्डल् / *verb* (अनौप) **swindle sb/sth (out of sth)** ठगना, ऐंठ लेना : *swindle an insurance company* ▸ **swindle** *noun* 1 ठगी, ख़रीद में धोखा 2 धोखेबाज़ी वाली वस्तु या व्यक्ति **swindler** *noun* ठग, धोखेबाज़।

swine / स्वाइन् / *noun* 1 (अनौप, अपमा) (घृणा में प्रयुक्त शब्द) : *You rotten swine!* 2 [*pl*] (अप्र) सूअर।

swing¹ / स्विङ् / *verb* (*pt, pp* **swung** / स्वङ् /) 1 झुलाना/झूलना, झूमना/झुमाना : *He swung his arms as he walked.* 2 गोलाई में मुड़ जाना, घूमना : *A car swung sharply round the corner.* 3 **swing (sth) (at sb/sth)** घूँसा तानना : *She swung at me with her fist.* 4 **swing around/round** अचानक विपरीत दिशा में घूम जाना : *He swung round to confront his accusers.* 5 **swing (sb) (from sth) to sth**; **swing (sb) around/round (to sth)** अचानक मत, मनोदशा का बदल जाना : *He swings from wild optimism to total despair.* ○ *Can you swing them round to my point of view?* ■ **swing into action** तुरंत प्रतिक्रिया देना/निर्णय लेना : *Immediately after the explosion, the anti-terrorist squad swung into action.*

swing² / स्विङ् / *noun* 1 झूलने वाली गति,

दोलन : *the swing of a pendulum* 2 झूला, हिंडोला, पेंग : *children playing/riding on the swings* 3 मत आदि के बदलाव की मात्रा : *Voting showed a 10% swing to Congress.* ○ *He is liable to abrupt swings of mood.* ■ **go with a swing** (अनौप) 1 (मनोरंजन) अच्छा और मज़ेदार होना 2 (संगीत, कविता आदि में) तेज़ लय होना **in full swing** ज़ोरों पर, भरपूर चालू।

swipe / स्वाइप् / *verb* (अनौप) 1 **swipe (at)** (sth/sb) तेज़ी से घुमाकर मारना या मारने की कोशिश करना : *He swiped at the ball and missed.* 2 (विशेषत: परि) चुरा लेना : *Who's swiped my tooth-brush?* ▸ **swipe** *noun* **swipe (at sb/sth)** (अनौप) 1 तेज़ प्रहार 2 शब्दों द्वारा प्रहार।

swirl / स्वर्ल् / *verb* (वायु, पानी आदि) भँवर में बहना, चक्कर खाते हुए चलना : *dust swirling (around) in the streets* ▸ **swirl** *noun* **swirl (of sth)** भँवर, चक्कर।

swish / स्विश् / *verb* सरसराहट की आवाज़ के साथ हवा में घुमाना : *The horse swished its tail from side to side.* ▸ **swish** *noun* [*sing*] सरसराने की आवाज़ या क्रिया : *the swish of curtains.*

switch / स्विच् / *noun* 1 बिजली का स्विच 2 पेड़ की टहनी (जानवरों को हाँकने में प्रयुक्त) 3 (अचानक का) बदलाव : *a switch in policy/opinion* ▸ **switch** *verb* 1 **switch (sth) (over) (from sth) (to sth)** अचानक बदल देना, बदल जाना : *switch to modern methods* 2 **switch (sth) (with sb/sth)**; **switch (sth) over/round** अदला–बदली करना, हो जाना : *Our glasses have been switched—this is mine.* ○ *You drive first and then we'll switch round/over.* ■ **switch off** (अनौप) रुचि, फुरती

आदि कम हो जाना : *I switch off when he starts talking about cars.* **switch (sth) on/off** बिजली का स्विच खोलना/बंद करना ▶ **switchboard** *noun* स्विचबोर्ड।

swivel / 'स्विवल् / *noun* (समासों में) एक प्रकार का छल्ला जो दो भागों को ऐसे जोड़ता है कि कोई भी भाग दूसरे को बिना मोड़े घूम सकता है; घुमाऊ लड़ी : *a swivel chair* ▶ **swivel** *verb* (-ll-; *US* -l-) **swivel (sth) (round)** इस प्रकार घूमना/ घुमाना : *She swivelled the telescope (round).*

swoon / स्वून् / *verb* **1 swoon (over sb/sth)** किसी से भावनात्मक रूप से प्रभावित होना : *All the girls are swooning over the new history teacher.* **2** (अप्र) मूर्च्छित हो जाना : *He almost swoons at the sight of blood.* ▶ **swoon** *noun* [sing] (अप्र) मूर्च्छा।

swoop / स्वूप् / *verb* **swoop (down) (on sb/sth)** झपट्टा मारना : *The owl swooped down on the mouse.* ▶ **swoop** *noun* **swoop (on sb/sth)** झपट्टा।

sword / सॉर्ड / *noun* तलवार, कटार।

swot / स्वॉट् / *verb* (-tt-) **swot (up) (on sth); swot (for sth); swot sth up** (अनौप) बहुत परिश्रम से पढ़ाई करना, विशेषत: परीक्षा की तैयारी के लिए : *swotting for the exams* ○ *I'm swotting up (on) my history.* ▶ **swot** *noun* (प्राय: अपमा) इस तरह पढ़ाई करने वाला व्यक्ति।

sycophant / 'सिकुफ़ैन्ट् / *noun* (औप, अपमा) चापलूस, चाटुकार।

syllable / 'सिलबल् / *noun* (व्या) अक्षर-समूह जिसमें एक स्वर ध्वनि के बाद/पहले व्यंजन ध्वनि हो, जैसे A-rith-me-tic में चार अक्षर-समूह हैं ▶ **syllabic** / सि 'लैबिक् / *adj* आक्षरिक।

syllabus / 'सिलबस् / *noun* (pl **sylla-buses** या **syllabi** / 'सिलबाइ /) पाठ्य-

क्रम; पाठ्यविवरण : *'Hamlet' is on this year's English literature syllabus.*

symbol / 'सिम्बल् / *noun* **1 symbol (of sth)** प्रतीक, चिह्न : *The lion is a symbol of courage.* **2 symbol (for sth)** प्रतीक चिह्न या निशान : *algebraic symbols* ▶ **symbolic** / सिम्'बॉलिक् / *adj* **symbolic (of sth)** प्रतीकात्मक : *a symbolic gesture of friendship* **symbolically** *adv* **symbolism** / 'सिम्बलिज़म् / *noun* प्रतीकवाद, प्रतीकार्थ, प्रतीकात्मकता : *poetry full of religious symbolism* **symbolize, -ise** / 'सिम्बलाइज़् / *verb* प्रतीक रूप में प्रयुक्त करना/होना : *More than any other figure, he symbolizes his country's struggle for independence.*

symmetrical / सि'मेट्रिक्ल् / *adj* सममित (किसी भी विभाजक रेखा के दोनों ओर बिलकुल एक से डिज़ाइन वाला) : *the symmetrical arrangement of the gardens.*

symmetry / 'सिमट्रि / *noun* **1** वस्तु के दो आधे भागों के आकार-प्रकार में यथार्थ समानता : *the perfect symmetry of the building* **2** भागों में व्यवस्थित होने का आकर्षक, नियमित तरीका : *the symmetry of her features.*

sympathetic / ,सिम्प'थेटिक् / *adj* **1 sympathetic (to/towards/with sb)** हमदर्द, सहानुभूतिपूर्ण : *a sympathetic look* **2 sympathetic (to sth/sb)** पसंद आने वाला, प्रियकर।

sympathy / 'सिम्पथि / *noun* (pl **sym-pathies**) **1 sympathy (for/towards sb)** समवेदना, सहानुभूति : *feel great sympathy for sb* **2 sympathies** [pl] हमदर्दी (की अभिव्यक्ति) **3 sympathy (between sb and sb)** समान पसंदों के व्यक्तियों के बीच मित्रता, हमदर्दी : *A bond of sympathy developed between* members of the group. ▸ **sympathize, -ise** /'सिम्पथ़ाइज़/ verb **sympathize (with sb/sth)** सहानुभूति दिखाना, करुणा के साथ अनुभव करना, समर्थन दिखाना।

symphony /'सिम्फ़नि/ noun (pl **symphonies**) स्वरसंगति, सुरीलापन : Beethoven's ninth symphony.

symposium /सिम्'पोज़िअम्/ noun (pl **symposia** /सिम्'पोज़िआ/ या **symposiums**) 1 किसी विशेष विषय पर विचार के लिए छोटा सम्मेलन 2 किसी विशेष विषय पर निबंधों का संग्रह।

symptom /'सिम्प्टम्/ noun 1 रोग के लक्षण : the rash that is a symptom of measles 2 चिह्न, आसार : The demonstration is a symptom of discontent among the students.

synagogue /'सिनगॉग्/ noun यहूदियों का प्रार्थना भवन।

synchronize, -ise /'सिङ्क्रनाइज़/ verb **synchronize (sth) (with sth)** एक ही समय में घटित होने देना; समकालिक होना/करना : The sound in a movie must synchronize with the action.

synchronous /'सिङ्क्रनस्/ adj (औप) समकालिक, तुल्यकालिक।

syndicate /'सिन्डिकट्/ noun सिंडिकेट, व्यवसाय संघ।

syndrome /'सिन्ड्रोम्/ noun 1 (चिकि) रोग के अलग-अलग समुच्चयगत लक्षण 2 समुच्चयगत मत, विचार, घटनाएँ आदि जो किसी स्थिति की विशेषता दर्शाती हों : Unemployment, inflation and low wages are all part of the same economic syndrome.

synonym /'सिननिम्/ noun पर्यायशब्द, समानार्थी शब्द : 'Shut' and 'close' are synonyms. ▸ **synonymous** /सि'नॉनिमस्/ adj **synonymous (with sth)** समानार्थी।

synopsis /सि'नॉप्सिस्/ noun (pl **synopses** /सि'नॉप्सीज़/) पुस्तक, शोध-प्रबंध आदि की रूपरेखा; सारांश : The programme gives a brief synopsis of the plot.

syntax /'सिन्टैक्स्/ noun (भाषा विज्ञान) वाक्य रचना, वाक्य विज्ञान ▸ **syntactic** /सिन्'टैक्टिक्/ adj : syntactic differences between English and French.

synthesis /'सिन्थ़सिस्/ noun (pl **syntheses** /'सिन्थ़सीज़/) 1 सम्मिश्रण, संयोजन : develop a new theory by the synthesis of several other theories 2 संयोजन द्वारा बनी वस्तु : Her art is a synthesis of modern and traditional techniques. 3 रासायनिक पदार्थ का उत्पादन ▸ **synthesize, -ise** /'सिन्थ़साइज़/ verb 1 सम्मिश्रण करना : The two elements are synthesized by a chemical process. 2 रासायनिक पदार्थ बनाना।

synthetic /सिन्'थ़ेटिक/ adj 1 कृत्रिम रीति से बना : synthetic fabrics/chemicals 2 (अनौप, अपमा) अप्राकृतिक; झूठा : the salesman's synthetic friendliness.

syringe /सि'रिन्ज़/ noun पिचकारी, इंजेक्शन की सुई ▸ **syringe** verb पिचकारी से द्रव डालना/छिड़कना या साफ़ करना : syringe a wound.

syrup /'सिरप्/ noun 1 चाशनी, शीरा 2 कोई भी गाढ़ा मीठा द्रव : maple syrup on pancakes.

system /'सिस्टम्/ noun 1 तंत्र : a railway system ○ the nervous system 2 सिद्धांतों, विचारों की प्रक्रिया का सेट; समुच्चय : a system of philosophy 3 **the system** [sing] (अनौप, सामान्यत: अपमा) समाज, संस्था आदि की व्यवस्था, योजना : You can't beat the system.
■ **get sth out of one's system**

(अनौप) किसी प्रभावशाली भाव/इच्छा को व्यक्त/पूरा करके उससे पीछा छुड़ाना : *Why don't you tell me what's wrong? You'll feel better when you've got it out of your system.* ▸ **systematic** / ˌसिस्ट 'मैटिक् / *adj* 1 सुव्यवस्थित, योजनानुसार : *a series of systematic experiments* 2 (अपमा) पूर्वनियोजित (षड्यंत्र आदि) **systematically** / ˌसिस्ट 'मैटिक्लि / *adv.*

Tt

tab / टैब् / noun 1 विशेषत:पकड़ने, टाँगने, बाँधने या पहचानने के लिए किसी वस्तु से जुड़ा और बाहर की तरफ़ निकलता हुआ कपड़े/धातु/काग़ज़ का टुकड़ा : To open, pull tab. ० a name-tab 2 (US) (**tabulator** भी) कंप्यूटर/टाइपराइटर की कुंजी-पटल पर सारणी बनाने का उपकरण 3 (US) बिल या क़ीमत ■ **keep tabs on sb/sth** (अनौप) नियमित रूप से/लगातार निरीक्षण या नियंत्रण में रखना : keep tabs on private phone calls made by members of staff.

table / टेब्ल् / noun 1 मेज़ 2 मेज़ पर बैठे व्यक्ति : His jokes amused the whole table. 3 तालिका, सारणी (तथ्यों आदि की सूची) : a table of contents 4 (गणित का) पहाड़ा : Do you know your six times table? ■ **on the table** 1 विचार या चर्चा के लिए प्रस्तुत 2 भविष्य में विचार-विमर्श के लिए स्थगित **turn the tables (on sb)** स्वयं को श्रेष्ठ अवस्था में लाने के लिए स्थिति को विपरीत करना ▸ **table** verb चर्चा के लिए कुछ औपचारिक रूप से प्रस्तुत करना **tablecloth** noun मेज़पोश **tablespoon** noun बड़ी चम्मच **table tennis** (अनौप ping-pong भी) noun टेबल टेनिस (का खेल)।

tableau / टैब्लो / noun (pl **tableaux** / टैब्लो या टैब्लोज़/) प्रभावशाली, नाटकीय दृश्य; झाँकी : a tableau in which the dancers form themselves into the shape of a heart.

tablet / टैब्लट् / noun 1 दवा की गोली 2 पट्टी, पटिया जिस पर शब्द अंकित किए गए हों : a memorial tablet engraved with the name of the school's founder.

tabloid / टैब्लॉइड् / noun छोटे आकार का लोकप्रिय समाचार-पत्र जो चित्रों और सनसनीख़ेज़ ख़बरों से भरपूर हो।

taboo / टब्बू / noun (pl **taboos**) **taboo (against/on sth)** संस्कृति या धर्म द्वारा निषेध/वर्जित वस्तु या कार्य : tribal taboos ▸ **taboo** adj निषिद्ध : Sex is no longer the taboo subject it was.

tabular / टैब्युलर् / adj (औप) सारणी/ तालिका में व्यवस्थित या प्रस्तुत किया गया।

tabulate / टैब्युलेट् / verb सारणी या तालिका में क्रमबद्ध करना ▸ **tabulation** noun.

tacit / टैसिट् / adj मौन, अनकहा; उप-लक्षित : give tacit agreement/support.

taciturn / टैसिटर्न् / adj चुप्पा, अल्प-भाषी ▸ **taciturnity** noun.

tack / टैक् / noun 1 [sing] किसी के कार्यों, शब्दों, विचारों की सामान्य प्रवृत्ति : be on the right/wrong tack 2 चपटी कील, बिरिंजी : a carpet tack 3 (सिलाई में) कच्चा टाँका, तोपा ▸ **tack** verb 1 बिरिंजी से जोड़ना : tack a poster to the wall 2 कच्चे टाँके लगाना, तुरुपना 3 (जहाज़ का) टेढ़े-मेढ़े चलना : The yacht tacked towards the mainland.

tackle / टैक्ल् / verb 1 समस्या का समाधान ढूँढ़ना : tackle a problem head on 2 (फुटबाल/हॉकी में) विरोधी से गेंद छीनने का प्रयास करना : He was tackled just outside the penalty area. 3 **tackle sb (about/on sth)** किसी अप्रिय या कठिन विषय पर किसी से बात करना : When are you going to tackle your brother about that money he owes me? ▸ **tackle** / टैक्ल् / noun 1 (फुटबाल में) विरोधी से गेंद छीनना 2 (तक) भारी वस्तु उठाने, खींचने आदि के लिए रस्सी और अन्य उपकरण 3 साज़-सामान, उपकरण : fishing tackle.

tact / टैक्ट् / noun व्यवहार-कौशल : *Criticizing one's colleagues requires tact and diplomacy.* ▸ **tactful** *adj* व्यवहार-कुशल **tactless** *adj.*

tactic / ' टैक्टिक् / noun 1 (प्राय: *pl*) (प्राय: प्रतिद्वंद्वी के विरुद्ध) कुछ पाने के लिए अपनाया गया तरीका 2 चाल, रणनीति : *skilled in tactics.*

tadpole /'टैड्पोल् / noun बेंगची, मेंढक का बच्चा।

tag / टैग्/ noun 1 (प्राय: समासों में) मूल्य, पता आदि दर्शाने वाला लेबल : *put name-tags on all one's belongings* 2 किसी का वर्णन करने के लिए प्रयुक्त शब्द या वाक्य 3 (व्या) वाक्य के अंत में जोड़ा गया शब्द या उपवाक्य जैसे *I do* वाक्य *Yes, I do.* में ▸ **tag** *verb* (-gg-) **tag (with sth)** 1 टैग लगाना : *I've tagged the relevant pages with yellow stickers.* 2 किसी व्यक्ति/वस्तु को उसके गुण आदि दर्शाने वाला नाम देना : *The president wishes to avoid being tagged as a lame duck.* ■ **tag along (behind/with sb)** पीछे-पीछे/साथ में चलना **tag sth on (to sth)** कुछ अतिरिक्त जोड़ना : *a postscript tagged on at the end of a letter.*

tail / टेल्/ noun 1 पूँछ, दुम 2 पूँछनुमा; पूँछ की स्थिति में (अंतःस्थिति में) : *the tail of a comet/kite* 3 (अनौप) पिछलगा व्यक्ति; छिपकर पीछा करने वाला 4 **tails** सिक्के का वह भाग जिस पर मानव या अन्य आकृति नहीं होती है ▸ **tail** *verb* पीछा करना ■ **tail off/away** आकार, संख्या, गुण आदि में कम हो जाना : *The number of tourists starts to tail off in October.*

tailor / 'टेलर्/ noun दर्ज़ी, टेलर ▸ **tailor** *verb* **tailor sth to/for sb/sth** किसी विशेष व्यक्ति, उद्देश्य आदि के लिए तैयार करना/अनुकूल बनाना : *homes tailored to the needs of the elderly* **tailor-made** *adj* 1 दर्ज़ी द्वारा तैयार 2 **tailor-**

made (for sth/sb) किसी ख़ास व्यक्ति, उद्देश्य के लिए बनाया गया : *He seems tailor-made for the job.*

taint / टेन्ट्/ noun (प्राय: *sing*) **taint of (sth)** रोग/दुर्गुण का अवशेष ▸ **taint** *verb* **taint sth (with sth)** छूत लगना/लगाना, दूषित होना/करना : *His reputation was tainted by the scandal.*

take / टेक् / verb (*pt* **took** / टुक् /; *pp* **taken** / 'टेकन् /) 1 **take sth/sb (with one); take sth (to sb)** ले जाना, किसी के साथ जाना : *She takes her children to school by car.* 2 लेना, पकड़ना, ग्रहण करना : *Free newspapers: please take one.* 3 ग़लती से या बिना अनुमति के ले जाना : *Someone has taken my gloves.* 4 **take sth (from sb)** अधिकार करना, जीत लेना, क़ब्ज़ा करना 5 स्वीकार करना; ग्राहक बनना : *If they offer me the job, I will take it.* 6 सहन करना; संभाल पाना : *She can't take criticism.* 7 **take sth as sth** समझना, अर्थ लगाना : *What did you take his comments to mean?* 8 **take sb/sth for sb/sth** (विशेषत: ग़लत तरीके से) मान लेना, समझना : *Do you take me for a fool?* 9 रहने के लिए जगह ढूँढ़ना : *We're taking a cottage in Nainital for a month.* 10 पता लगाकर लेखा-जोखा रखना : *The policeman took my name and address.* 11 किसी कार्य विशेष के लिए निर्धारित समय, गुण, व्यक्ति आदि की आवश्यकता होना : *It took her three hours to mend her bike.* 12 उपाधि पाने के लिए परीक्षा में बैठना : *When are you taking your driving test?* 13 यातायात साधन विशेष द्वारा जाना : *take the bus/train/plane* 14 मत या दृष्टिकोण रखना : *The government is taking a tough line on drug abuse.* ■ **take after sb** सदृश होना, परिवार के बड़े सदस्य से शकल, स्वभाव आदि मिलना **take it**

from me (that...) *(अनौप)* मेरी बात पर पूरा भरोसा कर सकते हो **take it/sth out on sb** किसी और पर गुस्सा निकालना **take it (that....)** कुछ मान लेना/समझना : *Are we to take it that you refuse to cooperate?* **take off** 1 हवाई जहाज़ का उड़ान भरना 2 कूदते समय धरती से संपर्क छोड़ना 3 अचानक तेज़ी से चलने/भागने लगना **take (sb) in** अतिथि रूप में लेना; चालाकी से लाभ उठाना **take sb off** नक़ल उतार कर मज़ाक़ बनाना **take sb on** 1 व्यक्ति को नौकरी देना, काम में लगाना 2 प्रतिद्वंद्वी के रूप में स्वीकार करना 3 कर्म- चारियों को काम में लगाना **take sb out** निमंत्रित व्यक्ति को बाहर ले जाना **take (sth) in** 1 शरीर में सोख लेना : *Fish take in oxygen through their gills.* 2 समझना 3 ध्यानपूर्वक देखना 4 कपड़े की लंबाई- चौड़ाई आदि घटाना **take sth out** लाइसेंस/ बीमा पॉलिसि आदि लेना **take (sth) over** प्रबंध/नियंत्रण में ले लेना **take sth up** 1 कोई काम/क्रिया सीखना शुरू करना 2 (विशेषत: नौकरी) शुरू करना 3 समर्थन देते हुए भाग लेना 4 रुके हुए को जारी करना 5 उपलब्ध वस्तु को स्वीकार करना **take sth up with sb** किसी से सहायता के लिए बातचीत करना **take to...** बचाव के लिए किसी स्थान पर जाना : *take to the for- ests/hills* **take to sb/sth** पसंद करना : *He hasn't taken to his new school.* **take to sth/doing sth** आदत बना लेना: *She's taken to drink.* **take up sth** समय लेना या स्थान घेरना : *Her time is fully taken up with writing.* ▸ **take- away** (US **takeout**) *noun* पकाया भोजन जो रेस्तरां से ख़रीद कर कहीं और खाया जा सके; ऐसा भोजन उपलब्ध कराने वाला भोजनालय **take home pay** *noun* कर और बाक़ी योगदान काटने के बाद बचा वेतन।

takings / 'टेकिङ्ज़् / *noun [pl]* आय, (व्यापार में) प्राप्ति : *count the day's takings.*

talcum powder / 'टैल्कम् पाउडर् / (**talc** / 'टैल्क् / भी) *noun* त्वचा पर लगाने के लिए मुलायम सुगंधित पाउडर।

tale / टेल् / *noun* 1 कहानी, क़िस्सा : *tales of adventure* 2 सत्य घटनाओं का विवरण या वर्णन : *He told me the tale of how he escaped from prison.* 3 अफ़वाह; मनगढ़ंत क़िस्सा।

talent / 'टैलन्ट् / *noun* 1 **talent (for sth)** प्रतिभा, प्रकृतिदत्त योग्यता : *have im- mense artistic talent* 2 प्रतिभाशाली व्यक्ति : *There's always room for new/fresh talent in the music busi- ness.* ▸ **talented** *adj* प्रतिभा संपन्न; प्रवीण : *a highly talented musician.*

talisman / 'टैलिज़्मन् / *noun* तावीज़, तंत्र-मंत्र का कवच।

talk¹ / टॉक् / *verb* 1 **talk (to/with sb) (about/of sth/sb)** बातचीत करना, बोलना; विचार-विमर्श करना : *We talked for almost an hour.* 2 बोलने की शक्ति/ समझ रखना : *children learning to talk* 3 शब्दों में व्यक्त करना 4 दूसरों के बारे में बातें करना 5 मानव भाषा की नक़ल कर सकना : *You can teach some parrots to talk.* ■ **talk back (to sb)** किसी अधिकारिक निर्देश/निंदा का अशिष्टता से जवाब देना **talk down to sb** किसी को कम बुद्धिमान या महत्त्वपूर्ण समझते हुए बात करना **talk sb into/out of doing sth** किसी को कुछ करने/न करने के लिए राज़ी करना **talk sb round (to sth)** स्वीकार करने/सहमत होने के लिए राज़ी करना : *We finally managed to talk them round.* **talk (sth) over) (with sb)** विचार-विमर्श करना ▸ **talkative** / 'टॉक- टिव्/ *adj* बातूनी, बक्की : *a very talka- tive child.*

talk² / टॉक् / *noun* 1 बातचीत, चर्चा 2 बातें, विशेषत: बिना काररवाई, परिणाम या सही सूचना के; अफ़वाह : *There's talk of a general election.* 3 भाषण;

अनौपचारिक वार्ता : *She gave a talk on her visit to China.* **4 talks** [*pl*] (समझौता-) वार्ता : *arms talks* ■ **the talk of sth** किसी स्थान पर बातचीत का मुख्य विषय : *Her resignation was the talk of the office.*

tall / टॉल् / *adj* (**-er, -est**) **1** (व्यक्ति/वस्तु) लंबा **2** लंबाई विशेष का : *Rajiv is over six feet tall.* ▸ **tall order** *noun* [*sing*] (अनौप) बेतुकी या अनुचित माँग; कठिन कार्य **tall story** *noun* (अनौप) अविश्वसनीय बात।

tallow / 'टैलो / *noun* चरबी (विशेषत: पशुओं की) जो मोमबत्ती, साबुन आदि बनाने में काम आती है।

tally / 'टैलि / *verb* (*pt, pp* tallied) **tally (with sth)** (कथन, मात्रा, हिसाब आदि का) मेल खाना, अनुरूप होना : *These figures don't tally.* ▸ **tally** *noun* हिसाब, लेखा : *a match tally of 14 points.*

talon / 'टैलन् / *noun* (प्राय: *pl*) पंजा, चंगुल : *an eagle's talons.*

tamarind / 'टैमरिन्ड् / *noun* इमली।

tambourine / टैम्ब'रीन् / *noun* (संगीत) डफली, खंजरी।

tame / टेम् / *adj* (**-r, -st**) **1** (पशु-पक्षी) पालतू, घरेलू (न कि जंगली) **2** (परि) (व्यक्ति) (दुम दबा कर) आज्ञापालन को तैयार : *She gets her tame husband to help her with domestic chores.* **3** नीरस, फीका : *a novel with rather a tame ending* ▸ **tame** *verb* पालतू बनाना : *taming wild animals.*

tamper / 'टैम्पर् / *verb* ■ **tamper with sth** बिना अधिकार के हस्तक्षेप करना, दस्तंदाज़ी/छेड़छाड़ करना : *The records of the meeting had been tampered with.*

tan / टैन् / *verb* (**-nn-**) **1** (व्यक्ति/त्वचा) सूर्य की धूप में अधिक रहने से ताँबे जैसा रंग हो जाना या करना : *My skin tans easily.*

2 पशुओं की खाल को काम लाने योग्य चमड़ा बनाना ▸ **tan** *noun, adj* भूरा रंग, पिंगल **tanner** *noun* चर्मशोधक **tannery** *noun* चर्मशोधन का स्थान।

tang / टैङ् / *noun* (प्राय: *sing*) तीखा स्वाद; तीक्ष्ण गंध : *a sauce with a tang of lemon juice.*

tangent / 'टैन्जन्ट् / *noun* (ज्यामिति) स्पर्श रेखा ■ **go/fly off at a tangent** अचानक विषय, काररवाई, व्यवहार आदि बदल देना : *Stick to the point—don't keep going off at a tangent.*

tangible / 'टैन्जब्ल् / *adj* **1** स्पष्ट और निश्चित; वास्तविक : *tangible proof* **2** स्पर्शनीय : *the tangible world.*

tangle / 'टैङ्ग्ल् / *noun* **1** बालों/धागों आदि की गुत्थी जिसे सुलझाना मुश्किल हो : *a tangle of branches* **2** गुत्थी, उलझन की स्थिति : *His financial affairs are in a complete tangle.* **3** (अनौप) झगड़ा या बहस : *They got into a tangle about politics and started shouting at each other.* ▸ **tangle** *verb* **tangle (sth) (up)** उलझाना, जटिल बनाना।

tank / टैङ्क् / *noun* **1** बड़ी टंकी, हौज़; द्रव या गैस रखने का बड़ा पात्र : *the petrol-tank of a car* **2** सेना का टैंक ▸ **tanker** *noun* टैंकर जहाज़ (तेल-पोत); टैंकर लॉरी/ हवाई जहाज़।

tantalize, -ise / 'टैन्टलाइज़् / *verb* तरसाना, ललचाना : *Give the dog the bone—don't tantalize him.* ▸ **tantalizing, -ising** *adj* : *a tantalizing prospect/smell of food.*

tantamount / 'टैन्टमाउन्ट् / *adj* **tantamount to sth** प्रभाव में बराबर, तुल्य : *Her statement is tantamount to a confession of guilt.*

tantrum / 'टैन्ट्रम् / *noun* अचानक आवेश, क्रोध में आने की क्रिया, विशेषकर बच्चों द्वारा

या बच्चों की तरह : *have/throw a tantrum*.

tap¹ / टैप् / *noun* 1 (*US* **faucet** भी) नल की टोंटी 2 गुप्त रूप से फ़ोन सुनने के लिए लगाया गया उपकरण : *put a tap on sb's phone* ▸ **tap** *verb* (**-pp-**) 1 टोंटी में से द्रव निकालना/निकलने देना : *tap a cask of cider* 2 पेड़ की छाल में से गोंद या रस निकालने के लिए चीरा लगाना : *tap rubber-trees* 3 किसी चीज़ के स्रोत में से आपूर्ति निकालना 4 फ़ोन में टैप लगाना।

tap² / टैप् / *verb* (**-pp-**) 1 थपकी देना; धीमे से खटखटाना : *Who's that tapping at the window?* 2 हलके-से मारना : *tapping her fingers on the table* ▸ **tap** *noun* थपकी।

tape / टेप् / *noun* 1 फ़ीता (कुछ बाँधने के लिए) : *a metre of linen tape* 2 टेप-रिकॉर्डर का टेप; कैसेट-टेप 3 वस्तुएँ चिपकाने के लिए पतले काग़ज़ या अन्य लचीले पदार्थ की पट्टी ▸ **tape** *verb* 1 फ़ीते से बाँधना; टेप से चिपकाना : *tape (up) a bundle* 2 टेप पर कुछ रिकॉर्ड करना : *tape a concert (off/from the radio)* **tape-measure** (**measuring tape** भी) *noun* इंची-टेप।

taper / टेप्र / *verb* 1 **taper (sth) (off) (to sth)** क्रमशः संकरा होता जाना या बना देना : *a blade that tapers (off) to a fine point* 2 **taper (sth) off** क्रमशः कम होते जाना या बना देना : *taper off production of an old model.*

tapestry / टैपिस्ट्रि / *noun* (*pl* **tapestries**) कपड़े का विशाल टुकड़ा जिसमें डिज़ाइन बनाने के लिए रंगीन ऊन के धागे सिल या बुन दिए जाते हैं : *a tapestry cushion cover.*

tar / टार् / *noun* 1 तारकोल 2 तंबाकू जलाने पर प्राप्त एक वैसा ही पदार्थ : *low-tar cigarettes* ▸ **tar** *verb* (**-rr-**) तारकोल डालना : *a tarred road.*

tardy / टार्डि / *adj* (औप) 1 धीमी, मंद गति से होने/चलने वाला : *be tardy in offering help* 2 सुस्त, देर से पहुँचने वाला : *a tardy arrival* ▸ **tardily** *adv.*

target / टार्गिट् / *noun* 1 लक्ष्य, निशाना : *shoot off target* 2 **target (for sth)** नापसंदगी, निंदा आदि का निशाना (व्यक्ति) : *become a target for scorn/hate* 3 उद्देश्य, लक्ष्य : *meet one's export targets* ▸ **target** *verb* (**-t-**) **target sth (at/on sth/sb)** किसी को निशाना/लक्ष्य बनाना : *missiles targeted on Iraq.* ○ *A new magazine that targets the elderly.*

tariff / टैरिफ़् / *noun* 1 होटल में भोजन-आवास आदि की दर सूची 2 आयातित सामान पर लगने वाले शुल्कों की सूची; शुल्क दर : *raise tariff barriers against foreign goods.*

tarmac / टार्मैक् / *noun* पक्की सड़क।

tarnish / टार्निश् / *verb* 1 धूप या नमी के कारण (धातु का) बदरंग हो जाना या धब्बा पड़ जाना : *The brasswork needs polishing—it's badly tarnished.* 2 किसी की इज़्ज़त ख़राब करना, कलंक लगाना, छवि बिगाड़ना : *a tarnished image.*

tarpaulin / टार्'पॉलिन् / *noun* तिरपाल (मोटा जलरोधी कपड़ा)।

tarry / टैरि / *verb* (*pt, pp* **tarried**) (अप्र या साहि) अधिक समय तक ठहरना/रहना; आने जाने में देर लगाना।

tart¹ / टार्ट् / *adj* 1 अम्ल, तीक्ष्ण खट्टा/खटास 2 व्यंग्यात्मक, कटु, कठोर : *a tart reply/tone* ▸ **tartly** *adv.*

tart² / टार्ट् / *noun* एक प्रकार की पेस्ट्री।

tart³ / टार्ट् / *noun* वेश्या।

task / टास्क्; *US* टैस्क् / *noun* नियत कार्य, विशेषतः कठिन या अप्रिय कार्य : *a daunting/thankless task* ■ **take sb to task (about/for/over sth)** डाँटना।

taskmaster / टास्कमास्टर; *US* टास्क्-मैस्टर् / *noun* कठोर अधिकारी।

tassel / 'टैस्ल् / noun फुँदा/फुँदना, (धागों का) झब्बा।

taste¹ / टेस्ट् / noun 1 स्वाद, ज़ायक़ा : Sugar has a sweet taste. 2 स्वाद, ज़ायक़ा पहचानने की शक्ति : Having a bad cold affects one's sense of taste. 3 (प्राय: sing) चखने के लिए लिया गया अल्पमात्रा में भोजन या पेय : Just have a taste of this cheese. 4 [sing] संक्षिप्त अनुभव : It was my first taste of life in a big city. 5 **taste (for sth)** किसी चीज़ के लिए पसंद : have expensive tastes in clothes 6 गुण, औचित्य आदि को पहचानने और उपभोग करने की योग्यता : have excellent taste in art/music ■ **(be) in good, bad, poor, the best of, the worst of, etc taste** सुरुचिपूर्ण/कुरुचिपूर्ण, भद्दा ▸ **tasteful** adj सुरुचिसंपन्न : tasteful furniture **tastefully** adv **tasteless** adj 1 स्वादहीन, रुचिहीन 2 फीका : a tasteless soup **tasty** / टेस्टि / adj (-ier, -iest) स्वादिष्ट : a tasty dish/meal.

taste² / टेस्ट् / verb 1 स्वाद अनुभव कर सकना; चखना : Can you taste the garlic in the stew? 2 **taste (of sth)** कोई विशेष स्वाद होना : taste sour/bitter/sweet 3 चख कर स्वाद लेना 4 अनुभव करना : taste freedom/power.

tattered / टैटई / adj फटा-पुराना : tattered jeans.

tatters / टैटर्ज़् / noun [pl] फटे-पुराने कपड़े, लत्ता/चिथड़ा : His clothes hung in tatters. ■ **in tatters** नष्ट अवस्था मे : The court case left his reputation in tatters.

tattoo / ट'टू; US टै'टू / noun (pl tattoos) शरीर पर गोदे गए चित्र आदि ▸ **tattoo** verb गोदना।

taunt / टॉन्ट् / verb **taunt sb (with sth)** ताना मारना, फबती कसना : The other children taunted him with remarks about his size. ▸ **taunt** noun (प्राय: pl) ताना, फबती।

Taurus / 'टॉरस् / noun राशिचक्र की दूसरी राशि, वृष या वृषभ; इस राशि का व्यक्ति।

taut / टॉट् / adj 1 कस कर खिंचा हुआ : a taut string ○ taut skin 2 (मांसपेशियाँ या नसें) तनी हुई, कसी हुई : a taut body.

tavern / 'टैवर्न् / noun (प्रा या साहि) सराय; शराबख़ाना।

tawdry / 'टॉड्रि / adj 1 आकर्षक बनाने के इरादे से किंतु भड़कीला और कुरुचिपूर्ण : tawdry jewellery 2 नैतिक दृष्टि से घृणित/कुत्सित : a tawdry affair.

tax / टैक्स् / noun टैक्स, कर : a property/sales tax ■ **a tax on sth** भार, बोझा : a tax on one's health ▸ **tax** verb 1 कर लगाना : tax luxury goods 2 कर अदा करना 3 बोझा बनना; भारी माँग रखना : All these questions are beginning to tax my patience. ■ **tax sb with sth/doing sth** दोष या आरोप लगाना ▸ **taxable** adj कर-योग्य : taxable income **taxing** adj थकाने या उबाने वाला; जिसके लिए बहुत परिश्रम की ज़रूरत हो : a taxing job.

taxation / टैक्'सेशन् / noun 1 कर पद्धति : the separate taxation of husbands and wives 2 दिया जाने वाला कर।

taxi / 'टैक्सि / (taxi-cab, cab भी) noun (pl taxies) किराए की मोटर, टैक्सी ▸ **taxi** verb (हवाई जहाज़ का) धरती पर पहियों के बल चलना : The plane was taxiing along the runway.

tea / टी / noun 1 चाय (की पत्ती); चाय (पेय) 2 (तीसरे पहर की) चाय।

teach / टीच् / verb (pt, pp **taught** / टॉट् /) 1 पढ़ाना; जानकारी देना; सिखाना : teach French/history/judo 2 तथ्य, सिद्धांत आदि की शिक्षा देना : Christ taught forgiveness. ▸ **teaching**

noun 1 अध्यापक का कार्य 2 (प्राय: *pl*) शिक्षा, जो पढ़ाया गया है।

teacher /'टीचर्/ *noun* शिक्षक, अध्यापक।

teak / टीक् / *noun* सागौन (की लकड़ी)।

team / टीम् / *noun* 1 खिलाड़ियों का दल, टीम : *Which team do you play for?* 2 एक साथ काम करने वाले लोगों का दल/ टोली : *a sales team* ▸ **team** *verb* ■ **team up (with sb)** किसी और के साथ काम करना, विशेषत: समान उद्देश्य के लिए ▸ **team spirit** *noun* पूरे दल, न कि व्यक्ति विशेष, के हित में कार्य करने की इच्छा

teamwork *noun* संगठित प्रयत्न : *The success of the project was largely the result of good teamwork.*

tear[1] / टेअर् / *verb* (*pt* **tore** / टॉर् /; *pp* **torn** / टॉर्न् /) 1 फाड़ना, चीरना : *tear a sheet of paper in two* 2 उखाड़ना, नोचना : *He tore his clothes off and dived into the lake.* 3 फट जाना : *This material tears easily.* 4 खिंचने से मांसपेशियों को हानि पहुँचना 5 उतावली में/ वेग से जाना : *cars tearing past* ■ **be torn between A and B** दो वस्तुओं/ व्यक्तियों में से किसी एक को चुनने की कठिन स्थिति में होना **tear at sth (with sth)** (विशेषत: काट कर या फाड़ कर) हिंसात्मक हमला करना : *He tore at the meat with his bare hands.* **tear sth apart, to shreds, to bits, etc** पूरी तरह नष्ट कर देना/हटा देना **tear sth down** ढा देना ▸ **tear** *noun* चीरा, खोंच : *The sheet has a tear in it.*

tear[2] / टिअर् / *noun* (प्राय: *pl*) आँसू : *She was in tears over the death of her puppy.* ▸ **tearful** *adj* अश्रुपूर्ण, दुखद।

tease / टीज़् / *verb* 1 छेड़ना, चिढ़ाना : *The other boys used to tease him because of his accent.* 2 किसी को यौनाकर्षित करना : *flirting and teasing* ▸ **teasingly** *adv.*

technical /'टेक्निकल्/ *adj* 1 तकनीकी, तकनीक से संबंधित : *a technical education* 2 (पुस्तक आदि) विशिष्ट ज्ञान की आवश्यकता वाली : *The article is rather technical in places.* 3 क़ानून या नियमों की विशेष जानकारी से ही समझ में आने वाला : *a crucial technical point* ▸ **technicality** /,टेक्नि'कैलटि / *noun* (*pl* **technicalities**) 1 विषय-संबंधी शब्द 2 बिना ख़ास महत्त्व का विवरण : *a mere technicality* **technically** / ,टेक्निक्लि / *adv* 1 तकनीक के संदर्भ में 2 सुनिश्चित, पक्के तौर पर।

technician / टेक्'निशन् / *noun* अपनी विशेष विधि में विशेषज्ञ : *laboratory technicians.*

technique / टेक्'नीक् / *noun* तकनीक, विशेष कौशल से संपन्न करने की विधि : *applying modern techniques to a traditional craft.*

technology / टेक्'नॉलजि / *noun* (*pl* **technologies**) प्रायोगिक विज्ञान का उद्योग, व्यापार आदि में उपयोग; प्रौद्योगिकी; तकनीकी विधियाँ : *new computer technologies.*

teddy bear /'टेडि बेअर् / *noun* (**teddy** भी) कपड़े या रूई जैसी मुलायम वस्तु से बना रीछ की शकल का खिलौना।

tedious /'टीडिअस् / *adj* अत्यधिक लंबा, थकाऊ और जी-ऊबाऊ : *The work is tedious.*

teem / टीम् / *verb* ■ **teem with sth** बड़ी संख्या में होना या रखना : *His mind is teeming with bright ideas.*

teenager /'टीनेजर् / *noun* 13 से 19 वर्ष का लड़का या लड़की : *music popular with teenagers.*

teens / टीन्ज़् / *noun* [*pl*] 13 से 19 वर्ष की उम्र, किशोरावस्था : *be in one's teens.*

teethe / टीद् / *verb* (बच्चे के) दाँत निकलना : *Babies like to chew something when they're teething.*

▸ **teething troubles (teething problems** भी) *noun [pl]* प्रारंभिक चरणों में छोटी कठिनाइयाँ।

teetotaller (*US* **teetotaler**) / टी'टो-ट्लर् / *noun* शराब का कभी न सेवन करने वाला व्यक्ति।

tel(e)- *pref* (*पूर्वपद*) **1** दूर- : *telepathy/telescopic* **2** टी वी विषयक : *telefilm* **3** दूरसंचार विषयक : *teleordering* ◦ *telemarketing.*

telecast / 'टेलिकास्ट् / *noun* टेलिविज़न कार्यक्रम का प्रसारण ▸ **telecast** *verb* टेलिविज़न कार्यक्रम प्रसारित करना।

telecommunications / टेलिक म्युनि 'केश्न्ज़् / (*अनौप* **telecoms** / 'टेलिकॉम्ज़् / भी) *noun [pl]* दूर-संचार; संचार विज्ञान तथा प्रौद्योगिकी का उपयोग।

telegram / 'टेलिग्रैम् / *noun* (**telemessage** भी) तार।

telegraph / 'टेलि'ग्राफ़; *US* 'टेलिग्रैफ़् / *noun* टेलीग्राफ़, तार भेजने का उपकरण ▸ **telegraph** *verb* तार भेजना **telegraphic** / टेलि'ग्रैफ़िक् / *adj* तार से भेजने योग्य/तार से भेजा गया : *telegraphic message.*

telepathy / ट'लेपथि / *noun* बिना बातचीत के दूर स्थित एक मस्तिष्क का दूसरे मस्तिष्क पर प्रभाव; दूरसंवेदन, दूरबोध : *She felt there was some telepathy between them.*

telephone / 'टेलिफ़ोन् / *noun* टेलिफ़ोन ▸ **telephone** (**phone** भी) *verb* टेलिफ़ोन द्वारा बात करना : *He telephoned to say he'd be late.*

telescope / 'टेलिस्कोप् / *noun* दूरबीन।

television / 'टेलिविश्न् / *noun* टेलिविज़न (टी वी) ▸ **televise** / 'टेलिवाइज़् / *verb* टी वी के माध्यम से संचार करना : *televise the Olympic Games.*

telex / 'टेलेक्स् / *noun* विशिष्ट मशीनों के माध्यम से संदेश भेजने की व्यवस्था (एक मशीन में संदेश टाइप किया जाता है जो टेलिफ़ोन द्वारा दूसरी मशीन तक पहुँचता है और दूसरी मशीन टंकित रूप में संदेश को निकाल देती है); इस प्रकार भेजा या पाया गया संदेश।

tell / टेल् / *verb* (*pt, pp* **told** / टोल्ड् /) **1 tell sth (to sb)** कहना, बताना, सुनाना : *tell jokes/stories* **2** जानकारी प्रदान करना **3** शब्दों में व्यक्त करना **4** भेद बताना, रहस्य खोलना : *Promise you won't tell.* **5** तय/निर्धारित करना; निश्चित रूप से जानना : *You can tell he's angry when he starts shouting a lot.* **6 tell A from B** (विशेषत: **can/could/be able to** के साथ) एक व्यक्ति/वस्तु को दूसरे से अलग पहचान पाना : *Can you tell Praveen from his twin brother?* **7 tell (on sb)** प्रत्यक्ष, स्पष्ट प्रभाव दिखाई पड़ना : *The strain was beginning to tell (on the rescue team).* **8** आदेश, निर्देश या सलाह देना : *Tell him to wait.* ■ **all told** सब कुछ/सबको गिन कर और मिला कर **tell on sb** (*अनौप*) विशेषत: अधिकारी को किसी की गतिविधियों के बारे में बताना : *Sridhar caught his sister smoking and told on her.* **tell (sb) off (for sth/doing sth)** (*अनौप*) किसी को ग़लत काम के लिए डाँटना **tell tales (about sb)** किसी व्यक्ति के भेद, अवगुण आदि के बारे में जानकारी देना **there's no knowing/saying/telling** यह कहना/भविष्यवाणी करना मुश्किल/असंभव है : *There's absolutely no telling how he'll react.* ▸ **telling** *adj* प्रभावकारी : *a telling argument/example.*

temper¹ / 'टेम्पर् / *noun* **1** मनोदशा, मिज़ाज, तबीयत : *be in a bad/good temper* **2** (प्राय: *sing*) जल्दी क्रोधित होने की प्रवृत्ति : *learn to control one's temper* ■ **keep/lose one's temper** क्रोध पर नियंत्रण रखने में सफल/असफल होना ▸ **-tempered** / -'टेम्पर्ड् / (समासों

में) विशेष मिज़ाज का होना : *a hot-tempered man.*

temper² / टेम्पर् / *verb* 1 स्टील (फ़ौलाद) को अपेक्षित कड़ापन आदि देना 2 **temper sth (with sth)** प्रभाव कम या मंद करना : *temper justice with mercy.*

temperament / टेम्परमन्ट् / *noun* व्यक्ति का स्वभाव जो उसकी सोच, आचरण आदि को प्रभावित करता है : *a man with an artistic temperament* ▸ **temperamental** *adj.*

temperance / टेम्परन्स् / *noun* 1 संयम, मिताचार 2 मिताहार, शराब आदि न पीना : *a temperance society.*

temperate / टेम्परट् / *adj* 1 (औप) संयमी, मिताहारी : *Please be more temperate in your language.* 2 (भूगोल) न तो बहुत गरम और न ही बहुत ठंडा (प्रदेश) : *temperate zones.*

temperature / टेम्प्रचर् / *noun* ताप-मान, ताप ▪ **get/have/run a temperature** ज्वर आना।

tempest / टेम्पिस्ट् / *noun* (औप या साहि) तूफ़ान ▸ **tempestuous** / टेम्पेस्चुअस् / *adj* 1 (औप या साहि) तूफ़ान से प्रभावित 2 उग्र/तीव्र रूप से उत्तेजित : *a tempestuous love-affair.*

template / टेम्प्लेट् / *noun* (पतले गत्ते, प्लास्टिक या धातु का) साँचा जिसके आधार पर कपड़ा, लकड़ी, पत्थर या धातु काटा/काटी जा सके।

temple¹ / टेम्प्ल् / *noun* मंदिर : *the temple of the Sun God at Konark.*

temple² / टेम्प्ल् / *noun* कनपटी।

tempo / टेम्पो / *noun* (*pl* **tempos** / टेम्पोज़्/) 1 किसी प्रक्रिया या आंदोलन की गति, रफ़्तार : *the exhausting tempo of city life* 2 संगीत के अंश की ताल या लय : *in waltz tempo.*

temporal / टेम्परल् / *adj* 1 (औप) समय-संबंधी : *a universe which has spatial and temporal dimensions*

2 (औप) ऐहलौकिक, सांसारिक (न कि आध्यात्मिक) : *one's temporal desires/needs.*

temporary / टेम्परेरि / *adj* अस्थायी : *temporary accommodation.*

tempt / टेम्प्ट् / *verb* 1 **tempt sb (into sth/doing sth)** कोई कार्य करने के लिए प्रलोभन देना, बहकाना : *They tried to tempt her (into staying) with offers of promotion.* 2 आकर्षित करना, इच्छा जाग्रत करना : *The warm weather tempted us into going for a swim.* ▸ **tempting** *adj* आकर्षक, मनमोहक, ललचाने वाला : *That cake looks very tempting.*

temptation / टेम्प्टेश्न् / *noun* 1 प्रलोभन 2 प्रलोभन देने वाली वस्तु।

ten / टेन् / *noun, pron, det* दस (अंक) ▸ **tenth** / टेन्थ् / *pron, det* दसवाँ, दसवाँ अंश।

tenacious / टनेशस् / *adj* 1 वस्तु, सिद्धांत, विशेष दिशा आदि मज़बूती/दृढ़ता से पकड़े हुए; पक्का, हठी/अड़ियल : *a tenacious adversary* 2 (विचार, प्रभाव आदि) जिससे बचना मुश्किल हो : *a tenacious belief in a discredited myth* ▸ **tenacity** / टनैसिटि / *noun.*

tenant / टेनन्ट् / *noun* (मकान, कमरे आदि का) किराएदार; (भूमि आदि का) काश्तकार, आसामी : *evict tenants for non-payment of rent* ▸ **tenancy** / टेनन्सि / *noun* 1 काश्तकारी 2 काश्तकारी की अवधि।

tend¹ / टेन्ड् / *verb* 1 रखवाली करना; सेवा-सुश्रूषा करना : *nurses tending the injured* 2 (US) दुकान, मधुशाला आदि में ग्राहकों की सेवा करना : *tend the store.*

tend² / टेन्ड् / *verb* 1 प्रवृत्त होना, झुकाव होना : *Women tend to live longer than men.* 2 **tend to/towards sth** किसी विशेष दिशा की ओर अग्रसर होना :

He tends towards extreme views.
▸ **tendency** / टेन्डन्सि / *noun* **1 tendency (to/towards sth) (to do sth)** झुकाव, प्रवृत्ति, रुझान : *a tendency towards fatness* **2** बदलने की दिशा, गति की दिशा : *Prices continued to show an upward tendency.*

tender¹ / टेन्डर् / *adj* (-er, -est) **1** संवेदनशील, दयालु/सदय : *have a tender heart* **2** स्नेही, सौम्य : *bid sb a tender farewell* **3** (खाद्य पदार्थ) मुलायम, नरम : *tender meat* **4** नाजुक; आसानी से नष्ट/ख़राब हो जाने वाला **5** छूने से दर्दभरा, संवेदनशील : *My leg is still very tender where it was bruised.*
▸ **tenderly** *adv* **tenderness** *noun.*

tender² / टेन्डर् / *verb* **1 tender (for sth)** (सामान आपूर्ति करने का) ठेका लेना : *Firms were invited to tender for the construction of the new motorway.* **2 tender sth (to sb)** (औप) औपचारिक रूप से प्रस्तुत करना/ देना : *He has tendered his resignation.* ▸ **tender** *noun* **1** (*US* **bid** भी) निविदा (सामान आपूर्ति करने के मूल्य की सूची) : *submit a tender for sth* **2 legal tender** धन का वह रूप जो क़ानूनन प्रचलित है।

tendon / टेन्डन् / *noun* कंडरा, मांसपेशी को हड्डी से जोड़ने वाली नस।

tendril / टेन्ड्रल् / *noun* प्रतान, लताओं के पतले धागे या सूत जैसे अंश जो अपने आधार को पकड़ते हैं।

tenement / टेनमन्ट् / (*US* **tenement-house** भी) *noun* बड़ा आहाता या चाल जिसमें अनेक परिवार रहते हैं : *a tenement block.*

tenet / टेनिट् / *noun* सिद्धांत, मत, धारणा : *This is one of the basic tenets of the Christian faith.*

tennis / टेनिस् / (**lawn tennis** भी) *noun* टेनिस (खेल

tenor¹ / टेनर् / *noun* [sing] **the tenor of sth 1** व्यक्ति/वस्तु का सामान्य दस्तूर, दिशा या स्वभाव : *At this point, the whole tenor of the meeting changed.* **2** सामान्य अर्थ।

tenor² / टेनर् / *noun* (संगीत) सामान्य पुरुष का उच्चतम स्वर; ऐसे स्वर वाला पुरुष।

tense¹ / टेन्स् / *adj* **1** (व्यक्ति) तनावग्रस्त, क्षुब्ध/बेचैन : *He's a very tense person.* **2** (स्थिति, काल, घटना आदि) तनाव-पूर्ण : *a tense moment* **3** (मांसपेशियाँ) तनी/खिंची हुई **4** (वस्तु) कस कर फैलाई हुई : *a tense wire* ▸ **tense** *verb* **tense (sth) (up)** तनाव से ग्रस्त हो जाना/ करना **tensely** *adv* **tenseness** *noun.*

tense² / टेन्स् / *noun* (व्या) क्रिया का काल : *the present/past/future tense.*

tension / टेन्शन् / *noun* **1** भौतिक तनाव, खिंचाव : *Massage helps relieve the tension in one's muscles.* **2** मानसिक, भावनात्मक तनाव, उत्तेजना : *suffer from (nervous) tension* **3** (प्राय: *pl*) **tension (between A and B)** आपसी तनातनी, तीव्र विरोध की स्थिति : *social tensions.*

tent / टेन्ट् / *noun* तंबू/ख़ेमा; शिविर : *put up/take down a tent.*

tentacle / टेन्टक्ल् / *noun* **1** स्पर्शक, कुछ प्राणियों के लंबे पतले लचीले अवयव **2 tentacles** [*pl*] (प्राय: अप्रमा) स्थान, संघ या तंत्र का प्रभाव जिसके चंगुल से निकलना मुश्किल हो : *the spreading tentacles of government bureaucracy.*

tentative / टेन्टटिव् / *adj* बिना पूर्ण निश्चय के साथ कहा/किया गया, प्रयोगात्मक; आरंभिक : *a tentative suggestion* ▸ **tentatively** *adv.*

tenterhooks / टेन्टरहुक्स् / *noun* [*pl*]
■ **(be) on tenterhooks** ख़बर या निर्णय जानने की उत्सुकतापूर्ण प्रतीक्षा की स्थिति; बेचैनी : *We were kept on tenter-*

hooks for hours while the judges were deciding the winners.

tenuous / 'टेन्युअस् / *adj* 1 काफ़ी नाज़ुक या कमज़ोर (जोड़, तर्क आदि): *a rather tenuous argument* ○ *keep a tenuous hold on life* 2 बारीक, पतला : *the tenuous threads of a spider's webs.*

tenure / 'टेन्यर् / *noun* 1 महत्त्वपूर्ण कार्य-काल या कार्यकाल की अवधि : *The tenure of the US Presidency is four years.* 2 भूमि को प्रयोग में लाने की क़ानूनी अवधि।

tepid / 'टेपिड् / *adj* 1 (पानी) गुनगुना 2 उत्साहीन : *His campaign received only tepid support.*

term / टर्म् / *noun* 1 शब्द, पदबंध आदि (विशेष विषय में प्रयुक्त) : *technical/legal/scientific terms* 2 अवधि; निश्चित समय 3 (स्कूल, कालेज का) सत्र : *the autumn/spring term* 4 समया-वधि-विशेष की समाप्ति : *a pregnancy approaching its term* 5 (*गणित*) शृंखला, अनुपात आदि में प्रत्येक संख्या या अभिव्यक्ति 6 **terms** [*pl*] निश्चित शर्तें: *get credit on easy terms* ■ **(be) on good, friendly, bad, etc terms (with sb)** अच्छे, मैत्रीपूर्ण, ख़राब संबंध होना **come to/make terms (with sb)** समझौता करना **come to terms with sth** अवधि के दौरान कुछ अप्रिय स्वीकार करना **in terms of sth; in sth terms** 1 कुछ विशेष से संबंधित : *The job is great in terms of salary but there are disadvantages.* 2 किसी के आधार पर **in the long/short term** निकट/दूर भविष्य में; निकट/दूर भविष्य तक की अवधि : *policies effective only in the short term* **on one's own/on sb's terms** निर्धारित की गई शर्तों पर ▸ **term** *verb* (*औप*) नाम रखना, शब्द के प्रयोग से वर्णन करना/कहना : *He has often been*

termed a genius **terms of reference** *noun* [*pl*] विचारार्ध-विषय।

terminal / 'टर्मिनल् / *adj* 1 (बीमारी) क्रमशः मौत की ओर ले जाती हुई, संघातक: लाइलाज : *terminal cancer* 2 अंत या विनाश में निश्चित परिणति वाला, आख़िरी : *an industry in terminal decline* ▸ **terminal** *noun* 1 (रेल या बस का) अंतिम स्टेशन 2 बिजली के तार के सिरे : *the positive/negative terminals.*

terminate / 'टर्मिनेट् / *verb* 1 (*औप*) समाप्त होना, समाप्त करना : *The meeting terminated in disorder.* 2 (बस या ट्रेन का) यात्रा समाप्त करना ▸ **termination** *noun* 1 समाप्ति 2 (*चिकि*) गर्भपात।

terminology / ,टर्मि 'नॉलजि / *noun* परिभाषिक शब्दावली।

terminus / 'टर्मिनस् / *noun* (*pl* **termini** / 'टर्मिनाइ / या **terminuses** / 'टर्मिन-सिज् /) रेल या बस का अंतिम स्टेशन।

termite / 'टर्माइट् / *noun* दीमक।

terrace / 'टेरस् / *noun* 1 (ढाल पर बने) एक-दूसरे से जुड़े मकानों की शृंखला 2 मकान या रेस्राँ के बग़ल में फ़र्शदार जगह 3 ढाल पर की चौरस भूमि जिस पर पेड़-पौधे उगाए जा सकें ▸ **terraced** *adj* टेरसयुक्त; शृंखला में/का हिस्सा : *a terraced garden/house.*

terracotta / ,टेर 'कॉटा / *noun* 1 पक्की मिट्टी—बरतन या मूर्ति बनाने के लिए : *a terracotta vase* 2 गहरा भूरा रंग जैसे पक्की मिट्टी का।

terrain / ट'रेन् / *noun* भूमि का भाग, उसकी भौतिक विशेषताओं के संदर्भ में : *hilly/marshy/rough terrain.*

terrestrial / ट'रेस्ट्रिअल् / *adj* 1 स्थल-चर; ज़मीन का या ज़मीन पर रहने वाला : *terrestrial species* 2 पृथ्वी का (आकाश के वैषम्य में)।

terrible / 'टेरब्ल् / *adj* 1 भयानक, अति गंभीर, संगीन, दुखी कर देने वाला : *a terrible war/accident* 2 निम्नस्तरीय,

निकृष्ट : *What a terrible meal!* 3 बहुत अधिक : *make a terrible fuss about nothing* ▸ **terribly** / टेरब्लि / *adv* 1 अत्यधिक : *a terribly good book* 2 बहुत बुरी तरह से : *She suffered terribly when her son was killed.*

terrier / टेरिअर / *noun* एक छोटे कद वाली नसल का कुत्ता।

terrific / ट'रिफ़िक़ / *adj* 1 बहुत महान/ विशाल, अत्यंत : *a terrific storm* 2 (अनौप) श्रेष्ठ; बहुत बढ़िया : *He's doing a terrific job.*

terrify / टेरिफ़ाइ / *verb* (*pt, pp* **terrified**) बहुत डरा देना, डर से भर देना : *The risks involved terrify me.*

territory / टेरट्रि / *noun* (*pl* **territories**) 1 राज्यक्षेत्र : *Turkish territory* 2 भूमि-विशेष : *fertile territory* 3 चर्चा, ज्ञान या कार्य का क्षेत्र : *Legal problems are Amit's territory.* ▸ **territorial** / टेर'टॉरिअल / *adj* राज्यक्षेत्र-विषयक : *territorial possessions* **territorial waters** *noun* [*pl*] देश का तटवर्ती समुद्र **the Territorial Army** *noun* अंशकालीन सैनिकों की सेना।

terror / टेरर / *noun* 1 अत्यधिक भय/ आतंक : *run away in terror* 2 अत्यधिक आतंक फैलाने वाला व्यक्ति/वस्तु : *street gangs that are the terror of the neighbourhood* ▸ **terrorize, -ise** / टेरराइज़ / *verb* उग्र होकर डर फैलाना।

terrorism / टेररिज़म / *noun* आतंकवाद, विशेषतः राजनीतिक उद्देश्यों के लिए आतंक का प्रयोग ▸ **terrorist** *noun* आतंकवादी।

terse / टर्स / *adj* संक्षिप्त और रूखा : *written in a terse style.*

tertiary / टर्शरि; *US* टर्शिएरि; / *adj* क्रम, दर्जे, चरण, महत्त्व आदि में तीसरा : *tertiary education ∘ tertiary burns.*

test¹ / टेस्ट / *noun* 1 योग्यता या जानकारी की परीक्षा : *an IQ/intelligence test* 2 जाँच के लिए चिकित्सकीय परीक्षण : *a*

test for AIDS/cancer 3 परीक्षण, परख, प्रयोग : *carry out tests on a new product* 4 (अनौप) टेस्ट-मैच ■ **put sb/sth to the test** किसी के गुणों का परीक्षण करना **stand the test of time, etc** लंबी अवधि के दौरान भरोसेमंद और टिकाऊ साबित होना।

test² / टेस्ट / *verb* **test (sb/sth) (for sth); test sb/sth (on sth)** परीक्षण करना, जाँचना; परीक्षण होना : *test for pollution in the water* ▸ **test-drive** *noun* वाहन के गुण या निष्पादन को परखने के लिए उसमें की गई सैर **test pilot** *noun* परीक्षण-उड़ान भरने वाला चालक **test-tube** *noun* परखनली।

testament / टेस्टमन्ट / *noun* (औप) 1 (प्रायः *sing*) **testament (to sth)** किसी बात का स्पष्ट प्रमाण : *The new model is a testament to the skill and dedication of the workforce.* 2 वसीयतनामा 3 **Old Testament, New Testament** बाइबिल के दो मुख्य विभाग।

testify / टेस्टिफ़ाइ / *verb* (*pt, pp* **testified**) 1 **testify (to sth); testify (against/for/in favour of sb)** गवाही देना, औपचारिक बयान देना : *summoned to testify in court* 2 **testify to sth** (औप) प्रमाणित करना, सिद्ध करना; साक्ष्य होना।

testimonial / टेस्टि'मोनिअल / *noun* 1 किसी व्यक्ति की योग्यता को प्रमाणित करने वाला लिखित कथन, संस्तुति-पत्र 2 सेवाओं/ उपलब्धियों के उपलक्ष में प्रदत्त कोई वस्तु/ प्रदर्शन : *a testimonial match.*

testimony / टेस्टिमनि / *noun* (*pl* **testimonies**) 1 सबूत का लिखित या मौखिक विवरण, विशेषतः गवाह द्वारा न्यायालय में दिया गया : *first-hand testimonies* 2 [*sing*] **testimony (to sth)** किसी बात/वस्तु का प्रमाण या प्रदर्शन : *The pyramids are (a) testimony to the*

Ancient Egyptians' engineering skills.

tetanus / टेटनस् / *noun* टेटनस, एक प्रकार का घातक रोग जिसमें कुछ या सभी मांसपेशियाँ अकड़ जाती हैं।

tether / टेद्र / *verb* **tether sth (to sth)** पगहे से बाँधना : *He tethered his horse (to a tree).* ▸ **tether** *noun* चराते समय पशुओं को बाँधा गया पगहा ▪ **at the end of one's tether** आत्मनियंत्रण या साधनों की समाप्ति के पास।

text / टेक्स्ट / *noun* **1** मूल पाठ : *too much text and not enough pictures* **2** भाषण, नाटक आदि का लिखित रूप : *the full text of the President's speech* **3** उद्धरण, अवतरण **4** परीक्षा के लिए पढ़ी जाने वाली पुस्तक ▸ **textbook** *noun* पाठ्य पुस्तक : *a grammar textbook.*

textile / टेक्स्टाइल / *noun* वस्त्र, बुना हुआ वस्त्र : *factories producing a range of textiles.*

texture / टेक्स्चर् / *noun* **1** देखने या छूने पर कपड़े, पदार्थ या सतह की बुनावट/बनावट का ढंग : *the texture of wool* **2** देखने या चखने पर खाद्य पदार्थ की बनावट : *a sauce with a creamy texture.*

than / दन्; दैन् / *conj* (तुलना को व्यक्त करने में प्रयुक्त) : *He learns more quickly than the others.* ▸ **than** *prep* **1** (तुलना दिखाने के लिए संज्ञा/सर्वनाम से पहले प्रयुक्त) : *I'm older than her.* **2** (राशि, संख्याएँ, फासलों की तुलना में more और less के बाद प्रयुक्त) : *It cost me more than Rs 1000.* **3** (no sooner, hardly, barely या scarcely के साथ शुरू होते हुए उपवाक्यों के बाद प्रयुक्त) : *Hardly had we arrived than the problems started.*

thank / थैङ्क् / *verb* **thank sb (for sth/doing sth)** धन्यवाद देना : *There's no need to thank me—I was only doing my job.* ▸ **thankful** *adj*

1 thankful to do sth; thankful (that.....) खुश और चिंतामुक्त (कुछ अच्छा होने के बाद) : *You should be thankful for having escaped with only minor injuries.* **2 thankful (for sth)** कृतज्ञ : *I am thankful for your enthusiasm and commitment.* **thankfully** *adv* **thankless** *adj* (क्रिया) व्यर्थ, अप्रिय : *perform a thankless task* **thanks** *noun* [*pl*] धन्यवाद ▪ **thanks (to sb) (for sth)** धन्यवाद ▪ **thanks to sb/ sth** के कारण, के फलस्वरूप : *The fête was a great success, thanks to the fine weather and a lot of hard work.* ▸ **thanksgiving** *noun* धन्यवाद-ज्ञापन (विशेषत: ईश्वर को)।

that¹ / दैट् / *det, pron* (*pl* **those** / दोज़/) **1** (कहीं दूर स्थित व्यक्ति/वस्तु को वर्णित करने में प्रयुक्त) : *Look at that man standing there.* **2** (पूर्वोल्लिखित व्यक्ति/वस्तु के संदर्भ में प्रयुक्त) : *That was a really stupid thing to say.* ▪ **that is (to say)** (अतिरिक्त जानकारी देने के लिए प्रयुक्त) **that's that** इस मामले में और कुछ किया या कहा नहीं जा सकता।

that² / दैट् / *pron* (संबंधवाचक उप-वाक्यों के शुरू में प्रयुक्त) पूर्वोल्लिखित व्यक्ति/ वस्तु : *The letter that came this morning was from my father.*

that³ / दैट् / *conj* क्रिया के कर्ता या कर्म के रूप में काम कर रहे उपवाक्य के शुरू में प्रयुक्त : *She said that the book was based on a true story.*

thatch / थैच् / *noun* **1** (प्राय: *sing*) छप्पर, फूस की छत : *Light gleamed beneath the overhanging thatch.* **2** [*sing*] (अनौप) सिर पर घने बाल ▸ **thatch** *verb* छप्पर डालना : *a hut thatched with palm leaves.*

thaw / थॉ / *verb* **1 thaw (sth) (out)** बर्फ या अन्य जमे द्रव का पिघलना/पिघलाना : *All the snow has thawed.* **2** (it के साथ

प्रयुक्त) (मौसम) बर्फ़ पिघलाने लायक गरम होना : *It's starting to thaw.* 3 (व्यक्तियों का) मैत्रीपूर्ण संबंध बनाने लगना : *Anglo-French relations have thawed considerably since the dispute over farming quotas.* ▸ **thaw** *noun* (प्राय: sing) 1 बर्फ़ पिघलाने वाला मौसम 2 व्यक्तियों, देशों आदि के बीच तनाव कम होने की स्थिति या अवधि : *a gradual thaw in relations with China.*

the / द्; दि; द्री / *def art* (a, an दोनों indefinite articles हैं) 1 (उपर्युक्त या ज्ञात को दर्शाने के लिए प्रयुक्त) : *A car hit the tree and the driver was killed.* 2 (विशेष व्यक्ति/वस्तु को दर्शाने के लिए प्रयुक्त) : *the house at the end of the street* 3 (उत्तमता-सूचक) : *the hottest day of the summer* 4 (यह दिखाना कि अपनी किस्म का केवल एक ही है) : *the Pacific Ocean* 5 (समान व्यक्तियों के समूह दर्शाने वाले विशेषणों के पहले प्रयुक्त) : *the poor* 6 (वस्तुओं आदि को सामान्य तौर पर दर्शाने के लिए प्रयुक्त) : *I heard it on the radio.* 7 (किसी का महत्त्व या लोकप्रियता दर्शाने के लिए प्रयुक्त) : *The family reunion was the social event of the year.* ■**the more, less, etc... the more, less etc...** उस मात्रा तक : *The more he has, the more he wants.*

theatre (*US* **theater**) / 'थ़िअटर् / *noun* 1 रंगशाला, थिएटर : *an open-air theatre* 2 **the theatre** [*sing*] ड्रामा, नाटक ▸ **theatrical** / थि'ऐट्रिक्ल् / *adj* 1 रंग-शाला-विषयक : *theatrical performances* 2 (व्यवहार) अतिनाटकीय, अतिशयोक्तिपूर्ण; कृत्रिम : *theatrical gestures.*

theft / थ़ेफ़्ट् / *noun* चोरी : *A number of thefts have been reported recently.*

their / द्रेअर् / *possess det* 1 उनका : *Their parties are always fun.* 2 (his या her की जगह प्रयुक्त जब व्यक्ति का लिंग पता न हो या अप्रासंगिक हो) : *If anyone telephones ask for their number so I can call back.* ▸ **theirs** / द्रेअर्ज़् / *possess pron* उनका : *It's a favourite place of theirs.*

them / द्रम्; द्रेम् / *pers pron* 1 they का कर्मकारक रूप : *Tell them the news.* 2 (him या her की जगह प्रयुक्त जब व्यक्ति का लिंग पता न हो या अप्रासंगिक हो) : *If anyone comes in, ask them to wait.* ▸ **themselves** / द्रम्'सेल्व्ज़् / *pron* 1 (reflex) (जब किसी क्रिया का कर्ता पर ही प्रभाव पड़े, यह दिखाने के लिए प्रयुक्त) : *The children were arguing amongst themselves.* 2 (emph) (them या they पर महत्त्व डालने के लिए प्रयुक्त)।

theme / थ़ीम् / *noun* 1 विषय; प्रसंग : *The theme of our discussion was 'World Peace'.* 2 (संगीत) टेक की धुन : *variations on a theme.*

then / द्रेन् / *adv* 1 (भूत/भविष्यकाल के संदर्भ में) तब, उस समय : *We were living in Kashmir then.* 2 अगला, उसके बाद : *I'll have soup first and then chicken.* 3 उस स्थिति में, इसलिए : *You'll be looking for a new secretary then?* 4 (सूची में) भी : *We'll invite Hema and Raghu, Narayan and Jyoti, and then there's Vinita and Vidya.*

thence / द्रेन्स् / *adv* (अप्रचल या औप) वहाँ से : *They travelled by rail to the coast and thence by boat to America.*

thenceforward / द्रेन्स्'फ़ॉर्वई् / (**thenceforth** भी) *adv* (औप) उस समय के बाद से : *He decided that thenceforward he would look at all incoming orders.*

theology / थ़ि'ऑलजि / *noun* (*pl* **theologies**) 1 ईश्वर की प्रकृति और

धार्मिक विश्वासों के आधार का अध्ययन
2 धार्मिक विश्वास : *rival theologies.*

theorem / 'थ्रिअरम्/ *noun* (गणित में)
सिद्धांत या नियम; तर्क द्वारा सिद्ध किया जा
सकने वाला प्रमेय या साध्य : *Pythagoras'*
theorem.

theoretical / 'थ्रिअ 'रेटिकल्/ *adj*
1 सैद्धांतिक (न कि व्यावहारिक) : *a theo-*
retical physicist 2 सिद्धांतजन्य; संभवत:
सत्य (पर प्रयोग या अनुभव से उत्पन्न नहीं) :
theoretical knowledge ▸ **theoreti-**
cally *adv.*

theory / 'थ्रिअरि/ *noun* (pl **theories**)
1 सिद्धांत, प्रतिपादित मत : *Darwin's*
theory of evolution 2 अध्ययन विषय
के आधारभूत सिद्धांत : *economic theory*
3 वाद, मत, अनिवार्यत: तर्क पर आधारित
नहीं : *different theories about how*
to bring up children ▸ **theorize,**
-ise / थ्रिअराइज़्/ *verb* किसी विषय पर
सिद्धांत बनाना।

therapeutic / थेर'प्यूटिक्/ *adj* स्वास्थ्य
ठीक रखने या रोग हरने से संबंधित : *the*
therapeutic properties of foods
○ *the therapeutic effects of sea air.*

therapy / 'थेरपि / *noun* उपचार,
चिकित्सा : *natural/alternative thera-*
pies ▸ **therapist** *noun.*

there¹ / देअर्/ *adv* (here के वैषम्य में)
1 वहाँ, उस स्थान पर/में : *It's there, right*
in front of you. 2 किसी का स्थान दिखाने
के लिए वाक्य के आरंभ में प्रयुक्त : *There's*
the statue I was telling you about.
3 किसी घटना आदि के विशेष पड़ाव के
संबंध में : *Don't stop there. What did*
you do next? ■ **there and then; then**
and there उसी स्थान और समय पर;
तुरंत : *I took one look at the car and*
offered to buy it there and then.

there you go/go again किसी को उसके
विशिष्ट व्यवहार की निंदा करने के लिए
प्रयुक्त : *There you go again—jump-*

ing to conclusions on the slightest
evidence. ▸ **there** *interj* (सफलता
की खुशी, क्रोध, प्रोत्साहन दिखाने में
प्रयुक्त) : *There! You've gone and*
woken the baby!

there² / देअर्/ *adv* (be और कुछ अन्य
क्रियाओं के कर्ता के रूप में प्रयुक्त, विशेषत:
किसी का पहली बार उल्लेख करने के
लिए) : *There's a man at the bus-*
stop.

thereabouts / देअर'बाउट्स्/ *adv* लग-
भग : *I'll be home at 8 o'clock or*
thereabouts.

thereafter / देअर 'आफ़्टर्; *US* देअर
'ऐफ़्टर / *adv* (औप) उसके बाद : *She*
retired in 1953 and died shortly
thereafter.

thereby / देअर 'बाइ / *adv* (औप) उस
रीति से : *They paid cash, thereby*
avoiding any problems with tax.

therefore / 'देअरफ़ॉर्/ *adv* इसलिए : *He*
is out of the country and therefore
unable to attend the meeting.

thereupon / देअर'पॉन् / *adv* (औप)
एकदम उसके बाद, तत्काल, फलस्वरूप :
Thereupon he got up and walked
out.

therm / थर्म्/ *noun* ऊष्मा की इकाई, थर्म
(विशेषत: गैस आपूर्ति को मापने में प्रयुक्त)।

thermal / 'थर्मल्/ *adj* 1 ऊष्मा से संबं-
धित : *thermal energy* 2 गरम रखने के
लिए (कपड़े आदि) : *thermal insula-*
tion/underwear.

thermometer / थर 'मॉमिटर्/ *noun*
थर्मामीटर; ज्वर/तापमान मापने का उपकरण।

thermostat / 'थर्मस्टैट्/ *noun* ताप को
नियंत्रण में रखने के लिए स्वचालित उप-
करण : *adjust/turn down the ther-*
mostat.

thesaurus / थ्रि 'सॉरस्/ *noun* (pl
thesauruses / थ्रि 'सॉरसिज़् / या **the-**
sauri / थ्रि'सॉराइ /) पर्याय शब्दकोश।

these / द्रीज़् / adj, pron (**those** के वैषम्य में) : *Look at these men over here.*

thesis / 'थ्रीसिस् / noun (pl **theses** / 'थ्रीसीज़्/) 1 तर्कों द्वारा समर्थित एवं प्रतिपादित सिद्धांत या कथन : *The author's central thesis is that freedom is incompatible with equality.* 2 विश्वविद्यालय की उपाधि के लिए प्रस्तुत शोध प्रबंध : *a Ph.D. thesis.*

they / द्रे / pers pron वे : *They went for a walk.*

thick / थ्रिक् / adj (**-er, -est**) 1 (**thin** के विपरीत अर्थ में) मोटा : *a thick slice of bread* ○ *a thick book* 2 **thick** (with sb/sth) घना : *a thick forest/crowd* 3 (द्रव या द्रव जैसा) गाढ़ा : *thick soup/ paint/glue* 4 (हवा या वातावरण में विद्यमान पदार्थ) काफ़ी मात्रा में : *thick fog* 5 (अनौप) मंदबुद्धि : *He's a bit thick.* 6 **thick with sb** (अनौप) घनिष्ठ, निकटतम (मित्र) : *Rajiv is very thick with Neena.* ▸ **thick** noun ■ **in the thick of sth** घना भाग, जहाँ सबसे अधिक सक्रियता हो : *We were in the thick of the fight.* **through thick and thin** सभी मुश्किलों के बावजूद ▸ **thicken** / 'थ्रिकन् / verb घना/गाढ़ा करना : *Use flour to thicken the gravy.* **thickly** adv **thickness** noun 1 मोटाई : *Snow fell to a thickness of several centimetres.* 2 परत 3 दो सतहों के बीच की मोटाई : *steps cut into the thickness of the wall* **thick-skinned** adj निंदा या अपमान से अप्रभावित।

thicket / 'थ्रिकिट् / noun झुरमुट, झाड़ी।

thief / थ्रीफ़् / noun (pl **thieves** / थ्रीज़्/) चोर ▸ **thieve** / थ्रीव् / verb (अनौप) चुराना : *You have been thieving again, haven't you?*

thigh / थ्राइ / noun जाँघ : *the thigh-bone.*

thimble / 'थ्रिम्बल् / noun दर्ज़ी द्वारा प्रयुक्त अंगुश्ताना।

thin / थ्रिन् / adj (**-nner, -nnest**) 1 (**thick** के विपरीत अर्थ में) पतला, महीन, बारीक : *a thin line/wire* 2 (कभी-कभी अपमा) छरहरा, दुबला-पतला : *have thin legs* 3 (पदार्थ में) द्रव की मात्रा अधिक होना : *thin gravy* 4 कमज़ोर; शक्ति एवं आत्मविश्वास से रहित : *a thin voice/ smile* 5 (वायु या वातावरण में विद्यमान पदार्थ) बड़ी मात्रा में न होना : *thin clouds* 6 कम वस्तुएँ, भाग या लोग होना : *a region with a thin population* 7 गुणों में निम्न ■ **vanish into thin air** पूर्णतः अदृश्य हो जाना, प्रायः अचानक या रहस्यमय ढंग से ▸ **thin** verb (**-nn-**) **thin** (sth) (**out**); **thin** (sth) (**down**) पतला करना, महीन बनाना/होना : *His hair is thinning on top.* **thinly** adv **thinness** noun **thin-skinned** adj निंदा या अपमान से जल्दी प्रभावित।

thing / थ्रिङ् / noun 1 वस्तु : *There wasn't a thing to eat.* 2 **things** [pl] किसी उद्देश्य के लिए प्रयुक्त आवश्यक वस्तुएँ : *Don't forget your swimming things.* 3 कोई परिस्थिति, घटना, क्रिया, गतिविधि या तथ्य : *I find the whole thing very boring.* 4 **things** [pl] अनिश्चित परिस्थितियाँ, शर्तें या बातें, सामान्य स्थिति : *Things are going from bad to worse.* ■ **first things first** ज़्यादा ज़रूरी मामले पहले निपटाए जाने चाहिए **have a thing about sb/sth** (अनौप) 1 (प्रायः अनुचित हद तक) किसी की तरफ़ आकर्षित होना 2 किसी के लिए गहरी और अनुचित नापसंदगी होना **make a thing of sth** (अनौप) बात का बतंगड़ बनाना।

think / थ्रिङ्क् / verb (pt, pp **thought** / थ़ॉट् /) 1 **think** (about sth) सोचना, विचार करना : *Are animals able to think?* 2 विचार या मत विशेष रखना : *I* *think this is their house.* 3 योजना या इरादा होना या बनाना 4 धारणा बनाना, कल्पना करना : *We couldn't think where you'd gone.* 5 *(अनौप)* विचार आदि एक दिशा में/विषय पर केंद्रित करना : *Let's think positive.* ■ **think aloud** सूझते हुए विचारों को व्यक्त करना **think better of it/of doing sth** पुनर्विचार के बाद कुछ करने का विचार त्याग देना : *Reshma was about to protest but thought better of it.* **think sth over** निर्णय पर पहुँचने से पहले पुन: विचार करना : *Please think over what I've said.* **think straight** तर्कपूर्वक और स्पष्ट ढंग से सोचना **think (the) better of sb** किसी के बारे में उच्च राय होना **think the world, highly, a lot, not much, poorly, little, etc of sb/sth** (किसी व्यक्ति/वस्तु की) बहुत अच्छी/बेकार धारणा रखना, किसी को ऐसा समझना : *His work is highly thought of by the critics.* **think twice about (doing) sth** कुछ करने से पहले ध्यानपूर्वक सोचना ► **think-tank** *noun* राजनीतिक, सामाजिक या आर्थिक मामलों पर राय देने के लिए विशेषज्ञों का समूह।

thinker / 'थिङ्कर् / *noun* 1 दर्शनशास्त्र, विज्ञान आदि विषयों पर गंभीरता से सोचने या लिखने वाला व्यक्ति : *Einstein was one of the greatest thinkers of the 20th century.* 2 गंभीर सोच-विचार करने वाला व्यक्ति : *Rashmi's a charming woman but she's not much of a thinker.*

thinking / 'थिङ्किङ् / *adj* गंभीर व महत्त्वपूर्ण विषयों पर विचार करने का सामर्थ्य : *All thinking people must hate violence.* ► **thinking** *noun* सोच-विचार करने की क्रिया **thinking-cap** *noun* ■ **put one's thinking-cap on** *(अनौप)* किसी समस्या को सोच-विचार कर सुलझाने की कोशिश करना।

third / थर्ड् / *pron, det* तीसरा, तीसरे स्थान पर ► **third** *noun* 1 तीन बराबर भागों में, एक (तिहाई) 2 **third (in sth)** तृतीय श्रेणी **third-class** *adj* *(अपमा)* निम्नतम स्तर, निकृष्ट **third-rate** *adj* घटिया क़िस्म का : *a third rate film/actor.*

thirst / थर्स्ट् / *noun* 1 [*sing*] प्यास; प्यास से व्याकुल : *They lost their way in the desert and died of thirst.* 2 [*sing*] **thirst (for sth)** (कुछ जानने/पाने की) तीव्र जिज्ञासा, इच्छा : *a thirst for knowledge* ► **thirst** *verb* *(अप्र)* प्यास लगना ■ **thirst for sth** कुछ करने के लिए व्याकुल होना : *thirsting for revenge* ► **thirsty** *adj* (-ier, -iest) 1 **thirsty (for sth)** प्यासा 2 *(अनौप)* प्यास उत्पन्न करने वाला **thirstily** *adv.*

thirteen / थर्'टीन् / *noun, pron, det* तेरह (का अंक) ► **thirteenth** *noun, pron, det* तेरहवाँ; 1/13.

thirty / 'थर्टि / *noun, pron, det* 1 तीस (का अंक) 2 **the thirties** [*pl*] 30 से 39 तक के अंक, वर्ष, तापमान ► **thirtieth** / 'थर्टिअथ् / *noun, pron, det* तीसवाँ, तीसवाँ अंश, 1/30.

this / दिस् / *det, pron* (*pl* **these** / दीज़् /) 1 (that के वैषम्य में) इस, यह : *Come here and look at this picture.* 2 (पूर्व उल्लिखित को संकेत करने के लिए): *What are these men doing?* 3 (कुछ प्रस्तुत करने के लिए प्रयुक्त): *This is my husband.* 4 (वर्तमान से संबंधित दिनों या समय की अवधियों के साथ प्रयुक्त): *this morning.*

thistle / 'थिस्ल् / *noun* भट-कटैया का पौधा ► **thistledown** *noun* भट-कटैया के पौधे के बीज।

thorax / 'थॉरैक्स् / *noun* (*pl* **thoraxes** या **thoraces** / 'थॉरसीज़्/) 1 छाती, सीना 2 (जीव विज्ञान) कीट के शरीर का बीच का भाग, वक्ष।

thorn / थॉर्न् / *noun* 1 काँटा 2 काँटेदार

झाड़ी : *hedges of thorn* ▸ **thorny** *adj*
(**-ier, -iest**) **1** काँटेदार : *a thorny bush*
2 कठिनाई/असहमति उत्पन्न करने वाला : *a*
thorny problem.

thorough / 'थ़रा; *US* थ़र्रो / *adj* **1** सभी
प्रकार से पूर्ण; पक्का, अत्यधिक सावधानी से
किया गया : *give the room a thorough*
cleaning **2** (व्यक्ति) जो इस प्रकार काम
करे : *He is a slow worker but very*
thorough. **3** (अपमा) पूरा-पूरा, पूर्ण :
That woman is a thorough nui-
sance. ▸ **thoroughly** *adv* **thor-**
oughness *noun.*

thoroughbred / 'थ़रब्रेड् / *noun, adj*
असली नसल का (घोड़ा आदि)।

thoroughfare / 'थ़रफ़ेअर् / *noun* आम
रास्ता।

those / द़ोज़् / *det, pron* (**these** के वैषम्य
में) उन, वे : *Those men are the tallest.*

though (थो' भी) / द़ो / *conj* **1** यद्यपि :
The food was delicious, though
expensive. **2** हालाँकि, फिर भी : *He'll*
probably say no, though it's worth
asking. ▸ **though** *adv* के बावजूद; भले
ही।

thought / थ़ॉट् / *noun* **1** (प्राय: *pl*)
विचार, राय; ध्यान : *Let me have your*
thoughts on the subject. **2** चिंतन
(सोचने की शक्ति, प्रक्रिया या रीति) : *be*
deep/lost in thought **3** (प्राय: *pl*)
thought of (doing) sth इरादा : *The*
thought of resigning never crossed
my mind. **4** किसी विषय/व्यक्ति से जुड़े
विशेष विचार/मत : *modern/scientific/*
Greek thought ■ **second thoughts;**
(*US*) **second thought** पुनर्विचार के
बाद धारणा/मत में बदलाव ▸ **thoughtful**
adj **1** विचारपूर्ण, विचारमग्न : *You're*
looking very thoughtful. **2** विचार-
सूचक, सावधानी से विचार करने वाला : *a*
player who has a thoughtful ap-
proach to the game **3** औरों का ध्यान

रखने वाला : *It was very thoughtful of*
you to send the flowers. **thought-**
fully *adv* **thoughtless** *adj* **1** स्वार्थी
2 बेपरवाह, बेलिहाज़ : *a thoughtless*
remark **thoughtlessness** *noun*
thoughtlessly *adv* **thought-provok-**
ing *adj* विचार करने के लिए उकसाने वाला।

thousand / 'थ़ाउज़्न्ड् / *noun, pron,*
det (*pl* अपरिवर्तित या **thousands**)
1 हज़ार, सहस्र **2** (प्राय: **thousands**
[*pl*]) बहुत अधिक/सारे : *We're giving*
away thousands of prizes. ▸ **thou-**
sandth *noun, pron, det* हज़ारवाँ,
हज़ारवाँ अंश, 1/1000.

thrash / थ़्रैश् / *verb* **1** छड़ी या कोड़े से
पीटना **2** (अनौप) पराजित करना : *Mohan*
Bagan were thrashed 3-0 by Rail-
ways. ■ **thrash sth out 1** गहराई से
विचार-विमर्श द्वारा (समस्या का) समाधान
करना : *call a meeting to thrash out*
the problem **2** चर्चा द्वारा (योजना आदि)
बनाना : *After much argument we*
thrashed out a plan. ▸ **thrashing**
noun **1** पिटाई **2** करारी हार।

thread / थ़्रेड् / *noun* **1** तागा/धागा, सूत :
a needle and thread **2** **thread (of**
sth) धागे से मिलती-जुलती पतली चीज़ : *A*
thread of light emerged from the
keyhole. **3** (प्राय: *pl*) विचार, प्रसंग या
विशेषता जो किसी बड़े का अंश हो : *pick*
up the thread(s) of a conversation
▸ **thread** *verb* **1** सूई में तागा डालना;
माला पिरोना/गूँथना : *thread a needle*
2 thread (sth) between/through sth
बारबार भीड़ में से बाहर आना और भीतर
जाना : *threading his way through*
the crowded streets **threadbare**
/ 'थ़्रेड्बेअर् / *adj* (कपड़ा) फटा-पुराना,
घिसा-पिटा; (तर्क) अपर्याप्त, अप्रभावी : *a*
threadbare carpet/coat ○ *a thread-*
bare argument.

threat / थ़्रेट् / *noun* **1 threat (to do sth)**

धमकी : *They did not carry out their threat to cut off the water supply.* 2 (प्राय: *sing*) मुसीबत या ख़तरे की आशंका : *The factory is under threat of closure.* 3 (प्राय: *sing*) व्यक्ति/वस्तु जो मुसीबत, ख़तरा पैदा कर सके : *Terrorism poses a threat to the whole country.*

threaten / थ्रेट्न् / *verb* 1 **threaten sb (with sth)** धमकी देना; धमकी से प्रभावित करने की कोशिश करना : *threaten an employee with dismissal* 2 अशुभ की संभावना होना : *When war threatens, people act irrationally.* ▶ **threatening** *adj* 1 हानि या हिंसा की धमकी व्यक्त करते हुए : *threatening behaviour* 2 ख़राब मौसम की संभावना दिखाते हुए **threateningly** *adv*.

three / थ्री / *noun, pron, det* तीन (का अंक)।

thresh / थ्रेश् / *verb* धान या खलिहान के अनाज को कूट-पीट कर निकालना, दाँवना।

threshold / थ्रेशहोल्ड् / *noun* 1 (द्वार की) दहलीज़; प्रवेश मार्ग, देहली : *standing at/on the threshold* 2 (प्राय: *sing*) नई स्थिति का आरंभ : *be on the threshold of victory* 3 कोई विशेष स्तर या मापदंड।

thrice / थ्राइस् / *adv* (अप्र) तीन बार।

thrift / थ्रिफ्ट् / *noun* 1 किफ़ायत, कमख़र्ची 2 (**thrift institution** भी) धन बचाने एवं उधार देने की सुविधा प्रदान करने वाली संस्था ▶ **thrifty** *adj* (**-ier, -iest**) कमख़र्च।

thrill / थ्रिल् / *noun* 1 रोमांच, पुलक : *He gets his thrills from rock-climbing.* 2 कँपकँपी, धड़कन : *feel a thrill of fear/horror* ▶ **thrill** *verb* रोमांच उत्पन्न/अनुभव करना : *The film is thrilling audiences all over the world.* **thriller** *noun* रोमांच उत्पन्न करने वाली कहानी, सनसनीख़ेज़ उपन्यास आदि **thrilling** *adj* रोमांच उत्पन्न करने वाला।

thrive / थ्राइव् / *verb* **thrive (on sth)** फलना-फूलना, सफल होना : *a thriving industry* ○ *These animals rarely thrive in captivity.*

throat / थ्रोट् / *noun* 1 कंठ, गला : *I've got a sore throat.* 2 आहार-नली।

throb / थ्रॉब् / *verb* (**-bb-**) **throb (with sth)** 1 (दिल, नबज़ या किसी अन्य अंग का) धड़कना; दर्द करना : *His head throbbed.* 2 धड़कने वाली गति/ध्वनि से चलना : *a throbbing pain/drumbeat* ▶ **throb** *noun* धड़कन, स्पंदन : *the throb of distant drums.*

throes / थ्रोज़ / *noun* [*pl*] ■ **in the throes of sth/of doing sth** किसी कठिन या कष्टप्रद कार्य या स्थिति में उलझा हुआ : *be in the throes of childbirth/of moving house.*

throne / थ्रोन् / *noun* 1 (राज) सिंहासन, राजगद्दी 2 **the throne** [*sing*] राजा/रानी का पद : *come to/ascend the throne.*

throng / थ्रॉङ्ग् / *noun* भीड़ : *throngs of busy shoppers* ▶ **throng** *verb* 1 भीड़ कर देना, भीड़ बना कर आना/जाना : *The children thronged into the assembly hall.* 2 **throng sth (with sb/sth)** भीड़ से भर देना : *Crowds thronged the main square of the city.*

throttle / थ्रॉट्ल् / *verb* 1 गला घोंटना : *He throttled the guard with his bare hands.* 2 कार्य करने या अस्तित्व में बनाए रखने वाली आवश्यक वस्तु को ले जाना/छीन लेना : *The city is being throttled by traffic congestion.* ▶ **throttle** *noun* मोटरकार का एक विशेष वॉल्व, थ्रॉटल।

through / थ्रू / *prep* 1 आर-पार, इस पार से उस पार : *The train is going through a tunnel.* 2 के बीच से : *The path led through the trees to the river.* 3 (स्थिति, कार्य या समय की अवधि के)

शुरू से अंत तक : *He will not live through the night.* 4 तब तक : *stay in Pune Tuesday through Friday* 5 के कारण; द्वारा : *You can only achieve success through hard work.* 6 कोई परीक्षा या चरण सफलतापूर्वक पार कर लेना : *get a Bill through Parliament* ▸ **through** *adv* 1 आर-पार : *The onlookers stood aside to let the doctor through.* 2 शुरू से अंत तक : *The baby slept right through (the night).* 3 किसी चरण/परीक्षा से सफलतापूर्वक गुज़रना : *Our team is through to the semifinals.* 4 टेलिफ़ोन द्वारा मिलाना : *I tried to ring you but I couldn't get through.* 5 **through (with sth/sb)** (कार्य/संबंध समाप्त होने/करने के संकेत देते हुए) : *Are you through with that newspaper?*

throughout / थ्रूआउट्/ *adv, prep* पूरी तरह से; शुरू से अंत तक; सर्वत्र : *The house was painted white throughout.*

throw¹ / थ्रो / *verb* (*pt* **threw** / थ्रू /; *pp* **thrown** /थ्रोन्/) 1 फेंकना 2 शरीर के अंगों को घुमाना या झटका देना; हाथ-पैर पटकना : *She threw up her hands in horror at the idea.* 3 **throw sth around/over sb/sth; throw sth on/off** (कपड़े आदि) उतार डालना : *She threw off the coat.* 4 किसी को अचानक या ज़ोर से पटक देना : *Two jockeys were thrown in the second race.* 5 किसी विशेष स्थिति में लाना : *We were thrown into confusion by the news.* ■ **throw oneself/sth into sth** पूरी शक्ति के साथ भाग लेना : *throwing themselves into their work* **throw open (a challenge/competition)** खोल देना; जनता के लिए खोल देना **throw sb over** (मित्र आदि) छोड़ देना : *When he became rich he threw over all*

his old friends. **throw sth away** गँवा देना, उड़ा डालना **throw sth/sb off** पीछा छुड़ाना **throw sth out** सुझाव देना, यों ही संकेत देना **throw (sth) up** वमन करना; पद त्याग करना।

throw² / थ्रो / *noun* 1 फेंकने की क्रिया : *a well aimed throw* 2 फेंकने की दूरी : *a throw of 70 metres.*

thrush / थ्रश् / *noun* एक प्रकार की गाने वाली चिड़िया।

thrust / थ्रस्ट् / *verb* (*pt, pp* **thrust**) 1 धकेलना/ज़ोर से रखना : *thrust a tip into the waiter's hand* 2 **thrust at sb (with sth)/thrust sth at sb** तलवार आदि घुसेड़ना : *He thrust a knife at me.* ■ **thrust sth/sb on/upon sb** किसी को कुछ स्वीकार करने के लिए विवश करना ▸ **thrust** *noun* 1 प्रहार, आक्रमण 2 रॉकेट, इंजिन द्वारा आगे की ओर उत्पन्न शक्ति।

thud / थड् / *verb* (-dd-) धम से गिरना, धब-धब करना ▸ **thud** *noun* धम या धब-धब की आवाज़ : *He fell off the ladder with a dull thud.*

thug / थग् / *noun* आक्रामक व्यक्ति; हिंसात्मक अपराधी ▸ **thuggery** *noun.*

thumb / थम् / *noun* अँगूठा **under sb's thumb** पूर्णतः किसी के प्रभाव/नियंत्रण में होना ▸ **thumb** *verb* ■ **thumb a lift** अँगूठे से इशारा कर वाहन में मुफ़्त सवारी माँगना **thumb through sth** किताब के पन्ने पलटना।

thump / थम्प् / *verb* 1 (मुट्ठी से) ठोकना, ज़ोर से खटखटाना : *Someone thumped on the door.* 2 ज़ोर-ज़ोर से धड़कना/ पीटना : *My heart was thumping (with excitement).* ▸ **thump** *noun* आघात; धमाका : *give sb a thump.*

thunder / 'थन्डर् / *noun* 1 (बिजली चमकने के बाद की) कड़क, गरज : *a crash/peal/roll of thunder* 2 [*sing*] बुलंद आवाज़, गरज : *the thunder of* *applause* ▸ **thunder** *verb* 1 (it के साथ) गरजना, कड़कना : *It thundered all night.* 2 **thunder against sth/ at sb** (व्यक्ति का) गरज कर बोलना; धमकी देना **thunderbolt** / 'थ़न्डर्बोल्ट् / *noun* बिजली (गिरना), गाज, वज्रपात **thunderstorm** / 'थ़न्डरस्टॉर्म् / *noun* बिजली और गरज के साथ होने वाली भारी वर्षा।

thunderstruck / 'थ़न्डरस्ट्रक् / *adj* हक्का-बक्का, आश्चर्य से जड़।

Thursday / 'थ़र्ज़्डे / *noun* बृहस्पतिवार।

thus / द़स् / *adv* (औप) 1 इस प्रकार, इस तरह से : *Hold the wheel in both hands, thus.* 2 इसलिए, इस कारण : *He is the eldest son and thus heir to the title.* ■ **thus far** इस सीमा तक।

thwart / थ़्वाट् / *verb* **thwart sb (in sth)** (किसी की योजना, प्रगति आदि में) अड़चन डालना; कार्य निष्फल कर देना : *He was thwarted (in his aims) by bad luck.*

tick¹ / टिक् / *noun* 1 (घड़ी की) टिक-टिक ध्वनि 2 (*US* check) विशेष चिह्न √ (सही का चिह्न) ▸ **tick** *verb* 1 **tick (away)** (घड़ी का) टिक-टिक की ध्वनि करना 2 **tick sth (off)** सही का चिह्न लगाना : *tick (off) the names of those present* ■ **tick sb off** (अनौप) गलती के लिए डाँटना।

tick² / टिक् / *noun* 1 (कुत्ते आदि को लगने वाली) किलनी 2 (अनौप) अप्रिय एवं बेकार व्यक्ति।

ticket / 'टिकिट् / *noun* 1 टिकट 2 लेबल ▸ **ticket** *verb* लेबल लगाना।

tickle / 'टिक्ल् / *verb* 1 गुदगुदाना : *tickle sb in the ribs* 2 चुनचुनाना, झुनझुनी होना : *My nose tickles.* 3 खुश करना, भाव प्रेरित करना : *The idea tickled her curiosity.* ▸ **tickle** *noun* गुदगुदी, चुनचुनाहट।

tidal / 'टाइड्ल् / *adj* ज्वार-भाटा विषयक :

a tidal river/estuary ▸ **tidal wave** *noun* 1 समुद्री बड़ी लहर 2 **tidal wave (of sth)** लोकप्रिय उत्साह या विरोध की लहर।

tide / टाइड् / *noun* 1 ज्वार-भाटा; ज्वार का पानी : *Swimmers should beware of strong tides.* 2 (प्राय: *sing*) (राय या मत की) दिशा, बाढ़ : *a rising tide of discontent* ■ **go, swim, etc with/ against the tide** अधिकांश लोगों के मत, धारणाओं आदि का समर्थन/विरोध करना ▸ **tide** *verb* **tide sb over (sth)** आपूर्ति कर किसी की मुश्किल समय में सहायता करना।

tidings / 'टाइडिङ्ज़् / *noun* [*pl*] (अप्र या परि) ख़बर : *Have you heard the good tidings?*

tidy / 'टाइडि / *adj* (-ier, -iest) 1 ठीक-ठाक, सुव्यवस्थित : *a tidy room* 2 (अनौप) (धनराशि) काफ़ी बड़ी : *She left a tidy fortune when she died.* ▸ **tidy** *verb* (*pt, pp* tidied) **tidy (sth/ sb/oneself) (up)** ठीक-ठाक/सुव्यवस्थित करना : *You'd better tidy this room (up) before the guests arrive.* **tidily** *adv* **tidiness** *noun.*

tie¹ / टाइ / *noun* 1 (**necktie** भी) टाई, नेकटाई 2 बंध, फीता : *ties for sealing plastic bags* 3 (प्राय: *pl*) (अलं) मैत्री संबंध, बंधन : *the ties of friendship* 4 खेल या प्रतियोगिता में दोनों प्रतिभागियों के बराबर अंक होने की स्थिति : *The match ended in a tie.* 5 खेलकूद में प्रतियोगियों के बीच खेल, मैच 6 व्यक्ति की स्वतंत्रता को सीमित करने वाली वस्तु।

tie² / टाइ / *verb* (*pt, pp* tied; *pres p* tying) 1 बाँधना : *tie a dog to a lamp-post* 2 **tie sth (on)** धागे से बाँध देना : *tie on a label* 3 गाँठ लगाना : *tie a ribbon* 4 **tie (sb) (with sb) (for sth)** (दो खिलाड़ियों या दो खिलाड़ी दलों का) समान अंक पाना : *The two teams tied (with* *each other).* **5 tie sth to sth** किसी से जोड़ना, संबद्ध करना ■ **tie sb/oneself down (to sth)** किसी/स्वयं को (परिस्थितियों, जगह, नौकरी आदि के संदर्भ में) सीमित कर देना **tie sb up 1** रस्सी से बाँध देना **2** किसी कार्य आदि में अत्यधिक व्यस्त कर देना **tie the knot** *(अनौप)* विवाह करना।

tier / टिअर् / *noun* ऊपर–नीचे बने ख़ाने (शेल्फ़) या बैठने का स्थान; इस प्रकार की संरचना : *the third tier of local government administration.*

tiff / टिफ़् / *noun* दोस्तों के बीच मामूली–सा झगड़ा : *She's had a tiff with her boy-friend.*

tiger / टाइगर् / *noun* बाघ।

tight / टाइट् / *adj* (-er, -est) **1** कसा, दृढ़ : *a tight knot* **2** चुस्त, तंग : *These shoes are too tight for me.* **3** ठसाठस : *a tight mass of fibres* **4** (स्थिति) मुश्किल/ख़तरनाक : *in a tight corner/spot* **5** (नियंत्रण) कड़ा, सख़्त : *tight security/constraints/sanctions* **6** कस कर ताना हुआ : *a tight rope/rein* **7** कमख़र्ची, कंजूस; (धन की) कमी : *She's very tight with her money.* ▶ **tighten** / टाइट्न् / *verb* **tighten (sth) (up) 1** कसना, जकड़ना : *tighten (up) the ropes* **2** सख़्ती से पेश आना/सख़्त होना या करना : *tighten up security* **tight-fisted** *adj* कंजूस **tight-lipped** *adj* होंठ सी लेना **tightly** *adv* **tightness** *noun.*

tights / टाइट्स् / *noun* [pl] चुस्त कपड़े (जैसे कलाबाज़ या नर्तक पहनते हैं) : *a pair of cotton tights.*

tigress / टाइग्रस् / *noun* बाघिन।

tile / टाइल् / *noun* टाइल; वर्गाकार या आयताकार पकी मिट्टी (या पत्थर) का खपड़ा (प्रायः दीवार या छत पर लगाने के लिए) : *cover the wall with cork tiles.*

till[1] / टिल् / *conj* = until.

till[2] / टिल् / *noun* दराज़, (ख़ज़ांची की) ड्राअर।

till[3] / टिल् / *verb* जोतना, हल चलाना।

tiller / टिलर् / *noun* पतवार का डंडा।

tilt / टिल्ट् / *verb* झुकाना/झुकना, तिरछा करना/होना : *This table tends to tilt (to one side/over).* ■ **tilt at sb/sth** भाषण या लेख में किसी को निशाना बनाना ▶ **tilt** *noun* (प्रायः sing) **1** झुकाव : *with a tilt of his head* **2** विरोधियों का मिलन; भाषण या लेख में आक्रमण : *have a tilt at sb* ■ **(at) full tilt/pelt/speed** पूरे वेग और शक्ति से।

timber / टिम्बर् / *noun* **1** (US **lumber** भी) इमारती लकड़ी : *a timber-merchant* **2** (प्रायः pl) (छत की) शहतीर, धरन।

time[1] / टाइम् / *noun* **1** समय (भूत, वर्तमान, भविष्य सभी के लिए प्रयुक्त शब्द) : *past/present/future time* **2** समय की अवधि, काल, वक़्त : *That will take time.* **3** सामान्यतया मापा गया समय; दिन के घंटों और मिनटों में व्यक्त समय : *Time in California is eight hours behind London.* ○ *What time is it?* **4** इकाई में मापी गई समय की अवधि : *The winner's time was 11.6 seconds.* **5** कुछ करने के लिए उपयुक्त/प्रयुक्त/उपलब्ध समय का क्षण या अवधि : *lunch time* **6** (प्रायः pl) विशेष घटनाओं/व्यक्तियों/अनुभवों के साथ जुड़ी समय की अवधि : *in ancient/prehistoric/recent times* **7** (संगीत में) ताल, लय **8** अवसर, मौक़ा : *this/that/last time* ■ **ahead of time** अपेक्षित समय से पहले **(all) in good time** उचित समय पर **all the time 1** कुछ घटित होने की पूरी अवधि के दौरान : *That letter I was searching for was in my pocket all the time.* **2** हमेशा **at a time** क्रम में, पृथक **at all times** हमेशा **at one time** अतीत में कोई अवधि **at the time** अतीत में कोई

विशेष क्षण/अवधि **at times** कभी-कभी **behind the times** विचार आदि पुराने ढंग के;दक़ियानूसी **every time** जब भी मुमकिन हो **for the time being** फ़िलहाल **from time to time** यदा-कदा **have a hard, rough, tough, etc time (of it)** कठिनाइयों-भरी अवधि से गुज़रना **have no time for sb/sth** किसी काम में/व्यक्ति के साथ समय न लगा/बिता पाना; कुछ नापसंद होना **have the time of one's life** (अनौप) अत्यधिक खुश या उत्तेजित होना : *The children had the time of their lives at the circus.* **in good time** ठीक समय पर; समय से पूर्व **in (less than) no time** बहुत जल्दी **in time** कभी-न-कभी **in time (for sth/to do sth)** देर से नहीं; समय पर **(it is) high/about time** भूतकाल में कोई समय जब कुछ कर लेना चाहिए था **keep with the times** प्रचलन के साथ विचार, दृष्टिकोण बदलना **on time** न जल्दी न देर से **take one's time (over sth/to do sth/doing sth)** बिना जल्दबाज़ी के काम करना **time after time; time and (time) again** बार-बार, समय-समय पर ▸ **time-consuming** *adj* बहुत समय लेने वाला : *Some of the more time-consuming jobs can be done by machines.* **time frame** *noun* कुछ करने के लिए उपलब्ध/प्रयुक्त समय/अवधि **time limit** *noun* समय सीमा **timetable** *noun* समय सारणी।

time² / टाइम् / *verb* 1 किसी घटना के लिए समय निश्चित करना, समय का प्रबंध करना : *You've timed your trip well.* 2 (खेल में) गेंद आदि को किसी विशेष क्षण पर मारना/धकेलना : *He timed that shot beautifully.* 3 समय नापना : *The winner was timed at 4 minutes 3.56 seconds.* ▸ **timing** *noun* 1 कुछ घटित होने का समय निर्धारित/नियंत्रित करने की क्रिया : *The timing of the an-*

nouncement was rather unexpected. 2 कुछ घटित होने का विशेष समय/अवधि : *Please check your flight timings carefully.*

timeless / टाइम्लस् / *adj* (औप या साहि) 1 समय के गुज़रने से अप्रभावित : *His work has a timeless quality.* 2 हमेशा क़ायम रहने वाला; अनंत : *Certain truths are timeless.* ▸ **timelessly** *adv* **timelessness** *noun*.

timely / टाइम्लि / *adj* आवश्यकता के समय होने वाला : *I was grateful for your timely intervention.*

timid / टिमिड् / *adj* कायर; भीरू : *as timid as a rabbit* ▸ **timidity** *noun* **timidly** *adv*.

timorous / टिमरस् / *adj* (औप) कायर एवं भ्रांत ▸ **timorously** *adv* **timorousness** *noun*.

tin / टिन् / *noun* 1 (प्रतीक **Sn**) टिन धातु 2 (**tin can** भी; *US* **can**) टीन, धातु का बना डिब्बा : *Open a tin of beans.* ▸ **tin** (*US* **can** भी) *verb* (-nn-) संरक्षण के लिए टीन के डिब्बे में बंद करना।

tinge / टिन्ज् / *verb* **tinge sth (with sth)** 1 हलका रंग चढ़ाना : *hair tinged with grey* 2 गुण-विशेष की थोड़ी-सी मात्रा जोड़ देना : *admiration tinged with envy* ▸ **tinge** *noun* (विशेषत: *sing*) **tinge (of sth)** आभा, झलक : *There was a tinge of melancholy in her voice.*

tingle / टिङ्ग्ल् / *verb* **tingle (with sth)** 1 (व्यक्ति के शरीर या अंग में) झुनझुनी चढ़ना : *fingers tingling with cold* 2 किसी भाव से प्रभावित या उत्तेजित होना : *tingling with indignation* ▸ **tingle** *noun* (प्राय: *sing*) झुनझुनी।

tinker / टिङ्कर् / *noun* 1 ख़ानाबदोश 2 घूम-घूम कर बरतन-भाँडे आदि ठीक करने वाला व्यक्ति ▸ **tinker** *verb* **tinker (with sth)** बिना पक्की जानकारी के मरम्मत

करना : He likes tinkering with old radios.

tinkle / 'टिङ्क्ल् / noun (प्राय: sing) 1 (tinkling भी) घंटियों की ध्वनि : the tinkle of a small bell 2 (अनौप) फ़ोन कॉल ▶ tinkle verb ऐसी ध्वनि करना।

tinsel / 'टिन्स्ल् / noun सजावट में प्रयुक्त चमकदार धातु का टुकड़ा या धागा : decorate a Christmas tree with tinsel.

tint / टिन्ट् / noun 1 रंग की छाया, झलक : tints of green in the sky at dawn 2 बालों को रँगने का रंग; बाल रँगने की क्रिया : She had a tint. ▶ tint verb हलका-सा रंग देना।

tiny / 'टाइनि / adj (-ier, -iest) बहुत छोटा, नन्हा : a tiny baby/cottage.

tip[1] / टिप् / noun 1 किसी वस्तु की नोक, सिरा, अग्रभाग : the tips of one's toes/ fingers 2 नोक पर रखी या लगी छोटी वस्तु : the tip of an arrow ■ on the tip of one's tongue (शब्द आदि) लगभग याद आते हुए the tip of the iceberg किसी जटिल समस्या का छोटा–सा सुस्पष्ट भाग ▶ tip verb (-pp-) tip sth (with sth) नोक पर कुछ लगाना/चढ़ाना : The table-legs were tipped with rubber.

tip[2] / टिप् / verb (-pp-) 1 tip sth (up/ over) उलट देना, झुकाना/तिरछा करना : She tipped over a chair in her rush to leave. 2 झुका कर पात्र में से वस्तु बाहर निकाल देना : He tipped the dirty water down the drain. 3 किनारा छू कर निकल जाना : The ball just tipped (the edge of) his racket.

tip[3] / टिप् / verb (-pp-) 1 टिप (बख्शिश, इनाम) देना : tip the taxi-driver 2 tip sb/sth (as sth/to do sth) कोई उपयोगी राय देना; होने वाली घटना के बारे में सलाह/ संकेत देना; भविष्यवाणी करना ■ tip sb off (अनौप) किसी घटना/परिस्थिति से संबंधित पहले से जानकारी देना : He tipped off

the police about the robbery. ▶ tip noun 1 बख्शिश, इनाम, टिप : He left a tip under his plate. 2 युक्ति; महत्त्वपूर्ण सूचना : a handy tip for removing grease stains.

tipsy / 'टिप्सि / adj (अनौप) शराब के गुलाबी नशे/हलके सुरूर में।

tiptoe / टिप्टो / noun ■ on tiptoe पंजों के बल खड़ा होना/चलना : walk on tiptoe so as not to wake the baby ▶ tiptoe verb पंजों के बल बिना आवाज़ किए सावधानी से चलना : She tiptoed (across) to the bed where Neha lay asleep.

tirade / टाइ 'रेड्; US 'टाइरेड् / noun tirade (against sb/sth) लंबा उत्तेजित आलोचना भरा भाषण : He launched into a long tirade against the government.

tire / 'टाइअर् / verb 1 थक जाना, ऊब जाना : She's got so much energy she never seems to tire. 2 थका/ऊबा देना : The long walk tired me. ■ tire of (doing) sth किसी चीज़ में रुचि खो देना tire sb/oneself out बहुत थक जाना/ थका देना ▶ tired / 'टाइअई / adj 1 थका हुआ 2 tired of sb/sth; tired of doing sth ऊबा हुआ, बोर हो चुका : I'm sick and tired of your criticisms. tireless adj अथक; शक्ति से भरपूर : a tireless campaigner tiresome / 'टाइअर्सम् / adj कष्टकर, ऊबाऊ; नीरस : Selling your house can be a tiresome business. tiring / 'टाइ- अरिङ् / adj थका देने वाला : a tiring journey.

tissue / 'टिश्; 'टिस्यू / noun 1 ऊतक : muscle/nerve/brain tissue 2 (tissue paper भी) पतले मुलायम काग़ज़ का रुमाल 3 महीन बुना हुआ कपड़ा।

tit[1] / टिट् / noun (अप) (विशेषत: pl) (स्त्री की) छाती; निपल।

tit² / टिट् / *noun* ■ **tit for tat** जैसे को तैसा : *a series of tit-for-tat killings by rival gangs.*

titbit / 'टिट्बिट् / (*US* **tidbit** / 'टिड्-बिट् /) *noun* 1 चटपटे आहार का टुकड़ा 2 **titbit (of sth)** छोटी लेकिन मज़ेदार ख़बर : *titbits of scandal.*

title / 'टाइट्ल् / *noun* 1 पुस्तक, कविता, चित्र आदि का शीर्षक 2 किसी मुद्रित किताब/ समाचार-पत्र आदि की सभी प्रतियाँ : *The company publishes about 20 new titles each year.* 3 उपाधि, ख़िताब; पदवी : *He inherited the title of Duke from his father.* 4 **title (to sth/to do sth)** (क़ानून) (संपत्ति का) स्वामित्व, अधिकार : *disputing the country's title to govern the islands* 5 (खेल में) सर्वश्रेष्ठ खिलाड़ी होने का आधिकारिक पद : *heavyweight title* ▸ **title** *verb* शीर्षक देना **title-deed** *noun* स्वामित्व का लिखित क़ानूनी अधिकार-पत्र **title-page** *noun* (किताब का शीर्षक और लेखक का नाम देते हुए) मुखपृष्ठ।

to¹ / टु; टू / *prep* 1 दिशा की ओर : *walk to the office* 2 जहाँ तक : *The garden extends to the river bank.* 3 (से) तक : *count (from 1) to 10* 4 एक समय से दूसरे समय तक; कुछ शुरू होने से पहले : *from Monday to Friday* ○ *How long is it to lunch?* 5 घड़ी के ठीक घंटे से पहले : *ten (minutes) to two* 6 किसी का; किसी के लिए : *the key to the door* 7 किसी से संबंधित : *his claim to the throne* 8 (तुलना में दूसरी वस्तु प्रस्तुत करने में प्रयुक्त) : *I prefer walking to climbing.* 9 संबंधवाची : *She's married to an Italian.*

to² / टु; टू / *adv part* (सामान्यत: दरवाज़ा) बंद स्थिति में : *Push the door to.* ■ **to and fro** इधर-उधर, आगे-पीछे : *walking to and fro.*

toad / टोड / *noun* 1 टोड, एक प्रकार का मेंढक 2 गाली के रूप में प्रयुक्त शब्द।

toadstool / 'टोड्स्टूल् / *noun* छतरी के आकार जैसा छोटा कुकुरमुत्ता।

toast¹ / टोस्ट् / *noun* सेंकी हुई डबलरोटी ▸ **toast** *verb* 1 डबलरोटी सेंकना : *He toasted a few slices of the bread.* 2 आग तापना।

toast² / टोस्ट् / *verb* शुभकामना/सलामती का जाम पीना : *toast the bride and groom* ▸ **toast** *noun* 1 शुभकामना का जाम उठाने की क्रिया 2 व्यक्ति जिसे शुभ-कामना दी जा रही है; लोकप्रिय व्यक्ति।

tobacco / ट'बैको / *noun* (*pl* **tobaccos**) तंबाकू : *tobacco smoke* ▸ **tobacconist** / ट'बैकनिस्ट् / *noun* तंबाकू बेचने वाला।

today / ट'डे / *noun* 1 आज : *Today is her 100th birthday.* 2 वर्तमान/मौजूदा समय/अवधि/काल : *today's young people* ▸ **today** *adv* आज; वर्तमान समय में।

toddle / 'टॉड्ल् / *verb* 1 छोटे, अस्थिर क़दम लेकर (विशेषत: बच्चे का) चलना : *Has she started toddling yet?* 2 (अनौप) चलना या जाना : *toddle round to see a friend* ▸ **toddler** / 'टॉड्लर् / *noun* नन्हा बच्चा जो चलना सीख रहा हो या जिसने अभी-अभी चलना सीखा हो।

toe / टो / *noun* 1 पैर की अँगुली; जानवर का खुर या सुम : *I stubbed my toe on the chair leg.* 2 जूते/मोज़े का पंजा ■ **on one's toes** क्रिया के लिए तैयार; चौकन्ना/ चौकस ▸ **toe** *verb* (*pt, pp* **toed**; *pres p* **toeing**) पंजा लगाना, पंजे से छूना ■ **toe the (party) line** (*US* **toe the mark** भी) (दल के) मान्य, परंपरा, मानदंड का पालन करना।

toffee / 'टॉफ़ि / *noun* टॉफ़ी।

together / ट'गेद्र् / *adv part* 1 साथ में, साथ-साथ : *They've gone for a walk together.* 2 सम्मिश्रित; जुड़े हुए 3 सह-मति में : *The party is absolutely* *together on this issue.* **4** इकट्ठे; एक ही साथ/समय : *All my troubles seem to come together.* ▶ **togetherness** *noun.*

toil / टॉइल् / *verb* **1** (विशेषतः *साहि*) toil (away) (at/over sth) कड़ा परिश्रम करना : *peasants toiling in the fields* **2** बड़ी कठिनाई से आगे बढ़ना : *The bus toiled up the steep hill.* ▶ **toil** *noun* (विशेषतः *साहि*) कठोर परिश्रम : *after a hard day's toil.*

toilet / टॉइलट् / *noun* **1** शौचघर **2** (*अप्र*) केश प्रसाधन (बालों को धोना, सजाना आदि); इसके लिए प्रयुक्त वस्तु : *toilet soap* ▶ **toiletries** *noun* [*pl*] प्रसाधन सामग्री।

token / टोकन् / *noun* **1** धातु या प्लास्टिक की गोल सिक्के जैसी वस्तु जिसे मशीनों को चलाने या भुगतान के रूप में प्रयोग में लाया जाता है : *a car-park token* **2** काग़ज़ का टुकड़ा जिसके बदले में किसी विशेष दुकान से कोई वस्तु ली जा सकती है : *a gift token* **3** चिह्न, साक्ष्य, गारंटी आदि दिखाने के लिए, प्रमाणस्वरूप : *Please accept this small gift in token of my affection.* ▶ **token** *adj* केवल प्रतीकात्मक : *put in a token appearance at the office party.*

tolerate / टॉलरेट् / *verb* **1** सहना, बरदाश्त करना (बिना विरोध के) : *tolerate heat/noise/pain* **2** नापसंद होने पर भी कुछ जारी रहने देना : *Bad language will not be tolerated.* ▶ **tolerable** / टॉल-रब्ल् / *adj* **1** सहनीय **2** पर्याप्त, ठीक, अच्छा : *a tolerable price* **tolerance** / टॉलरन्स् / *noun* tolerance (of/for sb/sth) सहिष्णुता (दूसरों के मन, रिवाज आदि स्वीकार करने की शक्ति) : *religious tolerance* **tolerant** / टॉलरन्ट् / *adj* tolerant (of/towards sb/ sth) सहिष्णु **toleration** *noun.*

toll¹ / टोल् / *noun* **1** सड़क/पुल आदि प्रयोग करने का महसूल, मार्ग-कर **2** किसी परिस्थिति-विशेष में मारे गए व्यक्तियों/पशुओं की संख्या : *the death-toll in the earthquake* ■ **take a heavy toll/ take its toll (of sth)** हानि पहुँचाना : *The war took a heavy toll of human life.*

toll² / टोल् / *verb* **1** toll (for sb/sth) धीरे-धीरे नियमित ढंग से घंटा बजाना (विशेषतः मृत्यु या अंत्येष्टि के समय गिरजाघर में) : *The church sexton tolled the bell.* **2** toll (for sb/sth) इस प्रकार घंटा बजना : *The church bell tolled the hour.* ▶ **toll** *noun* [*sing*] ऐसी ध्वनि।

tomato / ट॒माटो / *US* ट॒मेटो / *noun* (*pl* **tomatoes**) टमाटर।

tomb / टूम् / *noun* क़ब्र, मक़बरा/समाधि।

tomboy / टॉम्बाइ / *noun* लड़कों की तरह पेश आने का शौक़ रखने वाली लड़की।

tombstone / टूम्स्टोन् / *noun* क़ब्र या समाधि के ऊपर खड़ा किया गया पत्थर जिस पर मृतक व्यक्ति का नाम आदि लिखा रहता है।

tomorrow / ट॒मॉरो / *noun* **1** आने वाला कल **2** आगामी भविष्य, निकट भविष्य : *tomorrow's world* ▶ **tomorrow** *adv* कल (को) : *She's getting married tomorrow.*

ton / टन् / *noun* **1** भार की इकाई, इंग्लैंड में (लगभग) 1016 किलोग्राम, अमेरिका में (लगभग) 998 किलोग्राम→ **tonne** देखिए **2** tons [*pl*] tons (of sth) अत्यधिक : *They've got tons of money.*

tone¹ / टोन् / *noun* **1** स्वर-शैली, अभिव्यक्ति शैली; लहजा : *the ringing tones of an orator's voice* **2** किसी वस्तु का सामान्य स्वभाव **3** (रंगों का) शेड, रंगत, आभा : *a carpet in warm tones of brown and orange* **4** (संगीत) तान, सुर **5** (भाषा विज्ञान) स्वर का उतार-चढ़ाव : *rising/ falling tone* **6** (शरीर का) मज़बूत, ठोस होना : *good muscular tone* ▶ **tone-**

less *adj* नीरस, फीका, निर्जीव : *answer in a toneless voice* **tonelessly** *adv.*

tone² / टोन् / *verb* ▪ **tone sth down** 1 तीव्रता कम करना (अभिव्यक्ति, स्वर आदि की) : *You'd better tone down the more outspoken passages in your article.* 2 रंग की चमक कम करना **tone sth up** शरीर को मज़बूत, तंदुरुस्त बनाना।

tongs / टॉङ्ज़् / *noun* [pl] चिमटा, सँडसी : *(a pair of) sugar/coal/salad tongs.*

tongue / टङ् / *noun* 1 जीभ 2 (औप या साहि) भाषा : *He speaks English but his native tongue is German.* 3 (प्राय: sing) बोलने की शैली/लहजा : *She has a very sharp tongue.* 4 जीभ के आकार जैसी वस्तु : *the tongue of a shoe* ▪ **hold one's tongue** चुप रहना **mother tongue** मातृभाषा **with (one's) tongue in (one's) cheek** गंभीर न होने के इरादे से ▸ **-tongued** (समासों में) बोलचाल का विशेष ढंग होना : *sharp-tongued* **tongue-tied** *adj* शर्म या घबराहट के कारण बोल न पाना **tongue-twister** *noun* उच्चारण करने में मुश्किल शब्द या वाक्यांश।

tonic / टॉनिक् / *noun* 1 स्फूर्ति देने वाली दवा, टॉनिक 2 (प्राय: sing) स्फूर्ति एवं प्रसन्नता प्रदान करने वाली वस्तु : *The good news was a tonic for us all.*

tonight / ट'नाइट् / *noun* आज रात; आज की शाम/रात : *Tonight will be cloudy.* ▸ **tonight** *adv* आज (की) शाम/रात को : *Are you doing anything to-night?*

tonnage / 'टनिज् / *noun* 1 (टन में मापा) माल का कुल भार : *the total tonnage of bombs dropped in the war* 2 देश के व्यापारिक जहाज़ों का टन भार।

tonne / टन् / *noun* (pl **tonnes** या **tonne**) मीट्रिक टन (1000 किलोग्राम)।

tonsil / 'टॉन्सल् / *noun* गलसुआ; गले की ग्रंथि।

tonsure / 'टॉन्शर् / *noun* मुंडन।

too / टू / *adv* 1 भी; इसके अतिरिक्त : *He speaks Tamil, Kannada and Bangla too.* 2 अपेक्षा से अधिक : *drive too fast* 3 बहुत; पूर्णत : *You are really too kind.*

tool / टूल् / *noun* 1 कारीगर का औज़ार 2 कोई भी वस्तु जो कार्य में सहायक हो : *research tools like questionnaires* 3 वह व्यक्ति जो दूसरे के लाभ के लिए काम में लाया/शोषित किया जाता है।

toot / टूट् / *noun* भोंपू; सीटी ▸ **toot** *verb* भोंपू बजाना।

tooth / टूथ् / *noun* (pl **teeth** / टीथ् /) 1 दाँत 2 किसी वस्तु का दाँतनुमा अंग (जैसे कंघे के दाँत) : *the teeth of a saw/gear* ▪ **fight, etc tooth and nail** पूरी शक्ति से लड़ना ▸ **toothache** / 'टूथ्एक् / *noun* दाँत का दर्द।

top¹ / टॉप् / *noun* 1 (विशेषत: sing) चोटी, शिखर; ऊपरी सतह : *at the top of the stairs* ∘ *polish the top of the table* 2 [sing] **top (of sth)** पराकाष्ठा, सर्वोच्च स्थिति या पद : *reach the top* 3 ऊपरी भाग या परत : *the top of the milk* 4 ढक्कन : *Where's the top for this can of paint?* 5 शरीर के ऊपरी भाग के लिए वस्त्र : *I need a top to go with these shorts.* ▪ **at the top of one's voice** जितनी हो सके उतनी ऊँची आवाज़ में **be/feel on top of the world** सफलता या सौभाग्य के कारण बहुत खुश होना **from top to bottom** पूर्णत:; अच्छी तरह से **from top to toe** पूर्णत:; सर्वत्र **get on top of sth** कुछ करने में सफल होना : *How will I ever get on top of all this work?* **on top of sth/sb** 1 किसी के ऊपर 2 इसके अतिरिक्त : *He gets commission on top of his salary.* ▸ **top** *adj* पद या स्तर में सर्वोच्च : *a room* *on the top floor* **top-heavy** *adj* शिखर पर सर्वाधिक भारी; असंतुलित।

top² / टॉप् / *verb* (-pp-) **1** सर्वोपरि होना/रहना : *His latest book is topping the best-sellers list.* **2** ढकना; शिखर बनना: *ice-cream topped with chocolate sauce* **3** (पेड़ों) को छाँटना; भोजन के रूप में लेते समय फलों आदि का ऊपरी सिरा काटना : *top and tail gooseberries.*

top³ / टॉप् / *noun* लट्टू।

topaz / टोपैज़् / *noun* पुखराज।

topic / टॉपिक् / *noun* विचार-विषय : *a topic of conversation* ▸ **topical** *adj* सामयिक, वर्तमान रुचि का : *a topical theme.*

topography / ट'पॉग्रफ़ि / *noun* किसी स्थान की विशेष आकृति; वहाँ की नदियों, पहाड़ों, सड़कों, इमारतों आदि का विवरण : *describe the local topography* ▸ **topographical** *adj* : *a topographical map* **topographically** *adv.*

topple / टॉप्ल् / *verb* **1** topple (over) अस्थिर होकर लुढ़क जाना/अस्थिर करके लुढ़का देना : *The pile of books toppled over onto the floor.* **2** सत्ताधारी या अधिकारी को पद से हटा देना/सत्ता से लुढ़का देना : *The crisis threatens to topple the government (from power).*

topsy-turvy / टॉप्सि'टर्वि / *adj, adv* (अनौप) उलटा-पुलटा, अव्यवस्थित : *This sudden development turned all our plans topsy-turvy.*

torch / टॉर्च् / *noun* **1** (*US* flashlight भी) (बैटरी की) टॉर्च **2** मशाल ▸ **torch** *verb* जानबूझ कर आग लगाना : *buses torched by rioters.*

torment / टॉर्मेन्ट् / *noun* **1** सताए जाने का कारण (व्यक्ति या वस्तु) : *His shyness made public speaking a constant torment to him.* **2** तीव्र मानसिक या शारीरिक वेदना/तड़प : *be in great torment* ▸ **torment** / टॉर्'मेन्ट् / *verb* सताना, तड़पाना : *be tormented by hunger.*

tornado / टॉर्'नेडो / *noun* (*pl* tornadoes) बवंडर, तेज़ तूफ़ान : *The town was hit by a tornado.*

torpedo / टॉर्'पीडो / *noun* (*pl* torpedoes) एक विशेष बम जो किसी जहाज़ या पनडुब्बी से छोड़ा जाता है और जो अन्य जहाज़ पर हमला करके उसे डुबाने के काम में लाया जाता है, नौसैनी ▸ **torpedo** *verb* (*pt, pp* torpedoed; *pres p* torpedoing) **1** टॉरपीडो से हमला करना **2** किसी संस्था, नीति या घटना को नष्ट कर देना ▸ **torpedo boat** *noun* नौसेना का छोटा जहाज़ जिससे टॉरपीडो छोड़े जाते हैं।

torrent / टॉरन्ट् / *noun* **1** तेज़, ज़ोरदार प्रवाह : *rain pouring down in torrents* **2** अचानक तीव्रता से छोड़ी गई वस्तु की बड़ी मात्रा; बौछार : *a torrent of abuse* ▸ **torrential** / ट'रेन्श्ल् / *adj* वेगवान, वेगवती : *torrential rain.*

torrid / टॉरिड् / *adj* **1** बहुत गरम और सूखा (मौसम, देश) : *a torrid summer* **2** तीव्र, विशेषत: कामुक, भाव भरा : *a torrid love affair.*

torso / टॉर्सो / *noun* (*pl* torsos) शरीर का मुख्य भाग, सर, बाँहों और टाँगों के अलावा; धड़।

tortoise / टॉर्टस् / *noun* कछुआ।

tortuous / टॉर्चुअस् / *adj* **1** टेढ़ा-मेढ़ा, चक्करदार : *a tortuous mountain track* **2** (प्राय: अपमा) (नीति) वक्र, कपटी : *a tortuous argument.*

torture / टॉर्चर् / *noun* **1** यंत्रणा, घोर कष्ट **2** मानसिक/शारीरिक संताप/पीड़ा ▸ **torture** *verb* **1** यंत्रणा देना, अति कष्ट देना : *Political prisoners are regularly tortured.* **2** अत्यधिक मानसिक या शारीरिक पीड़ा देना/होना : *be tortured by fear.*

toss / टॉस् / verb 1 उछालना, दिशा विशेष में हलके/लापरवाही से फेंकना : toss the ducks some bread 2 निरंतर झटका देना, हिलना-डुलना : branches tossing (about) in the wind 3 सिर को झटका देना (तिरस्कार सूचक) : She just tossed her head and walked off. 4 toss up; toss (sb) for sth सिक्का उछाल कर संयोग के आधार पर निर्णय लेना ▸ toss noun उछाल/झटका।

total / 'टोटल् / adj 1 पूर्ण/समग्र (धनराशि या अन्य वस्तु) : The firm made a total profit of Rs 2,00,000. 2 पूर्ण/समग्र; निरा : total silence ▸ total noun पूर्ण जोड़ : What does the total come to? total verb (-ll-; US -l-) total sb/sth (up) जोड़ होना/कुल होना; जोड़ निकालना : The scores were totalled up and the winner announced. totally / 'टोटलि / adv पूरी तरह से : totally blind.

totalitarian / टो,टैल 'टेअरिअन् / adj (प्राय: अपमा) ऐसा राज्य जहाँ एक ही राजनीतिक दल का पूरा अधिकार हो और दूसरे दल न हों : a totalitarian regime.

totter / 'टॉटर् / verb 1 लड़खड़ाना : The child tottered across the room. 2 डगमगाना : The building tottered briefly and then collapsed.

touch¹ / टच् / verb 1 छूना, स्पर्श करना : Don't touch that dish—it's very hot! 2 भावना या चिंता का विषय बनना, प्रभावित करना : a sad story that touched us all deeply 3 (विशेषत: नकारात्मक वाक्यों में) गुण, निपुणता आदि में किसी के समान होना : No one can touch him as a designer. 4 निर्धारित/निश्चित स्तर तक पहुँचना : touch the depths of despair ∎ touch down वायुयान का धरती पर उतरना touch on/upon sth (विषय का) उल्लेख करना,

विषय छूना touch sth up गौण परिवर्तनों द्वारा किसी वस्तु में सुधार करना।

touch² / टच् / noun 1 (प्राय: sing) स्पर्श, छूना 2 स्पर्शजन्य संवेदन : Blind people rely a lot on (their sense of) touch. 3 [sing] a touch (of sth) पुट, थोड़ी-सी मात्रा : There's a touch of frost in the air. 4 एक सूक्ष्म अभिव्यक्ति ∎ in/out of touch (with sb) संपर्क में/संपर्क से बाहर in/out of touch (with sth) किसी के बारे में जानकारी होना/न होना ▸ touch-and-go adj (अनौप) परिणाम के बारे में बिलकुल अनिश्चित।

touching / 'टचिङ् / adj मर्मस्पर्शी, कारुणिक : a touching story/sight.

touchy / 'टचि / adj 1 तुनक-मिज़ाज : He's very touchy about his baldness. 2 (विषय, परिस्थिति आदि) जो जल्दी ही क्रोधित या नाराज़ कर दे।

tough / टफ् / adj (-er, -est) 1 सरलता से न कटने या फटने वाला : tough leather boots 2 मज़बूत; कठिनाइयों या दर्द सहन कर सकने वाला : He should recover—he's pretty tough. 3 (अपमा) (खाना, गोश्त) सख़्त, कड़ा 4 कष्टसाध्य : a tough assignment/problem 5 tough (on sb) (अनौप) दुर्भाग्यपूर्ण : It's rather tough on him getting ill just before his holiday. 6 tough (on/with sb/sth) व्यवहार या दृष्टिकोण में सख़्त या कड़ा : tough measures to deal with terrorism ▸ tough noun (अप्र या अनौप) गुंडा-बदमाश toughen / 'टफ़न् / verb toughen (sth/sb) (up) मज़बूत/ सख़्त बनाना/बनना : The government plans to toughen the immigration laws.

tour / टुअर् / noun टूर, दौरा, यात्रा : a round-the-world tour ▸ tour verb tour (in sth) यात्रा करना : They are touring (in) India.

tourism / 'टुअरिज़म् / *noun* पर्यटन
▶ **tourist** / 'टुअरिस्ट् / पर्यटक।

tournament / 'टुअर्नमन्ट् / *noun* खेल
प्रतियोगिता (टूर्नामेंट) : *a tennis tour-nament.*

tow / टो / *verb* (जहाज़, नाव, कार आदि
को) रस्सी या ज़ंजीर से खींचना : *tow a
caravan* ▶ **tow** *noun* (प्राय: *sing*)
खिंचाई, खिंचाव ■ **in tow 1** (*अनौप*) कुछ
पीछे आते हुए **2** (नाव आदि को) खींचना :
The trawler took us in tow.

towards / ट'वॉर्ड्ज़् / (**toward** / ट'वॉर्ड /
भी) *prep* **1** दिशा विशेष की ओर, किसी की
दिशा में : *walk towards the river* **2**
प्राप्ति के नज़दीक : *a first step towards
political unity* **3** कुछ पाने/योगदान करने
के इरादे से : *The money will go
towards (the cost of) a new school.*
4 किसी के संबंध में : *The local people
are always very friendly towards
tourists.* **5** (समय) के आसपास : *It
gets cooler towards evening.*

towel / 'टाउअल् / *noun* तौलिया : *a
hand-/bath-towel.*

tower / 'टाउअर् / *noun* मीनार, टावर ▶ **to-wer** *verb* ■ **tower above/over sb/
sth** आसपास की वस्तुओं से बहुत ऊँचा होना
(लंबाई, गुणों, प्रसिद्धि आदि में) : *The
mountain towered above us.*

town / टाउन् / *noun* **1** क़सबा (गाँव से बड़ी
और नगर से छोटी बस्ती) **2** वहाँ के लोग :
The whole town turned out to wel-come the team home. **3** व्यापारिक
स्थल : *I'm going into town—do you
want me to get you anything?*
▶ **town hall** *noun* टाउन हॉल (स्थानीय
शासन का भवन, कार्यालय आदि)।

toxic / 'टॉक्सिक् / *adj* ज़हरीला : *toxic
drugs* ▶ **toxicity** *noun* (*pl* **toxi-cities**) ज़हरीलापन : *substances with
low/high toxicity.*

toxin / 'टॉक्सिन् / *noun* ज़हरीला पदार्थ,
विशेषत: जीवाणु द्वारा बना/बनाया हुआ और
कोई विशेष बीमारी उत्पन्न करने वाला :
eliminate toxins from the body.

toy[1] / टॉइ / *noun* **1** खिलौना **2** (प्राय:
अपमा) मनोरंजन की, न कि गंभीरता से ली
जाने वाली, वस्तु : *His latest toy is a
personal computer.*

toy[2] / टॉइ / *verb* ■ **toy with sth 1** ला-परवाही से बिना सोचे-समझे वस्तु का प्रयोग
करना : *She was just toying with her
food, as if she wasn't really hun-gry.* **2** बिना गंभीरता के सोचना : *I've
been toying with the idea of mov-ing abroad.*

trace[1] / ट्रेस् / *noun* **1** चिह्न, संकेत, अव-शेष : *traces of prehistoric habita-tion* **2** बहुत थोड़ी मात्रा, लवलेश : *speak
without a trace of bitterness.*

trace[2] / ट्रेस् / *verb* **1** **trace sb/sth (to
sth)** खोज निकालना : *attempts to trace
a missing 5-year-old* **2** **trace sth
(back) (to sth)** आरंभ/स्रोत खोज निका-लना : *The cause of the fire was
traced to a faulty fuse-box.* **3** चिह्नों,
निशानों पर चलना : *They traced the
footprints to an old shed.* **4** **trace
sth (out)** ख़ाका उतारना, रूपरेखा खींचना
5 पारदर्शी काग़ज़ से मानचित्र की नक़ल
करना, अनुरेखण करना ▶ **tracing** *noun*
अनुरेखण।

track / ट्रैक् / *noun* **1** (प्राय: *pl*) पद चिह्न;
गाड़ी आदि के चलने से बने निशान : *tyre
tracks in the mud* **2** लीक, बहुत प्रयोग
से बना चिह्न : *a muddy track through
the forest* **3** किसी चीज़ द्वारा ली गई विशेष
दिशा : *the track of a storm/comet/
satellite* **4** रेल की पटरी : *lay some
new track* **5** ट्रैक (दौड़ के लिए चूने से
बनी रेखाओं वाला मैदान) : *a cycling
track* ■ **keep/lose track of sb/sth**
किसी के बारे में नियमित रूप से जानकारी
रखना/न रखना : *It's hard to keep

track of all one's old school friends. **on the right/wrong track** उचित/ग़लत तरीक़े से सोचते/कुछ करते हुए ▶ **track** *verb* **track sb/sth (to sth)** खोज पर चलना, पीछे जाना : *track a satellite* **track events** *noun* [*pl*] दौड़ आदि खेल-कूद प्रतियोगिताएँ।

tract¹ / ट्रैक्ट् / *noun* 1 भूभाग, विशाल इलाक़ा : *huge tracts of forests* 2 नलिका जैसे जुड़े हुए अंगों का तंत्र : *the digestive/urinary tract.*

tract² / ट्रैक्ट् / *noun* विशेषतः धार्मिक या राजनीतिक विषय पर छोटा निबंध।

traction / 'ट्रैक्श्न् / *noun* 1 सतह पर खींचने की क्रिया; इस क्रिया में प्रयोग की गई शक्ति : *electric/steam traction* 2 (चिकि) बाँह, टाँग आदि का खींच के द्वारा उपचार : *She's injured her back and is in traction for a month.*

tractor / 'ट्रैक्टर् / *noun* खेत जोतने के लिए प्रयुक्त मोटर युक्त गाड़ी।

trade¹ / ट्रेड् / *noun* 1 **trade (with sb/sth)** व्यापार, लेन-देन : *a trade agreement/deficit* 2 **trade (in sth)** व्यापार विशेष : *be in the cotton trade* 3 व्यवसाय, पेशा : *be a carpenter/tailor by trade* 4 **the trade** व्यापार-व्यवसाय में लगे लोग या संस्थाएँ : *offer discounts to the trade* ▶ **trademark** *noun* मार्का, व्यापारिक चिह्न, ट्रेडमार्क **tradesman** *noun* व्यापारी **trade wind** *noun* (भूगोल) पहले मध्य रेखा और फिर पश्चिम की ओर चलती हुई ज़ोरदार पवन **trade union** *noun* श्रमिक संघ।

trade² / ट्रेड् / *verb* 1 **trade (in sth) (with sb)** व्यापार करना : *trade in arms/textiles/grain* 2 **trade at sth** दुकान-विशेष से सामान ख़रीदना 3 **trade sth/sb (for sth)** बदले में कुछ देना/लेना : *I'll trade you my stamp collection for your model boat.* ■ **trade on sth** (विशेषतः *अपमा*) अनुचित लाभ उठाना

trade sth in (for sth) नई वस्तु के भुगतान के अंश के रूप में पुरानी प्रयुक्त वस्तु देना ▶ **trader** *noun* व्यापारी, दुकानदार।

tradition / ट्रॅडिश्न् / *noun* 1 परंपरा : *We decided to break with tradition and not send any cards this Christmas.* 2 परंपरा द्वारा स्थापित विश्वास या रीति : *literary traditions* ▶ **traditional** / ट्रॅ'डिशन्ल् / *adj* परंपरा के अनुसार/परंपरागत : *country people in their traditional outfits* **traditionally** *adv.*

traffic / 'ट्रैफ़िक् / *noun* 1 ट्रैफ़िक, सड़कों पर लोगों और वाहनों का यातायात : *heavy/light traffic* 2 (रेल, जहाज़, वायुयान आदि का) मार्ग पर यातायात : *commercial air traffic* 3 **traffic (in sth)** तस्करी आदि अवैध/अनुचित व्यापार : *the traffic in drugs/arms* ▶ **traffic** *verb* **(-ck-) traffic (in sth)** व्यापार (विशेषतः अवैध व्यापार)।

tragedy / 'ट्रैजडि / *noun* (pl **tragedies**) 1 दुखद घटना : *The whole affair ended in tragedy.* 2 त्रासदी, दुखांत नाटक : *Shakespeare's tragedies and comedies* ▶ **tragic** *adj* दुखद; दुखांत नाटक जैसा : *a tragic story* **tragically** *adv* : *a tragically short life.*

trail / ट्रेल् / *noun* 1 पदचिह्न; अवशेष : *The police are still on the trail of the escaped prisoner.* 2 निशान, चिह्न : *The hurricane left a trail of destruction.* 3 पगडंडी : *a trail through the forest* 4 विशेष उद्देश्य के लिए बनाया मार्ग : *a tourist trail* ▶ **trail** *verb* 1 घसीटना, खींचना : *a bird trailing a broken wing* 2 थके-थके से घिसटते हुए चलना 3 (पौधों का) फैल जाना : *roses trailing over the walls* 4 **trail sb/sth (to sth)** पीछा करना, पीछे-पीछे जाना।

trailer / 'ट्रेलर् / *noun* 1 किसी अन्य गाड़ी

द्वारा खींची जाने वाली गाड़ी : *a car towing a trailer* **2** लोकप्रिय करने के लिए फ़िल्म आदि के प्रदर्शन से पहले ही दिखाए गए लघु अंश।

train¹ / ट्रेन् / *noun* **1** रेलगाड़ी **2** कतार, ताँता : *a camel train* **3** (प्राय: *sing*) **train (of sth)** (विचारों या घटनाओं की) शृंखला, सिलसिला : *His phone call interrupted my train of thought.*

train² / ट्रेन् / *verb* **1** **train sb (as sth/ in sth)** प्रशिक्षण देना, सिखाना : *He was trained as an engineer.* **2 train (sb/ sth) (for sth)** व्यायाम, खुराक आदि द्वारा व्यक्ति या जानवर के शरीर को पुष्ट बनाना/ रखना : *My aunt trains horses.* **3** पौधों को किसी एक ही दिशा में फैलने देना : *train roses against the wall* ■ **train sth on sb/sth** बंदूक/कैमरे आदि का निशाना बाँधना ▶ **trainee** *noun* प्रशिक्षण ले रहा व्यक्ति **trainer** *noun* प्रशिक्षक, प्रशिक्षण देने वाला **training** *noun* प्रशिक्षण : *be in training for a competition* **training college** *noun* प्रशिक्षण महा-विद्यालय।

trait / ट्रेट / *noun* विशेषता, विशेषक-गुण : *personality traits.*

traitor / ट्रेटर् / *noun* **traitor (to sb/sth)** विश्वासघाती; देशद्रोही ▶ **traitorous** / 'ट्रेटरस् / *adj* (औप) विश्वासघातक : *traitorous behaviour.*

trajectory / ट्र'जेक्टरि / *noun* (*pl* **trajectories**) (हवा में फेंकी गई चीज़ का) उड़ान-पथ, प्रक्षेप-पथ : *a bullet's trajectory.*

tram / ट्रैम् / *noun* (**tramcar** भी) ट्राम गाड़ी।

tramp¹ / ट्रैम्प् / *verb* **1** धब-धब करते हुए चलना : *We could hear him tramping about upstairs.* **2** (लंबी दूरी की) पदयात्रा : *tramping over the moors.*

tramp² / ट्रैम्प् / *noun* **1** आवारा, घुमक्कड़ **2** (प्राय: *sing*) लंबी पद यात्रा : *go for a*

tramp **3** [*sing*] **the tramp of sb/sth** धब-धब की ध्वनि।

trample / 'ट्रैम्पल् / *verb* **1 trample sth/sb (down)** कुचलना, रौंदना : *The campers had trampled the corn (down).* **2 trample on/upon sth/sb** कुचल कर नष्ट करना, मसलना; भावनाओं, अधिकारों आदि की क़दर न करना; घृणा से देखना।

trampoline / 'ट्रैम्पलीन् / *noun* ठोस पदार्थ से बनी और ढाँचे के साथ बंधी चादर, जिसे हवा में ऊँची छलांग लगाने के लिए प्रयोग में लाया जाता है।

trance / ट्रान्स्; *US* ट्रैन्स् / *noun* **1** सुषुप्ति की अवस्था, बेहोशी **2** समाधि की अवस्था; गहन ध्यान/मग्न अवस्था : *She's been in a trance all day.*

tranquil / 'ट्रैइक्विल् / *adj* प्रशांत; नि-स्तब्ध : *lead a tranquil life in the country* ▶ **tranquillity** (*US* **tranquility** भी) / ट्रैइ'क्विलटि / *noun.*

trans- *pref* (पूर्वपद) **1** के उस पार, उस पार : *trans-atlantic* **2** दूसरे स्थान पर या दूसरी अवस्था में : *transplant/trans-form.*

transact / ट्रैन्'ज़ैक्ट् / *verb* **transact sth (with sb)** (औप) कारोबार करना।

transaction / ट्रैन्'ज़ैक्श्न् / *noun* **1 transaction (of sth)** कारोबार करने की क्रिया **2** सौदा, किया गया कारोबार : *cash transactions.*

transcend / ट्रैन्'सेन्ड् / *verb* (औप) सामान्य सीमा के बाहर जाना/होना : *issues that transcend party politics.*

transcendent / ट्रैन्'सेन्डन्ट् / *adj* अति श्रेष्ठ, अत्युत्तम : *a writer of transcend-ent genius.*

transcribe / ट्रैन्'स्क्राइब् / *verb* **1 tran-scribe sth (into sth)** लिखना/मुद्रित रूप में परिवर्तित करना : *transcribe a tune into musical notation* **2 tran-scribe sth (from sth)** प्रतिलिपि करना,

कापी पर नक़्ल करना : *a novel transcribed from the author's manuscript* ▸ transcription / ट्रैन्स्क्रिप्श्न् / noun 1 प्रतिलेखन 2 प्रतिलिखित अभिलेख।

transfer¹ / ट्रैन्स्'फ़र् / verb (-rr-) 1 transfer sth/sb (from ....) (to ....) स्थानांतरण करना : *The patient was transferred to another hospital.* 2 स्थान बदलना 3 transfer sth (to sb) (संपत्ति आदि) दूसरे के नाम लिखवाना : *He transferred ownership of the land to his nephew.* 4 transfer (sth) (from sth) (to sth) किसी भिन्न माध्यम में व्यक्त/नक़्ल करना : *transfer computer data from disk to tape.*

transfer² / 'ट्रैन्स्फ़र् / noun बदली/ स्थानांतरण; हस्तांतरण : *be on the transfer list.*

transfix / ट्रैन्स्'फ़िक्स् / verb (औप) डर या आश्चर्य के कारण हक्का-बक्का हो जाना, स्तंभित रह जाना या कर देना : *be transfixed with disbelief.*

transform / ट्रैन्स्'फ़ॉर्म् / verb transform sth/sb (from sth) (into sth) आकृति, गुण, प्रकृति आदि बदल देना; रूपांतरण कर देना : *A fresh coat of paint can transform a room.* ▸ transformation / ट्रैन्स्फ़र्'मेश्न् / noun रूपांतरण : *the country's transformation from dictatorship to democracy* transformer noun बिजली का ट्रांसफ़ॉर्मर।

transfusion / ट्रैन्स्'फ़्यूश्न् / (blood transfusion भी) noun बीमारी में रोगी के शरीर में दूसरे का ख़ून चढ़ाने की क्रिया/ प्रक्रिया।

transgress / ट्रैन्स्'ग्रेस्; US ट्रैन्स्'ग्रेस् / verb 1 (औप) नैतिक या क़ानून की सीमा के बाहर जाना : *transgress the bounds of decency* 2 transgress (against sth) (अप्र) नैतिक या धार्मिक नियम का

उल्लंघन करना ▸ transgression noun transgressor noun (औप) उल्लंघन-कर्ता; अपराधी।

transient / 'ट्रैन्ज़िअन्ट्; US ट्रैन्श्न् / adj अल्प, कुछ समय के लिए : *transient mood/problems.*

transistor / ट्रैन्'ज़िस्टर् / noun 1 ट्रांज़िस्टर, एक इलेक्ट्रॉनिक युक्ति 2 (transistor radio भी) रेडियो (ट्रांज़िस्टर)।

transit / 'ट्रैन्ज़िट्; ट्रैन्सिट् / noun एक स्थान से दूसरे स्थान पर ले जाने की प्रक्रिया : *goods delayed or lost in transit.*

transition / ट्रैन्'ज़िश्न्; ट्रैन्'सिश्न् / noun transition (from sth) (to sth); transition (between sth and sth) संक्रमण (एक स्थिति से दूसरी में पहुँचना) : *the transition from childhood to adult life* ▸ transitional adj.

transitive / 'ट्रैन्सटिव् / adj (व्या) (क्रिया) सकर्मक ▸ transitively adv.

translate / ट्रैन्स्'लेट् / verb 1 translate (sth) (from sth) (into sth) अनुवाद करना : *translate an article into Malayalam* 2 translate (sth) into sth पृथक, विशेषत:सक्रिय और व्यावहारिक, रूप में व्यक्त करना : *It's time to translate our ideas into action.* ▸ translation noun अनुवाद translator noun अनुवादकर्ता, अनुवादक।

translucent / ट्रैन्स्'लूस्न्ट् / adj पारभासी (ऐसा पारदर्शी होना कि प्रकाश तो जा सके पर उस पार की वस्तु, प्राणी आदि दिखाई न पड़े) : *windows made of translucent glass* ▸ translucence noun.

transmission / ट्रैन्स्'मिश्न् / noun 1 भेजने, दूसरे/दूसरों को देने की क्रिया : *the transmission of computer data along telephone lines* ∘ *the transmission of disease* 2 रेडियो या टेलिविज़न प्रसारण : *a live transmission from Mumbai.*

transmit / ट्रैन्स्'मिट् / verb (-tt-)
1 transmit sth/itself (from...) आगे बढ़ाना, एक से दूसरे को देना : *sexually transmitted diseases* **2** transmit sth (from...) (to ...) (रेडियो द्वारा) प्रसारित करना; संप्रेषित करना : *signals transmitted from a satellite.*

transparent / ट्रैन्स्'पैरन्ट् / adj **1** पारदर्शी (जिसमें से आर-पार देखा जा सके) : *the pure, transparent waters of the lake* **2** स्पष्ट, निःसंदिग्ध : *transparent lie* **3** सुबोध, सरल : *a transparent style of writing* ▸ **transparency** / ट्रैन्स्'पैरन्सि / noun **1** पारदर्शिता : *a plastic with the transparency of glass* **2** फ़ोटो जो पारदर्शी प्लास्टिक पर हो ताकि रोशनी पार होने पर देखी जा सके; स्लाइड।

transplant / ट्रैन्स्'प्लान्ट्; US ट्रैन्स्'प्लैन्ट् / verb **1** transplant sth (in/into sth) छोटे पौधे को एक स्थान से उखाड़ कर दूसरे स्थान पर लगाना **2** transplant sth (from sb/sth) (to/into sb/sth) शरीर के अंग या ऊतकों को दूसरे के शरीर में लगाना : *transplant a kidney into a 10-year-old boy* ▸ **transplant** / ट्रैन्स्प्लान्ट्; US ट्रैन्स्प्लैन्ट् / noun प्रतिरोपण : *a heart transplant.*

transport[1] / ट्रैन्स्'पॉर्ट् / verb **1** वहन करना, ले जाना, ढोना : *She was transported to hospital by helicopter.* **2** (पूर्व में) दंड के रूप में निष्कासित करके दूरस्थ स्थान पर भेज देना।

transport[2] / 'ट्रैन्स्पॉर्ट् / noun **1** (US transportation भी) परिवहन : *rail/road transport* **2** सैनिकों का परिवहन करने वाला जहाज़/वायुयान : *Military transports were used to evacuate the civilian population.*

transpose / ट्रैन्स्'पोज़् / verb **1** वस्तुओं का स्थान परिवर्तन करना, एक के स्थान पर दूसरे को रख देना : *Two letters were accidentally transposed and 'hand' got printed as 'hnad'.* **2** transpose sth (from....) to...; transpose sth into sth भिन्न वातावरण में अनुकूलन करना ▸ **transposition** noun.

transverse / 'ट्रैन्स्वर्स्; 'ट्रैन्ज़्वर्स् / adj आड़ा, तिरछा कटा; अनुप्रस्थ : *a transverse bar joining two parts.*

trap / ट्रैप् / noun **1** हानि पहुँचाने, पकड़ने या ढूँढ़ निकालने की योजना : *The thieves were caught in a police trap.* **2** (प्रायः sing) अप्रिय परिस्थिति जिसमें से बच निकलना मुश्किल हो : *Some women see marriage as a trap.* **3** फंदा, घात : *lay/set/bait a trap* **4** (अप) मुँह : *Shut your trap!* ▸ **trap** verb (-pp-) **1** जाल में पकड़ना/फँसाना : *It's cruel to trap birds.* **2** फँस जाना, अटक जाना : *My jacket was trapped in the car door.* **3** किसी स्थान से मुक्त होने से रोकना : *The filter traps dust from the air.* **4** trap sb (into sth/doing sth) किसी को छल द्वारा पकड़ना **trapper** noun फंदा शिकारी।

trapeze / ट्र'पीज़्; US ट्रै'पीज़् / noun व्यायाम अथवा कलाबाज़ी के लिए झूला।

trash / ट्रैश् / noun **1** (अपमा) (विचार, रचना, वस्तु आदि) रद्दी, बेकार : *He dismisses a lot of modern art as trash.* **2** (घर का) कूड़ा-करकट; घास-पात।

trauma / 'ट्रॉमा; US'ट्राउमा / noun (pl traumas) **1** (मनो) हानिकारक मानसिक आघात, सदमा; (प्रायः pl) (अनौप) अप्रिय अनुभव की वजह से उत्पन्न मानसिक वेदना, चिंता : *going through the trauma(s) of divorce* **2** (चिकि) चोट ▸ **traumatic** adj **traumatize**, **-ise** verb.

travail / 'ट्रैवेल्; ट्र'वेल्; / noun (प्रायः pl) (प्रायः या साहि) कष्टदायक व अप्रिय

अनुभव या स्थिति : *the country's economic travails.*

travel / ट्रैवॅल् / *verb* (-ll-; *US* -l-) 1 यात्रा/सफ़र करना 2 चलना, गति करना : *Light travels faster than sound.* 3 (*अनौप*) बहुत तेज़ चलना ▸ **travel** *noun* 1 यात्रा : *rail/space travel* 2 **travels** [*pl*] यात्राएँ, विशेषतः विदेशों की : *She wrote an account of her travels in China.* **traveller** (*US* **traveler**) *noun* यात्री; बेघर व्यक्ति।

traverse / ट्रॅ'वर्स् / *verb* यात्रा करना या कुछ तानना : *skiers traversing the slopes.*

travesty / 'ट्रैव्रिस्ट / *noun* (*pl* **travesties**) **travesty** (of sth) (*प्रायः अपमा*) उपहास्यास्पद नक़ल; तमाशा; उपहासात्मक विचार : *The trial was a travesty of justice.* ▸ **travesty** *verb* (*pt, pp* **travestied**) उपहास्यास्पद होना या बनाना।

trawl / ट्रॉल् / *verb* 1 **trawl** (through) sth (for sth/sb) किसी व्यक्ति या वस्तु विशेष की तलाश में बहुत-से लोग या सामान छान डालना : *The police are trawling (through) their files for similar cases.* 2 **trawl** (for sth) बड़े जाल से समुद्री मछलियों को पकड़ना : *trawling for mackerel* ▸ **trawler** *noun* इस काम में आने वाला जल-पोत/नाव।

tray / ट्रे / *noun* ट्रे, किश्ती : *a tea-tray/baking tray.*

treacherous / 'ट्रेचरस् / *adj* 1 विश्वास-घाती : *a treacherous person* 2 ख़तर-नाक, अविश्वसनीय, विशेषतः जब दिखने में सुरक्षित लगे : *treacherous currents* ▸ **treachery** / 'ट्रेचरि / *noun* (*pl* **treacheries**) विश्वासघात, धोखा।

treacle / 'ट्रीकॅल् / (*US* **molasses**) *noun* शीरा; राब ▸ **treacly** *adj* 1 शीरे जैसा 2 (*अपमा*) अति भावुक : *treacly music.*

tread / ट्रेड् / *verb* (*pt* **trod** / ट्रॉड् /; *pp* **trodden** / 'ट्रॉड्न् / या **trod**) 1 **tread** (on sth/sb) पैर रखना : *You're treading on my toe.* 2 **tread** sth (in/down/out) कुचल देना : *tread grapes* (*ie to make wine*) 3 चल-चल कर मार्ग बना देना ▸ **tread** *noun* 1 [*sing*] चाल, पग-ध्वनि : *walk with a heavy tread* 2 सीढ़ी या जीने की पौड़ी की ऊपरी सतह 3 (*टायर की*) गुड्डी।

treadle / 'ट्रेडॅल् / *noun* यंत्र/मशीन का पैर से चलाया जाने वाला पुरज़ा, पायदान : *a treadle sewing machine.*

treason / 'ट्रीज़्न् / (**high treason** भी) *noun* राजद्रोह, देश से ग़द्दारी/विश्वासघात ▸ **treasonable** *adj* राजद्रोहात्मक : *a treasonable offence.*

treasure / 'ट्रेश़र् / *noun* 1 चाँदी, सोना, हीरे जवाहरात; ख़ज़ाना/कोष : *buried treasure* 2 (*विशेषतः pl*) मूल्यवान वस्तु 3 बहुत प्यारा या महत्त्वपूर्ण व्यक्ति ▸ **treasure** *verb* 1 बहुमूल्य समझना/समझा जाना : *I treasure his friendship.* 2 मूल्यवान या अति प्रिय समझ कर संचित करना/रखना, याद रखना : *I shall always treasure the memory of our time together.*

treasurer / 'ट्रेश़रर् / *noun* ख़ज़ांची, कोषपाल।

treasury / 'ट्रेश़रि / *noun* (*pl* **treasuries**) 1 **the Treasury** राजकोष, ख़ज़ाना 2 कोषागार, ख़ज़ाना; संस्था या संगठन की निधि।

treat / ट्रीट् / *verb* 1 **treat** sb (as/like sth) व्यवहार-विशेष करना, बरताव करना : *I hate people who treat animals badly.* 2 **treat** sth **as** sth समझना, मानना : *I decided to treat his remark as a joke.* 3 विषय आदि पर विचार-विमर्श करना : *The question is treated at greater length in the next chapter.* 4 **treat** sb/sth; **treat** sb (for sth)

इलाज करना, चिकित्सा करना : *She was treated for malaria.* **5 treat sth (with sth)** संसाधित करना, परिरक्षा करने के लिए कुछ लगाना : *treat crops with insecticide* **6 treat sb/oneself (to sth)** स्वयं के खर्चे पर कुछ आनंददायक, जैसे दावत, देना ■ **treat sb like dirt/a dog** (अनौप) बिलकुल भी सम्मान न देना : *They treat their workers like dirt.* ▶ **treat** *noun* 1 ऐसा आनंद जो प्रायः विरले ही मिलता है : *The concert is a real treat for lovers of Indian classical music.* 2 दावत।

treatise / 'ट्रीटिस; 'ट्रीटिज़ / *noun* **treatise (on sth)** शोधात्मक पुस्तक।

treatment / 'ट्रीट्मन्ट / *noun* 1 व्यवहार; 2 चिकित्सा; समाधान : *receive treatment for shock.*

treaty / 'ट्रीटि / *noun* (pl treaties) 1 (देशों के बीच) औपचारिक संधि, सुलह-नामा : *the Treaty of Rome* 2 (तक) व्यक्तियों के बीच औपचारिक संधि (विशेषतः ख़रीद-फ़रोख़्त के समय), संधि-पत्र।

treble[1] / 'ट्रेब्ल् / *verb* तीन गुना करना : *He's trebled his earnings in two years.* ▶ **treble** *det, adj* तीन गुना, तिगुना : *He earns treble my salary.*

treble[2] / 'ट्रेब्ल् / *noun* 1 (संगीत में) उच्च स्वर 2 गायक लड़के का उच्च स्वर ▶ **treble** *adj* लय में उच्च स्वर वाला : *a treble voice.*

tree / ट्री / *noun* पेड़, वृक्ष।

trek / ट्रेक् / *noun* लंबी यात्रा (विशेषतः पैदल) : *a Himalayan trek* ▶ **trek** *verb* (-kk-) लंबी यात्रा करना : *go trekking in Nepal.*

tremble / 'ट्रेम्ब्ल् / *verb* 1 **tremble (with sth)** भय, कमज़ोरी या ठंड से काँपना, थरथराना : *His voice trembled with rage.* 2 चिंतित, उद्विग्न या भयभीत होना : *She trembled to think what might*

have happened to him. ▶ **tremble** *noun* कँपकँपी, उद्विग्नता।

tremendous / ट्र'मेन्डस् / *adj* 1 अत्यधिक, विशाल : *a tremendous explosion* 2 (अनौप) बहुत अच्छा, असामान्य : *a tremendous experience/film* ▶ **tremendously** *adv.*

tremor / 'ट्रेमर् / *noun* 1 कंप, कँपकँपी : *earth tremors* 2 उत्तेजित भाव की तरंग/लहर : *tremors of fear/delight.*

tremulous / 'ट्रेम्यलस् / *adj* (औप) उत्तेजना, आशंका, घबराहट या कमज़ोरी की वजह से काँपता हुआ : *in a tremulous voice* ○ *with a tremulous hand.*

trench / ट्रेन्च् / *noun* खाई।

trend / ट्रेन्ड् / *noun* सामान्य प्रवृत्ति; झुकाव/दिशा : *follow the latest trends in fashion* ▶ **trendy** *adj* (-ier, -iest) (अनौप) प्रचलित, फ़ैशनेबल : *trendy clothes/shops.*

trepidation / ट्रेपि'डेशन् / *noun* घबराहट, संत्रास : *I waited for my exam results with some trepidation.*

trespass / 'ट्रेस्पस् / *verb* 1 **trespass (on sth)** अनधिकार प्रवेश करना 2 **trespass (against sb)** (अप्र) अपराध/पाप करना ■ **trespass on sth** (औप) ग़लत/अनुचित प्रयोग करना; फ़ायदा उठाना : *I mustn't trespass on your time any longer.* ▶ **trespass** *noun* अनधिकार प्रवेश; अतिक्रमण : *an accidental trespass.*

tresses / 'ट्रेसिज़् / *noun* [pl] (साहि) विशेषतः महिला के लंबे बाल; लट।

tri- *pref* (पूर्वपद) तीन : *triangle/ tricolour.*

trial / 'ट्राइअल् / *noun* 1 मुक़दमा, न्यायालय में साक्ष्यों आदि की जाँच : *face trial on drug trafficking charges* 2 योग्यता, गुण आदि का परीक्षण, परख : *put a car through safety trials* 3 **trial (to sb)** दुर्बोध/परेशान करने वाला व्यक्ति ■ **trial**

and error विभिन्न प्रणालियों का प्रयोग करते हुए और ग़लतियों से सीखते हुए समस्या का समाधान पाने की क्रिया ▶ **trial run** noun किसी वस्तु के गुण, लोकप्रियता, निष्पादन आदि का परीक्षण।

triangle / ट्राइऐड्ग्ल् / noun (ज्यामिति) त्रिकोण; त्रिकोण जैसी आकृति वाला : a triangle of grass beside the path ▶ **triangular** / ट्राइ ऐड्ग्यलर् / adj 1 त्रिकोणीय : a triangular garden 2 त्रिपक्षीय : a triangular contest in an election.

tribe / ट्राइब् / noun 1 जनजाति 2 (प्राय: अपमा) लोगों का समूह/वर्ग : Politicians! I hate the whole tribe of them. ▶ **tribal** adj जनजातीय : tribal languages/wars.

tribulation / ट्रिब्यु लेशन् / noun (साहि या परि) मुसीबत, विपत्ति : the tribulations of modern life.

tribunal / ट्राइ ब्यूनल् / noun विशेष न्यायालय : a rent tribunal.

tributary / ट्रिब्यट्रि; US ट्रिब्यटेरि / noun (pl **tributaries**) सहायक नदी : The Sutlej is a tributary of the Indus. ▶ **tributary** adj सहायक : tributary streams/rivers.

tribute / ट्रिब्यूट् / noun 1 (विशेषत: पूर्व समय में) (प्राय: नियमित) ख़िराज, नज़र, भेंट/उपहार 2 श्रद्धांजलि, प्रशंसा : floral tributes 3 [sing] a tribute (to sth/sb) कुछ प्रभावशाली होने का संकेत : His recovery is a tribute to the doctor's skills.

trick / ट्रिक् / noun 1 चाल, दाँव-पेंच; छल-कपट : They had to think of a trick to get past the guards. 2 मनो-रंजन के लिए करतब, इंद्रजाल : conjuring tricks ○ card tricks 3 चारित्रिक विशेषता 4 (विशेषत: sing) कुछ करने की उत्तम या ठीक प्रणाली; कौशल; शैली ▶ **trick** verb 1 चाल से धोखा देना 2 **trick sb into sth/**

doing sth चालबाज़ी से कुछ करा लेना : She tricked him into marriage.

trickery / ट्रिकरि / noun धोखा, छल।

trickle / ट्रिक्ल् / verb 1 बूँद-बूँद टपक-ना : tears trickling down her cheeks 2 धीमे-धीमे गति करना/कराना : People have began trickling into the hall. ▶ **trickle** noun 1 द्रव की क्षीण धारा 2 (प्राय: sing) **trickle (of sth)** आती/जाती हुई किसी वस्तु आदि की ज़रा-सी मात्रा : a trickle of information.

tricky / ट्रिकि / adj (**-ier, -iest**) 1 (कार्य) जटिल, पेचीदा : a tricky situation/problem 2 (व्यक्ति, कार्य) कपटपूर्ण; कपटी।

tricycle / ट्राइसिकल् / (अनौप **trike** भी) noun तीन पहियों की साइकिल।

trident / ट्राइडन्ट् / noun त्रिशूल।

trifle / ट्राइफ्ल् / noun 1 महत्त्व की दृष्टि से नगण्य, तुच्छ : He busies himself with trifles and avoids doing what's really important. 2 अत्यल्प धनराशि ■ **a trifle** थोड़ा-सा : You acted a trifle hastily. ▶ **trifle** verb ■ **trifle with sb/sth** (विशेषत: नकारात्मक वाक्यों में) सम्मान/ध्यान देने योग्य व्यक्ति/वस्तु के साथ खिलवाड़ करना, चंचलतापूर्ण कार्य करना : He's not a man to be trifled with. ▶ **trifling** adj महत्त्वहीन, मामूली : a few trifling errors.

trigger / ट्रिगर् / noun 1 (पिस्तौल, बंदूक़ आदि का) घोड़ा 2 **trigger (for sth)** किसी प्रतिक्रिया का कारण (घटना/वस्तु) : the trigger for change ▶ **trigger** verb **trigger sth (off)** तीव्र क्रिया की शुरुआत का कारण होना/बनना : The smoke triggered off the alarm.

trigonometry / ट्रिग नॉमट्रि / noun त्रिकोणमिति (गणित की एक शाखा)।

trillion / ट्रिल्यन् / noun, pron, det 1 US में एक लाख करोड़ (10^{12}) की

संख्या 2 UK में एक करोड़ ख़रब (10^{18}) की संख्या।

trilogy / ट्रिलजि / *noun* (*pl* **trilogies**) तीन संबंधित उपन्यासों, गीति-नाट्यों आदि का समूह।

trim¹ / ट्रिम् / *verb* (-mm-) 1 काट-छाँट कर ठीक करना, सँवारना : *trim the top of a hedge* 2 **trim sth (with sth)** सजाना, सँवारना : *trim a dress with lace/ flowers* ▸ **trim** *noun* 1 सुव्यवस्था : *be in excellent trim* 2 (प्राय: *sing*) बालों आदि को थोड़ा-सा काटने की क्रिया **trimming** *noun* सजावट, गोटा-पट्टी।

trim² / ट्रिम् / *adj* 1 ठीक-ठीक, छरहरा एवं फ़िट : *a trim waistline/figure* 2 सु- व्यवस्थित : *a trim garden.*

trinity / ट्रिनिटि / *noun* 1 **the Trinity** (ईसाई धर्म में) Father, Son एवं Holy Spirit का संयुक्त स्वरूप ईश्वर 2 (औप) त्रिक, तीन का समूह।

trio / ट्रीओ / *noun* (*pl* **trios**) 1 (संगीत में) त्रिवादक या त्रिगायक : *a piano trio* 2 तीन का समूह, तिगड्डा : *A trio of number 9 buses came by.*

trip / ट्रिप् / *verb* (-pp-) 1 **trip (over/ up)**; **trip (over/on sth)** लड़खड़ाना, ठोकर खा कर गिरने लगना : *She tripped (over the cat) and fell.* 2 फुदकना, थिरकना 3 स्विच खोल कर कोई मशीन चलाना : *trip the shutter of a camera* ■ **trip (sb) up**, भेद खोलना; भूल करना, भूल करने देना : *I tripped up in the interview and said something rather silly.* ▸ **trip** *noun* 1 सैर, आमोद यात्रा : *a day- trip to the seaside* 2 लड़खड़ाहट, पतन **tripper** *noun* सैर करने वाला, घुमक्कड़।

triple / ट्रिप्ल् / *adj* 1 तीन अंशों/तीन व्यक्तियों से बना हुआ, त्रिपक्षीय : *The plan has a triple purpose.* 2 तिगुना, तिहरा : *travelling at triple the speed* ▸ **triple** *verb* तिगुना करना या होना : *Output has tripled in two years.*

triplet / ट्रिप्लट् / *noun* 1 एक साथ हुए तीन बच्चों में से कोई एक 2 तीन वस्तुओं का समूह।

tripod / ट्राइपॉड् / *noun* तिपाई, (कैमरे, दूरबीन आदि के लिए) तीन टाँगों वाला स्टैंड।

trite / ट्राइट् / *adj* (मुहावरा या मत/विचार) घिसा-पिटा, नया या मौलिक नहीं।

triumph / ट्राइअम्फ् / *noun* 1 विज- योल्लास, सफलता/जीत की खुशी : *shouts of triumph* 2 सफलता, कामयाबी : *the triumphs of modern science* ▸ **tri- umph** *verb* **triumph (over sb/sth)** जीतना, सफल होना : *Commonsense triumphed in the end.* **triumphant** *adj* विजयी, उल्लसित : *a triumphant cheer.*

trivia / ट्रिविआ / *noun* [*pl*] (प्राय: अपमा) मामूली, महत्त्वहीन, तुच्छ आदि बातें या वस्तुएँ।

trivial / ट्रिविअल् / *adj* (प्राय: अपमा) नगण्य, महत्त्वहीन वस्तुओं से संबंधित : *a trivial matter/offence* ▸ **triviality** / ट्रिवि ऐलटि / *noun* (*pl* **trivialities**) (अपमा) ओछापन; तुच्छ बात : *waste time on trivialities.*

trolley / ट्रॉलि / *noun* (*pl* **trolleys**) 1 ट्रॉली (दो या चार पहियों की हाथगाड़ी) : *a luggage trolley* 2 ट्राम गाड़ी।

trombone / ट्रॉम्बोन् / *noun* तुरही (बाजा) ▸ **trombonist** *noun.*

troop / ट्रूप् / *noun* 1 **troops** [*pl*] सेना, फ़ौज 2 दल, (विशेषत: चलती हुई) टोली : *a troop of school children* 3 रिसाला, घुड़सवार सेना का एक यूनिट 4 स्काउट का स्थानीय दल ▸ **troop** *verb* दल/टोली बना कर आना **trooper** *noun* 1 घुड़- सवार सैनिक 2 (US) राज्य पुलिस बल सदस्य **troop-ship** *noun* सेनावाहक जहाज़।

trophy / ट्रोफ़ि / *noun* (*pl* **trophies**) 1 ट्रॉफ़ी, विजयोपहार : *the Wimbledon tennis trophy* 2 शिकार या युद्ध की

सफलता की प्रतीक वस्तु : *a set of antlers and other trophies.*

tropic / 'ट्रॉपिक् / *noun* 1 (प्राय: *sing*) भूमध्य रेखा के उत्तर या दक्षिण की निश्चित अक्षांश रेखा (उत्तर में **the tropic of Cancer** कर्क रेखा; दक्षिण में **the tropic of Capricorn** मकर रेखा) 2 **the tropics** [*pl*] इन रेखाओं के बीच का भू-प्रदेश ▸ **tropical** *adj* : *tropical forests/diseases.*

trot / ट्रॉट् / *verb* (-tt-) 1 (घोड़ों का) दुलकी चाल चलना 2 (व्यक्ति का) जल्दी चलना : *The child was trotting beside its parents.* ▸ **trot** *noun* [*sing*] 1 ऐसे क़दम : *go at a steady trot* 2 इस प्रकार चलते रहने की अवधि : *go for a trot.*

trouble / 'ट्रब्ल् / *noun* 1 चिंता, कष्ट, परेशानी या इन सबका कारण : *My teeth are giving me trouble.* 2 **trouble (to sb)** अतिरिक्त कार्य/प्रयल, कठिनाई : *I don't want to be any trouble (to you).* 3 झगड़ा-फ़साद, झंझट : *the troubles in Kashmir* ∎ **get into trouble** झंझट में पड़ जाना **get sb into trouble** किसी को मुश्किल में डाल देना **take trouble over sth/with sth/to do sth** पर्याप्त सावधानी और प्रयल के साथ करना : *We took a lot of trouble to find the right person for the job.* ▸ **trouble** *verb* 1 दुखी होना/करना, चिंतित होना/करना : *be troubled by illness* 2 **trouble (about sth)** दुखी करना, कष्ट देना, असुविधा उत्पन्न करना : *He rushed into the room without even troubling to knock.* **troublesome** / 'ट्रब्लसम् / *adj* उपद्रवी, ऊधमी/ कष्टकर : *a troublesome child.*

trough / ट्रॉफ़् / *noun* 1 (पशुओं को खिलाने या पिलाने की) आयताकार नांद 2 आर्थिक मंदी या निष्क्रियता का दौर : *the trough of recession* 3 (मौसम विज्ञान में) दो उच्च दाब के क्षेत्रों के बीच कम दाब का क्षेत्र 4 दो लहरों आदि के बीच का निचला क्षेत्र।

trounce / ट्राउन्स् / *verb* बुरी तरह हराना : *Maharashtra were trounced 5-0 by Delhi.*

trousers / 'ट्राउज़र्ज़् / (*US* **pants** भी) *noun* [*pl*] पतलून।

trousseau / 'टूसो / *noun* (*pl* **trousseaus** या **trousseaux** / 'टूसोज़् /) (अप्र) दुलहन का साज-सामान (वस्त्र आदि)।

trout / ट्राउट् / *noun* (*pl* अपरिवर्तित) नदी, ताल आदि में पाई जाने वाली एक प्रकार की मछली।

trowel / 'ट्राउअल् / *noun* 1 करनी, मकान बनाने वाले राज का औज़ार 2 माली द्वारा प्रयुक्त खुरपी जैसा औज़ार।

truant / 'टूअन्ट् / *noun* 1 स्कूल से भागने वाला बच्चा 2 अपने काम/ज़िम्मेदारी से बचने वाला व्यक्ति ∎ **play truant** भगोड़ा हो जाना ▸ **truancy** *noun* : *an increase in truancy rates.*

truce / टूस् / *noun* युद्धविराम : *a three-day truce.*

truck / ट्रक् / *noun* 1 मालगाड़ी का खुला डिब्बा 2 सामान ढोने वाली मोटर, लॉरी 3 ठेला गाड़ी 4 सामान ढोने के लिए पीछे से खुली गाड़ी : *an army truck.*

trudge / ट्रज् / *verb* पैर घसीट कर चलना, थकावट के कारण धीरे-धीरे चलना : *trudging (along) through the deep snow.*

true / टू / *adj* (-r, -st) 1 सच्चा, तथ्य के अनुसार सही : *a true story* 2 वास्तविक, असली (न कि नक़ली), ख़रा : *He claimed to be the true heir.* 3 यथार्थ, सही-सही : *a true copy of a document* 4 **true (to sth)** स्वामिभक्त, निष्ठावान : *a true friend* ∎ **come true** (इच्छा, आशा आदि) सच हो जाना **one's true colours** (प्राय: अपमा) किसी का

वास्तविक स्वभाव **true to sth** अपेक्षा में खरा उतरना : *The movie is true to life.*

truly / टूलि / *adv* 1 ईमानदारी से : *truly grateful* 2 सच्चाई से, सच-सच : *Tell me truly what you think.* 3 पूर्णत:, वास्तव में : *a truly generous act.*

trumpet / ट्रम्पिट् / *noun* 1 तुरही (बाजा): *play the trumpet* 2 तुरही के आकार की वस्तु ■ **blow one's own trumpet** (अनौप) आत्मप्रशंसा करना, अपने मुँह मियाँ मिट्ठू बनना ▸ **trumpet** *verb* 1 (प्राय: अपमा) सार्वजनिक रूप से ज़ोर से कुछ सुनाना : *He's always trumpeting his opinions.* 2 हाथी का चिंघाड़ना।

truncate / ट्रङ्केट् / *verb* सिरा छाँट कर छोटा कर देना : *a truncated pyramid.*

truncheon / ट्रन्चन् / (**baton** भी) *noun* हथियार की तरह प्रयुक्त छोटी, पतली छड़ी।

trundle / ट्रन्ड्ल् / *verb* (किसी भारी एवं बेढंगी वस्तु का) लुढ़कना/लुढ़काना : *She was trundling a wheelbarrow along the path.*

trunk / ट्रङ्क् / *noun* 1 पेड़ का तना 2 शरीर का मध्य-भाग, धड़ 3 बक्सा, ट्रंक 4 हाथी की सूँड 5 **trunks** [*pl*] तैरने, कुश्ती लड़ने समय पहने जाने वाली निकर ▸ **trunk call** *noun* (अप्र) ट्रंककाल।

trust¹ / ट्रस्ट् / *noun* 1 **trust (in sb/sth)** विश्वास, भरोसा : *I put my trust in you.* 2 उत्तरदायित्व, ज़िम्मेदारी : *a position of great trust* 3 (क़ानून) न्यास, ट्रस्ट : *The project is financed by a charitable trust.* 4 अमानत, धरोहर ■ **take sth on trust** विश्वास पर लेना, सही मान लेना ▸ **trusting** *adj* विश्वासी : *have a trusting nature* **trustworthy** *adj* विश्वसनीय, जिस पर भरोसा किया जा सके : *I have always found her honest and trustworthy.*

trust² / ट्रस्ट् / *verb* 1 विश्वास/आस्था रखना : *I trust you implicitly.* 2 अमा-नत के रूप में देना, सौंपना : *I'd trust him with my life.* 3 (औप) आशा करना : *I trust (that) she's not seriously ill.*

trustee / ट्रस्टी / *noun* 1 न्यासी : *I've been asked to act as (a) trustee for my godson.* 2 (किसी संस्था, संस्थान आदि की) प्रबंधक समिति का सदस्य : *a trustee of the National Gallery.*

truth / ट्रूथ् / *noun* (*pl* **truths** / ट्रूद्ज़् /) 1 सच्चाई, सत्यता : *There's no truth in what he says.* 2 सत्य : *the search for (the) truth* 3 यथार्थ तथ्य ▸ **truthful** *adj* 1 सत्यवादी (व्यक्ति) 2 (कथन) सत्य **truthfully** *adv.*

try¹ / ट्राइ / *verb* (*pt, pp* **tried**) 1 प्रयत्न करना, कोशिश करना : *Try to be here on time.* 2 आज़माना, परखना : *I've tried this new detergent, with excellent results.* 3 **try sb (for sth)** मुक़दमा चलाया जाना; न्यायालय द्वारा अभियोग की जाँच किया जाना : *He was tried for murder.* 4 सहना मुश्किल होना : *Three hours of unnecessary delay had sorely tried my patience.* ■ **try one's hand (at sth)** कुछ करने का पहला प्रयास करना : *I'd like to try my hand at water-skiing.* **try sth on** कपड़े पहन कर उनकी शोभा परखना **try sb/sth out (on sb)** परीक्षण करना ▸ **trying** *adj* कष्टकर।

try² / ट्राइ / *noun* **try (at sth/doing sth)** प्रयास, प्रयत्न : *give it a try.*

tryst / ट्रिस्ट् / *noun* अभिसार, पूर्वनिश्चित भेंट।

tub / टब् / *noun* टब।

tuba / ट्यूबा; *US* टूबा / *noun* लंबा, पीतल का वाद्य।

tube / ट्यूब्; *US* टूब् / *noun* 1 रबड़, काँच, धातु की नली : *a laboratory full of jars and tubes* 2 **tube (of sth)** पतले लचीले धातु/प्लास्टिक से बना और गाढ़े द्रव से भरा ढक्कनदार पात्र : *squeeze* *toothpaste from/out of a tube* **3 the tube (the underground** भी) *(अनौप)* लंदन में भूमिगत रेलवे ▸ **tubing** *noun* ट्यूब का टुकड़ा : *two metres of copper tubing.*

tuber / 'ट्यूबर; *US* 'टूबर / *noun* कंद (जैसे आलू, जिमीकंद, शकरकंद आदि) ▸ **tuberous** *adj* **1** कंद वाला **2** कंद जैसा।

tuberculosis / ट्यू,बर्क्यु 'लोसिस / *noun* *(संक्षि* TB) तपेदिक, क्षय रोग।

tuck¹ / टक् / *verb* **1 tuck sth into sth; tuck sth in/up** (कपड़े में) चुनट डालना; कपड़े (शर्ट आदि को) छिपाने या स्थिर रखने के लिए मोड़ना; काग़ज़ को मोड़ कर रखना : *Tuck your jeans into your boots.* ◦ *tuck the flap of an envelope in* **2** किसी वस्तु को सुरक्षित/ आरामदेह स्थान पर रखना : *He tucked the map away in a drawer.* **3** (ठंडक आदि दूर करने के लिए) चारों ओर से अच्छी तरह लपेटना : *tuck a blanket round sb's knees.*

tuck² / टक् / *noun* **1** चुनट, तह : *a tuck in the waist of a dress* **2** *(अप्र, अनौप)* बच्चों की पसंदीदा मिठाई, केक आदि : *a school tuck shop.*

Tuesday / 'ट्यूज़्डे / *noun* मंगलवार।

tuft / टफ़्ट् / *noun* (बालों आदि का) गुच्छा ▸ **tufted** *adj* गुच्छेदार।

tug / टग् / *verb* (-gg-) **tug (at) sth** झटके से खींचना : *tug at sb's elbow* ▸ **tug** *noun* **1** झटका : *I felt a tug at my sleeve.* **2** (**tugboat** भी) खींचने वाली नाव-विशेष।

tuition / ट्यु 'इश्न्; *US* टु 'इश्न् / *noun* *(औप)* अध्यापन (विशेषत: व्यक्ति विशेष या छोटे समूह का); शिक्षण शुल्क।

tulip / 'ट्यूलिप्; *US* 'टूलिप् / *noun* कप के आकार के बड़े रंगीन फूलों वाला पौधा।

tumble / 'टम्ब्ल् / *verb* **1** धड़ाम से गिरना; (क़ीमत या महत्व) अचानक गिर

जाना : *Share prices tumbled on the stock market.* **2 tumble into/out of sth; tumble in/out** अव्यवस्थित ढंग से दिशा-विशेष में हड़बड़ी से जाना : *I threw off my clothes and tumbled into bed.* **3** ऊपर-नीचे, आगे-पीछे लुढ़कना : *The water tumbled over the rocks.* ■ **tumble down** नष्ट होना, ढह जाना **tumble to sth** *(अनौप)* परिस्थिति, छुपा अर्थ समझना ▸ **tumble** *noun.*

tumbler / 'टम्ब्लर् / *noun* गिलास।

tumour (*US* **tumor**) / 'ट्यूमर्; *US* 'टूमर् / *noun* शरीर के किसी भाग के ऊतक में असामान्य वृद्धि; गाँठ, रसौली : *benign/ malignant tumours.*

tumult / 'ट्यूमल्ट; *US* 'टूमल्ट् / *noun* *[sing]* *(औप)* **1** हंगामा, शोरगुल : *struggle to be heard above the tumult* **2** अशांत, अव्यवस्थित मनोदशा : *Her mind was in a tumult.* ▸ **tumultuous** / ट्यू'मल्चुअस् / *adj* **1** उप- द्रवी, उत्पाती : *tumultuous crowds* **2** शोरगुल-भरा : *receive a tumultuous applause/welcome.*

tuna / 'ट्यूना; *US* 'टूना / *noun* (*pl* अपरि- वर्तित या **tunas**) बड़ी, समुद्री मछली।

tune / ट्यून; *US* टून् / *noun* धुन, राग : *whistle a catchy tune* ■ **in/out of tune (with sb/sth)** स्वर संगति में होना/ न होना : *The violin is not quite in tune with the piano.* ▸ **tune** *verb* **1** वाद्ययंत्र मिलाना; ट्यून करना : *tune a guitar* **2** उद्देश्य-विशेष के लिए तैयार/ अनुकूलित करना : *His speech was finely tuned (to what the audience wanted to hear)* ■ **tune in (to sth)** रेडियो में स्टेशन लगाना ▸ **tuneful** *adj* रुचिकर, मधुर **tuneless** *adj.*

tunic / 'ट्यूनिक्; *US* 'टूनिक् / *noun* **1** बिना बाँहों का घुटनों तक लबादा/चोगा **2** पुलिस अफ़सरों, सैनिकों द्वारा पहने जाने वाला कोट।

tunnel / 'टन्ल् / noun सुरंग; पशुओं/ जानवरों की सुरंग/बिल : *The train went into a tunnel.* ▶ **tunnel** *verb* (**-ll-**) सुरंग खोदना : *The engineers had to tunnel through solid rock.*

turban / 'टर्बन् / noun पगड़ी, साफ़ा।

turbine / 'टर्बाइन् / noun टरबाइन (इंजिन या मोटर)।

turbulent / 'टर्ब्यलन्ट् / adj 1 अस्त-व्यस्त, गड़बड़ी या संघर्ष की स्थिति में : *turbulent crowds* 2 विक्षुब्ध; उग्र : *turbulent emotions* 3 (वायु या जल) तेज़, उपद्रवी ढंग से चलना।

turf / टर्फ़ / noun (*pl* **turfs** या **turves** / ट्र्व्ज़ /) 1 घास का मैदान; घास की थिगली : *soft, springy turf* 2 **the turf** [*sing*] घुड़दौड़ या घुड़दौड़ का मैदान।

turkey / 'टर्कि / noun (*pl* **turkeys**) एक बड़ी चिड़िया।

turmoil / 'टर्मॉइल् / noun [*sing*] शोर-गुल; खलबली, अनिश्चितता की स्थिति : *The country was in (a) turmoil during the strike.*

turn¹ / टर्न् / verb 1 मोड़ना, मुड़ना; घूमना/ घुमाना : *The hands of a clock turn very slowly.* 2 **turn (sb/sth) (over)** मुँह घुमाना; वस्तु का घूम जाना : *The car skidded, turned over and burst into flames.* 3 स्वभाव, गुण आदि में परिवर्तन होना/करना : *The milk turned sour in the heat.* 4 एक निश्चित आयु/ समय पर पहुँचना या पार करना : *She turned forty last June.* 5 **turn (sb/ sth) (from A) to/into B** एक अवस्था से दूसरी में जाना : *Caterpillars turn into butterflies.* ■ **turn out** घटना पर उप-स्थित होना; एकत्र होना, भाग लेना : *Not many men turned out for duty.* **turn out to be sb/sth; turn out that...** कुछ होना सिद्ध होना : *She turned out to be a friend of my sister.* **turn sb away (from sth)** घुसने न देना; मदद

करने से इनकार करना **turn (sb) off** (*अनौप*) रुचि खो देना; किसी को नीरस और ऊबाऊ अनुभव करवाना : *I'm afraid I turned off when they started talk-ing about pig-farming.* **turn (sb/ sth) back** वापस उसी रास्ते लौटना **turn sb/sth down** प्रस्ताव आदि/प्रस्ताव पेश करने वाले व्यक्ति को ठुकरा देना **turn sth down** कुकर/रेडियो के भाप/आवाज़ आदि को कम करना **turn sth off** 1 बिजली, पानी आदि का प्रवाह स्विच, नल आदि द्वारा रोकना 2 स्विच, बटन द्वारा टी वी, रेडियो बंद करना **turn sth on** कुकर, रेडियो आदि चालू करना **turn sth up** 1 रेडियो, टेलि-विज़न की आवाज़ बढ़ाना 2 वस्त्र को नीचे से मोड़ कर लंबाई छोटी करना 3 खोद कर खोजना **turn to sb/sth** सहायता, सलाह के लिए किसी के पास जाना **turn up** 1 विशेषत: संयोग से मिलना 2 आगमन करना; किसी स्थान पर पहुचना 3 (अवसर) संयोग से आना।

turn² / टर्न् / noun 1 मोड़ : *a lane full of twists and turns* 2 मोड़ मुड़ने की क्रिया 3 दिशा-परिवर्तन : *take a left turn* 4 स्थिति में परिवर्तन : *an unfortunate turn of events* 5 मौक़ा, क्रम, बारी : *Please wait for your turn to be served.* 6 (प्राय: *sing*) दौर, पारी, शिफ़्ट : *Whose turn is it to do the washing-up?* ■ **do sb a good/bad turn** सहायता/बाधा के लिए कुछ करना **in (his, its, etc) turn** एक के बाद एक : *The girls called out their names in turn.* **out of turn** 1 बिना पारी के 2 अनुचित समय पर **take turns (at sth); take sth in turns** एक के बाद एक कुछ करना।

turnip / 'टर्निप् / noun शलजम (सब्ज़ी)।

turpentine / 'टर्पन्टाइन् / (*अनौप* **turps** भी) noun तारपीन का तेल।

turquoise / 'टर्क्वॉइज़् / noun 1 फ़ीरोज़ा (नग) 2 फ़ीरोज़ी रंग।

turret / 'टरट् / noun 1 बुर्ज, कँगूरा 2 टैंक, युद्धपोत आदि के घुमाऊ लोहे के कँगूरे (तोपों को ढकने के लिए) : a warship armed with twin turrets.

turtle / 'टर्ट्ल / noun समुद्री कछुआ ■ **turn turtle** (अनौप) (जहाज़ का) उलट जाना।

tusk / टस्क् / noun (हाथी) दाँत।

tussle / 'टस्ल् / noun (अनौप) कुछ पाने के लिए संघर्ष; हाथापाई : We had a real tussle with the travel agent to get our money refunded. ▶ **tussle** verb **tussle (with sb)** झगड़ा/हाथापाई करना।

tutor / 'ट्यूटर; US 'टूटर् / noun 1 निजी शिक्षक : a tutor in a private language school 2 विश्वविद्यालय का शिक्षक; (US) सहायक प्राध्यापक ▶ **tutor** verb **tutor sb (in sth)** किसी को शिक्षा देना/पढ़ाना; ट्यूटर के रूप में कार्य करना।

tutorial / ट्यू 'टॉरिअल; US टू 'टॉरिअल् / adj शिक्षकीय : tutorial classes ▶ **tutorial** noun ट्यूटर के साथ बिताया हुआ शिक्षण का समय : have/give/miss a tutorial.

tweak / ट्वीक् / verb 1 चिकोटी काटना, उमेठना : She tweaked his ear playfully. 2 (अनौप) मशीन को समर्जित करना ▶ **tweak** noun चिकोटी।

tweed / ट्वीड् / noun ट्वीड, एक प्रकार का ऊनी कपड़ा : a tweed jacket.

tweezers / 'ट्वीज़र्ज़ / noun [pl] चिमटी : a pair of tweezers.

twelve / ट्वेल्व् / noun, pron, det बारह (का अंक) ▶ **twelfth** / 'ट्वेल्फ़्थ् / noun, pron, det बारहवाँ, बारहवाँ अंश (1/12).

twenty / 'ट्वेन्टि / noun, pron, det बीस (का अंक) ▶ **twentieth** / 'ट्वेन्टिअथ् / noun, pron, det बीसवाँ, बीसवाँ भाग (1/20).

twice / ट्वाइस् / adv 1 दो बार : I've already seen the show twice. 2 दुगना : He's twice her age.

twiddle / 'ट्विड्ल् / verb **twiddle (with)** sth बेचैनी या ऊब के कारण कुछ उमेठना, घुमाना : She sat twiddling the ring on her finger.

twig / ट्विग् / noun टहनी : Use dry twigs to start a fire.

twilight / 'ट्वाइलाइट् / noun 1 संध्या का प्रकाश, झुटपुटा 2 **the twilight (of sth)** (साहि) अंतकाल, जब महत्त्व या शक्ति कम हो जाती है : in the twilight of his career.

twin / ट्विन् / noun 1 जुड़वाँ बच्चों में से एक : my twin brother/sister 2 दो समान प्रकार की वस्तुओं में से एक, जोड़े में से एक।

twine / ट्वाइन् / noun सुतली, डोरी : ball of twine ▶ **twine** verb **twine (sth) round/around/ through sth** बटना, गूँथना, लपेटना।

twinge / ट्विन्ज् / noun 1 टीस, अचानक उठा दर्द : get occasional twinges of rheumatism 2 हूक : a twinge of conscience/guilt.

twinkle / 'ट्विङ्क्ल् / verb 1 टिमटिमाना 2 **twinkle (with sth) (at sb)** (व्यक्ति या आँखें) खुशी, शरारत आदि के कारण चमकना ▶ **twinkle** noun 1 टिमटिमाती रोशनी 2 आँखों की चमक।

twirl / ट्वर्ल् / verb 1 चक्कर खिलाना, घुमाना : twirl the cane in the air 2 अँगुलियों से नचाना : He kept twirling his moustache.

twist[1] / ट्विस्ट् / verb 1 **twist sth (round sth/round)** लपेटना : I twisted the bandage round her knee. 2 **twist sth (into sth)** (डोरा) बटना : We twisted the bed sheets into a rope and escaped by climbing down it. 3 विकृत करना, मरोड़ना : He twisted his face into a grin.

4 (सड़क) घुमावदार होना 5 अचानक घुमाव के कारण शरीर के अंग को चोट पहुँचना 6 शब्दों का अर्थ तोड़-मरोड़ कर पेश करना : *The papers twisted everything I said.*

twist² / ट्विस्ट् / *noun* 1 ऐंठन, मरोड़ : *He gave my arm a twist.* 2 घुमाव, ऐंठ; स्थान जहाँ सड़क आदि मुड़ती हो 3 बदलाव, विकास : *The story has an odd twist at the end.*

twitch / ट्विच् / *verb* 1 फड़कन के साथ गति करना : *The dog's nose twitched as it smelt the meat.* 2 (ज़ोर से) खींचना ▶ **twitch** *noun* 1 मांसपेशियों की अचानक की फड़कन : *I thought the mouse was dead, but then it gave a slight twitch.* 2 अचानक का खिंचाव : *I felt a twitch at my sleeve.*

twitter / ट्विटर् / *verb* चिड़ियों का चहकना/चहचहाना।

two / टू / *noun, pron, det* दो (का अंक)।

tycoon / टाइ'कून् / *noun (अनौप)* शक्तिशाली पूँजीपति : *publishing tycoons.*

type¹ / टाइप् / *noun* 1 **type (of sth)** जाति, प्रारूप : *different social types* 2 **type (of sth)** नमूना, प्रकार : *not the*

type of party I enjoy 3 विशेष गुणों का व्यक्ति : *a brainy type.*

type² / टाइप् / *verb* मुद्रण/टंकण करना ▶ **type** *noun* मुद्रण या टंकण का टाइप : *bold/italic type* **typewriter** *noun* टाइपराइटर **typewritten** *adj* टंकित **typist** *noun* टाइपिस्ट (टंकक)।

typhoid / 'टाइफ़ॉइड् / (**typhoid fever** भी) *noun* टाइफ़ॉइड ज्वर।

typhoon / टाइ'फून् / *noun* तूफ़ान।

typical / 'टिपिकल् / *adj* **typical (of sth/sb)** 1 प्रतिनिधिक, नमूने के रूप में : *a typical Gujarati meal* 2 व्यक्ति/वस्तु विशेष के लक्षणों वाला : *It was typical of her to refuse.* ▶ **typically** *adv.*

typify / 'टिपिफ़ाइ / *verb* (*pt, pp* **typified**) प्रतीक होना : *Now a millionaire, he typifies the self-made man.*

tyranny / 'टिरनि / *noun* (*pl* **tyrannies**) तानाशाही, प्रजा-पीड़न : *victims of tyranny* ▶ **tyrannical** / टि'रैनिकल् / (और **tyrannous** / 'टिरनस् / भी) *adj* अत्याचारपूर्ण : *a tyrannical regime.*

tyrant / 'टाइरन्ट् / *noun* अत्याचारी (शासक): *Her boss is a complete tyrant.*

tyre (*US* **tire**) / 'टाइअर् / *noun* पहिये का टायर।

Uu

udder / ˈअडर् / noun (गाय, बकरी, भैंस आदि पशुओं के) थन।

ugly / ˈअग्लि / adj (-ier, -iest) 1 (beautiful के वैषम्य में) कुरूप, बदसूरत : an ugly face 2 अनिष्ट सूचक : ugly threats/rumours.

ulcer / ˈअल्सर् / noun फोड़ा, व्रण : a gastric ulcer.

ulterior / अल्ˈटिअरिअर् / adj (औप) परवर्ती; अप्रत्यक्ष/परोक्ष : Vijay had an ulterior motive in inviting me to dinner—he wanted to borrow my van.

ultimate / ˈअल्टिमट् / adj 1 अंतिम : our ultimate aim/goal 2 (अनौप) चरम (अच्छा या बुरा) : suffer the ultimate embarrassment of public ridicule 3 आधार-भूत, मौलिक : the ultimate truths of philosophy and science.

ultimatum / ˌअल्टिˈमेटम् / noun (pl ultimatums) कठोर प्रतिक्रिया की धमकी के साथ अंतिम चेतावनी : to issue an ultimatum.

ultra- pref (पूर्वपद) अति-, परा-, पार-, सूक्ष्म-, चरम : ultra-conservative/ultra-modern/ultraviolet.

ultrasonic / ˌअल्ट्राˈसॉनिक् / adj परा-ध्वनिक, पराश्रव्यकी, पराश्रव्य : ultrasonic waves.

ultrasound / ˈअल्ट्रासाउन्ड् / noun अल्ट्रासाउन्ड।

umbilical cord / अम्ˌबिलिकल् ˈकॉर्ड् / noun नाभि-नाड़ी, नाला।

umbrage / ˈअम्ब्रिज् / noun ■ take umbrage (at sth) (औप या परि) बुरा मानना, यह अनुभव करना कि समुचित आदर नहीं दिया गया।

umbrella / अम्ˈब्रेला / noun 1 छाता 2 (अलं) रक्षक शक्ति या प्रभाव : The police operated under the umbrella of the security forces.

umpire / ˈअम्पाइअर् / noun (कुछ खेलों में) निर्णायक, मध्यस्थ ▶ umpire verb निर्णायक के रूप में कार्य करना : We need someone to umpire.

umpteen / ˌअम्प्ˈटीन् / pron, det बहुत बार, बहुत सारे : I've told this story umpteen times.

un- pref (उपसर्ग) 1 (विशेषण, क्रिया-विशेषण, संज्ञा के पहले) नकारात्मक अर्थ में : unable/unconsciously/untruth 2 (क्रिया के पहले) विपरीत कार्य सूचक; क्रिया द्वारा सूचित का विपरीत करना : unlock/undo/unfold 3 संज्ञा के पहले ऐसी क्रिया बनाने में सहायक जिससे कुछ हटाने का आभास हो : unearth ○ unmask.

unable / अन्ˈएब्ल् / adj unable to do sth (प्रायः औप) कोई कार्य करने की शक्ति, सामर्थ्य, अधिकार न होना।

unacceptable / ˌअनक्ˈसेप्टब्ल् / adj जो स्वीकार्य, ग्राह्य न हो : unacceptable terms/arguments.

unaccompanied / ˌअनˈकम्पनिड् / adj (औप) बेसंगत; किसी व्यक्ति का (विशेषतः बच्चों का) अकेले कहीं जाना/सफ़र करना; कोई सामान यात्री के साथ नहीं परंतु अलग भेजना : Children unaccompanied by an adult will not be admitted. ○ unaccompanied luggage/baggage.

unanimous / युˈनैनिमस् / adj 1 unanimous (in sth) एकमत : The environmental lobby is unanimous in its opposition to the proposed new bypass. 2 सर्वसम्मत : The decision was unanimous. ▶ unanimity / ˌयून ˈनिमिटि / noun मतैक्य या सर्वसम्मति unanimously adv.

unarmed /अन्'आर्म्ड्/ adj निरस्त्र, बिना हथियारों का।

unashamed /अन्'शेम्ड्/ adj निः-संकोच : unashamed delight/fervour.

unassuming /अन्'स्यूमिङ्; US अन्'सूमिङ्/ adj निरहंकारी, विनीत, विनम्र : a gentle and unassuming person.

unattached /अन्'टैच्ट्/ adj 1 बिना किसी से जुड़े हुए, असंलग्न, असंबद्ध : be unattached to any political organization 2 अविवाहित।

unattended /अन्'टेन्डिड्/ adj 1 बिना मालिक की उपस्थिति के : unattended vehicles/baggage 2 unattended (to) किसी चीज़ को बिना ध्यान दिए (छोड़ना) : leave the shop counter/telephone unattended ○ old correspondence still unattended to.

unauthorized, -ised /अन्'ऑथराइज्ड्/ adj अनधिकृत, अवैध : unauthorized entry.

unavoidable /अन्'वॉइडबल्/ adj जिससे बचा ना जा सके।

unaware /अन्'वेअर/ adj unaware (of sth/that....) अनजान, अज्ञानी : He was unaware of my presence. ○ be socially/ politically unaware.

unawares /अन्'वेअर्ज़्/ adv अनजाने में, अकस्मात् : His violent outburst caught/took me unawares.

unbalanced /अन्'बैलन्स्ट्/ adj 1 ज़रूरत से ज़्यादा या कम; असंतुलित : an unbalanced diet 2 मानसिक रूप से अस्वस्थ, पागल : mentally unbalanced.

unbearable /अन्'बेअरबल्/ adj असह-नीय : unbearable pain ○ I find his rudeness/the heat unbearable. ▸ **unbearably** adv : unbearably hot/selfish.

unbelievable /अन्बि'लीव्बल्/ adj अविश्वसनीय।

unborn /अन्'बॉर्न्/ adj अजन्मा; जो अभी पैदा न हुआ हो : unborn children/calves.

unbreakable /अन्'ब्रेकबल्/ adj जिसे तोड़ा ना जा सके या जो न टूटे : unbreakable toys.

unbroken /अन्'ब्रोकन्/ adj 1 जिसमें बाधा न आई हो, शांत : ten hours of unbroken sleep 2 (खेल आदि में) ऐसा रेकॉर्ड जो अटूट हो।

unburden /अन्'बर्डन्/ verb unburden oneself/sth (of sth) (to sb) (औप) अपना दुखड़ा कहकर हलकापन अनुभव करना : She preferred to unburden herself to me rather than to her husband.

uncalled-for /अन्'कॉल्ड्फ़ॉर्/ adj अ-प्रार्थित और अनावश्यक; अनुचित : Your rude remarks were quite uncalled-for.

uncanny /अन्'कैनि/ adj 1 रहस्यमय, अस्वाभाविक : The silence was uncanny. 2 असामान्य : The resemblance between them is uncanny.

uncertain /अन्'सर्ट्न्/ adj अनिश्चित, किसी कार्य के बारे में संदेह होना ▸ **uncertainty** noun.

uncharacteristic /अन्कैरक्ट'रिस्टिक्/ adj uncharacteristic (of sb) अस्वाभाविक : make an uncharacteristic mistake.

uncle /'अङ्क्ल्/ noun 1 चाचा, मामा, फूफा, मौसा : my uncle Jim 2 (अनौप) बच्चों द्वारा वयस्क पुरुषों के लिए प्रयुक्त संबोधन।

uncomfortable /अन्'कम्फ़र्टबल्/ adj 1 बिना आराम के 2 बेचैन।

uncommon /अन्'कॉमन्/ adj असाधारण, सामान्य से हट कर : an uncommon sighting/occurrence.

uncompromising / अन्'कॉम्प्रमाइ-ज़िइ/ *adj* अपना रुख, दृष्टिकोण बदलने को बिलकुल भी तैयार न होना, हठी।

unconcerned /,अन्कन्'सर्न्ड्/ *adj* बिना परवाह या चिंता किए; रुचिहीन; उदासीन।

unconditional /,अन्कन्'डिशन्ल्/ *adj* बिना किसी शर्त के।

unconscious /अन्'कॉन्शस्/ *adj* 1 बेहोश, बेसुध, अचेत : *She was unconscious for days after the accident.* 2 **unconscious of sb/sth** अनजान : *be unconscious of any change* ▸ **unconsciously** *adv* अनजाने में।

uncontrollable /,अन्कन्'ट्रोलब्ल्/ *adj* जिसे नियंत्रित न किया जा सके; असंचालनीय।

unconventional /,अन्कन्'वेन्शन्ल्/ *adj* अपरंपरागत, रूढ़िविरोधी।

uncountable / अन्'काउन्टब्ल्/ *adj* अनगिनत, असंख्य : *uncountable galaxies.*

uncouth / अन्'कूथ्/ *adj* गँवार/असभ्य; अपरिष्कृत : *an uncouth young man.*

uncover / अन्'कवर्/ *verb* 1 किसी चीज़ का ढक्कन खोलना; उघाड़ना 2 रहस्य, भेद पाना : *uncover the truth.*

undecided / अन्डि'साइडिड्/ *adj* 1 जिसका निर्णय अभी न हुआ हो : *The outcome of the match is still undecided.* 2 **undecided (about sth/sb)** किसी चीज़/व्यक्ति के बारे में निर्णय न लिया हो : *I'm still undecided about who to vote for.*

undeniable / अन्डि'नाइअब्ल्/ *adj* जिसे नकारा न जा सके, जिसका खंडन न किया जा सके : *undeniable facts.*

under / 'अन्डर्/ *prep* 1 नीचे : *Have you looked under the bed?* 2 कम : *Nobody under eighteen is allowed to buy alcohol.* 3 व्यक्ति या विभाग के अधीन 4 विचाराधीन : *under discus-*

sion 5 आच्छन्न ▸ **under** *adv part* नीचे।

under- *prefix (पूर्वपद)* 1 (संज्ञा के पूर्व) नीचे के, भीतर के : *undergrowth* ॰ *undercurrent* 2 (विशेषण और क्रिया के पूर्व) आवश्यकता से कम : *underripe* ॰ *undercooked* 3 पद या स्थिति में नीचे: *under-secretary/under-graduate.*

undercover /अन्डर्'कवर्/ *adj* गुप्त रूप से, जासूसी : *undercover payments* ॰ *undercover agents/activities.*

undercurrent / 'अन्डरकरन्ट् /*noun* **undercurrent (of sth)** प्रच्छन्न या गुप्त (विचार या भावना की) प्रवृत्ति : *I detect an undercurrent of resentment towards the new proposals.*

undercut /,अन्डर्'कट्/ *verb* (-tt-; *pt, pp* **undercut**) 1 कम दाम पर बेचना : *They're undercutting us by 5%.* 2 कमज़ोर बनाना, कम मज़बूत बना देना : *concessions made to try and undercut the opposition.*

underdog / 'अन्डर्डॉग्/ *noun* (युद्ध या वाद-विवाद में) हारने की संभावना वाला दल या व्यक्ति : *Before the match we were definitely the underdogs.*

underdone /,अन्डर्'डन्/ *adj* अधपका (भोजन) : *underdone vegetables.*

underestimate /,अन्डर्'एस्टिमेट्/ *verb* वास्तविकता से कम आँकना, ज़्यादा महत्त्व न देना।

undergo /,अन्डर्'गो/ *verb* (*pt* **underwent**; *pp* **undergone**) 1 सहना, भुगतना : *undergo great hardship* 2 (प्रक्रिया से) गुज़रना : *undergo major surgery/reform/repair.*

undergraduate /,अन्डर्'ग्रैजुअट्/ *noun* पूर्व-स्नातक: *undergraduate courses.*

underground / अन्डर्'ग्राउन्ड् / *adv* 1 भूमिगत 2 छुपी हुई जगह पर : *He went underground to avoid capture.* ▸ **underground** / 'अन्डर्ग्राउन्ड् / *adj*

1 भूमिगत 2 गुप्त, प्राय: ग़ैर-क़ानूनी और सरकार-विरोधी।

undergrowth / 'अन्डरग्रोथ् / *noun* बड़े पेड़ के नीचे उगी झाड़ी आदि; झाड़-झंकार।

underhand / अन्डर्'हैन्ड् / *adj (अपमा)* गुप्त या बेईमानीपूर्ण तरीक़े से : *employ underhand tactics.*

underlie / अन्डर्'लाइ / *verb (pt* **underlay;** *pp* **underlain)** *(औप)* आधारभूत होना, मूल में होना : *A similar theme underlies much of his work.*

underline / अन्डर्'लाइन् / *(under-score* भी *) verb* 1 (शब्द या पंक्ति को) रेखांकित करना 2 बल देना, महत्त्व देना : *The huge response to our appeal underlines how much the public really care.*

undermine / अन्डर्'माइन् / *verb* 1 भीतर से खोखला करना, जड़ें खोदना : *cliffs undermined by the sea* 2 धीरे-धीरे दुर्बल/क्षीण करना : *undermine sb's position/authority.*

underneath / अन्डर्'नीथ् / *prep, adv* नीचे, तले : *The coin rolled underneath the piano.* ○ *This jacket's too big, even with a sweater underneath.*

underpay / अन्डर्'पे / *verb (pt, pp* **underpaid) underpay sb (for sth)** कर्मचारी को योग्यतानुसार वेतन से कम देना।

underplay / अन्डर्'प्ले / *verb* किसी चीज़ का महत्त्व कम करना : *The government is trying to underplay the significance of opinion polls.*

underprivileged / अन्डर्'प्रिविलिज्ड् / *adj* अल्प अधिकार वाले।

underrate / अन्डर्'रेट् / *verb* जितना है उससे कम समझना, महत्त्व न देना : *underrate an opponent/achievement.*

underscore / अन्डर्'स्कॉर् / *verb* (शब्द या पंक्ति को) रेखांकित करना।

undersigned / अन्डर्'साइन्ड् / *noun*

the undersigned *(pl* अपरिवर्तित*) (औप)* जिसने (जिन्होंने) नीचे हस्ताक्षर किए हैं, अधोहस्ताक्षरी : *We, the undersigned declare that... .*

understand / अन्डर्'स्टैन्ड् / *verb (pt, pp* **understood)** 1 समझना : *understand the instructions/rules/conditions* 2 (प्राय: औप) (प्राप्त सूचना से) जानना : *I understand (that) she is in Paris.* 3 किसी चीज़ की जानकारी रखना सहानुभूति रखना : *understand children/machinery* ■ **make oneself understood** अपना अर्थ स्पष्ट करन ▸ **understandable** *adj* जिसे समझा ज सके, बोधगम्य; स्वाभाविक या उचित।

understanding / अन्डर्'स्टैन्डिङ् / *noun* 1 समझ, विवेक: *mysteries beyond human understanding* 2 समझदारी, दूसरे के दृष्टिकोण को समझन की क्षमता 3 समझौता करना : *come to reach an understanding.*

understatement / 'अन्डर्स्टेट्मन्ट् / *noun* न्यूनोक्ति।

understudy / 'अन्डर्स्टडि / *noun* un **derstudy (to sb)** (किसी दूसरे के स्था पर काम करने के लिए) अभ्यास या अध्यय करने वाला, अभिनेता/अभिनेत्री।

undertake / अन्डर्'टेक् / *verb (p* **undertook;** *pp* **undertaken)** *(औप* 1 भार ग्रहण करना, बीड़ा उठाना : *under take a mission/project* 2 किसी का को करने के लिए सहमत होना या उसको पू करने के लिए वचन देना : *He undertoo to finish the job by Friday.* ▸ **ur dertaking** *noun* 1 कार्य पूरा करने क ज़िम्मेदारी, उत्तरदायित्व; वाणिज्यिक उप क्रम : *a commercial undertakin* 2 **undertaking (that.../to do st** *(औप)* (कार्य पूरा करने का) आश्वास वचन : *a written undertaking the the loan would be repaid.*

undertaker / 'अन्डर्टेकर् / *(US mor*

cian भी) *noun* अंत्येष्टि का प्रबंध करने वाला।

undertone / 'अन्डर्टोन् / *noun* 1 (प्राय: pl) मंद स्वर : *speak in an undertone* 2 **undertone** (of sth) छिपी भावना, अर्थ या गुण 3 हलका रंग : *pink with an undertone of mauve.*

underwater / ˌअन्डर्'वॉटर् / *adj* पानी के नीचे का : *underwater caves/explorers/cameras* ▸ **underwater** *adv* पानी के नीचे : *The seal disappeared underwater.*

underwear / 'अन्डर्वेअर् / *noun* बनियाइन, जाँघिया, चोली आदि नीचे पहनने के कपड़े।

underweight / ˌअन्डर्'वेट् / *adj* सामान्य वज़न से कम।

underworld / 'अन्डर्वर्ल्ड् / *noun* 1 समाज का वह वर्ग जो दुराचार और अपराध करके धनार्जन करता है : *police contacts in the London underworld* 2 the **underworld** (पौराणिक कथाओं में) पाताल लोक।

underwrite / ˌअन्डर्'राइट् / *verb* (pt **underwrote**; pp **underwritten**) 1 बीमा करना 2 किसी परियोजना/उद्यम के लिए भुगतान करने का वादा करना : *The government underwrote the initial costs of the scheme.*

undesirable / ˌअन्डि'ज़ाइअरब्ल् / *adj* 1 अनचाहा, हानिकारक : *The drug has no undesirable side-effects.* ○ *Military intervention is highly undesirable.* 2 (लोग या उनकी आदतें) अस्वीकार्य : *She's a most undesirable influence.*

undivided / ˌअन्डि'वाइडिड् / *adj* छोटे-छोटे भागों में न बँटा हुआ, संपूर्ण।

undo / अन्'डू / *verb* (pt **undid**; pp **undone**) 1 (गाँठ) खोलना, बटन खोलना : *My zip has come undone.* 2 किए हुए को बिगाड़ देना, व्यर्थ कर देना : *He undid*

most of the good work of his predecessor.

undoubted / अन्'डाउटिड् / *adj* जिसमें कोई संदेह न हो : *her undoubted ability/talent as an athlete* ▸ **undoubtedly** *adv.*

undress / अन्'ड्रेस् / *verb* कपड़े उतारना।

undue / ˌअन्'ड्यू / *adj* (औप) उचित से अधिक, अनुचित; अत्यधिक : *undue haste* ○ *put undue pressure on sb* ▸ **unduly** *adv.*

undulate / 'अन्ड्युलेट् / *verb* लहराना, लहरदार होना : *undulating hills.*

unearth / अन्'अर्थ् / *verb* 1 **unearth sth** (from sth) खोदकर निकालना : *unearth buried treasure* 2 खोजकर प्रकाश में लाना।

unearthly / अन्'अर्थ्लि / *adj* रहस्यमय, भयानक; अलौकिक : *wild, unearthly music* ○ *The silence was unearthly.* ■ **at an unearthly hour** (अनौप) समय के पूर्व होने के कारण असुविधाजनक।

uneasy / अन्'ईज़ि / *adj* 1 **uneasy** (about/at sth) बेचैन, चिंतित : *have an uneasy conscience* 2 असुरक्षित : *an uneasy truce/silence* ▸ **uneasily** *adv.*

uneconomical / ˌअन्ˌईक'नॉमिक्ल् / *adj* उतना मितव्ययी, किफ़ायती नहीं जितना हो सकता है; अलाभकर।

uneducated / अन्'एजुकेटिड् / *adj* अ-शिक्षित।

unemployed / ˌअनिम्'प्लॉइड् / *adj* बे-रोज़गार, बेकार।

unemployment / ˌअनिम्'प्लॉइमन्ट् / *noun* बेरोज़गारी, बेरोज़गारी की अवस्था।

unending / अन्'एन्डिङ् / *adj* अनंत, बार-बार।

unequal / ˌअन्'ईक्वल् / *adj* असमान, अ-संतुलित।

unequivocal / ˌअनि'क्विवक्ल् / *adj*

(औप) सिर्फ़ एक अर्थ वाला, साफ़-साफ़ : *an unequivocal statement.*

unerring / अन्'अरिङ् / *adj* ठीक, अचूक : *her unerring accuracy/good taste.*

unethical / अन्'एथ्किल् / *adj* अनैतिक, नैतिकता के आधार पर नहीं : *unethical decisions/practices.*

uneven / अन्'ईवन् / *adj* 1 समतल नहीं, खुरदरा : *an uneven pavement/ floor/surface* 2 असंगत, अनियमित : *work of uneven quality* ∘ *have an uneven pulse* ▶ **unevenly** *adv.*

uneventful / अनि'वेन्ट्फ़ुल् / *adj* जिसमें कुछ असाधारण, असामान्य, उत्तेजक न घटे : *an uneventful journey.*

unexpected / अनिक्'स्पेक्टिड् / *adj* अ-प्रत्याशित, जिसकी आशा नहीं की गई : *un-expected guests/changes/results.*

unexplained / अनिक्'स्प्लेन्ड् / *adj* अस्पष्ट, रहस्यमय : *unexplained reasons/motives* ∘ *The disappearance of the aircraft remains unexplained.*

unfair / अन्'फ़ेअर् / *adj* 1 **unfair (on/ to sb)** पक्षपातपूर्ण, अन्यायपूर्ण : *unfair treatment* ∘ *an unfair decision* 2 अनुचित, बेजा : *unfair play* ▶ **unfairly** *adv* : *be treated unfairly* **unfairness** *noun.*

unfaithful / अन्'फ़ेथ्फ़ुल् / *adj* **unfaithful (to sb/sth)** 1 बेवफ़ा 2 (अप्र) नमकहराम, अविश्वस्त : *an unfaithful servant.*

unfamiliar / अन्फ़'मिलिअर् / *adj* 1 **unfamiliar (to sb)** अपरिचित 2 **unfa-miliar with sth** (औप) जानकारी/अनु-भवहीन : *I am unfamiliar with this type of computer.*

unfashionable / अन्'फ़ैश्नब्ल् / *adj* अप्रचलित, लोकप्रिय नहीं : *live in an unfashionable part of town.*

unfasten / अन्'फ़ास्न् / *verb* बंधी हुई चीज़ जैसे पेटी आदि को खोलना : *unfasten one's belt/watch.*

unfavourable (*US* **unfavorable**) / अन्'फ़ेव्रबल् / *adj* **unfavourable (to/ for sb/sth)** प्रतिकूल, अस्वीकार्य, अनुप-युक्त : *an unfavourable impression* ∘ *The play received unfavourable reviews.* ∘ *Conditions are unfa-vourable for sailing.*

unfit / अन्'फ़िट् / *adj* **unfit (for sth/to do sth)** 1 अयोग्य, बेकार; अनुपयुक्त : *food unfit for human consumption* ∘ *houses unfit for people to live in* ∘ *She is unfit for public office.* 2 अस्वस्थ : *Lack of exercise made him very unfit.*

unfold / अन्'फ़ोल्ड् / *verb* 1 फैलाना (खोलकर) : *unfold a map/table cloth* 2 (योजना आदि) प्रकट करना : *She un-folded her plans (to us).*

unforeseen / अन्फ़ॉर्'सीन् / *adj* पहले से जानकारी न होना; अप्रत्याशित : *unfore-seen circumstances/developments/ difficulties.*

unforgettable / अन्फ़र्'गेटब्ल् / *adj* जिसे कभी भूला न जा सके : *an unforget-table experience/moment.*

unforgivable / अन्फ़र्'गिव्बल् / *adj* जो माफ़ न किया जा सके।

unforgiving / अन्फ़र्'गिविङ् / *adj* माफ़ करने को तैयार न होना।

unfortunate / अन्'फ़ॉर्चनट् / *adj* 1 दुर्भाग्यपूर्ण : *an unfortunate start to the trip* 2 पसंद से विपरीत, खेदजनक : *a most unfortunate choice of words* ▶ **unfortunately** *adv* **unfortunately (for sb)** : *Unfortunately for him, he was proved wrong.*

unfounded / अन्'फ़ाउन्डिड् / *adj* निरा-धार, बेबुनियाद : *Her worries were proved largely unfounded.*

ungainly / अन्'गेनलि / adj भद्दा, उजड्डु : He walked in long ungainly strides.

ungrateful / अन्'ग्रेट्फ़ुल् / adj ungrateful (to sb) (for sth) एहसान न मानने वाला, अकृतज्ञ।

unguarded / अन्'गार्डिड् / adj 1 अ-रक्षित : The prisoner was left unguarded. 2 (कथन आदि) असावधानी से दिया हुआ : unguarded gossip.

unhappy / अन्'हैपि / adj (-ier, -iest) 1 दुखी 2 unhappy (about/at/with sth) अप्रसन्न 3 अभागा, बदक़िस्मत : an unhappy coincidence/chance ▸ **unhappiness** noun दुःख।

unhealthy / अन्'हेल्थि / adj 1 अ-स्वस्थ : an unhealthy complexion 2 स्वास्थ्य के लिए हानिकारक : an unhealthy climate/diet.

unheard / अन्'हर्ड् / adj 1 जिसे सुना न जाए और जिस पर कोई कार्रवाई न की जाए : My protests went unheard. 2 जो पहले न सुना हो : a previously unheard piece of music ▸ **unheard-of** / अन्'हर्ड् ऑव् / adj अभूतपूर्व, असाधा-रण।

unicorn / 'यूनिकॉर्न् / noun (पुरानी पाश्चात्य कहानियों में) घोड़ानुमा पशु जिसके माथे पर एक सीधा सींग होता है।

unidentified / ˌअनाइ'डेन्टिफ़ाइड् / adj जिसकी पहचान न हो सके : an unidentified species of insect.

uniform[1] / 'यूनिफ़ॉर्म् / adj एकसमान, एकरूप : of uniform length/size/shape/colour ▸ **uniformity** / ˌयूनि'फ़ॉर्मिटि / noun : the drab uniformity of the modern world **uniformly** adv.

uniform[2] / 'यूनिफ़ॉर्म् / noun पोशाक जो समान हो, वरदी : a military/police uniform ○ The tie is part of the school uniform.

unify / 'यूनिफ़ाइ / verb (pt, pp unified)

एक कर देना; एकरूप कर देना : an attempt to unify the nation ▸ **unification** noun एकीकरण : the unification of Germany.

unilateral / ˌयूनि'लैटरल् / adj किसी एक व्यक्ति, वर्ग, श्रेणी, देश की तरफ़ से : take unilateral action.

union / 'यूनिअन् / noun 1 संघ, यूनि-यन : a trade union 2 union (of A with B/between A and B) संयोजन, सम्मिलन : work towards monetary union 3 सामंजस्य, मेल-मिलाप : live together in perfect union.

unique / यू'नीक् / adj 1 एकमात्र; अनन्य : a unique design 2 अनुपम, अद्वितीय : a unique opportunity/ability/achievement.

unison / 'यूनिसन् / noun ■ in unison (with sb/sth) स्वरमेल में।

unit / 'यूनिट् / noun 1 इकाई, एकक, मात्र-क : a unit of currency 2 एकल वस्तु, व्यक्ति या समूह : a family unit.

unite / यु'नाइट् / verb 1 unite (sb/sth) (with sb/sth) जोड़ना, एक करना या होना : The two parties have united to form a coalition. 2 unite (in sth/doing sth) साथ काम करना : We should unite in fighting poverty and disease. ▸ **united** adj संयुक्त।

unity / 'यूनिटि / noun 1 एकता : political/national unity 2 (कला में) संपूर्णता प्रस्तुत करने की अवस्था।

universal / ˌयूनि'वर्सल् / adj सार्वभौमिक: universal suffrage ○ Such beliefs are by no means universal. ▸ **universally** adv.

universe / 'यूनिवर्स् / noun 1 the universe विश्व 2 ब्रह्मांड।

university / ˌयूनि'वर्सटि / noun विश्व-विद्यालय।

unjust / ˌअन्'जस्ट् / adj अनुचित, अन्याय-पूर्ण, अन्यायी।

unkempt / अन्'केम्प्ट् / adj (कपड़े या बाल) अव्यवस्थित, मैले-कुचैले : a long unkempt beard.

unkind / अन्'काइन्ड् / adj unkind (to sb/sth) निर्दयी, रूखा ▶ **unkindly** adv **unkindness** noun.

unknown / अन्'नोन् / adj unknown (to sb) 1 अज्ञात : The accident was due to unknown causes. 2 प्रसिद्ध या जाना पहचाना नहीं ▶ **unknown** noun.

unlawful / अन्'लॉफ़ुल् / adj (औप) गैर-क़ानूनी, अवैध : be charged with unlawful possession of drugs.

unleaded / अन्'लेडिड् / adj बिना सीसे का पेट्रोल।

unless / अन्'लेस् / conj यदि नहीं; जब तक नहीं... : You'll fail in your exams unless you work harder.

unlike / अन्'लाइक् / adj भिन्न, असमान : They're so unlike that nobody would think they're sisters. ▶ **unlike** prep से भिन्न : Her latest novel is quite unlike her earlier work.

unlikely / अन्'लाइकलि /adj (-ier, -iest) 1 संभावना न होना : It is unlikely to rain/that it will rain. 2 अविश्वस-नीय : an unlikely story.

unlimited / अन्'लिमिटिड् / adj असीमित, बहुत।

unload / अन्'लोड् / verb 1 unload (sth) (from sth) वाहन या जहाज़ से माल उतारना 2 बंदूक से गोली या कैमरे से फ़िल्म निकालना।

unlock / अन्'लॉक् / verb 1 चाबी से ताला खोलना 2 प्रकट होने में सहायक होना : attempt to unlock the creative talents of young people.

unlucky / अन्'लकि / adj अभागा, बद-क़िस्मत ▶ **unluckily** adv बदक़िस्मती से।

unmarried / अन्'मैरिड् /adj अविवाहित।

unmistakable / अन्मि'स्टेकब्ल् / adj साफ़, सुस्पष्ट : The family resemblance is unmistakable.

unnatural /अन्'नैच्रल्/ adj 1 अप्राकृतिक, असामान्य : unnatural behaviour 2 अस्वाभाविक : unnatural desires/vice 3 नक़ली; बनावटी : an unnatural laugh/voice.

unnecessary / अन्'नेसरि; US अन्'ने-ससेरि / adj अनावश्यक, अत्यधिक ▶ **unnecessarily** adv.

unnerve / अन्'नर्व् / verb हिम्मत छूट जाना, हिम्मत छुड़ा देना : His silence unnerved me.

unnoticed /अन्'नोटिस्ट्/ adj बिना किसी के ध्यान गए; अलक्षित : She slipped out of the meeting unnoticed.

unobtrusive / अनब्'ट्रूसिव् / adj जो आसानी से नज़र न आए : an unobtrusive design ० a shy, unobtrusive man.

unofficial /अन्'फ़िश्ल्/ adj बिना अधि-कारियों की मान्यता के, अशासकीय, गैर-सरकारी : unofficial strike/statement.

unorthodox / अन्'ऑर्थडॉक्स् / adj रूढ़ि-विरुद्ध, अपरंपरागत, असामान्य।

unpack / अन्'पैक् / verb unpack (A from) B; unpack (A) बैग, सूटकेस आदि से सामान ख़ाली करना।

unpaid / अन्'पेड् / adj 1 जिसके लिए रक़म अदा न की गई हो : an unpaid bill/debt 2 बिना वेतन के : take unpaid leave.

unpleasant / अन्'प्लेज़न्ट् / adj अप्रिय, अप्रीतिकर : unpleasant smells/weather ▶ **unpleasantness** noun मनोमालिन्य, अनबन : I don't want any unpleasantness with the neighbours.

unplug / अन्'प्लग् / verb (-gg-) किसी विद्युत यंत्र का प्लग निकालना।

unpopular / अन्'पॉप्यलर् / adj unpopular (with sb) अप्रिय : an unpopular author/design/leader.

unprecedented /अन्प्रेसिडेन्टिड्/ adj अभूतपूर्व : *crime on an unprecedented scale* ○ *unprecedented levels of unemployment.*

unpredictable /अन्प्रि डिक्टब्ल्/ adj जिस चीज़ या (व्यक्ति के) व्यवहार के बारे में अंदाज़ा न लगाया जा सके : *unpredictable weather* ○ *You never know how she'll react : she's so unpredictable.*

unprepared /अन्प्रि पेअर्ड/ adj तैयार न होना : *I was completely unprepared for his reaction.*

unpretentious /अन्प्रि टेन्शस्/ adj निरहंकार, विनीत : *He's one of the most unpretentious people I've ever met.*

unprofessional /अन्प्र फ़ेशन्ल्/ adj 1 अव्यावसायिक 2 व्यवहार जो किसी पेशे के लिए अनुपयुक्त हो।

unprovoked /अन्प्र वोक्ट्/ adj बिना भड़काए हमला होना : *unprovoked aggression/assaults.*

unqualified /अन् क्वॉलिफ़ाइड्/ adj 1 unqualified (as sth/for sth/to do sth) क़ानूनी या शासकीय मान्यता के बिना : *unqualified instructors/staff* 2 unqualified (to do sth) (अनौप) बिना योग्यता, दक्षता के : *an unqualified opinion.*

unquestionable /अन् क्वेस्चनब्ल्/ adj निस्संदेह, निर्विवाद, निश्चित : *unquestionable honesty/integrity/authority* ▶ **unquestionably** adv : *This design is unquestionably the best.*

unravel /अन् रैव्ल्/ verb (-ll-; US -l-) 1 (गुत्थी) सुलझाना; अलग-अलग करना : *try to unravel a great tangle of string* 2 रहस्योद्घाटन करना।

unreal /अन्रिअल्; US अन्रीअल्/ adj (अनुभव) अवास्तविक।

unreasonable /अन् रीज़नब्ल्/ adj (व्यक्ति या व्यवहार) हठी, अनुचित; बहुत अधिक प्रत्याशा करते हुए : *take an unreasonable risk* ○ *Am I being unreasonable in asking you to help me?*

unreliable /अन्रि लाइअब्ल्/ adj जिस पर भरोसा न किया जा सके : *an unreliable memory.*

unremitting /अन्रि मिटिङ्/ adj निरंतर, अविरल : *He will be remembered for his unremitting efforts to protect wildlife.*

unrest /अन् रेस्ट्/ noun अशांति, उप-द्रव : *political/social unrest.*

unripe /अन् राइप्/ adj कच्चा; फल आदि जो अभी पूरी तरह पका न हो : *unripe bananas.*

unrivalled (US unrivaled) /अन् राइव्ल्ड्/ adj अतुल्य, उच्चतम, अद्वितीय, बेजोड़ : *have an unrivalled knowledge of antiques.*

unroll /अन् रोल्/ verb 1 लिपटी हुई किसी चीज़ को खोलना या उसका खुल जाना : *unroll a carpet/map/sleeping-bag* 2 महत्वपूर्ण घटनाओं का एक के बाद एक घटित होना : *watch events/history unroll.*

unruly /अन् रूलि/ adj उपद्रवी/बेक़ाबू; उच्छृंखल : *an unruly child/crowd.*

unsafe /अन् सेफ़्/ adj असुरक्षित, ख़तर-नाक : *The water is unsafe to swim in.*

unsaid /अन् सेड्/ adj अनकहा : *Some things are better left unsaid.*

unsatisfactory /अन् सैटिस् फ़ैक्टरि/ adj संतोषजनक नहीं, अपर्याप्त : *His work is highly unsatisfactory.*

unsavoury (US unsavory) /अन् सेव्रि/ adj 1 (लोग या उनका व्यवहार) अप्रिय, आक्रामक : *unsavoury habits* 2 अप्रिय गंध या स्वाद वाला।

unscathed / अन्'स्केद्ड् / *adj* बिना घायल हुए : *The hostages emerged from their ordeal unscathed.*

unscrew /अन्'स्क्रू / *verb* 1 किसी चीज़ को घुमाकर या पेच निकालकर खोलना 2 किसी चीज़ का घुमाने से खुल जाना जैसे बोतल का ढक्कन।

unscrupulous / अन्'स्क्रूप्यलस् / *adj* बिना नैतिकता या सिद्धांत के, कपटी : *unscrupulous business methods/practices.*

unsettle / अन्'सेट्ल् / *verb* शांति भंग होना या करना, अस्थिर कर देना।

unshaven /अन्'शेवन् / *adj* बिना दाढ़ी बनाए।

unsightly / अन्'साइट्लि / *adj* कुरूप : *an unsightly scar.*

unskilled /अन्'स्किल्ड् / *adj* बिना किसी योग्यता व प्रशिक्षण के : *unskilled workers/labourers.*

unsolicited /अन्स्'लिसिटिड्/ *adj* जिसे माँगा न गया हो : *unsolicited help/advice/support* ० *unsolicited comments/criticisms.*

unsound /अन्'साउन्ड् / *adj* 1 निकृष्ट दशा में, कमज़ोर : *The roof is (structurally) unsound.* 2 ग़लतियों से भरा, अविश्वसनीय ■ *of unsound mind* (क़ानून) पागल।

unspeakable / अन्'स्पीकबल् / *adj* (प्रायः *अपमा*) अकथ्य, अकथनीय ः *unspeakable cruelty/suffering.*

unstable / अन्'स्टेबल् / *adj* 1 जो कभी भी हिल या गिर सकता है; अस्थायी 2 जिसमें जल्दी से परिवर्तन आए : *be emotionally/mentally unstable* ० *unstable share prices.*

unsteady / अन्'स्टेडि / *adj* 1 जो कभी भी हिल या गिर सकता है, जो काँपता हो : *an unsteady hand/voice* ०*an unsteady ladder* 2 अनियमित, असामान्य : *an*

unsteady pulse ० *His work is rather unsteady.*

unsuccessful /,अन्सक्'सेस्फ़ुल् / *adj* असफल ▶ **unsuccessfully** *adv.*

unsuitable / अन्'सूटबल् / *adj* **unsuitable (for sb/sth)** अनुपयुक्त; जो ठीक, उचित या सही न हो ▶ **unsuitably** *adv* अयोग्यता से, अनुचित ढंग से।

unsure /,अन्'शुअर् / *adj* 1 **unsure (of oneself)** अपने पर ज़्यादा भरोसा न होना 2 **unsure (about/of sth)** अनिश्चित, संदेहपूर्ण, संदिग्ध।

unsuspecting /,अन्स्'स्पेक्टिङ् / *adj* निःसंदेह; ख़तरे के बारे में अनजान।

untamed /अन्'टेम्ड् / *adj* 1 परती भूमि जिस पर खेती न की गई हो 2 (जानवर) जंगली, जिसे सधाया न गया हो 3 (व्यक्ति) अनियंत्रित और दूसरों से अप्रभावित।

untangle /,अन्'टैङ्ग्ल् / *verb* 1 उलझे हुए धागे, ऊन आदि को खोलना/सुलझाना 2 किसी जटिल मुद्दे को सरल या पूरी तरह समझने योग्य बनाना : *untangle a mystery.*

unthinkable / अन्'थ्रिङ्कबल् / *adj* कल्पनातीत, असंभव : *Defeat was unthinkable.*

unthinking / अन्'थ्रिङ्किङ् / *adj* लापरवाह; (कार्य) अविचारित : *unthinking remarks/criticism.*

untidy / अन्'टाइडि / *adj* (-ier, -iest) 1 बेढंगे रूप से किसी चीज़ का पड़े रहना : *an untidy desk/kitchen/cupboard* 2 (व्यक्ति) सुव्यवस्थित नहीं ▶ **untidily** *adv* **untidiness** *noun.*

untie / अन्'टाइ / *verb* बंधी हुई किसी चीज़ को खोलना : *untie a dog/parcel/prisoner* ० *untie a rope/ribbon/string.*

until / अन्'टिल् / *conj, prep* (**till** भी) तक : *Let's wait until the rain stops.* ० *wait until tomorrow.*

untimely /अन्'टाइम्लि/ *adj* 1 असामयिक,

असमय : *her untimely death at 25* **2** कुसमय, अनुपयुक्त समय पर : *an untimely arrival/remark.*

unto / 'अन्टु / *prep* (प्रा) तब तक।

untold / अन्'टोल्ड / *adj* **1** असंख्य, असीम : *untold suffering/damage* ○ *man of untold wealth* **2** अकथित : *Theirs is an untold story.*

untouchable / अन्'टचब्ल् / *adj* **1** जिसे छुआ न जा सके, जिस तक पहुँचा न जा सके : *an untouchable world record* **2** अछूत, हरिजन जाति से संबंधित ▸ **untouchable** *noun* अछूत, हरिजन जाति का सदस्य।

untouched / अन्'टच्ट् / *adj* **1 untouched (by sth)** अछूता, अप्रभावित, अपरिवर्तित : *an island untouched by progress* **2** अक्षत : *Some buildings were left untouched by the hurricane.* **3** (खाना) बिना छुए छोड़ना : *He left his meal untouched.*

untoward / अन्ट्'वॉर्ड; *US* अन्'टाई / *adj* (औप) अप्रत्याशित; दुर्भाग्यपूर्ण; परेशान करने वाला : *untoward occurrences* ○ *We all behaved as if nothing untoward had happened.*

untrue / अन्'टू / *adj* **1** झूठा : *The allegations were shown to be untrue.* **2 untrue (to sb/sth)** (औप) विश्वासघाती, निष्ठाहीन।

untruth / अन्'टूथ् / *noun* (*pl* **untruths** / अन्'टूदज़् /) (औप) **1** झूठ **2** जिसमें सच न हो ▸ **untruthful** / अन्'टूथ्फ़ुल् / *adj* जो झूठा हो : *an untruthful man* ○ *untruthful claims.*

unused¹ / अन्'यूज़्ड् / *adj* जो कभी इस्तेमाल न हुआ हो : *an unused envelope/ stamp.*

unused² / अन्'यूज़्ड् / *adj* **unused to sth/doing sth** जिसका ज़्यादा या बिलकुल अनुभव न हो : *We were unused to city life and found it strange at first.*

unusual / अन्'यूशुअल् / *adj* **1** अनूठा, असाधारण : *This bird is an unusual winter visitor in these parts.* **2** औरों से भिन्न होने के कारण आकर्षक या प्रशंसा के योग्य ▸ **unusually** *adv* **1** असाधारण तरीक़े से **2** सामान्य से हटकर : *an unusually high/low rainfall for January.*

unutterable / अन्'अटरब्ल् / *adj* (औप) अकथनीय : *unutterable sadness.*

unveil / अन्'वेल् / *verb* **1** किसी चीज़, विशेषत: किसी कलाकृति, के ऊपर से परदा हटाकर उसका उद्घाटन करना : *unveil a statue/monument/plaque/portrait* **2** घूँघट, परदा उठाना : *The bride unveiled (herself) at the end of the wedding ceremony.*

unwanted / अन्'वॉन्टिड् / *adj* जिसे कोई न चाहे, अनचाहा, अनावश्यक : *feel unwanted.*

unwelcome / अन्'वेल्कम् / *adj* अनचाहा, जिसका स्वागत न हो : *an unwelcome visitor.*

unwell / अन्'वेल् / *adj* बीमार।

unwieldy / अन्'वील्डि / *adj* **1** भारी-भरकम, बोझिल (वस्तु) : *long, unwieldy poles* **2** (तंत्र या समूह/संघ) कुव्यवस्थित : *the unwieldy bureaucracy of centralized government.*

unwilling / अन्'विलिङ् / *adj* **unwilling (to do sth)** अनिच्छुक ▸ **unwillingly** *adv* : *agree unwillingly to a request* **unwillingness** *noun*.

unwind / अन्'वाइन्ड् / *verb* (*pt, pp* **unwound** / अन्'वॉउन्ड् /) **1 unwind (sth) (from sth)** धागे, ऊन आदि के लिपटे होने की अवस्था से खुल जाना या खोल देना : *unwind a ball of wool/a reel of thread/a roll of bandage* **2** खिंचाव, तनाव की स्थिति में होने के बाद, आराम करना : *Music helps me unwind after a hard day's work.*

unwitting / अन्'विटिङ्/ adj (औप) अनजान; अनभिज्ञ : unwitting accomplices in the crime ▶ **unwittingly** adv.

unwrap /अन्'रैप्/ verb (लिपटे हुए को) खोलना, अनावृत करना : unwrap a parcel/present.

up¹ /अप्/ adv part 1 सीधा : I stood up to ask a question. 2 ऊपर, ऊपर की ओर : Lift your head up. ○ Prices are still going up. ○ The sun was coming up as we left. 3 पूरी तरह से : The stream has dried up. 4 सो कर उठना : It's time to get up. ■ not be up to much बहुत अच्छा नहीं : His work isn't up to much. up to sth (विशेषत: ग़लत काम) करने में लगा हुआ : I'm sure he's up to no good. what's up? (अनौप) क्या बात है? ▶ up noun ■ ups and downs (जीवन के) उतार-चढ़ाव : We've certainly had our ups and downs.

up² /अप्/ prep ऊपर, ऊपर की ओर : run up the stairs.

up- pref (पूर्वपद) : ऊपर की दिशा में : upland/upgrade.

upbeat /अप्बीट्/ adj प्रसन्न तथा उत्साह-पूर्ण : be in an upbeat mood ○ The conference ended on a distinctly upbeat note.

upbraid / अप्'ब्रेड् / verb upbraid sb (for sth/doing sth) डाँटना, झिड़कना।

upbringing /'अपब्रिङिङ्/ noun (प्राय: sing) शिक्षा, लिखाई-पढ़ाई तथा पालन-पोषण : a strict religious upbringing.

upcoming /'अप्कमिङ्/ adj जो शीघ्र ही शुरू होना वाला हो : a review of upcoming events.

update /अप्'डेट्/ verb सूचना को आज के दिन तक की बनाना; और अधिक आधुनिक करना; अद्यतन करना।

upgrade /अप्'ग्रेड्/ verb किसी व्यक्ति की पदोन्नति होना या वस्तु को उच्चस्तर की बनाना।

upheaval / अप्'हीव्ल् / noun क्रांति, काया पलट; उथल-पुथल : social/political upheavals.

uphill /अप्'हिल्/ adj 1 ऊपर, ऊपर की ओर : uphill road/climb 2 कठिन, श्रमसाध्य : an uphill task ▶ **uphill** adv.

uphold / अप्'होल्ड् / verb (pt, pp upheld) 1 (निर्णय का) अनुमोदन/समर्थन करना : uphold a verdict ○ uphold a policy/principle 2 प्रथा जारी रखना : uphold ancient traditions.

upholster /अप्'होल्स्टर्/ verb upholster sth (in/with sth) (कुर्सी में) गद्दी लगाना : upholster a sofa (in leather).

upholstery /अप्'होल्स्टरि/ noun कमरे का साज-सामान, गद्देदार सामान आदि।

upkeep / 'अपकीप् / noun किसी स्थिति में रखने का ख़र्च; रख-रखाव : I can't afford the upkeep of a large house and garden.

upland / 'अप्लन्ड् / noun (अक्सर pl) उच्च भूमि।

uplifting /अप्'लिफ्टिङ्/ adj आशा या ख़ुशी की भावना उत्पन्न करने वाला : an uplifting speech.

upon / अ'पॉन्/ prep (औप) = on.

upper /'अपर्/ adj 1 ऊपरी : the upper lip/jaw/arm ○ one of the upper floors/rooms/windows 2 पद/मर्यादा में ऊपर : the upper levels of society ▶ **upper** noun तले के ऊपर का जूते का भाग।

uppermost / 'अपर्मोस्ट् / adj सर्वोच्च; प्रमुख : the uppermost branches of a tree ○ executives in the uppermost levels ▶ **uppermost** adv किसी चीज़ को सबसे ऊपर की तरफ़ रखना या सबसे महत्त्वपूर्ण समझना : Put the box down with this side uppermost. ○ She has *always placed her career upper-most.*

upright /'अप्राइट्/ *adj* 1 खड़ा; सीधा : *his upright bearing/posture/stance* 2 खरा, ईमानदार : *an upright citizen* ▶ **upright** *adv* सीधी स्थिति में : *sit upright* **upright** *noun* खड़ा खंभा।

uprising /'अप्राइज़िङ्/ *noun* विद्रोह, बग़ावत।

uproar /'अप्रॉर्/ *noun* 1 हंगामा, हुल्लड़ : *The meeting ended in (an) uproar.* 2 (निंदा/तर्क-वितर्क का) कोहराम : *There was (an) uproar over the tax increases.* ▶ **uproarious** /अप्रॉरिअस्/ *adj* कोलाहलपूर्ण; कहकहा, ठहाका।

uproot /ˌअप्'रूट्/ *verb* 1 उखाड़ना : *trees uprooted by the floods* 2 **uproot oneself/sb (from sth...)** वह जगह छोड़ना या छुड़वाना जहाँ बहुत समय से बसे हों।

upset /ˌअप्'सेट्/ *verb* (-tt-; *pt, pp* **upset**) 1 गड़बड़ा देना : *The sight of animals suffering always upsets me.* 2 अस्त-व्यस्त कर देना : *upset the balance of power* 3 उलट देना, विशेषत: संयोग से : *upset one's cup/the milk* 4 पेट में गड़बड़ हो जाना ▶ **upset** *noun* गड़बड़ी।

upshot /'अप्शॉट्/ *noun* **the upshot (of sth)** परिणाम, निष्कर्ष।

upside-down (**upside down** भी) /ˌअप्साइड्'डाउन्/ *adj, adv* 1 ऊपर का भाग नीचे की ओर : *The picture is upside down.* 2 उलटा-पुलटा : *Burglars had turned the house up-side-down.*

upstairs /अप्'स्टेअर्ज़्/ *adv* सीढ़ियों से ऊपर जाना; ऊपरी मंजिल पर : *walk/go upstairs* ○ *I thought I heard a noise upstairs.*

upstart /'अप्स्टार्ट्/ *noun* (अपमा) वह

व्यक्ति जो अचानक रईस बन गया हो या किसी महत्त्वपूर्ण पद पर पहुँच गया हो और इसलिए दंभी हो गया हो : *upstart bureaucrats.*

upstream /ˌअप्'स्ट्रीम्/ *adv* जलधारा की प्रतिकूल दिशा में : *swim upstream* ▶ **upstream** *adj.*

uptake /'अप्टेक्/ *noun* [sing] पदार्थ ग्रहण करना/लेना ■ **quick/slow on the uptake** तुरंत/मंद समझने वाला।

uptight /ˌअप्'टाइट्/ *adj* **uptight (about sth)** (अनौप) 1 आशंकित या भयभीत होना : *get uptight about exams/interviews* 2 किसी चीज़ से चिढ़ जाना : *He gets very uptight at the mere mention of the subject.*

up-to-date /ˌअप् ट 'डेट्/ *adj* 1 आधुनिकतम, नवीनतम क़िस्म का : *up-to-date clothes/ideas/books/methods* 2 ऐसा जिसमें हाल की सूचना को शामिल किया गया हो : *up-to-date report.*

upward /'अप्वर्ड्/ *adj* ऊपर की ओर (चलता हुआ) : *an upward glance/climb* ▶ **upward** (**upwards** भी) *adv* उच्चतर स्थान की ओर **upwards of** *prep* से अधिक : *Upwards of a hundred people came to the meeting.*

urban /'अर्बन्/ *adj* नगरीय, शहरी : *urban areas* ▶ **urbanize, -ise** *verb* नगरीय बनना/बनाना : *urbanized localities* **urbanization, -isation** *noun.*

urbane /अर्'बेन्/ *adj* (औप) विनम्र; सुसभ्य : *an urbane man/manner* ▶ **urbanely** *adv* **urbanity** /अर्'बैनिटि/ *noun.*

urchin /'अर्चिन्/ *noun* (**street urchin** भी) (सड़कों पर खेलने वाला) गंदा नटखट बच्चा : *little urchins.*

urge /अर्ज्/ *verb* 1 (किसी व्यक्ति को) कुछ करने के लिए समझाना : *She urged me to reconsider my decision.* 2 **urge sth (on/upon sb/sth)** सुझाव देना, प्रेरित करना ▶ **urge** *noun* आवेग,

लालसा, ललक : *feel a sudden urge to travel.*

urgent / 'अर्जन्ट् / *adj* तुरंत निर्णय या काररवाई की अपेक्षा करने वाला; आवश्यकता प्रकट करने वाला : *an urgent message* ▸ **urgency** / 'अर्जन्सि / *noun* तुरंत कार्य करने की आवश्यकता या महत्ता : *a matter of the greatest urgency* **urgently** *adv.*

urine / 'युअरिन् / *noun* पेशाब, मूत्र ▸ **urinal** *noun* पेशाबघर **urinate** *verb* पेशाब करना।

urn / अर्न् / *noun* 1 अस्थिकलश, भस्म–कलश 2 चाय या कॉफ़ी के लिए धातु का बना पात्र।

us / अस् / *pers pron* we का कर्मकारक रूप : *She gave us a picture.*

usage / 'यूज़िज़्; 'यूसिज़् / *noun* 1 व्यवहार, शब्दों आदि का प्रयोग : *current English usage* 2 लोकोक्ति, आम रिवाज़।

use¹ / यूज़ / *verb* (*pt, pp* used / यूज़्ड् /) 1 use sth (for sth/doing sth) किसी काम के लिए प्रयोग करना : *May I use your phone?* 2 अपने लाभ के लिए किसी का उपयोग/शोषण करना : *He felt he'd been used.* 3 प्रयोग में/उपयोग में ले लेना, जिससे वस्तु की मात्रा कम हो जाए : *Use the milk sparingly, there's not much left.* ◾ **use sth up** जो था वह समाप्त हो जाना : *use up all one's strength/energy.*

use² / यूस् / *noun* 1 use (of sth) प्रयोग/उपयोग : *the use of electricity for heating* 2 प्रयोजन : *find a (new) use for sth* 3 लाभ, फ़ायदा : *What's the use of worrying about it?* 4 use (of sth) प्रयोग करने की शक्ति; उपभोग करने का अधिकार : *allow a tenant use of the garden* ◾ **come into use** काम में आने लगना **go out of use** पुराना/अप्रचलित हो जाना **make use of sth/sb** उपयोग में लाना, विशेषत: किसी लाभ के लिए।

used¹ / यूज़्ड् / *adj* पुरानी (वस्तु), नई नहीं : *used clothes.*

used² / यूस्ट् / *adj* ◾ used to sth/doing sth अभ्यस्त, परिचित : *be quite used to hard work.*

used to / 'यूस्ट ट / *modal verb* (किसी अन्य क्रिया के साथ) अतीत में उस क्रिया को किया करना : *I used to live in New Delhi.*

useful / 'यूस्फ़ुल् / *adj* 1 उपयोगी, लाभ–दायक : *a useful gadget/book/hint* 2 (अनौप) अच्छा, संतोषजनक ▸ **usefully** *adv* **usefulness** *noun.*

useless / 'यूस्लस् / *adj* 1 तुच्छ, बेकार : *All our efforts were useless.* 2 useless (doing sth/to do sth) कुशलता/योग्यता रहित : *I realized that it was useless to protest.* ▸ **uselessly** *adv* **uselessness** *noun.*

user / 'यूज़र / *noun* उपभोक्ता, वस्तु या सेवा को काम में लाने वाला : *users of public transport* ▸ **user-friendly** *adj* (मशीनों, पुस्तकों आदि के संदर्भ में) जिनका प्रयोग व्यक्ति सरलता से कर सके।

usher / 'अशर् / *noun* 1 प्रवेशक (वह व्यक्ति जो थिएटर, सिनेमा हॉल आदि में व्यक्ति को उसका स्थान बताता है) 2 कचहरी में लोगों को आने/जाने की अनुमति देने वाला कर्मचारी ▸ **usher** *verb* अंदर ले जाना, जगह पर पहुँचाना : *The girl ushered me along the aisle to my seat.*

usherette / अश्'रेट् / *noun* महिला प्र–वेशिका।

usual / 'यूश्अल् / *adj* सामान्य, साधारण; प्रथा के अनुसार : *make all the usual excuses ○ He wasn't his usual self. ○ When the accident happened, the usual crowd gathered.* ◾ **as usual** सामान्यतया ▸ **usually** *adv.*

usurp / यु'ज़र्प् / *verb* (औप) अधिकार या शक्ति हड़प लेना : *usurp the throne* ▸ **usurper** *noun.*

usury / 'यूशरि / *noun* (*अप्र*) सूदख़ोरी (ऊँचे ब्याज पर रुपया उठाना) ▸ **usurer** / 'यूशरर् / *noun* सूदख़ोर।

utensil / यू 'टेन्स्ल् / *noun* (घर के) बरतन-भाँडे : *cooking/kitchen utensils.*

utilitarian / यूटिलि'टेअरिअन् / *adj* प्रयोग के लिए (न कि विलास या सजावट के लिए): *The furniture throughout is plain and utilitarian.*

utility / यू'टिलटि / *noun* (*pl* **utilities**) 1 उपयोगिता : *the utility value of a dishwasher* 2 जनोपयोगी सेवाएँ जैसे पानी, बिजली, गैस आदि : *the administration of public utilities.*

utilize, -ise / 'यूटलाइज़् / *verb* (*औप*) उपयोग करना/प्रयोग में लाना : *utilize all available resources ∘ utilize solar power as a source of energy* ▸ **utilization, -isation** / यूटलाइ'ज़ेश्न् / *noun.*

utmost / 'अट्मोस्ट् / *adj* (**uttermost** भी) परम/चरम; सर्वाधिक : *of the utmost importance* ▸ **the utmost** (**uttermost** भी) *noun* भरसक : *My patience was tested to the uttermost.*

Utopia / यू 'टोपिआ / *noun* रामराज्य, (काल्पनिक) आदर्श समाज/राज्य।

utter[1] / 'अटर् / *adj* पूरा; निरा : *utter despair/nonsense/confusion* ▸ **utterly** *adv.*

utter[2] / 'अटर् / *verb* 1 उच्चारण करना, आवाज़ निकालना : *utter a sigh/a cry of pain* 2 कहना, बोलना : *He never uttered a word (of protest).* ▸ **utterance** *noun* (*औप*) 1 अभिव्यक्ति 2 कथन, उद्गार : *private/public utterances.*

U-turn / यू'टर्न् / *noun* 1 सड़क पर वाहन को ऐसे मोड़ना कि उसी दिशा में चलने लगे जिस दिशा से आया था 2 (*औप*) योजना या कार्यान्वयन में एकदम पलट कर विपरीत दिशा में गति।

Vv

vacancy / 'वेकन्सि / noun (pl **vacancies**) 1 ख़ाली जगह 2 **vacancy (for sb/ sth)** नौकरी के लिए ख़ाली पद।

vacant / 'वेकन्ट् / adj 1 ख़ाली, रिक्त : a vacant position 2 विचार या रुचि के किसी संकेत से विहीन : a vacant mind ▶ **vacantly** adv.

vacate / व'केट् / verb (औप) (मकान) ख़ाली करना; अपना स्थान/पद ख़ाली छोड़ना : vacate one's seat/hotel room.

vacation / व'केशन् / noun 1 (न्यायालय, विश्वविद्यालय या स्कूल में) लंबा अवकाश : the Christmas vacation 2 अवकाश की अवधि; छुट्टी।

vaccinate / 'वेक्सिनेट् / verb **vaccinate sb/sth (against sth)** (चेचक आदि का) टीका लगाना ▶ **vaccination** noun : have a polio vaccination.

vaccine / 'वैक्सीन् / noun टीके की दवाई।

vacuum / 'वेक्युअम् / noun 1 शून्य, ख़ाली जगह 2 (प्राय: sing) किसी व्यक्ति/ वस्तु की अनुपस्थिति से उत्पन्न रिक्तता ▶ **vacuum cleaner** noun सफ़ाई करने में प्रयुक्त विद्युत उपकरण जो धूल, मिट्टी आदि को खींच लेता है **vacuum flask** noun फ़्लास्क (ऐसी बोतल जिसमें ठंडी वस्तु ठंडी तथा गरम वस्तु गरम बनी रहती है)।

vagabond / 'वैगबॉन्ड् / noun (अप्र, प्राय: अपमा) आवारा, घुमक्कड़।

vagrant / 'वेग्रन्ट् / noun (औप या क़ानून) आवारा ▶ **vagrancy** / 'वेग्रन्सि / noun आवारगी।

vague / वेग् / adj (-r, -st) 1 अस्पष्ट, धुँधला : vague memories 2 (व्यक्ति या योजना) अनिश्चित : be vague about one's plans ▶ **vaguely** adv अस्पष्ट तौर से **vagueness** noun.

vain / वेन् / adj (-er, -est) 1 व्यर्थ, बेकार, निष्फल : a vain attempt 2 दंभी, घमंडी 3 (अप्र या अलं) ख़ाली, महत्त्वहीन : vain promises ■ **in vain** व्यर्थ; निष्फल ▶ **vainly** adv.

valentine / 'वैलन्टाइन् / 1 (**valentine card** भी) प्रेमी/प्रेमिका को सेंट वैलेंटाइन दिवस पर भेजा गया कार्ड 2 व्यक्ति जिसे ऐसा कार्ड भेजा गया हो : Will you be my valentine?

valet / 'वैले / noun ख़िदमतगार।

valiant / 'वैलिअन्ट् / adj (औप या साहि) शूरवीर : valiant warriors ▶ **valiantly** adv.

valid / 'वैलिड् / adj 1 (क़ानून) वैध, प्रभावकारी : a valid claim 2 (तर्क, कारण आदि) पक्के आधार पर, ठोस : raise valid objections to a plan 3 (समझौता आदि) क़ानूनी तौर पर माननीय : a valid passport ▶ **validity** / व'लिडटि / noun वैधता, विधिमान्यता **validly** adv.

valley / 'वैलि / noun घाटी (प्राय: जिसके बीच में से नदी बह रही हो)।

valour (US **valor**) / 'वैलर् / noun (औप या साहि) पराक्रम, बहादुरी : soldiers decorated for valour.

valuable / 'वैल्युअब्ल् / adj 1 बहुमूल्य, क़ीमती 2 अत्यंत उपयोगी या महत्त्वपूर्ण ▶ **valuables** noun [pl] बहुमूल्य वस्तुएँ (जैसे हीरे-जवाहरात)।

valuation / ,वैल्यु'एश्न् / noun किसी चीज़ का मूल्य या क़ीमत निर्धारित करने की क्रिया : property/land/stock valuation.

value / 'वैल्यू / noun 1 मूल्य, क़ीमत : rising property values 2 (गणित) मान, मूल्य : Find the value of x. 3 महत्त्व 4 **values** [pl] नैतिक मूल्य, आदर्श : social/cultural values ▶ **value** verb 1 **value sth (at sth)** क़ीमत निर्धारित करना 2 महत्त्व देना, सम्मान करना : value sb's advice.

valve / व़ैल्व़ / *noun* 1 (मशीन आदि का) वाल्व 2 हृदय का वाल्व।

vampire / व़ैम्पाइअर / *noun* खून चूसने वाला भूत; नरपिशाच।

van / व़ैन् / *noun* 1 व्यक्तियों या माल के परिवहन के लिए बंद मोटर गाड़ी : *a police van* 2 रेल का बंद माल डिब्बा : *the luggage van.*

vandal / व़ैन्ड्ल् / *noun* बर्बर; कलाकृतियों, सार्वजनिक संपत्ति आदि का ध्वंस करने वाला ▸ **vandalism** *noun* बर्बरता, विध्वंसक प्रवृत्ति/कार्य।

vane / व़ेन / *noun* 1 (प्राय: ऊँचे भवनों पर लगा हुआ) हवा की दिशा सूचित करने वाला तीर 2 पवन चक्की का फलक।

vanguard / व़ैन्गाई / *noun* 1 युद्ध में सेना की अग्रिम टुकड़ी 2 आंदोलन या फ़ैशन के अग्रणी, नेता : *in the vanguard of social change.*

vanilla / व़ 'निला / *noun* आइसक्रीम, मिठाई आदि में डाली जाने वाली एक प्रकार की सुगंधि : *vanilla ice-cream/essence.*

vanish / व़ैनिश् / *verb* 1 अचानक ग़ायब हो जाना, लुप्त हो जाना : *The thief vanished into the crowd.* 2 मिट जाना, शून्य हो जाना : *Our hopes of success have vanished.*

vanity / व़ैनटि / *noun* (*pl* **vanities**) 1 दंभ, मिथ्याभिमान 2 (औप) खोखलापन, असंतुष्टि : *the vanity of human ambitions.*

vanquish / व़ैङ्क्विश् / *verb* (औप) पराजित करना, हराना।

vapour (*US* **vapor**) / व़ेपर् / *noun* 1 भाप, वाष्प (द्रव या ठोस पदार्थ का गैस रूप) 2 कोहरा 3 बफ़ारा (जैसे गला ख़राब होने पर इलाज के रूप में) ▸ **vaporize, -ise** *verb* भाप/वाष्प में बदल देना।

variable / व़ेअरिअब्ल् / *adj* परिवर्तनीय; परिवर्तनशील : *variable pressure/rainfall/weather/speed.*

variance / व़ेअरिअन्स् / *noun* भिन्नता की सीमा ■ **at variance (with sb/sth)** असहमत होकर।

variant / व़ेअरिअन्ट / *noun* भिन्न या वैकल्पिक रूप : *The story has many variants.* ▸ **variant** *adj* वैकल्पिक या भिन्न।

variation / व़ेअरि 'ऐश्न् / *noun* भिन्नता/ परिवर्तन की मात्रा।

varied / व़ेअरिड / *adj* 1 विभिन्न प्रकार के : *varied opinions* 2 निरंतर या प्राय: परिवर्तनशील : *lead a full and varied life.*

variety / व़ 'राइअटि / *noun* (*pl* **varieties**) 1 विविधता : *offer/show/lack variety* 2 [*sing*] **variety (of sth)** (विभिन्न वस्तुओं का) संग्रह : *a wide variety of patterns to choose from* 3 **variety (of sth)** वस्तुओं की वह श्रेणी जो उसी प्रकार की अन्य सामान्य श्रेणी की वस्तुओं से भिन्न हो : *different varieties of orchids.*

various / व़ेअरिअस् / *adj* 1 विभिन्न, विविध 2 अनेक, कई : *for various reasons.*

varnish / व़ार्निश् / *noun* वार्निश ▸ **varnish** *verb* वार्निश करना।

vary / व़ेअरि / *verb* (*pt, pp* **varied**) 1 **vary (in sth)** आकार, आयतन या शक्ति में भिन्न होना : *These fish vary in weight from 1 kg to 2 kg.* ○ *Opinions vary widely on this point.* 2 **vary (with sth); vary (from sth to sth)** परिवर्तित होना या करना : *Prices vary with the seasons.*

vase / व़ाज़् / *noun* शीशे या चीनी मिट्टी का पुष्प-पात्र (गुलदान)।

Vaseline / व़ैसलीन् / *noun* (ट्रेडमार्क) एक गाढ़ा, हलके पीले रंग का पदार्थ, जो होठों आदि पर क्रीम की तरह लगाया जाता है; पेट्रोलियम जेली।

vassal / व़ैस्ल् / *noun* 1 (पूर्व में)

जागीरदार 2 दूसरे पर निर्भर व्यक्ति या देश : *vassal states.*

vast / व्रास्ट्; US व्रैस्ट् / *adj* 1 विशाल, विस्तृत : *a vast expanse of desert* 2 (अनौप) बहुत अधिक/बड़ा, व्यापक : *make a vast difference.*

vat / व्रैट् / *noun* टंकी; द्रव रखने के लिए प्रयुक्त एक विशाल पात्र : *distilling vats.*

vault¹ / व्रॉल्ट् / *noun* 1 मेहराबी छत 2 (शराब आदि रखने के लिए) तहख़ाना : *wine-vaults* 3 बैंक आदि में बहुमूल्य वस्तु सुरक्षित रखने के लिए कमरा 4 शव-कक्ष ▶ **vaulted** *adj* मेहराबदार : *a vaulted roof.*

vault² / व्रॉल्ट् / *verb* **vault (over sth)** लग्गे (पोल) के सहारे छलांग भरना, लाँघ-ना : *vault (over) a fence* ▶ **vault** *noun* ऐसी छलांग।

veer / व्रिअर् / *verb* 1 दिशा बदलना : *The plane veered wildly.* 2 (बातचीत या मत का) रुख़ बदलना : *Her mood veered between shame and anger.*

vegetable / 'व्रेज्टब्ल् / *noun* सब्ज़ी, तरकारी–भाजी।

vegetarian / ˌव्रेज्'टेअरिअन् / *noun* शाकाहारी (मांस आदि न खाने वाला) : *a vegetarian meal.*

vegetation / ˌव्रेज्'टेश्न् / *noun* सभी प्रकार के पौधे, वनस्पति; क्षेत्र विशेष में उगने वाले पौधे : *the luxuriant vegetation of tropical rain forests.*

vehement / 'व्रीअमन्ट् / *adj* (भावना, व्यक्ति) प्रचंड, उग्र : *a vehement protest* ▶ **vehemence** / 'व्रीअमन्स् / *noun.*

vehicle / 'व्रीअकुल्; US 'व्रीहिकुल् / *noun* 1 (विशेषत: औप) वाहन (व्यक्तियों या सामान वहन करने के लिए प्रयुक्त गाड़ी) 2 **vehicle (for sth)** अभिव्यक्ति का माध्यम : *Art may be used as a vehicle for propaganda.* ▶ **vehicular** *adj.*

veil / व्रेल् / *noun* 1 परदा, घूँघट 2 [*sing*]

आवरण, परदा : *a veil of mist over the hills* ■ **take the veil** नन बनना ▶ **veil** *verb* घूँघट काढ़ना; छिपना/छिपाना : *She veiled her eyes with her hand.*

vein / व्रेन् / *noun* 1 शिरा (दिल में ख़ून वापस ले जाने वाली नस) 2 पत्तों, कीटों के पंखों आदि की नसें 3 चट्टानी पत्थर में रग जैसे निशान 4 **vein (of sth)** स्पष्ट लक्षण या गुण : *have a vein of melancholy in one's character* 5 तबीयत, मनोदशा : *in lighter/more serious vein.*

velocity / व्र'लॉसटि / *noun* (*pl* **velocities**) (तक) वेग : *the velocity of light.*

velvet / 'व्रेल्व्रिट् / *noun* मख़मल ▶ **velvety** *adj* मख़मली : *a horse's velvety nose.*

vendetta / व्रेन्'डेडा / *noun* 1 एक व्यक्ति द्वारा दूसरे के प्रति की जाने वाली हानिकारक या आक्रमक कारखाई 2 दो परिवारों के बीच वैमनस्य, कुलबैर।

vendor / 'व्रेन्डर् / *noun* 1 छोटा दुकान-दार, जो प्राय: खुले में दुकान लगाकर वस्तुएँ बेचता है 2 (क़ानून) संपत्ति बेचने वाला।

veneer / व्र'निअर् / *noun* 1 मामूली लकड़ी के फ़र्नीचर पर बढ़िया लकड़ी की ऊपरी चिपकी परत : *maple/walnut veneer* 2 [*sing*] **veneer (of sth)** (प्राय: अपमा) असली स्वभाव को ढकने वाला ऊपरी नम्रतापूर्ण आचरण ▶ **veneer** *verb* **veneer sth (with sth)** ऊपरी परत चढ़ाना।

venerable / 'व्रेनरब्ल् / *adj* 1 (औप) पूजनीय, श्रद्धेय : *a venerable scholar* 2 पूजनीय व्यक्ति को प्रदत्त पदवी/उपाधि।

venerate / 'व्रेनरेट् / *verb* **venerate sb/sth (as sth)** (औप) समादर करना, श्रद्धा करना ▶ **veneration** *noun* श्रद्धा।

vengeance / 'व्रेन्जन्स् / *noun* **vengeance (on/upon sb)** प्रतिशोध, बदला : *take/seek/wreak vengeance for the bombing* ■ **with a vengeance** (अनौप) अपेक्षा से अधिक मात्रा के साथ।

venom / 'वेनम् / noun 1 (सर्प आदि का) विष 2 द्वेष, घृणा : There was anger and venom in her voice. ▸ **venomous** adj विषैला; विद्वेषपूर्ण।

vent / वेन्ट् / noun निकास : air/heating vents ■ **give (full) vent to sth** मुक्त अभिव्यक्ति करना ▸ **vent** verb **vent sth (on sb)** दबी भावनाओं की अभिव्यक्ति।

ventilate / 'वेन्टिलेट् / verb 1 हवा को मुक्त रूप से आने-जाने देना 2 (औप) (किसी प्रश्न पर) खुले आम चर्चा करना : These issues have been well ventilated in the press. ▸ **ventilation** noun **ventilator** noun रोशनदान, वातायन।

venture / 'वेन्चर् / noun साहसिक कार्य, जोखिम का काम : embark on a new venture ▸ **venture** verb (औप) जोखिम उठाना; साहस करना : venture into the water **venturesome** adj (औप) साहसिक, निडर : young children becoming more venturesome in their use of language.

venue / 'वेन्यू / noun जिस स्थान पर लोग एकत्र होते हैं, विशेषत: किसी खेल प्रतियोगिता, संगीत-समारोह आदि के लिए : a last-minute change of venue.

Venus / 'वीनस् / noun शुक्र ग्रह।

veracity / व 'रैसटि / noun (औप) सच्चाई : I don't doubt the veracity of your story.

veranda (verandah भी) / व 'रैन्डा / noun बरामदा, दालान।

verb / वर्ब् / noun (व्या) क्रिया, जैसे bring, happen, exist.

verbal / 'वर्ब्ल् / adj 1 शाब्दिक, शब्द-संबंधी : verbal skills 2 मौखिक (न कि लिखित) : a verbal explanation/agreement/reminder 3 (व्या) क्रिया-संबंधी ▸ **verbal noun (gerund भी)** noun (व्या) क्रियार्थक संज्ञा, -ing से बनी

संज्ञा, जैसे swimming वाक्य 'Swimming is a good form of exercise.' में।

verbatim / वर् 'बेटिम् / adj, adv शब्दश: एक-एक शब्द जैसे बोला या लिखा गया था : a verbatim report.

verdant / 'वर्डन्ट् / adj (औप या साहि) (मैदान, खेत, घास आदि) हरा-भरा।

verdict / 'वर्डिक्ट् / noun 1 (न्यायालय द्वारा दिया गया) निर्णय 2 **verdict (on sth/sb)** (परीक्षण के बाद दी गई) राय : The coroner recorded a verdict of accidental death.

verge / वर्ज / noun सड़क के किनारे की ज़मीन; रास्ते के छोर पर घास की पट्टी ■ **on/to the verge of sth/doing sth** कर्ता द्वारा किसी क्रिया को बस शुरू कर ही देना/ करने ही लगना; कोई घटना जो बस होने ही वाली हो : on the verge of war/success/bankruptcy ▸ **verge** verb ■ **verge on/upon sth** समीप होना।

verify / 'वेरिफ़ाइ / verb (pt, pp **verified**) 1 परीक्षण द्वारा कथन की यथार्थता या तथ्य की सत्यता जाँचना : verify statements/allegations/facts 2 पूर्वकथित सच्चाई किसी घटना आदि से प्रदर्शित करना ▸ **verification** / ‚वेरिफ़ि'केश्न् / noun जाँच, सत्यापन।

vermilion / वर् 'मिलिअन् / noun सिंदूर ▸ **vermilion** adj सिंदूरी।

vermin / 'वर्मिन् / noun 1 पौधों और पशु-पक्षियों को हानि पहुँचाने वाले जीव : Rats, foxes, moles and rabbits are usually treated as vermin. 2 कीड़े-मकोड़े।

vernacular / वर् 'नैक्यलर् / noun (प्राय: **the vernacular**) 1 देशी बोली 2 देशी स्थापत्य कला ▸ **vernacular** adj देश या जनपद की (भाषा आदि) : vernacular idioms/buildings.

versatile / 'वर्सटाइल् / adj सर्वतोमुखी प्रतिभा वाला : a versatile mind ▸ **versatility** / ‚वर्स'टिलिटि / noun.

verse / वर्स् / noun 1 पद्य (न कि गद्य)
कविता, छंदबद्ध करना : *Most of the play
is written in verse, but some of it is
in prose.* 2 पद, श्लोक।

versed / वर्स्ड् / adj versed in sth में
अनुभवी, अच्छा जानकार : *well versed in
the art of cooking.*

version / वर्शन्; वर्श़न् / noun 1 किसी
घटना का विवरण, बयान या वृत्तांत (किसी
एक व्यक्ति के दृष्टि से) : *There were
contradictory versions of what actually happened.* 2 ऐसी प्रति जो मूल
प्रति से थोड़ी अलग हो : *the deluxe
version of a car.*

versus / वर्सस् / prep (संक्षि v, vs)
(खेल या क़ानून में) प्रति, विरुद्ध; बनाम :
India versus Australia.

vertebra / वर्टिब्रा / noun (pl vertebrae / वर्टिब्री / रीढ़ की हड्डी का एक-
एक अंश : *the cervical vertebrae*
▶ **vertebrate** / वर्टिब्रट् / noun, adj
(जीव) रीढ़ की हड्डी वाला : *Mammals,
birds, reptiles, amphibians and
fishes are vertebrates.*

vertical / वर्टिकल् / adj (रेखा, स्तंभ
आदि) खड़ा, सीधा : *the vertical axis of
a graph* ▶ **vertical** noun **vertically** adv.

vertigo / वर्टिगो / noun चक्कर आने का
अनुभव, विशेषत: बहुत ऊँचाई से नीचे देखने
पर।

very[1] / वेरि / adv 1 अत्यधिक, बड़ी मात्रा
में : *very small/hot/useful* 2 पूर्ण अर्थ
में : *the very best quality.*

very[2] / वेरि / adj 1 वही (न कि कोई और):
This is the very book I want.
2 बिलकुल छोर पर : *at the very begin-
ning/end.*

vessel / वेस्ल् / noun 1 (औप) जहाज़
या बड़ी नाव : *cargo vessels* 2 (औप)
(द्रव का) पात्र, जैसे प्याला, कटोरा, बोतल
आदि 3 शरीर में नलिकाकार रचना : *blood
vessels.*

vest / वेस्ट् / noun 1 बनियान आदि 2 शरीर
के ऊपरी भाग को ढकने वाला वस्त्र-
विशेष : *a bullet-proof vest.*

vested interest / वेस्टिड् इन्ट्रस्ट् /
noun निहित स्वार्थ।

vestige / वेस्टिज् / noun 1 अवशेष,
निशानी : *the last vestiges of the old
colonial regime* 2 अत्यल्प मात्रा ▶ **ves-
tigial** adj.

vet[1] / वेट् / noun (औप **veterinary
surgeon** भी) पशुचिकित्सक।

vet[2] / वेट् / verb (-tt-) जाँच करना, गहराई
और सूक्ष्मता से देखना : *All new staff are
carefully vetted for security reasons.*

veteran / वेटरन् / noun 1 (व्यक्ति)
अनुभवी, दक्ष (विशेषत: सैनिक) : *war
veterans* 2 सेना का भूतपूर्व सदस्य।

veterinary / वेट्रनरि / adj पशुओं के रोगों
से संबद्ध : *veterinary medicine/stud-
ies* ▶ **veterinary surgeon** noun
(औप) पशुचिकित्सक।

veto / वीटो / noun (pl **vetoes**) veto
(on sth) 1 किसी वस्तु को रोकने का
अधिकार, निषेधाधिकार : *use the presidential veto* 2 निषेध, मनाही ▶ **veto**
verb (pres p **vetoing**) निषेधाधिकार
प्रयोग करना; मना करना।

vex / वेक्स् / verb (अप्र या औप) चिढ़ाना,
खिजाना ▶ **vexation** / वेक्'सेशन् / noun
(अप्र या औप) खीज, परेशानी : *life's
little vexations* **vexatious** adj.

via / वाइआ / prep (लैटिन) के रास्ते : *go
from London to Washington via
New York.*

viable / वाइअब्ल् / adj (कार्य) जो संभव
हो : *a viable plant proposition.*

viaduct / वाइअडक्ट् / noun सड़क या
रेल का नीची भूमि पर या घाटी के बीच बना
पुल।

vibrant / वाइब्रन्ट् / adj 1 जीवंत और
उत्साहपूर्ण : *a vibrant atmosphere*

2 (विशेषत: रंगों के लिए प्रयुक्त) चमकीले और आकर्षक।

vibrate / व़ाइ'ब्रेट / *verb* **1** दोलन करना, दोलायमान होना **2** कँपाना, काँपना; कंपन करना : *The strings of a piano vibrate when the keys are struck.*
▶ **vibration** / व़ाइ'ब्रेश्न् / *noun* कंपन; दोलन।

vicar / व़िकर् / *noun* (इंग्लैंड के चर्च में) पादरी।

vice¹ / व़ाइस् / *noun* **1** पापाचार, व्यसन : *Greed is a terrible vice.* **2** (अनौप) बुरी आदत, ख़राबी **3** विशेष आपराधिक व्यवहार।

vice² / व़ाइस् / *noun* शिकंजा (बढ़ई आदि द्वारा प्रयुक्त)।

vice- *pref* **1** दूसरे के स्थान पर कार्य करने वाला; उप-/सहायक- : *vice-president* **2** पद में ठीक उससे नीचे : *vice admiral.*

vice versa / व़ाइस् व़र्सा / *adv* (लैटिन) इसका विपरीत भी सत्य है, यह दर्शाने के लिए प्रयुक्त: *We help them and vice versa.*

vicinity / व़'सिनटि / *noun* the vicinity (of sth) समीपता; आस-पास का क्षेत्र; पास-पड़ोस : *There's no hospital in the immediate vicinity.*

vicious / व़िशस् / *adj* **1** कटु, द्वेषपूर्ण : *a vicious assault* **2** (जानवर) ख़तरनाक : *a vicious dog* **3** (औप) दूषित; पापमय; भ्रष्ट ■ **a vicious circle** ऐसी स्थिति कि जिसमें एक समस्या से दूसरी का जन्म होता है और दूसरी समस्या पहले की स्थिति को और ख़राब कर देती है।

victim / व़िक्टिम् / *noun* **1** शिकार **2** पीड़ित/ सताया हुआ व्यक्ति : *the victim of a hoax* **3** बली (पशु) : *a sacrificial victim.*

victimize, -ise / व़िक्टिमाइज़् / *verb* **victimize sb (for sth)** सताना, दंडित करना।

victor / व़िक्टर् / *noun* (औप) विजेता।

Victorian / व़िक'टॉरिअन् / *adj* ब्रिटिश रानी विक्टोरिया (1837-1901) के समय का, पुराने ढंग का : *Victorian novels/ poets/houses.*

victory / व़िक्टरि / *noun* (*pl* **victories**) विजय, सफलता : *celebrate victory*
▶ **victorious** / व़िक्'टॉरिअस् / *adj* **victorious (in sth); victorious (over sb/sth)** विजयी।

victuals / व़िट्ल्ज़् / *noun* [*pl*] (अप्र) खाद्य-सामग्री।

video / व़िडिओ / *noun* **1** चित्रमुद्रण **2** वीडियो कैसट/टेप/फ़िल्म, वीडियो कैसट रिकार्डर (VCR) ▶ **video** *verb* प्रसारण हेतु दृश्य चित्रण करना।

view¹ / व्यू / *noun* **1** दृष्टि, नज़र : *The lake came into view.* **2** दृश्य (विशेषत: प्राकृतिक दृश्य) : *a room with a view of the sea* **3** (विशेषत: *pl*) **view (about/on sth)** राय, मत, विचार ■ **a bird's-eye view (of sth)** बहुत ऊपर से (जैसे आसमान से) नीचे का दृश्य **in full view (of sb/sth)** सब के/किसी चीज़ के सामने **in view of sth** ध्यान में रखते हुए **on view** प्रदर्शित **with a view to doing sth** (औप) के उद्देश्य से, के विचार से।

view² / व्यू / *verb* (औप) **1** विचार करना, समझना : *How do you view your chances of success?* **2** देखना; निहारना
▶ **viewer** / व्यूअर् / *noun* दर्शक : *suitable for adult/younger viewers.*

vigil / व़िजिल् / *noun* निगरानी या प्रार्थना के लिए जागते रहने की अवधि : *hold a candlelight vigil for peace.*

vigilant / व़िजिलन्ट् / *adj* (औप) सतर्क, सावधान ▶ **vigilance** *noun* सतर्कता, चौकसी : *police vigilance.*

vigour (*US* **vigor**) / व़िगर् / *noun* **1** बल, उत्साह : *feeling full of vigour* **2** भाषा, विचार आदि में ओज/तेज़ ▶ **vigorous** *adj* हष्ट-पुष्ट; कर्मठ (व्यक्ति); सशक्त, ज़ोरदार (प्रयत्न, भाषा आदि)।

vile / व़ाइल / adj (-r, -st) 1 बहुत घटिया, एकदम रद्दी : a vile smell/taste ○ use vile language 2 कमीना, नीच : Bribery is a vile practice.

villa / 'व़िला / noun 1 शहर के बाहर उपवन वाला मकान 2 बड़े बग़ीचे वाला देहात में मकान (विशेषत: दक्षिण युरोप में)।

village / 'व़िलिज़ / noun 1 गाँव : We visited towns and villages all over India. 2 समुदाय के रूप में ग्रामवासी : The whole village is in a festive mood. ▶ **villager** noun ग्रामवासी।

villain / 'व़िलन / noun 1 दुर्जन, दुष्ट व्यक्ति 2 (फ़िल्म, नाटक आदि में) खलनायक : a tragic villain ▶ **villainous** adj दुष्टतापूर्ण; दुष्ट **villainy** noun (औप) दुष्टता, बदमाशी।

vindictive / व़िन्'डिक्टिव़् / adj क्षमा न करने वाला; प्रतिशोध का भाव रखने वाला : a vindictive person ▶ **vindictively** adv.

vine / व़ाइन् / noun अंगूर की बेल।

vinegar / 'व़िनिगर् / noun सिरका।

vineyard / 'व़िन्यई / noun अंगूर का बाग़।

violate / 'व़ाइअलेट् / verb 1 उल्लंघन करना : violate international law 2 तिरस्कार या उपेक्षा करना; धार्मिक स्थान में सेंध लगाकर घुसना : violate a shrine 3 (औप) बलात्कार करना ▶ **violation** noun.

violent / 'व़ाइअलन्ट् / adj 1 ज़बरदस्त हिंसापूर्ण : a violent assault 2 उग्र, प्रचंड : fly into a violent rage 3 अत्यधिक प्रचंड/तीक्ष्ण : violent winds/storms ○ violent toothache ▶ **violence** / 'व़ाइअलन्स् / noun हिंसा; प्रचंड शक्ति **violently** adv.

violet / 'व़ाइअलट् / noun 1 एक छोटा जंगली पौधा 2 बैंगनी रंग ▶ **violet** adj बैंगनी रंग का।

violin / व़ाइअ'लिन् / noun वायलिन, बेला ▶ **violinist** noun बेलावादक।

VIP / व़ी आई 'पी / noun (औप) (very important person का संक्षिप्त रूप) प्रतिष्ठा या प्रभाव की दृष्टि से अत्यंत महत्त्वपूर्ण व्यक्ति।

viper / 'व़ाइपर् / noun एक छोटा विषैला साँप।

virgin / 'व़र्जिन् / noun 1 कुमारी 2 the (Blessed) Virgin [sing] ईसा की माता, मेरी ▶ **virgin** adj 1 शुद्ध और अछूता : virgin olive oil 2 अप्रयुक्त, न भोगी हुई वस्तु : virgin soil/forest ▶ **virginity** noun.

Virgo / 'व़र्गो / noun कन्या राशि; इस राशि का व्यक्ति।

virile / 'व़िराइल् / adj 1 (पुरुष) सशक्त, बलशाली : virile young males 2 मर्दाना, पुरुषोचित : virile sports/games ▶ **virility** noun.

virtual / 'व़र्चुअल् / adj क़रीब-क़रीब, लगभग वैसा ही जैसा वर्णित परंतु पूर्णत: नहीं : He's become a virtual recluse since his wife died. ▶ **virtually** adv.

virtue / 'व़र्चू / noun 1 सद्गुण : lead a life of virtue 2 लाभ, आकर्षक गुण : The plan has the great virtue of being flexible. ■ **by virtue of sth** किसी के आधार पर, के कारण ▶ **virtuous** adj गुणवान, सद्गुणी : virtuous behaviour.

virulent / 'व़िरलन्ट् / adj 1 (बीमारी या विष) बहुत तेज़/हानिप्रद : a virulent form of flu 2 (औप) कटु, द्वेषपूर्ण : virulent criticism ▶ **virulence** noun.

virus / 'व़ाइरस् / noun 1 वाइरस, विषाणु जिनसे कई छूत के रोग होते हैं : the flu/AIDS virus 2 कंप्यूटर प्रोग्राम में गुप्त संकेत जिससे एकत्रित सूचना नष्ट हो जाती है (कंप्यूटर रोग)।

visa / 'व़ीज़ा / noun वीज़ा, देश में आने या जाने की अनुमति।

vis-à-vis / व्रीज़ आ 'वी / *prep* (फ़्रेंच) 1 के संबंध में। 2 की तुलना में।

visible / 'व्रिज़बल् / *adj* visible (to sb/ sth) 1 दृष्टिगोचर : *This star is not visible to the naked eye.* 2 प्रत्यक्ष, स्पष्ट : *visible improvements/ changes* ▸ **visibility** / ,व्रिज़ 'बिलटि / *noun* 1 दृष्टिगोचर होने की स्थिति : *companies trying to increase their visibility* 2 जितनी दूर तक साफ़-साफ़ देखा जा सके और जो दृष्टि मौसम आदि के हालात पर निर्भर हो : *Planes were grounded because of poor/low/ bad visibility.*

vision / 'व्रिश्न् / *noun* 1 दृष्टि; कल्पना-शक्ति : *a statesman of (great breadth of) vision* 2 स्वप्न या उस जैसा ही अलौकिक अनुभव : *Jesus came to Paul in a vision.* 3 भविष्य के बारे में कल्पना की गई योजना/दृष्टि : *an economic vision.*

visionary / 'व्रिश्नरि / *adj* 1 भविष्य के बारे में गहरी सोच-विचार का सामर्थ्य रखने वाला : *visionary leaders* 2 स्वप्नदर्शी; द्रष्टा : *visionary poetry.*

visit / 'व्रिज़िट् / *verb* 1 किसी व्यक्ति से मिलने जाना; किसी स्थान पर सैर करने के लिए जाना : *visit friends/relatives* 2 किसी स्थान पर अस्थायी रूप से ठहरना; किसी व्यक्ति के पास ठहरना ▸ **visit** *noun* visit (to sb/sth) (from sb/sth) मिलने की क्रिया; मिलने का समय : *pay a visit to a friend/doctor.*

visitor / 'व्रिज़िटर् / *noun* (visitor to sb/ sth) मुलाकाती; पर्यटक : *Rome welcomes millions of visitors each year.*

visor / 'व्राइज़र् / *noun* आँखों को चोट से बचाने वाला या चेहरा ढकने वाला हेल्मेट का भाग।

vista / 'व्रिस्टा / *noun* (औप) 1 दूर का खूबसूरत दृश्य 2 (अलं) सिंहावलोकन : *This discovery opens up new vistas of research for scientists.*

visual / 'व्रिश़्अल् / *adj* दृष्टि-संबंधी : *visual images* ▸ **visualize, -ise** / 'व्रिश़्अलाइज़् / *verb* मन में स्पष्ट रूप से देखना।

vital / 'व्राइट्ल् / *adj* 1 vital (to/for sth) सर्वोच्च, उच्चतम : *vital information* 2 जीवन के लिए आवश्यक : *vital bodily functions* ▸ **vitally** *adv.*

vitality / व्राइ'टैलटि / *noun* जीवन-शक्ति; तेजस्विता : *She is bursting with vitality and new ideas.*

vitamin / 'व्रिटेमिन् / *noun* विटामिन, स्वास्थ्य के लिए आवश्यक पदार्थ।

vitiate / 'व्रिशिएट् / *verb* (औप) 1 दूषित या विकृत कर देना 2 बल क्षीण कर देना।

vivacious / व्रि'वेशस् / *adj* सजीव, ज़िंदा-दिल : *a vivacious laugh* ▸ **vivacity** / व्रि'वैसटि / *noun.*

viva voce / व्राइवा 'वोचि / *noun* मौखिक परीक्षा।

vivid / 'व्रिव्रिड् / *adj* 1 (प्रकाश या रंग) चमकीला, चटकीला 2 (चित्रण, वर्णन) स्पष्ट और जीवंत : *a vivid description* 3 आसानी से विचार, छवि उत्पन्न करने वाला : *a vivid imagination* ▸ **vividly** *adv* **vividness** *noun.*

vixen / 'व्रिक्स्न् / *noun* मादा लोमड़ी।

viz / व्रिज़् / *abbr* (लैटिन videlicet, प्रायः इसे **namely** पढ़ते हैं) अर्थात्, यानी; दूसरे शब्दों में : *I shall confine my remarks to a certain class of creative persons, viz authors.*

vocabulary / व्र 'कैब्यलरि / *noun* 1 शब्दावली, शब्द समूह 2 (व्यक्ति, किताब आदि का) शब्दभंडार : *a rich vocabulary.*

vocal / 'व्रोक्ल् / *adj* 1 मौखिक; वाचिक : *vocal cords* 2 मुखरित; अभिव्यक्ति में सशक्त एवं बेबाक : *He is a very vocal critic of the govern-*

ment's transport policy. ▸ **vocalist** *noun* गायक।

vocation / वो'केश्न् / *noun* vocation (for/to sth) स्वप्रेरणा से चुना योग्यतानुसार पेशा : *Nursing is a vocation as well as a profession.* ▸ **vocational** *adj.*

vodka / वॉड्का /*noun* वोदका, रूसी शराब।

vogue / वोग् / *noun* vogue (for sth) फ़ैशन, लोकप्रिय प्रचलन : *a vogue for unusual pets.*

voice / वॉइस् / *noun* 1 वाणी, बोलते या गाते समय निकली ध्वनि : *Keep your voice down.* 2 voice (in sth) बोलने का अधिकार, राय : *The workers want a voice in the decision-making process.* ▸ **voice** *verb* भावनाओं को शब्दों में व्यक्त करना : *nervous about voicing their opinions.*

void / वाइड् / *adj (औप)* 1 ख़ाली 2 void (of sth) अभाव में, बिना : *Her face was void of all interest.* 3 *(क़ानून)* (समझौता आदि) अमान्य, अवैध : *The agreement was declared void.*

volatile /'वॉल्टाइल्/ *adj* 1 *(तक)* वाष्पशील, ऐसा द्रव जो सहज में ही गैस या वाष्प बन जाए 2 *(विशेषत: अपमा)* चंचल, चुलबुला *(व्यक्ति)*; तेज़ी से बदलने वाली *(स्थिति)*: *a volatile political situation.*

volcano / वॉल्'केनो / *noun (pl* volcanoes) ज्वालामुखी ▸ **volcanic** *adj* ज्वालामुखी-सदृश; ज्वालामुखी जनित : *a volcanic island.*

volition / व'लिश्न् / *noun (औप)* इच्छा शक्ति, संकल्प शक्ति।

volley / 'वॉलि / *noun* 1 पत्थरों, तीरों, गोलियों आदि की बौछार 2 *(अलं)* सवालों, टिप्पणियों की झड़ी : *a volley of abuse/ insults.*

volt / वोल्ट् / *noun (संक्षि V)* विद्युत बल

की इकाई, वोल्ट ▸ **voltage** / वोल्टिज़् / *noun* वोल्टेज : *high/low voltage.*

volte-face / वॉल्ट् 'फ़ास् / *noun (प्राय: sing) (औप) (फ्रेंच)* विचार, मत, दृष्टिकोण, नीति में पूर्ण रूप से बदलाव; कायापलट।

voluble / 'वॉल्युब्ल् / *adj (औप)* बातूनी; अधिक बोलने वाला/अधिक शब्दों में व्यक्त : *voluble protests* ▸ **volubly** *adv.*

volume / 'वॉल्यूम् / *noun* 1 कई खंडों वाली पुस्तक का एक खंड : *an encyclopedia in 20 volumes* 2 आयतन (ठोस, द्रव्य या गैस द्वारा घेरा स्थान) 3 ढेर, राशि : *the sheer volume of work* 4 *(ध्वनि की)* प्रबलता।

voluntary / 'वॉलन्ट्रि / *adj* 1 स्वैच्छिक : *Attendance is purely voluntary.* 2 स्वयंसेवा, बिना पैसा लिए किया गया *(कार्य)* : *fund-raising by voluntary groups* 3 *(शरीर क्रिया)* इच्छा से नियंत्रित : *voluntary muscles* ▸ **voluntarily** *adv.*

volunteer / वॉलन 'टिअर / *noun* 1 स्वयंसेवक : *Few volunteers came forward.* 2 स्वयंसेवक सैनिक : *volunteer troops* ▸ **volunteer** *verb* 1 volunteer (to do sth); volunteer (sth) (for sth) स्वयंसेवक के रूप में आगे आना; सेवाएँ समर्पित करना 2 बिना पूछे सुझाव पेश करना : *volunteer advice* 3 volunteer (for sth) स्वयंसेवक सैनिक बनना : *volunteer for military service.*

vomit /'वॉमिट् / *verb* vomit sth (up) 1 उलटी करना, वमन करना 2 *(अलं)* बड़ी मात्रा में बाहर निकालना : *factory chimneys vomiting forth black smoke* ▸ **vomit** *noun* उलटी, वमन।

voracious / व'रेशस् / *adj* 1 खाऊ, पेटू : *a voracious eater* 2 जानकारी की तीव्र इच्छा वाला; ज्ञानपिपासु : *a voracious reader.*

vote / व़ोट् / *noun* **1 vote (for/against
sb/sth)** मतदान **2 the vote** [*sing*]
(विशेषतया राजनीतिक दलों द्वारा) चुनावों में
प्राप्त वोट : *attempts to win the teenage vote* **3 the vote** [*sing*] मताधिकार
▸ **vote** *verb* **1 vote (for/against sb/
sth); vote (on sth)** पक्ष या विरोध में
मतदान करना **2** वोट/मतदान द्वारा चुनना या
समर्थन करना : *I was voted chairman.*
voter *noun* मतदाता **voting** *noun*
मतदान।

vouch / व़ाउच् / *verb* ■ **vouch for sb/
sth** (किसी का) ज़िम्मा लेना; ईमानदारी का
आश्वासन देना; निश्चित और दृढ़तापूर्वक
कहना : *I can vouch for him.*

voucher / 'व़ाउचर् / *noun* ख़र्च का पुरज़ा,
ख़र्च का प्रमाण-पत्र।

vouchsafe / व़ाउच्'सेफ़् / *verb* **vouchsafe sth (to sb)** (*अप्र या औप*) कृपापूर्वक
देना या कुछ कार्य करना : *He vouchsafed
to me certain family secrets.*

vow / व़ाउ / *noun* प्रतिज्ञा, वादा : *keep
one's marriage vows* ▸ **vow** *verb*
व्रत लेना : *They vowed revenge.*

vowel / 'व़ाउअल् / *noun* स्वर (अ, आ, इ,
ई, आदि)।

voyage / 'व़ॉइइज् / *noun* लंबी, अधिक
समय लेने वाली यात्रा जैसे समुद्री या अंतरिक्ष
यात्रा ▸ **voyage** *verb* (*औप*) लंबी यात्रा
करना : *voyaging across the Indian
Ocean* **voyager** / 'व़ॉइइजर् / सामान्यतया
खोज यात्री।

vulgar / 'व़ल्गर् / *adj* **1** असभ्य, गँवार :
a vulgar display of wealth **2** भद्दा,
अश्लील : *a vulgar joke* ▸ **vulgarity**
/ व़ल्'गैरटि / *noun* अभद्रता; कुरुचि।

vulnerable / 'व़ल्नरब्ल् / *adj* **vulnerable (to sth/sb)** असुरक्षित, जिसे आसानी
से चोट पहुँचाई जा सके/घायल किया जा
सके : *be vulnerable to blackmail*
▸ **vulnerability** *noun*.

vulture / 'व़ल्चर् / *noun* **1** गिद्ध **2** दूसरों
की मुसीबतों से लाभ उठाने वाला
(व्यक्ति)।

Ww

wad / वॉड् / noun 1 गद्दी; छेद भरने के लिए प्रयुक्त मुलायम वस्तु : *a wad of cotton wool* 2 (नोटों की) गड्डी ▸ **wad** verb गद्दीदार तह लगाना; मोटा अस्तर लगाना।

wadding / वॉडिङ् / noun पैकिंग के लिए प्रयुक्त रूई आदि।

wade / वेड् / verb 1 **wade (across/ through) (sth)** पानी को पैदल पार करना; (अलं) कठिनाई से कार्य करना 2 (US) पानी में खेलना : *children wading in the pool.*

wafer / वेफ़र् / noun कुरकुरे-मिठास लिए बिस्कुट जैसे पतले खाद्य पदार्थ; वेफ़र।

waft / वॉफ़्ट्; US वैफ़्ट् / verb हवा में उड़ा ले जाना/बिखेरना : *Delicious smells wafted up from the kitchen.*

wag / वैग् / verb (-gg-) अग़ल-बग़ल या ऊपर-नीचे हिलाना : *The dog wagged its tail.* ▸ **wag** noun इस प्रकार की गति।

wage¹ / वेज् / noun (प्राय: pl) मज़दूरी, वेतन : *Wages are paid on Fridays.*

wage² / वेज् / verb **wage sth (against/ on sth)** (युद्ध, आंदोलन आदि) छेड़ना।

wager / वेजर् / verb (अप्र या औप) **wager on sth** शर्त बदना; **wager (sth) (on sth)** दाँव लगाना : *wager Rs 1,000 (on a horse).*

wagon (waggon भी) / वैगन् / noun 1 वैगन, मालगाड़ी का खुला डिब्बा 2 चार पहिए की गाड़ी जैसे बैलगाड़ी।

waif / वेफ़् / noun 1 दुबला-पतला छोटा व्यक्ति, विशेषत: बच्चा : *She's such a poor little waif—I don't think she eats enough.* 2 बेघर व्यक्ति, परित्यक्त बालक।

wail / वेल् / verb 1 **wail (about/over sth)** बिलख-बिलखकर रोना 2 हवा का साँय-साँय करना : *You can hear the wind wailing in the chimney.* ▸ **wail** noun 1 विलाप, चिल्लाहट 2 साँय-साँय की ध्वनि।

waist / वेस्ट् / noun कमर।

waistcoat / वेस्कोट् / (US **vest** भी) noun वास्कट।

wait¹ / वेट् / verb 1 **wait (for sb/sth)** प्रतीक्षा करना; राह देखना : *I've been waiting for twenty minutes.* 2 अपनी बारी की प्रतीक्षा करना ■ **wait and see** धैर्य के साथ काम करना **wait up (for sb)** (किसी की प्रतीक्षा में) रात में जागते रहना ▸ **waiting-room** noun प्रतीक्षालय।

wait² / वेट् / noun [sing] **wait (for sb/ sth)** प्रतीक्षा, इंतज़ार : *We had a long wait for the bus.*

wait³ / वेट् / verb ■ **wait at table** भोजन परोसना; प्लेट आदि हटाकर ले जाना **wait upon sb** सेवा-टहल करना; परिचर्या करना।

waiter / वेटर् / noun (fem **waitress** / वेट्रस् /) वेटर, बैरा।

waive / वेव् / verb (औप) (अधिकार, दावा आदि) छोड़ देना : *waive a claim.*

wake¹ / वेक् / verb (pt **woke** / वोक् / ; pp **woken** / वोकन् /) 1 **wake (up) (to sth)** जागना : *I woke early this morning.* 2 **wake sb (up)** उठाना, सचेत करना, जगाना 3 (अलं या औप) दबी हुई भावनाएँ जाग्रत करना ▸ **wakeful** adj जागा हुआ; सोने में असमर्थ; (रात में अवधि) अनिद्र, विनिद्र : *The children were still wakeful even though it was well past their bedtime.* **waken** / वेकन् / verb 1 जगाना, उठाना 2 भावनाएँ जाग्रत करना : *waken a deep concern in people.*

wake² / वेक् / noun पानी में जहाज़ के चलने से बना चिह्न ■ **in the wake of sth** के परिणामस्वरूप : *Outbreaks of disease occurred in the wake of the drought.*

walk¹ /वॉक्/ verb 1 (व्यक्ति का) चलना, टहलना: The baby is learning to walk. 2 (पशु आदि को) चलाना 3 पैदल चलना : walk the moors ■ **walk away/off with sth** चुराना, चुपके से ले जाना; आसानी से इनाम जीतना : She walked away with the gold medal. **walk out (of sth)** सभा आदि समाप्त होने से पहले ही अचानक उठकर चले जाना (विशेषत: असहमति व्यक्त करते हुए) **walk out on sb** (अनौप) किसी को बेसहारा छोड़कर चले जाना ▸ **walk-out** noun बहिर्गमन **walk-over** noun (अनौप) 1 सहज विजय 2 प्रतिद्वंद्वी के न आने से प्राप्त विजय।

walk² /वॉक्/ noun 1 पैदल यात्रा; भ्रमण 2 रास्ता, पथ : There are some lovely walks in the countryside. 3 चलने का ढंग।

walkie-talkie /वॉकि 'टॉकि / noun (अनौप) सूचना प्राप्त करने या भेजने के लिए छोटा रेडियो जैसा उपकरण।

wall / वॉल्/ noun 1 दीवार 2 अवरोध 3 (किसी अंग आदि की) बाह्य सतह : the abdominal wall ■ **have one's back to the wall** विकट स्थिति में जहाँ से पीछे हटना असंभव हो **walls have ears** (कहा) दीवारों के भी कान होते हैं ▸ **wall** verb दीवार से घेरना, दीवार चुनकर बंद करना : a walled city/garden.

wallet /'वॉलिट्/ noun बटुआ, मुड़ने वाला जेबी बटुआ।

wallow /'वॉलो / verb 1 **wallow (about/around) (in sth)** कीचड़ या पानी में लोटना : wallow in a hot bath 2 गुलछर्रे उड़ाना, भोग-विलास में रहना; आकंठ डूबना : wallow in grief.

walnut /'वॉल्नट् / noun अखरोट।

walrus / 'वॉल्रस्/ noun एक बड़ा समुद्री पशु।

waltz /वॉल्स्; US वॉल्ट्स्/ noun संगीत के साथ एक नाच-विशेष ▸ **waltz** verb वॉल्स् नृत्य करना; नृत्य की मुद्रा में चलना।

wan /वॉन्/ adj 1 (व्यक्ति) पीला, थका हुआ-सा 2 (अभिव्यक्ति) बीमारों जैसी, अप्रसन्न : a wan smile ▸ **wanly** adv.

wand /वॉन्ड् / noun 1 (**magic wand** भी) जादूगर की (या कहानियों में परियों की) छड़ी 2 कोई भी छोटी पतली छड़ी।

wander /'वॉन्डर् / verb 1 (निष्प्रयोजन) घूमना 2 **wander (from/off sth)**; **wander (away/off)** रास्ते से भटक जाना, पथभ्रष्ट हो जाना : The child wandered off and got lost. 3 बहकी-बहकी बातें करना ▸ **wanderer** noun.

wane / वेन्/ verb 1 (चंद्रमा का) घटना 2 क्षीण होना, निर्बल होना : The power of the landowners waned during this period. ▸ **wane** noun ■ **on the wane** क्षय, क्षीणता : His political influence was on the wane.

want¹ / वॉन्ट् / verb 1 जरूरत पड़ना, आवश्यकता होना : How many copies do you want? 2 इच्छा रखना, चाहना 3 चाहिए 4 (औप) अभाव होना : He doesn't want courage. ■ **want for sth** (औप) किसी चीज़ के अभाव से पीड़ित होना।

want² / वॉन्ट् / noun 1 इच्छा, चाहत; जरूरत, आवश्यकता 2 **want of sth** कमी, अभाव : a want of food supplies.

wanting / वॉन्टिङ् /adj **wanting (in sth)** (औप) से रहित, की अनुपस्थिति में : She's certainly not wanting in confidence.

wanton /'वॉन्टन् / adj 1 चंचल : in a wanton mood 2 (कार्य आदि) बिना किसी उद्देश्य के, अकारण : wanton cruelty 3 (अप्र) मनमाना या अनियंत्रित व्यवहार ▸ **wantonly** adv.

war / वॉर्/ noun 1 युद्ध, लड़ाई : the horrors of war 2 शत्रुता, प्रतियोगिता या संघर्ष की स्थिति : a trade war ▸ **war** verb (-rr-) लड़ना, युद्ध करना : warring tribes **warfare** / 'वॉर्फ़ेअर / noun

1 संघर्ष, युद्ध : *guerrilla warfare* 2 युद्ध की स्थिति **warlike** *adj* 1 युद्धप्रिय, लड़ने को तैयार 2 लड़ाकू **warpath** *noun*
■ **(be/go) on the warpath** *(अनौप)* संघर्ष में लगा हुआ।

warble / 'वॉर्बल् / *verb* 1 (पक्षियों का) कूजना, चहचहाना 2 (व्यक्ति का) चहककर बोलना : *warble a few songs.*

ward / वॉर्ड / *noun* 1 (जेल या अस्पताल आदि में) वार्ड, अलग विभाग या कमरा : *a children's ward* 2 शहर का प्रशासनार्थ विभाजन/विभाग 3 आश्रित व्यक्ति, किसी बड़ी आयु के पुरुष के संरक्षण में बालक: *The child was made a ward of court.* ▸ **ward** *verb* ■ **ward sb/sth off** बचाव करना, रोकना।

warden / 'वॉर्ड्न् / *noun* छात्रावास का वार्डन।

warder / वॉर्डर् / *noun* (*fem* **wardress**) जेल का वार्डर (महिला–वार्डर।)

wardrobe / 'वॉर्ड्रोब् / *noun* 1 कपड़े रखने/टाँगने की अलमारी 2 व्यक्ति के अपने कपड़ों का संग्रह : *a new winter wardrobe.*

ware / वेअर् / *noun* 1 (समासों में) बना माल : *ironware* ◦ *handmade ware* 2 **wares** [*pl*] बेचने के लिए प्रस्तुत माल : *peddle one's wares* 3 बरतन विशेष : *porcelain ware* ▸ **warehouse** *noun* मालगोदाम।

warm¹ / वॉर्म् / *adj* (**-er, -est**) 1 (**cool** और **hot** के बीच) शरीर को अच्छी लगने वाली गरमाहट : *gusts of warm air* 2 (कपड़े) शरीर को समुचित तापमान पर रखने में सहायक 3 प्रेमपूर्ण एवं हार्दिक (व्यवहार) : *He has a warm heart.* ▸ **warm-blooded** *adj* गरम खून वाले प्राणी (सरीसृप एवं मछली आदि के विपरीत) **warm-hearted** *adj* सहृदय, दयालु **warmth** / वॉर्म्थ् / *noun* 1 गरमाहट 2 (अल) स्नेह; आवेश : *He was touched*

by the warmth of their welcome. **warmly** *adv.*

warm² / वॉर्म् / *verb* **warm (sth/sb) (up)** गरम करना या होना।

warn / वॉर्न् / *verb* 1 **warn sb (of sth); warn sb about/against sb/sth; warn sb against doing sth** चेतावनी देना, सचेत करना 2 कुछ न करने की सलाह देना : *They were warned not to climb the mountain in such bad weather.* ▸ **warning** *noun* पूर्व सूचना, चेतावनी।

warrant / 'वॉरन्ट् / *noun* 1 **warrant (for sth)** (गिरफ़्तारी, तलाशी, रिहाई आदि का) आज्ञापत्र, वारंट : *a warrant for sb's arrest* 2 **warrant for sth/doing sth** (औप) किसी कार्य को सही सिद्ध करने वाला कारण 3 अधिकार पत्र; नियुक्ति पत्र ▸ **warrant** *verb* (औप) सही सिद्ध करना; सामान के गुण आदि का आश्वासन देना **warranty** *noun* किसी वस्तु को ख़रीदते समय लिखित आश्वासन कि टूट जाने या काम न करने पर उसे ठीक या बदल दिया जाएगा।

warrior / 'वॉरिअर् / *noun* 1 (औप या अप्र) योद्धा, सैनिक 2 अपने क़बीले के लिए लड़ने वाला सदस्य : *a Zulu warrior.*

wart / वॉर्ट् / *noun* मस्सा।

wary / 'वेअरि / *adj* (**-ier, -iest**) **wary (of sb/sth)** सावधान, संकटों की ओर से सतर्क/ख़बरदार : *She is wary of strangers.* ▸ **warily** *adv.*

wash¹ / वॉश् / *verb* 1 धोना (पानी या अन्य द्रव से साफ़ करना) 2 (पानी) बहना : *Water washed over the deck.* 3 (पानी का) बहा ले जाना; (समुद्र या नदी में) बह जाना : *He was washed overboard in the storm.* 4 पानी डालना
■ **wash one's hands of sb/sth** ज़िम्मेदारी लेने से इनकार करना; पीछा छुड़ाना **wash (sth) out/off** धोकर साफ़ करना **wash up** (विशेषत: भोजन के बरतन)

wash² ▶ washable *adj* **wash-out** *noun* 1 बाढ़ या अतिवर्षा से बहकर आई मिट्टी, गिट्टी आदि जो रेल-पटरी या अन्य मार्ग या चैनल में रुकावट डाल देते हैं 2 *(अनौप)* असफल, बेकार *(व्यक्ति/घटना)।*

wash² / वॉश् / *noun* 1 धुलाई : *have a wash and brush up* 2 **the wash** [*sing*] धुलाई के कपड़े; धुलाई-स्थान 3 [*sing*] जहाज से उत्पन्न तरंगें एवं विचलित जल 4 (समास में) विशेष सफ़ाई का घोल : *mouthwash.*

washing / वॉशिङ् / *noun* धुलाई के कपड़े।

washstand / वॉश्स्टैन्ड् / *noun (प्रा)* कमरे में हाथ आदि धोने के लिए चिलमची, जग आदि।

wasp / वॉस्प् / *noun* बर्र, ततैया, भिड़।

wastage / वेस्टिज् / *noun* 1 हानि, क्षति : *food wastage* 2 अपव्यय।

waste¹ / वेस्ट् / *noun* 1 [*sing*] बरबादी, ख़राब करने की क्रिया : *a waste of time/ money* 2 बेकार, रद्दी : *nuclear/toxic waste* 3 (प्राय: *pl*) परती या बंजर भूमि : *desert wastes* ▶ **wasteful** *adj* ख़र्चीला; अपव्यय करने वाला।

waste² / वेस्ट् / *verb* 1 **waste sth (on sb/sth)** फ़ज़ूल इस्तेमाल करना; आवश्यकता से अधिक व्यर्थ में प्रयुक्त करना 2 बेकार करना, उपयोग में न ला सकना : *We had a wasted journey.* ■ **waste away** घिस जाना, छीजना।

waste³ / वेस्ट् / *adj* 1 परती/बंजर भूमि : *waste ground* 2 बेकार, रद्दी : *waste water.*

watch¹ / वॉच् / *verb* 1 ध्यान से देखना : *watch television* 2 **watch (over) sb/sth** रखवाली करना, चौकसी करना 3 कड़ी निगाह रखना, सतर्क रहना : *Watch what you say!* ■ **watch for sb/sth** प्रतीक्षा करना **watch out for sb/sth** 1 ध्यानपूर्वक सावधानी से देखना 2 सावधानी से कोई क्रिया करना ताकि कोई अहित न हो जाए।

watch² / वॉच् / *noun* 1 हाथ या जेब की घड़ी 2 निगरानी, सतर्कता : *The police put a watch on the suspect's house.* ■ **keep watch (for sb/sth)** पहरा देना ▶ **watchful** *adj* सतर्क, सावधान।

watchdog / वॉच्डॉग् / *noun* व्यक्ति या व्यक्तियों का समूह जिसका/जिनका कार्य मानवाधिकार हनन से लोगों को बचाना है।

watchman / वॉच्मन् / *noun* पहरेदार।

watchword / वॉच्वर्ड् / *noun* संकेत-शब्द; आदर्श वाक्य : *Safety is our watchword.*

water¹ / वॉटर् / *noun* 1 पानी 2 **waters** [*pl*] जल-राशि : *the clear blue waters of the Mediterranean* 3 ज्वार-भाटा : *(at) high/low water* 4 किसी पदार्थ का पानी वाला घोल : *mineral water* ■ **hold water** *(अनौप)* विश्वास करने लायक सही या वास्तविक लगना ▶ **water-closet** *noun (अप्र)* शौचघर **water-colour** *noun* 1 [*pl*] पानी में घुलने वाले चित्रकला के रंग 2 इन रंगों से रँगा चित्र **watercourse** *noun* छोटी नदी, नहर, नाला आदि; जल मार्ग **waterfall** *noun* झरना, विशेषत: ऊँची पहाड़ी से नदी में गिरने वाला प्रपात **waterfront** *noun* नदी, झील या समुद्र की ओर का नगर-भाग : *cafés on the waterfront* **waterproof** *adj* जलरुद्ध, जिसमें बाहर से पानी अंदर न जा सके **watershed** *noun (भूगोल)* दो नदियों के बीच की ऊँची भूमि **watertight** *adj* जलरोधी, जलरुद्ध : *a watertight compartment.*

water² / वॉटर् / *verb* 1 पानी डालना, सिंचाई करना 2 (पशुओं को) पानी पिलाना : *water the horses* 3 (आँखें) डबडबाना; (मुँह में) पानी भर आना 4 (शराब आदि में) पानी मिलाना ■ **water sth down** किसी द्रव में पानी मिलाकर उसे पतला बनाना ▶ **watering place** *noun (अप्र)* समुद्र तट का नगर जहाँ छुट्टी में लोग जाते हैं।

watery / वॉटरि / *adj* पानी जैसा; पनीला;

(प्राय: *अपमा*) पतला : *watery soup/ gravy.*

watt / वॉट् / *noun* (*संक्षि* W) वाट, विद्युत की इकाई : *a 60-watt light bulb.*

wave¹ / वेव् / *verb* 1 (हवा में) लह- राना : *a flag waving in the breeze* 2 **wave (at/to sb); wave sth (at sb); wave sth** संकेत देना, हाथ हिलाकर ध्यान आकर्षित करना : *He waved when he saw us.* ○ *The demonstrators were waving banners and placards (at passers-by).* 3 (बालों का) लहरियादार या छल्लेदार होना ■ **wave sth aside** किसी कथन को तुच्छ मानकर अमान्य करना।

wave² / वेव् / *noun* 1 लहर, तरंग 2 (संबोधन के रूप में) हाथ हिलाना : *With a quick wave of his hand, he was gone.* 3 बालों की लहरियादार शकल 4 किसी भाव का अचानक वर्धन और विकास : *a wave of anger* 5 ताप, प्रकाश, ध्वनि, विद्युत आदि की तरंग ▶ **wavy** / 'वेवि / *adj* (**-ier, -iest**) तरंगित, लहर- दार।

wavelength / 'वेव्लेङ्थ् / *noun* तरंग- दैर्घ्य।

waver / 'वेव्र् / *verb* 1 डगमगाना, डाँवाँ- डोल होना : *His voice wavered with emotion.* 2 **waver (between sth and sth)** हिचकिचाना, आगा-पीछा करना 3 (प्रकाश का) हिलना।

wax¹ / वैक्स् / *verb* (चंद्रमा की कलाओं का) बढ़ना ■ **wax and wane** कालावधि में शक्ति या महत्त्व की दृष्टि से घटना या बढ़ना → **wane** देखिए।

wax² / वैक्स् / *noun* 1 (**beeswax** भी) मोम 2 मोमबत्ती, मॉडेल आदि में प्रयुक्त साफ़ किया मोम : *a wax candle* 3 पैराफ़ीन मोम ▶ **waxwork** *noun* मोम से बनी (मानव आदि की) आकृति।

way / वे / *noun* 1 रास्ता, मार्ग : *a way across the fields* 2 (विशेषत: समास में) मार्ग, पथ : *railway/waterway*

3 [*sing*] दिशा : *Which way did he go?* 4 व्यवहार-रीति, ढंग; रीति-रिवाज : *speak in a kindly way* 5 [*sing*] दूरी : *We are a long way from the coast.* 6 दृष्टि, पहलू : *Can I help you in any way?* 7 योजना, कार्यरीति : *There are several ways of doing it.* 8 रास्ता, गति की गुंजाइश : *Find a way through the undergrowth.* 9 प्रगति, उन्नति ■ **all the way** 1 पूरी यात्रा के दौरान 2 पूरी तरह से : *We'll support you all the way.* **by the way** (बातचीत के दौरान) प्रसंगवश **by way of/in the way of sth** के अभिप्राय से, के तौर पर **give way (to sb/sth)** टूट जाना; झुक जाना : *We must not give way to their demands.* **go out of one's way (to do sth)** विशेष ध्यान देकर या कष्ट सहकर कोई कार्य करना **have/get one's own way** अपनी बात मनवाना **in a bad way** बुरी स्थिति में; बहुत बीमार **in a big/small way** बड़े/छोटे पैमाने पर **in a way; in one way; in some ways** कुछ सीमा तक **look the other way** जानबूझकर अनदेखा करना **make way (for sb/sth)** किसी को आगे जाने देना/रास्ता देना **no way** (*अनौप*) किसी भी स्थिति में नहीं **one way or the other; either way** कोई भी विकल्प लेकर, किसी भी रीति द्वारा **the other way round** विपरीत दिशा की ओर **ways and means** आवश्यकता पूर्ति के लिए (धन प्राप्ति के) उपाय, युक्तियाँ।

wayfarer / 'वेफ़ेअरर् / *noun* पैदल चलने वाला व्यक्ति।

waylay / वे'ले / *verb* (*pt, pp* **waylaid**) किसी की घात में बैठना; घात करने के लिए प्रतीक्षा करना।

wayside / 'वेसाइड् / *noun* सड़क के किनारे स्थित : *a wayside hotel.*

wayward / 'वेवर्ड् / *adj* ज़िद्दी/अड़ियल; झक्की : *a wayward child.*

we / वी / *pers pron* 1 हम : *We've*

moved to Hyderabad. **2** सामान्य लोग, आम जनता।

weak / वीक् / *adj* (**-er, -est**) **1** (**strong** के विपरीत) कमज़ोर, निर्बल : *He was too weak to walk far.* **2** (व्यक्ति का चरित्र) सशक्त नहीं, दुर्बल : *In a weak moment, I said he could borrow the car.* **3** (घोल) पतला : *weak tea* **4** निम्न-स्तरीय, कुशलता रहित : *a weak team* **5** कमज़ोर, सामान्य से कम : *a weak heart* ▸ **weaken** / वीकन् / *verb* **1** कमज़ोर करना या होना : *The fall in productivity has weakened the economy.* **2** धैर्य, साहस आदि तोड़ना **weakling** / वीक्लिङ् / *noun* कमज़ोर मनुष्य या पशु **weak-minded** *adj* सहज में ही दूसरे से प्रभावित होने वाला व्यक्ति, बोदा **weakness** *noun* **1** कमज़ोरी, दुर्बलता : *weakness of character* **2** चरित्रगत दोष **3 weakness (for sth/sb)** के प्रति विशेष आकर्षण, चस्का : *weakness for chocolate.*

wealth / वेल्थ् / *noun* **1** धन-सम्पत्ति **2** [*sing*] **wealth of sth** प्रचुरता, बड़ी संख्या या मात्रा : *a wealth of opportunity* ▸ **wealthy** *adj* (**-ier, -iest**) धनवान।

wean / वीन् / *verb* **wean sb/sth (off sth)** (छोटे बच्चे का) धीरे-धीरे माँ का दूध छुड़ाना (यानी कि बाहर का दूध पिलाने लगना)।

weapon / वेप्न् / *noun* शस्त्र, हथियार : *a deadly weapon.*

wear[1] / वेअर् / *verb* (*pt* **wore** / वॉर् /; *pp* **worn** / वॉर्न् /) **1** पहनना, धारण करना : *wear a beard/coat* **2** घिस जाना, छीजना, जीर्ण हो जाना : *The sheets have worn thin.* **3** अच्छी स्थिति में बने रहना, लगातार प्रयोग में आते रहना : *You should choose a fabric that wears (well).* **4** सहन करना, अनमना होकर स्वीकार करना ■ **wear on** समय का जैसे-तैसे बीत जाना **wear oneself/sb out** थका देना, थक

जाना : *Just listening to his silly chatter wears me out.* **wear sth off** धीरे-धीरे समाप्त हो जाना ▸ **wearable** *adj.*

wear[2] / वेअर् / *noun* **1** पहनावा : *casual clothes for everyday wear* **2** (समास में विशेषतः) पहनने वाली वस्तु : *children's/ladies' wear* **3** इस्तेमाल से कट-पिट जाना : *My shoes are showing (signs of) wear.* **4** टिकाऊपन ■ **the worse for wear** अच्छी स्थिति में न होना **wear and tear** टूट-फूट; सामान्य प्रयोग से वस्तु के मूल्य में क्षति।

weary / विअरि / *adj* (**-ier, -iest**) **1** थका-माँदा : *weary in body and mind* **2 weary of sth/doing sth** ऊबा हुआ, उकताया हुआ **3** थकाने/ऊबाने वाला : *a weary journey* ▸ **wearily** *adv* **weariness** *noun* **wearisome** *adj* थकाऊ; ऊबाऊ : *wearisome complaints/tasks* **weary** *verb* **weary sb (with sth)** **1** थकना, थकाना : *She was wearied by the constant noise.* **2 weary of sb/sth; weary of doing sth** (औप) ऊबना, उकताना।

weather[1] / वेदर् / *noun* मौसम, ऋतु (किसी समय किसी स्थान का तापमान, पवन-गति, वर्षा-मात्रा, आर्द्रता आदि) : *cold/windy weather* ▸ **weathercock/-vane** *noun* वायु की दिशा और गति का सूचक (मुर्गानुमा) तीर।

weather[2] / वेदर् / *verb* **1** मौसम से प्रभावित होकर आकार, रंग आदि बदलना; क्षीण होना : *rocks weathered by wind and water* **2** तूफ़ान या संघर्ष के बाद सही-सलामत निकल आना : *weather a crisis.*

weave / वीव् / *verb* (*pt* **wove** / वोव् /; *pp* **woven** / वोवन् / या **weaved**) **1** (कपड़ा) बुनना **2** चटाई बुनना, (माला) पिरोना : *weave a garland (out of primroses)* **3 weave sth (into sth)**

कहानी की रचना करना ▸ **weave** *noun* बुनावट **weaver** *noun* जुलाहा, बुनकर।

web / वेब् / *noun* 1 मकड़ी आदि का जाला 2 **web (of sth)** जाल : *a web of lies/ intrigue* 3 मेंढक, चमगादड़ आदि की वह झिल्ली जो पंजों को जोड़ती है, पाद-जाल ▸ **webbed** *adj* पादजाल वाले (प्राणी)।

webbing / वेबिङ् / *noun* पलंग आदि की निवार (मोटी बुनी पट्टी)।

website / वेब्साइट् / *noun* इंटरनेट संचार-व्यवस्था में सूचना सामग्री के भंडारण-स्थल जिनसे संपर्क कर सूचना प्राप्त की जा सकती है।

wed / वेड् / *verb* (*pt, pp* **wedded** या **wed**) (*अप्र*) विवाह करना।

wedding / वेडिङ् / *noun* विवाह समारोह : *a wedding dress/reception.*

wedge / वेज् / *noun* 1 फन्नी, पच्चर (V-आकार का धातु या लकड़ी का टुकड़ा जो लकड़ी आदि को फाड़ने में प्रयुक्त होता है): *Put a wedge under the door to keep it open.* 2 वेज की आकृति वाला गोल्फ़-क्लब ▸ **wedge** *verb* पच्चर लगाकर फाड़ना; पच्चर लगाना : *wedge a door open.*

wedlock / वेड्लॉक् / *noun* (औप या क़ानून) विवाहित अवस्था; दांपत्य स्थिति।

Wednesday / वेन्ज़्डे / *noun* (*संक्षि* **Wed, Weds**) बुधवार।

wee / वी / *adj* 1 बहुत छोटा, नन्हा : *the poor wee fellow* 2 (*अनौप*) मात्रा या प्रसार में बहुत ज़रा-सा।

weed / वीड् / *noun* खेत या बग़ीचे आदि में उगा जंगली पौधा ▸ **weed** *verb* निराई करना, ऐसे पौधों को उखाड़ना ■ **weed sth/sb out** छाँटना, अवांछित व्यक्तियों या व्यर्थ की वस्तुओं को निकालकर बाहर करना : *weed out the weakest plants* ▸ **weedy** *adj* (-ier, -iest) 1 जंगली पौधों से भरा हुआ 2 (*अनौप, अपमा*) दुबला-

पतला कमज़ोर व्यक्ति : *a weedy little man.*

week / वीक् / *noun* 1 सप्ताह, हफ़्ता 2 विभिन्न संस्थाओं में काम होने के दिन : *During the week the road is very busy, but there is very little traffic on Sundays.* ▸ **weekend** / वीक्'एन्ड् / *noun* शनिवार और इत-वार (आराम करने के दिन): *He has to work (at) weekends.* **weekly** *adj, adv* साप्ताहिक, सप्ताह में एक बार घटित होने वाला : *weekly payments* **weekly** *noun* साप्ताहिक पत्रिका/पत्र।

weep / वीप् / *verb* (*pt, pp* **wept** / वेप्ट् /) 1 **weep (for/over sb/sth)** रोना : *The music made me weep.* 2 घाव का बहना, शरीर के किसी अंग से मवाद निकलना।

weigh / वे / *verb* 1 तौलना, वज़न करना : *He weighed the stone in his hand.* 2 वज़न या भार होना : *How much do you weigh?* 3 **weigh sth (with/ against sth)** तुलना करना, मिलान करना : *weigh the advantages of the investment against the risks in-volved* 4 **weigh (with sb) (against sb/sth)** महत्त्वपूर्ण लगना, प्रभाव डालना 5 लंगर उठाना, यात्रा आरंभ करना : *weigh anchor* ■ **weigh one's words** सावधानी से कुछ व्यक्त करना; भला-बुरा विचार कर कहना **weigh on (sb/sth)** भार बनना, परेशान करना।

weight¹ / वेट् / *noun* 1 वज़न, भार 2 **weight (of sth)** भार, बोझ 3 तौलने का बाट 4 महत्त्व या प्रभाव : *Your opinion carries weight with the chairman.* ▸ **weightless** *adj* **weightlifting** *noun* व्यायाम या खेल के रूप में कोई भार उठाना **weighty** *adj* (-ier, -iest) बहुत भारी; (*अलं*) बहुत महत्त्वपूर्ण।

weight² / वेट् / *verb* 1 **weight sth**

(down) (with sth) बाट रखना; भारी करना : *weighted doors* 2 पक्षपातपूर्ण तरीक़े से प्रबंध या योजनाबद्ध करना।

weir / विअर् / *noun* 1 नदी के किनारे की दीवार, बाँध 2 मछली पकड़ने के लिए नदी के आर–पार टहनियाँ डालकर बनाया गया तालाब।

weird / विअर्ड / *adj* (**-er, -est**) 1 अलौकिक और प्राय: भयानक : *Weird shrieks were heard in the darkness.* 2 (*अनौप, प्राय: अपमा*) समझने-समझाने में कठिन; अजीबोग़रीब : *weird clothes.*

welcome / वेल्कम् / *adj* 1 अभिनंदन योग्य, सुखदायी : *a welcome change* 2 **welcome to sth/to do sth** कुछ करने/ हिस्सा लेने के लिए स्वागत है ■ **make sb welcome** स्वागत करना ▸ **welcome** *noun* स्वागत, आवभगत : *a hearty welcome* **welcome** *verb* **welcome sb (to sth)** स्वागत करना; अभिनंदन करना : *a welcoming smile.*

weld / वेल्ड् / *verb* 1 **weld A and B (together); weld A (on) to B** धातु के दो टुकड़ों को ठोक-पीटकर या पक्की तरह से जोड़ देना 2 **weld sb/sth into sth** (लोगों को) एक कर देना : *weld a bunch of untrained recruits into an efficient fighting force* ▸ **weld** *noun* (धातु के दो टुकड़ों का) ऐसा जोड़ **welder** *noun.*

welfare / वेल्फ़ेअर् / *noun* 1 कुशलक्षेम, ख़ैरियत 2 कल्याण : *student welfare.*

well¹ / वेल् / *noun* 1 कुआँ 2 तेल का कुआँ ▸ **well** *verb* **well (out/up)** उमड़ जाना, बहना : *Anger was welling up inside him.*

well² / वेल् / *adj* (**better** / बेटर् /; **best** / बेस्ट् /) 1 अच्छे स्वास्थ्य में : *I don't feel very well.* 2 संतोषजनक स्थिति में या पद पर : *It seems that all is not well at home.* 3 उचित, इच्छित : *It would be well to start early.*

well³ / वेल् / *adv* (**better** / बेटर् /; **best** / बेस्ट् /) 1 भली-भाँति, संतोषजनक ढंग से : *The children behaved well.* 2 प्रशंसा से : *She spoke well of the nurses and the way she had been looked after.* 3 पूर्णत: और ख़ूब : *Shake the mixture well.* 4 ठीक ही : *You may well be right.* 5 काफ़ी हद तक : *lean well forward in one's chair* ■ **as well (as sb/sth)** के अतिरिक्त **do well** 1 सफल होना 2 बीमारी के बाद स्वस्थ होना **leave/let well alone** संतोषजनक स्थिति में हस्तक्षेप न करना **well off** अच्छी आर्थिक स्थिति में ▸ **well-behaved** *adj* सभ्य **well-being** *noun* कल्याण; कुशलक्षेम **well-born** *adj* कुलीन **well-built** *adj* (व्यक्ति) सुडौल **well-defined** *adj* आसानी से और स्पष्टता से समझ में आने वाला; स्पष्ट रूप से दिखाई पड़ने वाला **well-informed** *adj* विस्तृत ज्ञान/सूचना प्राप्त **well-known** *adj* प्रसिद्ध **well-meaning** *adj* भला चाहने वाला **well-read** *adj* अधिक ज्ञान प्राप्त किया हुआ; पंडित **well-timed** *adj* उचित अवसर पर कहा या किया हुआ : *Your remarks were certainly well-timed.* **well-to-do** *adj* ख़ुशहाल, धनी **well-tried** *adj* परीक्षित एवं उपयोगितापूर्ण (रीति आदि) **well-wisher** *noun* शुभचिंतक।

well⁴ / वेल् / *interj* 1 (आश्चर्य या गुस्से की अभिव्यक्ति में) : *Well, what a thing to say!* 2 (संतोष एवं चैन की सांस को व्यक्त करने के लिए) : *Well, thank goodness that's over!* 3 (सहमति व्यक्त करने के लिए) : *Very well, then, I'll accept your offer.*

wend / वेन्ड् / *verb* (औप या साहि) जाना: *It's time we were wending our way home.*

west / वेस्ट् / *noun* [sing] (संक्षि W) 1 (प्राय: the West) पश्चिम दिशा 2 **the West** यूरोप, उत्तरी अमेरिका और कनाडा

▶ **west** *adj* 1 पश्चिम में/की ओर : *West Africa* 2 (वायु, पवन) पश्चिमी दिशा से **westerly** *adj* 1 पश्चिम में/की ओर 2 (हवा) पछवाँ, पश्चिमी **westerly** *noun* पछवाँ हवा, पश्चिम से आ रही पवन **west-ward** *adj* पश्चिम की ओर **westwards** (**westward** भी) *adv.*

western / 'वेस्टर्न् / *adj* पश्चिमी : *west-ern customs* ▶ **westernize, -ise** / 'वेस्टर्नाइज़् / *verb* पश्चिमी सभ्यता में रँगना; पाश्चात्य ढंग का बना देना : *The island became fully westernized after the war.*

wet / वेट् / *adj* (**-tter, -ttest**) 1 गीला, तर : *wet clothes* 2 (मौसम) बरसाती : *a wet day* 3 (स्याही, पेंट, सीमेंट आदि) ताज़ा लगाया हुआ ▶ **wet** *noun* 1 **the wet** [*sing*] वर्षा का मौसम 2 द्रव, पानी 3 नीरस या दुर्बल व्यक्ति **wet** *verb* (*pt, pp* **wetted** या **wet**) तर करना।

whack / वैक् / *verb* (अनौप) ज़ोर से मारना या पीटना ▶ **whack** *noun* 1 मारने/पीटने की आवाज़ 2 **whack** (**at sth**) (अनौप) प्रयास।

whale / वेल् / *noun* सबसे बड़ा समुद्री जंतु जो मछली जैसा दिखता है।

wharf / वॉर्फ़ / *noun* (*pl* **wharfs** या **wharves** / वॉर्व्ज़ /) जहाज़ घाट, घाट।

what / वॉट् / *interrog det* क्या; कौन; कौन-सा : *What time/date is it?* ▶ **what** *interrog pron* क्या : *What did you say?* ∎ **what for?** किस-लिए?

whatever / वॉट्'एवर् / *pron, adj* जो कुछ, जो भी : *Whatever we do, some people will criticize it.* ▶ **what-ever** (**whatsoever** भी) *adv* निस्संदेह : *There can be no doubt whatever about it.*

wheat / वीट् / *noun* गेहूँ।

wheel / वील् / *noun* 1 पहिया 2 स्टिअरिंग वील : *at the wheel* 3 **wheels** [*pl*] (अनौप) मोटर गाड़ी ▶ **wheel** *verb* 1 पहिए द्वारा खींचना या ठेलना : *wheel the barrow (across the garden)* 2 गोलाई में घूमना/घुमाना **wheelbarrow** *noun* एक पहिया ठेला **wheelchair** *noun* पहियों वाली कुर्सी (विशेषत: अपाहिज या बीमार लोगों के लिए)।

wheeze / वीज़् / *verb* घरघर करते हुए साँस लेना।

when / व्हेन् / *interrog adv* कब, किस समय : *When can you come?* ▶ **when** *rel adv* 1 पर, उस समय : *Sunday is the day when I can relax.* 2 जिस समय, जिस अवसर पर : *The last time I went to Scotland was in May, when the weather was beautiful.* **when** *pron* कब तक, किस समय: *Until when can you stay?* **when** *conj* 1 जब, उस समय : *When he saw me, he waved.* 2 क्योंकि, चूँकि 3 यद्यपि।

whence / व्हेन्स् / *adv* (अप्र या औप) जहाँ से : *They returned whence they came.*

whenever / व्हेन्'एवर् / *conj* जब-जब (भी); कभी भी।

where / वेअर् / *interrog adv* कहाँ, कौन-सी जगह : *Where do you live?* ▶ **where** *rel adv* 1 जिस जगह पर/में/को : *the place where you last saw it* 2 जिस स्थान पर **whereabouts** *interrog adv* कहाँ, किस जगह : *Whereabouts did you find it?* **whereabouts** *noun* पता-ठिकाना **whereby** *rel adv* (औप) जिससे **whereupon** *adv* जिस पर; तत्पश्चात : *She laughed at him, whereupon he walked out.*

whereas / वेअर्'ऐज़् / *conj* क्योंकि, जबकि; (तुलना में) : *He earns Rs 5,00,000 a year whereas she gets at least Rs 10,00,000.*

wherefore / 'वेअर्फ़ॉर् / noun ■ **the whys and wherefores** क्यों; जिस कारण।

wherever / वेअर्'एवर् / adv, conj जहाँ कहीं; कहीं भी।

whet / वेट् / verb (-tt-) 1 (चाकू आदि को) तेज़ करना, सान चढ़ाना 2 इच्छाएँ भड़काना : whet sb's appetite.

whether / 'वेदर् / conj कि : I don't know whether I'll be able to come.

which / विच् / interrog det कौन-सा : Which languages did you study at school? ▶ **which** interrog pron कौन-सा : Which is your favourite subject? **which** rel pron जो, जो कि : Houses which overlook the lake cost more.

whichever / विच्'एवर् / det, pron 1 जो कोई : Take whichever hat suits you. 2 चाहे जो : Whichever you buy, there's a six-month guarantee.

whiff / विफ़् / noun **whiff (of sth)** 1 (सिगरेट आदि का) कश, फूँक 2 संकेत, निशान : a whiff of danger.

while¹ / वाइल् / conj 1 जब, उस समय जब, ज्यों ही : He fell asleep while watching television. 2 वैषम्य, अंतर आदि दिखाने के लिए प्रयुक्त : I prefer black coffee while Rishi prefers it with milk. 3 (औप) हालाँकि, यद्यपि : While I admit that there are problems, I don't agree that they cannot be solved.

while² / वाइल् / noun [sing] समय की अवधि : I'll be back in a little while. ▶ **while** verb ■ **while sth away** समय काटना, गुज़ारना : We whiled away the time at the airport reading magazines.

whim / विम् / noun मौज, सनक : follow the whims of fashion.

whimper / 'विम्पर् / verb पिनपिनाना, तुनकना : A child in a bed nearby

began to whimper. ▶ **whimper** noun तुनक, पिनपिनाहट।

whimsical / 'विम्ज़िक्ल् / adj मौजी, झक्की; सनकी : a whimsical sense of humour.

whine / वाइन् / verb 1 कुत्ते का रिरियाना, धीमी आवाज़ से कराहते हुए-सा रोना; (मशीन का) धीमा ऊबाऊ शोर करना : In the background, a drill whined. 2 व्यर्थ की बात की शिकायत करना ▶ **whine** noun 1 रिरियाहट, कराहना या मशीन का शोर 2 शिकायत (बेकार की)।

whip¹ / विप् / noun 1 कोड़ा, चाबुक 2 राजनीतिक दल में अनुशासन बनाए रखने वाला अधिकारी : the chief whip.

whip² / विप् / verb (-pp-) 1 कोड़े मारना : Prisoners were whipped to get confessions out of them. 2 झटके से खींचना या निकालना : The intruder whipped out a knife. ▶ **whipping** noun कोड़ों की मार (दंड स्वरूप)।

whirl / वर्ल् / verb 1 तेज़ी से घूमना; वेग से चक्कर खाना/खिलाना 2 बहुत तेज़ी से गुज़रना : The houses whirled past us as the train gathered speed. 3 (दिमाग़ का) तेज़ी से चलना ▶ **whirl** noun 1 इस प्रकार की गति 2 एक के बाद एक तेज़ गतिविधि 3 भ्रमित अवस्था।

whirlpool / 'वर्लपूल् / noun पानी का भँवर।

whirlwind / 'वर्ल्विन्ड् / noun भँवर, बवंडर।

whisk / विस्क् / noun 1 झाड़ू; अंडे फेंटने का उपकरण 2 (घोड़े की पूँछ जैसी वस्तु का) झटका : a whisk of the horse's tail 3 चँवर, चामर ▶ **whisk** verb 1 तेज़ी से चले जाना; तेज़ी से कुछ ले जाना : The waiter whisked away the plates before we had finished. 2 (धूल आदि) झाड़ना; मक्खी आदि उड़ा देना।

whisker / 'विस्कर् / noun 1 (बिल्ली,

चूहे आदि की) मूँछ 2 **whiskers** [pl]
(अप्र या परि)कनपटी वाली दाढ़ी, गलमुच्छ।

whisky, whiskey / 'विस्कि / *noun*
ह्विस्की, एक तेज़ शराब।

whisper / 'विस्पर् / *verb* 1 फुसफुसाना
2 (पत्तियों का) सरसराना ▸ **whisper**
noun.

whistle / 'विस्ल् / *noun* 1 सीटी आदि से
निकली ध्वनि : *the shrill whistle of a
steam engine* 2 सीटी ▸ **whistle** *verb*
1 सीटी बजाना 2 सीटी बजाकर गाना 3 सीटी
जैसी आवाज़ के साथ गुज़रना : *A bullet
whistled past his head.*

white¹ / वाइट् / *adj* (-r, -st) 1 सफ़ेद रंग
का 2 सफ़ेद रंग वाली जाति (के लोग) : *His
attacker was a white youth.* 3 **white**
(with sth) (डर या भावुकता के कारण)
पीला ▸ **white elephant** *noun* बहुत
अधिक ख़र्च माँगने वाली किंतु काम में न आने
वाली संपत्ति **white flag** *noun* आत्मसमर्पण
का प्रतीक **whitewash** *noun* चूने से
दीवारों की पुताई **whitewash** *verb*
1 पुताई करना 2 दोषों पर परदा डालकर
निर्दोष ठहराना।

white² / वाइट् / *noun* 1 सफ़ेद रंग; सफ़ेद
कपड़े 2 गोरे लोग 3 अंडे की सफ़ेदी।

whittle / 'विट्ल् / *verb* **whittle A (from
B)** लकड़ी की छोटी-छोटी चपड़ी काटना
■ **whittle sth away** धीरे-धीरे समाप्त या
कम कर देना **whittle sth down** क्रमश:
आकार या मात्रा घटा देना : *The number of
employees is being whittled down.*

whizz (whiz भी) / विज़् / *verb* (हवा में)
सनसनाना : *A bullet whizzed past my
ear.* ▸ **whizz** *noun* सनसनाहट की ध्वनि।

who / हू / *interrog pron* कौन : *Who is
the woman in the black hat?* ▸ **who**
rel pron जो, जो कि : *the man who
wanted to meet you.*

whoever / हू 'एवर् / *pron* जो कोई, जो
भी : *Whoever says that is a liar.*

whole / होल् / *adj* 1 पूर्ण, समग्र : *three*

whole days ○ *Tell me the whole
truth.* 2 अखंड, अविकल : *cook something whole* ▸ **whole** *noun* 1 संपूर्ण;
पूर्णता : *Four quarters make a whole.*
2 **whole of sth** जितना है, सब **whole-
hearted** *adj* पूरे मन/उत्साह से **whole-
heartedly** *adv* **whole number** *noun*
(गणित) बिना भिन्न वाली संख्या **wholly**
/ 'होल्लि / *adv* पूर्ण रूप से, बिलकुल : *not
a wholly successful book.*

wholesale / 'होल्सेल् / *adv, adj* थोक
बिक्री से संबंधित।

wholesome / 'होल्सम् / *adj* स्वास्थ्य के
लिए हितकर : *plain but wholesome
meals.*

why / वाइ / *interrog adv* क्यों : *Why
were you late?* ▸ **why** *rel adv* क्यों,
जिस कारण से : *the reason why he left
her* **why** *interj* (आश्चर्यसूचक): *Why,
it's easy—a child could do it!*

wick / विक् / *noun* मोमबत्ती का धागा; अन्य
दीपों, लैंपों की बत्ती।

wicked / 'विकिड् / *adj* (-er, -est) 1 दुष्ट,
चरित्रहीन (व्यक्ति) 2 हानिकारक, द्वेषपूर्ण :
a wicked blow 3 मज़ाक़ में धक्का
पहुँचाने वाला : *a wicked sense of
humour* ▸ **wickedly** *adv* **wicked-
ness** *noun.*

wicker / 'विकर् / *noun* टोकरा/टोकरी बुनने
वाली खपची : *a wicker chair.*

wickerwork / 'विकर्वर्क् / *noun* तीली,
खपची आदि से तैयार वस्तु।

wicket / 'विकिट् / *noun* (क्रिकेट) विकेट;
दोनों ओर के विकेटों के बीच की भूमि :
Don't walk on the wicket. ▸ **wicket-
keeper** *noun* विकेट रक्षक।

wide / वाइड् / *adj* (-r, -st) 1 चौड़ा,
विस्तीर्ण : *a wide river* 2 विशाल, व्या-
पक : *the whole wide world* 3 पूर्णत:
खुला 4 **wide (of sth)** लक्ष्य से दूर : *Her
shot was wide (of the target).*
■ **give sb/sth a wide berth** किसी चीज़

या व्यक्ति से दूरी बनाकर रखना, सुरक्षित दूरी पर रहना ► **wide** adv 1 काफ़ी सीमा तक; पूर्णत: : *with legs wide apart* 2 लक्ष्य से बहुत दूर : *fall wide* **widely** adv.

widen / वाइडन् / verb और अधिक चौड़ा/ विस्तृत होना या करना : *The road is being widened.*

widespread / वाइड्स्प्रेड् / adj व्यापक, फैला हुआ।

widow / विडो / noun विधवा।

widower / विडोअर् / noun विधुर।

width / विड्थ् / noun 1 चौड़ाई : *10 metres in width* 2 विस्तार।

wield / वील्ड् / verb 1 पकड़ना और हथियार की तरह इस्तेमाल करना : *wield an axe* 2 अधिकार (शक्ति) रखना और प्रयोग कर सकना : *wield authority.*

wife / वाइफ़् / noun (pl **wives** / वा-इव्ज़् /) पत्नी।

wig / विग् / noun (नकली) बालों की टोपी जैसी रचना।

wiggle / विग्ल् / verb (अनौप) हिलना-डुलना।

wild / वाइल्ड् / adj (-er, -est) 1 (पशु) जंगली, (पेड़-पौधे) जंगली, न कि बोकर उगाया हुआ 2 (व्यक्ति, जाति) असभ्य 3 (भूमि) जहाँ खेती न हो सकती हो, बीहड़ : *a wild mountain region* 4 (मौसम) उग्र, तूफ़ानी 5 उच्छृंखल, निरंकुश : *He led a wild life in his youth.* 6 उत्तेजित, क्रोधित 7 बिना सावधानी से विचार किया हुआ 8 **wild about sth/sb** अति उत्साहित ► **wild** noun 1 **the wild** [sing] जंगल, नैसर्गिक क्षेत्र 2 **the wilds** [pl] उजाड़ बंजर भूमि **wildly** adv **wildness** noun.

wilderness / विल्डरनस् / noun 1 ऊसर, बीहड़ स्थल; रेगिस्तान 2 **wilderness (of sth)** ऐसा स्थान जहाँ घास और झाड़-झंखाड़ उगे हों।

wildfire / वाइल्ड्फ़ाइअर् / noun ■ **spread like wildfire** बड़ी तेज़ी से फैलना।

wiles / वाइल्ज़् / noun (प्राय: pl) चाल, छल-कपट।

wilful (US **willful** भी) / विल्फ़ुल् / adj 1 जानबूझकर किया (कुकर्म) : *wilful damage* 2 (व्यक्ति) ज़िद्दी, दुराग्रही ► **wilfully** adv **wilfulness** noun.

will¹ / विल् / modal verb (लघु रूप 'll; pt **would**) 1 भविष्य काल बनाने में सहायक क्रिया : *He'll start school this year, won't he?* 2 संकल्प, सहमति वाचक क्रिया : *I will admit that it wasn't a very sensible thing to do.* 3 निवेदन में प्रयुक्त : *Will you send this letter for me, please?* 4 आज्ञार्थक : *Will you be quiet!*

will² / विल् / verb (अप्र या औप) इच्छा करना : *Call it what you will.*

will³ / विल् / verb 1 कुछ करने या प्राप्त करने में मानसिक शक्ति का प्रयोग करना; इच्छावाचक : *Closing his eyes, he willed himself to relax.* 2 **will sth (to sb)** वसीयत में छोड़ना : *He willed most of his money to charity.*

will⁴ / विल् / noun 1 संकल्प शक्ति, इच्छा शक्ति 2 (**will-power** भी) आत्म संयम की शक्ति : *have a strong will* 3 दृढ़ता; तीव्र इच्छा 4 भावना : *bear sb no ill will* 5 वसीयतनामा ■ **against sb's will** किसी की इच्छा के विरुद्ध, ज़बरदस्ती **at will** इच्छानुसार, जब चाहे तब : *Come and go at will.*

willing / विलिङ् / adj 1 सहायता को तत्पर : *willing assistants* 2 बिना हिचकिचाहट के तुरंत दिया या किया हुआ : *willing cooperation* 3 **willing (to do sth)** करने को तैयार ► **willingly** adv **willingness** noun.

willow / विलो / noun एक प्रकार का पेड़ जिसकी लकड़ी से क्रिकेट के बल्ले बनाए जाते हैं।

wilt / विल्ट् / verb 1 (पौधों का) मुरझाना, कुम्हलाना 2 दुर्बल होना; उत्साह खो देना।

wily / 'वाइलि / adj (-ier, -iest) चालाक, धूर्त : as wily as a fox.

win / विन् / verb (-nn-; pt, pp won / वन् /) 1 जीतना 2 win sth (from sb) हासिल करना, जीतकर पाना; प्रयत्न से पाना : India won three silver medals. ■ win sb over/round to sth तर्कों से मना लेना, क़ायल करना : She's against the idea, but I'm sure I can win her over. ▸ win noun जीत, विजय winner noun विजेता; सफल वस्तु या विचार winning adj 1 जीतने वाला, जीता हुआ : the winning horse 2 आकर्षक और मोहक (व्यवहार, व्यक्तित्व) : a winning smile winnings noun [pl] दाँव में जीती धनराशि।

wince / विन्स् / verb wince (at sth) चौंक जाना (भय, दर्द आदि से); चेहरे पर (दर्द या शर्म से) झिझक का भाव लाना : He winced (with pain).

wind[1] / विन्ड् / noun 1 हवा : a light wind 2 साँस : be short of wind 3 (पेट में विकार उत्पन्न करने वाली) वायु, वात 4 वाद्य यंत्र : music for wind and strings ▸ windfall noun हवा से गिरा फल; (अलं) अप्रत्याशित लाभ wind instrument noun बिगुल, तुरही आदि windmill noun पवनचक्की windpipe noun श्वसनली windscreen noun कार आदि का सामने का शीशा windy adj (-ier, -iest) 1 बहुत अधिक हवादार 2 (भाषा) लंबे-लंबे शब्दों से भरी : windy phrases.

wind[2] / विन्ड् / verb (pt winded) 1 साँस फूलना/फुला देना : We were winded by the steep climb. 2 हवा/वायु ख़ारिज करने में (बच्चे आदि की) मदद करना।

wind[3] / वाइन्ड् / verb (pt, pp wound / वाउन्ड् /) 1 घुमावदार रास्ते (से जाना) : winding alleys and backstreets 2 लपेटना; धागे आदि की लच्छी या गोला बनाना 3 हैंडिल घुमाना : You operate the trapdoor by winding this handle. 4 (घड़ी में) चाभी देना : wind one's watch ■ wind sb/sth up (अलं) उत्तेजना या तनाव से भर देना wind (sth) up समाप्त करना या होना ▸ wind noun मोड़ या घुमाव winding-sheet noun कफ़न।

windlass / 'विन्डलस् / noun बेलन-चरख़ा।

window / 'विन्डो / noun 1 खिड़की : He opened the bedroom window. 2 कंप्यूटर में स्क्रीन का वह भाग जहाँ विशिष्ट सूचना-आंकड़े स्थित होते हैं ▸ window-pane noun खिड़की में लगा काँच का पल्ला window-shopping noun दुकान की बड़ी-बड़ी खिड़कियों से भीतर के सामान को देखने की प्रक्रिया, चाहे उस समय ख़रीदने की कोई योजना न भी हो।

wine / वाइन् / noun 1 अंगूर से बनी शराब 2 (wine red भी) गहरा लाल रंग : a wine dress.

wing / विङ् / noun 1 चिड़िया का पंख; कीटों के पंख 2 हवाई जहाज़ का पंख 3 किसी भवन का खंड : the east/west wing of a house 4 the wings [pl] (रंगमंच का) पार्श्व भाग ■ on the wing उड़ान पर (wait, etc) in the wings किसी कार्य के लिए तैयार, कार्यभार संभालने के लिए तैयार।

wink / विङ्क् / verb 1 wink (at sb) पलक मारना, इशारे के रूप में आँख मारना : He winked at me to show he was playing a joke on the others. 2 (साहि) (प्रकाश, तारे आदि का) टिम-टिमाना ▸ wink noun पलक की झपक।

winnow / 'विनो / verb winnow sth (from sth) सूप से फटकना, ओसाना।

winter / 'विन्टर् / noun शीतकाल ▸ wintry adj 1 ठंडा, शीतल : a wintry landscape 2 अमित्रवत् : a wintry smile.

wipe / वाइप् / verb 1 wipe sth (on sth) (कपड़े आदि से) पोंछना 2 wipe sth from/off sth; wipe sth away/off/up पोंछकर साफ़ करना : wipe the writing *off the blackboard* ■ **wipe sth out** 1 भीतर से साफ़ करना 2 पूरी तरह नष्ट कर देना : *the campaign to wipe out malaria* ▸ **wipe** *noun* पोंछन।

wire / वाइअर / *noun* 1 तार; विद्युतवाही तार 2 *(अनौप)* तार : *send sb a wire* ▸ **wire** *verb* 1 **wire A and B together** तार से बाँधना/जोड़ना 2 तार डालना : *The house is not wired yet.* 3 *(अनौप, विशेषत: US)* तार भेजना **wiry** / वाइअरि / *adj* (-ier, -iest) 1 *(व्यक्ति)* दुबला-पतला परंतु बलशाली 2 तार जैसा मज़बूत और लचीला : *wiry hair.*

wireless / वाइअरलस् / *noun* *(अप्र)* बेतार (का तार); रेडियो।

wisdom / विज़्डम् / *noun* 1 बुद्धि; बुद्धिमानी : *moral wisdom* 2 बुद्धिमत्तापूर्ण विचार, उक्तियाँ आदि : *listen to sb's pearls of wisdom.*

wise / वाइज़् / *adj* (-er, -est) बुद्धिमान, समझदार ▸ **wisely** *adv.*

wish / विश् / *verb* 1 चाहना : *Do you wish me to leave now?* 2 अतृप्त इच्छा रखना : *I wish I were rich.* 3 **wish (for sth)** अभिलाषा या आशा करना; लालसा रखना : *What more could one wish for?* 4 शुभकामना करना : *We wish you a Merry Christmas!* ■ **wish sb well** सफलता की शुभकामना देना, मंगलकामना करना ▸ **wish** *noun* 1 **wish (to do sth)**; **wish (for sth)** कामना, लालसा 2 **wishes** *[pl]* शुभकामनाएँ ■ **with all good wishes** शुभकामनाओं सहित।

wisp / विस्प् / *noun* **wisp (of sth)** 1 पूली, आँटी : *a wisp of hay* 2 दुबला-पतला छोटा व्यक्ति : *a wisp of a girl* ▸ **wispy** *adj.*

wistful / विस्ट्फ़ुल् / *adj* उत्कंठित; उदास : *wistful eyes/mood* ▸ **wistfully** *adv* अतीत या अप्राप्त के प्रति उदास एवं अभिलाषापूर्ण अभिव्यक्ति **wistfulness** *noun.*

wit / विट् / *noun* 1 बुद्धि; हाज़िरजवाबी : *have a quick wit* 2 **(wits** *[pl]* भी) बुद्धि की तीव्रता : *a battle of wits* 3 हाज़िरजवाब व्यक्ति ■ **at one's wits' end** किंकर्तव्यविमूढ होना **have one's wits about one** प्रत्युत्पन्नमति रहना ▸ **witticism** *noun* **wittily** *adv* **witty** / विटि / *adj* (-ier, -iest) विनोदपूर्ण : *a witty speaker.*

witch / विच् / *noun* *(पूर्व समय में)* चुड़ैल, डाइन; जादूगरनी ▸ **witchcraft** *noun* जादू-टोना **witch-doctor** *noun* ओझा।

with / विद्; विध् / *prep* 1 के साथ/की उपस्थिति में : *She lives with her parents.* 2 किसी वस्तु/व्यक्ति के गुण/विशेषता का सूचक : *a girl with red hair* 3 (साधनसूचक) : *feed the baby with a spoon* 4 पक्ष में, समर्थन में : *Are you with us on this issue?* 5 के विरोध में/ से : *fight with sb* 6 के कारण, के फलस्वरूप 7 साथ-साथ; उसी दिशा में : *sail with the wind.*

withdraw / विद्'ड्रॉ / *verb* (*pt* **withdrew** / विद्'ड्रू /; *pp* **withdrawn** / विद् 'ड्रॉन्/) 1 **withdraw sb/sth (from sth)** पीछे खींच लेना, पीछे हटा लेना; बैंक से पैसा निकालना : *The old coins have been withdrawn from circulation.* ○ *I'd like to withdraw Rs 10,000 please.* 2 वादे से मुकर जाना, प्रस्ताव करके पीछे हट जाना 3 **withdraw (from sth)** वापस होना या भेजना : *Heavy bombardment forced the army to withdraw.* ▸ **withdrawal** *noun* **withdrawn** *adj.*

wither / विद्र / *verb* 1 (पौधों का) मुरझाना, कुम्हलाना 2 **wither (away)** कमज़ोर होना, क्षीण हो जाना : *Their hopes gradually withered away.*

withhold / विद्'होल्ड् / *verb* (*pt, pp* **withheld** / विद्'हेल्ड् /) **withhold sth**

(from sb/ sth) रोक रखना; देने से इनकार करना : *withhold one's consent.*

within / विदिन् / *prep* 1 (समयावधि की) सीमा के अंदर : *I should be back within an hour.* 2 सीमा/विस्तार के भीतर/अंदर : *He finds it hard to live within his income.* ○ *within hearing* ▸ **within** *adv* (औप) भीतर : *Cleaner required. Apply within.*

without / विद्राउट् / *prep* 1 के बिना, से रहित : *Don't go without me.* 2 से ख़ाली/रहित : *two days without food* 3 किसी वस्तु का प्रयोग न करते हुए ▸ **without** *adv part* से रहित/ख़ाली/ बिना।

withstand / विद्स्टैन्ड्; विथ्स्टैन्ड् / *verb* (*pt, pp* **withstood**) रोकना, प्रतिरोध करना; सहन करना : *withstand attacks/pressure.*

witness / विट्नस् / *noun* 1 (**eye-witness** भी) प्रत्यक्षदर्शी, चश्मदीद गवाह 2 (न्यायालय में) गवाह, साक्षी व्यक्ति 3 (औप) किसी व्यक्ति या वस्तु के लिए कहा कथन : *give witness on behalf of an accused person* 4 लिखित हस्ताक्षर को प्रमाणित करने वाला व्यक्ति ■ **bear witness** साक्ष्य देना ▸ **witness** *verb* 1 घटना का साक्षी होना 2 (किसी समझौते या प्रलेख का) साक्ष्य देना 3 **witness to sth** (क़ानून या औप) न्यायालय में गवाही देना।

wittingly / विटिङ्ग्लि / *adv* जानबूझकर, प्रयोजन से : *He offended her wittingly.*

wizard / विज़र्ड् / *noun* 1 (कहानियों आदि में) जादूगर, ओझा 2 अत्यंत निपुण व्यक्ति, उस्ताद : *a financial wizard.*

wizened / विज़्न्ड् / *adj* (चेहरा) झुर्री पड़ा, बूढ़ा : *a face wizened with age.*

wobble / वॉब्ल् / *verb* **wobble sth** (about/around) लड़खड़ाना, ढुलमुल होना या करना : *This table wobbles.* ▸ **wobbly** / वॉब्लि / *adj* ढुलमुल।

woe / वो / *noun* (अप्र, औप) 1 व्यथा, घनी पीड़ा : *a tale of woe* 2 **woes** [*pl*] दुखदायी वस्तु : *economic woes* ▸ **woeful** *adj* दुखमय, दयनीय।

wolf / वुल्फ् / *noun* (*pl* **wolves** / वुल्व्ज़् /) भेड़िया।

woman / वुमन् / *noun* (*pl* **women** / विमिन् /) 1 नारी, महिला 2 पत्नी, प्रेमिका ▸ **womanhood** *noun* नारीत्व : *reach womanhood.*

womb / वूम् / *noun* गर्भ; बच्चेदानी; कोख ।

wonder / वन्डर् / *noun* आश्चर्य; आश्चर्यजनक घटना आदि : *the wonders of modern technology* ▸ **wonder** *verb* 1 **wonder (about sth)** आश्चर्य का अनुभव करना 2 **wonder (at sth)** आश्चर्यचकित होना, उत्सुक होना **wonderful** *adj* आश्चर्यजनक; प्रशंसनीय, उत्तम।

wont / वोन्ट् / *adj* **wont (to do sth)** (अप्र या साहि) आदी।

woo / वू / *verb* (*pt, pp* **wooed**) 1 प्रणय निवेदन करना 2 समर्थन पाने की कोशिश करना; (यश, संपत्ति आदि) पाने का यत्न करना : *woo the voters.*

wood / वुड् / *noun* 1 लकड़ी 2 (प्रायः *pl*) वन, जंगल : *go for a walk in the wood(s)* 3 लकड़ी का गोल्फ़ क्लब ▸ **wooded** *adj* जंगल से भरा : *a wooded valley* **wooden** *adj* 1 लकड़ी का बना 2 (अलं) (व्यवहार) भावशून्य, रूखा और भद्दा **woodland** *noun* वनस्थली **woodwork** *noun* 1 लकड़ी का काम 2 बढ़ई-गिरी **woody** *adj* पेड़ों से ढका हुआ : *a woody hillside.*

woodcutter / वुड्कटर् / *noun* (अप्र) लकड़हारा।

woodpecker / वुड्पेकर् / *noun* कठफोड़वा।

woof / वुफ़ / *interj, noun* (अनौप) कुत्ते की भौंकने की आवाज़।

wool / वूल् / *noun* ऊन; ऊनी वस्त्र : *a wool coat* ▸ **woollen** (US **woolen** भी) / 'वुलन् / *adj* ऊनी : *woollen gloves* **woolly** (US **wooly**) *adj* 1 ऊन से भरा हुआ : *woolly sheep* 2 ऊनी सामान।

word / वर्ड् / *noun* 1 (व्या) शब्द 2 कथन, बातचीत : *a word of advice* 3 समाचार, ख़बर 4 वादा, वचन : *I never doubted her word.* 5 (प्राय: the word) आदेश या संकेत : *Stay hidden until I give the word.* ■ **have a word with sb** से बातचीत करना **have words (with sb/ about sth)** झगड़ पड़ना/तर्क करना **in other words** दूसरे शब्दों में... **put in/ say a good word for sb** किसी के समर्थन में कुछ कहना **take sb at their word** इस विश्वास पर चलना कि जो वह कहता है वही करेगा ▸ **word** *verb* शब्दों में व्यक्त करना : *a carefully worded reminder* **wording** *noun* [*sing*] वाक्य रचना **wordless** *adj* **word processor** *noun* कंप्यूटर जिसमें पत्र, रिपोर्ट, लेख आदि लिखने का प्रोग्राम होता है; इसमें लिखित मैटर को बार-बार संपादित करने की सुविधा होती है।

work¹ / वर्क् / *noun* 1 कार्य, काम 2 काम जो करना है, कृत्य : *There is plenty of work to be done in the garden.* 3 कृति, बनाई वस्तु : *an exhibition of the work of young sculptors* 4 (किसी कार्य को पूरा करने के लिए) अपेक्षित वस्तुएँ 5 जीविकोपार्जन का धंधा, काम : *She has been out of work for a year.* 6 रचना, बुद्धि या कल्पना की कृति : *the collected works of Tolstoy* 7 **the works** [*pl*] मशीन के चलनशील पुर्ज़े 8 **works** [*pl*] (समासों में) भवन निर्माण या मरम्मत कार्य : *roadwork ○ publicworks* ■ **at work (on sth)** काम पर व्यस्त **get/set to work** काम

करना आरंभ करना **make short work of sth** तुरंत समाप्त करना ▸ **work-bag, work-basket, workbox** *noun* औज़ार-पेटी **workman** *noun* मज़दूर, कारीगर **workmanlike** *adj* कार्यकुशल **work-manship** *noun* कारीगरी : *They admired her workmanship.* **work-shop** *noun* कारख़ाना।

work² / वर्क् / *verb* 1 **work (away) (at/ on sth); work (under sb)** काम करना 2 **work (for sb/sth)** नौकरी करना 3 (मशीन, शरीर के अंगों का) अपेक्षित कार्य करना : *The gears work smoothly.* 4 **work (on sb/sth)** (प्रभाव) उत्पन्न करना; (योजना का) फलीभूत होना 5 काम कराना; चालू करना : *It works by electricity.* 6 लाभ प्राप्ति के लिए कुछ करना : *work a mine/an oil well* 7 **work sth (into sth)** ठोक-पीटकर आकार में लाना : *work gold* 8 **work sth (on sth)** सिलाई करना ■ **work sb/oneself up (into sth)** भड़काना **work sth off** 1 ऋण चुकाने के लिए धन कमाना 2 मात्रा या प्रभाव कम करना **work sth out** 1 हिसाब लगाना 2 समस्या सुलझाना/का हल निकालना 3 योजना बनाना **work (sth) up** धीरे-धीरे सुधारना **work towards sth** लक्ष्य को प्राप्त करने की चेष्टा करना।

workable / 'वर्कबल् / *adj* 1 व्याव-हारिक : *a workable solution* 2 संचालन योग्य।

worker / 'वर्कर् / *noun* मज़दूर, कामगार।

world / वर्ल्ड् / *noun* 1 **the world** [*sing*] दुनिया, संसार 2 **the world** [*sing*] जगत 3 किसी विशेष गतिविधि आदि में रुचि रखने वाले सभी लोग : *the world of art/sport* ■ **be worlds apart** व्यवहार, रवैया, विचार आदि में बिलकुल भिन्न होना **out of this world** (अनौप) आश्चर्यजनक, अत्यधिक सुंदर, शानदार ▸ **worldliness** *noun* **worldly** *adj* 1 भौतिक (धन, संपत्ति आदि से संबद्ध) : *one's worldly goods*

2 लौकिक, ऐहलौकिक (न कि आध्यात्मिक): *worldly pleasures.* **worldwide** *adj,* *adv* विश्वभर में।

worm / वर्म् / *noun* 1 कीड़ा; **worms** [*pl*] कृमि 2 (*अपमा*) अनैतिक और बेईमान व्यक्ति ▸ **worm** *verb* 1 पशुओं को कृमि की दवाई देना 2 धीरे-धीरे (जैसे कि रेंगते हुए) कहीं जाना : *They had to worm their way through the narrow tunnel.* ■ **worm one's way/oneself into sth** (*अपमा*) धीरे-धीरे कुछ पाना।

worry / 'वरि / *verb* (*pt, pp* **worried**) 1 **worry** (**about/over sb/sth**) परेशान होना या करना; चिंता में पड़ना, चिंतित होना 2 **worry sb** (**with sth**) किसी को परेशान या तंग करना : *The noise doesn't seem to worry them.* ▸ **worried** *adj* **worried** (**about sb/sth**); **worried** (**that...**) चिंतित, परेशान **worry** *noun* (*pl* **worries**) 1 चिंता, चिंतित होने की स्थिति 2 चिंता का कारण : *He has a lot of financial worries at the moment.*

worse / वर्स / *adj* (**bad** का तुलनात्मक रूप) **worse** (**than sth/doing sth**) बदतर (स्थिति या स्वास्थ्य) : *The weather got worse during the day.* ■ **go from bad to worse** स्थिति या हालात का पहले से बदतर होना ▸ **worse** *adv* ■ **worse off** और बुरी हालत में ▸ **worsen** / 'वर्स्न् / *verb* बदतर अथवा अत्यंत गिरी हुई स्थिति उत्पन्न करना या होना : *worsening economic situation.*

worship / 'वर्शिप् / *noun* 1 पूजा, पूजन : *bow one's head in worship* 2 भक्ति, आराधना; समादर : *hero worship* ▸ **worship** *verb* (-**pp**-; *US* -**p**-) 1 पूजा करना 2 चर्च सर्विस के लिए जाना 3 समादर देना **worshipper** *noun.*

worst / वर्स्ट / *adj* (**bad** का उत्तमावस्था) सबसे बुरा : *It was the worst storm for years.* ▸ **worst** *noun* सबसे बुरा भाग, समय आदि ■ **get the worst of it** हार

जाना **if the worst comes to the worst** यदि स्थिति जितनी ख़राब हो सकती है उतनी हो जाए : *If the worst comes to the worst, we'll just have to sell the house.*

worth / वर्थ् / *adj* 1 **be worth sth** किसी विशेष मूल्य वाला, क़ीमत का 2 **worth sth/doing sth** संतोषजनक लाभ देने वाला; श्रम के अनुसार तृप्ति/लाभ देने वाला : *It's not worth the trouble.* ■ **for all one/it is worth** पूरी क्षमता एवं शक्ति के साथ **worth sb's while** (जितना समय, श्रम आदि लगाया है उसके अनुसार) लाभकर ▸ **worth** *noun* 1 **worth of sth** मूल्य : *The thieves stole Rs 10,000 worth of jewellery.* 2 योग्यता **worthless** *adj* **worthwhile** *adj* लाभकर, सार्थक : *Nursing is a very worthwhile career.*

worthy / 'वर्दि / *adj* (-**ier**, -**iest**) 1 **worthy of sth/to do sth** के योग्य : *a statement worthy of contempt* 2 आदर के योग्य : *a worthy cause* 3 **worthy of sb/sth** (किसी के लिए) उचित; विशिष्ट : *It was a performance worthy of a master.* ▸ **worthily** *adv* **worthiness** *noun.*

would / वुड् / *modal verb* (लघु रूप '**d**) 1 (भूतकाल की क्रियाओं के साथ **will** के स्थान पर प्रयुक्त) : *He said he would be here at 8 o'clock.* 2 (काल्पनिक घटना के परिणाम के वर्णन में) : *If you went to see him, he would be delighted.* 3 (प्रश्नों या प्रतिबंधित वाक्यों में) : *If I had seen the advertisement in time, I would have applied for the job.* 4 (नम्रतापूर्ण व्यवहार में) : *Would you have dinner with me on Friday?* ∘ *Would you open the door for me, please?* 5 (स्वभाव अथवा पहले के व्यवहार के अनुसार): *He would always be the first to offer help.* ▸ **would-**

be *adj* जो कोई व्यक्ति बनना तो बहुत चाहता है किंतु है नहीं : *a would-be artist.*

wound / वून्ड् / *noun* 1 घाव, ज़ख़्म 2 wound (to sth) भावनाओं को पहुँचने वाली ठेस : *deep psychological wounds* ▸ **wound** *verb* 1 घाव करना/होना 2 ठेस पहुँचाना।

wow / वाउ / *interj* (अनौप) आश्चर्य, विस्मय, प्रशंसा आदि व्यक्त करने के लिए प्रयुक्त शब्द।

wrangle / 'रैङ्ग्ल् / *noun* wrangle (with sb) (about/over sth) कहा-सुनी, तकरार/झगड़ा ▸ **wrangle** *verb* wrangle (with sb) (about/over sth) कहा-सुनी होना, तकरार/झगड़ा होना या करना।

wrap / रैप् / *verb* (-pp-) 1 wrap sth (up) (in sth) (काग़ज़, प्लास्टिक आदि से) लपेटना, पूर्णत: ढक लेना : *individually wrapped chocolates* 2 wrap sth round/around sb/sth (शाल आदि) चारों ओर लपेट लेना/देना, गरम कपड़े ओढ़ लेना ■ be wrapped up in sb/sth तल्लीन होना, पूरी-पूरी रुचि दिखाना wrap sth up (अनौप) (विचार-विमर्श, विवाद आदि) संतोषजनक रूप से समाप्त करना ▸ **wrap** *noun* 1 शाल, गुलूबंद, कंबल आदि 2 लपेटने में प्रयुक्त काग़ज़, प्लास्टिक आदि **wrapper** / 'रैपर् / *noun* चॉकलेट, किताब, कॉपी आदि का रैपर **wrapping** *noun* लपेटने में प्रयुक्त सामान।

wrath / रॉथ् / *noun* (अप्र, साहि) रोष, गहरा क्रोध।

wreak / रीक् / *verb* wreak sth (on sb) (औप) अधिक क्षति पहुँचाना, नष्ट कर देना : *wreak one's fury on sb.*

wreath / रीथ् / *noun* (pl wreaths / रीद्ज़् /) 1 (फूलों की) माला, हार : *a funeral wreath* 2 (धुएँ आदि के) छल्ले : *wreaths of mist.*

wreck / रेक् / *noun* 1 क्षतिग्रस्त जहाज़ 2 बुरी तरह क्षतिग्रस्त कार; गिरे हुए हवाई जहाज़ या खंडहर का मलबा 3 (प्राय:

sing) (अनौप) शारीरिक/मानसिक रूप से विक्षत व्यक्ति : *a nervous/gibbering wreck* ▸ **wreck** *verb* 1 जहाज़ को क्षतिग्रस्त करना 2 पूरी तरह नष्ट करना; ख़राब कर देना **wreckage** / 'रेकिज् / *noun* मलबा : *A few survivors were pulled from the wreckage.*

wrench / रेन्च् / *verb* 1 wrench sth off (sth) झटके से मरोड़ना या खींचना : *wrench a door off its hinges* 2 मरोड़कर कंधे या टखने में चोट पहुँचाना या खाना ▸ **wrench** *noun* 1 मरोड़, झटका 2 [sing] बिछड़ने की पीड़ा या व्यथा : *Leaving home was a terrible wrench for me.* 3 रिंच (ढिबरी आदि कसने का औज़ार)।

wrest / रेस्ट् / *verb* ■ wrest sth from sb/sth (औप) झटके से खींचना/छीनना : *He wrested the gun from me.*

wrestle / 'रेस्ल् / *verb* wrestle (with sb) कुश्ती लड़ना ■ wrestle with sth किसी समस्या से जूझना; संघर्ष करना : *wrestle with a problem* ▸ **wrestler** / 'रेस्लर् / *noun* पहलवान।

wretch / रेच् / *noun* 1 अभागा, कम-बख़्त : *a poor half-starved wretch* 2 (प्राय: परि) नीच, कमीना व्यक्ति।

wretched / 'रेचिड् / *adj* 1 बदनसीब, दयनीय : *His migraine made him feel wretched.* 2 घटिया, असंतोषजनक।

wriggle / 'रिग्ल् / *verb* छटपटाना, तड़पना; ऐंठना, मरोड़ना : *The baby was wriggling its toes.* ○ *The fish wriggled out of my fingers.* ○ *The thieves left her tied up but she wriggled (her arms/herself) free.*

wring / रिङ् / *verb* (pt, pp wrung / रङ् /) 1 wring sth (out) ऐंठना, मरोड़ना (द्रव निकालने के लिए); (कपड़ों में से) पानी निचोड़ना 2 पक्षी को मारने के लिए गरदन मरोड़ना ▸ **wringer** *noun* कपड़ों में से पानी निचोड़ने वाली मशीन।

wrinkle / 'रिङ्क्ल् / *noun* 1 (प्राय: pl)

चेहरे आदि पर झुर्री : *She's beginning to get wrinkles around her eyes.* 2 (कपड़ों में) शिकन ▸ **wrinkle** *verb* 1 चेहरे पर शिकन लाना/डालना : *She wrinkled her nose in distaste.* 2 शिकन डालना/पड़ना **wrinkled** *adj* : *his old wrinkled face.*

wrist / रिस्ट् / *noun* (हाथ की) कलाई ▸ **wristwatch**/'रिस्टवॉच्/*noun* कलाई की घड़ी।

writ/रिट्/*noun* writ (for sth) (क़ानून) रिट, न्यायादेश।

write / राइट् / *verb* (*pt* wrote / रोट्/; *pp* written /'रिट्न्/) 1 लिखना 2 लिखकर रचना करना : *write a book/speech* 3 write sth (to sb) पत्र लिखना 4 write (about/on sth) लेखक या पत्रकार के रूप में काम करना 5 (कलम, पेंसिल आदि का) लिखने योग्य होना : *This pen won't write.* ■ **write back (to sb)** पत्र का उत्तर देना **write sth off** ऋण नहीं लौटेगा यह मानकर उसे समाप्त करना **write sb/sth off** पूर्णतया विफलता देख आगे कार्य न बढ़ाना।

writer /'राइटर् / *noun* लेखक, पत्रकार।

writhe /राइद्/*verb* (पीड़ा से) छटपटाना, तड़पना; (*अलं*) मनोव्यथा से छटपटाना।

writing/'राइटिङ्ग्/*noun* 1 लेख, किताब आदि लिखने, रचने की प्रक्रिया 2 **writings** [*pl*] रचनाएँ, कृतियाँ 3 हाथ की लिखावट ■ **in writing** लिखित रूप में।

wrong¹/रॉङ्/*adj* 1 असत्य, ग़लत : *He got the answer wrong.* 2 **wrong (about sth/sb); wrong (to do sth)** (व्यक्ति) ग़लती करना, ग़लत होना 3 अनु-

पयुक्त; ख़राब : *We were on the wrong train.* 4 **wrong (of/for sb) (to do sth)** अनैतिक; अन्यायपूर्ण ▸ **wrong** *verb* (औप) किसी के साथ ग़लत व्यवहार करना : *a wronged wife* **wrongful** *adj* अन्यायपूर्ण; अवैध **wrongfully** *adv* **wrongly** *adv* ग़लत रूप/रीति से : *wrongly spelt/translated.*

wrong²/रॉङ्/*adv* ग़लत ढंग से : *You've spelt my name wrong.* ■ **get sb wrong** (अनौप) किसी को ग़लत समझना **go wrong** 1 गड़बड़ होना, ग़लती करना 2 (मशीन आदि का) ख़राब हो जाना : *The car radio has gone wrong again.* 3 पथभ्रष्ट होना, चरित्रहीन हो जाना **in the wrong** दोषी होना।

wrong³/रॉङ्/*noun* ग़लत काम या कार्य; (औप) ऐसा काम जो नैतिक दृष्टि से ग़लत हो : *They have done us a great wrong.* ■ **in the wrong** दोषी होना।

wrongdoing /'रॉङ्डूइङ्/ *noun* अधर्म, अन्याय; पापाचार।

wrought/रॉट्/*verb* (औप, साहि, अप्र) (**work** का *pp*) कृत, घटित : *changes wrought in our society* ▸ **wrought** *adj* उत्पादित; (धातु) पीटकर आकार में लाई गई **wrought iron** *noun* गढ़ा हुआ लोहा **wrought up** *adj* व्यग्र, उत्तेजित।

wry / राइ / *adj* 1 स्थिति की समझ की चतुरतापूर्ण भाव वाली अभिव्यक्ति (चेहरे पर): *a wry grin/smile* 2 निराशा, नाराज़गी आदि दिखाने के लिए टेढ़ा किया हुआ (चेहरा) : *pull a wry face* ▸ **wryly** *adv.*

Xx

xenophobia / ˌzen'fəʊbɪə / *noun*
विदेशियों या अजनबियों से भय-द्वेष।

Xerox / 'ज़िअरॉक्स् / *noun* (ट्रेडमार्क)
मशीन जो फोटोकॉपी निकालती है ।

Xmas / 'क्रिस्मस्; 'ऐक्स्मस् / *noun*
(अनौप) क्रिसमस पर्व, क्रिसमस/एक्समस/

बड़ा दिन।

X-ray / 'ऐक्स् रे / *noun* (*pl* **X-rays**)
एक्स-रे; एक्स-रे की फ़ोटो।

xylophone / 'ज़ाइलफ़ोन् / *noun*
लकड़ी का बना हुआ एक प्रकार का वाद्य
यंत्र।

Yy

yacht / यॉट् / *noun* नौका-दौड़ की नाव; नौका-विहार के लिए आरामदेह नाव : *a yacht club/race* ▸ **yachting** *noun.*

yam / यैम् / *noun* घुइयाँ, रतालू; (US) एक प्रकार की शकरकंद।

yank / यैङ्क् / *verb* (अनौप) झटके के साथ खींचना : *She yanked (on) the rope and it broke.*

yard¹ / याई / *noun* 1 (*संक्षि* yd) गज़ (= 36 इंच) 2 जहाज़ के पाल में लगा डंडा ▸ **yardage** *noun* गज़ में मापा आकार-क्षेत्र।

yard² / याई / *noun* 1 अहाता, प्रांगण; बाड़ा : *Children were playing ball in the yard at the back of the house.* 2 प्रयोजन-विशेष के लिए प्रयुक्त भू-क्षेत्र : *a railway yard.*

yardstick / 'याईस्टिक् / *noun* तुलना करने का आधार।

yarn / यार्न् / *noun* 1 सूत, तागा 2 (अनौप) गपशप, मनढंत किस्सा : *spin a yarn* (किस्सा गढ़ना)।

yawn / यॉन् / *verb* 1 जँभाई लेना 2 (छेद आदि) फैला हुआ होना : (*अलं*) *a yawning gap between rich and poor* ▸ **yawn** *noun* 1 जँभाई 2 (प्राय: *sing*) (अनौप, अपमा) उबाऊ कहानी, घटना, समारोह आदि।

yeah / येआ / *adv* (अनौप) हाँ।

year / यिअर् / *noun* 1 साल, वर्ष 2 (प्राय: *pl*) उम्र; जीवन अवधि : *be twenty years old* ■ *year after year* अनेक सालों तक लगातार ▸ **yearly** *adj, adv* वार्षिक : *a yearly conference.*

yearn / यर्न् / *verb* **yearn (for sb/sth)** ललकना, लालायित होना, रहना : *He yearned for his home.* ▸ **yearning** / 'यर्निङ् / *noun* **yearning (for sb/sth)**; **yearning (to do sth)** उत्कंठा, ललक **yearningly** *adv.*

yeast / यीस्ट् / *noun* ख़मीर, यीस्ट।

yell / येल् / *verb* 1 **yell (out) (in/with sth)** चिल्लाना, चीख़ना : *yell out in pain* 2 **yell (at sb) (about/for sth)** चिल्लाकर कहना; किसी पर चिल्लाना : *She yelled at the child to get down off the wall.* ▸ **yell** *noun* चिल्लाहट; चीख़।

yellow / 'येलो / *adj* पीले रंग का, पीला ▸ **yellow** *noun* पीला रंग, पीलापन; पीली वस्तु या पीतांबर **yellow** *verb* पीला होना या करना : *yellowing leaves* **yellow fever** *noun* पीतज्वर (एक प्रकार का बुख़ार)।

yelp / येल्प् / *verb* (कुत्ते का) चीख़ना ▸ **yelp** *noun* चीख़ (कुत्ते की)।

yes / येस् / *interj* (सहमति सूचक) हाँ : *'Isn't she sweet?' 'Yes.'*

yesterday / 'येस्टर्डे / *adv* बीता हुआ कल : *He only arrived yesterday.* ▸ **yesterday** *noun* 1 कल : *Yesterday was Sunday.* 2 निकट भूतकाल : *dressed in yesterday's fashions.*

yet / येट् / *adv* 1 तब तक : *They won't arrive for at least two hours yet.* 2 अब तक : *I haven't received a letter from him yet.* 3 उस समय तक : *We may win yet.* ▸ **yet** *conj* फिर भी, किंतु।

yield / यील्ड् / *verb* 1 फल देना, फ़सल देना 2 **yield (to sb/sth)** (औप) आत्मसमर्पण करना; शक्ति के आगे झुक जाना : *She yielded to temptation and had another chocolate.* 3 दबाव से मुड़ जाना या टूट जाना 4 **yield to sth** से स्थानांतरित हो जाना या कर दिया जाना ▸ **yield** *noun* उपज, पैदावार : *a good/poor yield of wheat* **yielding** *adj* आज्ञाकारी, दबने वाला; (पदार्थ) मुड़ने या टूटने वाला, मुलायम।

yoga / 'योगा / *noun* योग; योग-व्यायाम, श्वास क्रिया।

yogurt (yoghurt, yoghourt भी) / 'यॉगर्ट; US 'योगर्ट / noun दही।

yoke / योक् / noun 1 (हल का) जुआ/जूआ 2 **yoke (of sth/sb)** (और) असहनीय कठोर व्यवहार एवं पराधीनता : throw off the yoke of slavery ▸ **yoke** verb 1 **yoke sth (to sth)** (बैलों पर) जुआ रखना 2 (और) **yoke A and B (together) (in sth)** व्यक्तियों, विचारों को जोड़ना, सन्नद्ध करना : companies yoked (together) in a trilateral deal.

yolk / योक् / noun अंडे की ज़रदी (पीला भाग)।

yonder / 'यॉन्डर् / det, adj, adv (अप्र) वहाँ, उधर : Whose is that farm (over) yonder?

you / यू / pers pron 1 तू, तुम, आप : You said you knew the way. 2 कोई भी व्यक्ति : You learn a language better if you visit the country where it is spoken.

young / यङ् / adj (-er, -est) 1 अल्प-वयस्क, किशोर; जवान 2 अपरिपक्व, अनुभवहीन : My daughter's thirteen but she's young for her age. 3 (अलं) आरंभिक स्थिति में : The night is still young. ▸ **young** noun [pl] 1 जानवरों के बच्चे 2 **the young** बच्चा/बच्चे : a film that appeals to the young **youngster** / 'यङ्ग्स्टर् / noun छोकरा/छोकरी, बच्चा।

your / यॉर् / possess det 1 तेरा, तुम्हारा, आपका : Excuse me, is this your seat? 2 किसी का : In Japan you are taught great respect for your elders. ▸ **yours** / यॉर्ज़् / possess pron 1 तेरा, तुम्हारा, आपका : Is that book yours? 2 (प्राय: **Yours**) (पत्र के अंत में प्रयुक्त) : Yours faithfully/sincerely/truly.

yourself / यॉर्'सेल्फ् / pron (pl **yourselves**) 1 (reflex) स्वयं : Have you hurt yourself? 2 (emph) आप ही : You yourself are one of the chief offenders.

youth / यूथ् / noun (pl **youths** / यूद्ज़् /) 1 किशोरावस्था, यौवन, जवानी 2 (प्राय: अपमा) जवान, किशोर : The fight was started by some youths who had been drinking. 3 (**the youth** भी) जवान लोग, युवक-युवतियाँ : the country's youth ▸ **youthful** adj तरुण; तरुणवत् : a youthful appearance.

yuck (yuk भी) / यक् / interj (अप) घृणा, अरुचि, नापसंदगी आदि व्यक्त करने के लिए प्रयुक्त।

Yule / यूल् / noun (**Yule-tide** भी) (अप्र) क्रिसमस।

yummy / 'यमि / adj (अनौप) स्वादिष्ट : Mum's made us a yummy chocolate cake.

yuppie (yuppy भी) / 'यपि / noun (अनौप, अक्सर अपमा) महत्त्वाकांक्षी और धनपिपासु तरुण व्यावसायिक।

Zz

zeal / ज़ील् / *noun* zeal (for/in sth); zeal (to do sth) (*औप*) उत्साह, जोश : *revolutionary/missionary zeal* ▸ **zealous** /'ज़ेलस्/ *adj* उत्साही।

zebra / 'ज़ेब्रा; 'ज़ीब्रा / *noun* (*pl* अपरिवर्तित या **zebras**) ज़ेब्रा (चितीदार घोड़े जैसा पशु) ▸ **zebra crossing** *noun* बड़ी सड़कों पर सफेद काली पट्टियाँ जो पैदल चलने वालों को सड़क पार करने का प्रथमाधिकार देती हैं।

zenith /'ज़ेनिथ्/ *noun* 1 आकाश का वह बिंदु जो ठीक सिर के ऊपर हो 2 (*अलं*) चरम सीमा, पराकाष्ठा : *reach the zenith of one's career.*

zero /'ज़िअरो/ *noun, pron, det* 1 शून्य (का अंक), 0 2 (+) और (–) के बीच का शून्यांक 3 निम्नतम बिंदु, कुछ नहीं : *zero inflation/growth.*

zest / ज़ेस्ट् / *noun* 1 मज़ा, रस 2 **zest** (for sth) रुचि, उत्साह : *have a zest for life* ▸ **zestful** *adj.*

zigzag /'ज़िग्ज़ैग्/ *noun* टेढ़ी-मेढ़ी रेखा ▸ **zigzag** *adj* टेढ़ा-मेढ़ा : *a zigzag road* **zigzag** *verb* (-gg-) टेढ़ी-मेढ़ी रीति से चलना।

zinc / ज़िंक् / *noun* (प्रतीक Zn) जस्ता, एक प्रकार की धातु।

zip / ज़िप् / *noun* (**zip-fastener** भी) ज़िप (कपड़े के दो हिस्सों को पास रखने वाली चेन, ज़िप)।

zodiac / 'ज़ोडिऐक् / *noun* राशिचक्र (आकाश के कुछ नक्षत्रों का बारह राशियों में विभाजन)।

zone / ज़ोन् / *noun* 1 क्षेत्र विशेष : *smoke-less zone* 2 मेखला, पेटी 3 (*भूगोल*) पृथ्वी के पाँच कटिबंधों में से कोई : *the tropical/torrid zone.*

zoo / ज़ू / *noun* (*pl* **zoos**) (*औप* **zoo-logical gardens** [*pl*] भी) चिड़ियाघर।

zoology /ज़ो'ऑलजि; जु'ऑलजि/ *noun* प्राणिशास्त्र, जीवविज्ञान ▸ **zoological** *adj* प्राणिविज्ञान विषयक **zoologist** / ज़ो'ऑलजिस्ट्; जु'ऑलजिस्ट् / *noun* जीवविज्ञानी।

zoom / ज़ूम् / *verb* 1 (वायुयान, गाड़ी आदि का) आवाज़ करते हुए तेज़ी से गुज़रना 2 (*अनौप*) (क़ीमतें आदि) अचानक तेज़ी से बढ़ जाना : *Overnight trading caused share prices to zoom (up).* 3 (कंप्यूटर) दृश्य को अत्यधिक बड़ा कर देना।

Appendix 1
Irregular Verbs

Infinitive	Past Tense	Past Participle
arise	arose	arisen
awake	awoke	awoken
be	was/were	been
bear	bore	borne
beat	beat	beaten
become	became	become
befall	befell	befallen
begin	began	begun
bend	bent	bent
bet	bet, betted	bet, betted
bid	bid, bade	bid, bidden
bind	bound	bound
bite	bit	bitten
bleed	bled	bled
blow	blew	blown, blowed
break	broke	broken
breed	bred	bred
bring	brought	brought
broadcast	broadcast	broadcast
build	built	built
burn	burnt, burned	burnt, burned
burst	burst	burst
bust	bust, busted	bust, busted
buy	bought	bought
cast	cast	cast
catch	caught	caught
choose	chose	chosen
cling	clung	clung
come	came	come
cost	cost	cost
creep	crept	crept
cut	cut	cut
deal	dealt	dealt
dig	dug	dug
dive	dived; (US) dove	dived
do	did	done
draw	drew	drawn
dream	dreamt, dreamed	dreamt, dreamed
drink	drank	drunk
drive	drove	driven
dwell	dwelt, dwelled	dwelt, dwelled
eat	ate	eaten
fall	fell	fallen
feed	fed	fed
feel	felt	felt
fight	fought	fought
find	found	found
flee	fled	fled
fling	flung	flung

fly	flew	flown
forbid	forbade	forbidden
forecast	forecast, forecasted	forecast, forecasted
foresee	foresaw	foreseen
foretell	foretold	foretold
forget	forgot	forgotten
forgive	forgave	forgiven
forsake	forsook	forsaken
freeze	froze	frozen
get	got	got; *(US)* gotten
give	gave	given
go	went	gone
grind	ground	ground
grow	grew	grown
hang	hung, hanged	hung, hanged
have	had	had
hear	heard	heard
hew	hewed	hewed, hewn
hide	hid	hidden
hit	hit	hit
hold	held	held
hurt	hurt	hurt
input	input, inputted	input, inputted
keep	kept	kept
kneel	knelt; *(esp US)* kneeled	knelt; *(esp US)* kneeled
know	knew	known
lay	laid	laid
lead	led	led
lean	leant, leaned	leant, leaned
leap	leapt, leaped	leapt, leaped
learn	learnt, learned	learnt, learned
leave	left	left
lend	lent	lent
let	let	let
lie	lay	lain
light	lighted, lit	lighted, lit
lose	lost	lost
make	made	made
mean	meant	meant
meet	met	met
mislay	mislaid	mislaid
mislead	misled	misled
misread	misread	misread
misspell	misspelt, misspelled	misspelt, misspelled
mistake	mistook	mistaken
misunderstand	misunderstood	misunderstood
mow	mowed	mown, mowed
outdo	outdid	outdone
outgrow	outgrew	outgrown
overcome	overcame	overcome
overdo	overdid	overdone
overhang	overhung	overhung
overhear	overheard	overheard

override	overrode	overridden
overrun	overran	overrun
oversee	oversaw	overseen
oversleep	overslept	overslept
overtake	overtook	overtaken
overthrow	overthrew	overthrown
pay	paid	paid
prove	proved	proved; *(US)* proven
put	put	put
quit	quit, quitted	quit, quitted
read	read	read
rebuild	rebuilt	rebuilt
repay	repaid	repaid
rewrite	rewrote	rewritten
rid	rid	rid
ride	rode	ridden
ring	rang	rung
rise	rose	risen
run	ran	run
saw	sawed	sawn; *(US)* sawed
say	said	said
see	saw	seen
seek	sought	sought
sell	sold	sold
send	sent	sent
set	set	set
sew	sewed	sewn, sewed
shake	shook	shaken
shear	sheared	shorn, sheared
shed	shed	shed
shine	shone	shone
shoe	shod	shod
shoot	shot	shot
show	showed	shown, showed
shrink	shrank, shrunk	shrunk
shut	shut	shut
sing	sang	sung
sink	sank	sunk
sit	sat	sat
slay	slew	slain
sleep	slept	slept
slide	slid	slid
sling	slung	slung
slink	slunk	slunk
slit	slit	slit
smell	smelt, smelled	smelt, smelled
sow	sowed	sown, sowed
speak	spoke	spoken
speed	sped, speeded	sped, speeded
spell	spelt, spelled	spelt, spelled
spend	spent	spent
spill	spilt, spilled	spilt, spilled
spin	spun	spun

spit	spat; (*US* also) spit	spat; (*US* also) spit
split	split	split
spoil	spoilt, spoiled	spoilt, spoiled
spread	spread	spread
spring	sprang	sprung
stand	stood	stood
steal	stole	stolen
stick	stuck	stuck
sting	stung	stung
stink	stank, stunk	stunk
stride	strode	stridden
strike	struck	struck
string	strung	strung
strive	strove	striven
swear	swore	sworn
sweep	swept	swept
swell	swelled	swollen, swelled
swim	swam	swum
swing	swung	swung
take	took	taken
teach	taught	taught
tear	tore	torn
tell	told	told
think	thought	thought
thrive	thrived, throve	thrived
throw	threw	thrown
thrust	thrust	thrust
tread	trod	trodden, trod
undercut	undercut	undercut
undergo	underwent	undergone
underpay	underpaid	underpaid
understand	understood	understood
undertake	undertook	undertaken
undo	undid	undone
unwind	unwound	unwound
uphold	upheld	upheld
upset	upset	upset
wake	woke	woken
wear	wore	worn
weave	wove, weaved	woven, weaved
weep	wept	wept
wet	wet, wetted	wet, wetted
win	won	won
wind	wound	wound
withdraw	withdrew	withdrawn
withhold	withheld	withheld
withstand	withstood	withstood
wring	wrung	wrung
write	wrote	written

Appendix 2

Measurements and SI Units

Metric measures (with approximate non-metric equivalents)

	Metric		Non-metric
Length	10 millimetres (mm)	= 1 centimetre (cm)	= 0.394 inch
	100 centimetres	= 1 metre (m)	= 39.4 inches/1.094 yards
	1000 metres	= 1 kilometre (km)	= 0.6214 mile
Area	100 square metres (m²)	= 1 are (a)	= 0.025 acre
	100 ares	= 1 hectare (ha)	= 2.471 acres
	100 hectares	= 1 square kilometre (km²)	= 0.386 square mile
Weight	1000 milligrams (mg)	= 1 gram (g)	= 15.43 grains
	1000 grams	= 1 kilogram (kg)	= 2.205 pounds
	1000 kilograms	= 1 tonne	= 19.688 hundredweight
Capacity	10 millilitres (ml)	= 1 centilitre	= 0.018 pint (0.021 US pint)
	100 centilitres (cl)	= 1 litre (l)	= 1.76 pints (2.1 US pints)
	10 litres	= 1 decalitre (dal)	= 2.2 gallons (2.63 US gallons)

SI Units

	Physical quantity	Name	Symbol
Base units	length	metre	m
	mass	kilogram	kg
	time	second	s
	electric current	ampere	A
	thermodynamic temperature	kelvin	K
	luminous intensity	candela	cd
	amount of substance	mole	mol
Supplementary units	plane angle	radian	rad
	solid angle	steradian	sr

Appendix 3

Roman Numerals

I	=	1	XIV	=	14	XC	=	90
II	=	2	XV	=	15	C	=	100
III	=	3	XVI	=	16	CC	=	200
IV	=	4	XVII	=	17	CCC	=	300
V	=	5	XVIII	=	18	CD	=	400
VI	=	6	XIX	=	19	D	=	500
VII	=	7	XX	=	20	DC	=	600
VIII	=	8	XXX	=	30	DCC	=	700
IX	=	9	XL	=	40	DCCC	=	800
X	=	10	L	=	50	CM	=	900
XI	=	11	LX	=	60	M	=	1000
XII	=	12	LXX	=	70	MM	=	2000
XIII	=	13	LXXX	=	80			

Appendix 4
Chemical Elements

Element	Symbol	Atomic number	Element	Symbol	Atomic number
actinium	Ac	89	mercury	Hg	80
aluminium	Al	13	molybdenum	Mo	42
americium	Am	95	neodymium	Nd	60
antimony	Sb	51	neon	Ne	10
argon	Ar	18	neptunium	Np	93
arsenic	As	33	nickel	Ni	28
astatine	At	85	niobium	Nb	41
barium	Ba	56	nitrogen	N	7
berkelium	Bk	97	nobelium	No	102
beryllium	Be	4	osmium	Os	76
bismuth	Bi	83	oxygen	O	8
boron	B	5	palladium	Pd	46
bromine	Br	35	phosphorus	P	15
cadmium	Cd	48	platinum	Pt	78
caesium	Cs	55	plutonium	Pu	94
calcium	Ca	20	polonium	Po	84
californium	Cf	98	potassium	K	19
carbon	C	6	praseodymium	Pr	59
cerium	Ce	58	promethium	Pm	61
chlorine	Cl	17	protactinium	Pa	91
chromium	Cr	24	radium	Ra	88
cobalt	Co	27	radon	Rn	86
copper	Cu	29	rhenium	Re	75
curium	Cm	96	rhodium	Rh	45
dysprosium	Dy	66	rubidium	Rb	37
einsteinium	Es	99	ruthenium	Ru	44
erbium	Er	68	rutherfordium	Rf	104
europium	Eu	63	samarium	Sm	62
fermium	Fm	100	scandium	Sc	21
fluorine	F	9	selenium	Se	34
francium	Fr	87	silicon	Si	14
gadolinium	Gd	64	silver	Ag	47
gallium	Ga	31	sodium	Na	11
germanium	Ge	32	strontium	Sr	38
gold	Au	79	sulphur	S	16
hafnium	Hf	72	tantalum	Ta	73
hahnium	Ha	105	technetium	Tc	43
helium	He	2	tellurium	Te	52
holmium	Ho	67	terbium	Tb	65
hydrogen	H	1	thallium	Tl	81
indium	In	49	thorium	Th	90
iodine	I	53	thulium	Tm	69
iridium	Ir	77	tin	Sn	50
iron	Fe	26	titanium	Ti	22
krypton	Kr	36	tungsten	W	74
lanthanum	La	57	uranium	U	92
lawrencium	Lr	103	vanadium	V	23
lead	Pb	82	xenon	Xe	54
lithium	Li	3	ytterbium	Yb	70
lutetium	Lu	71	yttrium	Y	39
magnesium	Mg	12	zinc	Zn	30
manganese	Mn	25	zirconium	Zr	40
mendelevium	Md	101			